GOODE'S
WORLD ATLAS
TWENTY-SECOND EDITION

Editor

Howard Veregin, Ph.D.

Editorial Advisory Board

Robert W. Christopherson, M.A.
American River College (Emeritus)

Francis Galgano, Ph.D.
Villanova University

Alberto Giordano, Ph.D.
Texas State University, San Marcos

Sallie A. Marston, Ph.D.
University of Arizona

Virginia Thompson, Ph.D.
Towson University

Introduction

5	Foreword
6	Goode's Atlas Through Time
7	Preface
8	Basic Earth Properties
9	Cartography and Geospatial Technology
10	Map Scale
11	Map Projections
12	Map Projections Used in Goode's World Atlas
14	Thematic Map Types in Goode's World Atlas
16	Reference Map Legend
17	Solar System / The Seasons

The World

18	World • Political
20	World • Physical
22	World • Plate Tectonics / Volcanoes / Earthquakes
24	World • Landforms / Gravity Anomaly
26	Indian and Pacific Oceans Floor
28	Atlantic Ocean Floor
29	Arctic Ocean Floor
30	World • Climate Regions
32	World • January, July Temperature
33	World • Temperature Range / Polar Region Temperature
34	World • January Pressure, Winds / Seasonal Precipitation
35	World • July Pressure, Winds / Seasonal Precipitation
36	World • Annual Precipitation and Ocean Currents / Precipitation Change / Variability of Precipitation
38	World • Temperature Change / Sea Level Change
39	World • CO_2 Emissions / Kyoto Protocol
40	World • Oceanic Environments / Sea Ice
42	World • Natural Vegetation
44	World • Soil Taxonomy
46	World • Terrestrial Biomes
48	World • Population Density
50	World • Birth Rate / Death Rate
51	World • Natural Increase / Urbanized Population
52	World • Gross Domestic Product / Literacy
53	World • Languages / Religions
54	World • HIV Infection / Tuberculosis
55	World • Malaria / Physicians
56	World • Life Expectancy / Undernourishment
57	World • Food Aid / Drinking Water
58	World • Agricultural Production / Agricultural Yield
59	World • Wheat / Tea, Rye
60	World • Maize (Corn) / Coffee, Oats
61	World • Barley, Cocoa Beans / Rice, Millet and Grain Sorghum
62	World • Potatoes, Cassava / Sugar, Spices
63	World • Fruits / Tobacco, Fisheries
64	World • Vegetable Oils
65	World • Natural Fibers, Rubber / Beer and Wine
66	World • Cattle / Pigs
67	World • Sheep / Poultry
68	World • Copper / Tin, Bauxite
69	World • Lead, Lithium / Zinc, Coltan
70	World • Iron Ore and Ferroalloys
71	World • Steel / Precious Metals
72	World • Energy Balance / Electrical Energy Production
73	World • Hydroelectricity / Alternative Energy
74	World • Petroleum / Natural Gas
75	World • Coal / Uranium
76	World • Wood Production / Humid Tropical Forest Loss
77	World • Exports / Imports
78	World • Drug Use / Prison Population
79	World • Military Power / Women's Rights
80	World • Alliances
81	World • Refugees / Major Conflicts
82	World • Telecommunications / Internet / Shipping Lanes
84	World • Time Zones / Hours of Daylight

North America

85	North America • Political
86	North America • Physical
87	North America • Land Cover
88	North America • Satellite Image / Precipitation / Landforms / Vegetation
89	North America • Population Density / Natural Hazards / Energy / Minerals, Agriculture
90	United States and Canada • Temperature / Precipitation / Evapotranspiration
91	United States and Canada • Solar Radiation / Wind Speed / El Niño / Sea Level Rise / Tornadoes / Storm Frequency
92	United States and Canada • Natural Vegetation
94	United States and Canada • Agriculture
96	United States and Canada • Geology
98	United States and Canada • Federal Lands and Interstate Highways
100	United States and Canada • Transportation / Territorial Expansion
101	United States and Canada • Minerals
102	United States and Canada • Population Density
103	United States • Demographics
106	United States • Environmental Issues
107	United States • Labor Structure / Manufacturing

108 | United States • Political
110 | United States • Physical
112 | Northwestern United States
114 | North Central United States
116 | Northeastern United States
118 | Southwestern United States / San Diego
120 | Central United States
122 | South Central United States / Houston
124 | Southeastern United States
126 | Alaska
127 | Hawaii • Precipitation / Vegetation / Population Density / Environments
128 | Canada • Political
130 | Canada • Physical
132 | Southwestern Canada / Vancouver
134 | South Central Canada
136 | Southeastern Canada
138 | Eastern Canada / Québec
140 | Middle America / Aruba-Netherlands Antilles / Bermuda
142 | The West Indies / Lesser Antilles / Puerto Rico
144 | Mexico
146 | Central Mexico
148 | Yucatan Peninsula, Guatemala, Belize and El Salvador
149 | Honduras, Nicaragua and Costa Rica
150 | Panama / Panama Canal
151 | United States Cities • Las Vegas / Los Angeles / Portland / Sacramento / San Francisco / Seattle
152 | United States Cities • Atlanta / Boston / Cleveland / New York-Philadelphia / Pittsburgh / Washington-Baltimore
154 | United States Cities • Chicago-Milwaukee / Detroit / Kansas City / Minneapolis-St. Paul / St. Louis
155 | United States Cities • Dallas-Ft. Worth / Denver / Miami / Orlando / Phoenix / Tampa-St. Petersburg
156 | Canada Cities • Calgary / Edmonton / Montréal / Ottawa / Toronto / Winnipeg
157 | Middle America Cities and Regional • Guadalajara / Guatemala City / Havana / Mexico City / Monterrey / St. Croix / San Juan / Virgin Islands

South America

158 | South America • Political
159 | South America • Physical
160 | South America • Land Cover
161 | South America • Satellite Image / Precipitation / Landforms / Vegetation
162 | South America • Population Density / Natural Hazards / Energy / Minerals, Agriculture
163 | South America Cities • Bogotá-Medellín / Caracas / Lima / Recife / Santiago
164 | Northern South America
166 | Amazon Basin
168 | Central South America / Buenos Aires
170 | Peru and Ecuador / Galapagos Islands
171 | Southern South America
172 | Southeastern Brazil / Rio de Janeiro / São Paulo
173 | Río de la Plata Region

Europe

174 | Europe • Political
176 | Europe • Physical
178 | Europe • Land Cover
180 | Europe • Satellite Image / Precipitation / Landforms / Vegetation
181 | Europe • Population Density / Natural Hazards / Energy / Minerals, Agriculture
182 | Europe • Geology
184 | Western Europe
186 | Eastern Europe
188 | Southern Europe and the Mediterranean
190 | The British Isles and Iceland / Faroe Islands / London / Shetland Islands-Orkney Islands
192 | Southern Scandinavia and the Baltic States
194 | Central Europe
196 | France / Marseille / Paris / The Riviera
198 | Spain and Portugal / Azores / Canary Islands / Lisbon / Madrid
200 | Italy, Greece and the Balkans / Crete / Malta
202 | Western Russia and the Dnieper Basin
204 | Europe Cities • Athens / Berlin / Birmingham-Nottingham / Copenhagen / İstanbul / Manchester-Liverpool / Naples / Rome / Vienna
205 | Europe Cities • Amsterdam-Rotterdam / Antwerp-Brussels / Essen-Düsseldorf / Moscow / St. Petersburg

Asia

206 | Asia • Political
208 | Asia • Physical
210 | Asia • Land Cover
212 | Asia • Satellite Image / Landforms
213 | Asia • Precipitation / Vegetation
214 | Asia • Population Density / Energy
215 | Asia • Natural Hazards / Minerals, Agriculture
216 | Northern Eurasia • Population Density / Ethnicity
217 | Middle East • Population Density / Ethnicity
218 | Russia
220 | Southwestern Asia
222 | Eastern Asia
224 | Southeastern Asia / Taiwan
226 | Central Asia

227 The Caucasus

228 The Middle East

230 The Persian Gulf

232 Iran, Pakistan and Afghanistan

234 Northern India

236 Southern India and Sri Lanka

237 India, Pakistan, Bangladesh and Sri Lanka • Population Density / Minerals, Agriculture

238 Southern China

240 Northeastern China

242 China and Taiwan • Population Density / Minerals, Agriculture

243 Korea

244 Japan / Okinawa

245 Southern Japan / Tōkyō / Ōsaka

246 Southeast Asia / Singapore

248 Malaysia and Central Indonesia

250 The Philippines / Batan Islands-Babuyan Islands

251 Asia Cities • Baghdād / Delhi / Karāchi / Kolkata / Kuala Lumpur / Manila / Mumbai / Seoul / T'aipei / Tehrān

252 Asia Cities • Bangkok / Beijing / Dhaka / Hong Kong / Jakarta / Jerusalem-Tel Aviv / Shanghai

Africa

253 Africa • Political

254 Africa • Physical

255 Africa • Land Cover

256 Africa • Satellite Image / Precipitation / Landforms / Vegetation

257 Africa • Population Density / Natural Hazards / Energy / Minerals, Agriculture

258 Northwestern Africa

260 Western Africa / Southern Nigeria

262 Central Africa

264 Southern Africa / Mauritius-Reunion

266 Northeastern Africa

267 The Rift Valley

268 Africa Cities and Regional • Cairo / Lagos / Nile Valley / Suez Canal

269 Africa Cities • Addis Ababa / Algiers / Casablanca / Johannesburg

Australia, New Zealand and Oceania

270 Australia and New Zealand • Political

272 Australia and New Zealand • Physical

274 Australia and New Zealand • Land Cover / Natural Hazards / Energy

275 Australia • Satellite Image / Precipitation / Landforms / Vegetation / Population Density / Minerals, Agriculture

276 Southeastern Australia

277 Northeastern Australia and Papua New Guinea

278 New Zealand / Auckland / Melbourne / Sydney / Wellington

279 Pacific Islands • Fiji / Guam / New Caledonia-Vanuatu / Sakishimi Shotō / Samoa-American Samoa / Solomon Islands / Tahiti

280 Oceania

The Oceans and Polar Regions

282 Pacific Ocean

284 Atlantic Ocean

286 Indian Ocean

287 Southern Ocean and Antarctica

288 Arctic Ocean

Tables and Indexes

289 World Political Information Table

294 World Comparisons

295 Principal Cities of the World

296 Glossary of Foreign Geographic Terms

297 Abbreviations of Geographic Names and Terms / Pronunciation of Geographic Names

298 Sources

300 Subject Index

301 Pronouncing Index

Goode's World Atlas

Copyright ©2010 by Rand McNally

Copyright ©1922, 1923, 1932, 1933, 1937, 1939, 1943, 1946, 1949, 1954, 1957, 1960, 1964, 1970, 1974, 1978, 1982, 1986, 1990, 1995, 2000, 2005 by Rand McNally. All rights reserved.

Formerly *Goode's School Atlas*

Made in U.S.A.

Library of Congress Catalog Card Number 99-38535

Cover Image

Top half. Blue Marble Next Generation monthly composite image for August. Blue Marble Next Generation images are derived from MODIS data at a spatial resolution of 500 meters. MODIS (Moderate Resolution Imaging Spectroradiometer) sensors on board the Terra and Aqua satellites provide global coverage every one to two days in 36 spectral bands. Source: NASA Visible Earth program (http://visibleearth.nasa.gov/).

Bottom half. Map of humid tropical forest loss for the period 2000-2005, derived from MODIS and Landsat imagery. Humid tropical forest loss is estimated to be over 27 million hectares for this period. Source: Hansen, M.C., Stehman, S.V., Potapov, P.V., Loveland, T.R., Townshend, J.R.G., DeFries, R.S., Pittman, K.W., Stolle, F., Steininger, M.K., Carroll, M., and Dimiceli, C. (2008). Humid tropical forest clearing from 2000 to 2005 quantified using multi-temporal and multi-resolution remotely sensed data. PNAS,105(27), 9439-9444. (http://globalmonitoring.sdstate.edu/projects/gfm/humidtropics/data.html).

The cover image illustrates how remote sensing data, coupled with geographic information systems for analysis and display, are increasingly being used to map and monitor changes in the global environment.

Interest in geography has increased dramatically in the last few decades.

Perhaps it is because of efforts by those who teach geography or study it. Perhaps, because of instant global communications and the Internet, we're all more aware of global events. Maybe it's globalization, or recent wars, or global terrorism. Perhaps, because of environmental concerns, we feel a responsibility to better understand and manage Earth and its resources.

Whatever the reasons, this renewed interest in geography is serious. Billions of dollars are being spent every year collecting geographic data. Globally, tens of thousands of organizations of all kinds — government, business, academic, non-profit — have recognized that many of the problems they face must be understood geographically.

In emergencies, government agencies at every level need geographic information about the hurricanes, wildfires, earthquakes, tsunamis, storm surges, and floods they must respond to. They also need to know about the geography of political trouble spots, famines, droughts, terrorism, the narcotics trade, energy resources, shipping, war fighting, and a long list of other topics.

But spending for geographic information goes far beyond governments. Geographic information is also essential to understanding commerce, business, history, military campaigns, migrations, exploration, evangelization, cultural diffusion, origins of civilizations, distribution of organisms and their ecology, agriculture, climate change, natural resources, transportation patterns, productivity, epidemiology, conservation, election results, and many, many other topics. Organizations throughout the world recognize this, pay for geographic information, and hire people to manage and analyze it for them.

Geography matters! The community of people who rely on it is growing every day.

Geography today is a multidisciplinary science. Our ability to collect geographic data scientifically is exploding and we have begun to acquire the methods needed to effectively manage this data explosion for the entire planet. This includes new tools like satellite images of Earth, geographic information system (GIS) software to process and display enormous volumes of data, and global positioning system (GPS) devices that can accurately determine locations anywhere on Earth.

Goode's World Atlas is part of this revolutionary growth. The atlas has long been a staple of the college classroom, educating students about important geographic issues of the day. The current 22nd edition, which you hold in your hands, makes extensive use of digital geographic information of the kind I refer to above. It focuses on important contemporary issues like globalization, global climate change, food security, and environmental degradation. It uses GIS to integrate information and render it for cartographic display.

Goode's World Atlas helps us understand our world and our place in it. It helps us interpret stories in the news, understand international conflicts, evaluate foreign competition for jobs, make informed decisions about free trade or immigration, respond to changing oil prices or possible climate change, and think through complex domestic and foreign policy issues.

Goode's World Atlas is an essential guidebook to the new geography, helping us sort through and decipher patterns in a flood of geographic data. It helps us make sense of these data, and it provides authoritative cartographic interpretations of complex geographic issues.

I have studied and worked with geographic information for more than forty years. My experiences have given me insights into what our world was and is, and what we can make of it in the future. I think that geography can give us new eyes with which to see the world, so that — as the poet remarked — after all our traveling we return home and see it for the first time. I believe that Goode's World Atlas is an invaluable component of this learning process. The Atlas continues to evolve and adapt, but remains rooted in its original function — helping us develop geographic understanding and knowledge as a way to make sense of our world.

Jack Dangermond
President, ESRI

Goode's Atlas is named for John Paul Goode, who created the atlas and served as its editor for many editions. Goode was one of the first U.S. academic cartographers. He was born in rural Minnesota in 1862, received his bachelor's degree from the University of Minnesota in 1889, and earned his doctorate in economic geography from the University of Pennsylvania in 1903. He spent much of his professional career at the University of Chicago. Among his many accomplishments he is perhaps best known for the development of the Interrupted Homolosine projection, which he first presented at the Association of American Geographers meeting in 1923, and which has been used extensively in Goode's Atlas and in many other geographic publications to the present day.

The Homolosine is a composite of two projections, the Mollweide (Homolographic) and the Sinusoidal. Goode interrupted the Homolosine over the oceans to minimize distortion of shapes over continental land masses. Lines of latitude on the Homolosine are straight lines, to facilitate analysis of comparative latitudes. Also, the projection is equal area. Goode was a strong proponent of equal area projections and an equally strong opponent of the Mercator projection, widely used in the early part of the 20th century for world maps. As Goode stated in the introduction to the 1st edition of the atlas (1923, p. x), the distortion of area on the Mercator projection is so extreme that "it becomes pedagogically a crime to use Mercator's map" for studies of areal distributions such as population density, rainfall, or sizes of countries.

Under Goode's editorship the atlas doubled in size. The 1st edition of Goode's School Atlas contained 96 pages of maps. The 4th edition (1932), the last edition that Goode would edit before his death, contained 174 pages of maps. Goode introduced many of the thematic map topics that are still found in the atlas today, including world economic maps of agricultural commodities, minerals, energy, and international trade. These topics reflect Goode's interest and training in economic geography.

Goode remained the only name on Goode's School Atlas until the 8th edition (1949), on which Edward B. Espenshade, Jr., was credited with numerous updates and revisions. Espenshade was then named editor for the 9th edition (1953). Espenshade was one of Goode's students and spent his academic career at Northwestern University in Evanston, Illinois. The 9th edition was significant in many respects. It boasted a new title, Goode's World Atlas, and contained many of the features of the modern atlas.

John Paul Goode

In particular, Espenshade made extensive use of maps compiled by experts in specific subdisciplines of geography. Examples include natural vegetation by A. W. Küchler, physiography by Erwin Raisz, climate regions by Glenn Trewartha, and agricultural regions by Derwent Whittlesey. By relying on the research of these and other scholars, Espenshade was able to incorporate the latest advances in the study of geographical phenomena. Espenshade also oversaw the creation of a new reference map series, which included hand-drawn shaded relief for the first time in the atlas. These reference maps were introduced in the 11th edition (1960).

Joel L. Morrison, then at the University of Wisconsin, joined Espenshade as associate editor on the 14th edition (1974). Morrison, who had a distinguished career in academia and the federal government, was affiliated with the atlas through the 19th edition (1995). In the 1970s and 1980s the atlas saw numerous innovations, including the introduction of ocean floor shaded relief maps, reference maps of major world cities, a continent environments map series, and the first use of cartograms.

The 19th edition was Espenshade's last as editor. On that edition, John C. Hudson assumed the role of associate editor. Hudson, a distinguished academic geographer at Northwestern University, then took on the role of editor for the 20th edition. Hudson introduced many new thematic maps, including world ecoregions, origins of plants, refugees, conflicts, and oceanic environments.

Howard Veregin was named editor for the 21st edition. Veregin was on the geography faculty at the University of Minnesota, then moved to Rand McNally where he currently serves as director of geographic information services. Veregin created the Goode's Editorial Board to help reorient the atlas in relation to modern geographic scholarship and pedagogy. With the 22nd edition the atlas became all-digital for the first time, with most maps produced using geographic information systems (GIS) technology. Major innovations for the 22nd edition include a new digital reference map series (the first new series since the 11th edition), many new thematic maps, and an updated design.

Throughout its history Goode's Atlas has adapted to changes in cartographic technology, map design, and geographic curricula. However, it has always maintained the pedagogical foundation that John Paul Goode established in the 1st edition in 1923. It should be seen first and foremost as a work of scholarship, incorporating the latest insights into geographical research and knowledge. It is also a fascinating portrait of almost nine decades of evolution in geography and cartography.

Robert B. McMaster, Ph.D.
Susanna A. McMaster, Ph.D.
University of Minnesota

The 22nd edition of Goode's World Atlas blends dramatic new maps and exceptional cartography with the strong traditions that have made Goode's Atlas a standard for over 85 years.

The 22nd edition features new thematic maps that focus on topics important to modern geography, including global climate change, sea level rise, CO_2 emissions, polar ice fluctuations, forest loss, extreme weather events, infectious diseases, water resources, and energy production. These maps have been produced with the latest digital sources integrated within geographic information systems (GIS) technology to deliver a contemporary portrait of the planet. We have also retained and updated the new maps introduced in the 21st edition, including HIV infection, military power, women's rights, and food aid. Other thematic maps and graphs have been updated using the same standards and quality requirements that have always been a defining feature of Goode's World Atlas.

The 22nd edition also delivers over 160 pages of new, digitally produced reference maps, providing detailed coverage of all continents. We have paid particular attention to expanding our coverage of Africa, Asia, and Central and South America. The new reference maps were produced using state-of-the-art GIS technology to integrate digital data sources and render them for cartographic display. Underlying these maps is Rand McNally's proprietary digital world database, the same trusted source used in many of our other world atlases.

At Rand McNally we take pride in the quality of our cartography and the rigorous standards we set for the research underlying each map. For the 22nd edition we worked closely with our Editorial Advisory Board to select new map topics, assess cartographic approaches, and identify new atlas features. Longtime Goode's users will see numerous changes to the atlas, including the use of more contemporary color palettes and graphic treatments to improve clarity, readability, and aesthetics. In addition we have implemented changes that bring more consistency to each section of the atlas.

Needless to say this atlas would not have been possible without the efforts of a very talented cartographic development team, who conducted basic research, developed new thematic maps, created the new reference maps, designed the maps and page layouts, performed quality assurance, and helped work through countless editorial decisions. I include their names here in alphabetical order.

Robert Argersinger, Greg Babiak, Genna Davis, Marzee Eckhoff, Brett Gover, Justin Griffin, Rob Harris, Michael Healy, Susan Hudson, Valbona Kokoshi, Marc Kugel, Brian Lash, Felix A. Lopez, Andy Lotter, Nina Lusterman, Donna McGrath, Rob Merrill, Joerg Metzner, Angela Mrotek, Darren Raffel, Amy J. Ruggles, Damon Sather, Dave Simmons, Andy Skinner, Jeff Thomas, Raymond T. Tobiaski, Tom Vitacco, Steve Wiertz, Yanyan Zhang

A brief acknowledgment such as this cannot really do justice to the thousands of hours of effort expended by these and other Rand McNally subject matter experts. Nor does this list include Rand McNally employees who worked on previous editions of the atlas, and to whom the current atlas owes much.

I would also like to acknowledge the work of the Editorial Advisory Board, who participated in discussions of the new directions we were planning to take, and made significant contributions in terms of content and design. We are indebted to the Board for helping us refocus Goode's Atlas in relation to modern geographic scholarship and teaching. The Goode's Editorial Advisory Board members are listed on the title page of this atlas.

While Goode's Atlas continues to change with the times, it remains the same accurate and reliable educational resource that J. Paul Goode originally intended it to be. We at Rand McNally remain committed to providing you with the most trusted tools to help you and your students open your classrooms to the world.

Howard Veregin

Howard Veregin, Ph.D., Editor
Skokie, Illinois

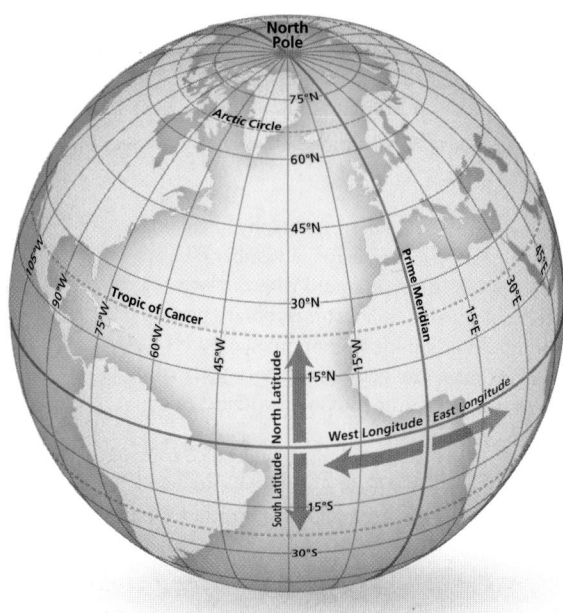

View of Earth centered on 30° N, 30° W

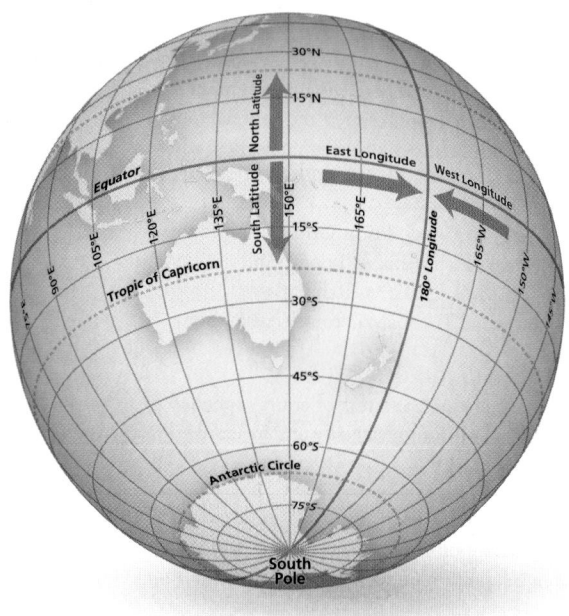

View of Earth centered on 30° S, 150° E

Basic Earth Properties

Earth is essentially spherical in shape. The North and South Poles are aligned with Earth's axis of rotation. The Equator is equidistant between the Poles and divides Earth into northern and southern hemispheres.

Latitude and longitude identify the locations of features on Earth's surface. Latitude is the angle north or south of the Equator. Longitude is the angle east or west of the Prime (Greenwich) Meridian. A meridian is a line of longitude extending from the North Pole to the South Pole. The Prime Meridian is the meridian passing through the Royal Observatory in Greenwich, England. This location for the Prime Meridian was adopted at the International Meridian Conference in Washington, D.C., in 1884.

Latitude and longitude are usually given in degrees, minutes and seconds. There are 60 minutes in a degree and 60 seconds in a minute. The symbols °, ' and " represent degrees, minutes and seconds, respectively. For latitude the symbols N and S indicate degrees north or south of the Equator. The latitude of the Equator is 0° and the latitudes of the North and South Poles are 90° N and 90° S. For longitude the symbols E and W indicate degrees east or west of the Prime Meridian. Longitude ranges from 0° at the Prime Meridian to 180° E or W. The meridian at 180° E is the same as the meridian at 180° W, and this meridian is the approximate location of the International Date Line. This meridian and the Prime Meridian divide Earth into eastern and western hemispheres.

A latitude-longitude coordinate pair defines the location of a feature on Earth. As an example, the Rand McNally building in Skokie, Illinois, has the coordinates 42° 3' 37" N, 87° 45' 39" W. Often the number of seconds are omitted from the coordinates if a high level of precision is not required.

Lines of latitude are also known as parallels. Two parallels of special importance are the Tropic of Cancer and the Tropic of Capricorn, at approximately 23° 30' N and S respectively. This angle coincides with the inclination of Earth's axis relative to its orbital plane around the Sun. The Tropics are the lines of latitude where the noon sun is directly overhead on the solstices. Two other important parallels are the Arctic Circle and the Antarctic Circle, at approximately 66° 30' N and S respectively. These lines mark the most northerly and southerly points at which the Sun can be seen on the solstices.

The Geographic Grid

The geographic grid is the grid of latitude-longitude lines on Earth. The following are some important characteristics of the grid.

Lines of longitude (meridians) are equal in length and meet at the Poles.

Lines of latitude (parallels) are parallel to each other and equally spaced along meridians.

The length of parallels decreases as one gets closer to the Poles. For example, the length of the parallel at 60° latitude is one-half the length of the Equator.

Meridians get closer together with increasing distance from the Equator, and finally converge at the Poles.

Parallels and meridians meet at right angles.

Cartography and Geospatial Technology

Geography's subject matter includes the people, landforms, climate, and other physical and human phenomena that make up Earth's environments and give unique character to different places. Geographers construct maps to visualize how these phenomena vary over geographic space. Maps help geographers understand and explain phenomena and their interactions.

The art and science of mapmaking is known as cartography. Although maps were once drawn by hand, they are now usually created using digital technology. This technology includes GIS (geographic information systems), as well as GPS (global positioning system) and remote sensing. Collectively these are known as geospatial technologies.

GIS is a specialized type of software that enables the integration, processing, analysis, and display of digital geographic information. It combines an underlying database with spatial analysis tools and cartographic rendering capabilities. First developed in the 1960s, GIS has evolved rapidly in the last decade with advances in computer processing power and the increased availability of digital geographic information. Applications of GIS have also diversified rapidly as more users have recognized its utility for solving geographic problems.

In cartography, GIS has redefined how maps are made. Since the underlying data for a map is stored in a database, a map is just one of many possible data representations. Many different maps can be produced from one database, based on different permutations of attributes, for different map scales, geographic areas, or time periods, and using different map treatments. GIS also enhances the efficiency of map production. For example, map symbology can be driven off stored attributes, selection and generalization can be conducted using defined rules, map text can be placed automatically, and index creation can be automated. All of the maps in this edition of Goode's World Atlas are digital, and the vast majority have been created using GIS software.

GIS also greatly enhances the ability to integrate data from a variety of sources and process these data for specific mapping purposes. In this sense GIS is closely related to other geospatial technologies such as GPS and remote sensing. GPS is a satellite-based system for capturing precise information about locations on Earth's surface. Originally developed by and for the military, GPS is now the underlying technology behind personal navigation devices and location-based services. GPS has revolutionized the field of surveying and is used in a wide variety of fields where accurate coordinates are needed.

Remote sensing refers to the collection of data about Earth from satellites and aircraft. Advances in remote sensing have greatly magnified the volume and types of geographic data available for mapping. Many of the maps in this atlas are derived from remote sensing imagery, including the maps of land cover, gravity, sea level change, sea ice, and forest loss. Modern remote sensing systems are designed to focus on specific portions of the electromagnetic spectrum, some of which cannot be seen by the human eye. This capability allows very specific geographic phenomena to be imaged and analyzed.

The diagram below illustrates how geospatial technology can be used to map and monitor changes in the global environment. This edition of Goode's World Atlas reflects this growing awareness and capability by incorporating the latest digital data sources wherever possible.

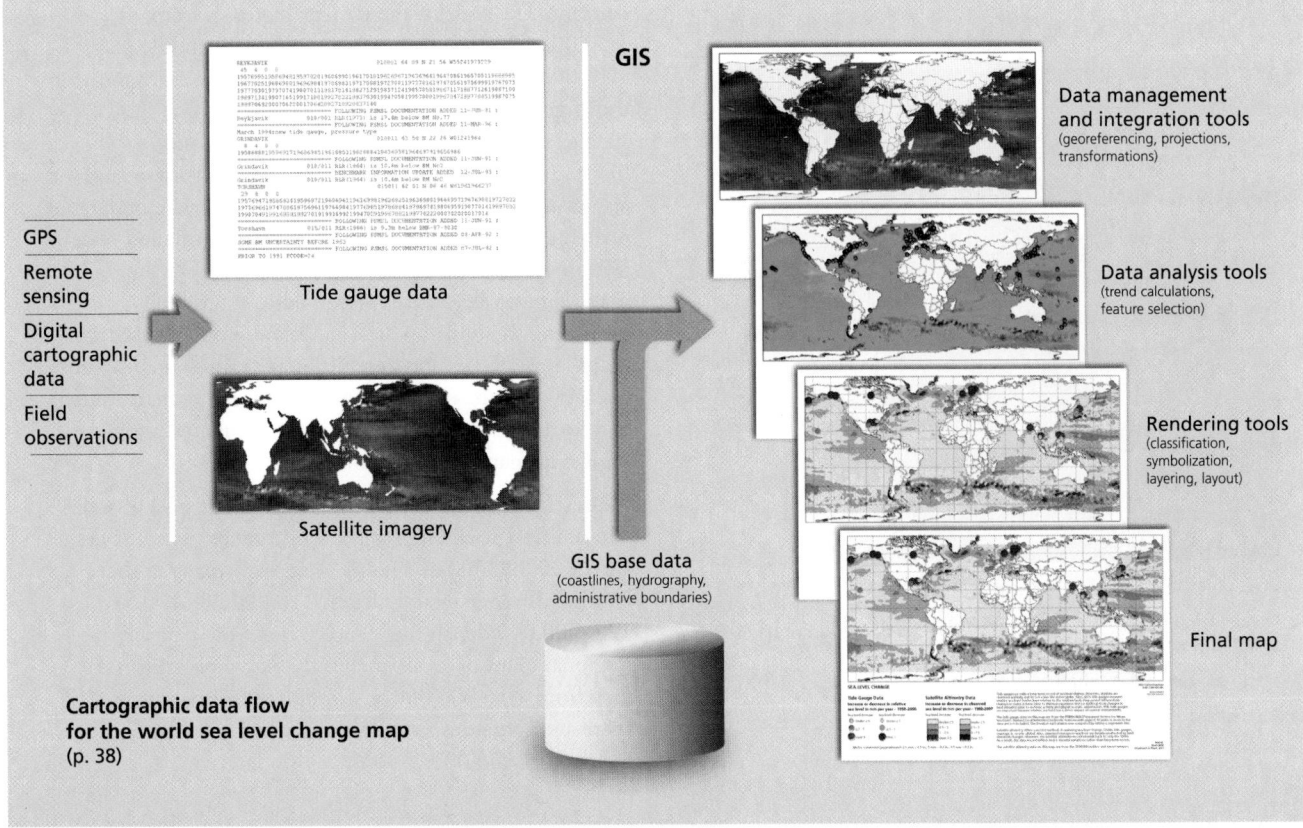

GIS

GPS

Remote sensing

Digital cartographic data

Field observations

Tide gauge data

Satellite imagery

GIS base data
(coastlines, hydrography, administrative boundaries)

Data management and integration tools
(georeferencing, projections, transformations)

Data analysis tools
(trend calculations, feature selection)

Rendering tools
(classification, symbolization, layering, layout)

Final map

Cartographic data flow for the world sea level change map (p. 38)

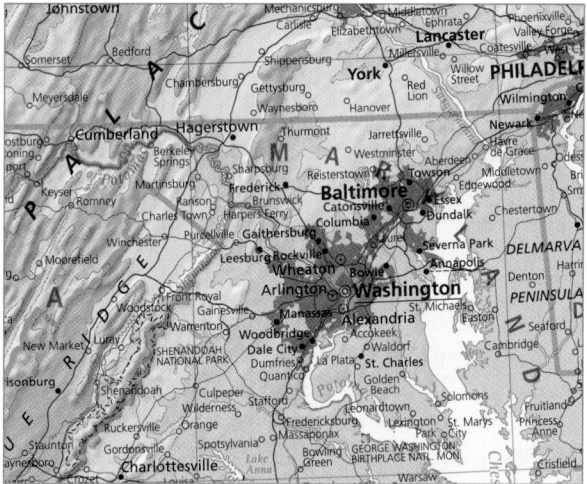

1:40,000,000 scale

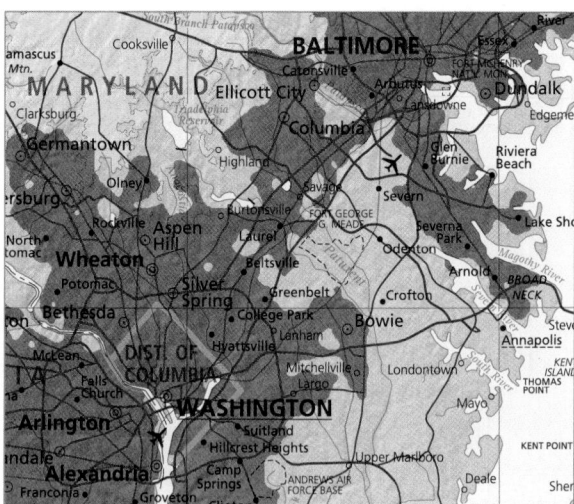

1:4,000,000 scale

1:1,000,000 scale

Map Scale

Map scale is the ratio of distance on a map to distance on Earth's surface. For example, if two towns on a map are separated by a distance of 1 inch, and these towns are actually 1 mile apart, then the scale of the map is 1 inch to 1 mile.

The statement "1 inch to 1 mile" is a verbal scale. Verbal scales are simple and intuitive, but it can be difficult to compare verbal scales for different maps on which different linear units are used, such as kilometers instead of miles. A more flexible way to express map scale is the representative fraction. To construct a representative fraction, the numerator and denominator are first converted to the same units. For example, since there are 63,360 inches in a mile, the verbal scale "1 inch to 1 mile" can be expressed as "1 inch to 63,360 inches". Next the unit names are dropped and the scale is expressed as a ratio, in this case 1:63,360. This means that 1 linear unit on the map represents 63,360 linear units on Earth, whether those units are inches, miles, kilometers, or some other unit of measurement.

Map scale can also be represented in graphical form. Many maps contain a graphic scale (or bar scale) showing real-world units such as miles or kilometers. The bar scale is usually subdivided to allow easy calculation of distance on the map. However, using a bar scale to measure distance can result in significant errors, especially on small-scale maps covering large areas. This is due to the distortion of distances on the map, as discussed in the map projection section below.

Map scale determines the amount of detail that can be portrayed on a map. The maps on this page illustrate this concept. The scale of these maps increases from 1:40,000,000 (top map) to 1:4,000,000 (middle map) to 1:1,000,000 (bottom map). On small-scale maps, only the largest and most important features can be shown, such as large cities, major rivers and lakes, and international boundaries. Features on small-scale maps are also smaller and more generalized than they are on larger-scale maps. For example, on the top map (smallest scale), Washington, D.C., appears as a small dot. On the middle map (larger scale), it is represented by a red blob indicating the built-up area of Washington. The bottom map (largest scale) shows additional detail that could not be shown on the other maps. This change in map content and feature complexity as a function of map scale is known as map generalization.

Maps in Goode's World Atlas have a wide range of scales. The smallest scales are for the world maps, where scales are 1:100,000,000 or smaller. Overview maps of the continents range in scale from 1:16,000,000 to 1:40,000,000 depending on the size of the continent. Regional maps of areas smaller than a whole continent vary from 1:16,000,000 to 1:4,000,000. In addition there are numerous inset maps of cities and islands at a scale of 1:1,000,000.

Map Projections

A map projection is a geometric representation of Earth's surface on a flat surface. Since Earth is roughly spherical, a map projection is needed to produce any flat map, whether a page in this atlas or a computer-generated map of driving directions on www.RandMcNally.com. Hundreds of projections have been developed since the dawn of cartography. A limitation of all of these projections is that they introduce geometric distortion. Some projections distort shape, others distort area, and all distort distance to some degree.

In order to choose an appropriate projection for a particular map, cartographers must pay careful attention to the properties that are distorted and the properties that are preserved by the projection. If shape is preserved, the projection is "conformal." On conformal projections the shapes of geographic features agree with their shapes on Earth. However, a limitation of conformal projections is that they necessarily distort area. This means that the sizes of the geographic features on the map will not be directly comparable. Some will be too large and others too small.

If areas are correctly represented, the projection is "equal area." On equal area projections the sizes of features on the map are directly comparable and in correct proportion to their sizes on Earth. However, in order to achieve this effect, equal area projections distort shape. No projection can preserve both shape and area simultaneously. Some projections preserve neither shape nor area, but instead balance shape and area distortion, creating a compromise projection.

The term "equidistant" is often used for projections that preserve distance. However this can be misleading since distance can only be preserved selectively, such as along specific meridians or parallels. No projection correctly preserves distance in all directions at all locations. Since distance is closely related to scale, one implication is that map scale is often only approximate and may not apply to the entire coverage area of a map. This problem is especially acute for small-scale maps covering large areas.

The projection selected for a particular map depends on the relative importance of different types of distortion, which in turn depends on the purpose of the map. For example, world maps showing phenomena that vary with area, such as population density, often use an equal area projection to give an accurate depiction of the importance of each region.

Map projections are created using mathematical procedures. To illustrate the general principles of projections without using mathematics, we can view a projection as the geometric transfer of information from a globe to a flat projection surface, such as a sheet of paper. If we allow the paper to be rolled in different ways, we can derive three basic types of map projections called cylindrical, conic, and azimuthal.

For cylindrical projections, the sheet of paper is rolled into a tube and wrapped around the globe so that it is tangent (touching) along a circle such as the Equator (see figure below). Information from the globe is transferred to the tube, and the tube is then unrolled to produce the final flat map.

Conic projections use a cone rather than a cylinder. The figure shows the cone tangent to the globe along a line of latitude with the apex of the cone over the North Pole. The line of tangency is called the standard parallel of the projection. Azimuthal projections use a flat projection surface that is tangent to the globe at a single point, such as the North Pole (see figure below).

In general, map distortion increases with distance away from the point or line of tangency. This is why maps of equatorial, mid-latitude, and polar regions often use cylindrical, conic and azimuthal projections, respectively.

The projection surface model is useful for illustrating how projections are developed. However, each of the three projection surfaces actually represents scores of individual projections. There are, for example, many projections with the term "cylindrical" in the name, each of which has the same basic rectangular shape, but different spacings of parallels and meridians.

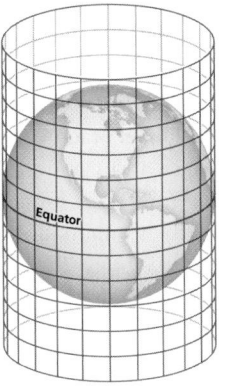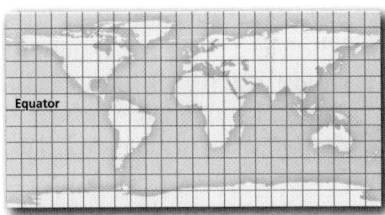

Cylindrical Projection

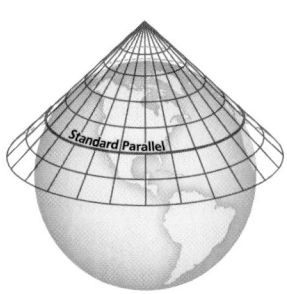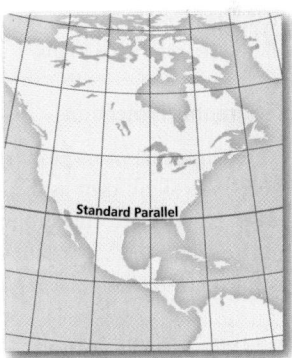

Conic Projection

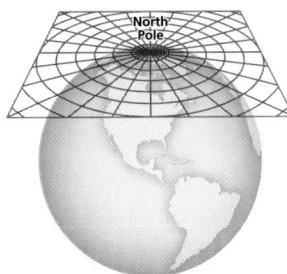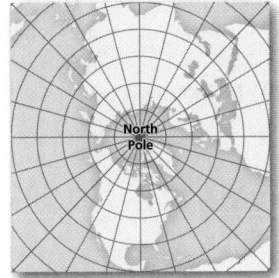

Azimuthal Projection

Map Projections Used in Goode's World Atlas

Of the hundreds of projections that have been developed, only a fraction are in everyday use. The main projections used in Goode's World Atlas are described below.

Lambert Conformal Conic Projection

On this conic projection, spacing between parallels increases with distance away from the standard parallel, which allows the geometric property of shape (but not area) to be preserved. The projection is named after Johann Lambert, an 18th century mathematician who developed some of the most important projections in use today. It became widely used in the United States in the 20th century following its adoption for many state mapping programs. This projection is used extensively in Goode's World Atlas for larger-scale reference maps.

Albers Equal Area Conic Projection

On this conic projection, spacing between parallels decreases with distance away from the standard parallel, which allows the geometric property of area (but not shape) to be preserved. The projection is named after Heinrich Albers, who developed it in 1805. It became widely used in the 20th century, when the United States Coast and Geodetic Survey made it a standard for equal area maps of the United States. This projection is used in Goode's World Atlas for continent thematic maps where the equal area property is important.

Lambert Azimuthal Equal Area Projection

On this azimuthal projection, area is preserved, but at the expense of significant shape distortion as distance from the point of tangency increases. This projection is most appropriate for areas of roughly circular shape. This projection, like the Lambert Conformal Conic, is named after Johann Lambert. It is used in Goode's World Atlas for smaller-scale reference maps.

Stereographic Projection

On this azimuthal projection, shape is preserved, but distortion of area becomes significant as distance from the point of tangency increases. As a result, this projection is often used for areas that are roughly circular in shape. This projection is used in Goode's World Atlas for maps of the polar regions.

Miller Cylindrical Projection

This cylindrical projection is neither conformal nor equal area. However, it is a useful compromise projection to show Earth in a simple, rectangular form. One problem is that polar areas exhibit significant exaggeration of area, a problem common to many cylindrical projections. The projection is named after Osborn Miller, director of the American Geographical Society, who developed it in 1942. The projection is used in Goode's World Atlas for many of the world climate maps.

Lambert Conformal Conic Projection

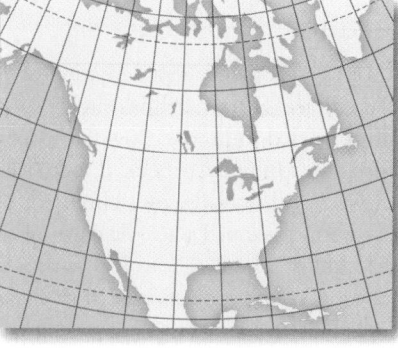

Albers Equal Area Conic Projection

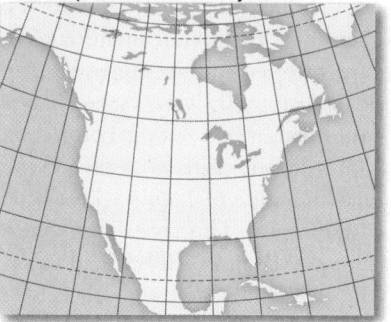

Lambert Azimuthal Equal Area Projection

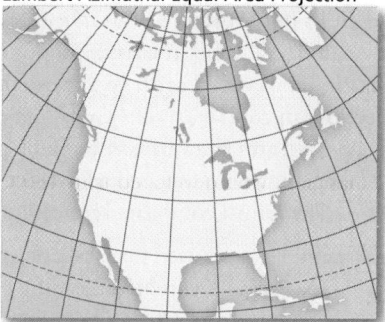

Stereographic Projection

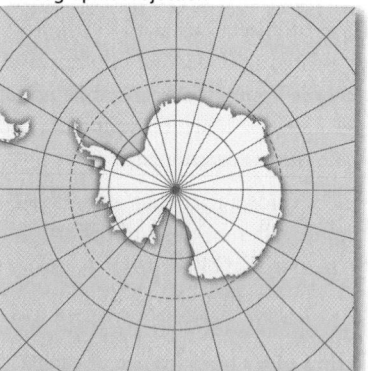

Miller Cylindrical Projection

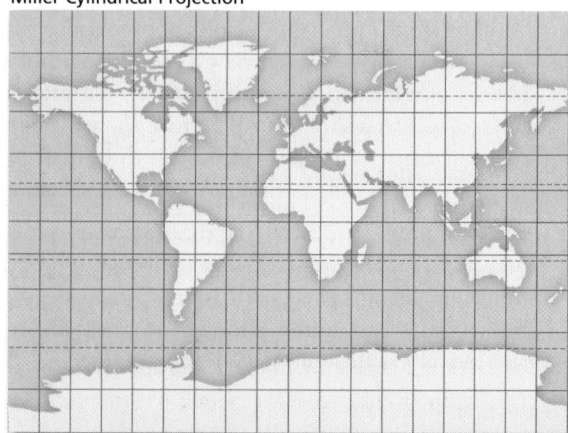

Plate Carrée Projection

This cylindrical projection is neither conformal nor equal area. Its main utility lies in the fact that it shows lines of latitude as evenly spaced lines on the map. This allows for effective thematic map display for phenomena that are measured at regular intervals of latitude. The projection is used in Goode's World Atlas for world climate change maps.

Sinusoidal Projection

The straight, evenly-spaced parallels on this pseudocylindrical projection resemble the parallels on cylindrical projections. Unlike cylindrical projections, however, meridians are curved and converge at the poles. This causes significant shape distortion in polar regions. The projection is therefore not conformal, although it is equal area. The Sinusoidal is the oldest-known pseudocylindrical projection, dating to the 16th century. It is not used extensively in Goode's World Atlas. However, along with the Mollweide projection, it is the basis for the Goode's Interrupted Homolosine projection described below.

Mollweide Projection

The Mollweide (or Homolographic) projection resembles the Sinusoidal but has less shape distortion in polar areas due to its elliptical form. Like the Sinusoidal projection, it is equal area but not conformal. It is one of several pseudocylindrical projections developed in the 19th century, and is named after Karl Mollweide, an astronomer and mathematician, who developed it in 1805. It is not used extensively in Goode's World Atlas. However, along with the Sinusoidal projection, it is the basis for the Goode's Interrupted Homolosine projection described below.

Goode's Interrupted Homolosine Equal Area Projection

This projection is a fusion of the Sinusoidal projection between 40° 44' N and S, and the Mollweide projection between these parallels and the Poles. The projection is equal area but not conformal. The unique appearance of the projection is due to the introduction of discontinuities in oceanic regions, the goal of which is to reduce distortion for continental land masses. A condensed version of the projection also exists in which the Atlantic Ocean is compressed to help maximize the scale of the map on the page. The Goode's Interrupted Homolosine projection is named after J. Paul Goode of the University of Chicago, who developed it in 1923. Goode was an advocate of interrupted projections and, as editor of Goode's School Atlas, promoted their use in education. This projection is used extensively in Goode's World Atlas for world thematic maps.

Robinson Projection

This pseudocylindrical projection resembles the Mollweide projection except that polar regions are flattened and stretched out. While neither conformal nor equal area, the Robinson projection manages to balance shape and area distortion in an effective way. The projection was developed in 1963 by Arthur Robinson of the University of Wisconsin, at the request of Rand McNally. The Robinson projection is widely used in Goode's World Atlas for world thematic maps where the interrupted nature of the Goode's Homolosine projection would be inappropriate.

Plate Carrée Projection

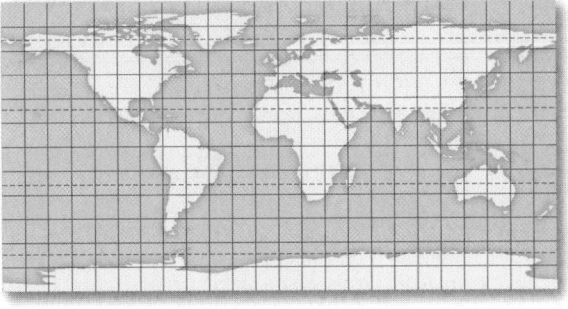

Sinusoidal Projection

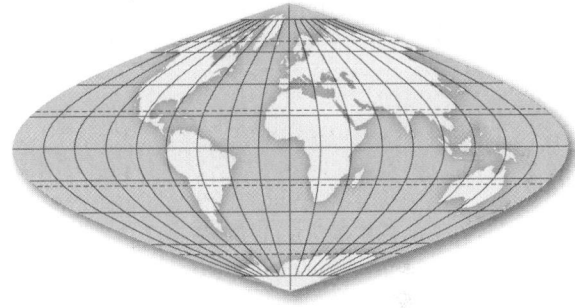

Mollweide Projection

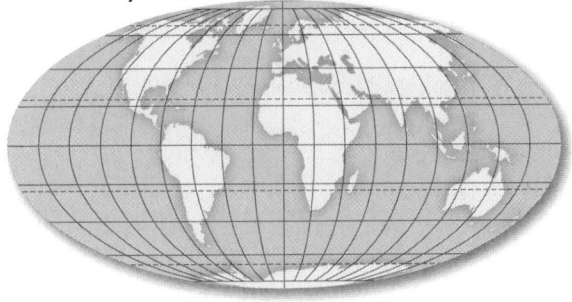

Goode's Interrupted Homolosine Equal Area Projection

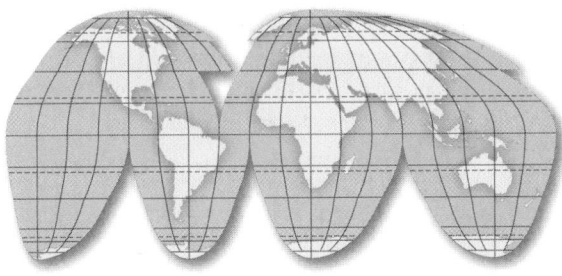

Robinson Projection

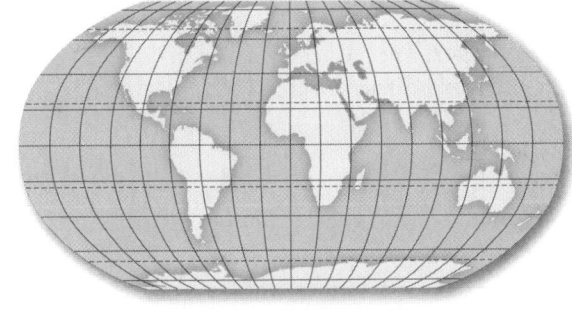

Point symbol map: Detail of Zinc and Coltan (p. 69)

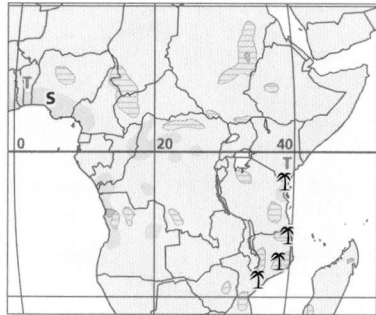

Area symbol map: Detail of Vegetable Oils (p. 64)

Dot map: Detail of Sugar, Spices (p. 62)

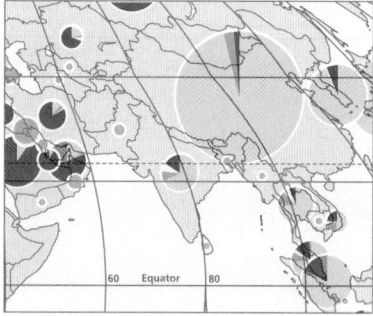

Proportional symbol map: Detail of Exports (p. 77)

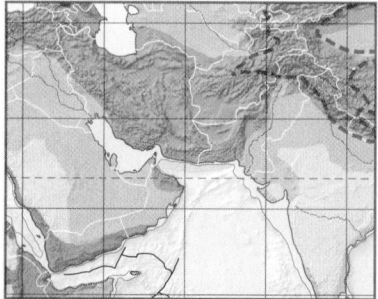

Area class map: Detail of Landforms (pp. 24-25)

Thematic Map Types in Goode's World Atlas

Thematic maps depict a single theme such as population density, agricultural productivity or annual precipitation. The selected theme is presented on a base of locational information, such as coastlines, country boundaries, and major drainage features.

Goode's World Atlas contains many different types of thematic maps. The characteristics of each are summarized below.

Point Symbol Maps

Point symbol maps are perhaps the simplest type of thematic map. They show features that occur at discrete locations. Examples include earthquakes, nuclear power plants, and mineral-producing areas. The Zinc and Coltan map (p. 69) is an example of a point symbol map. Different colors represent the two different materials, and various symbol sizes show relative importance.

Area Symbol Maps

Area symbol maps are useful for delineating regions of interest. For example, the Vegetable Oils maps (p. 64) show major oil-producing regions in different colors. Some point symbols also appear on this map, for less extensive oil crops.

Dot Maps

Dot maps show a distribution using a pattern of dots, where each dot represents a certain quantity or amount. For example, on the Sugar and Spice map (p. 62), each dot represents 20,000 metric tons of sugar produced. The different dot colors represent different sources of sugar (cane vs. beet). Dot maps are an effective way of representing the variable density of geographic phenomena.

Proportional Symbol Maps

Proportional symbol maps portray numeric quantities, such as total toxic chemical releases per state, or the total value of agricultural goods produced by country. The symbols on these maps — usually circles — are drawn such that the size the symbol is proportional to the value at that location. For example, the Exports map (p. 77) shows the value of goods exported by each country in the world, in billions of U.S. dollars. Proportional symbols are frequently subdivided based on the percentage of individual components making up the total. The Exports map uses wedges of different color to show the percentages of various types of exports, such as manufactured articles and raw materials.

Area Class Maps

Area class maps divide Earth into zones based on categories of a particular geographic phenomenon. For example, the Landforms map (pp. 24-25) divides Earth into seven unique structural regions based on landform type and origin. Other examples of area class maps in Goode's World Atlas include soil taxonomy (pp. 44-45), terrestrial biomes (pp. 46-47), and natural vegetation (pp. 42-43).

Flow Line Maps

Flow line maps show flows between locations. Usually the thickness of the flow lines is proportional to the volume of the flow. Flows may be physical commodities like petroleum or less tangible quantities like information. The flow lines on the Communication Network Infrastructure map (pp. 82-83) represent bandwidth usage in gigabits per second. Note that the locations of flow lines may not accurately represent the actual physical route.

Choropleth Maps

Choropleth maps apply distinctive colors to predefined areas, such as counties or states, to represent different quantities in each area. The quantities shown are usually rates, percentages, or densities. For example, the Birth Rate map (p. 50) shows the annual number of births per one thousand people for each country.

Isoline Maps

Isoline maps are used to portray quantities that vary continuously over space. These maps are frequently used for climate variables such as precipitation and temperature. For example, the January Temperature map for the North Polar region (p. 33) contains isolines at intervals of 5° C. Colors are also used to assist map interpretation.

Grid-Based Maps

Grid-based maps rely on data points occurring at regular intervals in a two-dimensional grid. Some grid-based maps are actually digital images, analogous to the pictures captured by digital cameras. These maps are created from a very fine grid of cells called pixels, each of which is assigned a color that corresponds to a specific value or range of values. The population density maps in this atlas (pp. 48-49, for example) are examples of this type. Other grid-based maps are based on data integrated over a coarser grid, such as the map showing temperature change for 5-degree grid cells (p. 38) and the tornado map showing the frequency of tornadoes within 1-degree grid cells (p. 91). Grid-based mapping is increasingly being used to map environmental phenomena observable from remote sensing systems.

Cartograms

Cartograms are maps on which shapes and areas have been deliberately distorted. The cartograms in this atlas draw each country as a rectangle whose size is proportional to the population of the country. This means that the countries with the largest areas are those with the largest populations, regardless of actual country area. Cartograms make explicit the relationship between the mapped variable and the size of the affected population. As an example, consider the HIV cartogram (p. 54). Both Chad and Nigeria have relatively high rates of HIV infection, but Nigeria is much larger than Chad on the cartogram, since Nigeria's population is much larger. This informs the cartogram reader that the population affected by HIV is much larger in Nigeria.

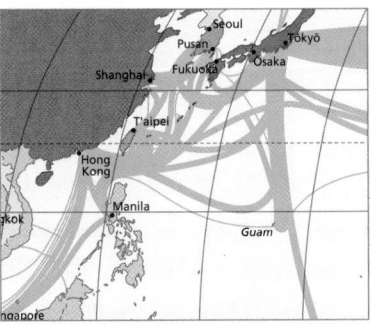

Flow line map: Detail of Communication Network Infrastructure (pp. 82-83)

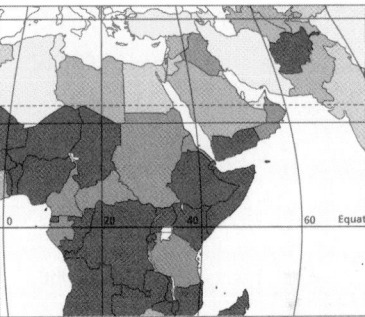

Choropleth map: Detail of Birth Rate (p. 50)

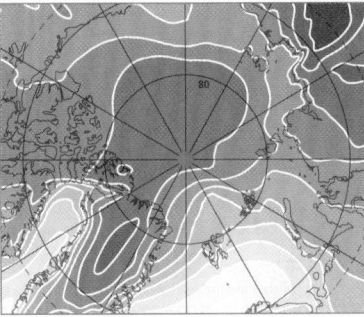

Isoline map: Detail of January Temperature (p. 33)

Grid-based map: Detail of Population Density (pp. 48-49)

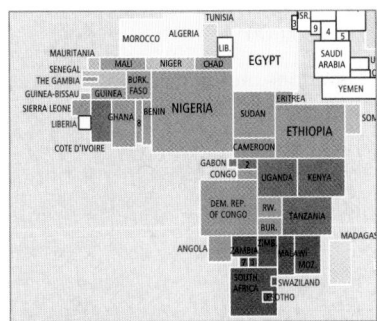

Cartogram: Detail of HIV Infection (p. 54)

Political Boundaries

	International
	Disputed or Unrecognized
	Secondary (State, Provincial, etc.)
– – –	International Boundary over Water
– – –	Secondary Boundary over Water
⌐ ¬	Park, Indian Reservation, Area of Interest
	Urbanized Area

Populated Places

TŌKYŌ	National Capital
Boise	Secondary Capital

1:2,000,000, 1:1,000,000 and 1:500,000 Inset Maps

⊙	1,000,000 and over
◎	100,000 to 1,000,000
⊙	50,000 to 100,000
•	10,000 to 50,000
○	Under 10,000
□	Neighborhood, Section of City

Other Reference Maps

⊙	1,000,000 and over
◎	250,000 to 1,000,000
⊙	100,000 to 250,000
•	25,000 to 100,000
○	Under 25,000

Note: Type size indicates the relative importance of the city. On the continent physical maps, city populations and relative importance are not differentiated.

Cultural Features

	Dam
⌂	Point of Interest
∴	Ruins
PALESTINE	Cultural or Historic Region

Transportation

——	Major Road
——	Minor Road
——	Railroad
✈	Airport

Land Features

△	Peak, Spot Height
≍	Pass
	Sand
	Contours

Elevation

Meters	Feet
3048	10,000
1524	5000
610	2000
305	1000
152.5	500
0	Sea Level

Below Sea level

152.5	500
3048	10,000
6096	20,000
9144	30,000

Note: The 500 foot contour is not shown on the small-scale oceans and polar regions maps.

Lakes and Reservoirs

	Fresh Water
	Fresh Water: Intermittent
	Dry Lake
	Salt Water
	Salt Water: Intermittent

Other Water features

	Swamp
	Glacier
	Ice Cap
	River
	Intermittent River
	Canal (navigable)
	Falls
	Springs
	Reef
→	Warm Ocean Current
→	Cold Ocean Current

The legend above shows the symbols used for reference maps in Goode's World Atlas.

To portray relative areas correctly, uniform map scales have been used wherever possible:

Continents – Between 1:16,000,000 and 1:40,000,000

Countries and regions – Between 1:4,000,000 and 1:16,000,000

World, polar areas and oceans – 1:40,000,000 and smaller

City and island inset maps – 1:500,000, 1:1,000,000 and 1:2,000,000

Elevations on the maps are shown using a combination of shaded relief and hypsometric tints. Shaded relief (or hill-shading) gives a three-dimensional impression of the landscape, while hypsometric tints show elevation ranges in different colors.

The choice of names for mapped features is complicated by the fact that a variety of languages and alphabets are used throughout the world. A local-names policy is used in Goode's World Atlas for populated places and local physical features. For some major features, an English form of the name is used with the local name, e.g., Vienna (Wien) and Naples (Napoli). In countries where more than one official language is used, names are given in the dominant local language. For large physical features spanning international borders, the conventional English form of the name is used. In cases where a non-Roman alphabet is used, names have been transliterated according to accepted practice.

Selected features are also listed in the Index, which includes a pronunciation guide. A list of foreign geographic terms is provided in the Glossary.

THE SOLAR SYSTEM

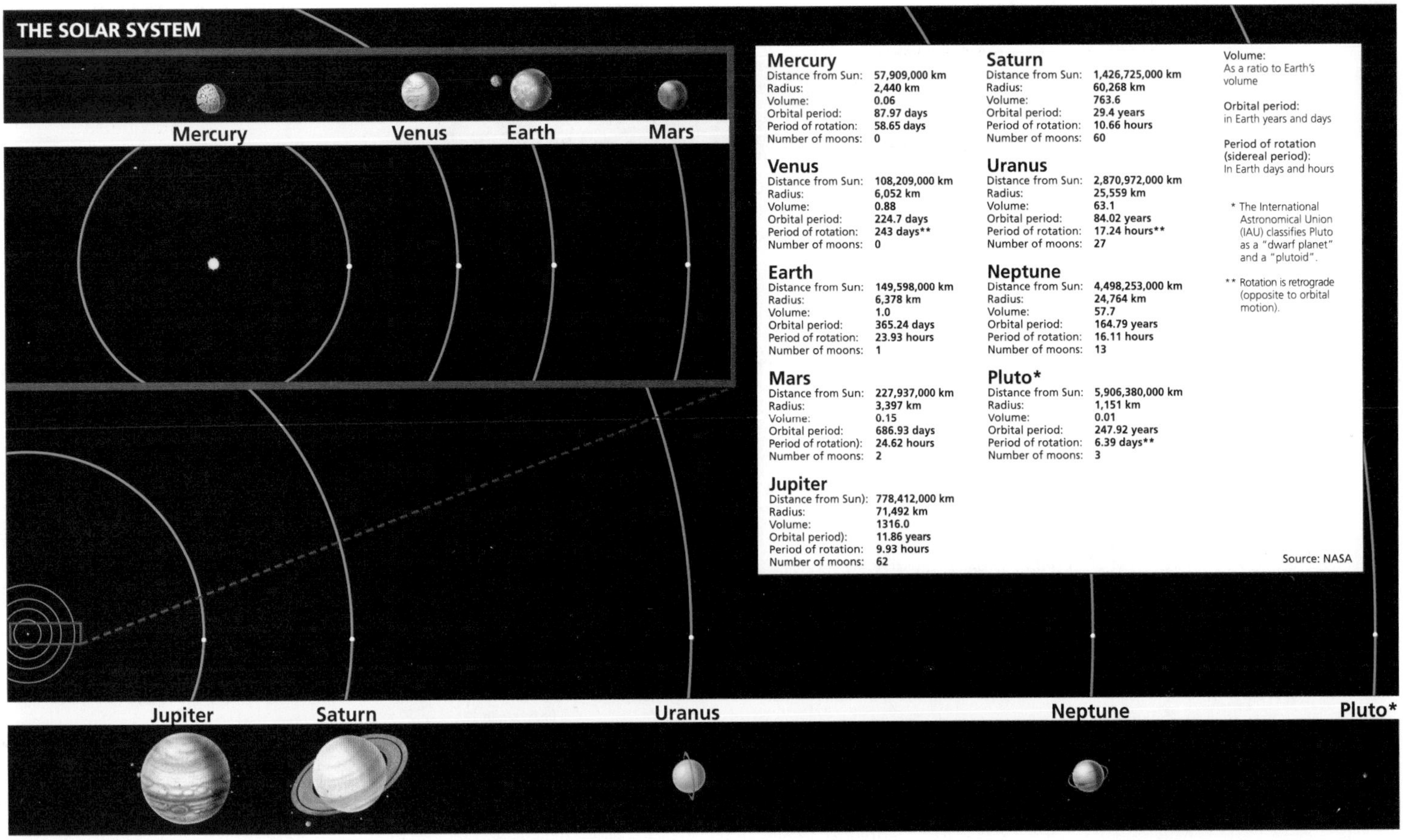

Mercury | Venus | Earth | Mars

Mercury
Distance from Sun: 57,909,000 km
Radius: 2,440 km
Volume: 0.06
Orbital period: 87.97 days
Period of rotation: 58.65 days
Number of moons: 0

Venus
Distance from Sun: 108,209,000 km
Radius: 6,052 km
Volume: 0.88
Orbital period: 224.7 days
Period of rotation: 243 days**
Number of moons: 0

Earth
Distance from Sun: 149,598,000 km
Radius: 6,378 km
Volume: 1.0
Orbital period: 365.24 days
Period of rotation: 23.93 hours
Number of moons: 1

Mars
Distance from Sun: 227,937,000 km
Radius: 3,397 km
Volume: 0.15
Orbital period: 686.93 days
Period of rotation: 24.62 hours
Number of moons: 2

Jupiter
Distance from Sun: 778,412,000 km
Radius: 71,492 km
Volume: 1316.0
Orbital period: 11.86 years
Period of rotation: 9.93 hours
Number of moons: 62

Saturn
Distance from Sun: 1,426,725,000 km
Radius: 60,268 km
Volume: 763.6
Orbital period: 29.4 years
Period of rotation: 10.66 hours
Number of moons: 60

Uranus
Distance from Sun: 2,870,972,000 km
Radius: 25,559 km
Volume: 63.1
Orbital period: 84.02 years
Period of rotation: 17.24 hours**
Number of moons: 27

Neptune
Distance from Sun: 4,498,253,000 km
Radius: 24,764 km
Volume: 57.7
Orbital period: 164.79 years
Period of rotation: 16.11 hours
Number of moons: 13

Pluto*
Distance from Sun: 5,906,380,000 km
Radius: 1,151 km
Volume: 0.01
Orbital period: 247.92 years
Period of rotation: 6.39 days**
Number of moons: 3

Volume:
As a ratio to Earth's volume

Orbital period:
in Earth years and days

Period of rotation (sidereal period):
In Earth days and hours

* The International Astronomical Union (IAU) classifies Pluto as a "dwarf planet" and a "plutoid".

** Rotation is retrograde (opposite to orbital motion).

Source: NASA

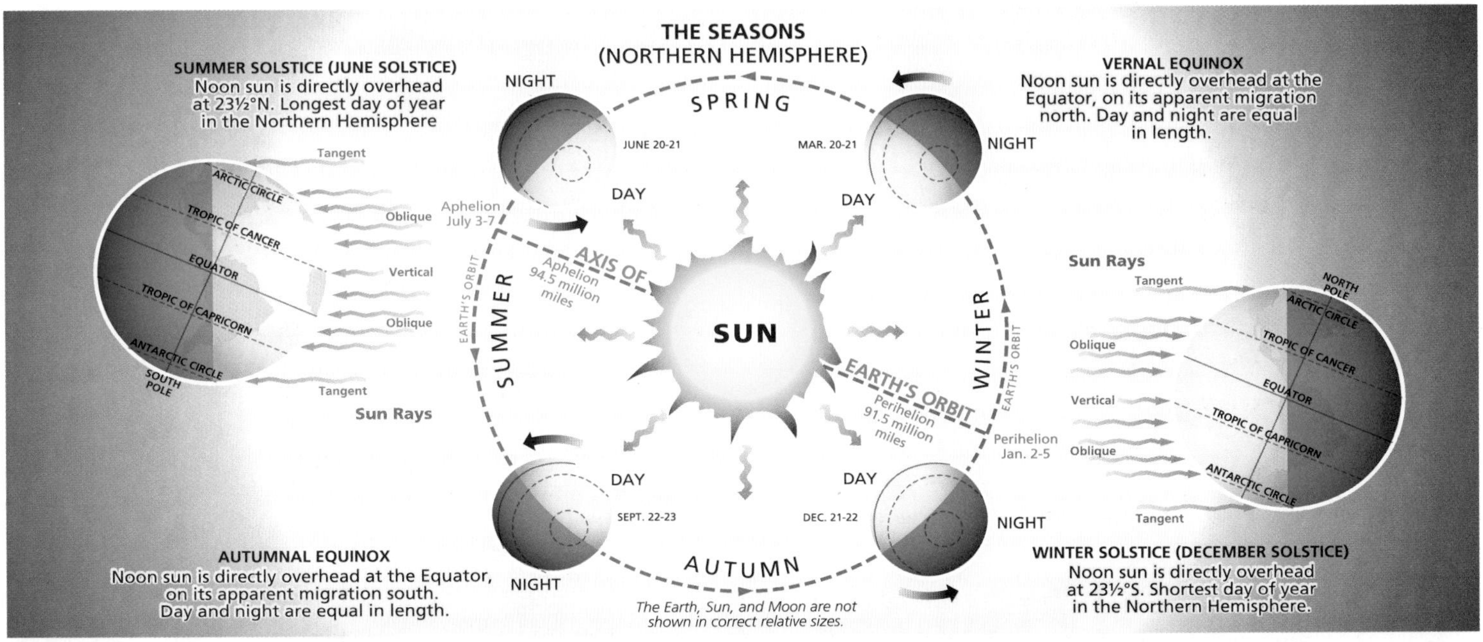

Jupiter | Saturn | Uranus | Neptune | Pluto*

THE SEASONS
(NORTHERN HEMISPHERE)

SUMMER SOLSTICE (JUNE SOLSTICE)
Noon sun is directly overhead at 23½°N. Longest day of year in the Northern Hemisphere

VERNAL EQUINOX
Noon sun is directly overhead at the Equator, on its apparent migration north. Day and night are equal in length.

AUTUMNAL EQUINOX
Noon sun is directly overhead at the Equator, on its apparent migration south. Day and night are equal in length.

WINTER SOLSTICE (DECEMBER SOLSTICE)
Noon sun is directly overhead at 23½°S. Shortest day of year in the Northern Hemisphere.

SPRING
NIGHT
DAY
JUNE 20-21
MAR. 20-21
NIGHT
DAY

Aphelion July 3-7
AXIS OF
Aphelion 94.5 million miles
SUMMER
EARTH'S ORBIT
SUN
WINTER
EARTH'S ORBIT
EARTH'S ORBIT
Perihelion 91.5 million miles
Perihelion Jan. 2-5

DAY
SEPT. 22-23
DEC. 21-22
DAY
NIGHT
NIGHT
AUTUMN

The Earth, Sun, and Moon are not shown in correct relative sizes.

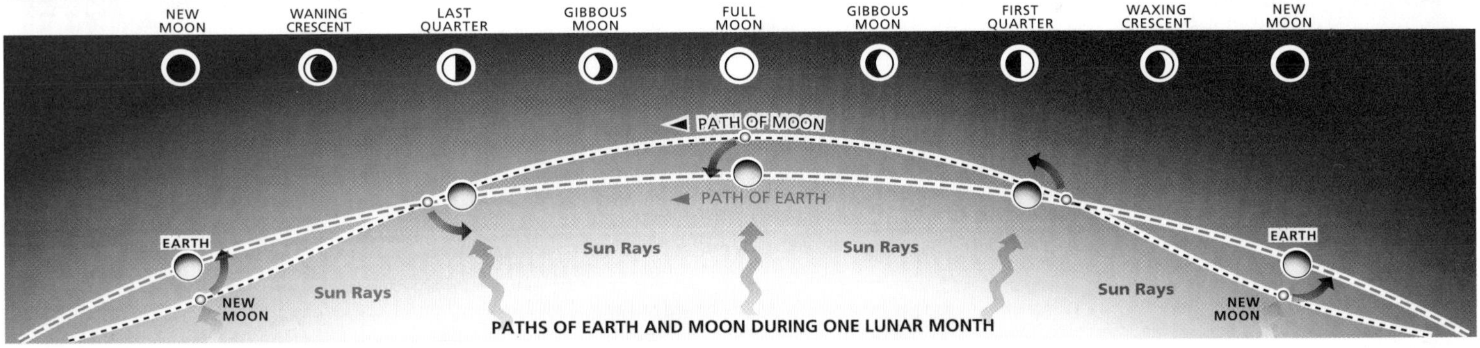

ARCTIC CIRCLE
TROPIC OF CANCER
EQUATOR
TROPIC OF CAPRICORN
ANTARCTIC CIRCLE
SOUTH POLE
Tangent
Oblique
Vertical
Oblique
Tangent
Sun Rays

Sun Rays
Tangent
Oblique
Vertical
Oblique
Tangent
NORTH POLE
ARCTIC CIRCLE
TROPIC OF CANCER
EQUATOR
TROPIC OF CAPRICORN
ANTARCTIC CIRCLE

NEW MOON | WANING CRESCENT | LAST QUARTER | GIBBOUS MOON | FULL MOON | GIBBOUS MOON | FIRST QUARTER | WAXING CRESCENT | NEW MOON

PATH OF MOON
PATH OF EARTH
EARTH
EARTH
NEW MOON
Sun Rays
Sun Rays
Sun Rays
Sun Rays
Sun Rays
NEW MOON

PATHS OF EARTH AND MOON DURING ONE LUNAR MONTH

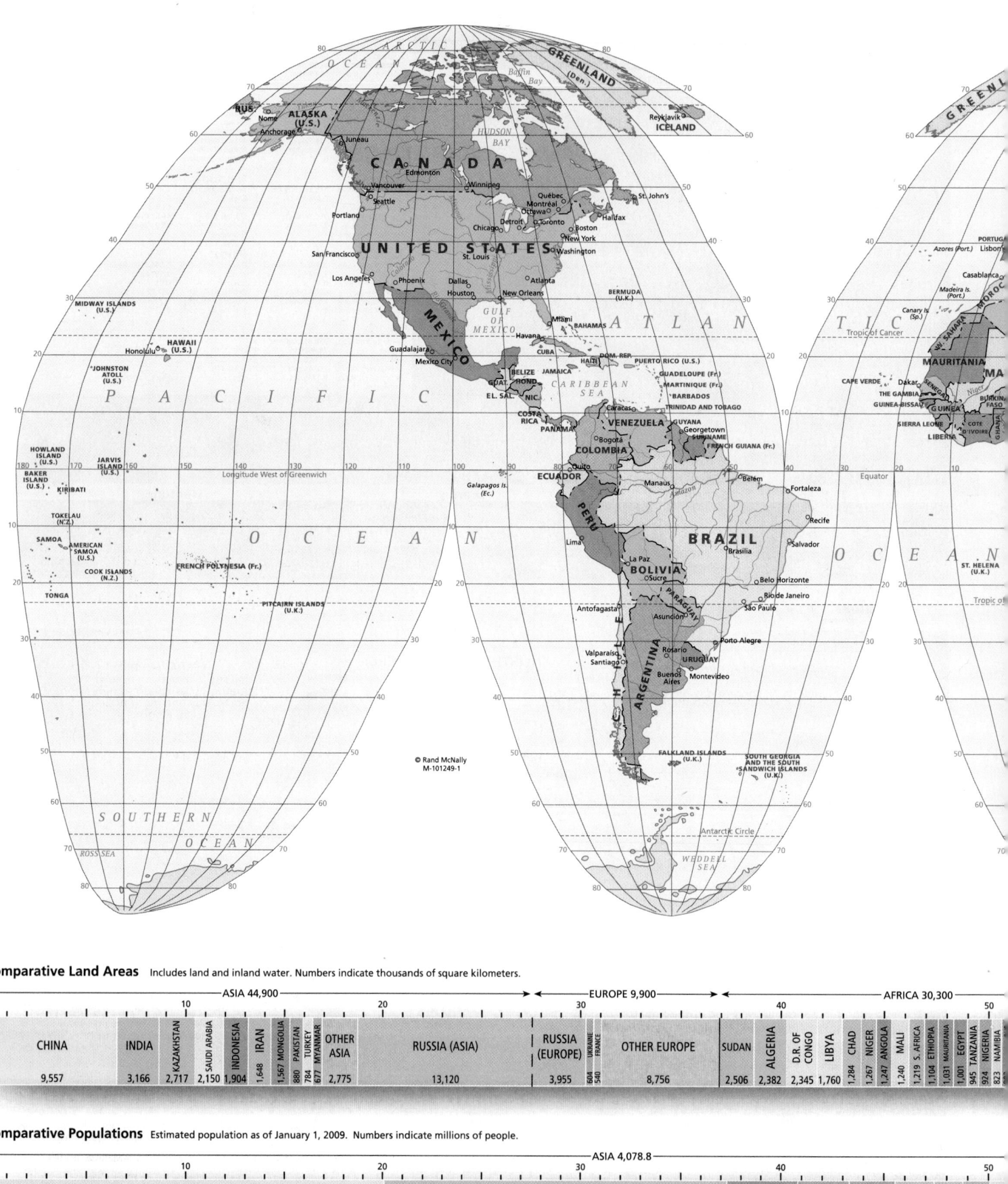

© Rand McNally
M-101249-1

Comparative Land Areas Includes land and inland water. Numbers indicate thousands of square kilometers.

	ASIA 44,900												EUROPE 9,900			AFRICA 30,300													
CHINA	INDIA	KAZAKHSTAN	SAUDI ARABIA	INDONESIA	IRAN	MONGOLIA	PAKISTAN	TURKEY	MYANMAR	OTHER ASIA	RUSSIA (ASIA)	RUSSIA (EUROPE)	UKRAINE	FRANCE	OTHER EUROPE	SUDAN	ALGERIA	D.R. OF CONGO	LIBYA	CHAD	NIGER	ANGOLA	MALI	S. AFRICA	ETHIOPIA	MAURITANIA	EGYPT	TANZANIA	NIGERIA	NAMIBIA
9,557	3,166	2,717	2,150	1,904	1,648	1,567	880	784	677	2,775	13,120	3,955	604	540	8,756	2,506	2,382	2,345	1,760	1,284	1,267	1,247	1,240	1,219	1,104	1,031	1,001	945	924	823

Comparative Populations Estimated population as of January 1, 2009. Numbers indicate millions of people.

	ASIA 4,078.8							
CHINA	INDIA	INDONESIA	PAKISTAN	BANGLA-DESH	JAPAN	PHILIPPINES	VIETNAM	TURKEY
1,341.8	1,157.1	238.9	174.5	155.0	127.2	97.0	86.5	76.1

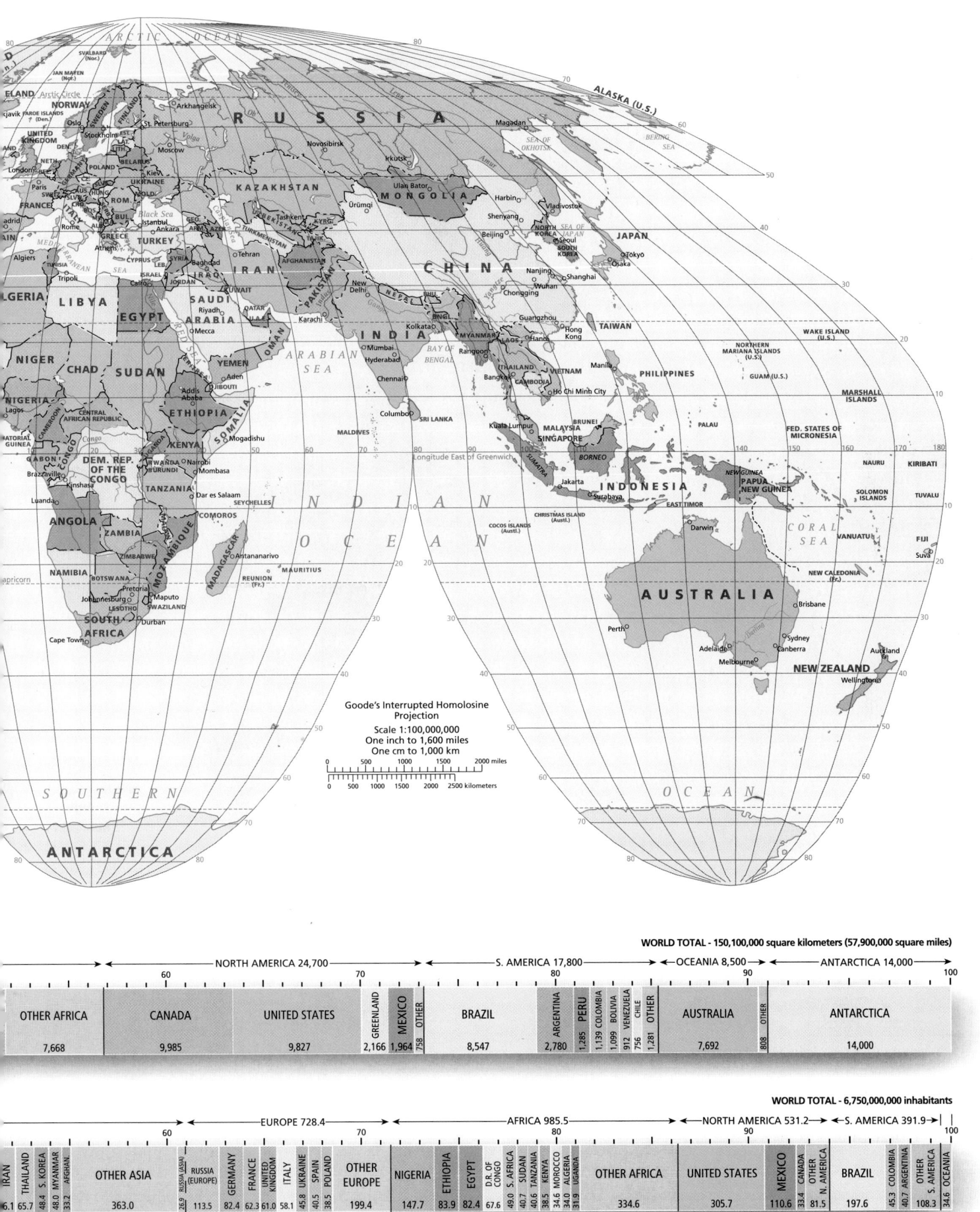

Goode's Interrupted Homolosine
Projection

Scale 1:100,000,000
One inch to 1,600 miles
One cm to 1,000 km

0   500   1000   1500   2000 miles

0   500 1000 1500 2000 2500 kilometers

WORLD TOTAL - 150,100,000 square kilometers (57,900,000 square miles)

	NORTH AMERICA 24,700			S. AMERICA 17,800		OCEANIA 8,500	ANTARCTICA 14,000

OTHER AFRICA	CANADA	UNITED STATES	GREENLAND	MEXICO	OTHER	BRAZIL	ARGENTINA	PERU	COLOMBIA	BOLIVIA	VENEZUELA	CHILE	OTHER	AUSTRALIA	OTHER	ANTARCTICA
7,668	9,985	9,827	2,166	1,964	758	8,547	2,780	1,285	1,139	1,099	912	756	1,281	7,692	808	14,000

WORLD TOTAL - 6,750,000,000 inhabitants

			EUROPE 728.4									AFRICA 985.5										NORTH AMERICA 531.2			S. AMERICA 391.9

IRAN	THAILAND	S. KOREA	MYANMAR	OTHER ASIA	RUSSIA (ASIA)	RUSSIA (EUROPE)	GERMANY	FRANCE	UNITED KINGDOM	ITALY	UKRAINE	SPAIN	POLAND	OTHER EUROPE	NIGERIA	ETHIOPIA	EGYPT	D.R. OF CONGO	S. AFRICA	SUDAN	TANZANIA	KENYA	MOROCCO	ALGERIA	UGANDA	OTHER AFRICA	UNITED STATES	MEXICO	CANADA	OTHER N. AMERICA	BRAZIL	COLOMBIA	ARGENTINA	OTHER S. AMERICA	OCEANIA
6.1	65.7	48.4	48.0	33.2	363.0	26.9	113.5	82.4	62.3	61.0	58.1	45.8	40.5	38.5	199.4	147.7	83.9	82.4	67.6	49.0	40.7	40.6	38.5	34.6	34.0	31.9	334.6	305.7	110.6	33.4	81.5	197.6	45.3	40.7	108.3	34.6

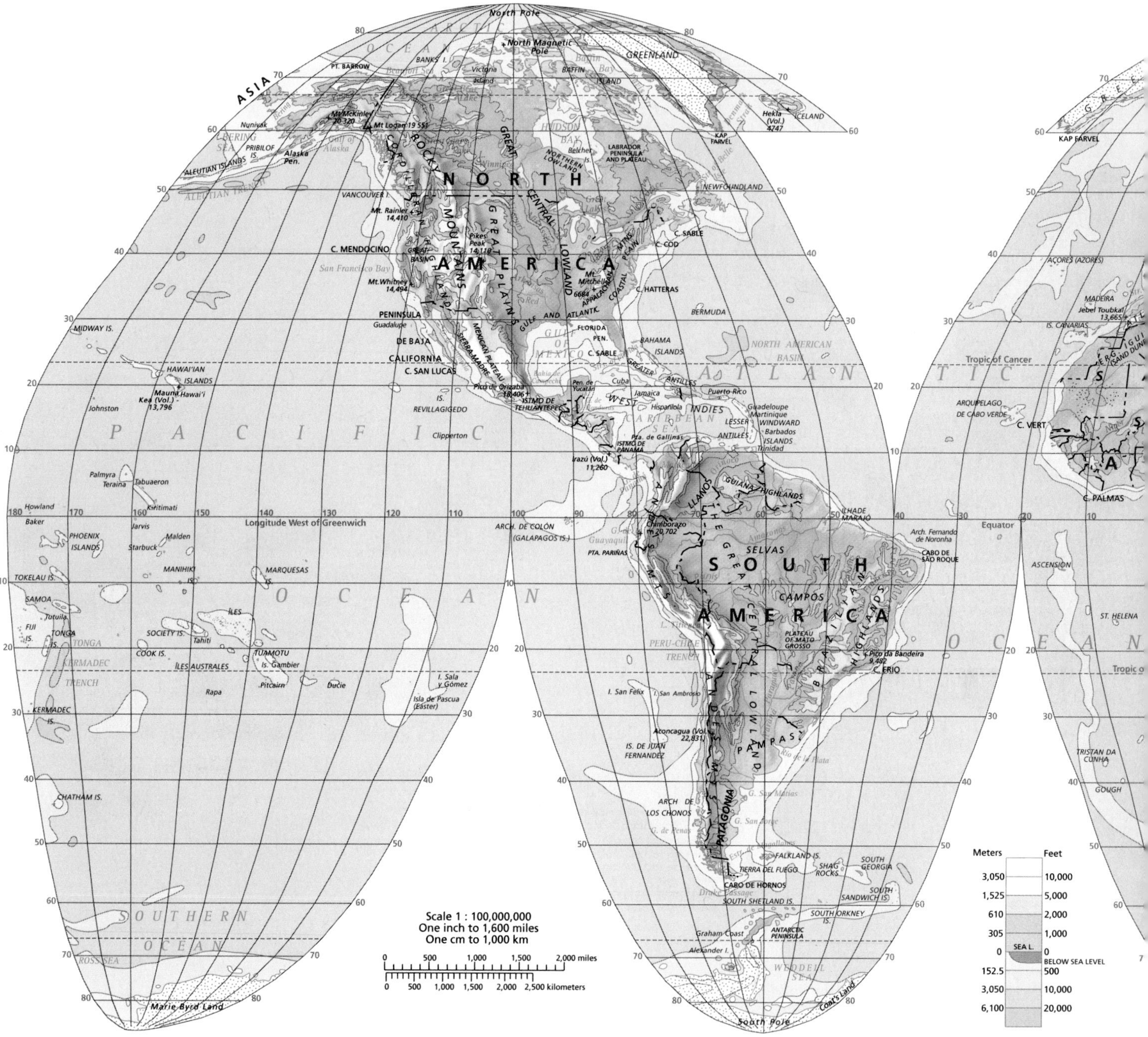

Scale 1 : 100,000,000
One inch to 1,600 miles
One cm to 1,000 km

Meters		Feet
3,050		10,000
1,525		5,000
610		2,000
305		1,000
0	SEA L.	0
		BELOW SEA LEVEL
152.5		500
3,050		10,000
6,100		20,000

Land Elevations in Profile

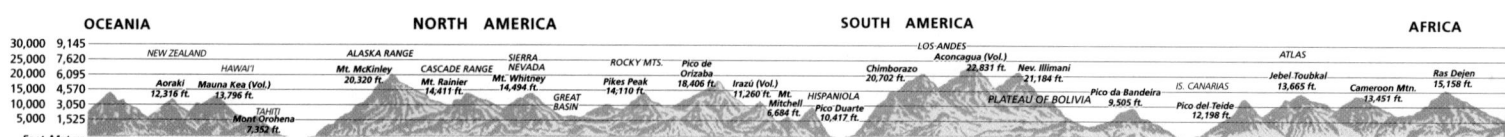

Ocean Depths in Profile

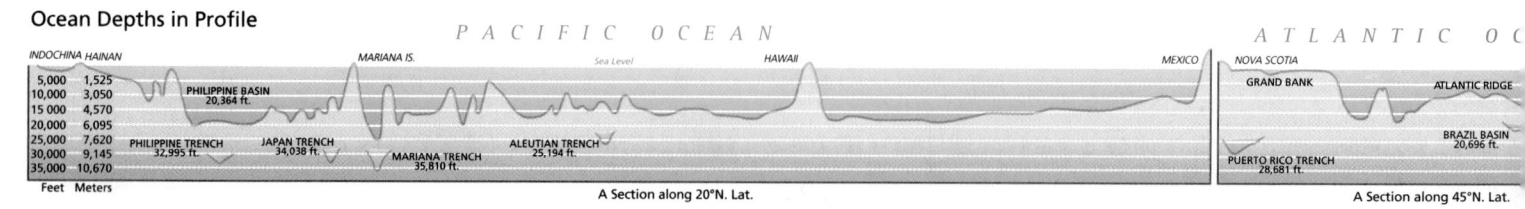

A Section along 20°N. Lat.

A Section along 45°N. Lat.

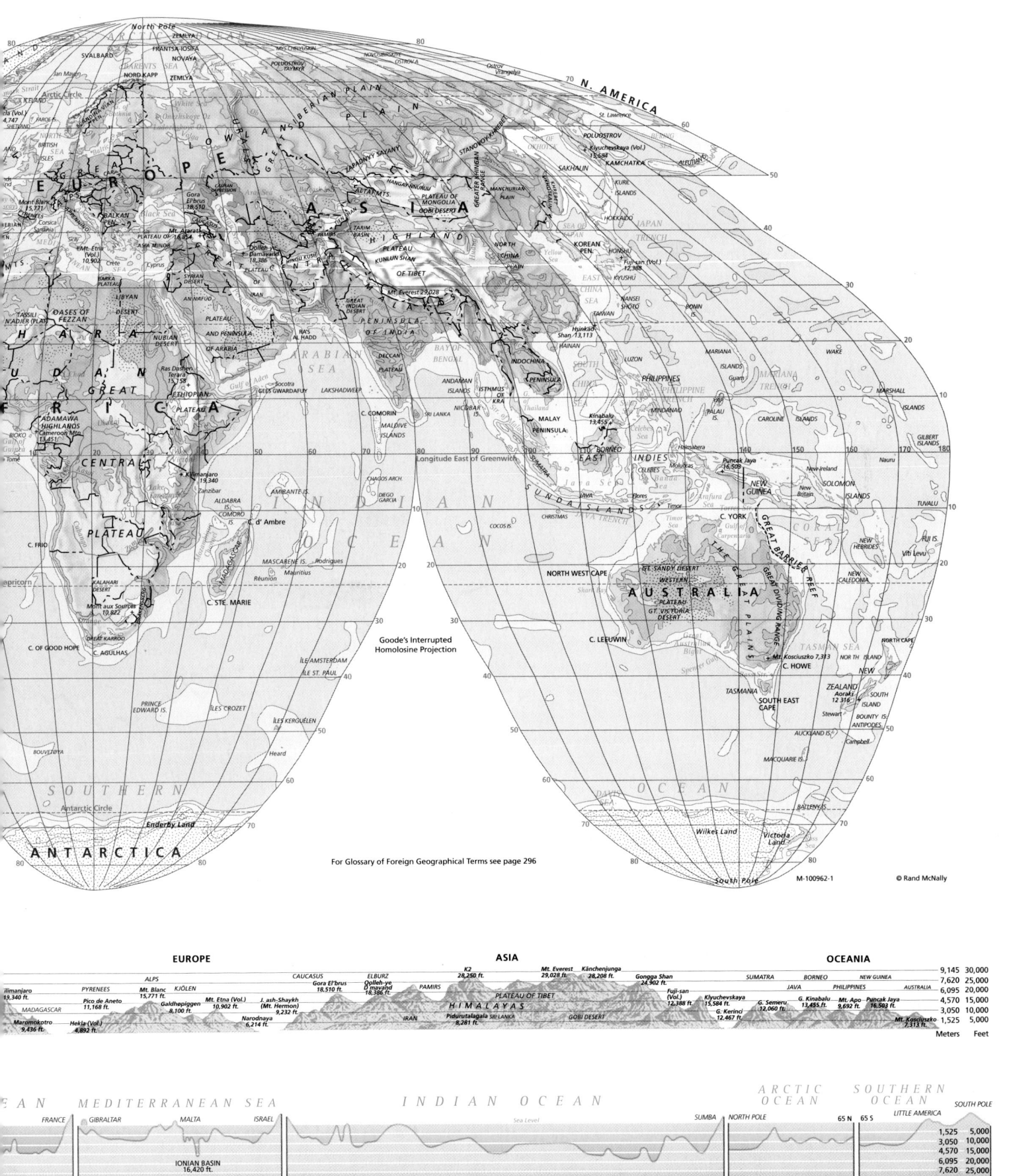

Goode's Interrupted
Homolosine Projection

For Glossary of Foreign Geographical Terms see page 296

M-100962-1

© Rand McNally

A Section along 10°S. Lat.

EVOLUTION OF THE CONTINENTS

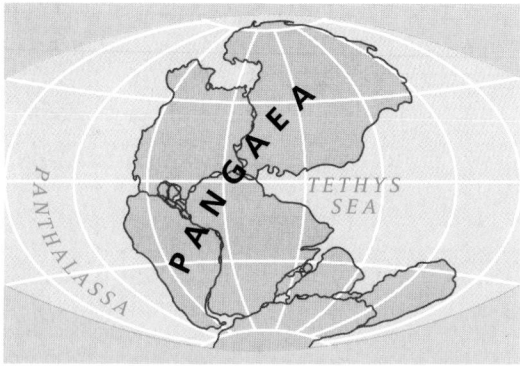

225 million years ago
The supercontinent of Pangaea exists and Panthalassa forms the ancestral ocean. Tethys Sea separates Eurasia and Africa.

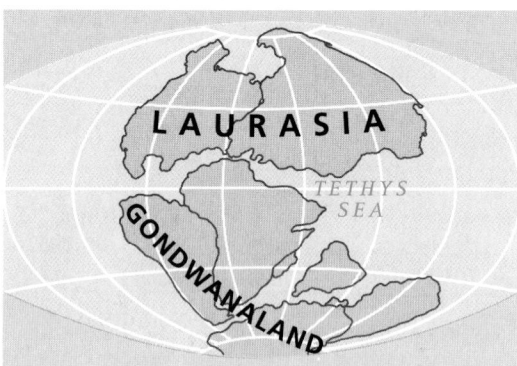

180 million years ago
Pangaea splits, Laurasia drifts north. Gondwanaland breaks into South America/Africa, India, and Australia/Antarctica.

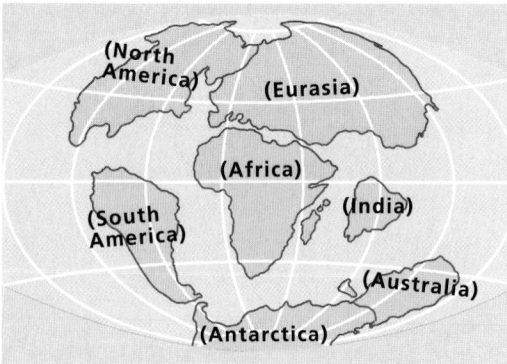

65 million years ago
Ocean basins take shape as South America and India move from Africa and the Tethys Sea closes to form the Mediterranean Sea.

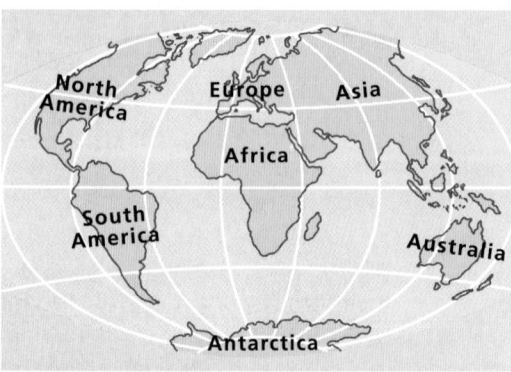

The present day
India has merged with Asia, Australia is free of Antarctica, and North America is free of Eurasia.

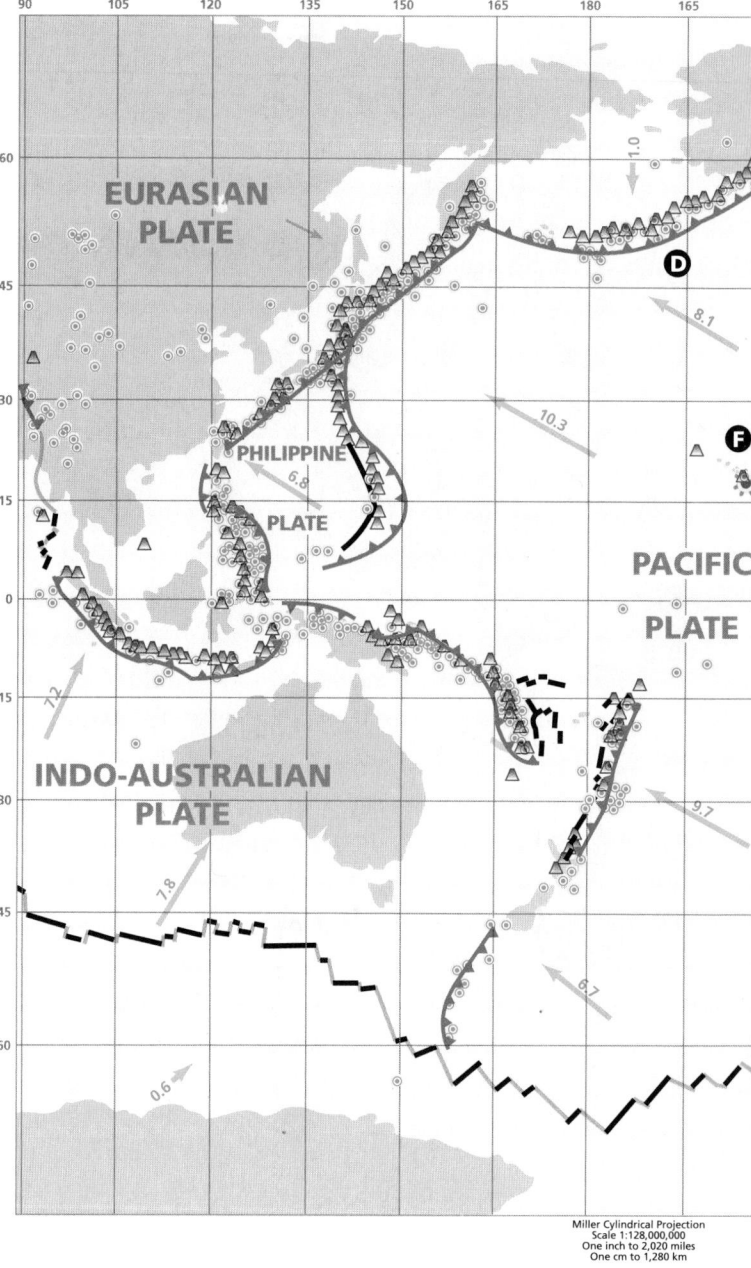

Miller Cylindrical Projection
Scale 1:128,000,000
One inch to 2,020 miles
One cm to 1,280 km

PLATE TECTONICS

Types of plate boundaries
See text at right for explanation

———— Divergent

▲▲▲ Convergent

———— Transform

Other map symbols

→ Direction of plate movement

6.7   Length of arrow is proportional to the amount of plate movement (number indicates centimeters of movement per year)

◉   Earthquake of magnitude 7.5 and above (from 10 A.D. to the present)

△   Volcano (eruption since 1900)

☀   Selected hot spots

A   Key to text descriptions and diagrams

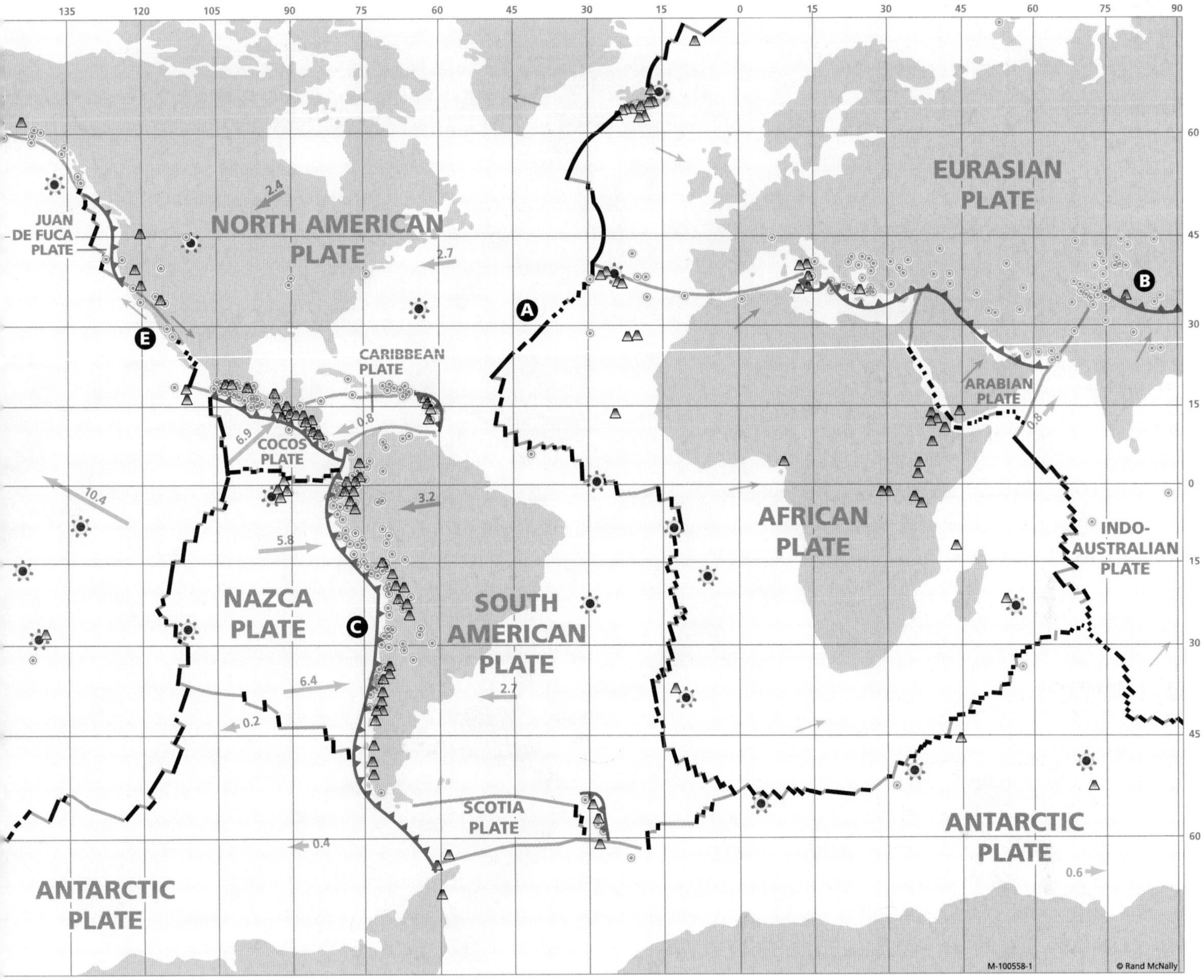

EURASIAN PLATE

JUAN DE FUCA PLATE

NORTH AMERICAN PLATE

2.4

2.7

Ⓔ

CARIBBEAN PLATE

Ⓐ

ARABIAN PLATE

6.9

0.8

0.8

COCOS PLATE

10.4

NAZCA PLATE

3.2

AFRICAN PLATE

INDO-AUSTRALIAN PLATE

5.8

Ⓒ

SOUTH AMERICAN PLATE

6.4

2.7

0.2

SCOTIA PLATE

ANTARCTIC PLATE

0.4

0.6

ANTARCTIC PLATE

Ⓑ

M-100558-1   © Rand McNally

Plate tectonic theory describes the motions of the lithosphere, the outer surface of which forms the Earth's crust. The theory originated with scientist Alfred Wegener's work on continental drift in the early part of the 20th century. According to plate tectonic theory, the lithosphere is composed of distinct plates that move relative to each other as a result of convection currents deep within the Earth's mantle. The largest of these plates and their movements are shown on the map above.

There are three main types of plate boundaries.

Divergent plate boundaries occur where two adjacent plates move away from each other. As the plates separate, upwelling magma from the mantle solidifies, and new crust is formed. (See diagram to the right.) These boundaries frequently make up oceanic ridge zones, such as the Mid-Atlantic Ridge (symbol A on map above). This spreading explains why North and South America have separated from Eurasia and Africa over time, as shown on the map series to the left. The Mid-Atlantic Ridge is actually part of a much larger subaqueous divergent boundary system that encircles the Earth.

Convergent plate boundaries occur where two adjacent plates collide with one another. When two continental plates collide, the resulting compression of lithospheric material causes large mountain ranges to form. The Himalayas, for example, were formed by the collision of the Eurasian and Indo-Australian Plates (symbol B on map above).

In other cases one plate is forced (subducted) under the other and the lithospheric material from the descending plate is recycled within the mantle. These areas are called **subduction zones**.

Subduction zones occur when a continental plate collides with an oceanic plate. An example occurs along the west coast of South America

where the Nazca Plate is being subducted under the South American Plate, creating the long, deep Peru-Chile trench and the Andes mountain chain (symbol C on map above). This area is part of a much larger ring of convergent plate boundaries circling the Pacific and known as the Ring of Fire. Volcanoes and earthquakes are common features in this region.

Subduction zones can also occur when two oceanic plates collide. Intense volcanic activity in these areas eventually results in the formation of long, volcanic island chains. (See diagram to the right.) The Aleutian Islands of Alaska are one example (symbol D on map above).

Transform boundaries occur when two plates slide laterally past each other with no divergence or convergence. Commonly they offset the active spreading ridges of divergent boundaries on the ocean floor. The San Andreas fault zone of California is an example of a terrestrial transform boundary (symbol E on map above).

Volcanoes and earthquakes do not occur only at plate boundaries. At certain isolated **hot spots**, upwelling magma rises to the surface to create tall volcanoes. Over time, as the plate moves, long islands chains are formed. The Hawai'ian Islands are one such example (symbol F on map above).

The rate of movement of tectonic plates is very slow, on the order of several centimeters per year. Over geological time, these small movements accumulate and cause fragmentation and reformation of continental land masses, as shown in the map series to the left. The process is still underway, which implies that the arrangement of the continents millions of years from now will be quite different from what it is today.

Convergent plate boundary
Island arc subduction zone
(symbol Ⓓ on map)

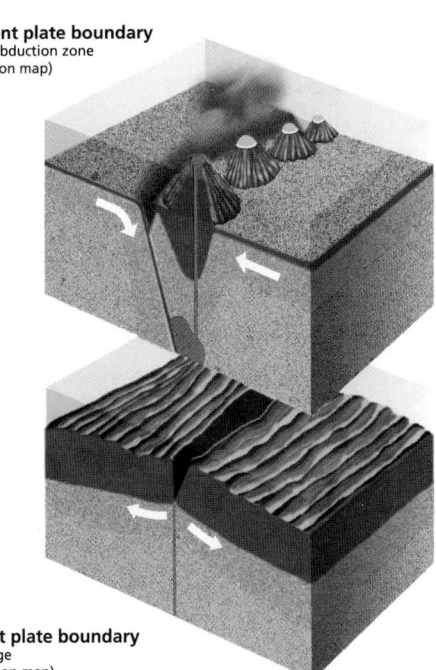

Divergent plate boundary
Oceanic ridge
(symbol Ⓐ on map)

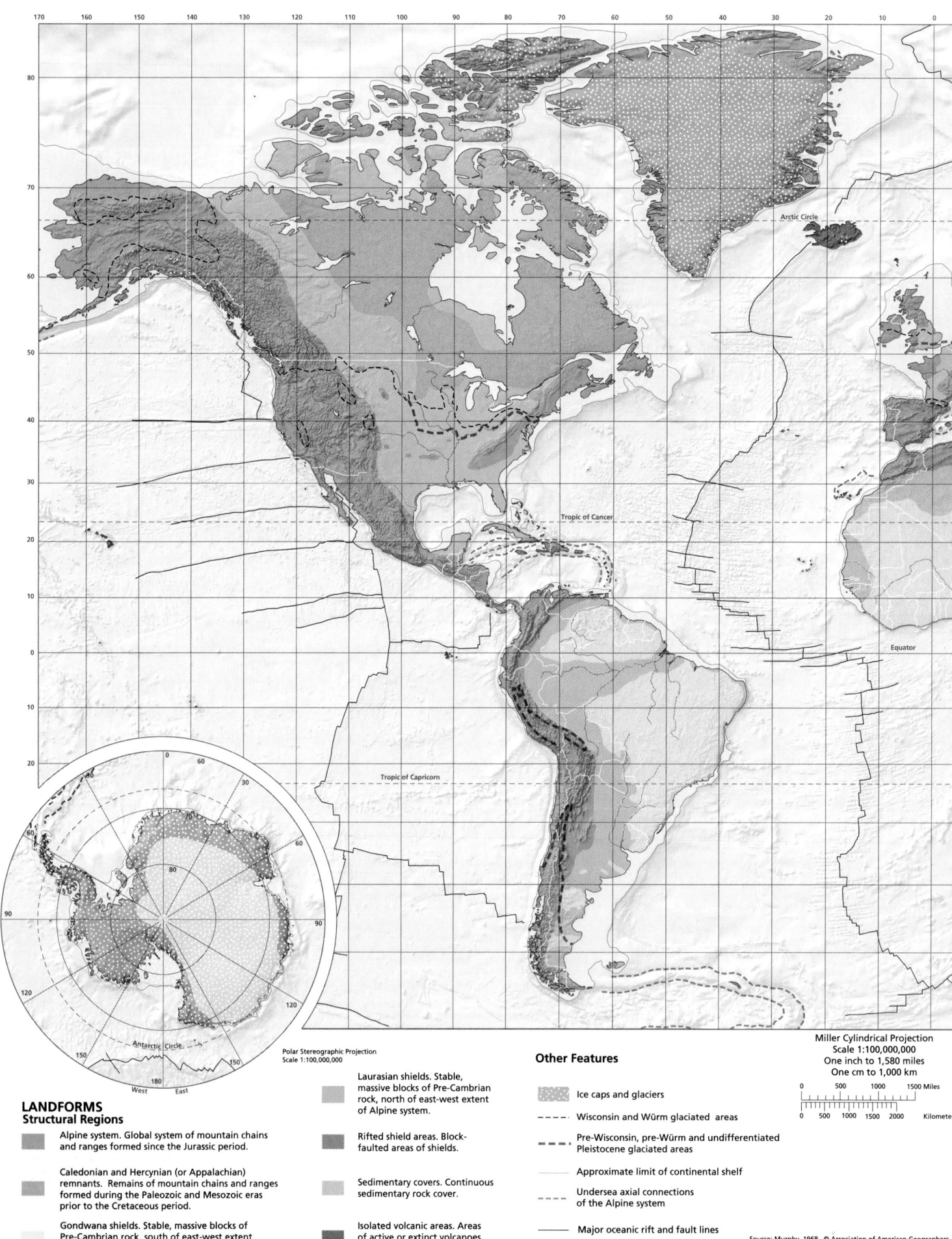

LANDFORMS
Structural Regions

Alpine system. Global system of mountain chains and ranges formed since the Jurassic period.

Caledonian and Hercynian (or Appalachian) remnants. Remains of mountain chains and ranges formed during the Paleozoic and Mesozoic eras prior to the Cretaceous period.

Gondwana shields. Stable, massive blocks of Pre-Cambrian rock, south of east-west extent of Alpine system.

Laurasian shields. Stable, massive blocks of Pre-Cambrian rock, north of east-west extent of Alpine system.

Rifted shield areas. Block-faulted areas of shields.

Sedimentary covers. Continuous sedimentary rock cover.

Isolated volcanic areas. Areas of active or extinct volcanoes and associated features.

Other Features

Ice caps and glaciers

- - - - Wisconsin and Würm glaciated areas

▬ ▬ ▬ Pre-Wisconsin, pre-Würm and undifferentiated Pleistocene glaciated areas

Approximate limit of continental shelf

- - - - Undersea axial connections of the Alpine system

Major oceanic rift and fault lines

Polar Stereographic Projection
Scale 1:100,000,000

Miller Cylindrical Projection
Scale 1:100,000,000
One inch to 1,580 miles
One cm to 1,000 km

| 0 | 500 | 1000 | 1500 Miles |
| 0 | 500 | 1000 | 1500 | 2000 Kilometers |

Source: Murphy, 1968. © Association of American Geographers.
Published by Taylor & Francis. Adapted with permission of the Association of American Geographers.

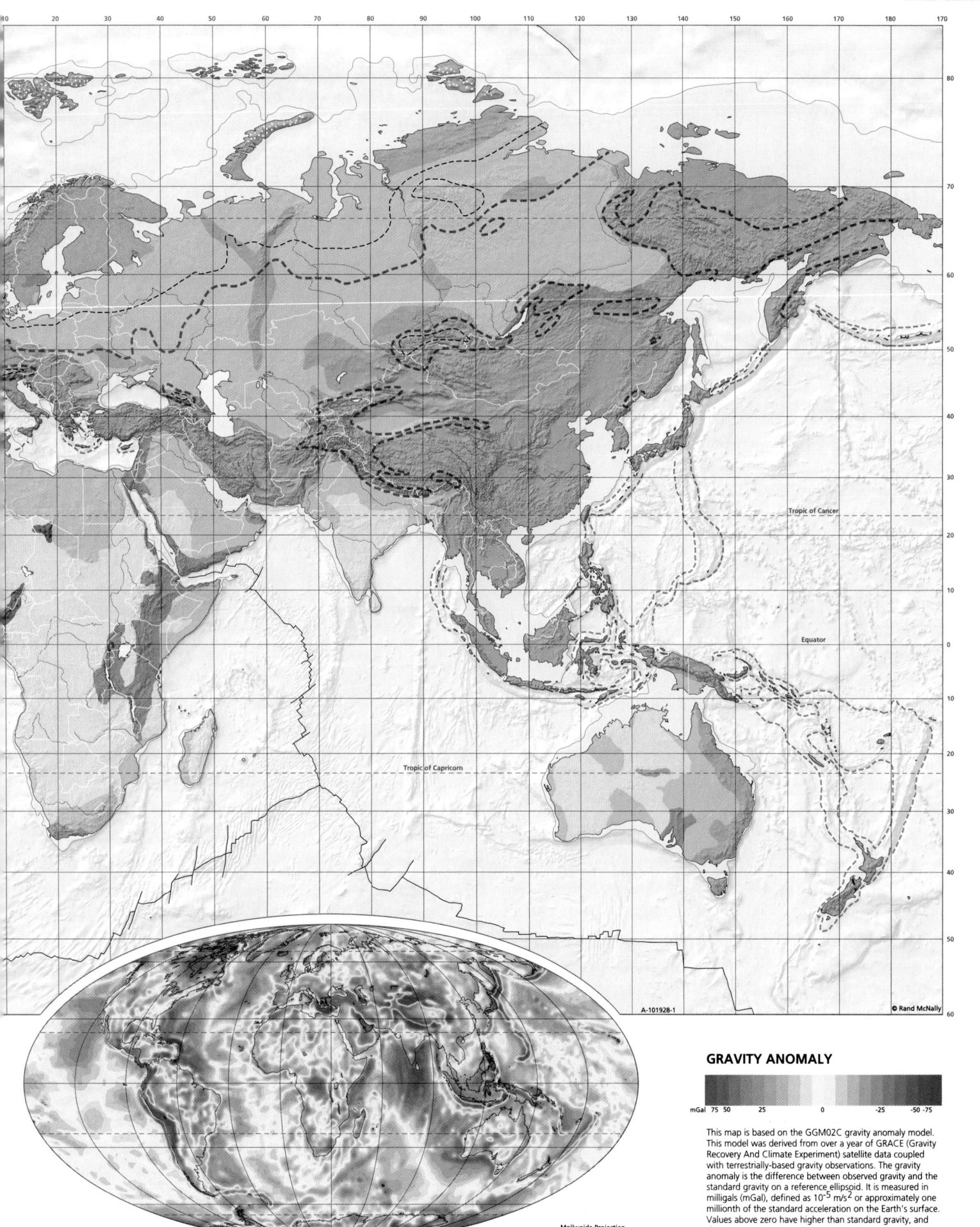

Mollweide Projection
Scale 1:275,000,000
Source: Tapley et al., 2005

A-101928-1

© Rand McNally

GRAVITY ANOMALY

mGal 75 50   25   0   -25   -50 -75

This map is based on the GGM02C gravity anomaly model.
This model was derived from over a year of GRACE (Gravity
Recovery And Climate Experiment) satellite data coupled
with terrestrially-based gravity observations. The gravity
anomaly is the difference between observed gravity and the
standard gravity on a reference ellipsoid. It is measured in
milligals (mGal), defined as 10^{-5} m/s^2 or approximately one
millionth of the standard acceleration on the Earth's surface.
Values above zero have higher than standard gravity, and
vice versa.

Chukchi Sea

Anadyr

Bering Strait

UNITED STATES

Anchorage

Aleutian Basin

Bering Sea

ALEUTIAN ISLANDS

Aleutian Trench

Gulf of Alaska

Prince Rupert

Gulf of Alaska Seamount Province

Seattle

CANADA

NORTH AMERICA

Hudson Bay

GREENLAND (Denmark)

Arctic Circle

Irminger Basin

Labrador Sea

Labrador Basin

NEWFOUNDLAND

Emperor Seamounts

Mendocino Fracture Zone

San Francisco

Los Angeles

Columbia

Missouri

Chicago

New York

Washington

ATLANTIC OCEAN

North American Basin

PACIFIC

OCEAN

Musicians Seamounts

Murray Fracture Zone

UNITED STATES

Mississippi

BERMUDA (Br.)

Hawaiian Ridge

Honolulu

HAWAIIAN ISLANDS

Molokai Fracture Zone

UNITED STATES

MEXICO

New Orleans

Gulf of Mexico

Mexico Basin

Havana

BAHAMAS

Tropic of Cancer

Mexico City

Campeche Bank

CUBA

HAITI

DOM. REP.

Blake Plateau

Mountains

Christmas Ridge

Clarion Fracture Zone

BELIZE

GUAT. HOND.

NIC.

Caribbean Sea

Venezuelan Basin

MARSHALL ISLANDS

Central Pacific Basin

Clipperton Fracture Zone

Middle America Trench

Guatemala Basin

COSTA RICA

PANAMA

VENEZUELA

Colón Ridge

Cocos Ridge

Panama Basin

Bogotá

COLOMBIA

NAURU

KIRIBATI

LINE ISLANDS

GALAPAGOS ISLANDS (Ec.)

ECUADOR

Equator

SOUTH

PHOENIX ISLANDS

PERU

BRAZIL

SOLOMON ISLANDS

TUVALU

TOKELAU (N.Z.)

AMERICA

SANTA CRUZ ISLANDS

WALLIS AND FUTUNA (Fr.)

SAMOA

COOK ISLANDS (N.Z.)

Lima

NUATU

North Fiji Basin

AMER. SAMOA

FRENCH POLYNESIA

Peru Basin

NEW HEBRIDES

FIJI

NIUE (N.Z.)

Tuamotu Ridge

TAHITI

Nazca Ridge

BOLIVIA

Tropic of Capricorn

NEW CALEDONIA (Fr.)

South Fiji Basin

TONGA

PITCAIRN (Br.)

Sala y Gomez Ridge

EASTER ISLAND (Chile)

EAST PACIFIC RISE

Peru-Chile Trench

CHILE

NORFOLK ISLAND (Austl.)

Lau Ridge

Tonga Ridge

Austral Seamounts

ARCHIPIÉLAGO JUAN FERNANDEZ (Chile)

Santiago

New Caledonia Basin

New Hebrides Trench

Kermadec Ridge

Kermadec Trench

Tonga Trench

Southwest Pacific Basin

PACIFIC

OCEAN

Chile Rise

Peru-Chile Trench

ARGENTINA

we Rise

Norfolk Ridge

Louisville Ridge

POLYNESIA

Auckland

NEW ZEALAND

NORTH ISLAND

Chatham Rise

SOUTH ISLAND

Bounty Trough

Campbell Plateau

BOUNTY ISLANDS

ANTIPODES ISLANDS

CAMPBELL ISLAND

Southwest Pacific Basin

Argentine Basin

FALKLAND ISLANDS (Br.)

Scotia Ridge

JCKLAND ISLANDS

Pacific - Antarctic Ridge

SOUTH SHETLAND ISLANDS (Br.)

Balleny Basin

OCEAN

Ross Sea

Amundsen Sea

Southeast Pacific Basin

Weddell Sea

Atlantic - Indian Basin

Antarctic Circle

Aptarctic Peninsula

M-100932-1

© Rand McNally

Robinson Projection
Scale 1:73,000,000
One inch to 1,200 miles
One cm to 730 km

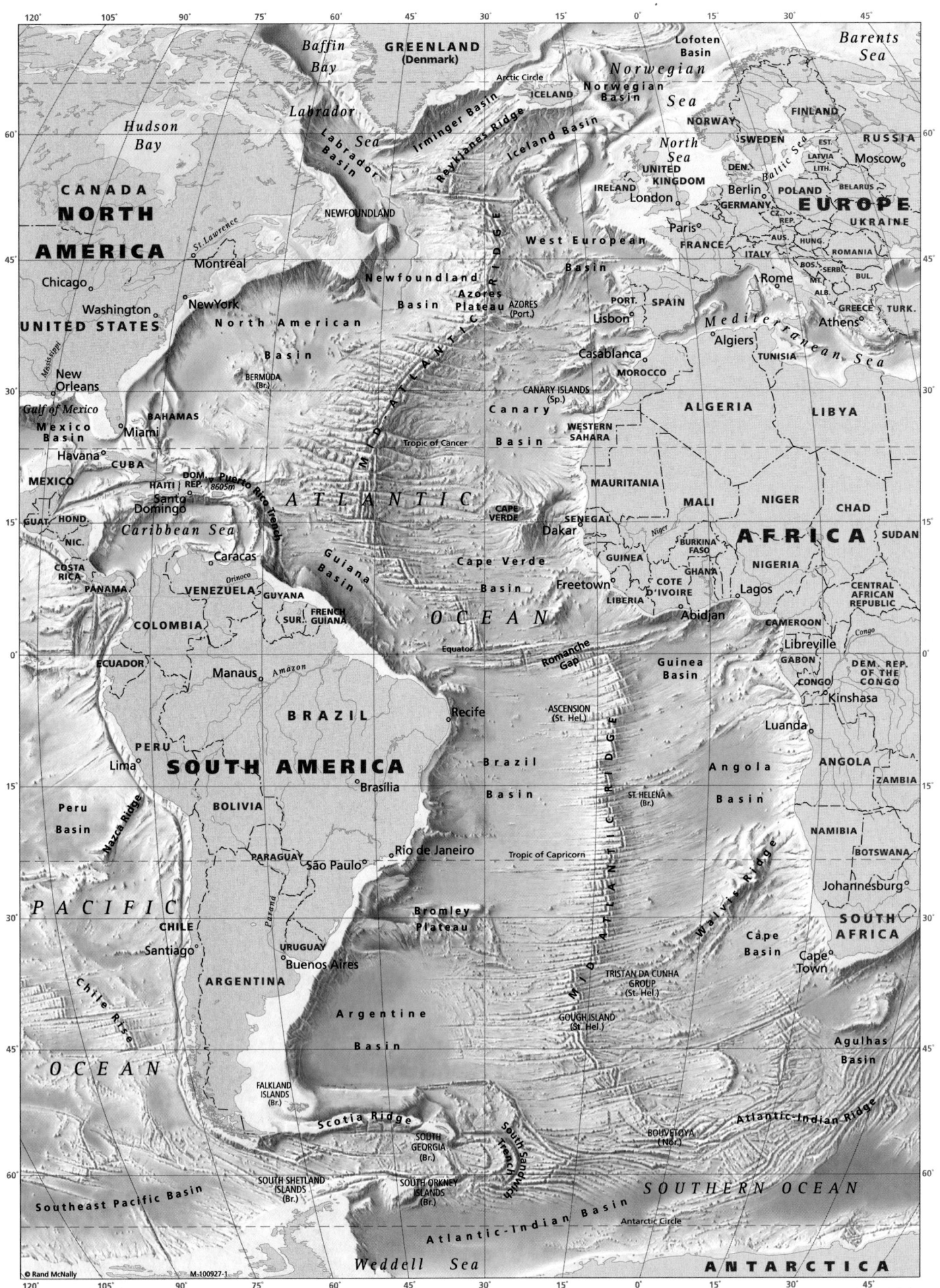

Robinson Projection
Scale 1:73,000,000
One inch to 1,200 miles
One cm to 730 km

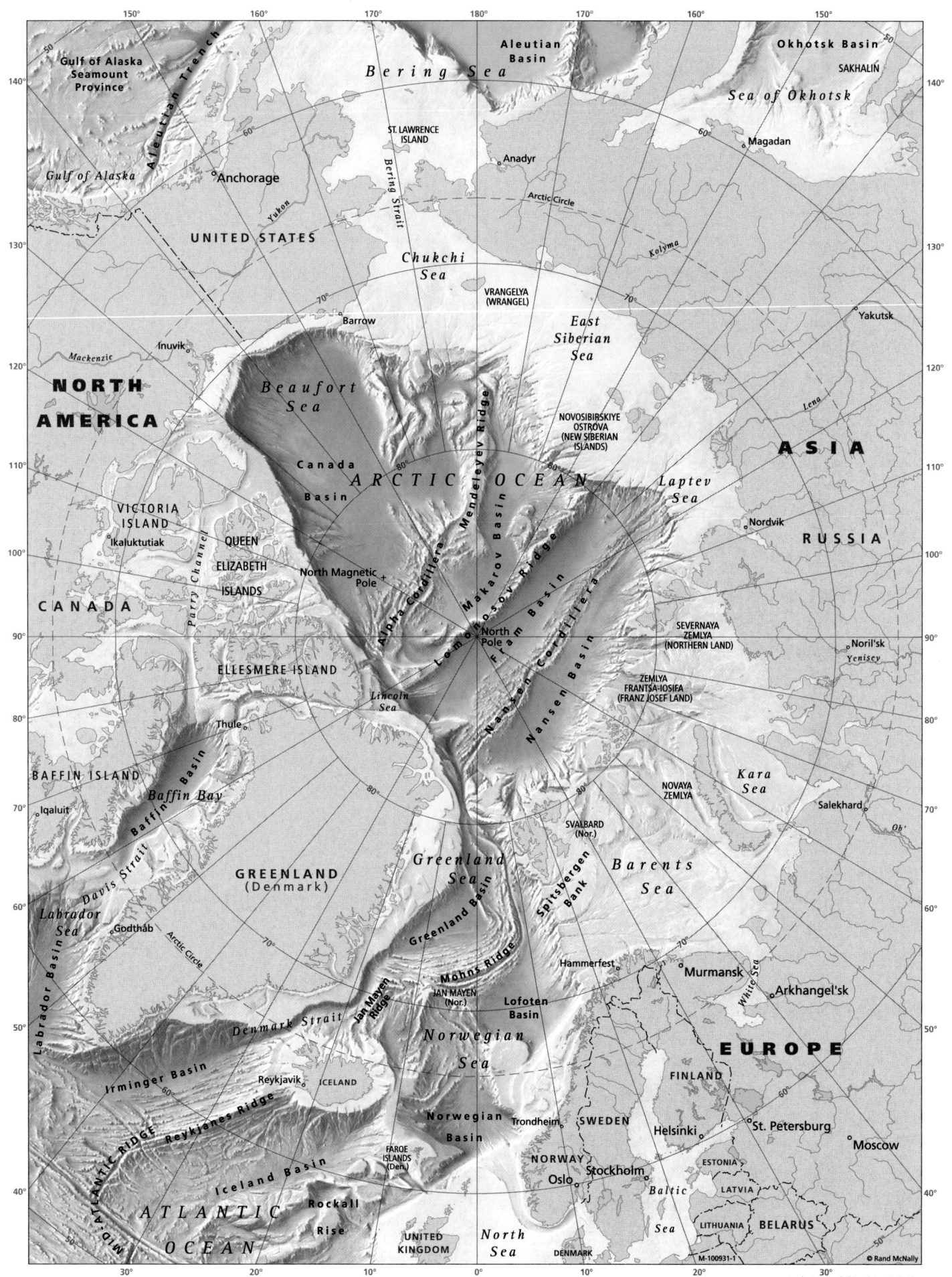

Lambert Azimuthal Equal Area Projection
Scale 1:30,000,000
One inch to 500 miles
One cm to 300 cm

© Rand McNally

M-100931-1

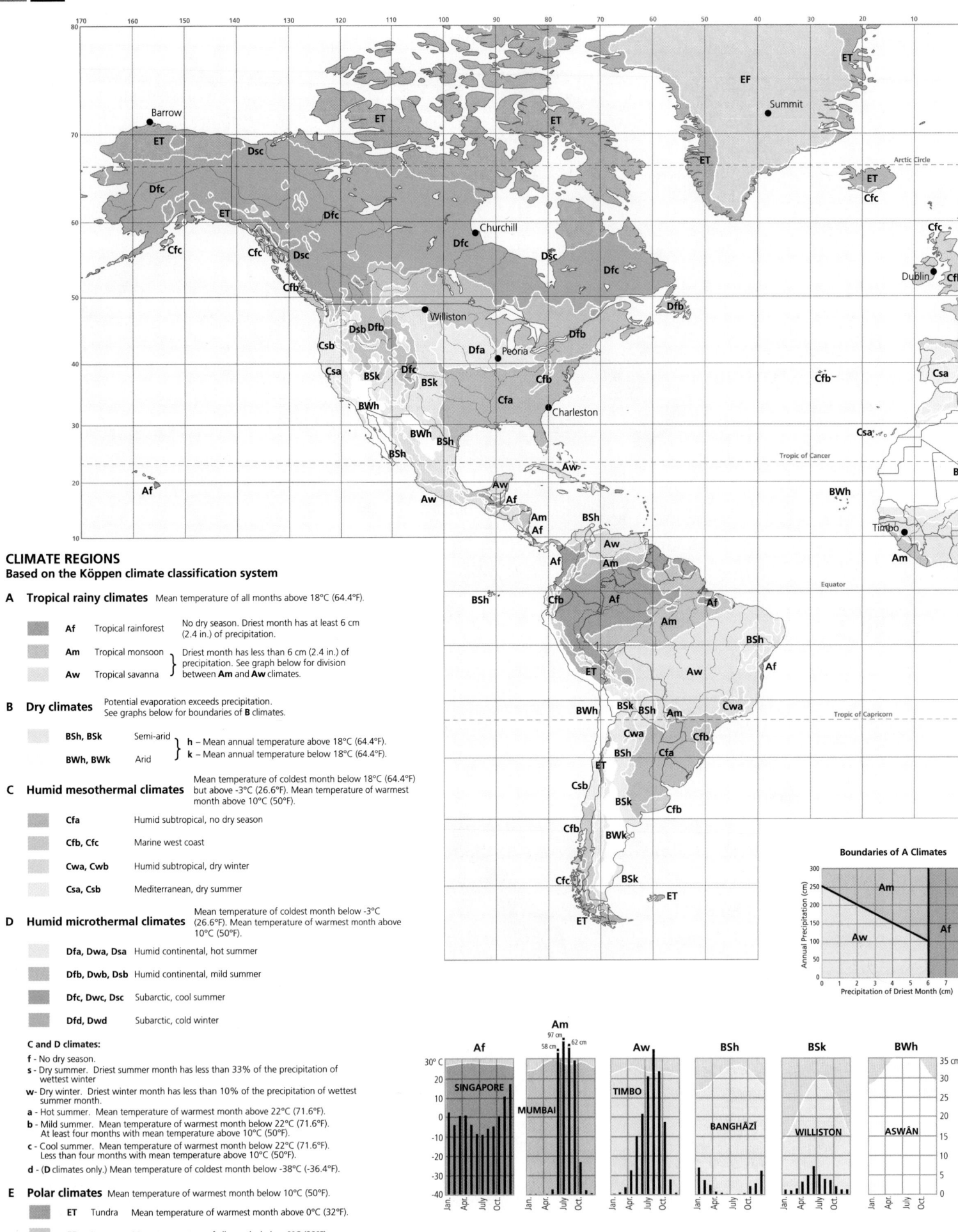

CLIMATE REGIONS
Based on the Köppen climate classification system

A Tropical rainy climates Mean temperature of all months above 18°C (64.4°F).

	Af	Tropical rainforest	No dry season. Driest month has at least 6 cm (2.4 in.) of precipitation.
	Am	Tropical monsoon	Driest month has less than 6 cm (2.4 in.) of precipitation. See graph below for division between **Am** and **Aw** climates.
	Aw	Tropical savanna	

B Dry climates Potential evaporation exceeds precipitation. See graphs below for boundaries of **B** climates.

	BSh, BSk	Semi-arid	h – Mean annual temperature above 18°C (64.4°F).
	BWh, BWk	Arid	k – Mean annual temperature below 18°C (64.4°F).

C Humid mesothermal climates Mean temperature of coldest month below 18°C (64.4°F) but above -3°C (26.6°F). Mean temperature of warmest month above 10°C (50°F).

	Cfa	Humid subtropical, no dry season
	Cfb, Cfc	Marine west coast
	Cwa, Cwb	Humid subtropical, dry winter
	Csa, Csb	Mediterranean, dry summer

D Humid microthermal climates Mean temperature of coldest month below -3°C (26.6°F). Mean temperature of warmest month above 10°C (50°F).

	Dfa, Dwa, Dsa	Humid continental, hot summer
	Dfb, Dwb, Dsb	Humid continental, mild summer
	Dfc, Dwc, Dsc	Subarctic, cool summer
	Dfd, Dwd	Subarctic, cold winter

C and D climates:

f - No dry season.
s - Dry summer. Driest summer month has less than 33% of the precipitation of wettest winter
w - Dry winter. Driest winter month has less than 10% of the precipitation of wettest summer month.
a - Hot summer. Mean temperature of warmest month above 22°C (71.6°F).
b - Mild summer. Mean temperature of warmest month below 22°C (71.6°F). At least four months with mean temperature above 10°C (50°F).
c - Cool summer. Mean temperature of warmest month below 22°C (71.6°F). Less than four months with mean temperature above 10°C (50°F).
d - (D climates only.) Mean temperature of coldest month below -38°C (-36.4°F).

E Polar climates Mean temperature of warmest month below 10°C (50°F).

	ET	Tundra	Mean temperature of warmest month above 0°C (32°F).
	EF	Icecap	Mean temperature of all months below 0°C (32°F).

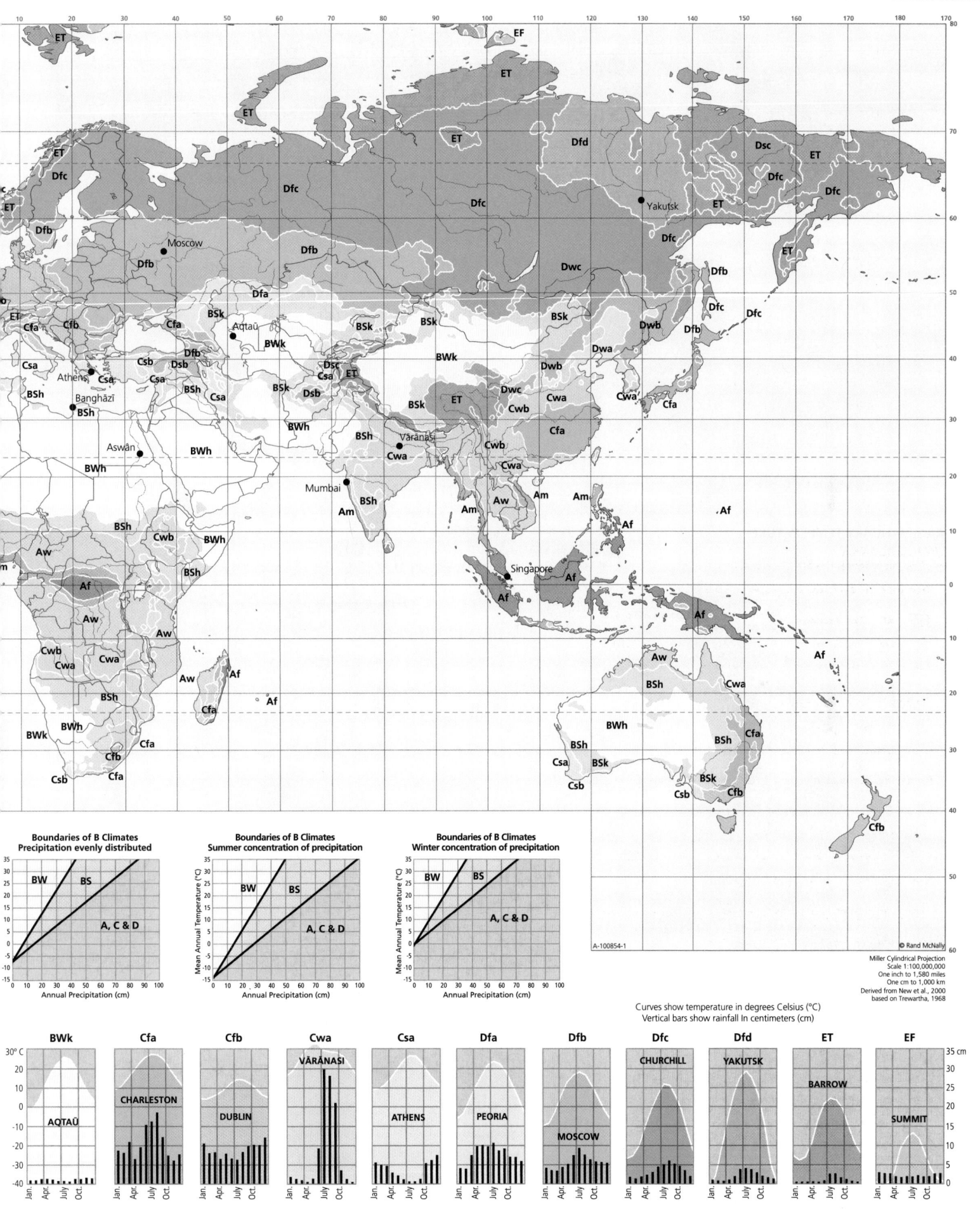

Boundaries of B Climates
Precipitation evenly distributed

Boundaries of B Climates
Summer concentration of precipitation

Boundaries of B Climates
Winter concentration of precipitation

A-100854-1   © Rand McNally

Miller Cylindrical Projection
Scale 1:100,000,000
One inch to 1,580 miles
One cm to 1,000 km
Derived from New et al., 2000
based on Trewartha, 1968

Curves show temperature in degrees Celsius (°C)
Vertical bars show rainfall In centimeters (cm)

BWk — AQTAŪ
Cfa — CHARLESTON
Cfb — DUBLIN
Cwa — VĀRĀNASI
Csa — ATHENS
Dfa — PEORIA
Dfb — MOSCOW
Dfc — CHURCHILL
Dfd — YAKUTSK
ET — BARROW
EF — SUMMIT

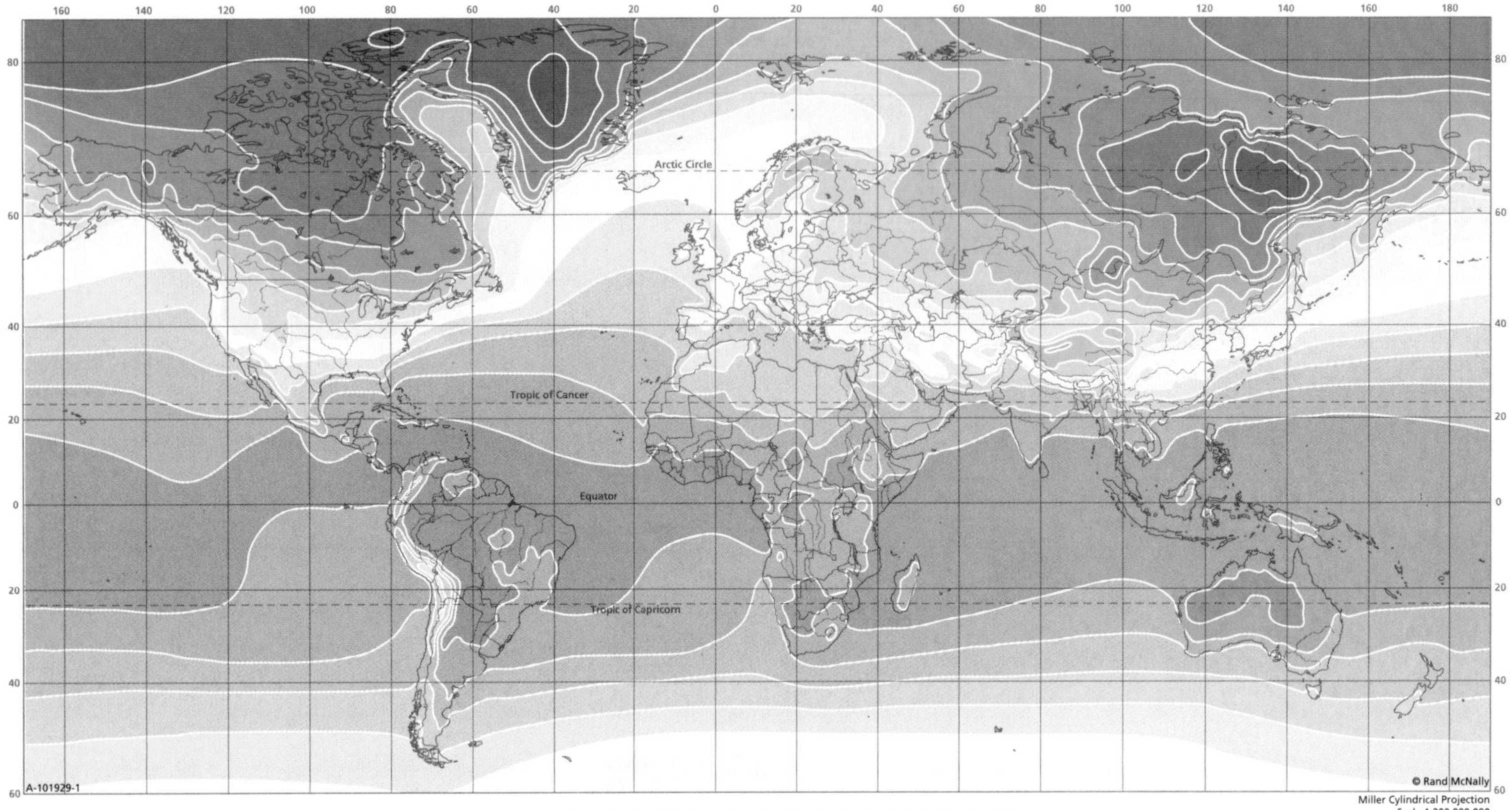

AVERAGE JANUARY TEMPERATURE

A-101929-1

© Rand McNally

Miller Cylindrical Projection
Scale 1:200,000,000
Sources: New et al., 2000; NOAA

°C	-45	-40	-35	-30	-25	-20	-15	-10	-5	0	5	10	15	20	25	30
°F	-49	-40	-31	-22	-13	-4	5	14	23	32	41	50	59	68	77	86

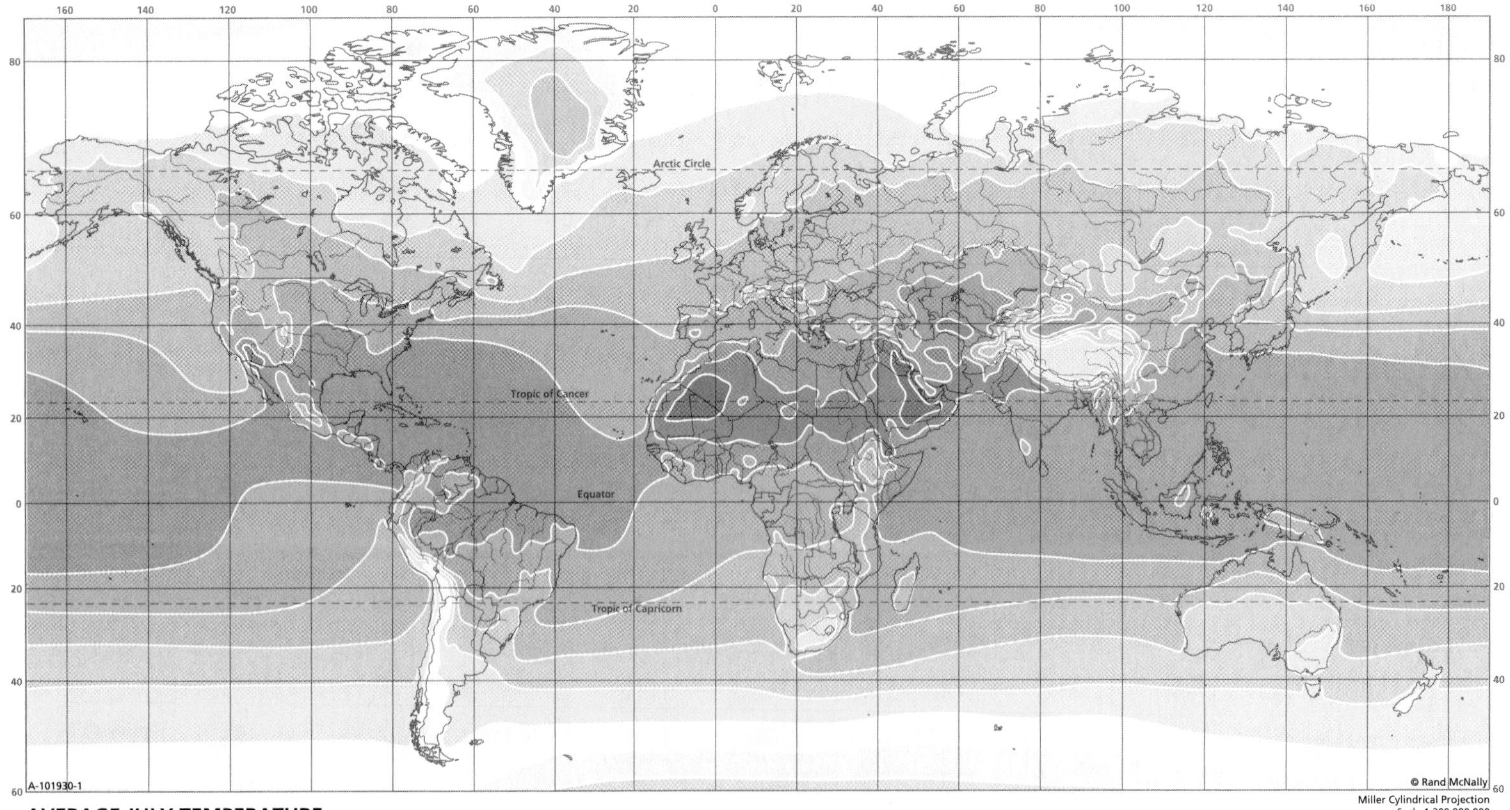

AVERAGE JULY TEMPERATURE

A-101930-1

© Rand McNally

Miller Cylindrical Projection
Scale 1:200,000,000
Sources: New et al., 2000; NOAA

°C	-10	-5	0	5	10	15	20	25	30	35
°F		14	23	32	41	50	59	68	77	86	95

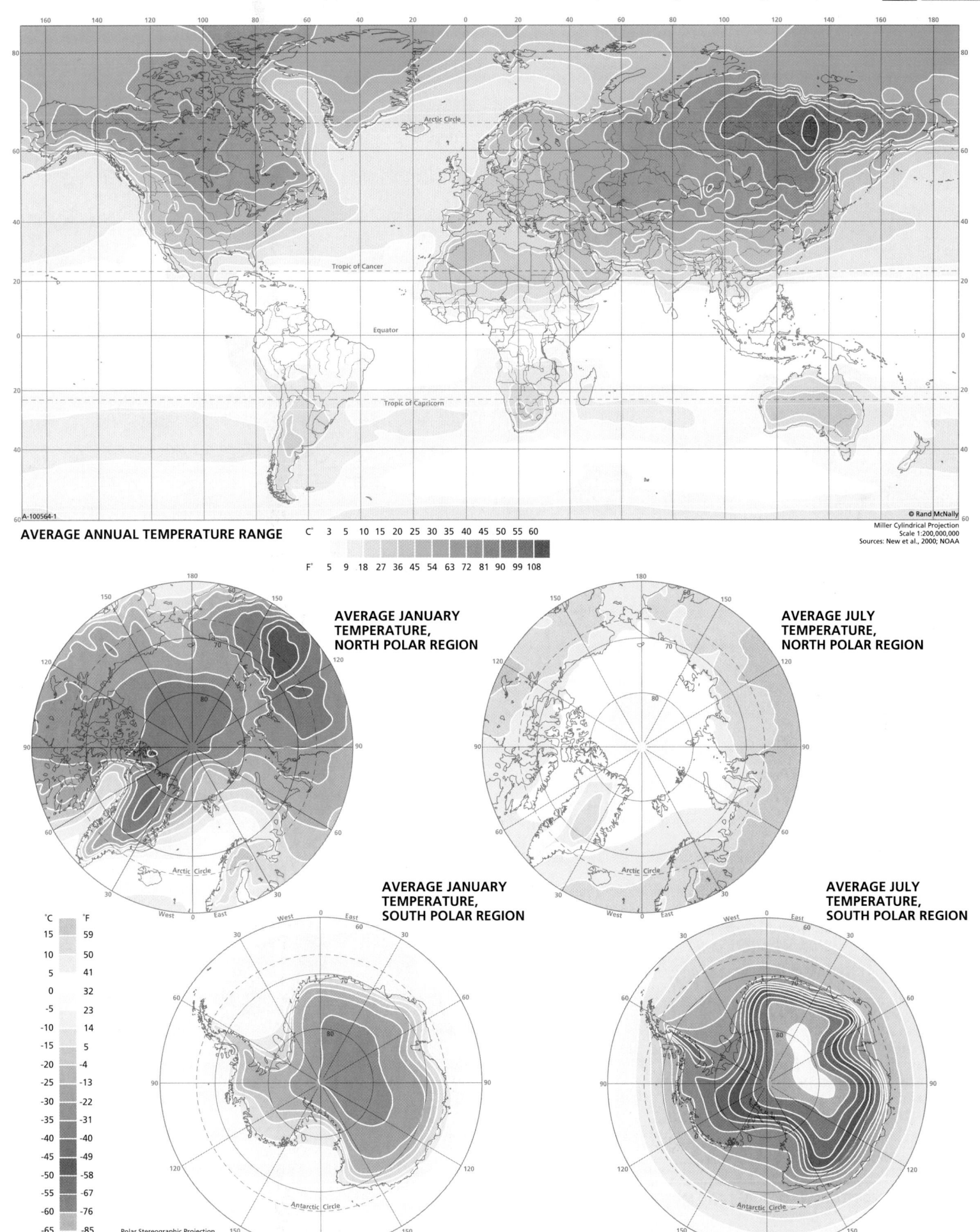

AVERAGE ANNUAL TEMPERATURE RANGE

C°	3	5	10	15	20	25	30	35	40	45	50	55	60

F°	5	9	18	27	36	45	54	63	72	81	90	99	108

Miller Cylindrical Projection
Scale 1:200,000,000
Sources: New et al., 2000; NOAA

© Rand McNally

A-100564-1

AVERAGE JANUARY TEMPERATURE, NORTH POLAR REGION

AVERAGE JULY TEMPERATURE, NORTH POLAR REGION

AVERAGE JANUARY TEMPERATURE, SOUTH POLAR REGION

AVERAGE JULY TEMPERATURE, SOUTH POLAR REGION

°C	°F
15	59
10	50
5	41
0	32
-5	23
-10	14
-15	5
-20	-4
-25	-13
-30	-22
-35	-31
-40	-40
-45	-49
-50	-58
-55	-67
-60	-76
-65	-85

Polar Stereographic Projection
Scale 1:100,000,000
Sources: New et al., 2000; NOAA

© Rand McNally
A-101983-1

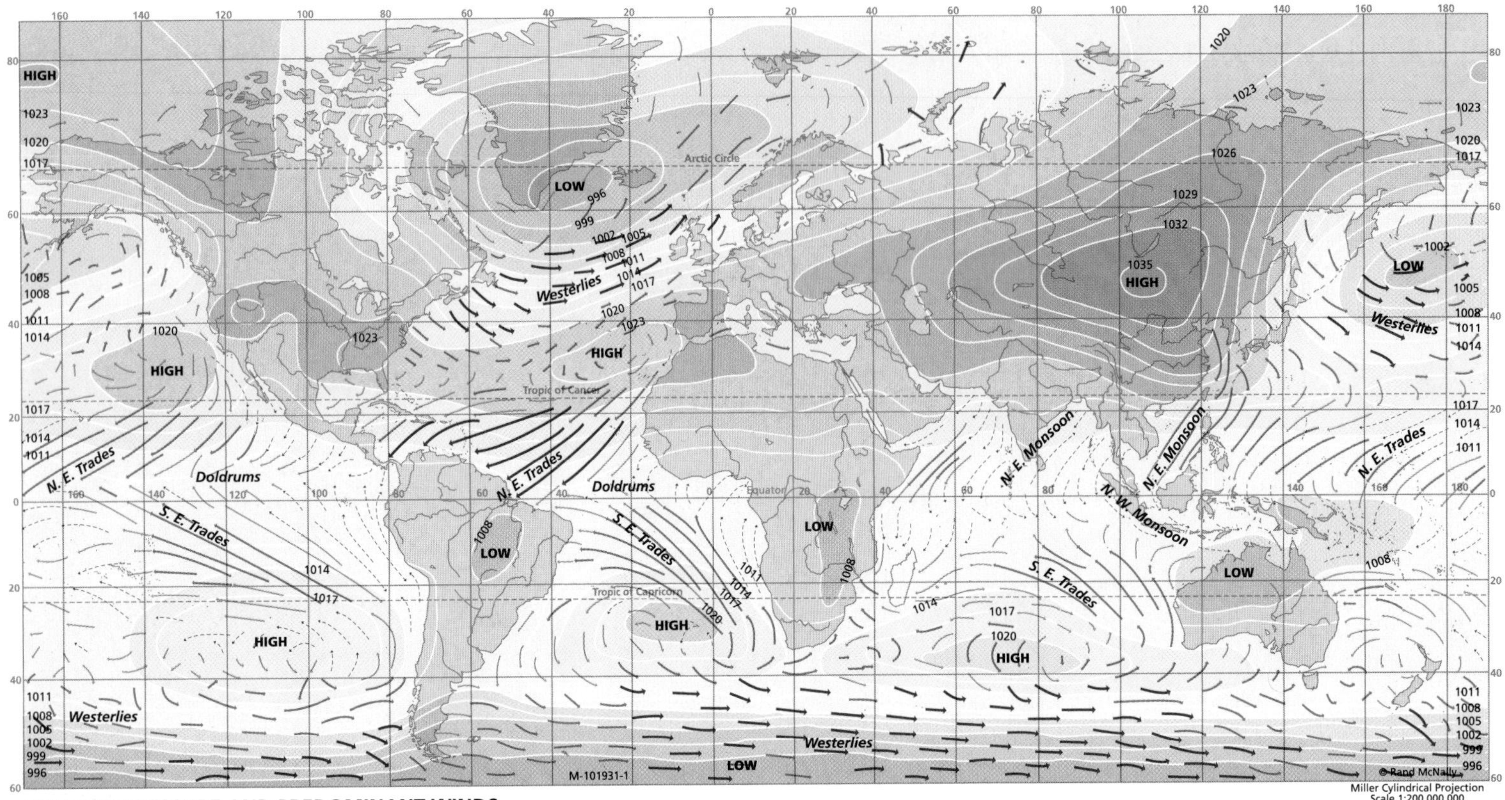

JANUARY PRESSURE AND PREDOMINANT WINDS

Atmospheric Pressure
in millibars (mb)

↓ Normal sea-level pressure (1013.25 mb)

| 1032 | 1026 | 1020 | 1014 | 1008 | 1002 | 996 |

Isobars on map at intervals of 3 millibars

Wind Speed

Kilometers per hour (kph)	Miles per hour (mph)
0-16	0-10
19-24	10-15
24-40	15-25
Over 40	Over 25

Direction of arrow indicates dominant wind direction.
Length of arrow indicates steadiness of wind.

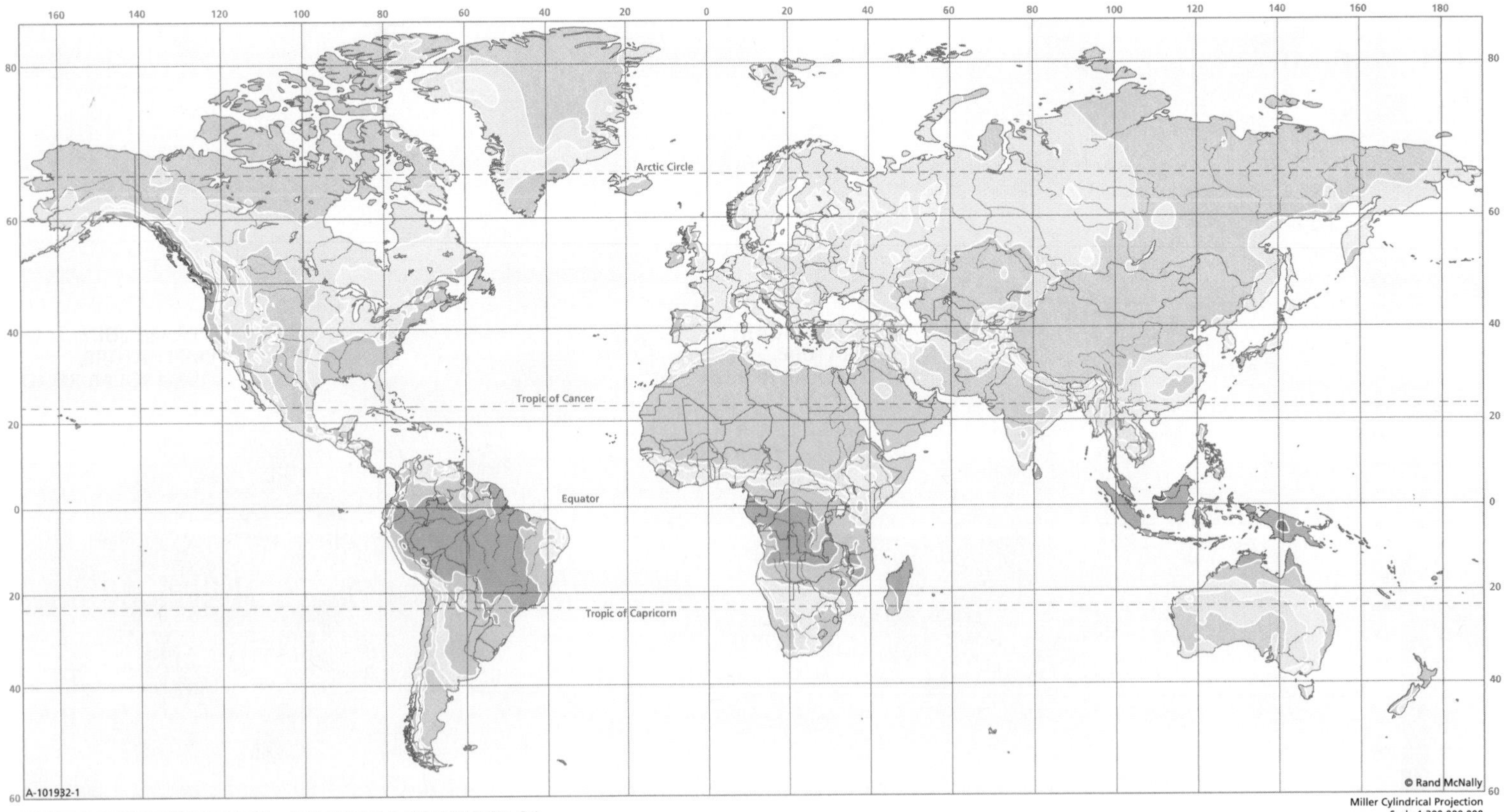

AVERAGE PRECIPITATION - OCTOBER 1 TO MARCH 31

12.5	25	50	100	200	Centimeters
5	10	20	40	80	Inches

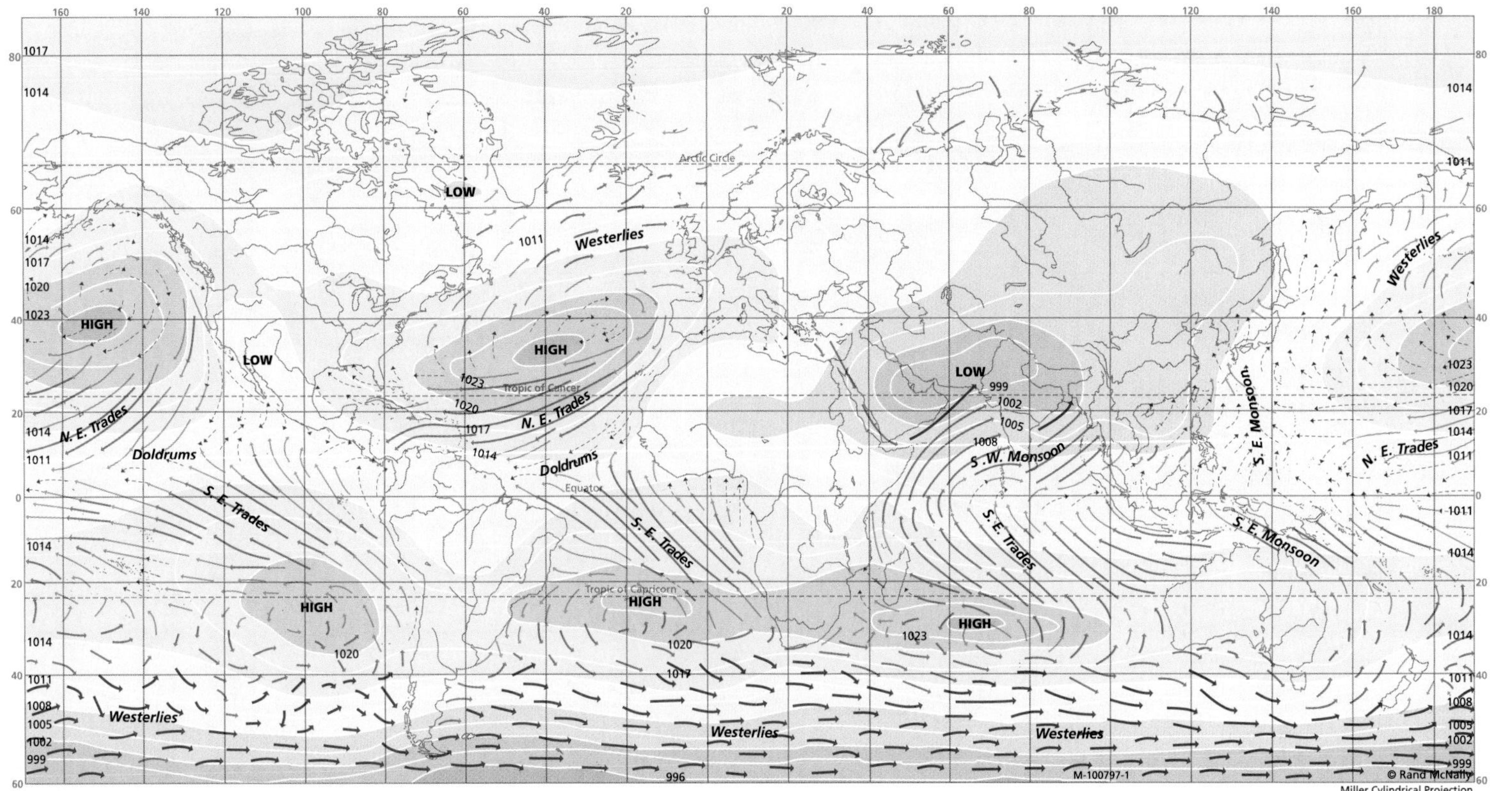

JULY PRESSURE AND PREDOMINANT WINDS

Atmospheric Pressure
in millibars (mb)

Normal sea-level pressure (1013.25 mb)

1026 1020 1014 1008 1002 996

Isobars on map at intervals of 3 millibars

Wind Speed

Kilometers per hour (kph)	Miles per hour (mph)
0-16	0-10
19-24	10-15
24-40	15-25
Over 40	Over 25

Direction of arrow indicates dominant wind direction.
Length of arrow indicates steadiness of wind.

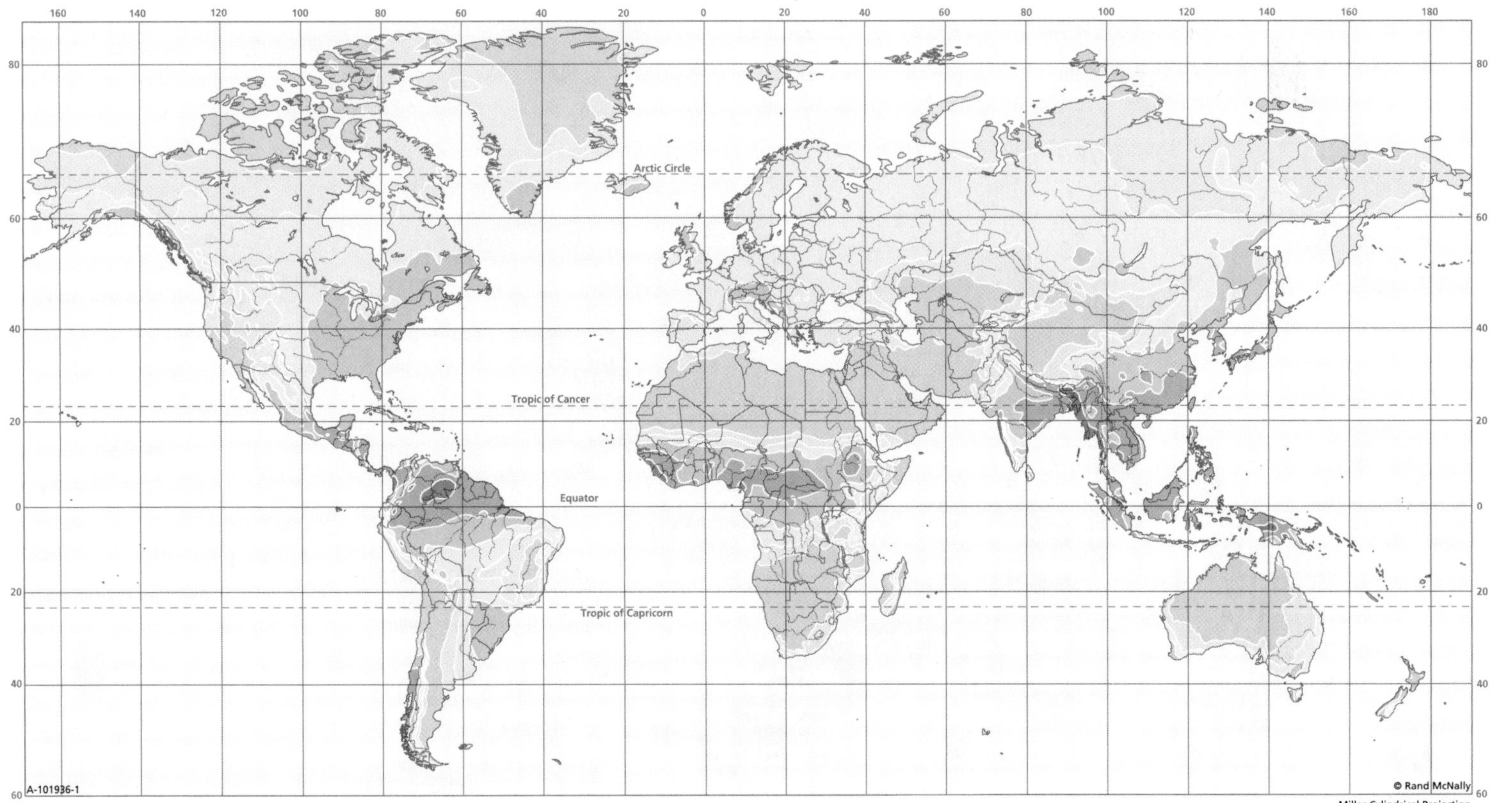

Miller Cylindrical Projection
Scale 1:200,000,000

© Rand McNally

AVERAGE PRECIPITATION - APRIL 1 TO SEPTEMBER 30

12.5 25 50 100 200 Centimeters

5 10 20 40 80 Inches

Miller Cylindrical Projection
Scale 1:200,000,000
Source: New et al., 2000

© Rand McNally

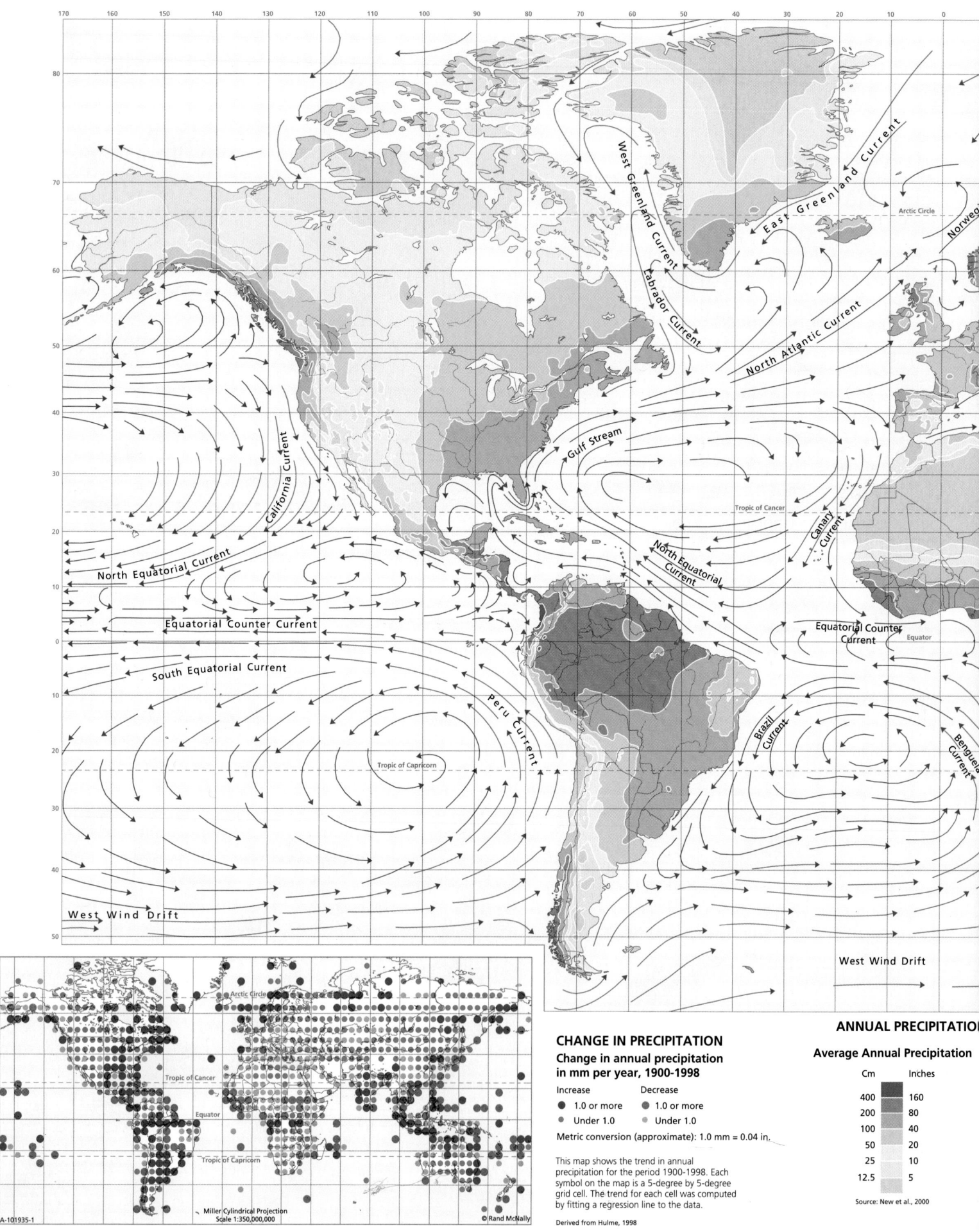

CHANGE IN PRECIPITATION

**Change in annual precipitation
in mm per year, 1900-1998**

Increase	Decrease
● 1.0 or more	● 1.0 or more
● Under 1.0	● Under 1.0

Metric conversion (approximate): 1.0 mm = 0.04 in.

This map shows the trend in annual
precipitation for the period 1900-1998. Each
symbol on the map is a 5-degree by 5-degree
grid cell. The trend for each cell was computed
by fitting a regression line to the data.

Derived from Hulme, 1998

ANNUAL PRECIPITATIO

Average Annual Precipitation

Cm	Inches
400	160
200	80
100	40
50	20
25	10
12.5	5

Source: New et al., 2000

Miller Cylindrical Projection
Scale 1:350,000,000

A-101935-1   © Rand McNally

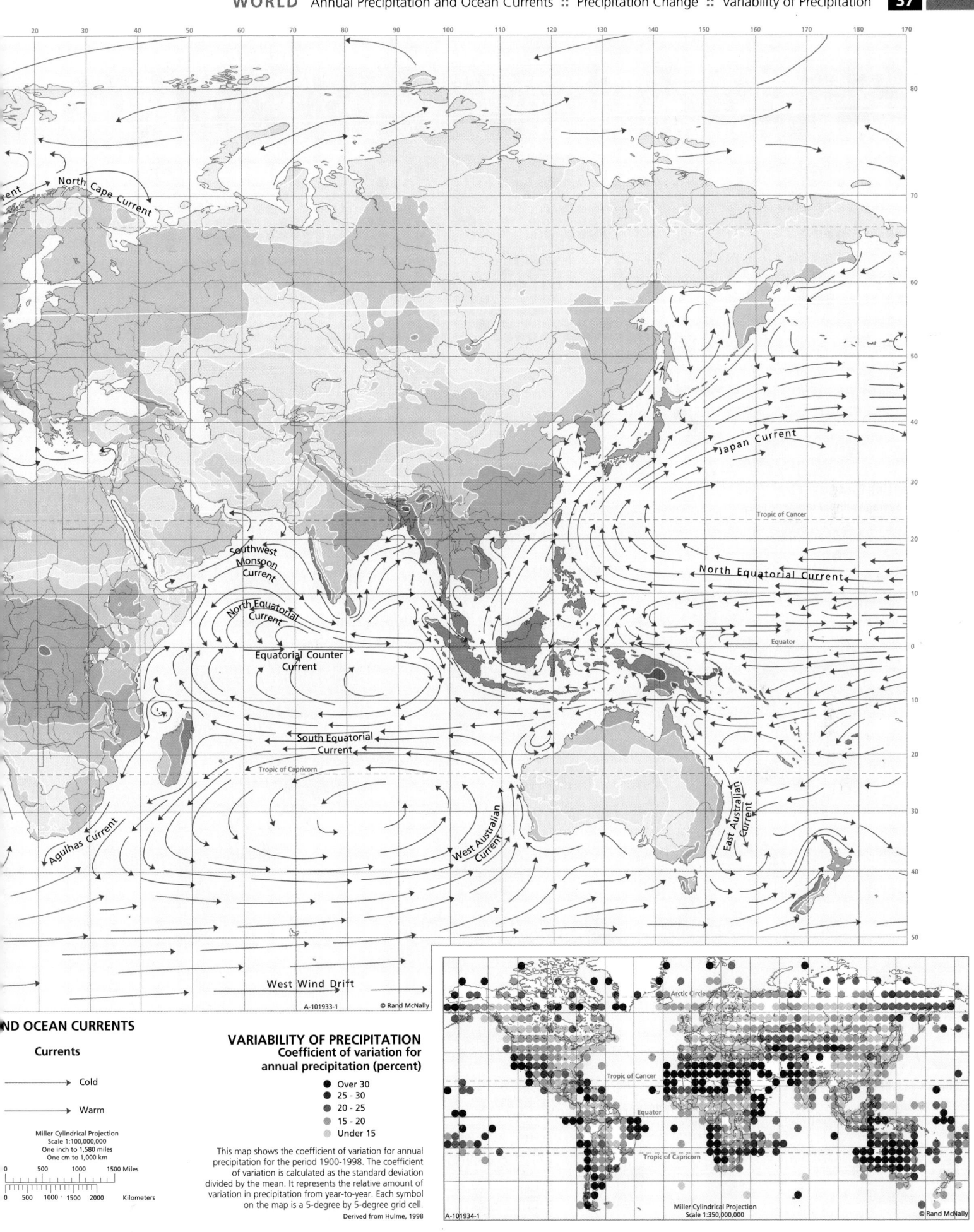

North Cape Current

Japan Current

Tropic of Cancer

Southwest
Monsoon
Current

North Equatorial Current

North Equatorial
Current

Equator

Equatorial Counter
Current

South Equatorial
Current

Tropic of Capricorn

West Australian
Current

East Australian
Current

Agulhas Current

West Wind Drift

A-101933-1   © Rand McNally

ND OCEAN CURRENTS

Currents

→ Cold

→ Warm

Miller Cylindrical Projection
Scale 1:100,000,000
One inch to 1,580 miles
One cm to 1,000 km

0   500   1000   1500 Miles

0   500 1000 1500 2000   Kilometers

VARIABILITY OF PRECIPITATION
Coefficient of variation for
annual precipitation (percent)

● Over 30
● 25 - 30
● 20 - 25
● 15 - 20
● Under 15

This map shows the coefficient of variation for annual
precipitation for the period 1900-1998. The coefficient
of variation is calculated as the standard deviation
divided by the mean. It represents the relative amount of
variation in precipitation from year-to-year. Each symbol
on the map is a 5-degree by 5-degree grid cell.

Derived from Hulme, 1998

Arctic Circle

Tropic of Cancer

Equator

Tropic of Capricorn

Miller Cylindrical Projection
Scale 1:350,000,000

A-101934-1   © Rand McNally

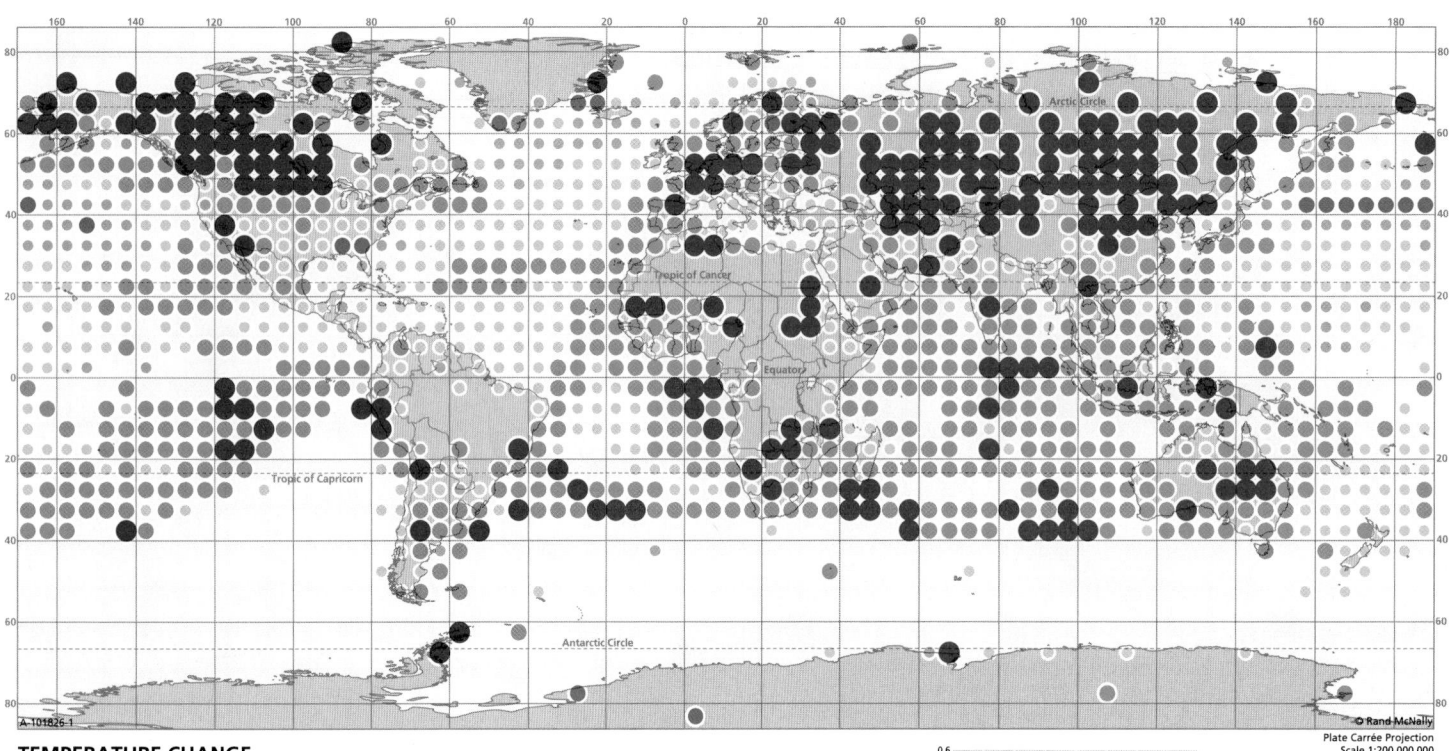

TEMPERATURE CHANGE

Change in average annual temperature
in Celsius degrees (C°) per decade, 1950-2006

Temperature increase	Temperature decrease
⬤ Over 0.2	⬤ Over 0.1
⬤ 0.1 - 0.2	⬤ Under 0.1
⬤ Under 0.1	

Temperature conversion (approximate): 0.1 C° = 0.18 F°; 0.2 C° = 0.36 F°

This map is derived from the HadCRUT3 temperature anomaly dataset. The anomaly for a given year is the difference in temperature from the baseline period of 1961-1990. Each symbol on the map is a 5-degree by 5-degree grid cell. Cells with a gap of 10 years or more in the record are not included. The trend for each cell was computed by fitting a regression line to the data.

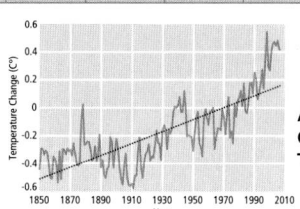

**Average Annual
Global Temperature
Trend, 1850-2007**

Plate Carrée Projection
Scale 1:200,000,000
Derived from Brohan et al., 2006

SEA LEVEL CHANGE

Tide Gauge Data
Change in relative sea level
in mm per year, 1950-2006

Sea level increase	Sea level decrease
⬤ Over 5.0	⬤ Over 5.0
⬤ 2.5 - 5.0	⬤ 2.5 - 5.0
⬤ Under 2.5	⬤ Under 2.5

Satellite Altimetry Data
Change in observed sea level
in mm per year, 1992-2007

Sea level increase	Sea level decrease
Over 7.5	Over 7.5
5.0 - 7.5	5.0 - 7.5
2.5 - 5.0	2.5 - 5.0
Under 2.5	Under 2.5

Metric conversion (approximate): 2.5 mm = 0.1 in.; 5.0 mm = 0.2 in.; 7.5 mm = 0.3 in.

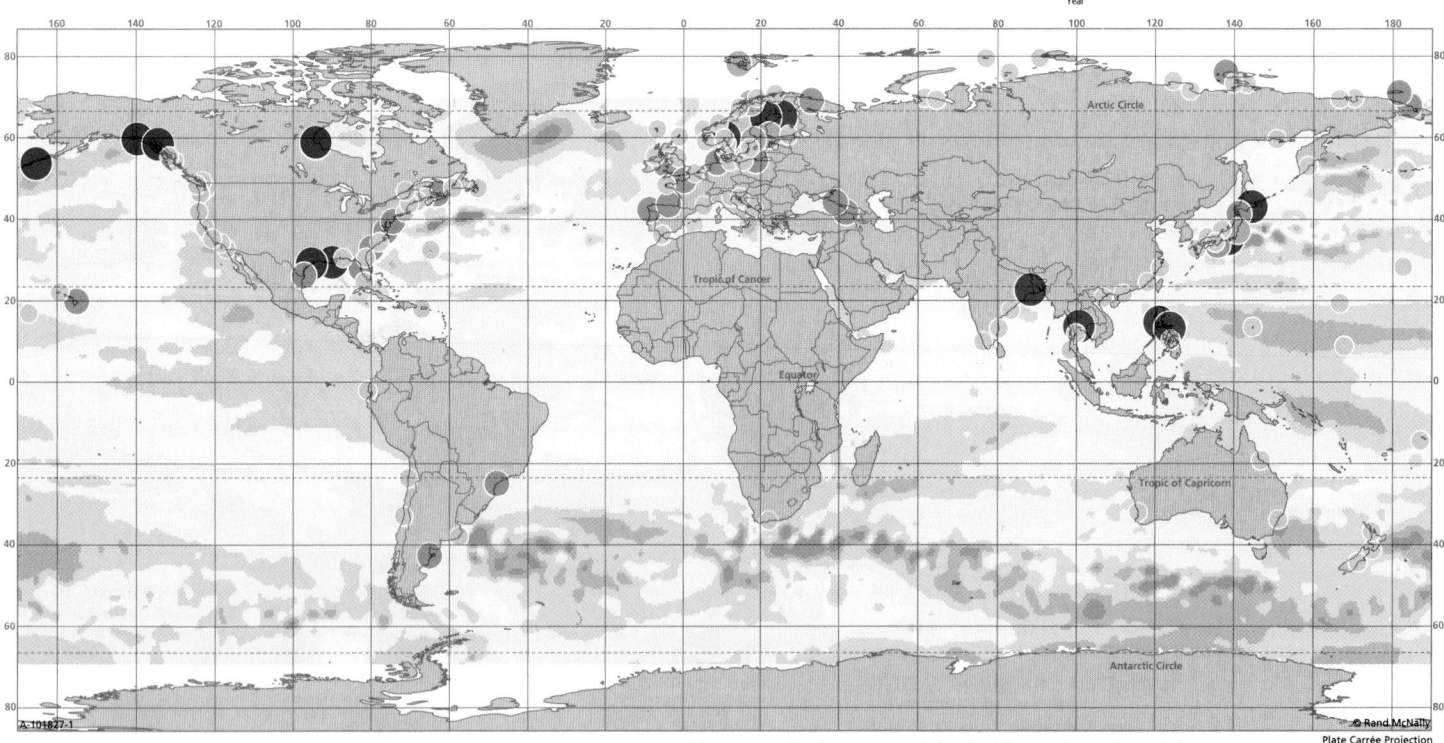

Tide gauges provide a long-term record of sea level change. The record extends for 200 years in some cases. However, stations are clustered spatially and do not cover the entire globe. Also, since tide gauges measure relative sea level (water level relative to the land surface), they cannot differentiate changes in water volume (due to thermal expansion and ice melting) from changes in land elevation (due to tectonic activity and glacial isostatic adjustment). Still, tide gauges are important because relative sea level has a direct impact on coastal environments.

The tide gauge data on this map are from the PSMSL-RLR (Permanent Service for Mean Sea Level - Revised Local Reference) network. Stations with gaps of 10 years or more in the data are not included. The trend at each station was computed by fitting a regression line.

Satellite altimetry offers a second method of assessing sea level change. Unlike tide gauges, coverage is nearly global. Also, observed changes in sea level are largely unaffected by land elevation changes. However, the satellite altimetry record extends back to only the 1990s. As a result, the data record reflects major decadal variations rather than long-term trends.

The satellite altimetry data on this map are from the TOPEX/Poseidon and Jason1 sensors.

Plate Carrée Projection
Scale 1:200,000,000
Sources: NOAA Laboratory
for Satellite Altimetry;
Woodworth and Player, 2003

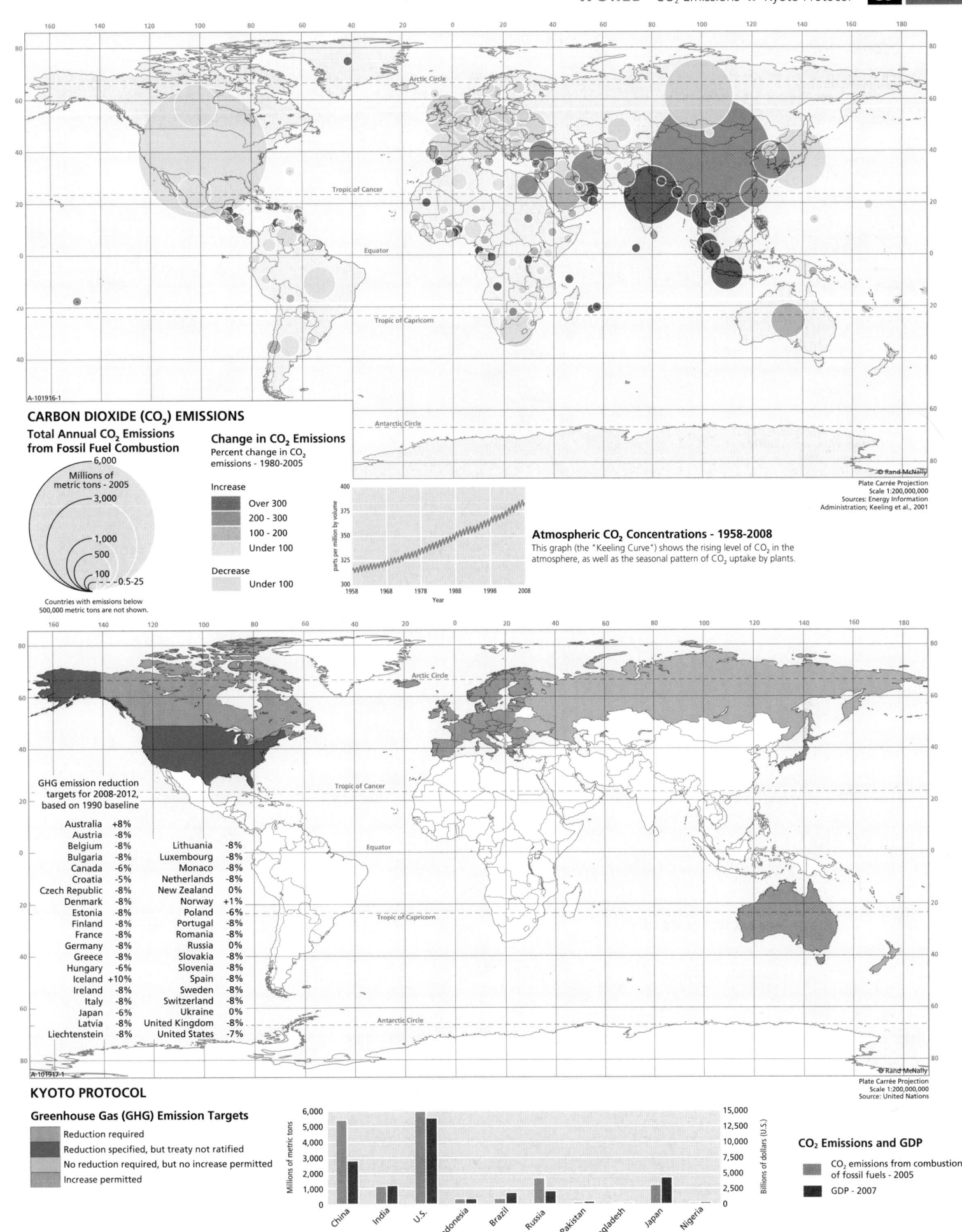

CARBON DIOXIDE (CO₂) EMISSIONS

Total Annual CO₂ Emissions from Fossil Fuel Combustion

Millions of metric tons - 2005

6,000
3,000
1,000
500
100
0.5-25

Countries with emissions below 500,000 metric tons are not shown.

Change in CO₂ Emissions

Percent change in CO₂ emissions - 1980-2005

Increase

Over 300
200 - 300
100 - 200
Under 100

Decrease

Under 100

Atmospheric CO₂ Concentrations - 1958-2008

This graph (the "Keeling Curve") shows the rising level of CO₂ in the atmosphere, as well as the seasonal pattern of CO₂ uptake by plants.

Plate Carrée Projection
Scale 1:200,000,000
Sources: Energy Information
Administration; Keeling et al., 2001

KYOTO PROTOCOL

GHG emission reduction targets for 2008-2012, based on 1990 baseline

Australia	+8%		
Austria	-8%		
Belgium	-8%	Lithuania	-8%
Bulgaria	-8%	Luxembourg	-8%
Canada	-6%	Monaco	-8%
Croatia	-5%	Netherlands	-8%
Czech Republic	-8%	New Zealand	0%
Denmark	-8%	Norway	+1%
Estonia	-8%	Poland	-6%
Finland	-8%	Portugal	-8%
France	-8%	Romania	-8%
Germany	-8%	Russia	0%
Greece	-8%	Slovakia	-8%
Hungary	-6%	Slovenia	-8%
Iceland	+10%	Spain	-8%
Ireland	-8%	Sweden	-8%
Italy	-8%	Switzerland	-8%
Japan	-6%	Ukraine	0%
Latvia	-8%	United Kingdom	-8%
Liechtenstein	-8%	United States	-7%

Plate Carrée Projection
Scale 1:200,000,000
Source: United Nations

Greenhouse Gas (GHG) Emission Targets

Reduction required
Reduction specified, but treaty not ratified
No reduction required, but no increase permitted
Increase permitted

(World's largest countries, 2000)

CO₂ Emissions and GDP

CO₂ emissions from combustion of fossil fuels - 2005
GDP - 2007

OCEANIC ENVIRONMENTS

Marine Productivity
Milligrams of carbon per square meter per day

	Over 500
	250-500
	150-250
	100-150
	Under 100

Velocity of current
Nautical miles per day

→	Over 36
→	24 - 36
→	12 - 24
→	Under 12
	Areas of upwelling cold water
	Average limits of sea ice or drift ice
	Coral reefs

Atmospheric heat gain (or loss) by contact with ocean surface
Calories per square centimeter per year

	+ 80,000
	+ 60,000
	+ 40,000
	0
	- 40,000
	- 60,000

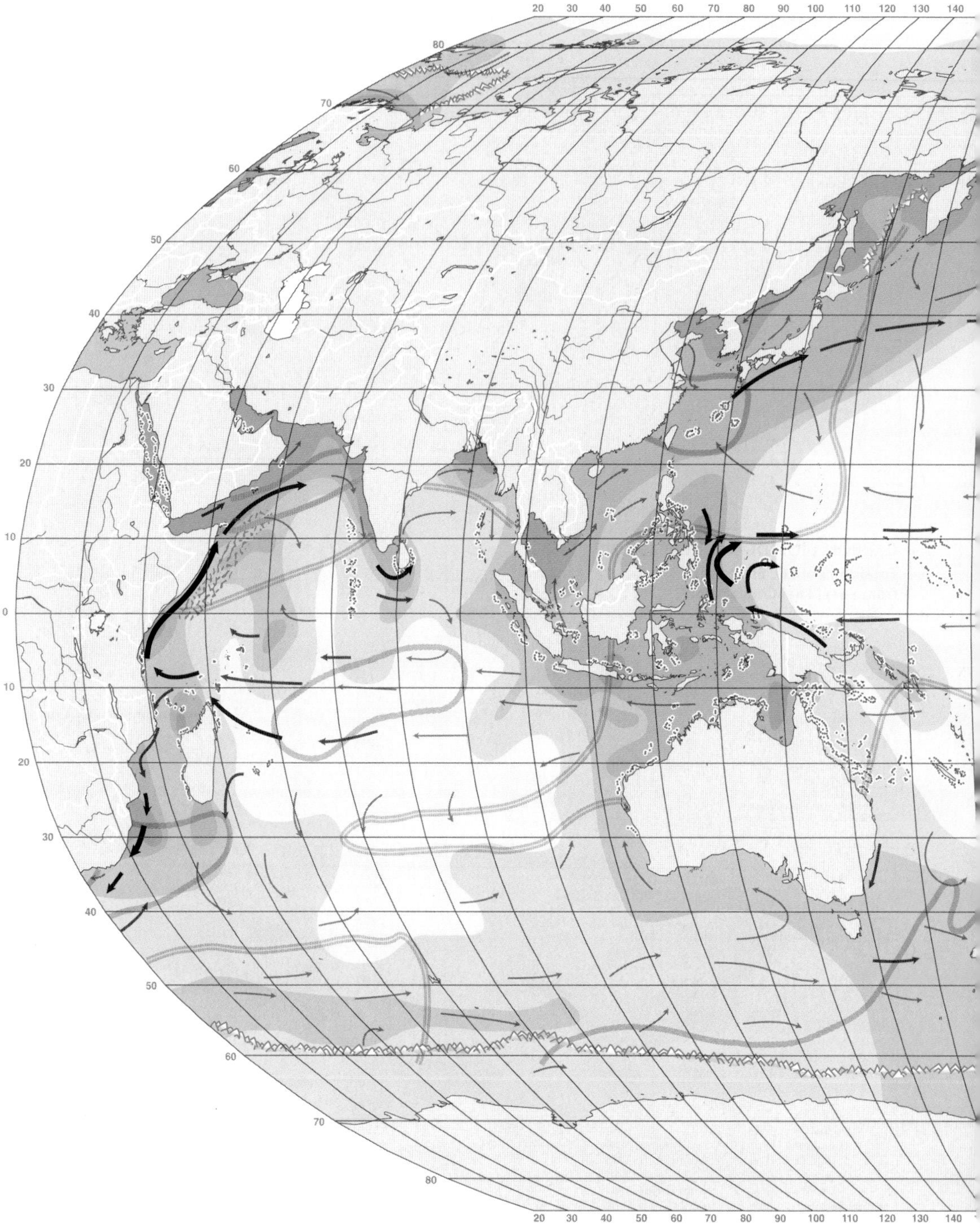

Robinson Projection
Scale 1:110,000,000
One inch to 1,750 miles
One cm to 1,100 km

0 500 1000 1500 2000 Miles
0 1000 2000 3000 Kilometers

CHANGE IN ARCTIC SEA ICE EXTENT

	Monthly sea ice extent
	Median monthly sea ice extent, 1979-2000
	Ice sheets, ice caps, and glaciers

March, 2008

September, 2007

Polar Stereographic Projection
Scale 1:140,000,000
Source: National Snow and Ice Data Center
© Rand McNally A-101961-1

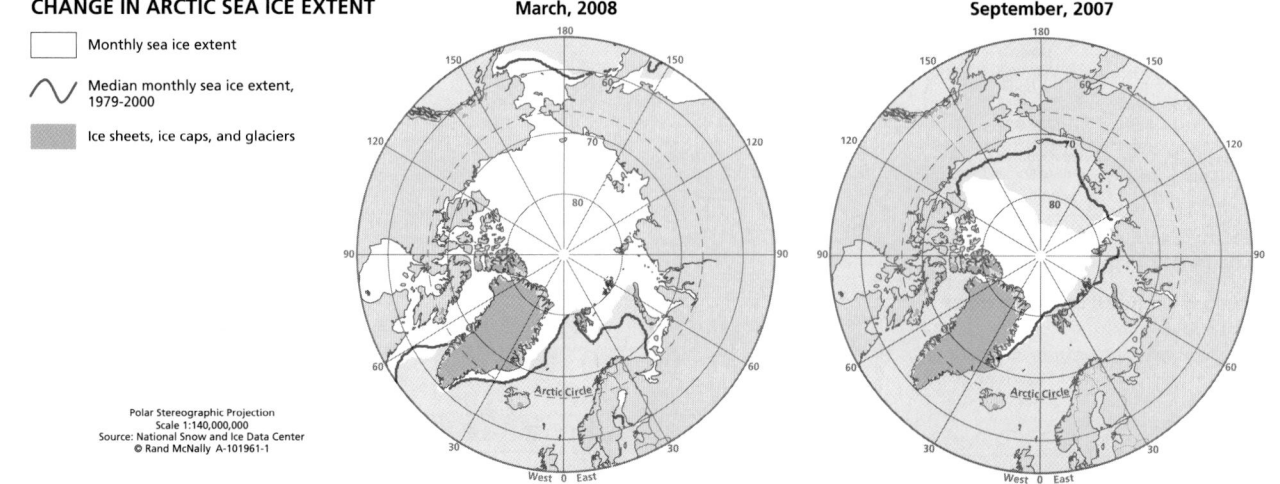

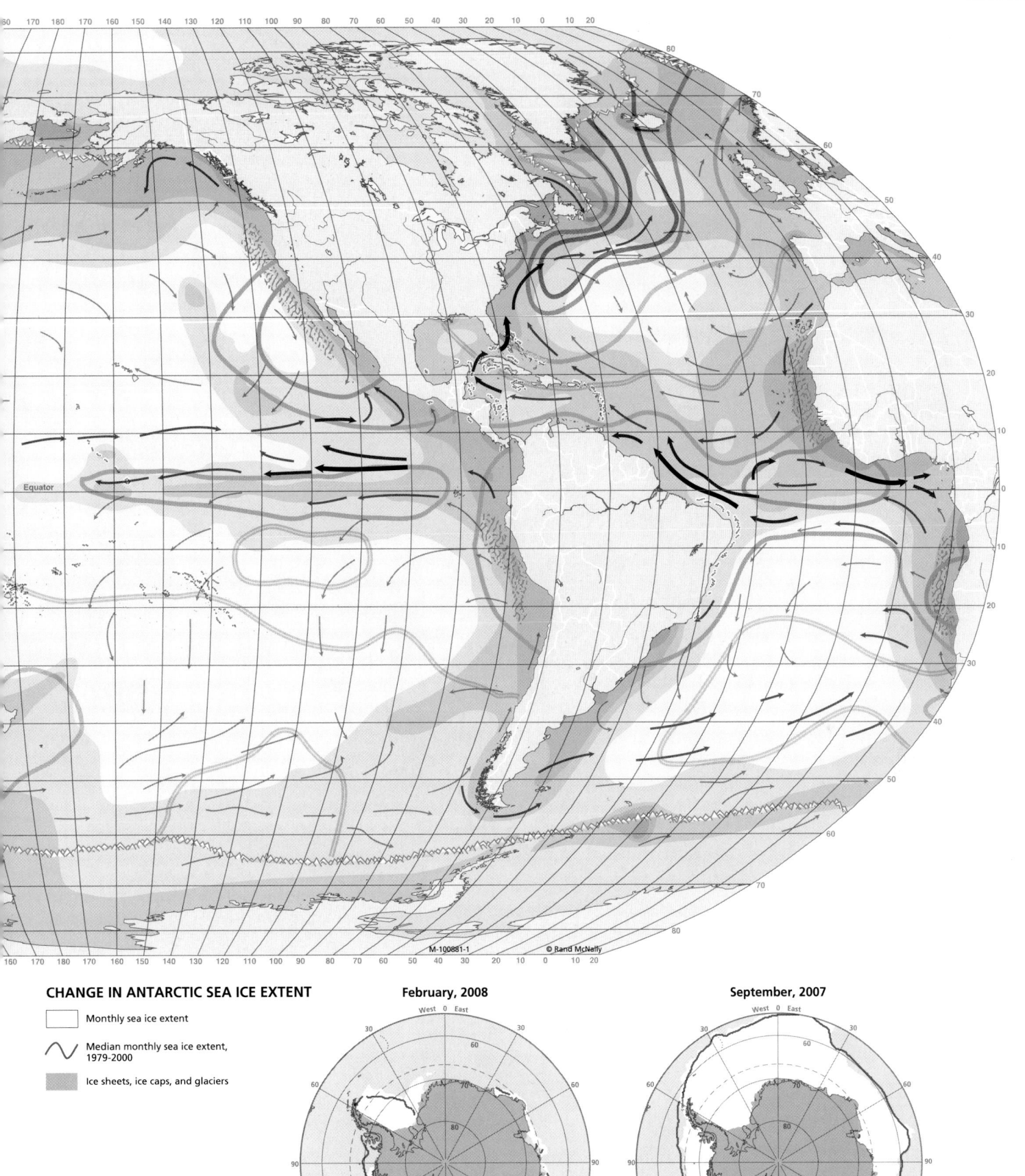

CHANGE IN ANTARCTIC SEA ICE EXTENT

☐ Monthly sea ice extent

〰 Median monthly sea ice extent,
1979-2000

▨ Ice sheets, ice caps, and glaciers

February, 2008

West 0 East

September, 2007

West 0 East

Polar Stereographic Projection
Scale 1:140,000,000
Source: National Snow and Ice Data Center
© Rand McNally A-101962-1

M-100881-1   © Rand McNally

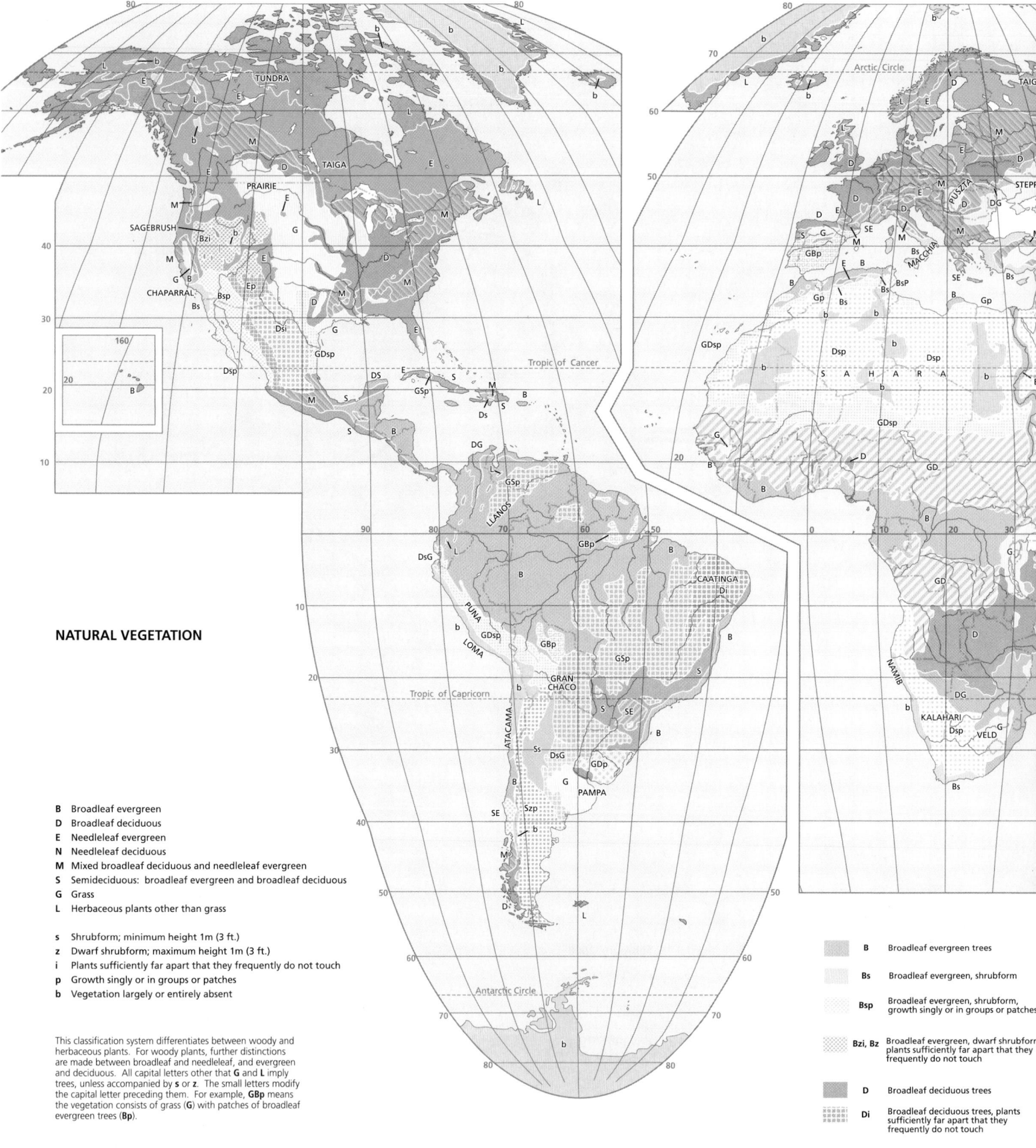

NATURAL VEGETATION

B   Broadleaf evergreen
D   Broadleaf deciduous
E   Needleleaf evergreen
N   Needleleaf deciduous
M   Mixed broadleaf deciduous and needleleaf evergreen
S   Semideciduous: broadleaf evergreen and broadleaf deciduous
G   Grass
L   Herbaceous plants other than grass

s   Shrubform; minimum height 1m (3 ft.)
z   Dwarf shrubform; maximum height 1m (3 ft.)
i   Plants sufficiently far apart that they frequently do not touch
p   Growth singly or in groups or patches
b   Vegetation largely or entirely absent

This classification system differentiates between woody and
herbaceous plants. For woody plants, further distinctions
are made between broadleaf and needleleaf, and evergreen
and deciduous. All capital letters other that **G** and **L** imply
trees, unless accompanied by **s** or **z**. The small letters modify
the capital letter preceding them. For example, **GBp** means
the vegetation consists of grass (**G**) with patches of broadleaf
evergreen trees (**Bp**).

	B	Broadleaf evergreen trees
	Bs	Broadleaf evergreen, shrubform
	Bsp	Broadleaf evergreen, shrubform, growth singly or in groups or patches
	Bzi, Bz	Broadleaf evergreen, dwarf shrubform plants sufficiently far apart that they frequently do not touch
	D	Broadleaf deciduous trees
	Di	Broadleaf deciduous trees, plants sufficiently far apart that they frequently do not touch

Goode's Interrupted Homolosine Projection (Condensed)
Scale 1: 78,000,000
One inch to 1,230 miles
One cm to 780 km

Source: Küchler, 1949. © Association of American Geographers
Published by Taylor & Francis. Adapted with permission
of the Association of American Geographers.

M-100836-1   © Rand McNally

Ds	Broadleaf deciduous, shrubform	
Dsi	Broadleaf deciduous, shrubform, plants sufficiently far apart that they frequently do not touch	
Dsp	Broadleaf deciduous, shrubform, growth singly or in groups or patches	
Dzp	Broadleaf deciduous, dwarf shrubform, growth singly or in groups or patches	
DsG	Broadleaf deciduous, shrubform Grass and other herbaceous plants	
DG	Broadleaf deciduous trees Grass and other herbaceous plants	
DBs	Broadleaf deciduous trees Broadleaf evergreen, shrubform	

E	Needleleaf evergreen trees
Ep	Needleleaf evergreen trees, growth singly or in groups or patches
G	Grass and other herbaceous plants
Gp	Grass and other herbaceous plants, growth singly or in groups or patches
GBp	Grass and other herbaceous plants Broadleaf evergreen trees, growth singly or in groups or patches
GD	Grass and other herbaceous plants Broadleaf deciduous trees
GDp	Grass and other herbaceous plants Broadleaf deciduous trees, growth singly or in groups or patches

GDsp	Grass and other herbaceous plants Broadleaf deciduous, shrubform, growth singly or in groups or patches
GSp	Grass and other herbaceous plants Semideciduous: broadleaf evergreen and broadleaf deciduous trees, growth singly or in groups or patches
L	Herbaceous plants other than grass
M	Mixed broadleaf deciduous and needleleaf evergreen trees
N	Needleleaf deciduous trees
ND	Needleleaf deciduous trees Broadleaf deciduous trees

S	Semideciduous: broadleaf evergreen and broadleaf deciduous trees
Ss	Semideciduous: broadleaf evergreen and broadleaf deciduous, shrubform
SsG	Semideciduous: broadleaf evergreen and broadleaf deciduous, shrubform Grass and other herbaceous plants
Szp	Semideciduous: broadleaf evergeen and broadleaf deciduous, dwarf shrubform, growth singly or in groups or patches
SE	Semideciduous: broadleaf evergreen and broadleaf deciduous trees Needleleaf evergreen trees
b	Vegetation largely or entirely absent

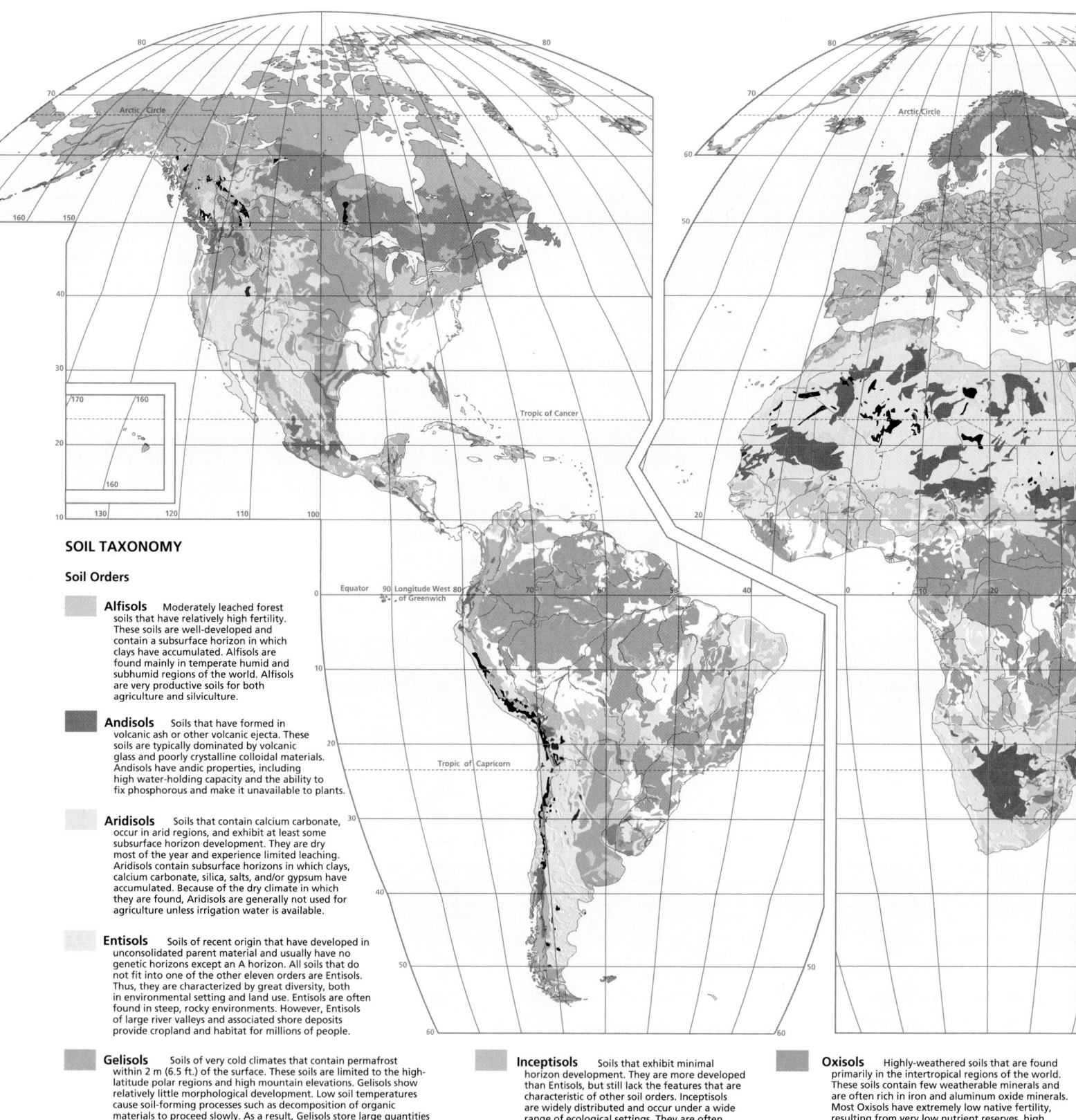

SOIL TAXONOMY

Soil Orders

Alfisols Moderately leached forest soils that have relatively high fertility. These soils are well-developed and contain a subsurface horizon in which clays have accumulated. Alfisols are found mainly in temperate humid and subhumid regions of the world. Alfisols are very productive soils for both agriculture and silviculture.

Andisols Soils that have formed in volcanic ash or other volcanic ejecta. These soils are typically dominated by volcanic glass and poorly crystalline colloidal materials. Andisols have andic properties, including high water-holding capacity and the ability to fix phosphorous and make it unavailable to plants.

Aridisols Soils that contain calcium carbonate, occur in arid regions, and exhibit at least some subsurface horizon development. They are dry most of the year and experience limited leaching. Aridisols contain subsurface horizons in which clays, calcium carbonate, silica, salts, and/or gypsum have accumulated. Because of the dry climate in which they are found, Aridisols are generally not used for agriculture unless irrigation water is available.

Entisols Soils of recent origin that have developed in unconsolidated parent material and usually have no genetic horizons except an A horizon. All soils that do not fit into one of the other eleven orders are Entisols. Thus, they are characterized by great diversity, both in environmental setting and land use. Entisols are often found in steep, rocky environments. However, Entisols of large river valleys and associated shore deposits provide cropland and habitat for millions of people.

Gelisols Soils of very cold climates that contain permafrost within 2 m (6.5 ft.) of the surface. These soils are limited to the high-latitude polar regions and high mountain elevations. Gelisols show relatively little morphological development. Low soil temperatures cause soil-forming processes such as decomposition of organic materials to proceed slowly. As a result, Gelisols store large quantities of organic carbon. Because of the extreme environment in which they are found, Gelisols support only a small fraction of the world's population. The frozen condition of Gelisol landscapes makes them sensitive to human activities.

Histosols Soils that are composed mainly of organic materials. They contain at least 20 to 30 percent organic matter by weight and are more than 40 cm (15.75 in.) thick. Most Histosols form in settings such as wetlands where restricted drainage inhibits the decomposition of plant and animal remains, allowing these organic materials to accumulate over time. As a result, Histosols are ecologically important because of the large quantities of carbon they contain. Histosols are often referred to as peats and mucks and are mined for fuel and horticultural products.

Inceptisols Soils that exhibit minimal horizon development. They are more developed than Entisols, but still lack the features that are characteristic of other soil orders. Inceptisols are widely distributed and occur under a wide range of ecological settings. They are often found on fairly steep slopes, young geomorphic surfaces, and on resistant parent materials. Land use varies considerably with Inceptisols.

Mollisols Soils of grassland ecosystems. These soils are characterized by a thick, dark surface horizon that results from the long-term addition of organic materials derived from plant roots. Mollisols primarily occur in the mid-latitudes and are extensive in prairie regions. Mollisols are among some of the most important and productive agricultural soils in the world.

Oxisols Highly-weathered soils that are found primarily in the intertropical regions of the world. These soils contain few weatherable minerals and are often rich in iron and aluminum oxide minerals. Most Oxisols have extremely low native fertility, resulting from very low nutrient reserves, high phosphorus retention by oxide minerals, and low cation exchange capacity. Oxisols can be quite productive with inputs of lime and fertilizers.

Spodosols Acid soils characterized by a subsurface accumulation of humus that is complexed with aluminum and iron. Spodosols often occur under coniferous forest in cool, moist climates. Because they are naturally infertile, Spodosols require additions of lime in order to be productive agriculturally.

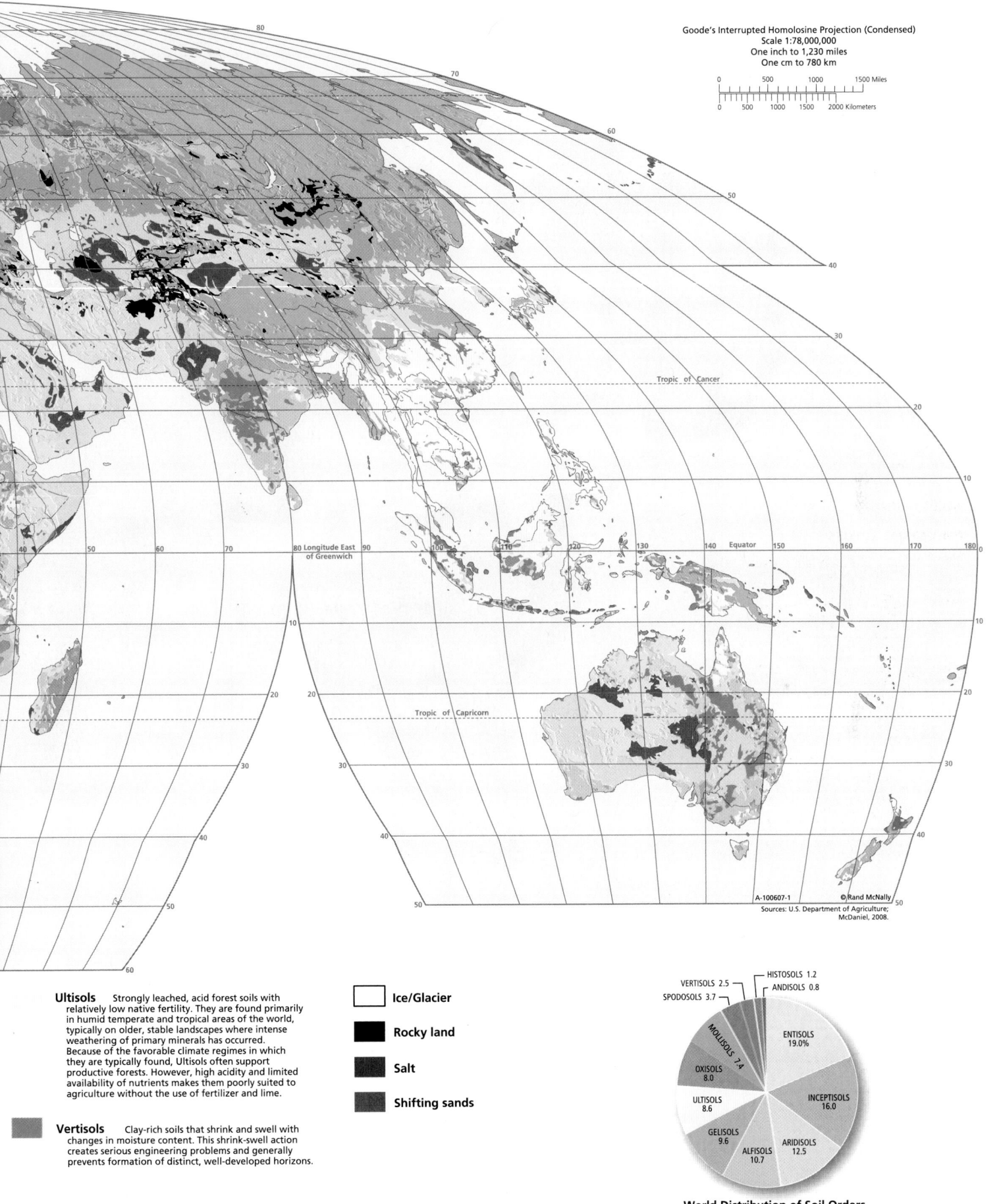

Goode's Interrupted Homolosine Projection (Condensed)
Scale 1:78,000,000
One inch to 1,230 miles
One cm to 780 km

Tropic of Cancer

80 Longitude East
of Greenwich

Equator

Tropic of Capricorn

A-100607-1   © Rand McNally

Sources: U.S. Department of Agriculture;
McDaniel, 2008.

Ultisols   Strongly leached, acid forest soils with
relatively low native fertility. They are found primarily
in humid temperate and tropical areas of the world,
typically on older, stable landscapes where intense
weathering of primary minerals has occurred.
Because of the favorable climate regimes in which
they are typically found, Ultisols often support
productive forests. However, high acidity and limited
availability of nutrients makes them poorly suited to
agriculture without the use of fertilizer and lime.

Vertisols   Clay-rich soils that shrink and swell with
changes in moisture content. This shrink-swell action
creates serious engineering problems and generally
prevents formation of distinct, well-developed horizons.

Ice/Glacier

Rocky land

Salt

Shifting sands

HISTOSOLS 1.2
ANDISOLS 0.8
VERTISOLS 2.5
SPODOSOLS 3.7
MOLLISOLS 7.4
OXISOLS 8.0
ULTISOLS 8.6
GELISOLS 9.6
ALFISOLS 10.7
ARIDISOLS 12.5
INCEPTISOLS 16.0
ENTISOLS 19.0%

World Distribution of Soil Orders
World Total - 123,826,000 sq. km

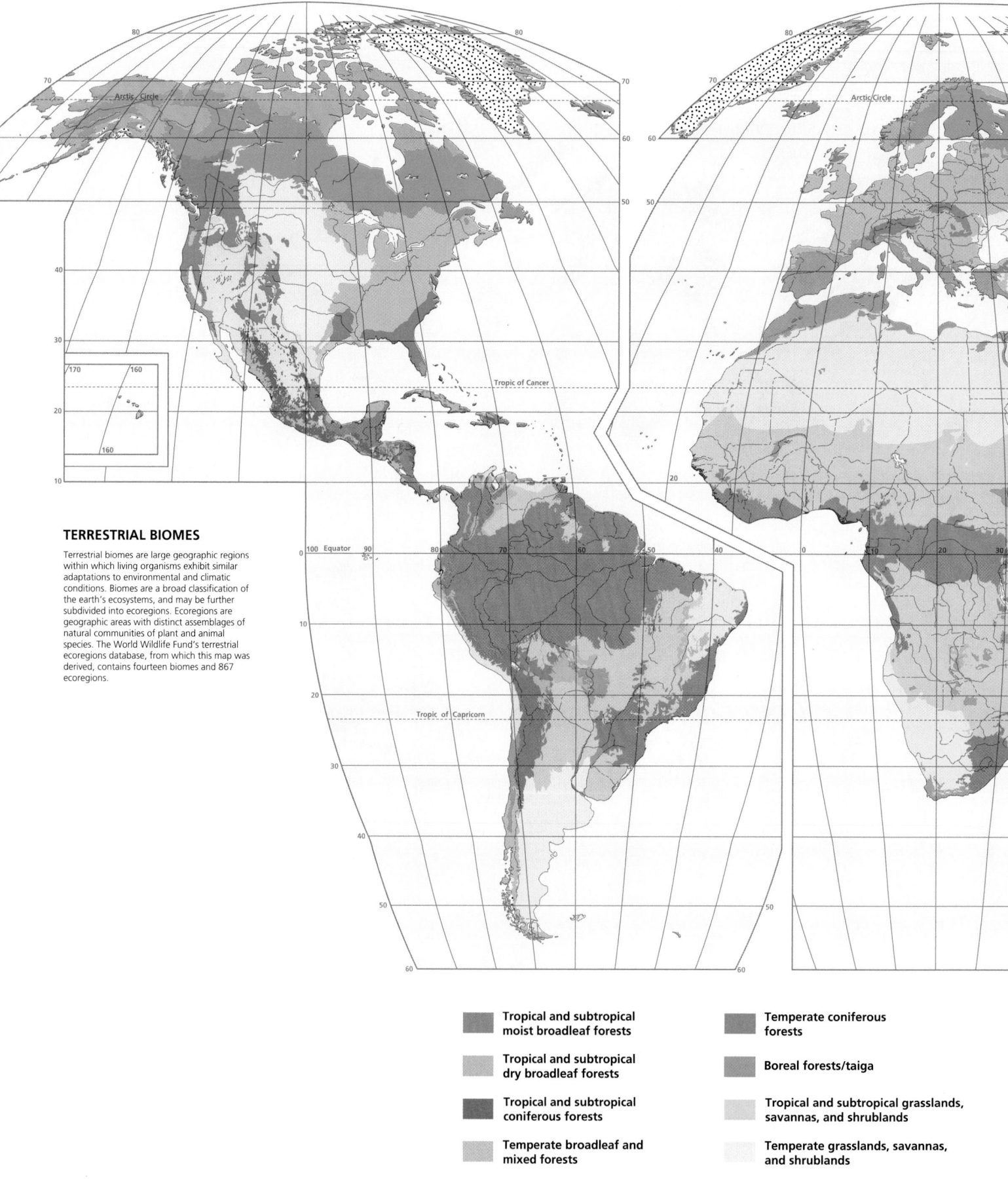

TERRESTRIAL BIOMES

Terrestrial biomes are large geographic regions within which living organisms exhibit similar adaptations to environmental and climatic conditions. Biomes are a broad classification of the earth's ecosystems, and may be further subdivided into ecoregions. Ecoregions are geographic areas with distinct assemblages of natural communities of plant and animal species. The World Wildlife Fund's terrestrial ecoregions database, from which this map was derived, contains fourteen biomes and 867 ecoregions.

Tropical and subtropical moist broadleaf forests

Tropical and subtropical dry broadleaf forests

Tropical and subtropical coniferous forests

Temperate broadleaf and mixed forests

Temperate coniferous forests

Boreal forests/taiga

Tropical and subtropical grasslands, savannas, and shrublands

Temperate grasslands, savannas, and shrublands

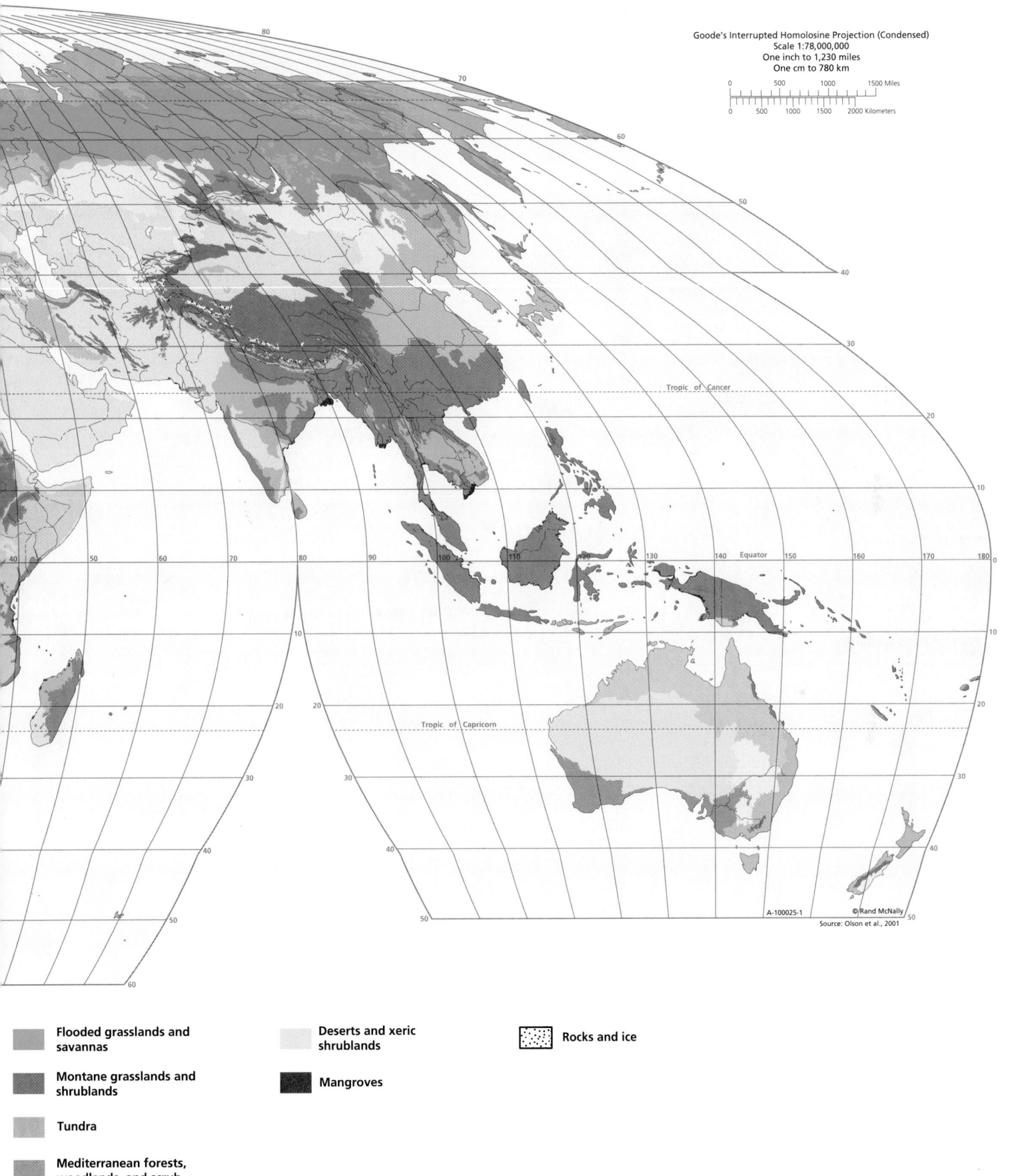

Goode's Interrupted Homolosine Projection (Condensed)
Scale 1:78,000,000
One inch to 1,230 miles
One cm to 780 km

A-100025-1
© Rand McNally
Source: Olson et al., 2001

Flooded grasslands and savannas

Montane grasslands and shrublands

Tundra

Mediterranean forests, woodlands, and scrub

Deserts and xeric shrublands

Mangroves

Rocks and ice

POPULATION DENSITY

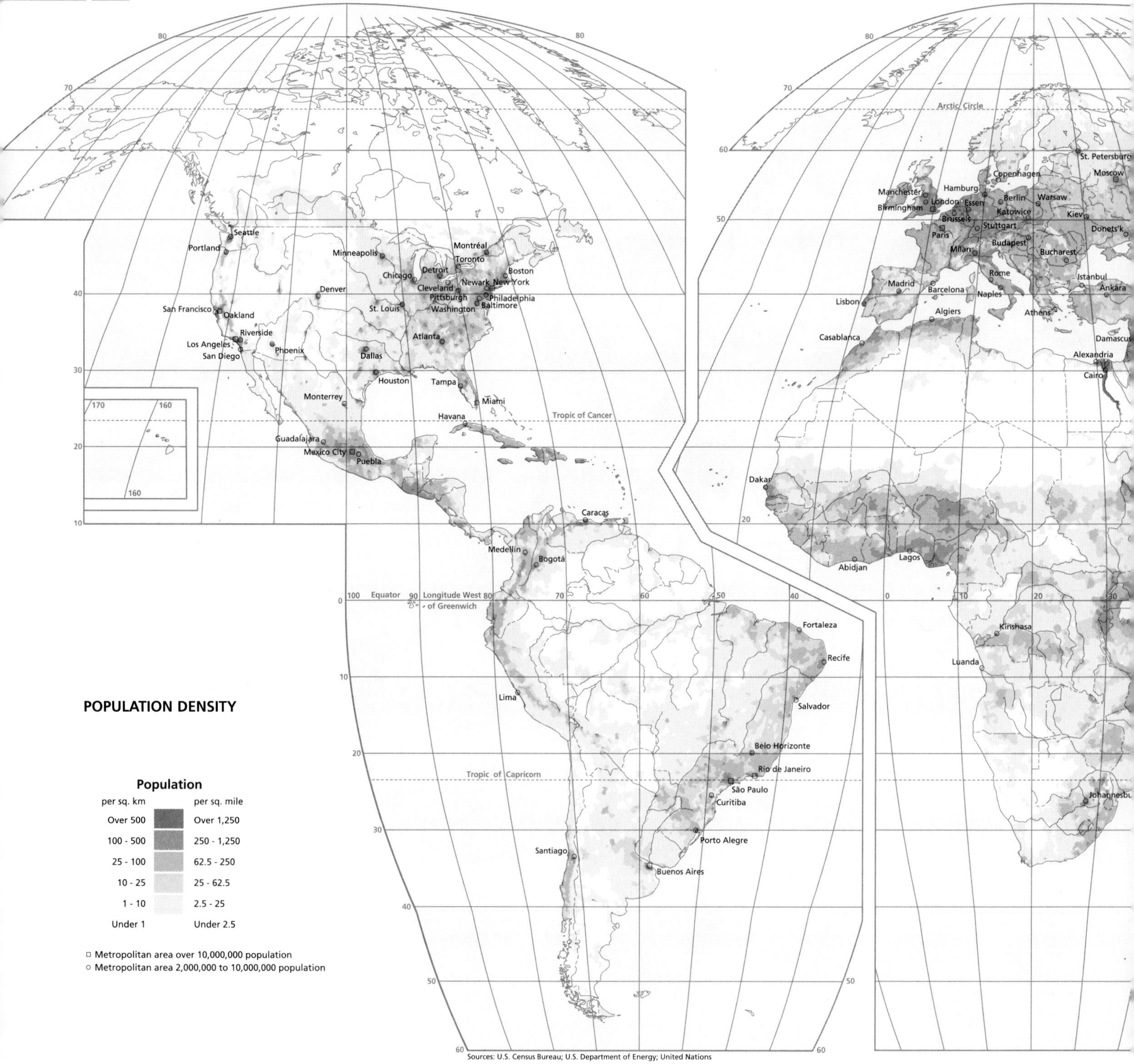

Population

per sq. km	per sq. mile
Over 500	Over 1,250
100 - 500	250 - 1,250
25 - 100	62.5 - 250
10 - 25	25 - 62.5
1 - 10	2.5 - 25
Under 1	Under 2.5

□ Metropolitan area over 10,000,000 population
○ Metropolitan area 2,000,000 to 10,000,000 population

Sources: U.S. Census Bureau; U.S. Department of Energy; United Nations

Arctic Circle
Tropic of Cancer
Equator
Longitude West of Greenwich
Tropic of Capricorn

Seattle, Portland, Minneapolis, Montréal, Toronto, Boston, Chicago, Detroit, Cleveland, Newark, New York, Denver, Pittsburgh, Philadelphia, San Francisco, Oakland, St. Louis, Washington, Baltimore, Riverside, Los Angeles, Phoenix, Atlanta, San Diego, Dallas, Houston, Tampa, Miami, Monterrey, Havana, Guadalajara, Mexico City, Puebla, Caracas, Medellín, Bogotá, Lima, Fortaleza, Recife, Salvador, Belo Horizonte, Rio de Janeiro, São Paulo, Curitiba, Porto Alegre, Santiago, Buenos Aires

St. Petersburg, Copenhagen, Moscow, Manchester, Hamburg, Warsaw, Birmingham, London, Essen, Berlin, Katowice, Kiev, Brussels, Stuttgart, Donets'k, Paris, Milan, Budapest, Bucharest, Madrid, Barcelona, Rome, Istanbul, Lisbon, Naples, Ankara, Algiers, Athens, Casablanca, Damascus, Alexandria, Cairo, Dakar, Abidjan, Lagos, Kinshasa, Luanda, Johannesburg

Largest Countries of the World 1950, 2000, 2050

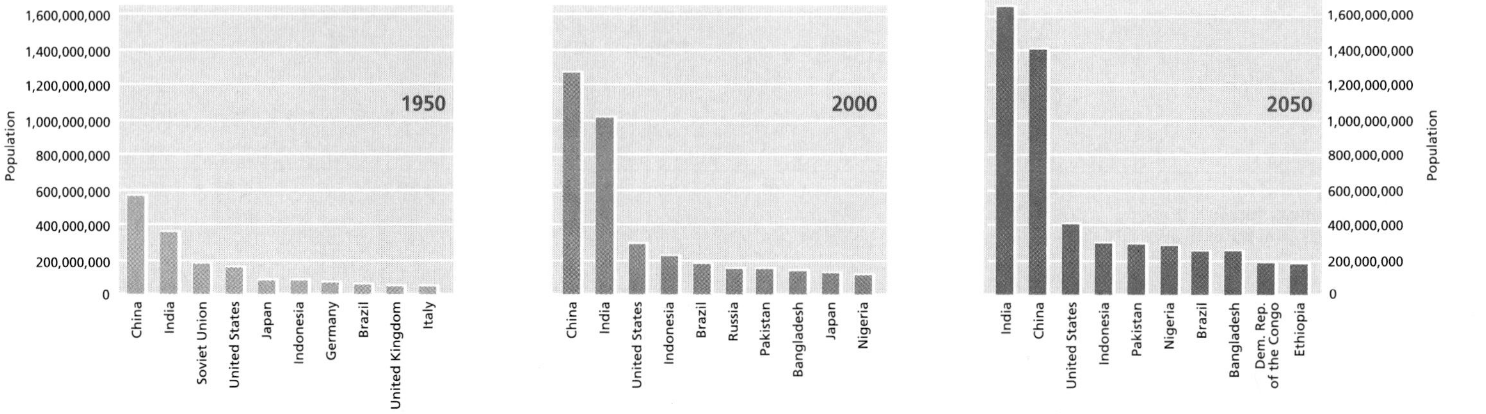

1950
China, India, Soviet Union, United States, Japan, Indonesia, Germany, Brazil, United Kingdom, Italy

2000
China, India, United States, Indonesia, Brazil, Russia, Pakistan, Bangladesh, Japan, Nigeria

2050
India, China, United States, Indonesia, Pakistan, Nigeria, Brazil, Bangladesh, Dem. Rep. of the Congo, Ethiopia

Population axis: 0, 200,000,000, 400,000,000, 600,000,000, 800,000,000, 1,000,000,000, 1,200,000,000, 1,400,000,000, 1,600,000,000

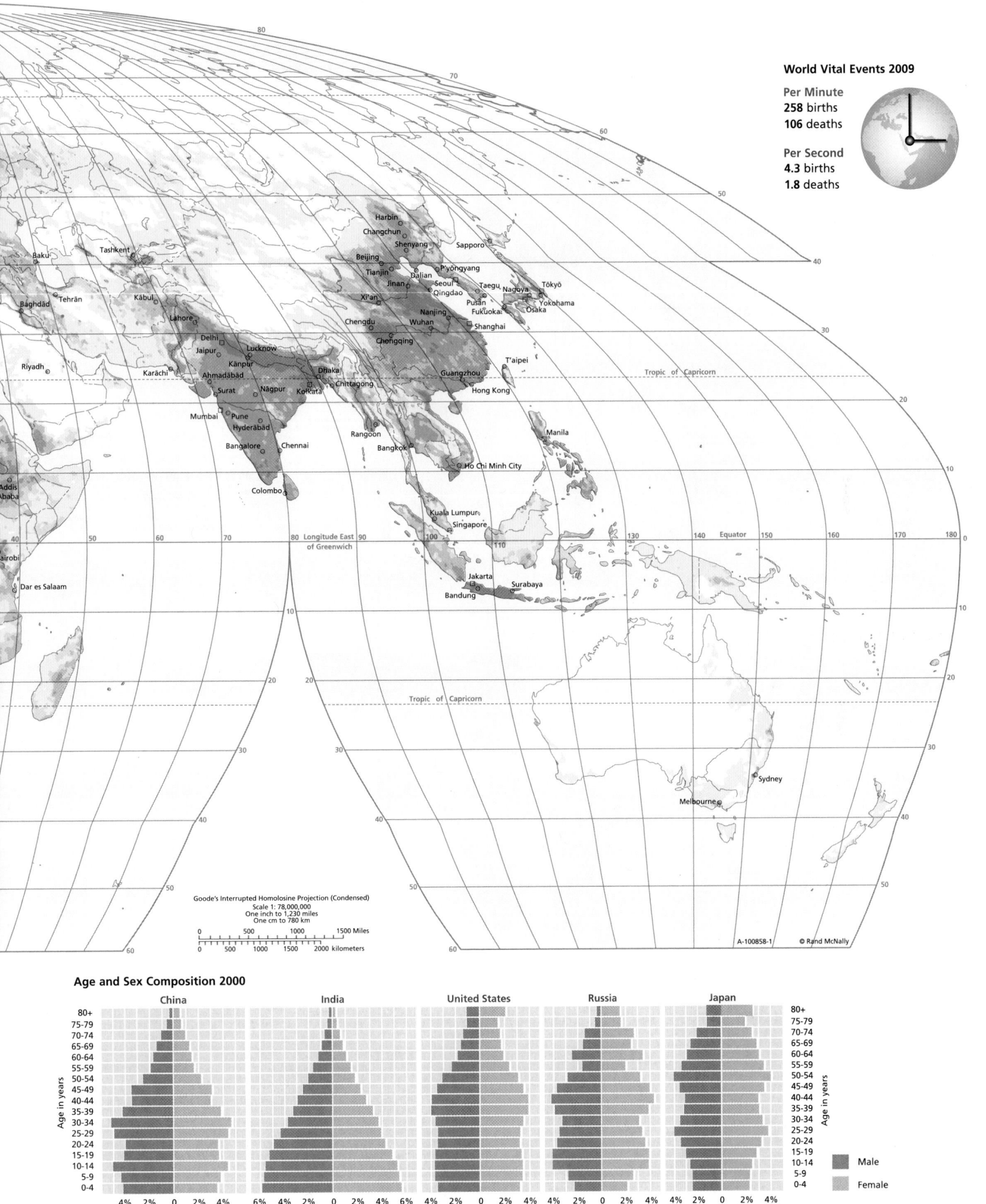

World Vital Events 2009

Per Minute
258 births
106 deaths

Per Second
4.3 births
1.8 deaths

Goode's Interrupted Homolosine Projection (Condensed)
Scale 1: 78,000,000
One inch to 1,230 miles
One cm to 780 km

0   500   1000   1500 Miles

0   500   1000   1500   2000 kilometers

Longitude East
of Greenwich

A-100858-1   © Rand McNally

Age and Sex Composition 2000

China

India

United States

Russia

Japan

Age in years

80+
75-79
70-74
65-69
60-64
55-59
50-54
45-49
40-44
35-39
30-34
25-29
20-24
15-19
10-14
5-9
0-4

Male
Female

Percent of total population

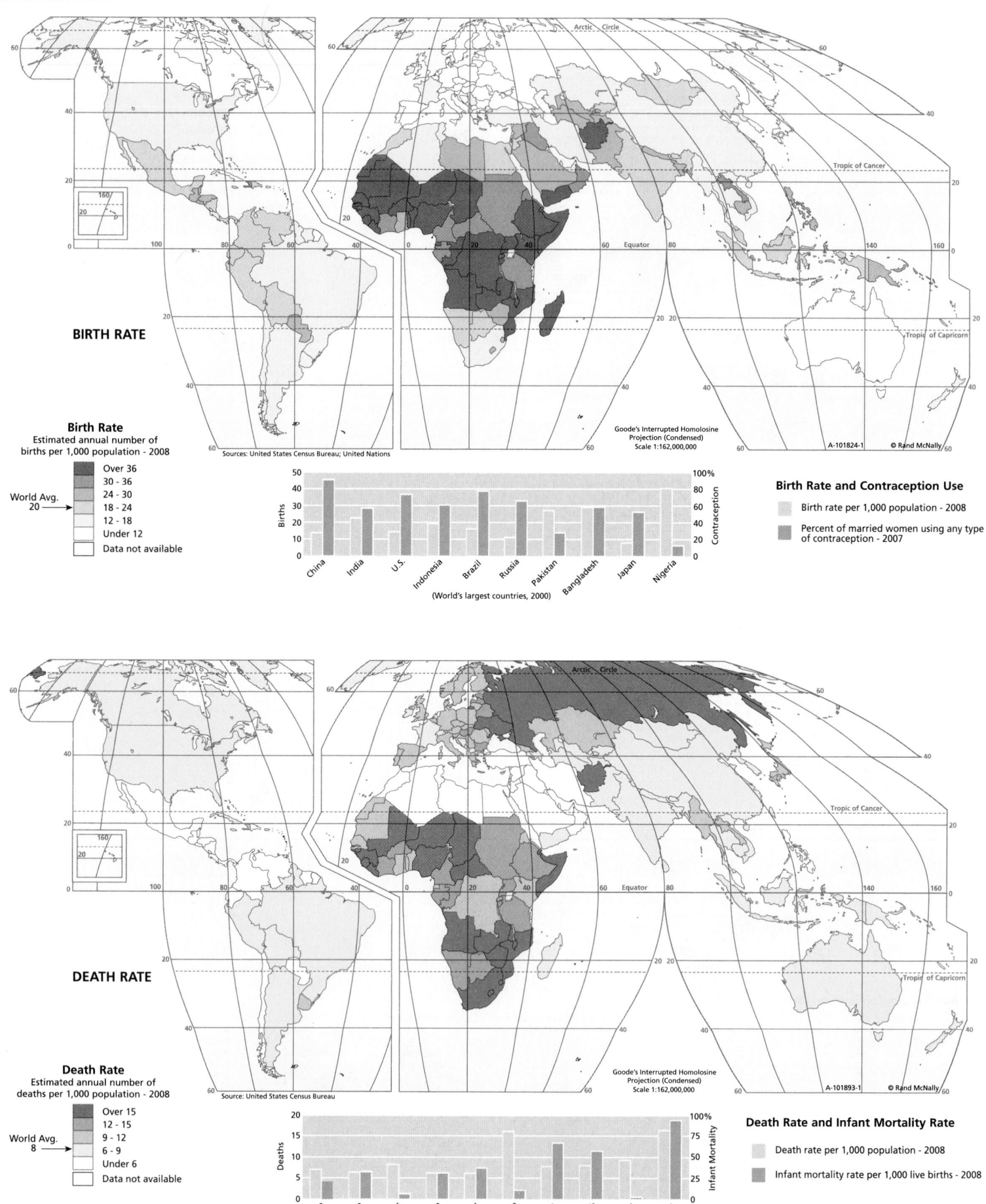

BIRTH RATE

Birth Rate
Estimated annual number of
births per 1,000 population - 2008

Over 36
30 - 36
24 - 30
World Avg.
20
18 - 24
12 - 18
Under 12
Data not available

Sources: United States Census Bureau; United Nations

Goode's Interrupted Homolosine
Projection (Condensed)
Scale 1:162,000,000

A-101824-1   © Rand McNally

Birth Rate and Contraception Use

Birth rate per 1,000 population - 2008

Percent of married women using any type
of contraception - 2007

(World's largest countries, 2000)

China India U.S. Indonesia Brazil Russia Pakistan Bangladesh Japan Nigeria

DEATH RATE

Death Rate
Estimated annual number of
deaths per 1,000 population - 2008

Over 15
12 - 15
9 - 12
World Avg.
8
6 - 9
Under 6
Data not available

Source: United States Census Bureau

Goode's Interrupted Homolosine
Projection (Condensed)
Scale 1:162,000,000

A-101893-1   © Rand McNally

Death Rate and Infant Mortality Rate

Death rate per 1,000 population - 2008

Infant mortality rate per 1,000 live births - 2008

(World's largest countries, 2000)

China India U.S. Indonesia Brazil Russia Pakistan Bangladesh Japan Nigeria

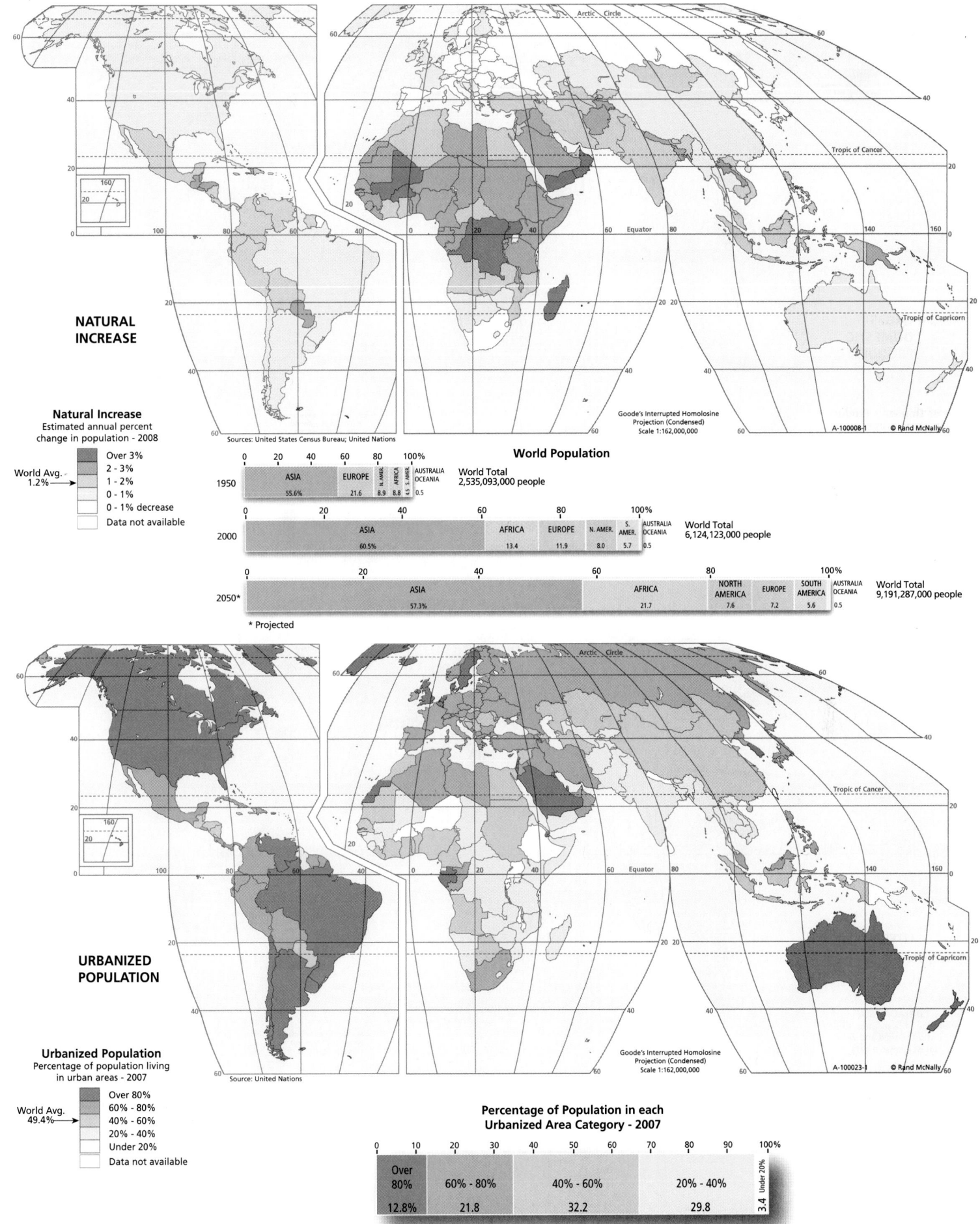

NATURAL INCREASE

Natural Increase
Estimated annual percent
change in population - 2008

- Over 3%
- 2 - 3%
- 1 - 2% ← World Avg. 1.2%
- 0 - 1%
- 0 - 1% decrease
- Data not available

Sources: United States Census Bureau; United Nations

Goode's Interrupted Homolosine
Projection (Condensed)
Scale 1:162,000,000

A-100008-1 © Rand McNally

World Population

1950					World Total 2,535,093,000 people
ASIA 55.6%	EUROPE 21.6	N. AMER. 8.9	AFRICA 8.8	S. AMER. 4.5	AUSTRALIA OCEANIA 0.5

2000						World Total 6,124,123,000 people
ASIA 60.5%	AFRICA 13.4	EUROPE 11.9	N. AMER. 8.0	S. AMER. 5.7	AUSTRALIA OCEANIA 0.5	

2050*						World Total 9,191,287,000 people
ASIA 57.3%	AFRICA 21.7	NORTH AMERICA 7.6	EUROPE 7.2	SOUTH AMERICA 5.6	AUSTRALIA OCEANIA 0.5	

* Projected

URBANIZED POPULATION

Urbanized Population
Percentage of population living
in urban areas - 2007

- Over 80%
- 60% - 80%
- 40% - 60% ← World Avg. 49.4%
- 20% - 40%
- Under 20%
- Data not available

Source: United Nations

Goode's Interrupted Homolosine
Projection (Condensed)
Scale 1:162,000,000

A-100023-1 © Rand McNally

**Percentage of Population in each
Urbanized Area Category - 2007**

Over 80% 12.8%	60% - 80% 21.8	40% - 60% 32.2	20% - 40% 29.8	Under 20% 3.4

GROSS DOMESTIC PRODUCT

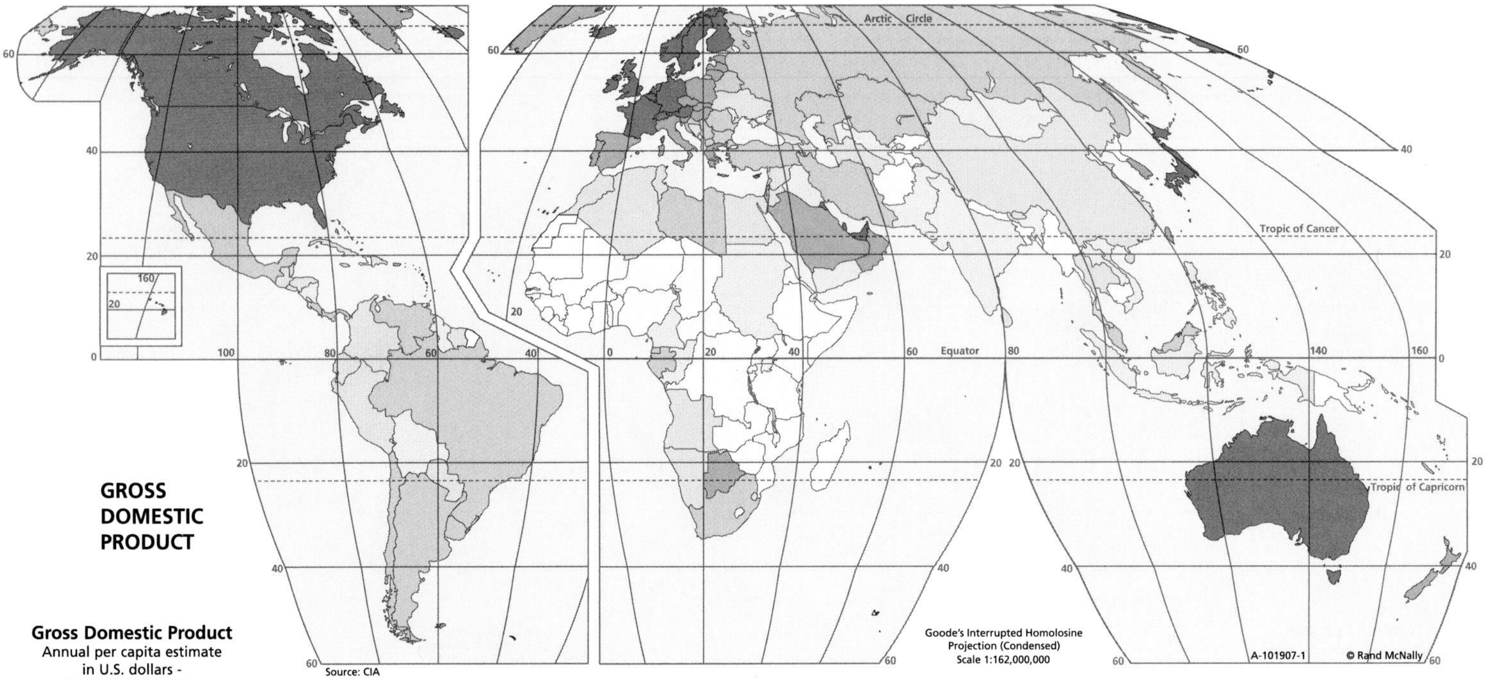
Arctic Circle
Tropic of Cancer
Equator
Tropic of Capricorn
Goode's Interrupted Homolosine Projection (Condensed)
Scale 1:162,000,000
A-101907-1
© Rand McNally
Source: CIA

Gross Domestic Product
Annual per capita estimate in U.S. dollars - latest available data

- Over $32,000
- $16,000 - $32,000
- $8,000 - $16,000
- $4,000 - $8,000
- $2,000 - $4,000
- Under $2,000
- Data not available

World Avg. $10,000

Percentage of World Population in each Per Capita GDP Category

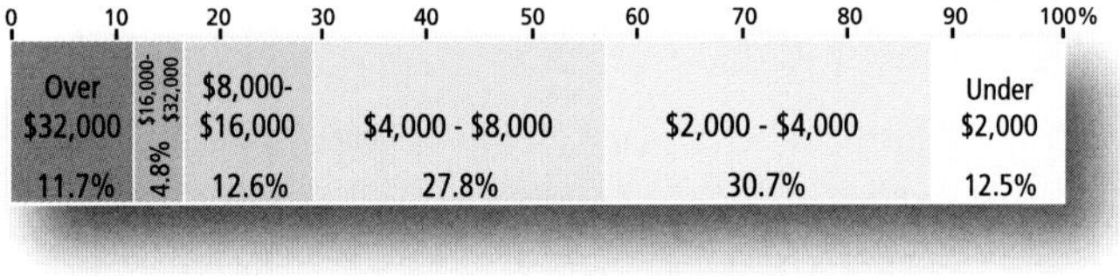
0
10
20
30
40
50
60
70
80
90
100%
Over $32,000
11.7%
$16,000-$32,000
4.8%
$8,000-$16,000
12.6%
$4,000 - $8,000
27.8%
$2,000 - $4,000
30.7%
Under $2,000
12.5%

LITERACY

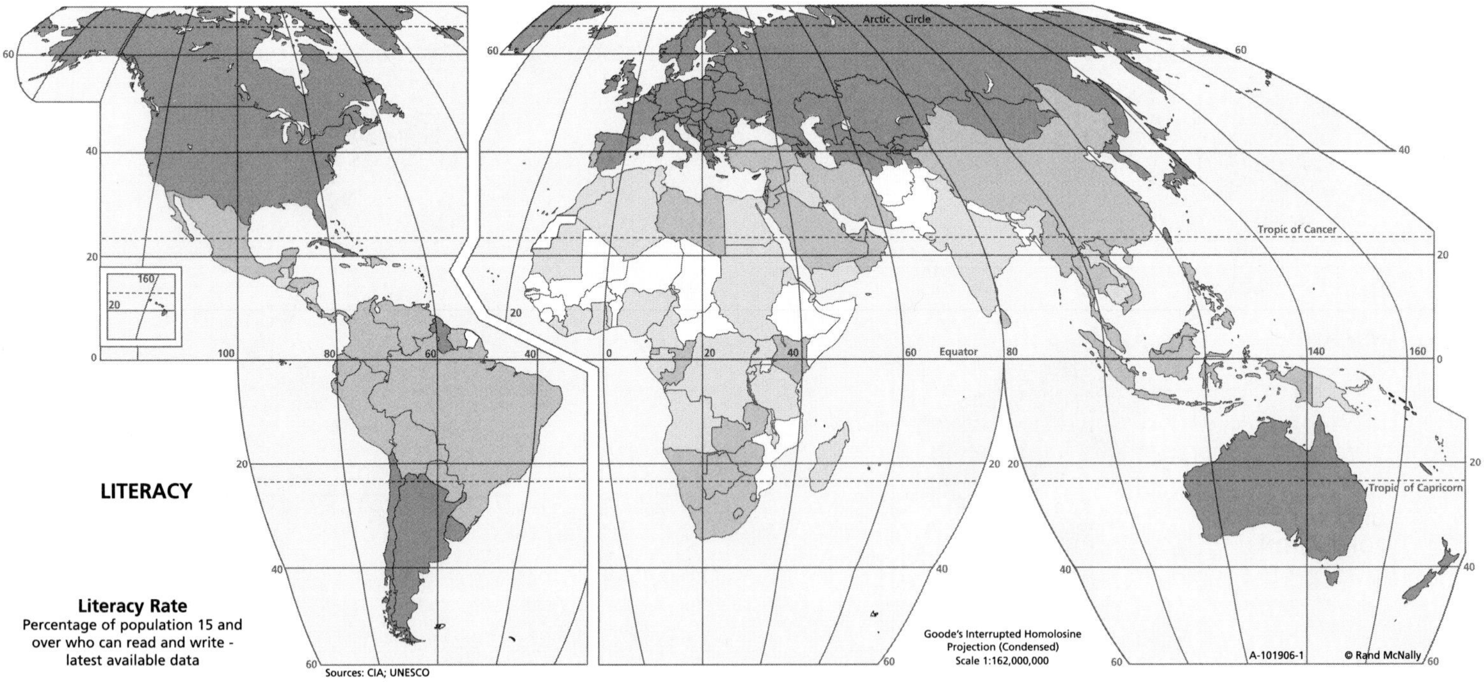
Arctic Circle
Tropic of Cancer
Equator
Tropic of Capricorn
Goode's Interrupted Homolosine Projection (Condensed)
Scale 1:162,000,000
A-101906-1
© Rand McNally
Sources: CIA; UNESCO

Literacy Rate
Percentage of population 15 and over who can read and write - latest available data

- Over 95%
- 75 - 95%
- 50 - 75%
- Under 50%
- Data not available

World Avg. 82%

Literacy and Compulsory Education

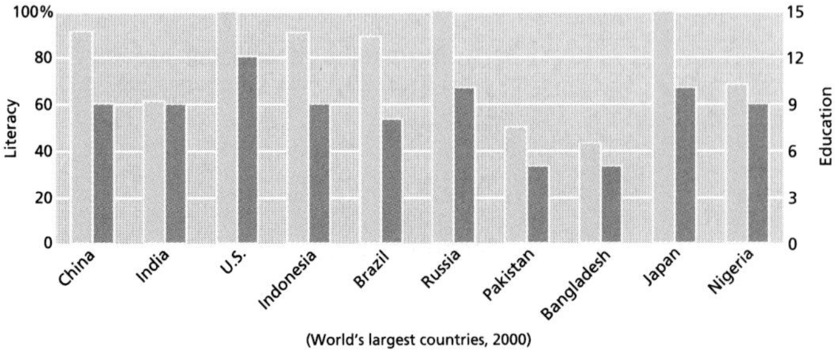
Literacy
Education
100%
80
60
40
20
0
15
12
9
6
3
China
India
U.S.
Indonesia
Brazil
Russia
Pakistan
Bangladesh
Japan
Nigeria
(World's largest countries, 2000)

- Literacy rate
- Years of compulsory education

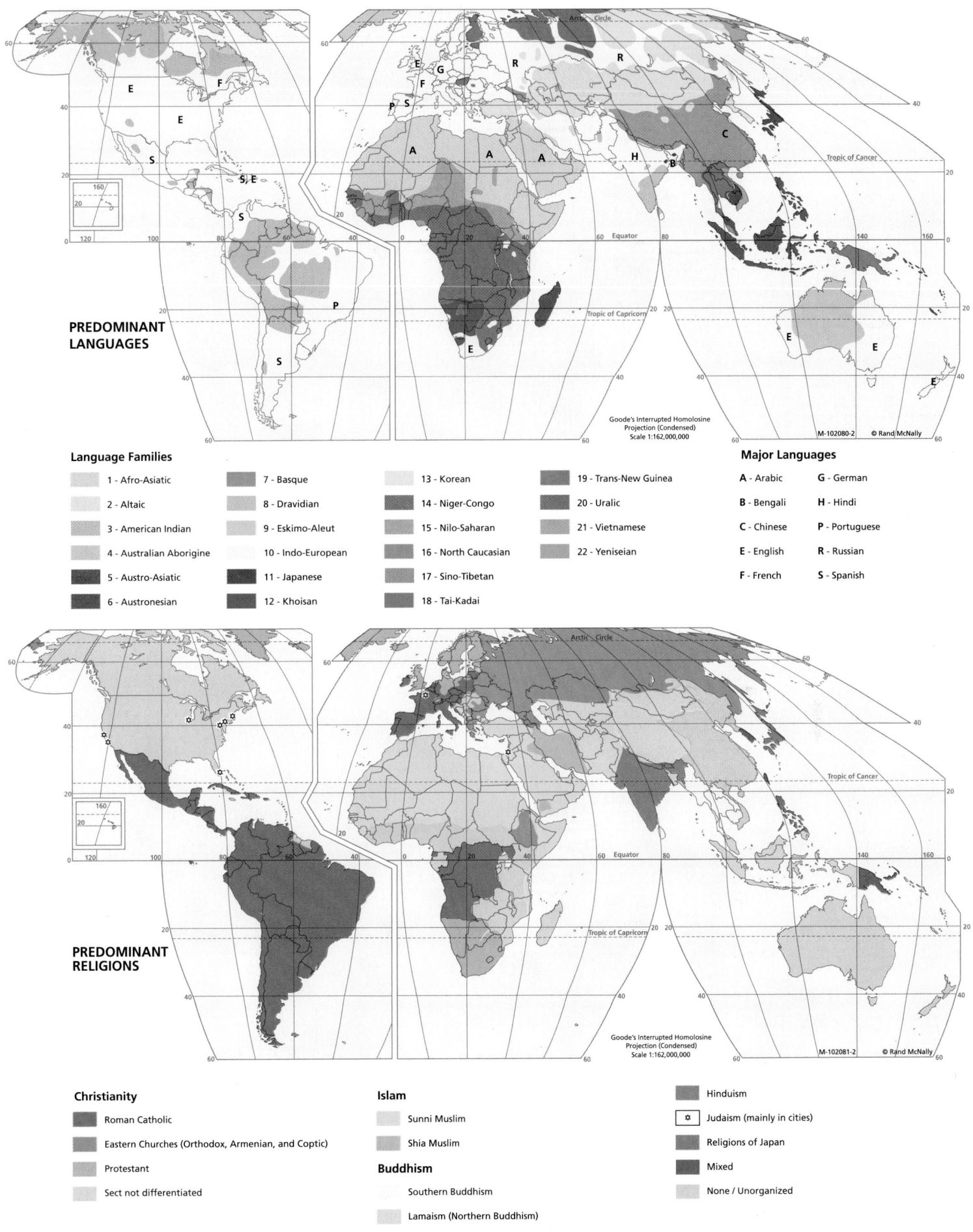

PREDOMINANT LANGUAGES

Language Families

1 - Afro-Asiatic	7 - Basque
2 - Altaic	8 - Dravidian
3 - American Indian	9 - Eskimo-Aleut
4 - Australian Aborigine	10 - Indo-European
5 - Austro-Asiatic	11 - Japanese
6 - Austronesian	12 - Khoisan

13 - Korean	19 - Trans-New Guinea
14 - Niger-Congo	20 - Uralic
15 - Nilo-Saharan	21 - Vietnamese
16 - North Caucasian	22 - Yeniseian
17 - Sino-Tibetan	
18 - Tai-Kadai	

Major Languages

A - Arabic	**G** - German
B - Bengali	**H** - Hindi
C - Chinese	**P** - Portuguese
E - English	**R** - Russian
F - French	**S** - Spanish

Goode's Interrupted Homolosine
Projection (Condensed)
Scale 1:162,000,000

M-102080-2   © Rand McNally

PREDOMINANT RELIGIONS

Christianity

- Roman Catholic
- Eastern Churches (Orthodox, Armenian, and Coptic)
- Protestant
- Sect not differentiated

Islam

- Sunni Muslim
- Shia Muslim

Buddhism

- Southern Buddhism
- Lamaism (Northern Buddhism)

- Hinduism
- ✡ Judaism (mainly in cities)
- Religions of Japan
- Mixed
- None / Unorganized

Goode's Interrupted Homolosine
Projection (Condensed)
Scale 1:162,000,000

M-102081-2   © Rand McNally

HIV INFECTION

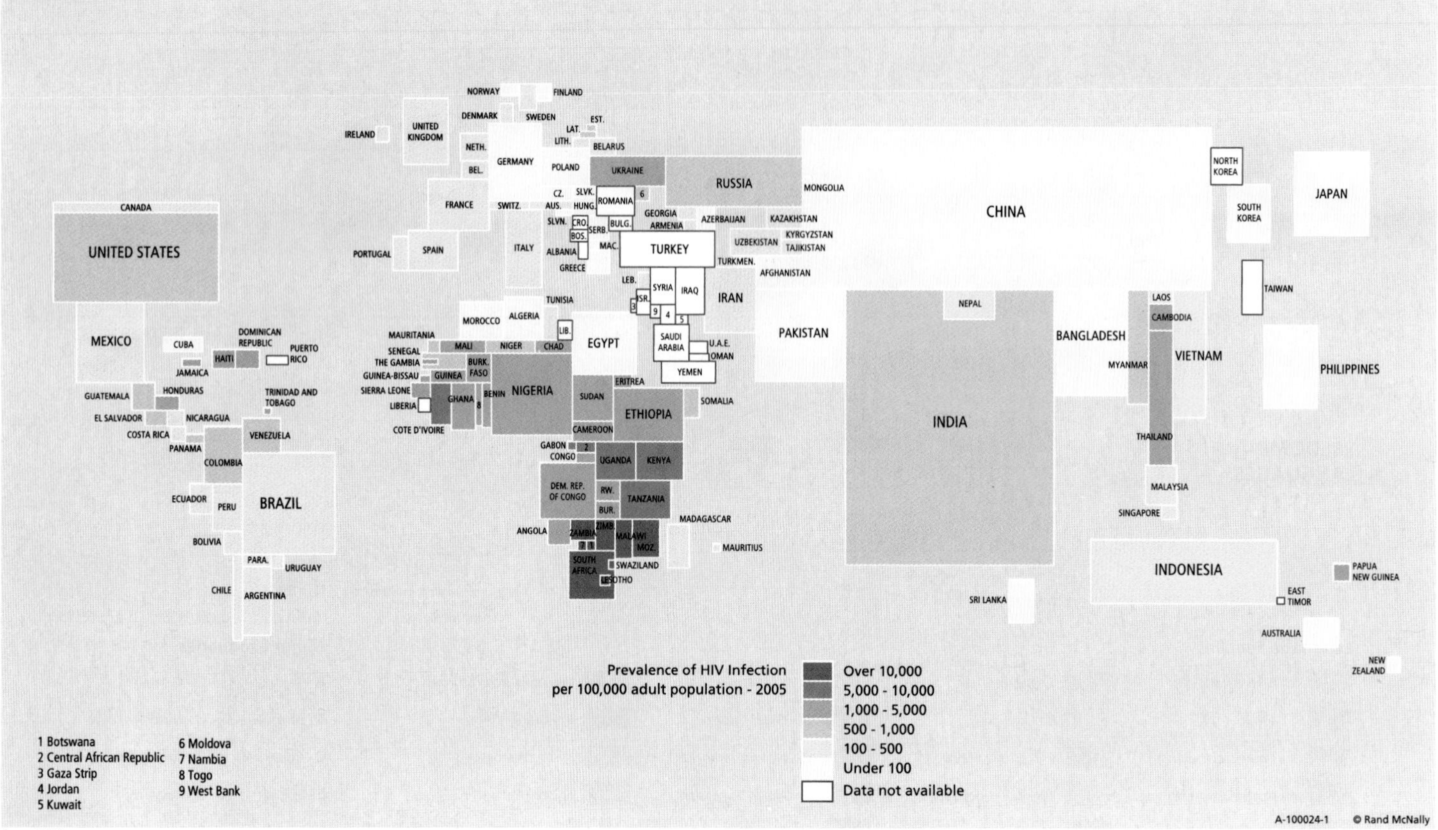

NORWAY FINLAND
IRELAND UNITED KINGDOM SWEDEN DENMARK EST.
NETH. LAT. LITH. BELARUS
BEL. GERMANY POLAND UKRAINE RUSSIA MONGOLIA
CANADA FRANCE SWITZ. CZ. SLVK. HUNG. ROMANIA GEORGIA AZERBAIJAN KAZAKHSTAN
SLVN. CRO. SERB. BULG. ARMENIA UZBEKISTAN KYRGYZSTAN TAJIKISTAN CHINA NORTH KOREA JAPAN
UNITED STATES PORTUGAL SPAIN ITALY ALBANIA MAC. TURKEY TURKMEN. SOUTH KOREA
GREECE LEB. SYRIA IRAQ IRAN AFGHANISTAN TAIWAN
ISR. 9 4 5
MEXICO CUBA DOMINICAN REPUBLIC PUERTO RICO MOROCCO ALGERIA TUNISIA LIB. EGYPT SAUDI ARABIA U.A.E. OMAN PAKISTAN NEPAL BANGLADESH LAOS CAMBODIA PHILIPPINES
JAMAICA HAITI MAURITANIA MALI NIGER CHAD YEMEN MYANMAR VIETNAM
GUATEMALA HONDURAS TRINIDAD AND TOBAGO SENEGAL THE GAMBIA BURK. FASO ERITREA SOMALIA INDIA
EL SALVADOR NICARAGUA GUINEA-BISSAU GUINEA SUDAN THAILAND
COSTA RICA PANAMA VENEZUELA SIERRA LEONE LIBERIA GHANA BENIN NIGERIA ETHIOPIA
COLOMBIA COTE D'IVOIRE CAMEROON MALAYSIA
ECUADOR PERU BRAZIL GABON CONGO 2 UGANDA KENYA SINGAPORE
DEM. REP. OF CONGO RW. TANZANIA
BOLIVIA BUR. INDONESIA PAPUA NEW GUINEA
PARA. URUGUAY ANGOLA ZAMBIA ZIM. MALAWI MOZ. MADAGASCAR MAURITIUS EAST TIMOR
CHILE SOUTH AFRICA SWAZILAND AUSTRALIA
ARGENTINA LESOTHO SRI LANKA NEW ZEALAND

Prevalence of HIV Infection
per 100,000 adult population - 2005

	Over 10,000
	5,000 - 10,000
	1,000 - 5,000
	500 - 1,000
	100 - 500
	Under 100
	Data not available

1 Botswana   6 Moldova
2 Central African Republic   7 Nambia
3 Gaza Strip   8 Togo
4 Jordan   9 West Bank
5 Kuwait

Source: WHO

A-100024-1   © Rand McNally

Size of each country is proportional to its population

☐ = 25,000,000 people

Countries with populations under 1,000,000 are not shown.

TUBERCULOSIS

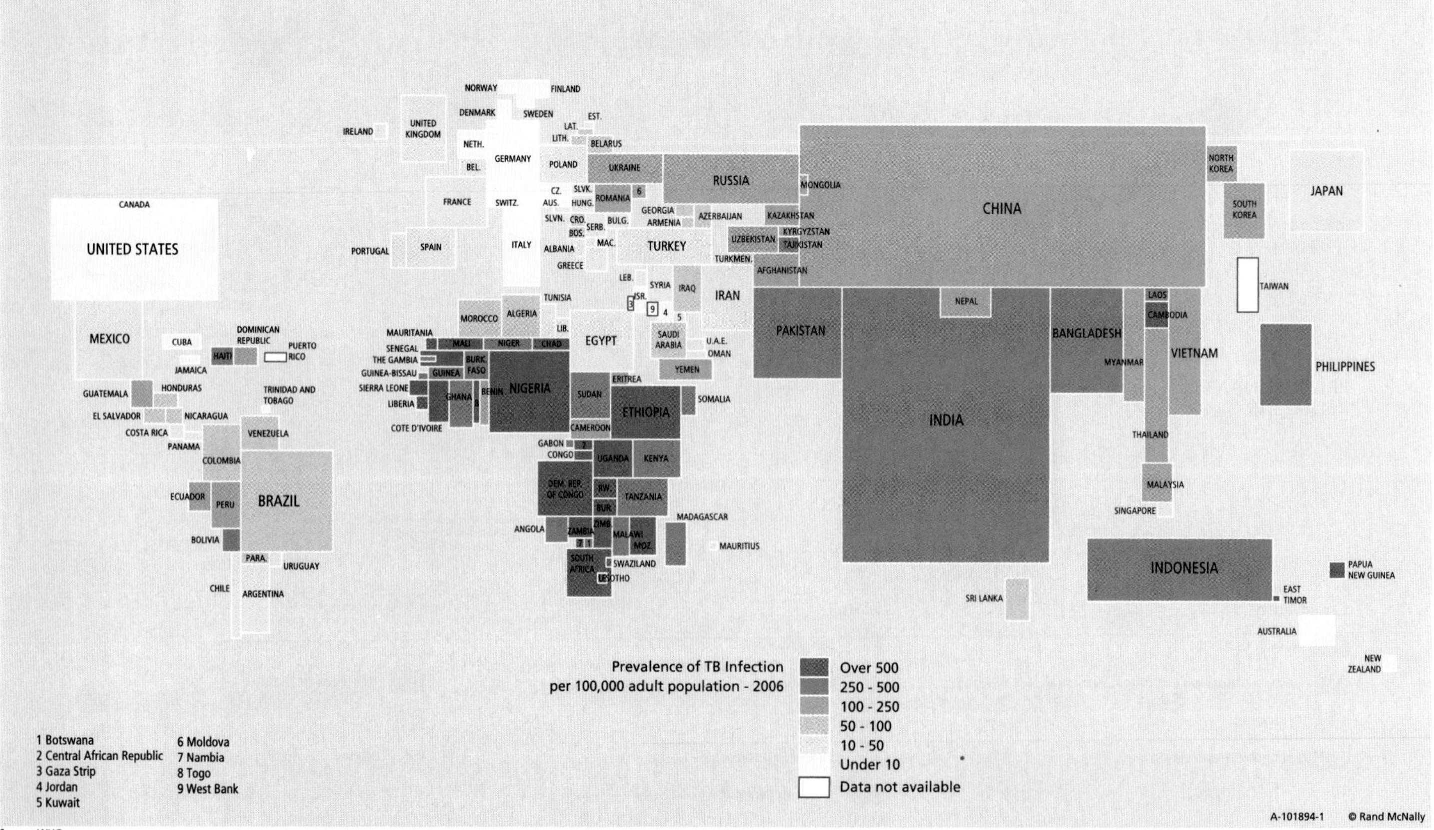

NORWAY FINLAND
IRELAND UNITED KINGDOM DENMARK SWEDEN EST.
NETH. LAT. LITH. BELARUS
BEL. GERMANY POLAND UKRAINE RUSSIA MONGOLIA
FRANCE SWITZ. CZ. SLVK. HUNG. ROMANIA GEORGIA AZERBAIJAN KAZAKHSTAN NORTH KOREA
CANADA SLVN. CRO. SERB. BULG. ARMENIA UZBEKISTAN KYRGYZSTAN CHINA JAPAN
PORTUGAL SPAIN ITALY ALBANIA MAC. TURKEY TURKMEN. TAJIKISTAN SOUTH KOREA
UNITED STATES GREECE LEB. SYRIA IRAQ IRAN AFGHANISTAN TAIWAN
ISR. 3 4 5
MEXICO CUBA DOMINICAN REPUBLIC PUERTO RICO MOROCCO ALGERIA LIB. EGYPT SAUDI ARABIA U.A.E. OMAN PAKISTAN NEPAL BANGLADESH LAOS CAMBODIA PHILIPPINES
JAMAICA HAITI MAURITANIA NIGER CHAD YEMEN MYANMAR VIETNAM
GUATEMALA HONDURAS SENEGAL MALI BURK. FASO ERITREA
TRINIDAD AND TOBAGO THE GAMBIA INDIA THAILAND
EL SALVADOR NICARAGUA GUINEA-BISSAU GUINEA SUDAN
COSTA RICA PANAMA SIERRA LEONE LIBERIA GHANA BENIN NIGERIA ETHIOPIA SOMALIA MALAYSIA
VENEZUELA COTE D'IVOIRE CAMEROON SINGAPORE
COLOMBIA GABON CONGO 2 UGANDA KENYA
ECUADOR PERU BRAZIL DEM. REP. OF CONGO RW. TANZANIA INDONESIA PAPUA NEW GUINEA
BOLIVIA BUR. EAST TIMOR
PARA. ANGOLA ZAMBIA ZIM. MALAWI MOZ. MADAGASCAR MAURITIUS
URUGUAY SOUTH AFRICA SWAZILAND AUSTRALIA
CHILE ARGENTINA LESOTHO SRI LANKA NEW ZEALAND

Prevalence of TB Infection
per 100,000 adult population - 2006

	Over 500
	250 - 500
	100 - 250
	50 - 100
	10 - 50
	Under 10
	Data not available

1 Botswana   6 Moldova
2 Central African Republic   7 Nambia
3 Gaza Strip   8 Togo
4 Jordan   9 West Bank
5 Kuwait

Source: WHO

A-101894-1   © Rand McNally

MALARIA

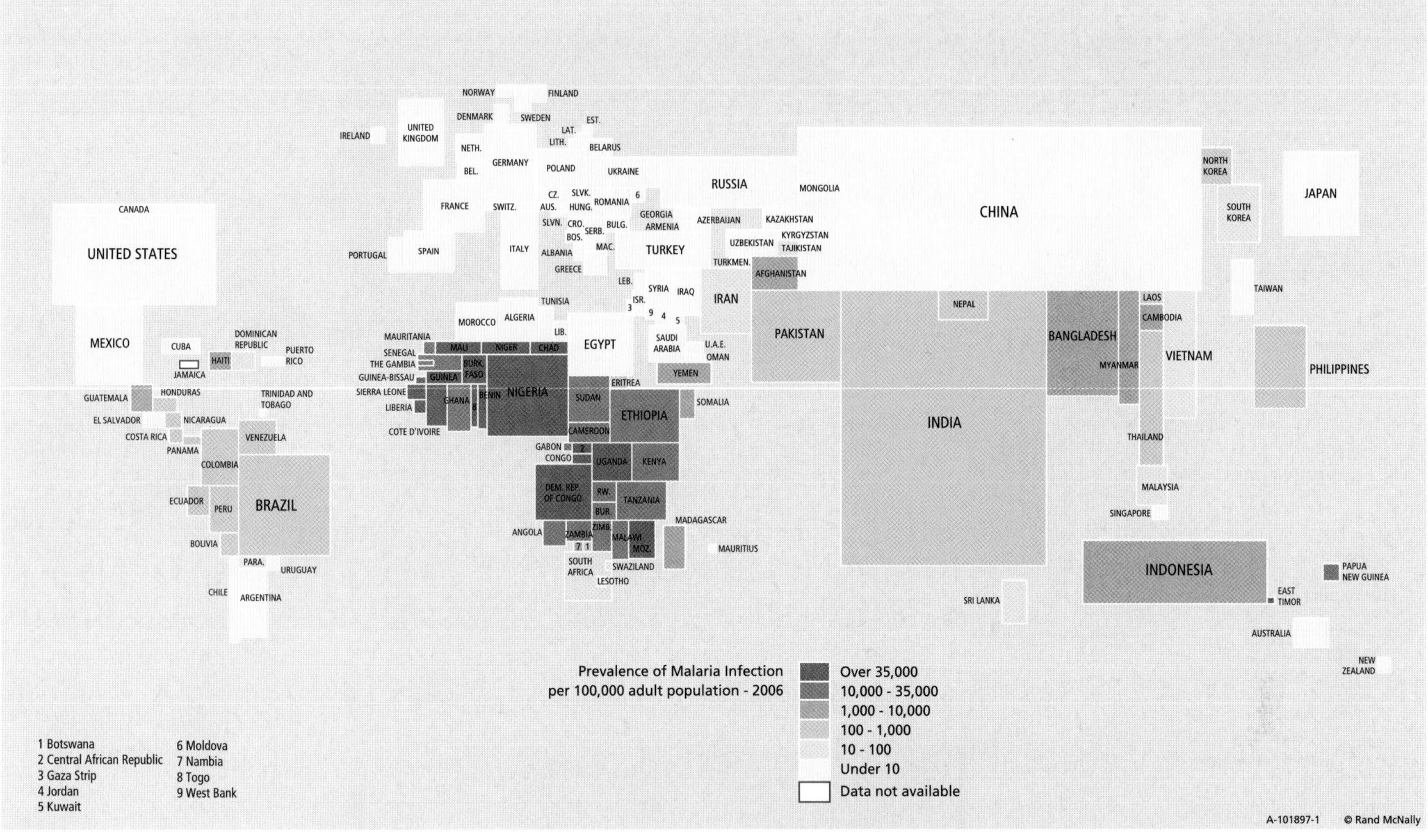

Prevalence of Malaria Infection
per 100,000 adult population - 2006

- Over 35,000
- 10,000 - 35,000
- 1,000 - 10,000
- 100 - 1,000
- 10 - 100
- Under 10
- Data not available

1 Botswana
2 Central African Republic
3 Gaza Strip
4 Jordan
5 Kuwait
6 Moldova
7 Namibia
8 Togo
9 West Bank

A-101897-1   © Rand McNally

Source: WHO

The maps on these two pages are called **cartograms**. On these cartograms, the size of each country is proportional to its total population. This means that the countries with the largest areas are those with the largest populations. The shapes of countries must be distorted in order to achieve this proportional representation. Here, each country is shown as a rectangle in order to facilitate size comparisons.

One advantage of these cartograms is that they reveal the relationship between the mapped variable and the affected population. Consider the example of Chad and Nigeria. Both have rela-tively high rates of HIV infection (between 1,000 and 5,000 cases per 100,000 population). But Nigeria is much larger than Chad on the cartogram, which informs the reader that the population affected by HIV is much larger in Nigeria.

PHYSICIANS

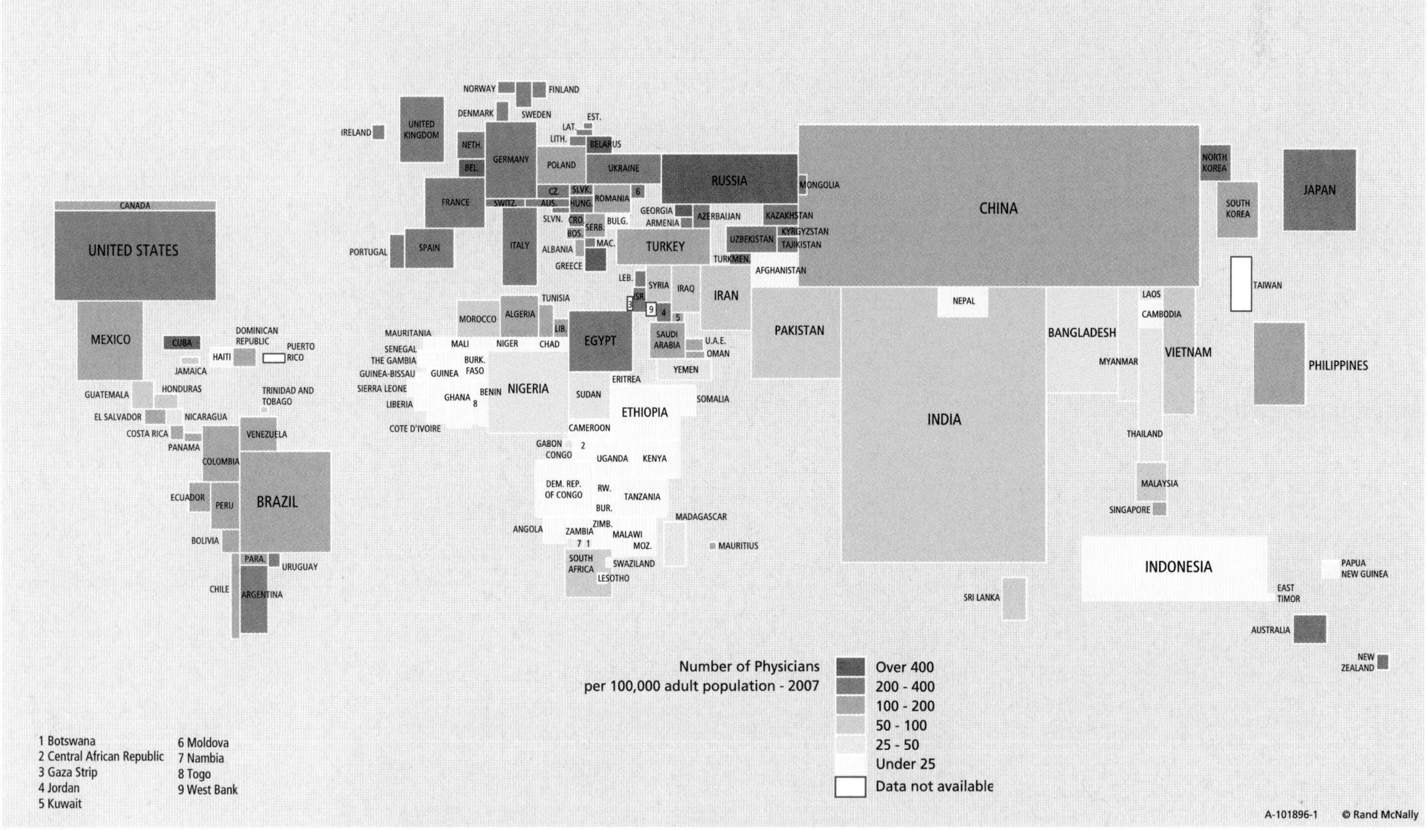

Number of Physicians
per 100,000 adult population - 2007

- Over 400
- 200 - 400
- 100 - 200
- 50 - 100
- 25 - 50
- Under 25
- Data not available

1 Botswana
2 Central African Republic
3 Gaza Strip
4 Jordan
5 Kuwait
6 Moldova
7 Namibia
8 Togo
9 West Bank

A-101896-1   © Rand McNally

Source: WHO

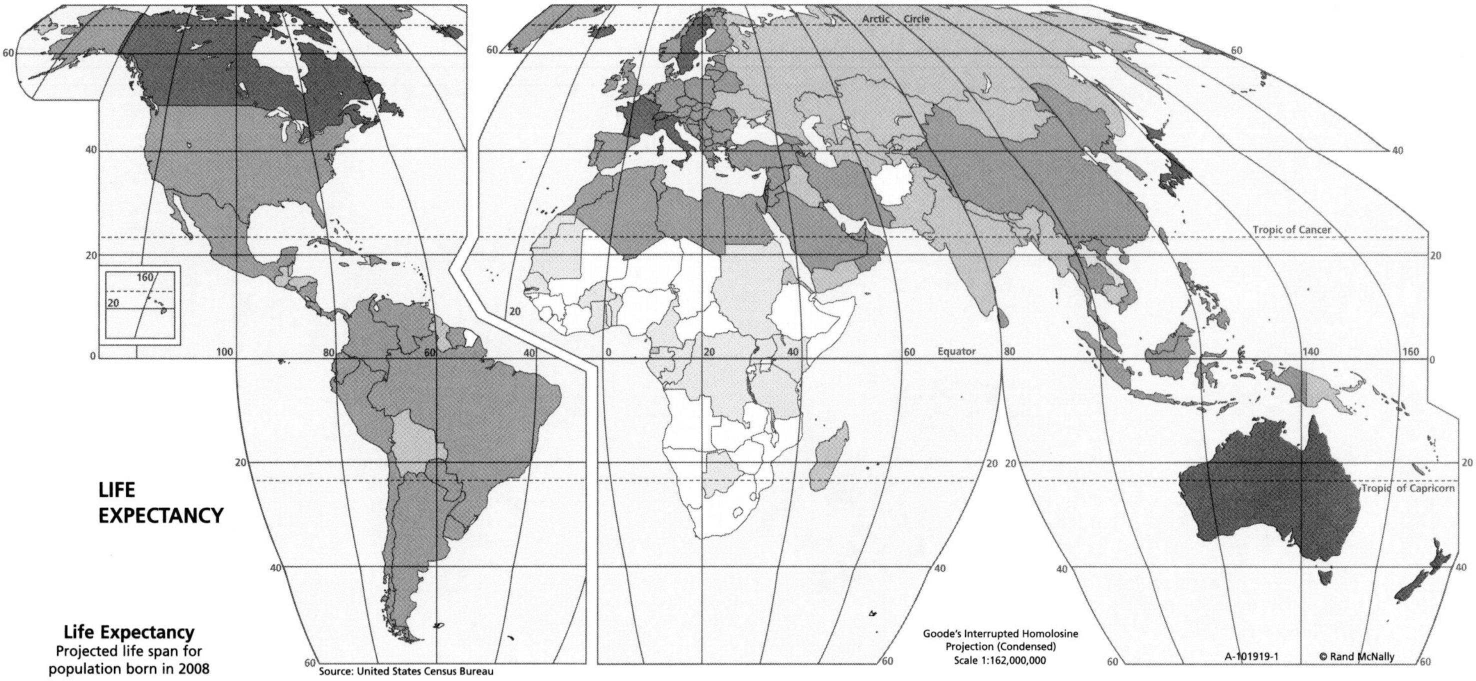

LIFE EXPECTANCY

Goode's Interrupted Homolosine
Projection (Condensed)
Scale 1:162,000,000

A-101919-1   © Rand McNally

Source: United States Census Bureau

Life Expectancy
Projected life span for
population born in 2008

World Avg.
66 →

- Over 80
- 70 - 80
- 60 - 70
- 50 - 60
- Under 50
- Data not available

Percentage of Births in each Life Expectancy Category - 2008

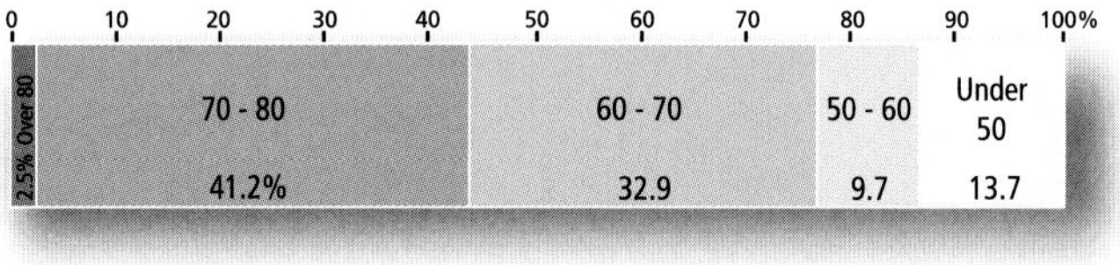

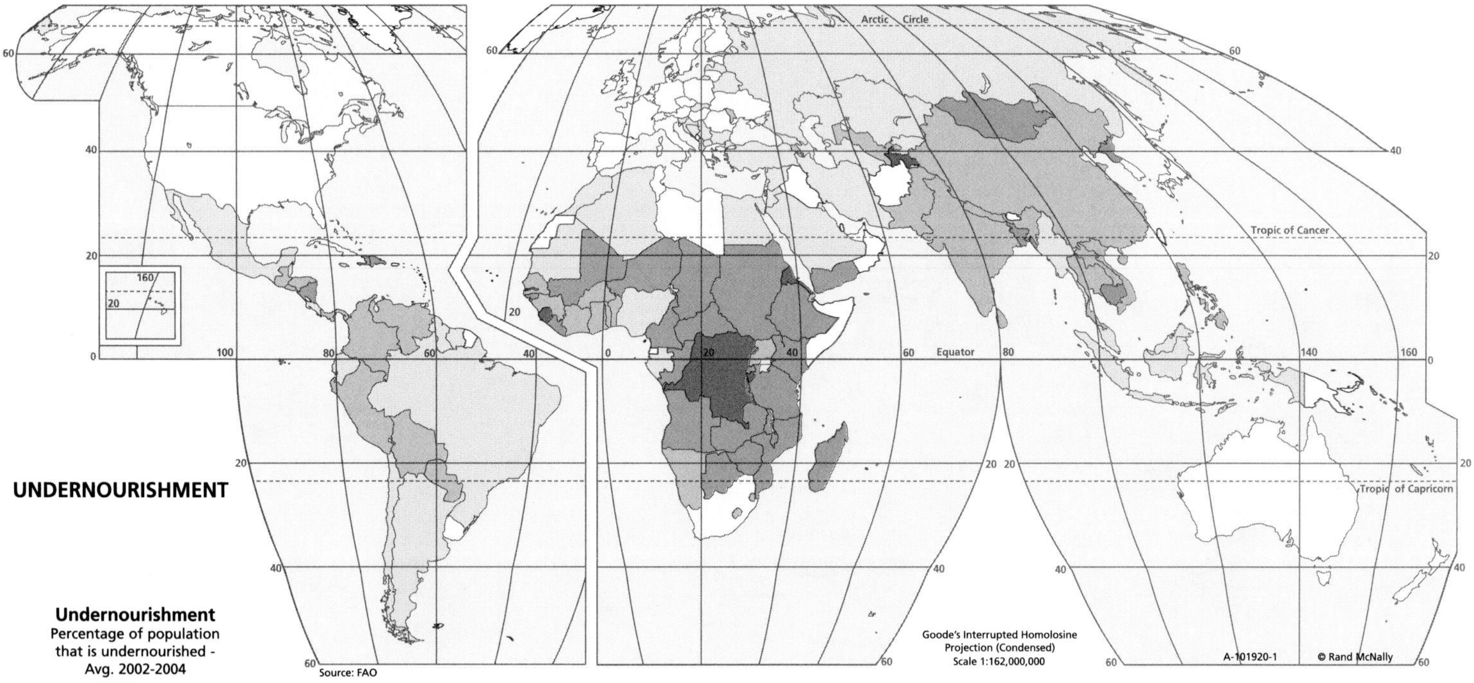

0	10	20	30	40	50	60	70	80	90	100%

Over 80 2.5%	70 - 80	60 - 70	50 - 60	Under 50
	41.2%	32.9	9.7	13.7

UNDERNOURISHMENT

Goode's Interrupted Homolosine
Projection (Condensed)
Scale 1:162,000,000

A-101920-1   © Rand McNally

Source: FAO

Undernourishment
Percentage of population
that is undernourished -
Avg. 2002-2004

- Over 50%
- 25% - 50%
- 10% - 25%
- 2.5% - 10%
- Under 2.5%
- Data not available

Undernourished People   World Total* - 825,900,000 people - Avg. 2002-2004

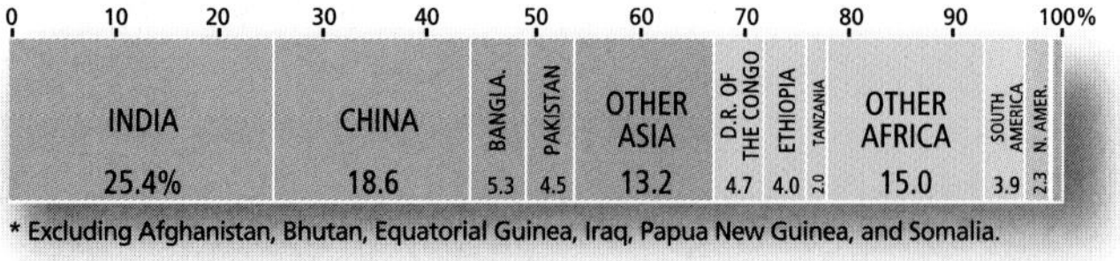

0	10	20	30	40	50	60	70	80	90	100%

INDIA	CHINA	BANGLA.	PAKISTAN	OTHER ASIA	D.R. OF THE CONGO	ETHIOPIA	TANZANIA	OTHER AFRICA	SOUTH AMERICA	N. AMER.
25.4%	18.6	5.3	4.5	13.2	4.7	4.0	2.0	15.0	3.9	2.3

* Excluding Afghanistan, Bhutan, Equatorial Guinea, Iraq, Papua New Guinea, and Somalia.

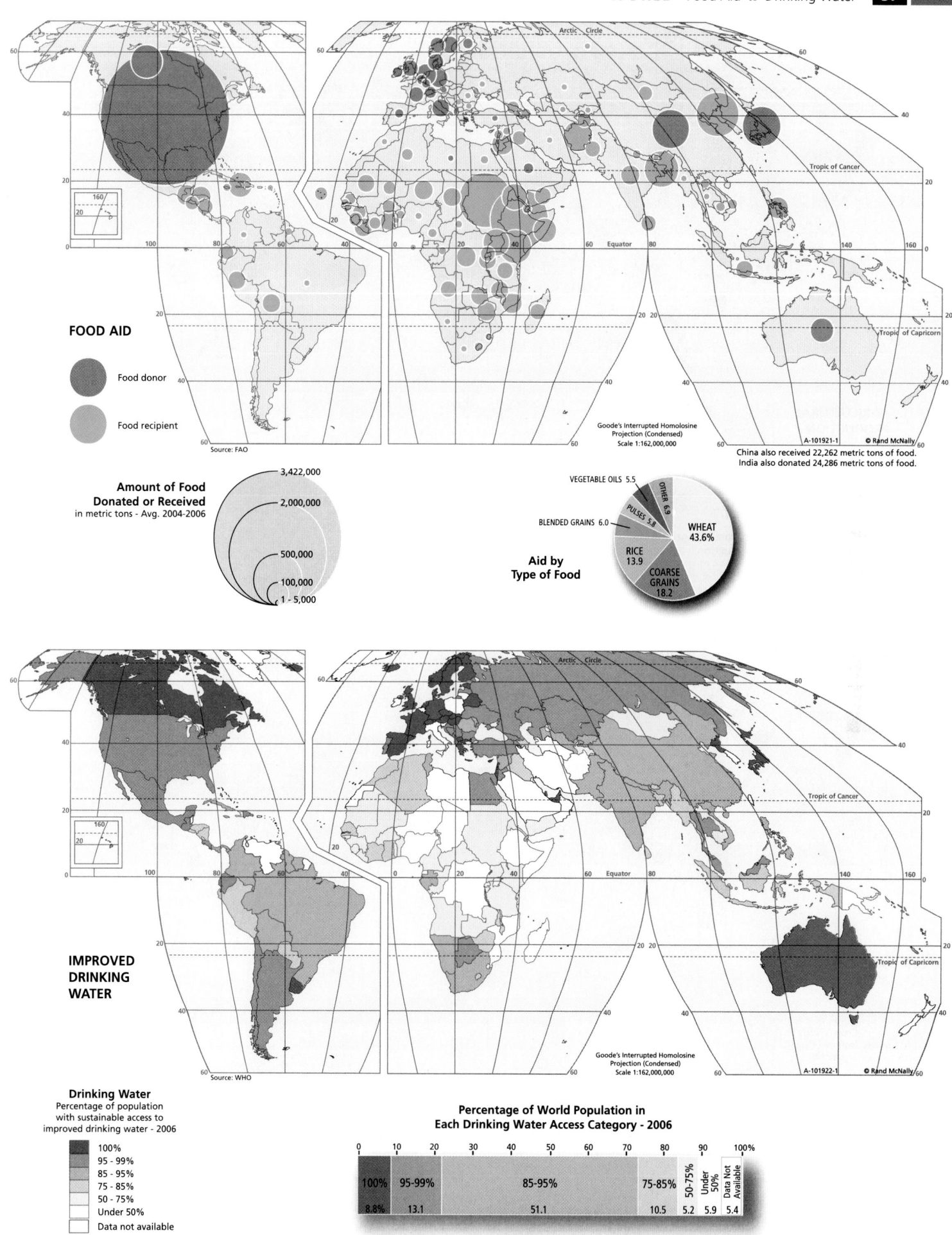

FOOD AID

Food donor

Food recipient

Source: FAO

Goode's Interrupted Homolosine
Projection (Condensed)
Scale 1:162,000,000

A-101921-1   © Rand McNally

China also received 22,262 metric tons of food.
India also donated 24,286 metric tons of food.

**Amount of Food
Donated or Received**
in metric tons - Avg. 2004-2006

3,422,000
2,000,000
500,000
100,000
1 - 5,000

**Aid by
Type of Food**

VEGETABLE OILS 5.5
OTHER 6.9
BLENDED GRAINS 6.0
PULSES 5.8
WHEAT 43.6%
RICE 13.9
COARSE GRAINS 18.2

**IMPROVED
DRINKING
WATER**

Source: WHO

Goode's Interrupted Homolosine
Projection (Condensed)
Scale 1:162,000,000

A-101922-1   © Rand McNally

Drinking Water
Percentage of population
with sustainable access to
improved drinking water - 2006

100%
95 - 99%
85 - 95%
75 - 85%
50 - 75%
Under 50%
Data not available

**Percentage of World Population in
Each Drinking Water Access Category - 2006**

0	10	20	30	40	50	60	70	80	90	100%

100%	95-99%	85-95%	75-85%	50-75%	Under 50%	Data Not Available
8.8%	13.1	51.1	10.5	5.2	5.9	5.4

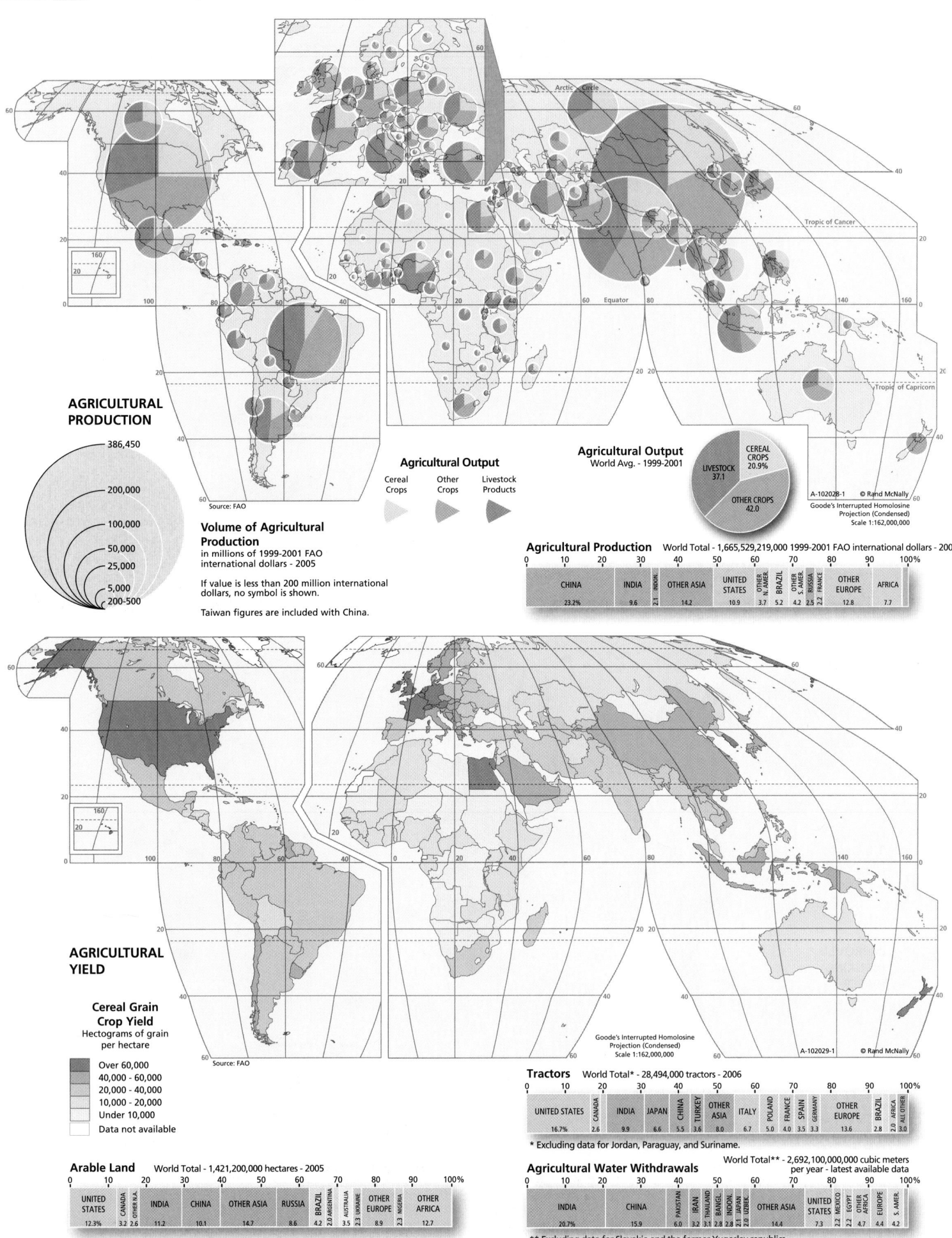

AGRICULTURAL PRODUCTION

386,450
200,000
100,000
50,000
25,000
5,000
200-500

160
20

Source: FAO

Volume of Agricultural Production
in millions of 1999-2001 FAO international dollars - 2005

If value is less than 200 million international dollars, no symbol is shown.

Taiwan figures are included with China.

Agricultural Output

Cereal Crops / Other Crops / Livestock Products

Agricultural Output
World Avg. - 1999-2001

CEREAL CROPS 20.9%
LIVESTOCK 37.1
OTHER CROPS 42.0

A-102028-1   © Rand McNally
Goode's Interrupted Homolosine
Projection (Condensed)
Scale 1:162,000,000

Agricultural Production   World Total - 1,665,529,219,000 1999-2001 FAO international dollars - 2005

0	10	20	30	40	50	60	70	80	90	100%
CHINA	INDIA	INDON.	OTHER ASIA	UNITED STATES	OTHER N. AMER.	BRAZIL	OTHER S. AMER.	RUSSIA	FRANCE	OTHER EUROPE	AFRICA
23.2%	9.6	2.1	14.2	10.9	3.7	5.2	4.2	2.5	2.2	12.8	7.7

AGRICULTURAL YIELD

Cereal Grain Crop Yield
Hectograms of grain per hectare

160
20

Source: FAO

- Over 60,000
- 40,000 - 60,000
- 20,000 - 40,000
- 10,000 - 20,000
- Under 10,000
- Data not available

Goode's Interrupted Homolosine
Projection (Condensed)
Scale 1:162,000,000

A-102029-1   © Rand McNally

Tractors   World Total* - 28,494,000 tractors - 2006

0	10	20	30	40	50	60	70	80	90	100%
UNITED STATES	CANADA	INDIA	JAPAN	CHINA	TURKEY	OTHER ASIA	ITALY	POLAND	FRANCE	SPAIN	GERMANY	OTHER EUROPE	BRAZIL	AFRICA	ALL OTHER
16.7%	2.6	9.9	6.6	5.5	3.6	8.0	6.7	5.0	4.0	3.5	3.3	13.6	2.8	2.0	3.0

* Excluding data for Jordan, Paraguay, and Suriname.

Arable Land   World Total - 1,421,200,000 hectares - 2005

0	10	20	30	40	50	60	70	80	90	100%
UNITED STATES	CANADA	OTHER N.A.	INDIA	CHINA	OTHER ASIA	RUSSIA	BRAZIL	ARGENTINA	AUSTRALIA	UKRAINE	OTHER EUROPE	NIGERIA	OTHER AFRICA
12.3%	3.2	2.6	11.2	10.1	14.7	8.6	4.2	2.0	3.5	2.3	8.9	2.3	12.7

Agricultural Water Withdrawals   World Total** - 2,692,100,000,000 cubic meters per year - latest available data

0	10	20	30	40	50	60	70	80	90	100%
INDIA	CHINA	PAKISTAN	IRAN	THAILAND	INDON.	BANGL.	JAPAN	UZBEK.	OTHER ASIA	UNITED STATES	MEXICO	EGYPT	OTHER AFRICA	EUROPE	S. AMER.
20.7%	15.9	6.0	3.2	3.1	2.8	2.8	2.1	2.0	14.4	7.3	2.2	2.2	4.7	4.4	4.2

** Excluding data for Slovakia and the former Yugoslav republics.

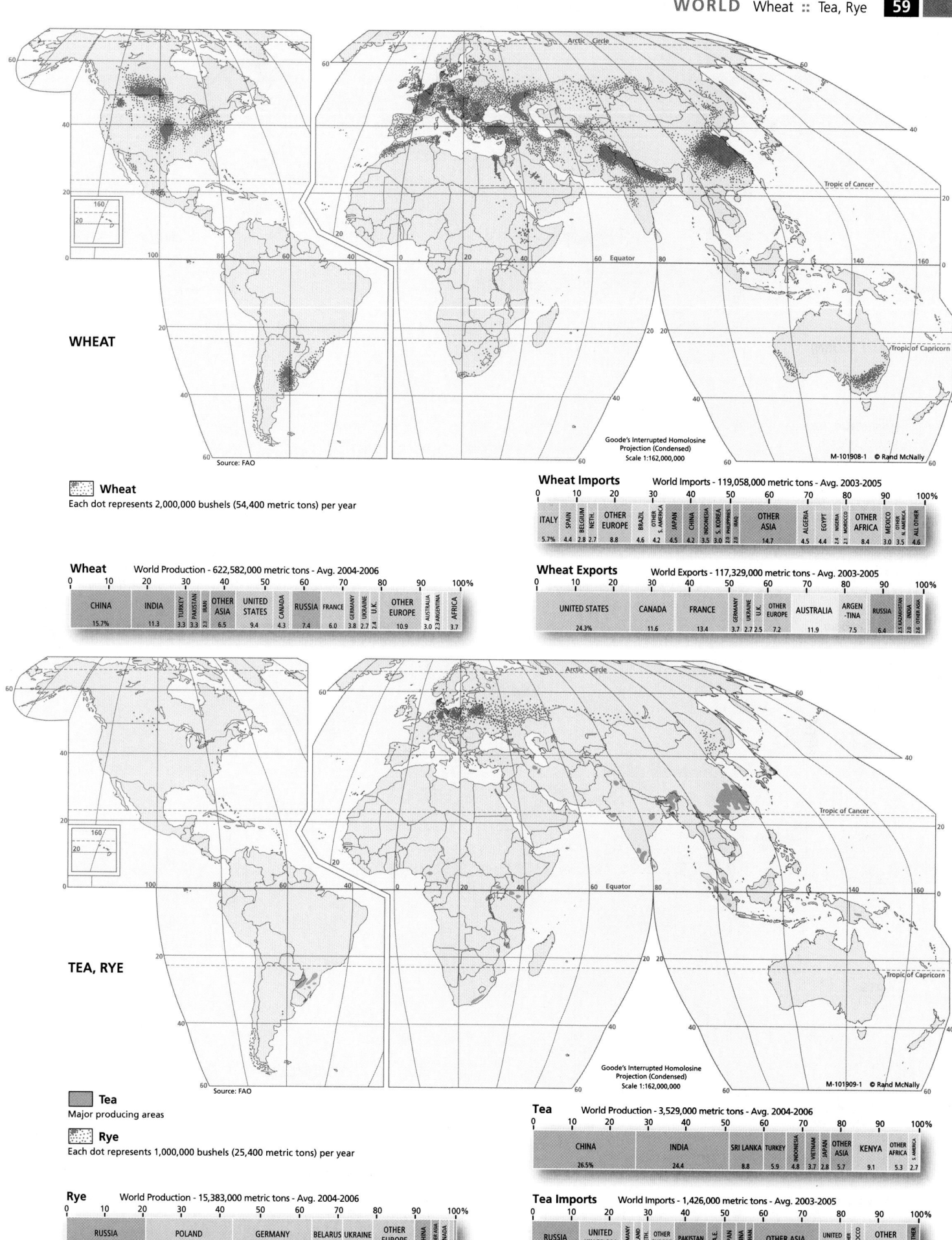

WHEAT

Goode's Interrupted Homolosine
Projection (Condensed)
Scale 1:162,000,000

Source: FAO

M-101908-1 © Rand McNally

Wheat
Each dot represents 2,000,000 bushels (54,400 metric tons) per year

Wheat Imports   World Imports - 119,058,000 metric tons - Avg. 2003-2005

0	10	20	30	40	50	60	70	80	90	100%
ITALY	SPAIN	BELGIUM	NETH.	OTHER EUROPE	BRAZIL	OTHER S. AMERICA	JAPAN	CHINA	INDONESIA	S. KOREA	PHILIPPINES	IRAQ	OTHER ASIA	ALGERIA	EGYPT	NIGERIA	MOROCCO	OTHER AFRICA	MEXICO	OTHER N. AMERICA	ALL OTHER
5.7%	4.4	2.8	2.7	8.8	4.6	4.2	4.5	4.2	3.5	3.0	2.0	2.0	14.7	4.5	4.4	2.4	2.1	8.4	3.0	3.5	4.6

Wheat   World Production - 622,582,000 metric tons - Avg. 2004-2006

0	10	20	30	40	50	60	70	80	90	100%
CHINA	INDIA	TURKEY	PAKISTAN	IRAN	OTHER ASIA	UNITED STATES	CANADA	RUSSIA	FRANCE	GERMANY	UKRAINE	U.K.	OTHER EUROPE	AUSTRALIA	ARGENTINA	AFRICA
15.7%	11.3	3.3	3.3	2.3	6.5	9.4	4.3	7.4	6.0	3.8	2.4	2.4	10.9	3.0	2.3	3.7

Wheat Exports   World Exports - 117,329,000 metric tons - Avg. 2003-2005

0	10	20	30	40	50	60	70	80	90	100%
UNITED STATES	CANADA	FRANCE	GERMANY	UKRAINE	U.K.	OTHER EUROPE	AUSTRALIA	ARGEN-TINA	RUSSIA	KAZAKHSTAN	INDIA	OTHER ASIA
24.3%	11.6	13.4	3.7	2.7	2.5	7.2	11.9	7.5	6.4	2.5	2.3	2.6

TEA, RYE

Goode's Interrupted Homolosine
Projection (Condensed)
Scale 1:162,000,000

Source: FAO

M-101909-1 © Rand McNally

Tea
Major producing areas

Rye
Each dot represents 1,000,000 bushels (25,400 metric tons) per year

Tea   World Production - 3,529,000 metric tons - Avg. 2004-2006

0	10	20	30	40	50	60	70	80	90	100%
CHINA	INDIA	SRI LANKA	TURKEY	INDONESIA	VIETNAM	JAPAN	OTHER ASIA	KENYA	OTHER AFRICA	S. AMERICA
26.5%	24.4	8.8	5.9	4.8	3.7	2.8	11.5	9.1	5.3	2.7

Rye   World Production - 15,383,000 metric tons - Avg. 2004-2006

0	10	20	30	40	50	60	70	80	90	100%
RUSSIA	POLAND	GERMANY	BELARUS	UKRAINE	OTHER EUROPE	CHINA	OTHER ASIA	CANADA
20.5%	22.3	20.1	7.9	7.7	10.7	4.2	2.2	2.3

Tea Imports   World Imports - 1,426,000 metric tons - Avg. 2003-2005

0	10	20	30	40	50	60	70	80	90	100%
RUSSIA	UNITED KINGDOM	GERMANY	POLAND	NETH.	OTHER EUROPE	PAKISTAN	U.A.E.	JAPAN	CHINA	AFGHAN.	OTHER ASIA	UNITED STATES	MOROCCO	OTHER AFRICA	ALL OTHER
12.2%	10.9	3.1	2.2	2.0	6.5	8.4	3.9	3.6	2.0	2.0	16.8	6.9	3.5	3.3	10.8	3.4

MAIZE (CORN)

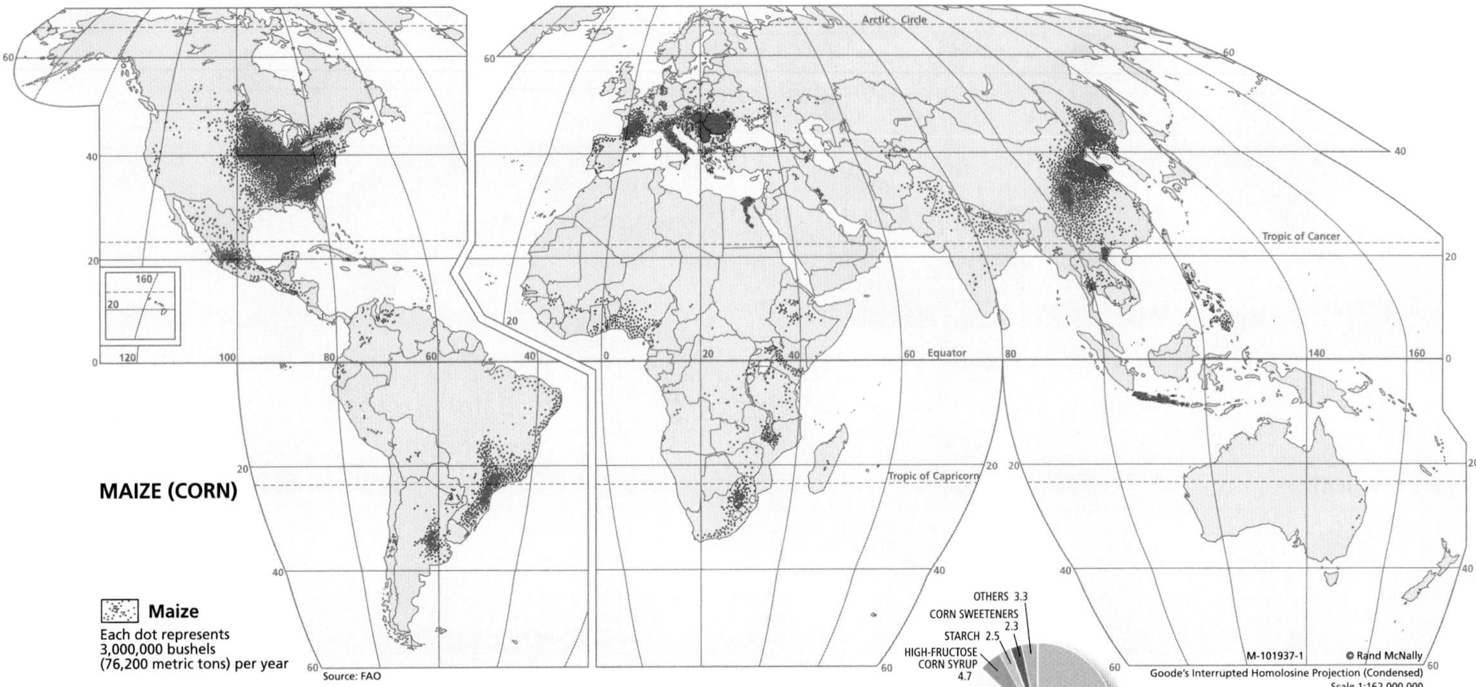

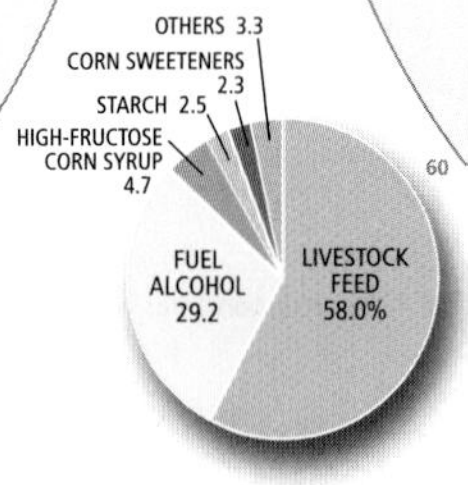

Arctic Circle
Tropic of Cancer
Equator
Tropic of Capricorn
Maize
Each dot represents
3,000,000 bushels
(76,200 metric tons) per year
Source: FAO
M-101937-1
© Rand McNally
Goode's Interrupted Homolosine Projection (Condensed)
Scale 1:162,000,000

OTHERS 3.3
CORN SWEETENERS 2.3
STARCH 2.5
HIGH-FRUCTOSE CORN SYRUP 4.7
FUEL ALCOHOL 29.2
LIVESTOCK FEED 58.0%

U.S. Maize Utilization - 2007

Maize World Production - 711,807,000 metric tons - Avg. 2004-2006

UNITED STATES 39.8%
MEXICO 2.9
OTHER N.A. 1.8
CHINA 19.5
INDIA 2.1
OTHER ASIA 5.9
BRAZIL 5.6
ARGENTINA 2.3
FRANCE 2.0
OTHER EUROPE 9.6
AFRICA 6.7

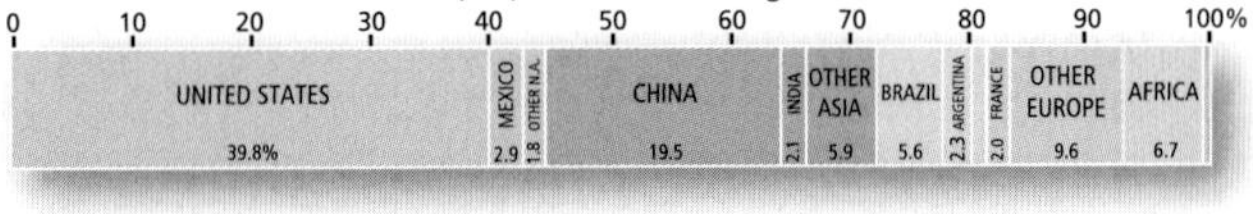

Maize Imports World Imports - 87,858,000 metric tons - Avg. 2003-2005

JAPAN 19.0%
S. KOREA 9.7
CHINA 5.8
MALAYSIA 3.4
IRAN 2.7
OTHER ASIA 9.0
MEXICO 6.5
CANADA 3.0
OTHER N. AMER. 4.7
EGYPT 4.5
ALGERIA 2.2
OTHER AFRICA 5.6
SPAIN 4.1
NETH. 2.4
OTHER EUROPE 9.7
COLOMBIA 2.4
OTHER S. AMER. 4.2

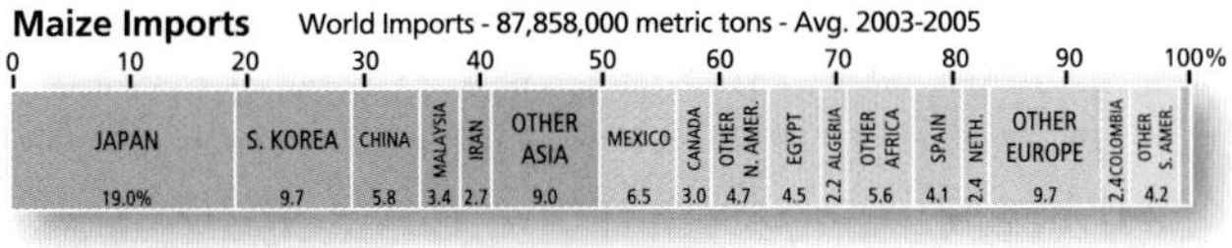

Maize Exports World Exports - 88,648,000 metric tons - Avg. 2003-2005

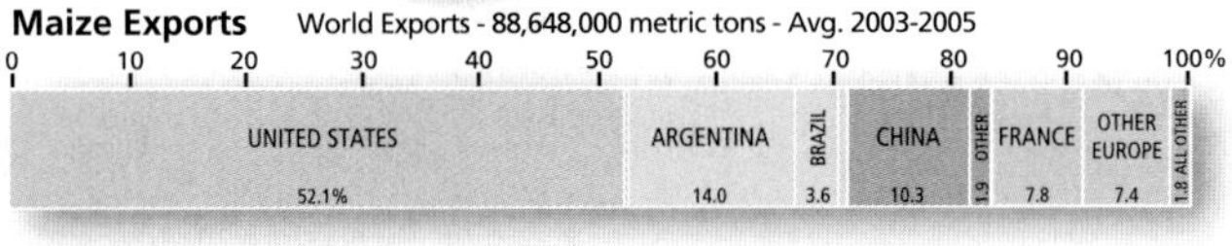

UNITED STATES 52.1%
ARGENTINA 14.0
BRAZIL 3.6
CHINA 10.3
OTHER 1.9
FRANCE 7.8
OTHER EUROPE 7.4
ALL OTHER 1.8

COFFEE, OATS

Arctic Circle
Tropic of Cancer
Equator
Tropic of Capricorn
Source: FAO
Goode's Interrupted Homolosine Projection (Condensed)
Scale 1:162,000,000
M-101938-1
© Rand McNally
Coffee
Major producing areas
Oats
Each dot represents 1,000,000 bushels (14,500 metric tons) per year

Coffee World Production - 7,612,900 metric tons - Avg. 2004-2006

BRAZIL 31.5%
COLOMBIA 9.1
PERU 2.5
OTHER S.A. 2.6
VIETNAM 10.7
INDONESIA 8.5
INDIA 3.6
OTHER ASIA 3.8
MEXICO 3.9
GUATEMALA 3.2
HONDURAS 2.5
OTHER N.A. 5.1
COTE D'IVOIRE 2.8
ETHIOPIA 2.6
UGANDA 2.0
OTHER AFRICA 4.7

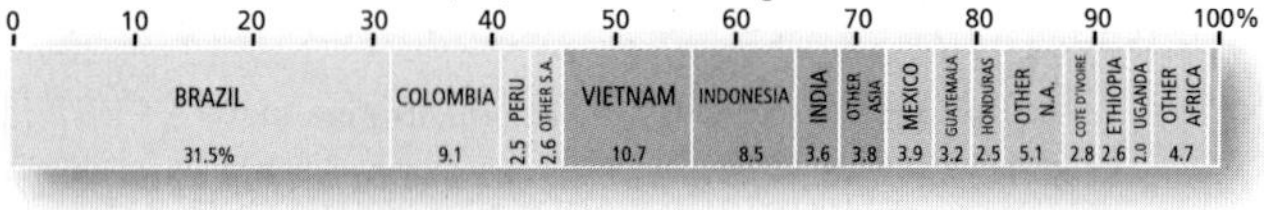

Oats World Production - 24,311,000 metric tons - Avg. 2004-2006

RUSSIA 19.7%
CANADA 14.7
UNITED STATES 6.5
POLAND 5.2
FINLAND 4.3
GERMANY 4.1
SPAIN 3.4
UKRAINE 3.4
SWEEDEN 3.2
BELARUS 2.6
U.K. 2.6
FRANCE 2.2
OTHER EUROPE 11.6
AUSTRALIA 4.6
CHINA 3.4
OTHER ASIA 1.9
SOUTH AMERICA 5.3

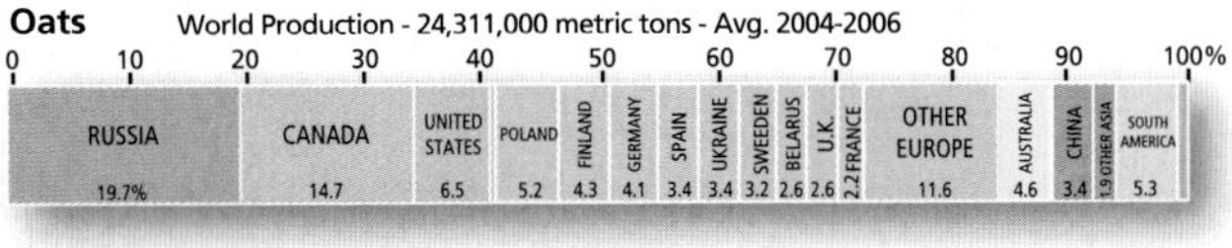

Coffee Imports World Imports - 5,392,000 metric tons - Avg. 2003-2005

UNITED STATES 22.7%
CANADA 2.3
GERMANY 16.9
ITALY 7.4
FRANCE 4.6
SPAIN 4.3
BELGIUM 3.6
NETH. 2.5
U.K. 2.1
OTHER EUROPE 13.6
JAPAN 7.4
OTHER ASIA 5.6
ALGERIA 2.1
OTHER 1.9
ALL OTHER 2.7

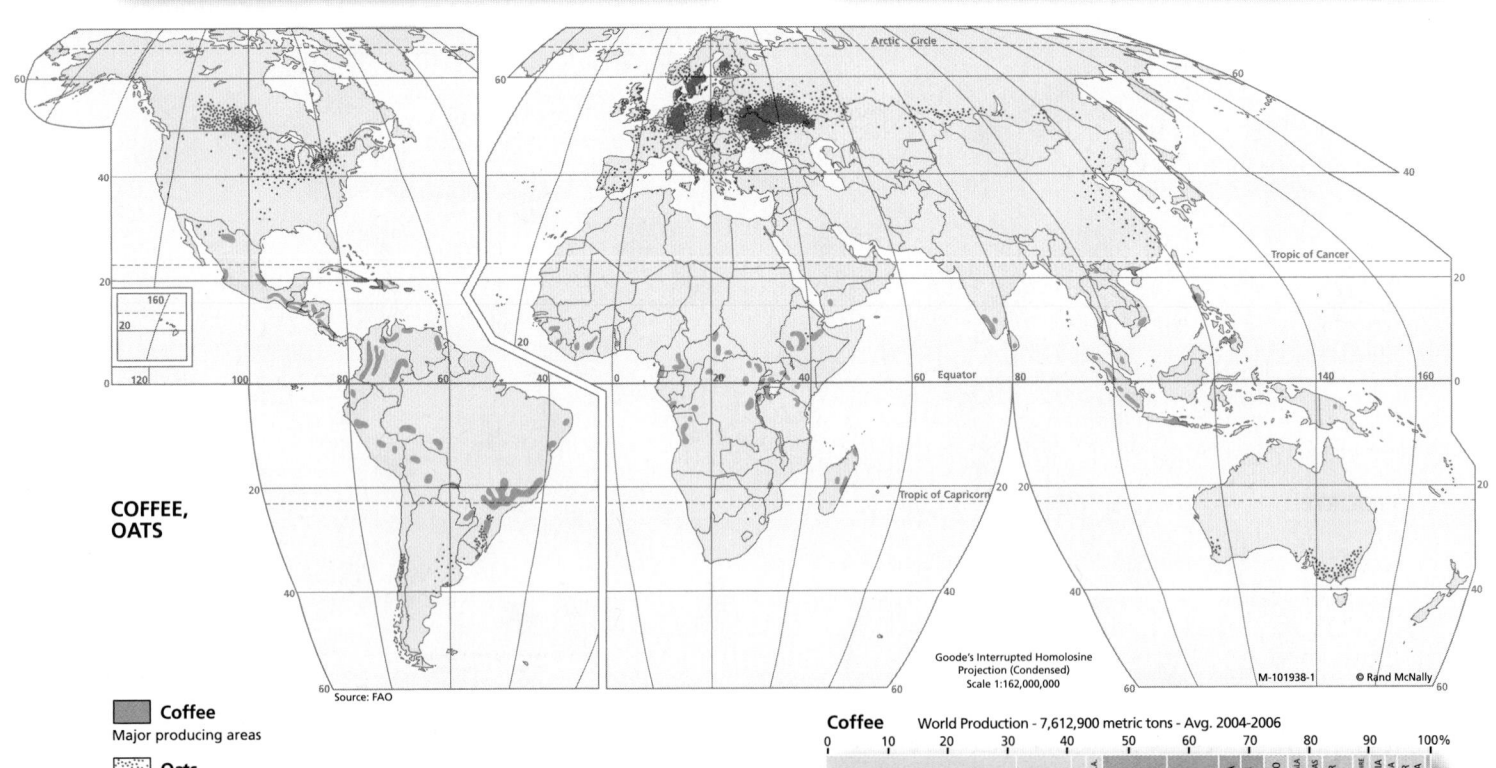

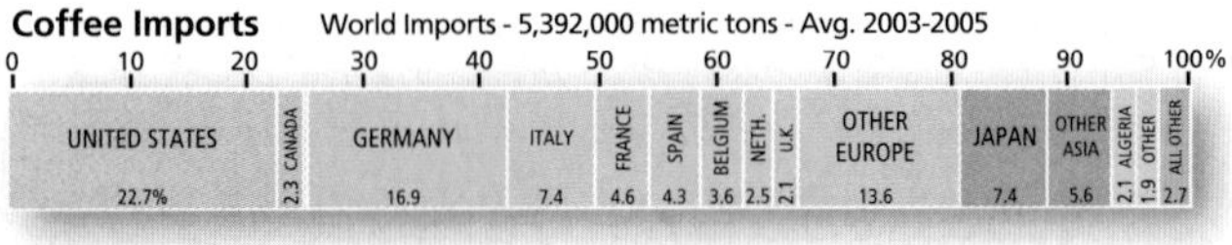

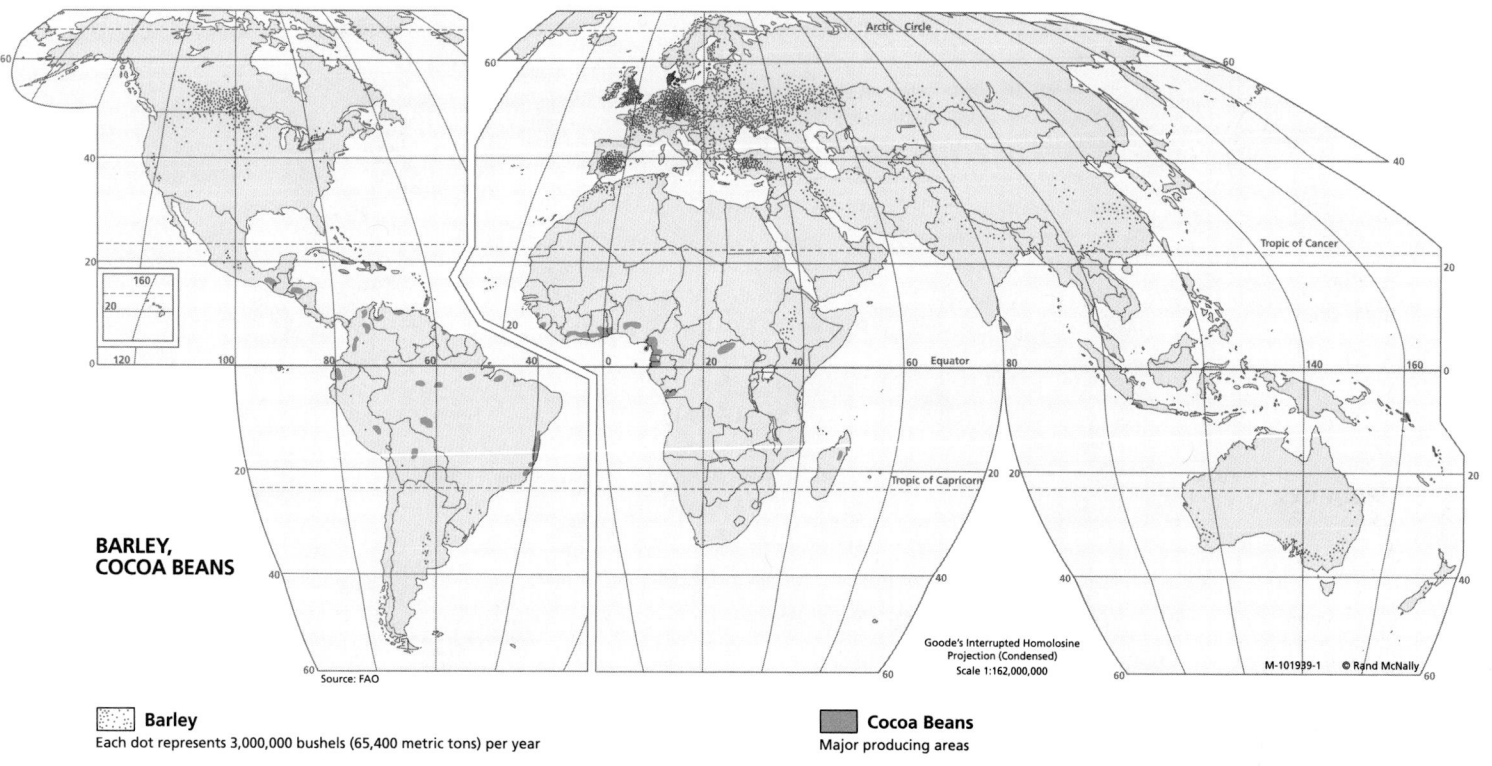

Goode's Interrupted Homolosine
Projection (Condensed)
Scale 1:162,000,000

M-101939-1 © Rand McNally

Source: FAO

BARLEY, COCOA BEANS

Barley
Each dot represents 3,000,000 bushels (65,400 metric tons) per year

Cocoa Beans
Major producing areas

Barley World Production - 144,809,000 metric tons - Avg. 2004-2006

	0	10	20	30	40	50	60	70	80	90	100%

RUSSIA	GERMANY	FRANCE	UKRAINE	SPAIN	U.K.	DENMARK 2.5	POLAND 2.4	OTHER EUROPE	CANADA	UNITED STATES	TURKEY	CHINA 2.3	IRAN 2.0	OTHER ASIA	AUSTRALIA	AFRICA	ALL OTHER 1.6
11.8%	8.4	7.3	7.2	5.4	3.8			13.0	8.2	3.7	6.5			4.4	4.9	3.9	

Cocoa Beans World Production - 4,017,000 metric tons - Avg. 2004-2006

	0	10	20	30	40	50	60	70	80	90	100%

COTE D'IVOIRE	GHANA	NIGERIA	CAMEROON 4.2	OTHER AF. 2.7	INDONESIA	OTHER ASIA 0.8	BRAZIL	ECUADOR 2.3	OTHER S.A. 2.1	N. AMERICA 2.3	ALL OTHER 0.2
34.6%	18.3	11.1			14.9		5.0				

Goode's Interrupted Homolosine
Projection (Condensed)
Scale 1:162,000,000

M-101940-1 © Rand McNally

Source: FAO

RICE, MILLET AND GRAIN SORGHUM

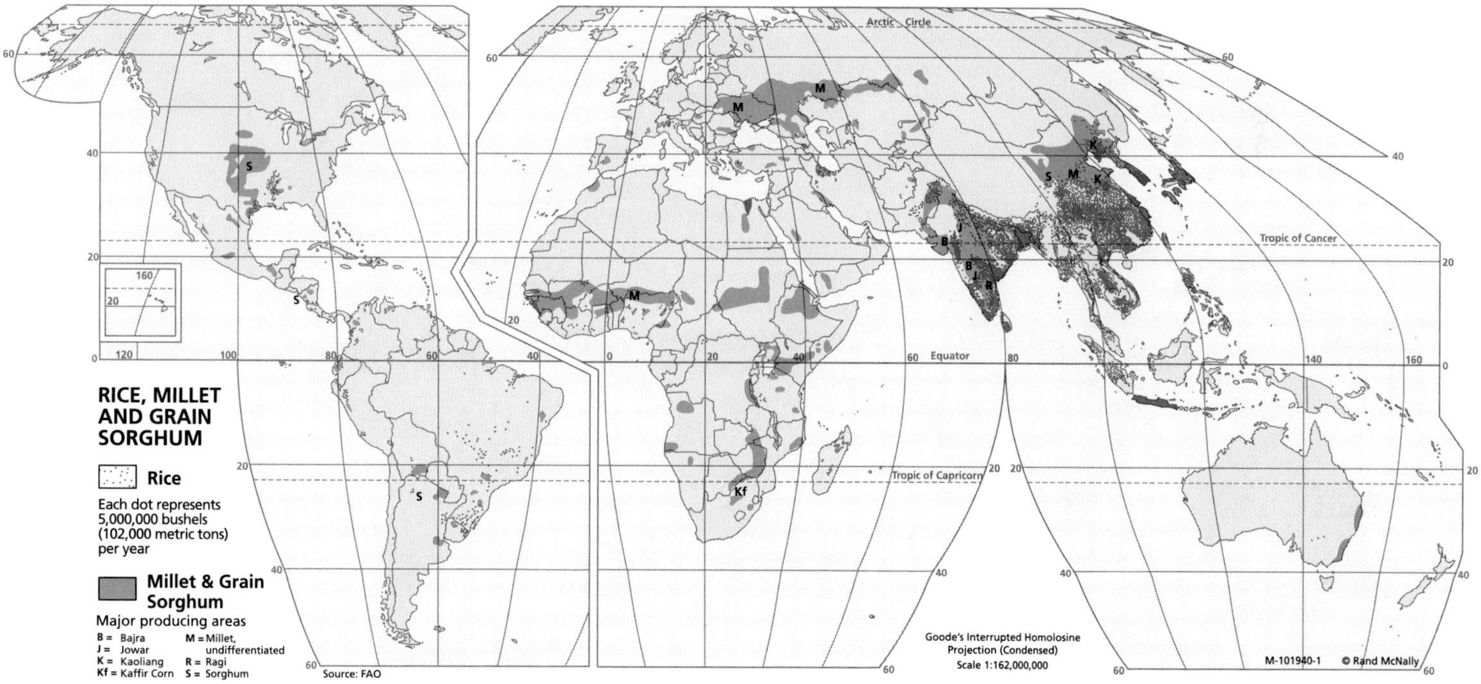

Rice
Each dot represents 5,000,000 bushels (102,000 metric tons) per year

Millet & Grain Sorghum
Major producing areas
B = Bajra   M = Millet, undifferentiated
J = Jowar
K = Kaoliang   R = Ragi
Kf = Kaffir Corn   S = Sorghum

Rice World Production - 624,479,000 metric tons - Avg. 2004-2006

	0	10	20	30	40	50	60	70	80	90	100%

CHINA	INDIA	INDONESIA	BANGL.	VIETNAM	THAILAND	MYANMAR	OTHER ASIA	BRAZIL 2.0	OTHER S.A. 1.7	AFRICA 3.2	ALL OTHER 2.5
28.9%	21.3	8.7	6.4	5.8	4.7	4.2	8.4				

Rice Imports World Imports - 26,906,000 metric tons - Avg. 2003-2005

	0	10	20	30	40	50	60	70	80	90	100%

NIGERIA	SENEGAL	S. AFRICA	COTE D'IVOIRE	OTHER AFRICA	PHILIPPINES	IRAN	BNGL.	S. ARABIA	N. KOREA	INDONESIA	JAPAN	CHINA	IRAQ	OTHER ASIA	BRAZIL	U.K.	OTHER EUROPE	CUBA	OTHER N. AMER.	ALL OTHER
5.2%	3.2	2.8	2.8	15.4	4.1	3.8	3.5	2.7	2.4	2.4	2.4			14.5	2.1		9.0	2.0	7.9	3.1

Millet & Grain Sorghum World Production - 88,629,000 metric tons - Avg. 2004-2006

	0	10	20	30	40	50	60	70	80	90	100%

INDIA	CHINA	OTHER	NIGERIA	SUDAN	NIGER	BURKINA F.	ETHIOPIA 2.0	OTHER AFRICA	UNITED STATES	MEXICO	ARGENTINA 2.0	BRAZIL	ALL OTHER
19.8%	4.8	3.1	18.5	5.3	3.8	2.9		9.8	11.1	6.8		2.0	3.8

Rice Exports* World Exports - 28,749,000 metric tons - Avg. 2003-2005

	0	10	20	30	40	50	60	70	80	90	100%

THAILAND	VIETNAM	INDIA	PAKISTAN	CHINA	OTHER ASIA	UNITED STATES	EGYPT	ITALY	OTHER	OTHER
30.1%	15.2	14.2	7.6	4.8	3.1	12.4	2.9	2.3	3.1	2.3

* including reexports

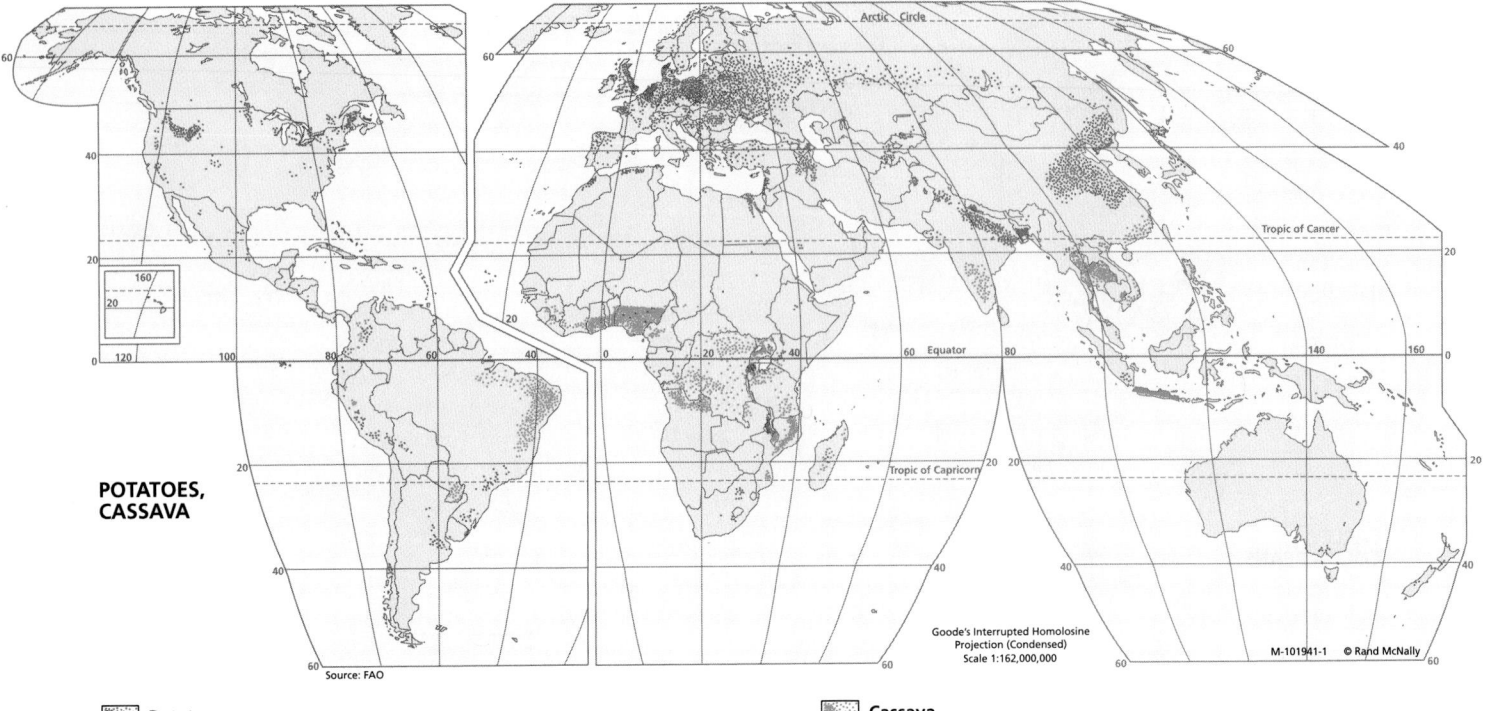

POTATOES, CASSAVA

Arctic Circle
Tropic of Cancer
Equator
Tropic of Capricorn
Goode's Interrupted Homolosine Projection (Condensed)
Scale 1:162,000,000
M-101941-1 © Rand McNally
Source: FAO

Potatoes
Each dot represents 100,000 metric tons average annual production

Cassava
Each dot represents 100,000 metric tons average annual production

Potatoes World Production - 323,418,000 metric tons - Avg. 2004-2006

CHINA	INDIA	OTHER ASIA	RUSSIA	UKRAINE	GERMANY	POLAND	BELARUS	NETH.	FRANCE	OTHER EUROPE	UNITED STATES	OTHER N.A.	AFRICA	SOUTH AMERICA
22.3%	7.3	11.1	11.5	6.2	3.6	3.4	2.7	2.1	2.1	9.8	6.1	2.2	5.0	4.1

Cassava World Production - 214,400,000 metric tons - Avg. 2004-2006

NIGERIA	DEM. REP. OF THE CONGO	MOZ.	GHANA	ANGOLA	TANZANIA	UGANDA	OTHER AFRICA	BRAZIL	PARAGUAY	OTHER S.A.	THAILAND	INDONESIA	VIETNAM	INDIA	CHINA	OTHER ASIA
19.6%	7.0	4.6	4.5	4.0	3.1	2.5	9.3	11.9	2.3	1.9	9.5	9.1	3.1	3.0	2.0	1.7

SUGAR, SPICES

Arctic Circle
Tropic of Cancer
Equator
Tropic of Capricorn
M-101942-1 © Rand McNally
Goode's Interrupted Homolosine Projection (Condensed)
Scale 1:162,000,000
Source: FAO

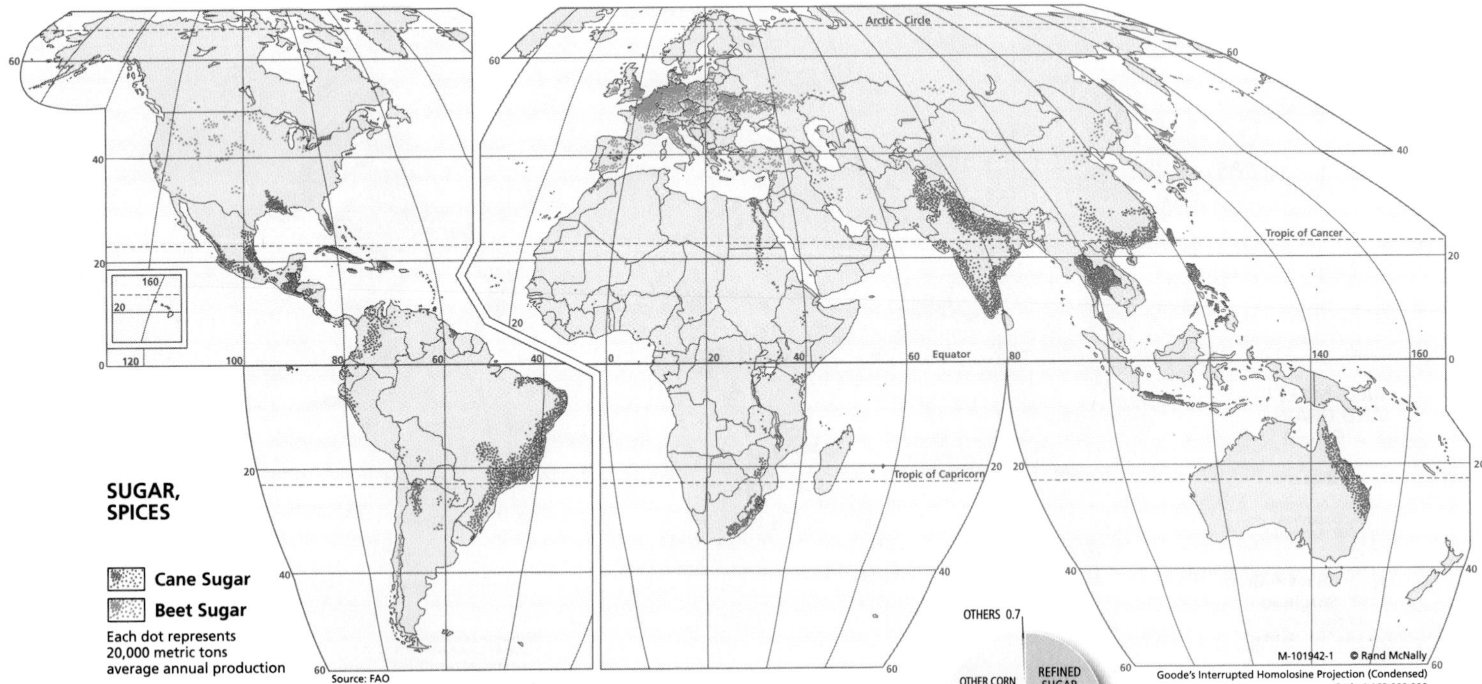

Cane Sugar
Beet Sugar
Each dot represents 20,000 metric tons average annual production

Cane Sugar World Production - 112,294,000 metric tons - Avg. 2004-2006

BRAZIL	COLOMBIA	OTHER S.A.	INDIA	CHINA	THAILAND	PAKISTAN	PHILIPPINES	OTHER ASIA	MEXICO	U.S.	OTHER N.A.	AUSTRALIA	RUSSIA	SOUTH AFRICA	OTHER AFRICA
25.9%	2.3	4.3	15.0	8.6	5.4	3.1	2.0	3.9	4.8	2.7	5.9	4.5	2.5	2.1	6.3

Beet Sugar World Production - 36,870,000 metric tons - Avg. 2004-2006

UNITED STATES	FRANCE	GERMANY	UKRAINE	POLAND	U.K.	ITALY	NETH.	BELGIUM	SPAIN	OTHER EUROPE	RUSSIA	TURKEY	CHINA	JAPAN	OTHER ASIA	AFRICA
11.8%	11.3	10.9	6.2	5.7	3.9	3.5	2.9	2.8	2.8	13.9	7.2	6.0	2.5	2.2	2.6	2.4

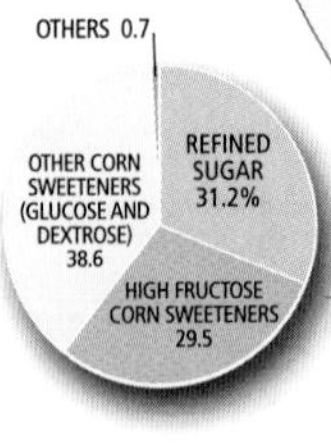

OTHERS 0.7
REFINED SUGAR 31.2%
OTHER CORN SWEETENERS (GLUCOSE AND DEXTROSE) 38.6
HIGH FRUCTOSE CORN SWEETENERS 29.5

U.S. Sweetener Consumption Per Person
Total - 90.9 kilograms - Avg. 2004-2006

Spices World Total - 7,306,000 metric tons - Avg. 2004-2006

INDIA	CHINA	INDONESIA	BANGL.	NEPAL	VIETNAM	OTHER ASIA	NIGERIA	ETHIOPIA	OTHER AFRICA	PERU	OTHER S.A.	EUROPE	NORTH AMERICA
45.2%	10.3	6.2	3.7	2.6	2.1	9.8	2.4	2.0	5.9	2.1	1.5	3.3	2.8

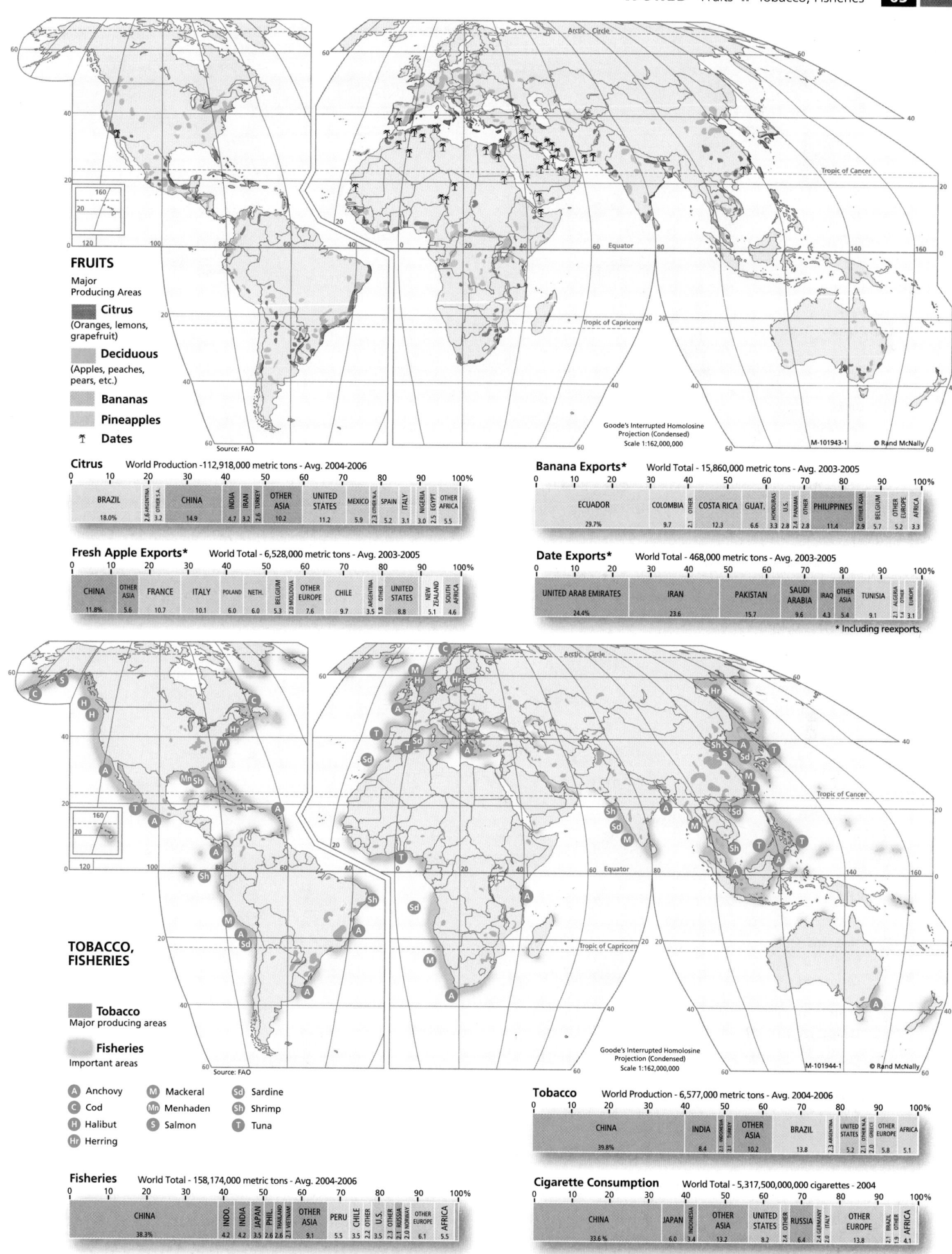

FRUITS

Major Producing Areas

Citrus
(Oranges, lemons, grapefruit)

Deciduous
(Apples, peaches, pears, etc.)

Bananas

Pineapples

Dates

Source: FAO

Goode's Interrupted Homolosine Projection (Condensed)
Scale 1:162,000,000
M-101943-1 © Rand McNally

Citrus
World Production -112,918,000 metric tons - Avg. 2004-2006

BRAZIL 18.0%	2.6 ARGENTINA	OTHER S.A. 3.2	CHINA 14.9	INDIA 4.7	IRAN 3.2	TURKEY 2.6	OTHER ASIA 10.2	UNITED STATES 11.2	MEXICO 5.9	SPAIN 2.3 OTHER N.A. / ITALY 5.2	NIGERIA 3.1 / EGYPT 3.0 / 2.5 SOUTH AFRICA	OTHER AFRICA 5.5

Fresh Apple Exports*
World Total - 6,528,000 metric tons - Avg. 2003-2005

CHINA 11.8%	OTHER ASIA 5.6	FRANCE 10.7	ITALY 10.1	POLAND 6.0	NETH. 6.0	BELGIUM 2.0 MOLDOVA	OTHER EUROPE 7.6	CHILE 9.7	ARGENTINA 3.5 OTHER 1.8	UNITED STATES 8.8	NEW ZEALAND 5.1	SOUTH AFRICA 4.6

Banana Exports*
World Total - 15,860,000 metric tons - Avg. 2003-2005

ECUADOR 29.7%	COLOMBIA 9.7	OTHER 2.1	COSTA RICA 12.3	GUAT. 6.6	HONDURAS 3.3 / U.S. 2.8 / PANAMA 2.8 / OTHER 2.4	PHILIPPINES 11.4	OTHER ASIA 2.9	BELGIUM 5.7	OTHER EUROPE 5.2	AFRICA 3.3

Date Exports*
World Total - 468,000 metric tons - Avg. 2003-2005

UNITED ARAB EMIRATES 24.4%	IRAN 23.6	PAKISTAN 15.7	SAUDI ARABIA 9.6	IRAQ 4.3	OTHER ASIA 5.4	TUNISIA 9.1	ALGERIA 2.1 / 1.9 OTHER	OTHER EUROPE 3.1

*Including reexports.

TOBACCO, FISHERIES

Tobacco
Major producing areas

Fisheries
Important areas

Source: FAO

Goode's Interrupted Homolosine Projection (Condensed)
Scale 1:162,000,000
M-101944-1 © Rand McNally

- Ⓐ Anchovy
- Ⓒ Cod
- Ⓗ Halibut
- Ⓗⁱ Herring
- Ⓜ Mackeral
- Ⓜⁿ Menhaden
- Ⓢ Salmon
- Ⓢⁱ Sardine
- Ⓢʰ Shrimp
- Ⓣ Tuna

Fisheries
World Total - 158,174,000 metric tons - Avg. 2004-2006

CHINA 38.3%	INDO. 4.2	INDIA 4.2	JAPAN 3.5	PHIL. 2.6	THAILAND 2.6	VIETNAM 2.1	OTHER ASIA 9.1	PERU 5.5	CHILE 3.5	OTHER 2.2	U.S. 2.3	RUSSIA 2.1 / NORWAY 2.0	OTHER EUROPE 6.1	AFRICA 5.5

Tobacco
World Production - 6,577,000 metric tons - Avg. 2004-2006

CHINA 39.8%	INDIA 8.4	INDONESIA 2.1 / TURKEY 2.1	OTHER ASIA 10.2	BRAZIL 13.8	ARGENTINA 2.3	UNITED STATES 5.2	OTHER N.A. 2.0 / GREECE 2.0	OTHER EUROPE 5.8	AFRICA 5.1

Cigarette Consumption
World Total - 5,317,500,000,000 cigarettes - 2004

CHINA 33.6%	JAPAN 6.0	INDONESIA 3.4	OTHER ASIA 13.2	UNITED STATES 8.2	OTHER 2.4	RUSSIA 6.4	GERMANY 2.4 / ITALY 2.1	OTHER EUROPE 13.8	BRAZIL 2.1 / 1.9 OTHER / AFRICA 4.1

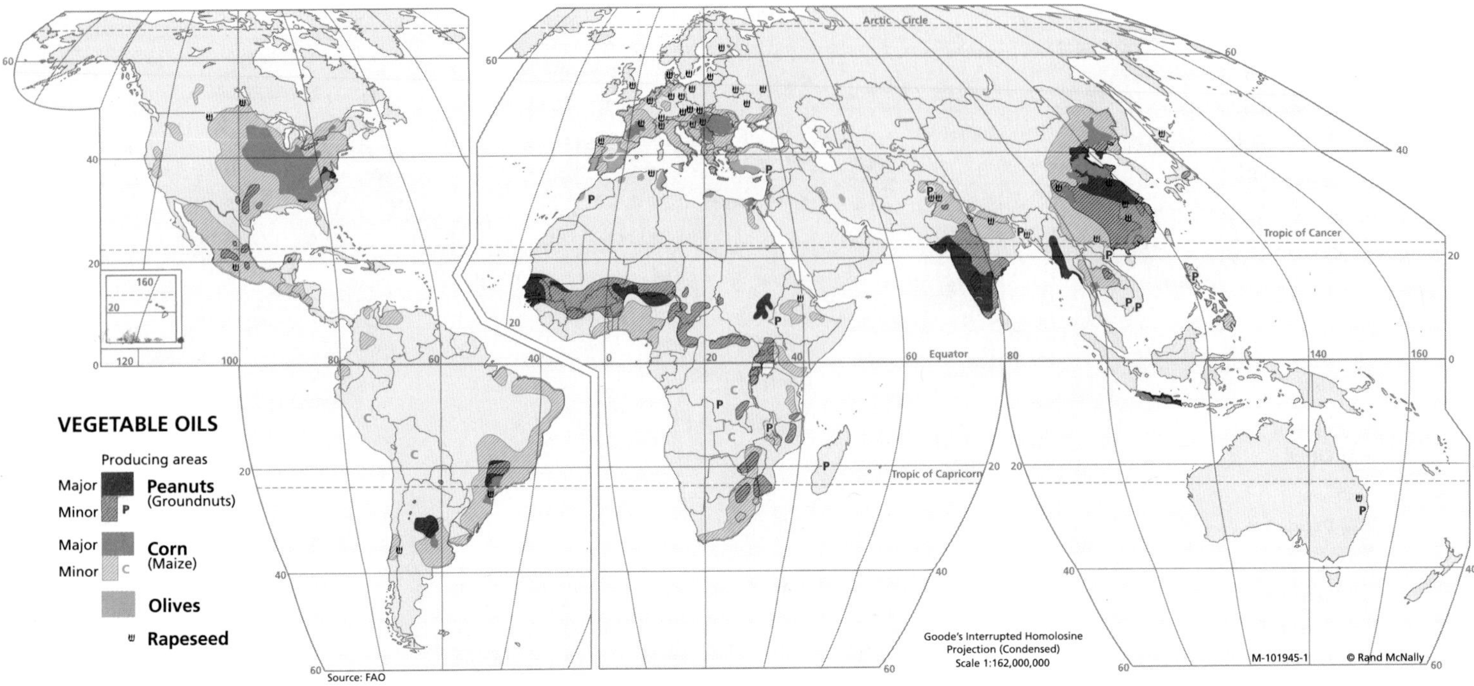

VEGETABLE OILS

Producing areas

Major / Minor **P** **Peanuts** (Groundnuts)

Major / Minor **C** **Corn** (Maize)

Olives

ш **Rapeseed**

Source: FAO

Goode's Interrupted Homolosine Projection (Condensed)
Scale 1:162,000,000

M-101945-1   © Rand McNally

Peanut Oil — World Production - 5,190,000 metric tons - Avg. 2004-2006

CHINA	INDIA	MYANMAR	OTHER ASIA	NIGERIA	SUDAN	OTHER AFRICA	ALL OTHER
39.8%	25.0	3.3	2.1	11.1	3.9	10.6	4.2

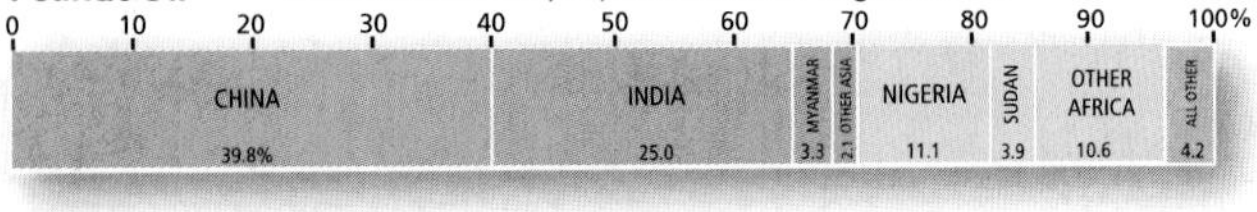

Canola (Rapeseed) Oil — World Production - 16,019,000 metric tons - Avg. 2004-2006

CHINA	INDIA	JAPAN	OTHER ASIA	GERMANY	FRANCE	U.K.	POLAND	OTHER EUROPE	CANADA	MEXICO	U.S.	ALL OTHER
28.4%	14.8	5.9	2.2	12.9	5.5	4.2	2.3	7.9	8.8	2.9	2.3	1.9

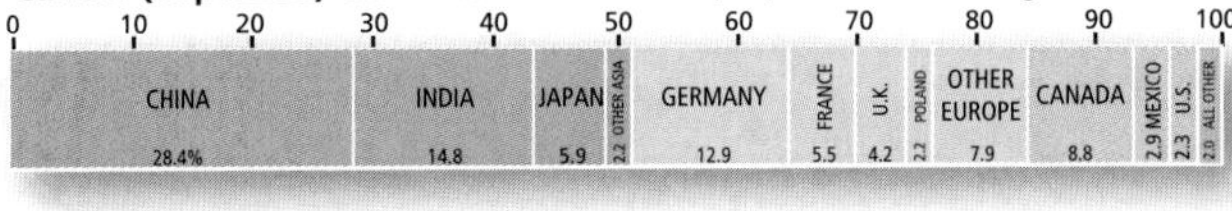

Corn Oil — World Production - 2,078,000 metric tons - Avg. 2004-2006

UNITED STATES	CANADA	CHINA	JAPAN	TURKEY	OTHER ASIA	S. AFRICA	OTHER AFRICA	BRAZIL	OTHER S.A.	ITALY	FRANCE	OTHER EUROPE
54.2%	2.1	6.0	4.7	3.3	3.4	3.4	3.4	4.7	2.7	2.1	6.3	

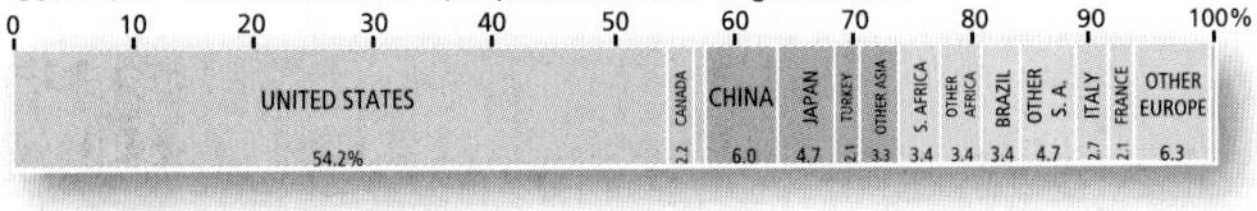

Olive Oil — World Production - 2,686,000 metric tons - Avg. 2004-2006

SPAIN	ITALY	GREECE	OTHER EUROPE	TUNISIA	MOROCCO	OTHER ASIA	SYRIA	TURKEY	OTHER ASIA
34.5%	26.0	14.2	1.8	6.2	2.9	1.5	5.5	4.2	2.0

VEGETABLE OILS

Producing areas

Major / Minor **S** **Soybeans**

Major / Minor **T** **Cottonseed**

Oil Palm Fruit

☙ **Sunflower Seed**

⚓ **Coconuts** (Copra)

Source: FAO

Goode's Interrupted Homolosine Projection (Condensed)
Scale 1:162,000,000

M-101946-1   © Rand McNally

Soybean Oil — World Production - 33,054,000 metric tons - Avg. 2004-2006

UNITED STATES	OTHER N.A.	CHINA	INDIA	OTHER ASIA	BRAZIL	ARGENTINA	GERMANY	OTHER EUROPE
26.2%	2.1	17.5	4.7	5.1	16.9	16.3	1.8 2.1	6.5

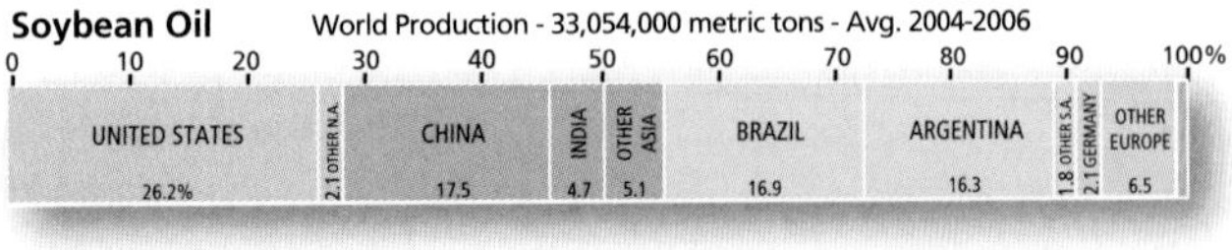

Palm Oil — World Production - 34,219,000 metric tons - Avg. 2004-2006

MALAYSIA	INDONESIA	THAILAND	OTHER AFRICA	NIGERIA	COLOMBIA	ALL OTHER
43.7%	41.0	2.0	3.5	3.0	2.0	2.6

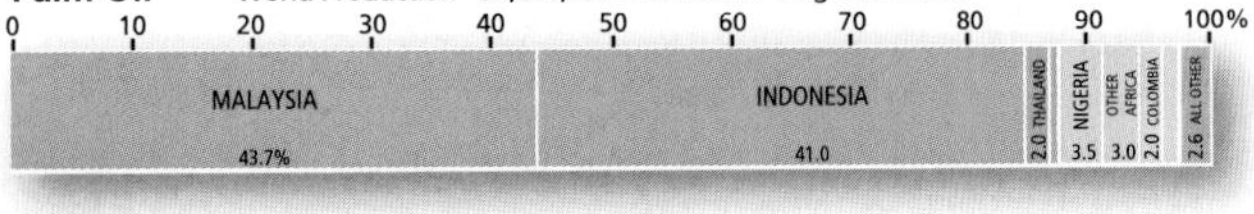

Sunflower Oil — World Production - 9,925,000 metric tons - Avg. 2004-2006

RUSSIA	UKRAINE	FRANCE	ROMANIA	SPAIN	NETH.	OTHER EUROPE	ARGENTINA	TURKEY	INDIA	CHINA	OTHER ASIA	S. AMERICA
21.4%	16.5	4.7	3.7	2.6	2.3	8.8	14.0	5.2	4.4	3.2	5.1	2.1

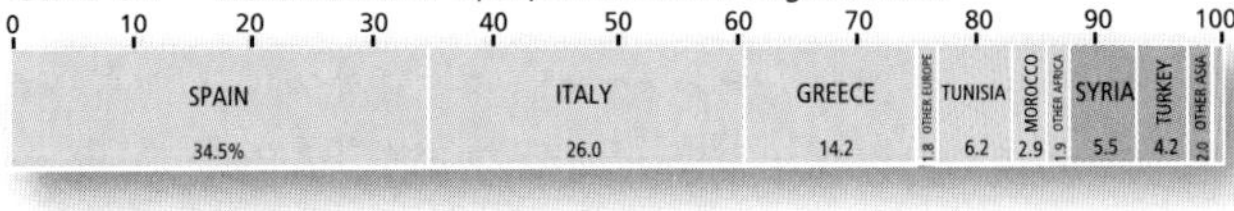

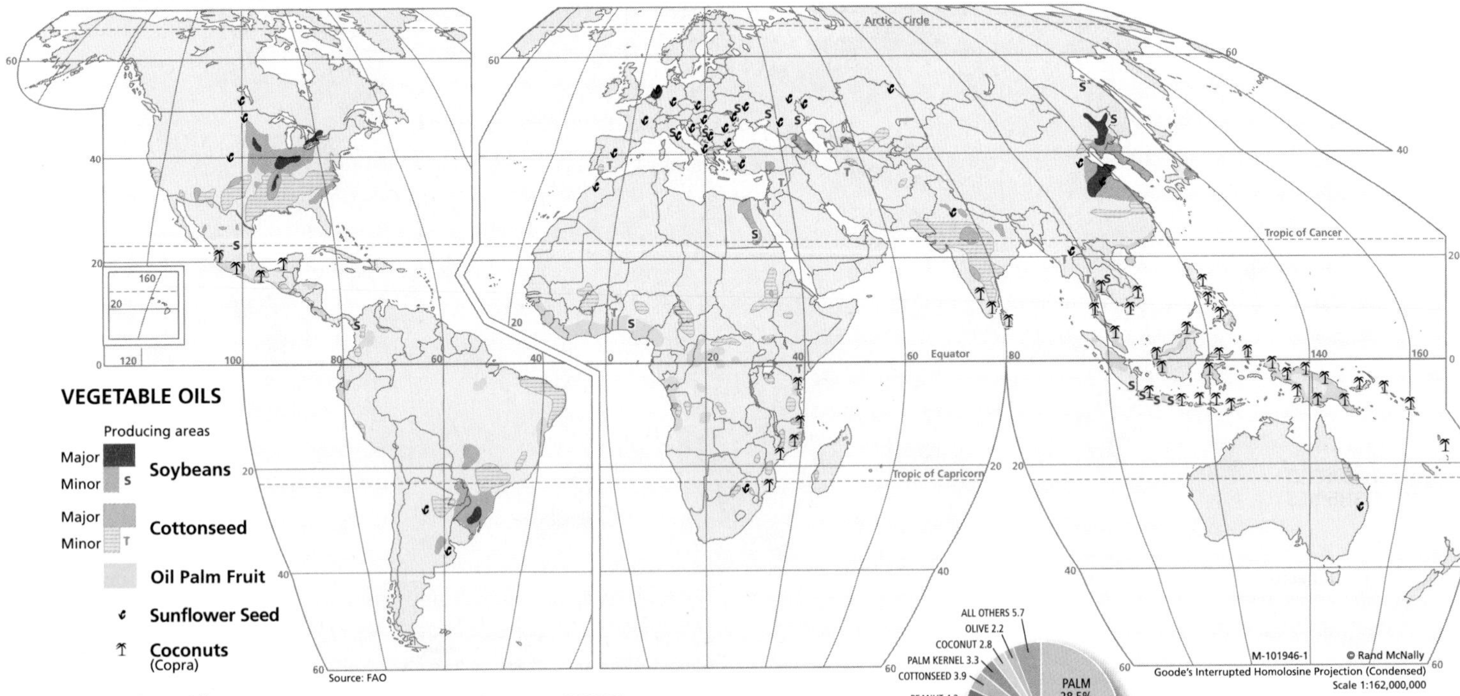

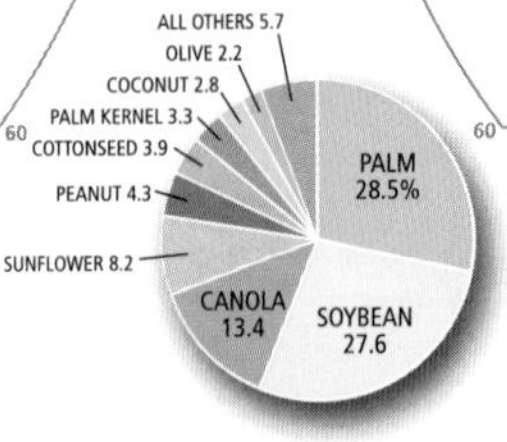

Vegetable Oils
World Production - 119,860,000 metric tons - Avg. 2004-2006

Pie chart:
- PALM 28.5%
- SOYBEAN 27.6
- CANOLA 13.4
- SUNFLOWER 8.2
- PEANUT 4.3
- COTTONSEED 3.9
- PALM KERNEL 3.3
- COCONUT 2.8
- OLIVE 2.2
- ALL OTHERS 5.7

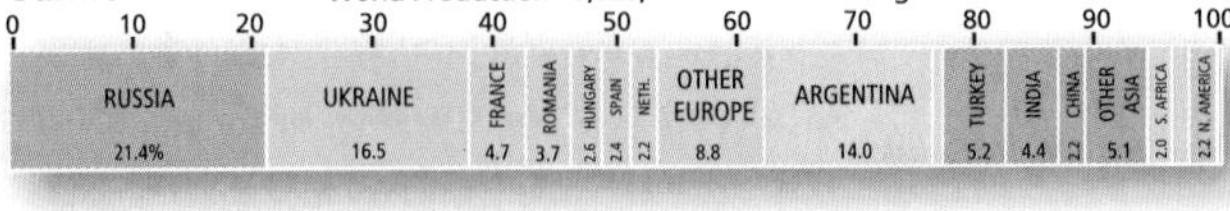

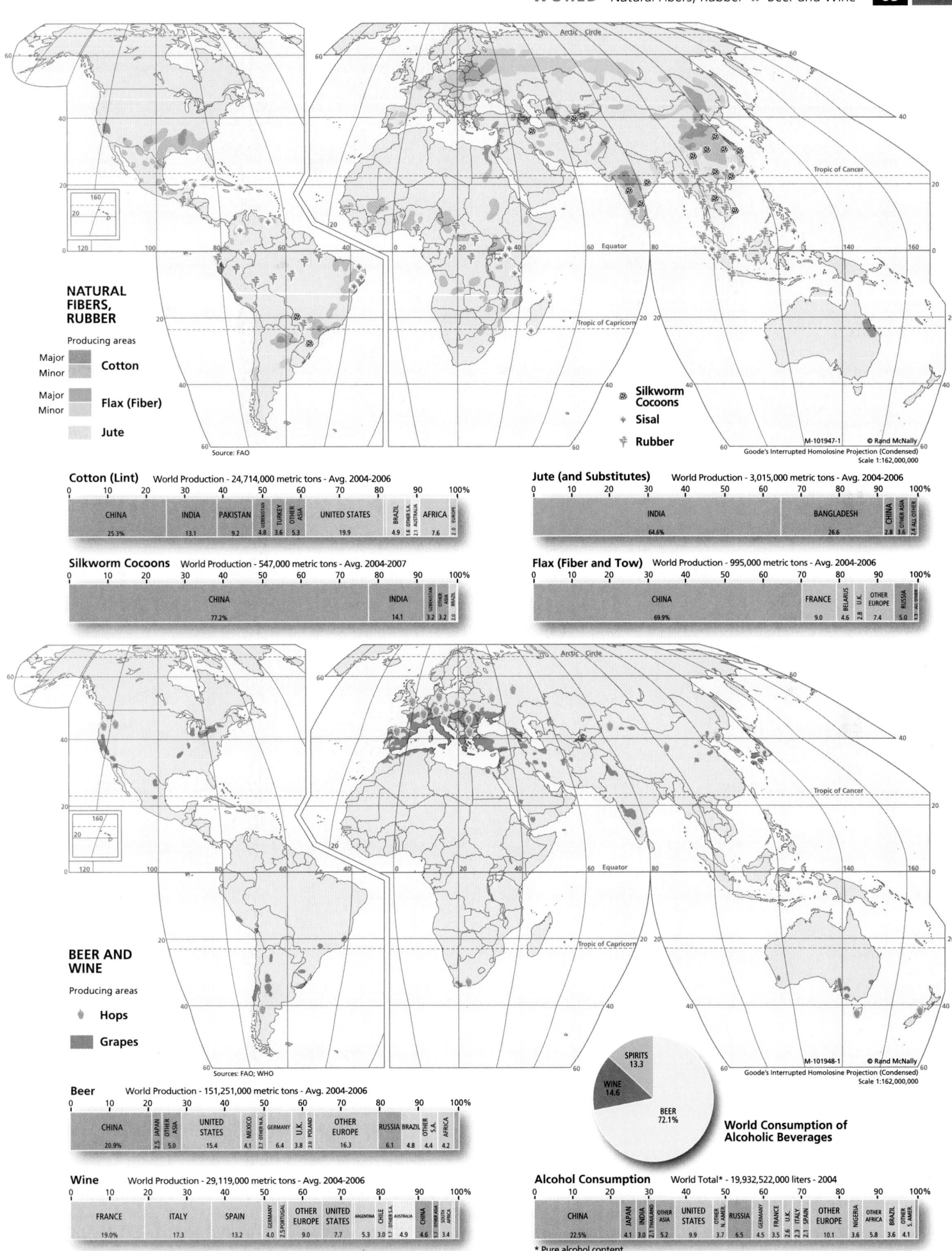

NATURAL FIBERS, RUBBER

Producing areas

Major / Minor	Cotton
Major / Minor	Flax (Fiber)
	Jute

Source: FAO

⚜ Silkworm Cocoons
✦ Sisal
🌴 Rubber

M-101947-1 © Rand McNally
Goode's Interrupted Homolosine Projection (Condensed)
Scale 1:162,000,000

Cotton (Lint) World Production - 24,714,000 metric tons - Avg. 2004-2006

CHINA	INDIA	PAKISTAN	UZBEKISTAN	TURKEY	OTHER ASIA	UNITED STATES	BRAZIL	OTHER S.A.	AUSTRALIA	AFRICA	EUROPE
25.3%	13.1	9.2	4.8	3.6	5.3	19.9	4.9	1.6	2.1	7.6	2.0

Silkworm Cocoons World Production - 547,000 metric tons - Avg. 2004-2007

CHINA	INDIA	UZBEKISTAN	OTHER ASIA	BRAZIL
77.2%	14.1	3.2	3.2	2.0

Jute (and Substitutes) World Production - 3,015,000 metric tons - Avg. 2004-2006

INDIA	BANGLADESH	CHINA	OTHER ASIA	ALL OTHER
64.6%	26.6	2.8	3.6	2.4

Flax (Fiber and Tow) World Production - 995,000 metric tons - Avg. 2004-2006

CHINA	FRANCE	BELARUS	U.K.	OTHER EUROPE	RUSSIA	
69.9%	9.0	4.6	2.8	7.4	5.0	1.3

BEER AND WINE

Producing areas

🍃 Hops
▇ Grapes

Sources: FAO; WHO

M-101948-1 © Rand McNally
Goode's Interrupted Homolosine Projection (Condensed)
Scale 1:162,000,000

Beer World Production - 151,251,000 metric tons - Avg. 2004-2006

CHINA	JAPAN	OTHER ASIA	UNITED STATES	MEXICO	OTHER N.A.	GERMANY	U.K.	POLAND	OTHER EUROPE	RUSSIA	BRAZIL	OTHER S.A.	AFRICA
20.9%	2.5	5.0	15.4	4.1	2.7	6.4	3.8	2.0	16.3	6.1	4.8	4.4	4.2

Wine World Production - 29,119,000 metric tons - Avg. 2004-2006

FRANCE	ITALY	SPAIN	GERMANY	PORTUGAL	OTHER EUROPE	UNITED STATES	ARGENTINA	CHILE	OTHER S.A.	AUSTRALIA	CHINA	OTHER ASIA	SOUTH AFRICA
19.0%	17.3	13.2	4.0	2.5	9.0	7.7	5.3	3.3	1.2	4.9	4.6	1.3	3.4

World Consumption of Alcoholic Beverages

- SPIRITS 13.3
- WINE 14.6
- BEER 72.1%

Alcohol Consumption World Total* - 19,932,522,000 liters - 2004

CHINA	JAPAN	INDIA	THAILAND	OTHER ASIA	UNITED STATES	OTHER N. AMER.	RUSSIA	GERMANY	FRANCE	U.K.	ITALY	SPAIN	OTHER EUROPE	NIGERIA	OTHER AFRICA	BRAZIL	OTHER S. AMER.
22.5%	4.1	3.0	2.1	5.2	9.9	3.7	6.5	4.5	3.5	2.6	2.1	2.1	10.1	3.6	5.8	3.6	4.1

* Pure alcohol content

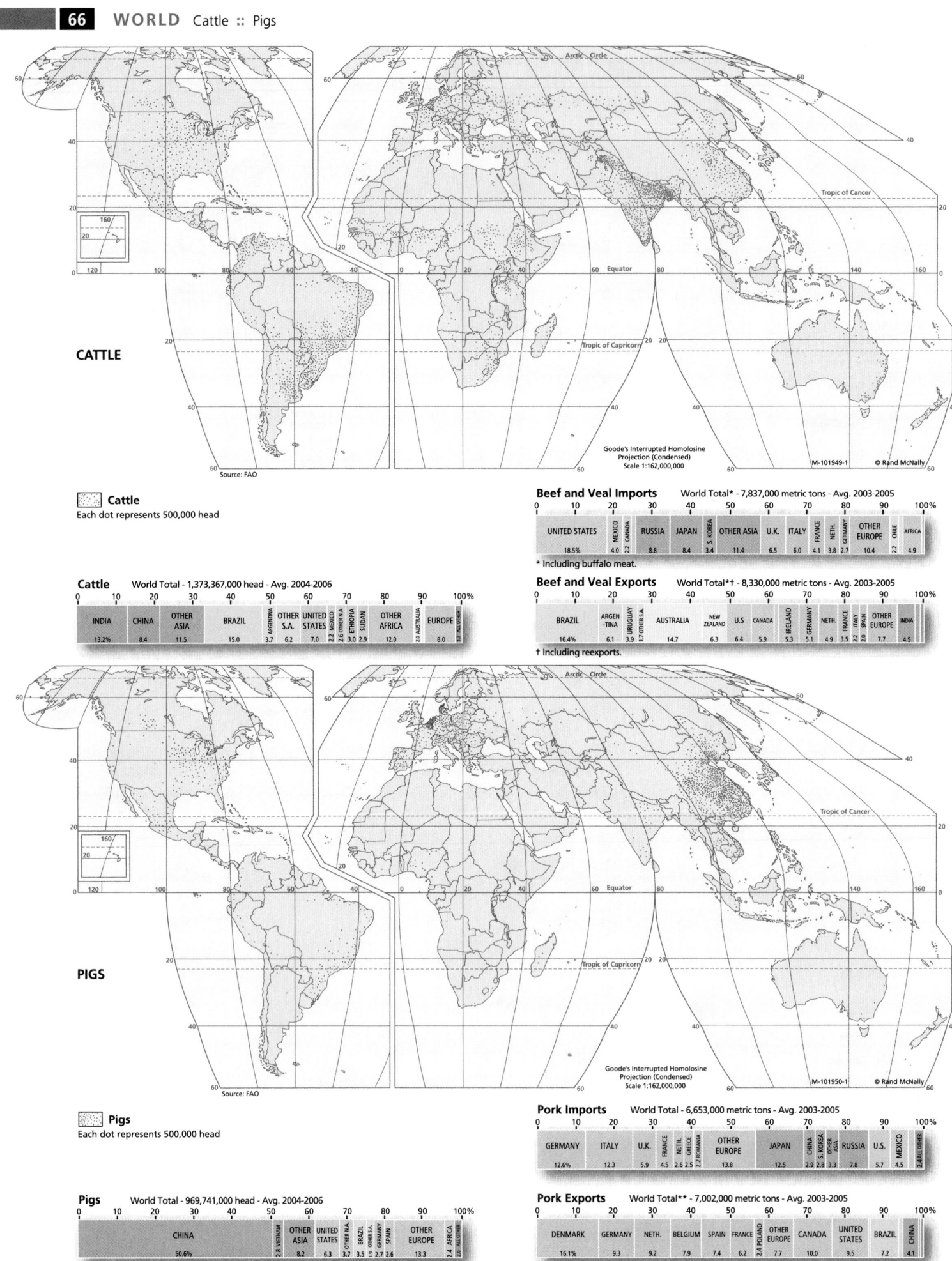

CATTLE

Source: FAO

Goode's Interrupted Homolosine Projection (Condensed)
Scale 1:162,000,000

M-101949-1 © Rand McNally

Cattle
Each dot represents 500,000 head

Cattle World Total - 1,373,367,000 head - Avg. 2004-2006

| | 0 | 10 | 20 | 30 | 40 | 50 | 60 | 70 | 80 | 90 | 100% |

INDIA	CHINA	OTHER ASIA	BRAZIL	ARGENTINA	OTHER S.A.	UNITED STATES	MEXICO	OTHER N.A.	ETHIOPIA	SUDAN	OTHER AFRICA	AUSTRALIA	EUROPE	ALL OTHER
13.2%	8.4	11.5	15.0	3.7	6.2	7.0	2.2	2.6	3.0	2.9	12.0	2.0	8.0	1.7

Beef and Veal Imports World Total* - 7,837,000 metric tons - Avg. 2003-2005

| | 0 | 10 | 20 | 30 | 40 | 50 | 60 | 70 | 80 | 90 | 100% |

UNITED STATES	MEXICO	CANADA	RUSSIA	JAPAN	S. KOREA	OTHER ASIA	U.K.	ITALY	FRANCE	GERMANY	NETH.	OTHER EUROPE	CHILE	AFRICA
18.5%	4.0	2.2	8.8	8.4	3.4	11.4	6.5	6.0	4.1	3.8	2.7	10.4	2.2	4.9

* Including buffalo meat.

Beef and Veal Exports World Total*† - 8,330,000 metric tons - Avg. 2003-2005

| | 0 | 10 | 20 | 30 | 40 | 50 | 60 | 70 | 80 | 90 | 100% |

BRAZIL	ARGEN-TINA	URUGUAY	OTHER S.A.	AUSTRALIA	NEW ZEALAND	U.S	CANADA	IRELAND	GERMANY	NETH.	FRANCE	ITALY	SPAIN	OTHER EUROPE	INDIA
16.4%	6.1	3.9	1.7	14.7	6.3	6.4	5.9	5.3	5.1	4.9	3.5	2.2	2.0	7.7	4.5

† Including reexports.

PIGS

Source: FAO

Goode's Interrupted Homolosine Projection (Condensed)
Scale 1:162,000,000

M-101950-1 © Rand McNally

Pigs
Each dot represents 500,000 head

Pigs World Total - 969,741,000 head - Avg. 2004-2006

| | 0 | 10 | 20 | 30 | 40 | 50 | 60 | 70 | 80 | 90 | 100% |

CHINA	VIETNAM	OTHER ASIA	UNITED STATES	BRAZIL	OTHER S.A.	GERMANY	SPAIN	OTHER EUROPE	AFRICA	ALL OTHER
50.6%	2.8	8.2	6.3	3.7	3.5	1.9	2.6	13.3	2.4	3.8

Pork Imports World Total - 6,653,000 metric tons - Avg. 2003-2005

| | 0 | 10 | 20 | 30 | 40 | 50 | 60 | 70 | 80 | 90 | 100% |

GERMANY	ITALY	U.K.	FRANCE	NETH.	GREECE	ROMANIA	OTHER EUROPE	JAPAN	CHINA	S. KOREA	OTHER ASIA	RUSSIA	U.S.	MEXICO	ALL OTHER
12.6%	12.3	5.9	4.5	2.6	2.5		13.8	12.5	2.9	2.8	3.3	7.8	5.7	4.5	2.4

Pork Exports World Total** - 7,002,000 metric tons - Avg. 2003-2005

| | 0 | 10 | 20 | 30 | 40 | 50 | 60 | 70 | 80 | 90 | 100% |

DENMARK	GERMANY	NETH.	BELGIUM	SPAIN	FRANCE	POLAND	OTHER EUROPE	CANADA	UNITED STATES	BRAZIL	CHINA
16.1%	9.3	9.2	7.9	7.4	6.2	2.4	7.7	10.0	9.5	7.2	4.1

** Including reexports.

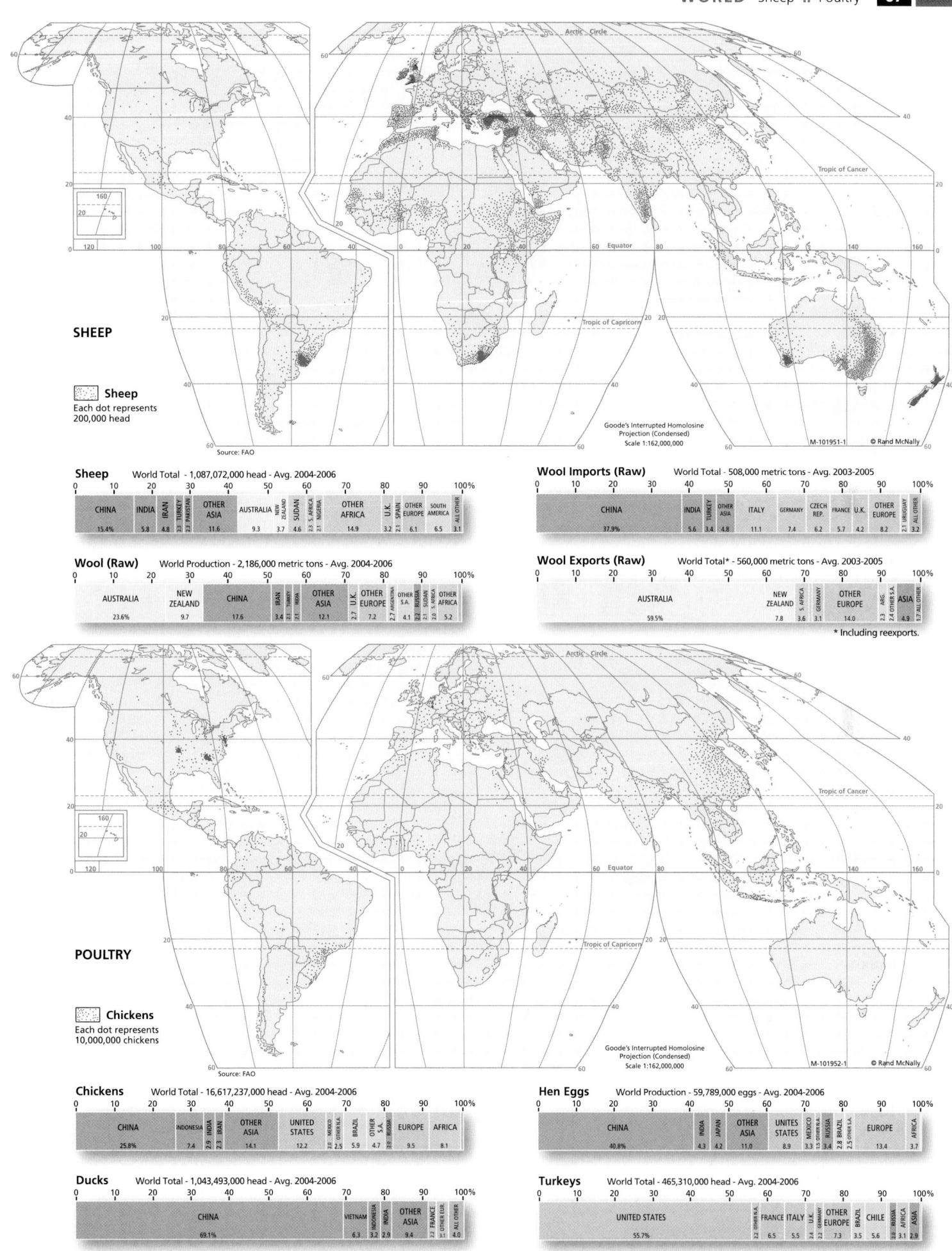

SHEEP

Sheep
Each dot represents
200,000 head

Source: FAO

Goode's Interrupted Homolosine
Projection (Condensed)
Scale 1:162,000,000

M-101951-1 © Rand McNally

Sheep World Total - 1,087,072,000 head - Avg. 2004-2006

CHINA	INDIA	IRAN	TURKEY	PAKISTAN	OTHER ASIA	AUSTRALIA	NEW ZEALAND	SUDAN	S. AFRICA	NIGERIA	OTHER AFRICA	U.K.	SPAIN	OTHER EUROPE	SOUTH AMERICA	ALL OTHER
15.4%	5.8	4.8	2.3	2.2	11.6	9.3	3.7	4.6	2.3	2.1	14.9	3.2	2.1	6.1	6.5	3.1

Wool (Raw) World Production - 2,186,000 metric tons - Avg. 2004-2006

AUSTRALIA	NEW ZEALAND	CHINA	IRAN	TURKEY	INDIA	OTHER ASIA	U.K.	OTHER EUROPE	ARGENTINA	OTHER S.A.	RUSSIA	SUDAN	S. AFRICA	OTHER AFRICA
23.6%	9.7	17.6	3.4	2.3	2.1	12.1	2.7	7.2	2.7	4.1	2.2	2.0	5.2	

Wool Imports (Raw) World Total - 508,000 metric tons - Avg. 2003-2005

CHINA	INDIA	TURKEY	OTHER ASIA	ITALY	GERMANY	CZECH REP.	FRANCE	U.K.	OTHER EUROPE	URUGUAY	ALL OTHER
37.9%	5.6	3.4	4.8	11.1	7.4	6.2	5.7	4.2	8.2	2.1	3.2

Wool Exports (Raw) World Total* - 560,000 metric tons - Avg. 2003-2005

AUSTRALIA	NEW ZEALAND	S. AFRICA	GERMANY	OTHER EUROPE	ARG.	OTHER S.A.	ASIA	ALL OTHER
59.5%	7.8	3.6	3.1	14.0	2.3	2.4	4.9	1.7

* Including reexports.

POULTRY

Chickens
Each dot represents
10,000,000 chickens

Source: FAO

Goode's Interrupted Homolosine
Projection (Condensed)
Scale 1:162,000,000

M-101952-1 © Rand McNally

Chickens World Total - 16,617,237,000 head - Avg. 2004-2006

CHINA	INDONESIA	INDIA	IRAN	OTHER ASIA	UNITED STATES	MEXICO	OTHER N.A.	BRAZIL	OTHER S.A.	RUSSIA	EUROPE	AFRICA
25.8%	7.4	2.9	2.3	14.1	12.2	2.0	2.5	5.9	4.7	2.0	9.5	8.1

Hen Eggs World Production - 59,789,000 eggs - Avg. 2004-2006

CHINA	INDIA	JAPAN	OTHER ASIA	UNITES STATES	MEXICO	OTHER N.A.	RUSSIA	BRAZIL	OTHER S.A.	EUROPE	AFRICA
40.8%	4.3	4.2	11.0	8.9	2.5	1.5	2.8	2.5		13.4	3.7

Ducks World Total - 1,043,493,000 head - Avg. 2004-2006

CHINA	VIETNAM	INDONESIA	INDIA	OTHER ASIA	FRANCE	OTHER EUR	ALL OTHER
69.1%	6.3	3.2	2.9	9.4	2.2		4.0

Turkeys World Total - 465,310,000 head - Avg. 2004-2006

UNITED STATES	OTHER N.A.	FRANCE	ITALY	U.K.	GERMANY	OTHER EUROPE	BRAZIL	CHILE	RUSSIA	AFRICA	ASIA
55.7%	2.2	6.5	5.5	2.4	2.2	7.3	3.5	5.6	2.0	3.1	2.9

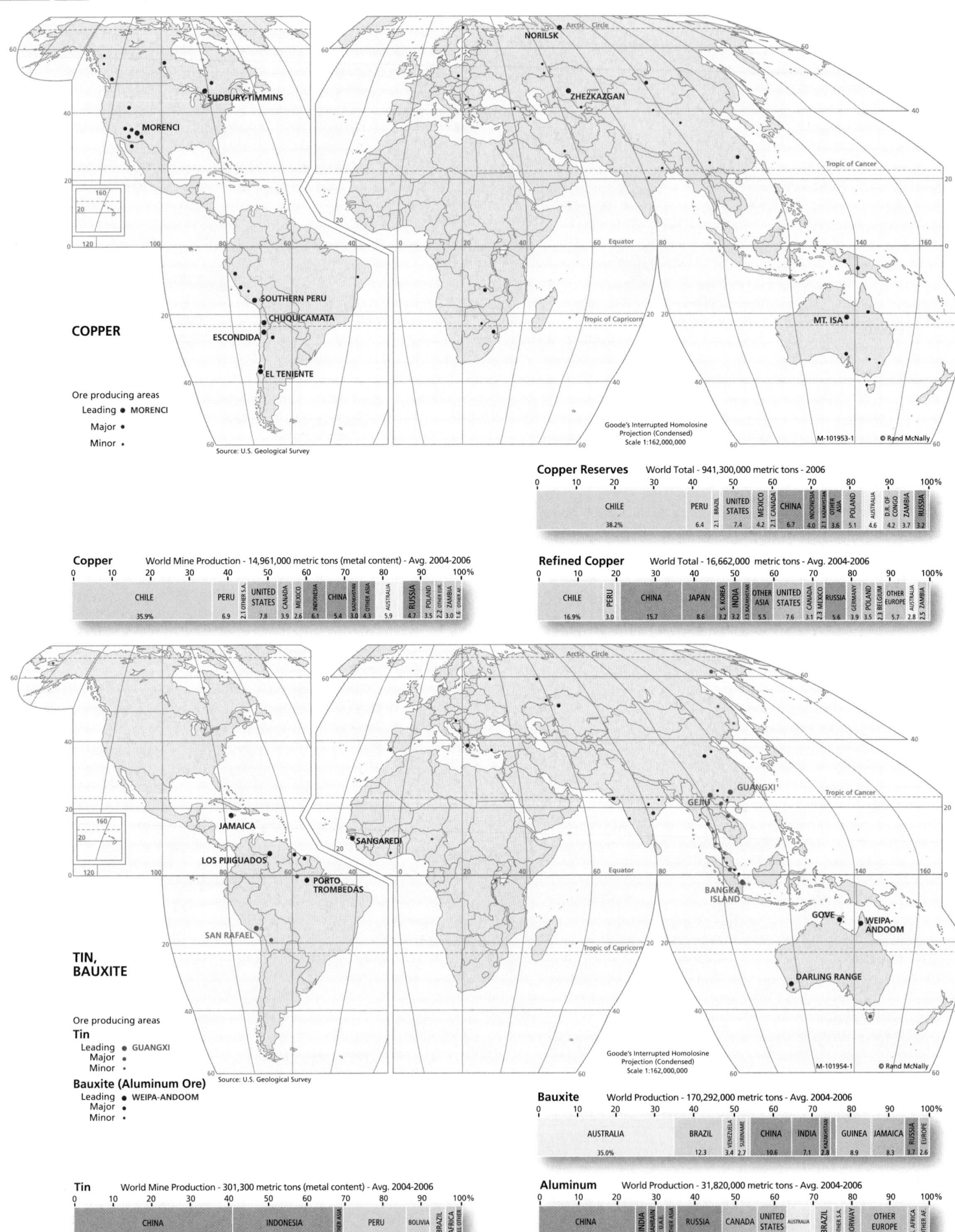

COPPER

NORILSK
ZHEZKAZGAN
SUDBURY-TIMMINS
MORENCI
SOUTHERN PERU
CHUQUICAMATA
ESCONDIDA
EL TENIENTE
MT. ISA

Ore producing areas
Leading ● MORENCI
Major •
Minor ·

Source: U.S. Geological Survey

Goode's Interrupted Homolosine
Projection (Condensed)
Scale 1:162,000,000

M-101953-1 © Rand McNally

Copper Reserves World Total - 941,300,000 metric tons - 2006

0	10	20	30	40	50	60	70	80	90	100%

| CHILE | PERU | BRAZIL | UNITED STATES | MEXICO | CANADA | CHINA | INDONESIA | KAZAKHSTAN | OTHER ASIA | POLAND | AUSTRALIA | D.R. OF CONGO | ZAMBIA | RUSSIA |
| 38.2% | 6.4 | 2.1 | 7.4 | 4.2 | 2.1 | 6.7 | 4.0 | 2.1 | 3.6 | 5.1 | 4.6 | 4.2 | 3.7 | 3.2 |

Copper World Mine Production - 14,961,000 metric tons (metal content) - Avg. 2004-2006

0	10	20	30	40	50	60	70	80	90	100%

| CHILE | PERU | OTHER S.A. | UNITED STATES | CANADA | MEXICO | INDONESIA | CHINA | KAZAKHSTAN | OTHER ASIA | AUSTRALIA | RUSSIA | POLAND | OTHER EUR. | ZAMBIA | OTHER AF. |
| 35.9% | 6.9 | 2.1 | 7.8 | 3.9 | 2.6 | 6.1 | 5.4 | 3.0 | 4.3 | 5.9 | 4.7 | 3.5 | 2.2 | 3.0 | 1.6 |

Refined Copper World Total - 16,662,000 metric tons - Avg. 2004-2006

0	10	20	30	40	50	60	70	80	90	100%

| CHILE | PERU | CHINA | JAPAN | S. KOREA | INDIA | KAZAKHSTAN | OTHER ASIA | UNITED STATES | CANADA | MEXICO | RUSSIA | GERMANY | POLAND | BELGIUM | OTHER EUROPE | ZAMBIA |
| 16.9% | 3.0 | 15.7 | 8.6 | 3.2 | 2.3 | 5.5 | 7.6 | 2.1 | 5.6 | 3.9 | 3.5 | 5.7 | 2.8 |

TIN, BAUXITE

GUANGXI
GEJIU
JAMAICA
SANGAREDI
LOS PIJIGUADOS
PORTO TROMBEDAS
BANGKA ISLAND
GOVE
WEIPA-ANDOOM
SAN RAFAEL
DARLING RANGE

Source: U.S. Geological Survey

Ore producing areas
Tin
Leading ● GUANGXI
Major •
Minor ·

Bauxite (Aluminum Ore)
Leading ● WEIPA-ANDOOM
Major •
Minor ·

Goode's Interrupted Homolosine
Projection (Condensed)
Scale 1:162,000,000

M-101954-1 © Rand McNally

Bauxite World Production - 170,292,000 metric tons - Avg. 2004-2006

0	10	20	30	40	50	60	70	80	90	100%

| AUSTRALIA | BRAZIL | VENEZUELA | SURINAME | CHINA | INDIA | KAZAKHSTAN | GUINEA | JAMAICA | RUSSIA | EUROPE |
| 35.0% | 12.3 | 3.4 | 2.7 | 10.6 | 7.1 | 2.8 | 8.9 | 8.3 | 3.7 | 2.6 |

Tin World Mine Production - 301,300 metric tons (metal content) - Avg. 2004-2006

0	10	20	30	40	50	60	70	80	90	100%

| CHINA | INDONESIA | OTHER ASIA | PERU | BOLIVIA | BRAZIL | AFRICA | ALL OTHER |
| 40.8% | 26.1 | 2.5 | 16.4 | 6.0 | 4.0 | 2.6 | 1.7 |

Aluminum World Production - 31,820,000 metric tons - Avg. 2004-2006

0	10	20	30	40	50	60	70	80	90	100%

| CHINA | INDIA | BAHRAIN | U.A.E. | RUSSIA | CANADA | UNITED STATES | AUSTRALIA | BRAZIL | OTHER S.A. | NORWAY | OTHER EUROPE | S. AFRICA | OTHER AF. |
| 24.9% | 3.0 | 2.3 | 2.7 | 3.0 | 11.5 | 8.9 | 7.6 | 6.0 | 4.7 | 2.8 | 4.2 | 12.2 | 2.7 | 2.8 |

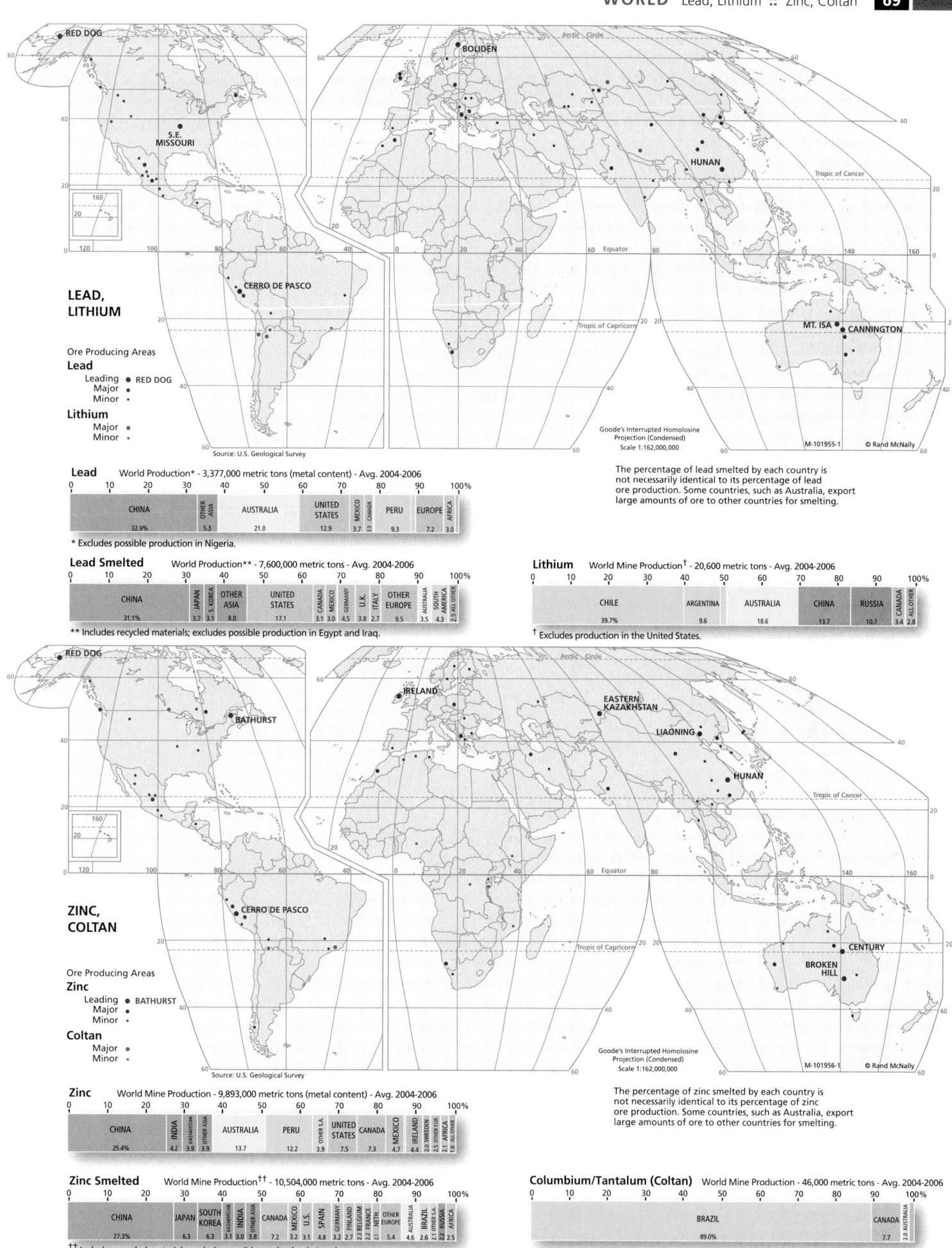

LEAD, LITHIUM

Ore Producing Areas

Lead
- Leading ● RED DOG
- Major ●
- Minor ·

Lithium
- Major ●
- Minor ·

Source: U.S. Geological Survey

Goode's Interrupted Homolosine
Projection (Condensed)
Scale 1:162,000,000

M-101955-1   © Rand McNally

The percentage of lead smelted by each country is
not necessarily identical to its percentage of lead
ore production. Some countries, such as Australia, export
large amounts of ore to other countries for smelting.

Lead   World Production* - 3,377,000 metric tons (metal content) - Avg. 2004-2006

CHINA	OTHER ASIA	AUSTRALIA	UNITED STATES	MEXICO	CANADA	PERU	EUROPE	AFRICA
32.9%	5.3	21.0	12.9	3.7	2.3	9.3	7.2	3.0

* Excludes possible production in Nigeria.

Lead Smelted   World Production** - 7,600,000 metric tons - Avg. 2004-2006

CHINA	JAPAN	S. KOREA	OTHER ASIA	UNITED STATES	CANADA	MEXICO	U.K.	ITALY	OTHER EUROPE	AUSTRALIA	SOUTH AMERICA	ALL OTHER
31.1%	3.7	3.1	8.0	17.1	3.1	3.0	3.8	2.7	9.5	3.5	4.3	2.5

** Includes recycled materials; excludes possible production in Egypt and Iraq.

Lithium   World Mine Production† - 20,600 metric tons - Avg. 2004-2006

CHILE	ARGENTINA	AUSTRALIA	CHINA	RUSSIA	CANADA	ALL OTHER
39.7%	9.6	18.6	13.7	10.7	3.4	2.8

† Excludes production in the United States.

ZINC, COLTAN

Ore Producing Areas

Zinc
- Leading ● BATHURST
- Major ●
- Minor ·

Coltan
- Major ●
- Minor ·

Source: U.S. Geological Survey

Goode's Interrupted Homolosine
Projection (Condensed)
Scale 1:162,000,000

M-101956-1   © Rand McNally

The percentage of zinc smelted by each country is
not necessarily identical to its percentage of zinc
ore production. Some countries, such as Australia, export
large amounts of ore to other countries for smelting.

Zinc   World Mine Production - 9,893,000 metric tons (metal content) - Avg. 2004-2006

CHINA	INDIA	KAZAKHSTAN	OTHER ASIA	AUSTRALIA	PERU	OTHER S.A.	UNITED STATES	CANADA	MEXICO	IRELAND	SWEDEN	OTHER EUR.	AFRICA	ALL OTHER
25.4%	4.2	3.9	3.9	13.7	12.2	3.9	7.5	7.3	4.7	4.4	2.0	2.5	2.1	—

Zinc Smelted   World Mine Production†† - 10,504,000 metric tons - Avg. 2004-2006

CHINA	JAPAN	SOUTH KOREA	KAZAKHSTAN	INDIA	OTHER ASIA	CANADA	MEXICO	U.S.	SPAIN	GERMANY	FINLAND	BELGIUM	FRANCE	NETH.	OTHER EUROPE	AUSTRALIA	BRAZIL	OTHER S.A.	RUSSIA	AFRICA
27.3%	6.3	6.3	3.1	3.8	3.1	7.2	3.3	3.1	4.8	3.2	2.7	2.3	2.2	2.1	5.4	4.6	2.6	2.1	2.2	2.5

†† Includes recycled materials; excludes possible production in Israel.

Columbium/Tantalum (Coltan)   World Mine Production - 46,000 metric tons - Avg. 2004-2006

BRAZIL	CANADA	AUSTRALIA
89.0%	7.7	2.0

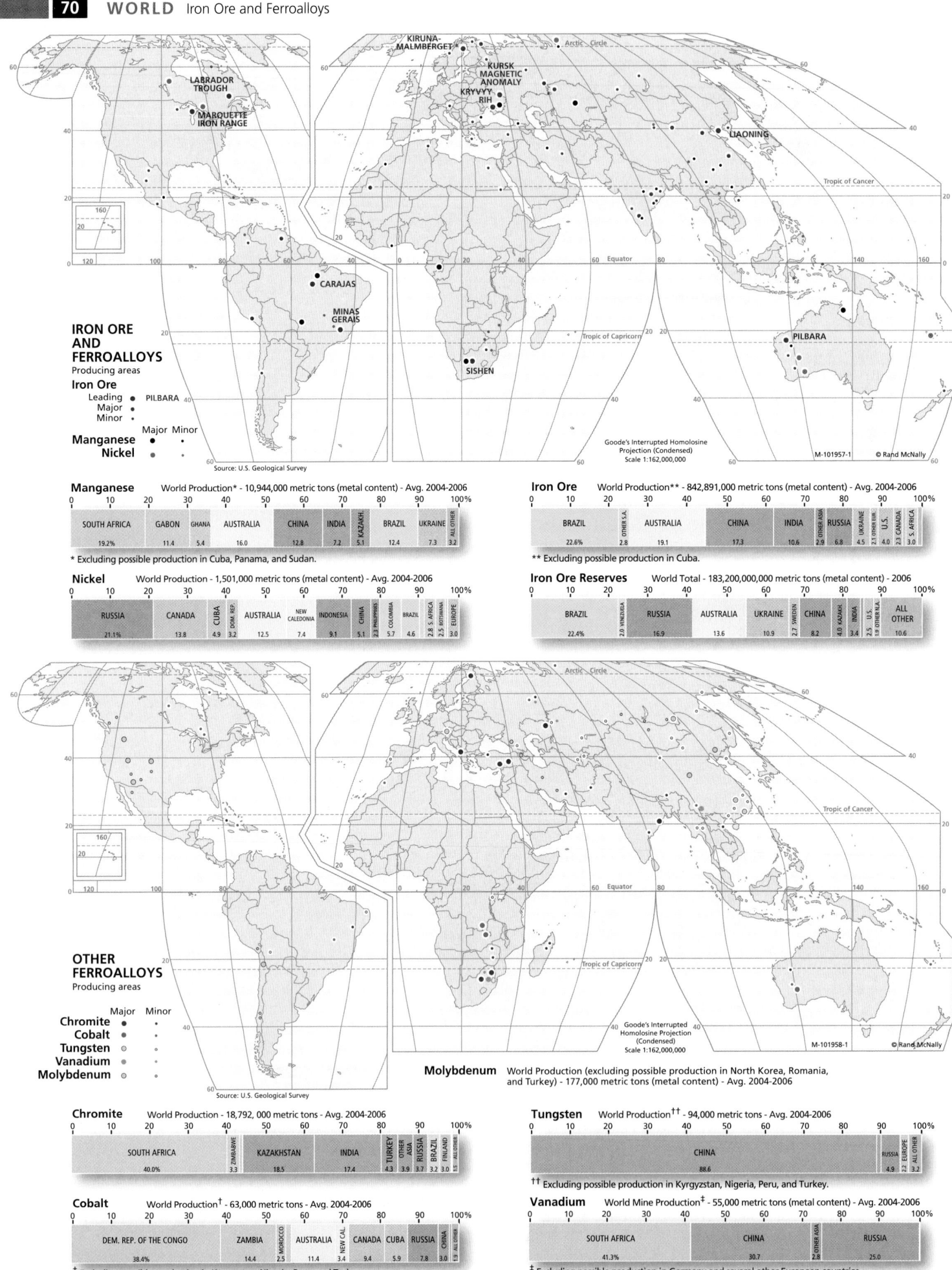

IRON ORE AND FERROALLOYS
Producing areas

Iron Ore
- Leading ● PILBARA
- Major ●
- Minor ·

Manganese ● Major · Minor
Nickel ●

Source: U.S. Geological Survey

Goode's Interrupted Homolosine
Projection (Condensed)
Scale 1:162,000,000

M-101957-1   © Rand McNally

Manganese   World Production* - 10,944,000 metric tons (metal content) - Avg. 2004-2006

SOUTH AFRICA	GABON	GHANA	AUSTRALIA	CHINA	INDIA	KAZAKH	BRAZIL	UKRAINE	ALL OTHER
19.2%	11.4	5.4	16.0	12.8	7.2	5.1	12.4	7.3	3.2

* Excluding possible production in Cuba, Panama, and Sudan.

Nickel   World Production - 1,501,000 metric tons (metal content) - Avg. 2004-2006

RUSSIA	CANADA	CUBA	DOM. REP.	AUSTRALIA	NEW CALEDONIA	INDONESIA	CHINA	PHILIPPINES	COLOMBIA	BRAZIL	S. AFRICA	BOTSWANA	EUROPE
21.1%	13.8	4.9	3.2	12.5	7.4	9.1	5.1	2.3	5.7	4.6	2.8	2.5	3.0

Iron Ore   World Production** - 842,891,000 metric tons (metal content) - Avg. 2004-2006

BRAZIL	OTHER S.A.	AUSTRALIA	CHINA	INDIA	OTHER ASIA	RUSSIA	UKRAINE	OTHER EUR.	U.S.	CANADA	S. AFRICA
22.6%		19.1	17.3	10.6	2.9	6.8	4.5	2.1	4.0	2.3	3.0

** Excluding possible production in Cuba.

Iron Ore Reserves   World Total - 183,200,000,000 metric tons (metal content) - 2006

BRAZIL	VENEZUELA	RUSSIA	AUSTRALIA	UKRAINE	SWEDEN	CHINA	KAZAKH	INDIA	U.S.	OTHER N.A.	ALL OTHER
22.4%	2.0	16.9	13.6	10.9	2.7	8.2	4.0	3.4	2.5	1.9	10.6

OTHER FERROALLOYS
Producing areas

	Major	Minor
Chromite	●	·
Cobalt	●	·
Tungsten	◎	◦
Vanadium	◉	◦
Molybdenum	◉	◦

Source: U.S. Geological Survey

Goode's Interrupted
Homolosine Projection
(Condensed)
Scale 1:162,000,000

M-101958-1   © Rand McNally

Molybdenum   World Production (excluding possible production in North Korea, Romania, and Turkey) - 177,000 metric tons (metal content) - Avg. 2004-2006

Chromite   World Production - 18,792, 000 metric tons - Avg. 2004-2006

SOUTH AFRICA	ZIMBABWE	KAZAKHSTAN	INDIA	TURKEY	OTHER ASIA	RUSSIA	BRAZIL	FINLAND	ALL OTHER
40.0%	3.3	18.5	17.4	4.3	3.9	3.7	3.2	3.0	

Cobalt   World Production† - 63,000 metric tons - Avg. 2004-2006

DEM. REP. OF THE CONGO	ZAMBIA	MOROCCO	AUSTRALIA	NEW CAL	CANADA	CUBA	RUSSIA	CHINA	ALL OTHER
38.4%	14.4	2.5	11.4	3.4	9.4	5.9	7.8	3.0	

† Excluding possible production in Kyrgyzstan, Nigeria, Peru, and Turkey.

Tungsten   World Production†† - 94,000 metric tons - Avg. 2004-2006

CHINA	RUSSIA	EUROPE	ALL OTHER
88.6	4.9	2.2	3.2

†† Excluding possible production in Kyrgyzstan, Nigeria, Peru, and Turkey.

Vanadium   World Mine Production‡ - 55,000 metric tons (metal content) - Avg. 2004-2006

SOUTH AFRICA	CHINA	OTHER ASIA	RUSSIA
41.3%	30.7	2.8	25.0

‡ Excluding possible production in Germany and several other European countries.

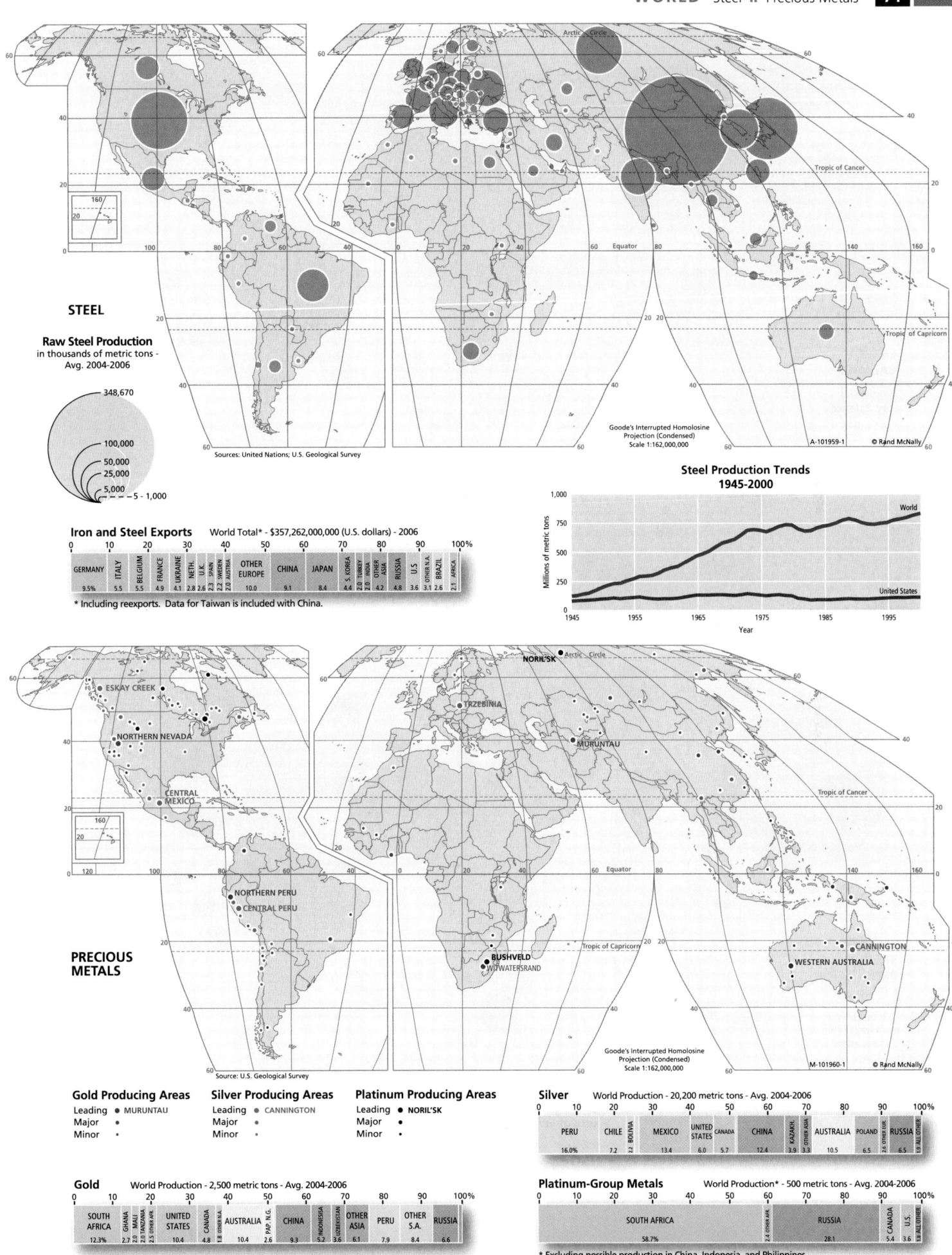

STEEL

Raw Steel Production
in thousands of metric tons -
Avg. 2004-2006

348,670
100,000
50,000
25,000
5,000
5 - 1,000

Sources: United Nations; U.S. Geological Survey

Iron and Steel Exports
World Total* - $357,262,000,000 (U.S. dollars) - 2006

GERMANY	ITALY	BELGIUM	FRANCE	UKRAINE	NETH.	SPAIN	SWEDEN	AUSTRIA	OTHER EUROPE	CHINA	JAPAN	S. KOREA	TURKEY	INDIA	OTHER ASIA	RUSSIA	U.S	OTHER N.A.	BRAZIL	AFRICA
9.5%	5.5	5.5	4.9	4.1	2.8	2.2	2.2	2.0	10.0	9.1	8.4	4.4	2.0	2.0	4.2	4.8	3.6	3.1	2.6	2.1

*Including reexports. Data for Taiwan is included with China.

Steel Production Trends 1945-2000

Goode's Interrupted Homolosine
Projection (Condensed)
Scale 1:162,000,000
A-101959-1 © Rand McNally

PRECIOUS METALS

Goode's Interrupted Homolosine
Projection (Condensed)
Scale 1:162,000,000
M-101960-1 © Rand McNally

Source: U.S. Geological Survey

Gold Producing Areas
Leading ● MURUNTAU
Major ●
Minor ·

Silver Producing Areas
Leading ● CANNINGTON
Major ●
Minor ·

Platinum Producing Areas
Leading ● NORIL'SK
Major ●
Minor ·

Silver
World Production - 20,200 metric tons - Avg. 2004-2006

PERU	CHILE	BOLIVIA	MEXICO	UNITED STATES	CANADA	CHINA	KAZAKH.	OTHER ASIA	AUSTRALIA	POLAND	RUSSIA	ALL OTHER
16.0%	7.2	2.2	13.4	6.0	5.7	12.4	3.9	3.3	10.5	6.5	6.5	1.9

Gold
World Production - 2,500 metric tons - Avg. 2004-2006

SOUTH AFRICA	GHANA	MALI	TANZANIA	OTHER AFR.	UNITED STATES	CANADA	AUSTRALIA	PAP. N.G.	CHINA	INDONESIA	UZBEKISTAN	OTHER ASIA	PERU	OTHER S.A.	RUSSIA
12.3%	2.7	2.0	2.0	2.5	10.4	4.8	10.4	2.6	9.3	3.6	2.6	6.1	7.9	8.4	6.6

Platinum-Group Metals
World Production* - 500 metric tons - Avg. 2004-2006

SOUTH AFRICA	OTHER AFR.	RUSSIA	CANADA	U.S.	ALL OTHER
58.7%	2.4	28.1	5.4	3.6	1.8

*Excluding possible production in China, Indonesia, and Philippines.

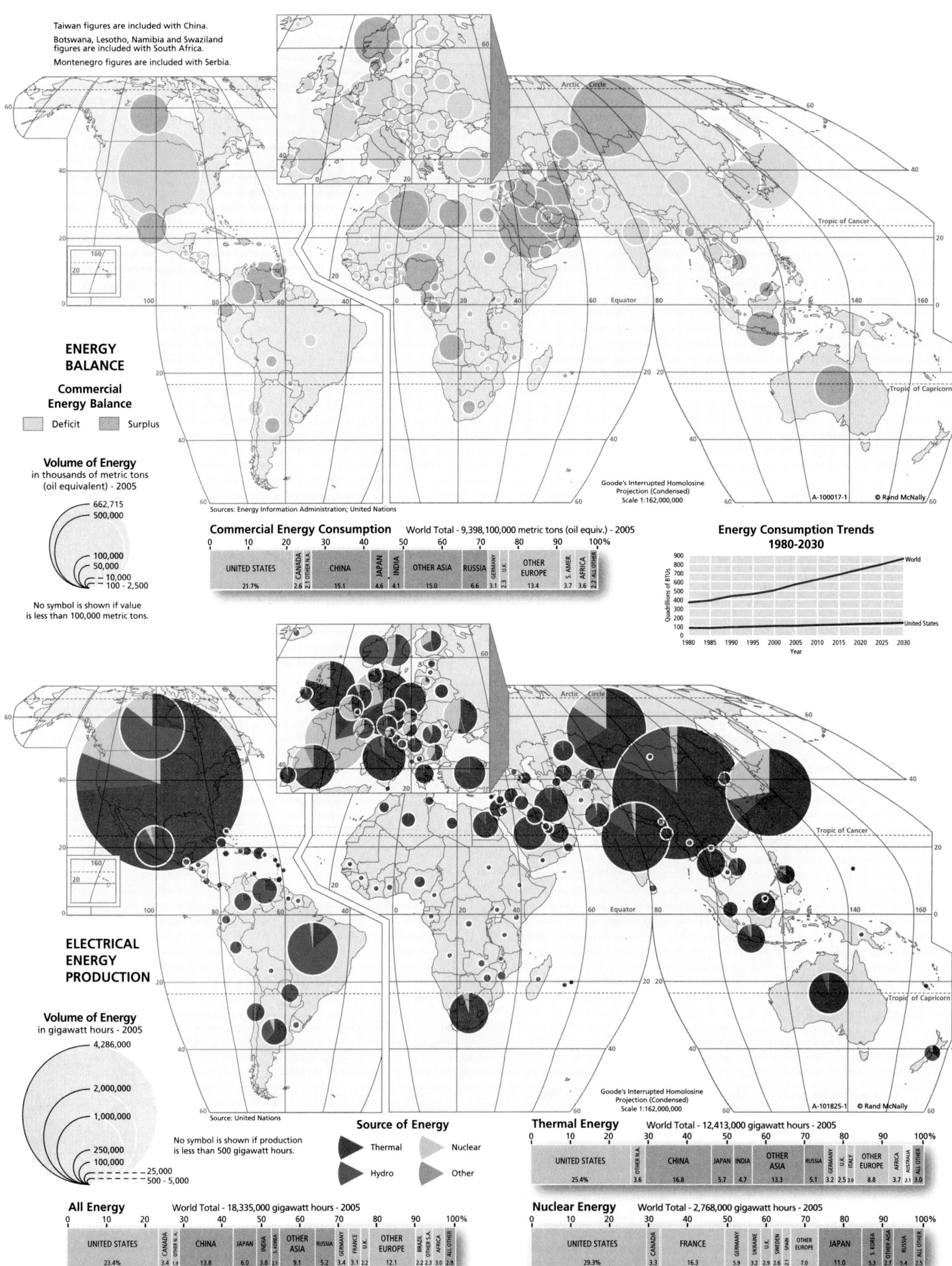

Taiwan figures are included with China.

Botswana, Lesotho, Namibia and Swaziland figures are included with South Africa.

Montenegro figures are included with Serbia.

ENERGY BALANCE

Commercial Energy Balance

Deficit   Surplus

Volume of Energy
in thousands of metric tons
(oil equivalent) - 2005

662,715
500,000
100,000
50,000
10,000
100 - 2,500

No symbol is shown if value
is less than 100,000 metric tons.

Sources: Energy Information Administration; United Nations

Goode's Interrupted Homolosine
Projection (Condensed)
Scale 1:162,000,000

A-100017-1   © Rand McNally

Commercial Energy Consumption
World Total - 9,398,100,000 metric tons (oil equiv.) - 2005

0	10	20	30	40	50	60	70	80	90	100%			

UNITED STATES	CANADA 2.6	OTHER N.A. 2.1	CHINA	JAPAN 4.6	INDIA 4.1	OTHER ASIA	RUSSIA 6.6	GERMANY 3.1	U.K. 2.3	OTHER EUROPE	S. AMER. 3.7	AFRICA 3.6	ALL OTHER 2.2
21.7%			15.1			15.0				13.4			

Energy Consumption Trends 1980-2030

World
United States

Quadrillions of BTUs: 900, 800, 700, 600, 500, 400, 300, 200, 100

Year: 1980 1985 1990 1995 2000 2005 2010 2015 2020 2025 2030

ELECTRICAL ENERGY PRODUCTION

Volume of Energy
in gigawatt hours - 2005

4,286,000
2,000,000
1,000,000
250,000
100,000
25,000
500 - 5,000

No symbol is shown if production
is less than 500 gigawatt hours.

Source: United Nations

Goode's Interrupted Homolosine
Projection (Condensed)
Scale 1:162,000,000

A-101825-1   © Rand McNally

Source of Energy

Thermal   Nuclear

Hydro   Other

Thermal Energy
World Total - 12,413,000 gigawatt hours - 2005

0	10	20	30	40	50	60	70	80	90	100%

UNITED STATES	OTHER N.A. 3.6	CHINA	JAPAN 5.7	INDIA 4.7	OTHER ASIA	RUSSIA 5.1	GERMANY 3.2	U.K. 2.5	ITALY 2.0	OTHER EUROPE	AFRICA 3.7	AUSTRALIA 2.1	ALL OTHER 3.0
25.4%		16.8			13.3					8.8			

All Energy
World Total - 18,335,000 gigawatt hours - 2005

0	10	20	30	40	50	60	70	80	90	100%

UNITED STATES	CANADA 3.4	OTHER N.A. 1.9	CHINA	JAPAN 6.0	INDIA 3.8	OTHER ASIA	RUSSIA 5.2	GERMANY 3.4	FRANCE 3.1	U.K. 2.2	OTHER EUROPE	BRAZIL 2.2	OTHER S.A. 2.3	AFRICA 3.0	ALL OTHER 2.9
23.4%			13.8			9.1					12.1				

Nuclear Energy
World Total - 2,768,000 gigawatt hours - 2005

0	10	20	30	40	50	60	70	80	90	100%

UNITED STATES	CANADA 3.3	FRANCE	GERMANY 5.9	UKRAINE 3.2	U.K. 2.9	SWEDEN 2.3	SPAIN 2.1	OTHER EUROPE	JAPAN	S. KOREA 5.3	OTHER ASIA 2.7	RUSSIA 5.4	ALL OTHER 2.5
29.3%		16.3						7.0	11.0				

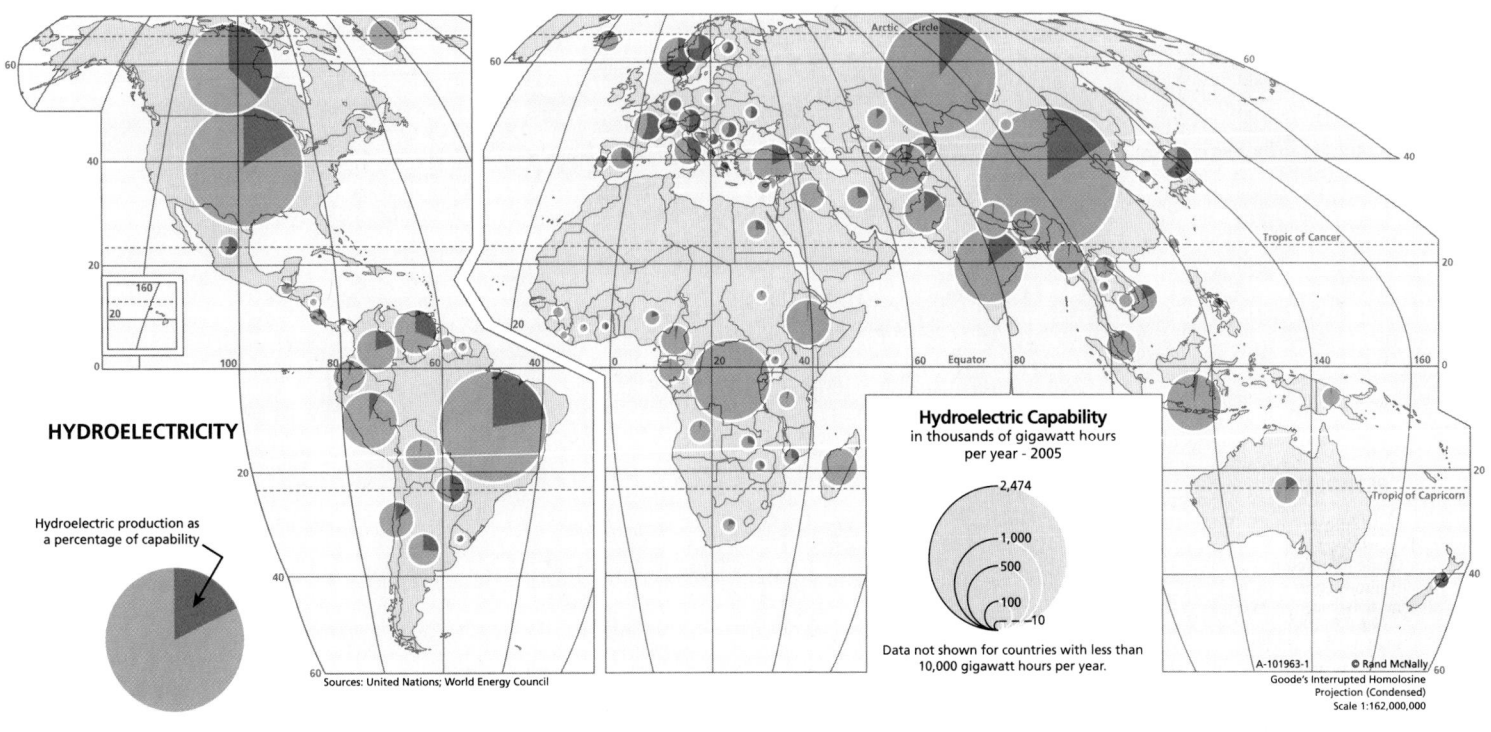

HYDROELECTRICITY

Hydroelectric production as a percentage of capability

Hydroelectric Capability
in thousands of gigawatt hours per year - 2005

2,474
1,000
500
100
10

Data not shown for countries with less than 10,000 gigawatt hours per year.

Sources: United Nations; World Energy Council

A-101963-1 © Rand McNally
Goode's Interrupted Homolosine
Projection (Condensed)
Scale 1:162,000,000

Hydroelectric Capability
World Total* - 16,494,000 gigawatt hours/year

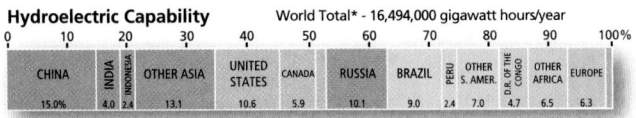

CHINA	INDIA	INDONESIA	OTHER ASIA	UNITED STATES	CANADA	RUSSIA	BRAZIL	PERU	OTHER S. AMER.	D.R. OF THE CONGO	OTHER AFRICA	EUROPE
15.0%	4.0	2.4	13.1	10.6	5.9	10.1	9.0	2.4	7.0	4.7	6.5	6.3

* Technically exploitable capability.

Hydroelectricity
World Production - 2,996,000 gigawatt hours - 2005

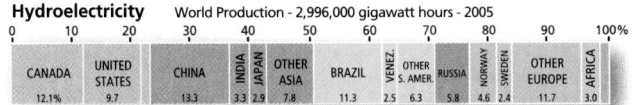

CANADA	UNITED STATES	CHINA	INDIA	JAPAN	OTHER ASIA	BRAZIL	VENEZ.	OTHER S. AMER.	RUSSIA	NORWAY	SWEDEN	OTHER EUROPE	AFRICA
12.1%	9.7	13.3	3.3	2.9	7.8	11.3	2.5	6.3	5.8	4.6	2.4	11.7	3.0

ALTERNATIVE ENERGY

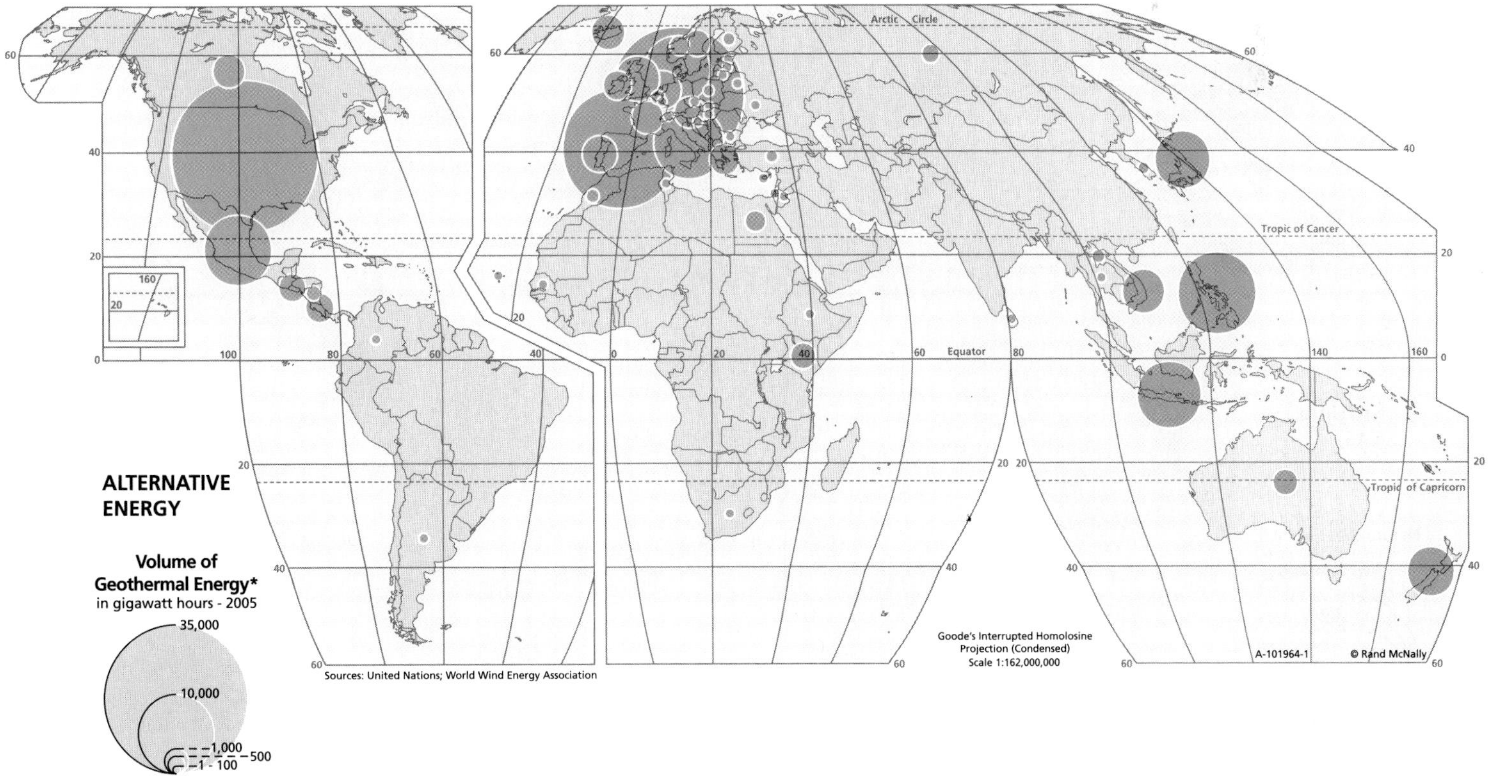

Volume of Geothermal Energy*
in gigawatt hours - 2005

35,000
10,000
1,000
500
100
1

Sources: United Nations; World Wind Energy Association

Goode's Interrupted Homolosine
Projection (Condensed)
Scale 1:162,000,000

A-101964-1 © Rand McNally

Geothermal Energy
World Production* - 158,000 gigawatt hours - 2005

UNITED STATES	MEXICO	OTHER N.A.	GERMANY	SPAIN	ITALY	DENMARK	OTHER EUROPE	PHIL.	INDON.	JAPAN	OTHER ASIA	N.Z.
22.3%	4.7	2.5	18.0	13.5	4.9	4.2	10.2	6.3	4.2	3.0	2.1	2.2

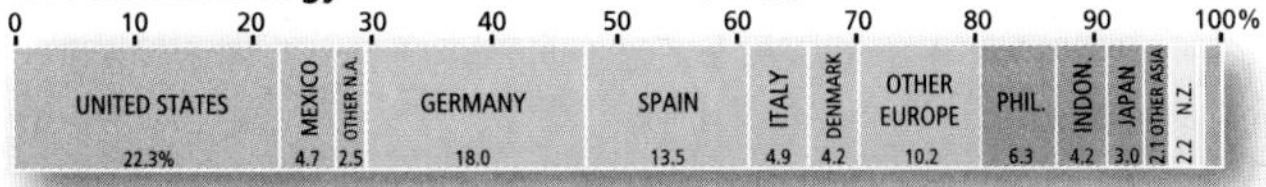

* May include other sources of energy, such as solar or wind energy.

Wind Energy
World Installed Capacity - 59 gigawatts - 2005

GERMANY	SPAIN	DENMARK	ITALY	U.K.	NETH.	OTHER EUROPE	UNITED STATES	INDIA	CHINA	OTHER ASIA
31.2%	17.0	5.3	2.9	2.3	2.1	8.5	15.5	7.5	2.1	2.3

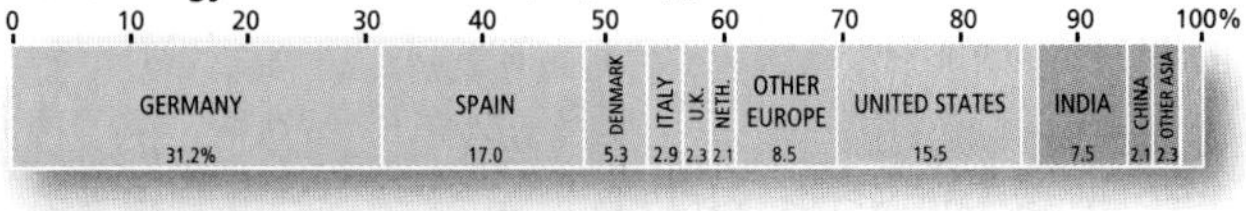

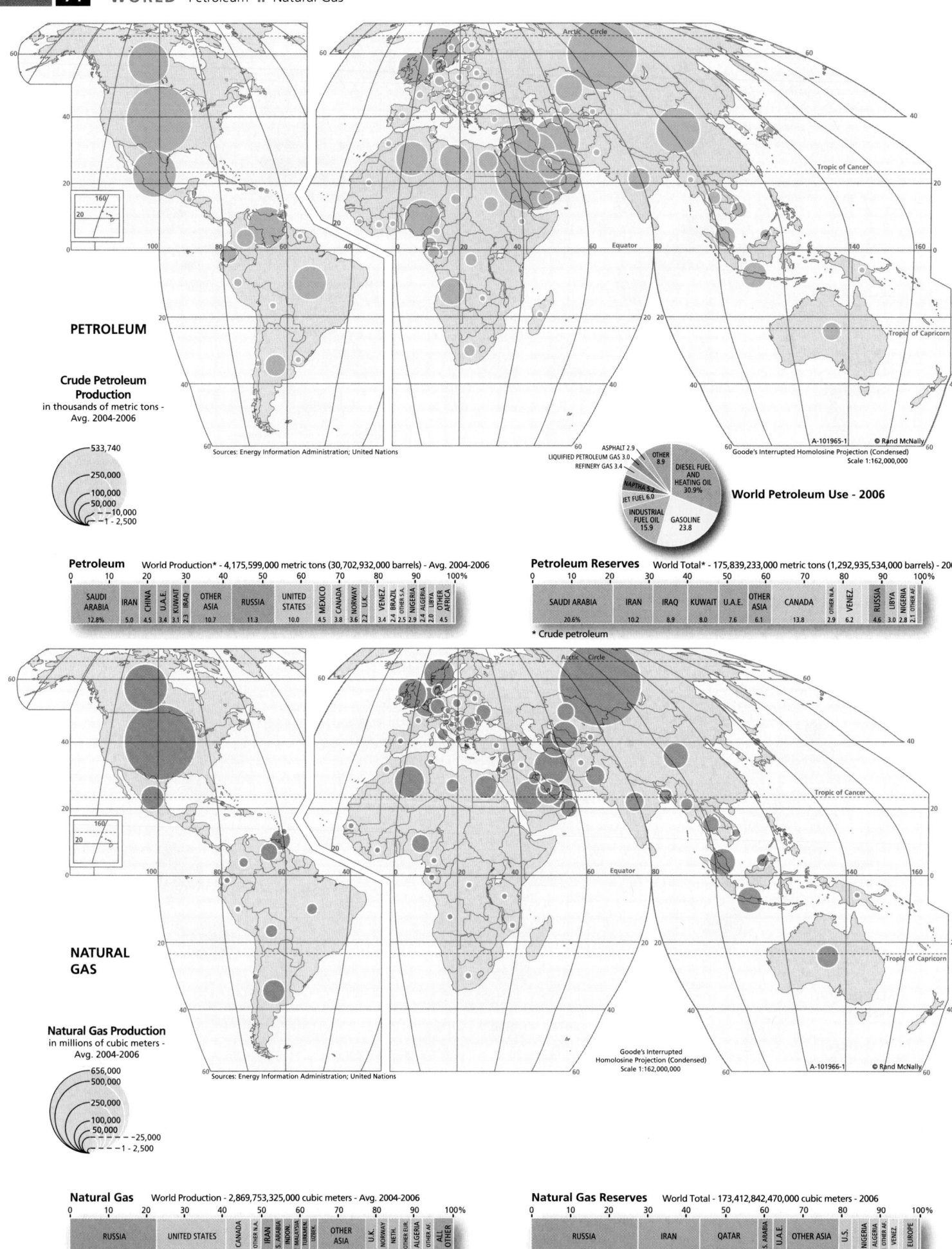

PETROLEUM

Crude Petroleum Production
in thousands of metric tons -
Avg. 2004-2006

533,740
250,000
100,000
50,000
10,000
1 - 2,500

Sources: Energy Information Administration; United Nations

ASPHALT 2.9
LIQUIFIED PETROLEUM GAS 3.0
REFINERY GAS 3.4
OTHER 8.9
DIESEL FUEL AND HEATING OIL 30.9%
NAPTHA 5.2
JET FUEL 6.0
INDUSTRIAL FUEL OIL 15.9
GASOLINE 23.8

World Petroleum Use - 2006

A-101965-1   © Rand McNally
Goode's Interrupted Homolosine Projection (Condensed)
Scale 1:162,000,000

Petroleum   World Production* - 4,175,599,000 metric tons (30,702,932,000 barrels) - Avg. 2004-2006

0	10	20	30	40	50	60	70	80	90	100%

SAUDI ARABIA	IRAN	CHINA	U.A.E.	KUWAIT	IRAQ	OTHER ASIA	RUSSIA	UNITED STATES	MEXICO	CANADA	NORWAY	U.K.	VENEZ.	BRAZIL	OTHER S.A.	NIGERIA	ALGERIA	LIBYA	OTHER AFRICA
12.8%	5.0	4.5	3.4	3.1	2.3	10.7	11.3	10.0	4.5	3.8	3.6	2.2	3.4	2.4	2.5	2.9	2.4	2.0	4.5

Petroleum Reserves   World Total* - 175,839,233,000 metric tons (1,292,935,534,000 barrels) - 2006

0	10	20	30	40	50	60	70	80	90	100%

SAUDI ARABIA	IRAN	IRAQ	KUWAIT	U.A.E.	OTHER ASIA	CANADA	OTHER N.A.	VENEZ.	RUSSIA	LIBYA	NIGERIA	OTHER AF.
20.6%	10.2	8.9	8.0	7.6	6.1	13.8	2.9	6.2	4.6	3.0	2.8	2.1

* Crude petroleum

NATURAL GAS

Natural Gas Production
in millions of cubic meters -
Avg. 2004-2006

656,000
500,000
250,000
100,000
50,000
25,000
1 - 2,500

Sources: Energy Information Administration; United Nations

Goode's Interrupted Homolosine Projection (Condensed)
Scale 1:162,000,000

A-101966-1   © Rand McNally

Natural Gas   World Production - 2,869,753,325,000 cubic meters - Avg. 2004-2006

0	10	20	30	40	50	60	70	80	90	100%

RUSSIA	UNITED STATES	CANADA	OTHER N.A.	IRAN	S. ARABIA	INDON.	MALAYSIA	TURKMEN.	UZBEK.	OTHER ASIA	U.K.	NORWAY	NETH.	OTHER EUR.	ALGERIA	OTHER AF.	ALL OTHER
22.4%	18.1	6.4	2.7	3.4	2.4	2.2	2.1	2.1		12.5	3.1	3.0	2.8	3.1	3.0	3.0	5.2

Natural Gas Reserves   World Total - 173,412,842,470,000 cubic meters - 2006

0	10	20	30	40	50	60	70	80	90	100%

RUSSIA	IRAN	QATAR	S. ARABIA	U.A.E.	OTHER ASIA	U.S.	NIGERIA	ALGERIA	OTHER AF.	VENEZ.	EUROPE
27.4%	15.9	14.9	3.9	3.5	13.3	3.3	3.0	2.6	2.3	2.5	3.9

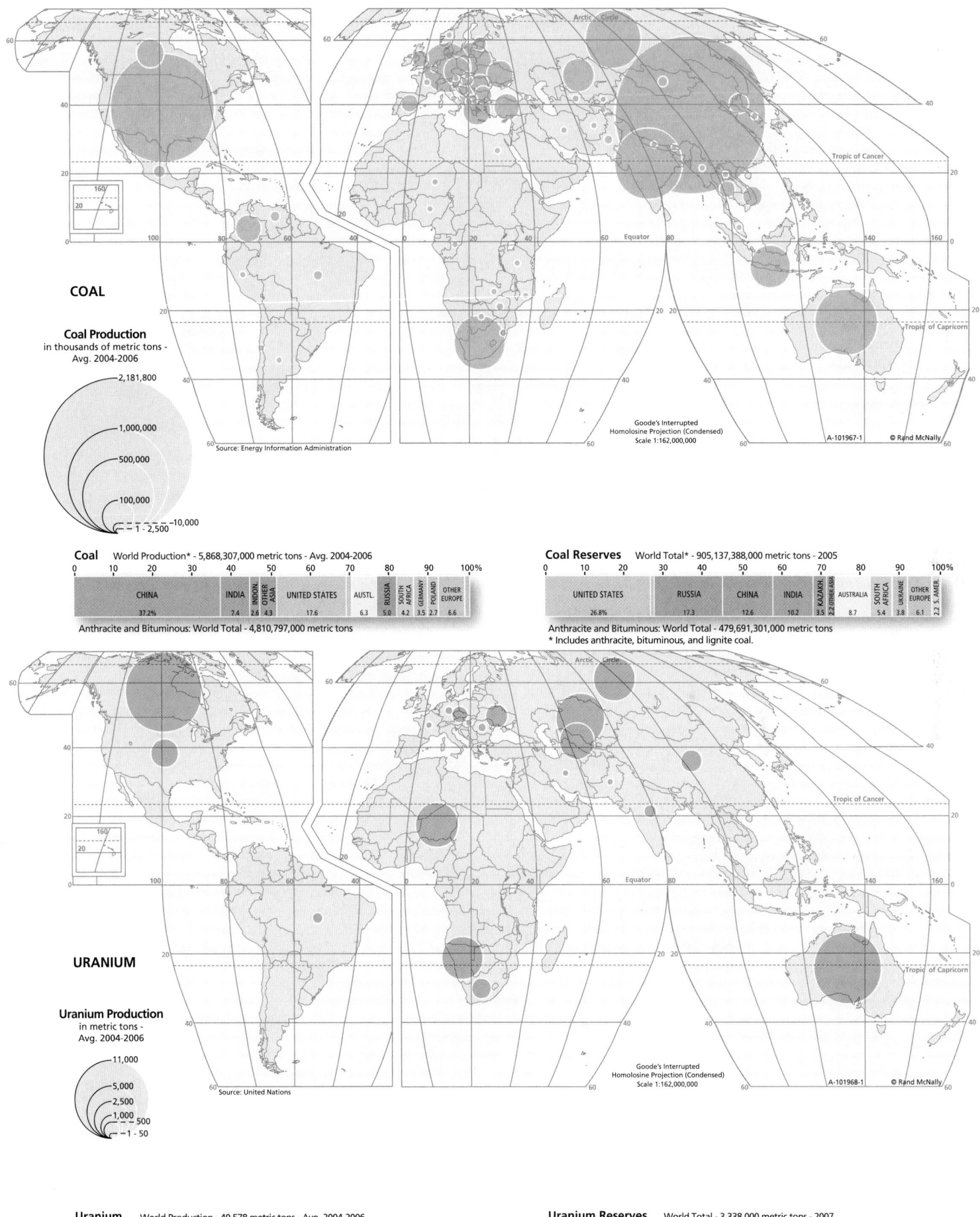

COAL

Coal Production
in thousands of metric tons -
Avg. 2004-2006

2,181,800
1,000,000
500,000
100,000
10,000
1 - 2,500

Source: Energy Information Administration

Goode's Interrupted
Homolosine Projection (Condensed)
Scale 1:162,000,000

A-101967-1 © Rand McNally

Coal World Production* - 5,868,307,000 metric tons - Avg. 2004-2006

CHINA	INDIA	INDON.	OTHER ASIA	UNITED STATES	AUSTL.	RUSSIA	SOUTH AFRICA	GERMANY	POLAND	OTHER EUROPE
37.2%	7.4	2.6	4.3	17.6	6.3	5.0	4.2	3.5	2.7	6.6

Anthracite and Bituminous: World Total - 4,810,797,000 metric tons

Coal Reserves World Total* - 905,137,388,000 metric tons - 2005

UNITED STATES	RUSSIA	CHINA	INDIA	KAZAKH.	OTHER ASIA	AUSTRALIA	SOUTH AFRICA	UKRAINE	OTHER EUROPE	S. AMER.
26.8%	17.3	12.6	10.2	3.5	2.2	8.7	5.4	3.8	6.1	2.2

Anthracite and Bituminous: World Total - 479,691,301,000 metric tons
* Includes anthracite, bituminous, and lignite coal.

URANIUM

Uranium Production
in metric tons -
Avg. 2004-2006

11,000
5,000
2,500
1,000
500
1 - 50

Source: United Nations

Goode's Interrupted
Homolosine Projection (Condensed)
Scale 1:162,000,000

A-101968-1 © Rand McNally

Uranium World Production - 40,578 metric tons - Avg. 2004-2006

CANADA	U.S.	AUSTRALIA	KAZAKHSTAN	UZBEK.	OTHER ASIA	NIGER	NAMIBIA	RUSSIA	UKRAINE
27.2%	3.2	21.4	11.0	5.5	2.5	8.2	7.6	8.0	2.0

Uranium Reserves World Total - 3,338,000 metric tons - 2007

AUSTRALIA	KAZAKHSTAN	UZBEK.	OTHER ASIA	UNITED STATES	CANADA	SOUTH AFRICA	NIGER	NAMIBIA	RUSSIA	BRAZIL	UKRAINE
21.7%	11.3	2.2	6.2	10.2	9.9	8.5	7.3	5.3	5.2	4.7	4.0

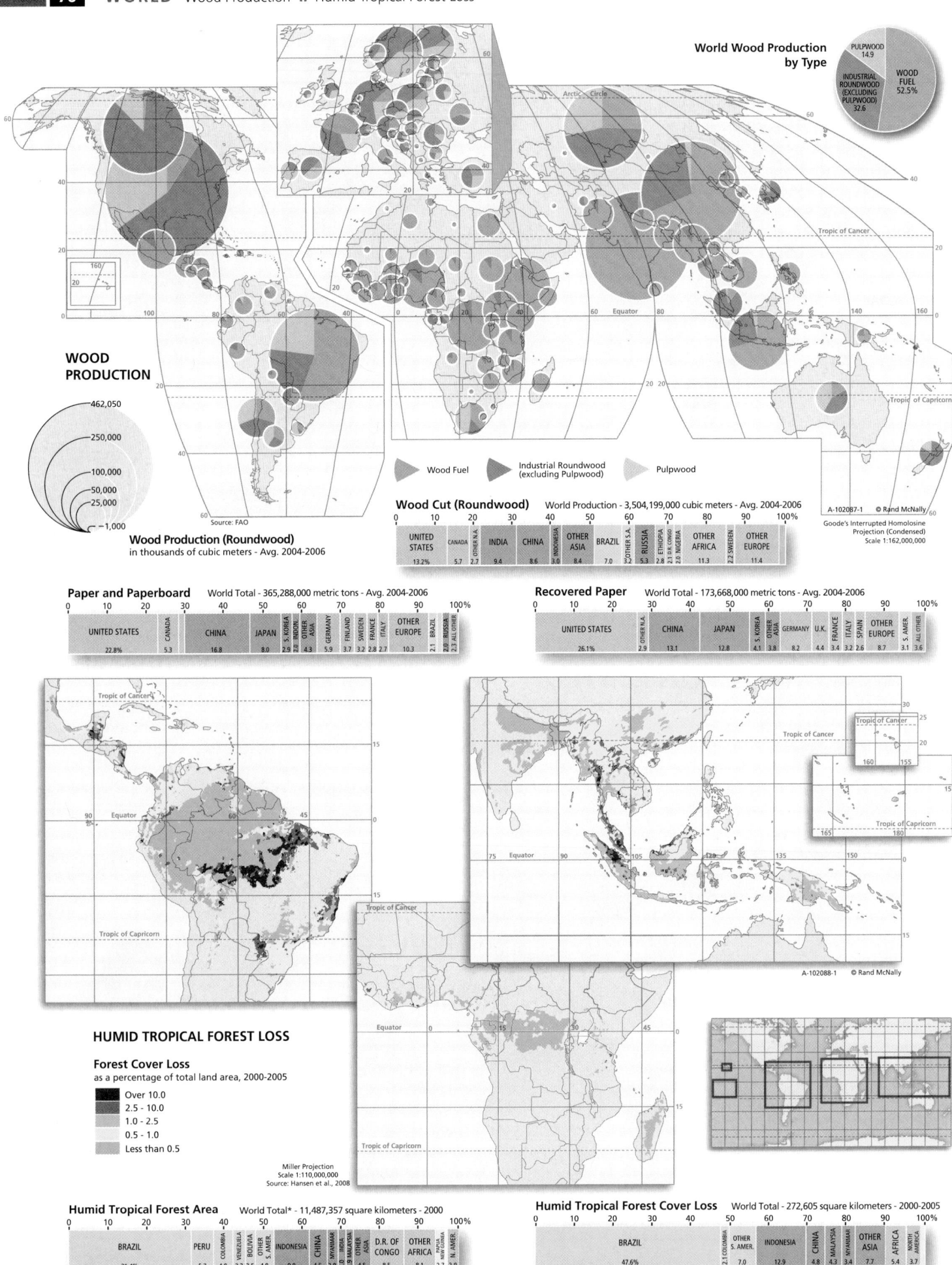

World Wood Production by Type

- PULPWOOD 14.9
- INDUSTRIAL ROUNDWOOD (EXCLUDING PULPWOOD) 32.6
- WOOD FUEL 52.5%

WOOD PRODUCTION

462,050
250,000
100,000
50,000
25,000
1,000

Source: FAO

Wood Production (Roundwood)
in thousands of cubic meters - Avg. 2004-2006

Wood Fuel | Industrial Roundwood (excluding Pulpwood) | Pulpwood

A-102087-1 © Rand McNally

Goode's Interrupted Homolosine Projection (Condensed)
Scale 1:162,000,000

Wood Cut (Roundwood)
World Production - 3,504,199,000 cubic meters - Avg. 2004-2006

UNITED STATES	CANADA	OTHER N.A.	INDIA	CHINA	INDONESIA	OTHER ASIA	BRAZIL	OTHER S.A.	RUSSIA	ETHIOPIA	D.R. CONGO	NIGERIA	OTHER AFRICA	SWEDEN	OTHER EUROPE
13.2%	5.7	2.7	9.4	8.6	3.0	8.4	7.0	2.1	5.3	2.1	2.1	2.0	11.3	2.2	11.4

Paper and Paperboard
World Total - 365,288,000 metric tons - Avg. 2004-2006

UNITED STATES	CANADA	CHINA	JAPAN	S. KOREA	INDON.	OTHER ASIA	GERMANY	FINLAND	SWEDEN	FRANCE	ITALY	OTHER EUROPE	BRAZIL	RUSSIA	ALL OTHER
22.8%	5.3	16.8	8.0	2.9	2.0	4.3	5.9	3.7	3.2	2.8	2.7	10.3	2.1	2.0	2.3

Recovered Paper
World Total - 173,668,000 metric tons - Avg. 2004-2006

UNITED STATES	OTHER N.A.	CHINA	JAPAN	S. KOREA	OTHER ASIA	GERMANY	U.K.	FRANCE	ITALY	SPAIN	OTHER EUROPE	S. AMER.	ALL OTHER
26.1%	2.9	13.1	12.8	4.1	3.8	8.2	4.4	3.4	3.2	2.6	8.7	3.1	3.6

A-102088-1 © Rand McNally

HUMID TROPICAL FOREST LOSS

Forest Cover Loss
as a percentage of total land area, 2000-2005

- Over 10.0
- 2.5 - 10.0
- 1.0 - 2.5
- 0.5 - 1.0
- Less than 0.5

Miller Projection
Scale 1:110,000,000
Source: Hansen et al., 2008

Humid Tropical Forest Area
World Total* - 11,487,357 square kilometers - 2000

BRAZIL	PERU	COLOMBIA	VENEZUELA	BOLIVIA	OTHER S. AMER.	INDONESIA	CHINA	MYANMAR	INDIA	MALAYSIA	OTHER ASIA	D.R. OF CONGO	OTHER AFRICA	PAPUA NEW GUINEA	N. AMER.
31.4%	5.7	4.9	3.3	2.5	4.8	9.0	4.5	2.8	2.0	1.9	4.5	8.5	8.1	2.1	2.9

*Defined as areas with tree canopy cover of 25% or more.

Humid Tropical Forest Cover Loss
World Total - 272,605 square kilometers - 2000-2005

BRAZIL	COLOMBIA	OTHER S. AMER.	INDONESIA	CHINA	MALAYSIA	MYANMAR	OTHER ASIA	AFRICA	NORTH AMERICA
47.6%	2.1	7.0	12.9	4.8	4.3	3.4	7.7	5.4	3.7

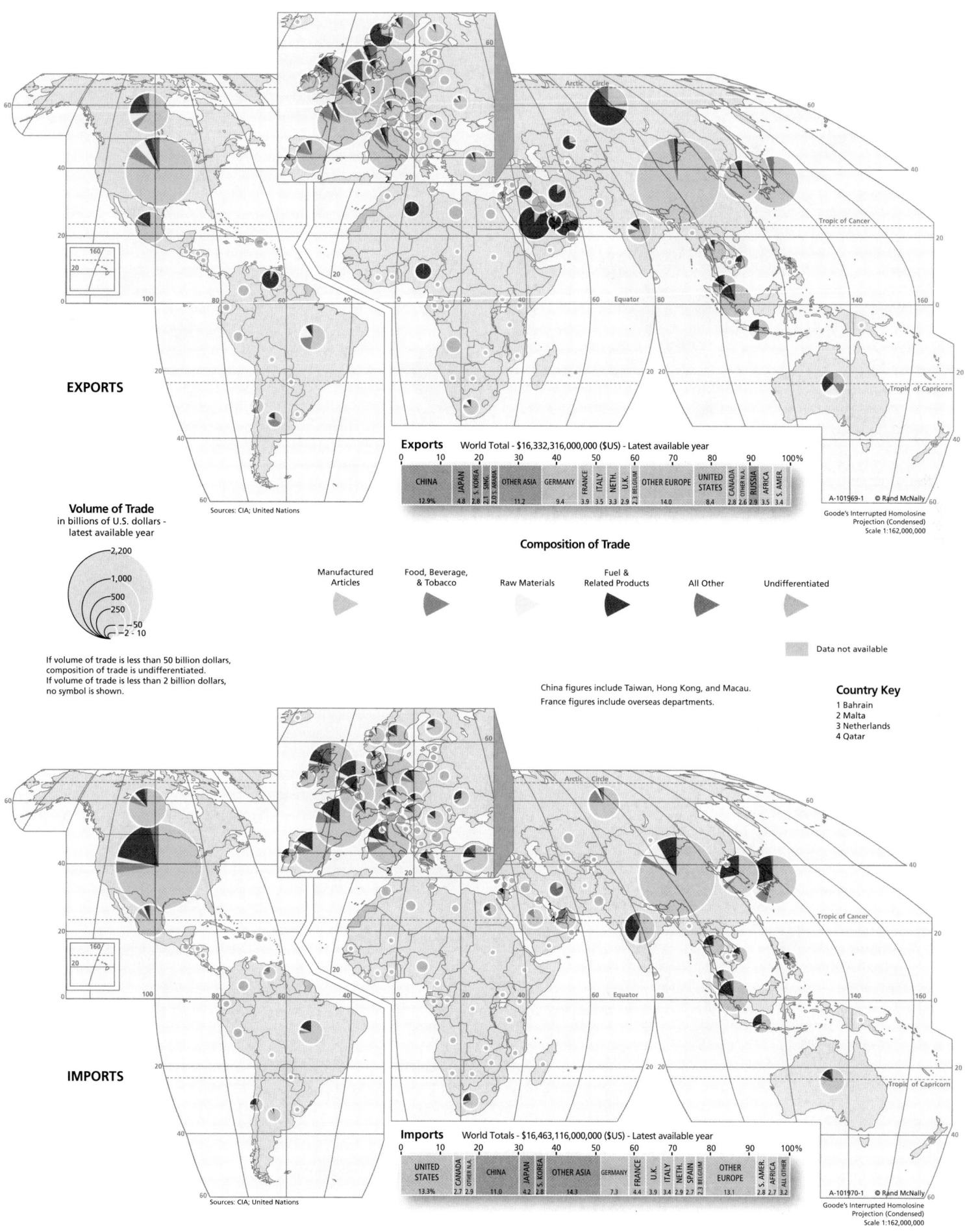

EXPORTS

Volume of Trade
in billions of U.S. dollars -
latest available year

2,200
1,000
500
250
50
2 - 10

If volume of trade is less than 50 billion dollars,
composition of trade is undifferentiated.
If volume of trade is less than 2 billion dollars,
no symbol is shown.

Sources: CIA; United Nations

Exports World Total - $16,332,316,000,000 ($US) - Latest available year

0	10	20	30	40	50	60	70	80	90	100%

CHINA	JAPAN	S. KOREA	SING.	S. ARABIA	OTHER ASIA	GERMANY	FRANCE	ITALY	NETH.	U.K.	BELGIUM	OTHER EUROPE	UNITED STATES	CANADA	OTHER N.A.	RUSSIA	AFRICA	S. AMER.
12.9%	4.8	2.8	2.3	2.0	11.2	9.4	3.9	3.5	3.3	2.9	2.3	14.0	8.4	2.8	2.6	2.9	3.5	3.4

A-101969-1 © Rand McNally

Goode's Interrupted Homolosine
Projection (Condensed)
Scale 1:162,000,000

Composition of Trade

Manufactured Articles   Food, Beverage, & Tobacco   Raw Materials   Fuel & Related Products   All Other   Undifferentiated

Data not available

China figures include Taiwan, Hong Kong, and Macau.
France figures include overseas departments.

Country Key
1 Bahrain
2 Malta
3 Netherlands
4 Qatar

IMPORTS

Sources: CIA; United Nations

Imports World Totals - $16,463,116,000,000 ($US) - Latest available year

0	10	20	30	40	50	60	70	80	90	100%

UNITED STATES	CANADA	OTHER N.A.	CHINA	JAPAN	S. KOREA	OTHER ASIA	GERMANY	FRANCE	U.K.	ITALY	NETH.	SPAIN	BELGIUM	OTHER EUROPE	S. AMER.	AFRICA	ALL OTHER
13.3%	2.7	2.9	11.0	4.2	2.8	14.3	7.3	4.4	3.9	3.4	2.9	2.7	2.3	13.1	2.8	2.7	3.2

A-101970-1 © Rand McNally

Goode's Interrupted Homolosine
Projection (Condensed)
Scale 1:162,000,000

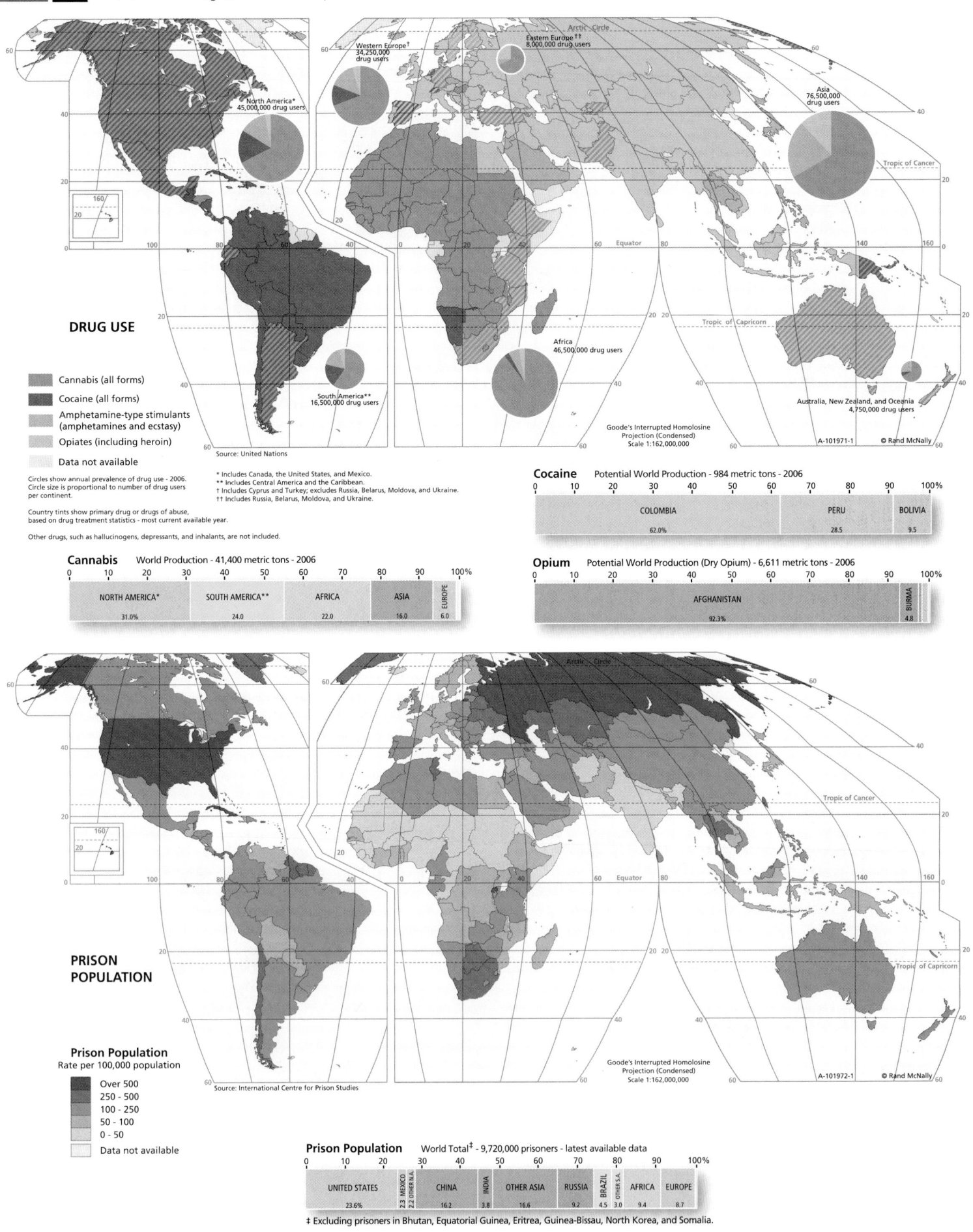

DRUG USE

- Cannabis (all forms)
- Cocaine (all forms)
- Amphetamine-type stimulants (amphetamines and ecstasy)
- Opiates (including heroin)
- Data not available

Circles show annual prevalence of drug use - 2006.
Circle size is proportional to number of drug users per continent.

Country tints show primary drug or drugs of abuse, based on drug treatment statistics - most current available year.

Other drugs, such as hallucinogens, depressants, and inhalants, are not included.

* Includes Canada, the United States, and Mexico.
** Includes Central America and the Caribbean.
† Includes Cyprus and Turkey; excludes Russia, Belarus, Moldova, and Ukraine.
†† Includes Russia, Belarus, Moldova, and Ukraine.

Source: United Nations

North America*
45,000,000 drug users

Western Europe†
34,250,000 drug users

Eastern Europe††
8,000,000 drug users

Asia
76,500,000 drug users

Africa
46,500,000 drug users

South America**
16,500,000 drug users

Australia, New Zealand, and Oceania
4,750,000 drug users

Goode's Interrupted Homolosine Projection (Condensed)
Scale 1:162,000,000

A-101971-1 © Rand McNally

Cannabis — World Production - 41,400 metric tons - 2006

0	10	20	30	40	50	60	70	80	90	100%

NORTH AMERICA*	SOUTH AMERICA**	AFRICA	ASIA	EUROPE
31.0%	24.0	22.0	16.0	6.0

Cocaine — Potential World Production - 984 metric tons - 2006

0	10	20	30	40	50	60	70	80	90	100%

COLOMBIA	PERU	BOLIVIA
62.0%	28.5	9.5

Opium — Potential World Production (Dry Opium) - 6,611 metric tons - 2006

0	10	20	30	40	50	60	70	80	90	100%

AFGHANISTAN	BURMA
92.3%	4.8

PRISON POPULATION

Prison Population
Rate per 100,000 population

- Over 500
- 250 - 500
- 100 - 250
- 50 - 100
- 0 - 50
- Data not available

Source: International Centre for Prison Studies

Goode's Interrupted Homolosine Projection (Condensed)
Scale 1:162,000,000

A-101972-1 © Rand McNally

Prison Population — World Total‡ - 9,720,000 prisoners - latest available data

0	10	20	30	40	50	60	70	80	90	100%

UNITED STATES	MEXICO	OTHER N.A.	CHINA	INDIA	OTHER ASIA	RUSSIA	BRAZIL	OTHER S.A.	AFRICA	EUROPE
23.6%	2.3	2.2	16.2	3.8	16.6	9.2	4.5	3.0	9.4	8.7

‡ Excluding prisoners in Bhutan, Equatorial Guinea, Eritrea, Guinea-Bissau, North Korea, and Somalia.

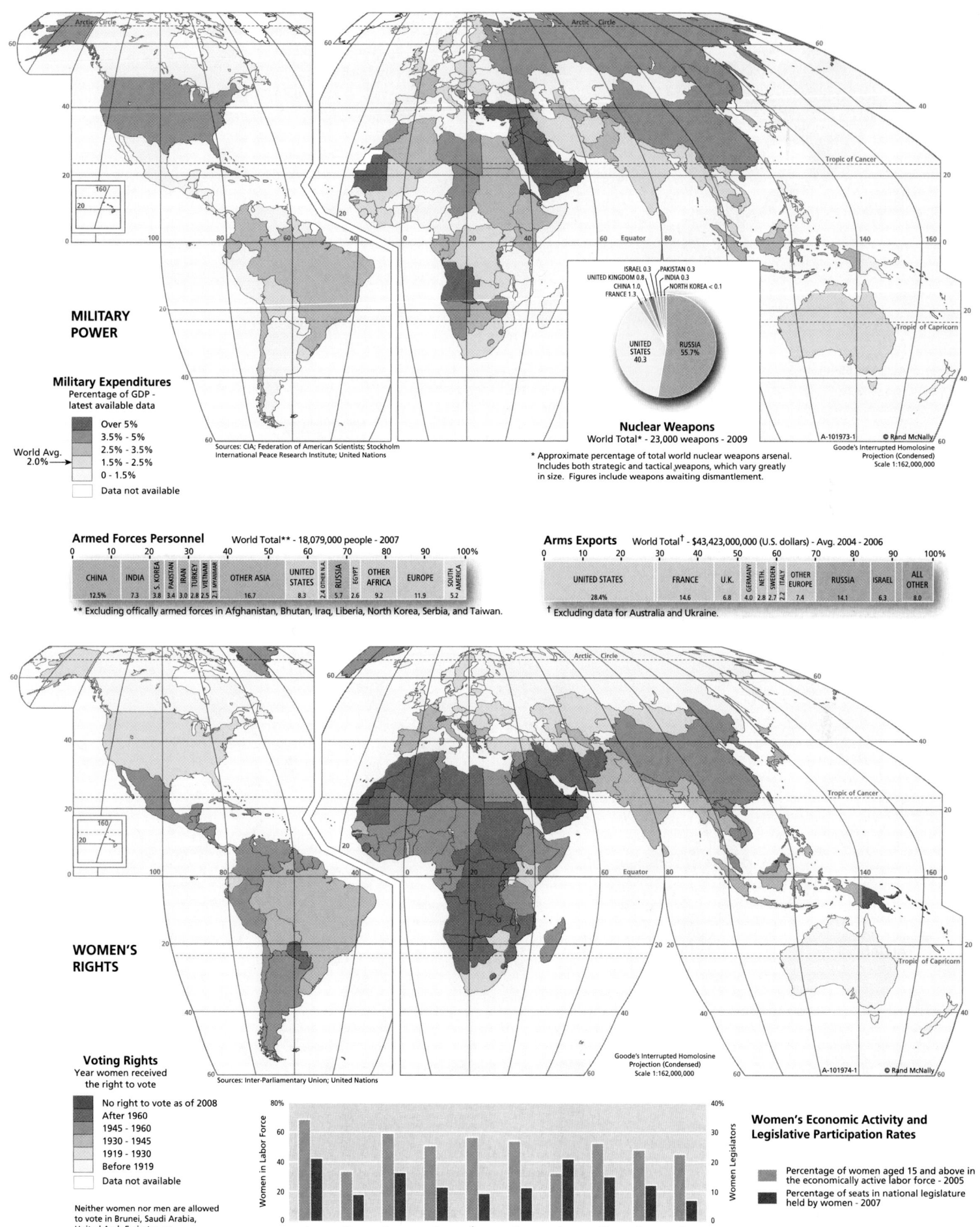

MILITARY POWER

Military Expenditures
Percentage of GDP -
latest available data

- Over 5%
- 3.5% - 5%
- 2.5% - 3.5%
- 1.5% - 2.5%
- 0 - 1.5%
- Data not available

World Avg. 2.0% →

Sources: CIA; Federation of American Scientists; Stockholm International Peace Research Institute; United Nations

Nuclear Weapons
World Total* - 23,000 weapons - 2009

ISRAEL 0.3 PAKISTAN 0.3
UNITED KINGDOM 0.8 INDIA 0.3
CHINA 1.0 NORTH KOREA < 0.1
FRANCE 1.3

UNITED STATES 40.3
RUSSIA 55.7%

* Approximate percentage of total world nuclear weapons arsenal. Includes both strategic and tactical weapons, which vary greatly in size. Figures include weapons awaiting dismantlement.

A-101973-1 © Rand McNally
Goode's Interrupted Homolosine Projection (Condensed)
Scale 1:162,000,000

Armed Forces Personnel World Total** - 18,079,000 people - 2007

0	10	20	30	40	50	60	70	80	90	100%

CHINA	INDIA	S. KOREA	PAKISTAN	IRAN	TURKEY	VIETNAM	MYANMAR	OTHER ASIA	UNITED STATES	OTHER N.A.	RUSSIA	EGYPT	OTHER AFRICA	EUROPE	SOUTH AMERICA
12.5%	7.3	3.8	3.4	3.0	2.8	2.5	2.1	16.7	8.3	2.4	5.7		9.2	11.9	5.2

** Excluding offically armed forces in Afghanistan, Bhutan, Iraq, Liberia, North Korea, Serbia, and Taiwan.

Arms Exports World Total† - $43,423,000,000 (U.S. dollars) - Avg. 2004 - 2006

0	10	20	30	40	50	60	70	80	90	100%

UNITED STATES	FRANCE	U.K.	GERMANY	NETH.	SWEDEN	ITALY	OTHER EUROPE	RUSSIA	ISRAEL	ALL OTHER
28.4%	14.6	6.8	4.0	2.8	2.2		7.4	14.1	6.3	8.0

† Excluding data for Australia and Ukraine.

WOMEN'S RIGHTS

Sources: Inter-Parliamentary Union; United Nations

Goode's Interrupted Homolosine Projection (Condensed)
Scale 1:162,000,000

A-101974-1 © Rand McNally

Voting Rights
Year women received
the right to vote

- No right to vote as of 2008
- After 1960
- 1945 - 1960
- 1930 - 1945
- 1919 - 1930
- Before 1919
- Data not available

Neither women nor men are allowed to vote in Brunei, Saudi Arabia, United Arab Emirates, or Western Sahara.

Women's Economic Activity and Legislative Participation Rates

- Percentage of women aged 15 and above in the economically active labor force - 2005
- Percentage of seats in national legislature held by women - 2007

(World's largest countries, 2000)

China, India, U.S., Indonesia, Brazil, Russia, Pakistan, Bangladesh, Japan, Nigeria

Women in Labor Force

Women Legislators

POLITICAL AND MILITARY ALLIANCES

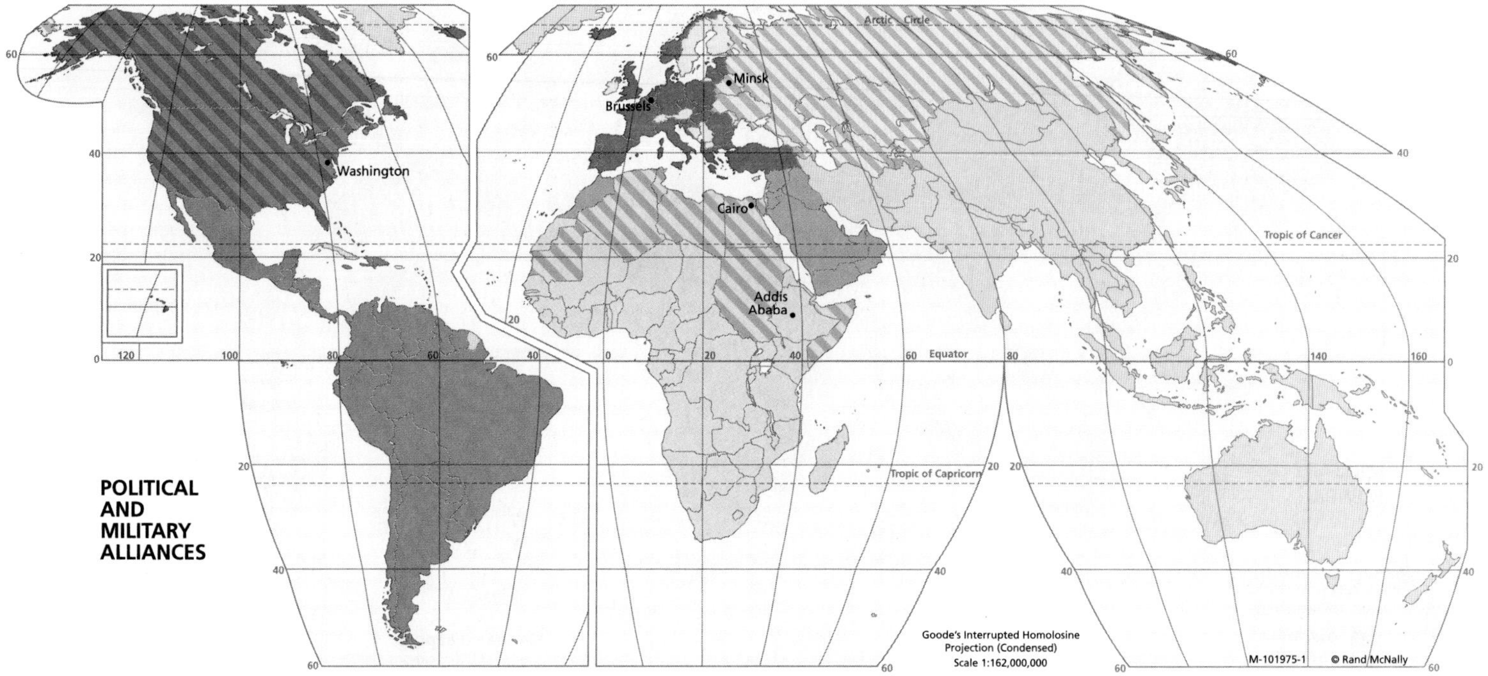
Arctic Circle
Minsk
Brussels
Washington
Cairo
Tropic of Cancer
Addis Ababa
Equator
Tropic of Capricorn
Goode's Interrupted Homolosine Projection (Condensed)
Scale 1:162,000,000
M-101975-1
© Rand McNally

AL	**Arab League** (League of Arab States) Founded 1945. Headquarters in Cairo, Egypt.
OAS	**Organization of American States** Founded 1948. Headquarters in Washington, D.C., United States.
NATO	**North Atlantic Treaty Organization** Founded 1949. Headquarters in Brussels, Belgium.
PFP	**Partnership for Peace Program**
CIS	**Commonwealth of Independent States** Founded 1991. Headquarters in Minsk, Belarus.
AU	**African Union** Founded 2000. Headquarters in Addis Ababa, Ethiopia.
	Not affiliated with above organizations.

ECONOMIC ALLIANCES

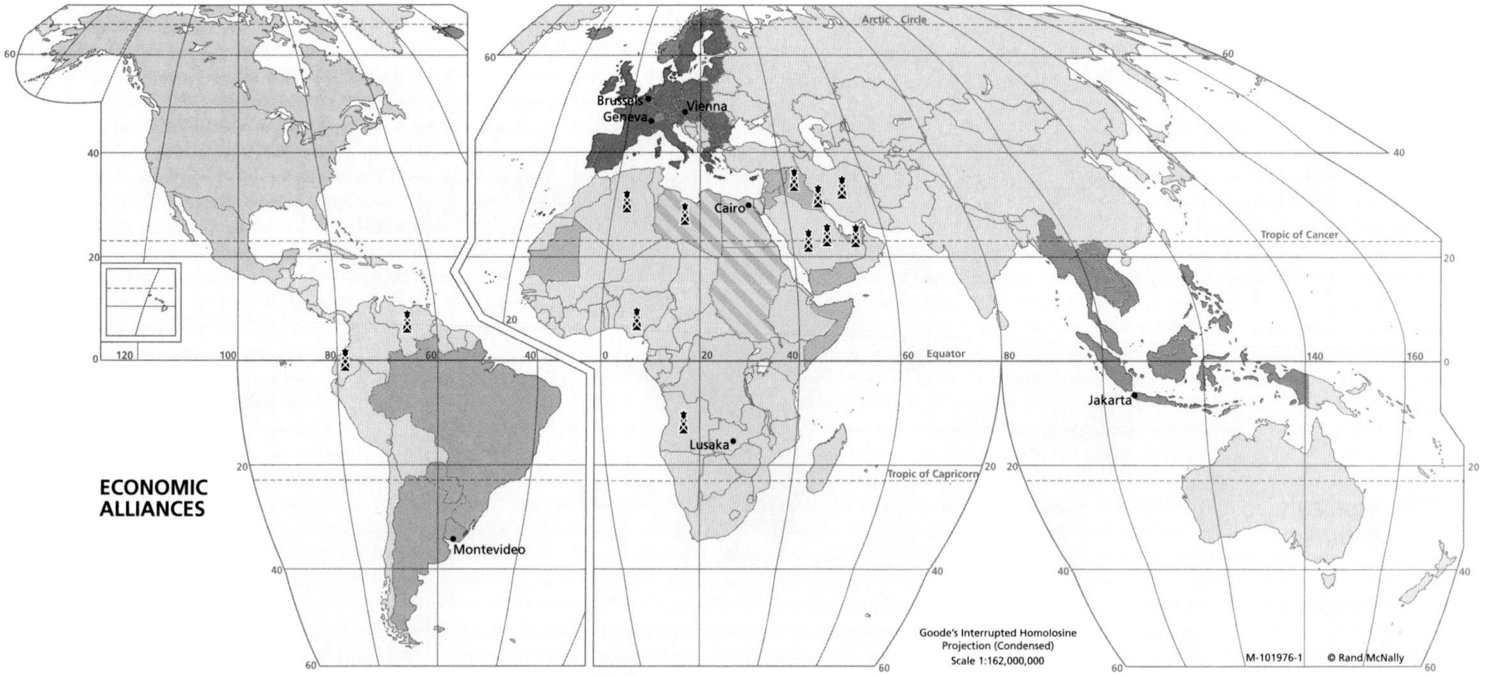
Arctic Circle
Brussels
Geneva
Vienna
Cairo
Tropic of Cancer
Equator
Jakarta
Lusaka
Tropic of Capricorn
Montevideo
Goode's Interrupted Homolosine Projection (Condensed)
Scale 1:162,000,000
M-101976-1
© Rand McNally

EU	**European Union** (Common Market) Founded 1957. Headquarters in Brussels, Belgium.
EFTA	**European Free Trade Association** Founded 1960. Headquarters in Geneva, Switzerland.
OPEC	**Organization of Petroleum Exporting Countries** Founded 1960. Headquarters in Vienna, Austria.
CAEU	**Council of Arab Economic Unity** Founded 1964. Headquarters in Cairo, Egypt. Includes Arab Common Market countries.
ASEAN	**Association of Southeast Asian Nations** Founded 1967. Headquarters in Jakarta, Indonesia.
MERCOSUR	**Southern Common Market** Founded 1991. Headquarters in Montevideo, Uruguay.
NAFTA	**North American Free Trade Agreement** Signed 1992.
COMESA	**Common Market for Eastern and Southern Africa** Founded 1994. Headquarters in Lusaka, Zambia.
	Not affiliated with above organizations.

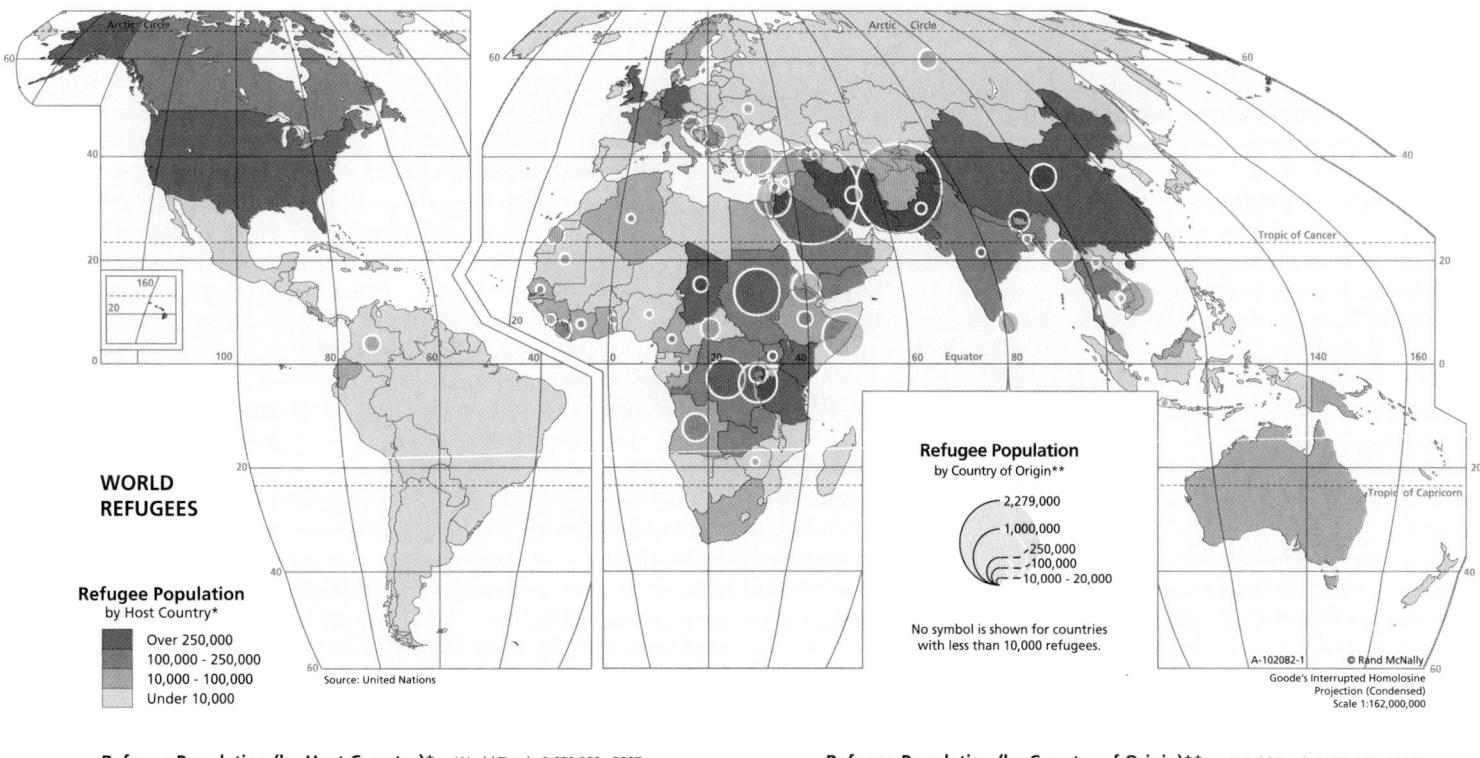

WORLD REFUGEES

Refugee Population
by Host Country*

- Over 250,000
- 100,000 - 250,000
- 10,000 - 100,000
- Under 10,000

Source: United Nations

Refugee Population
by Country of Origin**

- 2,279,000
- 1,000,000
- 250,000
- 100,000
- 10,000 - 20,000

No symbol is shown for countries
with less than 10,000 refugees.

A-102082-1 © Rand McNally
Goode's Interrupted Homolosine
Projection (Condensed)
Scale 1:162,000,000

Refugee Population (by Host Country)* World Total - 9,679,000 - 2007

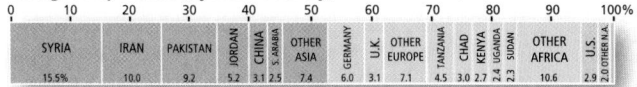

	0	10	20	30	40	50	60	70	80	90	100%
	SYRIA	IRAN	PAKISTAN	JORDAN	CHINA	S. ARABIA	OTHER ASIA	GERMANY	U.K.	OTHER EUROPE	TANZANIA	CHAD	KENYA	UGANDA	SUDAN	OTHER AFRICA	U.S.	OTHER N.A.
	15.5%	10.0	9.2	5.2	3.1	2.5	7.4	6.0	3.1	7.1	4.5	3.0	2.7	2.4	2.3	10.6	2.9	2.0

* People who have come to this country from another country.

Refugee Population (by Country of Origin)* World Total - 9,679,000 - 2007

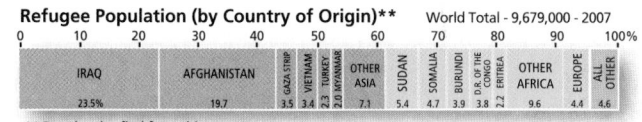

	0	10	20	30	40	50	60	70	80	90	100%
	IRAQ	AFGHANISTAN	GAZA STRIP	VIETNAM	TURKEY	MYANMAR	OTHER ASIA	SUDAN	SOMALIA	BURUNDI	D.R. OF THE CONGO	ERITREA	OTHER AFRICA	EUROPE	ALL OTHER
	23.5%	19.7	3.5	3.4	2.3	2.0	7.1	5.4	4.7	3.9	3.8	2.2	9.6	4.4	4.6

** People who fled from this country.

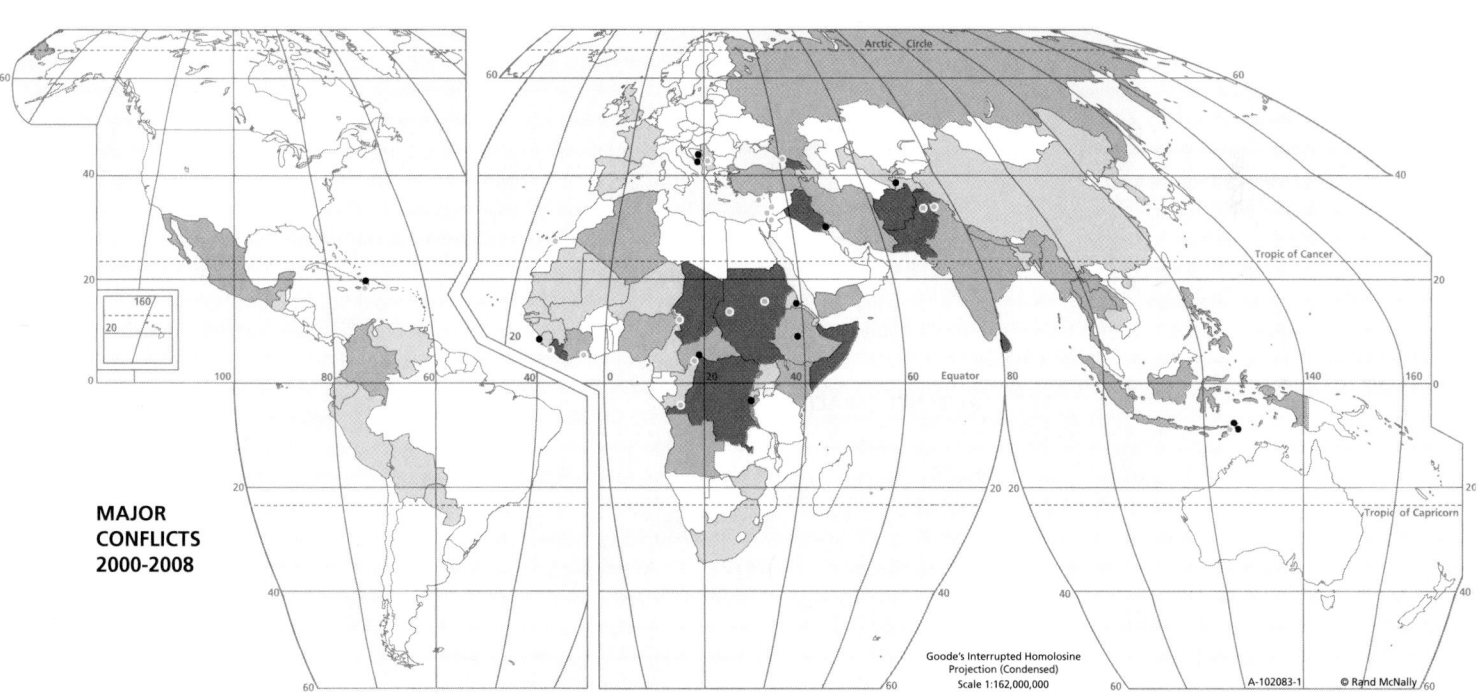

MAJOR CONFLICTS 2000-2008

Goode's Interrupted Homolosine
Projection (Condensed)
Scale 1:162,000,000

A-102083-1 © Rand McNally

- **Very Serious Conflict:** A sustained conflict in which organized, systematic, and continual violent force is used causing massive destruction.
- **Serious Conflict:** Severe crisis where organized violence is used regularly.
- **Hot Spot:** A tense situation in which at least one of the parties uses violence in sporadic incidents.

United Nations Peacekeeping Operations

- Ongoing Peacekeeping Missions
- Completed Peacekeeping Missions

COMMUNICATION NETWORK INFRASTRUCTURE

International Bandwidth Usage
Gigabits per second (Gbps) - 2007

- Over 1000
- 250 - 1000
- 50 - 250
- 1 - 50
- Less than 1

Capacity deployed by carriers, internet service providers (ISPs), and enterprises to carry internet, voice, and private network traffic across international borders.

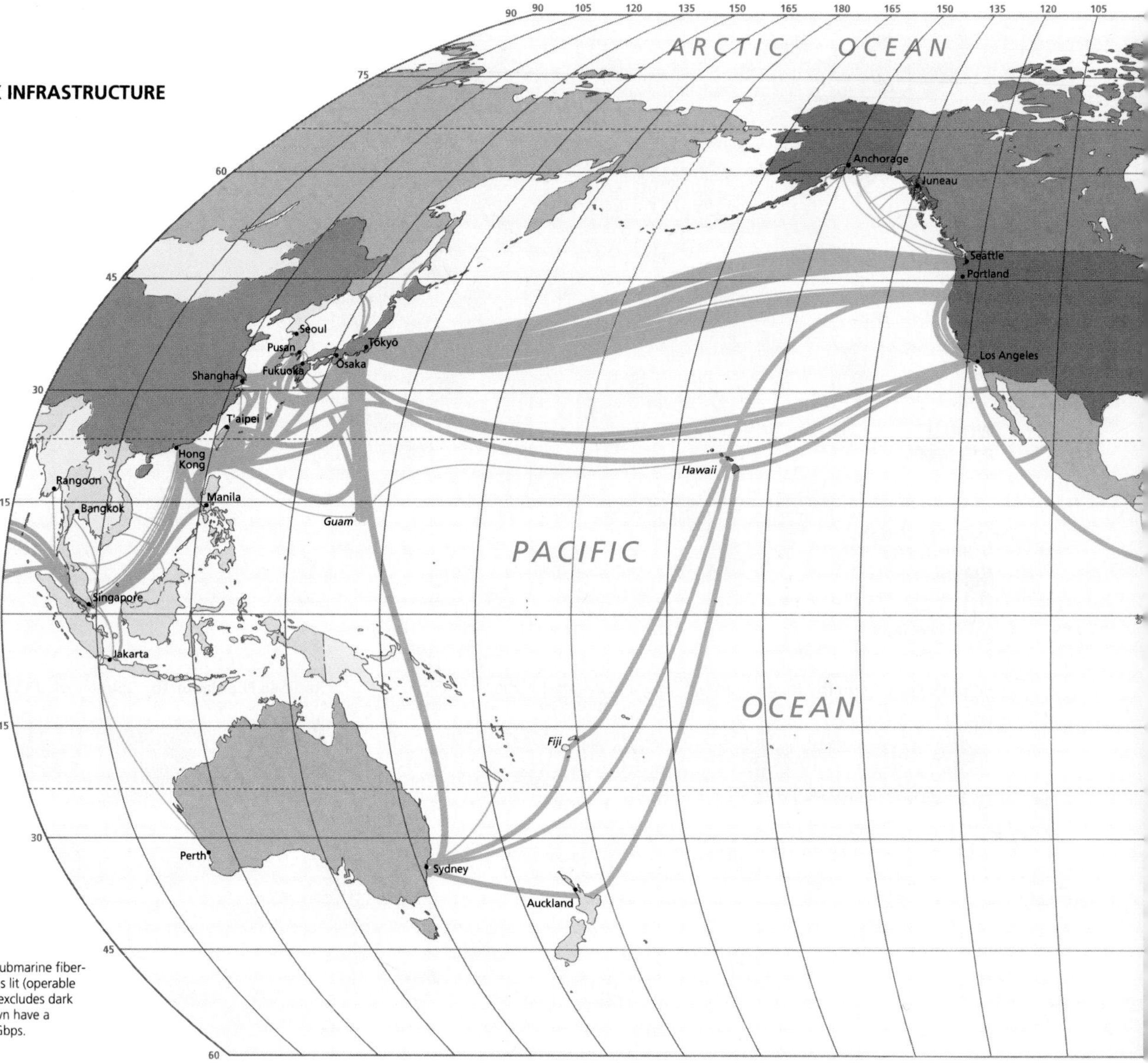

Submarine Cable Capacity
Lit capacity of submarine cables, in Gigabits per second (Gbps) - 2008

- Over 500
- 50 - 500
- 10 - 50

Line thickness is proportional to lit capacity of submarine fiber-optic cables. Lit capacity includes all cable that is lit (operable and capable of transmitting a light signal), but excludes dark fiber (inactive or inoperable cable). Cables shown have a maximum upgradeable capacity of at least 10 Gbps.

ARCTIC OCEAN

PACIFIC OCEAN

Anchorage, Juneau, Seattle, Portland, Los Angeles, Hawaii, Fiji, Auckland, Sydney, Perth, Jakarta, Singapore, Bangkok, Rangoon, Manila, Guam, Hong Kong, T'aipei, Shanghai, Fukuoka, Ōsaka, Tōkyō, Pusan, Seoul

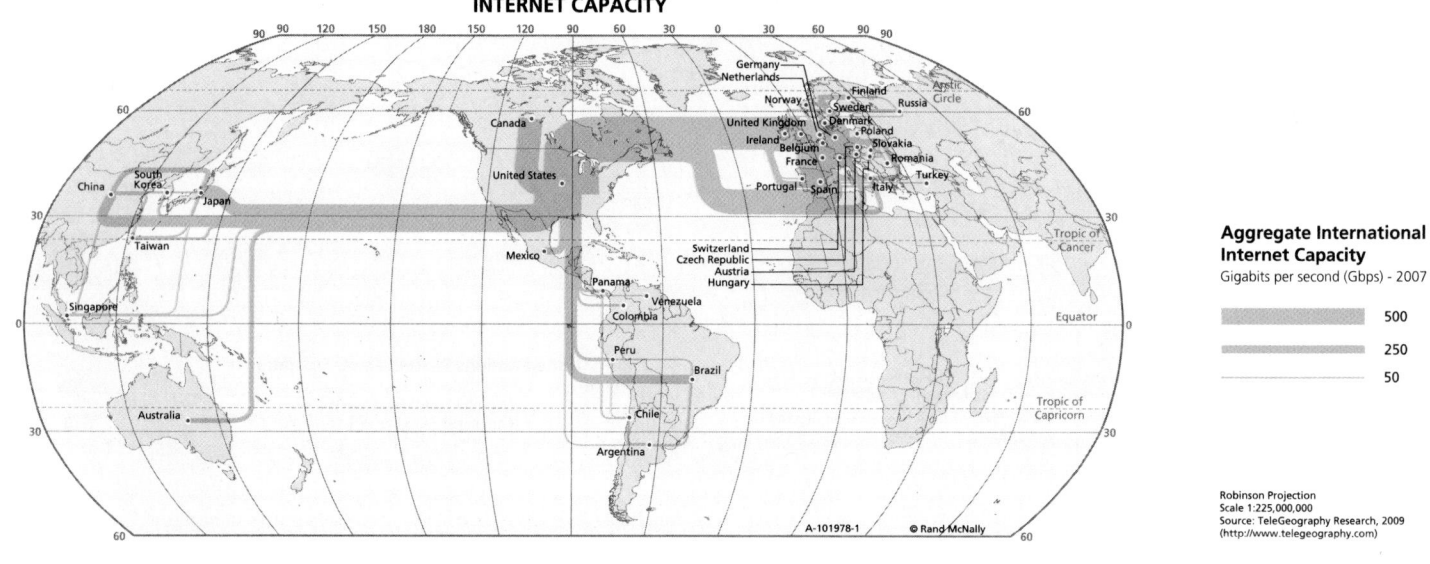

INTERNET CAPACITY

China, South Korea, Japan, Taiwan, Singapore, Australia, United States, Canada, Mexico, Panama, Venezuela, Colombia, Peru, Brazil, Chile, Argentina

Germany, Netherlands, Norway, United Kingdom, Ireland, Belgium, France, Portugal, Spain, Finland, Sweden, Denmark, Poland, Slovakia, Romania, Turkey, Italy, Russia, Switzerland, Czech Republic, Austria, Hungary

Arctic Circle, Tropic of Cancer, Equator, Tropic of Capricorn

Aggregate International Internet Capacity
Gigabits per second (Gbps) - 2007

- 500
- 250
- 50

A-101978-1   © Rand McNally

Robinson Projection
Scale 1:225,000,000
Source: TeleGeography Research, 2009
(http://www.telegeography.com)

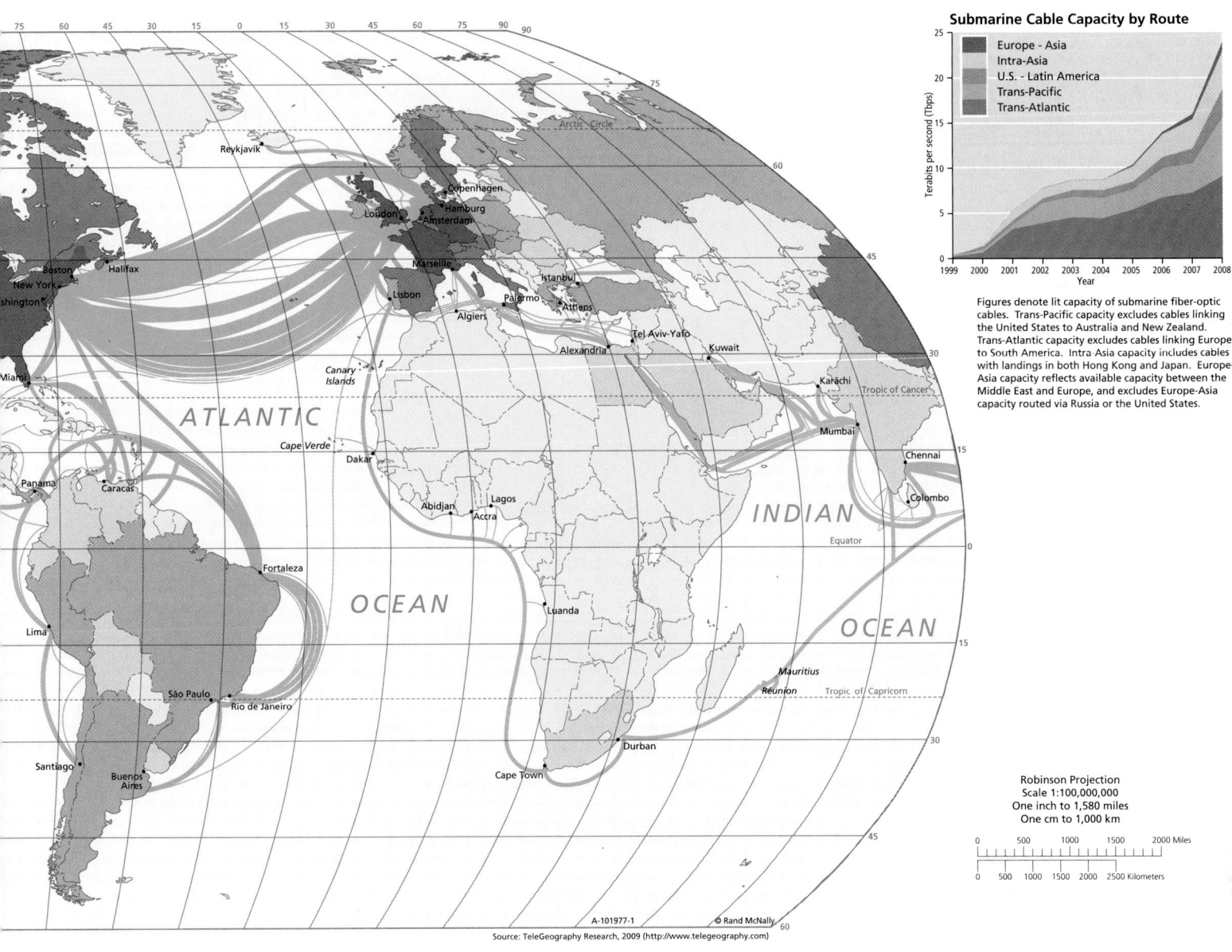

Submarine Cable Capacity by Route

Legend:
- Europe - Asia
- Intra-Asia
- U.S. - Latin America
- Trans-Pacific
- Trans-Atlantic

y-axis: Terabits per second (Tbps), x-axis: Year 1999–2008

Figures denote lit capacity of submarine fiber-optic cables. Trans-Pacific capacity excludes cables linking the United States to Australia and New Zealand. Trans-Atlantic capacity excludes cables linking Europe to South America. Intra Asia capacity includes cables with landings in both Hong Kong and Japan. Europe-Asia capacity reflects available capacity between the Middle East and Europe, and excludes Europe-Asia capacity routed via Russia or the United States.

Robinson Projection
Scale 1:100,000,000
One inch to 1,580 miles
One cm to 1,000 km

Source: TeleGeography Research, 2009 (http://www.telegeography.com)

A-101977-1   © Rand McNally

SHIPPING LANES

Relative Frequency of Ship Traffic

Highest

Lowest

This map shows the relative frequency of ship traffic over the world's oceans, for the period October 2004 through September 2005. Ship tracks were derived from the World Meteorological Association Voluntary Observing Ships Scheme, comprising over 3000 commercial and research vessels (equivalent to approximately 11% of the world commercial oceangoing fleet).

Robinson Projection
Scale 1:225,000,000
Source: Halpern et al., 2008

A-101980-1   © Rand McNally

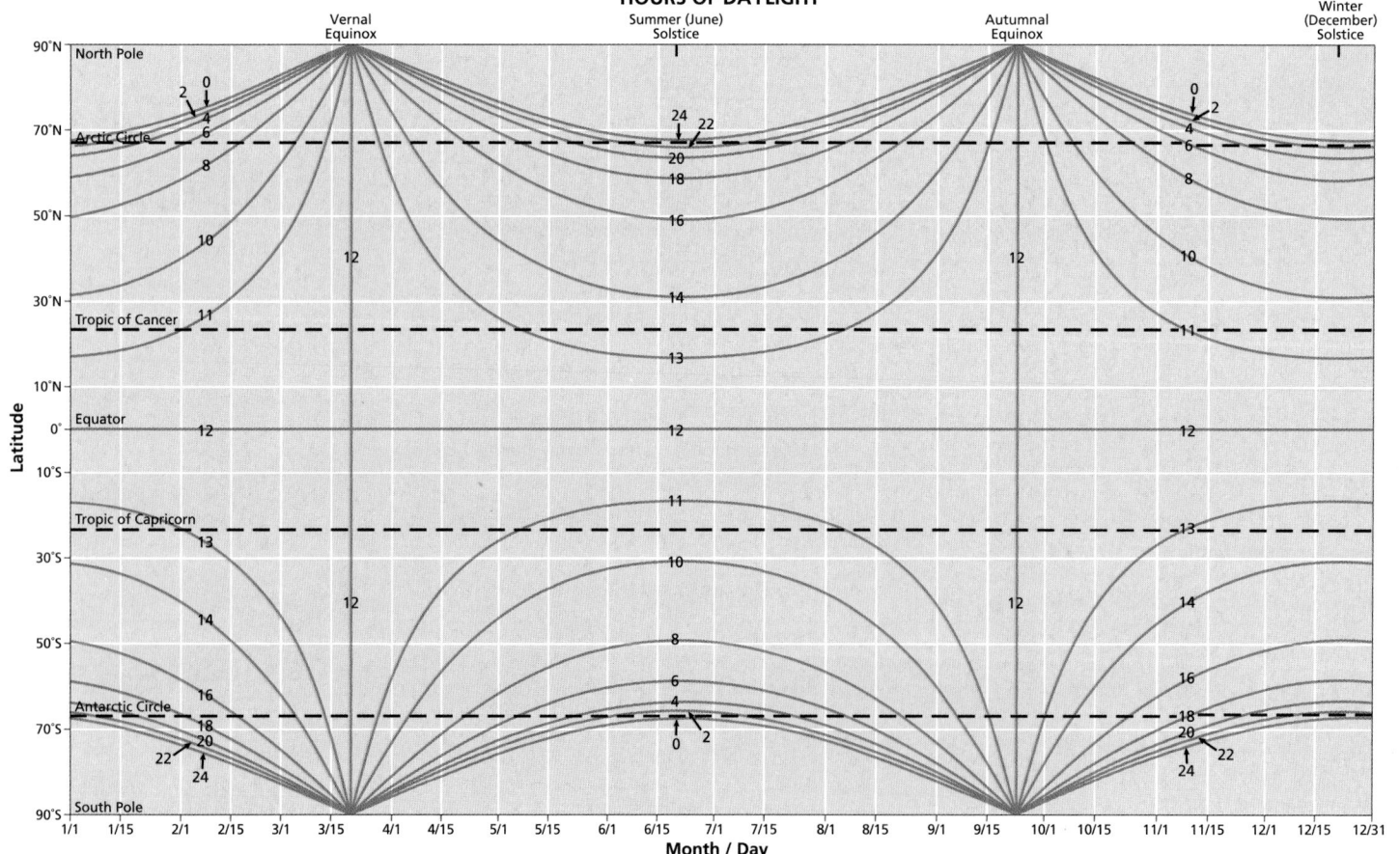

Miller Cylindrical Projection
Scale 1:225,000,000

M-100848-1 © Rand McNally

Time Zones

Coordinated Universal Time (UTC) is the standard for international time zones and the official reference for standard time across the world. Although UTC has officially replaced Greenwich Mean Time (GMT), both terms are widely employed and, in casual usage, are essentially synonymous. On the time zone map above, the numbers along the top and bottom edges indicate the time difference, in hours, from UTC. The first time zone, with a value of 0, is centered on the Prime Meridian running through Greenwich, England. To compute standard time at any location, add the value on the map to UTC at Greenwich. For example, Chicago is in time zone UTC -6, which means it is 6 hours earlier than UTC at Greenwich. This means that if it is noon at Greenwich then it is 6 a.m. in Chicago.

To ensure synchronization with the Sun's location, time zone boundaries should follow lines of longitude very precisely. However this is rarely the case, and most time zones boundaries are very irregular. They are often constrained to follow international or internal administrative boundaries, and may be shifted east or west for various reasons. Discontinuities sometimes exist where time changes by more than one hour across a zone boundary, and the UTC difference for some time zones is less than a full hour. To make matters even more complicated, these time zones do not account for Daylight Savings Time, which is observed in some jurisdictions for part of the year.

HOURS OF DAYLIGHT

This graph shows hours of daylight at various latitudes for each day of the year. The following are some important patterns evident on the graph.
- The Equator experiences 12 hours of daylight every day of the year.
- Every point on the Earth experiences 12 hours of daylight at the vernal and autumnal equinoxes.
- The greater the distance from the Equator, the greater the variability in daylight length over the year.
- In the northern hemisphere, daylight length is greater than 12 hours between the vernal and autumnal equinoxes (the northern hemisphere summer) and less than 12 hours between the autumnal and vernal equinoxes (the northern hemisphere winter). The opposite pattern occurs in the southern hemisphere.

- Areas north of the Arctic Circle and south of the Antarctic Circle experience an annual pattern with periods of total darkness and periods of continuous daylight.

The data used to create this graph do not account for refraction of the Sun's rays by the Earth's atmosphere, which lengthens the daylight period slightly. The calculations are based on the center of the Sun, and do not account for the size of the solar disk, which also extends the daylight period by several minutes.

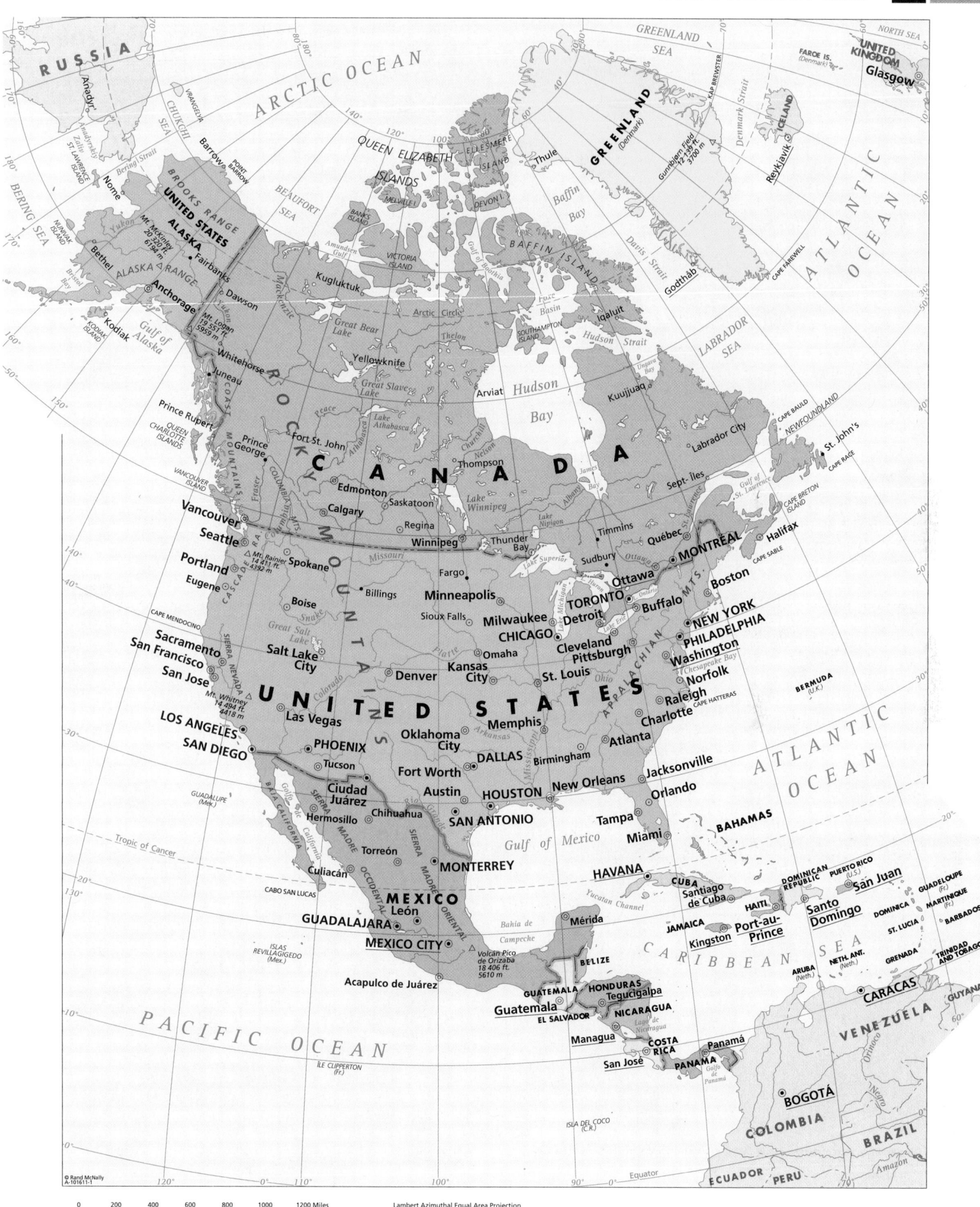

Lambert Azimuthal Equal Area Projection
Scale 1:40,000,000
One inch to 640 miles
One cm to 400 km

0 200 400 600 800 1000 1200 Miles

0 200 400 600 800 1000 1200 1400 1600 1800 2000 Kilometers

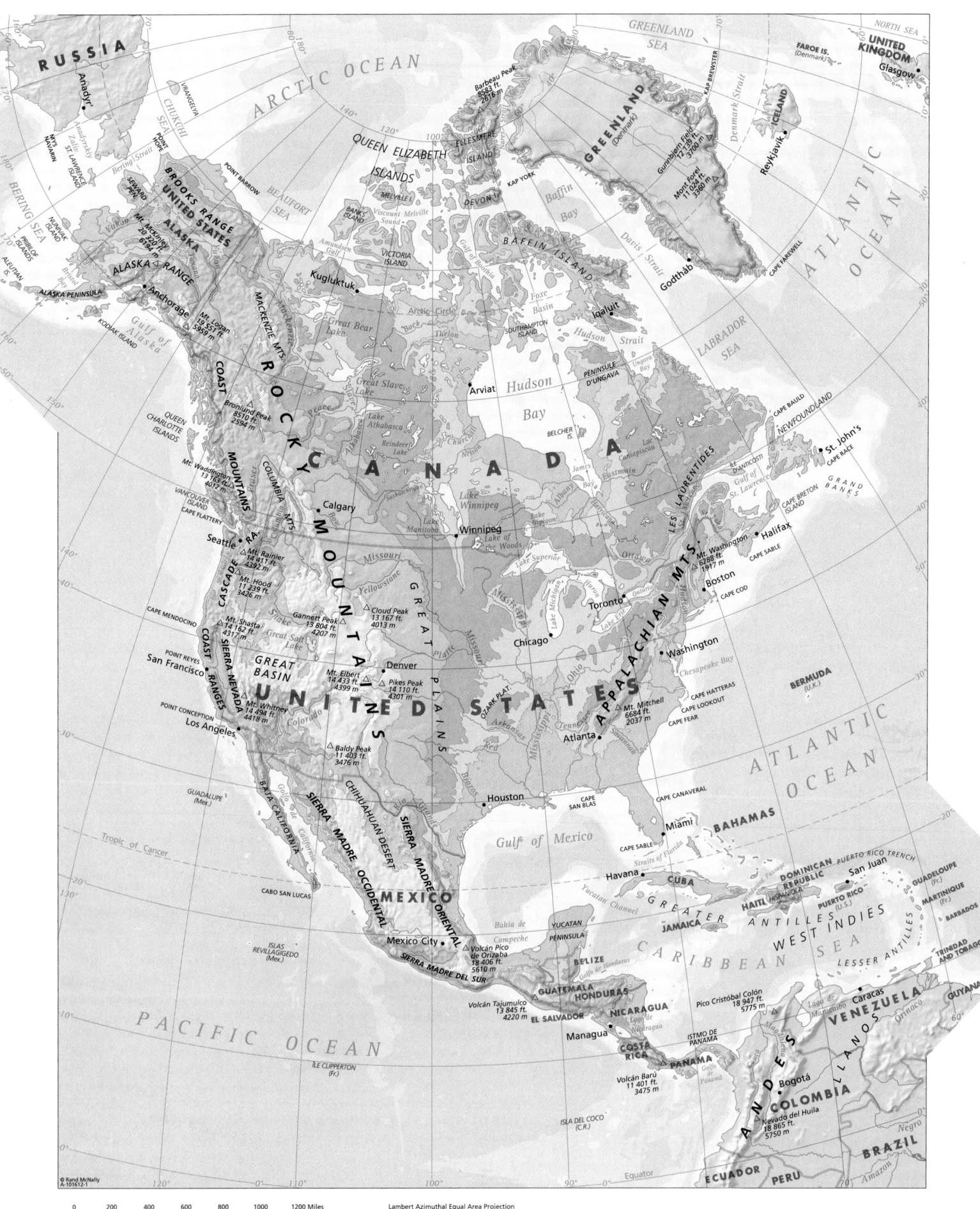

RUSSIA
Anadyr'

ARCTIC OCEAN

GREENLAND SEA

NORTH SEA

UNITED KINGDOM
Glasgow

FAROE IS. (Denmark)

ICELAND
Reykjavík

GREENLAND (Denmark)

Barbeau Peak 8583 ft. 2616 m

QUEEN ELIZABETH ISLANDS

ELLESMERE ISLAND

KAP YORK

Gunnbjørn Field 12 139 ft. 3700 m

Mont Forel 11 024 ft. 3360 m

Mont Forel

DEVON I.

KAP BREWSTER

Denmark Strait

BERING SEA

CHUKCHI SEA

BEAUFORT SEA

Baffin Bay

Davis Strait

ATLANTIC OCEAN

POINT BARROW

BANKS ISLAND

Viscount Melville Sound

BROOKS RANGE UNITED STATES

ALASKA

Mt. McKinley 20 320 ft. 6194 m

ALASKA RANGE

Anchorage

Mt. Logan 19 551 ft. 5959 m

MACKENZIE MTS.

Great Bear Lake

Kugluktuk

Amundsen Gulf

VICTORIA ISLAND

Gulf of Boothia

BAFFIN ISLAND

Foxe Basin

Godthåb

CAPE FAREWELL

SEWARD PEN.

ST. LAWRENCE ISLAND

NUNIVAK ISLAND

PRIBILOF ISLANDS

KODIAK ISLAND

ALASKA PENINSULA

Gulf of Alaska

Iqaluit

SOUTHAMPTON ISLAND

Hudson Strait

LABRADOR SEA

Arctic Circle

Mackenzie

Great Slave Lake

Back

Thelon

PÉNINSULE D'UNGAVA

Ungava Bay

CAPE BAULD

NEWFOUNDLAND

ALEUTIAN ISLANDS

COAST

ROCKY

Bronlund Peak 8510 ft. 2594 m

Peace

Lake Athabasca

Reindeer Lake

Churchill

Arviat

Hudson Bay

BELCHER IS.

Lac Caniapiscau

St. John's

CAPE RACE

D'ANTICOSTI

QUEEN CHARLOTTE ISLANDS

Mt. Waddington 13 163 ft. 4012 m

MOUNTAINS

C A N A D A

Nelson

Lake Winnipeg

James Bay

Eastmain

LES LAURENTIDES

Gulf of St. Lawrence

GRAND BANKS

CAPE BRETON ISLAND

VANCOUVER ISLAND

CAPE FLATTERY

COLUMBIA MTS.

Calgary

Saskatchewan

Lake Manitoba

Albany

Ottawa

Halifax

Seattle

Mt. Rainier 14 411 ft. 4392 m

Missouri

Winnipeg

Lake of the Woods

Lake Nipigon

CAPE SABLE

Mt. Washington 6288 ft. 1917 m

Boston

CASCADE RANGE

Mt. Hood 11 239 ft. 3426 m

Yellowstone

Snake

GREAT

Lake Superior

Lake Huron

Toronto

Lake Ontario

Hudson

CAPE COD

Mt. Shasta 14 162 ft. 4317 m

Gannett Peak 13 804 ft. 4207 m

Cloud Peak 13 167 ft. 4013 m

Great Salt Lake

Lake Michigan

Chicago

Lake Erie

APPALACHIAN MTS.

Washington

POINT REYES

San Francisco

GREAT BASIN

SIERRA NEVADA

COAST RANGES

Denver

Pikes Peak 14 110 ft. 4301 m

Mt. Elbert 14 433 ft. 4399 m

U N I T E D

PLAINS

S T A T E S

Platte

Missouri

OZARK PLAT.

Ohio

Chesapeake Bay

CAPE HATTERAS

BERMUDA (U.K.)

POINT CONCEPTION

Mt. Whitney 14 494 ft. 4418 m

Colorado

Arkansas

Glenn

Mt. Mitchell 6684 ft. 2037 m

CAPE LOOKOUT

Los Angeles

Baldy Peak 11 403 ft. 3476 m

Red

Brazos

Atlanta

Savannah

CAPE FEAR

GUADALUPE (Mex.)

BAJA CALIFORNIA

Rio Grande

Houston

CAPE SAN BLAS

CAPE CANAVERAL

ATLANTIC OCEAN

Tropic of Cancer

SIERRA MADRE OCCIDENTAL

CHIHUAHUAN DESERT

SIERRA MADRE ORIENTAL

CABO SAN LUCAS

Gulf of Mexico

CAPE SABLE

Miami

BAHAMAS

Straits of Florida

ISLAS REVILLAGIGEDO (Mex.)

Bahía de Campeche

MEXICO

Mexico City

Volcán Pico de Orizaba 18 406 ft. 5610 m

YUCATAN PENINSULA

Havana

CUBA

Yucatan Channel

Windward Passage

HAITI

DOMINICAN REPUBLIC

HISPANIOLA

PUERTO RICO TRENCH

San Juan

PUERTO RICO (U.S.)

GUADELOUPE (Fr.)

MARTINIQUE (Fr.)

GREATER ANTILLES

JAMAICA

WEST INDIES

BARBADOS

SIERRA MADRE DEL SUR

BELIZE

Golfo de Honduras

GUATEMALA

HONDURAS

CARIBBEAN SEA

LESSER ANTILLES

TRINIDAD AND TOBAGO

Volcán Tajumulco 13 845 ft. 4220 m

EL SALVADOR

NICARAGUA

Pico Cristóbal Colón 18 947 ft. 5775 m

Caracas

VENEZUELA

GUYANA

PACIFIC OCEAN

ÎLE CLIPPERTON (Fr.)

Managua

Lago de Nicaragua

COSTA RICA

PANAMA

ISTMO DE PANAMA

Golfo de Panamá

ANDES

LLANOS

Orinoco

Lago de Maracaibo

ISLA DEL COCO (C.R.)

Volcán Barú 11 401 ft. 3475 m

Bogotá

COLOMBIA

Nevado del Huila 18 865 ft. 5750 m

Magdalena

ECUADOR

PERU

Equator

BRAZIL

Negro

Amazon

© Rand McNally
A-101612-1

0 200 400 600 800 1000 1200 Miles

0 200 400 600 800 1000 1200 1400 1600 1800 2000 Kilometers

Lambert Azimuthal Equal Area Projection
Scale 1:40,000,000
One inch to 640 miles
One cm to 400 km

Land Cover

- Evergreen Needleleaf Forest
- Evergreen Broadleaf Forest
- Deciduous Broadleaf Forest
- Mixed Forest
- Woodland
- Wooded Grassland
- Closed Shrubland
- Open Shrubland
- Grassland
- Cropland
- Bare Ground (Desert and Ice)
- Urban and Built Up

A-102092-1
© Rand McNally

0 200 400 600 800 1000 1200 Miles
0 200 400 600 800 1000 1200 1400 1600 1800 2000 Kilometers

Lambert Azimuthal Equal Area Projection
Scale 1:40,000,000
One inch to 640 miles
One cm to 400 km

Source: CIESIN; Hansen et al., 2000

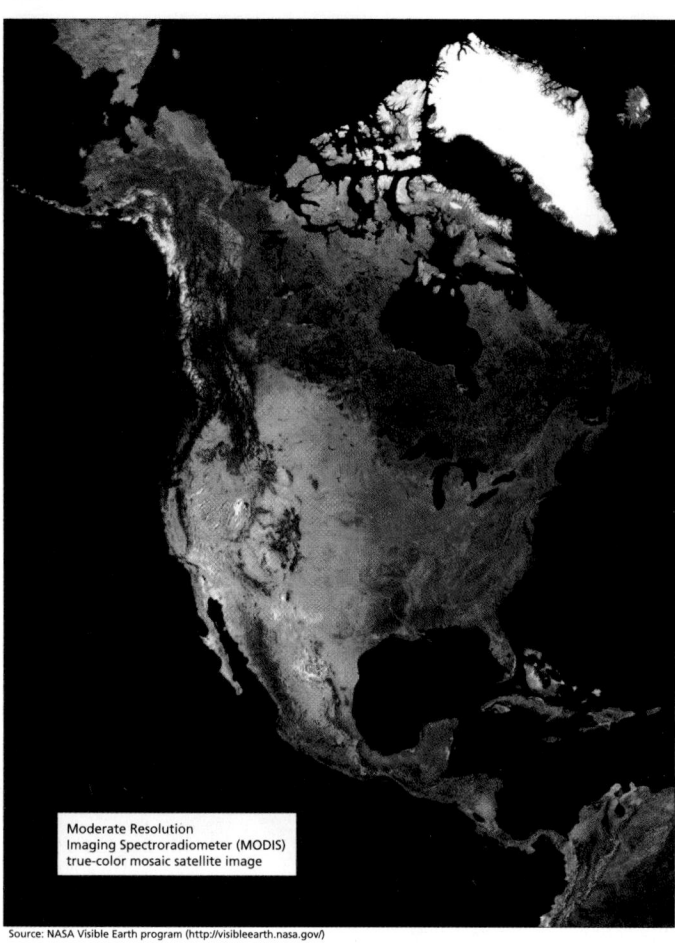

Moderate Resolution
Imaging Spectroradiometer (MODIS)
true-color mosaic satellite image

Source: NASA Visible Earth program (http://visibleearth.nasa.gov/)

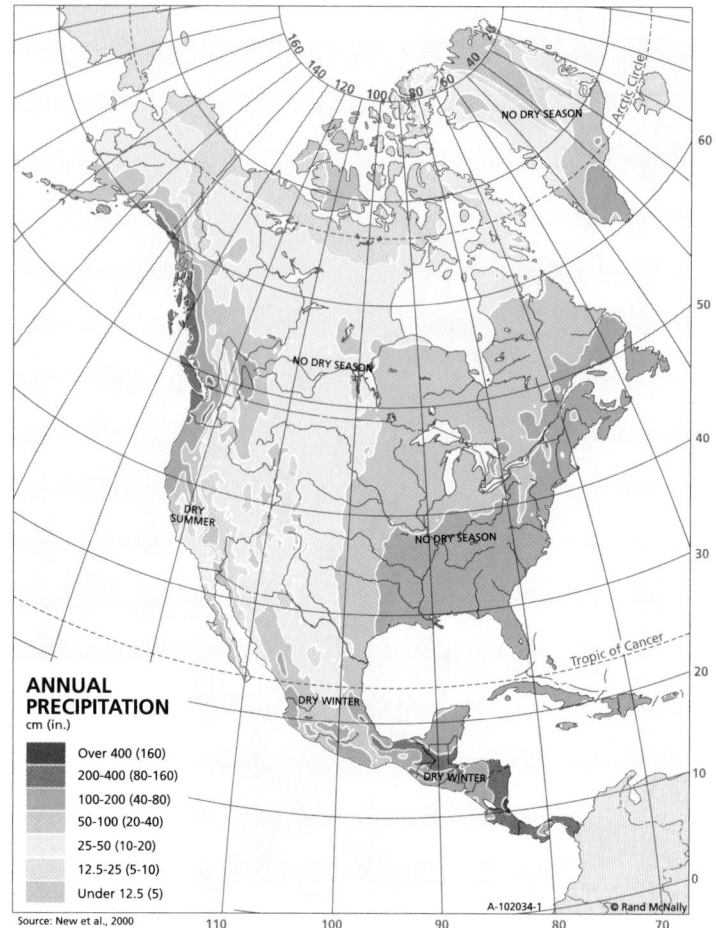

ANNUAL PRECIPITATION
cm (in.)

- Over 400 (160)
- 200-400 (80-160)
- 100-200 (40-80)
- 50-100 (20-40)
- 25-50 (10-20)
- 12.5-25 (5-10)
- Under 12.5 (5)

Source: New et al., 2000

A-102034-1
© Rand McNally

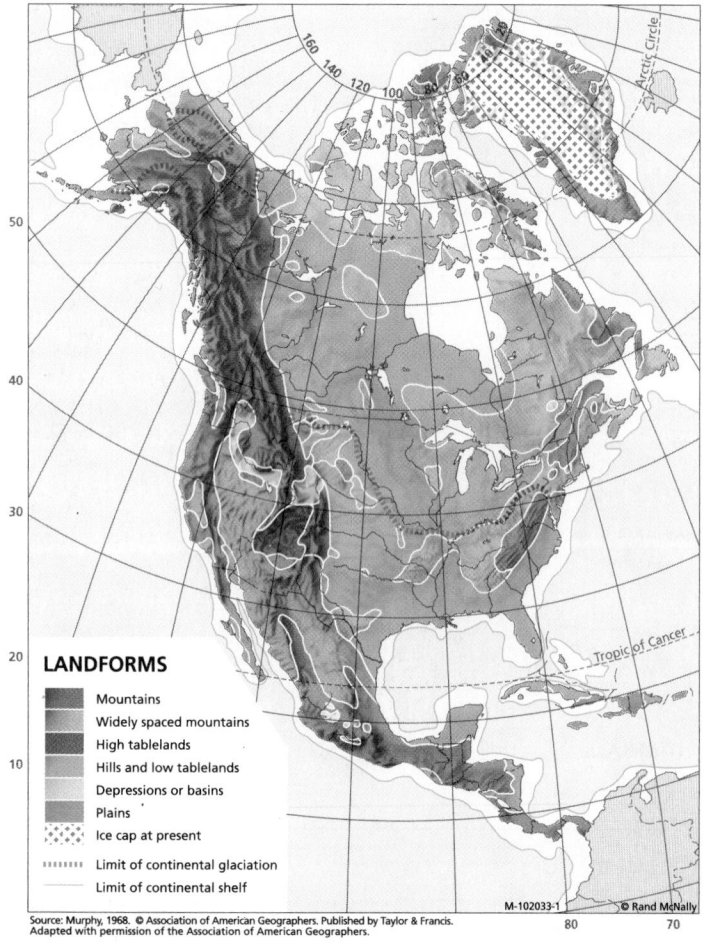

LANDFORMS

- Mountains
- Widely spaced mountains
- High tablelands
- Hills and low tablelands
- Depressions or basins
- Plains
- Ice cap at present
- Limit of continental glaciation
- Limit of continental shelf

Source: Murphy, 1968. © Association of American Geographers. Published by Taylor & Francis.
Adapted with permission of the Association of American Geographers.

M-102033-1
© Rand McNally

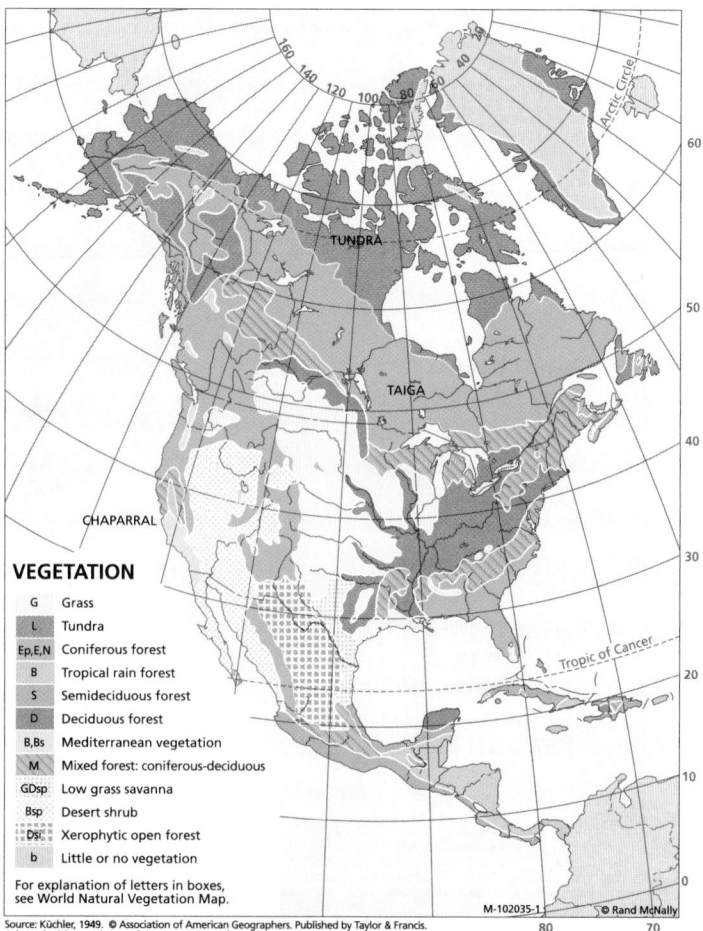

VEGETATION

G	Grass
L	Tundra
Ep,E,N	Coniferous forest
B	Tropical rain forest
S	Semideciduous forest
D	Deciduous forest
B,Bs	Mediterranean vegetation
M	Mixed forest: coniferous-deciduous
GDsp	Low grass savanna
Bsp	Desert shrub
Dsr	Xerophytic open forest
b	Little or no vegetation

For explanation of letters in boxes,
see World Natural Vegetation Map.

Source: Küchler, 1949. © Association of American Geographers. Published by Taylor & Francis.
Adapted with permission of the Association of American Geographers.

M-102035-1
© Rand McNally

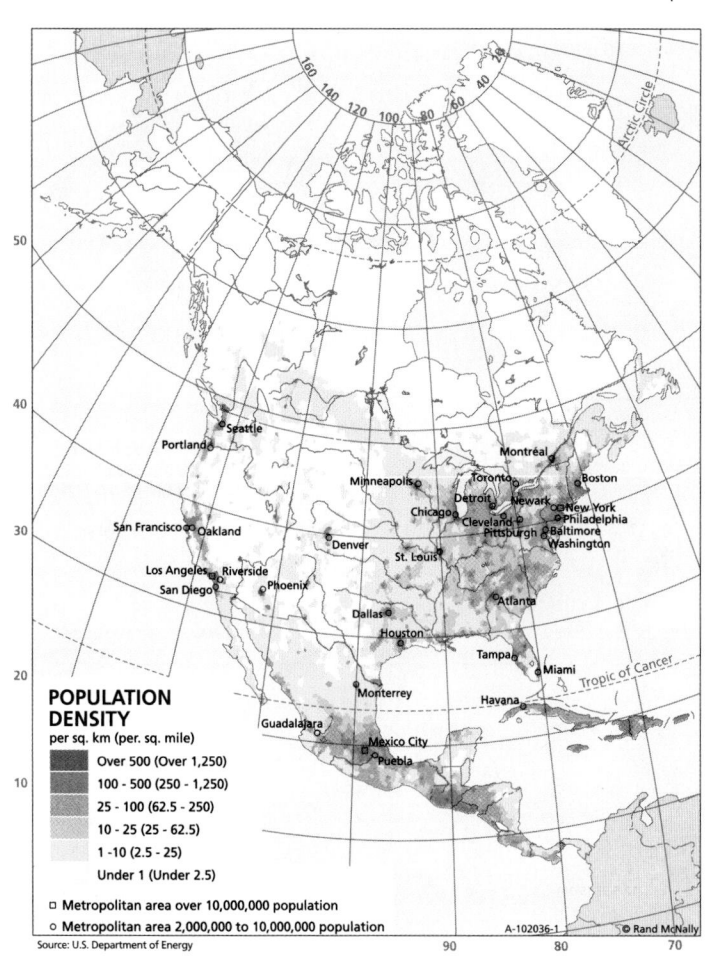

POPULATION DENSITY
per sq. km (per. sq. mile)

- Over 500 (Over 1,250)
- 100 - 500 (250 - 1,250)
- 25 - 100 (62.5 - 250)
- 10 - 25 (25 - 62.5)
- 1 -10 (2.5 - 25)
- Under 1 (Under 2.5)

□ Metropolitan area over 10,000,000 population
○ Metropolitan area 2,000,000 to 10,000,000 population

Source: U.S. Department of Energy

A-102036-1   © Rand McNally

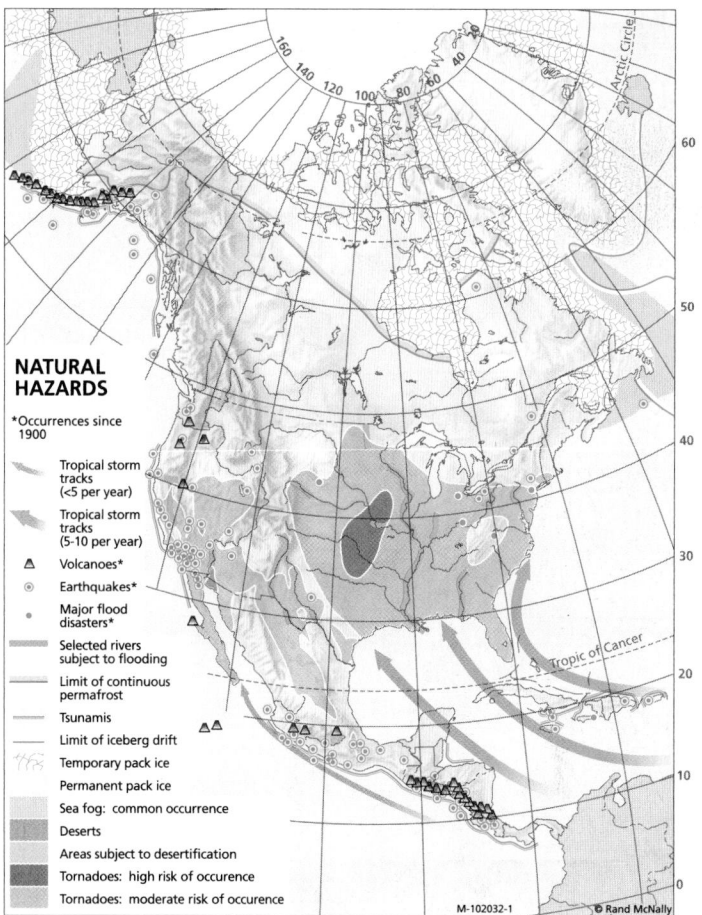

NATURAL HAZARDS

*Occurrences since 1900

Tropical storm tracks (<5 per year)

Tropical storm tracks (5-10 per year)

△ Volcanoes*

⊙ Earthquakes*

• Major flood disasters*

Selected rivers subject to flooding

Limit of continuous permafrost

Tsunamis

Limit of iceberg drift

Temporary pack ice

Permanent pack ice

Sea fog: common occurrence

Deserts

Areas subject to desertification

Tornadoes: high risk of occurence

Tornadoes: moderate risk of occurence

M-102032-1   © Rand McNally

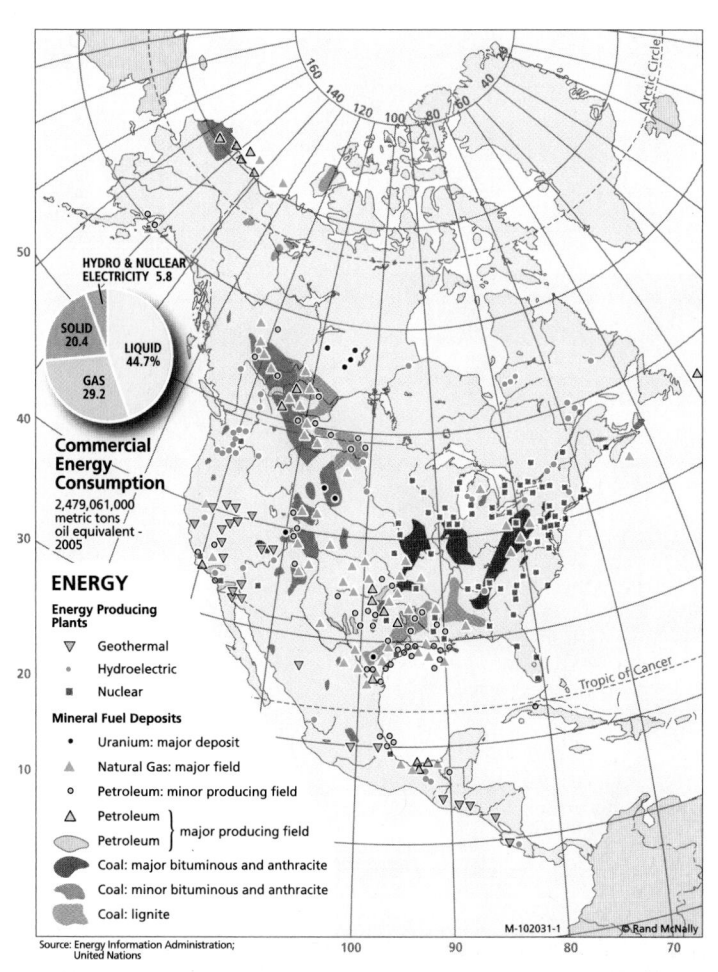

HYDRO & NUCLEAR ELECTRICITY 5.8

SOLID 20.4

LIQUID 44.7%

GAS 29.2

Commercial Energy Consumption
2,479,061,000 metric tons oil equivalent - 2005

ENERGY

Energy Producing Plants

▽ Geothermal

∘ Hydroelectric

■ Nuclear

Mineral Fuel Deposits

• Uranium: major deposit

▲ Natural Gas: major field

∘ Petroleum: minor producing field

△ Petroleum } major producing field
Petroleum

Coal: major bituminous and anthracite

Coal: minor bituminous and anthracite

Coal: lignite

Source: Energy Information Administration; United Nations

M-102031-1   © Rand McNally

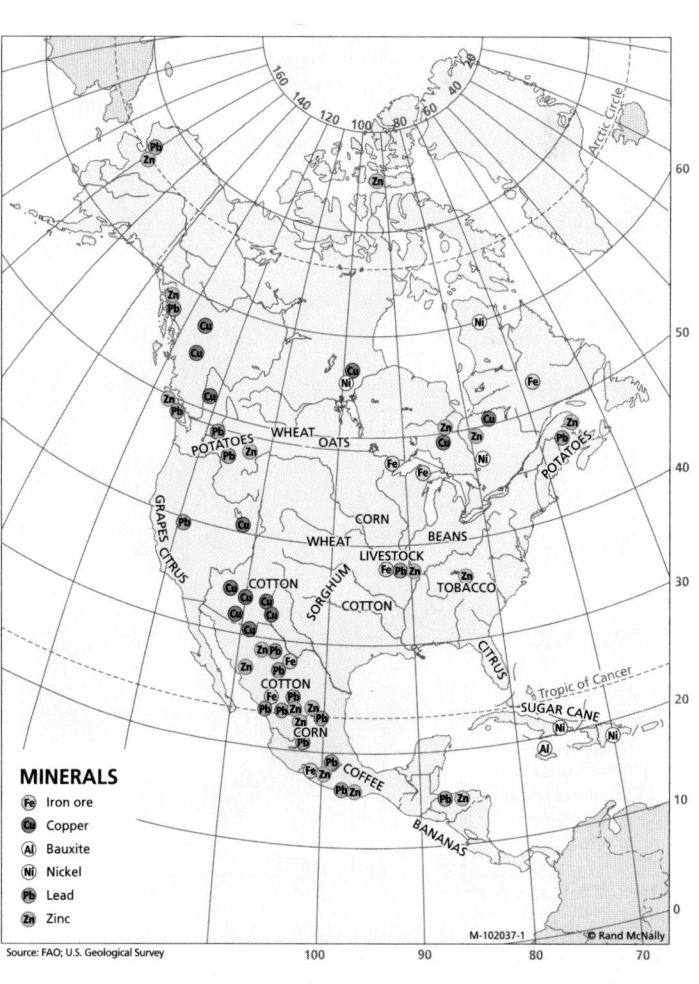

MINERALS

Fe Iron ore

Cu Copper

Al Bauxite

Ni Nickel

Pb Lead

Zn Zinc

Source: FAO; U.S. Geological Survey

M-102037-1   © Rand McNally

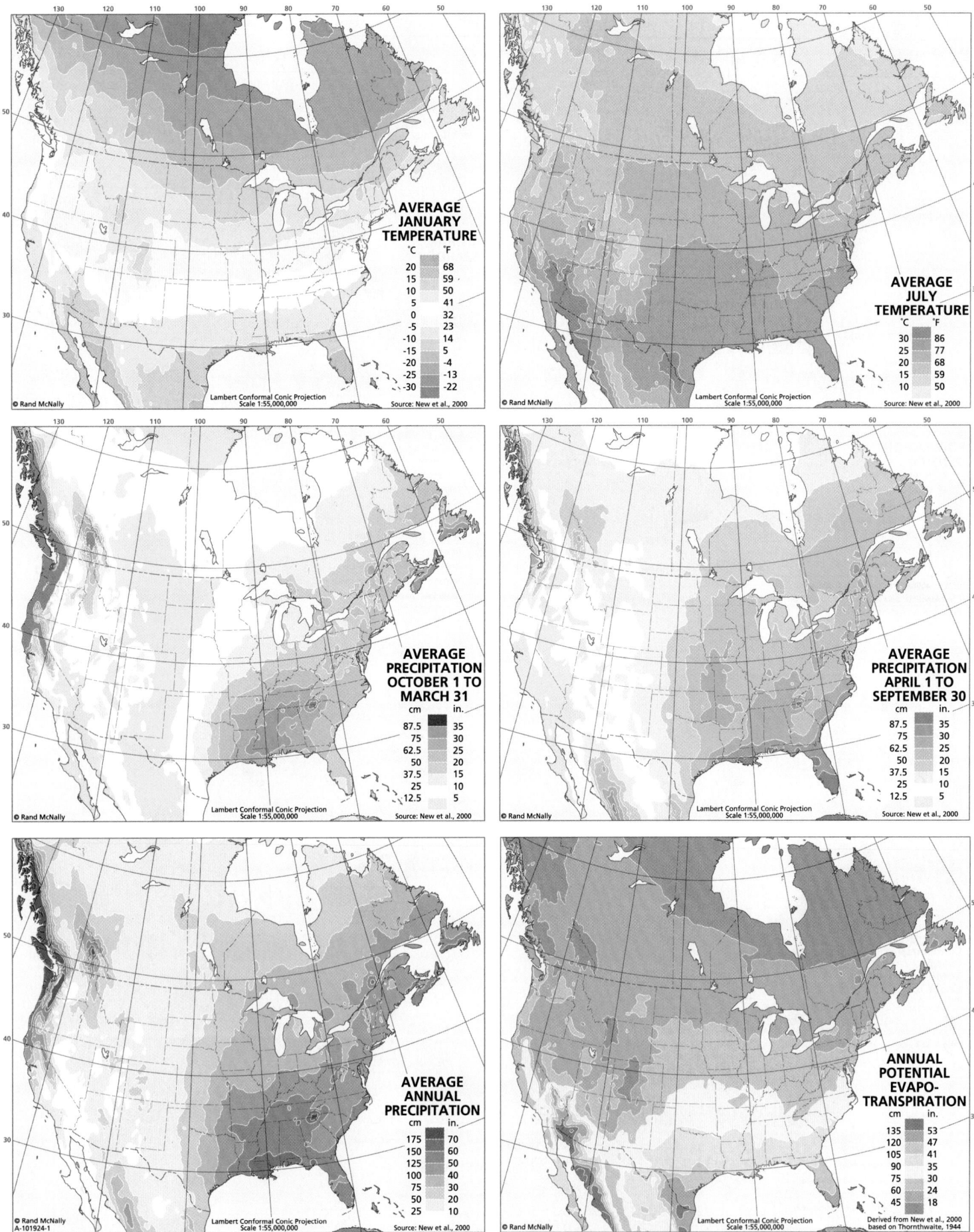

AVERAGE JANUARY TEMPERATURE

°C	°F
20	68
15	59
10	50
5	41
0	32
-5	23
-10	14
-15	5
-20	-4
-25	-13
-30	-22

Lambert Conformal Conic Projection
Scale 1:55,000,000
© Rand McNally
Source: New et al., 2000

AVERAGE JULY TEMPERATURE

°C	°F
30	86
25	77
20	68
15	59
10	50

Lambert Conformal Conic Projection
Scale 1:55,000,000
© Rand McNally
Source: New et al., 2000

AVERAGE PRECIPITATION OCTOBER 1 TO MARCH 31

cm	in.
87.5	35
75	30
62.5	25
50	20
37.5	15
25	10
12.5	5

Lambert Conformal Conic Projection
Scale 1:55,000,000
© Rand McNally
Source: New et al., 2000

AVERAGE PRECIPITATION APRIL 1 TO SEPTEMBER 30

cm	in.
87.5	35
75	30
62.5	25
50	20
37.5	15
25	10
12.5	5

Lambert Conformal Conic Projection
Scale 1:55,000,000
© Rand McNally
Source: New et al., 2000

AVERAGE ANNUAL PRECIPITATION

cm	in.
175	70
150	60
125	50
100	40
75	30
50	20
25	10

Lambert Conformal Conic Projection
Scale 1:55,000,000
© Rand McNally
A-101924-1
Source: New et al., 2000

ANNUAL POTENTIAL EVAPO-TRANSPIRATION

cm	in.
135	53
120	47
105	41
90	35
75	30
60	24
45	18

Lambert Conformal Conic Projection
Scale 1:55,000,000
© Rand McNally
Derived from New et al., 2000
based on Thornthwaite, 1944

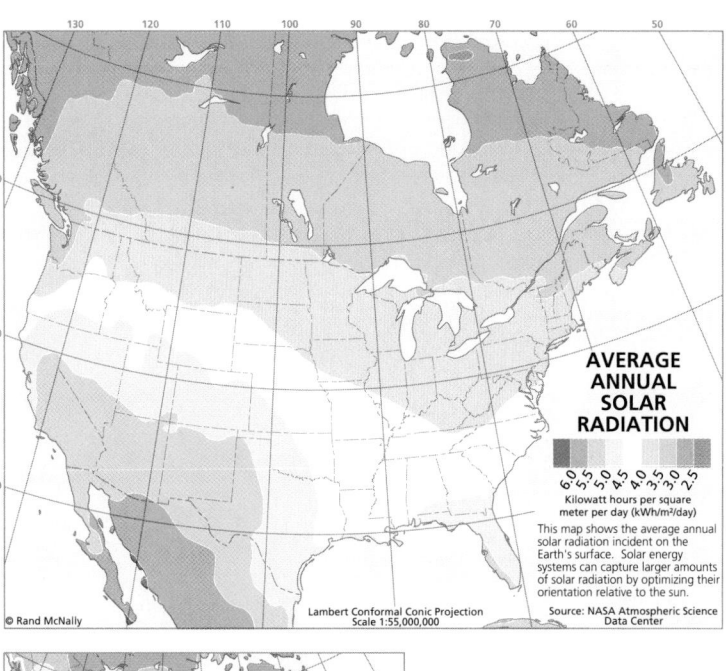

AVERAGE ANNUAL SOLAR RADIATION

Kilowatt hours per square meter per day (kWh/m²/day)

6.0 5.5 5.0 4.5 4.0 3.5 3.0 2.5

This map shows the average annual solar radiation incident on the Earth's surface. Solar energy systems can capture larger amounts of solar radiation by optimizing their orientation relative to the sun.

Source: NASA Atmospheric Science Data Center

© Rand McNally
Lambert Conformal Conic Projection
Scale 1:55,000,000

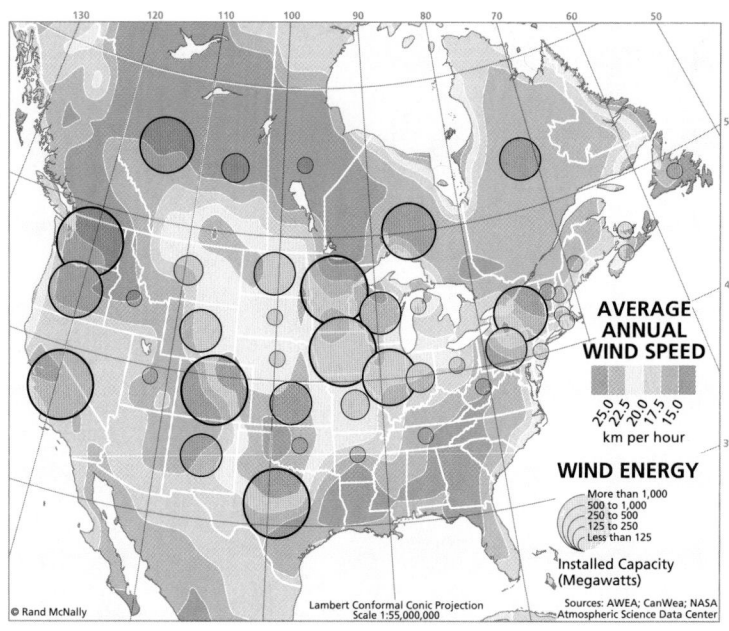

AVERAGE ANNUAL WIND SPEED

25.0 22.5 20.0 17.5 15.0
km per hour

WIND ENERGY
- More than 1,000
- 500 to 1,000
- 250 to 500
- 125 to 250
- Less than 125

Installed Capacity (Megawatts)

Sources: AWEA; CanWea; NASA Atmospheric Science Data Center

© Rand McNally
Lambert Conformal Conic Projection
Scale 1:55,000,000

EL NIÑO CLIMATE ANOMALIES

These two maps show temperature and precipitation anomalies associated with the 1982-83 El Niño-Southern Oscillation (ENSO) event, one of strongest such events on record. The maps compare temperature and precipitation values for the 1982-83 winter season (October 1, 1982 through March 31, 1983) to winter averages for the 1961-90 baseline period. A positive anomaly indicates a higher than average temperature or precipitation value for 1982-83, while a negative anomaly indicates a lower than average value.

Derived from Brohan et al., 2006, and Hulme, 1998

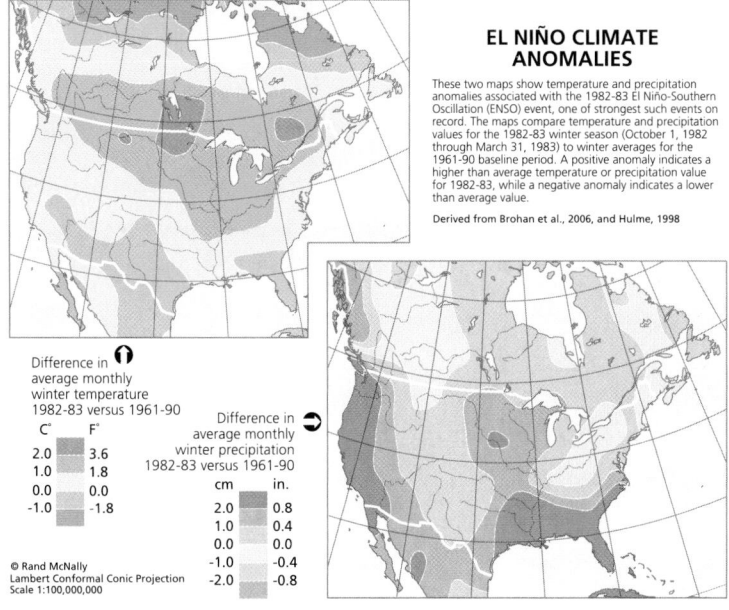

Difference in average monthly winter temperature 1982-83 versus 1961-90

C°	F°
2.0	3.6
1.0	1.8
0.0	0.0
-1.0	-1.8

Difference in average monthly winter precipitation 1982-83 versus 1961-90

cm	in.
2.0	0.8
1.0	0.4
0.0	0.0
-1.0	-0.4
-2.0	-0.8

© Rand McNally
Lambert Conformal Conic Projection
Scale 1:100,000,000

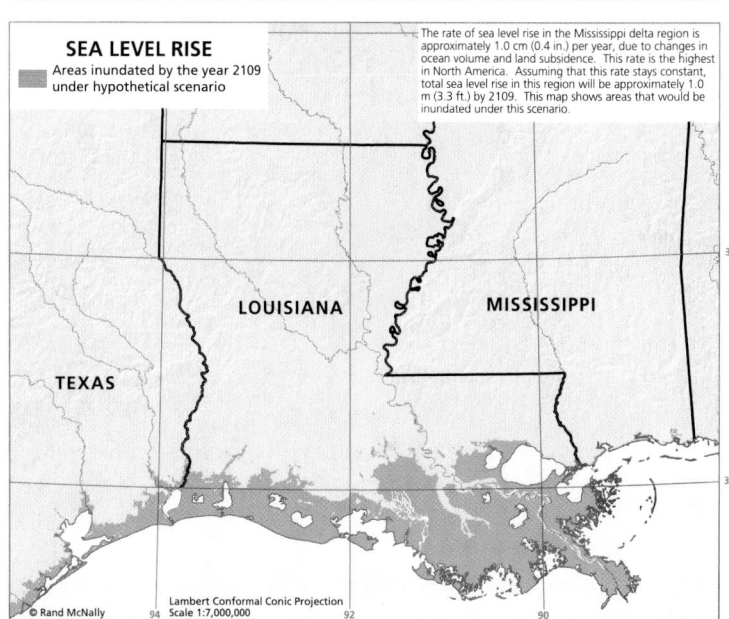

SEA LEVEL RISE

Areas inundated by the year 2109 under hypothetical scenario

The rate of sea level rise in the Mississippi delta region is approximately 1.0 cm (0.4 in.) per year, due to changes in ocean volume and land subsidence. This rate is the highest in North America. Assuming that this rate stays constant, total sea level rise in this region will be approximately 1.0 m (3.3 ft.) by 2109. This map shows areas that would be inundated under this scenario.

TEXAS   LOUISIANA   MISSISSIPPI

© Rand McNally
Lambert Conformal Conic Projection
Scale 1:7,000,000

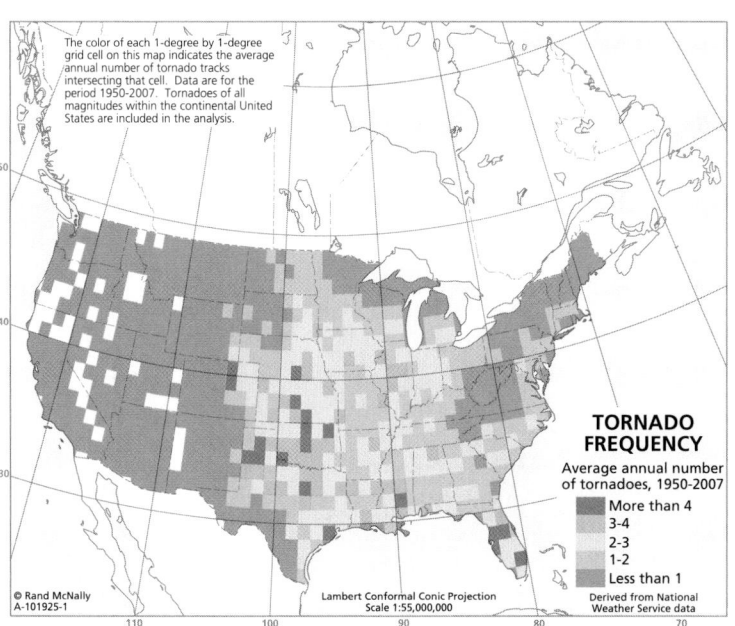

The color of each 1-degree by 1-degree grid cell on this map indicates the average annual number of tornado tracks intersecting that cell. Data are for the period 1950-2007. Tornadoes of all magnitudes within the continental United States are included in the analysis.

TORNADO FREQUENCY

Average annual number of tornadoes, 1950-2007

- More than 4
- 3-4
- 2-3
- 1-2
- Less than 1

© Rand McNally
A-101925-1
Lambert Conformal Conic Projection
Scale 1:55,000,000

Derived from National Weather Service data

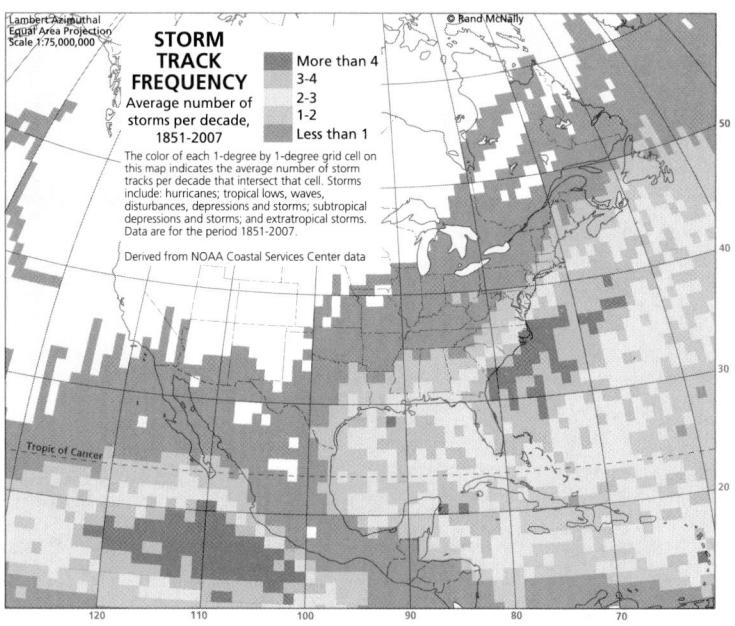

STORM TRACK FREQUENCY

Average number of storms per decade, 1851-2007

- More than 4
- 3-4
- 2-3
- 1-2
- Less than 1

The color of each 1-degree by 1-degree grid cell on this map indicates the average number of storm tracks per decade that intersect that cell. Storms include: hurricanes; tropical lows; waves; disturbances; depressions and storms; subtropical depressions and storms; and extratropical storms. Data are for the period 1851-2007.

Derived from NOAA Coastal Services Center data

Lambert Azimuthal Equal Area Projection
Scale 1:75,000,000

© Rand McNally

Tropic of Cancer

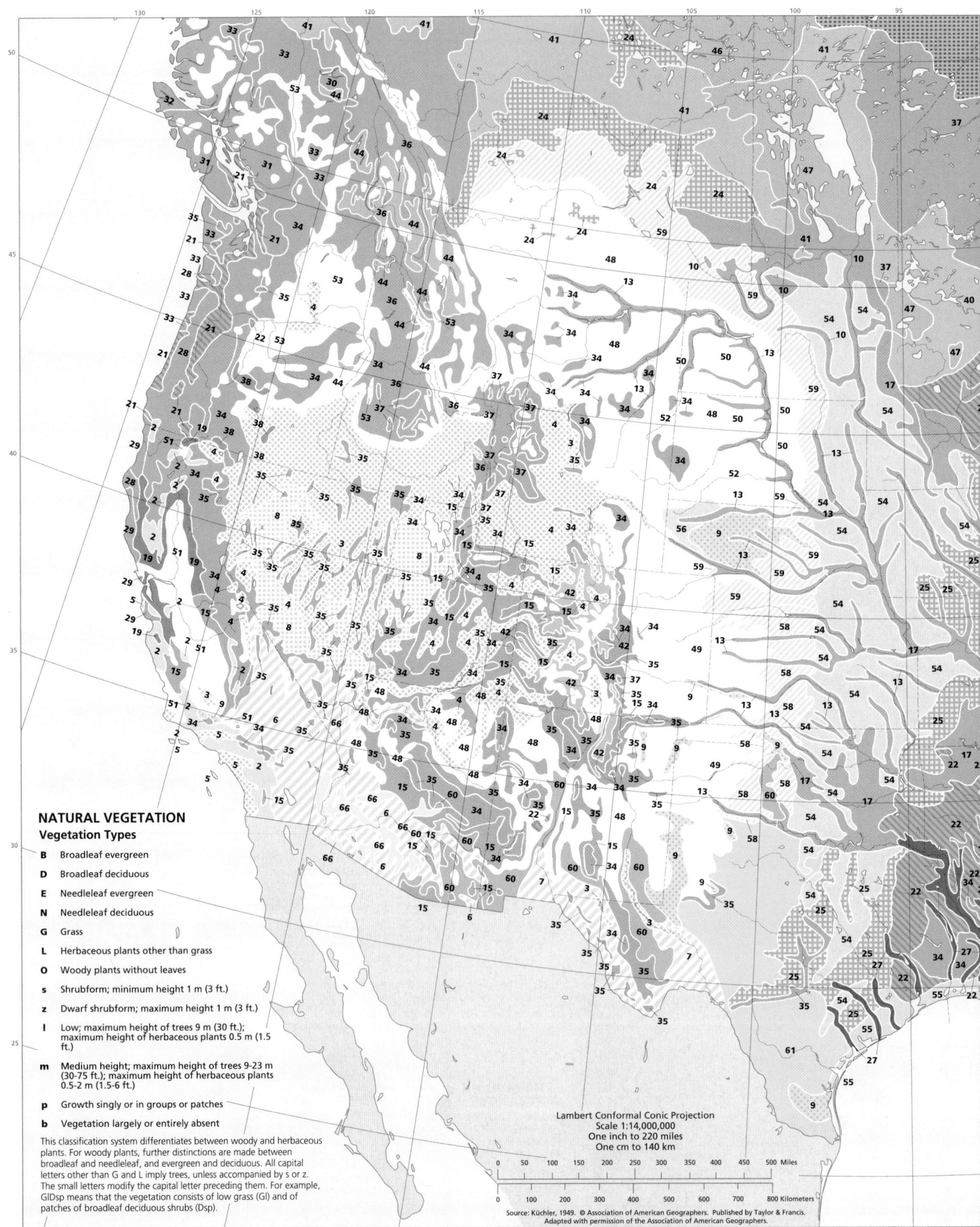

NATURAL VEGETATION
Vegetation Types

B Broadleaf evergreen

D Broadleaf deciduous

E Needleleaf evergreen

N Needleleaf deciduous

G Grass

L Herbaceous plants other than grass

O Woody plants without leaves

s Shrubform; minimum height 1 m (3 ft.)

z Dwarf shrubform; maximum height 1 m (3 ft.)

l Low; maximum height of trees 9 m (30 ft.); maximum height of herbaceous plants 0.5 m (1.5 ft.)

m Medium height; maximum height of trees 9-23 m (30-75 ft.); maximum height of herbaceous plants 0.5-2 m (1.5-6 ft.)

p Growth singly or in groups or patches

b Vegetation largely or entirely absent

This classification system differentiates between woody and herbaceous plants. For woody plants, further distinctions are made between broadleaf and needleleaf, and evergreen and deciduous. All capital letters other than G and L imply trees, unless accompanied by s or z. The small letters modify the capital letter preceding them. For example, GlDsp means that the vegetation consists of low grass (Gl) and of patches of broadleaf deciduous shrubs (Dsp).

Lambert Conformal Conic Projection
Scale 1:14,000,000
One inch to 220 miles
One cm to 140 km

0 50 100 150 200 250 300 350 400 450 500 Miles

0 100 200 300 400 500 600 700 800 Kilometers

Source: Küchler, 1949. © Association of American Geographers. Published by Taylor & Francis.
Adapted with permission of the Association of American Geographers.

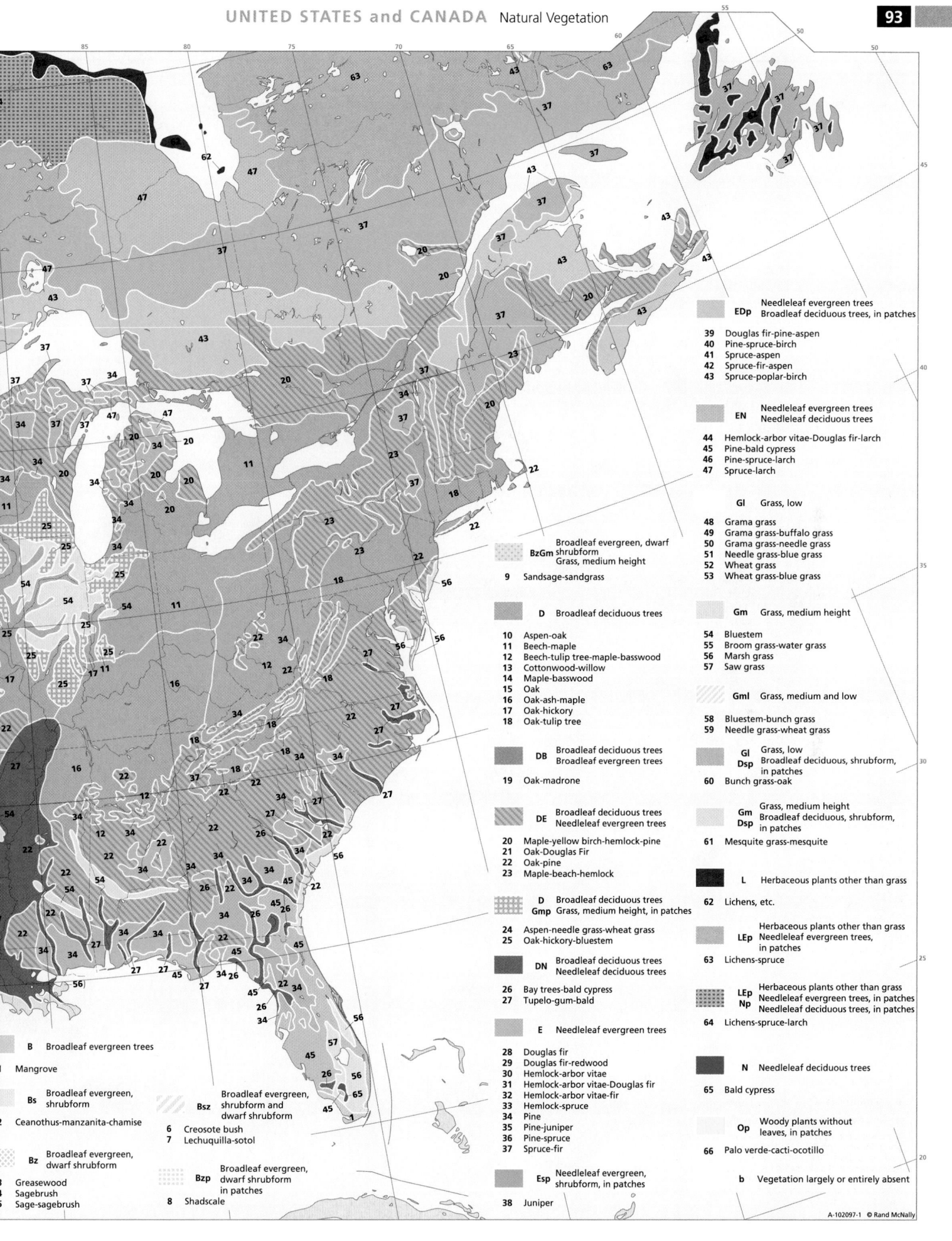

EDp Needleleaf evergreen trees / Broadleaf deciduous trees, in patches

39 Douglas fir-pine-aspen
40 Pine-spruce-birch
41 Spruce-aspen
42 Spruce-fir-aspen
43 Spruce-poplar-birch

EN Needleleaf evergreen trees / Needleleaf deciduous trees

44 Hemlock-arbor vitae-Douglas fir-larch
45 Pine-bald cypress
46 Pine-spruce-larch
47 Spruce-larch

Gl Grass, low

48 Grama grass
49 Grama grass-buffalo grass
50 Grama grass-needle grass
51 Needle grass-blue grass
52 Wheat grass
53 Wheat grass-blue grass

BzGm Broadleaf evergreen, dwarf shrubform / Grass, medium height

9 Sandsage-sandgrass

D Broadleaf deciduous trees

10 Aspen-oak
11 Beech-maple
12 Beech-tulip tree-maple-basswood
13 Cottonwood-willow
14 Maple-basswood
15 Oak
16 Oak-ash-maple
17 Oak-hickory
18 Oak-tulip tree

Gm Grass, medium height

54 Bluestem
55 Broom grass-water grass
56 Marsh grass
57 Saw grass

Gml Grass, medium and low

58 Bluestem-bunch grass
59 Needle grass-wheat grass

DB Broadleaf deciduous trees / Broadleaf evergreen trees

19 Oak-madrone

Gl Grass, low
Dsp Broadleaf deciduous, shrubform, in patches

60 Bunch grass-oak

DE Broadleaf deciduous trees / Needleleaf evergreen trees

20 Maple-yellow birch-hemlock-pine
21 Oak-Douglas Fir
22 Oak-pine
23 Maple-beach-hemlock

Gm Grass, medium height
Dsp Broadleaf deciduous, shrubform, in patches

61 Mesquite grass-mesquite

D Broadleaf deciduous trees
Gmp Grass, medium height, in patches

24 Aspen-needle grass-wheat grass
25 Oak-hickory-bluestem

L Herbaceous plants other than grass

62 Lichens, etc.

LEp Herbaceous plants other than grass / Needleleaf evergreen trees, in patches

63 Lichens-spruce

DN Broadleaf deciduous trees / Needleleaf deciduous trees

26 Bay trees-bald cypress
27 Tupelo-gum-bald

LEp Herbaceous plants other than grass / Needleleaf evergreen trees, in patches
Np Needleleaf deciduous trees, in patches

64 Lichens-spruce-larch

E Needleleaf evergreen trees

28 Douglas fir
29 Douglas fir-redwood
30 Hemlock-arbor vitae
31 Hemlock-arbor vitae-Douglas fir
32 Hemlock-arbor vitae-fir
33 Hemlock-spruce
34 Pine
35 Pine-juniper
36 Pine-spruce
37 Spruce-fir

N Needleleaf deciduous trees

65 Bald cypress

Op Woody plants without leaves, in patches

66 Palo verde-cacti-ocotillo

Esp Needleleaf evergreen, shrubform, in patches

38 Juniper

B Broadleaf evergreen trees

1 Mangrove

Bs Broadleaf evergreen, shrubform

2 Ceanothus-manzanita-chamise

Bsz Broadleaf evergreen, shrubform and dwarf shrubform

6 Creosote bush
7 Lechuquilla-sotol

Bz Broadleaf evergreen, dwarf shrubform

3 Greasewood
4 Sagebrush
5 Sage-sagebrush

Bzp Broadleaf evergreen, dwarf shrubform in patches

8 Shadscale

b Vegetation largely or entirely absent

A-102097-1   © Rand McNally

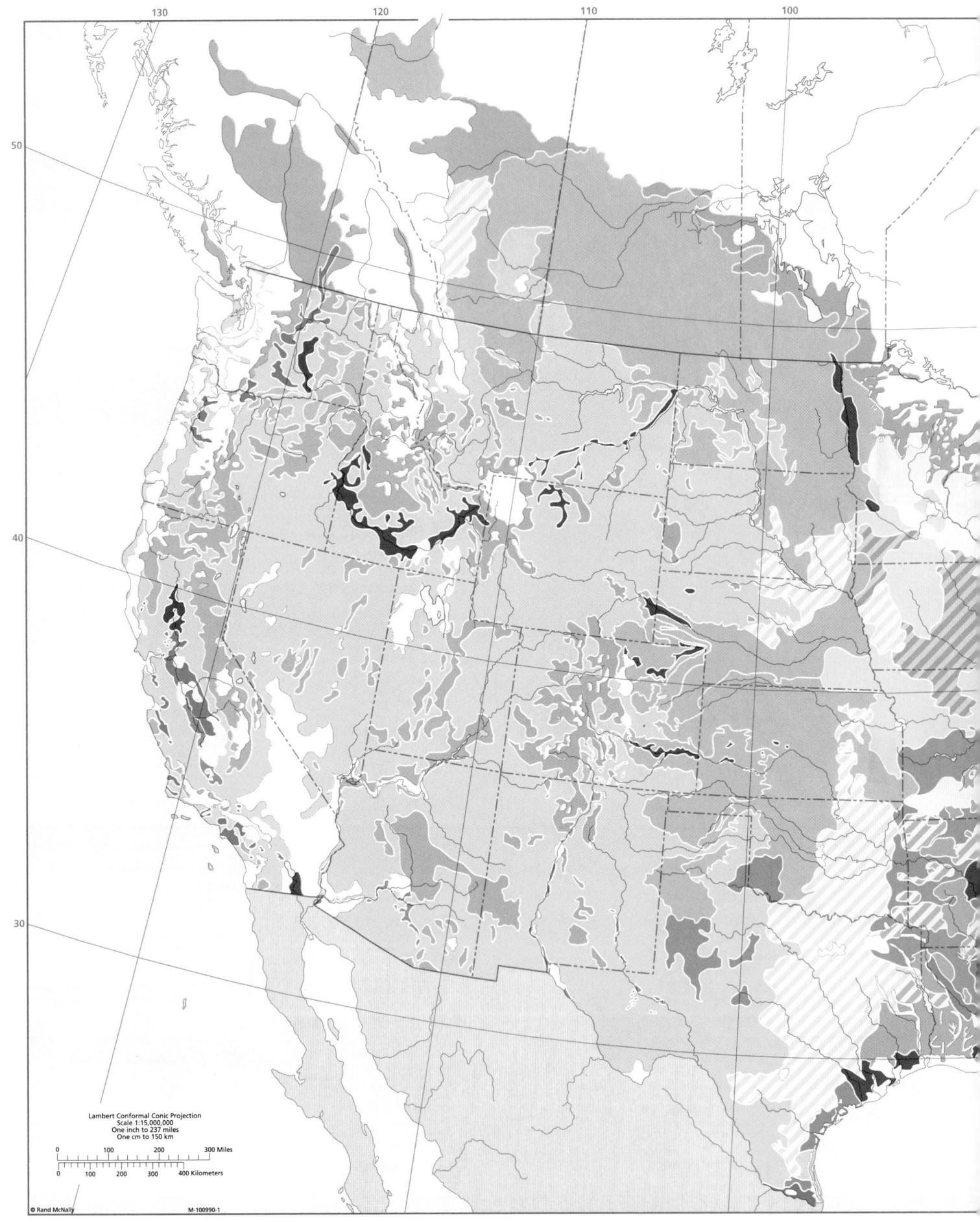

130 120 110 100

50

40

30

Lambert Conformal Conic Projection
Scale 1:15,000,000
One inch to 237 miles
One cm to 150 km

0 100 200 300 Miles

0 100 200 300 400 Kilometers

© Rand McNally   M-100990-1

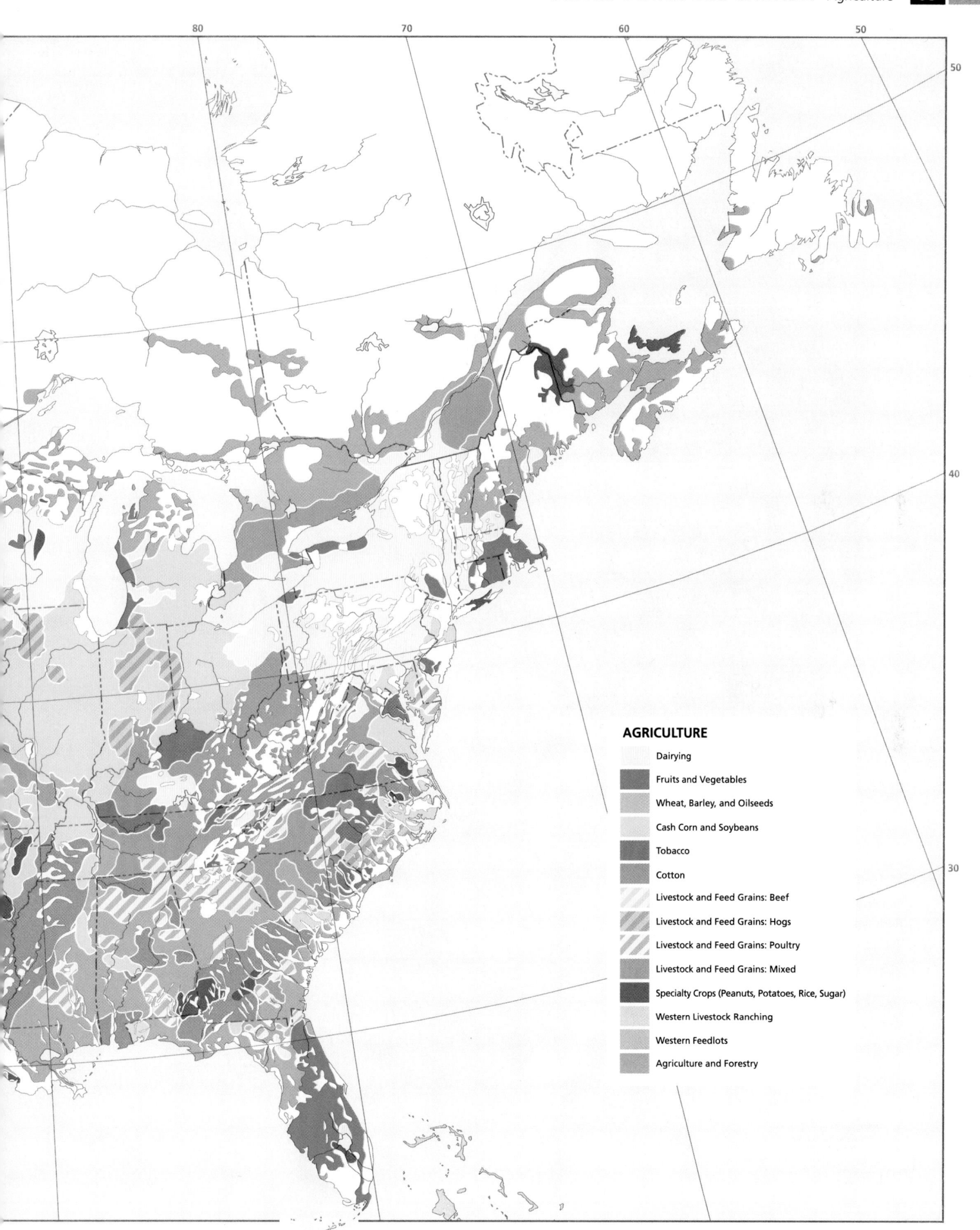

AGRICULTURE

Dairying

Fruits and Vegetables

Wheat, Barley, and Oilseeds

Cash Corn and Soybeans

Tobacco

Cotton

Livestock and Feed Grains: Beef

Livestock and Feed Grains: Hogs

Livestock and Feed Grains: Poultry

Livestock and Feed Grains: Mixed

Specialty Crops (Peanuts, Potatoes, Rice, Sugar)

Western Livestock Ranching

Western Feedlots

Agriculture and Forestry

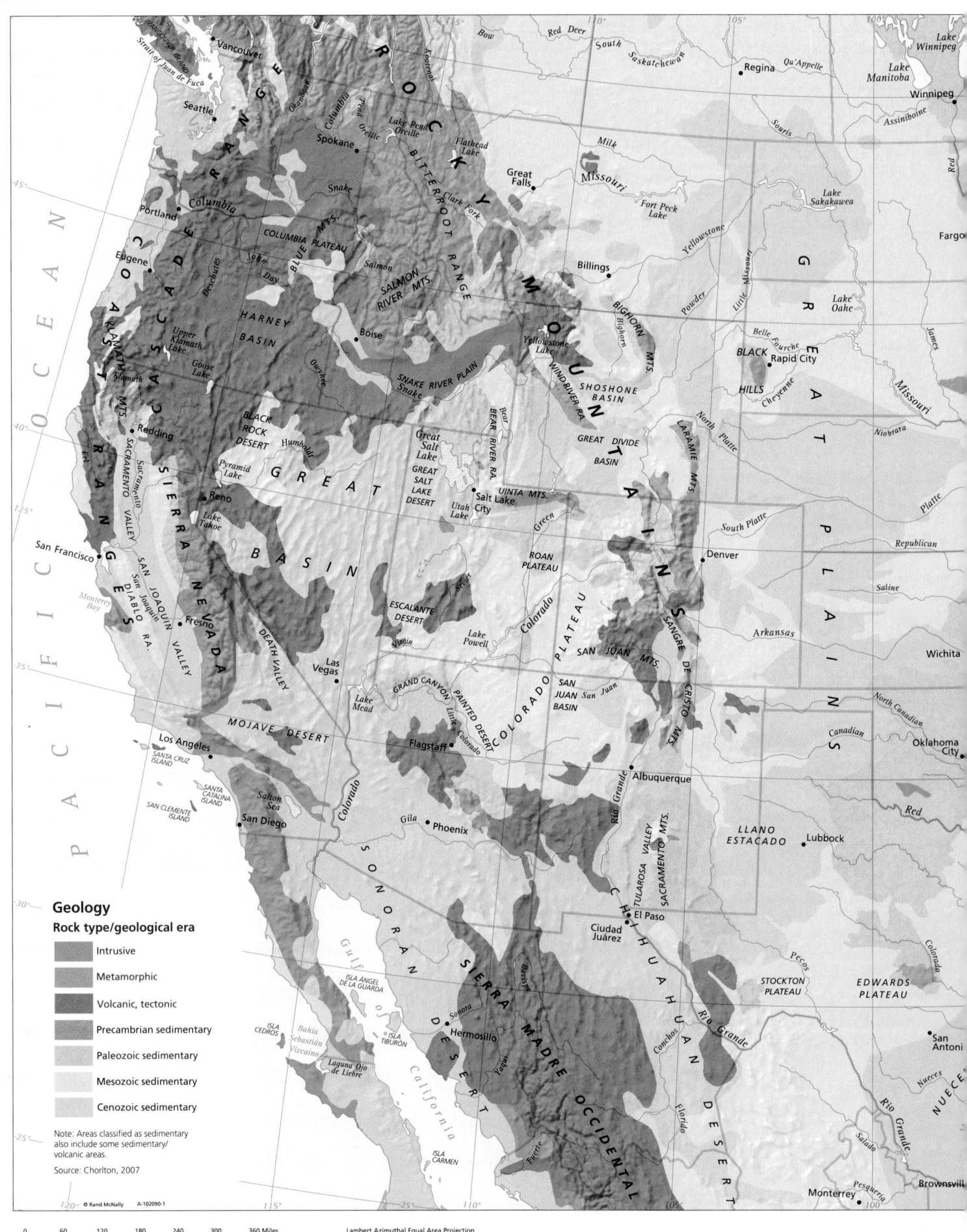

Geology

Rock type/geological era

- Intrusive
- Metamorphic
- Volcanic, tectonic
- Precambrian sedimentary
- Paleozoic sedimentary
- Mesozoic sedimentary
- Cenozoic sedimentary

Note: Areas classified as sedimentary also include some sedimentary/ volcanic areas.

Source: Chorlton, 2007

© Rand McNally   A-102090-1

0   60   120   180   240   300   360 Miles

0   60   120 180 240 300 360 420 480 540   600 Kilometers

Lambert Azimuthal Equal Area Projection
Scale 1:12,000,000
One inch to 190 miles
One cm to 120 km

The geological information on this map is highly generalized, and is intended for use at scales of 1:10,000,000 or smaller.

FEDERAL LANDS AND INTERSTATE HIGHWAYS
Selected highways and Federal Lands

National Parks, Monuments, Seashores, Preserves, Lakeshores, Recreation Areas

National Forests

National Grasslands

National Wildlife Refuges

Military Installations

Indian Reservations

—————— Interstate Highways

—————— Other Roads

U.S. Interstate Highways

Trans-Canada Highway

Canadian Autoroute

Other Canadian Roads

Albers Equal Area Conic Projection
Scale 1:12,000,000
One inch to 190 miles
One cm to 120 km

0 60 120 180 240 300 360 Miles

0 60 120 180 240 300 360 420 480 540 600 Kilometers

A-100036-1 © Rand McNally

Map 1: Railroads, Waterways, and Air Travel

PACIFIC TIME 9 A.M. — MOUNTAIN TIME 10 A.M. — CENTRAL TIME 11 A.M. — EASTERN TIME 12 A.M. — ATLANTIC TIME 1 A.M.

NEWF. TIME 1:30 P.M.

Edmonton, Calgary, Vancouver, Seattle-Tacoma, Portland, Spokane, Boise, Winnipeg, Montréal, Ottawa, Halifax

Reno, Sacramento, Oakland, San Francisco, San Jose, Las Vegas, Salt Lake City, Denver, Colorado Springs, Minneapolis-St. Paul, Milwaukee, Chicago-O'Hare, Chicago-Midway, Detroit, Toronto, Cleveland, Buffalo, Rochester, Syracuse, Albany, Boston, Manchester, Providence, Hartford, Bradley, La Guardia, Long Island, NY-Newark, NY-JFK, Pittsburgh, Philadelphia

Burbank, Los Angeles, Long Beach, San Diego, Ontario, Santa Ana, Phoenix, Tucson, Albuquerque, El Paso, Oklahoma City, Tulsa, Kansas City, St. Louis, Omaha, Indianapolis, Dayton, Columbus, Cincinnati, Washington, Dulles, Reagan Nat'l, Baltimore, Richmond, Norfolk, Louisville, Nashville, Greensboro, Raleigh-Durham, Charlotte, Memphis, Birmingham, Atlanta, Charleston

Dallas-Fort Worth, Dallas-Love, Austin, San Antonio, Houston, Houston-Hobby, Little Rock, New Orleans, Jacksonville, Orlando, Tampa, West Palm Beach, Ft. Lauderdale, Fort Myers, Miami

RAILROADS, WATERWAYS, AND AIR TRAVEL

Waterways
Controlling Depths
- 25 feet and over
- 12 to 25 feet
- 9 to 12 feet
- Less than 9 feet

Air Travel
Passengers Enplaned - 2007
- Over 15 million
- 5 million to 15 million
- 1 million to 5 million
- 500,000 to 1 million
- 250,000 to 500,000

Canada
38.5% / 19.7 / 12.7 / 14.5 / 14.7

United States
43.8% / 34.5 / 3.7 / 7.8 / 10.2

Railroad Freight
- Coal
- Other mine products
- Products of agriculture
- Forest products
- Manufactures and miscellaneous
- Major railroad

Total Metric Tons Hauled
In Canada - 281,755,800 - 2007
In U.S. - 1,759,929,200 - 2007

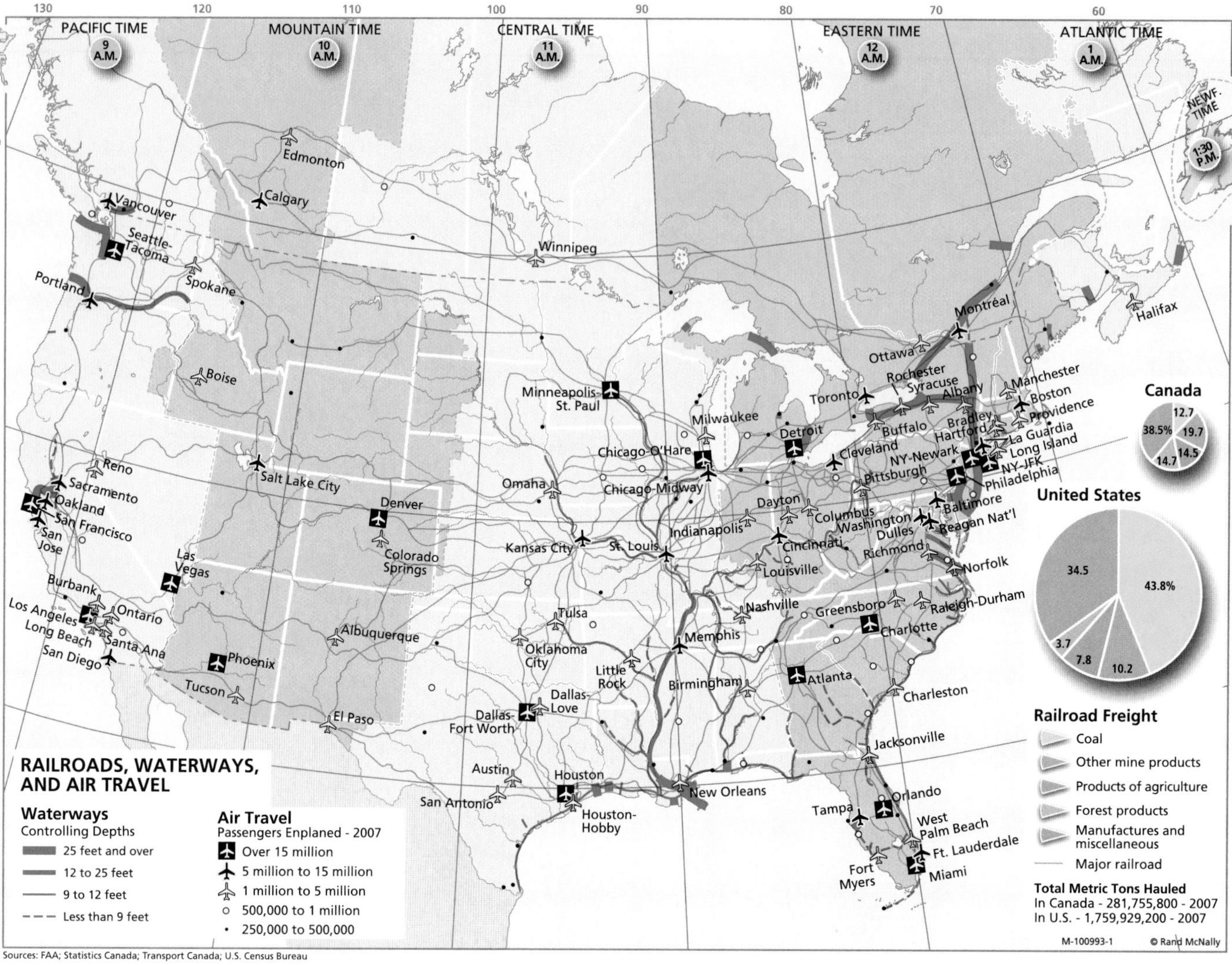

Sources: FAA; Statistics Canada; Transport Canada; U.S. Census Bureau

M-100993-1 © Rand McNally

Map 2: Canadian Territorial Evolution and Westward Expansion of the U.S., 1803-1860

BRITISH COLUMBIA 1871, Boundary Established 1846, Victoria, ALBERTA 1905, SASKATCHEWAN 1905, NORTHWEST TERRITORIES 1889, MANITOBA 1881, 1912, 1870, 1877, 1889, 1874, 1898, NEW BRUNSWICK 1867

Ft. Vancouver, WASHINGTON TERRITORY, Portland, Winnipeg, Title Established 1818, MINNESOTA 1856, QUEBEC 1867, Québec, BY TREATY 1842, Calais, MAINE 1820, Portland

OREGON 1859, OREGON COUNTRY 1846, Lewis and Clark Route, Ft. Union, NEBRASKA TERRITORY (Unorganized), ONTARIO 1867, Ottawa, Montréal, N.H., Oswego

Oregon Trail, California Trail, LOUISIANA PURCHASE 1803, MICHIGAN 1837, WISCONSIN 1848, Milwaukee, Chicago, Detroit, Toronto, Buffalo, NEW YORK, Albany, MASS., Boston, CONN., R.I.

Ft. Sutter, Salt Lake City, Ft. Bridger, UTAH TERRITORY, Ft. Laramie, Oregon Trail, Fremont Route, IOWA 1846, Mormon Trail, NORTHWEST TERRITORY, ILLINOIS 1818, INDIANA 1816, OHIO 1803, Cleveland, Cincinnati, PENNSYLVANIA, Pittsburgh, NJ, New York, Philadelphia, VT., N.H.

San Francisco, CEDED BY MEXICO 1848, Ft. Kearney, KANSAS TERRITORY, Zebulon Pike Route, Nauvoo, Independence, St. Louis, Louisville, Lexington, Washington, MARYLAND, DEL., VIRGINIA, Norfolk

CALIFORNIA 1850, Fremont Route, Los Angeles, Mormon Trail, California Trail, Santa Fe, NEW MEXICO TERRITORY, Santa Fe Trail, Ft. Union, INDIAN TERRITORY (Unorganized), MISSOURI 1821, KENTUCKY, Nashville, TENNESSEE, NORTH CAROLINA, SOUTH CAROLINA, Charleston

GADSDEN PURCHASE 1853, Santa Fe Trail, ARKANSAS 1836, Memphis, MISSISSIPPI TERRITORY, MISSISSIPPI 1817, ALABAMA 1818, GEORGIA, Atlanta, Savannah

TEXAS Annexed 1845, San Antonio, Galveston, LOUISIANA 1812, ANNEXED 1810, ANNEXED 1813, New Orleans, Mobile, Ceded by Spain 1819, St. Augustine, FLORIDA 1845

CANADIAN TERRITORIAL EVOLUTION AND WESTWARD EXPANSION OF THE U.S., 1803-1860

- ▲ Port Cities
- ● Other Cities
- ☐ States as of 1803
- Roads
- Canals
- Railroads

M-100989-1 © Rand McNally

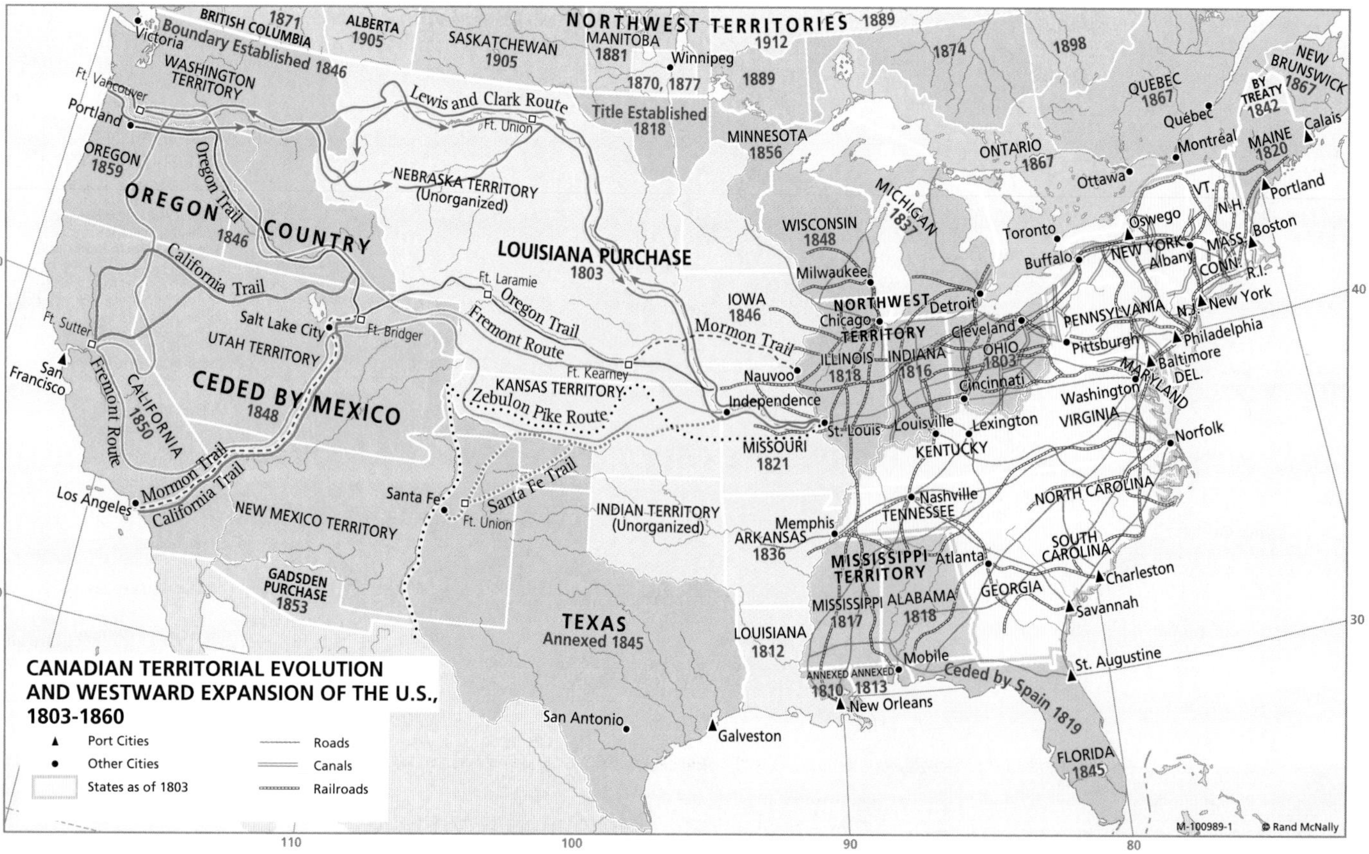

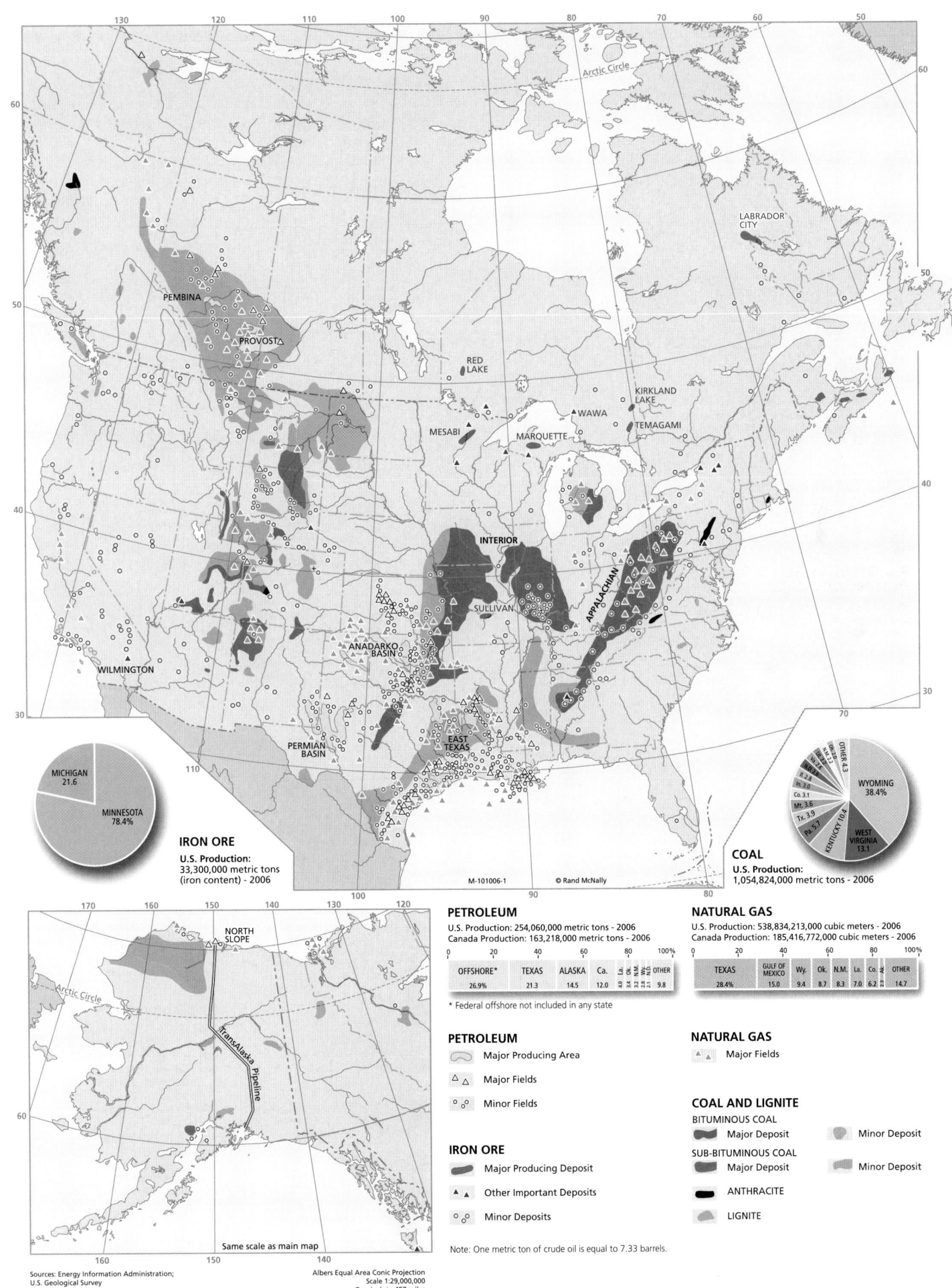

PEMBINA

PROVOST

LABRADOR CITY

RED LAKE

KIRKLAND LAKE

WAWA

TEMAGAMI

MESABI

MARQUETTE

INTERIOR

SULLIVAN

APPALACHIAN

ANADARKO BASIN

WILMINGTON

PERMIAN BASIN

EAST TEXAS

IRON ORE

MICHIGAN 21.6

MINNESOTA 78.4%

IRON ORE

U.S. Production:
33,300,000 metric tons
(iron content) - 2006

COAL

WYOMING 38.4%

WEST VIRGINIA 13.1

KENTUCKY 10.6

Pa. 5.7

Tx. 3.9

Mt. 3.6

Co. 3.1

In. 3.0

Il. 2.8

Va. 2.8

N.D. 2.3

Ut. 2.3

N.M. 2.3

OTHER 4.3

COAL

U.S. Production:
1,054,824,000 metric tons - 2006

M-101006-1 © Rand McNally

NORTH SLOPE

Arctic Circle

Trans Alaska Pipeline

Same scale as main map

Sources: Energy Information Administration;
U.S. Geological Survey

Albers Equal Area Conic Projection
Scale 1:29,000,000
One inch to 457 miles
One cm to 290 km

PETROLEUM

U.S. Production: 254,060,000 metric tons - 2006
Canada Production: 163,218,000 metric tons - 2006

0	20	40	60	80	100%

OFFSHORE*	TEXAS	ALASKA	Ca.	La.	Ok.	N.M.	Wy.	N.D.	OTHER
26.9%	21.3	14.5	12.0	4.0	3.4	3.2	2.8	2.1	9.8

* Federal offshore not included in any state

NATURAL GAS

U.S. Production: 538,834,213,000 cubic meters - 2006
Canada Production: 185,416,772,000 cubic meters - 2006

0	20	40	60	80	100%

TEXAS	GULF OF MEXICO	Wy.	Ok.	N.M.	La.	Co.	OTHER
28.4%	15.0	9.4	8.7	8.3	7.0	6.2	2.3	14.7

PETROLEUM

⬭ Major Producing Area

△ △ Major Fields

∘ ∘ Minor Fields

IRON ORE

⬬ Major Producing Deposit

▲ ▲ Other Important Deposits

∘ ∘ Minor Deposits

NATURAL GAS

▲ ▲ Major Fields

COAL AND LIGNITE

BITUMINOUS COAL

⬛ Major Deposit   ▨ Minor Deposit

SUB-BITUMINOUS COAL

⬛ Major Deposit   ▨ Minor Deposit

⬛ ANTHRACITE

▨ LIGNITE

Note: One metric ton of crude oil is equal to 7.33 barrels.

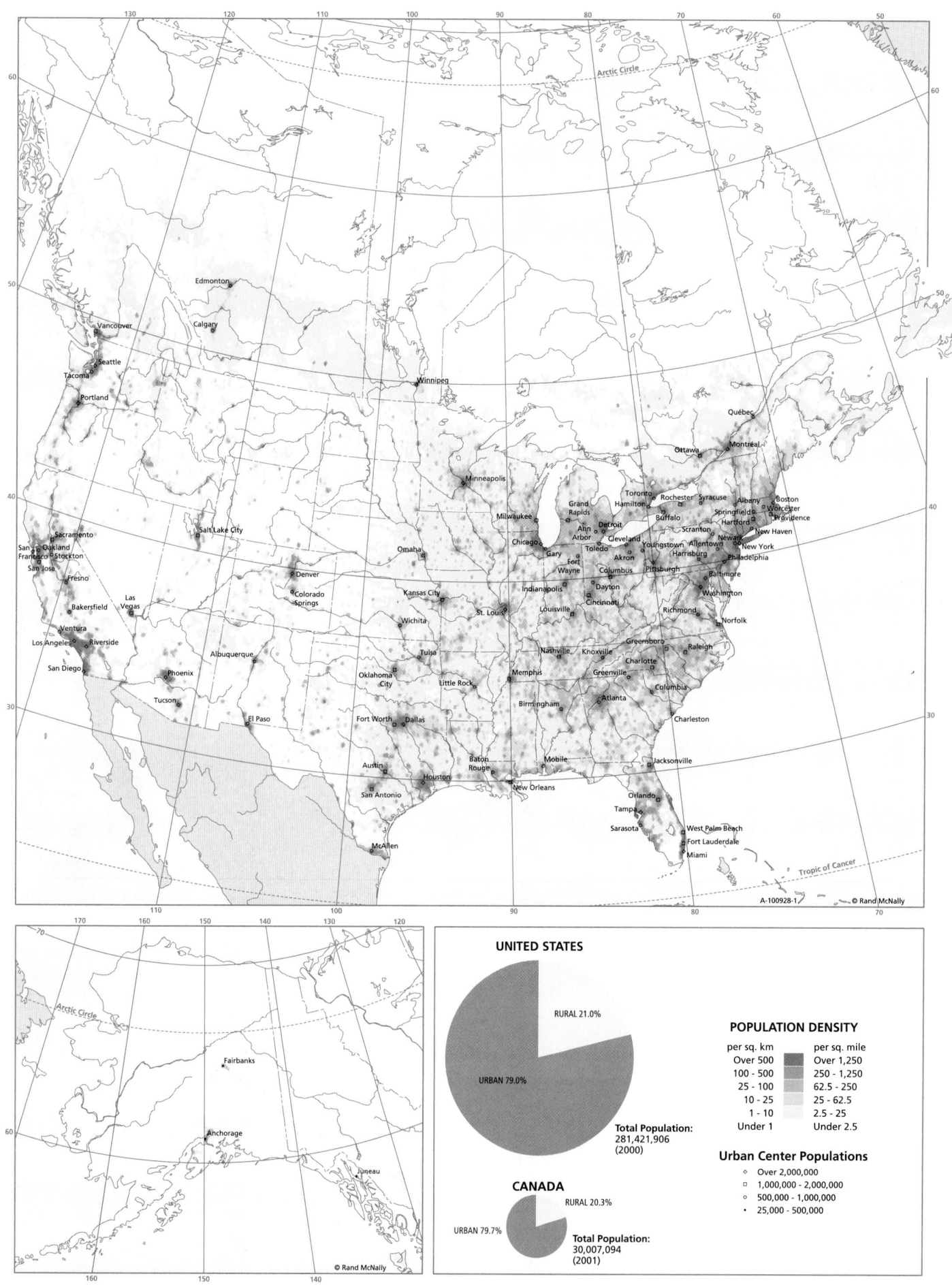

UNITED STATES

RURAL 21.0%

URBAN 79.0%

Total Population:
281,421,906
(2000)

CANADA

RURAL 20.3%

URBAN 79.7%

Total Population:
30,007,094
(2001)

POPULATION DENSITY

per sq. km	per sq. mile
Over 500	Over 1,250
100 - 500	250 - 1,250
25 - 100	62.5 - 250
10 - 25	25 - 62.5
1 - 10	2.5 - 25
Under 1	Under 2.5

Urban Center Populations

◇ Over 2,000,000
▢ 1,000,000 - 2,000,000
○ 500,000 - 1,000,000
· 25,000 - 500,000

Sources: Census of Canada; U.S. Census Bureau;
U.S. Department of Energy

Albers Equal Area Conic Projection
Scale 1:29,000,000
One inch to 457 miles
One cm to 290 km

© Rand McNally

A-100928-1

WHITE POPULATION

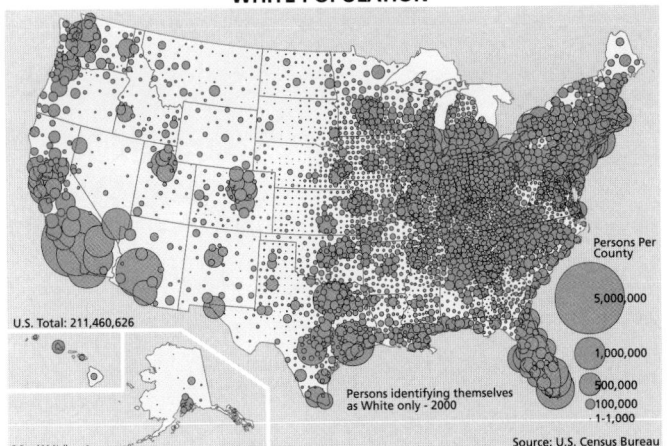

U.S. Total: 211,460,626

Persons Per County

5,000,000

1,000,000

500,000

100,000

1-1,000

Persons identifying themselves as White only - 2000

© Rand McNally

Source: U.S. Census Bureau

AFRICAN AMERICAN POPULATION

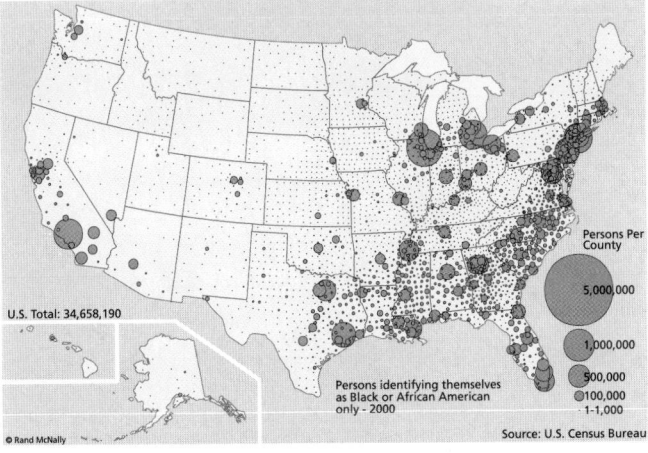

U.S. Total: 34,658,190

Persons Per County

5,000,000

1,000,000

500,000

100,000

1-1,000

Persons identifying themselves as Black or African American only - 2000

© Rand McNally

Source: U.S. Census Bureau

ASIAN POPULATION

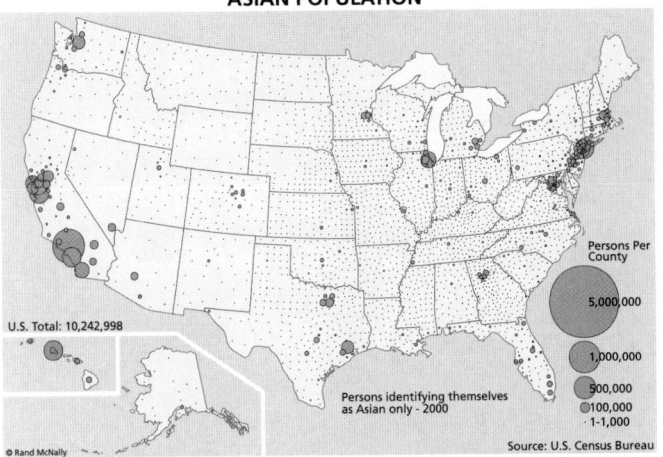

U.S. Total: 10,242,998

Persons Per County

5,000,000

1,000,000

500,000

100,000

1-1,000

Persons identifying themselves as Asian only - 2000

© Rand McNally

Source: U.S. Census Bureau

AMERICAN INDIAN AND ALASKA NATIVE POPULATION

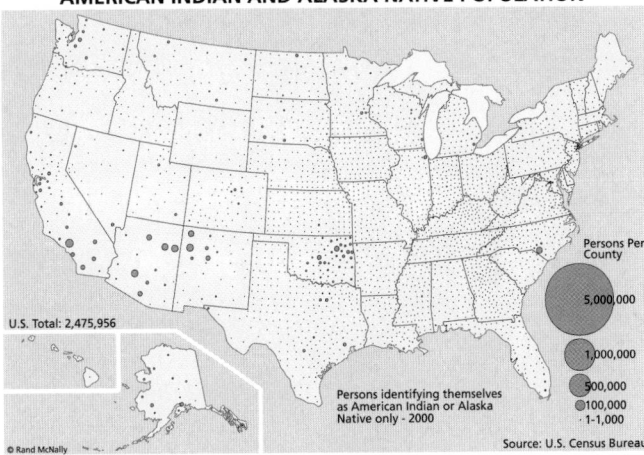

U.S. Total: 2,475,956

Persons Per County

5,000,000

1,000,000

500,000

100,000

1-1,000

Persons identifying themselves as American Indian or Alaska Native only - 2000

© Rand McNally

Source: U.S. Census Bureau

NATIVE HAWAIIAN AND PACIFIC ISLANDER POPULATION

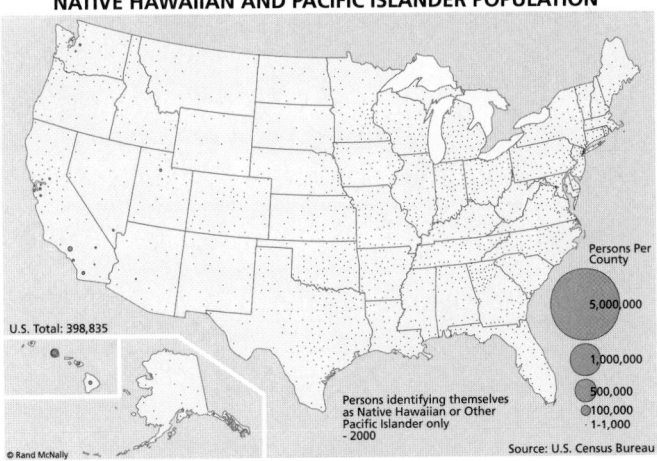

U.S. Total: 398,835

Persons Per County

5,000,000

1,000,000

500,000

100,000

1-1,000

Persons identifying themselves as Native Hawaiian or Other Pacific Islander only - 2000

© Rand McNally

Source: U.S. Census Bureau

SOME OTHER RACE

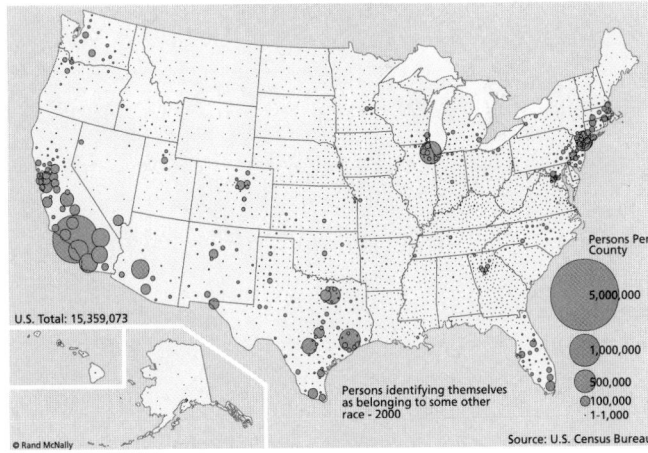

U.S. Total: 15,359,073

Persons Per County

5,000,000

1,000,000

500,000

100,000

1-1,000

Persons identifying themselves as belonging to some other race - 2000

© Rand McNally

Source: U.S. Census Bureau

TWO OR MORE RACES

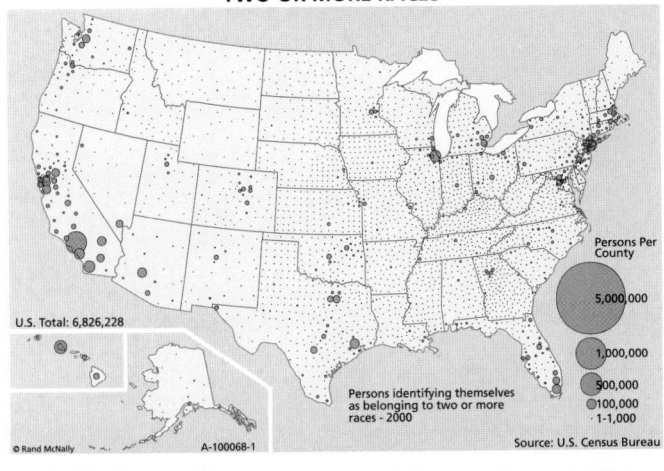

U.S. Total: 6,826,228

Persons Per County

5,000,000

1,000,000

500,000

100,000

1-1,000

Persons identifying themselves as belonging to two or more races - 2000

© Rand McNally   A-100068-1

Source: U.S. Census Bureau

HISPANIC POPULATION (ANY RACE)

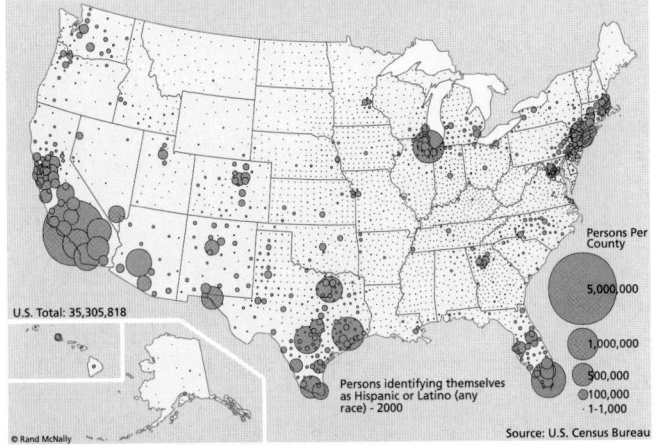

U.S. Total: 35,305,818

Persons Per County

5,000,000

1,000,000

500,000

100,000

1-1,000

Persons identifying themselves as Hispanic or Latino (any race) - 2000

© Rand McNally

Source: U.S. Census Bureau

POPULATION CHANGE

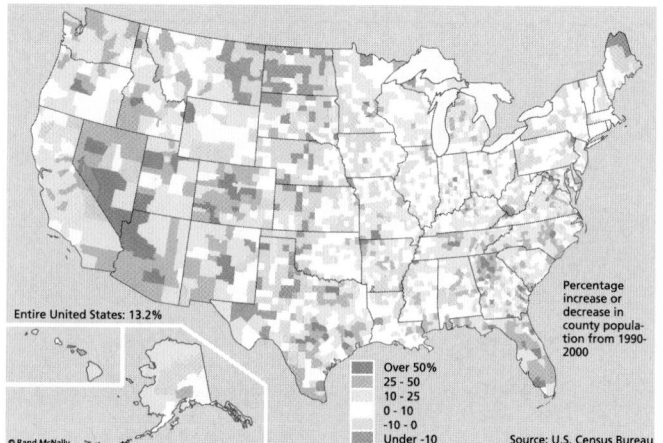

Entire United States: 13.2%

Percentage increase or decrease in county population from 1990-2000

Over 50%
25 - 50
10 - 25
0 - 10
-10 - 0
Under -10

© Rand McNally

Source: U.S. Census Bureau

INTER-STATE POPULATION SHIFTS

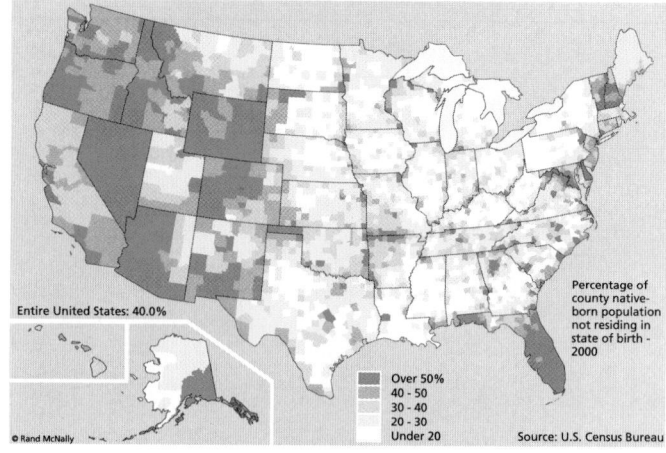

Entire United States: 40.0%

Percentage of county native-born population not residing in state of birth - 2000

Over 50%
40 - 50
30 - 40
20 - 30
Under 20

© Rand McNally

Source: U.S. Census Bureau

POPULATION UNDER 18

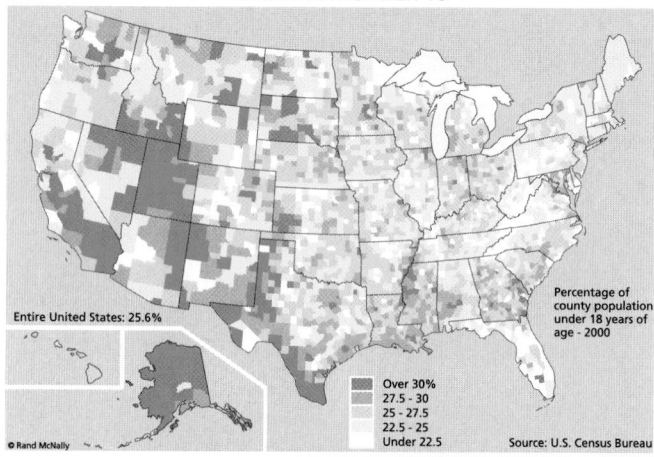

Entire United States: 25.6%

Percentage of county population under 18 years of age - 2000

Over 30%
27.5 - 30
25 - 27.5
22.5 - 25
Under 22.5

© Rand McNally

Source: U.S. Census Bureau

POPULATION 65 AND OVER

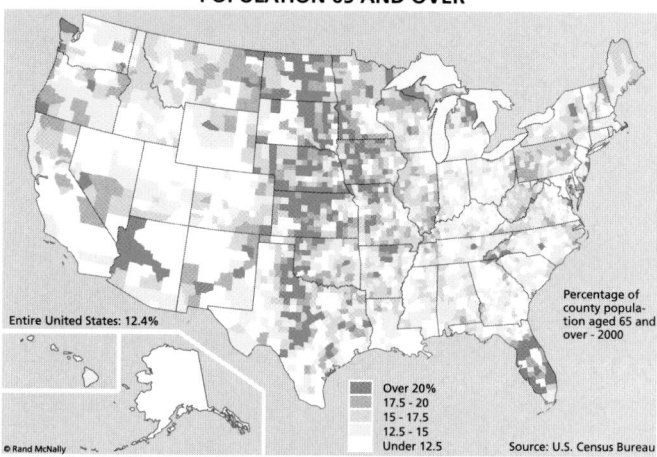

Entire United States: 12.4%

Percentage of county population aged 65 and over - 2000

Over 20%
17.5 - 20
15 - 17.5
12.5 - 15
Under 12.5

© Rand McNally

Source: U.S. Census Bureau

EDUCATIONAL ATTAINMENT RATE

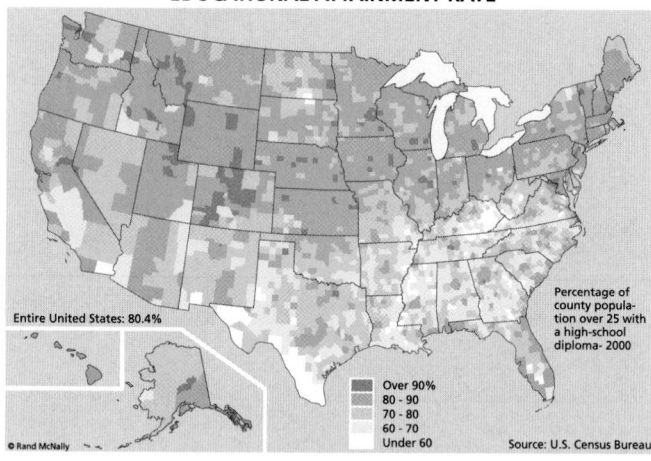

Entire United States: 80.4%

Percentage of county population over 25 with a high-school diploma- 2000

Over 90%
80 - 90
70 - 80
60 - 70
Under 60

© Rand McNally

Source: U.S. Census Bureau

COLLEGE ENROLLMENT RATE

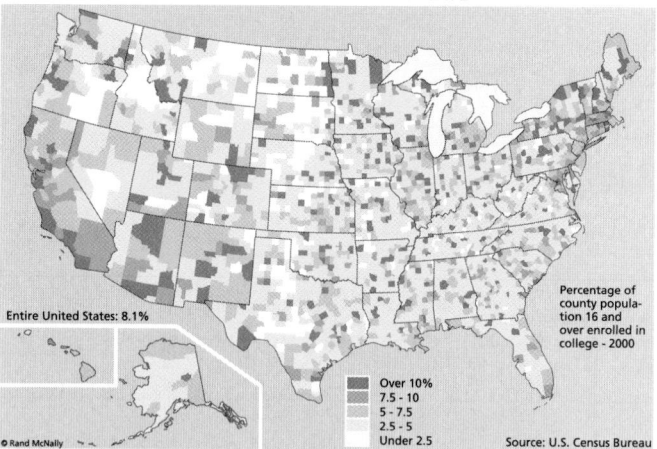

Entire United States: 8.1%

Percentage of county population 16 and over enrolled in college - 2000

Over 10%
7.5 - 10
5 - 7.5
2.5 - 5
Under 2.5

© Rand McNally

Source: U.S. Census Bureau

COMMUTING TIME

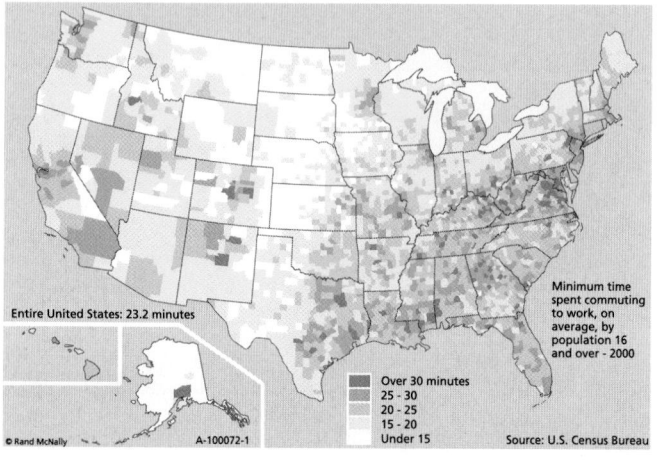

Entire United States: 23.2 minutes

Minimum time spent commuting to work, on average, by population 16 and over - 2000

Over 30 minutes
25 - 30
20 - 25
15 - 20
Under 15

© Rand McNally

A-100072-1

Source: U.S. Census Bureau

MEDIAN DECADE OF HOUSE CONSTRUCTION

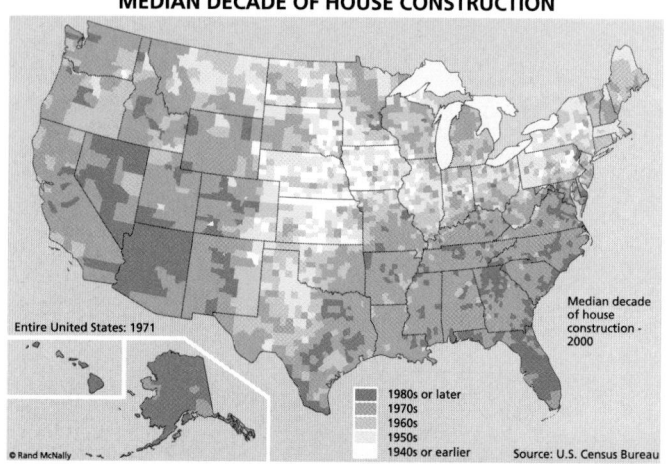

Entire United States: 1971

Median decade of house construction - 2000

1980s or later
1970s
1960s
1950s
1940s or earlier

© Rand McNally

Source: U.S. Census Bureau

WOMEN'S MEDIAN EARNINGS

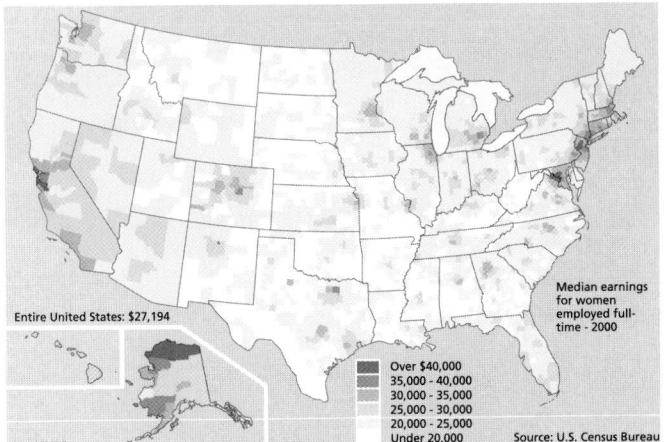

Entire United States: $27,194

Median earnings for women employed full-time - 2000

Over $40,000
35,000 - 40,000
30,000 - 35,000
25,000 - 30,000
20,000 - 25,000
Under 20,000

© Rand McNally

Source: U.S. Census Bureau

MEN'S MEDIAN EARNINGS

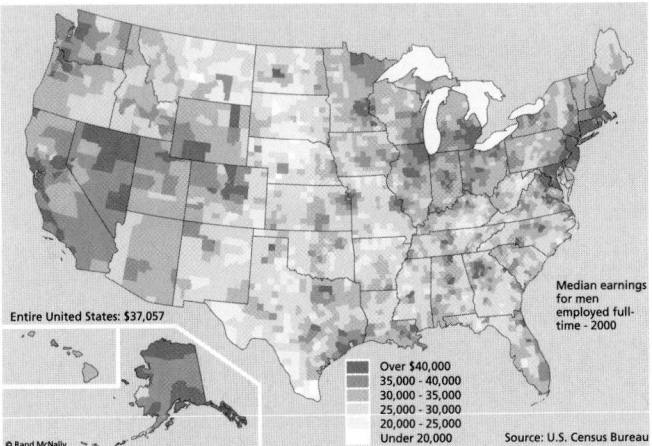

Entire United States: $37,057

Median earnings for men employed full-time - 2000

Over $40,000
35,000 - 40,000
30,000 - 35,000
25,000 - 30,000
20,000 - 25,000
Under 20,000

© Rand McNally

Source: U.S. Census Bureau

RATIO OF WOMEN'S TO MEN'S EARNINGS

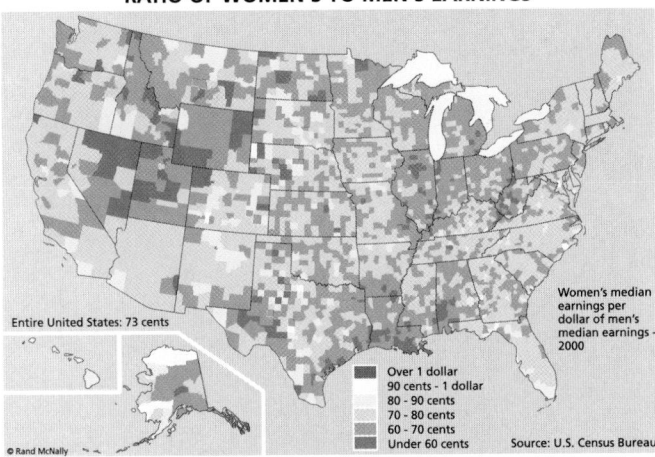

Entire United States: 73 cents

Women's median earnings per dollar of men's median earnings - 2000

Over 1 dollar
90 cents - 1 dollar
80 - 90 cents
70 - 80 cents
60 - 70 cents
Under 60 cents

© Rand McNally

Source: U.S. Census Bureau

MEDIAN HOUSEHOLD INCOME

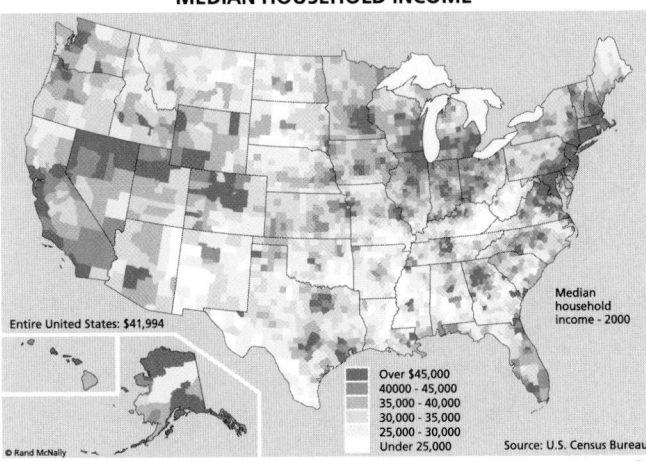

Entire United States: $41,994

Median household income - 2000

Over $45,000
40000 - 45,000
35,000 - 40,000
30,000 - 35,000
25,000 - 30,000
Under 25,000

© Rand McNally

Source: U.S. Census Bureau

HOUSEHOLDS HEADED BY WOMEN

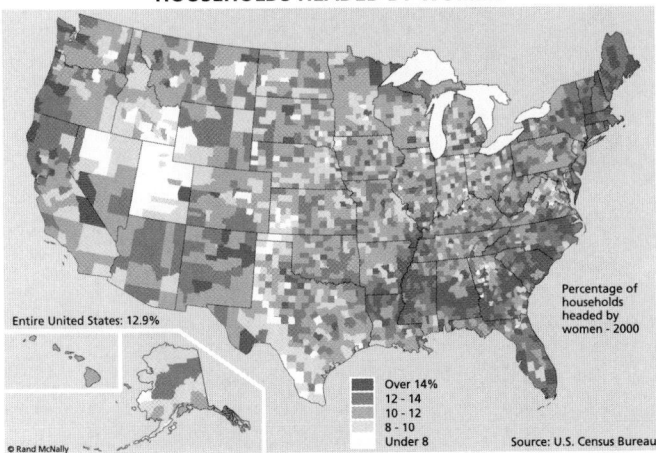

Entire United States: 12.9%

Percentage of households headed by women - 2000

Over 14%
12 - 14
10 - 12
8 - 10
Under 8

© Rand McNally

Source: U.S. Census Bureau

CHILDREN LIVING IN POVERTY

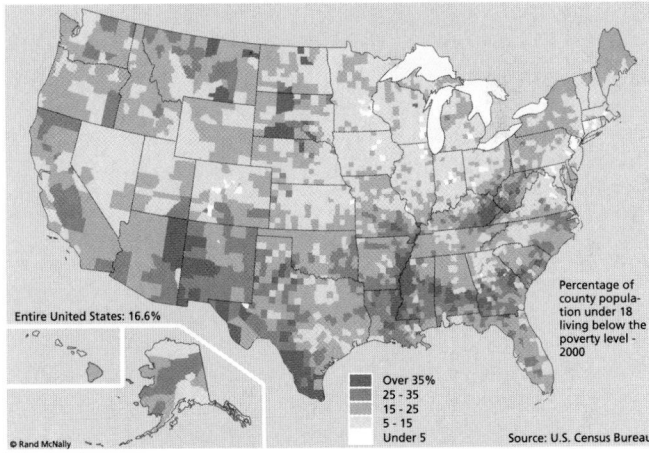

Entire United States: 16.6%

Percentage of county population under 18 living below the poverty level - 2000

Over 35%
25 - 35
15 - 25
5 - 15
Under 5

© Rand McNally

Source: U.S. Census Bureau

UNEMPLOYMENT RATE

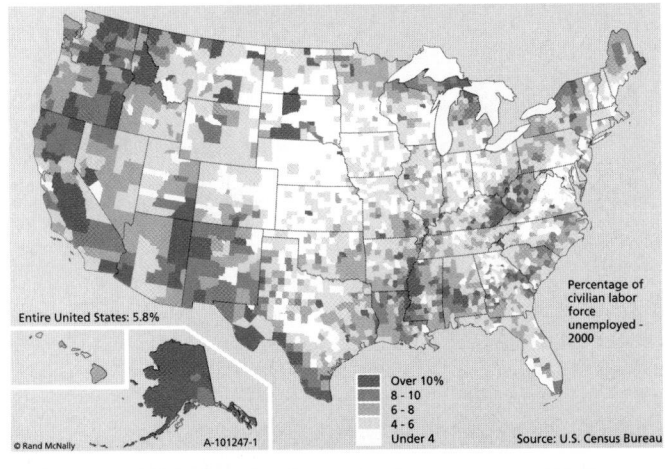

Entire United States: 5.8%

Percentage of civilian labor force unemployed - 2000

Over 10%
8 - 10
6 - 8
4 - 6
Under 4

© Rand McNally   A-101247-1

Source: U.S. Census Bureau

NON-ENGLISH SPEAKING HOUSEHOLDS

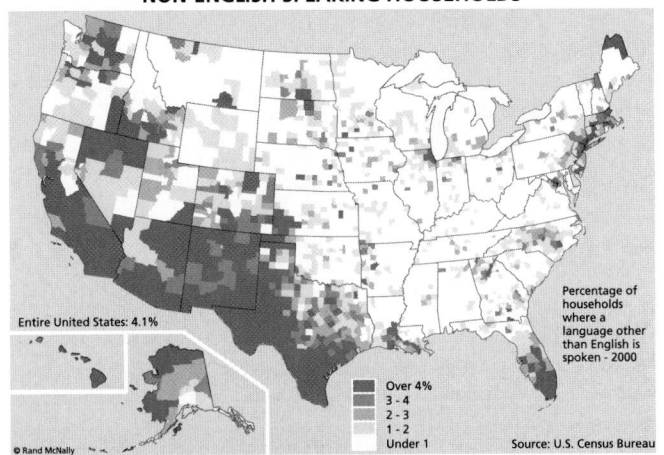

Entire United States: 4.1%

Percentage of households where a language other than English is spoken - 2000

Over 4%
3 - 4
2 - 3
1 - 2
Under 1

© Rand McNally

Source: U.S. Census Bureau

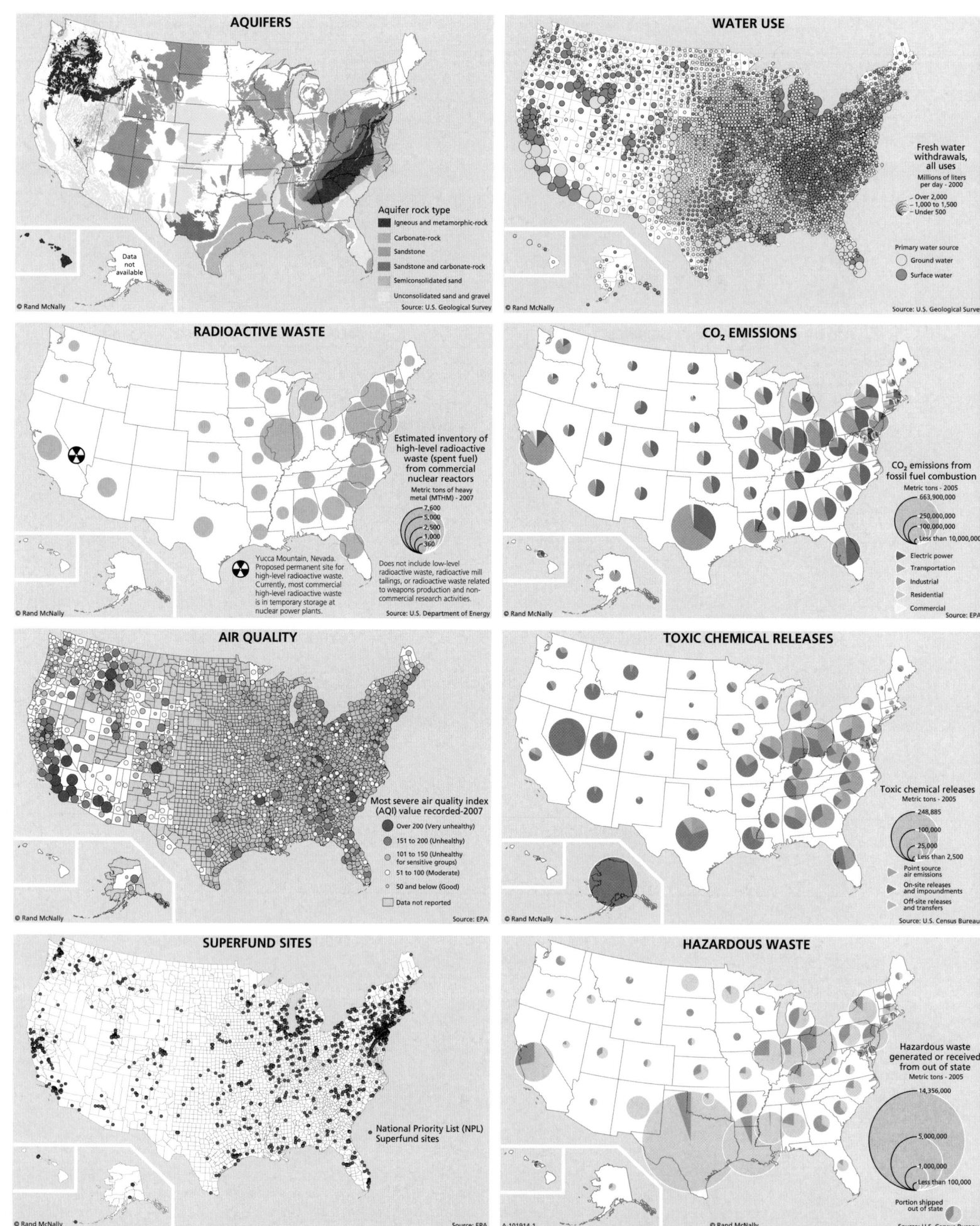

AQUIFERS

Aquifer rock type
- Igneous and metamorphic-rock
- Carbonate-rock
- Sandstone
- Sandstone and carbonate-rock
- Semiconsolidated sand
- Unconsolidated sand and gravel

Data not available

© Rand McNally
Source: U.S. Geological Survey

WATER USE

Fresh water withdrawals, all uses
Millions of liters per day - 2000
- Over 2,000
- 1,000 to 1,500
- Under 500

Primary water source
- Ground water
- Surface water

© Rand McNally
Source: U.S. Geological Survey

RADIOACTIVE WASTE

Estimated inventory of high-level radioactive waste (spent fuel) from commercial nuclear reactors
Metric tons of heavy metal (MTHM) - 2007
- 7,600
- 5,000
- 2,500
- 1,000
- 360

Yucca Mountain, Nevada. Proposed permanent site for high-level radioactive waste. Currently, most commercial high-level radioactive waste is in temporary storage at nuclear power plants.

Does not include low-level radioactive waste, radioactive mill tailings, or radioactive waste related to weapons production and non-commercial research activities.

© Rand McNally
Source: U.S. Department of Energy

CO₂ EMISSIONS

CO_2 emissions from fossil fuel combustion
Metric tons - 2005
- 663,900,000
- 250,000,000
- 100,000,000
- Less than 10,000,000

- Electric power
- Transportation
- Industrial
- Residential
- Commercial

© Rand McNally
Source: EPA

AIR QUALITY

Most severe air quality index (AQI) value recorded-2007
- Over 200 (Very unhealthy)
- 151 to 200 (Unhealthy)
- 101 to 150 (Unhealthy for sensitive groups)
- 51 to 100 (Moderate)
- 50 and below (Good)
- Data not reported

© Rand McNally
Source: EPA

TOXIC CHEMICAL RELEASES

Toxic chemical releases
Metric tons - 2005
- 248,885
- 100,000
- 25,000
- Less than 2,500

- Point source air emissions
- On-site releases and impoundments
- Off-site releases and transfers

© Rand McNally
Source: U.S. Census Bureau

SUPERFUND SITES

- National Priority List (NPL) Superfund sites

© Rand McNally
Source: EPA

A-101914-1

HAZARDOUS WASTE

Hazardous waste generated or received from out of state
Metric tons - 2005
- 14,356,000
- 5,000,000
- 1,000,000
- Less than 100,000

Portion shipped out of state

© Rand McNally
Source: U.S. Census Bureau

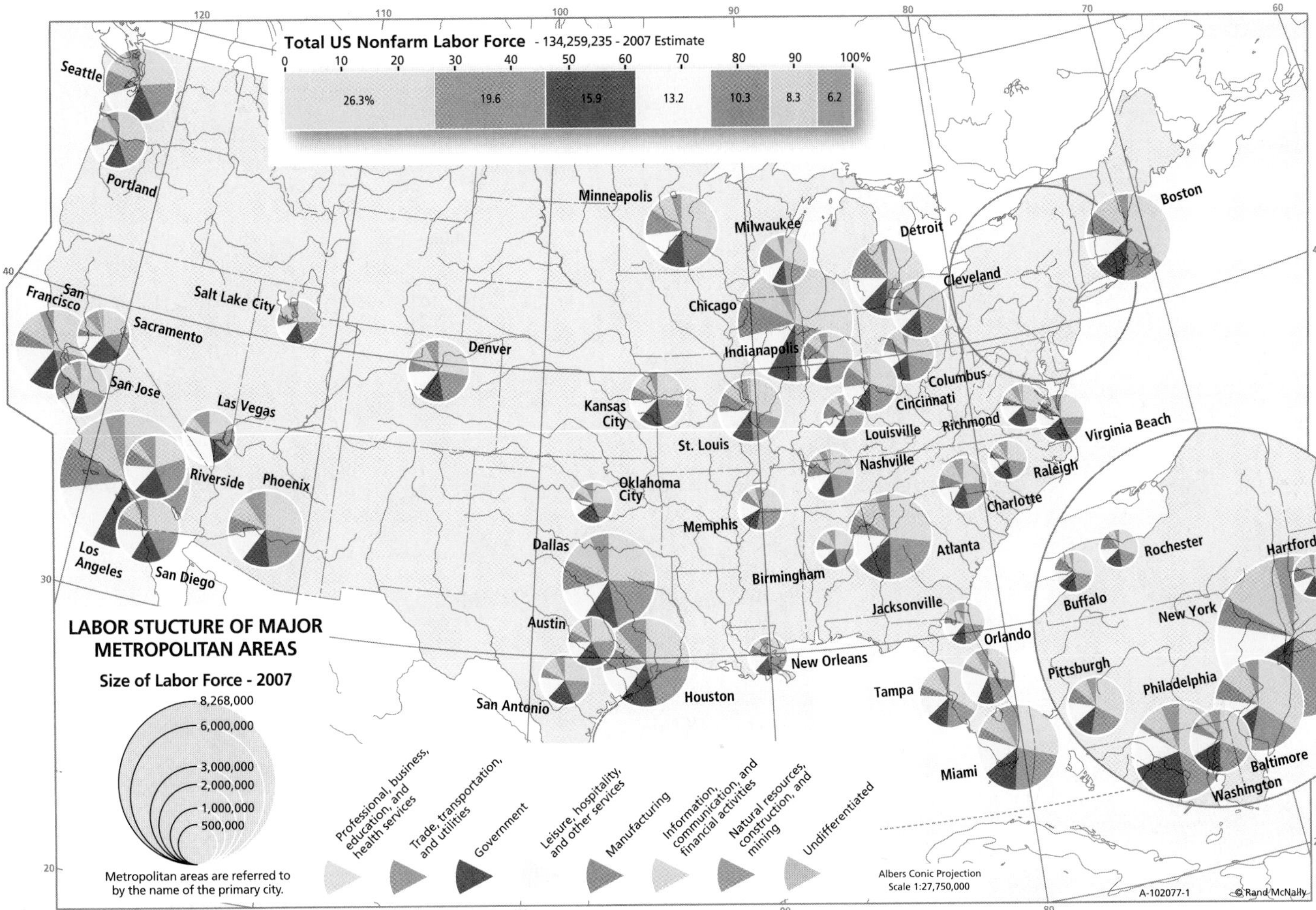

Total US Nonfarm Labor Force - 134,259,235 - 2007 Estimate

0	10	20	30	40	50	60	70	80	90	100%

26.3%	19.6	15.9	13.2	10.3	8.3	6.2

Seattle
Portland
San Francisco
Sacramento
Salt Lake City
San Jose
Las Vegas
Riverside
Phoenix
Los Angeles
San Diego
Denver
Minneapolis
Milwaukee
Chicago
Indianapolis
Kansas City
St. Louis
Oklahoma City
Dallas
Memphis
Austin
San Antonio
Houston
New Orleans
Detroit
Cleveland
Columbus
Cincinnati
Louisville
Richmond
Nashville
Charlotte
Atlanta
Birmingham
Jacksonville
Orlando
Tampa
Miami
Boston
Virginia Beach
Raleigh
Buffalo
Rochester
Hartford
New York
Providence
Pittsburgh
Philadelphia
Baltimore
Washington

LABOR STUCTURE OF MAJOR METROPOLITAN AREAS

Size of Labor Force - 2007

8,268,000
6,000,000
3,000,000
2,000,000
1,000,000
500,000

Metropolitan areas are referred to by the name of the primary city.

Professional, business, education, and health services
Trade, transportation, and utilities
Government
Leisure, hospitality, and other services
Manufacturing
Information, communication, and financial activities
Natural resources, construction, and mining
Undifferentiated

Albers Conic Projection
Scale 1:27,750,000

A-102077-1   © Rand McNally

Source: Bureau of Labor Statistics

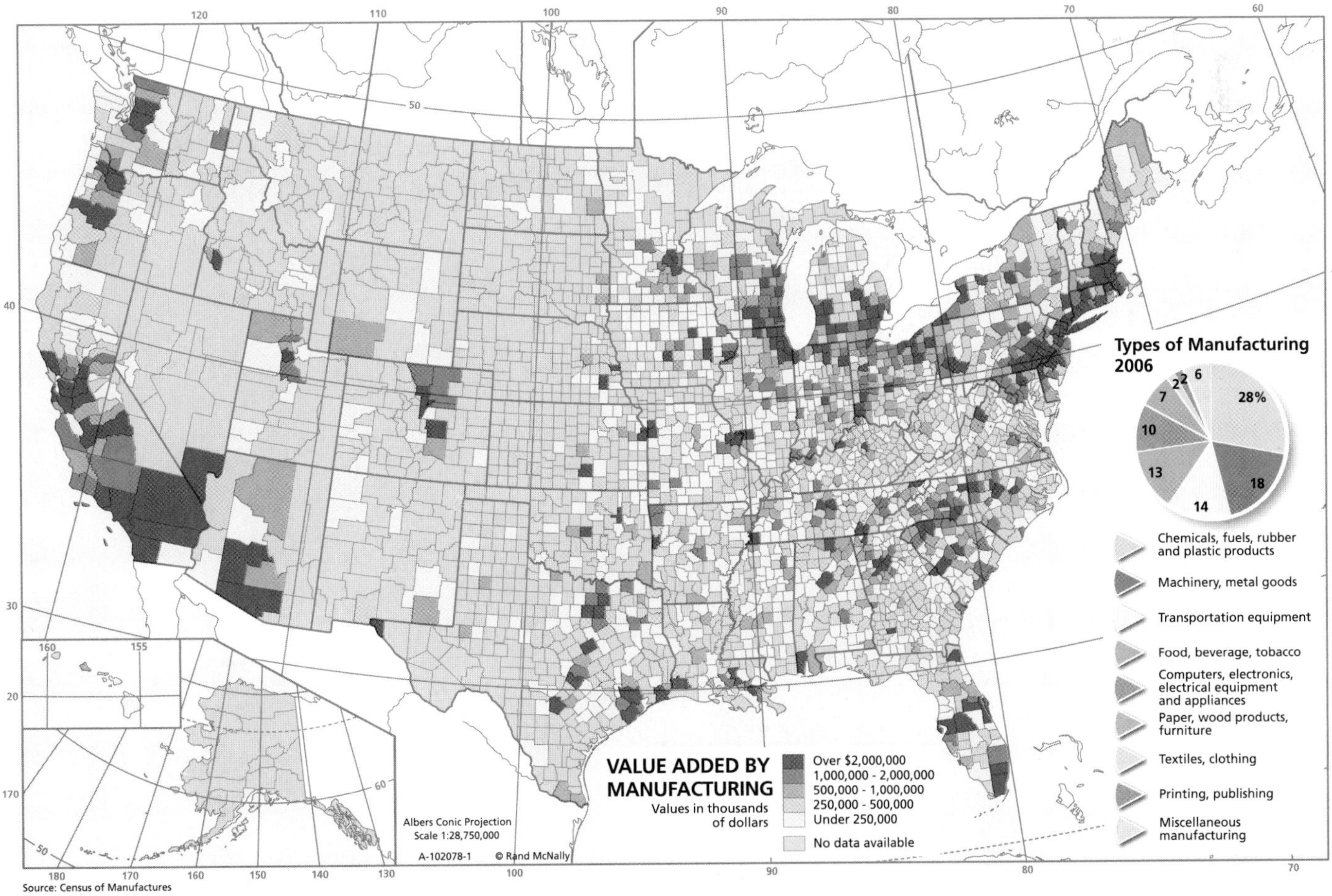

Types of Manufacturing 2006

2 2 6
7
28%
10
13
18
14

Chemicals, fuels, rubber and plastic products
Machinery, metal goods
Transportation equipment
Food, beverage, tobacco
Computers, electronics, electrical equipment and appliances
Paper, wood products, furniture
Textiles, clothing
Printing, publishing
Miscellaneous manufacturing

VALUE ADDED BY MANUFACTURING

Values in thousands of dollars

Over $2,000,000
1,000,000 - 2,000,000
500,000 - 1,000,000
250,000 - 500,000
Under 250,000
No data available

Albers Conic Projection
Scale 1:28,750,000

A-102078-1   © Rand McNally

Source: Census of Manufactures

Lambert Azimuthal Equal Area Projection
Scale 1:12,000,000
One inch to 190 miles
One cm to 120 km

© Rand McNally
A-101613-1

0   60   120   180   240   300   360 Miles
0   60   120 180 240 300 360 420 480 540 600 Kilometers

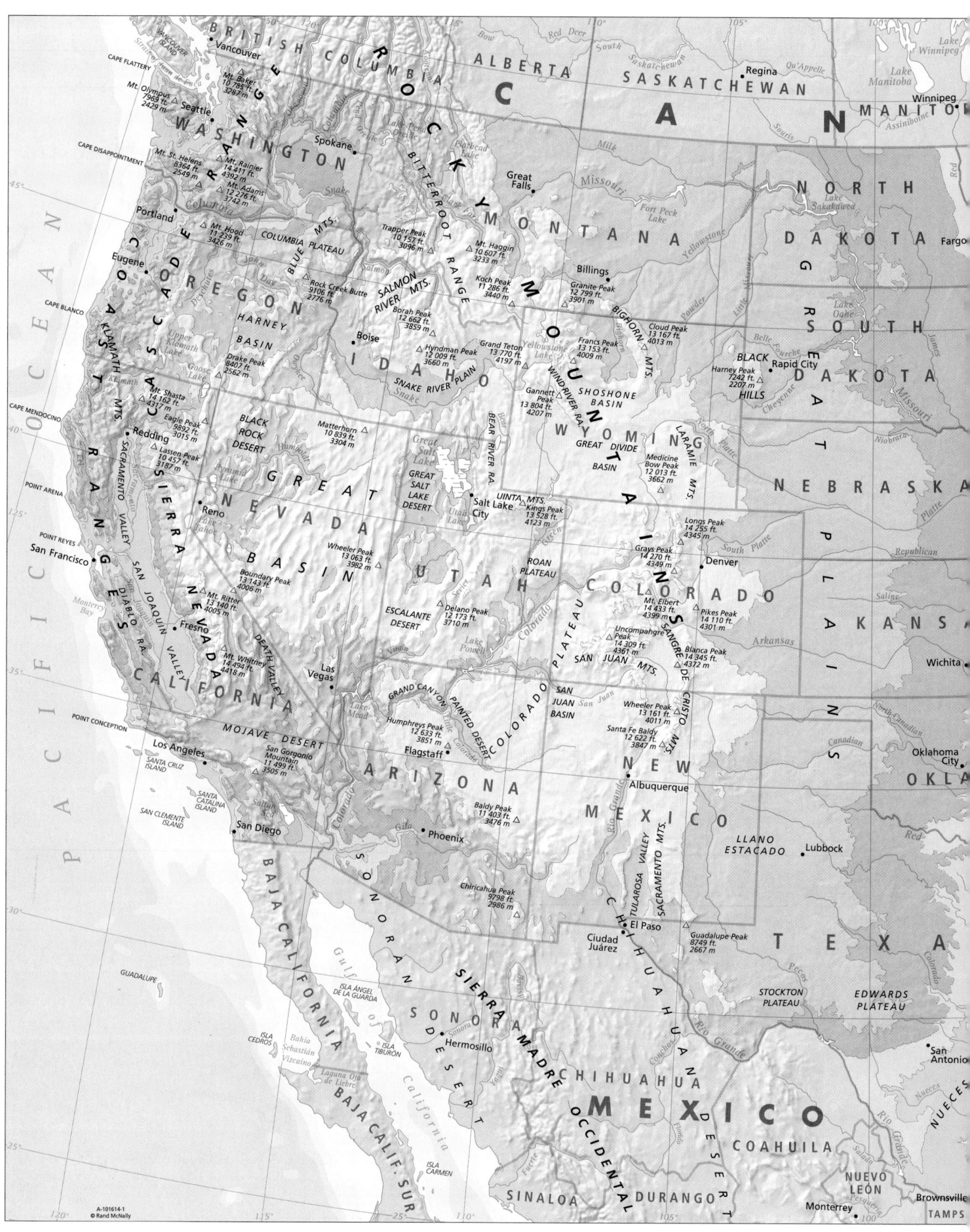

Lambert Azimuthal Equal Area Projection
Scale 1:12,000,000
One inch to 190 miles
One cm to 120 km

0   60   120   180   240   300   360 Miles
0 60 120 180 240 300 360 420 480 540 600 Kilometers

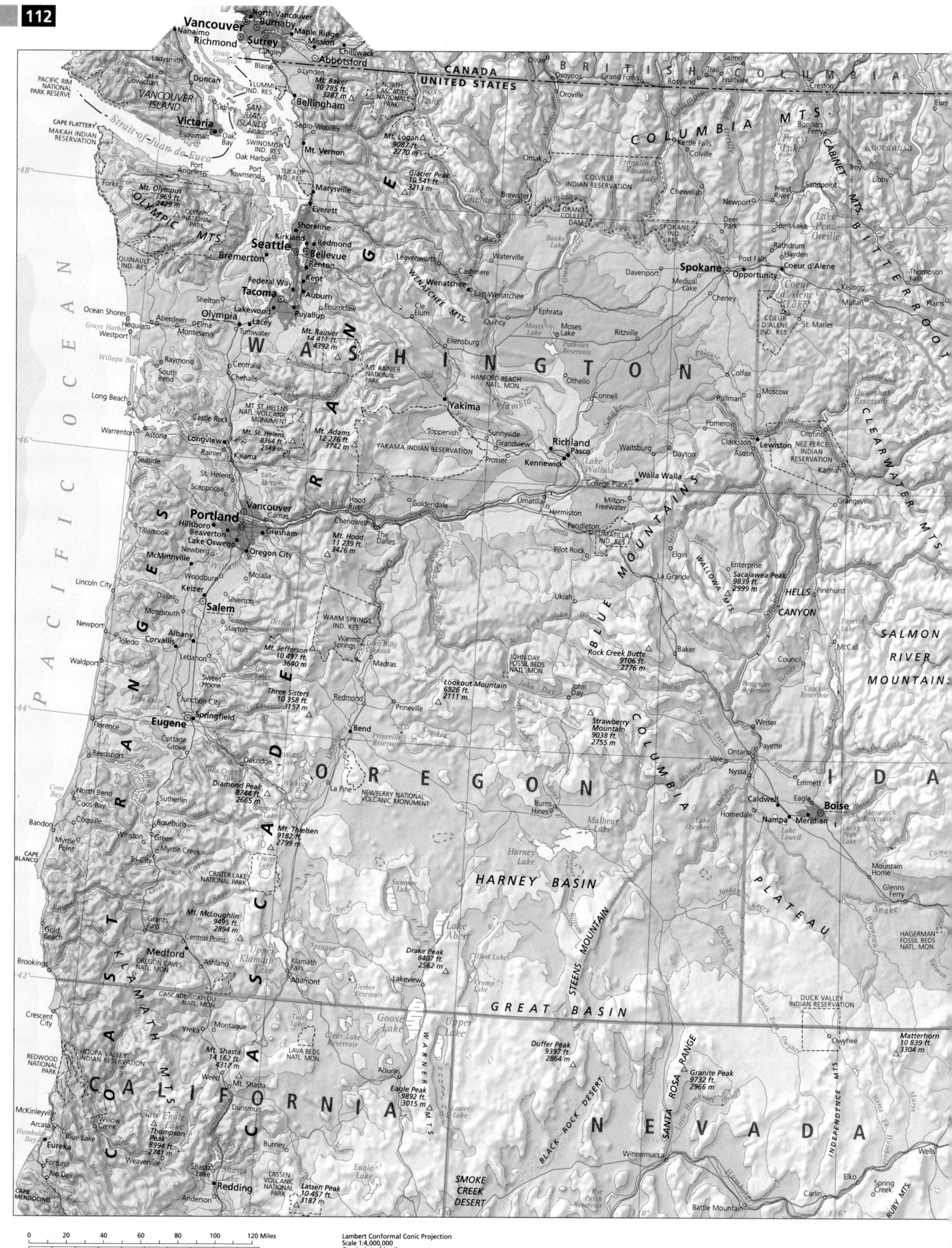

0 20 40 60 80 100 120 Miles

0 20 40 60 80 100 120 140 160 180 200 Kilometers

Lambert Conformal Conic Projection
Scale 1:4,000,000
One inch to 64 miles
One cm to 40 km

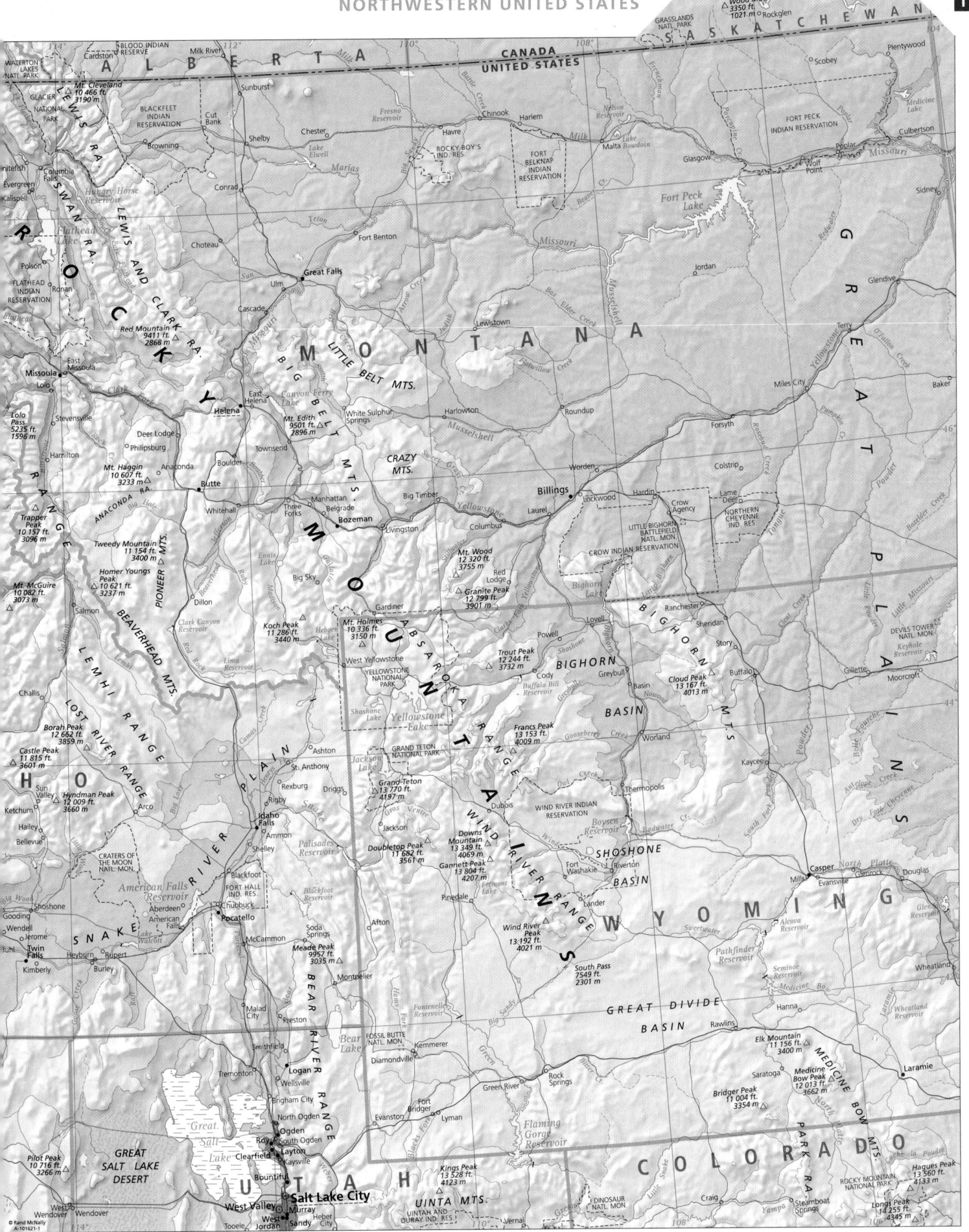

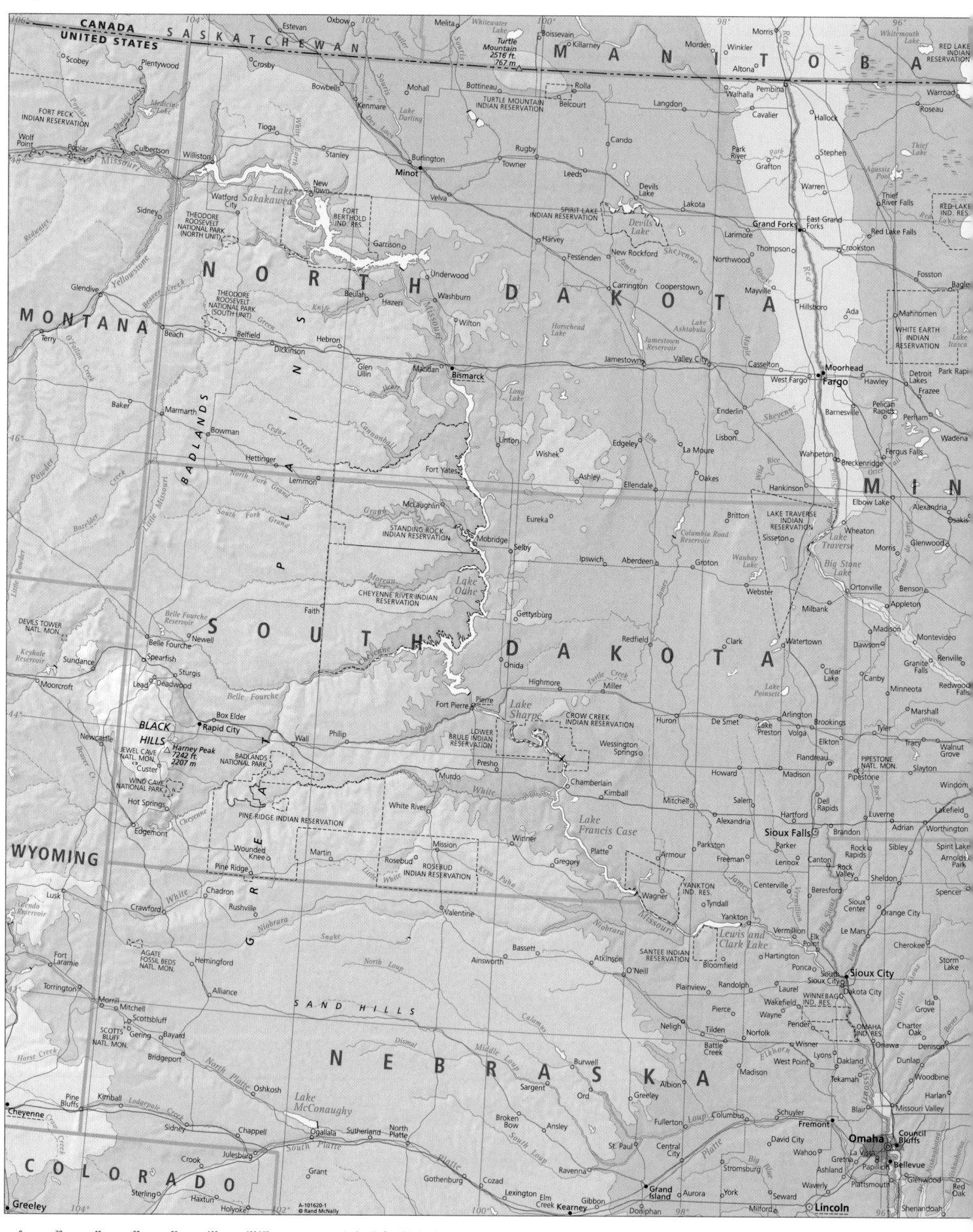

0 20 40 60 80 100 120 Miles

0 20 40 60 80 100 120 140 160 180 200 Kilometers

A-101620-1
© Rand McNally

Lambert Conformal Conic Projection
Scale 1:4,000,000
One inch to 64 miles
One cm to 40 km

0   20   40   60   80   100   120 Miles
0   20   40   60   80   100   120   140   160   180   200 Kilometers

Lambert Conformal Conic Projection
Scale 1:4,000,000
One inch to 64 miles
One cm to 40 km

Inset map a
Lambert Conformal Conic Projection
Scale 1:6,000,000
One inch to 96 miles
One cm to 60 km

Inset map a
Lambert Conformal Conic Projection
Scale 1:1,000,000
One inch to 16 miles
One cm to 10 km

Lambert Conformal Conic Projection
Scale 1:4,000,000
One inch to 64 miles
One cm to 40 km

0   20   40   60   80   100   120 Miles
0 20 40 60 80 100 120 140 160 180 200 Kilometers

Lambert Conformal Conic Projection
Scale 1:4,000,000
One inch to 64 miles
One cm to 40 km

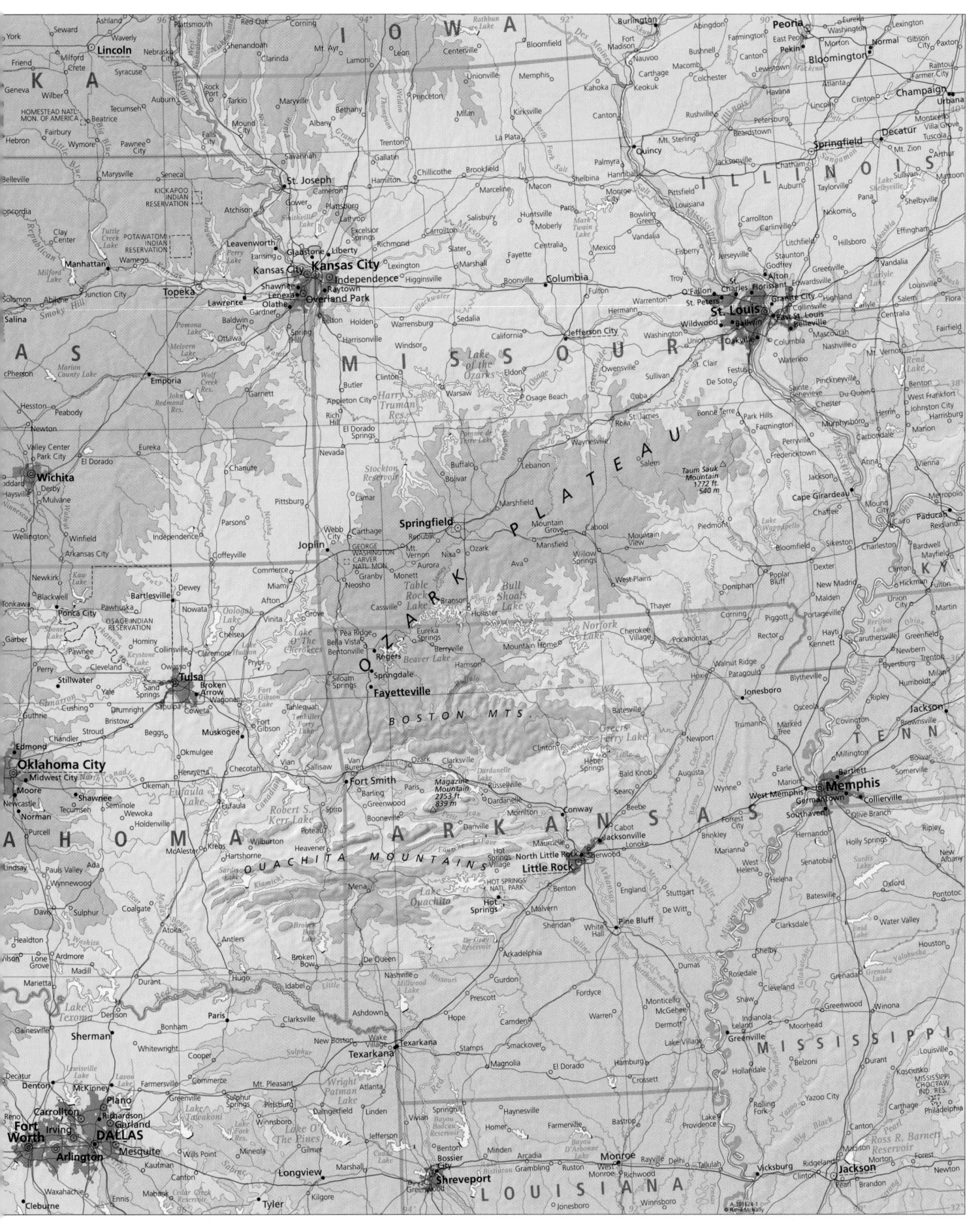

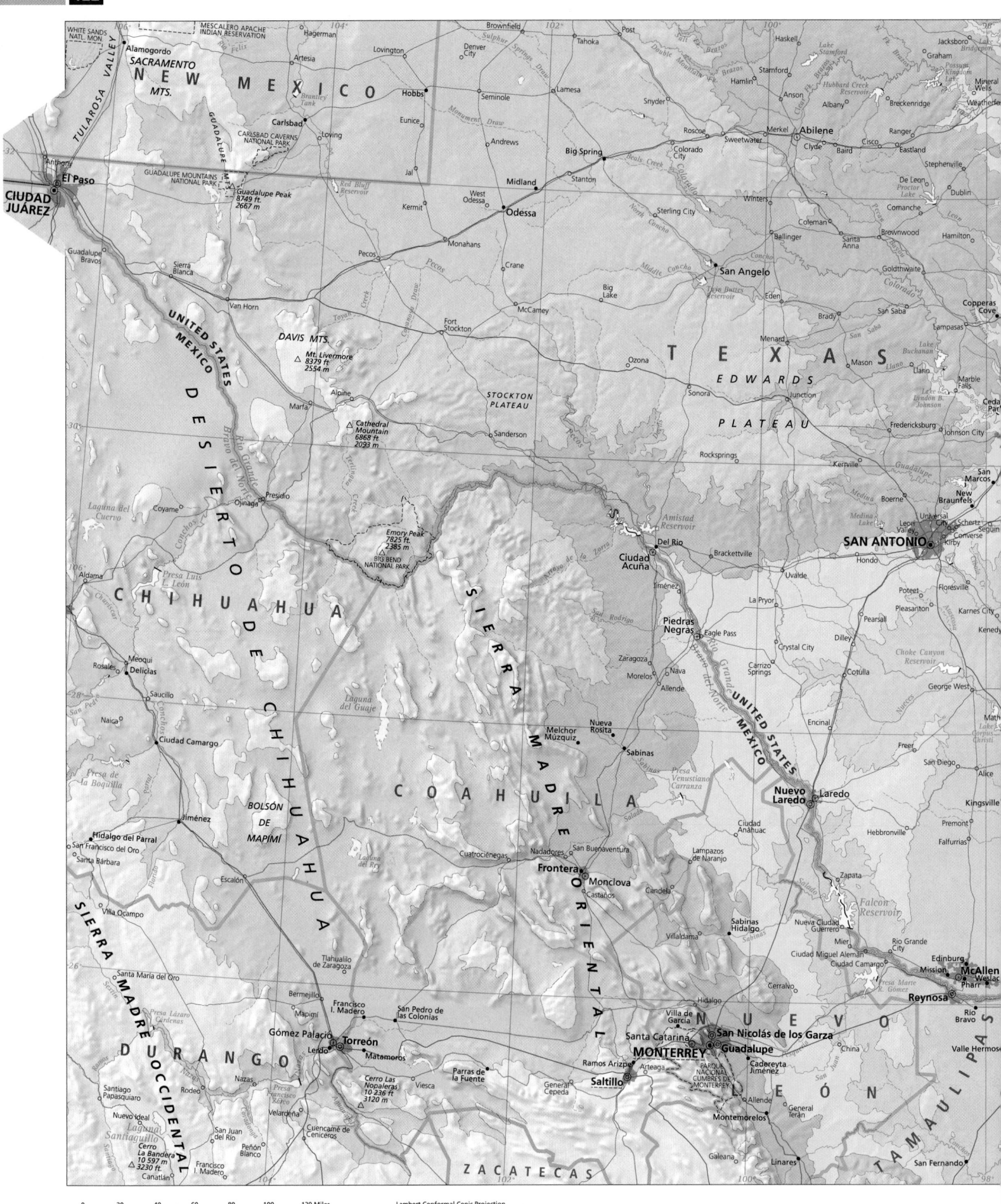

Lambert Conformal Conic Projection
Scale 1:4,000,000
One inch to 64 miles
One cm to 40 km

Inset map a
Lambert Conformal Conic Projection
Scale 1:1,000,000
One inch to 16 miles
One cm to 10 km

0   20   40   60   80   100   120 Miles
0   20   40   60   80   100   120   140   160   180   200 Kilometers

Lambert Conformal Conic Projection
Scale 1:4,000,000
One inch to 64 miles
One cm to 40 km

Inset map a
Lambert Conformal Conic Projection
Scale 1:4,000,000
One inch to 64 miles
One cm to 40 km

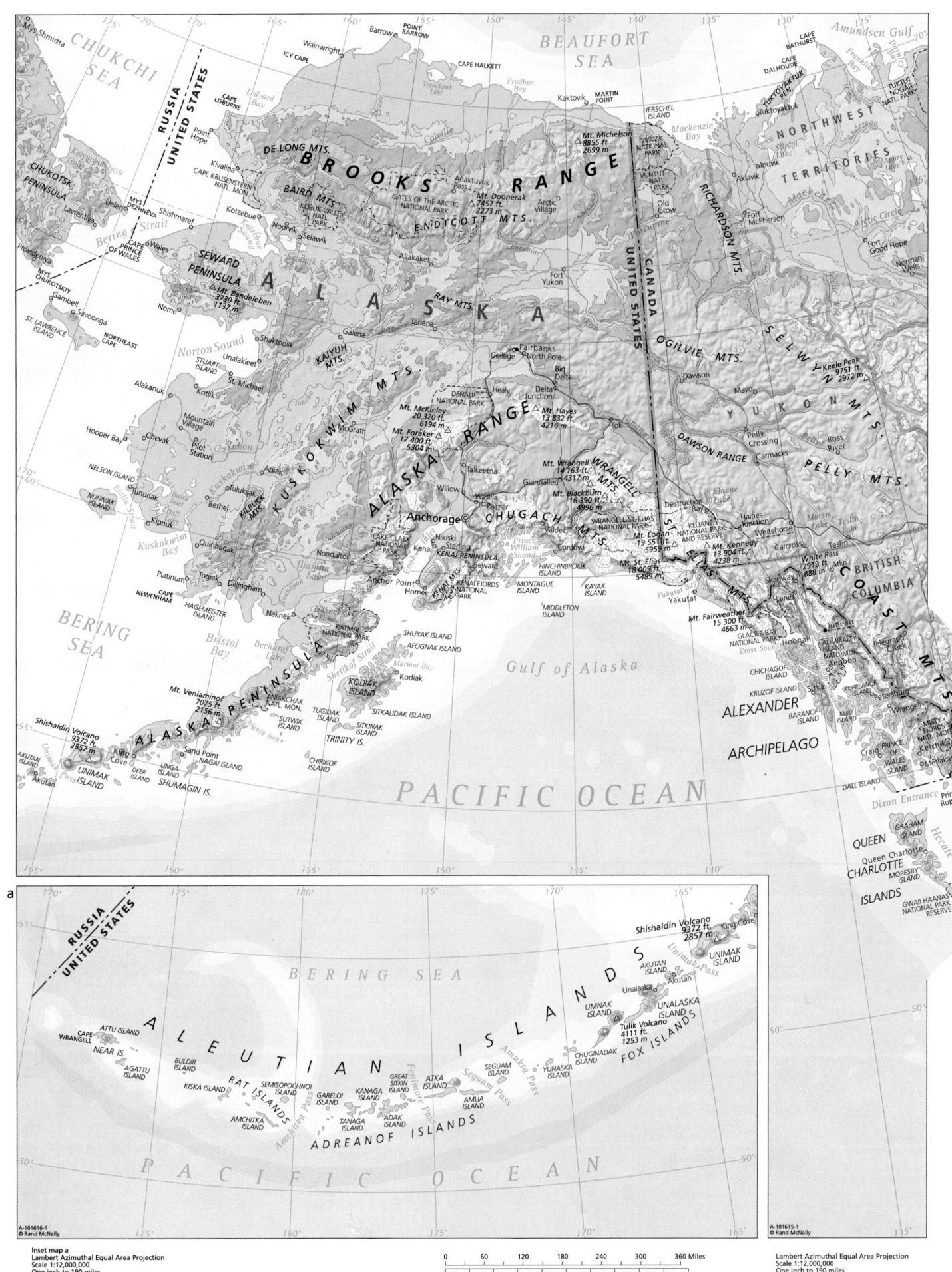

Inset map a
Lambert Azimuthal Equal Area Projection
Scale 1:12,000,000
One inch to 190 miles
One cm to 120 km

	0	60	120	180	240	300	360 Miles
0	60	120	180	240	360	420	480	540	600 Kilometers

Lambert Azimuthal Equal Area Projection
Scale 1:12,000,000
One inch to 190 miles
One cm to 120 km

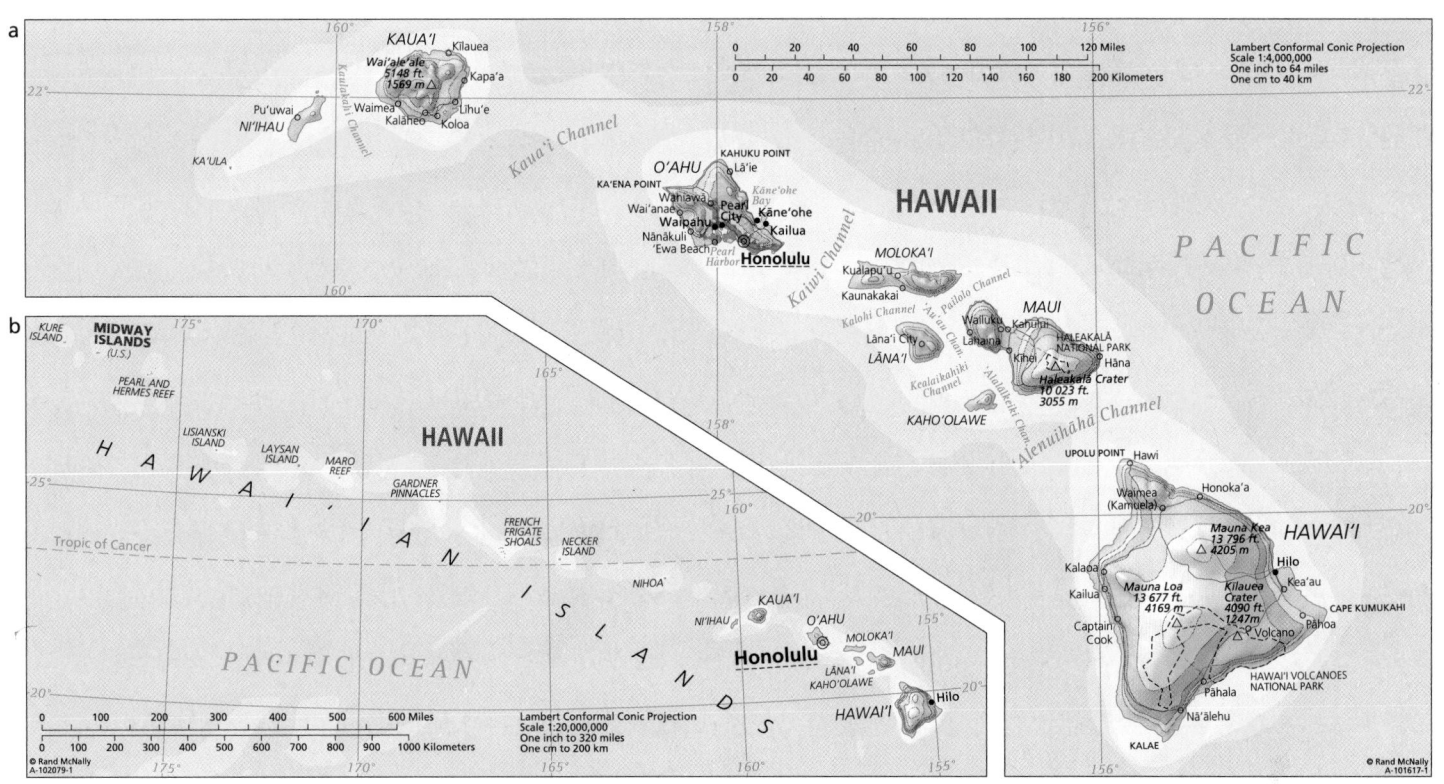

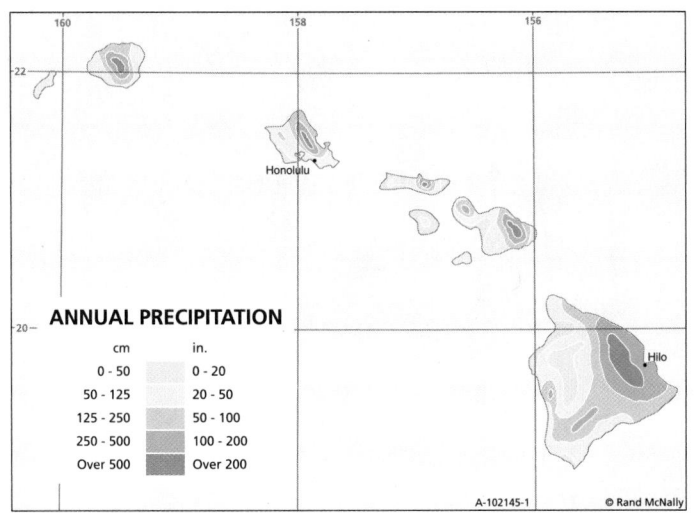

ANNUAL PRECIPITATION

cm	in.
0 - 50	0 - 20
50 - 125	20 - 50
125 - 250	50 - 100
250 - 500	100 - 200
Over 500	Over 200

A-102145-1   © Rand McNally

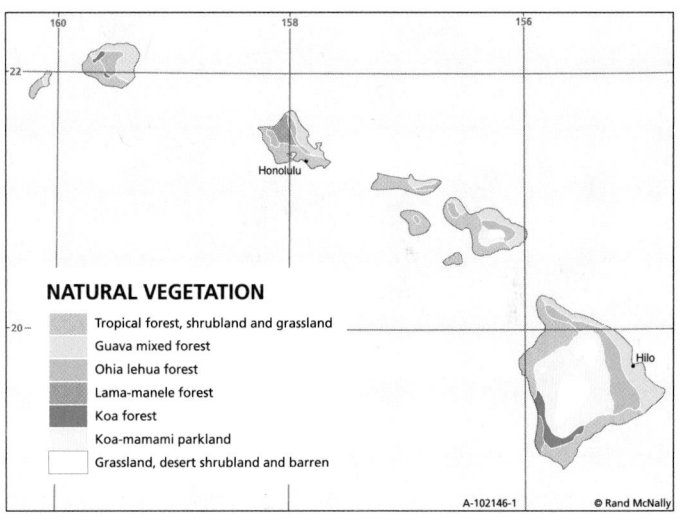

NATURAL VEGETATION

- Tropical forest, shrubland and grassland
- Guava mixed forest
- Ohia lehua forest
- Lama-manele forest
- Koa forest
- Koa-mamami parkland
- Grassland, desert shrubland and barren

A-102146-1   © Rand McNally

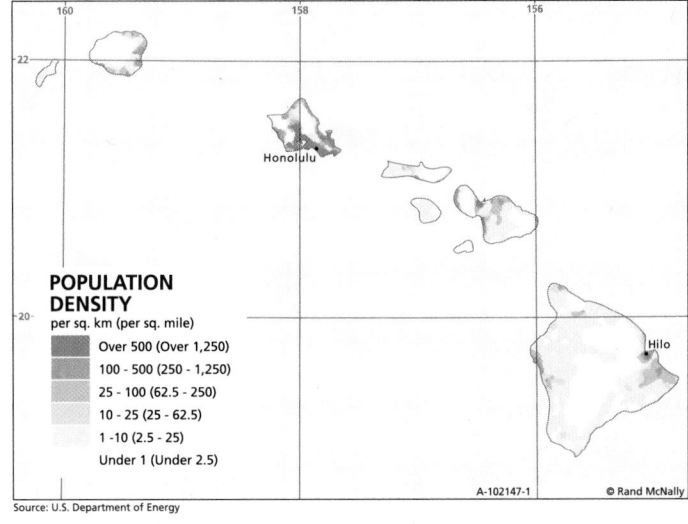

POPULATION DENSITY

per sq. km (per sq. mile)

- Over 500 (Over 1,250)
- 100 - 500 (250 - 1,250)
- 25 - 100 (62.5 - 250)
- 10 - 25 (25 - 62.5)
- 1 -10 (2.5 - 25)
- Under 1 (Under 2.5)

Source: U.S. Department of Energy

A-102147-1   © Rand McNally

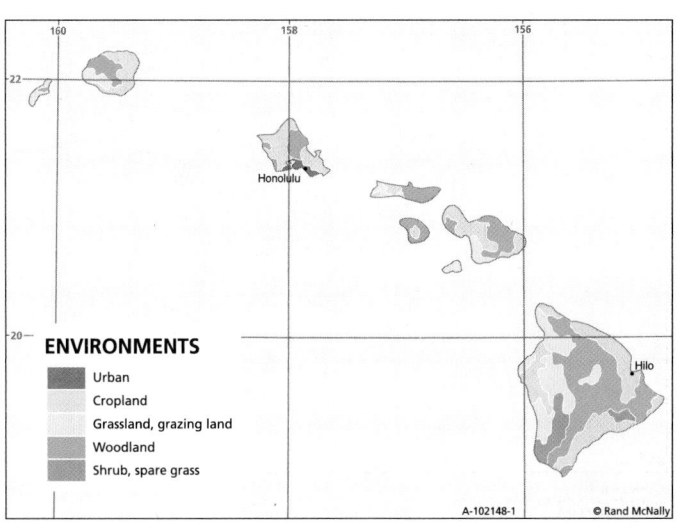

ENVIRONMENTS

- Urban
- Cropland
- Grassland, grazing land
- Woodland
- Shrub, spare grass

A-102148-1   © Rand McNally

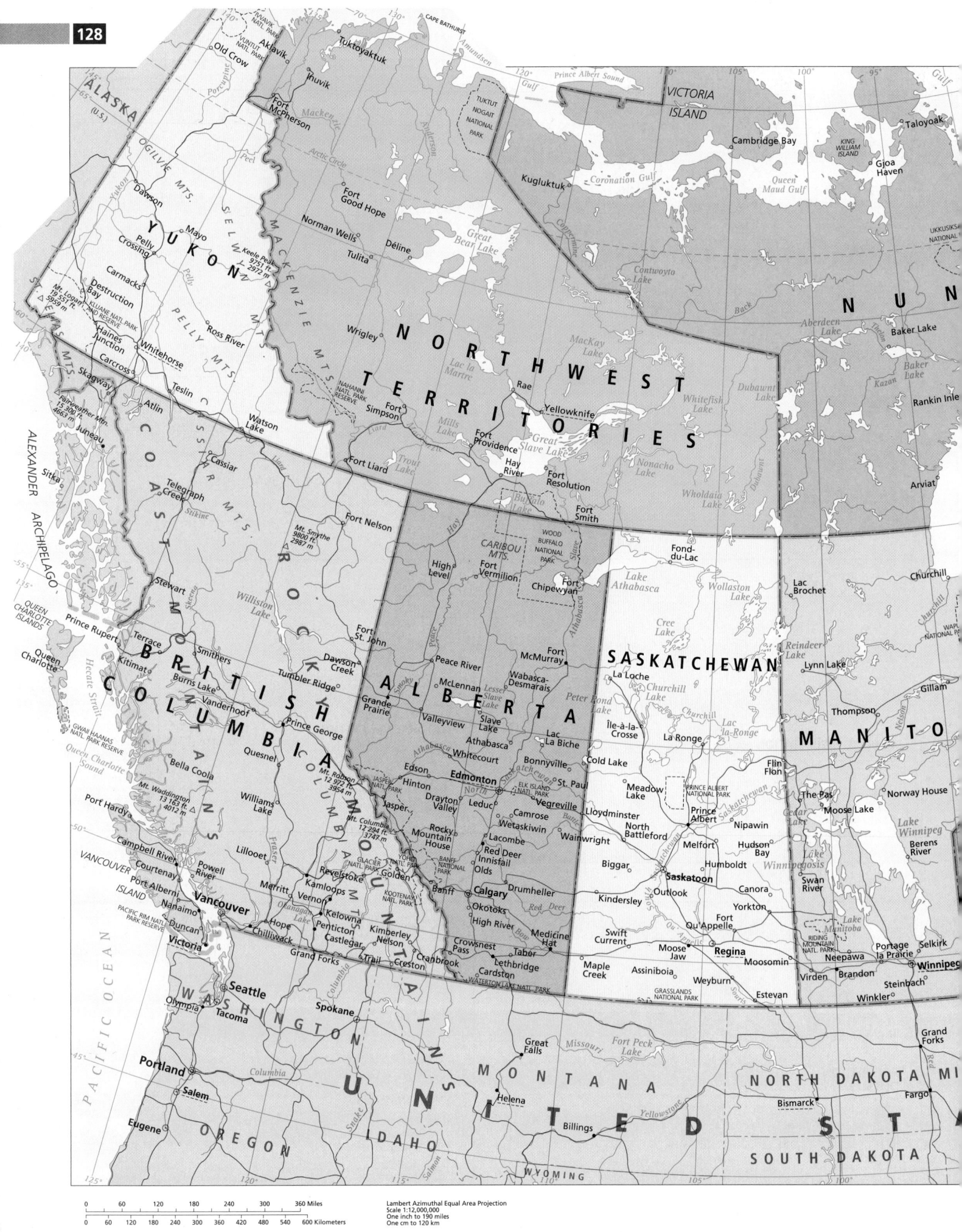

0   60   120   180   240   300   360 Miles

0   60 120 180 240 300 360 420 480 540 600 Kilometers

Lambert Azimuthal Equal Area Projection
Scale 1:12,000,000
One inch to 190 miles
One cm to 120 km

a

Saint-Augustin
St. Anthony
QUÉBEC
NEWFOUNDLAND
AND LABRADOR
LABRADOR SEA
CAPE BAULD

GROS MORNE
NATL. PARK
Gulf of St. Lawrence
Springdale
Corner Brook
Deer Lake
Bishop's Falls
Gander
Bonavista Bay
Bonavista
Grand Falls-Windsor
Stephenville
NEWFOUNDLAND
TERRA NOVA NATL. PARK
Notre Dame Bay
Trinity Bay
Carbonear
Channel-Port aux Basques
CAPE RAY
Cabot Strait
Grand Bank
Placentia Bay
St. John's
CAPE RACE
CAPE BRETON HIGHLANDS NATL. PARK
ST. PIERRE & MIQUELON (Fr.)
NOVA SCOTIA
Glace Bay
Sydney
ATLANTIC OCEAN
A-101659-1
© Rand McNally

Igloolik
NETTILLING LAKE
AUYUITTUQ NATL. PARK
Pangnirtung
ANGIJAK ISLAND
Repulse Bay
CAPE DORCHESTER
PRINCE CHARLES ISLAND
AIR FORCE ISLAND
BAFFIN ISLAND
AMADJUAK LAKE
Cumberland Sound
LABRADOR SEA
Arctic Circle
Cape Dorset
Igaluit
Frobisher Bay
RESOLUTION ISLAND
FOXE CHANNEL
CAPE DORSET
NUNAVUT
SOUTHAMPTON ISLAND
Coral Harbour
Chesterfield Inlet
COATS ISLAND
MANSEL ISLAND
Ivujivik
Salluit
AKPATOK ISLAND
Kangiqsujuaq
PÉNINSULE
Kangirsuk
Ungava Bay
Hudson Strait
Kangiqsualujjuaq
Mt. Caubvick Mont d'Iberville 5420 ft. 1652 m
Hebron
Povungnituk
Lac Couture
D'UNGAVA
Feuilles
Kuujjuaq
Nain
OTTAWA ISLANDS
Hopedale
CAPE HARRISON
Inukjuak
Hudson Bay
Lac Minto
NEWFOUNDLAND AND LABRADOR
Cartwright
Battle Harbour
BELCHER ISLANDS
Lac Bienville
Smallwood Reservoir
Schefferville
Happy Valley-Goose Bay
St. Anthony
Whapmagoostui
Réservoir La Grande Deux
Lac Caniapiscau
Churchill
Saint-Augustin
Springdale
GROS MORNE NATIONAL PARK
NEWFOUNDLAND
Deer Lake
York Factory
Fort Severn
Chisasibi
Réservoir Eastmain-Opinaca
Labrador City
Corner Brook
Stephenville
James Bay
Ekwan
AKIMISKI
Eastmain
Eastmain
Havre-Saint-Pierre
CAPE RAY
Channel-Port aux Basques
Cabot Strait
Missinaibi
Waskaganish
Lac Mistassini
QUÉBEC
Sept-Îles
ÎLE D'ANTICOSTI
PARC NATL. FORILLON
Gulf of St. Lawrence
Attawapiskat
Fort Albany
Chibougamau
Port-Cartier
Réservoir Manicouagan
Gaspé
ÎLES DE LA MADELEINE
CAPE BRETON HIGHLANDS NATL. PARK
Glace Bay
Moosonee
Baie-Comeau
Matane
Mont-Joli
Bonaventure
PRINCE EDWARD ISLAND
Sydney
ONTARIO
Harricana
Matagami
Réservoir Gouin
Rimouski
Campbellton
Bathurst
Miramichi
Summerside
Charlottetown
New Glasgow
Red Lake
Abitibi
La Sarre
Amos
Senneterre
Dolbeau-Mistassini
Alma
Rivière-du-Loup
Saguenay
Edmundston
KOUCHIBOUGUAC NATL. PARK
Moncton
Amherst
Truro
NOVA SCOTIA
Dartmouth
Kapuskasing
Lake Abitibi
Saint-Félicien
Roberval
La Malbaie
Baie-Saint-Paul
NEW BRUNSWICK
Fredericton
PRINCE EDWARD ISLAND NATL. PARK
Halifax
Armstrong
Hearst
Iroquois Falls
Val-d'Or
Rouyn-Noranda
La Tuque
Montmagny
Woodstock
Oromocto
FUNDY NATL. PARK
Bridgewater
Geraldton
Timmins
Kirkland Lake
Réservoir Gouin
Québec
Lévis
Saint John
KEJIMKUJIK NATL. PARK
Shelburne
Sioux Lookout
Nipigon
Marathon
Chapleau
New Liskeard
PARC NATIONAL DE LA MAURICIE
Shawinigan
Trois-Rivières
Drummondville
Victoriaville
Sherbrooke
Granby
St. Stephen
Bay of Fundy
Yarmouth
CAPE SABLE
Kenora
Lake of the Woods
Dryden
Lac Seul
Lake Nipigon
PUKASKWA NATL. PARK
Wawa
Mattawa
Lake Nipissing
Hawkesbury
Laval
MONTRÉAL
Cornwall
MAINE
Augusta
Atikokan
Fort Frances
Thunder Bay
Sault Sainte Marie
Elliot Lake
Espanola
Sudbury
North Bay
Pembroke
Renfrew
Ottawa
Ogdensburg
Montpelier
Portland
Gulf of Maine
Rainy River
International Falls
Houghton
Blind River
Georgian Bay
Parry Sound
Smiths Falls
Brockville
VT.
N.H.
Duluth
MINNESOTA
MICHIGAN
Midland
Orillia
Peterborough
Kingston
Concord
Boston
MASS.
St. Paul
WISCONSIN
LAKE SUPERIOR
Owen Sound
Barrie
Oshawa
Belleville
LAKE ONTARIO
Rochester
Albany
Providence
R.I.
Minneapolis
Green Bay
LAKE HURON
TORONTO
Niagara Falls
Hartford
CONN.
ATLANTIC OCEAN
Goderich
Kitchener
Hamilton
St. Catharines
Buffalo
NEW YORK
Grand Rapids
LAKE MICHIGAN
Sarnia
London
LAKE ERIE
Erie
PENN.
N.J.
NEW YORK
Milwaukee
Lansing
Detroit
Windsor
Chatham
Cleveland
OHIO
Toledo

Inset map a
Lambert Azimuthal Equal Area Projection
Scale 1:12,000,000
One inch to 190 miles
One cm to 120 km

A-101658-1
© Rand McNally

| 0 | 60 | 120 | 180 | 240 | 300 | 360 Miles |

| 0 | 60 | 120 | 180 | 240 | 300 | 360 | 420 | 480 | 540 | 600 Kilometers |

Lambert Azimuthal Equal Area Projection
Scale 1:12,000,000
One inch to 190 miles
One cm to 120 km

a

QUÉBEC
LABRADOR
SEA
CAPE BAULD
NEWFOUNDLAND
AND LABRADOR
CAPE
ST. JOHN
BELL ISLAND
FOGO ISLAND
CAPE FREELS
Strait of Belle Isle
Gulf of St. Lawrence
CAP WHITTLE
LONG RANGE MTS.
Notre Dame Bay
Bonavista Bay
Corner Brook
Deer Lake
Grand Lake
Trinity Bay
NEWFOUNDLAND
St. George's Bay
St. John's
CAPE RAY
CAPE SPEAR
Cabot Strait
MIQUELON
Placentia Bay
CAPE RACE
ST. PIERRE & MIQUELON (Fr.)
Saint-Pierre
CAPE BRETON ISLAND
NOVA SCOTIA
ATLANTIC OCEAN

A-101661-1
© Rand McNally

Inset map a
Lambert Azimuthal Equal Area Projection
Scale 1:12,000,000
One inch to 190 miles
One cm to 120 km

A-101660-1
© Rand McNally

Inset map a
Lambert Conformal Conic Projection
Scale 1:1,000,000
One inch to 16 miles
One cm to 10 km

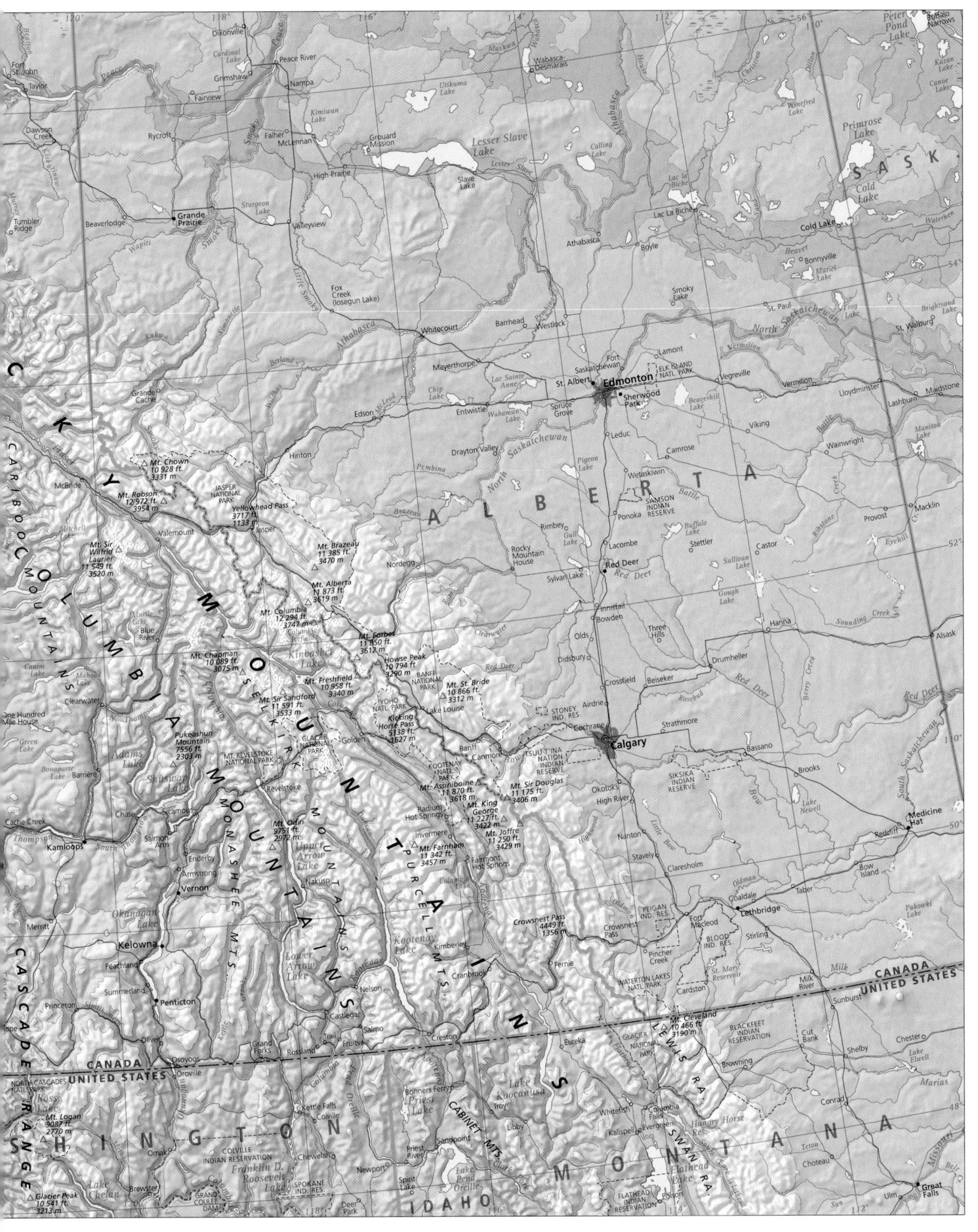

0   20   40   60   80   100   120 Miles
0 20 40 60 80 100 120 140 160 180 200 Kilometers

Lambert Conformal Conic Projection
Scale 1:4,000,000
One inch to 64 miles
One cm to 40 km

ALBERTA

SASKATCHEWAN

MANITOBA

MONTANA

NORTH DAKOTA

CANADA
UNITED STATES

Fort McMurray

Athabasca
Clearwater
Gordon Lake
La Loche
Lac La Loche
Turnor Lake
Winefred Lake
Careen Lake
Cree Lake
Black Birch Lake
Wasekamio Lake
Peter Pond Lake
Churchill Lake
Buffalo Narrows
Dillon
Churchill
Highrock Lake
Wathaman Lake
Reindeer Lake
Nokomis Lake
Goldsand Lake
Barrington Lake
Lynn Lake
South Indian Lake
Southern Indian Lake
Deception Lake
Macoun Lake
Kamuchawie Lake
Russell Lake
Granville Lake
Nelson House
Kazan Lake
Île-à-la-Crosse
Canoe Lake
Lac Île-à-la-Crosse
Pinehouse Lake
Foster
Black Bear Island Lake
Wintego Lake
Steephill Lake
Sisipuk Lake
Kississing Lake
Burntwood Lake
Wekusko Lake
Primrose Lake
Beauval
Lac la Plonge
Besnard Lake
Churchill
Pelican Narrows
Pelican Lake
Sherridon
Burntwood
Cold Lake
Keeley Lake
Doré Lake
La Ronge
Lac la Ronge
Egg Lake
Deschambault Lake
Wapawekka Lake
Big Sandy Lake
Suggi Lake
Namew Lake
Flin Flon
Athapapuskow
Cranberry Portage
Reed Lake
Cormorant Lake
Clearwater Lake
Bonnyville
St. Paul
Muriel Lake
Frog Lake
Green Lake
Meadow Lake
Sled Lake
Smoothstone Lake
Montreal Lake
Candle Lake
Torch
Choiceland
Mossy
Cumberland Lake
Cumberland House
The Pas
Denare Beach
Amisk Lake
North Moose Lake
South Moose Lake
Moose Lake
Cedar Lake
Grand Rapids
Vermilion
Lloydminster
St. Walburg
Brightsand Lake
Turtle Lake
Glaslyn
Spiritwood
Witchekan Lake
Big River
PRINCE ALBERT NATIONAL PARK
Delaronde Lake
White Fox
Nipawin
Carrot River
Wildcat Hill 2566 ft. 782 m
Red Deer Lake
Winnipegosis
Lashburn
Maidstone
Jackfish Lake
North Battleford
Redberry Lake
Shell Brook
Shellbrook
Duck Lake
Prince Albert
Saskatchewan
Birch Hills
Melfort
Tisdale
Hudson Bay
Swan Lake
Hart Mountain 2615 ft. 797 m
Pelican Rapids
Pelican Lake
Birch Island
Wainwright
Manitou Lake
Battle
Rosthorn
Wakaw
Basin Lake
Lenore Lake
Naicam
Kelvington
Swan River
Chitek Lake
Waterhen Lake
Provost
Macklin
Unity
Wilkie
Langham
Warman
Saskatoon
Bruno
Humboldt
Watson
Little Quill Lake
Wadena
Preeceville
Canora
Kamsack
DUCK MOUNTAIN
Baldy Mountain 2730 ft. 832 m
Ethelbert
Dauphin Lake
Kerrobert
Biggar
South Saskatchewan
Delisle
Lanigan
Big Quill Lake
Wynyard
Foam Lake
Yorkton
Roblin
Grandview
Dauphin
Sainte Rose du Lac
Kindersley
Alsask
Rosetown
Outlook
Kenaston
Watrous
TOUCHWOOD HILLS
Raymore
Ituna
Melville
Lake of the Prairies
Langenburg
Russell
RIDING MOUNTAIN NATL. PARK
RIDING MOUNTAIN
Erickson
Eston
GARDINER DAM
Davidson
Last Mountain Lake
Shoal Lake
Sounding Creek
Leader
Red Deer
Swift Current
QU'APPELLE DAM
Craik
Qu'Appelle
Regina Beach
Fort Qu'Appelle
Indian Head
Grenfell
Broadview
Wolseley
Esterhazy
Minnedosa
Neepawa
Lake Diefenbaker
Lumsden
Regina
Qu'Appelle
Rivers
Swift Current
Crane Lake
Gull Lake
Chaplin Lake
Moose Jaw
Old Wives Lake
Milestone
Yellow Grass
Weyburn
Kipling
Moosomin
Virden
Brandon
Carberry
Maple Creek
Gravelbourg
Assiniboia
Moose Mountain 2740 ft. 835 m
Stoughton
Carlyle
Wawota
Elkhorn
Souris
Shaunavon
Eastend
Pinto Butte 3442 ft. 1049 m
Wood Mountain 3350 ft. 1021 m
GRASSLANDS NATIONAL PARK
Rockglen
Radville
Midale
Lampman
Oxbow
Redvers
Melita
Minto
Boissevain
Killarney
Estevan
Whitewater Lake
Turtle Mountain 2516 ft. 767 m
TURTLE MOUNTAIN IND. RES.
Belcourt
Rolla
Bottineau
Chinook
Havre
Milk
Harlem
Scobey
Plentywood
Crosby
Kenmare
Mohall

Rand McNally A-101664-1

0 20 40 60 80 100 120 Miles
0 20 40 60 80 100 120 140 160 180 200 Kilometers

Lambert Conformal Conic Projection
Scale 1:4,000,000
One inch to 64 miles
One cm to 40 km

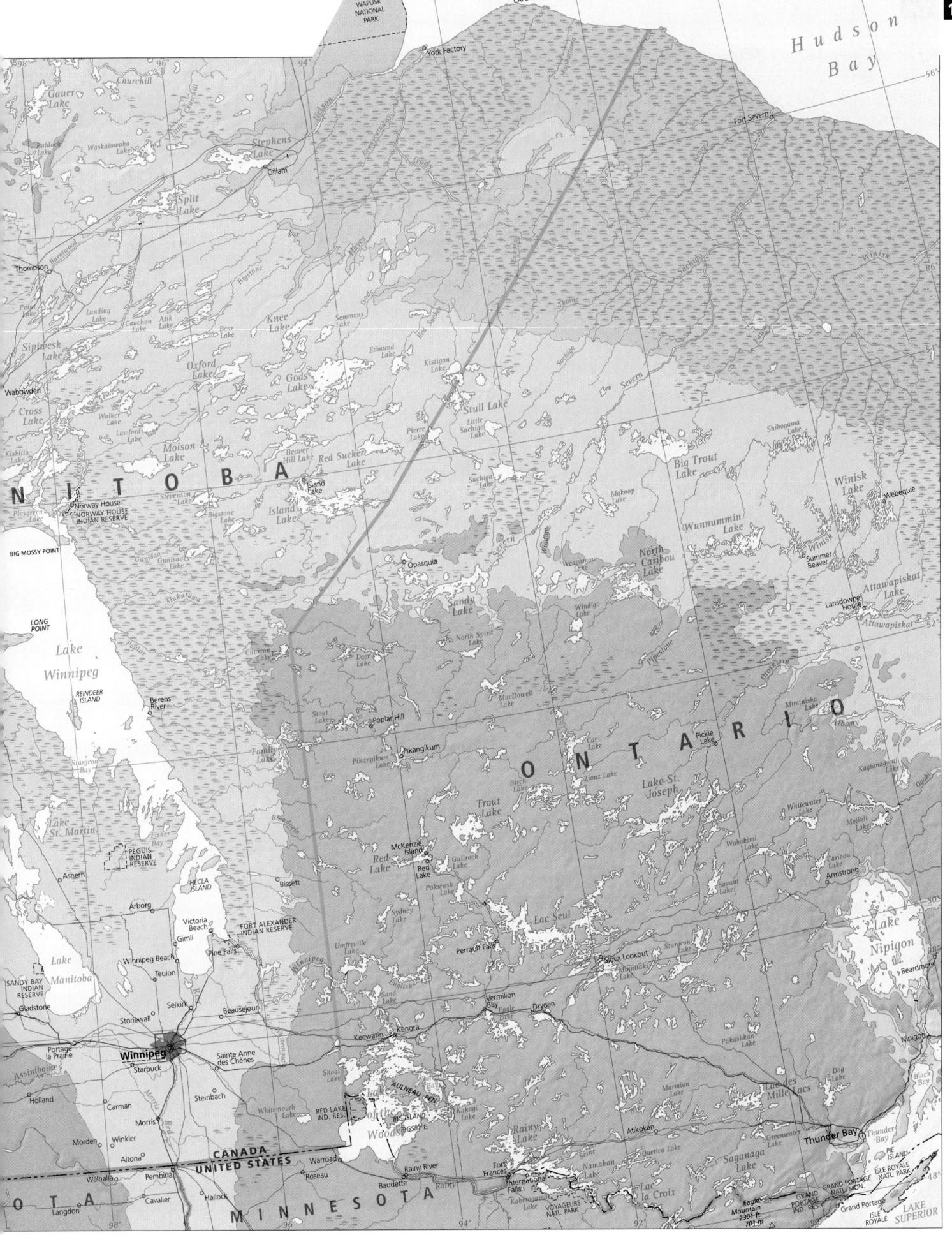

Hudson Bay

CAPE TATNAM

WAPUSK NATIONAL PARK

York Factory

Fort Severn

Churchill

Gauer Lake

Baldock Lake

Waskaiowaka Lake

Stephens Lake

Gillam

Split Lake

Thompson

Landing Lake

Pain Lake

Atik Lake

Cauchon Lake

Sipiwesk Lake

Knee Lake

Semmens Lake

Oxford Lake

Edmund Lake

Kistigan Lake

Waboiyden

Gods Lake

Cross Lake

Walker Lake

Lawford Lake

Stull Lake

Big Trout Lake

Kiskitto Lake

Molson Lake

Beaver Hill Lake

Red Sucker Lake

Pierce Lake

Little Sachigo Lake

Sachigo Lake

Shibogama Lake

M A N I T O B A

Stevenson Lake

Island Lake

Winisk Lake

Webequie

Norway House

NORWAY HOUSE INDIAN RESERVE

Bigstone Lake

Island Lake

Sachigo

Makoop Lake

Wunnummin Lake

Playgreen Lake

BIG MOSSY POINT

Gunisao Lake

Opasquia

Sandy Lake

Weagamow Lake

North Caribou Lake

Windigo Lake

Lansdowne House

Attawapiskat Lake

Mukutawa

Attawapiskat

LONG POINT

Lake Winnipeg

Chixxon Lake

Deer Lake

North Spirit Lake

Pipestone

Summer Beaver

REINDEER ISLAND

Poplar

Sioux Lookout

Berens River

Family Lake

Stout Lake

Poplar Hill

MacDowell Lake

Miminiska Lake

Oskikin

Albany

Sturgeon Bay

Pikangikum Lake

Pikangikum

O N T A R I O

Cat Lake

Pickle Lake

Kaginagami Lake

Lake St. Martin

Fisher Bay

Bloodvein

Birch Lake

Zionz Lake

Lake St. Joseph

Whitewater Lake

Mojikit Lake

Ashern

PEGUIS INDIAN RESERVE

Trout Lake

Wabakimi Lake

Caribou Lake

Arborg

Bissett

McKenzie Island

Gullrock Lake

Armstrong

Victoria Beach

Red Lake

Red Lake

Pakwash Lake

Savant Lake

Lake Nipigon

Gimli

FORT ALEXANDER INDIAN RESERVE

Sydney Lake

Lac Seul

Sturgeon Lake

Winnipeg Beach

Pine Falls

Umfreville Lake

Perrault Falls

Beardmore

Teulon

Winnipeg

Minnitaki Lake

Lake Manitoba

English

Sand Lake

Vermilion Bay

Dryden

SANDY BAY INDIAN RESERVE

Selkirk

Beausejour

Eagle Lake

Keewatin

Kenora

Nipigon

Gladstone

Stonewall

Pakashkan Lake

Black Bay

Portage la Prairie

Winnipeg

Sainte Anne des Chênes

Shoal Lake

Dog Lake

Starbuck

Assiniboine

Holland

Carman

Steinbach

Whitemouth Lake

RED LAKE IND. RES.

AULNEAU PEN.

BIG ISLAND

BIGSBY I.

Kakagi Lake

Marmion Lake

Lac des Mille Lacs

Thunder Bay

Thunder Bay

Morris

Morden

Winkler

CANADA

UNITED STATES

Warroad

Roseau

Rainy Lake

Atikokan

Quetico Prov. Park

Greenwater Lake

PIE ISLAND

Walhalla

Pembina

Roseau

Rainy River

Fort Frances

International Falls

Saganaga Lake

GRAND PORTAGE IND. RES.

GRAND PORTAGE NATL. MON.

ISLE ROYALE NATL. PARK

Langdon

Cavalier

Hallock

M I N N E S O T A

Baudette

Namakan Lake

Lac la Croix

Kabetogama

VOYAGEURS NATL. PARK

Eagle Mountain 2301 ft 701 m

Grand Portage

ISLE ROYALE

LAKE SUPERIOR

Assiniboine

Altona

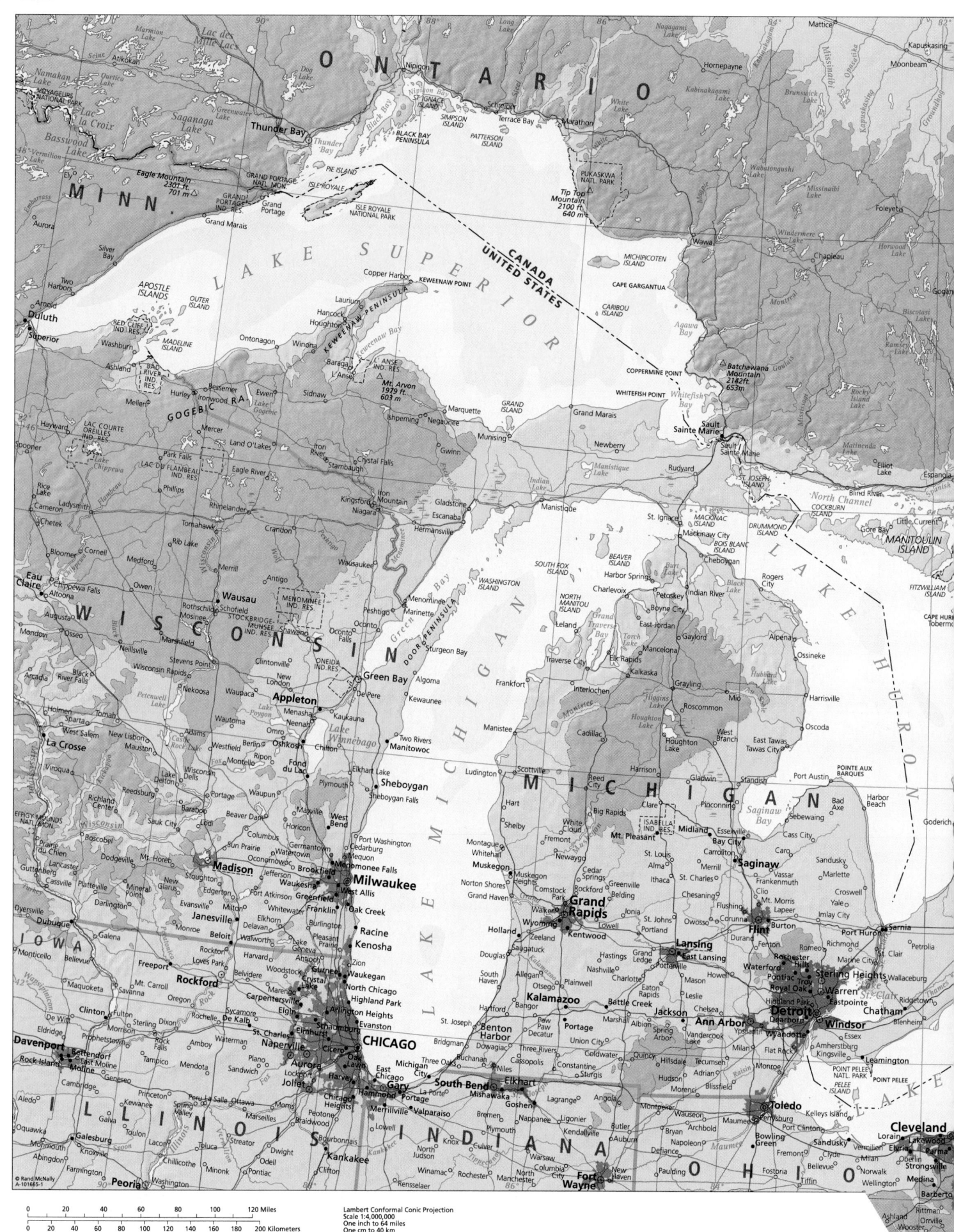

0 20 40 60 80 100 120 Miles
0 20 40 60 80 100 120 140 160 180 200 Kilometers

Lambert Conformal Conic Projection
Scale 1:4,000,000
One inch to 64 miles
One cm to 40 km

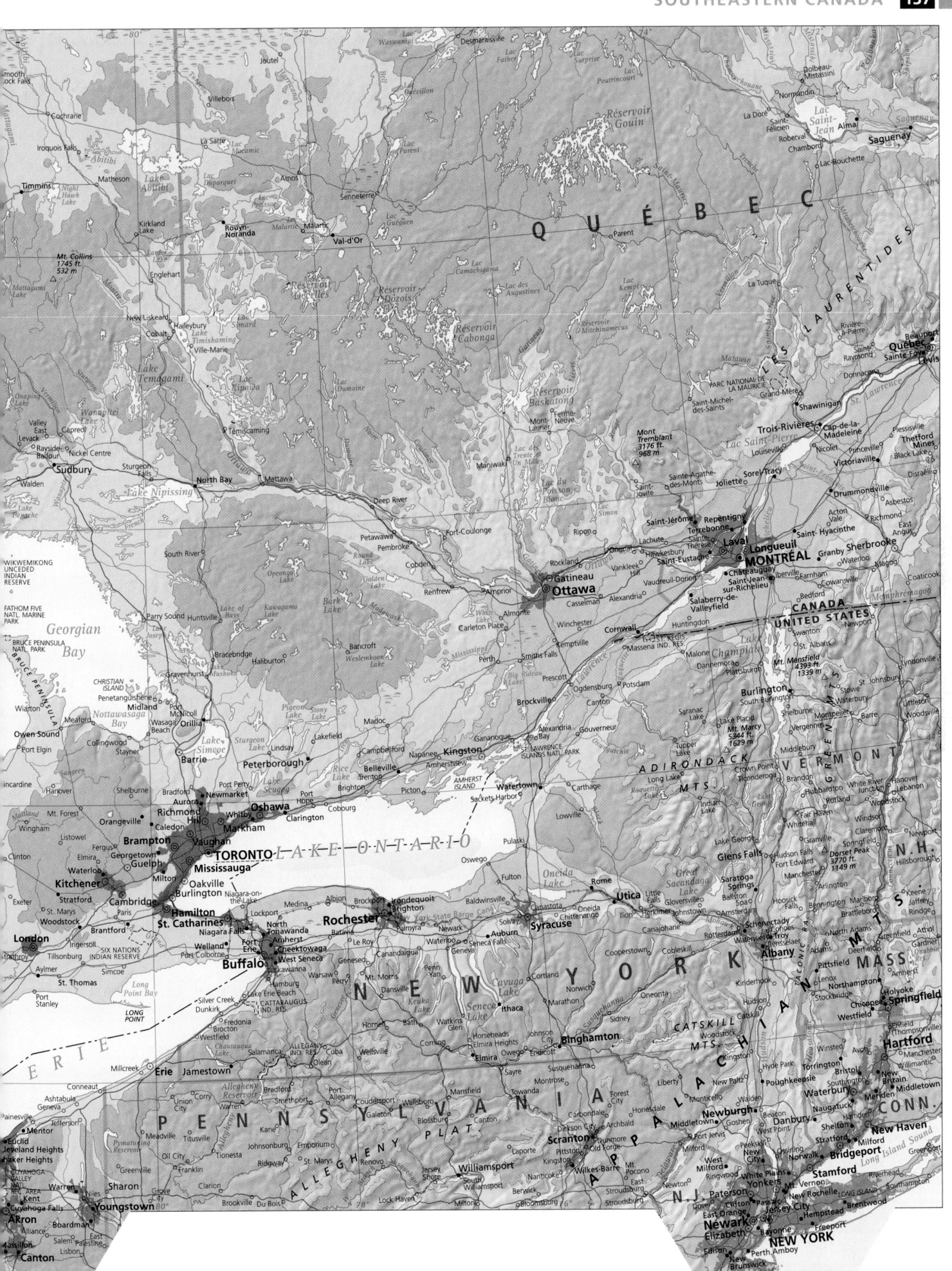

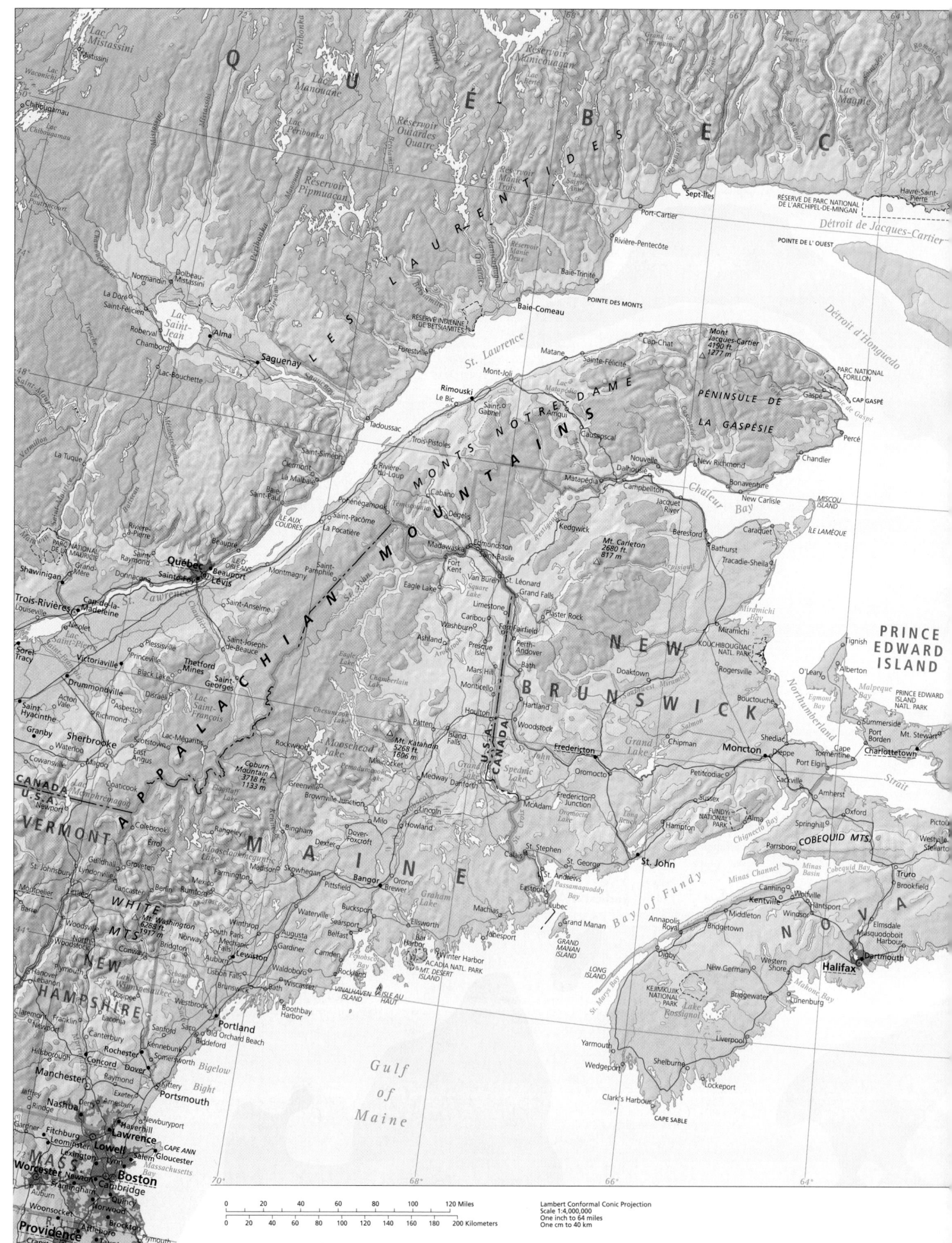

QUÉBEC

Lac Mistassini
Mistassini
Lac Waconichi
Chibougamau
Lac Chibougamau

Péribonka
Lac Manouane
Lac Péribonka
Reservoir Pipmuacan
Reservoir Outardes Quatre

Reservoir Manic Trois
Réservoir Manicouagan
Grand lac Germain

Lac Fournier
Lac Magpie

Havre-Saint-Pierre
RÉSERVE DE PARC NATIONAL DE L'ARCHIPEL-DE-MINGAN
Détroit de Jacques-Cartier
POINTE DE L'OUEST

Sept-Îles
Port-Cartier
Rivière-Pentecôte
Baie-Trinité
POINTE DES MONTS
Baie-Comeau
RÉSERVE INDIENNE DE BETSIAMITES
Forestville

Cap-Chat
Mont Jacques-Cartier 4190 ft. 1277 m
Détroit d'Honguedo
PARC NATIONAL FORILLON

Normandin
Dolbeau-Mistassini
La Doré
Saint-Félicien
Roberval
Chambord
Alma
Lac Saint-Jean
Lac-Bouchette
Saguenay

Matane
Sainte-Félicité
Mont-Joli
Lac Matapédia
Causapscal
PÉNINSULE DE LA GASPÉSIE
Gaspé
CAP GASPÉ
Baie de Gaspé
Percé

Rimouski
Le Bic
Saint-Gabriel
Amqui
Nouvelle
Dalhousie
New Richmond
Bonaventure
New Carlisle
Chandler

Tadoussac
Trois-Pistoles
Rivière-du-Loup
Cabano
Dégelis
Matapédia
Campbellton
Restigouche
Jacquet River
MISCOU ISLAND
ÎLE LAMÈQUE

MONTS NOTRE DAME MOUNTAINS

La Tuque
Clermont
La Malbaie
Baie-Saint-Paul
Rivière-à-Pierre
Pohénégamook
Témiscouata
Madawaska
Edmundston
Saint-Basile
Kedgwick
Mt. Carleton 2680 ft. 817 m
Beresford
Bathurst
Tracadie-Sheila
Caraquet

Beaupré
Saint-Raymond
ÎLE D'ORLÉANS
Saint-Pacôme
La Pocatière
Fort Kent
Van Buren
St. Léonard
Grand Falls

Chaleur Bay

PARC NATIONAL DE LA MAURICIE
Shawinigan
Grand-Mère
Donnacona
Sainte-Foy
Québec
Beauport
Lévis
Montmagny
Saint-Pamphile
Eagle Lake
Square Lake
Limestone
Caribou
Washburn
Perth-Andover
Bath
Plaster Rock
Hartland

NEW BRUNSWICK

PRINCE EDWARD ISLAND
Tignish
O'Leary
Alberton
Summerside
PRINCE EDWARD ISLAND NATL. PARK
Port Borden
Mt. Stewart
Charlottetown

KOUCHIBOUGUAC NATL. PARK
Rogersville
Miramichi
Miramichi Bay

Trois-Rivières
Cap-de-la-Madeleine
Louiseville
Nicolet
Lac Saint-Pierre
Plessisville
Princeville
Thetford Mines
Black Lake
Saint-Georges
Saint-Joseph-de-Beauce
Disraëli
Lac Saint-François
Ashland
Presque Isle
Fort Fairfield
Mars Hill
Monticello
Houlton
Woodstock

APPALACHIAN MOUNTAINS

Drummondville
Acton Vale
Asbestos
Richmond
Lac-Mégantic
Scotstown
East Angus
Eagle Lake
Chamberlain Lake
Chesuncook Lake
Patten
Island Falls
Fredericton
Chipman
Grand Lake
Moncton
Shediac
Dieppe
Port Elgin
Cape Tormentine
Northumberland Strait

Saint-Hyacinthe
Granby
Sherbrooke
Waterloo
Magog
Cowansville
Coaticook
Coburn Mountain 3718 ft. 1133 m
Eustis
Jackman
Rockwood
Moosehead Lake
Greenville
Brownville Junction
Mt. Katahdin 5268 ft. 1606 m
Millinocket
Pemadumcook Lake
Medway
Danforth
Spednic Lakes
McAdam
Oromocto
Fredericton Junction
Oromocto Lake
Petitcodiac
Sussex
Amherst
Oxford
Springhill
Parrsboro
COBEQUID MTS.
Pictou
Westville
Stellarton

CANADA U.S.A.
Newport
Lac Memphrémagog
VERMONT
St. Johnsbury
Colebrook
Errol

MAINE

Rangeley
Bingham
Dover-Foxcroft
Milo
Howland
Lincoln
Moxie Lake
Flagstaff Lake
Dexter
St. Croix
St. Stephen
St. Andrews
Passamaquoddy Bay
St. George
St. John
FUNDY NATIONAL PARK
Alma
Hampton
Long Reach
Sackville
Chignecto Bay
Minas Basin
Cobequid Bay
Truro
Brookfield
Canning
Kentville
Wolfville
Hantsport
Windsor
Elmsdale
Musquodoboit Harbour
NOVA SCOTIA

Montpelier
Barre
Woodsville
NEW HAMPSHIRE
WHITE MTS.
Mt. Washington 6288 ft. 1917 m
Lancaster
Berlin
Norway
Bridgton
Gorham
Conway
Mooselookmeguntic Lake
Mexico
Rumford
Farmington
Skowhegan
Pittsfield
Bangor
Orono
Brewer
Graham Lake
Ellsworth
Machias
Eastport
Lubec
Calais
St. John
St. Andrews
Grand Manan
GRAND MANAN ISLAND
Digby
Annapolis Royal
Bridgetown
Middleton
New Germany
Bridgewater
KEJIMKUJIK NATIONAL PARK
Lake Rossignol
Liverpool
Shelburne

Hanover
Lebanon
Plymouth
Laconia
Canterbury
Concord
Rochester
Dover
Somersworth
Manchester
Raymond
Exeter
Portsmouth
Kittery
Winthrop
Augusta
Mechanic Falls
Lewiston
Auburn
Gardiner
Waterville
Belfast
Camden
Rockland
Searsport
Penobscot Bay
VINALHAVEN ISLAND
ISLE AU HAUT
Bar Harbor
Winter Harbor
ACADIA NATL. PARK
MT. DESERT ISLAND
Jonesboro
Jaffrey
Rindge
Hillsborough
Henniker
Claremont
Newport
Franklin
Bigelow Bight
South Paris
Norridgewock
Winthrop
Lisbon Falls
Brunswick
Bath
Wiscasset
Boothbay Harbor
Damariscotta
Waldoboro
Portland
Old Orchard Beach
Biddeford
Saco
Kennebunk
Westbrook
Gorham
Sanford

Gulf of Maine

Yarmouth
Wedgeport
Clark's Harbour
CAPE SABLE
Lockeport
LONG ISLAND
St. Mary's Bay
Mahone Bay
Lunenburg

Nashua
Manchester
Keene
Peterborough
MASSACHUSETTS
Fitchburg
Leominster
Lowell
Lawrence
Haverhill
Newburyport
CAPE ANN
Gloucester
Salem
Lynn
Massachusetts Bay

Gardner
Worcester
Framingham
Newton
Cambridge
Boston
Quincy
Brockton
Woonsocket
R.I.
Providence
Cranston
Attleboro
Taunton
Plymouth
Auburn
Norwood
Milford

0   20   40   60   80   100   120 Miles
0   20   40   60   80   100   120   140   160   180   200 Kilometers

Lambert Conformal Conic Projection
Scale 1:4,000,000
One inch to 64 miles
One cm to 40 km

LABRADOR SEA

Red Bay 56° Pistolet Bay CAPE BAULD
L'ANSE-AUX-MEADOWS
St. Anthony
Hare Bay
GROAIS ISLAND
GREY ISLANDS
BELL ISLAND
HORSE ISLANDS

LABRADOR

Strait of Belle Isle
Saint-Augustin
Mutton Bay
CAP DU GROS MÉCATINA
Île du Petit Mécatina
La Romaine
Natashquan
CAP WHITTLE

St. John Island
Port Saunders
Blue Mountain 2129 ft. 649 m
Roddickton
White Bay
CAPE ST. JOHN 50°
La Scie
Notre Dame Bay
NEW WORLD ISLAND
FOGO ISLAND
Fogo
Durrell

ÎLE D'ANTICOSTI
POINTE DE L'EST

GROS MORNE NATIONAL PARK
Rocky Harbour Gros Morne 2644 ft. 806 m
Deer Lake
Springdale
Robert's Arm
Carmanville
CAPE FREELS

NEWFOUNDLAND

Bay of Islands
Lark Harbour
Corner Brook
Pasadena
Badger
Bishop's Falls
Glenwood
Gander
Hare Bay
New-Wes-Valley
Bonavista Bay

Gulf of St. Lawrence

LONG POINT
Port au Port Bay
Stephenville
CAPE ST. GEORGE

Grand Lake
Buchans
Grand Falls-Windsor
Gander Lake
Glovertown
Bonavista
Catalina

AND LABRADOR
NEWFOUNDLAND
Red Indian Lake

Victoria Lake
LONG RANGE MOUNTAINS
St. George's Bay
CAPE ANGUILLE 48°

Meelpaeg Lake
Jeddore Lake
Shoal Harbour
TERRA NOVA NATIONAL PARK
RANDOM ISLAND
GRATES POINT
Bay de Verde
Pouch Cove

CAPE RAY
Channel-Port aux Basques
Isle aux Morts
Burgeo
Hermitage Bay
Harbour Breton
Belle Bay
Placentia Bay
Trinity Bay
Carbonear
Harbour Grace
Brigus
Bay Roberts
Wabana
Torbay
St. John's
CAPE SPEAR
Concepción Bay
AVALON PENINSULA
Witless Bay

La Grosse Île
ÎLE DE L'EST
ÎLE DU CAP AUX MEULES
Cap-aux-Meules
ÎLES DE LA MADELEINE (Que.)
ÎLE DU HAVRE AUBERT

Cabot Strait

BRUNETTE ISLAND
Fortune Bay
BURIN PENINSULA
Fox Harbour

MIQUELON
Grand Bank
Fortune
Marystown
Burin
St. Lawrence
Branch
CAPE ST. MARY'S
St. Mary's Bay
St. Shotts
CAPE RACE

LANGLADE
Saint-Pierre
Saint-Pierre

SAINT PIERRE & MIQUELON (Fr.)

CAPE NORTH
Dingwall
Aspy Bay
CAPE BRETON HIGHLANDS NATL. PARK

Souris
Georgetown
Montague
Murray Harbour
Antigonish
w Glasgow
Port Hawkesbury

St. Ann's Bay
Sydney Mines
North Sydney
New Waterford
Glace Bay
SYDNEY
SCATARIE ISLAND
Louisbourg
CAPE BRETON ISLAND

Port Hood
St. Georges Bay
Bras d'Or Lake
St. Peters
ISLE MADAME
Chedabucto Bay
Canso

heet Harbour

ATLANTIC OCEAN

SABLE ISLAND (N.S.)

a

Inset map a
LES LAURENTIDES
Saint-Joachim
Sainte-Anne-de-Beaupré
Beaupré
Château-Richer
Lac-Beauport
L'Ange-Gardien
ÎLE D'ORLÉANS 47°
Saint-Raymond
Lac Saint-Joseph
Lac Saint-Charles
Boischatel
Sainte-Pétronille
Shannon
Charlesbourg
Beauport
Sainte-Catherine-de-la-Jacques-Cartier
Val-Bélair
Loretteville
Vanier
QUÉBEC
Beaumont
Chute-Panet
L'Ancienne-Lorette
Sainte-Foy
Lévis
St. Lawrence
Saint-Basile
Pont-Rouge
Cap-Rouge
Sillery
Saint-Romuald
Saint-Jean-Chrysostome
Neuville
Charny
Saint-Henri
Portneuf
Donnacona
Saint-Nicolas
Saint-Rédempteur
Saint-Antoine-de-Tilly
Saint-Apollinaire
Saint-Anselme
Cap-Santé
Sainte-Croix
Rivière-Bois-Clair
Saint-Agapit
Saint-Gilles
Laurier-Station
Saint-Flavien
Dosquet
Saint-Bernard 46°30'

Inset map a
Lambert Conformal Conic Projection
Scale 1:1,000,000
One inch to 16 miles
One cm to 10 km

© Rand McNally A-101666-1
© Rand McNally A-101667-1

PACIFIC OCEAN

Gulf of Mexico

M E X I C O

UNITED STATES

a

CARIBBEAN SEA

ARUBA
(Neth.)

NETHERLANDS
ANTILLES
(Neth.)

VENEZUELA

BONAIRE

CURAÇAO

Willemstad

FALCÓN

PENÍNSULA DE
PARAGUANA

© Rand McNally
A-101669-1

© Rand McNally
A-101668-1

Inset map a
Lambert Conformal Conic Projection
Scale 1:2,000,000
One inch to 32 miles
One cm to 20 km

b

BERMUDA
(U.K.)

ST. GEORGE'S ISLAND
ST. DAVID'S ISLAND
St. George
Harrington Sound
Castle Harbour
Flatts
Hamilton
Town Hill 259 ft. 79 m
Great Sound
SOMERSET ISLAND

HIGH POINT

ATLANTIC OCEAN

© Rand McNally A-101670-1

KENTUCKY
W. VA.
VIRGINIA
Roanoke
Richmond
Norfolk
Chesapeake Bay
Virginia Beach
Mt. Mitchell 6684 ft. 2037 m
Knoxville
Raleigh
SEE
Chattanooga
Charlotte NORTH CAROLINA
CAPE HATTERAS
Fayetteville
ALABAMA
Columbus
Atlanta
SOUTH CAROLINA
Columbia
CAPE LOOKOUT
GEORGIA
Wilmington
Montgomery
CAPE FEAR
Charleston
Savannah
Jacksonville
Tallahassee
FLORIDA
CAPE N BLAS
BERMUDA (U.K.)
Hamilton

ATLANTIC

OCEAN

Orlando
CAPE CANAVERAL
St. Petersburg Tampa
Lake Okeechobee
West Palm Beach
ABACO
GRAND BAHAMA
Fort Lauderdale
Miami
CAPE SABLE
Key West
Nassau ELEUTHERA
ANDROS NEW PROVIDENCE
CAT ISLAND
Tropic of Cancer
Straits of Florida
MANGROVE CAY
SAN SALVADOR
BAHAMAS
GREAT EXUMA
LONG ISLAND
CROOKED ISLAND
MAYAGUANA
HAVANA
Matanzas
CAYO COCO
ACKLINS
TURKS AND CAICOS ISLANDS (U.K.)
Pinar del Río
Santa Clara
CAYO ROMANO
Golfo de Batabanó
Cienfuegos
CUBA
CAYO GUAJABA
GREAT INAGUA
Grand Turk
CABO DE SAN ANTONIO
ISLA DE LA JUVENTUD
G R E A T E R
PUERTO RICO TRENCH
Camagüey
Holguín
CAYMAN ISLANDS (U.K.)
Manzanillo
Bayamo
Guantánamo
Cap-Haïtien
Santiago de los Caballeros
George Town
CABO CRUZ
Pico Turquino 6470 ft. 1972 m
Santiago de Cuba
Gonaïves
Pico Duarte 10 417 ft. 3175 m
DOMINICAN REPUBLIC
San Juan
VIRGIN ISLANDS (U.S.)
BRITISH VIRGIN ISLANDS (U.K.)
ANGUILLA
GRAND CAYMAN
HAITI
HISPANIOLA
Charlotte Amalie
L E E W A R D   I S L A N D S
ANTIGUA AND BARBUDA
Montego Bay
Port-au-Prince
Santo Domingo
San Pedro de Macorís
Ponce
PUERTO RICO (U.S)
ST. CROIX (U.S.)
ST. KITTS AND NEVIS
MONTSERRAT
GRANDE-TERRE
GUADELOUPE (Fr.)
JAMAICA
Kingston
Basse-Terre
BASSE-TERRE
MARIE-GALANTE
Spanish Town
A N T I L L E S
DOMINICA
Roseau
MARTINIQUE (Fr.)
W E S T   I N D I E S
Fort-de-France
HONDURAS
CABO GRACIAS A DIOS
Castries
ST. LUCIA
BARBADOS
Coco
C A R I B B E A N   S E A
Kingstown
Bridgetown
ISLA DE PROVIDENCIA (Col.)
ST. VINCENT AND THE GRENADINES
NICARAGUA
GRENADA
ISLA DE SAN ANDRÉS (Col.)
L E S S E R
ISLA BLANQUILLA
WINDWARD ISLANDS
Lago de Nicaragua
Bluefields
ARUBA (Neth.)
NETHERLANDS ANTILLES (Neth.)
A N T I L L E S
TOBAGO
PUNTA GALLINAS
BONAIRE
ISLA LA ORCHILA
TRINIDAD AND TOBAGO
COSTA RICA
Volcán Irazú 11 260 ft. 3432 m
Willemstad
CURAÇAO
ISLA DE MARGARITA
Port of Spain
Puntarenas
PEN. DE LA GUAJIRA
Punto Fijo
ISLA LA TORTUGA
Carúpano
Golfo de Paria
San José
Santa Marta
Puerto Cabello
Cumaná
TRINIDAD
Cerro Chirripó 12 530 ft. 3819 m
Barranquilla
MARACAIBO
CARACAS
Barcelona
Puerto Limón
Soledad
Pico Cristóbal Colón 18 947 ft. 5775 m
Cabimas
Barquisimeto
Colón
Cartagena
Golfo de Venezuela
Valle de la Pascua
Volcán Barú 11 401 ft. 3475 m
PANAMA CANAL
Sincelejo
Magangué
Acarigua
El Tigre
Ciudad Guayana
David
Panama
Santiago
Monteria
Mérida
Calabozo
Ciudad Bolívar
PEN. DE AZUERO
Golfo de Chiriquí
ISTMO DE PANAMÁ
Pico Bolívar 16 427 ft. 5007 m
San Fernando de Apure
ISLA DE COIBA
Golfo de Panamá
Ocaña
VENEZUELA
Georgetown
PUNTA MARIATO
Barrancabermeja
Cúcuta
San Cristóbal
Angel Falls
GUYANA
Bucaramanga
Mt. Roraima 9432 ft. 2875 m
MEDELLÍN
Sogamoso
Puerto Ayacucho
Cerro Marahuaca 8461 ft. 2579 m
GUIANA HIGHLANDS
CABO CORRIENTES
La Dorada
Tunja
PAKARAIMA MTS
ISLA DE MALPELO (Col.)
Manizales
Nevado del Tolima 17 110 ft. 5215 m
Villavicencio
San Fernando de Atabapo
Cerro Mato 6112 ft. 1863 m
SURINAME
Cartago
BOGOTÁ
B R A Z I L
Buenaventura
Ibagué
COLOMBIA
Boa Vista
CALI
Palmira
Nevado del Huila 18 865 ft. 5750 m

OCCIDENTAL
ORIENTAL
Meta
Vichada
Guaviare
Negro

0 80 160 240 320 400 480 Miles
0 80 160 240 320 400 480 560 640 720 800 Kilometers

Lambert Azimuthal Equal Area Projection
Scale 1:16,000,000
One inch to 256 miles
One cm to 160 km

Inset map b
Lambert Conformal Conic Projection
Scale 1:1,000,000
One inch to 16 miles
One cm to 10 km

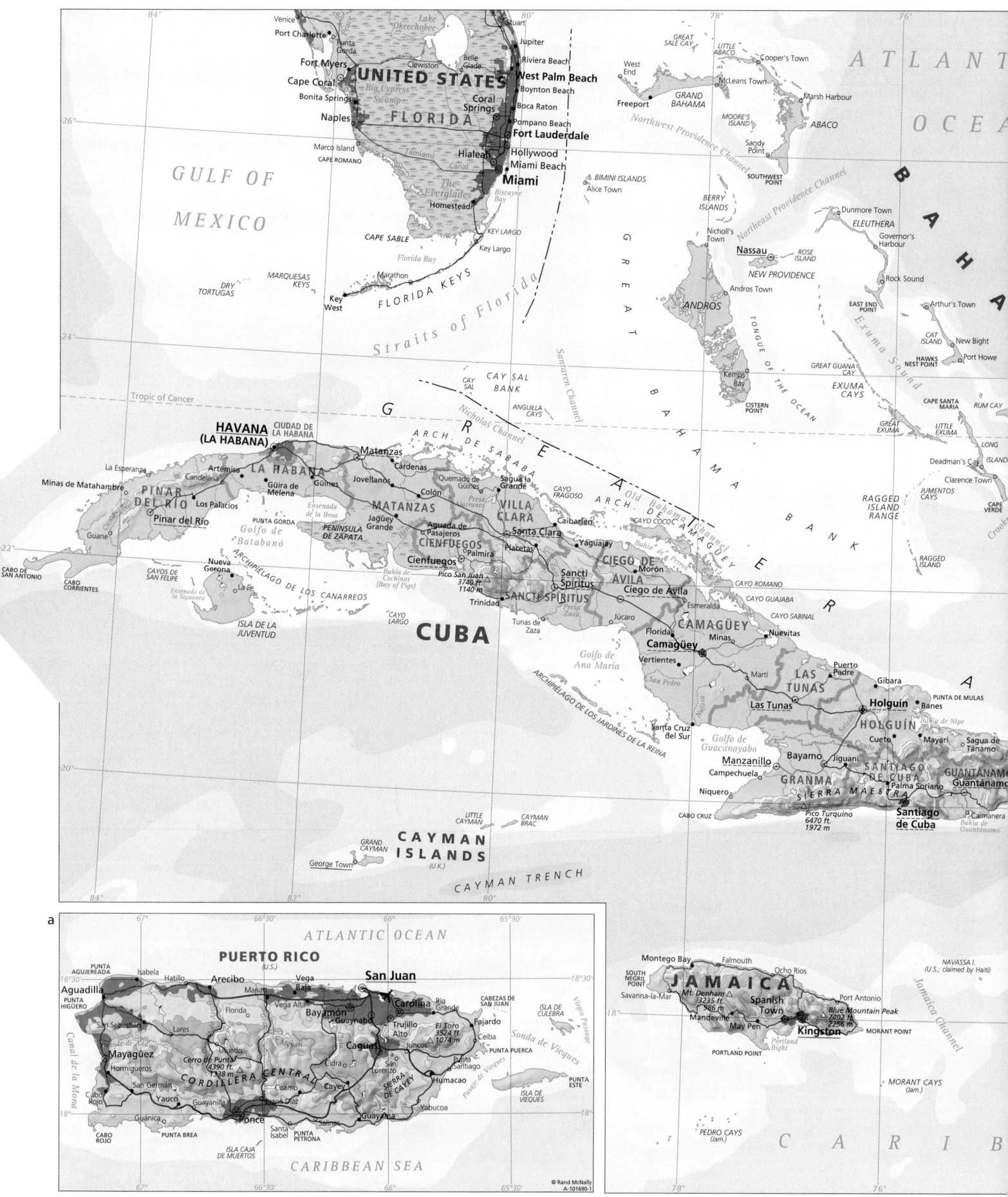

GULF OF MEXICO

UNITED STATES
FLORIDA

Venice
Port Charlotte
Punta Gorda
Fort Myers
Cape Coral
Bonita Springs
Naples
Big Cypress Swamp
Marco Island
CAPE ROMANO
The Everglades
Homestead
Tamiami Canal
Hialeah
Hollywood
Miami Beach
Miami
Biscayne Bay

Lake Okeechobee
Clewiston
Belle Glade
Stuart
Jupiter
Riviera Beach
West Palm Beach
Boynton Beach
Boca Raton
Pompano Beach
Fort Lauderdale
Coral Springs

CAPE SABLE
Key Largo
Key Largo
MARQUESAS KEYS
DRY TORTUGAS
Marathon
Key West
FLORIDA KEYS
Florida Bay

Straits of Florida

ATLANTIC OCEAN

GREAT SALE CAY
LITTLE ABACO
Cooper's Town
West End
McLeans Town
Freeport
GRAND BAHAMA
Marsh Harbour
ABACO
MOORE'S ISLAND
Sandy Point
Northwest Providence Channel
SOUTHWEST POINT
BERRY ISLANDS
Nicholl's Town
Alice Town
BIMINI ISLANDS
Northeast Providence Channel
Dunmore Town
ELEUTHERA
Governor's Harbour
Nassau
NEW PROVIDENCE
ROSE ISLAND
Rock Sound
Andros Town
ANDROS
EAST END POINT
Arthur's Town
CAT ISLAND
New Bight
Port Howe
HAWKS NEST POINT
TONGUE OF THE OCEAN
Kemps Bay
CISTERN POINT
GREAT GUANA CAY
EXUMA CAYS
CAPE SANTA MARIA
RUM CAY
GREAT EXUMA
LITTLE EXUMA
Exuma Sound
Deadman's Cay
LONG ISLAND
Clarence Town
JUMENTOS CAYS
CAPE VERDE
RAGGED ISLAND RANGE
RAGGED ISLAND

Tropic of Cancer

CAY SAL BANK
CAY SAL
Nicholas Channel
ANGUILLA CAYS
Santaren Channel
ARCH. DE SABANA
Old Bahama Channel
BAHAMA BANK

G R E A T

HAVANA (LA HABANA)
CIUDAD DE LA HABANA
La Esperanza
Minas de Matahambre
Candelaria
Artemisa
PINAR DEL RIO
Guane
Los Palacios
Pinar del Río
PUNTA GORDA
Golfo de Batabanó
Güira de Melena
LA HABANA
Güines
Jovellanos
Matanzas
Cárdenas
Colón
MATANZAS
Jagüey Grande
PENÍNSULA DE ZAPATA
Ensenada de la Broa
Aguada de Pasajeros
Quemado de Güines
Sagua la Grande
Santa Clara
VILLA CLARA
Placetas
Palmira
CIENFUEGOS
Cienfuegos
Bahía de Cochinos (Bay of Pigs)
Pico San Juan 3740 ft 1140 m
Trinidad
SANCTI SPÍRITUS
Sancti Spíritus
Tunas de Zaza
Presa Zaza
Yaguajay
Caibarién
CAYO FRAGOSO
ARCH. DE CAMAGÜEY
CAYO COCO
CAYO ROMANO
CAYO GUAJABA
CAYO SABINAL
CIEGO DE ÁVILA
Morón
Ciego de Ávila
Esmeralda
Júcaro
Bahía de Perros

CUBA
CAYO LARGO
ISLA DE LA JUVENTUD
Nueva Gerona
La Fe
CAYOS DE SAN FELIPE
Ensenada de la Siguanea
ARCHIPIÉLAGO DE LOS CANARREOS
CABO DE SAN ANTONIO
CABO CORRIENTES
Golfo de Ana María
ARCHIPIÉLAGO DE LOS JARDINES DE LA REINA
Golfo de Guacanayabo
Santa Cruz del Sur
San Pedro
Florida
CAMAGÜEY
Camagüey
Vertientes
Minas
Nuevitas
Martí
LAS TUNAS
Las Tunas
Puerto Padre
Gibara
PUNTA DE MULAS
Holguín
Banes
HOLGUÍN
Cueto
Mayarí
Sagua de Tánamo
Bahía de Nipe
Manzanillo
Bayamo
Jiguaní
GRANMA
Campechuela
Niquero
SIERRA MAESTRA
Pico Turquino 6470 ft 1972 m
CABO CRUZ
SANTIAGO DE CUBA
Palma Soriano
Santiago de Cuba
GUANTÁNAMO
Guantánamo
Caimanera
Bahía de Guantánamo

LITTLE CAYMAN
CAYMAN BRAC
GRAND CAYMAN
CAYMAN ISLANDS (U.K.)
George Town
CAYMAN TRENCH

a
ATLANTIC OCEAN
PUERTO RICO (U.S.)
PUNTA AGUJEREADA
PUNTA HIGÜERO
Aguadilla
Isabela
Hatillo
Arecibo
Manatí
Vega Baja
Vega
San Juan
Carolina
Bayamón
Guaynabo
Trujillo Alto
Río Grande
Fajardo
Ceiba
CABEZAS DE SAN JUAN
ISLA DE CULEBRA
Virgin Passage
Sonda de Vieques
San Sebastián
Lares
Florida
Vega Alta
El Toro 3524 ft 1074 m
PUNTA PUERCA
Canal de la Mona
Mayagüez
Hormigueros
San Germán
Cabo Rojo
Yauco
Guánica
CABO ROJO
PUNTA BREA
ISLA CAJA DE MUERTOS
Sabana Grande
Cerro de Punta (4390 ft) 1338 m
CORDILLERA CENTRAL
Utuado
Jayuya
Ciales
Cidra
Aibonito
Coamo
Cayey
SIERRA DE CAYEY
San Lorenzo
Humacao
Yabucoa
Juncos
Caguas
Ponce
Santa Isabel
PUNTA PETRONA
Salinas
Guayama
Guayanilla
Peñuelas
Juana Díaz
Las Piedras
PUNTA ESTE
ISLA DE VIEQUES
CARIBBEAN SEA

Montego Bay
Falmouth
Ocho Rios
NAVASSA I. (U.S.; claimed by Haiti)
SOUTH NEGRIL POINT
Savanna-la-Mar
JAMAICA
Mt. Denham 2235 ft 586 m
Spanish Town
Port Antonio
Jamaica Channel
Mandeville
May Pen
Blue Mountain Peak 7402 ft 2256 m
Kingston
MORANT POINT
PORTLAND POINT
Portland Bight
MORANT CAYS (Jam.)
PEDRO CAYS (Jam.)
CARIB

Inset map a
Lambert Conformal Conic Projection
Scale 1:2,000,000
One inch to 32 miles
One cm to 20 km

© Rand McNally   A-101690-1

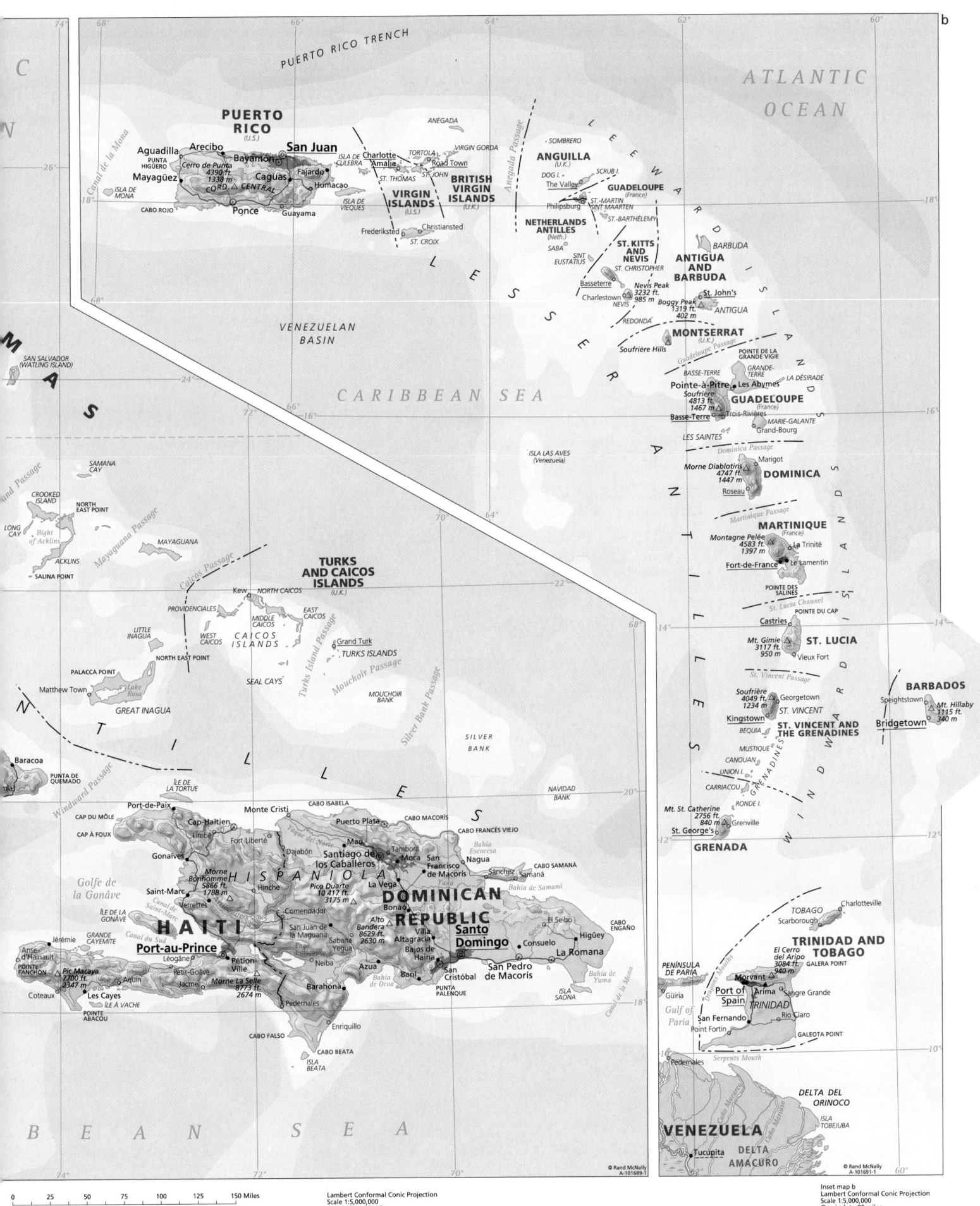

PUERTO RICO TRENCH

ATLANTIC OCEAN

C

PUERTO RICO
(U.S.)

Aguadilla
PUNTA HIGÜERO
Arecibo
Bayamón
San Juan
Mayagüez
Cerro de Punta
4390 ft.
1338 m
CORD.
CENTRAL
Caguas
Humacao
Ponce
Guayama

ISLA DE LA MONA
Canal de la Mona
ISLA DE MONA
CABO ROJO

ISLA DE CULEBRA
ISLA DE VIEQUES

Charlotte Amalie
ST. THOMAS
ST. JOHN
VIRGIN ISLANDS
(U.S.)
Frederiksted
Christiansted
ST. CROIX

ANEGADA
TORTOLA
Road Town
Virgin Gorda
BRITISH VIRGIN ISLANDS
(U.K.)

SOMBRERO
ANGUILLA
(U.K.)
DOG I.
The Valley
SCRUB I.
ST.-MARTIN
SINT MAARTEN
Philipsburg
GUADELOUPE
(France)
ST.-BARTHÉLEMY
NETHERLANDS ANTILLES
(Neth.)
SABA
SINT EUSTATIUS

ST. KITTS AND NEVIS
ST. CHRISTOPHER
Basseterre
Charlestown
NEVIS
Nevis Peak
3232 ft.
985 m
Boggy Peak
1319 ft.
402 m
St. John's
ANTIGUA
ANTIGUA AND BARBUDA
BARBUDA
REDONDA

MONTSERRAT
(U.K.)
Soufrière Hills

POINTE DE LA GRANDE VIGIE
GRANDE-TERRE
LA DÉSIRADE
BASSE-TERRE
Pointe-à-Pitre
Les Abymes
Soufrière
4813 ft.
1467 m
GUADELOUPE
(France)
Trois-Rivières
Basse-Terre
MARIE-GALANTE
Grand-Bourg
LES SAINTES

Dominica Passage
Marigot
Morne Diablotins
4747 ft.
1447 m
DOMINICA
Roseau

Martinique Passage
Montagne Pelée
4583 ft.
1397 m
MARTINIQUE
(France)
La Trinité
Fort-de-France
Le Lamentin

POINTE DES SALINES
St. Lucia Channel
POINTE DU CAP
Castries
Mt. Gimie
3117 ft.
950 m
ST. LUCIA
Vieux Fort

St. Vincent Passage
Soufrière
4049 ft.
1234 m
Georgetown
ST. VINCENT
Kingstown
ST. VINCENT AND THE GRENADINES
BEQUIA
MUSTIQUE
CANOUAN
UNION I.
CARRIACOU
RONDE I.

BARBADOS
Speightstown
Mt. Hillaby
1115 ft.
340 m
Bridgetown

VENEZUELAN BASIN

CARIBBEAN SEA

ISLA LAS AVES
(Venezuela)

SAN SALVADOR
(WATLING ISLAND)

M
A
S

Crooked Passage
SAMANA CAY
CROOKED ISLAND
NORTH EAST POINT
LONG CAY
Bight of Acklins
ACKLINS
SALINA POINT
MAYAGUANA
Mayaguana Passage

Caicos Passage
Kew
NORTH CAICOS
TURKS AND CAICOS ISLANDS
(U.K.)
PROVIDENCIALES
MIDDLE CAICOS
EAST CAICOS
WEST CAICOS
CAICOS ISLANDS
NORTH EAST POINT
Grand Turk
TURKS ISLANDS
Turks Island Passage

LITTLE INAGUA
PALACCA POINT
Matthew Town
Lake Rosa
GREAT INAGUA
NORTH EAST POINT

Mouchoir Passage
MOUCHOIR BANK

Silver Bank Passage
SILVER BANK

Baracoa
PUNTA DE QUEMADO

Windward Passage
CAP DU MÔLE
CAP À FOUX
Port-de-Paix
ÎLE DE LA TORTUE
Cap-Haïtien
Limbé
Fort-Liberté
Gonaïves
Saint-Marc
VERRETTES
Golfe de la Gonâve
ÎLE DE LA GONÂVE
GRANDE CAYEMITE
Jérémie
ANSE-D'HAINAULT
POINTE FANCHON
Pic Macaya
7700 ft.
2347 m
Coteaux
POINTE ABACOU
Les Cayes
ÎLE À VACHE
Aquin
Jacmel
Léogâne
Petit-Goâve
HAITI
Morne Bonhomme
5866 ft.
1788 m
Canal de Saint-Marc
Port-au-Prince
Pétion-Ville
Morne La Selle
8773 ft.
2674 m
Pedernales

Monte Cristi
Dajabón
Mao
Santiago de los Caballeros
Moca
Hinche
Comendador
San Juan de la Maguana
Azua
Neiba
Barahona
Enriquillo
CABO FALSO
CABO BETA
ISLA BETA

CABO ISABELA
Puerto Plata
CABO MACORÍS
Tamboril
Bonao
La Vega
Pico Duarte
10,417 ft.
3175 m
Alto Bandera
8629 ft.
2630 m
Sabana Yegua
HISPANIOLA
DOMINICAN REPUBLIC
San Cristóbal
Bajos de Haina
Baní
San José de Ocoa
Villa Altagracia
Santo Domingo
PUNTA PALENQUE
Bahía de Ocoa

CABO FRANCÉS VIEJO
Nagua
San Francisco de Macorís
Sánchez
Samaná
CABO SAMANÁ
Bahía de Samaná
Bahía Escocesa
El Seibo
Consuelo
La Romana
Higüey
San Pedro de Macorís
CABO ENGAÑO
Bahía de Yuma
ISLA SAONA
Canal de la Mona

Yaque del Norte
Yuna

Mt. St. Catherine
2756 ft.
840 m
Grenville
St. George's
GRENADA

TOBAGO
Charlotteville
Scarborough
TRINIDAD AND TOBAGO
El Cerro del Aripo
3084 ft.
940 m
GALERA POINT
Morvant
Arima
Sangre Grande
Port of Spain
TRINIDAD
Güiria
PENÍNSULA DE PARIA
San Fernando
Rio Claro
Point Fortin
GALEOTA POINT
Gulf of Paria
Serpents Mouth
Pedernales

VENEZUELA
Tucupita
DELTA AMACURO
DELTA DEL ORINOCO
ISLA TOBEJUBA

B E A N   S E A

© Rand McNally
A-101689-1

© Rand McNally
A-101691-1

PACIFIC OCEAN

| 0 | 40 | 80 | 120 | 160 | 200 | 240 Miles |
| 0 | 40 | 80 | 120 | 160 | 200 | 240 | 280 | 320 | 360 | 400 Kilometers |

Lambert Azimuthal Equal Area Projection
Scale 1:8,000,000
One inch to 128 miles
One cm to 80 km

UNITED STATES

Fort Worth · DALLAS · Cleburne · Tyler · Longview · Shreveport · Ruston · Monroe · Vicksburg · Jackson · MISSISSIPPI · Meridian · Troy · Albany · GEORGIA

Stamford · Abilene · Corsicana · Waco · Jacksonville · Nacogdoches · Natchitoches · Tallulah · Brookhaven · Laurel · Hattiesburg · Andalusia · Dothan · Bainbridge

San Angelo · Killeen · Temple · Lufkin · McComb · Natchez · McComb · Mobile · Pensacola · Fort Walton Beach · FLORIDA · Tallahassee

TEXAS · EDWARDS · Brady · Bryan · Huntsville · Conroe · De Ridder · LOUISIANA · Hammond · Bogalusa · Gulfport · Biloxi · Pascagoula · Panama City

Sonora · Fredericksburg · Austin · Bastrop · Opelousas · Baton Rouge · New Orleans · ST. GEORGE ISLAND · CAPE SAN BLAS

PLATEAU · Kerrville · San Marcos · Beaumont · Port Arthur · Lake Charles · Lafayette · New Iberia · Thibodaux · Houma · POINT AU FER ISLAND

Amistad Reservoir · Del Rio · Uvalde · HOUSTON · Baytown · Morgan City · MARSH ISLAND

Ciudad Acuña · Eagle Pass · San Antonio · Sugar Land · Texas City · Galveston

Piedras Negras · Allende · Cotulla · Lake Jackson · GALVESTON ISLAND · Freeport

Sabinas · Victoria · Beeville · MATAGORDA ISLAND

Nuevo Laredo · Laredo · Kingsville · Corpus Christi · SAN JOSE ISLAND

Ciudad Anáhuac · Zapata · PADRE ISLAND

Falcon Reservoir · Raymondville · Laguna Madre

Sabinas Hidalgo · McAllen · Harlingen

San Nicolás de los Garza · Reynosa · Brownsville

Guadalupe · Matamoros · Valle Hermoso

MONTERREY · Montemorelos · Barra de los Americanos

Saltillo · Linares · San Fernando · Laguna Madre

NUEVO LEÓN · Hidalgo · Abasolo

Matehuala · Charcas · Ciudad Victoria · Soto la Marina

TAMAULIPAS

GULF OF MEXICO

Tropic of Cancer

Cerritos · Ciudad Mante · Aldama · Cuauhtémoc

SAN LUIS POTOSÍ · Ciudad Valles · Tula · Tampico

San Luis Potosí · Rioverde · Pánuco · Laguna de Tamiahua

GUANAJUATO · Tantoyuca · CABO ROJO

San Luis de la Paz · Tamazunchale · Tamiahua

Guanajuato · Ixmiquilpan · Tuxpan de Rodríguez Cano

Irapuato · QUERÉTARO · Poza Rica de Hidalgo · Papantla de Olarte

Salamanca · HIDALGO · EL TAJÍN

Celaya · Querétaro · Pachuca de Soto · Martínez de la Torre

Acámbaro · Tulancingo · VERACRUZ

Morelia · MEXICO CITY · Ciudad Netzahualcóyotl · Teziutlán · Xalapa

Toluca de Lerdo · TLAXCALA · Tlaxcala de Xicohténcatl · Volcán Pico de Orizaba 18 406 ft. 5 610 m · Veracruz

Nevado de Toluca 15 387 ft. 4 690 m · MEXICO · Córdoba · Alvarado · PUNTA ROCA PARTIDA

Cuernavaca · PUEBLA DE ZARAGOZA · Orizaba · Tierra Blanca · San Andrés Tuxtla

Taxco de Alarcón · MORELOS · Tehuacán · Ciudad del Carmen

Huetamo de Núñez · Iguala · PUEBLA · Coatzacoalcos · Villahermosa · Sabancuy

GUERRERO · Huajuapan de León · Tuxtepec · Minatitlán · Paraíso · Frontera · Laguna de Términos

Chilpancingo de los Bravo · Tlapa de Comonfort · Asunción Nochixtlán · Emiliano Zapata

Petatlán · Putla de Guerrero · Oaxaca de Juárez · ISTMO DE TEHUANTEPEC · Tuxtla Gutiérrez · San Cristóbal de las Casas

Tecpan de Galeana · San Marcos · OAXACA · Tuxtla Gutiérrez · Teapa · Tenosique

Acapulco de Juárez · Ometepec · DEL SUR · Matías Romero · Cintalapa · CHIAPAS · Comitán de Domínguez

Miahuatlán de Porfirio Díaz · Ixtepec · Tonalá · SIERRA MADRE

Santiago Pinotepa Nacional · Santiago Jamiltepec · Juchitán de Zaragoza · Salina Cruz

MIDDLE AMERICA TRENCH · Puerto Escondido · PUNTA CORNETA · Puerto Ángel · Golfo de Tehuantepec · Mapastepec · Volcán Tajumulco 13 846 ft. 4 220 m

Huixtla · Quetzaltenango · Tapachula · Mazatenango · GUATEMALA

Bahía de Campeche · PUNTA MORRO · Seybaplaya · Champotón · CAMPECHE · Escárcega

Campeche · Hopelchén · Chetumal · Corozal · AMBERGRIS CAY

YUCATÁN · Progreso · Mérida · Hunucmá · Maxcanú · Temax · Tizimín · Cancún

Río Lagartos · Panabá · CABO CATOCHE

Dzibalchén · Tekax · Peto · Felipe Carrillo Puerto

CHICHÉN ITZÁ · UXMAL · Ticul · Valladolid · Playa del Carmen

YUCATÁN PENINSULA · QUINTANA ROO · Tulum · TULUM · ISLA COZUMEL · Cozumel

CARIBBEAN SEA

Bahía Chetumal

Belize City · TURNEFFE ISLANDS

TABASCO · Ionutá · Tenosique · TIKAL · Belmopan · Dangriga

PALENQUE · San Pedro · San Benito · BELIZE · ISLAS DE LA BAHÍA (Hond.)

La Libertad · Punta Gorda · Golfo de Honduras · Punta Negra · Livingston · La Ceiba

San Luis · Puerto Cortés · Tela

Cobán · El Estor · Puerto Barrios · San Pedro Sula · Santa Rosa de Copán · HONDURAS

Huehuetenango · Salamá · Zacapa · Chiquimula · Cerro El Pital 8 957 ft. 2 730 m · Siguatepeque · Comayagua

Pijijiapan · Guatemala · Cerro Las Minas 9 347 ft. 2 849 m · Yoro

GUATEMALA · Chiquimula · Copán · Santa Rosa de Copán

Escuintla · Jutiapa · EL SAL. · Tegucigalpa · Danlí

© Rand McNally · A-101672-1

PACIFIC

OCEAN

EAST PACIFIC RISE

MIDDLE AMERICA TRENCH

© Rand McNally
A-101672-1

Lambert Conformal Conic Projection
Scale 1:4,000,000
One inch to 64 miles
One cm to 40 km

0 20 40 60 80 100 120 Miles
0 20 40 60 80 100 120 140 160 180 200 Kilometers

GULF OF MEXICO

MEXICO BASIN

TAMAULIPAS

La Ascención
10 499 ft
3 200 m
Arramberri
Zaragoza
Hidalgo
Santander Jiménez
Abasolo
La Luz
Santiago de la Marina
BARRA DE LOS AMERICANOS
Laguna Madre
BARRA SOTO LA MARINA

Jaumave
Llera de Canales
Las Guayabas
La Pesca

Tula
Xicoténcatl
Aldama

Ciudad Mante
González
Laguna de San Andrés

Antiguo Morelos
Manuel
Cuauhtémoc

Ciudad del Malz
Ebano
Laguna Chía
Ciudad Madero
Tampico

Cárdenas
Pánuco
Ciudad Valles

San Ciro de Acosta
Ozuluama
Laguna de Tamiahua

Tamapatz
Tempoal de Sánchez
Magozal

Jalpan de Serra
Tantoyuca
CABO ROJO

Jacala
Cerro Azul
ISLA DE LOBOS

Zimapán
Chicontepec de Tejeda
Tamiahua

Tequisquiapan
Ixmiquilpan
Tuxpan de Rodríguez Cano

Huichapan
Poza Rica de Hidalgo
Santiago de la Peña

HIDALGO
Tihuatlán

Actopan
Papantla de Olarte
Gutiérrez Zamora

Tepeji de Ocampo
Pachuca de Soto
Huauchinango
EL TAJÍN

Nautla

Presa de Huapango
Tulancingo
Cuetzalan del Progreso
Martínez de la Torre

Santiago Teyahualco
Zacatlán
Teziutlán

Tlalnepantla
TEOTIHUACÁN
San Juan Teotihuacan
Chignahuapan
Misantla

MEXICO CITY
CD. DE MÉXICO
Ciudad Netzahualcóyotl
TLAXCALA
Libres
Perote
Xalapa

Toluca de Lerdo
San Martín Texmelucan
Apizaco
Cerro Cofre de Perote
13 944 ft
4250 m

DIST. FED.
Vol. Iztaccíhuatl
17 159 ft
5230 m
Tlaxcala de Xicohténcatl
Veracruz

Nev. de Toluca
15 387 ft
4690 m
Cholula de Rivadabia
PUEBLA DE ZARAGOZA
PUNTA ANTÓN LIZARDO

Cuernavaca
Amecameca de Juárez
San Andrés Cholula
Volcán Pico de Orizaba
18 406 ft
5610 m

Emiliano Zapata
Yautepec
Volcán Popocatépetl
17 930 ft
5465 m
Tecamachaco
Córdoba

MORELOS
Cuautla
Izucar de Matamoros
Orizaba
Tlacotalpan

Taxco de Alarcón
PUEBLA
Tepalcingo
Tecamachaco
Alvarado
PUNTA ROCA PARTIDA

Teloloapan
Iguala
Chiautla de Tapia
Tehuacán
Tierra Blanca
San Andrés Tuxtla

Huitzuco de los Figueroa
Acatlán de Osorio
San Gabriel Chilac
Cosamaloapan de Carpio
Cerro Santa Marta
5877 ft
1700 m

Bálsas Sur
Olinalá
Huajuapan de León
Huautla
Tuxtepec
San Juan Evangelista
Coatzacoalcos

Mezcala
Chilapa de Álvarez
Tlapa de Comonfort
Tamazulapan del Progreso
Cuicatlán
Playa Vicente
Acayucan
Minatitlán
Villahermosa

Chilpancingo de los Bravo
Silacayoapan
Asunción Nochixtlán
Ixtlán de Juárez
Jesús Carranza
Las Choapas
Macuspana

Tlalixtaquilla
Santa María Asunción Tlaxiaco
Huitzo
Santiago Choapan
ISTMO DE TEHUANTEPEC

Acapulco de Juárez
Metlatónoc
Malinaltepec
Cerro Pedro de Olla
10 991 ft
3350 m
Oaxaca de Juárez
OAXACA
Matías Romero
TABASCO

Ayutla de los Libres
Ometepec
Xochistlahuaca
Putla de Guerrero
Ocotlán de Morelos
Cerro Las Flores
7054 ft
2150 m
Ixtepec
Juchitán de Zaragoza
Ocozocuautla
San Cristóbal de las Casas

San Marcos
Cruz Grande
Cuajinicuilapa
Ejutla de Crespo
Nejapa de Madero
Miahuatlán de Porfirio Díaz
Santo Domingo Tehuantepec
Cintalapa
Tuxtla Gutiérrez
Chiapa de Corzo
CHIAPAS

Santiago Pinotepa Nacional
Santiago Jamiltepec
Río Grande
Santa María Colotepec
Puerto Escondido
San Pedro Pochutla
Puerto Ángel
PUNTA CORNETA
Salina Cruz
Golfo de Tehuantepec
Arriaga
Tonalá
Cerro Tres Picos
8366 ft
2550 m
Villa Flores
Pijijiapan
Cerro el Triunfo
8038 ft
2450 m
Mapastepec

Bahía de Campeche

Nuevo Progreso
Frontera
Paraíso
Comalcalco
Cárdenas
Teapa
Pichucalco
Petalcingo
Chilón
Simojovel
Copainalá
SIERRA MADRE DE CHIAPAS
Venustiano Carranza
Las Rosas
Revolución Mexicana
Chiapa de Corzo
Cerro Los Bolones
9154 ft
2790 m

CAMPECHE BANK

GULF OF MEXICO

CAYOS ARCAS

Bahía de Campeche

ISLA CONTOY
CABO CATOCHE
PUNTA HOLOHIT
Laguna de Yalahau
Isla Mujeres
ISLA MUJERES
PUNTA CANCUN

Río Lagartos
Panabá
Tizimín
Espita
Kantunilkin
Puerto Juárez
Cancún

Progreso
Dzilam González
Temax
Dzemul
Chicxulub
Hunucmá
Motul de Felipe Carrillo Puerto
Celestún
Estero Celestún
Umán
Mérida
Izamal
Tunkás
Dzitás
X-Can
Puerto Morelos

YUCATÁN
CHICHÉN ITZA
Valladolid
Chichimila
Chemax
COBÁ
Playa del Carmen

Maxcanú
Tekit
Muna
Ticul
Oxkutzcab
Chikindzonot
Cozumel
ISLA COZUMEL

Halachó
Becal
Calkiní
UXMAL
Tekax
Peto
Tzucacab
Tulum
TULUM

Dzitbalché
Hecelchakán
Bolonchén de Rejón
José María Morelos
Laguna Chichancanab

Tenabo
Campeche

PUNTA MORRO
Seybaplaya
Hopelchén
Iturbide
Chunhuhux
Felipe Carrillo Puerto
Bahía de la Ascensión

Champotón
Dzibalchén
QUINTANA ROO
Bahía del Espíritu Santo

Sabancuy
MEXICO
CAMPECHE
Escárcega
Nohbec

ISLA DEL CARMEN
Laguna de Términos
Laguna Bacalar
BANCO CHINCHORRO

Nuevo Progreso
Ciudad del Carmen
Frontera
Laguna del Pom
Palizada
Candelaria
CALAKMUL
Bahía Chetumal

Paraíso
Laguna Mecoacán
Chetumal
Corozal
Xcalak

Comalcalco
Laguna del Este
Nicolás Bravo
Caledonia
AMBERGRIS CAY

TABASCO
Jonuta
Emiliano Zapata
Multé
Orange Walk
San Pedro
CARIBBEAN SEA

Cárdenas
Villahermosa
PALENQUE
Palenque
Tenosique
Chuntuqui
Indian Church
CAY CORKER

Macuspana
San Pedro Tabasco
Piedras Negras
Hill Bank
Belize City

Pichucalco
Teapa
Laguna Chichen
TIKAL
El Encanto
Belmopan
NORTHERN CAY
Northern Lagoon

Petalcingo
Chilón
Ciudad Melchor de Mencos
BELIZE
Middlesex
TURNEFFE ISLANDS
LONG CAY
HALF MOON CAY

Copainalá
Simojovel
Ocosingo
Lago Petén Itzá
Flores
Dangriga

San Cristóbal de las Casas
San Benito
SOUTH WATER CAY

Ozocoautla
Chiapa de Corzo
Cerro Los Bolones 9154 ft. 2790 m
La Libertad
Victoria Peak 3675 ft. 1120 m
MAYA MOUNTAINS

Tuxtla Gutiérrez
CHIAPAS
La Florida
Sayaxché
Dolores
LAUGHING BIRD CAY

Venustiano Carranza
Las Rosas
Laguna Lacandón
San Luis
RANGUANA CAY

Villa Flores
Las Margaritas
PUNTA NEGRA
SAPODILLA CAYS
ISLA DE ROATÁN

Revolución Mexicana
Comitán de Domínguez
La Trinitaria
Punta Gorda
Gulf of Honduras
ISLA DE UTILA
ISLAS DE LA BAHÍA
Roatán
Utila

Presa de la Angostura
Las Delicias
CABO TRES PUNTAS
Bahía de Amatique

Pijijiapan
Barillas
Chisec
Livingston
Puerto Cortés
La Ceiba

Chicomuselo
Jacaltenango
Colorado

Cerro el Triunfo 8038 ft. 2450 m
El Pacayal
Concepción Huista
San Pedro Carchá
El Estor
Puerto Barrios
Baracoa
Tela
Pico Bonito 7989 ft. 2435 m

Mapastepec
Escuintla
Cobán
Panzós
QUIRIGUÁ
Choloma
San Pedro Sula
El Progreso
Olanchito

Motozintla de Mendoza
Huehuetenango
COPÁN
Cerro San Ildefonso 7310 ft. 2228 m
La Lima
Pico Pijol 7487 ft. 2282 m
Yoro

Huixtla
Volcán Tacaná 13,428 ft. 4093 m
San Andrés Sajcabajá
Salamá
San Jerónimo
Santa Rita
HONDURAS

Volcán Tajumulco 13,845 ft. 4220 m
San Pedro Sacatepéquez
Santa Cruz del Quiché
Chichicastenango
Zacapa
Santa Rosa de Copán
Santa Bárbara
Minas de Oro
San Ignacio
Salamá

Tapachula
Quetzaltenango
GUATEMALA
Chiquimula
Cerro Las Minas 9347 ft. 2849 m
CORDILLERA OPALACA
Siguatepeque
Comayagua
San Marcos de Colón
Guaimaca

Puerto Madero
Volcán Santa María 12,375 ft. 3772 m
Chimaltenango
Jalapa
San Luis Jilotepeque
Metapán
Cerro El Pital 8957 ft. 2730 m
La Esperanza
La Paz
Montaña El Chile 7402 ft. 2256 m

Champerico
Mazatenango
Antigua Guatemala
Lago de Atitlán
Guatemala
Villa Nueva
Cuilapa
Jutiapa
Santa Ana
Cojutepeque
San Francisco
Tegucigalpa
Danlí

Retalhuleu
Volcán de Fuego 12,346 ft. 3763 m
Escuintla
Barberena
Chalatenango
Yuscarán
Güinope

Puerto San José
Chiquimulilla
Santa Ana
Apopa
Sonsonate
Soyapango
San Salvador
Nueva San Salvador
Volcán de San Vicente 7156 ft. 2181 m
Sabanagrande
San Miguel

Acajutla
PUNTA REMEDIOS
San Vicente
Usulután
La Unión

MIDDLE AMERICA TRENCH
PACIFIC OCEAN
EL SALVADOR
Bahía de Jiquilisco
Golfo de Fonseca
Volcán Cosigüina 2818 ft. 859 m
Choluteca
El Corpus
NICARAGUA

© Rand McNally
A-101673-1

0 20 40 60 80 100 120 Miles
0 20 40 60 80 100 120 140 160 180 200 Kilometers

Lambert Conformal Conic Projection
Scale 1:4,000,000
One inch to 64 miles
One cm to 40 km

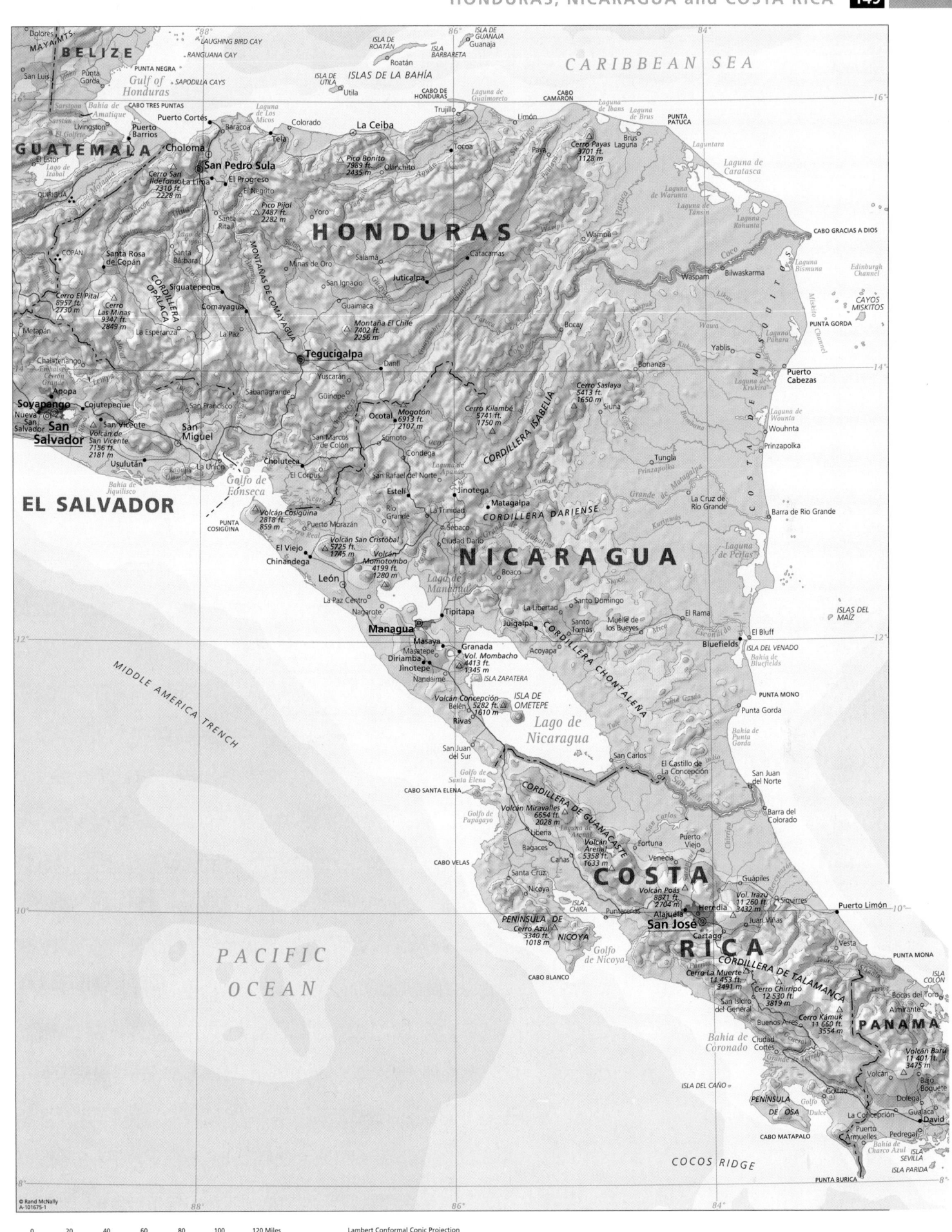

Dolores
MAYA MTS.
BELIZE
San Luis
Punta Gorda
PUNTA NEGRA
LAUGHING BIRD CAY
RANGUANA CAY
SAPODILLA CAYS
ISLA DE ROATÁN
Roatán
ISLA DE UTILA
Utila
ISLAS DE LA BAHÍA
ISLA BARBARETA
ISLA DE GUANAJA
Guanaja
CARIBBEAN SEA

Gulf of Honduras
Sarstoon
Bahía de Amatique
Livingston
CABO TRES PUNTAS
Puerto Barrios
El Golfete
Lago de Izabal
QUIRIGUÁ
El Estor
GUATEMALA

Puerto Cortés
Baracoa
Choloma
Cerro San Ildefonso 7310 ft. 2228 m
La Lima
San Pedro Sula
El Progreso
El Negrito
Tela
Laguna de Los Micos
Colorado
La Ceiba
Pico Bonito 7989 ft. 2435 m
Olanchito
Tocoa
Trujillo
CABO DE HONDURAS
Laguna de Guaimoreto
CABO CAMARÓN
Laguna de Ibans
Laguna de Brus
PUNTA PATUCA
Brus Laguna
Cerro Payas 3701 ft. 1128 m
Laguna de Caratasca

Santa Rita
Yoro
Pico Pijol 7487 ft. 2282 m
HONDURAS
Laguntara
CABO GRACIAS A DIOS

COPÁN
Santa Rosa de Copán
Santa Bárbara
Comayagua
MONTAÑAS DE COMAYAGUA
Minas de Oro
Salamá
San Ignacio
Catacamas
Juticalpa
Paya
Wampú
Laguna de Warunta
Laguna de Tansín
Edinburgh Channel

Cerro El Pital 8957 ft. 2730 m
CORDILLERA OPALACA
Cerro Las Minas 9347 ft. 2849 m
Siguatepeque
Guaimaca
Montaña El Chile 7402 ft. 2256 m
Bocay
Bonanza
Laguna de Rohusta
Bilwaskarma
CAYOS MISKITOS

Metapán
La Esperanza
La Paz
Tegucigalpa
Danlí
Waspam
PUNTA GORDA

Chalatenango
Cerro Grande
Apopa
Cojutepeque
San Francisco
Sabanagrande
Yuscarán
Güinope
Ocotal
Mogotón 6913 ft. 2107 m
Cerro Kilambé 5741 ft. 1750 m
Cerro Saslaya 5413 ft. 1650 m
Siuna
Tungla
Laguna de Krukira
Puerto Cabezas

Soyapango
Nueva San Salvador
San Salvador
San Vicente
Volcán de San Vicente 7156 ft. 2181 m
San Miguel
San Marcos de Colón
Somoto
Condega
CORDILLERA ISABELIA
Prinzapolka
Wouhnta
Prinzapolka
Laguna de Wounta

Usulután
La Unión
Choluteca
El Corpus
San Rafael del Norte
Estelí
Jinotega
Matagalpa
La Cruz de Río Grande
Barra de Río Grande

EL SALVADOR
Golfo de Fonseca
Bahía de Jiquilisco
El Real
Volcán Cosigüina 2818 ft. 859 m
PUNTA COSIGÜINA
Puerto Morazán
Río Grande
La Trinidad
Sébaco
Ciudad Darío
CORDILLERA DARIENSE
Grande de Matagalpa
Kurinwás

Volcán San Cristóbal 5725 ft. 1745 m
El Viejo
Chinandega
Volcán Momotombo 4199 ft. 1280 m
NICARAGUA
Boaco
Santo Domingo
Muelle de los Bueyes
El Rama
Laguna de Perlas
ISLAS DEL MAÍZ

León
La Paz Centro
Nagarote
Lago de Managua
Tipitapa
La Libertad
Santo Tomás
Juigalpa
Acoyapa
Mico
Escondido
El Bluff
Bluefields
ISLA DEL VENADO

MIDDLE AMERICA TRENCH
Managua
Masaya
Masatepe
Diriamba
Jinotepe
Nandaime
Granada
Vol. Mombacho 4413 ft. 1345 m
ISLA ZAPATERA
CORDILLERA CHONTALEÑA
Bahía de Bluefields
PUNTA MONO

Volcán Concepción 5282 ft. 1610 m
Belén
ISLA DE OMETEPE
Rivas
Lago de Nicaragua
Punta Gorda
Bahía de Punta Gorda

San Juan del Sur
Golfo de Santa Elena
ISLA DE PADRE
San Carlos
El Castillo de La Concepción
San Juan del Norte

CABO SANTA ELENA
Volcán Miravalles 6654 ft. 2028 m
CORDILLERA DE GUANACASTE
Liberia
Fortuna
Puerto Viejo
Barra del Colorado

PACIFIC OCEAN
Golfo de Papagayo
Bagaces
Cañas
Volcán Arenal 5358 ft. 1633 m
Venecia
Guápiles
Siquirres
Puerto Limón

CABO VELAS
Santa Cruz
Nicoya
Volcán Poás 8871 ft. 2704 m
Vol. Irazú 11 260 ft. 3432 m
Juan Viñas
Vesta

ISLA CHIRA
PENÍNSULA DE NICOYA
Cerro Azul 3340 ft. 1018 m
Puntarenas
Heredia
Alajuela
San José
Cartago
COSTA RICA
PUNTA MONA
ISLA COLÓN
Bocas del Toro

Golfo de Nicoya
CABO BLANCO
CORDILLERA DE TALAMANCA
Cerro La Muerte 11 453 ft. 3491 m
San Isidro del General
Cerro Chirripó 12 530 ft. 3819 m
Cerro Kamuk 11 660 ft. 3554 m
Buenos Aires
Almirante
PANAMA

Bahía de Coronado
Ciudad Cortés
Grande de Térraba
Volcán Barú 11 401 ft. 3475 m
Volcán
Bajo Boquete

PENÍNSULA DE OSA
Golfo Dulce
La Concepción
Golfito
Puerto Armuelles
Gualaca
David
Pedregal
ISLA SEVILLA
ISLA PARIDA

CABO MATAPALO
Bahía de Charco Azul
ISLA AZUL
COCOS RIDGE
PUNTA BURICA

© Rand McNally
A-101675-1

0 20 40 60 80 100 120 Miles
0 20 40 60 80 100 120 140 160 180 200 Kilometers

Lambert Conformal Conic Projection
Scale 1:4,000,000
One inch to 64 miles
One cm to 40 km

NICARAGUA

Laguna
Páhara
Puerto Cabezas

ISLA DE
PROVIDENCIA

SAN ANDRÉS
Y PROVIDENCIA
(Colombia)

ISLA DE
SAN ANDRÉS · San Andrés

CAYOS DEL
ESTE SUDESTE

ISLAS DEL MAÍZ
(Nicaragua)

CAYOS DE
ALBUQUERQUE

C A R I B B E A N
S E A

Inset map a

CARIBBEAN
SEA

PUNTA MANZANILLO

Portobelo
Nombre de Dios
Palenque
Miramar
Playa
Chiquita

Cerro Bruja
3212 ft.
979 m

María Chiquita

Coco
Solo
Colón · Cativá · Puerto Pilón
COLÓN
Cristóbal · Rainbow City
GATÚN
LOCKS · Margarita · Río Rita
Salamanca
Gatún
Gatuncillo
Lago
Alajuela
La Mesa

Nuevo Chagres
Palmas
Bellas

Buena Vista

P
A
N
A
M
A

Lago
Gatún
ISLA BARRO
COLORADO
Panama
Calzada
Larga

Escobal
Chilibre

D
E

Las Cumbres
Tocumen
Pacora

Bahía
Trinidad
Lagarterita
Gamboa
Paraíso
Pedro Miguel

Arenosa
PEDRO MIGUEL
LOCKS
Juan Díaz

Boca del
Río Indio
Cerro Cama
PANAMÁ
MIRAFLORES
LOCKS
San Miguelito

COCLÉ
La Zanguenga
Arraiján
Diablo
Heights
Panamá

Pueblo
Nuevo
Nuevo
Arraiján
Balboa

La Chorrera
Vacamonte

Ciri Grande
Lídice · Capira
Bahía de
Panamá

Río Indio
Taboga

©Rand McNally
A-101679-1

Puerto
Limón

COSTA RICA
Vesta
PUNTA
MONA
ISLA
COLÓN
ARCHIPIÉLAGO DE
BOCAS DEL TORO
PUNTA
MANZANILLO
Nombre
de Dios
El Porvenir
Golfo de San Blas
Ticantiquí

CORDILLERA DE
TALAMANCA
Almirante
Bocas del Toro
ISLA BASTIMENTOS
Portobelo
Panama Canal
(Canal de Panamá)
Colón
Cristóbal
ISTMO DE
PANAMÁ
SERRANÍA DE SAN BLAS

Cerro Kamuk
11 660 ft.
3554 m
Buenos Aires
ISLA POPA
Palmas Bellas
Lago
Gatún
Gamboa
Chepo
PUNTA MOSQUITO
Mansucum

Volcán Barú
11 401 ft.
3475 m
ISLA ESCUDO
DE VERAGUAS
Laguna de
Chiriquí
PEN.
VALIENTE
Golfo de los
Mosquitos
Lago Gatún
Paraíso
San Miguelito
Panamá
Pacora
CABO
TIBURÓN

Volcán
Bajo Boquete
Grande
La Chorrera
Capira
Bahía
de Panamá
Chimán
PUNTA
CARIBANA
Acandí
Golfo
de
Urabá

Golfito
La Concepción
Dolega
Gualaca
P A N A M A
Lídice
Bejuco
 SERRANÍA DEL DARIÉN

PEN.
DE
OSA
Golfo
Dulce
David
CORDILLERA CENTRAL
Penonomé
El Valle
Antón
San Carlos
San Miguel
La Palma
Yaviza

Puerto
Armuelles
Pedregal
Cerro
Santiago
9959 ft.
2121 m
Santa Fé
Natá
Río Hato
ISLA
SAN JOSÉ
ISLA
DEL REY
El Real de
Santa María
Turbo

CABO
MATAPALO
Bahía
de Charco
Azul
ISLA
SEVILLA
Remedios
Cañazas
Aguadulce
Golfo de
San Miguel
PUNTA
GARACHINÉ
Garachiné
ANTIOQUIA

PUNTA BURICA
ISLA PARIDA
ISLA BOCA
BRAVA
Golfo
de Chiriquí
Las
Palmas
Santa María
Santiago
Monagrillo
Bahía de
Parita
ARCHIPIÉLAGO
DE LAS PERLAS
Chigorodó

Soná
Montijo
Pesé
Chitré
Golfo de
Panamá
Jaqué
Ríosucio

Golfo
de
Montijo
Guararé
La Palma
Apartadó

ISLA DE
COIBA
ISLA DE
CEBACO
PENÍNSULA
DE AZUERO
Las Tablas
Pedasí
Salaquí
Salaquí
COLOMBIA

Tonosí
PUNTA MALA
CHOCÓ

ISLA JICARÓN
PUNTA MARIATO

PUNTA
MARZO
ANT.

PACIFIC
OCEAN
PANAMA BASIN
Golfo de
Cúpica
SERRANÍA DE BAUDÓ

Ensenada
de Tribugá
Quibdó
Nuquí

© Rand McNally
A-101677-1

| 0 | 20 | 40 | 60 | 80 | 100 | 120 Miles |

| 0 | 20 | 40 | 60 | 80 | 100 | 120 | 140 | 160 | 180 | 200 Kilometers |

Lambert Conformal Conic Projection
Scale 1:4,000,000
One inch to 64 miles
One cm to 40 km

Inset map a
Lambert Conformal Conic Projection
Scale 1:1,000,000
One inch to 16 miles
One cm to 10 km

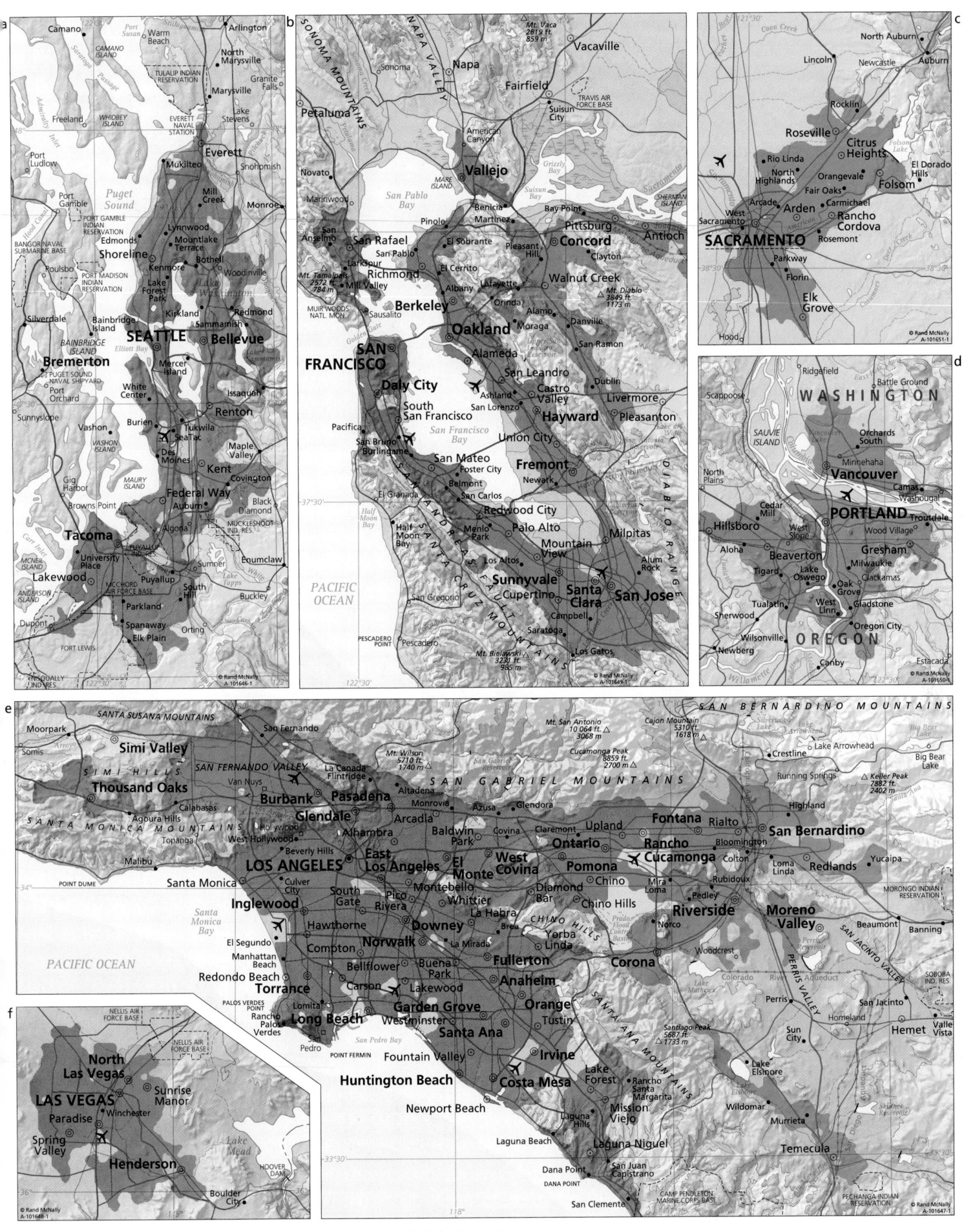

Lambert Conformal Conic Projection
Scale 1:1,000,000
One inch to 16 miles
One cm to 10 km

a

Lake Erie

CLEVELAND

Mentor On The Lake · Fairport Harbor · Painesville

Eastlake · Willowick · Willoughby · Mentor

Euclid · Willoughby Hills

Richmond Heights · East Cleveland · Chardon

Sheffield Lake · Bay Village · Rocky River · Lakewood · Mayfield Heights · Chesterland

Lorain · Avon Lake · Cleveland Heights · Beachwood · South Russell

Avon · Westlake · Brooklyn · Shaker Heights · Chagrin Falls

Sheffield · North Olmsted · Garfield Heights · Maple Heights · Solon

Amherst · North Ridgeville · Brook Park · Parma · Bedford · Reminderville

Elyria · Berea · Parma Heights · Broadview Heights · Aurora · Hiram

Oberlin · Eaton Estates · Strongsville · North Royalton · Brecksville · Macedonia · Twinsburg

Grafton · Brunswick · Hinckley · CUYAHOGA VALLEY NAT'L PARK · Mantua

Lagrange · Richfield · Hudson · Streetsboro

Wellington · Medina · Bath · Cuyahoga Falls · Stow · Ravenna · Lake Rockwell

West Salem · Chippewa Lake · Copley · Fairlawn · Kent · La Due Res.

Lodi · Creston · Akron · Tallmadge · Brimfield

Wadsworth · Norton · Barberton · Mogadore · Randolph · Magadore

Seville · Clinton · Suffield · Uniontown

Doylestown · Manchester · Portage Lakes · Greentown · Hartville

Rittman · Green

Madisonburg · Smithville · Canal Fulton · Lake Cable · North Canton

Wooster · Orrville · Dalton · Massillon · Perry Heights · Canton · East Canton · Louisville

Apple Creek · Richville

Brewster · Navarre · North Industry

MORICANVILLE DAM

© Rand McNally A-101629-1

b

White · Fairport Harbor · Gainesville · Chicopee · Lake Sidney Lanier

Ball Ground · Flowery Branch

North Canton · Canton · Cumming · Buford · BUFORD DAM

Emerson · Holly Springs · Sugar Hill · Suwanee

Cartersville · Woodstock · Alpharetta

Acworth · Roswell · Duluth · Auburn

Kennesaw · Sandy Springs · Norcross · Lawrenceville

Marietta · Dunwoody · Loganville

Dallas · Fair Oaks · Chamblee · Doraville · Snellville

Powder Springs · Smyrna · North Atlanta · Tucker · Stone Mountain

Hiram · Mableton · Austell · Decatur · Redan · Lithonia

Douglasville · ATLANTA · Conyers

East Point · Panthersville · Covington

College Park · Hapeville · Forest Park

Union City · Fairburn · Riverdale · Stockbridge

Palmetto · Jonesboro · McDonough

Sargent · Fayetteville · Hampton

Newnan · Peachtree City · Experiment

Moreland · Senoia · Jackson Lake

© Rand McNally A-101631-1

c

KITTATINNY MTN · Columbia · Pen Argyl · Bangor · Belvidere

Union Bridge · Westminster · Hereford · Forest Hill · Tamaqua · Lehighton · Palmerton · Washing...

Woodsboro · New Windsor · Upperco · Fallston · Slatington · Walnutport · Nazareth · Hampto...

Middleton · Walkersville · Libertytown · Finksburg · Cockeysville · Phoenix · Bel Air · BLUE MOUNTAIN · Schnecksville · Catasauqua · Northampton · Easton · Phillipsburg

Braddock Heights · Frederick · New Market · Sandyville · Reisterstown · Lutherville Timonium · Long Green · Pleasant Hills · Whitehall · Bethlehem · Wilson · Alpha · Clinton

Point of Rocks · Damascus · Mount Airy · Sykesville · Randallstown · Towson · Parkville · Perry Hall · Joppatowne · Edgewood · Allentown · Fountain Hill · Milford

Clarksburg · Cooksville · Pikesville · Overlea · Essex · Middle River · Emmaus · Hellertown · Coopersburg · Flemingto...

Dickerson · Germantown · Highland · BALTIMORE · Shoemakersville · Kutztown · Macungie · Quakertown

MARYLAND · Ellicott City · Catonsville · Arbutus · Dundalk · ABERDEEN PROVING GROUND · Reading · East Greenville · Red Hill · Perkasie

Poolesville · Columbia · Landsdowne · Edgemere · Laureldale · Boyertown · Gilbertsville · Telford · Plumsteadville · ...ambert

Gaithersburg · Olney · Savage · FORT GEORGE G. MEADE · Glen Burnie · Riviera Beach · Shillington · Fleetwood · Harleysville · Lansdale · New Hope

North Potomac · Rockville · Laurel · Severn · Severna Park · Lake Shore · Birdsboro · Stowe · Souderton · Doylestown

Ashburn · Wheaton · Aspen Hill · Beltsville · Odenton · Spring City · Royersford · Warminster · Richboro

Sterling · Potomac · Silver Spring · Greenbelt · College Park · Arnold · BROAD NECK · Phoenixville · Collegeville · Willow Grove

Herndon · Reston · Bethesda · Hyattsville · Crofton · Bowie · Stevensville · Honey Brook · Valley Forge · East Norriton · Norristown · Abington · Glenside · Croydon · Bristo...

VIRGINIA · McLean · DIST. OF COLUMBIA · Planham · KENT ISLAND · Exton · King of Prussia · Conshohocken · Cheltenham · Willingboro

Chantilly · Vienna · Falls Church · Mitchellville · Largo · Londontown · THOMAS POINT · Downingtown · Paoli · Ardmore · PHILADELPHIA

Centreville · Fairfax · Arlington · WASHINGTON · Suitland · Mayo · Eastern Bay · Newtown Square · Broomall · Havertown · Upper Darby

Manassas Park · Annandale · Hillcrest Heights · Camp Springs · KENT POINT · Coatesville · West Chester · Springfield

Burke · Franconia · Alexandria · Clinton · Wittman · Parkesburg · Darby · Camden · Haddonfield

Manassas · Springfield · Groveton · Rosaryville · Sherwood · Kennett Square · Chester · Bellmawr · Stratford

FORT BELVOIR · Mount Vernon · ANDREWS AIR FORCE BASE · Owings · TILGHMAN ISLAND · West Grove · Paulsboro · Lindenwo...

Lake Ridge · Fort Washington Forest · Bryans Road · Tilghman · Hockessin · Claymont · Gibbstown · Woodbury · Pine Hill

Woodbridge · Accokeek · Chesapeake Beach · Wilmington · Elsmere · Swedesboro · Manto · Berlin

Dale City · Potomac Heights · Waldorf · Huntingtown · Penns Grove · Glassboro

QUANTICO MARINE CORPS BASE · Dumfries · Marbury · St. Charles · Herring Bay · MARYLAND · DELAWARE · Pitman

Lunga Reservoir · Triangle · Quantico · La Plata · Prince Frederick · Chesapeake Bay · Golden Beach · Taylors Island

© Rand McNally A-101630-1

d

PENNSYLVANIA

SCALE

0 5 10 15 20 25 30 Miles
0 5 10 15 20 25 30 35 40 45 50 Kilometers

Lambert Conformal Conic Projection
Scale 1:1,000,000
One inch to 16 miles
One cm to 10 km

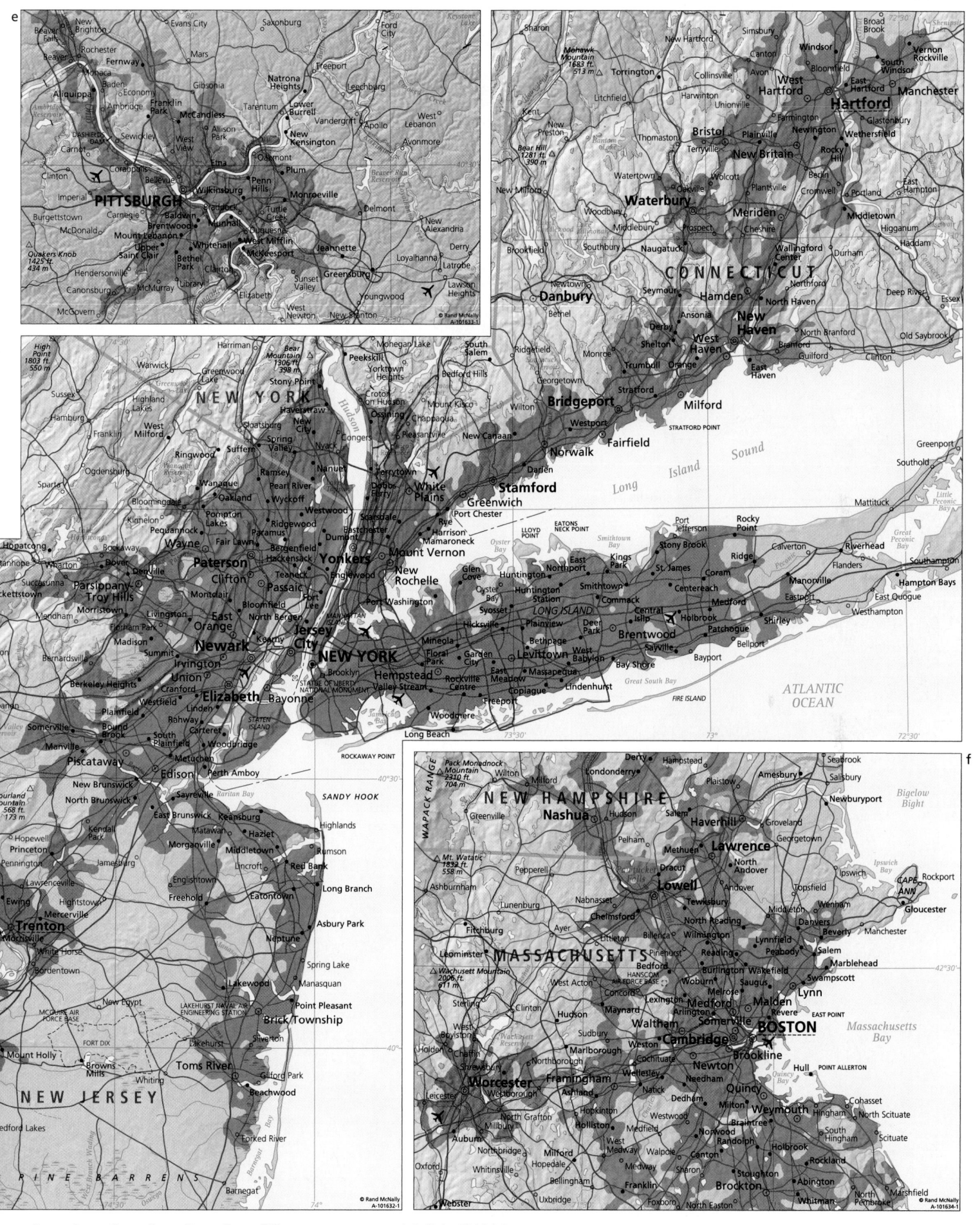

PITTSBURGH

CONNECTICUT

Hartford
Waterbury
New Haven
Bridgeport
Danbury
Stamford

NEW YORK

NEW YORK
Newark
Jersey City
Yonkers
Paterson
Elizabeth

NEW JERSEY

Trenton

LONG ISLAND

Long Island Sound

ATLANTIC OCEAN

NEW HAMPSHIRE
Nashua

MASSACHUSETTS

Lowell
Lawrence
Worcester
BOSTON
Cambridge
Quincy
Brockton

Massachusetts Bay

Lambert Conformal Conic Projection
Scale 1:1,000,000
One inch to 16 miles
One cm to 10 km

0 5 10 15 20 25 30 Miles
0 5 10 15 20 25 30 35 40 45 50 Kilometers

© Rand McNally

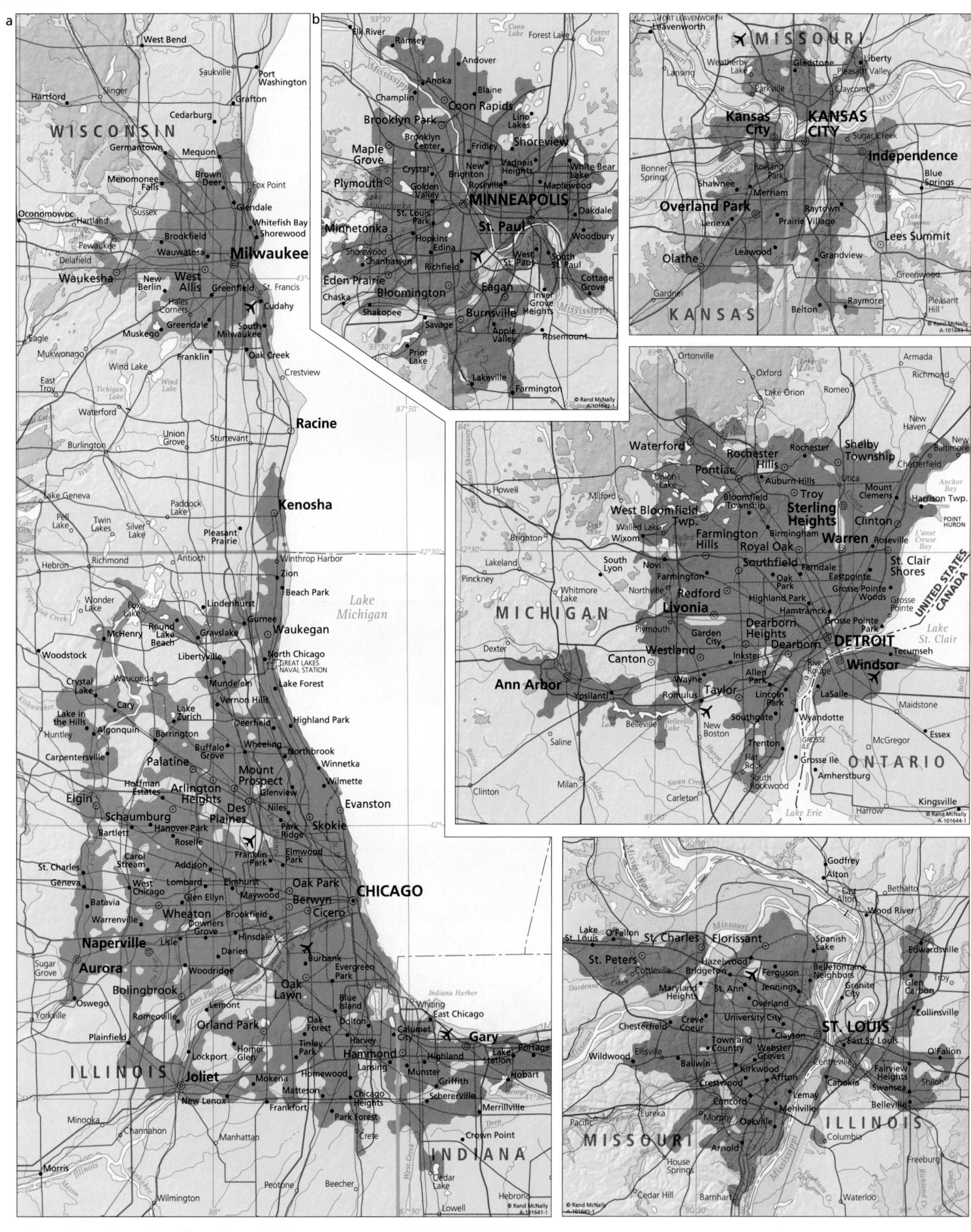

a

West Bend
Saukville
Port Washington
Slinger
Hartford
Grafton
Cedarburg
Germantown
Mequon
WISCONSIN
Menomonee Falls
Brown Deer
Fox Point
Oconomowoc
Hartland
Sussex
Glendale
Whitefish Bay
Delafield
Pewaukee
Brookfield
Wauwatosa
Shorewood
Waukesha
Milwaukee
Eagle
New Berlin
West Allis
Greenfield
St. Francis
Hales Corners
Cudahy
Muskego
Greendale
South Milwaukee
Mukwonago
Franklin
Oak Creek
East Troy
Wind Lake
Crestview
Waterford
Union Grove
Sturtevant
Racine
Burlington
Lake Geneva
Paddock Lake
Kenosha
Pell Lake
Twin Lakes
Silver Lake
Pleasant Prairie
Richmond
Antioch
Winthrop Harbor
Hebron
Zion
Beach Park
Wonder Lake
Lindenhurst
McHenry
Round Lake Beach
Grayslake
Gurnee
Waukegan
Woodstock
Wauconda
Libertyville
North Chicago
GREAT LAKES NAVAL STATION
Crystal Lake
Mundelein
Lake Forest
Lake in the Hills
Cary
Vernon Hills
Deerfield
Highland Park
Huntley
Algonquin
Lake Zurich
Carpentersville
Barrington
Wheeling
Northbrook
Buffalo Grove
Winnetka
Elgin
Palatine
Mount Prospect
Wilmette
Hoffman Estates
Arlington Heights
Glenview
Niles
Evanston
Schaumburg
Des Plaines
Bartlett
Hanover Park
Park Ridge
Skokie
Roselle
Elmwood Park
St. Charles
Carol Stream
Addison
Franklin Park
Geneva
West Chicago
Lombard
Elmhurst
Oak Park
Batavia
Glen Ellyn
Maywood
Berwyn
Warrenville
Wheaton
Brookfield
Cicero
CHICAGO
Naperville
Downers Grove
Hinsdale
Lisle
Darien
Burbank
Aurora
Woodridge
Evergreen Park
Bolingbrook
Oak Lawn
Sugar Grove
Romeoville
Lemont
Blue Island
Indiana Harbor
Yorkville
Oswego
Orland Park
Oak Forest
Dolton
Harvey
Whiting
East Chicago
Plainfield
Tinley Park
Homewood
Hammond
Gary
Lockport
Homer Glen
Lansing
Highland
Munster
Calumet City
Portage
Lake Station
Joliet
Mokena
Matteson
Chicago Heights
Griffith
Hobart
New Lenox
Schererville
Merrillville
Minooka
Frankfort
Park Forest
Crete
ILLINOIS
Channahon
Manhattan
INDIANA
Morris
Peotone
Beecher
Crown Point
Wilmington
Cedar Lake
Hebron
Lowell

b

Elk River
Ramsey
Coon Lake
Forest Lake
Forest Lake
Andover
Anoka
Blaine
Champlain
Coon Rapids
Lino Lakes
Brooklyn Park
Shoreview
Maple Grove
Brooklyn Center
Fridley
Vadnais Heights
White Bear Lake
Plymouth
Crystal
New Brighton
Roseville
Maplewood
Minnetonka
Golden Valley
St. Louis Park
MINNEAPOLIS
St. Paul
Oakdale
Shorewood
Hopkins
Edina
West St. Paul
Woodbury
Chanhassen
Richfield
South St. Paul
Eden Prairie
Cottage Grove
Chaska
Bloomington
Eagan
Inver Grove Heights
Shakopee
Burnsville
Savage
Apple Valley
Rosemount
Prior Lake
Lakeville
Farmington

Fort Leavenworth
Leavenworth
MISSOURI
Weatherby Lake
Gladstone
Liberty
Lansing
Pleasant Valley
Parkville
Claycomo
Kansas City
KANSAS CITY
Bonner Springs
Sugar Creek
Independence
Shawnee
Roeland Park
Blue Springs
Merriam
Overland Park
Raytown
Lenexa
Prairie Village
Lees Summit
Olathe
Leawood
Grandview
Greenwood
Gardner
KANSAS
Belton
Raymore
Pleasant Hill

Ortonville
Oxford
Lake Orion
Armada
Richmond
Waterford
Rochester Hills
Rochester
Shelby Township
New Baltimore
Howell
Pontiac
Auburn Hills
Utica
Chesterfield
Milford
Bloomfield Township
Troy
Mount Clemens
Harrison Twp.
West Bloomfield Twp.
Sterling Heights
Brighton
Walled Lake
Birmingham
Clinton
Roseville
Wixom
Farmington Hills
Warren
Lakeland
Royal Oak
MICHIGAN
South Lyon
Novi
Southfield
Farndale
Eastpointe
St. Clair Shores
Pinckney
Farmington
Oak Park
Highland Park
Grosse Pointe Woods
Whitmore Lake
Northville
Redford
Hamtramck
Grosse Pointe
Livonia
Dexter
Plymouth
Garden City
Dearborn Heights
Grosse Pointe Park
Westland
Dearborn
DETROIT
Canton
Inkster
Windsor
Ann Arbor
Wayne
Allen Park
Ypsilanti
Romulus
Taylor
Lincoln Park
LaSalle
Southgate
Maidstone
Saline
Belleville
New Boston
Wyandotte
Essex
Trenton
McGregor
Flat Rock
GROSSE ILE
Grosse Ile
ONTARIO
Clinton
Milan
Carleton
South Rockwood
Amherstburg
Kingsville
Harrow

Godfrey
Alton
Bethalto
Pacific
East Alton
Wood River
Lake St. Louis
O'Fallon
St. Charles
Florissant
Spanish Lake
St. Peters
Hazelwood
Bellefontaine Neighbors
Edwardsville
Cottleville
Bridgeton
Ferguson
Glen Carbon
Maryland Heights
St. Ann
Jennings
Granite City
Chesterfield
Overland
Troy
Creve Coeur
University City
Collinsville
Wildwood
Ellisville
Clayton
ST. LOUIS
Town and Country
Webster Groves
East St. Louis
O'Fallon
Ballwin
Kirkwood
Fairview Heights
Crestwood
Affton
Cahokia
Swansea
Eureka
Concord
Lemay
Mehlville
Belleville
Pacific
Murphy
Oakville
Shiloh
MISSOURI
House Springs
Arnold
ILLINOIS
Columbia
Cedar Hill
Barnhart
Freeburg
Waterloo

Lake Michigan

Lake St. Clair

Lake Erie

UNITED STATES
CANADA

© Rand McNally

0   5   10   15   20   25   30 Miles
0 5 10 15 20 25 30 35 40 45 50 Kilometers

Lambert Conformal Conic Projection
Scale 1:1,000,000
One inch to 16 miles
One cm to 10 km

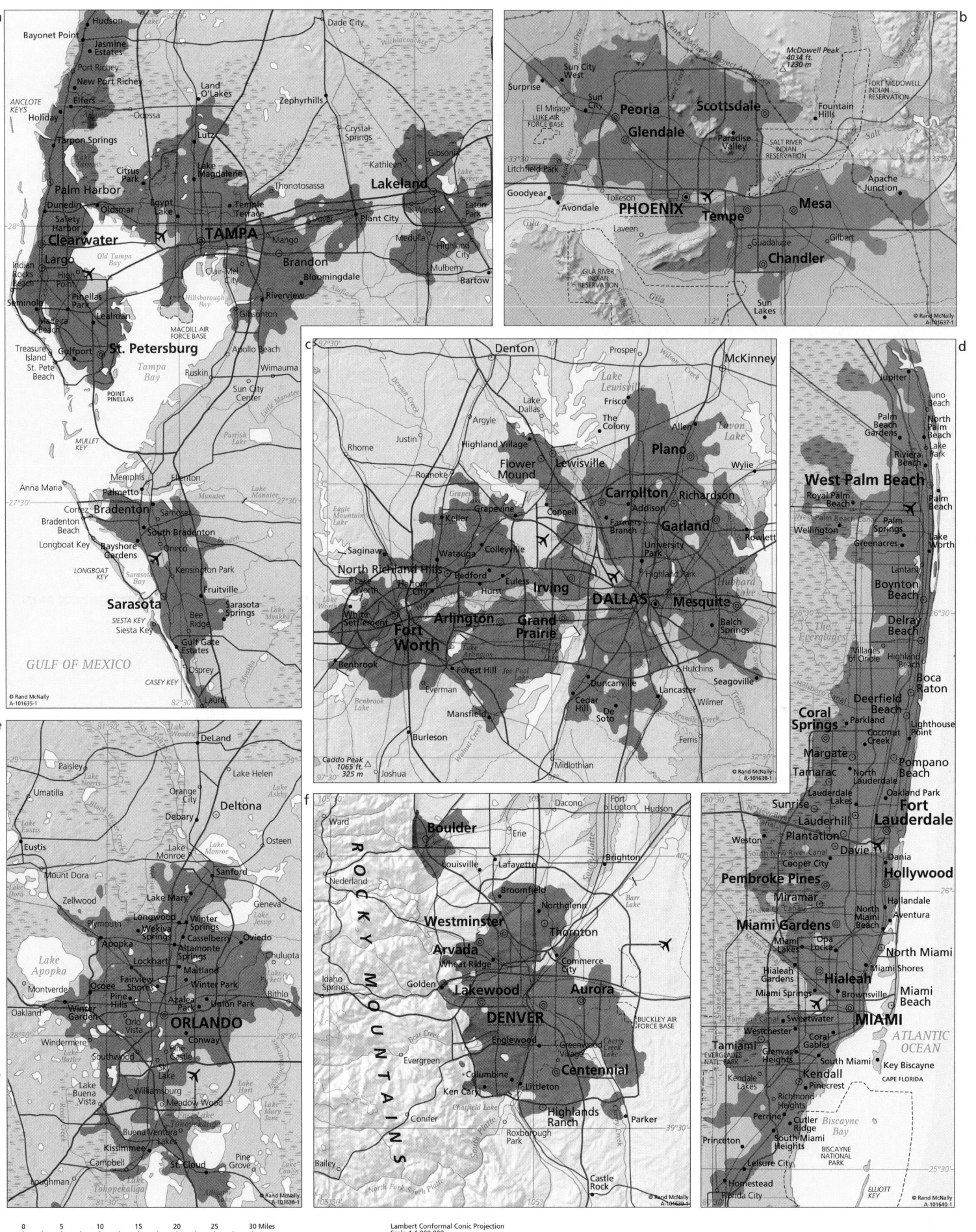

© Rand McNally
A-101637-1

© Rand McNally
A-101638-1

© Rand McNally
A-101635-1

© Rand McNally
A-101636-1

© Rand McNally
A-101639-1

© Rand McNally
A-101640-1

| 0 | 5 | 10 | 15 | 20 | 25 | 30 Miles |
| 0 | 5 | 10 | 15 | 20 | 25 | 30 | 35 | 40 | 45 | 50 Kilometers |

Lambert Conformal Conic Projection
Scale 1:1,000,000
One inch to 16 miles
One cm to 10 km

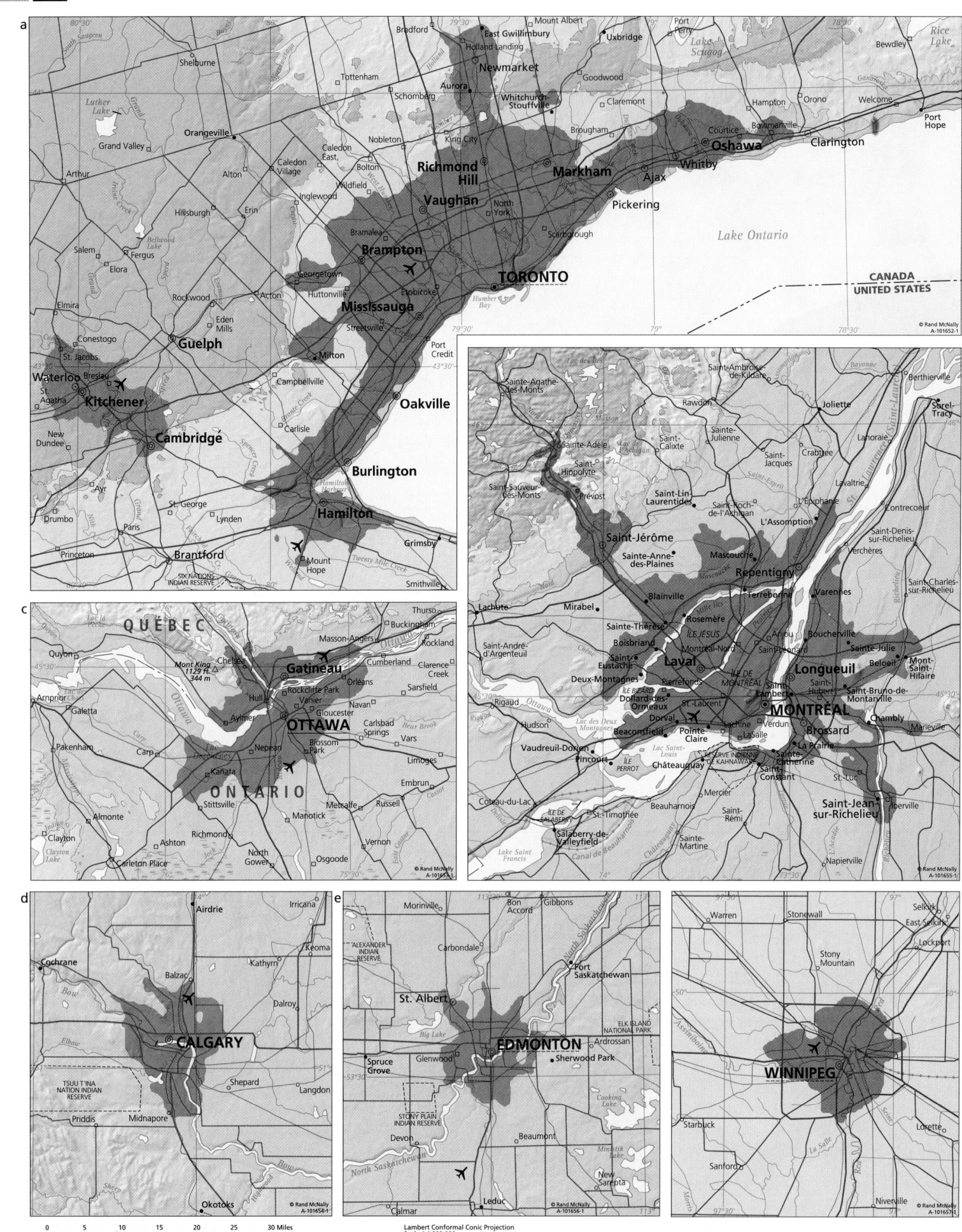

0   5   10   15   20   25   30 Miles
0   5   10   15   20   25   30   35   40   45   50 Kilometers

Lambert Conformal Conic Projection
Scale 1:1,000,000
One inch to 16 miles
One cm to 10 km

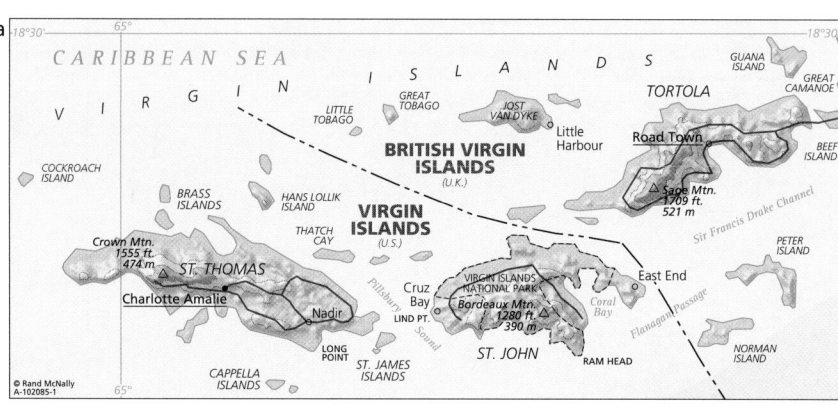

a

CARIBBEAN SEA

VIRGIN ISLANDS

BRITISH VIRGIN ISLANDS
(U.K.)

TORTOLA

GUANA ISLAND

GREAT CAMANOE

COCKROACH ISLAND

BRASS ISLANDS

HANS LOLLIK ISLAND

LITTLE TOBAGO

GREAT TOBAGO

JOST VAN DYKE

Little Harbour

Road Town

BEEF ISLAND

Little Tobago

THATCH CAY

VIRGIN ISLANDS
(U.S.)

Sage Mtn.
1709 ft.
521 m

Sir Francis Drake Channel

PETER ISLAND

Crown Mtn.
1555 ft.
474 m

ST. THOMAS

Charlotte Amalie

Nadir

Cruz Bay

LIND PT.

VIRGIN ISLANDS NATIONAL PARK
Bordeaux Mtn.
1280 ft.
390 m

Coral Bay

East End

Flanagan Passage

NORMAN ISLAND

Pillsbury Sound

LONG POINT

ST. JAMES ISLANDS

ST. JOHN

RAM HEAD

CAPPELLA ISLANDS

© Rand McNally
A-102085-1

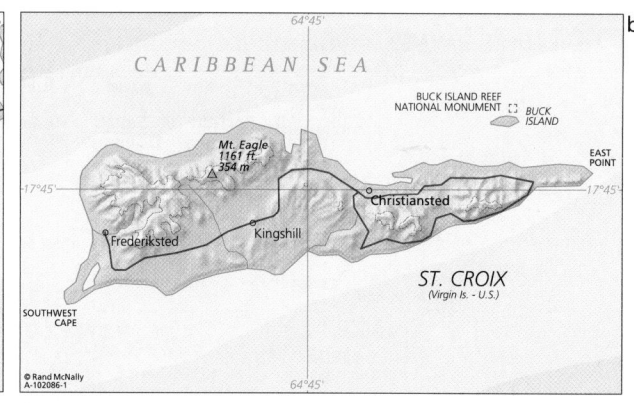

b

CARIBBEAN SEA

BUCK ISLAND REEF NATIONAL MONUMENT

BUCK ISLAND

EAST POINT

Mt. Eagle
1161 ft.
354 m

Christiansted

Frederiksted

Kingshill

ST. CROIX
(Virgin Is. - U.S.)

SOUTHWEST CAPE

© Rand McNally
A-102086-1

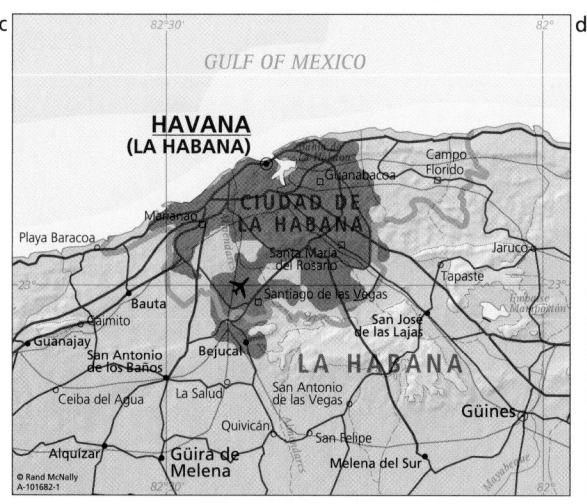

c

GULF OF MEXICO

HAVANA
(LA HABANA)

Guanabacoa

Campo Florido

Playa Baracoa

Marianao

Santa María del Rosario

Jaruco

CIUDAD DE LA HABANA

Bauta

Santiago de las Vegas

Tapaste

Güines

Guanajay

San Antonio de los Baños

Bejucal

San José de las Lajas

LA HABANA

Ceiba del Agua

La Salud

San Antonio de las Vegas

Quivicán

San Felipe

Alquízar

Güira de Melena

San Felipe

Mélena del Sur

© Rand McNally
A-101682-1

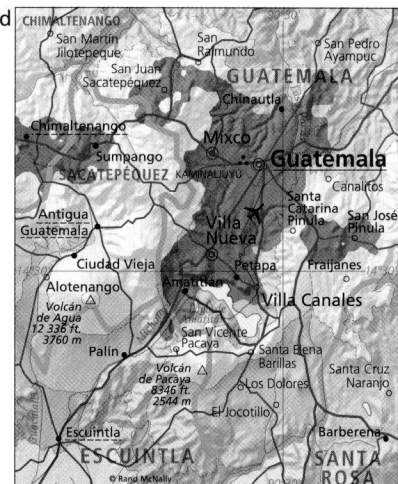

d

CHIMALTENANGO

San Martín Jilotepeque

San Raimundo

San Pedro Ayampuc

GUATEMALA

Chimaltenango

Mixco

Chinautla

San Juan Sacatepéquez

SACATEPÉQUEZ

Sumpango

KAMINALJUYÚ

Guatemala

Antigua Guatemala

Santa Catarina Pinula

San José Pinula

Ciudad Vieja

Villa Nueva

Petapa

Fraijanes

Alotenango

Amatitlán

Villa Canales

Volcán de Agua
12 336 ft.
3760 m

Palín

San Vicente Pacaya

Santa Elena Barillas

Santa Cruz Naranjo

Volcán de Pacaya
8346 ft.
2544 m

Los Dolores

Escuintla

El Jocotillo

Barberena

ESCUINTLA

SANTA ROSA

© Rand McNally
A-102084-1

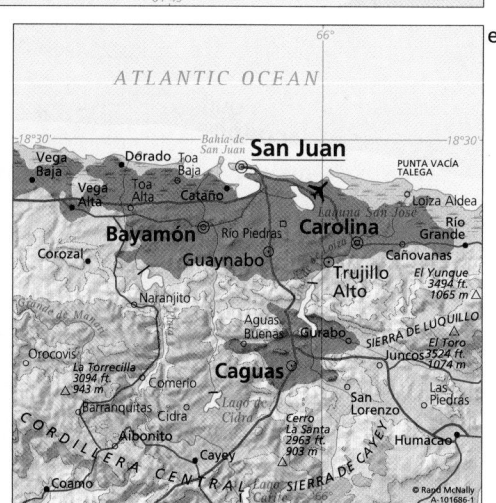

e

ATLANTIC OCEAN

Bahía de San Juan

San Juan

PUNTA VACÍA TALEGA

Vega Baja

Dorado

Toa Baja

Vega Alta

Toa Alta

Cataño

Loíza Aldea

Río Grande

Corozal

Bayamón

Río Piedras

Carolina

Cañovanas

Naranjito

Guaynabo

Trujillo Alto

El Yunque
3494 ft.
1065 m

SIERRA DE LUQUILLO

Orocovis

Aguas Buenas

Gurabo

El Toro
3524 ft.
1074 m

Juncos

La Torrecilla
3094 ft.
943 m

Comerío

Caguas

San Lorenzo

Las Piedras

Barranquitas

Cidra

Aibonito

Laguna Cidra

Cerro La Santa
2963 ft.
903 m

CORDILLERA CENTRAL

Cayey

SIERRA DE CA

Humacao

Coamo

Lago Carite

© Rand McNally
A-101686-1

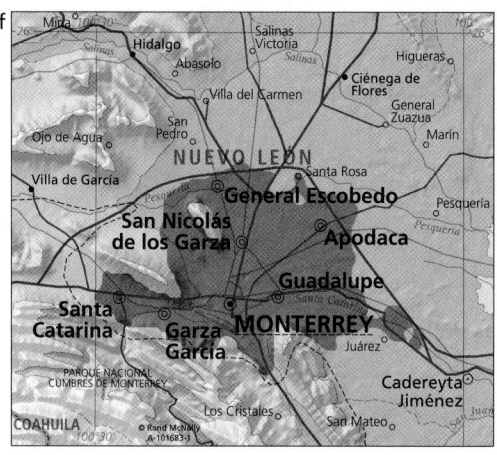

f

Mina

Hidalgo

Salinas Victoria

Higueras

Abasolo

Ciénega de Flores

Ojo de Agua

Villa del Carmen

General Zuazua

San Pedro

Marín

Villa de García

NUEVO LEÓN

Santa Rosa

General Escobedo

Pesquería

San Nicolás de los Garza

Apodaca

Guadalupe

Pesquería

Santa Catarina

Garza García

MONTERREY

Juárez

PARQUE NACIONAL CUMBRES DE MONTERREY

Los Cristales

Cadereyta Jiménez

COAHUILA

San Mateo

© Rand McNally
A-101683-1

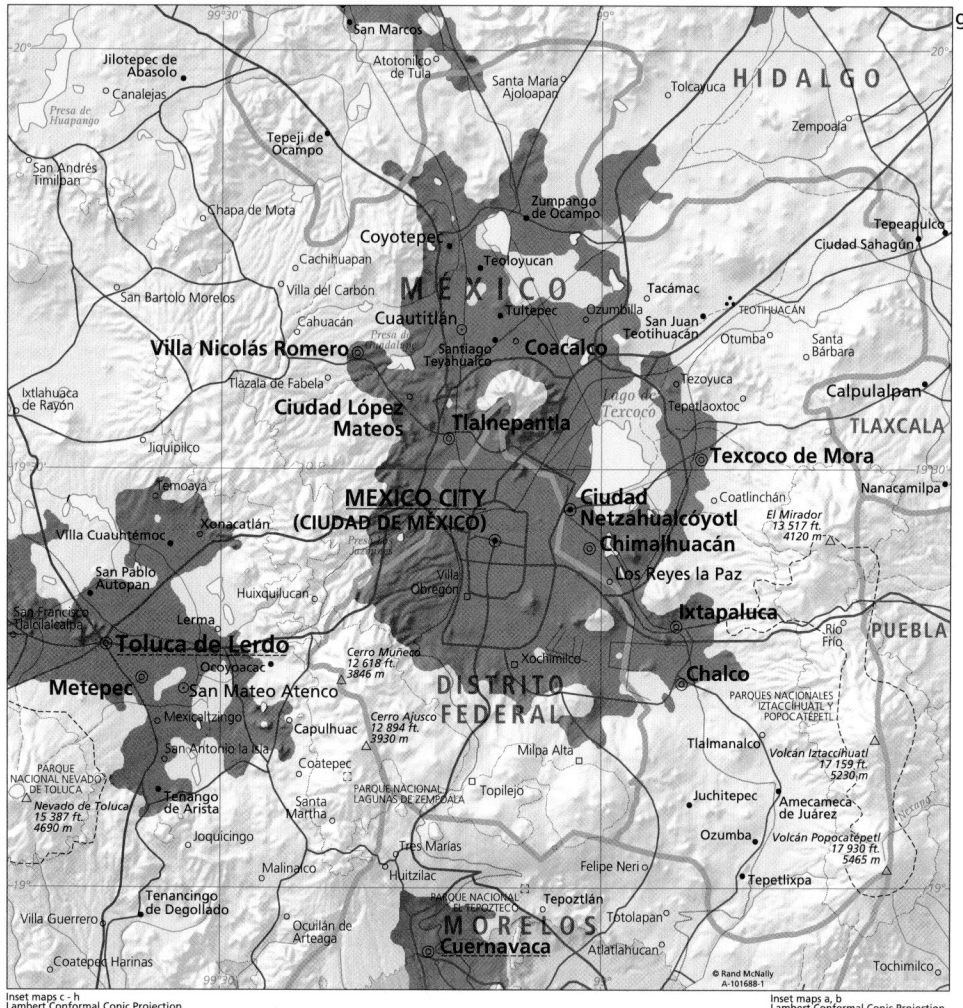

g

San Marcos

Jilotepec de Abasolo

Atotonilco de Tula

Santa María Ajoloapan

Tolcayuca

HIDALGO

Zempoala

Presa de Huapango

Canalejas

Tepeji de Ocampo

San Andrés Timilpan

Tepeapulco

Zumpango de Ocampo

Ciudad Sahagún

Chapa de Mota

Coyotepec

MÉXICO

Tacámac

Teoloyucan

Cachihuapan

Tultepec

Ozumbilla

San Juan Teotihuacán

TEOTIHUACÁN

Villa del Carbón

San Bartolo Morelos

Cuautitlán

Santiago Teyahualco

Tultepec

Otumba

Santa Bárbara

Cahuacán

Presa de Pacuya

Coacalco

Tezoyuca

Villa Nicolás Romero

Tezontepec

Tepetlaoxtoc

Calpulalpan

Ixtlahuaca de Rayón

Tlazala de Fabela

Tlalnepantla

TLAXCALA

Jiquipilco

Ciudad López Mateos

Texcoco de Mora

Lago de Texcoco

Nanacamilpa

Temoaya

Coatlinchán

MEXICO CITY
(CIUDAD DE MÉXICO)

Ciudad Netzahualcóyotl

El Mirador
13 517 ft.
4120 m

Villa Cuauhtémoc

Xonacatlán

Chimalhuacán

Villa Obregón

Los Reyes la Paz

San Pablo Autopan

Huixquilucan

Lerma

Ixtapaluca

Río Frío

PUEBLA

San Francisco Tlalcilalcalpa

Toluca de Lerdo

Cerro Muñeco
12 618 ft.
3846 m

Xochimilco

Chalco

Metepec

Ocoyoacac

San Mateo Atenco

Cerro Ajusco
12 894 ft.
3930 m

DISTRITO FEDERAL

PARQUES NACIONALES IZTACCÍHUATL Y POPOCATÉPETL

Tlalmanalco

Mexicaltzingo

Milpa Alta

Volcán Iztaccíhuatl
17 159 ft.
5230 m

San Antonio la Isla

Capulhuac

Juchitepec

Amecameca de Juárez

PARQUE NACIONAL NEVADO DE TOLUCA

Coatepec

PARQUE NACIONAL LAGUNAS DE ZEMPOALA

Topilejo

Ozumba

Volcán Popocatépetl
17 930 ft.
5465 m

Nevado de Toluca
15 387 ft.
4690 m

Tenango de Arista

Santa Martha

Tres Marías

Felipe Neri

Tepetlixpa

Ioquicingo

Malinalco

Tepoztlán

Tlotalpan

Tochimilco

Tenancingo de Degollado

Villa Guerrero

Ocuilán de Arteaga

MORELOS

Tepoztlán

Cuernavaca

Atlatlahucan

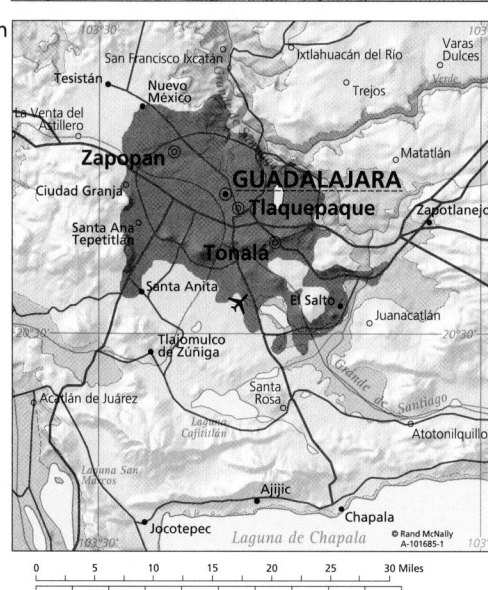

h

San Francisco Ixcatán

Ixtlahuacán del Río

Varas Dulces

Verde

Tesistán

Trejos

Nuevo México

La Venta del Astillero

Zapopan

Villa Cuauhtémoc

Matatlán

Ciudad Granja

GUADALAJARA

Santa Ana Tepetitlán

Tlaquepaque

Zapotlanejo

Tonalá

Santa Anita

El Salto

Juanacatlán

Tlajomulco de Zúñiga

Santa Rosa

Acatlán de Juárez

Ajijic

Chapala

Jocotepec

Laguna de Chapala

Laguna San Marcos

Atotonilquillo

© Rand McNally
A-101685-1

0	5	10	15	20	25	30 Miles
0	5	10	15	20	25 30 35 40 45	50 Kilometers

Inset maps c - h
Lambert Conformal Conic Projection
Scale 1:1,000,000
One inch to 16 miles
One cm to 10 km

Inset maps a, b
Lambert Conformal Conic Projection
Scale 1:500,000
One inch to 8 miles
One cm to 5 km

Gulf of Mexico

HAVANA **CUBA**

Mérida

HAITI DOMINICAN
REPUBLIC

**San
Juan**

JAMAICA
Kingston

**Port-au-
Prince**

**Santo
Domingo**

PUERTO
RICO
(U.S.)

MEXICO

BELIZE

GUATEMALA HONDURAS

Guatemala

EL SALVADOR NICARAGUA

Managua

COSTA
RICA Panamá

PANAMA

ISLA DEL
COCO
(C.R.)

C A R I B B E A N   S E A

GUADELOUPE
(Fr.)

MARTINIQUE
(Fr.)

ST. LUCIA

BARBADOS

ARUBA (Neth.)

GRENADA

TRINIDAD AND
TOBAGO

A T L A N T I C

O C E A N

Barranquilla **MARACAIBO** **CARACAS**

Cartagena Barquisimeto

Barcelona

Cúcuta San Cristóbal

Ciudad
Bolívar

Ciudad Guayana

MEDELLÍN

Bucaramanga

Manizales

BOGOTÁ

Llanos

Georgetown

Paramaribo

GUYANA

SURINAME

Cayenne

**FRENCH
GUIANA**
(Fr.)

CABO ORANGE

Buenaventura

CALI

VENEZUELA

Boa Vista

Esmeraldas

COLOMBIA

Orinoco

Pico da Neblina
9888 ft.
3014 m

Macapá

QUITO

Equator

ECUADOR

Chimborazo
20 702 ft.
6310 m

Negro

Amazon

Japurá

Putumayo

GUAYAQUIL

Cuenca

Iquitos

MANAUS

Santarém

Belém **São Luís**

Parnaíba

ARCHIPIÉLAGO DE COLÓN
(GALAPAGOS ISLANDS)
(Ec.)

Loja

Marañón

Içá

Juruá

Madeira

Purus

Tapajós

Xingu

Tocantins

Parnaíba

Fortaleza

Chiclayo Cajamarca

Ucayali

S E L V A S

Marabá

Teresina

CABO DE SÃO ROQUE

Trujillo

Pucallpa

Rio
Branco

Porto Velho

B R A Z I L

Campina
Grande **Natal**

Caruaru **João Pessoa**

Nevado Huascarán
22 133 ft.
6746 m

PERU

Huancayo

A
N
D
E
S

Juazeiro

RECIFE

Cusco

Lima

BOLIVIA

Guaporé

São Francisco

Represa de
Sobradinho

Maceió

Aracaju

PUNTA CARRETA Ica

Puno

La Paz • Trinidad

BRASÍLIA

SALVADOR

Arequipa

Cochabamba

Oruro

**SANTA CRUZ
DE LA SIERRA**

Cuiabá

GOIÂNIA

Itabuna

Arica

Sucre

Corumbá

BELO HORIZONTE

Montes
Claros

Potosí

Iquique

Tarija

Pico da Bandeira
9505 ft.
2897 m

Vitória

ILHAS
MARTIN VAZ
(Braz.)

PARAGUAY

GRAN

Campos

Antofagasta

ISLA SAN FÉLIX
(Chile)

Salta

CHACO

Asunción

SÃO PAULO

CABO FRIO

RIO DE JANEIRO

San Miguel de Tucumán

Corrientes

Posadas

Santos

CURITIBA

P A C I F I C

ARCHIPIÉLAGO JUAN
FERNÁNDEZ
(Chile)

Coquimbo

Santiago
del Estero

Salado

Santa
Maria

Florianópolis

PORTO ALEGRE

O C E A N

CÓRDOBA

Santa
Fe

Salto

Pelotas

Cerro Aconcagua
22 831 ft.
6959 m

Mendoza

Rosario

Paysandú

URUGUAY

Rio Grande

Valparaíso

SANTIAGO

BUENOS AIRES

La Plata

MONTEVIDEO

A R G E N T I N A

PAMPA

CABO SAN ANTONIO

Concepción

Neuquén

**Bahía
Blanca**

Mar del Plata

Valdivia

Negro

A T L A N T I C

Osorno

Golfo San Matías

O C E A N

Puerto Montt

C H I L E

ARCHIPIÉLAGO
DE LOS CHONOS

Comodoro Rivadavia

Golfo San
Jorge

Monte San Valentín
13 314 ft.
4058 m

PATAGONIA

CABO TRES PUNTAS

**FALKLAND
ISLANDS**
(U.K.)

Río
Gallegos

Stanley

Punta Arenas

S C O T I A

S E A

CAPE HORN

Drake Passage

**SOUTH GEORGIA
AND THE SOUTH
SANDWICH ISLANDS**
(U.K.)

SOUTH
SHETLAND IS.
(U.K.)

SOUTH
ORKNEY IS.
(U.K.)

ANTARCTIC PENINSULA

S O U T H E R N   O C E A N

Antarctic Circle

Tropic of Cancer

Tropic of Capricorn

© Rand McNally
A-101692-1

0	200	400	600	800	1000	1200 Miles

0	200	400	600	800	1000	1200	1400	1600	1800	2000 Kilometers

Lambert Azimuthal Equal Area Projection
Scale 1:40,000,000
One inch to 640 miles
One cm to 400 km

Gulf of Mexico
YUCATAN CHANNEL
Havana
CUBA
Tropic of Cancer
YUCATAN PENINSULA
GREATER
HAITI
DOMINICAN REPUBLIC
HISPANIOLA
PUERTO RICO TRENCH
MEXICO
JAMAICA
ANTILLES
PUERTO RICO (U.S.)
GUADELOUPE (Fr.)
ATLANTIC OCEAN
BELIZE
WEST INDIES
MARTINIQUE (Fr.)
GUATEMALA HONDURAS
CARIBBEAN SEA
LESSER ANTILLES
BARBADOS
EL SALVADOR
NICARAGUA
Lago de Nicaragua
Pico Cristóbal Colón 18 947 ft. 5775 m
TRINIDAD AND TOBAGO
COSTA RICA
ISTMO DE PANAMA
Maracaibo
Pico Bolívar 16 427 ft. 5007 m
Caracas
PANAMA
Golfo de Panamá
Lago de Maracaibo
VENEZUELA
Orinoco
GUYANA
Paramaribo
Mt. Roraima 9432 ft. 2875 m
SURINAME
FRENCH GUIANA (Fr.)
CABO ORANGE
ISLA DEL COCO (C.R.)
ISLA DE MALPELO (Col.)
Nevado del Tolima 17 110 ft. 5215 m
Bogotá
LLANOS
COLOMBIA
Pico da Neblina 9888 ft. 3014 m
PUNTA GALERA
Nevado del Huila 18 865 ft. 5750 m
Cayambe 18 996 ft. 5790 m
Negro
Japurá
Represa Balbina
Amazon
Belém
Equator
ECUADOR
Quito
Chimborazo 20 702 ft. 6310 m
Manaus
Fortaleza
ILHA FERNANDO DE NORONHA
ARCHIPIÉLAGO DE COLÓN (GALAPAGOS ISLANDS) (Ec.)
Golfo de Guayaquil
Iquitos
Putumayo
S E L V A S
Amazon
Madeira
Tapajós
CABO DE SAO ROQUE
PUNTA PARIÑAS
Marañón
Juruá
Purus
Xingu
PONTA DO SEIXAS
Nevado Huascarán 22 133 ft. 6746 m
B R A Z I L
Recife
PERU
Porto Velho
Represa de Sobradinho
Lima
Madre de Dios
Beni
Guaporé
PLANALTO DO MATO GROSSO
Pico das Almas 6024 ft. 1836 m
Salvador
PUNTA CARRETA
Lago Titicaca
Nevado Illampu 21 066 ft. 6421 m
Brasília
São Francisco
Nevado Coropuna 20 686 ft. 6305 m
La Paz
ALTIPLANO
BOLIVIA
Belo Horizonte
SERRA DO ESPINHAÇO
Nevado Sajama 21 463 ft. 6542 m
A N D E S
Volcán San Pedro 20 161 ft. 6145 m
CHACO
Paraná
Pico da Bandeira 9505 ft. 2897 m
ILHAS MARTIN VAZ (Braz.)
DESIERTO DE ATACAMA
Volcán Llullaillaco 22 110 ft. 6739 m
GRAN
PARAGUAY
Asunción
São Paulo
Rio de Janeiro
CABO FRIO
ISLA SAN FÉLIX (Chile)
Nevado Ojos del Salado 22 615 ft. 6893 m
San Miguel de Tucumán
Iguaçu Falls
PACIFIC OCEAN
PERU-CHILE TRENCH
CABO BASCUÑAN
Cerro General Manuel Belgrano 20 505 ft. 6250 m
Córdoba
Salado
Paraná
Uruguay
URUGUAY
Porto Alegre
Lagoa dos Patos
ARCHIPIÉLAGO JUAN FERNÁNDEZ (Chile)
Cerro Aconcagua 22 831 ft. 6959 m
Santiago
A R G E N T I N A
Montevideo
Tropic of Capricorn
Buenos Aires
Río de la Plata
PAMPA
CABO SAN ANTONIO
PUNTA LAVAPIÉ
Colorado
Bahía Blanca
C H I L E
Monte Tronador 11 453 ft. 3491 m
Negro
ATLANTIC OCEAN
Golfo San Matías
ISLA GRANDE DE CHILOE
A N D E S
CABO DOS BAHÍAS
ARCHIPIÉLAGO DE LOS CHONOS
Golfo San Jorge
CABO TRES PUNTAS
Monte San Valentín 13 314 ft. 4058 m
PATAGONIA
ISLA WELLINGTON
FALKLAND ISLANDS (U.K.)
EAST FALKLAND
ISLA DESOLACIÓN
Punta Arenas
TIERRA DEL FUEGO
WEST FALKLAND
ISLA SANTA INÉS
ISLA HOSTE
CAPE HORN (CABO DE HORNOS)
SCOTIA SEA
CAPE DISAPPOINTMENT
SOUTH GEORGIA
SOUTH SANDWICH TRENCH
Drake Passage
SOUTH SHETLAND IS. (U.K.)
SOUTH GEORGIA AND THE SOUTH SANDWICH ISLANDS (U.K.)
SOUTH ORKNEY IS. (U.K.)
SOUTH SANDWICH IS.
SOUTHERN
ANTARCTIC PENINSULA
OCEAN
Antarctic Circle

© Rand McNally
A-101693-1

0   200   400   600   800   1000   1200 Miles
0   200   400   600   800   1000   1200   1400   1600   1800   2000 Kilometers

Lambert Azimuthal Equal Area Projection
Scale 1:40,000,000
One inch to 640 miles
One cm to 400 km

Land Cover

- Evergreen Needleleaf Forest
- Evergreen Broadleaf Forest
- Deciduous Broadleaf Forest
- Mixed Forest
- Woodland
- Wooded Grassland
- Closed Shrubland
- Open Shrubland
- Grassland
- Cropland
- Bare Ground (Desert and Ice)
- Urban and Built Up

Source: CIESIN; Hansen et al., 2000

A-102093-1
© Rand McNally

0   200   400   600   800   1000   1200 Miles

0   200   400   600   800   1000   1200   1400   1600   1800   2000 Kilometers

Lambert Azimuthal Equal Area Projection
Scale 1:40,000,000
One inch to 640 miles
One cm to 400 km

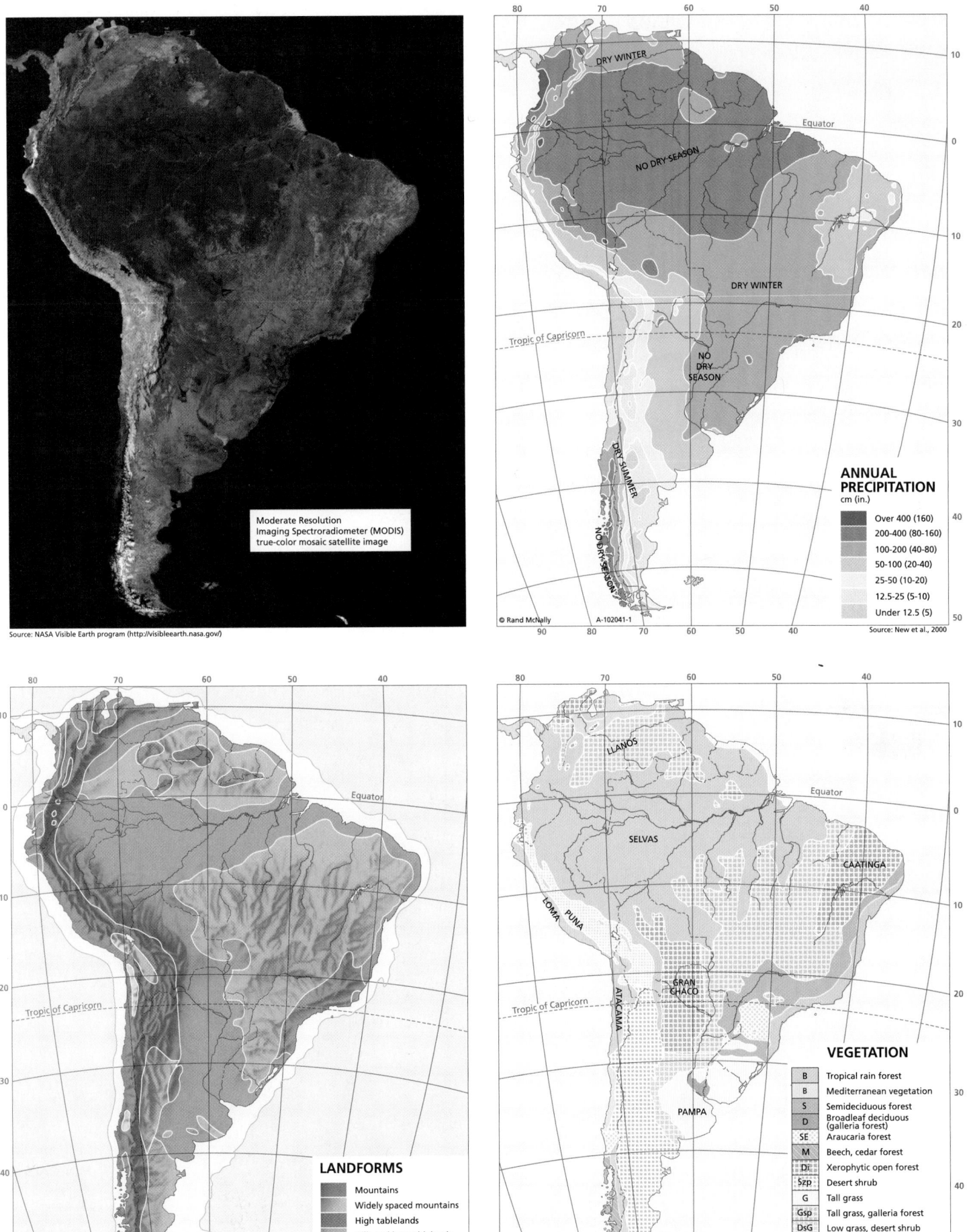

Moderate Resolution
Imaging Spectroradiometer (MODIS)
true-color mosaic satellite image

Source: NASA Visible Earth program (http://visibleearth.nasa.gov/)

DRY WINTER

Equator

NO DRY SEASON

DRY WINTER

Tropic of Capricorn

NO
DRY
SEASON

DRY SUMMER

NO DRY SEASON

**ANNUAL
PRECIPITATION**
cm (in.)

Over 400 (160)
200-400 (80-160)
100-200 (40-80)
50-100 (20-40)
25-50 (10-20)
12.5-25 (5-10)
Under 12.5 (5)

© Rand McNally   A-102041-1

Source: New et al., 2000

LANDFORMS

Mountains
Widely spaced mountains
High tablelands
Hills and low tablelands
Depressions or basins
Plains
Limit of continental shelf

Equator

Tropic of Capricorn

© Rand McNally   M-102038-1

Source: Murphy, 1968. © Association of American Geographers. Published by Taylor & Francis.
Adapted with permission of the Association of American Geographers.

LLANOS

SELVAS

CAATINGA

LOMA PUNA

GRAN
CHACO

ATACAMA

PAMPA

Equator

Tropic of Capricorn

VEGETATION

B	Tropical rain forest
B	Mediterranean vegetation
S	Semideciduous forest
D	Broadleaf deciduous (galleria forest)
SE	Araucaria forest
M	Beech, cedar forest
D	Xerophytic open forest
Szp	Desert shrub
G	Tall grass
Gsp	Tall grass, galleria forest
DsG	Low grass, desert shrub
GDsp	Montane grass, tola shrub
b	Little or no vegetation

For explanation of letters in boxes,
see World Natural Vegetation Map.

© Rand McNally   M-102042-1

Source: Küchler, 1949. © Association of American Geographers. Published by Taylor & Francis.
Adapted with permission of the Association of American Geographers.

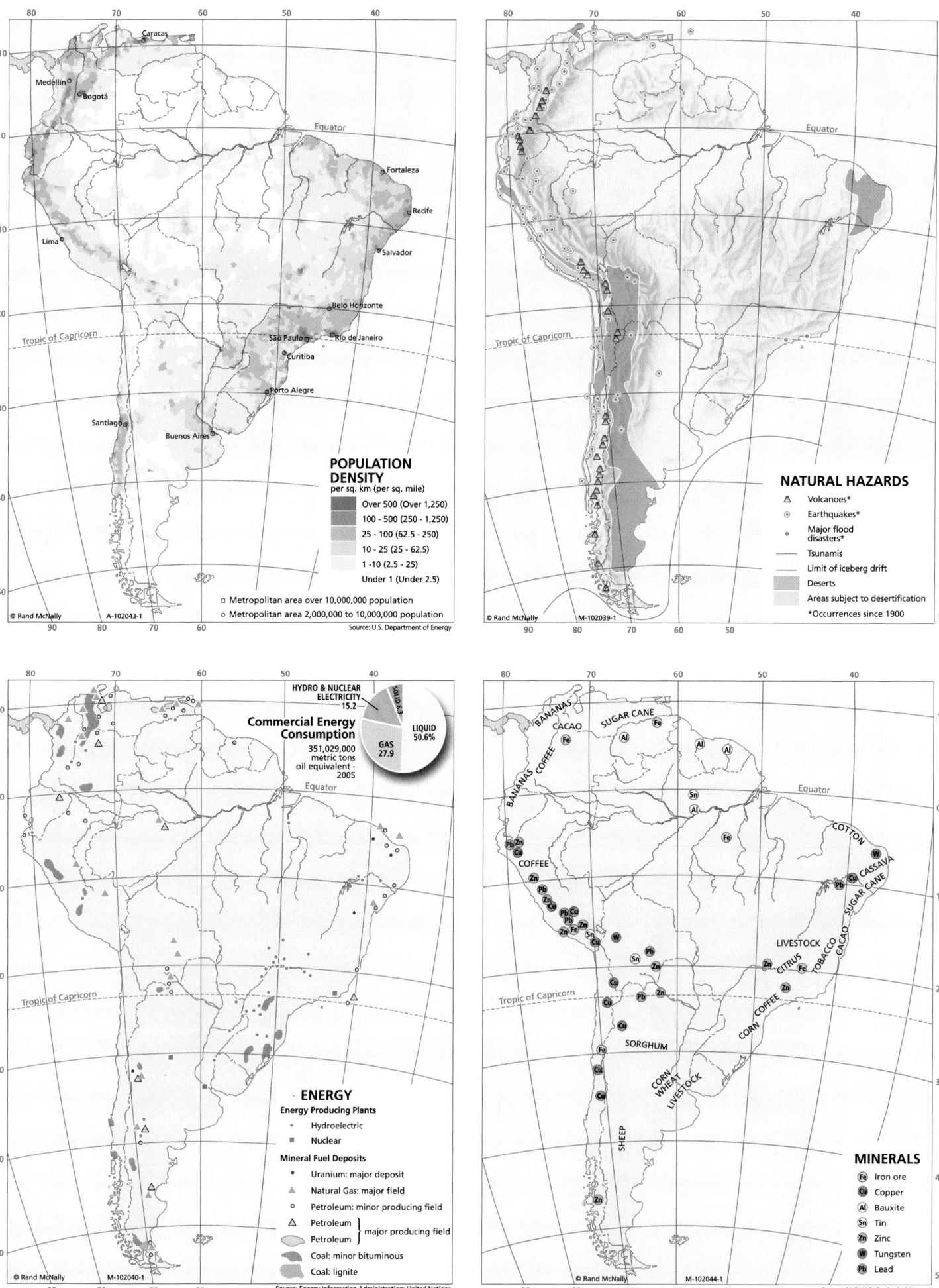

POPULATION DENSITY
per sq. km (per sq. mile)

- Over 500 (Over 1,250)
- 100 - 500 (250 - 1,250)
- 25 - 100 (62.5 - 250)
- 10 - 25 (25 - 62.5)
- 1 - 10 (2.5 - 25)
- Under 1 (Under 2.5)

□ Metropolitan area over 10,000,000 population
○ Metropolitan area 2,000,000 to 10,000,000 population

© Rand McNally   A-102043-1

Source: U.S. Department of Energy

Caracas · Medellín · Bogotá · Fortaleza · Recife · Lima · Salvador · Belo Horizonte · São Paulo · Rio de Janeiro · Curitiba · Porto Alegre · Santiago · Buenos Aires

NATURAL HAZARDS

- △ Volcanoes*
- ⊙ Earthquakes*
- · Major flood disasters*
- — Tsunamis
- — Limit of iceberg drift
- Deserts
- Areas subject to desertification

*Occurrences since 1900

© Rand McNally   M-102039-1

ENERGY

Energy Producing Plants
- · Hydroelectric
- ■ Nuclear

Mineral Fuel Deposits
- · Uranium: major deposit
- ▲ Natural Gas: major field
- ○ Petroleum: minor producing field
- △ Petroleum } major producing field
- ▲ Petroleum
- Coal: minor bituminous
- Coal: lignite

HYDRO & NUCLEAR ELECTRICITY 15.2

Commercial Energy Consumption

351,029,000 metric tons oil equivalent - 2005

SOLID 6.3
LIQUID 50.6%
GAS 27.9

© Rand McNally   M-102040-1

Source: Energy Information Administration; United Nations

MINERALS

- Fe Iron ore
- Cu Copper
- Al Bauxite
- Sn Tin
- Zn Zinc
- W Tungsten
- Pb Lead

BANANAS · CACAO · SUGAR CANE · BANANAS · COFFEE · COFFEE · COTTON · CASSAVA · SUGAR CANE · LIVESTOCK · TOBACCO · CACAO · SUGAR CANE · CITRUS · CORN · COFFEE · SORGHUM · CORN · WHEAT · LIVESTOCK · SHEEP

© Rand McNally   M-102044-1

Source: FAO; U.S. Geological Survey

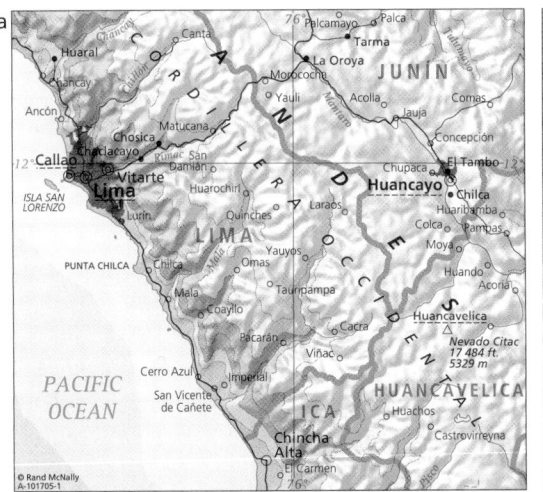
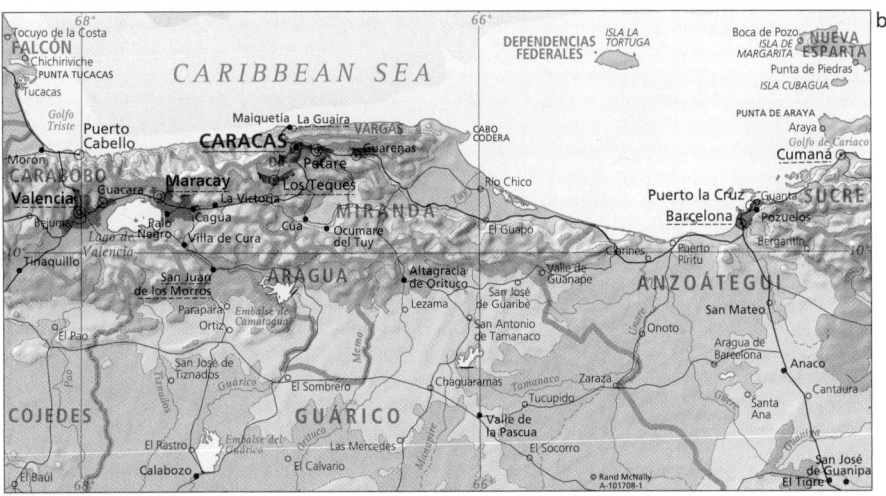
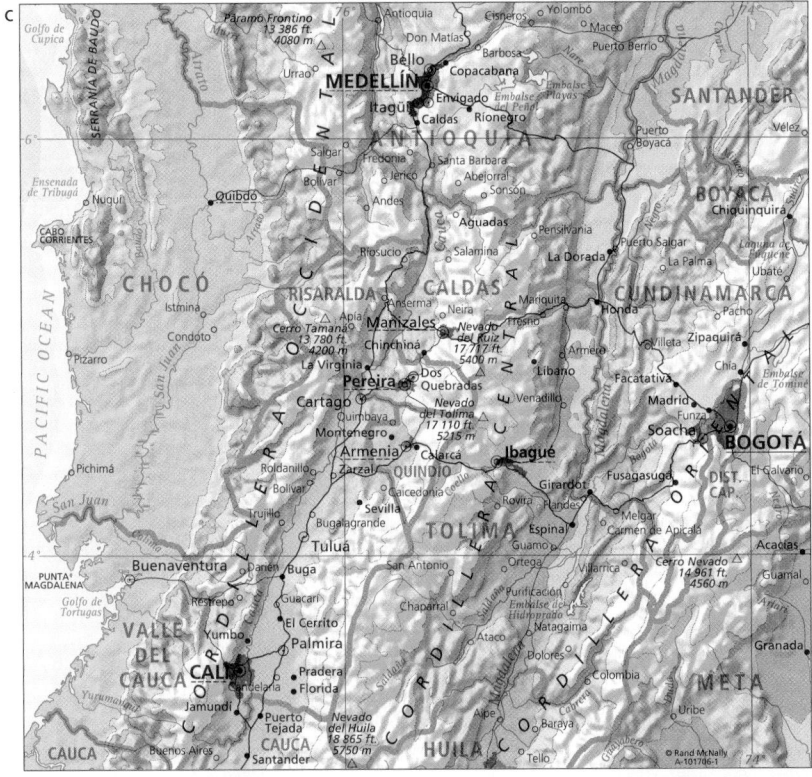
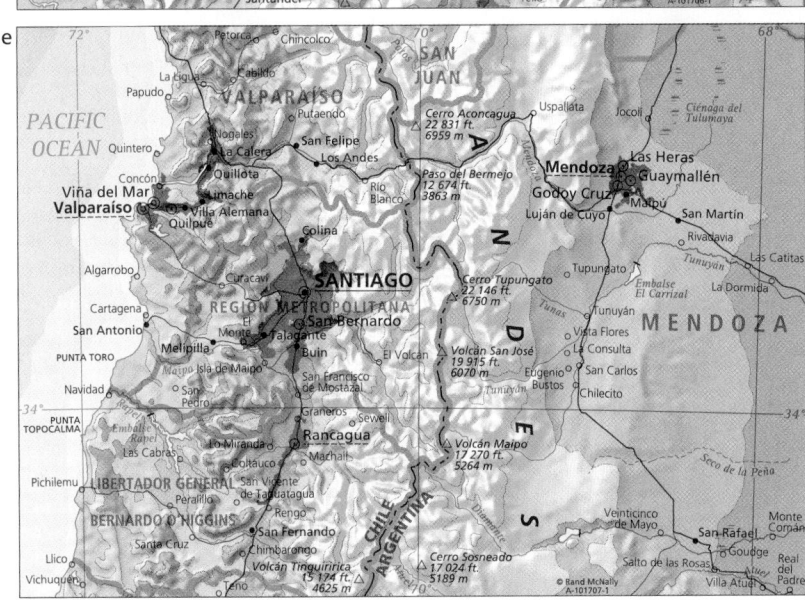
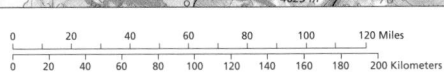

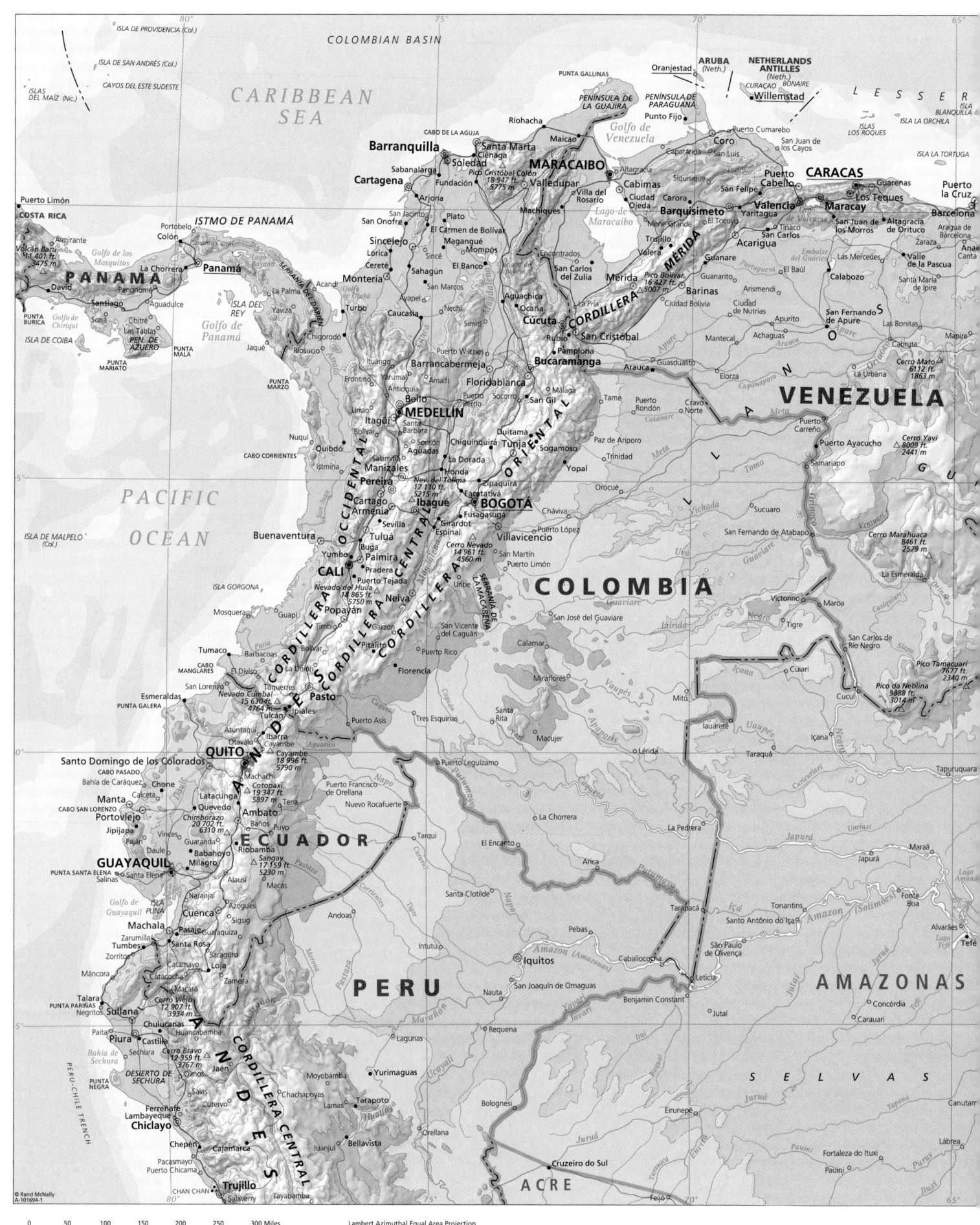

0   50   100   150   200   250   300 Miles
0 50 100 150 200 250 300 350 400 450 500 Kilometers

Lambert Azimuthal Equal Area Projection
Scale 1:10,000,000
One inch to 160 miles
One cm to 100 km

ATLANTIC OCEAN

ST. VINCENT
Kingstown
ST. VINCENT
AND THE
GRENADINES
BARBADOS
Bridgetown
GRENADA
St. George's

TOBAGO
Scarborough
TRINIDAD
AND
TOBAGO
Port of Spain
Arima
TRINIDAD
San Fernando

DE
ARGARITA
La Asunción
Porlamar
Carúpano
PENÍNSULA
DE PARIA
Güiria
Itapa
Golfo de
Paria
Caripito
Pedernales

mán
Juanípa
Jusepln
Maturín
Temblador
Tucupita
Barrancas
DELTA DEL ORINOCO
Boca
Grande

n José
Guanípa
gre

Orinoco
Morawhanna
Mabaruma
Ciudad Guayana
Upata
Ciudad
Bolívar
Ciudad Piar
Embalse
de Guri
Cerro Bolívar
2631 ft.
802 m.
a Paragua
Guasipati
El Callao
Tumeremo
Marlborough
Suddie
Georgetown
Hyde Park

El Dorado
Angel Falls
(Salto Ángel)
Luepa
Bartica
Rockstone
Linden
New Amsterdam
Paramaribo
Groningen
Moengo
Iracoubo
Sinnamary
Saint-Laurent
du Maroni
Kourou
Cayenne
Rémiré

Auyán Tepuy
9678 ft
2950 m
LA GRAN
SABANA
Mt. Roraima
9432 ft.
2875 m
GUYANA
Issano
Tumatumari
Corriverton
Nieuw
Nickerie
Onverwacht
Brokopondo
Saint-Élie
Saint-Georges

NA
HIGH
Conceição
do Maú
Uraricoera
Lethem
Dadanawa
PAKARAIMA MTS.
LANDS
SURINAME
WILHELMINA GEBERGTE
W.J. van
Blommesteln
Meer
Juliana Top
4035 ft.
1230 m
FRENCH
GUIANA
(France)
Saül
Vila Velha
Cunani
Calçoene
CABO ORANGE
Oiapoque

Boa Vista
Isherton
TUMUC-HUMAC MOUNTAINS
Amapá
ILHA DE MARACÁ
CABO NORTE
Sucuriju

RORAIMA
Caracaraí
ACARAI MOUNTAINS
AMAPÁ
Serra do Navio
Aporema
Ferreira Gomes
ILHA JANAUCU

São José
de Anauá
Porto Grande
Macapá
Porto Santana
Mazagão
ILHA CAVIANA DE FORA
ILHA MEXIANA
CABO
MAGUARI

Boiaçu
ILHA GRANDE
DO GURUPÁ
Itatupá
Boca do Jari
Anajás
Soure
Muraja
Maracanã
Salinópolis
Bragança
Capanema

Negro
Barcelos
Carvoeiro
Moura
Novo Airão
Represa
Balbina
Lago do
Erepecurú
Oriximiná
Óbidos
Alenquer
Monte
Alegre
Prainha
Gurupá
Porto de Moz
Veiros
São Miguel
dos Macacos
Muaná
Breves
Curralinho
Carrazedo
Portel
Belém
São Domingos
do Capim
Igarapé-
Açu
Irituia
Itamataré

Unini
Coari
Manacapuru
MANAUS
Itacoatiara
Careiro
Terra Santa
Faro
Juruti
Santarém
Cametá
Juaba
Carapajó
Acará
Tomé-Açu

Lago
Piorini
Codajás
Anori
Camará
Anamã
Nova Olinda
do Norte
Itapiranga
Urucará
Parintins
Barreirinha
Ariaú
ILHA TUPINAMBARANA
Vitória
Baião
Tucuruí
MARANHÃO

Abufari
Tapauá
Axinim
Canumã
Itaituba
Altamira
PARÁ
Jacundá
Açailândia

Coari
Aiapuá
Borba
Represa
de Tucuruí
Itupiranga
Marabá
Imperatriz
Amarante do
Maranhão

Abufari
Novo
Aripuanã
BRAZIL
Araguatins
Santa Isabel do Araguaia
Sítio
Novo

Tapauá
Marmelos
Manicoré
SERRA DOS CARAJÁS
Carajás
Xambioá
Montes Altos

Humaitá
Prainha
Nova
São Félix do Xingu
Araguaína
Babaçulândia
Carolina
Riachão

Samaúma
MATO
GROSSO
SERRA DO CACHIMBO
Gradaús
TOCANTINS
Conceição do Araguaia

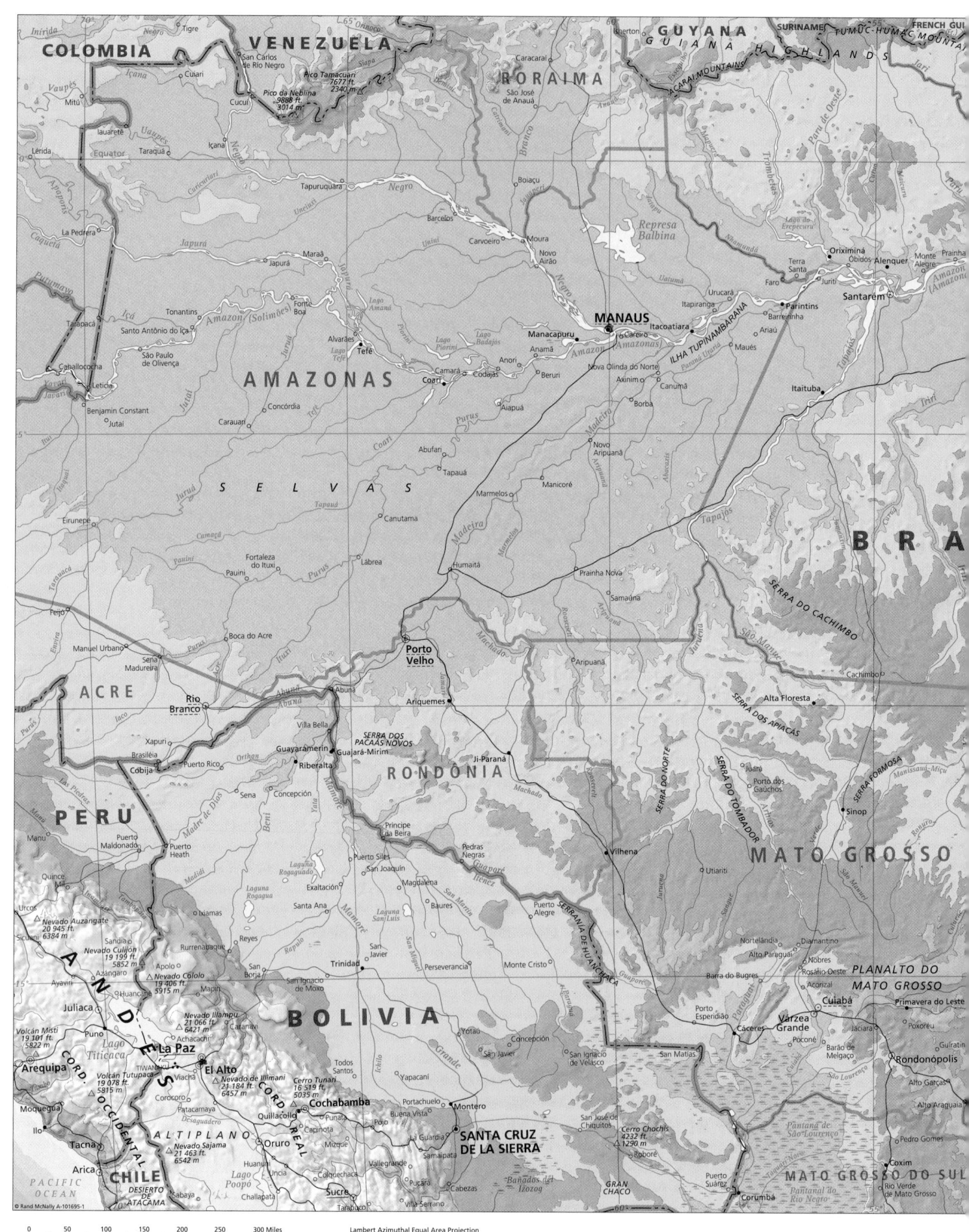

© Rand McNally A-101695-1

0   50   100   150   200   250   300 Miles
0   50   100   150   200   250   300   350   400   450   500 Kilometers

Lambert Azimuthal Equal Area Projection
Scale 1:10,000,000
One inch to 160 miles
One cm to 100 km

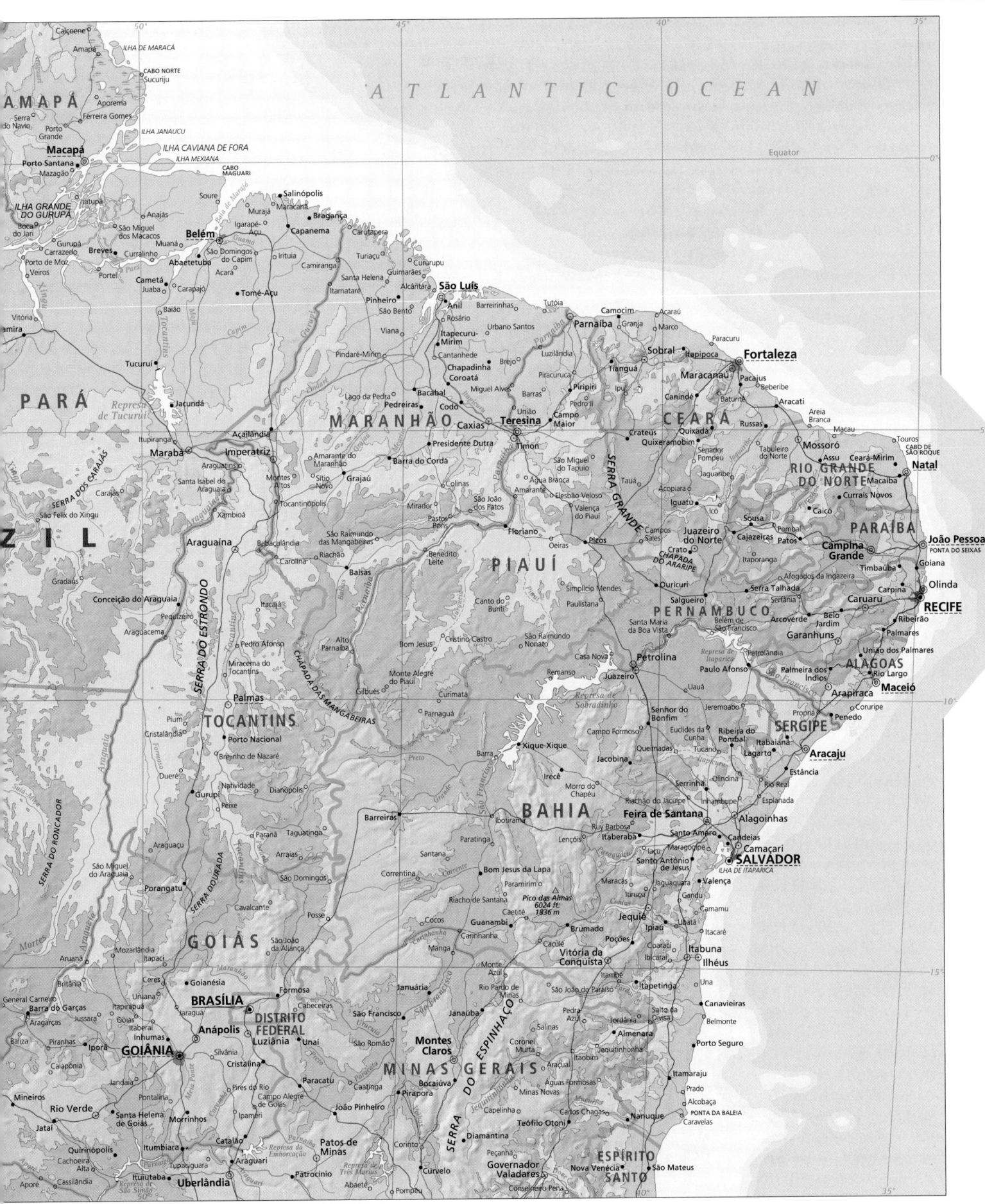

PERU
BOLIVIA
MATO GROSSO
PARAGUAY
CHILE
PACIFIC OCEAN
ARGENTINA
URUGUAY

GRAN CHACO
CORDILLERA OCCIDENTAL
DESIERTO DE ATACAMA
CORDILLERA DOMEYKO
ALTIPLANO
CORDILLERA REAL
A N D E S
SALAR DE UYUNI
SALAR DE ATACAMA
PUNA DE ATACAMA

JUJUY
SALTA
FORMOSA
CHACO
TUCUMÁN
CATAMARCA
SANTIAGO DEL ESTERO
SANTA FE
CORRIENTES
LA RIOJA
SAN JUAN
CÓRDOBA
ENTRE RÍOS
SAN LUIS
MENDOZA
LA PAMPA
BUENOS AIRES

Tropic of Capricorn
PERU-CHILE TRENCH

Lago Titicaca
La Paz
El Alto
Arequipa
Cochabamba
Oruro
SANTA CRUZ DE LA SIERRA
Sucre
Potosí
Asunción
Salta
San Miguel de Tucumán
Córdoba
Santiago del Estero
Corrientes
Posadas
Rosario
Santa Fe
Paraná
Mendoza
SANTIAGO
Valparaíso
Buenos Aires
La Plata
MONTEVIDEO

Lambert Azimuthal Equal Area Projection
Scale 1:10,000,000
One inch to 160 miles
One cm to 100 km

0 50 100 150 200 250 300 Miles
0 50 100 150 200 250 300 350 400 450 500 Kilometers

Inset map a
Lambert Conformal Conic Projection
Scale 1:1,000,000
One inch to 16 miles
One cm to 10 km

PACIFIC OCEAN

COLOMBIA

ECUADOR

AMAZONAS

BRAZIL

SELVAS

PERU

ACRE

BOLIVIA

CHILE

a

ISLA DARWIN

ISLA WOLF

PACIFIC OCEAN

ARCHIPIÉLAGO DE COLÓN
(GALAPAGOS ISLANDS)
(Ecuador)

ISLA PINTA

ISLA MARCHENA   ISLA GENOVESA

ISLA ISABELA   Volcán Wolf
5400 ft.
1646 m   Equator

Volcán La Cumbre   ISLA SANTIAGO
4800 ft.
1463 m
ISLA
FERNANDINA   Bahía   ISLA BALTA
Elizabeth
Volcán   ISLA SANTA CRUZ
Santo Tomás   Puerto
4888 ft.   Ayora
Cerro Azul   1490 m   ISLA
5541 ft.   SANTA FE
1689 m   Puerto Villamil   ISLA SAN
CRISTÓBAL
Puerto
Baquerizo
Moreno
ISLA SANTA
MARÍA   ISLA ESPAÑOLA

Inset map a
Lambert Conformal Conic Projection
Scale 1:6,000,000
One inch to 96 miles
One cm to 60 km

| 0 | 50 | 100 | 150 | 200 | 250 | 300 Miles |
| 0 | 50 100 150 | 200 250 | 300 350 | 400 | 450 | 500 Kilometers |

Lambert Azimuthal Equal Area Projection
Scale 1:10,000,000
One inch to 160 miles
One cm to 100 km

Lambert Azimuthal Equal Area Projection
Scale 1:10,000,000
One inch to 160 miles
One cm to 100 km

0   50   100   150   200   250   300 Miles
0 50 100 150 200 250 300 350 400 450 500 Kilometers

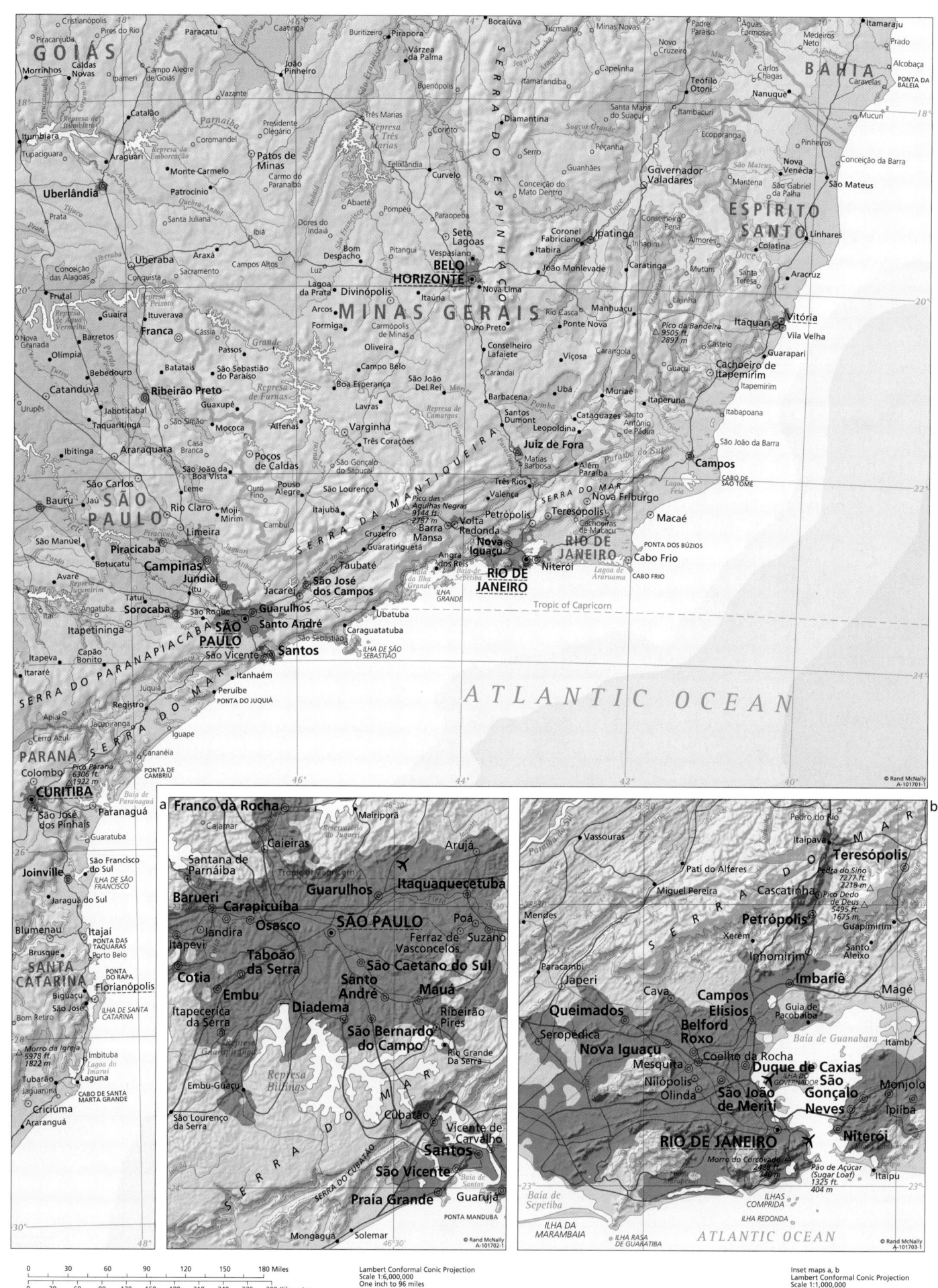

GOIÁS

Cristianópolis · 48° · Pires do Rio · Paracatu · Caatinga · Buritizeiro · Pirapora · Bocaiúva · Turmalina · Minas Novas · Itamaraju
Piracanjuba · Morrinhos · Caldas Novas · Ipameri · Campo Alegre de Goiás · João Pinheiro · Várzea da Palma · Novo Cruzeiro · Padre Paraíso · Medeiros Neto · Prado · Alcobaça
Itumbiara · Catalão · Ponta de Goiás · Vazante · Buenópolis · Itamarandiba · Mucuri · Carlos Chagas · Caravelas · PONTA DA BALEIA

BAHIA

Teófilo Otoni · Nanuque · Mucuri

Conceição das Alagoas · Uberlândia · Monte Carmelo · Patos de Minas · Carmo do Paranaíba · Três Marias · Diamantina · Suçuí Grande · Ecoporanga · Pinheiros · Conceição da Barra
Patrocínio · Araxá · Campos Altos · Represa de Três Marias · Corinto · Serro · Guanhães · Conselheiro Pena · São Gabriel da Palha · São Mateus

ESPÍRITO SANTO

BELO HORIZONTE

MINAS GERAIS

SÃO PAULO

ATLANTIC OCEAN

Tropic of Capricorn

RIO DE JANEIRO

CURITIBA

PARANÁ

SANTA CATARINA

Florianópolis

Inset a
Franco da Rocha

Guarulhos · **SÃO PAULO** · Itaquaquecetuba · Barueri · Carapicuíba · Osasco · Santana de Parnaíba · Caieiras · Mairiporã · Arujá
Diadema · Santo André · São Bernardo do Campo · Mauá · Cubatão · **Santos** · **São Vicente** · **Praia Grande** · Guarujá

Inset b

Teresópolis · Petrópolis · Nova Iguaçu · Duque de Caxias · São João de Meriti · **RIO DE JANEIRO** · Niterói · São Gonçalo · Magé

ATLANTIC OCEAN

0 30 60 90 120 150 180 Miles
0 30 60 90 120 150 180 210 240 270 300 Kilometers

Lambert Conformal Conic Projection
Scale 1:6,000,000
One inch to 96 miles
One cm to 60 km

Inset maps a, b
Lambert Conformal Conic Projection
Scale 1:1,000,000
One inch to 16 miles
One cm to 10 km

© Rand McNally

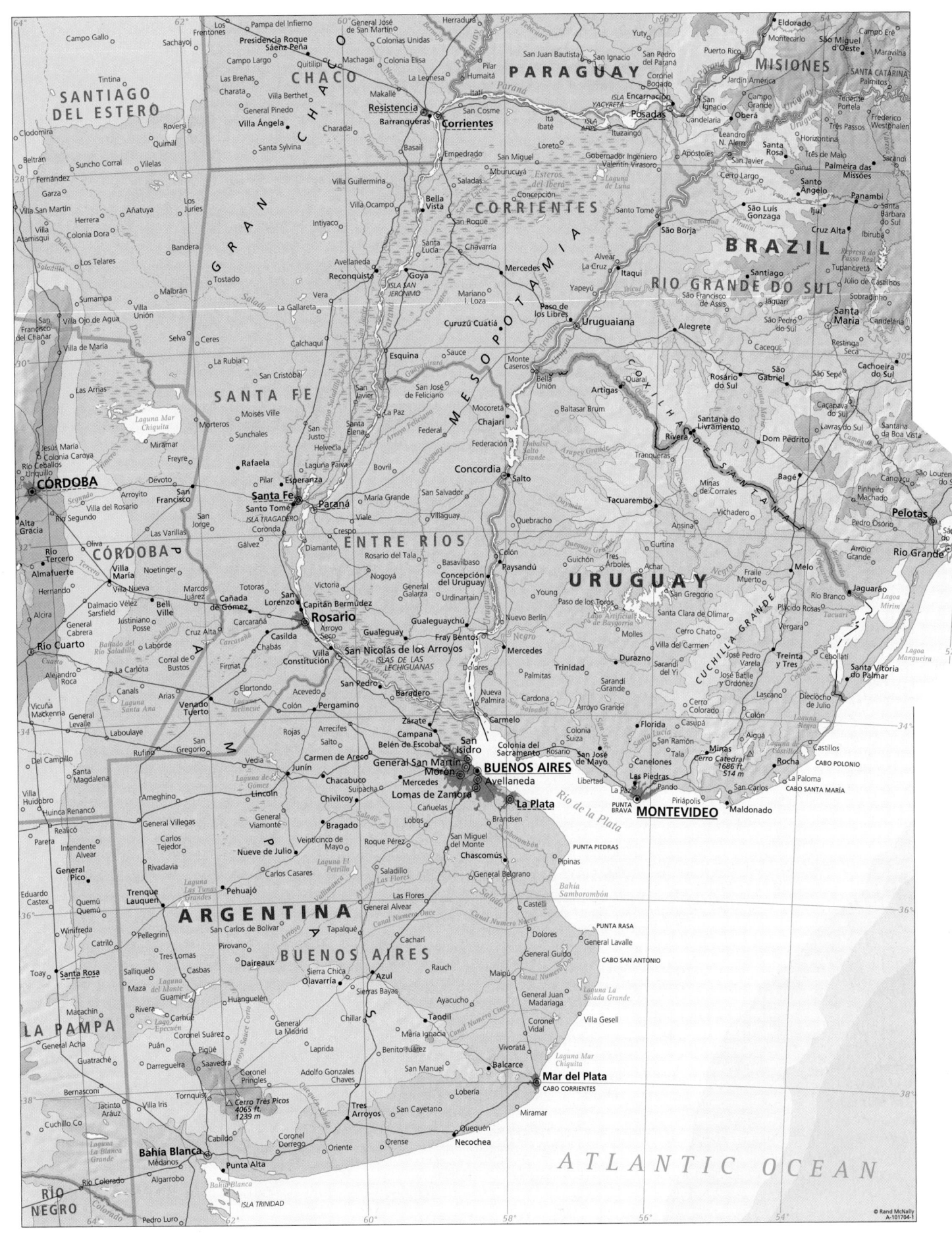

ATLANTIC OCEAN

Rand McNally
A-101704-1

0   30   60   90   120   150   180 Miles
0   30   60   90   120   150   180   210   240   270   300 Kilometers

Lambert Conformal Conic Projection
Scale 1:6,000,000
One inch to 96 miles
One cm to 60 km

| | 0 | 80 | 160 | 240 | 320 | 400 | 480 Miles |

| 0 | 80 | 160 | 240 | 320 | 400 | 480 | 560 | 640 | 720 | 800 Kilometers |

Lambert Conformal Conic Projection
Scale 1:16,000,000
One inch to 256 miles
One cm to 160 km

RUSSIA

KAZAKHSTAN

UKRAINE

TURKEY

IRAN

IRAQ

SYRIA

UZBEKISTAN

TURKMENISTAN

GEORGIA

ARMENIA

AZERBAIJAN

MOLDOVA

URAL MOUNTAINS

CAUCASUS MOUNTAINS

WHITE SEA

BLACK SEA

SEA OF AZOV

CASPIAN SEA

Aral Sea

Lake Balkhash (Balqash köli)

OSTROV KOLGUYEV

MYS KANIN NOS

Naryan-Mar · Inta · Usinsk · Pechora · Ukhta · Gora Narodnaya 6214ft 1894m

NOVOSIBIRSK · Barnaul · Semey · OMSK · Tyumen' · YEKATERINBURG · CHELYABINSK · Astana (Aqmola) · Qaraghandy

Severodvinsk · Arkhangel'sk · Segezha · Petrozavodsk · Syktyvkar · Kotlas

PETERSBURG (LENINGRAD) · Tikhvin · Cherepovets · Vologda · Novgorod · Borovichi · Rybinsk · Yaroslavl' · Ivanovo · Kostroma · Kirov · Solikamsk · Berezniki · PERM' · Kungur · Pervouralsk · Nizhniy Tagil · Glazov · Izhevsk · Zlatoust · Miass · Magnitogorsk

Vyshniy Volochëk · Tver' · Sergiyev Posad · Vladimir · Kovrov · Murom · Naberezhnye Chelny · UFA · Orsk

NIZHNIY NOVGOROD · Dzerzhinsk · KAZAN' · Cheboksary · Yoshkar-Ola · Al'met'yevsk · Oktyabrskiy · Sterlitamak · Salavat · Orenburg · Aqtöbe · Zhezqazghan

MOSCOW · Podolsk · Ryazan' · Kolomna · Saransk · Ulyanovsk · Dimitrovgrad · Tolyatti · SAMARA · Novokuybyshevsk · Oral · Atyraü

Serpukhov · Novomoskovsk · Penza · Syzran' · Balakovo · Kamyshin · Volzhskiy

Vicebsk · Smolensk · Kaluga · Tula · Michurinsk · Tambov · Saratov · Engel's · Balashov

Mahilëu · Bryansk · Orel · Elets · Lipetsk · Voronezh · Kursk · Staryy Oskol · Belgorod

Babrujsk · Homel' · Chernihiv

KIEV (KYÏV) · Sumy · KHARKIV · Poltava · DNIPROPETROVS'K · Horlivka · Luhans'k · Kamyshin

Zhytomyr · Vinnytsia · Kirovohrad · Kryvyi Rih · Zaporizhzhia · DONETS'K · VOLGOGRAD · Volgodonsk

Chisinău · Tiraspol · Mykolaiv · Mariupol' · Taganrog · ROSTOV-NA-DONU · Astrahan'

ODESA · Kherson · Kerch · Krasnodar · Armavir · Cherkessk · Pyatigorsk · Nalchik · Groznyy · Makhachkala · Derbent · Sumqayit

Galați · Simferopol' · Novorossiysk · Maykop · Gora El'brus 18 510 ft 5642 m · Vladikavkaz · BAKU (BAKI)

Constanța · Yalta · Sochi · GEORGIA · TBILISI · Gäncä · AZERBAIJAN

Varna · Burgas · ARMENIA · Yerevan · AZER. · TABRĪZ · Rasht · MASHHAD

İSTANBUL · ANKARA · BURSA · Van Gölü · TEHRĀN · Daryācheh-ye Namak

İZMIR · Tuz Gölü · Tigris · ESFAHĀN · Kermān

ADANA · Antalya · ALEPPO (HALAB) · Euphrates · IRAQ · Mosul · Kermānshāh · SHĪRĀZ · Bandar Abbās

Ródos · CYPRUS · Nicosia · LEBANON · Beirut (Bayrūt) · DAMASCUS (DIMASHQ) · BAGHDĀD · Basra · Ahvāz

KÁRPATHOS

Shymkent · TASHKENT · Nukus · Samarqand · Aşgabat · AFGHANISTAN

Kara-Kum Canal

Syr Darya · Amu Darya

HORN

ICELAND
Reykjavík
Hekla
4892 ft.
1491 m
Hvannadalshnúkur
6952 ft.
2119 m

NORWEGIAN SEA

Arctic Circle

NORWEGIAN BASIN

NORDKAPP
SØRØYA
Hammerfest
RINGVASSØYA
SENJA
Haltiatunturi
4357 ft.
1328 m
Murmansk
LOFOTEN
VESTERÅLEN
Kebnekaise
6926 ft.
2111 m
Sulitelma
6280 ft.
1914 m
LAPLAND

FAROE ISLANDS
(Denmark)

NORWAY
FRØYA
HITRA
SMØLA
Trondheim
Snøhetta
7500 ft.
2286 m
Helagsfjället
5892 ft.
1796 m
Oulu

SWEDEN
FINLAND

ATLANTIC OCEAN

SHETLAND ISLANDS
MAINLAND

RONA
ISLE OF LEWIS
CAPE WRATH
HEBRIDES
ISLAND OF SKYE
ISLAND OF MULL
JURA
ISLAY
Ben Nevis
4406 ft.
1343 m
Glasgow
ORKNEY ISLANDS
Moray Firth
KINNAIRD HEAD

Bergen
Galdhøpiggen
8100 ft.
2469 m
Glittertinden
8087 ft.
2465 m
Gaustatoppen
6178 ft.
1883 m
Oslo

Göteborg
Stockholm
GOTLAND
ÖLAND

Helsinki
St. Petersburg
(Leningrad)
ESTONIA
SAAREMAA
HIIUMAA
BALTIC
Gulf of Riga
LATVIA
Riga
LITHUANIA

NORTH SEA

THE NAZE
Skagerrak
Kattegat
DENMARK
Copenhagen
FYN
SJÆLLAND
LOLLAND
RÜGEN
BORNHOLM
SEA
Gdańsk
RUSSIA
Minsk

IRELAND
Dublin
Carrauntoohil
3406 ft.
1038 m
MIZEN HEAD
IRISH SEA
ISLE OF MAN
(U.K.)
GREAT BRITAIN
UNITED KINGDOM
Manchester
Snowdon
3560 ft.
1085 m
St. George's Channel
LAND'S END
London
English Channel
Strait of Dover
GUERNSEY
(U.K.)
JERSEY
(U.K.)
Brussels
BELGIUM
LUXEMBOURG
Paris
Seine

NETHERLANDS
IJsselmeer
Amsterdam
Waal
Hamburg
Elbe
Berlin
GERMANY
Frankfurt
am Main
Prague
CZECH REPUBLIC

POLAND
Warsaw
BELARUS
Pripyat'

WEST EUROPEAN BASIN

Bay of Biscay
CABO ORTEGAL
CABO DE FINISTERRA
FRANCE
Puy de Sancy
6184 ft.
1885 m
Lyon
MASSIF CENTRAL
Bordeaux
Loire

Munich
Inn
Zürich
SWITZERLAND
Mont Blanc
15,771 ft.
4807 m
Matterhorn
14,692 ft.
4478 m
Piz Bernina
13,287 ft.
4050 m
Milan
Po
LIECH.
ALPS
AUSTRIA
Großglockner
12,457 ft.
3797 m
Vienna
(Wien)
SLOVAKIA
Triglav
9396 ft.
2864 m
SLOVENIA
Zagreb
CROATIA
Budapest
HUNGARY
Drava
Danube
CARPATHIAN MOUNTAINS
Gerlachovský Štít
8711 ft.
2655 m
ROMANIA
Vârful Moldoveanu
8346 ft.
2544 m
TRANSYLVANIAN ALPS

PORTUGAL
Lisbon
(Lisboa)
CABO DE SÃO VICENTE
Madrid
Tagus
SPAIN
IBERIAN PENINSULA
CORDILLERA CANTÁBRICA
Bilbao
Duero
PYRENEES
Aneto
11,168 ft.
3404 m
ANDORRA
MONACO
Marseille
Golfe du Lion
CAP CORSE
CORSICA
(France)
Monte Cinto
8878 ft.
2706 m
ISOLA D'ELBA
LIGURIAN SEA
SAN MARINO
ITALY
APENNINES
Rome
(Roma)
Corno Grande
9560 ft.
2914 m
ADRIATIC SEA
BOSNIA AND HERZEGOVINA
Belgrade
(Beograd)
SERBIA
MONTENEGRO
BALKAN
Bucharest
Danube
BULGARIA
Sofia
Musala
9596 ft.
2925 m

SIERRA MORENA
Guadiana
Mulhacén
11,424 ft.
3482 m
Barcelona
València
Júcar
MALLORCA
MENORCA
EIVISSA
CAP DE LA NAO
BALEARIC ISLANDS
SARDINIA
(Italy)
CAPO SPARTIVENTO
Naples
(Napoli)
Vesuvius
4203 ft.
1281 m
Golfo di Taranto
PINDOS ÓROS
Mt. Olympus
9570 ft.
2917 m
ALBANIA
MACEDONIA
PENINSULA
AEGEAN
THASOS
LÍMNOS
LESVOS
CHÍOS
ÉVVOIA
GREECE
Parnassós
8061 ft.
2457 m
Athens
(Athína)
CYCLADES

Strait of Gibraltar
Gibraltar (U.K.)
Algiers
(Alger)
MEDITERRANEAN
TYRRHENIAN SEA
CAPO CABO
Palermo
SICILY
Monte Etna
10,902 ft.
3323 m
IONIAN ISLANDS
IONIAN SEA
ÁKRA TAÍNARO
KÝTHIRA
ÁKRA MALEAS
SEA OF CRETE

Casablanca
MOROCCO
ALGERIA
Chott ech Chergui
Chott Melrhir
TUNISIA
Tunis
CAP BON
MALTA
CAPO PASSERO
ISOLA DI LAMPEDUSA
(Italy)
SEA
CRETE

ATLAS MOUNTAINS
Irhil M'Goun
13,356 ft.
4071 m

© Rand McNally
A-101731-1

0   80   160   240   320   400   480 Miles
0   80   160   240   320   400   480   560   640   720   800 Kilometers

Lambert Conformal Conic Projection
Scale 1:16,000,000
One inch to 256 miles
One cm to 160 km

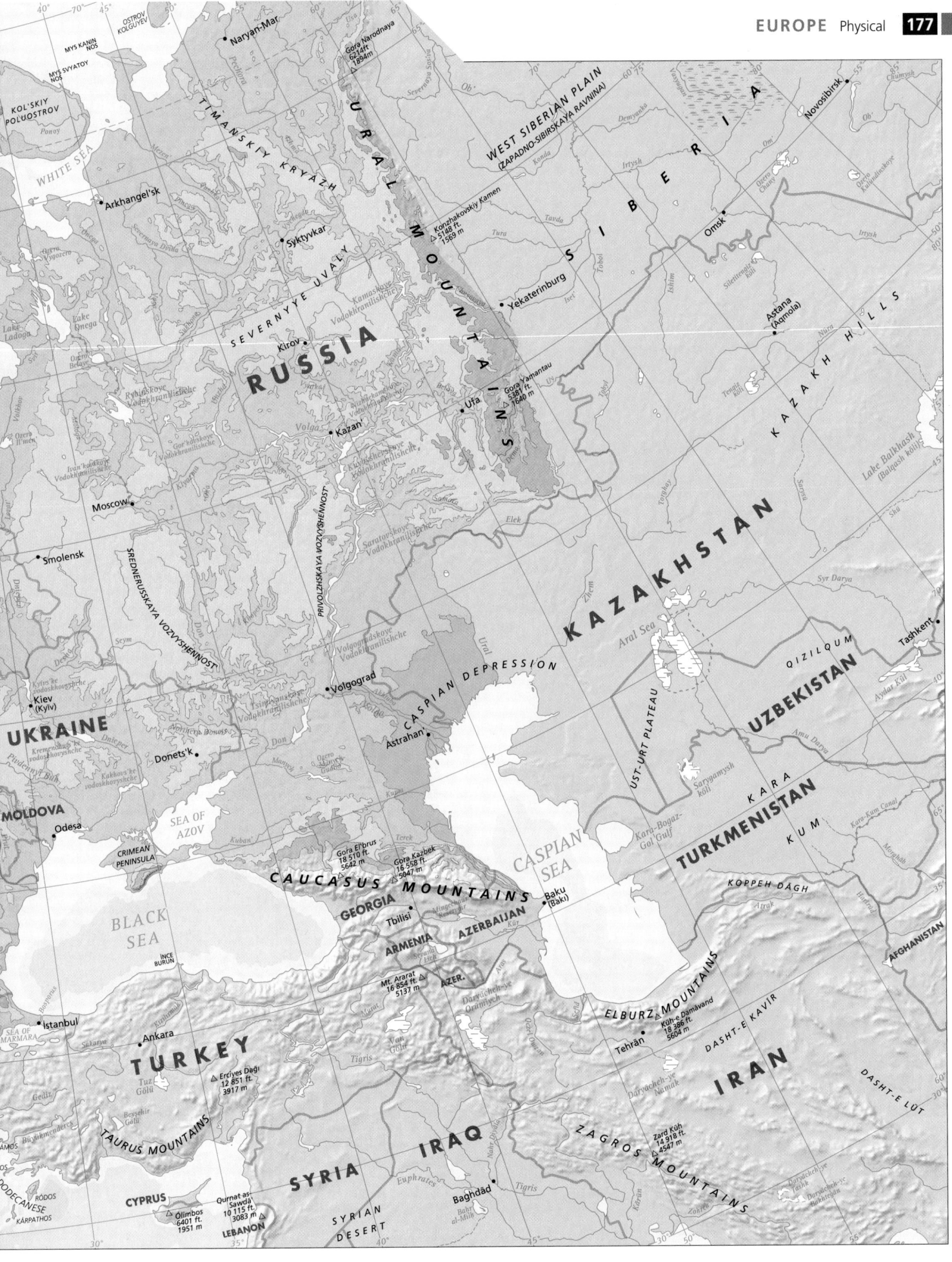

MYS KANIN NOS
MYS SVYATOY NOS
OSTROV KOLGUYEV
KOL'SKIY POLUOSTROV
Ponoy
Naryan-Mar
Gora Narodnaya
6214 ft
1894 m
WHITE SEA
Arkhangel'sk
TIMANSKIY KRYAZH
URAL MOUNTAINS
WEST SIBERIAN PLAIN
(ZAPADNO-SIBIRSKAYA RAVNINA)
Ob'
SIBERIA
Novosibirsk
Ob'
Syktyvkar
SEVERNYYE UVALY
Konzhakovskiy Kamen
5148 ft
1569 m
Omsk
Irtysh
Yekaterinburg
RUSSIA
Astana
(Aqmola)
KAZAKH HILLS
Kirov
Kazan'
Gora Yamantau
5381 ft
1640 m
Ufa
Lake Ladoga
Lake Onega
Moscow
KAZAKHSTAN
PRIVOLZHSKAYA VOZVYSHENNOST'
Smolensk
SREDNERUSSKAYA VOZVYSHENNOST'
Volgograd
Aral Sea
Syr Darya
QIZILQUM
UZBEKISTAN
Tashkent
Kiev
(Kyiv)
UKRAINE
Dnieper
CASPIAN DEPRESSION
UST-URT PLATEAU
Amu Darya
Astrahan'
Donets'k
Don
MOLDOVA
Odesa
SEA OF AZOV
CRIMEAN PENINSULA
Kuban'
Terek
CASPIAN SEA
Kara-Bogaz-Gol Gulf
KARA KUM
TURKMENISTAN
KOPPEH DAGH
Gora El'brus
18 510 ft
5642 m
Gora Kazbek
16 558 ft
5047 m
BLACK SEA
CAUCASUS MOUNTAINS
GEORGIA
Baku
(Bakı)
İNCE BURUN
Tbilisi
ARMENIA
AZERBAIJAN
AZER.
Istanbul
SEA OF MARMARA
Ankara
Mt. Ararat
16 854 ft
5137 m
ELBURZ MOUNTAINS
Küh-e Damāvand
18 386 ft
5604 m
AFGHANISTAN
Van Gölü
Tehrān
DASHT-E KAVĪR
TURKEY
Erciyes Dağı
12 851 ft
3917 m
Tuz Gölü
IRAN
DASHT-E LŪT
TAURUS MOUNTAINS
Tigris
ZAGROS MOUNTAINS
Zard Küh
14 918 ft
4547 m
SAMOS
DODECANESE
RÓDOS
KÁRPATHOS
CYPRUS
Ólimbos
6401 ft
1951 m
Qurnat as-Sawdā'
10 115 ft
3083 m
LEBANON
SYRIA
SYRIAN DESERT
IRAQ
Euphrates
Baghdād
Tigris

NORWEGIAN SEA

Arctic Circle

ATLANTIC
OCEAN

FAROE
ISLANDS

SHETLAND
ISLANDS

Trondheim

Gulf of Bothnia

HEBRIDES

ORKNEY
ISLANDS

NORTH
SEA

Oslo

Helsinki

St. Petersbur

Stockholm

BALTIC

Gulf of Finland

Glasgow

Göteborg

SAAREMAA

GOTLAND

Riga

Western Dvina

Dublin

IRISH SEA

Leeds

Copenhagen

ÖLAND

SEA

Manchester

BORNHOLM

Minsk

Birmingham

Hamburg

Elbe

Berlin

Warsaw

London

Amsterdam

Bug

Essen

Rhine

Łódź

English Channel

Brussels

Frankfurt
am Main

Prague

Oder

Katowice

Seine

Mannheim

Dniester

Paris

Stuttgart

Danube

CARPATHIAN MOUNTAINS

Bay of
Biscay

Loire

Munich

Vienna

Danube

Budapest

Bordeaux

MASSIF
CENTRAL

A

L

P

S

Danube

Lyon

Rhône

Turin

Milan

TRANSYLVANIAN ALPS

CORDILLERA CANTÁBRICA

PYRENEES

Marseille

LIGURIAN
SEA

A
P
E
N
N
I
N
E
S

ADRIATIC SEA

Belgrade

Bucharest

Porto

Ebro

Danube

Lisbon

Tagus

Madrid

Barcelona

CORSICA

Rome

Sofia

SIERRA MORENA

València

Sevilla

SARDINIA

Naples

PINDOS OROS

AEGEAN
SEA

BALEARIC ISLANDS

M E D I T E R R A N E A N

TYRRHENIAN
SEA

IONIAN
ISLANDS

Strait of Gibraltar

SICILY

IONIAN
SEA

Athens

CYCLADES

MALTA

S E A

SEA OF CRETE

CRETE

A-102094-1
© Rand McNally

| 0 | 80 | 160 | 240 | 320 | 400 | 480 Miles |

| 0 | 80 | 160 | 240 | 320 | 400 | 480 | 560 | 640 | 720 | 800 Kilometers |

Lambert Conformal Conic Projection
Scale 1:16,000,000
One inch to 256 miles
One cm to 160 km

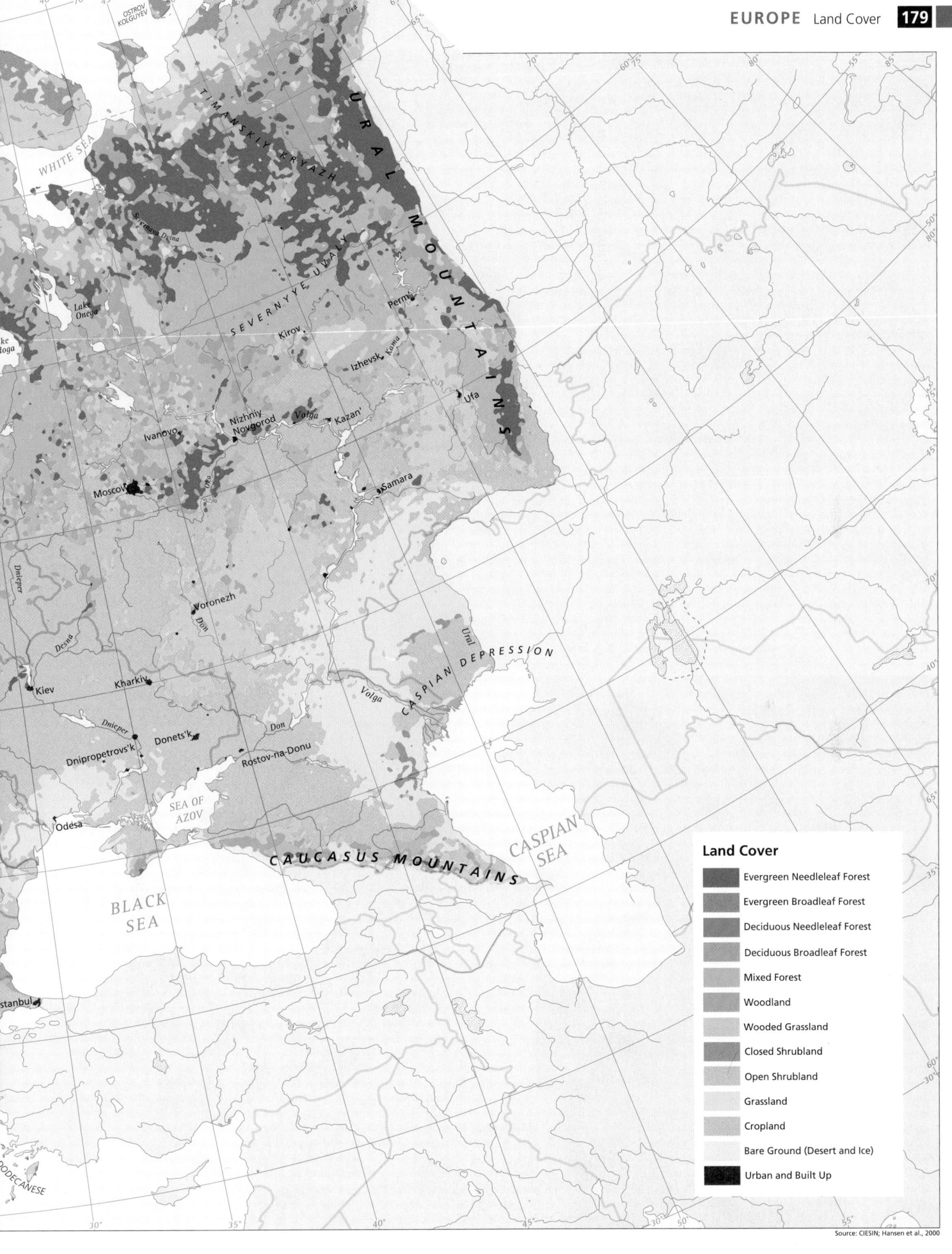

Land Cover

- Evergreen Needleleaf Forest
- Evergreen Broadleaf Forest
- Deciduous Needleleaf Forest
- Deciduous Broadleaf Forest
- Mixed Forest
- Woodland
- Wooded Grassland
- Closed Shrubland
- Open Shrubland
- Grassland
- Cropland
- Bare Ground (Desert and Ice)
- Urban and Built Up

Source: CIESIN; Hansen et al., 2000

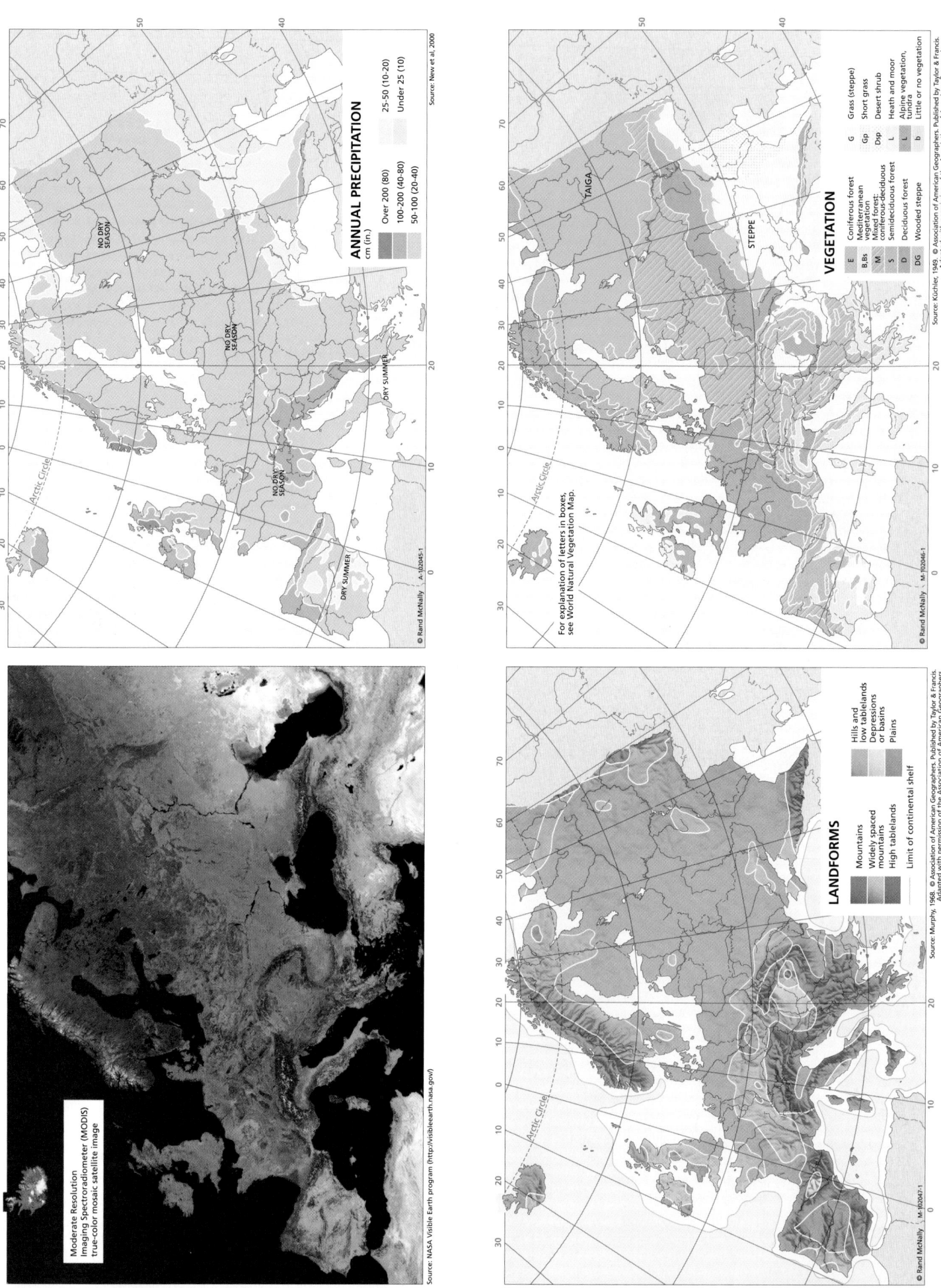

ANNUAL PRECIPITATION

cm (in.)

Over 200 (80)

100-200 (40-80)

50-100 (20-40)

25-50 (10-20)

Under 25 (10)

Source: New et al, 2000

NO DRY SEASON

NO DRY SEASON

DRY SUMMER

NO DRY SEASON

DRY SUMMER

© Rand McNally   A-1/2045-1

Moderate Resolution
Imaging Spectroradiometer (MODIS)
true-color mosaic satellite image

Source: NASA Visible Earth program (http://visibleearth.nasa.gov/)

VEGETATION

E   Coniferous forest

B, Bs   Mediterranean vegetation

M   Mixed forest: coniferous-deciduous

S   Semideciduous forest

D   Deciduous forest

DG   Wooded steppe

G   Grass (steppe)

Gp   Short grass

Dsp   Desert shrub

L   Heath and moor

L   Alpine vegetation, tundra

b   Little or no vegetation

For explanation of letters in boxes,
see World Natural Vegetation Map.

TAIGA

STEPPE

Source: Küchler, 1949. © Association of American Geographers. Published by Taylor & Francis.
Adapted with permission of the Association of American Geographers.

© Rand McNally   M-1/2046-1

LANDFORMS

Mountains

Widely spaced mountains

High tablelands

Hills and low tablelands

Depressions or basins

Plains

Limit of continental shelf

Source: Murphy, 1968. © Association of American Geographers. Published by Taylor & Francis.
Adapted with permission of the Association of American Geographers.

© Rand McNally   M-1/2047-1

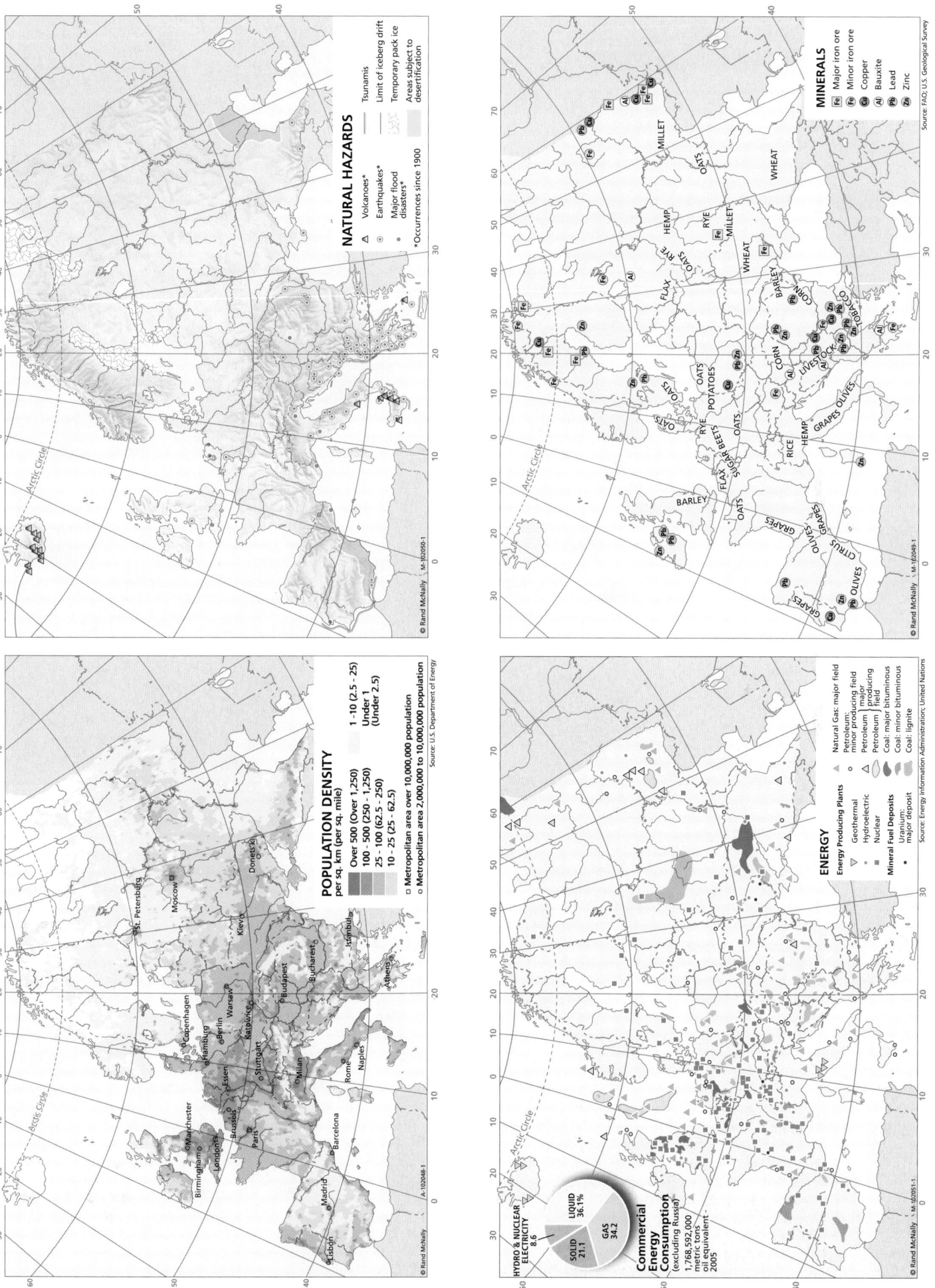

NATURAL HAZARDS

- △ Volcanoes*
- ⊙ Earthquakes*
- ● Major flood disasters*
- Tsunamis*
- Limit of iceberg drift
- Temporary pack ice
- Areas subject to desertification

*Occurrences since 1900

Source: U.S. Department of Energy

MINERALS

- Fe Major iron ore
- Fe Minor iron ore
- Cu Copper
- Al Bauxite
- Pb Lead
- Zn Zinc

Source: FAO; U.S. Geological Survey

POPULATION DENSITY
per sq. km (per sq. mile)

- Over 500 (Over 1,250)
- 100 - 500 (250 - 1,250)
- 25 - 100 (62.5 - 250)
- 10 - 25 (25 - 62.5)
- 1 - 10 (2.5 - 25)
- Under 1 (Under 2.5)

□ Metropolitan area over 10,000,000 population
○ Metropolitan area 2,000,000 to 10,000,000 population

Source: U.S. Department of Energy

ENERGY

Energy Producing Plants
- ▽ Geothermal
- ▽ Hydroelectric
- ▽ Nuclear

Mineral Fuel Deposits
- ● Uranium: major deposit

- ◐ Natural Gas: major field; minor producing field
- ○ Petroleum: major producing field
- ◑ Petroleum: minor field
- Coal: major bituminous
- Coal: minor bituminous
- Coal: lignite

Source: Energy Information Administration; United Nations

Commercial Energy Consumption
(excluding Russia)
1,768,592,000
metric tons
oil equivalent
2005

- SOLID 21.1
- LIQUID 36.1%
- GAS 34.2
- HYDRO & NUCLEAR ELECTRICITY 8.6

© Rand McNally

The geological information on this map is highly generalized, and is intended for use at scales of 1:10,000,000 or smaller.

Geology

Rock type/geological era

- Intrusive
- Metamorphic
- Volcanic, tectonic
- Precambrian sedimentary
- Paleozoic sedimentary
- Mesozoic sedimentary
- Cenozoic sedimentary

Note: Areas classified as sedimentary also include some sedimentary/volcanic areas.

Source: Chorlton, 2007

Reykjavik

NORWEGIAN SEA

Arctic Circle

Trondheim

Gulf of Bothnia

FAROE ISLANDS

SHETLAND ISLANDS

Oslo

Helsinki

Stockholm

St. Petersburg

Gulf of Finland

HEBRIDES

ORKNEY ISLANDS

BALTIC

Göteborg

SAAREMAA

Lake Peipus

Glasgow

NORTH SEA

GOTLAND

Riga

Western Dvina

Dublin

IRISH SEA

Leeds

Copenhagen

ÖLAND

SEA

Manchester

BORNHOLM

Birmingham

Minsk

London

Amsterdam

Hamburg

Elbe

Berlin

Warsaw

Vistula

ATLANTIC

Brussels

Essen

Łódź

Bug

English Channel

Rhine

Frankfurt am Main

Prague

Katowice

OCEAN

Seine

Paris

Mannheim

Oder

Bay of Biscay

Loire

Stuttgart

Danube

Munich

Vienna

CARPATHIAN MOUNTAINS

Dniester

Lyon

Budapest

Danube

Bordeaux

Dordogne

MASSIF CENTRAL

Rhône

A L P S

Drava

Sava

TRANSYLVANIAN ALPS

CORDILLERA CANTÁBRICA

Turin

Milan

Po

ADRIATIC SEA

Belgrade

Bucharest

Porto

PYRENEES

Marseille

Danube

Duero

LIGURIAN SEA

Madrid

Sofia

Lisbon

Tagus

CORSICA

A P E N N I N E S

Rome

PINDOS OROS

Barcelona

SIERRA MORENA

València

SARDINIA

Naples

AEGEAN SEA

Sevilla

BALEARIC ISLANDS

TYRRHENIAN SEA

IONIAN ISLANDS

Algiers

M E D I T E R

SICILY

IONIAN SEA

Athens

Casablanca

R A N E A N

CYCLADES

MALTA

SEA

SEA OF CRETE

A T L A S   M O U N T A I N S

CRETE

| 0 | 80 | 160 | 240 | 320 | 400 | 480 Miles |

| 0 | 80 | 160 | 240 | 320 | 400 | 480 | 560 | 640 | 720 | 800 Kilometers |

Lambert Conformal Conic Projection
Scale 1:16,000,000
One inch to 256 miles
One cm to 160 km

OSTROV KOLGUYEV

WHITE SEA

TIMANSKIY KRYAZH

URAL MOUNTAINS

WEST SIBERIAN PLAIN

SIBERIA

Novosibirsk

Ob'

Ob'

Usa

Pechora

Severnaya Dvina

Ozero Kulundinskoye

Irtysh

Omsk

Irtysh

Tobol

SEVERNYYE UVALY

Yekaterinburg

Perm'

Kirov

Astana

KAZAKH HILLS

Tobol

Izhevsk

Kama

Lake Onega

ake adoga

Ufa

Lake Balkhash

Nizhniy Novgorod

Volga

Kazan'

Zhem

Sha

Ivanovo

Oka

Samara

Moscow

Syr Darya

Aral Sea

QIZILOUM

Tashkent

Dnieper

Voronezh

Don

Desna

CASPIAN DEPRESSION

Ural

UST-URT PLATEAU

Kiev

Kharkiv

Northern Donets

Volga

Amu Darya

Dnieper

Donets'k

Don

KARA

Dnipropetrovs'k

Rostov-na-Donu

Kuma

KUM

Morghdb

SEA OF AZOV

Kuban'

Kara-Bogaz-Gol Gulf

CASPIAN SEA

Prut

Odesa

CAUCASUS MOUNTAINS

KOPPEH DAGH

Harrud

BLACK SEA

Tbilisi

ELBURZ MOUNTAINS

DASHT-E KAVIR

Istanbul

Kizilirmak

Aras

Sakarya

Ankara

Tehrān

DASHT-E LŪT

Tigris

TAURUS MOUNTAINS

ZAGROS MOUNTAINS

DODECANESE

CYPRUS

Euphrates

Karūn

Baghdad

Tigris

SYRIAN DESERT

© Rand McNally   A-102091-1

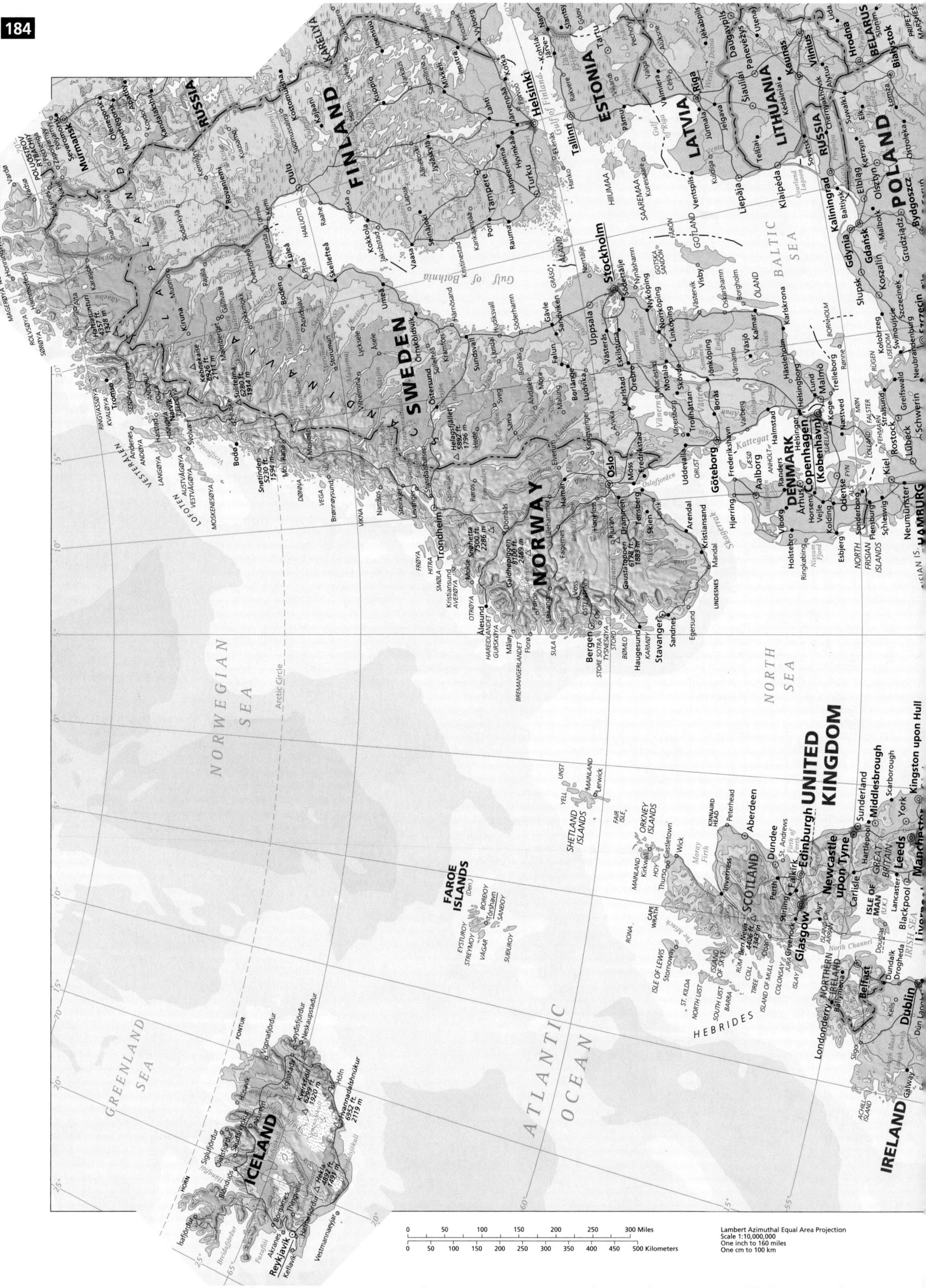

BARENTS SEA

RUSSIA

Murmansk

FINLAND

Helsinki

ESTONIA

Tallinn

LATVIA

Riga

LITHUANIA

RUSSIA

Kaliningrad

BELARUS

POLAND

Gulf of Finland

Gulf of Bothnia

Stockholm

BALTIC SEA

GOTLAND

ÖLAND

BORNHOLM

SWEDEN

Uppsala

Göteborg

Helgafjället
5892 ft.
1796 m

Kebnekaise
6926 ft.
2111 m

Sarektjåkkå
6880 ft.
2089 m

Snøhetta
7500 ft.
2286 m

Galdhøpiggen
8101 ft.
2469 m

Gaustatoppen
6178 ft.
1883 m

NORWAY

Oslo

Bergen

Stavanger

Trondheim

Ålesund

Bodø

Tromsø

LOFOTEN

VESTERÅLEN

DENMARK

Copenhagen
(København)

Aalborg

HAMBURG

NORTH SEA

NORWEGIAN SEA

Arctic Circle

GREENLAND SEA

ICELAND

Reykjavík

Hekla
4891 ft.
1491 m

FAROE ISLANDS
(Den.)

Tórshavn

SHETLAND ISLANDS

Lerwick

ORKNEY ISLANDS

Kirkwall

FAIR ISLE

UNITED KINGDOM

SCOTLAND

Edinburgh

Glasgow

Aberdeen

Inverness

Dundee

GREAT BRITAIN

Newcastle upon Tyne

Middlesbrough

Leeds

Manchester

Liverpool

Blackpool

York

Kingston upon Hull

Sunderland

ISLE OF MAN
(U.K.)

HEBRIDES

ISLE OF LEWIS

ISLE OF SKYE

Ben Nevis
4406 ft.
1343 m

NORTHERN IRELAND

Belfast

Londonderry

IRELAND

Dublin

ATLANTIC OCEAN

IRISH SEA

North Channel

Scale 1:10,000,000
One inch to 160 miles
One cm to 100 km
Lambert Azimuthal Equal Area Projection

| 0 | 50 | 100 | 150 | 200 | 250 | 300 Miles |

| 0 | 50 | 100 | 150 | 200 | 250 | 300 | 350 | 400 | 450 | 500 Kilometers |

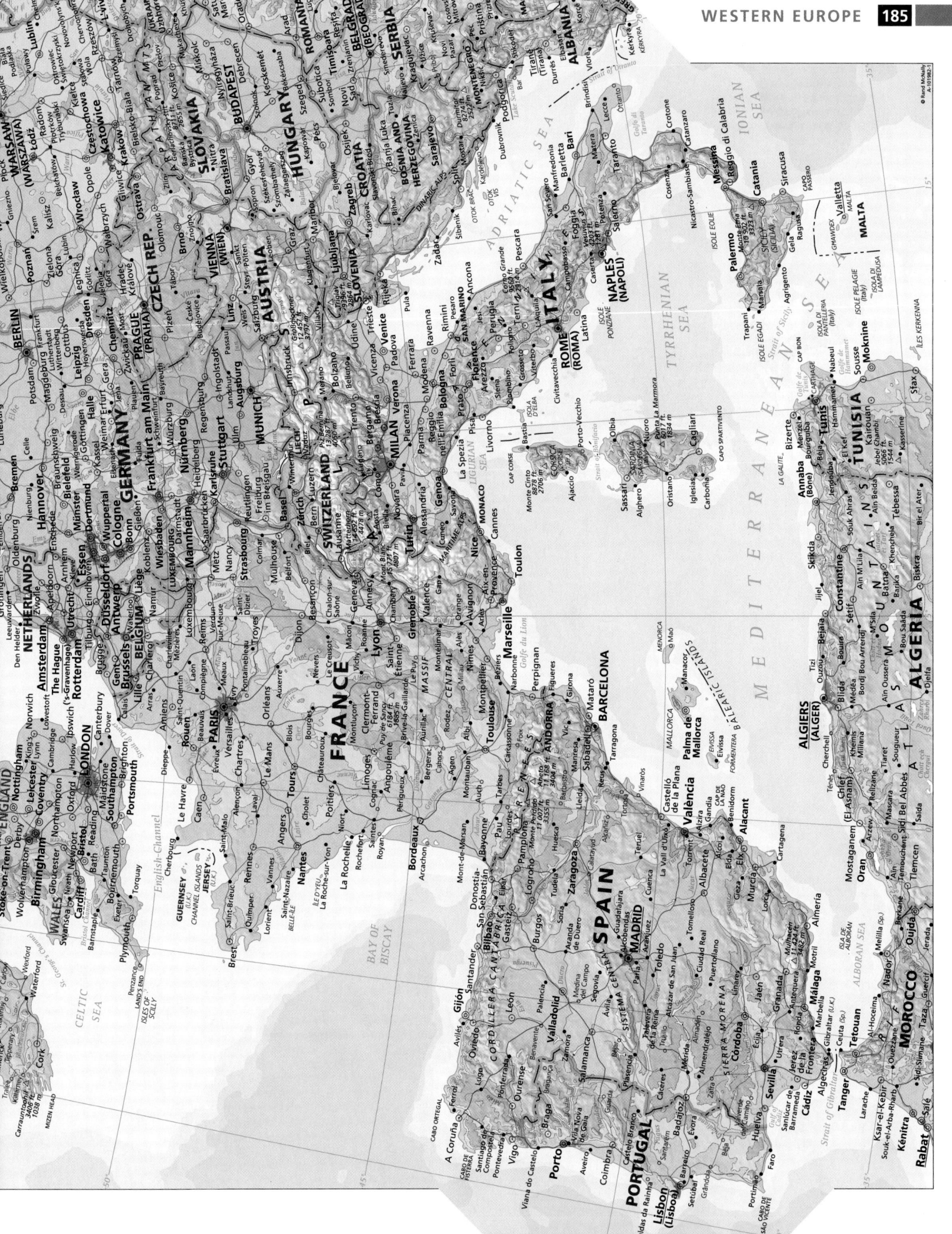

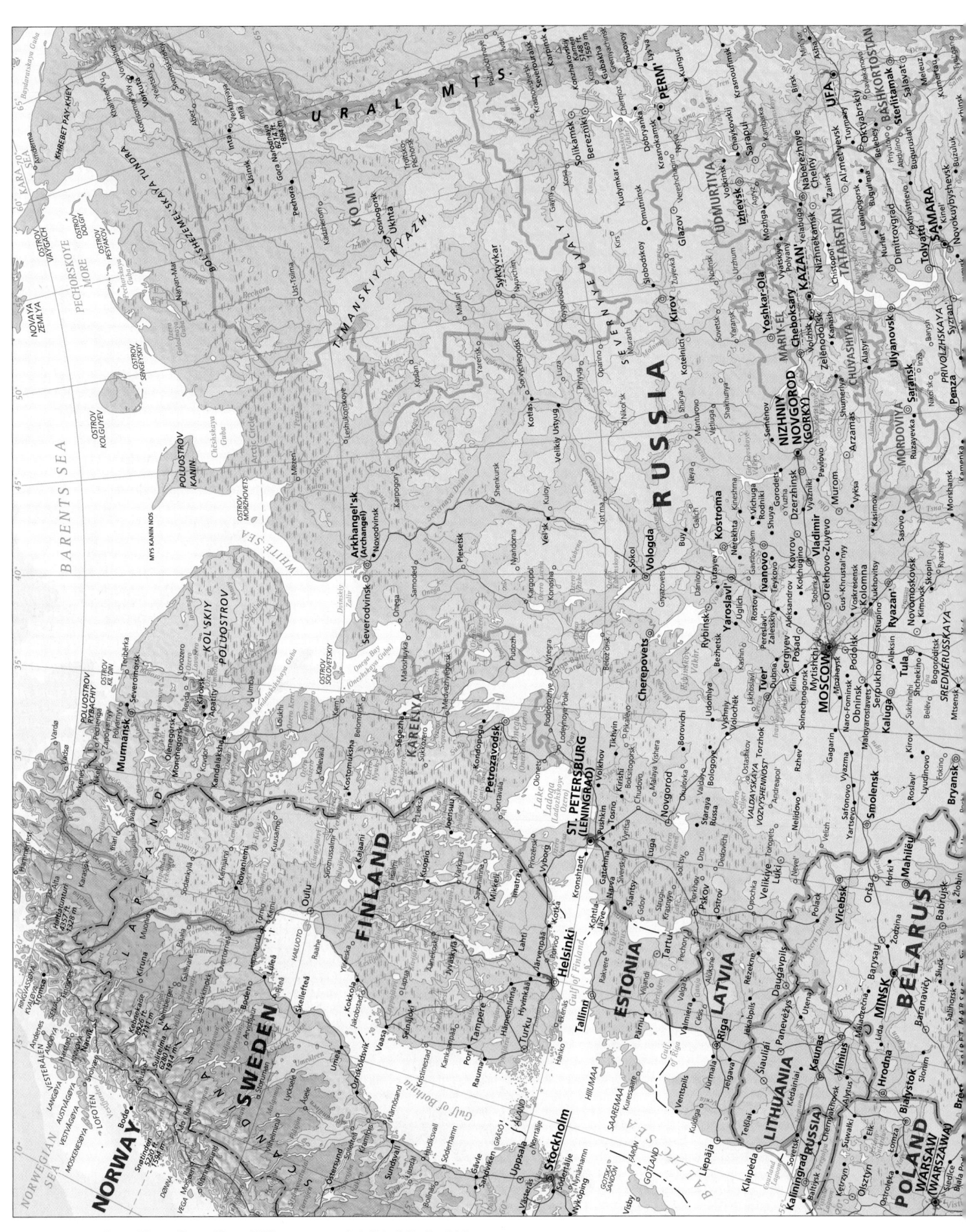

0   50   100   150   200   250   300 Miles

0   50   100   150   200   250   300   350   400   450   500 Kilometers

Lambert Azimuthal Equal Area Projection
Scale 1:10,000,000
One inch to 160 miles
One cm to 100 km

0   50   100   150   200   250   300 Miles
0 50 100 150 200 250 300 350 400 450 500 Kilometers

Lambert Azimuthal Equal Area Projection
Scale 1:10,000,000
One inch to 160 miles
One cm to 100 km

© Rand McNally
A-101877-1

a

GREENLAND SEA

Arctic Circle

ICELAND

Herðubreið
5518 ft.
1682 m

Askja
4954 ft.
1510 m

Kverkfjöll
6299 ft.
1920 m

Snæfell
6014 ft.
1833 m

Grímsvötn
5640 ft.
1719 m

Hvannadalshnúkur
6952 ft.
2119 m

Hekla
4892 ft.
1491 m

Reykjavík

REYKJANES

ATLANTIC OCEAN

© Rand McNally
A-101769-1

b

NORWEGIAN SEA

Slættaratindur
2894 ft.
882 m

FAROE ISLANDS
(Denmark)

ATLANTIC OCEAN

© Rand McNally
A-101763-1

c

SHETLAND ISLANDS
(U.K.)

St. Magnus Bay

ATLANTIC

OCEAN

FAIR ISLE

NORTH RONALDSAY

WESTRAY

ORKNEY ISLANDS
(U.K.)

MAINLAND

NORTH SEA

© Rand McNally
A-101764-1

ISLE OF LEWIS

HEBRIDES

SEA OF THE HEBRIDES

MALIN HEAD

Londonderry

NORTHERN IRELAND

Belfast

Dublin
(Baile Átha Cliath)

IRELAND

Lugnaquillia
Mountain
3031 ft.
924 m

Carrauntoohil
3406 ft.
1038 m

Cork

ATLANTIC

OCEAN

CELTIC

SEA

St. George's Channel

© Rand McNally
A-101759-1

| 0 | 20 | 40 | 60 | 80 | 100 | 120 Miles |
| 0 | 20 | 40 | 60 | 80 | 100 | 120 | 140 | 160 | 180 | 200 Kilometers |

Lambert Conformal Conic Projection
Scale 1:4,000,000
One inch to 64 miles
One cm to 40 km

d

Inset map d
Lambert Conformal Conic Projection
Scale 1:1,000,000
One inch to 16 miles
One cm to 10 km

0 20 40 60 80 100 120 Miles

0 20 40 60 80 100 120 140 160 180 200 Kilometers

Lambert Conformal Conic Projection
Scale 1:4,000,000
One inch to 64 miles
One cm to 40 km

Lambert Conformal Conic Projection
Scale 1:4,000,000
One inch to 64 miles
One cm to 40 km

0 20 40 60 80 100 120 Miles

0 20 40 60 80 100 120 140 160 180 200 Kilometers

Lambert Conformal Conic Projection
Scale 1:4,000,000
One inch to 64 miles
One cm to 40 km

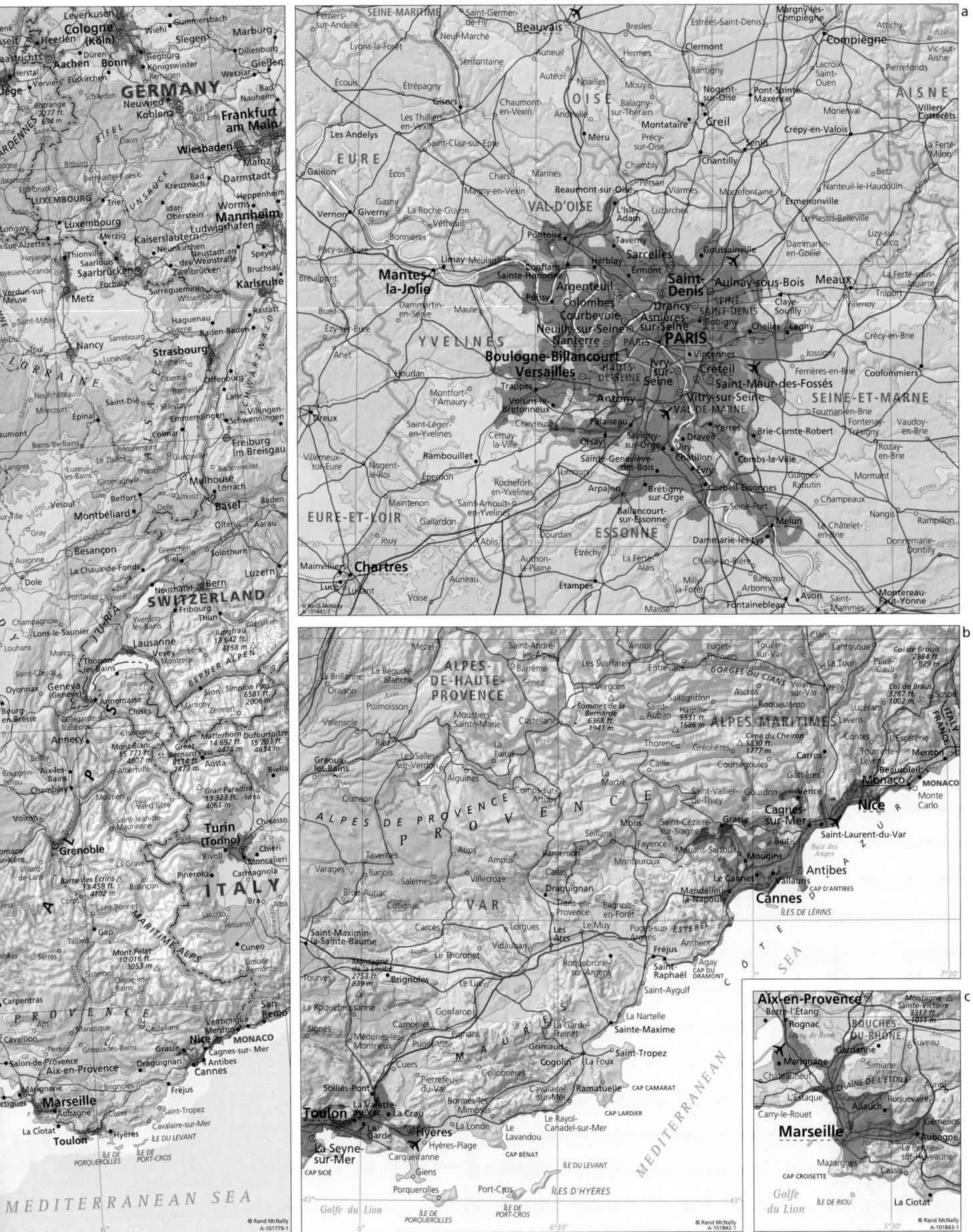

a

b

c

Inset maps a - c
Lambert Conformal Conic Projection
Scale 1:1,000,000
One inch to 16 miles
One cm to 10 km

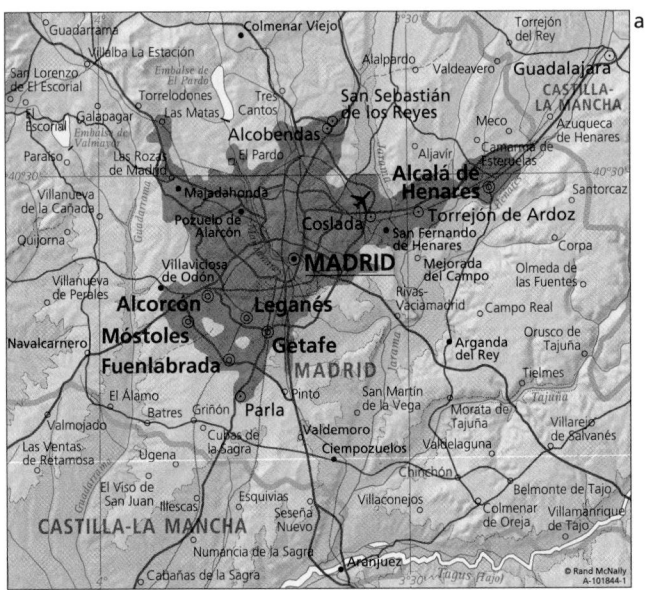

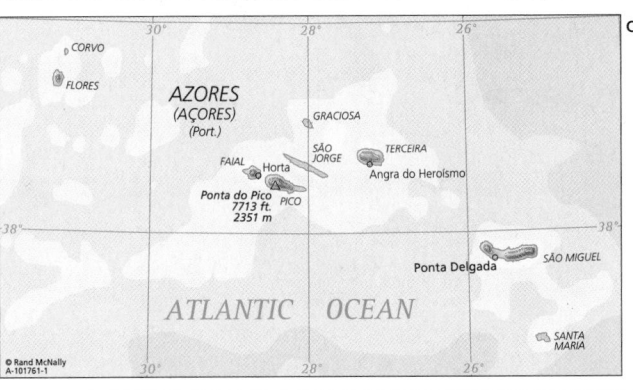

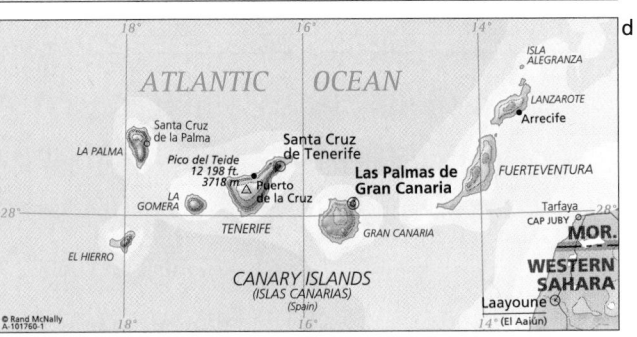

Lambert Conformal Conic Projection
Scale 1:4,000,000
One inch to 64 miles
One cm to 40 km

Inset maps a, b
Lambert Conformal Conic Projection
Scale 1:1,000,000
One inch to 16 miles
One cm to 10 km

Inset maps c, d
Lambert Conformal Conic Projection
Scale 1:8,000,000
One inch to 128 miles
One cm to 80 km

SWITZERLAND
AUSTRIA
HOHE TAUERN
HUN
SLOVENIA
Ljubljana
Zagreb
CROATIA
FRANCE
Turin (Torino)
MILAN (MILANO)
Venice (Venezia)
BOSNIA
AND
HERZEGOVINA
Genoa (Genova)
Bologna
Sarajevo
Monaco
Nice
LIGURIAN
SEA
Florence (Firenze)
SAN MARINO
ADRIATIC
Dubrovnik
CORSICA
CORSE
(France)
ITALY
SEA
VATICAN CITY
ROME (ROMA)
Pescara
SARDINIA
(SARDEGNA)
(Italy)
NAPLES (NAPOLI)
Bari
Taranto
TYRRHENIAN
SEA
Cagliari
Brindisi
Lecce
Kosovo unilaterally declared its
independence from Serbia in 2008.

SEA OF CRETE
Palermo
Messina
Reggio di Calabria
CRETE
(KRITI)
(Greece)
Marsala
SICILY
(SICILIA)
Catania
MEDITERRANEAN SEA

MEDITERRANEAN SEA
GOZO
Victoria
KEMMUNA
Skorba
Sliema
MALTA
Rabat
Valletta
MALTA
Birżebbuġa

© Rand McNally
A-101762-1

Lambert Conformal Conic Projection
Scale 1:4,500,000
One inch to 71 miles
One cm to 45 km

Inset map b
Lambert Conformal Conic Projection
Scale 1:2,000,000
One inch to 32 miles
One cm to 20 km

0 20 40 60 80 100 120 Miles
0 20 40 60 80 100 120 140 160 180 200 Kilometers

Lambert Conformal Conic Projection
Scale 1:4,000,000
One inch to 64 miles
One cm to 40 km

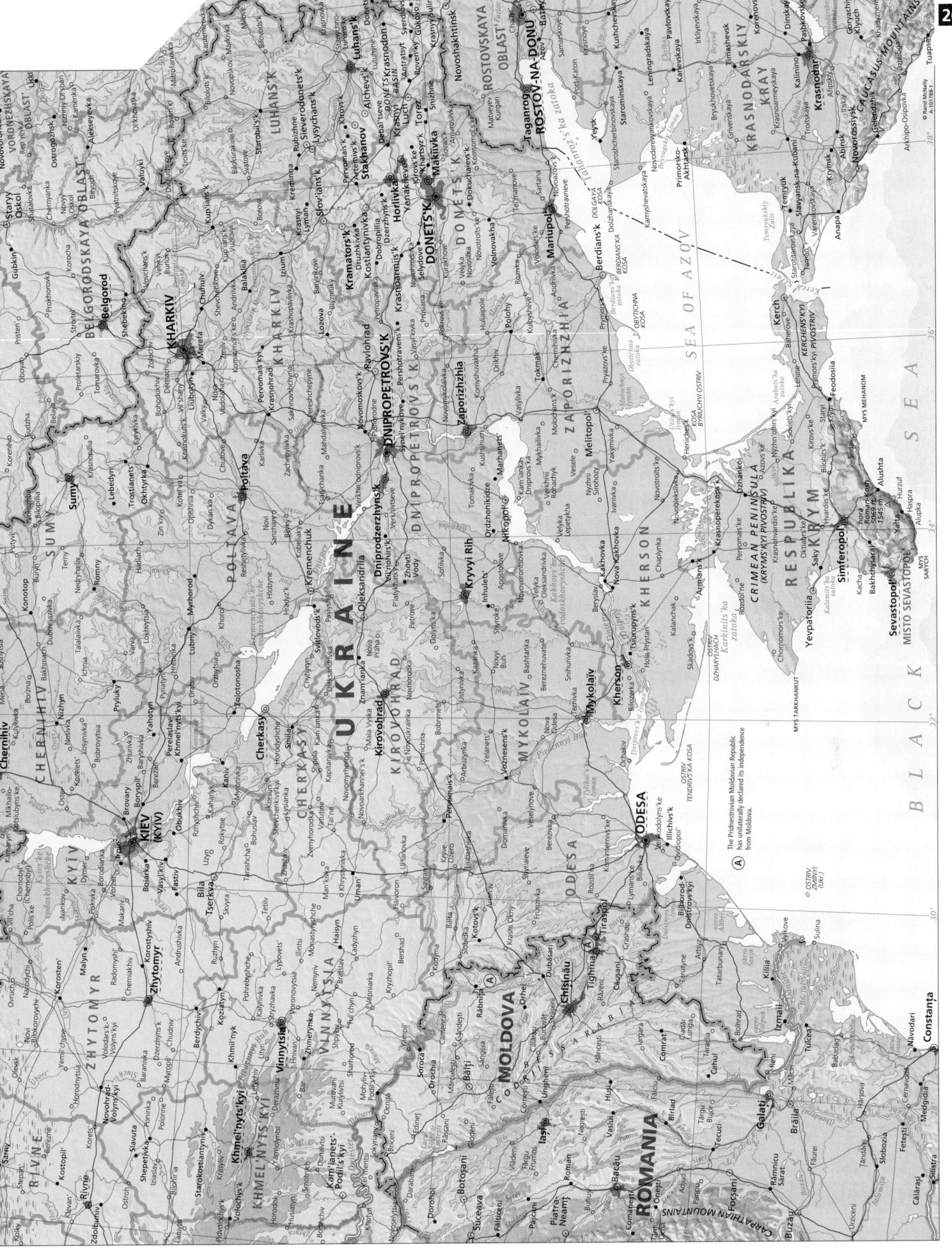

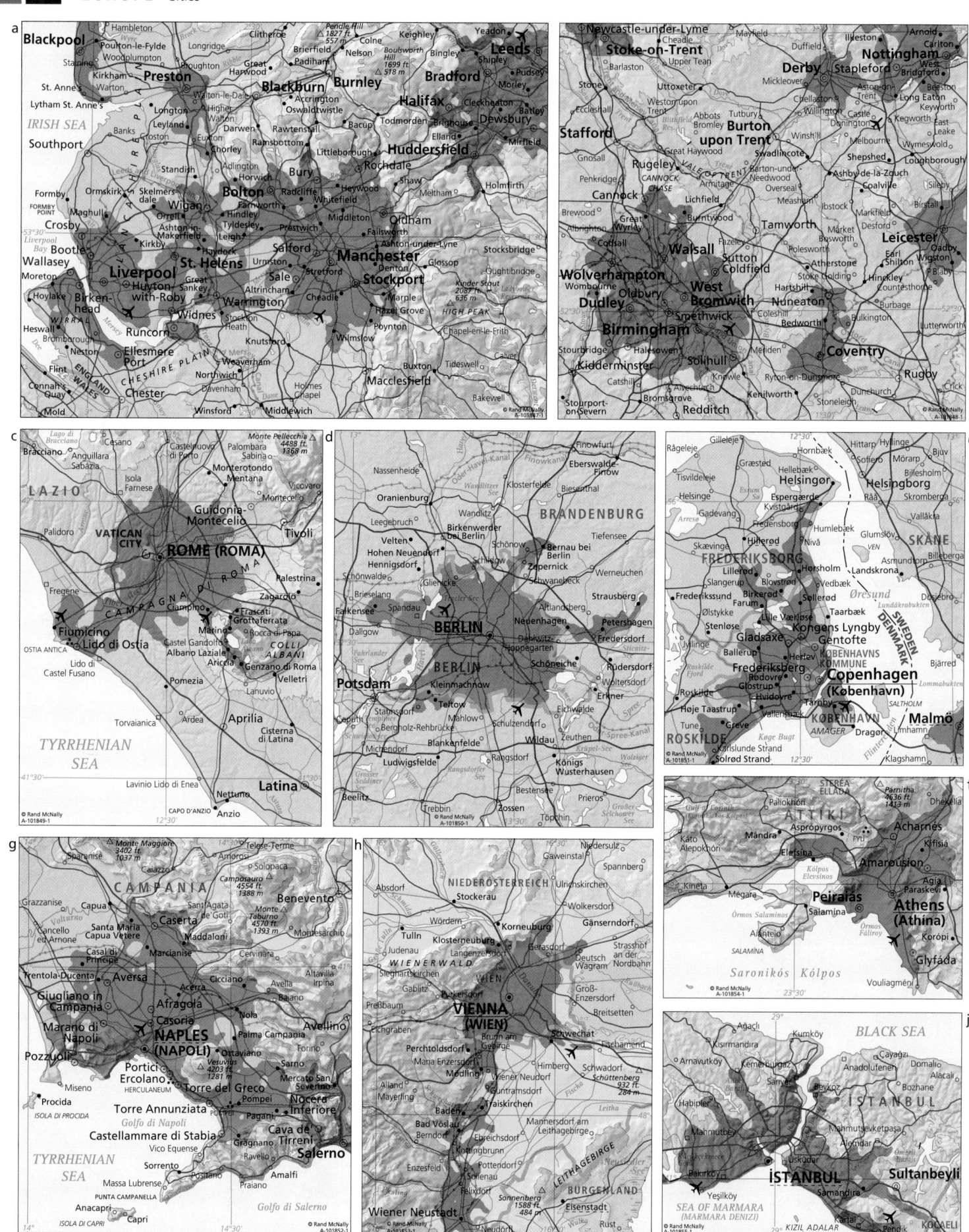

a

Blackpool
Hambleton
Poulton-le-Fylde
Woodplumpton
Longridge
Clitheroe
Pendle Hill
△ 1827 ft.
557 m
Keighley
Yeadon
Staining
Kirkham
Broughton
Great
Harwood
Brierfield
Nelson
Colne
Bingley
Shipley
Leeds
St. Anne's
Warton
Walton-le-Dale
Higher
Oswaldtwistle
Blackburn
Burnley
Boulsworth
Hill
△ 518 m
Pudsey
Morley
Bradford
Lytham St. Anne's
Longton
Leyland
Darwen
Ramsbottom
Rawtenstall
Bacup
Todmorden
Brighouse
Dewsbury
IRISH SEA
Banks
Croston
Chorley
Adlington
Horwich
Littleborough
Elland
Halifax
Southport
Formby
Ormskirk
Skelmersdale
Standish
Wigan
Bolton
Bury
Heywood
Rochdale
Shaw
Holmfirth
Huddersfield
Mirfield
53°30'
Maghull
Orrell
Ashton-in-Makerfield
Hindley
Tyldesley
Prestwich
Middleton
Failsworth
Oldham
Ashton-under-Lyne
Crosby
Kirkby
St. Helens
Leigh
Salford
Whitefield
Glossop
Liverpool Bay
Bootle
Wallasey
Moreton
Hoylake
Birken-head
Huyton-with-Roby
Great
Sankey
Altrincham
Sale
Stretford
Manchester
Stockport
Denton
Marple
Stocksbridge
Oughtibridge
Heswall
Widnes
Runcorn
Warrington
Cheadle
Hazel Grove
Kinder Scout
2087 ft.
636 m
HIGH PEAK
WIRRAL
Neston
Ellesmore
Port
Stockton
Heath
Knutsford
Wilmslow
Poynton
Chapel-en-le-Frith
Buxton
Flint
Bromborough
Northwich
Weaverham
Tideswell
Calver
Connah's Quay
Mold
ENGLAND
WALES
Chester
Davenham
Holmes
Chapel
Bakewell
CHESHIRE PLAIN
Winsford
Middlewich
Macclesfield
© Rand McNally
A-101847-1

b

Newcastle-under-Lyme
Cheadle
Mayfield
Duffield
Ilkeston
Arnold
Carlton
Nottingham
Stoke-on-Trent
Upper Tean
Derby
Stapleford
West
Bridgford
Barlaston
Stone
Weston upon
Trent
Mickleover
Chellaston
Aston-on-Trent
Long Eaton
Keyworth
Kegworth
Stafford
Eccleshall
Abbots
Bromley
Tutbury
Burton
upon Trent
Melbourne
Shepshed
Loughborough
Wymeswold
Gnosall
Great Haywood
Rugeley
Swadlincote
Ashby-de-la-Zouch
Barton-under-Needwood
Overseal
Coalville
Sileby
Penkridge
CANNOCK
CHASE
Lichfield
Measham
Ibstock
Markfield
Birstall
Cannock
Brewood
Great
Wyrley
Burntwood
Tamworth
Market
Bosworth
Desford
Leicester
Albrighton
Codsall
Fazeley
Polesworth
Atherstone
Earl
Shilton
Oadby
Wigston
Walsall
Sutton
Coldfield
Stoke Golding
Hinckley
Countesthorpe
Blaby
Wolverhampton
Wombourne
Oldbury
West
Bromwich
Smethwick
Coleshill
Bedworth
Nuneaton
Burbage
Lutterworth
Dudley
Birmingham
Solihull
Meriden
Ryton-on-Dunsmore
Coventry
Rugby
Stourbridge
Halesowen
Knowle
Kidderminster
Kenilworth
Stoneleigh
Dunchurch
Crick
Catshill
Alvechurch
Stourport-on-Severn
Bromsgrove
Redditch
© Rand McNally
A-101848-1

c

Lago di
Bracciano
Casano
Castelnuovo
di Porto
Palombara
Sabina
Monte Pellecchia
4488 ft.
1368 m
Bracciano
Anguillara
Sabázia
Monterotondo
Mentana
Vicovaro
LAZIO
Isola
Farnese
Montecelio
Tivoli
Palidoro
Guidonia-Montecelio
VATICAN
CITY
ROME (ROMA)
ROMA
Fregene
Palestrina
CAMPAGNA DI
Zagarolo
Ciampino
Frascati
Grottaferrata
Rocca di Papa
Fiumicino
Marino
Lido di Ostia
Castel Gandolfo
Albano Laziale
Ariccia
Genzano di Roma
COLLI
ALBANI
Velletri
OSTIA ANTICA
Lido di
Castel Fusano
Pomezia
Torvaianica
Ardea
Aprilia
Cisterna
di Latina
TYRRHENIAN
SEA
Lavinio Lido di Enea
41°30'
12°30'
Latina
Nettuno
CAPO D'ANZIO
Anzio
© Rand McNally
A-101849-1

d

Finowfurt
Nassenheide
Oder-Havel-Kanal
Finowkanal
Eberswalde-Finow
Oranienburg
Wandlitzer
See
Klosterfelde
Biesenthal
Leegebruch
Velten
Wandlitz
Birkenwerder
bei Berlin
Schönow
Bernau bei
Berlin
BRANDENBURG
Hohen Neuendorf
Hennigsdorf
Zepernick
Werneuchen
Schönwalde
Glienicke
Strausberg
Brieselang
Spandau
Neuenhagen
Altlandsberg
Falkensee
BERLIN
Petershagen
Dallgow
Fredersdorf
Fahrlander
See
Schöneiche
Rüdersdorf
Potsdam
BERLIN
Hoppegarten
Erkner
Kleinmachnow
Woltersdorf
Teltow
Eichwalde
Stahnsdorf
Mahlow
Schulzendorf
Wildau
Zeuthen
Caputh
Bergholz-Rehbrücke
Blankenfelde
Michendorf
Rangsdorf
Königs
Wusterhausen
Ludwigsfelde
Bestensee
Grosser
Seddiner
See
Beelitz
Trebbin
Zossen
Prieros
Grosser
Selchower
See
Töpchin
© Rand McNally
A-101850-1

e

12°30'
Rågeleje
Gilleleje
Hornbæk
Hittarp
Hyllinge
Bjuv
Tisvildeleje
Græsted
Hellebæk
Helsingør
Helsingborg
Sofiero
Mörarp
Helsinge
Esbergærde
Helsinge
Fredensborg
Niva
Humlebæk
Råå
Skromberga
FREDERIKSBORG
Hillerød
Kvistgaard
Glumslöv
VEN
SKÅNE
Asmundtorp
Billeberga
Frederikssund
Lillerød
Blovstrød
Birkerød
Hørsholm
Landskrona
Slangerup
Farum
Vedbæk
Øresund
Ølstykke
Stenløse
Søllerød
Taarbæk
Lundåkrabukten
Dösjebro
Jyllinge
Ballerup
Lille Værløse
Kongens Lyngby
Gentofte
SWEDEN
DENMARK
Roskilde
Fjord
Herlev
Gladsaxe
Bjärred
Rødovre
KØBENHAVNS
KOMMUNE
Frederiksberg
Glostrup
Copenhagen
(København)
Høje Taastrup
Hvidovre
Tårnby
SALTHOLM
Lommabukten
ROSKILDE
Vallensbæk
KØBENHAVN
AMAGER
Dragør
Malmö
Greve
Tune
Limhamn
Køge Bugt
Klagshamn
Solrød Strand
Karlslunde Strand
12°30'
Flintet
© Rand McNally
A-101851-1

f

STEREA
ELLADA
Párnitha
2636 ft.
1413 m
Dhekélia
Palliokhóri
ATTIKI
Káto
Alepokhóri
Aspropyrgos
FYLI
Acharnés
Kifisiá
Mándra
Eleffsina
Amaroússion
Agía
Paraskeví
Kólpos
Elevsínas
Kinéta
Mégara
Peiraías
Athens
(Athína)
Salamína
Órmos
Fáliron
Korópi
SALAMÍNA
Órmos Salamínas
Aiánteio
Glyfáda
Saronikós Kólpos
Vouliagméni
© Rand McNally
A-101854-1

g

Monte Maggiore
3402 ft.
1037 m
Telese-Terme
Spárnise
Amórosi
Solopaca
Camposauro
4554 ft.
1388 m
Niedersulz
Gaweinstal
Spannberg
Grazzanise
Capua
CAMPANIA
Sant'Agata
de'Goti
Benevento
Santa Maria
Capua Vetere
Caserta
Maddaloni
Monte
Taburno
4570 ft.
1393 m
Montesárchio
Cancello
ed Arnone
Casal di
Príncipe
Marcianise
Cervinara
Altavilla
Irpina
Trentola-Ducenta
Aversa
Cicciano
Avella
Baiano
Giugliano in
Campania
Acerra
Nola
Afragola
Palma Campania
Avellino
Forino
Marano di
Napoli
Casoria
NAPLES
(NAPOLI)
Ottaviano
Sarno
Mercato San
Severino
Pozzuoli
Portici
Ercolano
HERCULANEUM
Vesúvio
4203 ft.
1281 m
Pompei
Nocera
Inferiore
Pagani
Miseno
Torre del Greco
Cava de'
Tirreni
Procida
ISOLA DI PROCIDA
Torre Annunziata
Gragnano
Salerno
Castellammare di Stabia
Vico Equense
Ravello
Amalfi
TYRRHENIAN
SEA
Sorrento
Positano
Praiano
Golfo di Salerno
Massa Lubrense
PUNTA CAMPANELLA
Anacapri
Capri
ISOLA DI CAPRI
© Rand McNally
A-101852-1

h

Absdorf
Stockerau
Ulrichskirchen
Wördern
Korneuburg
Gänserndorf
Tulln
Klosterneuburg
Wolkersdorf
Judenau
Langenzersdorf
Gerasdorf
Strasshof
an der
Nordbahn
WIENERWALD
Sieghartskirchen
Deutsch
Wagram
Gablitz
WIEN
Gross-Enzersdorf
Preßbaum
Purkersdorf
VIENNA
(WIEN)
Breitsetten
Eichgraben
Brunn am
Gebirge
Schwechat
Perchtoldsdorf
Fischamend
Maria Enzersdorf
Mödling
Wiener Neudorf
Schwadorf
Schüttenberg
932 ft.
284 m
Alland
Mayerling
Guntramsdorf
Himberg
Mannersdorf am
Leithagebirge
Baden
Traiskirchen
Bad Vöslau
Ebreichsdorf
Berndorf
Leitha
Kottingbrunn
LEITHAGEBIRGE
BURGENLAND
Enzesfeld
Pottendorf
Sollenau
Eisenstadt
Sonnenberg
1588 ft.
484 m
Felixdorf
Wiener Neustadt
Neudörfl
Rust
© Rand McNally
A-101853-1

j

Ağaçlı
Kumköy
BLACK SEA
Kısırmandıra
Çayağzı
Arnavutköy
Kemerburgaz
Anadolufeneri
Domalıç
Sarıyer
Bozhane
Alaçalı
Habipler
Beykoz
İSTANBUL
Mahmutbey
Üsküdar
Mahmutşevketpaşa
Alemdar
Pakırköy
İSTANBUL
Sultanbeyli
Yeşilköy
SEA OF
MARMARA
(MARMARA DENİZİ)
Kartal
Pendik
KIZIL ADALAR
KOCAELİ
© Rand McNally
A-101855-1

0   5   10   15   20   25   30 Miles
0 5 10 15 20 25 30 35 40 45 50 Kilometers

Lambert Conformal Conic Projection
Scale 1:1,000,000
One inch to 16 miles
One cm to 10 km

Lambert Conformal Conic Projection
Scale 1:1,000,000
One inch to 16 miles
One cm to 10 km

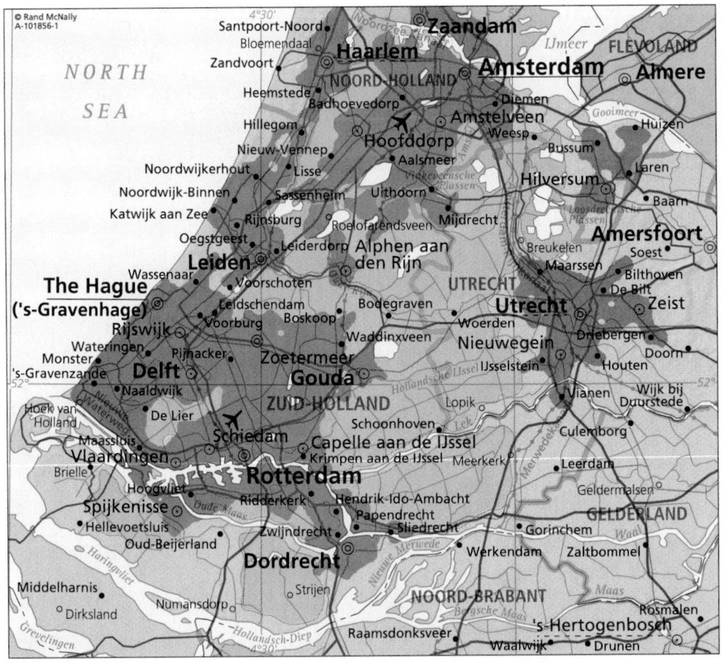

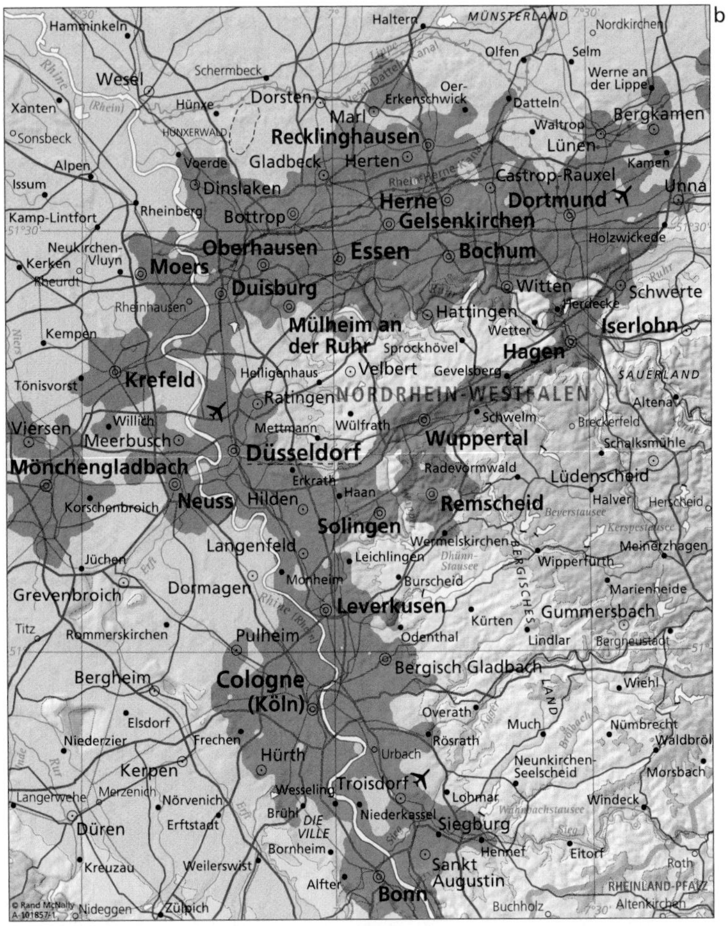

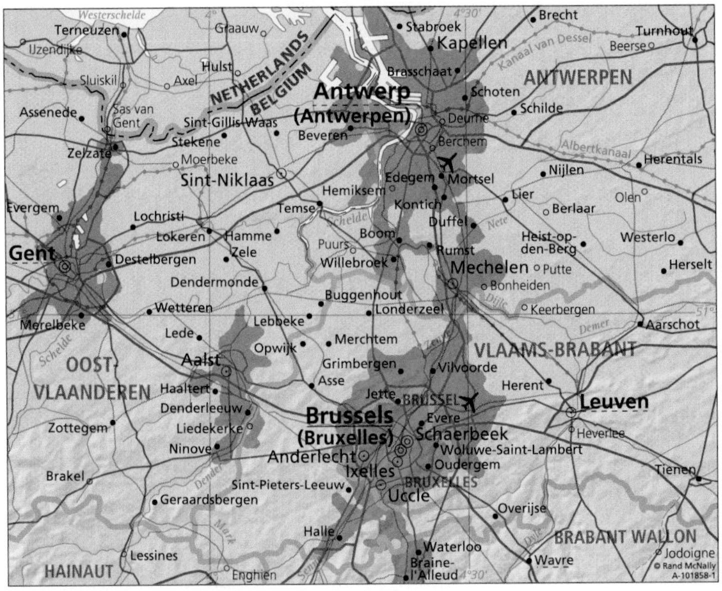

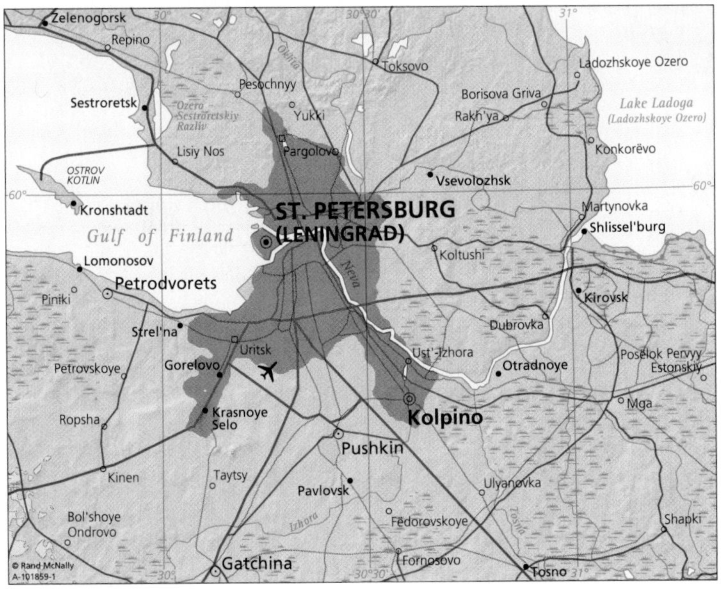

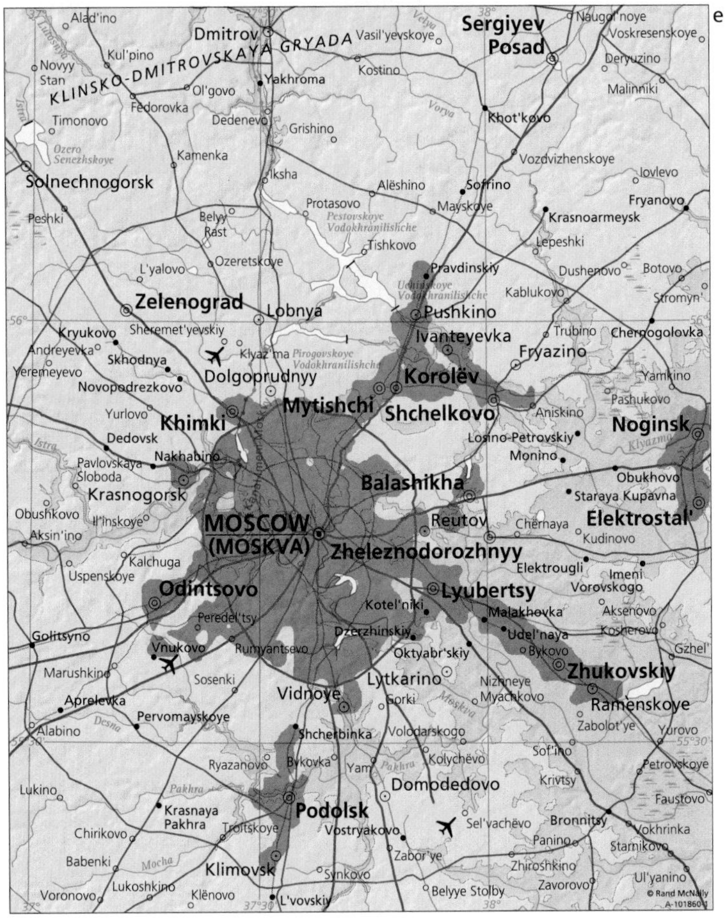

0 5 10 15 20 25 30 Miles
0 5 10 15 20 25 30 35 40 45 50 Kilometers

© Rand McNally
A-101856-1

© Rand McNally
A-101857-1

© Rand McNally
A-101858-1

© Rand McNally
A-101859-1

© Rand McNally
A-101860

ARCTIC OCEAN

SEVERNAYA
ZEMLYA

NORWEGIAN SEA

SVALBARD
(Norway)

FRANZ JOSEF
LAND

Arctic Circle

AZORES
(Port.)

ATLANTIC OCEAN

FAEROE
ISLANDS (Den.)

BARENTS
SEA

NOVAYA
ZEMLYA

KARA
SEA

OSTROV
KOLGUYEV

Khatanga

Dudinka   Noril'sk

IRELAND

UNITED
KINGDOM

NORTH
SEA

NORWAY

SWEDEN

FINLAND

Arkhangel'sk

Salekhard

Gora
Narodnaya
6214 ft
1894 m

R U S

LONDON

DENMARK

Stockholm

ST. PETERSBURG
(LENINGRAD)

Lake
Onega

Khanty-
Mansiysk

PARIS

NETH.
BELG.
GERMANY

BERLIN

BALTIC SEA

EST.
LATVIA
LITH.
RUS.

MOSCOW

YEKATERINBURG

Nizhniy Tagil

Tyumen'

Irtysh

Ob

Pechora

Yenisey

Pokamennaya

FRANCE

SWITZ.
AUSTRIA
CZECH
REP.

POLAND

BELARUS

KIEV

UKRAINE

Volga

Oka

Magnitogorsk

Orsk

CHELYABINSK

OMSK

Tomsk

Krasnoyarsk

NOVOSIBIRSK

Novokuzneck

SPAIN

MADRID

PORTUGAL

ITALY

SLVK.
HUNGARY

BUDAPEST

MOLD.

ROMANIA

BUCHAREST

Astana

Barnaul

ROME

CORSICA

SLVN.
CROATIA
BOS.
SERBIA
ALB.
BULGARIA

Don

Danube

Volga

Ural

Qaraghandy

Semey

Kyzyl

CASABLANCA

MOROCCO

SARDINIA

SICILY

MEDITERRANEAN

TUNIS

GREECE

NICE

BLACK SEA

Gora El'brus
18 510 ft
5642 m

CAUCASUS MTS.

Zhezqazghan

KAZAKHSTAN

Aral
Sea

Lake
Balqash

Balqash

ALGIERS

ALGERIA

TUNISIA

CRETE

İSTANBUL

ANKARA

TURKEY

GEORGIA

TBILISI

ARM.
Yerevan

AZER.

BAKU

Caspian Sea

Nukus

UZBEKISTAN

TASHKENT

ALMATY

Bishkek

KYRGYZSTAN

TIEN SHAN

ÜRÜMQI

IZMIR

ALEPPO

Nicosia

CYPRUS

SEA

TABRİZ

TURKMENISTAN

Aşgabat

MASHHAD

Dushanbe

Samarqand

TAJIKISTAN

Kashi

Tarim

KUNLUN SHAN

LIBYA

CAIRO

SYRIA

Beirut
LEBANON
ISRAEL
Jerusalem

DAMASCUS

Euphrates

Amman
JORDAN

IRAQ

BAGHDAD

TEHRĀN

Tigris

Basra

Kuwait

KUWAIT

ESFAHĀN

IRAN

Kūh-e Damvand
18 386 ft
5604 m

Kabul

AFGHANISTAN

Amu Darya

Syr Darya

Islāmābād

Quetta

K2
28 250 ft
8611 m

LAHORE

DELHI

New Delhi

Lhasa

NEPAL

EGYPT

NIGER

Lake Nasser

Tropic of Cancer

SAUDI

RIYADH

Medina

JIDDAH

Mecca

BAHRAIN

QATAR

Doha

Abu Dhabi

U.A.E.

Muscat

ARABIA

Nile

RED

SEA

Persian Gulf

RA'S AL-HADD

SHĪRĀZ

KARĀCHI

PAKISTAN

AHMADĀBĀD

HYDERĀBĀD

Indus

HIMALAYA

Mt. Everest
29 028 ft
8848 m

Kathmandu

Thimphu
BHUTAN

KĀNPUR

PATNA

Ganges

Brahmaputra

DHAKA

BNGL.

CHAD

Lake
Chad

Chari

KHARTOUM

SUDAN

ERITREA

YEMEN

SANAA

Aden

OMAN

INDIA

KOLKATA
(CALCUTTA)

NĀGPUR

Narmada

Godāvari

HYDERĀBĀD

CENTRAL
AFRICAN REPUBLIC

Blue Nile

White Nile

DJIBOUTI

Gulf of Aden

SOCOTRA

ARABIAN

SEA

MUMBAI
(BOMBAY)

Krishna

BAY OF
BENGAL

ADDIS
ABABA

ETHIOPIA

BENGALŪRU

CHENNAI
(MADRAS)

CONGO

Congo

Ubangi

Mountain Nile

SOMALIA

Cochin

SRI
LANKA

CAPE COMORIN

DONDRA HEAD

DEMOCRATIC
REPUBLIC
OF THE CONGO

Kasai

UGANDA

RWANDA

BURUNDI

Lake
Rudolf

KENYA

Lake
Victoria

NAIROBI

Equator

Colombo

Male'

MALDIVES

ANGOLA

ZAMBIA

TANZANIA

DAR ES SALAAM

Lake
Tanganyika

SEYCHELLES

CHAGOS ARCHIPELAGO
(B.I.O.T.)

INDIAN OCEAN

| 0 | 200 | 400 | 600 | 800 | 1000 | 1200 Miles |

| 0 | 200 | 400 | 600 | 800 | 1000 | 1200 | 1400 | 1600 | 1800 | 2000 Kilometers |

Lambert Azimuthal Equal Area Projection
Scale 1:40,000,000
One inch to 640 miles
One cm to 400 km

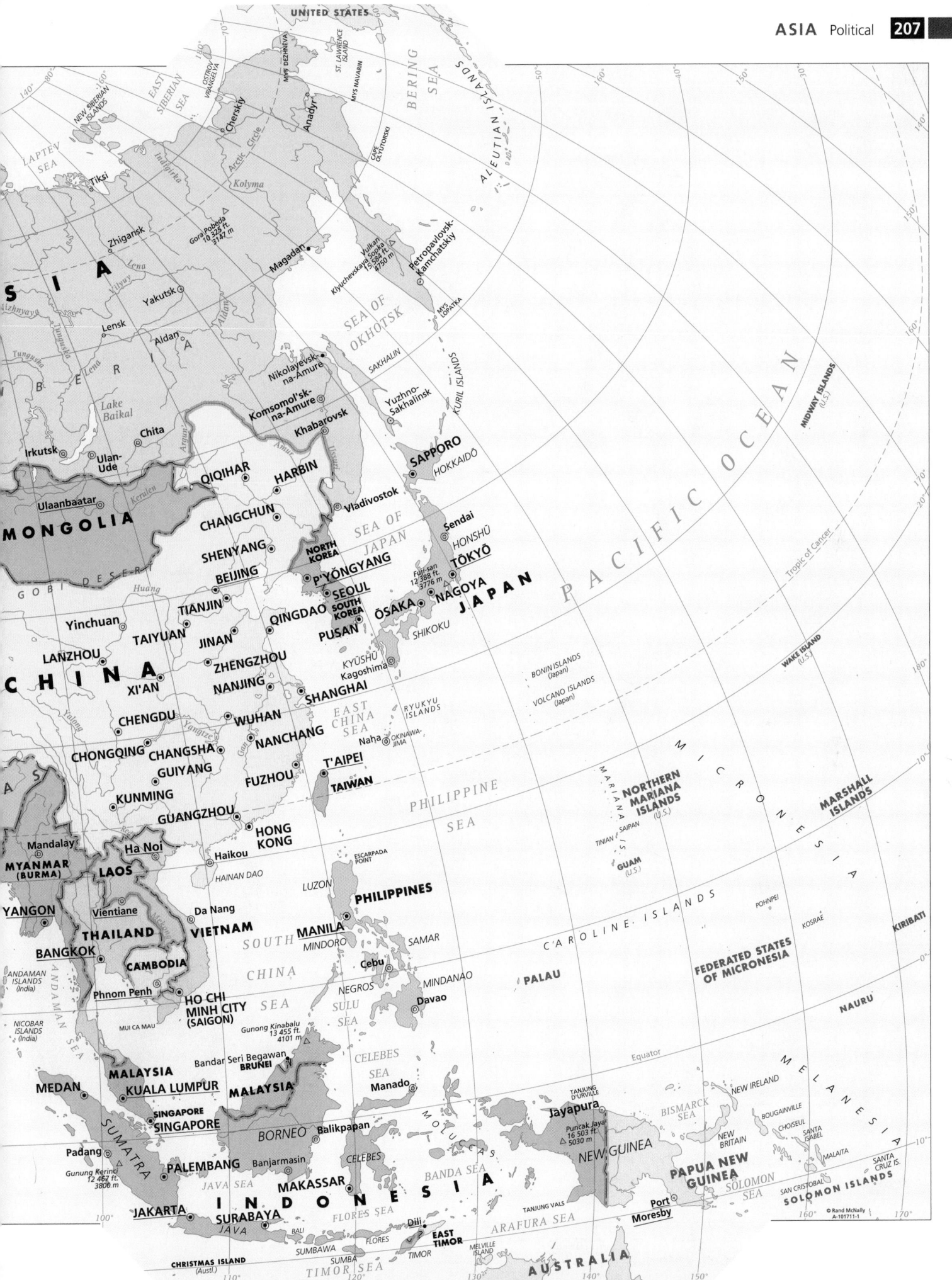

UNITED STATES

NEW SIBERIAN ISLANDS

OSTROV VRANGELYA

EAST SIBERIAN SEA

LAPTEV SEA

Tiksi

MYS DEZHNEVA

ST. LAWRENCE ISLAND

MYS NAVARIN

BERING SEA

ALEUTIAN ISLANDS

Cherskiy

Arctic Circle

Anadyr'

CAPE OLYUTORSKI

Zhigansk

Gora Pobeda 10 325 ft. 3147 m

Magadan

Vulkan Klyuchevskaya Sopka 15 584 ft. 4750 m

Petropavlovsk-Kamchatskiy

Indigirka

Kolyma

S I A

Yakutsk

Lena

Vilyuy

Aldan

Nikolayevsk-na-Amure

MYS LOPATKA

SEA OF OKHOTSK

Lensk

Tunguska

Aldan

Komsomol'sk-na-Amure

SAKHALIN

Nizhnyaya Tunguska

B E R I A

Lena

Khabarovsk

Yuzhno-Sakhalinsk

KURIL ISLANDS

Irkutsk

Lake Baikal

Chita

Argun

Ulan-Ude

Amur

Ussuri

Vladivostok

SAPPORO

HOKKAIDŌ

MONGOLIA

Ulaanbaatar

Kerulen

QIQIHAR

HARBIN

SEA OF JAPAN

Sendai

HONSHŪ

Tropic of Cancer

CHANGCHUN

NORTH KOREA

GOBI DESERT

SHENYANG

P'YŎNGYANG

TŌKYŌ

Fuji-san 12 388 ft. 3776 m

BEIJING

SEOUL

Huang

Yinchuan

TIANJIN

QINGDAO

SOUTH KOREA

ŌSAKA

NAGOYA

JAPAN

PACIFIC OCEAN

TAIYUAN

JINAN

PUSAN

SHIKOKU

LANZHOU

XI'AN

ZHENGZHOU

KYŪSHŪ

Kagoshima

C H I N A

NANJING

SHANGHAI

BONIN ISLANDS (Japan)

WAKE ISLAND (U.S.)

CHENGDU

WUHAN

EAST CHINA SEA

RYUKYU ISLANDS

VOLCANO ISLANDS (Japan)

Yangtze

CHONGQING

CHANGSHA

NANCHANG

Naha

OKINAWA-JIMA

Yalong

GUIYANG

FUZHOU

T'AIPEI

MARIANA ISLANDS

NORTHERN MARIANA ISLANDS (U.S.)

M I C R O N E S I A

MARSHALL ISLANDS

KUNMING

GUANGZHOU

TAIWAN

PHILIPPINE

SEA

Mandalay

Ha Noi

HONG KONG

TINIAN I.

SAIPAN

MYANMAR (BURMA)

LAOS

Haikou

HAINAN DAO

ESCARPADA POINT

GUAM (U.S.)

POHNPEI

YANGON

Vientiane

Da Nang

LUZON

C A R O L I N E   I S L A N D S

KOSRAE

KIRIBATI

THAILAND

VIETNAM

PHILIPPINES

ANDAMAN ISLANDS (India)

BANGKOK

CAMBODIA

SOUTH

MANILA

MINDORO

SAMAR

FEDERATED STATES OF MICRONESIA

PALAU

Phnom Penh

HO CHI MINH CITY (SAIGON)

CHINA

Cebu

NEGROS

MINDANAO

NAURU

NICOBAR ISLANDS (India)

MUI CA MAU

SEA

SULU SEA

Davao

Gunong Kinabalu 13 455 ft. 4101 m

CELEBES SEA

Equator

MALAYSIA

Bandar Seri Begawan

BRUNEI

MEDAN

KUALA LUMPUR

MALAYSIA

Manado

Jayapura

BISMARCK SEA

NEW IRELAND

M E L A N E S I A

SINGAPORE

SINGAPORE

BORNEO

Balikpapan

MOLUCCAS

Puncak Jaya 16 503 ft. 5030 m

NEW BRITAIN

BOUGAINVILLE

CHOISEUL

SANTA ISABEL

SUMATRA

Padang

PALEMBANG

Banjarmasin

CELEBES

NEW GUINEA

MALAITA

Gunung Kerinci 12 467 ft. 3800 m

JAVA SEA

MAKASSAR

BANDA SEA

PAPUA NEW GUINEA

SOLOMON SEA

SAN CRISTOBAL

SOLOMON ISLANDS

SANTA CRUZ IS.

JAKARTA

SURABAYA

I N D O N E S I A

JAVA

BALI

FLORES SEA

TANJUNG VALS

Dili

Port Moresby

ARAFURA SEA

© Rand McNally A-101711-1

CHRISTMAS ISLAND (Austl.)

SUMBAWA

SUMBA

FLORES

EAST TIMOR

TIMOR

MELVILLE ISLAND

TIMOR SEA

AUSTRALIA

ARCTIC OCEAN

ATLANTIC OCEAN

NORWEGIAN SEA

BARENTS SEA

KARA SEA

SVALBARD (Norway)

FRANZ JOSEF LAND

SEVERNAYA ZEMLYA

NOVAYA ZEMLYA

TAYMYR PENINSULA

AZORES (Port.)

FAROE ISLANDS (Den.)

MIZEN HEAD

IRELAND

UNITED KINGDOM

London

NORTH SEA

Arctic Circle

NORDKAPP

MYS KANIN NOS

OSTROV KOLGUYEV

YAMAL PENINSULA

Noril'sk

CABO DE FISTERRA

PORTUGAL

SÃO CABO DE VICENTE

SPAIN

Mulhacén 11,424 ft. 3482 m

Madrid

PYRENEES

France

Paris

Mont Blanc 15,771 ft. 4807 m

BELG.

NETH.

GERMANY

DENMARK

SWEDEN

NORWAY

Galdhøpiggen 8100 ft. 2469 m

BALTIC SEA

FINLAND

EST.

LATVIA

LITH.

St. Petersburg (Leningrad)

Lake Ladoga

Lake Onega

Pechora

Gora Narodnaya 6214 ft. 1894 m

R U S

URAL MTS.

WEST SIBERIAN PLAIN

Yekaterinburg

Novosibirsk

BELARUS

Moscow

POLAND

CZECH REP.

SWITZ.

ALPS

AUSTRIA

SLVK.

HUNGARY

CARPATHIAN MTS.

ROMANIA

UKRAINE

MOLD.

Dnieper

Don

Volga

Oka

Kama

Ural

Tobol

Ishim

Irtysh

SAYAN

KAZAKHSTAN

Qaraghandy

KAZAKH HILLS

Zhaysang Köli

Mt. Belukha 14,783 ft. 4506 m

ALTAY MTS.

CORSICA

SARDINIA

ITALY

Rome

Vesuvius 4203 ft. 1281 m

CROATIA

BOS.

SERBIA

MONT.

ALB.

MACE.

BULGARIA

Sea of Azov

Gora El'brus 18,510 ft. 5642 m

CAUCASUS MTS.

GEORGIA

ARM.

AZER.

Baku

CASPIAN DEPRESSION

Aral Sea

Syr Darya

Lake Balkhash

Almaty

Ürümqi

SAYAM

MOROCCO

ATLAS MOUNTAINS

ALGERIA

MEDITERRANEAN SEA

TUNISIA

Chott Melrir

Chott el Jerid

GREECE

Mt. Olympus 9570 ft. 2917 m

Monte Etna 10,902 ft. 3323 m

CRETE

Erciyes Dağı 12,851 ft. 3917 m

TURKEY

Istanbul

CYPRUS

Khalij Surt

CAUCASUS MTS.

Mt. Ararat 16,854 ft. 5137 m

SYRIA

LEBANON

ISRAEL

Damascus

Baghdad

IRAQ

JORDAN

Cairo

Tigris

Euphrates

Tehran

Kūh-e Damāvand 18,386 ft. 5604 m

DASHT-E KAVIR

Daryacheh-ye Namak

UZBEKISTAN

QIZILQUM

Tashkent

KARA KUM

TURKMENISTAN

Pik Imeni Ismail Samani 24,590 ft. 7495 m

TAJIKISTAN

PAMIRS

KYRGYZSTAN

TIEN SHAN

Jengish Chokusu 24,406 ft. 7439 m

TARIM PENDI

ALTUN SHAN

Tarim

Amu Darya

UST-URT PLAT.

CASPIAN SEA

K2 28,250 ft. 8611 m

HINDU KUSH

KUNLUN SHAN

PLATEAU OF TIBET

LIBYA

EGYPT

Lake Nasser

Tropic of Cancer

NIGER

CHAD

Lake Chad

Emi Koussi 11,204 ft. 3415 m

Jabal Marrah 10,072 ft. 3070 m

SUDAN

CENTRAL AFRICAN REPUBLIC

AN-NAFŪD

SAUDI ARABIA

ARABIAN PENINSULA

Riyadh

Jiddah

AL ḤIJĀZ

RED SEA

ASIR

RUB' AL-KHALI

KUWAIT

QATAR

U.A.E.

Jabal ash-Shām 9957 ft. 3035 m

Persian Gulf

ZAGROS MOUNTAINS

IRAN

DASHT-E LUT

AFGHANISTAN

Kabul

Lahore

PAKISTAN

GREAT INDIAN DESERT

Delhi

Annapurna 26,545 ft. 8091 m

Mt. Everest 29,028 ft. 8848 m

NEPAL

Lhasa

BHUTAN

H I M A L A Y A

INDIA

Dhaka

BNGL.

Kolkata (Calcutta)

Karāchi

RA'S AL-HADD

Gulf of Oman

OMAN

ARABIAN SEA

DECCAN

Narmada

Godāvari

Ganges

Brahmaputra

Chambal

Yamuna

Mumbai (Bombay)

WESTERN GHATS

EASTERN GHATS

ERITREA

Ras Dejen 15,158 ft. 4620 m

DJIBOUTI

YEMEN

Sanaa

RA'S FARTAK

Gulf of Aden

SOCOTRA (Yemen)

GEES GWARDAFUY

ETHIOPIA

Addis Ababa

SOMALIA

RA'S AL-HADD

LAKSHADWEEP

Ānai Mudi 8842 ft. 2695 m

Bengalūru

SRI LANKA

CAPE COMORIN

Colombo

Pidurutalagala 8281 ft. 2524 m

DONDRA HEAD

MALDIVES

BAY OF BENGAL

Krishna

CONGO

Mbomou

Ubangi

Congo

DEMOCRATIC REPUBLIC OF THE CONGO

Margherita Peak 16,763 ft. 5109 m

Lake Albert

UGANDA

Lake Edward

RWANDA

BURUNDI

Lake Tanganyika

Lake Rudolf

Lake Victoria

KENYA

Mt. Kenya 17,058 ft. 5199 m

Kilimanjaro 19,340 ft. 5895 m

TANZANIA

Dar es Salaam

Equator

INDIAN OCEAN

SEYCHELLES

CHAGOS ARCHIPELAGO (B.I.O.T.)

ANGOLA

ZAMBIA

Lake Mweru

Mountain Nile

White Nile

Blue Nile

Atbara

Sobat

Nile

Sankuru

Kasai

Lake Turkana

Lomami

Uele

0   200   400   600   800   1000   1200 Miles

0   200   400   600   800   1000   1200   1400   1600   1800   2000 Kilometers

Lambert Azimuthal Equal Area Projection
Scale 1:40,000,000
One inch to 640 miles
One cm to 400 km

UNITED STATES

OSTROV
VRANGELYA
NEW SIBERIAN
ISLANDS
CHUKOTSK PEN.
MYS
DEZHNYOVA
Gulf of
Anadyr'
• Anadyr'
MYS NAVARIN

EAST
SIBERIAN
SEA

LAPTEV
SEA

BERING
SEA

ALEUTIAN ISLANDS

ALEUTIAN TRENCH

Nizhnyaya

VERKHOYANSK MTS.

Indigirka

Gora Pobeda
10 325 ft.
△ 3 147 m

CHERSKIY MTS.

KAMCHATKA
PENINSULA

KOMANDORSKI
ISLANDS

CAPE WRANGELL

• Yakutsk

Gora Ledyanaya
8203 ft.
△ 2500 m
MYS
OLYUTORSKIY

A S I A

Vilyuy

Lena

DZHUGDZHUR RANGE

Vulkan
Klyuchevskaya Sopka
15 580 ft.
△ 4750 m

Magadan •

SEA
OF
OKHOTSK

S I B E R I A

Tunguska

Vitim

STANOVOY RANGE

Kyuchevskaya •
MYS
YELIZAVETY

KURIL TRENCH

STANOVOY
MTS.

Aldan

Petropavlovsk-
• Kamchatskiy

MYS LOPATKA

Lake
Baikal

Komsomol'sk-
na-Amure •

SIKHOTE-ALIN'

SAKHALIN

KURIL ISLANDS

• Irkutsk
M MTS.

Amur

Tatar Strait

MYS
TERPENIYA

Khanka

Sapporo •

JAVA TRENCH

Khilok

Lake
Khanka

• Harbin

HOKKAIDO

JAPAN TRENCH

MONGOLIA

Kerulen

GREATER KHINGAN RANGE

SEA
OF
JAPAN

Huang

NORTH
KOREA

HONSHŪ

• Ulaanbaatar

GOBI DESERT

• Beijing

Seoul •
CHENGSHAN
JIAO

Fuji-san
12 388 ft.
△ 3776 m

Tokyo •

JAPAN

Qinghai
Hu

Huang

SOUTH
KOREA

YELLOW
SEA

IZU TRENCH

C H I N A

Xi'an •
QIN LING

SHIKOKU

CHEJU-DO

IZU-SHOTO

Three
Gorges
Reservoir

KYŪSHŪ

Yalong

Chongqing •

Huai

Shanghai •

EAST
CHINA
SEA

BONIN IS.
(Japan)

VOLCANO ISLANDS
(Japan)

MARIANA TRENCH

Salween

T'aipei •

OKINAWA-JIMA

RYUKYU ISLANDS

RYUKYU TRENCH

A S

• Hong
Kong

TAIWAN
Yu Shan
13 114 ft.
△ 3997 m

Luzon Strait

PHILIPPINE
SEA

MARIANA ISLANDS

NORTHERN
MARIANA
ISLANDS
(U.S.)

PACIFIC OCEAN

MIDWAY ISLANDS
(U.S.)

HAWAI'IAN ISLANDS

NECKER RIDGE

Tropic of Cancer

WAKE ISLAND
(U.S.)

MYANMAR
(BURMA)

LAOS

HAINAN
DAO

ESCARPADA POINT

LUZON

Taiwan Strait

SAIPAN

TINIAN

M I C R O N E S I A

BIKINI

ENEWETAK

KWAJALEIN

MARSHALL
ISLANDS

MAJURO

• Yangon

THAILAND

Gulf of
Tonkin

Mekong

VIETNAM

SOUTH
CHINA
SEA

MINDORO

PHILIPPINES

SAMAR

GUAM
(U.S.)

CHALLENGER DEEP

YAP TRENCH

YAP

CAROLINE ISLANDS

CHUUK

POHNPEI

KOSRAE

KIRIBATI

TARAWA

ANDAMAN
ISLANDS
(India)

• Bangkok

CAMBODIA
Tonlé Sap

Manila •

PANAY

• Ho Chi
Minh City
(Saigon)

PALAWAN

NEGROS

Mt. Apo △
9692 ft.
△ 2954 m

MINDANAO

PALAU

FEDERATED STATES
OF MICRONESIA

NAURU

ANDAMAN
SEA

NICOBAR
ISLANDS
(India)

MUI CA MAU

MALAY PENINSULA

Gulf of
Thailand

Gunong Kinabalu
13 455 ft.
△ 4101 m

SULU
SEA

TINACA
POINT

BRUNEI

CELEBES
SEA

HALMAHERA

TANJUNG
D'URVILLE

PULAU
WAIGEO

BIAK

MANUS
ISLAND

NEW HANOVER

NEW IRELAND

M E L A N E S I A

PULAU
SIMEULUE

Strait of Malacca

MALAYSIA

IRAN MTS.

MALAYSIA

MOLUCCA
SEA

Jayapura •

BISMARCK
SEA

NEW
BRITAIN

BOUGAINVILLE

CHOISEUL

SANTA ISABEL

SOLOMON
ISLANDS

PULAU NIAS

SINGAPORE

Singapore •

BORNEO

Kapuas

CERAM

BURU

MOLUCCAS

Sepik

NEW GUINEA

Puncak Jaya
16 503 ft.
△ 5030 m

Mt. Wilhelm △
14 793 ft.
△ 4509 m

NEW BRITAIN TRENCH

NEW
GEORGIA

GUADALCANAL

MALAITA

SAN CRISTOBAL

S U M A T R A

Bukit Raya
7474 ft.
△ 2278 m

GREATER SUNDA ISLANDS

TANJUNG
PUTING

CELEBES

BANDA
SEA

PULAU
BUTON

KEPULAUAN
ARU

PAPUA NEW
GUINEA

SOLOMON SEA

SANTA CRUZ IS.

PULAU SIBERUT

Gunung Kerinci
12 467 ft.
△ 3800 m

Makassar •

TANJUNG SELATAN

Makassar Strait

JAVA
SEA

PULAU
WETAR

TANJUNG
YAMDENA

RENNELL

SAN CRISTOBAL
TRENCH

© Rand McNally
A-101712-1

I N D O N E S I A

JAVA TRENCH

• Jakarta

J A V A

Gunung Semeru
12 060 ft.
△ 3676 m

BALI

LOMBOK

SUMBAWA

LESSER SUNDA ISLANDS

FLORES

SUMBA

FLORES SEA

TIMOR

EAST
TIMOR

MELVILLE
ISLAND

TIMOR SEA

ARAFURA SEA

CAPE YORK

CAPE
ARNHEM

AUSTRALIA

CHRISTMAS
ISLAND
(Aust.)

ARCTIC OCEAN

SEVERNAYA
ZEMLYA

ATLANTIC OCEAN

BARENTS
SEA

KARA
SEA

Arctic Circle

Ob

WEST SIBERIAN
PLAIN

Yenisey

CEN

URAL MOUNTAINS

Yekaterinburg

Chelyabinsk

SAYAN

Ural

Irtysh

ALTAY MTS.

KAZAKH
HILLS

Istanbul

BLACK SEA

CAUCASUS MTS.

CASPIAN SEA

Aral Sea

Lake
Balkhash

S

MEDITERRANEAN SEA

Ankara

UST-URT
PLAT.

Syr Darya

QIZILQUM

TIEN SHAN

Almaty

KARA KUM

Tashkent

TARIM PENDI

ALTUN SHAN

Tabrīz

Tel Aviv-Yafo

Euphrates

Dushanbe

Damascus

Tigris

Tehrān

Mashhad

Amu Darya

PAMIRS

KUNLUN SHAN

'Ammān

Baghdād

DASHT-E KAVĪR

HINDU KUSH

PLATEAU OF
TIBET

ZAGROS MTS.

Eşfahān

Islāmābād

Tropic of Cancer

AN-NAFŪD

DASHT-E LŪT

HIMALAYA

Lahore

Indus

Brahmaputra

RED SEA

AL-HIJĀZ

Persian Gulf

GREAT INDIAN DESERT

Delhi

Kathmandu

Riyadh

Gulf of
Oman

Hyderābād

Kānpur

Ganges

Jiddah

Mecca

Karāchi

Dhaka

ASĪR

Ahmadābād

Kolkata

RUB' AL-KHALI

Indore

DECCAN

Mumbai

WESTERN GHATS

Hyderābād

EASTERN GHATS

BAY OF
BENGAL

Sanaa

Gulf of Aden

ARABIAN
SEA

Bengalūru

Chennai

Cochin

Colombo

Equator

INDIAN   OCEAN

A-102095-1
© Rand McNally

20°   30°   40°   50°   60°   70°   80°   90°

| 0 | 200 | 400 | 600 | 800 | 1000 | 1200 Miles |

| 0 | 200 | 400 | 600 | 800 | 1000 | 1200 | 1400 | 1600 | 1800 | 2000 Kilometers |

Lambert Azimuthal Equal Area Projection
Scale 1:40,000,000
One inch to 640 miles
One cm to 400 km

Land Cover

- Evergreen Needleleaf Forest
- Evergreen Broadleaf Forest
- Deciduous Needleleaf Forest
- Deciduous Broadleaf Forest
- Mixed Forest
- Woodland
- Wooded Grassland
- Closed Shrubland
- Open Shrubland
- Grassland
- Cropland
- Bare Ground (Desert and Ice)
- Urban and Built Up

Source: CIESIN; Hansen et al., 2000

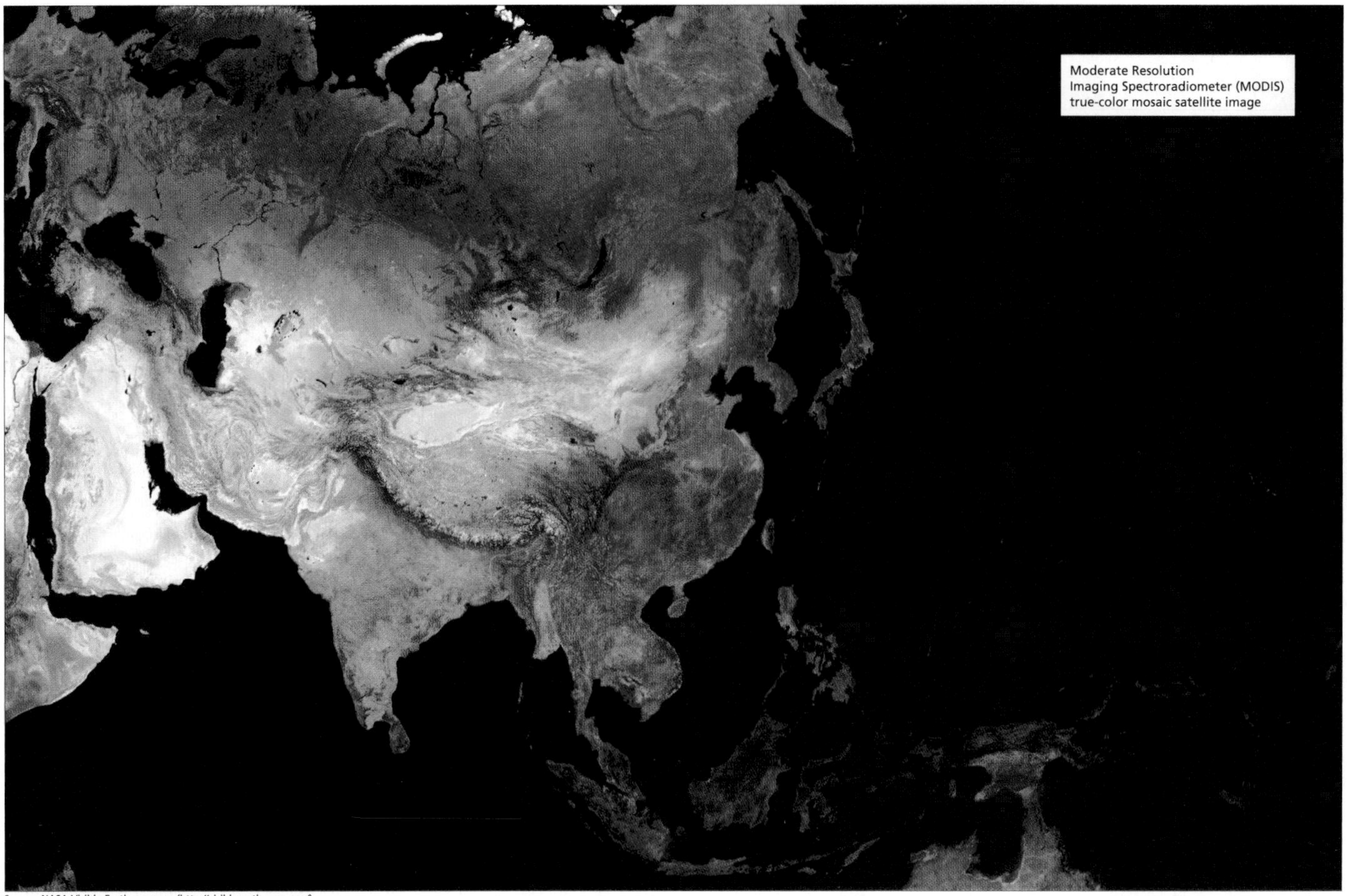

Moderate Resolution
Imaging Spectroradiometer (MODIS)
true-color mosaic satellite image

Source: NASA Visible Earth program (http://visibleearth.nasa.gov/)

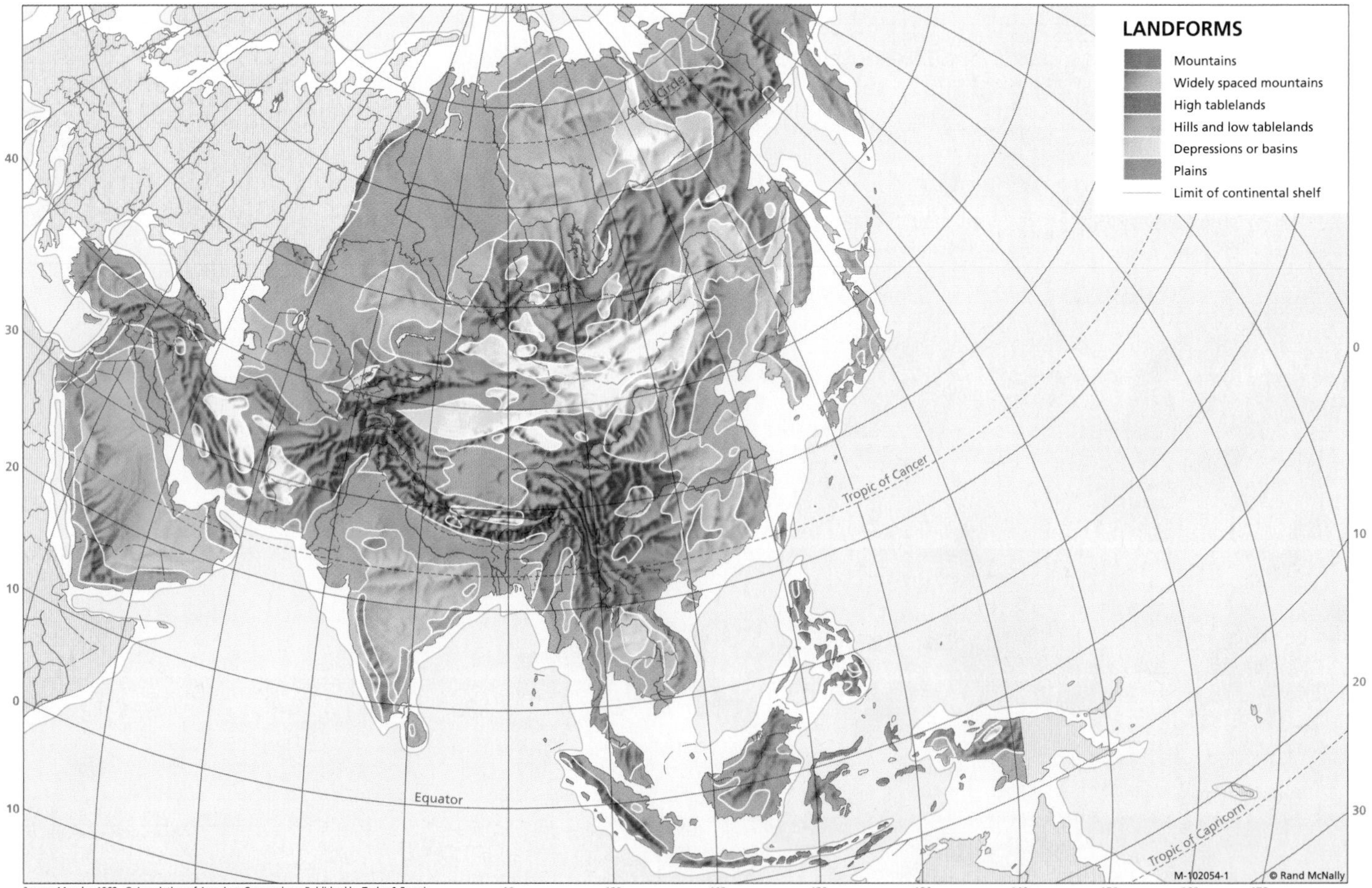

LANDFORMS

Mountains
Widely spaced mountains
High tablelands
Hills and low tablelands
Depressions or basins
Plains
Limit of continental shelf

Source: Murphy, 1968. © Association of American Geographers. Published by Taylor & Francis.
Adapted with permission of the Association of American Geographers.

M-102054-1   © Rand McNally

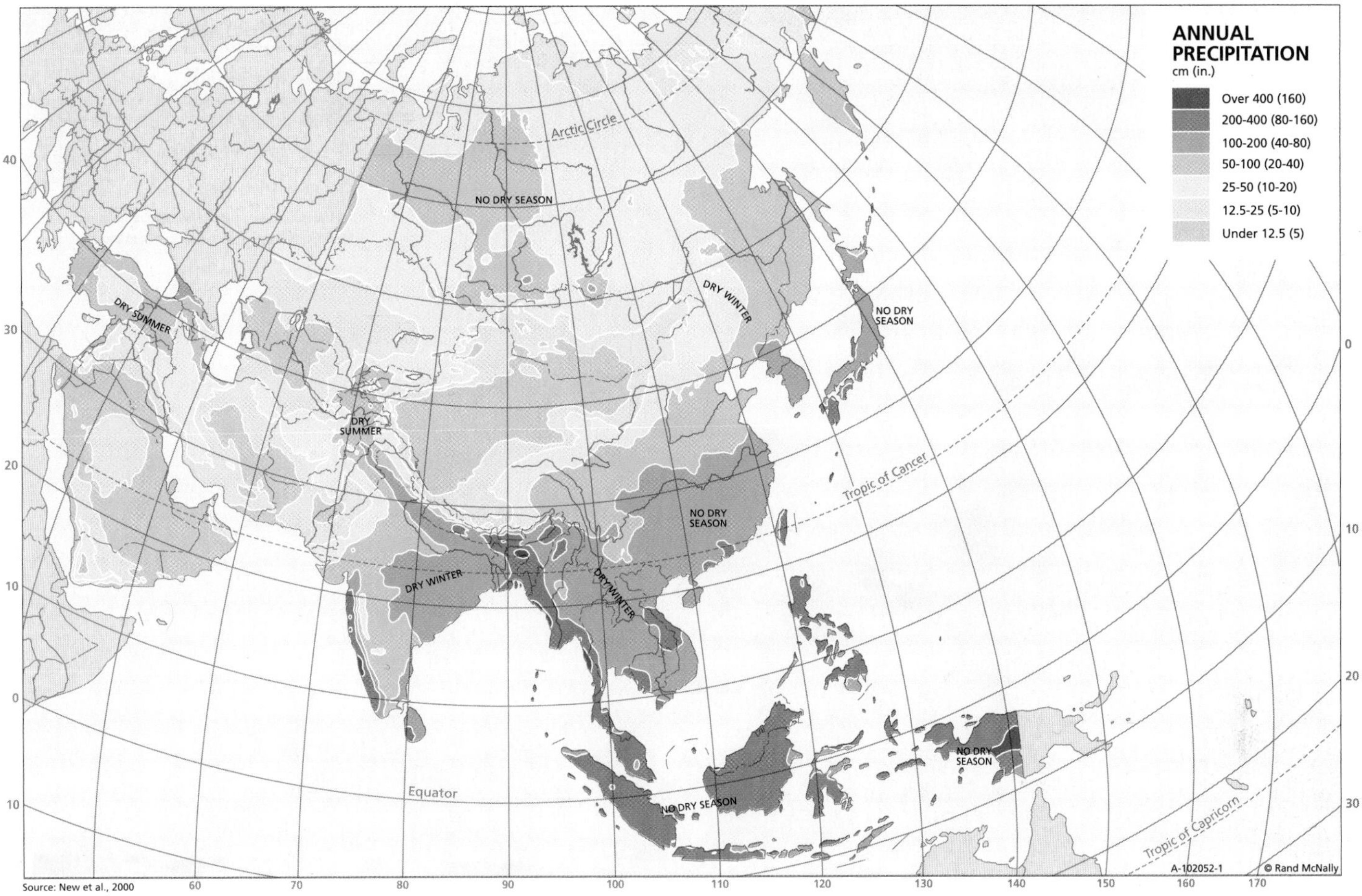

ANNUAL PRECIPITATION
cm (in.)

- Over 400 (160)
- 200-400 (80-160)
- 100-200 (40-80)
- 50-100 (20-40)
- 25-50 (10-20)
- 12.5-25 (5-10)
- Under 12.5 (5)

DRY SUMMER

NO DRY SEASON

DRY SUMMER

DRY WINTER

NO DRY SEASON

DRY SUMMER

NO DRY SEASON

DRY WINTER

DRY WINTER

DRY WINTER

Tropic of Cancer

NO DRY SEASON

NO DRY SEASON

Equator

Tropic of Capricorn

A-102052-1

© Rand McNally

Source: New et al., 2000

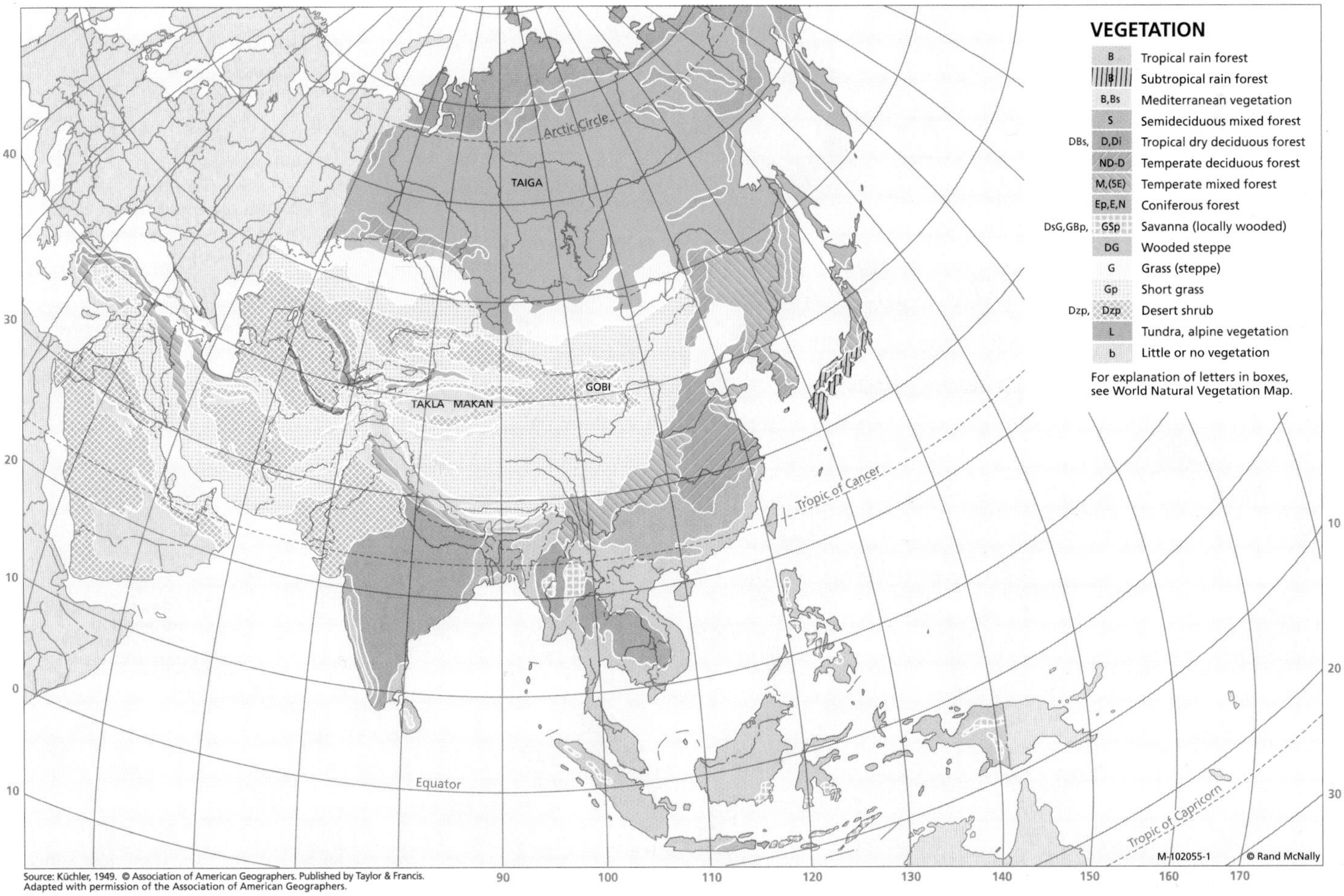

VEGETATION

B	Tropical rain forest
	Subtropical rain forest
B,Bs	Mediterranean vegetation
S	Semideciduous mixed forest
DBs, D,Di	Tropical dry deciduous forest
ND-D	Temperate deciduous forest
M,(SE)	Temperate mixed forest
Ep,E,N	Coniferous forest
DsG,GBp, GSp	Savanna (locally wooded)
DG	Wooded steppe
G	Grass (steppe)
Gp	Short grass
Dzp, Dzp	Desert shrub
L	Tundra, alpine vegetation
b	Little or no vegetation

For explanation of letters in boxes, see World Natural Vegetation Map.

Arctic Circle

TAIGA

GOBI

TAKLA MAKAN

Tropic of Cancer

Equator

Tropic of Capricorn

M-102055-1

© Rand McNally

Source: Küchler, 1949. © Association of American Geographers. Published by Taylor & Francis.
Adapted with permission of the Association of American Geographers.

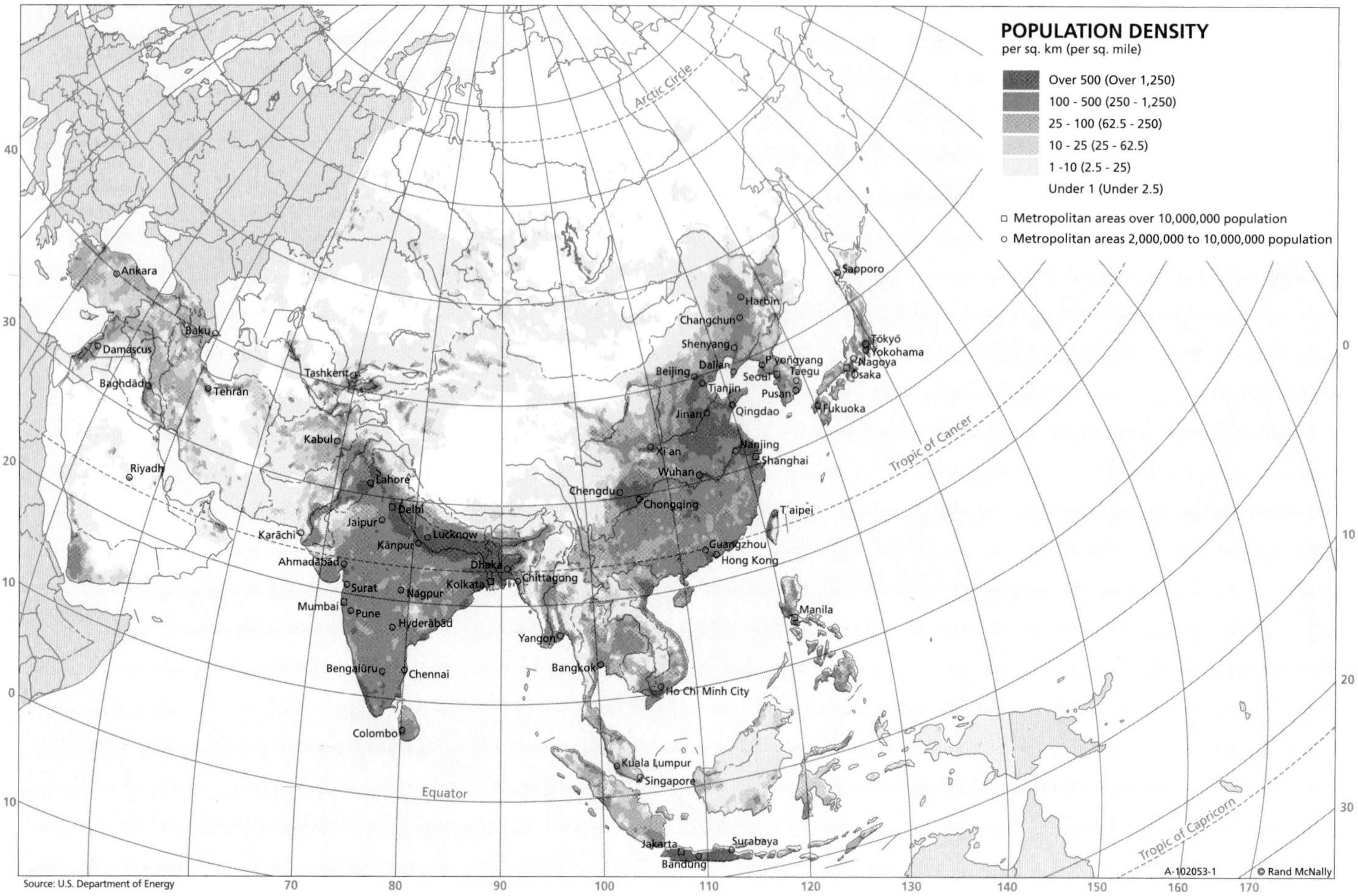

POPULATION DENSITY
per sq. km (per sq. mile)

- Over 500 (Over 1,250)
- 100 - 500 (250 - 1,250)
- 25 - 100 (62.5 - 250)
- 10 - 25 (25 - 62.5)
- 1 - 10 (2.5 - 25)
- Under 1 (Under 2.5)

□ Metropolitan areas over 10,000,000 population
○ Metropolitan areas 2,000,000 to 10,000,000 population

Ankara
Baku
Damascus
Baghdad
Tehran
Tashkent
Riyadh
Kabul
Lahore
Karachi
Delhi
Jaipur
Kanpur
Lucknow
Ahmadabad
Surat
Nagpur
Mumbai
Pune
Hyderabad
Bengaluru
Chennai
Colombo
Chengdu
Chongqing
Wuhan
Xi'an
Nanjing
Shanghai
Jinan
Qingdao
Beijing
Tianjin
Dalian
Seoul
Pusan
Pyongyang
Taegu
Fukuoka
Shenyang
Changchun
Harbin
Sapporo
Tōkyō
Yokohama
Nagoya
Osaka
T'aipei
Guangzhou
Hong Kong
Dhaka
Chittagong
Kolkata
Yangon
Bangkok
Ho Chi Minh City
Manila
Kuala Lumpur
Singapore
Jakarta
Bandung
Surabaya

Source: U.S. Department of Energy

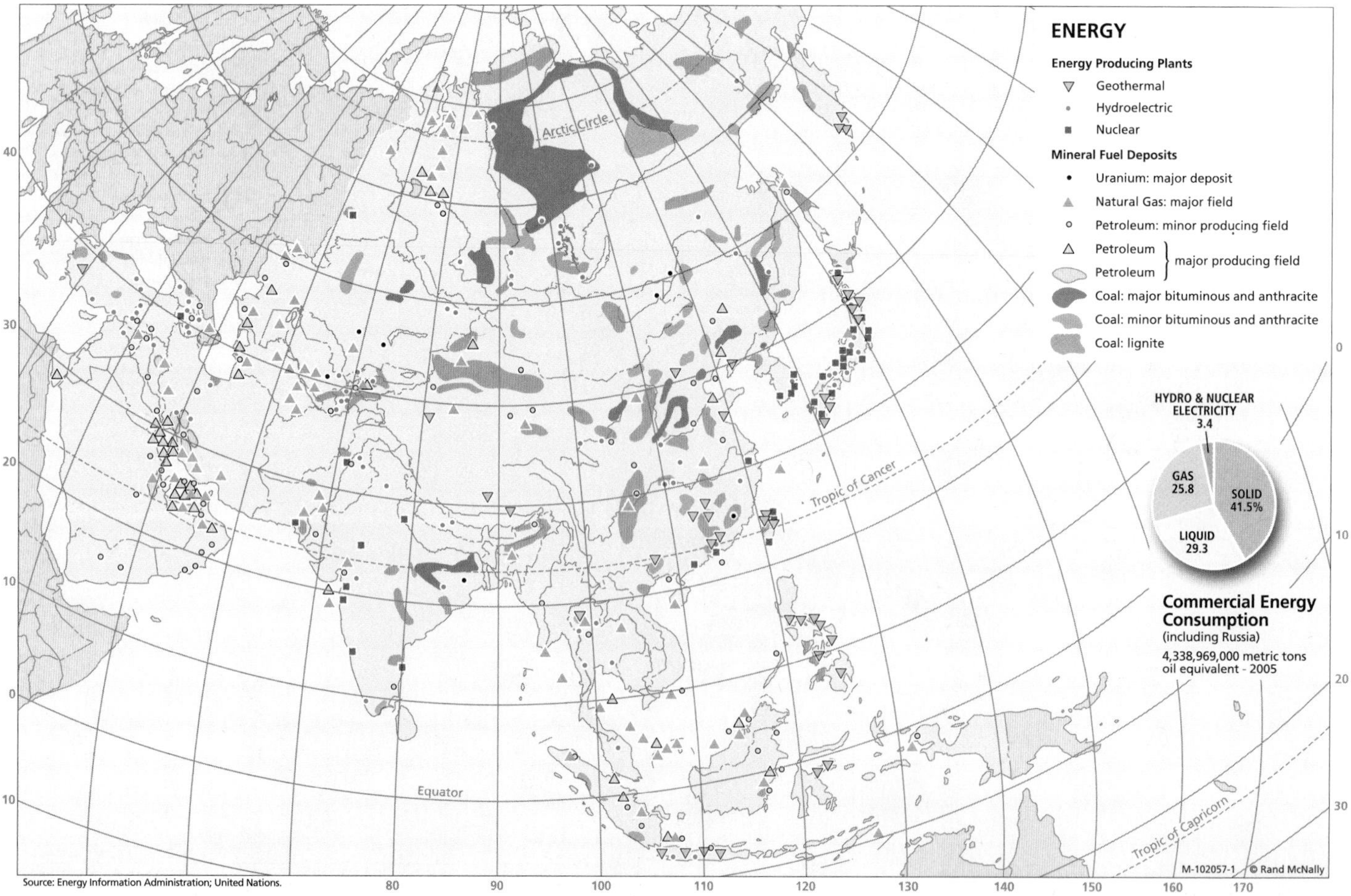

Arctic Circle
Tropic of Cancer
Equator
Tropic of Capricorn

A-102053-1   © Rand McNally

ENERGY

Energy Producing Plants
- ▽ Geothermal
- · Hydroelectric
- ■ Nuclear

Mineral Fuel Deposits
- • Uranium: major deposit
- ▲ Natural Gas: major field
- ○ Petroleum: minor producing field
- △ Petroleum } major producing field
- Petroleum
- Coal: major bituminous and anthracite
- Coal: minor bituminous and anthracite
- Coal: lignite

HYDRO & NUCLEAR ELECTRICITY 3.4
GAS 25.8
SOLID 41.5%
LIQUID 29.3

Commercial Energy Consumption
(including Russia)
4,338,969,000 metric tons oil equivalent - 2005

Arctic Circle
Tropic of Cancer
Equator
Tropic of Capricorn

Source: Energy Information Administration; United Nations.

M-102057-1   © Rand McNally

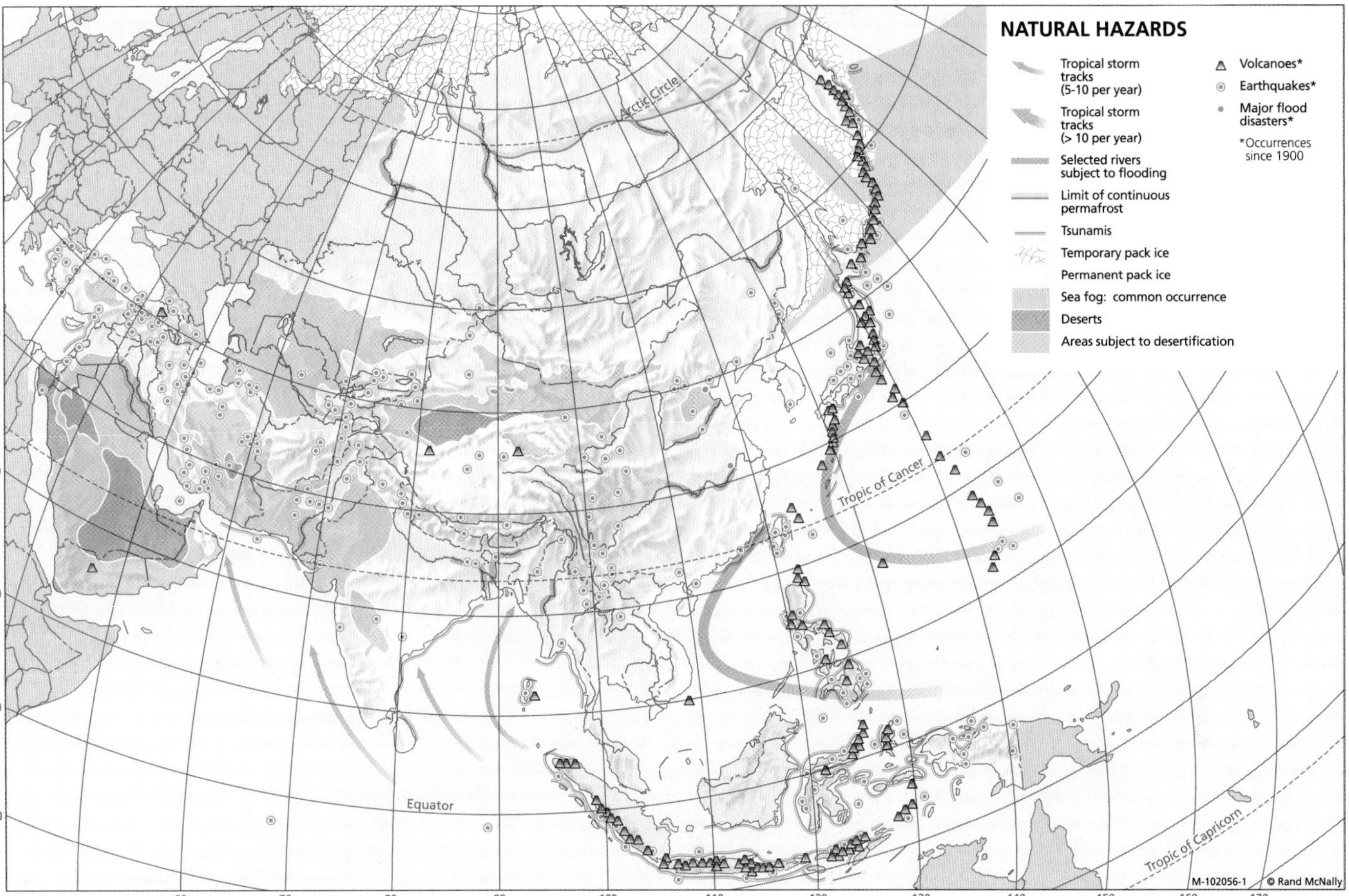

NATURAL HAZARDS

- Tropical storm tracks (5-10 per year)
- Tropical storm tracks (> 10 per year)
- Selected rivers subject to flooding
- Limit of continuous permafrost
- Tsunamis
- Temporary pack ice
- Permanent pack ice
- Sea fog: common occurrence
- Deserts
- Areas subject to desertification

△ Volcanoes*
⊙ Earthquakes*
• Major flood disasters*

*Occurrences since 1900

Arctic Circle
Tropic of Cancer
Equator
Tropic of Capricorn

M-102056-1 © Rand McNally

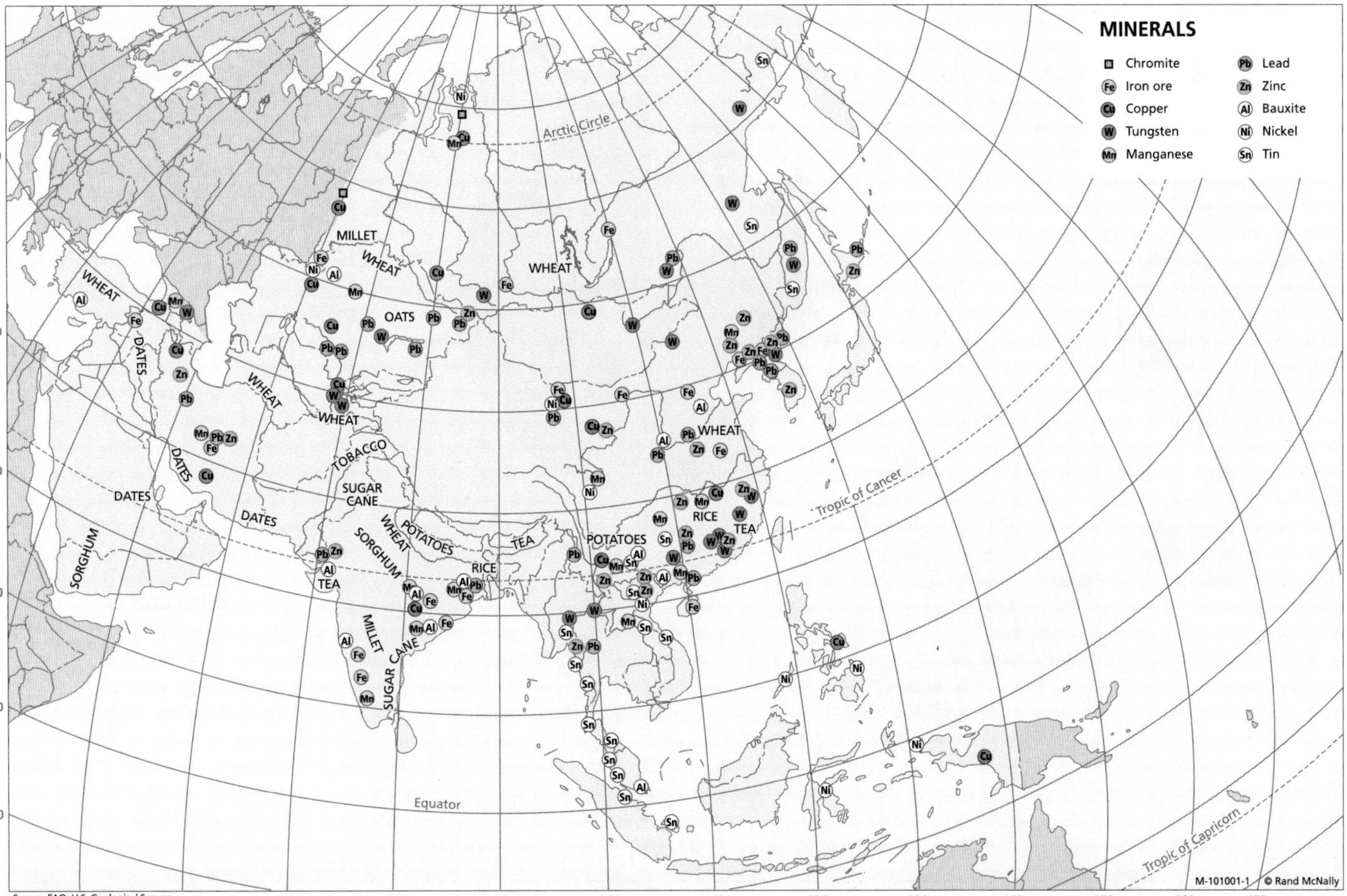

MINERALS

- ▣ Chromite
- Ⓕ Iron ore
- Ⓒ Copper
- Ⓦ Tungsten
- Ⓜ Manganese
- Ⓟ Lead
- Ⓩ Zinc
- Ⓐ Bauxite
- Ⓝ Nickel
- Ⓢ Tin

MILLET
WHEAT
WHEAT
WHEAT
OATS
DATES
WHEAT
WHEAT
TOBACCO
SUGAR CANE
POTATOES
TEA
RICE
DATES
DATES
DATES
SORGHUM
SORGHUM
WHEAT
RICE
POTATOES
TEA
RICE
TEA
TEA
SUGAR CANE
MILLET
SUGAR CANE

Arctic Circle
Tropic of Cancer
Equator
Tropic of Capricorn

Source: FAO; U.S. Geological Survey

M-101001-1 © Rand McNally

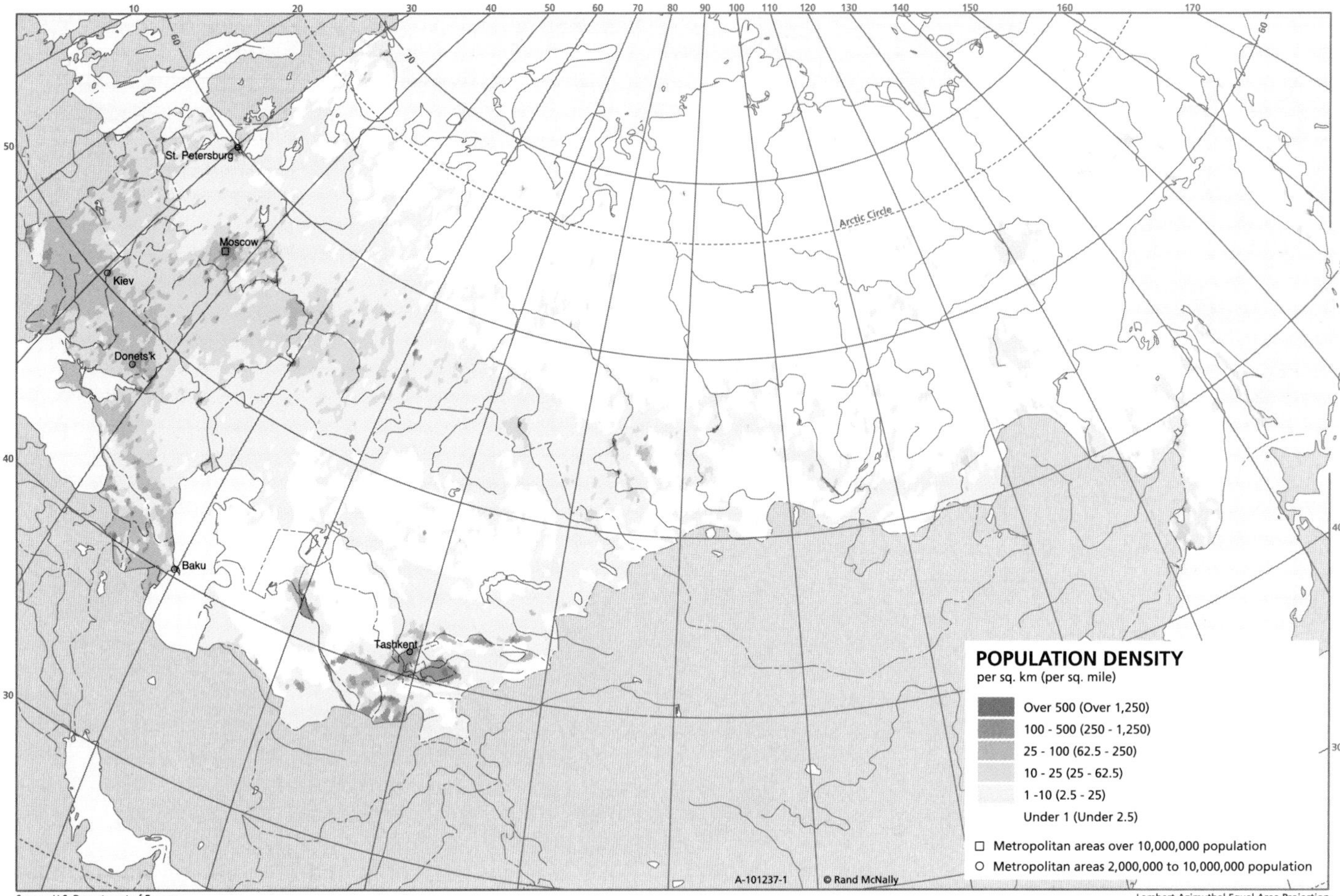
St. Petersburg
Moscow
Kiev
Donets'k
Baku
Tashkent
Arctic Circle
POPULATION DENSITY
per sq. km (per sq. mile)
Over 500 (Over 1,250)
100 - 500 (250 - 1,250)
25 - 100 (62.5 - 250)
10 - 25 (25 - 62.5)
1 -10 (2.5 - 25)
Under 1 (Under 2.5)
Metropolitan areas over 10,000,000 population
Metropolitan areas 2,000,000 to 10,000,000 population
A-101237-1
© Rand McNally

Source: U.S. Department of Energy

Lambert Azimuthal Equal Area Projection
Scale 1:45,000,000

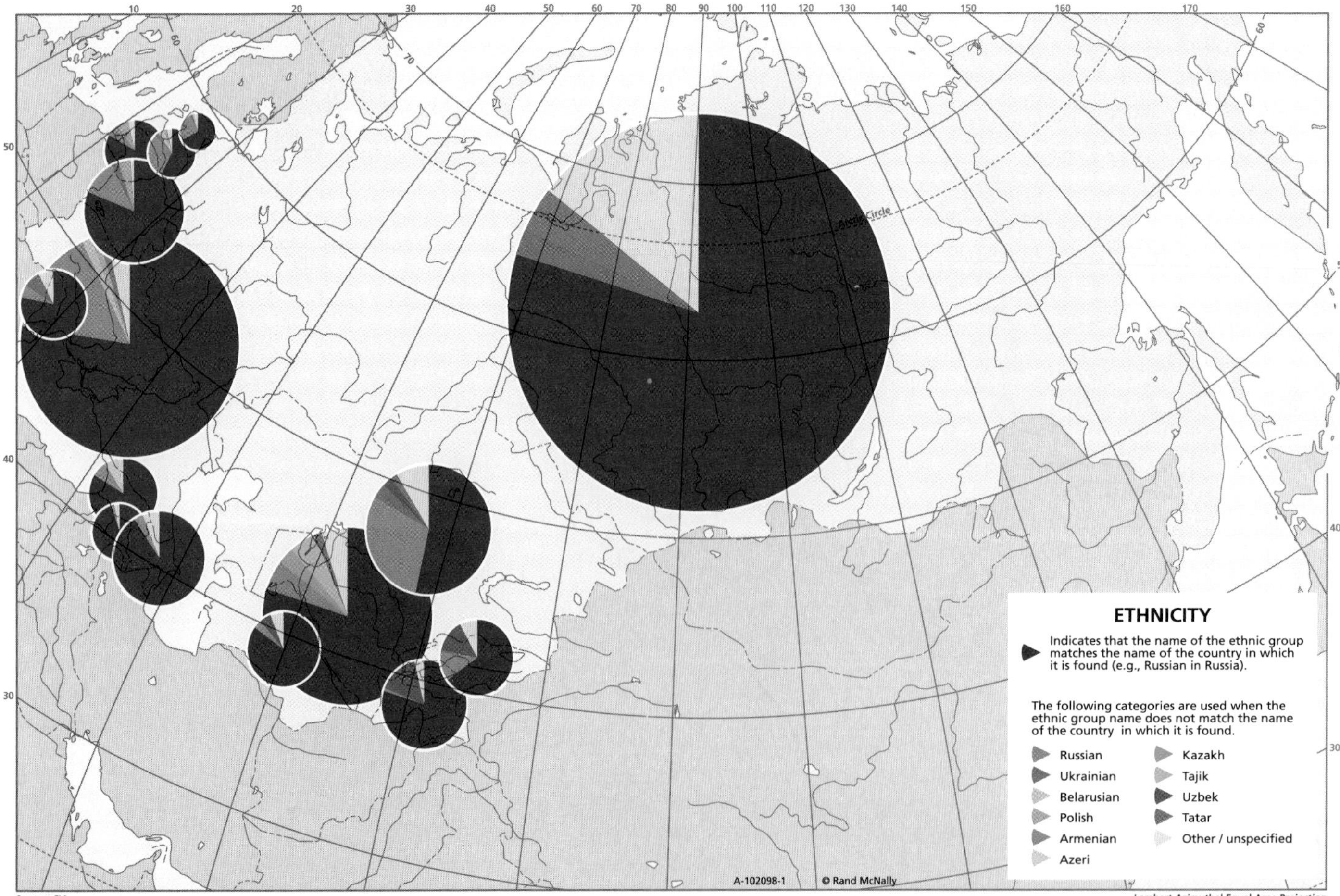
Arctic Circle
ETHNICITY
Indicates that the name of the ethnic group matches the name of the country in which it is found (e.g., Russian in Russia).
The following categories are used when the ethnic group name does not match the name of the country in which it is found.
Russian
Ukrainian
Belarusian
Polish
Armenian
Azeri
Kazakh
Tajik
Uzbek
Tatar
Other / unspecified
A-102098-1
© Rand McNally

Source: CIA

Lambert Azimuthal Equal Area Projection
Scale 1:45,000,000

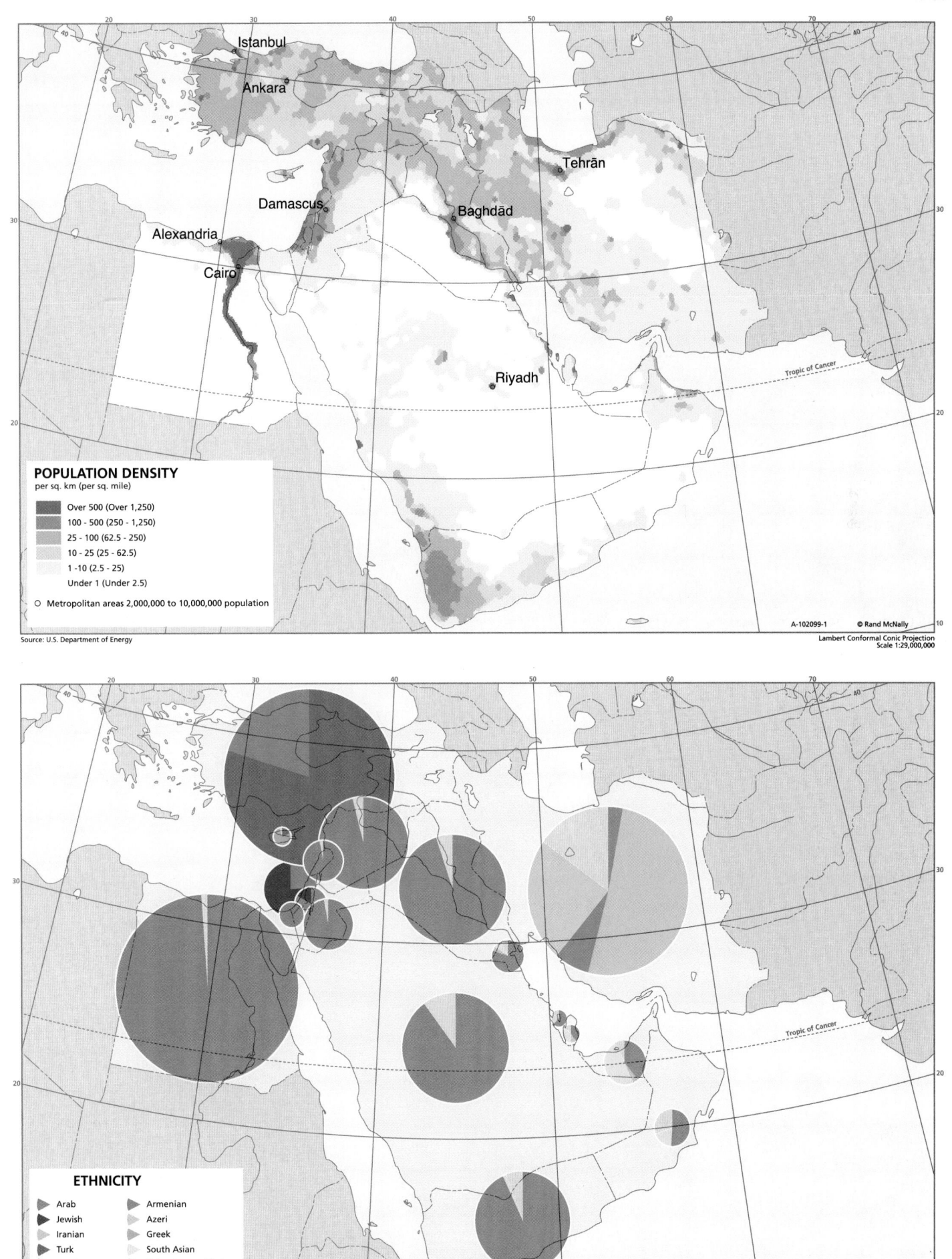

Source: U.S. Department of Energy

POPULATION DENSITY
per sq. km (per sq. mile)

- Over 500 (Over 1,250)
- 100 - 500 (250 - 1,250)
- 25 - 100 (62.5 - 250)
- 10 - 25 (25 - 62.5)
- 1 -10 (2.5 - 25)
- Under 1 (Under 2.5)

○ Metropolitan areas 2,000,000 to 10,000,000 population

Istanbul
Ankara
Damascus
Alexandria
Cairo
Tehrān
Baghdād
Riyadh

Tropic of Cancer

A-102099-1   © Rand McNally

Lambert Conformal Conic Projection
Scale 1:29,000,000

ETHNICITY

- Arab
- Jewish
- Iranian
- Turk
- Kurd
- Armenian
- Azeri
- Greek
- South Asian
- Other / unspecified

Tropic of Cancer

A-102100-1   © Rand McNally

Source: CIA

Lambert Conformal Conic Projection
Scale 1:29,000,000

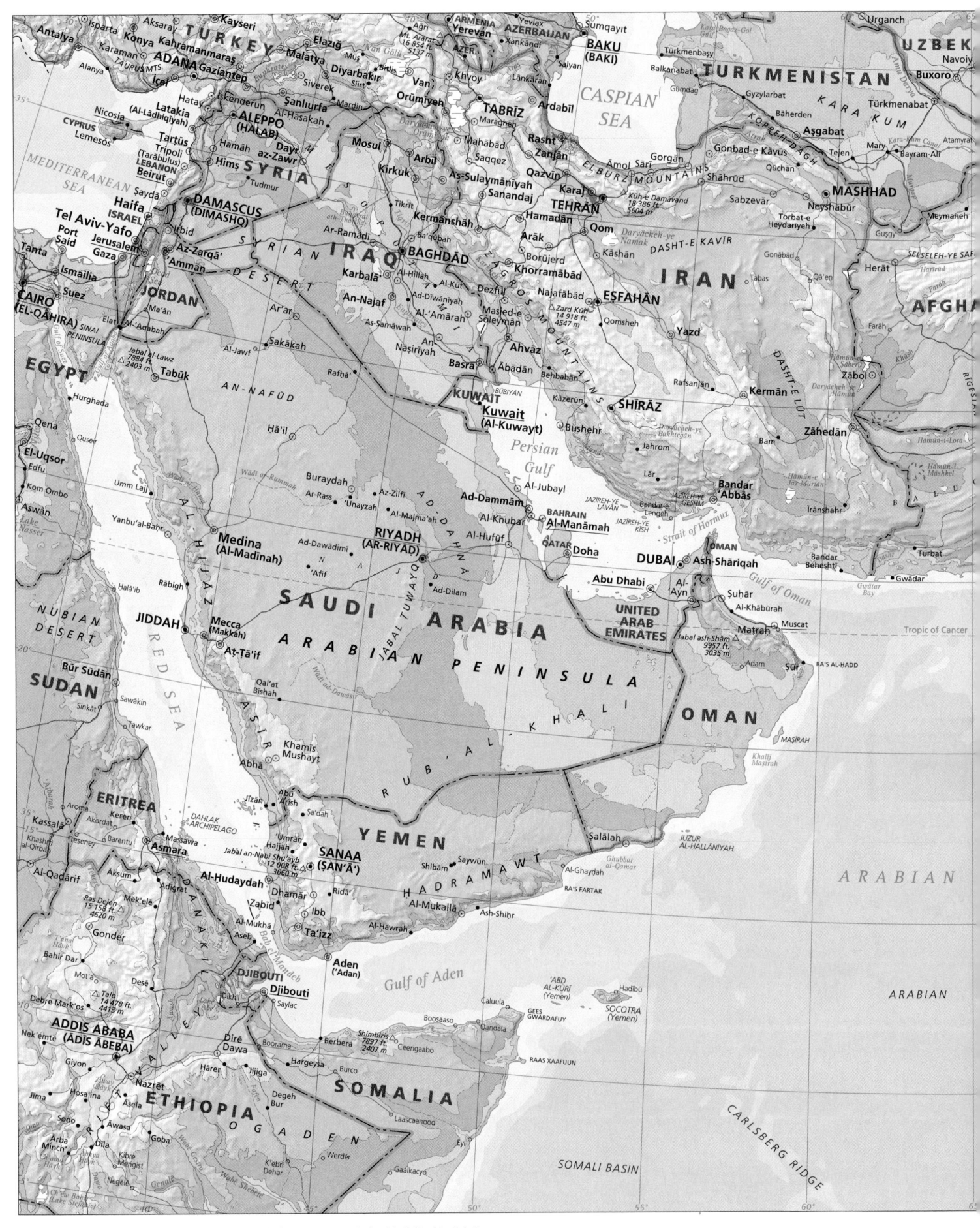

0　80　160　240　320　400　480 Miles

0　80　160　240　320　400　480　560　640　720　800 Kilometers

Lambert Azimuthal Equal Area Projection
Scale 1:16,000,000
One inch to 256 miles
One cm to 160 km

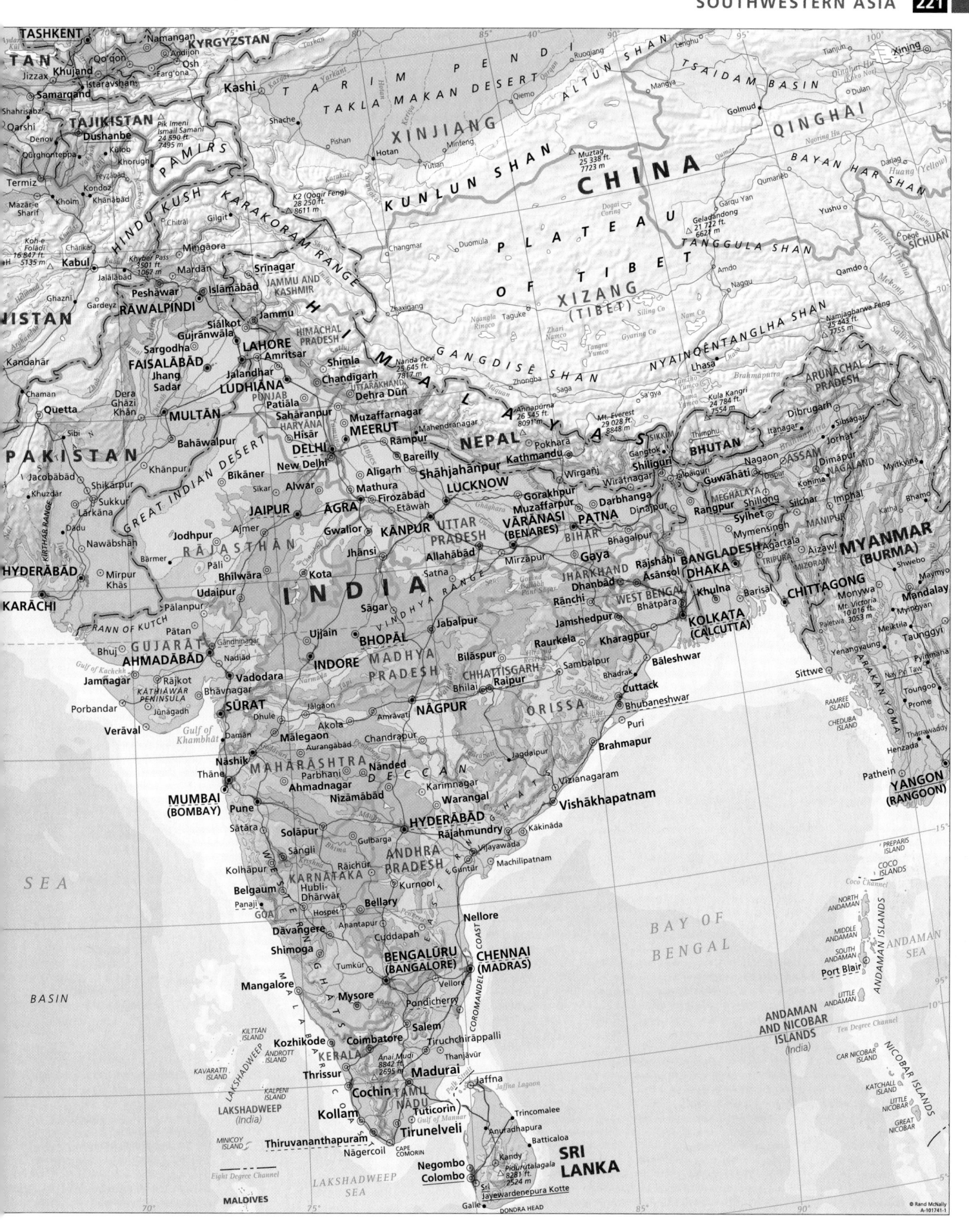

TASHKENT
KYRGYZSTAN
TAN
Namangan
Qo'qon
Andijon
Osh
Fargʻona
Jizzax
Khujand
Istaravshan
Samarqand
Kashi
Shahrisabz
Qarshi
TAJIKISTAN
Dushanbe
Denov
Qürghonteppa
Külob
PAMIRS
Pik Imeni
Ismail Samani
24 590 ft
7495 m
Termiz
Khorugh
Feyzabad
Kondoz
Mazar-e
Sharif
Kholm
Khanabad
HINDU KUSH
Chitral
Gilgit
KARAKORAM RANGE
K2 (Qogir Feng)
28 250 ft
8611 m
Koh-e
Foladi
16 847 ft
5135 m
Kabul
Ghazni
Gardez
Charikar
Jalalabad
Khyber Pass
3501 ft
1067 m
Mardan
Mingaora
Srinagar
JAMMU AND
KASHMIR
ISTAN
Peshawar
RAWALPINDI
Islamabad
Jammu
Sialkot
Gujranwala
HIMACHAL
PRADESH
Shimla
Chandigarh
Dera
Ghazi
Khan
LAHORE
Amritsar
Jalandhar
Jhang
Sadar
FAISALABAD
Sargodha
LUDHIANA
Patiala
PUNJAB
Dehra Dun
UTTARAKHAND
Nanda Devi
25 645 ft
7817 m
HIMALAYA
Annapurna
26 545 ft
8091 m
Mt. Everest
29 028 ft
8848 m
KARACHI
HYDERABAD
Quetta
Chaman
Kandahar
Sibi
KIRTHAR RANGE
Jacobabad
Shikarpur
Khuzdar
Larkana
Dadu
Sukkur
Nawabshah
Mirpur
Khas
Khanpur
Bahawalpur
MULTAN
Bikaner
GREAT INDIAN DESERT
RAJASTHAN
Barmer
Pali
Jodhpur
Ajmer
Sikar
Alwar
JAIPUR
Kota
Bhilwara
Udaipur
DELHI
New Delhi
Aligarh
Mathura
AGRA
Gwalior
Jhansi
Firozabad
Etawah
KANPUR
UTTAR
PRADESH
LUCKNOW
Shahjahanpur
Bareilly
Rampur
Saharanpur
Muzaffarnagar
MEERUT
HARYANA
Hisar
NEPAL
Pokhara
Kathmandu
Gorakhpur
Wirganj
Muzaffarpur
VARANASI
(BENARES)
PATNA
Allahabad
Mirzapur
Satna
Gaya
BIHAR
Bhagalpur
Darbhanga
Dinajpur
Pokhara
Ujjain
BHOPAL
INDORE
MADHYA
PRADESH
Jabalpur
Sagar
VINDHYA RANGE
Bilaspur
Raipur
CHHATTISGARH
Bhilai
Raurkela
Ranchi
Dhanbad
JHARKHAND
Jamshedpur
Rajshahi
Asansol
BANGLADESH
DHAKA
WEST BENGAL
Khulna
Bhatpara
KOLKATA
(CALCUTTA)
Kharagpur
Sambalpur
Bhadrak
Baleshwar
Cuttack
Bhubaneshwar
ORISSA
Puri
Brahmapur
MYANMAR
(BURMA)
CHITTAGONG
Mandalay
Monywa
Mt. Victoria
10 016 ft
3053 m
Paletwa
Sittwe
ARAKAN YOMA
AHMADABAD
GUJARAT
Nadiad
Vadodara
Rajkot
Jamnagar
Bhavnagar
Junagadh
KATHIAWAR
PENINSULA
Porbandar
Veraval
Bhuj
RANN OF KUTCH
Gulf of Kachchh
Gulf of
Khambhat
Daman
SURAT
Navsari
Dhule
Jalgaon
Malegaon
Akola
Amravati
NAGPUR
Chandrapur
INDIA
DECCAN
MAHARASHTRA
Nashik
Thane
MUMBAI
(BOMBAY)
Pune
Aurangabad
Ahmadnagar
Parbhani
Nanded
Nizamabad
Karimnagar
Warangal
Satara
Solapur
Sangli
Kolhapur
Gulbarga
Raichur
Bijapur
HYDERABAD
Rajahmundry
Kakinada
Vijayawada
Guntur
Machilipatnam
ANDHRA
PRADESH
Vishakhapatnam
Vizianagaram
Jagdalpur
Belgaum
Hubli-
Dharwar
Panaji
GOA
Bellary
Hospet
KARNATAKA
Davangere
Shimoga
Mangalore
Anantapur
Tumkur
BENGALURU
(BANGALORE)
Mysore
Kurnool
Cuddapah
Nellore
CHENNAI
(MADRAS)
Vellore
Pondicherry
Salem
Coimbatore
Tiruchchirappalli
Thanjavur
KERALA
Kozhikode
Thrissur
Anai Mudi
8842 ft
2695 m
Cochin
Madurai
TAMIL
NADU
Tuticorin
Tirunelveli
Kollam
Nagercoil
Thiruvananthapuram
CAPE
COMORIN
COROMANDEL
COAST
WESTERN GHATS
EASTERN GHATS

SRI
LANKA
Jaffna
Jaffna Lagoon
Trincomalee
Anuradhapura
Batticaloa
Kandy
Pidurutalagala
8281 ft
2524 m
Negombo
Colombo
Sri
Jayewardenepura Kotte
Galle
DONDRA HEAD
Gulf of Mannar
Palk Strait

SEA

BASIN

ARABIAN
SEA

BAY OF
BENGAL

LAKSHADWEEP
SEA

LAKSHADWEEP
(India)

KILTTAN
ISLAND
ANDROTT
ISLAND
KAVARATTI
ISLAND
KALPENI
ISLAND
MINICOY
ISLAND
Eight Degree Channel
Nine Degree Channel

ANDAMAN AND NICOBAR
ISLANDS
(India)

PREPARIS
ISLAND
COCO
ISLANDS
Coco Channel
NORTH
ANDAMAN
MIDDLE
ANDAMAN
SOUTH
ANDAMAN
Port Blair
LITTLE
ANDAMAN
ANDAMAN
SEA
Ten Degree Channel
CAR NICOBAR
ISLAND
KATCHALL
ISLAND
LITTLE
NICOBAR
GREAT
NICOBAR
NICOBAR ISLANDS

CHINA

XINJIANG
TARIM PENDI
TAKLA MAKAN DESERT
Yarkant
Shache
Pishan
Hotan
Minfeng
Qiemo
Ruoqiang
Lenghu
ALTUN SHAN
KUNLUN SHAN
Muztag
25 338 ft
7723 m
Yutian
QINGHAI
TSAIDAM BASIN
Golmud
Dulan
Mangya
BAYAN HAR SHAN
Qumarleb
Yushu
Dege
SICHUAN
Qamdo
PLATEAU
OF
TIBET
XIZANG
(TIBET)
Changmar
Duomula
Geladandong
21 722 ft
6621 m
TANGGULA SHAN
Amdo
Naggu
GANGDISE SHAN
Ngangla
Ringco
Taguke
Zhari
Namco
Siling Co
Nam Co
Lhasa
NYAINQENTANGLHA SHAN
Namjagbarwa Feng
24 784 ft
7554 m
Brahmaputra
ARUNACHAL
PRADESH
Dibrugarh
Sibsagar
Jorhat
ASSAM
Itanagar
Nagaon
Guwahati
Dimapur
NAGALAND
Kohima
Imphal
MANIPUR
MEGHALAYA
Shillong
Silchar
Aizawl
MIZORAM
TRIPURA
Agartala
Mymensingh
Sylhet
Rangpur
Shiliguri
Jalpaiguri
SIKKIM
Gangtok
BHUTAN
Thimphu

SRI LANKA

MALDIVES

PAKISTAN

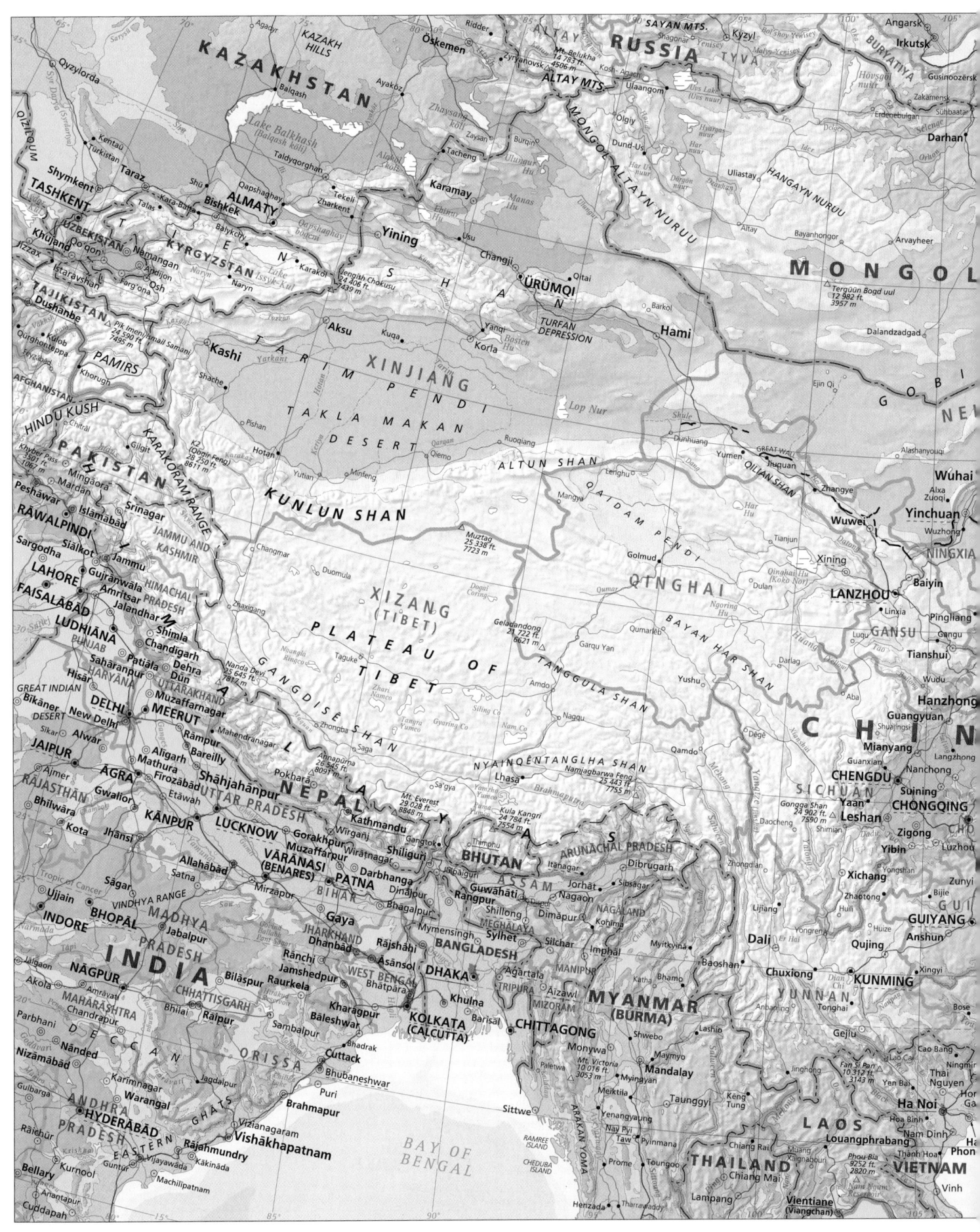

0   80   160   240   320   400   480 Miles
0   80   160   240   320   400   480   560   640   720   800 Kilometers

Lambert Azimuthal Equal Area Projection
Scale 1:16,000,000
One inch to 256 miles
One cm to 160 km

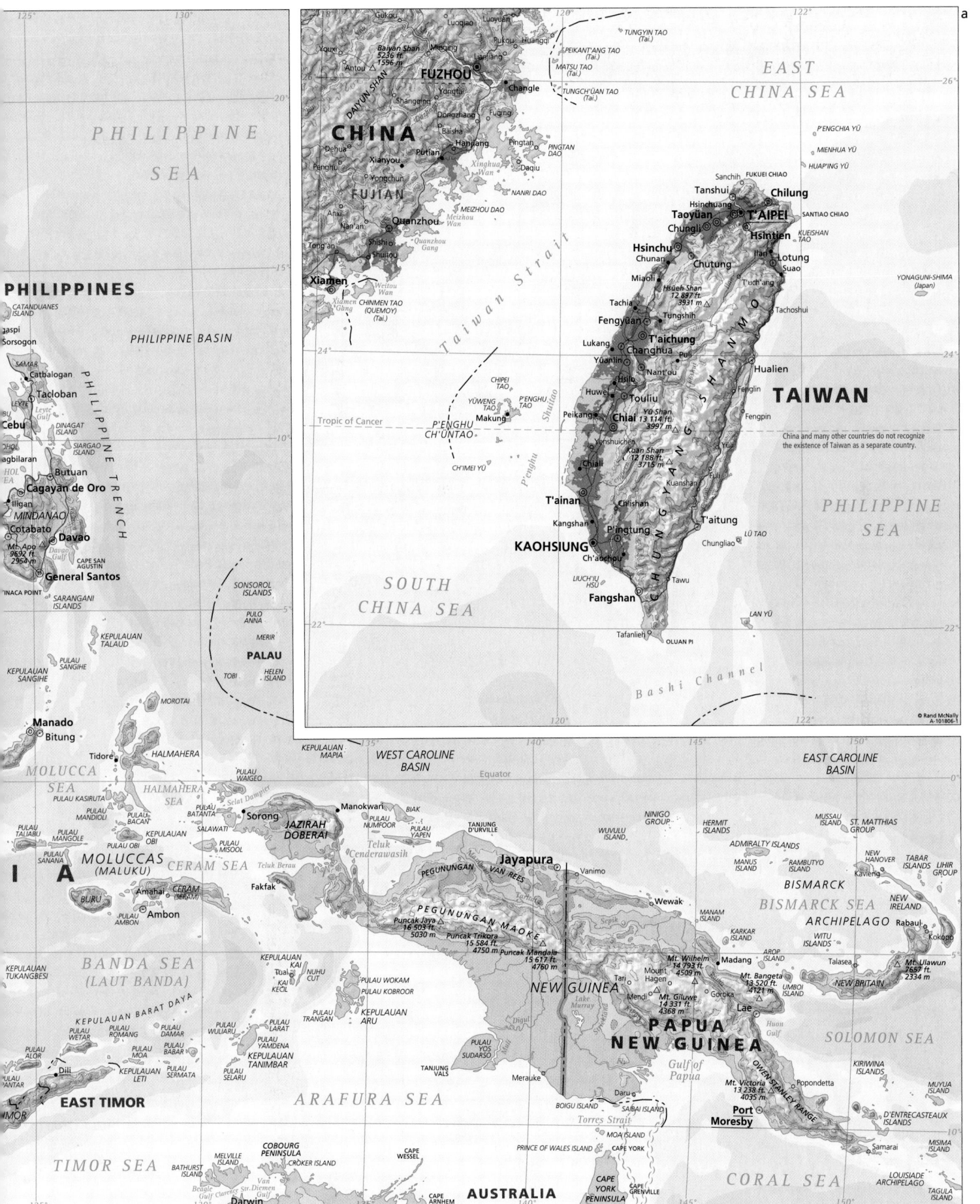

a

Inset map a (Taiwan)

CHINA

FUJIAN

FUZHOU

EAST CHINA SEA

PHILIPPINE SEA

Baiyun Shan 5236 ft. 1596 m

Xiamen

Quanzhou

Taiwan Strait

CHINMEN TAO (QUEMOY) (Tai.)

P'ENGHU CH'ÜNTAO

Makung

Tropic of Cancer

Tanshui
Hsinchuang
Taoyüan
Chungli
T'AIPEI
Chilung
Hsintien

Hsinchu
Chunan
Chutung
Chutung

Miaoli
Hüeh Shan 12 897 ft. 3931 m
T'uch'ang
Tachoshui

Fengyüan
Tungshih

Lukang
Yünlin
T'aichung
Changhua
Puli
Nant'ou

Huwei
Hsilo
Touliu
Yü Shan 13 114 ft. 3997 m
Chiai
Peikang
Yenshuichen
Kuan Shan 12 188 ft. 3715 m
Yüli

TAIWAN

Hualien

Fenglin

Fengpin

China and many other countries do not recognize the existence of Taiwan as a separate country.

Chiali
Kuanshan

T'ainan
Chishan

Kangshan
P'ingtung
T'aitung

KAOHSIUNG
Ch'aochou
Chungliao

LÜ TAO

PHILIPPINE SEA

LAN YÜ

Fangshan

SOUTH CHINA SEA

Tawu

Tafanlieh
OLUAN PI

Bashi Channel

© Rand McNally
A-101806-1

Main map

PHILIPPINE SEA

PHILIPPINE BASIN

PHILIPPINES

CATANDUANES ISLAND

Cebu

Butuan

Cagayan de Oro

Iligan
MINDANAO
Cotabato

Davao

Mt. Apo 9692 ft. 2954 m
CAPE SAN AGUSTIN

General Santos

SARANGANI ISLANDS

SONSOROL ISLANDS

PULO ANNA

MERIR

PALAU

TOBI
HELEN ISLAND

KEPULAUAN TALAUD

KEPULAUAN SANGIHE

Manado
Bitung

PULAU SANGIHE

MOROTAI

Tidore
HALMAHERA

MOLUCCA SEA

HALMAHERA SEA

PULAU WAIGEO

Manokwari
BIAK

Sorong

WEST CAROLINE BASIN

Equator

EAST CAROLINE BASIN

NINIGO GROUP

HERMIT ISLANDS

ADMIRALTY ISLANDS

MUSSAU ISLAND
ST. MATTHIAS GROUP

WUVULU ISLAND

MANUS ISLAND

RAMBUTYO ISLAND

NEW HANOVER

TABAR ISLANDS
LIHIR GROUP

Kavieng

BISMARCK ARCHIPELAGO

BISMARCK SEA

NEW IRELAND

Rabaul

WITU ISLANDS

Talasea

Mt. Ulawun 7657 ft. 2334 m

NEW BRITAIN

Kokopo

JAZIRAH DOBERAI

Teluk Cenderawasih

PULAU NUMFOOR

PULAU YAPEN

TANJUNG D'URVILLE

Vanimo

Jayapura

PEGUNUNGAN VAN REES

Wewak

MANAM ISLAND

KARKAR ISLAND

AROP ISLAND

Madang

MOLUCCAS (MALUKU)

CERAM SEA

Amahai
CERAM (SERAM)

Fakfak

PULAU MISOOL

PEGUNUNGAN MAOKE

Puncak Jaya 16 503 ft. 5030 m

Puncak Trikora 15 584 ft. 4750 m

Puncak Mandala 15 617 ft. 4760 m

Mt. Wilhelm 14 793 ft. 4509 m

Mt. Bangeta 13 520 ft. 4121 m

UMBOI ISLAND

Lae

SOLOMON SEA

Ambon

Ambon

BURU

PULAU SANANA

BANDA SEA

KEPULAUAN KAI

KEPULAUAN ARU

PULAU WOKAM

PULAU KOBROOR

NEW GUINEA

Lake Murray

Mt. Giluwe 14 331 ft. 4368 m

Mendi
Tari
Mount Hagen
Goroka

PAPUA NEW GUINEA

KIRIWINA ISLANDS

Gulf of Papua

Popondetta

D'ENTRECASTEAUX ISLANDS

MUYUA ISLAND

MISIMA ISLAND

Samarai

LOUISIADE ARCHIPELAGO

TAGULA ISLAND

KEPULAUAN BARAT DAYA

PULAU WETAR

Dili

EAST TIMOR

ARAFURA SEA

TANJUNG VALS

PULAU YOS SUDARSO

Merauke

Daru
BOIGU ISLAND
SAIBAI ISLAND

Torres Strait

Mt. Victoria 13 238 ft. 4035 m

OWEN STANLEY RANGE

Port Moresby

CORAL SEA

TIMOR SEA

MELVILLE ISLAND
BATHURST ISLAND

COBOURG PENINSULA

CROKER ISLAND

CAPE WESSEL

CAPE ARNHEM

PRINCE OF WALES ISLAND

CAPE YORK

MOA ISLAND

Darwin

AUSTRALIA

CAPE YORK PENINSULA

CAPE GRENVILLE

Inset map a
Lambert Conformal Conic Projection
Scale 1:4,000,000
One inch to 64 miles
One cm to 40 km

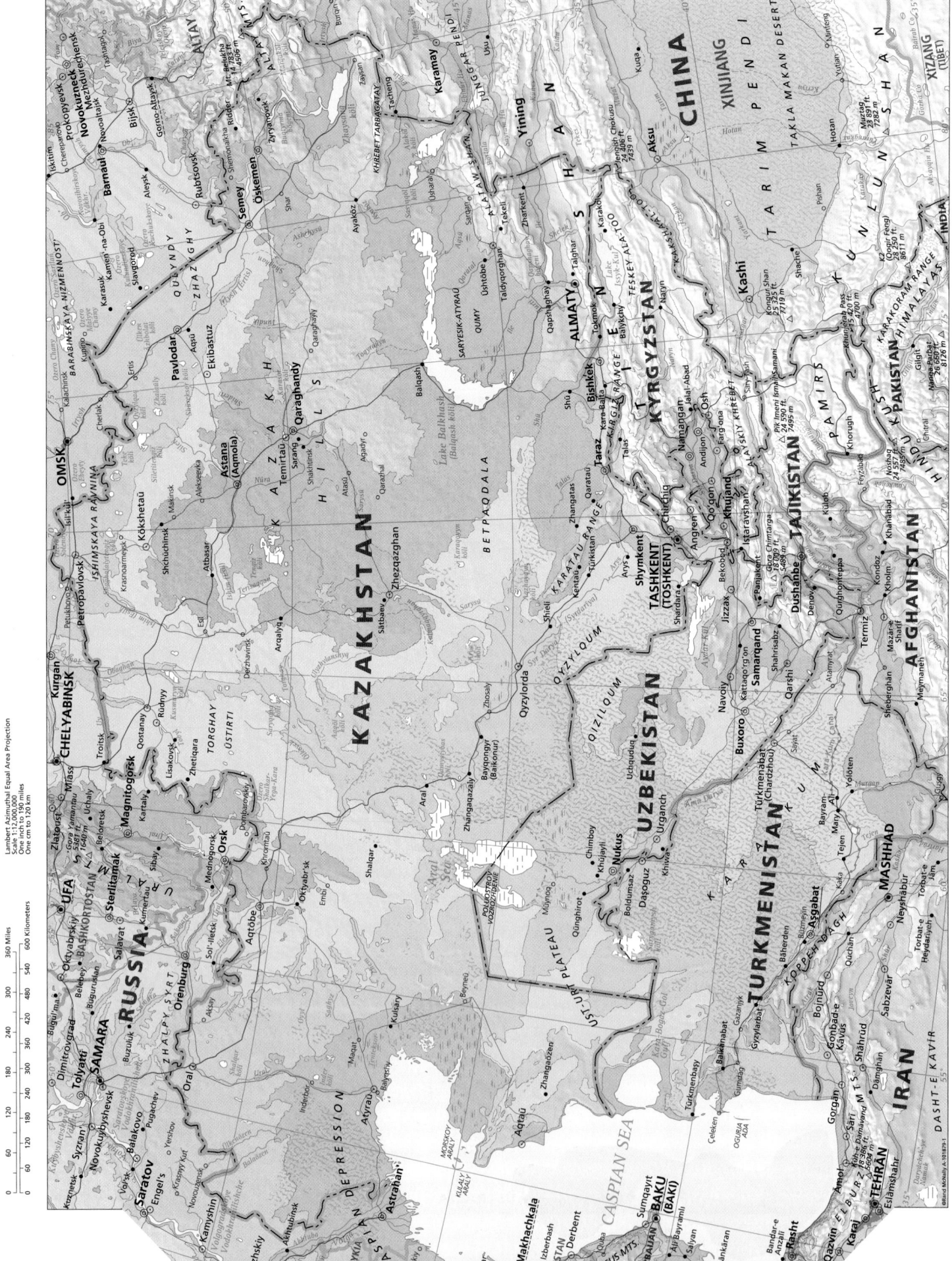

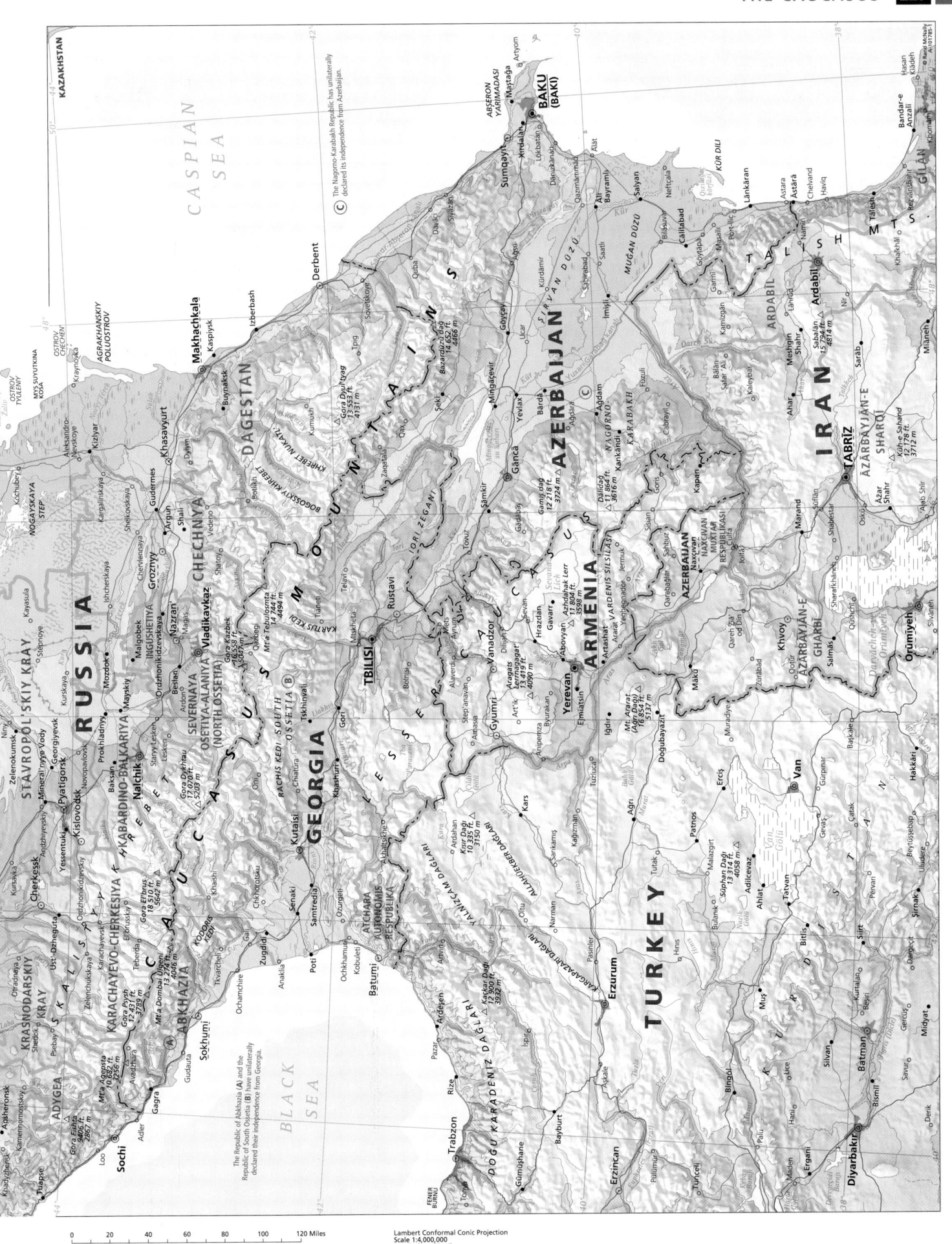

KAZAKHSTAN

C A S P I A N   S E A

© The Nagorno-Karabakh Republic has unilaterally declared its independence from Azerbaijan.

ABŞERON YARIMADASI
Maştağa
Artyom
BAKU (BAKI)
Sumqayıt
Xırdalan
Lökbatan

RUSSIA
STAVROPOL'SKIY KRAY
KRASNODARSKIY KRAY

Makhachkala
DAGESTAN

CHECHNYA
INGUSHETIYA
Vladikavkaz
SEVERNAYA OSETIYA-ALANIYA (NORTH OSSETIA)
SOUTH OSSETIA
KABARDINO-BALKARIYA
KARACHAYEVO-CHERKESIYA

ADYGEA
ABKHAZIA

C A U C A S U S   M O U N T A I N S

L E S S E R   C A U C A S U S

GEORGIA
TBILISI
Rustavi

ARMENIA
Yerevan
Gyumri

AZERBAIJAN
Gəncə
Şamkir
NAGORNO KARABAKH
Xankəndi
NAXÇIVAN MUXTAR RESPUBLİKASI
Naxçıvan

TURKEY
Erzurum
Kars
Van
Trabzon
Diyarbakır

IRAN
AZƏRBAYCAN-E SHARQI
TABRIZ
ARDABIL
Ardabil
Orūmiyeh

T A L I S H   M T S.

Black Sea

Lambert Conformal Conic Projection
Scale 1:4,000,000
One inch to 64 miles
One cm to 40 km

0   20   40   60   80   100   120 Miles
0   20   40   60   80   100   120   140   160   180   200 Kilometers

The Republic of Abkhazia (A) and the Republic of South Ossetia (B) have unilaterally declared their independence from Georgia.

TURKEY

Derik
Viranşehir
Şanlıurfa
Ceylanpınar
Ra's al-'Ay
Tall Tamir
Salūq 'Atīq
Dulq Maghār
Gaziantep
Nizip
Oğuzeli
Birecik
Sürüç
Kilis
Barak
Jarābulus
Manbij
Kırıkhan
A'zāz
Al-Bāb
ALEPPO (HALAB)
Tarsus
ADANA
İçel
Erdemli
Silifke
Mut
Kuzucubelen
Seyhan
İslâhiye
Hatay
Reyhanlı
Dār Ta'izzah
As-Safirah
Maskanah
Ar-Raqqah
Suwaydah
Euphrates

TAURUS MOUNTAIN

Alanya
Gazipaşa
Ermenek
Gülnar
Anamur
İskenderun
İskenderun Körfezi
Samandağı
AKINCI BURNU
RA'S AL-BASĪT
Idlib
Jisr ash-Shughūr
Idha
Al-Haffah
Ma'arrat an-Nu'mān
As-Saqlabiyah
Sūrān

Antalya Körfezi
ANAMUR BURNU

SYRIA

Dayr az-Zawr
Al-Kawm
Aṭ-Ţayyibah
Buşayrah
Al-Mayādin
Dab
As-Sukhnah

Latakia (Al-Lādhiqīyah)
Jablah
Bāniyās
Hamāh
Salamīyah
Tudmur
PALMYRA

North Cyprus declared itself an independent Turkish Republic in 1983.

KORUÇAM BURNU
Dipkarpaz
ZAFER BURNU
Ziyamet
Girne
İskele
CYPRUS
Güzelyurt Körfezi
Güzelyurt
Nicosia
Strovolos
Gazimağusa Körfezi
Gazimağusa
Néa Páfos
Lemesós
Olimbos 6401 ft. 1951 m
Lárnaka
Yermasóyia
Kólpos Lárnakas
Akrotíri
AKROTIRION PIDÁLION
AKROTIRION GÁTAS
Kólpos Khrisokhoús
Pólis

Tartūs
Ţall Kalakh
Buḩayrat Qaṭṭīnah
Shinshār
Furqlus
Ḩimş

Tripoli (Ṭarābulus)
Qurnat as-Sawdā' 10 115 ft. 3083 m
Al-Quşayr
Al-Hirmil
Al-Qaryatayn
Sab 'Ābār

LEBANON
Al-Batrūn
Jubayl
BYBLOS
Bsharri
Ba'labakk
BAALBEK
An-Nabk
Beirut (Bayrūt)
Jūnīyah
Zahlah
B'abda
BEKAA VALLEY
Az-Zabadānī
Al-Qutayfah
Khān Abū Shāmāt
Akāshāt

MEDITERRANEAN SEA

Şaydā
DAMASCUS (DIMASHQ)
Dūmā
Jaramānah
Darayyā
Al-Kiswah
At-Tanf
Mt. Hermon 9232 ft. 2914 m
Qaṭanā
Iwayyā
Qiryat'Shemona
Al-Qunayţirah
Al-Mismīyah
Lāhithah
At-Tall

Tyre (Şūr)
Har Meron 3963 ft. 1208 m
Zefat
GOLAN HEIGHTS
Nahariyya
Akko
Haifa (Ḩefa)
Tirat Karmel
Teverya
Fiq
Irbid
Dar'ā
As-Suwaydā'
Jabal ad-Durūz 5909 ft. 1801 m
Ar-Rutt

(A) Gaza Strip is administered by the Palestinian Authority following unilateral withdrawal by Israel in 2005.

(B) West Bank is controlled by Israel and parts are administered by the Palestinian Authority.

(C) Golan Heights has been unilaterally annexed by Israel.

Dor
Nazareth (Nazerat)
'Afula
Bet She'an
Ajlūn
Ar-Ramthā
Jarash
Al-Mafraq
Mahaṭṭat al-Ḩafīf

CAESAREA
Hadera
Netanya
Herzliyya
ISRAEL
Ţūlkarm
Tūbās
As-Salt
Az-Zarqā'
Ar-Ruşayfah
Tel Aviv-Yafo
Qalqilya
Nābulus
WEST BANK
Ariha (Jericho)
Amman
Rishon LeZiyyon
Petaḩ Tiqwa
Madabā
Rehovot
Ramallah (Bayt Lahm)
Al-Jīzah

D E S E R T
Jabal 'Unayzah 3084 ft. 940 m

Ashdod
Ashqelon
GAZA STRIP
Bethlehem (Bayt Laḩm)
Qiryat Gat
Jerusalem (Yerushalayim)
Azraq ash-Shīshān
Al-Hadithah

Gaza (Ghazzah)
Khān Yūnis
Al-Khalīl (Hebron)
Yaṭṭah
Dhībān
AL-HAMĀD
Port Said (Būr Sa'īd)
Būr Fu'ad
Khalīg el-Tīna
Rafah
Be'er Sheva
MASĀDA
'Arad
Al-Mazra'ah
Al-Qaţrānah

El-Arish
Rūmānī
Holot Haluza
Nizzana
Dimona
Yeroham
Al-Karak
Turayf
Al-'Isāwīyah

Ismailia
El-Qantara el-Sharqīya
Mizpé Ramon
At-Tafīlah
WADI AS-SIRHAN

EGYPT
El-Quseima
NEGEV
Gebel Yi'allaq 3589 ft. 1094 m
Wādī el-Arish
Ash-Shawbak
Sakbhat Hazawza

Suez (El-Suweis)
Bur Taufīq
El-Kuntilla
PETRA
Al-'Isāwīyah
Al-Jalāmīd

GEBEL EL-TĪH
El-Thamad
Ra's an-Naqb
Al-Jaff
QA' AL-JAFR
Ma'ān
Wādī Hadra

JORDAN
Nakhl
Ma'ān
Al-Busayṭā
Sakākah

SINAI PENINSULA
Abu Zenima
GEBEL EL-'IGMA
Ras el-Gineina 5335 ft. 1626 m
Elat
Al-'Aqabah
Jabal Ramm 5755 ft. 1754 m
Al-Jawf
Qāraḩ

Gulf of Suez (Khalīg el-Suweis)
Nuweiba
Al-Mudawwarah

Mt. Sinai (Gebel Musa) 7497 ft. 2285 m
Dahab
Haql
Al-Bi'r
AT-TAWIL
SAUDI
Gebel Abu Khashaba 4797 ft. 1462 m
El-Tūr
Maqna
Al-Bad'
Jabal al-Lawz 7884 ft. 2403 m

Sharm el-Sheikh
TIRAN
SANAFIR
RED SEA
Aynūnah
Ash-Sharmah
M I D Y A N
Tabūk
Al-Qalībah
AL-HUFRAH
AL-'URAYQ
RĀS MOHAMMED
Genisa

Gulf of Aqaba

0   20   40   60   80   100   120 Miles
0   20   40   60   80   100   120   140   160   180   200 Kilometers

Lambert Conformal Conic Projection
Scale 1:4,000,000
One inch to 64 miles
One cm to 40 km

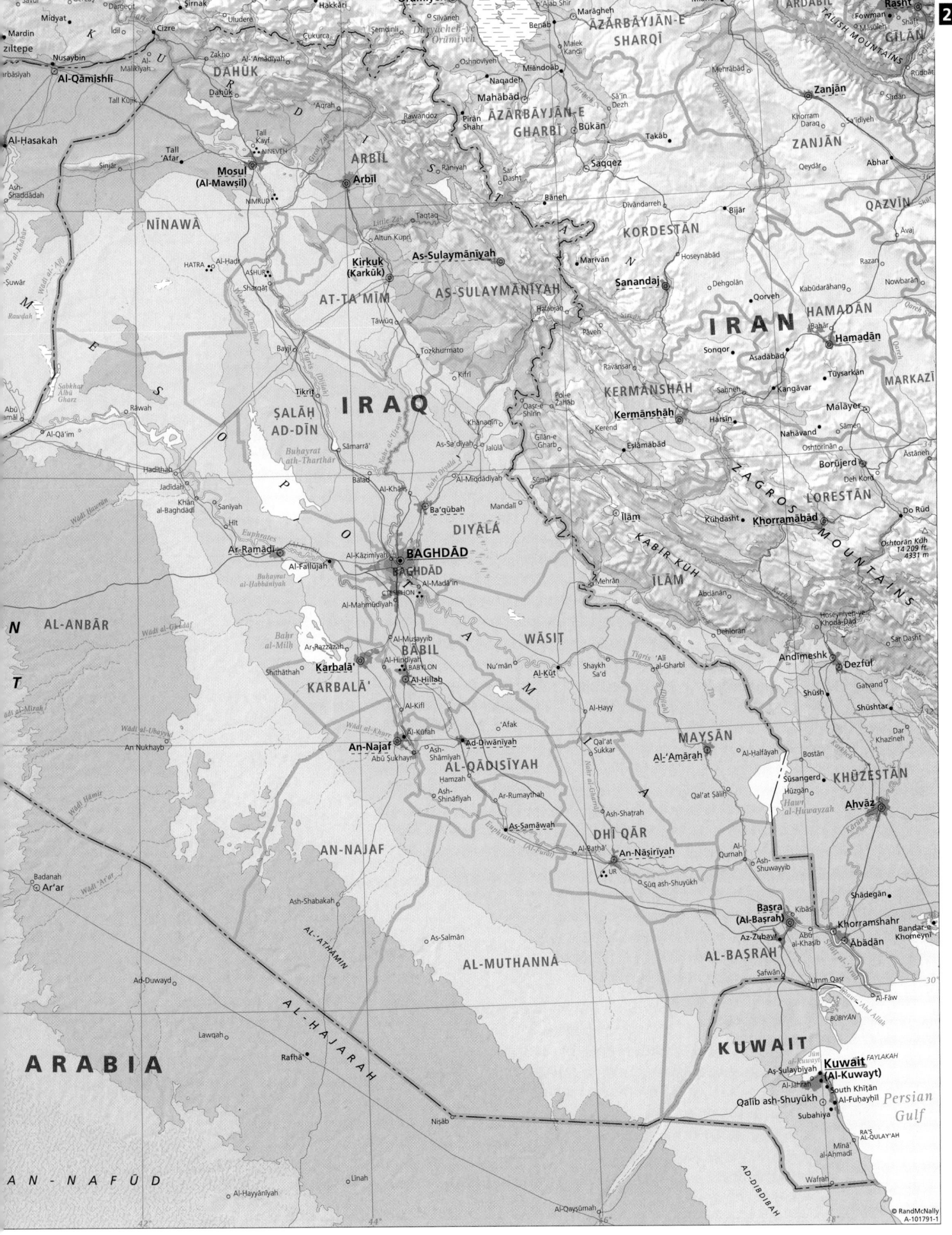

ARDABĪL
TALISH MOUNTAINS
GILĀN
Rasht
Fowman
Shaft
Khomām
Rūdbār

Savur
Gercüş
42
Béytüşşebap
Orūmīyeh
Ajab Shīr
Marāgheh
Mīāneh

Midyat
Hakkâri
Silvāneh
Daryācheh-ye
Orūmīyeh
Benāb
Malek Kandī
ĀZARBĀYJĀN-E SHARQĪ
Zanjān
Sindan
Sa'dīyeh

Mardin
Idil
Uludere
Çukurca
Şemdinli
Naqadeh
Mīāndoāb
Mehrābād
Khorram Daraq
Abhar
QAZVĪN

ziltepe
Nusaybin
Cizre
Zakho
Al-'Amādīyah
'Aqrah
Rawāndoz
Pīrān Shahr
Mahābād
ĀZARBĀYJĀN-E GHARBĪ
Būkān
Sā'īn Dezh
Takāb
Zanjān
Qeydār
Avaj

Al-Qāmishlī
Malikīyah
Tall Kūjik
DAHŪK
Dahūk
Tall Kayf
NINEVEH
Rānīyah
Sar Dasht
Saqqez
Bāneh
Dīvāndarreh
Bījār
Hoseynābād
Kabūdarāhang
Nowbarān

Al-Hasakah
Tall 'Afar
Sinjār
Mosul (Al-Mawşil)
NIMRŪD
ARBĪL
Arbīl
S
Mārīvān
Sanandaj
Dehgolān
Qorveh
Razan
Bahār
HAMADĀN

Ash-Shaddādah
NĪNAWĀ
HATRA
Al-Hadr
ASHUR
AT-TA'MĪM
Kirkuk (Karkūk)
As-Sulaymānīyah
AS-SULAYMĀNĪYAH
Halabjah
Pāveh
KORDESTĀN
Sonqor
Asadābād
IRAN
Hamadān
Tūysarkān
MARKAZĪ

Şuwār
M
Rawdah
Sharqāt
Tāwūq
Tozkhurmāto
Kifrī
Qaşr-e Shīrīn
Polīe Zahāb
Sahneh
Kangāvar
Nahāvand
Sāmen
Malāyer
Āstāneh

Abū amāl
E
S
Sabkhat Abū Ghar
Tikrīt
ŞALĀH AD-DĪN
Bayjī
IRAQ
As-Sa'dīyah
Jalūlā
Gīlān-e Gharb
Kerend
Eslāmābād
Oshtorīnān
Borūjerd
Deh Kord
Do Rūd

Al-Qā'im
Rāwah
P
Sāmarrā'
Nahr Dīyālá
Khānaqīn
Sūmār
Īlām
Kūhdasht
Khorramābād
LORESTĀN

Hadīthah
O
Bālad
Buhayrat ath-Tharthār
Al-Khāliş
Mandalī
ĪLĀM
Oshtorān Kūh 14 209 ft 4331 m

Jadīdah
Khān al-Baghdādī
Saniyah
Hīt
Ba'qūbah
DIYĀLĀ
Al-Miqdādīyah
Mehrān
Abdānān
KABĪR KŪH
Sar Dasht

Ar-Ramādī
Euphrates
Al-Kāzimīyah
BAGHDĀD
BAGHDĀD
Al-Madā'in
Dehlorān
Hoseynīyeh-ye Khoda-Dād

Khān al-Baghdādī
Al-Fallūjah
CTESIPHON
Al-Mahmūdīyah
WĀSIT
Andīmeshk
Dezful

Bahr al-Milh
Ar-Razzāzah
Al-Musayyib
BĀBIL
BABYLON
Nu'mān
Shaykh Sa'd
'Alī al-Gharbī
Shūsh
Shūshtar

AL-ANBĀR
Buhayrat al-Habbānīyah
Al-Hindīyah
Al-Hillah
Al-Kūt
M
Gatvand
Dar Khazīneh

N
Karbalā'
Shithāthah
KARBALĀ'
Al-Kifl
'Afak
Al-Hayy
Qal'at Sukkar
MAYSĀN
Al-'Amārah
Al-Halfāyah
Bostān
KHŪZESTĀN

T
Wādī al-'Ubayyid
Al-Kūfah
An-Najaf
Ad-Dīwānīyah
AL-QĀDISĪYAH
Qal'at Şālih
Şūsangerd
Hūzgān
Ahvāz

Wādī al-Mirah
An Nukhayb
Ash-Shāmīyah
Abū Şukhayr
Hamzah
Ar-Rumaythah
Ash-Shatrah
Hawr al-Huwayzah

Badanah
Ar'ar
Wādī 'Ar'ar
AL-'ATHĀMIN
Ash-Shinafīyah
Ash-Samāwah
DHĪ QĀR
An-Nāşirīyah
Al-Batha'
Al-Qurnah
Ash-Shuwayyib

Ash-Shabakah
AN-NAJAF
UR
Şūq ash-Shuyūkh
Shādegān

As-Salmān
Başra (Al-Başrah)
Kibāsī
Khorramshahr
Bandar-e Khomeynī

Ad-Duwayd
AL-MUTHANNĀ
Az-Zubayr
Abū al-Khaşīb
Ābādān

Lawqah
Rafhā'
AL-HAJARAH
Safwān
Umm Qasr
Al-Fāw
30

ARABIA
KUWAIT
Kuwait (Al-Kuwayt)
BŪBĪYĀN
FAYLAKAH

Nişāb
As-Sulaybīyah
Al-Jahrāh
South Khītān
Al-Fuhayhīl
Persian Gulf

AN-NAFŪD
Lînah
Al-Hayyānīyah
Al-Qayşūmah
Qālib ash-Shuyūkh
Subahīya
RA'S AL-QULAY'AH

AD-DIBDIBAH
Wafrah
Mīnā al-Ahmadī

© RandMcNally
A-101791-1

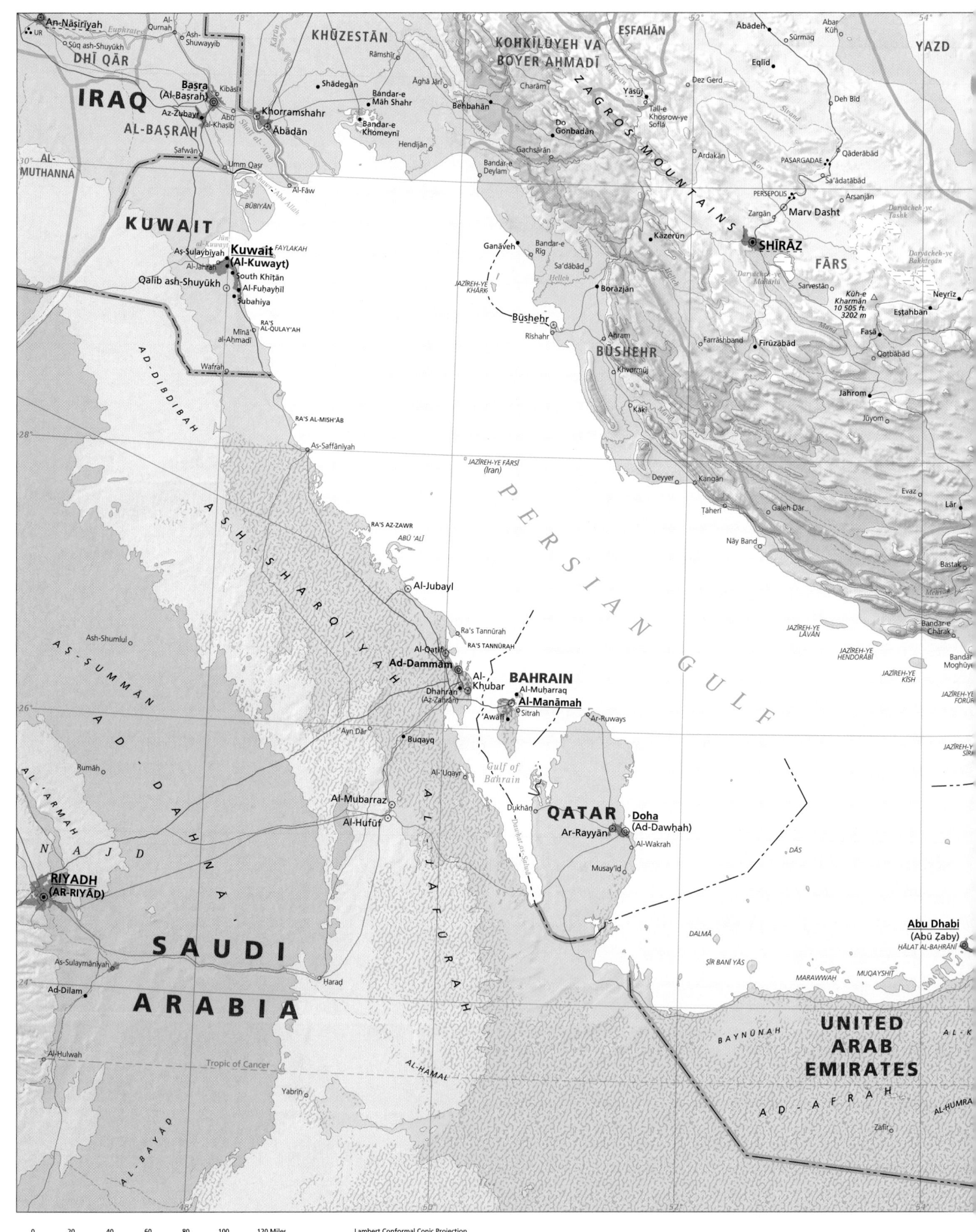

An-Nāṣirīyah
UR
Euphrates
Al-Qurnah
Ash-Shuwayyib
DHĪ QAR
Ṣūq ash-Shuyūkh
KHŪZESTĀN
Rāmshīr
ESFAHĀN
KOHKĪLŪYEH VA
BOYER AHMADĪ
Ābādeh
Abar
Kūh
Sūrmaq
YAZD

IRAQ
Baṣra (Al-Baṣrah)
Kibāsī
Shādegān
Bandar-e Māh Shahr
Aghā Jārī
Behbahān
Charām
Yāsūj
Do Gonbadān
Dez Gerd
Eqlīd
Deh Bīd

AL-BAṢRAH
Az-Zubayr
Al-Khaṣīb
Khorramshahr
Bandar-e Khomeynī
Tall-e Khosrow-ye Soflā
Ardakān
PASARGADAE
Qāderābād

Ṣafwān
Ābādān
Hendijān
Bandar-e Deylam
Gachsārān
Sa'ādatābād

AL-MUTHANNĀ
Umm Qaṣr
Al-Fāw
ZAGROS MOUNTAINS
PERSEPOLIS
Arsanjān
Daryācheh-ye Tashk

BŪBIYĀN
Jūn al-Kuwayt
Ganāveh
Bandar-e Rīg
Kāzerūn
Zargān
Marv Dasht

KUWAIT
FAYLAKAH
Sa'dābād
SHĪRĀZ

Kuwait (Al-Kuwayt)
As-Sulaybīyah
Al-Jahrāʼ
South Khīṭān
Būshehr
Borāzjān
Sarvestān
Kūh-e Kharmān
10 505 ft.
3202 m
Neyrīz

Qālib ash-Shuyūkh
Al-Fuḥayḥīl
Ṣubaḥiyah
Rīshahr
Aḥram
Eṣṭahbān
Fasā
FĀRS

Mīnāʼ al-Aḥmadī
RAʼS AL-QULAYʼAH
JAZĪREH-YE KHĀRK
Hellen
Khvormūj
Farrāshband
Fīrūzābād
Qoṭbābād

Wafrah
AD-DIBDIBAH
Kākī
Jahrom
Jūyom

RAʼS AL-MISHʼAB
JAZĪREH-YE FĀRSĪ (Iran)
Deyyer
Kangān

As-Saffānīyah
Ṭāherī
Galeh Dār
Evaz
Lār

ASH-SHARQĪYAH
RAʼS AZ-ZAWR
ABŪ ʼALĪ
Nāy Band
Bastak

PERSIAN GULF
JAZĪREH-YE LĀVĀN
Bandar-e Charak

Al-Jubayl
JAZĪREH-YE HENDORĀBĪ
Bandar Moghūyeh

Ash-Shumlul
Raʼs Tannūrah
RAʼS TANNŪRAH
JAZĪREH-YE KĪSH

AS-ṢUMMĀN
Al-Qaṭīf
Ad-Dammām
Al-Khubar
BAHRAIN
Al-Muḥarraq
JAZĪREH-YE FORŪR

AD-DAHNĀʼ
Dhahran (Az-Zahrān)
Al-Manāmah
Awālī
Sitrah
Ar-Ruways
JAZĪREH-YE SĪRĪ

Rumāh
'Ayn Dār
Gulf of Bahrain
DĀS

NAJD
Buqayq
Dukhān
QATAR
Doha (Ad-Dawḥah)

Al-Mubarraz
Al-'Uqayr
Ar-Rayyān
Al-Wakrah

AL-ARMAH
Al-Hufūf
AL-JAFŪRAH
DALMĀ
Abu Dhabi (Abū Ẓaby)
HĀLAT AL-BAḤRĀNĪ

RIYADH (AR-RIYĀD)
Musay'īd
ṢĪR BANĪ YĀS
MARAWWAH
MUQAYSHIT

SAUDI ARABIA
As-Sulaymānīyah
Harāḍ

Ad-Dilam
Tropic of Cancer
AL-HAMAL
BAYNŪNAH
UNITED ARAB EMIRATES
AL-K

Al-Hulwah
Yabrīn
AL-BAYAD
AD-AFRAH
AL-HUMRA

Zafīr

0   20   40   60   80   100   120 Miles
0   20   40   60   80   100   120   140   160   180   200 Kilometers

Lambert Conformal Conic Projection
Scale 1:4,000,000
One inch to 64 miles
One cm to 40 km

Ānār
Zarand
Rāvar
Lakar Kūh
9764 ft.
2976 m.

KHORĀSĀN-E
JONŪBĪ

Zābol
Sefid
Ābeh
Mohammadābād

DASHT-E
MĀRGOW

SĪSTĀN

Mīrābād
Chār
Borjak

Rodbār

Rafsanjān
Bāghīn
Kermān

Kūh-e Palvār
13 888 ft.
4233 m.

Noṣratābād

Kūh-e Malek Sīāh
5390 ft.
1643 m.

AFGHANISTAN

GOWD-E ZEREH

Shahr-e
Bābak

IRAN
KERMĀN

Mashīz
Rāyen

Golbāf

DASHT-E LUT

Zāhedān

Saindak

BALUCHISTAN

Sīrjān
Kūh-e Lāleh Zār
14 357 ft.
4376 m.

Kūh-e Hazār
14 649 ft.
4465 m.

Bāft

Bam

Fahraj

Mīrjāveh
Lādīz

Mashkī
Chāh

PAKISTAN

Nok
Kundi

ārāb
Kūh-e Khabīr
12 612 ft.
3844 m.

Esfandaqeh
Jīroft
Rīgān

Kūh-e Taftān
13 261 ft.
4042 m.

Khāsh

BALUCHISTĀN

Kūh-e
Qashqeh
9190 ft.
2801 m.

Fūrg

Dowlatābād

Do Sārī

Kūh-e Bazmān
11 453 ft.
3491 m.

Bazmān

Sarā-ye
Ahmadi
Golāshkerd

Bīzhanābād

SĪSTĀN VA BALŪCHESTĀN

Sarāvān
Dāvar
Panāh

Kol
LĀRISTĀN
Shamīl
Kahnūj

Hāmūn-e
Jaz Mūrīān
Bampūr
Bampūr
Īrānshahr
Zābolī
Sūrān

Qal'eh-ye
Deh-e Bārez
Manūjān

Bandar
'Abbās

Mīnāb
Maskūtān
Sarbāz

JAZĪREH-YE
HORMOZ
Qeshm

Remeshk

Kūh-e Būnīken
7169 ft.
2185 m.

Nahang

JAZĪREH-YE
LĀRAK

Angohrān
Bēnt
Nīkshahr
Rāsk
Īspīkān

Bāsa'īdū
JAZĪREH-YE
HENGĀM
Strait of Hormuz

RA'S
SHARĪTAH

Gevān
Jīnab
Gūr Kūh
6270 ft.
1911 m.

Qasā-e
Qand

Mand

Bandar-e
Lengeh
JAZĪREH-YE
QESHM

ABŪ
MŪSĀ

MŪSANDAM
PENINSULA

Kūmzār
Al-Khaṣab

OMAN

Gābrīk
Sūrak

Kārkīndar
Polān

Bāhū
Kalāt

PAKISTAN

Ra's al-Khaymah
Jabal al-Harim
6847 ft.
2087 m.

Jāsk
Hūmedān

Kohak

Umm al-Qaywayn
Dadnah
OMAN

RA'S-E
KŪH LAB

Bandar
Beheshtī

Gwātar
Bay
Jīwani

Gwādar
RĀS
NŪH

Ash-Shāriqah
'Ajmān
Al-Fujayrah

**DUBAI
(DUBAYY)**
Kalbā'

MAKRĀN C O A S T

Shināṣ

Al-Buraymī
Al-Buraymī
Ṣuḥār

Gulf of Oman

Al-'Ayn
Jabal Hafit
3806 ft.
1160 m.
Al-Qābil

Al-Ghurayfah
Al-Khābūrah

As-Suwayq

T A M

Dank
Maskin

Ar-Rustāq
Sama'īl

As-Sīb
Maṭraḥ
Muscat
(Masqaṭ)
Al-'Amrat

Bawshar
Sarūr
Qurayyāt

RA'S ABŪ DĀ'ŪD

Tropic of Cancer

A R A B I A N

S E A

Ibrī
Jabal ash-Shām
9957 ft.
3035 m.

AL HAJAR ASH-SHARQĪ

Fins

Tan'ām

Bahlā'
Nizwā
Izkī

Wādī Andam

Tiwī

Ibrā

OMAN

Al-Mudaybī
Ṣūr
RA'S AL-HADD
Al-Hadd

© Rand McNally
A-101797-1

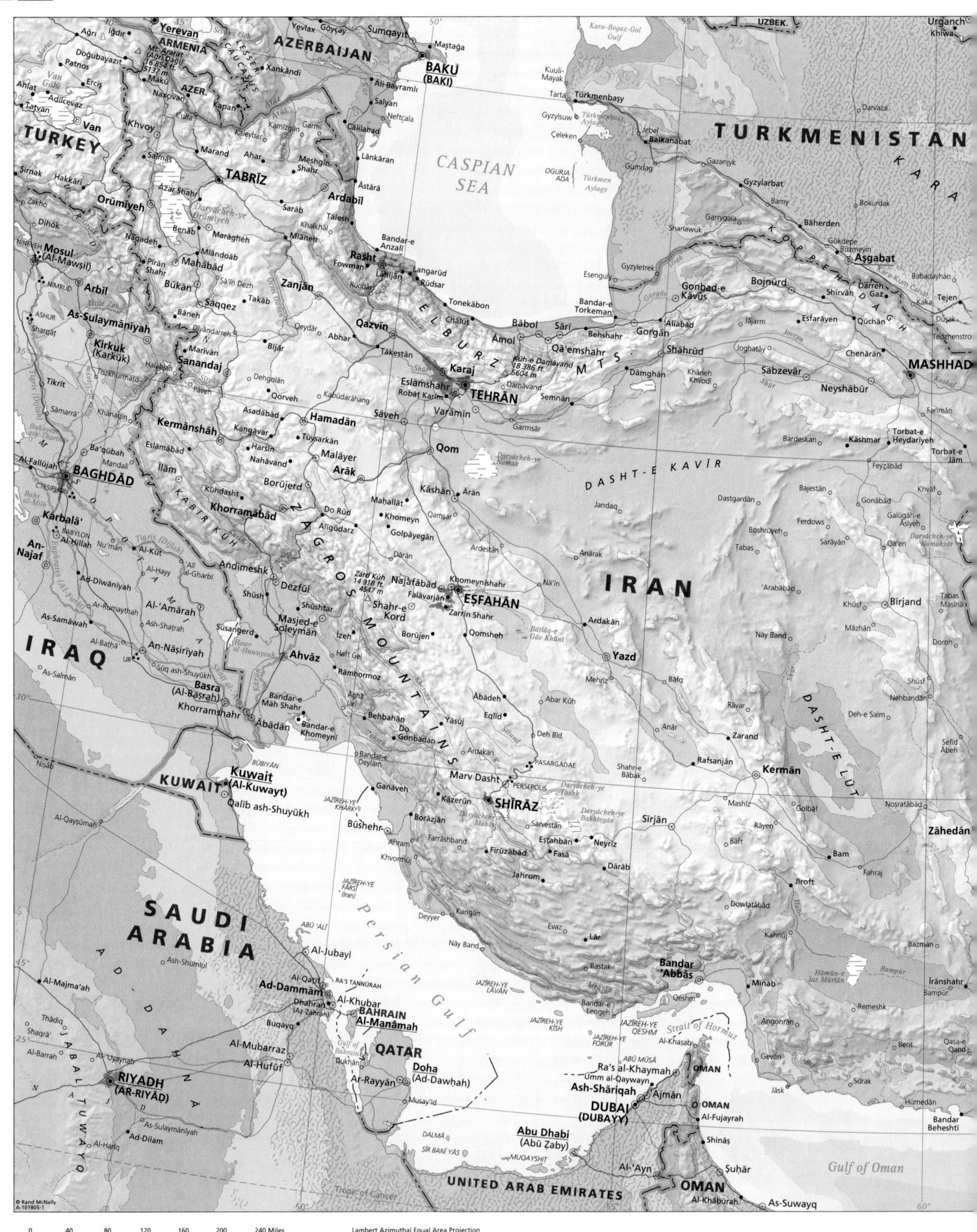

0 40 80 120 160 200 240 Miles

0 40 80 120 160 200 240 280 320 360 400 Kilometers

Lambert Azimuthal Equal Area Projection
Scale 1:8,000,000
One inch to 128 miles
One cm to 80 km

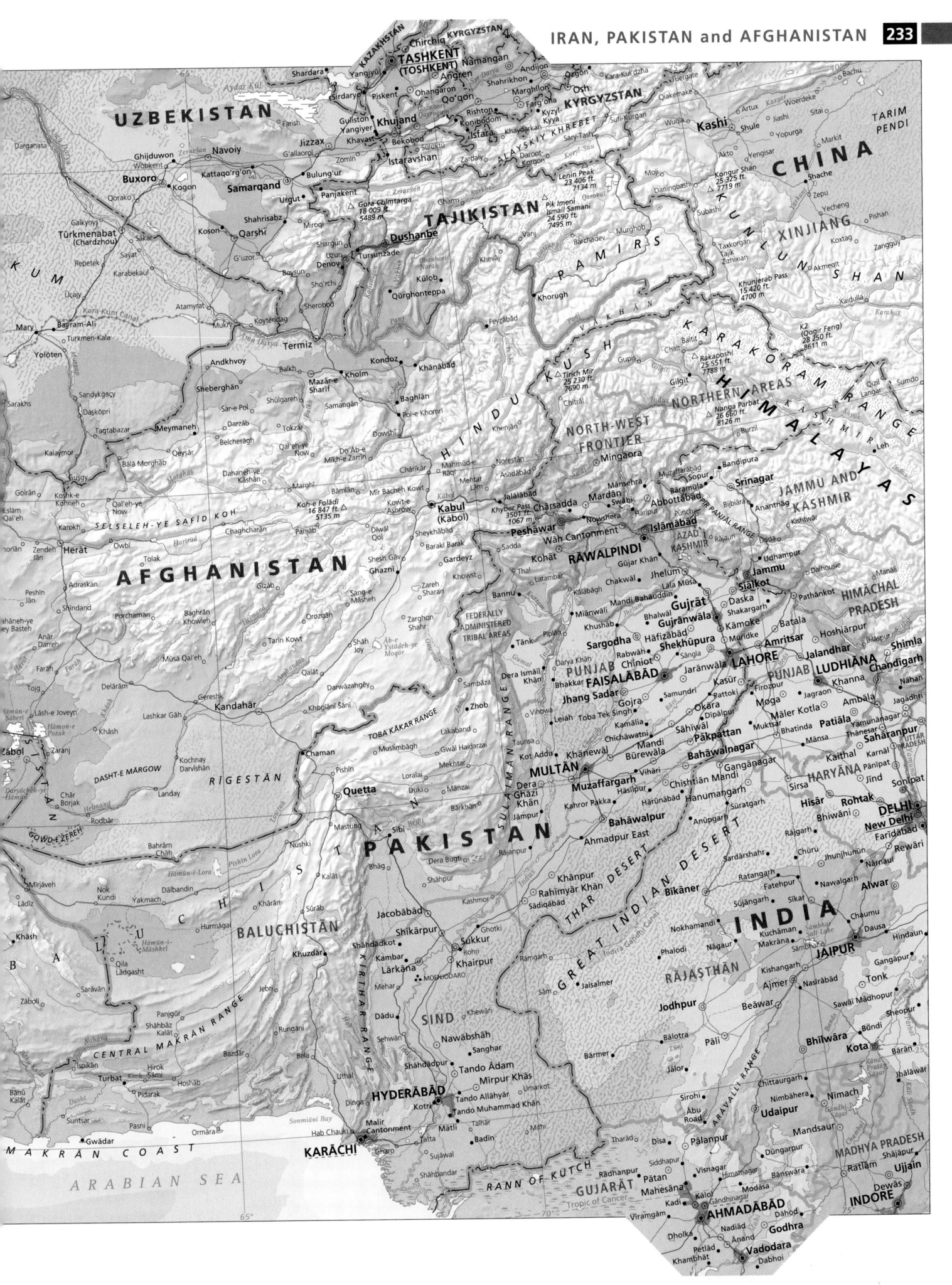

KAZAKHSTAN

KYRGYZSTAN

TASHKENT (TOSHKENT) · Shardara · Yangiyul · Angren · Namangan · Andijon · Ozgon · Kara-Kul'dzha

Chirchiq · Piskent · Ohangaron · Marghilon · Osh · Qiakemake · KYRGYZSTAN · Woerdeke · Sitai

UZBEKISTAN

Shardara · Yangiyul · Sirdaryo · Bekobod · Shahrikhon · Fargʻona · Rishton · Khaydarkan · Kyzyl-Suu · Sary-Tash · Wuqia · Kashi · Shule · Yopurga · Markit · Bachu

Farish · Guliston · Yangiyer · Konibodom · Isfara · Kyzyl-Kiya · Daroot-Korgon · Akto · Yengisar · Shache

Ghijduwon · Wobkent · Navoiy · Jizzax · Gʻallaorol · Zomin · Zardaly · Alayskiy Khrebet · Suli-Tash · Kargol · Artux · Jiashi · Zepu · Yecheng · Pishan

Buxoro · Kattaqoʻrgʻon · **Samarqand** · Bulungʻur · Urgut · Panjakent · Gora Chimtarga 18 009 ft. 5489 m · Gharm · Surkhob · Murghob · CHINA · XINJIANG · Koxtag

Qoraolʻ · Kogon · Qarshi · Shahrisabz · Koson · Miroqi · Shargun · **TAJIKISTAN** · Van · Barchadev · Subashi · Taxkorgan Tajik Zizhixian · Zanggui

KUM · Darganata · Zeravshan · Pik Imeni Ismail Samani 24 590 m 7495 m · PAMIRS · Kongur Shan 25 325 ft. 7719 m · K2 (Qogir Feng) 28 250 ft. 8611 m · Sumdo

Türkmenabat (Chardzhou) · Sakar · Repetek · Koson · Qaʻeh-ye Now · **Dushanbe** · Uzun · Tursunzade · Denov · Norak · Khevaj · Lenin Peak 23 406 ft. 7134 m · Khorug · Khunjerab Pass 15 420 ft. 4700 m · Rakaposhi 25 551 ft. 7788 m · KARAKORAM RANGE · Qizil Jangal

Galkynyş · Kogon · Boysun · Shoʻrchi · Kulob · Qurghonteppa · WAKHAN · Chalt · Baltit · KUNLUN SHAN · Xaidulla · Karakax

Mary · Bayram-Ali · Turkmen-Kala · Atamyrat · Mukry · Sayat · Karabekaul · Koytendag · Sherobod · Feyzabad · Gupis · Gilgit · Nanga Parbat 26 660 ft. 8126 m · Leh

Yoloten · Kara-Kum Canal · Termiz · Andkhvoy · Kholm · Kondoz · Khanabad · HINDU KUSH · Tirich Mir 25 230 ft. 7690 m · NORTHERN AREAS · Burzil · JAMMU AND KASHMIR

Sarakhs · Sandykgaçy · Daşköpri · Tagtabazar · Sheberghan · Balkh · **Mazar-e Sharif** · Samangan · Baghlan · Chitral · Gilgit · HIMALAYAS

Kalaýmor · Koshk-e · Qeysar · Sar-e Pol · Shulgareh · Pol-e Khomri · Dowshi · Khenjan · NORTH-WEST FRONTIER · Mingaora · Muzaffarabad · Sopur · Srinagar · Bandipura · Anantnag

Golran · Koshk-e Kohnan · Meymaneh · Darzab · Tokzar · Do Ab-e Mikh-e Zarrin · Mahmud-e Raqi · Norestan · Asadabad · Mansehra · Swabi · Abbottabad · Bijbiara · PIR PANJAL RANGE · Doda

Qaʻeh-ye · Bala Morghab · Belcheragh · Marghi · Koh Foladi 16 847 ft. 5135 m · Charikar · Mir Bacheh Kowt · Mehtar Lam · Jalalabad · Charsadda · Mardan · Haripur · Punch · Rajaun · Udhampur

Eslam Qaleh · Karokh · Chaghcharan · Panjab · Kowt-e Ashrow · Khyber Pass 3501 ft. 1067 m · Peshawar · Wah Cantonment · **Islamabad** · AZAD KASHMIR · Dalhousie

Zendeh Jan · **Herat** · Owbi · Harirud · Shesh Gav · Diwal Qol · **Kabul (Kabol)** · Sheykhabad · Baraki Barak · Sadda · Kohat · **Rawalpindi** · Gujar Khan · Jammu · Manali

Peshin · Adraskan · Tolak · SELSELEH-YE SAFID KOH · Ghazni · Gardeyz · Khowst · Thal · Latambar · Jhelum · Sialkot · HIMACHAL PRADESH

Shane-ye Basteh · **AFGHANISTAN** · Sange Masheh · Gizab · Zareh Sharan · Bannu · Kalabagh · Chakwal · Lala Musa · Pathankot · PRADESH

Anar Darreh · Porcheman · Baghran Khowleh · Orozgan · Zarghon Shahr · FEDERALLY ADMINISTERED TRIBAL AREAS · Mianwali · Mandi Bahauddin · Daska · Shakargarh · Batala · Shimla

Farah · Musa Qaleh · Tarin Kowt · Shah Joy · FEDERALLY ADMINISTERED TRIBAL AREAS · Tank · Khushab · **Gujranwala** · Kamoke · Muridke · Amritsar · Hoshiarpur · Bilaspur

Delaram · Shah Joy · Ab-e Ystadeh-ye Mogor · Zarghon Shahr · Darya Khan · Sargodha · Hafizabad · Chiniot · Sangla · **LAHORE** · Jalandhar · Ludhiana · Chandigarh · Nahan

Lashkar Gah · Gereshk · Kandahar · Khogiani Sani · Darwazaghey · Zhob · Sambaza · Piplan · Rabwah · Shekhupura · **FAISALABAD** · Jaranwala · Kasur · Firozpur · Moga · PUNJAB · **LUDHIANA** · Jagraon · Ambala · Jagadhri

Khash · Qalat · Chaman · TOBA KAKAR RANGE · Lakaband · Dera Ismail Khan · Jhang Sadar · Gojra · Toba Tek Singh · Rattoki · Dipalpur · Maler Kotla · Patiala · Yamunanagar

Zabol · Zaranj · DASHT-E MARGOW · RIGESTAN · Gwal Haidarzai · Gumal · Bhakkar · Leiah · Chichawatni · Kamalia · **Sahiwal** · Pakpattan · Muktsar · Bhatinda · **Patiala** · Mansa · Thanesar · SAHARANPUR

Chah Borjak · Rodbar · GOWD-E ZEREH · Muslimbagh · Loralai · Mekhtar · Manzai · Kot Addu · Khanewal · Mandi Burewala · Vihari · Chishtian Mandi · Bahawalnagar · Ganganagar · Kaithal · Jind · PRADESH

Mirjaveh · DARVACHEH-YE HAMUN · Landay · Pishin · Duki · Barkhan · **MULTAN** · Muzaffargarh · Hasilpur · Harunabad · Hanumangarh · Sirsa · Panipat · Sonipat · Yamuna

Nehbandan · Char Borjak · Bahram Chah · **Quetta** · Sibi · SULAIMAN RANGE · Dera Ghazi Khan · Kahror Pakka · **Bahawalpur** · Anupgarh · Suratgarh · HARYANA · Hisar · Rohtak · **DELHI**

Zabol · Zahedan · Bela · Mastung · Bolan · Jampur · Rajanpur · Ahmadpur East · Sardarshahr · Rajgarh · Bhiwani · **New Delhi** · Faridabad

Zahedan · Nok Kundi · Yakmach · Kharan · Surab · Bhag · Dera Bugti · Khanpur · Sadiqabad · THAR DESERT · Bikaner · Ratangarh · Churu · Jhunjhunun · Narnaul · Rewari

Ladiz · Kalat · Dalbandin · Nushki · Pishin Lora · Kashmor · Rahimyar Khan · Nokhamandi · Fatehpur · Sujangarh · Sikar · Nawalgarh · **Alwar**

Khash · Dalbandin · BALUCHISTAN · Jacobabad · Shahdadkot · Ghotki · Ramgarh · Phalodi · Nagaur · Makrana · Sambhar Salt Lake · Dausa · Hindaun

Mirjaveh · Qila Ladgasht · Kharan · Shikarpur · Sukkur · GREAT INDIAN DESERT · Nagaur · Kuchaman · **INDIA**

Saravan · Hurmagai · Khuzdar · Rohri · Khairpur · Jaisalmer · Kishangarh · Gangapur · Tonk

Panjgur · Hamun-i-Mashkel · Kambar · Larkana · MOENJODARO · Mehar · Sam · Ajmer · Nasirabad · **JAIPUR** · Tonk

Shahbaz Kalat · Jebri · KIRTHAR RANGE · Dadu · Khewari · Pali · Beawar · Sawai Madhopur · Sheopur

CENTRAL MAKRAN RANGE · Bazdar · Rungani · Bela · Sehwan · **Nawabshah** · Barmer · Jalor · **Jodhpur** · Balotra · Luni · Pali · RAJASTHAN · **Bhilwara** · Bundi · **Kota** · Baran

Nahang · Ispikan · Hirok · Sami · Shahdadpur · Sanghar · Jalor · Siroh · Chittaurgarh · Nimbahera · Nimach · Jhalawar

Turbat · Kech · Sami · Uthal · **Nawabshah** · Tando Adam · Siroh · Abu Road · Mandsaur · ARAVALI RANGE

Bahu Kalat · Pidarak · Dasht · SIND · Mirpur Khas · Umarkot · Udaipur · Dungarpur · MADHYA PRADESH

Suntsar · Pasni · Ormara · **HYDERABAD** · Tando Allahyar · Mithi · Disa · Palanpur · Ratlam · Ujjain

Gwadar · MAKRAN COAST · Kotri · Tando Muhammad Khan · Tharad · Siddhapur · Himatnagar · **INDORE** · Dewas

Malir Cantonment · Matli · Talhar · Badin · Radhanpur · Visnagar · Modasa · Dohad

Sonmiani Bay · Hab Chauki · Jati · Sujawal · Shahbandar · Mahesana · Kadi · Kalol · **AHMADABAD** · Godhra

KARACHI · Gharo · RANN OF KUTCH · GUJARAT · Tropic of Cancer · Viramgam · Dholka · Nadiad · Anand · **Vadodara**

ARABIAN SEA · GULF OF KUTCH · Dhandhuka · Petlad · Khambhat · Dabhoi

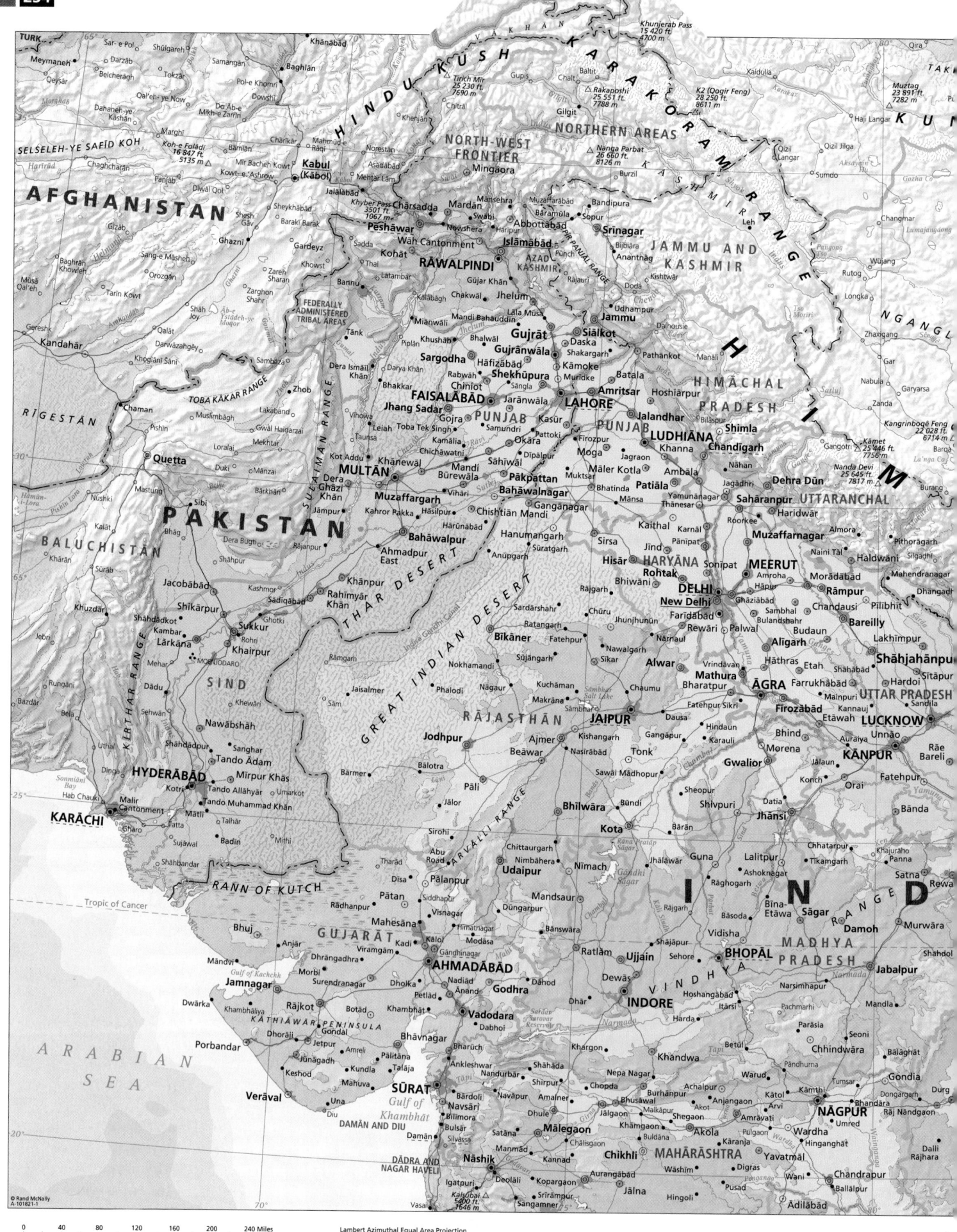

0   40   80   120   160   200   240 Miles
0 40 80 120 160 200 240 280 320 360 400 Kilometers

Lambert Azimuthal Equal Area Projection
Scale 1:8,000,000
One inch to 128 miles
One cm to 80 km

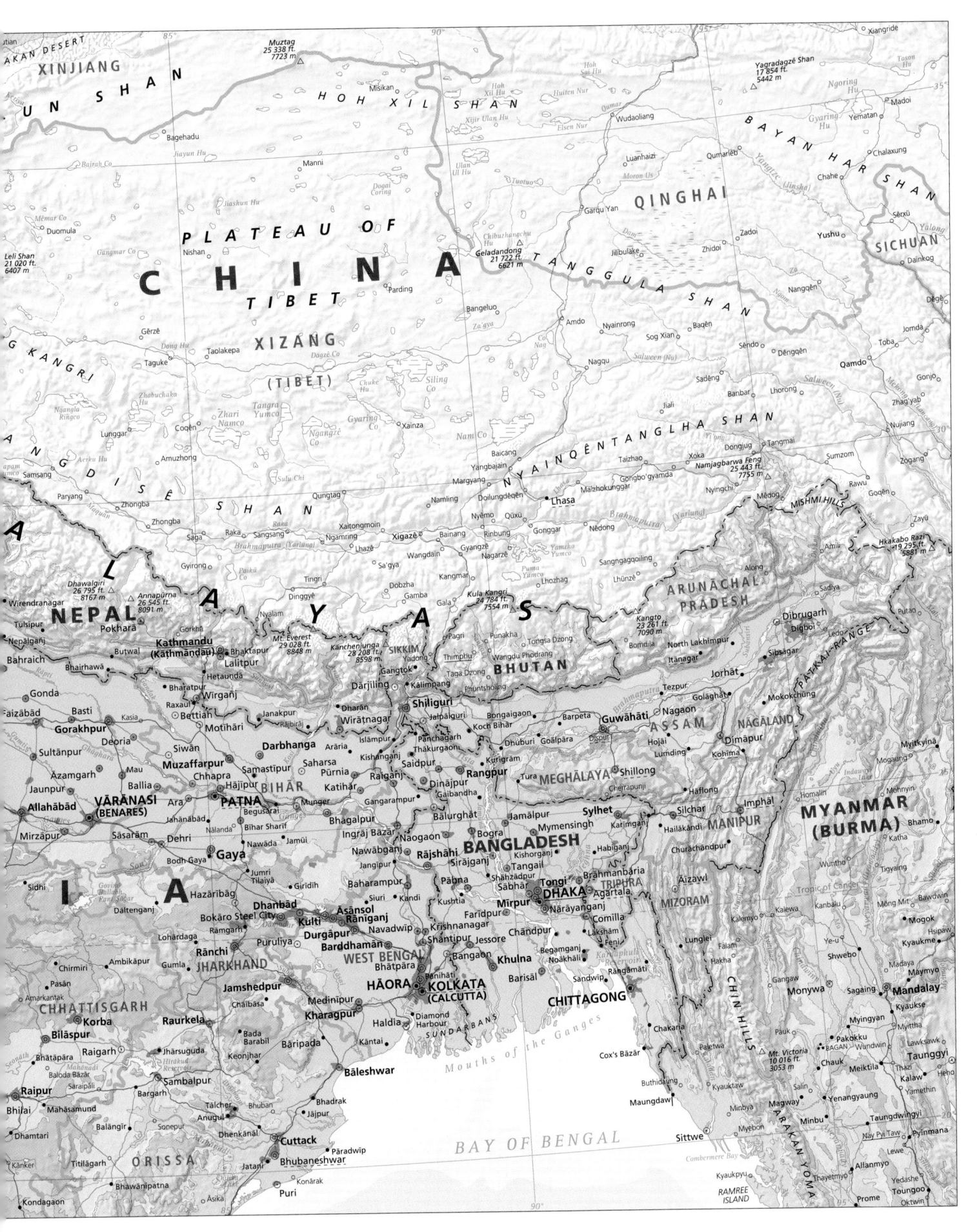

BAY OF BENGAL

© Rand McNally
A-101815-1

Lambert Azimuthal Equal Area Projection
Scale 1:8,000,000
One inch to 128 miles
One cm to 80 km

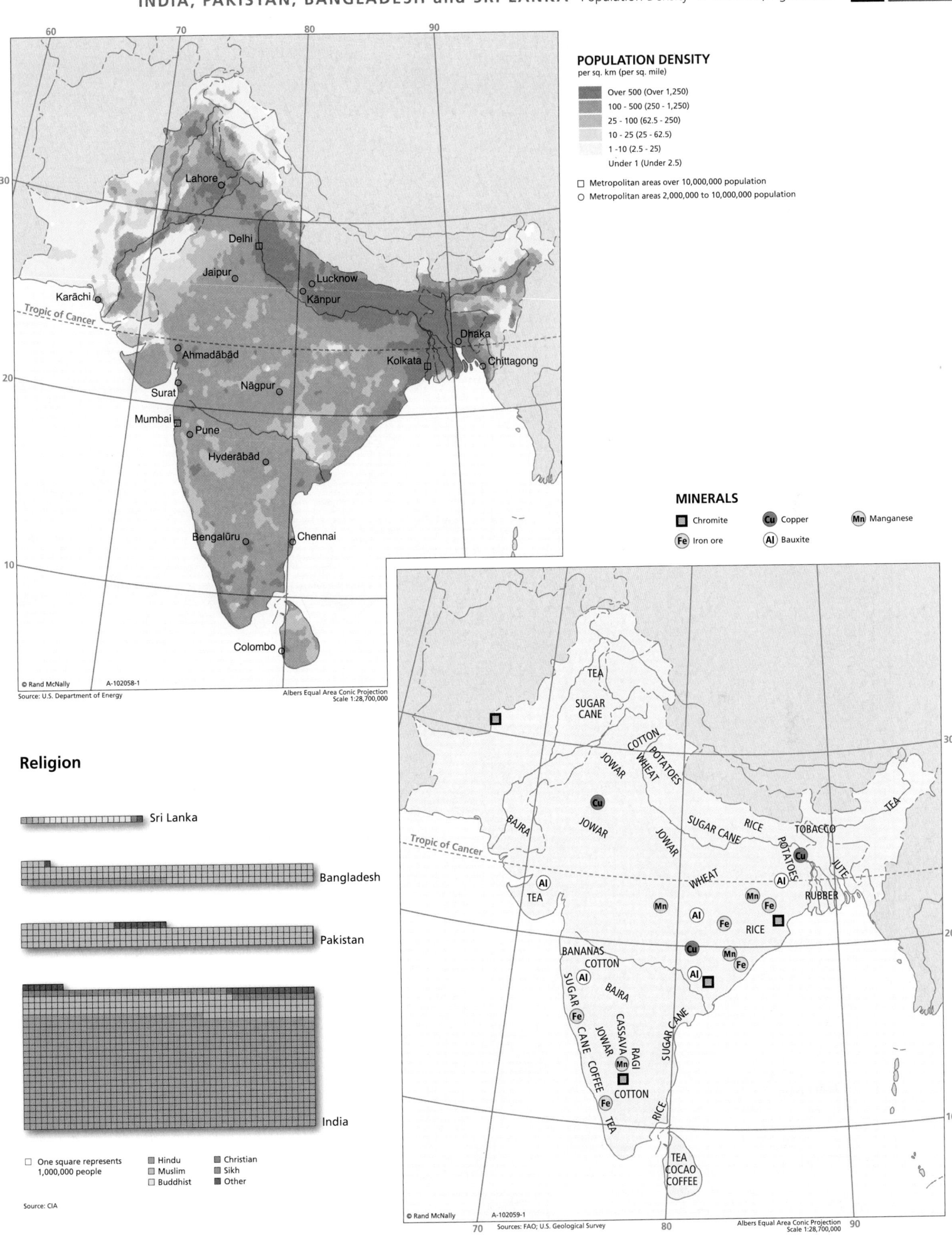

POPULATION DENSITY
per sq. km (per sq. mile)

- Over 500 (Over 1,250)
- 100 - 500 (250 - 1,250)
- 25 - 100 (62.5 - 250)
- 10 - 25 (25 - 62.5)
- 1 - 10 (2.5 - 25)
- Under 1 (Under 2.5)

□ Metropolitan areas over 10,000,000 population

○ Metropolitan areas 2,000,000 to 10,000,000 population

MINERALS

- ■ Chromite
- Cu Copper
- Mn Manganese
- Fe Iron ore
- Al Bauxite

Religion

Sri Lanka

Bangladesh

Pakistan

India

□ One square represents 1,000,000 people

- Hindu
- Christian
- Muslim
- Sikh
- Buddhist
- Other

Source: CIA

© Rand McNally   A-102058-1

Source: U.S. Department of Energy

Albers Equal Area Conic Projection
Scale 1:28,700,000

© Rand McNally   A-102059-1

Sources: FAO; U.S. Geological Survey

Albers Equal Area Conic Projection
Scale 1:28,700,000

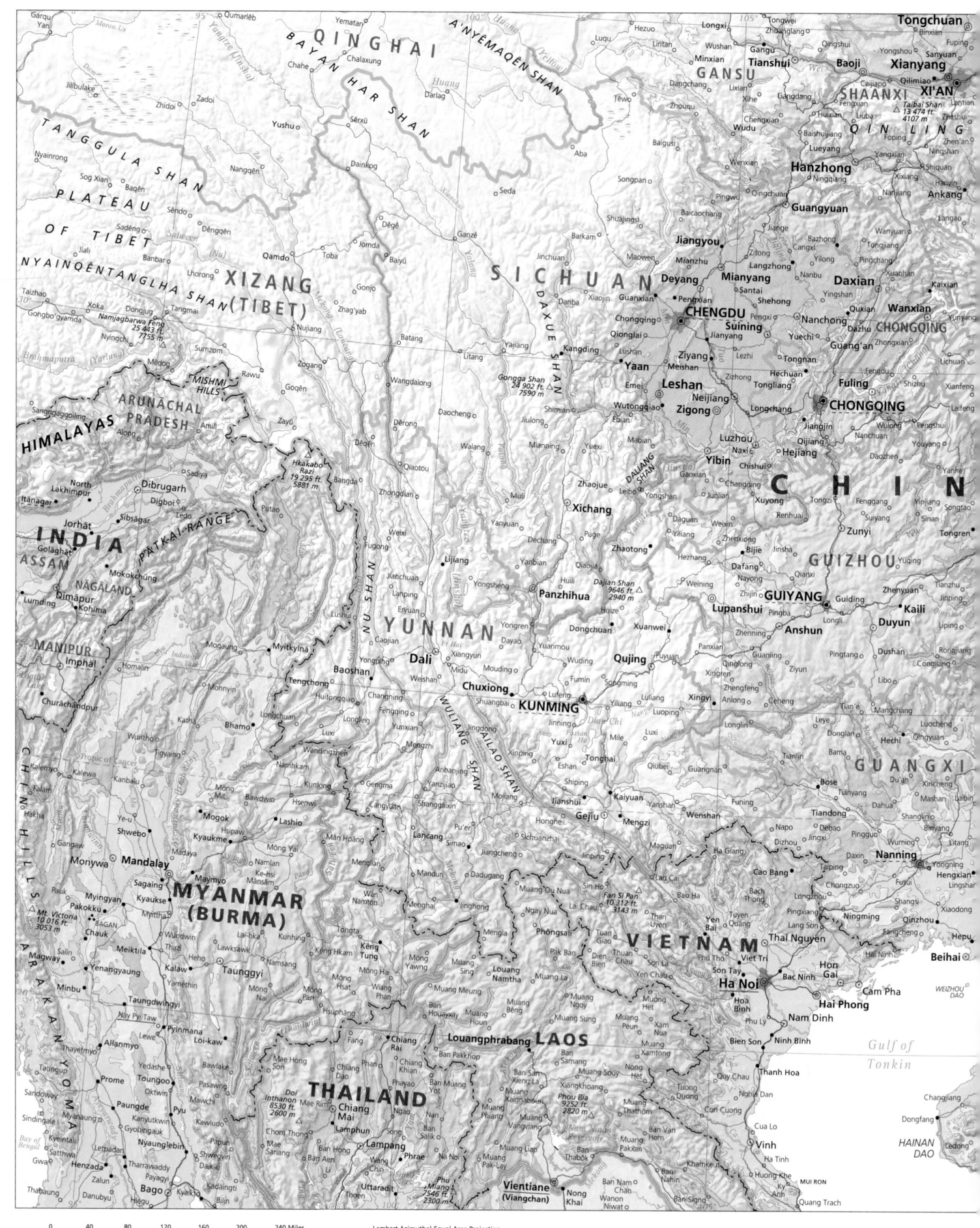

QINGHAI

A'NYEMAQEN SHAN

GANSU

SHAANXI

Tongchuan

Xianyang

XI'AN

QIN LING

Hanzhong

Ankang

SICHUAN

CHENGDU

CHONGQING

CHONGQING

XIZANG (TIBET)

PLATEAU OF TIBET

TANGGULA SHAN

NYAINQENTANGLHA SHAN

CHINA

GUIZHOU

GUIYANG

HIMALAYAS

ARUNACHAL PRADESH

INDIA

ASSAM

NAGALAND

MANIPUR

PAI KAI RANGE

YUNNAN

Dali

KUNMING

GUANGXI

Nanning

Beihai

CHIN HILLS

MYANMAR
(BURMA)

Mandalay

ARAKAN YOMA

Nay Pyi Taw

THAILAND

Chiang Mai

LAOS

Louangphrabang

VIETNAM

Ha Noi

Hai Phong

Vientiane
(Viangchan)

Gulf of
Tonkin

HAINAN
DAO

Bay of
Bengal

Scale 1:8,000,000
Lambert Azimuthal Equal Area Projection
One inch to 128 miles
One cm to 80 km

0   40   80   120   160   200   240 Miles
0 40 80 120 160 200 240 280 320 360 400 Kilometers

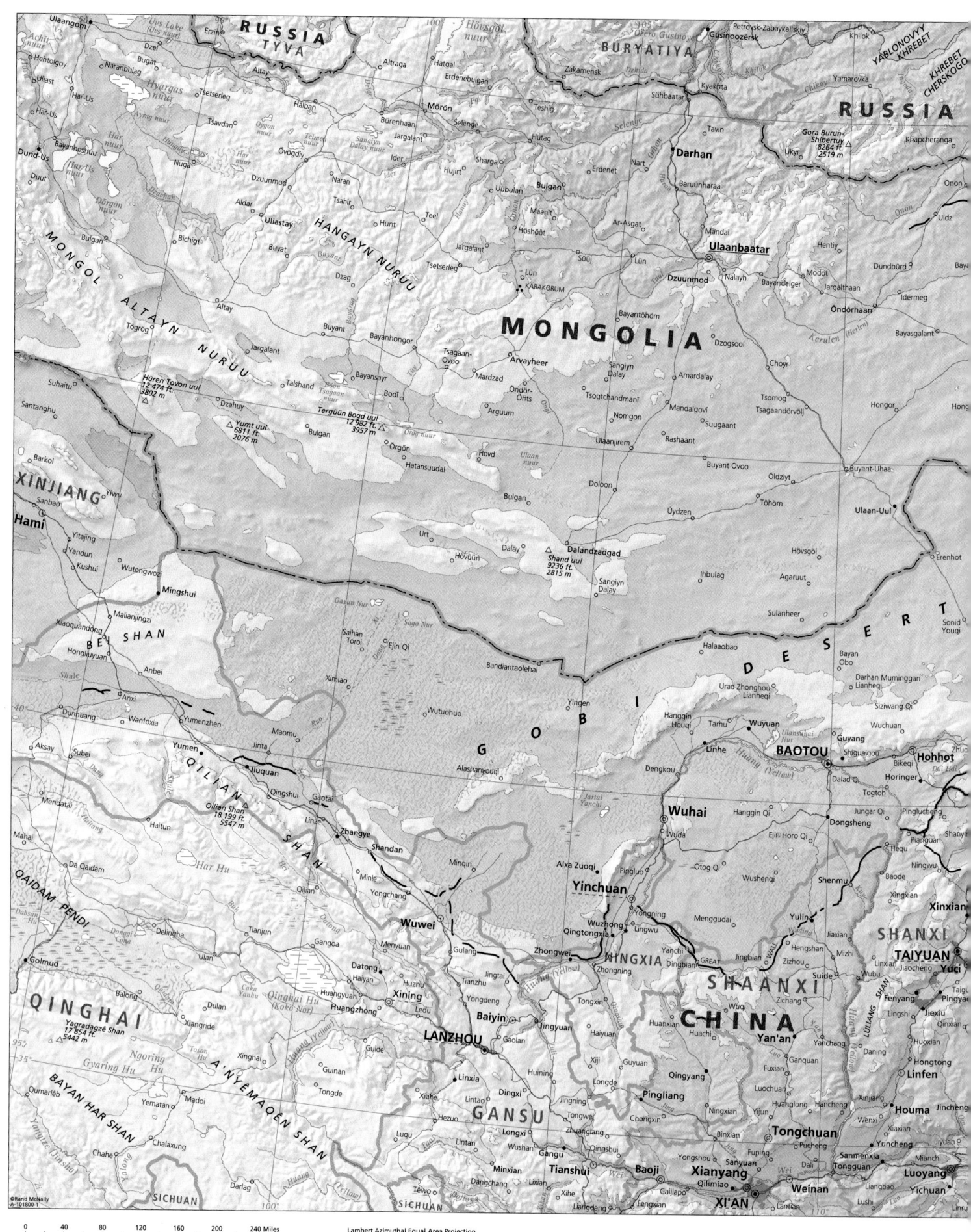

0	40	80	120	160	200	240 Miles

0	40	80	120	160	200	240	280	320	360	400 Kilometers

Lambert Azimuthal Equal Area Projection
Scale 1:8,000,000
One inch to 128 miles
One cm to 80 km

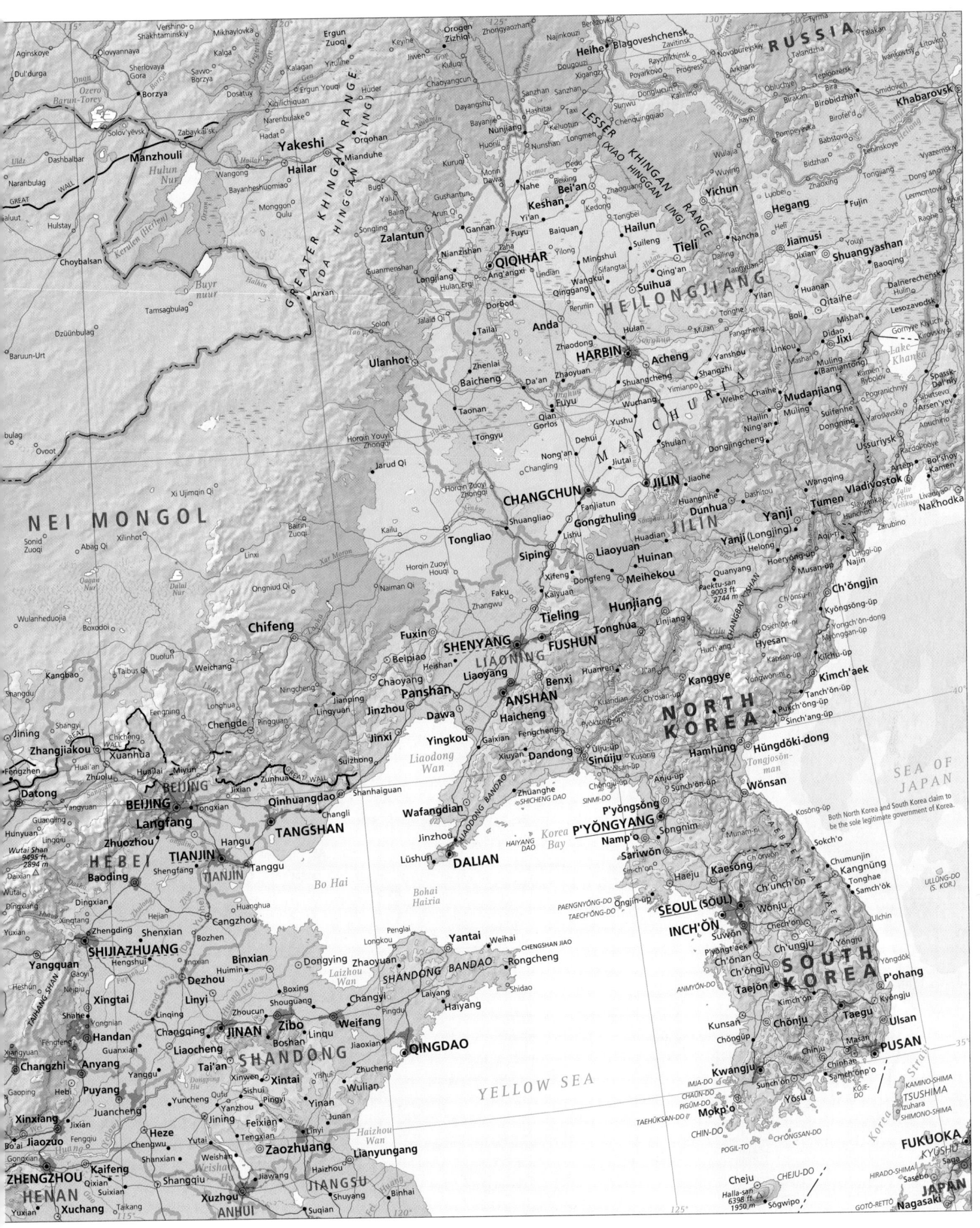

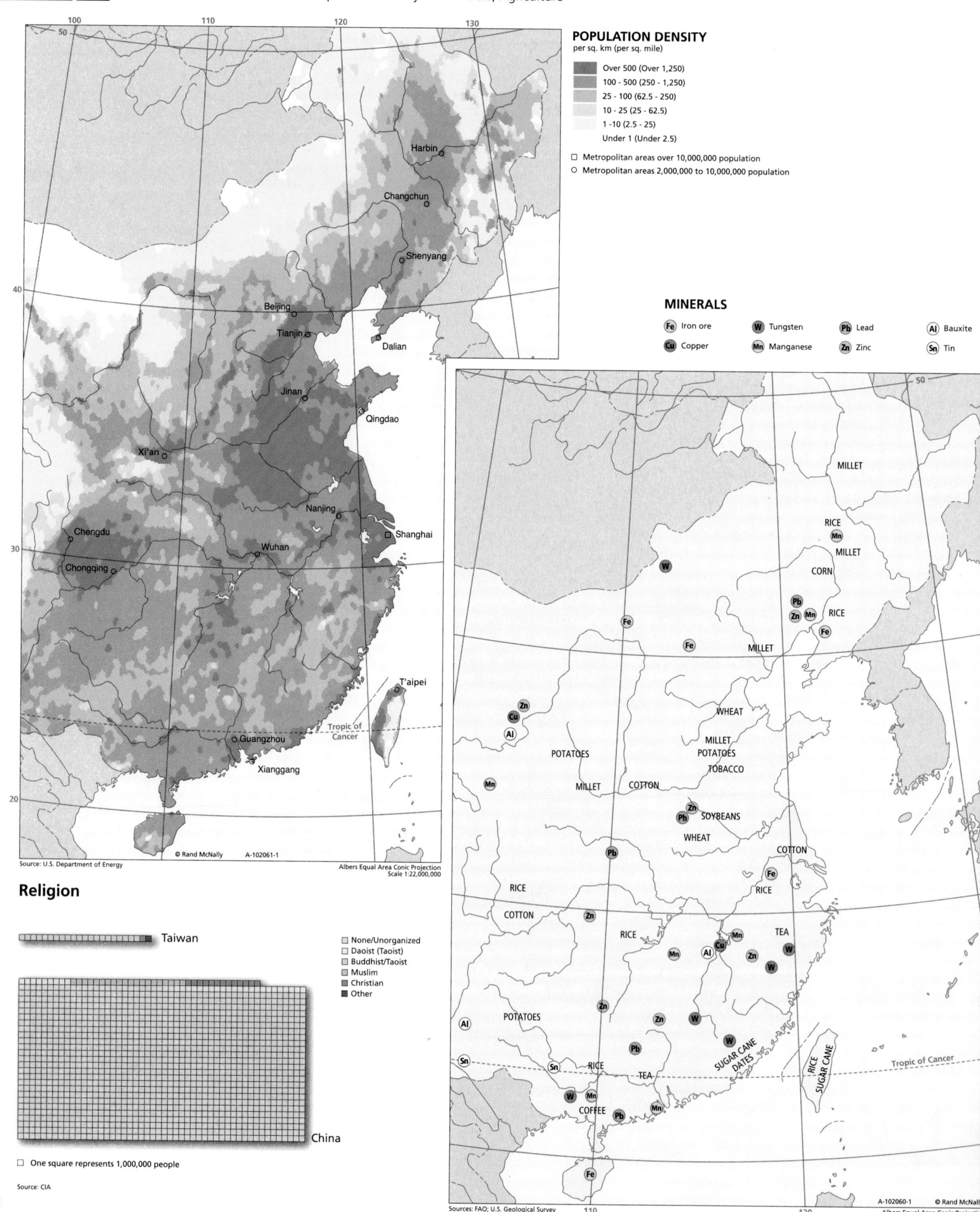

POPULATION DENSITY
per sq. km (per sq. mile)

- Over 500 (Over 1,250)
- 100 - 500 (250 - 1,250)
- 25 - 100 (62.5 - 250)
- 10 - 25 (25 - 62.5)
- 1 - 10 (2.5 - 25)
- Under 1 (Under 2.5)

□ Metropolitan areas over 10,000,000 population
○ Metropolitan areas 2,000,000 to 10,000,000 population

MINERALS

- Fe Iron ore
- Cu Copper
- W Tungsten
- Mn Manganese
- Pb Lead
- Zn Zinc
- Al Bauxite
- Sn Tin

Source: U.S. Department of Energy

© Rand McNally A-102061-1

Albers Equal Area Conic Projection
Scale 1:22,000,000

Religion

Taiwan

China

□ One square represents 1,000,000 people

□ None/Unorganized
□ Daoist (Taoist)
□ Buddhist/Taoist
□ Muslim
■ Christian
■ Other

Source: CIA

Sources: FAO; U.S. Geological Survey

A-102060-1   © Rand McNally

Albers Equal Area Conic Projectio
Scale 1:22,000,000

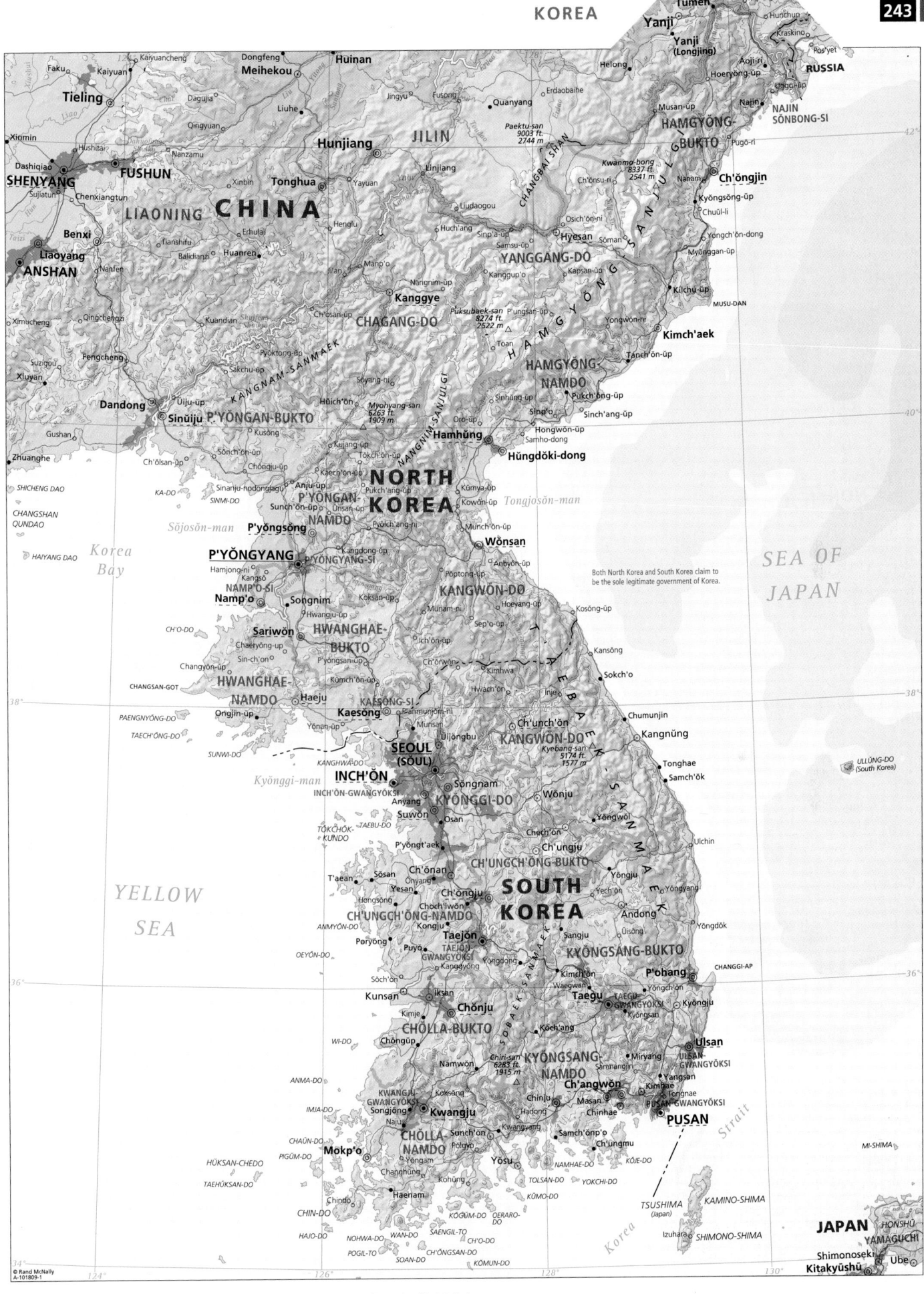

0 20 40 60 80 100 120 Miles
0 20 40 60 80 100 120 140 160 180 200 Kilometers

Lambert Conformal Conic Projection
Scale 1:4,000,000
One inch to 64 miles
One cm to 40 km

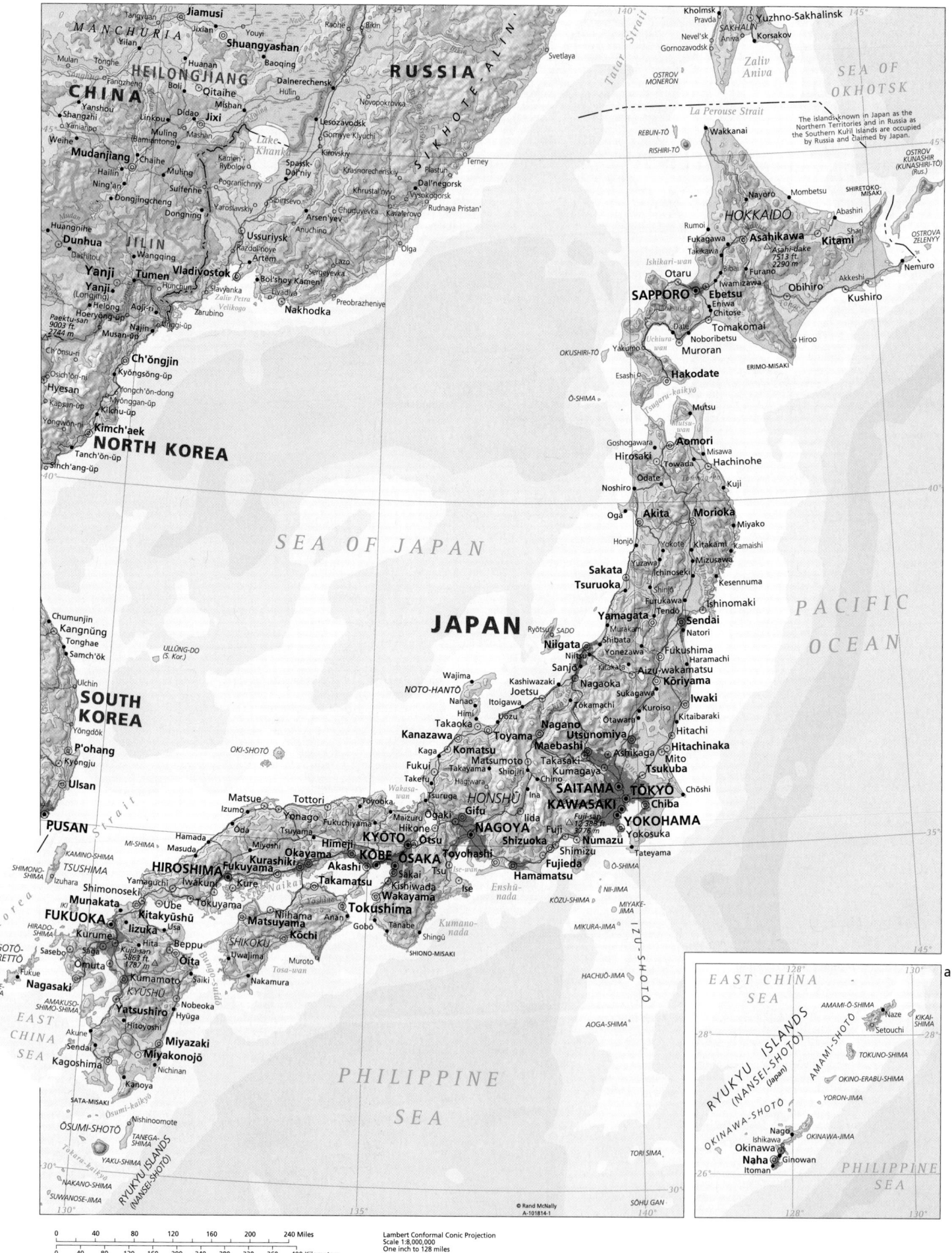

MANCHURIA

RUSSIA

SEA OF OKHOTSK

CHINA

HEILONGJIANG

JILIN

Jiamusi
Shuangyashan

SAKHALIN

Yuzhno-Sakhalinsk
Kholmsk
Korsakov

La Perouse Strait

The islands known in Japan as the Northern Territories and in Russia as the Southern Kuril Islands are occupied by Russia and claimed by Japan.

Wakkanai

HOKKAIDŌ

OSTROVA ZELENYY

OSTROV KUNASHIR (KUNASHIRI-TŌ) (Rus.)

NORTH KOREA

Vladivostok
Nakhodka

Asahikawa
Kitami
Nemuro

SAPPORO
Ebetsu
Kushiro

Muroran
Hakodate

SEA OF JAPAN

JAPAN

Aomori

PACIFIC OCEAN

Akita
Morioka

Sendai

HONSHŪ

Niigata
Fukushima
Kōriyama
Iwaki

Kanazawa
Nagano
Utsunomiya

SAITAMA
TOKYO
KAWASAKI
YOKOHAMA
Chiba

SOUTH KOREA

PUSAN

KYŌTO
NAGOYA
KŌBE
ŌSAKA

Fuji-san 12,388 ft 3776 m

HIROSHIMA

SHIKOKU

FUKUOKA

Nagasaki

KYŪSHŪ

Kagoshima

RYUKYU ISLANDS (NANSEI-SHOTŌ)

EAST CHINA SEA

PHILIPPINE SEA

© Rand McNally
A-101814-1

Lambert Conformal Conic Projection
Scale 1:8,000,000
One inch to 128 miles
One cm to 80 km

0 40 80 120 160 200 240 Miles
0 40 80 120 160 200 240 280 320 360 400 Kilometers

Inset map:

EAST CHINA SEA

128° 130° a

RYUKYU ISLANDS (NANSEI-SHOTŌ) (Japan)

AMAMI-Ō-SHIMA
Naze
KIKAI-SHIMA
Setouchi

AMAMI-SHOTŌ

TOKUNO-SHIMA

OKINO-ERABU-SHIMA

YORON-JIMA

OKINAWA-SHOTŌ

Nago
Ishikawa
OKINAWA-JIMA

Okinawa
Naha
Ginowan
Itoman

PHILIPPINE SEA

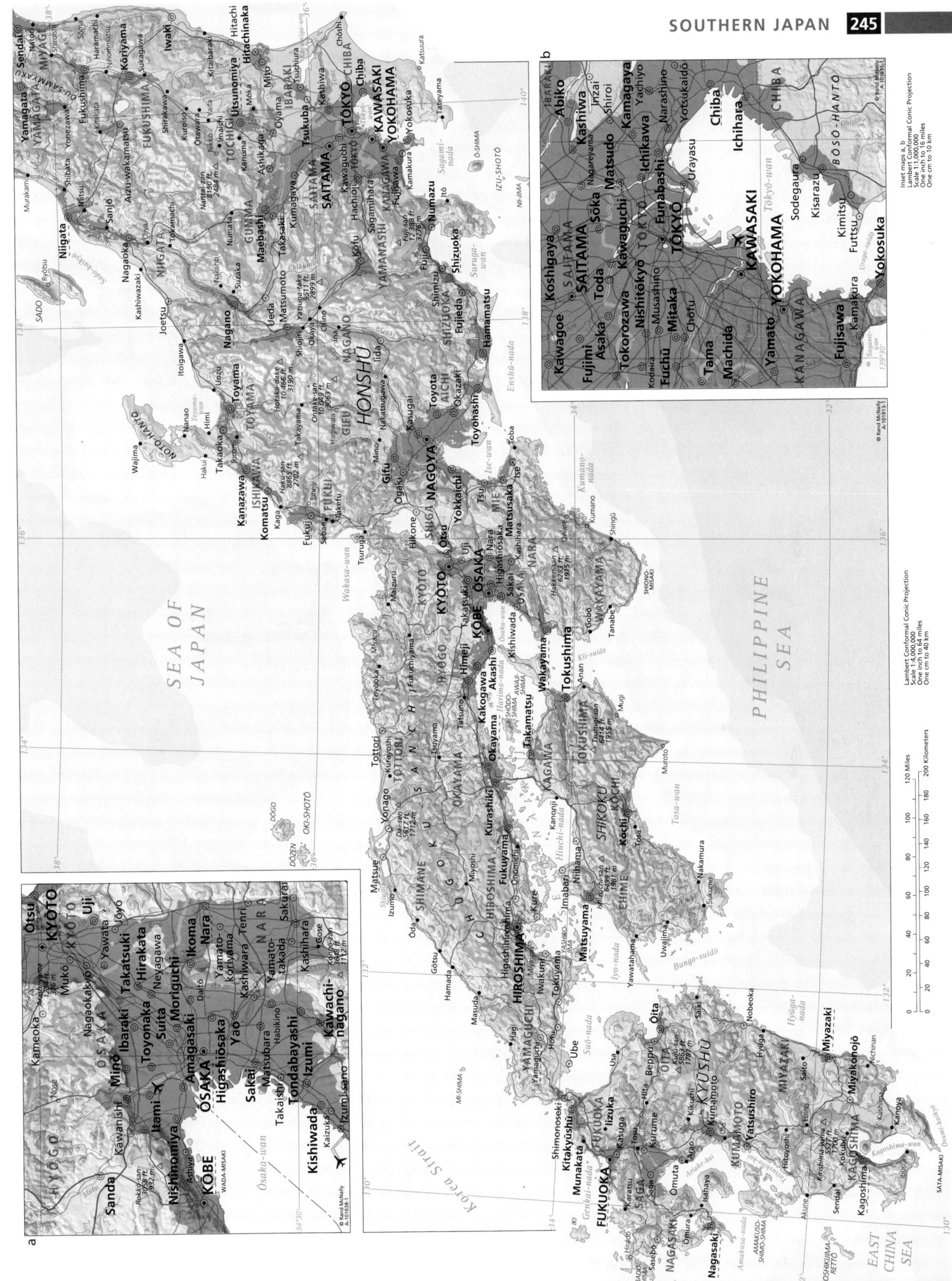

SEA OF JAPAN

HONSHŪ

PHILIPPINE SEA

EAST CHINA SEA

Korea Strait

Inset maps a, b
Lambert Conformal Conic Projection
Scale 1:1,000,000
One inch to 16 miles
One cm to 10 km

Lambert Conformal Conic Projection
Scale 1:4,000,000
One inch to 64 miles
One cm to 40 km

120 Miles   200 Kilometers

© Rand McNally
A-101813-1

Major Labels

GUANGXI
GUANGDONG
HAINAN
CHINA
YUNNAN
MYANMAR (BURMA)
LAOS
THAILAND
VIETNAM
CAMBODIA
INDOCHINA
INDIA
MIZORAM
CHITTAGONG
BNGL
CHIN HILLS
ARAKAN YOMA

Water Bodies

SOUTH CHINA SEA
Gulf of Tonkin
Gulf of Thailand
Gulf of Martaban
ANDAMAN SEA
BAY OF BENGAL
North Channel
Preparis South Channel
Coco Channel
Ten Degree Channel
Duncan Passage
MERGUI ARCHIPELAGO

Selected Cities and Towns

Guixian, Yulin, Nanning, Zhanjiang, Beihai, Haikou, Sanya, Cam Pha, Hon Gai, Hai Phong, Ha Nôi, Nam Dinh, Thanh Hoa, Vinh, Da Nang, Hue, Dong Ha, Quang Ngai, Quy Nhon, Nha Trang, Phan Rang, Phan Thiet, Da Lat, Bien Hoa, HO CHI MINH CITY (SAIGON), Vung Tau, My Tho, Can Tho, Ca Mau

Mandalay, Mogok, Lashio, Taunggyi, Monywa, Meiktila, Pyinmana, Toungoo, Bago, YANGON (RANGOON), Moulmein, Pathein, Sittwe, Mawlamyine, Dawei, Mergui, Kawthaung

Chiang Mai, Chiang Rai, Lampang, Uttaradit, Phitsanulok, Nakhon Sawan, Khon Kaen, Udon Thani, Nong Khai, Nakhon Ratchasima, BANGKOK (KRUNG THEP), Samut Prakan, Nakhon Pathom, Chon Buri, Rayong, Chanthaburi, Surat Thani, Chumphon, Hua Hin, Prachuap Khiri Khan, Ranong

Vientiane (Viangchan), Louangphrabang, Savannakhét, Pakxé, Ubon Ratchathani

Phnom Penh (Phnum Pénh), Siĕmréab, Bătdâmbâng, Kâmpóng Saôm, Krâchéh, Kâmpóng Cham

Port Blair, **ANDAMAN AND NICOBAR ISLANDS** (India)

Physical Features

△ Wuzhi Shan 6125 ft. 1867 m
△ Fan Si Pan 10312 ft. 3143 m
△ Phou Bia 9252 ft. 2820 m
△ Ngoc Linh 8524 ft. 2598 m
△ Phu Miang 7546 ft. 2300 m
△ Doi Inthanon 8530 ft. 2600 m
△ Three Pagodas Pass 3215 ft. 982 m
△ Mt. Victoria 10016 ft. 3053 m
△ Phnum Aôral 5948 ft. 1813 m

ANNAM PLATEAU
PHANOM DONGRAK RANGE
CHUÔR PHNUM KRAVANH
BILAUKTAUNG RANGE
DAWNA RANGE
Tropic of Cancer
ISTHMUS OF KRA
Mekong
Chao Phraya
Irrawaddy
Salween
Tonle Sap

Islands

HAINAN DAO, LEIZHOU BANDAO, WEIZHOU DAO
CON SON, DAO PHU QUOC, KO CHANG, KO KUT, KO SAMUI, KO PHANGAN, KO TAO
RAMREE ISLAND, CHEDUBA ISLAND, PAGODA POINT
COCO ISLANDS, NARCONDAM ISLAND, BARREN ISLAND
NORTH ANDAMAN, MIDDLE ANDAMAN, SOUTH ANDAMAN, LITTLE ANDAMAN, CAR NICOBAR ISLAND
KADAN KYUN, DAUNG KYUN, LANBI KYUN, CLARA ISLAND, ZADETKYI KYUN

---

0 40 80 120 160 200 240 Miles
0 40 80 120 160 200 240 280 320 360 400 Kilometers

Lambert Azimuthal Equal Area Projection
Scale 1:8,000,000
One inch to 128 miles
One cm to 80 km

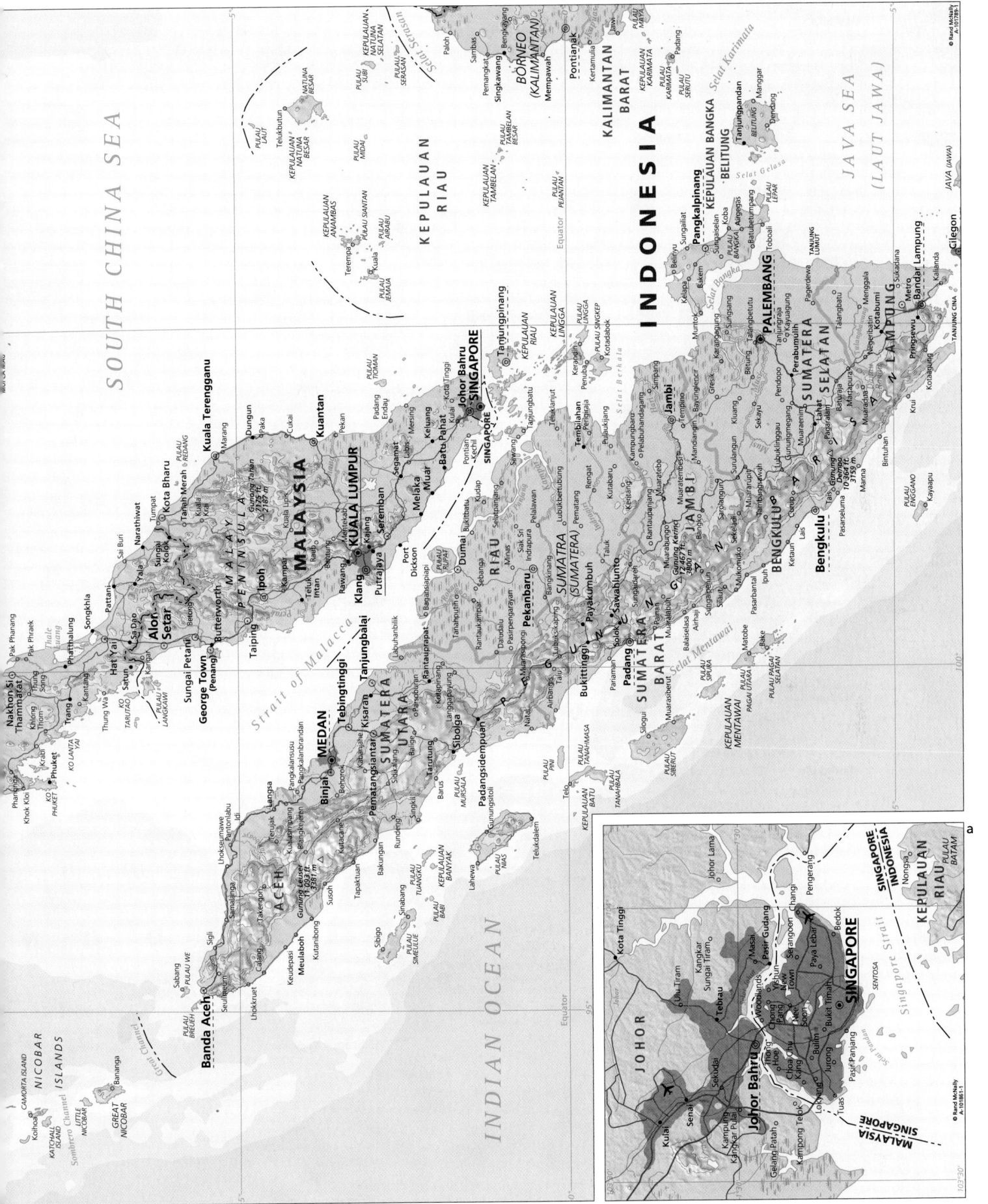

SOUTH CHINA SEA

INDONESIA

JAVA SEA
(LAUT JAWA)

JAVA (JAWA)

BORNEO
(KALIMANTAN)

KALIMANTAN
BARAT

KEPULAUAN
RIAU

KEPULAUAN BANGKA
BELITUNG

Pangkalpinang

PALEMBANG

SUMATERA
SELATAN

LAMPUNG

Bandar Lampung

Cilegon

MALAYSIA

MALAY PENINSULA

KUALA LUMPUR

Kuala Terengganu

SINGAPORE

Johor Bahru

Strait of Malacca

MEDAN

SUMATERA
UTARA

ACEH

Banda Aceh

SUMATERA
(SUMATERA)

RIAU

Pekanbaru

SUMATERA
BARAT

Padang

JAMBI

Jambi

BENGKULU

Bengkulu

INDIAN OCEAN

NICOBAR
ISLANDS

GREAT
NICOBAR

LITTLE
NICOBAR

Phuket

Equator

Inset map a
Lambert Conformal Conic Projection
Scale 1:1,000,000
One inch to 16 miles
One cm to 10 km

a

SINGAPORE

Johor Bahru

JOHOR

SINGAPORE
INDONESIA

MALAYSIA
SINGAPORE

KEPULAUAN
RIAU

PULAU
BATAM

Singapore Strait

THAILAND

SOUTH CHINA SEA

Thung Wa · Songkhla
Hat Yai
Satun · Sa Dao · Yala · Narathiwat
Pattani · Sai Buri
PULAU LANGKAWI
Sungai Petani
Alor Setar · Sungai Kolok · Tumpat · Kota Bharu
Betong · Tanah Merah
George Town (Penang) · Butterworth · Kuala Krai · Kuala Terengganu
PULAU REDANG
Taiping
MALAY PENINSULA · Marang
Ipoh · △ Gunong Tahan 7175 ft. 2187 m · Dungun
Kampar · Paka
Kuala Lipis · Cukai
MALAYSIA · **Kuantan**
Teluk Intan · Raub · Bentung
Rawang · Mentekab · Pekan
Klang · **KUALA LUMPUR** · Kajang · Padang · Endau
Tanjungbalai · Putrajaya · Seremban · PULAU TIOMAN
Labuhanbilik · Port Dickson · Segamat · Labis · Mersing
Rantauprapat · Bagansiapiapi · Melaka · Keluang
Kotapinang · Muar · Batu Pahat · Kota Tinggi
Langgapayung · PULAU RUPAT · Pontian Kechil · Kulai
SUMATERA UTARA · Tanahputih · Dumai · Bukitbatu · **Johor Bahru**
Daludalu · Sebanga · Kudap · **SINGAPORE**
Rantaukampar · SINGAPORE
RIAU · Minas · Siak Sri Indrapura · Selatpanjang · Sawang · Tanjungbatu · **Tanjungpinang**
Muarasipongi · Pasirpengaraian · Pelalawan
Pekanbaru · Telukjantan
Lubuksikaping · Lubukbertubung
Payakumbuh · KEPULAUAN LINGGA
Bukittinggi · Pematang · Tembilahan · Kerandin · Penuba · PULAU LINGGA
Pariaman · Taluk · Rengat · Perigiraja · Pulaukijang · Kotadabok
SUMATERA BARAT · Sawahlunto · Solok
Padang · Sungaidareh
Painan · △ Gunung Kerinci 12,467 ft. 3800 m
PULAU SIPURA · Muaralabuh · Rantaupanjang · Muarebo · Muaratembesi · Simpang · Belinyu
Balaiselasa · Airhaji · Sungaipenuh · **JAMBI** · Tempino · Kelapa · Sungailiat
PULAU PAGAI UTARA · Bangko · Mandiangin · Muntok · **Pangkalpinang**
Matobe · Sarolangun · Bayunglencir · Bakem
KEPULAUAN MENTAWAI · Silaut · Sekeladi · Gresik · Karangagung · Sungsang · **KEPULAUAN BANGKA BELITUNG**
Bake · Mukomuko · Pasarbantal · Muararupit · Kluang · Sungaiselan · Koba · Airgegas
BENGKULU · Ipuh · Tambangwah · Sekayu · Betung · **PALEMBANG** · Talangbetutu · Batubetumpang
Ketaun · Lubuklinggau · Pendopo · Talangbetutu · Toboali
Curup · Gunungmegang · Perabumulih · PULAU LEPAR
Bengkulu · Lais · Muaraenim · Kayuagung · Tanjungraja
Tais · △ Gunung Dempo 10,364 ft. 3159 m · Lahat · Pagerdewa
Pasarseluma · Pagaralam · Baturaja · Martapura · Talangbatu
Manna · Muaradua · Menggala
Bintuhan · Danau Ranau · Negeribatin · Kotabumi
PULAU ENGGANO · Krui · Kotaagung · Metro · Sukadana
Kayaapu · Pringsewu · **Bandar Lampung**
LAMPUNG · Kalianda
TANJUNG CINA · Cilegon
KRAKATOA · Serang
PULAU PANAITAN · Labuhan · **DEPOK** · Karawang
TANJUNG CANGKUANG · **BANTEN** · Bogor · Cikampek · Indramayu
Pelabuhanratu · Sukabumi · Cianjur · Klangenang · **Cirebon**
Jampang-kulon · **BANDUNG** · Majalaya · Garut · JAWA BARAT
Sindangbarang · Tasikmalaya · △ Gunung Slamet 11,247 ft. 3428 m
Karangnunggal · Cijulang · **Cilacap** · Purwokerto
Pacitan

KEPULAUAN RIAU

PULAU JEMAJA · Terempa · **KEPULAUAN ANAMBAS** · Telukbutun · **Miri**
PULAU LAUT · **KEPULAUAN NATUNA BESAR** · NATUNA BESAR · Niah
Kuala · PULAU SIANTAN · PULAU AIRABU · PULAU SUBI
PULAU AIRABU · PULAU MIDAI · PULAU SERASAN
KEPULAUAN RIAU · Selat Serasan · Lutong
KEPULAUAN NATUNA SELATAN · KEPULAUAN NATUNA SELATAN
Bintulu · Igan · Mukah · Tubau
PULAU BRUIT · Balingian · Belaga
SARAWAK · Paloh · TANJONG DATU · Sematan · Sarikei · Kapit
KEPULAUAN TAMBELAN · Sibu · **MALAYSIA**
PULAU TAMBELAN BESAR · Sambas · Siluas · Simonjan · Sri Aman · Betong
Kuching · Bau · **UPPER KAPUAS MTS.**
Singkawang · Bengkayang · △ Gunung Niut 5581 ft. 1701 m · Ngabang · Nangabadau · Nangaobat
Mempawah · Sosok · PEGUNUNGAN MULLER
PULAU PEJANTAN · **Pontianak** · Sanggau · Sintang · Longguntur
Equator · Meliau · Kertamula · **KALIMANTAN BARAT** · Nangapinoh · Nangaraun
Jawi · Kapuas · Teratak · PEGUNUNGAN SCHWANER · Tanjungpusu
PULAU MAYA · Telukbatang · Sandai · Kotabaru · Kalasin
KEPULAUAN KARIMATA · Sukadana · Nangatayap · Kualamanjual · △ Bukit Raya 7474 ft. 2278 m · Kualakurun
PULAU KARIMATA · Padang · Serengka · Panahan · Tewah
PULAU SERUTU · Teluk Sukadana · **KALIMANTAN TENGAH** · Batutinggi
Kualapesaguan · Memala · **Palangkaraya**
Kendawangan · Sukaraja · Mabau · Kotawaringin · Sampit
PULAU BAWAL · Kotawaringin · Telegapulang · Mendawai
Matua · **TANJUNG PUTING** · Kumai

JAVA SEA (LAUT JAWA)

GREATER SUNDA
KEPULAUAN KARIMUNJAWA · Tambak · PULAU BAWEAN
JAKARTA · **INDON**...
MADURA
Jepara · Pati · Rembang
SEMARANG · Kudus · Tuban · Bangkalan · Sumenep
Boja · Demak · Cepu · Blega · Pamekasan
Tegal · Pekalongan · **SURABAYA**
JAWA TENGAH · Salatiga · **Surakarta** · Jombang · Selat Madura
Magelang · Madiun · Kedin · **Pasuruan** · Probolinggo
Purworejo · JAWA TIMUR · **Malang** · Situbondo
Yogyakarta · Ponorogo · Kedin · Lumajang · Jember
YOGYAKARTA · Tulungagung · **Blitar** · △ Gunung Semeru 12,060 ft. 3676 m · Genteng

INDIAN OCEAN

JAVA (JAWA)

· Settlement

| 0 | 40 | 80 | 120 | 160 | 200 | 240 Miles |
| 0 | 40 | 80 | 120 | 160 | 200 | 240 | 280 | 320 | 360 | 400 Kilometers |

Lambert Azimuthal Equal Area Projection
Scale 1:8,000,000
One inch to 128 miles
One cm to 80 km

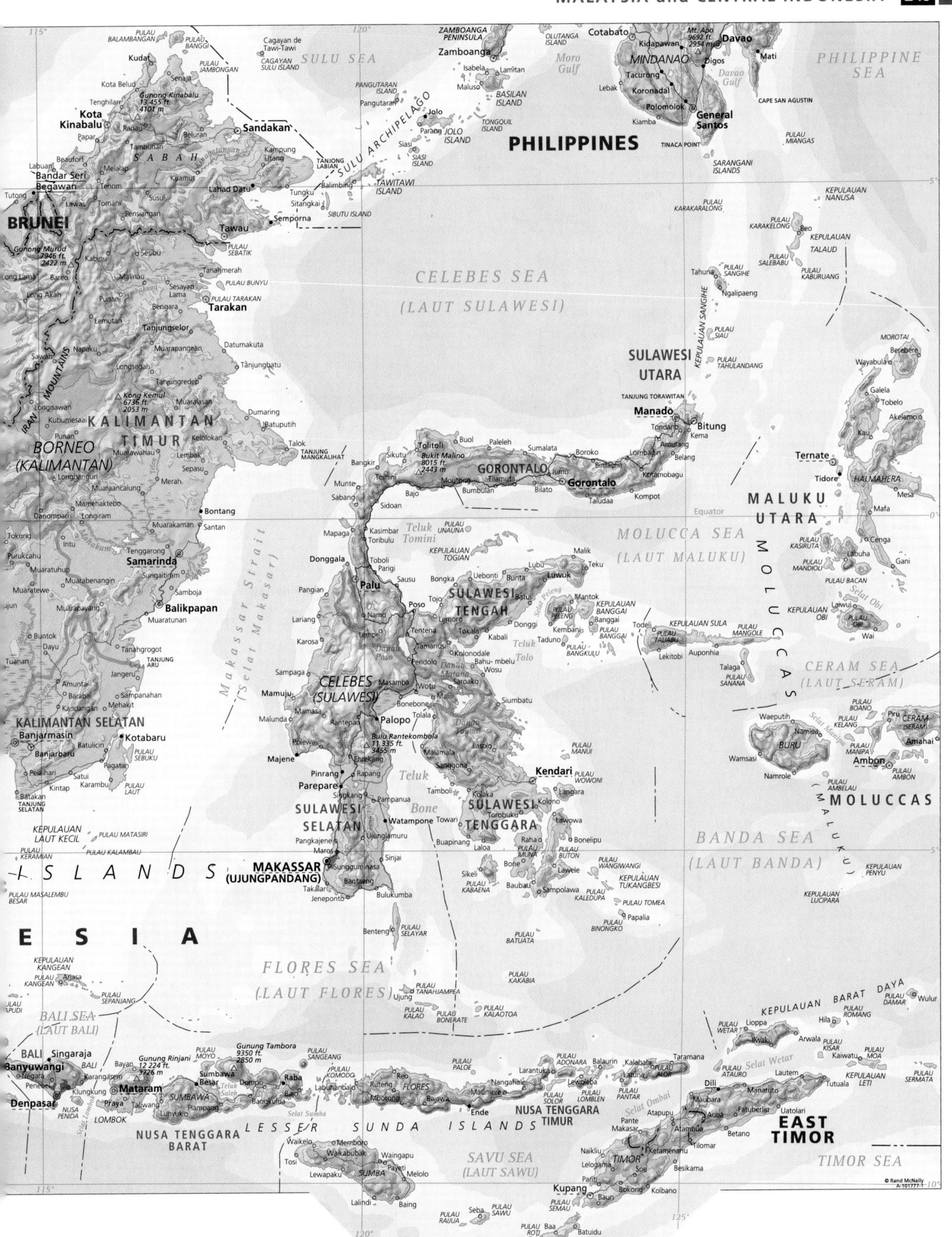

SOUTH CHINA SEA

PHILIPPINE SEA

SULU SEA

CELEBES SEA

PHILIPPINES

LUZON

MINDORO

PANAY

NEGROS

SAMAR

LEYTE

BOHOL

PALAWAN

MINDANAO

BORNEO

MALAYSIA

Inset (top right):

SOUTH CHINA SEA

BATAN ISLANDS
ITBAYAT ISLAND
Basco
BATAN ISLAND
Balintang Channel

AMIANAN ISLAND
Bashi Channel

Luzon Strait

BABUYAN ISLANDS
CALAYAN ISLAND
Calayan
DALUPIRI ISLAND
FUGA ISLAND
BABUYAN ISLAND
CAMIGUIN ISLAND

PHILIPPINE SEA

Pagudpud
Babuyan Channel
PALAUI ISLAND
CAPE BOJEADOR
ESCARPADA POINT
Laoag
San Nicolas
Batac
LUZON
Aparri
Gonzaga
Mt. Sicapoo
7329 ft.
2234 m

© Rand McNally
A-101808-1

Place names on main map (selection):

Pagudpud, CAPE BOJEADOR, Laoag, San Nicolas, Batac, Vigan, Bangued, Candon, Conner, Tabuk, Lubuagan, Aparri, Gonzaga, Tuguegarao City, Ilagan, Bontoc, Mt. Palanan 3976 ft. 1212 m, Mt. Sicapoo 7329 ft. 2234 m, Mt. Pulog 9626 ft. 2934 m, San Fernando, La Trinidad, Baguio, Agno, Lingayen, Dagupan, Santiago, Solano, Bayombong, Maddela, Santa Cruz, San Carlos, Camiling, Tarlac, Guimba, San Jose, Baler, CAPE SAN ILDEFONSO, Palauig, Iba, Angeles, Mt. Pinatubo 5840 ft. 1780 m, San Fernando, Malolos, Meycauayan, Quezon City, MANILA, Pasig, Cavite, Olongapo, Orani, BATAAN PENINSULA, Mariveles, Santa Cruz, San Pablo, Lucban, Balayan, Lipa, Batangas, Lucena, Daet, Naga, Iriga, Legaspi, Sorsogon, Bulusan, Mayon Volcano 8077 ft. 2462 m, Calapan, Mamburao, Mt. Halcon 8481 ft. 2585 m, Mt. Baco 8159 ft. 2487 m, Bongabong, San Jose, Roxas, Kalibo, Tibiao, Iloilo, Bacolod, San Carlos, La Carlota, La Castellana, Binalbagan, Kabankalan, Sipalay, Dumaguete, Bayawan, Tagbilaran, Masbate, Calbayog, Catbalogan, Tacloban, Ormoc, Baybay, Cebu, Mandaue, Lapu-Lapu, Maasin, Surigao, Dinagat, Butuan, Cabadbaran, Gingoog, Cagayan de Oro, Malaybalay, Iligan, Ozamis, Marawi, Pagadian, Dipolog, Zamboanga, Cotabato, Kidapawan, Davao, Tagum, Digos, General Santos, Mt. Apo 9692 ft. 2954 m, Mt. Kaatoan 9501 ft. 2896 m, Mt. Busa 6834 ft. 2083 m, Puerto Princesa, Mt. Mantalingajan 6841 ft. 2085 m, Victoria Peaks 5607 ft. 1709 m, Sandakan

SCARBOROUGH REEF

Scale bars:
0 30 60 90 120 150 180 Miles
0 30 60 90 120 150 180 210 240 270 300 Kilometers

Lambert Conformal Conic Projection
Scale 1:6,000,000
One inch to 96 miles
One cm to 60 km

© Rand McNally
A-101807-1

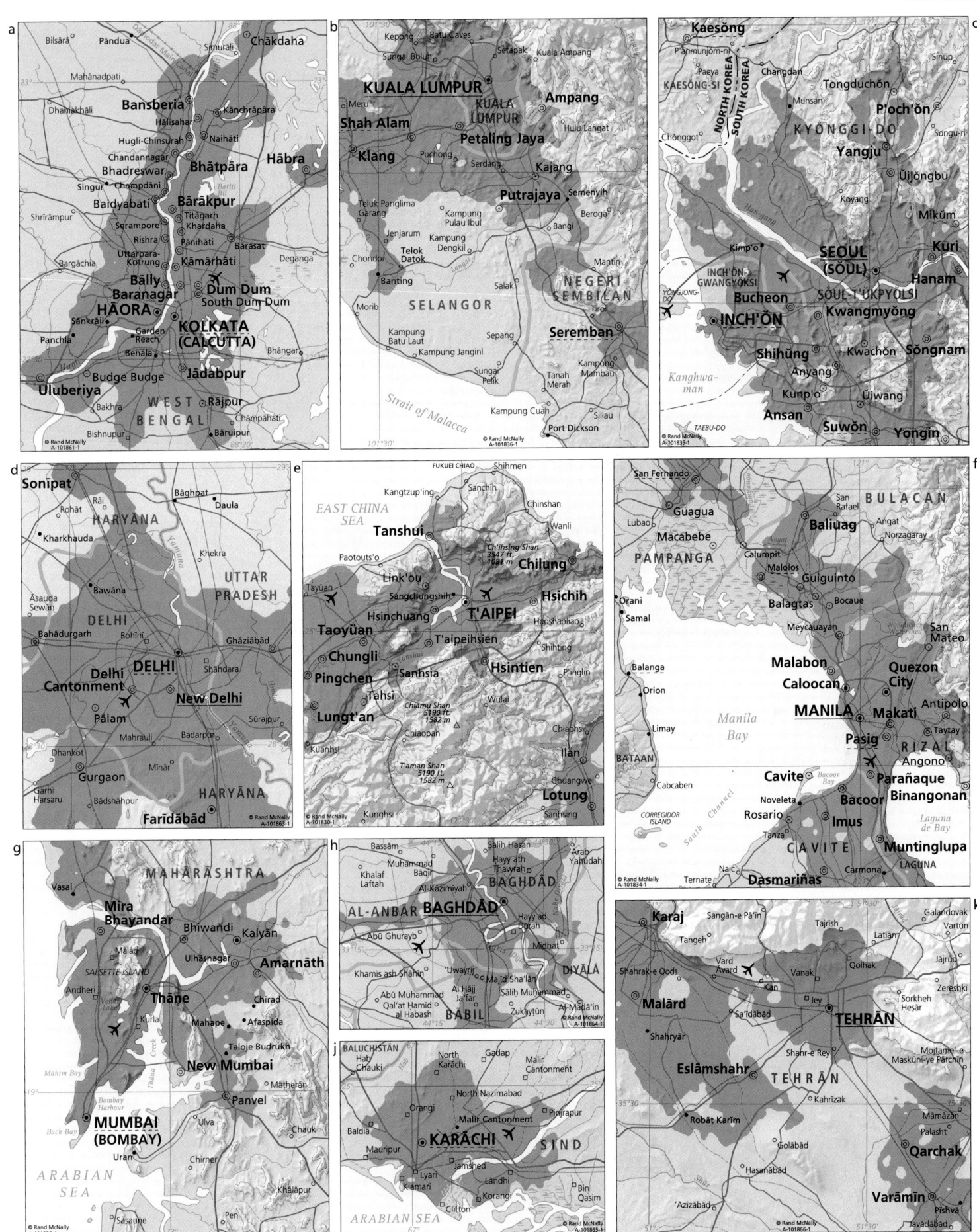

a Bilsárá · Pándua · Simurali · Chákdaha
Mahánadpati · 23° · Dhamákháli
Bansberia · Kánchrápára · Hálisahar · Naihati · Habra · Hugli-Chinsurah · Chandannagar · Bhátpára · Bhadreswar · Champdáni · Bárákpur · Singur · Baidyabáti · Serampore · Titágarh · Khardaha · Rishra · Pánihati · Bárasat · Uttarpára-Kotrung · Kámárháti · Deganga · Bargáchia · Bálly · Dum Dum · Baranagar · South Dum Dum · HÁORA · Sánkráil · KOLKATA (CALCUTTA) · Garden Reach · Panchla · Behála · Bhángar · Uluberia · Budge Budge · Jádabpur · Bakhra · Rájpur · WEST BENGAL · Champáhati · Bishnupur · Báruipur
© Rand McNally A-101861-1

b Kepong · Batu Caves · Batu Bblum · Sungai Bblum · Setapak · Kuala Ampang · Meru · **KUALA LUMPUR** · KUALA LUMPUR · **Ampang** · Hulu Langat · **Shah Alam** · Puchong · **Petaling Jaya** · **Klang** · Serdang · **Kajang** · Teluk Panglima Garang · Kampung Pulau Ibul · **Putrajaya** · Semenyih · Jenjarum · Kampung Dengkil · Bangi · Beroga · Chondoi · **Telok Datok** · Mantin · Salak · **NEGERI** · Banting · **SEMBILAN** · Morib · **SELANGOR** · Sepang · Tiroi · Kampung Batu Laut · Kampung Janginl · Sungai Pelik · **Seremban** · Kampung Mambau · Tanah Merah · Siliau · Kampung Cuah · Port Dickson
Strait of Malacca
© Rand McNally A-101836-1

c **Kaesŏng** · P'anmunjŏm-ni · Sinŭp · Paeya · Changdan · **KAESŎNG-SI** · NORTH KOREA · SOUTH KOREA · **Tongduchŏn** · Chŏnggot · Munsan · **P'och'ŏn** · Songu-ri · **KYŎNGGI-DO** · **Yangju** · Ŭijŏngbu · Koyang · Han-gang · **Mikŭm** · Kimp'o · **Kŭri** · YŎNGJONG-DO · **SEOUL** · Hanam · **INCH'ŎN-** · **(SŎUL)** · **GWANGYŎKSI** · Bucheon · **Kwangmyŏng** · **INCH'ŎN** · SŎUL-T'ŬKPYŎLSI · *Kanghwa-man* · **Shihŭng** · Kwachŏn · **Sŏngnam** · Anyang · **Ŭiwang** · Kunp'o · **Suwŏn** · TAEBU-DO · **Ansan** · **Yongin**
© Rand McNally A-101835-1

d **Sonīpat** · Rái · Bághpat · Daula · Rohát · HARYĀNA · Kharkhauda · Khekra · Ásauda Sewán · Bawána · UTTAR PRADESH · DELHI · **Ghāziābād** · Bahádurgarh · Rohīni · Shāhdara · **Delhi** · **DELHI** · **Cantonment** · Pálam · **New Delhi** · Mahrauli · Súrajpur · Dhankot · Badarpur · Garhi Harsaru · Minár · Gurgaon · Bádsháhpur · HARYĀNA · **Farīdābād**
© Rand McNally A-101863-1

e FUKUEI CHIAO · Shihmen · Kangtzup'ing · Sanchih · EAST CHINA SEA · **Tanshui** · Chinshan · Paotouts'o · Wanli · **Link'ou** · Ch'ihsing Shan 3547 ft, 1081 m · **Chilung** · Táyüan · Sängchungshih · **Hsichih** · **Hsinchuang** · **T'AIPEI** · Hupohaopliao · **Taoyüan** · T'aipeihsien · Shihting · **Chungli** · **Hsintien** · **Pingchen** · Sanhsia · P'inglin · Táhsi · Chiamu Shan 5190 ft, 1582 m · Wulai · **Lungt'an** · Chiaohsi · Chiaopan · Kuanhsi · **Ilan** · T'aman Shan 5190 ft, 1582 m · Ch'uangwei · **Lotung** · Kunghsi · Sanhsing
© Rand McNally A-101830-1

f San Fernando · **Guagua** · San Rafael · **Baliuag** · Lubao · **BULACAN** · Angat · Norzagaray · **Macabebe** · Calumpit · **PAMPANGA** · Malolos · **Guiguinto** · Orani · Balagtas · Bocaue · Samal · **Balanga** · Meycauayan · Nordhern Watershed · San Mateo · Orion · **Malabon** · **Quezon** · **Caloocan** · **City** · Limay · **MANILA** · **Makati** · Antipolo · *Manila Bay* · **Pasig** · RIZAL · Taytay · BATAAN · **Cavite** · Bacoor Bay · **Parañaque** · Angono · Cabcaben · Noveleta · **Bacoor** · **Binangonan** · **Imus** · Rosario · Tanza · *Laguna de Bay* · CORREGIDOR ISLAND · South Channel · CAVITE · **Muntinglupa** · Naic · Carmona · LAGUNA · Ternate · **Dasmariñas**
© Rand McNally A-101834-1

g MAHĀRĀSHTRA · Vasai · **Mira** · **Bhayandar** · **Bhiwandi** · **Kalyān** · Málád · Ulhásnagar · **Amarnáth** · SALSETTE ISLAND · Andheri · **Tháne** · Chirad · Vehār Lake · Kúrla · Mahape · Afaspida · Máhim Bay · **New Mumbai** · Taloje Budrukh · Kúrla · Mátherán · **Panvel** · Ulva · 19° · Bombay Harbour · Chauk · Back Bay · **MUMBAI** · **(BOMBAY)** · Uran · Chirner · Khálápur · *ARABIAN SEA* · Sásaune · Pen
© Rand McNally A-101833-1

h Bassám · Sálih Hasan · 'Arab Yahúdah · Muhammad Báqir · Hayy ath Thawrah · Khalaf Laftah · Al-Kázimīyah · **BAGHDĀD** · **AL-ANBĀR** · **BAGHDĀD** · Hayy ad · Abū Ghurayb · Durah · Khamis ash Shāhin · 'Uwayrij · Midhat · **DIYĀLĀ** · Abū Muhammad · Majid Sha'lán · Qal'at Hamid · Al Hājj · Sálih Muhammad · al Habash · Ja'far · Al-Mādā'in · **BĀBIL** · Zukáytún
© Rand McNally A-101864-1

j BALUCHISTĀN · Hab Chauki · Gadap · Gadap · North Karáchi · Malir Cantonment · North Nazimabad · **Orangi** · Pipriapur · Baldia · Malir Cantonment · **KARĀCHI** · **SIND** · Mauripur · Jamshed · Lyari · Lándhi · Kiamari · Korangi · Bin Qasim · *ARABIAN SEA* · 67° · Clifton
© Rand McNally A-101865-1

k **Karaj** · Sangān-e Pā'īn · Galandovak · Tangeh · Tajrish · Latián · Vartún · Vard Āvard · Jájrūd · Shahrak-e Qods · Qolhak · Vanak · Zereshkī · **Malārd** · Kan · Jey · Sorkheh Heşar · Sa'īdābād · **TEHRĀN** · Shahryār · Shahr-e Rey · Mojtame'-e · Maskūnī-ye Párchin · **Eslāmshahr** · **TEHRĀN** · Kahrīzak · Robāt Karīm · Mámázán · Golābād · Palasht · 'Azīzābād · Hasanābād · **Qarchak** · **Varāmīn** · Pishvā · 51° · 51°30' · Javādābād
© Rand McNally A-101866-1

0 5 10 15 20 25 30 Miles
0 5 10 15 20 25 30 35 40 45 50 Kilometers

Lambert Conformal Conic Projection
Scale 1:1,000,000
One inch to 16 miles
One cm to 10 km

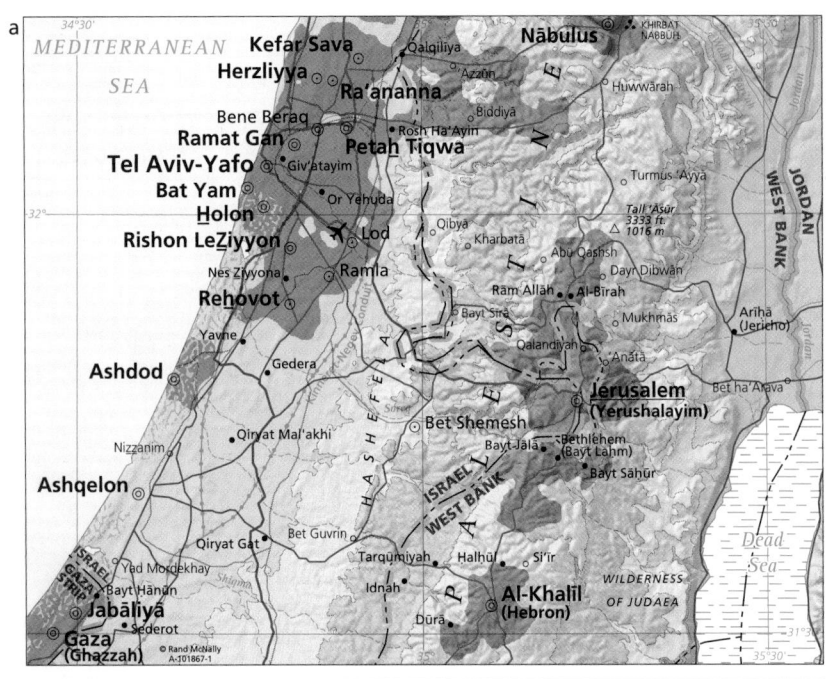

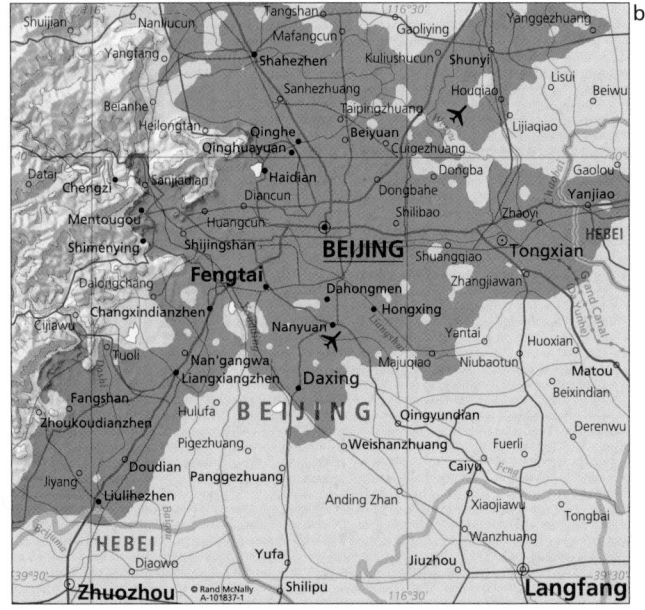

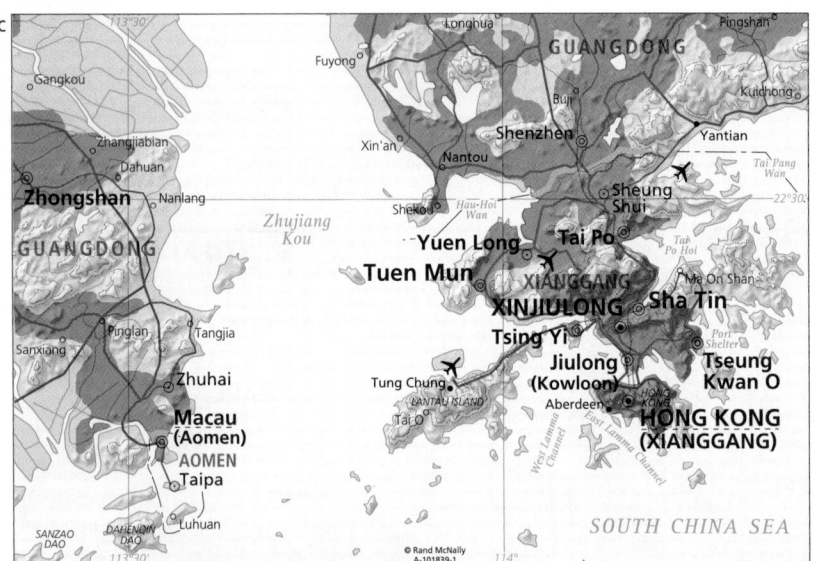

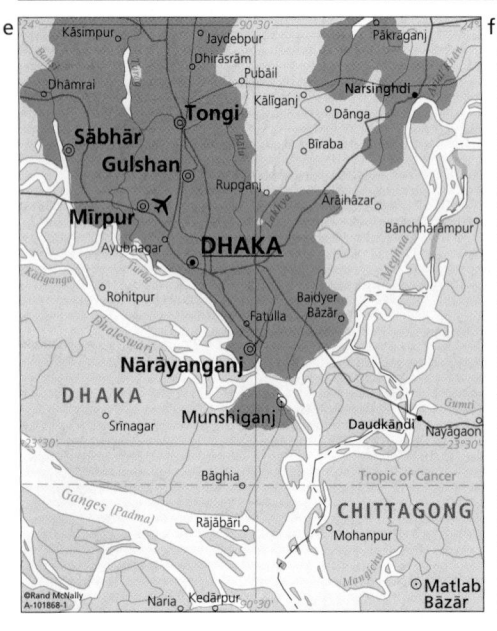

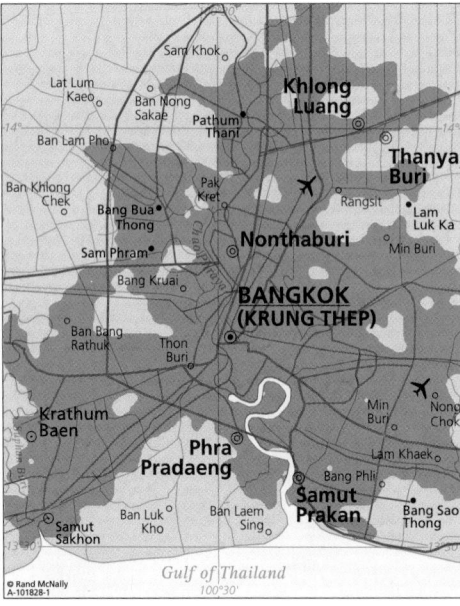

0	5	10	15	20	25	30 Miles
0	5	10	15	20	25	30 35 40 45 50 Kilometers

Lambert Conformal Conic Projection
Scale 1:1,000,000
One inch to 16 miles
One cm to 10 km

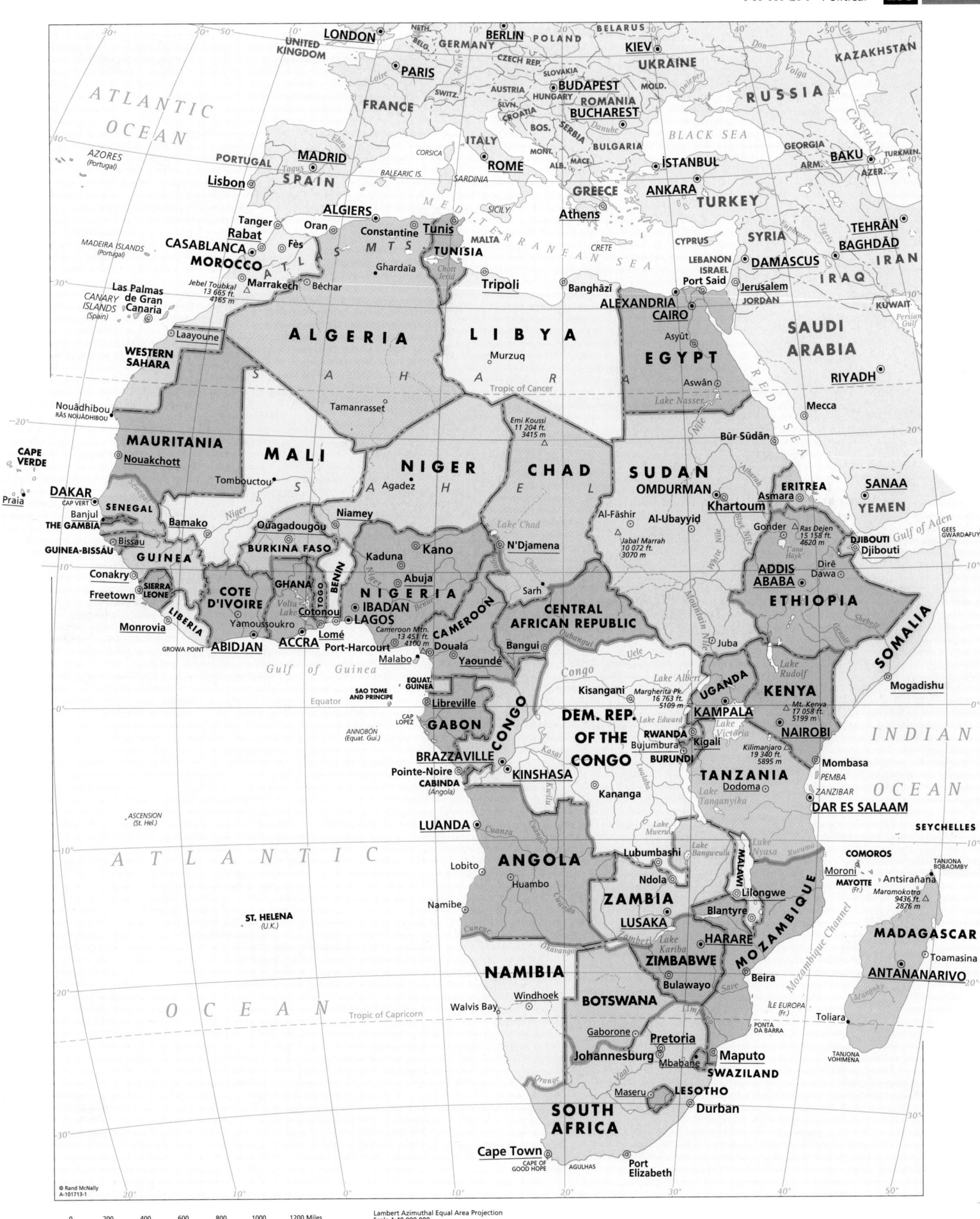

ATLANTIC OCEAN

LONDON
UNITED KINGDOM
PARIS
FRANCE
MADRID
SPAIN
Lisbon
PORTUGAL
AZORES (Portugal)
MADEIRA ISLANDS (Portugal)

BERLIN
GERMANY
NETH. BELG.
POLAND
CZECH REP.
SLOVAKIA
AUSTRIA
HUNGARY
BUDAPEST
ROMANIA
BUCHAREST
SWITZ.
SLVN.
CROATIA
BOS.
SERBIA
MONT.
ALB. MACE.
BULGARIA
ITALY
CORSICA
ROME
SARDINIA
SICILY
BALEARIC IS.
MALTA
CRETE
GREECE
Athens

BELARUS
UKRAINE
KIEV
RUSSIA
MOLD.
Danube
BLACK SEA
GEORGIA
İSTANBUL
ANKARA
TURKEY
ARM.
AZER.
BAKU
KAZAKHSTAN
TURKMEN.
CASPIAN SEA

MEDITERRANEAN SEA

TEHRÄN
BAGHDÄD
SYRIA
DAMASCUS
IRAN
IRAQ
LEBANON
ISRAEL
Jerusalem
JORDAN
KUWAIT
Persian Gulf

CYPRUS
Port Said
ALEXANDRIA
CAIRO

Tanger
Rabat
CASABLANCA
Oran
Fès
Constantine
Tunis
TUNISIA
Tripoli
Banghāzī
Ghardaïa

MOROCCO
Marrakech
Béchar
Jebel Toubkal 13 665 ft. 4165 m
Laayoune
WESTERN SAHARA
CANARY ISLANDS (Spain)
Las Palmas de Gran Canaria

ALGERIA
LIBYA
EGYPT
SAUDI ARABIA
RIYADH
Mecca

ATLAS MTS.
SAHARA
Tropic of Cancer
Murzuq
Asyūt
Aswân
Lake Nasser
RED SEA

Nouâdhibou
RÂS NOUÂDHIBOU
MAURITANIA
Nouakchott
MALI
Tombouctou
NIGER
CHAD
SUDAN
ERITREA
SANAA
YEMEN

Tamanrasset
Emi Koussi 11 204 ft. 3415 m
Bûr Sûdân
Agadez
Lake Chad
OMDURMAN
Khartoum
Asmara
DJIBOUTI
Gulf of Aden
GEES GWARDAFUY

SAHEL

CAPE VERDE
Praia
DAKAR
CAP VERT
SENEGAL
Banjul
THE GAMBIA
GUINEA-BISSAU
Bissau
GUINEA
Conakry
Bamako
Niger
BURKINA FASO
Ouagadougou
Niamey
Kaduna
Kano
N'Djamena
Jabal Marrah 10 072 ft. 3070 m
Al-Fāshir
Al-Ubayyid
Gonder
Ras Dejen 15 158 ft. 4620 m
T'ana Hayk'
Dirē Dawa
ADDIS ABABA
ETHIOPIA

SIERRA LEONE
Freetown
LIBERIA
Monrovia
COTE D'IVOIRE
Yamoussoukro
GHANA
TOGO
BENIN
ACCRA
Lomé
Cotonou
ABIDJAN
GROWA POINT
Volta Lake
NIGERIA
IBADAN
LAGOS
Abuja
Kaduna
Port-Harcourt
CAMEROON
Douala
Malabo
EQUAT. GUINEA
Yaoundé
CENTRAL AFRICAN REPUBLIC
Bangui
Sarh
Juba
SOMALIA
Mogadishu

Cameroon Mtn. 13 451 ft. 4100 m

SAO TOME AND PRINCIPE
Equator
CAP LOPEZ
ANNOBÓN (Equat. Gui.)
Libreville
GABON
CONGO
BRAZZAVILLE
Pointe-Noire
CABINDA (Angola)
KINSHASA
DEM. REP. OF THE CONGO
Kisangani
Margherita Pk. 16 763 ft. 5109 m
Lake Albert
UGANDA
KAMPALA
Lake Edward
RWANDA
Kigali
Bujumbura
BURUNDI
Lake Victoria
Lake Rudolf
KENYA
NAIROBI
Mt. Kenya 17 058 ft. 5199 m
Mombasa
Kilimanjaro 19 340 ft. 5895 m
PEMBA
ZANZIBAR
TANZANIA
Dodoma
DAR ES SALAAM
INDIAN OCEAN

Congo
Uele
Ubangui
Kasai
Kananga
Lake Tanganyika

LUANDA
ANGOLA
Lobito
Huambo
Namibe
ST. HELENA (U.K.)
ASCENSION (St. Hel.)
Lubumbashi
Ndola
ZAMBIA
LUSAKA
Lake Bangweulu
Lake Mweru
MALAWI
Lilongwe
Blantyre
COMOROS
Moroni
MAYOTTE (Fr.)
Antsirañana
TANJONA BOBAOMBY
Maromokotra 9436 ft. 2876 m
SEYCHELLES
Lake Nyasa

ATLANTIC OCEAN

NAMIBIA
Windhoek
Walvis Bay
BOTSWANA
Gaborone
ZIMBABWE
HARARE
Bulawayo
Beira
MOZAMBIQUE
Lake Kariba
Tropic of Capricorn
Johannesburg
Pretoria
Mbabane
SWAZILAND
Maputo
MADAGASCAR
Toamasina
ANTANANARIVO
ÎLE EUROPA (Fr.)
PONTA DA BARRA
TANJONA VOHIMENA
Toliara
Mozambique Channel

SOUTH AFRICA
Maseru
LESOTHO
Durban
Cape Town
CAPE OF GOOD HOPE
Port Elizabeth
AGULHAS

© Rand McNally
A-101713-1

Lambert Azimuthal Equal Area Projection
Scale 1:40,000,000
One inch to 640 miles
One cm to 400 km

0 200 400 600 800 1000 1200 Miles
0 200 400 600 800 1000 1200 1400 1600 1800 2000 Kilometers

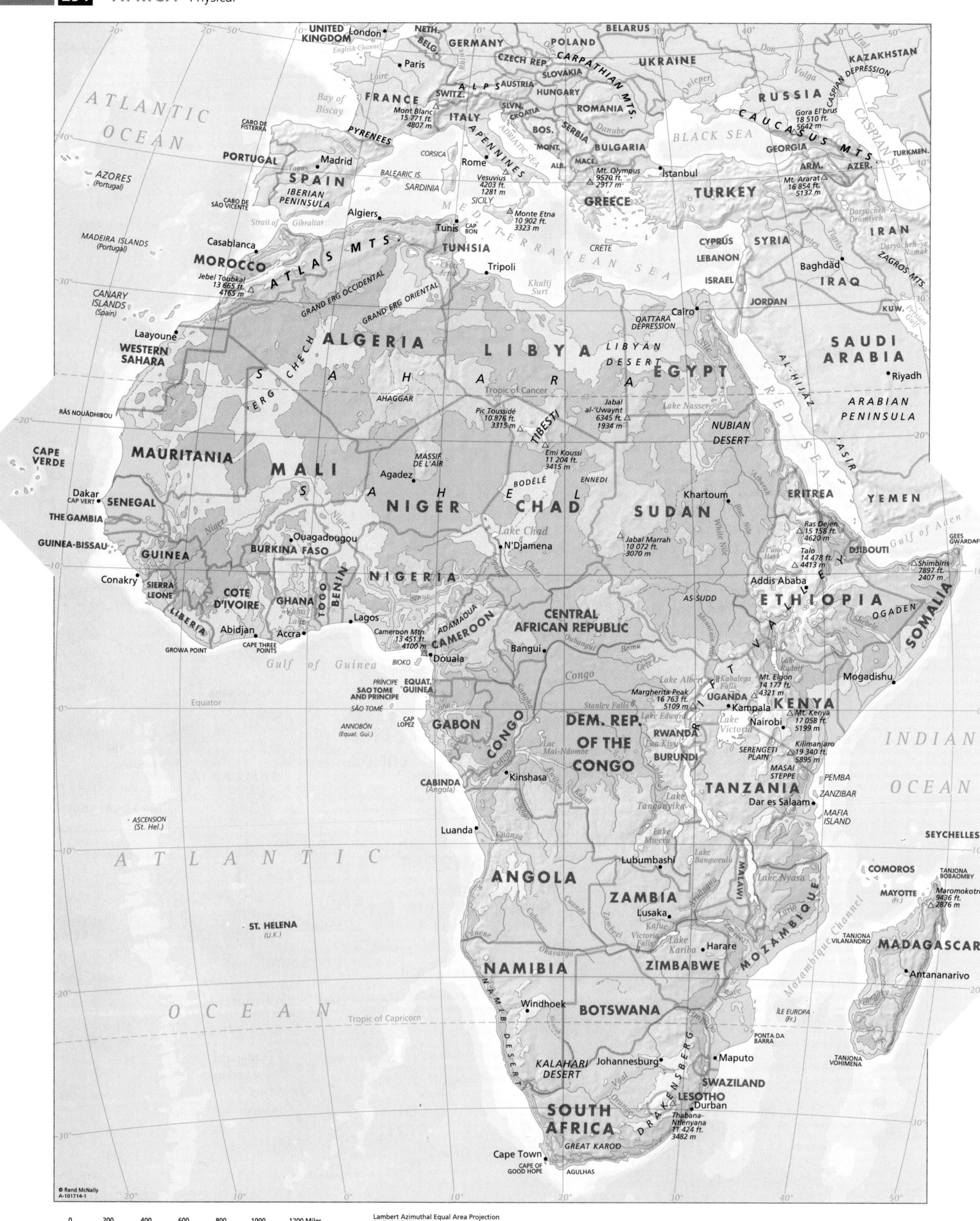

Lambert Azimuthal Equal Area Projection
Scale 1:40,000,000
One inch to 640 miles
One cm to 400 km

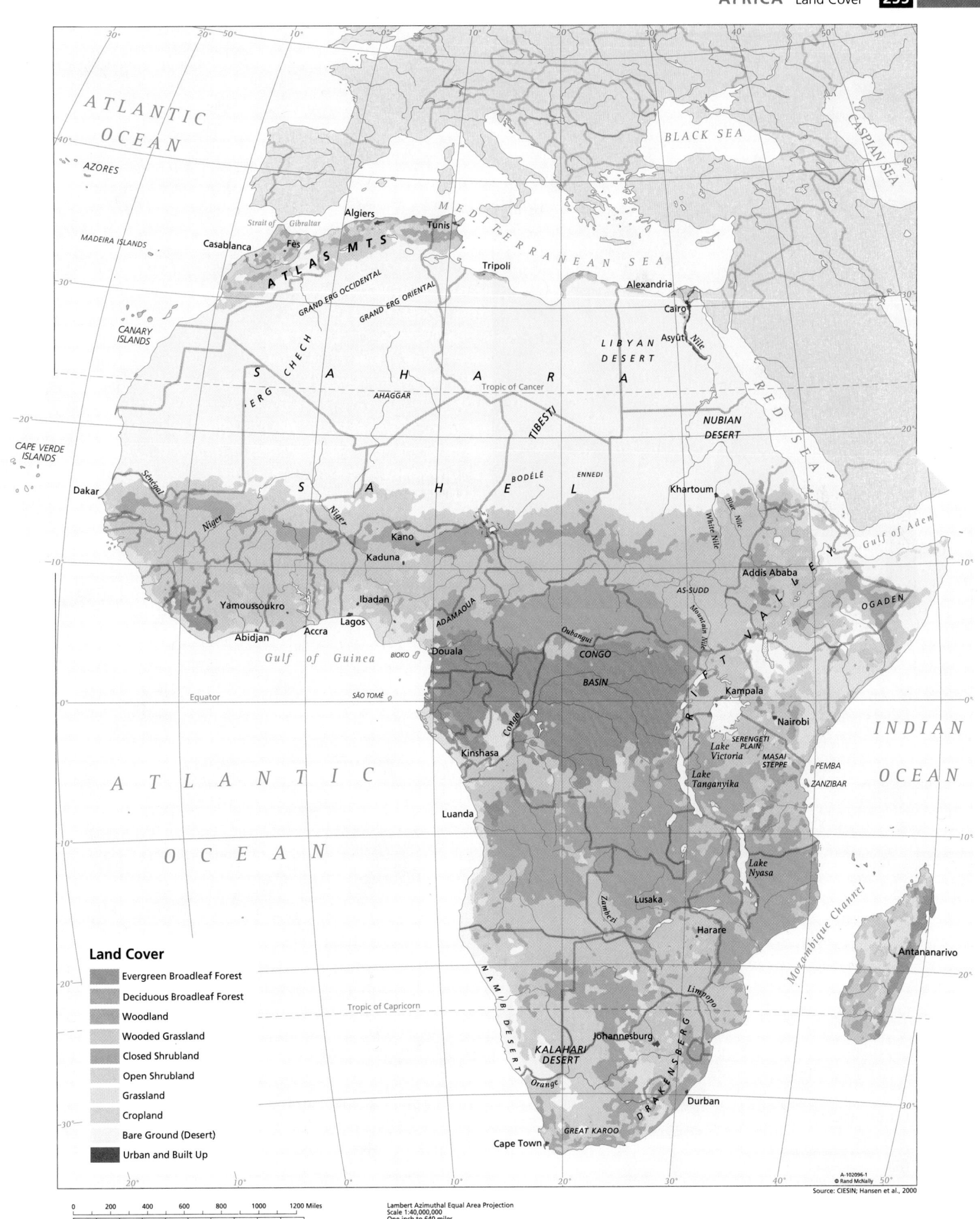

ATLANTIC OCEAN

AZORES

MADEIRA ISLANDS

CANARY ISLANDS

CAPE VERDE ISLANDS

BLACK SEA

CASPIAN SEA

MEDITERRANEAN SEA

Algiers
Tunis
Casablanca
Fès
Strait of Gibraltar
ATLAS MTS
Tripoli
Alexandria
Cairo
Asyût
Nile

GRAND ERG OCCIDENTAL
GRAND ERG ORIENTAL
LIBYAN DESERT
RED SEA

S A H A R A

ERG CHECH
AHAGGAR
Tropic of Cancer
TIBESTI
NUBIAN DESERT

Senégal
Dakar
Niger
Niger
BODÉLÉ
ENNEDI
Khartoum
Blue Nile
White Nile
Gulf of Aden

S A H E L

Kano
Kaduna
Addis Ababa
AS-SUDD
OGADEN

Yamoussoukro
Ibadan
Lagos
Abidjan
Accra
ADAMAOUA
BIOKO
Douala
Oubangui
CONGO BASIN
Mountain Nile
RIFT VALLEY

Gulf of Guinea
Equator
SÃO TOMÉ
Congo
Kampala
Nairobi
INDIAN OCEAN

Kinshasa
Lake Victoria
SERENGETI PLAIN
MASAI STEPPE
PEMBA
ZANZIBAR

A T L A N T I C
Lake Tanganyika

Luanda

O C E A N
Lake Nyasa

Zambezi
Lusaka

Harare

Antananarivo

Mozambique Channel

NAMIB DESERT
Limpopo

Tropic of Capricorn

KALAHARI DESERT
Johannesburg
DRAKENSBERG
Durban

Orange
GREAT KAROO
Cape Town

Land Cover

- Evergreen Broadleaf Forest
- Deciduous Broadleaf Forest
- Woodland
- Wooded Grassland
- Closed Shrubland
- Open Shrubland
- Grassland
- Cropland
- Bare Ground (Desert)
- Urban and Built Up

A-102096-1
© Rand McNally

Source: CIESIN; Hansen et al., 2000

0 200 400 600 800 1000 1200 Miles
0 200 400 600 800 1000 1200 1400 1600 1800 2000 Kilometers

Lambert Azimuthal Equal Area Projection
Scale 1:40,000,000
One inch to 640 miles
One cm to 400 km

Moderate Resolution
Imaging Spectroradiometer (MODIS)
true-color mosaic satellite image

Source: NASA Visible Earth program (http://visibleearth.nasa.gov/)

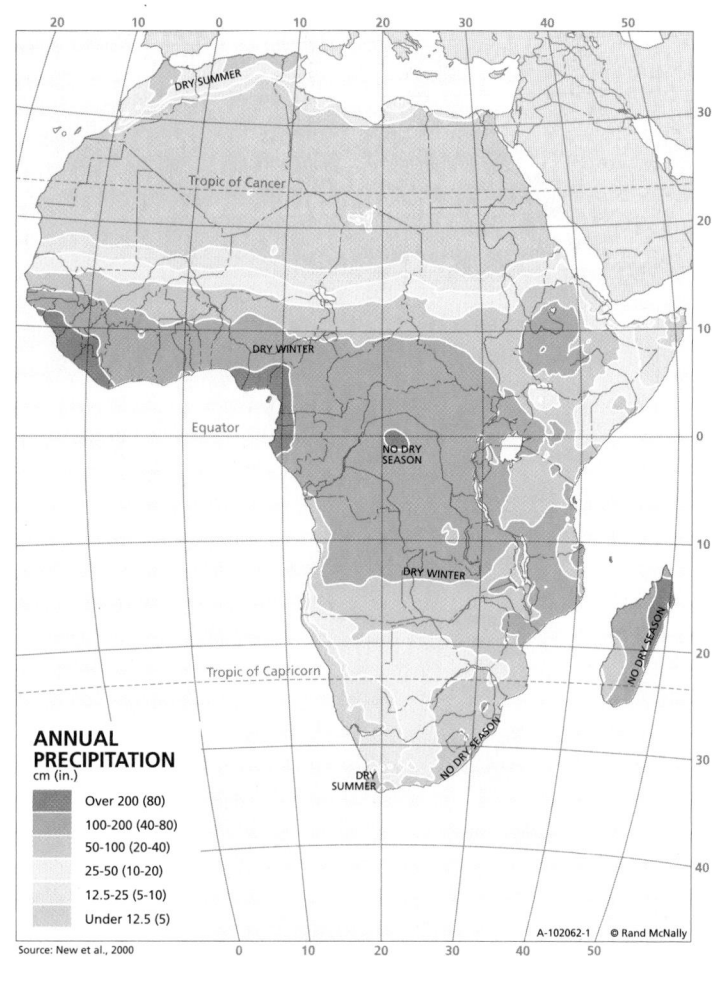

ANNUAL PRECIPITATION
cm (in.)

- Over 200 (80)
- 100-200 (40-80)
- 50-100 (20-40)
- 25-50 (10-20)
- 12.5-25 (5-10)
- Under 12.5 (5)

Source: New et al., 2000

A-102062-1   © Rand McNally

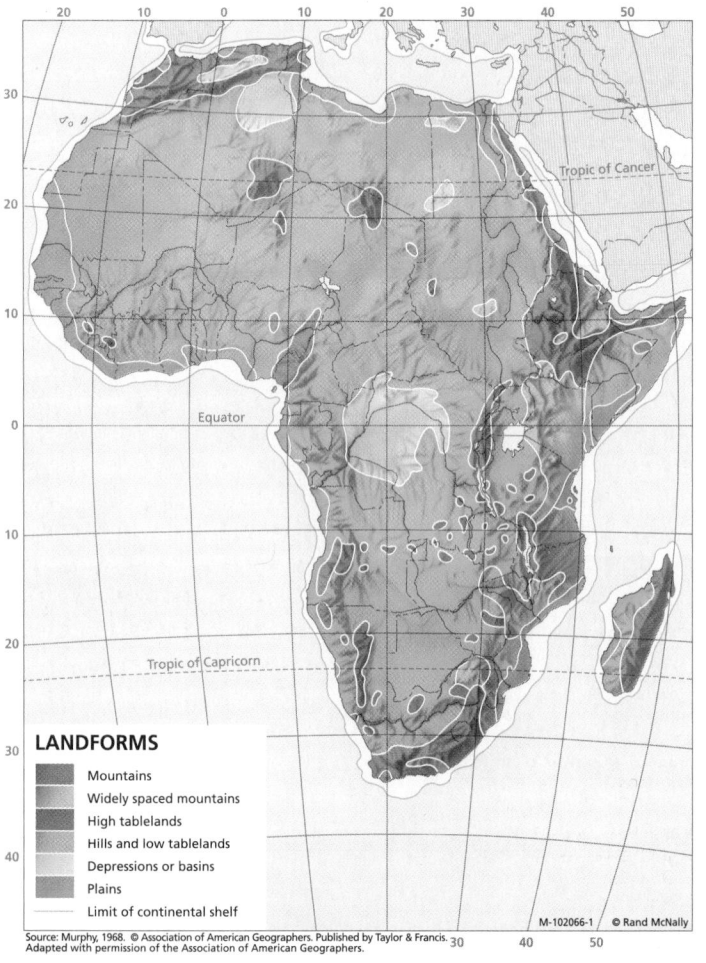

LANDFORMS

- Mountains
- Widely spaced mountains
- High tablelands
- Hills and low tablelands
- Depressions or basins
- Plains
- Limit of continental shelf

Source: Murphy, 1968. © Association of American Geographers. Published by Taylor & Francis.
Adapted with permission of the Association of American Geographers.

M-102066-1   © Rand McNally

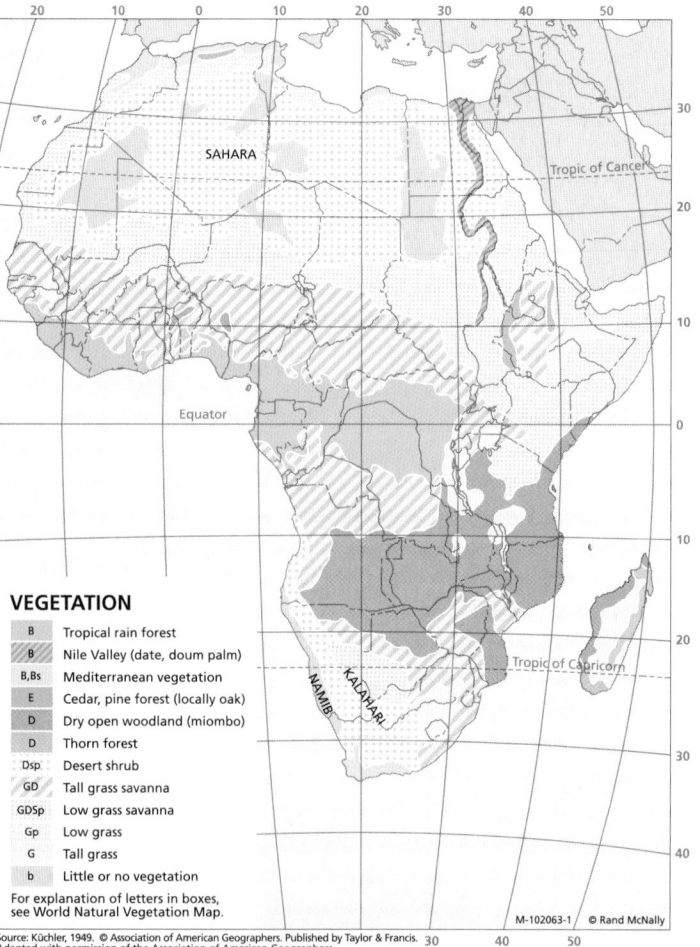

VEGETATION

B	Tropical rain forest
B	Nile Valley (date, doum palm)
B,Bs	Mediterranean vegetation
E	Cedar, pine forest (locally oak)
D	Dry open woodland (miombo)
D	Thorn forest
Dsp	Desert shrub
GD	Tall grass savanna
GDSp	Low grass savanna
Gp	Low grass
G	Tall grass
b	Little or no vegetation

For explanation of letters in boxes,
see World Natural Vegetation Map.

Source: Küchler, 1949. © Association of American Geographers. Published by Taylor & Francis.
Adapted with permission of the Association of American Geographers.

M-102063-1   © Rand McNally

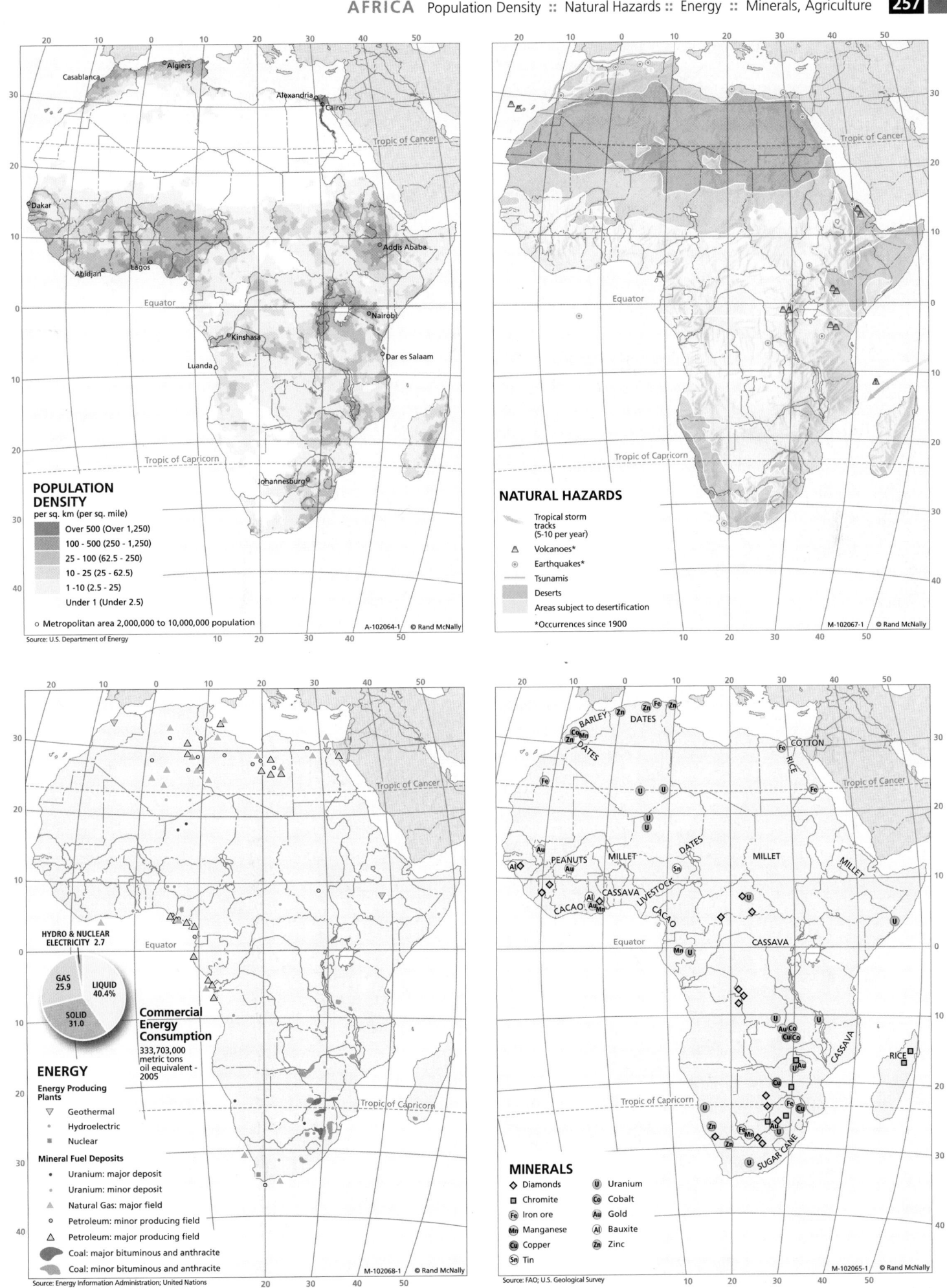

POPULATION DENSITY
per sq. km (per sq. mile)

- Over 500 (Over 1,250)
- 100 - 500 (250 - 1,250)
- 25 - 100 (62.5 - 250)
- 10 - 25 (25 - 62.5)
- 1 -10 (2.5 - 25)
- Under 1 (Under 2.5)

○ Metropolitan area 2,000,000 to 10,000,000 population

Source: U.S. Department of Energy

A-102064-1   © Rand McNally

NATURAL HAZARDS

- Tropical storm tracks (5-10 per year)
- △ Volcanoes*
- ⊙ Earthquakes*
- Tsunamis
- Deserts
- Areas subject to desertification

*Occurrences since 1900

M-102067-1   © Rand McNally

ENERGY

HYDRO & NUCLEAR ELECTRICITY 2.7

GAS 25.9
LIQUID 40.4%
SOLID 31.0

Commercial Energy Consumption
333,703,000 metric tons oil equivalent - 2005

Energy Producing Plants

- ▽ Geothermal
- • Hydroelectric
- ▪ Nuclear

Mineral Fuel Deposits

- • Uranium: major deposit
- • Uranium: minor deposit
- ▲ Natural Gas: major field
- ○ Petroleum: minor producing field
- △ Petroleum: major producing field
- Coal: major bituminous and anthracite
- Coal: minor bituminous and anthracite

Source: Energy Information Administration; United Nations

M-102068-1   © Rand McNally

MINERALS

- ◇ Diamonds
- ▢ Chromite
- Ⓕe Iron ore
- Ⓜn Manganese
- Ⓒu Copper
- Ⓢn Tin
- Ⓤ Uranium
- Ⓒo Cobalt
- Ⓐu Gold
- Ⓐl Bauxite
- Ⓩn Zinc

Source: FAO; U.S. Geological Survey

M-102065-1   © Rand McNally

PORTUGAL Huelva   SPAIN   Jaén   Cartagena   ALGIERS
CABO DE SÃO VICENTE Faro   Sevilla   Granada   Mulhacén   (ALGER)
                                              11 424 ft.
                                              3482 m   Almería
                        Cádiz   Málaga   Mostaganem   Chlef
                                 Gibraltar (U.K.)   ISLA DE   (El Asnam)   Médéa
                    Strait of Gibraltar Ceuta (Sp.)   ALBORÁN   Oran
                        Tanger   Al-   Melilla (Sp.)   Sidi Bel Abbès   Djelfa
                      Tetouan   Hoceima   Berkane   Zahrez
                                                                              Oujda   Rharbi
              Larache   Taza   Laghouat
                           Salé   Aïn   Chott ech
        MADEIRA ISLANDS   Rabat   Sefra   Chergui
       (ARQUIPÉLAGO DA MADEIRA) CASABLANCA   Meknès Fès   Djebel Aïssa
            (Portugal)   PORTO   El-Jadida   MOYEN ATLAS   7333 ft.   Ghardaïa
                          SANTO   Khouribga   2235 m
              Funchal MADEIRA   Safi   Beni-Mellal   Figuig
                                          Youssoufia   Er-Rachidia
                                                   Irhil M'Goun   El Golea
      ATLANTIC OCEAN   Essaouira   13 356 ft.   Béchar   GRAND ERG OCCIDENTAL
                              Marrákech   4071 m
                                       Jbel Toubkal   MOROCCO
         CANARY ISLANDS   CAP RHIR   13 665 ft.   ALGERIA
          (ISLAS CANARIAS)   Agadir   4165 m   Ouarzazate
              (Spain)   Sebkha de
     LA PALMA   LANZAROTE   Tiznit   Tlinatmoun
          TENERIFE   PLATEAU
       Santa Cruz   Arrecife   ANTI-ATLAS   DU TADEMAIT
       de Tenerife   FUERTEVENTURA   HAMADA DU DRÂA
    Pico del Teide   Tan-Tan   Tindouf   Adrar
    12 198 ft.   GRAN   Tarfaya   Aoulef
 EL HIERRO 3718 m Las Palmas   CAP JUBY   I-n-Salah
            de Gran Canaria   Oued Djaret
                      CAP BOJADOR   Laayoune (El Aaiún)
                                      Semara
                           Western Sahara has been
                           unilaterally annexed by Morocco.   Bîr
                                                       Mogrein
         Tropic of Cancer   Dakhla
                                                      EL HANK
      CAP BARBAS   WESTERN   Tessalit
                      SAHARA   Zouérat   IJÂFENE
                                                                              ADRAR DES IFÔGHAS
         Nouâdhibou   Atar ADRAR   OUARÂNE
         RÂS NOUÂDHIBOU
                           ET TÎDRA   Kidal
         RÂS TIMIRIST   MAURITANIA   AOUKÂR   MALI
         Nouakchott
                      Boutilimit   Tidjikja Tichît
                                                                  Tombouctou   Gao
              Rosso   Bogué   Kiffa   (Timbuktu)   Ménaka
      Saint-Louis   Kaédi   Hameud   KUMBI SALEH   Boû Gâdoûm   Goundam
           Louga   Vallée du Ferlo   'Adel Bagrou
      CAP VERT   SENEGAL   Nioro   Kayes   Ansongo
    DAKAR   Thiès
     Mbour Kaolack   Mopti
    Banjul (Bathurst)   PARC NATIONAL
    THE GAMBIA   Georgetown   DE LA BOUCLE
                Tambacounda   DU BAOULÉ   Djenné   Dori   Téra
     Ziguinchor Kolda   Ségou   San   Ouahigouya   Niamey
  Cacheu GUINEA- Kédougou   Kita   Bamako   White Volta   Dosso
  Bissau BISSAU   Kati Koutiala   BURKINA FASO
  ARQUIPÉLAGO   Mali   Sikasso   Koudougou Ouagadougou
  DOS BIJAGÓS   GUINEA   Labé Siguiri   BENIN

© Rand McNally
A-101816-1

0   60   120   180   240   300   360 Miles
0 60 120 180 240 300 360 420 480 540 600 Kilometers

Lambert Azimuthal Equal Area Projection
Scale 1:12,000,000
One inch to 190 miles
One cm to 120 km

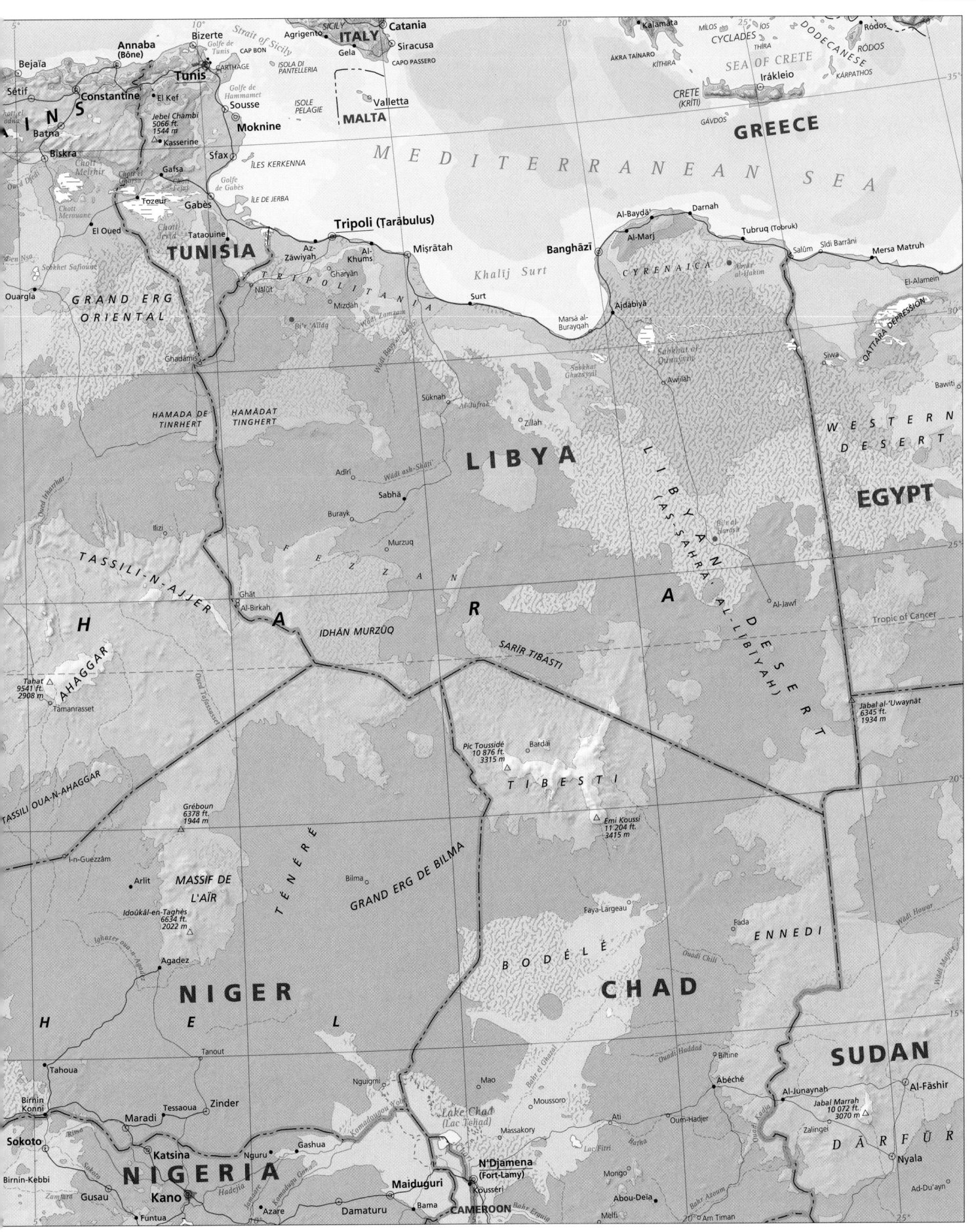

Bejaïa
Annaba (Bône)
Bizerte
Strait of Sicily
Agrigento
SICILY
Catania
ITALY
Sétif
Constantine
CAP BON
Golfe de Tunis
Gela
Siracusa
AINS
Batna
Tunis
CARTHAGE
ISOLA DI PANTELLERIA
CAPO PASSERO
El Kef
Jebel Chambi 5066 ft. 1544 m
Kasserine
Golfe de Hammamet
Sousse
ISOLE PELAGIE
Valletta
MALTA
Biskra
Chott Melrhir
Gafsa
Sfax
ÎLES KERKENNA
Oued Djedi
Chott el Gharsa
Tozeur
Gabès
ÎLE DE JERBA
Golfe de Gabès
Chott Meroane
El Oued
Chott Djerid
Tataouine
TUNISIA
Tripoli (Ṭarābulus)
Al-Khums
Miṣrātah
Surt
Khalīj Surt
Al-Baydāʾ
Darnah
Tubruq (Tobruk)
Sīdi Barrāni
Mersa Matruh
Ben Nsa
Sebkhet Safioune
Ouargla
GRAND ERG ORIENTAL
Az-Zāwiyah
Gharyān
Nālūt
TRIPOLITANIA
Mizdah
Al-Marj
Banghāzī
Ajdābiyā
Marsá al-Burayqah
CYRENAICA
Salūm
ʿUmar al-Ḥakim
El-Alamein
Ghadāmis
HAMADA DE TINRHERT
HAMĀDAT TINGHERT
Bi'r 'Allāq
Wadi Bey al-Kebir
Wādī Zamzam
Al-Jufrah
Sūknah
Zillah
Sabkhat al-Qunayyin
Sabkhat Ghuzzayil
Awjilah
WESTERN DESERT
Siwa
QATTARA DEPRESSION
Bawiti
Adīrī
Wādī ash-Shāṭiʾ
LIBYA
Sabhā
Burayk
Murzuq
Bi'r al-Ḥarash
EGYPT
LIBYAN (AS-SAHRĀʾ AL-LĪBIYAH)
Ilizi
Ghāt
Al-Birkah
TASSILI-N-AJJER
IDHĀN MURZŪQ
SARĪR TIBASTI
Al-Jawf
Tropic of Cancer
Jabal al-ʿUwaynāt 6345 ft. 1934 m
H
A
R
A
DESERT
Tahat 9541 ft. 2908 m
AHAGGAR
Tāmanrasset
Oued Tafassasset
Oued Mya Zhar
Pic Toussidé 10 876 ft. 3315 m
Bardaï
TIBESTI
TASSILI OUA-N-AHAGGAR
I-n-Guézzâm
Gréboun 6378 ft. 1944 m
Emi Koussi 11 204 ft. 3415 m
Arlit
MASSIF DE L'AÏR
Bilma
GRAND ERG DE BILMA
Idoûkâl-en-Taghès 6634 ft. 2022 m
Ighazer oua-n-Agadez
Agadez
TÉNÉRÉ
Faya-Largeau
Fada
ENNEDI
Ouadi Chili
Wadi Howar
NIGER
H
E
L
BODÉLÉ
CHAD
Wadi Maghrem
Tahoua
Tanout
Nguigmi
Mao
Bahr el Ghazal
Biltine
Ouadi Haddad
SUDAN
Birnin Konni
Tessaoua
Zinder
Moussoro
Ati
Oum-Hadjer
Abéché
Al-Junaynah
Jabal Marrah 10 072 ft. 3070 m
Al-Fāshir
Sokoto
Maradi
Nguru
Gashua
Massakory
Lac Fitri
Batha
Zalingei
Nyala
Birnin-Kebbi
Katsina
Komadougou Yobé
Lake Chad (Lac Tchad)
Mongo
Abou-Deïa
Ouadi Kadja
D A R F Ū R
Ad-Du'ayn
Zamfara
Gusau
Funtua
NIGERIA
Kano
Azare
Damaturu
Bama
CAMEROUN
Maiduguri
Hadejia
Jemere
Komadougou Gana
N'Djamena (Fort-Lamy)
Koussri
Bahr Erguig
Massenya
Melfi
Bahr Azoum
Am Timan

MEDITERRANEAN SEA

GREECE
Kalamáta
MILOS
ÍOS
CYCLADES
ÁKRA TAÍNARO
KÍTHIRA
THIRA
DODECANESE
RÓDOS
Irákleio
SEA OF CRETE
CRETE (KRÍTI)
GÁVDOS
KÁRPATHOS

Inset map a
Lambert Conformal Conic Projection
Scale 1:4,000,000
One inch to 64 miles
One cm to 40 km

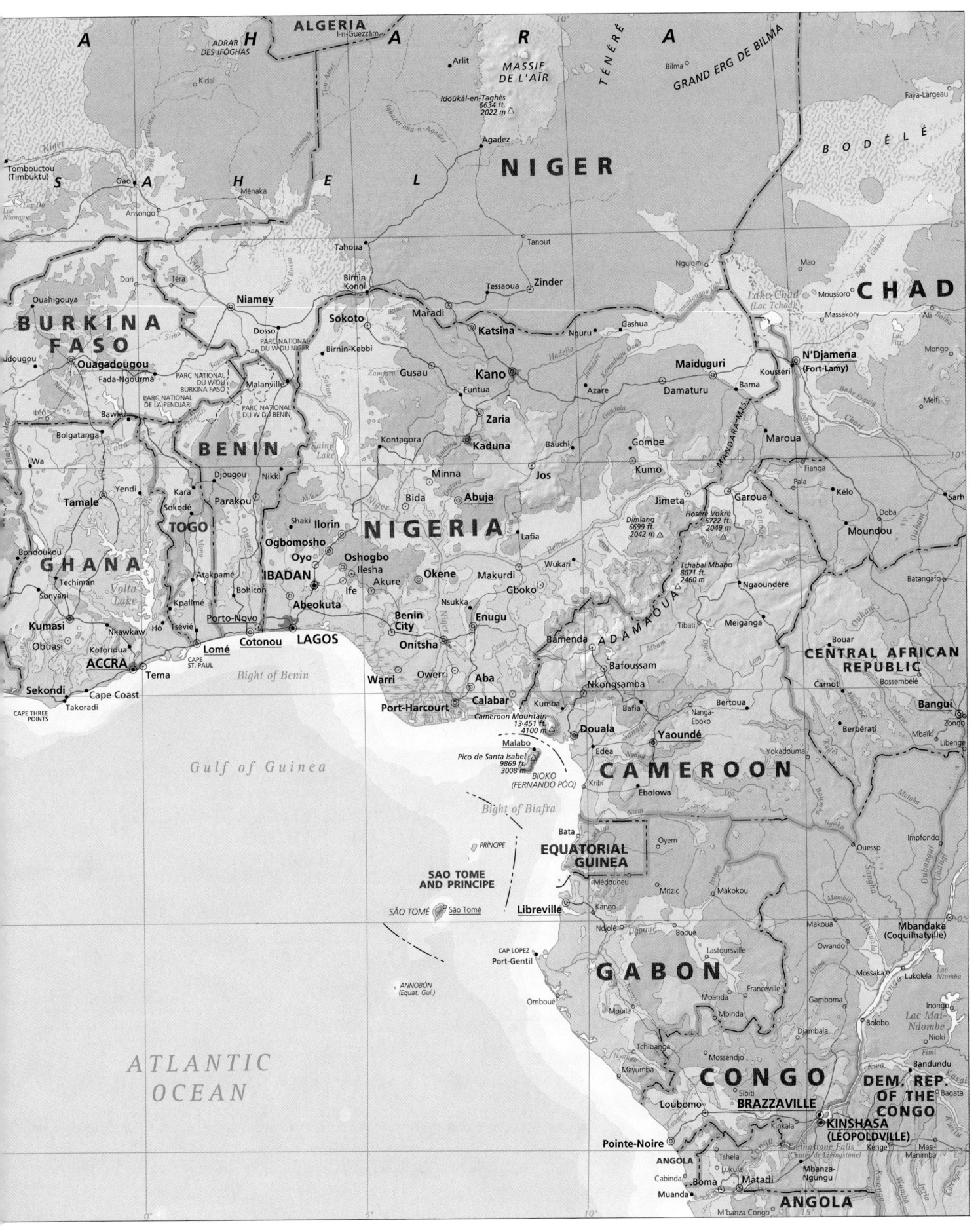

ALGERIA

ADRAR DES IFOGHAS

I-n-Guezzâm

S A H A R A

MASSIF DE L'AÏR

TÉNÉRÉ

GRAND ERG DE BILMA

Bilma

Faya-Largeau

BODÉLÉ

Arlit

Idoûkâl-en-Taghès
6634 ft.
2022 m

Kidal

Tombouctou
(Timbuktu)

Gao

Ménaka

Ansongo

Agadez

S A H E L

Tahoua

Tanout

Zinder

Nguigmi

Mao

Massakory

Moussoro

CHAD

Lac Fitri

Mongo

Ati

Melfi

N I G E R

Lake Chad
(Lac Tchad)

Lac Do Niangay

Dori

Téra

Birnin Konni

Tessaoua

Maradi

Gashua

Nguru

N'Djamena
(Fort-Lamy)

Kousséri

Bama

Ouahigouya

Niamey

Sokoto

Katsina

Azare

Damaturu

Maiduguri

Maroua

Fianga

Pala

Kélo

Doba

Sarh

BURKINA
FASO

Ouagadougou

Fada-Ngourma

Dosso

Birnin-Kebbi

Gusau

Kano

Funtua

Zaria

Bauchi

Kumo

Gombe

Garoua

Hosére Vokré
6722 ft.
2049 m

MANDARA MTS.

Dimlang
6699 ft.
2042 m

Jimeta

PARC NATIONAL DU W DU NIGER

PARC NATIONAL DU W DU BURKINA FASO

Malanville

Kontagora

Kaduna

Minna

Jos

Lafia

PARC NATIONAL DE LA PENDJARI

PARC NATIONAL DU W DU BENIN

BENIN

Djougou

Nikki

Bida

Abuja

NIGERIA

Wukari

Ngaoundéré

Tchabal Mbabo
8071 ft.
2460 m

Tibati

Meiganga

Bouar

Berbérati

CENTRAL AFRICAN
REPUBLIC

Bangui

Leo

Bolgatanga

Wa

Bawku

Tamale

Yendi

Kara

Sokodé

Shaki

Ilorin

Ogbomosho

Oyo

Oshogbo

Ilesha

Okene

Makurdi

Gboko

ADAMAOUA

Mham

Carnot

Bossembélé

TOGO

Parakou

Atakpamé

IBADAN

Ife

Akure

Nsukka

Bamenda

Bafoussam

GHANA

Kumasi

Obuasi

Techiman

Sunyani

Bondoukou

Nkawkaw

Koforidua

Kpalimé

Ho

Tsévié

Bohicon

Abeokuta

Porto-Novo

Benin
City

Onitsha

Enugu

Aba

Bafia

Nanga-Eboko

Bertoua

Berbérati

Mbaiki

Libenge

Zongo

ACCRA

Tema

Lomé

Cotonou

LAGOS

Warri

Owerri

Calabar

Kumba

Nkongsamba

Yaoundé

Yokadouma

Impfondo

Sekondi

Cape Coast

CAPE
ST. PAUL

Bight of Benin

Port-Harcourt

Cameroon Mountain
13,451 ft.
4100 m

Douala

Edéa

Ouesso

Takoradi

CAPE THREE
POINTS

Malabo

Pico de Santa Isabel
9869 ft.
3008 m

BIOKO
(FERNANDO PÓO)

Kribi

CAMEROON

Ebolowa

Makoua

Owando

Mbandaka
(Coquilhatville)

Gulf of Guinea

Bight of Biafra

Bata

CONGO

DEM. REP.
OF THE
CONGO

PRÍNCIPE

Oyem

Médouneu

Mitzic

Makokou

Lastoursville

EQUATORIAL
GUINEA

Kango

Boué

Mossendjo

Lukolela

SAO TOME
AND PRINCIPE

SÃO TOMÉ

São Tomé

Libreville

Ndjolé

Mayumba

Bandundu

CAP LOPEZ

Port-Gentil

Owendo

Lac Mai-
Ndombe

Nioki

ANNOBÓN
(Equat. Gui.)

Omboué

G A B O N

Franceville

Mossaka

Lukolela

Inongo

ATLANTIC
OCEAN

Tchibanga

Mouila

Moanda

Moanda

Gamboma

Bolobo

Mbinda

Djambala

Fimi

Sibiti

BRAZZAVILLE

KINSHASA
(LÉOPOLDVILLE)

Loubomo

Kinkala

Masi-
Manimba

Pointe-Noire

Livingstone Falls
(Chutes de Livingstone)

Kenge

ANGOLA

Tshela

Lukula

Mbanza-
Ngungu

Matadi

Bata

Cabinda

Boma

Muanda

M'banza Congo

ANGOLA

0 60 120 180 240 300 360 Miles

0 60 120 180 240 300 360 420 480 540 600 Kilometers

Lambert Azimuthal Equal Area Projection
Scale 1:12,000,000
One inch to 190 miles
One cm to 120 km

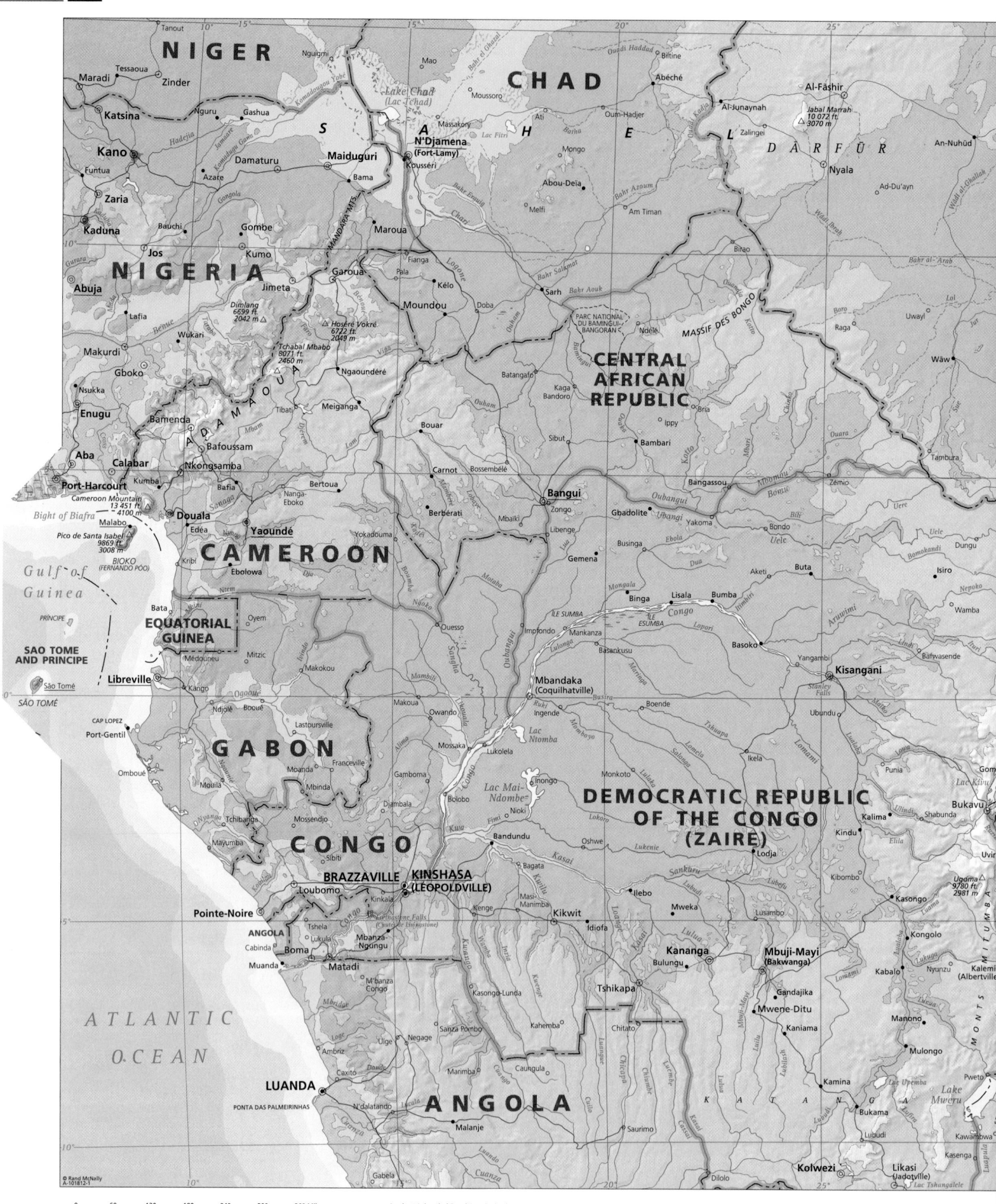

NIGER

CHAD

Tanout
Maradi   Tessaoua   Zinder   Nguigmi   Mao   Bahr el Ghazal   Ouadi Haddad   Biltine
Katsina   Nguru   Gashua   Massakory   Moussoro   Abéché   Al-Fâshir
Kano   Azare   Bama   Lac Fitri   Ati   Baïba   Oum-Hadjer   Al-Junaynah   Jabal Marrah 10 072 ft. 3070 m   Zalingei
Funtua   Damaturu   Maiduguri   N'Djamena (Fort-Lamy)   Kousséri   Mongo   DÂRFÛR   An-Nuhûd
Zaria   DÂRFÛR   Nyala   Ad-Du'ayn
Kaduna   Bauchi   Gombe   Maroua   Abou-Deïa   Melfi   Am Timan   Bîtao   Waâd Dunah   Wadi al-Ghallah

NIGERIA
Jos   Kumo   Garoua   Fianga   Kélo   Pala   Doba   Sarh   Bahr Salamat   Bahr Aouk   Boro   Raga   Uwayl   Wâw
Abuja   Jimeta   Dimlang 6699 ft. 2042 m   Moundou   PARC NATIONAL DU BAMINGUI-BANGORAN   Ndélé   MASSIF DES BONGO   Lol
Lafia   Hoséré Vokré 6722 ft. 2049 m   Batangafo   Kaga Bandoro   Ippy   Bria   Zémio   Uwayl
Wukari   Tchabal Mbabo 8071 ft. 2460 m   Ngaoundéré   CENTRAL AFRICAN REPUBLIC   Bambari
Makurdi   Tibati   Meiganga   Bouar   Sibut
Gboko   Bamenda   Bafoussam   Bertoua   Carnot   Bossembélé   Bangassou   Bômu   Tambura
Enugu   Nkongsamba   Nanga-Eboko   Berbérati   Mbaïki   Bangui   Zongo   Gbadolite   Ubangi   Yakoma   Bondo   Uere   Uele   Dungu
Aba   Calabar   Kumba   Bafia   Mbaïki   Libenge   Businga   Ebola   Gemena   Dua   Aketi   Buta   Isiro   Bafwasende
Port-Harcourt   Cameroon Mountain 13 451 ft. 4100 m   Douala   Yaoundé   CAMEROON   Ouesso   Impfondo   Mankanza   Binga   Lisala   Bumba   Basoko   Yangambi   Kisangani
Malabo   Pico de Santa Isabel 9869 ft. 3008 m   Edéa   Ebolowa   Yokadouma   ÎLE SUMBA   ÎLE ESUMBA   Congo   Lopori   Stanley Falls   Wamba
Bight of Biafra   BIOKO (FERNANDO PÓO)   Kribi   Mbandaka (Coquilhatville)   Ingende   Basankusu   Boende
PRÍNCIPE   Bata   Oyem   Mitzic   EQUATORIAL GUINEA   Makoua   Owando   Lac Ntomba   Busira   Ubundu
SAO TOME AND PRINCIPE   Médouneu   Makokou   Mossaka   Lukolela   Ikela   Punia   Lac Kivu
Libreville   Kango   Ndjolé   Booué   Lastoursville   Mbandaka   Bukavu
São Tomé   SÃO TOMÉ   CAP LOPEZ   Port-Gentil   GABON   Franceville   Gamboma   Lac Mai-Ndombe   Inongo   Monkoto   Ikela   Shabunda
Ombouė   Mouila   Moanda   Mbinda   Djambala   Bolobo   Nioki   DEMOCRATIC REPUBLIC OF THE CONGO (ZAIRE)   Kindu   Uvira
Tchibanga   Mossendjo   CONGO   Bandundu   Oshwe   Lodja   Kibombo   Kalima
Mayumba   Sibiti   BRAZZAVILLE   KINSHASA (LÉOPOLDVILLE)   Masi-Manimba   Kikwit   Ilebo   Mweka   Lusambo   Kasongo   Ugoma 9780 ft. 2981 m   Kongolo
Loubomo   Kinkala   Bagata   Idiofa   Kananga   Mbuji-Mayi (Bakwanga)   Kabalo   Nyunzu   Kalemie (Albertville)
Pointe-Noire   Livingstone Falls (Chute de Livingstone)   Kenge   Bulungu   Gandajika   Kamina
ANGOLA   Tshela   Mbanza-Ngungu   Kahemba   Tshikapa   Mwene-Ditu   Kaniama   Manono   Mulongo
Cabinda   Lukula   Boma   Matadi   Kasongo-Lunda   Chitato   Bukama   Lac Upemba   Pweto   Lake Mweru
Muanda   M'banza Congo   Kamina   Kasenga
ATLANTIC OCEAN   Negage   Sanza Pombo   Marimba   Caungula   Kolwezi   Likasi (Jadotville)   Lac Tshangalele
Uíge   Kasongo   Dilolo
Ambriz   Caxito   Uíge   Saurimo   Gabela
LUANDA   N'dalatando   Malanje   ANGOLA
PONTA DAS PALMEIRINHAS   Caála

© Rand McNally
A-101812-1

0   60   120   180   240   300   360 Miles
0   60   120   180   240   300   360   420   480   540   600 Kilometers

Lambert Azimuthal Equal Area Projection
Scale 1:12,000,000
One inch to 190 miles
One cm to 120 km

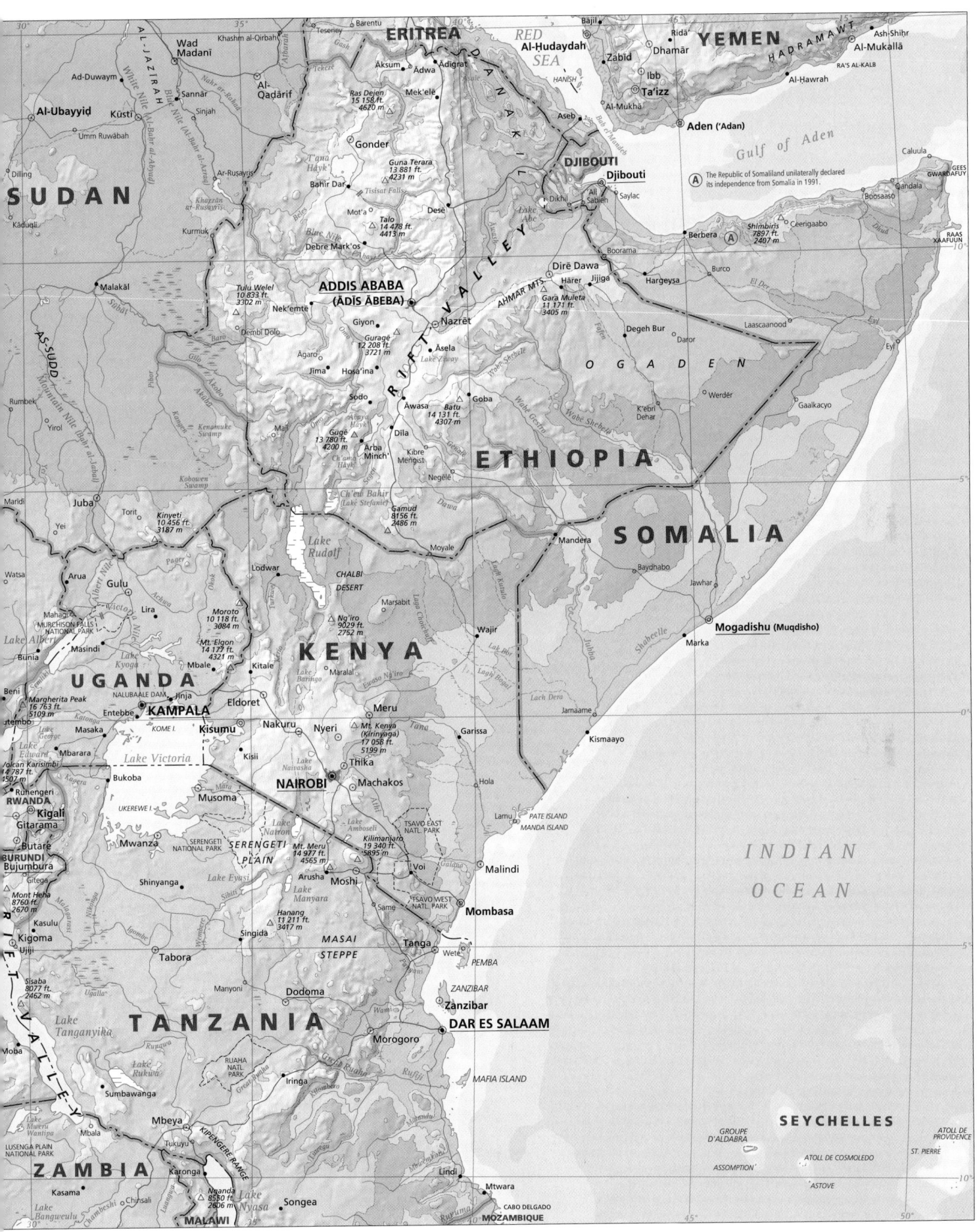

SUDAN

ERITREA

YEMEN

HADRAMAWT

RED SEA

DANAKIL

DJIBOUTI

Gulf of Aden

ETHIOPIA

SOMALIA

OGADEN

RIFT VALLEY

AHMAR MTS.

KENYA

UGANDA

RWANDA

BURUNDI

TANZANIA

INDIAN OCEAN

SEYCHELLES

ZAMBIA

MALAWI

MOZAMBIQUE

ADDIS ABABA (ĀDĪS ĀBEBA)

NAIROBI

KAMPALA

KIGALI

Bujumbura

DODOMA

DAR ES SALAAM

Mogadishu (Muqdisho)

Mombasa

Zanzibar

Al-Ubayyiḍ

Kūstī

Wad Madanī

Khashm al-Qirbah

Al-Ḥudaydah

Aden ('Adan)

Gonder

Bahir Dar

Djibouti

Berbera

Boosaaso

Qandala

RAAS XAAFUUN

GEES GWARDAFUY

Dirē Dawa

Hārer

Jijiga

Hargeysa

Burco

Laascaanood

Eyl

Gaalkacyo

Mandera

Baydhabo

Jawhar

Marka

Kismaayo

Lamu

PATE ISLAND

MANDA ISLAND

Malindi

Tanga

PEMBA

ZANZIBAR

MAFIA ISLAND

GROUPE D'ALDABRA

ATOLL DE COSMOLEDO

ASSUMPTION

ASTOVE

ST. PIERRE

ATOLL DE PROVIDENCE

CABO DELGADO

(A) The Republic of Somaliland unilaterally declared its independence from Somalia in 1991.

LUANDA
PONTA DAS PALMEIRINHAS
N'dalatando
Malanje

DEM. REP. OF THE CONGO
KATANGA
Kamina
Bukama
Lake Mweru
Kawambwa
LUSENGA
NAT. PARK
Kasenga

Gabela
Sumbe
Morro
de Móco
8596 ft.
2620 m.
Camacupa
Kuito
Caála
Huambo
(Nova Lisboa)

Benguela
Lobito
CABO DE SANTA MARIA
Cubal
Garida

PLANALTO
DO BIÉ

ANGOLA

Dilolo
Kolwezi
Likasi
(Jadotville)
Lubumbashi
(Élisabethville)
Solwezi
Chingola
Mufulira
Kitwe
Ndola
Luanshya
Kabwe

Luena
Luena

ZAMBIA

LUSAKA

Lubango
Namibe
Tombua
PONTA DA MARCA

Menongue

Mongu

Cubia

Mazabuka
Monze

Choma

Oshakati
Ondangwa
OVAMBOLAND
Rundu

CAPRIVI STRIP
Katima
Mulilo
Victoria
Falls
Livingstone

Lake
Kariba

Kadoma

Cape Fria
KAOKO VELD
ETOSHA
NATIONAL
PARK
Tsumeb
Grootfontein

KAUKAU VELD

Gumare

OKAVANGO
DELTA
Maun

VICTORIA FALLS
NATIONAL PARK
Hwange
HWANGE
NATIONAL
PARK

ZIMBA
Gweru

Khorixas
Brandberg
8461 ft.
2579 m
Omaruru
Erongo
7562 ft.
2305 m
Otjiwarongo

DAMARALAND
Okahandja
Swakop
Gobabis

NAMIBIA

Ghanzi

Lake
Ngami

MAKGADIKGADI

CENTRAL
KALAHARI
GAME RESERVE

Francistown

Selebi-
Phikwe

Bulawayo

Swakopmund
Walvis Bay

Windhoek
Rehoboth

NAMIB NAUKLUFT PARK

Serowe
Mahalapye

Palapye

BOTSWANA

Tropic of Capricorn

HOLLANDSBIRD
ISLAND

Mariental

KGALAGADI
TRANSFRONTIER PARK

GEMSBOK
NATIONAL
PARK

Molepolole

Khakhea

Mochudi

Kanye

Gaborone

Thabazimbi

Polokwane
(Pietersburg)

Makhad

ATLANTIC

OCEAN

Lüderitz

KALAHARI
GEMSBOK
NATIONAL PARK

GREAT

NAMAQUALAND

KALAHARI

DESERT

Tshabong

Mafikeng

Vryburg

Kanye

Rustenburg

Pretoria
(Tshwane)

Johannesburg
Soweto
Vereeniging

Withank

Keetmanshoop
Schroffenstein
7224 ft.
2202 m

Kuruman
Kuruman

Carletonville
Klerksdorp
Standerton

Kroonstad
Welkom

Newcastle

Karasburg

Upington
Kakamas

Kimberley

Warrenton

Bethlehem

Harrismith
Ladysmith

Oranjemund

AUGRABIES FALLS
NATIONAL PARK
Kenhardt

Prieska

Hopetown

Ficksburg

Estcourt

LITTLE
NAMAQUALAND

Springbok

Bloemfontein

Maseru

LESOTHO
Thabana
Ntlenyana
11 424 ft
3482 m

Kokstad

De Aar

Colesberg
Aliwal
North

SOUTH

Umtata

Carnarvon

Victoria
West

Middelburg
Kompasberg
8209 ft.
2502 m
Cradock

AFRICA

Queenstown

King
William's
Town

Lambert's Bay

Clanwilliam

NUWEVELDBERGE

Graaff-Reinet
Beaufort West

Somerset East

Grahamstown

Port Alfred

East London

Saldanha

Piketberg

GREAT KAROO

Willowmore

Oudtshoorn

ADDO ELEPHANT
NATIONAL PARK
Uitenhage

Port Elizabeth

Atlantis
Cape Town
Simon's Town

Paarl
Worcester
Swellendam
LITTLE KAROO
George

Mosselbaai

CAPE
ST. FRANCIS

CAPE OF
GOOD HOPE
AGULHAS

0 60 120 180 240 300 360 Miles
0 60 120 180 240 300 420 480 540 600 Kilometers

Lambert Azimuthal Equal Area Projection
Scale 1:12,000,000
One inch to 190 miles
One cm to 120 km

TANZANIA

Mbala
Mbeya
Tukuyu
Karonga
KIPENGERE RANGE
Kasama
Chinsali
 Nganda
8550 ft.
2606 m
Mzuzu
Songea
Lindi
Mtwara
CABO DELGADO
Mocímboa da Praia
Mjeda
Mpika
Kasungu
LIKOMA
ISLAND
SOUTH LUANGWA
NATIONAL PARK
Lichinga
Montepuez
Pemba
ILHA QUIRIMBA
Chipata
MALAWI
Lilongwe
Mangochi
Namapa
Nacala

Luangwa
Ulóngue
Lake Malombe
Cuamba
Nampula
Ilha de
Moçambique

Chinhoyi
HARARE
(SALISBURY)
Chitungwiza
Marondera
Cantandica
Inyangani
8504 ft.
2592 m
Rusape
Zomba
Blantyre
Sapitwa
9849 ft.
3002 m
Tete
Gurué
Nsanje
Mocuba
Moma
Angoche
ILHA ANGOCHE

MOZAMBIQUE
Marromeu
Quelimane

BWE
Mutare
Chimoio
Monte Binga
7995 ft.
2437 m
Dondo
Beira

Masvingo
GREAT ZIMBABWE
Chiredzi
vishavane
GONAREZHOU
NATIONAL PARK
Beitbridge
GREAT LIMPOPO
TRANSFRONTIER PARK
PARQUE
NACIONAL
DO LIMPOPO
ILHA DO BAZARUTO
Vilankulo
PONTA SÃO SEBASTIÃO

NOSY CHESTERFIELD
Île JUAN
DE NOVA
(France; claimed
by Madagascar)

COMOROS
Moroni
NJAZIDJA
NZWANI Mutsamudu
MWALI
MAYOTTE
(France; claimed by Comoros)
Mamoudzou

GROUPE
D'ALDABRA
SEYCHELLES
ASSOMPTION
ATOLL DE COSMOLEDO
ASSUMPTION
ST. PIERRE
ASTOVE
ATOLL DE
FARQUHAR
ATOLL DE
PROVIDENCE

Îles GLORIEUSES
(France; claimed by Madagascar)
NOSY MITSIO
NOSY BE
TANJONA BOBAOMBY
TANJONA ANORONTANY
Antsiranana
(Diégo-Suarez)
NOSY LAVA
Ambanja
Maromokotro
9436 ft.
2876 m
Sambava
Antsohihy
Antalaha
TANJONA ANGONTSY
SAIKANOSY
MASOALA

Mahajanga
Marovoay
TANJONA VILANANDRO
Besalampy
Farihy
Kinkony
Tsaratanana
Mananara
Avaratra
HELODRANO
ANTONGILA
NOSY SAINTE
MARIE
Soanierana
Ivongo
Amparafaravola
Ambatondrazaka

Maintirano
NOSY
BARREN
Tsiroanomandidy
Farihy
Alaotra
Toamasina

Belo Tsiribihina
Soavinandriana
Tsiafajavona
8668 ft.
2642 m
ANTANANARIVO
Antanifotsy
Mahanoro

Morondava
Antsirabe
Ambositra
Nosy-Varika
MADAGASCAR

Morombe
BASSAS DA INDIA
(France; claimed by Madagascar)
TANJONA ANKABOA
Île EUROPA
(France; claimed
by Madagascar)
Ankazoabo
Ihosy
Boby
8720 ft.
2658 m
Fianarantsoa
Mananjary
Manakara
Farafangana

PONTA DA BARRA FALSA
Massinga
Toliara
Betioky
Vangaindrano
Tropic of Capricorn

Maxixe
PONTA DA BARRA
Lagoa
Poelela
Chókwe
Chibuto
Xai-Xai
Tsiombe
Ambovombe
Tôlañaro
(Faradofay)
TANJONA
VOHIMENA

Zaneen
KRUGER
NATIONAL
PARK
Nelspruit
Die Berg
7648 ft.
2331 m
Matola
Mbabane
Lobamba
ILHA DA INHACA
Maputo
(Lourenço Marques)
SWAZILAND
Ermelo
Lake Sibayi
Vryheid
ZULULAND
Lake St. Lucia
Penfloio

Richards Bay
Pietermaritzburg
Durban
Port Shepstone

INDIAN
OCEAN

Mozambique Channel

© Rand McNally
A-101819-1

Inset map a
Lambert Conformal Conic Projection
Scale 1:4,000,000
One inch to 64 miles
One cm to 40 km

a

INDIAN OCEAN

POINTE L'HORTAL
Triolet
Rivière du Rempart
Port Louis
Rose Hill
Curepipe
Mahébourg
MAURITIUS

REUNION
(France)
Le Port
Saint-Denis
Saint-André
Saint-Paul
Saint-Benoît
Piton des Neiges
10 072 ft.
3070 m
Piton de la Fournaise
8635 ft.
2632 m
Saint-
Pierre
Saint-Louis
Saint-Joseph

MASCARENE ISLANDS

© Rand McNally
A-101782-1

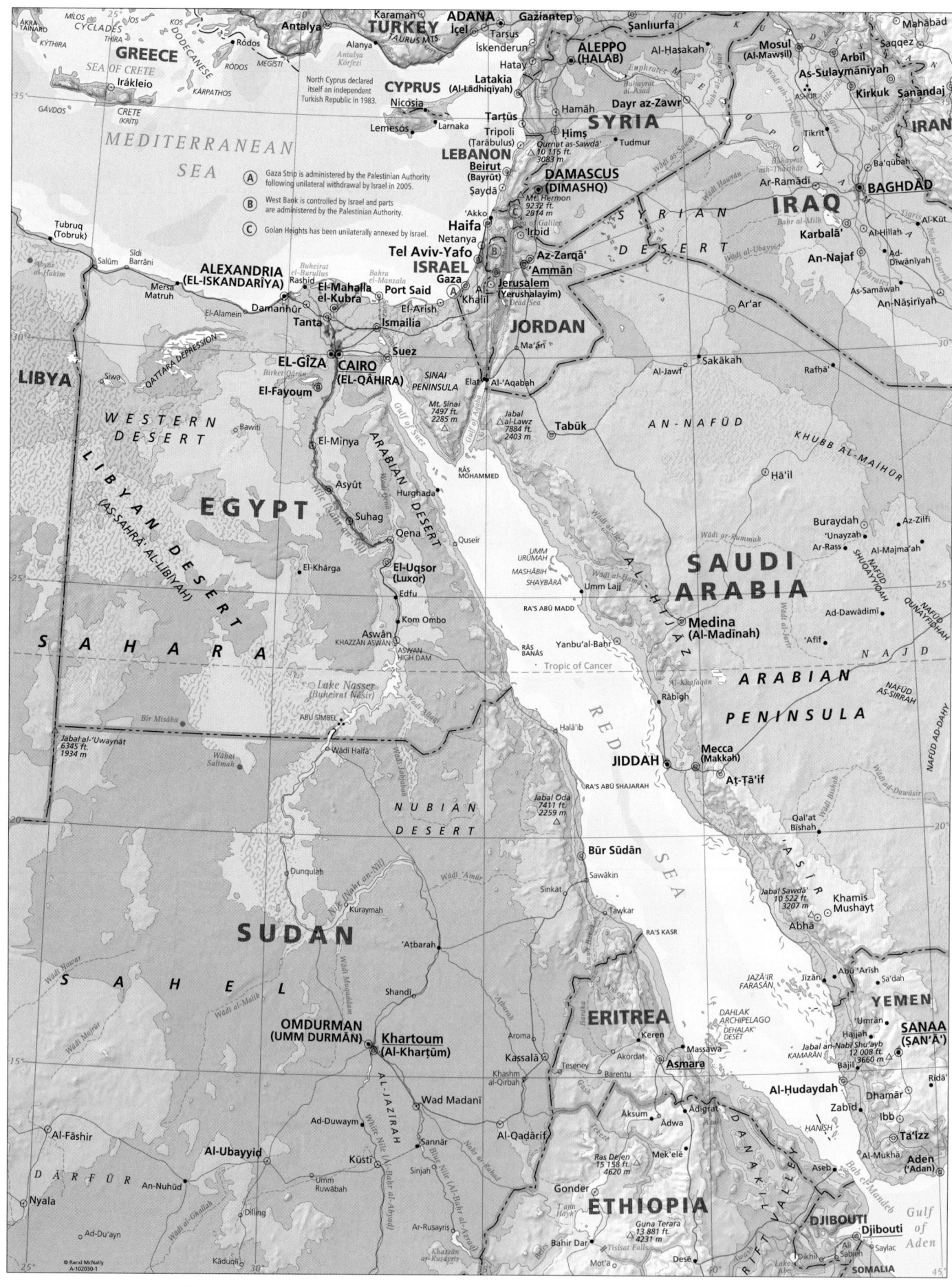

0 60 120 180 240 300 360 Miles

0 60 120 180 240 300 360 420 480 540 600 Kilometers

Lambert Azimuthal Equal Area Projection
Scale 1:12,000,000
One inch to 190 miles
One cm to 120 km

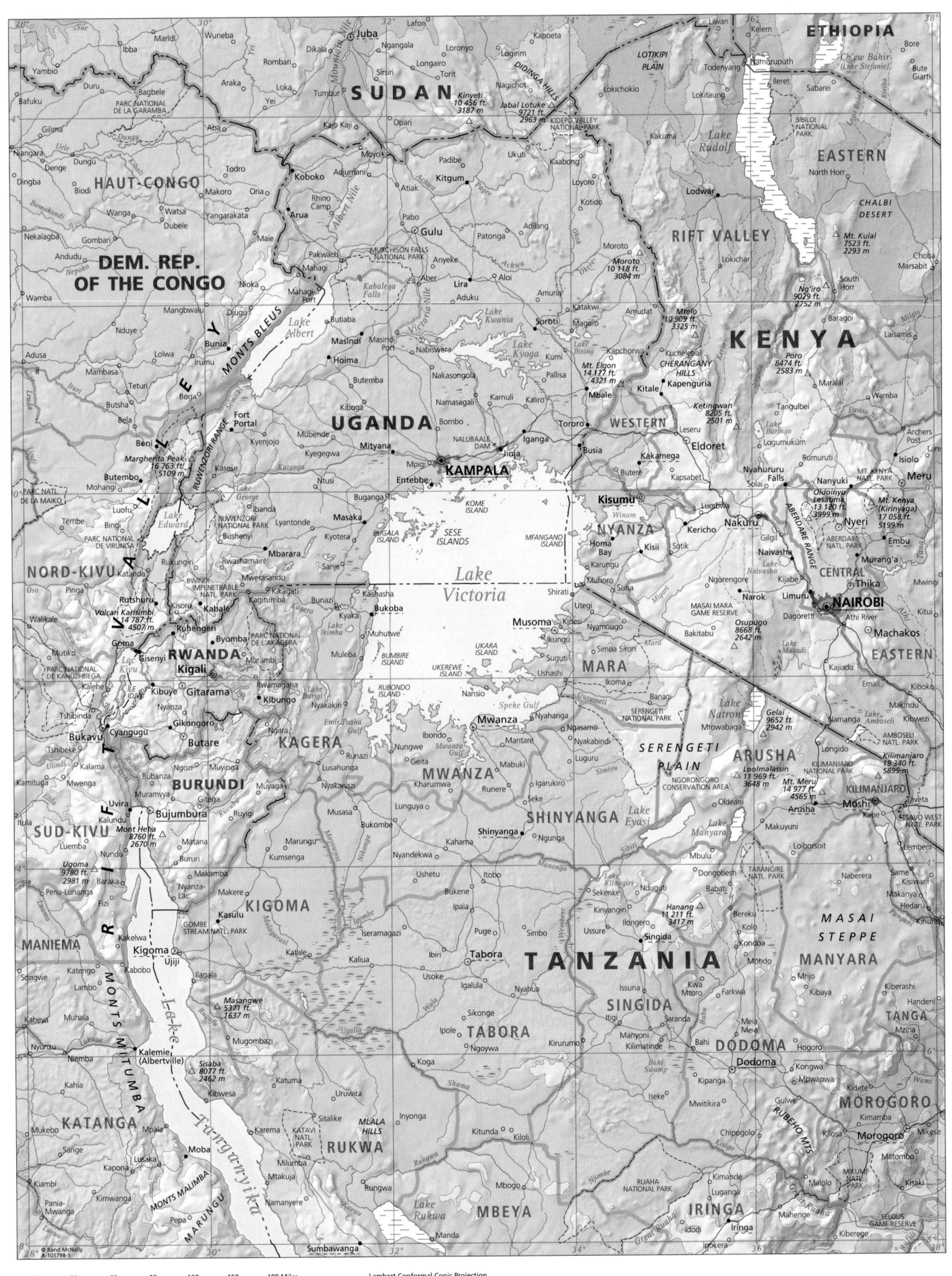

0   30   60   90   120   150   180 Miles

0   30   60   90   120   150   180   210   240   270   300 Kilometers

Lambert Conformal Conic Projection
Scale 1:6,000,000
One inch to 96 miles
One cm to 60 km

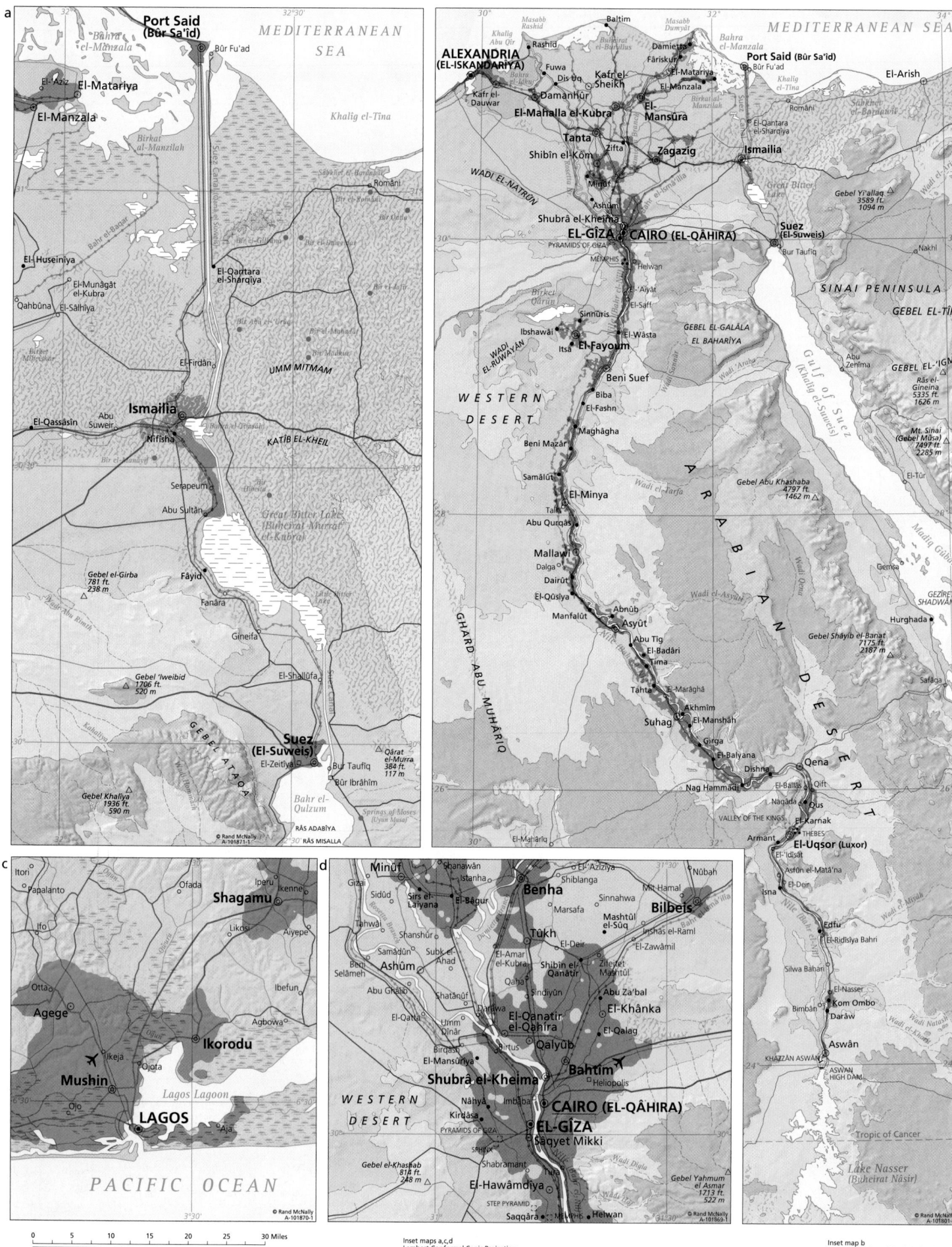

a

Port Said (Bûr Sa'îd)
Bûr Fu'ad

MEDITERRANEAN SEA

Bahra el-Manzala

El-Aziz
El-Matariya
El-Manzala

Khalig el-Tîna

Români

El-Huseinîya

El-Munâgât el-Kubra
Qahbûna
El-Sâlhîya
El-Qantara el-Sharqîya

El-Firdân

UMM MITMAM

Ismailia
El-Qassâsîn
Abu Suweir
Nifisha

KATÎB EL-KHEIL

Serapeum

Abu Sultân

Great Bitter Lake (Buheirat Murrat el-Kubrâ)

Gebel el-Girba
781 ft.
238 m
Fâyid
Fanâra

Gineifa

El-Shallûfa

Gebel 'Iweibid
1706 ft.
520 m

GEBEL ATAQA

Suez (El-Suweis)
El-Zeitiya
Bûr Taufiq

Gebel Khalîya
1936 ft.
590 m

Qârat el-Murra
384 ft.
117 m

Bûr Ibrâhîm

Bahr el-Qulzum

Springs of Moses (Uyûn Musa)

RÂS ADABÎYA
RÂS MISALLA

© Rand McNally
A-101871-1

b

MEDITERRANEAN SEA

Baltim
Rashîd
Damietta
Fâriskûr
El-Matariya
El-Manzala
Port Said (Bûr Sa'îd)
El-Arîsh

ALEXANDRIA (EL-ISKANDARÎYA)
Fuwa
Dis ûq
Kafr el-Sheikh
El-Qantara el-Sharqîya
Români

Kafr el-Dauwar
Damanhûr
El-Mahalla el-Kubra
El-Mansûra
Ismailia

Tanta
Zifta
Zagazig

Shibîn el-Kôm
Minûf

Ashûm
Suez (El-Suweis)
Bûr Taufiq

Shubrâ el-Kheima
EL-GÎZA CAIRO (EL-QÂHIRA)
PYRAMIDS OF GIZA
MEMPHIS
Helwan

Nakhl

El-'Aiyât
El-Saff

SINAI PENINSULA

Gebel Yi'allaq
3589 ft.
1094 m

Sinnûris
Ibshawâi
Itsa
El-Fayoum
El-Wâsta

GEBEL EL-GALÂLA EL BAHARÎYA

GEBEL EL-TÎH

Beni Suef

Biba
El-Fashn

Abu Zenîma

Râs el-Gineina
5335 ft.
1626 m

GEBEL EL-'IGMA

Maghâgha

WESTERN DESERT

Beni Mazâr

Samâlût

El-Minya
Talla
Abu Qurqâs

Gebel Abu Khashaba
4797 ft.
1462 m

El-Tûr

Mt. Sinai (Gebel Mûsa)
7497 ft.
2285 m

Mallawi
Dalga
Dairût
El-Qûsîya

WADI el-Asyûti

ARABIAN DESERT

Manfalût
Abnûb
Asyût
Abu Tîg
El-Badâri
Tima

Hurghada

Gemsa

GEZÎRET SHADWAN

Gebel Shâyib el-Banât
7175 ft.
2187 m

Tâhta
El-Marâghâ
Akhmîm
Suhag
El-Manshâh

Safâga

Girga

El-Balyana

Dishna
Qena

GHÂRD ABU MUHÂRIQ

Nag Hammâdi
El-Ballâs
Qift
Naqâda Qus
VALLEY OF THE KINGS
El-Karnak
THEBES
El-Uqsor (Luxor)
El-'Idîsât

Armant

© Rand McNally
A-101801-1

Inset map b
Lambert Conformal Conic Projection
Scale 1:4,000,000
One inch to 64 miles
One cm to 40 km

c

Itori
Papalanto
Ofada
Iperu
Ikenne

Ifo
Likosi
Aiyepe
Shagamu

Ibefun
Agbowa

Ottao
Agege
Ikeja
Ikorodu

Mushin
Ojota
Ojo

Lagos Lagoon

LAGOS
Aja

PACIFIC OCEAN

© Rand McNally
A-101870-1

d

Minûf
Shanawân
El-'Azîzîya
Shiblanga
Nûbah

Gizai
Sidûd
Istanha
Mit Hamal

Benha
Bilbeis

Tahwâl
Sirs el-Laiyana
El-Bâgur
Marsafa
Sinnuhwa
Mashtûl el-Sûq
Inshâs el-Raml

Shanshûr
Tûkh
El-Deir
El-Zawâmil

Samâdûn
Subk el-Ahad
El-Amar el-Kubra
Shibîn el-Qanâtir
Zifeiret Mashtûl

Ashûm
Qaha
Sindiyûn
Abu Za'bal

Abu Ghâlib
Shatânûf
Darawa
El-Qanâtir el-Qâhira
El-Khânka

El-Qatta
Umm Dînâr
Birtus
Qalyûb
El-Qalag

Birqash
El-Mansûrîya
Bahtîm
Heliopolis
Imbâba

Shubrâ el-Kheima
Kirdâsa
Nâhyâ

WESTERN DESERT

CAIRO (EL-QÂHIRA)
EL-GÎZA
Sâqyet Mikki
PYRAMIDS OF GIZA
SPHINX
Shabramant

Gebel el-Khashab
81 ft.
248 m

Gebel Yahmum el Asmar
1713 ft.
522 m

El-Hawâmdîya

STEP PYRAMID
Saqqâra
MEMPHIS
Helwan

© Rand McNally
A-101869-1

Inset maps a,c,d
Lambert Conformal Conic Projection
Scale 1:1,000,000
One inch to 16 miles
One cm to 10 km

Asfûn el-Matâ'na
El-Deir
Isna
El-Ridîsîya Bahri
Edfu
Silwa Bahâri
El-Nasser
Kôm Ombo
Birnbân
Darâw

Wadi Natash

KHAZZÂN ASWÂN
Aswân
ASWAN HIGH DAM

Tropic of Cancer

Lake Nasser (Buheirat Nâsir)

0 5 10 15 20 25 30 Miles
0 5 10 15 20 25 30 35 40 45 50 Kilometers

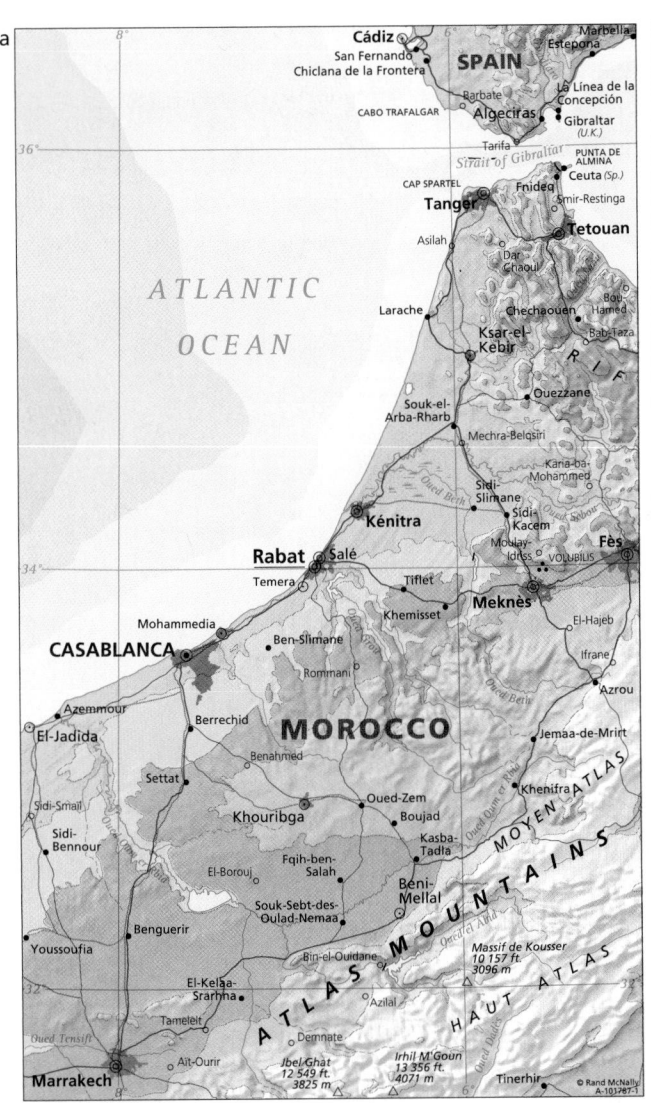

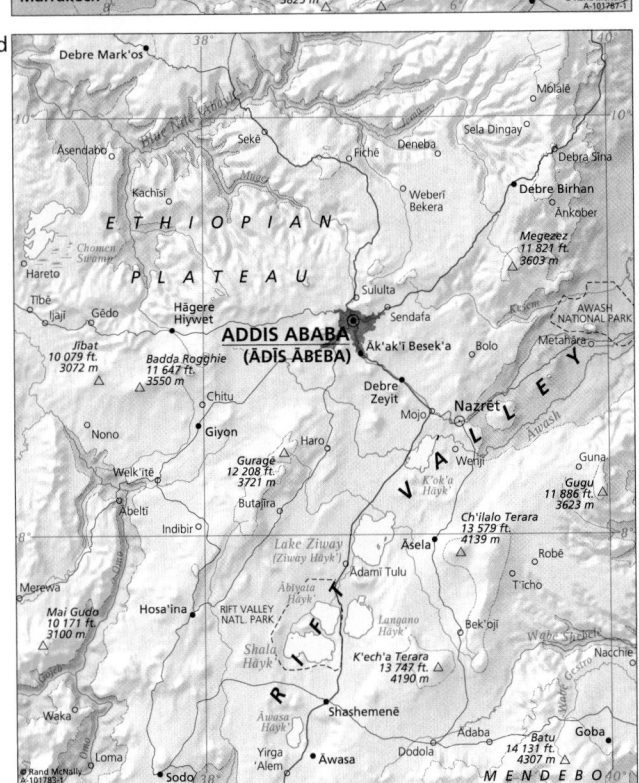

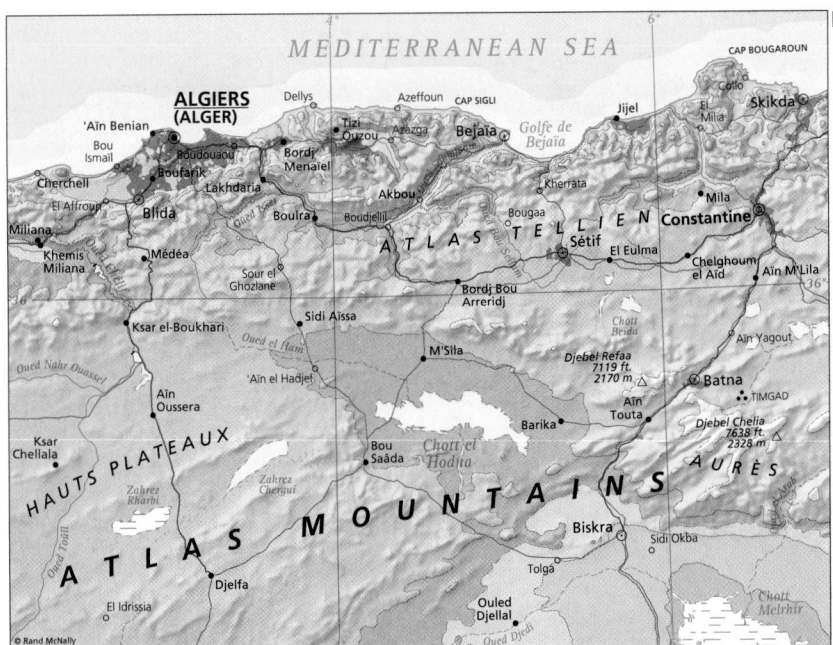

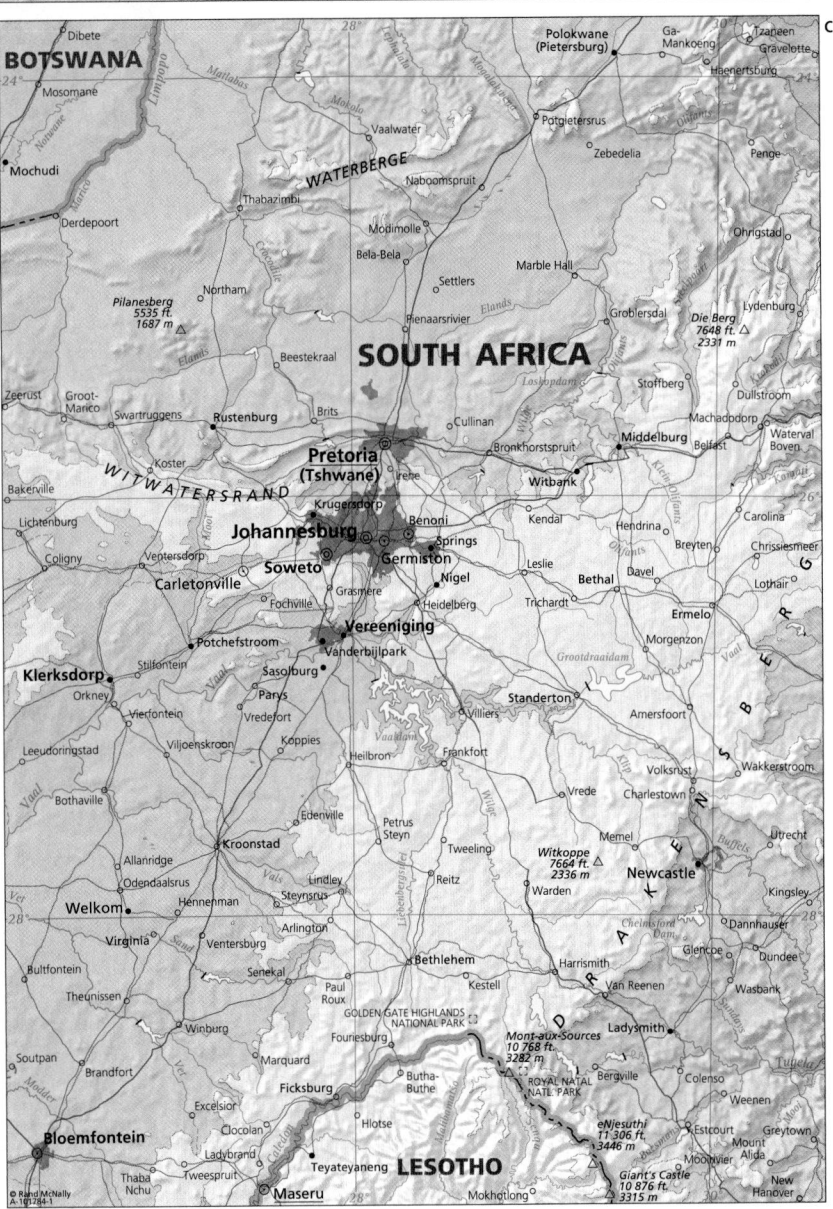

Lambert Azimuthal Equal Area Projection
Scale 1:4,000,000
One inch to 64 miles
One cm to 40 km

JAVA SEA
MADURA
SEMARANG
SURABAYA
BALI SEA
Malang
JAVA
(JAWA)
Denpasar
BALI
LOMBOK
Mataram
SUMBAWA
SUMBA
INDONESIA
LESSER SUNDA ISLANDS
FLORES
FLORES
SEA
PULAU
WETAR
Dili
TIMOR
PULAU
ALOR
EAST TIMOR
SAVU SEA
PULAU
ROTI
PULAU
BABAR
PULAU
YAMDENA
ARAFURA
SEA

TIMOR SEA

INDIAN OCEAN

ASHMORE
AND CARTIER
ISLANDS
(Austl.)

CAPE LONDONDERRY
Joseph
Bonaparte
Gulf

COBOURG
PENINSULA
MELVILLE
ISLAND
BATHURST
ISLAND
Beagle
Gulf
Van
Diemen
Gulf
Darwin
Pine
Creek
Katherine
ARNHEM
LAND
Daly
Roper
CAPE
WESSEL
CAPE ARNHEM
GROOTE
EYLANDT
GULF OF
CARPENTARIA
MORNINGTON
ISLAND
Burketown

Wyndham
Kununurra
Lake
Argyle
Collier
Bay
CAPE LEVEQUE
KIMBERLEY
Derby
Fitzroy
Broome
Fitzroy
Crossing
Halls
Creek
Victoria
Daly
Waters
Borroloola
BARKLY TABLELAND
Lake
Woods
TANAMI
DESERT
Tennant
Creek
Camooweal
Mount
Isa

Port
Hedland
Shay Gap
De Grey
Karratha
Roebourne
Marble Bar
BARROW
ISLAND
Onslow
NORTH WEST CAPE
Exmouth
Tom Price
Paraburdoo
Newman
Fortescue
Ashburton
GREAT SANDY
DESERT
Lake
Gregory
Lake
Dora
Lake
Auld
Lake
Disappointment
GIBSON
DESERT
Lake
Mackay
Lake
Wills
Lake
White
Lake
Macdonald
NORTHERN
TERRITORY
Barrow
Creek
AUSTRALIA
Boulia
Georgina
Mount Isa

Lake
Macleod
Carnarvon
SHARK
BAY
DIRK HARTOG
ISLAND
Denham
Gascoyne
WESTERN
AUSTRALIA
Lake
Carnegie
MACDONNELL
RANGES
Alice
Springs
Uluru
(Ayers Rock)
△ 2831 ft.
863 m
Mt. Woodroffe △
4708 ft.
1435 m
SIMPSON
DESERT
Birdsville
Eyre Creek
Oodnadatta
Macumba
Cooper

Tropic of Capricorn

Meekatharra
Murchison
Cue
Mount Magnet
Leonora
Lake
Barlee
Lake
Ballard
Laverton
Lake
Carey
GREAT VICTORIA DESERT
SOUTH
AUSTRALIA
Lake
Eyre
North
Lake
Eyre
South
Marree
Lake
Frome

Kalbarri
Northampton
Geraldton
Dongara
Mullewa
Yalgoo
Lake
Moore
Kalgoorlie-
Boulder
Coolgardie
Lake
Lefroy
Rawlinna
Ooldea
NULLARBOR PLAIN
Eucla
Ceduna
Woomera
Lake
Gairdner
Hawker
Kimba
EYRE
PENINSULA
Quorn
Whyalla
Peter-
borough

Moora
Northam
Wanneroo
York
Perth
Beverley
Fremantle
Brookton
Narrogin
Bunbury
DARLING RANGE
Collie
Katanning
CAPE NATURALISTE
Busselton
Augusta
CAPE LEEUWIN
Pemberton
Bridgetown
Mount Barker
Albany
Southern
Cross
Lake
Johnston
Lake
Cowan
Lake
Dundas
Norseman
Ravensthorpe
Esperance
GREAT AUSTRALIAN BIGHT
Elliston
Spencer
Gulf
Port
Lincoln
Port
Augusta
Port
Pirie
Wallaroo
Gulf St. Vincent
KANGAROO
ISLAND
Adelaide
Murray
Bridge
Encounter Bay
Kingston Southeast
Port
Elizabeth

INDIAN OCEAN

© Rand McNally
A-101715-1

0 80 160 240 320 400 480 Miles
0 80 160 240 320 400 480 560 640 720 800 Kilometers

Lambert Azimuthal Equal Area Projection
Scale 1:16,000,000
One inch to 256 miles
One cm to 160 km

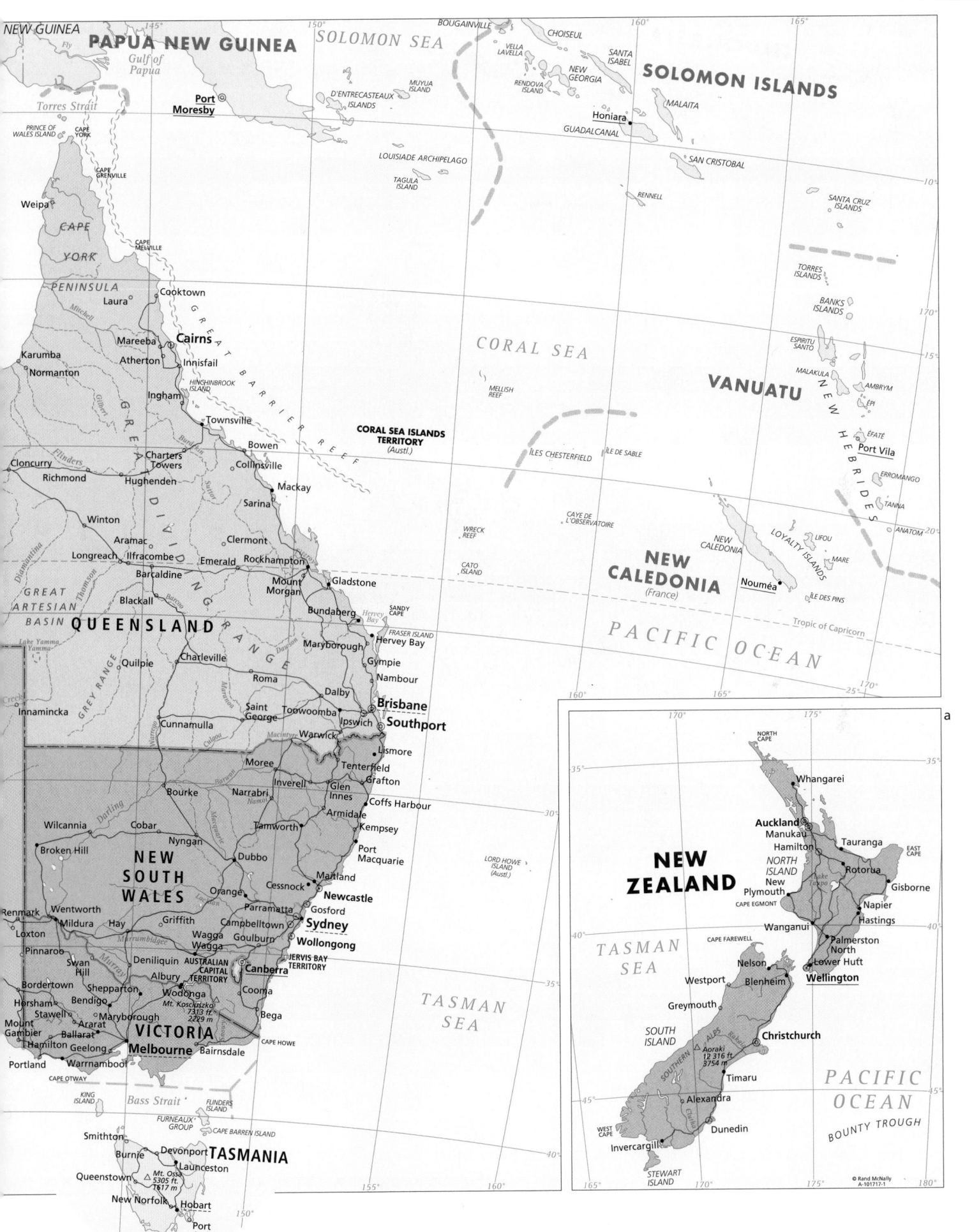

NEW GUINEA
PAPUA NEW GUINEA
Fly
Gulf of Papua
Port Moresby
Torres Strait
PRINCE OF WALES ISLAND
CAPE YORK
CAPE GRENVILLE

SOLOMON SEA
BOUGAINVILLE
CHOISEUL
VELLA LAVELLA
MUYUA ISLAND
D'ENTRECASTEAUX ISLANDS
RENDOVA ISLAND
NEW GEORGIA
SANTA ISABEL
SOLOMON ISLANDS
Honiara
GUADALCANAL
MALAITA
SAN CRISTOBAL
LOUISIADE ARCHIPELAGO
TAGULA ISLAND
RENNELL

TORRES ISLANDS
BANKS ISLANDS
SANTA CRUZ ISLANDS

Weipa
CAPE YORK
Laura
Cooktown
Karumba
Normanton
Mareeba
Atherton
Cairns
Innisfail
HINCHINBROOK ISLAND
Ingham
Townsville
Bowen
Cloncurry
Richmond
Hughenden
Charters Towers
Collinsville
Mackay
Winton
Sarina
Aramac
Clermont
Longreach Ilfracombe
Emerald
Rockhampton
Barcaldine
Mount Morgan
Gladstone
Blackall
QUEENSLAND
Bundaberg
SANDY CAPE
Quilpie
Maryborough
Hervey Bay
FRASER ISLAND
Charleville
Gympie
Roma
Nambour
Dalby
Innamincka
Cunnamulla
Saint George
Toowoomba
Warwick
Ipswich
Brisbane
Southport
Lismore
Moree
Tenterfield
Grafton
Inverell
Glen Innes
Coffs Harbour
Narrabri
Armidale
Bourke
Tamworth
Kempsey
Wilcannia
Cobar
Port Macquarie
Broken Hill
Nyngan
Dubbo
NEW SOUTH WALES
Orange
Maitland
Cessnock
Wentworth
Newcastle
Parramatta
Gosford
Renmark
Hay
Griffith
Sydney
Loxton
Campbelltown
Goulburn
Wollongong
Pinnaroo
Swan Hill
Deniliquin
Wagga Wagga
JERVIS BAY TERRITORY
Bordertown
Albury
AUSTRALIAN CAPITAL TERRITORY
Canberra
Horsham
Shepparton
Wodonga
Cooma
Stawell
Bendigo
Mt. Kosciuszko 7313 ft. 2229 m
Mount Gambier
Maryborough
Ararat
Bega
Ballarat
VICTORIA
Hamilton
Geelong
Melbourne
Bairnsdale
Portland
Warrnambool
CAPE HOWE
CAPE OTWAY
KING ISLAND
Bass Strait
FLINDERS ISLAND
FURNEAUX GROUP
CAPE BARREN ISLAND
Smithton
Burnie
Devonport
TASMANIA
Launceston
Queenstown
Mt. Ossa 5305 ft. 1617 m
New Norfolk
Hobart
Port Arthur
SOUTH EAST CAPE

CORAL SEA
MELLISH REEF
CORAL SEA ISLANDS TERRITORY (Austl.)
ÎLES CHESTERFIELD
ÎLE DE SABLE
WRECK REEF
CAYE DE L'OBSERVATOIRE
CATO ISLAND

VANUATU
ESPIRITU SANTO
MALAKULA
AMBRYM
EPI
ÉFATÉ
Port Vila
ERROMANGO
TANNA
ANATOM
NEW HEBRIDES
LOYALTY ISLANDS
LIFOU
MARE
NEW CALEDONIA (France)
NEW CALEDONIA
Nouméa
ÎLE DES PINS

PACIFIC OCEAN
Tropic of Capricorn

TASMAN SEA
LORD HOWE ISLAND (Austl.)

NEW ZEALAND (inset)
NORTH CAPE
Whangarei
Auckland
Manukau
Hamilton
Tauranga
EAST CAPE
NORTH ISLAND
Rotorua
New Plymouth
CAPE EGMONT
Gisborne
Napier
Hastings
Wanganui
Palmerston North
TASMAN SEA
CAPE FAREWELL
Nelson
Lower Hutt
Wellington
Westport
Blenheim
Greymouth
SOUTH ISLAND
SOUTHERN ALPS
Aoraki 12 316 ft 3754 m
Christchurch
Timaru
Alexandra
PACIFIC OCEAN
WEST CAPE
Dunedin
BOUNTY TROUGH
Invercargill
STEWART ISLAND

© Rand McNally
A-101717-1

0   80   160   240   320   400   480 Miles

0   80 160 240 320 400 480 560 640 720   800 Kilometers

Lambert Azimuthal Equal Area Projection
Scale 1:16,000,000
One inch to 256 miles
One cm to 160 km

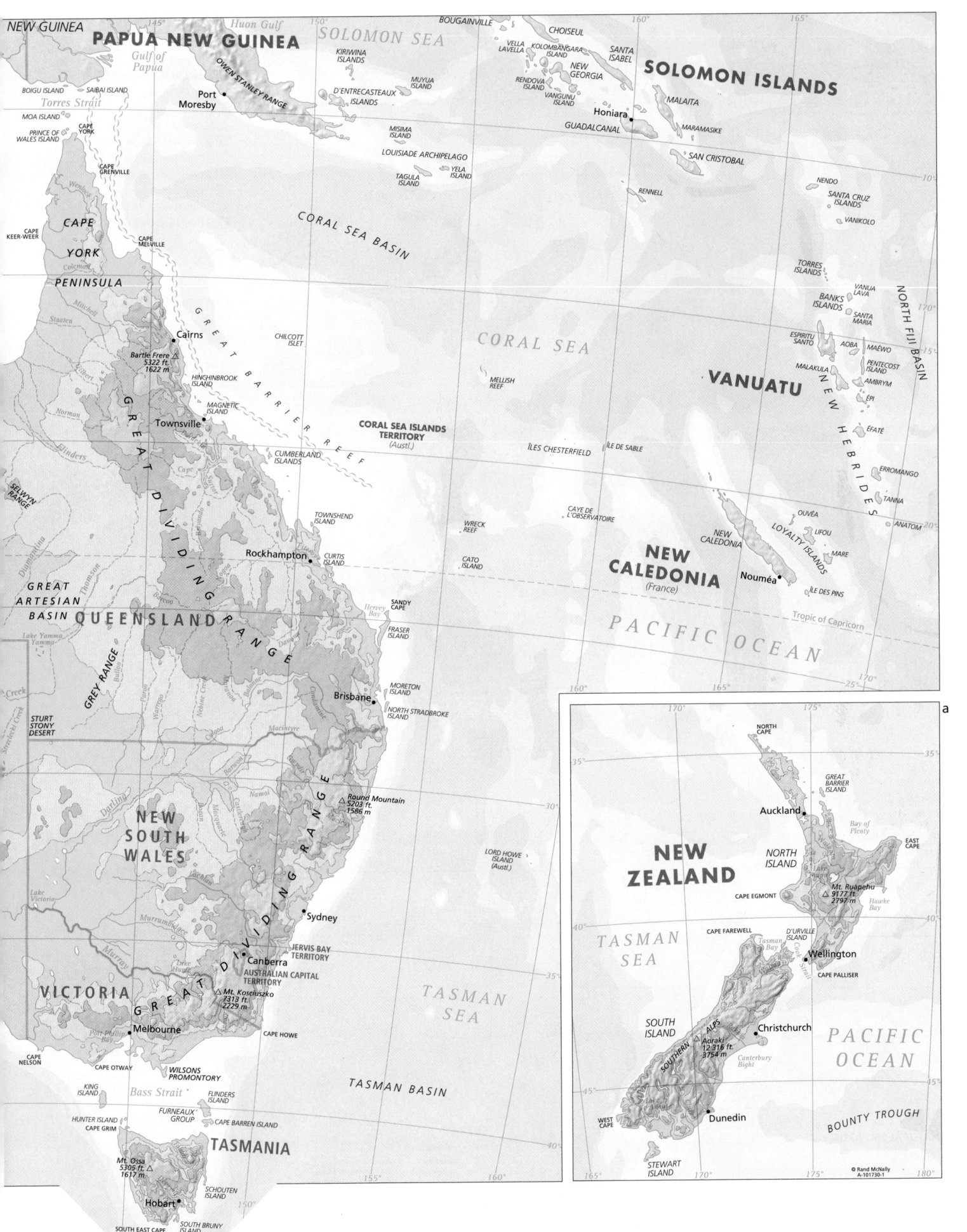

NEW GUINEA

PAPUA NEW GUINEA

Huon Gulf

SOLOMON SEA

BOUGAINVILLE

CHOISEUL

VELLA
LAVELLA · KOLOMBANGARA
ISLAND
NEW
GEORGIA

KIRIWINA
ISLANDS

SANTA
ISABEL

Gulf of
Papua

OWEN STANLEY RANGE

D'ENTRECASTEAUX
ISLANDS

RENDOVA
ISLAND
VANGUNU
ISLAND

SOLOMON ISLANDS

MUYUA
ISLAND

MALAITA

Port
Moresby

MISIMA
ISLAND

Honiara

MARAMASIKE

Torres Strait

LOUISIADE ARCHIPELAGO

GUADALCANAL

BOIGU ISLAND   SAIBAI ISLAND

TAGULA
ISLAND
YELA
ISLAND

SAN CRISTOBAL

MOA ISLAND

CAPE
YORK

PRINCE OF
WALES ISLAND

CAPE
GRENVILLE

RENNELL

NENDO

SANTA
CRUZ
ISLANDS

VANIKOLO

CAPE

Colmon

YORK

CAPE
MELVILLE

CORAL SEA BASIN

TORRES
ISLANDS

CAPE
KEER-WEER

PENINSULA

VANUA
LAVA

BANK'S
ISLANDS

SANTA
MARIA

NORTH FIJI BASIN

Staaten

CHILCOTT
ISLET

ESPIRITU
SANTO

AOBA
MAEWO

Cairns

CORAL SEA

Bartle Frere △
5322 ft.
1622 m

MALAKULA

PENTECOST
ISLAND

AMBRYM

Mitchell

HINCHINBROOK
ISLAND

MELLISH
REEF

VANUATU

EPI

Gilbert

MAGNETIC
ISLAND

Townsville

ÉFATÉ

Norman

**CORAL SEA ISLANDS
TERRITORY**
(Austl.)

ÎLES CHESTERFIELD

ÎLE DE SABLE

ERROMANGO

SELWYN
RANGE

CUMBERLAND
ISLANDS

TANNA

Flinders

TOWNSHEND
ISLAND

WRECK
REEF

CAYE DE
L'OBSERVATOIRE

OUVÉA

LIFOU

ANATOM

LOYALTY ISLANDS

Diamantina

Rockhampton

CURTIS
ISLAND

CATO
ISLAND

NEW
CALEDONIA

MARE

**GREAT
ARTESIAN
BASIN**

Thomson

Barcoo

SANDY
CAPE

**NEW
CALEDONIA**
(France)

Nouméa

QUEENSLAND

Hervey
Bay

FRASER
ISLAND

Tropic of Capricorn

ÎLE DES PINS

Lake Yamma
Yamma

**PACIFIC
OCEAN**

GREY RANGE

MORETON
ISLAND

Brisbane

Creek

NORTH STRADBROKE
ISLAND

STURT
STONY
DESERT

a

NORTH
CAPE

**NEW
SOUTH
WALES**

Round Mountain
5203 ft.
1586 m

GREAT
BARRIER
ISLAND

Auckland

LORD HOWE
ISLAND
(Austl.)

**NEW
ZEALAND**

**NORTH
ISLAND**

Bay of
Plenty

EAST
CAPE

Mt. Ruapehu
△ 9177 ft.
2797 m

CAPE EGMONT

Hawke
Bay

**TASMAN
SEA**

CAPE FAREWELL

D'URVILLE
ISLAND

Sydney

Tasman
Bay

Wellington

JERVIS BAY
TERRITORY

Canberra

CAPE PALLISER

**AUSTRALIAN CAPITAL
TERRITORY**

**TASMAN
SEA**

△ Mt. Kosciuszko
7313 ft.
2229 m

**SOUTH
ISLAND**

ALPS

Christchurch

VICTORIA

Aoraki
△ 12,316 ft.
3754 m

**PACIFIC
OCEAN**

Melbourne

SOUTHERN

Canterbury
Bight

CAPE HOWE

CAPE
NELSON

CAPE OTWAY

WILSONS
PROMONTORY

WEST
CAPE

Dunedin

KING
ISLAND

Bass Strait

FLINDERS
ISLAND

FURNEAUX
GROUP

CAPE BARREN ISLAND

TASMAN BASIN

BOUNTY TROUGH

HUNTER ISLAND

CAPE GRIM

TASMANIA

STEWART
ISLAND

Mt. Ossa
5305 ft. △
1617 m

SCHOUTEN
ISLAND

Hobart

© Rand McNally
A-101730-1

SOUTH BRUNY
ISLAND

SOUTH EAST CAPE

Land Cover

- Evergreen Broadleaf Forest
- Mixed Forest
- Woodland
- Wooded Grassland
- Closed Shrubland
- Open Shrubland
- Grassland
- Cropland
- Bare Ground (Desert)
- Urban and Built Up

PACIFIC OCEAN

Equator

NEW GUINEA

NEW BRITAIN

SOLOMON ISLANDS

ARAFURA SEA

SOLOMON SEA

TIMOR SEA

INDIAN OCEAN

ARNHEM LAND

Gulf of Carpentaria

CORAL SEA

KIMBERLEY

TANAMI DESERT

BARKLY TABLELAND

NEW HEBRIDES

GREAT SANDY DESERT

GIBSON DESERT

SIMPSON DESERT

GREAT ARTESIAN BASIN

NEW CALEDONIA

Tropic of Capricorn

GREAT DIVIDING RANGE

GREAT VICTORIA DESERT

Lake Eyre North

STURT STONY DESERT

Brisbane

NULLARBOR PLAIN

Darling

Sydney

Perth

DARLING RA.

GREAT AUSTRALIAN BIGHT

Adelaide

Murray

Melbourne

TASMAN SEA

INDIAN OCEAN

TASMANIA

NORTH ISLAND

Auckland

SOUTH ISLAND

SOUTHERN ALPS

Source: CIESIN; Hansen et al., 2000

A-102089-1 © Rand McNally

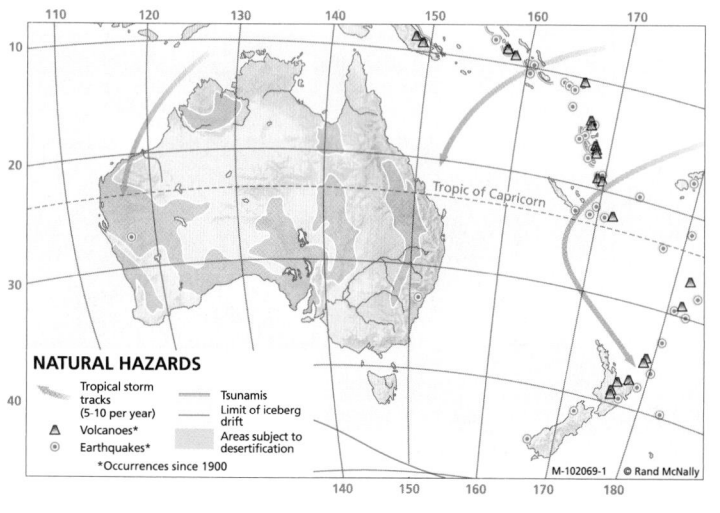

NATURAL HAZARDS

- Tropical storm tracks (5-10 per year)
- Volcanoes*
- Earthquakes*
- Tsunamis
- Limit of iceberg drift
- Areas subject to desertification

*Occurrences since 1900

Tropic of Capricorn

M-102069-1 © Rand McNally

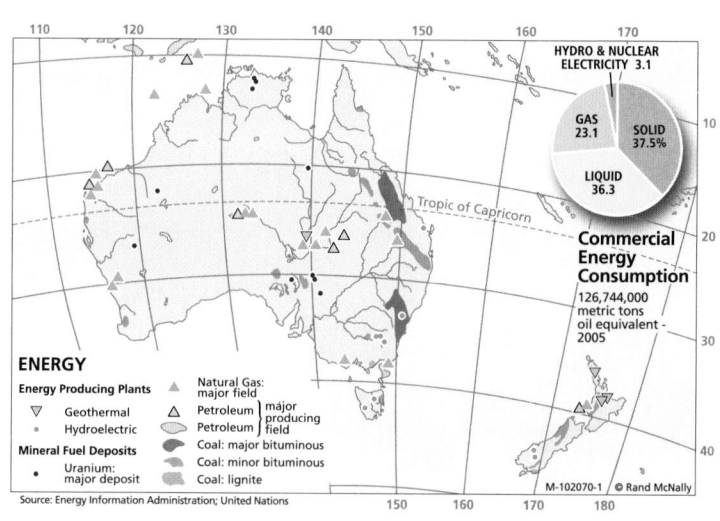

ENERGY

Energy Producing Plants
- Geothermal
- Hydroelectric

Mineral Fuel Deposits
- Uranium: major deposit

- Natural Gas: major field
- Petroleum: major producing field
- Petroleum
- Coal: major bituminous
- Coal: minor bituminous
- Coal: lignite

HYDRO & NUCLEAR ELECTRICITY 3.1

GAS 23.1
SOLID 37.5%
LIQUID 36.3

Commercial Energy Consumption

126,744,000 metric tons oil equivalent - 2005

Tropic of Capricorn

Source: Energy Information Administration; United Nations

M-102070-1 © Rand McNally

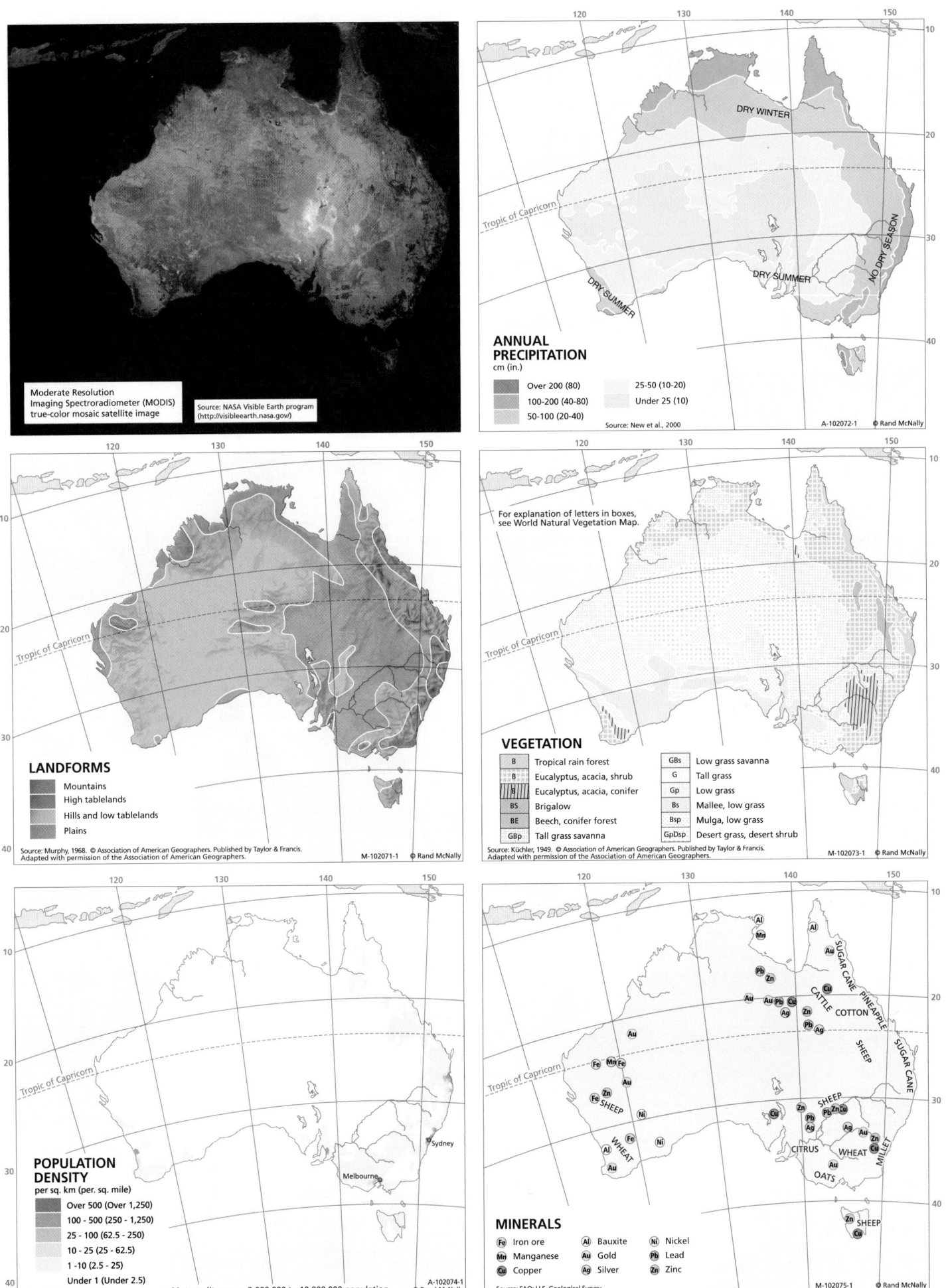

Moderate Resolution
Imaging Spectroradiometer (MODIS)
true-color mosaic satellite image

Source: NASA Visible Earth program
(http://visibleearth.nasa.gov/)

DRY WINTER

DRY SUMMER

DRY SUMMER

DRY SUMMER

NO DRY SEASON

Tropic of Capricorn

ANNUAL PRECIPITATION
cm (in.)

- Over 200 (80)
- 100-200 (40-80)
- 50-100 (20-40)
- 25-50 (10-20)
- Under 25 (10)

Source: New et al., 2000   A-102072-1   © Rand McNally

LANDFORMS

- Mountains
- High tablelands
- Hills and low tablelands
- Plains

Tropic of Capricorn

Source: Murphy, 1968. © Association of American Geographers. Published by Taylor & Francis.
Adapted with permission of the Association of American Geographers.   M-102071-1   © Rand McNally

VEGETATION

For explanation of letters in boxes,
see World Natural Vegetation Map.

Tropic of Capricorn

B	Tropical rain forest	GBs	Low grass savanna
B	Eucalyptus, acacia, shrub	G	Tall grass
B	Eucalyptus, acacia, conifer	Gp	Low grass
BS	Brigalow	Bs	Mallee, low grass
BE	Beech, conifer forest	Bsp	Mulga, low grass
GBp	Tall grass savanna	GpDsp	Desert grass, desert shrub

Source: Küchler, 1949. © Association of American Geographers. Published by Taylor & Francis.
Adapted with permission of the Association of American Geographers.   M-102073-1   © Rand McNally

POPULATION DENSITY
per sq. km (per. sq. mile)

- Over 500 (Over 1,250)
- 100 - 500 (250 - 1,250)
- 25 - 100 (62.5 - 250)
- 10 - 25 (25 - 62.5)
- 1 -10 (2.5 - 25)
- Under 1 (Under 2.5)

Tropic of Capricorn

Sydney
Melbourne

○ Metropolitan area 2,000,000 to 10,000,000 population

Source: U.S. Department of Energy   A-102074-1   © Rand McNally

MINERALS

Tropic of Capricorn

SUGAR CANE
PINEAPPLE
CATTLE
COTTON
SHEEP
SUGAR CANE
SHEEP
SHEEP
SHEEP
CITRUS
WHEAT
MILLET
OATS
WHEAT

Fe	Iron ore	Al	Bauxite	Ni	Nickel
Mn	Manganese	Au	Gold	Pb	Lead
Cu	Copper	Ag	Silver	Zn	Zinc

Source: FAO; U.S. Geological Survey   M-102075-1   © Rand McNally

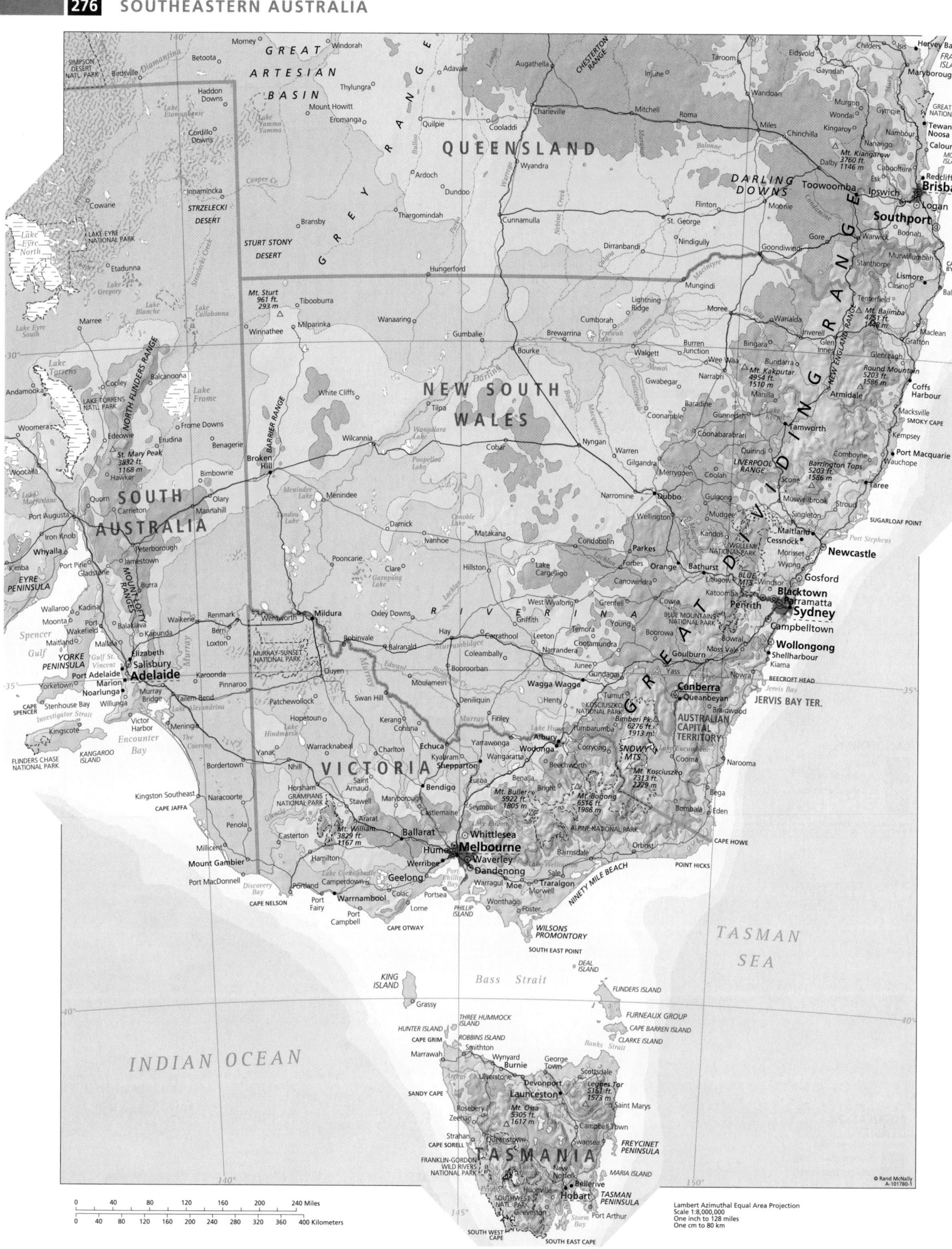

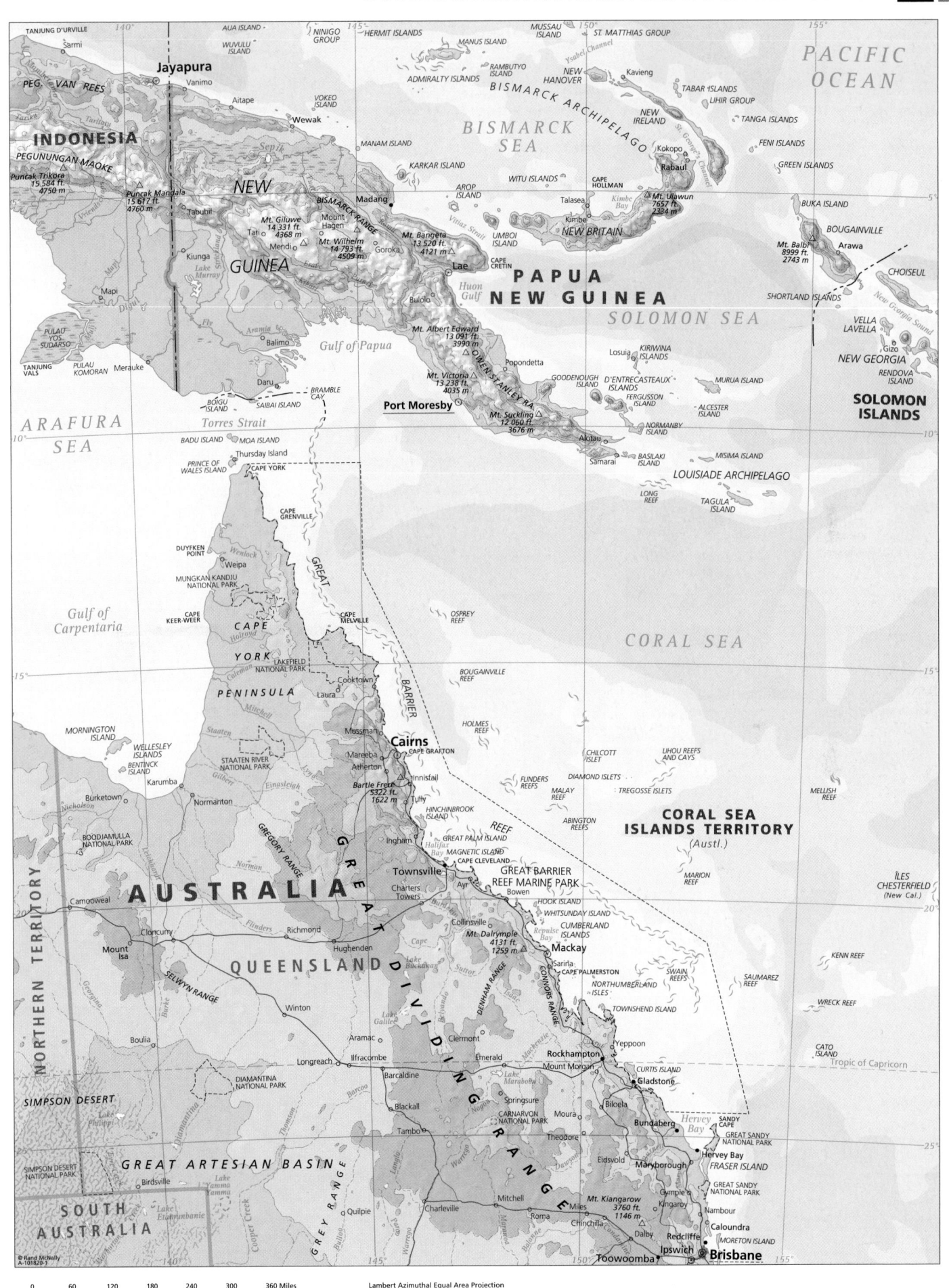

TANJUNG D'URVILLE
Sarmi
PEG. VAN REES
INDONESIA
PEGUNUNGAN MAOKE
Puncak Trikora
15,584 ft.
4750 m
Puncak Mandala
15,617 ft.
4760 m
Tabubil
Mt. Giluwe
14,331 ft.
4368 m
Tati
Mt. Wilhelm
14,793 ft.
4509 m
Mendi
NEW
GUINEA
Kiunga
Lake Murray
Mapi
Digul
PULAU YOS SUDARSO
TANJUNG VALS
PULAU KOMORAN
Merauke
Balimo
Daru
BOIGU ISLAND
SAIBAI ISLAND
BRAMBLE CAY
Torres Strait
ARAFURA SEA
BADU ISLAND
MOA ISLAND
Thursday Island
PRINCE OF WALES ISLAND
CAPE YORK

Jayapura
Vanimo
AUA ISLAND
WUVULU ISLAND
NINIGO GROUP
HERMIT ISLANDS
MANUS ISLAND
MUSSAU ISLAND
ST. MATTHIAS GROUP
Aitape
VOKEO ISLAND
Wewak
Sepik
MANAM ISLAND
KARKAR ISLAND
Madang
BISMARCK RANGE
Mount Hagen
Goroka
Mt. Bangeta
13,520 ft.
4121 m
Lae
CAPE CRETIN
Bulolo
Huon Gulf
Aramia
Fly
Gulf of Papua
Mt. Albert Edward
13,091 ft.
3990 m
Mt. Victoria
13,238 ft.
4035 m
Port Moresby
Mt. Suckling
12,060 ft.
3676 m
Popondetta
OWEN STANLEY RA.
Alotau
Samarai

ADMIRALTY ISLANDS
BISMARCK ARCHIPELAGO
NEW HANOVER
Kavieng
TABAR ISLANDS
LIHIR GROUP
NEW IRELAND
Kokopo
Rabaul
TANGA ISLANDS
FENI ISLANDS
GREEN ISLANDS
PACIFIC OCEAN
BISMARCK SEA
AROP ISLAND
WITU ISLANDS
CAPE HOLLMAN
Talasea
Kimbe Bay
Kimbe
UMBOI ISLAND
NEW BRITAIN
Mt. Ulawun
7657 ft.
2334 m
BUKA ISLAND
BOUGAINVILLE
Arawa
Mt. Balbi
8999 ft.
2743 m
CHOISEUL
SHORTLAND ISLANDS
SOLOMON SEA
PAPUA NEW GUINEA
KIRIWINA ISLANDS
Losuia
GOODENOUGH ISLAND
D'ENTRECASTEAUX ISLANDS
FERGUSSON ISLAND
MURUA ISLAND
ALCESTER ISLAND
NORMANBY ISLAND
BASILAKI ISLAND
MISIMA ISLAND
LOUISIADE ARCHIPELAGO
LONG REEF
TAGULA ISLAND
VELLA LAVELLA
Gizo
NEW GEORGIA
RENDOVA ISLAND
SOLOMON ISLANDS

CAPE GRENVILLE
DUYFKEN POINT
Weipa
MUNGKAN KANDJU NATIONAL PARK
CAPE KEER-WEER
CAPE YORK
PENINSULA
Holroyd
LAKEFIELD NATIONAL PARK
Cooktown
Laura
Gulf of Carpentaria
MORNINGTON ISLAND
WELLESLEY ISLANDS
BENTINCK ISLAND
Burketown
BOODJAMULLA NATIONAL PARK
Nicholson
Karumba
Normanton
STAATEN RIVER NATIONAL PARK
Staaten
Gilbert
Einasleigh
Mossman
Mareeba
Cairns
CAPE GRAFTON
Atherton
Innisfail
Bartle Frere
5322 ft.
1622 m
Tully
HINCHINBROOK ISLAND
Ingham
Halifax Bay
GREAT PALM ISLAND
MAGNETIC ISLAND
CAPE CLEVELAND
Townsville
Ayr
BARRIER
REEF
GREAT

OSPREY REEF
CORAL SEA
HOLMES REEF
BOUGAINVILLE REEF
CHILCOTT ISLET
LIHOU REEFS AND CAYS
DIAMOND ISLETS
FLINDERS REEFS
MALAY REEF
ABINGTON REEFS
TREGOSSE ISLETS
CORAL SEA ISLANDS TERRITORY
(Austl.)
MARION REEF
MELLISH REEF
ÎLES CHESTERFIELD
(New Cal.)

AUSTRALIA
Camooweal
Cloncurry
Mount Isa
SELWYN RANGE
QUEENSLAND
Richmond
Hughenden
Flinders
Cape
GREGORY RANGE
GREAT DIVIDING RANGE
Winton
Boulia
Aramac
Clermont
Emerald
Longreach
Ifracombe
Barcaldine
DIAMANTINA NATIONAL PARK
Blackall
Tambo
SIMPSON DESERT
Birdsville
SIMPSON DESERT NATIONAL PARK
GREAT ARTESIAN BASIN
Lake Yamma Yamma
SOUTH AUSTRALIA
Cooper Creek
Lake Eyrabanie
GREY RANGE
Quilpie
Charleville
Mitchell
Miles
Roma
Chinchilla
Dalby
Toowoomba

Charters Towers
Bowen
HOOK ISLAND
WHITSUNDAY ISLAND
Collinsville
CUMBERLAND ISLANDS
Mt. Dalrymple
4131 ft.
1259 m
Mackay
Sarina
CAPE PALMERSTON
NORTHUMBERLAND ISLES
DENHAM RANGE
CONNORS RANGE
TOWNSHEND ISLAND
SWAIN REEFS
SAUMAREZ REEF
KENN REEF
WRECK REEF
CATO ISLAND
Tropic of Capricorn
Yeppoon
Rockhampton
Mount Morgan
CURTIS ISLAND
Gladstone
Springsure
CARNARVON NATIONAL PARK
Moura
Theodore
Biloela
Eidsvold
Bundaberg
Hervey Bay
SANDY CAPE
GREAT SANDY NATIONAL PARK
Maryborough
FRASER ISLAND
GREAT SANDY NATIONAL PARK
Mt. Kiangarow
3760 ft.
1146 m
Gympie
Kingaroy
Nambour
Caloundra
MORETON ISLAND
Redcliffe
Ipswich
Brisbane
Gold Coast

© Rand McNally
A-101820-)

0   60   120   180   240   300   360 Miles
0   60   120   180   240   300   360   420   480   540   600 Kilometers

Lambert Azimuthal Equal Area Projection
Scale 1:12,000,000
One inch to 190 miles
One cm to 120 km

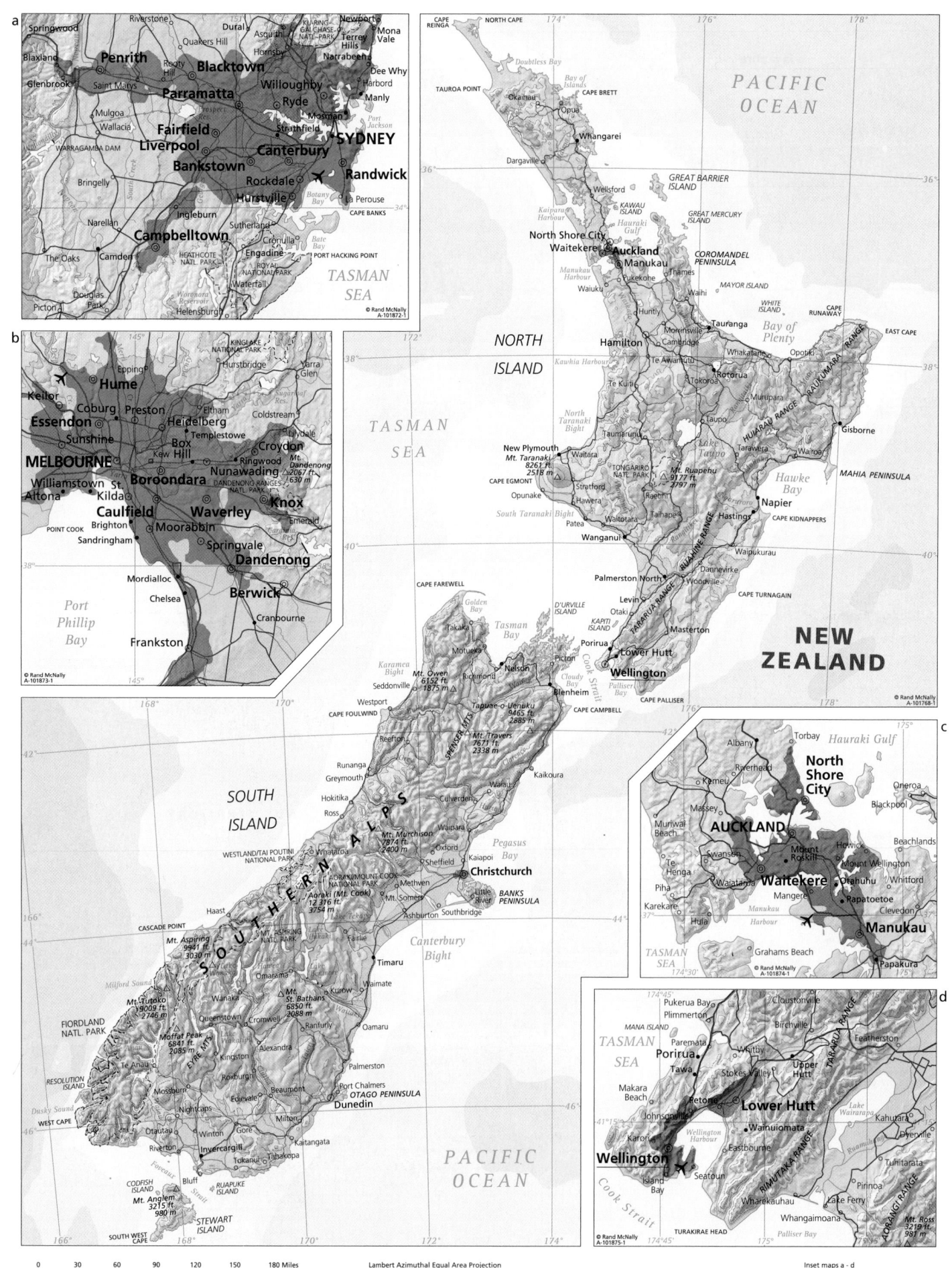

a

Springwood · Riverstone · Dural · Asquith · Newport · Mona Vale · Terrey Hills · Narrabeen
Blaxland · Quakers Hill · Hornsby · Dee Why · Harbord
Penrith · Rooty Hill · Saint Marys · Willoughby · Ryde · Manly · Mosman
Glenbrook · Mulgoa · Parramatta · Strathfield · Port Jackson
Blacktown
Fairfield · Liverpool · Canterbury · SYDNEY
Warragamba Dam · Bankstown · Rockdale · Randwick
Bringelly · Inglebum · Hurstville · La Perouse · CAPE BANKS
Narellan · Sutherland · Cronulla · Botany Bay · Bate Bay · PORT HACKING POINT
Campbelltown · Camden · Engadine
The Oaks · HEATHCOTE NATL. PARK · ROYAL NATIONAL PARK
Douglas Park · Waterfall · Helensburgh
Picton · Woronora Reservoir

TASMAN SEA

© Rand McNally
A-101872-1

b

KINGLAKE NATIONAL PARK
Epping · Hurstbridge · Yarra Glen
Keilor · Hume · Sugarloaf Res.
Essendon · Coburg · Preston · Heidelberg · Eltham · Coldstream
Sunshine · Templestowe · Lilydale
MELBOURNE · Box Hill · Kew · Ringwood · Croydon · Mt. Dandenong 2067 ft 630 m
Williamstown · St. Boroondara · Nunawading · DANDENONG RANGES NATL. PARK
Altona · Kilda · Waverley · Knox · Emerald
Caulfield · Brighton · Moorabbin · Springvale
POINT COOK · Sandringham · Dandenong
Mordialloc · Berwick
Port Phillip Bay · Chelsea · Cranbourne
Frankston

© Rand McNally
A-101873-1

NORTH ISLAND

PACIFIC OCEAN

CAPE REINGA · NORTH CAPE
Doubtless Bay
TAUROA POINT · CAPE BRETT
Okaihau · Opua · Bay of Islands
Dargaville · Whangarei
Wellsford · GREAT BARRIER ISLAND
KAWAU ISLAND · GREAT MERCURY ISLAND
Kaipara Harbour · Hauraki Gulf
North Shore City · Waitakere · Auckland · COROMANDEL PENINSULA
Manukau · Thames
Manukau Harbour · Waiuku · Pukekohe · Waihi · MAYOR ISLAND
Huntly · WHITE ISLAND · CAPE RUNAWAY
Morrinsville · Taranga · Bay of Plenty
Hamilton · Cambridge · Whakatane · Opotiki · EAST CAPE
Kawhia Harbour · Te Awamutu · RAUKUMARA RANGE
Te Kuiti · Rotorua · HUIARAU RANGE
North Taranaki Bight · Taumarunu · Lake Taupo · Taraweta · Wairoa · Gisborne
New Plymouth · Mt. Taranaki 8261 ft 2518 m · Waitara · TONGARIRO NATL. PARK · Mt. Ruapehu 9177 ft 2797 m · MAHIA PENINSULA
CAPE EGMONT · Stratford · Raetihi · Hawke Bay
Opunake · Hawera · Taihape · Hastings · Napier
South Taranaki Bight · Waitotara · Patea · CAPE KIDNAPPERS
Wanganui · Waipukurau · Dannevirke · CAPE TURNAGAIN
Palmerston North · Woodville
Levin · RUAHINE RANGE
D'URVILLE ISLAND · Otaki · TARARUA RANGE · Masterton
CAPE FAREWELL · KAPITI ISLAND · Porirua
Golden Bay · Takaka · Lower Hutt
Tasman Bay · Wellington · CAPE PALLISER
Motueka · Picton · Cook Strait · Palliser Bay

NEW ZEALAND

© Rand McNally
A-101768-1

TASMAN SEA

Karamea Bight · Mt. Owen 6152 ft 1875 m · Nelson · Richmond · Cloudy Bay · Blenheim
Seddonville · Tapuae-o-Uenuku 9465 ft 2885 m · CAPE CAMPBELL
Westport · Mt. Travers 7671 ft 2338 m
CAPE FOULWIND · SPENSER MTS.
Reefton · Runanga · Waiau · Kaikoura
Greymouth
Hokitika · Culverden · Pegasus Bay
Ross · Waipara
SOUTH ISLAND · Mt. Murchison 7874 ft 2400 m · Oxford · Kaiapoi
Whataroa · AORAKI/MOUNT COOK NATIONAL PARK · Sheffield · Christchurch
WESTLAND/TAI POUTINI NATIONAL PARK · Mt. Somers · Little River · BANKS PENINSULA
Aoraki (Mt. Cook) 12 316 ft 3754 m · Methven · Ashburton · Southbridge
Mt. Aspiring 9941 ft 3030 m · Faitlie · Canterbury Bight
MOUNT ASPIRING NATL. PARK · Timaru
CASCADE POINT · Omarama · Waimate
Mt. Tutoko 9009 ft 2746 m · Wanaka · Mt. St. Bathans 6850 ft 3088 m · Kurow · Oamaru
FIORDLAND NATL. PARK · Queenstown · Cromwell · Ranfurly · Palmerston
Milford Sound · Moffat Peak 6841 ft 2085 m · EYRE MTS. · Alexandra · Roxburgh · Beaumont · Port Chalmers · OTAGO PENINSULA
RESOLUTION ISLAND · Te Anau · Kingston · Edievale · Milton · Dunedin
WEST CAPE · Mossburn · Nightcaps · Gore · Kaitangata
Dusky Sound · Otautau · Winton · Riverton · Tokanui · Tokakopa
SOUTH WEST CAPE · Invercargill · Bluff · CODFISH ISLAND · RUAPUKE ISLAND
Mt. Anglem 3215 ft 980 m · STEWART ISLAND

PACIFIC OCEAN

c

Hauraki Gulf
Albany · Torbay
Riverhead · Kumeu · North Shore City · Oneroa
Massey · Blackpool
Muriwai Beach · AUCKLAND · Beachlands
Swanson · Mount Roskill · Howick · Mount Wellington · Whitford
Te Henga · Waitakere · Orahuhu
Piha · Mangere · Papatoetoe · Clevedon
Karekare · Manukau Harbour · Manukau
Hula · Papakura
TASMAN SEA · Grahams Beach

© Rand McNally
A-101874-1

d

Pukerua Bay · Cloustonville
MANA ISLAND · Plimmerton · Birchville · TARARUA RANGE · Featherston
TASMAN SEA · Paremata · Whitby
Porirua · Stokes Valley · Upper Hutt
Tawa · RIMUTAKA RANGE
Makara Beach · Petone · Lower Hutt · Lake Wairarapa · Kahutara
Johnsonville · Wainuiomata · Dyerville
Karori · Eastbourne · AORANGI RANGE
Wellington · Wellington Harbour · Pirinoa · Tuhitarata
Seatoun · Wharekauhau · Lake Ferry · Mt. Ross 3219 ft 981 m
Island Bay · Whangaimoana
Cook Strait · TURAKIRAE HEAD · Palliser Bay

© Rand McNally
A-101875-1

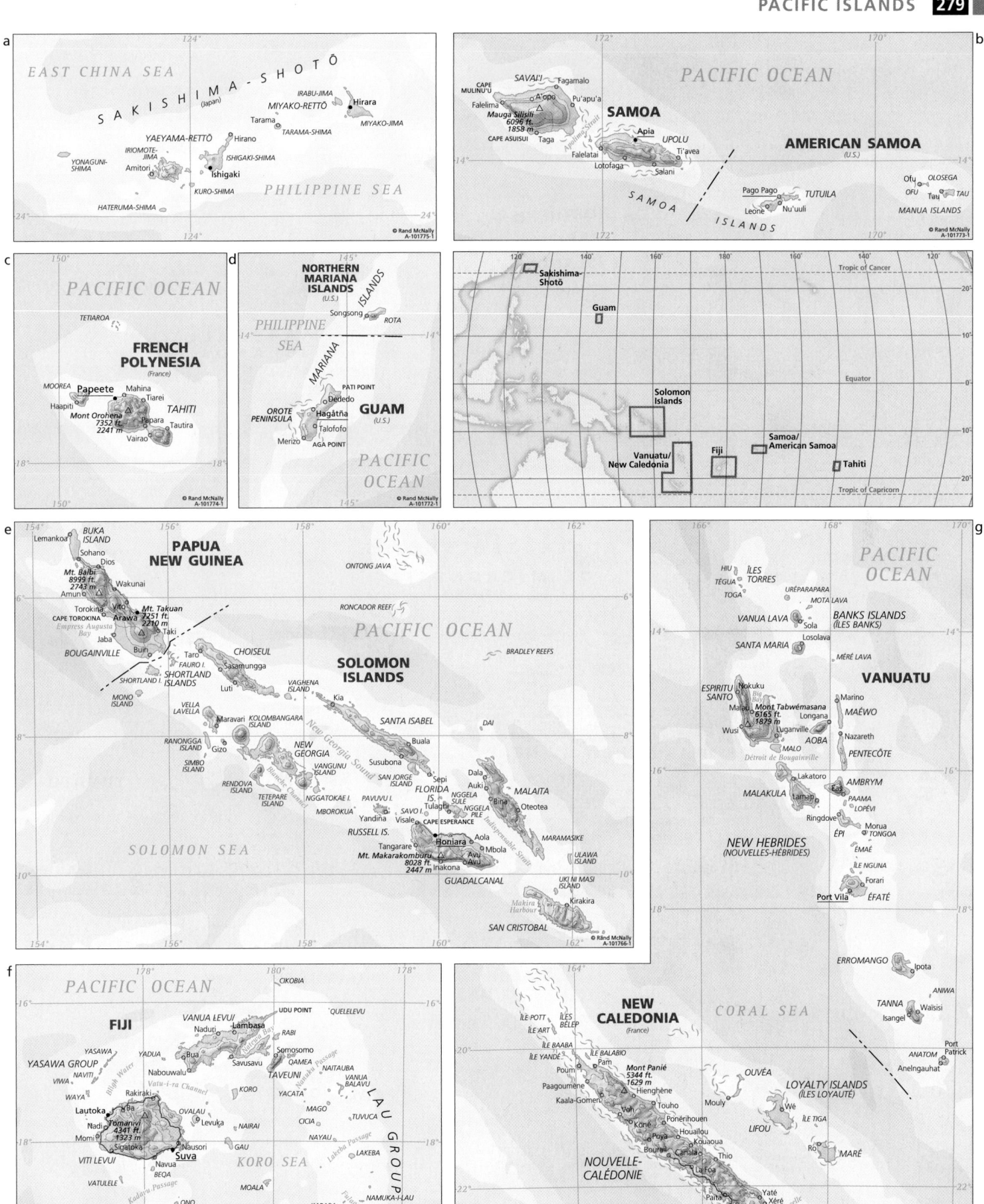

Inset maps a - d
Lambert Azimuthal Equal Area Projection
Scale 1:4,000,000
One inch to 64 miles
One cm to 40 km

Inset maps e - g
Lambert Azimuthal Equal Area Projection
Scale 1:8,000,000
One inch to 128 miles
One cm to 80 km

MINAMI-DAITŌ-JIMA (Jpn.)
OKINO-DAITŌ-JIMA (Jpn.)
HAHAJIMA-RETTŌ (Jpn.)
OGASAWARA-SHOTŌ (Jpn.)
MINAMI-IŌ-JIMA
KITA-IŌ-JIMA
IWO JIMA
KAZAN-RETTŌ
MARCUS ISLAND (Jpn.)

Tropic of Cancer

PHILIPPINE BASIN

OKINO-TORI-SHIMA (Jpn.)
FARALLON DE PAJAROS

PHILIPPINE SEA

ASUNCION ISLAND
AGRIHAN
PAGAN
ALAMAGAN
GUGUAN
ANATAHAN   SARIGAN
FARALLON DE MEDINILLA
SAIPAN
TINIAN
ROTA

NORTHERN MARIANA ISLANDS (U.S.)

WAKE ISLAND (U.S.)

MID-PACIFIC MOUNTAINS

INTERNATIONAL DATE LINE

M I C R

EAST MARIANA BASIN

TAONGI

MARSHALL ISLANDS

ENEWETAK   BIKINI
RONGELAP   UTRIK
BIKAR

Hagåtña
GUAM (U.S.)

Challenger Deep
-35 810 ft.
-10 915 m

YAP
ULITHI
GAFERUT
HALL ISLANDS
UJELANG
KWAJALEIN
LIB
WOTHO
MALOELAP
WOTJE

BABELDAOB Melekeok
BELILIOU
PALAU
SONSOROL ISLANDS
WOLEAI
EAURIPIK
LAMOTREK
CHUUK (TRUK ISLANDS)
LOSAP ATOLL
OROLUK
NAMOLOK ATOLL
SENYAVIN ISLANDS
Palikir
POHNPEI
MWOKIL
PINGELAP
KOSRAE
MAJURO
MILI
KILI
EBON

PULO ANNA   MERIR
CAROLINE ISLANDS
MORTLOCK ISLANDS
BUTARITARI

TOBI   HELEN ISLAND
WEST CAROLINE BASIN
NUKUORO
FEDERATED STATES
OF MICRONESIA
TARAWA

KEPULAUAN MAPIA
EAST CAROLINE BASIN
KAPINGAMARANGI
KURIA   ABEMAMA

Equator
PULAU WAIGEO
NONOUTI   NIKUNAU

Manokwari
BIAK
NINIGO GROUP
WUVULU ISLAND
MUSSAU ISLAND
MANUS ISLAND
NAURU
BANABA
BERU
ARORAE

Sorong JAZIRAH DOBERAI
TANJUNG D'URVILLE
PULAU YAPEN
ADMIRALTY ISLANDS
NEW HANOVER
Kavieng
TABAR ISLANDS
LIHIR GROUP
KIRIBATI

Fakfak
Jayapura
Aitape
Wewak
BISMARCK
NEW IRELAND
Rabaul

CERAM
PEGUNUNGAN VAN REES
BISMARCK SEA ARCHIPELAGO
WITU ISLANDS
Mt. Ulawun
7657 ft.
2334 m
NANUMEA
NIUTAO

PEGUNUNGAN MAOKE
Puncak Jaya
16 503 ft.
5030 m
Mt. Wilhelm
14 793 ft.
4509 m
Madang
NEW BRITAIN
BUKA ISLAND

KEPULAUAN KAI
NEW GUINEA
Mt. Giluwe
14 331 ft.
4368 m
PAPUA NEW GUINEA
Lae
BOUGAINVILLE
NIU   VAITUPU

BANDA SEA
KEPULAUAN ARU
SOLOMON
CHOISEUL
SOLOMON ISLANDS
TUVALU

INDONESIA
KEPULAUAN TANIMBAR
TANJUNG VALS
Merauke
Popondetta
KIRIWINA ISLANDS
VELLA LAVELLA
NEW GEORGIA
SANTA ISABEL
MALAITA
NANUMEA
FUNAFUTI

ARAFURA SEA
Gulf of Papua
Torres Strait
MUYUA ISLAND
VANGUNU I.
Honiara
SAN CRISTOBAL

MELVILLE ISLAND
CAPE YORK
Port Moresby
Samarai
D'ENTRECASTEAUX ISLANDS
MISIMA ISLAND
GUADALCANAL
RENNELL
NIULAKITA

Darwin
COBOURG PENINSULA
CAPE WESSEL
CAPE GRENVILLE
LOUISIADE ARCHIPELAGO
YELA ISLAND
TAGULA ISLAND
NENDO
SANTA CRUZ ISLANDS
VANIKOLO
ROTUMA

ARNHEM LAND
CAPE ARNHEM
GROOTE EYLANDT
Weipa   CAPE
CORAL SEA BASIN
TORRES ISLANDS
VANUA LAVA   BANKS ISLANDS
SANTA MARIA
NORTH FIJI BASIN

Katherine
Birdum
Gulf of Carpentaria
YORK
PENINSULA
Cooktown
CHILCOTT ISLET
ESPIRITU SANTO
MAEWO
PENTECÔTE
AMBRYM
FIJI
VANUA LEVU

WELLESLEY ISLANDS
Normanton
Cairns
Bartle Frere
5322 ft.
1622 m
MELLISH REEF
VANUATU
MALAKULA
ÉPI   ÉFATE
Port Vila
ERROMANGO
VITI LEVU
Suva
TAVEU

BARKLY TABLELAND
Tennant Creek
Townsville
Bowen
ÎLES CHESTERFIELD
ÎLE DE SABLE
TANNA   ANATOM
KANDAVU

TANAMI DESERT
Mount Isa
Charters Towers
Mackay
CAYE DE L'OBSERVATOIRE
NOUVELLE-CALÉDONIE
OUVÉA
LOYALTY ISLANDS
ÎLE HUNTER

Alice Springs
SIMPSON DESERT
Longreach
Rockhampton
Emerald
Gladstone
SANDY CAPE
NEW CALEDONIA (Fr.)
Nouméa
LIFOU
MARE
ÎLE DES PINS

GIBSON DESERT
AUSTRALIA
GREAT ARTESIAN BASIN
Charleville
Toowoomba
Brisbane
Southport
FRASER ISLAND
Harvey Bay
CATO ISLAND
SOUTH FIJI BASIN

Mt. Woodroffe
4708 ft.
1435 m
Tropic of Capricorn
Lake Eyre
Birdsville
Charleville
Moree
Lismore
Coffs Harbour

GREAT VICTORIA DESERT
NORFOLK ISLAND (Austl.)

0   150   300   450   600   750 Miles
0   150   300   450   600   750   900   1,050 Kilometers

Lambert Azimuthal Equal Area Projection
Scale 1:27,000,000
One inch to 426 miles
One cm to 270 km

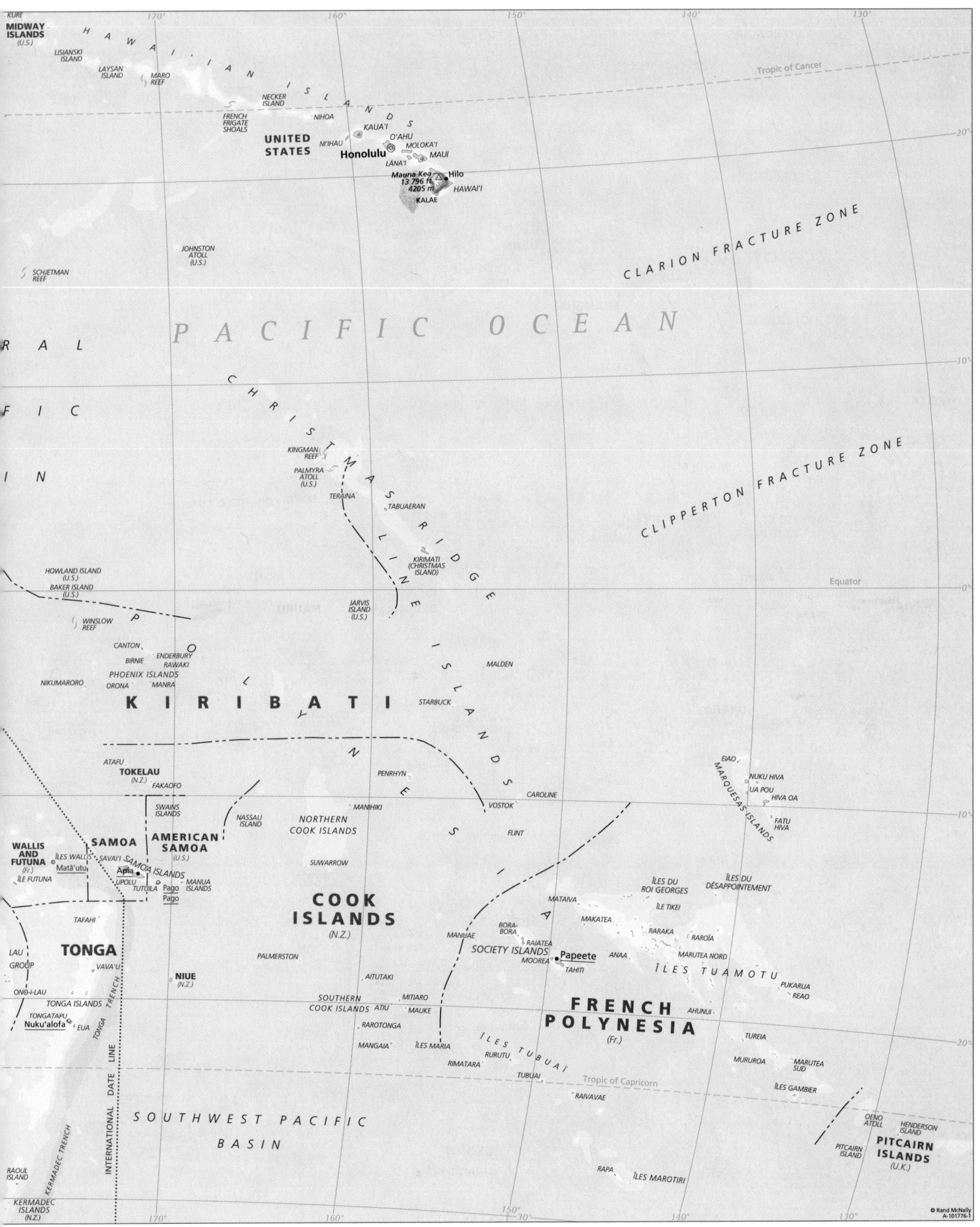

KURE
MIDWAY
ISLANDS
(U.S.)

LISIANSKI
ISLAND

LAYSAN
ISLAND

MARO
REEF

HA WA II AN ISLANDS

NECKER
ISLAND

NIHOA

FRENCH
FRIGATE
SHOALS

KAUA'I

NI'IHAU

O'AHU

MOLOKA'I

UNITED
STATES

Honolulu

LĀNA'I

MAUI

Mauna Kea
13 796 ft.
4205 m

Hilo

HAWAI'I

KALAE

Tropic of Cancer

20°

JOHNSTON
ATOLL
(U.S.)

SCHJETMAN
REEF

CLARION FRACTURE ZONE

PACIFIC OCEAN

10°

CHRISTMAS RIDGE

KINGMAN
REEF

PALMYRA
ATOLL
(U.S.)

TERAINA

TABUAERAN

CLIPPERTON FRACTURE ZONE

KIRIMATI
(CHRISTMAS
ISLAND)

Equator

0°

HOWLAND ISLAND
(U.S.)

BAKER ISLAND
(U.S.)

JARVIS
ISLAND
(U.S.)

CHRISTMAS LINE ISLANDS

WINSLOW
REEF

P O L Y N E S I A

CANTON

ENDERBURY

BIRNIE

RAWAKI

MALDEN

NIKUMARORO

PHOENIX ISLANDS

ORONA

MANRA

K I R I B A T I

STARBUCK

ATAFU
TOKELAU
(N.Z.)

FAKAOFO

PENRHYN

CAROLINE

10°

EIAO

NUKU HIVA

UA POU

HIVA OA

MARQUESAS ISLANDS

SWAINS
ISLANDS

NASSAU
ISLAND

MANIHIKI

VOSTOK

NORTHERN
COOK ISLANDS

FLINT

FATU
HIVA

WALLIS
AND
FUTUNA
(Fr.)

ÎLES WALLIS

Matā'utu

ÎLE FUTUNA

SAMOA

AMERICAN
SAMOA
(U.S.)

SAVAI'I

SAMOA ISLANDS

Apia

UPOLU

TUTUILA

MANUA
ISLANDS

Pago
Pago

SUWARROW

ÎLES DU
ROI GEORGES

ÎLES DU
DÉSAPPOINTEMENT

ÎLE TIKEI

MATAIVA

MAKATEA

RARAKA

RAROIA

TAFAHI

COOK
ISLANDS
(N.Z.)

MANUAE

BORA-
BORA

RAIATEA

SOCIETY ISLANDS

Papeete

MARUTEA NORD

ANAA

LAU
GROUP

TONGA

VAVA'U

PALMERSTON

MOOREA

TAHITI

ÎLES TUAMOTU

PUKARUA

REAO

NIUE
(N.Z.)

AITUTAKI

ON0-I-LAU

TONGA ISLANDS

SOUTHERN
COOK ISLANDS

MITIARO
ATIU

MAUKE

FRENCH
POLYNESIA
(Fr.)

AHUNUI

TUREIA

TONGATAPU

Nuku'alofa

EUA

RAROTONGA

MANGAIA

ÎLES MARIA

ÎLES TUBUAÏ

RURUTU

RIMATARA

TUBUAI

20°

MURUROA

MARUTEA
SUD

ÎLES GAMBIER

Tropic of Capricorn

RAIVAVAE

RAPA

ÎLES MAROTIRI

OENO
ATOLL

HENDERSON
ISLAND

SOUTHWEST PACIFIC
BASIN

PITCAIRN
ISLAND

PITCAIRN
ISLANDS
(U.K.)

RAOUL
ISLAND

KERMADEC TRENCH

INTERNATIONAL DATE LINE

KERMADEC
ISLANDS
(N.Z.)

TONGA TRENCH

© Rand McNally
A-101776-1

0   300   600   900   1200   1500 Miles

0   300   600   900   1200   1500   1800   2100 Kilometers

Mollweide Projection
Scale 1:55,000,000
One inch to 868 miles
One cm to 550 km

Mt. McKinley
20,320 ft.
6194 m RA.
Anchorage
Gulf of Alaska
KODIAK ISLAND
ALASKA
Yukon

COAST MTS.
Prince Rupert
QUEEN CHARLOTTE ISLANDS
VANCOUVER ISLAND
Vancouver
Seattle
Portland

CANADA
Edmonton
Calgary
Albany
Winnipeg
Nelson
Lake Superior

ROCKY MTS.
CASCADE RA.
Snake
Missouri
Great Salt Lake
Mississippi
GREAT PLAINS

LABRADOR CURRENT
NEWFOUNDLAND

UNITED KINGDOM
IRELAND

NORTH ATLANTIC CURRENT

MONTRÉAL
CAPE BRETON ISLAND
Ottawa
TORONTO
Lake Huron
Lake Michigan
CHICAGO
Lake Ontario
Lake Erie
Ohio
NEW YORK
PHILADELPHIA
Washington
APPALACHIAN MTS.

AZORES (PORT.)

San Francisco
UNITED STATES
SIERRA NEVADA
Colorado
CALIFORNIA CURRENT
CHANNEL IS.
LOS ANGELES
SAN DIEGO
DALLAS
Rio Grande
SIERRA MADRE OCCIDENTAL

GULF STREAM
BERMUDA (U.K.)

ATLANTIC OCEAN

Tropic of Cancer

HOUSTON
GULF OF MEXICO
Miami
MONTERREY
HAVANA
CUBA
BAHAMAS

HAWAI'IAN ISLANDS (U.S.)

MEXICO
GUADALAJARA
ISLAS REVILLAGIGEDO (Mex.)
MEXICO CITY
BELIZE
GUAT.
HONDURAS
Guatemala
EL SAL.
NICARAGUA
Managua
COSTA RICA
JAMAICA
HAITI
DOM. REP.
PUERTO RICO (U.S.)
SANTO DOMINGO
CARIBBEAN SEA
MARACAIBO
Panamá
PANAMA
CARACAS
TRINIDAD AND TOBAGO

NORTH EQUATORIAL CURRENT

NORTH EQUATORIAL CURRENT

CHRISTMAS ISLAND

MEDELLÍN
CALI
BOGOTÁ
COLOMBIA
GUY.
SUR.
FR. GUI. (fr.)
VENEZUELA

EQUATORIAL COUNTER CURRENT

QUITO
ECUADOR
GUAYAQUIL
GALAPAGOS ISLANDS (Ec.)
Equator
Amazon

LINE ISLANDS

SOUTH EQUATORIAL CURRENT

PERU
ANDES
BRAZIL
SELVAS
MANAUS

COOK IS.
VOSTOK
MARQUESAS ISLANDS
ÎLES DU ROI GEORGES
FLINT
SOCIETY IS.
TAHITI
ÎLES TUAMOTU
ÎLES DU DÉSAPPOINTEMENT

Lima
PERU CURRENT

SOUTHERN COOK IS.
ÎLES MARIA
ÎLES TUBUAI
FRENCH POLYNESIA (Fr.)

La Paz
BOLIVIA
BRASÍLIA

PITCAIRN ISLANDS (U.K.)
HENDERSON ISLAND

Tropic of Capricorn
Antofagasta
CHACO
PARAGUAY
PAMPA
GRAN
Asunción
SÃO PAULO

ISLA SALA Y GOMEZ (Chile)
EASTER ISLAND (ISLA DE PASCUA) (Chile)
ISLA SAN FÉLIX (Chile)
ISLA SAN AMBROSIO (Chile)

CHILE
ANDES
CÓRDOBA
ARGENTINA
URUG.
PORTO ALEGRE

ARCHIPIÉLAGO JUAN FERNÁNDEZ (Chile)
SANTIAGO
Cerro Aconcagua 22,831 ft. 6959 m
MONTEVIDEO
Concepción
PAMPA
BUENOS AIRES
Bahía Blanca

ISLA GRANDE DE CHILOÉ
PATAGONIA

ARCHIPIÉLAGO DE LOS CHONOS
Golfo San Jorge

ATLANTIC OCEAN

WEST WIND DRIFT

FALKLAND ISLANDS (U.K.)
SOUTH GEORGIA AND THE SOUTH SANDWICH ISLANDS (U.K.)
WEST WIND DRIFT

Punta Arenas
TIERRA DEL FUEGO
CABO DE HORNOS

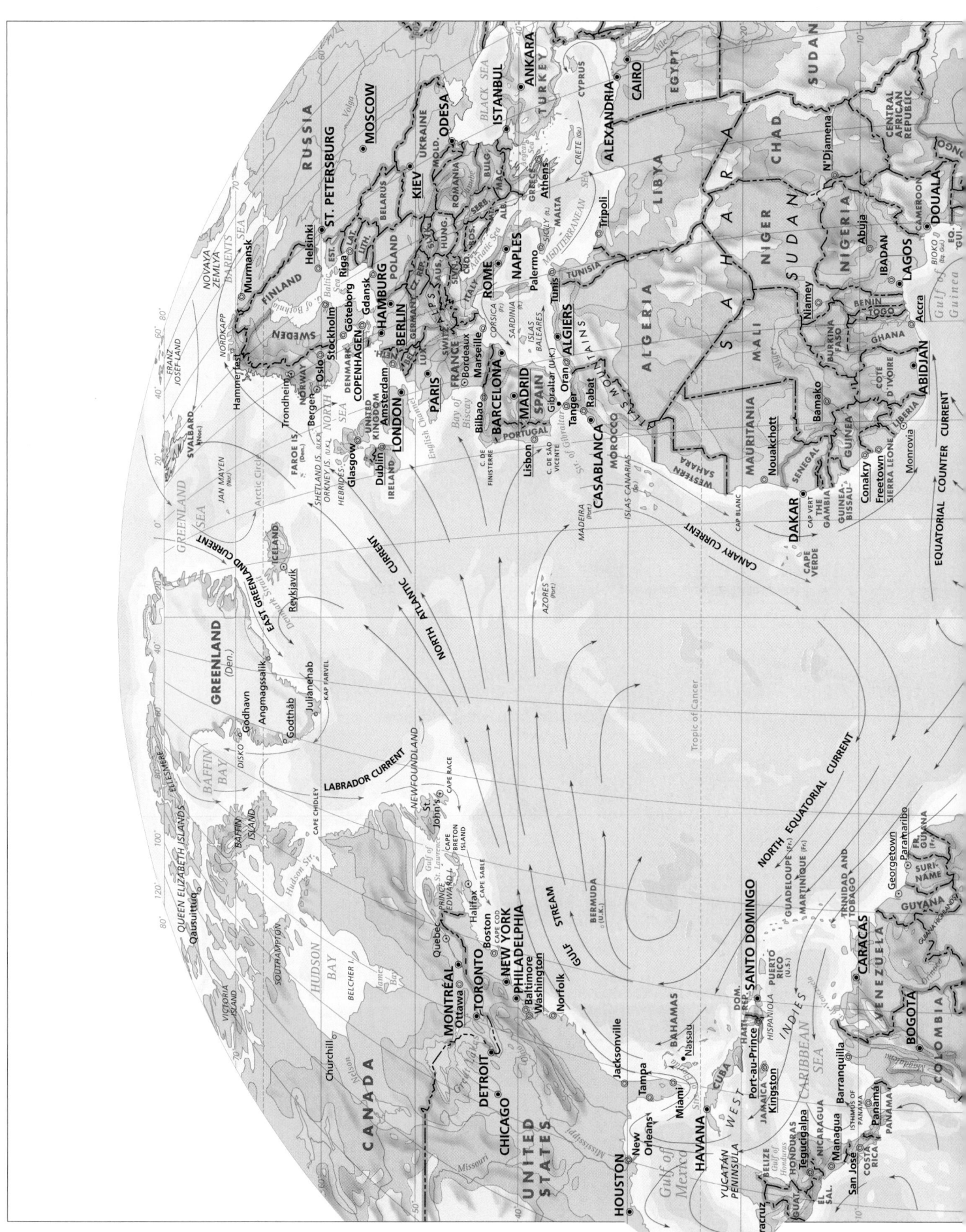

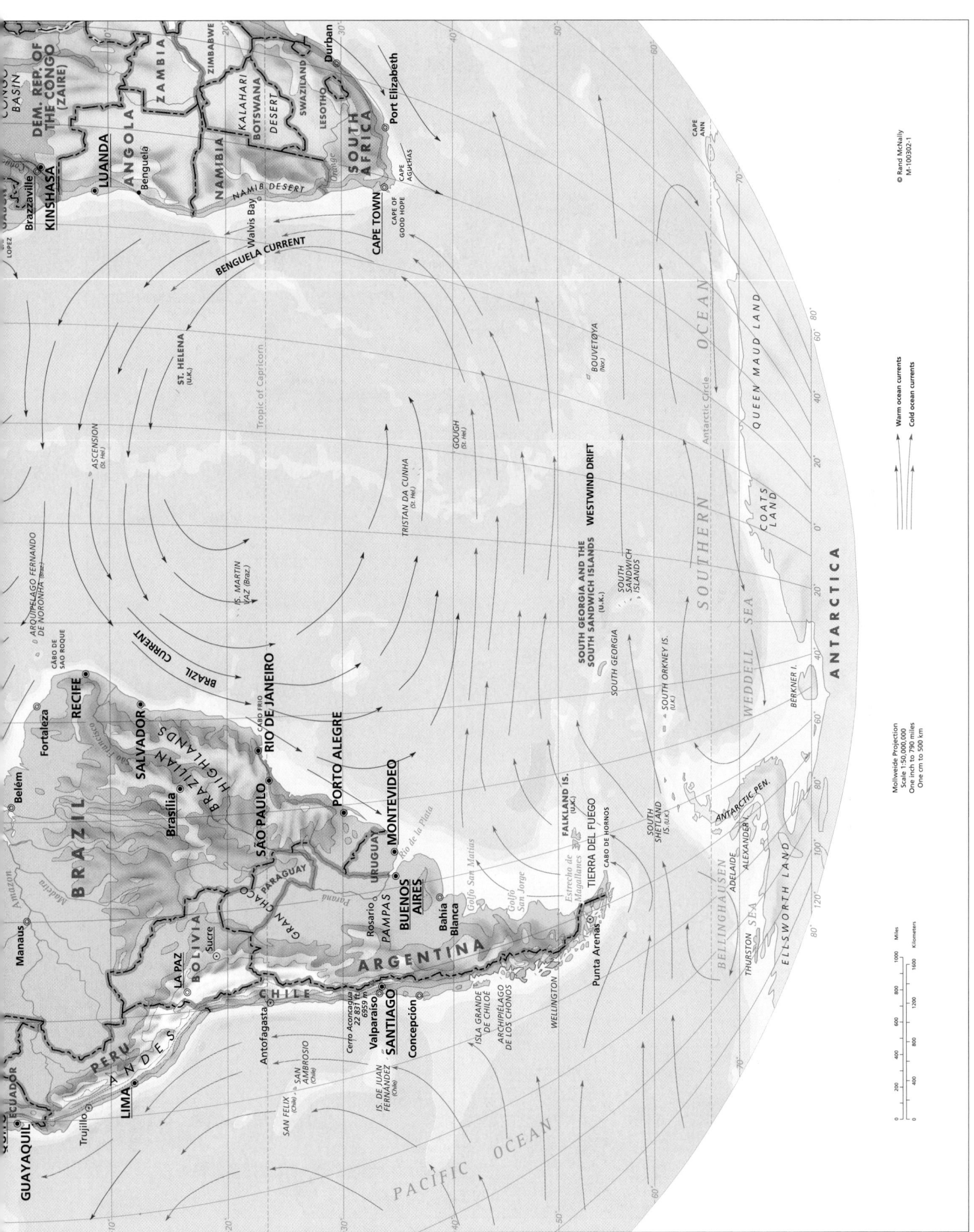

CONGO BASIN

DEM. REP. OF THE CONGO (ZAIRE)

Brazzaville

KINSHASA

LUANDA

ANGOLA

ZAMBIA

ZIMBABWE

KALAHARI DESERT

BOTSWANA

NAMIBIA

SWAZILAND

LESOTHO

Durban

SOUTH AFRICA

Port Elizabeth

CAPE ANN

Benguela

NAMIB DESERT

Walvis Bay

CAPE AGULHAS

CAPE TOWN

CAPE OF GOOD HOPE

BENGUELA CURRENT

LOPEZ

Orange

ST. HELENA (U.K.)

Tropic of Capricorn

BOUVETØYA (Nor.)

QUEEN MAUD LAND

OCEAN

Antarctic Circle

GUAYAQUIL

ECUADOR

Trujillo

LIMA

PERU

BOLIVIA

LA PAZ

Sucre

Manaus

Amazon

Madeira

BRAZIL

Belém

Fortaleza

RECIFE

CABO DE SAO ROQUE

SALVADOR

BRAZILIAN HIGHLANDS

Brasília

São Francisco

SÃO PAULO

RIO DE JANEIRO

CABO FRIO

PORTO ALEGRE

MONTEVIDEO

URUGUAY

PARAGUAY

GRAN CHACO

Rosario

Paraná

PAMPAS

BUENOS AIRES

Río de la Plata

Bahía Blanca

ARGENTINA

Golfo San Matías

Golfo San Jorge

ARQUIPÉLAGO FERNANDO DE NORONHA (Braz.)

IS. MARTIN VAZ (Braz.)

ASCENSION (St. Hel.)

TRISTAN DA CUNHA (St. Hel.)

GOUGH (St. Hel.)

SOUTH GEORGIA AND THE SOUTH SANDWICH ISLANDS

SOUTH GEORGIA

SOUTH SANDWICH ISLANDS

WESTWIND DRIFT

SOUTHERN

SEA

COATS LAND

ANTARCTICA

WEDDELL SEA

BERKNER I.

SOUTH ORKNEY IS. (U.K.)

FALKLAND IS. (U.K.)

Estrecho de Magallanes

TIERRA DEL FUEGO

CABO DE HORNOS

BRAZIL CURRENT

Antofagasta

Cerro Aconcagua 22,831 ft 6959 m

Valparaíso

SANTIAGO

Concepción

CHILE

ANDES

SAN FELIX (Chile)

SAN AMBROSIO (Chile)

IS. DE JUAN FERNÁNDEZ (Chile)

ISLA GRANDE DE CHILOÉ

ARCHIPIÉLAGO DE LOS CHONOS

WELLINGTON

Punta Arenas

SOUTH SHETLAND IS. (U.K.)

ANTARCTIC PEN.

Adelaide

ALEXANDER I.

BELLINGHAUSEN SEA

THURSTON I.

ELLSWORTH LAND

PACIFIC OCEAN

© Rand McNally M-100302-1

Mollweide Projection
Scale 1:50,000,000
One inch to 790 miles
One cm to 500 km

Warm ocean currents

Cold ocean currents

Miles
Kilometers

0   200   400   600   800   1000
0   400   800   1200   1600

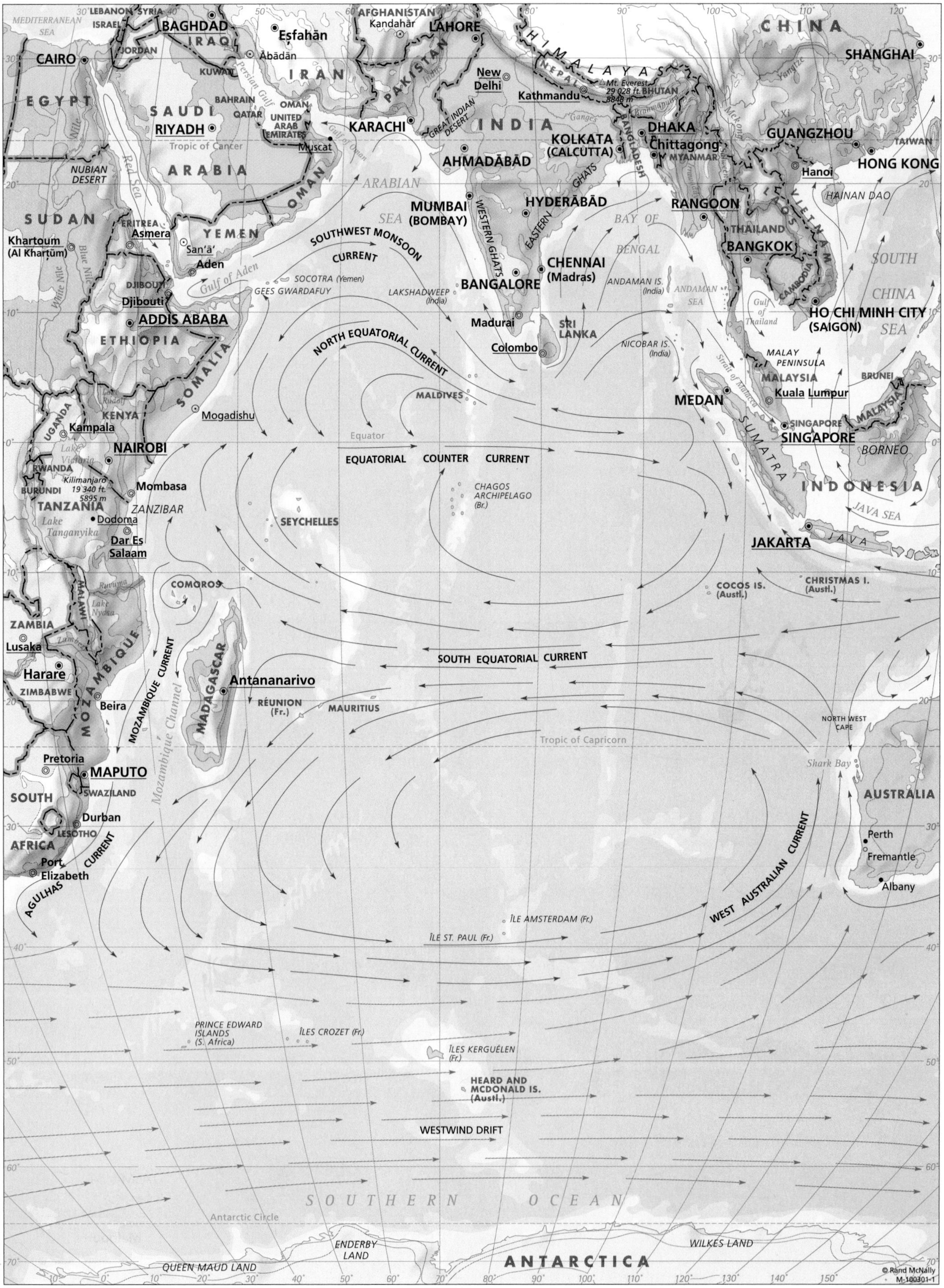

MEDITERRANEAN SEA
LEBANON SYRIA
ISRAEL
BAGHDAD
JORDAN
IRAQ
Eṣfahān
CAIRO
KUWAIT
IRAN
Ābādān
AFGHANISTAN
Kandahār
Kathmandu
LAHORE
HIMALAYAS
CHINA
SHANGHAI
EGYPT
SAUDI
RIYADH
BAHRAIN
QATAR
OMAN
UNITED ARAB EMIRATES
Muscat
Tropic of Cancer
PAKISTAN
New Delhi
Mt. Everest 29,028 ft 8848 m
NEPAL
BHUTAN
Ganges
Brahmaputra
KOLKATA (CALCUTTA)
DHAKA
Chittagong
BANGLADESH
MYANMAR
GUANGZHOU
TAIWAN
HONG KONG
HAINAN DAO
ARABIA
KARACHI
GREAT INDIAN DESERT
INDIA
Yangtze
Xi
NUBIAN DESERT
Red Sea
Gulf of Oman
Persian Gulf
Gulf of Aden
ARABIAN SEA
AHMADĀBĀD
MUMBAI (BOMBAY)
HYDERĀBĀD
WESTERN GHATS
EASTERN GHATS
RANGOON
Hanoi
SUDAN
YEMEN
San'ā'
Aden
SOUTHWEST MONSOON CURRENT
CHENNAI (Madras)
BAY OF BENGAL
THAILAND
BANGKOK
SOUTH CHINA SEA
Khartoum (Al Khartūm)
ERITREA
Asmera
SOCOTRA (Yemen)
GEES GWARDAFUY
LAKSHADWEEP (India)
BANGALORE
ANDAMAN IS. (India)
ANDAMAN SEA
Gulf of Thailand
CAMBODIA
HO CHI MINH CITY (SAIGON)
White Nile
Blue Nile
DJIBOUTI
Djibouti
Madurai
SRI LANKA
Colombo
NICOBAR IS. (India)
MALAY PENINSULA
MALAYSIA
Kuala Lumpur
BRUNEI
ADDIS ABABA
ETHIOPIA
SOMALIA
NORTH EQUATORIAL CURRENT
MALDIVES
MEDAN
SINGAPORE
SINGAPORE
MALAYSIA
UGANDA
KENYA
Kampala
Mogadishu
Equator
EQUATORIAL COUNTER CURRENT
CHAGOS ARCHIPELAGO (Br.)
SUMATRA
BORNEO
INDONESIA
NAIROBI
RWANDA
BURUNDI
Lake Victoria
Kilimanjaro 19,340 ft 5895 m
Mombasa
ZANZIBAR
SEYCHELLES
JAVA SEA
TANZANIA
Lake Tanganyika
Dodoma
Dar Es Salaam
JAKARTA
JAVA
COMOROS
COCOS IS. (Austl.)
CHRISTMAS I. (Austl.)
ZAMBIA
MALAWI
Lusaka
Lake Nyasa
Ruvuma
MOZAMBIQUE CURRENT
MADAGASCAR
SOUTH EQUATORIAL CURRENT
Harare
Zambezi
ZIMBABWE
Beira
Mozambique Channel
Antananarivo
RÉUNION (Fr.)
MAURITIUS
NORTH WEST CAPE
MOZAMBIQUE
Tropic of Capricorn
Shark Bay
Pretoria
MAPUTO
SWAZILAND
AUSTRALIA
SOUTH
Durban
LESOTHO
Perth
AFRICA
Port Elizabeth
AGULHAS CURRENT
WEST AUSTRALIAN CURRENT
Fremantle
Albany
ÎLE AMSTERDAM (Fr.)
ÎLE ST. PAUL (Fr.)
PRINCE EDWARD ISLANDS (S. Africa)
ÎLES CROZET (Fr.)
ÎLES KERGUÉLEN (Fr.)
HEARD AND MCDONALD IS. (Austl.)
WESTWIND DRIFT
SOUTHERN OCEAN
Antarctic Circle
QUEEN MAUD LAND
ENDERBY LAND
ANTARCTICA
WILKES LAND
© Rand McNally
M-100301-1

0 200 400 600 800 1000 Miles
0 400 800 1200 1600 Kilometers

Mollweide Projection
Scale 1:50,000,000
One inch to 790 miles
One cm to 500 km

Warm ocean currents

Cold ocean currents

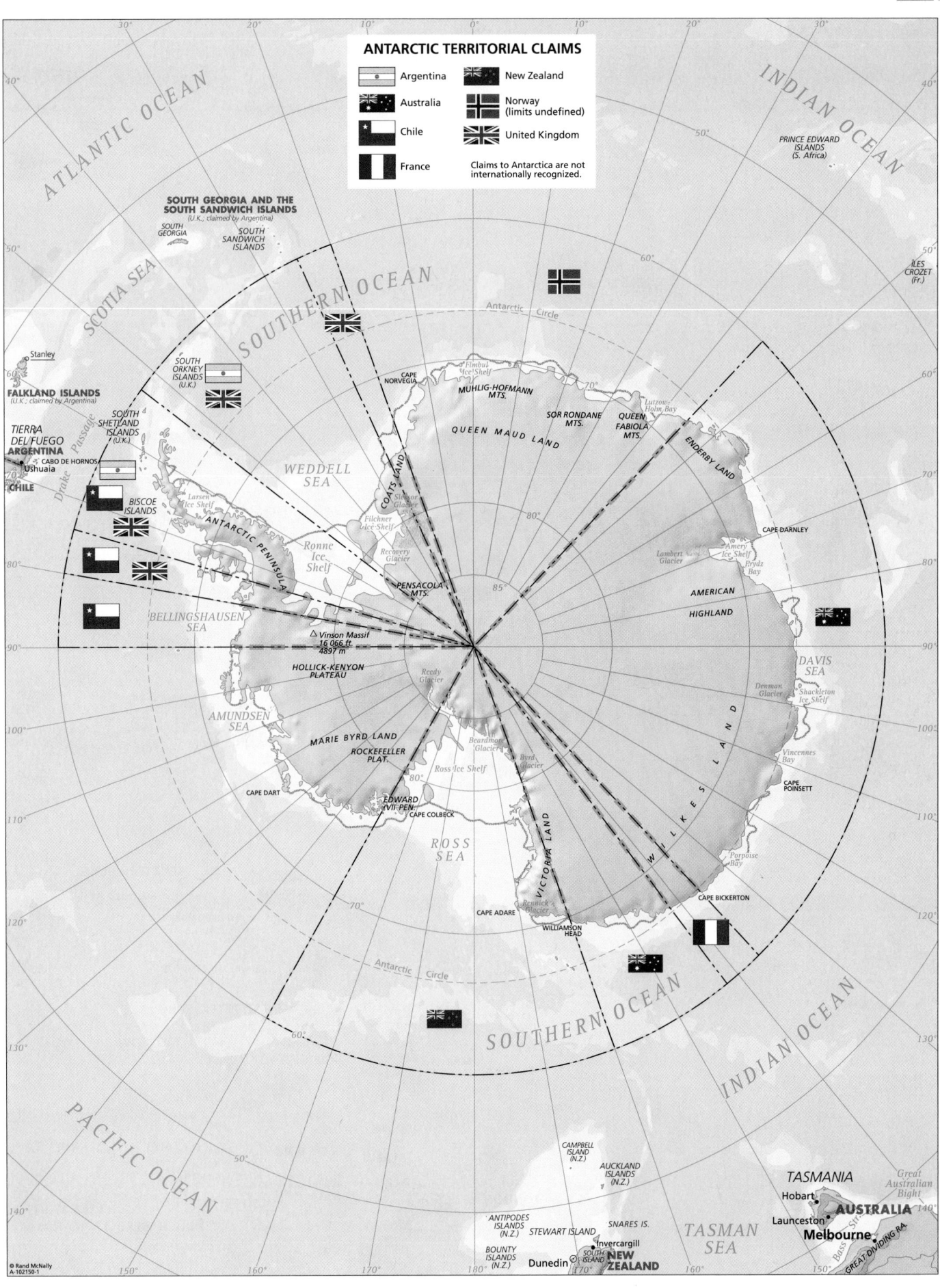

ANTARCTIC TERRITORIAL CLAIMS

Argentina
Australia
Chile
France
New Zealand
Norway (limits undefined)
United Kingdom

Claims to Antarctica are not internationally recognized.

ATLANTIC OCEAN

INDIAN OCEAN

PRINCE EDWARD ISLANDS (S. Africa)

SOUTH GEORGIA AND THE SOUTH SANDWICH ISLANDS (U.K.; claimed by Argentina)

SOUTH GEORGIA

SOUTH SANDWICH ISLANDS

SCOTIA SEA

SOUTHERN OCEAN

ÎLES CROZET (Fr.)

Antarctic Circle

Stanley

FALKLAND ISLANDS (U.K.; claimed by Argentina)

SOUTH ORKNEY ISLANDS (U.K.)

CAPE NORVEGIA

Fimbul Ice Shelf

MÜHLIG-HOFMANN MTS.

SOR RONDANE MTS.

Lützow-Holm Bay

QUEEN FABIOLA MTS.

ENDERBY LAND

TIERRA DEL FUEGO

ARGENTINA

CABO DE HORNOS
Ushuaia

CHILE

SOUTH SHETLAND ISLANDS (U.K.)

Drake Passage

WEDDELL SEA

COATS LAND

QUEEN MAUD LAND

CAPE DARNLEY

BISCOE ISLANDS

Larsen Ice Shelf

ANTARCTIC PENINSULA

Ronne Ice Shelf

Filchner Ice Shelf

Support Glacier

Recovery Glacier

PENSACOLA MTS.

Lambert Glacier

Amery Ice Shelf

Prydz Bay

AMERICAN HIGHLAND

DAVIS SEA

BELLINGSHAUSEN SEA

△ Vinson Massif 16,066 ft. 4,897 m

HOLLICK-KENYON PLATEAU

Reedy Glacier

Denman Glacier

Shackleton Ice Shelf

AMUNDSEN SEA

MARIE BYRD LAND

ROCKEFELLER PLAT.

Beardmore Glacier

Byrd Glacier

Ross Ice Shelf

WILKES LAND

Vincennes Bay

CAPE POINSETT

CAPE DART

EDWARD VII PEN.

CAPE COLBECK

VICTORIA LAND

Porpoise Bay

CAPE BICKERTON

ROSS SEA

Reunick Glacier

CAPE ADARE

WILLIAMSON HEAD

Antarctic Circle

SOUTHERN OCEAN

INDIAN OCEAN

PACIFIC OCEAN

CAMPBELL ISLAND (N.Z.)

AUCKLAND ISLANDS (N.Z.)

TASMANIA

Great Australian Bight

Hobart

AUSTRALIA

Launceston

Melbourne

ANTIPODES ISLANDS (N.Z.)

SNARES IS.

STEWART ISLAND

TASMAN SEA

Bass Strait

BOUNTY ISLANDS (N.Z.)

Invercargill

SOUTH ISLAND

NEW ZEALAND

Great Dividing Ra.

Dunedin

© Rand McNally
A-102150-1

| 0 | 200 | 400 | 600 | 800 | 1000 | 1200 Miles |

| 0 | 200 | 400 | 600 | 800 | 1000 | 1200 | 1400 | 1600 | 1800 | 2000 Kilometer |

Lambert Azimuthal Equal Area Projection
Scale 1:40,000,000
One inch to 640 miles
One cm to 400 km

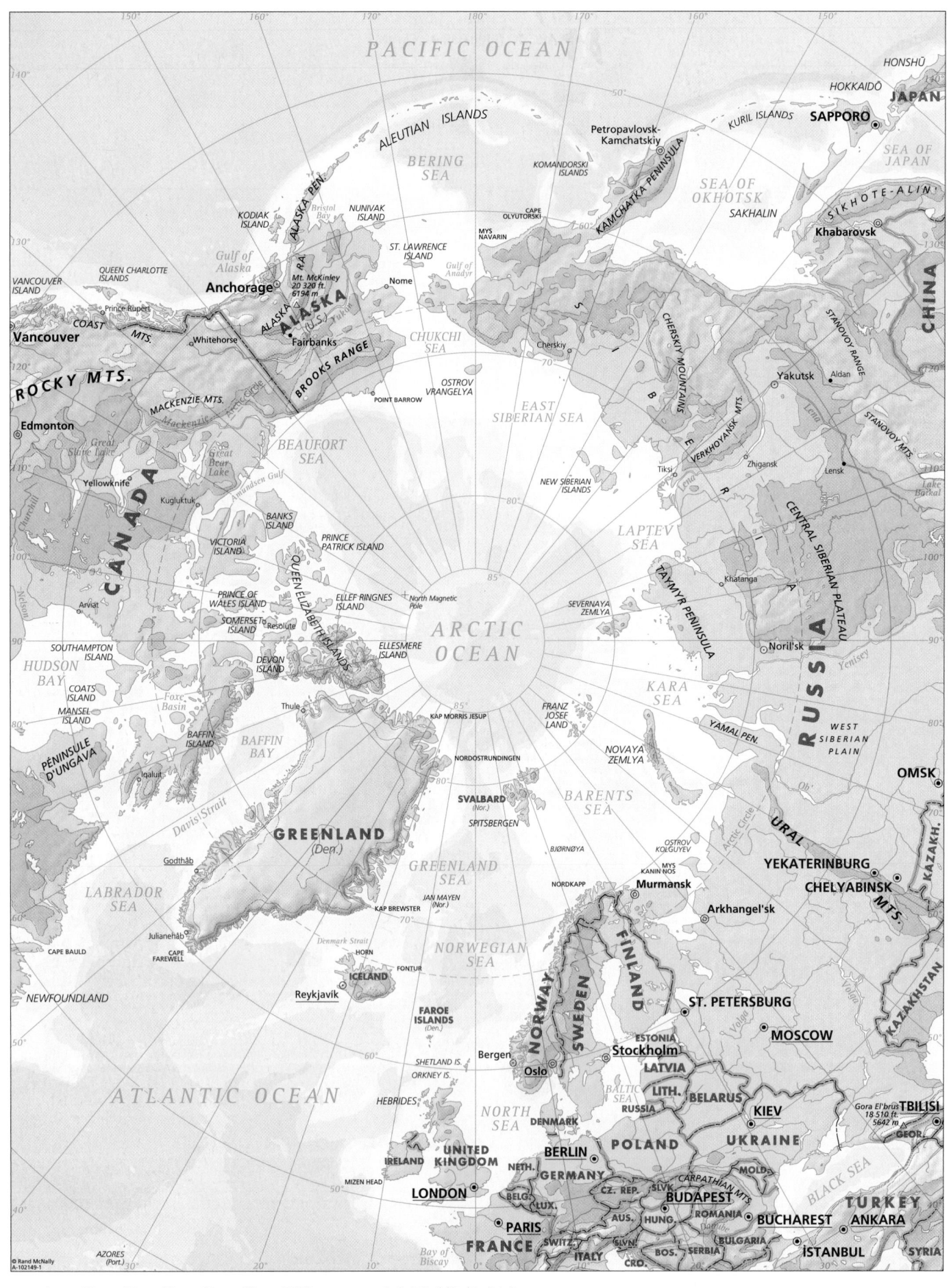

PACIFIC OCEAN

HONSHŪ
HOKKAIDŌ
JAPAN
SAPPORO

SEA OF JAPAN

Petropavlovsk-Kamchatskiy
KURIL ISLANDS

ALEUTIAN ISLANDS
BERING SEA
KOMANDORSKI ISLANDS
KAMCHATKA PENINSULA
SEA OF OKHOTSK
SAKHALIN
SIKHOTE-ALIN'

KODIAK ISLAND
ALASKA PEN.
Bristol Bay
NUNIVAK ISLAND
CAPE OLYUTORSKI
MYS NAVARIN

Khabarovsk

CHINA

Gulf of Alaska
Mt. McKinley 20,320 ft. 6194 m.
ST. LAWRENCE ISLAND
Gulf of Anadyr
Nome

QUEEN CHARLOTTE ISLANDS
VANCOUVER ISLAND
Prince Rupert
Anchorage
Fairbanks
CHUKCHI SEA
Cherskiy
STANOVOY RANGE
Yakutsk
Aldan
STANOVOY MTS.

Vancouver
COAST MTS.
Whitehorse
ALASKA (U.S.)
BROOKS RANGE
Yukon
OSTROV VRANGELYA
CHERSKY MOUNTAINS
Lake Baikal

ROCKY MTS.
MACKENZIE MTS.
Arctic Circle
Mackenzie
POINT BARROW
BEAUFORT SEA
EAST SIBERIAN SEA
VERKHOYANSK MTS.
Zhigansk
Lensk

Edmonton
Great Slave Lake
Tiksi
Lena
CENTRAL SIBERIAN PLATEAU

Yellowknife
Great Bear Lake
Amundsen Gulf
NEW SIBERIAN ISLANDS
LAPTEV SEA

CANADA
Kugluktuk
BANKS ISLAND
PRINCE PATRICK ISLAND
TAYMYR PENINSULA
Khatanga

Nelson
VICTORIA ISLAND
PRINCE OF WALES ISLAND
QUEEN ELIZABETH ISLANDS
ELLEF RINGNES ISLAND
North Magnetic Pole
SEVERNAYA ZEMLYA
Noril'sk

Arviat
SOMERSET ISLAND
Resolute
ARCTIC OCEAN
Yenisey

RUSSIA
WEST SIBERIAN PLAIN

SOUTHAMPTON ISLAND
DEVON ISLAND
ELLESMERE ISLAND
KARA SEA

HUDSON BAY
COATS ISLAND
MANSEL ISLAND
Foxe Basin
Thule
KAP MORRIS JESUP
FRANZ JOSEF LAND
YAMAL PEN.
Ob'

PÉNINSULE D'UNGAVA
BAFFIN ISLAND
BAFFIN BAY
NORDOSTRUNDINGEN
NOVAYA ZEMLYA
OMSK

Iqaluit
Davis Strait
SVALBARD (Nor.)
SPITSBERGEN
BARENTS SEA
URAL

GREENLAND (Den.)
Godthåb
BJØRNØYA
OSTROV KOLGUYEV
YEKATERINBURG
KAZAKH.

LABRADOR SEA
JAN MAYEN (Nor.)
GREENLAND SEA
MYS KANIN NOS
NORDKAPP
Murmansk
Arkhangel'sk
CHELYABINSK
URAL MTS.

Julianehåb
KAP BREWSTER
Denmark Strait
NORWEGIAN SEA
FINLAND
Volga
KAZAKHSTAN

CAPE BAULD
CAPE FAREWELL
HORN
FONTUR
ICELAND
NORWAY
SWEDEN
ST. PETERSBURG

NEWFOUNDLAND
Reykjavík
ESTONIA
Gora El'brus 18,510 ft. 5642 m.
TBILISI
GEOR.

FAROE ISLANDS (Den.)
Bergen
Oslo
Stockholm
LATVIA
MOSCOW

SHETLAND IS.
ORKNEY IS.
LITH.
BELARUS
Volga
RUSSIA

ATLANTIC OCEAN
HEBRIDES
NORTH SEA
DENMARK
BALTIC SEA
RUSSIA
KIEV
UKRAINE
Black Sea

IRELAND
UNITED KINGDOM
NETH.
BERLIN
GERMANY
POLAND
CARPATHIAN MTS.
MOLD.
BLACK SEA
TURKEY

MIZEN HEAD
LONDON
BELG.
LUX.
CZ. REP.
SLVK.
BUDAPEST
ROMANIA
BUCHAREST
ANKARA

AZORES (Port.)
PARIS
FRANCE
SWITZ.
AUS.
HUNG.
SLVN.
BULGARIA
SERBIA
İSTANBUL
SYRIA

Bay of Biscay
ITALY
BOS.
CRO.

© Rand McNally
A-102149-1

| 0 | 200 | 400 | 600 | 800 | 1000 | 1200 Miles |

| 0 | 200 | 400 | 600 | 800 | 1000 | 1200 | 1400 | 1600 | 1800 | 2000 Kilometers |

Lambert Azimuthal Equal Area Projection
Scale 1:40,000,000
One inch to 640 miles
One cm to 400 km

This table gives the area, population, population density, political status, capital, and predominant languages for every country in the world. The political units listed are categorized by political status in the 'Form of Government and Ruling Power' column of the table, as follows:

A independent countries;

B internally independent political entities which are under the protection of another country in matters of defense and foreign affairs;

C colonies and other dependent political units;

D the major administrative subdivisions of Australia, Canada, China, the United Kingdom, and the United States.

For comparison, the table also includes the continents and the world. All footnotes appear at the end of the table.

The populations are estimates for January 1, 2009, made by Rand McNally on the basis of official data, United States Census Bureau estimates, and other available information. Area figures include inland water.

Region or political division	Est. Pop. 1/1/09	Area sq. km.	Area sq. mi.	Pop. per sq. km.	Pop. per sq. mi.	Form of Government and Ruling Power	Political Status	Capital	Predominant Languages
Afars and Issas *see Djibouti*									
† Afghanistan	33,170,000	652,090	251,773	51	132	Transitional	A	Kabul (Kābol)	Dari, Pashto, Uzbek, Turkmen
Africa	985,490,000	30,300,000	11,700,000	33	84				
Alabama	4,685,000	135,765	52,419	35	89	State (U.S.)	D	Montgomery	English
Alaska	690,000	1,717,854	663,267	0.4	1.0	State (U.S.)	D	Juneau	English, indigenous
† Albania	3,630,000	28,748	11,100	126	327	Republic	A	Tiranë	Albanian, Greek
Alberta	3,570,000	661,848	255,541	5.4	14	Province (Canada)	D	Edmonton	English
† Algeria	33,975,000	2,381,741	919,595	14	37	Republic	A	Algiers (Alger)	Arabic, Berber dialects, French
American Samoa	65,000	199	77	327	844	Unincorporated territory (U.S.)	C	Pago Pago	Samoan, English
† Andorra	83,000	468	181	177	459	Parliamentary co-principality (Spanish and French)	B	Andorra la Vella	Catalan, Spanish (Castilian), French
† Angola	12,665,000	1,246,700	481,354	10	26	Republic	A	Luanda	Portuguese, indigenous
Anguilla	14,000	96	37	146	378	Overseas territory (U.K. protection)	B	The Valley	English
Anhui	61,865,000	139,000	53,668	445	1,153	Province (China)	D	Hefei	Chinese (Mandarin)
Antarctica	(1)	14,000,000	5,400,000						
† Antigua and Barbuda	85,000	442	171	192	497	Parliamentary state	A	St. John's	English, local dialects
Aomen *see Macau*									
† Argentina	40,700,000	2,780,400	1,073,519	15	38	Republic	A	Buenos Aires	Spanish, English, Italian, German, French
Arizona	6,535,000	295,254	113,998	22	57	State (U.S.)	D	Phoenix	English
Arkansas	2,870,000	137,732	53,179	21	54	State (U.S.)	D	Little Rock	English
† Armenia	2,965,000	29,800	11,506	99	258	Republic	A	Yerevan	Armenian, Russian
Aruba	100,000	193	75	518	1,333	Self-governing territory (Netherlands protection)	B	Oranjestad	Dutch, Papiamento, English, Spanish
Ascension	1,000	88	34	11	29	Dependency (St. Helena)	C	Georgetown	
Asia	4,078,790,000	44,900,000	17,300,000	91	236				
† Australia	21,135,000	7,692,030	2,969,910	2.7	7.1	Federal parliamentary state	A	Canberra	English, indigenous
Australian Capital Territory	340,000	2,360	911	144	373	Territory (Australia)	D	Canberra	English
† Austria	8,210,000	83,858	32,378	98	254	Federal republic	A	Vienna (Wien)	German
† Azerbaijan	8,205,000	86,600	33,437	95	245	Republic	A	Baku (Bakı)	Azeri, Russian, Armenian
† Bahamas	310,000	13,939	5,382	22	58	Parliamentary State	A	Nassau	English, Creole
† Bahrain	725,000	691	267	1,049	2,715	Monarchy	A	Manama (Al-Manāmah)	Arabic, English, Farsi, Urdu
† Bangladesh	155,045,000	143,998	55,598	1,077	2,789	Republic	A	Dhaka	Bangla, English
† Barbados	285,000	430	166	663	1,717	Parliamentary state	A	Bridgetown	English
Beijing (Peking)	16,010,000	16,800	6,487	953	2,468	Autonomous city (China)	D	Beijing	Chinese (Mandarin)
† Belarus	9,665,000	207,600	80,155	47	121	Republic	A	Minsk	Belarussian, Russian
Belau *see Palau*									
† Belgium	10,410,000	30,528	11,787	341	883	Constitutional monarchy	A	Brussels (Bruxelles)	Dutch (Flemish), French, German
† Belize	305,000	22,966	8,867	13	34	Parliamentary state	A	Belmopan	English, Spanish, Mayan, Garifuna
† Benin	8,660,000	112,622	43,484	77	199	Republic	A	Porto-Novo and Cotonou	French, Fon, Yoruba, indigenous
Bermuda	68,000	54	21	1,259	3,238	Overseas territory (U.K.)	C	Hamilton	English
† Bhutan	700,000	46,500	17,954	15	38	Monarchy (Indian protection)	B	Thimphu	Dzongkha, Tibetan and Nepalese dialects
† Bolivia	9,690,000	1,098,581	424,165	8.8	23	Republic	A	La Paz and Sucre	Aymara, Quechua, Spanish
† Bosnia and Herzegovina	4,605,000	51,197	19,767	90	233	Republic	A	Sarajevo	Bosnian, Croatian, Serbian
† Botswana	1,970,000	581,730	224,607	3.4	8.8	Republic	A	Gaborone	English, Tswana
† Brazil	197,550,000	8,547,404	3,300,172	23	60	Federal republic	A	Brasília	Portuguese, Spanish, English, French
British Columbia	4,380,000	944,735	364,764	4.6	12	Province (Canada)	D	Victoria	English
British Indian Ocean Territory	(1)	60	23			Overseas territory (U.K.)	C		English
British Virgin Islands	24,000	151	58	159	414	Overseas territory (U.K.)	C	Road Town	English
† Brunei	385,000	5,765	2,226	67	173	Monarchy	A	Bandar Seri Begawan	Malay, English, Chinese
† Bulgaria	7,235,000	110,994	42,855	65	169	Republic	A	Sofia (Sofiya)	Bulgarian, Turkish
† Burkina Faso	15,500,000	274,200	105,869	57	146	Republic	A	Ouagadougou	French, indigenous
Burma *see Myanmar*									
† Burundi	8,840,000	27,830	10,745	318	823	Republic	A	Bujumbura	French, Kirundi, Swahili
California	36,955,000	423,970	163,696	87	226	State (U.S.)	D	Sacramento	English
† Cambodia	14,365,000	181,035	69,898	79	206	Constitutional monarchy	A	Phnom Penh (Phnum Pénh)	Khmer, French
† Cameroon	18,670,000	475,440	183,568	39	102	Republic	A	Yaoundé	English, French, indigenous
† Canada	33,350,000	9,984,670	3,855,103	3.3	8.7	Federal parliamentary state	A	Ottawa	English, French
† Cape Verde	430,000	4,033	1,557	107	276	Republic	A	Praia	Portuguese, Crioulo
Cayman Islands	48,000	264	102	182	471	Overseas territory (U.K.)	C	George Town	English
† Central African Republic	4,480,000	622,984	240,536	7.2	19	Republic	A	Bangui	French, Sango, Arabic, indigenous
Ceylon *see Sri Lanka*									
† Chad	10,220,000	1,284,000	495,755	8.0	21	Republic	A	N'Djamena (Fort-Lamy)	Arabic, French, indigenous
Channel Islands	155,000	194	75	799	2,067	Two crown dependencies (U.K. protection)			English, French
† Chile	16,530,000	756,096	291,930	22	57	Republic	A	Santiago	Spanish
† China (incl. Hong Kong and Macau) (2)	1,341,820,000	9,557,172	3,690,045	140	364	Socialist republic	A	Beijing	Chinese dialects
Chongqing	28,430,000	82,400	31,815	345	894	Autonomous city (China)	D	Chongqing	Chinese (Mandarin)
Christmas Island	1,500	135	52	11	29	External territory (Australia)	C	Settlement	English, Chinese, Malay
Cocos (Keeling) Islands	600	14	5.4	43	111	External territory (Australia)	C	West Island	English, Cocos-Malay, Malay
† Colombia	45,330,000	1,138,914	439,737	40	103	Republic	A	Bogotá	Spanish
Colorado	4,965,000	269,601	104,094	18	48	State (U.S.)	D	Denver	English
† Comoros (excl. Mayotte)	740,000	2,235	863	331	857	Federal Islamic republic	A	Moroni	Arabic, French, Comoran
† Congo	3,960,000	342,000	132,047	12	30	Republic	A	Brazzaville	French, Lingala, Kikongo, indigenous
† Congo, Democratic Republic of the (Zaire)	67,590,000	2,345,095	905,446	29	75	Republic	A	Kinshasa (Léopoldville)	French, Kikongo, Lingala, Swahili, Tshiluba, Kingwana

Region or political division	Est. Pop. 1/1/09	Area sq. km.	Area sq. mi.	Pop. per sq. km.	Pop. per sq. mi.	Form of Government and Ruling Power	Political Status	Capital	Predominant Languages
Connecticut	3,520,000	14,357	5,543	245	635	State (U.S.)	D	Hartford	English
Cook Islands	12,000	236	91	51	132	Self-governing territory (New Zealand protection)	B	Avarua	English, Maori
† Costa Rica	4,225,000	51,100	19,730	83	214	Republic	A	San José	Spanish
† Cote d'Ivoire (Ivory Coast)	20,395,000	322,463	124,504	63	164	Republic	A	Abidjan and Yamoussoukro	French, Dioula and other indigenous
† Croatia	4,490,000	56,538	21,829	79	206	Republic	A	Zagreb	Croatian
† Cuba	11,440,000	110,861	42,804	103	267	Socialist republic	A	Havana (La Habana)	Spanish
† Cyprus	795,000	9,251	3,572	86	223	Republic	A	Nicosia	Greek, Turkish, English
† Czech Republic	10,215,000	78,866	30,450	130	335	Republic	A	Prague (Praha)	Czech, Slovak
Delaware	880,000	6,447	2,489	136	354	State (U.S.)	D	Dover	English
† Denmark	5,495,000	43,096	16,640	128	330	Constitutional monarchy	A	Copenhagen (København)	Danish
District of Columbia	595,000	177	68	3,362	8,750	Federal district (U.S.)	D	Washington	English
† Djibouti	510,000	23,200	8,958	22	57	Republic	A	Djibouti	French, Arabic, Somali, Afar
† Dominica	73,000	751	290	97	252	Republic	A	Roseau	English, French
† Dominican Republic	9,580,000	48,511	18,730	197	511	Republic	A	Santo Domingo	Spanish
† East Timor (Timor-Leste)	1,120,000	14,874	5,743	75	195	Republic	A	Dili	Portuguese, Tetum, Bahasa Indonesia (Malay)
† Ecuador	14,465,000	283,561	109,484	51	132	Republic	A	Quito	Spanish, Quechua, indigenous
† Egypt	82,400,000	1,001,449	386,662	82	213	Socialist republic	A	Cairo (El Qâhira)	Arabic
Ellice Islands *see Tuvalu*									
† El Salvador	7,125,000	21,041	8,124	339	877	Republic	A	San Salvador	Spanish, Nahua
England	51,135,000	130,422	50,356	392	1,015	Administrative division (U.K.)	D	London	English
† Equatorial Guinea	625,000	28,051	10,831	22	58	Republic	A	Malabo	Spanish, indigenous, English
† Eritrea	5,575,000	117,600	45,406	47	123	Republic	A	Asmera	Tigre, Kunama, Cushitic dialects, Nora Bana, Arabic
† Estonia	1,305,000	45,227	17,462	29	75	Republic	A	Tallinn	Estonian, Latvian, Lithuanian, Russian
† Ethiopia	83,870,000	1,104,300	426,373	76	197	Federal republic	A	Addis Ababa (Ādīs Ābeba)	Amharic, Tigrinya, Orominga, Guaraginga, Somali, Arabic
Europe	728,420,000	9,900,000	3,800,000	74	192				
Falkland Islands (3)	3,000	12,173	4,700	0.2	0.6	Overseas territory (U.K.)	C	Stanley	English
Faroe Islands	49,000	1,399	540	35	91	Self-governing territory (Danish protection)	B	Tórshavn	Danish, Faroese
† Fiji	940,000	18,274	7,056	51	133	Republic	A	Suva	English, Fijian, Hindustani
† Finland	5,250,000	338,145	130,559	16	40	Republic	A	Helsinki	Finnish, Swedish, Lapp, Russian
Florida	18,430,000	170,304	65,755	108	280	State (U.S.)	D	Tallahassee	English
† France (excl. Overseas Departments)	62,260,000	539,965	208,482	115	299	Republic	A	Paris	French
French Guiana	210,000	83,534	32,253	2.5	6.5	Overseas department (France)	C	Cayenne	French
French Polynesia	285,000	4,000	1,544	71	185	Overseas territory (France)	C	Papeete	French, Tahitian
Fujian	36,025,000	120,000	46,332	300	778	Province (China)	D	Fuzhou	Chinese dialects
† Gabon	1,500,000	267,668	103,347	5.6	15	Republic	A	Libreville	French, Fang, indigenous
† Gambia, The	1,760,000	10,689	4,127	165	426	Republic	A	Banjul (Bathurst)	English, Malinke, Wolof, Fula, indigenous
Gansu	26,385,000	450,000	173,746	59	152	Province (China)	D	Lanzhou	Chinese (Mandarin), Mongolian, Tibetan dialects
Gaza Strip	1,525,000	360	139	4,236	10,971	Israeli territory with limited self-government			Arabic
Georgia	9,740,000	153,910	59,425	63	164	State (U.S.)	D	Atlanta	English
† Georgia	4,625,000	69,700	26,911	66	172	Republic	A	Tbilisi	Georgian, Russian, Armenian, Azeri
† Germany	82,350,000	357,022	137,847	231	597	Federal republic	A	Berlin	German
† Ghana	23,610,000	238,533	92,098	99	256	Republic	A	Accra	English, Akan and other indigenous
Gibraltar	28,000	6.0	2.3	4,667	12,174	Overseas territory (U.K.)	C	Gibraltar	English, Spanish, Italian, Portuguese
Gilbert Islands *see Kiribati*									
Golan Heights	41,000	1,176	454	35	90	Occupied by Israel			Arabic, Hebrew
Great Britain *see United Kingdom*									
† Greece	10,730,000	131,957	50,949	81	211	Republic	A	Athens (Athína)	Greek, English, French
Greenland	58,000	2,166,086	836,331	0.03	0.07	Self-governing territory (Danish protection)	B	Godthåb	Danish, Greenlandic, Inuit dialects
† Grenada	91,000	344	133	265	684	Parliamentary state	A	St. George's	English, French
Guadeloupe (incl. St. Barthelemy and St. Martin)	465,000	1,780	687	261	677	Overseas department (France)	C	Basse-Terre	French, Creole
Guam	175,000	549	212	319	825	Unincorporated territory (U.S.)	C	Hagåtña	English, Chamorro, Japanese
Guangdong	94,205,000	177,800	68,649	530	1,372	Province (China)	D	Guangzhou (Canton)	Chinese dialects
Guangxi Zhuangzu	47,780,000	236,300	91,236	202	524	Autonomous region (China)	D	Nanning	Chinese dialects, Thai, Miao-Yao
† Guatemala	13,140,000	108,889	42,042	121	313	Republic	A	Guatemala	Spanish, Amerindian
Guernsey (incl. Dependencies)	66,000	78	30	846	2,200	Crown dependency (U.K. protection)	B	St. Peter Port	English, French
† Guinea	9,930,000	245,857	94,926	40	105	Republic	A	Conakry	French, indigenous
† Guinea-Bissau	1,520,000	36,125	13,948	42	109	Republic	A	Bissau	Portuguese, Crioulo, indigenous
Guizhou	38,040,000	170,000	65,637	224	580	Province (China)	D	Guiyang	Chinese (Mandarin), Thai, Miao-Yao
† Guyana	770,000	214,969	83,000	3.6	9.3	Republic	A	Georgetown	English, indigenous
Hainan	8,465,000	34,200	13,205	248	641	Province (China)	D	Haikou	Chinese, Min, Tai
† Haiti	8,955,000	27,750	10,714	323	836	Republic	A	Port-au-Prince	Creole, French
Hawaii	1,295,000	28,311	10,931	46	118	State (U.S.)	D	Honolulu	English, Hawaiian, Japanese
Hebei	69,845,000	190,000	73,359	368	952	Province (China)	D	Shijiazhuang	Chinese (Mandarin)
Heilongjiang	38,710,000	469,000	181,082	83	214	Province (China)	D	Harbin	Chinese dialects, Mongolian, Tungus
Henan	95,095,000	167,000	64,479	569	1,475	Province (China)	D	Zhengzhou	Chinese (Mandarin)
Holland *see Netherlands*									
† Honduras	7,715,000	112,088	43,277	69	178	Republic	A	Tegucigalpa	Spanish, indigenous
Hong Kong (Xianggang)	7,035,000	1,100	425	6,395	16,553	Special administrative region (China)	C	Hong Kong (Xianggang)	Chinese (Cantonese), English, Putonghua
Hubei	57,645,000	187,400	72,356	308	797	Province (China)	D	Wuhan	Chinese dialects
Hunan	64,215,000	210,000	81,082	306	792	Province (China)	D	Changsha	Chinese dialects, Miao-Yao
† Hungary	9,920,000	93,030	35,919	107	276	Republic	A	Budapest	Hungarian
† Iceland	305,000	103,000	39,769	3.0	7.7	Republic	A	Reykjavík	Icelandic
Idaho	1,530,000	216,446	83,570	7.1	18	State (U.S.)	D	Boise	English
Illinois	12,970,000	149,998	57,914	86	224	State (U.S.)	D	Springfield	English
† India (incl. part of Jammu and Kashmir)	1,157,055,000	3,166,285	1,222,510	365	946	Federal republic	A	New Delhi	English, Hindi, Telugu, Bengali, indigenous
Indiana	6,410,000	94,321	36,418	68	176	State (U.S.)	D	Indianapolis	English
† Indonesia	238,910,000	1,904,443	735,310	125	325	Republic	A	Jakarta	Bahasa Indonesia (Malay), English, Dutch, indigenous
Iowa	3,020,000	145,743	56,272	21	54	State (U.S.)	D	Des Moines	English

Region or political division	Est. Pop. 1/1/09	Area sq. km.	Area sq. mi.	Pop. per sq. km.	Pop. per sq. mi.	Form of Government and Ruling Power	Political Status	Capital	Predominant Languages
† Iran	66,135,000	1,648,195	636,372	40	104	Islamic republic	A	Tehrān	Farsi, Turkish dialects, Kurdish
† Iraq	28,585,000	438,317	169,235	65	169	Republic	A	Baghdād	Arabic, Kurdish, Assyrian, Armenian
† Ireland	4,180,000	70,273	27,133	59	154	Republic	A	Dublin (Baile Átha Cliath)	English, Irish Gaelic
Isle of Man	76,000	572	221	133	344	Crown dependency (U.K. protection)	B	Douglas	English, Manx Gaelic
† Israel (excl. Occupied Areas)	7,175,000	20,770	8,019	345	895	Republic	A	Jerusalem (Yerushalayim)	Hebrew, Arabic
† Italy	58,140,000	301,323	116,342	193	500	Republic	A	Rome (Roma)	Italian, German, French, Slovene
Ivory Coast *see Cote d'Ivoire*									
† Jamaica	2,815,000	10,991	4,244	256	663	Parliamentary state	A	Kingston	English, Creole
† Japan	127,200,000	377,750	145,850	337	872	Constitutional monarchy	A	Tōkyō	Japanese
Jersey	92,000	116	45	793	2,044	Crown dependency (U.K. protection)	B	St. Helier	English, French
Jiangsu	76,445,000	102,600	39,614	745	1,930	Province (China)	D	Nanjing	Chinese dialects
Jiangxi	43,935,000	166,600	64,325	264	683	Province (China)	D	Nanchang	Chinese dialects
Jilin	27,570,000	187,000	72,201	147	382	Province (China)	D	Changchun	Chinese (Mandarin), Mongolian, Korean
† Jordan	6,270,000	89,342	34,495	70	182	Constitutional monarchy	A	'Ammān	Arabic
Kansas	2,815,000	213,096	82,277	13	34	State (U.S.)	D	Topeka	English
† Kazakhstan	15,370,000	2,717,300	1,049,156	5.7	15	Republic	A	Astana (Aqmola)	Kazakh, Russian
Kentucky	4,290,000	104,659	40,409	41	106	State (U.S.)	D	Frankfort	English
† Kenya	38,475,000	582,646	224,961	66	171	Republic	A	Nairobi	English, Swahili, indigenous
† Kiribati	110,000	811	313	136	351	Republic	A	Bairiki	English, Gilbertese
† Korea, North	22,620,000	120,538	46,540	188	486	Socialist republic	A	P'yŏngyang	Korean
† Korea, South	48,445,000	99,268	38,328	488	1,264	Republic	A	Seoul (Sŏul)	Korean
Kosovo (4)	1,800,000	10,887	4,203	165	428	Republic	A	Priština	Albanian, Serbian
† Kuwait	2,645,000	17,818	6,880	148	384	Constitutional monarchy	A	Kuwait (Al-Kuwayt)	Arabic, English
† Kyrgyzstan	5,395,000	199,900	77,182	27	70	Republic	A	Bishkek	Kirghiz, Russian
† Laos	6,755,000	236,800	91,429	29	74	Socialist republic	A	Vientiane (Viangchan)	Lao, French, English
† Latvia	2,240,000	64,600	24,942	35	90	Republic	A	Rīga	Latvian, Russian, Lithuanian
† Lebanon	3,995,000	10,400	4,016	384	995	Republic	A	Beirut (Bayrūt)	Arabic, French, Armenian, English
† Lesotho	2,130,000	30,355	11,720	70	182	Constitutional monarchy	A	Maseru	English, Sesotho, Zulu, Xhosa
Liaoning	43,245,000	145,700	56,255	297	769	Province (China)	D	Shenyang	Chinese (Mandarin), Mongolian
† Liberia	3,395,000	111,369	43,000	30	79	Republic	A	Monrovia	English, indigenous
† Libya	6,240,000	1,759,540	679,362	3.5	9.2	Socialist republic	A	Tripoli (Tarābulus)	Arabic
† Liechtenstein	35,000	160	62	219	565	Constitutional monarchy	A	Vaduz	German
† Lithuania	3,560,000	65,300	25,213	55	141	Republic	A	Vilnius	Lithuanian, Polish, Russian
Louisiana	4,435,000	134,264	51,840	33	86	State (U.S.)	D	Baton Rouge	English
† Luxembourg	490,000	2,586	999	189	490	Constitutional monarchy	A	Luxembourg	French, Luxembourgish, German
Macau (Aomen)	555,000	18	6.9	30,833	80,435	Special administrative region (China)	C	Macau (Aomen)	Chinese (Cantonese), Portuguese
† Macedonia	2,065,000	25,713	9,928	80	208	Republic	A	Skopje	Macedonian, Albanian
† Madagascar	20,345,000	587,041	226,658	35	90	Republic	A	Antananarivo	Malagasy, French
Maine	1,325,000	91,646	35,385	14	37	State (U.S.)	D	Augusta	English
† Malawi	14,100,000	118,484	45,747	119	308	Republic	A	Lilongwe	Chichewa, English
† Malaysia	25,495,000	329,758	127,320	77	200	Federal constitutional monarchy	A	Kuala Lumpur and Putrajaya	Malay, Chinese dialects, English, Tamil
† Maldives	395,000	298	115	1,326	3,435	Republic	A	Male'	Divehi
† Mali	12,490,000	1,240,192	478,841	10	26	Republic	A	Bamako	French, Bambara, indigenous
† Malta	405,000	316	122	1,282	3,320	Republic	A	Valletta	English, Maltese
Manitoba	1,210,000	647,797	250,116	1.9	4.8	Province (Canada)	D	Winnipeg	English
† Marshall Islands	64,000	181	70	354	914	Republic (U.S. protection)	A	Majuro (island)	English, indigenous, Japanese
Martinique	445,000	1,100	425	405	1,047	Overseas department (France)	C	Fort-de-France	French, Creole
Maryland	5,665,000	32,133	12,407	176	457	State (U.S.)	D	Annapolis	English
Massachusetts	6,535,000	27,336	10,555	239	619	State (U.S.)	D	Boston	English
† Mauritania	3,090,000	1,030,700	397,956	3.0	7.8	Republic	A	Nouakchott	Arabic, Pular, Soninke, Wolof
† Mauritius (incl. Dependencies)	1,280,000	2,040	788	627	1,624	Republic	A	Port Louis	English, Creole, Bhojpuri, French, Hindi, Tamil, others
Mayotte (5)	220,000	374	144	588	1,528	Territorial collectivity (France)	C	Mamoudzou	French, Swahili (Mahorian)
† Mexico	110,585,000	1,964,382	758,452	56	146	Federal republic	A	Mexico City (Ciudad de México)	Spanish, indigenous
Michigan	10,060,000	250,494	96,716	40	104	State (U.S.)	D	Lansing	English
† Micronesia, Federated States of	110,000	702	271	157	406	Republic (U.S. protection)	A	Palikir	English, indigenous
Midway Islands	(1)	5.2	2.0	......	......	Unincorporated territory (U.S.)	C		English
Minnesota	5,250,000	225,171	86,939	23	60	State (U.S.)	D	St. Paul	English
Mississippi	2,955,000	125,434	48,430	24	61	State (U.S.)	D	Jackson	English
Missouri	5,945,000	180,533	69,704	33	85	State (U.S.)	D	Jefferson City	English
† Moldova	4,320,000	33,851	13,070	128	331	Republic	A	Chişinău	Romanian (Moldovan), Russian
† Monaco	33,000	2.0	0.8	16,500	41,250	Constitutional monarchy	A	Monaco	French, English, Italian, Monegasque
† Mongolia	3,020,000	1,566,500	604,829	1.9	5.0	Republic	A	Ulaanbaatar	Khalkha Mongol, Turkish dialects, Russian, Chinese
Montana	970,000	380,838	147,042	2.5	6.6	State (U.S.)	D	Helena	English
† Montenegro	675,000	13,812	5,333	49	127	Republic	A	Podgorica	Serbian, Albanian
Montserrat	5,000	102	39	49	128	Overseas territory (U.K.)	C	Plymouth (abandoned)	English
† Morocco (excl. Western Sahara)	34,600,000	446,550	172,414	77	201	Constitutional monarchy	A	Rabat	Arabic, Berber dialects, French
† Mozambique	21,475,000	801,590	309,496	27	69	Republic	A	Maputo (Lourenço Marques)	Portuguese, indigenous
† Myanmar (Burma)	47,950,000	676,578	261,228	71	184	Provisional military government	A	Yangon (Rangoon) and Nay Pyi Taw	Burmese, indigenous
† Namibia	2,100,000	823,144	317,818	2.6	6.6	Republic	A	Windhoek	English, Afrikaans, German, indigenous
† Nauru	14,000	21	8.1	667	1,728	Republic	A	Yaren District	Nauruan, English
Nebraska	1,795,000	200,345	77,354	9.0	23	State (U.S.)	D	Lincoln	English
Nei Mongol (Inner Mongolia)	24,270,000	1,183,000	456,759	21	53	Autonomous region (China)	D	Hohhot	Mongolian
† Nepal	28,380,000	147,181	56,827	193	499	Federal republic	A	Kathmandu (Kāṭhmāṇḍāū)	Nepali, Maithali, Bhojpuri, other indigenous
† Netherlands	16,680,000	41,864	16,164	398	1,032	Constitutional monarchy	A	Amsterdam and The Hague ('s-Gravenhage)	Dutch
Netherlands Antilles	225,000	800	309	281	728	Self-governing territory (Netherlands protection)	B	Willemstad	Dutch, Papiamento, English
Nevada	2,615,000	286,351	110,561	9.1	24	State (U.S.)	D	Carson City	English
New Brunswick	750,000	72,908	28,150	10	27	Province (Canada)	D	Fredericton	English, French
New Caledonia	225,000	18,575	7,172	12	31	Overseas territory (France)	C	Nouméa	French, indigenous
New Hampshire	1,325,000	24,216	9,350	55	142	State (U.S.)	D	Concord	English
New Hebrides *see Vanuatu*									
New Jersey	8,730,000	22,588	8,721	386	1,001	State (U.S.)	D	Trenton	English
New Mexico	1,995,000	314,915	121,590	6.3	16	State (U.S.)	D	Santa Fe	English, Spanish

Region or political division	Est. Pop. 1/1/09	Area sq. km.	Area sq. mi.	Pop. per sq. km.	Pop. per sq. mi.	Form of Government and Ruling Power	Political Status	Capital	Predominant Languages
New South Wales	6,960,000	800,640	309,129	8.7	23	State (Australia)	D	Sydney	English
New York	19,595,000	141,299	54,556	139	359	State (U.S.)	D	Albany	English
† New Zealand	4,195,000	270,534	104,454	16	40	Parliamentary state	A	Wellington	English, Maori
Newfoundland and Labrador	510,000	405,212	156,453	1.3	3.3	Province (Canada)	D	St. John's	English
† Nicaragua	5,840,000	129,640	50,054	45	117	Republic	A	Managua	Spanish, English, indigenous
† Niger	15,025,000	1,267,000	489,192	12	31	Provisional military government	A	Niamey	French, Hausa, Djerma, indigenous
† Nigeria	147,735,000	923,768	356,669	160	414	Transitional military government	A	Abuja	English, Hausa, Fulani, Yorbua, Ibo, indigenous
Ningxia Huizu	6,115,000	66,400	25,637	92	239	Autonomous region (China)	D	Yinchuan	Chinese (Mandarin)
Niue	1,500	259	100	5.8	15	Self-governing territory (New Zealand protection)	B	Alofi	English, indigenous
Norfolk Island	2,000	36	14	56	143	External territory (Australia)	C	Kingston	English, Norfolk
North America	531,180,000	24,700,000	9,500,000	22	56				
North Carolina	9,270,000	139,389	53,819	67	172	State (U.S.)	D	Raleigh	English
North Dakota	645,000	183,112	70,700	3.5	9.1	State (U.S.)	D	Bismarck	English
Northern Ireland	1,760,000	13,576	5,242	130	336	Administrative division (U.K.)	D	Belfast	English
Northern Mariana Islands	88,000	464	179	190	492	Commonwealth (U.S. protection)	B	Saipan (island)	English, Chamorro, Carolinian
Northern Territory	215,000	1,349,130	520,902	0.2	0.4	Territory (Australia)	D	Darwin	English, indigenous
Northwest Territories	43,000	1,346,106	519,735	0.03	0.08	Territory (Canada)	D	Yellowknife	English, indigenous
† Norway (incl. Jan Mayen and Svalbard)	4,655,000	323,877	125,050	14	37	Constitutional monarchy	A	Oslo	Norwegian, Lapp, Finnish
Nova Scotia	945,000	55,284	21,345	17	44	Province (Canada)	D	Halifax	English
Nunavut	30,000	2,093,190	808,185	0.01	0.04	Territory (Canada)	D	Iqaluit	English, indigenous
Oceania (incl. Australia)	34,605,000	8,500,000	3,300,000	4.1	10				
Ohio	11,550,000	116,096	44,825	99	258	State (U.S.)	D	Columbus	English
Oklahoma	3,660,000	181,036	69,898	20	52	State (U.S.)	D	Oklahoma City	English
† Oman	3,365,000	309,500	119,499	11	28	Monarchy	A	Muscat (Masqat)	Arabic, English, Baluchi, Urdu, Indian dialects
Ontario	12,950,000	1,076,395	415,599	12	31	Province (Canada)	D	Toronto	English
Oregon	3,810,000	254,805	98,381	15	39	State (U.S.)	D	Salem	English
† Pakistan (incl. part of Jammu and Kashmir)	174,525,000	879,902	339,732	198	514	Federal Islamic republic	A	Islāmābād	English, Urdu, Punjabi, Sindhi, Pashto
† Palau (Belau)	21,000	487	188	43	112	Republic	A	Melekeok	Angaur, English, Japanese, Palauan, Sonsorolese, Tobi
† Panama	3,335,000	75,517	29,157	44	114	Republic	A	Panamá	Spanish, English
† Papua New Guinea	5,995,000	462,840	178,704	13	34	Parliamentary state	A	Port Moresby	English, Motu, Pidgin, indigenous
† Paraguay	6,915,000	406,752	157,048	17	44	Republic	A	Asunción	Spanish, Guarani
Pennsylvania	12,515,000	119,282	46,055	105	272	State (U.S.)	D	Harrisburg	English
† Peru	29,365,000	1,285,216	496,225	23	59	Republic	A	Lima	Quechua, Spanish, Aymara
† Philippines	97,020,000	300,000	115,831	323	838	Republic	A	Manila	English, Pilipino, Tagalog
Pitcairn Islands (incl. Dependencies)	100	49	19	2.0	5.3	Overseas territory (U.K.)	C	Adamstown	English, Tahitian
† Poland	38,490,000	312,685	120,728	123	319	Republic	A	Warsaw (Warszawa)	Polish
† Portugal	10,695,000	91,985	35,516	116	301	Republic	A	Lisbon (Lisboa)	Portuguese
Prince Edward Island	140,000	5,660	2,185	25	64	Province (Canada)	D	Charlottetown	English
Puerto Rico	3,965,000	9,104	3,515	436	1,128	Commonwealth (U.S. protection)	B	San Juan	Spanish, English
† Qatar	830,000	11,427	4,412	73	188	Monarchy	A	Doha (Ad-Dawḩah)	Arabic, English
Qinghai	5,550,000	720,000	277,994	7.7	20	Province (China)	D	Xining	Tibetan dialects, Mongolian, Turkish dialects, Chinese (Mandarin)
Quebec	7,775,000	1,542,056	595,391	5.0	13	Province (Canada)	D	Québec	French, English
Queensland	4,180,000	1,730,650	668,208	2.4	6.3	State (Australia)	D	Brisbane	English
Reunion	815,000	2,510	969	325	841	Overseas department (France)	C	Saint-Denis	French, Creole
Rhode Island	1,055,000	4,002	1,545	264	683	State (U.S.)	D	Providence	English
Rhodesia see Zimbabwe									
† Romania	22,230,000	237,500	91,699	94	242	Republic	A	Bucharest (Bucureşti)	Romanian, Hungarian, German
† Russia	140,370,000	17,075,400	6,592,849	8.2	21	Federal republic	A	Moscow (Moskva)	Russian, Tatar, Ukrainian
† Rwanda	10,330,000	26,338	10,169	392	1,016	Republic	A	Kigali	French, Kinyarwanda, Kiswahili
St. Helena (incl. Dependencies)	7,500	314	121	24	62	Overseas territory (U.K.)	C	Jamestown	English
† St. Kitts and Nevis	40,000	261	101	153	396	Parliamentary state	A	Basseterre	English
† St. Lucia	160,000	616	238	260	672	Parliamentary state	A	Castries	English, French
St. Pierre and Miquelon	7,000	242	93	29	75	Territorial collectivity (France)	C	Saint-Pierre	French
† St. Vincent and the Grenadines	105,000	388	150	271	700	Parliamentary state	A	Kingstown	English, French
† Samoa	220,000	2,831	1,093	78	201	Constitutional monarchy	A	Apia	English, Samoan
† San Marino	30,000	61	24	492	1,250	Republic	A	San Marino	Italian
† Sao Tome and Principe	210,000	964	372	218	565	Republic	A	São Tomé	Portuguese, Fang
Saskatchewan	1,015,000	651,036	251,366	1.6	4.0	Province (Canada)	D	Regina	English
† Saudi Arabia	28,420,000	2,149,690	830,000	13	34	Monarchy	A	Riyadh (Ar-Riyāḍ)	Arabic
Scotland	5,150,000	78,133	30,167	66	171	Administrative division (U.K.)	D	Edinburgh	English, Scots Gaelic
† Senegal	13,525,000	196,712	75,951	69	178	Republic	A	Dakar	French, Wolof, Fulani, Serer, indigenous
† Serbia (excl. Kosovo)	7,395,000	77,474	29,913	95	247	Republic	A	Belgrade (Beograd)	Serbian
† Seychelles	87,000	455	176	191	494	Republic	A	Victoria	English, French, Creole
Shaanxi	37,815,000	205,000	79,151	184	478	Province (China)	D	Xi'an	Chinese (Mandarin)
Shandong	94,255,000	153,000	59,074	616	1,596	Province (China)	D	Jinan	Chinese (Mandarin)
Shanghai	18,375,000	6,200	2,394	2,964	7,675	Autonomous city (China)	D	Shanghai	Chinese (Wu)
Shanxi	34,170,000	156,000	60,232	219	567	Province (China)	D	Taiyuan	Chinese (Mandarin)
Sichuan	82,710,000	487,600	188,263	170	439	Province (China)	D	Chengdu	Chinese (Mandarin), Tibetan dialects, Miao-Yao
† Sierra Leone	6,365,000	71,740	27,699	89	230	Transitional military government	A	Freetown	English, Krio, Mende, Temne, indigenous
† Singapore	4,635,000	683	264	6,786	17,557	Republic	A	Singapore	Chinese (Mandarin), English, Malay, Tamil
† Slovakia	5,460,000	49,012	18,924	111	289	Republic	A	Bratislava	Slovak, Hungarian
† Slovenia	2,005,000	20,256	7,821	99	256	Republic	A	Ljubljana	Slovenian
† Solomon Islands	590,000	28,370	10,954	21	54	Parliamentary state	A	Honiara	English, indigenous
† Somalia	9,695,000	637,657	246,201	15	39	None	A	Mogadishu (Muqdisho)	Arabic, Somali, English, Italian
† South Africa	48,985,000	1,219,090	470,693	40	104	Republic	A	Pretoria (Tshwane), Cape Town and Bloemfontein	Afrikaans, English, Xhosa, Zulu, other indigenous
South America	391,890,000	17,800,000	6,900,000	22	57				
South Australia	1,600,000	983,480	379,724	1.6	4.2	State (Australia)	D	Adelaide	English
South Carolina	4,505,000	82,932	32,020	54	141	State (U.S.)	D	Columbia	English
South Dakota	810,000	199,731	77,117	4.1	11	State (U.S.)	D	Pierre	English
South Georgia and the South Sandwich Islands (3)	(1)	3,755	1,450	......	......	Overseas territory (U.K.)	C	Grytviken Harbour	English

Region or political division	Est. Pop. 1/1/09	Area sq. km.	Area sq. mi.	Pop. per sq. km.	Pop. per sq. mi.	Form of Government and Ruling Power	Political Status	Capital	Predominant Languages
South West Africa *see Namibia*	....	....	....	......	......	....		....	....
† Spain	40,510,000	504,750	194,885	80	208	Constitutional monarchy	A	Madrid	Spanish (Castilian), Catalan, Galician, Basque
Spanish North Africa (6)	150,000	32	12	4,688	12,500	Five possessions (Spain)	C		Spanish, Arabic, Berber dialects
Spanish Sahara *see Western Sahara*	....	....	....	......	......				
† Sri Lanka	21,230,000	65,610	25,332	324	838	Socialist republic	A	Colombo and Sri Jayewardenepura Kotte	English, Sinhala, Tamil
† Sudan	40,650,000	2,505,813	967,500	16	42	Provisional military government	A	Khartoum (Al-Khartūm)	Arabic, Nubian and other indigenous, English
† Suriname	480,000	163,265	63,037	2.9	7.6	Republic	A	Paramaribo	Dutch, Sranan Tongo, English, Hindustani, Javanese
† Swaziland	1,125,000	17,364	6,704	65	168	Monarchy	A	Mbabane and Lobamba	English, siSwati
† Sweden	9,050,000	449,964	173,732	20	52	Constitutional monarchy	A	Stockholm	Swedish, Lapp, Finnish
† Switzerland	7,595,000	41,293	15,943	184	476	Federal republic	A	Bern	German, French, Italian, Romansch
† Syria	19,965,000	185,180	71,498	108	279	Socialist republic	A	Damascus (Dimashq)	Arabic, Kurdish, Armenian, Aramaic, Circassian
Taiwan	22,950,000	36,002	13,901	637	1,651	Republic	A	T'aipei	Chinese (Mandarin), Taiwanese (Min), Hakka
† Tajikistan	7,280,000	143,100	55,251	51	132	Republic	A	Dushanbe	Tajik, Uzbek, Russian
† Tanzania	40,630,000	945,087	364,900	43	111	Republic	A	Dar es Salaam and Dodoma	English, Swahili, indigenous
Tasmania	500,000	68,400	26,409	7.3	19	State (Australia)	D	Hobart	English
Tennessee	6,250,000	109,151	42,143	57	148	State (U.S.)	D	Nashville	English
Texas	24,460,000	695,621	268,581	35	91	State (U.S.)	D	Austin	English, Spanish
† Thailand	65,705,000	513,115	198,115	128	332	Constitutional monarchy	A	Bangkok (Krung Thep)	Thai, indigenous
Tianjin (Tientsin)	10,885,000	11,300	4,363	963	2,495	Autonomous city (China)	D	Tianjin	Chinese (Mandarin)
Timor-Leste *see East Timor*	....	....	....	......	......				
† Togo	5,940,000	56,785	21,925	105	271	Provisional military government	A	Lomé	French, Ewe, Mina, Kabye, Dagomba
Tokelau	1,500	12	4.6	125	326	Island territory (New Zealand)	C		English, Tokelauan
† Tonga	120,000	650	251	185	478	Constitutional monarchy	A	Nuku'alofa	Tongan, English
† Trinidad and Tobago	1,230,000	5,128	1,980	240	621	Republic	A	Port of Spain	English, Hindi, French, Spanish
Tristan da Cunha	300	104	40	2.9	7.5	Dependency (St. Helena)	C	Edinburgh	English
† Tunisia	10,435,000	163,610	63,170	64	165	Republic	A	Tunis	Arabic, French
† Turkey	76,300,000	783,577	302,541	97	252	Republic	A	Ankara	Turkish, Kurdish, Arabic
† Turkmenistan	4,855,000	488,100	188,457	9.9	26	Republic	A	Aşgabat	Turkmen, Russian, Uzbek
Turks and Caicos Islands	23,000	430	166	53	139	Overseas territory (U.K.)	C	Grand Turk	English
† Tuvalu	12,000	26	10	462	1,200	Parliamentary state	A	Funafuti	Tuvaluan, English
† Uganda	31,935,000	241,038	93,065	132	343	Republic	A	Kampala	English, Luganda, Swahili, indigenous
† Ukraine	45,845,000	603,700	233,090	76	197	Republic	A	Kiev (Kyïv)	Ukrainian, Russian, Romanian, Polish
† United Arab Emirates	4,710,000	83,600	32,278	56	146	Federation of monarchs	A	Abu Dhabi (Abū Ẓaby)	Arabic, Farsi, English, Hindi, Urdu
† United Kingdom	61,030,000	242,910	93,788	251	651	Parliamentary monarchy	A	London	English, Welsh, Scots Gaelic
† United States	305,710,000	9,826,630	3,794,083	31	81	Federal republic	A	Washington	English, Spanish
Upper Volta *see Burkina Faso*	....	....	....	......	......				
† Uruguay	3,485,000	175,016	67,574	20	52	Republic	A	Montevideo	Spanish
Utah	2,750,000	219,887	84,899	13	32	State (U.S.)	D	Salt Lake City	English
† Uzbekistan	27,475,000	447,400	172,742	61	159	Republic	A	Tashkent (Toshkent)	Uzbek, Russian
† Vanuatu	215,000	12,190	4,707	18	46	Republic	A	Port Vila	Bislama, English, French
Vatican City	800	0.4	0.2	2,000	4,000	Monarchical-sacerdotal state	A	Vatican City	Italian, Latin, other
† Venezuela	26,615,000	912,050	352,145	29	76	Federal republic	A	Caracas	Spanish, Amerindian
Vermont	625,000	24,901	9,614	25	65	State (U.S.)	D	Montpelier	English
Victoria	5,235,000	227,420	87,807	23	60	State (Australia)	D	Melbourne	English
† Vietnam	86,545,000	331,689	128,066	261	676	Socialist republic	A	Ha Noi	Vietnamese, French, Chinese, English, Khmer, indigenous
Virginia	7,810,000	110,785	42,774	70	183	State (U.S.)	D	Richmond	English
Virgin Islands (U.S.)	110,000	347	134	317	821	Unincorporated territory (U.S.)	C	Charlotte Amalie	English, Spanish, Creole
Wake Island	(1)	7.8	3.0	......	......	Unincorporated territory (U.S.)	C		English
Wales	2,985,000	20,779	8,023	144	372	Administrative division (U.K.)	D	Cardiff	English, Welsh Gaelic
Wallis and Futuna	15,000	255	99	59	152	Overseas territory (France)	C	Matā'utu	French, Wallisian
Washington	6,585,000	184,665	71,300	36	92	State (U.S.)	D	Olympia	English
West Bank (incl. East Jerusalem)	2,435,000	5,860	2,263	416	1,076	Israeli territory with limited self-government			Arabic, Hebrew
Western Australia	2,105,000	2,529,880	976,792	0.8	2.2	State (Australia)	D	Perth	English
Western Sahara	400,000	266,000	102,703	1.5	3.9	Occupied by Morocco			Arabic
West Virginia	1,825,000	62,755	24,230	29	75	State (U.S.)	D	Charleston	English
Wisconsin	5,660,000	169,639	65,498	33	86	State (U.S.)	D	Madison	English
Wyoming	535,000	253,336	97,814	2.1	5.5	State (U.S.)	D	Cheyenne	English
Xianggang *see Hong Kong*	....	....	....	......	......				
Xinjiang Uygur (Sinkiang)	20,755,000	1,600,000	617,764	13	34	Autonomous region (China)	D	Ürümqi	Turkish dialects, Mongolian, Tungus, English
Xizang (Tibet)	2,845,000	1,220,000	471,045	2.3	6.0	Autonomous region (China)	D	Lhasa	Tibetan dialects
† Yemen	23,410,000	527,968	203,850	44	115	Republic	A	Sanaa (Ṣanʻāʼ)	Arabic
Yugoslavia *see Serbia*	....	....	....	......	......				
Yukon	32,000	482,443	186,272	0.07	0.2	Territory (Canada)	D	Whitehorse	English, Inuktitut, indigenous
Yunnan	45,390,000	394,000	152,124	115	298	Province (China)	D	Kunming	Chinese (Mandarin), Tibetan dialects, Khmer, Miao-Yao
Zaire *see Congo, Democratic Republic of the*	....	....	....	......	......				
† Zambia	11,765,000	752,614	290,586	16	40	Republic	A	Lusaka	English, Tonga, Lozi, other indigenous
Zhejiang	50,425,000	101,800	39,305	495	1,283	Province (China)	D	Hangzhou	Chinese dialects
† Zimbabwe	11,305,000	390,759	150,873	29	75	Republic	A	Harare (Salisbury)	English, Shona, Sindebele
WORLD	6,750,375,000	150,100,000	57,900,000	45	117				

(1) No Permanent Population.

(2) Population estimate includes 26,760,000 people not included in any province.

(3) Claimed by Argentina.

(4) Kosovo unilaterally declared its independence from Serbia in 2008.

(5) Claimed by Comoros.

(6) Comprises Ceuta, Melilla and several small islands.

† Member of the United Nations (2008)

... None, or not applicable.

General Information

Equatorial diameter of Earth . . . . . 12,756 km (7,926 mi.)
Polar diameter of Earth . . . . . 12,713 km (7,900 mi.)
Mean diameter of Earth . . . . . 12,742 km (7,918 mi.)
Equatorial circumference of Earth . . . . . 40,075 km (24,901 mi.)
Mean distance from Earth to Sun . . . . 149,598,000 km (92,955,900 mi.)
Mean distance from Earth to Moon . . . . . 384,403 km (238,857 mi.)
Total area of Earth . . . . . 510,100,000 sq. km (197,000,000 sq. mi.)
Highest elevation on Earth's surface, Mt. Everest, Asia . . . . . 8,848 m (29,028 ft.)
Lowest elevation on Earth's land surface, shores of the Dead Sea, Asia . . . . . 408 m (1,339 ft.) below sea level
Greatest known depth of the ocean, southwest of Guam, Pacific Ocean . . . . . 10,924 m (35,840 ft.)
Total land area of Earth (incl. inland water and Antarctica) . . . . . 150,100,000 sq. km (57,900,000 sq. mi.)
Area of Africa . . . . . 30,300,000 sq. km (11,700,000 sq. mi.)
Area of Antarctica . . . . . 14,000,000 sq. km (5,400,000 sq. mi.)
Area of Australia and Oceania . . 8,500,000 sq. km (3,300,000 sq. mi.)
Area of Asia . . . . . 44,900,000 sq. km (17,300,000 sq. mi.)
Area of Europe . . . . . 9,900,000 sq. km (3,800,000 sq. mi.)
Area of North America . . . . . 24,700,000 sq. km (9,500,000 sq. mi.)
Area of South America . . . . . 17,800,000 sq. km (6,900,000 sq. mi.)
World Population . . . . . (est. 1/1/09), 6,750,375,000

Principal Islands Area in sq. km (sq. mi.)

Baffin I., Nu., Can. 507,451 (195,928)
Banks I., N.T., Can. 70,028 (27,038)
Borneo, Asia 748,168 (288,869)
Bougainville, Pap. N. Gui. 9,317 (3,597)
Cape Breton I., N.S., Can. 10,311 (3,981)
Celebes, Indon. 180,680 (69,761)
Ceram, Indon. 17,454 (6,739)
Corsica, Fr. 8,741 (3,375)
Crete, Grc. 8,349 (3,224)
Cuba, Cuba 105,805 (40,852)
Cyprus, Cyp. 9,234 (3,565)
Devon I., Nu., Can. 55,247 (21,331)
Ellesmere I., Nu., Can. 196,236 (75,767)
Flores, Indon. 14,154 (5,465)
Great Britain, U.K. 226,000 (87,259)
Greenland, Green. 2,166,086 (836,330)
Guadalcanal, Sol. Is. 5,352 (2,066)
Hainan Dao, China 33,209 (12,822)
Hawai' i, Hi., U.S. 10,500 (4,054)
Hispaniola, N.A. 73,929 (28,544)
Hokkaidō, Japan 78,719 (30,394)
Honshū, Japan 225,800 (87,182)
Iceland, Ice. 101,826 (39,315)
Ireland, Ire.-U.K. 81,638 (31,521)
Jamaica, Jam. 11,189 (4,320)
Java, Indon. 138,793 (53,588)
Kodiak I., Ak., U.S. 9,578 (3,698)
Kyūshū, Japan 37,437 (14,455)
Leyte, Phil. 7,367 (2,844)
Long I., N.Y., U.S. 3,502 (1,352)
Luzon, Phil. 109,964 (42,457)
Madagascar, Madag. 587,713 (226,917)
Melville I., Can. 42,149 (16,274)
Mindanao, Phil. 97,530 (37,657)
Mindoro, Phil. 10,571 (4,081)
Negros, Phil. 13,074 (5,048)
New Britain, Pap. N. Gui. 35,144 (13,569)
New Caledonia, N. Cal. 16,648 (6,428)
Newfoundland, Nf., Can. 108,860 (42,031)
New Guinea, Asia-Oc. . . 785,753 (303,381)
North East Land, Nor. 14,247 (5,501)
North I., N.Z. 111,582 (43,082)
Palawan, Phil. 12,188 (4,706)
Panay, Phil. 12,011 (4,637)
Prince of Wales I., Nu., Can. 33,339 (12,872)
Puerto Rico, P.R. 8,733 (3,372)
Sakhalin, Russia 72,492 (27,989)
Samar, Phil. 12,849 (4,961)
Sardinia, Italy 23,949 (9,247)
Shikoku, Japan 18,544 (7,160)
Sicily, Italy 25,662 (9,908)
Southampton I., Nu., Can. 41,214 (15,913)
South I., N.Z. 145,836 (56,308)
Spitsbergen, Nor. 38,980 (15,050)
Sri Lanka, Sri L. 67,654 (26,121)
Sumatra, Indon. 443,065 (171,068)
Taiwan, Tai. 34,506 (13,323)
Tasmania, Austl. 65,519 (25,297)
Tierra del Fuego, S.A. . . . 47,401 (18,302)
Timor, Asia 28,418 (10,972)
Vancouver I., B.C., Can. . . 31,285 (12,079)
Victoria I., Can. 217,291 (83,896)
Vrangelya, Ostrov (Wrangel I.), Russia 7,865 (3,037)

Principal Lakes, Oceans and Seas Area in sq. km (sq. mi.)

Arabian Sea, Afr.-Asia 3,864,264 (1,492,000)
Aral Sea, Kaz.-Uzb. 17,158 (6,625)
Arctic Ocean . . . 14,056,000 (5,400,000)
Athabasca, L., Can. 7,935 (3,064)
Atlantic Ocean 76,762,000 (29,600,000)
Baikal, L., Russia 31,500 (12,162)
Balkhash, L., Kaz. 18,200 (7,027)
Baltic Sea, Eur. 422,168 (163,000)
Bering Sea, Asia-N.A. 2,291,900 (884,900)
Black Sea, Eur.-N.A. . . . 461,018 (178,000)
Caribbean Sea, N.A.-S.A. 2,754,000 (1,063,000)
Caspian Sea, Asia-Eur. 371,000 (143,244)
Chad, L., Afr. 1,540 (595)
Erie, L., Can.-U.S. 25,667 (9,910)
Eyre, L., Austl. 9,500 (3,668)
Great Bear Lake, Can.-U.S. 31,328 (12,096)
Great Salt Lake, U.S. 5,483 (2,117)
Great Slave Lake, Can. . . . 28,568 (11,030)
Hudson Bay, Can. . . 1,230,245 (475,000)
Huron, L., Can.-U.S. 59,570 (23,000)
Indian Ocean 68,556,000 (26,500,000)
Japan, Sea of, Asia 1,007,800 (389,100)
Kok Nor (Qinghai Hu), China 4,460 (1,722)
Ladoga, L., Russia 18,135 (7,002)
Manitoba, L., Can. 4,623 (1,785)
Maracaibo, L., Ven. 13,010 (5,023)
Mediterranean Sea 2,500,000 (965,000)
Mexico, Gulf of, N.A. 1,500,000 (600,000)
Michigan, L., U.S. 57,757 (22,300)
Nicaragua, Lago de, Nicaragua 8,150 (3,147)
North Sea, Eur. 574,978 (222,000)
Nyasa, L., Afr. 30,900 (11,931)
Onega, L., Russia 9,890 (3,819)
Ontario, L., Can.-U.S. 18,960 (7,320)
Pacific Ocean . . . 15,555,700 (6,000,000)
Red Sea, Afr.-Asia 437,708 (169,000)
Rudolf, L., Eth.-Kenya 6,750 (2,606)
Southern Ocean . . 20,327,000 (7,800,000)
Superior, L., Can.-U.S. . . . 82,100 (31,700)
Tanganyika. L., Afr. 32,000 (12,355)
Titicaca, Lago, Bol.-Peru . . 8,372 (3,232)
Torrens, L., Austl. 5,745 (2,218)
Vänern (L.), Swe. 5,648 (2,181)
Van Gölü (L.), Tur. 3,740 (1,444)
Victoria, L., Afr. 68,800 (26,564)
Winnipeg, L., Can. 24,387 (9,416)
Winnipegosis, L., Can. 5,374 (2,075)
Yellow Sea, Asia . . . 1,243,195 (480,000)

Principal Mountains Elevation in m (ft.)

Aconcagua, Cerro, Arg. . . 6,959 (22,831)
Annapūrṇa, Nepal 8,091 (26,545)
Aoraki (Mt. Cook), N.Z. . . 3,754 (12,316)
Apo, Mt., Phil. 2,954 (9,692)
Ararat, Mt., Tur. 5,137 (16,854)
Barú, Volcán, Pan. 3,475 (11,401)
Belukha, Mt., Asia 4,506 (14,783)
Bia, Phou, Laos 2,820 (9,252)
Blanc, Mont, Eur. 4,807 (15,771)
Blanca Pk., Co., U.S. 4,372 (14,345)
Bolívar, Pico, Ven. 5,007 (16,427)
Bonete Grande, Cerro, Arg. 6,872 (22,546)
Borah Pk., Id., U.S. 3,859 (12,662)
Boundary Pk., Nv., U.S. . . . 4,006 (13,143)
Cameroon Mtn., Camm. . . 4,100 (13,451)
Carrauntoohil, Ire. 1,038 (3,406)
Chaltel, Cerro, S.A. 3,340 (10,958)
Chimborazo, Ec. 6,310 (20,702)
Chirripó, Cerro, C.R. 3,819 (12,530)
Colima, Nevado de, Mex. 4,240 (13,911)
Cotopaxi, Ec. 5,897 (19,347)
Cristóbal Colón, Pico, Col. 5,775 (18,947)
Damāvand, Kūh-e, Iran . . 5,604 (18,386)
Dhawalāgiri, Nepal 8,167 (26,795)
Duarte, Pico, Dom. Rep. . . 3,175 (10,417)
Dufourspitze, Eur. 4,634 (15,203)
Elbert, Mt., Co., U.S. 4,399 (14,433)
El'brus, Gora, Russia 5,642 (18,510)
Elgon, Mt., Afr. 4,321 (14,177)
Erciyes Dağı, Tur. 3,917 (12,851)
Etna, Monte, Italy 3,323 (10,902)
Everest, Mt., Asia 8,848 (29,028)
Fairweather, Mt., N.A. . . . 4,663 (15,300)
Folādī, Koh-e, Afg. 5,135 (16,847)
Fuji-san, Japan 3,776 (12,388)
Galdhøpiggen, Nor. 2,469 (8,100)
Gannett Pk., Wy., U.S. . . . 4,207 (13,804)
Gerlachovský štít, Slvk. . . 2,655 (8,711)
Giluwe, Mt., Pap. N. Gui. . 4,368 (14,331)
Gongga Shan, China 7,590 (24,902)
Grand Teton, Wy., U.S. . . . 4,197 (13,770)
Großglockner, Aus. 3,797 (12,457)
Gunnbjørn Fjeld, Green. 3,700 (12,139)
Hekla, Ice. 1,491 (4,892)
Hkakabo Razi, Mya. 5,881 (19,295)
Hood, Mt., Or., U.S. 3,426 (11,239)
Huascarán, Nevado, Peru 6,746 (22,133)
Huila, Nevado del, Col. . . 5,750 (18,865)
Hvannadalshnúkur, Ice. . . 2,119 (6,952)
Illampu, Nevado, Bol. . . . 6,421 (21,066)
Illimani, Nevado de, Bol. 6,457 (21,184)
Imeni Ismail Samani, Pik (Communism Pk.), Taj. 7,495 (24,590)
Inthanon, Doi, Thai. 2,600 (8,530)
Jaya, Puncak, Indon. 5,030 (16,503)
Jungfrau, Switz. 4,158 (13,642)
K2 (Qogir Feng), Asia . . . 8,611 (28,250)
Kāmet, Asia 7,756 (25,446)
Kānchenjunga, Asia 8,598 (28,208)
Karisimbi, Volcan, Afr. . . . 4,507 (14,787)
Kebnekaise, Swe. 2,111 (6,926)
Kenya,Mt.,(Kirinyaga), Kenya 5,199 (17,058)
Kerinci, Gunung, Indon. . . 3,800 (12,467)
Kilimanjaro, Tan. 5,895 (19,340)
Kinabalu, Gunong, Malay. 4,101 (13,455)
Kinyeti, Sudan 3,187 (10,456)
Klyuchevskaya Sopka, Vulkan, Russia 4,750 (15,584)
Kosciuszko, Mt., Austl. . . . 2,229 (7,313)
Koussi, Emi, Chad 3,415 (11,204)
Kula Kangri, Bhu. 7,554 (24,784)
La Selle, Morne, Haiti . . . 2,674 (8,773)
Lassen Pk., Ca., U.S. 3,187 (10,457)
Llullaillaco, Volcán, S.A. . 6,739 (22,110)
Logan, Mt., Yk., Can. 5,959 (19,551)
Longs Pk., Co., U.S. 4,345 (14,255)
Margherita Pk., Afr. 5,109 (16,763)
Maromokotro, Madag. 2,876 (9,436)
Massive, Mt., Co., U.S. . . . 4,396 (14,421)
Matterhorn, Eur. 4,478 (14,692)
Mauna Kea, Hi., U.S. 4,205 (13,796)
Mauna Loa, Hi., U.S. 4,169 (13,677)
Mayon Volcano, Phil. 2,462 (8,077)
McKinley, Mt. (Denali), Ak., U.S. 6,194 (20,320)
Meru, Mt., Tan. 4,565 (14,977)
Misti, Volcán, Peru 5,822 (19,101)
Mitchell, Mt., N.C., U.S. . . . 2,037 (6,684)
Môco, Morro de, Ang. 2,620 (8,596)
Moldoveanu, Vârful, Rom. 2,544 (8,346)
Mulhacén, Spain 3,482 (11,424)
Musala, Blg. 2,925 (9,596)
Muztag, China 7,723 (25,338)
Namjagbarwa Feng, China 7,755 (25,443)
Nanda Devi, India 7,817 (25,645)
Nanga Parbat, Pak. 8,126 (26,660)
Nevis, Ben, Scot., U.K. 1,343 (4,406)
Ojos del Salado, Nevado, S.A. 6,893 (22,615)
Olympus, Mt., Grc. 2,917 (9,570)
Paektu-san, Asia 2,744 (9,003)
Paricutín, Mex. 2,800 (9,186)
Parnassós, Grc. 2,457 (8,061)
Pelée, Montagne, Mart. . . 1,397 (4,583)
Pico de Orizaba, Volcán, Mex. 5,610 (18,406)
Pidurutalagala, Sri L. 2,524 (8,281)
Pikes Pk., Co., U.S. 4,301 (14,110)
Pinatubo, Mt., Phil. 1,780 (5,840)
Pobeda, Gora Russia 3,147 (10,325)
Popocatépetl, Volcán, Mex. 5,465 (17,930)
Pulog, Mt., Phil. 2,934 (9,626)
Rainier, Mt., Wa., U.S. . . . 4,392 (14,411)
Ramm, Jabal, Jord. 1,754 (5,755)
Ras Dejen, Eth. 4,620 (15,158)
Rinjani, Gunung, Indon. . . 3,726 (12,224)
Robson, Mt., B.C., Can. . . . 3,954 (12,972)
Roraima, Mt., S.A. 2,875 (9,432)
Ruapehu, Mt., N.Z. 2,797 (9,177)
Ruiz, Nevado del, Col. . . 5,400 (17,717)
Saint Elias, Mt., N.A. . . . 5,489 (18,009)
Saint Helens, Mt., Wa., U.S. 2,549 (8,364)
Sajama, Nevado, Bol. . . . 6,542 (21,463)
Semeru, Gunung, Indon. 3,676 (12,060)
Shām, Jabal ash-, Oman . . 3,035 (9,957)
Shasta, Mt., Ca., U.S. 4,317 (14,162)
Snowdon, Wales, U.K. 1,085 (3,560)
Tahat, Alg. 2,908 (9,541)
Tajumulco, Volcán, Guat. 4,220 (13,845)
Tirich Mīr, Pak. 7,690 (25,230)
Toubkal, Jebel, Mor. 4,165 (13,665)
Triglav, Slvn. 2,864 (9,396)
Trikora, Puncak (Wilhelmina Pk.), Indon. 4,750 (15,584)
Tupungato, Cerro, S.A. . . 6,750 (22,146)
Turquino, Pico, Cuba 1,972 (6,470)
Uluru (Ayers Rock), Austl. . . 863 (2,831)
Uncompahgre Pk., Co., U.S. 4,361 (14,309)
Vesuvius, Italy 1,281 (4,203)
Vinson Massif, Ant. 4,897 (16,066)
Waddington, Mt., B.C., Can. 4,015 (13,173)
Washington, Mt., N.H., U.S. 1,917 (6,288)
Whitney, Mt., Ca., U.S. . . 4,418 (14,494)
Wilhelm, Mt., Pap. N. Gui. 4,509 (14,793)
Yü Shan, Tai. 3,997 (13,114)
Zugspitze, Eur. 2,962 (9,718)

Principal Rivers Length in km (mi.)

Albany, N.A. 982 (610)
Aldan, Asia 2,209 (1,373)
Amazonas-Ucayali, S.A. . 6,280 (3,902)
Amu Darya, Asia 1,687 (1,048)
Amur, Asia 2,820 (1,752)
Araguaia, S.A. 1,969 (1,223)
Arkansas, N.A. 2,350 (1,460)
Atchafalaya-Red, N.A. . . . 2,285 (1,420)
Athabasca, N.A. 1,231 (765)
Ayeyarwady, Asia 1,573 (977)
Brahmaputra, Asia 2,897 (1,800)
Brazos, N.A. 2,060 (1,280)
Canadian, N.A. 1,458 (906)
Churchill, N.A. 1,609 (1,000)
Colorado, N.A. (U.S.-Mex.) . . 2,334 (1,450)
Colorado, N.A. (TX) 1,387 (862)
Columbia, N.A. 2,000 (1,243)
Congo, Afr. 4,370 (2,715)
Danube, Eur. 2,860 (1,777)
Darling, Austl. 1,472 (915)
Dnieper, Eur. 2,285 (1,420)
Don, Eur. 1,907 (1,185)
Elbe, Eur. 1,091 (678)
Essequibo, S.A. 970 (603)
Euphrates, Asia 2,412 (1,499)
Fraser, N.A. 1,370 (851)
Ganges, Asia 3,000 (1,864)
Gila, N.A. 1,044 (649)
Godāvari, Asia 1,500 (932)
Huang (Yellow), Asia 4,667 (2,900)
Indigirka, Asia 1,726 (1,072)
Indus, Asia 3,180 (1,976)
Juruá, S.A. 2,758 (1,714)
Kama, Eur. 1,685 (1,047)
Kasai, Afr. 1,968 (1,223)
Kolyma, Asia 2,130 (1,324)
Lena, Asia 4,400 (2,734)
Limpopo, Afr. 1,212 (753)
Loire, Eur. 1,110 (690)
Mackenzie, N.A. 4,241 (2,635)
Madeira, S.A. 3,381 (2,101)
Magdalena, S.A. 1,530 (951)
Marañón, S.A. 1,546 (961)
Mekong, Asia 4,500 (2,796)
Mississippi, N.A. 3,766 (2,340)
Mississippi-Missouri, N.A. 6,420, (3,989)
Missouri, N.A. 4,088 (2,540)
Murray-Darling, Austl. . . . 2,844 (1,767)
Negro, S.A. 1,341 (833)
Nelson, N.A. 2,575 (1,600)
Niger, Afr. 4,160 (2,585)
Nile, Afr. 6,650 (4,132)
Ob', Asia 3,650 (2,268)
Oder, Eur. 906 (563)
Ohio, N.A. 2,108 (1,310)
Oka, Eur. 1,304 (810)
Orange, Afr. 2,300 (1,429)
Orinoco, S.A. 2,740 (1,703)
Ottawa, N.A. 1,271 (790)
Paraguay, S.A. 2,297 (1,427)
Paranaíba, S.A. 1,450 (901)
Peace, N.A. 1,923 (1,192)
Pechora, Eur. 1,810 (1,125)
Pecos, N.A. 1,490 (926)
Plata-Paraná, S.A. 4,700 (2,920)
Platte, N.A. 1,593 (990)
Purús, S.A. 2,588 (1,608)
Red, N.A. 2,076 (1,290)
Rhine, Eur. 1,320 (820)
Rhône, Eur 810 (503)
Rio Grande, N.A. 3,058 (1,900)
St. Lawrence, N.A. 3,058 (1,900)
Salado, S.A. 1,800 (1,118)
São Francisco, S.A. 2,800 (1,740)
Saskatchewan-Bow, N.A. 2,036 (1,265)
Severnaya Dvina (N. Dvina), Eur. 711 (442)
Snake, N.A. 1,674 (1,040)
Songhua (Sungari), Asia 872 (542)
Syr Darya, Asia 1,590 (988)
Tagus, Eur. 1,100 (684)
Tarim, Asia 964 (599)
Tennessee, N.A. 1,426 (886)
Tigris, Asia 1,752 (1,089)
Tisa, Eur. 881 (547)
Tocantins, S.A. 2,124 (1,320)
Ucayali, S.A. 1,484 (922)
Ural, Asia 2,102 (1,306)
Uruguay, S.A. 1,616 (1,004)
Vilyuy, Asia 2,446 (1,520)
Volga, Eur. 3,360 (2,088)
Volta, Afr. 1,600 (994)
Xiang, Asia 934 (580)
Xingu, S.A. 1,883 (1,170)
Yangtze (Chang), Asia 6,301 (3,915)
Yellowstone, N.A. 1,114 (692)
Yenisey, Asia 3,490 (2,169)
Yukon, N.A. 3,187 (1,980)
Zambezi, Afr. 2,660 (1,653)

Abidjan, Cote d'Ivoire 1,929,079
Abu Dhabi (Abū Ẓaby), United Arab Emirates 552,000
Accra, Ghana (1,390,000) 949,113
Ad-Dammām, Saudi Arabia (1,250,000) 525,000
Addis Ababa (Ādīs Ābeba), Ethiopia (2,200,000) 2,084,588
Ahmadābād, India (4,519,278) 3,515,361
Aleppo (Ḥalab), Syria (1,640,000) 1,591,400
Alexandria (El-Iskandarîya), Egypt (3,350,000) 2,926,859
Algiers (Alger), Algeria (2,547,983) 1,507,241
Almaty, Kazakhstan (1,190,000) 1,156,200
'Ammān, Jordan (1,500,000) 963,490
Amsterdam, Netherlands (1,121,303) 727,053
Ankara, Turkey (2,650,000) 2,559,471
Antananarivo, Madagascar 1,103,304
Antwerp (Antwerpen), Belgium (1,135,000) 453,030
Aşgabat, Turkmenistan 557,600
Asunción, Paraguay (700,000) 502,426
Athens (Athína), Greece (3,150,000) 772,072
Atlanta, United States (4,112,198) 416,474
Auckland, New Zealand (1,129,800) 380,154
Baghdād, Iraq 3,841,268
Baku (Bakı), Azerbaijan (2,020,000) 1,080,500
Bamako, Mali 658,275
Bandung, Indonesia (2,300,000) 2,136,260
Banghāzī, Libya (472,000) 446,250
Bangkok (Krung Thep), Thailand (7,360,000) 6,355,144
Bangui, Central African Republic 451,690
Barcelona, Spain (4,000,000) 1,496,266
Barranquilla, Colombia (1,260,000) 990,547
Beijing, China (7,320,000) 6,690,000
Beirut (Bayrūt), Lebanon (1,675,000) 509,000
Belfast, United Kingdom (730,000) 296,700
Belgrade (Beograd), Serbia (1,554,826) 1,136,786
Belo Horizonte, Brazil (4,055,000) 1,366,301
Bengalūru (Bangalore), India (5,686,844) 4,292,223
Berlin, Germany (4,220,000) 3,425,759
Birmingham, United Kingdom (2,705,000) . . . 965,928
Bishkek, Kyrgyzstan 631,300
Bogotá, Colombia (5,290,000) 4,931,796
Bonn, Germany (600,000) 304,841
Boston, United States (5,819,100) 589,141
Brasília, Brazil 1,947,133
Brazzaville, Congo 1,050,000
Brisbane, Australia (1,627,535) 888,449
Brussels (Bruxelles), Belgium (2,390,000) 133,845
Bucharest (București), Romania (2,300,000) 2,067,545
Budapest, Hungary (2,450,000) 1,906,798
Buenos Aires, Argentina (11,460,575) 2,776,138
Bulawayo, Zimbabwe 621,742
Cairo (El-Qâhira), Egypt (9,300,000) 6,068,695
Calgary, Canada (1,079,310) 987,969
Cali, Colombia (1,735,000) 1,641,498
Cape Town, South Africa (1,900,000) 854,616
Caracas, Venezuela (4,000,000) 1,822,465
Cardiff, United Kingdom (645,000) 272,129
Casablanca, Morocco (3,200,000) 2,761,975
Changchun, China 2,470,000
Chelyabinsk, Russia (1,310,000) 1,077,174
Chengdu, China 2,760,000
Chennai (Madras), India (6,424,624) 4,216,268
Chicago, United States (9,157,540) 2,896,016
Chișinău, Moldova 676,700
Chittagong, Bangladesh (2,342,662) 1,566,070
Chongqing, China 3,870,000
Cincinnati, United States (1,979,202) 331,285
Cleveland, United States (2,945,831) 478,403
Cologne (Köln), Germany (1,830,000) 964,311
Colombo, Sri Lanka (2,250,000) 642,163
Conakry, Guinea 950,000
Copenhagen (København), Denmark (2,030,000) 499,148
Córdoba, Argentina (1,368,301) 1,267,521
Cotonou, Benin (605,000) 536,827
Curitiba, Brazil (2,595,000) 1,586,848
Dakar, Senegal 1,490,450
Dalian, China 2,400,000
Dallas, United States (5,221,801) 1,188,580
Damascus (Dimashq), Syria (2,230,000) . . . 1,549,932
Dar es Salaam, Tanzania 2,497,940
Delhi, India (12,791,458) 9,817,439
Denver, United States (2,581,506) 554,636
Detroit, United States (5,456,428) 951,270
Dhaka, Bangladesh (6,537,308) 3,637,892
Dnipropetrovs'k, Ukraine (1,590,000) 1,147,000
Donets'k, Ukraine (2,090,000) 1,088,000
Douala, Cameroon 712,251
Dubai (Dubayy), United Arab Emirates . . . 1,171,000
Dublin (Baile Átha Cliath), Ireland (1,175,000) 481,854
Durban, South Africa (1,740,000) 715,669
Dushanbe, Tajikistan (800,000) 562,000
Düsseldorf, Germany (1,200,000) 529,062
Edinburgh, United Kingdom (640,000) 401,910
Edmonton, Canada (1,034,945) 730,372
El-Gîza, Egypt 1,883,189
Eşfahān, Iran (1,525,000) 1,266,072
Essen, Germany (5,040,000) 608,732
Faisalābād, Pakistan 2,008,861
Fortaleza, Brazil (2,780,000) 788,956
Frankfurt am Main, Germany (1,960,000) 643,469
Freetown, Sierra Leone (525,000) 469,776
Fukuoka, Japan (2,200,000) 1,302,454
Glasgow, United Kingdom (1,870,000) 662,954
Goiânia, Brazil 1,075,761
Guadalajara, Mexico (4,095,853) 1,600,894
Guangzhou (Canton), China 3,750,000
Guatemala, Guatemala (1,500,000) 823,301
Guayaquil, Ecuador 1,985,379
Hamburg, Germany (2,460,000) 1,704,731
Hannover, Germany (1,015,000) 520,670
Ha Noi, Vietnam (1,275,000) 905,939
Harare (Salisbury), Zimbabwe (1,470,000) 1,189,103
Harbin, China 3,120,000
Havana (La Habana), Cuba (2,285,000) 2,189,716
Helsinki, Finland (1,075,000) 512,686
Hiroshima, Japan (1,700,000) 1,113,786
Ho Chi Minh City (Saigon), Vietnam (3,300,000) 2,796,229
Hong Kong (Xianggang), China (4,770,000) 1,250,993
Honolulu, United States (876,156) 371,657
Houston, United States (4,669,571) 1,953,631
Hyderābād, India (5,533,640) 3,449,878
Ibadan, Nigeria 1,144,000
Islāmābād, Pakistan 529,180
İstanbul, Turkey (7,550,000) 6,620,241
İzmir, Turkey (1,900,000) 1,757,414
Jaipur, India 2,324,319
Jakarta, Indonesia (11,500,000) 8,347,083
Jerusalem (Yerushalayim), Israel (740,000) 680,500
Jiddah, Saudi Arabia 2,200,000
Jinan, China 2,150,000
Johannesburg, South Africa (4,000,000) 712,507
Kabul (Kābol), Afghanistan 1,424,400
Kampala, Uganda 1,208,544
Kānpur, India (2,690,486) 2,540,069
Kaohsiung, Taiwan (2,400,000) 1,509,510
Karāchi, Pakistan 9,339,023
Kathmandu (Kāṭhmāṇḍāū), Nepal (1,150,000) 671,846
Katowice, Poland (2,755,000) 327,032
Kharkiv, Ukraine (1,950,000) 1,555,000
Khartoum (Al-Kharṭūm), Sudan (2,950,000) 947,483
Kiev (Kyïv), Ukraine (3,250,000) 2,630,000
Kigali, Rwanda 603,049
Kingston, Jamaica (830,000) 516,500
Kinshasa (Léopoldville), Congo, Dem. Rep. of the 3,000,000
Kolkata (Calcutta), India (13,216,546) . . . 4,580,544
Kuala Lumpur, Malaysia (2,500,000) 1,297,526
Kuwait (Al-Kuwayt), Kuwait (1,126,000) 28,747
Lagos, Nigeria (3,800,000) 1,213,000
Lahore, Pakistan 5,143,495
La Paz, Bolivia (1,487,854) 789,585
Leeds, United Kingdom (1,530,000) 424,194
León, Mexico (1,425,210) 1,137,465
Lilongwe, Malawi 435,964
Lima, Peru (6,321,173) 340,422
Lisbon (Lisboa), Portugal (2,350,000) 663,394
Liverpool, United Kingdom (1,515,000) 481,786
Lomé, Togo 450,000
London, United Kingdom (12,000,000) 7,650,944
Los Angeles, United States (16,373,645) 3,694,820
Luanda, Angola 1,459,900
Lucknow, India (2,266,933) 2,207,340
Lusaka, Zambia 1,084,703
Lyon, France (1,648,216) 445,452
Madrid, Spain (4,690,000) 2,882,860
Managua, Nicaragua 864,201
Manaus, Brazil 1,394,724
Manchester, United Kingdom (2,760,000) . . 402,889
Manila, Philippines (11,200,000) 1,654,761
Mannheim, Germany (1,525,000) 310,475
Maputo (Lourenço Marques), Mozambique 966,837
Maracaibo, Venezuela 1,249,670
Marrakech, Morocco (760,000) 672,506
Marseille, France (1,516,340) 798,430
Mashhad, Iran 1,887,405
Mecca (Makkah), Saudi Arabia 1,025,000
Medan, Indonesia 1,904,273
Medellín, Colombia (2,290,000) 1,551,160
Melbourne, Australia (3,366,542) 67,784
Mexico City (Ciudad de México), Mexico (19,231,829) 8,720,916
Miami, United States (3,876,380) 362,470
Milan (Milano), Italy (3,790,000) 1,305,591
Milwaukee, United States (1,689,572) 596,974
Minneapolis, United States (2,968,806) 382,618
Minsk, Belarus (1,722,000) 1,661,000
Mogadishu (Muqdisho), Somalia 600,000
Mombasa, Kenya 665,018
Monrovia, Liberia 465,000
Monterrey, Mexico (3,664,331) 1,133,070
Montevideo, Uruguay (1,610,000) 1,269,552
Montréal, Canada (3,635,571) 1,620,693
Moscow (Moskva), Russia (13,500,000) 10,126,424
Mumbai (Bombay), India (16,368,084) 11,914,398
Munich (München), Germany (1,930,000) 1,205,923
Nagoya, Japan (5,280,000) 2,109,681
Nāgpur, India (2,122,965) 2,051,320
Nairobi, Kenya 2,143,254
Nanjing, China 2,490,000
Naples (Napoli), Italy (3,150,000) 1,046,987
N'Djamena (Fort-Lamy), Chad 546,572
Newcastle upon Tyne, United Kingdom (1,350,000) 189,150
New Delhi, India 294,783
New York, United States (21,199,865) 8,008,278
Nizhniy Novgorod (Gorky), Russia (1,900,000) 1,311,252
Nouakchott, Mauritania 558,195
Novosibirsk, Russia (1,530,000) 1,425,508
Nürnberg, Germany (1,065,000) 489,758
Odesa, Ukraine (1,150,000) 1,046,000
Omdurman (Umm Durmān), Sudan 1,271,403
Omsk, Russia (1,175,000) 1,134,016
Oran (Ouahran), Algeria 628,558
Ōsaka, Japan (16,500,000) 2,484,326
Oslo, Norway (773,498) 504,040
Ottawa, Canada (1,130,761) 648,480
Ouagadougou, Burkina Faso 709,700
Palembang, Indonesia 1,430,627
Panamá, Panama (995,000) 415,964
Paris, France (11,174,743) 2,125,246
Perm', Russia (1,100,000) 1,001,653
Perth, Australia (1,333,993) 13,463
Philadelphia, United States (6,188,463) . . . 1,517,550
Phnom Penh (Phnum Pénh), Cambodia 570,155
Phoenix, United States (3,251,876) 1,321,045
Port-au-Prince, Haiti (1,425,594) 846,247
Portland, United States (2,265,223) 529,121
Port Louis, Mauritius (500,000) 144,303
Port Moresby, Papua New Guinea 246,664
Porto, Portugal (1,230,000) 302,472
Porto Alegre, Brazil (3,375,000) 1,304,998
Prague (Praha), Czech Republic (1,328,000) 1,214,174
Pretoria (Tshwane), South Africa (1,100,000) 525,583
Puebla de Zaragoza, Mexico (2,109,049) . . . 1,399,519
Pune, India (3,755,525) 2,540,069
Pusan, Korea, South 3,797,566
P'yŏngyang, Korea, North 2,741,260
Qingdao, China 2,300,000
Québec, Canada (715,515) 490,614
Quezon City, Philippines 1,989,419
Quito, Ecuador (1,650,000) 1,399,378
Rabat, Morocco (1,210,000) 623,457
Recife, Brazil (3,160,000) 1,421,993
Rīga, Latvia (1,000,000) 874,200
Rio de Janeiro, Brazil (10,465,000) 5,851,914
Riyadh (Ar-Riyāḍ), Saudi Arabia 2,950,000
Rome (Roma), Italy (3,235,000) 2,649,765
Rosario, Argentina (1,161,188) 908,163
Rostov-na-Donu, Russia (1,220,000) 1,068,267
Rotterdam, Netherlands (1,089,979) 539,000
Sacramento, United States (1,796,857) 407,018
St. Louis, United States (2,603,607) 348,189
St. Petersburg (Leningrad), Russia (5,950,000) 4,661,219
Salvador, Brazil (2,855,000) 2,439,823
Samara, Russia (1,440,000) 1,157,880
San Diego, United States (2,813,833) 1,223,400
San Francisco, United States (7,039,362) . . . 776,733
San José, Costa Rica (996,194) 309,672
San Juan, Puerto Rico (2,450,292) 421,958
San Salvador, El Salvador (1,250,000) 415,346
Santiago, Chile (4,740,000) 4,295,593
Santo Domingo, Dominican Republic (2,005,000) 913,540
São Paulo, Brazil (17,380,000) 9,713,692
Sapporo, Japan (2,200,000) 1,822,992
Saratov, Russia (1,130,000) 873,055
Seattle, United States (3,554,760) 563,374
Seoul (Sŏul), Korea, South (15,850,000) 10,627,790
Shanghai, China (11,010,000) 8,930,000
Shenyang, China 4,050,000
Singapore, Singapore (4,800,000) 4,185,200
Sofia (Sofiya), Bulgaria (1,280,000) 1,190,126
Stockholm, Sweden (1,491,726) 674,452
Stuttgart, Germany (2,020,000) 585,274
Surabaya, Indonesia 2,599,796
Sūrat, India (2,811,466) 2,433,787
Sydney, Australia (3,997,321) 47,204
Tabrīz, Iran 1,191,043
T'aipei, Taiwan (6,800,000) 2,641,856
Tallinn, Estonia 403,981
Tashkent (Toshkent), Uzbekistan (2,325,000) 2,113,300
Tbilisi, Georgia (1,350,000) 1,081,678
Tegucigalpa, Honduras 769,061
Tehrān, Iran (8,800,000) 6,758,845
Tel Aviv-Yafo, Israel (2,000,000) 360,500
Tianjin, China 5,000,000
Tijuana, Mexico (1,483,992) 1,286,187
Tōkyō, Japan (32,000,000) 8,025,508
Toronto, Canada (5,113,149) 2,503,281
Tripoli (Ṭarābulus), Libya (960,000) 591,062
Tunis, Tunisia (1,350,000) 702,330
Turin (Torino), Italy (1,550,000) 921,485
Ufa, Russia (1,110,000) 1,042,437
Ulaanbaatar, Mongolia 649,797
Ürümqi, China 1,130,000
València, Spain (1,340,000) 739,014
Vancouver, Canada (2,116,581) 578,041
Vienna (Wien), Austria (1,950,000) 1,609,631
Vientiane (Viangchan), Laos 464,000
Vilnius, Lithuania 578,639
Volgograd, Russia (1,375,000) 1,011,417
Warsaw (Warszawa), Poland (2,400,000) 1,707,147
Washington, United States (7,608,070) 572,059
Winnipeg, Canada (694,668) 631,774
Wuhan, China 3,870,000
Xi'an, China 2,410,000
Yangon (Rangoon), Myanmar (2,800,000) 2,705,039
Yekaterinburg, Russia (1,550,000) 1,293,537
Yerevan, Armenia (1,320,000) 1,103,488
Yokohama, Japan 3,433,612
Zagreb, Croatia 867,865
Zürich, Switzerland (870,000) 365,043

Values are latest available city populations or recent estimates.
Metropolitan area populations are shown in parentheses.

Annam ... Annamese
Arab ... Arabic
Bantu ... Bantu
Bur ... Burmese
Camb ... Cambodian
Celt ... Celtic
Chn ... Chinese
Czech ... Czech
Dan ... Danish
Du ... Dutch
Fin ... Finnish
Fr ... French
Ger ... German
Gr ... Greek
Hung ... Hungarian
Ice ... Icelandic
India ... India
Indian ... American Indian
In don ... Indonesian
It ... Italian
Jap ... Japanese
Kor ... Korean
Mal ... Malayan
Mong ... Mongolian
Nor ... Norwegian
Per ... Persian
Pol ... Polish
Port ... Portuguese
Rom ... Romanian
Rus ... Russian
Serb ... Serbian
Siam ... Siamese
So. Slav ... Southern Slavonic
Sp ... Spanish
Swe ... Swedish
Tib ... Tibetan
Tur ... Turkish

å, Nor., Swe ... brook, river
aa, Dan., Nor ... brook
āb, Per ... water, river
abad, India, Per ... town, city
ada, Tur ... island
adrar, Berber ... mountain
ákra, Gr ... cape
älf, Swe ... river
alp, Ger ... mountain
altipiano, It ... plateau
alto, Sp ... height
archipel, Fr ... archipelago
archipiélago, Sp ... archipelago
arquipélago, Port ... archipelago
arroyo, Sp ... brook, stream
as, Nor., Swe ... ridge
austral, Sp ... southern
baai, Du ... bay
bab, Arab ... gate, port
bach, Ger ... brook, stream
backe, Swe ... Hill
bad, Ger ... bath, spa
bahía, Sp ... bay, gulf
bahr, Arab ... river, sea, lake
baia, It ... bay, gulf
baía, Port ... bay
baie, Fr ... bay, gulf
bajo, Sp ... depression
bak, Indon ... stream
bakke, Dan., Nor ... hill
balkan, Tur ... mountain range
bana, Jap ... point, cape
banco, Sp ... bank
bandao, Chn ... peninsula
bandar, Mal., Per .. town, port, harbor
bang, Siam ... village
bassin, Fr ... basin
batang, Indon., Mal ... river
bei, Chn ... north
ben, Celtic ... mountain, summit
bender, Arab ... harbor, port
bereg, Rus ... coast, shore
berg, Du., Ger., Nor., Swe ... mountain, hill
bir, Arab ... well
birkat, Arab ... lake, pond, pool
bit, Arab ... house
bjaerg, Dan., Nor ... mountain
bocche, It ... mouth
boğazı, Tur ... strait
bois, Fr ... forest, wood
bolsón, Sp ... flat-floored desert valley
boreal, Sp ... northern
borg, Dan., Nor., Swe ... castle, town
borgo, It ... town, suburb
bosch, Du ... forest, wood
bouche, Fr ... river mouth
bourg, Fr ... town, borough
bro, Dan., Nor., Swe ... bridge
brücke, Ger ... bridge
bucht, Ger ... bay, bight
bugt, Dan., Nor., Swe ... bay, gulf
bulu, Indon ... mountain
burg, Du., Ger ... castle, town
buri, Siam ... town
burun, burnu, Tur ... cape
by, Dan., Nor., Swe ... village
caatinga, Port. (Brazil) ... open brushland
cabezo, Sp ... summit
cabo, Port., Sp. ... cape
campo, It., Port., Sp ... plain, field
campos, Port. (Brazil) ... plains
cañón, Sp ... canyon
cap, Fr ... cape
capo, It ... cape
casa, It., Port., Sp ... house
castello, It., Port ... castle, fort
castillo, Sp ... castle
càte, Fr ... hill
çay, Tur ... stream, river
cayo, Sp ... rock, shoal, islet
cerro, Sp ... mountain, hill
champ, Fr ... field
château, Fr ... castle
chott, Arab ... salt lake
chu, Tib ... water, stream
cidade, Port ... town, city
cima, Sp ... summit, peak
città, It ... town, city
ciudad, Sp ... town, city
cochilha, Port ... ridge
col, Fr ... pass
colina, Sp ... hill
cordillera, Sp ... mountain chain
costa, It., Port., Sp ... coast
côte, Fr ... coast
cuchilla, Sp ... mountain ridge
dağ, Tur ... mountain(s)
dake, Jap ... peak, summit
dal, Dan., Du., Nor., Swe ... valley
dan, Kor ... point, cape
danau, Indon ... lake
dao, Chn ... island
dar, Arab ... house, abode, country
darya, Per ... river, sea
dasht, Per ... plain, desert
deniz, Tur ... sea
désert, Fr ... desert
deserto, It ... desert
desierto, Sp ... desert
détroit, Fr ... strait
dijk, Du ... dam, dike
djebel, Arab ... mountain
do, Kor ... island
dong, Chn ... east
dorf, Ger ... village
dorp, Du ... village
duin, Du ... dune
dzong, Tib . fort, administrative capital
eau, Fr ... water
ecuador, Sp ... equator
eiland, Du ... island
elv, Dan., Nor ... river, stream
embalse, Sp ... reservoir
erg, Arab ... dune, sandy desert
est, Fr., It ... east
estado, Sp ... state
este, Port., Sp ... east
estrecho, Sp ... strait
étang, Fr ... pond, lake
état, Fr ... state
eyjar, Ice ... islands
feld, Ger ... field, plain
festung, Ger ... fortress
fiume, It ... river
fjäll, Swe ... mountain
fjärd, Swe ... bay, inlet
fjeld, Nor ... mountain, hill
fjord, Dan., Nor ... fiord, inlet
fjördur, Ice ... fiord, inlet
fleuve, Fr ... river
flod, Dan., Swe ... river
flói, Ice ... bay, marshland
fluss, Ger ... river
foce, It ... river mouth
fontein, Du ... a spring
forêt, Fr ... forest
fors, Swe ... waterfall
forst, Ger ... forest
fos, Dan., Nor ... waterfall
fu, Chn ... town, residence
fuente, Sp ... spring, fountain
fuerte, Sp ... fort
furt, Ger ... ford
gang, Kor ... stream, river
gangri, Tib ... mountain
gat, Dan., Nor ... channel
gàve, Fr ... stream
gawa, Jap ... river
gebergte, Du ... mountain range
gebiet, Ger ... district, territory
gebirge, Ger ... mountains
ghat, India ... pass, mountain range
gobi, Mong ... desert
gol, Mong ... river
göl, gölü, Tur ... lake
golfe, Fr ... gulf, bay
golfo, It., Port., Sp ... gulf, bay
gomba, gompa, Tib ... monastery
gora, Rus., So. Slav ... mountain
góra, Pol ... mountain
gorod, Rus ... town
grad, Rus., So. Slav ... town
guba, Rus ... bay, gulf
gundung, Indon ... mountain
guntō, Jap ... archipelago
gunung, Mal ... mountain
haf, Swe ... sea, ocean
hafen, Ger ... port, harbor
haff, Ger ... gulf, inland sea
hai, Chn ... sea, lake
hama, Jap ... beach, shore
hamada, Arab ... rocky plateau
hamn, Swe ... harbor
hāmūn, Per ... swampy lake, plain
hantō, Jap ... peninsula
hassi, Arab ... well, spring
haus, Ger ... house
haut, Fr ... summit, top
hav, Dan., Nor ... sea, ocean
havn, Dan., Nor ... harbor, port
havre, Fr ... harbor, port
háza, Hung ... house, dwelling of
heim, Ger ... hamlet, home
hem, Swe ... hamlet, home
higashi, Jap ... east
hisar, Tur ... fortress
hissar, Arab ... fort
ho, Chn ... river
hoek, Du ... cape
hof, Ger ... court, farmhouse
höfn, Ice ... harbor
hoku, Jap ... north
holm, Dan., Nor., Swe ... island
hora, Czech ... mountain
horn, Ger ... peak
hoved, Dan., Nor ... cape
hu, Chn ... lake
huang, Chn ... yellow
hügel, Ger ... hill
huk, Dan., Swe ... point
hus, Dan., Nor., Swe ... house
île, Fr ... island
ilha, Port ... island
indsö, Dan., Nor ... lake
insel, Ger ... island
insjö, Swe ... lake
irmak, irmagi, Tur ... river
isla, Sp ... island
isola, It ... island
istmo, It., Sp ... isthmus
jarvi, jaur, Fin ... lake
jebel, Arab ... mountain
jiang, Chn ... river
jima, Jap ... island
jökel, Nor ... glacier
joki, Fin ... river
jökuli, Ice ... glacier
kaap, Du ... cape
kai, Jap ... bay, gulf, sea
kaikyō, Jap ... channel, strait
kalat, Per ... castle, fortress
kale, Tur ... fort
kali, Mal ... creek, river
kand, Per ... village
kap, Dan., Ger ... cape
kapp, Nor, Swe ... cape
kasr, Arab ... fort, castle
kawa, Jap ... river
kefr, Arab ... village
kei, Jap ... creek, river
ken, Jap ... prefecture
khor, Arab ... bay, inlet
khrebet, Rus ... mountain range
kita, Jap ... north
ko, Jap ... lake
köbstad, Dan ... market-town
kol, Mong ... lake
kólpos, Gr ... gulf
kong, Chn ... river
kopf, Ger ... head, summit, peak
köpstad, Swe ... market town
körfezi, Tur ... gulf
kosa, Rus ... spit
kou, Chn ... river mouth
köy, Tur ... village
kraal, Du. (Africa) ... native village
ksar, Arab ... fortified village
kuala, Mal ... bay, river mouth
kuh, Per ... mountain
kum, Tur ... sand
kuppe, Ger ... summit
küste, Ger ... coast
kyo, Jap ... town, capital
la, Tib ... mountain pass
labuan, Mal ... anchorage, port
lac, Fr ... lake
lago, It., Port., Sp ... lake
lagoa, Port ... lake, bay
laguna, It., Port., Sp ... lagoon, lake
lahti, Fin ... bay, gulf
lan, Swe ... county
landsby, Dan., Nor ... village
liman, Tur ... bay, port
ling, Chn ... pass, ridge, mountain
llanos, Sp ... plains
loch, Celt. (Scotland) ... lake, bay
loma, Sp ... long, low hill
lough, Celt. (Ireland) ... lake, bay
machi, Jap ... town
man, Kor ... bay
mar, Port., Sp ... sea
mare, It., Rom ... sea
marisma, Sp ... marsh, swamp
mark, Ger ... boundary limit
massif, Fr ... block of mountains
mato, Port ... forest, thicket
me, Siam ... river
meer, Du., Ger ... lake, sea
mer, Fr ... sea
mesa, Sp ... flat-topped mountain
meseta, Sp ... plateau
mina, Port., Sp ... mine
minami, Jap ... south
minato, Japan ... harbor, haven
misaki, Jap ... cape, headland
mont, Fr ... mount, mountain
montagna, It ... mountain
montagne, Fr ... mountain
montaña, Sp ... mountain
monte, It., Port., Sp .. mount, mountain
more, Rus., So. Slav ... sea
morro, Port., Sp ... hill, bluff
mühle, Ger ... mill
mund, Ger ... mouth, opening
mündung, Ger ... river mouth
mura, Jap ... township
myit, Bur ... river
mys, Rus ... cape
nada, Jap ... sea
nadi, India ... river, creek
naes, Dan., Nor ... cape
nafud, Arab ... desert of sand dunes
nagar, India ... town, city
nahr, Arab ... river
nam, Siam ... river, water
nan, Chn., Jap ... south
näs, Nor., Swe ... cape
nez, Fr ... point, cape
nishi, nisi, Jap ... west
njarga, Fin ... peninsula
nong, Siam ... marsh
noord, Du ... north
nor, Mong ... lake
nord, Dan., Fr., Ger., It., Nor., Swe .. north
norte, Port., Sp ... north
nos, Rus ... cape
nyasa, Bantu ... lake
ö, Dan., Nor., Swe ... island
occidental, Sp ... western
ocna, Rom ... salt mine
odde, Dan., Nor ... point, cape
oeste, Port., Sp ... west
oka, Jap ... hill
oost, Du ... east
oriental, Sp ... eastern
óros, Gr ... mountain
ost, Ger., Swe ... east
öster, Dan., Nor., Swe ... eastern
ostrov, Rus ... island
oued, Arab ... river, stream
ouest, Fr ... west
ozero, Rus ... lake
pää, Fin ... mountain
padang, Mal ... plain, field
pampas, Sp. (Argentina) ... grassy plains
pará, Indian (Brazil) ... river
pas, Fr ... channel, passage
paso, Sp ... mountain pass, passage
passo, It., Port ... mountain pass, passage, strait
patam, India ... city, town
pélagos, Gr ... open sea
pegunungan, Indon ... mountains
peña, Sp ... rock
pendi, Chn ... basin
pertuis, Fr ... strait
pic, Fr ... mountain peak
pico, Port., Sp ... mountain peak
piedra, Sp ... stone, rock
ping, Chn ... plain, flat
planalto, Port ... plateau
planina, Serb ... mountains
playa, Sp ... shore, beach
ploskogor'ye, Rus ... mountains
pnom, Camb ... mountain
pointe, Fr ... point
polder, Du., Ger ... reclaimed marsh
polje, So. Slav ... plain, field
poluostrov, Rus ... peninsula
pont, Fr ... bridge
ponta, Port ... point, headland
ponte, It., Port ... bridge
pore, India ... city, town
porthmós, Gr ... strait
porto, It., Port ... port, harbor
potamós, Gr ... river
prado, Sp ... field, meadow
presqu'île, Fr ... peninsula
proliv, Rus ... strait
pueblo, Sp ... town, village
puerto, Sp ... port, harbor
pulau, Indon ... island
punkt, Ger ... point
punt, Du ... point
punta, It., Sp ... point
pur, India ... city, town
puy, Fr ... peak
qal'a, qal'at, Arab ... fort, village
qasr, Arab ... fort, castle
rann, India ... wasteland
ra's, Arab ... cape, head
reka, Rus., So. Slav ... river
reprêsa, Port ... reservoir
rettō, Jap ... island chain
ría, Sp ... estuary
ribeira, Port ... stream
riberão, Port ... river
rio, It., Port ... stream, river
río, Sp ... river
rivière, Fr ... river
roca, Sp ... rock
rt, Serb ... cape
rūd, Per ... river
saari, Fin ... island
sable, Fr ... sand
sahara, Arab ... desert, plain
saki, Jap ... cape
sal, Sp ... salt
salar, Sp ... salt flat, salt lake
salto, Sp ... waterfall
san, Jap., Kor ... mountain, hill
sat, satul, Rom ... village
schloss, Ger ... castle
sebkha, Arab ... salt marsh
see, Ger ... lake, sea
şehir, Tur ... town, city
selat, Indon ... strait
selvas, Port., (Brazil) . tropical rain forests
seno, Sp ... bay
serra, Port ... mountain chain
serrania, Sp ... mountain ridge
seto, Jap ... strait
severnaya, Rus ... northern
shahr, Per ... town, city
shamo, Chn ... desert
shan, Chn ... mountain, hill, island
shatt, Arab ... river
shi, Jap, Chn ... city
shima, Jap ... island
shōtō, Jap ... archipelago
sierra, Sp ... mountain range
sjö, Nor., Swe ... lake, sea
sö, Dan., Nor ... lake, sea
söder, södra, Swe ... south
song, Annam ... river
sopka, Rus ... peak, volcano
source, Fr ... a spring
spitze, Ger ... summit, point
staat, Ger ... state
stad, Dan., Du., Nor., Swe ... city, town
stadt, Ger ... city, town
stato, It ... state
step', Rus ... treeless plain, steppe
straat, Du ... strait
strand, Dan., Du., Ger., Nor., Swe ... shore, beach
stretto, It ... strait
strom, Ger ... river, stream
ström, Dan., Nor., Swe .. stream, river
stroom, Du ... stream, river
su, suyu, Tur ... water, river
sud, Fr., Sp ... south
süd, Ger ... south
suidō, Jap ... channel
sul, Port ... south
sund, Dan., Nor., Swe ... sound
sungai, sungei, Indon., Mal ... river
sur, Sp ... south
syd, Dan., Nor., Swe ... south
tafelland, Ger. ... plateau
take, Jap ... peak, summit
tal, Ger ... valley
tanjung, tanjong, Mal ... cape
târg, târgul, Rom ... market, town
tell, Arab ... hill
teluk, Indon ... bay, gulf
terra, It ... land
terre, Fr ... earth, land
thal, Ger ... valley
tierra, Sp ... earth, land
tō, Jap ... east; island
tonle, Camb ... river, lake
top, Du ... peak
torp, Swe ... hamlet, cottage
tsangpo, Tib ... river
tso, Tib ... lake
tsu, Jap ... harbor, port
tundra, Rus ... treeless arctic plains
tuz, Tur ... salt
udde, Swe ... cape
ufer, Ger ... shore, riverbank
ujung, Indon ... point, cape
umi, Jap ... sea, gulf
ura, Jap ... bay, coast, creek
ust'ye, Rus ... river mouth
valle, It., Port., Sp ... valley
vallée, Fr ... valley
valli, It ... lake
vár, Hung ... fortress
város, Hung ... town
varoš, So. Slav ... town
veld, Du ... open plain, field
verkh, Rus ... top, summit
ves, Czech ... village
vest, Dan., Nor., Swe ... west
vik, Swe ... cove, bay
vila, Port ... town
villa, Sp ... town
villar, Sp ... village, hamlet
ville, Fr ... town, city
vodokhranilishche, Rus ... reservoir
vostok, Rus ... east
wad, wādī, Arab . intermittent stream
wald, Ger ... forest, woodland
wan, Chn., Jap ... bay, gulf
weiler, Ger ... hamlet, village
westersch, Ger ... western
wüste, Ger ... desert
xi, Chn ... west, western
yama, Jap ... mountain
yarimada, Tur ... peninsula
yug, Rus ... south
zaki, Jap ... cape
zaliv, Rus ... bay, gulf
zapad, Rus ... west
zee, Du ... sea
zemlya, Rus ... land
zuid, Du ... south

Abbreviations of Geographic Names and Terms

- **Ab., Can.** Alberta, Can.
- **Afg.** Afghanistan
- **Afr.** Africa
- **Ak., U.S.** Alaska, U.S.
- **Al., U.S.** Alabama, U.S.
- **Alb.** Albania
- **Alg.** Algeria
- **Am. Sam.** American Samoa
- **And.** Andorra
- **Ang.** Angola
- **Ant.** Antarctica
- **Antig.** Antigua and Barbuda
- **Ar., U.S.** Arkansas, U.S.
- **Arg.** Argentina
- **Arm.** Armenia
- **Aus.** Austria
- **Austl.** Australia
- **Az., U.S.** Arizona, U.S.
- **Azer.** Azerbaijan

- **b.** Bay, Gulf, Inlet, Lagoon
- **Bah.** Bahamas
- **Bahr.** Bahrain
- **Barb.** Barbados
- **bas.** Basin
- **B.C.,** British Columbia, Can.
- **Bdi.** Burundi
- **Bel.** Belgium
- **Bela.** Belarus
- **Ber.** Bermuda
- **Bhu.** Bhutan
- **B.I.O.T.** British Indian Ocean Territory
- **Blg.** Bulgaria
- **Bngl.** Bangladesh
- **Bol.** Bolivia
- **Bos.** Bosnia and Herzegovina
- **Bots.** Botswana
- **Braz.** Brazil
- **Bru.** Brunei
- **Br. Vir. Is.** British Virgin Islands
- **Burkina** Burkina Faso

- **c.** Cape, Point
- **Ca., U.S.** California, U.S.
- **Camb.** Cambodia
- **Camrn.** Cameroon
- **can.** Canal
- **Can.** Canada
- **C.A.R.** Central African Republic
- **Cay. Is.** Cayman Islands
- **C. Iv.** Cote d'Ivoire
- **clf.** Cliff, Escarpment
- **co.** County, Parish
- **Co., U.S.** Colorado, U.S.
- **Col.** Colombia
- **Com.** Comoros
- **cont.** Continent
- **Cook Is.** Cook Islands
- **C.R.** Costa Rica
- **Cro.** Croatia
- **cst.** Coast, Beach
- **Ct., U.S.** Connecticut, U.S.
- **C.V.** Cape Verde
- **Cyp.** Cyprus
- **Czech Rep.** Czech Republic

- **d.** Dam
- **D.C., U.S.** District of Columbia, U.S.
- **De., U.S.** Delaware, U.S.
- **del.** Delta
- **Den.** Denmark
- **dep.** Dependency, Colony
- **depr.** Depression
- **des.** Desert
- **Dji.** Djibouti
- **Dom.** Dominica
- **Dom. Rep.** Dominican Republic
- **D.R.C.** Democratic Republic of the Congo

- **Ec.** Ecuador
- **El Sal.** El Salvador
- **Eng., U.K.** England, U.K.
- **Eq. Gui.** Equatorial Guinea
- **Erit.** Eritrea
- **Est.** Estonia
- **est.** Estuary
- **Eth.** Ethiopia
- **E. Timor** East Timor
- **Eur.** Europe

- **Falk. Is.** Falkland Islands
- **Far. Is.** Faroe Islands
- **Fin.** Finland
- **Fl., U.S.** Florida, U.S.
- **for.** Forest, Moor
- **Fr.** France
- **Fr. Gu.** French Guiana
- **Fr. Poly.** French Polynesia

- **Ga., U.S.** Georgia, U.S.
- **Gam.** The Gambia
- **Gaza** Gaza Strip
- **Geor.** Georgia
- **Ger.** Germany
- **Gib.** Gibraltar
- **Grc.** Greece
- **Green.** Greenland
- **Gren.** Grenada
- **Guad.** Guadeloupe
- **Guat.** Guatemala
- **Guern.** Guernsey
- **Gui.** Guinea
- **Gui.-B.** Guinea-Bissau
- **Guy.** Guyana

- **Hi., U.S.** Hawaii, U.S.
- **hist.** Historic Site, Ruins
- **hist. reg.** Historic Region
- **Hond.** Honduras
- **Hung.** Hungary

- **i.** Island
- **Ia., U.S.** Iowa, U.S.
- **ice** Ice Feature, Glacier
- **Ice.** Iceland
- **Id., U.S.** Idaho, U.S.
- **Il., U.S.** Illinois, U.S.
- **In., U.S.** Indiana, U.S.
- **Indon.** Indonesia
- **ind. res.** Indian Reservation
- **I. of Man** Isle of Man
- **Ire.** Ireland
- **is.** Islands
- **Isr.** Israel
- **isth.** Isthmus

- **Jam.** Jamaica
- **Jord.** Jordan

- **Kaz.** Kazakhstan
- **Kir.** Kiribati
- **Kor., N.** Korea, North
- **Kor., S.** Korea, South
- **Ks., U.S.** Kansas, U.S.
- **Kuw.** Kuwait
- **Ky., U.S.** Kentucky, U.S.
- **Kyrg.** Kyrgyzstan

- **La., U.S.** Louisiana, U.S.
- **Lat.** Latvia
- **Leb.** Lebanon
- **Leso.** Lesotho
- **Lib.** Liberia
- **Liech.** Liechtenstein
- **Lith.** Lithuania
- **lk.** Lake
- **Lux.** Luxembourg

- **Ma., U.S.** Massachusetts, U.S.
- **Mac.** Macedonia
- **Madag.** Madagascar
- **Malay.** Malaysia
- **Mald.** Maldives
- **Marsh. Is.** Marshall Islands
- **Mart.** Martinique
- **Maur.** Mauritania
- **May.** Mayotte
- **Mb., Can.** Manitoba, Can.
- **Md., U.S.** Maryland, U.S.
- **Me., U.S.** Maine, U.S.
- **Mex.** Mexico
- **Mi., U.S.** Michigan, U.S.
- **Micron.** Micronesia, Federated States of
- **Mn., U.S.** Minnesota, U.S.
- **Mo., U.S.** Missouri, U.S.
- **Mol.** Moldova
- **Mong.** Mongolia
- **Mont.** Montenegro
- **Mor.** Morocco
- **Moz.** Mozambique
- **Ms., U.S.** Mississippi, U.S.
- **Mt., U.S.** Montana, U.S.
- **mth.** River Mouth or Channel
- **mtn.** Mountain
- **mts.** Mountains
- **Mya.** Myanmar

- **N.A.** North America
- **nat. cap.** National Capital
- **N.B., Can.** New Brunswick, Can.
- **N.C., U.S.** North Carolina, U.S.
- **N. Cal.** New Caledonia
- **N.D., U.S.** North Dakota, U.S.
- **Ne., U.S.** Nebraska, U.S.
- **Neth.** Netherlands
- **Neth. Ant.** Netherlands Antilles
- **Nf., Can.** Newfoundland, Can.
- **N.H., U.S.** New Hampshire, U.S.
- **Nic.** Nicaragua
- **Nig.** Nigeria
- **N. Ire., U.K.** Northern Ireland, U.K.
- **N.J., U.S.** New Jersey, U.S.
- **N.M., U.S.** New Mexico, U.S.
- **N. Mar. Is.** Northern Mariana Islands
- **Nmb.** Namibia
- **Nor.** Norway
- **n.p.** National Park or Monument
- **N.S., Can.** Nova Scotia, Can.
- **N.T., Can.** Northwest Territories, Can.
- **Nu., Can.** Nunavut, Can.
- **Nv., U.S.** Nevada, U.S.
- **N.Y., U.S.** New York, U.S.
- **N.Z.** New Zealand

- **oc.** Ocean
- **Oc.** Australia and Oceania
- **Oh., U.S.** Ohio, U.S.
- **Ok., U.S.** Oklahoma, U.S.
- **On., Can.** Ontario, Can.
- **Or., U.S.** Oregon, U.S.

- **p.** Pass
- **Pa., U.S.** Pennsylvania, U.S.
- **Pak.** Pakistan
- **Pan.** Panama
- **Pap. N. Gui.** Papua New Guinea
- **P.E., Can.** Prince Edward I., Can.
- **Para.** Paraguay
- **pen.** Peninsula
- **Phil.** Philippines
- **Pit.** Pitcairn
- **pk.** Park, Reserve
- **pl.** Plain, Flat
- **plat.** Plateau, Highland
- **p.o.i.** Point of Interest
- **Pol.** Poland
- **Port.** Portugal
- **P.R.** Puerto Rico

- **Qc., Can.** Québec, Can.

- **r.** Rock
- **rec.** Recreational Site, Park
- **reg.** Physical Region
- **res.** Reservoir
- **Reu.** Reunion
- **rf.** Reef, Shoal
- **R.I., U.S.** Rhode Island, U.S.
- **Rom.** Romania
- **Rw.** Rwanda

- **s.** Sea
- **S.A.** South America
- **S. Afr.** South Africa
- **Sau. Ar.** Saudi Arabia
- **S.C., U.S.** South Carolina, U.S.
- **Scot., U.K.** Scotland, U.K.
- **S.D., U.S.** South Dakota, U.S.
- **Sen.** Senegal
- **Serb.** Serbia
- **Sey.** Seychelles
- **S. Geor.** South Georgia
- **Sing.** Singapore
- **Sk., Can.** Saskatchewan, Can.
- **S.L.** Sierra Leone
- **Slvk.** Slovakia
- **Slvn.** Slovenia
- **S. Mar.** San Marino
- **Sol. Is.** Solomon Islands
- **Som.** Somalia
- **Sp. N. Afr.** Spanish North Africa
- **Sri L.** Sri Lanka
- **state** State, Province, Department, Region, etc.
- **St. Hel.** St. Helena
- **St. K./N.** St. Kitts and Nevis
- **St. Luc.** St. Lucia
- **stm.** River, Creek, Stream
- **St. P./M.** St. Pierre and Miquelon
- **S. Tom./P.** Sao Tome and Principe
- **strt.** Strait, Channel, Sound
- **St. Vin.** St. Vincent and the Grenadines
- **Sur.** Suriname
- **sw.** Swamp, Marsh
- **Swaz.** Swaziland
- **Swe.** Sweden
- **Switz.** Switzerland

- **Tai.** Taiwan
- **Taj.** Tajikistan
- **Tan.** Tanzania
- **T./C. Is.** Turks and Caicos Islands
- **Thai.** Thailand
- **Tn., U.S.** Tennessee, U.S.
- **Tok.** Tokelau
- **Trin.** Trinidad and Tobago
- **Tun.** Tunisia
- **Tur.** Turkey
- **Turkmen.** Turkmenistan
- **Tx., U.S.** Texas, U.S.

- **U.A.E.** United Arab Emirates
- **Ug.** Uganda
- **U.K.** United Kingdom
- **Ukr.** Ukraine
- **Ur.** Uruguay
- **U.S.** United States
- **Ut., U.S.** Utah, U.S.
- **Uzb.** Uzbekistan

- **Va., U.S.** Virginia, U.S.
- **val.** Valley, Watercourse
- **Ven.** Venezuela
- **Viet.** Vietnam
- **V.I.U.S.** Virgin Islands (U.S.)
- **vol.** Volcano
- **Vt., U.S.** Vermont, U.S.

- **Wa., U.S.** Washington, U.S.
- **Wal./F.** Wallis and Futuna
- **W.B.** West Bank
- **Wi., U.S.** Wisconsin, U.S.
- **W. Sah.** Western Sahara
- **wtfl.** Waterfall
- **W.V., U.S.** West Virginia, U.S.
- **Wy., U.S.** Wyoming, U.S.

- **Yk., Can.** Yukon, Can.

- **Zam.** Zambia
- **Zimb.** Zimbabwe

Pronunciation of Geographic Names

Key to the sound values of letters and symbols used in the index to indicate pronunciation

- ă — ăt; băttle
- *ă* — fin*ă*l; appe*ă*l
- ā — rāte; elāte
- å — senåte; inanimåte
- ä — ärm; cälm
- ȧ — ȧsk; bȧth
- *ȧ* — sof*ȧ*; m*ȧ*rine (short neutral or indeterminate sound)
- â — fâre; prepâre
- ch — choose; church
- dh — as th in other; either
- ē — bē; ēve
- e̊ — e̊vent; cre̊ate
- ĕ — bĕt; ĕnd
- *ĕ* — rec*ĕ*nt (short neutral or indeterminate sound)
- ẽ — cratẽr; cindẽr
- g — gō; gāme
- gh — guttural g
- ĭ — bĭt; wĭll
- *ĭ* — (short neutral or indeterminate sound)
- ī — rīde; bīte
- ᴋ — gutteral k as *ch* n German *ich*
- ng — sing
- ŋ — baŋk; liŋger
- ɴ — indicates nasalized
- ŏ — nŏd; ŏdd
- *ŏ* — c*ŏ*mmit; c*ŏ*nnect
- ō — ōld; bōld
- o̊ — o̊bey; ho̊tel
- ô — ôrder; lông
- oi — boil
- o͞o — fo͞od; ro͞ot
- ȯ — as oo in foot; wood
- ou — out; thou
- s — soft; so; sane
- sh — dish; finish
- th — thin; thick
- ū — pūre; cūre
- ů — ůnite; ůsůrp
- û — ûrn; fûr
- ŭ — stŭd; ŭp
- *ŭ* — circ*ŭ*s; s*ŭ*bmit
- ü — as in French tu
- zh — as z in azure
- ʼ — indeterminate vowel sound

In many cases the spelling of foreign geographical names does not even remotely indicate the pronunciation to an American, e.g., Słupsk in Poland is pronounced swȯpsk; Jujuy in Argentina is pronounced ho͞ohwē; La Spezia in Italy is lä-spĕ'zyä.

This condition is hardly surprising, however, when we consider that in our own language Worcester, Massachusetts, is pronounced wȯs'tẽr; Sioux City, Iowa, so͞o sĭ'te̊; Schuylkill Haven, Pennsylvania, sko͞ol'kĭl hā-vĕn; Poughkeepsie, New York, p*ŏ*-kĭp'se̊.

The indication of pronunciation of geographic names presents several peculiar problems:

1. Many foreign languages use sounds that are not present in the English language and which an American cannot normally articulate. Thus, though the nearest English equivalent sound has been indicated, only approximate results are possible.

2. There are several dialects in each foreign language that cause variation in the local pronunciation of names. This also occurs in identical names in the various divisions of a great language group.

3. Within the United States there are marked differences in pronunciation, not only of local geographic names, but also of common words, indicating that the sound and tone values for letters as well as the placing of the emphasis vary considerably from one part of the country to another.

4. A number of different letters and diacritical combinations could be used to indicate essentially the same or approximate pronunciations.

Some variation in pronunciation other than that indicated in this index may be encountered, but such a difference does not necessarily indicate that either is in error, and in many cases it is a matter of individual choice as to which is preferred. In fact, an exact indication of pronunciation of many foreign names using English letters and diacritical marks is extremely diffiicult and sometimes impossible.

The following sources have been consulted during the process of creating and updating the thematic maps and statistics for the 22nd Edition.

Andreassen, L., M. Beedle, E. Berthier, F. Cawkwell, N. Dickmann, E. Dolgova, A. Fountain, N. Glasser, E. Hansson, U. Haritashya, G. Hartman, C. Helm, L. Iacovelli, H. Jiskoot, G. Kapustin, T. Khromova, J. Kincaid, S. Kutuzov, I. Lavrentiev, X. Li, L. Mabileau, J. Meyer, P. Mool, A. Muravyev, G. Nosenko, F. Paul, A. Racoviteanu, F. Rau, A. Rivera, M. Schnirch, Y. Seliverstov, O. Sigurdsson, S. Taschner, P. Zenteno, and N. Zheltyhina. (2001-2008). *GLIMS Glacier Database*. National Snow and Ice Data Center/ World Data Center for Glaciology.

American Wind Energy Association (AWEA). (http://www.awea.org/)

Brohan, P., J.J. Kennedy, I. Harris, S.F.B. Tett, and P.D. Jones. (2006). Uncertainty estimates in regional and global observed temperature changes: A new dataset from 1850. *Journal of Geophysical Research*, 111, D12106, doi:10.1029/2005JD006548. (http://www.cru.uea.ac.uk/cru/data/temperature)

Brown, J., O.J. Ferrians, Jr., J.A. Heginbottom, and E.S. Melnikov. (1998). *Circum-Arctic Map of Permafrost and Ground Ice Conditions*. National Snow and Ice Data Center/ World Data Center for Glaciology.

Census of Canada. *Population Counts, for Canada, Provinces and Territories, and Census Divisions by Urban and Rural, 2001 Census.*

Center for International Earth Science Information Network (CIESIN), Columbia University; International Food Policy Research Institute (IFPRI); The World Bank; and Centro Internacional de Agricultural Tropical (CIAT). (2005). *Global Rural-Urban Mapping Project (GRUMP), Alpha Version.* Socioeconomic Data and Applications Center (SEDAC), Columbia University. (http://sedac.ciesin.columbia.edu/gpw/)

Center for Systemic Peace. *Major Episodes of Political Violence 1946-2007.*

Central Intelligence Agency (CIA). *World Factbook.* (https://www.cia.gov/library/publications/the-world-factbook/)

Chorlton, L B. (2007). *Generalized Geology of the World: Bedrock Domains and Major Faults in GIS Format: A Small-Scale World Geology Map with an Extended Geological Attribute Database.* Geological Survey of Canada, Open File 5529.

Coastal Services Center, National Oceanic and Atmospheric Administration. (http://www.csc.noaa.gov/)

Energy Information Administration (EIA), United States Department of Energy. *Coal Production and Number of Mines by State and Mine Type, 2007-2008.*

Energy Information Administration (EIA), United States Department of Energy. *International Energy Annual.*

Energy Information Administration (EIA), United States Department of Energy. *Natural Gas Annual 2006.*

Energy Information Administration (EIA), United States Department of Energy. *Petroleum Supply Annual 2006.*

Energy Information Administration (EIA), United States Department of Energy. *World Anthracite Coal Production, Most Recent Annual Estimates, 1980-2006.*

Energy Information Administration (EIA), United States Department of Energy. *World Bituminous Coal Production, Most Recent Annual Estimates, 1980-2006.*

Energy Information Administration (EIA), United States Department of Energy. *World Coal Production, Most Recent Annual Estimates, 1980-2007.*

Energy Information Administration (EIA), United States Department of Energy. *World Crude Oil Reserves, January 1, 1980 - January 1, 2008 Estimates.*

Energy Information Administration (EIA), United States Department of Energy. *World Dry Natural Gas Production, Most Recent Annual Estimates, 1980-2007.*

Energy Information Administration (EIA), United States Department of Energy. *World Production of Crude Oil, NGPL, and Other Liquids, and Refinery Processing Gain, Most Recent Annual Estimates, 1980-2007.*

Energy Information Administration (EIA), United States Department of Energy. *World Proved Natural Gas Reserves, January 1, 1980 - January 1, 2008 Estimates.*

Farr, T.G., P.A. Rosen, E. Caro, R. Crippen, R. Duren, S. Hensley, M. Kobrick, M. Paller, E. Rodriguez, L. Roth, D. Seal, S. Shaffer, J. Shimada, J. Umland, M. Werner, M. Oskin, D. Burbank, and D. Alsdorf. (2007). The Shuttle Radar Topography Mission. *Reviews of Geophysics*, 45, RG2004, doi:10.1029/2005RG000183.

Federal Aviation Administration (FAA). *CY 2007 Passenger Boarding and All-Cargo Data.*

Federation of American Scientists. *Status of World Nuclear Forces 2009.*

Fetterer, F. and K. Knowles. (2002). *Sea Ice Index.* National Snow and Ice Data Center.

Food and Agriculture Organization of the United Nations (FAO). *FAOSTAT.*

Global Volcanism Program, Smithsonian Institution. *Volcanoes of the World.*

Halpern, B.S., S. Walbridge, K.A. Selkoe, C.V. Kappel, F. Micheli, C. D'Agrosa, J.F. Bruno, K.S. Casey, C. Ebert, H.E. Fox, R. Fujita, D. Heinemann, H.S. Lenihan, E.M. P. Madin, M.T. Perry, E.R. Selig, M. Spalding, R. Steneck, and R. Watson. (2008). A global map of human impact on marine ecosystems. *Science*, 319(5865), pp. 948-952. doi: 10.1126/science.1149345.

Hansen, M., R. DeFries, J.R.G. Townshend, and R. Sohlberg. (2000). Global land cover classification at 1km resolution using a decision tree classifier. *International Journal of Remote Sensing*, 21, pp. 1331-1365.

Hansen, M.C., S.V. Stehman, P.V. Potapov, T.R. Loveland, J.R.G. Townshend, R.S. DeFries, K.W. Pittman, F. Stolle, M.K. Steininger, M. Carroll, and C. Dimiceli. (2008). Humid tropical forest clearing from 2000 to 2005 quantified using multi-temporal and multi-resolution remotely sensed data. *PNAS*, 105(27), pp. 9439-9444.

Heidelberg Institute for International Conflict Research. *Conflict Barometer.*

Heinrich J. , C. Klinke, and C.B. Schmidt. (1994). The Hop Atlas: *The History and Geography of the Cultivated Plant.* Nuremberg, Germany: Jon. Barth & Sohn.

Hulme, M. (1998). *Global Land Precipitation Dataset, Version 1.0.* Climatic Research Unit, University of East Anglia.

International Center for Prison Studies. (2009). *World Prison Population List, 8th Edition.* King's College, London.

International Lake Environment Committee. *World Lakes Database.*

International Water Power & Dam Construction. *Yearbook 2008.*

Inter-Parliamentary Union. *Women in National Parliaments.*

Inter-Parliamentary Union. *Women's Suffrage: A World Chronology of the Recognition of Women's Rights to Vote and to Stand for Election.*

Keeling, C.D., S.C. Piper, R.B. Bacastow, M. Wahlen, T.P. Whorf, M. Heimann, and H.A. Meijer. (2001). Exchanges of atmospheric CO_2 and $13CO_2$ with the terrestrial biosphere and oceans from 1978 to 2000. *I. Global Aspects, SIO Reference Series, No. 01-06.* Scripps Institution of Oceanography.

Kelly, T.D. and M.D. Fenton. (2003). *Iron and Steel Statistics.* United States Geological Survey.

Küchler, A.W. (1949). A physiognomic classification of vegetation. *Annals of the Association of American Geographers*, 39(3), pp. 201-210.

Laboratory for Satellite Altimetry, Satellite Oceanography and Climatology Division, National Oceanic and Atmospheric Administration. *Altimetry Data.* (http://ibis.grdl.noaa.gov/)

LakeNet Global Lake Database.

Mackay, J., M. Eriksen, and O. Shafey. (2006). *The Tobacco Atlas, 2nd Edition.* American Cancer Society.

McDaniel, P. (2008). *The Twelve Soil Orders.* (http://soils.ag.uidaho.edu/soilorders/index.htm/)

Murphy, R.E. (1968). Annals map supplement number 9. Landforms of the world. *Annals of the Association of American Geographers*, 58(1), pp. 198-200.

National Aeronautics and Space Administration (NASA), Atmospheric Science Data Center. (http://eosweb.larc.nasa.gov/)

National Aeronautics and Space Administration (NASA). (http://www.nasa.gov/)

National Oceanic and Atmospheric Administration (NOAA). (http://www.noaa.gov/)

National Snow and Ice Data Center. (http://nsidc.org/)

National Weather Service, National Oceanic and Atmospheric Administration. (http://www.spc.noaa.gov/)

Natural Resources Canada. *The Atlas of Canada.*

New, M., D. Lister, M. Hulme, and I. Makin. (2000). A high-resolution data set of surface climate over global land areas. *Climate Research*, 21, pp. 1-25.

Olson, D.M., E. Dinerstein, E.D. Wikramanayake, N.D. Burgess, G.V.N. Powell, E.C. Underwood, J.A. D'Amico, I. Itoua, H.E. Strand, J.C. Morrison, C.J. Loucks, T.F. Allnutt, T.H. Ricketts, Y. Kura, J.F. Lamoreux, W.W. Wettengel, P. Hedao, and K.R. Kassem. (2001). Terrestrial ecoregions of the world: A new map of life on earth. *BioScience*, 51(11), pp. 933-938.

Rand McNally. *The Rand McNally Road Atlas 2009.*

Statistics Canada. *Air Carrier Traffic at Canadian Airports.*

Stockholm International Peace Research Institute. *The Financial Value of National Arms Exports, 1998-2006.*

Tapley, B., J. Ries, S. Bettadpur, D. Chambers, M. Cheng, F. Condi, B. Gunter, Z. Kang, P.Nagel, R. Pastor, T. Pekker, S.Poole, and F. Wang, (2005). GGM02 - An improved Earth gravity field model from GRACE. *Journal of Geodesy*, doi 10.1007/s00190-005-0480-z. (http://www.csr.utexas.edu/grace/gravity/)

TeleGeography Research. (http://www.telegeography.com/)

The Canadian Wind Energy Association (CanWEA). (http://www.canwea.ca/)

Thornthwaite, C.W. (1944). Report of committee on transpiration and evaporation. *American Geophysical Union Transactions*, 25(5), pp. 683-693.

Transport Canada. *Transportation in Canada 2007.*

Trewartha, G.T. (1968). *An Introduction to Climate, 4th Edition.* New York: McGraw-Hill Book Company.

United Nations (UN). *Comtrade Database, SITC Rev.3. 2006.*

United Nations (UN). *Human Development Reports 2007/2008.*

United Nations (UN). *World Contraceptive Use 2007.*

United Nations (UN). *World Population Prospects Database: The 2006 Revision.*

United Nations Children's Fund (UNICEF). *Report on the Global AIDS Epidemic.*

United Nations Educational, Scientific and Cultural Organization (UNESCO), Institute for Statistics Data Centre. *Public Reports.*

United Nations Educational, Scientific and Cultural Organization (UNESCO), International Hydrological Programme. *World Water Resources and Their Use.*

United Nations Environment Program. *Global Resource Information Database.*

United Nations Environment Program. *Islands Directory.*

United Nations High Commissioner for Refugees (UNHCR). *2007 Global Trends: Refugees, Asylum-Seekers, Returnees, Internally Displaced and Stateless Persons.*

United Nations Peacekeeping. *List of Operations 1948-2008.*

United Nations, Department of Economic and Social Affairs. *2005 UN Energy Statistics Yearbook.*

United Nations, Department of Economic and Social Affairs. *World Urbanization Prospects, 2007 Revision.*

United Nations, Office on Drugs and Crime. *2008 World Drug Report.*

United Nations, Organization for Economic Co-operation and Development (OECD). *Uranium 2007: Resources, Production and Demand.*

United States Bureau of Labor Statistics. *Quarterly Census of Employment and Wages.*

United States Census Bureau. American FactFinder. *2006 Annual Survey of Manufactures.*

United States Census Bureau. *Census 2000 Summary Files.*

United States Census Bureau. *International Database.*

United States Census Bureau. *Statistical Abstract of the United States, 2008 Edition.*

United States Census Bureau. *Statistical Abstract of the United States, 2009 Edition.*

United States Department of Agriculture (USDA), Economic Research Service. *Sugar and Sweeteners Outlook, 2008.*

United States Department of Agriculture (USDA), Natural Resource Conservation Service. *Soil Taxonomy: A Basic System of Soil Classification for Making and Interpreting Soil Surveys.*

United States Department of Agriculture (USDA). *Chickens and Eggs-2007 Summary.*

United States Department of Agriculture (USDA). *Feed Grains Database.*

United States Department of Agriculture (USDA). *Poultry-Production and Value-2007 Summary.*

United States Department of Energy. *Landscan 2001 High Resolution Global Population Data Set.* © 2003 UT-Battelle, LLC. All rights reserved. Notice: These data were produced by UT-Battelle, LLC under Contract No. DE-AC05-00OR22725 with the Department of Energy. The Government has certain rigths in this data. Neither UT-Battelle, LLC nor the United States Department of Energy, nor any of their employees, makes any warranty, express or implied, or assumes any legal liability or responsibility for the accuracy, completeness, or usefulness of any data, apparatus, product, or process disclosed, or represents that its use would not infringe privately owned rights.

United States Environmental Protection Agency (EPA). (http://www.epa.gov/)

United States Environmental Protection Agency (EPA). *Great Lakes Factsheet No. 1.*

United States Geological Survey (USGS). *Lengths of Major Rivers.*

United States Geological Survey (USGS). *Mineral Commodity Summaries.*

United States Geological Survey (USGS). *Mineral Resources Data System (MRDS).*

United States Geological Survey (USGS). *Minerals Yearbook 2006.*

United States Geological Survey (USGS). *National Atlas of the United States.* (http://www.nationalatlas.gov/)

United States Geological Survey (USGS). *Significant Earthquakes of the World.*

Woodworth, P.L. and R. Player. (2003). The Permanent Service for Mean Sea Level: An update to the 21st century. *Journal of Coastal Research*, 19, pp. 287-295. (http://www.pol.ac.uk/psmsl/)

World Energy Council. *2007 Survey of Energy Resources.*

World Health Organization (WHO). *Global Atlas of the Health Workforce.*

World Health Organization (WHO). *Global Information System on Alcohol and Health.*

World Health Organization (WHO). *Global Status Report on Alcohol 2004.*

World Health Organization (WHO). *Statistical Information System (WHOSIS).* (http://www.who.int/whosis/)

World Health Organization (WHO). *World Malaria Report 2008.*

World Wind Energy Association. *Worldwide Wind Energy Installation Figures per Continent.*

The editor wishes to thank the individual scientists, research units, and organizations that made their datasets and research available for this edition of Goode's World Atlas.

Listed below are page references for major topics covered by the thematic maps and graphs, the introductory text, and the tables.

Agriculture 94-95, 237, 242
Agricultural production 58
Agricultural yield 58
Air quality 106
Air travel 100
Alcohol consumption 65
Alliances 80
Aluminum 68
Amphetamines 78
Anthracite .... See coal
Apples 63
Aquifers 106
Arable land 58
Armed forces 79
Arms exports 79
Atmospheric heat gain 40-41
Atmospheric pressure 34, 35
Bananas 63
Barley 61
Bauxite ... 68, 89, 162, 181, 215, 237, 242, 257, 275
Beef 66
Beer 65
Birth rate 49, 50
Bituminous coal .... See Coal
Cannabis 78
Canola oil 64
Capitals 289-93
Carbon dioxide, atmospheric concentration 39
Carbon dioxide, emissions 39, 106
Cartography and geospatial technology 9
Cassava 62
Cattle 66
Chickens 67
Chromite 70, 215, 237, 257
Cigarette consumption 63
Citrus fruit 63
Climate regions 30-31
Coal 75, 89, 101, 162, 181, 214, 257, 274
Cobalt 70, 257
Cocaine 78
Cocoa beans 61
Coconuts 64
Coffee 60
Coltan 69
Commuting time 104
Conflicts 81
Contraception use 50
Copper ... 68, 89, 162, 181, 215, 237, 242, 257, 275
Corn 60, 64
Corn oil 64
Cotton 65
Cottonseed 64
Currents .... See Ocean currents
Dates 63
Death rate 49, 50
Deciduous fruit 63
Desertification 89, 162, 181, 215, 257, 274
Diamonds 257
Drug use 78
Ducks 67
Earnings .... See Income
Earth properties 8
Earthquakes 22-23, 89, 162, 181, 215, 257, 274
Earth-sun relationships 17
Economic alliances .... See Alliances
Education 52, 104
Eggs 67
Electricity .... See Energy
El Niño/ENSO 91
Energy .... 72, 73, 89, 162, 181, 214, 257, 274. Also see specific energy generation methods (geothermal, hydroelectric, nuclear, thermal, and wind).
Environments 127
Ethnic groups .... See Race and ethnicity
Evapotranspiration 90
Exports 77
Federal lands 98-99
Fisheries 63
Flax 65
Floods 89, 162, 181, 215
Food aid 57
Forest cover 76
Forest loss 76
Fruit 63
Fuels .... 74-75, 89, 101, 162, 181, 214, 257, 274. Also see specific fuel types (coal, natural gas, petroleum, and uranium).
GDP .... See Gross Domestic Product
Geology 96-97, 182-83
Geothermal energy 73, 89, 181, 214, 257, 274
Glaciation 24-25
Gold 71, 257, 275
Government 289-293
Grain sorghum 61
Grapes 65
Gross Domestic Product 39, 52
Ground water 106
Hazardous waste sites 106
Highways 98-99
HIV infection 54
Hops 65
Hours of daylight 84
Housing 104
Hurricanes 91
Hydroelectric energy 73, 89, 162, 181, 214, 257, 274
Imports 77
Income 105
Indian reservations 98-99
Infant mortality 50
Internet 82
Interstate highways 98-99
Iron ore 70, 89, 101, 162, 181, 215, 237, 242, 257, 275
Jute 65
Kyoto Protocol 39
Labor force 107
Land areas 18-19
Land cover 87, 160, 178-79, 210-11, 255, 274
Land elevations 20-21
Landforms 24-25, 88, 161, 180, 212, 256, 275
Languages 53, 105
Lead 69, 89, 162, 181, 215, 242, 275
Life expectancy 56
Lignite .... See Coal
Literacy 52
Lithium 69
Maize .... See Corn
Malaria 55
Manganese 70, 215, 237, 242, 257, 275
Manufacturing 107
Map legend 16
Map projections 11-13
Map scale 10
Map symbols .... See Map legend
Marine productivity 40-41
Military alliances .... See Alliances
Military expenditures 79
Military installations 98-99
Millet 61
Minerals .... 68, 69, 70, 71, 89,162, 181, 215, 237, 242, 257, 275. Also see specific minerals.
Molybdenum 70
National parks 98-99
Natural gas 74, 89, 101, 162, 181, 214, 257, 274
Natural hazards 22-23, 89, 162, 181, 215, 257, 274
Natural increase 51
Natural vegetation .... See vegetation
Nickel 70, 89, 215, 275
Nuclear energy 72, 89, 162, 181, 214, 257
Nuclear weapons 79
Oats 60
Ocean currents 36-37, 40-41
Ocean depths 20-21
Ocean floor 26-27, 28, 29
Oil .... See petroleum
Oil palm fruit 64
Olive oil 64
Olives 64
Opiates 78
Palm oil 64
Paper 76
Peacekeeping operations 81
Peanut oil 64
Peanuts 64
Petroleum 74, 89, 101, 162, 181, 214, 257, 274
Physical features 294
Physicians 55
Pigs 66
Pineapples 63
Plate tectonics 22-23, 24-25
Platinum 71
Political alliances .... See Alliances
Population 18-19, 48-49, 51, 52, 57, 102, 103, 104, 105
Population change 104
Population density ... 48-49, 89, 102, 127, 162, 181, 214, 216, 217, 237, 242, 257, 275
Population growth .... See Natural increase
Population, age 104
Population, age-sex composition 49
Population, ethnic .... See Race and ethnicity
Population, urban .... See Urban population
Population, world 19, 51
Pork 66
Potatoes 62
Poultry 67
Poverty 105
Precipitation 34, 35, 36-37, 88, 90, 127, 161, 180, 213, 256, 275
Precipitation change 36
Precipitation variability 37
Prison population 78
Race and ethnicity 103, 216, 217
Radioactive waste 106
Railroads 100
Rapeseed 64
Refugees 81
Religions 53, 237, 242
Rice 61
Roundwood 76
Rubber 65
Rye 59
Satellite images 88, 161, 180, 212, 256, 275
Sea ice 40-41, 89, 162, 181, 215, 274
Sea level change 38, 91
Sheep 67
Shipping lanes 83
Silk 65
Silver 71, 275
Sisal 65
Soils 44-45
Solar insolation 91
Solar system 17
Soybean oil 64
Soybeans 64
Spices 62
Steel 71
Submarine cables 82-83
Sugar 62
Sunflower oil 64
Sunflower seeds 64
Superfund sites 106
Surface water 106
Tea 59
Telecommunications 82-83
Temperature 32, 33, 90
Temperature change 38
Temperature range 33
Temperature, polar 33
Terrestrial biomes 46-47
Territorial evolution 100
Thematic map types 14-15
Thermal energy 72
Time zones 84
Tin 68, 162, 215, 242, 257
Tobacco 63
Tornadoes 89, 91
Toxic chemicals 106
Tractors 58
Transportation 98-99, 100
Tropical storms 89, 91, 215, 257, 274
Tsunamis 89, 162, 181, 215, 257, 274
Tuberculosis 54
Tungsten 70, 162, 215, 242
Turkeys 67
Undernourishment 56
Unemployment 105
Uranium 75, 89, 162, 181, 214, 257, 274
Urban population 51, 295
Vanadium 70
Veal 66
Vegetable oils 64
Vegetation 42-43, 88, 92-93, 127, 161, 180, 213, 256, 275
Volcanoes 22-23, 89, 162, 181, 215, 257, 274
Water resources 106
Water, agricultural withdrawals 58
Water, drinking 57
Waterways 100
Wheat 59
Wind energy 73, 91
Winds 34, 35, 91
Wine 65
Women heads of household 105
Women's economic activity rate 79
Women's legislative participation rate 79
Women's voting rights 79
Wood production 76
Wool 67
Zinc 69, 89, 162, 181, 215, 242, 257, 275

This universal index includes in a single alphabetical list the names of selected features that appear on the reference maps. Each name is followed by a page number and geographical coordinates.

Abbreviation and Capitalization. Abbreviations of names on the maps have been standardized as much as possible. Names that are abbreviated on the maps are generally spelled out in full in the index.

Most initial letters of names are capitalized, except for a few Dutch names such as "s-Gravenhage". Capitalization of non-initial words in a name generally follows local practice.

Alphabetization. Names are alphabetized in the order of the letters of the English alphabet. Spanish *ll* and *ch*, for example, are not treated as separate letters. Furthermore, diacritical marks are disregarded in alphabetization – German or Scandinavian *ä* or *ö* are treated as *a* or *o*.

The names of physical features may appear inverted, since they are always alphabetized under the proper, not the generic, part of the name, thus: "Gibraltar, Strait of", not "Strait of Gibraltar". In this case "Gibraltar" is the proper part of the name and "Strait of" is the generic. Otherwise every entry, whether consisting of one word or more, is alphabetized as a single continuous entity on the basis of the proper part of the name. "Lakeland", for example, appears after "Lake Havasu City" and before "La Luz".

In the case of identical names, towns are listed first, then political divisions, then physical features.

Generic Terms. Except for cities, the names of all features are followed by terms that represent broad classes of features, for example, "Mississippi, stm." or "Alabama, state". A list of all abbreviations used in the index is on page 297.

Country names and the names of features that extend beyond the boundaries of one country are followed by the name of the continent in which each is located. Country designations follow the names of all other places in the index. The locations of places in the United States, Canada and the United Kingdom are further defined by abbreviations that include the state or political division in which each is located.

Pronunciations. Pronunciations are included for many of the names listed. An explanation of the pronunciation system used appears on page 297.

Page References and Geographical Coordinates. The page references and geographical coordinates are found in the last columns of each entry.

If a page contains several maps or insets, a lowercase letter identifies the specific map or inset.

Latitude and longitude coordinates for point features, such as cities and mountain peaks, indicate the location of the symbols. For extensive areal features, such as countries or mountain ranges, the locations are for the approximate center of the feature. For rivers, locations are given for the mouth.

Feature (Pronunciation)	Page	Lat.	Long.
A			
Aachen, Ger. (ä´kĕn)	194-95	50°46′N	6°06′E
Aalborg, Den. (ôl´bôr)	192-93	57°02′N	9°55′E
Aalen, Ger. (ä´lĕn)	194-95	48°50′N	10°06′E
Aali, Sadd el-, d., Egypt			
see Aswan High Dam	268b	23°59′N	32°53′E
Aarau, Switz. (ärôu)	194-95	47°24′N	8°03′E
Aba, China	238-39	33°06′N	101°59′E
Aba, Nig.	260a	5°07′N	7°22′E
Abacaxis, stm., Braz.	166-67	3°54′S	58°46′W
Abaco, i., Bah.	142-43	26°28′N	77°05′W
Ābādān, Iran (ä-bŭ-dän´)	228-29	30°21′N	48°17′E
Abadla, Alg.	188-89	31°01′N	2°41′W
Abaetetuba, Braz. (ä´bȧĕ-tĕ-tōō´bȧ)	166-67	1°44′S	48°53′W
Abagnar Qi, China see Xilinhot	240-41	43°56′N	116°03′E
Abag Qi, China	240-41	43°43′N	114°39′E
Abakan, Russia (ü-bá-kän´)	218-19	53°43′N	91°27′E
Abancay, Peru (ä-bän-kä´ē)	170	13°37′S	72°53′W
Abashiri, Japan (ä-bä-shē´rē)	244	44°01′N	144°16′E
Abasolo, Mex. (ä-bä-sō´lō)	146-47	24°04′N	98°22′W
Abay, stm., Afr. see Blue Nile	254	15°38′N	32°30′E
Ābaya Hāyk', l., Eth. (á-bä´yá)	262-63	6°18′N	37°52′E
Abbé, Lac, l., Afr. see Abe, Lake	262-63	11°10′N	41°48′E
Abbeville, Fr. (áb-vēl´)	196-97	50°07′N	1°50′E
Abbeville, Al., U.S. (ăb´ê-vĭl)	124-25	31°34′N	85°15′W
Abbeville, Ga., U.S. (ăb´ê-vĭl)	124-25	31°60′N	83°18′W
Abbeville, La., U.S. (ăb´ê-vĭl)	122-23	29°58′N	92°08′W
Abbeville, S.C., U.S. (ăb´ê-vĭl)	124-25	34°11′N	82°23′W
Abbotsford, B.C., Can. (ăb´ŭts-fērd)	132-33	49°03′N	122°17′W
Abbottābād, Pak.	232-33	34°09′N	73°13′E
'Abd al-Kūrī, i., Yemen (äbd-ĕl-kó´rê)	220-21	12°12′N	52°13′E
Abdulino, Russia (äb-dó-lē´nō)	186-87	53°41′N	53°40′E
Abe, Lake, l., Afr.	262-63	11°10′N	41°48′E
Abéché, Chad	258-59	13°50′N	20°50′E
Abemama, at., Kir.	280-81	0°26′N	173°54′E
Abengourou, C. Iv.	260-61	6°44′N	3°29′W
Abeokuta, Nig. (ä-bå-ô-kōō´tä)	260a	7°09′N	3°21′E
Aberdare, Wales, U.K. (ăb´ẽr-dâr´)	190-91	51°43′N	3°28′W
Aberdare National Park, n.p., Kenya	267	0°30′S	36°45′E
Aberdeen, Scot., U.K. (ăb-ẽr-dēn´)	190-91	57°09′N	2°06′W
Aberdeen, Id., U.S. (ăb-ẽr-dēn´)	112-13	42°57′N	112°51′W
Aberdeen, Md., U.S. (ăb-ẽr-dēn´)	116-17	39°31′N	76°10′W
Aberdeen, Ms., U.S. (ăb-ẽr-dēn´)	124-25	33°50′N	88°33′W
Aberdeen, S.D., U.S. (ăb-ẽr-dēn´)	114-15	45°28′N	98°29′W
Aberdeen, Wa., U.S. (ăb-ẽr-dēn´)	112-13	46°59′N	123°49′W
Aberdeen Lake, l., Nu., Can.	130-31	64°27′N	99°00′W
Aberystwyth, Wales, U.K. (ă-bĕr-ĭst´wĭth)	190-91	52°25′N	4°05′W
Abez', Russia	186-87	66°32′N	61°44′E
Abhā, Sau. Ar.	266	18°13′N	42°30′E
Abhé Bad, l., Afr. see Abe, Lake	262-63	11°10′N	41°48′E
Ābhē Bid Hāyk', l., Afr. see Abe, Lake	262-63	11°10′N	41°48′E
Abidjan, nat. cap., C. Iv. (ä-bēd-zhän´)	260-61	5°20′N	4°01′W
Abilene, Ks., U.S. (ăb´ĭ-lēn)	120-21	38°55′N	97°13′W
Abilene, Tx., U.S. (ăb´ĭ-lēn)	120-21	32°27′N	99°44′W
Abingdon, Il., U.S. (ăb´ĭng-dŭn)	114-15	40°48′N	90°23′W
Abingdon, Va., U.S. (ăb´ĭng-dŭn)	124-25	36°43′N	81°59′W
Abitibi, stm., On., Can.	130-31	51°03′N	80°55′W
Abitibi, Lac, l., Can. (läk äb-ĭ-tĭb´ĭ) see Abitibi, Lake	136-37	48°41′N	79°35′W
Abitibi, Lake, l., Can. (läk äb-ĭ-tĭb´ĭ)	136-37	48°41′N	79°35′W
Ābīyata Hāyk', l., Eth.	269d	7°36′N	38°36′E
Abkhazeti Autonomis Respublika, state, Geor. see Abkhazia	227	43°10′N	41°00′E
Abkhazia, state, Geor.	227	43°10′N	41°00′E
Åbo, Fin. see Turku	192-93	60°27′N	22°16′E
Abou-Deïa, Chad	258-59	11°27′N	19°17′E
Abou Simbel, hist., Egypt see Abu Simbel	266	22°22′N	31°38′E
Abovyan, Arm.	227	40°15′N	44°35′E
Abrantes, Port. (á-brän´tĕs)	198-99	39°28′N	8°12′W
Abra Pampa, Arg.	168-69	22°43′S	65°42′W
Abruka saar, i., Est. (ä-brò´kä-sä´är)	192-93	58°09′N	22°31′E
Abū 'Alī, i., Sau. Ar.	230-31	27°19′N	49°35′E
Abū 'Arīsh, Sau. Ar. (ä-bōō á-rēsh´)	266	16°58′N	42°50′E
Abu Dhabi, nat. cap., U.A.E. (ä´bōō dä´bē)	230-31	24°28′N	54°22′E
Abuja, nat. cap., Nig. (ä-bū´já)	260-61	9°12′N	7°11′E
Abū Kamāl, Syria	228-29	34°27′N	40°56′E
Abū Mūsā, i., Asia	230-31	25°52′N	55°02′E
Abū Mūsā, Jazīreh-ye, i., Asia see Abū Mūsā	230-31	25°52′N	55°02′E
Abunã, Braz.	166-67	9°41′S	65°22′W
Abuná, stm., S.A.	166-67	9°40′S	65°26′W
Abuná, stm., S.A. (á-bōō-nä´)	166-67	9°40′S	65°26′W
Ābu Road, India (á´bōō rŏd)	234-35	24°30′N	72°49′E
Abū Shajarah, Ra's, c., Sudan	266	21°05′N	37°13′E
Abu Simbel, hist., Egypt	266	22°22′N	31°38′E
Abū Sunbul, hist., Egypt see Abu Simbel	266	22°22′N	31°38′E
Abū Ẕaby, nat. cap., U.A.E. see Abu Dhabi	230-31	24°28′N	54°22′E
Abyaḍ, Al-Baḥr al-, stm., Sudan see White Nile	254	15°38′N	32°31′E
Abyssinia, nation, Afr. see Ethiopia	253	9°0′N	39°00′E
Acacías, Col. (ä-kä-sē´äs)	163c	4°00′N	73°45′W
Acadia National Park, n.p., Me., U.S. (ȧ-kā´dĭ-ȧ nãsh´ŭn-ăl pärk)	117a	44°20′N	68°14′W
Acajutla, El Sal. (ä-kä-hōōt´lä)	148	13°35′N	89°50′W
Acámbaro, Mex. (ä-käm´bä-rō)	146-47	20°03′N	100°43′W
Acaponeta, Mex. (ä-kä-pō-nā´tä)	146-47	22°29′N	105°22′W
Acaponeta, stm., Mex. (ä-kä-pō-nā´tä)	146-47	22°23′N	105°38′W
Acapulco de Juárez, Mex.	146-47	16°51′N	99°54′W
Acaraí, Serra, mts., S.A. see Acarai Mountains	164-65	1°30′N	58°15′W
Acarai Mountains, mts., S.A.	164-65	1°30′N	58°15′W
Acaraú, Braz.	166-67	2°53′S	40°07′W
Acarigua, Ven. (ä-kä-rē´gwä)	164-65	9°34′N	69°12′W
Acatlán de Osorio, Mex. (ä-kät-län´dä ô-sō´rē-ō)	146-47	18°13′N	98°03′W
Acayucan, Mex. (ä-kä-yōō´kän)	146-47	17°57′N	94°54′W
Accra, nat. cap., Ghana (ä´krà)	260-61	5°34′N	0°12′W
Acerra, Italy (ä-chĕ´r-rä)	200-01	40°57′N	14°22′E
Achacachi, Bol. (ä-chä-kä´chĕ)	168-69	16°02′S	68°41′W
Achalpur, India	234-35	21°18′N	77°31′E
Acheng, China	240-41	45°32′N	126°59′E
Achinsk, Russia (ä-chĕnsk´)	218-19	56°16′N	90°30′E
Acireale, Italy (ä-chē-rä-ä´lä)	200-01	37°37′N	15°10′E
Acklins, i., Bah. (äk´lĭns)	142-43	22°26′N	73°58′W
Acklins, Bight of, b., Bah.	142-43	22°32′N	74°08′W
Aconcagua, Cerro, mtn., Arg. (sĕ´r-rô ä-kôn-kä´gwä)	163e	32°39′S	70°02′W

n-sing; ŋ-baŋk; N-nasalized n; nŏd; cŏmmit; ōld; ŏbey; ôrder; oi-boil; fōōd; ò-as oo in foot; ou-out; s-soft; sh-dish; th-thin; pūre; ûnite; ûrn; stŭd; circŭs; ü-as in French tu; ´-indeterminate vowel.

Feature (Pronunciation)	Page	Lat.	Long.
Açores, is., Port. (ä-zō′rēs) *see* Azores	199c	38°30′N	28°00′W
A Coruña, Spain	198-99	43°22′N	8°25′W
Acoyapa, Nic. (ä-kô-yä′pä)	149	11°58′N	85°11′W
Acre, Isr. *see* 'Akko	228-29	32°55′N	35°06′E
Acre, state, Braz. (ä′krā)	166-67	9°0′S	70°00′W
Acre, stm., S.A. (ä′krā)	170	8°45′S	67°24′W
Actopan, Mex. (äk-tō-pän′)	146-47	20°16′N	98°57′W
Ada, Mn., U.S. (ā′dŭ)	114-15	47°18′N	96°31′W
Ada, Oh., U.S. (ā′dŭ)	116-17	40°46′N	83°49′W
Ada, Ok., U.S. (ā′dŭ)	120-21	34°47′N	96°41′W
Adak Island, i., Ak., U.S. (ă-dăk′ ī′lănd)	126a	51°43′N	176°43′W
Adam, Oman	220-21	22°23′N	57°31′E
Adama, Eth. *see* Nazrēt	269d	8°32′N	39°16′E
Adamaoua, mts., Afr.	260-61	7°0′N	12°00′E
Adamawa, mts., Afr. *see* Adamaoua	260-61	7°0′N	12°00′E
Adams, Ma., U.S. (ăd′ămz)	116-17	42°38′N	73°07′W
Adams, Wi., U.S. (ăd′ămz)	116-17	43°57′N	89°49′W
Adams, stm., B.C., Can. (ăd′ămz)	132-33	50°54′N	119°33′W
Adams, Mount, vol., Wa., U.S.	112-13	46°13′N	121°29′W
Adams Lake, lk., B.C., Can.	132-33	51°13′N	119°33′W
'Adan, Yemen *see* Aden	266	12°49′N	45°02′E
Adana, Tur. (ä′dä-nä)	228-29	37°00′N	35°20′E
Adapazarı, Tur. (ä-dä-pä-zä′rē) *see* Sakarya	186-87	40°47′N	30°24′E
Adare, Cape, c., Ant.	287	71°20′S	170°08′E
Adavale, Austl.	276	25°55′S	144°36′E
Ad-Dahnā', des., Sau. Ar.	220-21	24°30′N	48°10′E
Ad-Dammām, Sau. Ar.	230-31	26°26′N	50°07′E
Ad-Dawādimī, Sau. Ar.	266	24°28′N	44°18′E
Ad-Dawḥah, nat. cap., Qatar *see* Doha	230-31	25°17′N	51°32′E
Ad-Dilam, Sau. Ar.	230-31	23°56′N	47°06′E
Addis Ababa, nat. cap., Eth. (ä′dĭs ä′bä-bä)	269d	9°02′N	38°45′E
Ad-Dīwānīyah, Iraq	228-29	31°59′N	44°55′E
Addo Elephant National Park, n.p., S. Afr.	264-65	33°29′S	25°46′E
Ad-Du'ayn, Sudan	266	11°26′N	26°10′E
Ad-Duwaym, Sudan (ad-dò-ām′)	266	13°59′N	32°18′E
Adel, Ga., U.S. (ā-dĕl′)	124-25	31°08′N	83°25′W
Adel, Ia., U.S. (ā-dĕl′)	114-15	41°37′N	94°01′W
Adelaide, Austl. (ăd′ê-lād)	276	34°55′S	138°35′E
Adelaide Peninsula, pen., Nu., Can.	130-31	68°09′N	97°45′W
Aden, Yemen (ä′dĕn)	266	12°49′N	45°02′E
Aden, Gulf of, b., (gŭlf ŭv ä′dĕn)	220-21	12°40′N	48°07′E
Ādīgrat, Eth.	266	14°17′N	39°27′E
Ādilābād, India (ŭ-dĭl-ā-bäd′)	234-35	19°41′N	78°33′E
Adīrī, Libya	258-59	27°32′N	13°13′E
Adirondack Mountains, mts., N.Y., U.S. (ăd-ĭ-rŏn′dăk moun′tĭnz)	116-17	44°0′N	74°00′W
Ādīs Ābeba, nat. cap., Eth. (ä-dēs′ ä′bä-bä) *see* Addis Ababa	269d	9°02′N	38°45′E
Adjud, Rom. (äd′zhòd)	202-03	46°06′N	27°11′E
Adjuntas, Presa de las, res., Mex. *see* Vicente Guerrero, Presa	146-47	23°57′N	98°46′W
Admiralty Island National Monument, n.p., U.S. (ăd′mĭ-răl-tê ī′lănd năsh′ŭn-ăl mŏn′ū-mĕnt)	126	57°40′N	134°16′W
Admiralty Islands, is., Pap. N. Gui. (ăd′mĭ-răl-tê ī′lăndz)	277	2°10′S	147°00′E
Adolfo Gonzales Chaves, Arg.	173	38°01′S	60°08′W
Adonara, Pulau, i., Indon.	248-49	8°20′S	123°10′E
Ādoni, India	236	15°38′N	77°16′E
Adra, Spain (ä′drä)	198-99	36°45′N	3°01′W
Adrano, Italy (ä-drä′nō)	200-01	37°40′N	14°50′E
Adrar, Alg.	258-59	27°52′N	0°18′W
Adrâr, reg., Maur.	258-59	20°26′N	12°46′W
Adria, Italy (ä′drê-ä)	200-01	45°03′N	12°04′E
Adrian, Mi., U.S. (ā′drĭ-ăn)	116-17	41°53′N	84°02′W
Adrian, Mn., U.S. (ā′drĭ-ăn)	114-15	43°38′N	95°56′W
Adrianople, Tur. *see* Edirne	200-01	41°41′N	26°34′E
Adriatico, Mare, s., Eur. *see* Adriatic Sea	200-01	42°30′N	16°00′E
Adriatic Sea, s., Eur. (ā-drē-ă′tĭc sē)	200-01	42°30′N	16°00′E
Adriatik, Deti, s., Eur. *see* Adriatic Sea	200-01	42°30′N	16°00′E
Ādwa, Eth.	266	14°11′N	38°53′E
Adycha, stm., Russia (ä′dĭ-chà)	218-19	68°13′N	134°48′E
Adygea, state, Russia *see* Adygheya	186-87	45°0′N	40°00′E
Adygheya, state, Russia	186-87	45°0′N	40°00′E
Adz'va, stm., Russia (ädz′vá)	186-87	66°36′N	59°24′E
Aegean Sea, s., (ê-jē′ăn sē)	200-01	38°30′N	25°00′E
Afars and Issas, nation, Afr. *see* Djibouti	253	11°30′N	43°00′E
Affon, stm., Benin *see* Ouémé	260a	6°27′N	2°33′E
Afghānestān, nation, Asia *see* Afghanistan	206-07	33°0′N	65°00′E
Afghanistan, nation, Asia (ăf-găn-ĭ-stăn′)	206-07	33°0′N	65°00′E
'Afīf, Sau. Ar.	266	23°55′N	42°56′E
Afikpo, Nig.	260a	5°55′N	7°55′E
Aflou, Alg. (ä-flōō′)	188-89	34°07′N	2°06′E
Afognak Island, i., Ak., U.S. (ä-fŏg-năk′ ī′lănd)	126	58°14′N	152°39′W
Africa, cont., (ăf′rĭ-kă)	254	10°0′N	22°00′E
Afton, Ok., U.S. (ăf′tŭn)	120-21	36°42′N	94°58′W
Afton, Wy., U.S. (ăf′tŭn)	112-13	42°43′N	110°56′W
'Afula, Isr. (ä-fò′là)	228-29	32°36′N	35°18′E
Afyon, Tur. (ä-fê-ōn)	186-87	38°46′N	30°33′E
Afyonkarahisar, Tur. *see* Afyon	186-87	38°46′N	30°33′E
Agadez, Niger (ä′gȧ-dĕs)	258-59	16°58′N	7°59′E
Agadir, Mor. (ä-gȧ-dēr)	258-59	30°28′N	9°39′W
Agadyr, Kaz.	226	48°16′N	72°53′E
Agana, nat. cap., Guam *see* Hagåtña	279c	13°28′N	144°45′E
Āgaro, Eth.	262-63	7°50′N	36°40′E
Agartala, India	234-35	23°50′N	91°16′E
Agate Fossil Beds National Monument, n.p., Ne., U.S.	114-15	42°25′N	103°43′W
Ağdam, Azer. (äg′dăm)	227	39°59′N	46°56′E
Agde, Fr. (ägd)	196-97	43°19′N	3°28′E
Agen, Fr. (á-zhäɴ′)	196-97	44°12′N	0°38′E
Āghā Jārī, Iran	230-31	30°42′N	49°50′E
Agno, Phil. (äg′nō)	250	16°07′N	119°48′E
Agno, stm., Phil. (äg′nō)	250	16°02′N	120°09′E
Āgra, India (ä′grä)	234-35	27°11′N	78°00′E
Ağrı, Tur.	227	39°43′N	43°04′E
Ağrı Dağı, vol., Tur. *see* Ararat, Mount	227	39°42′N	44°18′E
Agrigento, Italy	200-01	37°18′N	13°35′E
Agrihan, i., N. Mar. Is.	280-81	18°46′N	145°40′E
Agryz, Russia	186-87	56°31′N	53°01′E
Aguadas, Col. (ä-gwä′dȧs)	163c	5°38′N	75°27′W
Aguadilla, P.R. (ä-gwä-dēl′yä)	142a	18°26′N	67°09′W
Aguadulce, Pan. (ä-gwä-dōōl′sä)	150	8°15′N	80°31′W
Aguán, stm., Hond. (ä-gwá′n)	149	15°58′N	85°44′W
Aguanaval, stm., Mex. (á-guä-nä-väl′)	144-45	25°25′N	102°49′W
Aguanish, stm., Qc., Can.	138-39	50°15′N	62°07′W
Agua Prieta, Mex.	144-45	31°19′N	109°33′W
Aguarico, stm., S.A.	170	0°58′S	75°11′W
Aguascalientes, Mex.	146-47	21°53′N	102°18′W
Aguascalientes, state, Mex. (ä′gwäs-käl-yĕn′tās)	146-47	22°0′N	102°30′W
Água Vermelha, Represa de, res., Braz.	168-69	20°0′S	50°00′W
Águilas, Spain (ä′gê-läs)	198-99	37°25′N	1°35′W
Aguililla, Mex. (ä-gē-lēl-yä)	146-47	18°44′N	102°44′W
Agulhas, c., S. Afr. (ä-gōōl′yäs)	264-65	34°49′S	20°03′E
Agusan, stm., Phil. (ä-gōō′sän)	250	9°01′N	125°31′E
Ahaggar, mts., Alg. (á-há-gär′)	258-59	23°0′N	6°30′E
Ahaggar, Tassili oua-n-, plat., Alg.	258-59	21°0′N	6°00′E
Ahar, Iran	227	38°28′N	47°04′E
Ahlen, Ger. (ä′lĕn)	194-95	51°46′N	7°54′E
Ahmadābād, India (ŭ-mĕd-ā-bäd′)	234-35	23°02′N	72°35′E
Ahmadnagar, India (ä′mûd-nû-gûr)	236	19°05′N	74°45′E
Aḥmar, Al-Baḥr al-, s., *see* Red Sea	266	20°0′N	38°00′E
Ahmar Mountains, mts., Eth.	262-63	9°14′N	41°25′E
Ahoskie, N.C., U.S. (ā-hŏs′kē)	124-25	36°17′N	76°59′W
Ahuacatlán, Mex. (ä-wä-kät-län′)	146-47	21°05′N	104°29′W
Ahumada, Mex.	144-45	30°37′N	106°31′W
Ahunui, at., Fr. Poly.	280-81	19°39′S	140°25′W
Åhus, Swe. (ô′hòs)	192-93	55°55′N	14°18′E
Ahvāz, Iran	228-29	31°19′N	48°42′E
Ahvenanmaa, is., Fin. (ä′vĕ-nån-mô) *see* Aland Islands	192-93	60°14′N	19°46′E
Aidar, stm., Eur.	202-03	48°44′N	39°16′E
Aigaíon Pélagos, s., *see* Aegean Sea	200-01	38°30′N	25°00′E
Aiken, S.C., U.S. (ā′kĕn)	124-25	33°33′N	81°43′W
Ailao Shan, mts., China	238-39	24°13′N	101°20′E
Aimorés, Braz.	172	19°30′S	41°05′W
Aïn Beni Mathar, Mor.	188-89	34°01′N	2°01′W
Aïn Sefra, Alg.	188-89	32°46′N	0°34′W
Ainsworth, Ne., U.S. (ānz′wûrth)	114-15	42°33′N	99°52′W
'Aïn Temouchent, Alg. (ä′ēntĕ-mōō-shăɴ′)	198-99	35°18′N	1°09′W
Aipe, Col. (ī′pĕ)	163c	3°13′N	75°14′W
Aïr, Massif de l', mts., Niger	258-59	18°0′N	8°30′E
Air Force Island, i., Nu., Can.	130-31	67°55′N	74°10′W
Aïssa, Djebel, mtn., Alg.	258-59	32°51′N	0°30′W
Aitape, Pap. N. Gui. (ä-ê-tä′pâ)	277	3°09′S	142°20′E
Aitkin, Mn., U.S. (āt′kĭn)	114-15	46°32′N	93°43′W
Aitutaki, at., Cook Is. (ī-tōō-tä′kē)	280-81	18°52′S	159°45′W
Aiud, Rom. (ä′ê-òd)	194-95	46°19′N	23°44′E
Aix-en-Provence, Fr. (ĕks-prô-vàɴs)	196-97	43°32′N	5°27′E
Aix-la-Chapelle, Ger. *see* Aachen	194-95	50°46′N	6°06′E
Aix-les-Bains, Fr. (ĕks′-lā-băɴ′)	196-97	45°42′N	5°55′E
Āīzawl, India	234-35	23°44′N	92°43′E
Aizu-wakamatsu, Japan	245	37°30′N	139°56′E
Ajaccio, Fr. (ä-yät′chō)	184-85	41°56′N	8°44′E
Ajdābiyā, Libya	188-89	30°45′N	20°14′E
Ajjer, Tassili-n-, plat., Alg.	258-59	25°41′N	7°29′E
'Ajmān, U.A.E.	230-31	25°24′N	55°28′E
Ajmer, India (ŭj-mēr′)	234-35	26°27′N	74°38′E
Ajo, Az., U.S. (ä′hô)	118-19	32°23′N	112°52′W
Akagera, stm., Afr. *see* Kagera	267	0°56′S	31°47′E
Akan-kokuritsu-kōen, n.p., Japan	244	43°30′N	144°15′E
Akashi, Japan (ä′kä-shē)	245	34°39′N	134°59′E
Akdeniz, s., *see* Mediterranean Sea	188-89	35°0′N	20°00′E
Aketi, D.R.C. (ä-kå-tē)	262-63	2°45′N	23°46′E
Akhaltsikhe, Geor. (äkå′l-tsĭ-kĕ)	227	41°38′N	42°59′E
Akhisar, Tur. (äk-hĭs-sär′)	200-01	38°56′N	27°50′E
Akhtuba, stm., Russia	186-87	46°40′N	48°08′E
Akhtubinsk, Russia	186-87	48°16′N	46°10′E
Akimiski Island, i., Nu., Can. (ä-kĭ-mĭ′skĭ ī′lănd)	130-31	53°0′N	81°20′W
Akita, Japan (ä′kê-tä)	244	39°43′N	140°07′E
Akkerman, Ukr. *see* Bilhorod-Dnistrovs'kyi	202-03	46°12′N	30°18′E
'Akko, Isr.	228-29	32°55′N	35°06′E
Aklavik, N.T., Can. (äk′lä-vĭk)	128-29	68°15′N	135°06′W
Ākobo, stm., Afr.	262-63	7°47′N	33°03′E
Akola, India (à-kō′lä)	234-35	20°43′N	77°00′E
Akordat, Erit.	266	15°32′N	37°53′E
Akpatok Island, i., Nu., Can. (ák′pȧ-tŏk ĭī′lănd))	130-31	60°25′N	67°60′W
Akron, Co., U.S. (ăk′rŭn)	120-21	40°10′N	103°13′W
Akron, Oh., U.S. (ăk′rŭn)	116-17	41°05′N	81°31′W
Aksaray, Tur. (äk-sȧ-rī′)	186-87	38°23′N	34°03′E
Akşehir, Tur. (äk′shå-hĕr)	186-87	38°21′N	31°25′E
Akşehir Gölü, lk., Tur. (äk′shå-hĕr)	186-87	38°32′N	31°27′E
Aksu, China (ä-kŭ-sōō)	226	41°08′N	80°15′E
Āksum, Eth.	266	14°08′N	38°43′E
Aktyubinsk, Kaz. *see* Aqtöbe	226	50°18′N	57°10′E
Akūbū, stm., Afr.	262-63	7°47′N	33°03′E
Akune, Japan (ä′kò-nå)	245	32°01′N	130°12′E
Akure, Nig.	260a	7°15′N	5°11′E
Akureyri, Ice. (ä-kò-rå′rē)	190a	65°39′N	18°07′W
Akyab, Mya. *see* Sittwe	246-47	20°09′N	92°54′E
Al-'Amārah, Iraq	228-29	31°50′N	47°09′E
Al-'Aqabah, Jord.	228-29	29°32′N	35°01′E
Al-'Arabīyah as-Su'ūdīyah, nation, Asia *see* Saudi Arabia	206-07	25°0′N	45°00′E
Al-'Ayn, U.A.E.	230-31	24°13′N	55°45′E
Al-'Azīzīyah, Libya	188-89	32°32′N	13°01′E
Al-'Irāq, nation, Asia *see* Iraq	206-07	33°0′N	44°00′E
Al-'Uqaylah, Libya	188-89	30°15′N	19°12′E
Alabama, state, U.S. (ăl-ȧ-băm′ȧ)	108-09	32°50′N	87°00′W
Alabama, stm., Al., U.S. (ăl-ȧ-băm′ȧ)	124-25	31°08′N	87°57′W
Alabat Island, i., Phil. (ä-lä-bät′ ī′lănd)	250	14°07′N	122°03′E
Alacant, Spain	198-99	38°21′N	0°30′W
Alagoa Grande, Braz.	163d	7°03′S	35°38′W
Alagoas, state, Braz. (ä-lä-gō′äzh)	163d	9°0′S	36°00′W
Alagoinhas, Braz. (ä-lä-gō-ēn′yäzh)	166-67	12°08′S	38°25′W
Alagón, stm., Spain (ä-lä-gōn′)	198-99	39°45′N	6°52′W
Alajuela, C.R. (ä-lä-hwa′lä)	149	10°01′N	84°13′W
Alajuela, Lago, res., Pan. (lä′gô-ä-lä-hwa′lä)	150	9°15′N	79°35′W
Alaköl köli, lk., Kaz.	226	46°10′N	81°45′E
Alamagan, i., N. Mar. Is.	280-81	17°36′N	145°50′E
Alamein, Egypt *see* El-Alamein	188-89	30°49′N	28°58′E
Alamo, Nv., U.S. (ä′lȧ-mō)	118-19	37°22′N	115°10′W
Alamogordo, N.M., U.S. (ăl-ȧ-mȧ-gôr′dō)	120-21	32°54′N	105°57′W
Alamosa, Co., U.S. (ăl-ȧ-mō′sȧ)	118-19	37°28′N	105°52′W
Aland Islands, is., Fin. (ô′lănd ī′lăndz)	192-93	60°14′N	19°46′E
Alanya, Tur.	228-29	36°33′N	32°01′E
Alaotra, Farihy, lk., Madag. (ä-lä-ō′trȧ)	264-65	17°25′S	48°33′E
Alappuzha, India	236	9°29′N	76°20′E
Alashanyouqi, China	240-41	40°04′N	103°33′E
Alaska, state, U.S. (ȧ-lăs′kȧ)	108-09	65°0′N	153°00′W
Alaska, Gulf of, b., Ak., U.S. (gŭlf ŭv ȧ-lăs′kȧ)	126	58°0′N	146°00′W
Alaska Peninsula, pen., Ak., U.S. (ȧ-lăs′kȧ pĕ-nĭn′sūlȧ)	126	57°0′N	158°00′W
Alaska Range, mts., Ak., U.S. (ȧ-lăs′kȧ rānj)	126	63°26′N	149°07′W
Alataw Shan, mts., Asia	226	45°0′N	81°00′E
Alatyr', Russia (ä′lä-tür)	186-87	54°51′N	46°34′E
Alausí, Ec.	170	2°13′S	78°51′W
Alayskiy khrebet, mts., Kyrg.	226	39°51′N	72°07′E

ăt; finăl; rāte; senâte; ärm; åsk; sofȧ; fâre; ch-choose; dh-as th in other; bē; êvent; bĕt; recĕnt; cratẽr; g-gō; gh-guttural g; bĭt; ĭ-short neutral; rīde; ĸ-guttural k as ch in German ich;

Feature (Pronunciation)	Page	Lat.	Long.
Alazeya, stm., Russia	218-19	70°51′N	153°39′E
Alba, Italy (äl′bä)	200-01	44°42′N	8°02′E
Albacete, Spain (äl-bä-thä′tä)	198-99	38°59′N	1°52′W
Al-Baḥrayn, nation, Asia see Bahrain	230-31	26°0′N	50°30′E
Albania, nation, Eur. (äl-bā′nǐ-á)	174-75	41°0′N	20°00′E
Albano Laziale, Italy			
(äl-bä′nō lät-zē-ä′lä)	200-01	41°44′N	12°39′E
Albany, Austl. (ôl′bá-nǐ)	270-71	35°01′s	117°53′E
Albany, Ga., U.S. (ôl′bá-nǐ)	124-25	31°34′N	84°09′W
Albany, Ky., U.S. (ôl′bá-nǐ)	124-25	36°41′N	85°08′W
Albany, Mo., U.S. (ôl′bá-nǐ)	120-21	40°15′N	94°20′W
Albany, N.Y., U.S. (ôl′bá-nǐ)	116-17	42°40′N	73°47′W
Albany, Or., U.S. (ôl′bá-nǐ)	112-13	44°38′N	123°05′W
Albany, Tx., U.S. (ôl′bá-nǐ)	120-21	32°44′N	99°17′W
Albany, stm., On., Can. (ôl′bá-nǐ)	130-31	52°17′N	81°32′W
Al-Başrah, Iraq see Basra	228-29	30°30′N	47°48′E
Al-Batrūn, Leb. (äl-bä-trōōn′)	228-29	34°15′N	35°40′E
Al-Bayḍā′, Libya	188-89	32°45′N	21°37′E
Albemarle, N.C., U.S. (äl′bě-märl)	124-25	35°14′N	80°12′W
Albemarle Island, i., Ec.			
see Isabela, Isla.	170a	0°30′s	91°06′W
Albemarle Sound, strt., N.C., U.S.			
(äl′bě-märl sound)	124-25	36°03′N	76°12′W
Albenga, Italy (äl-běn′gä)	200-01	44°03′N	8°13′E
Alberga Creek, stm., Austl.			
(äl-bûr′gá krěk)	272-73	27°07′s	135°30′E
Albert, Fr. (äl-bâr′)	196-97	49°60′N	2°39′E
Albert, Lac, lk., Afr. (läk ál-bâr′)			
see Albert, Lake	267	1°40′N	31°00′E
Albert, Lake, lk., Afr. (äl′bērt)	267	1°40′N	31°00′E
Alberta, state, Can. (äl-bûr′tá)	128-29	54°0′N	113°00′W
Alberta, Mount, mtn., Ab., Can.			
(mount äl-bûr′tá)	132-33	52°18′N	117°28′W
Albert Edward, Mount, mtn.,			
Pap. N. Gui. (mount äl′bĕrt ĕd′wĕrd)	277	8°24′s	147°22′E
Albert Lea, Mn., U.S. (äl′bĕrt lē′)	114-15	43°39′N	93°22′W
Albert Nile, stm., Ug. (ál-bâr′ nīl)	267	3°36′N	32°02′E
Alberton, P.E., Can. (äl′bēr-tŭn)	138-39	46°44′N	64°04′W
Albertville, D.R.C. see Kalemie	267	5°55′s	29°11′E
Albertville, Fr. (ál-bâr-vēl′)	196-97	45°40′N	6°23′E
Albertville, Al., U.S. (äl′bĕrt-vǐl)	124-25	34°16′N	86°13′W
Albi, Fr. (äl-bē′)	196-97	43°55′N	2°08′E
Albia, Ia., U.S. (äl-bǐ-á)	114-15	41°02′N	92°48′W
Albion, Il., U.S. (äl′bǐ-ŭn)	116-17	38°22′N	88°04′W
Albion, In., U.S. (äl′bǐ-ŭn)	116-17	41°23′N	85°24′W
Albion, Mi., U.S. (äl′bǐ-ŭn)	116-17	42°15′N	84°45′W
Albion, Ne., U.S. (äl′bǐ-ŭn)	114-15	41°41′N	98°00′W
Al-Birkah, Libya	258-59	24°52′N	10°12′E
Alborán, Isla de, i., Spain			
(ě′s-lä-däl-äl-bō-rä′n)	198-99	35°57′N	3°02′W
Alborz, Reshteh-ye Kūhhā-ye, mts.,			
Iran see Elburz Mountains	232-33	36°0′N	53°00′E
Albuquerque, N.M., U.S.			
(äl-bû-kûr′kě)	118-19	35°05′N	106°38′W
Albury, Austl. (äl′bēr-ě)	276	36°04′s	146°56′E
Alcalá de Henares, Spain			
(äl-kä-lä′ dä ä-na′räs)	198-99	40°29′N	3°22′W
Alcalá la Real, Spain (äl-kä-lä′lä rä-äl′)	198-99	37°28′N	3°56′W
Alcamo, Italy (äl′kä-mō)	200-01	37°59′N	12°58′E
Alcanar, Spain (äl-kä-när′)	198-99	40°33′N	0°29′E
Alcañiz, Spain (äl-kän-yěth′)	198-99	41°03′N	0°08′W
Alcântara, Braz. (äl-kän′tà-rà)	166-67	2°24′s	44°24′W
Alcázar de San Juan, Spain			
(äl-kä′thär dä sän hwän′)	198-99	39°23′N	3°12′W
Alcazarquivir, Mor. see Er-Rachidia	188-89	31°57′N	4°26′W
Alcazarquivir, Mor. see Ksar-el-Kebir	269a	35°01′N	5°54′W
Alcira, Spain (äl-thē′rä) see Alzira	198-99	39°09′N	0°26′W
Alcobaça, Braz.	172	17°31′s	39°13′W
Alcobendas, Spain (äl-kō-běn′dás)	198-99	40°33′N	3°38′W
Alcoi, Spain	198-99	38°42′N	0°28′W
Alcoy, Spain see Alcoi	198-99	38°42′N	0°28′W
Aldabra, Groupe d', is., Sey.			
(grūp-däl-dä′brä)	264-65	9°24′s	46°27′E
Aldama, Mex. (äl-dä′mä)	146-47	22°55′N	98°04′W
Aldama, Mex. (äl-dä′mä)	122-23	28°51′N	105°54′W
Aldan, Russia	218-19	58°36′N	125°24′E
Aldan, stm., Russia	218-19	63°26′N	129°26′E
Aldan Plateau, plat., Russia (ŭl-dän′)			
see Aldanskoye Nagor'ye	218-19	57°0′N	127°00′E
Aldanskoye Nagor'ye, plat., Russia	218-19	57°0′N	127°00′E
Alderney, i., Guern. (ôl′dēr-nǐ)	196-97	49°43′N	2°13′W
Aldershot, Eng., U.K. (ôl′dēr-shŏt)	190-91	51°15′N	0°46′W
Aledo, Il., U.S. (á-le′dō)	114-15	41°12′N	90°45′W
Alegranza, i., Spain	199d	29°24′N	13°30′W
Alegrete, Braz. (ä-lå-grā′tà)	173	29°47′s	55°47′W
Aleksandrov, Russia (ä-lyěk-sän′ drôf)	202-03	56°24′N	38°43′E

Feature (Pronunciation)	Page	Lat.	Long.
Aleksandrov-Gay, Russia	186-87	50°08′N	48°34′E
Aleksandrovsk-Sakhalinskiy, Russia	218-19	50°54′N	142°10′E
Aleksandrów Kujawski, Pol.			
(ä-lěk-säh′drōōv kōō-yav′skě)	194-95	52°52′N	18°43′E
Alekseevka, Kaz.	226	52°00′N	70°57′E
Alekseyevka, Russia			
(ä-lyěk-sā-yěf′kà)	202-03	50°38′N	38°41′E
Aleksin, Russia (äb′ing-tŭn)	202-03	54°30′N	37°05′E
Além Paraíba, Braz. (ä-lě′m-pá-räě′bá)	172	21°52′s	42°40′W
Alençon, Fr. (à-län-sôn′)	196-97	48°26′N	0°05′E
Alenquer, Braz. (ä-lěn-kěr′)	166-67	1°56′s	54°46′W
Alep, Syria see Aleppo	228-29	36°13′N	37°10′E
Aleppo, Syria (ä-lěp-ō)	228-29	36°13′N	37°10′E
Alès, Fr. (ä-lěs)	196-97	44°08′N	4°05′E
Alessandria, Italy (ä-lěs-sän′drě-ä)	200-01	44°55′N	8°37′E
Ålesund, Nor. (ő′lě-sòn′)	184-85	62°28′N	6°10′E
Aleutian Islands, is., Ak., U.S.			
(á-lu′shǎn ī′lándz)	126a	52°0′N	176°00′W
Alexander City, Al., U.S.			
(äl-ěg-zăn′dēr sǐ′tě)	124-25	32°57′N	85°57′W
Alexandra, N.Z.	278	45°15′s	169°23′E
Alexandretta, Tur. see İskenderun	228-29	36°35′N	36°11′E
Alexandretta, Gulf of, b., Tur.			
see İskenderun Körfezi	228-29	36°30′N	35°40′E
Alexandria, On., Can.			
(äl-ěg-zăn′drǐ-á)	136-37	45°18′N	74°38′W
Alexandria, Egypt (äl-ěg-zăn′drǐ-à)	268b	31°11′N	29°54′E
Alexandria, Rom. (äl-ěg-zăn′drǐ-à)	200-01	43°59′N	25°21′E
Alexandria, In., U.S. (äl-ěg-zăn′drǐ-à)	116-17	40°15′N	85°40′W
Alexandria, La., U.S. (äl-ěg-zăn′drǐ-à)	122-23	31°18′N	92°27′W
Alexandria, Mn., U.S.			
(äl-ěg-zăn′drǐ-à)	114-15	45°53′N	95°23′W
Alexandria, S.D., U.S.			
(äl-ěg-zăn′drǐ-à)	114-15	43°39′N	97°47′W
Alexandria, Va., U.S. (äl-ěg-zăn′drǐ-à)	116-17	38°48′N	77°03′W
Alexandria Bay, N.Y., U.S.			
(äl-ěg-zăn′drǐ-à bä)	116-17	44°20′N	75°55′W
Alexandrina, Lake, lk., Austl.	276	35°26′s	139°10′E
Alexandroúpoli, Grc.	200-01	40°52′N	25°53′E
Aleysk, Russia	226	52°29′N	82°46′E
Alfaro, Spain (äl-färō)	198-99	42°11′N	1°45′W
Al-Fāshir, Sudan (äl-fä′shēr)	266	13°38′N	25°21′E
Alfenas, Braz. (äl-fě′nás)	172	21°27′s	45°57′W
Al-Furāt, stm., Asia see Euphrates	208-09	30°60′N	47°27′E
Algeciras, Spain (äl-hä-thě′räs)	198-99	36°08′N	5°27′W
Alger, nat. cap., Alg. see Algiers	269b	36°46′N	3°03′E
Algeria, nation, Afr. (äl-gē′rǐ-à)	253	28°0′N	3°00′E
Algérie, nation, Afr. see Algeria	253	28°0′N	3°00′E
Al-Ghaydah, Yemen	220-21	16°13′N	52°12′E
Alghero, Italy (äl-gā′rō)	200-01	40°34′N	8°19′E
Algiers, nat. cap., Alg. (äl-jērs)	269b	36°46′N	3°03′E
Al-Ḥamād, pl., Sau. Ar.	228-29	32°0′N	39°30′E
Al-Ḥasakah, Syria	228-29	36°30′N	40°46′E
Al-Ḥawrah, Yemen	220-21	13°50′N	47°34′E
Al-Ḥayy, Iraq	228-29	32°10′N	46°03′E
Al-Ḥijāz, reg., Sau. Ar.	266	24°30′N	38°30′E
Al-Ḥillah, Iraq	228-29	32°29′N	44°26′E
Al-Hoceima, Mor.	198-99	35°15′N	3°56′W
Al-Ḥudaydah, Yemen	266	14°48′N	42°57′E
Al-Hufūf, Sau. Ar.	230-31	25°22′N	49°34′E
Alicante, Spain see Alacant	198-99	38°21′N	0°30′W
Alice, Tx., U.S. (äl′īs)	122-23	27°45′N	98°05′W
Alice Springs, Austl. (äl′īs springz)	270-71	23°42′s	133°52′E
Alīgarh, India (ä-lē-gŭr′)	234-35	27°54′N	78°04′E
Alima, stm., Congo	262-63	1°31′s	16°40′E
Al-Imārāt al-'Arabīyah al-Muttaḥidah,			
nation, Asia			
see United Arab Emirates	206-07	24°0′N	54°00′E
Alingsås, Swe. (á′lǐŋ-sôs)	192-93	57°56′N	12°32′E
'Ali Sabieh, Dji.	266	11°08′N	42°42′E
Aliwal North, S. Afr. (ä-lě-wäl′ nôrth)	264-65	30°42′s	26°43′E
Al-Jawf, Libya	258-59	24°12′N	23°17′E
Al-Jawf, Sau. Ar.	228-29	29°48′N	39°52′E
Al-Jazāʾir, nat. cap., Alg. see Algiers	269b	36°46′N	3°03′E
Al-Jazīrah, reg., Sudan	266	14°17′N	32°53′E
Aljezur, Port. (äl-zhä-zōōr′)	198-99	37°18′N	8°48′W
Al-Jubayl, Sau. Ar.	230-31	27°01′N	49°40′E
Al-Jufrah, well, Libya	258-59	29°06′N	15°57′E
Al-Junaynah, Sudan	262-63	13°27′N	22°27′E
Al-Karak, Jord. (äl-kě-räk′)	228-29	31°11′N	35°42′E
Al-Khābūrah, Oman	230-31	23°58′N	57°06′E
Al-Khalīl, W.B. see Hebron	228-29	31°32′N	35°06′E
Al-Kharṭūm, nat. cap., Sudan			
see Khartoum	266	15°35′N	32°32′E
Al-Khasab, Oman	230-31	26°12′N	56°15′E
Al-Khubar, Sau. Ar.	230-31	26°17′N	50°12′E

Feature (Pronunciation)	Page	Lat.	Long.
Al-Khums, Libya	188-89	32°39′N	14°16′E
Alkmaar, Neth. (älk-mär′)	190-91	52°38′N	4°45′E
Al-Kūt, Iraq	228-29	32°30′N	45°49′E
Al-Kuwayt, nation, Asia see Kuwait	206-07	29°30′N	47°45′E
Al-Kuwayt, nat. cap., Kuw. (äl-kōō-wit)			
see Kuwait	228-29	29°19′N	47°60′E
Al-Lādhiqīyah, Syria see Latakia	228-29	35°31′N	35°48′E
Allahābād, India (ŭl-ŭ-hä-bäd′)	234-35	25°26′N	81°51′E
Allakaket, Ak., U.S.	126	66°33′N	152°38′W
'Allāq, Bi'r, well, Libya	258-59	31°05′N	11°58′E
Allegan, Mi., U.S. (äl′ě-găn)	116-17	42°32′N	85°51′W
Allegheny Plateau, plat., U.S.			
(äl-ě-gā′nǐ plä-tō′)	116-17	41°30′N	78°00′W
Allendale, S.C., U.S. (äl′ěn-dāl)	124-25	33°00′N	81°19′W
Allende, Mex. (äl-yěn′då)	122-23	28°20′N	100°50′W
Allende, Mex. (äl-yěn′då)	122-23	25°17′N	100°01′W
Allenstein, Pol. see Olsztyn	194-95	53°47′N	20°29′E
Allentown, Pa., U.S.	116-17	40°37′N	75°29′W
Alleppey, India (á-lěp′ě)			
see Alappuzha	236	9°29′N	76°20′E
Aller, stm., Ger. (äl′ēr)	194-95	52°57′N	9°11′E
Alliance, Ne., U.S. (á-lī′áns)	114-15	42°06′N	102°52′W
Alliance, Oh., U.S. (á-lī′áns)	116-17	40°55′N	81°06′W
Allier, stm., Fr. (á-lyä′)	196-97	46°58′N	3°04′E
Allinge, Den. (äl′īŋ-ě)	194-95	55°16′N	14°48′E
Al-Lubnān, nation, Asia see Lebanon	206-07	34°0′N	36°00′E
Alma, N.B., Can. (äl′má)	138-39	45°36′N	64°57′W
Alma, Qc., Can. (äl′má)	136-37	48°33′N	71°39′W
Alma, Ga., U.S. (äl′má)	124-25	31°33′N	82°28′W
Alma, Mi., U.S. (äl′má)	116-17	43°23′N	84°39′W
Alma, Ne., U.S. (äl′má)	120-21	40°06′N	99°21′W
Alma, Wi., U.S. (äl′má)	114-15	44°20′N	91°54′W
Almadén, Spain (äl-mä-dhän)	198-99	38°49′N	4°49′W
Al-Madīnah, Sau. Ar. see Medina	266	24°28′N	39°37′E
Al-Maghrib, nation, Afr. see Morocco	253	32°0′N	5°00′W
Almagro, Spain (äl-mä′grō)	198-99	38°53′N	3°43′W
Al-Majma'ah, Sau. Ar.	232-33	25°55′N	45°21′E
Al-Makhā', Yemen see Mocha	266	13°19′N	43°15′E
Al-Manāmah, nat. cap., Bahr.			
(äl-mä-nä′má)	230-31	26°13′N	50°35′E
Almansa, Spain (äl-män′sä)	198-99	38°52′N	1°06′W
Al-Marj, Libya	188-89	32°30′N	20°53′E
Almas, Pico das, mtn., Braz.	166-67	13°33′s	41°56′W
Almaty, Kaz.	226	43°17′N	76°56′E
Al-Mawşil, Iraq see Mosul	228-29	36°20′N	43°08′E
Almazán, Spain (äl-mä-thän′)	198-99	41°29′N	2°32′W
Almelo, Neth. (äl′mě-lō)	190-91	52°22′N	6°39′E
Almenara, Braz.	168-69	16°12′s	40°41′W
Almendralejo, Spain			
(äl-män-drä-lä′hō)	198-99	38°41′N	6°24′W
Almería, Spain (äl-mä-rě′ä)	198-99	36°51′N	2°27′W
Almería, Golfo de, b., Spain			
(gôl-fô-dě-äl-mäī-rěn′)	198-99	36°46′N	2°30′W
Al'met'yevsk, Russia	186-87	54°54′N	52°19′E
Älmhult, Swe. (älm′hōōlt)	192-93	56°33′N	14°09′E
Almirante, Pan. (äl-mē-rän′tä)	150	9°17′N	82°24′W
Almonte, On., Can. (äl-mŏn′tě)	136-37	45°13′N	76°11′W
Almora, India	234-35	29°36′N	79°40′E
Al-Mubarraz, Sau. Ar.	230-31	25°25′N	49°35′E
Al-Muḥarraq, Bahr.	230-31	26°16′N	50°37′E
Al-Mukallā, Yemen	220-21	14°32′N	49°08′E
Almuñécar, Spain (äl-mōōn-yä′kär)	198-99	36°45′N	3°41′W
Alnön, i., Swe.	192-93	62°25′N	17°26′E
Alor, Pulau, i., Indon. (pōō-lou ä′lôr)	248-49	8°15′s	124°45′E
Alor Setar, Malay. (ä′lôr stär)	246-47	6°07′N	100°23′E
Alpen, mts., Eur. see Alps	184-85	46°25′N	10°00′E
Alpena, Mi., U.S. (äl-pē′ná)	116-17	45°03′N	83°26′W
Alpes, mts., Eur. see Alps	184-85	46°25′N	10°00′E
Alpi, mts., Eur. see Alps	184-85	46°25′N	10°00′E
Alpine, Az., U.S. (äl′pīn)	118-19	33°50′N	109°08′W
Alpine, Tx., U.S. (äl′pīn)	122-23	30°21′N	103°40′W
Alpine National Park, n.p., Austl.	276	36°57′s	147°12′E
Alps, mts., Eur. (älps)	194-95	46°25′N	10°00′E
Al-Qaḍārif, Sudan	266	14°02′N	35°23′E
Al-Qaṭīf, Sau. Ar.	230-31	26°33′N	50°01′E
Al-Quds, nat. cap., Isr. see Jerusalem	228-29	31°47′N	35°14′E
Als, i., Den. (äls)	194-95	54°59′N	9°55′E
Alsace, hist. reg., Fr. (äl-sá′s)	196-97	48°30′N	7°30′E
Alta Gracia, Arg. (äl′tä grä′sě-a)	173	31°45′s	64°26′W
Altagracia, Ven.	164-65	10°43′N	71°30′W
Altamaha, stm., Ga., U.S.			
(ôl-tá-má-hô′)	124-25	31°19′N	81°18′W
Altamira, Braz. (äl-tä-mē′rä)	166-67	3°13′s	52°12′W
Altamira, Chile	168-69	25°48′s	69°51′W
Altamura, Italy (äl-tä-mōō′rä)	200-01	40°50′N	16°33′E
Altavista, Va., U.S. (äl-tä-vǐs′tà)	124-25	37°07′N	79°18′W

Feature (Pronunciation)	Page	Lat.	Long.
Altay, Mong.	240-41	46°24'N	96°15'E
Altay, Mong.	240-41	49°42'N	96°24'E
Altay, state, Russia	226	51°0'N	86°00'E
Altay, mts., Asia *see* Altay Mountains	222-23	48°0'N	90°00'E
Altay Mountains, mts., Asia (äl'tī' moun'tĭnz)	222-23	48°0'N	90°00'E
Altay Shan, mts., Asia *see* Altay Mountains	222-23	48°0'N	90°00'E
Altenburg, Ger. (äl-tĕn-bo͝orgh)	194-95	50°59'N	12°26'E
Altiplano, plat., S.A. (äl-tē-plä'nō)	168-69	18°0'S	68°00'W
Alto Araguaia, Braz.	168-69	17°19'S	53°13'W
Alton, Il., U.S. (ôl'tŭn)	120-21	38°55'N	90°12'W
Altona, Mb., Can.	134-35	49°06'N	97°35'W
Altoona, Ia., U.S. (ăl-to͞o'nȧ)	114-15	41°38'N	93°28'W
Altoona, Pa., U.S. (ăl-to͞o'nȧ)	116-17	40°29'N	78°24'W
Altoona, Wi., U.S. (ăl-to͞o'nȧ)	114-15	44°48'N	91°26'W
Alto Parnaíba, Braz.	166-67	9°07'S	45°57'W
Alto Río Senguer, Arg.	171	45°03'S	70°51'W
Altun Shan, mts., China (äl-tòn shän)	222-23	38°0'N	88°00'E
Alturas, Ca., U.S. (ăl-to͞o'rȧs)	112-13	41°30'N	120°32'W
Altus, Ok., U.S. (ăl'tŭs)	120-21	34°38'N	99°20'W
Alu, i., Sol. Is. *see* Shortland Island	279e	7°04'S	155°43'E
Al-Ubayyiḍ, Sudan	266	13°11'N	30°13'E
Alūksne, Lat. (ä'lòks-nĕ)	192-93	57°25'N	27°04'E
Alula, Som. *see* Caluula	262-63	11°57'N	50°46'E
Al-Urdun, nation, Asia *see* Jordan	206-07	31°0'N	36°00'E
Al-Urdunn, stm., Asia *see* Jordan	228-29	31°46'N	35°34'E
Alushta, Ukr. (ä'lsho-tȧ)	202-03	44°41'N	34°24'E
Alva, Ok., U.S. (ăl'vȧ)	120-21	36°48'N	98°40'W
Alvarado, Mex. (äl-vä-rä'dhō)	146-47	18°46'N	95°46'W
Älvdalen, Swe. (ĕlv'dä-lĕn)	192-93	61°14'N	14°02'E
Alvear, Arg.	173	29°03'S	56°33'W
Alvesta, Swe. (äl-vĕs'tä)	192-93	56°54'N	14°33'E
Alwar, India (ŭl'wŭr)	234-35	27°34'N	76°37'E
Alxa Zuoqi, China	240-41	38°49'N	105°35'E
Al-Yaman, nation, Asia *see* Yemen	206-07	15°0'N	44°00'E
Alytus, Lith. (ä'lē-tòs)	194-95	54°24'N	24°04'E
Alzira, Spain	198-99	39°09'N	0°26'W
Amadjuak Lake, Ik., Nu., Can. (ä-mädj'wăk lăk)	130-31	65°0'N	71°00'W
Amahai, Indon.	248-49	3°20'S	128°56'E
Amakuso-Shimo-shima, i., Japan (ämä-ko͞o'sä shē-mō shē'mä)	245	32°20'N	130°05'E
Åmål, Swe. (ô'môl)	192-93	59°03'N	12°42'E
Amalfi, Col. (ä'mà'l-fē)	164-65	6°55'N	75°05'W
Amambaí, Braz.	168-69	23°07'S	55°13'W
Amami-Ō-shima, i., Japan	244a	28°15'N	129°20'E
Amami-shotō, is., Japan	244a	27°58'N	129°02'E
Amapá, Braz.	166-67	2°02'N	50°46'W
Amapá, state, Braz.	166-67	1°0'N	52°00'W
Amarante, Braz. (ä-mä-rän'tä)	166-67	6°14'S	42°50'W
Amarillo, Tx., U.S. (ăm-ȧ-rĭl'ō)	120-21	35°13'N	101°50'W
Amarkantak, India	234-35	22°40'N	81°46'E
Amaro, Monte, mtn., Italy (mòn-tĕ ä-mä'rō)	200-01	42°05'N	14°06'E
Amasya, Tur. (ä-mä'sē-à)	186-87	40°39'N	35°50'E
Amazon, stm., S.A. (ä'mȧ-zŏn)	164-65	0°04'S	49°15'W
Amazonas, state, Braz. (ä-mä-thō'näs)	166-67	5°0'S	63°00'W
Amazonas, stm., S.A. (ä-mä-thō'näs) *see* Amazon	164-65	0°04'S	49°15'W
Ambāla, India (ŭm-bä'lŭ)	234-35	30°21'N	76°49'E
Ambanja, Madag.	264-65	13°41'S	48°27'E
Ambargasta, Salinas de, pl., Arg.	168-69	29°15'S	64°30'W
Ambato, Ec. (äm-bä'tō)	170	1°15'S	78°37'W
Ambatondrazaka, Madag.	264-65	17°52'S	48°24'E
Ambelau, Pulau, i., Indon.	248-49	3°51'S	127°12'E
Amberg, Ger. (äm'bĕrgh)	194-95	49°27'N	11°52'E
Ambergris Cay, i., Belize (ăm'bēr-grēs kā)	148	18°03'N	87°55'W
Ambert, Fr. (äɴ-bĕr')	196-97	45°33'N	3°45'E
Ambikāpur, India	234-35	23°07'N	83°12'E
Amboina, Indon. *see* Ambon	248-49	3°44'S	128°11'E
Amboise, Fr. (äɴ-bwȧz')	196-97	47°24'N	0°60'E
Ambon, Indon.	248-49	3°44'S	128°11'E
Ambon, Pulau, i., Indon.	248-49	3°40'S	128°05'E
Amboseli National Park, n.p., Kenya	267	2°36'S	37°12'E
Ambositra, Madag. (äɴ-bō-sē'trä)	264-65	20°32'S	47°15'E
Ambovombe, Madag.	264-65	25°11'S	46°05'E
Amboy, Il., U.S. (ăm'boi)	116-17	41°43'N	89°20'W
Ambre, Cap d', c., Madag. *see* Bobaomby, Tanjona	264-65	11°58'S	49°15'E
Ambridge, Pa., U.S. (ăm'brĭdj)	116-17	40°36'N	80°13'W
Ambriz, Ang.	262-63	7°51'S	13°10'E
Ambrym, i., Vanuatu	279g	16°15'S	168°10'E
Amchitka Pass, strt., Ak., U.S. (ăm-chĭt'kȧ pȧs)	126a	51°30'N	179°30'W
Amderma, Russia	186-87	69°45'N	61°39'E
Amdo, China	234-35	32°17'N	91°44'E
Ameca, Mex. (ä-mĕ'kä)	146-47	20°33'N	104°02'W
Amecameca de Juárez, Mex.	146-47	19°07'N	98°46'W
Ameland, i., Neth.	190-91	53°27'N	5°45'E
Amelia Island, i., Fl., U.S.	124-25	30°37'N	81°27'W
American Falls, Id., U.S. (ȧ-mĕr'ĭ-kăn fôlz)	112-13	42°47'N	112°51'W
American Falls Reservoir, res., Id., U.S. (ȧ-mĕr'ĭ-kăn fôlz rĕ'sĕr-vwär)	112-13	42°57'N	112°44'W
American Fork, Ut., U.S. (ȧ-mĕr'ĭ-kăn fôrk)	118-19	40°24'N	111°48'W
American Highland, plat., Ant. (ȧ-mĕr'ĭ-kăn)	287	72°30'S	78°00'E
Americanos, Barra de los, i., Mex.	122-23	24°53'N	97°35'W
American Samoa, dep., Oc. (ȧ-mĕr'ĭ-kăn sȧ-mō'ȧ)	279b	14°20'S	170°00'W
Americus, Ga., U.S. (ȧ-mĕr'ĭ-kŭs)	124-25	32°05'N	84°14'W
Amerika Samoa, dep., Oc. *see* American Samoa	279b	14°20'S	170°00'W
Amersfoort, Neth. (ä'mĕrz-fōrt)	190-91	52°10'N	5°24'E
Ames, Ia., U.S. (āmz)	114-15	42°01'N	93°37'W
Amesbury, Ma., U.S. (āmz'bēr-ê)	116-17	42°52'N	70°56'W
Ámfissa, Grc. (ám-fĭ'sȧ)	200-01	38°32'N	22°23'E
Amga, Russia (ŭm-gä')	218-19	60°54'N	131°58'E
Amga, stm., Russia (ŭm-gä')	218-19	62°35'N	135°04'E
Amgun, stm., Russia	218-19	52°56'N	139°41'E
Amherst, N.S., Can. (ăm'hērst)	138-39	45°50'N	64°12'W
Amherst, Ma., U.S. (ăm'hērst)	116-17	42°23'N	72°31'W
Amherst, N.Y., U.S. (ăm'hērst)	116-17	42°58'N	78°47'W
Amherst, Va., U.S. (ăm'hērst)	116-17	37°35'N	79°04'W
Amiens, Fr. (ä-myăɴ')	196-97	49°54'N	2°18'E
Amistad, Presa de la, res., N.A. *see* Amistad Reservoir	122-23	29°28'N	101°07'W
Amistad Reservoir, res., N.A.	122-23	29°28'N	101°07'W
Amite, La., U.S. (ă-mēt')	124-25	30°43'N	90°31'W
Amite, stm., La., U.S. (ă-mēt')	124-25	30°13'N	90°36'W
Amlia Island, i., Ak., U.S. (ȧ'mlēȧ ī'lȧnd)	126a	52°07'N	173°34'W
'Ammān, nat. cap., Jord. (äm'mán)	228-29	31°57'N	35°56'E
Amnok-kang, stm., Asia *see* Yalu	243	39°57'N	124°22'E
Āmol, Iran	232-33	36°28'N	52°21'E
Amorgós, i., Grc. (ä-môr'gōs)	200-01	36°52'N	25°56'E
Amory, Ms., U.S. (āmô-rē)	124-25	33°59'N	88°29'W
Amos, Qc., Can. (ā'mŭs)	136-37	48°34'N	78°08'W
Amoy, China *see* Xiamen	225a	24°27'N	118°07'E
Amposta, Spain (äm-pōs'tä)	198-99	40°44'N	0°35'E
Amraoti, India *see* Amrāvati	234-35	20°56'N	77°46'E
Amrāvati, India	234-35	20°56'N	77°46'E
Amreli, India	234-35	21°36'N	71°13'E
Amritsar, India (ŭm-rĭt'sŭr)	234-35	31°38'N	74°52'E
Amroha, India	234-35	28°54'N	78°28'E
Amsterdam, N.Y., U.S. (ăm'stēr-dăm)	116-17	42°57'N	74°11'W
Amsterdam, nat. cap., Neth. (äm-stēr-däm')	190-91	52°22'N	4°54'E
Amstetten, Aus. (äm'stĕt-ĕn)	194-95	48°07'N	14°52'E
Am Timan, Chad (äm'tē-män')	258-59	11°02'N	20°17'E
Amu Darya, stm., Asia (ä-mò-dä'rēä)	226	44°14'N	59°41'E
Āmū Daryā, stm., Asia *see* Amu Darya	226	44°14'N	59°41'E
Amukta Pass, strt., Ak., U.S. (ä-mo͞ok'tȧ pȧs)	126a	52°26'N	171°51'W
Amundsen Gulf, b., Can. (ä'mŭn-sĕn-gŭlf')	86	71°0'N	124°00'W
Amundsen Sea, s., Ant. (ä'mŭn-sĕn sē)	287	72°30'S	112°00'W
Amuntai, Indon.	248-49	2°25'S	115°15'E
Amur, stm., Asia (ä-mo͞or')	218-19	52°57'N	141°10'E
Anaa, at., Fr. Poly.	280-81	17°26'S	145°31'W
Anabar, stm., Russia (ăn-ȧ-bär')	218-19	73°13'N	113°32'E
Anaco, Ven. (ä-nä'kô)	163b	9°25'N	64°28'W
Anaconda, Mt., U.S. (ăn-ȧ-kŏn'dȧ)	112-13	46°08'N	112°58'W
Anacortes, Wa., U.S. (ăn-ȧ-kôr'tĕz)	112-13	48°30'N	122°37'W
Anadarko, Ok., U.S. (ăn-ȧ-där'kō)	120-21	35°04'N	98°15'W
Anadyr', Russia (ŭ-nȧ-dĭr')	218-19	64°44'N	177°30'E
Anadyr', stm., Russia (ŭ-nȧ-dĭr')	218-19	64°52'N	176°15'E
Anadyr, Gulf of, b., Russia (gŭlf ŭv ä-nȧ-dyĭr')	218-19	64°0'N	179°00'W
Anadyr Mountains, plat., Russia (ä-nȧ-dyĭr' moun'tĭnz) *see* Anadyrskoye Ploskogor'ye	218-19	67°0'N	174°00'E
Anadyrskiy Zaliv, b., Russia *see* Anadyr, Gulf of	218-19	64°0'N	179°00'W
Anadyrskoye Ploskogor'ye, plat., Russia	218-19	67°0'N	174°00'E
Anaheim, Ca., U.S. (ăn'ȧ-hīm)	118-19	33°50'N	117°55'W
Ānai Mudi, mtn., India	236	10°10'N	77°04'E
Anaktuvuk Pass, Ak., U.S.	126	68°09'N	151°43'W
Anambas, Kepulauan, is., Indon. (ä-näm-bäs)	246-47	3°0'N	106°00'E
Anamosa, Ia., U.S. (ăn-ȧ-mō'sȧ)	114-15	42°06'N	91°16'W
Anamur, Tur.	228-29	36°04'N	32°50'E
Anantapur, India	236	14°41'N	77°36'E
Anantnāg, India	234-35	33°45'N	75°08'E
Anapa, Russia (á-nä'pä)	202-03	44°54'N	37°20'E
Anápolis, Braz. (ä-ná'pō-lēs)	168-69	16°21'S	48°57'W
Anatahan, i., N. Mar. Is.	280-81	16°22'N	145°40'E
Anatom, i., Vanuatu	279g	20°12'S	169°48'E
Añatuya, Arg. (á-nyä-to͞o'yá)	173	28°27'S	62°49'W
Anauá, stm., Braz.	166-67	0°58'N	61°22'W
Anbanjing, China	238-39	23°57'N	100°54'E
Anchiang, China *see* Qianyang	238-39	27°11'N	110°02'E
Anchorage, Ak., U.S. (ăŋ'kēr-āj)	126	61°12'N	149°53'W
Ancona, Italy (än-kō'nä)	200-01	43°37'N	13°31'E
Ancud, Chile (äŋ-ko͞odh')	171	41°53'S	73°49'W
Ancud, Golfo de, b., Chile (gôl-fō-dĕ-äŋ-ko͞odh')	171	42°05'S	73°00'W
Anda, China	240-41	46°24'N	125°19'E
Andalgalá, Arg.	168-69	27°35'S	66°19'W
Andalucía, hist. reg., Spain (än-dä-lo͞o-sē'ä)	198-99	37°15'N	4°30'W
Andalusia, Al., U.S. (ăn-dȧ-lo͞o'zhĭȧ)	124-25	31°19'N	86°29'W
Andaman and Nicobar Islands, state, India	246-47	11°0'N	93°00'E
Andaman Islands, is., India (ăn-dȧ-măn' ī'lȧndz)	246-47	12°0'N	92°45'E
Andaman Sea, s., Asia (ăn-dȧ-măn' sē)	246-47	10°0'N	95°00'E
Anderson, Ca., U.S. (ăn'dēr-sŭn)	112-13	40°29'N	122°22'W
Anderson, In., U.S. (ăn'dēr-sŭn)	116-17	40°05'N	85°41'W
Anderson, S.C., U.S. (ăn'dēr-sŭn)	124-25	34°30'N	82°39'W
Anderson, stm., N.T., Can. (ăn'dēr-sŭn)	130-31	69°42'N	128°54'W
Andes, mts., S.A. (ăn'dēz) (än'dās)	159	20°0'S	67°00'W
Andhra Pradesh, state, India	236	16°0'N	79°00'E
Andijon, Uzb.	232-33	40°47'N	72°21'E
Andkhvoy, Afg.	232-33	36°55'N	65°07'E
Andong, Kor., S. (än'dŭng')	243	36°34'N	128°43'E
Andorra, nation, Eur. (än-dôr'rä)	196-97	42°30'N	1°30'E
Andorra la Vella, nat. cap., And.	198-99	42°30'N	1°31'E
Andover, Mn., U.S. (ăn'dô-vēr)	114-15	45°14'N	93°17'W
Andøya, i., Nor. (änd-ûê)	184-85	69°08'N	15°54'E
Andradina, Braz.	168-69	20°55'S	51°23'W
Andrews, N.C., U.S. (ăn'dro͞oz)	124-25	35°12'N	83°49'W
Andrews, S.C., U.S. (ăn'dro͞oz)	124-25	33°27'N	79°34'W
Andrews, Tx., U.S. (ăn'dro͞oz)	120-21	32°19'N	102°33'W
Andria, Italy (än'drē-ä)	200-01	41°13'N	16°17'E
Andros, i., Bah. (ăn'drŏs)	142-43	24°26'N	77°57'W
Ándros, i., Grc. (àn'drôs)	200-01	37°50'N	24°53'E
Anegada, i., Br. Vir. Is.	143b	18°45'N	64°20'W
Aneto, mtn., Spain (ä-nĕ'tô)	198-99	42°38'N	0°40'E
Angamos, Punta, c., Chile	168-69	23°02'S	70°31'W
Ang'angxi, China (äŋ-äŋ-shyē)	240-41	47°09'N	123°48'E
Angara, stm., Russia	218-19	58°06'N	93°02'E
Angarsk, Russia	222-23	52°35'N	103°55'E
Ángel, Salto, wtfl., Ven. (säl'tō-á'n-hĕl) *see* Angel Falls	164-65	6°01'N	62°28'W
Ángel de la Guarda, Isla, i., Mex. (ē's-lä-á'n-hĕl-dĕ-lä-gwä'r-dä)	144-45	29°22'N	113°28'W
Angeles, Phil. (än'hā-lās)	250	15°08'N	120°36'E
Angel Falls, wtfl., Ven. (ăn'jĕl fôlz)	164-65	6°01'N	62°28'W
Ängelholm, Swe. (ĕng'ĕl-hôlm)	192-93	56°15'N	12°53'E
Angers, Fr.	196-97	47°28'N	0°33'W
Angicos, Braz.	163d	5°40'S	36°36'W
Angijak Island, i., Nu., Can.	130-31	65°40'N	62°15'W
Angkor Wat, hist., Camb. (äng'kôr)	246-47	13°26'N	103°52'E
Anglesey, i., Wales, U.K. (ăŋ'g'l-sê)	190-91	53°17'N	4°22'W
Angleton, Tx., U.S. (aŋ'g'l-tŭn)	122-23	29°10'N	95°26'W
Angmagssalik, Green. (àŋ-má'sà-lĭk)	284-85	65°35'N	37°50'W
Angoche, Moz.	264-65	16°14'S	39°55'E
Angoche, Ilha, i., Moz. (ē'lä-ăn-gō'chā)	264-65	16°21'S	39°51'E
Angol, Chile (aŋ-gōl')	171	37°48'S	72°43'W
Angola, In., U.S. (ăŋ-gō'lȧ)	116-17	41°38'N	84°59'W
Angola, nation, Afr. (ăŋ-gō'lȧ)	253	12°30'S	18°30'E
Angontsy, Tanjona, c., Madag.	264-65	15°13'S	50°27'E
Angora, nat. cap., Tur. *see* Ankara	186-87	39°56'N	32°53'E
Angostura, Ven. *see* Ciudad Bolívar	164-65	8°07'N	63°33'W
Angostura, Presa de la, res., Mex.	144-45	16°02'N	92°22'W
Angoulême, Fr. (äŋ-go͞o-lâm')	196-97	45°39'N	0°09'E
Angra dos Reis, Braz. (aŋ'grä dōs rä'ês)	172	23°01'S	44°19'W
Angren, Uzb.	232-33	41°01'N	70°08'E
Anguilla, dep., N.A. (ăŋ-gwĭl'ȧ)	140-41	18°15'N	63°05'W

ăt; finăl; rāte; senāte; ärm; àsk; sofȧ; fâre; ch-choose; dh-as th in other; bē; ēvent; bĕt; recĕnt; cratēr; g-gō; gh-guttural g; bĭt; ĭ-short neutral; rīde; ĸ-guttural k as ch in German ich;

Feature (Pronunciation)	Page	Lat.	Long.
Anguilla Cays, is., Bah. (ăŋ-gwĭl′ȧ kēs)	142-43	23°31′N	79°33′W
Anguille, Cape, c., Nf., Can. (kāp′-äŋ-gē′yě)	138-39	47°55′N	59°24′W
Anholt, i., Den. (än′hŏlt)	192-93	56°42′N	11°34′E
Anhui, state, China (än-hwā)	238-39	32°0′N	117°00′E
Anhwei, state, China *see* Anhui	238-39	32°0′N	117°00′E
Aniak, Ak., U.S. (ä-nyȧ′k)	126	61°35′N	159°33′W
Anina, Rom. (ä-nē′nä)	200-01	45°05′N	21°51′E
Anita, Pa., U.S. (ȧ-nē′ȧ)	116-17	41°0′N	78°58′W
Aniva, Zaliv, b., Russia (zä′lĭf ȧ-nē′vȧ)	244	46°16′N	142°48′E
Anjār, India	234-35	23°07′N	70°02′E
Anjouan, i., Com. *see* Nzwani	264-65	12°15′S	44°25′E
Anju-ŭp, Kor., N.	243	39°37′N	125°40′E
Ankaboa, Tanjona, c., Madag.	264-65	21°55′S	43°18′E
Ankang, China (än-käŋ)	238-39	32°41′N	109°01′E
Ankara, nat. cap., Tur. (än′kȧ-rȧ)	186-87	39°56′N	32°53′E
Ankazoabo, Madag.	264-65	22°18′S	44°31′E
Änkober, Eth.	269d	9°35′N	39°44′E
Anlong, China (än-loŋ)	238-39	25°07′N	105°28′E
Anlu, China (än′lōō′)	238-39	31°16′N	113°41′E
Anmyŏn-do, i., Kor., S.	243	36°30′N	126°22′E
Anna, Il., U.S. (ăn′ȧ)	116-17	37°27′N	89°14′W
Annaba, Alg.	184-85	36°54′N	7°46′E
An-Nafūd, des., Sau. Ar.	228-29	28°30′N	41°00′E
An-Najaf, Iraq (än nä-jäf′)	228-29	32°00′N	44°20′E
Annamitique, Chaîne, mts., Asia	246-47	17°0′N	106°00′E
Annapolis, Md., U.S. (ă-năp′ô-lĭs)	116-17	38°58′N	76°31′W
Annapūrṇa, mtn., Nepal	234-35	28°34′N	83°50′E
Ann Arbor, Mi., U.S. (ăn är′bẽr)	116-17	42°16′N	83°43′W
An-Nāṣirīyah, Iraq	228-29	31°03′N	46°15′E
An-Nawfalīyah, Libya	188-89	30°46′N	17°50′E
Annecy, Fr. (ȧn sē′)	196-97	45°54′N	6°07′E
Annemasse, Fr. (ȧn'mäs′)	196-97	46°12′N	6°14′E
An Nhon, Viet.	246-47	13°54′N	109°05′E
Anniston, Al., U.S. (ăn′ĭs-tŭn)	124-25	33°39′N	85°50′W
Annobón, i., Eq. Gui.	260-61	1°26′S	5°37′E
Annonay, Fr. (ȧn′ĭs-tsiŭn)	196-97	45°15′N	4°40′E
An-Nuhūd, Sudan	266	12°42′N	28°26′E
Anori, Braz.	166-67	3°45′S	61°42′W
Anorontany, Tanjona, c., Madag.	264-65	12°26′S	48°45′E
Anpu, China (än-pōō)	238-39	21°27′N	110°01′E
Anqing, China	238-39	30°30′N	117°02′E
Ansbach, Ger. (äns′bäk)	194-95	49°18′N	10°35′E
Anse-d'Hainault, Haiti (äns′dĕnō)	142-43	18°30′N	74°26′W
Anserma, Col. (á′n-sě′r-mȧ)	163c	5°14′N	75°48′W
Anshan, China	243	41°08′N	122°60′E
Anshun, China (än-shōōn′)	238-39	26°15′N	105°56′E
Anson, Tx., U.S. (ăn′sŭn)	120-21	32°44′N	99°53′W
Ansongo, Mali	258-59	15°40′N	0°30′E
Antakya, Tur. *see* Antioch	228-29	36°12′N	36°10′E
Antalaha, Madag.	264-65	14°55′S	50°17′E
Antalya, Tur. (än-tä′lē-ä) (ä-dä′lē-ä)	186-87	36°54′N	30°42′E
Antalya, Gulf of, b., Tur. *see* Antalya Körfezi	186-87	36°30′N	30°60′E
Antalya Körfezi, b., Tur.	186-87	36°30′N	30°60′E
Antananarivo, nat. cap., Madag. (än-tä′nä-nä-rēv)	264-65	18°55′S	47°32′E
An tAonach, Ire. *see* Nenagh	190-91	52°52′N	8°12′W
Antarctica, cont., (ănt-ärk′tĭ-kȧ)	287	87°0′S	60°00′E
Antarctic Peninsula, pen., Ant.	287	70°15′S	65°55′W
Antequera, Spain (än-tĕ-kĕ′rä)	198-99	37°01′N	4°33′W
Anthony, Tx., U.S. (ăn′thō-nė)	118-19	31°60′N	106°36′W
Anti-Atlas, mts., Mor.	258-59	30°0′N	8°30′W
Antibes, Fr. (än-tēb′)	196-97	43°35′N	7°07′E
Anticosti, Île d', i., Qc., Can. (ăn-tĭ-kŏs′tē)	138-39	49°30′N	63°00′W
Antigo, Wi., U.S. (ăn′tĭ-gō)	116-17	45°08′N	89°08′W
Antigonish, N.S., Can. (ăn-tĭ-gō-nêsh′)	138-39	45°37′N	61°60′W
Antigua, i., Antig.	143b	17°05′N	61°49′W
Antigua and Barbuda, nation, N.A. (ăn-tē′gwä ănd bär-bōō′dȧ)	140-41	17°03′N	61°48′W
Antigua Guatemala, Guat.	148	14°33′N	90°44′W
Antillas, Archipiélago de las, is., *see* West Indies	140-41	19°0′N	70°00′W
Antillas, Mar de las, s., *see* Caribbean Sea	140-41	15°0′N	73°00′W
Antillas Mayores, is., N.A. *see* Greater Antilles	142-43	20°0′N	74°00′W
Antillen, Nederlandse, dep., N.A. *see* Netherlands Antilles	140-41	12°15′N	68°45′W
Antilles, Grandes, is., N.A. *see* Greater Antilles	142-43	20°0′N	74°00′W
Antilles, Mer des, s., *see* Caribbean Sea	140-41	15°0′N	73°00′W
Antilles, Petites, is., *see* Lesser Antilles	143b	15°0′N	61°00′W
Antioch, Tur.	228-29	36°12′N	36°10′E
Antioch, Il., U.S. (ăn′tĭ-ŏk)	116-17	42°29′N	88°06′W
Antioquia, Col. (än-tē-ō′kēä)	163c	6°34′N	75°49′W
Antipodes Islands, is., N.Z.	287	49°40′S	178°47′E
Antlers, Ok., U.S. (ănt′lẽrz)	120-21	34°13′N	95°37′W
Antofagasta, Chile (än-tô-fä-gäs′tä)	168-69	23°39′S	70°23′W
Antón, Pan. (än-tōn′)	150	8°24′N	80°14′W
Antongila, Helodrano, b., Madag.	264-65	15°45′S	49°50′E
António Enes, Moz. (ăn-to′nyō ĕn′ēs) *see* Angoche	264-65	16°14′S	39°55′E
Antsirabe, Madag. (änt-sė-rä′bā)	264-65	19°52′S	47°02′E
Antsirañana, Madag.	264-65	12°17′S	49°17′E
Antsirane, Madag. *see* Antsirañana	264-65	12°17′S	49°17′E
Antsla, Est. (änt′slȧ)	192-93	57°50′N	26°32′E
Antsohihy, Madag.	264-65	14°49′S	48°03′E
Antung, China *see* Dandong	243	40°07′N	124°21′E
Antwerp, Bel. (ăn′twûrp)	190-91	51°13′N	4°25′E
Antwerpen, Bel. *see* Antwerp	190-91	51°13′N	4°25′E
Anugul, India	234-35	20°51′N	85°06′E
Anūpgarh, India (ŭ-nȯp′gŭr)	234-35	29°11′N	73°13′E
Anuradhapura, Sri L. (ŭ-nōō′rä-dŭ-pōō′rŭ)	236	8°21′N	80°24′E
Anvers, Bel. *see* Antwerp	190-91	51°13′N	4°25′E
Anvers Island, i., Ant.	287	64°33′S	63°35′W
Anxi, China (än-shyē)	225a	25°04′N	118°11′E
Anxi, China (än-shyē)	240-41	40°29′N	95°47′E
Anyang, China (än′yäng)	240-41	36°06′N	114°20′E
Anykščiai, Lith. (anīksh-chä′ė)	192-93	55°32′N	25°07′E
Anyuanyi, China *see* Tianzhu	240-41	36°60′N	103°07′E
Anzhero-Sudzhensk, Russia (än′zhâ-rô-sȯd′zhĕnsk)	218-19	56°05′N	86°01′E
Anzio, Italy (änt′zē-ō)	200-01	41°27′N	12°37′E
Aoba, i., Vanuatu	279g	15°25′S	167°50′E
Aoga-shima, i., Japan	244	32°28′N	139°46′E
Aomen, China	238-39	22°13′N	113°33′E
Aomori, Japan (äô-mō′rė)	244	40°49′N	140°45′E
Aoraki/Mount Cook National Park, n.p., N.Z.	278	43°35′S	170°15′E
Aoraki, mtn., N.Z.	278	43°36′S	170°10′E
Aôral, Phnum, mtn., Camb.	246-47	12°02′N	104°10′E
Aouk, Bahr, stm., Afr. (bär ä-ȯk′)	262-63	8°51′N	18°52′E
Aoukâr, reg., Maur.	258-59	18°0′N	9°30′W
Aoulef, Alg.	258-59	26°58′N	1°04′E
Apalachicola, Fl., U.S. (ăp-ȧ-lăch-ĭ-kō′lȧ)	124-25	29°44′N	84°60′W
Apalachicola, stm., Fl., U.S. (ăpȧ-lăch′ĭ-cōlā)	124-25	29°44′N	84°59′W
Apaporis, stm., S.A. (ä-pä-pō′rĭs)	170	1°21′S	69°25′W
Aparri, Phil. (ä-pär′rē)	250	18°20′N	121°40′E
Apatin, Serb. (ŏ′pŏ-tĭn)	200-01	45°40′N	18°59′E
Apatity, Russia	184-85	67°34′N	33°23′E
Apeldoorn, Neth. (ä′pĕl-dōōrn)	190-91	52°13′N	5°58′E
Apennines, mts., Italy (ă′-pȧ-nīnz)	200-01	43°0′N	13°00′E
Apía, Col. (ȧ-pē′ä)	163c	5°06′N	75°58′W
Apia, nat. cap., Samoa (ä′-pē-ȧ) (ä-pē′-ȧ)	279b	13°50′S	171°45′W
Apiacás, Serra dos, plat., Braz.	166-67	10°15′S	57°15′W
Apizaco, Mex. (ä-pė-zä′kō)	146-47	19°25′N	98°08′W
Apo, Mount, mtn., Phil. (mount ä′pō)	250	6°59′N	125°16′E
Apolo, Bol.	166-67	14°43′S	68°31′W
Aporé, stm., Braz.	168-69	19°28′S	50°56′W
Apostle Islands, is., Wi., U.S. (ä-pŏs′l ĭ′lȧndz)	114-15	46°50′N	90°30′W
Apóstoles, Arg.	173	27°55′S	55°48′W
Apostolove, Ukr.	202-03	47°39′N	33°43′E
Appalaches, Les, mts., N.A. *see* Appalachian Mountains	110-11	41°0′N	77°00′W
Appalachia, Va., U.S. (ăpȧ-lăch′ĭ-ȧ)	124-25	36°54′N	82°48′W
Appalachian Mountains, mts., N.A. (ăp-ȧ-lăch′ĭ-ăn moun′tĭnz)	110-11	41°0′N	77°00′W
Appennino, mts., Italy (äp-pĕn-nē′nō) *see* Apennines	200-01	43°0′N	13°00′E
Appleton, Mn., U.S. (ăp′l-tŭn)	114-15	45°12′N	96°01′W
Appleton, Wi., U.S. (ăp′l-tŭn)	116-17	44°15′N	88°25′W
Appleton City, Mo., U.S. (ăp′l-tŭn sĭ′tē)	120-21	38°11′N	94°02′W
Apt, Fr. (äpt)	196-97	43°52′N	5°24′E
Apucarana, Braz.	168-69	23°33′S	51°27′W
Apure, stm., Ven. (ä-pōō′rä)	164-65	7°37′N	66°23′W
Apurímac, stm., Peru (ä-pōō-rē-mäk′)	170	11°52′S	73°57′W
Aqaba, Gulf of, b., (gŭlf ŭv ä′kȧ-bȧ)	228-29	29°05′N	34°44′E
Aqmola, nat. cap., Kaz. *see* Astana	226	51°12′N	71°27′E
Aqtaū, Kaz.	186-87	43°38′N	51°11′E
Aqtöbe, Kaz.	226	50°18′N	57°10′E
Aquidauana, Braz. (ä-kē-däwä′nä)	168-69	20°29′S	55°48′W
Aquila, Italy *see* L'Aquila	200-01	42°21′N	13°24′E
Aquin, Haiti (ä-kän′)	142-43	18°17′N	73°24′W
Ar'ar, Sau. Ar.	228-29	30°56′N	41°04′E
Ara, India	234-35	25°34′N	84°40′E
Ara, stm., Japan (ä-rä)	245	35°40′N	139°51′E
Ara, stm., Japan (ä-rä)	245	38°09′N	139°25′E
'Arab, Baḥr al-, stm., Sudan	262-63	9°02′N	29°28′E
'Arab, Shaṭṭ al-, stm., Asia	228-29	29°57′N	48°33′E
Arabian Desert, des., Egypt (ȧ-rā′bĭ-ăn dĕs′ērt)	266	28°0′N	32°00′E
Arabian Gulf, b., Asia *see* Persian Gulf	230-31	27°0′N	51°00′E
Arabian Peninsula, pen., Asia (ȧ-rā′bĭ-ăn pĕ-nĭn′sūlȧ)	220-21	25°0′N	45°00′E
Arabian Sea, s., (ȧ-rā′bĭ-ăn sē)	220-21	15°0′N	65°00′E
Aracaju, Braz. (ä-rä′kä-zhōō′)	163d	10°54′S	37°04′W
Aracati, Braz. (ä-rä′kä-tē′)	166-67	4°34′S	37°46′W
Araçatuba, Braz. (ä-rä-sȧ-tōō′bä)	168-69	21°12′S	50°27′W
Aracruz, Braz. (ä-rä-krōō′s)	172	19°49′S	40°16′W
Araçuaí, Braz.	168-69	16°53′S	42°04′W
Arad, Rom. (ŏ′rŏd)	194-95	46°11′N	21°19′E
Arafura, Laut, s., *see* Arafura Sea	224-25	9°0′S	133°00′E
Arafura Sea, s., (ä-rä-fōō′rä sē)	224-25	9°0′S	133°00′E
Aragarças, Braz.	168-69	15°55′S	52°15′W
Aragón, hist. reg., Spain (ä-rä-gōn′)	198-99	41°30′N	1°00′W
Araguacema, Braz.	166-67	8°50′S	49°34′W
Aragua de Barcelona, Ven.	163b	9°27′N	64°50′W
Araguaia, stm., Braz. (ä-rä-gwä′yä)	166-67	5°20′S	48°42′W
Araguari, Braz. (ä-rä-gwä′rē)	172	18°39′S	48°12′W
Araguari, stm., Braz.	166-67	1°13′N	50°02′W
Araguatins, Braz. (ä-rä-gwä-tēns)	166-67	5°39′S	48°06′W
Arāk, Iran	232-33	34°05′N	49°41′E
Aral, Kaz.	226	46°48′N	61°40′E
Aral Sea, lk., Asia (ä′-rŭl sē)	226	45°0′N	60°00′E
Aral Tengizi, lk., Asia *see* Aral Sea	226	45°0′N	60°00′E
Aramac, Austl.	277	22°58′S	145°15′E
Aramberri, Mex. (ä-rȧm-bĕr-rē′)	146-47	24°06′N	99°49′W
Aranda de Duero, Spain (ä-rän′dä dā dwā′rō)	198-99	41°41′N	3°41′W
Arandas, Mex. (ä-rän′däs)	146-47	20°43′N	102°20′W
Aranjuez, Spain (ä-rän-hwāth′)	198-99	40°02′N	3°37′W
Aransas Pass, Tx., U.S. (ȧ-răn′sȧs pȧs)	122-23	27°54′N	97°09′W
Aranyaprathet, Thai.	246-47	13°41′N	102°31′E
Arapiraca, Braz.	163d	9°45′S	36°39′W
Araranguá, Braz.	172	28°56′S	49°29′W
Araraquara, Braz. (ä-rä-rä-kwä′rä)	172	21°47′S	48°10′W
Ararat, Austl. (ăr′ȧrăt)	276	37°17′S	142°56′E
Ararat, Mount, vol., Tur. (mount ăr′ȧrăt)	227	39°42′N	44°18′E
Araripe, Chapada do, plat., Braz. (shä-pä′dä-dō-ä-rä-rē′pĕ)	166-67	7°23′S	39°49′W
Araruama, Lagoa de, b., Braz. (lȧ-gô′ä-ä-rä-rōō-ä′mä)	172	22°53′S	42°12′W
Aras, stm., Asia (ä-räs)	227	40°01′N	48°28′E
Arauca, Col. (ä-rou′kä)	164-65	7°04′N	70°45′W
Arauca, stm., S.A. (ä-rou′kä)	164-65	7°25′N	66°31′W
Arāvalli Range, mts., India (ä-rä′vŭ-lė rānj)	234-35	24°42′N	73°19′E
Araxá, Braz.	172	19°36′S	46°55′W
Araya, Punta de, c., Ven. (pŭn′tȧ-dĕ-ä-rä′yȧ)	163b	10°38′N	64°17′W
Araz, stm., Asia	227	40°01′N	48°28′E
Ārba Minch', Eth.	262-63	6°01′N	37°34′E
Arbīl, Iraq	228-29	36°11′N	44°01′E
Arboga, Swe. (är-bō′gä)	192-93	59°24′N	15°51′E
Arboréa, Italy (är-bō-rĕ′ä)	200-01	39°46′N	8°35′E
Arbroath, Scot., U.K. (är-brōth′)	190-91	56°34′N	2°36′W
Arcachon, Fr. (är-kä-shôn′)	196-97	44°40′N	1°10′W
Arcadia, Fl., U.S. (är-kā′dĭ-ȧ)	125a	27°13′N	81°51′W
Arcadia, La., U.S. (är-kā′dĭ-ȧ)	120-21	32°34′N	92°56′W
Arcadia, Wi., U.S. (är-kā′dĭ-ȧ)	114-15	44°15′N	91°29′W
Arcata, Ca., U.S. (är-kȧ′tȧ)	112-13	40°53′N	124°05′W
Arc Dome, mtn., Nv., U.S. (ärk dōm)	118-19	38°50′N	117°21′W
Arcelia, Mex. (är-sā′lē-ä)	146-47	18°18′N	100°17′W
Archangel, Russia *see* Arkhangel'sk	186-87	64°32′N	40°25′E
Archbald, Pa., U.S. (ärch′bôld)	116-17	41°30′N	75°33′W
Archer Bend National Park, n.p., Austl. *see* Mungkan Kandju National Park	277	13°32′S	142°37′E
Arches National Park, n.p., Ut., U.S. (är′ches năsh′ŭn-ăl pärk)	118-19	38°43′N	109°36′W
Arco, Id., U.S. (är′kō)	112-13	43°39′N	113°18′W
Arcoverde, Braz.	163d	8°25′S	37°04′W
Arctic Ocean, oc., (ärk′tĭk ōshŭn)	288	85°0′N	170°00′E
Arctic Red, stm., N.T., Can.	130-31	67°27′N	133°45′W
Arctic Village, Ak., U.S.	126	68°05′N	145°31′W
Ardabīl, Iran	227	38°15′N	48°18′E
Ardahan, Tur. (är-dȧ-hän′)	227	41°06′N	42°43′E

n-sing; ŋ-baŋk; ɴ-nasalized n; nŏd; cŏmmit; ōld; ôbey; ôrder; oi-boil; fōōd; ȯ-as oo in foot; ou-out; s-soft; sh-dish; th-thin; pūre; ûnite; ûrn; stŭd; circŭs; ü-as in French tu; ′-indeterminate vowel.

Feature (Pronunciation)	Page	Lat.	Long.
Ardebil, Iran *see* Ardabīl	227	38°15'N	48°18'E
Ardennen, reg., Eur. *see* Ardennes	190-91	50°10'N	5°45'E
Ardennes, reg., Eur. (år-dĕn′)	190-91	50°10'N	5°45'E
Ardila, stm., Eur. (är-dē′lå)	198-99	38°10'N	7°29'W
Ardmore, Ok., U.S. (ärd′mōr)	120-21	34°10'N	97°09'W
Arecibo, P.R. (ä-rå-sē′bō)	142a	18°28'N	66°43'W
Areia Branca, Braz. (ä-rĕ′yä-brå′n-kă)	163d	4°56'S	37°07'W
Arena, Point, c., Ca., U.S. (point ä-rā′n*å*)	118-19	38°57'N	123°44'W
Arena, Punta, c., Mex.	144-45	23°34'N	109°28'W
Arendal, Nor. (ä′rĕn-däl)	192-93	58°27'N	8°48'E
Arequipa, Peru (ä-rå-kē′pä)	170	16°24'S	71°32'W
Arezzo, Italy (ä-rĕt′sō)	200-01	43°28'N	11°53'E
Argentan, Fr. (år-zhän-täN′)	196-97	48°45'N	0°01'W
Argenteuil, Fr. (är-zhäN-tû′y′)	196-97	48°57'N	2°14'E
Argentina, nation, S.A. (är-jĕn-tē′n*å*)	158	34°0'S	64°00'W
Argentino, Lago, lk., Arg. (lä′gô är-ĸĕn-tē′nō)	171	50°14'S	72°26'W
Argenton-sur-Creuse, Fr. (är-zhäN′tôN-sür-krôs)	196-97	46°35'N	1°31'E
Arghandāb, stm., Afg.	232-33	31°27'N	64°23'E
Argonne, reg., Fr. (ä′r-gôn)	196-97	49°07'N	5°14'E
Árgos, Grc. (är′gōs)	200-01	37°38'N	22°44'E
Arguello, Point, c., Ca., U.S. (point är-gwāl′yō)	118-19	34°35'N	120°38'W
Argun', stm., Asia (år-gōōn′)	218-19	53°19'N	121°27'E
Århus, Den. (ôr′hōōs)	192-93	56°09'N	10°13'E
Ariake-kai, b., Japan (ä′rē-ä′kå)	245	33°0'N	130°20'E
Arica, Chile (ä-rē′kä)	168-69	18°29'S	70°19'W
Arica, Col.	164-65	2°07'S	71°44'W
Arīḥā, W.B. *see* Jericho	228-29	31°52'N	35°27'E
Arima, Trin.	143b	10°37'N	61°17'W
Arinos, stm., Braz. (ä-rē′nôzsh)	166-67	10°26'S	58°20'W
Aripuanã, stm., Braz. (å-rê-pwän′y*å*)	166-67	5°07'S	60°23'W
Ariquemes, Braz.	166-67	9°54'S	63°05'W
Aristazabal Island, i., B.C., Can.	132-33	52°38'N	129°07'W
Arizona, Arg.	171	35°43'S	65°19'W
Arizona, state, U.S. (ăr-ĭ-zō′n*å*)	108-09	34°0'N	112°00'W
Arkadelphia, Ar., U.S. (är-k*å*-dĕl′fĭ-*å*)	120-21	34°07'N	93°04'W
Arkansas, state, U.S. (är′kăn-sô) (är-kăn′s*å*s)	108-09	34°50'N	92°30'W
Arkansas, stm., U.S. (är′kăn-sô) (är-kăn′s*å*s)	110-11	33°47'N	91°04'W
Arkansas City, Ks., U.S.	120-21	37°04'N	97°02'W
Arkhangel'sk, Russia (år-kän′gĕlsk)	186-87	64°32'N	40°25'E
Arkhangel'skoye, Russia (är-kän-gĕl′skô-yĕ)	202-03	53°16'N	37°42'E
Arles, Fr. (ärl)	196-97	43°41'N	4°38'E
Arlington, S.D., U.S. (är′lĕng-t*ŭ*n)	114-15	44°22'N	97°08'W
Arlington, Tx., U.S. (är′lĭng-t*ŭ*n)	120-21	32°45'N	97°07'W
Arlington, Va., U.S. (är′lĭng-t*ŭ*n)	116-17	38°52'N	77°07'W
Arlington, Vt., U.S. (är′lĭng-t*ŭ*n)	116-17	43°04'N	73°09'W
Arlington Heights, Il., U.S. (är′lĕng-t*ŭ*n hīts)	116-17	42°05'N	87°59'W
Arlit, Niger	258-59	18°45'N	7°21'E
Armant, Egypt (är-mänt′)	268b	25°37'N	32°32'E
Armavir, Russia (år-mȧ-vĭr′)	186-87	44°59'N	41°07'E
Armenia, Col. (är-mĕ′n*ĕå*)	163c	4°31'N	75°42'W
Armenia, nation, Asia (är-mē′nē-*å*)	227	40°0'N	45°00'E
Armeniya, nation, Asia *see* Armenia	227	40°0'N	45°00'E
Armentières, Fr. (år-mäN-tyâr′)	196-97	50°41'N	2°53'E
Armidale, Austl. (är′mĭ-dāl)	276	30°31'S	151°40'E
Armour, S.D., U.S. (är′mẽr)	114-15	43°19'N	98°21'W
Armstrong, On., Can.	134-35	50°19'N	89°04'W
Arnaud, stm., Qc., Can.	130-31	59°58'N	69°58'W
Arnedo, Spain (är-nā′dō)	198-99	42°14'N	2°07'W
Arnhem, Neth. (ärn′hĕm)	190-91	51°59'N	5°55'E
Arnhem, Cape, c., Austl. (kāp ärn′hĕm)	272-73	12°22'S	136°57'E
Arnhem Land, reg., Austl. (ärn′hĕm-lănd)	272-73	13°13'S	133°50'E
Arnold, Mn., U.S. (är′nŭld)	114-15	46°53'N	92°05'W
Arnprior, On., Can. (ärn-prī′ẽr)	136-37	45°26'N	76°21'W
Arnsberg, Ger. (ärns′bĕrgh)	194-95	51°24'N	8°04'E
Arnstadt, Ger. (ärn′shtät)	194-95	50°50'N	10°57'E
Aroma, Sudan	266	15°48'N	36°08'E
Aroostook, stm., N.A.	138-39	46°49'N	67°43'W
Arop Island, i., Pap. N. Gui.	277	5°20'S	147°05'E
Arorae, i., Kir.	280-81	2°38'S	176°49'E
Arqalyq, Kaz.	226	50°15'N	66°53'E
Arraias, Braz.	166-67	12°58'S	46°55'W
Ar-Ramādī, Iraq	228-29	33°26'N	43°19'E
Arran, Island of, i., Scot., U.K. (ī′l*ă*nd ŏv ă′răn)	190-91	55°35'N	5°15'W
Arras, Fr. (å-räs′)	196-97	50°17'N	2°47'E
Ar-Rass, Sau. Ar.	266	25°52'N	43°30'E
Arrecife, Spain	199d	28°57'N	13°33'W
Arrecifes, Arg. (är-rå-sē′fås)	173	34°04'S	60°06'W
Arriaga, Mex. (är-rêä′gä)	146-47	16°14'N	93°53'W
Ar-Riyāḍ, nat. cap., Sau. Ar. *see* Riyadh	230-31	24°38'N	46°43'E
Ar-Rub'al-Khālī, des., Asia *see* Rub'al-Khali	220-21	20°0'N	51°00'E
Ar-Ruṣayriṣ, Sudan	266	11°48'N	34°22'E
Ar-Ruṭbah, Iraq	228-29	33°02'N	40°17'E
Arsen'yev, Russia	244	44°09'N	133°17'E
Art, Île, i., N. Cal.	279g	19°43'S	163°39'E
Árta, Grc. (är′tä)	200-01	39°09'N	20°59'E
Arteaga, Mex. (är-tā-ä′gä)	146-47	18°20'N	102°18'W
Arteaga, Mex. (är-tā-ä′gä)	122-23	25°28'N	100°51'W
Artëm, Russia (*å*r-tyôm′)	244	43°21'N	132°11'E
Artemisa, Cuba (är-tå-mē′sä)	142-43	22°49'N	82°46'W
Artesia, N.M., U.S. (är-tē′sĭ-*å*)	120-21	32°51'N	104°24'W
Artibonite, stm., Haiti (är-tê-bô-nē′tā)	142-43	19°15'N	72°46'W
Artigas, Ur.	173	30°24'S	56°28'W
Artillery Lake, lk., N.T., Can.	130-31	63°09'N	107°52'W
Artvin, Tur.	227	41°10'N	41°50'E
Artyk, Russia	218-19	64°09'N	145°12'E
Aru, Kepulauan, is., Indon.	224-25	6°0'S	134°30'E
Aru, Tanjung, c., Indon.	248-49	2°11'S	116°35'E
Arua, Ug. (ä′rōō-ä)	267	3°01'N	30°55'E
Aruanã, Braz.	166-67	14°54'S	51°05'W
Aruba, dep., N.A. (ä-rōō′b*å*)	140-41	12°30'N	69°58'W
Arunāchal Pradesh, state, India	234-35	28°30'N	95°00'E
Aruppukkottai, India	236	9°31'N	78°06'E
Arusha, Tan. (å-rōō′shä)	267	3°22'S	36°41'E
Aruwimi, stm., D.R.C.	262-63	1°13'N	23°36'E
Arvayheer, Mong.	240-41	46°15'N	102°48'E
Arviat, Nu., Can.	128-29	61°08'N	94°07'W
Arvidsjaur, Swe.	184-85	65°36'N	19°07'E
Arvika, Swe. (är-vē′kå)	192-93	59°40'N	12°38'E
Arxan, China	240-41	47°11'N	119°57'E
Arys, Kaz.	226	42°26'N	68°48'E
Arzamas, Russia (är-zä-mäs′)	186-87	55°23'N	43°50'E
Aš, Czech Rep. (äsh′)	194-95	50°13'N	12°12'E
Asad, Buḥayrat al-, res., Syria	228-29	36°00'N	38°10'E
Asahi-dake, vol., Japan	244	43°40'N	142°51'E
Asahigawa, Japan *see* Asahikawa	244	43°46'N	142°22'E
Asahikawa, Japan	244	43°46'N	142°22'E
Āsānsol, India	234-35	23°41'N	86°59'E
Asbestos, Qc., Can. (ăs-bĕs′tōs)	136-37	45°46'N	71°57'W
Asbury Park, N.J., U.S. (ăz′bĕr-ĭ pärk)	116-17	40°13'N	74°01'W
Ascensión, Mex. (äs-sĕn-sê-ōn′)	144-45	31°06'N	107°60'W
Ascension, i., St. Hel. (å-sĕn′sh*ŭ*n)	254	7°57'S	14°22'W
Aschaffenburg, Ger. (ä-shäf′ĕn-bòrgh)	194-95	49°59'N	9°09'E
Aschersleben, Ger. (äsh′ĕrs-lā-bĕn)	194-95	51°46'N	11°28'E
Ascoli Piceno, Italy (äs′kô-lēpê-chā′nō)	200-01	42°52'N	13°35'E
Aseb, Erit.	266	12°58'N	42°42'E
Āsela, Eth.	269d	7°58'N	39°08'E
Åsele, Swe.	184-85	64°10'N	17°21'E
Aşgabat, nat. cap., Turkmen.	232-33	37°57'N	58°23'E
Asha, Russia (ä′shä)	186-87	55°00'N	57°16'E
Ashburn, Ga., U.S. (ăsh′b*ŭ*rn)	124-25	31°42'N	83°39'W
Ashburton, stm., Austl. (ăsh′bûr-t*ŭ*n)	272-73	21°42'S	114°55'E
Ashdown, Ar., U.S. (ăsh′doun)	120-21	33°41'N	94°08'W
Asheboro, N.C., U.S. (ăsh′bŭr-ô)	124-25	35°42'N	79°49'W
Asheville, N.C., U.S. (ăsh′vĭl)	124-25	35°36'N	82°34'W
Ashgabat, nat. cap., Turkmen. *see* Aşgabat	232-33	37°57'N	58°23'E
Ashikaga, Japan (ä′shê-kä′gå)	245	36°20'N	139°27'E
Ashkhabad, nat. cap., Turkmen. *see* Aşgabat	232-33	37°57'N	58°23'E
Ashland, Ky., U.S. (ăsh′l*ă*nd)	116-17	38°28'N	82°39'W
Ashland, Me., U.S. (ăsh′l*ă*nd)	117a	46°38'N	68°28'W
Ashland, Ne., U.S. (ăsh′l*ă*nd)	114-15	41°02'N	96°22'W
Ashland, Oh., U.S. (ăsh′l*ă*nd)	116-17	40°52'N	82°18'W
Ashland, Or., U.S. (ăsh′l*ă*nd)	112-13	42°12'N	122°42'W
Ashland, Va., U.S. (ăsh′l*ă*nd)	116-17	37°45'N	77°29'W
Ashland, Wi., U.S. (ăsh′l*ă*nd)	114-15	46°36'N	90°53'W
Ashley, N.D., U.S. (ăsh′lê)	114-15	46°02'N	99°22'W
Ashmore and Cartier Islands, dep., Oc.	224-25	12°25'S	123°20'E
Ashqelon, Isr. (äsh′kĕ-lōn)	228-29	31°40'N	34°35'E
Ash-Shāriqah, U.A.E. *see* Sharjah	230-31	25°22'N	55°24'E
Ash-Shiḥr, Yemen	220-21	14°46'N	49°37'E
Ashtabula, Oh., U.S. (ăsh-t*å*-bū′l*å*)	116-17	41°51'N	80°48'W
Ashton, Id., U.S. (ăsh′t*ŭ*n)	112-13	44°05'N	111°27'W
Ashur, hist., Iraq	228-29	35°30'N	43°16'E
Asia, cont., (ā′zh*å*)	208-09	50°0'N	100°00'E
Asinara, Golfo dell', b., Italy (gôl′fô-dĕl-ä-sē-nä′rä)	200-01	41°0'N	8°32'E
Asinara, Isola, i., Italy	200-01	41°04'N	8°16'E
Asino, Russia	218-19	56°60'N	86°08'E
'Asīr, reg., Sau. Ar. (ä-sēr′)	220-21	19°0'N	42°00'E
Askersund, Swe. (äs′kĕr-sònd)	192-93	58°53'N	14°54'E
Asmara, nat. cap., Erit. (äz-mä′-r*å*)	266	15°20'N	38°55'E
Asmera, nat. cap., Erit. (äs-mä′rä) *see* Asmara	266	15°20'N	38°55'E
Asotin, Wa., U.S. (*å*-sō′tĭn)	112-13	46°20'N	117°03'W
Aspen, Co., U.S. (ăs′p*ĕ*n)	118-19	39°12'N	106°49'W
Aspiring, Mount, mtn., N.Z.	278	44°23'S	168°44'E
Assab, Erit. *see* Aseb	266	12°58'N	42°42'E
Assam, state, India (ăs-săm′)	234-35	26°0'N	93°00'E
As-Samāwah, Iraq	228-29	31°19'N	45°17'E
Assateague Island, i., U.S.	116-17	38°05'N	75°12'W
Assens, Den. (äs′s*ĕ*ns)	192-93	55°16'N	9°55'E
Assiniboia, Sk., Can.	134-35	49°38'N	105°59'W
Assiniboine, stm., Can. (ă-sĭn′ĭ-boin)	134-35	49°53'N	97°08'W
Assiniboine, Mount, mtn., Can. (mount ă-sĭn′ĭ-boin)	132-33	50°52'N	115°39'W
Assis, Braz. (ä-sé′s)	168-69	22°40'S	50°26'W
Assomption, i., Sey.	264-65	9°44'S	46°30'E
As-Sūdān, nation, Afr. *see* Sudan	253	15°0'N	30°00'E
As-Sudd, reg., Sudan	262-63	8°0'N	31°00'E
As-Sulaymānīyah, Iraq	228-29	35°34'N	45°27'E
As-Sūrīyah, nation, Asia *see* Syria	206-07	35°0'N	38°00'E
As-Suwaydā', Syria	228-29	32°42'N	36°34'E
Astana, nat. cap., Kaz. (ä′stä-nä′)	226	51°12'N	71°27'E
Astara, Azer.	227	38°28'N	48°52'E
Asterābād, Iran *see* Gorgān	232-33	36°51'N	54°26'E
Asti, Italy (äs′tē)	200-01	44°55'N	8°13'E
Astorga, Spain (äs-tôr′gä)	198-99	42°28'N	6°03'W
Astoria, Or., U.S. (ăs-tō′rĭ-*å*)	112-13	46°11'N	123°50'W
Astove, i., Sey.	264-65	10°06'S	47°45'E
Astrakhan', Russia (äs-trå-kän′)	186-87	46°21'N	48°02'E
Asunción, nat. cap., Para. (ä-sōōn-syōn′)	168-69	25°16'S	57°39'W
Asuncion Island, i., N. Mar. Is.	280-81	19°42'N	145°24'E
Aswân, Egypt	268b	24°05'N	32°55'E
Aswan High Dam, d., Egypt	268b	23°59'N	32°53'E
Asyût, Egypt	268b	27°11'N	31°11'E
Atacama, Desierto de, des., Chile (dĕ-syĕ′r-tô-dĕ-ä-tä-kå′mä)	168-69	20°08'S	69°53'W
Atacama, Puna de, plat., S.A. (pōō′nä-dĕ-ä-tä-kå′mä)	168-69	23°46'S	67°45'W
Atacama, Salar de, pl., Chile (sȧ-lȧr′dĕ-ȧtä-kå′mä)	168-69	23°33'S	68°14'W
Atacama Desert, des., Chile (ä-tä-kä′mä) *see* Atacama, Desierto de	168-69	20°08'S	69°53'W
Ataco, Col. (ä-tä′kō)	163c	3°35'N	75°23'W
Atafu, at., Tok.	280-81	8°33'S	172°30'W
Atakpamé, Togo	260-61	7°32'N	1°09'E
Atamyrat, Turkmen.	232-33	37°50'N	65°13'E
Aṭar, Maur. (ä-tär′)	258-59	20°32'N	13°02'W
Atascadero, Ca., U.S. (ăt-ăs-k*å*-dâ′rō)	118-19	35°30'N	120°39'W
Atasū, Kaz.	226	48°41'N	71°39'E
Atbara, stm., Afr. *see* 'Aṭbarah	266	17°40'N	33°58'E
'Aṭbarah, Sudan (ät′bȧ-rä)	266	17°42'N	33°59'E
'Aṭbarah, stm., Afr.	266	17°40'N	33°58'E
Atbasar, Kaz. (ät′bä-sär′)	226	51°48'N	68°21'E
Atchafalaya, stm., La., U.S. (ăch-*å*-f*å*-lī′*å*)	124-25	29°28'N	91°16'W
Atchafalaya Bay, b., La., U.S. (ăch-*å*-f*å*-lī′*å* bā)	124-25	29°27'N	91°23'W
Atchara Autonomis Respublika, state, Geor.	227	41°40'N	42°00'E
Atchison, Ks., U.S. (ăch′ĭ-s*ŭ*n)	120-21	39°34'N	95°07'W
Athabasca, Ab., Can. (ăth-*å*-băs′k*å*)	132-33	54°42'N	113°17'W
Athabasca, stm., Ab., Can. (ăth-*å*-băs′k*å*)	130-31	58°40'N	110°55'W
Athabasca, Lake, lk., Can. (lāk ăth-*å*-băs′k*å*)	130-31	59°07'N	109°59'W
Athens, Al., U.S. (ăth′ĕnz)	124-25	34°48'N	86°58'W
Athens, Ga., U.S. (ăth′ĕnz)	124-25	33°57'N	83°22'W
Athens, Oh., U.S. (ăth′ĕnz)	116-17	39°20'N	82°06'W
Athens, Tn., U.S. (ăth′ĕnz)	124-25	35°27'N	84°36'W
Athens, Tx., U.S. (ăth′ĕnz)	122-23	32°13'N	95°51'W
Athens, nat. cap., Grc. (ăth′ĕnz)	200-01	37°59'N	23°44'E
Atherton, Austl.	277	17°16'S	145°30'E
Athi, stm., Kenya (ä′tē)	262-63	2°58'S	38°31'E
Athína, nat. cap., Grc. (ä-thē′nĕ) *see* Athens	200-01	37°59'N	23°44'E
Athos, Mount, mtn., Grc.	200-01	40°09'N	24°19'E
Athy, Ire. (*å*-thī)	190-91	52°60'N	6°59'W
Ati, Chad.	258-59	13°12'N	18°19'E

Feature (Pronunciation)	Page	Lat.	Long.
Atikokan, On., Can.	136-37	48°45'N	91°37'W
Atikonak Lake, lk., Nf., Can.	130-31	52°38'N	64°30'W
Atiu, i., Cook Is.	280-81	20°02'S	158°07'W
Atka, Russia	218-19	60°45'N	151°46'E
Atka Island, i., Ak., U.S. (ăt'kȧ ī'lȧnd)	126a	52°15'N	174°08'W
Atkarsk, Russia (åt-kärsk')	186-87	51°53'N	45°00'E
Atkinson, Ne., U.S. (ăt'kĭn-sŭn)	114-15	42°32'N	98°59'W
Atlanta, Ga., U.S. (ăt-lăn'tȧ)	124-25	33°46'N	84°25'W
Atlanta, Il., U.S. (ăt-lăn'tȧ)	116-17	40°16'N	89°14'W
Atlanta, Tx., U.S. (ăt-lăn'tȧ)	120-21	33°07'N	94°11'W
Atlantic, Ia., U.S. (ăt-lăn'tĭk)	114-15	41°24'N	95°01'W
Atlantic City, N.J., U.S. (ăt-lăn'tĭk sĭ'tē)	116-17	39°21'N	74°26'W
Atlantic Ocean, oc., (ăt-lăn'tĭk ōshŭn)	20-21	5°0'S	25°00'W
Atlantis, S. Afr.	264-65	33°32'S	18°29'E
Atlas Mountains, mts., Afr. (ăt'lăs moun'tĭnz)	258-59	33°0'N	2°00'W
Atlin, B.C., Can.	128-29	59°34'N	133°41'W
Atmore, Al., U.S. (ăt'mōr)	124-25	31°01'N	87°30'W
Atoka, Ok., U.S. (ȧ-tō'kȧ)	120-21	34°23'N	96°08'W
Atoui, Khaṭṭ, stm., Afr. (ȧ-tōō-ē')	258-59	20°03'N	15°58'W
Atoyac, stm., Mex. (ä-tô-yäk')	146-47	18°07'N	98°44'W
Atoyac de Álvarez, Mex. (ä-tô-yäk'dā äl'vä-rāz)	146-47	17°11'N	100°25'W
Atrak, stm., Asia	232-33	37°26'N	53°53'E
Atrato, stm., Col. (ä-trä'tō)	164-65	8°11'N	76°56'W
Atrek, stm., Asia see Atrak	232-33	37°26'N	53°53'E
Aṭ-Ṭā'if, Sau. Ar.	266	21°16'N	40°25'E
Attapu, Laos	246-47	14°48'N	106°51'E
Attawapiskat, On., Can.	128-29	52°56'N	82°25'W
Attawapiskat, stm., On., Can. (ăt'ȧ-wȧ-pĭs'kăt)	130-31	52°57'N	82°18'W
Attawapiskat Lake, lk., On., Can.	134-35	52°17'N	87°55'W
Attica, N.Y., U.S. (ăt'ĭ-kȧ)	116-17	42°52'N	78°17'W
Attleboro, Ma., U.S. (ăt''l-bŭr-ô)	116-17	41°57'N	71°17'W
Attu Island, i., Ak., U.S. (ăt-tōō' ī'lȧnd)	126a	52°55'N	173°00'E
Atuel, stm., Arg.	171	36°16'S	66°51'W
Åtvidaberg, Swe. (ôt-vē'dȧ-bĕrgh)	192-93	58°12'N	16°00'E
Atyraū, Kaz.	186-87	47°07'N	51°55'E
Aubagne, Fr. (ō-bän'y')	196-97	43°17'N	5°34'E
Aubry Lake, lk., N.T., Can.	130-31	67°22'N	126°27'W
Auburn, Al., U.S. (ô'bŭrn)	124-25	32°37'N	85°29'W
Auburn, Il., U.S. (ô'bŭrn)	120-21	39°35'N	89°45'W
Auburn, In., U.S. (ô'bŭrn)	116-17	41°22'N	85°03'W
Auburn, Ma., U.S. (ô'bŭrn)	116-17	42°12'N	71°50'W
Auburn, Ne., U.S. (ô'bŭrn)	120-21	40°23'N	95°51'W
Auburn, N.Y., U.S.	116-17	42°56'N	76°34'W
Auburn, Wa., U.S. (ô'bŭrn)	112-13	47°19'N	122°12'W
Aubusson, Fr. (ō-bü-sôɴ')	196-97	45°57'N	2°10'E
Auch, Fr. (ōsh)	196-97	43°39'N	0°35'E
Auckland, N.Z. (ôk'lănd)	278	36°51'S	174°45'E
Auckland Islands, is., N.Z. (ôk'lănd ī'lȧndz)	287	50°46'S	166°12'E
Audubon, Ia., U.S. (ô'dŏŏ-bŏn)	114-15	41°43'N	94°56'W
Augathella, Austl. (ôr'gȧ'thĕ-lȧ)	276	25°48'S	146°34'E
Augrabies Falls National Park, n.p., S. Afr.	264-65	28°35'S	20°19'E
Augsburg, Ger. (ouks'bŏŏrgh)	194-95	48°23'N	10°53'E
Augusta, Austl.	270-71	34°19'S	115°10'E
Augusta, Ar., U.S. (ô-gŭs'tȧ)	124-25	35°17'N	91°22'W
Augusta, Ga., U.S. (ô-gŭs'tȧ)	124-25	33°28'N	81°59'W
Augusta, Ky., U.S. (ô-gŭs'tȧ)	116-17	38°46'N	84°00'W
Augusta, Me., U.S.	117a	44°19'N	69°47'W
Augusta, Wi., U.S. (ô-gŭs'tȧ)	114-15	44°41'N	91°07'W
Augustus Island, i., Austl.	272-73	15°21'S	124°31'E
Auob, stm., Afr. (ä'wŏb)	264-65	26°26'S	20°37'E
Aurangābād, India (ou-rŭŋ-gä-bäd')	234-35	19°53'N	75°20'E
Aurillac, Fr. (ō-rē-yȧk')	196-97	44°55'N	2°26'E
Aurora, On., Can. (ô-rō'rȧ)	136-37	43°60'N	79°28'W
Aurora, Co., U.S. (ô-rō'rȧ)	120-21	39°44'N	104°52'W
Aurora, Il., U.S. (ô-rō'rȧ)	116-17	41°45'N	88°20'W
Aurora, In., U.S. (ô-rō'rȧ)	116-17	39°03'N	84°55'W
Aurora, Mn., U.S. (ô-rō'rȧ)	114-15	47°32'N	92°14'W
Aurora, Mo., U.S. (ô-rō'rȧ)	120-21	36°58'N	93°43'W
Aurora, Ne., U.S. (ô-rō'rȧ)	114-15	40°52'N	98°01'W
Au Sable, stm., Mi., U.S. (ô-sä'b'l)	116-17	44°24'N	83°19'W
Aussig, Czech Rep. see Ústí nad Labem	194-95	50°40'N	14°02'E
Austin, Mn., U.S. (ôs'tĭn)	114-15	43°40'N	92°58'W
Austin, Nv., U.S. (ôs'tĭn)	118-19	39°31'N	117°07'W
Austin, Tx., U.S. (ôs'tĭn)	122-23	30°16'N	97°42'W
Austin, Lake, lk., Austl.	272-73	27°40'S	118°00'E
Australia, nation, Oc. (ôs-trā'lĭ-ȧ)	270-71	25°0'S	135°00'E
Australian Capital Territory, state, Austl. (ôs-trā'lĭ-ăn)	276	35°30'S	149°00'E

Feature (Pronunciation)	Page	Lat.	Long.
Austral Islands, is., Fr. Poly. see Tubuaï, Îles	280-81	23°0'S	150°00'W
Austria, nation, Eur. (ôs'trĭ-ȧ)	174-75	47°20'N	13°20'E
Austvågøya, i., Nor.	184-85	68°21'N	14°38'E
Autlán de Navarro, Mex.	146-47	19°47'N	104°22'W
Autun, Fr. (ō-tŭɴ')	196-97	46°57'N	4°18'E
Auxerre, Fr. (ō-sâr')	196-97	47°48'N	3°34'E
Auyán Tepuy, mtn., Ven.	164-65	5°51'N	62°25'W
Auzangate, Nevado, mtn., Peru	170	13°48'S	71°14'W
Ava, Mo., U.S. (ā'vȧ)	120-21	36°57'N	92°40'W
Avallon, Fr. (ȧ-vȧ-lôɴ')	196-97	47°30'N	3°54'E
Avalon, Ca., U.S. (ăv'ȧ-lŏn)	118-19	33°20'N	118°19'W
Avaré, Braz.	172	23°07'S	48°55'W
Aveiro, Port. (ä-vā'rŏ)	198-99	40°38'N	8°39'W
Avellaneda, Arg. (ä-vĕl-yä-nā'dhä)	173	29°07'S	59°40'W
Avellaneda, Arg. (ä-vĕl-yä-nā'dhä)	173	34°40'S	58°23'W
Avellino, Italy (ä-vĕl-lē'nō)	200-01	40°55'N	14°47'E
Avesta, Swe. (ä-vĕs'tä)	192-93	60°09'N	16°11'E
Avezzano, Italy (ä-vät-sä'nō)	200-01	42°02'N	13°25'E
Avignon, Fr. (ȧ-vē-nyôɴ')	196-97	43°57'N	4°49'E
Ávila, Spain (ä-vē-lä)	198-99	40°40'N	4°42'W
Avilés, Spain (ä-vē-lās')	198-99	43°34'N	5°54'W
Avon, Ct., U.S. (ā'vŏn)	116-17	41°49'N	72°50'W
Avon, stm., Eng., U.K. (ā'vŭn)	190-91	50°44'N	1°47'W
Avon, stm., Eng., U.K. (ā'vŭn)	190-91	51°59'N	2°11'W
Avon Park, Fl., U.S. (ā'vŏn pärk')	125a	27°36'N	81°30'W
Avranches, Fr. (ȧ-vränsh')	196-97	48°41'N	1°22'W
Awaji-shima, i., Japan	245	34°21'N	134°51'E
Āwasa, Eth.	269d	6°56'N	38°32'E
Āwash, stm., Eth.	262-63	11°09'N	41°41'E
Awjilah, Libya	188-89	29°08'N	21°18'E
Axiós, stm., Eur.	200-01	40°31'N	22°43'E
Ax-les-Thermes, Fr. (äks'lā tĕrm')	196-97	42°43'N	1°51'E
Ayacucho, Arg. (ä-yä-kōō'chō)	173	37°09'S	58°29'W
Ayacucho, Peru	170	13°08'S	74°14'W
Ayaköz, Kaz.	226	47°57'N	80°26'E
Ayamonte, Spain (ä-yä-mô'n-tĕ)	198-99	37°13'N	7°24'W
Ayan, Russia (ȧ-yän')	218-19	56°26'N	138°13'E
Ayan, stm., Russia	218-19	70°10'N	95°47'E
Ayapel, Col.	164-65	8°19'N	75°09'W
Ayaviri, Peru (ä-yä-vē'rē)	170	14°53'S	70°35'W
Aydar, stm., Eur. (ī-där') see Aidar	202-03	48°44'N	39°16'E
Aydar Kŭl, lk., Uzb.	232-33	40°49'N	67°20'E
Ayden, N.C., U.S. (ā'dĕn)	124-25	35°28'N	77°25'W
Aydın, Tur. (āīy-dĕn)	200-01	37°51'N	27°50'E
Ayers Rock, mtn., Austl. see Uluru	272-73	25°20'S	130°60'E
Ayeyarwady, stm., Mya.	220-21	15°51'N	95°05'E
Aylesbury, Eng., U.K. (ālz'bĕr-ĭ)	190-91	51°49'N	0°50'W
Aylmer Lake, lk., N.T., Can. (āl'mēr lāk)	130-31	64°05'N	108°30'W
Ayon, Ostrov, i., Russia (ôs-trôf' ī-ôn')	218-19	69°47'N	168°41'E
Ayr, Austl.	277	19°34'S	147°24'E
Ayr, Scot., U.K. (âr)	190-91	55°28'N	4°38'W
Ayvalık, Tur. (āīy-wä-lĭk)	200-01	39°20'N	26°42'E
Azaouagh, stm., Afr.	258-59	15°30'N	3°18'E
Azärbaycan, nation, Asia see Azerbaijan	227	40°30'N	47°30'E
Azare, Nig.	260-61	11°41'N	10°11'E
Azemmour, Mor. (ȧ-zē-mōōr')	269a	33°18'N	8°21'W
Azerbaidzhan, nation, Asia see Azerbaijan	227	40°30'N	47°30'E
Azerbaijan, nation, Asia (ä'zĕr-bä-ē-jän')	227	40°30'N	47°30'E
Azogues, Ec. (ä-sō'gās)	170	2°44'S	78°50'W
Azores, is., Port. (ā'zōrz) (ȧ-zōrz')	199c	38°30'N	28°00'W
Azov, Russia (ȧ-zôf') (ä-zôf)	202-03	47°07'N	39°26'E
Azov, Sea of, s., Eur. (sē ŭv ä-zôf')	202-03	46°0'N	36°00'E
Azovs'ke more, s., Eur. (ȧ-zôf'skô-yĕ mô'rĕ) see Azov, Sea of	202-03	46°0'N	36°00'E
Azovskoye More, s., Eur. see Azov, Sea of	202-03	46°0'N	36°00'E
Azraq, Al-Baḥr al-, stm., Afr. see Blue Nile	254	15°38'N	32°30'E
Azrou, Mor.	269a	33°26'N	5°12'W
Aztec, N.M., U.S. (ăz'tĕk)	118-19	36°49'N	108°00'W
Azua, Dom. Rep. (ä'swä)	142-43	18°27'N	70°44'W
Azuaga, Spain (ä-thwä'gä)	198-99	38°15'N	5°40'W
Azuero, Península de, pen., Pan.	150	7°40'N	80°35'W
Azul, Arg. (ä-sōōl')	173	36°47'S	59°52'W
Az-Zahrān, Sau. Ar. see Dhahran	230-31	26°18'N	50°08'E
Az-Zarqā', Jord.	228-29	32°03'N	36°05'E
Az-Zāwiyah, Libya	188-89	32°47'N	12°44'E
Az-Zilfī, Sau. Ar.	266	26°18'N	44°49'E

B

Feature (Pronunciation)	Page	Lat.	Long.
Ba'qūbah, Iraq	228-29	33°45'N	44°40'E
Baaba, Île, i., N. Cal.	279g	20°03'S	163°58'E
Babadayhan, Turkmen.	232-33	37°42'N	60°24'E
Babaeski, Tur. (bä'bä-ĕs'kĭ)	200-01	41°26'N	27°06'E
Babahoyo, Ec. (bä-bä-ō'yō)	170	1°48'S	79°32'W
Babar, Pulau, i., Indon. (pōō-lou bä'bär)	224-25	7°55'S	129°45'E
Babeldaob, i., Palau	280-81	7°30'N	134°35'E
Bab el Mandeb, strt.,	266	12°44'N	43°21'E
Babelthuap, i., Palau see Babeldaob	280-81	7°30'N	134°35'E
Babi, Pulau, i., Indon.	246-47	2°05'N	96°39'E
Babine Lake, lk., B.C., Can. (băb'ēn lāk)	132-33	54°45'N	126°00'W
Bābol, Iran	232-33	36°33'N	52°41'E
Babrujsk, Bela.	202-03	53°08'N	29°14'E
Babuyan Island, i., Phil.	250a	19°32'N	121°57'E
Babuyan Islands, is., Phil. (bä-bōō-yän' ī'lȧndz)	250a	19°15'N	121°40'E
Bacabal, Braz.	166-67	4°14'S	44°47'W
Bacan, Pulau, i., Indon.	248-49	0°35'S	127°30'E
Bacău, Rom.	202-03	46°34'N	26°55'E
Bac Bo, Vinh, b., Asia see Tonkin, Gulf of	246-47	20°0'N	108°00'E
Back, stm., Nu., Can. (băk)	130-31	67°09'N	95°21'W
Bačka Palanka, Serb. (bäch'kä pälän-kä)	200-01	45°15'N	19°24'E
Bac Lieu, Viet.	246-47	9°17'N	105°43'E
Bac Ninh, Viet. (bäk'nēn'')	246-47	21°12'N	106°05'E
Baco, Mount, mtn., Phil. (mount bä'kō)	250	12°49'N	121°10'E
Bacolod, Phil. (bä-kō'lōd)	250	10°40'N	122°57'E
Badajoz, Spain (bȧ-dhä-hōth')	198-99	38°53'N	6°58'W
Badalona, Spain (bȧ-dhä-lō'nä)	198-99	41°28'N	2°16'E
Bad Axe, Mi., U.S. (băd' ăks)	116-17	43°48'N	82°59'W
Baden-Baden, Ger. (bä'dĕn-bä'dĕn)	194-95	48°46'N	8°14'E
Bad Hersfeld, Ger. (bät hĕrsh'fĕlt)	194-95	50°52'N	9°42'E
Bad Kissingen, Ger. (bät kĭs'ĭng-ĕn)	194-95	50°12'N	10°05'E
Badlands, hills, U.S. (băd' lănds)	114-15	46°14'N	103°37'W
Badlands National Park, n.p., S.D., U.S. (băd' lănds năsh'ŭn-ăl pärk)	114-15	43°50'N	102°21'W
Bad Reichenhall, Ger. (bät rī'kĕn-häl)	194-95	47°44'N	12°53'E
Bad River Indian Reservation, ind. res., Wi., U.S. (băd rĭv'ĕr ĭn'dĭ-ăn rĕ-sĕr-vā'shĕn)	114-15	46°33'N	90°40'W
Bad Tölz, Ger. (bät tûltz)	194-95	47°45'N	11°35'E
Badu Island, i., Austl.	277	10°07'S	142°08'E
Baena, Spain (bä-ā'nä)	198-99	37°37'N	4°19'W
Bafatá, Gui.-B.	260-61	12°10'N	14°41'W
Baffin Bay, b., N.A. (băf'ĭn bā)	86	73°0'N	66°00'W
Baffin Bugt, b., N.A. see Baffin Bay	86	73°0'N	66°00'W
Baffin Island, i., Nu., Can. (băf'ĭn ī'lȧnd)	86	68°0'N	70°00'W
Bafia, Camrn.	260-61	4°45'N	11°16'E
Bafing, stm., Afr.	260-61	13°47'N	10°50'W
Bafoussam, Camrn.	260-61	5°29'N	10°25'E
Bāfq, Iran (bäfk)	232-33	31°35'N	55°24'E
Bafra, Tur. (bäf'rä)	186-87	41°34'N	35°53'E
Bafwasende, D.R.C.	262-63	1°06'N	27°16'E
Bagan, hist., Mya.	246-47	21°13'N	94°54'E
Bagansiapiapi, Indon.	246-47	2°09'N	100°48'E
Bagata, D.R.C.	262-63	3°44'S	17°59'E
Bagdad, nat. cap., Iraq see Baghdād	228-29	33°21'N	44°25'E
Bagé, Braz.	173	31°19'S	54°06'W
Baghdād, nat. cap., Iraq (bȧgh-dȧd') (băg'dăd)	228-29	33°21'N	44°25'E
Bagheria, Italy (bä-gȧ-rē'ä)	200-01	38°05'N	13°30'E
Baghlān, Afg.	232-33	36°08'N	68°42'E
Bagley, Mn., U.S. (băg'lē)	114-15	47°30'N	95°23'W
Bagnères-de-Bigorre, Fr. (băn-yâr'dē-bē-gor')	196-97	43°04'N	0°09'E
Bago, Mya.	246-47	17°20'N	96°29'E
Bagoé, stm., Afr. (bȧ-gō'ā)	260-61	12°35'N	6°34'W
Baguio, Phil. (bä-gē-ō')	250	16°25'N	120°36'E
Bahama, Canal Viejo de, strt., N.A. see Old Bahama Channel	142-43	22°40'N	78°41'W
Bahama Islands, is., Bah.	20-21	24°15'N	76°00'W
Bahamas, nation, N.A. (bȧ-hā'mȧs)	140-41	24°15'N	76°00'W
Baharampur, India	234-35	24°06'N	88°15'E
Bahāwalpur, Pak. (bŭ-hä'wŭl-pōōr)	232-33	29°23'N	71°40'E
Bäherden, Turkmen.	232-33	38°26'N	57°26'E
Bahia, Braz. (bä-ē'ä) see Salvador	166-67	12°59'S	38°30'W
Bahia, state, Braz.	166-67	12°0'S	42°00'W
Bahía, Islas de la, is., Hond. (ē's-läs-dĕ-lä-bä-ē'ä)	149	16°20'N	86°30'W
Bahía Blanca, Arg. (bä-ē'ä blän'kä)	173	38°43'S	62°17'W

n-sing; ŋ-baŋk; ɴ-nasalized n; nŏd; cŏmmit; ōld; ôbey; ôrder; oi-boil; fōōd; ŏŏ-as oo in foot; ou-out; s-soft; sh-dish; th-thin; pūre; ûnite; ûrn; stŭd; circŭs; ü-as in French tu; '-indeterminate vowel.

Feature (Pronunciation)	Page	Lat.	Long.
Bahía de Caráquez, Ec. (bä-e´ä dä kä-rä´kĕz)	170	0°37′S	80°26′W
Bahir Dar, Eth.	266	11°35′N	37°24′E
Bahraich, India	234-35	27°35′N	81°36′E
Bahrain, nation, Asia (bä-rān´)	230-31	26°0′N	50°30′E
Baḩrānī, Ḩālat al-, i., U.A.E.	230-31	24°28′N	54°21′E
Baia Mare, Rom. (bä´yä mä´rā)	194-95	47°39′N	23°35′E
Baicheng, China	240-41	45°37′N	122°51′E
Baidoa, Som.	262-63	3°07′N	43°39′E
Baie-Comeau, Qc., Can.	138-39	49°13′N	68°10′W
Baie-Saint-Paul, Qc., Can. (bā-săn´-pôl´)	138-39	47°27′N	70°30′W
Baikal, Lake, lk., Russia (lăk bī-käl´)	218-19	53°0′N	107°40′E
Baile Átha Cliath, nat. cap., Ire. see Dublin	190-91	53°21′N	6°15′W
Bailén, Spain (bä-ê-lān´)	198-99	38°06′N	3°46′W
Băilești, Rom. (bă-ĭ-lĕsh´tê)	200-01	44°02′N	23°21′E
Bailong, stm., China	238-39	32°21′N	105°43′E
Bainbridge, Ga., U.S. (bān´brĭj)	124-25	30°54′N	84°34′W
Bainbridge, Oh., U.S. (bān´brĭj)	116-17	39°14′N	83°16′W
Baiquan, China (bī-chyuäŋ)	240-41	47°36′N	126°05′E
Baird, Tx., U.S. (bârd)	120-21	32°24′N	99°23′W
Bairin Zuoqi, China	240-41	43°59′N	119°23′E
Bairnsdale, Austl. (bârnz´dāl)	276	37°50′S	147°37′E
Baishuijiang, China	238-39	33°29′N	106°02′E
Baitou Shan, mtn., Asia see Paektu-san	243	41°59′N	128°07′E
Baiyin, China	240-41	36°33′N	104°12′E
Baja, Hung. (bŏ´yö)	194-95	46°11′N	18°57′E
Baja California, state, Mex. (bä-hä kăl-ĭ-fôr´nĭ-à)	144-45	30°0′N	115°00′W
Baja California, pen., Mex. (bä-hä kăl-ĭ-fôr´nĭ-à)	144-45	27°53′N	113°28′W
Baja California Norte, state, Mex. see Baja California	144-45	30°0′N	115°00′W
Baja California Sur, state, Mex. (bä-hä kăl-ĭ-fôr´nĭ-à sōōr´)	144-45	26°0′N	112°00′W
Bajestān, Iran	232-33	34°31′N	58°11′E
Bājil, Yemen	266	15°04′N	43°17′E
Bajo Boquete, Pan.	150	8°47′N	82°26′W
Baker, Ca., U.S. (bā´kẽr)	118-19	35°16′N	116°04′W
Baker, La., U.S. (bā´kẽr)	124-25	30°35′N	91°10′W
Baker, Mt., U.S. (bā´kẽr)	112-13	46°22′N	104°17′W
Baker, Or., U.S. (bā´kẽr)	112-13	44°47′N	117°50′W
Baker, Mount, vol., Wa., U.S. (mount bā´kẽr)	112-13	48°47′N	121°49′W
Baker Island, dep., Oc. (bā´kẽr ī´lănd)	280-81	0°15′N	176°27′W
Baker Island, i., Oc.	280-81	0°12′N	176°29′W
Baker Lake, Nu., Can.	128-29	64°18′N	95°55′W
Baker Lake, lk., Nu., Can. (bā´kẽr lăk)	130-31	64°10′N	95°30′W
Bakersfield, Ca., U.S. (bā´kẽrz-fēld)	118-19	35°22′N	119°01′W
Bakhmach, Ukr. (bàĸ-mäch´)	202-03	51°11′N	32°50′E
Bākhtarān, Iran see Kermānshāh	228-29	34°18′N	47°04′E
Bakhtegān, Daryācheh-ye, lk., Iran	230-31	29°20′N	54°05′E
Bakı, nat. cap., Azer. see Baku	227	40°23′N	49°51′E
Bakony, mts., Hung. (bà-kōn´y´)	194-95	47°01′N	17°45′E
Bakoy, stm., Afr. (bà-kô´ē)	258-59	13°48′N	10°49′W
Baku, nat. cap., Azer. (bà-kōō´)	227	40°23′N	49°51′E
Bakwanga, D.R.C. see Mbuji-Mayi	262-63	6°08′S	23°39′E
Balabac, Selat, strt., Asia see Balabac Strait	250	7°35′N	117°00′E
Balabac Island, i., Phil. (bä´lä-bäk ī´lănd)	250	7°57′N	117°01′E
Balabac Strait, strt., Asia (bä´lä-bäk strāt)	250	7°35′N	117°00′E
Balabanovo, Russia (bà-là-bä´nô-vô)	202-03	55°11′N	36°40′E
Balabio, Île, i., N. Cal.	279g	20°07′S	164°11′E
Bālāghāt, India	234-35	21°49′N	80°11′E
Balaguer, Spain (bä-lä-gĕr´)	198-99	41°48′N	0°49′E
Balakovo, Russia (bà´là-kô´vô)	186-87	52°01′N	47°47′E
Balambangan, Pulau, i., Malay.	248-49	7°16′N	116°55′E
Balāngīr, India	234-35	20°43′N	83°30′E
Balaözen, stm., Eur.	186-87	48°58′N	49°38′E
Balashov, Russia (bá´là-shôf)	186-87	51°32′N	43°10′E
Balasore, India (bä-là-sōr´) see Bāleshwar	234-35	21°29′N	86°57′E
Balassagyarmat, Hung. (bô´lôsh-shô-dyôr´môt)	194-95	48°04′N	19°19′E
Balaton, lk., Hung. (bô´lô-tôn)	194-95	46°50′N	17°45′E
Balayan, Phil. (bä-lä-yän´)	250	13°57′N	120°44′E
Balbina, Represa, res., Braz.	166-67	1°20′S	59°40′W
Balcarce, Arg. (bäl-kär´sā)	173	37°51′S	58°15′W
Baldock Lake, lk., Mb., Can.	134-35	56°33′N	97°57′W
Baldwinsville, N.Y., U.S. (bôld´wĭns-vĭl)	116-17	43°10′N	76°20′W
Baldy Peak, mtn., Az., U.S. (bôl´dê pēk)	118-19	33°55′N	109°35′W
Bâle, Switz. see Basel	194-95	47°33′N	7°36′E
Baleares, Islas, is., Spain see Balearic Islands	198-99	39°29′N	3°01′E
Balearic Islands, is., Spain (băl-ē-ă´-rĭk ī´lăndz)	198-99	39°29′N	3°01′E
Balears, Illes, is., Spain see Balearic Islands	198-99	39°29′N	3°01′E
Baler, Phil. (bä-lar´)	250	15°46′N	121°34′E
Bāleshwar, India	234-35	21°29′N	86°57′E
Baley, Russia (bál-yā´)	222-23	51°34′N	116°38′E
Bali, i., Indon. (bä´lē)	248-49	8°20′S	115°00′E
Bali, Laut, s., Indon. see Bali Sea	248-49	7°45′S	115°30′E
Balıkesir, Tur. (balĭk´ĭysĭr)	200-01	39°39′N	27°53′E
Balikpapan, Indon. (bä´lēk-pä´pän)	248-49	1°16′S	116°50′E
Balimo, Pap. N. Gui.	277	8°03′S	142°56′E
Balin, China	240-41	48°19′N	122°19′E
Balintang Channel, strt., Phil. (bä-lĭn-täng´ chăn´ĕl)	250a	19°59′N	121°51′E
Bali Sea, s., Indon. (bä´lē sē)	248-49	7°45′S	115°30′E
Balkanabat, Turkmen.	232-33	39°31′N	54°23′E
Balkan Peninsula, pen., Eur. (bôl´kăn pĕ-nĭn´sūlă)	200-01	44°0′N	23°00′E
Balkaria, state, Russia	227	43°30′N	43°30′E
Balkh, Afg. (bälk)	232-33	36°45′N	66°54′E
Balkh, stm., Afg.	232-33	36°38′N	66°56′E
Balkhash, Kaz. see Balqash	226	46°51′N	74°58′E
Balkhash, Lake, lk., Kaz. (lăk bal-käsh´)	226	46°0′N	74°00′E
Ballarat, Austl. (băl´ă-răt)	276	37°34′S	143°51′E
Ballard, Lake, lk., Austl. (lăk băl´ărd)	272-73	29°27′S	120°55′E
Ballia, India	234-35	25°45′N	84°09′E
Ballina, Austl. (băl-ĭ-nä´)	276	28°52′S	153°33′E
Ballinasloe, Ire. (băl´ĭ-nà-slō´)	190-91	53°20′N	8°14′W
Ballinger, Tx., U.S. (băl´ĭn-jẽr)	122-23	31°44′N	99°57′W
Ballston Spa, N.Y., U.S. (bôls´tŭn spä´)	116-17	43°00′N	73°51′W
Balonne, stm., Austl. (băl-ōn´)	276	28°37′S	148°10′E
Balqash, Kaz.	226	46°51′N	74°58′E
Balqash köli, lk., Kaz. see Balkhash, Lake	226	46°0′N	74°00′E
Balranald, Austl. (băl´-răn-ăld)	276	34°38′S	143°33′E
Balsas, Braz. (bäl´säs)	166-67	7°33′S	46°04′W
Balsas, stm., Braz.	166-67	7°14′S	44°34′W
Balsas, stm., Mex.	146-47	17°54′N	102°11′W
Balta, Ukr. (bál´tà)	202-03	47°56′N	29°40′E
Baltasar Brum, Ur.	173	30°42′S	57°19′W
Bălți, Mol.	202-03	47°46′N	27°55′E
Baltic Sea, s., Eur. (bôl´tĭk sē)	192-93	57°0′N	19°00′E
Baltijas jūra, s., Eur. see Baltic Sea	192-93	57°0′N	19°00′E
Baltijos jūra, s., Eur. see Baltic Sea	192-93	57°0′N	19°00′E
Baltim, Egypt (bál-tēm´)	268b	31°34′N	31°05′E
Baltimore, Md., U.S. (bôl´tĭ-mŏr)	116-17	39°17′N	76°37′W
Baltiysk, Russia (bäl-tēysk´)	194-95	54°39′N	19°55′E
Baltiyskoye More, s., Eur. see Baltic Sea	192-93	57°0′N	19°00′E
Bałtyckie, Morze, s., Eur. see Baltic Sea	192-93	57°0′N	19°00′E
Balūchestān, hist. reg., Asia see Baluchistan	232-33	28°0′N	63°00′E
Baluchistan, hist. reg., Asia	232-33	28°0′N	63°00′E
Baluchistān, hist. reg., Asia (bà-lò-chĭ-stän´) see Baluchistan	232-33	28°0′N	63°00′E
Balykchy, Kyrg.	226	42°28′N	76°12′E
Balyqshy, Kaz.	186-87	47°05′N	51°54′E
Bam, Iran	230-31	29°07′N	58°21′E
Bama, Nig.	260-61	11°32′N	13°41′E
Bamako, nat. cap., Mali (bä-mā-kō´)	258-59	12°39′N	7°60′W
Bambari, C.A.R. (bäm-bà-rē)	262-63	5°46′N	20°39′E
Bamberg, Ger. (bäm´bĕrgh)	194-95	49°54′N	10°54′E
Bamberg, S.C., U.S. (băm´bûrg)	124-25	33°18′N	81°02′W
Bamenda, Camrn.	260-61	5°58′N	10°09′E
Bāmīān, Afg.	232-33	34°50′N	67°49′E
Bamingui, stm., C.A.R.	262-63	8°34′N	19°04′E
Bamingui-Bangoran, Parc National du, n.p., C.A.R.	262-63	7°54′N	19°42′E
Bampūr, Iran (bŭm-pōōr´)	230-31	27°11′N	60°26′E
Banaba, i., Kir.	280-81	0°52′S	169°33′E
Banaras, India see Vārānasi	234-35	25°20′N	82°59′E
Banās, stm., India (băn-äs´)	234-35	25°55′N	76°44′E
Banâs, Râs, c., Egypt	266	23°54′N	35°47′E
Ban Bat, Viet.	246-47	13°13′N	108°40′E
Bancroft, On., Can. (băn´krŏft)	136-37	45°03′N	77°51′W
Bānda, India (bän´dä)	234-35	25°29′N	80°20′E
Banda, Laut, s., Indon. see Banda Sea	224-25	5°0′S	128°00′E
Banda Aceh, Indon.	246-47	5°33′N	95°19′E
Bandama, stm., C. Iv.	260-61	5°08′N	4°60′W
Bandar, India see Machilīpatnam	236	16°11′N	81°09′E
Bandar 'Abbās, Iran	230-31	27°11′N	56°16′E
Bandar Beheshtī, Iran	230-31	25°18′N	60°38′E
Bandar-e Anzalī, Iran	227	37°28′N	49°28′E
Bandar-e Khomeynī, Iran	228-29	30°26′N	49°06′E
Bandar-e Lengeh, Iran	230-31	26°34′N	54°53′E
Bandar-e Pahlavī, Iran see Bandar-e Anzalī	227	37°28′N	49°28′E
Bandar-e Shāhpūr, Iran see Bandar-e Khomeynī	228-29	30°26′N	49°06′E
Bandar-e Torkeman, Iran	232-33	36°54′N	54°04′E
Bandar Lampung, Indon.	246-47	5°26′S	105°16′E
Bandar Maharani, Malay. (bän-där´ mä-hä-rä´nê) see Muar	246-47	2°02′N	102°34′E
Bandar Penggaram, Malay. see Batu Pahat	246-47	1°51′N	102°56′E
Bandar Seri Begawan, nat. cap., Bru. (bän´där sĕr´ē bŭ´gä-wän)	248-49	4°56′N	114°56′E
Banda Sea, s., Indon. (bän´-dä sē) (băn´-dà sē)	224-25	5°0′S	128°00′E
Bandeira, Pico da, mtn., Braz. (pē´kô dä bän dā´rä)	172	20°26′S	41°47′W
Bandelier National Monument, n.p., N.M., U.S. (băn-dĕ-lēr´ năsh´ŭn-ăl mŏn´ū-mĕnt)	118-19	35°45′N	106°20′W
Bandera, Arg.	173	28°53′S	62°16′W
Banderas, Bahía de, b., Mex. (bä-ē´ä dĕ bän-dĕ´räs)	146-47	20°38′N	105°27′W
Bandiantaolehai, China	240-41	41°47′N	104°05′E
Bandırma, Tur. (bän-dĭr´mà)	200-01	40°22′N	27°59′E
Ban Don, Thai. see Surat Thani	246-47	9°06′N	99°18′E
Bandon, Or., U.S. (băn´dŭn)	112-13	43°07′N	124°23′W
Bandundu, D.R.C.	262-63	3°16′S	17°21′E
Bandung, Indon.	248-49	6°54′S	107°36′E
Banes, Cuba (bä´nās)	142-43	20°58′N	75°42′W
Banff, Ab., Can. (bănf)	132-33	51°10′N	115°36′W
Banff National Park, n.p., Ab., Can. (bănf năsh´ŭn-ăl pärk)	132-33	51°38′N	116°22′W
Banfora, Burkina	260-61	10°39′N	4°45′W
Bangalore, India (băŋ´gá´lôr) see Bengalūru	236	12°59′N	77°36′E
Bangassou, C.A.R. (bäŋ-gä-sōō´)	262-63	4°44′N	22°49′E
Banggai, Indon.	248-49	1°35′S	123°30′E
Banggai, Kepulauan, is., Indon. (băng-gī´)	248-49	1°30′S	123°15′E
Banggai, Pulau, i., Indon.	248-49	1°37′S	123°33′E
Banggi, Pulau, i., Malay.	248-49	7°16′N	117°10′E
Banggong Co, lk., Asia (bäŋ-gôŋ tswo) see Pangong Tso	234-35	33°45′N	78°42′E
Banghāzī, Libya (bĕn-gä´zē)	258-59	32°07′N	20°04′E
Bangka, Pulau, i., Indon. (pōō-lou bäŋ´kȧ)	246-47	2°15′S	106°00′E
Bangka, Selat, strt., Indon.	246-47	2°20′S	105°45′E
Bangkalan, Indon. (bäng-kȧ-län´)	248-49	7°02′S	112°45′E
Bangkok, nat. cap., Thai. (bäɴ´kŏk´)	246-47	13°45′N	100°31′E
Bangkulu, Pulau, i., Indon.	248-49	1°50′S	123°06′E
Bangladesh, nation, Asia (bän´-glă-dĕsh´)	206-07	24°0′N	90°00′E
Bangor, N. Ire., U.K. (băŋ´ŏr)	190-91	54°39′N	5°41′W
Bangor, Wales, U.K. (băŋ´ŏr)	190-91	53°14′N	4°09′W
Bangor, Me., U.S.	117a	44°48′N	68°47′W
Bangor, Mi., U.S. (băn´gẽr)	116-17	42°19′N	86°06′W
Bangor, Pa., U.S. (băn´gẽr)	116-17	40°51′N	75°13′W
Bangued, Phil. (bän-gād´)	250	17°36′N	120°37′E
Bangui, nat. cap., C.A.R. (bäɴ-gē´)	262-63	4°22′N	18°33′E
Bangweulu, Lake, lk., Zam. (lăk băng-wê-ōō´lōō)	264-65	11°04′S	29°53′E
Ban Hat Yai, Thai. see Hat Yai	246-47	7°01′N	100°28′E
Ban Houayxay, Laos	246-47	20°15′N	100°24′E
Baní, Dom. Rep. (bä´-nê)	142-43	18°17′N	70°19′W
Banifing, stm., Mali	260-61	14°29′N	4°13′W
Banja Luka, Bos. (bän-yä-lōō´kȧ)	200-01	44°46′N	17°12′E
Banjarbaru, Indon.	248-49	3°24′S	114°50′E
Banjarmasin, Indon. (bän-jẽr-mä´sĕn)	248-49	3°20′S	114°36′E
Banjul, nat. cap., Gam. (bôn-jōōl´)	260-61	13°27′N	16°36′W
Banks, Îles, is., Vanuatu see Banks Islands	279g	13°25′S	167°42′E
Banks Island, i., B.C., Can. (bănks ī´lănd)	132-33	53°25′N	130°10′W
Banks Island, i., N.T., Can. (bănks ī´lănd)	86	73°15′N	121°30′W
Banks Islands, is., Vanuatu	279g	13°25′S	167°42′E
Banks Peninsula, pen., N.Z. (bănks pĕ-nĭn´sūlă)	278	43°45′S	173°00′E
Banks Strait, strt., Austl. (bănks strāt)	276	40°40′S	148°07′E
Banningville, D.R.C. see Bandundu	262-63	3°16′S	17°21′E
Bannu, Pak.	232-33	32°59′N	70°37′E
Baños, Ec. (bä´-nyōs)	170	1°24′S	78°25′W

Feature (Pronunciation)	Page	Lat.	Long.
Bānswāra, India	234-35	23°33'N	74°27'E
Bantaeng, Indon.	248-49	5°32'S	119°56'E
Bantayan Island, i., Phil.	250	11°13'N	123°44'E
Bantry, Ire. (băn´trĭ)	190-91	51°41'N	9°27'W
Banyak, Kepulauan, is., Indon.	246-47	2°10'N	97°15'E
Banyuwangi, Indon. (bän-jô-wäŋ´gē)	248-49	8°12'S	114°21'E
Baode, China	240-41	39°01'N	111°05'E
Baoding, China (bou-dĭŋ)	240-41	38°51'N	115°29'E
Baoji, China (bou-jyē)	238-39	34°23'N	107°09'E
Bao Lac, Viet.	246-47	11°33'N	107°47'E
Baoshan, China (bou-shän)	238-39	25°07'N	99°10'E
Baoting, China	238-39	18°38'N	109°47'E
Baotou, China (bou-tō)	240-41	40°35'N	109°58'E
Baoying, China (bou-yĭŋ)	238-39	33°14'N	119°19'E
Baquedano, Chile	168-69	23°20'S	69°50'W
Bar, Mont.	200-01	42°05'N	19°06'E
Baraboo, Wi., U.S. (bâr´ȧ-bōō)	116-17	43°28'N	89°44'W
Baracoa, Cuba (bä-rä-kō´ä)	142-43	20°21'N	74°30'W
Baradero, Arg. (bä-rä-dĕ´ŏ)	173	33°48'S	59°31'W
Baragaon, India *see* Nālanda	234-35	25°08'N	85°24'E
Barahona, Dom. Rep. (bä-rä-ô´nä)	142-43	18°12'N	71°06'W
Baranavičy, Bela.	194-95	53°08'N	26°01'E
Baranof Island, i., Ak., U.S. (bä-rä´nôf ī´lȧnd)	126	57°0'N	135°00'W
Barão de Melgaço, Braz. (bä-roun-dĕ-mĕl-gä´sô)	168-69	16°13'S	55°58'W
Barat Daya, Kepulauan, is., Indon.	248-49	7°25'S	128°00'E
Baraya, Col. (bä-rá´yä)	163c	3°10'N	75°04'W
Barbacena, Braz. (bär-bä-sä´nȧ)	172	21°13'S	43°45'W
Barbacoas, Col. (bär-bä-kō´äs)	164-65	1°41'N	78°09'W
Barbados, nation, N.A. (bär-bā´dōz)	140-41	13°10'N	59°32'W
Barbas, Cap, c., W. Sah.	258-59	22°18'N	16°40'W
Barbastro, Spain (bär-bäs´trō)	198-99	42°02'N	0°08'E
Barberton, Oh., U.S. (bär´bēr-tŭn)	116-17	41°02'N	81°36'W
Barbosa, Col. (bär-bô´-sȧ)	163c	6°26'N	75°20'W
Barboursville, W.V., U.S. (bär´bērs-vĭl)	116-17	38°25'N	82°18'W
Barbuda, i., Antig. (bär-bōō´dȧ)	143b	17°38'N	61°48'W
Barcaldine, Austl. (bär´kôl-dīn)	277	23°34'S	145°18'E
Barce, Libya *see* Al-Marj	188-89	32°30'N	20°53'E
Barcelona, Spain (bär-thå-lō´nä)	198-99	41°24'N	2°10'E
Barcelona, Ven. (bär-så-lō´nä)	163b	10°08'N	64°41'W
Barcelos, Braz. (bär-sĕ´lôs)	166-67	0°59'S	62°54'W
Barcelos, Port. (bär-thĕ´lōs)	198-99	41°32'N	8°37'W
Barcoo, stm., Austl.	277	25°12'S	142°50'E
Bardaï, Chad	258-59	21°22'N	16°59'E
Barddhamān, India	234-35	23°14'N	87°52'E
Bardsey Island, i., Wales, U.K. (bärd´sē ī´lȧnd)	190-91	52°46'N	4°48'W
Bardstown, Ky., U.S. (bärds´toun)	116-17	37°49'N	85°28'W
Bardwell, Ky., U.S. (bärd´wĕl)	124-25	36°52'N	89°01'W
Bareilly, India	234-35	28°21'N	79°25'E
Barentsevo More, s., Eur. *see* Barents Sea	218-19	74°0'N	36°00'E
Barentshavet, s., Eur. *see* Barents Sea	218-19	74°0'N	36°00'E
Barents Sea, s., Eur. (bä´rĕnts sē)	218-19	74°0'N	36°00'E
Barentu, Erit. (bä-rĕn´tōō)	266	15°07'N	37°35'E
Barfleur, Pointe de, c., Fr. (pwănt´ dē bȧr-flûr´)	196-97	49°42'N	1°16'W
Barguzin, stm., Russia	218-19	53°25'N	108°59'E
Bar Harbor, Me., U.S. (bär här´bēr)	117a	44°23'N	68°13'W
Bari, Italy (bä´rē)	200-01	41°07'N	16°52'E
Bariloche, Arg. *see* San Carlos de Bariloche	171	41°09'S	71°18'W
Barinas, Ven. (bä-rē´näs)	164-65	8°38'N	70°13'W
Baring, Cape, c., N.T., Can. (kāp bâr´ĭng)	130-31	70°03'N	117°16'W
Bāripada, India	234-35	21°56'N	86°43'E
Barisāl, Bngl.	234-35	22°42'N	90°22'E
Barito, stm., Indon. (bä-rē´tō)	248-49	3°20'S	114°32'E
Barkley, Lake, res., U.S.	124-25	36°44'N	87°57'W
Barkley Sound, strt., B.C., Can.	132-33	48°53'N	125°20'W
Barkly Tableland, plat., Austl. (bär´klē tā´-bĕl-lănd)	272-73	18°0'S	136°00'E
Barkol, China (bär-kûl)	240-41	43°33'N	93°02'E
Bar-le-Duc, Fr. (bär-lē-dük´)	196-97	48°47'N	5°10'E
Barlee, Lake, lk., Austl. (lăk bär-lē´)	272-73	29°10'S	119°30'E
Barletta, Italy (bär-lĕt´tä)	200-01	41°19'N	16°17'E
Bārmer, India	234-35	25°44'N	71°24'E
Barnaul, Russia (bär-nä-ōl´)	226	53°22'N	83°45'E
Barnesville, Ga., U.S. (bärnz´vĭl)	124-25	33°03'N	84°10'W
Barnesville, Mn., U.S. (bärnz´vĭl)	114-15	46°39'N	96°25'W
Barnsley, Eng., U.K. (bärnz´lĭ)	190-91	53°34'N	1°29'W
Barnstaple, Eng., U.K. (bärn´stā-p'l)	190-91	51°05'N	4°03'W
Barnwell, S.C., U.S. (bärn´wĕl)	124-25	33°14'N	81°22'W
Baro, stm., Afr.	262-63	8°26'N	33°13'E
Baroda, India (bär-rō´dä) *see* Vadodara	234-35	22°18'N	73°11'E
Barpeta, India	234-35	26°19'N	91°00'E
Barqah, hist. reg., Libya *see* Cyrenaica	258-59	31°0'N	22°30'E
Barquisimeto, Ven. (bär-kē-sē-mā´tō)	164-65	10°05'N	69°19'W
Barra, Braz. (bär´rä)	166-67	11°05'S	43°09'W
Barra, Ponta da, c., Moz.	264-65	23°48'S	35°31'E
Barra do Corda, Braz. (bär´rä dô cōr-dä)	166-67	5°31'S	45°15'W
Barra Falsa, Ponta da, c., Moz.	264-65	22°54'S	35°34'E
Barra Mansa, Braz. (bär´rä män´sä)	172	22°33'S	44°10'W
Barranca, Peru	170	10°45'S	77°46'W
Barrancabermeja, Col. (bär-räŋ´kä-bēr-mā´hä)	164-65	7°04'N	73°51'W
Barrancas, Ven.	164-65	8°44'N	62°11'W
Barranquilla, Col. (bär-rän-kēl´yä)	164-65	10°59'N	74°48'W
Barras, Braz. (bȧ´r-räs)	166-67	4°15'S	42°18'W
Barre, Vt., U.S. (băr´ē)	116-17	44°12'N	72°30'W
Barreiras, Braz. (bär-rā´räs)	166-67	12°09'S	45°01'W
Barreiro, Port. (bär-rĕ´ê-rò)	198-99	38°39'N	9°04'W
Barreiros, Braz.	163d	8°49'S	35°12'W
Barren, Nosy, is., Madag.	264-65	18°30'S	43°53'E
Barretos, Braz. (bär-rā´tōs)	172	20°34'S	48°34'W
Barrhead, Ab., Can. (băr´ĭd)	132-33	54°07'N	114°24'W
Barrie, On., Can. (băr´ĭ)	136-37	44°23'N	79°41'W
Barrington Tops, mtn., Austl. (bă-rĕng-tŏn tŏps)	276	32°0'S	151°28'E
Barron, Wi., U.S. (băr´ŭn)	114-15	45°24'N	91°51'W
Barrow, Ak., U.S. (băr´ō)	126	71°18'N	156°38'W
Barrow, stm., Ire. (bȧ-rå)	190-91	52°17'N	7°00'W
Barrow, Point, c., Ak., U.S. (point băr´ō)	126	71°23'N	156°29'W
Barrow Creek, Austl.	270-71	21°31'S	133°55'E
Barrow Island, i., Austl.	272-73	20°48'S	115°23'E
Bārsi, India	236	18°14'N	75°42'E
Barstow, Ca., U.S. (bär´stō)	118-19	34°54'N	117°01'W
Bartica, Guy. (bär´tĭ-kȧ)	164-65	6°24'N	58°37'W
Bartın, Tur. (bär´tĭn)	186-87	41°38'N	32°21'E
Bartle Frere, mtn., Austl. (bärt´'l frēr´)	277	17°23'S	145°49'E
Bartlesville, Ok., U.S. (bär´tlz-vĭl)	120-21	36°45'N	95°59'W
Bartlett, Tn., U.S. (bärt´lĕt)	124-25	35°13'N	89°52'W
Bartlett, Tx., U.S. (bärt´lĕt)	122-23	30°48'N	97°26'W
Bartoszyce, Pol. (bär-tō-shĭ´tsȧ)	194-95	54°15'N	20°49'E
Bartow, Fl., U.S. (bär´tō)	125a	27°54'N	81°50'W
Bārū, stm., Afr. *see* Baro	262-63	8°26'N	33°13'E
Barú, Volcán, vol., Pan.	150	8°48'N	82°33'W
Baruun-Urt, Mong.	240-41	46°41'N	113°17'E
Barwon, stm., Austl. (bär´wŭn)	276	30°08'S	147°23'E
Barycz, stm., Pol. (bä´rĭch)	194-95	51°41'N	16°15'E
Barysaŭ, Bela.	192-93	54°14'N	28°31'E
Barysh, Russia	186-87	53°39'N	47°07'E
Basankusu, D.R.C. (bä-sän-kōō´sōō)	262-63	1°13'N	19°48'E
Basarabia, hist. reg., Eur. *see* Bessarabia	202-03	46°53'N	28°44'E
Basco, Phil.	250a	20°27'N	121°58'E
Bascuñán, Cabo, c., Chile	168-69	28°52'S	71°29'W
Basel, Switz. (bä´z'l)	194-95	47°33'N	7°36'E
Basey, Phil.	250	11°18'N	125°04'E
Bashi Channel, strt., Asia (băsh´ē chăn´ĕl)	222-23	22°0'N	121°00'E
Bashkortostan, state, Russia	186-87	54°0'N	56°00'E
Bashtanka, Ukr. (bȧsh-tän´kȧ)	202-03	47°24'N	32°27'E
Basilaki Island, i., Pap. N. Gui.	277	10°37'S	150°60'E
Basilan, Phil. *see* Isabela	250	6°41'N	121°58'E
Basilan Island, i., Phil.	250	6°34'N	122°03'E
Basin, Wy., U.S. (bā´s'n)	112-13	44°23'N	108°03'W
Basingstoke, Eng., U.K. (bă´zĭng-stōk)	190-91	51°16'N	1°07'W
Başkale, Tur. (bäsh-kä´lĕ)	227	38°03'N	44°01'E
Baskatong, Réservoir, res., Qc., Can.	136-37	46°46'N	75°50'W
Basoko, D.R.C. (bȧ-sō´kō)	262-63	1°14'N	23°36'E
Bas Qafqaz Silsilasi, mts., *see* Caucasus Mountains	227	42°38'N	45°00'E
Basra, Iraq (bŭs´-rä)	228-29	30°30'N	47°48'E
Bassano, Ab., Can. (bäs-sän´ō)	132-33	50°47'N	112°27'W
Bassein, Mya. *see* Pathein	246-47	16°46'N	94°44'E
Basse-Terre, i., Guad. (bȧs´ târ´)	143b	16°10'N	61°40'W
Basse-Terre, nat. cap., Guad. (bȧs´ târ´)	143b	16°00'N	61°43'W
Basseterre, nat. cap., St. K./N.	143b	17°18'N	62°44'W
Bassett, Ne., U.S. (băs´sĕt)	114-15	42°35'N	99°32'W
Bassett, Va., U.S. (băs´sĕt)	124-25	36°46'N	79°59'W
Bass Strait, strt., Austl. (băs strāt)	276	39°20'S	145°30'E
Båstad, Swe. (bô´stät)	192-93	56°25'N	12°52'E
Bastia, Fr. (bäs´tē-ä)	184-85	42°42'N	9°27'E
Bastrop, La., U.S. (băs´trŭp)	120-21	32°47'N	91°55'W
Bastrop, Tx., U.S. (băs´trŭp)	122-23	30°06'N	97°18'W
Basutoland, nation, Afr. *see* Lesotho	253	29°30'S	28°30'E
Bata, Eq. Gui. (bä´tä)	260-61	1°52'N	9°46'E
Batabanó, Golfo de, b., Cuba (gôl-fô-dĕ-bä-tä-bȧ´nô)	142-43	22°15'N	82°30'W
Batagay, Russia	218-19	67°40'N	134°40'E
Batagay-Alyta, Russia	218-19	67°48'N	130°25'E
Batala, India	234-35	31°49'N	75°13'E
Batang, China (bä-täŋ)	238-39	30°02'N	99°11'E
Batangafo, C.A.R.	262-63	7°19'N	18°18'E
Batangas, Phil. (bä-tän´gäs)	250	13°46'N	121°04'E
Batan Island, i., Phil.	250	13°15'N	124°00'E
Batan Island, i., Phil.	250a	20°27'N	121°59'E
Batan Islands, is., Phil. (bä-tän´ ī´lȧndz)	250a	20°30'N	121°50'E
Batanta, Pulau, i., Indon.	224-25	0°52'S	130°39'E
Batavia, Il., U.S. (bȧ-tā´vĭ-ȧ)	116-17	41°51'N	88°19'W
Batavia, Oh., U.S. (bȧ-tā´vĭ-ȧ)	116-17	39°05'N	84°11'W
Batavia, nat. cap., Indon. *see* Jakarta	248-49	6°11'S	106°50'E
Bataysk, Russia (bȧ-tīsk´)	202-03	47°08'N	39°46'E
Bătdâmbâng, Camb. (bȧt-tȧm-bāng´)	246-47	13°06'N	103°12'E
Batesville, Ar., U.S. (bāts´vĭl)	124-25	35°47'N	91°39'W
Batesville, In., U.S. (bāts´vĭl)	116-17	39°18'N	85°13'W
Batesville, Ms., U.S. (bāts´vĭl)	124-25	34°19'N	89°57'W
Bath, N.B., Can. (bȧth)	138-39	46°31'N	67°35'W
Bath, Eng., U.K. (bȧth)	190-91	51°23'N	2°22'W
Bathurst, Austl. (băth´ŭrst)	276	33°25'S	149°35'E
Bathurst, N.B., Can.	138-39	47°36'N	65°39'W
Bathurst, nat. cap., Gam. *see* Banjul	260-61	13°27'N	16°36'W
Bathurst, Cape, c., N.T., Can. (kāp bath´-ûrst)	130-31	70°35'N	128°00'W
Bathurst Island, i., Austl. (bȧth´ŭrst ī´lȧnd)	272-73	11°37'S	130°17'E
Batna, Alg. (băt´nä)	269b	35°34'N	6°11'E
Baton Rouge, La., U.S. (băt´ŭn rōōzh´)	124-25	30°27'N	91°08'W
Battambang, Camb. *see* Bătdâmbâng	246-47	13°06'N	103°12'E
Batticaloa, Sri L.	236	7°43'N	81°42'E
Battle, stm., Can.	130-31	52°42'N	108°15'W
Battle Creek, Mi., U.S. (băt´'l krēk´)	116-17	42°19'N	85°11'W
Battle Creek, Ne., U.S. (băt´'l krēk´)	114-15	42°00'N	97°36'W
Battle Harbour, Nf., Can. (băt´'l här´bēr)	128-29	52°16'N	55°35'W
Battle Mountain, Nv., U.S. (băt´'l moun´tĭn)	112-13	40°39'N	116°55'W
Batu, mtn., Eth.	269d	6°55'N	39°46'E
Batu, Kepulauan, is., Indon. (bä´tōō)	246-47	0°18'S	98°28'E
Batuata, Pulau, i., Indon.	248-49	6°12'S	122°42'E
Batumi, Geor. (bŭ-tōō´mē)	227	41°39'N	41°39'E
Batu Pahat, Malay.	246-47	1°51'N	102°56'E
Baturaja, Indon.	246-47	4°08'S	104°09'E
Baturité, Braz.	166-67	4°20'S	38°53'W
Baubau, Indon.	248-49	5°28'S	122°37'E
Bauchi, Nig. (bȧ-ōō´chē)	260-61	10°19'N	9°50'E
Bauld, Cape, c., Nf., Can.	138-39	51°38'N	55°26'W
Bauru, Braz. (bou-rōō´)	172	22°19'S	49°04'W
Bauska, Lat. (bou´skȧ)	192-93	56°24'N	24°14'E
Bautzen, Ger. (bout´sĕn)	194-95	51°11'N	14°26'E
Bavaria, hist. reg., Ger. (bȧ-vâ-rĭ-ȧ)	194-95	48°30'N	11°30'E
Bawdwin, Mya.	246-47	23°07'N	97°15'E
Bawean, Pulau, i., Indon. (pōō-lou bä´vē-än)	248-49	5°46'S	112°40'E
Bawiti, Egypt	188-89	28°21'N	28°52'E
Bawku, Ghana	260-61	11°04'N	0°15'W
Baxley, Ga., U.S. (băks´lĭ)	124-25	31°47'N	82°21'W
Bay, Laguna de, lk., Phil. (lä-gōō´nä dā bä´ē)	250	14°23'N	121°15'E
Bayamo, Cuba (bä-yä´mō)	142-43	20°23'N	76°38'W
Bayan Har Shan, mts., China	238-39	33°47'N	97°54'E
Bayanhongor, Mong.	240-41	46°10'N	100°42'E
Bayano, Lago, res., Pan.	150	9°12'N	78°44'W
Bayan Obo, China	240-41	41°59'N	110°08'E
Bayard, Ne., U.S. (bā´ērd)	114-15	41°46'N	103°20'W
Bayard, N.M., U.S. (bā´ērd)	118-19	32°46'N	108°08'W
Bayburt, Tur. (bä´ī-bȯrt)	227	40°16'N	40°14'E
Bay City, Mi., U.S. (bā sĭ´tē)	116-17	43°36'N	83°53'W
Bay City, Tx., U.S. (bā sĭ´tĭ)	122-23	28°59'N	95°58'W
Baydhabo, Som. *see* Baidoa	262-63	3°07'N	43°39'E
Baydrag, stm., Mong.	240-41	45°37'N	99°15'E
Bayern, hist. reg., Ger. (bī´ērn) *see* Bavaria	194-95	48°30'N	11°30'E
Bayeux, Fr. (bȧ-yû´)	196-97	49°17'N	0°42'W
Baykal, Ozero, lk., Russia *see* Baikal, Lake	218-19	53°0'N	107°40'E
Baykit, Russia (bī-kēt´)	218-19	61°41'N	96°25'E
Baykonur, Kaz. *see* Bayqongyr	226	45°38'N	63°18'E
Bay Minette, Al., U.S. (bā´mĭn-ĕt´)	124-25	30°53'N	87°47'W
Bayombong, Phil. (bä-yȯm-bŏng´)	250	16°29'N	121°09'E
Bayonne, Fr. (bȧ-yŏn´)	196-97	43°30'N	1°29'W
Bayonne, N.J., U.S. (bā-yōn´)	116-17	40°40'N	74°07'W

n-sing; ŋ-baŋk; ɴ-nasalized n; nŏd; cŏmmit; ōld; ôbey; ôrder; oi-boil; fōōd; ŏŏ-as oo in foot; ou-out; s-soft; sh-dish; th-thin; pūre; ûnite; ûrn; stŭd; circŭs; ü-as in French tu; ´-indeterminate vowel.

Feature (Pronunciation)	Page	Lat.	Long.
Bayou Bodcau Reservoir, res., La., U.S. (bī′yōō bŏd′kō rĕ′sĕr-vwär)	**120-21**	32°48′N	93°27′W
Bayqongyr, Kaz.	**226**	45°38′N	63°18′E
Bayram-Ali, Turkmen.	**232-33**	37°37′N	62°10′E
Bayreuth, Ger. (bī-roit′)	**194-95**	49°57′N	11°34′E
Bay Roberts, Nf., Can. (bā rŏb′ērts)	**138-39**	47°35′N	53°18′W
Bayrūt, nat. cap., Leb. *see* Beirut	**228-29**	33°53′N	35°30′E
Bays, Lake of, lk., On., Can. (lāk ŭv bās)	**136-37**	45°15′N	78°60′W
Bay Saint Louis, Ms., U.S. (bā′ sānt lōō′ĭs)	**124-25**	30°19′N	89°20′W
Bayt Laḥm, W.B. *see* Bethlehem	**228-29**	31°43′N	35°12′E
Baytown, Tx., U.S. (bā′town)	**122-23**	29°44′N	94°59′W
Baza, Spain (bä′thä)	**198-99**	37°29′N	2°46′W
Bazaruto, Ilha do, i., Moz. (ē′lä-dô-bä-zä-rōō′tō)	**264-65**	21°41′S	35°28′E
Be, Nosy, i., Madag.	**264-65**	13°20′S	48°15′E
Beach, N.D., U.S. (bēch)	**114-15**	46°55′N	104°00′W
Beachy Head, c., Eng., U.K. (bēchē hĕd)	**190-91**	50°45′N	0°15′E
Beacon, N.Y., U.S. (bē′kŭn)	**116-17**	41°31′N	73°58′W
Beagle Gulf, b., Austl.	**272-73**	12°0′S	130°20′E
Beardmore, On., Can.	**134-35**	49°36′N	87°58′W
Beardstown, Il., U.S. (bērds′toun)	**120-21**	40°01′N	90°26′W
Bear Island, i., Nor. (bâr ī′lănd) *see* Bjørnøya	**218-19**	74°27′N	19°02′E
Bear Lake, lk., Mb., Can. (bâr lāk)	**134-35**	55°08′N	96°00′W
Bear Lake, lk., U.S. (bâr lāk)	**112-13**	42°0′N	111°20′W
Bear River Range, mts., U.S. (bâr rĭv′ēr rānj)	**112-13**	41°29′N	111°41′W
Beata, Cabo, c., Dom. Rep. (kȧ′bô-bĕ-ä′tä)	**142-43**	17°37′N	71°25′W
Beata, Isla, i., Dom. Rep.	**142-43**	17°35′N	71°31′W
Beatrice, Ne., U.S. (bē′ȧ-trĭs)	**120-21**	40°16′N	96°45′W
Beatton, stm., B.C., Can.	**132-33**	56°05′N	120°22′W
Beatty, Nv., U.S. (bēt′ė)	**118-19**	36°55′N	116°45′W
Beattyville, Ky., U.S. (bēt′ė-vĭl)	**116-17**	37°34′N	83°43′W
Beaucaire, Fr. (bō-kâr′)	**196-97**	43°48′N	4°39′E
Beaufort, Malay.	**248-49**	5°22′N	115°44′E
Beaufort, N.C., U.S. (bō′fōrt)	**124-25**	34°43′N	76°40′W
Beaufort, S.C., U.S. (bō′fōrt)	**124-25**	32°24′N	80°44′W
Beaufort Sea, s., N.A. (bō′fōrt sē)	**86**	73°0′N	140°00′W
Beaufort West, S. Afr.	**264-65**	32°21′S	22°35′E
Beaumont, Tx., U.S. (bō′mŏnt)	**122-23**	30°05′N	94°08′W
Beaune, Fr. (bōn)	**196-97**	47°01′N	4°50′E
Beauport, Qc., Can. (bō-pôr′)	**136-37**	46°52′N	71°10′W
Beaupré, Qc., Can.	**138-39**	47°02′N	70°54′W
Beausejour, Mb., Can.	**134-35**	50°04′N	96°31′W
Beauvais, Fr. (bō-vĕ′)	**196-97**	49°26′N	2°05′E
Beaver, Ok., U.S. (bē′vēr)	**120-21**	36°49′N	100°31′W
Beaver, Ut., U.S. (bē′vēr)	**118-19**	38°17′N	112°38′W
Beaver, stm., Can.	**130-31**	55°26′N	107°47′W
Beaver Dam, Wi., U.S. (bē′vēr dăm)	**116-17**	43°27′N	88°50′W
Beaverhead Mountains, mts., U.S. (bē′vēr-hĕd moun′tĭnz)	**112-13**	44°58′N	113°26′W
Beaver Island, i., Mi., U.S. (bē′vēr ī′lănd)	**116-17**	45°40′N	85°32′W
Beaverton, Or., U.S. (bē′vēr-tŭn)	**112-13**	45°29′N	122°49′W
Beāwar, India	**234-35**	26°06′N	74°19′E
Bečej, Serb. (bĕc′chā)	**200-01**	45°37′N	20°03′E
Béchar, Alg.	**258-59**	31°37′N	2°14′W
Bechuanaland, nation, Afr. *see* Botswana	**253**	22°0′S	24°00′E
Beckley, W.V., U.S. (bĕk′lĭ)	**116-17**	37°48′N	81°11′W
Bedford, Qc., Can. (bĕd′fērd)	**136-37**	45°07′N	72°59′W
Bedford, In., U.S. (bĕd′fērd)	**116-17**	38°51′N	86°29′W
Bedford, Va., U.S. (bĕd′fērd)	**124-25**	37°20′N	79°31′W
Beebe, Ar., U.S. (bē′bē)	**124-25**	35°04′N	91°53′W
Beecroft Head, c., Austl. (bē′krûft hĕd)	**276**	35°00′S	150°51′E
Beersheba, Isr.	**228-29**	31°14′N	34°48′E
Be'er Sheva', Isr. (bēr-shē′bȧ) *see* Beersheba	**228-29**	31°14′N	34°48′E
Beeville, Tx., U.S. (bē′vĭl)	**122-23**	28°24′N	97°45′W
Bega, Austl. (bā′gȧ)	**276**	36°41′S	149°51′E
Beggs, Ok., U.S. (bĕgz)	**120-21**	35°45′N	96°05′W
Behbahān, Iran	**230-31**	30°35′N	50°14′E
Bei, stm., China (bā)	**238-39**	23°09′N	112°49′E
Bei'an, China (bā-än)	**240-41**	48°14′N	126°31′E
Beibu Wan, b., Asia *see* Tonkin, Gulf of	**246-47**	20°0′N	108°00′E
Beida, Libya *see* Al-Bayḍā'	**188-89**	32°45′N	21°37′E
Beihai, China (bā-hī)	**238-39**	21°27′N	109°05′E
Beijing, state, China	**240-41**	40°15′N	116°30′E
Beijing, nat. cap., China (bā-jyĭŋ)	**240-41**	39°55′N	116°22′E
Beipan, stm., China	**238-39**	25°01′N	106°04′E
Beipiao, China	**240-41**	41°48′N	120°46′E
Beira, Moz. (bā′rȧ)	**264-65**	19°50′S	34°50′E
Beirut, nat. cap., Leb. (bā-rōōt′)	**228-29**	33°53′N	35°30′E
Beitbridge, Zimb.	**264-65**	22°12′S	30°01′E
Beja, Port. (bā′zhä)	**198-99**	38°01′N	7°52′W
Béja, Tun.	**184-85**	36°44′N	9°11′E
Bejaïa, Alg.	**269b**	36°45′N	5°04′E
Bejuco, Pan. (bĕ-κōō′kō)	**150**	8°36′N	79°53′W
Bekdash, Turkmen. *see* Karabogaz	**186-87**	41°32′N	52°35′E
Békés, Hung. (bā′kāsh)	**194-95**	46°46′N	21°08′E
Békéscsaba, Hung. (bā′kāsh-chô′bô)	**194-95**	46°40′N	21°05′E
Bekobod, Uzb.	**232-33**	40°13′N	69°11′E
Bela, Pak.	**232-33**	26°13′N	66°18′E
Bela-Bela, S. Afr.	**269c**	24°53′S	28°19′E
Bela Crkva, Serb. (bĕ′lä tsĕrk′vä)	**200-01**	44°54′N	21°26′E
Belaga, Malay.	**248-49**	2°43′N	113°47′E
Belarus, nation, Eur. (byĕ-lä-rōōs′) (bē-lă-rōōs′)	**174-75**	53°50′N	28°00′E
Belau, nation, Oc. *see* Palau	**280-81**	5°0′N	137°00′E
Bela Vista, Braz.	**168-69**	22°06′S	56°32′W
Belaya, stm., Russia (byĕ′lȧ-yȧ)	**227**	45°06′N	39°29′E
Belaya, stm., Russia (byĕ′lȧ-yȧ)	**186-87**	55°47′N	54°04′E
Belaya Tserkov, Ukr. *see* Bila Tserkva	**202-03**	49°48′N	30°08′E
Belcher Islands, is., Nu., Can. (bĕl′chēr ī′lăndz)	**130-31**	56°20′N	79°30′W
Belding, Mi., U.S. (bĕl′dĭng)	**116-17**	43°06′N	85°13′W
Belebey, Russia (byĕ′lĕ-bâ′ĭ)	**186-87**	54°06′N	54°08′E
Belém, Braz. (bā-lĕɴ)	**166-67**	1°27′S	48°29′W
Belén, Para. (bā-lān′)	**168-69**	23°28′S	57°15′W
Belen, N.M., U.S. (bĕ-lån′)	**118-19**	34°40′N	106°46′W
Belëv, Russia (byĕl′yĕf)	**202-03**	53°48′N	36°09′E
Belfast, S. Afr.	**269c**	25°43′S	30°04′E
Belfast, N. Ire., U.K. (bĕl′făst)	**190-91**	54°36′N	5°56′W
Belfort, Fr. (bā-fôr′)	**196-97**	47°38′N	6°51′E
Belgaum, India	**236**	15°51′N	74°31′E
België, nation, Eur. *see* Belgium	**174-75**	50°50′N	4°00′E
Belgique, nation, Eur. *see* Belgium	**174-75**	50°50′N	4°00′E
Belgium, nation, Eur. (bĕl′jĭ-ŭm)	**174-75**	50°50′N	4°00′E
Belgorod, Russia (byĕl′gŭ-rut)	**202-03**	50°37′N	36°35′E
Belgrade, nat. cap., Serb. (bĕl′grăd)	**200-01**	44°50′N	20°28′E
Belhaven, N.C., U.S. (bĕl′hā-vĕn)	**124-25**	35°32′N	76°37′W
Beliliou, i., Palau	**280-81**	7°00′N	134°15′E
Belitung, i., Indon.	**246-47**	2°50′S	107°55′E
Belize, nation, N.A. (bĕ-lēz′)	**85**	17°15′N	88°45′W
Belize, stm., Belize (bĕ-lēz′)	**148**	17°30′N	88°11′W
Belize City, Belize (bĕ-lēz′ sĭ′tē)	**148**	17°30′N	88°11′W
Bel'kovskiy, Ostrov, i., Russia (ôs-trôf′ byĕl-kôf′skĭ)	**218-19**	75°32′N	135°44′E
Bella Bella, B.C., Can.	**132-33**	52°09′N	128°07′W
Bella Coola, B.C., Can.	**132-33**	52°21′N	126°46′W
Bellary, India (bĕl-lä′rē)	**236**	15°09′N	76°55′E
Bella Unión, Ur. (bĕ′l-yȧ-ōō-nyô′n)	**173**	30°15′S	57°35′W
Bella Vista, Arg. (bā′lyȧ vēs′tȧ)	**168-69**	27°02′S	65°18′W
Bella Vista, Arg. (bā′lyȧ vēs′tȧ)	**173**	28°30′S	59°02′W
Bellavista, Peru	**170**	7°04′S	76°35′W
Belle Bay, b., Nf., Can. (bĕl bā)	**138-39**	47°36′N	55°18′W
Bellefontaine, Oh., U.S. (bel-fŏn′tăn)	**116-17**	40°21′N	83°45′W
Belle Fourche, S.D., U.S. (bĕl′ fōōrsh′)	**114-15**	44°40′N	103°51′W
Belle Glade, Fl., U.S. (bĕl glād)	**125a**	26°42′N	80°40′W
Belle Isle, Strait of, strt., Nf., Can.	**130-31**	51°36′N	56°28′W
Belle Plaine, Ia., U.S. (bĕl plān′)	**114-15**	41°54′N	92°17′W
Belleville, On., Can. (bĕl′vĭl)	**136-37**	44°10′N	77°23′W
Belleville, Il., U.S. (bĕl′vĭl)	**120-21**	38°31′N	89°59′W
Belleville, Ks., U.S. (bĕl′vĭl)	**120-21**	39°49′N	97°38′W
Bellevue, Ia., U.S. (bĕl′vū)	**114-15**	42°15′N	90°25′W
Bellevue, Id., U.S. (bĕl′vū)	**112-13**	43°28′N	114°16′W
Bellevue, Ne., U.S. (bĕl′vū)	**114-15**	41°09′N	95°55′W
Bellevue, Oh., U.S. (bĕl′vū)	**116-17**	41°16′N	82°50′W
Bellevue, Wa., U.S. (bĕl′vū)	**112-13**	47°37′N	122°12′W
Belley, Fr. (bĕ-lē′)	**196-97**	45°46′N	5°41′E
Bellingham, Wa., U.S. (bĕl′ĭng-hăm)	**112-13**	48°46′N	122°29′W
Bellingshausen Sea, s., Ant. (bĕl′ĭngz houz′n sē)	**287**	71°0′S	85°00′W
Bellinzona, Switz. (bĕl-ĭn-tsō′nä)	**194-95**	46°11′N	9°01′E
Bell Island, i., Nf., Can. (bĕl ī′lănd)	**138-39**	50°44′N	55°35′W
Bello, Col. (bĕ′l-yô)	**163c**	6°20′N	75°34′W
Bell Peninsula, pen., Nu., Can. (bĕl pĕ-nĭn′sūlȧ)	**130-31**	63°50′N	81°60′W
Belluno, Italy (bĕl-lōō′nō)	**200-01**	46°09′N	12°13′E
Bell Ville, Arg. (bĕl vēl′)	**173**	32°39′S	62°41′W
Belmond, Ia., U.S. (bĕl′mŏnd)	**114-15**	42°51′N	93°37′W
Belmonte, Braz. (bĕl-mōn′tȧ)	**168-69**	15°54′S	38°53′W
Belmopan, nat. cap., Belize (bĕl-mō-pän′)	**148**	17°14′N	88°47′W
Belogorsk, Russia	**222-23**	50°54′N	128°30′E
Belo Horizonte, Braz. (bĕ′lôre-sô′n-tĕ)	**172**	19°55′S	43°56′W
Beloit, Ks., U.S. (bē-loit′)	**120-21**	39°27′N	98°06′W
Beloit, Wi., U.S. (bē-loit′)	**116-17**	42°31′N	89°02′W
Belomorsk, Russia (byĕl-ō-môrsk′)	**186-87**	64°32′N	34°45′E
Belorechensk, Russia	**186-87**	44°46′N	39°52′E
Beloretsk, Russia (byĕ′lō-rĕtsk)	**226**	53°58′N	58°24′E
Belorussia, nation, Eur. *see* Belarus	**174-75**	53°50′N	28°00′E
Belorussiya, nation, Eur. *see* Belarus	**174-75**	53°50′N	28°00′E
Belo Tsiribihina, Madag.	**264-65**	19°42′S	44°33′E
Belovo, Russia (bvĕ′lŭ-vû)	**218-19**	54°25′N	86°19′E
Beloye, Ozero, lk., Russia	**186-87**	60°11′N	37°37′E
Beloye More, s., Russia *see* White Sea	**186-87**	65°37′N	37°52′E
Beloz'orsk, Russia	**186-87**	60°02′N	37°48′E
Belton, Mo., U.S. (bĕl′tŭn)	**120-21**	38°48′N	94°32′W
Belton, Tx., U.S. (bĕl′tŭn)	**122-23**	31°03′N	97°27′W
Belts, Mol. *see* Bălţi	**202-03**	47°46′N	27°55′E
Beltsy, Mol. *see* Bălţi	**202-03**	47°46′N	27°55′E
Belukha, Gora, mtn., Asia *see* Belukha, Mount	**226**	49°51′N	86°29′E
Belukha, Mount, mtn., Asia (mount byĭ-lōō′-khŭ)	**226**	49°51′N	86°29′E
Belvidere, Il., U.S. (bĕl-vē-dēr′)	**116-17**	42°15′N	88°49′W
Belzoni, Ms., U.S. (bĕl-zō′nē)	**124-25**	33°11′N	90°29′W
Bembézar, stm., Spain (bĕm-bā-thär′)	**198-99**	37°45′N	5°12′W
Bemidji, Mn., U.S. (bē-mĭj′ĭ)	**114-15**	47°29′N	94°54′W
Benalla, Austl. (bĕn-ăl′ȧ)	**276**	36°33′S	145°59′E
Benares, India *see* Vārānasi	**234-35**	25°20′N	82°59′E
Benavente, Spain (bā-nä-vĕn′tā)	**198-99**	42°00′N	5°40′W
Bend, Or., U.S. (bĕnd)	**112-13**	44°04′N	121°18′W
Bender, Mol. *see* Tighina	**202-03**	46°50′N	29°29′E
Bender Cassim, Som.	**262-63**	11°17′N	49°11′E
Bendery, Mol. *see* Tighina	**202-03**	46°50′N	29°29′E
Bendigo, Austl. (bĕn′dĭ-gō)	**276**	36°46′S	144°17′E
Benedito Leite, Braz.	**166-67**	7°13′S	44°34′W
Benešov, Czech Rep. (bĕn′ĕ-shôf)	**194-95**	49°47′N	14°43′E
Benevento, Italy (bā-nä-vĕn′tō)	**200-01**	41°08′N	14°46′E
Bengal, Bay of, b., Asia (bā ŭv bĕn-gôl′)	**220-21**	15°0′N	90°00′E
Bengalūru, India	**236**	12°59′N	77°36′E
Bengbu, China (bŭŋ-bōō)	**238-39**	32°57′N	117°21′E
Bengkulu, Indon.	**246-47**	3°48′S	102°16′E
Benguela, Ang. (bĕn-gĕl′ȧ)	**264-65**	12°35′S	13°25′E
Beni, D.R.C.	**267**	0°30′N	29°28′E
Beni, stm., Bol. (bā′nē)	**166-67**	10°59′S	66°07′W
Beni Abbes, Alg.	**188-89**	30°08′N	2°10′W
Beni Mazâr, Egypt	**268b**	28°29′N	30°48′E
Beni-Mellal, Mor.	**269a**	32°21′N	6°22′W
Benin, nation, Afr. (bĕn-ēn′)	**253**	9°30′N	2°15′E
Benin, stm., Nig. (bĕn-ēn′)	**260a**	5°45′N	5°04′E
Benin, Bight of, b., Afr. (bīt ŭv bĕn-ēn′)	**260-61**	5°30′N	3°00′E
Bénin, Golfe de, b., Afr. *see* Benin, Bight of	**260-61**	5°30′N	3°00′E
Benin City, Nig. (bĕn-ēn′ sĭ′tē)	**260a**	6°20′N	5°38′E
Beni Saf, Alg. (bā′nē säf′)	**198-99**	35°18′N	1°23′W
Beni Suef, Egypt	**268b**	29°04′N	31°06′E
Benito Juárez, Arg.	**173**	37°41′S	59°48′W
Benjamín, Isla, i., Chile	**171**	44°40′S	74°08′W
Benjamin Constant, Braz.	**166-67**	4°28′S	70°01′W
Benkelman, Ne., U.S. (bĕn-kĕl-măn)	**120-21**	40°03′N	101°32′W
Bennetta, Ostrov, i., Russia	**218-19**	76°41′N	149°06′E
Bennettsville, S.C., U.S. (bĕn′ĕts vĭl)	**124-25**	34°37′N	79°41′W
Benoni, S. Afr. (bĕ-nō′nī)	**269c**	26°11′S	28°19′E
Bénoué, stm., Afr.	**260-61**	7°48′N	6°46′E
Benson, Az., U.S. (bĕn-sŭn)	**118-19**	31°58′N	110°18′W
Benson, Mn., U.S. (bĕn-sŭn)	**114-15**	45°19′N	95°36′W
Bentinck Island, i., Austl.	**277**	17°04′S	139°30′E
Benton, Ar., U.S. (bĕn′tŭn)	**120-21**	34°34′N	92°36′W
Benton, Il., U.S. (bĕn′tŭn)	**116-17**	37°60′N	88°55′W
Benton, Ky., U.S. (bĕn′tŭn)	**124-25**	36°52′N	88°21′W
Benton, La., U.S. (bĕn′tŭn)	**120-21**	32°42′N	93°45′W
Benton Harbor, Mi., U.S. (bĕn′tŭn här′bēr)	**116-17**	42°06′N	86°28′W
Bentonville, Ar., U.S. (bĕn′tŭn-vĭl)	**120-21**	36°22′N	94°12′W
Benue, stm., Afr. (bā′nōō-å)	**260-61**	7°48′N	6°46′E
Benxi, China (bŭn-shyē)	**243**	41°18′N	123°45′E
Beograd, nat. cap., Serb. (bĕ-ŏ′gräd) *see* Belgrade	**200-01**	44°50′N	20°28′E
Beppu, Japan (bĕ′pōō)	**245**	33°17′N	131°30′E
Bequia, i., St. Vin. (bĕk-ē′ä)	**143b**	13°02′N	61°13′W
Berau, Teluk, b., Indon.	**224-25**	2°30′S	132°30′E
Berbera, Som. (bûr′bûr-ȧ)	**262-63**	10°26′N	45°01′E
Berbérati, C.A.R.	**262-63**	4°14′N	15°48′E
Berbice, stm., Guy.	**164-65**	6°15′N	57°32′W
Berck, Fr. (bĕrk)	**196-97**	50°25′N	1°35′E
Berdians'k, Ukr.	**202-03**	46°45′N	36°49′E
Berdigestyakh, Russia	**218-19**	62°06′N	126°41′E

Feature (Pronunciation)	Page	Lat.	Long.
Berdychiv, Ukr.	202-03	49°54'N	28°37'E
Berea, Ky., U.S. (bĕ-rē´*á*)	116-17	37°34'N	84°18'W
Berens River, Mb., Can. (bĕrĕnz rĭv´ĕr)	134-35	52°22'N	97°02'W
Beresford, S.D., U.S. (bĕr´ĕs-fẽrd)	114-15	43°05'N	96°47'W
Berettyóújfalu, Hung. (bĕ´rĕt-tyō-ōō´y'fō-lōō)	194-95	47°13'N	21°33'E
Berezhany, Ukr. (bĕr-yĕ´zhá-nĕ)	194-95	49°27'N	24°57'E
Berezniki, Russia (bĕr-yôz´nyē-kē)	186-87	59°24'N	56°46'E
Berga, Spain (bĕr´gä)	198-99	42°06'N	1°51'E
Bergama, Tur. (bĕr´gä-mä)	200-01	39°08'N	27°11'E
Bergamo, Italy (bĕr´gä-mō)	200-01	45°42'N	9°41'E
Bergantín, Ven. (bĕr-gän-tē´n)	163b	10°01'N	64°21'W
Bergen, Nor. (bĕr´gĕn)	192-93	60°22'N	5°21'E
Bergerac, Fr. (bĕr-zhĕ-rák´)	196-97	44°51'N	0°29'E
Bergville, S. Afr. (bĕrg´vĭl)	269c	28°44'S	29°21'E
Berhala, Selat, strt., Indon.	246-47	0°48'S	104°25'E
Beringa, Ostrov, i., Russia	218-19	54°54'N	166°24'E
Beringovo More, s., *see* Bering Sea	126	60°0'N	175°00'W
Beringov Proliv, strt., *see* Bering Strait	126	65°30'N	169°00'W
Beringovskiy, Russia	218-19	63°04'N	179°22'E
Bering Sea, s., (bē´rĭng sē)	126	60°0'N	175°00'W
Bering Strait, strt., (bē´rĭng strāt)	126	65°30'N	169°00'W
Berja, Spain (bĕr´hä)	198-99	36°51'N	2°57'W
Berkakit, Russia	218-19	56°34'N	124°48'E
Berkane, Mor.	198-99	34°56'N	2°19'W
Berkeley, Ca., U.S. (bûrk´lĭ)	118-19	37°52'N	122°16'W
Berkeley Springs, W.V., U.S. (bûrk´lĭ sprĭngz)	116-17	39°37'N	78°15'W
Berlenga, i., Port. (bĕr-lĕn´gäzh)	198-99	39°25'N	9°30'W
Berlin, Md., U.S. (bûr-lĭn)	116-17	38°19'N	75°13'W
Berlin, N.H., U.S. (bûr-lĭn)	116-17	44°28'N	71°10'W
Berlin, Wi., U.S. (bûr-lĭn´)	116-17	43°58'N	88°57'W
Berlin, nat. cap., Ger. (bĕr-lēn´)	194-95	52°31'N	13°26'E
Bermejo, stm., Arg.	168-69	32°17'S	67°22'W
Bermejo, stm., S.A. (bĕr-mā´hō)	168-69	26°52'S	58°22'W
Bermejo, Paso del, p., S.A.	163e	32°49'S	70°05'W
Bermeo, Spain (bĕr-mā´yō)	198-99	43°25'N	2°44'W
Bermuda, dep., N.A. (bûr-myū´-d*ā*)	140-41	32°20'N	64°45'W
Bermuda Islands, is., Ber.	140-41	32°21'N	64°46'W
Bern, nat. cap., Switz. (bĕrn)	194-95	46°57'N	7°26'E
Bernasconi, Arg.	173	37°54'S	63°44'W
Berne, In., U.S. (bûrn)	116-17	40°39'N	84°57'W
Berne, nat. cap., Switz. *see* Bern	194-95	46°57'N	7°26'E
Bernier Island, i., Austl. (bĕr-nēr´ ī´l*ă*nd)	272-73	24°52'S	113°08'E
Bernina, Piz, mtn., Eur.	194-95	46°22'N	9°51'E
Bernina, Pizzo, mtn., Eur. *see* Bernina, Piz	194-95	46°22'N	9°51'E
Beroun, Czech Rep. (bā´rōn)	194-95	49°58'N	14°04'E
Berryville, Ar., U.S. (bĕr´ē-vĭl)	120-21	36°22'N	93°35'W
Bershad', Ukr. (byĕr´shät)	202-03	48°23'N	29°34'E
Bertoua, Camrn.	260-61	4°35'N	13°41'E
Beru, i., Kir.	280-81	1°20'S	176°00'E
Berwick, Pa., U.S. (bûr´wĭk)	116-17	41°04'N	76°15'W
Berwick-upon-Tweed, Eng., U.K. (bûr´ĭk-ŭp´ŏn-twēd)	190-91	55°47'N	2°01'W
Besalampy, Madag. (bĕz-á-lám-pē´)	264-65	16°45'S	44°30'E
Besançon, Fr. (bē-säɴ-sôn)	196-97	47°15'N	6°02'E
Bessarabia, hist. reg., Eur.	202-03	46°53'N	28°44'E
Bessemer, Al., U.S. (bĕs´ē-mẽr)	124-25	33°23'N	86°57'W
Bessemer, Mi., U.S. (bĕs´ē-mẽr)	114-15	46°29'N	90°03'W
Bessemer City, N.C., U.S. (bĕs´ē-mẽr sĭ´tē)	124-25	35°17'N	81°17'W
Betanzos, Spain (bĕ-tän´thōs)	198-99	43°17'N	8°12'W
Bethal, S. Afr. (bĕth´*ă*l)	269c	26°27'S	29°28'E
Bethel, Ak., U.S. (bĕth´*ĕ*l)	126	60°48'N	161°46'W
Bethlehem, S. Afr.	269c	28°14'S	28°19'E
Bethlehem, Pa., U.S. (bĕth´lē-hĕm)	116-17	40°38'N	75°23'W
Bethlehem, W.B. (bĕth´lē-hĕm)	228-29	31°43'N	35°12'E
Béthune, Fr. (bā-tün´)	196-97	50°32'N	2°39'E
Betioky, Madag.	264-65	23°43'S	44°23'E
Betpaqdala, des., Kaz.	226	46°0'N	70°00'E
Betsiamites, stm., Qc., Can.	138-39	48°56'N	68°37'W
Betsiboka, stm., Madag. (bĕt-sĭ-bō´ká)	264-65	16°03'S	46°35'E
Betūl, India	234-35	21°54'N	77°54'E
Beuthen, Pol. *see* Bytom	194-95	50°21'N	18°55'E
Beverley, Austl.	270-71	32°07'S	116°55'E
Bexhill, Eng., U.K. (bĕks´hĭl)	190-91	50°51'N	0°28'E
Beyneū, Kaz.	226	45°25'N	55°09'E
Beypazarı, Tur. (bā-pá-zä´rĭ)	186-87	40°10'N	31°56'E
Beyşehir Gölü, lk., Tur.	186-87	37°40'N	31°30'E
Bezhetsk, Russia (byĕ-zhĕtsk´)	202-03	57°48'N	36°42'E
Béziers, Fr. (bā-zyā´)	196-97	43°21'N	3°13'E
Bezwada, India *see* Vijayawāda	236	16°31'N	80°37'E
Bhadrak, India	234-35	21°03'N	86°30'E
Bhadrāvati, India	236	13°50'N	75°42'E
Bhāgalpur, India (bä´g*ŭ*l-pŏŏr)	234-35	25°15'N	86°59'E
Bhaktapur, Nepal	234-35	27°41'N	85°26'E
Bhamo, Mya. (bŭ-mō´)	238-39	24°17'N	97°15'E
Bhandāra, India	234-35	21°09'N	79°39'E
Bharat, nation, Asia *see* India	206-07	20°0'N	77°00'E
Bharatpur, India (bērt´pŏŏr)	234-35	27°13'N	77°29'E
Bharūch, India	234-35	21°43'N	72°60'E
Bhatinda, India (bŭ-tĭn-dá)	234-35	30°12'N	74°57'E
Bhātpāra, India	234-35	22°52'N	88°24'E
Bhāvnagar, India	234-35	21°46'N	72°08'E
Bhawānipatna, India	234-35	19°55'N	83°10'E
Bhilai, India	234-35	21°13'N	81°26'E
Bhilainagar, India *see* Bhilai	234-35	21°13'N	81°26'E
Bhīlwāra, India	234-35	25°21'N	74°38'E
Bhīma, stm., India (bē´má)	236	16°24'N	77°17'E
Bhind, India	234-35	26°34'N	78°47'E
Bhiwāni, India	234-35	28°47'N	76°08'E
Bhopāl, India (bō-päl)	234-35	23°15'N	77°24'E
Bhubaneshwar, India	234-35	20°14'N	85°50'E
Bhuj, India (bŏŏj)	234-35	23°15'N	69°40'E
Bhusāwal, India	234-35	21°03'N	75°47'E
Bhutan, nation, Asia (bōō-tän´)	206-07	27°30'N	90°30'E
Bia, Phou, mtn., Laos	246-47	18°59'N	103°09'E
Biafra, Bahía de, b., Afr. *see* Biafra, Bight of	260-61	4°0'N	8°00'E
Biafra, Bight of, b., Afr.	260-61	4°0'N	8°00'E
Biafra, Golfe de, b., Afr. *see* Biafra, Bight of	260-61	4°0'N	8°00'E
Biak, i., Indon. (bē´ăk)	224-25	1°0'S	136°00'E
Biała Podlaska, Pol. (byä´wä pōd-läs´kä)	194-95	52°02'N	23°08'E
Białystok, Pol. (byä-wĭs´tōk)	194-95	53°08'N	23°09'E
Bianco, Monte, mtn., Eur. *see* Blanc, Mont	196-97	45°50'N	6°52'E
Biarritz, Fr. (byä-rēts´)	196-97	43°29'N	1°33'W
Bickerton, Cape, c., Ant.	287	66°20'S	136°56'E
Bicknell, In., U.S. (bĭk´n*ĕ*l)	116-17	38°46'N	87°18'W
Bida, Nig. (bē´dä)	260-61	9°05'N	5°60'E
Bīdar, India	236	17°54'N	77°31'E
Biddeford, Me., U.S. (bĭd´ē-fẽrd)	116-17	43°30'N	70°27'W
Bié, Planalto do, plat., Ang.	264-65	13°30'S	17°02'E
Biebrza, stm., Pol. (byĕb´zhá)	194-95	53°13'N	22°26'E
Bielefeld, Ger. (bē´lē-fĕlt)	194-95	52°01'N	8°32'E
Biella, Italy (byĕl´lä)	200-01	45°34'N	8°04'E
Bielsko-Biała, Pol.	194-95	49°49'N	19°03'E
Bielsk Podlaski, Pol. (byĕlsk pŭd-lä´skĭ)	194-95	52°46'N	23°12'E
Bien Dong, s., Asia *see* South China Sea	224-25	10°0'N	113°00'E
Bien Hoa, Viet.	246-47	10°57'N	106°50'E
Bienville, Lac, lk., Qc., Can.	130-31	55°05'N	72°40'W
Biga, Tur. (bē´ghá)	200-01	40°14'N	27°15'E
Big Belt Mountains, mts., Mt., U.S. (bĭg bĕlt moun´tĭnz)	112-13	46°40'N	111°25'W
Big Bend National Park, n.p., Tx., U.S. (bĭg bĕnd năsh´ŭn-*ă*l pärk)	122-23	29°12'N	103°12'W
Big Black, stm., Ms., U.S. (bĭg blăk)	124-25	32°03'N	91°04'W
Big Cypress Indian Reservation, ind. res., Fl., U.S. (bĭg sī´prĕs ĭn´dĭ-*ă*n rĕ-sẽr-vā´shĕn)	125a	26°17'N	80°59'W
Big Cypress Swamp, sw., Fl., U.S. (bĭg sī´prĕs swŏmp)	125a	26°10'N	81°38'W
Big Delta, Ak., U.S. (bĭg dĕl´t*á*)	126	64°09'N	145°47'W
Biggar, Sk., Can.	134-35	52°03'N	107°58'W
Bigge Island, i., Austl.	272-73	14°35'S	125°10'E
Bighorn, stm., U.S. (bĭg hôrn)	110-11	46°09'N	107°29'W
Bighorn Mountains, mts., U.S. (bĭg hôrn moun´tĭnz)	112-13	43°59'N	107°04'W
Big Island, i., Nu., Can. (bĭg ī´l*ă*nd)	130-31	62°43'N	70°43'W
Big Island, i., On., Can. (bĭg ī´l*ă*nd)	134-35	49°09'N	94°37'W
Big Lake, Tx., U.S. (bĭg lāk)	122-23	31°11'N	101°28'W
Big Quill Lake, lk., Sk., Can.	134-35	51°55'N	104°22'W
Big Rapids, Mi., U.S. (bĭg răp´ĭdz)	116-17	43°42'N	85°29'W
Big River, Sk., Can. (bĭg rĭv´ẽr)	134-35	53°51'N	107°01'W
Big Sandy, stm., Wy., U.S. (bĭg sănd´ē)	112-13	41°52'N	109°47'W
Big Sioux, stm., U.S. (bĭg sōō)	114-15	42°29'N	96°28'W
Big Spring, Tx., U.S. (bĭg sprĭng)	120-21	32°15'N	101°29'W
Big Stone Gap, Va., U.S. (bĭg stōn)	124-25	36°52'N	82°47'W
Big Timber, Mt., U.S. (bĭg tĭm´-bẽr)	112-13	45°50'N	109°57'W
Big Trout Lake, lk., On., Can.	134-35	53°44'N	89°57'W
Bihār, state, India (bē-här´)	234-35	25°0'N	86°00'E
Bīhar Sharīf, India	234-35	25°12'N	85°32'E
Bijagós, Arquipélago dos, is., Gui.-B.	260-61	11°22'N	16°18'W
Bij-Chem, stm., Russia *see* Bol'shoy Yenisey	218-19	51°44'N	94°28'E
Bijie, China (bē-jyĕ)	238-39	27°18'N	105°17'E
Bīkāner, India (bĭ-kă´nûr)	234-35	28°01'N	73°19'E
Bikar, at., Marsh. Is.	280-81	12°14'N	170°08'E
Bikeqi, China	240-41	40°43'N	111°17'E
Bikin, Russia (bē-kēn´)	244	46°49'N	134°17'E
Bikin, stm., Russia (bē-kēn´)	244	46°51'N	134°02'E
Bikini, at., Marsh. Is.	280-81	11°35'N	165°23'E
Bilāspur, India (bē-läs´pōōr)	234-35	22°05'N	82°10'E
Bilāspur, India (bē-läs´pōōr)	234-35	31°18'N	76°46'E
Bila Tserkva, Ukr.	202-03	49°48'N	30°08'E
Bilauktaung Range, mts., Asia	246-47	13°0'N	99°00'E
Bilbao, Spain (bĭl-bä´ō)	198-99	43°15'N	2°56'W
Bilecik, Tur. (bē-lĕd-zhĕk´)	200-01	40°10'N	29°59'E
Biłgoraj, Pol. (bēw-gō´rī)	194-95	50°33'N	22°42'E
Bilhorod-Dnistrovs'kyi, Ukr.	202-03	46°12'N	30°18'E
Bili, stm., D.R.C.	262-63	4°08'N	22°29'E
Bilibino, Russia	218-19	68°04'N	166°21'E
Biliran Island, i., Phil.	250	11°36'N	124°29'E
Billabong Creek, stm., Austl. (bĭl´ă-bŏng krēk)	276	35°06'S	144°02'E
Billings, Mt., U.S. (bĭl´ĭngz)	112-13	45°47'N	108°31'W
Billiton, i., Indon. *see* Belitung	246-47	2°50'S	107°55'E
Bilma, Niger (bēl´mä)	258-59	18°41'N	12°56'E
Biloela, Austl.	277	24°24'S	150°30'E
Biloxi, Ms., U.S. (bĭ-lŏk´sĭ)	124-25	30°24'N	88°53'W
Biltine, Chad	258-59	14°32'N	20°55'E
Bimberi Peak, mtn., Austl. (bĭm´bĕrĭ pēk)	276	35°40'S	148°47'E
Bimini Islands, is., Bah.	142-43	25°42'N	79°15'W
Binga, D.R.C.	262-63	2°22'N	20°31'E
Binga, Monte, mtn., Afr.	264-65	19°47'S	33°03'E
Binga, Mount, mtn., Afr. *see* Binga, Monte	264-65	19°47'S	33°03'E
Binghamton, N.Y., U.S. (bĭng´*ă*m-t*ŭ*n)	116-17	42°06'N	75°55'W
Binhai, China	238-39	34°00'N	119°50'E
Binjai, Indon.	246-47	3°36'N	98°30'E
Binongko, Pulau, i., Indon.	248-49	5°57'S	124°02'E
Bintimani, mtn., S.L.	260-61	9°13'N	11°07'W
Bintulu, Malay. (bēn´tōō-lōō)	248-49	3°10'N	113°02'E
Binxian, China (bĭn-shyän)	238-39	35°02'N	108°06'E
Binxian, China (bĭn-shyän)	240-41	37°28'N	117°58'E
Binzert, Tun. *see* Bizerte	184-85	37°16'N	9°52'E
Bioko, i., Eq. Gui. (bē-ō´-kō)	260-61	3°30'N	8°40'E
Bīr, India	236	18°60'N	75°46'E
Bira, Russia (bē´rá)	240-41	48°60'N	132°28'E
Bira, stm., Russia (bē´rá)	240-41	48°10'N	133°17'E
Birao, C.A.R.	262-63	10°17'N	22°48'E
Birch Mountains, hills, Ab., Can. (bûrch moun´tĭnz)	130-31	57°34'N	113°07'W
Birdsville, Austl. (bûrdz´vĭl)	276	25°54'S	139°21'E
Birecik, Tur. (bē-rĕd-zhĕk´)	228-29	37°03'N	38°03'E
Bīrjand, Iran (bēr´jänd)	232-33	32°53'N	59°13'E
Bîrlad, Rom.	202-03	46°14'N	27°40'E
Birmingham, Eng., U.K.	190-91	52°28'N	1°53'W
Birmingham, Al., U.S. (bûr´mĭng-häm)	124-25	33°31'N	86°49'W
Bîr Mogreïn, Maur.	258-59	25°14'N	11°35'W
Birnie, at., Kir.	280-81	3°35'S	171°31'W
Birnin-Kebbi, Nig.	260-61	12°28'N	4°12'E
Birnin Konni, Niger	258-59	13°48'N	5°15'E
Birobidzhan, Russia (bē´rō-bē-jän´)	240-41	48°47'N	132°55'E
Birsk, Russia (bĭrsk)	186-87	55°25'N	55°34'E
Biryusa, stm., Russia (bēr-yōō´sä)	218-19	57°43'N	95°27'E
Biržai, Lith. (bêr-zhä´ê)	192-93	56°12'N	24°46'E
Bisbee, Az., U.S. (bĭz´bē)	118-19	31°27'N	109°55'W
Biscay, Bay of, b., Eur. (bĭs´kā´ bā)	196-97	44°0'N	4°00'W
Biscayne Bay, b., Fl., U.S. (bĭs-kān´ bā)	125a	25°33'N	80°15'W
Biscayne National Park, n.p., Fl., U.S.	125a	25°25'N	80°12'W
Biscoe Islands, is., Ant.	287	65°60'S	66°30'W
Bishkek, nat. cap., Kyrg. (bĭsh-kĕk´)	226	42°52'N	74°35'E
Bishop, Ca., U.S. (bĭsh´*ŭ*p)	118-19	37°22'N	118°23'W
Bishop, Tx., U.S. (bĭsh´*ŭ*p)	122-23	27°35'N	97°47'W
Bishop's Falls, Nf., Can.	138-39	49°02'N	55°30'W
Bishopville, S.C., U.S. (bĭsh´*ŭ*p-vĭl)	124-25	34°13'N	80°15'W
Biskra, Alg.	269b	34°50'N	5°43'E
Bislig, Phil.	250	8°13'N	126°19'E
Bismarck, N.D., U.S. (bĭz´märk)	114-15	46°48'N	100°48'W
Bismarck Archipelago, is., Pap. N. Gui. (bĭz´märk är´kå-pĕ´-å-gō)	277	5°0'S	150°00'E
Bismarck Range, mts., Pap. N. Gui. (bĭz´märk rānj)	277	5°30'S	144°45'E
Bismarck Sea, s., Pap. N. Gui. (bĭz´märk sē)	277	4°0'S	148°00'E
Bissagos, is., Gui.-B. *see* Bijagós, Arquipélago dos	260-61	11°22'N	16°18'W

n-sing; ŋ-baŋk; ɴ-nasalized n; nŏd; c*ŏ*mmit; ōld; ôbey; ôrder; oi-boil; fōōd; ŏŏ-as oo in foot; ou-out; s-soft; sh-dish; th-thin; pūre; ûnite; ûrn; stŭd; circ*ŭ*s; ü-as in French tu; ´-indeterminate vowel.

Feature (Pronunciation)	Page	Lat.	Long.
Bissau, nat. cap., Gui.-B. (bē-sa′o͞o)	260-61	11°52′N	15°36′W
Bissett, Mb., Can.	134-35	51°02′N	95°40′W
Bistcho Lake, lk., Ab., Can.	130-31	59°44′N	118°46′W
Bistineau, Lake, res., La., U.S. (lāk bĭs-tĭ-nō′)	120-21	32°25′N	93°22′W
Bistrița, Rom. (bĭs-trĭt-sȧ)	194-95	47°08′N	24°30′E
Bistrița, stm., Rom. (bĭs-trĭt-sȧ)	188-89	46°28′N	26°57′E
Bitlis, Tur. (bĭt-lēs′)	227	38°22′N	42°06′E
Bitola, Mac. (bē′tô-lä) (mô′nä-stēr)	200-01	41°02′N	21°20′E
Bitolj, Mac. *see* Bitola	200-01	41°02′N	21°20′E
Bitonto, Italy (bē-tôn′tō)	200-01	41°06′N	16°42′E
Bitra Island, i., India	236	11°36′N	72°11′E
Bitterfeld, Ger. (bĭt′ēr-fĕlt)	194-95	51°37′N	12°19′E
Bitterroot Range, mts., U.S. (bĭt′ēr-o͞ot rānj)	110-11	47°06′N	115°10′W
Bitung, Indon.	248-49	1°26′N	125°08′E
Bityug, stm., Russia (bĭt′yo͝og)	186-87	50°38′N	39°56′E
Biwa-ko, lk., Japan (bē-wä′kō)	245	35°15′N	136°05′E
Biya, stm., Russia (bĭ′yȧ)	218-19	52°26′N	85°00′E
Biysk, Russia (bēsk)	226	52°34′N	85°15′E
Bizerte, Tun. (bē-zĕrt′)	184-85	37°16′N	9°52′E
Bjarèzina, stm., Bela. (bĕr-yĕ′zē-nȧ)	202-03	52°33′N	30°14′E
Bjelovar, Cro. (byĕ-lō′vär)	200-01	45°54′N	16°50′E
Björneborg, Fin. *see* Pori	192-93	61°29′N	21°47′E
Bjørnøya, i., Nor.	218-19	74°27′N	19°02′E
Black, stm., Asia (blăk)	246-47	21°15′N	105°21′E
Black, stm., Ar., U.S. (blăk)	120-21	35°38′N	91°19′W
Blackall, Austl. (blăk′ăl)	277	24°26′S	145°28′E
Black Bay, b., On., Can. (blăk bā)	136-37	48°34′N	88°32′W
Blackburn, Eng., U.K. (blăk′bûrn)	190-91	53°45′N	2°29′W
Black Canyon of the Gunnison National Park, n.p., Co., U.S.	118-19	38°34′N	107°44′W
Blackduck, Mn., U.S. (blăk′dŭk)	114-15	47°43′N	94°32′W
Blackfeet Indian Reservation, ind. res., Mt., U.S. (blăk′fēt ĭn′dĭ-ăn rĕ-sēr-vā′shĕn)	112-13	48°40′N	113°00′W
Blackfoot, Id., U.S. (blăk′fŏŏt)	112-13	43°12′N	112°21′W
Black Forest, mts., Ger. *see* Schwarzwald	194-95	48°21′N	8°11′E
Black Hills, mts., U.S. (blăk hĭlz)	114-15	44°0′N	104°00′W
Black Lake, Qc., Can. (blăk lāk)	136-37	46°03′N	71°22′W
Blackpool, Eng., U.K. (blăk′po͞ol)	190-91	53°50′N	3°02′W
Black Range, mts., N.M., U.S. (blăk rānj)	118-19	33°20′N	107°50′W
Black River Falls, Wi., U.S. (blăk rĭv′ēr fôlz)	114-15	44°18′N	90°50′W
Black Rock Desert, des., Nv., U.S. (blăk rŏk dĕs′ērt)	112-13	41°06′N	118°51′W
Blacksburg, Va., U.S. (blăks′bûrg)	124-25	37°14′N	80°25′W
Black Sea, s., (blăk sē)	186-87	43°0′N	35°00′E
Blackshear, Ga., U.S. (blăk′shĭr)	124-25	31°18′N	82°15′W
Blackstone, Va., U.S. (blăk′stŏn)	124-25	37°05′N	77°60′W
Blacktown, Austl. (blăk′toun)	276	33°46′S	150°54′E
Black Volta, stm., Afr. (blăk vôl′tȧ)	260-61	8°41′N	0°60′W
Blackwell, Ok., U.S. (blăk′wĕl)	120-21	36°48′N	97°18′W
Blagodarnoye, Russia (blä′gô-där-nō′yĕ)	186-87	45°06′N	43°25′E
Blagoveshchensk, Russia	240-41	50°17′N	127°33′E
Blaine, Mn., U.S. (blān)	114-15	45°11′N	93°15′W
Blaine, Wa., U.S. (blān)	112-13	48°60′N	122°45′W
Blair, Ne., U.S. (blâr)	114-15	41°33′N	96°08′W
Blairsville, Pa., U.S. (blârs′vĭl)	116-17	40°26′N	79°16′W
Blakely, Ga., U.S. (blāk′lē)	124-25	31°23′N	84°56′W
Blanc, Cap, c., Afr. *see* Nouâdhibou, Râs	258-59	20°47′N	17°03′W
Blanc, Mont, mtn., Eur. (môn bläɴ)	196-97	45°50′N	6°52′E
Blanca, Bahía, b., Arg. (bä-ē′ä-blan′kä)	173	38°55′S	62°10′W
Blanca Peak, mtn., Co., U.S. (blăŋ′kȧ pēk)	120-21	37°35′N	105°29′W
Blanche, Lake, lk., Austl. (lāk blănch)	276	29°15′S	139°39′E
Blanco, Cabo, c., C.R. (kȧ′bô-blăŋ′kō)	149	9°34′N	85°07′W
Blanco, Cape, c., Or., U.S. (kāp blăn′kō)	112-13	42°50′N	124°33′W
Blanquilla, Isla, i., Ven.	164-65	11°51′N	64°37′W
Blantyre, Malawi (blăn-tīyr)	264-65	15°47′S	35°01′E
Blenheim, N.Z.	278	41°31′S	173°58′E
Bleus, Monts, mts., D.R.C.	267	1°37′N	30°28′E
Blida, Alg.	269b	36°29′N	2°49′E
Blind River, On., Can. (blīnd rĭv′ēr)	136-37	46°11′N	82°56′W
Blissfield, Mi., U.S. (blĭs-fēld)	116-17	41°50′N	83°52′W
Blitar, Indon.	248-49	8°06′S	112°10′E
Bloemfontein, S. Afr.	269c	29°07′S	26°12′E
Blois, Fr. (blwä)	196-97	47°35′N	1°20′E
Bloodvein, stm., Can.	134-35	51°48′N	96°53′W
Bloomer, Wi., U.S. (blo͞om′ēr)	114-15	45°06′N	91°29′W
Bloomfield, Ia., U.S. (blo͞om′fēld)	114-15	40°46′N	92°25′W
Bloomfield, In., U.S. (blo͞om′fēld)	116-17	39°01′N	86°56′W
Bloomfield, Mo., U.S. (blo͞om′fēld)	124-25	36°53′N	89°56′W
Bloomfield, Ne., U.S. (blo͞om′fēld)	114-15	42°36′N	97°39′W
Blooming Prairie, Mn., U.S. (blo͞om′ĭng prâ′rĭ)	114-15	43°52′N	93°03′W
Bloomington, Il., U.S. (blo͞om′ĭng-tŭn)	116-17	40°29′N	88°60′W
Bloomington, In., U.S. (blo͞om′ĭng-tŭn)	116-17	39°09′N	86°32′W
Bloomington, Mn., U.S. (blo͞om′ĭng-tŭn)	114-15	44°50′N	93°19′W
Bloomsburg, Pa., U.S. (blo͞omz′bûrg)	116-17	40°60′N	76°27′W
Blossburg, Pa., U.S. (blŏs′bûrg)	116-17	41°41′N	77°05′W
Blountstown, Fl., U.S. (blŭnts′tun)	124-25	30°27′N	85°03′W
Bludenz, Aus. (blo͞o-dĕnts′)	194-95	47°09′N	9°50′E
Blue Earth, Mn., U.S. (blo͞o ûrth)	114-15	43°38′N	94°06′W
Bluefield, W.V., U.S. (blo͞o′fēld)	124-25	37°15′N	81°14′W
Bluefields, Nic. (blo͞o′fēldz)	149	12°01′N	83°46′W
Blue Mountain, mtn., Nf., Can. (blo͞o moun′tĭn)	138-39	50°24′N	57°10′W
Blue Mountain Peak, mtn., Jam.	142-43	18°03′N	76°35′W
Blue Mountains, mts., Austl. (blo͞o moun′tĭnz)	276	33°37′S	150°17′E
Blue Mountains, mts., U.S. (blo͞o moun′tĭnz)	112-13	45°16′N	118°42′W
Blue Mountains National Park, n.p., Austl.	276	33°47′S	150°23′E
Blue Nile, stm., Afr. (blo͞o nīl)	254	15°38′N	32°30′E
Bluenose Lake, lk., Nu., Can.	130-31	68°25′N	119°45′W
Blue Ridge, mts., U.S. (blo͞o rĭj)	124-25	37°0′N	82°00′W
Blue River, B.C., Can. (blo͞o rĭv′ēr)	132-33	52°06′N	119°20′W
Bluff, Ut., U.S. (blŭf)	118-19	37°17′N	109°33′W
Bluffton, In., U.S. (blŭf-tŭn)	116-17	40°44′N	85°10′W
Blumenau, Braz. (blo͞o′mĕn-ou)	172	26°56′S	49°05′W
Blyth, Eng., U.K. (blĭth)	190-91	55°08′N	1°31′W
Blytheville, Ar., U.S. (blīth′vĭl)	124-25	35°56′N	89°55′W
Bo, S.L.	260-61	7°59′N	11°44′W
Boaco, Nic. (bô-ä′kō)	149	12°29′N	85°39′W
Bo'ai, China (bwo-ī)	240-41	35°10′N	113°04′E
Boano, Pulau, i., Indon.	248-49	2°58′S	127°56′E
Boa Vista, i., C.V. (bō-ä-vēsh′tȧ)	260-61	16°05′N	22°50′W
Bobaomby, Tanjona, c., Madag.	264-65	11°58′S	49°15′E
Bobbili, India	236	18°35′N	83°22′E
Bobo-Dioulasso, Burkina (bō′bō-dyo͞o-lȧs-sō′)	260-61	11°11′N	4°18′W
Bobruysk, Bela. *see* Babrujsk	202-03	53°08′N	29°14′E
Boby, mtn., Madag.	264-65	22°13′S	46°55′E
Boca do Acre, Braz.	166-67	8°45′S	67°23′W
Bocas del Toro, Pan. (bō′käs dĕl tō′rō)	150	9°20′N	82°15′W
Bochnia, Pol. (bōĸ′nyä)	194-95	49°58′N	20°25′E
Bocholt, Ger. (bō′ĸōlt)	194-95	51°50′N	6°37′E
Bodaybo, Russia (bō-dī′bō)	218-19	57°51′N	114°11′E
Bodélé, reg., Chad (bō-dȧ-lā′)	258-59	16°30′N	16°30′E
Boden, Swe.	184-85	65°50′N	21°43′E
Bodh Gaya, India	234-35	24°42′N	84°58′E
Bodmin, Eng., U.K. (bŏd′mĭn)	190-91	50°29′N	4°43′W
Bodø, Nor.	184-85	67°17′N	14°24′E
Bodrum, Tur.	200-01	37°02′N	27°26′E
Boende, D.R.C. (bô-ĕn′dȧ)	262-63	0°14′S	20°52′E
Boerne, Tx., U.S. (bō′ĕrn)	122-23	29°47′N	98°43′W
Bōfu, Japan (bō′fo͞o) *see* Hōfu	245	34°03′N	131°35′E
Bogal, Lagh, stm., Kenya	262-63	0°46′N	40°50′E
Bogale, Mya.	246-47	16°17′N	95°24′E
Bogalusa, La., U.S. (bō-gȧ-lo͞o′sȧ)	124-25	30°47′N	89°51′W
Bogan, stm., Austl. (bō′gĕn)	276	29°58′S	146°20′E
Bogo, Phil.	250	11°02′N	124°01′E
Bogong, Mount, mtn., Austl.	276	36°44′S	147°18′E
Bogor, Indon.	248-49	6°35′S	106°47′E
Bogoroditsk, Russia (bō-gō′rō-dĭtsk)	202-03	53°47′N	38°08′E
Bogotá, nat. cap., Col. (bō-gō-tä′)	163c	4°37′N	74°06′W
Bogra, Bngl.	234-35	24°50′N	89°22′E
Boguchany, Russia	218-19	58°23′N	97°29′E
Bogué, Maur.	258-59	16°35′N	14°16′W
Bo Hai, b., China	240-41	38°30′N	120°02′E
Bohai Haixia, strt., China (bwo-hī hī-shyä)	240-41	38°15′N	121°00′E
Bohain-en-Vermandois, Fr. (bô-ăɴ-ŏɴ-vâr-măɴ-dwä′)	196-97	49°59′N	3°27′E
Bohea Hills, mts., China *see* Wuyi Shan	238-39	27°42′N	117°09′E
Bohemia, hist. reg., Czech Rep.	194-95	49°50′N	14°00′E
Bohol, i., Phil. (bô-hôl′)	250	9°55′N	123°44′E
Bohol Sea, s., Phil.	250	9°10′N	124°25′E
Boipeba, Ilha de, i., Braz.	166-67	13°38′S	38°56′W
Bois, Lac des, lk., N.T., Can.	130-31	66°46′N	125°08′W
Boise, Id., U.S. (boi′zē)	112-13	43°37′N	116°13′W
Boise City, Ok., U.S. (boi′zē sĭ′tē)	120-21	36°44′N	102°30′W
Boissevain, Mb., Can. (bois′vān)	134-35	49°14′N	100°03′W
Bojeador, Cape, c., Phil.	250	18°30′N	120°35′E
Bojnūrd, Iran	232-33	37°29′N	57°20′E
Boksitogorsk, Russia	186-87	59°28′N	33°52′E
Bokurdak, Turkmen.	232-33	38°46′N	58°29′E
Bolbec, Fr. (bôl-bĕk′)	196-97	49°34′N	0°29′E
Bolgatanga, Ghana	260-61	10°48′N	0°51′W
Boli, China (bwo-lē)	244	45°45′N	130°34′E
Bolívar, Col.	163c	4°21′N	76°10′W
Bolivar, Mo., U.S. (bŏl′ĭ-vȧr)	120-21	37°37′N	93°25′W
Bolivar, Tn., U.S. (bŏl′ĭ-vȧr)	124-25	35°16′N	88°59′W
Bolívar, Cerro, mtn., Ven.	164-65	7°28′N	63°25′W
Bolívar, Pico, mtn., Ven.	164-65	8°33′N	71°01′W
Bolivar Peninsula, pen., Tx., U.S. (bŏl′ĭ-vȧr pĕ-nĭn′sūlȧ)	122-23	29°27′N	94°39′W
Bolivia, nation, S.A. (bō-lĭv′ĭ-ȧ)	158	17°0′S	65°00′W
Bolkhov, Russia (bŏl-ĸôf′)	202-03	53°27′N	36°00′E
Bollnäs, Swe. (bôl′nĕs)	192-93	61°21′N	16°24′E
Bolmen, lk., Swe. (bôl′mĕn)	192-93	56°55′N	13°40′E
Bolobo, D.R.C. (bō′lō-bō)	262-63	2°11′S	16°15′E
Bologna, Italy (bō-lōn′yä)	200-01	44°30′N	11°20′E
Bologoye, Russia (bŏ-lō-gô′yĕ)	202-03	57°54′N	34°03′E
Bol'shevik, Ostrov, i., Russia	218-19	78°40′N	102°30′E
Bol'shezemel'skaya Tundra, reg., Russia	186-87	67°30′N	55°60′E
Bol'shoy Begichëv, Ostrov, i., Russia	218-19	74°20′N	112°30′E
Bol'shoy Kavkaz, mts., *see* Caucasus Mountains	227	42°38′N	45°00′E
Bol'shoy Lyakhovskiy, Ostrov, i., Russia	218-19	73°35′N	142°00′E
Bol'shoy Uzen', stm., Eur. *see* Ülkenözen	186-87	48°60′N	49°59′E
Bol'shoy Yenisey, stm., Russia	218-19	51°44′N	94°28′E
Bolu, Tur. (bō′lŏ)	186-87	40°44′N	31°36′E
Bolzano, Italy (bôl-tsä′nō)	200-01	46°30′N	11°21′E
Boma, D.R.C. (bō′mä)	262-63	5°51′S	13°04′E
Bombala, Austl. (bŭm-bä′lă)	276	36°55′S	149°14′E
Bombay, India *see* Mumbai	236	18°57′N	72°50′E
Bom Jesus da Lapa, Braz.	166-67	13°15′S	43°25′W
Bømlo, i., Nor. (bûmlō)	192-93	59°47′N	5°12′E
Bomokandi, stm., D.R.C.	262-63	3°39′N	26°08′E
Bomu, stm., Afr.	262-63	4°09′N	22°29′E
Bon, Cap, c., Tun. (kȧp bôɴ)	258-59	37°05′N	11°03′E
Bonaire, i., Neth. Ant. (bō-nâr′)	140a	12°10′N	68°15′W
Bonaventure, Qc., Can.	138-39	48°02′N	65°30′W
Bonavista, Nf., Can. (bō-nȧ-vĭs′tȧ)	138-39	48°39′N	53°07′W
Bonavista Bay, b., Nf., Can. (bō-nȧ-vĭs′tȧ bā)	138-39	48°50′N	53°21′W
Bondo, D.R.C. (bôn′dō)	262-63	3°49′N	23°41′E
Bondoc Peninsula, pen., Phil. (bôn-dŏk′ pĕ-nĭn′sūlȧ)	250	13°30′N	122°30′E
Bondoukou, C. Iv. (bŏn-do͞o′ko͞o)	260-61	8°02′N	2°48′W
Bône, Alg. *see* Annaba	184-85	36°54′N	7°46′E
Bone, Indon. *see* Watampone	248-49	4°32′S	120°19′E
Bone, Teluk, b., Indon.	248-49	4°0′S	120°40′E
Bonerate, Pulau, i., Indon.	248-49	7°21′S	121°07′E
Bonete Grande, Cerro, mtn., Arg. (sĕ′r-rō bô′nĕtĕh grăn′dĕ)	168-69	27°57′S	68°45′W
Bongo, Massif des, mts., C.A.R.	262-63	8°36′N	22°50′E
Bonham, Tx., U.S. (bŏn′ăm)	120-21	33°35′N	96°11′W
Bonifacio, Bouches de, strt., Eur. *see* Bonifacio, Strait of	200-01	41°18′N	9°15′E
Bonifacio, Strait of, strt., Eur. (strāt ŭv bō-nē-fä′chō)	200-01	41°18′N	9°15′E
Bonifay, Fl., U.S. (bŏn-ĭ-fā′)	124-25	30°47′N	85°41′W
Bonin Islands, is., Japan (bō′nĭn ī′lăndz)	282-83	26°58′N	142°14′E
Bonn, Ger. (bōn)	194-95	50°44′N	7°05′E
Bonners Ferry, Id., U.S. (bonērz fĕr′ē)	112-13	48°41′N	116°19′W
Bonne Terre, Mo., U.S. (bŏn târ′)	120-21	37°55′N	90°33′W
Bonny, Nig. (bŏn′ē)	260a	4°26′N	7°10′E
Bonnyville, Ab., Can. (bŏnē-vĭl)	132-33	54°16′N	110°44′W
Bontang, Indon.	248-49	0°08′N	117°30′E
Bontoc, Phil. (bōn-tŏk′)	250	17°05′N	120°60′E
Boodjamulla National Park, n.p., Austl.	277	18°45′S	138°27′E
Booker T. Washington National Monument, n.p., Va., U.S. (bo͝ok′ēr tē wŏsh′ĭng-tŭn năsh′ŭn-ăl mŏn′ū-mĕnt)	124-25	37°01′N	79°45′W
Boonah, Austl.	276	28°00′S	152°41′E
Boone, Ia., U.S. (bo͞on)	114-15	42°04′N	93°53′W
Boone, N.C., U.S. (bo͞on)	124-25	36°13′N	81°41′W
Booneville, Ar., U.S. (bo͞on′vĭl)	120-21	35°08′N	93°56′W
Booneville, Ms., U.S. (bo͞on′vĭl)	124-25	34°39′N	88°34′W
Boonville, In., U.S. (bo͞on′vĭl)	116-17	38°03′N	87°17′W
Boonville, Mo., U.S. (bo͞on′vĭl)	120-21	38°58′N	92°45′W

ăt; finăl; rāte; senâte; ärm; ȧsk; sofȧ; fâre; ch-choose; dh-as th in other; bē; ēvent; bĕt; recĕnt; cratẽr; g-gō; gh-guttural g; bĭt; ĭ-short neutral; rīde; ĸ-guttural k as ch in German ich;

Feature (Pronunciation)	Page	Lat.	Long.
Boorama, Som.	262-63	9°58′N	43°09′E
Boosaaso, Som. *see* Bender Cassim	262-63	11°17′N	49°11′E
Boothbay Harbor, Me., U.S. (bo͞oth′bā här′bẽr)	117a	43°51′N	69°38′W
Boothia, Gulf of, b., Nu., Can. (gŭlf ŭv bo͞o′thĭ-*à*)	86	71°0′N	91°00′W
Boothia Peninsula, pen., Nu., Can.	130-31	70°30′N	95°00′W
Booué, Gabon	260-61	0°06′S	11°57′E
Bordoy, i., Far. Is.	190b	62°17′N	6°33′W
Bora-Bora, i., Fr. Poly.	280-81	16°30′S	151°45′W
Borah Peak, mtn., Id., U.S. (bō′rä pēk)	112-13	44°08′N	113°48′W
Borås, Swe. (bô′rōs)	192-93	57°44′N	12°57′E
Borāzjān, Iran (bō-räz-jän′)	230-31	29°16′N	51°12′E
Borba, Braz. (bôr′bä)	166-67	4°23′S	59°35′W
Bordeaux, Fr. (bôr-dō′)	196-97	44°50′N	0°34′W
Bordentown, N.J., U.S. (bôr′dĕn-toun)	116-17	40°08′N	74°44′W
Bordertown, Austl.	276	36°19′S	140°46′E
Bordj Bou Arreridj, Alg. (bôrj-bo͞o-à-rä-rēj′)	269b	36°04′N	4°46′E
Borgå, Fin. *see* Porvoo	192-93	60°24′N	25°40′E
Borgarnes, Ice.	190a	64°34′N	21°55′W
Borger, Tx., U.S. (bôr′gẽr)	120-21	35°40′N	101°24′W
Borgholm, Swe. (bôrg-hōlm′)	192-93	56°52′N	16°40′E
Borgne, Lake, b., La., U.S. (lāk bôrn′y′)	124-25	30°05′N	89°35′W
Borgomanero, Italy (bôr′gō-mä-nâ′rō)	200-01	45°42′N	8°28′E
Borgo Val di Taro, Italy (bô′r-zhō-väl-dē-tá′rō)	200-01	44°29′N	9°46′E
Borisoglebsk, Russia (bŏ-rē sô-glyĕpsk′)	186-87	51°22′N	42°06′E
Borken, Ger. (bōr′kĕn)	194-95	51°51′N	6°52′E
Borkum, i., Ger. (bōr′ko͝om)	194-95	53°36′N	6°42′E
Borlänge, Swe. (bôr-lĕn′gĕ)	192-93	60°29′N	15°27′E
Borneo, i., Asia (bôr′-nē-ō)	248-49	0°30′N	114°00′E
Bornholm, i., Den. (bôrn-hôlm)	192-93	55°09′N	14°55′E
Boro, stm., Sudan	262-63	8°51′N	26°11′E
Borogontsy, Russia	218-19	62°41′N	131°09′E
Borovichi, Russia (bŏ-rô-vē′chē)	202-03	58°23′N	33°55′E
Borroloola, Austl. (bŏr-rō-lo͞o′l*à*)	270-71	16°05′S	136°17′E
Borūjerd, Iran	228-29	33°53′N	48°45′E
Borzna, Ukr. (bôrz′nà)	202-03	51°15′N	32°26′E
Borzya, Russia (bôrz′yà)	240-41	50°22′N	116°31′E
Bosa, Italy (bō′sä)	200-01	40°18′N	8°30′E
Bosanska Gradiška, Bos. (bō′sän-skä grä-dĭsh′kä)	200-01	45°09′N	17°15′E
Bosanski Novi, Bos. (bō′s sän-skĭ nō′vē)	200-01	45°04′N	16°23′E
Boscobel, Wi., U.S. (bŏs′kô-bĕl)	114-15	43°08′N	90°42′W
Bose, China (bwo-sŭ)	238-39	23°55′N	106°38′E
Boshan, China (bwo-shan)	240-41	36°29′N	117°51′E
Bosna, stm., Bos.	200-01	45°04′N	18°28′E
Bosna i Hercegovina, nation, Eur. *see* Bosnia and Herzegovina	174-75	44°15′N	17°50′E
Bosnia and Hercegovina, nation, Eur. *see* Bosnia and Herzegovina	174-75	44°15′N	17°50′E
Bosnia and Herzegovina, nation, Eur. (bŏs′nĭ-à ănd hĕr-tsĕ-gô′vē-nà)	174-75	44°15′N	17°50′E
Bosporus, strt., Tur. (bŏs′p*ŏ*-rŭs)	200-01	41°06′N	29°04′E
Bossembélé, C.A.R.	262-63	5°16′N	17°39′E
Bossier City, La., U.S. (bŏsh′ẽr sĭ′tĭ)	120-21	32°31′N	93°44′W
Bosso, Dallol, stm., Niger	258-59	12°24′N	2°52′E
Bosten Hu, lk., China (bwo-stŭn ho͞o)	222-23	42°0′N	87°00′E
Boston, Ma., U.S. (bôs′t*ŭ*n)	116-17	42°22′N	71°03′W
Boston Mountains, mts., Ar., U.S. (bôs′t*ŭ*n moun′tĭnz)	120-21	35°50′N	93°20′W
Boteti, stm., Bots.	264-65	20°09′S	23°23′E
Bothaville, S. Afr. (bō′tā-vĭl)	269c	27°24′S	26°37′E
Bothnia, Gulf of, b., Eur. (gŭlf ŭv bŏth′nĭ-à)	184-85	63°0′N	20°00′E
Botoşani, Rom. (bō-tō-shän′ĭ)	194-95	47°45′N	26°40′E
Botswana, nation, Afr. (bŏtswănă)	253	22°0′S	24°00′E
Bottineau, N.D., U.S. (bŏt-ĭ-nō′)	114-15	48°49′N	100°27′W
Bottniska Viken, b., Eur. *see* Bothnia, Gulf of	184-85	63°0′N	20°00′E
Botucatu, Braz.	172	22°52′S	48°27′W
Botwood, Nf., Can. (bŏt′wo͝od)	138-39	49°09′N	55°22′W
Bouaké, C. Iv.	260-61	7°42′N	5°02′W
Bouar, C.A.R. (bo͞o-är)	262-63	5°57′N	15°36′E
Boufarik, Alg. (bo͞o-fà-rēk′)	269b	36°35′N	2°54′E
Bougainville, i., Pap. N. Gui. (bo͞o-găN-vēl′)	279e	6°0′S	155°00′E
Bougie, Alg. *see* Bejaïa	269b	36°45′N	5°04′E
Bouira, Alg. (boo-ē′rà)	269b	36°23′N	3°54′E
Boujdour, Cap, c., W. Sah.	258-59	26°08′N	14°29′W
Boulder, Co., U.S. (bōld′ẽr)	118-19	40°02′N	105°15′W
Boulder, Mt., U.S. (bōld′ẽr)	112-13	46°14′N	112°08′W
Boulder, stm., Mt., U.S. (bōld′ẽr)	112-13	45°52′N	111°57′W
Boulder City, Nv., U.S. (bōld′ẽr sĭ′tē)	118-19	35°59′N	114°50′W
Boulia, Austl.	277	22°55′S	139°55′E
Boulogne-Billancourt, Fr. (bo͞o-lôn′y′-bē-yän-ko͞or′)	196-97	48°51′N	2°15′E
Boulogne-sur-Mer, Fr. (bo͞o-lôn′y-sür-mâr′)	196-97	50°43′N	1°36′E
Boundary Peak, mtn., Nv., U.S.	118-19	37°51′N	118°21′W
Bountiful, Ut., U.S. (boun′tĭ-fo͝ol)	112-13	40°53′N	111°53′W
Bounty Islands, is., N.Z.	287	47°42′S	179°04′E
Bourg-en-Bresse, Fr. (bo͞or-gĕN-brĕs′)	196-97	46°13′N	5°13′E
Bourges, Fr. (bo͞orzh)	196-97	47°05′N	2°24′E
Bourke, Austl. (bŭrk)	276	30°06′S	145°56′E
Bournemouth, Eng., U.K. (bôrn′m*ŭ*th)	190-91	50°44′N	1°52′W
Bou Saâda, Alg. (bo͞o-sä′dä)	269b	35°13′N	4°11′E
Boutilimit, Maur.	258-59	17°33′N	14°42′W
Bouvetøya, i., Afr.	284-85	54°26′S	3°24′E
Bow, stm., Ab., Can. (bō)	132-33	49°56′N	111°42′W
Bowbells, N.D., U.S. (bō′bĕls)	114-15	48°48′N	102°15′W
Bowen, Austl. (bō′ĕn)	277	20°01′S	148°14′E
Bowie, Md., U.S. (bo͞o′ĭ) (bō′ē)	116-17	39°00′N	76°46′W
Bowie, Tx., U.S. (bo͞o′ĭ) (bō′ē)	120-21	33°34′N	97°51′W
Bowling Green, Ky., U.S. (bōlĭng grēn)	124-25	36°59′N	86°27′W
Bowling Green, Mo., U.S. (bōlĭng grēn)	120-21	39°21′N	91°12′W
Bowling Green, Oh., U.S. (bōlĭng grēn)	116-17	41°22′N	83°39′W
Bowling Green, Va., U.S. (bōlĭng grēn)	116-17	38°03′N	77°21′W
Bowman, N.D., U.S. (bō′m*ă*n)	114-15	46°11′N	103°24′W
Bowral, Austl.	276	34°28′S	150°26′E
Bowron, stm., B.C., Can. (bō′r*ŭ*n)	132-33	54°03′N	121°50′W
Boxing, China (bwo-shyĭŋ)	240-41	37°08′N	118°07′E
Boyang, China (bwo-yäŋ)	238-39	28°60′N	116°40′E
Boyle, Ire. (boil)	190-91	53°59′N	8°18′W
Boyoma Falls, wtfl., D.R.C. *see* Stanley Falls	262-63	0°29′N	25°13′E
Boysun, Uzb.	232-33	38°12′N	67°12′E
Bozeman, Mt., U.S. (bōz′m*ă*n)	112-13	45°41′N	111°03′W
Bozen, Italy *see* Bolzano	200-01	46°30′N	11°21′E
Bozhen, China (bwo-jŭn)	240-41	38°05′N	116°33′E
Bozhou, China	238-39	33°52′N	115°46′E
Bra, Italy (brä)	200-01	44°41′N	7°51′E
Bracebridge, On., Can. (brās′brĭj)	136-37	45°02′N	79°18′W
Brackettville, Tx., U.S. (brăk′ĕt-vĭl)	122-23	29°18′N	100°25′W
Bradano, stm., Italy (brä-dä′nō)	200-01	40°23′N	16°51′E
Bradenton, Fl., U.S. (brā′dĕn-tŭn)	125a	27°30′N	82°33′W
Bradford, Eng., U.K. (brăd′fẽrd)	190-91	53°48′N	1°45′W
Bradley, Il., U.S. (brăd′lĭ)	116-17	41°08′N	87°51′W
Brady, Tx., U.S. (brā′dĭ)	122-23	31°08′N	99°20′W
Braga, Port. (brä′gä)	198-99	41°33′N	8°26′W
Bragado, Arg. (brä-gä′dō)	173	35°08′S	60°30′W
Bragança, Braz. (brä-gän′sä)	166-67	1°03′S	46°46′W
Bragança, Port.	198-99	41°49′N	6°45′W
Brāhmanbāria, Bngl.	234-35	23°59′N	91°07′E
Brāhmani, stm., India	234-35	20°47′N	87°01′E
Brahmapur, India	236	19°18′N	84°49′E
Brahmaputra, stm., Asia (brä′mȧ-po͞o′trȧ)	234-35	24°02′N	91°00′E
Braidwood, Il., U.S. (brād′wo͝od)	116-17	41°16′N	88°12′W
Brăila, Rom. (brē′ēlȧ)	202-03	45°16′N	27°58′E
Brainerd, Mn., U.S. (brān′ẽrd)	114-15	46°21′N	94°12′W
Brampton, On., Can. (brămp′t*ŭ*n)	136-37	43°42′N	79°45′W
Branco, stm., Braz. (bräŋ′kō)	164-65	1°24′S	61°52′W
Brandberg, mtn., Nmb.	264-65	21°10′S	14°33′E
Brandenburg, Ger. (brän′dĕn-bo͝orgh)	194-95	52°25′N	12°33′E
Brandfort, S. Afr. (brăn′d-fôrt)	269c	28°42′S	26°28′E
Brandon, Mb., Can. (brăn′d*ŭ*n)	134-35	49°50′N	99°58′W
Brandon, Ms., U.S. (brăn′d*ŭ*n)	124-25	32°16′N	89°59′W
Brandon, S.D., U.S. (brăn′d*ŭ*n)	114-15	43°36′N	96°34′W
Brandon, Vt., U.S. (brăn′d*ŭ*n)	116-17	43°48′N	73°05′W
Braniewo, Pol. (brä-nyĕ′vô)	194-95	54°23′N	19°50′E
Brantford, On., Can. (brănt′fẽrd)	136-37	43°09′N	80°15′W
Bras d'Or Lake, lk., N.S., Can. (brä-dôr′ lāk)	138-39	45°52′N	60°50′W
Brasil, nation, S.A. *see* Brazil	158	10°0′S	55°00′W
Brasiléia, Braz.	166-67	10°60′S	68°45′W
Brasília, nat. cap., Braz. (brä-sē′lvä)	168-69	15°48′S	47°53′W
Braşov, Rom.	194-95	45°39′N	25°37′E
Brass, Nig. (brăs)	260a	4°19′N	6°15′E
Brassó, Rom. *see* Braşov	194-95	45°39′N	25°37′E
Bratislava, nat. cap., Slvk. (brä′tĭs-lä-vä)	194-95	48°09′N	17°07′E
Bratsk, Russia (brätsk)	218-19	56°08′N	101°39′E
Bratskoye Vodokhranilishche, res., Russia	218-19	55°57′N	101°52′E
Bratsk Reservoir, res., Russia (brätsk rĕ′sẽr-vwär) *see* Bratskoye Vodokhranilishche	218-19	55°57′N	101°52′E
Bratslav, Ukr. (brät′slȧf)	202-03	48°49′N	28°57′E
Brattleboro, Vt., U.S. (brăt′'l-bŭr-ô)	116-17	42°51′N	72°34′W
Braunschweig, Ger. (broun′shvīgh)	194-95	52°16′N	10°31′E
Brava, i., C.V.	260-61	14°52′N	24°43′W
Bravo, stm., N.A. *see* Rio Grande	110-11	25°57′N	97°09′W
Bravo del Norte, stm., N.A. *see* Rio Grande	110-11	25°57′N	97°09′W
Brawley, Ca., U.S. (brô′lĭ)	118-19	32°59′N	115°33′W
Brazeau, stm., Ab., Can.	132-33	52°55′N	115°14′W
Brazeau, Mount, mtn., Ab., Can. (mount brȧ-zō′)	132-33	52°33′N	117°21′W
Brazil, In., U.S. (br*ȧ*-zĭl′)	116-17	39°31′N	87°07′W
Brazil, nation, S.A. (br*ȧ*-zĭl′)	158	10°0′S	55°00′W
Brazos, stm., Tx., U.S. (brä′zōs)	122-23	33°15′N	100°00′W
Brazos, Salt Fork, stm., U.S. (sôlt fôrk)	120-21	33°16′N	100°01′W
Brazzaville, nat. cap., Congo (brȧ-zȧ-vēl′)	262-63	4°16′S	15°17′E
Brčko, Bos. (bĕrch′kô)	200-01	44°52′N	18°49′E
Breckenridge, Mn., U.S. (brĕk′ĕn-rĭj)	114-15	46°15′N	96°34′W
Breckenridge, Tx., U.S. (brĕk′ĕn-rĭj)	120-21	32°45′N	98°55′W
Břeclav, Czech Rep. (brzhĕl′lȧf)	194-95	48°46′N	16°54′E
Breda, Neth. (brā-dä′)	190-91	51°35′N	4°46′E
Bregenz, Aus. (brā′gĕnts)	194-95	47°30′N	9°46′E
Bregovo, Blg. (brĕ′gō-vō)	200-01	44°10′N	22°39′E
Breiđafjörđur, b., Ice.	190a	65°15′N	23°15′W
Brejo, Braz. (brå′zhô)	166-67	3°41′S	42°47′W
Bremen, Ger. (brā-m*ĕ*n)	194-95	53°04′N	8°51′E
Bremen, Ga., U.S. (brē′m*ĕ*n)	124-25	33°43′N	85°09′W
Bremen, In., U.S. (brē′mĕn)	116-17	41°27′N	86°08′W
Bremerhaven, Ger. (brām-ẽr-hä′f*ĕ*n)	194-95	53°32′N	8°36′E
Bremerton, Wa., U.S. (brĕm′ẽr-t*ŭ*n)	112-13	47°34′N	122°39′W
Brenham, Tx., U.S. (brĕn′*ă*m)	122-23	30°10′N	96°24′W
Brentwood, N.Y., U.S. (brĕnt′wo͝od)	116-17	40°47′N	73°15′W
Brentwood, Tn., U.S. (brĕnt′wo͝od)	124-25	36°02′N	86°47′W
Brescia, Italy (brā′shä)	200-01	45°33′N	10°13′E
Breslau, Pol. *see* Wrocław	194-95	51°07′N	17°02′E
Bressanone, Italy (brĕs-sä-nō′nā)	200-01	46°43′N	11°39′E
Bressuire, Fr. (grĕ-swēr′)	196-97	46°50′N	0°29′W
Brèst, Bela.	194-95	52°07′N	23°42′E
Brest, Fr. (brĕst)	196-97	48°24′N	4°30′W
Bretagne, hist. reg., Fr. (brĕ-tän′y*ĕ*) *see* Brittany	196-97	48°0′N	3°00′W
Breton Sound, strt., La., U.S. (brĕt′*ŭ*n sound)	124-25	29°34′N	89°16′W
Brevard, N.C., U.S. (brė-värd′)	124-25	35°14′N	82°44′W
Breves, Braz. (brā′vĕzh)	166-67	1°40′S	50°29′W
Brewarrina, Austl. (bro͞o-ẽr-rē′n*á*)	276	29°57′S	146°52′E
Brewster, Wa., U.S. (bro͞o′stẽr)	112-13	48°06′N	119°47′W
Brewster, Kap, c., Green.	86	70°09′N	22°06′W
Brewton, Al., U.S. (bro͞o′t*ŭ*n)	124-25	31°07′N	87°05′W
Brezhnev, Russia *see* Naberezhnye Chelny	186-87	55°42′N	52°19′E
Bria, C.A.R.	262-63	6°33′N	21°58′E
Briançon, Fr. (brē-äN-sôN′)	196-97	44°54′N	6°37′E
Bridgeport, Al., U.S. (brĭj′pôrt)	124-25	34°57′N	85°43′W
Bridgeport, Ca., U.S. (brĭj′pôrt)	118-19	38°16′N	119°14′W
Bridgeport, Ct., U.S. (brĭj′pôrt)	116-17	41°11′N	73°14′W
Bridgeport, Il., U.S. (brĭj′pôrt)	116-17	38°42′N	87°46′W
Bridgeport, Ne., U.S. (brĭj′pôrt)	114-15	41°40′N	103°05′W
Bridgeport, Tx., U.S. (brĭj′pôrt)	120-21	33°13′N	97°46′W
Bridgetown, Austl.	270-71	33°58′S	116°08′E
Bridgetown, N.S., Can. (brĭj′ toun)	138-39	44°52′N	65°16′W
Bridgetown, nat. cap., Barb. (brĭj′ toun)	143b	13°06′N	59°37′W
Bridgewater, N.S., Can.	138-39	44°22′N	64°31′W
Bridgton, Me., U.S. (brĭj′t*ŭ*n)	116-17	44°04′N	70°42′W
Bridlington, Eng., U.K. (brĭd′lĭng-t*ŭ*n)	190-91	54°05′N	0°12′W
Brig, Switz. (brēg)	194-95	46°19′N	8°00′E
Brigham City, Ut., U.S. (brĭg′*ă*m sĭ′tē)	112-13	41°31′N	112°01′W
Bright, Austl. (brīt)	276	36°44′S	146°58′E
Brighton, Eng., U.K. (brī′t*ŭ*n)	190-91	50°50′N	0°08′W
Brighton, Co., U.S. (brīt′*ŭ*n)	120-21	39°59′N	104°49′W
Brighton, N.Y., U.S. (brīt′*ŭ*n)	116-17	43°09′N	77°33′W
Brindisi, Italy (brēn′dē-zē)	200-01	40°38′N	17°56′E
Brinkley, Ar., U.S. (brĭŋk′lĭ)	124-25	34°54′N	91°11′W
Brioude, Fr. (brē-o͞od′)	196-97	45°18′N	3°23′E
Brisbane, Austl. (brĭz′băn)	276	27°28′S	153°02′E
Bristol, Eng., U.K.	190-91	51°27′N	2°36′W
Bristol, Ct., U.S. (brĭs′tŭl)	116-17	41°41′N	72°57′W
Bristol, R.I., U.S. (brĭs′tŭl)	116-17	41°40′N	71°16′W

n-sing; ŋ-baŋk; N-nasalized n; nŏd; cŏmmit; ōld; ôbey; ôrder; oi-boil; fo͞od; ŏ-as oo in foot; ou-out; s-soft; sh-dish; th-thin; pūre; ûnite; ûrn; stŭd; circ*ŭ*s; ü-as in French tu; ′-indeterminate vowel.

Feature (Pronunciation)	Page	Lat.	Long.
Bristol, Tn., U.S. (brĭs´tŭl)	**124-25**	36°35′N	82°11′W
Bristol, Va., U.S. (brĭs´tŭl)	**124-25**	36°36′N	82°11′W
Bristol Bay, b., Ak., U.S. (brĭs´tŭl bā)	**126**	58°0′N	159°00′W
Bristol Channel, strt., U.K.	**190-91**	51°23′N	4°01′W
Bristow, Ok., U.S. (brĭs´tō)	**120-21**	35°50′N	96°24′W
British Columbia, state, Can. (brĭt´ĭsh kŏl´ŭm-bĭ-ȧ)	**128-29**	54°0′N	125°00′W
British Guiana, nation, S.A. *see* Guyana	**158**	5°0′N	59°00′W
British Honduras, nation, N.A. *see* Belize	**85**	17°15′N	88°45′W
British Indian Ocean Territory, dep., Afr.	**206-07**	7°0′S	72°00′E
British Solomon Islands, nation, Oc. *see* Solomon Islands	**279e**	8°0′S	159°00′E
British Virgin Islands, dep., N.A.	**140-41**	18°30′N	64°30′W
Britt, Ia., U.S. (brĭt)	**114-15**	43°06′N	93°49′W
Brittany, hist. reg., Fr.	**196-97**	48°0′N	3°00′W
Britton, S.D., U.S. (brĭt´ŭn)	**114-15**	45°48′N	97°45′W
Brive-la-Gaillarde, Fr. (brēv-lä-gī-yärd´ĕ)	**196-97**	45°09′N	1°32′E
Brixen, Italy *see* Bressanone	**200-01**	46°43′N	11°39′E
Brno, Czech Rep. (b'r´nô)	**194-95**	49°12′N	16°37′E
Brockport, N.Y., U.S. (brŏk´pōrt)	**116-17**	43°13′N	77°56′W
Brockton, Ma., U.S. (brŏk´tŭn)	**116-17**	42°05′N	71°01′W
Brockville, On., Can. (brŏk´vĭl)	**136-37**	44°36′N	75°41′W
Brodnica, Pol. (brôd´nĭt-sȧ)	**194-95**	53°15′N	19°24′E
Brody, Ukr. (brô´dĭ)	**194-95**	50°05′N	25°10′E
Broken Arrow, Ok., U.S. (brō´kĕn ăr´ō)	**120-21**	36°03′N	95°47′W
Broken Bow, Ne., U.S. (brō´kĕn bō)	**114-15**	41°24′N	99°39′W
Broken Bow, Ok., U.S. (brō´kĕn bō)	**120-21**	34°02′N	94°44′W
Broken Hill, Austl. (brōk´ĕn hĭl)	**276**	31°58′S	141°27′E
Broken Hill, Zam. *see* Kabwe	**264-65**	14°27′S	28°27′E
Brokopondo, Sur.	**164-65**	5°04′N	54°59′W
Brokopondo Stuwmeer, res., Sur. *see* W.J. van Blommestein Meer	**164-65**	4°49′N	55°04′W
Bromberg, Pol. *see* Bydgoszcz	**194-95**	53°07′N	18°01′E
Bronlund Peak, mtn., B.C., Can.	**130-31**	57°26′N	126°38′W
Brookfield, Mo., U.S. (brŏŏk´fēld)	**120-21**	39°48′N	93°05′W
Brookfield, Wi., U.S. (brŏŏk´fēld)	**116-17**	43°04′N	88°07′W
Brookhaven, Ms., U.S. (brŏŏk´hāv'n)	**124-25**	31°34′N	90°27′W
Brookings, Or., U.S. (brŏŏk´ĭngs)	**112-13**	42°04′N	124°17′W
Brookings, S.D., U.S. (brŏŏk´ĭngs)	**114-15**	44°19′N	96°48′W
Brooklyn Park, Mn., U.S. (brŏŏk´lĭn pärk)	**114-15**	45°07′N	93°20′W
Brooks, Ab., Can. (brŏŏks)	**132-33**	50°34′N	111°54′W
Brooks Range, mts., Ak., U.S. (brŏŏks rānj)	**126**	68°0′N	154°00′W
Brooksville, Fl., U.S. (brŏŏks´vĭl)	**125a**	28°33′N	82°24′W
Brookton, Austl.	**270-71**	32°22′S	117°01′E
Broome, Austl. (bro͞om)	**270-71**	17°58′S	122°14′E
Brownfield, Tx., U.S. (broun´fēld)	**120-21**	33°11′N	102°16′W
Browning, Mt., U.S. (broun´ĭng)	**112-13**	48°33′N	112°60′W
Brownstown, In., U.S. (brounz´toun)	**116-17**	38°53′N	86°03′W
Brownsville, Tn., U.S. (brounz´vĭl)	**124-25**	35°36′N	89°16′W
Brownsville, Tx., U.S. (brounz´vĭl)	**122-23**	25°56′N	97°29′W
Brownwood, Tx., U.S. (broun´wŏŏd)	**122-23**	31°43′N	98°59′W
Bruce, Mount, mtn., Austl. (mount bro͞os)	**272-73**	22°35′S	118°08′E
Bruchsal, Ger. (brŏŏk´zäl)	**194-95**	49°08′N	8°36′E
Bruit, Pulau, i., Malay.	**248-49**	2°35′N	111°20′E
Bruneau, stm., U.S. (bro͞o-nō´)	**112-13**	42°57′N	115°57′W
Brunei, nation, Asia (brŏŏ-nī´)	**206-07**	4°30′N	114°40′E
Brunei, nat. cap., Bru. *see* Bandar Seri Begawan	**248-49**	4°56′N	114°56′E
Brünn, Czech Rep. *see* Brno	**194-95**	49°12′N	16°37′E
Brunswick, Ger. *see* Braunschweig	**194-95**	52°16′N	10°31′E
Brunswick, Ga., U.S. (brŭnz´wĭk)	**124-25**	31°11′N	81°30′W
Brunswick, Md., U.S. (brŭnz´wĭk)	**116-17**	39°19′N	77°38′W
Brunswick, Me., U.S. (brŭnz´wĭk)	**117a**	43°55′N	69°58′W
Brunswick, Península, pen., Chile	**171**	53°11′S	71°11′W
Brush, Co., U.S. (brŭsh)	**120-21**	40°15′N	103°38′W
Brusque, Braz. (bro͞o´s-ko͞oĕ)	**172**	27°07′S	48°56′W
Brussel, nat. cap., Bel. *see* Brussels	**190-91**	50°50′N	4°22′E
Brussels, nat. cap., Bel. (brŭs´ĕls)	**190-91**	50°50′N	4°22′E
Brüx, Czech Rep. *see* Most	**194-95**	50°31′N	13°39′E
Bruxelles, nat. cap., Bel. (brü-sĕl´) *see* Brussels	**190-91**	50°50′N	4°22′E
Bryan, Oh., U.S. (brī´ăn)	**116-17**	41°28′N	84°33′W
Bryan, Tx., U.S. (brī´ăn)	**122-23**	30°41′N	96°23′W
Bryansk, Russia	**202-03**	53°14′N	34°22′E
Bryce Canyon National Park, n.p., Ut., U.S. (brīs kăn´yŭn năsh´ŭn-ăl pärk)	**118-19**	37°29′N	112°15′W
Bryson City, N.C., U.S. (brīs´ŭn sĭ´tē)	**124-25**	35°26′N	83°27′W
Bryukhovetskaya, Russia (b'ryŭk´ô-vyĕt-skä´yä)	**202-03**	45°49′N	39°00′E
Bua Yai, Thai.	**246-47**	15°35′N	102°26′E
Būbiyān, i., Kuw.	**230-31**	29°45′N	48°15′E
Bucaramanga, Col. (bo͞o-kä´rä-mäŋ´gä)	**164-65**	7°03′N	73°05′W
Buchach, Ukr. (bŏŏ´chȧch)	**194-95**	49°04′N	25°25′E
Buchanan, Lib. (bů-kăn´ăn)	**260-61**	5°53′N	10°02′W
Buchanan, Mi., U.S. (bû-kăn´ăn)	**116-17**	41°49′N	86°22′W
Buchanan, Va., U.S. (bû-kăn´ăn)	**116-17**	37°31′N	79°41′W
Buchanan, Lake, lk., Tx., U.S. (lāk bû-kăn´ăn)	**122-23**	30°48′N	98°25′W
Buchans, Nf., Can.	**138-39**	48°49′N	56°52′W
Bucharest, nat. cap., Rom. (bo͞o-kȧ-rĕst´)	**200-01**	44°26′N	26°06′E
Buckhannon, W.V., U.S. (bŭk-hăn´ŭn)	**116-17**	38°59′N	80°14′W
Buckhaven, Scot., U.K. (bŭk-hā´v'n)	**190-91**	56°11′N	3°03′W
Buckie, Scot., U.K. (bŭk´ĭ)	**190-91**	57°40′N	2°59′W
Bucksport, Me., U.S. (bŭks´pôrt)	**117a**	44°34′N	68°48′W
București, nat. cap., Rom. (bo͞o-kŏŏ-rĕsh´tĭ) *see* Bucharest	**200-01**	44°26′N	26°06′E
Bucyrus, Oh., U.S. (bů-sī´rŭs)	**116-17**	40°48′N	82°58′W
Budapest, nat. cap., Hung. (bo͞o´dȧ-pĕsht´)	**194-95**	47°30′N	19°05′E
Budaun, India	**234-35**	28°02′N	79°08′E
Budennovsk, Russia	**186-87**	44°47′N	44°09′E
Budweis, Czech Rep. *see* České Budějovice	**194-95**	48°59′N	14°28′E
Buena Esperanza, Arg.	**171**	34°45′S	65°16′W
Buenaventura, Col. (bwā´nä-vĕn-to͞o´rȧ)	**163c**	3°53′N	77°04′W
Buenaventura, Mex.	**144-45**	29°51′N	107°28′W
Buena Vista, Bol.	**168-69**	17°27′S	63°40′W
Buena Vista, Co., U.S. (bū´nȧ vĭs´tȧ)	**118-19**	38°50′N	106°09′W
Buena Vista, Va., U.S. (bū´nȧ vĭs´tȧ)	**116-17**	37°44′N	79°21′W
Buenos Aires, state, Arg. (bwā´nōs ī´rās)	**173**	36°0′S	60°00′W
Buenos Aires, nat. cap., Arg. (bwā´nōs ī´rās)	**173**	34°37′S	58°23′W
Buenos Aires, Lago, lk., S.A. (lä´gô-bwā´nōs ī´rās)	**171**	46°26′S	71°40′W
Buffalo, Mn., U.S. (buf´ȧ-lō)	**114-15**	45°11′N	93°53′W
Buffalo, Mo., U.S. (buf´ȧ-lō)	**120-21**	37°39′N	93°06′W
Buffalo, N.Y., U.S. (buf´ȧ-lō)	**116-17**	42°53′N	78°52′W
Buffalo, Ok., U.S. (buf´ȧ-lō)	**120-21**	36°50′N	99°38′W
Buffalo, Tx., U.S. (buf´ȧ-lō)	**122-23**	31°27′N	96°04′W
Buffalo, Wy., U.S. (buf´ȧ-lō)	**112-13**	44°22′N	106°42′W
Buffalo, stm., Tn., U.S. (buf´ȧ-lō)	**124-25**	35°60′N	87°50′W
Buffalo Lake, lk., N.T., Can.	**130-31**	60°10′N	115°30′W
Buford, Ga., U.S. (bū´fĕrd)	**124-25**	34°07′N	84°00′W
Buga, Col. (bo͞o´gä)	**163c**	3°54′N	76°18′W
Bugojno, Bos. (bŏŏ-gō ĭ nô)	**200-01**	44°03′N	17°27′E
Bugsuk Island, i., Phil.	**250**	8°15′N	117°18′E
Bugt, China	**240-41**	48°46′N	121°54′E
Bugul'ma, Russia (bŏŏ-gŏŏl´mȧ)	**186-87**	54°31′N	52°47′E
Buguma, Nig.	**260a**	4°43′N	6°53′E
Buguruslan, Russia (bŏŏ-gŏŏ-rŏŏs-lȧn´)	**186-87**	53°39′N	52°27′E
Buhl, Id., U.S. (būl)	**112-13**	42°37′N	114°46′W
Buin, Chile (bŏŏ-ēn´)	**163e**	33°42′S	70°43′W
Buir Nur, lk., Asia (bo͞o-ēr no͞or)	**240-41**	47°48′N	117°42′E
Buitenzorg, Indon. *see* Bogor	**248-49**	6°35′S	106°47′E
Bujumbura, nat. cap., Bdi. (bo͞o-jŭm-bo͞o´rȧ)	**267**	3°23′S	29°22′E
Buka Island, i., Pap. N. Gui.	**279e**	5°15′S	154°35′E
Bukama, D.R.C. (bo͞o-kä´mä)	**262-63**	9°12′S	25°51′E
Bukavu, D.R.C.	**267**	2°30′S	28°51′E
Bukhara, Uzb. (bŏŏ-kä´rä) *see* Buxoro	**232-33**	39°46′N	64°26′E
Bukittinggi, Indon.	**246-47**	0°18′S	100°22′E
Bukoba, Tan.	**267**	1°19′S	31°48′E
Bulan, Phil.	**250**	12°40′N	123°53′E
Bulawayo, Zimb. (bo͞o-lȧ-wă´yō)	**264-65**	20°10′S	28°35′E
Bulgan, Mong.	**240-41**	48°49′N	103°33′E
Bulgaria, nation, Eur. (bŏŏl-gā´rĭ-ă)	**174-75**	43°0′N	25°00′E
Bŭlgariya, nation, Eur. *see* Bulgaria	**174-75**	43°0′N	25°00′E
Bulkley Ranges, mts., B.C., Can. (bŭlk´lē rānjĕz)	**132-33**	54°30′N	127°30′W
Bulloo, stm., Austl.	**272-73**	28°40′S	142°31′E
Bull Shoals Lake, res., U.S. (bŏŏl shōlz lāk)	**120-21**	36°29′N	92°47′W
Bultfontein, S. Afr. (bŏŏlt´fōn-tān´)	**269c**	28°17′S	26°09′E
Bulungu, D.R.C. (bo͞o-lŏŏŋ´go͞o)	**262-63**	6°03′S	21°53′E
Bumba, D.R.C. (bŏŏm´bȧ)	**262-63**	2°11′N	22°28′E
Bumbire Island, i., Tan.	**267**	1°39′S	31°53′E
Bunbury, Austl. (bŭn´bŭrĭ)	**270-71**	33°19′S	115°38′E
Bundaberg, Austl. (bŭn´dȧ-bûrg)	**277**	24°52′S	152°20′E
Būndi, India	**234-35**	25°27′N	75°38′E
Bungo-suidō, strt., Japan	**245**	33°0′N	132°13′E
Bunia, D.R.C.	**267**	1°32′N	30°15′E
Bunkie, La., U.S. (bŭŋ´kĭ)	**124-25**	30°57′N	92°11′W
Buntok, Indon.	**248-49**	1°44′S	114°50′E
Buon Ma Thuot, Viet.	**246-47**	12°40′N	108°03′E
Buqayq, Sau. Ar.	**230-31**	25°56′N	49°40′E
Burang, China	**234-35**	30°14′N	81°11′E
Buraydah, Sau. Ar.	**266**	26°19′N	43°59′E
Burayk, Libya	**258-59**	26°37′N	13°07′E
Burbank, Ca., U.S. (bûr´bănk)	**118-19**	34°11′N	118°19′W
Burco, Som.	**262-63**	9°32′N	45°33′E
Burdur, Tur. (bo͞or-dŏŏr´)	**186-87**	37°43′N	30°17′E
Bureya, stm., Russia (bŏŏ-rā´yä)	**240-41**	49°25′N	129°32′E
Burgas, Blg. (bŏŏr-gäs´)	**200-01**	42°31′N	27°28′E
Burgaw, N.C., U.S. (bûr´gô)	**124-25**	34°33′N	77°56′W
Burgos, Spain (bo͞o´r-gôs)	**198-99**	42°21′N	3°42′W
Burgsvik, Swe. (bŏŏrgs´vĭk)	**192-93**	57°02′N	18°18′E
Burhānpur, India (bŏŏr´hȧn-po͞or)	**234-35**	21°18′N	76°14′E
Burias Island, i., Phil. (bo͞o´rē-äs ī´lȧnd)	**250**	12°57′N	123°08′E
Burica, Punta, c., N.A. (po͞o´n-tä-bo͞o´rē-kä)	**150**	8°03′N	82°52′W
Burin, Nf., Can. (bûr´ĭn)	**138-39**	47°02′N	55°11′W
Burkburnett, Tx., U.S. (bûrk-bûr´nĕt)	**120-21**	34°06′N	98°34′W
Burke, stm., Austl.	**277**	23°12′S	139°34′E
Burketown, Austl. (bûrk´toun)	**277**	17°44′S	139°33′E
Burkina Faso, nation, Afr. (bo͞or-kē´-nȧ fä´sō)	**253**	13°0′N	1°30′W
Burley, Id., U.S. (bûr´lĭ)	**112-13**	42°33′N	113°47′W
Burlington, On., Can. (bûr´lĭng-tŭn)	**136-37**	43°19′N	79°48′W
Burlington, Co., U.S. (bûr´lĭng-tŭn)	**120-21**	39°18′N	102°16′W
Burlington, Ia., U.S. (bûr´lĭng-tŭn)	**114-15**	40°48′N	91°06′W
Burlington, N.C., U.S. (bûr´lĭng-tŭn)	**124-25**	36°06′N	79°26′W
Burlington, N.D., U.S. (bûr´lĭng-tŭn)	**114-15**	48°16′N	101°25′W
Burlington, Vt., U.S.	**116-17**	44°29′N	73°12′W
Burlington, Wi., U.S. (bûr´lĭng-tŭn)	**116-17**	42°41′N	88°16′W
Burma, nation, Asia *see* Bhutan	**206-07**	22°0′N	98°00′E
Burnie, Austl. (bûr´nē)	**276**	41°04′S	145°54′E
Burnley, Eng., U.K. (bûrn´lĕ)	**190-91**	53°48′N	2°15′W
Burns, Or., U.S. (bûrnz)	**112-13**	43°36′N	119°03′W
Burnside, stm., Nu., Can.	**130-31**	66°51′N	108°12′W
Burns Lake, B.C., Can. (bûrnz lāk)	**132-33**	54°14′N	125°46′W
Burntwood, stm., Mb., Can.	**134-35**	56°08′N	96°20′W
Burqin, China	**226**	47°43′N	86°54′E
Burra, Austl.	**276**	33°40′S	138°55′E
Bursa, Tur. (bo͞or´sȧ)	**200-01**	40°12′N	29°04′E
Bûr Sa'îd, Egypt *see* Port Said	**268b**	31°16′N	32°18′E
Būr Sūdān, Sudan *see* Port Sudan	**266**	19°37′N	37°13′E
Burton, Mi., U.S. (bûr´tŭn)	**116-17**	43°00′N	83°35′W
Burton upon Trent, Eng., U.K. (bŭr´tŭn-ŭp´-ŏn-trĕnt)	**190-91**	52°49′N	1°38′W
Buru, i., Indon.	**248-49**	3°24′S	126°40′E
Burundi, nation, Afr. (bū-rūn´-dē)	**253**	3°15′S	30°00′E
Burun-Shibertuy, Gora, mtn., Russia	**240-41**	49°42′N	109°58′E
Burwell, Ne., U.S. (bûr´wĕl)	**114-15**	41°46′N	99°08′W
Buryatia, state, Russia	**222-23**	53°0′N	109°00′E
Buryatiya, state, Russia *see* Buryatia	**222-23**	53°0′N	109°00′E
Bury Saint Edmunds, Eng., U.K. (bĕr´ī-sānt ĕd´mŭndz)	**190-91**	52°15′N	0°42′E
Busan, Kor., S. *see* Pusan	**243**	35°05′N	129°03′E
Būshehr, Iran	**230-31**	28°58′N	50°51′E
Bushire, Iran *see* Būshehr	**230-31**	28°58′N	50°51′E
Bushnell, Il., U.S. (bŏŏsh´nĕl)	**120-21**	40°33′N	90°30′W
Businga, D.R.C. (bŏŏ-sĭŋ´gȧ)	**262-63**	3°20′N	20°53′E
Busselton, Austl. (bûs´l-tŭn)	**270-71**	33°39′S	115°21′E
Busto Arsizio, Italy (bo͞os´tō är-sēd´zē-ō)	**200-01**	45°37′N	8°51′E
Busuanga Island, i., Phil. (bo͞o-swäŋ´gä ī´lȧnd)	**250**	12°05′N	120°05′E
Buta, D.R.C. (bo͞o´tȧ)	**262-63**	2°49′N	24°45′E
Butare, Rw.	**267**	2°36′S	29°44′E
Butaritari, at., Kir.	**280-81**	3°06′N	172°50′E
Bute Inlet, b., B.C., Can.	**132-33**	50°37′N	124°53′W
Butembo, D.R.C.	**267**	0°08′N	29°18′E
Butere, Kenya	**267**	0°13′N	34°30′E
Butha-Buthe, Leso. (bo͞o-thȧ-bo͞o´thȧ)	**269c**	28°45′S	28°16′E
Butha Qi, China *see* Zalantun	**240-41**	47°60′N	122°45′E
Butler, In., U.S. (bŭt´lẽr)	**116-17**	41°25′N	84°52′W
Butler, Mo., U.S. (bŭt´lẽr)	**120-21**	38°15′N	94°20′W
Butler, Pa., U.S.	**116-17**	40°51′N	79°54′W
Buton, Pulau, i., Indon.	**248-49**	5°02′S	122°53′E
Butte, Mt., U.S. (būt)	**112-13**	45°60′N	112°32′W
Butterworth, Malay.	**246-47**	5°24′N	100°23′E
Butuan, Phil. (bo͞o-to͞o´än)	**250**	8°57′N	125°32′E
Buṭwal, Nepal	**234-35**	27°43′N	83°28′E
Buxoro, Uzb.	**232-33**	39°46′N	64°26′E
Buy, Russia (bwē)	**186-87**	58°29′N	41°33′E
Buyant-Uhaa, Mong.	**240-41**	44°55′N	110°09′E
Buynaksk, Russia	**227**	42°50′N	47°06′E
Buyr nuur, lk., Asia *see* Buir Nur	**240-41**	47°48′N	117°42′E

ăt; finăl; rāte; senåte; ärm; åsk; sofȧ; fâre; ch-choose; dh-as th in other; bē; ėvent; bĕt; recĕnt; cratẽr; g-gō; gh-guttural g; bĭt; ĭ-short neutral; rīde; ĸ-guttural k as ch in German ich;

Feature (Pronunciation)	Page	Lat.	Long.
Büyük Ağrı Dağı, vol., Tur. see Ararat, Mount	227	39°42'N	44°18'E
Buzău, Rom. (bōō-zĕ'ŏ)	202-03	45°09'N	26°50'E
Búzi, stm., Moz.	264-65	19°53'S	34°45'E
Buzuluk, Russia (bŏ-zŏ-lŏk')	186-87	52°47'N	52°15'E
Byala Slatina, Blg. (byä'la slä'tēnä)	200-01	43°28'N	23°58'E
Byblos, Leb. see Jubayl	228-29	34°08'N	35°40'E
Bydgoszcz, Pol. (bĭd'gôshch)	194-95	53°07'N	18°01'E
Byelorussia, nation, Eur. see Belarus	174-75	53°50'N	28°00'E
Bytantay, stm., Russia (byän'täy)	218-19	68°45'N	134°27'E
Bytom, Pol. (bĭ'tŭm)	194-95	50°21'N	18°55'E
Byumba, Rw.	267	1°36'S	30°04'E
Byzantium, Tur. see İstanbul	200-01	41°02'N	28°59'E

C

Feature (Pronunciation)	Page	Lat.	Long.
Ca, stm., Asia	246-47	18°44'N	105°45'E
Caacupé, Para.	168-69	25°22'S	57°08'W
Caála, Ang.	264-65	12°51'S	15°33'E
Caazapá, Para.	168-69	26°11'S	56°22'W
Cabanatuan, Phil. (kä-bä-nä-twän')	250	15°29'N	120°59'E
Cabano, Qc., Can. (kä-bä-nō')	138-39	47°41'N	68°53'W
Cabedelo, Braz. (kä-bē-dā'lŏ)	163d	6°58'S	34°50'W
Cabeza del Buey, Spain (kȧ-bā'thä dĕl bwā')	198-99	38°43'N	5°13'W
Cabimas, Ven. (kä-bē'mäs)	164-65	10°24'N	71°26'W
Cabinda, Ang. (kä-bĭn'dȧ)	260-61	5°33'S	12°12'E
Cabinet Mountains, mts., U.S. (kăb'ĭ-nĕt moun'tĭnz)	112-13	48°19'N	116°12'W
Cabo, Braz.	163d	8°17'S	35°02'W
Cabo Frio, Braz. (kä'bō-frē'ŏ)	172	22°53'S	42°02'W
Cabonga, Réservoir, res., Qc., Can.	136-37	47°17'N	76°33'W
Caborca, Mex.	144-45	30°43'N	112°09'W
Cabot Strait, strt., Can. (kăb'ŭt strāt)	138-39	47°20'N	59°30'W
Cabo Verde, nation, Afr. see Cape Verde	253	16°0'N	24°00'W
Cabra, Spain (käb'rä)	198-99	37°29'N	4°27'W
Cabrera, Illa de, i., Spain	198-99	39°09'N	2°57'E
Cabrera, Isla de, i., Spain see Cabrera, Illa de	198-99	39°09'N	2°57'E
Cabriel, stm., Spain (kä-brē-ĕl')	198-99	39°14'N	1°03'W
Caçador, Braz.	168-69	26°47'S	51°01'W
Čačak, Serb. (chä'chȧk)	200-01	43°54'N	20°21'E
Cáceres, Braz. (kȧ'sĕ-rĕs)	168-69	16°04'S	57°42'W
Cáceres, Spain (kȧ'thȧ-rās)	198-99	39°28'N	6°22'W
Cache, stm., Ar., U.S. (kȧsh)	124-25	34°42'N	91°20'W
Cache Creek, B.C., Can. (kăsh krēk)	132-33	50°49'N	121°19'W
Cachimbo, Serra do, mts., Braz.	166-67	8°25'S	55°45'W
Cachoeira do Sul, Braz. (kä-shō-ā'rä-dŏ-sōō'l)	173	30°02'S	52°54'W
Cachoeiras de Macacu, Braz. (kä-shō-ā'räs-dĕ-mä-kȧ'kōō)	172	22°28'S	42°39'W
Cachoeiro de Itapemirim, Braz.	172	20°51'S	41°08'W
Cadereyta Jiménez, Mex. (kä-dä-rā'tä hē-mā'nāz)	122-23	25°35'N	99°60'W
Cadillac, Mi., U.S. (kăd'ĭ-lăk)	116-17	44°15'N	85°24'W
Cádiz, Spain (kȧ'dēz)	198-99	36°31'N	6°17'W
Cadiz, Ky., U.S. (kā'dĭz)	124-25	36°52'N	87°50'W
Cadiz, Oh., U.S. (kā'dĭz)	116-17	40°16'N	80°60'W
Cádiz, Golfo de, b., Eur. (gôl-fô-dĕ-kȧ'dēz) see Cadiz, Gulf of	198-99	36°50'N	7°10'W
Cadiz, Gulf of, b., Eur. (gŭlf ŭv kā'dĭz)	198-99	36°50'N	7°10'W
Caen, Fr. (kän)	196-97	49°11'N	0°21'W
Caetité, Braz.	166-67	14°04'S	42°29'W
Cafayate, Arg.	168-69	26°04'S	65°59'W
Cagayan, stm., Phil.	250	18°22'N	121°37'E
Cagayan de Oro, Phil.	250	8°29'N	124°38'E
Cagayan Islands, is., Phil.	250	9°40'N	121°16'E
Cagayan Sulu Island, i., Phil.	250	7°01'N	118°30'E
Cagliari, Italy (käl'yä-rē)	200-01	39°14'N	9°07'E
Cagliari, Golfo di, b., Italy (gôl-fô-dē-käl'yä-rē)	200-01	39°08'N	9°11'E
Cagua, Ven. (kä'gwä)	163b	10°12'N	67°26'W
Caguas, P.R. (kä'gwäs)	142a	18°14'N	66°02'W
Cahaba, stm., Al., U.S. (kȧ hä-bä)	124-25	32°20'N	87°06'W
Cahors, Fr. (kȧ-ôr')	196-97	44°27'N	1°26'E
Cahul, Mol.	202-03	45°55'N	28°12'E
Caibarién, Cuba (kī-bä-rē-ĕn')	142-43	22°31'N	79°28'W
Caicedonia, Col. (kī-sĕ-dŏ-nēä)	163c	4°19'N	75°48'W
Caicó, Braz.	163d	6°27'S	37°06'W
Caicos Islands, is., T./C. Is. (kī'kōs ī'lȧndz)	142-43	21°42'N	71°54'W
Caicos Passage, strt., N.A. (kī'kōs păs'ĭj)	142-43	22°00'N	72°30'W
Caimanera, Cuba (kī-mä-nā'rä)	142-43	19°59'N	75°10'W
Cairns, Austl. (kârnz)	277	16°56'S	145°45'E
Cairo, Ga., U.S. (kā'rō)	124-25	30°53'N	84°13'W
Cairo, Il., U.S. (kā'rō)	124-25	37°00'N	89°11'W
Cairo, nat. cap., Egypt (kī'rŏ)	268b	30°03'N	31°14'E
Cajamarca, Peru (kä-hä-mär'kä)	170	7°10'S	78°31'W
Cajazeiras, Braz.	166-67	6°54'S	38°34'W
Čakovec, Cro. (chȧ'kō-vĕts)	200-01	46°23'N	16°26'E
Calabar, Nig. (kăl-ȧ-bär')	260a	4°58'N	8°19'E
Calabozo, Ven. (kä-lä-bō'zō)	163b	8°55'N	67°26'W
Calafat, Rom. (kȧ-lȧ-fȧt')	200-01	43°59'N	22°57'E
Calagua Islands, is., Phil. (kä-gä-yän ī'lȧndz)	250	14°27'N	122°55'E
Calahorra, Spain (kä-lä-ôr'rä)	198-99	42°18'N	1°58'W
Calais, Fr. (kȧ-lĕ')	196-97	50°58'N	1°51'E
Calais, Me., U.S.	117a	45°11'N	67°16'W
Calais, Pas de, strt., Eur. see Dover, Strait of	190-91	50°59'N	1°31'E
Calama, Chile (kä-lä'mä)	168-69	22°27'S	68°55'W
Calamar, Col. (kä-lä-mär')	164-65	1°58'N	72°42'W
Calamian Group, is., Phil. (kä-lä-myän' grōōp)	250	12°0'N	120°00'E
Calapan, Phil. (kä-lä-pän')	250	13°24'N	121°11'E
Călăraşi, Rom. (kŭ-lŭ-rȧsh'ĭ)	202-03	44°13'N	27°19'E
Calatayud, Spain (kä-lä-tä-yōōdh')	198-99	41°21'N	1°38'W
Calayan Island, i., Phil.	250a	19°20'N	121°27'E
Calbayog, Phil.	250	12°04'N	124°34'E
Calcasieu, stm., La., U.S. (kăl'kȧ-shū)	122-23	30°03'N	93°19'W
Calcasieu Lake, lk., La., U.S. (kăl'kȧ-shū lăk)	122-23	29°56'N	93°16'W
Calçoene, Braz.	166-67	2°30'N	50°57'W
Calcutta, India (kăl-kŭt'ȧ) see Kolkata	234-35	22°32'N	88°22'E
Caldas, Col. (kȧ'l-däs)	163c	6°04'N	75°38'W
Caldas da Rainha, Port. (käl'däs dä rīn'yă)	198-99	39°24'N	9°08'W
Caldera, Chile (käl-dā'rä)	168-69	27°04'S	70°50'W
Caldwell, Id., U.S. (kôld'wĕl)	112-13	43°40'N	116°41'W
Caldwell, Oh., U.S. (kôld'wĕl)	116-17	39°44'N	81°31'W
Caldwell, Tx., U.S. (kôld'wĕl)	122-23	30°31'N	96°42'W
Caledonia, Mn., U.S. (kăl-ē-dō'nĭ-ȧ)	114-15	43°39'N	91°31'W
Calella, Spain (kä-lĕl'yä)	198-99	41°37'N	2°40'E
Calexico, Ca., U.S. (kȧ-lĕk'sĭ-kō)	118-19	32°41'N	115°30'W
Calgary, Ab., Can. (kăl'gȧ-rĭ)	132-33	51°03'N	114°05'W
Calhoun, Ga., U.S. (kăl-hōōn')	124-25	34°30'N	84°58'W
Calhoun, Ky., U.S. (kăl-hōōn')	116-17	37°32'N	87°15'W
Cali, Col. (kä'lē)	164-65	3°27'N	76°31'W
Calicut, India see Kozhikode	236	11°16'N	75°47'E
California, Mo., U.S. (kăl-ĭ-fôr'nĭ-ȧ)	120-21	38°38'N	92°34'W
California, state, U.S. (kăl-ĭ-fôr'nĭ-ȧ)	108-09	37°30'N	119°30'W
California, Golfo de, b., Mex. (gôl-fô-dĕ-kä-lē-fôr-nyä)	144-45	28°0'N	112°00'W
California, Gulf of, b., Mex. (gŭlf ŭv kăl-ĭ-fôr'nĭ-ȧ) see California, Golfo de	144-45	28°0'N	112°00'W
Calimere, Point, c., India	236	10°17'N	79°52'E
Calipatria, Ca., U.S. (kăl-ĭ-pàt'rĭ-ȧ)	118-19	33°08'N	115°31'W
Calkiní, Mex. (käl-kē-nē')	148	20°23'N	90°02'W
Callabonna, Lake, lk., Austl. (lăk călă'bŏnȧ)	276	29°41'S	140°03'E
Callao, Peru (käl-yä'ŏ)	163a	12°04'S	77°08'W
Calling Lake, lk., Ab., Can. (kôl'ĭng lăk)	132-33	55°13'N	113°15'W
Calmar, Swe. see Kalmar	192-93	56°40'N	16°22'E
Caloosahatchee, stm., Fl., U.S. (kȧ-loo-sȧ-hăch'ē)	125a	26°32'N	82°01'W
Caltagirone, Italy (käl-tä-jē-rō'nȧ)	200-01	37°14'N	14°31'E
Caltanissetta, Italy (käl-tä-nē-sĕt'tä)	200-01	37°29'N	14°04'E
Caluula, Som.	262-63	11°57'N	50°46'E
Calvert Island, i., B.C., Can.	132-33	51°33'N	128°02'W
Calvillo, Mex. (käl-vēl'yō)	146-47	21°51'N	102°43'W
Calvinia, S. Afr. (kăl-vĭn'ĭ-ȧ)	264-65	31°28'S	19°46'E
Camacupa, Ang.	264-65	12°01'S	17°28'E
Camagüey, Cuba (kä-mä-gwā')	142-43	21°22'N	77°55'W
Camagüey, state, Cuba (kä-mä-gwā')	142-43	21°30'N	78°00'W
Camaná, Peru	170	16°37'S	72°42'W
Camaquã, Braz.	168-69	30°51'S	51°49'W
Camará, Braz.	166-67	3°55'S	62°44'W
Camarón, Cabo, c., Hond. (kȧ'bô-kä-mä-rōn')	149	15°59'N	85°02'W
Camarones, Arg.	171	44°48'S	65°43'W
Camas, Wa., U.S. (kăm'ȧs)	112-13	45°35'N	122°24'W
Ca Mau, Viet.	246-47	9°11'N	105°09'E
Ca Mau, Mui, c., Viet.	246-47	8°37'N	104°43'E
Cambodia, nation, Asia (kăm-bō'dē-ȧ)	206-07	13°0'N	105°00'E
Camborne, Eng., U.K. (kăm'bôrn)	190-91	50°13'N	5°18'W
Cambrai, Fr. (kän-brĕ')	196-97	50°11'N	3°15'E
Cambrian Mountains, mts., Wales, U.K. (kăm'brĭ-ăn moun'tĭnz)	190-91	52°35'N	3°35'W
Cambridge, On., Can. (kăm'brĭj)	136-37	43°21'N	80°18'W
Cambridge, Eng., U.K. (kăm'brĭj)	190-91	52°13'N	0°08'E
Cambridge, Il., U.S. (kăm'brĭj)	114-15	41°18'N	90°11'W
Cambridge, Ma., U.S.	116-17	42°22'N	71°06'W
Cambridge, Md., U.S.	116-17	38°33'N	76°04'W
Cambridge, Mn., U.S. (kăm'brĭj)	114-15	45°34'N	93°13'W
Cambridge, Ne., U.S. (kăm'brĭj)	120-21	40°17'N	100°10'W
Cambridge, Oh., U.S. (kăm'brĭj)	116-17	40°02'N	81°35'W
Cambridge Bay, Nu., Can.	128-29	69°07'N	105°04'W
Cambridge City, In., U.S. (kăm'brĭj sĭ'tē)	116-17	39°49'N	85°11'W
Camden, Al., U.S. (kăm'dĕn)	124-25	31°59'N	87°17'W
Camden, Ar., U.S. (kăm'dĕn)	120-21	33°36'N	92°50'W
Camden, Me., U.S. (kăm'dĕn)	117a	44°13'N	69°05'W
Camden, N.J., U.S.	116-17	39°56'N	75°07'W
Camden, S.C., U.S. (kăm'dĕn)	124-25	34°15'N	80°36'W
Cameron, Mo., U.S. (kăm'ēr-ŭn)	120-21	39°44'N	94°14'W
Cameron, Tx., U.S. (kăm'ēr-ŭn)	122-23	30°51'N	96°59'W
Cameron, Wi., U.S. (kăm'ēr-ŭn)	114-15	45°25'N	91°45'W
Cameroon, nation, Afr. (kă'mă-rōōn')	253	6°0'N	12°00'E
Cameroon Mountain, vol., Camrn.	260-61	4°12'N	9°11'E
Cameroun, nation, Afr. see Cameroon	253	6°0'N	12°00'E
Cametá, Braz.	166-67	2°15'S	49°31'W
Camiguin Island, i., Phil.	250a	18°56'N	121°55'E
Camiling, Phil. (kä-mē-lĭng')	250	15°41'N	120°25'E
Camilla, Ga., U.S. (kȧ-mĭl'ȧ)	124-25	31°14'N	84°12'W
Caminha, Port. (kä-mĭn'yȧ)	198-99	41°52'N	8°49'W
Camiranga, Braz.	166-67	1°49'S	46°16'W
Camiri, Bol.	168-69	20°03'S	63°31'W
Camocim, Braz. (kä-mô-sĕn')	166-67	2°54'S	40°51'W
Camooweal, Austl.	277	19°55'S	138°08'E
Campana, Arg. (käm-pä'nä)	173	34°10'S	58°57'W
Campana, Isla, i., Chile (ē's-lä-käm-pän'yä)	171	48°20'S	75°15'W
Campbell Island, i., N.Z.	287	52°33'S	169°08'E
Campbell River, B.C., Can.	132-33	50°01'N	125°15'W
Campbellsville, Ky., U.S. (kăm'bĕlz-vĭl)	124-25	37°21'N	85°21'W
Campbellton, N.B., Can. (kăm'bĕl-tŭn)	138-39	47°60'N	66°41'W
Campbelltown, Austl. (kăm'bĕl-toun)	276	34°04'S	150°49'E
Campeche, Mex. (käm-pā'chȧ)	148	19°50'N	90°31'W
Campeche, state, Mex. (käm-pā'chȧ)	148	19°0'N	90°30'W
Campechuela, Cuba (käm-pȧ-chwā'lä)	142-43	20°14'N	77°17'W
Cam Pha, Viet.	246-47	21°02'N	107°21'E
Campina Grande, Braz. (käm-pē'nä grän'dĕ)	163d	7°13'S	35°53'W
Campinas, Braz. (käm-pē'näzh)	172	22°55'S	47°05'W
Campo Alegre de Goiás, Braz.	172	17°38'S	47°46'W
Campobasso, Italy (käm'pô-bäs'sō)	200-01	41°34'N	14°40'E
Campo Belo, Braz.	172	20°54'S	45°16'W
Campo de Criptana, Spain (käm'pō dā krēp-tä'nä)	198-99	39°24'N	3°07'W
Campo Gallo, Arg.	173	26°34'S	62°50'W
Campo Grande, Braz. (käm-pŏ grän'dĕ)	168-69	20°28'S	54°38'W
Campo Maior, Braz. (käm-pŏ mä-yôr')	166-67	4°49'S	42°10'W
Campo Mourão, Braz.	168-69	24°02'S	52°24'W
Campos, Braz. (kä'm-pôs)	172	21°45'S	41°21'W
Camrose, Ab., Can. (kăm-rōz)	132-33	53°01'N	112°50'W
Canada, nation, N.A. (kăn'ȧ-dȧ)	85	60°0'N	95°00'W
Cañada de Gómez, Arg. (kä-nyä'dä-dĕ-gô'mĕz)	173	32°49'S	61°24'W
Canadian, Tx., U.S. (kȧ-nā'dĭ-ăn)	120-21	35°55'N	100°23'W
Canadian, stm., U.S. (kȧ-nā'dĭ-ăn)	110-11	35°27'N	95°05'W
Canajoharie, N.Y., U.S. (kăn-ȧ-jō-hăr'ē)	116-17	42°54'N	74°35'W
Çanakkale, Tur. (chä-näk-kä'lĕ)	200-01	40°09'N	26°25'E
Çanakkale Boğazı, strt., Tur. see Dardanelles	200-01	40°17'N	26°33'E
Canandaigua, N.Y., U.S. (kăn-ăn-dā'gwȧ)	116-17	42°53'N	77°17'W
Cananea, Mex. (kä-nä-nĕ'ä)	144-45	30°59'N	110°18'W
Canarias, Islas, is., Spain (ē's-läs-kä-nä'ryäs) see Canary Islands	199d	28°01'N	15°35'W
Canary Islands, is., Spain (kȧ-nā'rē ī'lȧndz)	199d	28°01'N	15°35'W
Cañas, C.R. (kä'-nyäs)	149	10°25'N	85°06'W
Canastota, N.Y., U.S. (kăn-ȧs-tō'tȧ)	116-17	43°05'N	75°46'W
Canatlán, Mex. (kä-nät-län')	146-47	24°31'N	104°46'W
Canaveral, Cape, c., Fl., U.S.	125a	28°27'N	80°32'W

n-sing; ŋ-baŋk; N-nasalized n; nŏd; cŏmmit; ōld; ôbey; ôrder; oi-boil; fōōd; ŏ-as oo in foot; ou-out; s-soft; sh-dish; th-thin; pūre; ûnite; ûrn; stŭd; circŭs; ü-as in French tu; '-indeterminate vowel.

Feature (Pronunciation)	Page	Lat.	Long.
Canavieiras, Braz. (kä-ná-vē-ā´räs)	168-69	15°39′S	38°57′W
Canberra, nat. cap., Austl. (kăn´bĕr-*á*)	276	35°17′S	149°08′E
Canby, Mn., U.S. (kăn´bĭ)	114-15	44°43′N	96°17′W
Cancún, Mex.	148	21°08′N	86°51′W
Candala, Som. *see* Qandala	262-63	11°28′N	49°52′E
Candeias, Braz.	166-67	12°40′S	38°32′W
Candelaria, Cuba (kän-dĕ-lä´ryä)	142-43	22°45′N	82°58′W
Candelaria, stm., Mex. (kän-dĕ-lä-ryä)	148	18°38′N	91°17′W
Cando, N.D., U.S. (kăn´dō)	114-15	48°29′N	99°13′W
Candon, Phil. (kän-dōn´)	250	17°11′N	120°27′E
Canea, Grc. *see* Chaniá	200a	35°31′N	24°01′E
Canelones, Ur. (kä-nĕ-lô-nĕs)	173	34°32′S	56°17′W
Cangas, Spain (kän´gäs)	198-99	42°16′N	8°47′W
Cangas de Narcea, Spain (kä´n-gäs-dĕ-när-sĕ-ä)	198-99	43°11′N	6°33′W
Cangkuang, Tanjung, c., Indon.	248-49	6°50′S	105°15′E
Canguçu, Braz.	173	31°21′S	52°37′W
Cangzhou, China (tsäŋ-jō)	240-41	38°18′N	116°52′E
Caniapiscau, stm., Qc., Can.	130-31	57°41′N	69°29′W
Caniapiscau, Réservoir de, res., Qc., Can. *see* Caniapiscau, Lac	130-31	0°0′	0°00′
Caniapiscau, Lac, res., Qc., Can.	130-31	54°09′N	69°51′W
Canicattì, Italy (kä-nē-kät´tē)	200-01	37°21′N	13°51′E
Çankırı, Tur.	186-87	40°36′N	33°37′E
Cannanore, India	236	11°52′N	75°22′E
Cannelton, In., U.S. (kăn´*ĕ*l-t*ŭ*n)	116-17	37°55′N	86°45′W
Cannes, Fr. (kán)	196-97	43°33′N	7°01′E
Canning, N.S., Can. (kăn´ĭng)	138-39	45°09′N	64°25′W
Canoas, stm., Braz.	168-69	27°37′S	51°26′W
Canon City, Co., U.S. (kăn´y*ŭ*n sĭ´tē)	120-21	38°27′N	105°15′W
Canonsburg, Pa., U.S. (kăn´*ŭ*nz-bûrg)	116-17	40°16′N	80°11′W
Canora, Sk., Can. (k*á*-nōr*á*)	134-35	51°37′N	102°26′W
Canouan, i., St. Vin.	143b	12°43′N	61°20′W
Canso, N.S., Can. (kăn´sō)	138-39	45°20′N	61°00′W
Cantabrian Mountains, mts., Spain (kăn-tā´brē-*ă*n moun´tĭnz) *see* Cantábrica, Cordillera	198-99	43°0′N	5°00′W
Cantábrica, Cordillera, mts., Spain	198-99	43°0′N	5°00′W
Cantandica, Moz.	264-65	18°02′S	33°08′E
Cantanhede, Port. (kän-tän-yā´dā)	198-99	40°21′N	8°36′W
Cantaura, Ven.	163b	9°18′N	64°21′W
Canterbury, Eng., U.K. (kăn´tĕr-bĕr-ē)	190-91	51°17′N	1°05′E
Canterbury Bight, b., N.Z.	278	44°15′S	171°38′E
Can Tho, Viet.	246-47	10°02′N	105°47′E
Canton, China *see* Guangzhou	238-39	23°08′N	113°16′E
Canton, Ms., U.S.	124-25	32°37′N	90°02′W
Canton, Oh., U.S.	116-17	40°48′N	81°23′W
Canton, i., Kir.	280-81	2°49′S	171°41′W
Cañuelas, Arg. (kä-nyòĕ´-läs)	173	35°03′S	58°45′W
Canutama, Braz.	166-67	6°31′S	64°21′W
Canyon, Tx., U.S. (kăn´y*ŭ*n)	120-21	34°59′N	101°55′W
Canyon de Chelly National Monument, n.p., Az., U.S.	118-19	36°07′N	109°27′W
Canyonlands National Park, n.p., Ut., U.S. (kăn´y*ŭ*n-ländz năsh´ŭn-*ă*l pärk)	118-19	38°10′N	110°00′W
Cao Bang, Viet.	246-47	22°40′N	106°15′E
Capanaparo, stm., S.A.	164-65	7°03′N	67°04′W
Cap aux Meules, Île du, i., Qc., Can.	138-39	47°23′N	61°55′W
Cap-Chat, Qc., Can. (kȧp-shä´)	138-39	49°05′N	66°41′W
Cap-de-la-Madeleine, Qc., Can. (kȧp dē lȧ mȧ-d'lĕn´)	136-37	46°22′N	72°31′W
Cape Barren Island, i., Austl.	276	40°25′S	148°12′E
Cape Breton Highlands National Park, n.p., N.S., Can.	138-39	46°45′N	60°45′W
Cape Breton Island, i., N.S., Can. (kāp brĕt´*ŭ*n ī´l*ă*nd)	138-39	46°04′N	60°30′W
Cape Charles, Va., U.S. (kāp chärlz)	124-25	37°16′N	76°01′W
Cape Coast, Ghana	260-61	5°07′N	1°16′W
Cape Dorset, Nu., Can.	128-29	64°14′N	76°33′W
Cape Fear, stm., N.C., U.S. (kāp fēr)	124-25	33°53′N	78°01′W
Cape Girardeau, Mo., U.S. (kāp jē-rär-dō´)	120-21	37°18′N	89°32′W
Cape May, N.J., U.S. (kāp mā)	116-17	38°56′N	74°56′W
Cape Town, nat. cap., S. Afr. (kāp toun)	264-65	33°55′S	18°30′E
Cape Verde, nation, Afr. (kāp vûrd´) (kāp vĕr´dē)	253	16°0′N	24°00′W
Cape York Peninsula, pen., Austl. (kāp yôrk pĕ-nĭn´sūl*ă*)	277	14°0′S	142°30′E
Cap-Haïtien, Haiti (kȧp ȧ-ē-syăn´)	142-43	19°45′N	72°12′W
Capim, stm., Braz.	166-67	1°41′S	47°47′W
Capitol Reef National Park, n.p., Ut., U.S. (kăp´ĭ-tŏl rēf năsh´ŭn-*ă*l pärk)	118-19	38°15′N	111°10′W
Capiz, Phil. *see* Roxas	250	11°35′N	122°45′E
Caprara, Punta, c., Italy (pōō´n-tä-kä-prä´rä)	200-01	41°07′N	8°19′E
Capreol, On., Can.	136-37	46°42′N	80°55′W
Capri, Isola di, i., Italy (ē´-sō-lä-dē-kä´prē)	200-01	40°33′N	14°13′E
Caprivi Strip, hist. reg., Nmb.	264-65	17°59′S	23°00′E
Cap Saint Jacques, Viet. *see* Vung Tau	246-47	10°21′N	107°05′E
Capulin Volcano National Monument, n.p., N.M., U.S. (ká-pū´lĭn vŏl-kā´nō năsh´ŭn-*ă*l mŏn´*ū*-m*ĕ*nt)	120-21	36°47′N	103°56′W
Caquetá, stm., S.A.	166-67	3°08′S	64°46′W
Caracal, Rom. (ká-rá-kál´)	200-01	44°07′N	24°22′E
Caracaraí, Braz.	166-67	1°50′N	61°08′W
Caracas, nat. cap., Ven. (kä-rä´käs)	164-65	10°30′N	66°56′W
Caraguatatuba, Braz. (kä-rä-gwä-tä-tōō´bä)	172	23°37′S	45°25′W
Caraïbes, Îles des, is., *see* West Indies	140-41	19°0′N	70°00′W
Caraïbes, Mer des, s., *see* Caribbean Sea	140-41	15°0′N	73°00′W
Carajás, Braz.	166-67	6°06′S	50°23′W
Carajás, Serra dos, hills, Braz. (sĕ´r-rä-dôs-kä-rä-zhá´s)	166-67	6°16′S	51°21′W
Carangola, Braz. (kä-rän´gō´lä)	172	20°43′S	42°02′W
Caraquet, N.B., Can. (kă-rȧ-kĕt´)	138-39	47°47′N	64°57′W
Caratasca, Laguna de, b., Hond. (lä-gò´nä-dĕ-kä-rä-täs´kä)	149	15°24′N	83°54′W
Caratinga, Braz.	172	19°47′S	42°09′W
Carauari, Braz.	166-67	4°52′S	66°52′W
Caravelas, Braz. (kȧ-rä-vĕl´äzh)	172	17°44′S	39°15′W
Carazinho, Braz. (kä-rá´zē-ny*ō*)	168-69	28°17′S	52°46′W
Carballo, Spain (kär-bäl´yō)	198-99	43°13′N	8°41′W
Carberry, Mb., Can.	134-35	49°52′N	99°21′W
Carbonara, Capo, c., Italy (kä´pō är-bō-nä´rä)	200-01	39°06′N	9°31′E
Carbondale, Il., U.S. (kär´bŏn-dāl)	116-17	37°43′N	89°13′W
Carbondale, Pa., U.S. (kär´bŏn-dāl)	116-17	41°35′N	75°30′W
Carbonear, Nf., Can. (kär-bō-nēr´)	138-39	47°45′N	53°14′W
Carbon Hill, Al., U.S. (kär´bŏn hĭl)	124-25	33°54′N	87°32′W
Carcassonne, Fr. (kȧr-kȧ-sŏn´)	196-97	43°13′N	2°21′E
Carcross, Yk., Can. (kär´krôs)	128-29	60°11′N	134°42′W
Cárdenas, Cuba (kär´dā-näs)	142-43	23°02′N	81°12′W
Cárdenas, Mex. (ká´r-dĕ-näs)	146-47	18°00′N	93°22′W
Cárdenas, Mex. (ká´r-dĕ-näs)	146-47	21°60′N	99°39′W
Cardiel, Lago, lk., Arg.	171	48°55′S	71°15′W
Cardiff, Wales, U.K. (kär´dĭf)	190-91	51°29′N	3°11′W
Cardigan, Wales, U.K. (kär´dĭ-g*ă*n)	190-91	52°05′N	4°39′W
Cardston, Ab., Can. (kärds´tŭn)	132-33	49°12′N	113°18′W
Carei, Rom. (kä-rĕ´)	194-95	47°41′N	22°28′E
Careiro, Braz.	166-67	3°14′S	59°46′W
Careiro, Ilha do, i., Braz.	166-67	3°09′S	59°48′W
Carey, Oh., U.S. (kā´rē)	116-17	40°57′N	83°23′W
Carey, Lake, lk., Austl. (lāk kâr´ē)	272-73	29°04′S	122°19′E
Caribbean Sea, s., (kăr-ĭ-bē´*ă*n sē)	140-41	15°0′N	73°00′W
Caribe, Mar, s., *see* Caribbean Sea	140-41	15°0′N	73°00′W
Caribische Zee, s., *see* Caribbean Sea	140-41	15°0′N	73°00′W
Cariboo Mountains, mts., B.C., Can. (kă´rĭ-bōō moun´tĭnz)	132-33	53°0′N	121°00′W
Caribou, Me., U.S.	117a	46°51′N	68°00′W
Caribou Mountains, mts., Ab., Can.	130-31	59°06′N	115°10′W
Caricyn, Russia *see* Volgograd	186-87	48°44′N	44°25′E
Carinhanha, Braz. (kä-rĭ-nyän´yä)	166-67	14°19′S	43°48′W
Caripito, Ven.	164-65	10°06′N	63°06′W
Carleton, Mount, mtn., N.B., Can.	138-39	47°23′N	66°53′W
Carleton Place, On., Can. (kärl´tŭn plās)	136-37	45°09′N	76°09′W
Carletonville, S. Afr.	269c	26°21′S	27°24′E
Carlinville, Il., U.S. (kär´lĭn-vĭl)	120-21	39°16′N	89°53′W
Carlisle, Eng., U.K. (kär-līl´)	190-91	54°54′N	2°56′W
Carlos Casares, Arg. (kär-lôs-kä-sá´rĕs)	173	35°38′S	61°21′W
Carlow, Ire. (kär´lō)	190-91	52°50′N	6°55′W
Carlsbad, Czech Rep. *see* Karlovy Vary	194-95	50°14′N	12°53′E
Carlsbad, Ca., U.S. (kärlz´băd)	118-19	33°09′N	117°20′W
Carlsbad, N.M., U.S. (kärlz´băd)	120-21	32°25′N	104°14′W
Carlsbad Caverns National Park, n.p., N.M., U.S. (kärlz´băd kăv´ĕrnz năsh´ŭn-*ă*l pärk)	120-21	32°08′N	104°35′W
Carlyle, Il., U.S. (kärlīl´)	116-17	38°36′N	89°22′W
Carmacks, Yk., Can.	128-29	62°05′N	136°15′W
Carman, Mb., Can. (kär´măn)	134-35	49°31′N	97°59′W
Carmarthen, Wales, U.K. (kär-mär´th*ĕ*n)	190-91	51°52′N	4°19′W
Carmaux, Fr. (kär-mō´)	196-97	44°03′N	2°10′E
Carmel, In., U.S. (kär´m*ĕ*l)	116-17	39°58′N	86°07′W
Carmelo, Ur. (kär-mĕ´lo)	173	33°60′S	58°17′W
Carmen, Mex. *see* Ciudad del Carmen	148	18°39′N	91°49′W
Carmen, Isla, i., Mex.	144-45	26°00′N	111°08′W
Carmen, Isla del, i., Mex. (ē´s-lä-dĕl-kä´r-mĕn)	148	18°43′N	91°40′W
Carmen de Areco, Arg. (kär´mĕn´ dā ä-rā´kō)	173	34°23′S	59°50′W
Carmi, Il., U.S. (kär´mī)	116-17	38°05′N	88°10′W
Carnarvon, Austl. (kär-när´v*ŭ*n)	270-71	24°52′S	113°40′E
Carnarvon, S. Afr.	264-65	30°58′S	22°08′E
Carnarvon National Park, n.p., Austl.	277	24°42′S	147°55′E
Carnegie, Ok., U.S. (kär-nĕg´ĭ)	120-21	35°07′N	98°35′W
Carnegie, Lake, lk., Austl.	272-73	26°11′S	122°31′E
Carnot, C.A.R.	262-63	4°56′N	15°53′E
Carnsore Point, c., Ire. (kärn´sôr point)	190-91	52°11′N	6°22′W
Caro, Mi., U.S. (kâ´rō)	116-17	43°29′N	83°23′W
Carolina, Braz. (kä-rō-lē´nä)	166-67	7°21′S	47°25′W
Carolina, S. Afr. (kăr-ô-lī´n*á*)	269c	26°04′S	30°08′E
Caroline, at., Kir.	280-81	9°58′S	150°13′W
Caroline Islands, is., Oc. (kă´-rō-līn´ ī´l*ă*ndz)	280-81	8°0′N	147°00′E
Caroní, stm., Ven. (kä-rō´nē)	164-65	8°21′N	62°48′W
Carora, Ven. (kä-rō´rä)	164-65	10°10′N	70°05′W
Carpathian Mountains, mts., Eur. (kär-pā´thĭ-*ă*n moun´tĭnz)	186-87	48°0′N	24°00′E
Carpaţii, mts., Eur. *see* Carpathian Mountains	186-87	48°0′N	24°00′E
Carpaţii Meridionali, mts., Rom. *see* Transylvanian Alps	200-01	45°25′N	23°33′E
Carpentaria, Gulf of, b., Austl. (gŭlf ŭv kär-pĕn-târ´ĭ*ă*)	272-73	14°0′S	139°00′E
Carpentras, Fr. (kär-päɴ-träs´)	196-97	44°04′N	5°03′E
Carranza, Cabo, c., Chile	171	35°36′S	72°38′W
Carrara, Italy (kä-rä´rä)	200-01	44°05′N	10°06′E
Carrauntoohil, mtn., Ire.	190-91	51°59′N	9°45′W
Carreta, Punta, c., Peru (pōō´n-tä-kär-rĕ´tĕ´rȧ)	170	14°11′S	76°17′W
Carriacou, i., Gren.	143b	12°30′N	61°26′W
Carrington, N.D., U.S. (kăr´ĭng-t*ŭ*n)	114-15	47°27′N	99°07′W
Carrizal Bajo, Chile	168-69	28°06′S	71°09′W
Carrizozo, N.M., U.S. (kär-rē-zō´zō)	120-21	33°39′N	105°53′W
Carroll, Ia., U.S. (kăr´*ŭ*l)	114-15	42°04′N	94°52′W
Carrollton, Ga., U.S. (kăr-*ŭ*l-t*ŭ*n)	124-25	33°35′N	85°05′W
Carrollton, Il., U.S. (kăr-*ŭ*l-t*ŭ*n)	120-21	39°18′N	90°24′W
Carrollton, Ky., U.S. (kăr-*ŭ*l-t*ŭ*n)	116-17	38°41′N	85°11′W
Carrollton, Mi., U.S. (kăr-*ŭ*l-t*ŭ*n)	116-17	43°27′N	83°57′W
Carrollton, Mo., U.S. (kăr-*ŭ*l-t*ŭ*n)	120-21	39°22′N	93°30′W
Carrollton, Tx., U.S. (kăr-*ŭ*l-t*ŭ*n)	120-21	32°58′N	96°53′W
Carrot, stm., Can.	134-35	53°50′N	101°19′W
Carson City, Nv., U.S.	118-19	39°10′N	119°46′W
Cartagena, Col. (kär-tä-hā´nä)	164-65	10°25′N	75°30′W
Cartagena, Spain (kär-tä-κĕ´nä)	198-99	37°37′N	0°59′W
Cartago, Col. (kär-tä´gō)	163c	4°45′N	75°55′W
Cartago, C.R.	149	9°51′N	83°55′W
Cartersville, Ga., U.S. (kär´tĕrs-vĭl)	124-25	34°10′N	84°48′W
Carthage, Il., U.S. (kär´thåj)	120-21	40°25′N	91°08′W
Carthage, Mo., U.S. (kär´thåj)	120-21	37°11′N	94°19′W
Carthage, Ms., U.S. (kär´thåj)	124-25	32°44′N	89°32′W
Carthage, N.Y., U.S. (kär´thåj)	116-17	43°59′N	75°37′W
Carthage, Tx., U.S. (kär´thåj)	122-23	32°09′N	94°22′W
Cartwright, Nf., Can. (kärt´rīt)	128-29	53°41′N	56°60′W
Caruaru, Braz. (kä-rò-á-rōō´)	163d	8°17′S	35°58′W
Carúpano, Ven. (kä-rōō´pä-nō)	164-65	10°40′N	63°15′W
Carutapera, Braz.	166-67	1°13′S	46°00′W
Caruthersville, Mo., U.S. (k*á*-rŭdh´ĕrz-vĭl)	124-25	36°11′N	89°40′W
Carvoeiro, Braz.	166-67	1°26′S	61°60′W
Carvoeiro, Cabo, c., Port. (ká´bō-kär-vō-ĕ´y-rō)	198-99	39°21′N	9°24′W
Cary, N.C., U.S. (kā´rē)	124-25	35°47′N	78°47′W
Casablanca, Mor. (kä-sä-bläŋ´kä)	269a	33°36′N	7°36′W
Casa Branca, Braz. (ká´sä-brá´ɴ-kä)	172	21°48′S	47°04′W
Casa Grande, Az., U.S. (kä´sä grän´dā)	118-19	32°53′N	111°45′W
Casa Grande Ruins National Monument, n.p., Az., U.S.	118-19	32°59′N	111°32′W
Casamance, stm., Sen. (kä-sä-mäɴs´)	260-61	12°33′N	16°45′W
Casanare, stm., Col.	164-65	6°02′N	69°51′W
Cascade Mountains, mts., N.A. (kăs-kād´ moun´tĭnz)	110-11	45°14′N	121°56′W
Cascade Point, c., N.Z. (kăs-kād´ point)	278	44°00′S	168°22′E
Cascade Range, mts., N.A. (kăs-kād´ rānj) *see* Cascade Range	110-11	45°14′N	121°56′W
Cascais, Port. (käs-k*á*-ēzh)	198-99	38°42′N	9°25′W
Cascavel, Braz.	168-69	24°58′S	53°27′W
Caserta, Italy (kä-zĕr´tä)	200-01	41°05′N	14°19′E
Casey, Il., U.S. (kā´sĭ)	116-17	39°18′N	87°60′W

ăt; fin*ă*l; rāte; senåte; ärm; ȧsk; sof*á*; fâre; ch-choose; dh-as th in other; bē; ėvent; bĕt; recĕnt; cratẽr; g-gō; gh-guttural g; bĭt; ĭ-short neutral; rīde; κ-guttural k as ch in German ich;

Feature (Pronunciation)	Page	Lat.	Long.
Caseyr, c., Som. see Gwardafuy, Gees	262-63	11°50'N	51°17'E
Cashmere, Wa., U.S. (kăsh'mîr)	112-13	47°31'N	120°27'W
Casilda, Arg. (kä-sē'l-dä)	173	33°03'S	61°11'W
Casino, Austl. (kȧ-sē'nō)	276	28°52'S	153°03'E
Casiquiare, stm., Ven. (kä-sē-kyä'rä)	164-65	1°60'N	67°08'W
Caspe, Spain (käs'på)	198-99	41°14'N	0°03'W
Casper, Wy., U.S. (kăs'pẽr)	112-13	42°51'N	106°20'W
Caspian Depression, pl., (kăs'pĭ-ăn dĭ-prĕ'shŭn)	186-87	48°0'N	52°00'E
Caspian Sea, lk., (kăs'pĭ-ăn sē)	226	41°18'N	50°59'E
Cass, W.V., U.S. (kăs)	116-17	38°24'N	79°55'W
Cassai, stm., Afr. (kä-sä'ē)	262-63	3°02'S	16°56'E
Cass City, Mi., U.S. (kăs sĭ'tē)	116-17	43°36'N	83°10'W
Casselman, On., Can. (kăs''l-măn)	136-37	45°19'N	75°06'W
Casselton, N.D., U.S. (kăs''l-tŭn)	114-15	46°54'N	97°13'W
Cássia, Braz. (kȧ'syä)	172	20°33'S	46°56'W
Cassiar, B.C., Can.	128-29	59°16'N	129°43'W
Cassiar Mountains, mts., Can.	130-31	59°0'N	129°00'W
Cassino, Italy (käs-sē'nō)	200-01	41°30'N	13°51'E
Cass Lake, Mn., U.S. (kăs lāk)	114-15	47°22'N	94°37'W
Cassopolis, Mi., U.S. (kăs-ŏ'pō-lĭs)	116-17	41°55'N	86°01'W
Cassville, Mo., U.S. (kăs'vĭl)	120-21	36°41'N	93°52'W
Cassville, Wi., U.S. (kăs'vĭl)	114-15	42°43'N	90°59'W
Castelli, Arg. (kȧs-tĕ'zhē)	173	36°06'S	57°49'W
Castelli, Arg. (kȧs-tĕ'zhē)	168-69	25°57'S	60°37'W
Castelló de la Plana, Spain	198-99	39°59'N	0°02'W
Castellón de la Plana, Spain see Castelló de la Plana	198-99	39°59'N	0°02'W
Castelnaudary, Fr. (kȧs'tĕl-nō-dȧ-rē')	196-97	43°19'N	1°57'E
Castelo, Braz. (käs-tĕ'lô)	172	20°35'S	41°13'W
Castelo Branco, Port.	198-99	39°49'N	7°29'W
Castelsarrasin, Fr. (kȧs'tĕl-sȧ-rȧ-zăN')	196-97	44°02'N	1°06'E
Castelvetrano, Italy (käs'tĕl-vĕ-trä'nō)	200-01	37°41'N	12°47'E
Castilla, Peru (kȧs-tē'l-yä)	170	5°12'S	80°37'W
Castillo de San Marcos National Monument, n.p., Fl., U.S. (käs-tē'lyä de-sän mär-kōs năsh'ŭn-ăl mŏn'ū-mĕnt)	124-25	29°55'N	81°19'W
Castillos, Ur.	173	34°13'S	53°50'W
Castle Dale, Ut., U.S. (kȧs'l dāl)	118-19	39°24'N	110°27'W
Castlegar, B.C., Can. (kȧs''l-gär)	132-33	49°19'N	117°40'W
Castlemaine, Austl. (kȧs''l-mān)	276	37°04'S	144°13'E
Castle Peak, mtn., Co., U.S. (kȧs''l pēk)	118-19	39°01'N	106°52'W
Castle Peak, mtn., Id., U.S. (kȧs''l pēk)	112-13	44°02'N	114°35'W
Castlereagh, stm., Austl.	276	30°12'S	147°31'E
Castle Rock, Co., U.S. (kȧs''l rŏk)	120-21	39°23'N	104°51'W
Castle Rock, Wa., U.S. (kȧs''l rŏk)	112-13	46°17'N	122°54'W
Castres, Fr. (kȧs'tr')	196-97	43°36'N	2°15'E
Castries, nat. cap., St. Luc. (kȧs-trē')	143b	14°01'N	60°59'W
Castro, Braz. (käs'trō)	168-69	24°47'S	49°60'W
Castro, Chile (käs'tro)	171	42°29'S	73°46'W
Castro Verde, Port. (käs-trō vĕr'dĕ)	198-99	37°41'N	8°05'W
Castrovillari, Italy (käs'trō-vēl-lyä'rē)	200-01	39°49'N	16°13'E
Catacamas, Hond. (kä-tä-kȧ'mäs)	149	14°51'N	85°54'W
Catahoula Lake, lk., La., U.S. (kăt-ȧ-hō'lȧ lāk)	124-25	31°30'N	92°08'W
Catalão, Braz. (kä-tä-louN')	172	18°11'S	47°56'W
Catalina, Chile	168-69	25°13'S	69°44'W
Catalina, i., Ca., U.S. see Santa Catalina Island	118-19	33°23'N	118°24'W
Catamarca, state, Arg. (kä-tä-mär'kä)	168-69	27°0'S	67°00'W
Catanduanes Island, i., Phil. (kä-tän-dwä'nĕs ī'lănd)	250	13°45'N	124°15'E
Catanduva, Braz. (kä-tȧn-dōō'vä)	172	21°08'S	48°58'W
Catania, Italy (kä-tä'nyä)	200-01	37°30'N	15°06'E
Catanzaro, Italy (kä-tän-dzä'rō)	200-01	38°54'N	16°36'E
Catarman, Phil.	250	12°30'N	124°38'E
Catbalogan, Phil. (kät-bä-lō'gän)	250	11°50'N	124°51'E
Cathedral Mountain, mtn., Tx., U.S. (kȧ-thē'drăl moun'tĭn)	122-23	30°10'N	103°40'W
Cat Island, i., Bah.	142-43	24°26'N	75°32'W
Catlettsburg, Ky., U.S. (kăt'lĕts-bûrg)	116-17	38°25'N	82°37'W
Catoche, Cabo, c., Mex. (kȧ'bô kä-tō'chĕ)	148	21°36'N	87°06'W
Catonsville, Md., U.S. (kā'tŭnz-vĭl)	116-17	39°17'N	76°44'W
Catorce, Mex. (kä-tôr'sȧ)	146-47	23°42'N	100°56'W
Catriló, Arg.	173	36°24'S	63°25'W
Catrimani, stm., Braz.	166-67	0°28'N	61°43'W
Catskill, N.Y., U.S. (kăts'kĭl)	116-17	42°14'N	73°52'W
Catskill Mountains, mts., N.Y., U.S. (kăts'kĭl moun'tĭnz)	116-17	42°10'N	74°30'W
Cattaraugus Indian Reservation, ind. res., N.Y., U.S. (kăt'tȧ-rȧ-gŭs ĭn'dĭ-ăn rĕ-sẽr-vā'shĕn)	116-17	42°32'N	78°59'W
Catumbela, stm., Ang. (kä'tŏm-bĕl'ȧ)	264-65	12°27'S	13°30'E
Caubvick, Mount, mtn., Can.	130-31	58°53'N	63°43'W
Cauca, stm., Col. (kou'kä)	164-65	8°54'N	74°28'W
Caucasus Mountains, mts., (kô'kȧ-sŭs moun'tĭnz)	227	42°38'N	45°00'E
Caungula, Ang.	262-63	8°26'S	18°38'E
Cauquenes, Chile (kou-kā'nās)	171	35°58'S	72°19'W
Caura, stm., Ven. (kou'rä)	164-65	7°38'N	64°53'W
Caution, Cape, c., B.C., Can. (kăp kô'shŭn)	132-33	51°10'N	127°46'W
Cauto, stm., Cuba (kou'tō)	142-43	20°33'N	77°14'W
Cavalcante, Braz. (kä-väl-kän'tä)	166-67	13°47'S	47°30'W
Cavalier, N.D., U.S. (kăv-ȧ-lēr')	114-15	48°47'N	97°37'W
Cavalla, stm., Afr.	260-61	4°21'N	7°31'W
Cavally, stm., Afr.	260-61	4°21'N	7°31'W
Cavan, Ire. (kăv'ăn)	190-91	53°59'N	7°22'W
Caviana de Fora, Ilha, i., Braz.	166-67	0°10'N	50°10'W
Cavite, Phil. (kä-vē'tä)	250	14°29'N	120°54'E
Cawnpore, India see Kānpur	234-35	26°28'N	80°19'E
Caxias, Braz. (kä'shē-äzh)	166-67	4°50'S	43°21'W
Caxias do Sul, Braz. (kä'shē-äzh-dō-sōō'l)	168-69	29°11'S	51°11'W
Caxito, Ang. (kä-shē'tō)	262-63	8°33'S	13°36'E
Cayambe, Ec. (kȧ-īä'm-bĕ)	170	0°03'N	78°09'W
Cayambe, vol., Ec.	170	0°02'N	77°59'W
Cayenne, nat. cap., Fr. Gu. (kā-ĕn')	164-65	4°56'N	52°19'W
Cayman Brac, i., Cay. Is. (kā-män' brȧk)	142-43	19°43'N	79°49'W
Cayman Islands, dep., N.A. (kā'măn ī'lăndz) (kī-män' ī'lăndz)	140-41	19°30'N	80°40'W
Ceará, Braz. see Fortaleza	166-67	3°44'S	38°30'W
Ceará, state, Braz.	166-67	5°0'S	40°00'W
Ceará-Mirim, Braz. (sā-ä-rä'mē-rē'N)	163d	5°38'S	35°26'W
Ceatharlach, Ire. see Carlow	190-91	52°50'N	6°55'W
Cebaco, Isla de, i., Pan. (ē's-lä-dĕ-sȧ-bä'kō)	150	7°32'N	81°09'W
Cebu, Phil. (sā-bōō')	250	10°19'N	123°54'E
Cebu, i., Phil.	250	10°20'N	123°45'E
Čechy, hist. reg., Czech Rep. see Bohemia	194-95	49°50'N	14°00'E
Cedar, stm., U.S. (sē'dẽr)	114-15	41°17'N	91°20'W
Cedar Breaks National Monument, n.p., Ut., U.S. (sē'dẽr brāks năsh'ŭn-ăl mŏn'ū-mĕnt)	118-19	37°38'N	112°50'W
Cedarburg, Wi., U.S. (sē'dẽr bûrg)	116-17	43°17'N	87°59'W
Cedar City, Ut., U.S. (sē'dẽr sĭ'tē)	118-19	37°41'N	113°04'W
Cedar Falls, Ia., U.S. (sē'dẽr fôlz)	114-15	42°31'N	92°27'W
Cedar Lake, res., Mb., Can. (sē'dẽr lāk)	134-35	53°15'N	100°10'W
Cedar Rapids, Ia., U.S. (sē'dẽr răp'ĭdz)	114-15	41°58'N	91°40'W
Cedar Springs, Mi., U.S. (sē'dẽr sprĭngz)	116-17	43°13'N	85°33'W
Cedartown, Ga., U.S. (sē'dẽr-toun)	124-25	34°02'N	85°14'W
Cedros, Isla, i., Mex.	144-45	28°11'N	115°13'W
Ceduna, Austl. (sē-dō'nȧ)	270-71	32°07'S	133°41'E
Ceerigaabo, Som.	262-63	10°37'N	47°22'E
Cegléd, Hung. (tsā'glād)	194-95	47°10'N	19°48'E
Celaya, Mex. (sā-lä'yä)	146-47	20°31'N	100°49'W
Celebes, i., Indon. (sĕl'ē-bēz)	248-49	2°0'S	121°00'E
Celebes Sea, s., Asia (sĕ'-lē-bēz sē)	248-49	3°0'N	122°00'E
Çeleken, Turkmen.	232-33	39°26'N	53°07'E
Celestún, Mex. (sĕ-lĕs-tōō'n)	148	20°52'N	90°23'W
Celina, Oh., U.S. (sĕlī'na)	116-17	40°33'N	84°34'W
Celje, Slvn. (tsĕl'yĕ)	200-01	46°14'N	15°16'E
Celle, Ger. (tsĕl'ē)	194-95	52°37'N	10°05'E
Celtic Sea, s., Eur.	190-91	51°0'N	6°30'W
Cenderawasih, Teluk, b., Indon.	224-25	2°30'S	135°20'E
Center, Tx., U.S. (sĕn'tẽr)	122-23	31°48'N	94°10'W
Centerville, Ia., U.S. (sĕn'tẽr-vĭl)	114-15	40°44'N	92°52'W
Centerville, Pa., U.S. (sĕn'tẽr-vĭl)	116-17	40°03'N	79°59'W
Centerville, S.D., U.S. (sĕn'tẽr-vĭl)	114-15	43°07'N	96°60'W
Central, Cordillera, mts., Phil. (kôr-dēl-yĕ'rä-sĕn-träl)	250	17°02'N	120°53'E
Central, Massif, mts., Fr.	196-97	44°42'N	3°19'E
Central, Sistema, mts., Spain	198-99	40°34'N	4°29'W
Central African Republic, nation, Afr. (sĕn'trăl ăf'rĭ-kăn rē-pŭb'lĭk)	253	7°0'N	21°00'E
Central City, Ky., U.S. (sĕn'trăl sĭ'tĭ)	124-25	37°18'N	87°08'W
Central City, Ne., U.S. (sĕn'trăl sĭ'tē)	114-15	41°07'N	97°60'W
Centralia, Il., U.S. (sĕn-trā'lĭ-ȧ)	116-17	38°32'N	89°08'W
Centralia, Mo., U.S. (sĕn-trā'lĭ-ȧ)	120-21	39°13'N	92°08'W
Centralia, Wa., U.S. (sĕn-trā'lĭ-ȧ)	112-13	46°43'N	122°57'W
Central Kalahari Game Reserve, pk., Bots.	264-65	22°15'S	23°45'E
Central Russian Upland, plat., Russia (sĕn'trăl rŭsh'ăn ŭp'lănd) see Srednerusskaya Vozvyshennost'	202-03	52°0'N	38°00'E
Centreville, Al., U.S. (sĕn'tẽr-vĭl)	124-25	32°57'N	87°08'W
Century, Fl., U.S. (sĕn'tū-rĭ)	124-25	30°58'N	87°16'W
Ceram, i., Indon. (sārăm') (sā'räm)	224-25	3°0'S	129°00'E
Ceram Sea, s., Indon. (sārăm' sē) (sā'räm sē)	224-25	2°30'S	128°00'E
Cerignola, Italy (chā-rē-nyô'lä)	200-01	41°17'N	15°54'E
Cernăuţi, Ukr. see Chernivtsi	194-95	48°17'N	25°58'E
Cerralvo, Mex. (sĕr-räl'vō)	122-23	26°06'N	99°36'W
Cerralvo, Isla, i., Mex. (ē's-lä-sĕr-räl'vō)	144-45	24°14'N	109°52'W
Cerritos, Mex. (sĕr-rē'tôs)	146-47	22°26'N	100°17'W
Cerro de Pasco, Peru (sĕr'rō dā päs'kō)	170	10°41'S	76°16'W
Cervino, mtn., Eur. see Matterhorn	194-95	45°59'N	7°43'E
Cesena, Italy (chĕ'sĕ-nä)	200-01	44°09'N	12°15'E
Cēsis, Lat. (sā'sĭs)	192-93	57°19'N	25°17'E
Česká Lípa, Czech Rep. (chĕs'kä lē'pa)	194-95	50°41'N	14°32'E
Česká Republika, nation, Eur. see Czech Republic	174-75	49°40'N	15°10'E
České Budějovice, Czech Rep. (chĕs'kā bōō'dyĕ-yô-vēt-sĕ)	194-95	48°59'N	14°28'E
Çeşme, Tur. (chĕsh'mĕ)	200-01	38°18'N	26°19'E
Cessnock, Austl.	276	32°50'S	151°21'E
Cestos, stm., Lib.	260-61	5°29'N	9°33'W
Cetatea Albă, Ukr. see Bilhorod-Dnistrovs'kyi	202-03	46°12'N	30°18'E
Cetinje, Mont.	200-01	42°24'N	18°56'E
Ceuta, Sp. N. Afr. (thā-ōō'tä)	269a	35°54'N	5°19'W
Cévennes, reg., Fr. (sā-vĕn')	196-97	44°07'N	3°32'E
Ceylon, nation, Asia see Sri Lanka	206-07	7°0'N	81°00'E
Chacabuco, Arg. (chä-kä-bōō'kō)	173	34°38'S	60°29'W
Chachapoyas, Peru (chä-chä-poi'yäs)	170	6°13'S	77°52'W
Chaco, state, Arg. (chä'kō)	173	26°0'S	60°30'W
Chad, nation, Afr. (chăd)	253	15°0'N	19°00'E
Chad, Lake, lk., Afr. (lāk chăd)	258-59	13°03'N	14°33'E
Chadbourn, N.C., U.S. (chăd'bŭn)	124-25	34°19'N	78°50'W
Chadileuvu, stm., Arg. see Salado	171	38°49'S	64°59'W
Chadron, Ne., U.S. (chăd'rŭn)	114-15	42°50'N	103°00'W
Chaffee, Mo., U.S. (chăf'ē)	124-25	37°11'N	89°39'W
Chagos Archipelago, is., B.I.O.T. (chä'-gōs är'kȧ-pĕ'-ȧ-gō)	208-09	6°0'S	72°00'E
Chahanwusu, China see Dulan	240-41	36°10'N	98°22'E
Chaiyaphum, Thai.	246-47	15°48'N	102°02'E
Chalatenango, El Sal. (chäl-ä-tĕ-näŋ'gō)	148	14°02'N	88°56'W
Chalbi Desert, des., Kenya	267	3°00'N	37°20'E
Chalcis, Grc. see Chalkída	200-01	38°28'N	23°36'E
Chalkida, Grc.	200-01	38°28'N	23°36'E
Chalmette, La., U.S. (shäl-mĕt')	124-25	29°56'N	89°58'W
Chaltel, Cerro, mtn., S.A. (sĕ'r-rō-chäl'tĕl)	171	49°17'S	73°05'W
Chālūs, Iran	232-33	36°39'N	51°25'E
Chaman, Pak. (chŭm-än')	232-33	30°55'N	66°27'E
Chambal, stm., India (chŭm-bäl')	234-35	26°29'N	79°15'E
Chamberlain, S.D., U.S. (chäm'bẽr-lĭn)	114-15	43°49'N	99°19'W
Chambersburg, Pa., U.S.	116-17	39°56'N	77°40'W
Chambéry, Fr. (shäm-bā-rē')	196-97	45°35'N	5°55'E
Chambi, Jebel, mtn., Tun.	258-59	35°13'N	8°40'E
Chamical, Arg.	168-69	30°21'S	66°18'W
Ch'amo Hāyk', lk., Eth.	262-63	5°50'N	37°34'E
Chamonix-Mont-Blanc, Fr. (shȧ-mô-nē'-môn-bläN)	196-97	45°56'N	6°52'E
Champagne, hist. reg., Fr. (shäm-pän'yē)	196-97	49°0'N	4°30'E
Champaign, Il., U.S. (shăm-pān')	116-17	40°07'N	88°15'W
Champdoré, Lac, lk., Qc., Can.	130-31	55°55'N	65°48'W
Champerico, Guat. (chăm-pȧ-rē'kō)	148	14°17'N	91°55'W
Champlain, Lac, lk., N.A. see Champlain, Lake	116-17	44°45'N	73°15'W
Champlain, Lake, lk., N.A. (lăk shăm-plān')	116-17	44°45'N	73°15'W
Champotón, Mex. (chäm-pō-tōn')	148	19°21'N	90°43'W
Chañaral, Chile (chän-yä-räl')	168-69	26°21'S	70°37'W
Chan Chan, hist., Peru	170	8°03'S	79°08'W
Chanchan, Ruinas de, hist., Peru see Chan Chan	170	8°03'S	79°08'W
Chandalar, stm., Ak., U.S.	126	66°38'N	146°02'W
Chandeleur Islands, is., La., U.S. (shăn-dē-lōōr' ī'lăndz)	124-25	29°49'N	88°54'W
Chandīgarh, India	234-35	30°44'N	76°54'E
Chandīgarh, state, India	234-35	30°45'N	76°50'E
Chandler, Qc., Can. (chăn'dlẽr)	138-39	48°21'N	64°41'W
Chandler, Az., U.S. (chăn'dlẽr)	118-19	33°18'N	111°53'W
Chandler, Ok., U.S. (chăn'dlẽr)	120-21	35°42'N	96°53'W
Chāndpur, Bngl.	234-35	23°13'N	90°40'E
Chandrapur, India	234-35	19°57'N	79°18'E
Chang, stm., China see Yangtze	238-39	31°24'N	121°54'E
Changan, China see Xi'an	238-39	34°15'N	108°52'E

n-sing; ŋ-baŋk; N-nasalized n; nŏd; cŏmmit; ōld; ōbey; ôrder; oi-boil; fōōd; ŏŏ-as oo in foot; ou-out; s-soft; sh-dish; th-thin; pūre; ûnite; ûrn; stŭd; circŭs; ü-as in French tu; '-indeterminate vowel.

Feature (Pronunciation)	Page	Lat.	Long.
Changane, stm., Moz.	**264-65**	24°44'S	33°32'E
Changbaek-sanjulgi, mts., Asia see Changbai Shan	**243**	41°53'N	128°02'E
Changbai Shan, mts., Asia	**243**	41°53'N	128°02'E
Chang Cheng, p.o.i., China see Great Wall	**240-41**	40°0'N	112°30'E
Changchun, China (chäŋ-chòn)	**240-41**	43°53'N	125°19'E
Changde, China (chäŋ-dŭ)	**238-39**	29°02'N	111°41'E
Changhua, Tai. (chäng'hwä')	**225a**	24°04'N	120°30'E
Changji, China	**222-23**	44°01'N	87°18'E
Changjiang, China	**238-39**	19°16'N	109°02'E
Changkiakow, China see Zhangjiakou	**240-41**	40°49'N	114°53'E
Changli, China (chäŋ-lē)	**240-41**	39°42'N	119°10'E
Changmar, China	**234-35**	34°16'N	79°57'E
Changning, China (chäŋ-nĭŋ)	**238-39**	24°58'N	99°43'E
Changning, China (chäŋ-nĭŋ)	**238-39**	26°19'N	112°21'E
Changning, China (chäŋ-nĭŋ)	**238-39**	28°21'N	104°53'E
Changqing, China (chäŋ-chyĭŋ)	**240-41**	36°33'N	116°44'E
Changsha, China	**238-39**	28°12'N	112°58'E
Changshu, China (chäŋ-shōō)	**238-39**	31°38'N	120°44'E
Changting, China	**238-39**	25°50'N	116°21'E
Changyi, China (chäŋ-yē)	**240-41**	36°52'N	119°24'E
Changzhi, China (chäŋ-jr)	**240-41**	36°11'N	113°07'E
Changzhou, China (chäŋ-jō)	**238-39**	31°47'N	119°57'E
Chaniá, Grc.	**200a**	35°31'N	24°01'E
Chankiang, China see Zhanjiang	**238-39**	21°12'N	110°23'E
Channel Islands, is. Eur (chăn'ĕl ī'lăndz)	**196-197**	49°20'N	2°20'W
Channel Islands, is., Ca., U.S. (chăn'ĕl ī'lăndz)	**118-19**	34°0'N	120°00'W
Channel Islands National Park, n.p., Ca., U.S.	**118-19**	33°28'N	119°02'W
Channel-Port aux Basques, Nf., Can.	**138-39**	47°35'N	59°10'W
Chanthaburi, Thai.	**246-47**	12°37'N	102°07'E
Chantilly, Fr. (shäN-tē-yē')	**196-97**	49°12'N	2°28'E
Chanute, Ks., U.S. (shȧ-nōōt')	**120-21**	37°41'N	95°27'W
Chany, Ozero, lk., Russia (ô'zĕ-rô chä'nē)	**226**	54°50'N	77°30'E
Chao'an, China (chou-än)	**238-39**	23°40'N	116°39'E
Chao Hu, lk., China	**238-39**	31°31'N	117°33'E
Chao Phraya, stm., Thai.	**246-47**	13°32'N	100°36'E
Chaor, stm., China (chou-r)	**240-41**	46°48'N	123°35'E
Chaoxian, China (chou shyĕn)	**238-39**	31°35'N	117°51'E
Chaoyang, China (chou-yäŋ)	**238-39**	23°16'N	116°35'E
Chaoyang, China (chou-yäŋ)	**240-41**	41°35'N	120°28'E
Chapala, Mex. (chä-pä'lä)	**146-47**	20°17'N	103°11'W
Chapala, Laguna de, lk., Mex. (lä-ó'nä-dĕ-chä-pä'lä)	**146-47**	20°15'N	103°00'W
Chaparral, Col. (chä-pär-rä'l)	**163c**	3°44'N	75°28'W
Chapayevsk, Russia (châ-pī'ĕfsk)	**186-87**	52°58'N	49°42'E
Chapecó, Braz.	**168-69**	27°06'S	52°38'W
Chapel Hill, N.C., U.S. (chăp''l hĭl)	**124-25**	35°55'N	79°04'W
Chapleau, On., Can. (chăp-lō')	**136-37**	47°51'N	83°25'W
Chapman, Mount, mtn., B.C., Can. (mount chăp'măn)	**132-33**	51°50'N	118°20'W
Chappell, Ne., U.S. (chă-pĕl')	**114-15**	41°06'N	102°28'W
Charadai, Arg.	**173**	27°39'S	59°52'W
Chār Borjak, Afg.	**230-31**	30°18'N	62°01'E
Charcas, Mex. (chär'käs)	**146-47**	23°08'N	101°08'W
Chärdjew, Turkmen. see Türkmenabat	**232-33**	39°05'N	63°35'E
Chardzhou, Turkmen. see Türkmenabat	**232-33**	39°05'N	63°35'E
Chari, stm., Afr. (shä-rē')	**262-63**	12°56'N	14°34'E
Chārīkār, Afg.	**232-33**	35°01'N	69°10'E
Chariton, Ia., U.S. (chår'ĭ-tŭn)	**114-15**	41°01'N	93°19'W
Charkhlik, China see Ruoqiang	**220-21**	39°01'N	88°11'E
Charleroi, Bel. (shàr-lē-rwä')	**190-91**	50°25'N	4°26'E
Charleroi, Pa., U.S. (shär'lē-roi)	**116-17**	40°08'N	79°54'W
Charles, Cape, c., Va., U.S. (kāp chärlz)	**124-25**	37°08'N	75°58'W
Charles City, Ia., U.S. (chärlz sĭ'tē)	**114-15**	43°04'N	92°41'W
Charleston, Il., U.S. (chärlz'tŭn)	**116-17**	39°29'N	88°11'W
Charleston, Mo., U.S. (chärlz'tŭn)	**124-25**	36°55'N	89°21'W
Charleston, S.C., U.S. (chärlz'tŭn)	**124-25**	32°47'N	79°56'W
Charleston, W.V., U.S. (chärlz'tŭn)	**116-17**	38°21'N	81°38'W
Charlestown, In., U.S. (chärlz'toun)	**116-17**	38°27'N	85°40'W
Charleville, Austl. (chär'lē-vĭl)	**276**	26°24'S	146°14'E
Charlevoix, Mi., U.S. (shär'lē-voi)	**116-17**	45°18'N	85°15'W
Charlotte, Mi., U.S. (shär'lŏt)	**116-17**	42°33'N	84°50'W
Charlotte, N.C., U.S. (shär'lŏt)	**124-25**	35°14'N	80°51'W
Charlotte Amalie, nat. cap., V.I.U.S. (shär-lŏt'ĕ ä-mä'lĭ-å)	**143b**	18°21'N	64°56'W
Charlotte Harbor, b., Fl., U.S. (shär'lŏt här'bēr)	**125a**	26°45'N	82°11'W
Charlottenberg, Swe. (shär-lŭt'ĕn-bĕrg)	**192-93**	59°54'N	12°18'E
Charlottesville, Va., U.S. (shär'lŏtz-vĭl)	**116-17**	38°02'N	78°29'W
Charlottetown, P.E., Can.	**138-39**	46°14'N	63°08'W
Charlton Island, i., Nu., Can.	**130-31**	52°0'N	79°30'W
Chārsadda, Pak. (chŭr-sä'dä)	**232-33**	34°09'N	71°44'E
Charters Towers, Austl.	**277**	20°04'S	146°16'E
Chartres, Fr. (shärt'r')	**196-97**	48°27'N	1°29'E
Chascomús, Arg. (chäs-kō-mōōs')	**173**	35°35'S	58°01'W
Chase City, Va., U.S. (chās sĭ'tĭ)	**124-25**	36°47'N	78°28'W
Châteaudun, Fr. (shä-tō-däN')	**196-97**	48°04'N	1°20'E
Château-Gontier, Fr. (chå-tō'gôN'tyā')	**196-97**	47°50'N	0°42'W
Châteauguay, Qc., Can. (chå-tō-gā)	**136-37**	45°23'N	73°44'W
Châteauroux, Fr. (shå-tō-rōō')	**196-97**	46°48'N	1°42'E
Château-Thierry, Fr. (shå-tō'ty-ĕr-rē')	**196-97**	49°03'N	3°24'E
Châtellerault, Fr. (shä-tĕl-rō')	**196-97**	46°49'N	0°33'E
Chatham, On., Can. (chăt'ăm)	**136-37**	42°24'N	82°11'W
Chatham, Il., U.S. (chăt'ăm)	**116-17**	39°40'N	89°42'W
Chatham, i., Ec. see San Cristóbal, Isla	**170a**	0°50'S	89°26'W
Chatham, Isla, i., Chile	**171**	50°38'S	74°27'W
Chatham Sound, strt., B.C., Can. (chăt'ăm sound)	**132-33**	54°32'N	130°35'W
Chatham Strait, strt., Ak., U.S. (chăt'ăm strāt)	**126**	57°30'N	134°45'W
Chatrapur, India	**236**	19°21'N	84°60'E
Chattahoochee, Fl., U.S. (chăt-tȧ-hōō' chē)	**124-25**	30°42'N	84°51'W
Chattahoochee, stm., U.S. (chăt-tȧ-hōō' chē)	**110-11**	30°46'N	84°52'W
Chattanooga, Tn., U.S. (chăt-ȧ-nōō'gȧ)	**124-25**	35°03'N	85°18'W
Chaudière, stm., Qc., Can. (shō-dyĕr')	**138-39**	46°45'N	71°17'W
Chauk, Mya.	**246-47**	20°54'N	94°49'E
Chaumont, Fr. (shō-môN')	**196-97**	48°06'N	5°08'E
Chauny, Fr. (shō-nē')	**196-97**	49°37'N	3°13'E
Chaves, Port. (chä'vĕzh)	**198-99**	41°44'N	7°28'W
Chavin, hist., Peru	**170**	9°37'S	77°14'W
Chavin de Huantar, hist., Peru see Chavin	**170**	9°37'S	77°14'W
Chaykovskij, Russia	**186-87**	56°46'N	54°06'E
Cheb, Czech Rep. (κĕb)	**194-95**	50°05'N	12°22'E
Cheboksary, Russia (chyĕ-bôk-sä'rē)	**186-87**	56°08'N	47°15'E
Cheboygan, Mi., U.S. (shē-boi'găn)	**116-17**	45°38'N	84°29'W
Chech, 'Erg, des., Afr.	**258-59**	24°43'N	2°31'W
Chechen', Ostrov, i., Russia (ôs-trôf' chyĕch'ĕn)	**227**	43°59'N	47°41'E
Chechnya, state, Russia	**227**	43°20'N	45°45'E
Checotah, Ok., U.S. (chē-kō'tȧ)	**120-21**	35°29'N	95°31'W
Chedabucto Bay, b., N.S., Can. (chĕd-ȧ-bŭk-tō bā)	**138-39**	45°23'N	61°10'W
Cheduba Island, i., Mya.	**246-47**	18°48'N	93°38'E
Cheektowaga, N.Y., U.S. (chēk-tō-wä'gȧ)	**116-17**	42°54'N	78°45'W
Chefoo, China see Yantai	**240-41**	37°32'N	121°21'E
Chegdomyn, Russia	**218-19**	51°08'N	133°05'E
Chehalis, Wa., U.S. (chē-hā'lĭs)	**112-13**	46°40'N	122°58'W
Cheju, Kor., S. (chĕ'jōō')	**240-41**	33°30'N	126°32'E
Cheju-do, i., Kor., S. (chĕ'jōō')	**240-41**	33°22'N	126°30'E
Chekiang, state, China see Zhejiang	**238-39**	29°0'N	120°00'E
Chelan, Wa., U.S. (chē-lăn')	**112-13**	47°50'N	120°00'W
Chelif, Oued, stm., Alg. (wĕd shä-lēf)	**198-99**	36°03'N	0°08'E
Chełm, Pol. (κĕlm)	**194-95**	51°08'N	23°30'E
Chełmno, Pol. (κĕlm'nō)	**194-95**	53°21'N	18°27'E
Chelmsford, Eng., U.K. (chĕlm's-fērd)	**190-91**	51°44'N	0°28'E
Chelsea, Mi., U.S. (chĕl'sē)	**116-17**	42°19'N	84°01'W
Chelsea, Ok., U.S. (chĕl'sē)	**120-21**	36°32'N	95°26'W
Cheltenham, Eng., U.K. (chĕlt'nŭm)	**190-91**	51°54'N	2°04'W
Chelyabinsk, Russia (chĕl-yä-bĕnsk')	**226**	55°10'N	61°26'E
Chelyuskin, Mys, c., Russia (mĭs chĕl-yós'-kĭn)	**218-19**	77°45'N	104°20'E
Chemnitz, Ger.	**194-95**	50°50'N	12°56'E
Chemulpo, Kor., S. see Inch'ŏn	**243**	37°28'N	126°38'E
Chenāb, stm., Asia (chē-näb)	**232-33**	29°21'N	71°02'E
Cheney, Wa., U.S. (chē'nå)	**112-13**	47°29'N	117°35'W
Chengchow, China see Zhengzhou	**238-39**	34°46'N	113°39'E
Chengde, China (chŭŋ-dŭ)	**240-41**	40°58'N	117°56'E
Chengdu, China (chŭŋ-dōō)	**238-39**	30°39'N	104°04'E
Chengshan Jiao, c., China (jyou chŭŋ-shän)	**240-41**	37°23'N	122°42'E
Chennai, India	**236**	13°06'N	80°15'E
Chenyang, China see Shenyang	**243**	41°48'N	123°24'E
Chenzhou, China	**238-39**	25°48'N	112°59'E
Chepén, Peru (chĕ-pĕ'n)	**170**	7°14'S	79°25'W
Chepo, Pan. (chā'pō)	**150**	9°10'N	79°06'W
Cheraw, S.C., U.S. (chē'rô)	**124-25**	34°42'N	79°54'W
Cherbourg, Fr. (shär-bór')	**196-97**	49°39'N	1°38'W
Cheremkhovo, Russia (chĕr'yĕm-kô-vō)	**218-19**	53°09'N	103°04'E
Cherepanovo, Russia (chĕr'yĕ pä-nô'vō)	**226**	54°13'N	83°21'E
Cherepovets, Russia (chĕr-yĕ-pô'vyĕtz)	**202-03**	59°08'N	37°55'E
Chergui, Chott ech, lk., Alg. (chĕr-gē)	**258-59**	34°13'N	0°26'E
Cherkassy, Ukr. see Cherkasy	**202-03**	49°26'N	32°05'E
Cherkasy, Ukr.	**202-03**	49°26'N	32°05'E
Cherkessia, state, Russia	**227**	44°0'N	42°00'E
Cherkessk, Russia	**227**	44°13'N	42°04'E
Cherlak, Russia (chĭr-läk')	**226**	54°09'N	74°49'E
Chermoz, Russia (chĕr-môz')	**186-87**	58°47'N	56°09'E
Chernigov, Ukr. see Chernihiv	**202-03**	51°30'N	31°17'E
Chernihiv, Ukr.	**202-03**	51°30'N	31°17'E
Chernivtsi, Ukr.	**194-95**	48°17'N	25°58'E
Chernobyl, see Chornobyl', Ukr.	**202-203**	51°17'N	30°14'E
Cherno More, s., see Black Sea	**186-87**	43°0'N	35°00'E
Chernovtsy, Ukr. see Chernivtsi	**194-95**	48°17'N	25°58'E
Chernoye More, s., see Black Sea	**186-87**	43°0'N	35°00'E
Chernyakhovsk, Russia	**194-95**	54°38'N	21°49'E
Chernyanka, Russia (chĕrn-yäŋ'kä)	**202-03**	50°56'N	37°49'E
Cherokee, Ia., U.S. (chĕr-ô-kē')	**114-15**	42°45'N	95°33'W
Cherokee, Ok., U.S. (chĕr-ô-kē')	**120-21**	36°45'N	98°21'W
Cherrapunji, India	**234-35**	25°13'N	91°42'E
Cherryville, N.C., U.S. (chĕr'ĭ-vĭl)	**124-25**	35°23'N	81°23'W
Cherskiy, Russia	**218-19**	68°46'N	161°24'E
Cherskiy Mountains, mts., Russia (chĕr'skē moun'tĭnz) see Cherskogo, Khrebet	**218-19**	65°0'N	144°00'E
Cherskogo, Khrebet, mts., Russia	**218-19**	65°0'N	144°00'E
Cherson, Ukr. see Kherson	**202-03**	46°38'N	32°35'E
Chervonohrad, Ukr.	**194-95**	50°23'N	24°14'E
Chesaning, Mi., U.S. (chĕs'ȧ-nĭng)	**116-17**	43°11'N	84°07'W
Chesapeake, Va., U.S. (chĕs'ȧ-pēk)	**124-25**	36°48'N	76°16'W
Chesapeake Bay, b., U.S. (chĕs'á-pēk bā)	**116-17**	38°38'N	76°27'W
Chester, Eng., U.K. (chĕs'tēr)	**190-91**	53°12'N	2°54'W
Chester, Il., U.S. (chĕs'tēr)	**120-21**	37°55'N	89°49'W
Chester, Mt., U.S. (chĕs'tēr)	**112-13**	48°32'N	110°57'W
Chester, Pa., U.S. (chĕs'tēr)	**116-17**	39°51'N	75°21'W
Chester, S.C., U.S. (chĕs'tēr)	**124-25**	34°42'N	81°13'W
Chester, Va., U.S. (chĕs'tēr)	**116-17**	37°21'N	77°26'W
Chester, W.V., U.S. (chĕs'tēr)	**116-17**	40°36'N	80°33'W
Chesterfield, Eng., U.K. (chĕs'tēr-fēld)	**190-91**	53°14'N	1°26'W
Chesterfield, Îles, is., N. Cal.	**280-81**	19°30'S	158°00'E
Chesterfield, Nosy, i., Madag.	**264-65**	16°20'S	43°58'E
Chesterfield Inlet, Nu., Can.	**128-29**	63°21'N	90°43'W
Chetek, Wi., U.S. (chĕ'tĕk)	**114-15**	45°19'N	91°39'W
Chettlatt Island, i., India	**236**	11°41'N	72°42'E
Chetumal, Mex.	**148**	18°30'N	88°18'W
Chetumal, Bahía, b., N.A. (bä-ē-ä-chĕt-ōō-mäl')	**148**	18°39'N	88°06'W
Chevak, Ak., U.S.	**126**	61°39'N	165°17'W
Cheviot, Oh., U.S. (shĕv'ĭ-ŭt)	**116-17**	39°09'N	84°37'W
Ch'ew Bahir, lk., Afr.	**267**	4°40'N	36°50'E
Chewelah, Wa., U.S. (chē-wē'lä)	**112-13**	48°17'N	117°43'W
Cheyenne, Wy., U.S. (shī-ĕn')	**114-15**	41°10'N	104°48'W
Cheyenne, stm., U.S. (shī-ĕn')	**110-11**	44°47'N	100°44'W
Cheyenne River Indian Reservation, ind. res., S.D., U.S. (shī-ĕn' rĭv'ēr ĭn'dĭ-ăn rĕ-sēr-vā'shĕn)	**114-15**	45°0'N	100°40'W
Cheyenne Wells, Co., U.S. (shī-ĕn' wĕls)	**120-21**	38°49'N	102°21'W
Chhapra, India	**234-35**	25°47'N	84°45'E
Chhatarpur, India	**234-35**	24°55'N	79°36'E
Chhattisgarh, state, India	**234-35**	21°30'N	82°00'E
Chhindwāra, India	**234-35**	22°03'N	78°57'E
Chi, stm., Thai.	**246-47**	15°11'N	104°43'E
Chiai, Tai. (chĭ'ī')	**225a**	23°29'N	120°27'E
Chiang Mai, Thai.	**246-47**	18°48'N	99°00'E
Chiang Rai, Thai.	**246-47**	19°55'N	99°50'E
Chiapa de Corzo, Mex. (chē-ä'pä dā kôr'zō)	**146-47**	16°41'N	92°60'W
Chiapas, state, Mex. (chē-ä'päs)	**146-47**	16°30'N	92°30'W
Chiavari, Italy (kyä-vä'rē)	**200-01**	44°20'N	9°20'E
Chiba, Japan (chē'bä)	**245**	35°36'N	140°08'E
Chiba, state, Japan (chē'bȧ)	**245**	35°30'N	140°20'E
Chibougamau, Qc., Can. (chē-bōō'gä-mou)	**138-39**	49°55'N	74°22'W
Chibougamau, Lac, lk., Qc., Can. (läk chē-bōō'gä-mou)	**138-39**	49°50'N	74°15'W
Chibuto, Moz.	**264-65**	24°42'S	33°34'E
Chicago, Il., U.S. (shĭ-kô-gō) (chĭ-kä'gō)	**116-17**	41°52'N	87°38'W

ăt; finăl; rāte; senåte; ärm; åsk; sofȧ; fåre; ch-choose; dh-as th in other; bē; ēvent; bĕt; recĕnt; cratēr; g-gō; gh-guttural g; bĭt; ĭ-short neutral; rīde; κ-guttural k as ch in German ich;

Feature (Pronunciation)	Page	Lat.	Long.
Chicago Heights, Il., U.S. (shĭ-kô-gō hīts)	116-17	41°30′N	87°39′W
Chicapa, stm., Afr. (chē-kä′pä)	262-63	6°25′S	20°48′E
Chichagof Island, i., Ak., U.S. (chê-chä′gôf ī′lǎnd)	126	57°07′N	135°12′W
Chichén Itzá, hist., Mex.	148	20°40′N	88°35′W
Chichester, Eng., U.K. (chĭch′ĕs-tẽr)	190-91	50°51′N	0°47′W
Chichimilá, Mex. (chē-chē-mê′lä)	148	20°37′N	88°13′W
Chichiriviche, Ven. (chē-chē-rē-vē-chĕ)	163b	10°56′N	68°17′W
Chickamauga, Ga., U.S. (chĭk-ȧ-mô′gȧ)	124-25	34°53′N	85°18′W
Chickasawhay, stm., Ms., U.S. (chĭk-ȧ-sô′wā)	124-25	31°0′N	88°45′W
Chickasha, Ok., U.S. (chĭk′ȧ-shā)	120-21	35°03′N	97°57′W
Chiclana de la Frontera, Spain (chê-klä′nä dĕ-lä-frôn-tĕ′rä)	198-99	36°25′N	6°08′W
Chiclayo, Peru (chê-klä′yō)	170	6°46′S	79°51′W
Chico, Ca., U.S. (chē′kō)	118-19	39°44′N	121°49′W
Chico, stm., Arg.	171	43°49′S	66°26′W
Chico, stm., Arg.	171	49°52′S	68°35′W
Chicopee, Ma., U.S. (chĭk′ô-pē)	116-17	42°09′N	72°37′W
Chicoutimi, Qc., Can. (shē-kōō′tē-mē′)	136-37	48°26′N	71°04′W
Chicxulub, Mex. (chēk-sōō-lōō′b)	148	21°08′N	89°31′W
Chidambaram, India	236	11°24′N	79°42′E
Chiefland, Fl., U.S. (chēf′lǎnd)	124-25	29°29′N	82°52′W
Chieri, Italy (kyâ′rē)	200-01	45°01′N	7°49′E
Chieti, Italy (kyĕ′tē)	200-01	42°21′N	14°10′E
Chifeng, China (chr-fŭŋ)	240-41	42°16′N	118°58′E
Chignecto Bay, b., Can. (shĭg-nĕk′tō bā)	138-39	45°35′N	64°45′W
Chihli, Gulf of, b., China *see* Bo Hai	240-41	38°30′N	120°02′E
Chihuahua, Mex. (chê-wä′wä)	144-45	28°38′N	106°05′W
Chihuahua, state, Mex.	122-23	28°30′N	106°00′W
Chihuahua, Desierto de, des., N.A. *see* Chihuahuan Desert	144-45	35°0′N	106°00′W
Chihuahuan Desert, des., N.A.	144-45	35°0′N	106°00′W
Chikmagalūr, India	236	13°19′N	75°47′E
Chikoy, stm., Asia	240-41	51°02′N	106°38′E
Chilcotin, stm., B.C., Can. (chĭl-kō′tĭn)	132-33	51°44′N	122°24′W
Childers, Austl.	276	25°14′S	152°17′E
Childress, Tx., U.S. (chīld′rĕs)	120-21	34°26′N	100°13′W
Chile, nation, S.A. (chē′lā)	158	30°0′S	71°00′W
Chile Chico, Chile	171	46°33′S	71°44′W
Chilecito, Arg. (chê-lå-sē′tō)	168-69	29°10′S	67°30′W
Chilecito, Arg. (chê-lå-sē′tō)	163e	33°53′S	69°04′W
Chilika Lake, lk., India	234-35	19°45′N	85°25′E
Chilko, stm., B.C., Can. (chĭl′kō)	132-33	52°06′N	123°28′W
Chilko Lake, lk., B.C., Can.	132-33	51°17′N	124°04′W
Chillán, Chile (chēl-yän′)	171	36°36′S	72°07′W
Chillicothe, Il., U.S. (chĭl-ĭ-kŏth′ê)	116-17	40°55′N	89°29′W
Chillicothe, Mo., U.S. (chĭl-ĭ-kŏth′ê)	120-21	39°48′N	93°33′W
Chillicothe, Oh., U.S. (chĭl-ĭ-kŏth′ê)	116-17	39°20′N	82°59′W
Chilliwack, B.C., Can. (chĭl′ĭ-wăk)	132-33	49°10′N	121°57′W
Chiloé, Isla Grande de, i., Chile	171	42°30′S	73°55′W
Chilpancingo de los Bravo, Mex.	146-47	17°33′N	99°30′W
Chilton, Wi., U.S. (chĭl′tŭn)	116-17	44°02′N	88°09′W
Chilung, Tai. (chĭ′lung)	225a	25°08′N	121°44′E
Chilwa, Lake, lk., Afr.	264-65	15°20′S	35°43′E
Chimaltenango, Guat. (chê-mäl-tå-näŋ′gō)	148	14°40′N	90°49′W
Chimborazo, vol., Ec. (chêm-bô-rä′zō)	170	1°28′S	78°48′W
Chimbote, Peru (chêm-bō′tå)	170	9°04′S	78°35′W
Chimboy, Uzb.	226	42°56′N	59°47′E
Chimkent, Kaz. *see* Shymkent	226	42°18′N	69°36′E
Chimoio, Moz.	264-65	19°09′S	33°30′E
China, Mex. (chē′nä)	122-23	25°42′N	99°14′W
China, nation, Asia (chī′nȧ)	206-07	35°0′N	105°00′E
Chinandega, Nic. (chē-nän-dā′gä)	149	12°38′N	87°08′W
China Selatan, Laut, s., Asia *see* South China Sea	224-25	10°0′N	113°00′E
Chincha Alta, Peru (chĭn′chä äl′tä)	163a	13°26′S	76°08′W
Chinchilla, Austl. (chĭn-chĭl′ȧ)	276	26°45′S	150°38′E
Chin-do, i., Kor., S.	243	34°27′N	126°15′E
Chindwinn, stm., Mya. (chĭn-dwĭn)	238-39	21°24′N	95°16′E
Chingola, Zam. (chĭng-gōlä)	264-65	12°32′S	27°52′E
Chinhae, Kor., S.	243	35°08′N	128°40′E
Chin Hills, hills, Mya.	234-35	22°30′N	93°30′E
Chinhoyi, Zimb.	264-65	17°22′S	30°11′E
Chiniot, Pak.	232-33	31°43′N	72°59′E
Chinju, Kor., S. (chĭn′jōō)	243	35°10′N	128°05′E
Chinko, stm., C.A.R. (shĭn′kô)	262-63	4°51′N	23°53′E
Chinmen Tao, i., Tai.	225a	24°27′N	118°23′E
Chinnampo, Kor., N. *see* Namp'o	243	38°45′N	125°23′E
Chinon, Fr. (shē-nôɴ′)	196-97	47°11′N	0°15′E
Chinook, Mt., U.S. (shĭn-ŏk′)	112-13	48°36′N	109°14′W

Feature (Pronunciation)	Page	Lat.	Long.
Chinsali, Zam.	264-65	10°33′S	32°04′E
Chioggia, Italy (kyôd′jä)	200-01	45°13′N	12°17′E
Chíos, Grc. (kē′ôs)	200-01	38°23′N	26°09′E
Chíos, i., Grc.	200-01	38°23′N	26°04′E
Chipata, Zam.	264-65	13°37′S	32°38′E
Chipley, Fl., U.S. (chĭp′lĭ)	124-25	30°47′N	85°32′W
Chipman, N.B., Can. (chĭp′mȧn)	138-39	46°10′N	65°53′W
Chippewa, stm., Wi., U.S. (chĭp′ê-wä)	114-15	44°24′N	92°04′W
Chippewa Falls, Wi., U.S. (chĭp′ê-wä fôlz)	114-15	44°56′N	91°24′W
Chiquimula, Guat. (chē-kê-mōō′lä)	148	14°48′N	89°33′W
Chiquimulilla, Guat. (chē-kē-mōō-lê′l-yä)	148	14°05′N	90°23′W
Chiquinquirá, Col. (chê-kēŋ′kê-rä′)	163c	5°37′N	73°48′W
Chirchiq, Uzb.	232-33	41°28′N	69°35′E
Chire, stm., Afr. *see* Shire	264-65	17°42′S	35°19′E
Chiricahua National Monument, n.p., Az., U.S. (chĭ-rä-cä′hwä năsh′ŭn-ăl mŏn′ū-mĕnt)	118-19	31°59′N	109°22′W
Chiricahua Peak, mtn., Az., U.S.	118-19	31°52′N	109°20′W
Chiriquí Grande, Pan. (chē-rê-kē′ grän′dā)	150	8°57′N	82°08′W
Chiri-san, mtn., Kor., S. (chĭ′rĭ-sän′)	243	35°20′N	127°44′E
Chirripó, Cerro, mtn., C.R.	149	9°29′N	83°30′W
Chirua, Lago, lk., Afr. *see* Chilwa, Lake	264-65	15°20′S	35°43′E
Chisasibi, Qc., Can.	128-29	53°48′N	79°02′W
Chishima-rettō, is., Russia *see* Kuril Islands	218-19	47°14′N	152°18′E
Chisholm, Mn., U.S. (chĭz′ŭm)	114-15	47°29′N	92°53′W
Chisimayu, Som.	262-63	0°22′S	42°32′E
Chişinău, nat. cap., Mol.	202-03	47°02′N	28°50′E
Chistopol, Russia (chĭs-tô′pôl-y')	186-87	55°22′N	50°37′E
Chistyakovo, Ukr. *see* Torez	202-03	48°02′N	38°38′E
Chita, Russia (chê-tȧ′)	222-23	52°02′N	113°29′E
Chitato, Ang.	262-63	7°20′S	20°46′E
Chitradurga, India	236	14°14′N	76°24′E
Chitrāl, Pak. (chē-träl′)	232-33	35°52′N	71°49′E
Chitré, Pan.	150	7°58′N	80°26′W
Chittagong, Bngl. (chĭt-ȧ-gông′)	246-47	22°20′N	91°50′E
Chittaurgarh, India	234-35	24°54′N	74°37′E
Chittoor, India	236	13°13′N	79°06′E
Chiumbe, stm., Afr. (chê-ŏm′bå)	262-63	6°59′S	21°11′E
Chivasso, Italy (kê-väs′sō)	200-01	45°12′N	7°54′E
Chivilcoy, Arg. (chē-vêl-koi′)	173	34°54′S	60°02′W
Chkalov, Russia	186-87	51°48′N	55°06′E
Chlef, Alg.	198-99	36°10′N	1°20′E
Choâm Khsant, Camb.	246-47	14°13′N	104°56′E
Chochis, Cerro, mtn., Bol.	168-69	18°08′S	59°54′W
Chodzież, Pol. (kōj′yĕsh)	194-95	52°60′N	16°55′E
Choele Choel, Arg. (chô-ĕ′lĕ-chôĕ′l)	171	39°17′S	65°39′W
Choiseul, i., Sol. Is. (shwä-zûl′)	279e	7°05′S	157°00′E
Chojnice, Pol. (ĸōĭ-nē-tsĕ)	194-95	53°42′N	17°34′E
Chokurdakh, Russia	218-19	70°38′N	147°53′E
Chókwe, Moz.	264-65	24°33′S	32°60′E
Cholet, Fr. (shô-lĕ′)	196-97	47°04′N	0°53′W
Choluteca, Hond. (chō-lōō-tā′kä)	149	13°18′N	87°12′W
Choma, Zam.	264-65	16°49′S	26°59′E
Chomutov, Czech Rep. (kō′mò-tôf)	194-95	50°28′N	13°25′E
Chona, stm., Russia (chō′nä)	218-19	62°54′N	111°06′E
Ch'ŏnan, Kor., S.	243	36°48′N	127°10′E
Chon Buri, Thai.	246-47	13°22′N	101°00′E
Chone, Ec. (chô′nĕ)	170	0°42′S	80°05′W
Ch'ŏngjin, Kor., N. (chŭng-jĭn′)	243	41°47′N	129°48′E
Ch'ŏngju, Kor., S. (chŭng-jōō′)	243	36°38′N	127°30′E
Chongqing, China	238-39	29°34′N	106°34′E
Chongqing, state, China	238-39	30°0′N	108°00′E
Ch'ŏngsan-do, i., Kor., S.	243	34°11′N	126°54′E
Chongzuo, China	238-39	22°24′N	107°22′E
Chŏnju, Kor., S. (chŭn-jōō′)	243	35°49′N	127°09′E
Chonos, Archipiélago de los, is., Chile	171	45°0′S	74°00′W
Chorne more, s., *see* Black Sea	186-87	43°0′N	35°00′E
Chornobyl', Ukr.	202-03	51°17′N	30°14′E
Ch'ŏrwŏn, Kor., S.	243	38°17′N	127°14′E
Chōshi, Japan (chō′shē)	245	35°44′N	140°50′E
Chos Malal, Arg.	171	37°23′S	70°16′W
Chosŏn minjujuŭi-inmīn-konghwaguk, nation, Asia *see* North Korea	206-07	40°0′N	127°00′E
Choszczno, Pol. (chôsh′chnô)	194-95	53°10′N	15°25′E
Choteau, Mt., U.S. (shō′tō)	112-13	47°49′N	112°12′W
Chouk'ou, China *see* Shangshui	238-39	33°33′N	114°34′E
Choushan Islands, is., China *see* Zhoushan Qundao	238-39	30°0′N	122°00′E
Chown, Mount, mtn., Ab., Can. (mount choun)	132-33	53°24′N	119°22′W
Choybalsan, Mong.	240-41	48°04′N	114°32′E

Feature (Pronunciation)	Page	Lat.	Long.
Choyr, Mong.	240-41	46°22′N	108°22′E
Christchurch, N.Z. (krīst′chûrch)	278	43°32′S	172°39′E
Christiansburg, Va., U.S. (krĭs′chănz-bûrg)	124-25	37°08′N	80°25′W
Christina, stm., Ab., Can.	134-35	56°40′N	111°04′W
Christmas Island, dep., Oc. (krĭs′-mȧs ī′lǎnd)	248-49	10°30′S	105°40′E
Christmas Island, at., Kir. *see* Kiritimati	280-81	1°48′N	157°19′W
Chrudim, Czech Rep. (ĸrōō′dyĕm)	194-95	49°57′N	15°48′E
Chrzanów, Pol. (ĸzhä′nôf)	194-95	50°07′N	19°26′E
Chu, stm., Asia	246-47	19°53′N	105°45′E
Chubut, state, Arg. (chò-bōōt′)	171	44°0′S	69°00′W
Chubut, stm., Arg. (chò-bōōt′)	171	43°21′S	65°03′W
Chucunaque, stm., Pan. (chōō-kōō-nä′kå)	150	8°08′N	77°44′W
Chudovo, Russia (chò′dô-vô)	192-93	59°07′N	31°41′E
Chudskoye Ozero, lk., Eur. (chòt′skô-yĕ ôzê-rô) *see* Peipus, Lake	192-93	58°45′N	27°25′E
Chuguyevka, Russia (chò-gōō′yĕf-kå)	244	44°09′N	133°52′E
Chukchi Sea, s., (chōōk′chē sē)	126	69°0′N	171°00′W
Chukotskiy, Mys, c., Russia	126	64°16′N	173°07′W
Chukotskiy Poluostrov, pen., Russia *see* Chukotsk Peninsula	218-19	66°0′N	175°00′W
Chukotskoye More, s., *see* Chukchi Sea	126	69°0′N	171°00′W
Chukotsk Peninsula, pen., Russia	218-19	66°0′N	175°00′W
Chula Vista, Ca., U.S. (chōō′lå vĭs′tå)	118-19	32°38′N	117°05′W
Chul'man, Russia	218-19	56°51′N	124°53′E
Chulucanas, Peru	170	5°06′S	80°09′W
Chulym, stm., Russia	218-19	57°42′N	83°52′E
Chumbicha, Arg.	168-69	28°52′S	66°14′W
Chumphon, Thai.	246-47	10°30′N	99°08′E
Chumysh, stm., Russia	226	53°31′N	83°10′E
Chuna, stm., Russia	218-19	57°44′N	95°27′E
Ch'unch'ŏn, Kor., S. (chòn-chŭn′)	243	37°52′N	127°44′E
Ch'ungju, Kor., S. (chŭng′jōō′)	243	36°58′N	127°56′E
Chungking, China *see* Chongqing	238-39	29°34′N	106°34′E
Chungking, state, China *see* Chongqing	238-39	30°0′N	108°00′E
Chunya, stm., Russia (chòn′yä′)	218-19	61°37′N	96°32′E
Chuquicamata, Chile (chōō-kê-kä-mä′tä)	168-69	22°19′S	68°56′W
Chur, Switz. (kōōr)	194-95	46°51′N	9°31′E
Churchill, Mb., Can. (chûrch′ĭl)	128-29	58°47′N	94°10′W
Churchill, stm., Can. (chûrch′ĭl)	130-31	58°49′N	94°11′W
Churchill, Cape, c., Mb., Can. (kāp chûrch′ĭl)	130-31	58°46′N	93°14′W
Churchill Lake, lk., Sk., Can. (chûrch′ĭl lāk)	134-35	55°55′N	108°20′W
Chūru, India	234-35	28°18′N	74°58′E
Chusovaya, stm., Russia (chōō-sô-vä′yȧ)	176-77	58°09′N	57°03′E
Chusovoy, Russia (chōō-sô-vôy′)	186-87	58°18′N	57°49′E
Chuuk, is., Micron.	280-81	7°16′N	151°44′E
Chuvashia, state, Russia	186-87	55°30′N	47°00′E
Chuvashiya, state, Russia *see* Chuvashia	186-87	55°30′N	47°00′E
Chuxian, China (chōō shyĕn)	238-39	32°19′N	118°18′E
Chuxiong, China (chōō-shyôŋ)	238-39	25°03′N	101°33′E
Chüy, stm., Asia *see* Shū	226	45°00′N	67°45′E
Cianjur, Indon.	248-49	6°48′S	107°08′E
Cicero, Il., U.S. (sĭs′ẽr-ō)	116-17	41°51′N	87°45′W
Cicia, i., Fiji	279f	17°45′S	179°18′W
Ciechanów, Pol. (tsyĕ-kä′nôf)	194-95	52°53′N	20°37′E
Ciego de Ávila, Cuba (syā′gō-dĕ-ä′vê-lä)	142-43	21°51′N	78°46′W
Ciego de Ávila, state, Cuba (syā′gō-dĕ-ä′vê-lä)	142-43	22°0′N	78°40′W
Ciempozuelos, Spain (thyĕm-pô-thwā′lōs)	198-99	40°10′N	3°37′W
Ciénaga, Col. (syā′nä-gä)	164-65	11°00′N	74°15′W
Cienfuegos, Cuba (syĕn-fwā′gōs)	142-43	22°10′N	80°26′W
Cienfuegos, state, Cuba (syĕn-fwā′gōs)	142-43	22°10′N	80°30′W
Cieszyn, Pol. (tsyĕ′shĕn)	194-95	49°45′N	18°38′E
Cieza, Spain (thyā′thä)	198-99	38°14′N	1°25′W
Cihuatlán, Mex. (sē-wä-tlä′n)	146-47	19°14′N	104°34′W
Cikobia, i., Fiji	279f	15°43′S	179°58′W
Cilacap, Indon.	248-49	7°44′S	109°01′E
Cill Chainnigh, Ire. *see* Kilkenny	190-91	52°39′N	7°15′W
Cimarron, stm., U.S. (sĭm-ȧ-rōn′)	120-21	36°10′N	96°17′W
Cina Selatan, Laut, s., Asia *see* South China Sea	224-25	10°0′N	113°00′E
Cincinnati, Oh., U.S. (sĭn-sĭ-nát′ĭ)	116-17	39°11′N	84°28′W
Cintalapa, Mex. (sĕn-tä-lä′pä)	146-47	16°41′N	93°43′W

n-sing; ŋ-baŋk; ɴ-nasalized n; nŏd; cŏmmit; ōld; ôbey; ôrder; oi-boil; fōōd; ò-as oo in foot; ou-out; s-soft; sh-dish; th-thin; pūre; ûnite; ûrn; stŭd; circŭs; ü-as in French tu; ′-indeterminate vowel.

Feature (Pronunciation)	Page	Lat.	Long.
Cinto, Monte, mtn., Fr. (môɴ chēn´tō)	**184-85**	42°23′N	8°56′E
Cipolletti, Arg.	**171**	38°56′S	67°59′W
Circleville, Oh., U.S. (sûr´k'l-vĭl)	**116-17**	39°36′N	82°57′W
Circleville, Ut., U.S. (sûr´k'l-vĭl)	**118-19**	38°10′N	112°16′W
Cirebon, Indon.	**248-49**	6°45′S	108°34′E
Cisco, Tx., U.S. (sĭs´kō)	**120-21**	32°24′N	98°59′W
Cisneros, Col. (sês-nĕ´rôs)	**163c**	6°33′N	75°04′W
Cisterna di Latina, Italy (chēs-tĕ´r-nä-dē-lä-tē´nä)	**200-01**	41°36′N	12°49′E
Citlaltépetl, Volcán, vol., Mex. *see* Pico de Orizaba, Volcán	**146-47**	19°01′N	97°16′W
Citronelle, Al., U.S. (cĭt-rô´nĕl)	**124-25**	31°06′N	88°14′W
Città di Castello, Italy (chēt-tä´dē käs-tĕl´lō)	**200-01**	43°28′N	12°15′E
Ciudad Acuña, Mex.	**122-23**	29°19′N	100°56′W
Ciudad Altamirano, Mex. (syo͞o-dä´d-äl-tä-mē-rä´nô)	**146-47**	18°21′N	100°39′W
Ciudad Bolívar, Ven. (syo͞o-dhädh´ bô-lē´vär)	**164-65**	8°07′N	63°33′W
Ciudad Camargo, Mex.	**122-23**	27°42′N	105°10′W
Ciudad Cortés, C.R.	**149**	8°58′N	83°32′W
Ciudad Darío, Nic. (syo͞o-dhädh´dä´rē-ō)	**149**	12°43′N	86°07′W
Ciudad del Carmen, Mex. (syo͞o-dä´d-dĕl-kà´r-mĕn)	**148**	18°39′N	91°49′W
Ciudad del Maíz, Mex. (syo͞o-dhädh´del mä-ēz´)	**146-47**	22°24′N	99°36′W
Ciudad de México, nat. cap., Mex. *see* Mexico City	**146-47**	19°24′N	99°09′W
Ciudad de Nutrias, Ven.	**164-65**	8°05′N	69°17′W
Ciudad Guayana, Ven.	**164-65**	8°21′N	62°39′W
Ciudad Hidalgo, Mex. (syo͞o-dä´d-ē-dä´l-gô)	**146-47**	19°41′N	100°34′W
Ciudad Jiménez, Mex. *see* Jiménez	**122-23**	27°08′N	104°56′W
Ciudad Juárez, Mex. (syo͞o-dhädh hwä´rāz)	**122-23**	31°45′N	106°28′W
Ciudad Lerdo, Mex. *see* Lerdo	**122-23**	25°32′N	103°31′W
Ciudad Madero, Mex. (syo͞o-dä´d-mä-dĕ´rô)	**146-47**	22°16′N	97°50′W
Ciudad Mante, Mex. (syo͞o-dä´d-màn´tĕ)	**146-47**	22°44′N	98°58′W
Ciudad Netzahualcóyotl, Mex.	**146-47**	19°27′N	99°03′W
Ciudad Obregón, Mex. (syo͞o-dhädh-ô-brĕ-gô´n)	**144-45**	27°29′N	109°57′W
Ciudad Ojeda, Ven.	**164-65**	10°13′N	71°19′W
Ciudad Real, Spain (thyo͞o-dhädh´rā-äl´)	**198-99**	38°59′N	3°55′W
Ciudad Rodrigo, Spain (thyo͞o-dhädh´rô-drē´gō)	**198-99**	40°36′N	6°32′W
Ciudad Valles, Mex.	**146-47**	21°59′N	99°00′W
Ciudad Victoria, Mex. (syo͞o-dhädh´vêk-tō´rē-ä)	**146-47**	23°44′N	99°08′W
Civitavecchia, Italy (chē´vē-tä-vĕk´kyä)	**200-01**	42°06′N	11°48′E
Clairton, Pa., U.S. (klârtŭn)	**116-17**	40°18′N	79°53′W
Clanton, Al., U.S. (klăn´tŭn)	**124-25**	32°51′N	86°38′W
Clanwilliam, S. Afr.	**264-65**	32°10′S	18°54′E
Clare, Mi., U.S. (klâr)	**116-17**	43°49′N	84°45′W
Claremont, N.H., U.S. (klâr´mŏnt)	**116-17**	43°22′N	72°20′W
Claremore, Ok., U.S. (klâr´mōr)	**120-21**	36°19′N	95°37′W
Claremorris, Ire. (klâr-mŏr´ĭs)	**190-91**	53°43′N	8°60′W
Clarence, Isla, i., Chile	**171**	54°11′S	71°49′W
Clarence Island, i., Ant.	**287**	61°11′S	54°03′W
Clarence Strait, strt., Austl. (klăr´ĕns strāt)	**272-73**	12°0′S	131°00′E
Clarendon, Tx., U.S. (klâr´ĕn-dŭn)	**120-21**	34°56′N	100°54′W
Claresholm, Ab., Can. (klâr´ĕs-hōlm)	**132-33**	50°01′N	113°35′W
Clarinda, Ia., U.S. (klȧ-rĭn´dȧ)	**120-21**	40°44′N	95°02′W
Clarines, Ven. (klä-rē´nĕs)	**163b**	9°58′N	65°09′W
Clarion, Ia., U.S. (klăr´ĭ-ŭn)	**114-15**	42°44′N	93°44′W
Clarion, Pa., U.S. (klăr´ĭ-ŭn)	**116-17**	41°13′N	79°23′W
Clarión, Isla, i., Mex.	**144-45**	18°22′N	114°44′W
Clark, S.D., U.S. (klärk)	**114-15**	44°53′N	97°44′W
Clarke Island, i., Austl.	**276**	40°33′S	148°10′E
Clarksburg, W.V., U.S. (klärkz´bûrg)	**116-17**	39°16′N	80°20′W
Clarksdale, Ms., U.S. (klärks-dāl)	**124-25**	34°12′N	90°34′W
Clark's Harbour, N.S., Can. (klärks här´bēr)	**138-39**	43°28′N	65°38′W
Clarks Hill Lake, res., U.S. (klärks hĭl lāk) *see* J. Strom Thurmond Reservoir	**124-25**	33°45′N	82°16′W
Clarkston, Wa., U.S. (klärks´tŭn)	**112-13**	46°25′N	117°04′W
Clarksville, Ar., U.S. (klärks-vĭl)	**120-21**	35°28′N	93°28′W
Clarksville, Tn., U.S. (klärks-vĭl)	**124-25**	36°31′N	87°21′W
Clarksville, Tx., U.S. (klärks-vĭl)	**120-21**	33°37′N	95°04′W
Claxton, Ga., U.S. (klăks´tŭn)	**124-25**	32°10′N	81°54′W
Clay Center, Ks., U.S. (klā sĕn´tēr)	**120-21**	39°23′N	97°07′W
Clay City, Ky., U.S. (klā sĭ´tĭ)	**116-17**	37°52′N	83°57′W
Clayton, Ga., U.S. (klā´tŭn)	**124-25**	34°53′N	83°23′W
Clayton, N.C., U.S. (klā´tŭn)	**124-25**	35°39′N	78°28′W
Clayton, N.M., U.S. (klā´tŭn)	**120-21**	36°27′N	103°11′W
Clearfield, Ut., U.S. (klēr-fēld)	**112-13**	41°07′N	112°01′W
Clear Lake, Ia., U.S. (klēr lāk)	**114-15**	43°08′N	93°23′W
Clear Lake, S.D., U.S. (klēr lāk)	**114-15**	44°45′N	96°42′W
Clear Lake, lk., Ca., U.S. (klēr lāk)	**118-19**	39°02′N	122°50′W
Clearwater, Fl., U.S. (klēr-wô´tēr)	**125a**	27°58′N	82°47′W
Clearwater, stm., Can. (klēr-wô´tēr)	**134-35**	56°45′N	111°23′W
Clearwater, stm., Ab., Can. (klēr-wô´tēr)	**132-33**	52°22′N	114°57′W
Clearwater Mountains, mts., Id., U.S. (klēr-wô´tēr moun´tĭnz)	**112-13**	46°00′N	115°30′W
Cleburne, Tx., U.S. (klē´bŭrn)	**120-21**	32°22′N	97°24′W
Cle Elum, Wa., U.S. (klē ĕl´ŭm)	**112-13**	47°12′N	120°56′W
Clermont, Austl. (klēr´mŏnt)	**277**	22°49′S	147°40′E
Clermont-Ferrand, Fr. (klĕr-môɴ´fĕr-räɴ´)	**196-97**	45°47′N	3°06′E
Cleveland, Ms., U.S. (klēv´lănd)	**124-25**	33°45′N	90°43′W
Cleveland, Oh., U.S. (klēv´lănd)	**116-17**	41°29′N	81°42′W
Cleveland, Ok., U.S. (klēv´lănd)	**120-21**	36°19′N	96°28′W
Cleveland, Tn., U.S. (klēv´lănd)	**124-25**	35°10′N	84°52′W
Cleveland, Tx., U.S. (klēv´lănd)	**122-23**	30°21′N	95°05′W
Cleveland, Cape, c., Austl.	**277**	19°13′S	147°02′E
Cleveland Heights, Oh., U.S. (klēv´lănd hīts)	**116-17**	41°30′N	81°36′W
Cleves, Ger. *see* Kleve	**194-95**	51°47′N	6°09′E
Clewiston, Fl., U.S. (klē´wis-tŭn)	**125a**	26°45′N	80°54′W
Clifden, Ire. (klĭf´dĕn)	**190-91**	53°29′N	10°01′W
Clifton, Az., U.S. (klĭf´tŭn)	**118-19**	33°04′N	109°18′W
Clifton, Il., U.S. (klĭf´tŭn)	**116-17**	40°56′N	87°56′W
Clifton, N.J., U.S. (klĭf´tŭn)	**116-17**	40°53′N	74°10′W
Clifton, Tx., U.S. (klĭf´tŭn)	**122-23**	31°46′N	97°35′W
Clifton Forge, Va., U.S. (klĭf´tŭn fôrj)	**116-17**	37°49′N	79°50′W
Clinch, stm., U.S. (klĭnch)	**124-25**	35°53′N	84°30′W
Clingmans Dome, mtn., U.S. (klĭng´măns dōm)	**124-25**	35°35′N	83°30′W
Clinton, B.C., Can. (klĭn-´tŭn)	**132-33**	51°05′N	121°37′W
Clinton, On., Can. (klĭn-´tŭn)	**136-37**	43°37′N	81°32′W
Clinton, Ar., U.S. (klĭn-´tŭn)	**120-21**	35°36′N	92°28′W
Clinton, Ia., U.S. (klĭn-´tŭn)	**114-15**	41°51′N	90°12′W
Clinton, Il., U.S. (klĭn-´tŭn)	**116-17**	40°09′N	88°57′W
Clinton, In., U.S. (klĭn-´tŭn)	**116-17**	39°39′N	87°24′W
Clinton, Ky., U.S. (klĭn-´tŭn)	**124-25**	36°40′N	89°00′W
Clinton, Mo., U.S. (klĭn-´tŭn)	**120-21**	38°22′N	93°46′W
Clinton, Ms., U.S. (klĭn-´tŭn)	**124-25**	32°21′N	90°19′W
Clinton, N.C., U.S. (klĭn-´tŭn)	**124-25**	34°59′N	78°19′W
Clinton, Ok., U.S. (klĭn-´tŭn)	**120-21**	35°31′N	98°58′W
Clinton, S.C., U.S. (klĭn-´tŭn)	**124-25**	34°28′N	81°53′W
Clinton, Tn., U.S. (klĭn-´tŭn)	**124-25**	36°06′N	84°08′W
Clintonville, Wi., U.S. (klĭn´tŭn-vĭl)	**116-17**	44°36′N	88°46′W
Clio, Mi., U.S. (klē´ō)	**116-17**	43°10′N	83°44′W
Clipperton, Île, at., Oc.	**140-41**	10°18′N	109°13′W
Clipperton Island, at., Oc. *see* Clipperton, Île	**140-41**	10°18′N	109°13′W
Clodomira, Arg.	**173**	27°33′S	64°07′W
Cloncurry, Austl. (klŏn-kŭr´ē)	**277**	20°43′S	140°30′E
Cloquet, Mn., U.S. (klô-kā´)	**114-15**	46°43′N	92°28′W
Cloud Peak, mtn., Wy., U.S. (kloud pēk)	**112-13**	44°25′N	107°10′W
Clover, S.C., U.S. (klō´vēr)	**124-25**	35°07′N	81°14′W
Cloverdale, Ca., U.S. (klō´vēr-dāl)	**118-19**	38°48′N	123°01′W
Clovis, Ca., U.S. (klō´vĭs)	**118-19**	36°50′N	119°42′W
Clovis, N.M., U.S. (klō´vĭs)	**120-21**	34°24′N	103°13′W
Cluj-Napoca, Rom.	**194-95**	46°47′N	23°36′E
Cluny, Fr. (klü-nē´)	**196-97**	46°26′N	4°39′E
Clyde, Oh., U.S. (klīd)	**116-17**	41°18′N	82°58′W
Clyde, Tx., U.S. (klīd)	**120-21**	32°25′N	99°29′W
Cnossus, hist., Grc. *see* Knossos	**200a**	35°17′N	25°12′E
Côa, stm., Port. (kô´ä)	**198-99**	41°05′N	7°06′W
Coahuila, state, Mex. (kō-ä-wē´lä)	**122-23**	27°20′N	102°00′W
Coalcomán de Matamoros, Mex.	**146-47**	18°47′N	103°09′W
Coaldale, Ab., Can. (kōl´dāl)	**132-33**	49°44′N	112°37′W
Coalgate, Ok., U.S. (kōl´gāt)	**120-21**	34°32′N	96°14′W
Coalinga, Ca., U.S. (kō-ȧ-lĭŋ´gȧ)	**118-19**	36°09′N	120°22′W
Coari, Braz. (kō-är´ē)	**166-67**	4°06′S	63°07′W
Coari, stm., Braz.	**166-67**	4°27′S	63°29′W
Coast Mountains, mts., N.A. (kōst moun´tĭnz)	**130-31**	55°0′N	129°00′W
Coast Ranges, mts., U.S. (kōst rānj´ĕz)	**110-11**	40°46′N	123°38′W
Coatesville, Pa., U.S. (kōts´vĭl)	**116-17**	39°59′N	75°49′W
Coaticook, Qc., Can. (kō´tĭ-ko͝ok)	**136-37**	45°08′N	71°48′W
Coats Island, i., Nu., Can. (kōts ī´lănd)	**130-31**	62°30′N	82°60′W
Coats Land, reg., Ant. (kōts lănd)	**287**	77°0′S	28°00′W
Coatzacoalcos, Mex.	**146-47**	18°08′N	94°26′W
Cobá, hist., Mex. (kô´bä)	**148**	20°36′N	87°35′W
Cobalt, On., Can. (kō´bôlt)	**136-37**	47°24′N	79°41′W
Cobán, Guat. (kō-bän´)	**148**	15°28′N	90°22′W
Cobar, Austl.	**276**	31°30′S	145°50′E
Cobija, Bol. (kô-bē´hä)	**166-67**	11°02′S	68°44′W
Coblenz, Ger. *see* Koblenz	**194-95**	50°21′N	7°35′E
Cobourg, On., Can. (kō´bôrgh)	**136-37**	43°58′N	78°09′W
Cobourg Peninsula, pen., Austl.	**272-73**	11°22′S	132°17′E
Coburg, Ger. (kō´bo͝org)	**194-95**	50°16′N	10°58′E
Cocanada, India *see* Kākināda	**236**	16°57′N	82°15′E
Cochabamba, Bol.	**168-69**	17°23′S	66°10′W
Cochin, India	**236**	9°56′N	76°15′E
Cochran, Ga., U.S. (kŏk´răn)	**124-25**	32°23′N	83°21′W
Cochrane, Ab., Can. (kŏk´răn)	**132-33**	51°11′N	114°29′W
Cochrane, On., Can. (kŏk´răn)	**136-37**	49°04′N	81°02′W
Cochrane, Lago, lk., S.A.	**171**	47°21′S	71°56′W
Cockburn Island, i., On., Can. (kŏk-bûrn ī´lănd)	**136-37**	45°55′N	83°22′W
Cockburn Town, nat. cap., T./C. Is. *see* Grand Turk	**142-43**	21°27′N	71°08′W
Coco, stm., N.A. (kô-kô)	**149**	14°59′N	83°11′W
Coco, Cayo, i., Cuba (kä´-yō-kô´kô)	**142-43**	22°29′N	78°28′W
Coco, Isla del, i., C.R. (ē´s-lä-dĕl-kô-kô)	**86**	5°32′N	87°04′W
Cocoa, Fl., U.S. (kō´kō)	**125a**	28°22′N	80°44′W
Cocoa Beach, Fl., U.S. (kō´kō bēch)	**125a**	28°19′N	80°37′W
Coco Channel, strt., Asia	**246-47**	13°45′N	93°01′E
Coco Islands, is., Mya.	**246-47**	14°09′N	93°25′E
Cocos Islands, dep., Oc. (kō´kōs ī´lăndz)	**224-25**	12°10′S	96°55′E
Cocula, Mex. (kō-ko͞o´lä)	**146-47**	20°23′N	103°50′W
Cod, Cape, pen., Ma., U.S. (kăp kŏd)	**116-17**	41°42′N	70°15′W
Codajás, Braz. (kō-dä-häzh´)	**166-67**	3°49′S	62°05′W
Codera, Cabo, c., Ven. (kà´bô-kō-dĕ´rä)	**163b**	10°34′N	66°03′W
Codó, Braz.	**166-67**	4°29′S	43°53′W
Cody, Wy., U.S. (kō´dĭ)	**112-13**	44°32′N	109°03′W
Coeur d'Alene, Id., U.S. (kûr dȧ-lān´)	**112-13**	47°41′N	116°47′W
Coeur d'Alene Indian Reservation, ind. res., Id., U.S. (kûr dȧ-lān´ ĭn´dĭ-ăn rĕ-sĕr-vā´shĕn)	**112-13**	47°18′N	116°45′W
Coffeyville, Ks., U.S. (kŏf´ĭ-vĭl)	**120-21**	37°02′N	95°37′W
Coffs Harbour, Austl.	**276**	30°19′S	153°08′E
Cognac, Fr. (kôn-yak´)	**196-97**	45°42′N	0°20′W
Cohoes, N.Y., U.S. (kô-hōz´)	**116-17**	42°47′N	73°42′W
Coiba, Isla de, i., Pan.	**150**	7°27′N	81°45′W
Coig, stm., Arg. (kô´ēk)	**171**	50°57′S	69°09′W
Coihaique, Chile	**171**	45°34′S	72°04′W
Coimbatore, India (kô-ēm-bá-tôr´)	**236**	10°60′N	76°58′E
Coimbra, Port. (kô-ēm´brä)	**198-99**	40°13′N	8°25′W
Coín, Spain (kô-ēn´)	**198-99**	36°40′N	4°46′W
Coire, Switz. *see* Chur	**194-95**	46°51′N	9°31′E
Cojutepeque, El Sal. (kô-hô-tĕ-pā´kā)	**148**	13°43′N	88°56′W
Cokato, Mn., U.S. (kô-kā´tō)	**114-15**	45°04′N	94°12′W
Colac, Austl. (kŏ´lăc)	**276**	38°21′S	143°35′E
Colatina, Braz. (kō-lä-tē´nä)	**172**	19°32′S	40°39′W
Colbeck, Cape, c., Ant.	**287**	77°25′S	157°33′W
Colby, Ks., U.S. (kōl´bĭ)	**120-21**	39°24′N	101°03′W
Colchester, Eng., U.K. (kōl´chĕs-tēr)	**190-91**	51°53′N	0°54′E
Cold Lake, Ab., Can.	**132-33**	54°27′N	110°10′W
Cold Lake, lk., Can. (kōld lāk)	**132-33**	54°33′N	110°05′W
Coldwater, Mi., U.S. (kōld´wô-tēr)	**116-17**	41°57′N	85°00′W
Coleman, Tx., U.S. (kōl´măn)	**122-23**	31°50′N	99°25′W
Colenso, S. Afr. (kŏ-lĕnz´ō)	**269c**	28°45′S	29°50′E
Coleraine, Mn., U.S. (kōl-rān´)	**114-15**	47°17′N	93°26′W
Colesberg, S. Afr.	**264-65**	30°43′S	25°06′E
Colfax, Ia., U.S. (kōl´făks)	**114-15**	41°41′N	93°15′W
Colfax, La., U.S. (kōl´făks)	**122-23**	31°31′N	92°42′W
Colfax, Wa., U.S. (kōl´făks)	**112-13**	46°53′N	117°22′W
Colhué Huapi, Lago, lk., Arg. (lä´gō kōl-wā´ōá´pē)	**171**	45°32′S	68°46′W
Colima, Mex.	**146-47**	19°14′N	103°44′W
Colima, state, Mex. (kōlē´mä)	**146-47**	19°10′N	104°00′W
Colima, Nevado de, vol., Mex. (nĕ-vä´dô-dĕ-kô-lē´mä)	**146-47**	19°33′N	103°38′W
Colinas, Braz.	**166-67**	6°02′S	44°14′W
Coll, i., Scot., U.K. (kōl)	**190-91**	56°38′N	6°34′W
College, Ak., U.S. (kŏl´ĕj)	**126**	64°51′N	147°46′W
College Park, Ga., U.S. (kŏl´ĕj pärk)	**124-25**	33°39′N	84°27′W
Collie, Austl. (kŏl´ē)	**270-71**	33°21′S	116°09′E
Collier Bay, b., Austl. (kŏl-yēr bā)	**272-73**	16°10′S	124°15′E
Collingwood, On., Can. (kŏl´ĭng-wo͝od)	**136-37**	44°29′N	80°12′W
Collins, Ms., U.S. (kŏl´ĭns)	**124-25**	31°38′N	89°34′W
Collinsville, Austl.	**277**	20°34′S	147°51′E
Collinsville, Il., U.S. (kŏl´ĭnz-vĭl)	**120-21**	38°41′N	89°58′W
Collinsville, Ok., U.S. (kŏl´ĭnz-vĭl)	**120-21**	36°22′N	95°50′W
Collipulli, Chile	**171**	37°57′S	72°26′W
Colmar, Fr. (kôl´mär)	**196-97**	48°05′N	7°22′E

ăt; finăl; rāte; senāte; ärm; åsk; sofȧ; fâre; ch-choose; dh-as th in other; bē; ēvent; bĕt; recĕnt; cratēr; g-gō; gh-guttural g; bĭt; ĭ-short neutral; rīde; ĸ-guttural k as ch in German ich;

Feature (Pronunciation)	Page	Lat.	Long.
Colmenar Viejo, Spain (kôl-mā-när´vyā´hō)	**198-99**	40°40'N	3°46'W
Cologne, Ger. (kū-lōn´)	**194-95**	50°56'N	6°57'E
Colomb-Béchar, Alg. *see* Béchar	**258-59**	31°37'N	2°14'W
Colombia, Col. (kô-lôm´bē-ä)	**163c**	3°24'N	74°48'W
Colombia, nation, S.A. (kô-lôm´bē-ä)	**158**	4°0'N	72°00'W
Colombo, nat. cap., Sri L. (kô-lôm´bō)	**236**	6°55'N	79°52'E
Colón, Arg. (kō-lōn´)	**173**	32°16'S	58°08'W
Colón, Arg. (kō-lōn´)	**173**	33°55'S	61°04'W
Colón, Cuba (kô-lô´n)	**142-43**	22°43'N	80°54'W
Colón, Pan. (kō-lô´n)	**150**	9°22'N	79°54'W
Colón, Archipiélago de, is., Ec.	**170a**	0°43'N	91°30'W
Colonia Alvear Norte, Arg. *see* General Alvear	**171**	34°59'S	67°42'W
Colonia del Sacramento, Ur.	**173**	34°29'S	57°50'W
Colonia Dora, Arg.	**173**	28°37'S	62°57'W
Colonia Suiza, Ur. (kô-lô´nēä-sōē´zä)	**173**	34°18'S	57°14'W
Colorado, state, U.S. (kŏl-ô-rä´dō)	**108-09**	39°0'N	105°30'W
Colorado, stm., Arg.	**171**	39°52'S	62°09'W
Colorado, stm., N.A. (kŏl-ô-rä´dō)	**110-11**	31°55'N	114°58'W
Colorado, stm., Tx., U.S. (kŏl-ô-rä´dō)	**122-23**	28°36'N	95°59'W
Colorado City, Tx., U.S. (kŏl-ô-rä´dō sĭ´tĭ)	**120-21**	32°23'N	100°52'W
Colorado National Monument, n.p., Co., U.S. (kŏl-ô-rä´dō năsh´ŭn-ăl mŏn´ū-mĕnt)	**118-19**	39°03'N	108°41'W
Colorado Plateau, plat., U.S. (kŏl-ô-rä´dō plă-tō´)	**118-19**	38°0'N	109°00'W
Colorado Springs, Co., U.S. (kŏl-ô-rä´dō sprĭngz)	**120-21**	38°50'N	104°49'W
Colotepec, stm., Mex. (kô-lô´tĕ-pĕk)	**146-47**	15°48'N	97°01'W
Colotlán, Mex. (kô-lô-tlän´)	**146-47**	22°06'N	103°15'W
Colquechaca, Bol. (kôl-kä-chä´kä)	**168-69**	18°41'S	66°02'W
Colstrip, Mt., U.S. (kōl´strip)	**112-13**	45°53'N	106°39'W
Columbia, Il., U.S. (kô-lŭm´bĭ-*à*)	**120-21**	38°26'N	90°11'W
Columbia, Ky., U.S. (kô-lŭm´bĭ-*à*)	**124-25**	37°06'N	85°18'W
Columbia, Md., U.S. (kô-lŭm´bĭ-*à*)	**116-17**	39°14'N	76°50'W
Columbia, Mo., U.S. (kô-lŭm´bĭ-*à*)	**120-21**	38°57'N	92°21'W
Columbia, Ms., U.S. (kô-lŭm´bĭ-*à*)	**124-25**	31°15'N	89°50'W
Columbia, S.C., U.S. (kô-lŭm´bĭ-*à*)	**124-25**	34°00'N	81°02'W
Columbia, Tn., U.S. (kô-lŭm´bĭ-*à*)	**124-25**	35°37'N	87°02'W
Columbia, stm., N.A. (kô-lŭm´bĭ-*à*)	**130-31**	46°14'N	124°06'W
Columbia, Mount, mtn., Ab., Can. (mount kô-lŭm´bĭ-*à*)	**132-33**	52°09'N	117°25'W
Columbia City, In., U.S. (kô-lŭm´bĭ-*à* sĭ´tē)	**116-17**	41°09'N	85°28'W
Columbia Icefield, ice, Can. (kô-lŭm´bĭ-*à* ī´fēld)	**132-33**	52°08'N	117°27'W
Columbia Mountains, mts., N.A. (kô-lŭm´bĭ-*à* moun´tĭnz)	**130-31**	52°0'N	119°00'W
Columbiana, Al., U.S. (kô-ŭm-bĭ-ă´n*à*)	**124-25**	33°11'N	86°36'W
Columbus, Ga., U.S. (kô-lŭm´b*ŭs*)	**124-25**	32°28'N	84°58'W
Columbus, In., U.S. (kô-lŭm´b*ŭs*)	**116-17**	39°12'N	85°55'W
Columbus, Ms., U.S. (kô-lŭm´b*ŭs*)	**124-25**	33°29'N	88°25'W
Columbus, Mt., U.S. (kô-lŭm´b*ŭs*)	**112-13**	45°39'N	109°16'W
Columbus, Ne., U.S. (kô-lŭm´b*ŭs*)	**114-15**	41°26'N	97°22'W
Columbus, N.M., U.S. (kô-lŭm´b*ŭs*)	**118-19**	31°50'N	107°38'W
Columbus, Oh., U.S.	**116-17**	39°58'N	82°60'W
Columbus, Tx., U.S. (kô-lŭm´b*ŭs*)	**122-23**	29°42'N	96°32'W
Columbus, Wi., U.S. (kô-lŭm´b*ŭs*)	**116-17**	43°21'N	89°01'W
Colusa, Ca., U.S. (kô-lū´s*à*)	**118-19**	39°12'N	122°01'W
Colville, Wa., U.S. (kŏl´vĭl)	**112-13**	48°33'N	117°54'W
Colville, stm., Ak., U.S. (kŏl´vĭl)	**126**	70°27'N	150°18'W
Colville Indian Reservation, ind. res., Wa., U.S. (kŏl´vĭl ĭn´dĭ-*ă*n rĕ-sĕr-vā´shēn)	**112-13**	48°15'N	119°00'W
Comacchio, Italy (kô-mäk´kyō)	**200-01**	44°43'N	12°11'E
Comala, Mex. (kō-mä-lä´)	**146-47**	19°19'N	103°45'W
Comalcalco, Mex. (kō-mäl-käl´kō)	**146-47**	18°16'N	93°12'W
Comanche, Ok., U.S. (kô-măn´chē)	**120-21**	34°21'N	97°58'W
Comanche, Tx., U.S. (kô-măn´chē)	**122-23**	31°54'N	98°36'W
Comandante Fontana, Arg.	**168-69**	25°19'S	59°40'W
Comayagua, Hond. (kō-mä-yä´gwä)	**149**	14°27'N	87°39'W
Combarbalá, Chile	**168-69**	31°11'S	71°03'W
Comilla, Bngl. (kô-mĭl´ä)	**234-35**	23°27'N	91°11'E
Comino, Capo, c., Italy (kä´pō kô-mē´nō)	**200-01**	40°32'N	9°49'E
Comitán de Domínguez, Mex.	**148**	16°15'N	92°07'W
Commentry, Fr. (kô-mäN-trē´)	**196-97**	46°17'N	2°44'E
Commerce, Ga., U.S. (kŏm´ērs)	**124-25**	34°12'N	83°27'W
Commerce, Ok., U.S. (kŏm´ērs)	**120-21**	36°56'N	94°52'W
Commerce, Tx., U.S. (kŏm´ērs)	**120-21**	33°16'N	95°54'W
Committee Bay, b., Nu., Can.	**130-31**	68°30'N	86°30'W
Communism Peak, mtn., Taj. *see* Imeni Ismail Samani, Pik	**226**	38°57'N	72°01'E
Como, Italy (kō´mō)	**200-01**	45°47'N	9°05'E
Comodoro Rivadavia, Arg.	**171**	45°52'S	67°30'W
Comoé, Parc National de la, n.p., C. Iv.	**260-61**	9°0'N	3°30'W
Comores, nation, Afr. *see* Comoros	**264-65**	12°10'S	44°15'E
Comores, Archipel des, is., Afr.	**264-65**	12°07'S	44°03'E
Comorin, Cape, c., India (kăp kŏ´mô-rĭn)	**236**	8°05'N	77°34'E
Comoros, nation, Afr. (kŏm´ō-rōz) (k*à*-mō´-rōz)	**264-65**	12°10'S	44°15'E
Comox, B.C., Can. (kō´mŏks)	**132-33**	49°41'N	124°56'W
Compiègne, Fr. (kôN-pyĕn´y')	**196-97**	49°25'N	2°49'E
Compostela, Mex. (kŏm-pô-stä´lä)	**146-47**	21°14'N	104°53'W
Conakry, nat. cap., Gui. (kô-ná-krē´)	**260-61**	9°31'N	13°43'W
Concarneau, Fr. (kôN-kär-nō´)	**196-97**	47°52'N	3°55'W
Conceição do Araguaia, Braz.	**166-67**	8°15'S	49°19'W
Concepción, Bol. (kôn-sĕp´syōn´)	**166-67**	11°29'S	66°36'W
Concepción, Bol. (kôn-sĕp´syōn´)	**168-69**	16°15'S	62°04'W
Concepción, Chile	**171**	36°49'S	73°05'W
Concepción, Para.	**168-69**	23°24'S	57°25'W
Concepción del Oro, Mex. (kôn-sĕp-syōn´ dĕl ō´rō)	**146-47**	24°37'N	101°24'W
Concepción del Uruguay, Arg. (kôn-sĕp-syô´n-dĕl-ōō-rōō-gwī´)	**173**	32°29'S	58°14'W
Conception Bay, b., Nf., Can. (kŏn-sĕp´sh*ŭ*n bā)	**138-39**	47°44'N	52°59'W
Conchos, stm., Mex. (kōn´chōs)	**144-45**	24°56'N	97°38'W
Conchos, stm., Mex. (kōn´chōs)	**144-45**	29°34'N	104°24'W
Concord, Ca., U.S. (kŏŋ´k*ŏ*rd)	**118-19**	37°59'N	122°02'W
Concord, N.C., U.S. (kŏŋ´k*ŏ*rd)	**124-25**	35°24'N	80°36'W
Concord, N.H., U.S.	**116-17**	43°12'N	71°32'W
Concordia, Arg. (kŏn-kôr´dĭ-*à*)	**173**	31°23'S	58°01'W
Concórdia, Braz.	**168-69**	27°14'S	52°02'W
Concordia, Mex. (kôn-kô´r-dyä)	**146-47**	23°16'N	106°04'W
Concordia, Ks., U.S. (kôn-kô´r-dyä)	**120-21**	39°34'N	97°40'W
Condega, Nic. (kŏn-dĕ´gä)	**149**	13°22'N	86°24'W
Condobolin, Austl.	**276**	33°05'S	147°09'E
Condoto, Col.	**163c**	5°05'N	76°38'W
Conegliano, Italy (kō-nâl-yä´nō)	**200-01**	45°53'N	12°18'E
Conghua, China (tsôŋ-hwä)	**238-39**	23°33'N	113°35'E
Congo, nation, Afr. (kŏn´gō)	**253**	1°0'S	15°00'E
Congo, stm., Afr. (kŏn´gō)	**262-63**	5°58'S	12°44'E
Congo, Democratic Republic of the, nation, Afr. (dĕ-mō-kră´tĭc rē-pŭb´lĭk ŭv th*à* kŏn´gō)	**253**	4°0'S	25°00'E
Congo, République démocratique du, nation, Afr. *see* Congo, Democratic Republic of the	**253**	4°0'S	25°00'E
Conjeeveram, India *see* Kānchipuram	**236**	12°50'N	79°43'E
Conneaut, Oh., U.S. (kŏn-ē-ôt´)	**116-17**	41°57'N	80°34'W
Connecticut, state, U.S. (kŏ-nĕt´ĭ-k*ŭ*t)	**108-09**	41°45'N	72°45'W
Connecticut, stm., U.S.	**110-11**	41°16'N	72°20'W
Connellsville, Pa., U.S. (kŏn´nĕlz-vĭl)	**116-17**	40°01'N	79°36'W
Connersville, In., U.S. (kŏn´ērz-vĭl)	**116-17**	39°39'N	85°08'W
Connors Range, mts., Austl. (kŏn´n*ŏ*rs rānj)	**277**	21°40'S	149°10'E
Conrad, Mt., U.S. (kŏn´răd)	**112-13**	48°10'N	111°56'W
Conroe, Tx., U.S. (kŏn´rō)	**122-23**	30°19'N	95°28'W
Conselheiro Lafaiete, Braz.	**172**	20°40'S	43°47'W
Conshohocken, Pa., U.S. (kŏn-shô-hŏk´*ĕ*n)	**116-17**	40°05'N	75°18'W
Constance, Ger. *see* Konstanz	**194-95**	47°40'N	9°10'E
Constance, Lake, lk., Eur. (lāk kŏn´st*ă*ns)	**194-95**	47°39'N	8°54'E
Constanța, Rom. (kōn-stán´tsá)	**202-03**	44°11'N	28°38'E
Constantine, Alg. (kôN-stäN´tēn´)	**269b**	36°22'N	6°37'E
Constantine, Mi., U.S. (kŏn´st*ă*n-tēn)	**116-17**	41°50'N	85°39'W
Constantinople, Tur. *see* İstanbul	**200-01**	41°02'N	28°59'E
Constitución, Chile (kôn´stĭ-tōō-syōn´)	**171**	35°19'S	72°25'W
Contreras, Isla, i., Chile	**171**	51°52'S	74°57'W
Contwoyto Lake, lk., Can.	**130-31**	65°42'N	110°50'W
Converse, Tx., U.S. (kŏn´vĕrs)	**122-23**	29°31'N	98°18'W
Conway, Ar., U.S. (kŏn´wā)	**120-21**	35°05'N	92°27'W
Conway, N.H., U.S. (kŏn´wā)	**116-17**	43°59'N	71°07'W
Conway, S.C., U.S. (kŏn´wā)	**124-25**	33°50'N	79°03'W
Cook, Cape, c., B.C., Can. (kăp kŏok)	**132-33**	50°07'N	127°54'W
Cook, Mount, mtn., N.Z. (mount kŏok) *see* Aoraki	**278**	43°36'S	170°10'E
Cookeville, Tn., U.S. (kŏok´vĭl)	**124-25**	36°10'N	85°31'W
Cook Inlet, b., Ak., U.S. (kŏok ĭn´lĕt)	**126**	60°32'N	151°40'W
Cook Islands, dep., Oc. (kŏok ī´l*ă*ndz)	**280-81**	20°0'S	158°00'W
Cook Strait, strt., N.Z. (kŏok strāt)	**278**	41°15'S	174°30'E
Cooktown, Austl. (kŏok´toun)	**277**	15°29'S	145°15'E
Coolgardie, Austl. (kōōl-gär´dē)	**270-71**	30°57'S	121°10'E
Cooma, Austl. (kōō´m*á*)	**276**	36°14'S	149°08'E
Coonabarabran, Austl.	**276**	31°16'S	149°17'E
Coonamble, Austl. (kōō-năm´b'l)	**276**	30°58'S	148°23'E
Coonoor, India	**236**	11°20'N	76°48'E
Coon Rapids, Mn., U.S. (kōn răp´ĭdz)	**114-15**	45°10'N	93°20'W
Cooper, Tx., U.S. (kōōp´ēr)	**120-21**	33°23'N	95°41'W
Cooper Creek, stm., Austl.	**276**	28°18'S	137°29'E
Cooperstown, N.D., U.S. (kōōp´ērs-toun)	**114-15**	47°27'N	98°07'W
Coosa, stm., U.S. (kōō´s*á*)	**124-25**	32°30'N	86°16'W
Coos Bay, Or., U.S. (kōōs bā)	**112-13**	43°22'N	124°13'W
Cootamundra, Austl. (kŏt*ă*-m*ŭ*nd´r*ă*)	**276**	34°39'S	148°01'E
Copan, hist., Hond.	**149**	14°50'N	89°09'W
Copenhagen, nat. cap., Den. (kō´p*ĕ*n-hā´g*ĕ*n)	**192-93**	55°41'N	12°34'E
Copiapó, Chile (kō-pyä-pō´)	**168-69**	27°22'S	70°20'W
Copley, Austl.	**276**	30°33'S	138°26'E
Copper, stm., Ak., U.S. (kŏp´ēr)	**126**	60°33'N	144°52'W
Copper Harbor, Mi., U.S. (kŏp´ēr här´bēr)	**114-15**	47°28'N	87°55'W
Coppermine, Nu., Can. *see* Kugluktuk	**128-29**	67°47'N	115°11'W
Coppermine, stm., Can. (kŏp´ēr mīn)	**130-31**	67°48'N	115°08'W
Coquilhatville, D.R.C. *see* Mbandaka	**262-63**	0°02'N	18°15'E
Coquimbo, Chile (kô-kēm´bō)	**168-69**	29°58'S	71°20'W
Corabia, Rom. (kô-rä´bĭ-*á*)	**200-01**	43°47'N	24°31'E
Corail, Mer de, s., Oc. *see* Coral Sea	**272-73**	20°0'S	158°00'E
Coral Harbour, Nu., Can.	**128-29**	64°08'N	83°12'W
Coral Sea, s., Oc. (kŏr´ăl sē)	**272-73**	20°0'S	158°00'E
Corangamite, Lake, lk., Austl. (lāk cŏr-ăŋ´á-mīt)	**276**	38°10'S	143°25'E
Corato, Italy (kō´rä-tô)	**200-01**	41°09'N	16°25'E
Corbin, Ky., U.S. (kôr´bĭn)	**124-25**	36°57'N	84°06'W
Corby, Eng., U.K. (kôr´bĭ)	**190-91**	52°29'N	0°40'W
Corcaigh, Ire. *see* Cork	**190-91**	51°54'N	8°28'W
Corcovado, Golfo, b., Chile (gôl-fô-kôr-kô-vä´dhō)	**171**	43°30'S	73°30'W
Corcovado, Volcán, vol., Chile	**171**	43°12'S	72°48'W
Cordele, Ga., U.S. (kôr-dēl´)	**124-25**	31°58'N	83°47'W
Cordell, Ok., U.S. (kôr-dĕl´)	**120-21**	35°18'N	98°59'W
Córdoba, Arg. (kôr´dô-vä)	**173**	31°24'S	64°12'W
Córdoba, Mex. (kô´r-dô-bä)	**146-47**	18°53'N	96°56'W
Córdoba, Spain (kô´r-dô-bä)	**198-99**	37°54'N	4°47'W
Córdoba, state, Arg. (kôr´dô-vä)	**173**	32°0'S	64°00'W
Cordova, Spain *see* Córdoba	**198-99**	37°54'N	4°47'W
Cordova, Ak., U.S. (kôr´dô-vä)	**126**	60°33'N	145°45'W
Cordova, Al., U.S. (kôr´dō-*á*)	**124-25**	33°46'N	87°11'W
Corfu, i., Grc. *see* Kérkyra	**200-01**	39°40'N	19°45'E
Corinth, Grc.	**200-01**	37°56'N	22°58'E
Corinth, Ms., U.S. (kŏr´ĭnth)	**124-25**	34°56'N	88°31'W
Corinto, Braz. (kô-rē´n-tō)	**172**	18°23'S	44°27'W
Cork, Ire. (kôrk)	**190-91**	51°54'N	8°28'W
Corleone, Italy (kôr-lå-ō´nā)	**200-01**	37°49'N	13°18'E
Cornelia, Ga., U.S. (kôr-nē´ly*á*)	**124-25**	34°31'N	83°32'W
Cornell, Wi., U.S. (kôr-nĕl´)	**114-15**	45°10'N	91°09'W
Corner Brook, Nf., Can. (kôr´nēr brŏok)	**138-39**	48°57'N	57°58'W
Corning, Ar., U.S. (kôr´nĭng)	**124-25**	36°25'N	90°35'W
Corning, Ia., U.S. (kôr´nĭng)	**114-15**	40°60'N	94°45'W
Corning, N.Y., U.S. (kôr´nĭng)	**116-17**	42°09'N	77°03'W
Corno Grande, mtn., Italy (kôr´nō grän´dĕ)	**200-01**	42°28'N	13°34'E
Cornwall, On., Can. (kôrn´wôl)	**136-37**	45°02'N	74°44'W
Coro, Ven. (kō´rô)	**164-65**	11°27'N	69°40'W
Corocoro, Bol. (kō-rô-kō´rô)	**168-69**	17°11'S	68°27'W
Coromandel Coast, cst., India (kŏr-ô-man´dĕl kōst)	**236**	13°30'N	80°30'E
Coronado, Ca., U.S. (kŏr-ô-nä´dō)	**118-19**	32°41'N	117°11'W
Coronado, Bahía de, b., C.R. (bä-ē´ä-dĕ-kô-rô-nä´dō)	**149**	9°0'N	83°50'W
Coronation Gulf, b., Nu., Can. (kŏr-ô-nā´sh*ŭ*n gŭlf)	**130-31**	68°24'N	109°56'W
Coronel, Chile (kō-rô-nĕl´)	**171**	37°01'S	73°08'W
Coronel Dorrego, Arg. (kŏ-rô-nĕl-dôr-rĕ´gô)	**173**	38°43'S	61°17'W
Coronel Fabriciano, Braz.	**172**	19°31'S	42°39'W
Coronel Oviedo, Para. (kŏ-rô-nĕl-ô-vē̇´dô)	**168-69**	25°27'S	56°26'W
Coronel Pringles, Arg. (kŏ-rô-nĕl-prēn´glĕs)	**173**	37°59'S	61°22'W
Coronel Suárez, Arg. (kŏ-rô-nĕl-swä´răs)	**173**	37°27'S	61°56'W
Coropuna, Nevado, vol., Peru (nĕ-vä-dô-kō-rō-pōō´nä)	**170**	15°31'S	72°42'W
Corozal, Belize (cŏr-ŏth-äl´)	**148**	18°24'N	88°24'W
Corpus Christi, Tx., U.S. (kôr´p*ŭs* krĭstē)	**122-23**	27°48'N	97°24'W
Corpus Christi, Lake, res., Tx., U.S. (lāk kôr´p*ŭs* krĭstē)	**122-23**	28°10'N	97°55'W
Corpus Christi Bay, b., Tx., U.S. (kôr´p*ŭs* krĭstē bā)	**122-23**	27°48'N	97°20'W

n-sing; ŋ-baŋk; N-nasalized n; nŏd; cŏmmit; ōld; ôbey; ôrder; oi-boil; fōōd; ŏo-as oo in foot; ou-out; s-soft; sh-dish; th-thin; pūre; ûnite; ûrn; stŭd; circŭs; ü-as in French tu; ´-indeterminate vowel.

Feature (Pronunciation)	Page	Lat.	Long.
Corral, Chile (kô-räl´)	171	39°53′s	73°28′w
Corral de Almaguer, Spain			
(kô-räl´dä äl-mä-gär´)	198-99	39°45′N	3°10′w
Corrente, stm., Braz.	166-67	13°08′s	43°28′w
Correntina, Braz. (kô-rěn-tē-nä)	166-67	13°21′s	44°39′w
Corrientes, Arg. (kô-ryěn´täs)	173	27°29′s	58°50′w
Corrientes, state, Arg. (kô-ryěn´tās)	173	29°0′s	58°00′w
Corrientes, stm., S.A.	170	3°44′s	74°33′w
Corrientes, Cabo, c., Col.			
(ká´bô-kô-ryěn´täs)	163c	5°30′N	77°32′w
Corrientes, Cabo, c., Cuba			
(ká´bô-kôr-rē-čn´těs)	142-43	21°46′N	84°31′w
Corrientes, Cabo, c., Mex.	146-47	20°24′N	105°41′w
Corriverton, Guy.	164-65	5°53′N	57°09′w
Corry, Pa., U.S. (kôr´ĭ)	116-17	41°55′N	79°38′w
Corse, i., Fr. *see Corsica*	184-85	42°0′N	9°00′E
Corse, Cap, c., Fr. (káp kôrs)	184-85	43°01′N	9°25′E
Corsica, i., Fr. (kô´r-sē-kä)	184-85	42°0′N	9°00′E
Corsicana, Tx., U.S. (kôr-sĭ-kăn´á)	122-23	32°06′N	96°29′w
Cortazar, Mex. (kôr-tä-zär´)	146-47	20°29′N	100°56′w
Cortés, Mar de, b., Mex.			
see California, Golfo de	144-45	28°0′N	112°00′w
Cortez, Co., U.S.	118-19	37°21′N	108°35′w
Cortez, Sea of, b., Mex.			
see California, Golfo de	144-45	28°0′N	112°00′w
Corubal, Afr.	258-59	11°57′N	15°03′w
Coruche, Port. (kô-rōō´she)	198-99	38°58′N	8°31′w
Çorum, Tur. (chô-rōōm´)	186-87	40°33′N	34°57′E
Corumbá, Braz.	168-69	19°01′s	57°39′w
Corumbá, Braz.	168-69	18°19′s	48°54′w
Corunna, Spain *see A Coruña*	198-99	43°22′N	8°25′w
Corunna, Mi., U.S. (kô-rŭn´á)	116-17	42°59′N	84°07′w
Coruripe, Braz. (kō-rô-rē´pī)	163d	10°09′s	36°10′w
Corvallis, Or., U.S. (kôr-văl´ĭs)	112-13	44°35′N	123°16′w
Corvo, i., Port.	199c	39°42′N	31°06′w
Corydon, In., U.S. (kôr´ĭ-dŭn)	116-17	38°13′N	86°07′w
Cos, i., Grc. *see Kos*	200-01	36°50′N	27°10′E
Cosenza, Italy (kô-zěnt´sä)	200-01	39°17′N	16°15′E
Coshocton, Oh., U.S. (kô-shŏk´tŭn)	116-17	40°16′N	81°51′w
Cosmoledo, Atoll de, at., Sey.			
(kôs-mô-lä´dô)	264-65	9°42′s	47°31′E
Cosne-sur-Loire, Fr. (kōn-sür-lwär´)	196-97	47°24′N	2°56′E
Costa Rica, nation, N.A. (kôs´tá rē´ká)	85	10°0′N	84°00′w
Costermansville, D.R.C. *see Bukavu*	267	2°30′s	28°51′E
Cotabato, Phil. (kô-tä-bä´tō)	250	7°12′N	124°14′E
Cote d'Ivoire, nation, Afr. (kôt-dē-vwär´)	253	8°0′N	5°00′w
Cotija de la Paz, Mex.			
(kô-tē´-kä-dě-lä-pá´z)	146-47	19°49′N	102°43′w
Cotonou, nat. cap., Benin (kô-tô-nōō´)	260a	6°22′N	2°26′E
Cotopaxi, vol., Ec. (kō-tô-päk´sě)	170	0°41′s	78°27′w
Cotswold Hills, hills, Eng., U.K.			
(kŭtz´wŏld hĭlz)	190-91	51°49′N	1°57′w
Cottage Grove, Or., U.S. (kŏt´áj grōv)	112-13	43°48′N	123°03′w
Cottbus, Ger. (kŏtt´bōōs)	194-95	51°45′N	14°19′E
Cotulla, Tx., U.S. (kô-tŭl´lá)	122-23	28°26′N	99°14′w
Coudersport, Pa., U.S. (koū´dērz-port)	116-17	41°46′N	78°01′w
Coudres, Île aux, i., Qc., Can.	138-39	47°24′N	70°23′w
Coulommiers, Fr. (kōō-lô-myä´)	196-97	48°49′N	3°05′E
Council Bluffs, Ia., U.S.			
(koun´sĭl blŭfs)	114-15	41°16′N	95°51′w
Courtenay, B.C., Can. (cōōrt-nä´)	132-33	49°41′N	124°60′w
Coushatta, La., U.S. (kou-shät´á)	122-23	32°01′N	93°21′w
Couture, Lac, lk., Qc., Can.	130-31	60°07′N	75°20′w
Coventry, Eng., U.K. (kŭv´ěn-trĭ)	190-91	52°25′N	1°30′w
Covington, Ga., U.S. (kŭv´ĭng-tŭn)	124-25	33°36′N	83°51′w
Covington, In., U.S. (kŭv´ĭng-tŭn)	116-17	40°08′N	87°23′w
Covington, Ky., U.S. (kŭv´ĭng-tŭn)	116-17	39°05′N	84°31′w
Covington, La., U.S. (kŭv´ĭng-tŭn)	124-25	30°28′N	90°06′w
Covington, Tn., U.S. (kŭv´ĭng-tŭn)	124-25	35°34′N	89°39′w
Covington, Va., U.S. (kŭv´ĭng-tŭn)	116-17	37°48′N	79°60′w
Cowan, Lake, lk., Austl. (läk kou´án)	272-73	31°50′s	121°50′E
Cowes, Eng., U.K. (kouz)	190-91	50°46′N	1°18′w
Cowra, Austl. (kou´rá)	276	33°50′s	148°41′E
Coxim, Braz. (kō-shēn´)	168-69	18°30′s	54°45′w
Cox's Bāzār, Bngl.	246-47	21°26′N	91°58′E
Coyame, Mex. (kô-yä´mä)	122-23	29°28′N	105°07′w
Coyle, stm., Arg. *see Coig.*	171	50°57′s	69°09′w
Coyuca de Benítez, Mex.			
(kô-yōō´kä dä bā-nē´tāz)	146-47	17°01′N	100°05′w
Coyuca de Catalán, Mex.			
(kô-yōō´kä dä kä-tä-län´)	146-47	18°19′N	100°42′w
Cozad, Ne., U.S. (kō´zăd)	114-15	40°52′N	99°59′w
Cozumel, Mex. (kô-zōō-mě´l)	148	20°31′N	86°55′w
Cozumel, Isla, i., Mex.			
(ē´s-lä-kô-zōō-mě´l)	148	20°25′s	86°55′w
Cracow, Pol. *see Kraków.*	194-95	50°04′N	19°58′E

Feature (Pronunciation)	Page	Lat.	Long.
Cradock, S. Afr. (krä´dŭk)	264-65	32°10′s	25°37′E
Craig, Ak., U.S. (krăg)	126	55°28′N	133°06′w
Craig, Co., U.S. (krăg)	112-13	40°31′N	107°32′w
Craiova, Rom. (krá-yō´vá)	200-01	44°19′N	23°48′E
Cranbrook, B.C., Can. (krăn´brók)	132-33	49°31′N	115°46′w
Crandon, Wi., U.S. (krăn´dŭn)	116-17	45°34′N	88°54′w
Cranston, R.I., U.S. (krăns´tŭn)	116-17	41°48′N	71°26′w
Crater Lake, lk., Or., U.S. (krä´těr läk)	112-13	42°56′N	122°06′w
Crater Lake National Park, n.p., Or., U.S.			
(krä´těr läk näsh´ŭn-ál pärk)	112-13	42°52′N	122°10′w
Craters of the Moon National Monument and Preserve, n.p., Id., U.S. (krä´těrz ŭv thá mōōn näsh´ŭn-ál mŏn´ŭ-měnt ănd prī-zûrv)	112-13	43°25′N	113°33′w
Crateús, Braz. (krä-tå-ōōzh´)	166-67	5°10′s	40°40′w
Crato, Braz. (krä´tô)	166-67	7°14′s	39°23′w
Crawford, Ne., U.S. (krô´fěrd)	114-15	42°41′N	103°25′w
Crawfordsville, In., U.S. (krô´fěrdz-vīl)	116-17	40°02′N	86°54′w
Crazy Mountains, mts., Mt., U.S. (krä´zī moun´tīnz)	112-13	46°08′N	110°20′w
Cree, stm., Sk., Can.	130-31	58°55′N	105°46′w
Cree Lake, lk., Sk., Can. (krē läk)	130-31	57°30′N	106°30′w
Creil, Fr. (krě´y)	196-97	49°16′N	2°29′E
Crema, Italy (krā´mä)	200-01	45°22′N	9°42′E
Cremona, Italy (krā-mô´nä)	200-01	45°09′N	10°01′E
Crépy-en-Valois, Fr. (krā-pē´ěn-vä-lwä´)	196-97	49°14′N	2°54′E
Crescent City, Ca., U.S.	112-13	41°46′N	124°12′w
Cresco, Ia., U.S. (krěs´kō)	114-15	43°22′N	92°07′w
Crestline, Oh., U.S. (krěst-līn)	116-17	40°47′N	82°44′w
Creston, B.C., Can. (krěs´tŭn)	132-33	49°06′N	116°31′w
Creston, Ia., U.S. (krěs´tŭn)	114-15	41°04′N	94°22′w
Crestview, Fl., U.S. (krěst´vū)	124-25	30°46′N	86°34′w
Crestwood, Ky., U.S. (krěst´wòd)	116-17	38°19′N	85°28′w
Crete, Ne., U.S. (krēt)	120-21	40°37′N	96°58′w
Crete, i., Grc. (krēt)	200a	35°13′N	25°00′E
Crete, Sea of, s., Grc. (sē ŭv krēt)	188-89	35°54′N	25°01′E
Crewe, Eng., U.K. (krōō)	190-91	53°06′N	2°27′w
Criciúma, Braz.	172	28°41′s	49°24′w
Crimea, pen., Ukr.			
see Crimean Peninsula.	202-03	45°0′N	34°00′E
Crimean Peninsula, pen., Ukr.	202-03	45°0′N	34°00′E
Cripple Creek, Co., U.S. (krĭp´'l krěk)	120-21	38°45′N	105°11′w
Crisfield, Md., U.S. (krĭs-fēld)	116-17	37°59′N	75°51′w
Cristalândia, Braz.	166-67	10°36′s	49°12′w
Cristóbal Colón, Pico, mtn., Col. (pē´kô-krēs-tō´bäl-kō-lôn´)	164-65	10°50′N	73°41′w
Crna Gora, nation, Eur.			
see Montenegro	174-75	42°30′N	19°18′E
Croatia, nation, Eur. (krō-ä´-shá)	174-75	45°10′N	15°30′E
Crockett, Tx., U.S. (krŏk´ět)	122-23	31°18′N	95°28′w
Crocodile, stm., S. Afr.	269c	24°11′s	26°53′E
Crooked, stm., B.C., Can. (krōōk´ěd)	132-33	54°50′N	122°53′w
Crooked Island, i., Bah.	142-43	22°45′N	74°13′w
Crooked Island Passage, strt., Bah. (krōōk´ěd ĭ´lánd päs´ĭj)	142-43	22°43′N	74°35′w
Crookston, Mn., U.S. (króks´tŭn)	114-15	47°47′N	96°37′w
Crosby, Mn., U.S. (krôz´bī)	114-15	46°29′N	93°58′w
Crosby, N.D., U.S. (krôz´bī)	114-15	48°55′N	103°18′w
Cross, stm., Afr. (krôs)	260a	4°49′N	8°15′E
Cross City, Fl., U.S. (krôs sī´tī)	124-25	29°38′N	83°07′w
Crossett, Ar., U.S. (krôs´ět)	122-23	33°08′N	91°58′w
Cross Lake, res., Mb., Can.	134-35	54°45′N	97°30′w
Cross Sound, strt., Ak., U.S. (krôs sound)	126	58°10′N	136°30′w
Crotone, Italy (krō-tô´ně)	200-01	39°05′N	17°07′E
Crow Creek Indian Reservation, ind. res., S.D., U.S. (krō krěk ĭn´dĭ-án rě-sěr-vä´shěn)	114-15	44°11′N	99°30′w
Crow Indian Reservation, ind. res., Mt., U.S. (ĭn´dĭ-án rě-sěr-vä´shěn)	112-13	45°27′N	108°00′w
Crowley, La., U.S. (krou´lē)	122-23	30°13′N	92°23′w
Crown Point, N.Y., U.S. (kroun point´)	116-17	43°57′N	73°26′w
Crowsnest Pass, Ab., Can.	132-33	49°37′N	114°25′w
Crozet, Archipel, is., Afr.			
see Crozet, Îles.	287	46°0′s	52°00′E
Crozet, Îles, is., Afr. (ēl-krô-zě´)	287	46°0′s	52°00′E
Cruz, Cabo, c., Cuba (ká´-bô-krōōz)	142-43	19°51′N	77°44′w
Cruz Alta, Braz. (krōōz äl␣tä)	173	28°37′s	53°36′w
Cruz del Eje, Arg. (krōōz-s-děl-č-kě)	168-69	30°43′s	64°49′w
Cruzeiro, Braz. (krōō-zā´rò)	172	22°35′s	44°58′w
Cruzeiro do Sul, Braz. (krōō-zā´rò dò sōōl)	170	7°39′s	72°41′w
Crystal City, Tx., U.S. (krĭs´tăl sī´tī)	122-23	28°41′N	99°50′w
Crystal Falls, Mi., U.S. (krĭs´tăl fôlz)	114-15	46°06′N	88°19′w

Feature (Pronunciation)	Page	Lat.	Long.
Crystal Lake, Il., U.S. (krĭs´tăl läk läk)	116-17	42°14′N	88°17′w
Crystal Springs, Ms., U.S. (krĭs´tăl sprĭngz)	124-25	31°59′N	90°22′w
Csongrád, Hung. (chôn´gräd)	194-95	46°43′N	20°09′E
Cúa, Ven. (kōō´ä)	163b	10°09′N	66°53′w
Cua Lo, Viet.	246-47	18°49′N	105°43′E
Cuamba, Moz.	264-65	14°47′s	36°32′E
Cuando, stm., Afr.	264-65	18°30′s	23°36′E
Cuango, stm., Afr.	262-63	3°13′s	17°23′E
Cuanza, stm., Ang. (kwän´zä)	264-65	9°21′s	13°09′E
Cuatrociénegas, Mex. (kwä´trô syä´nå-gäs)	122-23	26°60′N	102°04′w
Cuauhtémoc, Mex. (kwä-ōō-tě-môk´)	146-47	22°33′N	98°09′w
Cuauhtémoc, Mex. (kwä-ōō-tě-môk´)	144-45	28°25′N	106°52′w
Cuautitlán, Mex. (kwä-ōō-tět-län´)	146-47	19°27′N	104°21′w
Cuautla, Mex. (kwä-ōō´tlá)	146-47	18°49′N	98°57′w
Cuba, nation, N.A. (kū´bá)	140-41	21°30′N	80°00′w
Cubagua, Isla, i., Ven. (ē´-lä-kōō-bä´gwä)	163b	10°49′N	64°11′w
Cubal, Ang.	264-65	13°03′s	14°17′E
Cubango, stm., Afr. (kōō-bän´gō)	264-65	18°57′s	22°25′E
Cubia, stm., Afr.	264-65	16°01′s	21°43′E
Cúcuta, Col. (kōō´kōō-tä)	164-65	7°53′N	72°29′w
Cuddalore, India (kŭd´á-lōr´)	236	11°45′N	79°46′E
Cuddapah, India (kŭd´á-pä)	236	14°28′N	78°49′E
Cue, Austl. (kū)	270-71	27°26′s	117°54′E
Cuenca, Ec. (kwěn´kä)	170	2°53′s	79°00′w
Cuenca, Spain (kwěn´kä)	198-99	40°05′N	2°08′w
Cuencamé de Ceniceros, Mex.	122-23	24°52′N	103°42′w
Cuernavaca, Mex. (kwěr-nä-vä´kä)	146-47	18°55′N	99°14′w
Cuero, Tx., U.S. (kwä´rō)	122-23	29°06′N	97°17′w
Cuiabá, Braz.	168-69	15°36′s	56°05′w
Cuiabá, stm., Braz.	166-67	17°54′s	57°28′w
Cuicatlán, Mex. (kwē-kä-tlän´)	146-47	17°46′N	96°58′w
Cuilapa, Guat. (kô-ē-lä´pä)	148	14°17′N	90°18′w
Cuilo, stm., Afr.	262-63	5°53′s	16°35′E
Cuilo, stm., Afr.	260-61	3°23′s	17°23′E
Cuíto, stm., Ang. (kōō-ē-´tō)	264-65	18°01′s	20°47′E
Cuitzeo, Lago de, lk., Mex. (lä´gô-dě-kwět´zä-ō)	146-47	19°55′N	101°05′w
Culebra, Isla de, i., P.R. (ē´s-lä-dě-kōō-lä´brä)	142a	18°19′N	65°17′w
Culfa, Azer.	227	38°58′N	45°38′E
Culgoa, stm., Austl. (kŭl-gō´á)	276	29°59′s	146°07′E
Culiacán, Mex. (kōō-lyä-ká´n)	146-47	24°04′N	107°05′w
Culiacán, Mex.	144-45	24°49′N	107°24′w
Culion Island, i., Phil.	250	11°51′N	119°57′E
Cullera, Spain (kōō-lyä´rä)	198-99	39°10′N	0°14′w
Cullinan, S. Afr. (kô´lĭ-nán)	269c	25°40′s	28°33′E
Cullman, Al., U.S. (kŭl´mán)	124-25	34°10′N	86°51′w
Culpeper, Va., U.S. (kŭl´pěp-ěr)	116-17	38°27′N	77°60′w
Culuene, stm., Braz.	166-67	12°56′s	52°50′w
Culver, In., U.S. (kŭl´věr)	116-17	41°13′N	86°25′w
Cumaná, Ven.	163b	10°27′N	64°11′w
Cumbal, Nevado, vol., Col.	164-65	0°57′N	77°52′w
Cumberland, Md., U.S.	116-17	39°39′N	78°46′w
Cumberland, Wi., U.S. (kŭm´běr-lánd)	114-15	45°32′N	92°01′w
Cumberland, stm., U.S. (kŭm´běr-lánd)	110-11	37°08′N	88°25′w
Cumberland, Lake, res., Ky., U.S. (läk kŭm´běr-lánd)	124-25	36°57′N	84°55′w
Cumberland Peninsula, pen., Nu., Can. (kŭm´běr-lánd pě-nĭn´sûlá)	130-31	66°32′N	64°13′w
Cumberland Plateau, plat., U.S. (kŭm´běr-lánd plä-tō´)	124-25	36°0′N	85°00′w
Cumberland Sound, strt., Nu., Can. (kŭm´běr-lánd sound)	130-31	65°10′N	65°30′w
Cumbres de Monterrey, Parque Nacional, n.p., Mex.	122-23	25°30′N	100°25′w
Cunani, Braz.	164-65	2°52′N	51°06′w
Cunco, Chile	171	38°56′s	72°02′w
Cunene, stm., Afr.	264-65	17°15′s	11°45′E
Cunnamulla, Austl. (kŭn-á-mŭl-á)	276	28°04′s	145°41′E
Curaçao, i., Neth. Ant. (kōō-rä-sä´ō)	140a	12°11′N	69°00′w
Curacautín, Chile (kä-rä-käō-tē´n).	171	38°25′s	71°56′w
Curacó, stm., Arg. *see Salado.*	171	38°49′s	64°59′w
Curanilahue, Chile	171	37°28′s	73°21′w
Curaray, stm., S.A.	170	2°26′s	74°04′w
Curepipe, Mauritius	265a	20°19′s	57°31′E
Curicó, Chile	171	34°59′s	71°14′w
Curitiba, Braz. (kōō-rē-tē´bá)	172	25°26′s	49°16′w
Currais Novos, Braz. (kōōr-rä´ēs nô-vôs)	163d	6°15′s	36°31′w
Curralinho, Braz.	166-67	1°48′s	49°47′w
Current, stm., U.S. (kûr´ěnt)	120-21	36°15′N	90°55′w
Curtis Island, i., Austl.	277	23°38′s	151°09′E

ăt; fìnál; räte; senåte; ärm; ásk; sofá; fåre; ch-choose; dh-as th in other; bē; ĕvent; bĕt; recĕnt; cratēr; g-gō; gh-guttural g; bĭt; ĭ-short neutral; rīde; ĸ-guttural k as ch in German ich;

Feature (Pronunciation)	Page	Lat.	Long.
Curuá, stm., Braz.	166-67	1°57'S	55°08'W
Curuá, stm., Braz.	166-67	5°21'S	54°28'W
Cururupu, Braz. (kōō-rò-rò-pōō')	166-67	1°50'S	44°52'W
Curuzú Cuatiá, Arg.	173	29°48'S	58°03'W
Curvelo, Braz. (kòr-věl'ò)	172	18°45'S	44°27'W
Cusco, Peru	170	13°31'S	71°59'W
Cushing, Ok., U.S. (kŭsh'ĭng)	120-21	35°59'N	96°46'W
Custer, S.D., U.S. (kŭs'tẽr)	114-15	43°45'N	103°36'W
Cut, Nuhu, i., Indon.	224-25	5°29'S	133°06'E
Cut Bank, Mt., U.S. (kŭt bănk)	112-13	48°38'N	112°20'W
Cuthbert, Ga., U.S. (kŭth'bẽrt)	124-25	31°46'N	84°47'W
Cuttack, India (kŭ-tăk')	234-35	20°30'N	85°50'E
Cutzamalá, stm., Mex. (kōō-tzä-mä-lä')	146-47	18°23'N	100°41'W
Cuvo, stm., Ang. (kōō'vō)	264-65	10°52'S	13°48'E
Cuyabá, Braz. *see* Cuiabá	168-69	15°36'S	56°05'W
Cuyahoga Falls, Oh., U.S. (kī-*ȧ*-hō'*gȧ* fôlz)	116-17	41°08'N	81°29'W
Cuyo Islands, is., Phil. (kōō'yō ī'l*ȧ*ndz)	250	11°04'N	120°57'E
Cuyuni, stm., S.A. (kōō-yōō'nē)	164-65	6°23'N	58°40'W
Cyangugu, Rw.	267	2°29'S	28°54'E
Cyclades, is., Grc. (sĭ'cl*ȧ*-dēz)	200-01	37°30'N	25°00'E
Cynthiana, Ky., U.S. (sĭn-thĭ-ăn'*ȧ*)	116-17	38°23'N	84°18'W
Cyprus, nation, Asia (sī'prŭs)	228-29	35°0'N	33°00'E
Cyrenaica, hist. reg., Libya (sĭr-*ȧ*-nā'ĭ-k*ȧ*)	258-59	31°0'N	22°30'E
Czech Republic, nation, Eur. (chěk rě-pŭb'lĭk)	174-75	49°40'N	15°10'E
Czernowitz, Ukr. *see* Chernivtsi	194-95	48°17'N	25°58'E
Częstochowa, Pol. (chăN-stô kô'vȧ)	194-95	50°49'N	19°08'E

D

Feature (Pronunciation)	Page	Lat.	Long.
Da, Song, stm., Asia *see* Black	246-47	21°15'N	105°21'E
Da'an, China (dä-än)	240-41	45°30'N	124°18'E
Dabhoi, India	234-35	22°08'N	73°25'E
Dabie Shan, mts., China (dä-bĭĕ shän)	238-39	31°06'N	115°56'E
Dacca, nat. cap., Bngl. *see* Dhaka	234-35	23°43'N	90°25'E
Dac Glei, Viet.	246-47	15°11'N	107°48'E
Dachau, Ger. (dä'kou)	194-95	48°15'N	11°27'E
Dade City, Fl., U.S. (dād sĭ'tĭ)	125a	28°22'N	82°11'W
Dadeville, Al., U.S. (dād'vĭl)	124-25	32°50'N	85°46'W
Dadiangas, Phil. *see* General Santos	250	6°07'N	125°10'E
Dādra and Nagar Haveli, state, India	234-35	20°05'N	73°00'E
Dādu, Pak.	232-33	26°44'N	67°46'E
Dadu, stm., China (dä-dōō)	238-39	29°33'N	103°46'E
Daegu, Kor., S. *see* Taegu	243	35°52'N	128°35'E
Daejeon, Kor., S. *see* Taejŏn	243	36°20'N	127°26'E
Daet, Phil.	250	14°07'N	122°57'E
Dagestan, state, Russia (dä-gěs-tän')	227	43°0'N	47°00'E
Dagupan, Phil. (dä-gōō'pän)	250	16°02'N	120°21'E
Da Hinggan Ling, mts., China (dä hĭŋ-gän lĭŋ) *see* Greater Khingan Range	222-23	49°0'N	122°00'E
Dahlak Archipelago, is., Erit. (dä-läk' är'kȧ-pĕ'-ȧ-gō)	266	15°45'N	40°30'E
Dahlak Kebir, i., Erit. *see* Dehalak' Desēt	266	15°40'N	40°06'E
Dahomey, nation, Afr. *see* Benin	253	9°30'N	2°15'E
Daḥy, Nafūd ad-, des., Sau. Ar.	266	22°20'N	45°35'E
Daireaux, Arg.	173	36°36'S	61°45'W
Dairen, China *see* Dalian	240-41	38°54'N	121°34'E
Dairût, Egypt	268b	27°33'N	30°49'E
Dai-sen, vol., Japan (dī'sĕn')	245	35°22'N	133°33'E
Dajabón, Dom. Rep. (dä-kä-bô'n)	142-43	19°33'N	71°42'W
Dajian Shan, mtn., China	238-39	26°42'N	103°34'E
Dakar, nat. cap., Sen. (dȧ-kär')	260-61	14°41'N	17°27'W
Dakhla, W. Sah.	258-59	23°43'N	15°56'W
Dalälven, stm., Swe.	192-93	60°38'N	17°27'E
Dalandzadgad, Mong.	240-41	43°35'N	104°25'E
Da Lat, Viet.	246-47	11°58'N	108°27'E
Dālbandin, Pak.	232-33	28°53'N	64°25'E
Dalby, Austl. (dôl'bē)	276	27°11'S	151°16'E
Dale, Nor. (dä'lĕ)	192-93	61°22'N	5°25'E
Dale Hollow Lake, res., U.S. (dāl hŏl'ō lāk)	124-25	36°37'N	85°20'W
Dalhart, Tx., U.S. (dăl härt)	120-21	36°04'N	102°31'W
Dalhousie, N.B., Can. (dăl-hōō'zē)	138-39	48°04'N	66°24'W
Dalhousie, India	234-35	32°34'N	75°58'E
Dalhousie, Cape, c., N.T., Can.	130-31	70°14'N	129°42'W
Dali, China (dä-lē)	238-39	34°47'N	109°57'E
Dali, China (dä-lē)	238-39	25°36'N	100°13'E
Dalian, China (dä-lĭĕn)	240-41	38°54'N	121°34'E
Daliang Shan, mts., China	238-39	28°0'N	103°00'E

Feature (Pronunciation)	Page	Lat.	Long.
Dallas, Or., U.S. (dăl'l*ȧ*s)	112-13	44°55'N	123°18'W
Dallas, Tx., U.S. (dăl'l*ȧ*s)	120-21	32°47'N	96°46'W
Dall Island, i., Ak., U.S. (dăl ī'*ă*nd ī'l*ȧ*nd)	126	54°57'N	133°01'W
Dalmā, i., U.A.E.	230-31	24°31'N	52°19'E
Dal'negorsk, Russia	244	44°33'N	135°34'E
Dalnerechensk, Russia	244	45°56'N	133°44'E
Daloa, C. Iv.	260-61	6°53'N	6°27'W
Dalrymple, Mount, mtn., Austl. (mount dăl'rĭm-p'l)	277	21°02'S	148°38'E
Dāltenganj, India	234-35	24°03'N	84°04'E
Dalton, Ga., U.S. (dôl't*ŭ*n)	124-25	34°46'N	84°58'W
Dalupiri Island, i., Phil.	250a	19°05'N	121°14'E
Daly, stm., Austl. (dā'lĭ)	272-73	13°19'S	130°16'E
Daly Waters, Austl.	270-71	16°15'S	133°22'E
Damān, India	234-35	20°25'N	72°51'E
Damān and Diu, state, India	234-35	20°25'N	72°50'E
Damanhûr, Egypt	268b	31°02'N	30°28'E
Damar, Pulau, i., Indon.	248-49	1°01'S	128°23'E
Damaraland, hist. reg., Nmb. (dă'n*ȧ*-r*ȧ*-lănd)	264-65	22°11'S	17°35'E
Damas, nat. cap., Syria *see* Damascus	228-29	33°31'N	36°18'E
Damascus, nat. cap., Syria (d*ȧ*-măs'kŭs)	228-29	33°31'N	36°18'E
Damāvand, Kūh-e, vol., Iran	232-33	35°56'N	52°08'E
Dāmghān, Iran (dām-gän')	232-33	36°10'N	54°21'E
Damietta, Egypt	268b	31°25'N	31°49'E
Dāmodar, stm., India	234-35	22°17'N	88°06'E
Damoh, India	234-35	23°51'N	79°27'E
Dampier, Selat, strt., Indon. (sȧ-lät' dăm'pēr)	224-25	0°40'S	130°40'E
Danakil, reg., Afr.	266	13°0'N	41°00'E
Da Nang, Viet.	246-47	16°03'N	108°12'E
Danbury, Ct., U.S. (dăn'bẽr-ĭ)	116-17	41°23'N	73°27'W
Dandenong, Austl. (dăn'dē-nông)	276	38°00'S	145°13'E
Dandong, China (dän-dôŋ)	243	40°07'N	124°21'E
Dang, stm., China	240-41	40°26'N	94°34'E
Dângrêk, Chuŏr Phnum, mts., Asia *see* Phanom Dongrak Range	246-47	14°25'N	103°30'E
Dangriga, Belize	148	16°58'N	88°13'W
Danilov, Russia (dä'nē-lôf)	202-03	58°11'N	40°11'E
Dankov, Russia (däŋ'kôf)	202-03	53°16'N	39°09'E
Danmark, nation, Eur. *see* Denmark	174-75	56°0'N	10°00'E
Danmarksstrædet, strt., *see* Denmark Strait	86	67°0'N	25°00'W
Dannemora, N.Y., U.S. (dăn-ē-mō'r*ȧ*)	116-17	44°43'N	73°43'W
Dannhauser, S. Afr. (dän'hou-zẽr)	269c	28°02'S	30°04'E
Dansville, N.Y., U.S. (dănz'vĭl)	116-17	42°33'N	77°41'W
Danube, stm., Eur. (dăn'ūb)	188-89	45°23'N	29°36'E
Danville, Ar., U.S. (dăn'vĭl)	120-21	35°04'N	93°23'W
Danville, Il., U.S. (dăn'vĭl)	116-17	40°08'N	87°38'W
Danville, In., U.S. (dăn'vĭl)	116-17	39°45'N	86°31'W
Danville, Ky., U.S. (dăn'vĭl)	116-17	37°39'N	84°47'W
Danville, Va., U.S. (dăn'vĭl)	124-25	36°35'N	79°24'W
Danxian, China (dän shyĕn)	238-39	19°31'N	109°33'E
Danzig, Pol. *see* Gdańsk	194-95	54°21'N	18°38'E
Daocheng, China	238-39	29°04'N	100°36'E
Daoxian, China (dou shyĕn)	238-39	25°35'N	111°27'E
Da Qaidam, China	240-41	37°53'N	95°19'E
Darabani, Rom. (dă-ră-băn'*ĭ*)	194-95	48°11'N	26°36'E
Darbhanga, India (dŭr-bŭŋ'gä)	234-35	26°09'N	85°54'E
Dardanelles, strt., Tur. (där-d*ȧ*-nělz')	200-01	40°17'N	26°33'E
Dar-el-Beida, Mor. *see* Casablanca	269a	33°36'N	7°36'W
Dar es Salaam, nat. cap., Tan. (där ěs s*ȧ*-läm')	262-63	6°49'S	39°16'E
Dārfūr, hist. reg., Sudan (där-fōōr')	262-63	13°30'N	23°30'E
Darganata, Turkmen.	232-33	40°29'N	62°10'E
Darhan, Mong.	240-41	49°29'N	105°56'E
Darién, Col. (dä-rē-ĕn')	163c	3°56'N	76°30'W
Darlag, China	238-39	33°46'N	99°40'E
Darling, stm., Austl. (där'lĭng)	276	34°07'S	141°55'E
Darling Downs, reg., Austl. (där'lĭng dounz)	276	27°30'S	150°30'E
Darling Range, mts., Austl. (där'lĭng rānj)	272-73	32°31'S	116°21'E
Darlington, Eng., U.K. (där'lĭng-t*ŭ*n)	190-91	54°32'N	1°34'W
Darlington, S.C., U.S. (där'lĭng-t*ŭ*n)	124-25	34°18'N	79°52'W
Darlington, Wi., U.S. (där'lĭng-t*ŭ*n)	116-17	42°41'N	90°07'W
Darmstadt, Ger. (därm'shtät)	194-95	49°52'N	8°39'E
Darnah, Libya	188-89	32°46'N	22°39'E
Darnley, Cape, c., Ant.	287	67°43'S	69°30'E
Daror, Eth.	262-63	8°14'N	44°41'E
Dart, Cape, c., Ant.	287	73°06'S	126°20'W
Dartmoor, for., Eng., U.K. (därt'mōōr)	190-91	50°35'N	3°55'W
Dartmouth, N.S., Can. (därt'mŭth)	138-39	44°41'N	63°34'W
Daru, Pap. N. Gui. (dä'rōō)	277	9°05'S	143°14'E
Daruvar, Cro. (där'rōō-vär)	200-01	45°36'N	17°13'E

Feature (Pronunciation)	Page	Lat.	Long.
Darvaza, Turkmen.	232-33	40°10'N	58°29'E
Darwin, Austl. (där'wĭn)	224-25	12°27'S	130°50'E
Dasht, stm., Pak. (dŭsht)	230-31	25°13'N	61°42'E
Daşköpri, Turkmen.	232-33	36°17'N	62°38'E
Daşoguz, Turkmen.	226	41°50'N	59°58'E
Datia, India	234-35	25°40'N	78°27'E
Datong, China (dä-tôŋ)	240-41	37°03'N	101°36'E
Datong, China (dä-tôŋ)	240-41	40°05'N	113°17'E
Datong, stm., China	240-41	36°20'N	102°50'E
Datu Piang, Phil.	250	7°02'N	124°29'E
Daua, stm., Afr. *see* Dawa	262-63	4°10'N	42°06'E
Daugava, stm., Eur. *see* Western Dvina	192-93	57°04'N	24°03'E
Daugavpils, Lat. (dä'ŏ-gäv-pēls)	192-93	55°53'N	26°32'E
Daule, stm., Ec.	170	2°18'S	79°50'W
Daung Kyun, i., Mya.	246-47	12°14'N	98°05'E
Dauphin, Mb., Can. (dô'fĭn)	134-35	51°09'N	100°03'W
Dauphin Lake, lk., Mb., Can. (dô'fĭn lāk)	134-35	51°17'N	99°48'W
Dāvangere, India	236	14°28'N	75°55'E
Davao, Phil. (dä'vä-ô)	250	7°04'N	125°35'E
Davao Gulf, b., Phil.	250	6°40'N	125°55'E
Davenport, Ia., U.S. (dăv'*ĕ*n-pōrt)	114-15	41°31'N	90°35'W
Davenport, Wa., U.S. (dăv'*ĕ*n-pōrt)	112-13	47°39'N	118°08'W
David, Pan. (d*ȧ*-vēdh')	150	8°26'N	82°26'W
David City, Ne., U.S. (dā'vĭd sĭ'tē)	114-15	41°15'N	97°08'W
Davis, Ca., U.S. (dā'vĭs)	118-19	38°33'N	121°44'W
Davis, Ok., U.S. (dā'vĭs)	120-21	34°30'N	97°07'W
Davis Mountains, mts., Tx., U.S. (dā'vĭs moun'tĭnz)	122-23	30°42'N	104°10'W
Davis Sea, s., Ant.	287	66°0'S	92°00'E
Davisstrædet, strt., N.A. *see* Davis Strait	86	67°0'N	57°00'W
Davis Strait, strt., N.A. (dā'vĭs strāt)	86	67°0'N	57°00'W
Davlekanovo, Russia	186-87	54°13'N	55°02'E
Davos, Switz. (dä'vōs)	194-95	46°48'N	9°49'E
Dawa, stm., Afr.	262-63	4°10'N	42°06'E
Dawāsir, Wādī ad-, stm., Sau. Ar.	220-21	20°26'N	45°35'E
Dawei, Mya.	246-47	14°05'N	98°13'E
Dawna Range, mts., Mya. (dô'n*ȧ* rānj)	246-47	16°50'N	98°15'E
Dawson, Yk., Can. (dô's*ŭ*n)	128-29	64°03'N	139°24'W
Dawson, Ga., U.S. (dô's*ŭ*n)	124-25	31°47'N	84°26'W
Dawson, Mn., U.S. (dô's*ŭ*n)	114-15	44°56'N	96°04'W
Dawson, stm., Austl. (dô's*ŭ*n)	277	23°38'S	149°46'E
Dawson, Isla, i., Chile	171	53°55'S	70°43'W
Dawson Creek, B.C., Can. (dô's*ŭ*n krēk)	132-33	55°47'N	120°20'W
Dawson Springs, Ky., U.S. (dô's*ŭ*n sprĭngz)	124-25	37°10'N	87°41'W
Dawu, China (dä-wōō)	238-39	31°33'N	114°07'E
Dax, Fr. (d*ȧ*ks)	196-97	43°43'N	1°03'W
Daxian, China (dä-shyĕn)	238-39	31°13'N	107°30'E
Daxue Shan, mts., China	238-39	30°30'N	101°46'E
Dayr az-Zawr, Syria (dȧ-ēr̄ēz-zôr')	228-29	35°21'N	40°09'E
Dayton, Oh., U.S. (dā't*ŭ*n)	116-17	39°45'N	84°12'W
Dayton, Tn., U.S. (dā't*ŭ*n)	124-25	35°30'N	85°01'W
Dayton, Tx., U.S. (dā't*ŭ*n)	122-23	30°03'N	94°54'W
Dayton, Wa., U.S. (dā't*ŭ*n)	112-13	46°19'N	117°58'W
Daytona Beach, Fl., U.S. (dā-tō'n*ȧ* bēch)	124-25	29°13'N	81°02'W
Dayu, China (dä-yōō)	238-39	25°24'N	114°22'E
Da Yunhe, can., China (dä yòn-hŭ) *see* Grand Canal	240-41	32°11'N	119°33'E
De Aar, S. Afr. (dē-är')	264-65	30°39'S	24°01'E
Dead Sea, lk., Asia (dĕd sē)	228-29	31°30'N	35°30'E
Deadwood, S.D., U.S. (dĕd'wòd)	114-15	44°23'N	103°44'W
Deal Island, i., Austl.	276	39°28'S	147°20'E
Dean, stm., B.C., Can. (dēn)	132-33	52°48'N	126°59'W
Dean Channel, strt., B.C., Can. (dēn chăn'ĕl)	132-33	52°33'N	127°13'W
Deán Funes, Arg. (dĕ-á'n-fōō-nĕs)	173	30°25'S	64°21'W
Dearborn, Mi., U.S. (dēr'b*ŭ*rn)	116-17	42°19'N	83°10'W
Dearg, Beinn, mtn., Scot., U.K. (bĕn dŭrg)	190-91	57°47'N	4°56'W
Dease, stm., B.C., Can.	130-31	59°55'N	128°29'W
Death Valley, Ca., U.S. (dĕth văl'ē)	118-19	36°19'N	116°25'W
Death Valley, val., Ca., U.S. (dĕth văl'ē)	118-19	36°30'N	117°00'W
Death Valley National Park, n.p., U.S. (dĕth văl'ē năsh'ŭn-*ă*l pärk)	118-19	36°25'N	116°56'W
Debao, China (dŭ-bou)	238-39	23°20'N	106°37'E
Dęblin, Pol. (dăN'blĭn)	194-95	51°35'N	21°53'E
Dębno, Pol. (dĕb-nō')	194-95	52°44'N	14°43'E
Debrecen, Hung. (dĕ'brĕ-tsĕn)	194-95	47°32'N	21°38'E
Debre Mark'os, Eth.	269d	10°20'N	37°44'E
Decatur, Al., U.S. (dē-kā't*ŭ*r)	124-25	34°36'N	86°59'W
Decatur, Il., U.S. (dē-kā't*ŭ*r)	116-17	39°50'N	88°57'W

n-sing; ŋ-baŋk; N-nasalized n; nŏd; c*ŏ*mmit; ōld; ôbey; ôrder; oi-boil; fōōd; ò-as oo in foot; ou-out; s-soft; sh-dish; th-thin; pūre; ůnite; ûrn; stŭd; circ*ŭ*s; ü-as in French tu; '-indeterminate vowel.

Feature (Pronunciation)	Page	Lat.	Long.
Decatur, In., U.S. (dê-kā′tŭr)	116-17	40°50′N	84°55′W
Decatur, Mi., U.S. (dê-kā′tŭr)	116-17	42°06′N	85°58′W
Decatur, Tx., U.S. (dê-kā′tŭr)	120-21	33°14′N	97°35′W
Decazeville, Fr. (dē-käz′vēl′)	196-97	44°34′N	2°15′E
Deccan, plat., India (děk′ăn)	236	17°0′N	78°00′E
Deception Lake, lk., Sk., Can. (dê-sěp′shŭn lāk)	134-35	56°33′N	104°10′W
Decorah, Ia., U.S. (dê-kō′rá)	114-15	43°18′N	91°47′W
Dee, stm., Scot., U.K. (dē)	190-91	57°08′N	2°05′W
Deep River, On., Can. (dēp rĭv′ēr)	136-37	46°06′N	77°30′W
Deerfield, Ma., U.S. (dēr′fēld)	116-17	42°33′N	72°36′W
Deer Lake, Nf., Can. (dēr lāk)	138-39	49°11′N	57°26′W
Deer Lake, lk., On., Can. (dēr lāk)	134-35	52°39′N	94°29′W
Deer Lodge, Mt., U.S. (dēr lŏj)	112-13	46°24′N	112°44′W
Deer Park, Wa., U.S. (dēr pärk)	112-13	47°57′N	117°28′W
Deer River, Mn., U.S. (dēr rĭv′ēr)	114-15	47°19′N	93°48′W
Defiance, Oh., U.S. (dē-fī′ăns)	116-17	41°16′N	84°22′W
Defuniak Springs, Fl., U.S. (dê fū′nĭ-ăk sprĭngz)	124-25	30°43′N	86°07′W
Dêgê, China	238-39	31°50′N	98°40′E
Degeh Bur, Eth.	262-63	8°13′N	43°33′E
Deggendorf, Ger. (dě′ghěn-dôrf)	194-95	48°51′N	12°58′E
Dehalak′ Desēt, i., Erit.	266	15°40′N	40°06′E
Dehiwala-Mount Lavinia, Sri L.	236	6°52′N	79°52′E
Dehra Dūn, India (dā′rŭ dūn)	234-35	30°19′N	78°02′E
Dehri, India	234-35	24°54′N	84°11′E
Dehua, China (dŭ-hwä)	225a	25°30′N	118°14′E
Dehui, China	240-41	44°32′N	125°43′E
Dej, Rom. (dāzh)	194-95	47°09′N	23°53′E
De Kalb, Il., U.S. (dê kălb′)	116-17	41°56′N	88°45′W
DeLand, Fl., U.S. (dē lănd′)	124-25	29°02′N	81°18′W
Delano, Ca., U.S. (děl′á-nō)	118-19	35°47′N	119°15′W
Delavan, Wi., U.S. (děl′á-văn)	116-17	42°38′N	88°39′W
Delaware, Oh., U.S. (děl′á-wâr)	116-17	40°18′N	83°04′W
Delaware, state, U.S. (děl′á-wâr)	108-09	39°10′N	75°30′W
Delaware, stm., Ks., U.S. (děl′á-wâr)	120-21	39°04′N	95°25′W
Delaware, stm., U.S.	116-117	39°20′N	75°25′E
Delaware Bay, b., U.S. (děl′á-wâr bā)	116-17	39°05′N	75°15′W
De Leon, Tx., U.S. (dê lê-ŏn′)	122-23	32°07′N	98°33′W
Delft, Neth. (dělft)	190-91	52°01′N	4°22′E
Delgado, Cabo, c., Moz. (kà′bô-děl-gä′dō)	264-65	10°41′S	40°38′E
Delger, stm., Mong.	240-41	49°17′N	100°42′E
Delhi, India (děl′hī)	234-35	28°40′N	77°14′E
Delhi, La., U.S. (děl′hī)	124-25	32°28′N	91°30′W
Delhi, state, India (děl′hī)	234-35	28°37′N	77°10′E
Delicias, Mex.	122-23	28°12′N	105°29′W
Déline, N.T., Can.	128-29	65°11′N	123°25′W
Delingha, China	240-41	37°15′N	97°11′E
Dell Rapids, S.D., U.S. (děl răp′ĭdz)	114-15	43°49′N	96°43′W
Delmarva Peninsula, pen., U.S.	116-17	38°30′N	75°30′W
Delmenhorst, Ger. (děl′mĕn-hôrst)	194-95	53°04′N	8°38′E
De Long Mountains, mts., Ak., U.S. (dē′lŏng moun′tĭnz)	126	68°20′N	162°00′W
Delphi, In., U.S. (děl′fī)	116-17	40°35′N	86°40′W
Delphos, Oh., U.S. (děl′fŏs)	116-17	40°51′N	84°21′W
Del Rio, Tx., U.S. (děl rē′ō)	122-23	29°22′N	100°54′W
Delta Junction, Ak., U.S.	126	64°02′N	145°44′W
Dëma, stm., Russia (dyěm′ä)	176-77	54°44′N	55°54′E
Dembī Dolo, Eth.	262-63	8°32′N	34°48′E
Demidov, Russia (dzyě′mê-dô′f)	192-93	55°16′N	31°32′E
Deming, N.M., U.S. (děm′ĭng)	118-19	32°16′N	107°45′W
Demini, stm., Braz.	166-67	0°46′S	62°56′W
Demopolis, Al., U.S. (dê-mŏp′ô-lĭs)	124-25	32°31′N	87°50′W
Dempo, Gunung, vol., Indon. (gōō-nŏng děm′pô)	246-47	4°00′S	103°09′E
Demyanka, stm., Russia (dyěm-yän′kä)	218-19	59°31′N	69°05′E
Demyansk, Russia (dyěm-yänsk′)	192-93	57°38′N	32°28′E
Denakil, reg., Afr. *see* Danakil	266	13°0′N	41°00′E
Denali, mtn., Ak., U.S. *see* McKinley, Mount	126	63°04′N	151°00′W
Denali National Park and Preserve, n.p., Ak., U.S.	126	63°15′N	150°30′W
Dêngqên, China	238-39	31°27′N	95°27′E
Denham, Austl.	270-71	25°55′S	113°33′E
Denham, Mount, mtn., Jam.	142-43	18°13′N	77°32′W
Denham Range, mts., Austl.	277	21°41′S	147°55′E
Deniliquin, Austl. (dě-nĭl′ĭ-kwĭn)	276	35°32′S	144°58′E
Denison, Ia., U.S. (děn′ĭ-sŭn)	114-15	42°01′N	95°22′W
Denison, Tx., U.S. (děn′ĭ-sŭn)	120-21	33°45′N	96°33′W
Denizli, Tur. (děn-ĭz-lē′)	200-01	37°47′N	29°05′E
Denmark, S.C., U.S. (děn′märk)	124-25	33°20′N	81°09′W
Denmark, nation, Eur. (děn′märk)	174-75	56°0′N	10°00′E
Denmark Strait, strt., (děn′märk strāt)	86	67°0′N	25°00′W
Denov, Uzb.	232-33	38°16′N	67°54′E
Denpasar, Indon.	248-49	8°39′S	115°13′E
Denton, Tx., U.S. (děn′tŭn)	120-21	33°14′N	97°08′W
D'Entrecasteaux Islands, is., Pap. N. Gui. (dän-tr′-kás-tō′ ī′lándz)	277	9°27′S	150°32′E
Denver, Co., U.S. (děn′vēr)	120-21	39°44′N	104°58′W
Deolāli, India	234-35	19°57′N	73°50′E
De Pere, Wi., U.S. (dê pēr′)	116-17	44°26′N	88°03′W
Dêqên, China	238-39	28°38′N	98°52′E
De Queen, Ar., U.S. (dê kwēn′)	120-21	34°03′N	94°21′W
De Quincy, La., U.S. (dê kwĭn′sĭ)	122-23	30°27′N	93°26′W
Dera, Lach, stm., Afr. (dā′rä)	262-63	0°13′N	42°18′E
Dera Ghāzi Khān, Pak. (dā′rū gä-zē′ kan′)	232-33	30°03′N	70°38′E
Dera Ismāīl Khān, Pak. (dā′rū ĭs-mä-ēl′ kan′)	232-33	31°49′N	70°55′E
Derbent, Russia (děr-běnt′)	227	42°03′N	48°17′E
Derby, Austl. (där′bê) (dûr′bê)	270-71	17°20′S	123°38′E
Derby, Eng., U.K. (där′bê)	190-91	52°55′N	1°29′W
Derby, Ks., U.S. (dûr′bê)	120-21	37°32′N	97°15′W
De Ridder, La., U.S. (dê rĭd′ēr)	122-23	30°51′N	93°18′W
Dermott, Ar., U.S. (dûr′mŏt)	124-25	33°32′N	91°26′W
Derry, N. Ire., U.K. *see* Londonderry	190-91	54°59′N	7°20′W
Derry, N.H., U.S. (dâr′ĭ)	116-17	42°53′N	71°20′W
Derventa, Bos. (děr′ven-tà)	200-01	44°59′N	17°54′E
Derzhavinsk, Kaz.	226	51°06′N	66°19′E
Desaguadero, stm., S.A.	170	18°04′S	67°06′W
Désappointement, Îles du, is., Fr. Poly.	280-81	14°10′S	141°20′W
Deschambault Lake, lk., Sk., Can.	134-35	54°40′N	103°35′W
Deschutes, stm., Or., U.S. (dā-shōōt′)	112-13	45°39′N	120°55′W
Desē, Eth.	266	11°09′N	39°38′E
Deseado, stm., Arg. (dā-sā-ä′dhō)	171	47°46′S	65°53′W
Desengaño, Punta, c., Arg.	171	49°15′S	67°37′W
De Smet, S.D., U.S. (dê smět′)	114-15	44°23′N	97°33′W
Des Moines, Ia., U.S. (dē moin′)	114-15	41°34′N	93°36′W
Des Moines, stm., U.S. (dē moin′)	110-11	40°22′N	91°26′W
Desna, stm., Eur. (dyěs-nà′)	202-03	50°33′N	30°34′E
Desolación, Isla, i., Chile (ě′s-lä-dě-sô-lä-syô′n)	171	53°00′S	74°09′W
De Soto, Mo., U.S. (dê sō′tō)	120-21	38°08′N	90°34′W
Dessau, Ger. (děsou)	194-95	51°50′N	12°14′E
Destruction Bay, Yk., Can.	128-29	61°14′N	138°50′W
Detmold, Ger. (dět′mōld)	194-95	51°56′N	8°53′E
Detroit, Mi., U.S. (dê-troit′)	116-17	42°21′N	83°04′W
Detroit Lakes, Mn., U.S. (dê-troit′ lākz)	114-15	46°49′N	95°51′W
Detva, Slvk. (dyět′vá)	194-95	48°32′N	19°29′E
Deutschland, nation, Eur. *see* Germany	174-75	51°0′N	10°00′E
Deva, Rom. (dā′vä)	194-95	45°53′N	22°55′E
Deventer, Neth. (děv′ěn-tēr)	190-91	52°16′N	6°10′E
Devils, stm., Tx., U.S. (děv′'lz)	122-23	29°32′N	100°59′W
Devils Lake, N.D., U.S. (děv′'lz lāk)	114-15	48°07′N	98°52′W
Devils Postpile National Monument, n.p., Ca., U.S. (děv′'lz pōst-pīl năsh′ŭn-ăl mŏn′ŭ-měnt)	118-19	37°37′N	119°05′W
Devils Tower National Monument, n.p., Wy., U.S. (děv′'lz tou′ēr năsh′ŭn-ăl mŏn′ŭ-měnt)	112-13	44°36′N	104°43′W
Devon Island, i., Nu., Can.	86	75°0′N	87°00′W
Devonport, Austl. (děv′ŭn-pôrt)	276	41°11′S	146°21′E
Dewās, India	234-35	22°58′N	76°03′E
Dewey, Ok., U.S. (dū′ĭ)	120-21	36°48′N	95°56′W
De Witt, Ar., U.S. (dê wĭt′)	124-25	34°18′N	91°20′W
De Witt, Ia., U.S. (dê wĭt′)	114-15	41°49′N	90°32′W
Dexter, Me., U.S. (děks′tēr)	117a	45°02′N	69°17′W
Dexter, Mo., U.S. (děks′tēr)	124-25	36°48′N	89°58′W
Dexter, N.M., U.S. (děks′tēr)	120-21	33°12′N	104°22′W
Dezfūl, Iran	228-29	32°23′N	48°24′E
Dezhnëva, Mys, c., Russia (mĭs dyězh′nyĭf)	126	66°08′N	169°41′W
Dezhou, China (dŭ-jō)	240-41	37°27′N	116°17′E
Dhahran, Sau. Ar.	230-31	26°18′N	50°08′E
Dhaka, nat. cap., Bngl. (dä′kä) (dăk′à)	234-35	23°43′N	90°25′E
Dhamār, Yemen	266	14°33′N	44°24′E
Dhanbād, India	234-35	23°48′N	86°26′E
Dhār, India	234-35	22°36′N	75°18′E
Dhawalāgiri, mtn., Nepal	234-35	28°42′N	83°30′E
Dhuburi, India	234-35	26°01′N	89°59′E
Dhule, India	234-35	20°54′N	74°46′E
Diablo, Pico del, mtn., Mex.	144-45	30°59′N	115°45′W
Diablo Range, mts., Ca., U.S. (dyä′blô rānj)	118-19	37°0′N	121°20′W
Diamante, Arg.	173	32°04′S	60°39′W
Diamantina, Braz.	172	18°15′S	43°37′W
Diamantina, stm., Austl. (dī′man-tē′ná)	277	26°58′S	138°49′E
Diamantina National Park, n.p., Austl.	277	23°43′S	141°11′E
Diamantino, Braz. (dà-à-män-tē′no)	166-67	14°25′S	56°27′W
Dian Chi, lk., China (dĭěn chē)	238-39	24°50′N	102°42′E
Dianópolis, Braz.	166-67	11°38′S	46°50′W
D' Iberville, Mont, mtn., Can. *see* Caubvick, Mount	130-31	58°53′N	63°43′W
Dibrugarh, India	234-35	27°29′N	94°55′E
Dickinson, N.D., U.S. (dĭk′ĭn-sŭn)	114-15	46°53′N	102°47′W
Dickson, Tn., U.S. (dĭk′sŭn)	124-25	36°04′N	87°22′W
Dickson City, Pa., U.S. (dĭk′sŭn sĭ′tê)	116-17	41°28′N	75°37′W
Dicle, stm., Asia *see* Tigris	208-09	30°60′N	47°27′E
Diego de Almagro, Isla, i., Chile	171	51°28′S	75°11′W
Diégo-Suarez, Madag. *see* Antsirañana	264-65	12°17′S	49°17′E
Dien Bien, Viet.	246-47	21°23′N	103°01′E
Dien Bien Phu, Viet. *see* Dien Bien	246-47	21°23′N	103°01′E
Dieppe, N.B., Can. (dê-ěp′)	138-39	46°06′N	64°44′W
Dieppe, Fr.	196-97	49°56′N	1°05′E
Difuri, i., Mald.	236	5°24′N	73°38′E
Digboi, India	234-35	27°23′N	95°38′E
Digby, N.S., Can. (dĭg′bĭ)	138-39	44°37′N	65°46′W
Digul, stm., Indon.	277	7°10′S	138°41′E
Dijlah, stm., Asia *see* Tigris	208-09	30°60′N	47°27′E
Dijon, Fr. (dē-zhŏn′)	196-97	47°19′N	5°02′E
Dikhil, Dji.	266	11°06′N	42°22′E
Dikson, Russia (dĭk′sŏn)	218-19	73°30′N	80°33′E
Dīla, Eth.	262-63	6°19′N	38°14′E
Dili, nat. cap., E. Timor (dĭl′ê)	248-49	8°35′S	125°35′E
Dilling, Sudan	266	12°02′N	29°40′E
Dillingham, Ak., U.S. (dĭl′ĕng-hăm)	126	59°03′N	158°28′W
Dillon, Mt., U.S. (dĭl′ŭn)	112-13	45°13′N	112°38′W
Dillon, S.C., U.S. (dĭl′ŭn)	124-25	34°25′N	79°22′W
Dilolo, D.R.C. (dê-lō′lō)	262-63	10°42′S	22°21′E
Dimāpur, India	234-35	25°55′N	93°44′E
Dimashq, nat. cap., Syria *see* Damascus	228-29	33°31′N	36°18′E
Dimitrovgrad, Blg.	200-01	42°03′N	25°37′E
Dimitrovgrad, Russia	186-87	54°13′N	49°36′E
Dimlang, mtn., Nig.	260-61	8°24′N	11°47′E
Dinagat Island, i., Phil.	250	10°12′N	125°35′E
Dinājpur, Bngl.	234-35	25°38′N	88°38′E
Dinan, Fr. (dē-nän′)	196-97	48°28′N	2°03′W
Dinant, Bel. (dē-nän′)	190-91	50°16′N	4°55′E
Dinara Planina, mts., Eur. (dê′nä-rä plä′nê-na) *see* Dinaric Alps	200-01	43°55′N	16°38′E
Dinaric Alps, mts., Eur.	200-01	43°55′N	16°38′E
Dinariche, Alpi, mts., Eur. *see* Dinaric Alps	200-01	43°55′N	16°38′E
Dindigul, India	236	10°22′N	77°59′E
Dingalan Bay, b., Phil. (dĭŋ-gä′län bā)	250	15°18′N	121°25′E
Dinggyê, China	234-35	28°35′N	86°37′E
Dinghai, China	238-39	30°01′N	122°06′E
Dingwall, Scot., U.K. (dĭng′wôl)	190-91	57°36′N	4°26′W
Dingxi, China	240-41	35°33′N	104°32′E
Dingxian, China (dĭŋ shyĕn)	240-41	38°31′N	114°60′E
Dingyuan, China (dĭŋ-yüän)	238-39	32°32′N	117°40′E
Dinosaur National Monument, n.p., U.S. (dī′nô-sŏr năsh′ŭn-ăl mŏn′ŭ-měnt)	112-13	40°32′N	108°58′W
Dipolog, Phil.	250	8°35′N	123°21′E
Dirē Dawa, Eth.	262-63	9°35′N	41°52′E
Diriamba, Nic. (dēr-yäm′bä)	149	11°51′N	86°15′W
Dirj, Libya	188-89	30°10′N	10°28′E
Dirranbandi, Austl. (dĭ-rà-băn′dê)	276	28°35′S	148°14′E
Disappointment Islands, is., Fr. Poly. (dĭs′á-point′ment ī′lándz) *see* Désappointement, Îles du	280-81	14°10′S	141°20′W
Dispur, India	234-35	26°08′N	91°48′E
Disraëli, Qc., Can. (dĭs-rā′lĭ)	136-37	45°54′N	71°21′W
District of Columbia, state, U.S.	108-09	38°54′N	77°01′W
Distrito Federal, state, Braz. (dēs-trē′tô-fĕ-dĕ-rä′l)	168-69	15°45′S	47°45′W
Distrito Federal, state, Mex.	146-47	19°15′N	99°10′W
Dis ûq, Egypt	268b	31°08′N	30°39′E
Diu, India (dē′ōō)	234-35	20°43′N	70°59′E
Divinópolis, Braz. (dē-vē-nô′pō-lēs)	172	20°09′S	44°53′W
Divnoye, Russia	186-87	45°55′N	43°22′E
Divo, C. Iv.	260-61	5°50′N	5°22′W
Dixon, Il., U.S. (dĭks′ŭn)	116-17	41°50′N	89°29′W
Dixon Entrance, strt., N.A.	126	54°25′N	132°30′W
Diyarbakır, Tur. (dê-yär-běk′ĭr)	227	37°55′N	40°14′E
Dja, stm., Afr.	260-61	2°02′N	15°12′E
Djajapura, Indon. *see* Jayapura	277	2°32′S	140°43′E
Djakarta, nat. cap., Indon. *see* Jakarta	248-49	6°11′S	106°50′E
Djambala, Congo	262-63	2°33′S	14°46′E
Djedi, Oued, stm., Alg.	258-59	34°28′N	6°06′E
Djelfa, Alg.	269b	34°41′N	3°15′E

Feature (Pronunciation)	Page	Lat.	Long.
Djenné, Mali	258-59	13°54'N	4°33'W
Djérem, stm., Camrn.	260-61	5°19'N	13°24'E
Djibouti, nation, Afr. (jē-bōō-tē´)	253	11°30'N	43°00'E
Djibouti, nat. cap., Dji. (jē-bōō-tē´)	266	11°34'N	43°09'E
Djokjakarta, Indon. *see* Yogyakarta	248-49	7°48'S	110°22'E
Djougou, Benin	260-61	9°42'N	1°40'E
Djugu, D.R.C.	267	1°58'N	30°30'E
Dmitrov, Russia (d'mē´trôf)	202-03	56°21'N	37°31'E
Dnepr, stm., Eur. *see* Dnieper	202-03	46°31'N	32°22'E
Dneprodzerzhinsk, Ukr. *see* Dniprodzerzhyns'k	202-03	48°29'N	34°41'E
Dnestr, stm., Eur. *see* Dniester	188-89	46°19'N	30°17'E
Dnieper, stm., Eur. (nē´pûr)	202-03	46°31'N	32°22'E
Dniester, stm., Eur. (nēs´-tẽr)	188-89	46°19'N	30°17'E
Dnipro, stm., Eur. *see* Dnieper	202-03	46°31'N	32°22'E
Dniprodzerzhyns'k, Ukr.	202-03	48°29'N	34°41'E
Dnipropetrovs'k, Ukr.	202-03	48°28'N	34°58'E
Dnister, stm., Eur. *see* Dniester	188-89	46°19'N	30°17'E
Dnjapro, stm., Eur. *see* Dnieper	202-03	46°31'N	32°22'E
Dno, Russia (d'nô´)	192-93	57°49'N	29°59'E
Doba, Chad	262-63	8°39'N	16°51'E
Doberai, Jazirah, pen., Indon.	224-25	1°30'S	132°30'E
Doboj, Bos. (dō´boi)	200-01	44°44'N	18°06'E
Dobrich, Blg.	200-01	43°35'N	27°50'E
Dobryanka, Russia (dôb-ryän´kȧ)	186-87	58°28'N	56°25'E
Doce, stm., Braz. (dō´sȧ)	172	19°39'S	39°49'W
Doctor Arroyo, Mex. (dŏk-tōr´ är-rō´yŏ)	146-47	23°42'N	100°11'W
Dodecanese, is., Grc. (dō´dĕ-kȧ-nēs´)	200-01	36°30'N	27°00'E
Dodekanisoy, is., Grc. *see* Dodecanese	200-01	36°30'N	27°00'E
Dodge City, Ks., U.S. (dŏj sĭ´tē)	120-21	37°45'N	100°01'W
Dodgeville, Wi., U.S. (dŏj´vĭl)	116-17	42°58'N	90°08'W
Dodola, Eth.	269d	7°00'N	39°07'E
Dodoma, nat. cap., Tan. (dō´dô-mȧ)	267	6°11'S	35°45'E
Dogai Coring, lk., China	234-35	34°35'N	88°59'E
Dog Island, i., Anguilla	143b	18°17'N	63°15'W
Dog Lake, lk., On., Can. (dŏg lāk)	136-37	48°46'N	89°33'W
Dōgo, i., Japan	245	36°15'N	133°16'E
Doğu Karadeniz Dağları, mts., Tur.	227	40°30'N	40°30'E
Doha, nat. cap., Qatar (dō´hȧ)	230-31	25°17'N	51°32'E
Dolbeau-Mistassini, Qc., Can.	136-37	48°53'N	72°13'W
Dole, Fr. (dōl)	196-97	47°06'N	5°29'E
Dolgaya Kosa, spit, Russia (dôl-gä´yȧ kô´sȧ)	202-03	46°41'N	37°43'E
Dolinsk, Russia (dȧ-lēnsk´)	222-23	47°20'N	142°48'E
Dolisie, Congo *see* Loubomo	262-63	4°11'S	12°40'E
Dolores, Arg. (dô-lō´rĕs)	173	36°20'S	57°41'W
Dolores, Ur.	173	33°32'S	58°12'W
Dolores Hidalgo, Mex. (dô-lô´rĕs-ē-däl´gō)	146-47	21°09'N	100°56'W
Domažlice, Czech Rep. (dō´mäzh-lē-tsĕ)	194-95	49°27'N	12°56'E
Dombarovskiy, Russia	226	50°46'N	59°32'E
Dombås, Nor.	192-93	62°05'N	9°08'E
Dombóvár, Hung. (dŏm´bō-vär)	194-95	46°22'N	18°08'E
Domeyko, Chile	168-69	28°57'S	70°54'W
Domeyko, Cordillera, mts., Chile (kôr-dēl-yĕ´rä-dô-mā´kō)	168-69	24°45'S	69°09'W
Dominica, nation, N.A. (dŏ-mĭ-nē´kȧ)	140-41	15°30'N	61°20'W
Dominican Republic, nation, N.A. (dô-mĭn´ĭ-kăn rē-pŭb´lĭk)	140-41	19°0'N	70°40'W
Dominion, Cape, c., Nu., Can.	130-31	66°09'N	74°27'W
Dominique, Canal de la, strt., N.A. *see* Martinique Passage	143b	15°10'N	61°15'W
Domodedovo, Russia (dô-mô-dyĕ´do-vô)	202-03	55°26'N	37°47'E
Dom Pedrito, Braz.	173	30°59'S	54°40'W
Domuyo, Volcán, vol., Arg.	171	36°38'S	70°26'W
Don, stm., Russia (dŏn)	186-87	47°05'N	39°15'E
Don, stm., Scot., U.K. (dŏn)	190-91	57°11'N	2°06'W
Donaldsonville, La., U.S. (dŏn´ăld-sŭn-vĭl)	124-25	30°06'N	90°60'W
Donau, stm., Eur. *see* Danube	188-89	45°23'N	29°36'E
Don Benito, Spain (dōn´bā-nē´tō)	198-99	38°57'N	5°52'W
Doncaster, Eng., U.K. (doŋ´kăs-tẽr)	190-91	53°32'N	1°08'W
Dondo, Moz.	264-65	19°35'S	34°44'E
Dondra Head, c., Sri L.	236	5°55'N	80°35'E
Donegal, Ire. (dŏn-ē-gôl´)	190-91	54°39'N	8°07'W
Donegal Bay, b., Ire. (dŏn-ē-gôl´ bā)	190-91	54°30'N	8°30'W
Donets'k, Ukr.	202-03	47°60'N	37°48'E
Dong, stm., China (dôŋ)	238-39	23°05'N	113°60'E
Dong, stm., China (dôŋ)	240-41	42°17'N	101°06'E
Dongara, Austl. (dôn-gä´rȧ)	270-71	29°15'S	114°58'E
Dongfang, China (dôŋ-fäŋ)	238-39	19°05'N	108°38'E
Donggala, Indon. (dôn-gä´lä)	248-49	0°41'S	119°44'E
Dongguan, China (dôŋ-gůän)	238-39	23°03'N	113°44'E
Dong Hai, s., Asia *see* East China Sea	222-23	30°0'N	126°00'E
Donghai Dao, i., China	238-39	21°02'N	110°25'E
Dong Hoi, Viet. (dông-hô-ē´)	246-47	17°29'N	106°37'E
Dong Nai, stm., Viet.	246-47	10°44'N	106°46'E
Dongola, Sudan *see* Dunqulah	266	19°11'N	30°28'E
Dong San Shen, hist. reg., China *see* Manchuria	240-41	47°0'N	125°00'E
Dongting Hu, lk., China (dôŋ-tĭŋ hōō)	238-39	29°20'N	112°54'E
Dongyang, China	238-39	29°16'N	120°14'E
Dongzhi, China	238-39	30°07'N	117°01'E
Doniphan, Mo., U.S. (dŏn´ĭ-făn)	124-25	36°37'N	90°50'W
Doniphan, Ne., U.S. (dŏn´ĭ-făn)	114-15	40°46'N	98°23'W
Donostia, Spain *see* Donostia-San Sebastián	198-99	43°19'N	1°60'W
Donostia-San Sebastián, Spain	198-99	43°19'N	1°60'W
Door Peninsula, pen., Wi., U.S. (dōr pĕ-nĭn´sūlȧ)	116-17	44°55'N	87°20'W
Dorchester, Eng., U.K. (dôr´chĕs-tẽr)	190-91	50°43'N	2°27'W
Dorchester, Cape, c., Nu., Can.	130-31	65°27'N	77°26'W
Dordogne, stm., Fr. (dôr-dôn´yẽ)	196-97	45°02'N	0°35'W
Dore Lake, lk., Sk., Can.	134-35	54°46'N	107°17'W
Dores do Indaiá, Braz.	172	19°28'S	45°36'W
Dori, Burkina	260-61	14°02'N	0°02'W
Dornbirn, Aus. (dôrn´bĕrn)	194-95	47°25'N	9°45'E
Dorogobuzh, Russia (dôrôgô´-bōō´zh)	202-03	54°55'N	33°18'E
Dorohoi, Rom. (dō-rô-hoi´)	194-95	47°57'N	26°24'E
Dorpat, Est. *see* Tartu	192-93	58°23'N	26°43'E
Dorre Island, i., Austl. (dôr ī´lȧnd)	272-73	25°07'S	113°06'E
Dortmund, Ger. (dôrt´mŏŏnt)	194-95	51°31'N	7°28'E
Dörtyol, Tur. (dûrt´yôl)	228-29	36°52'N	36°13'E
Dosatuy, Russia	240-41	50°22'N	118°34'E
Dos Bahías, Cabo, c., Arg. (kȧ´bô-dōs-bä-ē´äs)	171	44°56'S	65°33'W
Dos Hermanas, Spain (dōsĕr-mä´näs)	198-99	37°17'N	5°55'W
Dosso, Niger (dōs-ō´)	258-59	13°03'N	3°12'E
Dossor, Kaz.	186-87	47°32'N	52°59'E
Dothan, Al., U.S. (dō´thăn)	124-25	31°13'N	85°24'W
Douai, Fr. (dōō-ā´)	196-97	50°22'N	3°05'E
Douala, Camrn. (dōō-ä´lä)	260-61	4°03'N	9°42'E
Douarnenez, Fr. (dōō-är nē-nĕs´)	196-97	48°06'N	4°20'W
Douglas, Az., U.S. (dŭg´lăs)	118-19	31°20'N	109°34'W
Douglas, Ga., U.S. (dŭg´lăs)	124-25	31°30'N	82°51'W
Douglas, Mi., U.S. (dŭg´lăs)	116-17	42°39'N	86°12'W
Douglas, Wy., U.S. (dŭg´lăs)	112-13	42°45'N	105°23'W
Douglas, nat. cap., I. of Man (dŭg´lăs)	190-91	54°10'N	4°29'W
Douglas Channel, strt., B.C., Can. (dŭg´lăs chăn´ĕl)	132-33	53°30'N	129°12'W
Douglasville, Ga., U.S. (dŭg´lăs-vĭl)	124-25	33°45'N	84°45'W
Dourada, Serra, plat., Braz. (sĕ´r-rä-dōōō-rȧ´dȧ)	166-67	13°10'S	48°34'W
Dourados, Braz.	168-69	22°13'S	54°49'W
Douro, stm., Eur. (dô´ô-rŏ)	198-99	41°09'N	8°41'W
Dover, Eng., U.K. (dō vẽr)	190-91	51°08'N	1°18'E
Dover, De., U.S.	116-17	39°09'N	75°31'W
Dover, N.H., U.S.	116-17	43°12'N	70°53'W
Dover, N.J., U.S. (dō vẽr)	116-17	40°54'N	74°32'W
Dover, Oh., U.S. (dō vẽr)	116-17	40°31'N	81°28'W
Dover, Strait of, strt., Eur. (strāt ŭv dō vẽr)	190-91	50°59'N	1°31'E
Dover-Foxcroft, Me., U.S. (dō´vẽr fŏks´krôft)	117a	45°11'N	69°14'W
Dovrefjell, mts., Nor. (dŏv´rĕ fyĕl´)	192-93	62°06'N	9°25'E
Dowagiac, Mi., U.S. (dô-wô´jăk)	116-17	41°59'N	86°06'W
Drâa, Hamada du, des., Alg.	258-59	29°0'N	6°45'W
Drâa, Oued, stm., Afr. (wĕd drȧ)	258-59	28°41'N	11°07'W
Drăgăşani, Rom. (drä-gȧ-shän´ĭ)	200-01	44°40'N	24°16'E
Draguignan, Fr. (drä-gēn-yäɴ´)	196-97	43°33'N	6°28'E
Drake, Pasaje de, strt., *see* Drake Passage	287	58°0'S	70°00'W
Drakensberg, mts., Afr. (drä´kĕnz-bĕrgh)	264-65	27°0'S	30°00'E
Drake Passage, strt., (drāk păs´ĭj)	287	58°0'S	70°00'W
Dráma, Grc. (drä´mä)	200-01	41°09'N	24°09'E
Drammen, Nor. (dräm´ĕn)	192-93	59°45'N	10°13'E
Drau, stm., Eur. (drou) *see* Drava	200-01	45°33'N	18°56'E
Drava, stm., Eur. (drä´vä)	200-01	45°33'N	18°56'E
Drayton Valley, Ab., Can. (drā´tŭn văl´ē)	132-33	53°14'N	114°59'W
Dresden, Ger. (drās´dĕn)	194-95	51°03'N	13°44'E
Dreux, Fr. (drû)	196-97	48°44'N	1°22'E
Drin, stm., Alb. (drēn)	200-01	41°45'N	19°35'E
Drina, stm., Eur. (drē´nä)	200-01	44°54'N	19°21'E
Drøbak, Nor. (drû´bäk)	192-93	59°39'N	10°39'E
Drohobych, Ukr.	194-95	49°21'N	23°31'E
Druc', stm., Bela. (drōōt)	202-03	53°04'N	30°02'E
Druk-Yul, nation, Asia *see* Bhutan	206-07	27°30'N	90°30'E
Drumheller, Ab., Can. (drŭm-hĕl-ẽr)	132-33	51°28'N	112°42'W
Drummond Island, i., Mi., U.S. (drŭm´ŭnd ī´lȧnd)	116-17	46°0'N	83°40'W
Drummondville, Qc., Can. (drŭm´ŭnd-vĭl)	136-37	45°53'N	72°30'W
Drumright, Ok., U.S. (drŭm´rīt)	120-21	35°60'N	96°36'W
Drwęca, stm., Pol. (d'r-vän´tsȧ)	194-95	52°60'N	18°41'E
Dryden, On., Can. (drī-dĕn)	134-35	49°47'N	92°51'W
Dry Tortugas, is., Fl., U.S. (drī tôr-tōō´gäz)	125a	24°38'N	82°55'W
Dry Tortugas National Park, n.p., Fl., U.S. (drī tôr-tōō´gäz năsh´ŭn-ăl pärk)	125a	24°37'N	82°54'W
Duala, Camrn. *see* Douala	260-61	4°03'N	9°42'E
Duarte, Pico, mtn., Dom. Rep. (pēcô dŭŭ´ärtēh)	142-43	19°02'N	70°59'W
Dubai, U.A.E.	230-31	25°16'N	55°19'E
Dubawnt, stm., Can. (dōō-bônt´)	130-31	64°31'N	100°05'W
Dubawnt Lake, lk., Can. (dōō-bônt´ lāk)	130-31	63°08'N	101°30'W
Dubayy, U.A.E. *see* Dubai	230-31	25°16'N	55°19'E
Dubbo, Austl. (dŭb´ō)	276	32°15'S	148°36'E
Dublin, Ga., U.S. (dŭb´lĭn)	124-25	32°32'N	82°54'W
Dublin, Oh., U.S. (dŭb´lĭn)	116-17	40°06'N	83°07'W
Dublin, Tx., U.S. (dŭb´lĭn)	122-23	32°05'N	98°20'W
Dublin, nat. cap., Ire. (dŭb´lĭn)	190-91	53°21'N	6°15'W
Dubno, Ukr. (dōō´b-nô)	194-95	50°24'N	25°45'E
Du Bois, Pa., U.S. (dȯ-bois´)	116-17	41°07'N	78°46'W
Dubovka, Russia (dȯ-bôf´kȧ)	186-87	49°04'N	44°49'E
Dubrovka, Russia (dōō-brôf´kȧ)	202-03	53°42'N	33°31'E
Dubrovnik, Cro. (dȯ´brôv-nĕk)	200-01	42°39'N	18°06'E
Dubuque, Ia., U.S. (dȯ-būk´)	114-15	42°30'N	90°41'W
Duchesne, Ut., U.S. (dȯ-shān´)	118-19	40°10'N	110°24'W
Duck Lake, Sk., Can. (dŭk lāk)	134-35	52°49'N	106°14'W
Duck Valley Indian Reservation, ind. res., U.S. (dŭk văl´ē ĭn´dĭ-ăn rĕ-sẽr-vā´shĕn)	112-13	42°00'N	116°10'W
Dudinka, Russia (dōō-dĭn´kȧ)	218-19	69°24'N	86°11'E
Dudley, Eng., U.K. (dŭd´lĭ)	190-91	52°30'N	2°05'W
Duero, stm., Eur.	198-99	41°09'N	8°41'W
Dufourspitze, mtn., Eur.	194-95	45°55'N	7°52'E
Dugi Otok, i., Cro. (dōō´gē o´tôk)	200-01	43°59'N	15°04'E
Duisburg, Ger. (dōō´ĭs-bȯrgh)	194-95	51°26'N	6°47'E
Duitama, Col.	164-65	5°50'N	73°02'W
Dukhān, Qatar	230-31	25°25'N	50°48'E
Dukhovshchina, Russia (dōō-kôfsh-´chēnȧ)	202-03	55°12'N	32°25'E
Dulan, China	240-41	36°10'N	98°22'E
Dulce, Golfo, b., C.R. (gōl´fô dōōl´sä)	149	8°32'N	83°14'W
Duluth, Mn., U.S. (dȯ-lōōth´)	114-15	46°46'N	92°09'W
Dumaguete, Phil.	250	9°18'N	123°18'E
Dumai, Indon.	246-47	1°40'N	101°27'E
Dumali Point, c., Phil. (dōō-mä´lē point)	250	13°07'N	121°33'E
Dumaran Island, i., Phil.	250	10°33'N	119°51'E
Dumaring, Indon.	248-49	1°32'N	118°13'E
Dumfries, Scot., U.K. (dŭm-frēs´)	190-91	55°04'N	3°37'W
Duna, stm., Eur. *see* Danube	188-89	45°23'N	29°36'E
Dünaburg, Lat. *see* Daugavpils	192-93	55°53'N	26°32'E
Dunai, stm., Eur. *see* Danube	188-89	45°23'N	29°36'E
Dunaj, stm., Eur. *see* Danube	188-89	45°23'N	29°36'E
Dunărea, stm., Eur. *see* Danube	188-89	45°23'N	29°36'E
Dunav, stm., Eur. *see* Danube	188-89	45°23'N	29°36'E
Duncan, B.C., Can. (dŭŋ´kăn)	132-33	48°47'N	123°42'W
Duncan, Ok., U.S. (dŭŋ´kăn)	120-21	34°30'N	97°57'W
Duncan, stm., B.C., Can. (dŭŋ´kăn)	132-33	50°11'N	116°57'W
Duncansby Head, c., Scot., U.K. (dŭn´kănz-bĭ hĕd)	190-91	58°39'N	3°02'W
Dundalk, Ire. (dŭn´kôk)	190-91	54°01'N	6°24'W
Dundas, Lake, lk., Austl. (lāk dŭn-dȧs)	272-73	32°35'S	121°50'E
Dundas Island, i., B.C., Can. (dŭn-dăs´ ī´lȧnd)	132-33	54°33'N	130°55'W
Dún Dealgan, Ire. *see* Dundalk	190-91	54°01'N	6°24'W
Dundee, S. Afr.	269c	28°09'S	30°15'E
Dundee, Scot., U.K.	190-91	56°29'N	2°59'W
Dund-Us, Mong.	240-41	47°60'N	91°38'E
Dunedin, N.Z.	278	45°52'S	170°29'E
Dunfermline, Scot., U.K. (dŭn-fẽrm´lĭn)	190-91	56°04'N	3°29'W
Dūngarpur, India	234-35	23°50'N	73°43'E
Dungarvan, Ire. (dŭn-gár´văn)	190-91	52°06'N	7°38'W
Dungu, D.R.C.	267	3°37'N	28°34'E
Dunhua, China (dȯn-hwä)	244	43°22'N	128°14'E
Dunhuang, China	240-41	40°08'N	94°40'E
Dunkerque, Fr. (dŭɴ-kĕrk´)	196-97	51°03'N	2°23'E
Dunkirk, Fr. *see* Dunkerque	196-97	51°03'N	2°23'E
Dunkirk, In., U.S. (dŭn´kûrk)	116-17	40°22'N	85°12'W

n-sing; ŋ-baŋk; ɴ-nasalized n; nŏd; cŏmmit; ōld; ôbey; ôrder; oi-boil; fōōd; ȯ-as oo in foot; ou-out; s-soft; sh-dish; th-thin; pūre; ůnite; ûrn; stŭd; circŭs; ü-as in French tu; ´-indeterminate vowel.

Feature (Pronunciation)	Page	Lat.	Long.
Dunkirk, N.Y., U.S. (dŭn´kûrk)	**116-17**	42°29'N	79°19'W
Dún Laoghaire, Ire. (dŭn-lâ´rĕ)	**190-91**	53°17'N	6°08'W
Dunlap, Ia., U.S. (dŭn´l*ă*p)	**114-15**	41°51'N	95°36'W
Dunlap, Tn., U.S. (dŭn´l*ă*p)	**124-25**	35°22'N	85°23'W
Dunleary, Ire. see Dún Laoghaire	**190-91**	53°17'N	6°08'W
Dunmore, Pa., U.S. (dŭn´mōr)	**116-17**	41°27'N	75°38'W
Dunn, N.C., U.S. (dŭn)	**124-25**	35°18'N	78°37'W
Dunqulah, Sudan	**266**	19°11'N	30°28'E
Dunsmuir, Ca., U.S. (dŭnz´mūr)	**112-13**	41°13'N	122°17'W
Duolun, China (dwô-lo͞on)	**240-41**	42°12'N	116°28'E
Duomula, China	**234-35**	34°07'N	82°30'E
Duque de York, Isla, i., Chile	**171**	50°40'S	75°20'W
Duquesne, Pa., U.S. (do͝o-kān´)	**116-17**	40°22'N	79°51'W
Du Quoin, Il., U.S. (do͝o-kwoin´)	**116-17**	38°01'N	89°15'W
Durand, Mi., U.S. (dů-rănd´)	**116-17**	42°55'N	83°59'W
Durand, Wi., U.S. (dů-rănd´)	**114-15**	44°37'N	91°57'W
Durango, Mex. (do͞o-rä´n-gô)	**146-47**	24°02'N	104°41'W
Durango, Co., U.S. (do͝o-răŋ´gō)	**118-19**	37°17'N	107°52'W
Durango, state, Mex. (do͞o-rä´n-gô)	**122-23**	24°50'N	104°50'W
Durant, Ms., U.S. (dů-rănt´)	**124-25**	33°05'N	89°52'W
Durant, Ok., U.S. (dů-rănt´)	**120-21**	33°60'N	96°23'W
Durazno, Ur. (do͞o-räz´nō)	**173**	33°25'S	56°30'W
Durazzo, Alb. see Durrës	**200-01**	41°19'N	19°27'E
Durban, S. Afr. (dûr´b*ă*n)	**264-65**	29°55'S	30°56'E
Durbe, Lat. (do͞or´bĕ)	**192-93**	56°35'N	21°21'E
Düren, Ger. (dü´r*ĕ*n)	**194-95**	50°48'N	6°29'E
Durg, India	**234-35**	21°11'N	81°17'E
Durham, Eng., U.K. (dûr´ăm)	**190-91**	54°47'N	1°34'W
Durham, N.C., U.S.	**124-25**	35°60'N	78°54'W
Durmitor, mtn., Mont	**200-01**	43°08'N	19°01'E
Durrës, Alb. (dòr´ĕs)	**200-01**	41°19'N	19°27'E
Durrësi, Alb. see Durrës	**200-01**	41°19'N	19°27'E
D'Urville, Tanjung, c., Indon.	**277**	1°28'S	137°54'E
D'Urville Island, i., N.Z.	**278**	40°50'S	173°52'E
Dushan, China (do͞o-shän)	**238-39**	25°50'N	107°32'E
Dushanbe, nat. cap., Taj. (dū-shän´-b*ä*) (dū-shän-bă´)	**232-33**	38°34'N	68°47'E
Düsseldorf, Ger. (düs´*ĕ*l-dôrf)	**194-95**	51°14'N	6°48'E
Duyfken Point, c., Austl.	**277**	12°34'S	141°38'E
Duyun, China (do͞o-yòn)	**238-39**	26°16'N	107°30'E
Dwārka, India	**234-35**	22°14'N	68°59'E
Dwight, Il., U.S. (dwīt)	**116-17**	41°05'N	88°25'W
Dyat'kovo, Russia (dyät´kō-vō)	**202-03**	53°35'N	34°21'E
Dyersburg, Tn., U.S. (dī´ērz-bûrg)	**124-25**	36°02'N	89°23'W
Dyersville, Ia., U.S. (dī´ērz-vĭl)	**114-15**	42°29'N	91°07'W
Dzavhan, stm., Mong	**240-41**	48°53'N	93°26'E
Dzerzhinsk, Russia	**186-87**	56°15'N	43°24'E
Dzhambul, Kaz. see Taraz	**226**	42°54'N	71°21'E
Dzhankoi, Ukr.	**202-03**	45°43'N	34°23'E
Dzharylhach, ostriv, i., Ukr.	**202-03**	46°02'N	32°55'E
Dzhebariki-Khaya, Russia	**218-19**	62°11'N	135°46'E
Dzhezkazgan, Kaz. see Zhezqazghan	**226**	47°47'N	67°41'E
Dzhugdzhur, Khrebet, mts., Russia	**218-19**	58°0'N	136°00'E
Dzhugdzhur Range, mts., Russia (jo͞og-jo͞or´ rānj) see Dzhugdzhur, Khrebet	**218-19**	58°0'N	136°00'E
Dzhungarian Alatau Mountains, mts., Asia see Alataw Shan	**226**	45°0'N	81°00'E
Dzibalchén, Mex. (zē-bäl-chĕ´n)	**148**	19°28'N	89°44'W
Dzilam González, Mex. (zē-lä´m-gôn-zä´lĕz)	**148**	21°17'N	88°56'W
Dzitás, Mex. (zē-tá´s)	**148**	20°51'N	88°31'W
Dzuunmod, Mong.	**240-41**	47°43'N	106°57'E
E			
Eagle, Id., U.S. (ē´gl)	**112-13**	43°41'N	116°19'W
Eagle Grove, Ia., U.S. (ē´gl grōv)	**114-15**	42°40'N	93°54'W
Eagle Lake, Me., U.S. (ē´gl lāk)	**117a**	47°02'N	68°36'W
Eagle Lake, Tx., U.S. (ē´gl lāk)	**122-23**	29°35'N	96°20'W
Eagle Pass, Tx., U.S. (ē´gl pås)	**122-23**	28°42'N	100°29'W
Earle, Ar., U.S. (ûrl)	**124-25**	35°16'N	90°28'W
Earlington, Ky., U.S. (ûr´lĭng-t*ŭ*n)	**124-25**	37°16'N	87°31'W
Easley, S.C., U.S. (ēz´lĭ)	**124-25**	34°50'N	82°35'W
East Angus, Qc., Can. (ēst ăŋ´g*ŭ*s)	**136-37**	45°29'N	71°40'W
Eastbourne, Eng., U.K. (ēst´bôrn)	**190-91**	50°46'N	0°17'E
East Caicos, i., T./C. Is. (ēst kī´kōs)	**142-43**	21°42'N	71°29'W
East Cape, c., N.Z.	**278**	37°41'S	178°33'E
East Chicago, In., U.S. (ēst shĭ-kô´gō)	**116-17**	41°39'N	87°26'W
East China Sea, s., Asia (ēst chī´n*á* sē)	**222-23**	30°0'N	126°00'E
East Detroit, Mi., U.S. (ēst dê-troit´) see Eastpointe	**116-17**	42°28'N	82°57'W
Easter Island, i., Chile (ē´stēr ī´l*ă*nd) see Pascua, Isla de	**282-83**	27°07'S	109°22'W
Eastern Desert, des., Egypt see Arabian Desert	**266**	28°0'N	32°00'E
Eastern Ghāts, mts., India (ē´stērn ghäts) (ē´stērn ghôts)	**236**	14°0'N	78°50'E
East Falkland, i., Falk. Is.	**171**	51°53'S	59°11'W
East Grand Forks, Mn., U.S. (ēst grănd fôrks)	**114-15**	47°55'N	97°00'W
East Helena, Mt., U.S. (ēst hĕ-hē´n*á*)	**112-13**	46°35'N	111°55'W
East Jordan, Mi., U.S. (ēst jôr´d*ă*n)	**116-17**	45°09'N	85°07'W
Eastland, Tx., U.S. (ēst´l*ă*nd)	**120-21**	32°24'N	98°49'W
East Lansing, Mi., U.S. (ēst lăn´sĭng)	**116-17**	42°44'N	84°29'W
East Liverpool, Oh., U.S. (ēst lĭv´ēr-po͞ol)	**116-17**	40°38'N	80°35'W
East London, S. Afr. (ēst ŭn´d*ŭ*n)	**264-65**	32°60'S	27°54'E
Eastmain, Qc., Can.	**128-29**	52°13'N	78°33'W
Eastmain, stm., Qc., Can. (ēst´mān)	**130-31**	52°15'N	78°35'W
Eastmain-Opinaca, Réservoir, res., Qc., Can.	**130-31**	52°23'N	76°35'W
Eastman, Ga., U.S. (ēst´m*ă*n)	**124-25**	32°12'N	83°10'W
East Moline, Il., U.S. (ēst mô-lēn´)	**114-15**	41°32'N	90°25'W
East Nishnabotna, stm., Ia., U.S. (ēst nĭsh-n*á*-bŏt´n*á*)	**120-21**	40°39'N	95°38'W
East Orange, N.J., U.S. (ēst ŏr´ĕnj)	**116-17**	40°46'N	74°12'W
East Pakistan, nation, Asia see Bangladesh	**206-07**	24°0'N	90°00'E
East Peoria, Il., U.S. (ēst pē-ō´rĭ-*á*)	**116-17**	40°40'N	89°35'W
Eastpointe, Mi., U.S.	**116-17**	42°28'N	82°57'W
Eastport, Me., U.S. (ēst´pōrt)	**117a**	44°54'N	66°60'W
East Providence, R.I., U.S. (ēst prŏv´ĭ-dĕns)	**116-17**	41°49'N	71°23'W
East Saint Louis, Il., U.S.	**120-21**	38°37'N	90°09'W
East Sea, s., Asia see Japan, Sea of	**222-23**	40°0'N	135°00'E
East Siberian Sea, s., Russia (ēst sī-bĭr´y´n sē)	**218-19**	74°0'N	166°00'E
East Stroudsburg, Pa., U.S. (ēst stroudz´bûrg)	**116-17**	41°00'N	75°11'W
East Tawas, Mi., U.S. (ēst tô´w*ă*s)	**116-17**	44°17'N	83°28'W
East Timor, nation, Asia (ēst tē-mōr´)	**248-49**	8°35'S	126°00'E
Eaton, Oh., U.S. (ē´t*ŭ*n)	**116-17**	39°45'N	84°38'W
Eaton Rapids, Mi., U.S. (ē´t*ŭ*n răp´ĭdz)	**116-17**	42°30'N	84°39'W
Eatonton, Ga., U.S. (ētŭn-tŭn)	**124-25**	33°20'N	83°23'W
Eau Claire, Wi., U.S. (ō klâr´)	**114-15**	44°49'N	91°30'W
Eau Claire, Lac à l', lk., Qc., Can.	**130-31**	56°11'N	74°26'W
Eauripik, at., Micron.	**280-81**	6°41'N	143°03'E
Ebinur Hu, lk., China	**226**	44°56'N	82°52'E
Eboli, Italy (ĕb´ô-lē)	**200-01**	40°38'N	15°04'E
Ebolowa, Camrn.	**260-61**	2°55'N	11°09'E
Echoing, stm., Can. (ĕk´ō-ĭng)	**134-35**	55°51'N	92°04'W
Echuca, Austl. (ê-chò´kå)	**276**	36°08'S	144°45'E
Écija, Spain (ā´thē-hä)	**198-99**	37°32'N	5°05'W
Ecuador, nation, S.A. (ĕk´w*á*-dôr)	**158**	2°0'S	77°30'W
Eddyville, Ia., U.S. (ĕd´ĭ-vĭl)	**114-15**	41°09'N	92°38'W
Eddyville, Ky., U.S. (ĕd´ĭ-vĭl)	**124-25**	37°06'N	88°05'W
Ede, Nig.	**260a**	7°44'N	4°25'E
Edéa, Camrn. (ĕ-dā´ä)	**260-61**	3°48'N	10°08'E
Eden, Austl.	**276**	37°04'S	149°54'E
Eden, N.C., U.S. (ē´d*ĕ*n)	**124-25**	36°29'N	79°46'W
Eden, Tx., U.S. (ē´d*ĕ*n)	**122-23**	31°13'N	99°51'W
Eden Prairie, Mn., U.S. (ē´d*ĕ*n prâr´ĭ)	**114-15**	44°51'N	93°28'W
Edenton, N.C., U.S. (ē´d*ĕ*n-t*ŭ*n)	**124-25**	36°04'N	76°37'W
Edenville, S. Afr. (ē´d'n-vĭl)	**269c**	27°34'S	27°41'E
Edfu, Egypt	**268b**	24°58'N	32°52'E
Edgefield, S.C., U.S. (ĕj´fēld)	**124-25**	33°47'N	81°56'W
Edgeley, N.D., U.S. (ĕj´lĭ)	**114-15**	46°21'N	98°43'W
Edgemont, S.D., U.S. (ĕj´mŏnt)	**114-15**	43°18'N	103°48'W
Edgerton, Wi., U.S. (ĕj´ēr-t*ŭ*n)	**116-17**	42°50'N	89°04'W
Edinburg, Tx., U.S. (ĕd´'n-bûrg)	**122-23**	26°18'N	98°10'W
Edinburgh, Scot., U.K. (ĕd´'n-bŭr-ô)	**190-91**	55°57'N	3°13'W
Edirne, Tur.	**200-01**	41°41'N	26°34'E
Edmond, Ok., U.S. (ĕd´m*ŭ*nd)	**120-21**	35°39'N	97°29'W
Edmonton, Ab., Can. (ĕd´m*ŭ*n-t*ŭ*n)	**132-33**	53°33'N	113°30'W
Edmundston, N.B., Can. (ĕd´m*ŭ*n-st*ŭ*n)	**138-39**	47°22'N	68°19'W
Edna, Tx., U.S. (ĕd´n*á*)	**122-23**	28°59'N	96°39'W
Édouard, Lac, lk., Afr. see Edward, Lake	**267**	0°23'S	29°36'E
Edremit, Tur. (ĕd-rĕ-mēt´)	**200-01**	39°36'N	27°01'E
Edson, Ab., Can. (ĕd´sŭn)	**132-33**	53°35'N	116°26'W
Eduardo Castex, Arg.	**173**	35°55'S	64°18'W
Edward, Lake, lk., Afr. (lăk ĕd´wērd)	**267**	0°23'S	29°36'E
Edwards Plateau, plat., Tx., U.S.	**122-23**	30°46'N	100°47'W
Edwardsville, Il., U.S. (ĕd´wērdz-vĭl)	**120-21**	38°48'N	89°57'W
Edward VII Peninsula, pen., Ant.	**287**	77°40'S	154°60'W
Eel, stm., Ca., U.S. (ēl)	**110-11**	40°38'N	124°20'W
Eesti, nation, Eur. see Estonia	**174-75**	59°0'N	26°00'E
Éfaté, i., Vanuatu (å-fä´tā)	**279g**	17°40'S	168°25'E
Effigy Mounds National Monument, n.p., Ia., U.S. (ĕf´ĭ-jŭ mounds năsh´ŭn-*ă*l mŏn´*ū*-m*ĕ*nt)	**114-15**	43°06'N	91°13'W
Effingham, Il., U.S. (ĕf´ĭng-hăm)	**116-17**	39°07'N	88°33'W
Eg, stm., Mong.	**240-41**	49°23'N	103°38'E
Egadi, Isole, is., Italy (ĕ´sō-lĕ-ĕ´gä-dē)	**200-01**	37°58'N	12°16'E
Ege Denizi, s., see Aegean Sea	**200-01**	38°30'N	25°00'E
Eger, Czech Rep. see Cheb	**194-95**	50°05'N	12°22'E
Eger, Hung. (ĕ gĕr)	**194-95**	47°54'N	20°23'E
Egersund, Nor. (ĕ´ghĕr-sòn')	**192-93**	58°27'N	6°00'E
Egmont, Cape, c., N.Z. (kāp ĕg´mŏnt)	**278**	39°17'S	173°45'E
Eğridir Gölü, lk., Tur.	**186-87**	38°02'N	30°53'E
Egum Atoll, at., Pap. N. Gui.	**277**	9°25'S	151°55'E
Egvekinot, Russia	**218-19**	66°18'N	179°11'W
Egypt, nation, Afr. (ē´jĭpt)	**253**	27°0'N	30°00'E
Eichstätt, Ger. (īk´shtät)	**194-95**	48°54'N	11°11'E
Eidfjord, Nor. (ĕĭd´fyōr)	**192-93**	60°28'N	7°05'E
Eidsvoll, Nor. (ĭdhs´vôl)	**192-93**	60°19'N	11°14'E
Eifel, mts., Ger. (ī´f*ĕ*l)	**194-95**	50°14'N	6°42'E
Eight Degree Channel, strt., Asia	**236**	8°0'N	73°00'E
Einbeck, Ger. (īn´bĕk)	**194-95**	51°49'N	9°52'E
Eindhoven, Neth. (ĭnd´hō-v*ĕ*n)	**190-91**	51°26'N	5°29'E
Éire, nation, Eur. see Ireland	**174-75**	53°0'N	8°00'W
Eirunepé, Braz.	**166-67**	6°39'S	69°52'W
Eisenach, Ger. (ī´zĕn-äκ)	**194-95**	50°59'N	10°19'E
Eivissa, Spain	**198-99**	38°55'N	1°25'E
Eivissa, i., Spain	**198-99**	39°0'N	1°25'E
Ejin Qi, China	**240-41**	41°52'N	100°56'E
Ejmiatsin, Arm.	**227**	40°10'N	44°18'E
Ejutla de Crespo, Mex. (å-hōt´lä dā krās´pō)	**146-47**	16°34'N	96°44'W
Ekenäs, Fin. (ĕ´kĕ-nâs)	**192-93**	59°58'N	23°26'E
Ekibastuz, Kaz.	**226**	51°43'N	75°20'E
Ekimchan, Russia	**218-19**	53°04'N	132°57'E
Eko, Nig. see Lagos	**260a**	6°27'N	3°24'E
Ekwan, stm., On., Can.	**130-31**	53°12'N	82°14'W
El Aaiún, nat. cap., W. Sah. see Laayoune	**258-59**	27°10'N	13°12'W
El Abiodh Sidi Cheikh, Alg.	**188-89**	32°53'N	0°32'E
El Affroun, Alg. (ĕl åf-froun´)	**269b**	36°28'N	2°37'E
El-Agheila, Libya see Al-'Uqaylah	**188-89**	30°15'N	19°12'E
El-Alamein, Egypt	**188-89**	30°49'N	28°58'E
Elands, stm., S. Afr. (ĕlånds)	**269c**	25°17'S	27°32'E
El-Arish, Egypt	**268b**	31°08'N	33°50'E
El Asnam, Alg. see Chlef	**198-99**	36°10'N	1°20'E
Elat, Isr.	**228-29**	29°33'N	34°57'E
Elat, Gulf of, b., see Aqaba, Gulf of	**228-29**	29°05'N	34°44'E
Elath, Isr. see Elat	**228-29**	29°33'N	34°57'E
Elazığ, Tur. (ĕl-ä´zĕz)	**186-87**	38°41'N	39°15'E
Elba, Al., U.S. (ĕl´bå)	**124-25**	31°25'N	86°04'W
Elba, Isola d', i., Italy (ê-sō lä-d-ĕl´b*á*)	**200-01**	42°46'N	10°17'E
El Banco, Col. (ĕl băn´cō)	**164-65**	9°01'N	73°58'W
Elbe, stm., Eur. (ĕl´bĕ)	**194-95**	53°53'N	9°01'E
Elbert, Mount, mtn., Co., U.S. (mount ĕl´bērt)	**118-19**	39°07'N	106°27'W
Elberton, Ga., U.S. (ĕl´bēr-t*ŭ*n)	**124-25**	34°07'N	82°51'W
Elbeuf, Fr. (ĕl-bûf´)	**196-97**	49°17'N	1°01'E
Elbing, Pol. see Elbląg	**194-95**	54°10'N	19°24'E
Elbistan, Tur. (ĕl-bē-stän´)	**186-87**	38°13'N	37°12'E
Elbląg, Pol. (ĕl´blăŋg)	**194-95**	54°10'N	19°24'E
El Bonillo, Spain (ĕl bō-nēl´yô)	**198-99**	38°57'N	2°33'W
Elbow Lake, Mn., U.S. (ĕl´bō lāk)	**114-15**	45°60'N	95°59'W
El'brus, Gora, mtn., Russia (gå-rä´ĕl´bròs´)	**227**	43°21'N	42°26'E
Elburz Mountains, mts., Iran (ĕl´bòrz´ moun´tĭnz)	**232-33**	36°0'N	53°00'E
El Cajon, Ca., U.S.	**118-19**	32°48'N	116°57'W
El Calafate, Arg.	**171**	50°21'S	72°17'W
El Campo, Tx., U.S. (ĕl-kăm´pō)	**122-23**	29°11'N	96°16'W
El Carmen de Bolívar, Col.	**164-65**	9°43'N	75°07'W
El Centro, Ca., U.S. (ĕl-sĕn´trô)	**118-19**	32°48'N	115°33'W
Elche, Spain see Elx	**198-99**	38°15'N	0°42'W
Elda, Spain (ĕl´dä)	**198-99**	38°29'N	0°47'W
El'dikan, Russia	**218-19**	60°46'N	135°09'E
El Djazaïr, nation, Afr. see Algeria	**253**	28°0'N	3°00'E
El Djazaïr, nat. cap., Alg. see Algiers	**269b**	36°46'N	3°03'E
Eldon, Mo., U.S. (ĕl-d*ŭ*n)	**120-21**	38°21'N	92°35'W
Eldora, Ia., U.S. (ĕl-dō´r*á*)	**114-15**	42°22'N	93°06'W
Eldorado, Arg.	**173**	26°24'S	54°38'W
El Dorado, Ar., U.S. (ĕl dô-rä´dō)	**120-21**	33°12'N	92°41'W
El Dorado, Ks., U.S. (ĕl dô-rä´dō)	**120-21**	37°49'N	96°51'W
Eldoret, Kenya (ĕl-dô-rĕt´)	**267**	0°31'N	35°17'E
Electra, Tx., U.S. (ê-lĕk´tr*á*)	**120-21**	34°03'N	98°55'W
Elek, stm., Asia	**186-87**	51°30'N	53°20'E
Elektrostal', Russia (ĕl-yĕk´trō-stál)	**202-03**	55°47'N	38°28'E

ăt; fināl; rāte; senåte; ärm; åsk; sofá; fâre; ch-choose; dh-as th in other; bē; êvent; bĕt; recĕnt; cratẽr; g-gō; gh-guttural g; bĭt; ĭ-short neutral; rīde; κ-guttural k as ch in German ich;

Feature (Pronunciation)	Page	Lat.	Long.
El Encanto, Col.	164-65	1°42′S	73°14′W
Elephant Butte Reservoir, res., N.M., U.S. (ĕl′ĕ-fănt būt rĕ′sĕr-vwär)	118-19	33°17′N	107°10′W
Elets, Russia	202-03	52°37′N	38°30′E
Eleuthera, i., Bah. (ē-lū′thēr-à)	142-43	25°11′N	76°13′W
El-Fayoum, Egypt	268b	29°19′N	30°50′E
El Ferrol del Caudillo, Spain see Ferrol	198-99	43°29′N	8°14′W
El Galpón, Arg.	168-69	25°24′S	64°38′W
Elgin, Scot., U.K. (ĕl′jĭn)	190-91	57°39′N	3°19′W
Elgin, Il., U.S. (ĕl′jĭn)	116-17	42°02′N	88°17′W
Elgin, Or., U.S. (ĕl′jĭn)	112-13	45°34′N	117°55′W
Elgin, Tx., U.S. (ĕl′jĭn)	122-23	30°21′N	97°22′W
El-Gîza, Egypt see Giza	268b	30°01′N	31°13′E
El Golea, Alg.	188-89	30°33′N	2°54′E
Elgon, Mount, mtn., Afr. (mount ĕl′gŏn)	267	1°08′N	34°33′E
El Guapo, Ven. (ĕl-gwá′pō)	163b	10°09′N	65°58′W
El Ḩank, clf., Afr.	258-59	24°23′N	6°36′W
El Hierro, i., Spain	199d	27°45′N	18°00′W
Elila, stm., D.R.C. (ĕ-lē′là)	262-63	2°44′S	25°53′E
Élisabethville, D.R.C. see Lubumbashi	262-63	11°41′S	27°28′E
Elisenvaara, Russia (ā-lē′sĕn-vä′rà)	192-93	61°24′N	29°46′E
El-Iskandarîya, Egypt see Alexandria	268b	31°11′N	29°54′E
Elista, Russia	186-87	46°19′N	44°16′E
Elizabeth, Austl.	276	34°43′S	138°40′E
Elizabeth City, N.C., U.S. (ē-lĭz′à-bĕth sĭ′tĭ)	124-25	36°18′N	76°13′W
Elizabethton, Tn., U.S. (ē-lĭz-à-bĕth′tŭn)	124-25	36°21′N	82°14′W
Elizabethtown, Ky., U.S. (ē-lĭz′ă-bĕth-toun)	116-17	37°42′N	85°52′W
Elizabethtown, Pa., U.S. (ē-lĭz′ă-bĕth-toun)	116-17	40°09′N	76°37′W
El-Jadida, Mor.	269a	33°15′N	8°31′W
Elk, stm., B.C., Can. (ĕlk)	132-33	49°10′N	115°14′W
Elk City, Ok., U.S. (ĕlk sĭ′tē)	120-21	35°25′N	99°25′W
El Kef, Tun. (ĕl-xĕf′)	184-85	36°11′N	8°43′E
El-Khârga, Egypt	266	25°27′N	30°33′E
Elkhart, In., U.S. (ĕlk′härt)	116-17	41°42′N	85°57′W
Elkhorn, Wi., U.S. (ĕlk′hôrn)	116-17	42°40′N	88°33′W
Elkin, N.C., U.S. (ĕl′kĭn)	124-25	36°15′N	80°51′W
Elk Island National Park, n.p., Ab., Can. (ĕlk ī′lànd năsh′ŭn-ăl pärk)	132-33	53°36′N	112°54′W
Elko, Nv., U.S. (ĕl′kō)	112-13	40°50′N	115°46′W
Elk Point, S.D., U.S. (ĕlk point)	114-15	42°41′N	96°41′W
Elk Rapids, Mi., U.S. (ĕlk răp′ĭdz)	116-17	44°53′N	85°24′W
Elk River, Mn., U.S. (ĕlk rĭv′ĕr)	114-15	45°18′N	93°35′W
Elkton, Ky., U.S. (ĕlk′tŭn)	124-25	36°49′N	87°09′W
Elkton, S.D., U.S. (ĕlk′tŭn)	114-15	44°14′N	96°29′W
Ellás, nation, Eur. see Greece	174-75	39°0′N	22°00′E
Ellendale, N.D., U.S. (ĕl′ĕn-dāl)	114-15	46°00′N	98°32′W
Ellensburg, Wa., U.S. (ĕl′ĕnz-bûrg)	112-13	46°60′N	120°32′W
Ellesmere Island, i., Nu., Can. (ĕlz′mēr ī′lănd)	86	81°0′N	80°00′W
Ellice Islands, nation, Oc. see Tuvalu	280-81	8°0′S	178°00′E
Elliot Lake, On., Can.	136-37	46°23′N	82°39′W
Elliston, Austl.	270-71	33°39′S	134°54′E
Ellisville, Ms., U.S. (ĕl′ĭs-vĭl)	124-25	31°36′N	89°12′W
Ellore, India see Elūru	236	16°43′N	81°07′E
Ellsworth, Ks., U.S. (ĕlz′wûrth)	120-21	38°44′N	98°13′W
Elma, Wa., U.S. (ĕl′mà)	112-13	47°00′N	123°24′W
El-Mahalla el-Kubra, Egypt	268b	30°58′N	31°10′E
El-Mansûra, Egypt	268b	31°02′N	31°23′E
Elmhurst, Il., U.S. (ĕlm′hûrst)	116-17	41°53′N	87°57′W
El-Minya, Egypt	268b	28°06′N	30°45′E
Elmira, N.Y., U.S.	116-17	42°05′N	76°48′W
Elmira Heights, N.Y., U.S. (ĕl-mī′rà hīts)	116-17	42°09′N	76°50′W
El Nevado, Cerro, mtn., Arg. see Nevado, Cerro	171	35°34′S	68°28′W
El-Obeid, Sudan see Al-Ubayyiḍ	266	13°11′N	30°13′E
El Oued, Alg.	188-89	33°21′N	6°53′E
El Pao, Ven. (ĕl pá′ō)	163b	9°38′N	68°08′W
El Paso, Tx., U.S. (ĕl-pas′ō)	118-19	31°48′N	106°27′W
El Paso de Robles, Ca., U.S. see Paso Robles	118-19	35°38′N	120°41′W
El Pital, Cerro, mtn., N.A.	148	14°23′N	89°08′W
El Porvenir, Pan. (ĕl-pôr-vä-nēr′)	150	9°33′N	78°59′W
El-Qâhira, nat. cap., Egypt see Cairo	268b	30°03′N	31°14′E
El Reno, Ok., U.S. (ĕl-rē′nō)	120-21	35°32′N	97°57′W
El Salto, Mex. (ĕl-säl′tō)	146-47	23°46′N	105°21′W
El Salvador, nation, N.A. (ĕl säl′vä-dôr)	85	13°50′N	88°55′W
Elsaß, hist. reg., Fr. see Alsace	196-97	48°30′N	7°30′E
Elsberry, Mo., U.S. (ĕlz′bĕr-ĭ)	120-21	39°10′N	90°48′W
Elsinore, Den. see Helsingør	192-93	56°02′N	12°37′E
El-Suweis, Egypt see Suez	268b	29°58′N	32°33′E
El Tajín, hist., Mex.	146-47	20°27′N	97°23′W
El Tigre, Ven. (ĕl-tē′grĕ)	163b	8°54′N	64°15′W
El-Uqsor, Egypt see Luxor	268b	25°42′N	32°39′E
Elūru, India	236	16°43′N	81°07′E
Elvas, Port. (ĕl′väzh)	198-99	38°53′N	7°10′W
Elverum, Nor. (ĕl′vĕ-rŏŏm)	192-93	60°53′N	11°34′E
El Viejo, Nic. (ĕl-vyĕ′kŏ)	149	12°40′N	87°10′W
Elwood, In., U.S. (ĕ′wŏŏd)	116-17	40°16′N	85°50′W
Elx, Spain	198-99	38°15′N	0°42′W
Ely, Mn., U.S. (ē′lĭ)	114-15	47°54′N	91°52′W
Ely, Nv., U.S.	118-19	39°15′N	114°53′W
Elyria, Oh., U.S. (ē-lĭr′ĭ-à)	116-17	41°22′N	82°06′W
Émaé, i., Vanuatu	279g	17°04′S	168°22′E
Emāmshahr, Iran see Shāhrūd	232-33	36°25′N	54°58′E
Embi, Kaz.	226	48°50′N	58°09′E
Embira, stm., Braz. see Envira	166-67	6°42′S	69°48′W
Embu, Kenya	267	0°32′S	37°27′E
Emden, Ger. (ĕm′dĕn)	194-95	53°22′N	7°12′E
Emerald, Austl.	277	23°31′S	148°10′E
Emiliano Zapata, Mex. (ĕ-mē-lyá′nô-zä-pá′tá)	148	17°45′N	91°46′W
Emiliano Zapata, Mex. (ĕ-mē-lyá′nô-zä-pá′tá)	146-47	18°51′N	99°11′W
Eminence, Ky., U.S. (ĕm′ĭ-nĕns)	116-17	38°22′N	85°11′W
Emmen, Neth. (ĕm′ĕn)	190-91	52°47′N	6°54′E
Emmetsburg, Ia., U.S. (ĕm′ĕts-bûrg)	114-15	43°07′N	94°41′W
Emmett, Id., U.S. (ĕm′ĕt)	112-13	43°53′N	116°30′W
Emory Peak, mtn., Tx., U.S. (ĕ′mŏ-rē pēk)	122-23	29°14′N	103°19′W
Empalme, Mex.	144-45	27°58′N	110°49′W
Empedrado, Arg.	173	27°57′S	58°48′W
Empoli, Italy (ām′pō-lē)	200-01	43°43′N	10°57′E
Emporia, Ks., U.S. (ĕm-pō′rĭ-à)	120-21	38°24′N	96°11′W
Emporia, Va., U.S. (ĕm-pō′rĭ-à)	124-25	36°42′N	77°33′W
Emporium, Pa., U.S. (ĕm-pō′rĭ-ŭm)	116-17	41°30′N	78°15′W
Empty Quarter, des., Asia see Rub'al-Khali	220-21	20°0′N	51°00′E
En, stm., Eur. see Inn	194-95	48°34′N	13°28′E
Encarnación, Para. (ĕn-kär-nä-syōn′)	173	27°20′S	55°52′W
Encinal, Tx., U.S. (ĕn′sĭ-nôl)	122-23	28°02′N	99°21′W
Encontrados, Ven. (ĕn-kōn-trä′dōs)	164-65	9°03′N	72°14′W
Encounter Bay, b., Austl. (ĕn-koun′tĕr bā)	276	35°35′S	138°44′E
Ende, Indon.	248-49	8°50′S	121°40′E
Enderbury, at., Kir. (ĕn′dĕr-bûrĭ)	280-81	3°08′S	171°05′W
Enderby Land, reg., Ant. (ĕn′dĕr-bĭĭ lănd)	287	68°05′S	52°53′E
Enderlin, N.D., U.S. (ĕn′dĕr-lĭn)	114-15	46°37′N	97°36′W
Endicott, N.Y., U.S. (ĕn′dĭ-kŏt)	116-17	42°07′N	76°04′W
Ene, stm., Peru	170	11°10′S	74°15′W
Enewetak, at., Marsh. Is.	280-81	11°39′N	162°17′E
Enfield, N.C., U.S. (ĕn′fēld)	124-25	36°11′N	77°40′W
Engaño, Cabo, c., Dom. Rep. (ká′-bô-ĕn-gä-nô)	142-43	18°37′N	68°20′W
Engel's, Russia (ĕn′gĕls)	186-87	51°29′N	46°08′E
Enggano, Pulau, i., Indon. (pōō-lou ĕng-gä′nō)	246-47	5°24′S	102°16′E
England, Ar., U.S. (ĭŋ′glănd)	124-25	34°33′N	91°58′W
England, state, U.K. (ĭŋ′glănd)	190-91	52°30′N	1°30′W
Englehart, On., Can.	136-37	47°49′N	79°52′W
Englewood, Co., U.S. (ĕn′g′l-wŏŏd)	120-21	39°39′N	104°59′W
English, stm., On., Can. (ĭn′glĭsh)	134-35	50°11′N	95°03′W
English Bāzār, India see Ingrāj Bāzār	234-35	24°60′N	88°09′E
English Channel, strt., Eur. (ĭn′glĭsh chăn′ĕl)	190-91	50°13′N	2°20′W
Enguri, stm., Geor. (ĕn-gôr′)	227	42°24′N	41°33′E
Enid, Ok., U.S. (ē′nĭd)	120-21	36°24′N	97°52′W
Eniwetok, at., Marsh. Is. see Enewetak	280-81	11°39′N	162°17′E
eNjesuthi, mtn., Afr.	269c	29°09′S	29°23′E
Enköping, Swe. (ĕn′kû-pĭng)	192-93	59°38′N	17°05′E
Ennedi, plat., Chad (ĕn-nĕd′ē)	258-59	17°15′N	22°00′E
Enniskillen, N. Ire., U.K. (ĕn-ĭs-kĭl′ĕn)	190-91	54°21′N	7°38′W
Enriquillo, Dom. Rep. (ĕn-rē-kē′l-yō)	142-43	17°53′N	71°16′W
Enriquillo, Lago, lk., Dom. Rep. (lä′gô-ĕn-rē-kē′l-yō)	142-43	18°29′N	71°38′W
Enschede, Neth. (ĕns′kà-dĕ)	190-91	52°13′N	6°54′E
Ensenada, Mex. (ĕn-sĕ-nä′dä)	144-45	31°52′N	116°37′W
Enshi, China (ŭn-shr)	238-39	30°14′N	109°27′E
Entebbe, Ug.	267	0°04′N	32°28′E
Enterprise, Or., U.S. (ĕn′tĕr-prīz)	112-13	45°26′N	117°17′W
Enugu, Nig. (ĕ-nōō′gōō)	260a	6°27′N	7°27′E
Enumclaw, Wa., U.S. (ĕn′ŭm-klô)	112-13	47°12′N	121°59′W
Enurmino, Russia	126	66°55′N	171°48′W
Envigado, Col. (ĕn-vē-gá′dō)	163c	6°10′N	75°35′W
Envira, stm., Braz.	166-67	6°42′S	69°48′W
Épernay, Fr. (ā-pĕr-nĕ′)	196-97	49°03′N	3°58′E
Ephraim, Ut., U.S. (ē′frā-ĭm)	118-19	39°22′N	111°35′W
Ephrata, Pa., U.S. (ĕfrā′tà)	116-17	40°11′N	76°11′W
Ephrata, Wa., U.S. (ĕfrā′tà)	112-13	47°19′N	119°33′W
Épi, i., Vanuatu	279g	16°43′S	168°16′E
Épinal, Fr. (ā-pē-nál′)	196-97	48°11′N	6°26′E
Equatorial Guinea, nation, Afr. (ĕ-kwä-tô′rĭ-ăl gĭn′ē)	253	2°0′N	9°00′E
Erciyes Dağı, vol., Tur.	186-87	38°32′N	35°28′E
Erdenebulgan, Mong.	240-41	50°06′N	101°35′E
Erding, Ger. (ĕr′dēng)	194-95	48°18′N	11°55′E
Erechim, Braz. (ĕ-rĕ-shē′n)	168-69	27°38′S	52°17′W
Ereğli, Tur. (ĕ-rå′ĭ-le)	186-87	37°31′N	34°04′E
Ereğli, Tur. (ĕ-rå′ĭ-le)	186-87	41°17′N	31°26′E
Erenhot, China	240-41	43°39′N	111°60′E
Erfoud, Mor.	188-89	31°26′N	4°14′W
Erfurt, Ger. (ĕr′fŏŏrt)	194-95	50°58′N	11°01′E
Erguig, Bahr, stm., Chad	260-61	11°21′N	15°24′E
Ergun, stm., Asia	240-41	53°19′N	121°27′E
Er Hai, lk., China	238-39	25°48′N	100°11′E
Erick, Ok., U.S. (âr′ĭk)	120-21	35°14′N	99°52′W
Erie, Pa., U.S.	116-17	42°07′N	80°03′W
Erie, Lake, lk., N.A. (lāk ē′rĭ)	116-17	42°15′N	80°60′W
Erimo-misaki, c., Japan (ā′rē-mō mē′sä-kē)	244	41°55′N	143°15′E
Eritrea, nation, Afr. (ā-rē-trā′à)	266	15°20′N	39°00′E
Erlangen, Ger. (ĕr′läng-ĕn)	194-95	49°36′N	11°01′E
Ermelo, S. Afr.	269c	26°31′S	29°59′E
Erne, Lower Lough, lk., N. Ire., U.K. (lō′ĕr lŏk ûrn)	190-91	54°28′N	7°45′W
Erode, India	236	11°21′N	77°44′E
Eromanga, Austl.	276	26°40′S	143°16′E
Er-Rachidia, Mor.	188-89	31°57′N	4°26′W
Erromango, i., Vanuatu	279g	18°45′S	169°05′E
Ertis, Kaz.	226	53°20′N	75°28′E
Ertis, stm., Asia see Irtysh	218-19	61°05′N	68°47′E
Ertix, stm., Asia see Irtysh	218-19	61°05′N	68°47′E
Ērtra, nation, Afr. see Eritrea	266	15°20′N	39°00′E
Erwin, Tn., U.S. (ûr′wĭn)	124-25	36°08′N	82°25′W
Erzin, Russia	240-41	50°15′N	95°09′E
Erzincan, Tur. (ĕr-zĭn-jän′)	227	39°44′N	39°31′E
Erzurum, Tur. (ĕrz′rōōm′)	227	39°54′N	41°17′E
Esashi, Japan (ĕs′ä-shē)	244	41°52′N	140°10′E
Esbjerg, Den. (ĕs′byĕrgh)	192-93	55°28′N	8°27′E
Escalante, Ut., U.S. (ĕs-kà-lăn′tē)	118-19	37°46′N	111°36′W
Escambia, stm., Fl., U.S. (ĕs-kăm′bĭ-à)	124-25	30°32′N	87°11′W
Escanaba, Mi., U.S. (ĕs-kà-nô′bà)	116-17	45°45′N	87°04′W
Escarpada Point, c., Phil.	250	18°31′N	122°13′E
Escondido, Ca., U.S. (ĕs-kŏn-dē′dō)	118-19	33°07′N	117°05′W
Escuinapa de Hidalgo, Mex.	146-47	22°51′N	105°48′W
Escuintla, Guat. (ĕs-kwēn′tlä)	148	14°18′N	90°47′W
Esenguly, Turkmen.	232-33	37°27′N	54°01′E
Eşfahān, Iran	232-33	32°39′N	51°40′E
Esh-Sham, nat. cap., Syria see Damascus	228-29	33°31′N	36°18′E
Esil, Kaz.	226	51°57′N	66°24′E
Esil, stm., Asia see Ishim	218-19	57°43′N	71°12′E
Eskifjördur, Ice. (ĕs′kē-fyŭr′dōōr)	190a	65°04′N	13°57′W
Eskilstuna, Swe. (ă′shĕl-stü-na)	192-93	59°22′N	16°31′E
Eskimo Point, Nu., Can. see Arviat	128-29	61°08′N	94°07′W
Eskişehir, Tur. (ĕs-kē-shĕ′h′r)	186-87	39°47′N	30°31′E
Esla, stm., Spain (ĕs-lä)	198-99	41°29′N	6°03′W
Eslāmshahr, Iran	232-33	35°33′N	51°14′E
Eslöv, Swe. (ĕs′lûv)	192-93	55°50′N	13°19′E
Esmeralda, Isla, i., Chile	171	48°57′S	75°25′W
Esmeraldas, Ec. (ĕs-mā-räl′däs)	170	0°57′N	79°39′W
España, nation, Eur. see Spain	174-75	40°0′N	4°00′W
Espanola, On., Can. (ĕs-pà-nō′là)	136-37	46°16′N	81°47′W
Española, Isla, i., Ec.	170a	1°23′S	89°42′W
Esperance, Austl. (ĕs′pē-răns)	270-71	33°51′S	121°53′E
Esperanza, Arg.	173	31°27′S	60°56′W
Espichel, Cabo, c., Port. (ká′bō-ĕs-pē-shĕl′)	198-99	38°25′N	9°13′W
Espinal, Col. (ĕs-pē-näl′)	163c	4°09′N	74°53′W
Espinhaço, Serra do, mts., Braz. (sĕ′r-rä-dô-ĕs-pē-nà-sō)	172	17°25′S	43°40′W
Espírito Santo, Braz. (ĕs-pē′rē-tô-sán′tô) see Vila Velha	172	20°20′S	40°17′W
Espírito Santo, state, Braz. (ĕs-pē′rē-tô-sán′tô)	172	19°30′S	40°30′W
Espiritu Santo, i., Vanuatu (ĕs-pē′rē-tōō sän′tō)	279g	15°15′S	166°50′E
Espíritu Santo, Isla del, i., Mex.	144-45	24°29′N	110°21′W
Espita, Mex. (ĕs-pē′tä)	148	21°02′N	88°18′W
Esposende, Port. (ĕs-pō-zĕn′dā)	198-99	41°32′N	8°47′W
Esquel, Arg. (ĕs-kĕ′l)	171	42°54′S	71°19′W

n-sing; ŋ-baŋk; ɴ-nasalized n; nŏd; cŏmmit; ōld; ôbey; ôrder; oi-boil; fōōd; ŏŏ-as oo in foot; ou-out; s-soft; sh-dish; th-thin; pūre; ūnite; ûrn; stŭd; circŭs; ü-as in French tu; ′-indeterminate vowel.

Feature (Pronunciation)	Page	Lat.	Long.
Esquimalt, B.C., Can. (ĕs-kwī´mŏlt)	**132-33**	48°26'N	123°24'W
Esquina, Arg.	**173**	30°01'S	59°32'W
Essaouira, Mor.	**258-59**	31°30'N	9°45'W
Essen, Ger. (ĕs´sĕn)	**194-95**	51°28'N	7°01'E
Essequibo, stm., Guy. (ĕs-ā-kē´bō)	**164-65**	7°04'N	58°26'W
Essex, Md., U.S. (ĕs´ĕks)	**116-17**	39°19'N	76°29'W
Essexville, Mi., U.S. (ĕs´ĕks-vĭl)	**116-17**	43°37'N	83°50'W
Est, Pointe de l', c., Qc., Can.	**138-39**	49°08'N	61°41'W
Estación Colonia Alvear Norte, Arg. *see* General Alvear	**171**	34°59'S	67°42'W
Estación Foguista J. F. Juárez, Arg. *see* El Galpón	**168-69**	25°24'S	64°38'W
Estación Gobernador Vera, Arg. *see* Vera	**173**	29°28'S	60°13'W
Estación J. J. Castelli, Arg. *see* Castelli	**168-69**	25°57'S	60°37'W
Estados, Isla de los, i., Arg.	**171**	54°48'S	64°33'W
Estância, Braz. (ĕs-tän´sĭ-ä)	**166-67**	11°16'S	37°26'W
Estarreja, Port. (ĕ-tär-rā´zhä)	**198-99**	40°45'N	8°34'W
Estcourt, S. Afr. (ĕst-coort)	**269c**	29°00'S	29°53'E
Estelí, Nic.	**149**	13°05'N	86°22'W
Estepona, Spain (ĕs-tå-pō´nä)	**198-99**	36°26'N	5°08'W
Esterhazy, Sk., Can. (ĕs´tĕr-hā-zē)	**134-35**	50°39'N	102°05'W
Estevan, Sk., Can. (ĕ-stē´văn)	**134-35**	49°08'N	103°00'W
Estherville, Ia., U.S. (ĕs´tĕr-vĭl)	**114-15**	43°25'N	94°50'W
Estill, S.C., U.S. (ĕs´tĭl)	**124-25**	32°45'N	81°14'W
Eston, Sk., Can.	**134-35**	51°10'N	108°46'W
Estonia, nation, Eur. (ĕs-tō´nĭ-å)	**174-75**	59°0'N	26°00'E
Estrela, mtn., Port. (ĕs-trā´lȧ)	**198-99**	40°19'N	7°37'W
Estremoz, Port. (ĕs-trā-mōzh´)	**198-99**	38°51'N	7°35'W
Estrondo, Serra do, plat., Braz. (sĕr´-rȧ dò ĕs-trôn´-dò)	**166-67**	9°0'S	48°45'W
Esumba, Île, i., D.R.C.	**262-63**	2°0'N	21°12'E
Eszék, Cro. *see* Osijek	**200-01**	45°33'N	18°42'E
Étampes, Fr. (ā-täNp´)	**196-97**	48°26'N	2°10'E
Étaples, Fr. (ā-täp´l')	**196-97**	50°31'N	1°38'E
Etāwah, India	**234-35**	26°46'N	79°01'E
Ethiopia, nation, Afr. (ē-thē-ō´pē-å)	**253**	9°0'N	39°00'E
Etna, Monte, vol., Italy (môn-tå ĕt´nȧ)	**200-01**	37°45'N	15°00'E
Etolin Strait, strt., Ak., U.S. (ĕt ō lĭn strāt)	**126**	60°20'N	165°15'W
Etorofu-tō, i., Russia *see* Iturup, Ostrov	**218-19**	44°51'N	147°27'E
Etosha National Park, n.p., Nmb.	**264-65**	18°60'S	15°07'E
Etosha Pan, pl., Nmb. (ētō´shä)	**264-65**	18°45'S	16°15'E
Etowah, Tn., U.S. (ĕt´ô-wä)	**124-25**	35°19'N	84°32'W
Et Tīdra, i., Maur.	**258-59**	19°44'N	16°24'W
Eua, i., Tonga	**280-81**	21°22'S	174°56'W
Euboea, i., Grc. *see* Évvoia	**200-01**	38°34'N	23°50'E
Eucla, Austl. (ū´klȧ)	**270-71**	31°42'S	128°54'E
Euclid, Oh., U.S. (ū´klĭd)	**116-17**	41°35'N	81°31'W
Eufaula, Al., U.S. (û-fô´lȧ)	**124-25**	31°54'N	85°09'W
Eufaula, Ok., U.S. (û-fô´lȧ)	**120-21**	35°16'N	95°36'W
Eugene, Or., U.S. (û-jēn´)	**112-13**	44°03'N	123°05'W
Eugenia, Punta, c., Mex.	**144-45**	27°51'N	115°05'W
Eunice, La., U.S. (ū´nĭs)	**122-23**	30°30'N	92°25'W
Eunice, N.M., U.S. (ū´nĭs)	**120-21**	32°26'N	103°10'W
Euphrates, stm., Asia (û-frā´tēz)	**208-09**	30°60'N	47°27'E
Eureka, Ca., U.S.	**112-13**	40°47'N	124°09'W
Eureka, Il., U.S. (û-rē´kȧ)	**116-17**	40°43'N	89°16'W
Eureka, Ks., U.S. (û-rē´kȧ)	**120-21**	37°50'N	96°18'W
Eureka, Mt., U.S. (û-rē´kȧ)	**112-13**	48°53'N	115°03'W
Eureka, S.D., U.S. (û-rē´kȧ)	**114-15**	45°46'N	99°38'W
Eureka Springs, Ar., U.S. (û-rē´kȧ sprĭngz)	**120-21**	36°24'N	93°45'W
Europa, Île, i., Reu.	**264-65**	22°20'S	40°21'E
Europa Island, i., Reu. *see* Europa, Île	**264-65**	22°20'S	40°21'E
Europe, cont., (ū´rŭp)	**20-21**	50°0'N	28°00'E
Eustis, Fl., U.S. (ūs´tĭs)	**124-25**	28°51'N	81°41'W
Eutaw, Al., U.S. (ū-tå)	**124-25**	32°50'N	87°53'W
Eutsuk Lake, lk., B.C., Can. (ōōt´sŭk lāk)	**132-33**	53°19'N	126°44'W
Evans, Lac, lk., Qc., Can.	**130-31**	50°55'N	77°00'W
Evanston, Il., U.S. (ĕv´ăn-stŭn)	**116-17**	42°01'N	87°41'W
Evanston, Wy., U.S. (ĕv´ăn-stŭn)	**112-13**	41°17'N	110°58'W
Evansville, In., U.S. (ĕv´ănz-vĭl)	**116-17**	37°59'N	87°35'W
Evansville, Wi., U.S. (ĕv´ănz-vĭl)	**116-17**	42°47'N	89°17'W
Evansville, Wy., U.S. (ĕv´ănz-vĭl)	**112-13**	42°50'N	106°15'W
Eva Perón, Arg. *see* La Plata	**173**	34°55'S	57°57'W
Eveleth, Mn., U.S. (ĕv´ē-lĕth)	**114-15**	47°28'N	92°32'W
Evensk, Russia	**218-19**	61°57'N	159°15'E
Everard, Lake, lk., Austl. (lāk ĕv´ĕr-ård)	**272-73**	31°25'S	135°06'E
Everest, Mount, mtn., Asia (mount ĕv´ĕr-ĕst)	**234-35**	27°59'N	86°56'E
Everett, Wa., U.S. (ĕv´ĕr-ĕt)	**112-13**	47°58'N	122°12'W
Everglades, The, sw., Fl., U.S. (thȧ ĕv´ĕr-glādz swŏmp)	**125a**	26°0'N	80°40'W
Everglades National Park, n.p., Fl., U.S. (ĕv´ĕr-glādz năsh´ŭn-ăl pärk)	**125a**	25°27'N	80°53'W
Evergreen, Al., U.S. (ĕv´ĕr-grēn)	**124-25**	31°26'N	86°57'W
Evergreen, Co., U.S. (ĕv´ĕr-grēn)	**118-19**	39°38'N	105°19'W
Evergreen, Mt., U.S. (ĕv´ĕr-grēn)	**112-13**	48°13'N	114°17'W
Évora, Port. (ĕv´ô-rä)	**198-99**	38°34'N	7°54'W
Evpatoria, Ukr. *see* Yevpatoriia	**202-03**	45°12'N	33°22'E
Évreux, Fr. (ā-vrû´)	**196-97**	49°01'N	1°09'E
Évvoia, i., Grc.	**200-01**	38°34'N	23°50'E
Exe, stm., Eng., U.K. (ĕks)	**190-91**	50°42'N	3°29'W
Exeter, Eng., U.K. (ĕk´sē-tĕr)	**190-91**	50°43'N	3°32'W
Exmoor, plat., Eng., U.K. (ĕks´mòr)	**190-91**	51°09'N	3°44'W
Exmouth, Austl.	**270-71**	21°56'S	114°07'E
Exmouth, Eng., U.K. (ĕks´mŭth)	**190-91**	50°38'N	3°24'W
Exmouth Gulf, b., Austl.	**272-73**	22°0'S	114°20'E
Exploits, stm., Nf., Can. (ĕks-ploits´)	**138-39**	49°05'N	55°18'W
Exuma Sound, strt., Bah. (ĕk-sōō´mä sound)	**142-43**	24°12'N	76°01'W
Eyasi, Lake, lk., Tan. (lāk å-yä´sē)	**267**	3°40'S	35°05'E
Eyl, Som.	**262-63**	7°59'N	49°49'E
Eyre Creek, stm., Austl.	**277**	26°38'S	138°59'E
Eyre North, Lake, lk., Austl. (lāk âr nôrth)	**272-73**	28°33'S	137°15'E
Eyre Peninsula, pen., Austl.	**272-73**	33°15'S	135°48'E
Eyre South, Lake, lk., Austl. (lāk âr south)	**276**	29°18'S	137°26'E
Eysturoy, i., Far. Is.	**190b**	62°12'N	6°55'W
Ezequiel Ramos Mexía, Embalse, res., Arg.	**171**	39°27'S	69°01'W
Ezine, Tur. (å´zĭ-nå)	**200-01**	39°47'N	26°20'E

F

Feature (Pronunciation)	Page	Lat.	Long.
Faaborg, Den. (fô´bòrg)	**194-95**	55°06'N	10°15'E
Fabriano, Italy (fä-brē-ä´nò)	**200-01**	43°21'N	12°54'E
Fada, Chad (fä´dä)	**258-59**	17°12'N	21°35'E
Fada-Ngourma, Burkina (fä´dä'n gōōr´mä)	**260-61**	12°03'N	0°22'E
Faddeyevskiy, Ostrov, i., Russia (ôs-trôf´ fȧd-yä´skĭ)	**218-19**	75°27'N	144°20'E
Faenza, Italy (fä-ĕnd´zä)	**200-01**	44°17'N	11°53'E
Færøerne, dep., Eur. *see* Faroe Islands	**174-75**	62°0'N	7°00'W
Fafen, stm., Eth.	**262-63**	5°39'N	44°08'E
Făgăraş, Rom. (fȧ-gä´räsh)	**194-95**	45°50'N	24°59'E
Fagernes, Nor.	**192-93**	60°59'N	9°15'E
Fagnano, Lago, lk., S.A. (lä´gô fäk-nä´nô)	**171**	54°34'S	67°58'W
Faguibine, Lac, lk., Mali	**258-59**	16°49'N	3°50'W
Faial, i., Port. (fä-yä´l)	**199c**	38°34'N	28°42'W
Fairbanks, Ak., U.S. (fâr´bănks)	**126**	64°51'N	147°42'W
Fairbury, Ne., U.S. (fâr´bĕr-ĭ)	**120-21**	40°09'N	97°11'W
Fairfax, Mn., U.S. (fâr´făks)	**114-15**	44°31'N	94°43'W
Fairfax, S.C., U.S. (fâr´făks)	**124-25**	32°57'N	81°14'W
Fairfield, Ia., U.S. (fâr´fēld)	**114-15**	41°01'N	91°58'W
Fairfield, Il., U.S. (fâr´fēld)	**116-17**	38°22'N	88°22'W
Fairfield, Oh., U.S. (fâr´fēld)	**116-17**	39°21'N	84°34'W
Fairfield, Tx., U.S. (fâr´fēld)	**122-23**	31°43'N	96°10'W
Fair Haven, Vt., U.S. (fâr ā´vĕn)	**116-17**	43°36'N	73°16'W
Fair Isle, i., Scot., U.K. (fâr ĭl)	**190c**	59°32'N	1°39'W
Fairmont, Mn., U.S. (fâr´mŏnt)	**114-15**	43°40'N	94°28'W
Fairmont, W.V., U.S. (fâr´mŏnt)	**116-17**	39°29'N	80°08'W
Fair Ness, c., Nu., Can.	**130-31**	63°25'N	72°02'W
Fairview, Ok., U.S. (fâr´vū)	**120-21**	36°16'N	98°29'W
Fairweather, Mount, mtn., N.A. (mount fâr-wĕdh´ĕr)	**126**	58°54'N	137°32'W
Fairweather Mountain, mtn., N.A. *see* Fairweather, Mount	**126**	58°54'N	137°32'W
Faisalābād, Pak.	**232-33**	31°25'N	73°05'E
Faith, S.D., U.S. (fāth)	**114-15**	45°01'N	102°01'W
Faiyum, Egypt *see* El-Fayoum	**268b**	29°19'N	30°50'E
Faizābād, India	**234-35**	26°47'N	82°08'E
Fakaofo, at., Tok.	**280-81**	9°22'S	171°14'W
Fakfak, Indon.	**224-25**	2°56'S	132°18'E
Faku, China (fä-kōō)	**243**	42°30'N	123°25'E
Falam, Mya.	**246-47**	22°54'N	93°41'E
Falémé, stm., Afr.	**258-59**	14°46'N	12°15'W
Falfurrias, Tx., U.S. (făl´fōō-rē´ås)	**122-23**	27°14'N	98°09'W
Falher, Ab., Can. (făl´ĕr)	**132-33**	55°44'N	117°13'W
Falkenberg, Swe. (fäl´kĕn-bĕrgh)	**192-93**	56°54'N	12°29'E
Falkensee, Ger. (fäl´kĕn-zā)	**194-95**	52°34'N	13°04'E
Falkirk, Scot., U.K. (fôl´kûrk)	**190-91**	56°00'N	3°47'W
Falkland Islands, dep., S.A. (fôk´lănd ī´lăndz)	**158**	51°45'S	59°00'W
Falkland Islands, is., Falk. Is. (fôk´lănd ī´lăndz)	**171**	51°41'S	59°08'W
Falkland Sound, strt., Falk. Is.	**171**	51°45'S	59°25'W
Falköping, Swe. (fäl´chûp-ĭng)	**192-93**	58°10'N	13°32'E
Fall River, Ma., U.S. (fôl rĭv´ĕr)	**116-17**	41°42'N	71°10'W
Falls City, Ne., U.S. (fôlz sĭ´tē)	**120-21**	40°04'N	95°37'W
Falmouth, Jam. (făl´mŭth)	**142-43**	18°29'N	77°39'W
Falmouth, Eng., U.K. (făl´mŭth)	**190-91**	50°09'N	5°03'W
Falmouth, Ky., U.S. (făl´mŭth)	**116-17**	38°41'N	84°20'W
False Divi Point, c., India	**236**	15°43'N	80°50'E
Falster, i., Den. (fäls´tĕr)	**192-93**	54°48'N	11°58'E
Fălticeni, Rom. (fŭl-tĕ-chân´y')	**194-95**	47°28'N	26°19'E
Falun, Swe. (fä-lōōn´)	**192-93**	60°36'N	15°38'E
Famagusta, Cyp. *see* Gazimağusa	**228-29**	35°07'N	33°57'E
Fanch'eng, China *see* Xiangfan	**238-39**	32°02'N	112°09'E
Fangxian, China (fäŋ-shyĕn)	**238-39**	32°03'N	110°44'E
Fanning Island, at., Kir. *see* Tabuaeran	**280-81**	3°51'N	159°18'W
Fano, Italy (fä´nō)	**200-01**	43°51'N	13°01'E
Fanø, i., Den. (făn´û)	**192-93**	55°25'N	8°25'E
Fan Si Pan, mtn., Viet.	**246-47**	22°15'N	103°46'E
Faradofay, Madag. *see* Tôlañaro	**264-65**	25°02'S	47°00'E
Farafangana, Madag. (fä-rä-fäŋ-gä´nä)	**264-65**	22°49'S	47°50'E
Farāh, Afg. (fä-rä´)	**232-33**	32°22'N	62°04'E
Farāh, stm., Afg.	**232-33**	31°27'N	61°27'E
Farallon de Medinilla, i., N. Mar. Is.	**280-81**	16°01'N	146°04'E
Farallon de Pajaros, i., N. Mar. Is.	**280-81**	20°32'N	144°54'E
Farasān, Jazā'ir, is., Sau. Ar.	**266**	16°48'N	41°54'E
Farewell, Cape, c., Green.	**86**	59°46'N	43°60'W
Farewell, Cape, c., N.Z. (kāp fâr-wĕl´)	**278**	40°30'S	172°41'E
Farg'ona, Uzb.	**232-33**	40°23'N	71°48'E
Fargo, N.D., U.S. (fär´gō)	**114-15**	46°52'N	96°49'W
Faribault, Mn., U.S. (fâ´rĭ-bō)	**114-15**	44°18'N	93°17'W
Farīdpur, Bngl.	**234-35**	23°36'N	89°51'E
Farmersburg, In., U.S. (fär´mĕrz-bûrg)	**116-17**	39°15'N	87°23'W
Farmersville, Tx., U.S. (fär´mĕrz-vĭl)	**120-21**	33°10'N	96°22'W
Farmington, Il., U.S. (färm-ĭng-tŭn)	**114-15**	40°42'N	90°00'W
Farmington, Mo., U.S. (färm-ĭng-tŭn)	**120-21**	37°47'N	90°25'W
Farmington, N.M., U.S. (färm-ĭng-tŭn)	**118-19**	36°44'N	108°12'W
Farmville, N.C., U.S. (färm-vĭl)	**124-25**	35°35'N	77°36'W
Farmville, Va., U.S. (färm-vĭl)	**124-25**	37°18'N	78°24'W
Farnham, Qc., Can. (fär´năm)	**136-37**	45°17'N	72°59'W
Faro, Braz. (fä´rò)	**166-67**	2°10'S	56°45'W
Faro, Port. (fä´rò)	**198-99**	37°01'N	7°56'W
Faro, stm., Afr.	**260-61**	9°20'N	12°54'E
Faroe Islands, dep., Eur. (fâr´ō ī´lăndz)	**174-75**	62°0'N	7°00'W
Fårön, i., Swe.	**192-93**	57°56'N	19°08'E
Farquhar, Atoll de, at., Sey.	**264-65**	10°10'S	51°10'E
Farrukhābād, India (fŭ-ròk-hä-bäd´)	**234-35**	27°24'N	79°35'E
Farsund, Nor. (fär´sòn)	**192-93**	58°05'N	6°48'E
Fartak, Ra's, c., Yemen	**220-21**	15°39'N	52°12'E
Farukolu, i., Mald.	**236**	6°12'N	73°16'E
Farvel, Kap, c., Green. *see* Farewell, Cape	**86**	59°46'N	43°60'W
Farwell, Tx., U.S. (fär´wĕl)	**120-21**	34°24'N	103°01'W
Fasano, Italy (fä-zä´nō)	**200-01**	40°50'N	17°21'E
Fatehpur Sīkri, India	**234-35**	27°06'N	77°40'E
Fauro Island, i., Sol. Is.	**279e**	6°55'S	156°04'E
Fauske, Nor.	**184-85**	67°16'N	15°24'E
Fawn, stm., On., Can.	**134-35**	55°22'N	88°20'W
Faxaflói, b., Ice.	**190a**	64°25'N	23°00'W
Faya-Largeau, Chad	**258-59**	17°56'N	19°07'E
Fayette, Al., U.S. (fâ-yĕt´)	**124-25**	33°41'N	87°50'W
Fayette, Mo., U.S. (fâ-yĕt´)	**120-21**	39°09'N	92°41'W
Fayette, Ms., U.S. (fâ-yĕt´)	**124-25**	31°43'N	91°04'W
Fayetteville, Ar., U.S. (fâ-yĕt´vĭl)	**120-21**	36°05'N	94°10'W
Fayetteville, N.C., U.S. (fâ-yĕt´vĭl)	**124-25**	35°03'N	78°53'W
Fayetteville, Tn., U.S. (fâ-yĕt´vĭl)	**124-25**	35°09'N	86°34'W
Fayetteville, W.V., U.S. (fâ-yĕt´vĭl)	**116-17**	38°03'N	81°06'W
Faylakah, i., Kuw.	**230-31**	29°26'N	48°20'E
Fayyum, Egypt *see* El-Fayoum	**268b**	29°19'N	30°50'E
Fazzān, hist. reg., Libya *see* Fezzan	**258-59**	26°0'N	14°00'E
Fear, Cape, c., N.C., U.S. (kāp fēr)	**124-25**	33°57'N	77°56'W
Fécamp, Fr. (fā-käN´)	**196-97**	49°46'N	0°23'E
Fedala, Mor. *see* Mohammedia	**269a**	33°42'N	7°23'W
Federal, Arg.	**173**	30°57'S	58°47'W
Federated States of Micronesia, nation, Oc. *see* Micronesia, Federated States of	**280-81**	5°0'N	152°00'E
Feia, Lagoa, b., Braz. (lä´gō-å fĕ´yä)	**172**	22°0'S	41°20'W
Feijó, Braz.	**166-67**	8°11'S	70°24'W

Feature (Pronunciation)	Page	Lat.	Long.
Feira de Santana, Braz. (fē´á-rä dä sänt-än´ä)	166-67	12°15'S	38°58'W
Feixian, China (fā-shyěn)	240-41	35°16'N	117°58'E
Fejaj, Chott, lk., Tun.	258-59	33°53'N	9°10'E
Felanitx, Spain (fā-lä-nēch´)	198-99	39°29'N	3°09'E
Feldkirch, Aus. (fělt´kĭrk)	194-95	47°14'N	9°36'E
Felipe Carrillo Puerto, Mex.	148	19°35'N	88°02'W
Felix, Cape, c., Nu., Can.	130-31	69°53'N	97°57'W
Feltre, Italy (fěl´trā)	200-01	46°01'N	11°54'E
Fen, stm., China	240-41	35°28'N	110°34'E
Fengcheng, China (fŭŋ-chŭŋ)	238-39	28°10'N	115°46'E
Fengcheng, China (fŭŋ-chŭŋ)	243	40°27'N	124°04'E
Fengdu, China (fŭŋ-dōō)	238-39	29°58'N	107°46'E
Fengfeng, China	240-41	36°29'N	114°14'E
Fengtien, China *see* Shenyang	243	41°48'N	123°24'E
Fengxian, China (fŭŋ-shyěn)	238-39	33°57'N	106°40'E
Fengyang, China (fŭng´yäng´)	238-39	32°52'N	117°33'E
Fengzhen, China (fŭŋ-jŭn)	240-41	40°26'N	113°09'E
Feni Islands, is., Pap. N. Gui.	277	4°04'S	153°38'E
Fenton, Mi., U.S. (fěn-tŭn)	116-17	42°48'N	83°42'W
Fenyang, China	240-41	37°16'N	111°47'E
Feodosiia, Ukr.	202-03	45°02'N	35°22'E
Ferdows, Iran	232-33	34°01'N	58°10'E
Fergus Falls, Mn., U.S. (fûr´gŭs fôlz)	114-15	46°17'N	96°05'W
Fergusson Island, i., Pap. N. Gui.	277	9°31'S	150°39'E
Ferlo, Vallée du, stm., Sen.	260-61	15°50'N	15°43'W
Fermo, Italy (fĕr´mō)	200-01	43°10'N	13°43'E
Fermoy, Ire. (fûr-moi´)	190-91	52°08'N	8°17'W
Fernandina, Isla, i., Ec.	170a	0°26'S	91°30'W
Fernandina Beach, Fl., U.S. (fûr-năn-dē´ná bēch)	124-25	30°40'N	81°27'W
Fernando de Noronha, Ilha, i., Braz.	159	3°51'S	32°25'W
Fernandópolis, Braz.	168-69	20°16'S	50°15'W
Fernando Póo, i., Eq. Gui. *see* Bioko	260-61	3°30'N	8°40'E
Fernie, B.C., Can. (fûr´nĭ)	132-33	49°30'N	115°03'W
Ferrara, Italy (fěr-rä´rä)	200-01	44°51'N	11°36'E
Ferrat, Cap, c., Alg. (kăp fěr-rät)	198-99	35°55'N	0°23'W
Ferreñafe, Peru (fěr-rěn-yá´fě)	170	6°38'S	79°47'W
Ferriday, La., U.S. (fěr´ĭ-dā)	124-25	31°38'N	91°33'W
Ferro, i., Spain *see* El Hierro	199d	27°45'N	18°00'W
Ferrol, Spain	198-99	43°29'N	8°14'W
Fès, Mor. (fěs)	269a	34°03'N	5°00'W
Fessenden, N.D., U.S. (fěs´ěn-děn)	114-15	47°39'N	99°38'W
Festus, Mo., U.S. (fěst´ŭs)	120-21	38°14'N	90°24'W
Fethiye, Tur. (fět-hē´yě)	200-01	36°37'N	29°08'E
Feuilles, stm., Qc., Can.	130-31	58°39'N	70°25'W
Feyẕābād, Afg.	232-33	37°08'N	70°34'E
Fez, Mor. *see* Fès	269a	34°03'N	5°00'W
Fezzan, hist. reg., Libya	258-59	26°0'N	14°00'E
Fianarantsoa, Madag. (fyá-nä´rán-tsō´á)	264-65	21°25'S	47°07'E
Fianga, Chad	262-63	9°55'N	15°09'E
Ficksburg, S. Afr. (fĭks´bûrg)	269c	28°52'S	27°53'E
Fife Ness, c., Scot., U.K. (fīf´nes´)	190-91	56°17'N	2°36'W
Figeac, Fr. (fē-zhák´)	196-97	44°37'N	2°02'E
Figueira da Foz, Port. (fē-gwěy-rä-dá-fō´z)	198-99	40°09'N	8°51'W
Figuig, Mor.	188-89	32°08'N	1°13'W
Fiji, nation, Oc. (fē´jē)	279f	18°0'S	178°00'E
Fiji, nation, Oc. (fē´jē)	279f	18°0'S	178°00'E
Filicudi, Isola, i., Italy (ē´-sō-lä fē´le-kōō´dē)	200-01	38°34'N	14°34'E
Fillmore, Ut., U.S. (fĭl´môr)	118-19	38°58'N	112°20'W
Fimi, stm., D.R.C.	262-63	3°02'S	16°56'E
Findlay, Oh., U.S. (fĭnd´lå)	116-17	41°02'N	83°38'W
Finisterre, Cabo de, c., Spain *see* Fisterra, Cabo de	198-99	42°53'N	9°16'W
Finland, nation, Eur. (fĭn´lănd)	174-75	64°0'N	26°00'E
Finland, Gulf of, b., Eur. (gŭlf ŭv fĭn´lănd)	192-93	60°0'N	27°00'E
Finskiy Zaliv, b., Eur. *see* Finland, Gulf of	192-93	60°0'N	27°00'E
Fiordland National Park, n.p., N.Z.	278	45°30'S	167°20'E
Fırat, stm., Asia *see* Euphrates	208-09	30°60'N	47°27'E
Firenze, Italy *see* Florence	200-01	43°47'N	11°14'E
Fīrozābād, India	234-35	27°09'N	78°24'E
Fīrozpur, India	234-35	30°55'N	74°37'E
Fisterra, Cabo de, c., Spain	198-99	42°53'N	9°16'W
Fitchburg, Ma., U.S. (fĭch´bûrg)	116-17	42°35'N	71°48'W
Fitzgerald, Ga., U.S. (fĭts-jěr´ăld)	124-25	31°43'N	83°15'W
Fitz Roy, Arg.	171	47°03'S	67°14'W
Fitz Roy, Monte, mtn., S.A.	171	49°17'S	73°05'W
Fitzroy Crossing, Austl.	270-71	18°12'S	125°34'E
Fiume, Cro. *see* Rijeka	200-01	45°20'N	14°27'E
Fizi, D.R.C.	267	4°19'S	28°56'E
Flagstaff, Az., U.S. (flăg-stáf)	118-19	35°11'N	111°39'W
Flaherty Island, i., Nu., Can.	130-31	56°14'N	79°17'W
Flåm, Nor. (flôm)	192-93	60°51'N	7°07'E
Flaming Gorge Reservoir, res., U.S. (flā´mĭng gôrj rě´sěr-vwär)	112-13	41°14'N	109°35'W
Flandreau, S.D., U.S. (flăn´drō)	114-15	44°03'N	96°36'W
Flathead Indian Reservation, ind. res., Mt., U.S. (flăt´hěd ĭn´dĭ-ăn rě-sěr-vā´shěn)	112-13	47°30'N	114°25'W
Flathead Lake, lk., Mt., U.S. (flăt´hěd lāk)	112-13	47°52'N	114°08'W
Flat Rock, Mi., U.S. (flăt rŏk)	116-17	42°06'N	83°17'W
Flattery, Cape, c., Wa., U.S. (kāp flăt´ẽr-ĭ)	112-13	48°23'N	124°43'W
Flekkefjord, Nor. (fläk´kě-fyôr)	192-93	58°18'N	6°41'E
Flemingsburg, Ky., U.S. (flěm´ĭngz-bûrg)	116-17	38°25'N	83°45'W
Flensburg, Ger. (flěns´bòrgh)	194-95	54°47'N	9°26'E
Flers, Fr. (flěr)	196-97	48°45'N	0°34'W
Flinders, stm., Austl. (flĭn´děrz)	277	17°36'S	140°36'E
Flinders Chase National Park, n.p., Austl.	276	35°58'S	136°44'E
Flinders Island, i., Austl. (flĭn´děrz ī´lănd)	276	40°0'S	148°00'E
Flin Flon, Mb., Can. (flĭn flŏn)	134-35	54°46'N	101°53'W
Flint, Mi., U.S. (flĭnt)	116-17	43°00'N	83°41'W
Flint, i., Kir.	280-81	11°25'S	151°48'W
Flint, stm., Ga., U.S. (flĭnt)	124-25	30°46'N	84°48'W
Flora, Il., U.S. (flō´rá)	116-17	38°40'N	88°29'W
Florala, Al., U.S. (flŏr-ăl´á)	124-25	31°00'N	86°20'W
Florence, Italy (flŏr´ěns)	200-01	43°47'N	11°14'E
Florence, Al., U.S. (flŏr´ěns)	124-25	34°48'N	87°41'W
Florence, Az., U.S. (flŏr´ěns)	118-19	33°02'N	111°23'W
Florence, Ky., U.S. (flŏr´ěns)	116-17	38°60'N	84°38'W
Florence, Or., U.S. (flŏr´ěns)	112-13	43°59'N	124°06'W
Florence, S.C., U.S. (flŏr´ěns)	124-25	34°11'N	79°46'W
Florencia, Col. (flō-rěn´sě-á)	164-65	1°36'N	75°36'W
Flores, i., Indon. (flō´rěs)	248-49	8°38'S	120°56'E
Flores, i., Port.	199c	39°26'N	31°13'W
Flores, Laut, s., Indon. *see* Flores Sea	248-49	8°0'S	120°00'E
Flores Island, i., B.C., Can.	132-33	49°20'N	126°10'W
Flores Sea, s., Indon. (flō´rěs sē)	248-49	8°0'S	120°00'E
Floresville, Tx., U.S. (flō´rěs-vĭl)	122-23	29°08'N	98°09'W
Floriano, Braz. (flō-rá-ä´nò)	166-67	6°47'S	43°01'W
Florianópolis, Braz. (flō-rē-ä-nō´pò-lěs)	172	27°35'S	48°32'W
Florida, Col. (flō-rē´dä)	163c	3°21'N	76°15'W
Florida, Ur. (flô-rē-dhä)	173	34°06'S	56°12'W
Florida, state, U.S. (flŏr´ĭ-dá)	108-09	28°0'N	82°00'W
Florida, Estrecho de la, strt., N.A. *see* Florida, Straits of	142-43	24°59'N	79°45'W
Florida, Straits of, strt., N.A. (strāts ŭv flŏr´ĭ-dá)	142-43	24°59'N	79°45'W
Florida Bay, b., Fl., U.S. (flŏr´ĭ-dá bā)	125a	24°58'N	80°48'W
Florida Keys, is., Fl., U.S. (flŏr´ĭ-dá kēs)	125a	24°47'N	81°06'W
Florido, stm., Mex. (flô-rē´dō)	144-45	27°43'N	105°11'W
Flórina, Grc. (flô-rē´nä)	200-01	40°47'N	21°24'E
Florissant, Mo., U.S. (flŏr´ĭ-sănt)	120-21	38°48'N	90°20'W
Florø, Nor.	192-93	61°35'N	5°01'E
Floydada, Tx., U.S. (floi-dā´dá)	120-21	33°59'N	101°20'W
Flushing, Mi., U.S. (flŭsh´ĭng)	116-17	43°04'N	83°50'W
Fly, stm., (flī)	277	8°14'S	142°09'E
Foča, Bos. (fō´chä)	200-01	43°30'N	18°47'E
Fochville, S. Afr. (fŏk´vĭl)	269c	26°29'S	27°31'E
Focşani, Rom. (fŏk-shä´nē)	202-03	45°42'N	27°12'E
Fogang, China (fwo-gäŋ)	238-39	23°52'N	113°32'E
Foggia, Italy (fôd´jä)	200-01	41°28'N	15°32'E
Fogo, Nf., Can. (fō´gō)	138-39	49°43'N	54°18'W
Fogo, i., C.V.	260-61	14°54'N	24°23'W
Fogo Island, i., Nf., Can. (fō´gō ī´lănd)	138-39	49°39'N	54°11'W
Foguista J. F. Juárez, Arg. *see* El Galpón	168-69	25°24'S	64°38'W
Foix, Fr. (fwä)	196-97	42°58'N	1°37'E
Fokino, Russia	202-03	53°26'N	34°26'E
Folādī, Koh-e, mtn., Afg.	232-33	34°38'N	67°32'E
Foley Island, i., Nu., Can.	130-31	68°32'N	75°07'W
Foligno, Italy (fō-lēn´yō)	200-01	42°58'N	12°42'E
Fond-du-Lac, Sk., Can.	128-29	59°20'N	107°10'W
Fond du Lac, Wi., U.S. (fŏn dū lăk´)	116-17	43°46'N	88°27'W
Fond du Lac Indian Reservation, ind. res., Mn., U.S. (fŏn dū lăk´ ĭn´dĭ-ăn rě-sěr-vā´shěn)	114-15	46°45'N	92°37'W
Fondi, Italy (fōn´dē)	200-01	41°22'N	13°26'E
Fonseca, Golfo de, b., N.A. (gôl-fô-dě-fōn-sä´kä)	149	13°10'N	87°40'W
Fontainebleau, Fr. (fôn-těn-blō´)	196-97	48°24'N	2°42'E
Fontana, Ca., U.S. (fŏn-tă´ná)	118-19	34°06'N	117°26'W
Fonte Boa, Braz. (fōn´tå bō´ă)	166-67	2°32'S	66°01'W
Fontenay-le-Comte, Fr. (fônt-ně´lē-kônt´)	196-97	46°28'N	0°48'W
Fontur, c., Ice.	190a	66°22'N	14°35'W
Foochow, China *see* Fuzhou	225a	26°06'N	119°17'E
Forbach, Fr. (fôr´bäk)	196-97	49°12'N	6°54'E
Forbes, Austl. (fôrbz)	276	33°23'S	148°00'E
Forchheim, Ger. (fôrk´hīm)	194-95	49°43'N	11°04'E
Fordyce, Ar., U.S. (fôr´dīs)	120-21	33°49'N	92°25'W
Forest, Ms., U.S. (fŏr´ěst)	124-25	32°22'N	89°28'W
Forest City, Ia., U.S. (fŏr´ěst sĭ´tē)	114-15	43°16'N	93°39'W
Forest City, N.C., U.S. (fŏr´ěst sĭ´tĭ)	124-25	35°20'N	81°52'W
Forest City, Pa., U.S. (fŏr´ěst sĭ´tē)	116-17	41°39'N	75°28'W
Forestville, Qc., Can. (fŏr´ěst-vĭl)	138-39	48°45'N	69°06'W
Forfar, Scot., U.K. (fôr´fár)	190-91	56°38'N	2°54'W
Forlì, Italy (fôr-lē´)	200-01	44°13'N	12°03'E
Formentera, i., Spain (fôr-měn-tā´rä)	198-99	38°42'N	1°28'E
Formiga, Braz. (fôr-mē´gá)	172	20°28'S	45°26'W
Formosa, Arg. (fôr-mō´sä)	168-69	26°10'S	58°12'W
Formosa, Braz.	168-69	15°32'S	47°20'W
Formosa, nation, Asia (fôr-mō´sá) *see* Taiwan	206-07	23°30'N	121°00'E
Formosa, state, Arg. (fôr-mō´sä)	168-69	25°0'S	60°00'W
Formosa, Serra, plat., Braz. (sě´r-rä fôr-mō´sä)	166-67	12°0'S	55°00'W
Formosa Strait, strt., Asia *see* Taiwan Strait	225a	24°0'N	119°00'E
Føroyar, dep., Eur. *see* Faroe Islands	174-75	62°0'N	7°00'W
Forrest City, Ar., U.S. (fŏr´ěst sĭ´tĭ)	124-25	35°00'N	90°48'W
Forsyth, Ga., U.S. (fôr-sīth´)	124-25	33°02'N	83°57'W
Forsyth, Mt., U.S. (fôr-sīth´)	112-13	46°16'N	106°41'W
Fort Albany, On., Can. (fôrt ôl´bá nĭ)	128-29	52°13'N	81°40'W
Fortaleza, Braz. (fôr´tä-lā´zá)	166-67	3°44'S	38°30'W
Fort-Archambault, Chad *see* Sarh	262-63	9°09'N	18°23'E
Fort Atkinson, Wi., U.S. (fôrt ăt´kĭn-sŭn)	116-17	42°55'N	88°51'W
Fort Bayard, China *see* Zhanjiang	238-39	21°12'N	110°23'E
Fort Benton, Mt., U.S. (fôrt běn´tŭn)	112-13	47°49'N	110°41'W
Fort Berthold Indian Reservation, ind. res., N.D., U.S. (fôrt bērth´ôld ĭn´dĭ-ăn rě-sěr-vā´shěn)	114-15	47°40'N	102°25'W
Fort Bragg, Ca., U.S.	118-19	39°27'N	123°48'W
Fort Branch, In., U.S. (fôrt brănch)	116-17	38°15'N	87°35'W
Fort Chipewyan, Ab., Can.	128-29	58°43'N	111°10'W
Fort Collins, Co., U.S. (fôrt kŏl´ĭns)	120-21	40°35'N	105°05'W
Fort-Dauphin, Madag. *see* Tôlañaro	264-65	25°02'S	47°00'E
Fort-de-France, nat. cap., Mart. (dē frāns)	143b	14°36'N	61°04'W
Fort Dodge, Ia., U.S. (fôrt dŏj)	114-15	42°30'N	94°11'W
Fort Edward, N.Y., U.S. (fôrt wẽrd)	116-17	43°16'N	73°35'W
Fortescue, stm., Austl. (fôr´těs-kū)	272-73	21°00'S	116°06'E
Fort-Foureau, Camrn. *see* Kousséri	260-61	12°05'N	15°02'E
Fort Frances, On., Can. (fôrt frăn´sěs)	134-35	48°37'N	93°24'W
Fort Franklin, N.T., Can. *see* Déline	128-29	65°11'N	123°25'W
Fort Frederica National Monument, n.p., Ga., U.S. (fôrt frěd´ě-rī-ká năsh´ŭn-ăl mŏn´ū-měnt)	124-25	31°12'N	81°26'W
Fort-George, Qc., Can. *see* Chisasibi	128-29	53°48'N	79°02'W
Fort Gibson, Ok., U.S. (fôrt gĭb´sŭn)	120-21	35°49'N	95°15'W
Fort Good Hope, N.T., Can. (fôrt gōōd hōp)	128-29	66°15'N	128°37'W
Forth, Firth of, b., Scot., U.K. (fûrth ŏv fôrth)	190-91	56°07'N	2°58'W
Fort Johnston, Malawi *see* Mangochi	264-65	14°28'S	35°15'E
Fort Kent, Me., U.S. (fôrt kěnt)	117a	47°15'N	68°35'W
Fort-Lamy, nat. cap., Chad *see* N'Djamena	258-59	12°07'N	15°03'E
Fort Lauderdale, Fl., U.S. (fôrt lô´dẽr-dāl)	125a	26°07'N	80°09'W
Fort Liard, N.T., Can.	128-29	60°14'N	123°27'W
Fort Lupton, Co., U.S. (fôrt lŭp´tŭn)	120-21	40°05'N	104°49'W
Fort Macleod, Ab., Can. (fôrt má-kloud´)	132-33	49°43'N	113°25'W
Fort Madison, Ia., U.S. (fôrt măd´ĭ-sŭn)	120-21	40°38'N	91°19'W
Fort McMurray, Ab., Can. (fôrt mák-mŭr´ĭ)	134-35	56°44'N	111°25'W
Fort McPherson, N.T., Can. (fôrt mák-fŭr´s'n)	128-29	67°25'N	134°52'W
Fort Meade, Fl., U.S. (fôrt mēd)	125a	27°46'N	81°48'W
Fort Mill, S.C., U.S. (fôrt mĭl)	124-25	35°00'N	80°57'W
Fort Mojave Indian Reservation, ind. res., Az., U.S. (fôrt mō-hä´vâ ĭn´dĭ-ăn rě-sěr-vā´shěn)	118-19	34°55'N	114°35'W
Fort Morgan, Co., U.S. (fôrt môr´găn)	120-21	40°15'N	103°48'W
Fort Myers, Fl., U.S. (fôrt mī´ěrz)	125a	26°38'N	81°52'W

Feature (Pronunciation)	Page	Lat.	Long.
Fort Nelson, B.C., Can. (fôrt nĕl′sŭn)	128-29	58°49′N	122°41′W
Fort Nelson, stm., B.C., Can. (fôrt nĕl′sŭn)	130-31	59°31′N	124°03′W
Fort Norman, N.T., Can. *see* Tulita	128-29	64°54′N	125°34′W
Fort Payne, Al., U.S. (fôrt pān)	124-25	34°27′N	85°43′W
Fort Peck Indian Reservation, ind. res., Mt., U.S. (fôrt pĕk ĭn′dĭ-ăn rĕ-sĕr-vā′shĕn)	112-13	48°22′N	105°40′W
Fort Peck Lake, res., Mt., U.S. (fôrt pĕk lāk)	112-13	47°45′N	106°45′W
Fort Pierce, Fl., U.S. (fôrt pērs)	125a	27°27′N	80°20′W
Fort Portal, Ug. (fôrt pôr′tál)	267	0°40′N	30°17′E
Fort Providence, N.T., Can. (fôrt prŏv′ĭ-dĕns)	128-29	61°21′N	117°35′W
Fort Pulaski National Monument, n.p., Ga., U.S. (fôrt pu-lăs′kĭ năsh′ŭn-ăl mŏn′ū-mĕnt)	124-25	32°01′N	80°55′W
Fort Qu'Appelle, Sk., Can.	134-35	50°46′N	103°48′W
Fort Resolution, N.T., Can. (fôrt rĕz′ō-lū′shŭn)	128-29	61°10′N	113°38′W
Fort Rosebery, Zam. *see* Mansa	264-65	11°12′S	28°53′E
Fort Saint James, B.C., Can. (fôrt sânt jāmz)	132-33	54°28′N	124°16′W
Fort Saint John, B.C., Can. (fôrt sânt jŏn)	132-33	56°17′N	120°54′W
Fort Saskatchewan, Ab., Can. (fôrt săs-kăt′choo-ån)	132-33	53°43′N	113°14′W
Fort Severn, On., Can. (fôrt sĕv′ĕrn)	134-35	55°60′N	87°38′W
Fort-Shevchenko, Kaz. (fôrt shĕv-chĕn′kô)	186-87	44°30′N	50°16′E
Fort Simpson, N.T., Can. (fôrt sĭmp′sŭn)	128-29	61°51′N	121°22′W
Fort Smith, N.T., Can. (fôrt smĭth)	128-29	60°01′N	111°54′W
Fort Smith, Ar., U.S. (fôrt smĭth)	120-21	35°23′N	94°25′W
Fort Stockton, Tx., U.S. (fôrt stŏk′tŭn)	122-23	30°54′N	102°53′W
Fort Sumner, N.M., U.S. (fôrt sŭm′nĕr)	120-21	34°29′N	104°14′W
Fort Sumter National Monument, n.p., S.C., U.S. (fôrt sŭm′tĕr năsh′ŭn-ăl mŏn′ū-mĕnt)	124-25	32°45′N	79°52′W
Fortuna, Ca., U.S. (fŏr-tū′nȧ)	112-13	40°36′N	124°09′W
Fortune, Nf., Can. (fôr′tŭn)	138-39	47°04′N	55°50′W
Fortune Bay, b., Nf., Can. (fôr′tŭn bā)	138-39	47°25′N	55°25′W
Fort Union National Monument, n.p., N.M., U.S. (fôrt ūn′yŭn năsh′ŭn-ăl mŏn′ū-mĕnt)	120-21	35°56′N	105°03′W
Fort Valley, Ga., U.S. (fôrt văl′ē)	124-25	32°33′N	83°53′W
Fort Vermilion, Ab., Can. (fôrt vĕr-mĭl′yŭn)	128-29	58°23′N	116°02′W
Fort Walton Beach, Fl., U.S.	124-25	30°25′N	86°36′W
Fort Wayne, In., U.S. (fôrt wān)	116-17	41°04′N	85°07′W
Fort William, Scot., U.K. (fôrt wĭl′yŭm)	190-91	56°49′N	5°06′W
Fort Worth, Tx., U.S. (fôrt wûrth)	120-21	32°45′N	97°21′W
Fort Yukon, Ak., U.S. (fôrt yoo′kŏn)	126	66°34′N	145°15′W
Forūr, Jazīreh-ye, i., Iran	230-31	26°17′N	54°31′E
Foshan, China	238-39	23°03′N	113°07′E
Fossano, Italy (fôs-sä′nō)	200-01	44°33′N	7°44′E
Fossil Butte National Monument, n.p., Wy., U.S.	112-13	41°50′N	110°40′W
Fosston, Mn., U.S. (fôs′tŭn)	114-15	47°34′N	95°45′W
Foster, Austl.	276	38°39′S	146°12′E
Foster, stm., Sk., Can.	134-35	55°47′N	105°48′W
Fostoria, Oh., U.S. (fŏs-tō′rĭ-ȧ)	116-17	41°10′N	83°24′W
Fougères, Fr. (foo-zhâr′)	196-97	48°21′N	1°12′W
Foulwind, Cape, c., N.Z. (kāp foul′wĭnd)	278	41°45′S	171°28′E
Fouriesburg, S. Afr. (fō′rēz-bûrg)	269c	28°37′S	28°13′E
Fourmies, Fr. (foor-mē′)	196-97	50°01′N	4°03′E
Foveaux Strait, strt., N.Z. (fō-vō′ strāt)	278	46°35′S	168°00′E
Fowler, In., U.S. (foul′ĕr)	116-17	40°37′N	87°19′W
Foxe Basin, b., Nu., Can. (fŏks bā′s′n)	130-31	68°25′N	76°60′W
Foxe Peninsula, pen., Nu., Can. (fŏks pĕ-nĭn′sūlȧ)	130-31	65°0′N	76°00′W
Foz do Iguaçu, Braz.	168-69	25°33′S	54°35′W
Fraga, Spain (frä′gä)	198-99	41°32′N	0°21′E
Franca, Braz. (frä′n-kä)	172	20°32′S	47°24′W
France, nation, Eur. (fråns)	174-75	46°0′N	2°00′E
Francés Viejo, Cabo, c., Dom. Rep. (kå′bô-frän′sås vyā′hō)	142-43	19°39′N	69°55′W
Franceville, Gabon (fräns-vēl′)	260-61	1°38′S	13°35′E
Francis Case, Lake, res., S.D., U.S. (lăk frăn′sĭs kās)	114-15	43°15′N	98°57′W
Francistown, Bots. (från′sĭs-toun)	264-65	21°10′S	27°30′E
Francois Lake, lk., B.C., Can.	132-33	54°02′N	125°43′W
Francs Peak, mtn., Wy., U.S.	112-13	43°58′N	109°20′W
Frankfort, S. Afr. (frănk′fōrt)	269c	27°17′S	28°31′E
Frankfort, In., U.S. (frăŋk′fŭrt)	116-17	40°17′N	86°30′W
Frankfort, Ky., U.S.	116-17	38°12′N	84°50′W
Frankfort, Mi., U.S. (frăŋk′fŭrt)	116-17	44°38′N	86°14′W
Frankfurt, Ger.	194-95	52°21′N	14°32′E
Frankfurt am Main, Ger.	194-95	50°07′N	8°40′E
Franklin, In., U.S. (frănk′lĭn)	116-17	39°28′N	86°03′W
Franklin, Ky., U.S. (frănk′lĭn)	124-25	36°43′N	86°35′W
Franklin, La., U.S. (frănk′lĭn)	124-25	29°47′N	91°30′W
Franklin, N.C., U.S. (frănk′lĭn)	124-25	35°11′N	83°23′W
Franklin, N.H., U.S. (frănk′lĭn)	116-17	43°27′N	71°40′W
Franklin, Tx., U.S. (frănk′lĭn)	122-23	31°01′N	96°29′W
Franklin, Va., U.S. (frănk′lĭn)	124-25	36°41′N	76°56′W
Franklin, Wi., U.S. (frănk′lĭn)	116-17	42°52′N	87°60′W
Franklin, W.V., U.S. (frănk′lĭn)	116-17	38°39′N	79°21′W
Franklin Mountains, mts., N.T., Can. (frănk′lĭn moun′tĭnz)	130-31	62°59′N	123°43′W
Franklinton, La., U.S. (frăŋk′lĭn-tŭn)	124-25	30°51′N	90°09′W
Frantsa-Iosifa, Zemlya, is., Russia *see* Franz Josef Land	218-19	81°0′N	55°00′E
Franz Josef Land, is., Russia	218-19	81°0′N	55°00′E
Frascati, Italy (fräs-kä′tē)	200-01	41°48′N	12°41′E
Fraser, stm., B.C., Can.	132-33	49°06′N	123°11′W
Fraserburgh, Scot., U.K. (frā′zĕr-bûrg)	190-91	57°42′N	2°01′W
Fraser Island, i., Austl.	276	25°15′S	153°10′E
Fraser Plateau, plat., B.C., Can.	132-33	52°0′N	123°00′W
Fray Bentos, Ur.	173	33°08′S	58°18′W
Frazee, Mn., U.S. (frā-zē′)	114-15	46°44′N	95°42′W
Fredericia, Den. (frĕdh-ĕ-rē′tsē-à)	192-93	55°35′N	9°46′E
Frederick, Ok., U.S. (frĕd′ĕr-ĭk)	120-21	34°23′N	99°01′W
Fredericksburg, Tx., U.S. (frĕd′ēr-ĭkz-bûrg)	122-23	30°16′N	98°52′W
Fredericksburg, Va., U.S. (frĕd′ēr-ĭkz-bûrg)	116-17	38°18′N	77°28′W
Fredericktown, Mo., U.S. (frĕd′ēr-ĭk-toun)	120-21	37°34′N	90°18′W
Fredericton, N.B., Can. (frĕd′-ēr-ĭk-tŭn)	138-39	45°57′N	66°39′W
Frederikshavn, Den. (frĕdh′ĕ-rĕks-houn)	192-93	57°26′N	10°32′E
Fredonia, Col. (frĕ-dō′nyá)	163c	5°56′N	75°40′W
Fredonia, N.Y., U.S. (frē-dō′nĭ-ȧ)	116-17	42°26′N	79°20′W
Fredrikstad, Nor. (frådh′rĕks-ståd)	192-93	59°12′N	10°56′E
Freels, Cape, c., Nf., Can. (kāp frēlz)	138-39	49°15′N	53°28′W
Freeport, Bah. (frē′pōrt)	142-43	26°31′N	78°39′W
Freeport, Il., U.S. (frē′pōrt)	116-17	42°18′N	89°37′W
Freeport, N.Y., U.S. (frē′pōrt)	116-17	40°39′N	73°35′W
Freeport, Tx., U.S. (frē′pōrt)	122-23	28°57′N	95°22′W
Freetown, nat. cap., S.L. (frē′toun)	260-61	8°29′N	13°13′W
Freiberg, Ger. (frī′bĕrgh)	194-95	50°55′N	13°21′E
Freirina, Chile (frå-ĭ-rē′nä)	168-69	28°30′S	71°06′W
Freising, Ger. (frī′zĭng)	194-95	48°24′N	11°44′E
Fréjus, Fr. (frā-zhüs′)	196-97	43°26′N	6°45′E
Fremantle, Austl. (frē′măn-t'l)	270-71	32°03′S	115°45′E
Fremont, Ca., U.S. (frē-mŏnt′)	118-19	37°33′N	121°59′W
Fremont, Mi., U.S. (frē′-mŏnt)	116-17	43°28′N	85°57′W
Fremont, Ne., U.S. (frē′-mŏnt)	114-15	41°27′N	96°30′W
Fremont, Oh., U.S. (frē′-mŏnt)	116-17	41°21′N	83°07′W
French Guiana, dep., S.A. (frĕnch gē-ä′nä)	158	4°0′N	53°00′W
French Lick, In., U.S. (frĕnch lĭk)	116-17	38°33′N	86°37′W
French Polynesia, dep., Oc. (frĕnch pŏl-ĭ-nē′zhȧ)	280-81	15°0′S	140°00′W
French Somaliland, nation, Afr. *see* Djibouti	253	11°30′N	43°00′E
Fresco, stm., Braz.	166-67	6°40′S	52°00′W
Freshfield, Mount, mtn., Can. (mount frĕsh′fēld)	132-33	51°44′N	116°57′W
Fresnillo, Mex. (frås-nēl′yō)	146-47	23°10′N	102°52′W
Fresno, Col. (frĕs′nô)	163c	5°09′N	75°01′W
Fresno, Ca., U.S.	118-19	36°45′N	119°46′W
Fria, Cape, c., Nmb. (kāp frĭȧ)	264-65	18°29′S	12°02′E
Frías, Arg. (frē′äs)	168-69	28°38′S	65°07′W
Friedberg, Ger. (frēd′bĕrgh)	194-95	48°22′N	10°59′E
Friedrichshafen, Ger. (frē-drēks-häf′ĕn)	194-95	47°40′N	9°29′E
Friend, Ne., U.S. (frĕnd)	120-21	40°39′N	97°17′W
Friesische Inseln, is., Eur. *see* Frisian Islands	190-91	53°27′N	5°50′E
Frio, Cabo, c., Braz. (kå′bō-frē′ō)	172	22°53′S	42°00′W
Frisian Islands, is., Eur. (frē′zhăn ī′lăndz)	190-91	53°27′N	5°50′E
Frobisher Bay, Nu., Can. *see* Iqaluit	128-29	63°44′N	68°28′W
Frobisher Bay, b., Nu., Can. (frŏb′ĭsh′ĕr bā)	130-31	62°30′N	65°60′W
Frobisher Lake, lk., Sk., Can. (frŏb′ĭsh′ĕr lāk)	134-35	56°22′N	108°17′W
Frolovo, Russia	186-87	49°47′N	43°39′E
Frome, Lake, lk., Austl. (lăk froom)	276	30°42′S	139°48′E
Frontera, Mex. (frôn-tā′rä)	146-47	18°32′N	92°38′W
Frontera, Mex. (frôn-tā′rä)	122-23	26°56′N	101°27′W
Front Royal, Va., U.S. (frŭnt roi′ăl)	116-17	38°55′N	78°12′W
Frosinone, Italy (frō-zē-nō′nå)	200-01	41°39′N	13°21′E
Frostburg, Md., U.S. (frôst′bûrg)	116-17	39°39′N	78°55′W
Frøya, i., Nor.	184-85	63°43′N	8°42′E
Fruita, Co., U.S. (froot-ȧ)	118-19	39°10′N	108°44′W
Fuchun, stm., China (foo-chòn)	238-39	30°06′N	120°10′E
Fuego, Volcán de, vol., Guat. (vôl-kä′n-dĕ-fwā′gō)	148	14°29′N	90°53′W
Fuente de Cantos, Spain (fwĕn′tå dā kän′tōs)	198-99	38°15′N	6°18′W
Fuerte, stm., Mex. (foo-ĕ′r-tĕ)	144-45	25°51′N	109°25′W
Fuerte Olimpo, Para. (fwĕr′tå ō-lēm-pō)	168-69	21°05′S	57°52′W
Fuerteventura, i., Spain (fwĕr′tå-vĕn-too′rä)	199d	28°20′N	14°00′W
Fuga Island, i., Phil.	250a	18°52′N	121°22′E
Fuji, Japan (foo′jē)	245	35°09′N	138°40′E
Fuji, stm., Japan (foo′jē)	245	35°07′N	138°39′E
Fujian, state, China (foo-jyĕn)	225a	26°0′N	118°00′E
Fujin, China (foo-jyĭn)	240-41	47°15′N	132°02′E
Fuji-san, vol., Japan (foo′jē-sän)	245	35°22′N	138°44′E
Fujiyama, vol., Japan *see* Fuji-san	245	35°22′N	138°44′E
Fukien, state, China *see* Fujian	225a	26°0′N	118°00′E
Fukuchiyama, Japan (fō′kò-chē-yä′ma)	245	35°18′N	135°07′E
Fukue-jima, i., Japan (fò-koo′ā jē′mȧ)	244	32°40′N	128°45′E
Fukui, Japan (foo′koo-ē)	245	36°04′N	136°13′E
Fukuoka, Japan	245	33°35′N	130°25′E
Fukushima, Japan (foo′kò-shē′má)	245	37°45′N	140°28′E
Fulaga, i., Fiji	279f	19°09′S	178°36′W
Fulaga Passage, strt., Fiji	279f	18°56′S	178°36′W
Fulda, Ger. (fòl′dä)	194-95	50°33′N	9°41′E
Fuling, China (foo-lĭŋ)	238-39	29°42′N	107°25′E
Fullerton, Ne., U.S. (fòl′ĕr-tŭn)	114-15	41°22′N	97°58′W
Fulton, Il., U.S. (fŭl′tŭn)	114-15	41°52′N	90°10′W
Fulton, Ky., U.S. (fŭl′tŭn)	124-25	36°31′N	88°53′W
Fulton, Mo., U.S. (fŭl′tŭn)	120-21	38°51′N	91°57′W
Fulton, Ms., U.S. (fŭl′tŭn)	124-25	34°14′N	88°24′W
Fulton, N.Y., U.S. (fŭl′tŭn)	116-17	43°19′N	76°25′W
Funafuti, at., Tuvalu	280-81	8°29′S	179°11′E
Funan, China *see* Fushun	243	41°52′N	123°54′E
Funchal, Port. (fòn-shäl′)	258-59	32°39′N	16°54′W
Fundación, Col. (foon-dä-syō′n)	164-65	10°31′N	74°11′W
Fundy, Bay of, b., Can. (bā ŭv fŭn′dĭ)	138-39	45°0′N	66°00′W
Fundy National Park, n.p., N.B., Can. (fŭn′dĭ năsh′ŭn-ăl pärk)	138-39	45°38′N	65°00′W
Fünfkirchen, Hung. *see* Pécs	194-95	46°04′N	18°13′E
Funing, China (foo-nĭŋ)	238-39	23°34′N	105°37′E
Furnas, Represa de, res., Braz.	172	21°12′S	45°57′W
Furneaux Group, is., Austl. (fûr′nō groop)	276	40°10′S	148°05′E
Fürstenwalde, Ger. (für′stĕn-väl-dĕ)	194-95	52°21′N	14°04′E
Fürth, Ger. (fürt)	194-95	49°28′N	10°59′E
Fusan, Kor., S. *see* Pusan	243	35°05′N	129°03′E
Fushun, China (foo′shoon′)	243	41°52′N	123°54′E
Fusong, China (foo-soŋ)	243	42°20′N	127°17′E
Fusui, China	238-39	22°38′N	107°55′E
Futuna, Île, i., Wal./F.	280-81	14°18′S	178°09′W
Fuxian, China (foo shyĕn)	240-41	36°02′N	109°22′E
Fuxian, China (foo shyĕn) *see* Wafangdian	240-41	39°37′N	122°01′E
Fuxian Hu, lk., China	238-39	24°29′N	102°53′E
Fuxin, China (foo-shyĭn)	240-41	42°08′N	121°45′E
Fuyang, China (foo-yäŋ)	238-39	32°54′N	115°49′E
Fuyang, stm., China (foo-yäŋ)	240-41	38°11′N	116°04′E
Fuyu, China (foo-yoo)	240-41	45°10′N	124°49′E
Fuyu, China (foo-yoo)	240-41	47°49′N	124°28′E
Fuzhou, China	225a	26°06′N	119°17′E
Fuzhou, China (foo-jō)	238-39	28°01′N	116°20′E
Fyn, i., Den. (fü′'n)	192-93	55°20′N	10°30′E

G

Feature (Pronunciation)	Page	Lat.	Long.
Gaalkacyo, Som.	262-63	6°46′N	47°26′E
Gabela, Ang.	264-65	10°51′S	14°22′E
Gaberones, nat. cap., Bots. *see* Gaborone	264-65	24°40′S	25°56′E
Gabès, Tun. (gä′bĕs)	188-89	33°54′N	10°06′E
Gabès, Golfe de, b., Tun. (gôlf-dĕ-gä′bĕs)	258-59	34°14′N	10°30′E

Feature (Pronunciation)	Page	Lat.	Long.
Gabon, nation, Afr. (gà-bôn´)	253	1°0's	11°45'E
Gaborone, nat. cap., Bots.			
(gà-bō-rō´-nä) (gà´bô-rōō-nä)	264-65	24°40's	25°56'E
Gabrovo, Blg. (gäb´rô-vō)	200-01	42°51'N	25°19'E
Gachsārān, Iran	230-31	30°12'N	50°47'E
Gacko, Bos. (gäts´kô)	200-01	43°10'N	18°32'E
Gadag, India	236	15°25'N	75°37'E
Gadsden, Al., U.S. (gădz´děn)	124-25	34°00'N	86°01'w
Găeşti, Rom. (gà-yĕsh´tě)	200-01	44°43'N	25°20'E
Gaeta, Italy (gä-ā´tä)	200-01	41°13'N	13°34'E
Gaferut, i., Micron.	280-81	9°12'N	145°23'E
Gaffney, S.C., U.S. (găf´nĭ)	124-25	35°04'N	81°39'w
Gafsa, Tun. (gäf´sä)	188-89	34°24'N	8°49'E
Gagnoa, C. Iv.	260-61	6°07'N	5°56'w
Gagra, Geor.	227	43°20'N	40°15'E
Gaillimh, Ire. see Galway	190-91	53°16'N	9°03'w
Gainesville, Fl., U.S. (gānz´vĭl)	124-25	29°39'N	82°18'w
Gainesville, Ga., U.S. (gānz´vĭl)	124-25	34°18'N	83°49'w
Gainesville, Tx., U.S. (gānz´vĭl)	120-21	33°38'N	97°09'w
Gainesville, Va., U.S. (gānz´vĭl)	116-17	38°47'N	77°38'w
Gairdner, Lake, lk., Austl.			
(lāk gärd´něr)	272-73	31°33's	135°57'E
Gaithersburg, Md., U.S.			
(gā´thěrs´bûrg)	116-17	39°08'N	77°12'w
Gaixian, China (gī-shyĕn)	240-41	40°24'N	122°22'E
Galán, Cerro, mtn., Arg.	168-69	25°57's	66°54'w
Galana, stm., Kenya	262-63	3°09's	40°08'E
Galapagos Islands, is., Ec.			
(gä-lä´-pä-gōs ī´lándz)			
see Colón, Archipiélago de	170a	0°43'N	91°30'w
Galashiels, Scot., U.K. (găl-á-shēlz)	190-91	55°38'N	2°50'w
Galaţi, Rom.	202-03	45°26'N	28°03'E
Galatina, Italy (gä-lä-tē´nä)	200-01	40°10'N	18°10'E
Galatz, Rom. see Galaţi	202-03	45°26'N	28°03'E
Galdhøpiggen, mtn., Nor.	192-93	61°37'N	8°17'E
Galeana, Mex. (gä-lå-ä´nä)	122-23	24°50'N	100°04'w
Galela, Indon.	248-49	1°50'N	127°50'E
Galena, Ak., U.S. (gá-lē´ná)	126	64°44'N	156°57'w
Galena, Il., U.S. (gá-lē´ná)	114-15	42°25'N	90°25'w
Galera, Punta, c., Chile	171	39°58's	73°40'w
Galera, Punta, c., Ec.	170	0°49'N	80°03'w
Galesburg, Il., U.S.	114-15	40°57'N	90°22'w
Galeton, Pa., U.S. (găl´tŭn)	116-17	41°44'N	77°39'w
Galich, Russia (gäl´ĭch)	186-87	58°23'N	42°22'E
Galicia, hist. reg., Eur. (gá-lĭsh´ĭ-á)	194-95	49°0'N	22°00'E
Galicja, hist. reg., Eur. see Galicia	194-95	49°0'N	22°00'E
Galilee, Sea of, lk., Isr. (sē ŭv găl´ĭ-lē)	228-29	32°48'N	35°35'E
Galion, Oh., U.S. (găl´ĭ-ŭn)	116-17	40°44'N	82°47'w
Galkynyş, Turkmen.	232-33	39°16'N	63°11'E
Gallatin, Mo., U.S. (găl´á-tĭn)	120-21	39°55'N	93°58'w
Gallatin, Tn., U.S. (găl´á-tĭn)	124-25	36°24'N	86°27'w
Galle, Sri L. (găl)	236	6°02'N	80°13'E
Gallinas, Punta, c., Col.			
(pōō´n-tä-gä-lyē´näs)	164-65	12°28'N	71°40'w
Gallipoli, Italy (găl-lē´pô-lē)	200-01	40°03'N	17°59'E
Gallipoli, Tur.	200-01	40°26'N	26°41'E
Gallipoli Peninsula, pen., Tur.			
(găl-lē´pô-lē pě-nĭn´sŭlá)	200-01	40°20'N	26°30'E
Gallipolis, Oh., U.S. (găl-ĭ-pô-lēs)	116-17	38°49'N	82°12'w
Gällivare, Swe. (yĕl-ĭ-vär´ĕ)	184-85	67°08'N	20°7'E
Gallup, N.M., U.S. (găl´ŭp)	118-19	35°32'N	108°45'w
Galva, Il., U.S. (găl´vá)	114-15	41°10'N	90°02'w
Galveston, Tx., U.S. (găl´věs-tŭn)	122-23	29°18'N	94°48'w
Galveston Bay, b., Tx., U.S.			
(găl´věs-tŭn bā)	122-23	29°36'N	94°57'w
Galveston Island, i., Tx., U.S.			
(găl´věs-tŭn ī´lánd)	122-23	29°13'N	94°55'w
Gálvez, Arg.	173	32°02's	61°13'w
Galway, Ire. (gôl´wā)	190-91	53°16'N	9°03'w
Gamba, China (gäm-bä)	234-35	28°17'N	88°31'E
Gambell, Ak., U.S.	126	63°47'N	171°44'w
Gambia, The, nation, Afr.			
(thá găm´bē-á)	253	13°30'N	15°30'w
Gambier, Îles, is., Fr. Poly.	280-81	23°08's	134°57'w
Gamboma, Congo (gäm-bō´mä)	262-63	1°53's	15°51'E
Gamlakarleby, Fin. see Kokkola	184-85	63°50'N	23°09'E
Gamleby, Swe. (gäm´lě-bü)	192-93	57°55'N	16°23'E
Gan, stm., China (gän)	222-23	49°11'N	125°10'E
Gananoque, On., Can.	136-37	44°20'N	76°10'w
Gäncä, Azer.	227	40°41'N	46°21'E
Ganda, Ang.	264-65	13°02's	14°39'E
Gandajika, D.R.C.	262-63	6°44's	23°57'E
Gander, Nf., Can. (găn´děr)	138-39	48°57'N	54°35'w
Gander, stm., Nf., Can. (găn´děr)	138-39	49°29'N	54°24'w
Gander Lake, lk., Nf., Can.			
(găn´děr lăk)	138-39	48°57'N	54°39'w

Feature (Pronunciation)	Page	Lat.	Long.
Gāndhinagar, India	234-35	23°13'N	72°40'E
Gandia, Spain	198-99	38°58'N	0°11'w
Ganga, stm., Asia see Ganges	234-35		
Gangānagar, India	234-35	29°55'N	73°52'E
Gangaw, Mya.	246-47	22°11'N	94°09'E
Gangdisê Shan, mts., China	234-35	31°0'N	82°00'E
Ganges, stm., Asia (găn´jēz)	234-35	21°58'N	90°57'E
Ganges, Mouths of the, mth., Asia			
(mouthz ŭv thá găn´jēz)	234-35	22°0'N	89°00'E
Gangneung, Kor., S. see Kangnŭng	243	37°46'N	128°54'E
Gangotri, India	234-35	30°60'N	78°59'E
Gangtok, India	234-35	27°19'N	88°38'E
Gangu, China	238-39	34°45'N	105°20'E
Gannan, China (găn-nän)	240-41	47°56'N	123°30'E
Gannett Peak, mtn., Wy., U.S.			
(găn´ět pēk)	112-13	43°11'N	109°39'w
Gansu, state, China (găn-sōō)	240-41	37°0'N	103°00'E
Ganzê, China	238-39	31°38'N	100°01'E
Ganzhou, China (gän-jō)	238-39	25°53'N	114°55'E
Gao, Mali (gä´ō)	258-59	16°16'N	0°02'w
Gao'an, China (gou-än)	238-39	28°26'N	115°23'E
Gaoyi, China (gou-yē)	240-41	37°37'N	114°36'E
Gaoyou, China (gou-yō)	238-39	32°47'N	119°26'E
Gaoyou Hu, lk., China (kä´ō-yōō´hōō)	238-39	32°50'N	119°20'E
Gap, Fr. (gáp)	196-97	44°34'N	6°05'E
Garabogazköl Aylagy, b., Turkmen.			
see Kara-Bogaz-Gol Gulf	232-33	41°15'N	53°24'E
Garagum, des., Turkmen.			
see Kara Kum	226	39°0'N	60°00'E
Garagum Kanaly, can., Turkmen.			
see Kara-Kum Canal	232-33	37°34'N	65°41'E
Garanhuns, Braz. (gä-rän-yónsh´)	163d	8°54's	36°29'w
Garber, Ok., U.S. (gär´běr)	120-21	36°26'N	97°35'w
Garden City, Ga., U.S. (gär´d'n sī´tě)	124-25	32°07'N	81°09'w
Garden City, Ks., U.S. (gär´d'n sī´tě)	120-21	37°58'N	100°52'w
Gardeyz, Afg.	232-33	33°36'N	69°13'E
Gardiner, Mt., U.S. (gärd´něr)	112-13	45°02'N	110°42'w
Gardner, Ks., U.S. (gärd´něr)	120-21	38°49'N	94°56'w
Gardner, Ma., U.S. (gärd´něr)	116-17	42°35'N	71°60'w
Gardner Canal, b., B.C., Can.			
(gärd´něr kä´nál)	132-33	53°28'N	128°18'w
Gardner Pinnacles, r., Hi., U.S.			
(gärd´něr pĭn´á-k'lz)	127	25°0'N	167°55'w
Garibaldi, Mount, vol., B.C., Can.			
(mount gär-ĭ-bäl´dĕ)	132-33	49°51'N	122°59'w
Garissa, Kenya	262-63	0°27's	39°39'E
Garland, Tx., U.S. (gär´länd)	120-21	32°56'N	96°38'w
Garmisch-Partenkirchen, Ger.			
(gär´měsh pär´těn-kēr´кěn)	194-95	47°30'N	11°06'E
Garnett, Ks., U.S. (gär´nět)	120-21	38°17'N	95°14'w
Garoua, Camrn. (gär´wä)	260-61	9°19'N	13°23'E
Garqu Yan, China	238-39	33°54'N	92°19'E
Garrett, In., U.S. (gär´ět)	116-17	41°21'N	85°07'w
Garrison, N.D., U.S. (gär´ĭ-sŭn)	114-15	47°39'N	101°25'w
Garry Lake, lk., Nu., Can. (gär´ĭ lǎk)	130-31	66°0'N	100°00'w
Garut, Indon.	248-49	7°12's	107°54'E
Garwolin, Pol. (gär-vō´lěn)	194-95	51°54'N	21°38'E
Gary, In., U.S. (gā´rĭ)	116-17	41°36'N	87°21'w
Garyarsa, China	234-35	31°43'N	80°20'E
Garzón, Col. (gär-thōn´)	164-65	2°12'N	75°38'w
Gas City, In., U.S. (gäs sī´tě)	116-17	40°29'N	85°37'w
Gascogne, Golfe de, b., Eur.			
see Biscay, Bay of	196-97	44°0'N	4°00'w
Gash, stm., Afr.	266	16°45'N	35°54'E
Gaspé, Qc., Can.	138-39	48°49'N	64°29'w
Gasteiz, Spain	198-99	42°51'N	2°40'w
Gastonia, N.C., U.S. (găs-tō´nĭ-á)	124-25	35°16'N	81°11'w
Gastre, Arg. (gäs-trě)	171	42°17's	69°14'w
Gata, Cabo de, c., Spain			
(kä´bô-dě-gä´tä)	198-99	36°44'N	2°11'w
Gata, Sierra de, mts., Spain			
(syěr´rá dä gä´tä)	198-99	40°16'N	6°44'w
Gatchina, Russia (gä-chē´ná)	192-93	59°33'N	30°08'E
Gates of the Arctic National Park			
and Preserve, n.p., Ak., U.S.	126	67°45'N	153°30'w
Gatesville, Tx., U.S. (gäts´vĭl)	122-23	31°25'N	97°44'w
Gatineau, Qc., Can. (gá´tě-nō)	136-37	45°29'N	75°38'w
Gatineau, stm., Qc., Can. (gá´tě-nō)	136-37	45°27'N	75°42'w
Gauer Lake, lk., Mb., Can.	134-35	57°0'N	97°50'w
Gauja, stm., Eur. (gä´ó-yä)	192-93	57°09'N	24°17'E
Gaustatoppen, mtn., Nor.	192-93	59°50'N	8°35'E
Gávdos, i., Grc. (gäv´dôs)	200a	34°50'N	24°06'E
Gävle, Swe. (yěv´lě)	192-93	60°40'N	17°10'E
Gavrilov-Yam, Russia			
(gá´vrě-lôf yäm´)	202-03	57°18'N	39°52'E

Feature (Pronunciation)	Page	Lat.	Long.
Gaxun Nur, lk., China	240-41	42°22'N	100°34'E
Gaya, India (gǔ´yä)(gī´á)	234-35	24°48'N	85°00'E
Gaylord, Mi., U.S. (gā´lôrd)	116-17	45°02'N	84°40'w
Gaylord, Mn., U.S. (gā´lôrd)	114-15	44°33'N	94°14'w
Gayndah, Austl. (gān´däh)	276	25°38's	151°36'E
Gayny, Russia	186-87	60°18'N	54°19'E
Gaza, Gaza (gä´zá) (gä´zá)	228-29	31°30'N	34°28'E
Gazanjyk, Turkmen.	232-33	39°15'N	55°32'E
Gaziantep, Tur. (gä-zē-än´těp)	228-29	37°04'N	37°23'E
Gazimağusa, Cyp.	228-29	35°13'N	33°57'E
Gbadolite, D.R.C.	262-63	4°15'N	21°00'E
Gbanga, Lib.	260-61	7°00'N	9°29'w
Gboko, Nig.	260-61	7°20'N	8°60'E
Gdańsk, Pol. (g´dänsk)	194-95	54°21'N	18°38'E
Gdov, Russia (g´dôf)	192-93	58°45'N	27°49'E
Gdynia, Pol. (g´děn´yá)	194-95	54°32'N	18°31'E
Geary, Ok., U.S. (gē´rĭ)	120-21	35°38'N	98°19'w
Gediz, stm., Tur.	200-01	38°35'N	26°48'E
Geelong, Austl. (jē-lông´)	276	38°08's	144°21'E
Geeveston, Austl.	276	43°10's	146°55'E
Gefle, Swe. see Gävle	192-93	60°40'N	17°10'E
Geita, Tan.	267	2°52's	32°10'E
Gejiu, China (gǔ-jīo)	238-39	23°22'N	103°09'E
Gela, Italy	200-01	37°04'N	14°15'E
Gelasa, Selat, strt., Indon.	246-47	2°55's	107°13'E
Gelibolu, Tur. (gě-lĭb´ô-lò)			
see Gallipoli	200-01	40°26'N	26°41'E
Gelibolu Yarımadası, pen., Tur.			
see Gallipoli Peninsula	200-01	40°20'N	26°30'E
Gemena, D.R.C.	262-63	3°14'N	19°47'E
Gemlik, Tur. (gěm´lĭk)	200-01	40°26'N	29°09'E
Gemsbok National Park, n.p., Bots.	264-65	25°15's	21°10'E
Gen, stm., China	240-41	50°15'N	119°21'E
Genalē, stm., Afr.	262-63	0°15's	42°39'E
General Acha, Arg.	173	37°23's	64°36'w
General Alvear, Arg.			
(hě-ně-rál´ ál-vě-ä´r)	171	34°59's	67°42'w
General Alvear, Arg.			
(hě-ně-rál´ äl-vě-á´r)	173	36°01's	60°01'w
General Belgrano, Arg.			
(hě-ně-rál´ běl-grá´nô)	173	35°46's	58°29'w
General Carrera, Lago, lk., S.A.	171	46°26's	71°40'w
General Cepeda, Mex.			
(hě-ně-rál´ sě-pě´dä)	122-23	25°23'N	101°28'w
General Conesa, Arg.	171	40°07's	64°26'w
General Eugenio A. Garay, Para.	168-69	20°35's	62°11'w
General Guido, Arg. (hě-ně-rál´ gē´dô)	173	36°40's	57°48'w
General Juan Madariaga, Arg.	173	37°00's	57°09'w
General La Madrid, Arg.	173	37°15's	61°17'w
General Lavalle, Arg.			
(hě-ně-rál´ lá-vä´l-yě)	173	36°25's	56°57'w
General Levalle, Arg.	173	34°01's	63°55'w
General Manuel Belgrano, Cerro,			
mtn., Arg.	168-69	29°01's	67°50'w
General Pico, Arg. (hě-ně-rál´ pē´kô)	173	35°40's	63°46'w
General Pinedo, Arg.	173	27°19's	61°17'w
General Roca, Arg. (hě-ně-rál´ rô-kä)	171	39°01's	67°35'w
General San Martín, Arg.			
(hě-ně-rál´ sän-mär-tē´n)	173	34°34's	58°33'w
General Santos, Phil.	250	6°07'N	125°10'E
General Viamonte, Arg.			
(hě-ně-rál´ vēä´môn-tě)	173	34°60's	61°02'w
General Villegas, Arg.	173	35°02's	63°01'w
Geneseo, Il., U.S. (jě-něsěō)	114-15	41°27'N	90°09'w
Geneva, Switz. (jě-ně´vá)	194-95	46°12'N	6°09'E
Geneva, Al., U.S. (jě-ně´vá)	124-25	31°02'N	85°52'w
Geneva, In., U.S. (jě-ně´vá)	116-17	40°35'N	84°57'w
Geneva, Ne., U.S. (jě-ně´vá)	120-21	40°32'N	97°36'w
Geneva, N.Y., U.S. (jě-ně´vá)	116-17	42°52'N	76°59'w
Geneva, Oh., U.S. (jě-ně´vá)	116-17	41°48'N	80°56'w
Geneva, Lake, lk., Eur. (lǎk jě-ně´vá)	194-95	46°26'N	6°22'E
Genève, Switz. see Geneva	194-95	46°12'N	6°09'E
Genève, Lac de, lk., Eur.			
see Geneva, Lake	194-95	46°24'N	6°22'E
Genf, Switz. see Geneva	194-95	46°12'N	6°09'E
Genil, stm., Spain (hä-nēl´)	198-99	37°42'N	5°19'w
Genoa, Italy (jen´ô-á)	200-01	44°25'N	8°57'E
Genova, Italy see Genoa	200-01	44°25'N	8°57'E
Genova, Golfo di, b., Italy			
(gôl-fô-dě-jěn´ō-vä)	200-01	44°10'N	8°55'E
Genovesa, Isla, i., Ec.			
(ě´s-lä-gě-nō-vě-sä)	170a	0°20'N	89°57'w
Gensan, Kor., N. see Wŏnsan	243	39°09'N	127°26'E
Geographe Bay, b., Austl.			
(jě-ô-graf´ bä)	272-73	33°35's	115°15'E

n-sing; ŋ-baŋk; N-nasalized n; nŏd; cŏmmit; ōld; ôbey; ôrder; oi-boil; fōōd; ó-as oo in foot; ou-out; s-soft; sh-dish; th-thin; pūre; ûnite; ûrn; stŭd; circŭs; u-as in French tu;　´-indeterminate vowel.

Feature (Pronunciation)	Page	Lat.	Long.
George, S. Afr.	264-65	33°58'S	22°27'E
George, stm., Qc., Can.	130-31	58°46'N	66°08'W
George, Lake, lk., Ug. (lăk jôrg)	267	0°02'N	30°12'E
George, Lake, lk., Fl., U.S. (lăk jôr-ĭj)	124-25	29°17'N	81°36'W
Georgetown, On., Can. (jôr-ĭj-toun)	136-37	43°39'N	79°55'W
Georgetown, P.E., Can. (jôr-ĭj-toun)	138-39	46°11'N	62°32'W
Georgetown, Gam.	260-61	13°33'N	14°46'W
George Town, Malay.	246-47	5°25'N	100°20'E
Georgetown, De., U.S. (jôrg-toun)	116-17	38°41'N	75°23'W
Georgetown, Il., U.S. (jôrg-toun)	116-17	39°58'N	87°38'W
Georgetown, Ky., U.S. (jôrg-toun)	116-17	38°12'N	84°34'W
Georgetown, Oh., U.S. (jôrg-toun)	116-17	38°51'N	83°52'W
Georgetown, S.C., U.S. (jôr-ĭj-toun)	124-25	33°23'N	79°18'W
Georgetown, Tx., U.S. (jôrg-toun)	122-23	30°38'N	97°41'W
George Town, nat. cap., Cay. Is. (jôr-ĭj-toun)	142-43	19°18'N	81°22'W
Georgetown, nat. cap., Guy. (jôrj'toun)	164-65	6°48'N	58°09'W
George Washington Birthplace National Monument, n.p., Va., U.S. (jôrj wŏsh'ĭng-tŭn bûrth'plās năsh'ŭn-ăl mŏn'ū-mĕnt)	116-17	38°11'N	76°56'W
George Washington Carver National Monument, n.p., Mo., U.S. (jôrg wăsh-ĭng-tŭn kär'vẽr năsh'ŭn-ăl mŏn'ū-mĕnt)	120-21	37°00'N	94°21'W
George West, Tx., U.S. (jôrg wĕst)	122-23	28°20'N	98°07'W
Georgia, nation, Asia (jôr'ji-ă)	227	42°0'N	44°00'E
Georgia, state, U.S. (jôr'jĭ-ă)	108-09	32°50'N	83°15'W
Georgiana, Al., U.S. (jôr-jē-ăn'ă)	124-25	31°38'N	86°45'W
Georgian Bay, b., On., Can.	136-37	45°15'N	80°50'W
Georgiyevsk, Russia (gyôr-gyĕfsk')	227	44°09'N	43°29'E
Gera, Ger. (gā'rä)	194-95	50°52'N	12°05'E
Geral, Serra, mts., Braz. (sĕr'ră zhă-räl')	168-69	26°30'S	50°30'W
Geraldton, Austl. (jĕr'ăld-tŭn)	270-71	28°46'S	114°37'E
Geraldton, On., Can.	128-29	49°41'N	86°60'W
Gereshk, Afg.	232-33	31°49'N	64°34'E
Gering, Ne., U.S. (gē'rĭng)	114-15	41°48'N	103°40'W
Gerlachovský štít, mtn., Slvk.	194-95	49°11'N	20°09'E
Germantown, Tn., U.S. (jûr'măn-toun)	124-25	35°06'N	89°49'W
Germantown, Wi., U.S. (jûr'măn-toun)	116-17	43°14'N	88°07'W
Germany, nation, Eur. (jûr'mă-nĭ)	174-75	51°0'N	10°00'E
Germiston, S. Afr. (jûr'mĭs-tŭn)	269c	26°13'S	28°11'E
Gerona, Spain *see* Girona	198-99	41°59'N	2°49'E
Getafe, Spain (hä-tä'fā)	198-99	40°19'N	3°44'W
Gettysburg, S.D., U.S. (gĕt'ĭs-bûrg)	114-15	45°01'N	99°57'W
Ghaapplato, plat., S. Afr.	264-65	27°29'S	24°19'E
Ghadāmis, Libya	188-89	30°12'N	9°33'E
Ghāghara, stm., Asia	234-35	25°45'N	84°48'E
Ghāghra, stm., Asia *see* Ghāghara	234-35	25°45'N	84°48'E
Ghana, nation, Afr. (gän'ä)	253	8°0'N	1°00'W
Ghanzi, Bots. (gän'zē)	264-65	21°42'S	21°39'E
Ghardaïa, Alg. (gär-dä'ē-ä)	258-59	32°33'N	3°40'E
Gharm, Taj.	232-33	39°02'N	70°23'E
Gharyān, Libya	188-89	32°10'N	13°01'E
Ghāt, Libya	258-59	24°56'N	10°12'E
Ghawdex, i., Malta *see* Gozo	200b	36°03'N	14°15'E
Ghazal, Bahr el, stm., Chad (bär ĕl ghä-zäl')	258-59	13°05'N	15°20'E
Ghāziābād, India	234-35	28°40'N	77°26'E
Ghaznī, Afg.	232-33	33°33'N	68°25'E
Ghazzah, Gaza (gä'ziä) *see* Gaza	228-29	31°30'N	34°28'E
Ghijduwon, Uzb.	232-33	40°06'N	64°41'E
Ghorīān, Afg.	232-33	34°21'N	61°29'E
Gibara, Cuba (hē-bä'rä)	142-43	21°07'N	76°08'W
Gibraleón, Spain (hē-brä-lå-ōn')	198-99	37°23'N	6°58'W
Gibraltar, dep., Eur. (gĭ-bräl-tă'r)	174-75	36°08'N	5°21'W
Gibraltar, nat. cap., Gib. (gĭ-bräl-tă'r)	198-99	36°08'N	5°21'W
Gibraltar, Estrecho de, strt., *see* Gibraltar, Strait of	198-99	35°57'N	5°36'W
Gibraltar, Strait of, strt., (stăt ŭv gĭ-bräl-tă'r)	198-99	35°57'N	5°36'W
Gibson City, Il., U.S. (gĭb'sŭn sĭ'tê)	116-17	40°28'N	88°22'W
Gibson Desert, des., Austl. (gĭb'sŭn dĕs'ẽrt)	272-73	24°30'S	126°00'E
Giddings, Tx., U.S. (gĭd'ĭngz)	122-23	30°11'N	96°56'W
Gien, Fr. (zhē-ăɴ')	196-97	47°41'N	2°38'E
Gießen, Ger. (gēs'sĕn)	194-95	50°35'N	8°40'E
Gifu, Japan (gē'fōō)	245	35°25'N	136°45'E
Gijón, Spain (hê-hōn')	198-99	43°32'N	5°40'W
Gila, stm., U.S. (hē'lă)	110-11	32°43'N	114°33'W
Gila Bend, Az., U.S. (hē'lă bĕnd)	118-19	32°57'N	112°43'W
Gila Cliff Dwellings National Monument, n.p., N.M., U.S. (hē'lă klĭf dwĕl'ĭngz năsh'ŭn-ăl mŏn'ū-mĕnt)	118-19	33°02'N	108°16'W
Gilbert, Mn., U.S. (gĭl'bẽrt)	114-15	47°29'N	92°28'W
Gilbert, Mount, mtn., B.C., Can. (mount gĭl-bẽrt)	132-33	50°54'N	124°17'W
Gilbert Islands, nation, Oc. *see* Kiribati	280-81	5°0'S	170°00'W
Gilbert Islands, is., Kir. (gĭl-bẽrt ī'lăndz) *see* Kiribati	280-81	0°30'S	174°00'E
Gilbués, Braz.	166-67	9°50'S	45°21'W
Gilford Island, i., B.C., Can. (gĭl'fẽrd ī'lănd)	132-33	50°45'N	126°20'W
Gilgandra, Austl.	276	31°43'S	148°40'E
Gilgit, Pak. (gĭl'gĭt)	232-33	35°53'N	74°21'E
Gilgit, stm., Pak.	232-33	35°42'N	74°38'E
Gil Island, i., B.C., Can. (gĭl ī'lănd)	132-33	53°11'N	129°15'W
Gillam, Mb., Can.	134-35	56°21'N	94°43'W
Gillette, Wy., U.S. (jĭ-lĕt')	112-13	44°18'N	105°30'W
Gillingham, Eng., U.K. (gĭl'ĭng ăm)	190-91	51°23'N	0°34'E
Gilman, Il., U.S. (gĭl'măn)	116-17	40°46'N	87°59'W
Gilmer, Tx., U.S. (gĭl'mẽr)	120-21	32°44'N	94°57'W
Gīlo, stm., Eth.	262-63	8°07'N	33°11'E
Gilroy, Ca., U.S. (gĭl-roi')	118-19	37°01'N	121°34'W
Giluwe, Mount, mtn., Pap. N. Gui.	277	6°02'S	143°51'E
Gilyuy, stm., Russia	218-19	53°59'N	127°27'E
Gimcheon, Kor., S. *see* Kimch'ŏn	243	36°07'N	128°07'E
Gimli, Mb., Can. (gĭm'lē)	134-35	50°38'N	96°59'W
Gioia del Colle, Italy (jô'yä dĕl kôl'lā)	200-01	40°48'N	16°55'E
Girardot, Col. (hē-rär-dōt')	163c	4°18'N	74°47'W
Giresun, Tur. (ghĕr'ĕ-sòn')	186-87	40°55'N	38°24'E
Girga, Egypt	268b	26°20'N	31°53'E
Girīdīh, India (jē-rē-dē)	234-35	24°11'N	86°18'E
Girona, Spain	198-99	41°59'N	2°49'E
Girvan, Scot., U.K. (gûr'văn)	190-91	55°15'N	4°52'W
Gisborne, N.Z. (gĭz'bŭrn)	278	38°40'S	178°01'E
Gisenyi, Rw.	267	1°42'S	29°16'E
Gisors, Fr. (zhē-zôr')	196-97	49°17'N	1°47'E
Gitarama, Rw.	267	2°04'S	29°44'E
Gitega, Bdi.	267	3°21'S	29°54'E
Giurgiu, Rom. (jòr'jò)	200-01	43°54'N	25°58'E
Givet, Fr. (zhē-vĕ')	196-97	50°08'N	4°50'E
Giyon, Eth.	269d	8°32'N	37°59'E
Giza, Egypt	268b	30°01'N	31°13'E
Gizo, Sol. Is.	279e	8°06'S	156°50'E
Giżycko, Pol. (gĭ'zhĭ-ko)	194-95	54°02'N	21°46'E
Gjoa Haven, Nu., Can.	128-29	68°39'N	95°55'W
Gjøvik, Nor. (gyû'vĕk)	192-93	60°48'N	10°41'E
Glace Bay, N.S., Can. (gläs bā)	138-39	46°13'N	59°58'W
Glacier Bay National Park and Preserve, n.p., Ak., U.S.	126	59°04'N	136°36'W
Glacier National Park, n.p., B.C., Can. (glā'shẽr năsh'ŭn-ăl pärk)	132-33	51°15'N	117°35'W
Glacier National Park, n.p., Mt., U.S.	112-13	48°35'N	113°40'W
Glacier Peak, vol., Wa., U.S. (glā'shẽr pēk) (glā'shẽr pēk)	112-13	48°07'N	121°07'W
Gladstone, Austl. (glăd'stōn)	277	23°51'S	151°15'E
Gladstone, Austl. (glăd'stōn)	276	33°17'S	138°21'E
Gladstone, Mi., U.S. (glăd'stōn)	116-17	45°51'N	87°01'W
Gladstone, Mo., U.S. (glăd'stōn)	120-21	39°14'N	94°35'W
Gladwin, Mi., U.S. (glăd'wĭn)	116-17	43°59'N	84°29'W
Glåma, stm., Nor. *see* Glomma	184-85	59°11'N	10°58'E
Glasgow, Scot., U.K. (glás'gō)	190-91	55°53'N	4°15'W
Glasgow, Ky., U.S.	124-25	37°00'N	85°55'W
Glasgow, Mt., U.S.	112-13	48°12'N	106°38'W
Glauchau, Ger. (glou'ĸou)	194-95	50°49'N	12°33'E
Glazov, Russia (glä'zôf)	186-87	58°08'N	52°39'E
Gleiwitz, Pol. *see* Gliwice	194-95	50°17'N	18°40'E
Glen Canyon, val., U.S. (glĕn kăn'yŭn)	118-19	37°10'N	110°50'W
Glencoe, S. Afr. (glĕn-cō)	269c	28°12'S	30°06'E
Glendale, Az., U.S. (glĕn'dāl)	118-19	33°32'N	112°12'W
Glendale, Ca., U.S. (glĕn'dāl)	118-19	34°08'N	118°14'W
Glendive, Mt., U.S. (glĕn'dīv)	112-13	47°06'N	104°43'W
Glen Innes, Austl. (glĕn ĭn'ĕs)	276	29°44'S	151°44'E
Glenns Ferry, Id., U.S. (glĕns fĕr'ē)	112-13	42°58'N	115°18'W
Glenrock, Wy., U.S. (glĕn'rŏk)	112-13	42°52'N	105°53'W
Glens Falls, N.Y., U.S. (glĕnz fôlz)	116-17	43°19'N	73°39'W
Glittertinden, mtn., Nor.	192-93	61°39'N	8°33'E
Gliwice, Pol. (gwĭ-wĭt'sĕ)	194-95	50°17'N	18°40'E
Globe, Az., U.S. (glōb)	118-19	33°24'N	110°47'W
Glomma, stm., Nor.	184-85	59°11'N	10°58'E
Glorieuses, Îles, is., Reu.	264-65	11°30'S	47°20'E
Glorioso Islands, is., Reu. *see* Glorieuses, Îles	264-65	11°30'S	47°20'E
Gloucester, Eng., U.K. (glŏs'tẽr)	190-91	51°53'N	2°14'W
Gloversville, N.Y., U.S. (glŭv'ẽrz-vĭl)	116-17	43°03'N	74°21'W
Glovertown, Nf., Can. (glŭv'ẽr-toun)	138-39	48°40'N	54°03'W
Glückstadt, Ger. (glük-shtät)	194-95	53°47'N	9°26'E
Gmunden, Aus. (g'mòn'dĕn)	194-95	47°55'N	13°47'E
Gnesen, Pol. *see* Gniezno	194-95	52°32'N	17°37'E
Gniezno, Pol. (g'nyåz'nō)	194-95	52°32'N	17°37'E
Gnjilane, Serb. (gnyē'lá-nĕ)	200-01	42°28'N	21°29'E
Goa, state, India (gō'á)	236	15°20'N	74°00'E
Goālpāra, India	234-35	26°10'N	90°37'E
Goba, Eth. (gō'bä)	269d	7°00'N	39°59'E
Gobabis, Nmb. (gō-bä'bĭs)	264-65	22°27'S	18°58'E
Gobernador Gregores, Arg.	171	48°46'S	70°15'W
Gobernador Vera, Arg. *see* Vera	173	29°28'S	60°13'W
Gobi Desert, des., Asia (gō'be dĕs'ẽrt)	240-41	43°0'N	105°00'E
Goch, Ger. (gôk)	194-95	51°41'N	6°09'E
Godāvari, stm., India (gô-dä'vŭ-rê)	236	16°59'N	81°47'E
Goderich, On., Can. (gōd'rĭch)	136-37	43°45'N	81°42'W
Godfrey, Il., U.S. (gŏd'frê)	120-21	38°57'N	90°11'W
Godhavn, Green. (gōdh'håvn)	284-85	69°15'N	53°33'W
Godhra, India	234-35	22°46'N	73°37'E
Godoy Cruz, Arg.	163e	32°55'S	68°50'W
Gods, stm., Mb., Can. (gŏdz)	134-35	56°23'N	92°51'W
Gods Lake, lk., Mb., Can.	134-35	54°43'N	94°14'W
Godthåb, nat. cap., Green. (gŏt'hòb)	284-85	64°11'N	51°44'W
Godwin Austen, mtn., Asia *see* K2	232-33	35°53'N	76°30'E
Goeie Hoop, Kaap die, c., S. Afr. *see* Good Hope, Cape of	264-65	34°21'S	18°28'E
Goiana, Braz.	163d	7°33'S	34°59'W
Goiânia, Braz. (gô-vá'nyä)	168-69	16°40'S	49°16'W
Goiás, Braz. (gô-yá's)	168-69	15°55'S	50°07'W
Goiás, state, Braz. (gô-yá's)	166-67	16°0'S	50°00'W
Gökçeada, i., Tur.	200-01	40°10'N	25°50'E
Gökova Körfezi, b., Tur.	200-01	36°54'N	27°51'E
Göksu, stm., Tur. (gûk'sōō')	228-29	36°19'N	34°03'E
Gol, Nor. (gûl)	192-93	60°42'N	8°57'E
Gold Coast, Austl. *see* Southport	276	27°58'S	153°25'E
Golden, B.C., Can. (gōl'dĕn)	132-33	51°18'N	116°58'W
Golden, Co., U.S. (gōl'dĕn)	118-19	39°45'N	105°13'W
Goldendale, Wa., U.S. (gōl'dĕn-dāl)	112-13	45°49'N	120°50'W
Golden Hinde, mtn., B.C., Can. (gōl'dĕn hīnd)	132-33	49°40'N	125°45'W
Goldsboro, N.C., U.S. (gōldz-bûr'ô)	124-25	35°23'N	77°60'W
Goldthwaite, Tx., U.S. (gōld'thwāt)	122-23	31°27'N	98°34'W
Golfito, C.R. (gôl-fē'tō)	149	8°38'N	83°10'W
Goliad, Tx., U.S. (gō-lĭ-ăd')	122-23	28°40'N	97°23'W
Golmud, China	240-41	36°25'N	94°54'E
Goma, D.R.C.	267	1°41'S	29°13'E
Gombe, Nig.	260-61	10°17'N	11°10'E
Gomel', Bela. *see* Homel'	202-03	52°26'N	30°59'E
Gómez Palacio, Mex. (gō'mĕz pä-lä'syō)	122-23	25°35'N	103°30'W
Gonābād, Iran	232-33	34°21'N	58°41'E
Gonaïves, Haiti (gō-nà-ēv')	142-43	19°27'N	72°41'W
Gonam, stm., Russia	218-19	57°19'N	131°15'E
Gonarezhou National Park, n.p., Zimb.	264-65	21°34'S	31°56'E
Gonâve, Île de la, i., Haiti (ēl-dē-lá-gô-náv')	142-43	18°51'N	73°03'W
Gonbad-e Kāvūs, Iran	232-33	37°15'N	55°10'E
Gonda, India	234-35	27°08'N	81°58'E
Gondar, Eth. *see* Gonder	266	12°37'N	37°28'E
Gonder, Eth.	266	12°37'N	37°28'E
Gondia, India	234-35	21°28'N	80°12'E
Gongbo'gyamda, China	238-39	29°55'N	93°26'E
Gongga Shan, mtn., China (gŏŋ-gä shän)	238-39	29°35'N	101°51'E
Gongola, stm., Nig.	260-61	9°29'N	12°03'E
Gongxian, China	240-41	34°48'N	113°03'E
Gongzhuling, China	240-41	43°30'N	124°49'E
Gonzales, La., U.S. (gŏn-zä'lĕz)	124-25	30°14'N	90°55'W
Gonzales, Tx., U.S. (gŏn-zä'lĕz)	122-23	29°30'N	97°27'W
Goodenough Island, i., Pap. N. Gui.	277	9°20'S	150°15'E
Good Hope, Cape of, c., S. Afr. (kāp ŏv gŏŏd hōp)	264-65	34°21'S	18°28'E
Good Hope Mountain, mtn., B.C., Can. (gŏŏd hōp moun'tĭn)	132-33	51°09'N	124°10'W
Gooding, Id., U.S. (gòd'ĭng)	112-13	42°57'N	114°43'W
Goodland, Ks., U.S. (gòd'lănd)	120-21	39°20'N	101°43'W
Goole, Eng., U.K. (gōōl)	190-91	53°42'N	0°53'W
Goondiwindi, Austl.	276	28°32'S	150°19'E
Goose Lake, lk., U.S. (gōōs lāk)	112-13	41°57'N	120°25'W
Goqên, China	238-39	29°09'N	97°14'E
Gorakhpur, India (gō'rŭk-pōōr)	234-35	26°46'N	83°22'E
Gorda, Punta, c., Cuba (pōō'n-tä-gôr-dä)	142-43	22°23'N	82°09'W
Gorgān, Iran	232-33	36°51'N	54°26'E
Gorgona, Isla, i., Col.	164-65	2°58'N	78°11'W

ăt; finăl; rāte; senāte; ärm; åsk; sofá; fâre; ch-choose; dh-as th in other; bē; ēvent; bĕt; recĕnt; cratẽr; g-gō; gh-guttural g; bĭt; ĭ-short neutral; rīde; ĸ-guttural k as ch in German ich;

Feature (Pronunciation)	Page	Lat.	Long.
Gorgona, Isola di, i., Italy (gôr-gō´nä)	**200-01**	43°26'N	9°54'E
Gori, Geor. (gō´rē)	**227**	41°59'N	44°06'E
Gorica, Italy *see* Gorizia	**200-01**	45°57'N	13°38'E
Gorinchem, Neth. (gō´rĭn-кĕm)	**190-91**	51°50'N	5°01'E
Gorizia, Italy (gô-rē´tsê-yä)	**200-01**	45°57'N	13°38'E
Gorkhā, Nepal	**234-35**	28°0'N	84°37'E
Gorky, Russia *see* Nizhniy Novgorod	**186-87**	56°19'N	44°01'E
Gorki Reservoir, res., Russia (gôr´kē rĕ´sĕr-vwär) *see* Gor'kovskoye Vodokhranilishche	**186-87**	57°02'N	43°10'E
Gor'kovskoye Vodokhranilishche, res., Russia	**186-87**	57°02'N	43°10'E
Gorlice, Pol. (gôr-lē´tsĕ)	**194-95**	49°39'N	21°10'E
Görlitz, Ger. (gür´lĭts)	**194-95**	51°09'N	14°59'E
Gorlovka, Ukr. *see* Horlivka	**202-03**	48°20'N	38°03'E
Gorna Oryakhovitsa, Blg. (gôr´nä-ôr-yĕk´ô-vē-tsá)	**200-01**	43°08'N	25°42'E
Gornji Milanovac, Serb. (gôrn´yē-mē´la-nô-väts)	**200-01**	44°01'N	20°27'E
Gorno-Altaysk, Russia (gôr´nŭ´ŭl-tīsk´)	**226**	51°58'N	85°51'E
Gornozavodsk, Russia	**244**	46°33'N	141°51'E
Gorodets, Russia	**186-87**	56°39'N	43°28'E
Goroka, Pap. N. Gui.	**277**	6°05'S	145°24'E
Gorontalo, Indon. (gō-rōn-tä´lo)	**248-49**	0°32'N	123°04'E
Görz, Italy *see* Gorizia	**200-01**	45°57'N	13°38'E
Gorzów Wielkopolski, Pol. (gō-zhōōv´vyĕl-ko-pōl´skē)	**194-95**	52°44'N	15°14'E
Gosford, Austl.	**276**	33°25'S	151°21'E
Goshen, In., U.S. (gō´shĕn)	**116-17**	41°35'N	85°49'W
Goslar, Ger. (gôs´lär)	**194-95**	51°55'N	10°26'E
Gostivar, Mac. (gos´tê-vär)	**200-01**	41°48'N	20°55'E
Gostynin, Pol. (gôs-tē´nĭn)	**194-95**	52°26'N	19°28'E
Göta, stm., Swe. (gōētä)	**192-93**	57°41'N	11°53'E
Göteborg, Swe.	**192-93**	57°43'N	11°58'E
Gotha, Ger. (gō´tȧ)	**194-95**	50°57'N	10°42'E
Gothenburg, Swe. *see* Göteborg	**192-93**	57°43'N	11°58'E
Gothenburg, Ne., U.S. (gŏth´ĕn-bûrg)	**114-15**	40°56'N	100°10'W
Gotland, i., Swe.	**192-93**	57°30'N	18°33'E
Gotō-rettō, is., Japan	**244**	32°50'N	129°00'E
Gotska Sandön, i., Swe.	**192-93**	58°22'N	19°16'E
Göttingen, Ger. (gŭt´ĭng-ĕn)	**194-95**	51°32'N	9°56'E
Gouda, Neth. (gou´dä)	**190-91**	52°01'N	4°42'E
Gouin, Réservoir, res., Qc., Can.	**136-37**	48°37'N	74°55'W
Goulburn, Austl. (gōl´bŭrn)	**276**	34°45'S	149°43'E
Goundam, Mali (gōōn-däɴ´)	**258-59**	16°25'N	3°40'W
Gouverneur, N.Y., U.S. (gŭv-ẽr-nōōr´)	**116-17**	44°20'N	75°28'W
Governador Valadares, Braz. (gô-vĕr-nä-dō-´r vä-lä-dä´rĕs)	**172**	18°53'S	41°58'W
Goya, Arg. (gō´yä)	**173**	29°09'S	59°15'W
Goyania, Braz. *see* Goiânia	**168-69**	16°40'S	49°16'W
Göyçay, Azer. (gĕ-ôk´chī)	**227**	40°39'N	47°45'E
Gozo, i., Malta	**200b**	36°03'N	14°15'E
Graaff-Reinet, S. Afr. (gräf´rī´nĕt)	**264-65**	32°16'S	24°33'E
Gračac, Cro. (grä´chäts)	**200-01**	44°18'N	15°50'E
Graceville, Fl., U.S. (grās´vĭl)	**124-25**	30°57'N	85°31'W
Gracias a Dios, Cabo, c., N.A.	**149**	14°60'N	83°10'W
Graciosa, i., Port. (grä-syô´sä)	**199c**	39°04'N	28°00'W
Gradačac, Bos. (gra-dä´chats)	**200-01**	44°53'N	18°26'E
Gradaús, Braz.	**166-67**	7°43'S	51°10'W
Grænlandshav, s., *see* Greenland Sea	**288**	77°0'N	1°00'W
Grænlandssund, strt., *see* Denmark Strait	**86**	67°0'N	25°00'W
Grafton, Austl. (graf´tŭn)	**276**	29°42'S	152°56'E
Grafton, N.D., U.S. (graf´tŭn)	**114-15**	48°25'N	97°25'W
Grafton, W.V., U.S. (graf´tŭn)	**116-17**	39°20'N	80°01'W
Grafton, Cape, c., Austl.	**277**	16°53'S	145°56'E
Graham, N.C., U.S. (grā´ăm)	**124-25**	36°04'N	79°24'W
Graham, Tx., U.S. (grā´ăm)	**120-21**	33°07'N	98°35'W
Graham Island, i., B.C., Can. (grā´ăm ī´lȧnd)	**132-33**	53°47'N	132°34'W
Grahamstad, S. Afr. *see* Grahamstown	**264-65**	33°18'S	26°31'E
Grahamstown, S. Afr. (grā´ăms´toun)	**264-65**	33°18'S	26°31'E
Grajaú, Braz.	**166-67**	5°47'S	46°07'W
Grajaú, stm., Braz.	**166-67**	3°41'S	44°49'W
Grajewo, Pol. (grä-yā´vo)	**194-95**	53°39'N	22°28'E
Grampian Mountains, mts., Scot., U.K. (grăm´pĭ-ăn moun´tĭnz)	**190-91**	56°55'N	4°00'W
Grampians National Park, n.p., Austl.	**276**	37°15'S	142°25'E
Granada, Nic. (grä-nä´dhä)	**149**	11°56'N	85°58'W
Granada, Spain (grä-nä´dä)	**198-99**	37°11'N	3°36'W
Granbury, Tx., U.S. (grăn´bĕr-ĭ)	**120-21**	32°27'N	97°48'W
Granby, Qc., Can. (grăn´bĭ)	**136-37**	45°24'N	72°43'W
Granby, Co., U.S. (grăn´bĭ)	**118-19**	40°06'N	105°57'W
Granby, Mo., U.S. (grăn´bĭ)	**120-21**	36°55'N	94°15'W
Gran Canaria, i., Spain (grän´kä-nä´rē-ä)	**199d**	27°52'N	15°37'W
Gran Chaco, reg., S.A. (grán´chá´kō)	**168-69**	23°0'S	60°00'W
Grand, stm., Can. (grănd)	**136-37**	42°52'N	79°34'W
Grand, stm., Mi., U.S. (grănd)	**116-17**	43°04'N	86°14'W
Grand Bahama, i., Bah. (grănd bȧ-hā´mȧ)	**142-43**	26°38'N	78°25'W
Grand Bank, Nf., Can. (grănd băngk)	**138-39**	47°06'N	55°45'W
Grand-Bassam, C. Iv. (grän bá-sän´)	**260-61**	5°13'N	3°45'W
Grand-Bourg, Guad. (grän bōōr´)	**143b**	15°54'N	61°19'W
Grand Canal, can., China (grănd kȧ´năl)	**240-41**	32°11'N	119°33'E
Grand Canyon, Az., U.S. (grănd kăn´yŭn)	**118-19**	36°02'N	112°10'W
Grand Canyon, val., Az., U.S. (grănd kăn´yŭn)	**118-19**	36°22'N	112°30'W
Grand Canyon National Park, n.p., Az., U.S. (grănd kăn´yŭn năsh´ŭn-ăl pärk)	**118-19**	36°20'N	112°53'W
Grand Canyon-Parashant National Monument, n.p., Az., U.S.	**118-19**	36°20'N	113°44'W
Grand Cayman, i., Cay. Is. (grănd kā´măn) (grănd kī-män´)	**142-43**	19°20'N	81°15'W
Grand Coulee Dam, d., Wa., U.S. (grănd kōō´lē dăm)	**112-13**	47°57'N	119°01'W
Grande, stm., Bol. (grän´dĕ)	**168-69**	15°50'S	64°47'W
Grande, stm., Braz. (grän´dĕ)	**166-67**	11°05'S	43°09'W
Grande, stm., Braz. (grän´dĕ)	**168-69**	20°08'S	51°00'W
Grande, Bahía, b., Arg. (bä-ē´ä-grán´dĕ)	**171**	51°15'S	68°31'W
Grande, Cuchilla, mts., Ur. (kōō-chē´l-yä grän´dĕ)	**173**	33°25'S	55°06'W
Grande, Ilha, i., Braz. (ē´lä-grän´dĕ)	**172**	23°09'S	44°14'W
Grande, Rio, stm., N.A. (rē´ō grän´dā) *see* Rio Grande	**110-11**	25°57'N	97°09'W
Grande Cayemite, i., Haiti	**142-43**	18°37'N	73°45'W
Grande Comore, i., Com. *see* Njazidja	**264-65**	11°35'S	43°20'E
Grande de Santiago, stm., Mex. (grä´n-dĕ-dĕ-sän-tyá´gô)	**146-47**	21°37'N	105°28'W
Grande do Gurupá, Ilha, i., Braz.	**166-67**	1°0'S	51°30'W
Grande Prairie, Ab., Can. (grănd prâr´ĭ)	**132-33**	55°10'N	118°48'W
Grand Erg de Bilma, des., Niger	**258-59**	18°30'N	14°00'E
Grand Erg Occidental, des., Alg.	**258-59**	30°56'N	1°35'E
Grand Erg Oriental, des., Alg.	**258-59**	30°30'N	7°00'E
Grandes, Salinas, pl., Arg.	**168-69**	30°06'S	65°14'W
Grandes Antillas, Islas, is., N.A. *see* Greater Antilles	**142-43**	20°0'N	74°00'W
Grande-Terre, i., Guad.	**143b**	16°19'N	61°22'W
Grand Falls, N.B., Can. (grănd fôlz)	**138-39**	47°03'N	67°44'W
Grand Falls-Windsor, Nf., Can.	**138-39**	48°56'N	55°39'W
Grandfather Mountain, mtn., N.C., U.S. (grănd-fä-thẽr moun´tĭn)	**124-25**	36°07'N	81°48'W
Grandfield, Ok., U.S. (grănd´fēld)	**120-21**	34°14'N	98°41'W
Grand Forks, B.C., Can. (grănd fôrks)	**132-33**	49°02'N	118°27'W
Grand Forks, N.D., U.S. (grănd fôrks)	**114-15**	47°55'N	97°03'W
Grand Haven, Mi., U.S. (grănd hā´v'n)	**116-17**	43°04'N	86°13'W
Grand Island, Ne., U.S. (grănd ī´lȧnd)	**114-15**	40°55'N	98°21'W
Grand Island, i., Mi., U.S. (grănd ī´lȧnd)	**114-15**	46°30'N	86°40'W
Grand Junction, Co., U.S. (grănd jŭngk´shŭn)	**118-19**	39°04'N	108°34'W
Grand Lake, lk., N.B., Can. (grănd lāk)	**138-39**	45°53'N	66°03'W
Grand Lake, lk., Nf., Can. (grănd lāk)	**138-39**	48°59'N	57°22'W
Grand Lake, lk., La., U.S. (grănd lāk)	**122-23**	29°53'N	92°45'W
Grand Ledge, Mi., U.S. (grănd lĕj)	**116-17**	42°45'N	84°44'W
Grand Manan Island, i., N.B., Can. (grănd mȧ-năn ī´lȧnd)	**138-39**	44°43'N	66°49'W
Grand-Mère, Qc., Can. (grän mâr´)	**136-37**	46°37'N	72°42'W
Grândola, Port. (grăn´dô-lȧ)	**198-99**	38°10'N	8°34'W
Grand Portage Indian Reservation, ind. res., Mn., U.S. (grănd pōr´tĭj ĭn´dĭ-ăn rĕ-sẽr-vā´shĕn)	**114-15**	47°58'N	89°47'W
Grand Rapids, Mb., Can. (grănd răp´ĭdz)	**134-35**	53°12'N	99°17'W
Grand Rapids, Mi., U.S. (grănd răp´ĭdz)	**116-17**	42°58'N	85°40'W
Grand Rapids, Mn., U.S. (grănd răp´ĭdz)	**114-15**	47°14'N	93°31'W
Grand-Sault, N.B., Can. *see* Grand Falls	**138-39**	47°03'N	67°44'W
Grand Staircase-Escalante National Monument, n.p., Ut., U.S.	**118-19**	37°30'N	111°30'W
Grand Teton, mtn., Wy., U.S. (grănd tē´tŏn)	**112-13**	43°44'N	110°48'W
Grand Teton National Park, n.p., Wy., U.S. (grănd tē´tŏn năsh´ŭn-ăl pärk)	**112-13**	43°56'N	110°46'W
Grand Traverse Bay, b., Mi., U.S. (grănd trăv´ẽrs bā)	**116-17**	45°02'N	85°30'W
Grand Turk, nat. cap., T./C. Is. (grănd tûrk)	**142-43**	21°27'N	71°08'W
Grandview, Mb., Can.	**134-35**	51°10'N	100°42'W
Grandview, Wa., U.S. (grănd´vyōō)	**112-13**	46°15'N	119°54'W
Grangeville, Id., U.S. (grānj´vĭl)	**112-13**	45°56'N	116°07'W
Granite City, Il., U.S. (grăn´ĭt sĭ´tê)	**120-21**	38°42'N	90°09'W
Granite Falls, Mn., U.S. (grăn´ĭt fôlz)	**114-15**	44°49'N	95°33'W
Granite Falls, N.C., U.S. (grăn´ĭt fôlz)	**124-25**	35°48'N	81°26'W
Granite Peak, mtn., Mt., U.S.	**112-13**	45°10'N	109°48'W
Gränna, Swe. (grĕn´á)	**192-93**	58°00'N	14°28'E
Granollers, Spain (grä-nôl-yĕrs´)	**198-99**	41°37'N	2°17'E
Grantham, Eng., U.K. (grăn´tȧm)	**190-91**	52°55'N	0°39'W
Grants, N.M., U.S.	**118-19**	35°10'N	107°51'W
Grants Pass, Or., U.S. (grȧnts păs)	**112-13**	42°26'N	123°19'W
Granville, Fr. (grän-vēl´)	**196-97**	48°51'N	1°35'W
Granville, N.Y., U.S. (grăn´vĭl)	**116-17**	43°24'N	73°16'W
Granville Lake, lk., Mb., Can.	**134-35**	56°17'N	100°30'W
Gräsö, i., Swe.	**192-93**	60°24'N	18°25'E
Grasse, Fr. (gräs)	**196-97**	43°40'N	6°55'E
Grasslands National Park, n.p., Sk., Can.	**134-35**	49°04'N	106°58'W
Grates Point, c., Nf., Can. (grāts point)	**138-39**	48°10'N	52°57'W
Graudenz, Pol. *see* Grudziądz	**194-95**	53°29'N	18°44'E
Gravatá, Braz.	**163d**	8°12'S	35°34'W
Gravelbourg, Sk., Can. (grăv´ĕl-bôrg)	**134-35**	49°52'N	106°34'W
Gravenhage, 's-, nat. cap., Neth. *see* Hague, The	**190-91**	52°06'N	4°18'E
Gray, Fr. (grå)	**196-97**	47°26'N	5°35'E
Grayling, Mi., U.S. (grā´lĭng)	**116-17**	44°39'N	84°42'W
Grays Peak, mtn., Co., U.S. (grāz pēk)	**118-19**	39°37'N	105°45'W
Graz, Aus. (gräts)	**194-95**	47°05'N	15°27'E
Great Artesian Basin, bas., Austl. (grāt är-tēzh-ȧn bā´s'n)	**272-73**	25°0'S	143°00'E
Great Australian Bight, b., Austl. (grāt ôs-trā´lĭ-ăn bīt)	**272-73**	35°0'S	130°00'E
Great Barrier Island, i., N.Z. (grāt băr´ĭ-ẽr ī´lȧnd)	**278**	36°10'S	175°25'E
Great Barrier Reef, rf., Austl.	**277**	18°0'S	146°50'E
Great Barrier Reef Marine Park, n.p., Austl.	**277**	18°0'S	146°50'E
Great Basin, bas., U.S. (grāt bā´s'n)	**110-11**	40°0'N	117°00'W
Great Basin National Park, n.p., Nv., U.S.	**118-19**	38°55'N	114°14'W
Great Bear Lake, lk., N.T., Can. (grāt bâr lāk)	**130-31**	66°0'N	120°00'W
Great Bend, Ks., U.S. (grāt bĕnd)	**120-21**	38°22'N	98°45'W
Great Britain, nation, Eur. *see* United Kingdom	**174-75**	54°0'N	2°00'W
Great Britain, i., U.K. (grāt brĭt´'n)	**190-91**	54°0'N	2°00'W
Great Channel, strt., Asia	**246-47**	6°25'N	94°20'E
Great Dismal Swamp, sw., U.S. (grāt dĭz´măl swŏmp)	**124-25**	36°28'N	76°28'W
Great Divide Basin, bas., Wy., U.S. (grāt dĭ-vīd´ bā´s'n)	**112-13**	42°0'N	108°10'W
Great Dividing Range, mts., Austl. (grāt dĭ-vī-dĭng rānj)	**270-71**	25°0'S	147°00'E
Greater Antilles, is., N.A. (grāt´ẽr ăn-tĭ´lēz)	**142-43**	20°0'N	74°00'W
Greater Khingan Range, mts., China (grāt´ẽr hĭŋ-gän rānj)	**222-23**	49°0'N	122°00'E
Greater Sunda Islands, is., Asia (grāt´ẽr sōōn´dȧ ī´lȧndz)	**248-49**	2°0'S	110°00'E
Great Exuma, i., Bah. (grāt ĕk-sōō´mä)	**142-43**	23°32'N	75°50'W
Great Falls, Mt., U.S. (grāt fôlz)	**112-13**	47°30'N	111°18'W
Great Falls, S.C., U.S. (grāt fôlz)	**124-25**	34°34'N	80°54'W
Great Grimsby, Eng., U.K. *see* Grimsby	**190-91**	53°35'N	0°05'W
Grimsby, Eng., U.K.	**190-91**	53°35'N	0°05'W
Great Guana Cay, i., Bah. (grāt gwä´nä kē)	**142-43**	24°0'N	76°20'W
Great Inagua, i., Bah. (grāt ê-nä´gwä)	**142-43**	21°05'N	73°18'W
Great Indian Desert, des., Asia (grāt ĭn´dĭ-ăn dĕs´ẽrt)	**232-33**	27°0'N	71°00'E
Great Karoo, plat., S. Afr.	**264-65**	32°47'S	22°32'E
Great Limpopo Transfrontier Park, n.p., Afr.	**264-65**	23°0'S	31°30'E
Great Namaqualand, hist. reg., Nmb.	**264-65**	25°0'S	17°00'E
Great Nicobar, i., India (grāt nĭk-ô-bär´)	**246-47**	7°0'N	93°50'E
Great Palm Island, i., Austl.	**277**	18°43'S	146°37'E
Great Pee Dee, stm., S.C., U.S. (grāt pē-dē´)	**124-25**	33°18'N	79°17'W

n-sing; ŋ-baŋk; ɴ-nasalized n; nŏd; cŏmmit; ōld; ôbey; ôrder; oi-boil; fōōd; ò-as oo in foot; ou-out; s-soft; sh-dish; th-thin; pūre; ûnite; ûrn; stŭd; circŭs; ü-as in French tu; ´-indeterminate vowel.

Feature (Pronunciation)	Page	Lat.	Long.
Great Plains, pl., U.S. (grāt plānz)	110-11	42°0'N	100°00'W
Great Ruaha, stm., Tan.	267	7°56'S	37°48'E
Great Salt Lake, lk., Ut., U.S. (grāt sôlt lāk)	112-13	41°10'N	112°30'W
Great Salt Lake Desert, des., Ut., U.S. (grāt sôlt lāk dĕs´ẽrt)	110-11	40°40'N	113°30'W
Great Sand Dunes National Park and Preserve, n.p., Co., U.S.	118-19	37°46'N	105°33'W
Great Sandy Desert, des., Austl. (grāt săn´dē dĕs´ẽrt)	272-73	21°30'S	125°00'E
Great Sandy National Park, n.p., Austl.	277	24°55'S	153°16'E
Great Slave Lake, lk., N.T., Can. (grāt slāv lāk)	130-31	61°30'N	114°00'W
Great Smoky Mountains National Park, n.p., U.S. (grāt smōk-ē moun´tĭnz năsh´ŭn-ăl pärk)	124-25	35°39'N	83°30'W
Great Victoria Desert, des., Austl. (grāt vĭk-tō´rĭ-ȧ dĕs´ẽrt)	272-73	28°30'S	127°45'E
Great Wall, p.o.i., China	240-41	40°0'N	112°30'E
Gréboun, mtn., Niger	258-59	20°0'N	8°35'E
Gredos, Sierra de, mts., Spain (syĕr´rä dā grā´dōs)	198-99	40°20'N	4°51'W
Greece, nation, Eur. (grēs)	174-75	39°0'N	22°00'E
Greeley, Co., U.S. (grē´lĭ)	114-15	40°24'N	104°41'W
Greeley, Ne., U.S. (grē´lĭ)	114-15	41°33'N	98°32'W
Green, stm., U.S. (grēn)	110-11	38°11'N	109°53'W
Green, stm., Ky., U.S. (grēn)	116-17	37°54'N	87°31'W
Green Bay, Wi., U.S. (grēn bā)	116-17	44°30'N	87°60'W
Green Bay, b., U.S. (grēn bā)	116-17	44°58'N	87°35'W
Greencastle, In., U.S. (grēn-kȧs´'l)	116-17	39°38'N	86°51'W
Green Cove Springs, Fl., U.S. (grēn kōv sprĭngz)	124-25	29°60'N	81°42'W
Greenfield, Ca., U.S. (grēn´fēld)	118-19	36°19'N	121°15'W
Greenfield, Ia., U.S. (grēn´fēld)	114-15	41°18'N	94°28'W
Greenfield, In., U.S. (grēn´fēld)	116-17	39°47'N	85°46'W
Greenfield, Oh., U.S. (grēn´fēld)	116-17	39°20'N	83°23'W
Greenfield, Tn., U.S. (grēn´fēld)	124-25	36°09'N	88°48'W
Greenfield, Wi., U.S. (grēn´fēld)	116-17	42°57'N	88°01'W
Green Islands, is., Pap. N. Gui.	277	4°30'S	154°10'E
Greenland, dep., N.A. (grēn´lănd)	85	70°0'N	40°00'W
Greenland, i., Green. (grēn´lănd)	86	70°0'N	40°00'W
Greenland Sea, s., (grēn´lănd sē)	288	77°0'N	1°00'W
Green Mountains, mts., N.A. (grēn moun´tĭnz)	116-17	43°45'N	72°45'W
Greenock, Scot., U.K. (grēn´ŭk)	190-91	55°57'N	4°45'W
Green River, Ut., U.S. (grēn rĭv´ẽr)	118-19	38°60'N	110°09'W
Green River, Wy., U.S. (grēn rĭv´ẽr)	112-13	41°32'N	109°28'W
Greensboro, Al., U.S. (grēnz´bŭro)	124-25	32°42'N	87°36'W
Greensboro, Ga., U.S. (grēns-bûr´ô)	124-25	33°35'N	83°11'W
Greensboro, N.C., U.S. (grēns-bûr´ô)	124-25	36°04'N	79°48'W
Greensburg, In., U.S. (grēnz´bûrg)	116-17	39°20'N	85°29'W
Greensburg, Ky., U.S. (grēns-bûrg)	124-25	37°16'N	85°30'W
Greenville, Lib. (grēn´vĭl)	260-61	5°02'N	9°03'W
Greenville, Al., U.S. (grēn´vĭl)	124-25	31°50'N	86°37'W
Greenville, Il., U.S. (grēn´vĭl)	116-17	38°53'N	89°25'W
Greenville, Ky., U.S. (grēn´vĭl)	124-25	37°12'N	87°11'W
Greenville, Me., U.S. (grēn´vĭl)	117a	45°27'N	69°34'W
Greenville, Mi., U.S. (grēn´vĭl)	116-17	43°11'N	85°15'W
Greenville, Ms., U.S. (grēn´vĭl)	124-25	33°25'N	91°03'W
Greenville, N.C., U.S. (grēn´vĭl)	124-25	35°37'N	77°22'W
Greenville, Oh., U.S. (grēn´vĭl)	116-17	40°06'N	84°38'W
Greenville, Pa., U.S. (grēn´vĭl)	116-17	41°24'N	80°23'W
Greenville, S.C., U.S. (grēn´vĭl)	124-25	34°51'N	82°24'W
Greenville, Tx., U.S. (grēn´vĭl)	120-21	33°09'N	96°07'W
Greenwood, Ar., U.S. (grēn-wŏŏd)	120-21	35°12'N	94°16'W
Greenwood, In., U.S. (grēn-wŏŏd)	116-17	39°36'N	86°05'W
Greenwood, La., U.S. (grēn-wŏŏd)	120-21	32°27'N	93°58'W
Greenwood, Ms., U.S. (grēn-wŏŏd)	124-25	33°31'N	90°11'W
Greenwood, S.C., U.S. (grēn-wŏŏd)	124-25	34°12'N	82°09'W
Greer, S.C., U.S. (grēr)	124-25	34°56'N	82°14'W
Gregory, S.D., U.S. (grĕg´ô-rĭ)	114-15	43°14'N	99°26'W
Gregory, Lake, lk., Austl. (lāk grĕg´ô-rē)	276	28°55'S	139°00'E
Gregory Range, mts., Austl.	277	19°0'S	143°05'E
Greifswald, Ger. (grīfs´vält)	194-95	54°05'N	13°23'E
Greiz, Ger. (grīts)	194-95	50°39'N	12°13'E
Gremyachinsk, Russia (grâ´myȧ-chĭnsk)	186-87	58°35'N	57°51'E
Grenada, Ms., U.S. (grē-nā´da)	124-25	33°46'N	89°49'W
Grenada, nation, N.A. (grē-nā´-dȧ)	140-41	12°07'N	61°40'W
Grenadines, is., N.A. (grĕn´ȧ-dēnz)	143b	12°40'N	61°15'W
Grenoble, Fr. (grē-nô´bl')	196-97	45°11'N	5°42'E
Grenville, Cape, c., Austl.	277	11°58'S	143°14'E
Gresham, Or., U.S. (grĕsh´ăm)	112-13	45°29'N	122°26'W
Gresik, Indon.	248-49	7°10'S	112°39'E
Gretna, La., U.S. (grĕt´nȧ)	124-25	29°55'N	90°04'W
Gretna, Ne., U.S. (grĕt´nȧ)	114-15	41°08'N	96°15'W
Grey, stm., Nf., Can. (grā)	138-39	47°33'N	57°08'W
Greybull, Wy., U.S. (grā´bŏŏl)	112-13	44°30'N	108°03'W
Grey Islands, is., Nf., Can.	138-39	50°50'N	55°37'W
Greymouth, N.Z. (grā´mouth)	278	42°28'S	171°13'E
Grey Range, mts., Austl. (grā rānj)	276	27°0'S	143°35'E
Greytown, S. Afr. (grā´toun)	269c	29°04'S	30°35'E
Gribanovskiy, Russia	186-87	51°27'N	41°58'E
Gribbel Island, i., B.C., Can.	132-33	53°25'N	129°00'W
Griffin, Ga., U.S. (grĭf´ĭn)	124-25	33°15'N	84°16'W
Griffith, Austl. (grĭf-ĭth)	276	34°17'S	146°03'E
Grim, Cape, c., Austl. (kāp grĭm)	276	40°39'S	144°43'E
Grímsey, i., Ice. (grĭms´â)	190a	66°33'N	18°01'W
Grimstad, Nor. (grĭm-städh)	192-93	58°20'N	8°36'E
Groesbeck, Tx., U.S. (grōs´bĕk)	122-23	31°31'N	96°32'W
Gronau, Ger. (grō´nou)	194-95	52°13'N	7°01'E
Groningen, Neth. (grō´nĭng-ĕn)	190-91	53°13'N	6°34'E
Grønland, dep., N.A. *see* Greenland	85	70°0'N	40°00'W
Grønland, i., Green. *see* Greenland	86	70°0'N	40°00'W
Grønlandshavet, s., *see* Greenland Sea	288	77°0'N	1°00'W
Groote Eylandt, i., Austl. (grō´tē ī´länt)	272-73	13°60'S	136°38'E
Grootfontein, Nmb. (grōt´fōn-tān´)	264-65	19°34'S	18°06'E
Groot Karroo, plat., S. Afr. *see* Great Karoo	264-65	32°47'S	22°32'E
Groot Namaland, hist. reg., Nmb. *see* Great Namaqualand	264-65	25°0'S	17°00'E
Gros Morne, mtn., Nf., Can. (grō môrn´)	138-39	49°36'N	57°48'W
Gros Morne National Park, n.p., Nf., Can. (grō môrn´ năsh´ŭn-ăl pärk)	138-39	49°40'N	57°45'W
Grosseto, Italy (grôs-sā´tō)	200-01	42°46'N	11°07'E
Großglockner, mtn., Aus.	194-95	47°04'N	12°42'E
Grosswardein, Rom. *see* Oradea	194-95	47°04'N	21°56'E
Groton, Ct., U.S. (grŏt´ŭn)	116-17	41°21'N	72°05'W
Groton, S.D., U.S. (grŏt´ŭn)	114-15	45°27'N	98°06'W
Grouard Mission, Ab., Can.	132-33	55°32'N	116°09'W
Groveton, N.H., U.S. (grōv´tŭn)	116-17	44°36'N	71°31'W
Growa Point, c., Lib.	260-61	4°21'N	7°36'W
Groznyy, Russia (grōz´nĭ)	227	43°19'N	45°41'E
Grudziądz, Pol. (grŏŏ´jyôɴts)	194-95	53°29'N	18°44'E
Grünberg, Pol. *see* Zielona Góra	194-95	51°56'N	15°31'E
Grundy Center, Ia., U.S. (grŭn´dĭ sĕn´tẽr)	114-15	42°21'N	92°47'W
Gruziya, nation, Asia *see* Georgia	227	42°0'N	44°00'E
Gryazi, Russia (gryä´zĭ)	186-87	52°29'N	39°57'E
Gryazovets, Russia (gryä´zô-vĕts)	186-87	58°53'N	40°15'E
Gryfice, Pol. (grĭ´fĭ-tsĕ)	194-95	53°55'N	15°12'E
Guacanayabo, Golfo de, b., Cuba (gôl-fô-dĕ-gwä-kä-nä-yä´bō)	142-43	20°28'N	77°30'W
Guacara, Ven. (gwá´kä-rä)	163b	10°14'N	67°53'W
Guadalajara, Mex. (gwä-dhä-lä-hä´rä)	146-47	20°40'N	103°20'W
Guadalajara, Spain (gwä-dä-lä-kä´rä)	198-99	40°38'N	3°10'W
Guadalcanal, i., Sol. Is. (gwä-dhäl-kä-näl´)	279e	9°32'S	160°12'E
Guadalquivir, stm., Spain (gwä-dhäl-kê-vēr´)	198-99	36°47'N	6°24'W
Guadalupe, Mex.	122-23	25°41'N	100°15'W
Guadalupe, stm., Tx., U.S. (gwä-dhä-lōō´pâ)	122-23	28°27'N	96°49'W
Guadalupe, Isla, i., Mex.	140-41	29°03'N	118°21'W
Guadalupe, Sierra de, mts., Spain (syĕr´rä dā gwä-dhä-lōō´pä)	198-99	39°29'N	5°28'W
Guadalupe Mountains, mts., U.S. (gwä-dhä-lōō´pȧ moun´tĭnz)	122-23	32°24'N	105°04'W
Guadalupe Mountains National Park, n.p., Tx., U.S.	122-23	31°55'N	104°55'W
Guadalupe Peak, mtn., Tx., U.S. (gwä-dhä-lōō´pȧ pēk)	122-23	31°50'N	104°52'W
Guadarrama, Sierra de, mts., Spain (syĕr´rä dā gwä-dhär-rä´mä)	198-99	40°51'N	4°01'W
Guadeloupe, dep., N.A. (gwä-dē-lōōp)	140-41	16°15'N	61°35'W
Guadiana, stm., Eur. (gwä-dvä´nä)	198-99	37°10'N	7°24'W
Guadix, Spain (gwä-dēsh´)	198-99	37°18'N	3°08'W
Guafo, Isla, i., Chile	171	43°36'S	74°43'W
Guaíra, Braz. (gwä-ē-rä)	172	20°19'S	48°18'W
Guaíra, Braz. (gwä-ē-rä)	168-69	24°06'S	54°15'W
Guajaba, Cayo, i., Cuba (kä´yō-gwä-hä´bä)	142-43	21°50'N	77°30'W
Guajará-Mirim, Braz. (gwä-zhä-rä´mē-rēn´)	166-67	10°48'S	65°22'W
Gualeguay, Arg. (gwä-lĕ-gwä´y)	173	33°09'S	59°20'W
Gualeguay, stm., Arg. (gwä-lĕ-gwä´y)	173	33°19'S	59°39'W
Gualeguaychú, Arg.	173	33°01'S	58°31'W
Guam, dep., Oc. (gwäm)	279c	13°28'N	144°47'E
Guam, i., Guam (gwäm)	279c	13°28'N	144°47'E
Guaminí, Arg.	173	37°01'S	62°25'W
Guamo, Col. (gwá´mō)	163c	4°02'N	74°58'W
Guanaja, Isla de, i., Hond.	149	16°29'N	85°53'W
Guanajuato, Mex. (gwä-nä-hwä´tō)	146-47	21°01'N	101°16'W
Guanajuato, state, Mex. (gwä-nä-hwä´tō)	146-47	21°0'N	101°00'W
Guanambi, Braz.	166-67	14°14'S	42°47'W
Guanare, Ven. (gwä-nä´rå)	164-65	9°03'N	69°46'W
Guandacol, Arg.	168-69	29°31'S	68°32'W
Guane, Cuba (gwä´nå)	142-43	22°12'N	84°05'W
Guang'an, China	238-39	30°28'N	106°38'E
Guangchang, China (gůäŋ-chäŋ)	238-39	26°51'N	116°19'E
Guangdong, state, China (gůäŋ-dôŋ)	287	23°0'N	113°00'E
Guanghua, China *see* Laohekou	238-39	32°25'N	111°36'E
Guangnan, China	238-39	24°10'N	105°06'E
Guangxi, state, China	238-39	24°0'N	109°00'E
Guangyuan, China	238-39	32°25'N	105°49'E
Guangzhou, China	238-39	23°08'N	113°16'E
Guanta, Ven. (gwän´tä)	163b	10°14'N	64°36'W
Guantánamo, Cuba (gwän-tä´nä-mô)	142-43	20°08'N	75°13'W
Guantánamo, state, Cuba (gwän-tä´nä-mô)	142-43	20°20'N	75°00'W
Guanxian, China (gůän-shyĕn)	238-39	31°00'N	103°36'E
Guanxian, China (gůän-shyĕn)	240-41	36°28'N	115°26'E
Guapí, Col.	164-65	2°36'N	77°54'W
Guápiles, C.R. (gwä-pē-lĕs)	149	10°12'N	83°47'W
Guaporé, stm., S.A. (gwä-pô-rā´)	166-67	11°55'S	65°00'W
Guarabira, Braz. (gwä-rä-bē´rȧ)	163d	6°51'S	35°29'W
Guaranda, Ec. (gwä-rán´dä)	170	1°36'S	78°60'W
Guarapari, Braz. (gwä-rä-pä´rē)	172	20°40'S	40°30'W
Guarapuava, Braz. (gwä-rä-pwä´vȧ)	168-69	25°23'S	51°29'W
Guarda, Port. (gwär´dä)	198-99	40°33'N	7°15'W
Guarulhos, Braz. (gwȧ-rō´l-yôs)	172	23°29'S	46°32'W
Guasave, Mex.	144-45	25°34'N	108°28'W
Guasdualito, Ven.	164-65	7°15'N	70°45'W
Guasipati, Ven. (gwä-sê-pä´tē)	164-65	7°29'N	61°53'W
Guastalla, Italy (gwäs-täl´lä)	200-01	44°55'N	10°39'E
Guatemala, nation, N.A. (guä-tȧ-mä´lä)	85	15°30'N	90°15'W
Guatemala, nat. cap., Guat. (guä-tȧ-mä´lä)	148	14°38'N	90°32'W
Guaviare, stm., Col.	164-65	4°04'N	67°43'W
Guaxupé, Braz.	172	21°18'S	46°42'W
Guayama, P.R. (gwä-yä´mä)	142a	17°59'N	66°07'W
Guayana, Ven. *see* Ciudad Guayana	164-65	8°21'N	62°39'W
Guayana, nation, S.A. *see* Guyana	158	5°0'N	59°00'W
Guayaquil, Ec. (gwī-ä-kēl´)	170	2°12'S	79°54'W
Guayaquil, Golfo de, b., S.A. (gôl-fô-dĕ gwī-ä-kēl´)	170	2°57'S	80°36'W
Guaymas, Mex. (gwá´y-mäs)	144-45	27°55'N	110°55'W
Gûbâi, Madîq, strt., Egypt	268b	27°40'N	33°55'E
Gubakha, Russia (gōō-bä´kȧ)	186-87	58°52'N	57°33'E
Gubbio, Italy (gōōb´byô)	200-01	43°21'N	12°34'E
Gubkin, Russia	202-03	51°17'N	37°33'E
Gucheng, China (gōō-chŭŋ)	238-39	32°18'N	111°35'E
Gudermes, Russia	227	43°21'N	46°06'E
Guebwiller, Fr. (gĕb-vē-lâr´)	196-97	47°55'N	7°12'E
Guelph, On., Can. (gwĕlf)	136-37	43°33'N	80°15'W
Guercif, Mor.	184-85	34°14'N	3°20'W
Guéret, Fr. (gā-rĕ´)	196-97	46°10'N	1°52'E
Guernesey, dep., Eur. *see* Guernsey	196-97	49°28'N	2°35'W
Guernsey, dep., Eur. (gûrn´zĭ)	196-97	49°28'N	2°35'W
Guerrero, Mex. (gĕr-rā´rō)	144-45	28°33'N	107°30'W
Guerrero, state, Mex. (gĕr-rā´rō)	146-47	17°40'N	100°00'W
Gugē, mtn., Eth.	262-63	6°11'N	37°24'E
Guguan, i., N. Mar. Is.	280-81	17°19'N	145°51'E
Guide, China	240-41	36°01'N	101°27'E
Guilin, China (gwā-lĭn)	238-39	25°17'N	110°17'E
Guimarães, Port. (gē-mä-rănsh´)	198-99	41°27'N	8°18'W
Guimaras Island, i., Phil.	250	10°35'N	122°37'E
Guiné, Golfo da, b., Afr. *see* Guinea, Gulf of	260-61	2°0'N	2°30'E
Guinea, nation, Afr. (gĭn´ē)	253	11°0'N	10°00'W
Guinea, Golfo de, b., Afr. *see* Guinea, Gulf of	260-61	2°0'N	2°30'E
Guinea, Gulf of, b., Afr. (gŭlf ŭv gĭn´ē)	260-61	2°0'N	2°30'E
Guinea-Bissau, nation, Afr. (gĭn´ē bē-sa´ōō)	253	12°0'N	15°00'W
Guinea Ecuatorial, nation, Afr. *see* Equatorial Guinea	253	2°0'N	9°00'E
Guiné-Bissau, nation, Afr. *see* Guinea-Bissau	253	12°0'N	15°00'W
Guinée, nation, Afr. *see* Guinea	253	11°0'N	10°00'W
Guinée, Golfe de, b., Afr. *see* Guinea, Gulf of	260-61	2°0'N	2°30'E
Güines, Cuba	142-43	22°51'N	82°02'W

ăt; finăl; rāte; senåte; ärm; åsk; sofȧ; fâre; ch-choose; dh-as th in other; bē; êvent; bĕt; recĕnt; cratẽr; g-gō; gh-guttural g; bĭt; ĭ-short neutral; rīde; ĸ-guttural k as ch in German ich;

Feature (Pronunciation)	Page	Lat.	Long.
Guingamp, Fr. (găn-gän´)	196-97	48°34'N	3°09'W
Guiping, China	238-39	23°23'N	110°04'E
Güira de Melena, Cuba (gwē´rä dĕ må-lā´nä)	142-43	22°48'N	82°30'W
Guiratinga, Braz.	168-69	16°21'S	53°45'W
Güiria, Ven. (gwê-rē´ä)	143b	10°35'N	62°18'W
Guiuan, Phil.	250	11°02'N	125°44'E
Guixian, China	238-39	23°06'N	109°39'E
Guiyang, China	238-39	26°35'N	106°43'E
Guizhou, state, China (gwā-jō)	238-39	27°0'N	107°00'E
Gujarāt, state, India	234-35	22°0'N	72°00'E
Gujrānwāla, Pak.	232-33	32°09'N	74°11'E
Gujrāt, Pak.	232-33	32°34'N	74°05'E
Gulbarga, India (gŏŏl-bûr´gá)	236	17°20'N	76°50'E
Gulbene, Lat. (gŏŏl-bă´nĕ)	192-93	57°10'N	26°46'E
Gulfport, Ms., U.S. (gŭlf´pōrt)	124-25	30°22'N	89°06'W
Gulian, China	222-23	52°56'N	122°19'E
Guliston, Uzb.	232-33	40°30'N	68°46'E
Gulja, China *see* Yining	226	43°55'N	81°18'E
Gull Lake, Sk., Can. (gŭl lāk)	134-35	50°08'N	108°27'W
Gull Lake, lk., Ab., Can. (gŭl lāk)	132-33	52°33'N	114°02'W
Gulu, Ug.	267	2°47'N	32°18'E
Gumaca, Phil. (gōō-mä-kä´)	250	13°55'N	122°06'E
Gumdag, Turkmen.	232-33	39°12'N	54°36'E
Gummersbach, Ger. (gŏŏm´ĕrs-bäk)	194-95	51°02'N	7°34'E
Gumti, stm., India	234-35	25°31'N	83°10'E
Gümüşhane, Tur.	227	40°28'N	39°28'E
Guna, India	234-35	24°39'N	77°18'E
Gundagai, Austl.	276	35°04'S	148°06'E
Gunisao, stm., Mb., Can. (gŭn-i-sä´ō)	134-35	53°53'N	97°60'W
Gunisao Lake, lk., Mb., Can. (gŭn-i-sä´ō lāk)	134-35	53°33'N	96°15'W
Gunnbjørn Fjeld, mtn., Green.	86	68°53'N	30°00'W
Gunnedah, Austl. (gŭ´nē-dä)	276	30°59'S	150°15'E
Gunnison, Co., U.S. (gŭn´ĭ-sŭn)	118-19	38°33'N	106°55'W
Gunnison, Ut., U.S. (gŭn´ĭ-sŭn)	118-19	39°09'N	111°49'W
Gunsan, Kor., S. *see* Kunsan	243	35°59'N	126°43'E
Guntersville, Al., U.S. (gŭn´tĕrz-vĭl)	124-25	34°22'N	86°18'W
Guntūr, India (gŏŏn´tōōr)	236	16°18'N	80°27'E
Gunungsitoli, Indon.	246-47	1°15'N	97°37'E
Guoyang, China (gwô-yäŋ)	238-39	33°30'N	116°12'E
Gurara, stm., Nig.	260-61	8°11'N	6°42'E
Gurdon, Ar., U.S. (gûr´dŭn)	120-21	33°55'N	93°10'W
Guri, Embalse de, res., Ven.	164-65	7°30'N	62°50'W
Gurnee, Il., U.S. (gûr´nē)	116-17	42°22'N	87°54'W
Gurué, Moz.	264-65	15°27'S	36°59'E
Gurupá, Braz.	166-67	1°25'S	51°39'W
Gurupi, Braz.	166-67	11°43'S	49°02'W
Gurupi, stm., Braz.	166-67	1°16'S	46°09'W
Guryev, Kaz. *see* Atyraū	186-87	47°07'N	51°55'E
Gusau, Nig. (gōō-zä´ōō)	260-61	12°10'N	6°40'E
Guşgy, Turkmen.	232-33	35°16'N	62°21'E
Gushi, China (gōō-shr)	238-39	32°11'N	115°41'E
Gusinoozërsk, Russia	240-41	51°17'N	106°31'E
Gus'-Khrustal'nyy, Russia (gōōs-krōō-stäl'ny')	186-87	55°37'N	40°40'E
Gütersloh, Ger. (gü´tĕrs-lo)	194-95	51°54'N	8°23'E
Guthrie, Ok., U.S. (gŭth´rĭ)	120-21	35°53'N	97°26'W
Gutian, China	238-39	26°36'N	118°46'E
Gutiérrez Zamora, Mex. (gōō-tē-âr´räz zä-mō´rä)	146-47	20°27'N	97°05'W
Guttenberg, Ia., U.S. (gŭt´ĕn-bûrg)	114-15	42°47'N	91°06'W
Guwāhāti, India	234-35	26°11'N	91°44'E
Guyana, nation, S.A. (gŭy´ănă)	158	5°0'N	59°00'W
Guyane, dep., S.A. *see* French Guiana	158	4°0'N	53°00'W
Guyang, China (gōō-yäŋ)	240-41	41°02'N	110°04'E
Guymon, Ok., U.S. (gī´mŏn)	120-21	36°41'N	101°29'W
Guyuan, China	240-41	35°59'N	106°18'E
Guzhen, China (gōō-jŭn)	238-39	33°19'N	117°19'E
Guzmán, Mex.	146-47	19°42'N	103°28'W
G'uzor, Uzb.	232-33	38°36'N	66°15'E
Gvardeysk, Russia (gvår-dĕysk´)	194-95	54°39'N	21°05'E
Gwādar, Pak. (gwä´dŭr)	230-31	25°08'N	62°20'E
Gwalior, India	234-35	26°13'N	78°09'E
Gwangju, Kor., S. *see* Kwangju	243	35°09'N	126°54'E
Gwardafuy, Gees, c., Som.	262-63	11°50'N	51°17'E
Gweru, Zimb.	264-65	19°27'S	29°49'E
Gwinn, Mi., U.S. (gwĭn)	114-15	46°17'N	87°25'W
Gyandzha, Azer. *see* Gäncä	227	40°41'N	46°21'E
Gyangzê, China	234-35	28°56'N	89°34'E
Gyaring Co, lk., China	234-35	31°05'N	88°24'E
Gyaring Hu, lk., China	240-41	34°54'N	97°15'E
Gyeongju, Kor., S. *see* Kyŏngju	243	35°51'N	129°13'E
Gympie, Austl. (gĭm´pē)	276	26°12'S	152°40'E
Gyöngyös, Hung. (dyûn´dyûsh)	194-95	47°47'N	19°56'E
Győr, Hung. (dyûr)	194-95	47°41'N	17°39'E

Feature (Pronunciation)	Page	Lat.	Long.
Gyula, Hung. (dyŏŏ´lä)	194-95	46°39'N	21°20'E
Gyumri, Arm.	227	40°47'N	43°51'E
Gyzylarbat, Turkmen.	232-33	38°59'N	56°16'E
Gyzyletrek, Turkmen.	232-33	37°36'N	54°47'E

H

Feature (Pronunciation)	Page	Lat.	Long.
Haapamäki, Fin. (häp´ä-mĕ-kĕ)	192-93	62°15'N	24°27'E
Haapsalu, Est. (häp´sä-lŏŏ)	192-93	58°56'N	23°33'E
Haar, Ger. (här)	194-95	48°06'N	11°44'E
Haarlem, Neth. (här´lĕm)	190-91	52°23'N	4°38'E
Hachijō-jima, i., Japan	244	33°05'N	139°48'E
Hachinohe, Japan (hä´chē-nō´hå)	244	40°30'N	141°29'E
Ḥadd, Ra's al-, c., Oman	230-31	22°32'N	59°48'E
Hadejia, stm., Nig.	260-61	12°50'N	10°51'E
Ḥadera, Isr. (kå-dĕ´rå)	228-29	32°27'N	34°55'E
Haderslev, Den. (hä´dhĕrs-lĕv)	192-93	55°15'N	9°30'E
Hadībū, Yemen	220-21	12°39'N	54°02'E
Ḥadīthah, Iraq	228-29	34°02'N	42°22'E
Ḥaḍramawt, reg., Yemen	220-21	15°0'N	50°00'E
Hadyai, Thai. *see* Hat Yai	246-47	7°01'N	100°28'E
Haeju, Kor., N. (hä´ĕ-jŭ)	243	38°03'N	125°43'E
Haft Gel, Iran	232-33	31°26'N	49°32'E
Hagåtña, nat. cap., Guam	279c	13°28'N	144°45'E
Hagen, Ger. (hä´gĕn)	194-95	51°22'N	7°28'E
Hagerstown, Md., U.S. (hā´gĕrz-toun)	116-17	39°39'N	77°43'W
Haggin, Mount, mtn., Mt., U.S.	112-13	46°05'N	113°05'W
Hagi, Japan (hä´gĭ)	245	34°24'N	131°24'E
Hague, Cap de la, c., Fr. (kåp dē lá åg´)	196-97	49°43'N	1°56'W
Hague, The, nat. cap., Neth.	190-91	52°06'N	4°18'E
Haguenau, Fr. (åg´nō´)	196-97	48°49'N	7°47'E
Hahajima-rettō, is., Japan	280-81	26°37'N	142°10'E
Haicheng, China (hī-chŭŋ)	240-41	40°51'N	122°46'E
Haifa, Isr. (hä´ĕ-få)	228-29	32°49'N	35°00'E
Haifeng, China (hä´ê-fĕng´)	238-39	22°58'N	115°20'E
Haikang, China	238-39	20°55'N	110°05'E
Haikou, China	238-39	20°03'N	110°22'E
Ḥā'il, Sau. Ar.	266	27°31'N	41°42'E
Hailar, China	240-41	49°11'N	119°44'E
Hailar, stm., China	240-41	49°30'N	117°51'E
Hailey, Id., U.S. (hā´lĭ)	112-13	43°32'N	114°19'W
Hailun, China (hä´ê-lōōn´)	240-41	47°27'N	126°58'E
Hailuoto, i., Fin.	184-85	65°02'N	24°42'E
Hainan, state, China (hī´-nän´)	238-39	19°0'N	109°30'E
Hainan Dao, i., China (hī-nän dou)	238-39	19°0'N	109°30'E
Hainan Strait, strt., China (hī´-nän´ strāt) *see* Qiongzhou Haixia	238-39	20°10'N	110°15'E
Haines, Ak., U.S. (hānz)	126	59°14'N	135°27'W
Haines City, Fl., U.S. (hānz sĭ´tĭ)	125a	28°07'N	81°38'W
Haines Junction, Yk., Can.	128-29	60°45'N	137°28'W
Hai Ninh, Viet.	246-47	21°32'N	107°56'E
Hai Phong, Viet. (hī´fŏng´)(hä´ĕp-hŏng)	246-47	20°52'N	106°41'E
Haiti, nation, N.A. (hā´tĭ)	140-41	19°0'N	72°25'W
Haïti, i., N.A. *see* Hispaniola	142-43	19°0'N	71°00'W
Haizhou, China	238-39	34°35'N	119°08'E
Hajdúböszörmény, Hung. (hôl´dŏŏ-bû´sûr-mān')	194-95	47°40'N	21°31'E
Hajdúnánás, Hung. (hô´ĭ-dŏŏ-nä´näsh)	194-95	47°50'N	21°27'E
Ḥajjah, Yemen	266	15°42'N	43°36'E
Ḥakīm, Abyār al-, well, Libya	258-59	31°36'N	23°29'E
Hakodate, Japan (hä-kō-dä´t å)	244	41°45'N	140°43'E
Haku-san, vol., Japan (hä´kōō-sän´)	245	36°09'N	136°46'E
Ḥalab, Syria *see* Aleppo	228-29	36°13'N	37°10'E
Ḥalā'ib, Sudan	266	22°13'N	36°38'E
Halberstadt, Ger. (häl´bĕr-shtät)	194-95	51°53'N	11°03'E
Halcon, Mount, mtn., Phil. (mount häl-kōn´)	250	13°16'N	121°00'E
Halden, Nor. (häl´dĕn)	192-93	59°08'N	11°23'E
Haleakalā National Park, n.p., Hi., U.S. (hä´lå-ä´kä-lä năsh´ŭn-ăl pärk)	127a	20°44'N	156°13'W
Haleyville, Al., U.S. (hā´lĭ-vĭl)	124-25	34°14'N	87°38'W
Halfway, stm., B.C., Can.	132-33	56°13'N	121°26'W
Halifax, N.S., Can. (hăl´ĭ-făks)	138-39	44°39'N	63°36'W
Halifax Bay, b., Austl. (hăl´ĭ-făx bā)	277	18°50'S	146°30'E
Halla-san, mtn., Kor., S. (häl´lä-sän´)	240-41	33°22'N	126°32'E
Halle, Ger.	194-95	51°29'N	11°58'E
Hallettsville, Tx., U.S. (hăl´ĕts-vĭl)	122-23	29°27'N	96°56'W
Hall Islands, is., Micron.	280-81	8°35'N	151°59'E
Hallock, Mn., U.S. (hăl´ŭk)	114-15	48°46'N	96°57'W
Hall Peninsula, pen., Nu., Can. (hôl pĕ-nĭn´sūlȧ)	130-31	63°30'N	66°00'W

Feature (Pronunciation)	Page	Lat.	Long.
Hallsberg, Swe. (häls´bĕrgh)	192-93	59°05'N	15°08'E
Halls Creek, Austl. (hôlz krēk)	270-71	18°15'S	127°40'E
Halmahera, i., Indon. (häl-mä-hā´rä)	248-49	1°0'N	128°00'E
Halmahera, Laut, s., Indon. *see* Halmahera Sea	224-25	1°0'S	129°00'E
Halmahera Sea, s., Indon. (häl-mä-hā´rä sē)	224-25	1°0'S	129°00'E
Halmstad, Swe. (hälm´städ)	192-93	56°40'N	12°53'E
Hälsingborg, Swe. *see* Helsingborg	192-93	56°03'N	12°42'E
Haltern, Ger. (häl´tĕrn)	194-95	51°45'N	7°11'E
Haltiatunturi, mtn., Eur.	184-85	69°18'N	21°16'E
Halton Hills, On., Can. *see* Georgetown	136-37	43°39'N	79°55'W
Halys, stm., Tur. *see* Kızılırmak	186-87	41°44'N	35°58'E
Hamada, Japan	245	34°53'N	132°05'E
Hamadān, Iran (hŭ-mŭ-dän´)	228-29	34°48'N	48°31'E
Ḥamāh, Syria (hä´mä)	228-29	35°08'N	36°45'E
Hamamatsu, Japan (hä´mä-mät´sŏŏ)	245	34°43'N	137°42'E
Hamar, Nor. (hä´mär)	192-93	60°48'N	11°05'E
Hamburg, Ger. (häm´bŏŏrgh)	194-95	53°33'N	9°59'E
Hamburg, Ar., U.S. (hăm´bûrg)	124-25	33°14'N	91°48'W
Hamburg, N.Y., U.S. (hăm´bûrg)	116-17	42°43'N	78°50'W
Hamden, Ct., U.S. (hăm´dĕn)	116-17	41°24'N	72°54'W
Hämeenlinna, Fin. (hĕ´mån-lĭn-nå)	192-93	60°58'N	24°31'E
HaMelaḥ, Yam, lk., Asia *see* Dead Sea	228-29	31°30'N	35°30'E
Hameln, Ger. (hä´mĕln)	194-95	52°06'N	9°22'E
Hamersley Range, mts., Austl. (hăm´ĕrz-lē rānj)	272-73	22°24'S	117°34'E
Hamhŭng, Kor., N. (häm´hŏŏng´)	243	39°55'N	127°32'E
Hami, China (hä-mē)	240-41	42°50'N	93°31'E
Hamilton, Austl. (hăm´ĭl-tŭn)	276	37°45'S	142°01'E
Hamilton, On., Can. (hăm´ĭl-tŭn)	136-37	43°15'N	79°51'W
Hamilton, N.Z. (hăm´ĭl-tŭn)	278	37°47'S	175°17'E
Hamilton, Al., U.S. (hăm´ĭl-tŭn)	124-25	34°08'N	87°59'W
Hamilton, Mo., U.S. (hăm´ĭl-tŭn)	120-21	39°45'N	94°00'W
Hamilton, Mt., U.S. (hăm´ĭl-tŭn)	112-13	46°14'N	114°10'W
Hamilton, Oh., U.S. (hăm´ĭl-tŭn)	116-17	39°24'N	84°34'W
Hamilton, Tx., U.S. (hăm´ĭl-tŭn)	122-23	31°41'N	98°08'W
Hamilton, nat. cap., Ber. (hăm´ĭl-tŭn)	140-41	32°18'N	64°48'W
Hamina, Fin. (hå´mē-nå)	192-93	60°34'N	27°19'E
Hamlet, N.C., U.S. (hăm´lĕt)	124-25	34°54'N	79°42'W
Hamlin, Tx., U.S. (hăm´lĭn)	120-21	32°53'N	100°08'W
Hamm, Ger. (häm)	194-95	51°41'N	7°49'E
Hammamet, Tun.	184-85	36°24'N	10°37'E
Hammamet, Golfe de, b., Tun.	258-59	36°05'N	10°40'E
Hammerfest, Nor. (hä´mĕr-fĕst)	184-85	70°40'N	23°42'E
Hammond, In., U.S. (hăm´ŭnd)	116-17	41°35'N	87°30'W
Hammond, La., U.S. (hăm´ŭnd)	124-25	30°30'N	90°28'W
Hammonton, N.J., U.S. (hăm´ŭn-tŭn)	116-17	39°38'N	74°48'W
Hampton, N.B., Can. (hămp´tŭn)	138-39	45°32'N	65°51'W
Hampton, Ia., U.S. (hămp´tŭn)	114-15	42°45'N	93°12'W
Hampton, S.C., U.S. (hămp´tŭn)	124-25	32°52'N	81°07'W
Hampton, Va., U.S. (hămp´tŭn)	124-25	37°02'N	76°21'W
Ḥamrā', Al-Ḥamādah al-, des., Libya	188-89	30°0'N	12°00'E
Hāmūn, Daryācheh-ye, lk., Iran	230-31	30°43'N	61°07'E
Han, stm., China (hän)	238-39	23°41'N	116°38'E
Han, stm., China (hän)	238-39	30°34'N	114°17'E
Hāna, Hi., U.S. (hä´nä)	127a	20°45'N	155°59'W
Hancheng, China	240-41	35°29'N	110°25'E
Hancock, Mi., U.S. (hăn´kŏk)	114-15	47°08'N	88°36'W
Handan, China (hän-dän)	240-41	36°37'N	114°28'E
Hanford, Ca., U.S. (hăn´fērd)	118-19	36°20'N	119°38'W
Hangayn nuruu, mts., Mong.	240-41	47°32'N	98°42'E
Hangchow, China *see* Hangzhou	238-39	30°15'N	120°10'E
Hanggin Houqi, China	240-41	40°57'N	107°14'E
Hanggin Qi, China	240-41	39°55'N	108°52'E
Hangö, Fin. (häng´gû) *see* Hanko	192-93	59°50'N	22°58'E
Hangzhou, China (häng´chō´)	238-39	30°15'N	120°10'E
Hanjiang, China	225a	25°30'N	119°06'E
Hankinson, N.D., U.S. (hăŋ´kĭn-sŭn)	114-15	46°04'N	96°55'W
Hanko, Fin.	192-93	59°50'N	22°58'E
Hankow, China *see* Wuhan	238-39	30°34'N	114°17'E
Hanna, Ab., Can. (hăn´á)	132-33	51°39'N	111°56'W
Hannibal, Mo., U.S. (hăn´ĭ băl)	120-21	39°42'N	91°22'W
Hannover, Ger. (hän-ō´vĕr)	194-95	52°24'N	9°44'E
Ha Noi, nat. cap., Viet. (hä-noi´)	246-47	21°02'N	105°50'E
Hanover, On., Can. (hăn´ô-vĕr)	136-37	44°09'N	81°01'W
Hanover, Ger. *see* Hannover	194-95	52°24'N	9°44'E
Hanover, N.H., U.S. (hăn´ô-vĕr)	116-17	43°42'N	72°17'W
Hanover, Pa., U.S. (hăn´ô-vĕr)	116-17	39°48'N	76°59'W
Hanover, Va., U.S. (hăn´ô-vĕr)	116-17	37°46'N	77°23'W
Hanover, Isla, i., Chile	171	50°58'S	74°45'W
Hantsport, N.S., Can. (hănts´pōrt)	138-39	45°04'N	64°12'W
Hanuy, stm., Mong.	240-41	49°21'N	102°22'E
Hanzhong, China (hän-jôŋ)	238-39	33°04'N	107°02'E

Feature (Pronunciation)	Page	Lat.	Long.
Hāora, India	**234-35**	22°35'N	88°20'E
Haparanda, Swe. (hä-pa-rän'dä)	**184-85**	65°50'N	24°06'E
Happy Valley-Goose Bay, Nf., Can.	**128-29**	53°20'N	60°25'W
Hāpur, India	**234-35**	28°44'N	77°47'E
Harare, nat. cap., Zimb. (hä-rä'-rē)	**264-65**	17°50'S	31°03'E
Ḥarash, Bi'r al-, well, Libya	**258-59**	25°39'N	22°08'E
Harbin, China	**240-41**	45°45'N	126°38'E
Harbor Beach, Mi., U.S. (här'bẽr bēch)	**116-17**	43°51'N	82°39'W
Harbour Breton, Nf., Can. (här'bẽr brĕt'ŭn) (brĕ-tôn')	**138-39**	47°30'N	55°49'W
Harbour Grace, Nf., Can. (här'bẽr grās)	**138-39**	47°44'N	53°15'W
Hardangerfjorden, b., Nor.	**192-93**	60°10'N	6°00'E
Hardin, Mt., U.S. (här'dĭn)	**112-13**	45°44'N	107°37'W
Hardoi, India	**234-35**	27°23'N	80°09'E
Hare Bay, b., Nf., Can. (hâr bā)	**138-39**	51°16'N	55°51'W
Hareidlandet, i., Nor.	**184-85**	62°21'N	5°57'E
Hārer, Eth.	**262-63**	9°18'N	42°08'E
Hargeysa, Som. (här-gā'ē-sȧ)	**262-63**	9°34'N	44°04'E
Har Horin, hist., Mong. see Karakorum	**240-41**	47°14'N	102°50'E
Har Hu, lk., China	**240-41**	38°15'N	97°40'E
Hari, stm., Indon.	**246-47**	1°04'S	104°12'E
Haridwār, India	**234-35**	29°56'N	78°07'E
Harīrūd, stm., Asia	**232-33**	37°24'N	60°31'E
Harlan, Ia., U.S. (här'lăn)	**114-15**	41°39'N	95°20'W
Harlan, Ky., U.S. (här'lăn)	**124-25**	36°51'N	83°19'W
Harlem, Mt., U.S. (hår'lĕm)	**112-13**	48°32'N	108°47'W
Harlingen, Neth. (här'lĭng-ĕn)	**190-91**	53°10'N	5°26'E
Harlingen, Tx., U.S. (här'lĭng-ĕn)	**122-23**	26°12'N	97°42'W
Harlow, Eng., U.K. (här'lō)	**190-91**	51°47'N	0°07'E
Harlowton, Mt., U.S. (här'lô-tun)	**112-13**	46°26'N	109°50'W
Harney Basin, bas., Or., U.S. (här'nĭ bā's'n)	**112-13**	43°15'N	119°00'W
Harney Peak, mtn., S.D., U.S. (här'nĭ pēk)	**114-15**	43°52'N	103°32'W
Härnösand, Swe. (hĕr-nû-sänd)	**184-85**	62°38'N	17°56'E
Haro, Spain (ä'rō)	**198-99**	42°36'N	2°52'W
Hārot, stm., Afg.	**232-33**	31°29'N	61°16'E
Harper, Lib. (här'pẽr)	**260-61**	4°23'N	7°43'W
Harpers Ferry, W.V., U.S. (här'pẽrz fĕr'ē)	**116-17**	39°19'N	77°45'W
Harricana, stm., Can.	**130-31**	51°10'N	79°47'W
Harriman, Tn., U.S. (hăr'ĭ-măn)	**124-25**	35°56'N	84°33'W
Harrington, De., U.S. (hăr'ĭng-tŭn)	**116-17**	38°56'N	75°34'W
Harris, Lake, lk., Austl.	**272-73**	31°06'S	135°11'E
Harrisburg, Il., U.S. (hăr'ĭs-bûrg)	**116-17**	37°44'N	88°32'W
Harrisburg, Pa., U.S.	**116-17**	40°16'N	76°54'W
Harrismith, S. Afr. (hă-rĭs'mĭth)	**269c**	28°17'S	29°08'E
Harrison, Ar., U.S. (hăr'ĭ-sŭn)	**120-21**	36°14'N	93°07'W
Harrison, Mi., U.S. (hăr'ĭ-sŭn)	**116-17**	44°01'N	84°48'W
Harrison, Cape, c., Nf., Can.	**130-31**	54°55'N	57°56'W
Harrisonburg, Va., U.S. (hăr'ĭ-sŭn-bûrg)	**116-17**	38°27'N	78°52'W
Harrison Lake, lk., B.C., Can. (hăr'ĭ-sŭn lăk)	**132-33**	49°33'N	121°52'W
Harrisonville, Mo., U.S. (hăr-ĭ-sŭn-vĭl)	**120-21**	38°39'N	94°21'W
Harrisville, Mi., U.S. (hăr'ĭs-vĭl)	**116-17**	44°39'N	83°18'W
Harrisville, W.V., U.S. (hăr'ĭs-vĭl)	**116-17**	39°13'N	81°03'W
Harrodsburg, Ky., U.S. (hăr'ŭdz-bûrg)	**116-17**	37°46'N	84°51'W
Harstad, Nor. (här'städh)	**184-85**	68°47'N	16°34'E
Hart, Mi., U.S. (härt)	**116-17**	43°42'N	86°22'W
Hartford, Ct., U.S. (härt'fẽrd)	**116-17**	41°46'N	72°41'W
Hartford, Ky., U.S. (härt'fẽrd)	**116-17**	37°27'N	86°54'W
Hartford, Mi., U.S. (härt'fẽrd)	**116-17**	42°12'N	86°10'W
Hartford, S.D., U.S. (härt'fẽrd)	**114-15**	43°38'N	96°58'W
Hartford City, In., U.S. (härt'fẽrd sĭ'tė)	**116-17**	40°27'N	85°22'W
Hartlepool, Eng., U.K. (här't'l-pōōl)	**190-91**	54°42'N	1°12'W
Hart Mountain, mtn., Mb., Can. (härt moun'tĭn)	**134-35**	52°29'N	101°25'W
Harts, stm., S. Afr.	**264-65**	28°24'S	24°17'E
Hartselle, Al., U.S. (härt'sĕl)	**124-25**	34°27'N	86°56'W
Hartshorne, Ok., U.S. (härts'hôrn)	**120-21**	34°51'N	95°34'W
Hartsville, S.C., U.S. (härts'vĭl)	**124-25**	34°22'N	80°05'W
Hartwell, Ga., U.S. (härt'wĕl)	**124-25**	34°21'N	82°55'W
Hartwell Lake, res., U.S. (härt'wĕl lăk)	**124-25**	34°28'N	82°51'W
Har Us nuur, lk., Mong.	**240-41**	48°0'N	92°10'E
Harvard, Il., U.S. (här'vȧrd)	**116-17**	42°25'N	88°37'W
Harvey, N.D., U.S.	**114-15**	47°46'N	99°55'W
Harwich, Eng., U.K. (här'wĭch)	**190-91**	51°57'N	1°17'E
Haryāna, state, India	**234-35**	29°20'N	76°20'E
Harz, mts., Ger. (härts)	**194-95**	51°45'N	10°30'E
Haskell, Tx., U.S. (hăs'kĕl)	**120-21**	33°09'N	99°44'W
Hassan, India	**236**	12°60'N	76°06'E
Hassi Messaoud, Alg.	**188-89**	31°41'N	6°04'E
Hässleholm, Swe. (häs'lĕ-hōlm)	**192-93**	56°09'N	13°46'E
Hastings, N.Z. (hās'tĭngz)	**278**	39°38'S	176°51'E
Hastings, Eng., U.K. (hās'tĭngz)	**190-91**	50°52'N	0°35'E
Hastings, Mi., U.S. (hās'tĭngz)	**116-17**	42°39'N	85°17'W
Hastings, Mn., U.S. (hās'tĭngz)	**114-15**	44°44'N	92°51'W
Hastings, Ne., U.S. (hās'tĭngz)	**120-21**	40°35'N	98°24'W
Hatay, Tur. see Antioch	**228-29**	36°12'N	36°10'E
Haţeg, Rom. (kät-sāg')	**200-01**	45°36'N	22°57'E
Hāthras, India	**234-35**	27°36'N	78°03'E
Ha Tinh, Viet.	**246-47**	18°20'N	105°54'E
Hatteras, Cape, c., N.C., U.S. (kāp hăt'ẽr-ȧs)	**124-25**	35°13'N	75°32'W
Hatteras Island, i., N.C., U.S.	**124-25**	35°25'N	75°29'W
Hattiesburg, Ms., U.S. (hăt'ĭz-bûrg)	**124-25**	31°20'N	89°17'W
Hatvan, Hung. (hôt'vôn)	**194-95**	47°40'N	19°41'E
Hat Yai, Thai.	**246-47**	7°01'N	100°28'E
Haugesund, Nor. (hou'gẽ-soon')	**192-93**	59°25'N	5°18'E
Hauraki Gulf, b., N.Z. (hä-ōō-rä'kē gŭlf)	**278**	36°35'S	175°05'E
Haut Atlas, mts., Mor.	**258-59**	31°47'N	6°04'W
Haute-Volta, nation, Afr. see Burkina Faso	**253**	13°0'N	1°30'W
Havana, Il., U.S. (hȧ-vă'nȧ)	**120-21**	40°18'N	90°03'W
Havana, nat. cap., Cuba (hȧ-vă'nȧ)	**142-43**	23°06'N	82°27'W
Havel, stm., Ger. (hä'fĕl)	**194-95**	52°53'N	12°01'E
Haverhill, Ma., U.S. (hā'vẽr-hĭl)	**116-17**	42°47'N	71°05'W
Havre, Fr. see Le Havre	**196-97**	49°29'N	0°08'E
Havre, Mt., U.S. (hăv'ẽr)	**112-13**	48°33'N	109°41'W
Havre Aubert, Île du, i., Qc., Can.	**138-39**	47°14'N	61°57'W
Havre de Grace, Md., U.S. (hăv'ẽr dē grās')	**116-17**	39°33'N	76°06'W
Havre-Saint-Pierre, Qc., Can.	**138-39**	50°15'N	63°36'W
Hawai'i, i., Hi., U.S. (hä-wī'ē)	**127a**	19°29'N	155°30'W
Hawai'ian Islands, is., Hi., U.S. (hä-wī'ăn ī'lăndz)	**127**	24°0'N	157°00'W
Hawai'i Volcanoes National Park, n.p., Hi., U.S.	**127a**	19°23'N	155°17'W
Hawaii, state, U.S. (hä wī'ē)	**108-09**	20°17'N	157°45'W
Hawi, Hi., U.S. (hä'wē)	**127a**	20°15'N	155°50'W
Hawick, Scot., U.K. (hô'ĭk)	**190-91**	55°25'N	2°47'W
Hawke Bay, b., N.Z. (hôk bā)	**278**	39°20'S	177°30'E
Hawker, Austl. (hô'kẽr)	**276**	31°53'S	138°25'E
Hawkesbury, On., Can. (hôks'bẽr-ĭ)	**136-37**	45°37'N	74°36'W
Hawkesbury Island, i., B.C., Can.	**132-33**	53°38'N	129°00'W
Hawkinsville, Ga., U.S. (hô'kĭnz-vĭl)	**124-25**	32°17'N	83°28'W
Hawley, Mn., U.S. (hô'lĭ)	**114-15**	46°53'N	96°19'W
Hawthorne, Nv., U.S.	**118-19**	38°32'N	118°37'W
Haxtun, Co., U.S. (hăks'tŭn)	**114-15**	40°38'N	102°38'W
Hay, Austl.	**276**	34°31'S	144°50'E
Hay, stm., Can. (hā)	**130-31**	60°52'N	115°44'W
HaYarden, stm., Asia see Jordan	**228-29**	31°46'N	35°34'E
Hayastan, nation, Asia see Armenia	**227**	40°0'N	45°00'E
Hayden, Id., U.S. (hā'dĕn)	**112-13**	47°46'N	116°47'W
Hayes, stm., Mb., Can. (hāz)	**134-35**	57°03'N	92°14'W
Hayes, Mount, mtn., Ak., U.S. (mount hāz)	**126**	63°37'N	146°43'W
Haynesville, La., U.S. (hānz'vĭl)	**120-21**	32°58'N	93°08'W
Hay River, N.T., Can. (hā rĭv'ẽr)	**128-29**	60°49'N	115°48'W
Hays, Ks., U.S. (hāz)	**120-21**	38°52'N	99°18'W
Hazard, Ky., U.S. (hăz'ȧrd)	**124-25**	37°15'N	83°12'W
Hazārībāg, India	**234-35**	23°60'N	85°22'E
Hazelton, B.C., Can. (hā'z'l-tŭn)	**132-33**	55°15'N	127°42'W
Hazelton Mountains, mts., B.C., Can. (hā'z'l-tŭn moun'tĭnz)	**132-33**	54°51'N	128°00'W
Hazleton, Pa., U.S. (hā'z'l-tŭn)	**116-17**	40°57'N	75°59'W
Headland, Al., U.S. (hĕd'lănd)	**124-25**	31°21'N	85°21'W
Healdsburg, Ca., U.S. (hēldz'bûrg)	**118-19**	38°37'N	122°52'W
Healdton, Ok., U.S. (hēld'tŭn)	**120-21**	34°14'N	97°29'W
Heard and McDonald Islands, dep., Oc.	**282-83**	53°05'S	73°00'E
Heard Island, i., Austl. (hûrd ī'lănd)	**286**	53°06'S	73°30'E
Hearne, Tx., U.S. (hûrn)	**122-23**	30°53'N	96°36'W
Hearst, On., Can. (hûrst)	**128-29**	49°41'N	83°42'W
Heavener, Ok., U.S. (hēv'nẽr)	**120-21**	34°54'N	94°36'W
Hebbronville, Tx., U.S. (hē'brŭn-vĭl)	**122-23**	27°18'N	98°41'W
Hebei, state, China (hŭ-bā)	**240-41**	38°0'N	116°00'E
Heber City, Ut., U.S. (hē'bẽr sĭ'tė)	**118-19**	40°31'N	111°25'W
Heber Springs, Ar., U.S. (hē'bẽr sprĭngz)	**124-25**	35°29'N	92°02'W
Hebi, China	**240-41**	35°58'N	114°09'E
Hebrides, is., Scot., U.K.	**190-91**	57°0'N	6°30'W
Hebron, Nf., Can. (hĕb'rŭn)	**128-29**	58°12'N	62°38'W
Hebron, N.D., U.S. (hĕb'rŭn)	**114-15**	46°54'N	102°03'W
Hebron, Ne., U.S. (hĕb'rŭn)	**120-21**	40°09'N	97°35'W
Hebron, W.B.	**228-29**	31°32'N	35°06'E
Hecate Strait, strt., B.C., Can. (hĕk'ȧ-tē strāt)	**132-33**	53°0'N	131°00'W
Hecelchakán, Mex. (ā-sĕl-chä-kän')	**148**	20°10'N	90°08'W
Hechi, China (hŭ-chr)	**238-39**	24°42'N	108°02'E
Hechuan, China (hŭ-chyuän)	**238-39**	29°60'N	106°16'E
Hedemora, Swe. (hĭ-dĕ-mō'rä)	**192-93**	60°17'N	15°59'E
Hefa, Isr. see Haifa	**228-29**	32°49'N	35°00'E
Hefei, China (hŭ-fā)	**238-39**	31°51'N	117°17'E
Heflin, Al., U.S. (hĕf'lĭn)	**124-25**	33°39'N	85°35'W
Hegang, China	**240-41**	47°19'N	130°16'E
Heho, Mya.	**246-47**	20°43'N	96°49'E
Heidelberg, Ger. (hīdĕl-bĕrgh)	**194-95**	49°25'N	8°42'E
Heihe, China	**240-41**	50°14'N	127°30'E
Heijō, nat. cap., Kor., N. see P'yŏngyang	**243**	39°01'N	125°44'E
Heilbron, S. Afr. (hīl'brōn)	**269c**	27°17'S	27°59'E
Heilbronn, Ger. (hīl'brōn)	**194-95**	49°08'N	9°12'E
Heilong, stm., Asia see Amur	**218-19**	52°57'N	141°10'E
Heilongjiang, state, China (hā-lôŋ-jyäŋ)	**240-41**	48°0'N	128°00'E
Heilongjiang, stm., Asia see Amur	**218-19**	52°57'N	141°10'E
Heilungkiang, state, China see Heilongjiang	**240-41**	48°0'N	128°00'E
Heinola, Fin. (hå-nō'lȧ)	**192-93**	61°12'N	26°03'E
Hejaz, reg., Sau. Ar. (hĕ-jăz') (hē-jäz') see Al-Ḥijāz	**266**	24°30'N	38°30'E
Hejian, China (hŭ-jyĕn)	**240-41**	38°26'N	116°05'E
Hekla, vol., Ice.	**190a**	64°0'N	19°39'W
Hel, Pol. (hāl)	**194-95**	54°37'N	18°48'E
Helagsfjället, mtn., Swe.	**184-85**	62°55'N	12°27'E
Helena, Ar., U.S. (hē-lē'nȧ)	**124-25**	34°32'N	90°36'W
Helena, Mt., U.S.	**112-13**	46°36'N	112°02'W
Helen Island, i., Palau	**280-81**	2°58'N	131°49'E
Helgoland, i., Ger. (hĕl'gō-länd)	**194-95**	54°11'N	7°52'E
Hellín, Spain (ĕl-yĕn')	**198-99**	38°30'N	1°42'W
Hells Canyon, val., U.S. (hĕls kăn'yŭn)	**112-13**	45°17'N	116°40'W
Helmand, stm., Asia (hĕl'mŭnd)	**232-33**	31°19'N	61°29'E
Helmond, Neth. (hĕl'mōnt) (ĕl'môn')	**190-91**	51°29'N	5°40'E
Helmstedt, Ger. (hĕlm'shtĕt)	**194-95**	52°13'N	11°01'E
Helsingborg, Swe. (hĕl'sĭng-bôrgh)	**192-93**	56°03'N	12°42'E
Helsingfors, nat. cap., Fin. see Helsinki	**192-93**	60°10'N	24°57'E
Helsingør, Den. (hĕl-sĭng-ûr')	**192-93**	56°02'N	12°37'E
Helsinki, nat. cap., Fin. (hĕl'sēn-kė)	**192-93**	60°10'N	24°57'E
Helvetia, nation, Eur. see Switzerland	**174-75**	47°0'N	8°00'E
Hemingford, Ne., U.S. (hĕm'ĭng-fẽrd)	**114-15**	42°19'N	103°05'W
Hempstead, N.Y., U.S. (hĕmp'stĕd)	**116-17**	40°42'N	73°41'W
Hempstead, Tx., U.S. (hĕmp'stĕd)	**122-23**	30°05'N	96°05'W
Hemse, Swe. (hĕm'sĕ)	**192-93**	57°14'N	18°23'E
Henan, state, China (hŭ-nän)	**238-39**	34°0'N	114°00'E
Henderson, Ky., U.S. (hĕn'dẽr-sŭn)	**116-17**	37°50'N	87°35'W
Henderson, N.C., U.S. (hĕn'dẽr-sŭn)	**124-25**	36°20'N	78°24'W
Henderson, Nv., U.S. (hĕn'dẽr-sŭn)	**118-19**	36°02'N	114°59'W
Henderson, Tn., U.S. (hĕn'dẽr-sŭn)	**124-25**	35°26'N	88°38'W
Henderson, Tx., U.S. (hĕn'dẽr-sŭn)	**122-23**	32°09'N	94°48'W
Henderson Island, i., Pit.	**280-81**	24°22'S	128°19'W
Hendersonville, N.C., U.S. (hĕn'dẽr-sŭn-vĭl)	**124-25**	35°19'N	82°28'W
Hendersonville, Tn., U.S. (hĕn'dẽr-sŭn-vĭl)	**124-25**	36°18'N	86°37'W
Hendorābī, Jazīreh-ye, i., Iran	**230-31**	26°41'N	53°38'E
Hendrina, S. Afr. (hĕn-drē'nȧ)	**269c**	26°10'S	29°44'E
Hendū Kosh, mts., Asia see Hindu Kush	**232-33**	36°0'N	71°30'E
Hengām, Jazīreh-ye, i., Iran	**230-31**	26°39'N	55°53'E
Hengelo, Neth. (hĕngĕ-lō)	**190-91**	52°16'N	6°48'E
Hengshan, China (hĕng'shän')	**238-39**	27°15'N	112°51'E
Hengshan, China (hĕng'shän')	**240-41**	37°57'N	109°18'E
Hengshui, China (hĕng'shōō-ē')	**240-41**	37°44'N	115°42'E
Hengxian, China (hŭŋ shyĕn)	**238-39**	22°41'N	109°12'E
Hengyang, China	**238-39**	26°54'N	112°36'E
Henlopen, Cape, c., De., U.S. (kāp hĕn-lō'pĕn)	**116-17**	38°47'N	75°06'W
Hennebont, Fr. (ĕn-bôn')	**196-97**	47°48'N	3°16'W
Hennessey, Ok., U.S. (hĕn'ĕ-sĭ)	**120-21**	36°07'N	97°54'W
Henrietta, Tx., U.S. (hen-rĭ-ĕ'tȧ)	**120-21**	33°49'N	98°12'W
Henrietta Maria, Cape, c., On., Can. (kāp hĕn-rĭ-ĕt'ȧ mȧ-rē'ȧ)	**130-31**	55°08'N	82°20'W
Henzada, Mya.	**246-47**	17°38'N	95°28'E
Hepu, China (hŭ-pōō)	**238-39**	21°41'N	109°11'E
Herāt, Afg. (hĕ-rät')	**232-33**	34°21'N	62°12'E
Heredia, C.R. (ā-rā'dhē-ä)	**149**	9°59'N	84°07'W
Hereford, Eng., U.K. (hĕrĕ'fẽrd)	**190-91**	52°04'N	2°43'W
Hereford, Tx., U.S. (hĕr'ĕ-fẽrd)	**120-21**	34°50'N	102°24'W
Herford, Ger. (hĕr'fôrt)	**194-95**	52°07'N	8°40'E
Herkimer, N.Y., U.S. (hûr'kĭ-mẽr)	**116-17**	43°02'N	74°58'W
Herlen, stm., Asia see Kerulen	**240-41**	48°44'N	117°03'E
Hermannstadt, Rom. see Sibiu	**194-95**	45°47'N	24°09'E
Hermansville, Mi., U.S. (hûr'mănz-vĭl)	**116-17**	45°42'N	87°36'W

ăt; finăl; rāte; senâte; ärm; ȧsk; sofȧ; fâre; ch-choose; dh-as th in other; bē; ėvent; bĕt; recĕnt; cratẽr; g-gō; gh-guttural g; bĭt; ĭ-short neutral; rīde; ᴋ-guttural k as ch in German ich;

Feature (Pronunciation)	Page	Lat.	Long.
Hermit Islands, is., Pap. N. Gui. (hûr′mĭt ī′lăndz)	277	1°30′S	145°05′E
Hermon, Mount, mtn., Asia	228-29	33°25′N	35°51′E
Hermosillo, Mex. (ĕr-mô-sē′l-yō)	144-45	29°05′N	110°58′W
Hermus, stm., Tur. *see* Gediz	200-01	38°36′N	26°48′E
Herning, Den. (hĕr′nĭng)	192-93	56°08′N	8°59′E
Herrin, Il., U.S. (hĕr′ĭn)	116-17	37°48′N	89°02′W
Herstal, Bel. (hĕr′stäl)	190-91	50°40′N	5°38′E
Hertford, N.C., U.S. (hûrt′fērd)	124-25	36°11′N	76°29′W
Hervey Bay, Austl.	276	25°17′S	152°50′E
Hervey Bay, b., Austl.	272-73	25°0′S	153°00′E
Hessen, hist. reg., Ger. (hĕs′ĕn)	194-95	50°30′N	9°15′E
Hettinger, N.D., U.S. (hĕt′ĭn-jēr)	114-15	46°00′N	102°38′W
Hexian, China (hŭ shyĕn)	238-39	24°18′N	111°39′E
Heyuan, China (hŭ-yüän)	238-39	23°43′N	114°42′E
Heze, China (hŭ-dzŭ)	240-41	35°15′N	115°27′E
Hialeah, Fl., U.S. (hī-à-lē′ăh)	125a	25°51′N	80°17′W
Hiawatha, Ia., U.S. (hī-ȧ-wô′thȧ)	114-15	42°02′N	91°41′W
Hibbing, Mn., U.S. (hĭb′ĭng)	114-15	47°25′N	92°56′W
Hickman, Ky., U.S. (hĭk′măn)	124-25	36°34′N	89°11′W
Hickory, N.C., U.S. (hĭk′ô-rĭ)	124-25	35°44′N	81°21′W
Hicks, Point, c., Austl.	276	37°48′S	149°16′E
Hidalgo, Mex. (ē-dhäl′gō)	146-47	24°15′N	99°26′W
Hidalgo, Mex. (ē-dhäl′gō)	122-23	25°58′N	100°27′W
Hidalgo, state, Mex. (ē-dhäl′gō)	146-47	20°30′N	99°00′W
Hidalgo del Parral, Mex. (ē-dä′l-gō-dĕl-pär-rä′l)	122-23	26°57′N	105°40′W
Higasi Sina Kai, s., Asia *see* East China Sea	222-23	30°0′N	126°00′E
Higginsville, Mo., U.S. (hĭg′ĭnz-vĭl)	120-21	39°05′N	93°43′W
Highland, Il., U.S. (hī′lănd)	120-21	38°44′N	89°41′W
Highland Park, Il., U.S. (hī′lănd pärk)	116-17	42°11′N	87°48′W
Highland Park, Mi., U.S. (hī′lănd pärk)	116-17	42°24′N	83°07′W
High Level, Ab., Can.	128-29	58°31′N	117°08′W
Highmore, S.D., U.S. (hī′mōr)	114-15	44°31′N	99°26′W
High Point, N.C., U.S. (hī point)	124-25	35°57′N	80°01′W
High Prairie, Ab., Can. (hī prā′rĭ)	132-33	55°26′N	116°29′W
High River, Ab., Can. (hī rĭv′ēr)	132-33	50°35′N	113°52′W
Hightstown, N.J., U.S. (hīts-toun)	116-17	40°17′N	74°32′W
High Wycombe, Eng., U.K. (hī wĭ-kŭm)	190-91	51°38′N	0°45′W
Higüey, Dom. Rep. (ē-gwĕ′y)	142-43	18°37′N	68°43′W
Hiiumaa, i., Est. (hē′ŏm-ô)	192-93	58°55′N	22°38′E
Hikone, Japan (hē′kô-nĕ)	245	35°15′N	136°15′E
Hildesheim, Ger. (hĭl′dĕs-hīm)	194-95	52°09′N	9°57′E
Hilla, Iraq *see* Al-Ḥillah	228-29	32°29′N	44°26′E
Hillaby, Mount, mtn., Barb. (mount hĭl′ȧ-bĭ)	143b	13°12′N	59°35′W
Hillerød, Den. (hē′lĕ-rûdh hĭl)	192-93	55°56′N	12°19′E
Hillsboro, Il., U.S. (hĭlz′bŭr-ō)	116-17	39°09′N	89°29′W
Hillsboro, N.D., U.S. (hĭlz′bŭr-ō)	114-15	47°24′N	97°04′W
Hillsboro, Oh., U.S. (hĭlz′bŭr-ō)	116-17	39°12′N	83°37′W
Hillsboro, Or., U.S. (hĭlz′bŭr-ō)	112-13	45°31′N	122°59′W
Hillsboro, Tx., U.S. (hĭlz′bŭr-ō)	122-23	32°01′N	97°08′W
Hillsboro, W.V., U.S. (hĭlz′bŭr-ō)	116-17	38°08′N	80°13′W
Hillsdale, Mi., U.S. (hĭls-dāl hĭlz)	116-17	41°55′N	84°38′W
Hillston, Austl.	276	33°29′S	145°33′E
Hilo, Hi., U.S. (hē′lō)	127a	19°43′N	155°05′W
Himāchal Pradesh, state, India	234-35	32°0′N	77°00′E
Himalayas, mts., Asia (hĭ-mä′lȧ-yȧz) (hĭ-mȧ-lā′-yȧz)	234-35	28°0′N	84°00′E
Himalaya Shan, mts., Asia *see* Himalayas	234-35	28°0′N	84°00′E
Himatnagar, India	234-35	23°35′N	72°58′E
Himeji, Japan (hē′mȧ-jē)	245	34°50′N	134°42′E
Ḥimṣ, Syria	228-29	34°45′N	36°44′E
Hinche, Haiti (hēn′chȧ) (äɴsh)	142-43	19°09′N	72°00′W
Hinchinbrook Island, i., Austl. (hĭn-chĭn-brŏŏk ī′lănd)	277	18°23′S	146°17′E
Hindenburg, Pol. *see* Zabrze	194-95	50°18′N	18°46′E
Hindu Kush, mts., Asia (hĭn′dōō kōōsh′)	232-33	36°0′N	71°30′E
Hindupur, India (hĭn′dōō-pōōr)	236	13°49′N	77°30′E
Hinnøya, i., Nor.	184-85	68°32′N	15°59′E
Hinton, Ab., Can. (hĭn′tŭn)	132-33	53°25′N	117°34′W
Hinton, W.V., U.S. (hĭn′tŭn)	116-17	37°40′N	80°53′W
Hirado-shima, i., Japan (hē′rä-dō shē′mä)	245	33°20′N	129°30′E
Hirara, Japan	279a	24°47′N	125°17′E
Hīrmand, stm., Asia *see* Helmand	232-33	31°19′N	61°29′E
Hirosaki, Japan (hē′rō-sä′kē)	244	40°36′N	140°29′E
Hiroshima, Japan (hē-rō-shē′mȧ)	245	34°24′N	132°28′E
Hirosima, Japan *see* Hiroshima	245	34°24′N	132°28′E
Hirschberg, Pol. *see* Jelenia Góra	194-95	50°54′N	15°44′E
Hirson, Fr. (ēr-sôɴ′)	196-97	49°56′N	4°05′E
Hisār, India	234-35	29°09′N	75°44′E
Hispaniola, i., N.A. (hĭ′spăn-ĭ-ō-lȧ)	142-43	19°0′N	71°00′W
Hitachi, Japan (hē-tä′chē)	245	36°36′N	140°39′E
Hitoyoshi, Japan (hē′tô-yō′shē)	245	32°12′N	130°46′E
Hitra, i., Nor. (hĭträ)	184-85	63°33′N	8°45′E
Hiu, i., Vanuatu	279g	13°08′S	166°33′E
Hiva Oa, i., Fr. Poly.	280-81	9°45′S	139°00′W
Hjo, Swe. (yō)	192-93	58°18′N	14°17′E
Hjørring, Den. (jûr′ĭng)	192-93	57°28′N	9°59′E
Hkakabo Razi, mtn., Mya.	238-39	28°17′N	97°46′E
Hlohovec, Slvk. (hlō′ho-vĕts)	194-95	48°26′N	17°48′E
Ho, Ghana	260-61	6°36′N	0°28′E
Hoa Binh, Viet.	246-47	20°50′N	105°20′E
Hobart, Austl. (hō′bȧrt)	276	42°52′S	147°18′E
Hobart, Ok., U.S. (hō′bȧrt)	120-21	35°02′N	99°06′W
Hobbs, N.M., U.S. (hŏbs)	120-21	32°42′N	103°08′W
Hobro, Den. (hô-brô′)	192-93	56°38′N	9°48′E
Ho Chi Minh City, Viet. (hō-chē-mĭn sĭ′tē)	246-47	10°45′N	106°40′E
Hodeida, Yemen *see* Al-Ḥudaydah	266	14°48′N	42°57′E
Hodgenville, Ky., U.S. (hŏj′ĕn-vĭl)	116-17	37°34′N	85°44′W
Hódmezővásárhely, Hung. (hōd′mĕ-zû-vô′shôr-hĕl-y′)	194-95	46°25′N	20°20′E
Hodna, Chott el, lk., Alg.	269b	35°25′N	4°45′E
Hodonín, Czech Rep. (hē′dô-nēn)	194-95	48°51′N	17°08′E
Hoei, Bel. *see* Huy	190-91	50°31′N	5°14′E
Hof, Ger. (hōf)	194-95	50°18′N	11°55′E
Hofsjökull, ice, Ice. (hôfs′yü′kōōl)	190a	64°50′N	18°54′W
Hōfu, Japan	245	34°03′N	131°35′E
Hofuf, Sau. Ar. *see* Al-Hufūf	230-31	25°22′N	49°34′E
Hogansville, Ga., U.S. (hō′gănz-vĭl)	124-25	33°11′N	84°55′W
Hoggar, mts., Alg. *see* Ahaggar	258-59	23°0′N	6°30′E
Hohensalza, Pol. *see* Inowrocław	194-95	52°48′N	18°15′E
Hohe Tauern, mts., Aus. (hō′ĕ tou′ērn)	194-95	47°06′N	12°56′E
Hohhot, China (hŭ-hōō-tŭ)	240-41	40°49′N	111°39′E
Hoihow, China *see* Haikou	238-39	20°03′N	110°22′E
Hoisington, Ks., U.S. (hoi′zĭng-tŭn)	120-21	38°31′N	98°46′W
Hokitika, N.Z. (hō-kĭ-tē′kä)	278	42°44′S	170°58′E
Hokkaidō, i., Japan (hôk′kĭ-dō)	244	44°0′N	143°00′E
Hola, Kenya	262-63	1°30′S	40°01′E
Holbrook, Az., U.S. (hōl′brŏŏk)	118-19	34°54′N	110°10′W
Holden, Mo., U.S. (hōl′dĕn)	120-21	38°43′N	93°60′W
Holden, W.V., U.S. (hōl′dĕn)	116-17	37°49′N	82°04′W
Holdenville, Ok., U.S. (hōl′dĕn-vĭl)	120-21	35°05′N	96°24′W
Holdrege, Ne., U.S. (hōl′drĕj)	120-21	40°27′N	99°22′W
Holguín, Cuba (ôl-gēn′)	142-43	20°53′N	76°15′W
Holguín, state, Cuba (ôl-gēn′)	142-43	20°55′N	75°50′W
Holland, Mi., U.S. (hŏl′ȧnd)	116-17	42°47′N	86°06′W
Holland, nation, Eur. *see* Netherlands	174-75	52°15′N	5°30′E
Hollandia, Indon. *see* Jayapura	277	2°32′S	140°43′E
Hollandsbird Island, i., Nmb.	264-65	24°39′S	14°32′E
Hollick-Kenyon Plateau, plat., Ant.	287	79°0′S	97°00′W
Hollis, Ok., U.S. (hŏl′ĭs)	120-21	34°41′N	99°55′W
Hollister, Mo., U.S. (hŏl′ĭs-tēr)	120-21	36°37′N	93°13′W
Holly Springs, Ms., U.S. (hŏl′ĭ sprĭngz)	124-25	34°46′N	89°27′W
Hollywood, Fl., U.S. (hŏl′ē-wŏŏd)	125a	26°01′N	80°09′W
Holmestrand, Nor. (hôl′mĕ-strän)	192-93	59°29′N	10°18′E
Holstebro, Den. (hôl′stĕ-brô)	192-93	56°22′N	8°38′E
Holyhead, Wales, U.K. (hŏl′ē-hĕd)	190-91	53°19′N	4°38′W
Holyoke, Co., U.S. (hōl′yōk)	114-15	40°35′N	102°18′W
Holyoke, Ma., U.S. (hōl′yōk)	116-17	42°12′N	72°37′W
Homa Bay, Kenya	267	0°31′S	34°27′E
Homalin, Mya.	238-39	24°51′N	94°56′E
Homel′, Bela.	202-03	52°26′N	30°59′E
Homer, Ak., U.S. (hō′mēr)	126	59°39′N	151°31′W
Homer, La., U.S. (hō′mēr)	120-21	32°48′N	93°04′W
Homestead, Fl., U.S. (hōm′stĕd)	125a	25°29′N	80°28′W
Homestead National Monument of America, n.p., Ne., U.S. (hōm′stĕd)	120-21	40°16′N	96°48′W
Homewood, Al., U.S. (hōm′wŏŏd)	124-25	33°28′N	86°48′W
Hominy, Ok., U.S. (hŏm′ĭ-nĭ)	120-21	36°25′N	96°24′W
Homs, Libya *see* Al-Khums	188-89	32°39′N	14°16′E
Homs, Syria *see* Ḥimṣ	228-29	34°45′N	36°44′E
Honan, state, China *see* Henan	238-39	34°0′N	114°00′E
Honda, Col. (hōn′dȧ)	163c	5°13′N	74°45′W
Hondo, stm., N.A. (hon-dō′)	148	18°29′N	88°18′W
Honduras, nation, N.A. (hŏn-dōō′rȧs)	85	15°0′N	86°30′W
Honduras, Golfo de, b., N.A. *see* Honduras, Gulf of	148	16°05′N	87°58′W
Honduras, Gulf of, b., N.A. (gŭlf ŭv hŏn-dōō′rȧs)	148	16°05′N	87°58′W
Hønefoss, Nor. (hē′nĕ-fōs)	192-93	60°11′N	10°15′E
Honesdale, Pa., U.S. (hōnz′dāl)	116-17	41°34′N	75°16′W
Honfleur, Fr. (ôɴ-flûr′)	196-97	49°25′N	0°14′E
Hong, Song, stm., Asia *see* Red	238-39	20°18′N	106°32′E
Hon Gai, Viet.	246-47	21°03′N	107°04′E
Hongjiang, China	238-39	27°04′N	109°58′E
Hong Kong, China (hông kông) (hŏng kŏng)	238-39	22°16′N	114°10′E
Hongliuyuan, China	240-41	41°02′N	95°25′E
Hongshui, stm., China (hôŋ-shwā)	238-39	23°48′N	109°32′E
Hongtong, China	240-41	36°17′N	111°40′E
Honguedo, Détroit d′, strt., Qc., Can.	138-39	49°15′N	64°00′W
Hongze Hu, lk., China	238-39	33°16′N	118°34′E
Honiara, nat. cap., Sol. Is. (hō-nē-ä′-rä)	279e	9°26′S	159°57′E
Honiton, Eng., U.K. (hŏn′ĭ-tŏn)	190-91	50°48′N	3°12′W
Honolulu, Hi., U.S. (hŏn-ō-lōō′lōō)	127a	21°19′N	157°52′W
Honshū, i., Japan (hŏn′-shōō)	244	36°0′N	138°00′E
Hood, i., Ec. *see* Española, Isla	170a	1°23′S	89°42′W
Hood, Mount, vol., Or., U.S. (mount hŏŏd)	112-13	45°23′N	121°42′W
Hood River, Or., U.S. (hŏŏd rĭv′ēr)	112-13	45°42′N	121°31′W
Hooker, Ok., U.S. (hŏŏk′ēr)	120-21	36°52′N	101°13′W
Hook Island, i., Austl.	277	20°08′S	148°55′E
Hoonah, Ak., U.S. (hōō′nȧ)	126	58°07′N	135°26′W
Hooper Bay, Ak., U.S. (hŏŏp′ēr bā)	126	61°31′N	166°06′W
Hoopeston, Il., U.S. (hōōps′tŭn)	116-17	40°28′N	87°39′W
Hoosick Falls, N.Y., U.S. (hōō′sĭk fôlz)	116-17	42°54′N	73°21′W
Hoover Dam, d., U.S. (hōō′vēr dăm)	118-19	36°02′N	114°43′W
Hope, B.C., Can.	132-33	49°23′N	121°26′W
Hope, Ar., U.S. (hōp)	120-21	33°40′N	93°35′W
Hope, Ben, mtn., Scot., U.K. (bĕn hōp)	190-91	58°24′N	4°37′W
Hopedale, Nf., Can. (hōp′dāl)	128-29	55°28′N	60°13′W
Hopeh, state, China *see* Hebei	240-41	38°0′N	116°00′E
Hopelchén, Mex. (o-pĕl-chĕ′n)	148	19°46′N	89°51′W
Hopes Advance, Cap, c., Qc., Can. (kȧp hōps ăd-vans′)	130-31	61°04′N	69°34′W
Hopetoun, Austl. (hōp′toun)	276	35°44′S	142°22′E
Hopetown, S. Afr. (hōp′toun)	264-65	29°35′S	24°04′E
Hopewell, Va., U.S. (hōp′wĕl)	124-25	37°18′N	77°17′W
Hopi Indian Reservation, ind. res., Az., U.S. (hō′pē ĭn′dĭ-ăn rĕ-sēr-vā′shĕn)	118-19	35°45′N	110°35′W
Hopkinsville, Ky., U.S. (hŏp′kĭns-vĭl)	124-25	36°52′N	87°29′W
Hoquiam, Wa., U.S. (hō′kwĭ-ăm)	112-13	46°59′N	123°53′W
Horicon, Wi., U.S. (hŏr′ĭ-kŏn)	116-17	43°27′N	88°37′W
Horlivka, Ukr.	202-03	48°20′N	38°03′E
Hormoz, Jazīreh-ye, i., Iran	230-31	27°04′N	56°28′E
Hormuz, Strait of, strt., Asia (strāt ŭv hôr′mŭz′)	230-31	26°34′N	56°15′E
Horn, c., Ice.	190a	66°28′N	22°28′W
Horn, Cape, c., Chile (kāp hôrn)	171	55°59′S	67°16′W
Hornavan, lk., Swe.	184-85	66°10′N	17°46′E
Hornell, N.Y., U.S. (hôr-nĕl′)	116-17	42°20′N	77°39′W
Hornepayne, On., Can.	136-37	49°12′N	84°47′W
Horn Island, i., Ms., U.S.	124-25	30°15′N	88°43′W
Hornos, Cabo de, c., Chile *see* Horn, Cape	171	55°59′S	67°16′W
Horn Plateau, plat., N.T., Can.	130-31	62°08′N	120°16′W
Horqin Youyi Qianqi, China *see* Ulanhot	240-41	46°04′N	122°04′E
Horqueta, Para. (ŏr-kĕ′tä)	168-69	23°20′S	57°03′W
Horse Islands, is., Nf., Can. (hôrs ī′lăndz)	138-39	50°13′N	55°45′W
Horsens, Den. (hôrs′ĕns)	192-93	55°52′N	9°52′E
Horsham, Austl. (hôr′shăm) (hôrs′ăm)	276	36°43′S	142°12′E
Horten, Nor. (hôr′tĕn)	192-93	59°25′N	10°29′E
Horton, stm., N.T., Can.	130-31	69°55′N	127°02′W
Hosa'ina, Eth.	269d	7°37′N	37°56′E
Hoséré Vokré, mtn., Camrn.	260-61	8°20′N	13°15′E
Hoshangābād, India	234-35	22°45′N	77°43′E
Hoshiārpur, India	234-35	31°32′N	75°55′E
Hospet, India	236	15°16′N	76°23′E
Hoste, Isla, i., Chile (ĕ′s-lä-ŏs′tā)	171	55°05′S	69°15′W
Hotan, China (hwō-tän)	226	37°07′N	79°55′E
Hotan, stm., China (hwō-tän)	226	40°30′N	80°56′E
Hot Springs, Ar., U.S. (hŏt sprĭngz)	120-21	34°30′N	93°04′W
Hot Springs, N.M., U.S. (hŏt sprĭngz) *see* Truth or Consequences	118-19	33°08′N	107°15′W
Hot Springs, S.D., U.S. (hŏt sprĭngz)	114-15	43°26′N	103°29′W
Hot Springs, Va., U.S. (hŏt sprĭngz)	116-17	37°60′N	79°49′W
Hot Springs National Park, n.p., Ar., U.S. (hŏt sprĭngz năsh′ŭn-ăl pärk)	120-21	34°31′N	93°02′W
Hottah Lake, lk., N.T., Can.	130-31	65°04′N	118°29′W
Houghton, Mi., U.S. (hō′tŭn)	114-15	47°06′N	88°36′W
Houghton Lake, lk., Mi., U.S. (hō′tŭn lāk)	116-17	44°20′N	84°45′W
Houlton, Me., U.S. (hōl′tŭn)	117a	46°08′N	67°50′W
Houma, China	240-41	35°37′N	111°21′E
Houma, La., U.S. (hōō′mȧ)	124-25	29°35′N	90°43′W

n-sing; ŋ-baŋk; ɴ-nasalized n; nŏd; cŏmmit; ōld; ōbey; ôrder; oi-boil; fōōd; ŏŏ-as oo in foot; ou-out; s-soft; sh-dish; th-thin; pūre; ûnite; ûrn; stŭd; circŭs; ü-as in French tu; ′-indeterminate vowel.

Feature (Pronunciation)	Page	Lat.	Long.
Houston, Ms., U.S. (hūs´tŭn)	124-25	33°54'N	88°60'W
Houston, Tx., U.S. (hūs´tŭn)	122-23	29°45'N	95°22'W
Hovd, Mong. *see* Dund-Us	240-41	47°60'N	91°38'E
Hovd, stm., Mong.	218-19	48°05'N	92°13'E
Hövsgöl nuur, lk., Mong.	240-41	51°0'N	100°30'E
Howard, S.D., U.S. (hou´ărd)	114-15	44°00'N	97°32'W
Howe, Cape, c., Austl. (kāp hou)	276	37°30'S	149°58'E
Howell, Mi., U.S. (hou´ĕl)	116-17	42°36'N	83°56'W
Howe Sound, strt., B.C., Can. (hou sound)	132-33	49°22'N	123°18'W
Howland Island, dep., Oc. (hou´lănd ī´lănd)	280-81	0°51'N	176°38'W
Howland Island, i., Oc. (hou´lănd ī´lănd)	280-81	0°48'N	176°38'W
Hoxie, Ar., U.S. (kŏh´sĭ)	124-25	36°03'N	90°59'W
Hradec Králové, Czech Rep.	194-95	50°12'N	15°50'E
Hranice, Czech Rep. (hrän´yĕ-tsĕ)	194-95	49°33'N	17°45'E
Hrodna, Bela.	194-95	53°41'N	23°50'E
Hrubieszów, Pol. (hrōō-byä´shōōf)	194-95	50°49'N	23°56'E
Hrvatska, nation, Eur. (hr-väts´kä) *see* Croatia	174-75	45°10'N	15°30'E
Hsinchu, Tai. (hsĭn´chōō´)	225a	24°48'N	120°58'E
Hsinhailien, China *see* Lianyungang	238-39	34°37'N	119°11'E
Hsipaw, Mya.	246-47	22°37'N	97°18'E
Huacho, Peru	170	11°08'S	77°37'W
Huadian, China (hwä-dĭĕn)	240-41	42°58'N	126°45'E
Hua Hin, Thai.	246-47	12°35'N	99°57'E
Huai'an, China (hwī-än)	238-39	33°31'N	119°08'E
Huai'an, China (hwī-än)	240-41	40°40'N	114°25'E
Huaicheng, China *see* Huai'an	238-39	33°31'N	119°08'E
Huaide, China *see* Gongzhuling	240-41	43°30'N	124°49'E
Huailai, China	240-41	40°23'N	115°34'E
Huainan, China	238-39	32°40'N	117°01'E
Huaiyang, China (hōōāī´yang)	238-39	33°44'N	114°53'E
Huajuapan de León, Mex. (wäj-wä´päm dā lā-ōn´)	146-47	17°49'N	97°45'W
Hualfín, Arg.	168-69	27°14'S	66°50'W
Hualien, Tai. (hwä´lyĕn´)	225a	23°58'N	121°35'E
Huallaga, stm., Peru (wäl-yä´gä)	170	5°06'S	75°36'W
Huallanca, Peru	170	8°49'S	77°52'W
Huambo, Ang.	264-65	12°46'S	15°44'E
Huancavelica, Peru (wän´kä-vā-lē´kä)	163a	12°47'S	75°01'W
Huancayo, Peru (wän-kä´yō)	163a	12°05'S	75°13'W
Huang, stm., China (hŭäŋ)	222-23	37°49'N	118°53'E
Huangchuan, China (hŭäŋ-chŭän)	238-39	32°08'N	115°03'E
Huang Hai, s., Asia *see* Yellow Sea	222-23	36°0'N	123°00'E
Huangho, stm., China *see* Huang	222-23	37°49'N	118°53'E
Huanghua, China (hŭäŋ-hwä)	240-41	38°22'N	117°21'E
Huangshan, China	238-39	29°45'N	118°18'E
Huangshi, China	238-39	30°13'N	115°05'E
Huangyuan, China (hŭäŋ-yŭän)	240-41	36°41'N	101°16'E
Huanren, China (hŭän-rŭn)	243	41°13'N	125°20'E
Huánuco, Peru (wä-nōō´kō)	170	9°56'S	76°15'W
Huanuni, Bol. (wä-nōō´nē)	168-69	18°17'S	66°50'W
Huaral, Peru (wä-rä'l)	163a	11°30'S	77°12'W
Huaraz, Peru	170	9°32'S	77°33'W
Huascarán, Nevado, mtn., Peru (nĕ-vä´dō wäs-kä-rän´)	170	9°07'S	77°37'W
Huasco, Chile (wäs´kō)	168-69	28°28'S	71°15'W
Huatabampo, Mex.	144-45	26°50'N	109°38'W
Huauchinango, Mex. (wä-ōō-chē-näŋ´gō)	146-47	20°11'N	98°03'W
Huautla, Mex. (wä-ōō´tlä)	146-47	18°08'N	96°50'W
Huaxian, China (hwä shyĕn)	238-39	23°23'N	113°12'E
Huaynamota, stm., Mex. (wäy-nä-mō´tä)	146-47	21°57'N	104°32'W
Hubbard, Tx., U.S. (hŭb´ērd)	122-23	31°50'N	96°48'W
Hubbard Creek Reservoir, lk., Tx., U.S. (hŭb´ērd krēk rĕ´sēr-vwär)	120-21	32°48'N	99°01'W
Hubei, state, China (hōō-bā)	238-39	31°0'N	112°00'E
Hubli-Dhārwār, India	236	15°21'N	75°09'E
Huddersfield, Eng., U.K. (hŭd´ērz-fēld)	190-91	53°39'N	1°47'W
Hudiksvall, Swe. (hōō´dĭks-väl)	192-93	61°44'N	17°07'E
Hudson, Mi., U.S. (hŭd´sŭn)	116-17	41°51'N	84°21'W
Hudson, Wi., U.S. (hŭd´sŭn)	114-15	44°59'N	92°45'W
Hudson, stm., U.S. (hŭd´sŭn)	110-11	40°41'N	74°02'W
Hudson, Détroit d', strt., Can. *see* Hudson Strait	130-31	62°30'N	71°60'W
Hudson Bay, Sk., Can. (hŭd´sŭn bā)	134-35	52°52'N	102°23'W
Hudson Bay, b., Can. (hŭd´sŭn bā)	130-31	60°0'N	86°00'W
Hudson Falls, N.Y., U.S. (hŭd´sŭn fôlz)	116-17	43°19'N	73°35'W
Hudson Strait, strt., Can. (hŭd´sŭn strāt)	130-31	62°30'N	71°60'W
Hue, Viet. (ü-ā´)	246-47	16°28'N	107°35'E
Huehuetenango, Guat. (wā-wå-tå-näŋ´gō)	148	15°21'N	91°27'W
Huejuquilla El Alto, Mex. (wā-hōō-kēl´yä ĕl äl´tō)	146-47	22°38'N	103°54'W
Huelva, Spain (wĕl´vä)	198-99	37°16'N	6°57'W
Huesca, Spain (wĕs-kä)	198-99	42°08'N	0°25'W
Huéscar, Spain (wās´kär)	198-99	37°48'N	2°33'W
Huetamo de Núñez, Mex.	146-47	18°35'N	100°53'W
Hughenden, Austl. (hū´ĕn-dĕn)	277	20°51'S	144°13'E
Hugli, stm., India (hōōg´lĭ)	234-35	21°36'N	87°60'E
Hugo, Ok., U.S. (hū´gō)	120-21	34°01'N	95°31'W
Hugoton, Ks., U.S. (hū´gō-tŭn)	120-21	37°11'N	101°21'W
Huhehot, China *see* Hohhot	240-41	40°49'N	111°39'E
Huichapan, Mex. (wē-chä-pän´)	146-47	20°22'N	99°40'W
Hŭich'ŏn, Kor., N.	243	40°10'N	126°17'E
Huila, Nevado del, vol., Col. (nĕ-vä-dō-del-wē´lä)	163c	2°59'N	75°58'W
Huili, China	238-39	26°40'N	102°14'E
Huimin, China (hōōĭ mĭn)	240-41	37°29'N	117°32'E
Huinan, China	243	42°41'N	126°02'E
Huixtla, Mex.	148	15°08'N	92°27'W
Huize, China	238-39	26°25'N	103°18'E
Huizhou, China	238-39	23°05'N	114°24'E
Hujirt, Mong.	240-41	48°53'N	101°14'E
Hukuoka, Japan *see* Fukuoka	245	33°35'N	130°25'E
Hulan, China (hōō´län´)	240-41	45°59'N	126°36'E
Hulan Ergi, China	240-41	47°12'N	123°38'E
Hulin, China (hōō´lĭn´)	244	45°46'N	132°59'E
Hulun, China *see* Hailar	240-41	49°11'N	119°44'E
Hulun Nur, lk., China (hōō-lòn nòr)	240-41	49°01'N	117°32'E
Humacao, P.R. (ōō-mä-kä´ō)	142a	18°09'N	65°49'W
Humahuaca, Arg.	168-69	23°12'S	65°21'W
Humaitá, Braz.	166-67	7°30'S	63°02'W
Humaitá, Para.	173	27°05'S	58°32'W
Humble, Tx., U.S. (hŭm´b'l)	122-23	29°59'N	95°16'W
Humboldt, Sk., Can. (hŭm´bōlt)	134-35	52°11'N	105°07'W
Humboldt, Ia., U.S. (hŭm´bōlt)	114-15	42°43'N	94°13'W
Humboldt, Tn., U.S. (hŭm´bōlt)	124-25	35°50'N	88°55'W
Humboldt, stm., Nv., U.S. (hŭm´bōlt)	110-11	40°01'N	118°33'W
Hume, Lake, res., Austl.	276	36°08'S	147°02'E
Humphreys Peak, mtn., Az., U.S. (hŭm´frĭs pēk)	118-19	35°20'N	111°40'W
Húnaflói, b., Ice. (hōō´nä-flō´ĭ)	190a	65°50'N	20°50'W
Hunan, state, China (hōō´nän´)	238-39	28°0'N	111°00'E
Hunchun, China (hòn-chŭn)	243	42°52'N	130°22'E
Hunedoara, Rom. (kōō´nĕd-wä´rȧ)	200-01	45°46'N	22°55'E
Hungary, nation, Eur. (hŭŋ´gȧ-rĭ)	174-75	47°0'N	20°00'E
Hŭngdŏki-dong, Kor., N.	243	39°50'N	127°38'E
Hungerford, Austl. (hŭn´gēr-fērd)	276	28°59'S	144°24'E
Hŭngnam, Kor., N. *see* Hŭngdŏki-dong	243	39°50'N	127°38'E
Hunjiang, China	243	41°57'N	126°28'E
Hunsrück, mts., Ger. (hōōns´rûk)	194-95	49°46'N	7°08'E
Hunter, Île, i., N. Cal.	280-81	22°24'S	172°06'E
Hunter Island, i., Austl.	276	40°32'S	144°45'E
Hunter Island, i., B.C., Can.	132-33	51°54'N	128°03'W
Huntingburg, In., U.S. (hŭnt´ĭng-bûrg)	116-17	38°18'N	86°57'W
Huntingdon, Qc., Can. (hŭnt´ĭng-dŭn)	136-37	45°06'N	74°10'W
Huntingdon, Tn., U.S. (hŭnt´ĭng-dŭn)	124-25	36°00'N	88°26'W
Huntington, In., U.S. (hŭnt´ĭng-tŭn)	116-17	40°52'N	85°28'W
Huntington, Ut., U.S. (hŭnt´ĭng-tŭn)	118-19	39°20'N	110°58'W
Huntington, W.V., U.S. (hŭnt´ĭng-tŭn)	116-17	38°25'N	82°26'W
Huntington Beach, Ca., U.S. (hŭnt´ĭng-tŭn bēch)	118-19	33°39'N	117°59'W
Huntsville, On., Can. (hŭnts´vĭl)	136-37	45°19'N	79°12'W
Huntsville, Al., U.S. (hŭnts´vĭl)	124-25	34°43'N	86°36'W
Huntsville, Mo., U.S. (hŭnts´vĭl)	120-21	39°26'N	92°33'W
Huntsville, Tx., U.S. (hŭnts´vĭl)	122-23	30°43'N	95°33'W
Hunucmá, Mex.	148	21°01'N	89°52'W
Hunyuan, China	240-41	39°42'N	113°41'E
Huong Thuy, Viet.	246-47	16°25'N	107°40'E
Huon Gulf, b., Pap. N. Gui.	277	7°10'S	147°25'E
Huonville, Austl.	276	43°01'S	147°02'E
Huoqiu, China (hwō-chyō)	238-39	32°20'N	116°16'E
Huoshan, China (hwō-shän)	238-39	31°24'N	116°20'E
Hurd, Cape, c., On., Can. (kāp hûrd)	136-37	45°14'N	81°42'W
Hurghada, Egypt	268b	27°14'N	33°50'E
Hurley, Wi., U.S. (hûr´lĭ)	114-15	46°27'N	90°11'W
Huron, S.D., U.S. (hū´rŏn)	114-15	44°22'N	98°13'W
Huron, Lake, lk., N.A. (lāk hū´rŏn)	116-17	44°30'N	82°15'W
Hurricane, Ut., U.S. (hŭr´ĭ-kān)	118-19	37°11'N	113°17'W
Húsavík, Ice.	190a	66°03'N	17°19'W
Huși, Rom. (kòsh')	202-03	46°41'N	28°04'E
Husum, Ger. (hōō´zòm)	194-95	54°28'N	9°04'E
Hutchinson, Ks., U.S. (hŭch´ĭn-sŭn)	120-21	38°03'N	97°55'W
Hutchinson, Mn., U.S. (hŭch´ĭn-sŭn)	114-15	44°53'N	94°23'W
Huy, Bel. (ü-ē´) (hū´ē)	190-91	50°31'N	5°14'E
Huzhou, China	238-39	30°52'N	120°06'E
Hvannadalshnúkur, mtn., Ice.	190a	64°01'N	16°41'W
Hvar, Otok, i., Cro. (ō´tŏk кhvär)	200-01	43°09'N	16°45'E
Hwaining, China *see* Anqing	238-39	30°30'N	117°02'E
Hwange, Zimb.	264-65	18°22'S	26°30'E
Hwange National Park, n.p., Zimb.	264-65	19°0'S	26°35'E
Hwang-hae, s., Asia *see* Yellow Sea	222-23	36°0'N	123°00'E
Hyargas nuur, lk., Mong.	240-41	49°12'N	93°24'E
Hyde Park, Guy.	164-65	6°30'N	58°16'W
Hyde Park, N.Y., U.S. (hīd pärk)	116-17	41°47'N	73°56'W
Hyderābād, India (hī-dēr-ȧ-băd´)	236	17°23'N	78°29'E
Hyderābād, Pak. (hī-dēr-ȧ-băd´)	232-33	25°23'N	68°21'E
Hyères, Fr. (ē-âr´)	196-97	43°08'N	6°08'E
Hyesan, Kor., N.	243	41°24'N	128°10'E
Hyndman Peak, mtn., Id., U.S. (hīnd´măn pēk)	112-13	43°45'N	114°08'W
Hyōgo, state, Japan (hĭyō´gō)	245	35°0'N	135°00'E
I			
Iaco, stm., S.A.	170	9°02'S	68°35'W
Iași, Rom. (yä´shē)	202-03	47°10'N	27°36'E
Iba, Phil. (ē´bä)	250	15°20'N	119°58'E
Ibadan, Nig. (ē-bä´dän)	260a	7°23'N	3°54'E
Ibagué, Col.	163c	4°27'N	75°15'W
Iban, Pegunungan, mts., Asia *see* Iran Mountains	248-49	2°05'N	114°55'E
Ibarra, Ec. (ē-bär´rä)	170	0°22'N	78°08'W
Ibb, Yemen	266	13°58'N	44°11'E
Iberian Peninsula, pen., Eur. (ī-bē´rĭ-ăn pĕ-nĭn´sū-lȧ)	176-77	40°0'N	5°00'W
Ibérica, Península, pen., Eur. *see* Iberian Peninsula	176-77	40°0'N	5°00'W
Iberville, Qc., Can. (ē-bår-vēl´) (ī´bēr-vĭl)	136-37	45°19'N	73°14'W
Ibiá, Braz.	172	19°29'S	46°32'W
Ibicaraí, Braz.	166-67	14°51'S	39°37'W
Ibicuí, stm., Braz.	173	29°25'S	56°47'W
Ibiza, Spain *see* Eivissa	198-99	38°55'N	1°25'E
Ibiza, i., Spain (ē-bē´thä) *see* Eivissa	198-99	39°0'N	1°25'E
Ica, Peru (ē´kȧ)	170	14°04'S	75°45'W
Içá, stm., S.A.	170	3°07'S	67°56'W
Içana, Braz. (ē-sä´nä)	166-67	0°21'N	67°19'W
İçel, Tur.	228-29	36°49'N	34°38'E
Iceland, nation, Eur. (īs´lănd)	174-75	65°0'N	18°00'W
Ichalkaranji, India	236	16°41'N	74°28'E
Ichilo, stm., Bol.	168-69	15°50'S	64°47'W
Icó, Braz.	166-67	6°24'S	38°51'W
Idabel, Ok., U.S. (ī´dȧ-bĕl)	120-21	33°53'N	94°49'W
Ida Grove, Ia., U.S. (ī´dȧ-grōv)	114-15	42°21'N	95°28'W
Idah, Nig. (ē´dä)	260a	7°07'N	6°45'E
Idaho, state, U.S. (ī´dȧ-hō)	108-09	45°0'N	115°00'W
Idaho Falls, Id., U.S. (ī´dȧ-hō fôlz)	112-13	43°30'N	112°03'W
Idaho Springs, Co., U.S. (ī´dȧ-hō sprĭngz)	118-19	39°44'N	105°31'W
Ider, stm., Mong.	240-41	49°16'N	100°41'E
Idi, Indon. (ē´dē)	246-47	4°57'N	97°46'E
Idi Amin Dada, Lac, lk., Afr. *see* Edward, Lake	267	0°23'S	29°36'E
Idiofa, D.R.C.	262-63	5°01'S	19°35'E
Ídi Óros, mtn., Grc.	200a	35°18'N	24°43'E
Idlib, Syria	228-29	35°56'N	36°39'E
Idoûkâl-en-Taghès, mtn., Niger	258-59	17°43'N	8°45'E
Iesi, Italy (yā´sē) *see* Jesi	200-01	43°31'N	13°14'E
Ife, Nig.	260a	7°28'N	4°33'E
Ifôghas, Adrar des, mts., Afr.	258-59	20°0'N	2°00'E
Igarka, Russia (ē-gär´kȧ)	218-19	67°28'N	86°38'E
Iglesias, Italy (ē-lā´syōs)	200-01	39°19'N	8°32'E
Igloolik, Nu., Can.	128-29	69°23'N	81°48'W
Igluligaarjuk, Nu., Can. *see* Chesterfield Inlet	128-29	63°21'N	90°43'W
Iglulik, Nu., Can. *see* Igloolik	128-29	69°23'N	81°48'W
Igombe, stm., Tan.	267	4°43'S	31°23'E
Iguaçu, stm., S.A. (ē-gwä-sōō´)	168-69	25°36'S	54°36'W
Iguaçu, Cataratas do, wtfl., S.A. *see* Iguassu Falls	168-69	25°42'S	54°27'W
Iguaçu, Saltos do, wtfl., S.A. *see* Iguassu Falls	168-69	25°42'S	54°27'W
Iguala, Mex. (ē-gwä´lä)	146-47	18°21'N	99°32'W
Igualada, Spain (ē-gwä-lä´dä)	198-99	41°35'N	1°39'E
Iguape, Braz.	172	24°43'S	47°34'W
Iguassu Falls, wtfl., S.A. (ē-gwä-sōō´ fôlz)	168-69	25°42'S	54°27'W

ăt; finăl; rāte; senåte; ärm; åsk; sofȧ; fâre; ch-choose; dh-as th in other; bē; ēvent; bĕt; recĕnt; cratēr; g-gō; gh-guttural g; bĭt; ĭ-short neutral; rīde; к-guttural k as ch in German ich;

Feature (Pronunciation)	Page	Lat.	Long.
Iguatu, Braz. (ē-gwä-tōō′)	166-67	6°22′S	39°18′W
Iguazú, stm., S.A. see Iguaçu	168-69	25°36′S	54°36′W
Iguazú, Cataratas del, wtfl., S.A. see Iguassu Falls	168-69	25°42′S	54°27′W
Ihosy, Madag.	264-65	22°24′S	46°07′E
Iida, Japan (ē′ē-dȧ)	245	35°31′N	137°50′E
Iisalmi, Fin.	184-85	63°32′N	27°17′E
Iizuka, Japan (ē′ē-zō-kȧ)	245	33°38′N	130°41′E
Ijâfene, des., Maur.	258-59	22°04′N	7°42′W
Ijebu-Ode, Nig. (ē-jĕ′bōō ōdȧ)	260a	6°49′N	3°56′E
IJsselmeer, lk., Neth. (ī′sĕl-mār)	190-91	52°45′N	5°25′E
Ijuí, Braz.	173	28°23′S	53°55′W
Ikaalinen, Fin. (ē′kä-lĭ-nĕn)	192-93	61°45′N	23°04′E
Ikaluktutiak, Nu., Can. see Cambridge Bay	128-29	69°07′N	105°04′W
Ikaría, i., Grc. (ē-kä′ryȧ)	200-01	37°36′N	26°09′E
Ikela, D.R.C.	262-63	1°11′S	23°17′E
Ikhtiman, Blg. (ēk′tē-män)	200-01	42°26′N	23°50′E
Iki, i., Japan (ē′kē)	245	33°47′N	129°43′E
Ikom, Nig.	260a	5°58′N	8°42′E
Ikoma, Tan. (ē-kō′mä)	267	2°05′S	34°38′E
Ikopa, stm., Madag.	264-65	17°00′S	46°45′E
Iksan, Kor., S.	243	35°56′N	126°57′E
Ilagan, Phil.	250	17°08′N	121°53′E
Ilam, nation, Asia see Sri Lanka	206-07	7°0′N	81°00′E
Ilan, Tai. (ē′län′)	225a	24°46′N	121°45′E
Ile, stm., Asia	226	45°20′N	74°05′E
Île-à-la-Crosse, Sk., Can.	134-35	55°26′N	107°55′W
Île-à-la-Crosse, Lac, lk., Sk., Can.	134-35	55°42′N	107°41′W
Ilebo, D.R.C.	262-63	4°20′S	20°36′E
Ilek, stm., Asia see Elek	186-87	51°30′N	53°20′E
Ilesha, Nig.	260a	7°38′N	4°45′E
Ilfracombe, Austl.	277	23°29′S	144°30′E
Ilfracombe, Eng., U.K. (ĭl-frȧ-kōōm′)	190-91	51°12′N	4°08′W
Ilha de Moçambique, Moz.	264-65	15°02′S	40°41′E
Ilha Grande, Baía da, b., Braz. (bäē′ä dĕ ēl′yȧ grän′dĕ)	172	23°09′S	44°30′W
Ílhavo, Port. (ēl′yȧ-vō)	198-99	40°36′N	8°40′W
Ilhéos, Braz. see Ilhéus	166-67	14°47′S	39°03′W
Ilhéus, Braz. (ē-lĕ′ōōs)	166-67	14°47′S	39°03′W
Ili, stm., Asia see Ile	226	45°20′N	74°05′E
Iliamna Lake, lk., Ak., U.S. (ē-lē-ăm′nȧ lăk)	126	59°37′N	154°49′W
Iligan, Phil.	250	8°15′N	124°16′E
Ilion, N.Y., U.S. (ĭl′ĭ-ŭn)	116-17	43°01′N	75°03′W
Ilizi, Alg.	258-59	26°29′N	8°29′E
Illampu, Nevado, mtn., Bol. (nĕ-vä′dō-ēl-yäm-pōō′)	168-69	15°50′S	68°34′W
Illapel, Chile (ē-zhä-pĕ′l)	168-69	31°37′S	71°09′W
Illimani, Nevado de, mtn., Bol. (nĕ-vä′dō-dĕ-ēl-yē-mä′nē)	168-69	16°50′S	67°54′W
Illinois, state, U.S. (ĭl-ĭ-noi′) (ĭl-ĭ-noiz′)	108-09	40°0′N	89°00′W
Illinois, stm., Il., U.S. (ĭl-ĭ-noi′) (ĭl-ĭ-noiz′)	110-11	38°58′N	90°25′W
Il'men', Ozero, lk., Russia (ô′zĕ-rô el′men′′) (ĭl′mĕn)	192-93	58°17′N	31°20′E
Ilo, Peru	170	17°38′S	71°20′W
Iloilo, Phil. (ē-lō-ē′lō)	250	10°42′N	122°34′E
Ilorin, Nig. (ē-lō-rēn′)	260a	8°30′N	4°33′E
Ilwaki, Indon.	248-49	7°55′S	126°25′E
Imabari, Japan (ē′mä-bä′rē)	245	34°04′N	133°00′E
Imandra, Ozero, lk., Russia (ô′zĕ-rô ē-män′drȧ)	186-87	67°33′N	33°00′E
Imatra, Fin.	192-93	61°10′N	28°46′E
Imbituba, Braz.	172	28°14′S	48°41′W
Imeni Ismail Samani, Pik, mtn., Taj.	226	38°57′N	72°01′E
Imlay City, Mi., U.S. (ĭm′lā sĭ′tē)	116-17	43°01′N	83°05′W
Imola, Italy (ē′mō-lä)	200-01	44°21′N	11°43′E
Imotski, Cro. (ē-mōts′kē)	200-01	43°27′N	17°13′E
Imperatriz, Braz.	166-67	5°31′S	47°28′W
Imperia, Italy (ēm-pā′rē-ä)	200-01	43°54′N	8°03′E
Imperial, Ne., U.S. (ĭm-pē′rĭ-ăl)	120-21	40°31′N	101°39′W
Impfondo, Congo (ĭmp-fōn′dō)	262-63	1°37′N	18°04′E
Imphāl, India (ĭmp′hŭl)	234-35	24°47′N	93°57′E
Inari, Fin.	184-85	68°54′N	26°60′E
Inari, lk., Fin. see Inarijärvi	186-87	69°0′N	28°00′E
Inarijärvi, lk., Fin.	186-87	69°0′N	28°00′E
Inca, Spain (ēŋ′kä)	198-99	39°43′N	2°55′E
Inca de Oro, Chile	168-69	26°45′S	69°54′W
İnce Burun, c., Tur. (ĭn′jȧ)	186-87	42°05′N	34°58′E
Inch'ŏn, Kor., S. (ĭn′chŭn)	243	37°28′N	126°38′E
Indefatigable, i., Ec. see Santa Cruz, Isla	170a	0°38′S	90°23′W
Independence, Ia., U.S. (ĭn-dē-pĕn′dĕns)	114-15	42°29′N	91°54′W
Independence, Ks., U.S. (ĭn-dē-pĕn′dĕns)	120-21	37°13′N	95°42′W
Independence, Ky., U.S. (ĭn-dē-pĕn′dĕns)	116-17	38°56′N	84°32′W
Independence, Mo., U.S. (ĭn-dē-pĕn′dĕns)	120-21	39°05′N	94°25′W
Independence Mountains, mts., Nv., U.S. (ĭn-dē-pĕn′dĕns moun′tĭnz)	112-13	41°18′N	116°00′W
Inderbor, Kaz.	186-87	48°32′N	51°42′E
India, nation, Asia (ĭn′dĭ-ȧ)	206-07	20°0′N	77°00′E
Indiana, Pa., U.S. (ĭn-dĭ-ăn′ȧ)	116-17	40°35′N	79°09′W
Indiana, state, U.S. (ĭn-dĭ-ăn′ȧ)	108-09	40°0′N	86°15′W
Indianapolis, In., U.S. (ĭn-dĭ-ăn-ăp′ō-lĭs)	116-17	39°46′N	86°08′W
Indian Head, Sk., Can. (ĭn′dĭ-ăn hĕd)	134-35	50°32′N	103°40′W
Indian Ocean, oc., (ĭn′dĭ-ăn ōshŭn)	20-21	10°0′S	70°00′E
Indianola, Ia., U.S. (ĭn-dĭ-ăn-ō′lȧ)	114-15	41°21′N	93°33′W
Indianola, Ms., U.S. (ĭn-dĭ-ăn-ō′lȧ)	124-25	33°27′N	90°39′W
Indian Springs, Nv., U.S. (ĭn′dĭ-ăn sprĭngz)	118-19	36°34′N	115°41′W
Indigirka, stm., Russia (ēn-dē-gēr′kȧ)	218-19	70°49′N	148°54′E
Indochina, reg., Asia (ĭn-dō-chī′nȧ)	246-47	16°0′N	107°00′E
Indonesia, nation, Asia (ĭn′dō-nē-zhȧ)	206-07	5°0′S	120°00′E
Indore, India (ĭn-dōr′)	234-35	22°43′N	75°52′E
Indragiri, stm., Indon. (ĭn-drȧ-jē′rē)	246-47	0°22′S	103°26′E
Indrāvati, stm., India (ĭn-drŭ-vä′tē)	236	18°44′N	80°17′E
Indus, stm., Asia (ĭn′dŭs)	208-09	24°60′N	68°16′E
Inferior, Laguna, b., Mex. (lä-gō′nä-ēn-fĕr-rôr)	146-47	16°17′N	94°40′W
Infiernillo, Presa del, res., Mex.	146-47	18°37′N	101°46′W
Ingende, D.R.C.	262-63	0°13′S	18°58′E
Ingersoll, On., Can. (ĭn′gēr-sŏl)	136-37	43°02′N	80°53′W
Ingham, Austl. (ĭng′ăm)	277	18°39′S	146°09′E
Ingoda, stm., Russia (ēn-gō′dȧ)	222-23	51°43′N	115°48′E
Ingolstadt, Ger. (ĭŋ′gôl-shtät)	194-95	48°46′N	11°26′E
Ingrāj Bāzār, India	234-35	24°60′N	88°09′E
I-n-Guezzâm, Alg.	258-59	19°27′N	5°48′E
Ingushetia, state, Russia	227	43°15′N	45°00′E
Ingushetiya, state, Russia see Ingushetia	227	43°15′N	45°00′E
Inhaca, Ilha da, i., Moz.	264-65	26°01′S	32°57′E
Inhambupe, Braz. (ēn-yäm-bōō′pä)	166-67	11°49′S	38°20′W
Inírida, stm., Col. (ē-nē-rē′dä)	164-65	3°55′N	67°51′W
Injune, Austl. (ĭn′jōn)	276	25°51′S	148°34′E
Inland Sea, s., Japan (ĭn′lănd sē) see Seto-naikai	245	34°22′N	133°37′E
Inn, stm., Eur. (ĭn)	194-95	48°34′N	13°28′E
Innamincka, Austl. (ĭnn-ȧ′mĭn-kȧ)	276	27°45′S	140°44′E
Inner Mongolia, state, China see Nei Mongol	240-41	43°0′N	115°00′E
Innisfail, Austl.	277	17°33′S	146°02′E
Innisfail, Ab., Can.	132-33	52°02′N	113°58′W
Innoko, stm., Ak., U.S.	126	62°11′N	159°44′W
Innsbruck, Aus. (ĭns′brŏŏk)	194-95	47°16′N	11°24′E
Inongo, D.R.C. (ē-nôŋ′gō)	262-63	1°55′S	18°18′E
Inowrocław, Pol. (ē-nô-vrôts′läf)	194-95	52°48′N	18°15′E
I-n-Salah, Alg.	258-59	27°11′N	2°29′E
Inta, Russia	186-87	66°02′N	60°09′E
International Falls, Mn., U.S. (ĭn′tĕr-năsh′ŭn-ăl fôlz)	114-15	48°36′N	93°25′W
Inthanon, Doi, mtn., Thai.	246-47	18°35′N	98°29′E
Intiyaco, Arg.	173	28°40′S	60°04′W
Inukjuak, Qc., Can.	128-29	58°28′N	78°06′W
Inuvik, N.T., Can.	128-29	68°20′N	133°39′W
Invercargill, N.Z.	278	46°25′S	168°22′E
Inverell, Austl.	276	29°47′S	151°07′E
Inverness, Scot., U.K. (ĭn-vĕr-nĕs′)	190-91	57°28′N	4°15′W
Inverness, Fl., U.S. (ĭn-vĕr-nĕs′)	124-25	28°50′N	82°20′W
Investigator Strait, strt., Austl. (ĭn-vĕst′ĭ′gā-tôr strāt)	276	35°25′S	137°10′E
Inyangani, mtn., Zimb. (ēn-yän-gä′nē)	264-65	18°17′S	32°50′E
Inza, Russia	186-87	53°51′N	46°22′E
Ioánnina, Grc. (yô-ä′nē-nȧ)	200-01	39°39′N	20°51′E
Iō-jima, i., Japan see Iwo Jima	280-81	24°47′N	141°20′E
Ionia, Mi., U.S. (ī-ō′nĭ-ȧ)	116-17	42°59′N	85°04′W
Ionian Islands, is., Grc. (ī-ō′nĭ-ăn ī′lăndz)	200-01	38°30′N	20°30′E
Ionian Sea, s., Eur. (ī-ō′nĭ-ăn sē)	200-01	39°0′N	19°00′E
Ionio, Mar, s., Eur. see Ionian Sea	200-01	39°0′N	19°00′E
Iónioi Nísoi, is., Grc. see Ionian Islands	200-01	38°30′N	20°30′E
Iónion Pélagos, s., Eur. see Ionian Sea	200-01	39°0′N	19°00′E
Íos, i., Grc. (ī′ŏs)	200-01	36°43′N	25°20′E
Iō-tō, i., Japan see Iwo Jima	280-81	24°47′N	141°20′E
Iowa, state, U.S. (ī′ō-wȧ)	108-09	42°15′N	93°15′W
Iowa, stm., Ia., U.S. (ī′ō-wȧ)	114-15	41°10′N	91°01′W
Iowa City, Ia., U.S. (ī′ō-wȧ sĭ′tē)	114-15	41°40′N	91°32′W
Iowa Falls, Ia., U.S. (ī′ō-wȧ fôlz)	114-15	42°32′N	93°16′W
Iowa Park, Tx., U.S. (ī′ō-wȧ pärk)	120-21	33°58′N	98°40′W
Ipameri, Braz.	172	17°43′S	48°09′W
Ipiales, Col. (ē-pē-ä′lås)	164-65	0°50′N	77°38′W
Ipiaú, Braz.	166-67	14°08′S	39°44′W
Ipoh, Malay.	246-47	4°36′N	101°04′E
Iporã, Braz.	168-69	16°27′S	51°07′W
Ippy, C.A.R.	262-63	6°16′N	21°12′E
Ipswich, Austl. (ĭps′wĭch)	276	27°37′S	152°47′E
Ipswich, Eng., U.K. (ĭps′wĭch)	190-91	52°04′N	1°09′E
Ipswich, S.D., U.S. (ĭps′wĭch)	114-15	45°27′N	99°02′W
Ipu, Braz. (ē-pōō)	166-67	4°20′S	40°42′W
Iqaluit, Nu., Can.	128-29	63°44′N	68°28′W
Iquique, Chile (ē-kē′kĕ)	168-69	20°13′S	70°09′W
Iquitos, Peru (ē-kē′tōs)	170	3°47′S	73°15′W
Irákleio, Grc.	200a	35°20′N	25°08′E
Iran, nation, Asia (ē-rän′)	206-07	32°0′N	53°00′E
Īrān, nation, Asia see Iran	206-07	32°0′N	53°00′E
Iran, Pegunungan, mts., Asia see Iran Mountains	248-49	2°05′N	114°55′E
Iran Mountains, mts., Asia (ē-rän′ moun′tĭnz)	248-49	2°05′N	114°55′E
Īrānshahr, Iran	230-31	27°13′N	60°42′E
Irapuato, Mex. (ē-rä-pwä′tō)	146-47	20°41′N	101°21′W
Iraq, nation, Asia (ē-räk′)	206-07	33°0′N	44°00′E
Irazú, Volcán, vol., C.R. (vôl-kȧ′n ē-rä-zōō′)	149	9°58′N	83°53′W
Irbid, Jord. (ēr-bēd′)	228-29	32°34′N	35°51′E
Irbīl, Iraq see Arbīl	228-29	36°11′N	44°01′E
Ireland, nation, Eur. (īr-lănd)	174-75	53°0′N	8°00′W
Irian, i., see New Guinea	277	5°0′S	140°00′E
Iringa, Tan. (ē-rĭŋ′gä)	267	7°47′S	35°42′E
Iriomote-jima, i., Japan (ērē′-ō-mō-tā jē′mȧ)	279a	24°20′N	123°50′E
Iriri, stm., Braz.	166-67	3°48′S	52°36′W
Irish Sea, s., Eur. (ī′rĭsh sē)	190-91	53°30′N	5°20′W
Irkutsk, Russia (ĭr-kōōtsk′)	222-23	52°18′N	104°17′E
Iron Knob, Austl. (ī-ăn nŏb)	276	32°44′S	137°08′E
Iron Mountain, Mi., U.S. (ī′ērn moun′tĭn)	116-17	45°49′N	88°03′W
Iron River, Mi., U.S. (ī′ērn rĭv′ēr)	114-15	46°06′N	88°39′W
Ironton, Oh., U.S. (ī′ērn-tŭn)	116-17	38°32′N	82°41′W
Ironwood, Mi., U.S. (ī′ērn-wŏd)	114-15	46°27′N	90°10′W
Ironwood Forest National Monument, n.p., Az., U.S.	118-19	32°27′N	111°30′W
Iroquois Falls, On., Can. (ĭr′ō-kwoi fôlz)	136-37	48°46′N	80°40′W
Irrawaddy, stm., Mya. (ĭr-ȧ-wäd′ē) see Ayeyarwady	220-21	15°51′N	95°05′E
Irtysh, stm., Asia (ĭr-tĭsh′)	218-19	61°05′N	68°47′E
Irumu, D.R.C. (ē-rō′mōō)	267	1°27′N	29°52′E
Irún, Spain (ē-rōōn′)	198-99	43°21′N	1°48′W
Iruña, Spain see Pamplona	198-99	42°49′N	1°39′W
Irvine, Ky., U.S. (ûr′vĭn)	116-17	37°42′N	83°58′W
Irving, Tx., U.S. (ûr′vēng)	120-21	32°49′N	96°57′W
Isabela, Phil.	250	6°41′N	121°58′E
Isabela, Cabo, c., Dom. Rep. (kȧ′bō-ē-sä-bĕ′lä)	142-43	19°55′N	71°01′W
Isabela, Isla, i., Ec. (ē′s-lä-ē-sä-bā′lä)	170a	0°30′S	91°06′W
Isabelia, Cordillera, mts., Nic. (kôr-dēl-yĕ′rä-ē-sä-bĕlyä)	149	13°30′N	85°32′W
Isabella Indian Reservation, ind. res., Mi., U.S. (ĭs-ȧ-bĕl′-lȧ ĭn′dĭ-ăn rē-sĕr-vā′shĕn)	116-17	43°41′N	84°48′W
Ísafjörður, Ice. (ēs′ȧ-fỹr-dōr)	190a	66°03′N	23°07′W
Ischia, Isola d', i., Italy (ē′-sō-lä-dĕ′sh-kyä)	200-01	40°43′N	13°54′E
Ise, Japan (ĭs′hĕ) (ū′gē-yä′mä′dȧ)	245	34°30′N	136°42′E
Isernia, Italy (ē-zĕr′nyä)	200-01	41°36′N	14°14′E
Iset', stm., Russia	218-19	56°36′N	66°17′E
Ise-wan, b., Japan (ē′sĕ wän)	245	34°43′N	136°43′E
Iseyin, Nig.	260a	7°58′N	3°36′E
Isfahan, Iran see Eşfahān	232-33	32°39′N	51°40′E
Ishigaki-shima, i., Japan	279a	24°24′N	124°12′E
Ishikari, stm., Japan	244	43°16′N	141°23′E
Ishikari-wan, b., Japan (ē′shē-kä-rē wän)	244	43°25′N	141°01′E
Ishim, Russia (ĭsh-ĕm′)	218-19	56°07′N	69°30′E
Ishim, stm., Asia (ĭsh-ĕm′)	218-19	57°43′N	71°12′E
Ishimskaya Ravnina, pl., Asia	226	55°0′N	70°00′E
Ishinomaki, Japan (ĭsh-nō-mä′kē)	244	38°25′N	141°18′E
Ishpeming, Mi., U.S. (ĭsh′pē-mĭng)	114-15	46°29′N	87°39′W
Isil'kul', Russia	226	54°54′N	71°16′E
Isiolo, Kenya	267	0°21′N	37°35′E
Isiro, D.R.C.	262-63	2°46′N	27°37′E
İskenderun, Tur. (ĭs-kĕn′dĕr-ōōn)	228-29	36°35′N	36°11′E

n-sing; ŋ-baŋk; ɴ-nasalized n; nŏd; cŏmmit; ōld; ōbey; ôrder; oi-boil; fōōd; ŏ-as oo in foot; ou-out; s-soft; sh-dish; th-thin; pūre; ůnite; ûrn; stŭd; circŭs; ü-as in French tu; ′-indeterminate vowel.

Feature (Pronunciation)	Page	Lat.	Long.
İskenderun Körfezi, b., Tur.	228-29	36°30'N	35°40'E
Iskitim, Russia	226	54°39'N	83°18'E
Iskŭr, stm., Blg. (ĭs'k'r)	200-01	43°45'N	24°26'E
Isla Cristina, Spain (ī'lä-krē-stē'nä)	198-99	37°12'N	7°19'W
Islāmābād, nat. cap., Pak. (ĭs'lä-mä-bäd') (ĭs-lä'-mä-bäd')	232-33	33°39'N	73°05'E
Isla Mujeres, Mex. (ē's-lä-mōō-kĕ'rĕs)	148	21°12'N	86°43'W
Ísland, nation, Eur. *see* Iceland	174-75	65°0'N	18°00'W
Island Lake, lk., Mb., Can. (ī'lǎnd lāk ī'lǎnd)	134-35	53°47'N	94°25'W
Islands, Bay of, b., Nf., Can. (bā ŭv ī'lǎndz)	138-39	49°10'N	58°15'W
Íslandshaf, s., Eur. *see* Norwegian Sea	184-85	70°0'N	2°00'E
Islay, i., Scot., U.K. (ī'lā)	190-91	55°49'N	6°17'W
Isle of Man, dep., Eur. (īl ŭv măn)	190-91	54°15'N	4°30'W
Isle Royale National Park, n.p., Mi., U.S. (īl'roi-ǎl' năsh'ŭn-ǎl pärk)	114-15	47°58'N	88°55'W
Ismailia, Egypt (ēs-mä-ēl'ēä)	268b	30°36'N	32°16'E
Isparta, Tur. (ē-spär'tá)	186-87	37°46'N	30°33'E
Israel, nation, Asia (ĭz'rē-ĕl)	206-07	31°30'N	34°45'E
Isrā'īl, nation, Asia *see* Israel	206-07	31°30'N	34°45'E
Issoire, Fr. (ē-swár')	196-97	45°33'N	3°15'E
Issoudun, Fr. (ē-sōō-dăn')	196-97	46°57'N	2°00'E
Issyk-Kul, Lake, lk., Kyrg. (lāk ē'-sĭk-kōōl')	226	42°25'N	77°15'E
İstanbul, Tur. (ē-stän-bōōl')	200-01	41°02'N	28°59'E
İstanbul Boğazı, strt., Tur. *see* Bosporus	200-01	41°06'N	29°04'E
Istaravshan, Taj.	232-33	39°54'N	69°00'E
Istiaía, Grc. (ĭs-tyī'yä)	200-01	38°57'N	23°09'E
Istmina, Col. (ēst-mē'nä)	163c	5°09'N	76°41'W
Istra, pen., Eur. (ē-strä)	200-01	45°17'N	13°57'E
Istria, pen., Eur. *see* Istra	200-01	45°17'N	13°57'E
Itabaiana, Braz. (ē-tä-bä-yá-nä)	163d	7°20'S	35°20'W
Itabaiana, Braz. (ē-tä-bä-yá-nä)	166-67	10°41'S	37°26'W
Itabapoana, Braz. (ē-tä'-bä-pôä'nä)	172	21°18'S	40°59'W
Itaberaí, Braz.	168-69	16°01'S	49°48'W
Itabira, Braz.	172	19°38'S	43°14'W
Itabuna, Braz. (ē-tä-bōō'ná)	166-67	14°47'S	39°17'W
Itacoatiara, Braz. (ē-tá-kwá-tyä'rá)	166-67	3°08'S	58°26'W
Itagüí, Col. (ē-tä'gwē)	163c	6°10'N	75°38'W
Itaipu, Represa de, res., S.A.	168-69	24°56'S	54°26'W
Itaipu Reservoir, res., S.A. (ē-tī'pōō rĕ'sĕr-vwär) *see* Itaipu, Represa de	168-69	24°56'S	54°26'W
Itaituba, Braz. (ē-tä'ī-tōō'bá)	166-67	4°15'S	55°59'W
Itajaí, Braz. (ē-tä-zhī')	172	26°54'S	48°40'W
Itajubá, Braz.	172	22°26'S	45°27'W
Italia, nation, Eur. *see* Italy	174-75	43°0'N	13°00'E
Italy, nation, Eur. (ĭt'á-lē)	174-75	43°0'N	13°00'E
Itämeri, s., Eur. *see* Baltic Sea	192-93	57°0'N	19°00'E
Itānagar, India	234-35	27°09'N	93°33'E
Itaparica, Ilha de, i., Braz.	166-67	13°0'S	38°42'W
Itapecuru-Mirim, Braz. (ē-tä-pĕ'kōō-rōō-mē-rēN')	166-67	3°24'S	44°20'W
Itapemirim, Braz.	172	21°01'S	40°49'W
Itaperuna, Braz. (ē-tá'pâ-rōō'nä)	172	21°12'S	41°54'W
Itapetinga, Braz.	168-69	15°15'S	40°16'W
Itapetininga, Braz. (ē-tä-pĕ-tē-nē'N-gä)	172	23°35'S	48°02'W
Itapicuru, stm., Braz.	166-67	2°51'S	44°12'W
Itapicuru, stm., Braz.	166-67	11°45'S	37°31'W
Itaquari, Braz.	172	20°20'S	40°23'W
Itaqui, Braz.	173	29°08'S	56°32'W
Itararé, Braz.	172	24°07'S	49°21'W
Itārsi, India	234-35	22°36'N	77°46'E
Itasca, Tx., U.S. (ī-tăs'ká)	122-23	32°10'N	97°09'W
Itaúna, Braz. (ē-tä-ōō'nä)	172	20°04'S	44°34'W
Itbayat Island, i., Phil.	250a	20°46'N	121°50'E
Itenes, stm., S.A. *see* Iténez	166-67	11°55'S	65°00'W
Iténez, stm., S.A.	166-67	11°55'S	65°00'W
Ithaca, Mi., U.S. (ĭth'á-ká)	116-17	43°17'N	84°36'W
Ithaca, N.Y., U.S. (ĭth'á-ká)	116-17	42°26'N	76°30'W
Itu, Braz. (ē-tōō')	172	23°16'S	47°18'W
Ituango, Col. (ē-twäŋ'gō)	164-65	7°06'N	75°44'W
Ituí, stm., Braz.	164-65	4°39'S	70°15'W
Ituiutaba, Braz. (ē-tōō-ēōō-tä'bä)	168-69	18°58'S	49°27'W
Itumbiara, Braz.	172	18°25'S	49°12'W
Iturbide, Mex. (ē'tōōr-bē'dhâ)	148	19°38'N	89°36'W
Ituri, stm., D.R.C.	262-63	1°40'N	27°02'E
Iturup, Ostrov, i., Russia (ôs-trôf' ē-tōō-rōōp')	218-19	44°51'N	147°27'E
Ituxi, stm., Braz.	166-67	7°18'S	64°51'W
Ituzaingó, Arg. (ē-tōō-zä-ē'n-gô)	173	27°36'S	56°40'W
Ītyop'iya, nation, Afr. *see* Ethiopia	253	9°0'N	39°00'E
Iuka, Ms., U.S. (ī-ū'ká)	124-25	34°49'N	88°11'W
Iul'tin, Russia	218-19	67°43'N	178°51'W
Ivaí, stm., Braz.	168-69	23°18'S	53°44'W
Ivalo, Fin. (ĭ'vä-lô)	184-85	68°40'N	27°32'E
Ivanhoe, Austl. (ĭv'ăn-hō)	276	32°55'S	144°19'E
Ivano-Frankivs'k, Ukr.	194-95	48°55'N	24°44'E
Ivanovo, Russia (ē-vä'nô-vō)	186-87	57°01'N	40°59'E
Ivanovo-Voznesensk, Russia *see* Ivanovo	186-87	57°01'N	40°59'E
Ivdel', Russia (ĭv'dyĕl)	186-87	60°41'N	60°27'E
Iviza, Spain *see* Eivissa	198-99	38°55'N	1°25'E
Ivory Coast, nation, Afr. *see* Cote d'Ivoire	253	8°0'N	5°00'W
Ivrea, Italy (ē-vrĕ'ä)	200-01	45°28'N	7°53'E
Ivujivik, Qc., Can.	128-29	62°23'N	77°55'W
Iwaki, Japan	245	37°03'N	140°55'E
Iwo, Nig.	260a	7°38'N	4°11'E
Iwo Jima, i., Japan (ē'wō jē'má)	280-81	24°47'N	141°20'E
Ixmiquilpan, Mex. (ēs-mē-kēl'pän)	146-47	20°29'N	99°13'W
Ixtepec, Mex. (ēks-tĕ'pĕk)	146-47	16°32'N	95°05'W
Ixtlán de Juárez, Mex. (ēs-tlän' dā hwä'râz)	146-47	17°20'N	96°30'W
Ixtlán del Río, Mex. (ēs-tlän'dĕl rē'ō)	146-47	21°02'N	104°22'W
Iyo-nada, s., Japan (ē'yō nä-dä)	245	33°40'N	132°20'E
Izabal, Lago de, lk., Guat. (lä'gô-dĕ-ē'zä-bäl')	148	15°30'N	89°10'W
Izamal, Mex. (ē-zä-mä'l)	148	20°56'N	89°01'W
Izberbash, Russia	227	42°33'N	47°52'E
Izhevsk, Russia (ē-zhyĕfsk')	186-87	56°50'N	53°12'E
Izhma, stm., Russia	186-87	65°19'N	52°55'E
Izium, Ukr.	202-03	49°13'N	37°17'E
Izmaïl, Ukr.	200-01	45°21'N	28°50'E
İzmir, Tur. (ĭz-mēr')	200-01	38°26'N	27°09'E
İzmit, Tur. (ĭz-mēt')	200-01	40°47'N	29°57'E
Izuhara, Japan (ē'zōō-hä'rä)	243	34°12'N	129°17'E
Izumo, Japan (ē'zōō-mō)	245	35°22'N	132°46'E
Izu-shotō, is., Japan	244	32°0'N	140°00'E

J

Feature (Pronunciation)	Page	Lat.	Long.
Jabal, Baḩr al-, stm., Sudan *see* Mountain Nile	262-63	9°30'N	30°30'E
Jabalpur, India	234-35	23°10'N	79°56'E
Jaboatão, Braz. (zhä-bô-á-touN)	163d	8°07'S	35°01'W
Jaca, Spain (hä'kä)	198-99	42°35'N	0°34'W
Jacala, Mex. (hä-ká'lä)	146-47	21°01'N	99°11'W
Jacaltenango, Guat. (hä-kál-tĕ-näŋ'gō)	148	15°40'N	91°44'W
Jacareí, Braz.	172	23°19'S	45°58'W
Jacarezinho, Braz. (zhä-kä-rĕ'zē-nyô)	168-69	23°10'S	49°59'W
Jacksboro, Tx., U.S. (jăks'bŭr-ô)	120-21	33°13'N	98°09'W
Jackson, Al., U.S. (jăk'sŭn)	124-25	31°31'N	87°54'W
Jackson, Ga., U.S. (jăk'sŭn)	124-25	33°18'N	83°58'W
Jackson, Ky., U.S. (jăk'sŭn)	116-17	37°33'N	83°24'W
Jackson, La., U.S. (jăk'sŭn)	124-25	30°50'N	91°13'W
Jackson, Mi., U.S. (jăk'sŭn)	116-17	42°15'N	84°24'W
Jackson, Mn., U.S. (jăk'sŭn)	114-15	43°37'N	94°59'W
Jackson, Mo., U.S. (jăk'sŭn)	120-21	37°23'N	89°40'W
Jackson, Ms., U.S. (jăk'sŭn)	124-25	32°19'N	90°11'W
Jackson, Oh., U.S. (jăk'sŭn)	116-17	39°03'N	82°39'W
Jackson, Tn., U.S. (jăk'sŭn)	124-25	35°37'N	88°49'W
Jackson, Wy., U.S. (jăk'sŭn)	112-13	43°29'N	110°45'W
Jackson Lake, lk., Wy., U.S. (jăk'sŭn lāk)	112-13	43°55'N	110°40'W
Jacksonville, Al., U.S. (jăk'sŭn-vĭl)	124-25	33°49'N	85°46'W
Jacksonville, Ar., U.S. (jăk'sŭn-vĭl)	120-21	34°52'N	92°07'W
Jacksonville, Fl., U.S. (jăk'sŭn-vĭl)	124-25	30°21'N	81°39'W
Jacksonville, Il., U.S. (jăk'sŭn-vĭl)	120-21	39°44'N	90°14'W
Jacksonville, N.C., U.S. (jăk'sŭn-vĭl)	124-25	34°45'N	77°25'W
Jacksonville, Tx., U.S. (jăk'sŭn-vĭl)	122-23	31°58'N	95°16'W
Jacksonville Beach, Fl., U.S. (jăk'sŭn-vĭl bēch)	124-25	30°17'N	81°24'W
Jacmel, Haiti (zhák-mĕl')	142-43	18°14'N	72°32'W
Jacobābād, Pak.	232-33	28°17'N	68°26'E
Jacobina, Braz. (zhä-kô-bē'ná)	166-67	11°11'S	40°31'W
Jacques-Cartier, Détroit de, strt., Qc., Can.	138-39	49°53'N	62°45'W
Jacques-Cartier, Mont, mtn., Qc., Can.	138-39	48°59'N	65°57'W
Jacquet River, N.B., Can. (zhá-kĕ' rĭv'ēr) (jăk'ĕt rĭv'ēr)	138-39	47°55'N	66°01'W
Jacuí, stm., Braz.	168-69	30°02'S	51°15'W
Jadotville, D.R.C. *see* Likasi	262-63	10°59'S	26°43'E
Jadransko more, s., Eur. *see* Adriatic Sea	200-01	42°30'N	16°00'E
Jadransko morje, s., Eur. *see* Adriatic Sea	200-01	42°30'N	16°00'E
Jaén, Peru (kä-ĕ'n)	170	5°43'S	78°47'W
Jaén, Spain	198-99	37°46'N	3°48'W
Jaffa, Cape, c., Austl. (kăp jăf'ā)	276	36°58'S	139°40'E
Jaffna, Sri L. (jăf'ná)	236	9°40'N	80°01'E
Jagādhri, India	234-35	30°10'N	77°18'E
Jagdalpur, India	236	19°05'N	82°02'E
Jägerndorf, Czech Rep. *see* Krnov	194-95	50°05'N	17°42'E
Jaguarão, Braz.	173	32°34'S	53°23'W
Jaguariaíva, Braz.	168-69	24°15'S	49°42'W
Jaguaribe, stm., Braz.	166-67	4°25'S	37°46'W
Jagüey Grande, Cuba (hä'gwā grän'dā)	142-43	22°32'N	81°08'W
Jahrom, Iran	230-31	28°29'N	53°33'E
Jaipur, India	234-35	26°55'N	75°48'E
Jaisalmer, India	234-35	26°55'N	70°55'E
Jajce, Bos. (yī'tsĕ)	200-01	44°20'N	17°17'E
Jājpur, India	234-35	20°51'N	86°20'E
Jakarta, nat. cap., Indon. (yä-kär'tä)	248-49	6°11'S	106°50'E
Jakobstad, Fin. (yá'kôb-stádh)	184-85	63°41'N	22°43'E
Jalālābād, Afg. (jŭ-lä-lá-bäd)	232-33	34°26'N	70°27'E
Jalal-Abad, Kyrg.	226	40°56'N	73°00'E
Jalandhar, India	234-35	31°19'N	75°35'E
Jalapa, Guat. (hä-lä'pá)	148	14°38'N	89°59'W
Jalapa, Mex. *see* Xalapa	146-47	19°32'N	96°55'W
Jālgaon, India	234-35	21°01'N	75°34'E
Jalisco, state, Mex. (hä-lēs'kō)	146-47	20°20'N	103°40'W
Jālna, India	234-35	19°51'N	75°54'E
Jalón, stm., Spain (hä-lōn')	198-99	41°47'N	1°03'W
Jālor, India	234-35	25°21'N	72°37'E
Jalostotitlán, Mex. (hä-lōs-tē-tlán')	146-47	21°11'N	102°27'W
Jalpa, Mex. (häl'pä)	146-47	21°38'N	102°60'W
Jalpāiguri, India	234-35	26°31'N	88°42'E
Jamaame, Som.	262-63	0°01'N	42°42'E
Jamaica, nation, N.A. (já-mā'ká)	140-41	18°15'N	77°30'W
Jamanxim, stm., Braz.	166-67	4°45'S	56°27'W
Jambi, Indon. (mäm'bē)	246-47	1°37'S	103°36'E
Jambongan, Pulau, i., Malay.	248-49	6°40'N	117°27'E
James, stm., U.S. (jāmz)	110-11	42°52'N	97°19'W
James, stm., Va., U.S. (jāmz)	116-17	36°56'N	76°26'W
James Bay, b., Can. (jāmz bā)	130-31	53°30'N	80°30'W
Jamestown, Austl.	276	33°12'S	138°36'E
Jamestown, Ky., U.S. (jāmz'toun)	124-25	36°59'N	85°04'W
Jamestown, N.D., U.S. (jāmz'toun)	114-15	46°54'N	98°42'W
Jamestown, N.Y., U.S. (jāmz'toun)	116-17	42°06'N	79°14'W
Jammu, India (jŭmū)	234-35	32°43'N	74°51'E
Jammu and Kashmir, state, India (jŭmū ănd kàsh-mēr')	234-35	34°0'N	76°00'E
Jammu and Kashmir, hist. reg., Asia	234-35	34°0'N	76°00'E
Jamnagar, India (jäm-nŭ'gŭr)	234-35	22°28'N	70°04'E
Jamshedpur, India (jäm'shād-pōōr)	234-35	22°48'N	86°11'E
Jamuna, stm., Bngl.	234-35	23°43'N	89°49'E
Janaucu, Ilha, i., Braz.	166-67	0°30'N	50°10'W
Janesville, Ca., U.S. (jānz'vĭl)	118-19	40°18'N	120°32'W
Janesville, Wi., U.S. (jānz'vĭl)	116-17	42°41'N	89°02'W
Jangīpur, India	234-35	24°28'N	88°04'E
Jan Mayen, dep., Eur. (yän mī'ĕn)	288	71°02'N	8°19'W
Jan Mayen, i., Nor. (yän mī'ĕn)	288	71°03'N	8°19'W
Januária, Braz. (zhä-nwä'rē-ä)	168-69	15°29'S	44°22'W
Japan, nation, Asia (já-păn')	206-07	36°0'N	138°00'E
Japan, Sea of, s., Asia (sē ŭv já-păn')	222-23	40°0'N	135°00'E
Japurá, stm., S.A.	166-67	3°08'S	64°46'W
Jaraguá do Sul, Braz.	172	26°29'S	49°05'W
Jarama, stm., Spain (hä-rä'mä)	198-99	40°02'N	3°39'W
Jari, stm., Braz. (zhä-rē)	166-67	1°09'S	51°53'W
Jarkand, China *see* Shache	226	38°25'N	77°15'E
Jarocin, Pol. (yä-rō'tsyēn)	194-95	51°58'N	17°30'E
Jarosław, Pol. (yá-rôs-wáf)	194-95	50°01'N	22°41'E
Jarud Qi, China (jya-lōō-tū shyē)	240-41	44°34'N	120°54'E
Jarvis Island, dep., Oc.	280-81	0°19'S	160°01'W
Jarvis Island, i., Oc.	280-81	0°23'S	160°01'W
Jāsk, Iran (jäsk)	230-31	25°39'N	57°47'E
Jasło, Pol. (yás'wō)	194-95	49°45'N	21°28'E
Jason Islands, is., Falk. Is.	171	51°09'S	60°54'W
Jasper, Ab., Can. (jăs'pēr)	132-33	52°52'N	118°05'W
Jasper, Al., U.S. (jăs'pēr)	124-25	33°50'N	87°17'W
Jasper, Fl., U.S. (jăs'pēr)	124-25	30°31'N	82°57'W
Jasper, Ga., U.S. (jăs'pēr)	124-25	34°28'N	84°25'W
Jasper, In., U.S. (jăs'pēr)	116-17	38°23'N	86°56'W
Jasper, Tx., U.S. (jăs'pēr)	122-23	30°54'N	94°00'W
Jasper National Park, n.p., Ab., Can. (jăs'pēr năsh'ŭn-ǎl pärk)	132-33	52°53'N	118°03'W
Jassy, Rom. *see* Iași	202-03	47°10'N	27°36'E
Jataí, Braz.	168-69	17°53'S	51°45'W
Jaú, Braz.	172	22°18'S	48°33'W

Feature (Pronunciation)	Page	Lat.	Long.
Jauja, Peru (kä-ó'k)	163a	11°47'S	75°29'W
Jaumave, Mex. (hou-mä'vå)	146-47	23°25'N	99°23'W
Jaunpur, India	234-35	25°44'N	82°41'E
Java, i., Indon. (jä'vȧ)	248-49	7°30'S	109°59'E
Javari, stm., S.A. (kȧ-vä-rē)	170	4°21'S	70°02'W
Java Sea, s., Indon. (jä'vȧ sē)	248-49	5°0'S	110°00'E
Javhlant, Mong. *see* Uliastay	240-41	47°44'N	96°51'E
Jawa, i., Indon. *see* Java	248-49	7°30'S	109°59'E
Jawa, Laut, s., Indon. *see* Java Sea	248-49	5°0'S	110°00'E
Jawhar, Som.	262-63	2°47'N	45°31'E
Jaworzno, Pol. (yä-vôzh'nô)	194-95	50°12'N	19°15'E
Jaya, Puncak, mtn., Indon.	224-25	4°05'S	137°11'E
Jayapura, Indon.	277	2°32'S	140°43'E
Jaz Mūrīān, Hāmūn-e, lk., Iran	230-31	27°14'N	58°49'E
Jeanerette, La., U.S. (jěn-ēr-et') (zhän-rět')	124-25	29°55'N	91°40'W
Jeddah, Sau. Ar. *see* Jiddah	266	21°30'N	39°12'E
Jędrzejów, Pol. (yăn-dzhā'yôf)	194-95	50°39'N	20°19'E
Jefferson, Ia., U.S. (jěf'ēr-sŭn)	114-15	42°01'N	94°23'W
Jefferson, Oh., U.S. (jěf'ēr-sŭn)	116-17	41°44'N	80°46'W
Jefferson, Tx., U.S. (jěf'ēr-sŭn)	120-21	32°45'N	94°21'W
Jefferson, Wi., U.S. (jěf'ēr-sŭn)	116-17	43°00'N	88°48'W
Jefferson, Mount, mtn., Nv., U.S. (mount jěf'ēr-sŭn)	118-19	38°46'N	116°55'W
Jefferson City, Mo., U.S.	120-21	38°33'N	92°10'W
Jefferson City, Tn., U.S. (jěf'ēr-sŭn sĭ'tē)	124-25	36°07'N	83°30'W
Jeffersontown, Ky., U.S. (jěf'ēr-sŭn-toun)	116-17	38°13'N	85°35'W
Jeffersonville, In., U.S. (jěf'ēr-sŭn-vĭl)	116-17	38°17'N	85°44'W
Jeju, Kor., S. *see* Cheju	240-41	33°30'N	126°32'E
Jēkabpils, Lat. (yěk'ȧb-pĭls)	192-93	56°30'N	25°52'E
Jelenia Góra, Pol. (yě-lěn'yȧ gō'rȧ)	194-95	50°54'N	15°44'E
Jelgava, Lat.	192-93	56°39'N	23°44'E
Jellico, Tn., U.S. (jěl'ĭ-kō)	124-25	36°35'N	84°08'W
Jemaja, Pulau, i., Indon.	246-47	2°55'N	105°45'E
Jember, Indon.	248-49	8°10'S	113°42'E
Jena, Ger. (yā'nä)	194-95	50°56'N	11°35'E
Jengish Chokusu, mtn., Asia	226	42°02'N	80°05'E
Jenkins, Ky., U.S. (jěŋ'kĭnz)	124-25	37°10'N	82°39'W
Jennings, La., U.S. (jěn'ĭngz)	122-23	30°13'N	92°39'W
Jeonju, Kor., S. *see* Chŏnju	243	35°49'N	127°09'E
Jequié, Braz.	166-67	13°52'S	40°05'W
Jequitinhonha, stm., Braz. (zhě-kē-těŋ-ŏ'n-yä)	168-69	15°51'S	38°53'W
Jerada, Mor.	184-85	34°19'N	2°10'W
Jerba, Île de, i., Tun.	258-59	33°48'N	10°54'E
Jérémie, Haiti (zhā-rȧ-mē')	142-43	18°39'N	74°07'W
Jeremoabo, Braz. (zhě-rā-mō-ȧ'bō)	166-67	10°06'S	38°19'W
Jerevan, nat. cap., Arm. *see* Yerevan	227	40°11'N	44°30'E
Jerez de la Frontera, Spain	198-99	36°42'N	6°08'W
Jericho, W.B.	228-29	31°52'N	35°27'E
Jerid, Chott, lk., Tun. (shôt jěr'ĭd)	258-59	33°42'N	8°26'E
Jerome, Id., U.S. (jě-rōm')	112-13	42°44'N	114°31'W
Jersey, dep., Eur. (jûr'zĭ)	196-97	49°15'N	2°10'W
Jersey City, N.J., U.S. (jûr'zĭ sĭ'tē)	116-17	40°44'N	74°04'W
Jersey Shore, Pa., U.S. (jûr'zĭ shōr)	116-17	41°12'N	77°15'W
Jerseyville, Il., U.S. (jēr'zē-vĭl)	120-21	39°07'N	90°20'W
Jerusalem, nat. cap., Isr. (jě-rōō'sȧ-lěm)	228-29	31°47'N	35°14'E
Jesi, Italy	200-01	43°31'N	13°14'E
Jesselton, Malay. *see* Kota Kinabalu	248-49	5°58'N	116°05'E
Jessore, Bngl.	234-35	23°10'N	89°13'E
Jesup, Ga., U.S. (jěs'ŭp)	124-25	31°36'N	81°53'W
Jesús Carranza, Mex. (hē-sōō's-kär-rȧ'n-zä)	146-47	17°24'N	95°02'W
Jesús María, Arg.	173	30°59'S	64°05'W
Jewel Cave National Monument, n.p., S.D., U.S. (jū'ěl kāv)	114-15	43°45'N	103°51'W
Jhālāwār, India	234-35	24°36'N	76°10'E
Jhang Sadar, Pak.	232-33	31°16'N	72°19'E
Jhānsi, India (jän'sē)	234-35	25°27'N	78°35'E
Jharkhand, state, India	234-35	23°30'N	85°00'E
Jhelum, Pak.	232-33	32°56'N	73°43'E
Jhelum, stm., Asia (jā'lŭm)	232-33	31°12'N	72°08'E
Jhunjhunūn, India	234-35	28°08'N	75°24'E
Jiading, China (jyä-dĭŋ)	238-39	31°23'N	121°14'E
Jiali, China	238-39	30°45'N	93°20'E
Jialing, China *see* Guangyuan	238-39	32°25'N	105°49'E
Jialing, stm., China (jyä-lĭŋ)	238-39	29°34'N	106°35'E
Jiamusi, China	244	46°48'N	130°22'E
Ji'an, China (jyē-än)	238-39	27°07'N	114°59'E
Ji'an, China (jyē-än)	243	41°06'N	126°10'E
Jianchuan, China	238-39	26°34'N	99°53'E
Jiangjin, China	238-39	29°17'N	106°15'E
Jiangkou, China	238-39	23°35'N	110°11'E
Jiangling, China (jyäŋ-lĭŋ)	238-39	30°19'N	112°12'E
Jiangmen, China	238-39	22°34'N	113°05'E
Jiangsu, state, China (jyäŋ-sōō)	238-39	33°0'N	120°00'E
Jiangxi, state, China (jyäŋ-shyē)	238-39	28°0'N	116°00'E
Jiangyin, China (jyäŋ-yĭn)	238-39	31°54'N	120°15'E
Jianli, China (jyěn-lē)	238-39	29°49'N	112°54'E
Jianning, China (jyěn-nĭŋ)	238-39	26°50'N	116°49'E
Jian'ou, China (jyěn-ō)	238-39	27°02'N	118°19'E
Jianshi, China (jyěn-shr)	238-39	30°36'N	109°44'E
Jianshui, China	238-39	23°37'N	102°49'E
Jiaohe, China (jyou-hŭ)	240-41	43°43'N	127°20'E
Jiaoxian, China (jyou shyěn)	240-41	36°17'N	119°60'E
Jiaozuo, China (jyou-dzwō)	240-41	35°15'N	113°14'E
Jiashan, China (jyä-shän)	238-39	32°46'N	117°59'E
Jiashun Hu, lk., China	234-35	34°24'N	85°47'E
Jiaxing, China (jyä-shyĭŋ)	238-39	30°46'N	120°45'E
Jiayu, China (jyä-yōō)	238-39	29°58'N	113°55'E
Jibuti, nat. cap., Dji. *see* Djibouti	266	11°34'N	43°09'E
Jicarilla Apache Indian Reservation, ind. res., N.M., U.S. (kē-kȧ-rēl'yȧ ĭn'dĭ-ăn rě-sēr-vā'shěn)	118-19	36°40'N	107°00'W
Jicarón, Isla, i., Pan. (ē's-lä-kē-kä-rōn')	150	7°16'N	81°49'W
Jiddah, Sau. Ar.	266	21°30'N	39°12'E
Jieyang, China (jyě-yäŋ)	238-39	23°33'N	116°21'E
Jiguaní, Cuba (kē-gwä-nē')	142-43	20°22'N	76°25'W
Jijiga, Eth.	262-63	9°21'N	42°48'E
Jilin, China (jyē-lĭn)	240-41	43°51'N	126°33'E
Jilin, state, China	240-41	44°0'N	126°00'E
Jīma, Eth.	262-63	7°38'N	36°50'E
Jiménez, Mex. (kê-mä'nåz)	122-23	27°08'N	104°56'W
Jiménez, Mex. (kê-mä'nåz)	122-23	29°02'N	100°41'W
Jiménez del Téul, Mex. (kê-mä'nåz děl tě-ōō'l)	146-47	23°14'N	103°49'W
Jimeta, Nig.	260-61	9°16'N	12°26'E
Jim Thorpe, Pa., U.S. (jĭm' thôrp')	116-17	40°52'N	75°44'W
Jinan, China (jyē-nän)	240-41	36°40'N	116°59'E
Jincheng, China (jyĭn-chŭŋ)	240-41	35°30'N	112°50'E
Jindřichuv Hradec, Czech Rep. (yēn'd'r-zhĭ-kōōf hrä'děts)	194-95	49°09'N	15°01'E
Jing, stm., China (jyĭŋ)	238-39	34°28'N	109°05'E
Jingdezhen, China (jyĭn-dŭ-jŭn)	238-39	29°17'N	117°12'E
Jinggangshan, China	238-39	26°36'N	114°05'E
Jinghong, China	238-39	21°59'N	100°49'E
Jingning, China (jyĭŋ-nĭŋ)	240-41	35°32'N	105°44'E
Jingxian, China (jyĭŋ shyěn)	238-39	26°40'N	109°25'E
Jingxian, China (jyĭŋ shyěn)	238-39	30°41'N	118°24'E
Jingxian, China (jyĭŋ shyěn)	240-41	37°41'N	116°16'E
Jinhae, Kor., S. *see* Chinhae	243	35°08'N	128°40'E
Jinhua, China (jyĭn-hwä)	238-39	29°07'N	119°39'E
Jining, China (jyē-nĭŋ)	240-41	35°24'N	116°34'E
Jining, China (jyē-nĭŋ)	240-41	41°02'N	113°06'E
Jinja, Ug. (jĭn'jä)	267	0°26'N	33°13'E
Jinju, Kor., S. *see* Chinju	243	35°10'N	128°05'E
Jinmu Jiao, c., China	238-39	18°11'N	109°35'E
Jinning, China	238-39	24°40'N	102°35'E
Jinotega, Nic. (kē-nō-tä'gä)	149	13°05'N	85°60'W
Jinotepe, Nic. (kē-nō-tä'på)	149	11°51'N	86°12'W
Jinsen, Kor., S. *see* Inch'ŏn	243	37°28'N	126°38'E
Jinsha, stm., China *see* Yangtze	238-39	31°24'N	121°54'E
Jinshi, China	238-39	29°38'N	111°52'E
Jinta, China (jyĭn-tä)	240-41	40°00'N	98°53'E
Jinxi, China	240-41	40°45'N	120°50'E
Jinyun, China (jyĭn-yòn)	238-39	28°40'N	120°03'E
Jinzhai, China (jyĭn-jī)	238-39	31°45'N	115°55'E
Jinzhou, China (jyĭn-jō)	240-41	39°06'N	121°43'E
Jinzhou, China (jyĭn-jō)	240-41	41°07'N	121°08'E
Ji-Paraná, Braz.	166-67	10°52'S	61°57'W
Jiparaná, stm., Braz. *see* Machado	166-67	8°02'S	62°53'W
Jipijapa, Ec. (kē-pē-hä'pä)	170	1°21'S	80°35'W
Jiujiang, China (jyô-jyän)	238-39	29°43'N	115°59'E
Jiulian Shan, mts., China	238-39	24°17'N	114°36'E
Jiuling Shan, mts., China	238-39	28°46'N	114°45'E
Jiuquan, China (jyô-chyän)	240-41	39°45'N	98°30'E
Jiutai, China	240-41	44°09'N	125°50'E
Jixi, China	244	45°17'N	130°58'E
Jixian, China (jyē shyěn)	244	46°43'N	131°08'E
Jixian, China (jyē shyěn)	240-41	35°25'N	114°04'E
Jixian, China (jyē shyěn)	240-41	40°02'N	117°24'E
Jīzān, Sau. Ar.	266	16°54'N	42°36'E
Jizzax, Uzb.	232-33	40°08'N	67°51'E
J. J. Castelli, Arg. *see* Castelli	168-69	25°57'S	60°37'W
João Belo, Moz. *see* Xai-Xai	264-65	25°03'S	33°39'E
João Pessoa, Braz.	163d	7°07'S	34°52'W
Joaquín V. González, Arg.	168-69	25°05'S	64°09'W
Jódar, Spain (hō'där)	198-99	37°50'N	3°21'W
Jodhpur, India (hōd'pōōr)	234-35	26°17'N	73°01'E
Joensuu, Fin. (yô-ěn'sōō)	184-85	62°36'N	29°47'E
Joetsu, Japan	245	37°09'N	138°15'E
Joffre, Mount, mtn., Can. (mount jō'f'r)	132-33	50°32'N	115°13'W
Jõgeva, Est. (yû'gě-vå)	192-93	58°45'N	26°24'E
Jogjakarta, Indon. *see* Yogyakarta	248-49	7°48'S	110°22'E
Johannesburg, S. Afr. (yô-hän'ěs-bòrgh)	269c	26°12'S	28°05'E
John Day, stm., Or., U.S. (jŏn' dā)	112-13	45°44'N	120°39'W
Johnsonburg, Pa., U.S. (jŏn'sŭn-bûrg)	116-17	41°29'N	78°41'W
Johnson City, N.Y., U.S. (jŏn'sŭn sĭ'tē)	116-17	42°07'N	75°58'W
Johnson City, Tn., U.S. (jŏn'sŭn sĭ'tē)	124-25	36°19'N	82°22'W
Johnson City, Tx., U.S. (jŏn'sŭn sĭ'tē)	122-23	30°16'N	98°24'W
Johnston, Lake, lk., Austl.	272-73	32°18'S	120°46'E
Johnston Atoll, dep., Oc.	280-81	16°45'N	169°32'W
Johnston Atoll, at., Oc. (jŏn'stŭn ă'tôl)	280-81	16°45'N	169°32'W
Johnstown, Pa., U.S. (jonz'toun)	116-17	40°19'N	78°55'W
Johor Bahru, Malay.	246-47	1°28'N	103°45'E
Joigny, Fr. (zhwȧn-yē')	196-97	47°59'N	3°24'E
Joinville, Braz.	172	26°18'S	48°50'W
Jokkmokk, Swe.	184-85	66°37'N	19°50'E
Joliet, Il., U.S. (jō-lĭ-ět')	116-17	41°31'N	88°04'W
Joliette, Qc., Can. (zhô-lyět')	136-37	46°02'N	73°25'W
Jolo, Phil. (hō-lō)	250	6°02'N	120°60'E
Jolo Group, is., Phil.	250	6°01'N	121°18'E
Jolo Island, i., Phil. (hō-lō ī'lănd)	250	5°58'N	121°06'E
Jomda, China	238-39	31°27'N	98°15'E
Jon, Deti, s., Eur. *see* Ionian Sea	200-01	39°0'N	19°00'E
Jonava, Lith. (yō-nä'vȧ)	192-93	55°05'N	24°17'E
Jonesboro, Ar., U.S. (jōnz'bûro)	124-25	35°51'N	90°42'W
Jonesboro, La., U.S. (jōnz'bûro)	120-21	32°14'N	92°43'W
Jonesville, La., U.S. (jōnz'vĭl)	124-25	31°37'N	91°49'W
Joniškis, Lith. (yô'nĭsh-kĭs)	192-93	56°14'N	23°38'E
Jönköping, Swe. (yûn'chû-pĭng)	192-93	57°47'N	14°11'E
Jonquière, Qc., Can. (zhôn-kyâr')	136-37	48°26'N	71°11'W
Jonuta, Mex. (hô-nōō'tä)	148	18°06'N	92°07'W
Joplin, Mo., U.S. (jŏp'lĭn)	120-21	37°05'N	94°31'W
Jordan, Mt., U.S.	112-13	47°20'N	106°57'W
Jordan, nation, Asia (jôr'dăn)	206-07	31°0'N	36°00'E
Jordan, stm., Asia (jôr'dăn)	228-29	31°46'N	35°34'E
Jorhāt, India (jôr-hät')	234-35	26°46'N	94°13'E
Jos, Nig.	260-61	9°56'N	8°53'E
José Batlle y Ordóñez, Ur.	173	33°29'S	55°08'W
José de San Martín, Arg.	171	44°02'S	70°29'W
Joseph Bonaparte Gulf, b., Austl. (jô'sěf bō'nȧ-pärt gŭlf)	272-73	14°15'S	128°30'E
Joshua Tree National Park, n.p., Ca., U.S. (jô'shū-ȧ trē năsh'ŭn-ăl pärk)	118-19	33°55'N	116°00'W
Jostedalsbreen, ice, Nor.	192-93	61°40'N	7°00'E
Jovellanos, Cuba (hō-věl-yä'nōs)	142-43	22°48'N	81°11'W
J. Strom Thurmond Reservoir, res., U.S.	124-25	33°45'N	82°16'W
Juan Aldama, Mex. (kòȧ'n-äl-dá'mä)	146-47	24°19'N	103°19'W
Juan de Fuca, Strait of, strt., N.A. (strāt ŭv hwän' dā fōō'kä)	112-13	48°18'N	124°00'W
Juan de Fuca Strait, strt., N.A. *see* Juan de Fuca, Strait of	112-13	48°18'N	124°00'W
Juan Fernández, Archipiélago, is., Chile	159	33°0'S	80°00'W
Juanjuí, Peru	170	7°10'S	76°45'W
Juárez, Arg. (hōōȧ'rěz) *see* Benito Juárez	173	37°41'S	59°48'W
Juazeiro, Braz. (zhōōȧ'zā'rô)	166-67	9°25'S	40°30'W
Juazeiro do Norte, Braz. (zhōōȧ'zā'rô-dô-nôr-tě)	166-67	7°12'S	39°20'W
Juba, Sudan	267	4°51'N	31°37'E
Jubal, Strait of, strt., Egypt *see* Gûbâl, Madîq	268b	27°40'N	33°55'E
Jubayl, Leb. (jōō-bĭl')	228-29	34°08'N	35°40'E
Jubba, stm., Afr.	262-63	0°15'S	42°39'E
Juby, Cap, c., Mor. (kăp yōō'bē)	258-59	27°57'N	12°55'W
Júcaro, Cuba (hōō'kȧ-rô)	142-43	21°38'N	78°51'W
Juchipila, Mex. (hōō-chē-pē'lȧ)	146-47	21°24'N	103°07'W
Juchitán de Zaragoza, Mex.	146-47	16°26'N	95°01'W
Juchitlán, Mex. (hōō-chē-tlän)	146-47	20°05'N	104°06'W
Juddah, Sau. Ar. *see* Jiddah	266	21°30'N	39°12'E
Juidongshan, China	238-39	23°44'N	117°30'E
Juigalpa, Nic. (hwē-gäl'pä)	149	12°06'N	85°22'W
Juiz de Fora, Braz. (zhò-ēzh' dā fō'rä)	172	21°45'S	43°22'W
Jujuy, Arg. (hōō-hwē') *see* San Salvador de Jujuy	168-69	24°12'S	65°18'W
Jujuy, state, Arg. (hōō-hwē')	168-69	23°0'S	66°00'W
Julesburg, Co., U.S. (jōōlz'bûrg)	114-15	40°59'N	102°17'W

n-sing; ŋ-baŋk; N-nasalized n; nŏd; cŏmmit; ōld; ôbey; ôrder; oi-boil; fōōd; ò-as oo in foot; ou-out; s-soft; sh-dish; th-thin; pūre; ůnite; ûrn; stŭd; circŭs; ü-as in French tu; ′-indeterminate vowel.

Feature (Pronunciation)	Page	Lat.	Long.
Juliaca, Peru (hōō-lē-ä′kä) 170	170	15°30′s	70°08′w
Juliana Top, mtn., Sur. 164-65	164-65	3°39′n	56°32′w
Julianehåb, Green. 284-85	284-85	60°44′n	46°02′w
Jumentos Cays, is., Bah.			
(hōō-měn′tōs kēs) 142-43	142-43	22°42′n	75°55′w
Jumilla, Spain (hōō-mēl′yä) 198-99	198-99	38°28′n	1°20′w
Jūnāgadh, India (jò-nä′gŭd) 234-35	234-35	21°31′n	70°27′E
Junction, Tx., U.S. (jŭŋk′shŭn) 122-23	122-23	30°29′n	99°47′w
Junction City, Ks., U.S.			
(jŭŋk′shŭn sĭ′tě) 120-21	120-21	39°02′n	96°50′w
Junction City, Or., U.S.			
(jŭŋk′shŭn sĭ′tě) 112-13	112-13	44°14′n	123°11′w
Jundiaí, Braz. 172	172	23°11′s	46°53′w
Juneau, Ak., U.S. (jōō′nō) 126	126	58°20′n	134°25′w
Junee, Austl. 276	276	34°52′s	147°35′E
Jungar Qi, China 240-41	240-41	39°49′n	111°10′E
Jungfrau, mtn., Switz. (yòng′frou) 194-95	194-95	46°32′n	7°58′E
Junín, Arg. (hōō-nē′n) 173	173	34°36′s	60°58′w
Junín de los Andes, Arg. 171	171	39°55′s	71°05′w
Jūniyah, Leb. (jōō-nē′ě) 228-29	228-29	33°60′n	35°39′E
Junxian, China 238-39	238-39	32°32′n	111°31′E
Juquiá, Braz. 172	172	24°19′s	47°38′w
Jur, stm., Sudan (jòr) 262-63	262-63	8°39′n	29°17′E
Jura, i., Scot., U.K. (jōō′rà) 190-91	190-91	56°01′n	5°56′w
Jura, mts., Eur. (zhŭ-rä′) 194-95	194-95	47°06′n	6°50′E
Jurbarkas, Lith. (yōōr-bär′käs) 192-93	192-93	55°05′n	22°47′E
Jūrmala, Lat. 192-93	192-93	56°58′n	23°42′E
Juruá, stm., S.A. 166-67	166-67	2°35′s	65°47′w
Juruena, stm., Braz. (zhōō-rōōě′nä) . .166-67	166-67	7°21′s	58°09′w
Justo Daract, Arg. 171	171	33°52′s	65°11′w
Jutaí, stm., Braz. 166-67	166-67	2°44′s	66°48′w
Jutiapa, Guat. (hōō-tě-ä′pä) 148	148	14°18′n	89°54′w
Juticalpa, Hond. (hōō-tě-käl′pä) 149	149	14°40′n	86°13′w
Jutland, reg., Den. see Jylland 192-93	192-93	56°0′n	9°15′E
Juventud, Isla de la, i., Cuba 142-43	142-43	21°40′n	82°50′w
Jyekundo, China see Yushu 238-39	238-39	33°00′n	97°00′E
Jylland, reg., Den. 192-93	192-93	56°0′n	9°15′E
Jyväskylä, Fin. 192-93	192-93	62°15′n	25°45′E

K

Feature (Pronunciation)	Page	Lat.	Long.
K2, mtn., Asia (kä-tōō) 232-33	232-33	35°53′n	76°30′E
Ka′ena Point, c., Hi., U.S.			
(kä′á-nä point) 127a	127a	21°35′n	158°17′w
Kaapstad, nat. cap., S. Afr.			
see Cape Town 264-65	264-65	33°55′s	18°30′E
Kaarlela, Fin. see Kokkola 184-85	184-85	63°50′n	23°09′E
Kaba, stm., Afr. see Little Scarcies . . .260-61	260-61	8°51′n	13°07′w
Kabaena, Pulau, i., Indon.			
(pōō-lou kä-bä-ĕ′nä) 248-49	248-49	5°15′s	121°55′E
Kabala, S.L. (kà-bá′là) 260-61	260-61	9°35′n	11°33′w
Kabale, Ug. 267	267	1°11′s	29°56′E
Kabalega Falls, wtfl., Ug. 267	267	2°17′n	31°42′E
Kabalo, D.R.C. (kä-bä′lō) 262-63	262-63	6°03′s	26°55′E
Kabara, i., Fiji 279f	279f	18°57′s	178°57′w
Kabardin-Balkaria, state, Russia			
see Balkaria 227	227	43°30′n	43°30′E
Kabardino-Balkariya, state, Russia			
see Balkaria 227	227	43°30′n	43°30′E
Kabīr Kūh, mts., Iran 228-29	228-29	33°36′n	46°12′E
Kābol, nat. cap., Afg. (kä′bōōl)			
see Kabul 232-33	232-33	34°32′n	69°10′E
Kābol, stm., Asia 232-33	232-33	33°55′n	72°14′E
Kabompo, stm., Zam. (kà-bŏm′pō) 264-65	264-65	14°12′s	23°11′E
Kabul, nat. cap., Afg. (kä′bōōl) 232-33	232-33	34°32′n	69°10′E
Kabul, stm., Asia (kä′bôl) see Kābol . .232-33	232-33	33°55′n	72°14′E
Kaburuang, Pulau, i., Indon. 248-49	248-49	3°48′n	126°48′E
Kabwe, Zam. 264-65	264-65	14°27′s	28°27′E
Kachchh, Gulf of, b., India 234-35	234-35	22°37′n	69°30′E
Kachchh, Rann of, reg., Asia			
see Kutch, Rann of 234-35	234-35	24°15′n	70°46′E
Kachul, Mol. see Cahul 202-03	202-03	45°55′n	28°12′E
Kadamatt Island, i., India 236	236	11°13′n	72°47′E
Kadan Kyun, i., Mya. 246-47	246-47	12°30′n	98°22′E
Kadéï, stm., Afr. 260-61	260-61	3°31′n	16°03′E
Kadina, Austl. 276	276	33°58′s	137°43′E
Kadiyevka, Ukr. see Stakhanov 202-03	202-03	48°34′n	38°40′E
Kadoma, Zimb. 264-65	264-65	18°21′s	29°54′E
Kaduna, Nig. (kä-dōō′nä) 260-61	260-61	10°32′n	7°25′E
Kaduna, stm., Nig. (kä-dōō′nä) 260-61	260-61	8°45′n	5°48′E
Kāduqlī, Sudan 266	266	10°60′n	29°43′E
Kadzherom, Russia 186-87	186-87	64°41′n	55°55′E
Kaédi, Maur. (kä-ā-dē′) 258-59	258-59	16°10′n	13°29′w

Feature (Pronunciation)	Page	Lat.	Long.
Kaesŏng, Kor., N. (kä′ě-sŭng) (kĭ′jō) 243	243	37°59′n	126°34′E
Kafue, stm., Zam. (kä′fōō) 264-65	264-65	15°56′s	28°57′E
Kafue National Park, n.p., Zam.			
(kä′fōō näsh′ŭn-ăl pärk) 264-65	264-65	15°22′s	25°25′E
Kaga Bandoro, C.A.R. 262-63	262-63	6°59′n	19°12′E
Kagera, stm., Afr. (kä-gä′rà) 267	267	0°56′s	31°47′E
Kagoshima, Japan (kä′gŏ-shē′má) 245	245	31°36′n	130°33′E
Kagoshima-wan, b., Japan			
(kä′gŏ-shē′mä wän) 245	245	31°24′n	130°38′E
Kahama, Tan. 267	267	3°49′s	32°36′E
Kahayan, stm., Indon. 248-49	248-49	1°34′s	114°06′E
Kahemba, D.R.C. 262-63	262-63	7°18′s	18°59′E
Kaho′olawe, i., Hi., U.S. (kä-hōō-lä′wē) . . . 127a	127a	20°33′n	156°37′w
Kahoka, Mo., U.S. (kà-hō′kà) 120-21	120-21	40°26′n	91°43′w
Kahramanmaraş, Tur. 186-87	186-87	37°35′n	36°57′E
Kahuku Point, c., Hi., U.S.			
(kä-hōō′kōō point) 127a	127a	21°43′n	157°59′w
Kai, Kepulauan, is., Indon. 224-25	224-25	5°35′s	132°45′E
Kaibab Indian Reservation, ind. res.,			
Az., U.S. (kä′ē-bäb			
ĭn′dĭ-ăn rĕ-sĕr-vā′shĕn) 118-19	118-19	36°55′n	112°40′w
Kaidu, stm., China (kī-dōō) 222-23	222-23	41°58′n	86°44′E
Kaifeng, China 238-39	238-39	34°47′n	114°21′E
Kaijo, Kor., N. see Kaesŏng 243	243	37°59′n	126°34′E
Kai Kecil, i., Indon. 224-25	224-25	5°46′s	132°43′E
Kailas, mtn., China			
see Kangrinboqê Feng 234-35	234-35	31°04′n	81°18′E
Kailas Range, mts., China (kī-läs′ränj)			
see Gangdisê Shan 234-35	234-35	31°0′n	82°00′E
Kailu, China 240-41	240-41	43°36′n	121°19′E
Kailua, Hi., U.S. (kä′ē-lōō′ä) 127a	127a	21°24′n	157°45′w
Kailua, Hi., U.S. (kä′ē-lōō′ä) 127a	127a	19°39′n	155°58′w
Kailua Kona, Hi., U.S. see Kailua 127a	127a	19°39′n	155°58′w
Kaiping, China 238-39	238-39	22°22′n	112°37′E
Kairouan, Tun. 184-85	184-85	35°41′n	10°07′E
Kaiserslautern, Ger. (kī-zěrs-lou′těrn) . .194-95	194-95	49°26′n	7°45′E
Kaiyuan, China (kū-yuän′) 243	243	42°32′n	124°02′E
Kaiyuan, China (kū-yuän′) 238-39	238-39	23°42′n	103°14′E
Kajaani, Fin. (kä′yà-ně) 184-85	184-85	64°14′n	27°45′E
Kaka, Turkmen. 232-33	232-33	37°20′n	59°37′E
Kakabia, Pulau, i., Indon. 248-49	248-49	6°54′s	122°13′E
Kakamas, S. Afr. 264-65	264-65	28°46′s	20°36′E
Kakamega, Kenya 267	267	0°17′n	34°45′E
Kakhovka, Ukr. (kä-kôf′kà) 202-03	202-03	46°49′n	33°30′E
Kakhovka Reservoir, res., Ukr			
see Kakhovs′ke vodoskhovyshche 202-03	202-03	47°28′n	34°06′E
Kakhovs′ke vodoskhovyshche,			
res., Ukr. 202-03	202-03	47°28′n	34°06′E
Kakhul, Mol. see Cahul 202-03	202-03	45°55′n	28°12′E
Kākināda, India 236	236	16°57′n	82°15′E
Kakshaal-Too, mts., Asia 226	226	41°0′n	78°00′E
Kaktovik, Ak., U.S. (kăk-tō′vĭk) 126	126	70°08′n	143°38′w
Kakuma, Kenya 267	267	3°42′n	34°52′E
Kalaallit Nunaat, dep., N.A.			
see Greenland 85	85	70°0′n	40°00′w
Kalabahi, Indon. 248-49	248-49	8°15′s	124°32′E
Kalach, Russia (kà-lách′) 186-87	186-87	50°25′n	41°00′E
Kalachinsk, Russia 226	226	55°02′n	74°35′E
Kalach-na-Donu, Russia 186-87	186-87	48°43′n	43°28′E
Kalae, stm., Hi., U.S. 127a	127a	18°55′n	155°41′w
Kalahari Desert, des., Afr.			
(kä-lä-hä′rě dĕs′ĕrt) 264-65	264-65	24°0′s	21°30′E
Kalahari Gemsbok National Park,			
n.p., S. Afr. 264-65	264-65	25°30′s	20°30′E
Kalama, Wa., U.S. (kà-lăm′à) 112-13	112-13	46°01′n	122°50′w
Kalamáta, Grc. 200-01	200-01	37°03′n	22°07′E
Kalamazoo, Mi., U.S. (kăl-à-má-zōō′) . . .116-17	116-17	42°17′n	85°35′w
Kalamazoo, stm., Mi., U.S.			
(kăl-à-má-zōō′) 116-17	116-17	42°40′n	86°12′w
Kalanchak, Ukr. (kä-län-chäk′) 202-03	202-03	46°15′n	33°18′E
Kalao, Pulau, i., Indon. 248-49	248-49	7°18′s	120°58′E
Kalaotoa, Pulau, i., Indon. 248-49	248-49	7°22′s	121°47′E
Kalāt, Pak. (kŭ-lät′) 232-33	232-33	29°02′n	66°35′E
Kalaw, Mya. 246-47	246-47	20°38′n	96°34′E
Kalbarri, Austl. 270-71	270-71	27°42′s	114°10′E
Kaledupa, Pulau, i., Indon. 248-49	248-49	5°32′s	123°47′E
Kalemie, D.R.C. 267	267	5°55′s	29°11′E
Kalemyo, Mya. 246-47	246-47	23°13′n	94°07′E
Kalevala, Russia 186-87	186-87	65°11′n	31°11′E
Kalewa, Mya. 246-47	246-47	23°12′n	94°18′E
Kalgoorlie-Boulder, Austl.			
(kăl-gōōr′lě-bōld′ĕr) 270-71	270-71	30°44′s	121°27′E
Kalibo, Phil. 250	250	11°43′n	122°23′E
Kalima, D.R.C. 262-63	262-63	2°36′s	26°37′E
Kalimantan, i., Asia see Borneo 248-49	248-49	0°30′n	114°00′E
Kālimpang, India 234-35	234-35	27°04′n	88°28′E

Feature (Pronunciation)	Page	Lat.	Long.
Kaliningrad, Russia (kä-lē-nēn′grät) 194-95	194-95	54°43′n	20°30′E
Kalisch, Pol. see Kalisz. 194-95	194-95	51°46′n	18°06′E
Kalispell, Mt., U.S. (kăl′ĭ-spěl) 112-13	112-13	48°12′n	114°19′w
Kalisz, Pol. (kä′lēsh) 194-95	194-95	51°46′n	18°06′E
Kalixälven, stm., Swe. 184-85	184-85	65°53′n	23°03′E
Kalmar, Swe. (käl′mär) 192-93	192-93	56°40′n	16°22′E
Kalmarsund, strt., Swe. (käl′mär) 192-93	192-93	56°40′n	16°25′E
Kal′mius, stm., Ukr. (käl″myōōs) 202-03	202-03	47°05′n	37°34′E
Kalmykia, state, Russia 186-87	186-87	46°30′n	45°30′E
Kalmykiya, state, Russia see Kalmykia . .186-87	186-87	46°30′n	45°30′E
Kalpeni Island, i., India 236	236	10°05′n	73°38′E
Kalsūbai, mtn., India 234-35	234-35	19°36′n	73°43′E
Kaluga, Russia (kä-lŏ′gä) 202-03	202-03	54°32′n	36°17′E
Kalundborg, Den. (kä-lòn″bôr′) 192-93	192-93	55°41′n	11°07′E
Kalush, Ukr. (kä′lòsh) 194-95	194-95	49°02′n	24°22′E
Kalyān, India. 236	236	19°16′n	73°08′E
Kalyazin, Russia (käl-yá′zēn) 202-03	202-03	57°14′n	37°54′E
Kálymnos, i., Grc. 200-01	200-01	37°0′n	27°00′E
Kama, stm., Russia (kä′mä) 186-87	186-87	55°35′n	51°29′E
Kamaishi, Japan (kä′mä-ē′shě) 244	244	39°16′n	141°53′E
Kamakura, Japan (kä′mä-kōō′rä) 245	245	35°19′n	139°33′E
Kama Reservoir, res., Russia			
(kä′mä rě′sĕr-vwär)			
see Kamskoye Vodokhranilishche. . . .186-87	186-87	58°52′n	56°15′E
Kambarka, Russia. 186-87	186-87	56°15′n	54°13′E
Kamchatka, Poluostrov, pen., Russia			
see Kamchatka Peninsula 218-19	218-19	56°0′n	160°00′E
Kamchatka Peninsula, pen., Russia			
(käm-chăt-kà′ pě-nĭn′sūlà) 218-19	218-19	56°0′n	160°00′E
Kamenjak, Rt, c., Cro. (kä′mě-nyäk) 200-01	200-01	44°46′n	13°55′E
Kamenka, Russia 186-87	186-87	53°11′n	44°03′E
Kamen′-na-Obi, Russia			
(kä-mĭny′nŭ ô′bē) 226	226	53°48′n	81°20′E
Kāmet, mtn., Asia. 234-35	234-35	30°54′n	79°37′E
Kam′ianets′-Podil′s′kyi, Ukr. 194-95	194-95	48°40′n	26°36′E
Kamina, D.R.C. 262-63	262-63	8°44′s	25°00′E
Kaminak Lake, lk., Nu., Can. 130-31	130-31	62°09′n	95°07′w
Kamino-shima, i., Japan 243	243	34°35′n	129°25′E
Kaminuriak Lake, lk., Nu., Can. 130-31	130-31	62°59′n	95°35′w
Kamituga, D.R.C. 267	267	3°02′s	28°14′E
Kamloops, B.C., Can. (kăm′lōōps) 132-33	132-33	50°40′n	120°20′w
Kampala, nat. cap., Ug. (käm-pä′lä) 267	267	0°19′n	32°34′E
Kampar, stm., Indon. (käm′pär) 246-47	246-47	0°14′n	102°42′E
Kamphaeng Phet, Thai. 246-47	246-47	16°28′n	99°32′E
Kâmpóng Cham, Camb. 246-47	246-47	12°0′n	105°27′E
Kâmpóng Chhnăng, Camb. 246-47	246-47	12°15′n	104°40′E
Kâmpóng Saôm, Camb. 246-47	246-47	10°38′n	103°31′E
Kâmpóng Saôm, Chhâk, b., Camb. 246-47	246-47	10°50′n	103°32′E
Kâmpóng Thum, Camb.			
(kŏm′pŏng-tŏm) 246-47	246-47	12°42′n	104°54′E
Kâmpôt, Camb. (käm′pŏt) 246-47	246-47	10°37′n	104°11′E
Kampuchea, nation, Asia			
see Cambodia 206-07	206-07	13°0′n	105°00′E
Kamsack, Sk., Can. (kăm′săk) 134-35	134-35	51°34′n	101°54′w
Kamskoye Vodokhranilishche,			
res., Russia. 186-87	186-87	58°52′n	56°15′E
Kamuela, Hi., U.S. see Waimea 127a	127a	20°02′n	155°40′w
Kámuk, Cerro, mtn., C.R.			
(sě′r-rŏ-kä-mōō′k). 149	149	9°17′n	83°01′w
Kamyshin, Russia (kä-mwēsh′ĭn) 186-87	186-87	50°07′n	45°24′E
Kanaaupscow, stm., Qc., Can. 130-31	130-31	53°40′n	76°44′w
Kanab, Ut., U.S. (kăn′äb) 118-19	118-19	37°03′n	112°32′w
Kanab Plateau, plat., U.S.			
(kăn′äb plä-tō′) 118-19	118-19	36°36′n	112°45′w
Kanagawa, state, Japan (kä′nä-gä′wä) . . . 245	245	35°30′n	139°15′E
Kananga, D.R.C. 262-63	262-63	5°54′s	22°25′E
Kanash, Russia 186-87	186-87	55°31′n	47°29′E
Kanawha, stm., W.V., U.S.			
(kà-nô′wá) 116-17	116-17	38°50′n	82°09′w
Kanazawa, Japan (kä′nä-zä′wä) 245	245	36°34′n	136°39′E
Kanchanjanggā, mtn., Asia			
see Kānchenjunga 234-35	234-35	27°41′n	88°10′E
Kānchenjunga, mtn., Asia			
(kĭn-chĭn-jòn′gä) 234-35	234-35	27°41′n	88°10′E
Kānchipuram, India 236	236	12°50′n	79°43′E
Kandahār, Afg. 232-33	232-33	31°37′n	65°43′E
Kandalaksha, Russia (kán-dá-läk′shá) . .184-85	184-85	67°09′n	32°24′E
Kandangan, Indon. 248-49	248-49	2°48′s	115°16′E
Kandavu, i., Fiji 279f	279f	19°00′s	178°11′E
Kandy, Sri L. (kän′dě) 236	236	7°18′n	80°38′E
Kane, Pa., U.S. (kān) 116-17	116-17	41°40′n	78°48′w
Kāne′ohe, Hi., U.S. (kä-nā-ō′hä) 127a	127a	21°25′n	157°48′w
Kanevskaya, Russia (kà-nyěf′skà) 202-03	202-03	46°05′n	38°58′E
Kangar, Malay. 246-47	246-47	6°27′n	100°12′E
Kangaroo Island, i., Austl.			
(kăŋ-gá-rō′ ī′lánd) 276	276	35°50′s	137°05′E

Feature (Pronunciation)	Page	Lat.	Long.
Kangāvar, Iran (kŭŋ´gä-vär)	228-29	34°30'N	47°58'E
Kangding, China	238-39	30°04'N	102°01'E
Kangean, Kepulauan, is., Indon. (käŋ´gê-än)	248-49	6°55'S	115°30'E
Kangean, Pulau, i., Indon.	248-49	6°54'S	115°20'E
Kanggye, Kor., N. (käng´gyĕ)	243	40°58'N	126°36'E
Kangiqsliniq, Nu., Can. see Rankin Inlet	128-29	62°49'N	92°10'W
Kangiqsualujjuaq, Qc., Can.	128-29	58°42'N	65°59'W
Kangiqsujuaq, Qc., Can.	128-29	61°35'N	71°58'W
Kangirsuk, Qc., Can.	128-29	60°02'N	70°01'W
Kangnŭng, Kor., S. (käng´nò ng)	243	37°46'N	128°54'E
Kango, Gabon (käɴ-gō)	260-61	0°11'N	10°05'E
Kangrinboqê Feng, mtn., China	234-35	31°04'N	81°18'E
Kangto, mtn., Asia	234-35	27°52'N	92°30'E
Kanhsien, China see Ganzhou	238-39	25°53'N	114°55'E
Kaniama, D.R.C.	262-63	7°33'S	24°10'E
Kanin, Poluostrov, pen., Russia	186-87	68°0'N	45°00'E
Kanin Nos, Mys, c., Russia	186-87	68°39'N	43°17'E
Kankakee, Il., U.S. (kăŋ-kȧ-kē´)	116-17	41°07'N	87°51'W
Kankan, Gui. (kän-käɴ) (kän-kän´)	260-61	10°23'N	9°18'W
Kankō, Kor., N. see Hamhŭng	243	39°55'N	127°32'E
Kanmaw Kyun, i., Mya.	246-47	11°40'N	98°28'E
Kannapolis, N.C., U.S. (kăn-ăp´ô-lĭs)	124-25	35°29'N	80°37'W
Kannur, India see Cannanore	236	11°52'N	75°22'E
Kano, Nig. (kä´nō)	260-61	12°01'N	8°30'E
Kānpur, India (kän´pûr)	234-35	26°28'N	80°19'E
Kansas, state, U.S. (kăn´zȧs)	108-09	38°45'N	98°15'W
Kansas City, Ks., U.S. (kăn´zȧs sĭ´tē)	120-21	39°07'N	94°38'W
Kansas City, Mo., U.S. (kăn´zȧs sĭ´tē)	120-21	39°06'N	94°34'W
Kansk, Russia	218-19	56°12'N	95°43'E
Kansu, state, China see Gansu	240-41	37°0'N	103°00'E
Kantang, Thai. (kän´täng´)	246-47	7°24'N	99°32'E
Kanton, i., Kir. see Canton	280-81	2°49'S	171°41'W
Kantunilkin, Mex. (kän-tōō-nēl-kē´n)	148	21°06'N	87°29'W
Kanye, Bots.	264-65	24°59'S	25°19'E
Kaohsiung, Tai. (kä-ô-syòng´)	225a	22°38'N	120°17'E
Kaoko Veld, plat., Nmb.	264-65	20°0'S	14°00'E
Kaolack, Sen.	260-61	14°09'N	16°04'W
Kaoma, Zam.	264-65	14°47'S	24°48'E
Kapenguria, Kenya	267	1°09'N	35°01'E
Kapfenberg, Aus. (kȧp´fĕn-bĕrgh)	194-95	47°27'N	15°17'E
Kapingamarangi, at., Micron.	280-81	1°04'N	154°46'E
Kapit, Malay.	248-49	2°00'N	112°56'E
Kapoeta, Sudan	267	4°47'N	33°35'E
Kaposvár, Hung. (kô´pôsh-vär)	194-95	46°22'N	17°48'E
Kapuas, stm., Indon.	248-49	0°09'S	109°08'E
Kapuas Hulu, Pegunungan, mts., Asia see Upper Kapuas Mountains	248-49	1°15'N	113°30'E
Kapuas Hulu, Pergunungan, mts., Asia see Upper Kapuas Mountains	248-49	1°15'N	113°30'E
Kapuskasing, On., Can.	136-37	49°25'N	82°25'W
Kapuskasing, stm., On., Can.	136-37	49°38'N	82°16'W
Kara, Togo	260-61	9°33'N	1°12'E
Kara, stm., Russia (kärȧ)	186-87	69°07'N	64°45'E
Kara-Balta, Kyrg.	226	42°48'N	73°51'E
Karabogaz, Turkmen.	186-87	41°32'N	52°35'E
Kara-Bogaz-Gol Gulf, b., Turkmen. (kȧ-rä´ bŭ-gäs´ gôl gŭlf)	232-33	41°15'N	53°24'E
Karabük, Tur.	186-87	41°13'N	32°37'E
Karachay, state, Russia see Cherkessia	227	44°0'N	42°00'E
Karachay-Cherkessia, state, Russia see Cherkessia	227	44°0'N	42°00'E
Karachayevo-Cherkesiya, state, Russia see Cherkessia	227	44°0'N	42°00'E
Karachev, Russia (kȧ-rȧ-chôf´)	202-03	53°07'N	34°59'E
Karāchi, Pak. (kȧ-rä´chē)	232-33	24°54'N	67°01'E
Kara Deniz, s., see Black Sea	186-87	43°0'N	35°00'E
Karaginskiy, Ostrov, i., Russia	218-19	58°50'N	164°00'E
Karaginskiy Zaliv, b., Russia	218-19	58°50'N	164°00'E
Karaj, Iran	232-33	35°50'N	50°59'E
Karakax, stm., China	226	38°03'N	80°32'E
Karakelong, Pulau, i., Indon.	248-49	4°16'N	126°49'E
Karakol, Kyrg.	226	42°29'N	78°23'E
Karakoram Range, mts., Asia (kä´rä kō´ròm rănj)	234-35	35°30'N	77°00'E
Karakorum, hist., Mong.	240-41	47°14'N	102°50'E
Karakorum Shan, mts., Asia see Karakoram Range	234-35	35°30'N	77°00'E
Kara Kum, des., Turkmen. (kärä-kōōm´)	226	39°0'N	60°00'E
Kara-Kum Canal, can., Turkmen. (kärä-kōōm´ kȧ´năl)	232-33	37°34'N	65°41'E
Karakumy, des., Turkmen. see Kara Kum	226	39°0'N	60°00'E
Karaman, Tur. (kä-rä-män´)	186-87	37°11'N	33°13'E
Karamay, China (kär-äm-ä)	226	45°36'N	84°51'E
Karamea Bight, b., N.Z. (kȧ-rȧ-mē´ȧ bīt)	278	41°30'S	171°40'E
Karasburg, Nmb.	264-65	28°01'S	18°45'E
Kara Sea, s., Russia (kärȧ sē)	218-19	76°0'N	80°00'E
Karasuk, Russia	226	53°43'N	78°03'E
Karatau Range, mts., Kaz.	226	43°36'N	68°52'E
Karatsu, Japan (kä´rȧ-tsōō)	245	33°26'N	129°59'E
Karawang, Indon.	248-49	6°18'S	107°18'E
Karbalā', Iraq	228-29	32°37'N	44°02'E
Karcag, Hung. (kär´tsäg)	194-95	47°19'N	20°56'E
Kardeljevo, Cro.	200-01	43°04'N	17°26'E
Kärdla, Est. (kĕrd´lȧ)	192-93	58°60'N	22°45'E
Kargasok, Russia	218-19	59°04'N	80°50'E
Kargopol', Russia (kär-gō-pōl´´)	186-87	61°30'N	38°58'E
Kariba, Zimb.	264-65	16°31'S	28°48'E
Kariba, Lake, res., Afr.	264-65	17°0'S	28°00'E
Karimata, Kepulauan, is., Indon. (kä-rê-mä´tȧ)	246-47	1°25'S	109°05'E
Karimata, Pulau, i., Indon.	246-47	1°36'S	108°55'E
Karimata, Selat, strt., Indon.	248-49	2°05'S	108°40'E
Karīmnagar, India	236	18°26'N	79°09'E
Karimunjawa, Kepulauan, is., Indon. (kä´rê-mōōn-yä´vä)	248-49	5°50'S	110°25'E
Karisimbi, Volcan, vol., Afr.	267	1°30'S	29°27'E
Karkar Island, i., Pap. N. Gui. (kär´kär ī´lȧnd)	277	4°40'S	146°00'E
Karkūk, Iraq see Kirkuk	228-29	35°28'N	44°24'E
Karleby, Fin. see Kokkola	184-85	63°50'N	23°09'E
Karl-Marx-Stadt, Ger. see Chemnitz	194-95	50°50'N	12°56'E
Karlovac, Cro. (kär´lô-vȧts)	200-01	45°29'N	15°33'E
Karlovo, Blg. (kär´lô-vō)	200-01	42°39'N	24°48'E
Karlovy Vary, Czech Rep. (kär´lô-vê vä´rê)	194-95	50°14'N	12°53'E
Karlshamn, Swe. (kärls´häm)	192-93	56°09'N	14°51'E
Karlskrona, Swe. (kärls´krô-nä)	192-93	56°10'N	15°36'E
Karlsruhe, Ger. (kärls´rōō-ĕ)	194-95	49°01'N	8°23'E
Karlstad, Swe. (kärl´städ)	192-93	59°23'N	13°31'E
Karmøy, i., Nor. (kärm-ûe)	192-93	59°15'N	5°15'E
Karnāl, India	234-35	29°41'N	76°59'E
Karnātaka, state, India	236	14°0'N	76°00'E
Karonga, Malawi (kȧ-rōŋ´gȧ)	264-65	9°55'S	33°56'E
Kárpathos, i., Grc.	188-89	35°41'N	27°09'E
Karpaty, mts., Eur. see Carpathian Mountains	186-87	48°0'N	24°00'E
Karpinsk, Russia (kär´pĭnsk)	186-87	59°46'N	60°00'E
Karpogory, Russia	186-87	64°00'N	44°23'E
Karratha, Austl.	270-71	20°43'S	116°48'E
Kars, Tur. (kärs)	227	40°36'N	43°05'E
Karshi, Uzb. (kär´shē) see Qarshi	232-33	38°52'N	65°48'E
Karskoye More, s., Russia see Kara Sea	218-19	76°0'N	80°00'E
Kartaly, Russia (kȧr´tä lȇ)	226	53°03'N	60°39'E
Karumba, Austl.	277	17°28'S	140°51'E
Karūr, India	236	10°57'N	78°05'E
Kārwār, India	236	14°48'N	74°08'E
Kasai, stm., Afr.	262-63	3°02'S	16°56'E
Kasama, Zam. (kȧ-sä´mȧ)	264-65	10°12'S	31°11'E
Kasar, Ras, c., Afr. see Kasr, Ra's	266	18°01'N	38°34'E
Kasba Lake, lk., Can.	130-31	60°18'N	102°07'W
Kasba-Tadla, Mor. (käs´bȧ-täd´lȧ)	269a	32°37'N	6°16'W
Kaschau, Slvk. see Košice	194-95	48°43'N	21°16'E
Kasenga, D.R.C. (kȧ-seŋ´gȧ)	262-63	10°22'S	28°37'E
Kasese, Ug.	267	0°10'N	30°05'E
Kāshān, Iran (kä-shän´)	232-33	33°59'N	51°26'E
Kashgar, China (käsh-gär) see Kashi	226	39°28'N	75°59'E
Kashi, China (kä-shr)	226	39°28'N	75°59'E
Kashihara, Japan (kä´shē-hä´rä)	245	34°30'N	135°48'E
Kashin, Russia (kä-shēn´)	202-03	57°22'N	37°37'E
Kashira, Russia (kä-shē´rȧ)	202-03	54°51'N	38°10'E
Kashiwazaki, Japan (kä´shē-wä-zä´kê)	245	37°22'N	138°33'E
Kāshmar, Iran	232-33	35°13'N	58°28'E
Kasia, India	234-35	26°45'N	83°55'E
Kasimov, Russia (kȧ-sē´môf)	186-87	54°56'N	41°23'E
Kaskaskia, stm., Il., U.S. (kăs-kăs´kĭ-ȧ)	120-21	37°58'N	89°57'W
Kaskattama, stm., Mb., Can. (kăs-kȧ-tä´mȧ)	134-35	57°03'N	90°05'W
Kasongo, D.R.C. (kä-sôŋ´gō)	262-63	4°27'S	26°40'E
Kasongo-Lunda, D.R.C.	262-63	6°29'S	16°50'E
Kaspīy Mangy oypaty, pl., see Caspian Depression	186-87	48°0'N	52°00'E
Kaspiysk, Russia	227	42°53'N	47°38'E
Kaspiyskiy, Russia	186-87	45°24'N	47°21'E
Kaspiyskoye More, lk., see Caspian Sea	226	41°18'N	50°59'E
Kasr, Ra's, c., Afr.	266	18°01'N	38°34'E
Kassa, Slvk. see Košice	194-95	48°43'N	21°16'E
Kassalā, Sudan	266	15°27'N	36°23'E
Kassel, Ger. (käs´ĕl)	194-95	51°19'N	9°29'E
Kasserine, Tun.	184-85	35°09'N	8°50'E
Kasson, Mn., U.S. (kăs´ŭn)	114-15	44°02'N	92°46'W
Kastamonu, Tur. (kä-stȧ-mō´nōō)	186-87	41°23'N	33°47'E
Kastellorizo, i., Grc. see Megísti	188-89	36°08'N	29°36'E
Kastoría, Grc. (kȧs-tō´rĭ-ȧ)	200-01	40°32'N	21°17'E
Kasulu, Tan.	267	4°34'S	30°06'E
Kasungu, Malawi	264-65	13°03'S	33°28'E
Kasūr, Pak.	232-33	31°07'N	74°27'E
Katahdin, Mount, mtn., Me., U.S. (mount kȧ-tä´dĭn)	117a	45°55'N	68°55'W
Katanda, D.R.C.	267	0°50'S	29°22'E
Katanga, hist. reg., D.R.C. (kȧ-täŋ´gȧ)	262-63	10°0'S	26°00'E
Katanga, stm., Russia	218-19	60°09'N	102°14'E
Katanning, Austl. (kȧ-tăn´ĭng)	270-71	33°42'S	117°33'E
Katchall Island, i., India	246-47	7°55'N	93°23'E
Katha, Mya.	238-39	24°10'N	96°20'E
Katherine, Austl. (kăth´ẽr-ĭn)	270-71	14°29'S	132°16'E
Kāthiāwār Peninsula, pen., India (kä´tyȧ-wär´ pĕ-nĭn´sūlȧ)	234-35	22°0'N	71°00'E
Kāṭhmāṇḍāū, nat. cap., Nepal see Kathmandu	234-35	27°42'N	85°19'E
Kathmandu, nat. cap., Nepal (kät-män-dōō´)	234-35	27°42'N	85°19'E
Katihār, India	234-35	25°33'N	87°34'E
Katima Mulilo, Nmb.	264-65	17°30'S	24°16'E
Ka Tiriti o te Moana, mts., N.Z. see Southern Alps	278	43°30'S	170°30'E
Katmai National Park and Preserve, n.p., Ak., U.S. (kăt´mī năsh´ŭn-ăl pärk ănd prĭ-zûrv´)	126	58°30'N	155°05'W
Kātmāndu, nat. cap., Nepal see Kathmandu	234-35	27°42'N	85°19'E
Katni, India see Murwāra	234-35	23°50'N	80°24'E
Katoomba, Austl.	276	33°43'S	150°18'E
Katowice, Pol.	194-95	50°16'N	19°01'E
Katrineholm, Swe. (kȧ-trē´nĕ-hōlm)	192-93	58°59'N	16°12'E
Katsina, Nig. (kät´sê-nȧ)	260-61	12°60'N	7°36'E
Kattaqo'rg'on, Uzb.	232-33	39°55'N	66°16'E
Kattegat, strt., Eur. (kăt´ĕ-găt)	192-93	57°0'N	11°00'E
Kattegatt, strt., Eur. see Kattegat	192-93	57°0'N	11°00'E
Kattowitz, Pol. see Katowice	194-95	50°16'N	19°01'E
Katun', stm., Russia (kȧ-tòn´)	226	52°26'N	85°00'E
Kaua'i, i., Hi., U.S.	127a	22°0'N	159°30'W
Kaufbeuren, Ger. (kouf´boi-rĕn)	194-95	47°53'N	10°37'E
Kaufman, Tx., U.S. (kôf´mȧn)	120-21	32°35'N	96°20'W
Kaukauna, Wi., U.S. (kô-kô´nȧ)	116-17	44°16'N	88°16'W
Kaukau Veld, plat., Afr.	264-65	19°30'S	20°30'E
Kaunakakai, Hi., U.S. (kä´ōō-nȧ-kä´kī)	127a	21°06'N	157°01'W
Kaunas, Lith. (kou´nȧs) (kôv´nô)	192-93	54°54'N	23°54'E
Kauriāla, stm., Asia see Ghāghara	234-35	25°45'N	84°48'E
Kau-ye Kyun, i., Mya.	246-47	10°60'N	98°31'E
Kavála, Grc. (kä-vä´lä)	200-01	40°57'N	24°24'E
Kavalerovo, Russia	244	44°16'N	135°03'E
Kavaratti Island, i., India	236	10°34'N	72°38'E
Kavieng, Pap. N. Gui. (kä-vê-ĕng´)	277	2°34'S	150°48'E
Kavīr, Dasht-e, des., Iran (dŭsht-ê-ka-vēr´)	232-33	34°40'N	54°30'E
Kavkasioni, mts., see Caucasus Mountains	227	42°38'N	45°00'E
Kawaguchi, Japan (kä-wä-gōō-chē)	245	35°48'N	139°43'E
Kawambwa, Zam.	264-65	9°48'S	29°05'E
Kawasaki, Japan (kä-wä-sä´kê)	245	35°32'N	139°42'E
Kaxgar, stm., China	226	39°25'N	76°26'E
Kayak Island, i., Ak., U.S.	126	59°54'N	144°27'W
Kayan, stm., Indon.	248-49	2°55'N	117°35'E
Kaycee, Wy., U.S. (kā-sē´)	112-13	43°43'N	106°40'W
Kayes, Mali (kāz)	258-59	14°27'N	11°26'W
Kayoa, Pulau, i., Indon.	248-49	0°04'S	127°24'E
Kayseri, Tur. (kī´sĕ-rē)	186-87	38°44'N	35°29'E
Kayuagung, Indon.	246-47	3°23'S	104°50'E
Kazakh Hills, hills, Kaz. (kä-zäk´ hĭlz)	226	49°0'N	72°00'E
Kazakhstan, nation, Asia (kä-zäk-stän´)	206-07	47°0'N	76°00'E
Kazan', Russia (kȧ-zän´)	186-87	55°51'N	49°04'E
Kazan, stm., Can.	130-31	64°10'N	95°22'W
Kazanka, Ukr. (kȧ-zän´kȧ)	202-03	47°50'N	32°50'E
Kazanlŭk, Blg. (kȧ´zȧn-lĕk)	200-01	42°37'N	25°24'E
Kazan-rettō, is., Japan	280-81	25°0'N	141°00'E
Kazbek, Gora, vol., (gȧ-rä´ kȧz-bĕk´)	227	42°42'N	44°31'E
Kāzerūn, Iran	230-31	29°37'N	51°39'E
Kazincbarcika, Hung. (kô´zĭnts-bôr-tsĭ-ko)	194-95	48°15'N	20°39'E
Kazvin, Iran see Qazvīn	232-33	36°16'N	49°58'E
Kazym, stm., Russia (kä-zēm´)	218-19	63°53'N	65°53'E

n-sing; ŋ-baŋk; ɴ-nasalized n; nŏd; cȯmmit; ōld; ôbey; ôrder; oi-boil; fōōd; ò-as oo in foot; ou-out; s-soft; sh-dish; th-thin; pūre; ûnite; ûrn; stŭd; circŭs; ü-as in French tu; ´-indeterminate vowel.

Feature (Pronunciation)	Page	Lat.	Long.
Kearney, Ne., U.S. (kär'nĭ)	114-15	40°42'N	99°05'W
Keban Barajı, res., Tur.	186-87	38°56'N	38°55'E
Kebnekaise, mtn., Swe. (kĕp'nĕ-kä-ēs'ĕ)	184-85	67°55'N	18°35'E
K'ebrī Dehar, Eth.	262-63	6°45'N	44°17'E
Kech, stm., Pak.	232-33	25°59'N	62°44'E
Kecskemét, Hung. (kĕch'kĕ-māt)	194-95	46°54'N	19°42'E
Kėdainiai, Lith. (kē-dī'nĭ-ī)	192-93	55°18'N	23°59'E
Kedgwick, N.B., Can. (kĕdj'wĭk)	138-39	47°38'N	67°23'W
Kediri, Indon.	248-49	7°49'S	112°01'E
Kédougou, Sen.	260-61	12°33'N	12°11'W
Keele Peak, mtn., Yk., Can.	130-31	63°26'N	130°19'W
Keeling Islands, dep., Oc. (kē'lĭng ī'lăndz) see Cocos Islands	224-25	12°10'S	96°55'E
Keelung, Tai. see Chilung	225a	25°08'N	121°44'E
Keene, N.H., U.S.	116-17	42°56'N	72°17'W
Keer-Weer, Cape, c., Austl.	277	13°51'S	141°29'E
Keetmanshoop, Nmb. (kāt'māns-hōp)	264-65	26°35'S	18°09'E
Keewatin, Mn., U.S. (kē-wä'tĭn)	114-15	47°24'N	93°04'W
Keflavík, Ice.	190a	64°01'N	22°35'W
Ke-hsi Mānsām, Mya.	246-47	21°56'N	97°51'E
Keijō, nat. cap., Kor., S. see Seoul	243	37°33'N	127°01'E
Keila, Est. (kā'lȧ)	192-93	59°18'N	24°26'E
Kelang, Pulau, i., Indon.	248-49	3°12'S	127°44'E
Kellogg, Id., U.S. (kĕl'ŏg)	112-13	47°32'N	116°08'W
Kelmė, Lith. (kĕl-må)	192-93	55°38'N	22°55'E
Kélo, Chad	262-63	9°19'N	15°49'E
Kelowna, B.C., Can.	132-33	49°53'N	119°29'W
Keluang, Malay.	246-47	2°02'N	103°20'E
Kem', Russia (kĕm)	186-87	64°57'N	34°36'E
Kemano, B.C., Can.	132-33	53°32'N	127°57'W
Kemerovo, Russia	218-19	55°23'N	86°03'E
Kemi, Fin. (kā'mē)	184-85	65°46'N	24°34'E
Kemijärvi, Fin. (kā'mē-yĕr-vē)	184-85	66°43'N	27°24'E
Kemijoki, stm., Fin. (kā'mē-yô'kē)	184-85	65°47'N	24°30'E
Kemmerer, Wy., U.S. (kĕm'ẽr-ẽr)	112-13	41°48'N	110°33'W
Kemper, Fr. see Quimper	196-97	47°60'N	4°06'W
Kempsey, Austl. (kĕmp'sē)	276	31°06'S	152°50'E
Kempt, Lac, lk., Qc., Can. (läk kĕmpt)	136-37	47°25'N	74°15'W
Kemul, Kong, mtn., Indon.	248-49	1°52'N	116°13'E
Kenadsa, Alg.	188-89	31°33'N	2°25'W
Kenai, Ak., U.S. (kĕ-nī')	126	60°34'N	151°13'W
Kenai Fjords National Park, n.p., Ak., U.S. (kĕ-nī' fē-ôrdz' năsh'ŭn-ăl pärk)	126	59°50'N	150°09'W
Kenai Peninsula, pen., Ak., U.S. (kĕ-nī' pĕ-nĭn'sūlă)	126	60°10'N	150°00'W
Kendal, Eng., U.K. (kĕn'dăl)	190-91	54°20'N	2°44'W
Kendall, Cape, c., Nu., Can.	130-31	63°36'N	87°09'W
Kendallville, In., U.S. (kĕn'dăl-vĭl)	116-17	41°26'N	85°15'W
Kendari, Indon.	248-49	3°57'S	122°36'E
Kenedy, Tx., U.S. (kĕn'ĕ-dĭ)	122-23	28°49'N	97°50'W
Kenema, S.L.	260-61	7°52'N	11°11'W
Kenge, D.R.C.	262-63	4°52'S	16°56'E
Kēng Tung, Mya.	246-47	21°17'N	99°36'E
Kenhardt, S. Afr.	264-65	29°20'S	21°09'E
Kénitra, Mor. (kĕ-nē'trȧ)	269a	34°16'N	6°35'W
Kenmare, N.D., U.S. (kĕn-mâr')	114-15	48°42'N	102°05'W
Kennebec, stm., Me., U.S. (kĕn-ē-bĕk')	117a	43°45'N	69°46'W
Kennebunk, Me., U.S. (kĕn-ē-buŋk')	116-17	43°23'N	70°33'W
Kennedy, Cape, c., Fl., U.S. see Canaveral, Cape	125a	28°27'N	80°32'W
Kenner, La., U.S. (kĕn'ẽr)	124-25	29°59'N	90°15'W
Kennett, Mo., U.S. (kĕn'ĕt)	124-25	36°14'N	90°02'W
Kennewick, Wa., U.S. (kĕn'ē-wĭk)	112-13	46°12'N	119°08'W
Kenney Dam, d., B.C., Can.	132-33	53°37'N	124°58'W
Kenora, On., Can. (kē-nō'rȧ)	134-35	49°46'N	94°29'W
Kenosha, Wi., U.S. (kĕ-nō'shȧ)	116-17	42°34'N	87°50'W
Kenova, W.V., U.S. (kē-nō'vȧ)	116-17	38°24'N	82°35'W
Kent, Oh., U.S. (kĕnt)	116-17	41°09'N	81°21'W
Kent, Wa., U.S. (kĕnt)	112-13	47°23'N	122°12'W
Kentaū, Kaz.	226	43°31'N	68°31'E
Kentland, In., U.S. (kĕnt'lănd)	116-17	40°46'N	87°27'W
Kenton, Oh., U.S. (kĕn'tŭn)	116-17	40°39'N	83°36'W
Kent Peninsula, pen., Nu., Can. (kĕnt pĕ-nĭn'sūlă)	130-31	68°30'N	107°00'W
Kentucky, state, U.S. (kĕn-tŭk'ĭ)	108-09	37°30'N	85°15'W
Kentucky, stm., Ky., U.S. (kĕn-tŭk'ĭ)	116-17	38°41'N	85°11'W
Kentucky Lake, res., U.S. (kĕn-tŭk'ĭ lāk)	124-25	36°41'N	88°04'W
Kentville, N.S., Can.	138-39	45°05'N	64°29'W
Kentwood, La., U.S. (kĕnt'wo͝od)	124-25	30°56'N	90°31'W
Kentwood, Mi., U.S. (kĕnt'wo͝od)	116-17	42°55'N	85°35'W
Kenya, nation, Afr. (kēn'yȧ)	253	1°0'N	38°00'E
Kenya, Mount, mtn., Kenya (mount kēn'yȧ)	267	0°09'S	37°19'E
Kenyon, Mn., U.S. (kĕn'yŭn)	114-15	44°17'N	93°00'W
Keokuk, Ia., U.S. (kē'ō-kŭk)	120-21	40°24'N	91°23'W
Kępno, Pol. (kăŋ'pnō)	194-95	51°17'N	18°00'E
Kerala, state, India	236	10°0'N	76°30'E
Keramian, Pulau, i., Indon.	248-49	5°05'S	114°36'E
Kerang, Austl. (kē-răng')	276	35°44'S	143°55'E
Kerbela, Iraq see Karbalā'	228-29	32°37'N	44°02'E
Kerch, Ukr.	202-03	45°21'N	36°28'E
Kerchens'ka protoka, strt., Eur. see Kerch Strait	202-03	45°23'N	36°41'E
Kerchenskiy Proliv, strt., Eur. (kĕr-chĕn'skĭ prô'lĭf) see Kerch Strait	202-03	45°23'N	36°41'E
Kerch Strait, strt., Eur.	202-03	45°23'N	36°41'E
Keren, Erit.	266	15°46'N	38°27'E
Kerguelen, Îles, i., Afr.	286	49°20'S	69°16'E
Kerguélen, Îles, is., Afr. (ēl-kĕr'gȧ-lĕn)	286	49°15'S	69°10'E
Kericho, Kenya	267	0°22'S	35°16'E
Kerinci, Gunung, vol., Indon.	246-47	1°42'S	101°16'E
Keriya, stm., China (kē'rē-yä)	234-35	35°17'N	81°34'E
Kerkenna, Îles, is., Tun. (ēl-dĕ-kĕr'kĕn-nä)	258-59	34°44'N	11°12'E
Kerki, Turkmen. (kĕr'kē) see Atamyrat	232-33	37°50'N	65°13'E
Kérkyra, Grc.	200-01	39°37'N	19°55'E
Kérkyra, i., Grc.	200-01	39°40'N	19°45'E
Kermadec Islands, is., N.Z. (kẽr-măd'ĕk ī'lăndz)	280-81	30°10'S	178°15'W
Kermān, Iran (kĕr-män')	230-31	30°17'N	57°04'E
Kermānshāh, Iran	228-29	34°18'N	47°04'E
Kerme, Gulf of, b., Tur. see Gökova Körfezi	200-01	36°54'N	27°51'E
Kerrobert, Sk., Can.	134-35	51°55'N	109°08'W
Kerrville, Tx., U.S. (kûr'vĭl)	122-23	30°03'N	99°08'W
Kerulen, stm., Asia (kĕr'o͞o-lĕn)	240-41	48°44'N	117°03'E
Keşan, Tur. (kĕ'shȧn)	200-01	40°52'N	26°39'E
Kesennuma, Japan	244	38°54'N	141°35'E
Keshan, China (kū-shän)	240-41	48°01'N	125°52'E
Keshod, India	234-35	21°18'N	70°14'E
Kestell, S. Afr. (kĕs'tĕl)	269c	28°18'S	28°38'E
Keszthely, Hung. (kĕst'hĕl-lĭ)	194-95	46°46'N	17°15'E
Ket', stm., Russia (kyĕt)	218-19	58°55'N	81°32'E
Keta, Ozero, lk., Russia	218-19	68°44'N	90°00'E
Ketapang, Indon. (kĕ-tȧ-päng')	248-49	1°52'S	109°58'E
Ketchikan, Ak., U.S. (kĕch-ĭ-kăn')	126	55°20'N	131°35'W
Ketchum, Id., U.S.	112-13	43°41'N	114°23'W
Ketoy, Ostrov, i., Russia	218-19	47°20'N	152°28'E
Kettering, Eng., U.K. (kĕt'ẽr-ĭng)	190-91	52°24'N	0°45'W
Kettering, Oh., U.S. (kĕt'ẽr-ĭng)	116-17	39°42'N	84°10'W
Kewanee, Il., U.S. (kē-wä'nē)	116-17	41°14'N	89°55'W
Kewaunee, Wi., U.S. (kē-wô'nē)	116-17	44°27'N	87°30'W
Keweenaw Peninsula, pen., Mi., U.S. (kē'wē-nô pĕ-nĭn'sūlă)	114-15	47°12'N	88°25'W
Keweenaw Point, c., Mi., U.S.	114-15	47°27'N	87°50'W
Key Largo, i., Fl., U.S.	125a	25°11'N	80°22'W
Keyser, W.V., U.S. (kī'sẽr)	116-17	39°26'N	78°59'W
Key West, Fl., U.S. (kē wĕst')	125a	24°33'N	81°47'W
Kgalagadi Transfrontier Park, n.p., Afr.	264-65	25°23'S	20°44'E
Khabarovsk, Russia (ĸä-bä'rôfsk)	240-41	48°26'N	135°08'E
Khairpur, Pak.	232-33	27°32'N	68°45'E
Khajurāho, India	234-35	24°50'N	79°58'E
Khakhea, Bots.	264-65	24°45'S	23°31'E
Khal'mer-Yu, Russia (kŭl-myĕr'-yo͞o')	186-87	67°57'N	64°45'E
Khambhāt, India	234-35	22°19'N	72°37'E
Khambhāt, Gulf of, b., India	234-35	20°57'N	72°26'E
Khamīs Mushayṭ, Sau. Ar.	266	18°18'N	42°44'E
Khammam, India	236	17°15'N	80°09'E
Khānābād, Afg.	232-33	36°41'N	69°07'E
Khandwa, India	234-35	21°49'N	76°21'E
Khandyga, Russia	218-19	62°40'N	135°32'E
Khānewāl, Pak.	232-33	30°18'N	71°56'E
Khanka, Lake, lk., Asia (läk ĸän'kȧ)	244	45°11'N	132°25'E
Khanka, Ozero, lk., Asia see Khanka, Lake	244	45°11'N	132°25'E
Khānpur, Pak.	232-33	28°38'N	70°40'E
Khantayskoye Vodokhranilishche, res., Russia	218-19	68°0'N	88°00'E
Khanty-Mansiysk, Russia (ĸŭn-te'mŭn-sĕsk')	218-19	60°59'N	69°01'E
Khao Laem Reservoir, res., Thai.	246-47	14°55'N	98°33'E
Khapcheranga, Russia	240-41	49°42'N	112°23'E
Kharagpur, India (kŭ-rŭg'po͝or)	234-35	22°20'N	87°20'E
Kharg Island, i., Iran see Khārk, Jazīreh-ye	230-31	29°15'N	50°19'E
Khargon, India	234-35	21°50'N	75°36'E
Khārk, Jazīreh-ye, i., Iran	230-31	29°15'N	50°19'E
Kharkiv, Ukr.	202-03	49°60'N	36°14'E
Kharkov, Ukr. see Kharkiv	202-03	49°60'N	36°14'E
Kharmanli, Blg. (ĸȧr-män'lē)	200-01	41°56'N	25°55'E
Khartoum, nat. cap., Sudan (kär-to͞om')	266	15°35'N	32°32'E
Khasavyurt, Russia	227	43°15'N	46°35'E
Khāsh, stm., Afg.	232-33	30°48'N	61°46'E
Khashm al-Qirbah, Sudan	266	14°58'N	35°55'E
Khaskovo, Blg. (ĸäs'kō-vō)	200-01	41°56'N	25°34'E
Khatanga, Russia (ĸȧ-tän'gȧ)	218-19	71°58'N	102°30'E
Khatangskiy Zaliv, b., Russia (kä-täŋ'g-skē zä'lĭf)	208-09	73°35'N	109°45'E
Khatt, Oued al, stm., W. Sah.	258-59	26°55'N	13°03'W
Khaybar, Kowtal-e, p., Asia see Khyber Pass	232-33	34°06'N	71°07'E
Khazar, Daryā-ye, lk., see Caspian Sea	226	41°18'N	50°59'E
Khemis Miliana, Alg.	269b	36°16'N	2°13'E
Khersān, stm., Iran	232-33	31°34'N	50°22'E
Kherson, Ukr. (ĸĕr-sôn')	202-03	46°38'N	32°35'E
Kherson, co., Ukr. (ĸĕr-sôn')	202-03	46°45'N	33°30'E
Kheta, stm., Russia	218-19	71°55'N	102°06'E
Khilok, Russia	240-41	51°21'N	110°27'E
Khilok, stm., Russia	240-41	51°19'N	106°59'E
Khimki, Russia (ĸēm'kĭ)	202-03	55°54'N	37°26'E
Khiwa, Uzb.	232-33	41°24'N	60°22'E
Khmel'nyts'kyi, Ukr.	194-95	49°26'N	27°01'E
Khodzheyli, Uzb. see Khŭjayli	226	42°48'N	59°25'E
Kholm, Afg.	232-33	36°41'N	67°42'E
Kholm, Russia (kôlm)	192-93	57°09'N	31°11'E
Kholmsk, Russia (kŭlmsk)	244	47°03'N	142°03'E
Khomeynīshahr, Iran	232-33	32°41'N	51°32'E
Khong, stm., Asia see Mekong	246-47	10°33'N	105°27'E
Khong, stm., Asia see Salween	208-09	16°33'N	97°40'E
Salween, stm., Asia	208-09	16°33'N	97°40'E
Khon Kaen, Thai.	246-47	16°27'N	102°50'E
Khoper, stm., Russia (ĸō'pẽr)	186-87	49°37'N	42°19'E
Khor, stm., Russia (ĸôr')	240-41	47°49'N	134°41'E
Khorixas, Nmb.	264-65	20°21'S	14°59'E
Khorol, Ukr. (ĸō'rôl)	202-03	49°47'N	33°17'E
Khorol, stm., Ukr. (ĸō'rôl)	202-03	49°28'N	33°47'E
Khorramābād, Iran	228-29	33°29'N	48°21'E
Khorramshahr, Iran (kō-ram'shär)	228-29	30°25'N	48°11'E
Khorugh, Taj.	232-33	37°29'N	71°33'E
Khouribga, Mor.	269a	32°53'N	6°55'W
Khromtaū, Kaz.	226	50°15'N	58°27'E
Khudzhand, Taj. see Khujand	232-33	40°17'N	69°39'E
Khujand, Taj.	232-33	40°17'N	69°39'E
Khŭjayli, Uzb.	226	42°48'N	59°25'E
Khulna, Bngl.	234-35	22°49'N	89°34'E
Khunjerab Pass, p., Asia	232-33	36°52'N	75°28'E
Khust, Ukr. (ĸōst)	194-95	48°11'N	23°18'E
Khuzdār, Pak.	232-33	27°48'N	66°37'E
Khvalynsk, Russia (ĸvȧ-lĭnsk')	186-87	52°29'N	48°05'E
Khvoy, Iran	227	38°33'N	44°58'E
Khyber Pass, p., Asia (kī'bẽr păs)	232-33	34°06'N	71°07'E
Kiamba, Phil.	250	5°60'N	124°37'E
Kiambi, D.R.C. (kyäm'bē)	267	7°19'S	28°01'E
Kiamichi, stm., Ok., U.S. (kyȧ-mē'chē)	120-21	33°57'N	95°14'W
Kiamusze, China see Jiamusi	244	46°48'N	130°22'E
Kiangarow, Mount, mtn., Austl.	276	26°50'S	151°32'E
Kiangsi, state, China see Jiangxi	238-39	28°0'N	116°00'E
Kiangsu, state, China see Jiangsu	238-39	33°0'N	120°00'E
Kiantajärvi, lk., Fin. (kyȧn'tȧ-yĕr-vē)	186-87	65°03'N	29°07'E
Kibombo, D.R.C.	262-63	3°54'S	25°55'E
Kibre Mengist, Eth.	262-63	5°52'N	39°00'E
Kıbrıs, nation, Asia see Cyprus	228-29	35°0'N	33°00'E
Kičevo, Mac. (kē'chĕ-vō)	200-01	41°32'N	20°57'E
Kıcık Qafqaz daqları, mts., Asia see Lesser Caucasus	227	40°60'N	44°35'E
Kicking Horse Pass, p., Can.	132-33	51°27'N	116°20'W
Kidal, Mali (kē-dȧl')	258-59	18°26'N	1°24'E
Kiel, Ger. (kēl)	194-95	54°19'N	10°07'E
Kiel Canal, can., Ger. (kēl kä-näl')	194-95	53°54'N	9°10'E
Kielce, Pol. (kyĕl'tsĕ)	194-95	50°53'N	20°38'E
Kiev, nat. cap., Ukr. (kē'ĕf) (kē'ĕv)	202-03	50°26'N	30°30'E
Kiev Reservoir, res., Ukr. (kē'ĕf rĕ'sẽr-vwär) (kē'ĕv rĕ'sẽr-vwär) see Kyïvs'ke vodoskhovyshche	202-03	50°51'N	30°32'E
Kiffa, Maur. (kēf'ȧ)	258-59	16°37'N	11°24'W
Kigali, nat. cap., Rw. (kē-gä'lē)	267	1°56'S	30°04'E
Kigoma, Tan. (kē-gō'mä)	267	4°53'S	29°37'E
Kiirun, Tai. see Chilung	225a	25°08'N	121°44'E
Kii-suidō, strt., Japan (kē so͞o-ē'dō)	245	33°55'N	134°55'E
Kikládes, is., Grc. see Cyclades	200-01	37°30'N	25°00'E
Kikori, stm., Pap. N. Gui.	277	7°22'S	144°14'E
Kikwit, D.R.C. (kē'kwēt)	262-63	5°02'S	18°49'E

ăt; fināl; rāte; senāte; ärm; ȧsk; sofȧ; fâre; ch-choose; dh-as th in other; bē; ēvent; bĕt; recĕnt; cratẽr; g-gō; gh-guttural g; bĭt; ĭ-short neutral; rīde; ĸ-guttural k as ch in German ich;

Feature (Pronunciation)	Page	Lat.	Long.
Kil, Swe. (kēl)	192-93	59°31'N	13°19'E
Kīlauea, Hi., U.S. (kē-lä-ōō-ā'ä)	127a	22°13'N	159°25'W
Kili, i., Marsh. Is.	280-81	5°39'N	169°07'E
Kilimanjaro, mtn., Tan. (kyl-ė-măn-jä'rō)	267	3°04'S	37°22'E
Kilimatinde, Tan. (kĭl-ė-mä-tĭn'då)	267	5°52'S	34°58'E
Kilingi-Nõmme, Est. (kē'lĭn-gė-nôm'mĕ)	192-93	58°09'N	24°58'E
Kilis, Tur. (kē'lēs)	228-29	36°43'N	37°07'E
Kilkenny, Ire. (kĭl-kĕn-ĭ)	190-91	52°39'N	7°15'W
Kilkís, Grc. (kĭl'kĭs)	200-01	40°59'N	22°53'E
Killala, Ire. (kĭ-lä'lȧ)	190-91	54°13'N	9°13'W
Killarney, Mb., Can.	134-35	49°12'N	99°42'W
Killeen, Tx., U.S.	122-23	31°06'N	97°42'W
Kilmarnock, Scot., U.K. (kĭl-mär'nŭk)	190-91	55°36'N	4°30'W
Kilombero, stm., Tan.	262-63	8°31'S	37°22'E
Kilosa, Tan.	267	6°50'S	36°59'E
Kilrush, Ire. (kĭl'rŭsh)	190-91	52°39'N	9°29'W
Kilttān Island, i., India	236	11°29'N	73°00'E
Kimamba, Tan.	267	6°46'S	37°08'E
Kimba, Austl. (kĭm'bȧ)	276	33°07'S	136°26'E
Kimball, Ne., U.S. (kĭm-băl)	114-15	41°14'N	103°40'W
Kimball, S.D., U.S. (kĭm-băl)	114-15	43°45'N	98°57'W
Kimberley, B.C., Can. (kĭm'bẽr-lĭ)	132-33	49°41'N	115°59'W
Kimberley, S. Afr. (kĭm'bẽr-lĭ)	264-65	28°44'S	24°45'E
Kimberley, plat., Austl.	272-73	17°0'S	127°00'E
Kimberley, reg., Austl.	272-73	16°0'S	127°00'E
Kimch'aek, Kor., N.	243	40°41'N	129°12'E
Kimch'ŏn, Kor., S.	243	36°07'N	128°07'E
Kimmirut, Nu., Can.	128-29	62°51'N	69°53'W
Kimovsk, Russia	202-03	53°58'N	38°32'E
Kimry, Russia (kĭm'rė)	202-03	56°52'N	37°22'E
Kinabalu, Gunong, mtn., Malay.	248-49	6°05'N	116°33'E
Kincardine, On., Can. (kĭn-kär'dĭn)	136-37	44°10'N	81°38'W
Kincolith, B.C., Can.	132-33	55°00'N	129°57'W
Kinder, La., U.S. (kĭn'dẽr)	122-23	30°29'N	92°51'W
Kindersley, Sk., Can. (kĭn'dẽrz-lė)	134-35	51°29'N	109°10'W
Kindia, Gui. (kĭn'dė-ȧ)	260-61	10°04'N	12°51'W
Kindu, D.R.C.	262-63	2°57'S	25°55'E
Kinel', Russia	186-87	53°14'N	50°38'E
Kineshma, Russia (kė-nĕsh'mȧ)	186-87	57°27'N	42°08'E
Kingaroy, Austl. (kĭŋ'gă-roi)	276	26°33'S	151°51'E
King City, Ca., U.S. (kĭng sĭ'tĭ)	118-19	36°12'N	121°08'W
Kingfisher, Ok., U.S. (kĭng'fĭsh-ẽr)	120-21	35°52'N	97°56'W
Kingisepp, Russia (kĭŋ-gė-sep')	192-93	59°22'N	28°37'E
King Island, i., Austl. (kĭng ī'lănd)	276	39°50'S	144°00'E
King Island, i., B.C., Can.	132-33	52°12'N	127°42'W
Kingman, Az., U.S. (kĭng'măn)	118-19	35°12'N	114°02'W
Kingman, Ks., U.S. (kĭng'măn)	120-21	37°39'N	98°07'W
Kings Canyon National Park, n.p., Ca., U.S. (kĭngz kăn'yŭn năsh'ŭn-ăl pärk)	118-19	36°56'N	118°35'W
Kingscote, Austl. (kĭngz'kŭt)	276	35°39'S	137°37'E
King's Lynn, Eng., U.K. (kĭngz lĭn')	190-91	52°46'N	0°24'E
Kings Mountain, N.C., U.S. (kĭngz moun'tĭn)	124-25	35°15'N	81°20'W
Kings Peak, mtn., Ut., U.S. (kĭngz pēk)	112-13	40°46'N	110°22'W
Kingsport, Tn., U.S. (kĭngz'pōrt)	124-25	36°33'N	82°34'W
Kingston, On., Can. (kĭngz'tŭn)	136-37	44°14'N	76°30'W
Kingston, N.Y., U.S.	116-17	41°56'N	74°00'W
Kingston, Pa., U.S. (kĭngz'tŭn)	116-17	41°15'N	75°54'W
Kingston, nat. cap., Jam. (kĭngz'tŭn)	142-43	18°00'N	76°48'W
Kingston Southeast, Austl.	276	36°50'S	139°51'E
Kingston upon Hull, Eng., U.K.	190-91	53°45'N	0°20'W
Kingstown, Ire. *see* Dún Laoghaire	190-91	53°17'N	6°08'W
Kingstown, nat. cap., St. Vin. (kĭngz'toun)	143b	13°09'N	61°14'W
Kingstree, S.C., U.S. (kĭngz'trē)	124-25	33°40'N	79°50'W
Kingsville, Tx., U.S. (kĭngz'vĭl)	122-23	27°31'N	97°51'W
King William Island, i., Nu., Can. (kĭng wĭl'yăm ī'lănd)	130-31	69°0'N	97°30'W
King William's Town, S. Afr. (kĭng-wĭl'-yŭmz-toun)	264-65	32°51'S	27°22'E
Kinkala, Congo	262-63	4°22'S	14°46'E
Kinkony, Farihy, lk., Madag.	264-65	16°08'S	45°50'E
Kinnaird Head, c., Scot., U.K. (kĭn-ård'hĕd)	190-91	57°42'N	2°01'W
Kinneret, Yam, lk., Isr. *see* Galilee, Sea of	228-29	32°48'N	35°35'E
Kinngait, Nu., Can. *see* Cape Dorset	128-29	64°14'N	76°33'W
Kinsale, Old Head of, c., Ire. (ōld hĕd ŏv kĭn-sāl)	190-91	51°37'N	8°32'W
Kinshasa, nat. cap., D.R.C. (kĭn-shä'sä)	262-63	4°21'S	15°18'E
Kinsley, Ks., U.S. (kĭnz'lĭ)	120-21	37°56'N	99°24'W
Kinston, N.C., U.S. (kĭnz'tŭn)	124-25	35°16'N	77°35'W
Kinyeti, mtn., Sudan	267	3°57'N	32°54'E
Kipawa, Lac, res., Qc., Can.	136-37	46°54'N	78°59'W
Kipengere Range, mts., Tan.	264-65	9°23'S	34°26'E
Kípros, nation, Asia *see* Cyprus	228-29	35°0'N	33°00'E
Kirby, Tx., U.S. (kŭr'bĭ)	122-23	29°29'N	98°22'W
Kirbyville, Tx., U.S. (kŭr'bĭ-vĭl)	122-23	30°40'N	93°54'W
Kirenga, stm., Russia (kė-rĕŋ'gȧ)	218-19	57°46'N	108°06'E
Kirensk, Russia (kē-rĕnsk')	218-19	57°48'N	108°10'E
Kirghizia, nation, Asia *see* Kyrgyzstan	226	41°30'N	75°00'E
Kirgiziya, nation, Asia *see* Kyrgyzstan	226	41°30'N	75°00'E
Kirgiz Range, mts., Asia	226	42°29'N	73°50'E
Kiribati, nation, Oc. (kē-rä-bäs)	280-81	5°0'S	170°00'W
Kiribati, is., Kir. (kē-rä-bäs)	280-81	0°30'S	174°00'E
Kırıkkale, Tur.	186-87	39°51'N	33°31'E
Kirin, state, China *see* Jilin	240-41	44°0'N	126°00'E
Kirinyaga, mtn., Kenya *see* Kenya, Mount	267	0°09'S	37°19'E
Kiritimati, at., Kir.	280-81	1°48'N	157°19'W
Kiriwina Islands, is., Pap. N. Gui.	277	8°35'S	151°05'E
Kirkcaldy, Scot., U.K. (kẽr-kô'dĭ)	190-91	56°07'N	3°10'W
Kirkenes, Nor.	184-85	69°43'N	30°02'E
Kirkland, Wa., U.S. (kûrk'lănd)	112-13	47°40'N	122°12'W
Kirkland Lake, On., Can.	136-37	48°10'N	80°01'W
Kırklareli, Tur. (kẽrk'lȧr-ĕ'lė)	200-01	41°45'N	27°14'E
Kirksville, Mo., U.S. (kûrks'vĭl)	120-21	40°12'N	92°34'W
Kirkuk, Iraq	228-29	35°28'N	44°24'E
Kirkwall, Scot., U.K. (kûrk'wôl)	190c	58°59'N	2°58'W
Kirov, Russia	202-03	54°04'N	34°19'E
Kirov, Russia	186-87	58°36'N	49°40'E
Kirov Bay, b., Azer. (kē'rŭf bä) *see* Qızılağaç körfäzi	227	39°05'N	49°01'E
Kirovohrad, Ukr.	202-03	48°31'N	32°16'E
Kirovsk, Russia (kė-rôfsk')	184-85	67°37'N	33°40'E
Kirs, Russia	186-87	59°21'N	52°15'E
Kirsanov, Russia (kẽr-sá'nôf)	186-87	52°39'N	42°45'E
Kırşehir, Tur. (kẽr-shĕ'hẽr)	186-87	39°09'N	34°10'E
Kīrthar Range, mts., Pak. (kĭr-tŭr rŭnj)	232-33	27°0'N	67°10'E
Kiruna, Swe. (kē-rōō'nä)	184-85	67°51'N	20°16'E
Kirzhach, Russia (kẽr-zhák')	202-03	56°09'N	38°52'E
Kisaki, Tan. (kē-sá'kē)	267	7°27'S	37°37'E
Kisangani, D.R.C.	262-63	0°32'N	25°12'E
Kisar, Pulau, i., Indon.	248-49	8°05'S	127°10'E
Kīsh, Jazīreh-ye, i., Iran	230-31	26°32'N	53°56'E
Kishinev, nat. cap., Mol. *see* Chişinău	202-03	47°02'N	28°50'E
Kisii, Kenya	267	0°40'S	34°46'E
Kiska Island, i., Ak., U.S. (kĭs'kä ī'lănd)	126a	51°60'N	177°31'E
Kiskitto Lake, lk., Mb., Can. (kĭs-kĭ'tō lăk)	134-35	54°16'N	98°34'W
Kiskunfélegyháza, Hung. (kĭsh'kŏn-fā'lĕd-y'hä'zô)	194-95	46°43'N	19°50'E
Kiskunhalas, Hung. (kĭsh'kŏn-hô'lôsh)	194-95	46°25'N	19°30'E
Kislovodsk, Russia	227	43°55'N	42°44'E
Kismaayo, Som. *see* Chisimayu	262-63	0°22'S	42°32'E
Kiso, stm., Japan (kē'sō)	245	35°04'N	136°44'E
Kissidougou, Gui. (kē'sē-dōō'gōō)	260-61	9°11'N	10°06'W
Kissimmee, Fl., U.S. (kĭ-sĭm'ė)	125a	28°18'N	81°24'W
Kissimmee, stm., Fl., U.S. (kĭ-sĭm'ė)	125a	27°08'N	80°52'W
Kisumu, Kenya (kē'sōō-mōō)	267	0°05'S	34°46'E
Kita, Mali (kē'tȧ)	258-59	13°02'N	9°30'W
Kita-Daitō-jima, i., Japan	222-23	25°57'N	131°18'E
Kita-Iō-jima, i., Japan	280-81	25°26'N	141°17'E
Kitakyūshū, Japan	245	33°54'N	130°51'E
Kitale, Kenya	267	1°01'N	34°60'E
Kitami, Japan	244	43°48'N	143°54'E
Kitchener, On., Can. (kĭch'ĕ-nẽr)	136-37	43°27'N	80°29'W
Kitega, Bdi. *see* Gitega	267	3°21'S	29°54'E
Kitgum, Ug. (kĭt'gŏm)	267	3°17'N	32°52'E
Kitimat, B.C., Can. (kĭ'tĭ-măt)	132-33	54°01'N	128°42'W
Kitimat Ranges, mts., B.C., Can. (kĭ'tĭ-măt rānjĕz)	132-33	53°30'N	128°50'W
Kittanning, Pa., U.S. (kĭ-tăn'ĭng)	116-17	40°49'N	79°31'W
Kittery, Me., U.S. (kĭt'ẽr-ĭ)	116-17	43°06'N	70°45'W
Kitty Hawk, N.C., U.S. (kĭt'tė hôk)	124-25	36°04'N	75°44'W
Kitui, Kenya	267	1°22'S	38°01'E
Kitwe, Zam.	264-65	12°49'S	28°13'E
Kivalina, Ak., U.S.	126	67°44'N	164°32'W
Kivu, Lac, lk., Afr.	267	2°03'S	28°54'E
Kiyev, nat. cap., Ukr. *see* Kiev	202-03	50°26'N	30°30'E
Kizel, Russia (kē'zĕl)	186-87	59°04'N	57°39'E
Kızılırmak, stm., Tur.	186-87	41°44'N	35°58'E
Kizlyar, Russia (kĭz-lyär')	227	43°51'N	46°42'E
Kladno, Czech Rep. (kläd'nō)	194-95	50°08'N	14°06'E
Klagenfurt, Aus. (klä'gĕn-fōrt)	194-95	46°38'N	14°19'E
Klaipėda, Lith. (klī'pȧ-dȧ)	192-93	55°43'N	21°08'E
Klamath, stm., U.S. (klăm'ăth)	110-11	41°33'N	124°06'W
Klamath Falls, Or., U.S. (klăm'ăth fôlz)	112-13	42°14'N	121°48'W
Klamath Mountains, mts., U.S. (klăm'ăth moun'tĭnz)	112-13	41°31'N	123°14'W
Klang, Malay.	246-47	3°03'N	101°27'E
Klatovy, Czech Rep. (klá'tô-vė)	194-95	49°24'N	13°18'E
Klausenburg, Rom. *see* Cluj-Napoca	194-95	46°47'N	23°36'E
Klein Karroo, plat., S. Afr. *see* Little Karoo	264-65	33°45'S	21°30'E
Klerksdorp, S. Afr. (klĕrks'dôrp)	269c	26°52'S	26°39'E
Kletnya, Russia (klyĕt'nyȧ)	202-03	53°23'N	33°13'E
Kleve, Ger. (klĕ'fĕ)	194-95	51°47'N	6°09'E
Klimovsk, Russia (klĭ'môfsk)	202-03	55°22'N	37°32'E
Klin, Russia (klēn)	202-03	56°20'N	36°43'E
Klintehamn, Swe. (klēn'tē-häm)	192-93	57°24'N	18°12'E
Klintsy, Russia (klĭn'tsĭ)	202-03	52°45'N	32°15'E
Klip, stm., S. Afr. (klĭp)	269c	27°03'S	29°04'E
Klosterneuburg, Aus. (klōs-tẽr-noi'bōōrgh)	194-95	48°18'N	16°21'E
Kluane National Park and Reserve, n.p., Yk., Can.	128-29	60°45'N	139°30'W
Kluczbork, Pol. (klōōch'bōrk)	194-95	50°58'N	18°14'E
Klyazma, stm., Russia (klyäz'mȧ)	186-87	56°10'N	42°58'E
Klyuchevskaya Sopka, Vulkan, vol., Russia (klyōō-chĕfskä'yä)	218-19	56°04'N	160°38'E
Klyuchi, Russia (klyōō'chĭ)	218-19	56°19'N	160°51'E
Knee Lake, lk., Mb., Can.	134-35	55°06'N	94°36'W
Knight Inlet, b., B.C., Can. (nīt ĭn'lĕt)	132-33	50°42'N	125°43'W
Knin, Cro. (knēn)	200-01	44°02'N	16°12'E
Knossos, hist., Grc.	200a	35°17'N	25°12'E
Knox, In., U.S. (nŏks)	116-17	41°17'N	86°37'W
Knox, Cape, c., B.C., Can.	132-33	54°11'N	133°04'W
Knoxville, Ia., U.S. (nŏks'vĭl)	114-15	41°19'N	93°06'W
Knoxville, Il., U.S. (nŏks'vĭl)	114-15	40°54'N	90°17'W
Knoxville, Tn., U.S. (nŏks'vĭl)	124-25	35°58'N	83°55'W
Kōbe, Japan (kō'bĕ)	245	34°41'N	135°10'E
København, nat. cap., Den. (kû-b'n-houn') *see* Copenhagen	192-93	55°41'N	12°34'E
Koblenz, Ger. (kō'blĕntz)	194-95	50°21'N	7°35'E
Kobroor, Pulau, i., Indon.	224-25	6°12'S	134°32'E
Kobryn, Bela. (kō'brĕn')	194-95	52°13'N	24°21'E
Kobuk, stm., Ak., U.S. (kō'bŭk)	126	66°34'N	161°33'W
Kobuk Valley National Park, n.p., Ak., U.S. (kō'bŭk văl'ē năsh'ŭn-ăl pärk)	126	67°20'N	159°00'W
Kobuleti, Geor. (kô-bŏ-lyā'tė)	227	41°49'N	41°48'E
Kocaeli, Tur. *see* İzmit	200-01	40°47'N	29°57'E
Kočevje, Slvn. (kô'chāv-ye)	200-01	45°38'N	14°52'E
Koch Bihār, India	234-35	26°19'N	89°27'E
Kochechum, stm., Russia	218-19	64°17'N	100°11'E
Kochi, India *see* Cochin	236	9°56'N	76°15'E
Kōchi, Japan	245	33°33'N	133°32'E
Kodiak, Ak., U.S. (kō'dyăk)	126	57°49'N	152°22'W
Kodiak Island, i., Ak., U.S. (kō'dyăk ī'lănd)	126	57°30'N	153°30'W
Koforidua, Ghana (kō fō-rĭ-dōō'ȧ)	260-61	6°05'N	0°17'W
Kōfu, Japan	245	35°39'N	138°34'E
Køge, Den. (kû'gĕ)	192-93	55°27'N	12°11'E
Kogon, Uzb.	232-33	39°43'N	64°33'E
Kŏgŭm-do, i., Kor., S.	243	34°27'N	127°11'E
Kohāt, Pak.	232-33	33°35'N	71°27'E
Kohīma, India (kō-ē'mȧ)	234-35	25°39'N	94°06'E
Kohtla-Järve, Est.	192-93	59°24'N	27°15'E
Koidu-Sefagu, S.L.	260-61	8°38'N	10°59'W
Kŏje-do, i., Kor., S. (kû'jĕ)	243	34°52'N	128°37'E
Kokiu, China *see* Gejiu	238-39	23°22'N	103°09'E
Kokkola, Fin. (kô'kô-lȧ)	184-85	63°50'N	23°09'E
Kokomo, In., U.S. (kō'kō-mō)	116-17	40°29'N	86°07'W
Koko Nor, lk., China (kō'kô nor) *see* Qinghai Hu	240-41	36°48'N	100°06'E
Kokopo, Pap. N. Gui. (kō-kō'pō)	277	4°20'S	152°14'E
Kökshetaū, Kaz.	226	53°17'N	69°24'E
Koksoak, stm., Qc., Can. (kōk'sō-ăk)	130-31	58°31'N	68°10'W
Kokstad, S. Afr. (kôk'shtät)	264-65	30°33'S	29°26'E
Kokubu, Japan (kō'kōō-bōō)	245	31°44'N	130°46'E
Kolaka, Indon.	248-49	4°05'S	121°37'E
Kola Peninsula, pen., Russia (kō'lȧ pĕ-nĭn'sūlă) *see* Kol'skiy Poluostrov	186-87	67°18'N	36°21'E
Kolār, India (kōl-är')	236	13°08'N	78°08'E
Kolberg, Pol. *see* Kołobrzeg	194-95	54°11'N	15°34'E
Kolchugino, Russia (kôl-chò'gė-nô)	202-03	56°18'N	39°23'E
Kolda, Sen.	260-61	12°53'N	14°57'W
Kolding, Den. (kŭl'dĭng)	192-93	55°30'N	9°28'E
Kolguyev, Ostrov, i., Russia (ôs-trôf' kôl-gò'yĕf)	186-87	69°05'N	49°15'E

n-sing; ŋ-baŋk; ɴ-nasalized n; nŏd; cŏmmit; ōld; ôbey; ôrder; oi-boil; fōōd; ò-as oo in foot; ou-out; s-soft; sh-dish; th-thin; pūre; ûnite; ûrn; stŭd; circŭs; ü-as in French tu; '-indeterminate vowel.

Feature (Pronunciation)	Page	Lat.	Long.
Kolhāpur, India	236	16°42'N	74°13'E
Koliba, stm., Afr. *see* Corubal	258-59	11°57'N	15°03'W
Kolín, Czech Rep. (kō'lēn)	194-95	50°01'N	15°12'E
Kolkasrags, c., Lat. (kôl-käs'rágz)	192-93	57°45'N	22°36'E
Kolkata, India	234-35	22°32'N	88°22'E
Kollam, India	236	8°53'N	76°35'E
Köln, Ger. *see* Cologne	194-95	50°56'N	6°57'E
Koło, Pol. (kô'wô)	194-95	52°12'N	18°39'E
Kołobrzeg, Pol. (kô-lôb'zhěk)	194-95	54°11'N	15°34'E
Kolombangara Island, i., Sol. Is.	279e	8°0'S	157°05'E
Kolomea, Ukr. *see* Kolomyia	194-95	48°32'N	25°03'E
Kolomna, Russia (kál-ôm'ná)	202-03	55°05'N	38°49'E
Kolomyia, Ukr.	194-95	48°32'N	25°03'E
Kolozsvár, Rom. *see* Cluj-Napoca	194-95	46°47'N	23°36'E
Kolpashevo, Russia (kŭl pá shô'vá)	218-19	58°20'N	82°56'E
Kolpino, Russia (kôl'pē-nô)	192-93	59°45'N	30°36'E
Kol'skiy Poluostrov, pen., Russia	186-87	67°18'N	36°21'E
Kolwezi, D.R.C. (kōl-wě'zē)	262-63	10°43'S	25°28'E
Kolyma, stm., Russia (kŭ-lĭ-mä')	218-19	69°38'N	161°18'E
Kom, Iran *see* Qom	232-33	34°39'N	50°53'E
Komadugu Gana, stm., Nig.	260-61	13°04'N	12°24'E
Komandorski Islands, is., Russia (kŭ-mŭn-dôr'-skē ī'lándz)	218-19	55°0'N	167°00'E
Komandorskiye Ostrova, is., Russia *see* Komandorski Islands	218-19	55°0'N	167°00'E
Komárno, Slvk. (kô'mär-nô)	194-95	47°45'N	18°09'E
Komárom, Hung. (kô'mä-rôm)	194-95	47°45'N	18°07'E
Komatsu, Japan (kō-mät'sōō)	245	36°24'N	136°27'E
Kome Island, i., Ug.	267	0°05'S	32°45'E
Komi, state, Russia (kômē)	186-87	64°0'N	54°00'E
Komodo, Pulau, i., Indon.	248-49	8°33'S	119°29'E
Komoé, stm., Afr.	260-61	5°12'N	3°43'W
Kom Ombo, Egypt	268b	24°28'N	32°57'E
Komorn, Slvk. *see* Komárno	194-95	47°45'N	18°09'E
Kompasberg, mtn., S. Afr.	264-65	31°45'S	24°32'E
Komsomolets, Ostrov, i., Russia	218-19	80°30'N	95°00'E
Komsomol'skiy, Russia	186-87	67°32'N	63°59'E
Komsomol'sk-na-Amure, Russia	218-19	50°34'N	137°01'E
Konan, Kor., N. *see* Hŭngdŏki-dong	243	39°50'N	127°38'E
Konārak, India	234-35	19°54'N	86°07'E
Konda, stm., Russia (kôn'dá)	218-19	60°43'N	69°40'E
Kondoa, Tan. (kôn-dō'á)	267	4°53'S	35°48'E
Kondopoga, Russia	186-87	62°12'N	34°17'E
Kondoz, Afg.	232-33	36°44'N	68°51'E
Kondoz, stm., Afg.	232-33	37°00'N	68°16'E
Kong, stm., Asia	246-47	13°32'N	105°57'E
Kongolo, D.R.C. (kôŋ'gō'lō)	262-63	5°23'S	27°01'E
Kongsberg, Nor. (kŭngs'běrg)	192-93	59°40'N	9°39'E
Kongsvinger, Nor. (kŭngs'vĭŋ-gēr)	192-93	60°12'N	12°00'E
Kongur Shan, mtn., China	226	38°37'N	75°20'E
Königgrätz, Czech Rep. *see* Hradec Králové	194-95	50°12'N	15°50'E
Königsberg, Russia *see* Kaliningrad	194-95	54°43'N	20°30'E
Konin, Pol. (kô'nyĕn)	194-95	52°14'N	18°16'E
Kónitsa, Grc. (kô'nyē'tsá)	200-01	40°03'N	20°45'E
Konjic, Bos. (kôn'yēts)	200-01	43°39'N	17°57'E
Konkouré, stm., Gui.	260-61	9°57'N	13°41'W
Konosha, Russia	186-87	60°58'N	40°16'E
Konotop, Ukr. (kô-nô-tôp')	202-03	51°14'N	33°12'E
Końskie, Pol. (koin''skyĕ)	194-95	51°12'N	20°25'E
Konstanz, Ger. (kôn'shtänts)	194-95	47°40'N	9°10'E
Kontagora, Nig. (kōn-tá-gō'rä)	260-61	10°24'N	5°27'E
Kon Tum, Viet.	246-47	14°21'N	108°01'E
Konya, Tur. (kōn'yà)	186-87	37°52'N	32°31'E
Konzhakovskiy Kamen, mtn., Russia	186-87	59°38'N	59°08'E
Kootenay Lake, lk., B.C., Can. (kōō'tē-nā lāk)	132-33	49°35'N	116°50'W
Kootenay National Park, n.p., B.C., Can. (kōō'tē-nā năsh'ŭn-ăl pärk)	132-33	51°0'N	116°00'W
Kopervik, Nor. (kô'pĕr-vēk)	192-93	59°17'N	5°18'E
Köpetdag, Gershi, mts., Asia *see* Koppeh Dāgh	232-33	37°50'N	58°00'E
Kopet Mountains, mts., Asia (kō-pĕt' moun'tĭnz) *see* Koppeh Dāgh	232-33	37°50'N	58°00'E
Köping, Swe. (chû'pĭng)	192-93	59°31'N	15°60'E
Koppeh Dāgh, mts., Asia	232-33	37°50'N	58°00'E
Koprivnica, Cro. (kô'prē-vnē'tsá)	200-01	46°10'N	16°50'E
Korāput, India	236	18°49'N	82°43'E
Korat, Thai. *see* Nakhon Ratchasima	246-47	14°58'N	102°06'E
Korça, Alb. *see* Korçë	200-01	40°37'N	20°47'E
Korçë, Alb.	200-01	40°37'N	20°47'E
Korčula, Otok, i., Cro. (ō'tŏk kôr'chōō-lá)	200-01	42°57'N	16°50'E
Kordestān, hist. reg., Asia *see* Kurdistan	228-29	37°0'N	45°00'E
Korea, North, nation, Asia (nôrth kô-rē' á)	206-07	40°0'N	127°00'E
Korea, South, nation, Asia (south kô-rē' á)	206-07	36°30'N	128°00'E
Korea Bay, b., Asia (kô-rē' á bā)	240-41	39°0'N	124°00'E
Korea Strait, strt., Asia (kô-rē-á strāt)	243	34°0'N	129°00'E
Korf, Russia	218-19	60°21'N	165°56'E
Korhogo, C. Iv. (kôr-hō'gō)	260-61	9°27'N	5°38'W
Kórinthos, Grc. (kô-rēn'thôs) (kŏr'ĭnth) *see* Corinth	200-01	37°56'N	22°58'E
Koritsa, Alb. *see* Korçë	200-01	40°37'N	20°47'E
Kōriyama, Japan (kō'rē-yä'mä)	245	37°24'N	140°23'E
Korla, China (kōr-lä)	222-23	41°44'N	86°09'E
Koro, i., Fiji	279f	17°16'S	179°24'E
Korocha, Russia (kô-rō'chá)	202-03	50°49'N	37°11'E
Koromere, c., N.Z. *see* East Cape	278	37°41'S	178°33'E
Korop, Ukr. (kō'rôp)	202-03	51°34'N	32°56'E
Koro Sea, s., Fiji	279f	18°00'S	179°50'E
Korosten', Ukr. (kô'rôs-tĕn)	202-03	50°57'N	28°39'E
Korsakov, Russia (kôr'sá-kôf')	244	46°38'N	142°47'E
Korsør, Den. (kôrs'ûr')	192-93	55°21'N	11°09'E
Koryak Mountains, mts., Russia *see* Koryakskoye Nagor'ye	218-19	62°30'N	172°00'E
Koryakskoye Nagor'ye, mts., Russia	218-19	62°30'N	172°00'E
Kos, i., Grc.	200-01	36°50'N	27°10'E
Kosa, Russia	186-87	59°57'N	54°59'E
Kościan, Pol. (kŭsh'tsyán)	194-95	52°05'N	16°39'E
Kosciusko, Ms., U.S. (kŏs-ĭ-ŭs'kō)	124-25	33°03'N	89°35'W
Kosciuszko, Mount, mtn., Austl. (mount kŏs-ĭ-ŭs'kō)	276	36°27'S	148°16'E
Kosciuszko National Park, n.p., Austl.	276	36°15'S	148°24'E
Kosh-Agach, Russia	222-23	50°01'N	88°45'E
Koshu, Kor., S. *see* Kwangju	243	35°09'N	126°54'E
Košice, Slvk. (kō'shē-tsĕ')	194-95	48°43'N	21°16'E
Koslan, Russia	186-87	63°29'N	48°41'E
Köslin, Pol. *see* Koszalin	194-95	54°11'N	16°12'E
Kosovska Mitrovica, Serb. (kô'sôv-skä' mē'trô-vē-tsä')	200-01	42°53'N	20°52'E
Kosrae, i., Micron.	280-81	5°19'N	162°59'E
Kossou, Lac de, res., C. Iv.	260-61	7°15'N	5°42'W
Kostiantynivka, Ukr.	202-03	48°32'N	37°44'E
Kostroma, Russia (kôs-trô-má')	186-87	57°46'N	40°57'E
Koszalin, Pol. (kô-shä'lĭn)	194-95	54°11'N	16°12'E
Kota, India	234-35	25°11'N	75°50'E
Kotabaru, Indon. *see* Jayapura	277	2°32'S	140°43'E
Kotabaru, Indon.	248-49	3°15'S	116°14'E
Kota Belud, Malay.	248-49	6°29'N	116°33'E
Kota Bharu, Malay.	246-47	6°08'N	102°15'E
Kotabumi, Indon.	246-47	4°49'S	104°53'E
Kotadabok, Indon.	246-47	0°33'S	104°31'E
Kota Kinabalu, Malay.	248-49	5°58'N	116°05'E
Kotamobagu, Indon.	248-49	0°43'N	124°18'E
Kotel, Blg. (kō-tĕl')	200-01	42°54'N	26°28'E
Kotelnich, Russia (kô-tyĕl'nĕch)	186-87	58°18'N	48°19'E
Kotel'nyy, Ostrov, i., Russia (ôs-trôf' kô-tyĕl'nē)	218-19	75°45'N	138°44'E
Kotka, Fin. (kŏt'ká)	192-93	60°28'N	26°56'E
Kotlas, Russia (kôt'lás)	186-87	61°15'N	46°39'E
Kotovs'k, Ukr.	202-03	47°45'N	29°32'E
Kottagūdem, India	236	17°32'N	80°38'E
Kottayam, India	236	9°35'N	76°32'E
Kotte, nat. cap., Sri L. *see* Sri Jayewardenepura Kotte	236	6°54'N	79°54'E
Kotto, stm., C.A.R.	262-63	4°14'N	22°03'E
Kotuy, stm., Russia (kô-tōō')	218-19	71°55'N	102°06'E
Kotzebue, Ak., U.S. (kôt'sĕ-bōō)	126	66°53'N	162°36'W
Kotzebue Sound, strt., Ak., U.S. (kôt'sĕ-bōō sound)	126	66°20'N	163°00'W
Koudougou, Burkina (kōō-dōō'gōō)	260-61	12°15'N	2°22'W
Kourou, Fr. Gu.	164-65	5°09'N	52°39'W
Kousséri, Camrn.	260-61	12°05'N	15°02'E
Koussi, Emi, mtn., Chad (ā'mē ĸōō-sē')	258-59	19°50'N	18°30'E
Koutiala, Mali (kōō-tē-ä'lä)	258-59	12°23'N	5°28'W
Kouvola, Fin. (kō'ō-vô-lä)	192-93	60°52'N	26°41'E
Kovel', Ukr. (kō'vĕl)	194-95	51°14'N	24°42'E
Kovrov, Russia (kôv-rôf')	186-87	56°22'N	41°20'E
Kowel, Ukr. *see* Kovel'	194-95	51°14'N	24°42'E
Kowie, S. Afr. *see* Port Alfred	264-65	33°36'S	26°54'E
Kowkcheh, stm., Afg.	232-33	37°10'N	69°24'E
Koygorodok, Russia	186-87	60°26'N	50°59'E
Koyukuk, stm., Ak., U.S. (kô-yōō'kôk)	126	64°56'N	157°30'W
Kozáni, Grc.	200-01	40°18'N	21°49'E
Kozelets', Ukr. (kôzĕ-lyĕts)	202-03	50°55'N	31°07'E
Kozhikode, India	236	11°16'N	75°47'E
Kozienice, Pol. (kō-zyĕ-nē'tsĕ)	194-95	51°35'N	21°33'E
Kozyrëvsk, Russia	218-19	56°05'N	159°53'E
Kpalimé, Togo	260-61	6°54'N	0°38'E
Kra, Isthmus of, isth., Asia	246-47	10°02'N	98°52'E
Kraai, stm., S. Afr. (krä'ē)	264-65	30°40'S	26°45'E
Krâchéh, Camb.	246-47	12°30'N	106°02'E
Kragujevac, Serb. (krä'gōō'yĕ-váts)	200-01	44°01'N	20°55'E
Krakatoa, i., Indon.	248-49	6°10'S	105°26'E
Kraków, Pol. (krä'kôf)	194-95	50°04'N	19°58'E
Kralendijk, Neth. Ant.	140a	12°09'N	68°16'W
Kraljevo, Serb. (kräl'ye-vô)	200-01	43°44'N	20°41'E
Kramators'k, Ukr.	202-03	48°44'N	37°32'E
Kramfors, Swe. (kräm'fôrs)	184-85	62°56'N	17°47'E
Kraśnik, Pol. (kräsh'nĭk)	194-95	50°56'N	22°13'E
Krasnoarmeysk, Kaz.	226	53°51'N	69°45'E
Krasnoarmeysk, Russia (kräs'nô-är-māsk')	186-87	51°02'N	45°42'E
Krasnoarmeysk, Russia (kräs'nô-är-māsk')	202-03	56°08'N	38°08'E
Krasnodar, Russia (kräs'nô-dár)	202-03	45°02'N	38°59'E
Krasnokamsk, Russia (kräs-nô-kämsk')	186-87	58°05'N	55°53'E
Krasnoslobodsk, Russia (kräs'nô-slôbôtsk')	186-87	48°43'N	44°34'E
Krasnoufimsk, Russia (krŭs-nŭ-ōō-fēmsk')	186-87	56°37'N	57°46'E
Krasnovishersk, Russia (kräs-nô-vêshersk')	186-87	60°24'N	57°05'E
Krasnovodsk, Turkmen. *see* Türkmenbaşy	232-33	40°01'N	52°58'E
Krasnoyarsk, Russia (kräs-nô-yársk')	218-19	56°01'N	92°53'E
Krasnyi Luch, Ukr.	202-03	48°09'N	38°55'E
Krasnystaw, Pol. (kräs-nē-stáf')	194-95	50°59'N	23°11'E
Krasnyy Kut, Russia (krás-nē kōōt')	186-87	50°57'N	46°58'E
Kremenchug, Ukr. *see* Kremenchuk	202-03	49°05'N	33°25'E
Kremenchug Reservoir, res., Ukr. (krĕ-mĕn-chōōk' rĕ'sĕr-vwär) *see* Kremenchuts'ke vodoskhovyshche	202-03	49°20'N	32°30'E
Kremenchuk, Ukr.	202-03	49°05'N	33°25'E
Kremenchuts'ke vodoskhovyshche, res., Ukr.	202-03	49°20'N	32°30'E
Kresttsy, Russia (krâst'sĕ)	192-93	58°15'N	32°31'E
Kresttsy, Russia (krâst'sĕ)	202-03	58°23'N	38°59'E
Kretinga, Lith. (krĕ-tĭŋ'gá)	192-93	55°53'N	21°15'E
Kribi, Camrn. (krē'bē)	260-61	2°55'N	9°54'E
Krishna, stm., India	236	15°51'N	80°52'E
Krishnanagar, India	234-35	23°24'N	88°30'E
Kristiania, nat. cap., Nor. *see* Oslo	192-93	59°55'N	10°45'E
Kristiansand, Nor. (krĭs-tyán-sän'')	192-93	58°10'N	8°00'E
Kristianstad, Swe. (krĭs-tyán-städ')	192-93	56°02'N	14°09'E
Kristiansund, Nor. (krĭs-tyán-sōn'')	184-85	63°07'N	7°47'E
Kristiinankaupunki, Fin. *see* Kristinestad	192-93	62°16'N	21°22'E
Kristinehamn, Swe. (krēs-tē'nĕ-häm')	192-93	59°20'N	14°08'E
Kristinestad, Fin. (krĭs-tē'nĕ-städh)	192-93	62°16'N	21°22'E
Kríti, i., Grc. *see* Crete	200a	35°13'N	25°00'E
Kritikón Pélagos, s., Grc. *see* Crete, Sea of	188-89	35°54'N	25°01'E
Kriva Palanka, Mac. (krē-vá-pá-läŋ'ká)	200-01	42°12'N	22°20'E
Krivoy Rog, Ukr. *see* Kryvyi Rih	202-03	47°54'N	33°22'E
Križevci, Cro. (krē'zhĕv-tsĭ)	200-01	46°04'N	16°34'E
Krnov, Czech Rep. (k'r'nôf)	194-95	50°05'N	17°42'E
Krokodil, stm., S. Afr. (krŏ'kō-dĭl) *see* Crocodile	269c	24°11'S	26°53'E
Kromy, Russia (krô'mē)	202-03	52°41'N	35°46'E
Krŏng Kaôh Kŏng, Camb.	246-47	11°37'N	102°59'E
Kronshtadt, Russia (krōn'shtät)	192-93	59°59'N	29°47'E
Kronstadt, Rom. *see* Braşov	194-95	45°39'N	25°37'E
Kroonstad, S. Afr. (krōn'shtät)	269c	27°40'S	27°14'E
Kropotkin, Russia (krá-pôt'kĭn)	186-87	45°26'N	40°34'E
Krosno, Pol. (krôs'nô)	194-95	49°42'N	21°46'E
Krotoszyn, Pol. (krô-tō'shĭn)	194-95	51°42'N	17°26'E
Krško, Slvn. (k'rsh'kô)	200-01	45°58'N	15°29'E
Kruger National Park, n.p., S. Afr.	264-65	23°56'S	31°33'E
Krugersdorp, S. Afr. (krōō'gĕrz-dôrp)	269c	26°05'S	27°47'E
Krui, Indon.	246-47	5°14'S	103°56'E
Krung Thep, nat. cap., Thai. *see* Bangkok	246-47	13°45'N	100°31'E
Kruševac, Serb. (krō'shĕ-váts)	200-01	43°35'N	21°20'E
Kruzof Island, i., Ak., U.S.	126	57°10'N	135°40'W
Kryms'kyi pivostriv, pen., Ukr. *see* Crimean Peninsula	202-03	45°0'N	34°00'E
Kryvyi Rih, Ukr.	202-03	47°54'N	33°22'E
Ksar-el-Kebir, Mor.	269a	35°01'N	5°54'W

Feature (Pronunciation)	Page	Lat.	Long.
Kualakapuas, Indon.	**248-49**	3°02'S	114°25'E
Kuala Lumpur, nat. cap., Malay. (kwä'lä lòm-pōōr')	**246-47**	3°10'N	101°42'E
Kuala Terengganu, Malay.	**246-47**	5°19'N	103°09'E
Kuandian, China (kůän-dĭĕn)	**243**	40°44'N	124°47'E
Kuantan, Malay.	**246-47**	3°49'N	103°20'E
Kuban', stm., Russia	**186-87**	45°21'N	37°25'E
Kuching, Malay. (kōō'chĭng)	**248-49**	1°34'N	110°20'E
Kudat, Malay. (kōō-dät')	**248-49**	6°53'N	116°46'E
Kudus, Indon.	**248-49**	6°48'S	110°50'E
Kudymkar, Russia (kōō-dĭm-kär')	**186-87**	59°01'N	54°39'E
Kufstein, Aus. (kōōf'shtīn)	**194-95**	47°35'N	12°10'E
Kugluktuk, Nu., Can.	**128-29**	67°47'N	115°11'W
Kuiseb, stm., S. Afr.	**264-65**	22°58'S	14°29'E
Kuito, Ang.	**264-65**	12°23'S	16°56'E
Kuiu Island, i., Ak., U.S.	**126**	56°45'N	134°10'W
Kujū-san, vol., Japan (kōō'jò-sän')	**245**	33°05'N	131°15'E
Kula Kangri, mtn., Bhu.	**234-35**	28°03'N	90°22'E
Kular, Russia	**218-19**	70°42'N	134°12'E
Kuldīga, Lat. (kòl'dē-gȧ)	**192-93**	56°58'N	21°60'E
Kuldja, China *see* Yining	**226**	43°55'N	81°18'E
Kulmbach, Ger. (klòlm'bäk)	**194-95**	50°06'N	11°27'E
Kŭlob, Taj.	**232-33**	37°55'N	69°47'E
Kuloy, Russia	**186-87**	61°02'N	42°29'E
Kulsary, Kaz.	**186-87**	46°59'N	53°59'E
Kulundinskaya Ravnina, pl., Asia *see* Qulyndy Zhazyghy	**226**	53°0'N	79°00'E
Kulundinskoye, Ozero, lk., Russia	**226**	53°0'N	79°36'E
Kuma, stm., Russia (kōō'mä)	**186-87**	44°57'N	46°27'E
Kumamoto, Japan (kōō'mä-mō'tô)	**245**	32°48'N	130°43'E
Kumanovo, Mac. (kò-mä'nô-vô)	**200-01**	42°08'N	21°43'E
Kumasi, Ghana (kōō-mä'sê)	**260-61**	6°41'N	1°38'W
Kumayri, Arm. *see* Gyumri	**227**	40°47'N	43°51'E
Kumba, Camrn. (kòm'bȧ)	**260-61**	4°38'N	9°26'E
Kumbakonam, India (kòm'bŭ-kō'nŭm)	**236**	10°57'N	79°23'E
Kumertau, Russia	**186-87**	52°46'N	55°48'E
Kŭm-gang, stm., Kor., S. (kòm gäng')	**243**	35°60'N	126°42'E
Kumo, Nig.	**260-61**	10°01'N	11°13'E
Kumul, China *see* Hami	**240-41**	42°50'N	93°31'E
Kunashir, Ostrov, i., Russia (ôs-trôf' kōō-nū-shēr')	**244**	44°10'N	146°00'E
Kunashiri-tō, i., Russia *see* Kunashir, Ostrov	**244**	44°10'N	146°00'E
Kunene, stm., Afr.	**264-65**	17°15'S	11°45'E
Kungälv, Swe. (kŭng'ĕlf)	**192-93**	57°52'N	11°60'E
Kunghit Island, i., B.C., Can.	**132-33**	52°06'N	131°04'W
Kungsbacka, Swe. (kŭngs'bä-kȧ)	**192-93**	57°28'N	12°05'E
Kungur, Russia (kòn-gōōr')	**186-87**	57°26'N	56°57'E
Kunjirap Daban, p., Asia *see* Khunjerab Pass	**232-33**	36°52'N	75°28'E
Kunlun Mountains, mts., China (kōōn-lōōn moun'tĭnz) *see* Kunlun Shan	**222-23**	36°30'N	88°00'E
Kunlun Shan, mts., China (kōōn-lōōn shän)	**222-23**	36°30'N	88°00'E
Kunming, China (kōōn-mĭŋ)	**238-39**	25°03'N	102°43'E
Kunsan, Kor., S. (kòn'sän')	**243**	35°59'N	126°43'E
Kununurra, Austl.	**270-71**	15°46'S	128°44'E
K'uo-k'o-sha-lo Ling, mts., Asia *see* Kakshaal-Too	**226**	41°0'N	78°00'E
Kuopio, Fin. (kò-ô'pē-ŏ)	**184-85**	62°54'N	27°43'E
Kupang, Indon.	**248-49**	10°11'S	123°35'E
Kup'ians'k, Ukr.	**202-03**	49°43'N	37°38'E
Kupino, Russia (kōō-pĭ'nŏ)	**226**	54°21'N	77°17'E
Kupiškis, Lith. (kò-pĭsh'kĭs)	**192-93**	55°50'N	24°59'E
Kupreanof Island, i., Ak., U.S.	**126**	56°45'N	133°31'W
Kuqa, China (kōō-chyä)	**226**	41°11'N	83°28'E
Kür, stm., Asia	**227**	39°17'N	49°26'E
Kura, stm., Asia	**227**	39°17'N	49°26'E
Kurashiki, Japan (kōō'rä-shē'kê)	**245**	34°36'N	133°46'E
Kuraymah, Sudan	**266**	18°34'N	31°51'E
Kurayoshi, Japan (kōō'rȧ-yō'shê)	**245**	35°26'N	133°49'E
Kurchatov, Russia	**202-03**	51°39'N	35°36'E
Kurdistan, hist. reg., Asia (kûrd'ĭ-stăn)	**228-29**	37°0'N	45°00'E
Kure, Japan (kōō'rĕ)	**245**	34°15'N	132°34'E
Kure Atoll, at., Hi., U.S.	**127**	28°25'N	178°25'W
Kuressaare, Est. (kò'rĕ-sä'rĕ)	**192-93**	58°15'N	22°30'E
Kureyka, stm., Russia	**218-19**	66°29'N	87°15'E
Kurgan, Russia (kòr-găn')	**226**	55°27'N	65°20'E
Kurgan-Tyube, Taj. (kòr-gän' työ'bĕ) *see* Qŭrghonteppa	**232-33**	37°50'N	68°47'E
Kuria, i., Kir.	**280-81**	0°12'N	173°24'E
Kuril Islands, is., Russia (kōō'rĭl ĭ'lăndz)	**218-19**	47°14'N	152°18'E
Kuril'skiye Ostrova, is., Russia *see* Kuril Islands	**218-19**	47°14'N	152°18'E
Kurmuk, Sudan (kòr'mōōk)	**262-63**	10°33'N	34°17'E
Kurnool, India (kòr-nōōl')	**236**	15°50'N	78°02'E
Kuršėnai, Lith. (kòr'shå-nī)	**192-93**	55°59'N	22°56'E
Kursk, Russia (kòrsk)	**202-03**	51°44'N	36°11'E
Kuruman, S. Afr. (kōō-rōō-män')	**264-65**	27°28'S	23°26'E
Kurume, Japan (kōō'rò-mĕ)	**245**	33°19'N	130°31'E
Kurunegala, Sri L.	**236**	7°29'N	80°22'E
Kushiro, Japan (kōō'shē-rō)	**244**	42°59'N	144°24'E
Kushka, Turkmen. *see* Guşgy	**232-33**	35°16'N	62°21'E
Kushtia, Bngl.	**234-35**	23°55'N	89°08'E
Kushui, China	**240-41**	42°10'N	94°22'E
Kuskokwim, stm., Ak., U.S. (kŭs'kô-kwĭm)	**126**	60°16'N	162°29'W
Kuskokwim Bay, b., Ak., U.S. (kŭs'kô-kwĭm bā)	**126**	59°32'N	162°52'W
Kuskokwim Mountains, mts., Ak., U.S. (kŭs'kô-kwĭm moun'tĭnz)	**126**	62°24'N	157°07'W
Kustanay, Kaz. *see* Qostanay	**226**	53°12'N	63°37'E
Kūstī, Sudan	**266**	13°10'N	32°40'E
Kütahya, Tur. (kû-tä'hyȧ)	**186-87**	39°26'N	29°58'E
Kutaisi, Geor. (kōō-tŭ-ē'sē)	**227**	42°16'N	42°42'E
Kūt al-Imāra, Iraq *see* Al-Kūt	**228-29**	32°30'N	45°49'E
Kutaradja, Indon. *see* Banda Aceh	**246-47**	5°33'N	95°19'E
Kutch, Gulf of, b., India *see* Kachchh, Gulf of	**234-35**	22°37'N	69°30'E
Kutch, Rann of, reg., Asia	**234-35**	24°15'N	70°46'E
Kutina, Cro. (kōō'tē-nȧ)	**200-01**	45°29'N	16°46'E
Kutno, Pol. (kòt'nô)	**194-95**	52°14'N	19°22'E
Kuujjuaq, Qc., Can.	**128-29**	58°06'N	68°25'W
Kuusamo, Fin. (kōō'sȧ-mô)	**184-85**	65°59'N	29°10'E
Kuvshinovo, Russia (kòv-shē'nô-vô)	**202-03**	57°01'N	34°11'E
Kuwait, nation, Asia (kōō-wāt')	**206-07**	29°30'N	47°45'E
Kuwait, nat. cap., Kuw. (kōō-wāt')	**228-29**	29°19'N	47°60'E
Kuybyshev, Russia *see* Samara	**186-87**	53°11'N	50°07'E
Kuybyshev, Russia	**218-19**	55°27'N	78°18'E
Kuybyshev Reservoir, res., Russia (kōō'ê-bĭ-shĭf rĕ'sĕr-vwär) *see* Kuybyshevskoye Vodokhranilishche	**186-87**	54°30'N	48°30'E
Kuybyshevskoye Vodokhranilishche, res., Russia	**186-87**	54°30'N	48°30'E
Kuzneck, Russia *see* Novokuznetsk	**226**	53°45'N	87°07'E
Kuznetsk, Russia (kōōz-nyĕtsk')	**186-87**	53°07'N	46°36'E
Kuznetsovka, Russia (kòz-nyĕt'sôf-kȧ)	**192-93**	56°19'N	28°34'E
Kvaløya, i., Nor.	**184-85**	69°40'N	18°30'E
Kwajalein, at., Marsh. Is.	**280-81**	9°06'N	167°21'E
Kwando, stm., Afr.	**264-65**	18°30'S	23°36'E
Kwangchow, China *see* Guangzhou	**238-39**	23°08'N	113°16'E
Kwangju, Kor., S.	**243**	35°09'N	126°54'E
Kwango, stm., Afr. (kwäng'ō')	**262-63**	3°13'S	17°23'E
Kwangsi Chuang, state, China *see* Guangxi	**238-39**	24°0'N	109°00'E
Kwangtung, state, China *see* Guangdong	**287**	23°0'N	113°00'E
Kweichow, state, China *see* Guizhou	**238-39**	27°0'N	107°00'E
Kweihwa, China *see* Hohhot	**240-41**	40°49'N	111°39'E
Kweiyang, China *see* Guiyang	**238-39**	26°35'N	106°43'E
Kwekwe, Zimb.	**264-65**	18°56'S	29°49'E
Kwilu, stm., Afr. (kwē'lōō) *see* Cuilo	**262-63**	5°53'S	16°35'E
Kwilu, stm., Afr. (kwē'lōō)	**260-61**	3°23'S	17°23'E
Kyakhta, Russia (kyäk'ta)	**240-41**	50°21'N	106°27'E
Kyaukpyu, Mya. (chouk'pyoo')	**246-47**	19°25'N	93°33'E
Kyauktaw, Mya.	**246-47**	20°49'N	92°59'E
Kyïv, nat. cap., Ukr. (kē'yĕf) *see* Kiev	**202-03**	50°26'N	30°30'E
Kyïvs'ke vodoskhovyshche, res., Ukr.	**202-03**	50°51'N	30°32'E
Kyoga, Lake, lk., Ug.	**267**	1°30'N	33°00'E
Kyŏmip'o, Kor., N. *see* Songnim	**243**	38°44'N	125°38'E
Kyŏngju, Kor., S. (kyŭng'yōō)	**243**	35°51'N	129°13'E
Kyŏngsŏng, nat. cap., Kor., S. *see* Seoul	**243**	37°33'N	127°01'E
Kyōto, Japan (kyō'tō')	**245**	34°60'N	135°45'E
Kyrgyz Ala Too, mts., Asia *see* Kirgiz Range	**226**	42°29'N	73°50'E
Kyrgyzstan, nation, Asia (kûr'-gĭ-stän')	**226**	41°30'N	75°00'E
Kyūshū, i., Japan (kyōō-shōō)	**245**	33°0'N	131°00'E
Kyustendil, Blg. (kyòs-tĕn-dĭl')	**200-01**	42°18'N	22°41'E
Kyzyl, Russia (kĭ zĭl)	**222-23**	51°43'N	94°24'E
Kyzylkum, des., Asia *see* Qyzylqum	**226**	42°0'N	64°00'E
Kyzyl-Kyya, Kyrg.	**232-33**	40°15'N	72°07'E

L

Feature (Pronunciation)	Page	Lat.	Long.
Läänemeri, s., Eur. *see* Baltic Sea	**192-93**	57°0'N	19°00'E
Laascaanood, Som.	**262-63**	8°29'N	47°21'E
La Asunción, Ven. (lä ä-sōōn-syōn')	**164-65**	11°01'N	63°52'W
Laayoune, nat. cap., W. Sah. (lā-yōōn') (lä-yōōn')	**258-59**	27°10'N	13°12'W
La Baie, Qc., Can.	**136-37**	48°20'N	70°53'W
La Banda, Arg. (lä bän'dä)	**168-69**	27°44'S	64°15'W
La Barca, Mex. (lä bär'kȧ)	**146-47**	20°17'N	102°33'W
Labé, Gui.	**260-61**	11°19'N	12°17'W
Labe, stm., Eur. (lä'bĕ) *see* Elbe	**194-95**	53°53'N	9°01'E
Labian, Tanjong, c., Malay.	**248-49**	5°19'N	119°16'E
Labinsk, Russia	**186-87**	44°38'N	40°44'E
Labis, Malay. (läb'ĭs)	**246-47**	2°23'N	103°01'E
Labouheyre, Fr. (lȧ-bōō-âr')	**196-97**	44°13'N	0°55'W
Laboulaye, Arg. (lä-bô'ōō-lä-yĕ)	**173**	34°07'S	63°24'W
Labrador City, Nf., Can.	**128-29**	52°56'N	66°54'W
Labrador Sea, s., N.A. (lăb'rȧ-dôr sē)	**86**	57°0'N	53°00'W
Lábrea, Braz. (lä-brā'ä)	**166-67**	7°16'S	64°47'W
Labuan, Malay.	**248-49**	5°17'N	115°15'E
Labuha, Indon.	**248-49**	0°39'S	127°30'E
Labuk, stm., Malay.	**248-49**	5°53'N	117°30'E
La Calera, Chile (lä-kä-lĕ-rä)	**163e**	32°46'S	71°12'W
Lacantum, stm., Mex. (lä-kän-tōō'm)	**148**	16°33'N	90°41'W
La Carlota, Arg.	**173**	33°26'S	63°17'W
La Carolina, Spain (lä kä-rô-lē'nä)	**198-99**	38°17'N	3°37'W
Laccadive, Minicoy and Amīndīvi Islands, state, India *see* Lakshadweep	**236**	10°0'N	73°00'E
Laccadive Islands, is., India *see* Lakshadweep	**236**	10°0'N	73°00'E
La Ceiba, Hond. (lȧ sēbä)	**149**	15°46'N	86°48'W
Lacha, Ozero, lk., Russia (ô'zĕ-rô lȧ'chä)	**186-87**	61°20'N	38°48'E
La Chaux-de-Fonds, Switz. (lȧ shō dē-fôn')	**194-95**	47°06'N	6°50'E
Lachlan, stm., Austl. (läk'lăn)	**276**	34°21'S	143°53'E
La Chorrera, Col.	**164-65**	1°12'S	72°55'W
La Chorrera, Pan. (làchôr-rā'rä)	**150**	8°53'N	79°47'W
Lachute, Qc., Can. (lȧ-shōōt')	**136-37**	45°39'N	74°21'W
La Ciotat, Fr. (lȧ syô-tá')	**196-97**	43°11'N	5°36'E
Lackawanna, N.Y., U.S. (lak-ȧ-wŏn'ă)	**116-17**	42°49'N	78°51'W
Lac La Biche, Ab., Can.	**132-33**	54°46'N	111°58'W
Lac-Mégantic, Qc., Can.	**138-39**	45°34'N	70°53'W
La Columna, mtn., Ven. *see* Bolívar, Pico	**164-65**	8°33'N	71°01'W
Lacombe, Ab., Can.	**132-33**	52°28'N	113°45'W
Laconia, N.H., U.S. (lȧ-kō'nĭ-ȧ)	**116-17**	43°32'N	71°28'W
La Coruña, Spain *see* A Coruña	**198-99**	43°22'N	8°25'W
La Crosse, Wi., U.S. (lȧ-krôs')	**114-15**	43°48'N	91°14'W
La Désirade, i., Guad.	**143b**	16°19'N	61°03'W
Ladispoli, Italy (lä-dē's-pô-lē)	**200-01**	41°57'N	12°05'E
Lādīz, Iran	**230-31**	28°55'N	61°18'E
Ladoga, Lake, lk., Russia (lăk lä'-dȧ-gȧ)	**192-93**	61°0'N	31°30'E
La Dorada, Col.	**163c**	5°27'N	74°41'W
Ladozhskoye Ozero, lk., Russia *see* Ladoga, Lake	**192-93**	61°0'N	31°30'E
Ladybrand, S. Afr.	**269c**	29°11'S	27°27'E
Ladysmith, B.C., Can. (lā'dĭ-smĭth)	**132-33**	48°58'N	123°48'W
Ladysmith, S. Afr. (lā'dĭ-smĭth)	**269c**	28°34'S	29°46'E
Ladysmith, Wi., U.S. (lā'dĭ-smĭth)	**114-15**	45°28'N	91°06'W
Lae, Pap. N. Gui. (lä'å)	**277**	6°43'S	146°59'E
Læsø, i., Den.	**192-93**	57°16'N	11°01'E
La Esperanza, Hond. (lä ĕs-pȧ-rän'zä)	**149**	14°19'N	88°11'W
Lafayette, Al., U.S. (lă-fā-yĕt')	**124-25**	32°54'N	85°24'W
Lafayette, Co., U.S. (lă-fā-yĕt')	**120-21**	39°60'N	105°05'W
Lafayette, In., U.S. (lă-fā-yĕt')	**116-17**	40°25'N	86°53'W
Lafayette, La., U.S. (lă-fā-yĕt')	**124-25**	30°13'N	92°02'W
Lafia, Nig.	**260-61**	8°30'N	8°31'E
La Flèche, Fr. (lȧ flāsh')	**196-97**	47°42'N	0°04'W
Lagan, stm., Swe.	**192-93**	56°33'N	12°56'E
Lågen, stm., Nor. (lô'ghĕn)	**192-93**	59°02'N	10°04'E
Lages, Braz.	**168-69**	27°49'S	50°18'W
Laghouat, Alg. (lä-gwät')	**188-89**	33°51'N	2°51'E
Lagoa da Prata, Braz. (lȧ-gô'ä-dȧ-prä'tȧ)	**172**	20°02'S	45°33'W
La Gomera, i., Spain	**199d**	28°07'N	17°11'W
Lagos, Nig. (lä'gōs)	**260a**	6°27'N	3°24'E
Lagos, Port. (lä'gōzh)	**198-99**	37°06'N	8°40'W
Lagos de Moreno, Mex. (lä'gōs dā mô-rā'nō)	**146-47**	21°22'N	101°54'W
La Grand'Combe, Fr. (lȧ grän kaɴb')	**196-97**	44°13'N	4°01'E
La Grande, Or., U.S. (lȧ grănd')	**112-13**	45°20'N	118°05'W
La Grande Deux, Réservoir, res., Qc., Can.	**130-31**	53°40'N	76°55'W
La Grande Quatre, Réservoir, res., Qc., Can.	**130-31**	54°0'N	73°15'W
Lagrange, Ga., U.S.	**124-25**	33°02'N	85°02'W
La Grange, Ky., U.S. (lä grănj)	**116-17**	38°24'N	85°23'W
La Gran Sabana, pl., Ven.	**164-65**	5°21'N	62°04'W

n-sing; ŋ-baŋk; ɴ-nasalized n; nŏd; cŏmmit; ōld; ôbey; ôrder; oi-boil; fōōd; ò-as oo in foot; ou-out; s-soft; sh-dish; th-thin; pūre; ůnite; ûrn; stŭd; circŭs; ü-as in French tu; '-indeterminate vowel.

Feature (Pronunciation)	Page	Lat.	Long.
La Guajira, Península de, pen., S.A.	164-65	12°0'N	71°40'W
Laguna, Braz. (lä-go͞o'nä)	172	28°28'S	48°47'W
Lagunillas, Bol. (lä-go͞o-nēl'yäs)	168-69	19°38'S	63°43'W
La Habana, nat. cap., Cuba (lä-ä-bá' nä) see Havana	142-43	23°06'N	82°27'W
Lahad Datu, Malay.	250	5°02'N	118°20'E
Lahaina, Hi., U.S. (lä-hä'ē-nä)	127a	20°53'N	156°40'W
Lahat, Indon.	246-47	3°48'S	103°32'E
Lāhījān, Iran	232-33	37°12'N	50°00'E
Laholm, Swe. (lä'hôlm)	192-93	56°31'N	13°03'E
Lahore, Pak. (lä-hōr')	232-33	31°35'N	74°20'E
Lahr, Ger. (lär)	194-95	48°21'N	7°52'E
Lahti, Fin. (lä'tē)	192-93	60°59'N	25°40'E
Laibach, nat. cap., Slvn. see Ljubljana	200-01	46°03'N	14°31'E
Laibin, China (lī-bĭn)	238-39	23°42'N	109°14'E
Laichow Bay, b., China see Laizhou Wan	240-41	37°20'N	119°19'E
L'Aigle, Fr. (lĕ'gl')	196-97	48°46'N	0°38'E
Laiwui, Indon.	248-49	1°21'S	127°39'E
Laiyang, China (lāī'yäng)	240-41	36°58'N	120°43'E
Laizhou Bay, b., China (lī-jō bā) see Laizhou Wan	240-41	37°20'N	119°19'E
Laizhou Wan, b., China (lī-jō wän)	240-41	37°20'N	119°19'E
Lajeado, Braz. (lä-zhĕá'dô)	168-69	29°24'S	51°57'W
Lajes, Braz. (lá'zhĕs)	163d	5°41'S	36°14'W
Lajinha, Braz. (lä-zhē'nyä)	172	20°09'S	41°37'W
La Junta, Co., U.S. (lȧ ho͝on'tȧ)	120-21	37°59'N	103°33'W
Lake Arthur, La., U.S. (lāk är'thŭr)	122-23	30°05'N	92°41'W
Lakeba, i., Fiji	279f	18°13'S	178°47'W
Lakeba Passage, strt., Fiji	279f	17°55'S	178°45'W
Lake Cargelligo, Austl.	276	33°19'S	146°22'E
Lake Charles, La., U.S. (lāk chärlz')	122-23	30°14'N	93°13'W
Lake City, Fl., U.S. (lāk sĭ'tĭ)	124-25	30°12'N	82°38'W
Lake City, Mn., U.S. (lāk sĭ'tē)	114-15	44°27'N	92°17'W
Lake City, S.C., U.S. (lāk sĭ'tĭ)	124-25	33°52'N	79°45'W
Lake Cowichan, B.C., Can. (lāk kou'ĭ-chȧn)	132-33	48°50'N	124°03'W
Lake Crystal, Mn., U.S. (lāk krĭs'tȧl)	114-15	44°07'N	94°13'W
Lake Geneva, Wi., U.S. (lāk jĕ-nē'vȧ)	116-17	42°36'N	88°26'W
Lake Harbour, Nu., Can. see Kimmirut	128-29	62°51'N	69°53'W
Lake Havasu City, Az., U.S. (lāk hăv'â-so͞o sĭ'tē)	118-19	34°29'N	114°21'W
Lakeland, Fl., U.S. (lāk wûrth')	125a	28°03'N	81°58'W
Lake Linden, Mi., U.S. (lāk lĭn'dĕn)	114-15	47°12'N	88°24'W
Lake Louise, Ab., Can. (lāk lo͞o-ēz')	132-33	51°27'N	116°13'W
Lake Mills, Ia., U.S. (lāk mĭlz')	114-15	43°25'N	93°32'W
Lake Oswego, Or., U.S. (lāk ŏs-wē'go)	112-13	45°25'N	122°43'W
Lake Placid, N.Y., U.S. (lāk plăs'ĭd)	116-17	44°17'N	73°59'W
Lake Preston, S.D., U.S. (lāk prĕs'tŭn)	114-15	44°22'N	97°23'W
Lake Providence, La., U.S. (lāk prŏv'ĭ-dĕns)	124-25	32°49'N	91°11'W
Lakeview, Or., U.S.	112-13	42°12'N	120°21'W
Lake Village, Ar., U.S. (lāk vĭl'āj)	124-25	33°19'N	91°17'W
Lake Wales, Fl., U.S. (lāk wālz')	125a	27°54'N	81°35'W
Lakewood, Co., U.S. (lāk'wo͝od)	120-21	39°44'N	105°07'W
Lakewood, N.J., U.S. (lāk'wo͝od)	116-17	40°07'N	74°14'W
Lakewood, Oh., U.S. (lāk'wo͝od)	116-17	41°29'N	81°48'W
Lakewood, Wa., U.S. (lāk'wo͝od)	112-13	47°11'N	122°31'W
Lake Worth, Fl., U.S. (lāk wûrth')	125a	26°37'N	80°03'W
Lakhdenpokh'ya, Russia (l'ăk-dĭe'npŏkyȧ)	192-93	61°31'N	30°12'E
Lakhīmpur, India	234-35	27°57'N	80°47'E
Lakota, N.D., U.S. (lȧ-kō'tȧ)	114-15	48°02'N	98°21'W
Lakshadweep, state, India	236	10°0'N	73°00'E
Lakshadweep, is., India	236	10°0'N	73°00'E
Lakshadweep Sea, s., Asia	236	7°0'N	76°00'E
La Libertad, Guat. (lä lē-bĕr-tädh')	148	16°47'N	90°07'W
La Ligua, Chile (lä lē'gwä)	163e	32°27'S	71°15'W
Lalitpur, India	234-35	24°41'N	78°25'E
Lalitpur, Nepal	234-35	27°40'N	85°19'E
La Loche, Sk., Can.	134-35	56°29'N	109°26'W
La Louvière, Bel. (lȧ lo͞o-vyâr')	190-91	50°29'N	4°12'E
La Luz, Mex. (lä lo͞oz')	146-47	24°12'N	97°52'W
Lama, Ozero, lk., Russia	218-19	69°32'N	90°27'E
La Madrid, Arg.	168-69	27°39'S	65°15'W
La Malbaie, Qc., Can. (lȧ mäl-bā')	138-39	47°40'N	70°09'W
La Mancha, reg., Spain (lä män'chä)	198-99	39°21'N	2°28'W
La Manche, strt., Eur. see English Channel	190-91	50°13'N	2°20'W
Lamar, Co., U.S. (lȧ-mär')	120-21	38°05'N	102°37'W
Lamar, Mo., U.S. (lȧ-mär')	120-21	37°30'N	94°16'W
La Marmora, Punta, mtn., Italy (pŏ'n-tä-lä-mä'r-mô-rä)	200-01	39°59'N	9°20'E
Lamas, Peru (lä'mäs)	170	6°25'S	76°35'W
Lamballe, Fr. (läɴ-bäl')	196-97	48°28'N	2°32'W
Lambayeque, Peru (läm-bä-yā'kå)	170	6°41'S	79°54'W
Lambertsbaai, S. Afr. see Lambert's Bay	264-65	32°06'S	18°19'E
Lambert's Bay, S. Afr.	264-65	32°06'S	18°19'E
Lame Deer, Mt., U.S. (lām dēr')	112-13	45°39'N	106°41'W
La Méditerranée, s., see Mediterranean Sea	188-89	35°0'N	20°00'E
Lamego, Port. (lä-mā'gō)	198-99	41°06'N	7°49'W
Lamesa, Tx., U.S.	120-21	32°45'N	101°58'W
Lamía, Grc. (lȧ-mē'ȧ)	200-01	38°54'N	22°26'E
Lamon Bay, b., Phil. (lä-mōn' bā)	250	14°28'N	122°01'E
Lamoni, Ia., U.S.	120-21	40°38'N	93°56'W
Lamotrek, at., Micron.	280-81	7°21'N	146°20'E
La Moure, N.D., U.S. (lȧ mo͞or')	114-15	46°20'N	98°17'W
Lampang, Thai.	246-47	18°17'N	99°29'E
Lampasas, Tx., U.S. (lăm-păs'ȧs)	122-23	31°04'N	98°11'W
Lampazos de Naranjo, Mex.	122-23	27°02'N	100°31'W
Lamphun, Thai.	246-47	18°35'N	99°01'E
Lamu, Kenya (lä'mo͞o)	262-63	2°17'S	40°53'E
Lan', stm., Bela. (lȧn')	194-95	52°09'N	27°17'E
Lāna'i, i., Hi., U.S. (lä-nä'ē)	127a	20°50'N	156°55'W
Lanark, Scot., U.K. (lăn'ȧrk)	190-91	55°41'N	3°47'W
Lancang, stm., Asia see Mekong	246-47	10°33'N	105°27'E
Lancaster, Eng., U.K.	190-91	54°03'N	2°50'W
Lancaster, Ca., U.S. (lăŋ'kăs-tē)	118-19	34°42'N	118°08'W
Lancaster, Ky., U.S. (lăŋ'kăs-tē)	116-17	37°37'N	84°35'W
Lancaster, Oh., U.S. (lăŋ'kăs-tē)	116-17	39°43'N	82°36'W
Lancaster, Pa., U.S.	116-17	40°03'N	76°19'W
Lancaster, S.C., U.S. (lăŋ'kăs-tē)	124-25	34°43'N	80°46'W
Lancaster, Wi., U.S. (lăŋ'kăs-tē)	114-15	42°51'N	90°43'W
Lanchow, China see Lanzhou	240-41	36°04'N	103°43'E
Lander, Wy., U.S. (lăn'dēr)	112-13	42°50'N	108°44'W
Landerneau, Fr. (läɴ-dĕr-nō')	196-97	48°27'N	4°16'W
Landes, reg., Fr. (läɴd)	196-97	44°10'N	0°52'W
Landsberg, Pol. see Gorzów Wielkopolski	194-95	52°44'N	15°14'E
Landsberg an der Warthe, Pol. see Gorzów Wielkopolski	194-95	52°44'N	15°14'E
Land's End, c., Eng., U.K. (lăndz ĕnd)	190-91	50°03'N	5°44'W
Landshut, Ger. (länts'ho͞ot)	194-95	48°33'N	12°09'E
Landskrona, Swe. (låns-krô'nȧ)	192-93	55°52'N	12°50'E
Lanett, Al., U.S. (lȧ-nĕt')	124-25	32°52'N	85°11'W
La'nga Co, lk., China (läŋ-lä tswo)	234-35	30°43'N	81°13'E
Langano Hāyk', lk., Eth.	269d	7°36'N	38°46'E
Langdon, N.D., U.S.	114-15	48°46'N	98°23'W
Langeland, i., Den.	192-93	55°00'N	10°51'E
Langeoog, i., Ger.	194-95	53°45'N	7°32'E
Langjökull, ice, Ice. (läng-yû'ko͞ol)	190a	64°42'N	20°12'W
Langkawi, Pulau, i., Malay.	246-47	6°24'N	99°50'E
Langley, B.C., Can. (lăng'lĭ)	132-33	49°06'N	122°39'W
Langon, Fr. (läɴ-gôɴ')	196-97	44°33'N	0°15'W
Langøya, i., Nor.	184-85	68°44'N	14°50'E
Langqên, stm., Asia see Sutlej	234-35	29°21'N	71°02'E
Langres, Fr. (läɴ'gr')	196-97	47°52'N	5°19'E
Langsa, Indon. (läng'sȧ)	246-47	4°28'N	97°58'E
Lang Son, Viet. (lăng'sŏn')	246-47	21°51'N	106°45'E
Langzhong, China (läŋ-jôŋ)	238-39	31°34'N	105°59'E
Lanigan, Sk., Can. (lăn'ĭ-gȧn)	134-35	51°52'N	105°02'W
Länkäran, Azer. (lĕn-kô-rän')	227	38°45'N	48°51'E
Lansdale, Pa., U.S. (lănz'dāl)	116-17	40°15'N	75°17'W
L'Anse, Mi., U.S. (låns)	114-15	46°45'N	88°26'W
Lansing, Mi., U.S.	116-17	42°45'N	84°33'W
Lanta Yai, Ko, i., Thai.	246-47	7°34'N	99°03'E
Lanxi, China	238-39	29°12'N	119°28'E
Lanzarote, i., Spain (län-zȧ-rō'tä)	199d	29°0'N	13°40'W
Lanzhou, China (län-jō)	240-41	36°04'N	103°43'E
Lao, nation, Asia see Laos	206-07	18°0'N	105°00'E
Laoag, Phil. (lä-wäg')	250	18°12'N	120°36'E
Laoang, Phil.	250	12°35'N	125°02'E
Lao Cai, Viet.	246-47	22°30'N	103°58'E
Laoha, stm., China	240-41	43°25'N	120°45'E
Laohekou, China	238-39	32°25'N	111°36'E
Laon, Fr. (läɴ)	196-97	49°34'N	3°39'E
La Orchila, Isla, i., Ven.	164-65	11°48'N	66°09'W
La Oroya, Peru (lä-ô-rō'yä)	163a	11°30'S	75°56'W
Laos, nation, Asia (lä-ōs) (lȧ-ōs')	206-07	18°0'N	105°00'E
La Palma, Pan. (lä-päl'mä)	150	7°42'N	80°11'W
La Palma, Pan.	150	8°24'N	78°09'W
La Palma, i., Spain (lä-päl'mä)	199d	28°40'N	17°52'W
La Paloma, Ur.	173	34°40'S	54°10'W
La Paragua, Ven.	164-65	6°51'N	63°19'W
La Paz, Arg. (lä päz')	173	30°44'S	59°38'W
La Paz, Arg. (lä päz')	171	33°27'S	67°34'W
La Paz, Hond. (lä-pá'z)	149	14°19'N	87°41'W
La Paz, Mex. (lä-pá'z)	146-47	23°41'N	100°43'W
La Paz, Mex.	144-45	24°10'N	110°18'W
La Paz, nat. cap., Bol. (lä-pá'z)	168-69	16°30'S	68°09'W
Lapeer, Mi., U.S. (lȧ-pēr')	116-17	43°03'N	83°18'W
Lapland, reg., Eur. (lăp'lȧnd)	184-85	68°0'N	25°00'E
La Plata, Arg. (lä plä'tä)	173	34°55'S	57°57'W
La Plata, Mo., U.S. (lȧ plä'tȧ)	120-21	40°02'N	92°29'W
La Pocatière, Qc., Can. (lȧ pô-kȧ-tyâr')	138-39	47°22'N	70°02'W
La Porte, In., U.S. (lȧ pōrt')	116-17	41°37'N	86°42'W
La Porte City, Ia., U.S. (lȧ pōrt' sĭ'tē)	114-15	42°19'N	92°11'W
Lappland, reg., Eur. see Lapland	184-85	68°0'N	25°00'E
Laptev Sea, s., Russia (läp'tyĭf sē)	208-09	76°0'N	126°00'E
Laptevykh, More, s., Russia see Laptev Sea	208-09	76°0'N	126°00'E
La Quiaca, Arg. (lä kē-ä'kä)	168-69	22°07'S	65°36'W
L'Aquila, Italy (lá'kē-lä)	200-01	42°21'N	13°24'E
Lār, Iran (lär)	230-31	27°40'N	54°20'E
Larache, Mor. (lä-räsh')	269a	35°12'N	6°09'W
Lārak, Jazīreh-ye, i., Iran	230-31	26°52'N	56°22'E
Laramie, Wy., U.S. (lăr'ȧ-mĭ)	112-13	41°19'N	105°35'W
Larantuka, Indon.	248-49	8°19'S	122°58'E
Larat, Pulau, i., Indon.	224-25	7°08'S	131°50'E
Laredo, Spain (lȧ-rā'dhō)	198-99	43°25'N	3°25'W
Laredo, Tx., U.S. (lȧ-rā'dhō)	122-23	27°31'N	99°28'W
Largo, Cayo, i., Cuba (kä'yō-lär'gō)	142-43	21°38'N	81°28'W
Larimore, N.D., U.S. (lăr'ĭ-môr)	114-15	47°54'N	97°38'W
La Rioja, Arg. (lä rē-ōhä)	168-69	29°25'S	66°51'W
La Rioja, state, Arg. (lä-rē-ô'kä)	168-69	30°0'S	67°30'W
Lárisa, Grc. (lä'rē-sȧ)	200-01	39°38'N	22°25'E
Larissa, Grc. see Lárisa	200-01	39°38'N	22°25'E
Lārkāna, Pak.	232-33	27°33'N	68°13'E
Larnaca, Cyp. see Larnaka	228-29	34°55'N	33°38'E
Larnaka, Cyp.	228-29	34°55'N	33°38'E
Larned, Ks., U.S. (lär'nĕd)	120-21	38°11'N	99°05'W
La Rochelle, Fr. (lȧ rô-shĕl')	196-97	46°10'N	1°10'W
La Roche-sur-Yon, Fr. (lȧ rôsh'sûr-yôɴ')	196-97	46°40'N	1°26'W
La Roda, Spain (lä rō'dä)	198-99	39°12'N	2°09'W
La Ronge, Sk., Can.	134-35	55°06'N	105°17'W
La Rubia, Arg.	173	30°08'S	61°48'W
Larvik, Nor. (lär'vēk)	192-93	59°04'N	10°01'E
La Salle, Il., U.S. (lȧ săl')	116-17	41°20'N	89°06'W
La Sarre, Qc., Can.	136-37	48°48'N	79°12'W
Las Aves, Isla, i., Ven.	143b	15°41'N	63°37'W
Lascano, Ur.	173	33°40'S	54°13'W
Las Cruces, N.M., U.S. (läs-kro͞o'sĕs)	118-19	32°19'N	106°47'W
La Selle, Morne, mtn., Haiti (mōrn lä'sĕl')	142-43	18°22'N	71°59'W
La Serena, Chile (lä-sĕ-rĕ'nä)	168-69	29°54'S	71°15'W
Las Flores, Arg. (läs flo'rĕs)	173	36°01'S	59°06'W
Las Heras, Arg.	171	46°31'S	68°56'W
Lashio, Mya. (lăsh'ē-ō)	246-47	22°57'N	97°45'E
Lashkar, India see Gwalior	234-35	26°13'N	78°09'E
Las Lajas, Arg.	171	38°30'S	70°22'W
Las Lomitas, Arg.	168-69	24°43'S	60°36'W
Las Minas, Cerro, mtn., Hond.	149	14°33'N	88°39'W
La Solana, Spain (lä-sô-lä-nä)	198-99	38°57'N	3°14'W
Las Palmas de Gran Canaria, Spain (läs päl'mäs)	199d	28°07'N	15°26'W
La Spezia, Italy (lä-spĕ'zyä)	200-01	44°07'N	9°50'E
Las Piedras, Ur. (läs-pyĕ'drȧs)	173	34°44'S	56°13'W
Las Piedras, stm., Peru	170	12°31'S	69°14'W
Las Plumas, Arg.	171	43°43'S	67°14'W
Las Rosas, Mex. (läs rō thäs)	146-47	16°22'N	92°22'W
Lassen Peak, vol., Ca., U.S. (lăs'ĕn pēk)	112-13	40°29'N	121°31'W
Lassen Volcanic National Park, n.p., Ca., U.S. (lăs'ĕn vŏl-kăn'ĭk năsh'ŭn-ăl pärk)	112-13	40°30'N	121°27'W
Las Tablas, Pan. (läs tä'bläs)	150	7°46'N	80°17'W
Last Mountain Lake, lk., Sk., Can. (lȧst moun'tĭn lāk)	134-35	51°06'N	105°15'W
Las Tórtolas, Cerro, mtn., S.A.	168-69	29°57'S	69°53'W
Lastoursville, Gabon (lȧs-to͞or-vēl')	260-61	0°48'S	12°42'E
Las Tunas, Cuba	142-43	20°58'N	76°57'W
Las Varillas, Arg.	173	31°52'S	62°42'W
Las Vegas, N.M., U.S. (läs vā'gäs)	120-21	35°36'N	105°13'W
Las Vegas, Nv., U.S. (läs vā'gäs)	118-19	36°11'N	115°08'W
Latacunga, Ec. (lä-tä-kòŋ'gä)	170	0°56'S	78°36'W
Latakia, Syria	228-29	35°31'N	35°48'E
La Teste-de-Buch, Fr. (lä-tĕst-dĕ-büsh)	196-97	44°38'N	1°09'W
Lathrop, Mo., U.S. (lā'thrŭp)	120-21	39°33'N	94°20'W
La Tortuga, Isla, i., Ven. (ē's-lä-lä-tôr-to͞o'gä)	163b	10°56'N	65°20'W
Latouche Treville, Cape, c., Austl.	272-73	18°28'S	121°50'E
La Tremblade, Fr. (lä-trĕɴ-bläd')	196-97	45°46'N	1°08'W

ăt; finăl; rāte; senâte; ärm; åsk; sofȧ; fâre; ch-choose; dh-as th in other; bē; ēvent; bĕt; recĕnt; cratēr; g-gō; gh-guttural g; bĭt; ĭ-short neutral; rīde; ĸ-guttural k as ch in German ich;

Feature (Pronunciation)	Page	Lat.	Long.
Latrobe, Pa., U.S. (lȧ-trōb´)	**116-17**	40°18'N	79°22'W
La Tuque, Qc., Can. (lȧ´tük´)	**136-37**	47°26'N	72°47'W
Lātūr, India (lä-to͞or´)	**236**	18°24'N	76°35'E
Latvia, nation, Eur. (lăt´vē-ȧ)	**174-75**	57°0'N	25°00'E
Latvija, nation, Eur. *see* Latvia	**174-75**	57°0'N	25°00'E
Lauenburg, Pol. *see* Lębork	**194-95**	54°32'N	17°46'E
Lau Group, is., Fiji	**279f**	18°20'S	178°30'W
Lauis, Switz. *see* Lugano	**194-95**	46°01'N	8°57'E
Launceston, Austl. (lôn´sĕs-tŭn)	**276**	41°25'S	147°08'E
La Unión, Chile (lä-o͞o-nyô´n)	**171**	40°18'S	73°05'W
La Unión, El Sal.	**148**	13°20'N	87°51'W
La Unión, Mex. (lä o͞on-nyōn´)	**146-47**	17°58'N	101°49'W
Laura, Austl. (lôrȧ)	**277**	15°33'S	144°26'E
Laurel, De., U.S. (lô´rĕl)	**116-17**	38°33'N	75°34'W
Laurel, Md., U.S. (lô´rĕl)	**116-17**	39°06'N	76°51'W
Laurel, Ms., U.S. (lô´rĕl)	**124-25**	31°42'N	89°08'W
Laurel, Mt., U.S. (lô´rĕl)	**112-13**	45°40'N	108°46'W
Laurel, Ne., U.S. (lô´rĕl)	**114-15**	42°26'N	97°06'W
Laurens, S.C., U.S. (lô´rĕnz)	**124-25**	34°30'N	82°01'W
Laurentides, Les, plat., Qc., Can.	**130-31**	48°0'N	71°00'W
Laurinburg, N.C., U.S. (lô´rĭn-bûrg)	**124-25**	34°47'N	79°28'W
Laurium, Mi., U.S. (lô´rĭ-ŭm)	**114-15**	47°14'N	88°26'W
Lausanne, Switz. (lō-zȧn´)	**194-95**	46°31'N	6°38'E
Lausitzer Neiße, stm., Eur. *see* Neisse	**194-95**	52°04'N	14°46'E
Laut, Pulau, i., Indon.	**248-49**	3°40'S	116°10'E
Lautaro, Chile (lou-tä´rô)	**171**	38°31'S	72°26'W
Laut Kecil, Kepulauan, is., Indon.	**248-49**	4°49'S	115°44'E
Lava, Nosy, i., Madag.	**264-65**	14°33'S	47°36'E
Lava Beds National Monument, n.p., Ca., U.S. (lä´vȧ bĕds năsh´ŭn-ăl mŏn´ū-mĕnt)	**112-13**	41°45'N	121°32'W
Laval, Qc., Can.	**136-37**	45°33'N	73°44'W
Laval, Fr. (lä-väl´)	**196-97**	48°04'N	0°46'W
Lāvān, Jazīreh-ye, i., Iran	**230-31**	26°49'N	53°15'E
Lavapié, Punta, c., Chile	**171**	37°09'S	73°35'W
La Vega, Dom. Rep. (lä-vĕ´gä)	**142-43**	19°13'N	70°31'W
Laverton, Austl. (lā´vēr-tŭn)	**270-71**	28°37'S	122°24'E
La Victoria, Ven. (lä vĕk-tō´rē-ä)	**163b**	10°13'N	67°20'W
Lavras, Braz. (lä´vräzh)	**172**	21°14'S	45°00'W
Lavrentiya, Russia	**126**	65°35'N	171°01'W
Lawas, Malay.	**248-49**	4°51'N	115°24'E
Lawn Hill National Park, n.p., Austl. *see* Boodjamulla National Park	**277**	18°45'S	138°27'E
Lawrence, In., U.S. (lô´rĕns)	**116-17**	39°50'N	86°01'W
Lawrence, Ks., U.S. (lô´rĕns)	**120-21**	38°57'N	95°15'W
Lawrence, Ma., U.S. (lô´rĕns)	**116-17**	42°42'N	71°10'W
Lawrenceburg, In., U.S. (lô´rĕnsbûrg)	**116-17**	39°05'N	84°52'W
Lawrenceburg, Ky., U.S. (lô´rĕnsbûrg)	**116-17**	38°03'N	84°54'W
Lawrenceburg, Tn., U.S. (lô´rĕnsbûrg)	**124-25**	35°15'N	87°20'W
Lawrenceville, Ga., U.S. (lô-rĕns-vĭl)	**124-25**	33°58'N	83°59'W
Lawrenceville, Il., U.S. (lô-rĕns-vĭl)	**116-17**	38°43'N	87°41'W
Lawrenceville, Va., U.S. (lô-rĕns-vĭl)	**124-25**	36°46'N	77°51'W
Lawton, Ok., U.S. (lô´tŭn)	**120-21**	34°36'N	98°24'W
Lawz, Jabal al-, mtn., Sau. Ar.	**228-29**	28°40'N	35°18'E
La'youn, nat. cap., W. Sah. *see* Laayoune	**258-59**	27°10'N	13°12'W
Laysan Island, i., Hi., U.S.	**127**	25°50'N	171°50'W
Layton, Ut., U.S. (lā´tŭn)	**112-13**	41°05'N	111°58'W
Lazarev, Russia	**218-19**	52°12'N	141°30'E
Lázaro Cárdenas, Mex.	**146-47**	17°57'N	102°12'W
Lazdijai, Lith. (läzh´dē-yī´)	**194-95**	54°14'N	23°32'E
Lead, S.D., U.S. (lēd)	**114-15**	44°21'N	103°46'W
Leader, Sk., Can.	**134-35**	50°53'N	109°31'W
Leadville, Co., U.S. (lĕd´vĭl)	**118-19**	39°15'N	106°18'W
Leaf, stm., Ms., U.S. (lēf)	**124-25**	31°0'N	88°45'W
League City, Tx., U.S. (lēg sĭ´tĭ)	**122-23**	29°30'N	95°06'W
Leamington, On., Can. (lĕm´ĭng-tŭn)	**136-37**	42°02'N	82°36'W
Leavenworth, Ks., U.S. (lĕv´ĕn-wûrth)	**120-21**	39°18'N	94°56'W
Leavenworth, Wa., U.S. (lĕv´ĕn-wûrth)	**112-13**	47°36'N	120°40'W
Łeba, Pol. (lā´bä)	**194-95**	54°45'N	17°33'E
Lebak, Phil.	**250**	6°31'N	124°02'E
Lebanon, In., U.S. (lĕb´ȧ-nŭn)	**116-17**	40°03'N	86°28'W
Lebanon, Ky., U.S. (lĕb´ȧ-nŭn)	**116-17**	37°34'N	85°15'W
Lebanon, Mo., U.S. (lĕb´ȧ-nŭn)	**120-21**	37°41'N	92°40'W
Lebanon, N.H., U.S. (lĕb´ȧ-nŭn)	**116-17**	43°39'N	72°15'W
Lebanon, Oh., U.S. (lĕb´ȧ-nŭn)	**116-17**	39°26'N	84°13'W
Lebanon, Or., U.S. (lĕb´ȧ-nŭn)	**112-13**	44°32'N	122°54'W
Lebanon, Tn., U.S. (lĕb´ȧ-nŭn)	**124-25**	36°13'N	86°17'W
Lebanon, Va., U.S. (lĕb´ȧ-nŭn)	**124-25**	36°54'N	82°05'W
Lebanon, nation, Asia (lĕb´ȧ-nŭn)	**206-07**	34°0'N	36°00'E
Lebedyan', Russia (lyĕ´bĕ-dyän´)	**202-03**	53°01'N	39°08'E
Lębork, Pol. (lăn-bôrk´)	**194-95**	54°32'N	17°46'E
Lebrija, Spain (lå-brē´hä)	**198-99**	36°56'N	6°04'W
Lebu, Chile	**171**	37°37'S	73°39'W
Lecce, Italy (lĕt´chā)	**200-01**	40°21'N	18°10'E
Lecco, Italy (lĕk´kō)	**200-01**	45°51'N	9°23'E
Le Creusot, Fr. (lĕkrû-zô)	**196-97**	46°48'N	4°26'E
Ledo, India	**234-35**	27°17'N	95°44'E
Ledu, China	**240-41**	36°28'N	102°24'E
Leduc, Ab., Can. (lĕ-do͞ok´)	**132-33**	53°15'N	113°32'W
Ledyanaya, Gora, mtn., Russia	**218-19**	61°53'N	171°09'E
Ledyard Bay, b., Ak., U.S.	**126**	69°14'N	164°31'W
Leech Lake, lk., Mn., U.S. (lēch lāk)	**114-15**	47°09'N	94°23'W
Leeds, Eng., U.K. (lēdz)	**190-91**	53°50'N	1°35'W
Leeds, N.D., U.S. (lēdz)	**114-15**	48°17'N	99°27'W
Leesburg, Fl., U.S. (lēz´bûrg)	**124-25**	28°49'N	81°53'W
Leesburg, Va., U.S. (lēz´bûrg)	**116-17**	39°06'N	77°34'W
Leesville, La., U.S. (lēz´vĭl)	**122-23**	31°08'N	93°16'W
Leeton, Austl.	**276**	34°33'S	146°24'E
Leeuwarden, Neth. (lā´wär-dĕn)	**190-91**	53°12'N	5°47'E
Leeuwin, Cape, c., Austl. (kāp o͞o´wĭn)	**272-73**	34°23'S	115°08'E
Leeward Islands, is., N.A. (lē´wērd ī´lăndz)	**143b**	17°0'N	63°00'W
Lefkáda, i., Grc.	**200-01**	38°42'N	20°39'E
Lefkoşa, nat. cap., Cyp. *see* Nicosia	**228-29**	35°10'N	33°22'E
Lefroy, Lake, lk., Austl. (lăk lē-froi´)	**272-73**	31°15'S	121°40'E
Leganés, Spain (lå-gä´nås)	**198-99**	40°20'N	3°46'W
Legaspi, Phil.	**250**	13°08'N	123°45'E
Leghorn, Italy *see* Livorno	**200-01**	43°34'N	10°19'E
Legnica, Pol. (lĕk-nĭt´sȧ)	**194-95**	51°13'N	16°10'E
Leh, India (lā)	**234-35**	34°10'N	77°35'E
Le Havre, Fr. (lē åv´r´)	**196-97**	49°29'N	0°08'E
Leicester, Eng., U.K. (lĕs´tēr)	**190-91**	52°39'N	1°08'W
Leikanger, Nor. (lī´käŋ´gēr)	**192-93**	61°12'N	6°50'E
Leine, stm., Ger. (lī´nĕ)	**194-95**	52°43'N	9°36'E
Leipzig, Ger. (līp´tsĭk)	**194-95**	51°20'N	12°23'E
Leiria, Port. (lā-rē´ä)	**198-99**	39°45'N	8°48'W
Leitchfield, Ky., U.S. (lēch´fēld)	**116-17**	37°29'N	86°18'W
Leizhou Bandao, pen., China (lā-jō bän-dou)	**238-39**	20°47'N	110°05'E
Leksand, Swe. (lĕk´sänd)	**192-93**	60°43'N	15°01'E
Leland, Mi., U.S. (lē´lănd)	**116-17**	45°01'N	85°46'W
Leland, Ms., U.S. (lē´lănd)	**124-25**	33°25'N	90°54'W
Leli Shan, mtn., China	**234-35**	33°26'N	81°42'E
Le Maire, Estrecho de, strt., Arg. (ĕs-trĕ´chô-dĕ-lĕ-mī´rĕ)	**171**	54°50'S	64°60'W
Léman, Lac, lk., Eur. *see* Geneva, Lake	**194-95**	46°24'N	6°22'E
Le Mans, Fr. (lē mäN´)	**196-97**	48°00'N	0°12'E
Le Mars, Ia., U.S. (lē märz´)	**114-15**	42°48'N	96°10'W
Lemesós, Cyp.	**228-29**	34°41'N	33°03'E
Lemhi Range, mts., Id., U.S. (lĕm´hī rānj)	**112-13**	44°33'N	113°36'W
Lemmon, S.D., U.S. (lĕm´ŭn)	**114-15**	45°56'N	102°10'W
Lemnos, i., Grc. *see* Límnos	**200-01**	39°55'N	25°18'E
Lempa, stm., N.A. (lĕm´pä)	**148**	13°15'N	88°49'W
Lena, stm., Russia (lē´nȧ) (lyĕ´nŭ)	**218-19**	72°25'N	126°40'E
Lençóis, Braz.	**166-67**	12°34'S	41°23'W
Lenexa, Ks., U.S. (lē´nĕx-ă)	**120-21**	38°58'N	94°44'W
Lenghu, China	**220-21**	38°50'N	93°26'E
Lenin, Qullai, mtn., Asia *see* Lenin Peak	**232-33**	39°20'N	72°55'E
Lenina, Pik, mtn., Asia *see* Lenin Peak	**232-33**	39°20'N	72°55'E
Lenin Atyndagy Choku, mtn., Asia *see* Lenin Peak	**232-33**	39°20'N	72°55'E
Leningrad, Russia *see* Saint Petersburg	**192-93**	59°57'N	30°15'E
Leningradskaya, Russia (lyĕ-nĭn-gräd´skȧ-yȧ)	**202-03**	46°19'N	39°23'E
Leninogor, Kaz. *see* Ridder	**226**	50°21'N	83°30'E
Leninogorsk, Russia	**186-87**	54°35'N	52°29'E
Lenin Peak, mtn., Asia	**232-33**	39°20'N	72°55'E
Leninsk, Kaz. *see* Bayqongyr	**226**	45°38'N	63°18'E
Leninsk-Kuznetskiy, Russia	**218-19**	54°41'N	86°12'E
Leninskoye, Russia	**240-41**	47°60'N	132°38'E
Lennox, S.D., U.S. (lĕn´ŭks)	**114-15**	43°21'N	96°55'W
Lennox, Isla, i., Chile	**171**	55°18'S	66°50'W
Lenoir, N.C., U.S. (lē-nōr´)	**124-25**	35°55'N	81°32'W
Lensk, Russia	**218-19**	60°44'N	114°56'E
Léo, Burkina	**260-61**	11°06'N	2°06'W
Leoben, Aus. (lå-ō´bĕn)	**194-95**	47°22'N	15°06'E
Léogâne, Haiti (lā-ō-gan´)	**142-43**	18°31'N	72°38'W
Leominster, Ma., U.S. (lĕm´ĭn-stēr)	**116-17**	42°32'N	71°45'W
León, Mex. (lå-ōn´)	**146-47**	21°07'N	101°42'W
León, Nic. (lĕ-ô´n)	**149**	12°26'N	86°52'W
León, Spain (lĕ-ô´n)	**198-99**	42°36'N	5°34'W
Leon, Ia., U.S. (lē´ŏn)	**114-15**	40°45'N	93°44'W
León, hist. reg., Spain (lĕ-ô´n)	**198-99**	42°0'N	6°00'W
Leon, stm., Tx., U.S. (lē´ŏn)	**122-23**	30°59'N	97°24'W
León de los Aldamas, Mex. *see* León	**146-47**	21°07'N	101°42'W
Leonforte, Italy (lā-ôn-fôr´tā)	**200-01**	37°38'N	14°23'E
Leonora, Austl.	**270-71**	28°53'S	121°20'E
Léopold II, Lac, lk., D.R.C. *see* Mai-Ndombe, Lac	**260-61**	2°25'S	18°18'E
Leopoldina, Braz. (lā-ô-pôl-dē´nä)	**172**	21°32'S	42°38'W
Léopoldville, nat. cap., D.R.C. *see* Kinshasa	**262-63**	4°21'S	15°18'E
Lepe, Spain (lā´pā)	**198-99**	37°15'N	7°12'W
Leping, China (lŭ-pĭŋ)	**238-39**	28°57'N	117°06'E
Le Port, Reu.	**265a**	20°55'S	55°18'E
Le Puy, Fr. (lē pwē´)	**196-97**	45°03'N	3°53'E
Lerdo, Mex. (lĕr´dō)	**122-23**	25°32'N	103°31'W
Lérida, Spain *see* Lleida	**198-99**	41°37'N	0°38'E
Lerma, stm., Mex. (lĕr´mä)	**146-47**	20°13'N	102°41'W
Le Roy, N.Y., U.S. (lē roi´)	**116-17**	42°58'N	77°59'W
Lerwick, Scot., U.K. (lĕr´ĭk) (lûr´wĭk)	**190c**	60°09'N	1°09'W
Lesbos, i., Grc. *see* Lésvos	**200-01**	39°10'N	26°20'E
Les Cayes, Haiti	**142-43**	18°12'N	73°45'W
Leshan, China (lŭ-shän)	**238-39**	29°34'N	103°45'E
Leshukonskoye, Russia	**186-87**	64°53'N	45°42'E
Leskovac, Serb. (lĕs´kō-vȧts)	**200-01**	43°01'N	21°57'E
Leslie, Mi., U.S. (lĕz´lĭ)	**116-17**	42°27'N	84°25'W
Lesosibirsk, Russia	**218-19**	58°14'N	92°29'E
Lesotho, nation, Afr. (lĕsō´thō)	**253**	29°30'S	28°30'E
Lesozavodsk, Russia (lyĕ-sô-zȧ-vôdsk´)	**244**	45°28'N	133°24'E
Les Sables-d'Olonne, Fr. (lā sȧ´bl'dô-lŭn´)	**196-97**	46°30'N	1°47'W
Les Saintes, is., Guad. (lā-săNt´)	**143b**	15°52'N	61°37'W
Lesser Antilles, is., (lĕs´ēr ăn-tĭ´lēz)	**143b**	15°0'N	61°00'W
Lesser Caucasus, mts., Asia	**227**	40°60'N	44°35'E
Lesser Khingan Range, mts., China	**240-41**	48°45'N	127°00'E
Lesser Slave, stm., Ab., Can. (lĕs´ēr slāv)	**132-33**	55°10'N	114°03'W
Lesser Slave Lake, lk., Ab., Can. (lĕs´ēr slāv lāk)	**132-33**	55°29'N	115°10'W
Lesser Sunda Islands, is., Asia (lĕs´ēr so͞on´dȧ ī´lăndz)	**248-49**	9°0'S	120°00'E
Le Sueur, Mn., U.S. (lē so͞or´)	**114-15**	44°28'N	93°55'W
Lésvos, i., Grc.	**200-01**	39°10'N	26°20'E
Leszno, Pol. (lĕsh´nô)	**194-95**	51°51'N	16°35'E
Lethbridge, Ab., Can. (lĕth´brĭj)	**132-33**	49°42'N	112°49'W
Lethem, Guy.	**164-65**	3°23'N	59°48'W
Leti, Kepulauan, is., Indon.	**248-49**	8°13'S	127°50'E
Leticia, Col. (lĕ-tē´syȧ)	**164-65**	4°10'S	69°56'W
Leucas, i., Grc. *see* Lefkáda	**200-01**	38°42'N	20°39'E
Levanger, Nor. (lĕ-văng´ĕr)	**184-85**	63°45'N	11°18'E
Leveque, Cape, c., Austl. (kāp lē-vĕk´)	**272-73**	16°26'S	122°56'E
Leverkusen, Ger. (lĕ´fĕr-ko͞o-zĕn)	**194-95**	51°03'N	6°59'E
Levice, Slvk. (lā´vĕt-sĕ)	**194-95**	48°13'N	18°37'E
Le Vigan, Fr. (lē vē-gäN´)	**196-97**	43°59'N	3°35'E
Lévis, Qc., Can. (lā-vē´) (lē´vĭs)	**136-37**	46°48'N	71°11'W
Levittown, Pa., U.S. (lĕ´vĭt-toun)	**116-17**	40°09'N	74°51'W
Levkosía, nat. cap., Cyp. *see* Nicosia	**228-29**	35°10'N	33°22'E
Lewes, De., U.S. (lo͞o´ĭs)	**116-17**	38°46'N	75°08'W
Lewis, Isle of, i., Scot., U.K. (ĭl ŏv lo͞o´ĭs)	**190-91**	58°08'N	6°45'W
Lewisburg, Tn., U.S. (lū´ĭs-bûrg)	**124-25**	35°27'N	86°48'W
Lewisburg, W.V., U.S. (lū´ĭs-bûrg)	**116-17**	37°48'N	80°27'W
Lewisporte, Nf., Can. (lū´ĭs-pōrt)	**138-39**	49°16'N	55°05'W
Lewiston, Id., U.S. (lū´ĭs-tŭn)	**112-13**	46°24'N	117°00'W
Lewiston, Me., U.S. (lū´ĭs-tŭn)	**116-17**	44°06'N	70°13'W
Lewistown, Il., U.S. (lū´ĭs-toun)	**120-21**	40°23'N	90°09'W
Lewistown, Mt., U.S. (lū´ĭs-toun)	**112-13**	47°04'N	109°26'W
Lexington, Il., U.S. (lĕk´sĭng-tŭn)	**116-17**	40°38'N	88°46'W
Lexington, Ky., U.S. (lĕk´sĭng-tŭn)	**116-17**	38°03'N	84°31'W
Lexington, Ma., U.S. (lĕk´sĭng-tŭn)	**116-17**	42°27'N	71°14'W
Lexington, Mo., U.S. (lĕk´sĭng-tŭn)	**120-21**	39°11'N	93°53'W
Lexington, N.C., U.S. (lĕk´sĭng-tŭn)	**124-25**	35°49'N	80°15'W
Lexington, Ne., U.S. (lĕk´sĭng-tŭn)	**114-15**	40°47'N	99°44'W
Lexington, Oh., U.S. (lĕk´sĭng-tŭn)	**116-17**	40°41'N	82°34'W
Lexington, Tn., U.S. (lĕk´sĭng-tŭn)	**124-25**	35°39'N	88°24'W
Lexington, Va., U.S. (lĕk´sĭng-tŭn)	**116-17**	37°46'N	79°27'W
Leyte, i., Phil. (lā´tā)	**250**	10°50'N	124°50'E
Leyte Gulf, b., Phil.	**250**	10°50'N	125°25'E
Leżajsk, Pol. (lĕ´zhä-ĭsk)	**194-95**	50°16'N	22°26'E
L'gov, Russia (lgôf)	**202-03**	51°39'N	35°16'E
Lhasa, China (läs´ä)	**234-35**	29°39'N	91°08'E
Lhasa, stm., China	**234-35**	29°20'N	90°46'E
Lhokseumawe, Indon.	**246-47**	5°11'N	97°08'E
Lhorong, China	**238-39**	30°47'N	95°51'E
Li, stm., China	**238-39**	29°12'N	112°11'E
Liangzhou, China *see* Wuwei	**240-41**	37°56'N	102°38'E
Lianjiang, China (lĭĕn-jyäŋ)	**225a**	26°12'N	119°31'E
Lianxian, China	**238-39**	24°47'N	112°21'E
Lianyungang, China (lĭĕn-yòn-gäŋ)	**238-39**	34°37'N	119°11'E
Lianzhou, China *see* Hepu	**238-39**	21°41'N	109°11'E
Liao, stm., China	**240-41**	40°41'N	122°09'E

n-sing; ŋ-baŋk; N-nasalized n; nŏd; cŏmmit; ōld; ôbey; ôrder; oi-boil; fo͞od; ò-as oo in foot; ou-out; s-soft; sh-dish; th-thin; pūre; ûnite; ûrn; stŭd; circŭs; ü-as in French tu; ´-indeterminate vowel.

Feature (Pronunciation)	Page	Lat.	Long.
Liaocheng, China (lĭou-chŭŋ)	**240-41**	36°27'N	115°59'E
Liaodong Bandao, pen., China (lĭou-dôŋ bän-dou)	**240-41**	39°55'N	122°19'E
Liaodong Wan, b., China (lĭou-dôŋ wäŋ)	**240-41**	40°30'N	121°30'E
Liaoning, state, China	**243**	41°0'N	123°00'E
Liaotung, Gulf of, b., China *see* Liaodong Wan	**240-41**	40°30'N	121°30'E
Liaotung Peninsula, pen., China *see* Liaodong Bandao	**240-41**	39°55'N	122°19'E
Liaoyang, China (lyä´ō-yäng´)	**243**	41°16'N	123°10'E
Liaoyuan, China (lĭou-yůän)	**240-41**	42°55'N	125°08'E
Liard, stm., Can. (lē-är´)	**130-31**	61°51'N	121°19'W
Lib, i., Marsh. Is.	**280-81**	8°19'N	167°25'E
Libagon, Phil.	**250**	10°18'N	125°03'E
Líbano, Col. (lē´bá-nô)	**163c**	4°56'N	75°04'W
Libau, Lat. *see* Liepāja	**192-93**	56°31'N	21°01'E
Libby, Mt., U.S. (lĭb´ē)	**112-13**	48°23'N	115°33'W
Libenge, D.R.C. (lē-bĕŋ´gä)	**262-63**	3°39'N	18°38'E
Liberal, Ks., U.S. (lĭb´ẽr-ăl)	**120-21**	37°02'N	100°56'W
Liberec, Czech Rep. (lē´bĕr-ĕts)	**194-95**	50°46'N	15°04'E
Liberia, C.R.	**149**	10°37'N	85°26'W
Liberia, nation, Afr. (lī-bē´rĭ-á)	**253**	6°30'N	9°30'W
Liberty, Ky., U.S. (lĭb´ẽr-tĭ)	**124-25**	37°19'N	84°56'W
Liberty, Mo., U.S. (lĭb´ẽr-tĭ)	**120-21**	39°15'N	94°25'W
Liberty, N.Y., U.S. (lĭb´ẽr-tĭ)	**116-17**	41°48'N	74°44'W
Liberty, S.C., U.S. (lĭb´ẽr-tĭ)	**124-25**	34°47'N	82°42'W
Liberty, Tx., U.S. (lĭb´ẽr-tĭ)	**122-23**	30°04'N	94°48'W
Lībiyā, nation, Afr. *see* Libya	**253**	27°0'N	17°00'E
Lībīyah, Aṣ-Ṣaḥrā' al-, des., Afr. *see* Libyan Desert	**254**	24°0'N	25°00'E
Libourne, Fr. (lē-bōōrn´)	**196-97**	44°55'N	0°14'W
Libres, Mex. (lē´brās)	**146-47**	19°28'N	97°41'W
Libreville, nat. cap., Gabon (lē-br'vēl´)	**260-61**	0°24'N	9°28'E
Libya, nation, Afr. (lĭb´ē-ä)	**253**	27°0'N	17°00'E
Libyan Desert, des., Afr. (lĭb´ē-ăn dĕs´ẽrt)	**254**	24°0'N	25°00'E
Licancábur, Volcán, vol., S.A.	**168-69**	22°50'S	67°50'W
Licantén, Chile (lē-kän-tĕ´n)	**171**	34°59'S	72°06'W
Lichinga, Moz.	**264-65**	13°17'S	35°15'E
Lichtenburg, S. Afr. (lĭk´tĕn-bĕrgh)	**269c**	26°10'S	26°10'E
Licking, stm., Ky., U.S. (lĭk´ĭng)	**116-17**	39°05'N	84°31'W
Licungo, stm., Moz.	**264-65**	17°38'S	37°22'E
Lida, Bela. (lē´dá)	**194-95**	53°54'N	25°18'E
Lidköping, Swe. (lēt´chû-pĭng)	**192-93**	58°30'N	13°11'E
Lidzbark, Pol. (lĭts´bärk)	**194-95**	53°16'N	19°50'E
Liechtenstein, nation, Eur. (lĕk´tĕn-shtīn)	**194-95**	47°09'N	9°35'E
Liège, Bel.	**190-91**	50°38'N	5°34'E
Liegnitz, Pol. *see* Legnica	**194-95**	51°13'N	16°10'E
Lienz, Aus. (lē-ĕnts´)	**194-95**	46°50'N	12°46'E
Liepāja, Lat. (le´pä-yä´)	**192-93**	56°31'N	21°01'E
Lietuva, nation, Eur. *see* Latvia	**174-75**	56°0'N	24°00'E
Lièvre, stm., Qc., Can.	**136-37**	45°31'N	75°26'W
Lifou, i., N. Cal.	**279g**	20°44'S	167°14'E
Ligao, Phil. (lē-gä´ō)	**250**	13°14'N	123°34'E
Ligonha, stm., Moz. (lē-gō´nyá)	**264-65**	16°53'S	39°08'E
Ligonier, In., U.S. (lĭg-ô-nēr)	**116-17**	41°28'N	85°34'W
Lihir Group, is., Pap. N. Gui.	**277**	2°55'S	152°36'E
Līhu'e, Hi., U.S. (lē-hōō´ā)	**127a**	21°59'N	159°22'W
Liivi laht, b., Eur. *see* Riga, Gulf of	**192-93**	57°30'N	23°35'E
Lijiang, China (lē-jyäŋ)	**238-39**	26°52'N	100°14'E
Likasi, D.R.C.	**262-63**	10°59'S	26°43'E
Likhoslavl, Russia (lyē-kôsläv´'l)	**202-03**	57°07'N	35°28'E
Likouala, stm., Congo	**262-63**	1°12'S	16°49'E
Lille, Fr. (lēl)	**196-97**	50°39'N	3°07'E
Lillehammer, Nor. (lēl´ĕ-häm´mẽr)	**192-93**	61°07'N	10°28'E
Lillesand, Nor. (lēl´ĕ-sän')	**192-93**	58°15'N	8°24'E
Lillestrøm, Nor. (lēl´ĕ-strûm)	**192-93**	59°58'N	11°04'E
Lillooet, B.C., Can. (lĭ´lōō-ĕt)	**132-33**	50°42'N	121°56'W
Lillooet, stm., B.C., Can. (lĭ´lōō-ĕt)	**132-33**	49°45'N	122°08'W
Lilongwe, nat. cap., Malawi (lē-lō-än)	**264-65**	13°59'S	33°44'E
Liloy, Phil.	**250**	8°07'N	122°40'E
Lima, Oh., U.S. (lī´má)	**116-17**	40°45'N	84°07'W
Lima, nat. cap., Peru (lē´mä)	**170**	12°04'S	77°03'W
Limassol, Cyp. *see* Lemesós	**228-29**	34°41'N	33°03'E
Limay, stm., Arg. (lē-mä´ē)	**171**	38°59'S	68°00'W
Limbaži, Lat. (lēm´bä-zĭ)	**192-93**	57°31'N	24°43'E
Limeira, Braz. (lē-mā´rä)	**172**	22°34'S	47°24'W
Limerick, Ire. (lĭm´nák)	**190-91**	52°40'N	8°38'W
Límnos, i., Grc.	**200-01**	39°55'N	25°18'E
Limoges, Fr.	**196-97**	45°50'N	1°15'E
Limón, Hond. (lē-mô´n)	**149**	15°51'N	85°31'W
Limon, Co., U.S. (lī´mŏn)	**120-21**	39°16'N	103°42'W
Limoux, Fr. (lē-mōō´)	**196-97**	43°04'N	2°12'E
Limpopo, stm., Afr. (lĭm-pō´pō)	**264-65**	25°12'S	33°31'E
Limpopo, Grande Parque Transfronteiriço do, n.p., Afr. *see* Great Limpopo Transfrontier Park	**264-65**	23°0'S	31°30'E
Limpopo, Parque Nacional do, n.p., Moz.	**264-65**	23°21'S	31°54'E
Linapacan Island, i., Phil.	**250**	11°27'N	119°49'E
Linares, Chile (lē-nä´rās)	**171**	35°50'S	71°36'W
Linares, Mex.	**122-23**	24°51'N	99°34'W
Linares, Spain (lē-nä´rĕs)	**198-99**	38°06'N	3°38'W
Lincoln, Arg. (lĭŋ´kŭn)	**173**	34°52'S	61°31'W
Lincoln, Eng., U.K. (lĭŋ´kŭn)	**190-91**	53°14'N	0°33'W
Lincoln, Il., U.S. (lĭŋ´kŭn)	**116-17**	40°09'N	89°22'W
Lincoln, Ks., U.S. (lĭŋ´kŭn)	**120-21**	39°02'N	98°09'W
Lincoln, Me., U.S. (lĭŋ´kŭn)	**117a**	45°22'N	68°31'W
Lincoln, Ne., U.S.	**114-15**	40°48'N	96°43'W
Lincoln, Mount, mtn., Co., U.S. (mount lĭŋ´kŭn)	**118-19**	39°21'N	106°07'W
Lincolnton, N.C., U.S. (lĭŋ´kŭn-tŭn)	**124-25**	35°28'N	81°15'W
Lindale, Ga., U.S. (lĭn´dāl)	**124-25**	34°12'N	85°11'W
Linden, Guy.	**164-65**	6°05'N	58°17'W
Linden, Al., U.S. (lĭn´dĕn)	**124-25**	32°19'N	87°48'W
Linden, Tx., U.S. (lĭn´dĕn)	**120-21**	33°01'N	94°22'W
Lindesberg, Swe. (lĭn´dĕs-bĕrgh)	**192-93**	59°36'N	15°13'E
Lindesnes, c., Nor. (lĭn´ĕs-nĕs)	**192-93**	58°0'N	7°02'E
Lindi, Tan. (lĭn´dē)	**264-65**	9°60'S	39°42'E
Lindi, stm., D.R.C.	**262-63**	0°33'N	25°05'E
Lindian, China (lĭn-dĭĕn)	**240-41**	47°11'N	124°52'E
Lindley, S. Afr. (lĭnd´lē)	**269c**	27°53'S	27°56'E
Lindsay, On., Can. (lĭn´zē)	**136-37**	44°21'N	78°44'W
Lindsay, Ok., U.S. (lĭn´zē)	**120-21**	34°50'N	97°37'W
Line Islands, is., Oc. (līn ī´lándz)	**280-81**	0°05'N	157°00'W
Linfen, China	**240-41**	36°05'N	111°31'E
Lingao, China (lĭn-gou)	**238-39**	19°54'N	109°40'E
Lingayen, Phil. (lĭŋ´gä-yān´)	**250**	16°01'N	120°14'E
Lingayen Gulf, b., Phil.	**250**	16°15'N	120°14'E
Lingen, Ger. (lĭŋ´gĕn)	**194-95**	52°31'N	7°19'E
Lingga, Kepulauan, is., Indon.	**246-47**	0°05'S	104°35'E
Lingling, China (lĭŋ-lĭŋ) *see* Yongzhou	**238-39**	26°13'N	111°37'E
Lingyuan, China (lĭŋ-yůän)	**240-41**	41°15'N	119°16'E
Linh, Ngoc, mtn., Viet.	**246-47**	15°04'N	107°59'E
Linhai, China	**238-39**	28°51'N	121°07'E
Linhe, China (lĭn-hŭ)	**240-41**	40°49'N	107°30'E
Linjiang, China (lĭn-jyäŋ)	**243**	41°49'N	126°55'E
Linköping, Swe. (lĭn´chû-pĭng)	**192-93**	58°25'N	15°37'E
Linkou, China	**244**	45°19'N	130°16'E
Linqing, China (lĭn-chyĭŋ)	**240-41**	36°51'N	115°42'E
Linqu, China (lĭn-chyōō)	**240-41**	36°31'N	118°32'E
Linru, China	**238-39**	34°10'N	112°50'E
Lins, Braz. (lē´ns)	**168-69**	21°40'S	49°45'W
Lintao, China	**240-41**	35°22'N	103°51'E
Linton, In., U.S. (lĭn´tŭn)	**116-17**	39°02'N	87°10'W
Linton, N.D., U.S. (lĭn´tŭn)	**114-15**	46°16'N	100°14'W
Linxi, China (lĭn-shyē)	**240-41**	43°36'N	118°03'E
Linxia, China	**240-41**	35°36'N	103°13'E
Linyi, China (lĭn-yē)	**240-41**	35°04'N	118°22'E
Linyi, China (lĭn-yē)	**240-41**	37°11'N	116°52'E
Linz, Aus. (lĭnts)	**194-95**	48°18'N	14°18'E
Lion, Golfe du, b., Fr.	**196-97**	43°0'N	4°00'E
Lipa, Phil. (lē-pä´)	**250**	13°56'N	121°10'E
Lipari, Isola, i., Italy (ē´-sō-lä-lē´pä-rē)	**200-01**	38°29'N	14°56'E
Lipetsk, Russia (lyē´pĕtsk)	**202-03**	52°37'N	39°37'E
Lípez, Cerro, mtn., Bol.	**168-69**	21°55'S	66°53'W
Liping, China (lē-pĭŋ)	**238-39**	26°17'N	108°60'E
Lippe, stm., Ger. (lĭp´ē)	**194-95**	51°39'N	6°37'E
Lippstadt, Ger. (lĭp´shtät)	**194-95**	51°40'N	8°20'E
Lipu, China (lē-pōō)	**238-39**	24°25'N	110°29'E
Lira, Ug.	**267**	2°15'N	32°54'E
Lisakovsk, Kaz.	**226**	52°32'N	62°33'E
Lisala, D.R.C. (lē-sä´lä)	**262-63**	2°09'N	21°31'E
Lisboa, nat. cap., Port. (lēzh-bō´ä) *see* Lisbon	**198-99**	38°43'N	9°08'W
Lisbon, N.D., U.S. (lĭz´bŭn)	**114-15**	46°26'N	97°41'W
Lisbon, Oh., U.S. (lĭz´bŭn)	**116-17**	40°46'N	80°46'W
Lisbon, nat. cap., Port. (lĭz´bŭn)	**198-99**	38°43'N	9°08'W
Lisbon Falls, Me., U.S. (lĭz´bŭn fôlz)	**116-17**	44°00'N	70°03'W
Lisburn, N. Ire., U.K. (lĭs´bŭrn)	**190-91**	54°31'N	6°03'W
Lisburne, Cape, c., Ak., U.S.	**126**	68°52'N	166°14'W
Lishui, China (lĭ´shwĭ´)	**238-39**	28°27'N	119°54'E
Lisianski Island, i., Hi., U.S.	**127**	26°02'N	174°00'W
Lisichansk, Ukr. *see* Lysychans'k	**202-03**	48°55'N	38°26'E
Lisieux, Fr. (lē-zyû´)	**196-97**	49°09'N	0°14'E
Liski, Russia (lyēs´kē)	**202-03**	50°59'N	39°31'E
Lismore, Austl. (lĭz´môr)	**276**	28°49'S	153°17'E
Litang, China	**238-39**	23°12'N	109°09'E
Litang, China	**238-39**	29°60'N	100°16'E
Litang, stm., China	**238-39**	28°03'N	101°32'E
Litchfield, Il., U.S. (lĭch´fēld)	**116-17**	39°10'N	89°39'W
Litchfield, Mn., U.S. (lĭch´fēld)	**114-15**	45°08'N	94°32'W
Lithgow, Austl. (lĭth´gō)	**276**	33°30'S	150°09'E
Lithuania, nation, Eur. (lĭth-ů-ā-´nĭ-á)	**174-75**	56°0'N	24°00'E
Litoměřice, Czech Rep. (lē´tô-myĕr´zhĭ-tsĕ)	**194-95**	50°33'N	14°08'E
Litovko, Russia	**240-41**	49°15'N	135°10'E
Little Abaco, i., Bah. (lĭt´'l ä´bä-kō)	**142-43**	26°54'N	77°43'W
Little Andaman, i., India (lĭt´'l ăn-dá-măn´)	**246-47**	10°45'N	92°30'E
Little Belt Mountains, mts., Mt., U.S. (lĭt´'l bĕlt moun´tĭnz)	**112-13**	46°45'N	110°35'W
Little Bighorn, stm., U.S. (lĭt´'l bĭg-hôrn)	**112-13**	45°44'N	107°34'W
Little Bighorn Battlefield National Monument, n.p., Mt., U.S. (lĭt´'l bĭg-hôrn băt´'l-fēld năsh´ŭn-ăl mŏn´ŭ-mĕnt)	**112-13**	45°32'N	107°20'W
Little Cayman, i., Cay. Is. (lĭt´'l kā´mán) (lĭt´'l kī-män´)	**142-43**	19°42'N	80°02'W
Little Current, On., Can.	**136-37**	45°58'N	81°55'W
Little Exuma, i., Bah. (lĭt´'l ĕk-sōō´mä)	**142-43**	23°27'N	75°37'W
Little Falls, Mn., U.S. (lĭt´'l fôlz)	**114-15**	45°59'N	94°22'W
Little Falls, N.Y., U.S. (lĭt´'l fôlz)	**116-17**	43°03'N	74°52'W
Littlefield, Tx., U.S. (lĭt´'l-fēld)	**120-21**	33°55'N	102°20'W
Little Inagua, i., Bah. (lĭt´'l ē-nä´gwä)	**142-43**	21°30'N	72°60'W
Little Karoo, plat., S. Afr.	**264-65**	33°45'S	21°30'E
Little Karroo, plat., S. Afr. (lĭt´'l kä-rōō) *see* Little Karoo	**264-65**	33°45'S	21°30'E
Little Missouri, stm., U.S. (lĭt´'l mĭ-sōō´rĭ)	**110-11**	47°36'N	102°17'W
Little Nicobar, i., India	**246-47**	7°20'N	93°40'E
Little Powder, stm., U.S. (lĭt´'l pou´dẽr)	**112-13**	45°28'N	105°21'W
Little Rock, Ar., U.S.	**120-21**	34°43'N	92°19'W
Little Scarcies, stm., Afr.	**260-61**	8°51'N	13°07'W
Little Sioux, stm., U.S. (lĭt´'l sōō)	**114-15**	41°49'N	96°06'W
Little Smoky, stm., Ab., Can. (lĭt´'l smōk´ĭ)	**132-33**	55°40'N	117°38'W
Littleton, Co., U.S. (lĭt´'l-tŭn)	**120-21**	39°35'N	105°01'W
Littleton, N.H., U.S. (lĭt´'l-tŭn)	**116-17**	44°18'N	71°46'W
Litzmannstadt, Pol. *see* Łódź	**194-95**	51°47'N	19°31'E
Liuaniua, at., Sol. Is. *see* Ontong Java	**279e**	5°19'S	159°16'E
Liubliana, nat. cap., Slvn. *see* Ljubljana	**200-01**	46°03'N	14°31'E
Liubotyn, Ukr.	**202-03**	49°56'N	35°57'E
Liuchow, China *see* Liuzhou	**238-39**	24°19'N	109°23'E
Liuyang, China (lyōō´yäng´)	**238-39**	28°08'N	113°38'E
Liuzhou, China (lĭō-jō)	**238-39**	24°19'N	109°23'E
Live Oak, Fl., U.S. (līv ōk)	**124-25**	30°18'N	82°59'W
Livermore, Ca., U.S. (lĭv´ẽr-mōr)	**118-19**	37°41'N	121°46'W
Livermore, Ky., U.S. (lĭv´ẽr-mōr)	**116-17**	37°29'N	87°08'W
Liverpool, N.S., Can. (lĭv´ẽr-pōōl)	**138-39**	44°03'N	64°43'W
Liverpool, Eng., U.K. (lĭv´ẽr-pōōl)	**190-91**	53°25'N	2°57'W
Liverpool Range, mts., Austl. (lĭv´ẽr-pōōl rānj)	**276**	31°51'S	150°18'E
Livingston, Guat.	**148**	15°50'N	88°46'W
Livingston, Al., U.S. (lĭv´ĭng-stŭn)	**124-25**	32°36'N	88°12'W
Livingston, Mt., U.S. (lĭv´ĭng-stŭn)	**112-13**	45°40'N	110°34'W
Livingston, Tn., U.S. (lĭv´ĭng-stŭn)	**124-25**	36°23'N	85°19'W
Livingston, Tx., U.S. (lĭv´ĭng-stŭn)	**122-23**	30°42'N	94°57'W
Livingston, Lake, res., Tx., U.S.	**122-23**	30°43'N	95°08'W
Livingstone, Zam. (lĭv-ĭng-stôn)	**264-65**	17°52'S	25°51'E
Livingstone, Chutes de, wtfl., Afr. *see* Livingstone Falls	**260-61**	4°51'S	14°29'E
Livingstone Falls, wtfl., Afr.	**260-61**	4°51'S	14°29'E
Livno, Bos. (lēv´nô)	**200-01**	43°50'N	17°00'E
Livny, Russia (lēv´nē)	**202-03**	52°25'N	37°37'E
Livorno, Italy (lē-vôr´nō) (lĕg´hôrn)	**200-01**	43°34'N	10°19'E
Livramento, Braz. (lē-vrá-mĕ´n-tô) *see* Santana do Livramento	**173**	30°53'S	55°31'W
Lixi, China	**238-39**	29°15'N	114°47'E
Lixian, China (lē shyĕn)	**238-39**	29°30'N	111°38'E
Lixian, China (lē shyĕn)	**238-39**	34°09'N	105°07'E
Lixian, stm., Asia *see* Black	**246-47**	21°15'N	105°21'E
Lizard Point, c., Eng., U.K. (lĭz´ard point)	**190-91**	49°58'N	5°13'W
Ljubljana, nat. cap., Slvn. (lyōō´blyä´na)	**200-01**	46°03'N	14°31'E
Ljungby, Swe. (lyông´bü)	**192-93**	56°50'N	13°56'E
Ljusdal, Swe. (lyōōs´däl)	**192-93**	61°50'N	16°06'E
Ljusnan, stm., Swe.	**184-85**	61°09'N	17°10'E
Llandudno, Wales, U.K. (lăn-düd´nō)	**190-91**	53°19'N	3°50'W
Llanelli, Wales, U.K. (lá-nĕl´ĭ)	**190-91**	51°41'N	4°09'W
Llanes, Spain (lyä´nâs)	**198-99**	43°25'N	4°45'W

ăt; finăl; rāte; senâte; ärm; åsk; sofá; fâre; ch-choose; dh-as th in other; bē; ēvent; bĕt; recĕnt; cratẽr; g-gō; gh-guttural g; bĭt; ĭ-short neutral; rīde; κ-guttural k as ch in German ich;

Feature (Pronunciation)	Page	Lat.	Long.
Llano, Tx., U.S. (lä′nō) (lyä′nō)	122-23	30°46′N	98°40′W
Llano, stm., Tx., U.S. (lä′nō) (lyä′nō)	122-23	30°39′N	98°25′W
Llanos, pl., S.A. (lyä′nōs)	164-65	5°0′N	70°00′W
Lleida, Spain	198-99	41°37′N	0°38′E
Lloydminster, Sk., Can.	132-33	53°17′N	110°01′W
Llullaillaco, Cerro, vol., S.A. see Llullaillaco, Volcán	168-69	24°43′S	68°33′W
Llullaillaco, Volcán, vol., S.A. (vôl-kä′n lyōō-lyī-lyä′kō)	168-69	24°43′S	68°33′W
Loa, stm., Chile	168-69	21°26′S	70°03′W
Loanda, Braz.	168-69	23°00′S	53°11′W
Loanda, nat. cap., Ang. see Luanda	264-65	8°49′S	13°14′E
Loange, stm., Afr. (lô-äŋ′gä)	262-63	4°17′S	20°02′E
Lobamba, nat. cap., Swaz. (lōō′-bäm-bä) (lō-bäm′-bä)	264-65	26°27′S	31°12′E
Lobaye, stm., C.A.R.	262-63	3°41′N	18°35′E
Lobería, Arg. (lô-bĕ′rē′ä)	173	38°09′S	58°47′W
Lobito, Ang. (lô-bē′tō)	264-65	12°21′S	13°33′E
Lobos, Arg. (lō′bôs)	173	35°11′S	59°06′W
Loches, Fr. (lôsh)	196-97	47°08′N	0°60′E
Lockhart, Tx., U.S. (lŏk′härt)	122-23	29°53′N	97°40′W
Lock Haven, Pa., U.S. (lŏk′hā-vĕn)	116-17	41°07′N	77°27′W
Loc Ninh, Viet. (lŏk′nĭng′)	246-47	11°53′N	106°37′E
Lodève, Fr. (lô-dĕv′)	196-97	43°43′N	3°19′E
Lodeynoye Pole, Russia (lô-dĕy-nô′yĕ)	192-93	60°44′N	33°34′E
Lodi, Italy (lô′dē)	200-01	45°19′N	9°30′E
Lodi, Ca., U.S. (lō′dī)	118-19	38°08′N	121°16′W
Lodi, Wi., U.S. (lō′dī)	116-17	43°19′N	89°31′W
Lodja, D.R.C.	262-63	3°26′S	23°27′E
Lodsch, Pol. see Łódź	194-95	51°47′N	19°31′E
Lodwar, Kenya	267	3°08′N	35°38′E
Łódź, Pol.	194-95	51°47′N	19°31′E
Loei, Thai.	246-47	17°27′N	101°31′E
Lofa, stm., Afr.	260-61	6°39′N	11°04′W
Loffa, stm., Afr. see Lofa	260-61	6°39′N	11°04′W
Lofoten, is., Nor. (lô′fō-tĕn)	184-85	68°08′N	14°10′E
Logan, N.M., U.S. (lō′găn)	120-21	35°22′N	103°25′W
Logan, Oh., U.S. (lō′găn)	116-17	39°32′N	82°25′W
Logan, Ut., U.S. (lō′găn)	112-13	41°45′N	111°50′W
Logan, W.V., U.S. (lō′găn)	116-17	37°51′N	81°60′W
Logan, Mount, mtn., Yk., Can. (mount lō′găn)	130-31	60°34′N	140°24′W
Logansport, In., U.S. (lō′gănz-pōrt)	116-17	40°45′N	86°21′W
Logone, stm., Afr. (lō-gō′nä) (lô-gôn′)	260-61	12°05′N	15°02′E
Logroño, Spain (lô-grō′nyō)	198-99	42°28′N	2°27′W
Løgstør, Den. (lügh-stûr′)	192-93	56°58′N	9°16′E
Loi-kaw, Mya.	246-47	19°40′N	97°13′E
Loire, stm., Fr. (lwår)	196-97	47°18′N	2°00′W
Loja, Ec. (lō′hä)	170	3°59′S	79°12′W
Loja, Spain (lô′-kä)	198-99	37°10′N	4°09′W
Lokoro, stm., D.R.C.	262-63	1°43′S	18°22′E
Lol, stm., Sudan (lōl)	262-63	9°13′N	28°59′E
Lolland, i., Den. (lôl′än′)	192-93	54°47′N	11°16′E
Lom, Blg. (lōm)	200-01	43°50′N	23°15′E
Lom, stm., Afr.	260-61	5°19′N	13°24′E
Lomami, stm., D.R.C.	262-63	0°47′N	24°17′E
Lomas de Zamora, Arg. (lō′mäs dā zä-mō′rä)	173	34°46′S	58°24′W
Lomblen, Pulau, i., Indon. (pōō-lou lŏm-blĕn′)	248-49	8°25′S	123°30′E
Lombok, i., Indon. (lŏm-bŏk′)	248-49	8°45′S	116°30′E
Lomé, nat. cap., Togo (lō′mē)	260-61	6°08′N	1°13′E
Lomela, stm., D.R.C. (lô-mā′lä)	262-63	0°18′S	20°45′E
Lomond, Loch, lk., Scot., U.K. (lŏk lō′mŭnd)	190-91	56°06′N	4°37′W
Lomonosov, Russia (lô-mô′nô-sof)	192-93	59°55′N	29°48′E
Lompoc, Ca., U.S. (lŏm-pōk′)	118-19	34°39′N	120°27′W
Łomża, Pol. (lôm′zhä)	194-95	53°11′N	22°05′E
Lonaconing, Md., U.S. (lō-nă-kō′nĭng)	116-17	39°34′N	78°58′W
Loncoche, Chile	171	39°22′S	72°38′W
London, On., Can. (lŭn′dŭn)	136-37	42°59′N	81°14′W
London, Ky., U.S. (lŭn′dŭn)	124-25	37°07′N	84°05′W
London, Oh., U.S. (lŭn′dŭn)	116-17	39°53′N	83°27′W
London, nat. cap., Eng., U.K. (lŭn′dŭn)	190-91	51°30′N	0°10′W
Londonderry, N. Ire., U.K.	190-91	54°59′N	7°20′W
Londonderry, Cape, c., Austl.	272-73	13°45′S	126°56′E
Londonderry, Isla, i., Chile	171	55°03′S	70°35′W
Londrina, Braz. (lôn-drē′nä)	168-69	23°19′S	51°10′W
Long Beach, Ca., U.S. (lông bēch)	118-19	33°46′N	118°12′W
Long Beach, Ms., U.S. (lông bēch)	124-25	30°21′N	89°10′W
Long Beach, Wa., U.S. (lông bēch)	112-13	46°22′N	124°03′W
Long Branch, N.J., U.S. (lông branch)	116-17	40°18′N	73°60′W
Long Cay, i., Bah. (lông kē)	142-43	22°35′N	74°22′W
Longchang, China	238-39	29°21′N	105°17′E
Long Eaton, Eng., U.K. (lông ē′tŭn)	190-91	52°53′N	1°16′W

Feature (Pronunciation)	Page	Lat.	Long.
Longford, Ire. (lŏng′fērd)	190-91	53°44′N	7°48′W
Long Island, i., Bah.	142-43	23°15′N	75°07′W
Long Island, i., N.S., Can. (lông ī′lănd)	138-39	44°20′N	66°16′W
Long Island, i., Nu., Can.	130-31	54°52′N	79°21′W
Long Island, i., Pap. N. Gui. (lông ī′lănd) see Arop Island	277	5°20′S	147°05′E
Long Island, i., N.Y., U.S. (lông ī′lănd)	116-17	40°47′N	73°17′W
Long Island Sound, strt., U.S. (lông ī′lănd sound)	116-17	41°05′N	72°58′W
Longjiang, China	240-41	47°20′N	123°11′E
Longkou, China (lôŋ-kō)	240-41	37°39′N	120°21′E
Long Lake, lk., On., Can. (lông lāk)	136-37	49°30′N	86°50′W
Longli, China	238-39	26°28′N	106°58′E
Longmont, Co., U.S. (lông′mŏnt)	120-21	40°10′N	105°06′W
Longnawan, Indon.	248-49	1°48′N	114°53′E
Long Point, c., Nf., Can. (lông point)	138-39	48°47′N	58°47′W
Long Point Bay, b., On., Can. (lông point bā)	136-37	42°40′N	80°14′W
Longquan, China	238-39	28°03′N	119°06′E
Long Range Mountains, mts., Nf., Can. (lông rānj moun′tĭnz)	138-39	49°20′N	57°39′W
Longreach, Austl. (lông′rēch)	277	23°27′S	144°15′E
Longs Peak, mtn., Co., U.S. (lôngz pēk)	112-13	40°16′N	105°37′W
Longueuil, Qc., Can. (lôN-gû′y′)	136-37	45°32′N	73°30′W
Longview, Tx., U.S. (lông-vū)	120-21	32°30′N	94°44′W
Longview, Wa., U.S. (lông-vū)	112-13	46°08′N	122°57′W
Longwy, Fr. (lôN-wē′)	196-97	49°31′N	5°47′E
Longxi, China (lôŋ-shyē)	238-39	34°57′N	104°42′E
Long Xuyen, Viet. (loung′ sōō′yĕn)	246-47	10°23′N	105°26′E
Longzhou, China (lôŋ-jō)	238-39	22°21′N	106°51′E
Lonoke, Ar., U.S. (lō′nōk)	124-25	34°48′N	91°54′W
Lons-le-Saunier, Fr. (lôN-lē-sō-nyā′)	196-97	46°41′N	5°32′E
Lookout, Cape, c., N.C., U.S. (kāp căp lòkòut)	124-25	34°36′N	76°32′W
Loop Head, c., Ire. (lōōp hĕd)	190-91	52°34′N	9°56′W
Lopatka, Mys, c., Russia (mĭs lô-pät′kå)	218-19	50°53′N	156°40′E
Lop Buri, Thai.	246-47	14°48′N	100°37′E
Lopévi, i., Vanuatu	279g	16°31′S	168°20′E
Lopez, Cap, c., Gabon	260-61	0°38′S	8°42′E
Lop Nor, lk., China see Lop Nur	222-23	40°29′N	90°16′E
Lop Nur, lk., China	222-23	40°29′N	90°16′E
Lopori, stm., D.R.C. (lō-pō′rē)	262-63	1°14′N	19°49′E
Lora, Hāmūn-i-, lk., Asia	232-33	29°17′N	64°47′E
Lorain, Oh., U.S. (lô-rān′)	116-17	41°28′N	82°11′W
Loralai, Pak. (lō-rŭ-lī′)	232-33	30°22′N	68°36′E
Lorca, Spain (lôr′kä)	198-99	37°41′N	1°41′W
Lord Howe Island, i., Austl. (lôrd hou ī′lănd)	272-73	31°34′S	159°06′E
Lordsburg, N.M., U.S. (lôrdz′bûrg)	118-19	32°21′N	108°42′W
Loreto, Mex.	144-45	26°01′N	111°21′W
Lorica, Col. (lô-rē′kä)	164-65	9°14′N	75°49′W
Lorient, Fr. (lô-rē′äN′)	196-97	47°45′N	3°22′W
Lörrach, Ger. (lûr′äk)	194-95	47°37′N	7°40′E
Lorraine, hist. reg., Fr.	196-97	49°0′N	6°00′E
Los Alamos, N.M., U.S. (lōs ăl-ă-mōs′)	118-19	35°53′N	106°18′W
Los Andes, Chile (lôs än′dĕs)	163e	32°50′S	70°36′W
Los Angeles, Chile (lôs äŋ′hå-lās)	171	37°27′S	72°19′W
Los Angeles, Ca., U.S. (lōs ăŋ′gĕl-ĕs)	118-19	34°03′N	118°14′W
Losap Atoll, at., Micron.	280-81	6°58′N	152°39′E
Los Gatos, Ca., U.S. (lōs gä′tōs)	118-19	37°13′N	121°59′W
Los Lagos, Chile	171	39°52′S	72°48′W
Los Mochis, Mex.	144-45	25°47′N	108°60′W
Los Roques, Islas, is., Ven.	164-65	11°50′N	66°45′W
Los Teques, Ven. (lôs tĕ′kĕs)	163b	10°21′N	67°02′W
Lost River Range, mts., Id., U.S. (lôst rĭv′ēr rānj)	112-13	44°10′N	113°35′W
Losuia, Pap. N. Gui.	277	8°33′S	151°03′E
Los Vilos, Chile (lôs vē′lôs)	168-69	31°53′S	71°29′W
Lota, Chile (lō′tä)	171	37°05′S	73°09′W
Lothringen, hist. reg., Fr. see Lorraine	196-97	49°0′N	6°00′E
Lotung, Tai.	225a	24°41′N	121°46′E
Louangphrabang, Laos (lōō-ang′prä-bäng′)	246-47	19°52′N	102°08′E
Loubomo, Congo	262-63	4°11′S	12°40′E
Loudon, Tn., U.S. (lou′dŭn)	124-25	35°44′N	84°21′W
Louga, Sen.	260-61	15°37′N	16°13′W
Louisa, Ky., U.S. (lōō′ēz-å)	116-17	38°06′N	82°37′W
Louisa, Va., U.S. (lōō′ēz-å)	116-17	38°01′N	78°00′W
Louise Island, i., B.C., Can.	132-33	52°58′N	131°50′W
Louisiade Archipelago, is., Pap. N. Gui.	277	11°0′S	153°00′E
Louisiana, Mo., U.S. (lōō-ē-zē-ăn′ă)	120-21	39°27′N	91°04′W
Louisiana, state, U.S. (lōō-ē-zē-ăn′ă)	108-09	31°15′N	92°15′W
Louis Trichardt, S. Afr. (lōō′ĭs trĭchårt) see Makhado	264-65	23°03′S	29°55′E

Feature (Pronunciation)	Page	Lat.	Long.
Louisville, Ga., U.S. (lōō′ē-vĭl)	124-25	32°60′N	82°24′W
Louisville, Il., U.S. (lōō′ē-vĭl)	116-17	38°46′N	88°31′W
Louisville, Ky., U.S. (lōō′ē-vĭl)	116-17	38°15′N	85°46′W
Louisville, Ms., U.S. (lōō′ē-vĭl)	124-25	33°07′N	89°03′W
Louis-XIV, Pointe, c., Qc., Can.	130-31	54°38′N	79°45′W
Loukhi, Russia	186-87	66°04′N	33°03′E
Louny, Czech Rep. (lō′nē)	194-95	50°21′N	13°48′E
Lourdes, Fr. (lōōrd)	196-97	43°06′N	0°03′W
Lourenço Marques, nat. cap., Moz. see Maputo	264-65	25°58′S	32°35′E
Louviers, Fr. (lōō-vyā′)	196-97	49°13′N	1°10′E
Lovat', stm., Russia	192-93	58°13′N	31°27′E
Lovech, Blg. (lō′vĕts)	200-01	43°08′N	24°43′E
Loveland, Co., U.S. (lŭv′lănd)	120-21	40°25′N	105°06′W
Lovell, Wy., U.S. (lŭv′ĕl)	112-13	44°50′N	108°24′W
Lovelock, Nv., U.S. (lŭv′lŏk)	118-19	40°11′N	118°28′W
Loviisa, Fin. (lô′vē-så)	192-93	60°27′N	26°13′E
Lovisa, Fin. see Loviisa	192-93	60°27′N	26°13′E
Low, Cape, c., Nu., Can. (kāp lō)	130-31	63°07′N	85°18′W
Lowa, stm., D.R.C. (lō′wå)	262-63	1°25′S	25°52′E
Lowell, Ma., U.S.	116-17	42°38′N	71°19′W
Lower Brule Indian Reservation, ind. res., S.D., U.S. (lō′ēr brü′lā ĭn′dĭ-ăn rĕ-sĕr-vā′shĕn)	114-15	44°05′N	99°54′W
Lower California, pen., Mex. see Baja California	144-45	27°53′N	113°28′W
Lower Hutt, N.Z. (lō′ēr hŭt)	278	41°13′S	174°56′E
Lower Post, B.C., Can.	128-29	59°56′N	128°29′W
Lower Red Lake, lk., Mn., U.S. (lō′ēr rĕd lāk)	114-15	47°57′N	95°01′W
Lower Zambezi National Park, n.p., Zam.	264-65	15°32′S	29°56′E
Lowestoft, Eng., U.K. (lō′stŏf)	190-91	52°29′N	1°44′E
Łowicz, Pol. (lô′vĭch)	194-95	52°06′N	19°57′E
Loxton, Austl. (lôks′tŭn)	276	34°27′S	140°34′E
Loyalty Islands, is., N. Cal.	279g	21°0′S	167°00′E
Loyauté, Îles, is., N. Cal. see Loyalty Islands	279g	21°0′S	167°00′E
Loznica, Serb. (lōz′nē-tså)	200-01	44°32′N	19°14′E
Lualaba, stm., D.R.C. (lōō-ă-lä′bă)	262-63	0°22′N	25°21′E
Luama, stm., D.R.C. (lōō′ä-må)	262-63	4°46′S	26°53′E
Lu'an, China (lōō-än)	238-39	31°44′N	116°29′E
Luan, stm., China	240-41	39°24′N	119°17′E
Luanda, nat. cap., Ang. (lōō-än′dä)	264-65	8°49′S	13°14′E
Luando, stm., Ang.	264-65	10°21′S	16°27′E
Luanginga, stm., Afr. see Luanguinga	264-65	15°12′S	22°55′E
Luang Prabang, Laos see Louangphrabang	246-47	19°52′N	102°08′E
Luangue, stm., Afr.	262-63	4°17′S	20°02′E
Luanguinga, stm., Afr. (lōō-ä-gĭŋ′gå)	264-65	15°12′S	22°55′E
Luangwa, Zam.	264-65	15°37′S	30°25′E
Luanshya, Zam.	264-65	13°08′S	28°24′E
Luapula, stm., Afr.	264-65	9°24′S	28°31′E
Lubaczów, Pol. (lōō-bä′chòf)	194-95	50°10′N	23°07′E
Lubań, Pol. (lōō′bän′)	194-95	51°07′N	15°18′E
Lubang, Phil. (lōō-bäng′)	250	13°51′N	120°07′E
Lubang Island, i., Phil.	250	13°46′N	120°11′E
Lubang Islands, is., Phil. (lōō-bäng′ ī′lăndz)	250	13°45′N	120°17′E
Lubango, Ang.	264-65	14°55′S	13°30′E
Lubāns, lk., Lat. (lōō-bä′nås)	192-93	56°46′N	26°53′E
Lubartów, Pol. (lōō-bär′tòf)	194-95	51°28′N	22°37′E
Lubbock, Tx., U.S. (lŭb′ŭk)	120-21	33°34′N	101°51′W
Lübeck, Ger. (lü′bĕk)	194-95	53°52′N	10°40′E
Lubiana, nat. cap., Slvn. see Ljubljana	200-01	46°03′N	14°31′E
Lubilash, stm., D.R.C. (lōō-bē-låsh′)	262-63	6°03′S	23°45′E
Lublin, Pol. (lyò′blēn′)	194-95	51°14′N	22°35′E
Lubnān, nation, Asia see Lebanon	206-07	34°0′N	36°00′E
Lubny, Ukr. (lòb′nē)	202-03	50°01′N	33°00′E
Lubuagan, Phil. (lō-bwä-gä′n)	250	17°22′N	121°10′E
Lubudi, D.R.C. (lò-bò′dē)	262-63	9°57′S	25°58′E
Lubudi, stm., D.R.C. (lò-bò′dē)	262-63	4°02′S	21°23′E
Lubudi, stm., D.R.C. (lò-bò′dē)	262-63	9°13′S	25°38′E
Lubumbashi, D.R.C. (lōō-bŭm-bä′shē)	262-63	11°41′S	27°28′E
Lucca, Italy (lōōk′kä)	200-01	43°51′N	10°30′E
Lucena, Phil. (lōō-sā′nä)	250	13°56′N	121°37′E
Lucena, Spain (lōō-thā′nä)	198-99	37°24′N	4°29′W
Lučenec, Slvk. (lōō′châ-nyĕts)	194-95	48°20′N	19°40′E
Lucera, Italy (lōō-châ′rä)	200-01	41°31′N	15°20′E
Lucerne, Switz. see Luzern	194-95	47°03′N	8°19′E
Lucipara, Kepulauan, is., Indon.	248-49	5°33′S	127°27′E
Lucknow, India (lŭk′nou)	234-35	26°52′N	80°55′E
Luçon, Fr. (lü-sôN′)	196-97	46°27′N	1°10′W
Lüda, China see Dalian	240-41	38°54′N	121°34′E
Lüderitz, Nmb. (lü′dēr-ĭts) (lü′dĕ-rĭts)	264-65	26°39′S	15°09′E

n-sing; ŋ-baŋk; N-nasalized n; nŏd; cŏmmit; ōld; ôbey; ôrder; oi-boil; fōōd; ò-as oo in foot; ou-out; s-soft; sh-dish; th-thin; pūre; ûnite; ûrn; stŭd; circŭs; ü-as in French tu; ′-indeterminate vowel.

Feature (Pronunciation)	Page	Lat.	Long.
Ludhiāna, India	234-35	30°54'N	75°51'E
Ludington, Mi., U.S. (lŭd'ĭng-tŭn)	116-17	43°57'N	86°26'W
Ludlow, Eng., U.K. (lŭd'lō)	190-91	52°22'N	2°43'W
Ludvika, Swe. (loodh-vē'kȧ)	192-93	60°08'N	15°11'E
Ludza, Lat. (lo͞od'zȧ)	192-93	56°32'N	27°44'E
Luena, Ang.	264-65	11°47'S	19°54'E
Luena, stm., Ang.	264-65	12°30'S	22°34'E
Lufeng, China	238-39	22°56'N	115°37'E
Lufira, stm., D.R.C. (lo͞o-fē'rȧ)	262-63	8°21'S	26°26'E
Lufkin, Tx., U.S. (lŭf'kĭn)	122-23	31°20'N	94°43'W
Luga, Russia (lo͞o'gȧ)	192-93	58°44'N	29°52'E
Luga, stm., Russia (lo͞o'gȧ)	192-93	59°40'N	28°18'E
Lugano, Switz. (lo͞o-gä'nō)	194-95	46°01'N	8°57'E
Lugenda, stm., Moz.	264-65	11°25'S	38°29'E
Lugo, Italy (lo͞o'gô)	200-01	44°25'N	11°55'E
Lugo, Spain (lo͞o'gō)	198-99	43°01'N	7°33'W
Luhans'k, Ukr.	202-03	48°34'N	39°20'E
Luik, Bel. see Liège	190-91	50°38'N	5°34'E
Luimneach, Ire. see Limerick	190-91	52°40'N	8°38'W
Lukanga Swamp, sw., Zam. (lo͞o-käŋ'gȧ swŏmp)	264-65	14°25'S	27°45'E
Lukenie, stm., D.R.C. (lo͞o-kā'nyȧ)	262-63	2°44'S	18°10'E
Lukolela, D.R.C.	262-63	1°04'S	17°11'E
Łuków, Pol. (wō'kof)	194-95	51°56'N	22°23'E
Lukuga, stm., D.R.C. (lo͞o-ko͞o'gȧ)	262-63	5°40'S	26°55'E
Lukula, D.R.C.	262-63	5°22'S	12°57'E
Lulaka, stm., D.R.C.	262-63	0°53'S	20°11'E
Luleå, Swe.	184-85	65°36'N	22°10'E
Lüleburgaz, Tur. (lü'lĕ-bor-gäs')	200-01	41°25'N	27°22'E
Lüliang Shan, mts., China	240-41	37°25'N	111°20'E
Luling, Tx., U.S. (lū'lĭng)	122-23	29°41'N	97°39'W
Lulonga, stm., D.R.C.	262-63	0°38'N	18°21'E
Lulua, stm., D.R.C.	262-63	5°02'S	21°06'E
Lumberton, Ms., U.S. (lŭm'bẽr-tŭn)	124-25	31°00'N	89°30'W
Lumberton, N.C., U.S. (lŭm'bẽr-tŭn)	124-25	34°38'N	79°01'W
Lumberton, Tx., U.S. (lŭm'bẽr-tŭn)	122-23	30°14'N	94°12'W
Lund, Swe. (lŭnd)	192-93	55°42'N	13°11'E
Lüneburg, Ger. (lü'nē-bōrgh)	194-95	53°16'N	10°25'E
Lunel, Fr. (lü-nĕl')	196-97	43°40'N	4°08'E
Lunenburg, N.S., Can. (lo͞o'nĕn-bûrg)	138-39	44°23'N	64°19'W
Lunéville, Fr. (lü-nā-vel')	196-97	48°36'N	6°30'E
Lunga, stm., Zam.	264-65	14°34'S	26°26'E
Lūni, stm., India	234-35	24°37'N	71°17'E
Lunsar, S.L.	260-61	8°41'N	12°32'W
Luo, stm., China	238-39	34°41'N	110°08'E
Luoding, China (lwô-dĭŋ)	238-39	22°47'N	111°33'E
Luohe, China (lwô-hŭ)	238-39	33°34'N	114°02'E
Luoyang, China (lwô-yäŋ)	238-39	34°41'N	112°27'E
Luqu, China	238-39	34°38'N	102°14'E
Luray, Va., U.S. (lū-rā')	116-17	38°39'N	78°28'W
Lurgan, N. Ire., U.K. (lûr'găn)	190-91	54°28'N	6°20'W
Lurín, Peru	163a	12°17'S	76°52'W
Lúrio, stm., Moz.	264-65	13°30'S	40°32'E
Lusaka, nat. cap., Zam. (lo-sä'kȧ)	264-65	15°24'S	28°17'E
Lusambo, D.R.C. (lo͞o-säm'bō)	262-63	4°57'S	23°30'E
Lushan, China	238-39	30°15'N	102°58'E
Lu Shan, mtn., China	238-39	29°31'N	115°58'E
Lüshun, China (lü-shŭn)	240-41	38°49'N	121°15'E
Lusk, Wy., U.S. (lŭsk)	114-15	42°46'N	104°27'W
Lūt, Dasht-e, des., Iran (dă'sht-ē-lo͞ot)	232-33	32°0'N	58°00'E
Lutherstadt Wittenberg, Ger.	194-95	51°52'N	12°39'E
Luton, Eng., U.K. (lū'tŭn)	190-91	51°53'N	0°25'W
Lutong, Malay.	248-49	4°28'N	113°60'E
Luts'k, Ukr.	194-95	50°45'N	25°20'E
Lutzow-Holm Bay, b., Ant.	287	69°10'S	37°30'E
Luverne, Al., U.S. (lū-vûn')	124-25	31°43'N	86°16'W
Luverne, Mn., U.S. (lū-vûn')	114-15	43°39'N	96°13'W
Luvua, stm., D.R.C.	262-63	6°45'S	26°57'E
Luwegu, stm., Tan.	262-63	8°31'S	37°23'E
Luwuk, Indon.	248-49	0°56'S	122°47'E
Luxembourg, nation, Eur. see Luxemburg	190-91	49°45'N	6°05'E
Luxembourg, nat. cap., Lux.	190-91	49°37'N	6°07'E
Luxemburg, nation, Eur. (lŭk'-sŭm-bûrg)	190-91	49°45'N	6°05'E
Luxi, China	238-39	24°21'N	98°23'E
Luxor, Egypt	268b	25°42'N	32°38'E
Luza, Russia	186-87	60°37'N	47°16'E
Luzern, Switz. (lo-tsĕrn)	194-95	47°03'N	8°19'E
Luzhou, China (lo͞o-jō)	238-39	28°53'N	105°27'E
Luziânia, Braz. (lo͞o-zyȧ'nēȧ)	168-69	16°15'S	47°55'W
Lužická Nisa, stm., Eur. see Neisse	194-95	52°04'N	14°46'E
Luzon, i., Phil. (lo͞o-zŏn')	250	16°0'N	121°00'E
Luzon Strait, strt., Asia (lo͞o-zŏn' strāt)	238-39	20°30'N	121°00'E
L'viv, Ukr.	194-95	49°51'N	24°02'E
Lwów, Ukr. see L'viv	194-95	49°51'N	24°02'E
Lyallpur, Pak. see Faisalābād	232-33	31°25'N	73°05'E
Lycksele, Swe.	184-85	64°36'N	18°41'E
Lydenburg, S. Afr. (lī'dĕn-bûrg)	269c	25°08'S	30°27'E
Lykens, Pa., U.S. (lī'kĕnz)	116-17	40°34'N	76°43'W
Lynchburg, Va., U.S. (lĭnch'bûrg)	124-25	37°25'N	79°09'W
Lyndonville, Vt., U.S. (lĭn'dŭn-vĭl)	116-17	44°32'N	72°00'W
Lynn, Ma., U.S. (lĭn)	116-17	42°28'N	70°57'W
Lynn Lake, Mb., Can. (lĭn lāk)	134-35	56°51'N	101°00'W
Lyon, Fr. (lē-ôN')	196-97	45°45'N	4°49'E
Lyons, Ga., U.S. (lī'ŭnz)	124-25	32°12'N	82°19'W
Lyons, Ks., U.S. (lī'ŭnz)	120-21	38°21'N	98°12'W
Lyons, Ne., U.S. (lī'ŭnz)	114-15	41°56'N	96°29'W
Lysekil, Swe. (lü'sĕ-kĕl)	192-93	58°17'N	11°27'E
Lys'va, Russia (lĭs'vȧ)	186-87	58°06'N	57°48'E
Lysychans'k, Ukr.	202-03	48°55'N	38°26'E
Lyuban', Russia (lyo͞o'bȧn)	192-93	59°21'N	31°15'E
Lyubertsy, Russia (lyo͞o'bĕr-tsĕ)	202-03	55°41'N	37°53'E
Lyudinovo, Russia (lū-dē'novō)	202-03	53°52'N	34°28'E

M

Feature (Pronunciation)	Page	Lat.	Long.
Ma, stm., Asia	246-47	19°47'N	105°52'E
Ma'ān, Jord. (mä-än')	228-29	30°12'N	35°44'E
Ma'anshan, China	238-39	31°42'N	118°30'E
Maastricht, Neth. (mäs'trĭκt)	190-91	50°52'N	5°42'E
Mabank, Tx., U.S. (mā'bănk)	120-21	32°23'N	96°06'W
Macaé, Braz.	172	22°24'S	41°47'W
MacAlpine Lake, lk., Nu., Can.	130-31	66°38'N	102°51'W
Macapá, Braz.	166-67	0°03'N	51°03'W
Macará, Ec.	170	4°22'S	79°56'W
Macau, Braz. (mä-kà'ô)	163d	5°07'S	36°38'W
Macclesfield, Eng., U.K. (măk''lz-fēld)	190-91	53°16'N	2°08'W
MacDonnell Ranges, mts., Austl. (măk-dŏn'ĕl rānjĕz)	272-73	23°52'S	133°14'E
MacDowell Lake, lk., On., Can. (măk-dou ĕl lāk)	134-35	52°15'N	92°45'W
Macdui, Ben, mtn., Scot., U.K. (bĕn măk-do͞o'ē)	190-91	57°05'N	3°39'W
Macedonia, nation, Eur. (măs-ê-dō'nĭ-ȧ)	174-75	41°50'N	22°00'E
Macedonia, hist. reg., Eur. (măs-ê-dō'nĭ-ȧ)	200-01	41°0'N	23°00'E
Maceió, Braz.	163d	9°40'S	35°43'W
Macerata, Italy (mä-chā-rä'tä)	200-01	43°18'N	13°27'E
Macfarlane, Lake, lk., Austl. (lāk măc'fär-lān)	276	31°58'S	136°43'E
Machado, stm., Braz.	166-67	8°02'S	62°53'W
Machagai, Arg.	173	26°56'S	60°02'W
Machakos, Kenya	267	1°31'S	37°16'E
Machala, Ec. (mä-chá'lä)	170	3°16'S	79°57'W
Machilīpatnam, India	236	16°11'N	81°09'E
Machiques, Ven.	164-65	10°04'N	72°32'W
Machu Picchu, hist., Peru	170	13°07'S	72°34'W
Măcin, Rom. (mȧ-chēn')	202-03	45°15'N	28°08'E
Mackay, Austl. (mȧ-kī')	277	21°10'S	149°12'E
MacKay Lake, lk., N.T., Can. (mă-kā' lāk)	130-31	63°54'N	110°23'W
Mackenzie, stm., N.T., Can. (mȧ-kĕn'zĭ)	130-31	58°60'N	111°25'W
Mackenzie Bay, b., Can. (mȧ-kĕn'zĭ bā)	126	69°0'N	136°30'W
Mackenzie Mountains, mts., Can. (mȧ-kĕn'zĭ moun'tĭnz)	130-31	64°0'N	130°00'W
Mackinaw City, Mi., U.S. (măk'ĭ-nô sĭ'tē)	116-17	45°46'N	84°43'W
Maclean, Austl.	276	29°28'S	153°13'E
Macleod, Lake, lk., Austl.	272-73	24°04'S	113°42'E
Macomb, Il., U.S. (mȧ-ko͞om')	120-21	40°28'N	90°40'W
Mâcon, Fr. (mä-kôN)	196-97	46°19'N	4°50'E
Macon, Ga., U.S. (mā'kŏn)	124-25	32°50'N	83°38'W
Macon, Mo., U.S. (mā'kŏn)	120-21	39°44'N	92°28'W
Macon, Ms., U.S. (mā'kŏn)	124-25	33°06'N	88°34'W
Macquarie, stm., Austl. (mȧ-kwŏr'ē)	276	30°08'S	147°23'E
Mada, stm., Nig.	260-61	7°59'N	7°58'E
Madagascar, nation, Afr. (măd-ȧ-găs'kȧr)	253	19°0'S	46°00'E
Madagasikara, nation, Afr. see Madagascar	253	19°0'S	46°00'E
Madame, Isle, i., N.S., Can. (ēl mȧ-dȧm')	138-39	45°33'N	61°02'W
Madang, Pap. N. Gui. (mä-däng')	277	5°17'S	145°45'E
Madawaska, stm., On., Can. (măd-ȧ-wôs'kȧ)	136-37	45°27'N	76°21'W
Madeira, i., Port. (mä-dā'rä)	258-59	32°44'N	17°00'W
Madeira, stm., S.A. (mä-dā'-rȧ)	166-67	3°22'S	58°45'W
Madeira, Arquipélago da, is., Port. (är-kē-pĕ'lä-gō-dä-mädĕy'-rä) see Madeira Islands	258-59	32°40'N	16°45'W
Madeira Islands, is., Port. (mä-dā'rä ī'lȧndz)	258-59	32°40'N	16°45'W
Madeleine, Îles de la, is., Qc., Can.	138-39	47°30'N	61°45'W
Madelia, Mn., U.S. (mȧ-dē'lĭ-ȧ)	114-15	44°03'N	94°25'W
Madhya Pradesh, state, India (mŭd'vŭ prŭ-dāsh')	234-35	23°0'N	79°00'E
Madidi, stm., Bol.	166-67	12°31'S	66°58'W
Madikeri, India	236	12°25'N	75°45'E
Madill, Ok., U.S. (mȧ-dĭl')	120-21	34°05'N	96°47'W
Madison, Al., U.S. (măd'ĭ-sŭn)	124-25	34°41'N	86°45'W
Madison, Fl., U.S. (măd'ĭ-sŭn)	124-25	30°28'N	83°25'W
Madison, Ga., U.S. (măd'ĭ-sŭn)	124-25	33°36'N	83°28'W
Madison, In., U.S. (măd'ĭ-sŭn)	116-17	38°44'N	85°23'W
Madison, Me., U.S. (măd'ĭ-sŭn)	116-17	44°48'N	69°53'W
Madison, Mn., U.S. (măd'ĭ-sŭn)	114-15	45°01'N	96°12'W
Madison, Ms., U.S. (măd'ĭ-sŭn)	124-25	32°28'N	90°07'W
Madison, N.C., U.S. (măd'ĭ-sŭn)	124-25	36°23'N	79°58'W
Madison, Ne., U.S. (măd'ĭ-sŭn)	114-15	41°50'N	97°27'W
Madison, S.D., U.S. (măd'ĭ-sŭn)	114-15	44°00'N	97°07'W
Madison, Wi., U.S. (măd'ĭ-sŭn)	116-17	43°05'N	89°22'W
Madison, W.V., U.S. (măd'ĭ-sŭn)	116-17	38°04'N	81°49'W
Madisonville, Ky., U.S. (măd'ĭ-sŭn-vĭl)	124-25	37°20'N	87°30'W
Madisonville, Tx., U.S. (măd'ĭ-sŭn-vĭl)	122-23	30°56'N	95°55'W
Madiun, Indon.	248-49	7°37'S	111°31'E
Madoi, China	240-41	34°55'N	98°12'E
Madona, Lat. (mȧ'dō'nȧ)	192-93	56°51'N	26°14'E
Madras, India see Chennai	236	13°06'N	80°15'E
Madras, state, India see Tamil Nādu	236	11°0'N	78°15'E
Madre, Laguna, b., Mex. (lä-ò'nä mä'drä)	122-23	25°01'N	97°40'W
Madre, Laguna, b., Tx., U.S.	122-23	26°58'N	97°26'W
Madre, Sierra, mts., Phil. (sē-ĕ'r-rä-mȧ'drē)	250	16°20'N	122°00'E
Madre de Dios, stm., S.A. (mä'drȧ dā dē-ōs')	166-67	10°24'S	65°24'W
Madre de Dios, Isla, i., Chile (ē's-lä-mȧ'drȧ dā dē-ōs')	171	50°15'S	75°05'W
Madre del Sur, Sierra, mts., Mex. (sē-ĕ'r-rä-mä'drȧ dĕl-so͞or')	146-47	17°0'N	100°00'W
Madre Occidental, Sierra, mts., Mex. (sē-ĕ'r-rä-mȧ'drĕ-äk-sĭ-dĕn'-tl)	144-45	25°0'N	105°00'W
Madre Oriental, Sierra, mts., Mex. (sē-ĕ'r-rä-mȧ'drĕ ō-rē-ĕn-täl')	144-45	21°26'N	99°50'W
Madrid, nat. cap., Spain (mä-drē'd)	198-99	40°24'N	3°41'W
Madridejos, Spain (mä-dhrē-dhā'hōs)	198-99	39°28'N	3°32'W
Madurai, India (mä-do͞o'rä)	236	9°55'N	78°08'E
Maebashi, Japan (mä-ĕ-bä'shē)	245	36°23'N	139°05'E
Mae Hong Son, Thai.	246-47	19°16'N	97°57'E
Mae Klong, stm., Thai.	246-47	13°22'N	99°60'E
Mae Sot, Thai.	246-47	16°43'N	98°35'E
Maestra, Sierra, mts., Cuba (sē-ĕ'r-rȧ-mä-ās'trä)	142-43	20°06'N	76°24'W
Maéwo, i., Vanuatu	279g	15°10'S	168°10'E
Mafeking, S. Afr. (mȧf'ĕ-kĭng) see Mafikeng	264-65	25°53'S	25°39'E
Mafia Island, i., Tan.	262-63	7°50'S	39°50'E
Mafikeng, S. Afr.	264-65	25°53'S	25°39'E
Mafra, Braz. (mä'frä)	168-69	26°08'S	49°49'W
Mafra, Port. (mäf'rȧ)	198-99	38°57'N	9°19'W
Magadan, Russia (mȧ-gȧ-dän')	218-19	59°35'N	150°50'E
Magallanes, Chile see Punta Arenas	171	53°09'S	70°55'W
Magallanes, Estrecho de, strt., S.A.	171	54°0'S	71°00'W
Magangué, Col.	164-65	9°18'N	74°48'W
Magat, stm., Phil. (mä-gät')	250	17°02'N	121°50'E
Magdagachi, Russia	222-23	53°27'N	125°49'E
Magdalena, Bol. (mäg-dä-lā'nä)	166-67	13°20'S	64°08'W
Magdalena, Mex. (mäg-dä-lā'nä)	146-47	20°54'N	103°57'W
Magdalena, N.M., U.S. (mäg-dä-lā'nä)	118-19	34°07'N	107°15'W
Magdalena, stm., Col. (mäg-dä-lā'nä)	164-65	11°06'N	74°51'W
Magdalena, Bahía, b., Mex. (bä-ē'ä-mäg-dä-lā'nä)	144-45	24°35'N	112°00'W
Magdalena, Isla, i., Chile (ē's-lä-mäg-dä-lā'nä)	171	44°40'S	73°10'W
Magdalena de Kino, Mex.	144-45	30°38'N	110°58'W
Magdeburg, Ger. (mäg'dĕ-bōrgh)	194-95	52°08'N	11°38'E
Magelang, Indon.	248-49	7°28'S	110°13'E
Magellan, Strait of, strt., S.A. (strāt ŭv mȧ-gĕl'-ăn) see Magallanes, Estrecho de	171	54°0'S	71°00'W
Magerøya, i., Nor.	184-85	71°02'N	25°42'E
Magnesia, Tur. see Manisa	200-01	38°37'N	27°26'E
Magnetic Island, i., Austl.	277	19°08'S	146°50'E

Feature (Pronunciation)	Page	Lat.	Long.
Magnitogorsk, Russia (mȧg-nyĕ´tô-gôrsk)	226	53°26′N	59°04′E
Magnolia, Ar., U.S. (măg-nō´lĭ-*ȧ*)	120-21	33°16′N	93°15′W
Magnolia, Ms., U.S. (măg-nō´lĭ-*ȧ*)	124-25	31°09′N	90°28′W
Mago, i., Fiji	279f	17°27′S	179°09′W
Magog, Qc., Can. (m*ȧ*-gŏg´)	136-37	45°16′N	72°09′W
Magpie, stm., On., Can. (Măg´pī)	136-37	47°56′N	84°50′W
Magpie, stm., Qc., Can. (Măg´pī)	138-39	50°19′N	64°27′W
Magpie, Lac, lk., Qc., Can. (läk măg´pī)	138-39	51°0′N	64°41′W
Maguari, Cabo, c., Braz.	166-67	0°18′S	48°22′W
Magway, Mya.	246-47	20°30′N	94°30′E
Magyarország, nation, Eur. see Hungary	174-75	47°0′N	20°00′E
Mahābād, Iran	228-29	36°46′N	45°44′E
Mahagi, D.R.C.	267	2°19′N	31°01′E
Mahajanga, Madag.	264-65	15°43′S	46°19′E
Mahakam, stm., Indon.	248-49	0°35′S	117°17′E
Mahalapye, Bots.	264-65	23°06′S	26°50′E
Mahalla el-Kubra, Egypt see El-Mahalla el-Kubra	268b	30°58′N	31°10′E
Mahānadi, stm., India	234-35	20°19′N	86°47′E
Mahanoro, Madag. (mȧ-hȧ-nō´rō)	264-65	19°55′S	48°48′E
Mahārāshtra, state, India	236	19°0′N	76°00′E
Maha Sarakham, Thai.	246-47	16°11′N	103°18′E
Mahbūbnagar, India	236	16°44′N	77°59′E
Mahe, India (mä-ā´)	236	11°42′N	75°32′E
Mahébourg, Mauritius.	265a	20°24′S	57°42′E
Mahendra Giri, mtn., India	236	18°58′N	84°21′E
Mahendranagar, Nepal	234-35	28°58′N	80°10′E
Mahenge, Tan. (mä-hĕŋ´gȧ)	267	7°38′S	36°16′E
Mahesāna, India	234-35	23°36′N	72°23′E
Mahilëu, Bela.	192-93	53°56′N	30°21′E
Mahnomen, Mn., U.S. (mô-nō´mĕn)	114-15	47°19′N	95°59′W
Mahón, Spain see Maó	198-99	39°53′N	4°16′E
Mahone Bay, b., N.S., Can. (m*ȧ*-hōn´ bā)	138-39	44°30′N	64°15′W
Maicuru, stm., Braz.	166-67	2°12′S	54°18′W
Maiduguri, Nig. (mä´ē-dȧ-gōō´rē)	260-61	11°51′N	13°09′E
Maiko, stm., D.R.C.	262-63	0°11′N	25°32′E
Maikop, Russia see Maykop	186-87	44°36′N	40°06′E
Mai-Ndombe, Lac, lk., D.R.C.	260-61	2°25′S	18°18′E
Maine, state, U.S. (mān)	108-09	45°15′N	69°15′W
Maine, Gulf of, b., N.A.	138-39	43°0′N	68°00′W
Mainland, i., Scot., U.K. (mān-lănd)	190c	60°16′N	1°16′W
Maintenon, Fr. (măN-t*ē*-nôN´)	196-97	48°35′N	1°35′E
Maintirano, Madag. (mä´ēn-tē-rä´nō)	264-65	18°03′S	44°02′E
Mainz, Ger. (mīnts)	194-95	50°00′N	8°16′E
Maio, i., C.V. (mä´yo)	260-61	15°11′N	23°10′W
Maipo, stm., Chile (mī´pô)	163e	33°37′S	71°38′W
Maipo, Volcán, vol., S.A. (vôl-kȧ´n mī´pô)	163e	34°10′S	69°50′W
Maipú, Arg.	173	36°52′S	57°54′W
Maiquetía, Ven. (mī-kĕ-tē´ä)	163b	10°36′N	66°58′W
Maitland, Austl. (māt´l*ă*nd)	276	32°44′S	151°33′E
Maitland, Austl. (māt´l*ă*nd)	276	34°23′S	137°40′E
Maíz, Islas del, is., Nic.	149	12°15′N	83°00′W
Maizuru, Japan (mä-ĭ´zōō-rōō)	245	35°28′N	135°24′E
Majene, Indon.	248-49	3°32′S	118°57′E
Majī, Eth.	262-63	6°11′N	35°35′E
Majorca, i., Spain (m*ȧ*-jôr´-k*ȧ*) see Mallorca	198-99	39°30′N	3°00′E
Majuro, at., Marsh. Is.	280-81	7°05′N	171°09′E
Makanya, Tan. (mä-kän´yä)	267	4°21′S	37°50′E
Makarov, Russia	222-23	48°38′N	142°46′E
Makarska, Cro. (mȧ´kär-skȧ)	200-01	43°17′N	17°01′E
Makasar, Selat, strt., Indon. see Makassar Strait	248-49	2°0′S	117°30′E
Makassar, Indon. (m*ȧ*-kă´-s*ŭr*)	248-49	5°08′S	119°25′E
Makassar Strait, strt., Indon. (m*ȧ*-kă´-s*ŭr* strāt)	248-49	2°0′S	117°30′E
Makatea, i., Fr. Poly.	280-81	15°50′S	148°16′W
Makedonija, nation, Eur. see Macedonia	174-75	41°50′N	22°00′E
Makedonija, hist. reg., Eur. see Macedonia	200-01	41°0′N	23°00′E
Makeni, S.L.	260-61	8°53′N	12°03′W
Makeyevka, Ukr. see Makiïvka	202-03	48°02′N	37°58′E
Makgadikgadi, pl., Bots.	264-65	20°17′S	25°43′E
Makhachkala, Russia (mäĸ´äch-kä´lä)	227	42°59′N	47°30′E
Makhado, S. Afr.	264-65	23°03′S	29°55′E
Makiïvka, Ukr.	202-03	48°02′N	37°58′E
Makindu, Kenya	267	2°16′S	37°50′E
Makinsk, Kaz.	226	52°39′N	70°25′E
Makkah, Sau. Ar. see Mecca	266	21°27′N	39°51′E
Makokou, Gabon (mȧ-kô-kōō´)	260-61	0°35′N	12°51′E
Makona, stm., Afr. see Moa	260-61	6°60′N	11°34′W
Makoua, Congo	262-63	0°00′S	15°38′E
Makung, Tai.	225a	23°34′N	119°34′E
Makurdi, Nig.	260-61	7°44′N	8°31′E
Mala, Punta, c., Pan. (pȯ´n-tä-mä´lä)	150	7°28′N	80°01′W
Malabang, Phil.	250	7°38′N	124°04′E
Malabar Coast, cst., India (măl´ȧ-bär kōst)	236	11°0′N	75°00′E
Malabo, nat. cap., Eq. Gui. (mä-lä´bō)	260-61	3°45′N	8°47′E
Malacca, Malay. see Kota Kinabalu	246-47	2°12′N	102°16′E
Malacca, Strait of, strt., Asia (strāt ŭv m*ȧ*-lăk´*ȧ*)	246-47	2°30′N	101°20′E
Malad City, Id., U.S. (m*ȧ*-lăd´ sĭ´tē)	112-13	42°12′N	112°15′W
Maladzečna, Bela.	194-95	54°19′N	26°52′E
Málaga, Col. (mȧ´lä-gȧ)	164-65	6°42′N	72°44′W
Málaga, Spain (mȧ´lä-gȧ)	198-99	36°44′N	4°25′W
Malagasy Republic, nation, Afr. see Madagascar	253	19°0′S	46°00′E
Malaita, i., Sol. Is. (m*ȧ*-lä´ē-t*ȧ*)	279e	9°0′S	161°00′E
Malaka, Malay. see Kota Kinabalu	246-47	2°12′N	102°16′E
Malaka, Selat, strt., Asia see Malacca, Strait of	246-47	2°30′N	101°20′E
Malakāl, Sudan (mȧ-lȧ-käl´)	262-63	9°31′N	31°39′E
Malakula, i., Vanuatu (mä-lä-kōō´lä)	279g	16°15′S	167°30′E
Malang, Indon.	248-49	7°59′S	112°38′E
Malanje, Ang. (mä-läŋ-gȧ)	264-65	9°32′S	16°20′E
Malanville, Benin	260-61	11°52′N	3°23′E
Mälaren, lk., Swe.	192-93	59°30′N	17°12′E
Malargüe, Arg.	171	35°28′S	69°35′W
Malartic, Qc., Can.	136-37	48°09′N	78°07′W
Malatya, Tur. (mȧ-lä´tyȧ)	186-87	38°21′N	38°18′E
Malawi, nation, Afr. (mä-lä´-wē)	253	13°30′S	34°00′E
Malawi, Lake, lk., Afr. (läk mä-lä´-wē) see Nyasa, Lake	264-65	12°0′S	34°30′E
Malaya Vishera, Russia	192-93	58°51′N	32°14′E
Malaybalay, Phil.	250	8°09′N	125°08′E
Malay Peninsula, pen., Asia (m*ȧ*-lā´ pĕ-nĭn´sūl*ȧ*) (mā´lā)	246-47	6°0′N	101°00′E
Malaysia, nation, Asia (mȧ-lā´zhȧ)	206-07	2°30′N	112°30′E
Malbork, Pol. (mäl´bôrk)	194-95	54°02′N	19°02′E
Malden, Mo., U.S. (môl´dĕn)	124-25	36°34′N	89°58′W
Malden, i., Kir. (môl´dĕn)	280-81	4°03′S	154°59′W
Maldive Islands, nation, Asia see Maldives	206-07	3°15′N	73°00′E
Maldives, nation, Asia (măl´dīvz) (môl´dēvz)	206-07	3°15′N	73°00′E
Maldonado, Ur. (mäl-dō-nȧ´dȯ)	173	34°55′S	54°57′W
Male', nat. cap., Mald. (mä-lā´)	236	4°10′N	73°30′E
Maléas, Ákra, c., Grc.	200-01	36°26′N	23°12′E
Male Atoll, at., Mald.	236	4°25′N	73°30′E
Mālegaon, India	234-35	20°33′N	74°32′E
Malheur Lake, lk., Or., U.S. (mȧ-lōōr´ lăk)	112-13	43°20′N	118°45′W
Mali, nation, Afr. (mä´-lē)	253	17°0′N	4°00′W
Mali, stm., Mya.	238-39	25°43′N	97°31′E
Malik, Wādī al-, stm., Sudan	266	18°03′N	30°58′E
Mali Kyun, i., Mya.	246-47	13°06′N	98°16′E
Malinaltepec, Mex. (mä-lē-näl-tȧ-pĕk´)	146-47	17°05′N	98°39′W
Malindi, Kenya (mä-lēn´dē)	262-63	3°13′S	40°06′E
Malino, Bukit, mtn., Indon.	248-49	0°42′N	120°51′E
Malkara, Tur. (mäl´kȧ-rȧ)	200-01	40°52′N	26°55′E
Malko Tŭrnovo, Blg. (mäl´kō-t'r´nō-vȧ)	200-01	41°59′N	27°32′E
Mallawi, Egypt	268b	27°44′N	30°51′E
Mallery Lake, lk., Nu., Can.	130-31	63°55′N	98°25′W
Mallorca, i., Spain	198-99	39°30′N	3°00′E
Malmö, Swe.	192-93	55°36′N	13°01′E
Maloelap, at., Marsh. Is.	280-81	8°45′N	171°03′E
Malolos, Phil. (mä-lô´lôs)	250	14°51′N	120°49′E
Maloshuyka, Russia	186-87	63°44′N	37°25′E
Måløy, Nor.	184-85	61°56′N	5°08′E
Maloyaroslavets, Russia (mä´lô-yä-rô-slä-vyĕts)	202-03	55°01′N	36°28′E
Malpelo, Isla de, i., Col. (ē´s-lä-dĕ-mäl-pā´lō)	164-65	3°59′N	81°35′W
Malpeque Bay, b., P.E., Can. (môl-pĕk´ bā)	138-39	46°30′N	63°47′W
Malta, Mt., U.S. (môl´t*ȧ*)	112-13	48°21′N	107°52′W
Malta, nation, Eur. (môl´t*ȧ*)	174-75	35°50′N	14°35′E
Malta, i., Malta	200b	35°53′N	14°27′E
Maluku, is., Indon. see Moluccas	248-49	2°0′S	128°00′E
Maluku, Laut, s., Indon. see Molucca Sea	248-49	0°13′N	125°10′E
Malvern, Ar., U.S. (măl´vērn)	120-21	34°22′N	92°49′W
Malyy Anyuy, stm., Russia	218-19	68°31′N	160°55′E
Malyye Derbety, Russia	186-87	47°58′N	44°43′E
Malyy Kavkaz, mts., Asia see Lesser Caucasus	227	40°60′N	44°35′E
Malyy Shantar, Ostrov, i., Russia	218-19	54°30′N	137°36′E
Malyy Taymyr, Ostrov, i., Russia	218-19	78°08′N	107°12′E
Malyy Uzen', stm., Eur. see Balaözen	186-87	48°58′N	49°38′E
Mamberamo, stm., Indon.	277	1°35′S	137°52′E
Mambéré, stm., C.A.R.	262-63	3°32′N	16°03′E
Mamburao, Phil. (mäm-bōō´rä-ō)	250	13°15′N	120°35′E
Mammoth Cave National Park, n.p., Ky., U.S. (măm´*ŏ*th kāv năsh´ŭn-*ă*l pärk)	124-25	37°11′N	86°08′W
Mamoré, stm., S.A.	166-67	10°24′S	65°23′W
Mamoudzou, nat. cap., May.	264-65	12°47′S	45°14′E
Mamry, Jezioro, lk., Pol. (mäm´rĭ)	194-95	54°07′N	21°44′E
Man, C. Iv.	260-61	7°24′N	7°33′W
Man, Isle of, dep., Eur. see Isle of Man	190-91	54°15′N	4°30′W
Manacapuru, Braz.	166-67	3°17′S	60°36′W
Manacor, Spain (mä-nä-kôr´)	198-99	39°34′N	3°12′E
Manado, Indon.	248-49	1°29′N	124°51′E
Managua, nat. cap., Nic. (mä-nä´gwä)	149	12°09′N	86°17′W
Managua, Lago de, lk., Nic. (lȧ´gô-dĕ-mä-nä´gwä)	149	12°20′N	86°20′W
Manakara, Madag. (mä-nä-kä´r*ŭ*)	264-65	22°09′S	48°01′E
Manāli, India	234-35	32°16′N	77°09′E
Manama, nat. cap., Bahr. (mä-nä´m*ȧ*) see Al-Manāmah	230-31	26°13′N	50°35′E
Manam Island, i., Pap. N. Gui.	277	4°05′S	145°02′E
Mananara, stm., Madag. (mä-nä-nä´r*ŭ*)	264-65	23°21′S	47°42′E
Mananara Avaratra, Madag.	264-65	16°10′S	49°46′E
Mananjary, Madag. (mä-nän-zhä´rē)	264-65	21°14′S	48°21′E
Manáos, Braz. see Manaus	166-67	3°07′S	60°01′W
Mana Pools National Park, n.p., Zimb.	264-65	15°52′S	29°15′E
Manas Hu, lk., China	226	45°43′N	85°54′E
Manassas, Va., U.S. (m*ȧ*-năs´*ȧ*s)	116-17	38°45′N	77°28′W
Manaus, Braz. (mä-nä´ōōzh)	166-67	3°07′S	60°01′W
Mancelona, Mi., U.S. (măn-sē-lō´nȧ)	116-17	44°54′N	85°04′W
Manchester, Eng., U.K. (măn´chĕs-tẽr)	190-91	53°27′N	2°15′W
Manchester, Ct., U.S. (măn´chĕs-tẽr)	116-17	41°47′N	72°31′W
Manchester, Ga., U.S. (măn´chĕs-tẽr)	124-25	32°51′N	84°37′W
Manchester, Ia., U.S. (măn´chĕs-tẽr)	114-15	42°29′N	91°28′W
Manchester, Ky., U.S. (măn´chĕs-tẽr)	124-25	37°09′N	83°47′W
Manchester, N.H., U.S.	116-17	42°59′N	71°28′W
Manchester, Tn., U.S. (măn´chĕs-tẽr)	124-25	35°29′N	86°05′W
Manchuria, hist. reg., China (măn-chōō´rē-ȧ)	240-41	47°0′N	125°00′E
Mand, stm., Iran	230-31	28°09′N	51°16′E
Manda Island, i., Kenya	262-63	2°15′S	40°57′E
Mandal, Nor. (män´däl)	192-93	58°02′N	7°27′E
Mandala, Puncak, mtn., Indon.	277	4°43′S	140°18′E
Mandalay, Mya. (măn´d*ȧ*-lā)	246-47	21°58′N	96°05′E
Mandalgovĭ, Mong.	240-41	45°46′N	106°16′E
Mandalī, Iraq	228-29	33°45′N	45°32′E
Mandan, N.D., U.S. (măn´dăn)	114-15	46°49′N	100°55′W
Mandara, Monts, mts., Afr. see Mandara Mountains	260-61	10°45′N	13°40′E
Mandara Mountains, mts., Afr. (män-dä´rä moun´tĭnz)	260-61	10°45′N	13°40′E
Mandeb, Bab el, strt., Asia (băb´ĕl măn-dĕb´) see Bab el Mandeb	266	12°44′N	43°21′E
Mandera, Kenya	262-63	3°56′N	41°52′E
Mandioli, Pulau, i., Indon.	248-49	0°44′S	127°14′E
Mandla, India	234-35	22°35′N	80°23′E
Mandsaur, India	234-35	24°03′N	75°05′E
Manduria, Italy (män-dōō´rē-ä)	200-01	40°24′N	17°38′E
Māndvi, India (mŭnd´vē)	234-35	22°51′N	69°22′E
Manfalût, Egypt	268b	27°19′N	30°58′E
Manfredonia, Italy (män-frā-dô´nyä)	200-01	41°38′N	15°55′E
Mangabeiras, Chapada das, hills, Braz.	166-67	9°55′S	46°32′W
Mangaia, i., Cook Is.	280-81	21°55′S	157°54′W
Mangalore, India (mŭŋ-gŭ-lōr´)	236	12°52′N	74°51′E
Mangchang, China	238-39	25°08′N	107°31′E
Mangkalihat, Tanjung, c., Indon.	248-49	1°02′N	118°59′E
Mangochi, Malawi	264-65	14°28′S	35°15′E
Mangoky, stm., Madag. (män-gō´kē)	264-65	21°20′S	43°32′E
Mangole, Pulau, i., Indon.	248-49	1°51′S	125°51′E
Mangshi, China see Luxi	238-39	24°21′N	98°23′E
Mangueira, Lagoa, b., Braz.	173	33°06′S	52°48′W
Mangum, Ok., U.S. (măŋ´gŭm)	120-21	34°53′N	99°30′W
Mangya, China	220-21	37°40′N	90°50′E
Manhattan, Ks., U.S. (măn-hăt´*ă*n)	120-21	39°11′N	96°34′W
Manhattan, Mt., U.S. (măn-hăt´*ă*n)	112-13	45°51′N	111°20′W
Manhuaçu, Braz. (män-ōȧ´sōō)	172	20°15′S	42°02′W

n-sing; ŋ-baŋk; ɴ-nasalized n; nŏd; c*ŏ*mmit; ōld; ôbey; ôrder; oi-boil; fōōd; ȯ-as oo in foot; ou-out; s-soft; sh-dish; th-thin; pūre; ûnite; ûrn; stŭd; circ*ŭ*s; ü-as in French tu; ´-indeterminate vowel.

Feature (Pronunciation)	Page	Lat.	Long.
Manicoré, Braz.	**166-67**	5°49'S	61°16'W
Manicouagan, stm., Qc., Can.	**138-39**	49°10'N	68°09'W
Manicouagan, Réservoir, res., Qc., Can.	**130-31**	51°22'N	68°44'W
Manihiki, at., Cook Is. (mä'nē-hē'kē)	**280-81**	10°24'S	161°01'W
Manila, nat. cap., Phil. (mȧ-nĭl'ȧ)	**250**	14°35'N	120°60'E
Manila Bay, b., Phil. (mȧ-nĭl'ȧ bā)	**250**	14°30'N	120°45'E
Manipa, Pulau, i., Indon.	**248-49**	3°18'S	127°33'E
Manipur, state, India	**234-35**	25°0'N	94°00'E
Manisa, Tur. (mä'nē-sȧ)	**200-01**	38°37'N	27°26'E
Manistee, Mi., U.S. (măn-ĭs-tē')	**116-17**	44°15'N	86°19'W
Manistique, Mi., U.S. (măn-ĭs-tēk')	**116-17**	45°58'N	86°14'W
Manitoba, state, Can. (măn-ĭ-tō'bȧ)	**128-29**	54°0'N	97°00'W
Manitoba, Lake, lk., Mb., Can. (lāk măn-ĭ-tō'bȧ)	**134-35**	50°47'N	98°43'W
Manitoulin Island, i., On., Can. (măn-ĭ-tōō'lĭn ī'lănd)	**136-37**	45°47'N	82°20'W
Manitou Springs, Co., U.S. (măn'ĭ-tōō sprĭngz)	**120-21**	38°52'N	104°54'W
Manitowoc, Wi., U.S. (măn-ĭ-tō-wŏk')	**116-17**	44°06'N	87°39'W
Maniwaki, Qc., Can.	**136-37**	46°23'N	75°59'W
Manizales, Col. (mä-nē-zä'lås)	**163c**	5°04'N	75°31'W
Mānjra, stm., India	**236**	18°49'N	77°52'E
Mankanza, D.R.C.	**262-63**	1°33'N	19°04'E
Mankato, Ks., U.S. (măn-kā'tō)	**120-21**	39°47'N	98°13'W
Mankato, Mn., U.S. (măn-kā'tō)	**114-15**	44°10'N	93°59'W
Manlleu, Spain (män-lyā'ōō)	**198-99**	42°0'N	2°17'E
Manna, Indon.	**246-47**	4°28'S	102°55'E
Mannar, Sri L. (mȧ-när')	**236**	8°59'N	79°55'E
Mannar, Gulf of, b., Asia	**236**	8°30'N	79°00'E
Mannar Island, i., Sri L.	**236**	9°03'N	79°50'E
Mannheim, Ger. (män'hīm)	**194-95**	49°30'N	8°28'E
Manning, S.C., U.S. (măn'ĭng)	**124-25**	33°42'N	80°13'W
Mannington, W.V., U.S. (măn'ĭng-tŭn)	**116-17**	39°31'N	80°23'W
Manokwari, Indon. (mȧ-nŏk-wä'rē)	**224-25**	0°51'S	134°05'E
Manono, D.R.C.	**262-63**	7°18'S	27°25'E
Manosque, Fr. (mȧ-nôsk')	**196-97**	43°50'N	5°47'E
Manouane, Lac, res., Qc., Can.	**138-39**	50°42'N	70°46'W
Manra, at., Kir.	**280-81**	4°27'S	171°15'W
Manresa, Spain (män-rā'sä)	**198-99**	41°44'N	1°49'E
Mansa, Zam.	**264-65**	11°12'S	28°53'E
Mansel Island, i., Nu., Can. (măn'sĕl ī'lănd)	**130-31**	61°60'N	79°50'W
Mansfield, Eng., U.K. (mănz'fēld)	**190-91**	53°09'N	1°12'W
Mansfield, La., U.S. (mănz'fēld)	**122-23**	32°02'N	93°43'W
Mansfield, Mo., U.S. (mănz'fēld)	**120-21**	37°06'N	92°35'W
Mansfield, Oh., U.S. (mănz'fēld)	**116-17**	40°45'N	82°31'W
Mansfield, Pa., U.S. (mănz'fēld)	**116-17**	41°48'N	77°04'W
Mansura, Egypt *see* El-Mansûra	**268b**	31°02'N	31°23'E
Manta, Ec. (män'tä)	**170**	0°57'S	80°43'W
Mantes-la-Jolie, Fr. (mänt-ĕ-lä-zhō-lē')	**196-97**	48°59'N	1°43'E
Mantiqueira, Serra da, mts., Braz.	**172**	22°14'S	44°53'W
Manturovo, Russia	**186-87**	58°20'N	44°47'E
Manuae, at., Cook Is.	**280-81**	19°21'S	158°56'W
Manuae, at., Fr. Poly.	**280-81**	16°30'S	154°40'W
Manua Islands, is., Am. Sam.	**279b**	14°13'S	169°35'W
Manuel Rodríguez, Isla, i., Chile	**171**	52°34'S	73°51'W
Manui, Pulau, i., Indon. (pōō-lou mä-nōō'ē)	**248-49**	3°35'S	123°08'E
Manukau, N.Z.	**278**	37°02'S	174°54'E
Manus Island, i., Pap. N. Gui. (mä'nōōs ī'lănd)	**277**	2°05'S	147°00'E
Manyame, stm., Afr.	**264-65**	15°37'S	30°39'E
Manyara, Lake, lk., Tan.	**267**	3°35'S	35°50'E
Manych, stm., Russia	**186-87**	47°15'N	40°15'E
Manyoni, Tan.	**267**	5°45'S	34°50'E
Manzanillo, Cuba (män'zä-nēl'yō)	**142-43**	20°21'N	77°07'W
Manzanillo, Mex.	**146-47**	19°03'N	104°20'W
Manzhouli, China (män-jō-lē)	**240-41**	49°35'N	117°27'E
Mao, Chad (mä'ō)	**258-59**	14°07'N	15°19'E
Maó, Spain	**198-99**	39°53'N	4°16'E
Maoke, Pegunungan, mts., Indon.	**277**	4°0'S	138°00'E
Maoming, China	**238-39**	21°41'N	110°51'E
Mapastepec, Mex. (ma-päs-tȧ-pĕk')	**146-47**	15°26'N	92°54'W
Mapi, Indon.	**277**	7°05'S	139°24'E
Mapimí, Mex. (mä-pē-mē')	**122-23**	25°49'N	103°51'W
Mapimí, Bolsón de, des., Mex. (bôl-sŏ'n-dĕ-mä-pē'mē)	**122-23**	26°30'N	104°00'W
Maple Creek, Sk., Can. (mā'p'l crēk krēk)	**134-35**	49°55'N	109°29'W
Maplewood, Mn., U.S. (mā'p'l wŏd)	**114-15**	45°01'N	93°04'W
Mapuera, stm., Braz.	**166-67**	1°05'S	57°03'W
Maputo, nat. cap., Moz. (mä-pōō'-tō)	**264-65**	25°58'S	32°35'E
Maqat, Kaz.	**186-87**	47°39'N	53°22'E
Maquan, stm., China	**234-35**	29°33'N	84°07'E
Maquinchao, Arg.	**171**	41°15'S	68°41'W
Maquoketa, Ia., U.S. (mȧ-kō-kē-tȧ)	**114-15**	42°04'N	90°40'W
Mar, Serra do, mts., Braz. (sĕr'rȧ dò mär')	**172**	23°30'S	45°30'W
Mara, stm., Afr.	**267**	1°32'S	33°59'E
Marabá, Braz.	**166-67**	5°21'S	49°06'W
Maracá, Ilha de, i., Braz.	**166-67**	2°05'N	50°25'W
Maracaibo, Ven. (mä-rä-kī'bō)	**164-65**	10°40'N	71°38'W
Maracaibo, Lago de, lk., Ven. (lä'gô-dĕ-mä-rä-kī'bō)	**164-65**	9°43'N	71°50'W
Maracaibo, Lake, lk., Ven. (lāk mä-rä-kī'bō) *see* Maracaibo, Lago de	**164-65**	9°43'N	71°50'W
Maracay, Ven. (mä-rä-kāy')	**163b**	10°16'N	67°37'W
Marādah, Libya	**188-89**	29°13'N	19°12'E
Maradi, Niger (mȧ-rȧ-dē')	**258-59**	13°29'N	7°06'E
Marāgheh, Iran	**228-29**	37°23'N	46°15'E
Maragogipe, Braz.	**166-67**	12°46'S	38°55'W
Marahuaca, Cerro, mtn., Ven.	**164-65**	3°35'N	65°27'W
Marajó, Baía de, b., Braz.	**166-67**	1°0'S	48°30'W
Maralal, Kenya	**267**	1°05'N	36°41'E
Maramasike, i., Sol. Is.	**279e**	9°32'S	161°27'E
Marand, Iran	**227**	38°26'N	45°46'E
Maranhão, state, Braz. (mä-rän-youɴ)	**166-67**	5°0'S	45°00'W
Maranoa, stm., Austl. (mä-rä-nō'ä)	**272-73**	27°44'S	148°44'E
Marañón, stm., Peru (mä-rä-nyōn')	**170**	4°29'S	73°30'W
Maraş, Tur. *see* Kahramanmaraş	**186-87**	37°35'N	36°57'E
Marathon, On., Can. (măr'ȧ-thŏn)	**136-37**	48°43'N	86°23'W
Marathon, Fl., U.S. (măr'ȧ-thŏn)	**125a**	24°42'N	81°06'W
Marathon, N.Y., U.S. (măr'ȧ-thŏn)	**116-17**	42°27'N	76°02'W
Marawwaḥ, i., U.A.E.	**230-31**	24°17'N	53°15'E
Marble Bar, Austl. (märb''l bär)	**270-71**	21°10'S	119°45'E
Marble Hall, S. Afr.	**269c**	24°57'S	29°14'E
Marburg an der Drau, Slvn. *see* Maribor	**200-01**	46°33'N	15°39'E
Marca, Ponta da, c., Ang.	**264-65**	16°31'S	11°42'E
Marceline, Mo., U.S. (mär-sē-lēn')	**120-21**	39°43'N	92°57'W
Marchena, Isla, i., Ec. (ē's-lä-mär-chĕ'nä)	**170a**	0°21'N	90°29'W
Mar Chiquita, Laguna, lk., Arg. (lä-gōō'nä-mär-chē-kē'tä)	**173**	30°42'S	62°36'W
Marcus Island, i., Japan (mär'kŭs ī'lănd)	**280-81**	24°18'N	153°58'E
Marcy, Mount, mtn., N.Y., U.S. (mount mär'sē)	**116-17**	44°07'N	73°56'W
Mardān, Pak.	**232-33**	34°12'N	72°03'E
Mar del Plata, Arg. (mär dĕl- plä'ta)	**173**	37°60'S	57°34'W
Mardin, Tur. (mär-dēn')	**228-29**	37°18'N	40°45'E
Maré, i., N. Cal. (mȧ-rā')	**279g**	21°30'S	167°59'E
Mareeba, Austl.	**277**	16°60'S	145°24'E
Marengo, Il., U.S. (mȧ-rĕŋ'gō)	**116-17**	42°15'N	88°37'W
Marfa, Tx., U.S. (mär'fȧ)	**122-23**	30°19'N	104°02'W
Margarita, Isla de, i., Ven. (ē's-lä dĕ mä-gȧ-rē'tä)	**163b**	11°0'N	64°00'W
Margate, Eng., U.K. (mär'gāt)	**190-91**	51°23'N	1°25'E
Margelan, Uzb. *see* Marghilon	**232-33**	40°28'N	71°44'E
Margherita, Som. *see* Jamaame	**262-63**	0°01'N	42°42'E
Margherita Peak, mtn., Afr.	**267**	0°22'N	29°51'E
Marghilon, Uzb.	**232-33**	40°28'N	71°44'E
Mārgow, Dasht-e, des., Afg.	**232-33**	30°45'N	63°10'E
Marguerite, Pic, mtn., Afr. *see* Margherita Peak	**267**	0°22'N	29°51'E
Marhanets', Ukr.	**202-03**	47°39'N	34°38'E
Maria, Îles, is., Fr. Poly.	**280-81**	21°44'S	154°38'W
María Cleofas, Isla, i., Mex.	**146-47**	21°18'N	106°15'W
María Elena, Chile	**168-69**	22°20'S	69°40'W
Maria Island, i., Austl.	**276**	42°39'S	148°04'E
María Madre, Isla, i., Mex.	**146-47**	21°37'N	106°35'W
María Magdalena, Isla, i., Mex.	**146-47**	21°27'N	106°26'W
Mariana Islands, is., Oc. (mä-ryä'nä ī'lăndz)	**280-81**	15°60'N	145°44'E
Marianna, Ar., U.S. (mā-rĭ-ăn'ȧ)	**124-25**	34°46'N	90°46'W
Marianna, Fl., U.S. (mā-rĭ-ăn'ȧ)	**124-25**	30°46'N	85°15'W
Mariánské Lázně, Czech Rep. (mär'yan-skě'läz'nyě)	**194-95**	49°58'N	12°42'E
Maria Theresiopel, Serb. *see* Subotica	**200-01**	46°06'N	19°41'E
Mariato, Punta, c., Pan.	**150**	7°13'N	80°53'W
Maribo, Den. (mä'rē-bō)	**194-95**	54°46'N	11°31'E
Maribor, Slvn. (mä're-bôr)	**200-01**	46°33'N	15°39'E
Marīdī, Sudan	**267**	4°55'N	29°28'E
Marie Byrd Land, reg., Ant.	**287**	80°0'S	120°00'W
Marie-Galante, i., Guad. (mȧ-rē' gȧ-länt')	**143b**	15°56'N	61°16'W
Mari El, state, Russia	**186-87**	56°30'N	48°00'E
Marienbad, Czech Rep. *see* Mariánské Lázně	**194-95**	49°58'N	12°42'E
Marienburg, Pol. *see* Malbork	**194-95**	54°02'N	19°02'E
Mariental, Nmb.	**264-65**	24°37'S	17°58'E
Mariestad, Swe. (mä-rē'ĕ-städ')	**192-93**	58°43'N	13°51'E
Marietta, Ga., U.S. (mā-rĭ-ĕt'ȧ)	**124-25**	33°57'N	84°33'W
Marietta, Oh., U.S. (mā-rĭ-ĕt'ȧ)	**116-17**	39°25'N	81°28'W
Marietta, Ok., U.S. (mā-rĭ-ĕt'ȧ)	**120-21**	33°56'N	97°07'W
Marília, Braz. (mä-rē'lyȧ)	**168-69**	22°13'S	49°57'W
Marimba, Ang.	**262-63**	8°22'S	16°59'E
Marinduque, i., Phil. (mä-rēn-dōō'kā)	**250**	13°24'N	121°58'E
Marine City, Mi., U.S. (mȧ-rēn' sĭ'tē)	**116-17**	42°43'N	82°29'W
Marinette, Wi., U.S. (măr-ĭ-nĕt')	**116-17**	45°06'N	87°37'W
Maringá, Braz.	**168-69**	23°25'S	51°56'W
Maringa, stm., D.R.C. (mă-riŋ'gä)	**262-63**	1°13'N	19°50'E
Marinha Grande, Port. (mä-rēn'yȧ grän'dĕ)	**198-99**	39°45'N	8°56'W
Marion, Al., U.S. (măr'ĭ-ŭn)	**124-25**	32°38'N	87°19'W
Marion, Ar., U.S. (măr'ĭ-ŭn)	**124-25**	35°13'N	90°12'W
Marion, Ia., U.S. (măr'ĭ-ŭn)	**114-15**	42°02'N	91°36'W
Marion, Il., U.S. (măr'ĭ-ŭn)	**116-17**	37°44'N	88°56'W
Marion, In., U.S. (măr'ĭ-ŭn)	**116-17**	40°33'N	85°39'W
Marion, Ky., U.S. (măr'ĭ-ŭn)	**124-25**	37°20'N	88°05'W
Marion, N.C., U.S. (măr'ĭ-ŭn)	**124-25**	35°41'N	82°01'W
Marion, Oh., U.S. (măr'ĭ-ŭn)	**116-17**	40°35'N	83°07'W
Marion, S.C., U.S. (măr'ĭ-ŭn)	**124-25**	34°11'N	79°24'W
Marion, Va., U.S. (măr'ĭ-ŭn)	**124-25**	36°50'N	81°31'W
Marion, Lake, res., S.C., U.S. (lāk măr'ĭ-ŭn)	**124-25**	33°32'N	80°29'W
Mariquita, Col. (mä-rē-kē'tä)	**163c**	5°11'N	74°54'W
Mariscal Estigarribia, Para.	**168-69**	22°02'S	60°37'W
Maritzburg, S. Afr. *see* Pietermaritzburg	**264-65**	29°36'S	30°23'E
Mariupol', Ukr.	**202-03**	47°06'N	37°34'E
Mariy-El, state, Russia *see* Mari El	**186-87**	56°30'N	48°00'E
Marka, Som.	**262-63**	1°43'N	44°46'E
Markaryd, Swe. (mär'kä-rüd)	**192-93**	56°28'N	13°35'E
Marked Tree, Ar., U.S. (märkt trē)	**124-25**	35°32'N	90°25'W
Markha, Russia	**218-19**	60°36'N	123°19'E
Markha, stm., Russia	**218-19**	63°27'N	118°53'E
Markham, On., Can. (märk'ȧm)	**136-37**	43°52'N	79°16'W
Markovo, Russia (mär'kô-vô)	**218-19**	64°40'N	170°27'E
Marks, Russia	**186-87**	51°42'N	46°44'E
Marksville, La., U.S. (märks'vĭl)	**124-25**	31°07'N	92°05'W
Marlette, Mi., U.S. (mär-lĕt')	**116-17**	43°20'N	83°04'W
Marlin, Tx., U.S. (mär'lĭn)	**122-23**	31°17'N	96°53'W
Marlinton, W.V., U.S. (mär'lĭn-tŭn)	**116-17**	38°14'N	80°06'W
Marlow, Ok., U.S. (mär'lō)	**120-21**	34°38'N	97°58'W
Marmande, Fr. (mȧr-mänd')	**196-97**	44°30'N	0°10'E
Marmara, Sea of, s., Tur. (mär'mȧ-rȧ)	**200-01**	40°40'N	28°15'E
Marmara Denizi, s., Tur. *see* Marmara, Sea of	**200-01**	40°40'N	28°15'E
Marmarth, N.D., U.S. (mär-mȧrth)	**114-15**	46°18'N	103°55'W
Marmelos, stm., Braz.	**166-67**	6°05'S	61°46'W
Maroa, Ven. (mä-rō'ä)	**164-65**	2°44'N	67°33'W
Maromokotro, mtn., Madag.	**264-65**	14°01'S	48°58'E
Marondera, Zimb.	**264-65**	18°10'S	31°32'E
Marosvásárhely, Rom. *see* Târgu Mureş	**194-95**	46°33'N	24°34'E
Marotiri, Îles, is., Fr. Poly.	**280-81**	27°53'S	143°21'W
Maroua, Camrn. (mär'wä)	**260-61**	10°37'N	14°19'E
Marovoay, Madag.	**264-65**	16°07'S	46°39'E
Marquesas Islands, is., Fr. Poly. (mär-kĕ'säs ī'lăndz)	**280-81**	8°59'S	139°31'W
Marquesas Keys, is., Fl., U.S. (mȧr-kē'zȧs kēs)	**125a**	24°34'N	82°08'W
Marquette, Mi., U.S.	**114-15**	46°32'N	87°23'W
Marquises, Îles, is., Fr. Poly. *see* Marquesas Islands	**280-81**	8°59'S	139°31'W
Marrah, Jabal, vol., Sudan (jĕb'ĕl mär'ä)	**262-63**	13°03'N	24°21'E
Marrakech, Mor. (mȧr-rä'kĕsh)	**269a**	31°38'N	8°01'W
Marrakesh, Mor. *see* Marrakech	**269a**	31°38'N	8°01'W
Marree, Austl. (mär'rē)	**276**	29°39'S	138°04'E
Marromeu, Moz.	**264-65**	18°16'S	35°52'E
Marsá al-Burayqah, Libya	**188-89**	30°23'N	19°36'E
Marsabit, Kenya	**267**	2°20'N	37°60'E
Marsala, Italy (mär-sä'lä)	**200-01**	37°48'N	12°26'E
Marseille, Fr. (mȧr-sâ'y')	**196-97**	43°18'N	5°24'E
Marseilles, Il., U.S. (mär-sĕlz')	**116-17**	41°20'N	88°42'W
Marshall, Il., U.S. (mär'shăl)	**116-17**	39°23'N	87°42'W
Marshall, Mi., U.S. (mär'shăl)	**116-17**	42°16'N	84°57'W
Marshall, Mn., U.S. (mär'shăl)	**114-15**	44°27'N	95°48'W
Marshall, Mo., U.S. (mär'shăl)	**120-21**	39°07'N	93°12'W
Marshall, Tx., U.S. (mär'shăl)	**120-21**	32°33'N	94°22'W

ăt; finăl; rāte; senāte; ärm; åsk; sofȧ; fâre; ch-choose; dh-as th in other; bē; ēvent; bĕt; recĕnt; cratẽr; g-gō; gh-guttural g; bĭt; ĭ-short neutral; rīde; ĸ-guttural k as ch in German ich;

Feature (Pronunciation)	Page	Lat.	Long.
Marshall Islands, nation, Oc. (mär´shăl ī´lăndz)	**280-81**	11°0'N	168°00'E
Marshalltown, Ia., U.S. (mär´shăl-toun)	**114-15**	42°03'N	92°54'W
Marshfield, Mo., U.S. (märsh´fēld)	**120-21**	37°20'N	92°54'W
Marshfield, Wi., U.S. (märsh´fēld)	**116-17**	44°40'N	90°10'W
Marsh Harbour, Bah. (mär´sh här´bēr)	**142-43**	26°32'N	77°04'W
Marsh Island, i., La., U.S.	**124-25**	29°35'N	91°53'W
Mart, Tx., U.S. (märt)	**122-23**	31°32'N	96°50'W
Martaban, Gulf of, b., Mya. (gŭlf ŭv mär-tŭ-bän´)	**246-47**	16°46'N	97°01'E
Martha's Vineyard, i., Ma., U.S. (mär´thȧz vĭn´yȧrd)	**116-17**	41°24'N	70°38'W
Martigny, Switz. (mȧr-tē-nyē´)	**194-95**	46°06'N	7°04'E
Martin, S.D., U.S. (mär´tĭn)	**114-15**	43°10'N	101°44'W
Martin, Tn., U.S. (mär´tĭn)	**124-25**	36°21'N	88°51'W
Martina Franca, Italy (mär-tē´nä fräŋ´kä)	**200-01**	40°42'N	17°20'E
Martinez, Ga., U.S. (mär-tē´nĕz)	**124-25**	33°31'N	82°05'W
Martinique, dep., N.A. (mȧr-tē-nēk´)	**140-41**	14°40'N	61°00'W
Martinique Passage, strt., N.A.	**143b**	15°10'N	61°15'W
Martinsburg, W.V., U.S. (mär´tĭnz-bûrg)	**116-17**	39°27'N	77°57'W
Martinsville, In., U.S. (mär´tĭnz-vĭl)	**116-17**	39°25'N	86°25'W
Martinsville, Va., U.S. (mär´tĭnz-vĭl)	**124-25**	36°41'N	79°52'W
Martin Vaz, Ilhas, is., Braz.	**159**	20°30'S	28°51'W
Martos, Spain (mär´tōs)	**198-99**	37°43'N	3°58'W
Martre, Lac la, lk., N.T., Can. (läk lä märtr)	**130-31**	63°15'N	117°55'W
Marungu, mts., D.R.C.	**267**	7°42'S	30°01'E
Mary, Turkmen. (mä´rē)	**232-33**	37°35'N	61°49'E
Maryborough, Austl. (mă´rĭ-bŭr-ō)	**276**	25°32'S	152°42'E
Maryborough, Austl. (mă´rĭ-bŭr-ō)	**276**	37°03'S	143°44'E
Maryland, state, U.S. (mĕr´ĭ-lănd)	**108-09**	39°0'N	76°45'W
Marystown, Nf., Can. (mâr´ĭz-toun)	**138-39**	47°11'N	55°10'W
Marysville, Ca., U.S.	**118-19**	39°09'N	121°35'W
Marysville, Ks., U.S. (mă´rĭz-vĭl)	**120-21**	39°50'N	96°39'W
Marysville, Oh., U.S. (mă´rĭz-vĭl)	**116-17**	40°14'N	83°22'W
Marysville, Wa., U.S. (mă´rĭz-vĭl)	**112-13**	48°04'N	122°10'W
Maryville, Mo., U.S. (mă´rĭ-vĭl)	**120-21**	40°21'N	94°52'W
Maryville, Tn., U.S. (mă´rĭ-vĭl)	**124-25**	35°46'N	83°58'W
Masai Mara Game Reserve, pk., Kenya	**267**	1°15'S	35°15'E
Masai Steppe, plat., Tan.	**267**	4°45'S	37°00'E
Masaka, Ug.	**267**	0°20'S	31°44'E
Masalembu Besar, Pulau, i., Indon.	**248-49**	5°34'S	114°26'E
Masan, Kor., S. (mä-sän´)	**243**	35°12'N	128°34'E
Masatepe, Nic. (mä-sä-tĕ´pĕ)	**149**	11°54'N	86°09'W
Masaya, Nic. (mä-sä´yä)	**149**	11°58'N	86°06'W
Masbate, Phil. (mäs-bä´tä)	**250**	12°22'N	123°38'E
Masbate, i., Phil. (mäs-bä´tä)	**250**	12°15'N	123°30'E
Mascara, Alg.	**198-99**	35°23'N	0°08'E
Mascareignes, Îles, is., Afr.	**265a**	21°0'S	57°00'E
Mascarene Islands, is., Afr. see Mascareignes, Îles	**265a**	21°0'S	57°00'E
Mascota, Mex. (mäs-kō´tä)	**146-47**	20°31'N	104°47'W
Mascoutah, Il., U.S. (mäs-kū´tä)	**120-21**	38°29'N	89°48'W
Maseru, nat. cap., Leso. (măz´ēr-ōō)	**269c**	29°19'S	27°29'E
Mashābih, i., Sau. Ar.	**266**	25°38'N	36°31'E
Mashhad, Iran	**232-33**	36°17'N	59°36'E
Māshkel, Hāmūn-i-, lk., Pak. (hä-mōōn´ē mäsh-kĕl´)	**232-33**	28°15'N	63°00'E
Masi-Manimba, D.R.C.	**262-63**	4°46'S	17°57'E
Masindi, Ug. (mä-sēn´dē)	**267**	1°41'N	31°43'E
Masira, Gulf of, b., Oman see Maşīrah, Khalīj	**220-21**	20°10'N	58°15'E
Maşīrah, i., Oman	**220-21**	20°27'N	58°48'E
Maşīrah, Khalīj, b., Oman	**220-21**	20°10'N	58°15'E
Masjed-e Soleymān, Iran	**232-33**	31°58'N	49°18'E
Masoala, Saikanosy, pen., Madag.	**264-65**	15°26'S	50°04'E
Mason, Mi., U.S. (mā´sŭn)	**116-17**	42°35'N	84°26'W
Mason, Tx., U.S. (mā´sŭn)	**122-23**	30°45'N	99°15'W
Mason City, Ia., U.S. (mā´sŭn sĭ´tĭ)	**114-15**	43°09'N	93°12'W
Masqaţ, nat. cap., Oman see Muscat	**230-31**	23°36'N	58°32'E
Massa, Italy (mäs´sä)	**200-01**	44°03'N	10°09'E
Massachusetts, state, U.S. (măs-ȧ-chōō´sĕts)	**108-09**	42°15'N	71°50'W
Massafra, Italy (mäs-sä´frä)	**200-01**	40°35'N	17°08'E
Massakory, Chad	**258-59**	12°60'N	15°44'E
Massawa, Erit.	**266**	15°37'N	39°26'E
Massena, N.Y., U.S. (mă-sē´nȧ)	**116-17**	44°56'N	74°53'W
Masset, B.C., Can. (măs´ĕt)	**132-33**	54°02'N	132°08'W
Massillon, Oh., U.S. (măs´ĭ-lŏn)	**116-17**	40°48'N	81°31'W
Massinga, Moz. (mä-sĭn´gä)	**264-65**	23°20'S	35°24'E
Massive, Mount, mtn., Co., U.S. (mount măs´ĭv)	**118-19**	39°12'N	106°28'W
Maştağa, Azer.	**227**	40°32'N	49°59'E
Mastung, Pak.	**232-33**	29°48'N	66°52'E
Masuda, Japan (mä-sōō´dȧ)	**245**	34°41'N	131°51'E
Masulipatam, India see Machilīpatnam	**236**	16°11'N	81°09'E
Masvingo, Zimb.	**264-65**	20°04'S	30°49'E
Matadi, D.R.C. (mȧ-tä´dē)	**262-63**	5°49'S	13°29'E
Matagalpa, Nic. (mä-tä-gäl´pä)	**149**	12°60'N	85°44'W
Matagami, Qc., Can.	**128-29**	49°45'N	77°39'W
Matagorda Island, i., Tx., U.S.	**122-23**	28°15'N	96°37'W
Mataiva, at., Fr. Poly.	**280-81**	14°53'S	148°40'W
Matamoros, Mex. (mä-tä-mō´rōs)	**122-23**	25°52'N	97°30'W
Matamoros, Mex. (mä-tä-mō´rōs)	**122-23**	25°32'N	103°14'W
Matandu, stm., Tan.	**262-63**	8°43'S	39°22'E
Matane, Qc., Can. (mȧ-tȧn´)	**138-39**	48°50'N	67°31'W
Matanzas, Cuba (mä-tän´zäs)	**142-43**	23°03'N	81°34'W
Matanzas, state, Cuba (mä-tän´zäs)	**142-43**	22°40'N	81°20'W
Matapalo, Cabo, c., C.R. (kȧ´bô-mä-tä-pä´lō)	**149**	8°23'N	83°17'W
Matapan, Cape, c., Grc. see Taínaro, Ákra	**200-01**	36°23'N	22°29'E
Matapédia, Qc., Can. (mă-tȧ-pā´dē-ȧ)	**138-39**	47°58'N	66°56'W
Matapédia, Lac, lk., Qc., Can. (läk mă-tȧ-pā´dē-ȧ)	**138-39**	48°33'N	67°33'W
Matara, Sri L. (mä-tä´rä)	**236**	5°57'N	80°34'E
Mataram, Indon.	**248-49**	8°35'S	116°07'E
Mataró, Spain	**198-99**	41°32'N	2°26'E
Matasiri, Pulau, i., Indon.	**248-49**	4°48'S	115°49'E
Matâ'utu, nat. cap., Wal./F.	**280-81**	13°17'S	176°09'W
Matehuala, Mex. (mä-tȧ-wä´lä)	**146-47**	23°40'N	100°38'W
Matera, Italy (mä-tâ´rä)	**200-01**	40°41'N	16°36'E
Mathura, India (mu-tó´rū)	**234-35**	27°30'N	77°41'E
Mathurai, India see Madurai	**236**	9°55'N	78°08'E
Matias Barbosa, Braz. (mä-tē´äs-bȧr-bô-sä)	**172**	21°53'S	43°19'W
Mato, Cerro, mtn., Ven.	**164-65**	7°16'N	65°15'W
Mato Grosso, state, Braz. (mät´ō grōs´ō)	**166-67**	12°0'S	57°00'W
Mato Grosso, Planalto do, plat., Braz. (plä-nȧl´tō-dō mät´ō grōs´ō)	**166-67**	14°59'S	53°37'W
Mato Grosso do Sul, state, Braz.	**168-69**	20°0'S	55°00'W
Matola, Moz.	**264-65**	25°49'S	32°27'E
Matosinhos, Port.	**198-99**	41°11'N	8°41'W
Maţraḩ, Oman (mȧ-trä´)	**230-31**	23°37'N	58°31'E
Matsue, Japan (mät´sōō-ĕ)	**245**	35°28'N	133°04'E
Matsumoto, Japan (mät´sŏŏ-mō´tō)	**245**	36°14'N	137°58'E
Matsu Tao, i., Tai.	**225a**	26°09'N	119°56'E
Matsuyama, Japan (mät´sŏŏ-yä´mä)	**245**	33°50'N	132°46'E
Mattawa, On., Can. (măt´ȧ-wȧ)	**136-37**	46°18'N	78°41'W
Matterhorn, mtn., Eur. (mät´ēr-hôrn)	**194-95**	45°59'N	7°43'E
Matthew Town, Bah. (măth´ū toun)	**142-43**	21°01'N	73°42'W
Mattoon, Il., U.S. (mă-tōōn´)	**116-17**	39°29'N	88°23'W
Maturín, Ven. (mä-tōō-rēn´)	**164-65**	9°44'N	63°11'W
Maubeuge, Fr. (mō-bûzh´)	**196-97**	50°17'N	3°58'E
Maués, Braz. (mȧ-wĕ´s)	**166-67**	3°22'S	57°43'W
Maui, i., Hi., U.S. (mä´ōō-ē)	**127a**	20°45'N	156°15'W
Maumee, Oh., U.S. (mô-mē´)	**116-17**	41°34'N	83°39'W
Maumee, stm., U.S. (mô-mē´)	**116-17**	41°42'N	83°27'W
Maun, Bots. (mä-ōn´)	**264-65**	19°60'S	23°25'E
Mauna Kea, vol., Hi., U.S. (mä´ō-näkä´ä)	**127a**	19°50'N	155°28'W
Mauna Loa, vol., Hi., U.S. (mä´ō-nälō´ä)	**127a**	19°29'N	155°36'W
Maunoir, Lac, lk., N.T., Can.	**130-31**	67°30'N	125°00'W
Maurepas, Lake, lk., La., U.S. (lăk mō-rē-pä´)	**124-25**	30°15'N	90°30'W
Mauritania, nation, Afr. (mô-rē-tā´nĭ-ȧ)	**253**	20°0'N	12°00'W
Mauritanie, nation, Afr. see Mauritania	**253**	20°0'N	12°00'W
Mauritius, nation, Afr. (mô-rĭsh´ĭ-ŭs)	**253**	20°17'S	57°33'E
Mauston, Wi., U.S. (môs´tŭn)	**116-17**	43°47'N	90°04'W
Mawlamyaing, Mya. see Mawlamyine	**246-47**	16°30'N	97°38'E
Mawlamyine, Mya.	**246-47**	16°30'N	97°38'E
Maxixe, Moz.	**264-65**	23°52'S	35°21'E
Maya, stm., Russia (mä´yä)	**218-19**	60°25'N	134°34'E
Mayaguana, i., Bah.	**142-43**	22°23'N	72°57'W
Mayagüez, P.R. (mä-yä-gwāz´)	**142a**	18°12'N	67°09'W
Mayfield, Ky., U.S. (mā´fēld)	**124-25**	36°45'N	88°38'W
Maykop, Russia	**186-87**	44°36'N	40°06'E
Maymyo, Mya. (mī´myō)	**246-47**	22°02'N	96°28'E
Mayo, Yk., Can. (mä-yō´)	**128-29**	63°36'N	135°51'W
Mayodan, N.C., U.S. (mā-yō´dăn)	**124-25**	36°24'N	79°59'W
Mayon Volcano, vol., Phil. (mä-yōn´ vŏl-kā´nō)	**250**	13°15'N	123°41'E
Mayotte, dep., Afr. (mȧ-yôt´)	**264-65**	12°50'S	45°10'E
Maysville, Ky., U.S. (māz´vĭl)	**116-17**	38°38'N	83°46'W
Mayumba, Gabon	**260-61**	3°22'S	10°40'E
Māyūram, India	**236**	11°06'N	79°39'E
Mayville, N.D., U.S. (mā´vĭl)	**114-15**	47°30'N	97°19'W
Mayville, Wi., U.S. (mā´vĭl)	**116-17**	43°30'N	88°32'W
Mayyit, Al-Baḩr al-, lk., Asia see Dead Sea	**228-29**	31°30'N	35°30'E
Maza, Arg.	**173**	36°48'S	63°20'W
Mazabuka, Zam. (mä-zä-bōō´kä)	**264-65**	15°51'S	27°46'E
Mazagan, Mor. see El-Jadida	**269a**	33°15'N	8°31'W
Mazagão, Braz. (mä-zȧ-gou´ɴ)	**166-67**	0°07'S	51°17'W
Mazara del Vallo, Italy (mät-sä´rä dĕl väl´lō)	**200-01**	37°39'N	12°36'E
Mazār-e Sharīf, Afg.	**232-33**	36°42'N	67°07'E
Mazarrón, Spain (mä-zär-rô´n)	**198-99**	37°36'N	1°19'W
Mazaruni, stm., Guy.	**164-65**	6°26'N	58°36'W
Mazatenango, Guat. (mä-zä-tȧ-näŋ´gō)	**148**	14°32'N	91°30'W
Mazatlán, Mex. (mä-zä-tlän´)	**146-47**	23°13'N	106°25'W
Mažeikiai, Lith. (mȧ-zhā´kē-ī)	**192-93**	56°19'N	22°21'E
Mazoe, stm., Afr. see Mazowe	**264-65**	16°32'S	33°26'E
Mazowe, stm., Afr.	**264-65**	16°32'S	33°26'E
Mazyr, Bela.	**202-03**	52°03'N	29°16'E
Mbabane, nat. cap., Swaz. (m'bä-bä´nē)	**264-65**	26°20'S	31°09'E
Mbaïki, C.A.R. (m'bȧ-ē´kē)	**262-63**	3°52'N	17°60'E
Mbala, Zam.	**264-65**	8°51'S	31°22'E
Mbale, Ug.	**267**	1°05'N	34°10'E
Mbandaka, D.R.C.	**262-63**	0°02'N	18°15'E
M'banza Congo, Ang.	**262-63**	6°16'S	14°15'E
Mbanza-Ngungu, D.R.C.	**262-63**	5°14'S	14°53'E
Mbarara, Ug.	**267**	0°36'S	30°38'E
Mbari, stm., C.A.R.	**262-63**	4°36'N	22°44'E
Mbeya, Tan.	**264-65**	8°54'S	33°30'E
Mbinda, Congo	**262-63**	2°07'S	12°53'E
Mbini, stm., Afr.	**260-61**	1°35'N	9°38'E
Mbomou, stm., Afr. (m'bō´mōō)	**262-63**	4°09'N	22°29'E
Mbour, Sen.	**260-61**	14°25'N	16°58'W
Mbuji-Mayi, D.R.C.	**262-63**	6°08'S	23°39'E
Mbuji-Mayi, stm., D.R.C.	**262-63**	6°02'S	23°44'E
McAdam, N.B., Can. (măk-ăd´ăm)	**138-39**	45°35'N	67°20'W
McAlester, Ok., U.S. (măk ăl´ĕs-tēr)	**120-21**	34°56'N	95°46'W
McAllen, Tx., U.S. (măk-ăl´ĕn)	**122-23**	26°12'N	98°14'W
McBride, B.C., Can. (măk-brīd´)	**132-33**	53°18'N	120°10'W
McCamey, Tx., U.S. (mȧ-kā´mĭ)	**122-23**	31°08'N	102°13'W
McCauley Island, i., B.C., Can.	**132-33**	53°40'N	130°15'W
McColl, S.C., U.S.	**124-25**	34°40'N	79°33'W
McComb, Ms., U.S. (mȧ-kōm´)	**124-25**	31°14'N	90°27'W
McCook, Ne., U.S. (mȧ-ko͝ok´)	**120-21**	40°12'N	100°37'W
McGehee, Ar., U.S. (mȧ-gē´)	**124-25**	33°38'N	91°24'W
McGill, Nv., U.S. (mȧ-gĭl´)	**118-19**	39°25'N	114°49'W
McGrath, Ak., U.S. (măk´grȧth)	**126**	62°58'N	155°38'W
McGregor, Tx., U.S. (măk-grĕg´ēr)	**122-23**	31°26'N	97°24'W
McGregor, stm., B.C., Can. (măk-grĕg´ēr)	**132-33**	54°10'N	122°01'W
McKeesport, Pa., U.S. (mȧ-kez´pōrt)	**116-17**	40°21'N	79°52'W
McKenzie, Tn., U.S. (mȧ-kĕn´zĭ)	**124-25**	36°08'N	88°31'W
McKinley, Mount, mtn., Ak., U.S. (mount mȧ-kĭn´lĭ)	**126**	63°04'N	151°00'W
McKinney, Tx., U.S. (mȧ-kĭn´ĭ)	**120-21**	33°12'N	96°37'W
McLaughlin, S.D., U.S. (măk-lŏf´lĭn)	**114-15**	45°49'N	100°48'W
McLennan, Ab., Can. (măk-lĭn´năn)	**132-33**	55°41'N	116°52'W
McLeod, stm., Ab., Can.	**132-33**	54°09'N	115°42'W
McLoughlin, Mount, mtn., Or., U.S. (mount măk-lŏk´lĭn)	**112-13**	42°27'N	122°19'W
McMinnville, Or., U.S. (măk-mĭn´vĭl)	**112-13**	45°13'N	123°11'W
McMinnville, Tn., U.S. (măk-mĭn´vĭl)	**124-25**	35°41'N	85°47'W
McPherson, Ks., U.S. (măk-fŭr´s'n)	**120-21**	38°22'N	97°40'W
McRae, Ga., U.S. (măk-rā´)	**124-25**	32°04'N	82°54'W
Mead, Lake, res., U.S. (lāk mēd)	**118-19**	36°08'N	114°26'W
Meade, stm., Ak., U.S.	**126**	70°55'N	156°00'W
Meadow Lake, Sk., Can. (mĕd´ō lāk)	**134-35**	54°08'N	108°26'W
Meadville, Pa., U.S.	**116-17**	41°39'N	80°09'W
Meaford, On., Can. (mē´fērd)	**136-37**	44°36'N	80°35'W
Meaux, Fr. (mō)	**196-97**	48°58'N	2°53'E
Mecca, Sau. Ar. (mĕk´ȧ)	**266**	21°27'N	39°51'E
Mechanic Falls, Me., U.S. (mē-kăn´ĭk fôlz)	**116-17**	44°07'N	70°24'W
Mechanicsburg, Pa., U.S. (mē-kăn´ĭks-bûrg)	**116-17**	40°12'N	77°01'W
Mechanicsville, Va., U.S. (mē-kăn´ĭks-vĭl)	**116-17**	37°36'N	77°22'W
Mecubúri, stm., Moz.	**264-65**	14°10'S	40°32'E
Medan, Indon. (mȧ-dän´)	**246-47**	3°35'N	98°41'E
Medanosa, Punta, c., Arg. (pōō´n-tä-mē-dä-nō´sä)	**171**	48°06'S	65°55'W
Médéa, Alg.	**269b**	36°12'N	2°51'E
Medellín, Col. (mā-dhĕl-yēn´)	**164-65**	6°15'N	75°35'W
Medenine, Tun. (mā-dē-nēn´)	**188-89**	33°20'N	10°30'E
Medford, Ok., U.S. (mĕd´fērd)	**120-21**	36°49'N	97°43'W
Medford, Or., U.S. (mĕd´fērd)	**112-13**	42°20'N	122°52'W

n-sing; ŋ-baŋk; ɴ-nasalized n; nŏd; cŏmmit; ōld; ôbey; ôrder; oi-boil; fōōd; ŏ-as oo in foot; ou-out; s-soft; sh-dish; th-thin; pūre; ůnite; ûrn; stŭd; circŭs; ü-as in French tu; ´-indeterminate vowel.

Feature (Pronunciation)	Page	Lat.	Long.
Medford, Wi., U.S. (mĕd´fẽrd)	**116-17**	45°08′N	90°20′W
Medgyes, Rom. *see* Mediaș	**194-95**	46°10′N	24°22′E
Mediaș, Rom. (mĕd-yäsh´)	**194-95**	46°10′N	24°22′E
Medical Lake, Wa., U.S. (mĕd´ĭ-kăl lăk)	**112-13**	47°37′N	117°43′W
Medicine Hat, Ab., Can. (mĕd´ĭ-sĭn hăt)	**132-33**	50°03′N	110°41′W
Medicine Lodge, Ks., U.S. (mĕd´ĭ-sĭn lŏj)	**120-21**	37°17′N	98°35′W
Medina, Sau. Ar. (må-dē´nȧ)	**266**	24°28′N	39°37′E
Medina, N.Y., U.S. (mē-dī´nȧ)	**116-17**	43°13′N	78°23′W
Medina, Oh., U.S. (mē-dī´nȧ)	**116-17**	41°08′N	81°51′W
Medina del Campo, Spain (må-dē´nä dĕl käm´pō)	**198-99**	41°19′N	4°55′W
Medina de Ríoseco, Spain (må-dē´nä dā rē-ô-sā´kô)	**198-99**	41°52′N	5°02′W
Medinīpur, India	**234-35**	22°26′N	87°20′E
Medio, Punta, c., Chile	**168-69**	27°07′S	70°56′W
Mediterranean Sea, s., (mĕd-ĭ-tẽr-ā´nē-ăn sē)	**188-89**	35°0′N	20°00′E
Méditerranée, Mer, s., *see* Mediterranean Sea	**188-89**	35°0′N	20°00′E
Mediterráneo, Mar, s., *see* Mediterranean Sea	**188-89**	35°0′N	20°00′E
Mediterraneo, Mar, s., *see* Mediterranean Sea	**188-89**	35°0′N	20°00′E
Mediterrània, Mar, s., *see* Mediterranean Sea	**188-89**	35°0′N	20°00′E
Mednogorsk, Russia	**226**	51°25′N	57°35′E
Médouneu, Gabon	**260-61**	0°59′N	10°55′E
Medveditsa, stm., Russia (mĕd-vyĕ´dē tså)	**186-87**	49°35′N	42°39′E
Medvezhyegorsk, Russia	**186-87**	62°55′N	34°28′E
Medyn', Russia (mĕ-dēn´)	**202-03**	54°57′N	35°53′E
Meekatharra, Austl. (mē-kȧ-thăr´ȧ)	**270-71**	26°35′S	118°30′E
Meeker, Co., U.S. (mēk´ẽr)	**118-19**	40°03′N	107°55′W
Meelpaeg Lake, res., Nf., Can. (mēl´pȧ-ĕg lāk)	**138-39**	48°16′N	56°35′W
Meerut, India (mē´rŭt)	**234-35**	28°59′N	77°42′E
Meghālaya, state, India	**234-35**	25°30′N	91°15′E
Meghna, stm., Bngl.	**234-35**	22°50′N	90°42′E
Megísti, i., Grc.	**188-89**	36°08′N	29°36′E
Mehun-sur-Yèvre, Fr. (mē-ŭN-sür-yĕvr´)	**196-97**	47°09′N	2°13′E
Meiganga, Camrn.	**260-61**	6°34′N	14°07′E
Meiktila, Mya.	**246-47**	20°52′N	95°52′E
Meixian, China *see* Meizhou	**238-39**	24°20′N	116°07′E
Meizhou, China	**238-39**	24°20′N	116°07′E
Mejillones, Chile (må-ĸē-lyō´nås)	**168-69**	23°06′S	70°27′W
Mek'elē, Eth.	**266**	13°30′N	39°28′E
Meknès, Mor. (mĕk´nĕs) (mĕk-nĕs´)	**269a**	33°54′N	5°33′W
Mekong, stm., Asia (mā-kông´)	**246-47**	10°33′N	105°27′E
Mékôngk, stm., Asia *see* Mekong	**246-47**	10°33′N	105°27′E
Mékrou, stm., Afr.	**260-61**	12°24′N	2°50′E
Melaka, Malay.	**246-47**	2°12′N	102°16′E
Melaka, Selat, strt., Asia *see* Malacca, Strait of	**246-47**	2°30′N	101°20′E
Melanesia, is., Oc. (mĕl-ȧ-nē´-zhȧ)	**280-81**	13°0′S	164°00′E
Mélanésie, is., Oc. *see* Melanesia	**280-81**	13°0′S	164°00′E
Melawi, stm., Indon.	**248-49**	0°05′N	111°29′E
Melbourne, Austl. (mĕl´bŭrn)	**276**	37°49′S	144°57′E
Melbourne, Fl., U.S. (mĕl´bŭrn)	**125a**	28°05′N	80°37′W
Melbourne Island, i., Nu., Can.	**130-31**	68°30′N	104°45′W
Melchor, Isla, i., Chile	**171**	45°08′S	73°57′W
Melekeok, nat. cap., Palau	**280-81**	7°29′N	134°37′E
Meleuz, Russia	**186-87**	52°58′N	55°56′E
Mélèzes, stm., Qc., Can.	**130-31**	57°41′N	69°29′W
Melfi, Chad	**258-59**	11°03′N	17°56′E
Melfort, Sk., Can. (mĕl´fôrt)	**134-35**	52°52′N	104°36′W
Melilla, Sp. N. Afr. (mā-lēl´yä)	**198-99**	35°18′N	2°57′W
Melipilla, Chile (må-lē-pē´lyä)	**163e**	33°41′S	71°13′W
Melita, Mb., Can.	**134-35**	49°16′N	100°59′W
Melitopol', Ukr. (mā-lē-tô´pôl-y')	**202-03**	46°51′N	35°21′E
Mellen, Wi., U.S. (mĕl´ĕn)	**114-15**	46°20′N	90°40′W
Mellerud, Swe. (mål´ĕ-rōōdh)	**192-93**	58°42′N	12°28′E
Melo, Ur. (mā´lō)	**173**	32°22′S	54°11′W
Melos, i., Grc. (mē´lŏs) *see* Mílos	**200-01**	36°41′N	24°28′E
Melrhir, Chott, lk., Alg.	**258-59**	34°18′N	6°17′E
Melrose, Mn., U.S. (mĕl´rōz)	**114-15**	45°40′N	94°49′W
Melton Mowbray, Eng., U.K. (mĕl´tŭn mō´brâ)	**190-91**	52°46′N	0°53′W
Melun, Fr. (mē-lŭN´)	**196-97**	48°32′N	2°40′E
Melville, Sk., Can. (mĕl´vĭl)	**134-35**	50°55′N	102°48′W
Melville, Cape, c., Austl. (kāp mĕl´vĭl)	**277**	14°11′S	144°30′E
Melville, Lake, lk., Nf., Can. (lāk mĕl´vĭl)	**130-31**	53°40′N	59°44′W
Melville Island, i., Austl. (mĕl´vĭl ī´lȧnd)	**272-73**	11°40′S	131°00′E
Melville Island, i., Can.	**86**	75°15′N	109°59′W
Melville Peninsula, pen., Nu., Can. (mĕl´vĭl pĕ-nĭn´sūlȧ)	**130-31**	68°0′N	84°00′W
Memel, Lith. *see* Klaipėda	**192-93**	55°43′N	21°08′E
Memel, S. Afr. (mĕ´mĕl)	**269c**	27°41′S	29°34′E
Memmingen, Ger. (mĕm´ĭng-ĕn)	**194-95**	47°59′N	10°11′E
Mempawah, Indon.	**246-47**	0°20′N	108°58′E
Memphis, Mo., U.S. (mĕm´fĭs)	**120-21**	40°28′N	92°10′W
Memphis, Tn., U.S. (mĕm´fĭs)	**124-25**	35°09′N	90°03′W
Memphis, Tx., U.S. (mĕm´fĭs)	**120-21**	34°44′N	100°33′W
Mena, Ukr. (mē-nä´)	**202-03**	51°31′N	32°14′E
Mena, Ar., U.S. (mē´nȧ)	**120-21**	34°35′N	94°15′W
Menado, Indon. *see* Manado	**248-49**	1°29′N	124°51′E
Ménaka, Mali	**258-59**	15°55′N	2°24′E
Menard, Tx., U.S. (mē-närd´)	**122-23**	30°55′N	99°47′W
Menasha, Wi., U.S. (mē-năsh´ȧ)	**116-17**	44°12′N	88°26′W
Mendawai, stm., Indon.	**248-49**	3°14′S	113°19′E
Mende, Fr. (mäNd)	**196-97**	44°30′N	3°30′E
Mendi, Pap. N. Gui.	**277**	6°10′S	143°40′E
Mendocino, Cape, c., Ca., U.S. (kāp mĕn´dô-sē´nō)	**112-13**	40°25′N	124°23′W
Mendota, Ca., U.S. (mĕn-dō´tȧ)	**118-19**	36°46′N	120°23′W
Mendota, Il., U.S. (mĕn-dō´tȧ)	**116-17**	41°33′N	89°07′W
Mendoza, Arg. (mĕn-dō´sä)	**163e**	32°53′S	68°49′W
Mendoza, state, Arg. (mĕn-dō´sä)	**163e**	34°30′S	68°30′W
Mengcheng, China (mŭŋ-chŭŋ)	**238-39**	33°16′N	116°33′E
Menggala, Indon.	**246-47**	4°29′S	105°15′E
Menghai, China	**238-39**	21°59′N	100°27′E
Menindee, Austl. (mĕ-nĭn-dē)	**276**	32°24′S	142°26′E
Menominee, Mi., U.S. (mē-nŏm´ĭ-nē)	**116-17**	45°08′N	87°37′W
Menominee, stm., U.S. (mē-nŏm´ĭ-nē)	**114-15**	45°06′N	87°36′W
Menongue, Ang.	**264-65**	14°39′S	17°41′E
Menorca, i., Spain (mĕ-nô´r-kä)	**198-99**	40°0′N	4°00′E
Mentawai, Selat, strt., Indon.	**246-47**	1°45′S	100°00′E
Menzel Bourguiba, Tun.	**184-85**	37°10′N	9°48′E
Meoqui, Mex.	**122-23**	28°16′N	105°29′W
Meppel, Neth. (mĕp´ĕl)	**190-91**	52°42′N	6°12′E
Meppen, Ger. (mĕp´ĕn)	**194-95**	52°42′N	7°18′E
Merauke, Indon. (må-rou´kä)	**277**	8°30′S	140°24′E
Merca, Som. *see* Marka	**262-63**	1°43′N	44°46′E
Merced, Ca., U.S. (mẽr-sĕd´)	**118-19**	37°18′N	120°29′W
Mercedario, Cerro, mtn., Arg. (sĕ´r-rô mĕr-så-dhä´rē-ō)	**168-69**	31°59′S	70°08′W
Mercedes, Arg. (mĕr-sā´dhās)	**173**	29°11′S	58°03′W
Mercedes, Arg. (mĕr-sā´dhās)	**173**	34°40′S	59°26′W
Mercedes, Ur.	**173**	33°15′S	58°02′W
Mercy, Cape, c., Nu., Can.	**130-31**	64°54′N	63°35′W
Merefa, Ukr. (må-rĕf´å)	**202-03**	49°51′N	36°05′E
Mergui, Mya. (mẽr-gē´)	**246-47**	12°26′N	98°37′E
Mergui Archipelago, is., Mya. (mẽr-gē´ är´kå-pĕ´-å-gō)	**246-47**	12°0′N	98°00′E
Mérida, Mex.	**148**	20°59′N	89°37′W
Mérida, Spain	**198-99**	38°55′N	6°20′W
Mérida, Ven. (mĕ´rē-dhä)	**164-65**	8°37′N	71°09′W
Meriden, Ct., U.S. (mĕr´ĭ-dĕn)	**116-17**	41°32′N	72°48′W
Meridian, Id., U.S. (mē-rĭd-ĭ-ăn)	**112-13**	43°36′N	116°21′W
Meridian, Ms., U.S. (mē-rĭd-ĭ-ăn)	**124-25**	32°22′N	88°42′W
Meridian, Tx., U.S. (mē-rĭd-ĭ-ăn)	**122-23**	31°55′N	97°40′W
Merikarvia, Fin. (mā´rē-kår´vē-å)	**192-93**	61°51′N	21°30′E
Merín, Laguna, b., S.A. *see* Mirim, Lagoa	**173**	32°45′S	52°50′W
Merir, i., Palau	**280-81**	4°19′N	132°19′E
Merkel, Tx., U.S. (mûr´kĕl)	**120-21**	32°28′N	100°01′W
Merrill, Mi., U.S. (mĕr´ĭl)	**116-17**	43°25′N	84°20′W
Merrill, Wi., U.S. (mĕr´ĭl)	**116-17**	45°11′N	89°41′W
Merritt, B.C., Can. (mĕr´ĭt)	**132-33**	50°06′N	120°46′W
Merryville, La., U.S. (mĕr´ĭ-vĭl)	**122-23**	30°45′N	93°33′W
Mersa Matruh, Egypt	**188-89**	31°21′N	27°14′E
Merseburg, Ger. (mĕr´zĕ-bŏŏrgh)	**194-95**	51°21′N	11°60′E
Mersin, Tur. *see* İçel	**228-29**	36°49′N	34°38′E
Merthyr Tydfil, Wales, U.K. (mûr´thẽr tĭd´vĭl)	**190-91**	51°46′N	3°23′W
Méru, Fr. (mā-rü´)	**196-97**	49°14′N	2°08′E
Meru, Kenya (mā´rōō)	**267**	0°03′N	37°39′E
Meru, Mount, vol., Tan.	**267**	3°14′S	36°45′E
Merzifon, Tur. (mĕr´ze-fōn)	**186-87**	40°52′N	35°27′E
Mesa, Az., U.S. (mā´sȧ)	**118-19**	33°24′N	111°49′W
Mesabi Range, hills, Mn., U.S. (mā-sŏb´bē rānj)	**114-15**	47°30′N	92°50′W
Mesagne, Italy (mā-sän´yå)	**200-01**	40°34′N	17°49′E
Mesa Verde National Park, n.p., Co., U.S. (mā´sȧ vẽr´dē năsh´ŭn-ăl pärk)	**118-19**	37°15′N	108°26′W
Mescalero Apache Indian Reservation, ind. res., N.M., U.S. (mĕs-kä-lā´rō ȧ-păch´ē ĭn´dĭ-ăn rĕ-sẽr-vā´shĕn)	**120-21**	33°12′N	105°40′W
Mesewa, Erit. *see* Massawa	**266**	15°37′N	39°26′E
Meshchovsk, Russia (myĕsh´chĕfsk)	**202-03**	54°19′N	35°17′E
Meshed, Iran *see* Mashhad	**232-33**	36°17′N	59°36′E
Mesogéios Thálassa, s., *see* Mediterranean Sea	**188-89**	35°0′N	20°00′E
Mesopotamia, hist. reg., Asia	**228-29**	34°0′N	44°00′E
Mesoyéios Thálassa, s., *see* Mediterranean Sea	**188-89**	35°0′N	20°00′E
Messalo, stm., Moz.	**264-65**	11°41′S	40°26′E
Messina, Italy (mĕ-sē´nȧ)	**200-01**	38°11′N	15°33′E
Messina, Stretto di, strt., Italy (strĕ´t-tô dē mĕ-sē´nȧ)	**200-01**	38°09′N	15°35′E
Meta, stm., S.A.	**164-65**	6°11′N	67°28′W
Métabetchouane, stm., Qc., Can. (mĕ-tȧ-bĕt-chōō-än´)	**136-37**	48°26′N	71°58′W
Meta Incognita Peninsula, pen., Nu., Can.	**130-31**	62°45′N	68°30′W
Metán, Arg. (mĕ-tȧ´n)	**168-69**	25°30′S	64°57′W
Metapán, El Sal. (må-täpän´)	**148**	14°20′N	89°26′W
Metković, Cro. (mĕt´kô-vĭch)	**200-01**	43°03′N	17°39′E
Metlakatla, Ak., U.S. (mĕt-lȧ-kăt´lȧ)	**126**	55°07′N	131°35′W
Metropolis, Il., U.S. (mē-trŏp´ô-lĭs)	**124-25**	37°09′N	88°44′W
Metter, Ga., U.S. (mĕt´ẽr)	**124-25**	32°24′N	82°04′W
Metz, Fr. (mĕtz)	**196-97**	49°08′N	6°10′E
Meulaboh, Indon.	**246-47**	4°09′N	96°08′E
Mexia, Tx., U.S. (må-hē´ä)	**122-23**	31°40′N	96°29′W
Mexiana, Ilha, i., Braz.	**166-67**	0°02′S	49°35′W
Mexicali, Mex. (mâk-sē-kä´lē)	**144-45**	32°39′N	115°30′W
Mexicana, Altiplanicie, plat., Mex.	**20-21**	25°29′N	104°00′W
Mexican Hat, Ut., U.S. (mĕk´sĭ-kăn hăt)	**118-19**	37°12′N	109°52′W
Mexico, Me., U.S. (mĕk´sĭ-kō)	**116-17**	44°34′N	70°33′W
Mexico, Mo., U.S. (mĕk´sĭ-kō)	**120-21**	39°10′N	91°53′W
Mexico, nation, N.A. (mĕk´sĭ-kō)	**85**	23°0′N	102°00′W
México, state, Mex.	**146-47**	19°20′N	99°45′W
México, Golfo de, b., N.A. *see* Mexico, Gulf of	**140-41**	25°0′N	90°00′W
Mexico, Gulf of, b., N.A. (gŭlf ŭv mĕk´sĭ-kō)	**140-41**	25°0′N	90°00′W
Mexico City, nat. cap., Mex. (mĕk´sĭ-kō sĭ´tē)	**146-47**	19°24′N	99°09′W
Meyersdale, Pa., U.S. (mī´ẽrz-dāl)	**116-17**	39°49′N	79°02′W
Meymaneh, Afg.	**232-33**	35°56′N	64°48′E
Mezen', Russia	**186-87**	65°50′N	44°15′E
Mezen', stm., Russia	**186-87**	65°53′N	44°09′E
Mézenc, Mont, mtn., Fr. (mŏN-mä-zĕN´)	**196-97**	44°55′N	4°11′E
Mezha, stm., Russia (myâ´zhȧ)	**202-03**	55°43′N	31°31′E
Mezhdurechensk, Russia	**226**	53°41′N	88°07′E
Mezőkövesd, Hung. (mĕ´zû-kû´vĕsht)	**194-95**	47°48′N	20°35′E
Mezőtúr, Hung. (mĕ´zû-tōōr)	**194-95**	47°00′N	20°37′E
Mezquital, Mex. (måz-kē-täl´)	**146-47**	23°29′N	104°22′W
Mfangano Island, i., Kenya	**267**	0°28′S	34°01′E
M'Goun, Irhil, mtn., Mor.	**258-59**	31°31′N	6°25′W
Miahuatlán de Porfirio Díaz, Mex.	**146-47**	16°19′N	96°36′W
Miajadas, Spain (mē-â-hä´dās)	**198-99**	39°09′N	5°54′W
Miami, Fl., U.S. (mī-ă´-mē)	**125a**	25°47′N	80°13′W
Miami Beach, Fl., U.S.	**125a**	25°48′N	80°08′W
Mīāneh, Iran	**228-29**	37°26′N	47°42′E
Mianyang, China	**238-39**	31°28′N	104°44′E
Miaoli, Tai. (mē-ou´lĭ)	**225a**	24°33′N	120°49′E
Miass, Russia (mī-äs´)	**226**	54°59′N	60°06′E
Michalovce, Slvk. (mē´kä-lôf´tsĕ)	**194-95**	48°46′N	21°56′E
Michelson, Mount, mtn., Ak., U.S. (mount mĭch´ĕl-sŭn)	**126**	69°19′N	144°17′W
Michigan, state, U.S. (mĭsh-´ĭ-găn)	**108-09**	44°0′N	85°00′W
Michigan, Lake, lk., U.S. (lāk mĭsh-´ĭ-găn)	**116-17**	44°0′N	87°00′W
Michigan City, In., U.S. (mĭsh-´ĭ-găn sĭ´tē)	**116-17**	41°43′N	86°53′W
Michipicoten Island, i., On., Can.	**136-37**	47°45′N	85°45′W
Michoacán, state, Mex.	**146-47**	19°10′N	101°50′W
Michurinsk, Russia (mĭ-chōō-rĭnsk´)	**186-87**	52°54′N	40°29′E
Micronesia, is., Oc. (mī-krō-nē´zhȧ)	**280-81**	11°0′N	159°00′E
Micronesia, Federated States of, nation, Oc. (fĕ´ẽr-ā´ĕd stāts ŭv mī-krō-nē´zhȧ)	**280-81**	5°0′N	152°00′E
Middelburg, S. Afr.	**264-65**	31°30′S	25°00′E
Middelfart, Den. (mēd´'l-färt)	**192-93**	55°30′N	9°45′E
Middle, stm., B.C., Can. (mĭd´'l)	**132-33**	54°52′N	125°08′W
Middle Andaman, i., India (mĭd´'l ăn-dȧ-măn´)	**246-47**	12°30′N	92°50′E

ăt; finăl; rāte; senåte; ärm; åsk; sofȧ; fâre; ch-choose; dh-as th in other; bē; ēvent; bĕt; recĕnt; cratẽr; g-gō; gh-guttural g; bĭt; ĭ-short neutral; rīde; ĸ-guttural k as ch in German ich;

Feature (Pronunciation)	Page	Lat.	Long.
Middle Caicos, i., T./C. Is.	142-43	21°48′N	71°47′W
Middlesboro, Ky., U.S. (mǐd′′lz-bŭr-ô)	124-25	36°36′N	83°43′W
Middlesbrough, Eng., U.K. (mǐd′′lz-brŭ)	190-91	54°34′N	1°14′W
Middleton, N.S., Can. (mǐd′′l-tŭn)	138-39	44°57′N	65°04′W
Middleton Island, i., Ak., U.S.	126	59°26′N	146°19′W
Middletown, Oh., U.S.	116-17	39°31′N	84°23′W
Midland, On., Can. (mǐd′lănd)	136-37	44°45′N	79°52′W
Midland, Mi., U.S.	116-17	43°36′N	84°14′W
Midland, Tx., U.S.	122-23	32°00′N	102°05′W
Midway, Ky., U.S. (mǐd′wā)	116-17	38°08′N	84°42′W
Midway Islands, dep., Oc. (mǐd′wä ī′lăndz)	280-81	28°13′N	177°22′W
Międzyrzecz, Pol. (myän-dzú′zhěch)	194-95	52°27′N	15°35′E
Mier, Mex. (myâr)	122-23	26°26′N	99°09′W
Mieres, Spain (myā′rās)	198-99	43°16′N	5°46′W
Mier y Noriega, Mex. (myâr′ĕ nô-rĕ-ā′gä)	146-47	23°25′N	100°08′W
Miguel Alemán, Presa, res., Mex. (prä′sä-mě-gäl′-älě-má′n)	146-47	18°13′N	96°32′W
Mikhaylov, Russia (mē-käy′lôf)	202-03	54°14′N	39°02′E
Mikhaylovka, Russia	186-87	50°04′N	43°15′E
Mikkeli, Fin. (měk′ě-lī)	192-93	61°42′N	27°12′E
Mikun′, Russia	186-87	62°22′N	50°05′E
Mikura-jima, i., Japan (mē′kōō-rä jē′má)	244	33°52′N	139°36′E
Milaca, Mn., U.S. (mē-lăk′à)	114-15	45°45′N	93°39′W
Milagro, Arg.	168-69	31°01′S	65°60′W
Milagro, Ec.	170	2°08′S	79°36′W
Milan, Italy (mē-län′)	200-01	45°28′N	9°12′E
Milan, Mi., U.S. (mī′lăn)	116-17	42°05′N	83°41′W
Milan, Mo., U.S. (mī′lăn)	120-21	40°12′N	93°07′W
Milan, Oh., U.S. (mī′lăn)	116-17	41°18′N	82°37′W
Milan, Tn., U.S. (mī′lăn)	124-25	35°55′N	88°46′W
Milano, Italy (mē-lä′nō) see Milan	200-01	45°28′N	9°12′E
Milâs, Tur. (mē′läs)	200-01	37°19′N	27°47′E
Milbank, S.D., U.S. (mǐl′băŋk)	114-15	45°13′N	96°38′W
Mildura, Austl. (mǐl-dū′rá)	276	34°12′S	142°10′E
Mile, China	238-39	24°26′N	103°27′E
Miles, Austl.	276	26°40′S	150°11′E
Miles City, Mt., U.S. (mīlz sǐ′tě)	112-13	46°25′N	105°50′W
Milford, Ct., U.S. (mǐl′ferd)	116-17	41°13′N	73°04′W
Milford, De., U.S. (mǐl′ferd)	116-17	38°55′N	75°26′W
Milford, Ne., U.S. (mǐl′ferd)	114-15	40°46′N	97°03′W
Milford, Ut., U.S. (mǐl′ferd)	118-19	38°24′N	113°01′W
Milford Sound, b., N.Z.	278	44°31′S	167°48′E
Milk, stm., N.A.	112-13	48°03′N	106°19′W
Mil′kovo, Russia	218-19	54°42′N	158°38′E
Millau, Fr. (mē-yô′)	196-97	44°06′N	3°05′E
Milledgeville, Ga., U.S. (mǐl′ěj-vǐl)	124-25	33°05′N	83°14′W
Mille Lacs, Lac des, lk., On., Can. (läk dĕ měl läks)	136-37	48°50′N	90°30′W
Mille Lacs Lake, lk., Mn., U.S.	114-15	46°15′N	93°40′W
Millen, Ga., U.S. (mǐl′ěn)	124-25	32°48′N	81°56′W
Millenium, at., Kir. see Caroline	280-81	9°58′S	150°13′W
Miller, S.D., U.S. (mǐl′ēr)	114-15	44°31′N	98°59′W
Millerovo, Russia (mǐl′ě-rô-vô)	186-87	48°56′N	40°24′E
Millersburg, Oh., U.S. (mǐl′ērz-bûrg)	116-17	40°33′N	81°54′W
Millicent, Austl. (mǐl-ĭ-sěnt)	276	37°36′S	140°20′E
Millinocket, Me., U.S. (mǐl-ĭ-nŏk′ět)	117a	45°40′N	68°42′W
Mills Lake, lk., N.T., Can.	130-31	61°30′N	118°10′W
Milos, i., Grc. (mē′lòs)	200-01	36°41′N	24°28′E
Milton, On., Can. (mǐl′tŭn)	136-37	43°31′N	79°53′W
Milton, Fl., U.S. (mǐl′tŭn)	124-25	30°38′N	87°02′W
Milton, Pa., U.S. (mǐl′tŭn)	116-17	41°01′N	76°51′W
Milton, Vt., U.S. (mǐl′tŭn)	116-17	42°47′N	88°56′W
Milwaukee, Wi., U.S. (mǐl-wô′kě)	116-17	43°01′N	87°56′W
Min, stm., China (měn)	222-23	26°04′N	119°33′E
Min, stm., China (měn)	238-39	28°46′N	104°38′E
Minami-Daitō-jima, i., Japan	222-23	25°50′N	131°15′E
Minami-lō-jima, i., Japan	280-81	24°14′N	141°28′E
Minami-Tori-shima, i., Japan see Marcus Island	280-81	24°18′N	153°58′E
Minas, Cuba (mē′näs)	142-43	21°29′N	77°36′W
Minas, Ur. (mē′näs)	173	34°23′S	55°14′W
Minas Basin, b., N.S., Can. (mī′năs bā′s′n)	138-39	45°20′N	64°00′W
Minas Channel, strt., N.S., Can. (mī′năs chăn′ěl)	138-39	45°15′N	64°45′W
Minas de Oro, Hond. (mē′näs-dě-ō-rô)	149	14°46′N	87°20′W
Minas Gerais, state, Braz.	172	18°0′S	44°00′W
Minas Novas, Braz. (mē′näzh nō′väzh)	172	17°15′S	42°30′W
Minatitlán, Mex. (mě-nä-tē-tlän′)	146-47	17°59′N	94°32′W
Mindanao, i., Phil. (mǐn-dä-nou′)	250	8°0′N	125°00′E

Feature (Pronunciation)	Page	Lat.	Long.
Mindanao Sea, s., Phil. (mǐn-dä-nou′ sē) see Bohol Sea	250	9°10′N	124°25′E
Mindelo, C.V.	260-61	16°52′N	24°60′W
Minden, Ger. (mǐn′děn)	194-95	52°18′N	8°55′E
Mindoro, i., Phil. (mǐn-dô′rō)	250	12°50′N	121°05′E
Mindoro Strait, strt., Phil. (mǐn-dô′rō strāt)	250	12°20′N	120°40′E
Mineiros, Braz.	168-69	17°34′S	52°34′W
Mineola, Tx., U.S. (mǐn-ē-ō′la)	120-21	32°40′N	95°29′W
Mineral′nyye Vody, Russia	227	44°12′N	43°08′E
Mineral Point, Wi., U.S. (mǐn′ēr-ăl point)	116-17	42°52′N	90°10′W
Mineral Wells, Tx., U.S. (mǐn′ēr-ăl wělz)	120-21	32°48′N	98°07′W
Minfeng, China	226	37°04′N	82°39′E
Mingäçevir, Azer.	227	40°46′N	47°02′E
Mingäçevir su anbarı, res., Azer.	227	40°55′N	46°48′E
Mingäora, Pak.	232-33	34°49′N	72°21′E
Mingechaur, Azer. see Mingäçevir.	227	40°46′N	47°02′E
Mingechaur Reservoir, res., Azer. see Mingäçevir su anbarı	227	40°55′N	46°48′E
Minicoy Island, i., India	236	8°16′N	73°03′E
Minigwal, Lake, lk., Austl.	272-73	29°35′S	123°12′E
Minle, China	240-41	38°28′N	100°56′E
Minna, Nig. (mǐn′à)	260-61	9°37′N	6°33′E
Minneapolis, Mn., U.S. (mǐn-ē-ăp′ô-lǐs)	114-15	44°59′N	93°17′W
Minnedosa, Mb., Can. (mǐn-ē-dō′sà)	134-35	50°14′N	99°49′W
Minneota, Mn., U.S. (mǐn-ē-ō′tá)	114-15	44°34′N	96°00′W
Minnesota, state, U.S.	108-09	46°0′N	94°15′W
Minnesota, stm., Mn., U.S.	114-15	44°54′N	93°11′W
Minnitaki Lake, lk., On., Can. (mǐ′nǐ-tä′kě läk)	134-35	49°58′N	92°00′W
Minonk, Il., U.S. (mǐ′nônk)	116-17	40°54′N	89°02′W
Minorca, i., Spain see Menorca	198-99	40°0′N	4°00′E
Minot, N.D., U.S.	114-15	48°14′N	101°18′W
Minsk, state, Bela. (měnsk)	194-95	53°45′N	27°45′E
Minsk, nat. cap., Bela. (měnsk)	194-95	53°54′N	27°33′E
Mińsk Mazowiecki, Pol. (měn′sk mä-zô-vyět′skī)	194-95	52°11′N	21°34′E
Minto, Lac, lk., Qc., Can.	130-31	57°12′N	74°58′W
Minturno, Italy (měn-tōōr′nō)	200-01	41°16′N	13°45′E
Minxian, China	238-39	34°26′N	104°02′E
Minya, Egypt see El-Minya	268b	28°06′N	30°45′E
Minya Konka, mtn., China see Gongga Shan	238-39	29°35′N	101°51′E
Min′yar, Russia	186-87	55°03′N	57°33′E
Miracema do Tocantins, Braz.	166-67	9°33′S	48°24′W
Mirador, Braz. (mē-rä-dōr′)	166-67	6°22′S	44°22′W
Miraflores, Col. (mē-rä-flō′räs)	164-65	1°25′N	72°17′W
Miramar, Arg.	173	38°16′S	57°51′W
Miramichi, N.B., Can.	138-39	47°02′N	65°28′W
Miramichi Bay, b., N.B., Can. (mǐr′á-mē′shě bä)	138-39	47°08′N	65°08′W
Miranda, Braz.	168-69	19°25′S	57°20′W
Miranda de Ebro, Spain (mē-rá′n-dě-dě-ě′brŏ)	198-99	42°42′N	2°56′W
Miranda do Douro, Port. (mě-rän′dä dò-dwě′rŏ)	198-99	41°30′N	6°16′W
Mirandela, Port. (mě-rän-dä′lá)	198-99	41°29′N	7°11′W
Mirecourt, Fr. (mēr-kōōr′)	196-97	48°18′N	6°08′E
Miri, Malay. (mē′rě)	248-49	4°23′N	113°59′E
Mirim, Lagoa, b., S.A. (lá-gô′ä-mē-rěN′)	173	32°45′S	52°50′W
Mirnyy, Russia	218-19	62°31′N	113°59′E
Mīrpur Khās, Pak. (měr′pōōr käs)	232-33	25°31′N	69°01′E
Mirzāpur, India (mēr′zä-pōōr)	234-35	25°08′N	82°34′E
Misāha, Bîr, well, Egypt	266	22°12′N	27°57′E
Misantla, Mex. (mě-sän′tlä)	146-47	19°56′N	96°50′W
Miscou Island, i., N.B., Can. (mǐs′kō ī′lánd)	138-39	47°57′N	64°32′W
Mishan, China (mǐ′shän)	244	45°32′N	131°52′E
Mishawaka, In., U.S. (mǐsh-à-wôk′á)	116-17	41°40′N	86°10′W
Mishmi Hills, hills, Asia	238-39	29°0′N	96°00′E
Misima Island, i., Pap. N. Gui.	277	10°42′S	152°45′E
Misiones, state, Arg. (mē-syō′näs)	173	27°0′S	55°00′W
Miskitos, Cayos, is., Nic.	149	14°23′N	82°46′W
Miskolc, Hung. (mǐsh′kôlts)	194-95	48°06′N	20°47′E
Misool, Pulau, i., Indon. (pōō-lou mē-sôl′)	224-25	1°52′S	130°10′E
Mişr, nation, Afr. see Egypt	253	27°0′N	30°00′E
Mişrātah, Libya	188-89	32°22′N	15°06′E
Missinaibi, stm., On., Can. (mǐs′ǐn-ä′ě-bě)	130-31	50°45′N	81°31′W
Missinaibi Lake, lk., On., Can. (mǐs′ǐn-ä′ě-bě läk)	136-37	48°21′N	83°43′W
Mission, S.D., U.S. (mǐsh′ŭn)	114-15	43°18′N	100°38′W

Feature (Pronunciation)	Page	Lat.	Long.
Mission, Tx., U.S. (mǐsh′ŭn)	122-23	26°13′N	98°19′W
Mississippi, state, U.S. (mǐs-ĭ-sǐp′ě)	108-09	32°50′N	89°30′W
Mississippi, stm., U.S. (mǐs-ĭ-sǐp′ě).	110-11	28°60′N	89°08′W
Mississippi River Delta, del., La., U.S.	110-11	29°10′N	89°15′W
Mississippi Sound, strt., U.S. (mǐs-ĭ-sǐp′ě sound)	124-25	30°15′N	88°40′W
Missoula, Mt., U.S. (mǐ-zōō′lá)	112-13	46°52′N	114°00′W
Missouri, state, U.S. (mǐ-sōō′rě)	108-09	38°30′N	93°30′W
Missouri, stm., U.S. (mǐ-sōō′rě).	110-11	38°49′N	90°07′W
Missouri City, Tx., U.S. (mǐ-sōō′rě sǐ′tǐ)	122-23	29°37′N	95°31′W
Missouri Valley, Ia., U.S. (mǐ-sōō′rě văl′ě)	114-15	41°33′N	95°54′W
Mistassibi, stm., Qc., Can.	136-37	48°53′N	72°14′W
Mistassini, Lac, lk., Qc., Can. (läk mǐs-tá-sī′ně)	130-31	51°0′N	73°37′W
Misti, Volcán, vol., Peru.	170	16°18′S	71°24′W
Mita, Punta de, c., Mex. (pōō′n-tä-dě-mē′tä)	146-47	20°47′N	105°32′W
Mitau, Lat. see Jelgava	192-93	56°39′N	23°44′E
Mitchell, Austl.	276	26°29′S	147°58′E
Mitchell, In., U.S. (mǐch′ěl)	116-17	38°44′N	86°29′W
Mitchell, Ne., U.S. (mǐch′ěl)	114-15	41°57′N	103°48′W
Mitchell, S.D., U.S. (mǐch′ěl)	114-15	43°43′N	98°02′W
Mitchell, Mount, mtn., N.C., U.S. (mount mǐch′ěl).	124-25	35°46′N	82°16′W
Mitiaro, i., Cook Is.	280-81	19°48′S	157°43′W
Mito, Japan	245	36°22′N	140°29′E
Mitsio, Nosy, i., Madag.	264-65	12°54′S	48°36′E
Mitsiwa, Erit. see Massawa	266	15°37′N	39°26′E
Mittellandkanal, can., Ger. (mǐt′ěl-länd kä-näl′)	194-95	52°14′N	11°43′E
Mitú, Col.	164-65	1°08′N	70°03′W
Mitumba, Monts, mts., D.R.C.	267	6°0′S	29°00′E
Mitzic, Gabon	260-61	0°47′N	11°34′E
Miyake-jima, i., Japan (mě′yä-kâ jě′má)	244	34°05′N	139°32′E
Miyako, Japan	244	39°38′N	141°57′E
Miyako-jima, i., Japan	279a	24°47′N	125°20′E
Miyakonojō, Japan	245	31°43′N	131°04′E
Miyazaki, Japan	245	31°54′N	131°26′E
Miyazu, Japan	245	35°32′N	135°11′E
Miyoshi, Japan (mě-yō′shě′)	245	34°49′N	132°51′E
Miyun, China	240-41	40°22′N	116°50′E
Mizdah, Libya (měz′dä)	188-89	31°26′N	12°59′E
Mizen Head, c., Ire.	190-91	51°27′N	9°49′W
Mizil, Rom. (mē′zǐl)	200-01	44°59′N	26°27′E
Mizoram, state, India	246-47	23°30′N	93°00′E
Mizque, Bol.	168-69	17°57′S	65°20′W
Mjölby, Swe. (myûl′bü)	192-93	58°20′N	15°09′E
Mjøsa, lk., Nor. (myûsä).	192-93	60°40′N	11°00′E
Mkinvartsveri, Mt'a, vol., see Kazbek, Gora.	227	42°42′N	44°31′E
Mladá Boleslav, Czech Rep. (mlä′dä bō′lě-sláf)	194-95	50°25′N	14°54′E
Mlanje Peak, mtn., Malawi see Sapitwa	264-65	15°57′S	35°36′E
Mława, Pol. (mwä′vä)	194-95	53°07′N	20°22′E
Moa, stm., Afr.	260-61	6°0′N	11°34′W
Moa, Pulau, i., Indon.	248-49	8°10′S	127°56′E
Moab, Ut., U.S. (mō′äb)	118-19	38°35′N	109°33′W
Moa Island, i., Austl.	277	10°12′S	142°16′E
Moala, i., Fiji	279f	18°36′S	179°53′E
Moanda, Gabon	260-61	1°34′S	13°13′E
Moba, D.R.C.	267	7°04′S	29°44′E
Moberly, Mo., U.S. (mō′běr-lǐ)	120-21	39°25′N	92°26′W
Mobile, Al., U.S. (mô-bēl′).	124-25	30°41′N	88°03′W
Mobile Bay, b., Al., U.S. (mô-bēl′ bä)	124-25	30°34′N	87°60′W
Mobridge, S.D., U.S. (mō′brǐj)	114-15	45°32′N	100°26′W
Mobutu Sese Seko, Lac, lk., Afr. see Albert, Lake	267	1°40′N	31°00′E
Moca, Dom. Rep. (mō′kä)	142-43	19°24′N	70°31′W
Moçambique, Moz. (mō-sän-bē′kě) see Ilha de Moçambique	264-65	15°02′S	40°41′E
Moçambique, nation, Afr. see Mozambique	253	18°15′S	35°00′E
Moçambique, Canal de, strt., Afr. see Mozambique Channel	264-65	19°0′S	41°00′E
Moçâmedes, Ang. (mô-zä-mě-děs) see Namibe	264-65	15°12′S	12°10′E
Mocha, Yemen	266	13°19′N	43°15′E
Mocha, Isla, i., Chile	171	38°22′S	73°55′W
Mochudi, Bots. (mō-chōō′dě)	269c	24°23′S	26°09′E
Mocímboa da Praia, Moz. (mô-sě′ěm-bò-ä prä′ēä)	264-65	11°20′S	40°22′E
Môco, Morro de, mtn., Ang.	264-65	12°28′S	15°10′E
Mococa, Braz. (mô-kô′kä)	172	21°28′S	46°60′W

n-sing; ŋ-baŋk; N-nasalized n; nŏd; cŏmmit; ōld; ôbey; ôrder; oi-boil; fōōd; ô-as oo in foot; ou-out; s-soft; sh-dish; th-thin; pūre; ûnite; ûrn; stŭd; circŭs; ü-as in French tu; ′-indeterminate vowel.

Feature (Pronunciation)	Page	Lat.	Long.
Mocorito, Mex.	**144-45**	25°29'N	107°55'W
Moctezuma, Mex. (mồk'tả-zōō'mä)	**144-45**	29°48'N	109°42'W
Mocuba, Moz.	**264-65**	16°51'S	36°60'E
Modder, stm., S. Afr.	**264-65**	29°03'S	24°38'E
Modena, Italy (mô'dĕ-nä)	**200-01**	44°39'N	10°55'E
Modesto, Ca., U.S.	**118-19**	37°39'N	120°60'W
Modimolle, S. Afr.	**269c**	24°42'S	28°25'E
Mödling, Aus. (mûd'lĭng)	**194-95**	48°05'N	16°18'E
Moe, Austl.	**276**	38°11'S	146°15'E
Moengo, Sur.	**164-65**	5°38'N	54°24'W
Moeris, Lake, lk., Egypt see Qârûn, Birket	**268b**	29°28'N	30°39'E
Moero, Lac, lk., Afr. see Mweru, Lake	**262-63**	9°0'S	28°45'E
Mogadishu, nat. cap., Som. (mŏg'*á*-dĭ'shōō)	**262-63**	2°03'N	45°20'E
Mogador, Mor. see Essaouira	**258-59**	31°30'N	9°45'W
Mogaung, Mya. (mô-gä'ông)	**238-39**	25°18'N	96°56'E
Mogilno, Pol. (mô-gēl'nô)	**194-95**	52°40'N	17°59'E
Mogocha, Russia	**218-19**	53°44'N	119°45'E
Mogok, Mya. (mô-gŏk')	**246-47**	22°56'N	96°31'E
Mogotón, mtn., N.A.	**149**	13°45'N	86°23'W
Moguer, Spain (mô-gĕr')	**198-99**	37°16'N	6°50'W
Mohács, Hung. (mô'häch)	**194-95**	46°00'N	18°41'E
Mohall, N.D., U.S. (mō'hôl)	**114-15**	48°46'N	101°30'W
Mohammedia, Mor.	**269a**	33°42'N	7°23'W
Mohe, China (mwo-hŭ)	**222-23**	53°29'N	122°20'E
Mohéli, i., Com. see Mwali	**264-65**	12°18'S	43°42'E
Mohyliv-Podil's'kyi, Ukr.	**202-03**	48°28'N	27°47'E
Mo i Rana, Nor.	**184-85**	66°19'N	14°10'E
Moisie, stm., Qc., Can.	**138-39**	50°15'N	66°05'W
Moissac, Fr. (mwä-sák')	**196-97**	44°06'N	1°05'E
Mojave, Ca., U.S. (mô-hä'vä)	**118-19**	35°04'N	118°10'W
Mojave Desert, des., Ca., U.S. (mô-hä'vä dĕs'ẽrt)	**118-19**	35°0'N	117°00'W
Mojiguaçu, stm., Braz. (mô-gê-gwá'sōō)	**172**	20°54'S	48°11'W
Moknine, Tun.	**184-85**	35°38'N	10°54'E
Mokp'o, Kor., S. (mồk'pō')	**243**	34°48'N	126°24'E
Moksha, stm., Russia	**186-87**	54°45'N	41°53'E
Moldavia, nation, Eur. see Moldova	**174-75**	47°0'N	29°00'E
Molde, Nor. (môl'dĕ)	**184-85**	62°45'N	7°11'E
Moldova, nation, Eur. (mäl-dō'v*á*)	**174-75**	47°0'N	29°00'E
Moldoveanu, Vârful, mtn., Rom.	**200-01**	45°36'N	24°44'E
Molepolole, Bots. (mō-lå-pô-lō'lå)	**264-65**	24°25'S	25°31'E
Molfetta, Italy (môl-fĕt'tä)	**200-01**	41°12'N	16°36'E
Molina, Chile (mŏ-lē'nä)	**171**	35°07'S	71°17'W
Molina de Aragón, Spain (mô-lē'nä dĕ ä-rä-gô'n)	**198-99**	40°51'N	1°53'W
Molina de Segura, Spain (mô-lē'nä dĕ sĕ-gōō'rä)	**198-99**	38°03'N	1°13'W
Moline, Il., U.S. (mô-lēn')	**114-15**	41°30'N	90°29'W
Mollendo, Peru (mô-lyĕn'dō)	**170**	17°01'S	72°02'W
Mölndal, Swe. (mûln'däl)	**192-93**	57°41'N	11°56'E
Moloka'i, i., Hi., U.S. (mō-lô kä'ē)	**127a**	21°07'N	157°00'W
Molopo, stm., Afr. (mō-lō-pô)	**264-65**	28°31'S	20°13'E
Molson Lake, lk., Mb., Can. (mōl's*ŭ*n lāk)	**134-35**	54°12'N	96°45'W
Moluccas, is., Indon. (mō-lŭk'ŭz)	**248-49**	2°0'S	128°00'E
Molucca Sea, s., Indon. (mō-lŭk'*á* sē)	**248-49**	0°13'N	125°10'E
Moma, Moz.	**264-65**	16°50'S	39°09'E
Mombasa, Kenya (mōm-bä'sä)	**262-63**	4°03'S	39°40'E
Mombetsu, Japan (môm'bĕt-sōō')	**244**	44°21'N	143°21'E
Mompós, Col. (mōm-pōs')	**164-65**	9°12'N	74°25'W
Møn, i., Den. (mûn)	**192-93**	55°00'N	12°20'E
Mona, Canal de la, strt., N.A. see Mona Passage	**143b**	18°30'N	67°45'W
Mona, Isla de, i., P.R.	**143b**	18°05'N	67°54'W
Monaco, nation, Eur. (mŏn'*á*-kō)	**196-97**	43°45'N	7°25'E
Mona Passage, strt., N.A. (mō'nä păs'ĭj)	**143b**	18°30'N	67°45'W
Monarch Mountain, mtn., B.C., Can. (mŏn'ẽrk moun'tĭn)	**132-33**	51°54'N	125°53'W
Monastir, Mac. see Bitola	**200-01**	41°02'N	21°20'E
Monastyrshchina, Russia (mô-nás-tērsh'chĭ-ná)	**202-03**	54°21'N	31°51'E
Monchegorsk, Russia (mōn'chĕ-gôrsk)	**184-85**	67°55'N	32°50'E
Monclova, Mex. (môn-klō'vä)	**122-23**	26°54'N	101°25'W
Moncton, N.B., Can. (mŭŋk't*ŭ*n)	**138-39**	46°06'N	64°48'W
Mondego, stm., Port. (mōn-dĕ'gō)	**198-99**	40°08'N	8°45'W
Mondego, Cabo, c., Port. (ká'bō mōn-dā'gō)	**198-99**	40°11'N	8°54'W
Mondovi, Wi., U.S. (mŏn-dō'vĭ)	**114-15**	44°34'N	91°39'W
Monett, Mo., U.S. (mô-nĕt')	**120-21**	36°55'N	93°56'W
Monforte de Lemos, Spain (môn-fôr'tä dĕ lĕ'môs)	**198-99**	42°32'N	7°30'W
Mongala, stm., D.R.C. (mŏŋ-gäl'*á*)	**262-63**	1°53'N	19°50'E
Möng Hsat, Mya.	**246-47**	20°31'N	99°13'E
Mongibello, vol., Italy see Etna, Monte	**200-01**	37°45'N	15°00'E
Mongo, Chad	**258-59**	12°11'N	18°42'E
Mongol Altayn nuruu, mts., Asia	**222-23**	46°30'N	93°00'E
Mongol Ard Uls, nation, Asia see Mongolia	**206-07**	46°0'N	105°00'E
Mongolia, nation, Asia (mŏŋ-gō'lĭ-*á*)	**206-07**	46°0'N	105°00'E
Mongu, Zam. (mŏŋ-gōō')	**264-65**	15°17'S	23°08'E
Monkoto, D.R.C. (môn-kō'tô)	**262-63**	1°37'S	20°40'E
Monmouth, Il., U.S. (mŏn'mŭth)(mŏn'mouth)	**114-15**	40°54'N	90°39'W
Monmouth, Or., U.S. (mŏn'mŭth)(mŏn'mouth)	**112-13**	44°51'N	123°14'W
Monmouth Mountain, mtn., B.C., Can. (mŏn'mŭth moun'tĭn)	**132-33**	51°0'N	123°47'W
Mono, stm., Afr.	**260-61**	6°16'N	1°49'E
Mono Island, i., Sol. Is.	**279e**	7°22'S	155°33'E
Mono Lake, lk., Ca., U.S. (mō'nō lāk)	**118-19**	38°0'N	119°00'W
Monon, In., U.S. (mō'nŏn)	**116-17**	40°52'N	86°52'W
Monongahela, Pa., U.S. (mô-nŏn-gå-hē'là)	**116-17**	40°11'N	79°55'W
Monopoli, Italy (mô-nô'pô-lē)	**200-01**	40°57'N	17°18'E
Monroe, Ga., U.S. (m*ŭ*n-rō')	**124-25**	33°48'N	83°43'W
Monroe, La., U.S. (m*ŭ*n-rō')	**120-21**	32°31'N	92°07'W
Monroe, Mi., U.S. (m*ŭ*n-rō')	**116-17**	41°55'N	83°25'W
Monroe, N.C., U.S. (m*ŭ*n-rō')	**124-25**	34°59'N	80°33'W
Monroe, Ut., U.S. (m*ŭ*n-rō')	**118-19**	38°38'N	112°07'W
Monroe, Wi., U.S. (m*ŭ*n-rō')	**116-17**	42°36'N	89°38'W
Monroe City, Mo., U.S. (m*ŭ*n-rō' sĭ'tê)	**120-21**	39°39'N	91°44'W
Monroeville, Al., U.S. (m*ŭ*n-rō'vĭl)	**124-25**	31°31'N	87°20'W
Monrovia, nat. cap., Lib. (mŏn-rō'vĭ-*á*)	**260-61**	6°19'N	10°47'W
Mönsterås, Swe. (mŭn'stĕr-ôs)	**192-93**	57°02'N	16°27'E
Montague, P.E., Can. (mŏn't*á*-gū)	**138-39**	46°10'N	62°39'W
Montague, Ca., U.S. (mŏn't*á*-gū)	**112-13**	41°44'N	122°31'W
Montague, Mi., U.S. (mŏn't*á*-gū)	**116-17**	43°25'N	86°21'W
Montague, Isla, i., Mex.	**144-45**	31°43'N	114°44'W
Montague Island, i., Ak., U.S. (mŏn't*á*-gū ī'l*á*nd)	**126**	60°10'N	147°18'W
Montana, state, U.S. (mŏn-tăn'*á*)	**108-09**	47°0'N	110°00'W
Montargis, Fr. (môɴ-tár-zhē')	**196-97**	48°00'N	2°44'E
Montauban, Fr.	**196-97**	44°01'N	1°21'E
Montauk, N.Y., U.S. (mŏn-tôk')	**116-17**	41°03'N	71°57'W
Montauk Point, c., N.Y., U.S. (mŏn-tôk' point)	**116-17**	41°04'N	71°52'W
Montbard, Fr. (môɴ-bár')	**196-97**	47°38'N	4°20'E
Montbéliard, Fr. (môɴ-bā-lyàr')	**196-97**	47°31'N	6°46'E
Montbrison, Fr. (môɴ-brē-zoɴ')	**196-97**	45°37'N	4°04'E
Mont-de-Marsan, Fr. (môɴ-dē-már-säɴ')	**196-97**	43°53'N	0°30'W
Montdidier, Fr. (môɴ-dē-dyā')	**196-97**	49°39'N	2°34'E
Monte Alegre, Braz.	**166-67**	2°00'S	54°05'W
Monte Azul, Braz.	**168-69**	15°09'S	42°52'W
Monte Caseros, Arg. (mŏ'n-tĕ-kä-sĕ'rôs)	**173**	30°15'S	57°39'W
Monte Comán, Arg.	**163e**	34°35'S	67°53'W
Monte Cristi, Dom. Rep. (mô'n-tĕ-krē's-tē)	**142-43**	19°51'N	71°38'W
Monte Escobedo, Mex. (mōn'tå ĕs-kô-bā'dhō)	**146-47**	22°18'N	103°32'W
Montego Bay, Jam. (mŏn-tē'gō bā)	**142-43**	18°28'N	77°55'W
Montélimar, Fr. (môɴ-tā-lē-mär')	**196-97**	44°34'N	4°45'E
Monte Lindo, stm., Para.	**168-69**	23°54'S	57°17'W
Montello, Wi., U.S. (mŏn-tĕl'ō)	**116-17**	43°48'N	89°20'W
Montemorelos, Mex. (mōn'tå-mō-rā'lōs)	**122-23**	25°11'N	99°50'W
Montemor-o-Novo, Port. (môɴ-tĕ-môr'ō-nô'vô)	**198-99**	38°38'N	8°13'W
Montenegro, nation, Eur. (môn-tå-nā'grō) (mōn-tē-nē'grō)	**174-75**	42°30'N	19°18'E
Montepuez, Moz.	**264-65**	13°07'S	38°60'E
Montepulciano, Italy (môn'tå-pōōl-chä'nō)	**200-01**	43°06'N	11°47'E
Monte Quemado, Arg.	**168-69**	25°48'S	62°49'W
Montereau-Faut-Yonne, Fr. (môn-t'rō'fō-yôn')	**196-97**	48°23'N	2°57'E
Monterey, Ca., U.S. (mŏn-t*ĕ*-rā')	**118-19**	36°36'N	121°54'W
Monterey, Tn., U.S. (mŏn-t*ĕ*-rā')	**124-25**	36°09'N	85°16'W
Monterey, Va., U.S. (mŏn-t*ĕ*-rā')	**116-17**	38°24'N	79°35'W
Monterey Bay, b., Ca., U.S. (mŏn-t*ĕ*-rā' bā)	**118-19**	36°48'N	121°55'W
Montería, Col. (mōn-tā-rā'ä)	**164-65**	8°45'N	75°53'W
Monteros, Arg. (mōn-tĕ'rôs)	**168-69**	27°10'S	65°30'W
Monterotondo, Italy (môn-tĕ-rô-tô'n-dō)	**200-01**	42°03'N	12°36'E
Monterrey, Mex. (mōn-tĕ-rā')	**122-23**	25°41'N	100°19'W
Montesano, Wa., U.S. (mŏn-tē-sä'nō)	**112-13**	46°59'N	123°35'W
Monte Sant'Angelo, Italy (mô'n-tĕ săn ă'n-gzhĕ-lô)	**200-01**	41°43'N	15°57'E
Montes Claros, Braz. (môn-tĕs-klä'rôs)	**168-69**	16°44'S	43°51'W
Montevallo, Al., U.S. (mŏn-tē-văl'ō)	**124-25**	33°06'N	86°51'W
Montevarchi, Italy (mōn-tå-vär'kē)	**200-01**	43°32'N	11°35'E
Montevideo, Mn., U.S. (mŏn'tå-vē-dhā'ō)	**114-15**	44°57'N	95°43'W
Montevideo, nat. cap., Ur. (mŏn'tå-vē-dhā'ō)	**173**	34°54'S	56°11'W
Monte Vista, Co., U.S. (mŏn'tē vĭs't*á*)	**118-19**	37°35'N	106°09'W
Montezuma, Ga., U.S. (mŏn-tē-zōō'm*á*)	**124-25**	32°18'N	84°03'W
Montgomery, Pak. see Sāhīwāl	**232-33**	30°40'N	73°06'E
Montgomery, Al., U.S. (mŏnt-gŭm'ẽr-ĭ)	**124-25**	32°23'N	86°18'W
Monticello, Ar., U.S. (mŏn-tĭ-sĕl'ō)	**124-25**	33°38'N	91°47'W
Monticello, Fl., U.S. (mŏn-tĭ-sĕl'ō)	**124-25**	30°32'N	83°52'W
Monticello, Ga., U.S. (mŏn-tĭ-sĕl'ō)	**124-25**	33°18'N	83°41'W
Monticello, Ia., U.S. (mŏn-tĭ-sĕl'ō)	**114-15**	42°14'N	91°12'W
Monticello, Il., U.S. (mŏn-tĭ-sĕl'ō)	**116-17**	40°00'N	88°35'W
Monticello, In., U.S. (mŏn-tĭ-sĕl'ō)	**116-17**	40°45'N	86°45'W
Monticello, Ky., U.S. (mŏn-tĭ-sĕl'ō)	**124-25**	36°50'N	84°52'W
Monticello, Mn., U.S. (mŏn-tĭ-sĕl'ō)	**114-15**	45°18'N	93°48'W
Monticello, Ut., U.S. (mŏn-tĭ-sĕl'ō)	**118-19**	37°53'N	109°21'W
Montijo, Port. (môn-tē'zhō)	**198-99**	38°42'N	8°58'W
Montijo, Spain (môn-tē'hō)	**198-99**	38°55'N	6°37'W
Montijo, Golfo de, b., Pan. (gôl-fô-dĕ-môn-tē'hō)	**150**	7°40'N	81°07'W
Mont-Joli, Qc., Can. (môɴ zhô-lē')	**138-39**	48°37'N	68°07'W
Mont-Laurier, Qc., Can.	**136-37**	46°32'N	75°30'W
Montluçon, Fr. (môɴ-lü-sôɴ')	**196-97**	46°20'N	2°36'E
Montmagny, Qc., Can. (môɴ-mán-yē')	**138-39**	46°59'N	70°33'W
Montmorillon, Fr. (môɴ'mô-rē-yôɴ')	**196-97**	46°26'N	0°52'E
Montpelier, Id., U.S. (mŏnt-pēl'yẽr)	**112-13**	42°20'N	111°18'W
Montpelier, Oh., U.S. (mŏnt-pēl'yẽr)	**116-17**	41°34'N	84°36'W
Montpelier, Vt., U.S.	**116-17**	44°16'N	72°35'W
Montpellier, Fr. (môɴ-pĕ-lyā')	**196-97**	43°37'N	3°52'E
Montréal, Qc., Can. (mŏn-trē-ôl')	**136-37**	45°29'N	73°34'W
Montreal, stm., On., Can. (mŏn-trē-ôl')	**136-37**	47°08'N	79°26'W
Montreal, stm., On., Can. (mŏn-trē-ôl')	**136-37**	47°15'N	84°39'W
Montreal Lake, lk., Sk., Can. (mŏn-trē-ôl' lăk)	**134-35**	54°20'N	105°40'W
Montreux, Switz. (môn-trû')	**194-95**	46°26'N	6°55'E
Montrose, Scot., U.K. (mŏnt-rōz')	**190-91**	56°43'N	2°28'W
Montrose, Co., U.S. (mŏn-trōz')	**118-19**	38°29'N	107°53'W
Monts, Pointe des, c., Qc., Can. (pwăɴt' dā môɴ')	**138-39**	49°20'N	67°23'W
Montserrat, dep., N.A. (mŏnt-sĕ-răt')	**140-41**	16°45'N	62°12'W
Monywa, Mya. (mŏn'yōō-wà)	**246-47**	22°06'N	95°08'E
Monza, Italy (mōn'tsä)	**200-01**	45°35'N	9°17'E
Monze, Zam.	**264-65**	16°17'S	27°29'E
Monzón, Spain (mōn-thōn')	**198-99**	41°55'N	0°12'E
Moody, Tx., U.S. (mōō'dĭ)	**122-23**	31°18'N	97°21'W
Mooi, stm., S. Afr. (mōō'ĭ)	**269c**	26°52'S	26°57'E
Mooi, stm., S. Afr. (mōō'ĭ)	**269c**	28°46'S	30°34'E
Moon, Mountains of the, mts., Afr. see Ruwenzori Range	**267**	0°20'N	29°53'E
Moonta, Austl. (mōōn'tà)	**276**	34°04'S	137°35'E
Moora, Austl. (mòr'*á*)	**270-71**	30°38'S	116°00'E
Moore, Lake, lk., Austl. (lăk mōr)	**272-73**	29°44'S	117°32'E
Moorea, i., Fr. Poly.	**279d**	17°32'S	149°50'W
Mooresville, In., U.S. (mōrz'vĭl)	**116-17**	39°36'N	86°22'W
Mooresville, N.C., U.S. (mōrz'vĭl)	**124-25**	35°35'N	80°49'W
Moorhead, Mn., U.S. (mōr'hĕd)	**114-15**	46°53'N	96°45'W
Moorhead, Ms., U.S. (mōr'hĕd)	**124-25**	33°28'N	90°31'W
Moosehead Lake, lk., Me., U.S.	**117a**	45°38'N	69°39'W
Moose Jaw, Sk., Can. (mōōs jô)	**134-35**	50°23'N	105°32'W
Moose Jaw, stm., Sk., Can. (mōōs jô)	**134-35**	50°34'N	105°17'W
Moose Lake, Mb., Can. (mōōs lăk)	**134-35**	53°42'N	100°21'W
Moosomin, Sk., Can. (mōō'sô-mĭn)	**134-35**	50°08'N	101°41'W
Moosonee, On., Can. (mōō'sô-nê)	**128-29**	51°17'N	80°40'W
Moppo, Kor., S. see Mokp'o	**243**	34°48'N	126°24'E
Mopti, Mali (mŏp'tê)	**258-59**	14°29'N	4°12'W
Moquegua, Peru (mô-kā'gwä)	**170**	17°12'S	70°57'W
Mora, Spain (mô-rä)	**198-99**	39°41'N	3°46'W
Mora, Swe. (mō'rä)	**192-93**	61°00'N	14°35'E
Mora, Mn., U.S. (mō'r*á*)	**114-15**	45°53'N	93°18'W
Mora, N.M., U.S. (mō'r*á*)	**120-21**	35°58'N	105°22'W
Morādābād, India (mô-rä-dä-bäd')	**234-35**	28°50'N	78°47'E
Moraleda, Canal, strt., Chile	**171**	44°30'S	73°30'W
Morant Cays, is., Jam.	**142-43**	17°24'N	75°59'W

ăt; finăl; rāte; senâte; ärm; åsk; sofá; fâre; ch-choose; dh-as th in other; bē; ēvent; bĕt; recĕnt; cratẽr; g-gō; gh-guttural g; bĭt; ĭ-short neutral; rīde; ᴋ-guttural k as ch in German ich;

Feature (Pronunciation)	Page	Lat.	Long.
Morant Point, c., Jam. (mô-rănt´ point)	142-43	17°55'N	76°11'W
Moratuwa, Sri L.	236	6°48'N	79°53'E
Morava, hist. reg., Czech Rep.	194-95	49°30'N	16°60'E
Moravská Ostrava, Czech Rep. *see* Ostrava	194-95	49°50'N	18°17'E
Morawhanna, Guy. (mô-rà-hwä´nà)	164-65	8°17'N	59°44'W
Moray Firth, b., Scot., U.K. (mŭr´å fûrth)	190-91	58°02'N	3°05'W
Morbi, India	234-35	22°49'N	70°50'E
Morden, Mb., Can. (môr´dĕn)	134-35	49°11'N	98°05'W
Moreau, stm., S.D., U.S. (mô-rō´)	114-15	45°19'N	100°20'W
Moree, Austl. (mō´rē)	276	29°28'S	149°51'E
Morehead, Ky., U.S. (mōr´hĕd)	116-17	38°11'N	83°27'W
Morehead City, N.C., U.S. (mōr´hĕd sĭ´tĭ)	124-25	34°43'N	76°45'W
Morelia, Mex. (mô-rā´lyä)	146-47	19°42'N	101°12'W
Morella, Spain (mô-rāl´yä)	198-99	40°37'N	0°07'W
Morelos, Mex. (mô-rā´lōs)	122-23	28°25'N	100°53'W
Morelos, state, Mex.	146-47	18°45'N	99°00'W
Morena, Sierra, mts., Spain (syĕr´rä mô-rā´nä)	198-99	38°0'N	5°00'W
Morenci, Mi., U.S. (mô-rĕn´sĭ)	116-17	41°43'N	84°13'W
Moresby Island, i., B.C., Can. (mōrz´bĭ ī´lănd)	132-33	52°50'N	131°55'W
Moreton Island, i., Austl. (môr´tŭn ī´lănd)	276	27°11'S	153°24'E
Morgan City, La., U.S. (môr´găn sĭ´tĭ)	124-25	29°42'N	91°12'W
Morganfield, Ky., U.S. (môr´găn-fēld)	116-17	37°41'N	87°55'W
Morganton, N.C., U.S. (môr´găn-tŭn)	124-25	35°45'N	81°41'W
Morgantown, Ky., U.S. (môr´găn-toun)	124-25	37°13'N	86°41'W
Morgantown, W.V., U.S. (môr´găn-toun)	116-17	39°38'N	79°57'W
Morgenzon, S. Afr. (môr´gănt-sŏn)	269c	26°44'S	29°37'E
Morghāb, stm., Asia	232-33	38°38'N	61°10'E
Morioka, Japan (mō´rē-ō´kà)	244	39°42'N	141°09'E
Morkoka, stm., Russia (môr-kô´kà)	218-19	65°11'N	115°51'E
Morlaix, Fr. (mŏr-lĕ´)	196-97	48°35'N	3°50'W
Mornington, Isla, i., Chile	171	49°45'S	75°23'W
Mornington Island, i., Austl.	277	16°33'S	139°24'E
Morocco, nation, Afr. (mô-rŏk´ō)	253	32°0'N	5°00'W
Morogoro, Tan. (mō-rō-gō´rō)	267	6°49'S	37°40'E
Moro Gulf, b., Phil.	250	6°51'N	123°00'E
Moroleón, Mex. (mō-rō-lā-ōn´)	146-47	20°08'N	101°12'W
Morombe, Madag. (mōō-rōōm´bā)	264-65	21°45'S	43°22'E
Morón, Arg. (mo-rō´n)	173	34°39'S	58°37'W
Morón, Cuba (mô-rōn´)	142-43	22°07'N	78°38'W
Mörön, Mong.	240-41	49°38'N	100°10'E
Morón, Ven. (mô-rō´n)	163b	10°29'N	68°12'W
Morona, stm., Peru	170	4°45'S	77°04'W
Morondava, Madag. (mô-rōn-dá´và)	264-65	20°18'S	44°17'E
Morón de la Frontera, Spain (mô-rōn´dā läf rôn-tā´rä)	198-99	37°07'N	5°27'W
Moroni, nat. cap., Com.	264-65	11°42'S	43°15'E
Moron Us, stm., China	234-35	34°40'N	94°56'E
Morozovsk, Russia	186-87	48°21'N	41°50'E
Morrill, Ne., U.S. (mŏr´ĭl)	114-15	41°57'N	103°57'W
Morrilton, Ar., U.S. (mŏr´ĭl-tŭn)	120-21	35°09'N	92°45'W
Morrinhos, Braz. (mô-rēn´yōzh)	172	17°44'S	49°06'W
Morris, Mb., Can. (mŏr´ĭs)	134-35	49°21'N	97°23'W
Morris, Il., U.S. (mŏr´ĭs)	116-17	41°22'N	88°26'W
Morris, Mn., U.S. (mŏr´ĭs)	114-15	45°35'N	95°55'W
Morris, stm., Mb., Can. (mŏr´ĭs)	134-35	49°21'N	97°21'W
Morrison, Il., U.S. (mŏr´ĭ-sŭn)	116-17	41°49'N	89°57'W
Morristown, Tn., U.S. (mŏr´rĭs-toun)	124-25	36°13'N	83°17'W
Morro do Chapéu, Braz. (môr-ò dò-shä-pĕ´ōō)	166-67	11°33'S	41°09'W
Morshansk, Russia (môr-shánsk´)	186-87	53°26'N	41°49'E
Morskoy araly, i., Kaz.	186-87	44°59'N	50°18'E
Morteros, Arg. (mōr-tĕ´tôs)	173	30°42'S	62°00'W
Mortes, stm., Braz.	166-67	11°43'S	50°43'W
Mortlock Islands, is., Micron.	280-81	5°28'N	153°41'E
Morwell, Austl.	276	38°14'S	146°24'E
Mosal'sk, Russia (mō-zálsk´)	202-03	54°30'N	34°58'E
Moscow, Id., U.S. (mŏs´kō)	112-13	46°44'N	117°00'W
Moscow, nat. cap., Russia (mŏs´kō)	202-03	55°45'N	37°38'E
Moscow, stm., Russia (mŏs´kō) *see* Moskva	202-03	55°04'N	38°51'E
Mosel, stm., Eur. (mō´sĕl) (mô-zĕl)	194-95	50°22'N	7°37'E
Moselle, stm., Eur.	194-95	50°22'N	7°37'E
Moshi, Tan. (mō´shē)	267	3°20'S	37°20'E
Mosjøen, Nor.	184-85	65°50'N	13°12'E
Moskenesøya, i., Nor.	184-85	67°60'N	13°06'E
Moskva, nat. cap., Russia (mŏs-kvä´) *see* Moscow	202-03	55°45'N	37°38'E
Moskva, stm., Russia (mŏs-kvä´)	202-03	55°04'N	38°51'E
Mosquera, Col.	164-65	2°30'N	78°26'W
Mosquito Coast, hist. reg., Nic. *see* Mosquitos, Costa de	149	13°0'N	83°45'W
Mosquitos, Costa de, hist. reg., Nic. (kôs-tä-dĕ-mōs-kē´tō)	149	13°0'N	83°45'W
Mosquitos, Golfo de los, b., Pan.	150	9°0'N	81°15'W
Moss, Nor. (môs)	192-93	59°26'N	10°42'E
Mossaka, Congo	262-63	1°09'S	16°50'E
Mosselbaai, S. Afr. (mô´sŭl bā)	264-65	34°11'S	22°08'E
Mossel Bay, S. Afr. *see* Mosselbaai	264-65	34°11'S	22°08'E
Mossendjo, Congo	262-63	2°53'S	12°40'E
Mossoró, Braz.	163d	5°11'S	37°20'W
Moss Point, Ms., U.S. (môs point)	124-25	30°23'N	88°33'W
Most, Czech Rep. (mōst)	194-95	50°31'N	13°39'E
Mostaganem, Alg.	198-99	35°56'N	0°05'E
Mostar, Bos. (môs´tär)	200-01	43°20'N	17°48'E
Mostardas, Braz.	168-69	31°07'S	50°57'W
Mosul, Iraq (mō´sŭl) (mōsōōl´)	228-29	36°20'N	43°08'E
Mot'a, Eth.	266	11°04'N	37°53'E
Motagua, stm., N.A. (mô-tä´gwä)	148	15°43'N	88°13'W
Motala, Swe. (mô-tô´lä)	192-93	58°32'N	15°04'E
Motherwell, Scot., U.K. (mŭdh´ēr-wĕl)	190-91	55°48'N	3°60'W
Motril, Spain (mô-trēl´)	198-99	36°45'N	3°31'W
Motygino, Russia	218-19	58°12'N	94°39'E
Mouhoun, stm., Afr. *see* Black Volta	260-61	8°41'N	0°60'W
Mouila, Gabon	260-61	1°52'S	11°00'E
Moulins, Fr. (mōō-lăN´)	196-97	46°34'N	3°20'E
Moulmein, Mya. *see* Mawlamyine	246-47	16°30'N	97°38'E
Moulouya, Oued, stm., Mor. (wĕd mōō-lōō´yá)	258-59	35°08'N	2°21'W
Moultrie, Ga., U.S. (mōl´trĭ)	124-25	31°11'N	83°47'W
Mound City, Il., U.S. (mound sĭ´tê)	124-25	37°05'N	89°10'W
Mound City, Mo., U.S. (mound sĭ´tê)	120-21	40°08'N	95°14'W
Moundou, Chad	262-63	8°34'N	16°05'E
Moundsville, W.V., U.S. (moundz´vĭl)	116-17	39°55'N	80°44'W
Mountain Brook, Al., U.S. (moun´tĭn brŏŏk)	124-25	33°29'N	86°42'W
Mountain Grove, Mo., U.S. (moun´tĭn grōv)	120-21	37°08'N	92°16'W
Mountain Home, Ar., U.S. (moun´tĭn hōm)	120-21	36°20'N	92°23'W
Mountain Home, Id., U.S. (moun´tĭn hōm)	112-13	43°08'N	115°41'W
Mountain Nile, stm., Sudan (moun´tĭn nīl)	262-63	9°30'N	30°30'E
Mountain View, Mo., U.S. (moun´tĭn vū)	124-25	36°60'N	91°42'W
Mountain Village, Ak., U.S.	126	62°05'N	163°44'W
Mount Airy, N.C., U.S. (mount âr´ĭ)	124-25	36°30'N	80°37'W
Mount Ayr, Ia., U.S. (mount âr)	120-21	40°43'N	94°14'W
Mount Barker, Austl.	270-71	34°38'S	117°40'E
Mount Carmel, Il., U.S. (mount kär´mĕl)	116-17	38°24'N	87°46'W
Mount Carmel, Pa., U.S. (mount kär´mĕl)	116-17	40°48'N	76°25'W
Mount Cook National Park, n.p., N.Z. *see* Aoraki/Mount Cook National Park	278	43°35'S	170°15'E
Mount Desert Island, i., Me., U.S. (mount dē-zûrt´ ī´lănd)	117a	44°20'N	68°20'W
Mount Dora, Fl., U.S. (mount dō´rà)	124-25	28°48'N	81°38'W
Mount Forest, On., Can. (mount fŏr´ĕst)	136-37	43°59'N	80°44'W
Mount Gambier, Austl. (mount găm´bēr)	276	37°50'S	140°47'E
Mount Gilead, Oh., U.S. (mount gĭl´ĕăd)	116-17	40°33'N	82°49'W
Mount Hagen, Pap. N. Gui.	277	5°52'S	144°14'E
Mount Isa, Austl. (mount ī´zà)	277	20°44'S	139°29'E
Mount Kenya National Park, n.p., Kenya	267	0°09'S	37°19'E
Mount Magnet, Austl. (mount măg-nĕt)	270-71	28°04'S	117°51'E
Mount McKinley National Park, n.p., Ak., U.S. *see* Denali National Park and Preserve	126	63°15'N	150°30'W
Mount Morgan, Austl. (mount môr-găn)	277	23°39'S	150°23'E
Mount Morris, Mi., U.S. (mount mŏr´ĭs)	116-17	43°07'N	83°42'W
Mount Morris, N.Y., U.S. (mount mŏr´ĭs)	116-17	42°44'N	77°52'W
Mount Olive, N.C., U.S. (mount ŏl´ĭv)	124-25	35°12'N	78°04'W
Mount Pleasant, Ia., U.S. (mount plĕz´ănt)	114-15	40°58'N	91°32'W
Mount Pleasant, Mi., U.S. (mount plĕz´ănt)	116-17	43°36'N	84°46'W
Mount Pleasant, S.C., U.S. (mount plĕz´ănt)	124-25	32°47'N	79°52'W
Mount Pleasant, Tn., U.S. (mount plĕz´ănt)	124-25	35°32'N	87°12'W
Mount Pleasant, Tx., U.S. (mount plĕz´ănt)	120-21	33°09'N	94°58'W
Mount Pleasant, Ut., U.S. (mount plĕz´ănt)	118-19	39°33'N	111°27'W
Mount Rainier National Park, n.p., Wa., U.S. (mount rå-nēr´ năsh´ŭn-ăl pärk)	112-13	46°52'N	121°43'W
Mount Shasta, Ca., U.S. (mount shăs´tà)	112-13	41°19'N	122°18'W
Mount Sterling, Il., U.S. (mount stûr´lĭng)	120-21	39°59'N	90°46'W
Mount Sterling, Ky., U.S. (mount stûr´lĭng)	116-17	38°03'N	83°57'W
Mount Stewart, P.E., Can. (mount stū´ărt)	138-39	46°22'N	62°53'W
Mount Vernon, Il., U.S. (mount vûr´nŭn)	116-17	38°19'N	88°55'W
Mount Vernon, In., U.S. (mount vûr´nŭn)	116-17	37°56'N	87°54'W
Mount Vernon, Ky., U.S. (mount vûr´nŭn)	124-25	37°21'N	84°22'W
Mount Vernon, Mo., U.S. (mount vûr´nŭn)	120-21	37°06'N	93°49'W
Mount Vernon, N.Y., U.S. (mount vûr´nŭn)	116-17	40°55'N	73°50'W
Mount Vernon, Oh., U.S. (mount vûr´nŭn)	116-17	40°23'N	82°29'W
Mount Vernon, Wa., U.S. (mount vûr´nŭn)	112-13	48°25'N	122°20'W
Moura, Braz. (mō´rá)	166-67	1°29'S	61°37'W
Mourne Mountains, mts., N. Ire., U.K. (môrn moun´tĭnz)	190-91	54°10'N	6°04'W
Moussoro, Chad	258-59	13°38'N	16°30'E
Moûtiers, Fr. (mōō-tyâr´)	196-97	45°29'N	6°31'E
Moutong, Indon.	248-49	0°29'N	121°14'E
Moyahua, Mex. (mô-yä´wä)	146-47	21°16'N	103°10'W
Moyale, Kenya (mô-yä´lä)	262-63	3°32'N	39°03'E
Moyen Atlas, mts., Mor.	258-59	33°30'N	5°00'W
Moyero, stm., Russia	218-19	68°44'N	103°38'E
Moyo, Pulau, i., Indon.	248-49	8°15'S	117°34'E
Moyobamba, Peru (mō-yō-bäm´bä)	170	6°04'S	76°56'W
Mozambique, nation, Afr. (mō-zăm-bēk´)	253	18°15'S	35°00'E
Mozambique, Canal du, strt., Afr. *see* Mozambique Channel	264-65	19°0'S	41°00'E
Mozambique Channel, strt., Afr. (mō-zăm-bek´ chăn´ĕl)	264-65	19°0'S	41°00'E
Mozdok, Russia (môz-dôk´)	227	43°44'N	44°39'E
Mozhaysk, Russia (mô-zhäysk´)	202-03	55°30'N	36°01'E
Mozhga, Russia	186-87	56°27'N	52°12'E
Mozyr, Bela. *see* Mazyr	202-03	52°03'N	29°16'E
Mpika, Zam.	264-65	11°51'S	31°27'E
Mpwapwa, Tan. ('m-pwä´pwä)	267	6°19'S	36°26'E
M'Sila, Alg. (m'sē´là)	269b	35°42'N	4°33'E
Msta, stm., Russia (m'stá´)	202-03	58°29'N	31°27'E
Mtkvari, stm., Asia *see* Kür	227	39°17'N	49°26'E
Mtsensk, Russia (m'tsĕnsk)	202-03	53°17'N	36°35'E
Mtwara, Tan.	264-65	10°21'S	40°15'E
Muanda, D.R.C.	262-63	5°57'S	12°22'E
Muang Khammouan, Laos	246-47	17°25'N	104°49'E
Muang Không, Laos	246-47	14°07'N	105°51'E
Muang Ngoy, Laos	246-47	20°42'N	102°40'E
Muang Pak-Lay, Laos	246-47	18°13'N	101°24'E
Muang Pakxan, Laos	246-47	18°25'N	103°39'E
Muang Sing, Laos	246-47	21°11'N	101°09'E
Muang Vangviang, Laos	246-47	18°55'N	102°26'E
Muang Xaignabouri, Laos	246-47	19°17'N	101°43'E
Muar, Malay.	246-47	2°02'N	102°34'E
Muaratewe, Indon.	248-49	0°56'S	114°52'E
Mubende, Ug.	267	0°35'N	31°24'E
Mucajaí, stm., Braz.	164-65	2°24'N	60°50'W
Muchinga Mountains, mts., Zam.	264-65	11°40'S	31°44'E
Mucuri, stm., Braz.	172	18°05'S	39°34'W
Mudan, stm., China (mōō-dän)	244	46°18'N	129°32'E
Mudanjiang, China (mōō-dän-jyäŋ)	244	44°35'N	129°36'E
Mudgee, Austl. (mŭ-jē)	276	32°36'S	149°35'E
Mueda, Moz.	264-65	11°40'S	39°34'E
Mufulira, Zam.	264-65	12°33'S	28°14'E
Muğla, Tur. (mōōg´lä)	200-01	37°13'N	28°22'E
Mühlhausen, Ger. (mül´hou-zĕn)	194-95	51°13'N	10°28'E
Muhlig-Hofmann Mountains, mts., Ant.	287	72°10'S	4°53'E

n-sing; ŋ-baŋk; N-nasalized n; nŏd; cŏmmit; ōld; ôbey; ôrder; oi-boil; fōōd; ŏ-as oo in foot; ou-out; s-soft; sh-dish; th-thin; pūre; ûnite; ûrn; stŭd; circŭs; ü-as in French tu; ´-indeterminate vowel.

Feature (Pronunciation)	Page	Lat.	Long.
Muhu, i., Est. (mōō'hōō)	192-93	58°37'N	23°13'E
Mukacheve, Ukr.	194-95	48°26'N	22°45'E
Mukah, Malay.	248-49	2°54'N	112°06'E
Mukalla, Yemen *see* Al-Mukallā	220-21	14°32'N	49°08'E
Mukden, China *see* Shenyang	243	41°48'N	123°24'E
Mukry, Turkmen.	232-33	37°36'N	65°43'E
Mula, Spain (mōō'lä)	198-99	38°03'N	1°30'W
Muladu, i., Mald.	236	7°01'N	72°59'E
Mulchatna, stm., Ak., U.S.	126	59°39'N	157°08'W
Mulhacén, mtn., Spain	198-99	37°03'N	3°19'W
Mulhouse, Fr. (mü-lōōz')	196-97	47°45'N	7°20'E
Muling, China (mōō-lĭŋ)	244	44°31'N	130°16'E
Muling, China (mōō-lĭŋ)	244	44°56'N	130°32'E
Muling, stm., China (mōō-lĭŋ)	244	45°52'N	133°30'E
Mull, Island of, i., Scot., U.K. (ī'lănd ŏv mŭl)	190-91	56°27'N	6°00'W
Mullan, Id., U.S. (mŭl'ăn)	112-13	47°28'N	115°48'W
Muller, Pegunungan, mts., Indon. (mül'ẽr)	248-49	0°40'N	113°50'E
Mullewa, Austl.	270-71	28°33'S	115°31'E
Mullins, S.C., U.S. (mŭl'ĭnz)	124-25	34°12'N	79°15'W
Mulongo, D.R.C.	262-63	7°49'S	26°60'E
Multān, Pak. (mŏŏ-tän')	232-33	30°11'N	71°27'E
Mulvane, Ks., U.S. (mŭl-vān')	120-21	37°28'N	97°15'W
Mumbai, India	236	18°57'N	72°50'E
Mumbwa, Zam. (mŏŏm'bwä)	264-65	14°59'S	27°04'E
Mun, stm., Thai.	246-47	15°19'N	105°31'E
Muna, Mex. (mōō'nä)	148	20°29'N	89°43'W
Muna, stm., Russia	218-19	67°53'N	123°05'E
Muna, Pulau, i., Indon.	248-49	4°53'S	122°27'E
München, Ger. *see* Munich	194-95	48°08'N	11°35'E
Muncie, In., U.S. (mŭn'sĭ)	116-17	40°11'N	85°22'W
Munger, India	234-35	25°23'N	86°28'E
Mungindi, Austl. (mŭn-gĭn'dē)	276	28°59'S	148°59'E
Mungkan Kandju National Park, n.p., Austl.	277	13°32'S	142°37'E
Munich, Ger. (mū'nĭk)	194-95	48°08'N	11°35'E
Munising, Mi., U.S. (mū'nĭ-sĭng)	114-15	46°24'N	86°39'W
Munkács, Ukr. *see* Mukacheve	194-95	48°26'N	22°45'E
Münster, Ger.	194-95	51°57'N	7°37'E
Muntok, Indon. (mŏn-tŏk')	246-47	2°04'S	105°10'E
Muonio, Fin.	184-85	67°58'N	23°40'E
Muqayshiṭ, i., U.A.E.	230-31	24°10'N	53°45'E
Muqdisho, nat. cap., Som. *see* Mogadishu	262-63	2°03'N	45°20'E
Muradiye, Tur. (mōō-rä'dē-yĕ)	227	38°59'N	43°50'E
Murashi, Russia	186-87	59°24'N	48°58'E
Murat, stm., Tur. (mōō-rät')	227	38°40'N	39°53'E
Murchison, stm., Austl. (mûr'chĭ-sŭn)	272-73	27°42'S	114°08'E
Murchison Falls, wtfl., Ug. *see* Kabalega Falls	267	2°17'N	31°42'E
Murchison Falls National Park, n.p., Ug.	267	2°15'N	31°50'E
Murcia, Spain (mōōr'thyä)	198-99	37°59'N	1°08'W
Mur-de-Barrez, Fr.	196-97	44°51'N	2°39'E
Murdo, S.D., U.S. (mûr'dō)	114-15	43°53'N	100°41'W
Muret, Fr. (mü-rĕ')	196-97	43°28'N	1°19'E
Murfreesboro, N.C., U.S. (mûr'frēz-bŭr-ō)	124-25	36°27'N	77°06'W
Murfreesboro, Tn., U.S. (mûr'frēz-bŭr-ō)	124-25	35°50'N	86°23'W
Murgap, stm., Asia (mōōr-gäp')	232-33	38°38'N	61°10'E
Murgon, Austl.	276	26°15'S	151°57'E
Mūrītāniyā, nation, Afr. *see* Mauritania	253	20°0'N	12°00'W
Murmansk, Russia (mōōr-mänsk')	184-85	68°58'N	33°05'E
Murom, Russia (mōō'rŏm)	186-87	55°34'N	42°02'E
Muroran, Japan (mōō'rō-rän)	244	42°19'N	140°59'E
Muros, Spain (mōō'rōs)	198-99	42°47'N	9°04'W
Murphy, N.C., U.S. (mŭr'fĭ)	124-25	35°05'N	84°02'W
Murphysboro, Il., U.S. (mŭr'fĭz-bŭr-ō)	116-17	37°46'N	89°20'W
Murray, Ky., U.S. (mŭr'ī)	124-25	36°37'N	88°19'W
Murray, Ut., U.S. (mŭr'ī)	112-13	40°39'N	111°54'W
Murray, stm., Austl. (mŭr'ī)	276	35°22'S	139°21'E
Murray, stm., B.C., Can. (mŭr'ī)	132-33	55°43'N	121°13'W
Murray, Lake, lk., Pap. N. Gui.	277	7°0'S	141°30'E
Murray Bridge, Austl. (mŭr'ī brĭj)	276	35°08'S	139°16'E
Murray Harbour, P.E., Can. (mŭr'ī här'bẽr)	138-39	45°60'N	62°32'W
Murray-Sunset National Park, n.p., Austl.	276	34°45'S	141°30'E
Murrumbidgee, stm., Austl. (mŭr-ŭm-bĭd'jē)	276	34°42'S	143°08'E
Murska Sobota, Slvn. (mōōr'skä sō'bō-tä)	200-01	46°40'N	16°10'E
Murua Island, i., Pap. N. Gui.	277	9°06'S	152°45'E
Murud, Gunong, mtn., Malay.	248-49	3°52'N	115°30'E
Mururoa, at., Fr. Poly.	280-81	21°52'S	138°55'W
Murwāra, India	234-35	23°50'N	80°24'E
Murwillumbah, Austl. (mŭr-wĭl'lŭm-bŭ)	276	28°21'S	153°24'E
Murzuq, Libya	258-59	25°56'N	13°55'E
Murzūq, Idhān, des., Libya	258-59	24°30'N	13°00'E
Mürzzuschlag, Aus. (mürts'tsōō-shlägh)	194-95	47°36'N	15°41'E
Muş, Tur. (mōōsh)	227	38°43'N	41°29'E
Musala, mtn., Blg.	200-01	42°11'N	23°34'E
Musay'īd, Qatar	230-31	24°59'N	51°33'E
Muscat, nat. cap., Oman (mŭs-kăt')	230-31	23°36'N	58°32'E
Muscat and Oman, nation, Asia *see* Oman	206-07	22°0'N	58°00'E
Muscatine, Ia., U.S. (mŭs-kȧ-tēn)	114-15	41°25'N	91°02'W
Muscle Shoals, Al., U.S. (mŭs''l shōlz)	124-25	34°44'N	87°40'W
Mushin, Nig.	260a	6°31'N	3°21'E
Musi, stm., Indon. (mōō'sē)	246-47	2°22'S	104°55'E
Muskegon, Mi., U.S. (mŭs-kē'gŭn)	116-17	43°14'N	86°15'W
Muskegon, stm., Mi., U.S. (mŭs-kē'gŭn)	116-17	43°13'N	86°19'W
Muskegon Heights, Mi., U.S. (mŭs-kē'gŭn hīts)	116-17	43°12'N	86°14'W
Muskingum, stm., Oh., U.S. (mŭs-kĭŋ'gŭm)	116-17	39°24'N	81°28'W
Muskogee, Ok., U.S. (mŭs-kō'gē)	120-21	35°44'N	95°22'W
Muskoka, Lake, lk., On., Can. (lăk mŭs-kō'kȧ)	136-37	45°02'N	79°25'W
Musoma, Tan.	267	1°30'S	33°48'E
Mussau Island, i., Pap. N. Gui. (mōō-sä'ōō ī'lănd)	277	1°27'S	149°37'E
Musselshell, stm., Mt., U.S. (mŭs''l-shĕl)	112-13	47°27'N	107°55'W
Mustvee, Est. (mōōst'vē-ĕ)	192-93	58°51'N	26°56'E
Musu-dan, c., Kor., N. (mō'sō dän)	243	40°51'N	129°43'E
Muswellbrook, Austl. (mŭs'wŭnl-brŏk)	276	32°16'S	150°54'E
Mutare, Zimb.	264-65	18°58'S	32°40'E
Mutsamudu, Com.	264-65	12°08'S	44°26'E
Mutsu, Japan	244	41°17'N	141°10'E
Mutsu-wan, b., Japan (mōōt'sōō wän)	244	41°05'N	140°55'E
Mutton Bay, Qc., Can. (mŭt''n bā)	138-39	50°47'N	59°02'W
Muttra, India *see* Mathura	234-35	27°30'N	77°41'E
Mutum, Braz. (mōō-tōō'm)	172	19°48'S	41°27'W
Muynak, Uzb. *see* Mŭynoq	226	43°46'N	59°02'E
Mŭynoq, Uzb.	226	43°46'N	59°02'E
Muyua Island, i., Pap. N. Gui. *see* Murua Island	277	9°06'S	152°45'E
Muzaffarnagar, India	234-35	29°28'N	77°42'E
Muzaffarpur, India	234-35	26°07'N	85°23'E
Muztag, mtn., China	234-35	36°03'N	80°07'E
Muztag, mtn., China	234-35	36°25'N	87°25'E
Muztaū bīīgi, mtn., Asia *see* Belukha, Mount	226	49°51'N	86°29'E
Mwali, i., Com.	264-65	12°18'S	43°42'E
Mwanza, Tan. (mwän'zä)	267	2°31'S	32°54'E
Mweka, D.R.C.	262-63	4°51'S	21°34'E
Mwene-Ditu, D.R.C.	262-63	7°03'S	23°27'E
Mweru, Lake, lk., Afr. (lăk mwĕ'rōō)	262-63	9°0'S	28°45'E
Mweru Wantipa, Lake, lk., Zam.	262-63	8°45'S	29°40'E
Mwokil, at., Micron.	280-81	6°39'N	159°47'E
Myanaung, Mya.	246-47	18°17'N	95°19'E
Myanmar, nation, Asia (myän-mär)	206-07	22°0'N	98°00'E
Myaundzha, Russia	218-19	63°03'N	147°11'E
Myaungmya, Mya.	246-47	16°35'N	94°55'E
Myingyan, Mya. (myĭng-yŭn')	246-47	21°27'N	95°23'E
Myitkyinā, Mya. (myĭ'chē-nȧ)	238-39	25°23'N	97°24'E
Mykolaïv, Ukr.	202-03	46°58'N	31°59'E
Mymensingh, Bngl.	234-35	24°45'N	90°24'E
Myohyang-san, mtn., Kor., N. (myō'hyang-sän')	243	40°01'N	126°21'E
Mýrdalsjökull, ice, Ice. (mür'däls-yû'kōl)	190a	63°40'N	19°05'W
Myrtle Beach, S.C., U.S. (mûr't'l bēch)	124-25	33°42'N	78°54'W
Mysore, India (mī-sōr')	236	12°18'N	76°39'E
Mysore, state, India *see* Karnātaka	236	14°0'N	76°00'E
Mys Shmidta, Russia	126	68°52'N	179°37'W
My Tho, Viet.	246-47	10°22'N	106°22'E
Mytilíni, Grc.	200-01	39°06'N	26°33'E
Mytishchi, Russia (mē-tēsh'chi)	202-03	55°55'N	37°46'E
Mzuzu, Malawi	264-65	11°24'S	33°57'E
N			
Naantali, Fin. (nän'tȧ-lē)	192-93	60°30'N	22°04'E
Naberezhnye Chelny, Russia	186-87	55°42'N	52°19'E
Nabeul, Tun. (nā-bûl')	184-85	36°27'N	10°46'E
Nabī Shu'ayb, Jabal an-, mtn., Yemen	220-21	15°17'N	43°59'E
Nābulus, W.B.	228-29	32°14'N	35°17'E
Nacala, Moz. (nă-kä'lȧ)	264-65	14°33'S	40°40'E
Náchod, Czech Rep. (näk'ôt)	194-95	50°25'N	16°11'E
Nacogdoches, Tx., U.S. (năk'ō-dō'chĕz)	122-23	31°35'N	94°39'W
Nacozari de García, Mex.	144-45	30°24'N	109°39'W
Nadadores, Mex. (nä-dä-dō'räs)	122-23	27°02'N	101°35'W
Nadiād, India	234-35	22°41'N	72°52'E
Nador, Mor.	198-99	35°11'N	2°56'W
Nadym, Russia	218-19	65°35'N	72°39'E
Nadym, stm., Russia (nȧ'dĭm)	218-19	66°13'N	72°00'E
Næstved, Den. (nĕst'vĭdh)	194-95	55°14'N	11°46'E
Naga, Phil. (nä'gä)	250	13°38'N	123°11'E
Nāgāland, state, India	234-35	26°0'N	95°00'E
Nagano, Japan (nä'gä-nō)	245	36°39'N	138°12'E
Nagaoka, Japan (nä'gȧ-ō'kȧ)	245	37°27'N	138°51'E
Nagaon, India	234-35	26°21'N	92°41'E
Nāgappattinam, India	236	10°46'N	79°51'E
Nagarote, Nic. (nä-gä-rô'tĕ)	149	12°16'N	86°34'W
Nagasaki, Japan (nä'gȧ-sä'kē)	245	32°45'N	129°53'E
Nāgaur, India	234-35	27°12'N	73°44'E
Nāgercoil, India	236	8°10'N	77°26'E
Nagorno-Karabakh, hist. reg., Azer. (nu-gôr'nŭ-kŭ-rŭ-bäk')	227	40°00'N	46°40'E
Nagoya, Japan	245	35°10'N	136°55'E
Nāgpur, India (näg'pōōr)	234-35	21°09'N	79°05'E
Nagqu, China	234-35	31°31'N	92°05'E
Nagua, Dom. Rep. (nȧ'gwä)	142-43	19°23'N	69°51'W
Naguna, Île, i., Vanuatu *see* Nguna, Île	279g	17°27'S	168°21'E
Nagybánya, Rom. *see* Baia Mare	194-95	47°39'N	23°35'E
Nagykanizsa, Hung. (nôd'y'kô'nē-shô)	194-95	46°27'N	16°60'E
Nagykőrös, Hung. (nôd'y'kū-rūsh)	194-95	47°02'N	19°46'E
Nagyvarad, Rom. *see* Oradea	194-95	47°04'N	21°56'E
Naha, Japan (nä'hä)	244a	26°13'N	127°42'E
Nāhan, India	234-35	30°32'N	77°17'E
Nahanni National Park Reserve, n.p., N.T., Can.	128-29	61°35'N	125°45'W
Nahe, China	240-41	48°29'N	124°53'E
Nahr al-Urdunn, stm., Asia *see* Jordan	228-29	31°46'N	35°34'E
Nahuel Huapi, Lago, lk., Arg. (lä'gō nä'wĕl wä'pē)	171	40°58'S	71°30'W
Naica, Mex. (nä-ē'kä)	122-23	27°51'N	105°30'W
Nain, Nf., Can. (nīn)	128-29	56°33'N	61°43'W
Nā'īn, Iran	232-33	32°52'N	53°05'E
Naini Tāl, India	234-35	29°24'N	79°26'E
Nairn, Scot., U.K. (nârn)	190-91	57°35'N	3°53'W
Nairobi, nat. cap., Kenya (nī-rō'bē)	267	1°16'S	36°49'E
Naitauba, i., Fiji	279f	17°01'S	179°16'W
Naivasha, Kenya (nī-vä'shȧ)	267	0°45'S	36°26'E
Najafābād, Iran	232-33	32°38'N	51°22'E
Najasa, stm., Cuba (nä-hä'sä)	142-43	20°43'N	77°59'W
Najd, hist. reg., Sau. Ar.	266	26°07'N	44°40'E
Najin, Kor., N. (nä'jĭn)	243	42°15'N	130°18'E
Naju, Kor., S. (nä'jōō')	243	35°02'N	126°43'E
Nakambé, stm., Afr. *see* White Volta	260-61	8°57'N	1°10'W
Nakanbe, stm., Afr. *see* White Volta	260-61	8°57'N	1°10'W
Nakano-shima, i., Japan	244	29°50'N	129°52'E
Nakhichevan, Azer. *see* Naxçıvan	227	39°13'N	45°25'E
Nakhodka, Russia (nŭ-kôt'kŭ)	244	42°49'N	132°53'E
Nakhon Pathom, Thai.	246-47	13°49'N	100°04'E
Nakhon Phanom, Thai.	246-47	17°24'N	104°47'E
Nakhon Ratchasima, Thai.	246-47	14°58'N	102°06'E
Nakhon Sawan, Thai.	246-47	15°42'N	100°06'E
Nakhon Si Thammarat, Thai.	246-47	8°26'N	99°58'E
Nakskov, Den. (näk'skou)	194-95	54°50'N	11°08'E
Nakuru, Kenya	267	0°17'S	36°04'E
Nālanda, India	234-35	25°08'N	85°24'E
Nalchik, Russia (nȧl-chēk')	227	43°29'N	43°37'E
Nalgonda, India	236	17°03'N	79°16'E
Nalubaale Dam, d., Ug.	267	0°27'N	33°11'E
Nālūt, Libya (nä-lōōt')	188-89	31°53'N	10°60'E
Namak, Daryācheh-ye, lk., Iran	232-33	34°30'N	51°50'E
Namangan, Uzb. (nȧ-mȧn-gän')	232-33	40°60'N	71°40'E
Namapa, Moz.	264-65	13°42'S	39°49'E
Nambour, Austl. (năm'bōr)	276	26°38'S	152°58'E
Namcha Barwa, mtn., China *see* Namjagbarwa Feng	238-39	29°38'N	95°04'E
Nam Co, lk., China (näm tswo)	234-35	30°41'N	90°32'E
Nam Dinh, Viet. (näm dĕnĸ')	246-47	20°26'N	106°10'E
Namhae-do, i., Kor., S. (näm'hī')	243	34°48'N	127°57'E
Namhkam, Mya.	238-39	23°50'N	97°41'E

Feature (Pronunciation)	Page	Lat.	Long.
Namib Desert, des., Nmb. (nä-mēb′ dĕs′ĕrt)	264-65	23°0′S	15°00′E
Namibe, Ang.	264-65	15°12′S	12°10′E
Namibia, nation, Afr. (nä-mĭ′-bē-ȧ)	253	22°0′S	17°00′E
Namib Naukluft Park, pk., Nmb.	264-65	24°40′S	15°17′E
Namjagbarwa Feng, mtn., China	238-39	29°38′N	95°04′E
Namlea, Indon.	248-49	3°16′S	127°06′E
Nam Ngum Reservoir, res., Laos	246-47	18°33′N	102°37′E
Namoi, stm., Austl. (nămôi)	276	30°00′S	148°04′E
Namolok Atoll, at., Micron.	280-81	5°55′N	153°08′E
Nampa, Id., U.S. (năm′pȧ)	112-13	43°35′N	116°33′W
Namp'o, Kor., N.	243	38°45′N	125°23′E
Nampula, Moz.	264-65	15°07′S	39°16′E
Namsang, Mya.	246-47	20°53′N	97°43′E
Namsos, Nor. (näm′sôs)	184-85	64°28′N	11°32′E
Namu, B.C., Can.	132-33	51°50′N	127°52′W
Namuka-i-Lau, i., Fiji	279f	18°51′S	178°38′W
Namyit Island, i., Asia	224-25	10°24′N	114°27′E
Nan, Thai.	246-47	18°46′N	100°46′E
Nan, stm., Thai.	246-47	15°42′N	100°09′E
Nanaimo, B.C., Can. (nȧ-nī′mō)	132-33	49°10′N	123°57′W
Nanam, Kor., N. (nä′nän′)	243	41°43′N	129°42′E
Nanango, Austl.	276	26°41′S	152°00′E
Nanao, Japan (nä′nä-ō)	245	37°03′N	136°58′E
Nanchang, China	238-39	28°41′N	115°53′E
Nancheng, China (nän-chäŋ) *see* Hanzhong	238-39	33°04′N	107°02′E
Nancheng, China (nän-chäŋ)	238-39	27°34′N	116°39′E
Nanchong, China (nän-chôŋ)	238-39	30°47′N	106°05′E
Nancy, Fr. (näN-sē′)	196-97	48°41′N	6°10′E
Nanda Devi, mtn., India (nän′dä dā′vē)	234-35	30°23′N	79°59′E
Nānded, India	236	19°09′N	77°18′E
Nanga-Eboko, Camrn.	260-61	4°40′N	12°22′E
Nanga Parbat, mtn., Pak.	232-33	35°15′N	74°36′E
Nangis, Fr. (näN-zhē′)	196-97	48°34′N	3°01′E
Nanhai, China *see* Foshan	238-39	23°03′N	113°07′E
Nan Hai, s., Asia *see* South China Sea	224-25	10°0′N	113°00′E
Nanjing, China (nän-jyĭŋ)	238-39	24°31′N	117°23′E
Nanjing, China (nän-jyĭŋ)	238-39	32°03′N	118°47′E
Nanking, China *see* Nanjing	238-39	32°03′N	118°47′E
Nan Ling, mts., China	238-39	25°0′N	112°00′E
Nanliu, stm., China (nän-lĭō)	238-39	21°40′N	109°05′E
Nanning, China (nän′nĭng′)	238-39	22°48′N	108°20′E
Nanpan, stm., China (nän-pän)	238-39	24°57′N	106°08′E
Nanping, China (nän-pĭŋ)	238-39	26°38′N	118°10′E
Nansei-shotō, is., Japan *see* Ryukyu Islands	244a	25°44′N	126°58′E
Nanshan Island, i., Asia	224-25	10°44′N	115°49′E
Nansio, Tan.	267	2°06′S	33°03′E
Nantai-zan, vol., Japan (nän-täē-zän)	245	36°46′N	139°30′E
Nantes, Fr. (näNt′)	196-97	47°14′N	1°33′W
Nanticoke, Pa., U.S. (năn′tĭ-kōk)	116-17	41°12′N	76°00′W
Nantong, China (nän-tôŋ)	238-39	32°01′N	120°51′E
Nantucket Island, i., Ma., U.S. (năn-tŭk′ĕt ī′lȧnd)	116-17	41°16′N	70°03′W
Nanumea, at., Tuvalu	280-81	5°42′S	176°09′E
Nanuque, Braz.	172	17°50′S	40°20′W
Nanxiong, China (nän-shôŋ)	238-39	25°07′N	114°20′E
Nanyang, China (nän-yäŋ)	238-39	33°00′N	112°32′E
Nanyuki, Kenya	267	0°01′N	37°05′E
Nao, Cabo de la, c., Spain *see* Nao, Cap de la	198-99	38°44′N	0°14′E
Nao, Cap de la, c., Spain	198-99	38°44′N	0°14′E
Náousa, Grc. (nä′o͞o-sȧ)	200-01	40°37′N	22°03′E
Napa, Ca., U.S. (năp′ȧ)	118-19	38°18′N	122°17′W
Napaktulik Lake, lk., Nu., Can.	130-31	66°15′N	113°05′W
Napanee, On., Can. (năp′ȧ-nē)	136-37	44°15′N	76°57′W
Naperville, Il., U.S. (nā′pĕr-vĭl)	116-17	41°46′N	88°09′W
Napier, N.Z. (nā′pĭ-ĕr)	278	39°29′S	176°54′E
Naples, Italy (nā′p'lz)	200-01	40°51′N	14°17′E
Naples, Fl., U.S. (nā′p'lz)	125a	26°09′N	81°48′W
Napo, stm., S.A. (nä′pō)	170	3°29′S	72°38′W
Napoleon, Oh., U.S. (nȧ-pō′lē-ŭn)	116-17	41°23′N	84°08′W
Napoli, Italy (nä′pô-lē) *see* Naples	200-01	40°51′N	14°17′E
Nappanee, In., U.S. (năp′ȧ-nē)	116-17	41°26′N	85°59′W
Nara, Japan (nä′rä)	245	34°41′N	135°50′E
Nara, state, Japan (nä′rä)	245	34°30′N	135°50′E
Naracoorte, Austl. (nȧ-rȧ-ko͞on′tē)	276	36°58′S	140°44′E
Naraụ, stm., Eur. *see* Narew	194-95	52°31′N	21°05′E
Nārāyanganj, Bngl.	234-35	23°37′N	90°30′E
Narbonne, Fr. (nȧr-bôn′)	196-97	43°11′N	2°60′E
Narborough, i., Ec. *see* Fernandina, Isla	170a	0°26′S	91°30′W
Nares Stræde, strt., N.A. *see* Nares Strait	86	80°30′N	68°00′W
Nares Strait, strt., N.A.	86	80°30′N	68°00′W
Narew, stm., Eur. (när′ĕf)	194-95	52°31′N	21°05′E
Narmada, stm., India	234-35	21°41′N	72°45′E
Nārnaul, India	234-35	28°03′N	76°06′E
Narodnaya, Gora, mtn., Russia (gȧ-rä′ nȧ-rôd′nȧ-yȧ)	186-87	65°04′N	60°09′E
Naro-Fominsk, Russia (nä′rô-mĕnsk′)	202-03	55°23′N	36°44′E
Narok, Kenya	267	1°05′S	35°52′E
Narrabri, Austl.	276	30°20′S	149°47′E
Narrandera, Austl. (nȧ-rȧn-dē′rȧ)	276	34°45′S	146°33′E
Narrogin, Austl. (năr′ô-gĭn)	270-71	32°56′S	117°11′E
Narromine, Austl.	276	32°14′S	148°14′E
Narsimhapur, India	234-35	22°57′N	79°12′E
Narva, Est. (nȧr′vȧ)	192-93	59°23′N	28°12′E
Narva laht, b., Eur.	192-93	59°30′N	27°40′E
Narvik, Nor. (när′vĕk)	184-85	68°26′N	17°25′E
Narvskiy Zaliv, b., Eur. (nȧr′vskĭ zä′lĭf) *see* Narva laht	192-93	59°30′N	27°40′E
Naryan-Mar, Russia (när′yȧn mär′)	186-87	67°37′N	52°60′E
Naryn, Kyrg.	226	41°26′N	75°59′E
Naryn, stm., Asia (nŭ-rĭn′)	226	41°46′N	73°13′E
Nasca, Peru	170	14°50′S	74°57′W
Nāshik, India	234-35	20°00′N	73°47′E
Nashua, Ia., U.S. (năsh′ū-ȧ)	114-15	42°57′N	92°33′W
Nashua, N.H., U.S.	116-17	42°46′N	71°28′W
Nashville, Ar., U.S. (năsh′vĭl)	120-21	33°57′N	93°51′W
Nashville, Ga., U.S. (năsh′vĭl)	124-25	31°12′N	83°15′W
Nashville, Il., U.S. (năsh′vĭl)	116-17	38°21′N	89°23′W
Nashville, Mi., U.S. (năsh′vĭl)	116-17	42°36′N	85°06′W
Nashville, Tn., U.S. (năsh′vĭl)	124-25	36°09′N	86°47′W
Našice, Cro. (nä′shĕ-tsĕ)	200-01	45°29′N	18°04′E
Nāşir, Buḩayrat, res., Afr. *see* Nasser, Lake	266	22°40′N	32°00′E
Nâsir, Buheirat, res., Afr. *see* Nasser, Lake	266	22°40′N	32°00′E
Nasirābād, Bngl. *see* Mymensingh	234-35	24°45′N	90°24′E
Nass, stm., B.C., Can. (năs)	132-33	54°59′N	129°40′W
Nassau, nat. cap., Bah. (năs′ô)	142-43	25°04′N	77°20′W
Nassau Island, i., Cook Is.	280-81	11°34′S	165°24′W
Nasser, Lake, res., Afr. (lăk nä-sĕr)	266	22°40′N	32°00′E
Natagaima, Col. (nä-tä-gī′mä)	163c	3°38′N	75°06′W
Natal, Braz. (nä-täl′)	163d	5°47′S	35°13′W
Natal, Indon.	246-47	0°34′N	99°07′E
Natashquan, Qc., Can. (nä-tăsh′kwän)	138-39	50°12′N	61°49′W
Natashquan, stm., Can.	138-39	50°11′N	61°35′W
Natchez, Ms., U.S. (năch′ĕz)	124-25	31°34′N	91°24′W
Natchitoches, La., U.S. (năk′ĭ-tŏsh)(nách-ĭ-tŏsh′)	122-23	31°46′N	93°06′W
National City, Ca., U.S. (năsh′ŭn-ăl sĭ′tĭ)	118-19	32°41′N	117°06′W
Natividade, Braz. (nä-tē-vē-dä′dĕ)	166-67	11°42′S	47°47′W
Natron, Lake, lk., Afr. (lāk nā′trŏn)	267	2°25′S	35°60′E
Natuna Besar, Kepulauan, is., Indon.	246-47	4°40′N	108°00′E
Natuna Selatan, Kepulauan, is., Indon.	246-47	2°45′N	109°00′E
Natural Bridges National Monument, n.p., Ut., U.S. (năt′ū-răl brĭj′ĕs năsh′ŭn-ăl mŏn′ū-mĕnt)	118-19	37°37′N	109°59′W
Naturaliste, Cape, c., Austl. (kāp năt-ū-rȧ-lĭst′)	272-73	33°33′S	115°01′E
Naugatuck, Ct., U.S. (nô′gȧ-tŭk)	116-17	41°29′N	73°03′W
Naujat, Nu., Can. *see* Repulse Bay	128-29	66°32′N	86°14′W
Naumburg, Ger. (noum′bôrgh)	194-95	51°10′N	11°48′E
Nauru, nation, Oc. (nä-o͞o′-ro͞o)	280-81	0°32′S	166°55′E
Nautla, Mex. (nä-o͞ot′lä)	146-47	20°13′N	96°47′W
Nava, Mex. (nä′vä)	122-23	28°25′N	100°46′W
Navadwīp, India	234-35	23°25′N	88°22′E
Navahermosa, Spain (nä-vä-ĕr-mō′sä)	198-99	39°38′N	4°28′W
Navajo Indian Reservation, ind. res., U.S. (năv′ȧ-hō ĭn′dĭ-ăn rĕ-sĕr-vā′shĕn)	118-19	36°39′N	109°46′W
Navajo National Monument, n.p., Az., U.S. (năv′ȧ-hō năsh′ŭn-ăl mŏn′ū-mĕnt)	118-19	36°44′N	110°29′W
Navanagar, India *see* Jamnagar	234-35	22°28′N	70°04′E
Navarin, Mys, c., Russia	218-19	62°17′N	179°06′E
Navarino, Isla, i., Chile (ĕ′s-lä-nȧ-vä-rē′nô)	171	55°05′S	67°49′W
Navasota, Tx., U.S. (năv-ȧ-sō′tȧ)	122-23	30°23′N	96°06′W
Navasota, stm., Tx., U.S. (năv-ȧạ-sō′tȧ)	122-23	30°20′N	96°09′W
Navassa Island, dep., N.A.	140-41	18°24′N	75°01′W
Navassa Island, i., N.A. (nȧ-văs′ȧ ī′lȧnd)	142-43	18°24′N	75°01′W
Navidad, Chile (nä-vē-dä′d)	163e	33°56′S	71°50′W
Naviti, i., Fiji	279f	17°07′S	177°15′E
Navoiy, Uzb.	232-33	40°07′N	65°23′E
Navojoa, Mex. (nä-vô-kô′ä)	144-45	27°05′N	109°27′W
Navsāri, India	234-35	20°57′N	72°56′E
Nawa, Japan *see* Naha	244a	26°13′N	127°42′E
Nawābshāh, Pak. (nȧ-wäb′shä)	232-33	26°14′N	68°24′E
Naxçıvan, Azer.	227	39°13′N	45°25′E
Naxçıvan Muxtar Respublikası, state, Azer.	227	39°20′N	45°30′E
Náxos, i., Grc. (nák′sôs)	200-01	37°03′N	25°31′E
Nayarit, state, Mex. (nä-yä-rēt′)	146-47	22°0′N	105°00′W
Nayau, i., Fiji	279f	17°58′S	179°03′W
Nayoro, Japan	244	44°21′N	142°28′E
Nay Pyi Taw, nat. cap., Mya.	246-47	19°45′N	96°07′E
Nazaré, Port.	198-99	39°36′N	9°04′W
Nazaré da Mata, Braz. (nä-zä-rĕ′ dä-mä-tä)	163d	7°44′S	35°14′W
Nazas, Mex. (nä′zäs)	122-23	25°14′N	104°08′W
Nazas, stm., Mex. (nä′zäs)	122-23	25°35′N	105°03′W
Naze, Japan	244a	28°22′N	129°30′E
Naze, The, c., Nor. *see* Lindesnes	192-93	58°0′N	7°02′E
Nazilli, Tur. (nȧ-zĭ-lē′)	200-01	37°55′N	28°20′E
Nazrēt, Eth.	269d	8°32′N	39°16′E
N'dalatando, Ang.	264-65	9°18′S	14°54′E
Ndélé, C.A.R.	262-63	8°25′N	20°39′E
N'Djamena, nat. cap., Chad (ŭn-jä-mē-nä′)	258-59	12°07′N	15°03′E
Ndjolé, Gabon	260-61	0°08′S	10°45′E
Ndola, Zam. (n'dō′lä)	264-65	12°57′S	28°38′E
Neagh, Lough, lk., N. Ire., U.K. (lŏk nā)	190-91	54°37′N	6°23′W
Neagră, Marea, s., *see* Black Sea	186-87	43°0′N	35°00′E
Near Islands, is., Ak., U.S. (nēr ī′lȧndz)	126a	52°37′N	173°03′E
Neath, Wales, U.K. (nēth)	190-91	51°40′N	3°48′W
Nebine Creek, stm., Austl. (nĕ-bēne′ krēk)	276	29°21′S	146°45′E
Neblina, Cerro de la, mtn., S.A. *see* Neblina, Pico da	164-65	0°50′N	65°59′W
Neblina, Pico da, mtn., S.A.	164-65	0°50′N	65°59′W
Nebraska, state, U.S. (nē-brăs′kȧ)	108-09	41°30′N	100°00′W
Nebraska City, Ne., U.S. (nē-brăs′kȧ sĭ′tē)	120-21	40°41′N	95°52′W
Nechako, stm., B.C., Can.	132-33	53°55′N	122°43′W
Nechako Plateau, plat., B.C., Can. (nĭ-chă′kō plă-tō′)	132-33	54°0′N	124°30′W
Nechako Range, mts., B.C., Can. (nĭ-chă′kō rānj)	132-33	53°21′N	124°37′W
Nechako Reservoir, res., B.C., Can. (nĭ-chă′kō rĕ′sĕr-vwär)	132-33	53°33′N	124°53′W
Neches, stm., Tx., U.S. (nĕch′ĕz)	122-23	29°59′N	93°52′W
Necker Island, i., Hi., U.S.	127	23°35′N	164°42′W
Necochea, Arg. (nā-kô-chā′ä)	173	38°34′S	58°44′W
Nederland, nation, Eur. *see* Netherlands	174-75	52°15′N	5°30′E
Nederlandse Antillen, dep., N.A. *see* Netherlands Antilles	140-41	12°15′N	68°45′W
Nêdong, China	234-35	29°13′N	91°47′E
Needles, Ca., U.S. (nē′d'lz)	118-19	34°50′N	114°36′W
Neenah, Wi., U.S. (nē′nȧ)	116-17	44°11′N	88°28′W
Neepawa, Mb., Can.	134-35	50°14′N	99°28′W
Neftçala, Azer.	227	39°24′N	49°15′E
Negage, Ang.	262-63	7°45′S	15°17′E
Negapatam, India *see* Nāgappattinam	236	10°46′N	79°51′E
Negaunee, Mi., U.S. (nē-gô′nē)	114-15	46°30′N	87°36′W
Negēlē, Eth.	262-63	5°20′N	39°35′E
Negombo, Sri L.	236	7°13′N	79°51′E
Negotin, Serb. (nĕ′gô-tēn)	200-01	44°13′N	22°33′E
Negra, Punta, c., Peru	170	6°05′S	81°06′W
Negritos, Peru	170	4°40′S	81°17′W
Negro, stm., Arg.	171	41°02′S	62°47′W
Negro, stm., S.A. (nā′grô)	164-65	3°08′S	59°55′W
Negro, stm., S.A. (nā′grô)	173	33°26′S	58°27′W
Negros, i., Phil. (nā′grōs)	250	10°0′N	123°00′E
Nehbandān, Iran	232-33	31°32′N	60°02′E
Neiba, Dom. Rep. (nȧ-ē′bä)	142-43	18°29′N	71°25′W
Neijiang, China (nā-jyäŋ)	238-39	29°35′N	105°03′E
Neillsville, Wi., U.S. (nēlz′vĭl)	114-15	44°34′N	90°35′W
Nei Mongol, state, China	240-41	43°0′N	115°00′E
Neiqiu, China (nā-chyō)	240-41	37°17′N	114°30′E
Neira, Col. (nā′rä)	163c	5°09′N	75°31′W
Neisse, stm., Eur. (nēs)	194-95	52°04′N	14°46′E
Neiva, Col. (nā-ē′vä)(nā′vä)	164-65	2°56′N	75°17′W
Nejd, hist. reg., Sau. Ar. *see* Najd	266	26°07′N	44°40′E
Nek'emtē, Eth.	262-63	9°02′N	36°29′E
Nekoosa, Wi., U.S. (nē-ko͞o′sȧ)	116-17	44°18′N	89°54′W
Nelidovo, Russia	202-03	56°13′N	32°47′E
Neligh, Ne., U.S. (nē′-lē)	114-15	42°08′N	98°02′W
Nellore, India (nĕl-lōr′)	236	14°27′N	79°59′E

Feature (Pronunciation)	Page	Lat.	Long.
Nelson, B.C., Can. (nĕl′sŭn)	132-33	49°29′N	117°18′W
Nelson, N.Z. (nĕl′sŭn)	278	41°18′S	173°15′E
Nelson, stm., Mb., Can. (nĕl′sŭn)	130-31	57°08′N	92°21′W
Nelson, Cape, c., Austl. (kāp nĕl′sŭn)	276	38°25′S	141°32′E
Nelspruit, S. Afr.	264-65	25°28′S	30°59′E
Neman, Russia (ŋĕ′-mȧn)	192-93	55°02′N	22°02′E
Neman, stm., Eur. (ŋĕ′-mȧn)	192-93	55°21′N	21°16′E
Nĕman, stm., Eur.	192-93	55°21′N	21°16′E
Nemunas, stm., Eur.	192-93	55°21′N	21°16′E
Nemuro, Japan (nā′mō-rō)	244	43°20′N	145°35′E
Nen, stm., China (nŭn)	240-41	45°26′N	124°39′E
Nenagh, Ire. (nē′nȧ)	190-91	52°52′N	8°12′W
Nendo, i., Sol. Is.	272-73	10°45′S	165°54′E
Neosho, Mo., U.S. (nē-ō′shō)	120-21	36°52′N	94°23′W
Neosho, stm., U.S. (nē-ō′shō)	120-21	35°48′N	95°18′W
Nepal, nation, Asia (nĕ-pôl′)	206-07	28°0′N	84°00′E
Nepāl, nation, Asia *see* Nepal	206-07	28°0′N	84°00′E
Nepālgañj, Nepal	234-35	28°04′N	81°37′E
Nephi, Ut., U.S. (nē′fī)	118-19	39°43′N	111°50′W
Nercha, stm., Russia	218-19	51°56′N	116°39′E
Nerchinsk, Russia (nyĕr′ chĕnsk)	222-23	51°59′N	116°35′E
Nerekhta, Russia (nyĕ-rĕĸ′tȧ)	202-03	57°28′N	40°34′E
Nerja, Spain (nĕr′hä)	198-99	36°45′N	3°52′W
Neskaupstaður, Ice.	190a	65°09′N	13°42′W
Ness, Loch, lk., Scot., U.K. (lŏĸ nĕs)	190-91	57°17′N	4°29′W
Ness City, Ks., U.S. (nĕs sĭ′tē)	120-21	38°27′N	99°54′W
Nesterov, Russia (nyĕs-tā′rôf)	192-93	54°38′N	22°35′E
Netanya, Isr.	228-29	32°21′N	34°52′E
Netherlands, nation, Eur. (nĕdh′ēr-lăndz)	174-75	52°15′N	5°30′E
Netherlands Antilles, dep., N.A. (nĕdh′ēr-lăndz ăn-tĭ′lēz)	140-41	12°15′N	68°45′W
Netherlands Guiana, nation, S.A. *see* Suriname	158	4°0′N	56°00′W
Nettuno, Italy (nĕt-tōō′nō)	200-01	41°28′N	12°39′E
Neubrandenburg, Ger. (noi-brän′dĕn-bòrgh)	194-95	53°33′N	13°15′E
Neudamm, Pol. *see* Dębno	194-95	52°44′N	14°43′E
Neufchâtel-en-Bray, Fr. (nû-shä-tĕl′ĕɴ-brā′)	196-97	49°44′N	1°27′E
Neumarkt, Rom. *see* Târgu Mureș	194-95	46°33′N	24°34′E
Neumünster, Ger. (noi′münstēr)	194-95	54°04′N	9°59′E
Neunkirchen, Aus. (noin′kĭrĸ-ĕn)	194-95	47°44′N	16°06′E
Neuquén, Arg. (nĕ-ò-kān′)	171	38°57′S	68°04′W
Neuquén, state, Arg. (nĕ-ò-kān′)	171	39°0′S	70°00′W
Neuquén, stm., Arg. (nĕ-ò-kān′)	171	38°59′S	68°00′W
Neuruppin, Ger. (noi′rōō-pēn)	194-95	52°55′N	12°49′E
Neusatz, Serb. *see* Novi Sad	200-01	45°15′N	19°50′E
Neuse, stm., N.C., U.S. (nūz)	124-25	35°09′N	76°31′W
Neustrelitz, Ger. (noi-strā′lĭts)	194-95	53°22′N	13°04′E
Neuwied, Ger. (noi′vēdt)	194-95	50°26′N	7°28′E
Nevada, Ia., U.S. (nē-vä′dȧ)	114-15	42°02′N	93°27′W
Nevada, Mo., U.S. (nē-vä′dȧ)	120-21	37°51′N	94°21′W
Nevada, state, U.S. (nē-vȧ′dȧ)	108-09	39°0′N	117°00′W
Nevada, Sierra, mts., Spain (syĕr′rä nā-vä′dhä)	198-99	37°05′N	3°10′W
Nevada, Sierra, mts., Ca., U.S. (sē-ĕ′r-rä nē-vä′dȧ)	118-19	38°0′N	119°15′W
Nevado, Cerro, mtn., Arg.	171	35°34′S	68°28′W
Nevado, Cerro, mtn., Col. (sĕ′r-rō-nē-vä′dō)	163c	3°59′N	74°04′W
Nevel′, Russia (nyĕ′vĕl)	192-93	56°01′N	29°56′E
Nevel′sk, Russia	244	46°40′N	141°52′E
Nevers, Fr. (nē-vâr′)	196-97	46°60′N	3°09′E
Nevinnomyssk, Russia	186-87	44°38′N	41°56′E
Nevis, i., St. K./N. (nē′vĭs)	143b	17°10′N	62°34′W
Nevis, Ben, mtn., Scot., U.K. (bĕn nē′vĭs)	190-91	56°48′N	5°01′W
Nevşehir, Tur. (nĕv-shĕ′hĕr)	186-87	38°37′N	34°43′E
New, stm., U.S. (nū)	110-11	38°09′N	81°12′W
New Albany, In., U.S. (nū ôl′bȧ-nĭ)	116-17	38°17′N	85°50′W
New Albany, Ms., U.S. (nū ôl′bȧ-nĭ)	124-25	34°30′N	89°01′W
New Amsterdam, Guy. (nū ăm′stēr-dăm)	164-65	6°15′N	57°30′W
Newark, De., U.S. (nōō′ärk)	116-17	39°41′N	75°45′W
Newark, N.J., U.S.	116-17	40°43′N	74°10′W
Newark, N.Y., U.S. (nū′ērk)	116-17	43°03′N	77°05′W
Newark, Oh., U.S. (nōō′ûrk)	116-17	40°03′N	82°24′W
Newaygo, Mi., U.S. (nū′wā-go)	116-17	43°25′N	85°48′W
New Bedford, Ma., U.S. (nū bĕd′fērd)	116-17	41°38′N	70°56′W
Newberg, Or., U.S. (nū′bûrg)	112-13	45°18′N	122°58′W
New Bern, N.C., U.S. (nū bûrn)	124-25	35°06′N	77°04′W
Newberry, Mi., U.S. (nū′bĕr-ĭ)	114-15	46°22′N	85°28′W
Newberry, S.C., U.S. (nū′bĕr-ĭ)	124-25	34°17′N	81°37′W
New Boston, Oh., U.S. (nū bôs′tŭn)	116-17	38°45′N	82°56′W
New Boston, Tx., U.S. (nū bôs′tŭn)	120-21	33°28′N	94°25′W
New Braunfels, Tx., U.S. (nū broun′fĕls)	122-23	29°42′N	98°07′W
New Britain, Ct., U.S. (nū brĭt′′n)	116-17	41°40′N	72°46′W
New Britain, i., Pap. N. Gui. (nū brĭt′′n)	277	6°0′S	150°00′E
New Brunswick, state, Can. (nū brŭnz′wĭk)	128-29	46°30′N	66°15′W
Newburgh, N.Y., U.S.	116-17	41°30′N	74°02′W
Newbury, Eng., U.K. (nū′bēr-ĭ)	190-91	51°24′N	1°19′W
Newburyport, Ma., U.S. (nū′bēr-ĭ-pōrt)	116-17	42°48′N	70°52′W
New Caledonia, dep., Oc. (nū kăl-ē-dō′nĭ-ȧ)	279g	21°30′S	165°30′E
New Caledonia, i., N. Cal. (nū kăl-ē-dō′nĭ-ȧ) *see* Nouvelle-Calédonie	279g	21°33′S	165°42′E
New Carlisle, Qc., Can. (nū kär-līl′)	138-39	48°01′N	65°21′W
Newcastle, Austl. (nū-kȧs′′l)	276	32°56′S	151°45′E
Newcastle, S. Afr.	269c	27°46′S	29°55′E
New Castle, De., U.S. (nū kȧs′′l)	116-17	39°40′N	75°33′W
New Castle, In., U.S. (nū kȧs′′l)	116-17	39°55′N	85°22′W
Newcastle, Ok., U.S. (nū-kȧs′′l)	120-21	35°14′N	97°36′W
New Castle, Pa., U.S.	116-17	40°60′N	80°21′W
Newcastle, Wy., U.S. (nū-kȧs′′l)	114-15	43°51′N	104°13′W
Newcastle upon Tyne, Eng., U.K.	190-91	54°59′N	1°40′W
New Delhi, nat. cap., India (nū dĕl′hī)	234-35	28°36′N	77°13′E
Newell, S.D., U.S. (nū′ĕl)	114-15	44°43′N	103°25′W
New England Range, mts., Austl. (nū ĭŋ′glănd rānj)	276	29°52′S	151°44′E
Newenham, Cape, c., Ak., U.S. (kāp ū-ĕn-hăm)	126	58°39′N	162°10′W
Newfoundland, i., Nf., Can. (nū-fĭn′lănd′) (nū′fŭnd-lănd) (nū′found-lănd′)	138-39	48°30′N	56°00′W
Newfoundland and Labrador, state, Can.	128-29	52°0′N	56°00′W
New Georgia, i., Sol. Is. (nū ôr′jĭ-ȧ)	279e	8°09′S	157°26′E
New Glasgow, N.S., Can. (nū glȧs′gō)	138-39	45°36′N	62°38′W
New Guinea, i., (nū gĭne)	277	5°0′S	140°00′E
New Hampshire, state, U.S. (nū hămp′shĭr)	108-09	43°35′N	71°40′W
New Hampton, Ia., U.S. (nū hămp′tŭn)	114-15	43°03′N	92°19′W
New Hanover, S. Afr. (nū hăn′ôvēr)	269c	29°21′S	30°31′E
New Hanover, i., Pap. N. Gui. (nū hăn′ôvēr)	277	2°30′S	150°15′E
New Harmony, In., U.S. (nū här′mō-nĭ)	116-17	38°08′N	87°56′W
New Haven, Ct., U.S. (nū hā′vĕn)	116-17	41°19′N	72°56′W
New Haven, In., U.S. (nū hāv′′n)	116-17	41°04′N	85°02′W
New Hazelton, B.C., Can.	132-33	55°15′N	127°35′W
New Hebrides, nation, Oc. *see* Vanuatu	279g	16°0′S	167°00′E
New Hebrides, is., Vanuatu (nū hĕ′brĭ-dēz)	279g	16°0′S	167°00′E
New Iberia, La., U.S. (nū jĭ-bē′rĭ-ȧ)	124-25	30°00′N	91°49′W
New Jersey, state, U.S. (nū jûr′zĭ)	108-09	40°15′N	74°30′W
Newkirk, Ok., U.S. (nū′kûrk)	120-21	36°53′N	97°03′W
New Kowloon, China *see* Xinjiulong	238-39	22°21′N	114°10′E
New Lexington, Oh., U.S. (nū lĕk′sĭng-tŭn)	116-17	39°42′N	82°13′W
New Lisbon, Wi., U.S. (nū lĭz′bŭn)	116-17	43°52′N	90°10′W
New Liskeard, On., Can.	136-37	47°31′N	79°40′W
New London, Ct., U.S. (nū lŭn′dŭn)	116-17	41°21′N	72°07′W
New London, Wi., U.S. (nū lŭn′dŭn)	116-17	44°23′N	88°44′W
New Madrid, Mo., U.S. (nū măd′rĭd)	124-25	36°35′N	89°32′W
Newmarket, On., Can. (nū′mär-kĕt)	136-37	44°03′N	79°27′W
New Martinsville, W.V., U.S. (nū mär′tĭnz-vĭl)	116-17	39°38′N	80°52′W
New Mexico, state, U.S. (nū mĕk′sĭ-kō)	108-09	34°30′N	106°00′W
Newnan, Ga., U.S. (nū′năn)	124-25	33°23′N	84°48′W
New Norfolk, Austl. (nū nôr′fŏk)	276	42°47′S	147°03′E
New Orleans, La., U.S. (nū ôr′lănz)	124-25	29°59′N	90°05′W
New Philadelphia, Oh., U.S. (nū fĭl-ȧ-dĕl′fĭ-ȧ)	116-17	40°30′N	81°27′W
New Plymouth, N.Z. (nū plĭm′ŭth)	278	39°04′S	174°05′E
Newport, Eng., U.K. (nū-pôrt)	190-91	50°42′N	1°18′W
Newport, Wales, U.K. (nū-pôrt)	190-91	51°35′N	3°00′W
Newport, Ar., U.S. (nū′pōrt)	124-25	35°37′N	91°17′W
Newport, In., U.S. (nū′pōrt)	116-17	39°53′N	87°25′W
Newport, Or., U.S. (nū′pōrt)	112-13	44°39′N	124°03′W
Newport, R.I., U.S. (nū′pōrt)	116-17	41°29′N	71°19′W
Newport, Tn., U.S. (nū′pōrt)	124-25	35°58′N	83°11′W
Newport, Wa., U.S. (nū′pōrt)	112-13	48°11′N	117°07′W
Newport News, Va., U.S. (nū′pōrt nūz)	124-25	36°59′N	76°25′W
New Providence, i., Bah. (nū prŏv′ĭ-dĕns)	142-43	25°02′N	77°24′W
New Richmond, Wi., U.S. (nū rĭch′mŭnd)	114-15	45°07′N	92°32′W
New Roads, La., U.S. (nū rōds)	124-25	30°42′N	91°27′W
New Rochelle, N.Y., U.S. (nū rū-shĕl′)	116-17	40°54′N	73°49′W
New Rockford, N.D., U.S. (nū rŏk′fērd)	114-15	47°41′N	99°09′W
New Siberian Islands, is., Russia (nū sī-bĭr′y′n ī′lăndz)	218-19	75°0′N	142°00′E
New Smyrna Beach, Fl., U.S. (nū smûr′nȧ bēch)	124-25	29°02′N	80°56′W
New South Wales, state, Austl. (nū south wālz)	276	33°0′S	146°00′E
Newton, Ia., U.S. (nū′tŭn)	114-15	41°42′N	93°03′W
Newton, Il., U.S. (nū′tŭn)	116-17	38°59′N	88°10′W
Newton, Ks., U.S. (nū′tŭn)	120-21	38°03′N	97°21′W
Newton, Ma., U.S. (nū′tŭn)	116-17	42°20′N	71°13′W
Newton, Ms., U.S. (nū′tŭn)	124-25	32°20′N	89°10′W
Newton, N.C., U.S. (nū′tŭn)	124-25	35°40′N	81°13′W
Newton, Tx., U.S. (nū′tŭn)	122-23	30°50′N	93°46′W
New Ulm, Mn., U.S. (nū ŭlm)	114-15	44°19′N	94°28′W
New Waterford, N.S., Can. (nū wô′tēr-fērd)	138-39	46°15′N	60°06′W
New York, N.Y., U.S. (nū yôrk)	116-17	40°43′N	74°01′W
New York, state, U.S. (nū yôrk)	108-09	43°0′N	75°00′W
New Zealand, nation, Oc. (nū zē′lȧnd)	278	41°0′S	174°00′E
Neyshābūr, Iran	232-33	36°11′N	58°52′E
Nezahualcóyotl, Presa, res., Mex.	146-47	17°10′N	93°40′W
Nez Perce Indian Reservation, ind. res., Id., U.S. (nĕz′ pûrs′ ĭn′dĭ-ăn rĕ-sēr-vā′shĕn)	112-13	46°20′N	116°30′W
Ngami, Lake, lk., Bots. (lăk n′gä′mē)	264-65	20°29′S	22°46′E
Ngangla Ringco, lk., China (ŋäŋ-lä rĭŋ-tswo)	234-35	31°34′N	83°01′E
Ngaoundéré, Camrn.	260-61	7°19′N	13°35′E
Ng′iro, Ewaso, stm., Kenya	262-63	0°28′N	39°55′E
Ngoring Hu, lk., China	240-41	34°53′N	97°41′E
Ngorongoro Conservation Area, pk., Tan.	267	3°0′S	35°30′E
Ngozi, Bdi.	267	2°54′S	29°53′E
Nguigmi, Niger (′n-gĕg′mē)	258-59	14°15′N	13°07′E
Nguna, Île, i., Vanuatu	279g	17°27′S	168°21′E
Nguru, Nig. (′n-gōō′rōō)	260-61	12°52′N	10°27′E
Nhamundá, stm., Braz.	166-67	1°58′S	56°58′W
Nha Trang, Viet. (nyä-träng′)	246-47	12°16′N	109°12′E
Ni′ihau, i., Hi., U.S. (nē′ē-ha′ōō)	127a	21°54′N	160°09′W
Niagara, Wi., U.S. (nī-ăg′ȧ-rȧ)	116-17	45°46′N	88°01′W
Niagara Falls, On., Can. (nī-ăg′ȧ-rȧ fôlz)	136-37	43°05′N	79°02′W
Niah, Malay.	248-49	3°52′N	113°43′E
Niamey, nat. cap., Niger (nē-ä-mā′)	258-59	13°31′N	2°07′E
Niangara, D.R.C. (nē-ăn-gȧ′rȧ)	267	3°42′N	27°54′E
Nias, Pulau, i., Indon. (pōō-lou nē′äs′)	246-47	1°05′N	97°35′E
Niassa, Lago, lk., Afr. *see* Nyasa, Lake	264-65	12°0′S	34°30′E
Nicaragua, nation, N.A. (nĭk-ȧ-rä′gwȧ)	85	13°0′N	85°00′W
Nicaragua, Lago de, lk., Nic. (lä′gô dĕ-nĭk-ȧ-rä′gwȧ)	149	11°39′N	85°26′W
Nicaragua, Lake, lk., Nic. (lāk nĭk-ȧ-rä′gwȧ) *see* Nicaragua, Lago de	149	11°39′N	85°26′W
Nice, Fr. (nēs)	196-97	43°43′N	7°16′E
Nichinan, Japan	245	31°36′N	131°23′E
Nicholas Channel, strt., N.A. (nĭk′ō-lȧs chăn′ĕl)	142-43	23°21′N	80°21′W
Nicholasville, Ky., U.S. (nĭk′ō-lȧs-vĭl)	116-17	37°53′N	84°35′W
Nicobar Islands, is., India (nĭk-ō-bär′ ī′lăndz)	246-47	8°0′N	93°30′E
Nicomedia, Tur. *see* İzmit	200-01	40°47′N	29°57′E
Nicosia, nat. cap., Cyp. (nē-kō-sē′ȧ)	228-29	35°10′N	33°22′E
Nicosia, nat. cap., Cyp. (nē-kô-zē′ă)	228-29	35°10′N	33°22′E
Nicoya, C.R. (nē-kō′yä)	149	10°09′N	85°27′W
Nicoya, Golfo de, b., C.R. (gôl-fô dĕ nē-kō′yä)	149	9°47′N	84°48′W
Nicoya, Península de, pen., C.R.	149	10°01′N	85°25′W
Nictheroy, Braz. *see* Niterói	172	22°54′S	43°07′W
Nidzica, Pol. (nē-jēt′sȧ)	194-95	53°22′N	20°26′E
Nienburg, Ger. (nē′ĕn-bòrgh)	194-95	52°38′N	9°13′E
Nieuw Nickerie, Sur. (nē′ū nē-nē′kĕ-rē′)	164-65	5°56′N	56°60′W
Niğde, Tur. (nĭg′dĕ)	186-87	37°60′N	34°44′E
Nigel, S. Afr. (nī′jĕl)	269c	26°26′S	28°28′E
Niger, nation, Afr. (nī′jēr)	253	16°0′N	8°00′E
Niger, stm., Afr. (nī′jēr) (nē-zhâr′)	260-61	4°17′N	6°04′E
Nigeria, nation, Afr. (nī-jē′rĭ-ȧ)	253	10°0′N	8°00′E
Nihoa, i., Hi., U.S.	127	23°03′N	161°56′W

ăt; finăl; rāte; senāte; ärm; ȧsk; sofȧ; fâre; ch-choose; dh-as th in other; bē; ēvent; bĕt; recĕnt; cratēr; g-gō; gh-guttural g; bĭt; ĭ-short neutral; rīde; ĸ-guttural k as ch in German ich;

Feature (Pronunciation)	Page	Lat.	Long.
Nihon, nation, Asia *see* Japan	206-07	36°0'N	138°00'E
Nihon-kai, s., Asia *see* Japan, Sea of	222-23	40°0'N	135°00'E
Niigata, Japan (nē'ē-gä'tá)	245	37°55'N	139°04'E
Nii-jima, i., Japan (nē jē'mȧ)	245	34°22'N	139°16'E
Nijmegen, Neth. (nī'mā-gĕn)	190-91	51°50'N	5°50'E
Nikel', Russia	184-85	69°25'N	30°15'E
Nikkō, Japan	245	36°45'N	139°37'E
Nikolayev, Ukr. *see* Mykolaïv	202-03	46°58'N	31°59'E
Nikolayevsk-na-Amure, Russia	218-19	53°09'N	140°44'E
Nikol'sk, Russia (nē-kôlsk')	186-87	53°42'N	46°05'E
Nikol'sk, Russia (nē-kôlsk')	186-87	59°32'N	45°27'E
Nikopol', Ukr.	202-03	47°34'N	34°24'E
Nikumaroro, at., Kir.	280-81	4°40'S	174°32'W
Nikunau, i., Kir.	280-81	1°22'S	176°27'E
Nīl, Bahr el-, stm., Afr. *see* Nile	266	30°10'N	31°07'E
Nīl, Nahr an-, stm., Afr. *see* Nile	266	30°10'N	31°07'E
Nile, stm., Afr. (nīl)	266	30°10'N	31°07'E
Niles, Mi., U.S. (nīlz)	116-17	41°50'N	86°15'W
Niles, Oh., U.S. (nīlz)	116-17	41°11'N	80°44'W
Nimba, Mont, mtn., Afr. (môn nĭm'bȧ)	260-61	7°37'N	8°25'W
Nimba, Mount, mtn., Afr. *see* Nimba, Mont	260-61	7°37'N	8°25'W
Nîmes, Fr. (nēm)	196-97	43°51'N	4°22'E
Nine Degree Channel, strt., India	236	9°0'N	73°00'E
Ninety Mile Beach, cst., Austl.	276	38°13'S	147°23'E
Ning'an, China (nĭŋ-än)	244	44°20'N	129°28'E
Ningbo, China (nĭŋ-bwo)	238-39	29°53'N	121°32'E
Ningcheng, China	240-41	41°33'N	119°20'E
Ningde, China (nĭŋ-dŭ)	238-39	26°43'N	119°33'E
Ningdu, China	238-39	26°31'N	115°58'E
Ningming, China	238-39	22°08'N	107°05'E
Ningshan, China	238-39	33°19'N	108°19'E
Ningsia Hui, state, China *see* Ningxia	240-41	37°0'N	106°00'E
Ningwu, China (nĭng'wōō')	240-41	39°03'N	112°12'E
Ningxia, state, China (nĭŋ-shyä)	240-41	37°0'N	106°00'E
Ninh Binh, Viet. (nēn bĕnk')	246-47	20°15'N	105°59'E
Ninigo Group, is., Pap. N. Gui.	224-25	1°15'S	144°15'E
Ninnescah, stm., Ks., U.S. (nĭn'ĕs-kä)	120-21	37°20'N	97°10'W
Nioaque, Braz. (nēô-á'-kĕ)	168-69	21°09'S	55°50'W
Niobrara, stm., U.S. (nī-ô-brâr'ȧ)	110-11	42°46'N	98°03'W
Nioki, D.R.C.	262-63	2°39'S	17°42'E
Nioro, Mali	258-59	15°14'N	9°35'W
Nipawin, Sk., Can.	134-35	53°22'N	104°00'W
Nipe, Bahía de, b., Cuba (bä-ē'ä-dĕ-nē'pā)	142-43	20°47'N	75°42'W
Nipigon, On., Can. (nĭp'ĭ-gŏn)	136-37	49°01'N	88°15'W
Nipigon, Lake, res., On., Can. (lăk nĭp'ĭ-gŏn)	134-35	49°40'N	88°34'W
Nipigon Bay, b., On., Can. (nĭp'ĭ-gŏn bā)	136-37	48°54'N	87°56'W
Nipissing, Lake, lk., On., Can. (lăk nĭp'ĭ-sĭng)	136-37	46°15'N	79°42'W
Niquero, Cuba (nē-kā'rō)	142-43	20°03'N	77°35'W
Niš, Serb.	200-01	43°19'N	21°54'E
Nisa, Port. (nē'sȧ)	198-99	39°30'N	7°39'W
Nish, Serb. *see* Niš	200-01	43°19'N	21°54'E
Nishapur, Iran *see* Neyshābūr	232-33	36°11'N	58°52'E
Nisser, lk., Nor. (nĭs'ĕr)	192-93	59°10'N	8°30'E
Nistru, stm., Eur. *see* Dniester	188-89	46°19'N	30°17'E
Niterói, Braz. (nē-tĕ-rô'ĭ)	172	22°54'S	43°07'W
Nitra, Slvk. (nē'trá)	194-95	48°19'N	18°06'E
Nitro, W.V., U.S. (nī'trō)	116-17	38°25'N	81°51'W
Niue, dep., Oc. (nĭ'ò)	280-81	19°02'S	169°52'W
Niulakita, i., Tuvalu	280-81	10°45'S	179°30'E
Niut, Gunung, mtn., Indon.	248-49	1°0'N	109°55'E
Niutao, i., Tuvalu	280-81	6°07'S	177°19'E
Nixon, Tx., U.S. (nĭk'sŭn)	122-23	29°16'N	97°46'W
Nizāmābād, India	236	18°40'N	78°06'E
Nizhnekamsk, Russia	186-87	55°33'N	51°58'E
Nizhnekamskoye Vodokhranilishche, res., Russia	186-87	55°50'N	53°00'E
Nizhneudinsk, Russia (nēzh'nyĭ-ōōdēnsk')	218-19	54°54'N	99°02'E
Nizhnevartovsk, Russia	218-19	60°56'N	76°34'E
Nizhniy Novgorod, Russia	186-87	56°19'N	44°01'E
Nizhniy Tagil, Russia (nyēzh'-nyē tŭgēl')	218-19	57°55'N	59°59'E
Nizhnyaya Tunguska, stm., Russia	218-19	65°46'N	87°54'E
Nizhyn, Ukr.	202-03	51°02'N	31°54'E
Njazidja, i., Com.	264-65	11°35'S	43°20'E
Njombe, stm., Tan.	267	6°56'S	35°06'E
Nkawkaw, Ghana	260-61	6°33'N	0°47'W
Nkongsamba, Camrn.	260-61	4°57'N	9°56'E
Nmai, stm., Mya.	238-39	25°43'N	97°31'E
Noākhāli, Bngl.	234-35	22°49'N	91°06'E
Noatak, stm., Ak., U.S. (nō-á'ták)	126	67°00'N	162°30'W
Nobeoka, Japan (nō-bå-ō'kȧ)	245	32°35'N	131°41'E
Noblesville, In., U.S. (nō'bl'z-vĭl)	116-17	40°02'N	86°00'W
Nochistlán, Mex. (nô-chēs-tlän')	146-47	21°22'N	102°51'W
Nogales, Mex. (nō-gä'lĕs)	144-45	31°19'N	110°56'W
Nogales, Az., U.S. (nô-gä'lĕs)	118-19	31°21'N	110°56'W
Nogent-le-Rotrou, Fr. (nō-zhôɴ-lē-rō-trōō')	196-97	48°19'N	0°49'E
Noginsk, Russia (nô-gēnsk')	202-03	55°52'N	38°28'E
Nogoyá, Arg.	173	32°24'S	59°48'W
Noir, Isla, i., Chile	171	54°29'S	73°01'W
Noirmoutier, Île de, i., Fr. (ēl-dē-nwȧr-mōō-tyā')	196-97	47°0'N	2°15'W
Nokomis, Il., U.S. (nô-kō'mĭs)	116-17	39°18'N	89°17'W
Nolinsk, Russia (nô-lēnsk')	186-87	57°33'N	49°57'E
Nombre de Dios, Mex. (nôm-brĕ-dĕ-dyô's)	146-47	23°50'N	104°14'W
Nombre de Dios, Pan. (nô'm-brĕ dĕ-dyô's)	150	9°35'N	79°28'W
Nome, Ak., U.S. (nōm)	126	64°30'N	165°24'W
Nonacho Lake, lk., N.T., Can.	130-31	61°42'N	109°40'W
Nondalton, Ak., U.S.	126	60°01'N	154°49'W
Nong'an, China (nôŋ-än)	240-41	44°26'N	125°11'E
Nong Khai, Thai.	246-47	17°52'N	102°45'E
Nonouti, at., Kir.	280-81	0°38'S	174°26'E
Noord Zee, s., Eur. *see* North Sea	184-85	56°0'N	3°00'E
Noorvik, Ak., U.S.	126	66°53'N	160°59'W
Nootka Island, i., B.C., Can. (nōōt'kȧ ī'lȧnd)	132-33	49°44'N	126°46'W
Nordegg, Ab., Can. (nûr'dĕg)	132-33	52°28'N	116°05'W
Norderney, i., Ger. (nōr'dĕr-nĕy)	194-95	53°43'N	7°11'E
Nordhausen, Ger. (nôrt'hau-zĕn)	194-95	51°30'N	10°48'E
Nordhorn, Ger. (nôrt'hōrn)	194-95	52°26'N	7°04'E
Nordkapp, c., Nor.	184-85	71°10'N	25°47'E
Nord-Ostsee-Kanal, can., Ger. (nōrd-ōzt-zā kä-näl') *see* Kiel Canal	194-95	53°54'N	9°10'E
Nordsee, s., Eur. *see* North Sea	184-85	56°0'N	3°00'E
Nordsjøen, s., Eur. *see* North Sea	184-85	56°0'N	3°00'E
Norfolk, Ne., U.S. (nôr'fŏk)	114-15	42°02'N	97°25'W
Norfolk, Va., U.S. (nôr'fŏk)	124-25	36°51'N	76°16'W
Norfolk Island, dep., Oc. (nôr-fŭk ī'lȧnd)	280-81	29°02'S	167°57'E
Norge, nation, Eur. *see* Norway	174-75	62°0'N	10°00'E
Noril'sk, Russia (nô rēlsk')	218-19	69°19'N	88°14'E
Norin, stm., Asia *see* Naryn	226	41°46'N	73°13'E
Normal, Il., U.S. (nôr'mȧl)	116-17	40°30'N	88°59'W
Norman, Ok., U.S.	120-21	35°13'N	97°26'W
Norman, stm., Austl. (nôr'mȧn)	277	17°28'S	140°50'E
Normanby Island, i., Pap. N. Gui.	277	10°05'S	151°05'E
Normandie, hist. reg., Fr. (nŏr-mäɴ-dē') *see* Normandy	196-97	49°0'N	0°05'W
Normandy, hist. reg., Fr. (nŏr-män-dē')	196-97	49°0'N	0°05'W
Normanton, Austl. (nôr'mȧn-tŭn)	277	17°40'S	141°05'E
Norman Wells, N.T., Can.	128-29	65°17'N	126°42'W
Ñorquinco, Arg.	171	41°51'S	70°55'W
Norristown, Pa., U.S. (nŏr'ĭs-toun)	116-17	40°07'N	75°21'W
Norrköping, Swe. (nôr'chûp'ĭng)	192-93	58°36'N	16°11'E
Norrtälje, Swe. (nôr-tĕl'yĕ)	192-93	59°46'N	18°44'E
Norseman, Austl. (nôrs'mȧn)	270-71	32°12'S	121°48'E
Norskehavet, s., Eur. *see* Norwegian Sea	184-85	70°0'N	2°00'E
Norte, Serra do, plat., Braz. (sĕ'r-rä-dô-nôr'te)	166-67	11°20'S	59°00'W
North, Cape, c., N.S., Can.	138-39	47°02'N	60°24'W
North Adams, Ma., U.S. (nôrth ăd'ămz)	116-17	42°42'N	73°07'W
Northam, Austl. (nôr-dhăm)	270-71	31°39'S	116°40'E
Northam, S. Afr. (nôr'thăm)	269c	25°03'S	27°11'E
North America, cont., (nôrth ȧ-mĕr'ĭ-kȧ)	20-21	45°0'N	100°00'W
Northampton, Austl. (nôr-thămp'tŭn)	270-71	28°21'S	114°38'E
Northampton, Eng., U.K. (nôrth-ămp'tŭn)	190-91	52°15'N	0°54'W
North Andaman, i., India (nôrth ăn-dȧ-măn')	246-47	13°15'N	92°55'E
North Battleford, Sk., Can. (nôrth ăt'l-fērd)	134-35	52°46'N	108°16'W
North Bay, On., Can.	136-37	46°19'N	79°26'W
North Bend, Or., U.S. (nôrth bĕnd)	112-13	43°24'N	124°13'W
North Caicos, i., T./C. Is. (nôrth kī'kôs)	142-43	21°56'N	71°59'W
North Cape, c., N.Z. (nôrth kāp)	278	34°24'S	173°02'E
North Caribou Lake, lk., On., Can.	134-35	52°50'N	90°40'W
North Carolina, state, U.S. (nôrth kăr-ô-lī'nȧ)	108-09	35°30'N	80°00'W
North Cascades National Park, n.p., Wa., U.S.	112-13	48°30'N	121°00'W
North Channel, strt., On., Can.	136-37	46°02'N	82°50'W
North Channel, strt., U.K.	190-91	55°10'N	5°40'W
North Charleston, S.C., U.S. (nôrth chärlz'tŭn)	124-25	32°53'N	79°60'W
North Chicago, Il., U.S. (nôrth shī-kô'gō)	116-17	42°18'N	87°52'W
North Dakota, state, U.S. (nôrth dȧ-kō'tȧ)	108-09	47°30'N	100°15'W
Northeast Providence Channel, strt., Bah. (nôr-thēst' prŏv'ĭ-dĕns chăn'ĕl)	142-43	25°40'N	77°09'W
Northeim, Ger. (nôrt'hīm)	194-95	51°42'N	10°00'E
Northern Cook Islands, is., Cook Is.	280-81	10°0'S	161°00'W
Northern Donets, stm., Eur. (nôr'thērn dŏn-ĕts')	186-87	47°36'N	40°54'E
Northern Indian Lake, lk., Mb., Can.	130-31	57°21'N	97°19'W
Northern Ireland, state, U.K. (nôr'thērn īr'lănd)	190-91	54°40'N	6°45'W
Northern Mariana Islands, dep., Oc. (nôr'thērn mä-rē-ä'nȧ ī'lȧndz)	280-81	16°0'N	149°00'E
Northern Sporades, is., Grc. *see* Vóreioi Sporades	200-01	39°15'N	23°55'E
Northern Territory, state, Austl.	270-71	20°0'S	134°00'E
Northfield, Mn., U.S. (nôrth'fēld)	114-15	44°28'N	93°10'W
North Island, i., N.Z. (nôrth ī'lȧnd)	278	39°0'S	176°00'E
North Judson, In., U.S. (nôrth jŭd'sŭn)	116-17	41°13'N	86°46'W
North Korea, nation, Asia (nôrth kō-rē'-ȧ)	206-07	40°0'N	127°00'E
North Lakhimpur, India	234-35	27°14'N	94°07'E
North Little Rock, Ar., U.S. (nôrth lĭt''l rŏk)	120-21	34°46'N	92°18'W
North Magnetic Pole, p.o.i.	288	81°18'N	110°48'W
North Manchester, In., U.S. (nôrth măn'chĕs-tēr)	116-17	40°60'N	85°46'W
North Ogden, Ut., U.S. (nôrth ŏg'dĕn)	112-13	41°19'N	111°58'W
North Ossetia, state, Russia	227	43°0'N	44°15'E
North Platte, Ne., U.S. (nôrth plăt)	114-15	41°08'N	100°45'W
North Platte, stm., U.S. (nôrth plăt)	110-11	41°07'N	100°42'W
Northport, Al., U.S. (nôrth'pōrt)	124-25	33°14'N	87°34'W
North Saskatchewan, stm., Can. (nôrth săn-kăch'ē-wăn)	130-31	53°14'N	105°05'W
North Sea, s., Eur. (nôrth sē)	184-85	56°0'N	3°00'E
North Shore City, N.Z.	278	36°48'S	174°47'E
North Siberian Lowland, pl., Russia (nôrth sī-bĭr'y'n lō'lȧnd) *see* Severo-Sibirskaya Nizmennost'	218-19	73°0'N	100°00'E
North Sydney, N.S., Can. (nôrth sĭd'nē)	138-39	46°13'N	60°16'W
North Thompson, stm., B.C., Can.	132-33	50°41'N	120°20'W
North Tonawanda, N.Y., U.S. (nôrth tŏn-ȧ-wŏn'dȧ)	116-17	43°02'N	78°52'W
Northumberland Strait, strt., Can. (nôr thŭm'bēr-lȧnd strāt)	138-39	46°0'N	63°30'W
North Vancouver, B.C., Can. (nôrth văn-kōō'vēr)	132-33	49°19'N	123°04'W
North Vernon, In., U.S. (nôrth vûr'nŭn)	116-17	39°00'N	85°38'W
North West Cape, c., Austl. (nôrth wĕst kāp)	272-73	21°48'S	114°10'E
Northwest Providence Channel, strt., Bah. (nôrth-wĕst' prŏv'ĭ-dĕns chăn'ĕl)	142-43	26°10'N	78°20'W
Northwest Territories, state, Can. (nôrth'wĕst tĕr'ĭ-tō'rĭs)	128-29	65°0'N	120°00'W
North Wilkesboro, N.C., U.S. (nôrth wĭlks'bûrô)	124-25	36°11'N	81°09'W
Northwood, Ia., U.S. (nôrth'wŏd)	114-15	43°27'N	93°13'W
Northwood, N.D., U.S. (nôrth'wŏd)	114-15	47°44'N	97°34'W
Norton, Ks., U.S. (nôr'tŭn)	120-21	39°50'N	99°53'W
Norton, Va., U.S. (nôr'tŭn)	124-25	36°56'N	82°38'W
Norton Sound, strt., Ak., U.S. (nôr'tŭn sound)	126	63°50'N	164°00'W
Norvegia, Cape, c., Ant.	287	71°25'S	12°18'W
Norwalk, Ct., U.S. (nôr'wôk)	116-17	41°07'N	73°25'W
Norwalk, Oh., U.S. (nôr'wôk)	116-17	41°15'N	82°36'W
Norway, Me., U.S. (nôr'wā)	116-17	44°13'N	70°32'W
Norway, nation, Eur. (nôr'wā)	174-75	62°0'N	10°00'E
Norway House, Mb., Can. (nôr'wā hous)	134-35	53°59'N	97°48'W
Norwegian Sea, s., Eur. (nôr-wē'jăn sē sē)	184-85	70°0'N	2°00'E
Norwich, Eng., U.K.	190-91	52°38'N	1°17'E
Norwich, Ct., U.S. (nôr'wĭch)	116-17	41°32'N	72°05'W
Norwood, Ma., U.S. (nôr'wŏŏd)	116-17	42°11'N	71°12'W
Norwood, Oh., U.S. (nôr'wŏŏd)	116-17	39°10'N	84°27'W
Noshiro, Japan (nō'shē-rō)	244	40°12'N	140°02'E

n-sing; ŋ-baŋk; ɴ-nasalized n; nŏd; cŏmmit; ōld; ôbey; ôrder; oi-boil; fōōd; ŏ-as oo in foot; ou-out; s-soft; sh-dish; th-thin; pūre; ûnite; ûrn; stŭd; circŭs; ü-as in French tu; '-indeterminate vowel.

Feature (Pronunciation)	Page	Lat.	Long.
Nosivka, Ukr. (nô´sôf-kȧ)	202-03	50°56'N	31°36'E
Nosop, stm., Afr.	264-65	26°53'S	20°41'E
Nossob, stm., Afr. (nŏ´sŏb)	264-65	26°53'S	20°41'E
Nosy-Varika, Madag.	264-65	20°35'S	48°32'E
Noteć, stm., Pol. (nô´tĕcn)	194-95	52°44'N	15°25'E
Notodden, Nor. (nōt´ôd'n)	192-93	59°34'N	9°16'E
Noto-hantō, pen., Japan	245	37°20'N	137°00'E
Notozero, Ozero, lk., Russia	186-87	66°28'N	32°05'E
Notre-Dame, Monts, mts., Qc., Can.	138-39	48°10'N	68°00'W
Notre Dame Bay, b., Nf., Can. (nō´t'r dȧm´ bā)	138-39	49°46'N	55°15'W
Nottawasaga Bay, b., On., Can. (nŏt´ȧ-wȧ-sä´gȧ bā)	136-37	44°35'N	80°15'W
Nottingham, Eng., U.K. (nŏt´ĭng-ăm)	190-91	52°57'N	1°07'W
Nottingham Island, i., Nu., Can.	130-31	63°20'N	77°55'W
Nouâdhibou, Maur.	258-59	20°55'N	17°02'W
Nouâdhibou, Râs, c., Afr.	258-59	20°47'N	17°03'W
Nouakchott, nat. cap., Maur. (nü-äk´-shôt)	258-59	18°06'N	15°58'W
Nouméa, nat. cap., N. Cal. (nōō-mā´ä)	279g	22°17'S	166°27'E
Nouvelle, Qc., Can. (nōō-vĕl´)	138-39	48°08'N	66°19'W
Nouvelle-Calédonie, dep., Oc. *see* New Caledonia	279g	21°30'S	165°30'E
Nouvelle-Calédonie, i., N. Cal.	279g	21°33'S	165°42'E
Nouvelle-France, Cap de, c., Qc., Can.	130-31	62°27'N	73°42'W
Nouvelles-Hébrides, nation, Oc. *see* Vanuatu	279g	16°0'S	167°00'E
Nouvelles-Hébrides, is., Vanuatu *see* New Hebrides	279g	16°0'S	167°00'E
Nova Freixo, Moz. *see* Cuamba	264-65	14°47'S	36°32'E
Nova Friburgo, Braz. (nō´vȧ frē-bōōr´gō)	172	22°16'S	42°32'W
Nova Goa, India *see* Panaji	236	15°30'N	73°50'E
Nova Iguaçu, Braz. (nō´vä-ē-gwä-sōō´)	172	22°45'S	43°27'W
Nova Kakhovka, Ukr.	202-03	46°45'N	33°25'E
Nova Lima, Braz. (nō´vȧ lē´mä)	172	19°60'S	43°51'W
Nova Lisboa, Ang. *see* Huambo	264-65	12°46'S	15°44'E
Novara, Italy (nō-vä´rä)	200-01	45°27'N	8°37'E
Nova Scotia, state, Can. (nō´vȧ skō´shȧ)	128-29	45°0'N	63°00'W
Novaya Ladoga, Russia (nô´vȧ-ya lȧ-dô-gȧ)	192-93	60°05'N	32°15'E
Novaya Sibir', Ostrov, i., Russia (ôs-trôf´ nô´vȧ-ya sê-bēr´)	218-19	75°0'N	149°00'E
Novaya Zemlya, is., Russia (nô´vȧ-ya zĕm-lyȧ´)	218-19	74°0'N	57°00'E
Nova Zagora, Blg. (nô´vä zä´gô-rȧ)	200-01	42°30'N	26°01'E
Novelda, Spain (nō-vĕl´dȧ)	198-99	38°23'N	0°46'W
Nové Zámky, Slvk. (nô´vě zäm´kě)	194-95	47°60'N	18°11'E
Novgorod, Russia (nôv´gô-rŏt)	192-93	58°32'N	31°18'E
Novi Pazar, Blg. (nō´vĭ pä-zär´)	200-01	43°21'N	27°12'E
Novi Pazar, Serb. (nō´vĭ pȧ-zär´)	200-01	43°08'N	20°31'E
Novi Sad, Serb. (nō´vĭ säd´)	200-01	45°15'N	19°50'E
Novoanninskiy, Russia	186-87	50°32'N	42°41'E
Novo Aripuanã, Braz.	166-67	5°08'S	60°21'W
Novocherkassk, Russia (nô´vô-chĕr-kȧsk´)	186-87	47°25'N	40°06'E
Novodvinsk, Russia	186-87	64°25'N	40°49'E
Novohrad-Volyns'kyi, Ukr.	194-95	50°36'N	27°38'E
Novokuybyshevsk, Russia	186-87	53°06'N	49°56'E
Novokuznetsk, Russia (nô´vô-kŏ´z-nyĕ´tsk)	226	53°45'N	87°07'E
Novo Mesto, Slvn. (nôvô măs´tô)	200-01	45°48'N	15°10'E
Novomoskovsk, Russia (nô´vô-môs-kôfsk´)	202-03	54°05'N	38°13'E
Novomoskovs'k, Ukr. (nô´vô-kŏ´z-nyĕ´tsk)	202-03	48°38'N	35°12'E
Novorossiysk, Russia (nô´vô-rô-sēsk´)	202-03	44°43'N	37°46'E
Novorzhev, Russia (nô´vô-rzhĕv´)	192-93	57°02'N	29°20'E
Novoshakhtinsk, Russia	202-03	47°48'N	39°54'E
Novosibirsk, Russia (nô´vô-sê-bērsk´)	218-19	55°01'N	82°53'E
Novosibirskiye Ostrova, is., Russia *see* New Siberian Islands	218-19	75°0'N	142°00'E
Novosibirskoye Vodokhranilishche, res., Russia	226	54°35'N	82°35'E
Novosil', Russia (nô´vô-sĭl)	202-03	52°58'N	37°03'E
Novosokol'niki, Russia (nô´vô-sô-kôl´nē-kē)	192-93	56°21'N	30°10'E
Novouzensk, Russia (nô-vô-ô-zĕnsk´)	186-87	50°29'N	48°10'E
Novovolyns'k, Ukr.	194-95	50°44'N	24°08'E
Novozybkov, Russia (nô´vô-zĕp´kôf)	202-03	52°32'N	31°56'E
Nový Jičín, Czech Rep. (nô´vē yē´chĕn)	194-95	49°36'N	18°01'E
Novyy Oskol, Russia (nô´vē ôs-kôl´)	202-03	50°46'N	37°53'E
Novyy Uzen, Kaz. *see* Zhangaözen	186-87	43°19'N	52°47'E
Nowata, Ok., U.S. (nô-wä´tȧ)	120-21	36°42'N	95°38'W
Nowra, Austl. (nou´rȧ)	276	34°53'S	150°36'E
Nowshera, Pak.	232-33	34°01'N	71°59'E
Nowy Dwór Mazowiecki, Pol. (nō´vĭ dvōōr mä-zo-vyĕts´ke)	194-95	52°26'N	20°43'E
Nowy Targ, Pol. (nō´vē tärk´)	194-95	49°28'N	20°03'E
Noxubee, stm., U.S. (nŏks´û-bē)	124-25	32°50'N	88°10'W
Nsanje, Malawi	264-65	16°58'S	35°12'E
Nsukka, Nig.	260a	6°51'N	7°24'E
Ntem, stm., Afr.	260-61	2°20'N	9°50'E
Ntomba, Lac, lk., D.R.C.	262-63	0°48'S	18°03'E
Nu, stm., Asia (nōō) *see* Salween	208-09	16°33'N	97°40'E
Nubian Desert, des., Sudan (nōō´bĭ-ăn dĕs´ērt)	266	20°30'N	33°00'E
Nueces, stm., Tx., U.S. (nů-ā´sȧs)	122-23	27°50'N	97°22'W
Nueltin Lake, lk., Can. (nwĕl´tin lāk)	130-31	60°19'N	99°40'W
Nueva, Isla, i., Chile	171	55°14'S	66°32'W
Nueva Gerona, Cuba (nwä´vä κĕ-rō´nä)	142-43	21°53'N	82°48'W
Nueva Imperial, Chile	171	38°44'S	72°57'W
Nueva Palmira, Ur. (nwä´vä päl-mē´rä)	173	33°52'S	58°23'W
Nueva Rosita, Mex. (nòĕ´vä rô-sĕ´tä)	122-23	27°57'N	101°13'W
Nueva Toltén, Chile	171	39°12'S	73°13'W
Nueve de Julio, Arg. (nwā´vå dā hōō´lyô)	173	35°27'S	60°53'W
Nuevitas, Cuba (nwä-vē´täs)	142-43	21°33'N	77°16'W
Nuevo, Cayo, i., Mex.	146-47	21°51'N	92°06'W
Nuevo, Golfo, b., Arg.	171	42°42'S	64°36'W
Nuevo Casas Grandes, Mex.	144-45	30°25'N	107°55'W
Nuevo Laredo, Mex. (nwā´vô lä-rā´dhō)	122-23	27°28'N	99°31'W
Nuevo León, state, Mex. (nwā´vô lå-ōn´)	122-23	25°40'N	100°00'W
Nuguria Islands, is., Pap. N. Gui.	277	3°21'S	154°41'E
Nui, at., Tuvalu	280-81	7°15'S	177°10'E
Nukha, Azer. *see* Şeki	227	41°10'N	47°10'E
Nuku'alofa, nat. cap., Tonga (nōō´-kōō-ä-lō´-fȧ)	280-81	21°08'S	175°13'W
Nukuoro, at., Micron.	280-81	3°51'N	154°58'E
Nukus, Uzb.	226	42°28'N	59°36'E
Nullarbor Plain, pl., Austl. (nŭ-lär´bôr plān)	272-73	31°0'S	129°00'E
Numara, i., Mald.	236	6°25'N	73°04'E
Numazu, Japan (nōō´mä-zōō)	245	35°06'N	138°52'E
Numedalslågen, stm., Nor. *see* Lågen	192-93	59°02'N	10°04'E
Numfoor, Pulau, i., Indon.	224-25	1°03'S	134°54'E
Nunavut, state, Can.	128-29	70°0'N	95°00'W
Nunivak Island, i., Ak., U.S. (nōō´nĭ-văk ī´lȧnd)	126	60°00'N	166°29'W
Nunjiang, China	240-41	49°10'N	125°14'E
Nuomin, stm., China	240-41	48°13'N	124°31'E
Nuoro, Italy (nwô´rō)	200-01	40°20'N	9°20'E
Nūra, stm., Kaz.	226	50°22'N	69°15'E
Nuremberg, Ger. *see* Nürnberg	194-95	49°27'N	11°04'E
Nürnberg, Ger. (nürn´bĕrgh)	194-95	49°27'N	11°04'E
Nushagak, stm., Ak., U.S. (nū-shă-găk´)	126	59°03'N	158°24'W
Nu Shan, mts., China	238-39	27°0'N	99°00'E
Nushki, Pak. (nŭsh´kē)	232-33	29°35'N	66°04'E
Nuuk, nat. cap., Green. *see* Godthåb	284-85	64°11'N	51°44'W
Nuweveldberge, mts., S. Afr.	264-65	32°14'S	21°48'E
Nyahururu Falls, Kenya	267	0°02'N	36°22'E
Nyainqêntanglha Shan, mts., China (nyä-ĭn-chyŭn-täŋ-lä shän)	234-35	30°0'N	90°00'E
Nyala, Sudan	266	12°03'N	24°54'E
Nyandoma, Russia	186-87	61°40'N	40°13'E
Nyanza, Rw.	267	2°21'S	29°45'E
Nyasa, Lake, lk., Afr. (lăk nyä´sȧ)	264-65	12°0'S	34°30'E
Nyasaland, nation, Afr. *see* Malawi	253	13°30'S	34°00'E
Nyborg, Den. (nü´bôr'')	192-93	55°19'N	10°47'E
Nybro, Swe. (nü´brô)	192-93	56°45'N	15°55'E
Nyeri, Kenya	267	0°25'S	36°57'E
Nyíregyháza, Hung. (nyē´rĕd-y'hä´zä)	194-95	47°57'N	21°43'E
Nyköping, Swe. (nü´chû-pĭng)	192-93	58°45'N	16°60'E
Nylstroom, S. Afr. (nĭl´strōm) *see* Modimolle	269c	24°42'S	28°25'E
Nynäshamn, Swe. (nü-nĕs-häm'n)	192-93	58°55'N	17°57'E
Nyngan, Austl. (nĭŋ´gȧn)	276	31°33'S	147°10'E
Nyong, stm., Camrn. (nyông)	260-61	3°16'N	9°55'E
Nysa Łużycka, stm., Eur. *see* Neisse	194-95	52°04'N	14°46'E
Nyslott, Fin. *see* Savonlinna	192-93	61°52'N	28°54'E
Nytva, Russia	186-87	57°56'N	55°20'E
Nyunzu, D.R.C.	267	5°58'S	28°02'E
Nyurba, Russia	218-19	63°17'N	118°20'E
Nyuvchim, Russia	186-87	61°23'N	50°36'E
Nyuya, stm., Russia (nyōō´yȧ)	218-19	60°32'N	116°18'E
Nzérékoré, Gui.	260-61	7°45'N	8°49'W
Nzwani, i., Com. (än-zhwän)	264-65	12°15'S	44°25'E

O

Feature (Pronunciation)	Page	Lat.	Long.
O'ahu, i., Hi., U.S. (ō-ä´hōō) (ō-ä´hü)	127a	21°30'N	158°00'W
Oahe, Lake, res., U.S.	114-15	45°29'N	100°20'W
Oak Bay, B.C., Can. (ōk bā)	132-33	48°27'N	123°18'W
Oak Creek, Wi., U.S. (ōk krēk´)	116-17	42°52'N	87°54'W
Oakdale, La., U.S. (ōk´dāl)	122-23	30°49'N	92°40'W
Oakes, N.D., U.S. (ōks)	114-15	46°08'N	98°06'W
Oak Grove, Ky., U.S. (ōk grōv)	124-25	36°40'N	87°26'W
Oak Harbor, Wa., U.S. (ōk här´bēr)	112-13	48°18'N	122°40'W
Oakland, Ca., U.S. (ōk´lănd)	118-19	37°48'N	122°17'W
Oakland, Md., U.S. (ōk´lănd)	116-17	39°24'N	79°24'W
Oakland, Ne., U.S. (ōk´lănd)	114-15	41°50'N	96°28'W
Oak Lawn, Il., U.S. (ōk lôn)	116-17	41°43'N	87°45'W
Oakley, Ks., U.S. (ōk´lĭ)	120-21	39°08'N	100°51'W
Oak Ridge, Tn., U.S. (ōk rĭj)	124-25	36°01'N	84°15'W
Oakville, On., Can. (ōk´vĭl)	136-37	43°27'N	79°40'W
Oakville, Mo., U.S. (ōk´vĭl)	120-21	38°28'N	90°19'W
Oaxaca, state, Mex. (wä-hä´kä)	146-47	17°0'N	96°30'W
Oaxaca de Juárez, Mex.	146-47	17°03'N	96°43'W
Ob', stm., Russia (ôb)	218-19	66°47'N	68°56'E
Oban, Scot., U.K. (ō´băn)	190-91	56°25'N	5°28'W
Oberlin, Ks., U.S. (o´bēr-lĭn)	120-21	39°49'N	100°32'W
Oberlin, Oh., U.S. (o´bēr-lĭn)	116-17	41°17'N	82°13'W
Obi, Kepulauan, is., Indon. (ō´bē)	248-49	1°27'S	127°38'E
Obi, Pulau, i., Indon.	248-49	1°30'S	127°45'E
Óbidos, Braz. (ō´bē-dōzh)	166-67	1°54'S	55°31'W
Obihiro, Japan (ō´bē-hē´rō)	244	42°55'N	143°12'E
Obluchye, Russia	240-41	49°01'N	131°04'E
Obninsk, Russia	202-03	55°06'N	36°37'E
Oboyan, Russia (ô-bô-yän´)	202-03	51°13'N	36°17'E
Observatoire, Caye de l', i., N. Cal.	272-73	21°25'S	158°50'E
Obsgchiy Syrt, mts., Eur. *see* Zhalpy Syrt	186-87	52°0'N	51°30'E
Obskaya Guba, b., Russia	218-19	69°0'N	73°00'E
Obuasi, Ghana	260-61	6°13'N	1°41'W
Ocala, Fl., U.S. (ô-kä´lȧ)	124-25	29°11'N	82°08'W
Ocampo, Mex. (ô-käm´pō)	144-45	28°11'N	108°23'W
Ocaña, Col. (ō-kän´yä)	164-65	8°14'N	73°21'W
Ocaña, Spain (ô-kä´n-yä)	198-99	39°57'N	3°30'W
Occidental, Cordillera, mts., Col.	164-65	5°0'N	76°00'W
Ocean City, Md., U.S. (ō´shăn sĭ´tē)	116-17	38°20'N	75°05'W
Ocean City, N.J., U.S. (ō´shăn sĭ´tē)	116-17	39°17'N	74°35'W
Ocean Falls, B.C., Can. (ō´shăn fôlz)	132-33	52°21'N	127°41'W
Ocean Grove, N.J., U.S. (ō´shăn grōv)	116-17	40°13'N	74°00'W
Ocean Island, i., Kir. *see* Banaba	280-81	0°52'S	169°33'E
Oceanside, Ca., U.S. (ō´shăn-sīd)	118-19	33°12'N	117°22'W
Ocean Springs, Ms., U.S. (ō´shăn sprĭngs sprĭngz)	124-25	30°26'N	88°50'W
Ochlockonee, stm., U.S. (ŏk-lô-kō´nē)	124-25	29°59'N	84°26'W
Ocilla, Ga., U.S. (ô-sĭl´ȧ)	124-25	31°36'N	83°15'W
Ockelbo, Swe. (ôk´ĕl-bô)	192-93	60°54'N	16°44'E
Ocmulgee National Monument, n.p., Ga., U.S. (ôk-mŭl´gē năsh´ŭn-ăl mŏn´ŭ-mĕnt)	124-25	32°43'N	83°38'W
Oconee, stm., Ga., U.S. (ô-kō´nē)	124-25	31°58'N	82°32'W
Oconomowoc, Wi., U.S. (ô-kŏn´ô-mô-wŏk´)	116-17	43°06'N	88°29'W
Oconto, Wi., U.S. (ô-kŏn´tō)	116-17	44°54'N	87°52'W
Oconto Falls, Wi., U.S. (ô-kŏn´tō fôlz)	116-17	44°52'N	88°08'W
Ocosingo, Mex.	148	16°55'N	92°06'W
Ocotal, Nic. (ō-kō-täl´)	149	13°38'N	86°28'W
Ocotlán, Mex. (ō-kō-tlän´)	146-47	20°21'N	102°47'W
Ocotlán de Morelos, Mex. (ō-kō-tlän´ dā mō-rā´lōs)	146-47	16°47'N	96°40'W
Ocracoke Island, i., N.C., U.S.	124-25	35°06'N	75°59'W
October Revolution Island, i., Russia *see* Oktyabr'skoy Revolyutsii, Ostrov	218-19	79°30'N	96°60'E
Ocumare del Tuy, Ven. (ō-kōō-mä´rä del twē´)	163b	10°07'N	66°46'W
Oda, Jabal, mtn., Sudan	266	20°21'N	36°39'E
Odda, Nor. (ôdh-ȧ)	192-93	60°04'N	6°32'E
Odemira, Port. (ō-dȧ-mē´rȧ)	198-99	37°35'N	8°38'W
Ödemiş, Tur. (û´dĕ-mēsh)	200-01	38°14'N	27°59'E
Odendaalsrus, S. Afr. (ō´dĕn-däls-rûs´)	269c	27°52'S	26°42'E
Odense, Den. (ō´dhĕn-sĕ)	192-93	55°24'N	10°23'E
Oder, stm., Eur. (ō´dēr)	194-95	53°55'N	14°17'E
Odesa, Ukr.	202-03	46°29'N	30°42'E
Odessa, De., U.S. (ô-dĕs´ȧ)	116-17	39°27'N	75°40'W
Odessa, Tx., U.S. (ô-dĕs´ȧ)	122-23	31°51'N	102°22'W
Odin, Mount, mtn., B.C., Can.	132-33	50°33'N	118°08'W
Odintsovo, Russia (ô-dĕn´tsô-vô)	202-03	55°40'N	37°16'E
Odra, stm., Eur. (ô´drȧ) *see* Oder	194-95	53°55'N	14°17'E
Odrzywół, Pol.	194-95	51°32'N	20°33'E
Oeiras, Braz. (wå-ê-räzh´)	166-67	7°01'S	42°08'W
Oelwein, Ia., U.S. (ōl´wīn)	114-15	42°40'N	91°55'W

ăt; finăl; rāte; senâte; ärm; åsk; sofȧ; fâre; ch-choose; dh-as th in other; bē; ēvent; bĕt; recĕnt; cratẽr; g-gō; gh-guttural g; bĭt; ĭ-short neutral; rīde; κ-guttural k as ch in German ich;

Feature (Pronunciation)	Page	Lat.	Long.
Oeno Atoll, at., Pit.	280-81	23°55'S	130°44'W
O'Fallon, Mo., U.S. (ō-făl'ŭn)	120-21	38°49'N	90°42'W
Offenburg, Ger. (ôf'ĕn-bòrgh)	194-95	48°28'N	7°57'E
Ofu, i., Am. Sam.	279b	14°10'S	169°40'W
Ogaadeen, reg., Afr. see Ogaden	262-63	8°0'N	44°00'E
Ogaden, reg., Afr. (ō-gä'dĕn)	262-63	8°0'N	44°00'E
Ogallala, Ne., U.S. (ō-gä-lä'lä)	114-15	41°08'N	101°43'W
Ogasawara-guntō, is., Japan see Bonin Islands	282-83	26°58'N	142°14'E
Ogasawara-shotō, is., Japan	280-81	26°0'N	142°00'E
Ogbomosho, Nig. (ŏg-bō-mō'shō)	260a	8°08'N	4°15'E
Ogden, Ia., U.S. (ŏg'dĕn)	114-15	42°03'N	94°02'W
Ogden, Ut., U.S. (ŏg'dĕn)	112-13	41°14'N	111°57'W
Ogdensburg, N.Y., U.S. (ŏg'dĕnz-bûrg)	116-17	44°42'N	75°30'W
Ogea Levu, i., Fiji	279f	19°08'S	178°24'W
Ogeechee, stm., Ga., U.S. (ō-gē'chē)	124-25	31°51'N	81°05'W
Ogilvie Mountains, mts., Yk., Can. (ō'g'l-vĭ moun'tĭnz)	130-31	65°03'N	139°29'W
Ogooué, stm., Afr.	260-61	0°49'S	9°00'E
Ogulin, Cro. (ō-gōō-lēn')	200-01	45°16'N	15°14'E
Ogurja Ada, i., Turkmen.	226	38°57'N	53°03'E
O'Higgins, Lago, lk., S.A.	171	48°53'S	72°39'W
Ohio, state, U.S. (ō'hī'ō)	108-09	40°15'N	82°45'W
Ohio, stm., U.S. (ō'hī'ō)	110-11	36°59'N	89°09'W
Ohlau, Pol. see Oława	194-95	50°56'N	17°19'E
Ohōtuku-kai, s., Asia see Okhotsk, Sea of	218-19	53°0'N	150°00'E
Ohrid, Mac. (ō'krēd)	200-01	41°07'N	20°49'E
Oiapoque, Braz.	164-65	3°51'N	51°49'W
Oiapoque, stm., S.A.	164-65	4°10'N	51°37'W
Oil City, Pa., U.S. (oil sĭ'tĭ sĭ'tē)	116-17	41°26'N	79°42'W
Ōita, Japan (ō'ē-tä)	245	33°14'N	131°37'E
Ojinaga, Mex. (ō-kē-nä'gä)	122-23	29°33'N	104°25'W
Ojocaliente, Mex. (ō-kô-kä-lyĕ'n-tĕ)	146-47	22°33'N	102°13'W
Ojos del Salado, Cerro, mtn., S.A. see Ojos del Salado, Nevado	168-69	27°06'S	68°32'W
Ojos del Salado, Nevado, mtn., S.A.	168-69	27°06'S	68°32'W
Oka, stm., Russia (ô-kä')	218-19	55°16'N	102°18'E
Oka, stm., Russia (ô-kä')	186-87	56°20'N	43°59'E
Okahandja, Nmb.	264-65	21°58'S	16°54'E
Okanagan, stm., N.A. (ō'kȧ-näg'ăn) see Okanogan	132-33	48°06'N	119°44'W
Okanagan Lake, lk., B.C., Can. (ō'kȧ-näg'ăn lāk)	132-33	49°55'N	119°31'W
Okanogan, stm., N.A.	132-33	48°06'N	119°44'W
Okāra, Pak.	232-33	30°48'N	73°27'E
Okavango, stm., Afr. (ō-kȧ-vän'gō)	264-65	18°57'S	22°25'E
Okavango Delta, del., Bots.	264-65	19°29'S	22°32'E
Okavango Swamp, del., Bots. see Okavango Delta	264-65	19°29'S	22°32'E
Okaya, Japan (ō'kȧ-yȧ)	245	36°04'N	138°03'E
Okayama, Japan (ō'kȧ-yä'mȧ)	245	34°40'N	133°55'E
Okazaki, Japan (ō'kȧ-zä'kē)	245	34°57'N	137°10'E
Okeechobee, Fl., U.S. (ō-kē-chō'bē)	125a	27°15'N	80°50'W
Okeechobee, Lake, lk., Fl., U.S. (lāk ō-kē-chō'bē)	125a	26°55'N	80°45'W
Okefenokee Swamp, sw., U.S. (ō'kē-fē-nō'kē swŏmp)	124-25	30°42'N	82°20'W
Okemah, Ok., U.S. (ō-kē'mä)	120-21	35°26'N	96°18'W
Okene, Nig.	260a	7°29'N	6°15'E
Okha, Russia (ŭ-kä')	218-19	53°35'N	142°57'E
Okhota, stm., Russia	218-19	59°20'N	143°04'E
Okhotsk, Russia (ô-kôtsk')	218-19	59°22'N	143°18'E
Okhotsk, Sea of, s., Asia (sē ŭv ô-kôtsk')	218-19	53°0'N	150°00'E
Okhotskoye More, s., Asia see Okhotsk, Sea of	218-19	53°0'N	150°00'E
Okhtyrka, Ukr.	202-03	50°18'N	34°54'E
Okinawa-jima, i., Japan	244a	26°32'N	127°60'E
Okino-Daitō-jima, i., Japan	222-23	24°28'N	131°11'E
Okino-Tori-shima, i., Japan	222-23	20°27'N	136°04'E
Oki-shotō, is., Japan	245	36°11'N	133°11'E
Oklahoma, state, U.S. (ō-klȧ-hō'mȧ)	108-09	35°30'N	98°00'W
Oklahoma City, Ok., U.S. (ō-klȧ-hō'mȧ sĭ'tĭ)	120-21	35°29'N	97°29'W
Okmulgee, Ok., U.S. (ōk-mŭl'gē)	120-21	35°36'N	95°58'W
Okolona, Ms., U.S. (ō-kō-lō'nȧ)	124-25	33°60'N	88°45'W
Okotoks, Ab., Can.	132-33	50°44'N	113°59'W
Oktyabr'sk, Kaz.	226	49°28'N	57°25'E
Oktyabrskiy, Russia	186-87	54°29'N	53°29'E
Oktyabr'skiy, Russia	218-19	52°41'N	156°13'E
Oktyabr'skoy Revolyutsii, Ostrov, i., Russia	218-19	79°30'N	96°60'E
Okushiri-tō, i., Japan (ō'koo-shē'rē tō)	244	42°10'N	139°27'E
Ola, Russia	218-19	59°37'N	151°20'E
Olanchito, Hond. (ō'län-chē'tō)	149	15°29'N	86°34'W
Öland, i., Swe. (û-länd')	192-93	56°45'N	16°38'E
Olary, Austl.	276	32°17'S	140°19'E
Olathe, Ks., U.S. (ō-lā'thē)	120-21	38°53'N	94°49'W
Olavarría, Arg. (ō-lä-vär-rē'ä)	173	36°54'S	60°19'W
Oława, Pol. (ô-lä'vä)	194-95	50°56'N	17°19'E
Olbia, Italy (ô'l-byä)	200-01	40°56'N	9°30'E
Old Bahama Channel, strt., N.A. (ōld bȧ-hā'mȧ chăn'ĕl)	142-43	22°40'N	78°41'W
Old Crow, Yk., Can. (ōld crō)	128-29	67°36'N	139°49'W
Oldenburg, Ger. (ôl'dĕn-bòrgh)	194-95	53°09'N	8°13'E
Old Forge, Pa., U.S. (ōld fôrj)	116-17	41°22'N	75°44'W
Olds, Ab., Can. (ōldz)	132-33	51°47'N	114°05'W
Old Wives Lake, lk., Sk., Can. (ōld wīvz lāk)	134-35	50°06'N	106°00'W
Olean, N.Y., U.S. (ō-lē-ăn')	116-17	42°05'N	78°26'W
Olekma, stm., Russia (ô-lyĕk-mȧ')	218-19	60°23'N	120°41'E
Olëkminsk, Russia (ô-lyĕk-mēnsk')	218-19	60°22'N	120°26'E
Oleksandriia, Ukr.	202-03	48°40'N	33°07'E
Olenegorsk, Russia	184-85	68°09'N	33°14'E
Olenëk, stm., Russia (ô-lyĕ-nyôk')	208-09	73°00'N	119°45'E
Olga, Russia (ôl'gȧ)	244	43°44'N	135°17'E
Ölgiy, Mong.	222-23	48°58'N	89°58'E
Olhão, Port. (ôl-youN')	198-99	37°02'N	7°51'W
Ólimbos, mtn., Cyp.	228-29	34°56'N	32°51'E
Olímpia, Braz.	172	20°44'S	48°55'W
Olinda, Braz. (ô-lē'n-dä)	163d	8°01'S	34°51'W
Oliva, Arg.	173	32°03'S	63°34'W
Oliva, Spain (ô-lē'vä)	198-99	38°55'N	0°07'W
Olive Hill, Ky., U.S. (ŏl'ĭv hĭl)	116-17	38°18'N	83°11'W
Oliveira, Braz. (ô-lē-vā'rä)	172	20°42'S	44°49'W
Oliver, B.C., Can. (ŏ'lĭ-vẽr)	132-33	49°11'N	119°33'W
Olivia, Mn., U.S. (ō-lĭv'ē-ȧ)	114-15	44°47'N	94°59'W
Ollagüe, Chile (ô-lyä'gå)	168-69	21°13'S	68°16'W
Olmaliq, Uzb.	232-33	40°51'N	69°35'E
Olmos, Peru	170	5°56'S	79°46'W
Olmütz, Czech Rep. see Olomouc	194-95	49°36'N	17°16'E
Olney, Il., U.S. (ŏl'nĭ)	116-17	38°43'N	88°06'W
Olney, Tx., U.S. (ŏl'nē)	120-21	33°22'N	98°45'W
Olomane, stm., Qc., Can. (ō'lō mȧ'nĕ)	138-39	50°14'N	60°38'W
Olomouc, Czech Rep. (ô'lô-mōts)	194-95	49°36'N	17°16'E
Olonets, Russia (ô-lô'nĕts)	192-93	60°59'N	32°59'E
Olongapo, Phil.	250	14°52'N	120°17'E
Oloron-Sainte-Marie, Fr. (ō-lō-rôNt'sănt mȧ-rē')	196-97	43°11'N	0°36'W
Olot, Spain (ô-lōt')	198-99	42°11'N	2°29'E
Olovyannaya, Russia	240-41	50°57'N	115°34'E
Olsztyn, Pol. (ôl'shtĭn)	194-95	53°47'N	20°29'E
Olt, stm., Rom.	186-87	43°43'N	24°48'E
Olten, Switz. (ôl'tĕn)	194-95	47°21'N	7°54'E
Oltenița, Rom. (ôl-tā'nĭ-tsȧ)	200-01	44°05'N	26°38'E
Olutanga Island, i., Phil.	250	7°22'N	122°52'E
Olvera, Spain (ôl-vĕ'rä)	198-99	36°56'N	5°16'W
Olympia, Wa., U.S.	112-13	47°02'N	122°53'W
Olympic Mountains, mts., Wa., U.S. (ō-lĭm'pĭk moun'tĭnz)	112-13	47°50'N	123°45'W
Olympic National Park, n.p., Wa., U.S. (ō-lĭm'pĭk năsh'ŭn-ăl pärk)	112-13	47°51'N	123°44'W
Ólympos, mtn., Grc. see Olympus, Mount	200-01	40°05'N	22°21'E
Olympus, mtn., Cyp. see Ólimbos	228-29	34°56'N	32°51'E
Olympus, Mount, mtn., Grc. (mount ō-lĭm'pŭs)	200-01	40°05'N	22°21'E
Olympus, Mount, mtn., Wa., U.S. (mount ō-lĭm'pŭs)	112-13	47°48'N	123°43'W
Olyutorski, Cape, c., Russia (kāp ŭl-yōō'tôr-skē) see Olyutorskiy, Mys	218-19	59°57'N	170°22'E
Olyutorskiy, Mys, c., Russia (mĭs ŭl-yōō'tŏr-skē)	218-19	59°57'N	170°22'E
Olyutorskiy Zaliv, b., Russia	218-19	60°15'N	168°30'E
Om', stm., Russia	218-19	54°59'N	73°22'E
Omagh, N. Ire., U.K. (ō'mä)	190-91	54°36'N	7°18'W
Omaha, Ne., U.S. (ō'mȧ-hä)	114-15	41°15'N	95°56'W
Omaha Indian Reservation, ind. res., Ne., U.S. (ō'mȧ-hä ĭn'dĭ-ăn rĕ-sẽr-vā'shŭn)	114-15	42°07'N	96°32'W
Omak, Wa., U.S.	112-13	48°25'N	119°31'W
Oman, nation, Asia (ō-män')	206-07	22°0'N	58°00'E
'Omān, Daryā-ye, b., Asia see Oman, Gulf of	230-31	24°30'N	58°30'E
Oman, Gulf of, b., Asia (gŭlf ŭv ō-män')	230-31	24°30'N	58°30'E
Omaruru, Nmb. (ō-mä-rōō'rōō)	264-65	21°26'S	15°57'E
Omatako, stm., Nmb.	264-65	17°57'S	20°28'E
Omboué, Gabon	260-61	1°37'S	9°16'E
Omdurman, Sudan (ŏm-dûr-măn')	266	15°39'N	32°29'E
Ometepe, Isla de, i., Nic. (ē's-lä-dĕ-ō-mĕ-tā'pā)	149	11°30'N	85°35'W
Ometepec, Mex. (ō-mā-tå-pĕk')	146-47	16°41'N	98°24'W
Ōminato, Japan see Mutsu	244	41°17'N	141°10'E
Omineca, stm., B.C., Can. (ō-mĭ-nĕk'ȧ)	132-33	56°07'N	124°28'W
Omineca Mountains, mts., B.C., Can.	130-31	56°0'N	125°00'W
Omo, stm., Afr. (ō'mō)	262-63	4°31'N	36°03'E
Omolon, stm., Russia (ō'mō)	218-19	68°42'N	158°43'E
Omro, Wi., U.S. (ŏm'rō)	116-17	44°02'N	88°45'W
Omsk, Russia (ômsk)	226	54°57'N	73°23'E
Omsukchan, Russia	218-19	62°30'N	155°46'E
Ōmura, Japan (ō'mōō-rȧ)	245	32°55'N	129°58'E
Ōmuta, Japan (ō-mò-tȧ)	245	33°01'N	130°27'E
Omutninsk, Russia (ô'mōō-tnēnsk)	186-87	58°39'N	52°11'E
Onawa, Ia., U.S. (ŏn-ȧ-wȧ)	114-15	42°02'N	96°06'W
Onda, Spain (ōn'dä)	198-99	39°58'N	0°15'W
Ondangwa, Nmb.	264-65	17°56'S	16°00'E
Ondo, Nig.	260a	7°06'N	4°50'E
Öndörhaan, Mong.	240-41	47°20'N	110°40'E
Onega, Russia (ô-nyĕ'gȧ)	186-87	63°55'N	38°06'E
Onega, stm., Russia (ô-nyĕ'gȧ)	186-87	63°57'N	37°57'E
Onega, Lake, lk., Russia (lāk ô-nyĕ'-gȧ)	186-87	61°30'N	35°45'E
Oneida, N.Y., U.S. (ō-nī'dȧ)	116-17	43°06'N	75°39'W
O'Neill, Ne., U.S. (ō-nēl')	114-15	42°28'N	98°39'W
Onekotan, Ostrov, i., Russia	218-19	49°21'N	154°42'E
Oneonta, Al., U.S. (ō-nē-ŏn'tȧ)	124-25	33°57'N	86°28'W
Oneonta, N.Y., U.S. (ō-nē-ŏn'tȧ)	116-17	42°28'N	75°04'W
Onezhskoye Ozero, lk., Russia see Onega, Lake	186-87	61°30'N	35°45'E
Ongi, stm., Mong.	240-41	44°31'N	103°40'E
Onitsha, Nig. (ō-nĭt'shȧ)	260a	6°09'N	6°47'E
Ono-i-Lau, i., Fiji	280-81	20°39'S	178°42'W
Onomichi, Japan (ō'nō-mē'chē)	245	34°25'N	133°12'E
Onon, stm., Asia (ō'nōn)	222-23	51°42'N	115°49'E
Onoto, Ven. (ō-nŏ'tō)	163b	9°36'N	65°11'W
Onotoa, at., Kir.	280-81	1°53'S	175°34'E
Onslow, Austl. (ŏnz'lō)	270-71	21°39'S	115°07'E
Onslow Bay, b., N.C., U.S. (ŏnz'lō bā)	124-25	34°20'N	77°20'W
Ontake-san, vol., Japan (ōn'tä-kȧ-sän)	245	35°53'N	137°29'E
Ontario, Or., U.S. (ŏn-tā'rĭ-ō)	112-13	44°02'N	116°57'W
Ontario, state, Can. (ŏn-tā'rĭ-ō)	128-29	51°0'N	85°00'W
Ontario, Lake, lk., N.A. (lāk ŏn-tā'rĭ-ō)	116-17	43°45'N	78°00'W
Ontonagon, Mi., U.S. (ŏn-tō-năg'ŏn)	114-15	46°52'N	89°19'W
Ontong Java, at., Sol. Is.	279e	5°19'S	159°16'E
Onverwacht, Sur.	164-65	5°36'N	55°12'W
Oodnadatta, Austl. (ōōd'nȧ-dȧ'tȧ)	270-71	27°33'S	135°27'E
Ooldea, Austl.	270-71	30°28'S	131°51'E
Oos-Londen, S. Afr. see East London	264-65	32°60'S	27°54'E
Oostende, Bel. (ōst-ĕn'dĕ)	190-91	51°14'N	2°55'E
Opalaca, Cordillera, mts., Hond. (kôr-dēl-yĕ'rä-ō-pä-lä'kä)	149	14°30'N	88°20'W
Oparino, Russia	186-87	59°51'N	48°17'E
Opasquia, On., Can. (ō-păs'kwē-ȧ)	134-35	53°16'N	93°35'W
Opelika, Al., U.S. (ŏp-ē-lī'kȧ)	124-25	32°38'N	85°23'W
Opelousas, La., U.S. (ŏp-ē-lōō'sȧs)	124-25	30°32'N	92°05'W
Opeongo Lake, lk., On., Can. (ŏp-ē-ŏŋ'gō lāk)	136-37	45°42'N	78°24'W
Opobo, Nig.	260a	4°35'N	7°34'E
Opochka, Russia (ō-pôch'kȧ)	192-93	56°43'N	28°40'E
Opoczno, Pol. (ō-pôch'nō)	194-95	51°23'N	20°18'E
Opole, Pol. (ō-pôl'ä)	194-95	50°40'N	17°57'E
Oporto, Port. see Porto	198-99	41°09'N	8°37'W
Opp, Al., U.S. (ŏp)	124-25	31°17'N	86°15'W
Oppeln, Pol. see Opole	194-95	50°40'N	17°57'E
Opportunity, Wa., U.S. (ŏp-ŏr tū'nĭ tĭ)	112-13	47°40'N	117°13'W
Opuwo, Nmb.	264-65	18°02'S	13°41'E
Oqsuqtooq, Nu., Can. see Gjoa Haven	128-29	68°39'N	95°55'W
Oradea, Rom. (ō-räd'yä)	194-95	47°04'N	21°56'E
Orai, India	234-35	25°59'N	79°28'E
Oral, Kaz.	186-87	51°13'N	51°22'E
Oral Dengizi, lk., Asia see Aral Sea	226	45°0'N	60°00'E
Oran, Alg. (ō-rän)(ō-räN')	198-99	35°41'N	0°39'W
Orange, Austl. (ŏr'ĕnj)	276	33°18'S	149°05'E
Orange, Fr. (ō-ranzh')	196-97	44°08'N	4°49'E
Orange, Tx., U.S. (ŏr'ĕnj)	122-23	30°06'N	93°44'W
Orange, Va., U.S. (ŏr'ĕnj)	116-17	38°15'N	78°06'W
Orange, stm., Afr. (ŏr'ĕnj)	264-65	28°35'S	16°28'E
Orange, Cabo, c., Braz. (kȧ'bō-rȧ'n-zhĕ)	159	4°22'N	51°33'W
Orangeburg, S.C., U.S. (ŏr'ĕnj-bûrg)	124-25	33°30'N	80°51'W
Orange City, Ia., U.S. (ŏr'ĕnj sĭ'tē)	114-15	43°00'N	96°03'W
Orangeville, On., Can. (ŏr'ĕnj-vĭl)	136-37	43°55'N	80°05'W
Orange Walk, Belize (ŏr'ĕnj wôl'k)	148	18°06'N	88°33'W

Feature (Pronunciation)	Page	Lat.	Long.
Orani, Phil. (ō-rä′nē)	250	14°49′N	120°31′E
Oranienburg, Ger. (ō-rä′nē-ĕn-bòrgh)	194-95	52°45′N	13°15′E
Oranje, stm., Afr. *see* Orange	264-65	28°35′S	16°28′E
Oranjemund, Nmb.	264-65	28°34′S	16°28′E
Oranjestad, nat. cap., Aruba	140a	12°32′N	70°01′W
Orăștie, Rom. (ô-rûsh′tyå)	194-95	45°50′N	23°13′E
Orașul Stalin, Rom. *see* Brașov	194-95	45°39′N	25°37′E
Orbetello, Italy (ôr-bå-tĕl′lō)	200-01	42°27′N	11°13′E
Orbost, Austl. (ôr′bŭst)	276	37°42′S	148°28′E
Ord, Ne., U.S. (ôrd)	114-15	41°36′N	98°56′W
Ordu, Tur. (ôr′dò)	186-87	40°59′N	37°52′E
Ordzhonikidze, Russia *see* Vladikavkaz	227	43°03′N	44°39′E
Örebro, Swe. (û′rē-brō)	192-93	59°17′N	15°12′E
Oregon, state, U.S.	108-09	44°0′N	121°00′W
Oregon City, Or., U.S.	112-13	45°21′N	122°36′W
Orekhovo-Zuyevo, Russia (ôr-yĕ′ĸô-vô zò′yĕ-vô)	202-03	55°48′N	38°58′E
Orël, Russia	202-03	52°59′N	36°04′E
Orem, Ut., U.S. (ō′rĕm)	118-19	40°16′N	111°41′W
Orense, Spain *see* Ourense	198-99	42°20′N	7°52′W
Organ Pipe Cactus National Monument, n.p., Az., U.S. (ôr′găn pīp kăk′tŭs năsh′ŭn-ăl mŏn′ū-mĕnt)	118-19	32°0′N	112°55′W
Orhon, stm., Mong.	240-41	50°14′N	106°08′E
Oriental, Cordillera, mts., Col. (kôr-dēl-yĕ′rä ō-rē-ĕn-täl′)	164-65	6°0′N	73°00′W
Oriental, Cordillera, mts., Peru	170	11°0′S	74°00′W
Orillia, On., Can. (ô-rĭl′ĭ-à)	136-37	44°36′N	79°25′W
Orinoco, stm., S.A. (ō-rĭ-nō′kō)	164-65	8°47′N	60°40′W
Orissa, state, India (ō-rĭs′à)	234-35	20°0′N	84°00′E
Oristano, Italy (ô-rēs-tä′nō)	200-01	39°54′N	8°36′E
Oriximiná, Braz.	166-67	1°45′S	55°52′W
Orizaba, Mex. (ô-rē-zä′bä)	146-47	18°51′N	97°06′W
Orkla, stm., Nor. (ôr′klå)	184-85	63°19′N	9°51′E
Orkney, S. Afr. (ôrk′nĭ)	269c	26°59′S	26°41′E
Orkney Islands, is., Scot., U.K.	190c	59°0′N	3°00′W
Orlando, Fl., U.S. (ôr-lăn′dō)	125a	28°32′N	81°23′W
Orléans, Fr. (ôr-lā-äN′)	196-97	47°55′N	1°55′E
Orleans, In., U.S. (ôr-lēnz′)	116-17	38°40′N	86°27′W
Ormāra, Pak.	232-33	25°13′N	64°38′E
Ormoc, Phil.	250	11°01′N	124°37′E
Ormond Beach, Fl., U.S. (ôr′mŏnd bēch)	124-25	29°17′N	81°04′W
Örnsköldsvik, Swe. (ûrn′skôlts-vēk)	184-85	63°18′N	18°43′E
Orocué, Col.	164-65	4°49′N	71°20′W
Oroluk, at., Micron.	280-81	7°31′N	155°18′E
Oromocto, N.B., Can.	138-39	45°51′N	66°28′W
Orosháza, Hung. (ô-rôsh-hä′sô)	194-95	46°34′N	20°40′E
Orotukan, Russia	218-19	62°16′N	151°38′E
Oroville, Ca., U.S. (ōr′ô-vĭl)	118-19	39°31′N	121°33′W
Oroville, Wa., U.S. (ōr′ô-vĭl)	112-13	48°56′N	119°26′W
Oroville, Lake, res., Ca., U.S. (lāk ōr′ô-vĭl)	118-19	39°38′N	121°30′W
Orrville, Oh., U.S. (ôr′vĭl)	116-17	40°50′N	81°46′W
Orša, Bela.	192-93	54°31′N	30°25′E
Orsa, Swe. (ōr′sä)	192-93	61°08′N	14°37′E
Orsha, Bela. (ôr′shå) *see* Orša	192-93	54°31′N	30°25′E
Orsk, Russia (ôrsk)	226	51°12′N	58°34′E
Orșova, Rom. (ôr′shô-vä)	200-01	44°43′N	22°25′E
Ortega, Col. (ôr-tĕ′gä)	163c	3°56′N	75°13′W
Ortegal, Cabo, c., Spain (ká′bô-ôr-tå-gäl′)	198-99	43°46′N	7°54′W
Orthez, Fr. (ôr-tĕz′)	196-97	43°30′N	0°46′W
Orthon, stm., Bol.	166-67	10°49′S	66°04′W
Ortigueira, Spain (ôr-tē-gā′ē-rä)	198-99	43°41′N	7°50′W
Ortonville, Mn., U.S. (ôr-tŭn-vĭl)	114-15	45°19′N	96°27′W
Orūmīyeh, Iran	228-29	37°32′N	45°05′E
Orūmīyeh, Daryācheh-ye, lk., Iran	227	37°40′N	45°30′E
Oruro, Bol. (ô-rōō′rō)	168-69	17°58′S	67°07′W
Orust, i., Swe.	192-93	58°10′N	11°38′E
Orvieto, Italy (ôr-vyå′tō)	200-01	42°44′N	12°06′E
Orxon, stm., China	240-41	48°56′N	117°46′E
Osa, Península de, pen., C.R. (pĕ-nē′n-sōō-lä ō′sä)	149	8°34′N	83°31′W
Osage, Ia., U.S. (ō′sāj)	114-15	43°17′N	92°49′W
Osage, stm., Mo., U.S. (ō′sāj)	120-21	38°36′N	91°56′W
Ōsaka, Japan (ō′sä-kä)	245	34°41′N	135°31′E
Ōsaka-wan, b., Japan (ō′sä-kä wän)	245	34°30′N	135°18′E
Osakis, Mn., U.S. (ô-sā′kĭs)	114-15	45°52′N	95°09′W
Osceola, Ar., U.S. (ŏs-ē-ō′là)	124-25	35°43′N	89°58′W
Osceola, Ia., U.S. (ŏs-ē-ō′là)	114-15	41°02′N	93°46′W
Oscoda, Mi., U.S. (ŏs-kō′dá)	116-17	44°25′N	83°19′W
Osh, Kyrg. (ôsh)	232-33	40°32′N	72°48′E
Oshakati, Nmb.	264-65	17°47′S	15°41′E
Oshawa, On., Can. (ŏsh′á-wá)	136-37	43°54′N	78°51′W
Ō-shima, i., Japan (ō′shē′mä)	245	34°44′N	139°25′E
Oshkosh, Ne., U.S. (ŏsh′kŏsh)	114-15	41°25′N	102°21′W
Oshkosh, Wi., U.S. (ŏsh′kŏsh)	116-17	44°00′N	88°33′W
Oshogbo, Nig.	260a	7°46′N	4°33′E
Oshwe, D.R.C.	262-63	3°22′S	19°30′E
Osijek, Cro. (ôs′ĭ-yĕk)	200-01	45°33′N	18°42′E
Osipenko, Ukr. *see* Berdians'k	202-03	46°45′N	36°49′E
Oskaloosa, Ia., U.S. (ŏs-kà-lōō′sà)	114-15	41°18′N	92°39′W
Oskarshamn, Swe.	192-93	57°16′N	16°29′E
Oskarström, Swe. (ôs′kärs-strûm)	192-93	56°48′N	12°58′E
Öskemen, Kaz.	226	49°57′N	82°38′E
Oslo, nat. cap., Nor. (ŏs′lō)	192-93	59°55′N	10°45′E
Osmānābād, India	236	18°10′N	76°02′E
Osnabrück, Ger. (ôs-nä-brük′)	194-95	52°17′N	8°03′E
Osorno, Chile (ô-sō′r-nō)	171	40°35′S	73°07′W
Ossa, Mount, mtn., Austl. (mount ŏsà)	276	41°54′S	146°01′E
Osse, stm., Nig.	260a	5°55′N	5°16′E
Osseo, Wi., U.S. (ŏs′sē-ō)	114-15	44°35′N	91°14′W
Ossining, N.Y., U.S. (ŏs′ĭ-nĭng)	116-17	41°10′N	73°52′W
Ossipee, N.H., U.S. (ŏs′ĭ-pē)	116-17	43°42′N	71°07′W
Ossora, Russia	218-19	59°18′N	163°09′E
Ostashkov, Russia (ôs-täsh′kôf)	202-03	57°08′N	33°08′E
Ostende, Bel. *see* Oostende	190-91	51°14′N	2°55′E
Oster, Ukr. (ōs′tĕr)	202-03	50°57′N	30°53′E
Österreich, nation, Eur. *see* Austria	174-75	47°20′N	13°20′E
Östersjön, s., Eur. *see* Baltic Sea	192-93	57°0′N	19°00′E
Østersøen, s., Eur. *see* Baltic Sea	192-93	57°0′N	19°00′E
Östersund, Swe. (ûs′tĕr-sōōnd)	184-85	63°11′N	14°39′E
Östhammar, Swe. (ûst′häm′är)	192-93	60°15′N	18°22′E
Ostrau, Czech Rep. *see* Ostrava	194-95	49°50′N	18°17′E
Ostrava, Czech Rep.	194-95	49°50′N	18°17′E
Ostrogozhsk, Russia (ôs-tr-gôzhk′)	202-03	50°52′N	39°04′E
Ostrołęka, Pol. (ôs-trô-woN′kà)	194-95	53°05′N	21°35′E
Ostrov, Russia (ôs-trôf′)	192-93	57°21′N	28°20′E
Ostrowiec Świętokrzyski, Pol. (ôs-trō′vyĕts shvyĕN-tō-kzhĭ′ske)	194-95	50°56′N	21°24′E
Ostrów Mazowiecka, Pol. (ôs′tròf mä-zô-vyĕt′skä)	194-95	52°48′N	21°54′E
Ostrów Wielkopolski, Pol. (ôs′trōōf vyĕl-kō-pōl′skē)	194-95	51°39′N	17°48′E
Ostsee, s., Eur. *see* Baltic Sea	192-93	57°0′N	19°00′E
Ostuni, Italy (ôs-tōō′nē)	200-01	40°45′N	17°33′E
Ōsumi-shotō, is., Japan	244	30°29′N	130°39′E
Osuna, Spain (ô-sōō′nä)	198-99	37°14′N	5°06′W
Oswego, N.Y., U.S.	116-17	43°27′N	76°31′W
Otaru, Japan (ō′tå-rò)	244	43°12′N	140°60′E
Otavalo, Ec. (ōtä-vä′lō)	170	0°14′N	78°16′W
Othonoí, i., Grc.	200-01	39°51′N	19°24′E
Oti, stm., Afr.	260-61	8°30′N	0°06′E
Otjiwarongo, Nmb. (ŏt-jē-wá-rôn′gō)	264-65	20°27′S	16°38′E
Otočac, Cro. (ō′tô-cháts)	200-01	44°52′N	15°13′E
Otoskwin, stm., On., Can.	134-35	52°11′N	87°45′W
Otra, stm., Nor.	192-93	58°09′N	8°01′E
Ótranto, Italy (ô′trän-tō) (ô-trän′tō)	200-01	40°09′N	18°28′E
Otranto, Canale d', strt., Eur. *see* Otranto, Strait of	200-01	40°0′N	19°00′E
Otranto, Strait of, strt., Eur. (strāt ŭv ô′trän-tô) (ô-trän′tō)	200-01	40°0′N	19°00′E
Otsego, Mi., U.S. (ŏt-sē′gō)	116-17	42°28′N	85°41′W
Ōtsu, Japan (ō′tsò)	245	35°00′N	135°52′E
Ottawa, Il., U.S. (ŏt′á-wá)	116-17	41°21′N	88°51′W
Ottawa, Ks., U.S. (ŏt′á-wá)	120-21	38°37′N	95°16′W
Ottawa, Oh., U.S. (ŏt′á-wá)	116-17	41°01′N	84°02′W
Ottawa, nat. cap., On., Can. (ŏt′á-wá)	136-37	45°25′N	75°41′W
Ottawa, stm., Can. (ŏt′á-wá)	136-37	45°20′N	73°58′W
Ottawa Islands, is., Nu., Can.	130-31	59°30′N	80°10′W
Ottumwa, Ia., U.S. (ô-tŭm′wá)	114-15	41°01′N	92°24′W
Otway, Cape, c., Austl. (kāp ŏt′wā)	276	38°51′S	143°30′E
Otwock, Pol. (ôt′vôtsk)	194-95	52°07′N	21°16′E
Ou, stm., Laos	246-47	20°03′N	102°13′E
Ouachita Mountains, mts., U.S. (wŏsh′ĭ-tô moun′tĭnz)	120-21	34°40′N	94°25′W
Ouagadougou, nat. cap., Burkina (wä′gá-dōō′gōō)	260-61	12°23′N	1°32′W
Ouahigouya, Burkina (wä-ē-gōō′yä)	260-61	13°35′N	2°25′W
Ouahran, Alg. *see* Oran	198-99	35°41′N	0°39′W
Ouaka, stm., C.A.R.	262-63	4°59′N	19°56′E
Ouandja, stm., C.A.R.	262-63	9°34′N	21°39′E
Ouara, stm., C.A.R.	262-63	5°06′N	24°29′E
Ouarâne, reg., Maur.	258-59	21°0′N	10°30′W
Ouargla, Alg.	188-89	31°56′N	5°22′E
Ouarzazate, Mor.	258-59	30°56′N	6°54′W
Oubangui, stm., Afr. (ōō-bän′gē)	262-63	0°25′S	17°47′E
Oudtshoorn, S. Afr. (outs′hōrn)	264-65	33°36′S	22°12′E
Oued-Zem, Mor. (wĕd-zĕm′)	269a	32°52′N	6°35′W
Ouémé, stm., Benin	260a	6°27′N	2°33′E
Ouesso, Congo	262-63	1°37′N	16°04′E
Ouezzane, Mor. (wĕ-zan′)	269a	34°48′N	5°34′W
Ouham, stm., Afr.	260-61	9°17′N	18°16′E
Oujda, Mor.	184-85	34°41′N	1°54′W
Oulu, Fin. (ō′lò)	184-85	65°01′N	25°28′E
Oulujärvi, lk., Fin.	184-85	64°18′N	27°08′E
Oulujoki, stm., Fin.	184-85	65°01′N	25°29′E
Oum er Rbia, Oued, stm., Mor.	269a	33°20′N	8°20′W
Ouray, Co., U.S. (ōō-rā′)	118-19	38°02′N	107°40′W
Ourense, Spain	198-99	42°20′N	7°52′W
Ourinhos, Braz. (ôò-rē′nyôs)	168-69	22°59′S	49°52′W
Ouro Fino, Braz. (ōŭ-rô-fē′nō)	172	22°17′S	46°22′W
Ouro Preto, Braz. (ō′rò prā′tò)	172	20°23′S	43°30′W
Outaouais, stm., Can. *see* Ottawa	136-37	45°20′N	73°58′W
Outardes, stm., Qc., Can.	138-39	49°03′N	68°30′W
Outlook, Sk., Can.	134-35	51°30′N	107°03′W
Ouvéa, i., N. Cal.	279g	20°33′S	166°34′E
Ouyen, Austl. (ōō-ĕn)	276	35°04′S	142°19′E
Ovalau, i., Fiji	279f	17°40′S	178°48′E
Ovalle, Chile (ō-väl′yā)	168-69	30°36′S	71°12′W
Ovar, Port. (ô-vär′)	198-99	40°52′N	8°37′W
Övertorneå, Swe.	184-85	66°23′N	23°39′E
Oviedo, Spain (ō-vē-å′dhō)	198-99	43°22′N	5°51′W
Owando, Congo	262-63	0°29′S	15°55′E
Owase, Japan (ō′wä-shē)	245	34°04′N	136°12′E
Owego, N.Y., U.S. (ō-wē′gō)	116-17	42°07′N	76°16′W
Owen, Wi., U.S. (ō′ĕn)	114-15	44°57′N	90°33′W
Owen Falls Dam, d., Ug. *see* Nalubaale Dam	267	0°27′N	33°11′E
Owensboro, Ky., U.S. (ō′ĕnz-bŭr-ô)	116-17	37°46′N	87°06′W
Owen Sound, On., Can. (ō′ĕn sound)	136-37	44°34′N	80°56′W
Owen Stanley Range, mts., Pap. N. Gui. (ō′ĕn stăn′lē rānj)	277	9°20′S	147°55′E
Owensville, Mo., U.S. (ō′ĕnz-vĭl)	120-21	38°21′N	91°30′W
Owenton, Ky., U.S. (ō′ĕn-tŭn)	116-17	38°32′N	84°50′W
Owerri, Nig. (ô-wĕr′ē)	260a	5°29′N	7°01′E
Owo, Nig.	260a	7°12′N	5°35′E
Owosso, Mi., U.S. (ô-wŏs′ō)	116-17	42°60′N	84°10′W
Owyhee, stm., U.S. (ô-wī′hē)	112-13	43°48′N	117°02′W
Oxbow, Sk., Can.	134-35	49°14′N	102°11′W
Oxford, N.S., Can. (ŏks′fērd)	138-39	45°43′N	63°53′W
Oxford, Eng., U.K. (ŏks′fērd)	190-91	51°46′N	1°16′W
Oxford, Al., U.S. (ŏks′fērd)	124-25	33°36′N	85°50′W
Oxford, Ms., U.S. (ŏks′fērd)	124-25	34°21′N	89°33′W
Oxford, N.C., U.S. (ŏks′fērd)	124-25	36°19′N	78°35′W
Oxford, Oh., U.S. (ŏks′fērd)	116-17	39°30′N	84°45′W
Oxford Lake, lk., Mb., Can. (ŏks′fērd lāk)	134-35	54°49′N	95°29′W
Oxkutzcab, Mex. (ŏx-kōō′tz-käb)	148	20°18′N	89°25′W
Oxnard, Ca., U.S. (ŏks′närd)	118-19	34°12′N	119°11′W
Oxus, stm., Asia *see* Amu Darya	226	44°14′N	59°41′E
Oyapok, stm., S.A. (ō-yá-pŏk′)	164-65	4°10′N	51°37′W
Oyem, Gabon	260-61	1°36′N	11°35′E
Oyo, Nig. (ō′yō)	260a	7°50′N	3°56′E
Oyonnax, Fr. (ō-yô-náks′)	196-97	46°16′N	5°39′E
Oyyl, stm., Kaz.	226	48°33′N	52°25′E
Ozamis, Phil.	250	8°09′N	123°49′E
Ozark, Al., U.S. (ō′zärk)	124-25	31°28′N	85°38′W
Ozark, Ar., U.S. (ō′zärk)	120-21	35°29′N	93°50′W
Ozark, Mo., U.S. (ō′zärk)	120-21	37°01′N	93°12′W
Ozark Plateau, plat., U.S. (ō′zärk plă-tō′)	120-21	37°0′N	93°00′W
Ozarks, Lake of the, res., Mo., U.S. (lāk ŭv thá ō′zärksz)	120-21	38°06′N	92°44′W
Ozernovskiy, Russia	218-19	51°30′N	156°31′E
Ozery, Russia (ô-zyô′rē)	202-03	54°51′N	38°33′E
Ozorków, Pol. (ô-zôr′kôf)	194-95	51°58′N	19°18′E

P

Feature (Pronunciation)	Page	Lat.	Long.
Paama, i., Vanuatu	279g	16°29′S	168°14′E
Paarl, S. Afr. (pärl)	264-65	33°44′S	18°58′E
Pabianice, Pol. (pä-byá-nē′tsĕ)	194-95	51°40′N	19°21′E
Pābna, Bngl.	234-35	24°00′N	89°14′E
Pacaraima, Serra, mts., S.A. (sĕr′rá pä-kä-rä-ē′má) *see* Pakaraima Mountains	164-65	5°06′N	60°39′W
Pacaraima, Sierra de, mts., S.A. *see* Pakaraima Mountains	164-65	5°06′N	60°39′W
Pacasmayo, Peru (pä-käs-mä′yō)	170	7°24′S	79°33′W
Pachmarhi, India	234-35	22°28′N	78°26′E
Pachuca de Soto, Mex.	146-47	20°06′N	98°45′W
Pacific Ocean, oc., (pá-sĭf′ĭk ōshŭn)	20-21	10°0′S	150°00′W

ăt; finăl; rāte; senâte; ärm; åsk; sofá; fâre; ch-choose; dh-as th in other; bē; êvent; bĕt; recĕnt; cratẽr; g-gō; gh-guttural g; bĭt; ĭ-short neutral; rīde; ĸ-guttural k as ch in German ich;

Feature (Pronunciation)	Page	Lat.	Long.
Pacific Ranges, mts., B.C., Can. (pȧ-sĭf´ĭk rānjĕz)	132-33	51°11'N	125°33'W
Pacific Rim National Park Reserve, n.p., B.C., Can. (pȧ-sĭf´ĭk rĭm năsh´ŭn-ăl pärk rĭ-zûrv´)	132-33	48°45'N	125°06'W
Padang, Indon.	246-47	0°57'S	100°22'E
Padang, Indon. (pä-däng´)	246-47	1°39'S	108°55'E
Padangsidempuan, Indon.	246-47	1°23'N	99°16'E
Paden City, W.V., U.S. (pā´dĕn sĭ´tĭ)	116-17	39°37'N	80°51'W
Paderborn, Ger. (pä-dĕr-bôrn´)	194-95	51°43'N	8°45'E
Padma, stm., Asia *see* Ganges	234-35	21°58'N	90°57'E
Padova, Italy (pä´dô-vä)	200-01	45°24'N	11°52'E
Padre Island, i., Tx., U.S. (pä´drā ī´lȧnd)	122-23	27°01'N	97°23'W
Padua, Italy (păd´ū-ȧ) *see* Padova	200-01	45°24'N	11°52'E
Paducah, Ky., U.S.	124-25	37°05'N	88°37'W
Paektu-san, mtn., Asia (pâk´tōō-sän´)	243	41°59'N	128°07'E
Pagadian, Phil.	250	7°50'N	123°25'E
Pagalu, i., Eq. Gui. *see* Annobón	260-61	1°26'S	5°37'E
Pagan, i., N. Mar. Is.	280-81	18°07'N	145°46'E
Pago Pago, nat. cap., Am. Sam. (pän´-gō pän´-gō)	279b	14°16'S	170°42'W
Pagosa Springs, Co., U.S. (pȧ-gō´sȧ sprĭngz)	118-19	37°16'N	107°02'W
Pāhala, Hi., U.S. (pä-hä´lä)	127a	19°12'N	155°28'W
Pahang, stm., Malay.	246-47	3°30'N	103°24'E
Pahlevī, Iran *see* Bandar-e Anzalī	227	37°28'N	49°28'E
Paide, Est. (pī´dĕ)	192-93	58°54'N	25°35'E
Päijänne, lk., Fin. (pĕ´ē-yĕn-nĕ)	192-93	61°35'N	25°30'E
Painesville, Oh., U.S. (pānz´vĭl)	116-17	41°43'N	81°15'W
Painted Desert, des., Az., U.S. (pānt´ĕd dĕs´ẽrt)	118-19	35°45'N	111°07'W
Paintsville, Ky., U.S. (pānts´vĭl)	116-17	37°48'N	82°49'W
Paisley, Scot., U.K. (pāz´lĭ)	190-91	55°51'N	4°25'W
Paita, Peru (pä-ē´tä)	170	5°06'S	81°06'W
Pajala, Swe.	184-85	67°13'N	23°23'E
Pakaraima Mountains, mts., S.A.	164-65	5°06'N	60°39'W
Pakistan, nation, Asia (pä´-kĭ-stän)	206-07	30°0'N	70°00'E
Pakistan, East, nation, Asia *see* Bangladesh	206-07	24°0'N	90°00'E
Pakokku, Mya. (pȧ-kŏk´kŏ)	246-47	21°19'N	95°06'E
Paks, Hung. (pôksh)	194-95	46°39'N	18°53'E
Pak Sane, Laos *see* Muang Pakxan	246-47	18°25'N	103°39'E
Pakxé, Laos	246-47	15°08'N	105°48'E
Pala, Chad	262-63	9°21'N	14°54'E
Palacios, Tx., U.S. (pä-lä´syōs)	122-23	28°42'N	96°13'W
Palaiseau, Fr. (pȧ-lĕ-zō´)	196-97	48°43'N	2°16'E
Palana, Russia	218-19	59°05'N	159°59'E
Palangkaraya, Indon.	248-49	2°10'S	113°54'E
Palani, India	236	10°27'N	77°31'E
Pālanpur, India (pä´lŭn-pōōr)	234-35	24°10'N	72°27'E
Palapye, Bots. (pȧ-läp´yĕ)	264-65	22°34'S	27°07'E
Palatka, Russia	218-19	60°06'N	150°57'E
Palatka, Fl., U.S. (pȧ-lăt´kȧ)	124-25	29°39'N	81°39'W
Palau, nation, Oc. (pä-lä´ŏ)	280-81	5°0'N	137°00'E
Palauig, Phil. (pȧ-lou´ĕg)	250	15°26'N	119°56'E
Palawan, i., Phil. (pä-lä´wan)	250	9°30'N	118°30'E
Paldiski, Est. (päl´dĭ-skĭ)	192-93	59°20'N	24°06'E
Palembang, Indon. (pä-lĕm-bäng´)	246-47	2°58'S	104°46'E
Palencia, Spain (pä-lĕ´n-syä)	198-99	42°01'N	4°32'W
Palenque, Mex. (pä-lĕŋ´kå)	148	17°31'N	91°57'W
Palenque, hist., Mex.	148	17°30'N	91°60'W
Palenque, Punta, c., Dom. Rep. (pōō´n-tä pä-lĕŋ´kå)	142-43	18°15'N	70°09'W
Palermo, Italy (pä-lĕr´mô)	200-01	38°07'N	13°21'E
Palesse, reg., Eur. *see* Pripet Marshes	194-95	52°0'N	27°00'E
Palestine, Tx., U.S. (păl´ĕs-tīn)	122-23	31°45'N	95°38'W
Paletwa, Mya. (pŭ-lĕt´wä)	246-47	21°18'N	92°51'E
Pālghāt, India	236	10°46'N	76°39'E
Pāli, India	234-35	25°47'N	73°20'E
Palikir, nat. cap., Micron.	280-81	6°58'N	158°13'E
Pālitāna, India	234-35	21°31'N	71°49'E
Palizada, Mex. (pä-lē-zä´dä)	148	18°15'N	92°05'W
Palk Strait, strt., Asia (pôk strāt)	236	10°0'N	79°45'E
Palliser, Cape, c., N.Z.	278	41°37'S	175°17'E
Palma de Mallorca, Spain	198-99	39°34'N	2°39'E
Palmares, Braz. (päl-mä´rĕs)	163d	8°41'S	35°36'W
Palmas, Braz. (päl´mäs)	168-69	26°30'S	52°01'W
Palmas, Braz.	166-67	10°06'S	48°20'W
Palma Soriano, Cuba (päl´mä-sô-rē-ä´nō)	142-43	20°13'N	75°59'W
Palmeira dos Índios, Braz. (pä-mā´rä-dôs-ē´n-dyôs)	163d	9°25'S	36°37'W
Palmeirinhas, Ponta das, c., Ang.	264-65	9°05'S	12°60'E
Palmer, Ak., U.S. (päm´ẽr)	126	61°32'N	149°05'W
Palmerston, at., Cook Is.	280-81	18°03'S	163°10'W
Palmerston, Cape, c., Austl.	277	21°33'S	149°28'E
Palmerston North, N.Z. (päm´ẽr-stŭn nôrth)	278	40°21'S	175°37'E
Palmetto, Fl., U.S. (pȧl-mĕt´ō)	125a	27°31'N	82°35'W
Palmi, Italy (päl´mē)	200-01	38°21'N	15°51'E
Palmira, Col. (päl-mē´rä)	163c	3°33'N	76°18'W
Palm Springs, Ca., U.S.	118-19	33°50'N	116°32'W
Palmyra, Syria *see* Tudmur	228-29	34°33'N	38°17'E
Palmyra, Mo., U.S. (păl-mī´rȧ)	120-21	39°48'N	91°31'W
Palmyra, N.Y., U.S. (păl-mī´rȧ)	116-17	43°03'N	77°14'W
Palmyra Atoll, at., Oc.	280-81	5°51'N	162°05'W
Palo Alto, Ca., U.S. (pä´lō äl´tō)	118-19	37°26'N	122°08'W
Paloe, Pulau, i., Indon.	248-49	8°20'S	121°43'E
Palopo, Indon.	248-49	3°00'S	120°11'E
Palos, Cabo de, c., Spain (kȧ´bô-dĕ-pä´lôs)	198-99	37°38'N	0°41'W
Palu, Indon.	248-49	0°54'S	119°52'E
Palu, Tur. (pä-loo´)	227	38°41'N	39°60'E
Paluan, Phil. (pä-lōō´än)	250	13°26'N	120°27'E
Pāmban Island, i., India	236	9°16'N	79°19'E
Pamekasan, Indon.	248-49	7°10'S	113°29'E
Pamiers, Fr. (pȧ-myā´)	196-97	43°07'N	1°36'E
Pamir, mts., Asia *see* Pamirs	232-33	38°0'N	73°00'E
Pāmīr, Daryā-ye, mts., Asia *see* Pamirs	232-33	38°0'N	73°00'E
Pamirs, mts., Asia (pä-mērz)	232-33	38°0'N	73°00'E
Pamlico Sound, strt., N.C., U.S. (păm´lĭ-kō sound)	124-25	35°20'N	75°55'W
Pampa, Tx., U.S. (păm´pȧ)	120-21	35°32'N	100°58'W
Pampa, reg., Arg. (păm´pȧ) *see* Pampas	173	35°0'S	63°00'W
Pampanga, stm., Phil. (päm-päŋ´gä)	250	14°46'N	120°39'E
Pampas, reg., Arg. (päm´päs)	173	35°0'S	63°00'W
Pampas, stm., Peru	170	13°25'S	73°13'W
Pampeluna, Spain *see* Pamplona	198-99	42°49'N	1°39'W
Pamplona, Col. (päm-plō´nä)	164-65	7°22'N	72°38'W
Pamplona, Spain (päm-plô´nä)	198-99	42°49'N	1°39'W
Pana, Il., U.S. (pā´nȧ)	116-17	39°23'N	89°05'W
Panagyurishte, Blg. (pȧ-nȧ-gyōō´rĕsh-tĕ)	200-01	42°30'N	24°12'E
Panaitan, Pulau, i., Indon.	248-49	6°36'S	105°12'E
Panaji, India	236	15°30'N	73°50'E
Panama, nation, N.A. (păn-ȧ-mä´ sĭ´tĭ)	85	9°0'N	80°00'W
Panamá, nat. cap., Pan. (păn-ȧ-mä´)	150	8°58'N	79°32'W
Panamá, Golfo de, b., Pan.	150	8°0'N	79°30'W
Panama, Gulf of, b., Pan. *see* Panamá, Golfo de	150	8°0'N	79°30'W
Panama, Isthmus of, isth., Pan. *see* Panamá, Istmo de	150	9°0'N	80°00'W
Panamá, Istmo de, isth., Pan.	150	9°0'N	80°00'W
Panama Canal, can., Pan.	150	9°23'N	79°56'W
Panama City, Fl., U.S. (păn-ȧ-mä´ sĭ´tĭ)	124-25	30°10'N	85°40'W
Panay, i., Phil. (pä-nī´)	250	11°15'N	122°30'E
Panay Gulf, b., Phil.	250	10°15'N	122°15'E
Pančevo, Serb. (pȧn´chĕ-vô)	200-01	44°53'N	20°40'E
Panevėžys, Lith. (pä´nyĕ-vāzh´ēs)	192-93	55°44'N	24°23'E
Pangani, stm., Tan. (pän-gä´nē)	262-63	5°24'S	38°57'E
Pangkalanbuun, Indon.	248-49	2°42'S	111°38'E
Pangkalpinang, Indon. (päng-käl´pē-näng´)	246-47	2°08'S	106°06'E
Pangnirtung, Nu., Can.	128-29	66°08'N	65°43'W
Pangong Tso, lk., Asia	234-35	33°45'N	78°42'E
Panguitch, Ut., U.S. (pän´gwĭch)	118-19	37°50'N	112°26'W
Pangutaran Group, is., Phil.	250	6°14'N	120°39'E
Panhame, stm., Afr. *see* Manyame	264-65	15°37'S	30°39'E
Pānīpat, India	234-35	29°23'N	76°58'E
Panj, stm., Asia	232-33	37°00'N	68°16'E
Panjgūr, Pak.	232-33	26°58'N	64°05'E
Panjim, India *see* Panaji	236	15°30'N	73°50'E
Panna, India	234-35	24°43'N	80°11'E
Pannirtuuq, Nu., Can. *see* Pangnirtung	128-29	66°08'N	65°43'W
Pantar, Pulau, i., Indon. (pōō-lou pän´tär)	248-49	8°25'S	124°07'E
Pantelleria, Isola di, i., Italy (ē´sō-lä-dē-pän-tĕl-lå-rē´ä)	200-01	36°47'N	12°00'E
Pante Makasar, E. Timor	248-49	9°13'S	124°21'E
Pánuco, Mex. (pä´nōō-kô)	146-47	22°02'N	98°11'W
Pánuco, stm., Mex. (pä´nōō-kô)	146-47	22°16'N	97°47'W
Panxian, China	238-39	25°49'N	104°35'E
Panzós, Guat. (pä-zōs´)	148	15°24'N	89°39'W
Paoli, In., U.S. (pȧ-ō´lĭ)	116-17	38°33'N	86°28'W
Pápa, Hung. (pä´pô)	194-95	47°20'N	17°28'E
Papagayo, Golfo de, b., C.R. (gôl-fô-dĕ-pä-pä-gá´yō)	149	10°42'N	85°50'W
Papantla de Olarte, Mex. (pä-pän´tlä dā-ô-lä´r-tĕ)	146-47	20°27'N	97°19'W
Papeete, nat. cap., Fr. Poly. (pä-pĕ´-tē)	279d	17°32'S	149°34'W
Papenburg, Ger. (päp´ĕn-bôrgh)	194-95	53°06'N	7°24'E
Papua, Gulf of, b., Pap. N. Gui. (gŭlf ŭv păp-ōō-ȧ)	277	8°30'S	145°00'E
Papua New Guinea, nation, Oc. (păp-ōō-ȧ nū gĭne)	277	6°0'S	147°00'E
Papudo, Chile (pä-pōō´dô)	163e	32°31'S	71°28'W
Papun, Mya.	246-47	18°04'N	97°27'E
Pará, Braz. *see* Belém	166-67	1°27'S	48°29'W
Pará, state, Braz.	166-67	4°0'S	53°00'W
Pará, stm., Braz.	166-67	1°29'S	48°49'W
Paraburdoo, Austl.	270-71	23°12'S	117°44'E
Paracatu, Braz. (pä-rä-kä-tōō´)	172	17°14'S	46°52'W
Paracatu, stm., Braz.	168-69	16°35'S	45°06'W
Paracel Islands, is., China	224-25	15°46'N	112°17'E
Paraćin, Serb. (pá´rä-chēn)	200-01	43°52'N	21°25'E
Pāradwīp, India	234-35	20°17'N	86°41'E
Paragould, Ar., U.S. (păr´ȧ-gōōld)	124-25	36°04'N	90°30'W
Paraguá, stm., Bol.	166-67	13°32'S	61°49'W
Paragua, stm., Ven.	164-65	6°56'N	62°55'W
Paraguaçu, stm., Braz. (pä-rä-gwä-zōō´)	166-67	12°50'S	38°48'W
Paraguay, stm., S.A. (pä-rä-gwä´y)	173	27°19'S	58°36'W
Paraguai, stm., S.A. *see* Paraguay	173	27°19'S	58°36'W
Paraguaná, Península de, pen., Ven.	164-65	11°56'N	70°03'W
Paraguarí, Para.	168-69	25°37'S	57°09'W
Paraguay, nation, S.A. (păr´ȧ-gwā)	158	23°0'S	58°00'W
Parahyba, Braz. *see* João Pessoa	163d	7°07'S	34°52'W
Paraíba, Braz. *see* João Pessoa	163d	7°07'S	34°52'W
Paraíba, state, Braz. (pä-rä-ē´bä)	163d	7°15'S	36°30'W
Paraíba do Sul, stm., Braz.	172	21°37'S	41°02'W
Paraíso, Mex.	146-47	18°23'N	93°14'W
Paraíso, Pan. (pä-rä-ē´sō)	150	9°03'N	79°38'W
Parakou, Benin (pȧ-rȧ-kōō´)	260-61	9°20'N	2°37'E
Paramaribo, nat. cap., Sur. (pȧ-rȧ-mȧ´rē-bō)	164-65	5°49'N	55°10'W
Paramirim, Braz.	166-67	13°27'S	42°14'W
Paramushir, Ostrov, i., Russia	218-19	50°25'N	155°50'E
Paraná, Arg. (pä-rä-nä´)	173	31°44'S	60°31'W
Paranã, Braz.	166-67	12°33'S	47°52'W
Paraná, state, Braz.	168-69	24°0'S	51°00'W
Paranã, stm., Braz.	166-67	12°30'S	48°14'W
Paraná, stm., S.A. (pä-rä-nä´)	168-69	33°48'S	59°14'W
Paranaguá, Braz.	172	25°31'S	48°31'W
Paranaguá, Baía de, b., Braz.	172	25°27'S	48°22'W
Paranaíba, Braz. (pä-rä-nȧ-ē´bȧ)	168-69	19°41'S	51°11'W
Paranaíba, stm., Braz. (pä-rä-nȧ-ē´bȧ)	168-69	20°08'S	51°00'W
Paranapanema, stm., Braz. (pä-rä´nȧ´pä-nĕ-mä)	168-69	22°42'S	53°10'W
Paranavaí, Braz.	168-69	23°04'S	52°29'W
Parapara, Ven. (pä-rä-pä-rä)	163b	9°44'N	67°17'W
Paray-le-Monial, Fr. (pȧ-rĕ´lē-mô-nyäl´)	196-97	46°27'N	4°07'E
Pārbat, stm., India	234-35	25°51'N	76°33'E
Parbhani, India	236	19°16'N	76°46'E
Pardo, stm., Braz. (pär´dō)	166-67	15°39'S	38°57'W
Pardo, stm., Braz. (pär´dō)	172	20°09'S	48°37'W
Pardubice, Czech Rep. (pär´dŏ-bĭt-sĕ)	194-95	50°02'N	15°46'E
Parece Vela, i., Japan *see* Okino-Tori-shima	222-23	20°27'N	136°04'E
Parent, Qc., Can.	136-37	47°56'N	74°37'W
Parepare, Indon.	248-49	4°01'S	119°38'E
Paria, Golfo de, b., (gôl-fô-dĕ-bĕr-pä-rē-ä) *see* Paria, Gulf of	140-41	10°20'N	62°00'W
Paria, Gulf of, b.,	140-41	10°20'N	62°00'W
Paricutín, vol., Mex.	146-47	19°28'N	102°15'W
Parima, Serra, mts., S.A. (sĕr´rȧ pä-rē´mȧ) *see* Parima, Sierra	164-65	3°24'N	64°10'W
Parima, Sierra, mts., S.A.	164-65	3°24'N	64°10'W
Pariñas, Punta, c., Peru (pōō´n-tä-pä-rē´n-yäs)	170	4°40'S	81°20'W
Parintins, Braz. (pä-rĭn-tĭnzh´)	166-67	2°37'S	56°45'W
Paris, Ar., U.S. (păr´ĭs)	120-21	35°18'N	93°44'W
Paris, Il., U.S. (păr´ĭs)	116-17	39°37'N	87°42'W
Paris, Ky., U.S. (păr´ĭs)	116-17	38°12'N	84°16'W
Paris, Mo., U.S. (păr´ĭs)	120-21	39°29'N	92°00'W
Paris, Tn., U.S. (păr´ĭs)	124-25	36°18'N	88°20'W
Paris, Tx., U.S. (păr´ĭs)	120-21	33°40'N	95°33'W
Paris, nat. cap., Fr. (pȧ-rē´)	196-97	48°52'N	2°21'E
Parita, Bahía de, b., Pan. (bä-ē´ä-dĕ-pä-rē´tä)	150	8°08'N	80°24'W
Park City, Ks., U.S. (pärk sĭ´tē)	120-21	37°48'N	97°18'W
Parker, Co., U.S. (pär´kẽr pärk)	120-21	39°31'N	104°46'W
Parker, S.D., U.S. (pär´kẽr pärk)	114-15	43°24'N	97°08'W

Feature (Pronunciation)	Page	Lat.	Long.
Parkersburg, W.V., U.S. (pär´kẽrz-bûrg)	116-17	39°15'N	81°33'W
Parkes, Austl. (pärks)	276	33°09'S	148°10'E
Park Falls, Wi., U.S. (pärk fôlz)	114-15	45°56'N	90°26'W
Park Range, mts., Co., U.S. (pärk rānj)	112-13	40°40'N	106°40'W
Park Rapids, Mn., U.S. (pärk răp´ĭdz)	114-15	46°55'N	95°04'W
Park River, N.D., U.S. (pärk rĭv´ẽr)	114-15	48°24'N	97°45'W
Parkston, S.D., U.S. (pärks´tŭn)	114-15	43°24'N	97°59'W
Parla, Spain (pär´lä)	198-99	40°14'N	3°46'W
Parlākimidi, India	236	18°47'N	84°06'E
Parma, Italy (pär´mä)	200-01	44°49'N	10°20'E
Parnaguá, Braz.	166-67	10°13'S	44°38'W
Parnaíba, Braz. (pär-nä-ē´bä)	166-67	2°54'S	41°47'W
Parnaíba, stm., Braz. (pär-nä-ē´bä)	166-67	2°46'S	41°50'W
Parnassós, mtn., Grc.	200-01	38°32'N	22°35'E
Pärnu, Est. (pĕr´nōō)	192-93	58°22'N	24°33'E
Paroo, stm., Austl. (pä´rōō)	276	30°23'S	143°59'E
Parowan, Ut., U.S. (păr´ō-wăn)	118-19	37°51'N	112°50'W
Parral, Chile (pär-rä´l)	171	36°09'S	71°50'W
Parramatta, Austl.	276	33°49'S	151°00'E
Parras de la Fuente, Mex.	122-23	25°27'N	102°10'W
Parrsboro, N.S., Can. (pärz´bŭr-ō)	138-39	45°25'N	64°20'W
Parry, Cape, c., N.T., Can.	130-31	70°08'N	124°24'W
Parry, Mount, mtn., B.C., Can. (mount păr´ĭ)	132-33	52°53'N	128°45'W
Parry Sound, On., Can. (păr´ĭ sound)	136-37	45°20'N	80°02'W
Parsnip, stm., B.C., Can. (pärs´nĭp)	132-33	55°10'N	123°02'W
Parsons, Ks., U.S. (pär´s'nz)	120-21	37°20'N	95°16'W
Parsons, W.V., U.S. (pär´s'nz)	116-17	39°06'N	79°41'W
Parthenay, Fr. (pȧr-t'nĕ´)	196-97	46°39'N	0°15'W
Partinico, Italy (pär-tē´nē-kô)	200-01	38°03'N	13°07'E
Paru, stm., Braz.	166-67	1°35'S	52°31'W
Parys, S. Afr. (pȧ-rĭs´)	269c	26°54'S	27°28'E
Pasadena, Ca., U.S. (păs-ȧ-dē´nȧ)	118-19	34°09'N	118°09'W
Pasaje, Ec.	170	3°20'S	79°48'W
Pa Sak, stm., Thai.	246-47	14°21'N	100°35'E
Pascagoula, Ms., U.S. (păs-kȧ-gōō´lȧ)	124-25	30°22'N	88°33'W
Pascagoula, stm., Ms., U.S. (păs-kȧ-gōō´lȧ)	124-25	30°22'N	88°37'W
Paşcani, Rom. (päsh-kän´)	194-95	47°15'N	26°44'E
Pasco, Wa., U.S. (păs´kō)	112-13	46°14'N	119°05'W
Pascua, Isla de, i., Chile	282-83	27°07'S	109°22'W
Pasni, Pak.	232-33	25°16'N	63°27'E
Paso de Indios, Arg.	171	43°51'S	68°56'W
Paso de los Libres, Arg. (pä-sō-dĕ-lôs-lē´brĕs)	173	29°42'S	57°09'W
Paso de los Toros, Ur. (pä-sō-dĕ-lôs tō´rôs)	173	32°49'S	56°31'W
Paso Robles, Ca., U.S. (pä´sō rō´blĕs)	118-19	35°38'N	120°41'W
Passaic, N.J., U.S. (pă-sā´ĭk)	116-17	40°52'N	74°08'W
Passau, Ger. (päsou)	194-95	48°34'N	13°27'E
Passero, Capo, c., Italy (kä´pō päs-sĕ´rō)	200-01	36°40'N	15°09'E
Passo Fundo, Braz. (pä´sō fōn´dō)	168-69	28°15'S	52°25'W
Passos, Braz. (pä´s-sōs)	172	20°43'S	46°37'W
Pastaza, stm., S.A. (päs-tä´zä)	170	4°55'S	76°24'W
Pasto, Col. (päs´tō)	164-65	1°12'N	77°16'W
Pasuruan, Indon.	248-49	7°38'S	112°54'E
Pasvalys, Lith. (päs-vä-lēs´)	192-93	56°04'N	24°24'E
Patagonia, reg., Arg. (păt-ȧ-gō´nĭ-ȧ)	171	44°0'S	68°00'W
Pātan, India	234-35	23°51'N	72°07'E
Pate Island, i., Kenya	262-63	2°06'S	41°03'E
Paterson, N.J., U.S. (păt´ẽr-sŭn)	116-17	40°55'N	74°10'W
Pathānkot, India	234-35	32°16'N	75°39'E
Pathein, Mya.	246-47	16°46'N	94°44'E
Pathfinder Reservoir, res., Wy., U.S. (păth´fīn-dẽr rĕ´sẽr-vwär)	112-13	42°25'N	106°55'W
Patiāla, India (pŭt-ē-ä´lŭ)	234-35	30°19'N	76°23'E
Pātkai Range, mts., Asia	238-39	27°0'N	96°00'E
Patna, India	234-35	25°36'N	85°07'E
Patnanongan Island, i., Phil. (pät-nä-nōŋ´gän ī´lȧnd)	250	14°48'N	122°11'E
Pato Branco, Braz.	168-69	26°14'S	52°41'W
Patos, Braz. (pä´tōzh)	163d	7°01'S	37°16'W
Patos, Lagoa dos, b., Braz. (lä´gō-ȧ dozh pä´tōzh)	168-69	31°06'S	51°15'W
Patos de Minas, Braz. (pä´tōzh dĕ-mē´näzh)	172	18°35'S	46°31'W
Patquía, Arg.	168-69	30°02'S	66°52'W
Pátra, Grc.	200-01	38°14'N	21°44'E
Patricio Lynch, Isla, i., Chile	171	48°37'S	75°26'W
Patrocínio, Braz. (pä-trō-sē´nē-ō)	172	18°56'S	46°60'W
Pattani, Thai. (pät´ȧ-nē)	246-47	6°52'N	101°15'E
Patten, Me., U.S. (păt´'n)	117a	45°59'N	68°27'W
Patterson, La., U.S. (păt´ẽr-sŭn)	124-25	29°42'N	91°18'W
Patuca, stm., Hond.	149	15°48'N	84°18'W
Patuca, Punta, c., Hond. (pōō´n-tä-pä-tōō´kä)	149	15°49'N	84°18'W
Pátzcuaro, Mex. (päts´kwä-rō)	146-47	19°31'N	101°37'W
Pau, Fr. (pō)	196-97	43°18'N	0°22'W
Pauini, stm., Braz.	166-67	7°47'S	67°05'W
Pauk, Mya.	246-47	21°27'N	94°28'E
Paulding, Oh., U.S. (pôl´dĭng)	116-17	41°08'N	84°35'W
Paulis, D.R.C. *see* Isiro	262-63	2°46'N	27°37'E
Paulistana, Braz.	166-67	8°09'S	41°09'W
Paulo Afonso, Braz.	166-67	9°21'S	38°14'W
Paul Roux, S. Afr. (pôrl rōō)	269c	28°18'S	27°58'E
Pauls Valley, Ok., U.S. (pôlz văl´ē)	120-21	34°44'N	97°13'W
Paungde, Mya.	246-47	18°29'N	95°30'E
Pavia, Italy (pä-vē´ä)	200-01	45°12'N	9°10'E
Pavlodar, Kaz. (pȧv-lō-dȧr´)	226	52°17'N	76°59'E
Pavlovo, Russia	186-87	55°57'N	43°04'E
Pavuvu Island, i., Sol. Is.	279e	9°03'S	159°06'E
Pawan, stm., Indon.	248-49	1°51'S	109°56'E
Pawhuska, Ok., U.S. (pô-hŭs´kȧ)	120-21	36°40'N	96°20'W
Pawnee, Ok., U.S. (pô-nē´)	120-21	36°20'N	96°48'W
Pawnee, stm., Ks., U.S. (pô-nē´)	120-21	38°10'N	99°06'W
Pawnee City, Ne., U.S. (pô-nē´ sĭ´tē)	120-21	40°07'N	96°09'W
Paw Paw, Mi., U.S. (pô pô)	116-17	42°13'N	85°53'W
Pawtucket, R.I., U.S. (pô-tŭk´ĕt)	116-17	41°53'N	71°23'W
Paxton, Il., U.S. (păks´tŭn)	116-17	40°27'N	88°05'W
Payakumbuh, Indon.	246-47	0°14'S	100°38'E
Payette, Id., U.S. (pȧ-ĕt´)	112-13	44°05'N	116°56'W
Pay-Khey, Khrebet, mts., Russia	186-87	69°0'N	63°00'E
Paynesville, Mn., U.S. (pānz´vĭl)	114-15	45°23'N	94°43'W
Paysandú, Ur. (pī-sän-dōō´)	173	32°20'S	58°05'W
Payson, Az., U.S. (pā´s'n)	118-19	34°10'N	111°19'W
Pazardzhik, Blg. (pä-zȧr-dzhek´)	200-01	42°12'N	24°20'E
Peabody, Ks., U.S. (pē´bŏd-ĭ)	120-21	38°10'N	97°06'W
Peace, stm., Can. (pēs)	130-31	58°60'N	111°25'W
Peace, stm., Fl., U.S. (pēs)	125a	26°58'N	82°01'W
Peace River, Ab., Can. (pēs rĭv´ẽr)	132-33	56°15'N	117°16'W
Pearl, stm., U.S. (pûrl)	124-25	30°11'N	89°32'W
Pearland, Tx., U.S. (pûrl´ănd)	122-23	29°33'N	95°17'W
Pearl and Hermes Atoll, at., Hi., U.S.	127	27°55'N	175°45'W
Pearl Harbor, b., Hi., U.S. (pûrl här´bẽr)	127a	21°22'N	157°59'W
Pearsall, Tx., U.S. (pẽr´sôl)	122-23	28°54'N	99°06'W
Pebble Island, i., Falk. Is.	171	51°20'S	59°34'W
Peçanha, Braz. (pā-kän´yȧ)	172	18°32'S	42°34'W
Pechenga, Russia (pyĕ´chĕŋ-gȧ)	184-85	69°34'N	31°14'E
Pechora, Russia	186-87	65°08'N	57°09'E
Pechora, stm., Russia (pyĕ-chô´rȧ)	186-87	67°59'N	53°56'E
Pechorskoye More, s., Russia	186-87	70°0'N	54°00'E
Pecos, Tx., U.S. (pā´kōs)	122-23	31°25'N	103°30'W
Pecos, stm., U.S. (pā´kōs)	110-11	29°42'N	101°22'W
Pécs, Hung. (pāch)	194-95	46°04'N	18°13'E
Pedernales, Ven.	143b	9°57'N	62°15'W
Pedra Azul, Braz. (pā´drä-zōō´l)	168-69	15°60'S	41°17'W
Pedreiras, Braz. (pĕ-drā´räs)	166-67	4°34'S	44°39'W
Pedro Afonso, Braz.	166-67	8°60'S	48°10'W
Pedro II, Braz. (pā´drō sĕ-gōn´dō)	166-67	4°25'S	41°28'W
Pedro Juan Caballero, Para. (pĕ´drō hōȧ´n-kä-bäl-yĕ´rō)	168-69	22°33'S	55°45'W
Peebles, Scot., U.K. (pē´b'lz)	190-91	55°39'N	3°12'W
Peekskill, N.Y., U.S. (pēks´kĭl)	116-17	41°17'N	73°55'W
Peel, stm., Can.	130-31	67°42'N	134°31'W
Pegasus Bay, b., N.Z. (pĕg´ȧ-sŭs bā)	278	43°20'S	173°00'E
Pegu, Mya. *see* Bago	246-47	17°20'N	96°29'E
Peiching, nat. cap., China *see* Beijing	240-41	39°55'N	116°22'E
Peipsi järv, lk., Eur. *see* Peipus, Lake	192-93	58°45'N	27°25'E
Peipus, Lake, lk., Eur. (lāk pī´pŭs)	192-93	58°45'N	27°25'E
Peiraiás, Grc.	200-01	37°57'N	23°39'E
Peixe, stm., Braz.	168-69	21°30'S	51°57'W
Pekalongan, Indon.	248-49	6°53'S	109°40'E
Pekanbaru, Indon.	246-47	0°31'N	101°27'E
Pekin, Il., U.S. (pē´kĭn)	116-17	40°34'N	89°39'W
Peking, nat. cap., China *see* Beijing	240-41	39°55'N	116°22'E
Pelagie, Isole, is., Italy	184-85	35°40'N	12°40'E
Pelat, Mont, mtn., Fr. (môɴ pē-lȧ´)	196-97	44°16'N	6°42'E
Peleduy, Russia (pyĕl-yĭ-dōō´ē)	218-19	59°39'N	112°44'E
Pelée, Montagne, vol., Mart. (môɴ-pē-lā´ pȧ-lē´)	143b	14°48'N	61°10'W
Pelee Island, i., On., Can. (pē´lē ī´lȧnd)	136-37	41°46'N	82°39'W
Peleliu, i., Palau *see* Beliliou	280-81	7°00'N	134°15'E
Peleng, Pulau, i., Indon.	248-49	1°15'S	123°08'E
Pelham, Ga., U.S. (pĕl´hăm)	124-25	31°08'N	84°09'W
Pelican Rapids, Mn., U.S. (pĕl´ĭ-kăn răp´ĭdz)	114-15	46°35'N	96°04'W
Pella, Ia., U.S. (pĕl´ȧ)	114-15	41°25'N	92°55'W
Pellworm, i., Ger. (pĕl´vōrm)	194-95	54°31'N	8°38'E
Pelly, stm., Yk., Can. (pĕl´ĭ)	130-31	62°46'N	137°20'W
Pelly Crossing, Yk., Can.	128-29	62°50'N	136°35'W
Pelly Mountains, mts., Yk., Can. (pĕl´ĭ moun´tĭnz)	130-31	62°0'N	133°00'W
Peloponnesus, pen., Grc.	200-01	37°30'N	22°00'E
Pelopónnisos, pen., Grc. *see* Peloponnesus	200-01	37°30'N	22°00'E
Pelotas, Braz. (pȧ-lō´tăzh)	173	31°45'S	52°19'W
Pelotas, stm., Braz.	168-69	27°28'S	51°54'W
Pematangsiantar, Indon.	246-47	2°57'N	99°04'E
Pemba, Moz. (pĕm´bȧ)	264-65	13°01'S	40°32'E
Pemba, i., Tan. (pĕm´bȧ)	262-63	5°10'S	39°48'E
Pemberton, Austl.	270-71	34°27'S	116°01'E
Pembina, N.D., U.S. (pĕm´bĭ-nȧ)	114-15	48°58'N	97°15'W
Pembina, stm., Ab., Can. (pĕm´bĭ-nȧ)	132-33	54°45'N	114°17'W
Pembroke, On., Can. (pĕm´brōk)	136-37	45°49'N	77°07'W
Pembroke, Cape, c., Nu., Can.	130-31	62°56'N	81°56'W
Pembuang, stm., Indon.	248-49	3°21'S	112°33'E
Peñalara, Pico de, mtn., Spain (pĕ´kō-dĕ-pā-nyä-lä´rä)	198-99	40°51'N	3°57'W
Penang, Malay. *see* George Town	246-47	5°25'N	100°20'E
Peñarroya-Pueblonuevo, Spain (pĕn-yär-rō´yä-pwĕ´blō-nwĕ´vō)	198-99	38°18'N	5°16'W
Peñas, Cabo de, c., Spain (kȧ´bō-dĕ-pā´nyäs)	198-99	43°39'N	5°51'W
Penas, Golfo de, b., Chile (gôl-fō-dĕ-pĕ´n-äs)	171	47°22'S	74°50'W
Pender, Ne., U.S. (pĕn´dẽr)	114-15	42°07'N	96°43'W
Pendjari, stm., Afr.	260-61	10°55'N	0°50'E
Pendleton, Or., U.S. (pĕn´d'l-tŭn)	112-13	45°40'N	118°48'W
Pend Oreille, Lake, lk., Id., U.S. (lāk pŏn-dō-rā´) (lāk pĕn-dō-rĕl´)	112-13	48°10'N	116°17'W
Penedo, Braz. (pȧ-nā´dō)	163d	10°16'S	36°35'W
Penetanguishene, On., Can. (pĕn´ē-tăŋ-gĭ-shēn´)	136-37	44°46'N	79°56'W
Penganga, stm., India	236	19°54'N	79°10'E
P'enghu, Tai. *see* Makung	225a	23°34'N	119°34'E
P'enghu Ch'üntao, is., Tai.	225a	23°30'N	119°30'E
Penglai, China (pŭŋ-lī)	240-41	37°48'N	120°43'E
Pengshui, China	238-39	29°18'N	108°09'E
Pengxian, China	238-39	30°59'N	103°56'E
Peniche, Port. (pĕ-nē´chå)	198-99	39°21'N	9°22'W
Penida, Nusa, i., Indon.	248-49	8°44'S	115°32'E
Pennines, mts., Eng., U.K. (pĕn-īn')	190-91	54°11'N	2°02'W
Pennsylvania, state, U.S. (pĕn-sĭl-vā´nĭ-ȧ)	108-09	40°45'N	77°30'W
Penn Yan, N.Y., U.S. (pĕn yăn´)	116-17	42°40'N	77°03'W
Penobscot, stm., Me., U.S.	117a	44°29'N	68°48'W
Penobscot Bay, b., Me., U.S. (pē-nŏb´skŏt bā)	117a	44°15'N	68°52'W
Penola, Austl.	276	37°23'S	140°50'E
Penonomé, Pan.	150	8°31'N	80°22'W
Penrhyn, at., Cook Is.	280-81	9°0'S	158°00'W
Pensacola, Fl., U.S. (pĕn-sȧ-kō´lȧ)	124-25	30°25'N	87°13'W
Pensacola Mountains, mts., Ant.	287	84°21'S	47°02'W
Pensilvania, Col. (pĕn-sĕl-vá´nyä)	163c	5°32'N	75°03'W
Pentecost Island, i., Vanuatu (pĕn´tē-kŏst ī´lȧnd) *see* Pentecôte	279g	15°42'S	168°10'E
Pentecôte, i., Vanuatu	279g	15°42'S	168°10'E
Penticton, B.C., Can.	132-33	49°30'N	119°35'W
Pentland Firth, strt., Scot., U.K. (pĕnt´lănd fûrth)	190-91	58°44'N	3°07'W
Penyu, Kepulauan, is., Indon.	248-49	5°22'S	127°46'E
Penza, Russia (pĕn´zȧ)	186-87	53°12'N	45°00'E
Penzance, Eng., U.K. (pĕn-zăns´)	190-91	50°07'N	5°33'W
Penzhina, stm., Russia (pyĭn-zē-nŭ)	218-19	62°29'N	165°15'E
People's Democratic Republic of Korea, nation, Asia *see* Korea, North	206-07	40°0'N	127°00'E
Peoria, Il., U.S. (pē-ō´rĭ-ȧ)	116-17	40°41'N	89°36'W
Peotone, Il., U.S. (pē´ō-tôn)	116-17	41°20'N	87°47'W
Pequeñas Antillas, is., *see* Lesser Antilles	143b	15°0'N	61°00'W
Perabumulih, Indon.	246-47	3°27'S	104°15'E
Perak, stm., Malay.	246-47	3°58'N	100°53'E
Perdido, Monte, mtn., Spain (mōn-tȧ-pĕr-dē´dō)	198-99	42°40'N	0°05'E
Pereira, Col. (pā-rā´rä)	163c	4°50'N	75°42'W
Pereslavl'-Zalesskiy, Russia (pȧ-rȧ-slȧv´'l zȧ-lyĕs´kĭ)	202-03	56°44'N	38°51'E
Pergamino, Arg. (pĕr-gä-mē´nō)	173	33°54'S	60°35'W
Perham, Mn., U.S. (pẽr´hăm)	114-15	46°36'N	95°35'W
Péribonka, stm., Qc., Can.	130-31	48°46'N	72°03'W
Périgueux, Fr. (pā-rē-gû´)	196-97	45°11'N	0°43'E
Perito Moreno, Arg.	171	46°36'S	70°55'W
Perlas, Laguna de, b., Nic. (lä-gō´nä-dĕ-läs-pĕr´läs)	149	12°30'N	83°40'W
Perleberg, Ger. (pĕr´lē-bĕrg)	194-95	53°05'N	11°52'E

ăt; finăl; rāte; senȧte; ärm; ȧsk; sofȧ; fâre; ch-choose; dh-as th in other; bē; ēvent; bĕt; recĕnt; cratẽr; g-gō; gh-guttural g; bĭt; ĭ-short neutral; rīde; ĸ-guttural k as ch in German ich;

Feature (Pronunciation)	Page	Lat.	Long.
Perm', Russia (pĕrm)	186-87	58°00'N	56°16'E
Pernambuco, Braz. *see* Recife	163d	8°03'S	34°54'W
Pernambuco, state, Braz. (pĕr-näm-bōō'kō)	166-67	8°0'S	37°00'W
Pernik, Blg. (pĕr-nēk')	200-01	42°37'N	23°03'E
Péronne, Fr. (pā-rôn')	196-97	49°56'N	2°56'E
Perote, Mex. (pĕ-rō'tĕ)	146-47	19°34'N	97°15'W
Perpignan, Fr. (pĕr-pē-nyäɴ')	196-97	42°42'N	2°53'E
Perros, Bahía de, strt., Cuba (bä-ē'ä-dĕ-pā'rōs)	142-43	22°21'N	78°31'W
Perry, Fl., U.S. (pĕr'ĭ)	124-25	30°07'N	83°35'W
Perry, Ga., U.S. (pĕr'ĭ)	124-25	32°28'N	83°44'W
Perry, Ia., U.S. (pĕr'ĭ)	114-15	41°51'N	94°07'W
Perry, N.Y., U.S. (pĕr'ĭ)	116-17	42°43'N	78°01'W
Perry, Ok., U.S. (pĕr'ĭ)	120-21	36°17'N	97°17'W
Perrysburg, Oh., U.S. (pĕr ĭz-bûrg)	116-17	41°34'N	83°37'W
Perryton, Tx., U.S. (pĕr'ĭ-tŭn)	120-21	36°23'N	100°48'W
Perryville, Mo., U.S. (pĕr-ĭ-vĭl)	120-21	37°43'N	89°52'W
Persepolis, hist., Iran (pēr-sĕpŏ-lĭs)	230-31	29°57'N	52°52'E
Persia, nation, Asia *see* Iran	206-07	32°0'N	53°00'E
Persian Gulf, b., Asia (pûr'zhăn gŭlf)	230-31	27°0'N	51°00'E
Perth, Austl. (pûrth)	270-71	31°57'S	115°51'E
Perth, On., Can. (pûrth)	136-37	44°55'N	76°15'W
Perth, Scot., U.K. (pûrth)	190-91	56°24'N	3°27'W
Perth Amboy, N.J., U.S. (pûrth ăm'boi)	116-17	40°31'N	74°14'W
Pertuis, Fr. (pĕr-tüē')	196-97	43°42'N	5°30'E
Peru, Il., U.S. (pē-rōō')	116-17	41°20'N	89°07'W
Peru, In., U.S. (pē-rōō')	116-17	40°45'N	86°03'W
Peru, nation, S.A. (pē-rōō')	158	10°0'S	76°00'W
Perugia, Italy (pā-rōō'jä)	200-01	43°07'N	12°22'E
Pervomais'k, Ukr.	202-03	48°03'N	30°51'E
Pervouralsk, Russia (pĕr-vô-ŏ-rälsk')	218-19	56°55'N	59°57'E
Pesaro, Italy (pā'zä-rō)	200-01	43°55'N	12°55'E
Pescadores, is., Tai. *see* P'enghu Ch'üntao	225a	23°30'N	119°30'E
Pescara, Italy (pās-kä'rä)	200-01	42°29'N	14°12'E
Peshāwar, Pak. (pĕ-shä'wŭr)	232-33	33°60'N	71°33'E
Peshtigo, Wi., U.S. (pĕsh'tē-gō)	116-17	45°03'N	87°44'W
Pesqueira, Braz.	163d	8°22'S	36°42'W
Pesyakov, Ostrov, i., Russia	186-87	68°45'N	57°41'E
Petacalco, Bahía, b., Mex. (bä-ē'ä-dĕ-pĕ-tä-käl'kō)	146-47	17°56'N	101°57'W
Petah Tiqwa, Isr.	228-29	32°06'N	34°54'E
Petaluma, Ca., U.S. (pĕt-ȧ-lō'mȧ)	118-19	38°14'N	122°38'W
Petare, Ven. (pĕ-tä'rĕ)	163b	10°29'N	66°49'W
Petatlán, Mex. (pā-tä-tlän')	146-47	17°31'N	101°16'W
Peterborough, Austl.	276	32°58'S	138°50'E
Peterborough, On., Can. (pē'tēr-bŭr-ō)	136-37	44°18'N	78°20'W
Peterhead, Scot., U.K. (pē-tēr-hĕd')	190-91	57°31'N	1°47'W
Peter Pond Lake, lk., Sk., Can. (pē'tēr pŏnd lāk)	134-35	56°06'N	109°06'W
Petersburg, Ak., U.S. (pē'tērz-bûrg)	126	56°48'N	132°57'W
Petersburg, Il., U.S. (pē'tērz-bûrg)	120-21	40°00'N	89°50'W
Petersburg, In., U.S. (pē'tērz-bûrg)	116-17	38°29'N	87°17'W
Petersburg, Va., U.S. (pē'tērz-bûrg)	124-25	37°14'N	77°24'W
Petersburg, W.V., U.S. (pē'tērz-bûrg)	116-17	38°59'N	79°08'W
Peter the Great Bay, b., Russia *see* Petra Velikogo, Zaliv	244	42°40'N	132°00'E
Petitcodiac, N.B., Can. (pē-tē-kō-dyăk')	138-39	45°56'N	65°11'W
Petit-Goâve, Haiti (pē-tē' gō-äv')	142-43	18°26'N	72°51'W
Petlalcingo, Mex. (pĕ-tläl-sĕŋ'gō)	146-47	18°04'N	97°56'W
Peto, Mex. (pĕ'tō)	148	20°08'N	88°54'W
Petorca, Chile (pā-tōr'kä)	163e	32°15'S	70°57'W
Petoskey, Mi., U.S. (pē-tŏs-kĭ)	116-17	45°22'N	84°57'W
Petra Velikogo, Zaliv, b., Russia	244	42°40'N	132°00'E
Petrich, Blg. (pā'trĭch)	200-01	41°24'N	23°13'E
Petrified Forest National Park, n.p., Az., U.S. (pĕt'rĭ-fīd fŏr'ĕst năsh'ŭn-ăl pärk)	118-19	34°54'N	109°47'W
Petrinja, Cro. (pā'trēn-yȧ)	200-01	45°27'N	16°16'E
Petrodvorets, Russia (pyĕ-trô-dvô-ryĕts')	192-93	59°53'N	29°52'E
Petrolia, On., Can. (pē-trō'lĭ-ȧ)	136-37	42°53'N	82°09'W
Petrolina, Braz. (pĕ-trō-lē'nȧ)	166-67	9°24'S	40°30'W
Petropavlovsk, Kaz. (pyĕ-trô-päv'lôvsk)	226	54°52'N	69°09'E
Petropavlovsk-Kamchatskiy, Russia (pyĕ-trô-päv'lôvsk käm-chät'skĭ)	218-19	53°01'N	158°41'E
Petrópolis, Braz. (på-trô-pô-lēzh')	172	22°31'S	43°10'W
Petroșani, Rom.	200-01	45°25'N	23°23'E
Petrovgrad, Serb. *see* Zhovti Vody	200-01	45°23'N	20°24'E
Petrovsk, Russia (pyĕ-trôfsk')	186-87	52°19'N	45°23'E
Petrovsk-Zabaykal'skiy, Russia (pyĕ-trôfskzä-bī-käl'skĭ)	240-41	51°16'N	108°50'E
Petrozavodsk, Russia (pyā'trō-zá-vôtsk')	186-87	61°47'N	34°21'E
Petrozsény, Rom. *see* Petroșani	200-01	45°25'N	23°23'E
Petukhovo, Russia	226	55°04'N	67°54'E
Pevek, Russia	218-19	69°41'N	170°21'E
Peza, stm., Russia (pyå'zå)	186-87	65°36'N	44°37'E
Pézenas, Fr. (pā-zē-nä')	196-97	43°27'N	3°26'E
Pforzheim, Ger. (pfōrts'hīm)	194-95	48°54'N	8°42'E
Pha-an, Mya.	246-47	16°53'N	97°38'E
Phangan, Ko, i., Thai.	246-47	9°45'N	100°01'E
Phangnga, Thai.	246-47	8°27'N	98°32'E
Phanom Dong Rak, Thiu Khao, mts., Asia *see* Phanom Dongrak Range	246-47	14°25'N	103°30'E
Phanom Dongrak Range, mts., Asia	246-47	14°25'N	103°30'E
Phan Rang, Viet.	246-47	11°34'N	108°60'E
Phan Si Pan, mtn., Viet. *see* Fan Si Pan	246-47	22°15'N	103°46'E
Phan Thiet, Viet.	246-47	10°56'N	108°06'E
Phenix City, Al., U.S. (fē'nĭks sĭ'tĭ)	124-25	32°28'N	85°01'W
Phetchabun, Thiu Khao, mts., Thai.	246-47	16°32'N	100°55'E
Philadelphia, Ms., U.S. (fĭl-ȧ-dĕl'phĭ-ȧ)	124-25	32°46'N	89°07'W
Philadelphia, Pa., U.S. (fĭl-ȧ-dĕl'phĭ-ȧ)	116-17	39°57'N	75°10'W
Philip, S.D., U.S. (fĭl'ĭp)	114-15	44°02'N	101°39'W
Philippeville, Alg. *see* Skikda	269b	36°53'N	6°55'E
Philippines, nation, Asia (fĭl'ĭ-pēnz)	206-07	13°0'N	122°00'E
Philippine Sea, s., (fĭl'ĭ-pēn sē)	222-23	20°0'N	135°00'E
Philipsburg, Mt., U.S. (fĭl'lĭps-bērg)	112-13	46°20'N	113°18'W
Phillip Island, i., Austl. (fĭl'ĭp ī'lȧnd)	276	38°29'S	145°14'E
Phillips, Wi., U.S. (fĭl'ĭps)	116-17	45°42'N	90°24'W
Phillipsburg, Ks., U.S. (fĭl'lĭps-bērg)	120-21	39°45'N	99°19'W
Phillipsburg, N.J., U.S. (fĭl'lĭps-bērg)	116-17	40°42'N	75°11'W
Phitsanulok, Thai.	246-47	16°50'N	100°16'E
Phnom Penh, nat. cap., Camb. (nŏm'pĕn')	246-47	11°34'N	104°54'E
Phnum Pénh, nat. cap., Camb. (nŏm'pĕn') *see* Phnom Penh	246-47	11°34'N	104°54'E
Phoenix, Az., U.S. (fē'nĭks)	118-19	33°26'N	112°03'W
Phoenix Islands, is., Kir. (fē'nĭks ī'lȧndz)	280-81	4°0'S	172°00'W
Phoenixville, Pa., U.S. (fē'nĭks-vĭl)	116-17	40°08'N	75°31'W
Phôngsali, Laos	246-47	21°43'N	102°07'E
Phra Chedi Sam Ong, p., Asia *see* Three Pagodas Pass	246-47	15°18'N	98°22'E
Phrae, Thai.	246-47	18°08'N	100°09'E
Phra Nakhon, nat. cap., Thai. *see* Bangkok	246-47	13°45'N	100°31'E
Phra Nakhon Si Ayutthaya, Thai.	246-47	14°21'N	100°34'E
Phuket, Thai.	246-47	7°52'N	98°23'E
Phuket, Ko, i., Thai.	246-47	8°0'N	98°22'E
Phu Ly, Viet.	246-47	20°31'N	105°56'E
Phu Quoc, Dao, i., Viet.	246-47	10°12'N	104°00'E
Piacenza, Italy (pyä-chĕnt'sä)	200-01	45°03'N	9°42'E
Piatra-Neamț, Rom.	194-95	46°57'N	26°24'E
Piauí, state, Braz.	166-67	7°0'S	43°00'W
Piazza Armerina, Italy (pyät'sä är-må-rē'nä)	200-01	37°23'N	14°22'E
Pic, stm., On., Can. (pēk)	136-37	48°36'N	86°18'W
Picayune, Ms., U.S. (pĭk'ȧ yōōn)	124-25	30°32'N	89°42'W
Pichanal, Arg.	168-69	23°18'S	64°14'W
Pichilemu, Chile (pē-chē-lĕ'mōō)	163e	34°23'S	72°00'W
Pichucalco, Mex. (pē-chōō-käl'kō)	146-47	17°30'N	93°10'W
Pickle Lake, On., Can.	134-35	51°30'N	90°04'W
Pico, i., Port. (pē'kō)	199c	38°28'N	28°20'W
Pico de Orizaba, Volcán, vol., Mex. (vôl-kä'n-pē'kō-dĕ-ō-rē-zä'bä)	146-47	19°01'N	97°16'W
Picos, Braz. (pē'kōzh)	166-67	7°05'S	41°28'W
Picton, On., Can. (pĭk'tŭn)	136-37	43°60'N	77°08'W
Picton, Isla, i., Chile	171	55°03'S	66°55'W
Pictou, N.S., Can. (pĭk-tōō')	138-39	45°41'N	62°42'W
Pidurutalagala, mtn., Sri L. (pē'dō-rō-tä'lȧ-gä'lȧ)	236	6°60'N	80°46'E
Piedmont, Al., U.S. (pēd'mŏnt)	124-25	33°55'N	85°37'W
Piedmont, Mo., U.S. (pēd'mŏnt)	124-25	37°09'N	90°42'W
Piedra del Águila, Arg.	171	40°03'S	70°03'W
Piedras, Punta, c., Arg. (pōō'n-tä-pyĕ'dräs)	173	35°26'S	57°07'W
Piedras Negras, Mex. (pyā'dräs nā'gräs)	122-23	28°42'N	100°31'W
Pierce, Ne., U.S. (pērs)	114-15	42°12'N	97°32'W
Pierre, S.D., U.S. (pēr)	114-15	44°22'N	100°21'W
Pietarsaari, Fin. *see* Jakobstad	184-85	63°41'N	22°43'E
Pietermaritzburg, S. Afr. (pē-tēr-mȧ-rĭts-bûrg)	264-65	29°36'S	30°23'E
Pietersburg, S. Afr. (pē'tērz-bûrg) *see* Polokwane	269c	23°53'S	29°26'E
Pigeon Lake, lk., Ab., Can. (pĭj'ŭn lāk)	132-33	53°0'N	114°00'W
Pigeon Lake, lk., On., Can. (pĭj'ŭn lāk)	136-37	44°30'N	78°30'W
Piggott, Ar., U.S. (pĭg-ŭt)	124-25	36°23'N	90°12'W
Pigüé, Arg.	173	37°37'S	62°25'W
Pihkva järv, lk., Eur. *see* Pskov, Lake	192-93	58°0'N	28°00'E
Pijijiapan, Mex. (pēkē-kē-ä'pän)	146-47	15°42'N	93°13'W
Pikalëvo, Russia	186-87	59°31'N	34°11'E
Pikes Peak, mtn., Co., U.S. (pīks pēk)	120-21	38°51'N	105°03'W
Piketberg, S. Afr.	264-65	32°55'S	18°46'E
Pikeville, Ky., U.S. (pĭk'vĭl)	116-17	37°30'N	82°33'W
Piła, Pol. (pē'lȧ)	194-95	53°09'N	16°44'E
Pilanesberg, hill, S. Afr. (pē'ȧns'bûrg)	269c	25°12'S	27°05'E
Pilar, Arg. (pē'lär)	173	31°26'S	61°16'W
Pilar, Para.	173	26°54'S	58°19'W
Pilcomayo, stm., S.A. (pēl-cō-mī'ō)	168-69	25°17'S	57°40'W
Pili, Phil. (pē'lē)	250	13°32'N	123°17'E
Pīlībhīt, India	234-35	28°38'N	79°48'E
Pilica, stm., Pol. (pē-lēt'sä)	194-95	51°52'N	21°17'E
Pilipinas, nation, Asia *see* Philippines	206-07	13°0'N	122°00'E
Pilsen, Czech Rep. *see* Plzeň	194-95	49°45'N	13°23'E
Pinamalayan, Phil. (pē-nä-mä-lä'yän)	250	13°02'N	121°29'E
Pinang, Malay. *see* George Town	246-47	5°25'N	100°20'E
Pinar del Río, Cuba (pē-när' dĕl rē'ō)	142-43	22°25'N	83°41'W
Pinar del Río, state, Cuba (pē-när' dĕl rē'ō)	142-43	22°30'N	83°45'W
Pinatubo, Mount, vol., Phil. (mount pē-nä-tōō'bō)	250	15°08'N	120°21'E
Pincher Creek, Ab., Can. (pĭn'chēr krēk)	132-33	49°29'N	113°57'W
Pinckneyville, Il., U.S. (pĭnk'nĭ-vĭl)	116-17	38°05'N	89°23'W
Pindaré, stm., Braz.	166-67	3°18'S	44°47'W
Píndos Óros, mts., Grc.	200-01	39°49'N	21°14'E
Pindus Mountains, mts., Grc. (pĭn'dŭs moun'tĭnz) *see* Píndos Óros	200-01	39°49'N	21°14'E
Pine, stm., B.C., Can. (pīn)	132-33	56°09'N	120°44'W
Pine Bluff, Ar., U.S. (pīn blŭf)	124-25	34°14'N	92°02'W
Pine City, Mn., U.S. (pīn sĭ'tē)	114-15	45°50'N	92°58'W
Pine Creek, Austl. (pīn crēk krēk)	270-71	13°48'S	131°50'E
Pine Falls, Mb., Can. (pīn fôlz)	134-35	50°34'N	96°14'W
Pinega, stm., Russia (pē-nyĕ'gȧ)	186-87	64°08'N	41°54'E
Pinehouse Lake, lk., Sk., Can.	134-35	55°34'N	106°31'W
Pine Ridge, S.D., U.S. (pīn rĭj)	114-15	43°01'N	102°33'W
Pinerolo, Italy (pē-nå-rô'lō)	200-01	44°54'N	7°20'E
Pines, Isle of, i., Cuba (īl ŭv pīnz) *see* Juventud, Isla de la	142-43	21°40'N	82°50'W
Pineville, Ky., U.S. (pīn'vĭl)	124-25	36°45'N	83°42'W
Pineville, La., U.S. (pīn'vĭl)	122-23	31°20'N	92°26'W
Ping, stm., Thai.	246-47	15°42'N	100°09'E
Pingdingshan, China	238-39	33°45'N	113°18'E
Pingdu, China (pĭŋ-dōō)	240-41	36°47'N	119°56'E
Pingelap, at., Micron.	280-81	6°13'N	160°42'E
Pingjiang, China	238-39	28°42'N	113°35'E
Pingle, China (pĭŋ-lŭ)	238-39	24°38'N	110°40'E
Pingliang, China (pĭng'lyăng')	240-41	35°33'N	106°42'E
Pingquan, China (pĭŋ-chyůän)	240-41	40°59'N	118°39'E
Pingtan, China (pĭŋ-tän)	225a	25°31'N	119°47'E
Pingtan Dao, i., China (pĭŋ-tän dou)	225a	25°33'N	119°48'E
P'ingtung, Tai.	225a	22°40'N	120°29'E
Pingwu, China (pĭŋ-wōō)	238-39	32°25'N	104°33'E
Pingxiang, China (pĭŋ-shyäŋ)	238-39	22°08'N	106°44'E
Pingxiang, China (pĭŋ-shyäŋ)	238-39	27°38'N	113°50'E
Pingyao, China	240-41	37°16'N	112°14'E
Pingyi, China (pĭŋ-yē)	240-41	35°30'N	117°38'E
Pingyuan, China (pĭŋ-yůän)	238-39	24°36'N	115°55'E
Pinheiro, Braz.	166-67	2°31'S	45°05'W
Pinnacles National Monument, n.p., Ca., U.S. (pĭn'ȧ-k'lz năsh'ŭn-ăl mŏn'ū-mĕnt)	118-19	36°30'N	121°11'W
Pinnaroo, Austl.	276	35°16'S	140°54'E
Pinos, Isla de, i., Cuba *see* Juventud, Isla de la	142-43	21°40'N	82°50'W
Pinrang, Indon.	248-49	3°48'S	119°39'E
Pins, Île des, i., N. Cal.	279g	22°37'S	167°28'E
Pinsk, Bela. (pēn'sk)	194-95	52°07'N	26°07'E
Pinsk Marshes, reg., Eur. *see* Pripet Marshes	194-95	52°0'N	27°00'E
Pinta, Isla, i., Ec.	170a	0°35'N	90°44'W
Pinyug, Russia	186-87	60°15'N	47°47'E
Piombino, Italy (pyôm-bē'nō)	200-01	42°56'N	10°32'E
Pioneer Mountains, mts., Mt., U.S. (pī'ō-nēr' moun'tĭnz)	112-13	45°31'N	112°60'W
Pioner, Ostrov, i., Russia	218-19	79°50'N	92°30'E

n-sing; ŋ-baŋk; ɴ-nasalized n; nŏd; cŏmmit; ōld; ôbey; ôrder; oi-boil; fōōd; ŏ-as oo in foot; ou-out; s-soft; sh-dish; th-thin; pūre; ûnite; ûrn; stŭd; circŭs; ü-as in French tu; '-indeterminate vowel.

Feature (Pronunciation)	Page	Lat.	Long.
Piorini, stm., Braz.	**166-67**	3°23'S	63°30'W
Piotrków Trybunalski, Pol. (pyōtr'ko͞of trĭ-bo͞o-nal'skē)	**194-95**	51°24'N	19°42'E
Pipe Spring National Monument, n.p., Az., U.S. (pīp sprĭng năsh'ŭn-ăl mŏn'ū-mĕnt)	**118-19**	36°50'N	112°49'W
Pipestone, Mn., U.S. (pīp'stōn)	**114-15**	43°60'N	96°19'W
Pipestone, stm., On., Can.	**134-35**	52°54'N	89°15'W
Pipestone National Monument, n.p., Mn., U.S. (pīp'stōn năsh'ŭn-ăl mŏn'ū-mĕnt)	**114-15**	44°0'N	96°18'W
Pipinas, Arg.	**173**	35°32'S	57°19'W
Pipmuacan, Réservoir, res., Qc., Can. (pĭp-mä-kän')	**138-39**	49°37'N	70°27'W
Piqua, Oh., U.S. (pĭk'wà)	**116-17**	40°09'N	84°15'W
Piracicaba, Braz. (pē-rä-sē-kä'bä)	**172**	22°43'S	47°36'W
Piraeus, Grc. see Peiraiás	**200-01**	37°57'N	23°39'E
Piran, Slvn. (pē-rå'n)	**200-01**	45°32'N	13°34'E
Pirané, Arg.	**168-69**	25°43'S	59°05'W
Pirapora, Braz. (pē-rà-pō'rà)	**172**	17°21'S	44°56'W
Pires do Rio, Braz.	**172**	17°18'S	48°17'W
Piriápolis, Ur.	**173**	34°52'S	55°16'W
Pirineos, mts., Eur. see Pyrenees	**196-97**	42°40'N	1°00'E
Pirna, Ger. (pĭr'nä)	**194-95**	50°58'N	13°57'E
Pirot, Serb. (pē'rōt)	**200-01**	43°10'N	22°35'E
Piru, Indon. (pē-ro͞o')	**248-49**	3°03'S	128°11'E
Pisa, Italy (pē'sä)	**200-01**	43°44'N	10°24'E
Pisagua, Chile (pē-sä'gwä)	**168-69**	19°34'S	70°12'W
Pisco, Peru (pēs'kō)	**170**	13°42'S	76°12'W
Písek, Czech Rep. (pē'sĕk)	**194-95**	49°19'N	14°09'E
Pishan, China	**226**	37°37'N	78°16'E
Pisticci, Italy (pēs-tē'chē)	**200-01**	40°23'N	16°34'E
Pistoia, Italy (pēs-tô'yä)	**200-01**	43°56'N	10°55'E
Pisuerga, stm., Spain (pē-swĕr'gä)	**198-99**	41°33'N	4°52'W
Pitalito, Col. (pē-tä-lē'tō)	**164-65**	1°52'N	76°01'W
Pitanga, Braz.	**168-69**	24°44'S	51°45'W
Pitcairn Island, i., Pit.	**280-81**	25°04'S	130°06'W
Pitcairn Islands, dep., Oc. (pĭt'kârn ī'lăndz)	**280-81**	25°04'S	130°05'W
Piteå, Swe.	**184-85**	65°19'N	21°29'E
Piteälven, stm., Swe.	**184-85**	65°23'N	21°19'E
Pitești, Rom. (pē-tĕsht'')	**200-01**	44°51'N	24°52'E
Pithiviers, Fr. (pē-tē-vyā')	**196-97**	48°10'N	2°15'E
Pitti Island, i., India	**236**	10°50'N	72°37'E
Pitt Island, i., B.C., Can. (pĭt ī'lănd)	**132-33**	53°35'N	129°45'W
Pittsburg, Ks., U.S. (pĭts'bûrg)	**120-21**	37°25'N	94°42'W
Pittsburg, Tx., U.S. (pĭts'bûrg)	**120-21**	33°00'N	94°58'W
Pittsburgh, Pa., U.S. (pĭts'bûrg)	**116-17**	40°27'N	80°01'W
Pittsfield, Il., U.S. (pĭts'fēld)	**120-21**	39°36'N	90°48'W
Pittston, Pa., U.S. (pĭts'tŭn)	**116-17**	41°20'N	75°47'W
Pium, Braz.	**166-67**	10°27'S	49°11'W
Piura, Peru (pē-o͞o'rä)	**170**	5°11'S	80°38'W
Pivdennyi Buh, stm., Ukr. see Southern Bug	**202-03**	46°39'N	31°56'E
Placentia Bay, b., Nf., Can.	**138-39**	47°15'N	54°30'W
Placerville, Ca., U.S. (plăs'ēr-vĭl)	**118-19**	38°44'N	120°48'W
Placetas, Cuba (plä-thā'täs)	**142-43**	22°19'N	79°39'W
Plainview, Mn., U.S. (plān'vū)	**114-15**	44°10'N	92°09'W
Plainview, Ne., U.S. (plān'vū)	**114-15**	42°21'N	97°47'W
Plainview, Tx., U.S. (plān'vū)	**120-21**	34°11'N	101°42'W
Plainwell, Mi., U.S. (plan'wĕl)	**116-17**	42°26'N	85°38'W
Plano, Il., U.S. (plā'nō)	**116-17**	41°40'N	88°32'W
Plano, Tx., U.S. (plā'nō)	**120-21**	33°03'N	96°41'W
Plant City, Fl., U.S. (plånt sĭ'tĭ)	**125a**	28°01'N	82°07'W
Plaquemine, La., U.S. (plăk'mēn')	**124-25**	30°17'N	91°14'W
Plasencia, Spain (plä-sĕn'thē-ä)	**198-99**	40°02'N	6°05'W
Plaster Rock, N.B., Can. (plås'tēr rŏk)	**138-39**	46°55'N	67°24'W
Plastun, Russia (plås-to͞on')	**244**	44°45'N	136°18'E
Plata, Río de la, est., S.A. (rē'ō dälä plä'tä)	**173**	35°0'S	57°00'W
Platinum, Ak., U.S. (plăt'ĭ-nŭm)	**126**	59°01'N	161°49'W
Plato, Col. (plä'tō)	**164-65**	9°48'N	74°47'W
Platte, S.D., U.S. (plăt)	**114-15**	43°23'N	98°51'W
Platte, stm., U.S. (plăt)	**120-21**	39°16'N	94°51'W
Platte, stm., Ne., U.S. (plăt)	**110-11**	41°04'N	95°53'W
Platteville, Wi., U.S. (plăt'vĭl)	**114-15**	42°44'N	90°29'W
Plattsburg, Mo., U.S. (plăts'bûrg)	**120-21**	39°34'N	94°27'W
Plattsburgh, N.Y., U.S.	**116-17**	44°42'N	73°28'W
Plattsmouth, Ne., U.S. (plăts'mŭth)	**114-15**	41°01'N	95°54'W
Plauen, Ger. (plou'ĕn)	**194-95**	50°30'N	12°08'E
Playa Vicente, Mex. (plä-yä vē-sĕn'tå)	**146-47**	17°48'N	95°49'W
Play Ku, Viet.	**246-47**	13°59'N	108°01'E
Pleasanton, Tx., U.S. (plĕz'ăn-tŭn)	**122-23**	28°58'N	98°29'W
Pleiku, Viet. see Play Ku	**246-47**	13°59'N	108°01'E
Plenty, Bay of, b., N.Z. (bā ŭv plĕn'tē)	**278**	37°40'S	177°00'E
Plentywood, Mt., U.S. (plĕn'tē-wŏd)	**112-13**	48°46'N	104°32'W
Plesetsk, Russia	**186-87**	62°43'N	40°18'E
Plessisville, Qc., Can. (plĕ-sē'vēl')	**136-37**	46°13'N	71°46'W
Pleszew, Pol. (plĕ'zhĕf)	**194-95**	51°54'N	17°47'E
Płock, Pol. (pwôtsk)	**194-95**	52°33'N	19°42'E
Ploërmel, Fr. (plô-ĕr-mĕl')	**196-97**	47°56'N	2°24'W
Ploești, Rom. see Ploiești	**200-01**	44°57'N	26°02'E
Ploiești, Rom. (plô-yĕsht'')	**200-01**	44°57'N	26°02'E
Plomb du Cantal, mtn., Fr. (plôn'dü-kän-täl')	**196-97**	45°04'N	2°45'E
Plonge, Lac la, lk., Sk., Can. (läk lä plōnzh)	**134-35**	55°08'N	107°17'W
Plovdiv, Blg. (plôv'dĭf) (fĭl-ĭp-ŏp'ô-lĭs)	**200-01**	42°09'N	24°45'E
Plungė, Lith. (plŏn'gā)	**192-93**	55°54'N	21°52'E
Plyeven, Blg.	**200-01**	43°25'N	24°37'E
Plymouth, Eng., U.K. (plĭm'ŭth)	**190-91**	50°23'N	4°10'W
Plymouth, In., U.S. (plĭm'ŭth)	**116-17**	41°20'N	86°18'W
Plymouth, N.C., U.S. (plĭm'ŭth)	**124-25**	35°52'N	76°45'W
Plymouth, N.H., U.S. (plĭm'ŭth)	**116-17**	43°46'N	71°41'W
Plymouth, Pa., U.S. (plĭm'ŭth)	**116-17**	41°14'N	75°58'W
Plymouth, Vt., U.S. (plĭm'ŭth)	**116-17**	43°33'N	72°44'W
Plymouth, Wi., U.S. (plĭm'ŭth)	**116-17**	43°46'N	87°59'W
Plzeň, Czech Rep.	**194-95**	49°45'N	13°23'E
Po, stm., Italy	**200-01**	44°59'N	12°03'E
Pobeda, Gora, mtn., Russia	**218-19**	65°12'N	146°12'E
Pobedy, Pik, mtn., Asia see Jengish Chokusu	**226**	42°02'N	80°05'E
Pocahontas, Ar., U.S. (pō-kà-hŏn'tàs)	**124-25**	36°16'N	90°58'W
Pocahontas, Ia., U.S. (pō-kà-hŏn'tàs)	**114-15**	42°44'N	94°40'W
Pocatello, Id., U.S. (pō-kà-tĕl'ō)	**112-13**	42°53'N	112°29'W
Pochëp, Russia (pô-chĕp')	**202-03**	52°55'N	33°29'E
Pocomoke City, Md., U.S. (pō-kō-mōk' sĭ'tē)	**116-17**	38°04'N	75°33'W
Poços de Caldas, Braz. (pō-sôs-dĕ-käl'dås)	**172**	21°47'S	46°34'W
Podgorica, nat. cap., Mont.	**200-01**	42°27'N	19°16'E
Podkamennaya Tunguska, stm., Russia	**218-19**	61°36'N	90°09'E
Podolsk, Russia (pô-dôl''sk)	**202-03**	55°26'N	37°34'E
Podporozhye, Russia	**192-93**	60°55'N	34°10'E
Poggibonsi, Italy (pôd-jē-bôn'sē)	**200-01**	43°28'N	11°09'E
Pogranichnyy, Russia	**244**	44°24'N	131°23'E
P'ohang, Kor., S.	**243**	36°03'N	129°22'E
Pohjanlahti, b., Eur. see Bothnia, Gulf of	**184-85**	63°0'N	20°00'E
Pohnpei, i., Micron.	**280-81**	6°55'N	158°15'E
Poinsett, Cape, c., Ant.	**287**	65°48'S	113°10'E
Point Au Fer Island, i., La., U.S.	**124-25**	29°15'N	91°15'W
Pointe-à-Pitre, Guad. (pwănt' à pē-tr')	**143b**	16°15'N	61°32'W
Pointe-des-Galets, Reu. see Le Port	**265a**	20°55'S	55°18'E
Pointe-Noire, Congo	**262-63**	4°48'S	11°52'E
Point Hope, Ak., U.S. (point hōp)	**126**	68°21'N	166°41'W
Point Pleasant, Oh., U.S. (point plĕz'ănt)	**116-17**	38°54'N	84°14'W
Point Pleasant, W.V., U.S. (point plĕz'ănt)	**116-17**	38°52'N	82°08'W
Poitiers, Fr. (pwà-tyā')	**196-97**	46°35'N	0°20'E
Pokharā, Nepal	**234-35**	28°13'N	83°60'E
Pokhvistnevo, Russia	**186-87**	53°39'N	52°08'E
Pokrovsk, Russia	**218-19**	61°31'N	129°11'E
Pokrovskoye, Russia (pô-krôf'skô-yĕ)	**202-03**	52°37'N	36°51'E
Polack, Bela.	**192-93**	55°30'N	28°47'E
Poland, nation, Eur. (pō'lănd)	**174-75**	52°0'N	19°00'E
Polatlı, Tur.	**186-87**	39°36'N	32°10'E
Polessk, Russia (pô'lĕsk)	**192-93**	54°52'N	21°05'E
Polesye, reg., Eur. see Pripet Marshes	**194-95**	52°0'N	27°00'E
Polillo Island, i., Phil.	**250**	14°50'N	121°57'E
Polillo Islands, is., Phil. (pô-lēl'yō ī'lăndz)	**250**	14°50'N	122°05'E
Polissya, reg., Eur. see Pripet Marshes	**194-95**	52°0'N	27°00'E
Pollāchi, India	**236**	10°39'N	77°01'E
Polokwane, S. Afr.	**269c**	23°53'S	29°26'E
Polonnaruwa, Sri L.	**236**	7°56'N	81°01'E
Polotsk, Bela. see Polack	**192-93**	55°30'N	28°47'E
Polska, nation, Eur. see Poland	**174-75**	52°0'N	19°00'E
Polson, Mt., U.S. (pōl'sŭn)	**112-13**	47°41'N	114°09'W
Poltava, Ukr. (pôl-tä'vä)	**202-03**	49°36'N	34°31'E
Põltsamaa, Est. (pôlt'så-mä)	**192-93**	58°39'N	25°58'E
Polunochnoye, Russia (pô-lo͞o-nô'ch-nô'yĕ)	**186-87**	60°52'N	60°26'E
Polyarnyy, Russia (pŭl-yär'nē)	**218-19**	69°06'N	178°39'E
Polyarnyy, Russia (pŭl-yär'nē)	**184-85**	69°11'N	33°28'E
Polynesia, is., Oc. (pŏl-ĭ-nē'zhà)	**280-81**	4°0'S	156°00'W
Polynésie, is., Oc. see Polynesia	**280-81**	4°0'S	156°00'W
Polynésie française, dep., Oc. see French Polynesia	**280-81**	15°0'S	140°00'W
Pomerania, hist. reg., Eur. (pŏm-ē-rā'nĭ-à)	**194-95**	54°0'N	16°00'E
Pomeroy, Oh., U.S. (pŏm'ēr-oi)	**116-17**	39°02'N	82°01'W
Pomeroy, Wa., U.S. (pŏm'ēr-oi)	**112-13**	46°28'N	117°35'W
Pommern, hist. reg., Eur. see Pomerania	**194-95**	54°0'N	16°00'E
Pomona, Ca., U.S. (pô-mō'nà)	**118-19**	34°03'N	117°45'W
Pomorze, hist. reg., Eur. see Pomerania	**194-95**	54°0'N	16°00'E
Pompano Beach, Fl., U.S. (pŏm'pă-nô bēch)	**125a**	26°14'N	80°08'W
Pompei, hist., Italy	**200-01**	40°45'N	14°30'E
Pompeii, hist., Italy see Pompei	**200-01**	40°45'N	14°30'E
Ponape, i., Micron. see Pohnpei	**280-81**	6°55'N	158°15'E
Ponca, Ne., U.S. (pŏn'kà)	**114-15**	42°33'N	96°43'W
Ponca City, Ok., U.S. (pŏn'kà sĭ'tĭ)	**120-21**	36°42'N	97°05'W
Ponce, P.R. (pōn'sā)	**142a**	18°01'N	66°37'W
Pondicherry, India	**236**	11°56'N	79°50'E
Pondicherry, state, India see Puducherry	**236**	11°56'N	79°50'E
Ponferrada, Spain (pôn-fĕr-rä'dhä)	**198-99**	42°33'N	6°35'W
Pongolo, stm., S. Afr.	**264-65**	26°52'S	32°21'E
Ponoka, Ab., Can. (pŏ-nō'kà)	**132-33**	52°40'N	113°35'W
Ponoy, Russia	**186-87**	66°60'N	41°16'E
Ponta Delgada, Port. (pōn'tà dĕl-gä'dà)	**199c**	37°45'N	25°40'W
Ponta Grossa, Braz. (pôn'tä grō'sà)	**168-69**	25°05'S	50°10'W
Ponta Porã, Braz.	**168-69**	22°33'S	55°42'W
Pontarlier, Fr. (pôn'tàr-lyā')	**196-97**	46°54'N	6°22'E
Pont-Audemer, Fr. (pôn'tōd'mâr')	**196-97**	49°21'N	0°31'E
Pontchartrain, Lake, lk., La., U.S. (lāk pôn-shàr-trăn')	**124-25**	30°10'N	90°10'W
Pontedera, Italy (pōn-tå-dā'rä)	**200-01**	43°40'N	10°38'E
Ponte Nova, Braz. (pô'n-tĕ-nō'vå)	**172**	20°25'S	42°54'W
Pontevedra, Spain (pôn-tĕ-vĕ-drä)	**198-99**	42°25'N	8°38'W
Pontiac, Il., U.S. (pŏn'tĭ-ăk)	**116-17**	40°53'N	88°37'W
Pontiac, Mi., U.S. (pŏn'tĭ-ăk)	**116-17**	42°38'N	83°18'W
Pontianak, Indon. (pôn-tē-ä'nák)	**246-47**	0°01'S	109°20'E
Pontine, Isole, is., Italy see Ponziane, Isole	**200-01**	40°55'N	12°57'E
Pontine Islands, is., Italy see Ponziane, Isole	**200-01**	40°55'N	12°57'E
Pontivy, Fr. (pôn-tē-vē')	**196-97**	48°04'N	2°58'W
Pontoise, Fr. (pôn-twáz')	**196-97**	49°03'N	2°05'E
Pontotoc, Ms., U.S. (pŏn-tô-tŏk')	**124-25**	34°15'N	88°60'W
Pontremoli, Italy (pôn-trĕm'ô-lē)	**200-01**	44°23'N	9°53'E
Pontus Mountains, mts., Tur. see Doğu Karadeniz Dağları	**227**	40°30'N	40°30'E
Ponziane, Isole, is., Italy	**200-01**	40°55'N	12°57'E
Poole, Eng., U.K. (po͞ol)	**190-91**	50°44'N	1°59'W
Poona, India see Pune	**236**	18°32'N	73°52'E
Poopó, Lago, lk., Bol.	**168-69**	18°47'S	67°05'W
Popayán, Col. (pō-pä-yän')	**164-65**	2°27'N	76°36'W
Popigay, stm., Russia	**218-19**	72°57'N	106°10'E
Poplar, Mt., U.S. (pŏp'lēr)	**112-13**	48°06'N	105°13'W
Poplar, stm., Can.	**134-35**	53°02'N	97°27'W
Poplar Bluff, Mo., U.S. (pŏp'lēr blŭf)	**124-25**	36°45'N	90°24'W
Poplar Plains, Ky., U.S. (pŏp'lēr plānz)	**116-17**	38°22'N	83°40'W
Poplarville, Ms., U.S. (pŏp'lēr-vĭl)	**124-25**	30°51'N	89°34'W
Popocatépetl, Volcán, vol., Mex.	**146-47**	19°01'N	98°37'W
Popondetta, Pap. N. Gui.	**277**	8°47'S	148°13'E
Popovo, Blg. (pô'pô-vō)	**200-01**	43°21'N	26°14'E
Poprad, Slvk.	**194-95**	49°03'N	20°19'E
Porangatu, Braz.	**166-67**	13°26'S	49°12'W
Porbandar, India (pōr-bŭn'dŭr)	**234-35**	21°39'N	69°37'E
Porcher Island, i., B.C., Can. (pôr'kēr ī'lănd)	**132-33**	53°57'N	130°30'W
Porcupine, stm., N.A.	**126**	66°34'N	145°21'W
Pordenone, Italy (pōr-då-nō'nå)	**200-01**	45°58'N	12°39'E
Pori, Fin. (pô'rē)	**192-93**	61°29'N	21°47'E
Porkhov, Russia (pôr'κôf)	**192-93**	57°46'N	29°34'E
Porlamar, Ven. (pôr-lä-mär')	**164-65**	10°57'N	63°51'W
Pornic, Fr. (pôr-nēk')	**196-97**	47°07'N	2°06'W
Poronaysk, Russia (pô'rô-nīsk)	**218-19**	49°14'N	143°06'E
Porpoise Bay, b., Ant.	**287**	66°30'S	128°30'E
Porsgrunn, Nor. (pôrs'grôn')	**192-93**	59°09'N	9°40'E
Port, Reu. see Le Port	**265a**	20°55'S	55°18'E
Portachuelo, Bol. (pôrt-ä-chwä'lō)	**168-69**	17°21'S	63°24'W
Portage, In., U.S. (pôr'tāj)	**116-17**	41°35'N	87°11'W
Portage, Mi., U.S. (pôr'tāj)	**116-17**	42°12'N	85°36'W
Portage, Pa., U.S. (pôr'tāj)	**116-17**	40°23'N	78°40'W
Portage, Wi., U.S. (pôr'tāj)	**116-17**	43°33'N	89°28'W
Portage la Prairie, Mb., Can. (pōr'tĭj lä-prā'rĭ)	**134-35**	49°58'N	98°18'W
Port Alberni, B.C., Can. (pōr äl-bĕr-nē')	**132-33**	49°15'N	124°48'W
Portalegre, Port. (pôr-tä-lā'grĕ)	**198-99**	39°17'N	7°25'W

ăt; finăl; rāte; senåte; ärm; åsk; sofȧ; fâre; ch-choose; dh-as th in other; bē; ēvent; bĕt; recĕnt; cratēr; g-gō; gh-guttural g; bĭt; ĭ-short neutral; rīde; κ-guttural k as ch in German ich;

Feature (Pronunciation)	Page	Lat.	Long.
Portales, N.M., U.S. (pôr-tä'lĕs)	**120-21**	34°11'N	103°20'W
Port Alfred, S. Afr.	**264-65**	33°36'S	26°54'E
Port Alice, B.C., Can. (pōrt ăl'ĭs)	**132-33**	50°23'N	127°26'W
Port Allegany, Pa., U.S. (pōrt ăl-ē-gā'nĭ)	**116-17**	41°49'N	78°17'W
Port Angeles, Wa., U.S. (pōrt ăn'jē-lĕs)	**112-13**	48°07'N	123°26'W
Port Antonio, Jam.	**142-43**	18°10'N	76°27'W
Port Arthur, Austl.	**276**	43°09'S	147°50'E
Port Arthur, China *see* Lüshun	**240-41**	38°49'N	121°15'E
Port Arthur, Tx., U.S.	**122-23**	29°54'N	93°56'W
Port Augusta, Austl. (pōrt ô-gŭs'tă)	**276**	32°30'S	137°46'E
Port au Port Bay, b., Nf., Can. (pôr'tō pōr' bā)	**138-39**	48°40'N	58°45'W
Port-au-Prince, nat. cap., Haiti (pôr'tō präNs')	**142-43**	18°32'N	72°20'W
Port Austin, Mi., U.S. (pōrt ôs'tĭn)	**116-17**	44°02'N	83°00'W
Port Blair, India (pōrt blâr)	**246-47**	11°39'N	92°45'E
Port Borden, P.E., Can. (pōrt bôr'dĕn)	**138-39**	46°15'N	63°42'W
Port-Cartier, Qc., Can.	**138-39**	50°02'N	66°52'W
Port Clinton, Oh., U.S. (pōrt klĭn'tŭn)	**116-17**	41°30'N	82°58'W
Port-de-Paix, Haiti (pôrt dē pĕ)	**142-43**	19°56'N	72°49'W
Port Dickson, Malay. (pōrt dĭk'sŭn)	**246-47**	2°31'N	101°49'E
Port Edward, China *see* Weihai	**240-41**	37°30'N	122°07'E
Portel, Braz.	**166-67**	1°58'S	50°48'W
Port Elgin, N.B., Can. (pōrt ĕl'jĭn)	**138-39**	46°03'N	64°06'W
Port Elgin, On., Can. (pōrt ĕl'jĭn)	**136-37**	44°26'N	81°23'W
Port Elizabeth, S. Afr. (pōrt ē-lĭz'á-bĕth)	**264-65**	33°56'S	25°34'E
Porterville, Ca., U.S. (pōr'tēr-vĭl)	**118-19**	36°05'N	119°02'W
Port Fairy, Austl.	**276**	38°23'S	142°14'E
Port-Francqui, D.R.C. *see* Ilebo	**262-63**	4°20'S	20°36'E
Port-Gentil, Gabon (pôr-zhäN-tē')	**260-61**	0°43'S	8°47'E
Port-Harcourt, Nig. (pōrt här'kŭrt)	**260a**	4°47'N	7°01'E
Port Hardy, B.C., Can. (pōrt här'dĭ)	**132-33**	50°43'N	127°30'W
Port Hedland, Austl. (pōrt hĕd'lănd)	**270-71**	20°19'S	118°36'E
Port Hood, N.S., Can. (pōrt hòd)	**138-39**	46°01'N	61°32'W
Port Hope, On., Can. (pōrt hōp)	**136-37**	43°57'N	78°17'W
Port Huron, Mi., U.S. (pōrt hū'rŏn)	**116-17**	42°58'N	82°26'W
Portimão, Port. (pôr-tē-mouN)	**198-99**	37°08'N	8°32'W
Port Jervis, N.Y., U.S. (pōrt jûr'vĭs)	**116-17**	41°23'N	74°42'W
Port Lairge, Ire. *see* Waterford	**190-91**	52°15'N	7°06'W
Portland, Austl. (pōrt'lănd)	**276**	38°21'S	141°36'E
Portland, In., U.S. (pōrt'lănd)	**116-17**	40°26'N	84°59'W
Portland, Me., U.S. (pōrt'lănd)	**116-17**	43°40'N	70°17'W
Portland, Mi., U.S. (pōrt'lănd)	**116-17**	42°52'N	84°54'W
Portland, Or., U.S. (pōrt'lănd)	**112-13**	45°32'N	122°40'W
Portland, Tn., U.S. (pōrt'lănd)	**124-25**	36°35'N	86°31'W
Portland, Tx., U.S. (pōrt'lănd)	**122-23**	27°53'N	97°19'W
Portland Bight, b., Jam. (pōrt'lănd bĭt)	**142-43**	17°50'N	77°06'W
Portland Inlet, b., B.C., Can. (pōrt'lănd ĭn'lĕt)	**132-33**	54°50'N	130°14'W
Portland Point, c., Jam. (pōrt'lănd point)	**142-43**	17°43'N	77°11'W
Port Lavaca, Tx., U.S. (pōrt lá-vä'ká)	**122-23**	28°37'N	96°38'W
Port Lincoln, Austl. (pōrt lĭŋ-kŭn)	**270-71**	34°44'S	135°52'E
Port Louis, nat. cap., Mauritius	**265a**	20°10'S	57°30'E
Port-Lyautey, Mor. *see* Kénitra	**269a**	34°16'N	6°35'W
Port Macquarie, Austl. (pōrt má-kwŏ'rĭ)	**276**	31°27'S	152°55'E
Port Moresby, nat. cap., Pap. N. Gui. (pōrt mōrz'bē)	**277**	9°28'S	147°12'E
Port Neches, Tx., U.S. (pōrt nĕch'ĕz)	**122-23**	29°59'N	93°57'W
Porto, Port. (pōr'tò)	**198-99**	41°09'N	8°37'W
Porto Alegre, Braz. (pōr'tō ä-lā'grĕ)	**168-69**	30°03'S	51°12'W
Porto Amélia, Moz. *see* Pemba	**264-65**	13°01'S	40°32'E
Portobelo, Pan. (pôr'tô-bā'lô)	**150**	9°33'N	79°39'W
Porto de Moz, Braz.	**166-67**	1°44'S	52°14'W
Porto de Pedras, Braz. (pōr'tō pā'dräzh)	**163d**	9°09'S	35°17'W
Porto Esperança, Braz.	**168-69**	19°37'S	57°27'W
Porto Esperidião, Braz.	**168-69**	15°51'S	58°28'W
Portoferraio, Italy (pōr'tō-fĕr-rä'yō)	**200-01**	42°49'N	10°19'E
Port of Spain, nat. cap., Trin. (pōrt ŭv spān')	**143b**	10°39'N	61°30'W
Portogruaro, Italy (pōr'tō-grò-ä'rō)	**200-01**	45°47'N	12°50'E
Porto Murtinho, Braz. (pōr'tō mòr-tēn'yò)	**168-69**	21°42'S	57°52'W
Porto Nacional, Braz. (pōr'tō ná-syō-näl')	**166-67**	10°42'S	48°25'W
Porto-Novo, nat. cap., Benin (pōr'tō-nō'vō)	**260a**	6°29'N	2°37'E
Porto Santo, i., Port. (pōr'tò sän'tò)	**258-59**	33°04'N	16°20'W
Porto Seguro, Braz. (pōr'tō sā-gōō'rò)	**168-69**	16°26'S	39°04'W
Porto Torres, Italy (pōr'tō tôr'rĕs)	**200-01**	40°50'N	8°24'E
Porto União, Braz.	**168-69**	26°15'S	51°04'W
Porto-Vecchio, Fr. (pōr'tō-vĕk'ē-ō)	**184-85**	41°36'N	9°16'E
Porto Velho, Braz. (pōr'tō vāl'yò)	**166-67**	8°46'S	63°54'W
Portoviejo, Ec. (pôr-tō-vyā'hō)	**170**	1°03'S	80°27'W
Port Phillip Bay, b., Austl. (pōrt fĭl'ĭp bā)	**276**	38°07'S	144°48'E
Port Pirie, Austl. (pōrt pĭ'rē)	**276**	33°12'S	138°00'E
Port Said, Egypt (pōrt sä-ēd')	**268b**	31°16'N	32°18'E
Port Saint Lucie, Fl., U.S. (pōrt sānt lū'sē)	**125a**	27°20'N	80°20'W
Port Shepstone, S. Afr. (pōrt hĕps'tŭn)	**264-65**	30°45'S	30°25'E
Portsmouth, Eng., U.K. (pôrts'mŭth)	**190-91**	50°48'N	1°05'W
Portsmouth, N.H., U.S. (pôrts'mŭth)	**116-17**	43°04'N	70°46'W
Portsmouth, Oh., U.S. (pôrts'mŭth)	**116-17**	38°44'N	82°60'W
Portsmouth, Va., U.S. (pôrts'mŭth)	**124-25**	36°50'N	76°19'W
Port Stanley, nat. cap., Falk. Is. *see* Stanley	**171**	51°43'S	57°49'W
Port Sudan, Sudan (pōrt sōō-dän')	**266**	19°37'N	37°13'E
Port Sulphur, La., U.S. (pōrt sŭl'fēr)	**124-25**	29°29'N	89°42'W
Port Townsend, Wa., U.S. (pōrt tounz'ĕnd)	**112-13**	48°07'N	122°46'W
Portugal, nation, Eur. (pōr'tu-găl)	**174-75**	39°30'N	8°00'W
Portugalete, Spain (pōr-tōō-gä-lā'tā)	**198-99**	43°19'N	3°01'W
Portuguese Guinea, nation, Afr. *see* Guinea-Bissau	**253**	12°0'N	15°00'W
Port Vila, nat. cap., Vanuatu (port vē'lá)	**279g**	17°45'S	168°19'E
Port Wakefield, Austl. (pōrt wāk'fēld)	**276**	34°11'S	138°01'E
Port Washington, Wi., U.S. (pōrt wôsh'ĭng-tŭn)	**116-17**	43°23'N	87°53'W
Porvenir, Chile	**171**	53°18'S	70°22'W
Porvoo, Fin.	**192-93**	60°24'N	25°40'E
Posadas, Arg. (pō-sä'dhäs)	**173**	27°22'S	55°54'W
Posen, Pol. *see* Poznań	**194-95**	52°24'N	16°54'E
Poso, Indon.	**248-49**	1°23'S	120°46'E
Poso, Danau, lk., Indon. (pō'sō)	**248-49**	1°52'S	120°35'E
Posse, Braz.	**166-67**	14°06'S	46°22'W
Post, Tx., U.S. (pōst)	**120-21**	33°11'N	101°23'W
Postojna, Slvn. (pōs-tōyná)	**200-01**	45°47'N	14°13'E
Pos'yet, Russia (pos-yĕt')	**243**	42°39'N	130°49'E
Potawatomi Indian Reservation, ind. res., Ks., U.S. (pŏt-å-wä'tō-mē ĭn'dĭ-ăn rĕ-sĕr-vā'shĕn)	**120-21**	39°20'N	95°50'W
Potchefstroom, S. Afr. (pŏch'ĕf-strōm)	**269c**	26°43'S	27°07'E
Poteau, Ok., U.S. (pō-tō')	**120-21**	35°04'N	94°38'W
Poteet, Tx., U.S. (pō-tēt)	**122-23**	29°02'N	98°34'W
Potenza, Italy (pō-tĕnt'sä)	**200-01**	40°39'N	15°48'E
Potgietersrus, S. Afr. (pōt-ĸē'tērs-rûs)	**269c**	24°11'S	29°01'E
Poti, Geor. (pô'tē)	**227**	42°09'N	41°40'E
Potomac, stm., U.S. (pō-tō'măk)	**110-11**	37°59'N	76°18'W
Potosí, Bol.	**168-69**	19°35'S	65°45'W
Potrerillos, Chile	**168-69**	26°26'S	69°29'W
Potsdam, Ger. (pōts'däm)	**194-95**	52°24'N	13°04'E
Potsdam, N.Y., U.S. (pōts'dăm)	**116-17**	44°40'N	74°59'W
Pott, Île, i., N. Cal.	**279g**	19°35'S	163°35'E
Pottstown, Pa., U.S. (pōts'toun)	**116-17**	40°16'N	75°39'W
Pottsville, Pa., U.S. (pōts'vĭl)	**116-17**	40°41'N	76°12'W
Poughkeepsie, N.Y., U.S. (pŏ-kĭp'sē)	**116-17**	41°42'N	73°56'W
Pouso Alegre, Braz. (pō'zò ä-lā'grĕ)	**172**	22°14'S	45°56'W
Poŭthĭsăt, Camb.	**246-47**	12°32'N	103°56'E
Póvoa de Varzim, Port. (pō-vō'á dā vär'zēN)	**198-99**	41°23'N	8°45'W
Povorino, Russia	**186-87**	51°12'N	42°16'E
Povungnituk, Qc., Can.	**128-29**	60°03'N	77°19'W
Povungnituk, stm., Qc., Can.	**130-31**	60°01'N	77°23'W
Powder, stm., U.S. (pou'dēr)	**110-11**	46°44'N	105°27'W
Powell, Wy., U.S. (pou'ĕl)	**112-13**	44°45'N	108°45'W
Powell, Lake, res., U.S. (lāk pou'ĕl)	**118-19**	37°29'N	110°44'W
Powell Lake, lk., B.C., Can. (pou'ĕl lāk)	**132-33**	50°11'N	124°24'W
Powell River, B.C., Can. (pou'ĕl rĭv'ēr)	**132-33**	49°53'N	124°33'W
Poxoréu, Braz.	**168-69**	15°50'S	54°23'W
Poyang Hu, lk., China	**238-39**	29°0'N	116°25'E
Poyarkovo, Russia	**240-41**	49°38'N	128°39'E
Požarevac, Serb. (pô'zhá'rĕ-váts)	**200-01**	44°38'N	21°11'E
Poznań, Pol.	**194-95**	52°24'N	16°54'E
Pozoblanco, Spain (pō-thō-blän'kō)	**198-99**	38°23'N	4°51'W
Pozsony, nat. cap., Slvk. *see* Bratislava	**194-95**	48°09'N	17°07'E
Pozuelo de Alarcón, Spain (pō-thwā'lō dā ä-lär-kōn')	**198-99**	40°27'N	3°46'W
Pra, stm., Ghana (prá)	**260-61**	5°0'N	1°38'W
Prachin Buri, Thai. (prä'chĕn)	**246-47**	14°03'N	101°23'E
Prachuap Khiri Khan, Thai.	**246-47**	11°49'N	99°48'E
Pradera, Col. (prä-dĕ'rä)	**163c**	3°25'N	76°15'W
Prades, Fr. (pråd)	**196-97**	42°37'N	2°26'E
Prado, Braz.	**172**	17°18'S	39°15'W
Prague, nat. cap., Czech Rep. (präg)	**194-95**	50°05'N	14°26'E
Praha, nat. cap., Czech Rep. (prä'hà) *see* Prague	**194-95**	50°05'N	14°26'E
Praia, nat. cap., C.V. (prä'yà)	**260-61**	14°55'N	23°31'W
Prainha Nova, Braz.	**166-67**	7°29'S	60°38'W
Prairie du Chien, Wi., U.S. (prā'rĭ dò shēn')	**114-15**	43°03'N	91°08'W
Pratas Island, i., Tai.	**222-23**	20°42'N	116°43'E
Prathet Thai, nation, Asia *see* Thailand	**206-07**	15°0'N	100°00'E
Prato, Italy (prä'tō)	**200-01**	43°53'N	11°06'E
Pratt, Ks., U.S. (prăt)	**120-21**	37°39'N	98°44'W
Prattville, Al., U.S. (prăt'vĭl)	**124-25**	32°28'N	86°28'W
Praya, Indon.	**248-49**	8°43'S	116°17'E
Pregolya, stm., Russia (prĕ-gô'lă)	**194-95**	54°41'N	20°23'E
Premont, Tx., U.S. (prē-mŏnt')	**122-23**	27°22'N	98°07'W
Prenzlau, Ger. (prĕnts'lou)	**194-95**	53°19'N	13°52'E
Preparis Island, i., Mya.	**246-47**	14°53'N	93°41'E
Preparis North Channel, strt., Mya.	**246-47**	15°32'N	94°06'E
Preparis South Channel, strt., Mya.	**246-47**	14°37'N	93°53'E
Přerov, Czech Rep. (przhĕ'rôf)	**194-95**	49°27'N	17°28'E
Prescott, On., Can. (prĕs'kŭt)	**136-37**	44°43'N	75°31'W
Prescott, Ar., U.S. (prĕs'kŏt)	**120-21**	33°49'N	93°23'W
Prescott, Az., U.S. (prĕs'kŏt)	**118-19**	34°33'N	112°28'W
Presho, S.D., U.S. (prĕsh'ō)	**114-15**	43°55'N	100°04'W
Presidencia Roque Sáenz Peña, Arg.	**173**	26°47'S	60°26'W
Presidente Epitácio, Braz. (prā-sē-dĕn'tĕ å-pē-tä'syò)	**168-69**	21°46'S	52°07'W
Presidente Prudente, Braz.	**168-69**	22°07'S	51°24'W
Presidio, Tx., U.S. (prĕ-sĭ'dĭ-ō)	**122-23**	29°34'N	104°23'W
Presidio, stm., Mex. (prĕ-sē'dyô)	**146-47**	23°05'N	106°17'W
Prešov, Slvk. (prĕ'shôf)	**194-95**	48°59'N	21°15'E
Presque Isle, Me., U.S. (prĕsk-ēl')	**117a**	46°41'N	68°01'W
Preßburg, nat. cap., Slvk. *see* Bratislava	**194-95**	48°09'N	17°07'E
Preston, Eng., U.K. (prĕs'tŭn)	**190-91**	53°46'N	2°42'W
Preston, Id., U.S. (prĕs'tŭn)	**112-13**	42°06'N	111°53'W
Preto, stm., Braz.	**166-67**	11°21'S	43°52'W
Pretoria, nat. cap., S. Afr. (prĕ-tō'rĭ-á)	**269c**	25°45'S	28°11'E
Préveza, Grc. (prĕ'vå-zä)	**200-01**	38°57'N	20°45'E
Priboj, Serb. (prē'boi)	**200-01**	43°35'N	19°32'E
Price, Ut., U.S. (prīs)	**118-19**	39°36'N	110°48'W
Price Island, i., B.C., Can.	**132-33**	52°23'N	128°41'W
Prichard, Al., U.S. (prĭt'chârd)	**124-25**	30°44'N	88°05'W
Prienai, Lith. (prē-ĕn'ī)	**192-93**	54°38'N	23°57'E
Prieska, S. Afr. (prē-ĕs'ká)	**264-65**	29°40'S	22°44'E
Prijedor, Bos. (prē'yĕ-dôr)	**200-01**	44°59'N	16°42'E
Prijepolje, Serb. (prē'yĕ-pô'lyĕ)	**200-01**	43°24'N	19°39'E
Prikaspiyskaya Nizmennost', pl., *see* Caspian Depression	**186-87**	48°0'N	52°00'E
Prilep, Mac. (prē'lĕp)	**200-01**	41°21'N	21°34'E
Primorsk, Russia (prē-môrsk')	**192-93**	60°22'N	28°38'E
Primrose Lake, lk., Can.	**132-33**	54°55'N	109°45'W
Prince Albert, Sk., Can. (prĭns ăl'bērt)	**134-35**	53°13'N	105°45'W
Prince Albert National Park, n.p., Sk., Can. (prĭns ăl'bērt năsh'ŭn-ăl pärk)	**134-35**	54°0'N	106°25'W
Prince Albert Sound, b., N.T., Can. (prĭns ăl'bērt sound)	**130-31**	70°27'N	114°50'W
Prince Charles Island, i., Nu., Can. (prĭns chärlz ī'lănd)	**130-31**	67°47'N	76°06'W
Prince Edward Island, state, Can. (prĭns ĕd'wērd ī'lănd)	**128-29**	46°20'N	63°20'W
Prince Edward Island, i., P.E., Can.	**130-31**	46°20'N	63°20'W
Prince Edward Island National Park, n.p., P.E., Can.	**138-39**	46°30'N	63°25'W
Prince Edward Islands, is., S. Afr. (prĭns ĕd'wērd ī'lăndz)	**287**	46°45'S	37°49'E
Prince George, B.C., Can. (prĭns jôrj)	**132-33**	53°54'N	122°46'W
Prince of Wales, Cape, c., Ak., U.S. (kāp prĭns ŭv wālz)	**126**	65°40'N	168°07'W
Prince of Wales Island, i., Austl. (prĭns ŭv wālz ī'lănd)	**277**	10°40'S	142°10'E
Prince of Wales Island, i., Nu., Can. (prĭns ŭv wālz ī'lănd)	**288**	72°40'N	99°00'W
Prince of Wales Island, i., Ak., U.S. (prĭns ŭv wālz ī'lănd)	**126**	55°47'N	132°50'W
Prince Rupert, B.C., Can. (prĭns roo'pērt)	**132-33**	54°19'N	130°17'W
Princess Royal Island, i., B.C., Can.	**132-33**	52°57'N	128°49'W
Princeton, B.C., Can. (prĭns'tŭn)	**132-33**	49°27'N	120°31'W
Princeton, Il., U.S. (prĭns'tŭn)	**116-17**	41°22'N	89°28'W
Princeton, In., U.S. (prĭns'tŭn)	**116-17**	38°21'N	87°35'W
Princeton, Ky., U.S. (prĭns'tŭn)	**124-25**	37°07'N	87°53'W
Princeton, Mn., U.S. (prĭns'tŭn)	**114-15**	45°34'N	93°35'W
Princeton, Mo., U.S. (prĭns'tŭn)	**120-21**	40°24'N	93°35'W

n-sing; ŋ-baŋk; N-nasalized n; nŏd; cŏmmit; ōld; ôbey; ôrder; oi-boil; fōōd; ò-as oo in foot; ou-out; s-soft; sh-dish; th-thin; pūre; ûnite; ûrn; stŭd; circŭs; ü-as in French tu; '-indeterminate vowel.

Feature (Pronunciation)	Page	Lat.	Long.
Princeton, N.J., U.S. (prĭns´tŭn)	116-17	40°22'N	74°39'W
Princeton, W.V., U.S. (prĭns´tŭn)	124-25	37°22'N	81°06'W
Prince William Sound, strt., Ak., U.S. (prĭns wĭl´yăm sound)	126	60°42'N	147°07'W
Príncipe, i., S. Tom./P. (prēn´sē-pě)	260-61	1°37'N	7°25'E
Principe Channel, strt., B.C., Can. (prĭn´sĭ-pē chăn´ĕl)	132-33	53°28'N	130°00'W
Príncipe da Beira, Braz.	166-67	12°25'S	64°25'W
Prineville, Or., U.S. (prīn´vĭl)	112-13	44°18'N	120°51'W
Prinzapolka, stm., Nic. (prēn-zä-pōl´kä)	149	13°24'N	83°34'W
Priozërsk, Russia (prĭ-ô´zěrsk)	192-93	61°02'N	30°09'E
Pripet Marshes, reg., Eur.	194-95	52°0'N	27°00'E
Priština, Serb. (prēsh´tĭ-nä)	200-01	42°40'N	21°10'E
Pritzwalk, Ger. (prēts´välk)	194-95	53°09'N	12°10'E
Privas, Fr. (prē-väs´)	196-97	44°44'N	4°37'E
Privolzhskaya Vozvyshennost', plat., Russia	186-87	52°0'N	46°00'E
Privolzhskiy, Russia	186-87	51°24'N	46°02'E
Priyutovo, Russia	186-87	53°53'N	53°56'E
Prizren, Serb. (prē´zrěn)	200-01	42°13'N	20°45'E
Probolinggo, Indon.	248-49	7°45'S	113°13'E
Proctor, Mn., U.S. (prŏk´tẽr)	114-15	46°44'N	92°14'W
Proddatūr, India	236	14°45'N	78°33'E
Progreso, Mex. (prô-grā´sō)	148	21°16'N	89°39'W
Prokopyevsk, Russia	226	53°54'N	86°44'E
Prokuplje, Serb. (prô´kòp'l-yě)	200-01	43°14'N	21°36'E
Prome, Mya.	246-47	18°49'N	95°13'E
Pronja, stm., Bela. (prô´nyä)	192-93	53°27'N	31°01'E
Propriá, Braz.	163d	10°13'S	36°50'W
Prosser, Wa., U.S. (prŏs´ẽr)	112-13	46°12'N	119°46'W
Prostějov, Czech Rep. (prôs´tyě-yôf)	194-95	49°29'N	17°07'E
Protoka, stm., Russia (prôt´ô-kȧ)	202-03	45°44'N	37°47'E
Providence, R.I., U.S. (prŏv´ĭ-děns)	116-17	41°50'N	71°25'W
Providence, Atoll de, at., Sey.	264-65	9°14'S	51°03'E
Providencia, Isla de, i., Col.	164-65	13°21'N	81°22'W
Providenciales, i., T./C. Is.	142-43	21°47'N	72°17'W
Provideniya, Russia (prô-vĭ-dä´nĭ-yȧ)	126	64°23'N	173°18'W
Provo, Ut., U.S. (prō´vō)	118-19	40°13'N	111°38'W
Prudhoe Bay, b., Ak., U.S.	126	70°21'N	148°22'W
Prudnik, Pol. (pròd´nĭk)	194-95	50°19'N	17°35'E
Pruszków, Pol. (pròsh´kòf)	194-95	52°10'N	20°49'E
Prut, stm., Eur. (prōōt)	186-87	45°28'N	28°13'E
Prydz Bay, b., Ant.	287	69°0'S	76°00'E
Pryluky, Ukr.	202-03	50°36'N	32°23'E
Pryor, Ok., U.S. (prī´ẽr)	120-21	36°19'N	95°19'W
Przemyśl, Pol. (pzhě´mĭsh´l)	194-95	49°47'N	22°47'E
Przhevalsk, Kyrg. (p'r-zhĭ-välsk´) see Karakol	226	42°29'N	78°23'E
Pskov, Russia (pskôf)	192-93	57°49'N	28°22'E
Pskov, Lake, lk., Eur. (lāk pskôf)	192-93	58°0'N	28°00'E
Pskovskoye Ozero, lk., Eur. (p'skôv´skô´yě ôzě-rô) see Pskov, Lake	192-93	58°0'N	28°00'E
Ptuj, Slvn. (ptōō´ē)	200-01	46°26'N	15°52'E
Pucallpa, Peru	170	8°23'S	74°32'W
Pucheng, China (pōō-chŭŋ)	238-39	27°55'N	118°32'E
Pucheng, China (pōō-chŭŋ)	238-39	34°58'N	109°35'E
Puck, Pol. (pòtsk)	194-95	54°43'N	18°24'E
Pudozh, Russia (pōō´dòzh)	186-87	61°48'N	36°34'E
Puducherry, India see Pondicherry	236	11°56'N	79°50'E
Puducherry, state, India	236	11°56'N	79°50'E
Pudukkottai, India	236	10°23'N	78°49'E
Puebla, state, Mex. (pwā´blä)	146-47	18°50'N	98°00'W
Puebla de Zaragoza, Mex.	146-47	19°03'N	98°12'W
Pueblo, Co., U.S. (pwā´blō)	120-21	38°16'N	104°38'W
Puente Genil, Spain (pwěn´tā-hå-nēl´)	198-99	37°24'N	4°47'W
Puerto Aisén, Chile (pwě´r-tō ä´y-sě´n)	171	45°15'S	72°15'W
Puerto Ángel, Mex. (pwě´r-tō äŋ´hål)	146-47	15°40'N	96°29'W
Puerto Armuelles, Pan. (pwe´r-tô är-mōō-ā´lyās)	150	8°17'N	82°52'W
Puerto Asís, Col.	164-65	0°31'N	76°31'W
Puerto Ayacucho, Ven.	164-65	5°40'N	67°38'W
Puerto Baquerizo Moreno, Ec.	170a	0°54'S	89°36'W
Puerto Barrios, Guat. (pwě´r-tō bär´rē-ōs)	148	15°43'N	88°35'W
Puerto Bermúdez, Peru (pwě´r-tō běr-mōō´dāz)	170	10°20'S	74°54'W
Puerto Berrío, Col. (pwě´r-tō běr-rē´ō)	163c	6°28'N	74°26'W
Puerto Cabello, Ven. (pwě´r-tô kä-běl´yō)	163b	10°28'N	68°01'W
Puerto Cabezas, Nic. (pwě´r-tô kä-bā´zäs)	149	14°01'N	83°23'W
Puerto Carreño, Col.	164-65	6°11'N	67°30'W
Puerto Chicama, Peru (pwě´r-tō chē-kä´mä)	170	7°42'S	79°25'W
Puerto Cortés, Hond. (pwě´r-tô kôr-tās´)	149	15°51'N	87°57'W

Feature (Pronunciation)	Page	Lat.	Long.
Puerto Cumarebo, Ven. (pwě´r-tō kōō-mä-rě´bô)	164-65	11°29'N	69°21'W
Puerto de la Cruz, Spain	199d	28°23'N	16°33'W
Puerto Deseado, Arg. (pwě´r-tō dā-så-ä´dhō)	171	47°44'S	65°54'W
Puerto Juárez, Mex.	148	21°10'N	86°49'W
Puerto la Cruz, Ven. (pwě´r-tō lä krōō´z)	163b	10°13'N	64°38'W
Puerto Leguízamo, Col.	164-65	0°11'S	74°46'W
Puerto Libertad, Mex.	144-45	29°55'N	112°41'W
Puerto Limón, C.R.	149	9°59'N	83°02'W
Puertollano, Spain (pwě-tôl-yä´nō)	198-99	38°41'N	4°06'W
Puerto Madryn, Arg. (pwě´r-tō mä-drēn´)	171	42°46'S	65°03'W
Puerto Maldonado, Peru (pwě´r-tō mäl-dō-nä´dô)	170	12°36'S	69°12'W
Puerto Montt, Chile (pwě´r-tō mô´nt)	171	41°28'S	72°57'W
Puerto Morazán, Nic.	149	12°50'N	87°11'W
Puerto Natales, Chile (pwě´r-tō nä-tá´lěs)	171	51°42'S	72°29'W
Puerto Padre, Cuba (pwě´r-tō pä´drā)	142-43	21°12'N	76°36'W
Puerto Peñasco, Mex. (pwě´r-tô pěn-yä´s-kô)	144-45	31°19'N	113°32'W
Puerto Pinasco, Para. (pwě´r-tō pē-ná´s-kô)	168-69	22°37'S	57°49'W
Puerto Pirámides, Arg.	171	42°34'S	64°15'W
Puerto Píritu, Ven. (pwě´r-tō pē´rē-tōō)	163b	10°02'N	65°02'W
Puerto Plata, Dom. Rep. (pwě´r-tô plä´tä)	142-43	19°45'N	70°39'W
Puerto Princesa, Phil.	250	9°44'N	118°45'E
Puerto Rico, Bol.	166-67	11°06'S	67°32'W
Puerto Rico, dep., N.A. (pwěr´tô rē´kō)	140-41	18°15'N	66°30'W
Puerto Rico, i., P.R. (pwěr´tô rē´kō)	142a	18°15'N	66°30'W
Puerto Salgar, Col. (pwě´r-tō säl-gär´)	163c	5°28'N	74°39'W
Puerto San José, Guat.	148	13°56'N	90°49'W
Puerto San Julián, Arg.	171	49°18'S	67°43'W
Puerto Santa Cruz, Arg. (pwě´r-tō sän´tä krōōz´)	171	50°01'S	68°34'W
Puerto Sastre, Para.	168-69	22°02'S	58°01'W
Puerto Suárez, Bol. (pwě´r-tō swä´råz)	168-69	18°57'S	57°51'W
Puerto Tejada, Col. (pwě´r-tō tě-κä´dä)	163c	3°14'N	76°25'W
Puerto Vallarta, Mex. (pwě´r-tō väl-yär´tä)	146-47	20°37'N	105°14'W
Puerto Varas, Chile (pwě´r-tō vä´räs)	171	41°20'S	72°58'W
Puerto Villamil, Ec.	170a	0°56'S	91°01'W
Puerto Wilches, Col. (pwě´r-tō vēl´c-hěs)	164-65	7°20'N	73°54'W
Pueyrredón, Lago, lk., S.A.	171	47°21'S	71°56'W
Puget Sound, b. Wa., U.S.	112-113	47°49'N	122°27'W
Pugachev, Russia (pōō´gȧ-chyôf)	186-87	52°02'N	48°49'E
Puhi-waero, c., N.Z. see South West Cape	278	47°17'S	167°28'E
Pukch'ŏng-ŭp, Kor., N.	243	40°14'N	128°19'E
Pukou, China	238-39	32°06'N	118°43'E
Pula, Cro. (pōō´lä)	200-01	44°52'N	13°51'E
Pulacayo, Bol. (pōō-lä-kä´yō)	168-69	20°23'S	66°42'W
Pulaski, N.Y., U.S. (pů-lăs´kĭ)	116-17	43°34'N	76°07'W
Pulaski, Tn., U.S. (pů-lăs´kĭ)	124-25	35°12'N	87°02'W
Pulaski, Va., U.S. (pů-lăs´kĭ)	124-25	37°03'N	80°47'W
Puławy, Pol. (pò-wä´vě)	194-95	51°25'N	21°59'E
Pullman, Wa., U.S. (pòl´măn)	112-13	46°44'N	117°10'W
Pulo Anna, i., Palau	280-81	4°40'N	131°58'E
Pulog, Mount, mtn., Phil. (mount pōō´lôg)	250	16°36'N	120°54'E
Puma Yumco, lk., China (pōō-mä yōōm-tswo)	234-35	28°33'N	90°24'E
Puná, Isla, i., Ec.	170	2°47'S	80°08'W
Punakha, Bhu. (pōō-nŭk´ŭ)	234-35	27°37'N	89°52'E
Punata, Bol. (pōō-nä´tä)	168-69	17°33'S	65°50'W
Pune, India	236	18°32'N	73°52'E
Punia, D.R.C.	262-63	1°28'S	26°27'E
Punjab, state, India (pŭn´jäb´)	234-35	31°0'N	75°30'E
Puno, Peru (pōō´nô)	170	15°51'S	70°02'W
Punta Alta, Arg.	173	38°53'S	62°04'W
Punta Arenas, Chile (pōō´n-tä-rě´näs)	171	53°09'S	70°55'W
Punta de Piedras, Ven. (pōō´n-tä dě pyě´dräs)	163b	10°54'N	64°06'W
Punta Gorda, Belize (pòn´tä gôr´dä)	148	16°06'N	88°48'W
Punta Gorda, Fl., U.S. (pŭn´tȧ gôr´dȧ)	125a	26°56'N	82°03'W
Puntarenas, C.R. (pònt-ä-rä´näs)	149	9°58'N	84°50'W
Punto Fijo, Ven. (pōō´n-tô fē´κô)	164-65	11°43'N	70°12'W
Punxsutawney, Pa., U.S. (pŭnk-sŭ-tô´nē)	116-17	40°56'N	78°58'W
Puqi, China	238-39	29°43'N	113°53'E
Puquio, Peru (pōō´kyô)	170	14°42'S	74°09'W

Feature (Pronunciation)	Page	Lat.	Long.
Pur, stm., Russia	218-19	67°21'N	77°55'E
Purcell, Ok., U.S. (pûr-sěl´)	120-21	35°02'N	97°22'W
Puri, India (pò´rē)	234-35	19°48'N	85°51'E
Purificación, Col. (pōō-rē-fē-kä-syōn´)	163c	3°51'N	74°55'W
Purificación, Mex. (pōō-rē-fē-kä-syô´n)	146-47	19°43'N	104°36'W
Pūrnia, India	234-35	25°47'N	87°29'E
Pursat, Camb. see Poŭthĭsăt	246-47	12°32'N	103°56'E
Purus, stm., S.A.	166-67	3°41'S	61°28'W
Purús, stm., S.A. (pōō-rōō´s)	166-67	3°41'S	61°28'W
Purwokerto, Indon.	248-49	7°25'S	109°14'E
Pusan, Kor., S. (pōō´sän´)	243	35°05'N	129°03'E
Pushkin, Russia (pòsh´kĭn)	192-93	59°43'N	30°26'E
Pustoshka, Russia (pûs-tôsh´kȧ)	192-93	56°20'N	29°22'E
Putaendo, Chile (pōō-tä-ěn-dô)	163e	32°37'S	70°44'W
Putao, Mya.	238-39	27°21'N	97°24'E
Putian, China (pōō-tĭěn)	225a	25°26'N	119°00'E
Puting, Tanjung, c., Indon.	248-49	3°32'S	111°49'E
Putla de Guerrero, Mex. (pōō´tlä-dě-gěr-rě´rō)	146-47	17°00'N	97°54'W
Putnam, Ct., U.S. (pŭt´nȧm)	116-17	41°55'N	71°54'W
Putorana, Gory, plat., Russia	218-19	69°0'N	95°00'E
Putrajaya, nat. cap., Malay.	246-47	2°56'N	101°43'E
Puttalam, Sri L.	236	8°01'N	79°51'E
Putumayo, stm., S.A. (pò-tōō-mä´yō)	170	3°07'S	67°56'W
Puyallup, Wa., U.S. (pū-ăl´ŭp)	112-13	47°11'N	122°17'W
Puyang, China (pōō-yäŋ)	240-41	35°42'N	115°00'E
Puyo, Ec.	170	1°29'S	77°59'W
Pweto, D.R.C. (pwā´tō)	262-63	8°28'S	28°54'E
Pyakupur, stm., Russia	218-19	64°56'N	77°44'E
Pyandzh, stm., Asia see Panj	232-33	37°00'N	68°16'E
Pyasina, stm., Russia (pyä-sē´nȧ)	218-19	73°52'N	87°09'E
Pyasino, Ozero, lk., Russia	218-19	69°45'N	87°45'E
Pyatigorsk, Russia (pyȧ-tē-gôrsk´)	227	44°04'N	43°04'E
Pyè, Mya. see Prome	246-47	18°49'N	95°13'E
Pyinmana, Mya. (pyēn-mä´nȧ)	246-47	19°44'N	96°13'E
P'yŏngyang, nat. cap., Kor., N. (pyŭng´gäng´)	243	39°01'N	125°44'E
Pyramid Lake, lk., Nv., U.S. (pĭ´rȧ-mĭd lāk)	118-19	40°01'N	119°35'W
Pyramid Lake Indian Reservation, ind. res., Nv., U.S. (pĭ´rȧ-mĭd lāk ĭn´dĭ-ăn rě-sẽr-vā´shěn)	118-19	40°13'N	119°36'W
Pyrenees, mts., Eur. (pĭr-e-nēz´)	196-97	42°40'N	1°00'E
Pýrgos, Grc.	200-01	37°40'N	21°27'E
Pyritz, Pol. see Pyrzyce	194-95	53°09'N	14°53'E
Pyrzyce, Pol. (pězhĭ´tsě)	194-95	53°09'N	14°53'E

Q

Feature (Pronunciation)	Page	Lat.	Long.
Qā'en, Iran	232-33	33°44'N	59°10'E
Qaidam, stm., China	240-41	36°52'N	95°57'E
Qaidam Pendi, bas., China	222-23	37°0'N	95°00'E
Qal'at Bīshah, Sau. Ar.	266	19°60'N	42°36'E
Qalāt, Afg.	232-33	32°07'N	66°54'E
Qamani'tuaq, Nu., Can. see Baker Lake	128-29	64°18'N	95°55'W
Qamar, Ghubbat al-, b., Yemen	220-21	16°0'N	52°30'E
Qamdo, China (chyäm-dwō)	238-39	31°10'N	97°09'E
Qamea, i., Fiji	279f	16°46'S	179°46'W
Qandahār, Afg. see Kandahār	232-33	31°37'N	65°43'E
Qandala, Som.	262-63	11°28'N	49°52'E
Qapshaghay, Kaz.	226	43°52'N	77°04'E
Qapshaghay bögeni, res., Kaz.	226	43°49'N	77°42'E
Qaqortoq, Green. see Julianehåb	284-85	60°44'N	46°02'W
Qaraghandy, Kaz.	226	49°53'N	73°10'E
Qarataū, Kaz.	226	43°10'N	70°28'E
Qarataū zhotasy, mts., Kaz. see Karatau Range	226	43°36'N	68°52'E
Qaraton, Kaz.	186-87	46°26'N	53°31'E
Qarazhal, Kaz.	226	48°01'N	70°49'E
Qarqan, stm., China	222-23	39°26'N	88°22'E
Qarshi, Uzb.	232-33	38°52'N	65°48'E
Qârûn, Birket, lk., Egypt	268b	29°28'N	30°39'E
Qāsh, Nahr al-, stm., Afr. see Gash	266	16°45'N	35°54'E
Qatar, nation, Asia (kä´tàr)	206-07	25°0'N	51°10'E
Qattâra, Munkhafad el-, depr., Egypt see Qattara Depression	266	30°0'N	27°30'E
Qattara Depression, depr., Egypt (kä-tä´rȧ dĭ-prě´shŭn)	266	30°0'N	27°30'E
Qazaqstan, nation, Asia see Kazakhstan	206-07	47°0'N	76°00'E
Qazaqtyng usaqshoqylyghy, hills, Kaz. see Kazakh Hills	226	49°0'N	72°00'E

Feature (Pronunciation)	Page	Lat.	Long.
Qazımämmäd, Azer.	227	40°02'N	48°56'E
Qazvīn, Iran	232-33	36°16'N	49°58'E
Qena, Egypt	268b	26°11'N	32°43'E
Qeqertarsuaq, Green. *see* Godhavn	284-85	69°15'N	53°33'W
Qeshm, Jazīreh-ye, i., Iran	230-31	26°45'N	55°45'E
Qezel Owzan, stm., Iran	228-29	36°47'N	49°09'E
Qianyang, China	238-39	27°11'N	110°02'E
Qiemo, China	220-21	38°10'N	85°30'E
Qijiang, China (chyē-jyäŋ)	238-39	29°02'N	106°39'E
Qilian Shan, mts., China (chyē-lĭĕn shän)	240-41	39°06'N	98°40'E
Qing'an, China (chyĭŋ-än)	240-41	46°52'N	127°30'E
Qingdao, China (chyĭn-dou)	240-41	36°05'N	120°20'E
Qinghai, state, China (chyĭŋ-hī)	240-41	36°0'N	96°00'E
Qinghai Hu, lk., China (chyĭŋ-hī hōō)	240-41	36°48'N	100°06'E
Qingjiang, China (chyĭŋ-jyäŋ)	238-39	33°36'N	119°01'E
Qingshui, stm., China	238-39	27°08'N	109°37'E
Qingshui, stm., China	240-41	37°28'N	105°32'E
Qingtang, China	238-39	24°12'N	113°51'E
Qingyang, China (chyĭŋ-yäŋ)	238-39	30°38'N	117°51'E
Qingyang, China (chyĭŋ-yäŋ)	240-41	36°01'N	107°52'E
Qingyuan, China (chyĭŋ-yöän) *see* Baoding	240-41	38°51'N	115°29'E
Qingyuan, China (chyĭŋ-yöän)	238-39	23°42'N	113°02'E
Qingyuan, China (chyĭŋ-yöän)	238-39	27°37'N	119°06'E
Qingyuan, China (chyĭŋ-yöän)	243	42°07'N	124°58'E
Qingyuan, China (chyĭŋ-yöän)	238-39	24°35'N	108°45'E
Qing Zang Gaoyuan, plat., China *see* Tibet, Plateau of	222-23	33°0'N	92°00'E
Qinhuangdao, China (chyĭn-huaŋ-dou)	240-41	39°56'N	119°36'E
Qin Ling, mts., China (chyĭn lĭŋ)	238-39	34°0'N	108°00'E
Qinzhou, China (chyĭn-jō)	238-39	21°58'N	108°37'E
Qionghai, China (chyôŋ-hī)	238-39	19°16'N	110°28'E
Qionglai, China	238-39	30°25'N	103°28'E
Qiongzhong, China	238-39	19°02'N	109°48'E
Qiongzhou Haixia, strt., China	238-39	20°10'N	110°15'E
Qiqihar, China (chyē-chyē-här)	240-41	47°20'N	123°58'E
Qitai, China (chyē-tī)	222-23	44°01'N	89°35'E
Qixian, China (chyē-shyĕn)	238-39	34°33'N	114°47'E
Qiyang, China (chyē-yäŋ)	238-39	26°29'N	111°43'E
Qızılağaç körfäzi, b., Azer.	227	39°05'N	49°01'E
Qizilqum, des., Asia	226	42°0'N	64°00'E
Qo'qon, Uzb.	232-33	40°32'N	70°56'E
Qogir Feng, mtn., Asia *see* K2	232-33	35°53'N	76°30'E
Qom, Iran	232-33	34°39'N	50°53'E
Qomolangma Feng, mtn., Asia *see* Everest, Mount	234-35	27°59'N	86°56'E
Qomsheh, Iran	232-33	32°00'N	51°52'E
Qondūz, Afg. *see* Kondoz	232-33	36°44'N	68°51'E
Qorako'l, Uzb.	232-33	39°32'N	63°55'E
Qosshaghyl, Kaz.	186-87	46°51'N	53°48'E
Qostanay, Kaz.	226	53°12'N	63°37'E
Quadra Island, i., B.C., Can.	132-33	50°12'N	125°16'W
Quakertown, Pa., U.S. (kwā'kēr-toun)	116-17	40°27'N	75°21'W
Quanah, Tx., U.S. (kwä'nȧ)	120-21	34°18'N	99°45'W
Quang Ngai, Viet. (kwäng n'gä'ē)	246-47	15°07'N	108°47'E
Quan Long, Viet. *see* Ca Mau	246-47	9°11'N	105°09'E
Quanzhou, China (chyuän-jō)	225a	24°55'N	118°35'E
Qu'Appelle, stm., Can.	134-35	50°26'N	101°20'W
Quartu Sant'Elena, Italy (kwär-tōō' sänt ā'lā-nä)	200-01	39°15'N	9°11'E
Quatsino Sound, strt., B.C., Can. (kwŏt-sē'nō sound)	132-33	50°26'N	127°59'W
Quba, Azer. (kōō'bȧ)	227	41°22'N	48°31'E
Qūchān, Iran	232-33	37°06'N	58°31'E
Queanbeyan, Austl.	276	35°21'S	149°14'E
Québec, Qc., Can. (kwē-bĕk') (kȧ-bĕk')	136-37	46°49'N	71°13'W
Québec, state, Can. (kwē-bĕk') (kē-bĕk')	128-29	52°0'N	72°00'W
Quedlinburg, Ger. (kvĕd'lĕn-bŏŏrgh)	194-95	51°47'N	11°09'E
Queen Charlotte, B.C., Can.	132-33	53°16'N	132°05'W
Queen Charlotte Islands, is., B.C., Can. (kwēn shär'lŏt ī'lăndz)	132-33	53°0'N	132°00'W
Queen Charlotte Mountains, mts., B.C., Can. (kwēn shär'lŏt moun'tĭnz)	132-33	53°0'N	132°00'W
Queen Charlotte Sound, strt., B.C., Can. (kwēn shär'lŏt sound)	132-33	51°30'N	129°30'W
Queen Charlotte Strait, strt., B.C., Can. (kwēn shär'lŏt strāt)	132-33	50°50'N	127°25'W
Queen Fabiola Mountains, mts., Ant.	287	71°30'S	35°40'E
Queen Maud Gulf, b., Nu., Can. (kwēn mäd gŭlf)	130-31	68°25'N	102°30'W
Queen Maud Land, reg., Ant. (kwēn mäd lănd)	287	74°59'S	15°51'E
Queensland, state, Austl. (kwēnz'lănd)	277	22°0'S	145°00'E

Feature (Pronunciation)	Page	Lat.	Long.
Queenstown, Austl. (kwēnz'toun)	276	42°04'S	145°33'E
Queenstown, S. Afr.	264-65	31°54'S	26°53'E
Queleleveu, i., Fiji	279f	16°05'S	179°09'W
Quelimane, Moz. (kā-lē-mä'nĕ)	264-65	17°53'S	36°53'E
Quelpart Island, i., Kor., S. *see* Cheju-do	240-41	33°22'N	126°30'E
Quemado de Güines, Cuba (kā-mä'dhä-dĕ-gwē'nĕs)	142-43	22°48'N	80°15'W
Quemoy, i., Tai. *see* Chinmen Tao	225a	24°27'N	118°23'E
Querétaro, Mex. (kå-rā'tä-rō)	146-47	20°35'N	100°23'W
Querétaro, state, Mex. (kå-rā'tä-rō)	146-47	21°0'N	99°55'W
Quesnel, B.C., Can. (kā-nĕl')	132-33	52°58'N	122°29'W
Quesnel, stm., B.C., Can. (kā-nĕl')	132-33	52°58'N	122°30'W
Quesnel Lake, lk., B.C., Can. (kā-nĕl' lāk)	132-33	52°32'N	121°05'W
Quetta, Pak. (kwĕt'ä)	232-33	30°13'N	67°01'E
Quetzaltenango, Guat.	148	14°50'N	91°31'W
Quevedo, Ec.	170	1°01'S	79°27'W
Quezon City, Phil. (kā-zōn sī'tē)	250	14°38'N	121°03'E
Qufu, China (chyōō-fōō)	240-41	35°36'N	117°02'E
Quibdó, Col. (kēb'dō)	163c	5°42'N	76°39'W
Quila, Mex.	146-47	24°25'N	107°13'W
Quillacollo, Bol.	168-69	17°26'S	66°17'W
Quillota, Chile (kēl-yō'tä)	163e	32°51'S	71°14'W
Quilon, India (kwē-lōn') *see* Kollam	236	8°53'N	76°35'E
Quilpie, Austl. (kwĭl'pē)	276	26°37'S	144°16'E
Quimbaya, Col. (kēm-bä'yä)	163c	4°38'N	75°46'W
Quimilí, Arg.	173	27°38'S	62°25'W
Quimper, Fr. (kăn-pĕr')	196-97	47°60'N	4°06'W
Quince Mil, Peru	170	13°15'S	70°37'W
Quincy, Fl., U.S. (kwĭn'sē)	124-25	30°35'N	84°35'W
Quincy, Il., U.S. (kwĭn'sē)	120-21	39°56'N	91°24'W
Quincy, Ma., U.S. (kwĭn'sē)	116-17	42°15'N	71°02'W
Quincy, Mi., U.S. (kwĭn'sē)	116-17	41°57'N	84°53'W
Quincy, Wa., U.S. (kwĭn'sē)	112-13	47°14'N	119°51'W
Quines, Arg.	168-69	32°14'S	65°47'W
Quintana Roo, state, Mex. (kēn-tä-nä rô'ô)	148	19°40'N	88°30'W
Quintero, Chile (kēn-tě'rô)	163e	32°47'S	71°32'W
Quirihue, Chile	171	36°17'S	72°33'W
Quirimba, Ilha, i., Moz.	264-65	12°20'S	40°36'E
Quiroga, Mex. (kē-rô'gä)	146-47	19°40'N	101°32'W
Quitman, Ga., U.S. (kwĭt'măn)	124-25	30°47'N	83°34'W
Quitman, Ms., U.S. (kwĭt'măn)	124-25	32°02'N	88°44'W
Quito, nat. cap., Ec. (kē'tō)	170	0°12'S	78°30'W
Quixadá, Braz.	166-67	4°58'S	39°01'W
Qujing, China	238-39	25°35'N	103°50'E
Qulyndy Zhazyghy, pl., Asia	226	53°0'N	79°00'E
Qum, Iran *see* Qom	232-33	34°39'N	50°53'E
Qumarlêb, China	238-39	34°30'N	95°21'E
Qŭnghirot, Uzb.	226	43°03'N	58°51'E
Quorn, Austl. (kwôrn)	276	32°21'S	138°03'E
Qŭrghonteppa, Taj.	232-33	37°50'N	68°47'E
Quseir, Egypt	266	26°07'N	34°17'E
Quxian, China (chyōō-shyĕn)	238-39	30°51'N	106°58'E
Quy Nhon, Viet.	246-47	13°46'N	109°15'E
Quzhou, China (chyoō-jō)	238-39	28°57'N	118°52'E
Qyrghyz zhotasy, mts., Asia *see* Kirgiz Range	226	42°29'N	73°50'E
Qyzylorda, Kaz. (kzĕl-ôr'dȧ)	226	44°51'N	65°30'E
Qyzylqum, des., Asia	226	42°0'N	64°00'E

R

Feature (Pronunciation)	Page	Lat.	Long.
Raab, Hung. *see* Győr	194-95	47°41'N	17°39'E
Raahe, Fin. (rä'ĕ)	184-85	64°41'N	24°31'E
Raba, Indon.	248-49	8°29'S	118°45'E
Rabat, nat. cap., Mor. (rȧ-bät')	269a	34°01'N	6°50'W
Rabaul, Pap. N. Gui. (rä'boul)	277	4°12'S	152°11'E
Rabi, i., Fiji	279f	16°30'S	179°58'W
Rābigh, Sau. Ar.	266	22°48'N	39°02'E
Race, Cape, c., Nf., Can. (kāp rās)	138-39	46°40'N	53°06'W
Rach Gia, Viet.	246-47	10°01'N	105°06'E
Racine, Wi., U.S. (rȧ-sēn')	116-17	42°43'N	87°47'W
Radford, Va., U.S. (răd'fērd)	124-25	37°07'N	80°35'W
Radom, Pol. (rä'dôm)	194-95	51°24'N	21°09'E
Radomsko, Pol. (rä-dôm'skô)	194-95	51°04'N	19°27'E
Radomyshl', Ukr. (rä-dô-mēsh''l)	202-03	50°30'N	29°15'E
Radviliškis, Lith. (räd'vē-lēsh'kēs)	192-93	55°49'N	23°33'E
Radzyń Podlaski, Pol. (räd'zēn-y' pŭd-lä'skĭ)	194-95	51°47'N	22°36'E
Rae, N.T., Can.	128-29	62°50'N	116°02'W
Rāe Bareli, India	234-35	26°13'N	81°14'E

Feature (Pronunciation)	Page	Lat.	Long.
Raeford, N.C., U.S. (rā'fērd)	124-25	34°58'N	79°16'W
Rafaela, Arg. (rä-fä-å'lä)	173	31°15'S	61°29'W
Rafḥā', Sau. Ar.	228-29	29°41'N	43°28'E
Rafsanjān, Iran	230-31	30°24'N	55°59'E
Raga, Sudan	262-63	8°28'N	25°41'E
Ragay Gulf, b., Phil.	250	13°30'N	122°45'E
Ragged Island, i., Bah.	142-43	22°14'N	75°44'W
Ragged Island Range, is., Bah.	142-43	22°34'N	75°52'W
Ragusa, Italy (rä-gōō'sä)	200-01	36°55'N	14°44'E
Rāichūr, India (rä'ē-chōōr')	236	16°12'N	77°21'E
Raigarh, India (rī'gŭr)	234-35	21°54'N	83°24'E
Rainbow Bridge National Monument, n.p., Ut., U.S. (rān'bō brĭj năsh'ŭn-ăl mŏn'ū-mĕnt)	118-19	37°06'N	110°57'W
Rainier, Mount, vol., Wa., U.S. (mount rā-nēr')	112-13	46°51'N	121°45'W
Rainy Lake, lk., N.A. (rān'ē lāk)	134-35	48°39'N	93°17'W
Rainy River, On., Can. (rān'ē rĭv'ēr)	134-35	48°44'N	94°34'W
Raipur, India	234-35	21°15'N	81°39'E
Raivavae, i., Fr. Poly.	280-81	23°52'S	147°40'W
Rājahmundry, India (räj-ŭ-mŭn'drē)	236	17°01'N	81°47'E
Rajang, stm., Malay.	248-49	2°10'N	111°21'E
Rājapālaiyam, India	236	9°27'N	77°34'E
Rājasthān, state, India (rä'jŭs-tän)	234-35	27°0'N	74°00'E
Rājgarh, India	234-35	23°55'N	76°55'E
Rājkot, India (räj'kôt)	234-35	22°18'N	70°48'E
Rājshāhi, Bngl.	234-35	24°22'N	88°36'E
Rakaposhi, mtn., Pak.	232-33	36°10'N	74°30'E
Rakata, Pulau, i., Indon. *see* Krakatoa	248-49	6°10'S	105°26'E
Rakiura, i., N.Z. *see* Stewart Island	278	47°0'S	167°50'E
Rakvere, Est. (rák'vě-rě)	192-93	59°21'N	26°22'E
Raleigh, N.C., U.S.	124-25	35°47'N	78°39'W
Rambouillet, Fr. (räN-bōō-yĕ')	196-97	48°39'N	1°50'E
Rambutyo Island, i., Pap. N. Gui.	277	2°18'S	147°49'E
Rāmeswaram, India	236	9°17'N	79°19'E
Ramm, Jabal, mtn., Jord.	228-29	29°35'N	35°24'E
Ramos, Mex. (rä'mōs)	146-47	22°50'N	101°55'W
Ramos Arizpe, Mex. (rä'mōs ä-rēz'pā)	122-23	25°32'N	100°57'W
Rāmpur, India (räm'pōōr)	234-35	28°48'N	79°01'E
Rampur Boalia, Bngl. *see* Rājshāhi	234-35	24°22'N	88°36'E
Ramree Island, i., Mya. (räm'rē' ī'lănd)	246-47	19°06'N	93°48'E
Ramsey Lake, lk., On., Can. (răm'zē lāk)	136-37	47°15'N	82°16'W
Ramsgate, Eng., U.K. (rămz''gāt)	190-91	51°20'N	1°24'E
Ramu, stm., Pap. N. Gui. (rä'mōō)	277	4°03'S	144°40'E
Ranau, Malay.	248-49	5°57'N	116°41'E
Rancagua, Chile (rän-kä'gwä)	163e	34°10'S	70°44'W
Rānchi, India	234-35	23°21'N	85°20'E
Randers, Den. (rän'ĕrs)	192-93	56°28'N	10°03'E
Randleman, N.C., U.S. (răn'd'l-măn)	124-25	35°49'N	79°49'W
Randolph, Ne., U.S. (răn'dôlf)	114-15	42°23'N	97°21'W
Random Island, i., Nf., Can. (răn'dŭm ī'lănd)	138-39	48°08'N	53°45'W
Rāngāmāti, Bngl.	246-47	22°42'N	92°08'E
Rangeley, Me., U.S. (rānj'lē rānj)	116-17	44°58'N	70°39'W
Ranger, Tx., U.S. (rān'jēr rānj)	120-21	32°29'N	98°41'W
Rangoon, nat. cap., Mya. (ráŋ-gōōn') *see* Yangon	246-47	16°47'N	96°12'E
Rangpur, Bngl. (rŭng'pōōr)	234-35	25°45'N	89°16'E
Rānīganj, India (rä-nē-gŭnj')	234-35	23°36'N	87°07'E
Rankin Inlet, Nu., Can.	128-29	62°49'N	92°10'W
Rann of Kutch, reg., Asia *see* Kutch, Rann of	234-35	24°15'N	70°46'E
Ranongga Island, i., Sol. Is.	279e	8°05'S	156°34'E
Rantauprapat, Indon.	246-47	2°06'N	99°49'E
Rantekombola, Bulu, mtn., Indon.	248-49	3°24'S	120°02'E
Rantoul, Il., U.S. (răn-tōōl')	116-17	40°18'N	88°09'W
Raoul Island, i., N.Z.	280-81	29°16'S	177°55'W
Rapa, i., Fr. Poly.	280-81	27°36'S	144°20'W
Rapallo, Italy (rä-päl'lô)	200-01	44°21'N	9°14'E
Rapel, stm., Chile (rä-pål')	163e	33°54'S	71°50'W
Rapid City, S.D., U.S. (răp'ĭd sĭ'tē)	114-15	44°04'N	103°13'W
Rapla, Est. (räp'lȧ)	192-93	59°00'N	24°47'E
Rappahannock, stm., Va., U.S. (răp'ȧ-hăn'ŭk)	116-17	37°35'N	76°18'W
Rapu Rapu Island, i., Phil.	250	13°12'N	124°09'E
Raraka, at., Fr. Poly.	280-81	16°10'S	144°54'W
Raroïa, i., Fr. Poly.	280-81	16°01'S	142°27'W
Rarotonga, i., Cook Is.	280-81	21°14'S	159°46'W
Ras Dashen Terara, mtn., Eth. (räs dä-shän') *see* Ras Dejen	266	13°16'N	38°24'E
Ras Dejen, mtn., Eth.	266	13°16'N	38°24'E
Raseiniai, Lith. (rä-syā'nyĭ)	192-93	55°23'N	23°08'E
Rashid, Egypt *see* Rosetta	268b	31°24'N	30°25'E
Rashin, Kor., N. *see* Najin	243	42°15'N	130°18'E

n-sing; ŋ-baŋk; N-nasalized n; nŏd; cŏmmit; ōld; ōbey; ôrder; oi-boil; fōōd; ŏŏ-as oo in foot; ou-out; s-soft; sh-dish; th-thin; pūre; ûnite; ûrn; stŭd; circŭs; ü-as in French tu; '-indeterminate vowel.

Feature (Pronunciation)	Page	Lat.	Long.
Rasht, Iran	228-29	37°17'N	49°35'E
Rasshua, Ostrov, i., Russia	218-19	47°45'N	153°01'E
Rasskazovo, Russia (räs-kä'sô-vô)	186-87	52°40'N	41°53'E
Rastatt, Ger. (rä-shtät)	194-95	48°51'N	8°12'E
Ratangarh, India (rŭ-tŭn'gŭr)	234-35	28°05'N	74°37'E
Rathenow, Ger. (rä'tĕ-nō)	194-95	52°36'N	12°20'E
Rat Islands, is., Ak., U.S. (răt ī'lăndz)	126a	52°0'N	178°00'E
Ratlām, India	234-35	23°20'N	75°02'E
Ratnāgiri, India	236	16°59'N	73°18'E
Raton, N.M., U.S. (rá-tōn')	120-21	36°55'N	104°26'W
Rättvik, Swe. (rĕt'vēk)	192-93	60°53'N	15°07'E
Rauch, Arg. (rá'ōōch)	173	36°47'S	59°06'W
Rauma, Fin. (rä'ò-mȧ)	192-93	61°08'N	21°30'E
Raurkela, India	234-35	22°13'N	84°52'E
Ravenna, Italy (rä-vĕn'nä)	200-01	44°25'N	12°12'E
Ravenna, Ne., U.S. (rȧ-vĕn'ȧ)	114-15	41°02'N	98°55'W
Ravensburg, Ger. (rä'vĕns-bōōrgh)	194-95	47°47'N	9°37'E
Ravensthorpe, Austl. (rā'vĕns-thôrp)	270-71	33°35'S	120°03'E
Ravenswood, W.V., U.S. (rā'vĕnz-wòd)	116-17	38°57'N	81°46'W
Rāvi, stm., Asia	232-33	30°37'N	71°53'E
Rawaki, at., Kir.	280-81	3°43'S	170°43'W
Rāwalpindi, Pak. (rä-wŭl-pēn'dē)	232-33	33°36'N	73°04'E
Rawicz, Pol. (rä'vēch)	194-95	51°37'N	16°52'E
Rawlinna, Austl.	270-71	31°02'S	125°18'E
Rawlins, Wy., U.S. (rô'lĭnz)	112-13	41°47'N	107°14'W
Rawson, Arg.	171	43°19'S	65°06'W
Raxaul, India	234-35	26°59'N	84°50'E
Ray, Cape, c., Nf., Can. (kāp rā)	138-39	47°38'N	59°18'W
Raya, Bukit, mtn., Indon.	248-49	0°40'S	112°41'E
Raychikhinsk, Russia	240-41	49°48'N	129°24'E
Raymond, N.H., U.S. (rā'mŭnd)	116-17	43°02'N	71°11'W
Raymond, Wa., U.S. (rā'mŭnd)	112-13	46°41'N	123°44'W
Raymondville, Tx., U.S. (rā'mŭnd-vĭl)	122-23	26°29'N	97°46'W
Rayne, La., U.S. (rān)	122-23	30°14'N	92°16'W
Raytown, Mo., U.S. (rā'toun)	120-21	38°59'N	94°28'W
Rayville, La., U.S. (rā-vĭl)	124-25	32°29'N	91°46'W
Raz, Pointe du, c., Fr. (pwänt dü rä)	196-97	48°03'N	4°44'W
Razdol'noye, Russia (räz-dôl'nô-yĕ)	244	43°30'N	131°49'E
Razlog, Blg. (räz'lôk)	200-01	41°53'N	23°29'E
Razorback Mountain, mtn., B.C., Can. (rā'zēr-băk moun'tĭn)	132-33	51°35'N	124°42'W
Ré, Île de, i., Fr.	196-97	46°12'N	1°24'W
Reading, Eng., U.K. (rĕd'ĭng)	190-91	51°28'N	0°59'W
Reading, Pa., U.S.	116-17	40°20'N	75°56'W
Real, Cordillera, mts., S.A.	168-69	16°50'S	66°34'W
Realicó, Arg.	173	35°02'S	64°14'W
Rebun-tō, i., Japan (rē'bōōn tō)	244	45°23'N	141°02'E
Recife, Braz. (rå-sē'fĕ)	166-67	8°03'S	34°54'W
Reconquista, Arg. (rā-kôn-kēs'tä)	173	29°09'S	59°38'W
Recreo, Arg.	168-69	29°17'S	65°04'W
Rector, Ar., U.S. (rĕk'tēr)	124-25	36°16'N	90°18'W
Rèčyča, Bela.	202-03	52°22'N	30°25'E
Red, stm., Asia (rĕd)	238-39	20°18'N	106°32'E
Red, stm., N.A. (rĕd)	110-11	50°25'N	96°47'W
Red, stm., U.S. (rĕd)	110-11	29°49'N	91°23'W
Red, stm., Ky., U.S. (rĕd)	116-17	37°50'N	84°06'W
Redang, Pulau, i., Malay.	246-47	5°46'N	103°01'E
Red Bank, Tn., U.S. (rĕd băngk)	124-25	35°07'N	85°17'W
Red Bluff, Ca., U.S.	118-19	40°11'N	122°14'W
Red Bluff Reservoir, res., U.S. (rĕd blŭf rĕ'sēr-vwär)	122-23	31°57'N	103°56'W
Redcliff, Ab., Can. (rĕd'clĭf)	132-33	50°05'N	110°47'W
Redcliffe, Austl. (rĕd'clĭf)	276	27°14'S	153°07'E
Red Cloud, Ne., U.S. (rĕd kloud)	120-21	40°05'N	98°31'W
Red Deer, Ab., Can. (rĕd dēr)	132-33	52°16'N	113°49'W
Red Deer, stm., Can. (rĕd dēr)	132-33	50°55'N	109°53'W
Red Deer, stm., Can. (rĕd dēr)	134-35	52°59'N	100°52'W
Red Deer Lake, lk., Mb., Can. (rĕd dēr lāk)	134-35	52°56'N	101°20'W
Redding, Ca., U.S.	112-13	40°35'N	122°23'W
Redfield, S.D., U.S. (rĕd'fēld)	114-15	44°52'N	98°31'W
Red Indian Lake, lk., Nf., Can. (rĕd ĭn'dĭ-ăn lāk)	138-39	48°39'N	56°50'W
Red Lake, On., Can. (rĕd lāk)	134-35	51°01'N	93°49'W
Red Lake, lk., On., Can.	134-35	51°01'N	94°05'W
Red Lake Falls, Mn., U.S. (rĕd lāk fôlz)	114-15	47°53'N	96°16'W
Red Lake Indian Reservation, ind. res., Mn., U.S. (rĕd lāk ĭn'dĭ-ăn rĕ-sēr-vā'shĕn)	114-15	48°03'N	94°59'W
Red Lion, Pa., U.S. (rĕd lī'ŭn)	116-17	39°54'N	76°36'W
Redmond, Or., U.S. (rĕd'mŭnd)	112-13	44°17'N	121°10'W
Redmond, Wa., U.S. (rĕd'mŭnd)	112-13	47°40'N	122°07'W
Red Oak, Ia., U.S. (rĕd ōk)	114-15	41°01'N	95°14'W
Redon, Fr. (rē-dôn')	196-97	47°39'N	2°05'W
Redonda, i., Antig. (rĕ-dŏn'dȧ)	143b	16°56'N	62°21'W
Red Sea, s., (rĕd sē)	266	20°0'N	38°00'E
Red Sucker Lake, lk., Mb., Can. (rĕd sŭk'ēr lāk)	134-35	54°09'N	93°40'W
Red Wing, Mn., U.S.	114-15	44°34'N	92°32'W
Redwood Falls, Mn., U.S. (rĕd'wòd fôlz)	114-15	44°32'N	95°07'W
Redwood National Park, n.p., Ca., U.S. (rĕd'wòd năsh'ŭn-ăl pärk)	112-13	41°20'N	124°02'W
Reed City, Mi., U.S. (rēd sĭ'tē)	116-17	43°53'N	85°32'W
Reed Lake, lk., Mb., Can. (rēd lāk)	134-35	54°38'N	100°30'W
Reedley, Ca., U.S. (rēd'lē)	118-19	36°35'N	119°26'W
Reedsburg, Wi., U.S. (rēdz'bûrg)	116-17	43°32'N	89°59'W
Reedsport, Or., U.S. (rēdz'pôrt)	112-13	43°42'N	124°06'W
Reform, Al., U.S. (rē-fôrm')	124-25	33°23'N	88°01'W
Refugio, Tx., U.S. (rå-fōō'hyô) (rĕ-fū'jō)	122-23	28°18'N	97°17'W
Rega, stm., Pol. (rĕ-gä)	194-95	54°09'N	15°17'E
Regensburg, Ger. (rā'ghĕns-bòrgh)	194-95	49°01'N	12°06'E
Reggio di Calabria, Italy (rĕ'jô dē kä-lä'brē-ä)	200-01	38°07'N	15°39'E
Reghin, Rom. (rå-gēn')	194-95	46°47'N	24°43'E
Regina, Sk., Can. (rē-jī'nȧ)	134-35	50°27'N	104°38'W
Registan, reg., Afg. *see* Rīgestān	232-33	31°0'N	65°00'E
Rehoboth, Nmb.	264-65	23°19'S	17°05'E
Rehovot, Isr.	228-29	31°54'N	34°49'E
Reidsville, N.C., U.S. (rēdz'vĭl)	124-25	36°21'N	79°40'W
Reims, Fr. (răns)	196-97	49°15'N	4°02'E
Reindeer Lake, lk., Can. (rān'dēr lāk)	134-35	57°16'N	102°15'W
Reinosa, Spain (rå-ē-nō'sä)	198-99	42°60'N	4°08'W
Remada, Tun.	188-89	32°19'N	10°23'E
Remanso, Braz.	166-67	9°37'S	42°07'W
Remedios, Pan. (rĕ-mĕ'dyōs)	150	8°13'N	81°50'W
Remiremont, Fr. (rē-mēr-môn')	196-97	48°01'N	6°36'E
Rendova Island, i., Sol. Is. (rĕn'dô-vȧ ī'lănd)	279e	8°32'S	157°20'E
Rendsburg, Ger. (rĕnts'bòrgh)	194-95	54°18'N	9°40'E
Renfrew, On., Can. (rĕn'frōō)	136-37	45°29'N	76°42'W
Rengo, Chile (rĕn'gō)	163e	34°29'S	70°53'W
Reni, Ukr. (ran')	200-01	45°28'N	28°17'E
Renmark, Austl. (rĕn'märk)	276	34°11'S	140°45'E
Rennell, i., Sol. Is. (rĕn-nĕl')	272-73	11°33'S	160°05'E
Rennes, Fr. (rĕn)	196-97	48°07'N	1°41'W
Reno, Nv., U.S. (rē'nō)	118-19	39°32'N	119°49'W
Reno, Tx., U.S. (rē'nō)	120-21	32°56'N	97°35'W
Renovo, Pa., U.S. (rē-nō'vō)	116-17	41°20'N	77°45'W
Rensselaer, In., U.S. (rĕn'sē-lâr)	116-17	40°57'N	87°09'W
Rensselaer, N.Y., U.S. (rĕn'sē-lâr)	116-17	42°40'N	73°45'W
Renton, Wa., U.S. (rĕn'tŭn)	112-13	47°30'N	122°11'W
Reo, Indon.	248-49	8°19'S	120°29'E
Repetek, Turkmen.	232-33	38°34'N	63°11'E
Republic, Mo., U.S. (rē-pŭb'lĭk)	120-21	37°08'N	93°29'W
República Dominicana, nation, N.A. *see* Dominican Republic	140-41	19°0'N	70°40'W
Republican, stm., U.S. (rē-pŭb'lĭ-kăn)	110-11	39°03'N	96°48'W
Republican, South Fork, stm., U.S. (south fôrk rē-pŭb'lĭ-kăn)	120-21	40°04'N	101°31'W
Republic of Korea, nation, Asia	206-07	36°30'N	128°00'E
République centrafricaine, nation, Afr. *see* Central African Republic	253	7°0'N	21°00'E
Repulse Bay, Nu., Can.	128-29	66°32'N	86°14'W
Repulse Bay, b., Austl. (rē-pŭls' bā)	277	20°36'S	148°43'E
Requena, Spain (rå-kā'nä)	198-99	39°29'N	1°06'W
Resht, Iran *see* Rasht	228-29	37°17'N	49°35'E
Resistencia, Arg. (rā-sēs-tĕn'syä)	173	27°27'S	59°00'W
Reşiţa, Rom. (rå'shē-tȧ)	200-01	45°18'N	21°53'E
Resolution Island, i., Nu., Can. (rĕz-ô-lū'shŭn ī'lănd)	130-31	61°30'N	65°00'W
Resolution Island, i., N.Z. (rĕz-ŏl-ûshûn ī'lănd)	278	45°40'S	166°40'E
Restrepo, Col. (rĕs-trĕ'pô)	163c	3°48'N	76°31'W
Retalhuleu, Guat. (rā-täl-ōō-lān')	148	14°32'N	91°41'W
Rethel, Fr. (r-tl')	196-97	49°31'N	4°22'E
Reunion, dep., Afr. (rā-ü-nyôn')	265a	21°06'S	55°36'E
Réunion, dep., Afr. *see* Reunion	265a	21°06'S	55°36'E
Reus, Spain (rā'ōōs)	198-99	41°09'N	1°07'E
Reutlingen, Ger. (roit'lĭng-ĕn)	194-95	48°30'N	9°12'E
Reval, nat. cap., Est. *see* Tallinn	192-93	59°26'N	24°48'E
Revda, Russia (ryâv'dȧ)	186-87	67°58'N	34°34'E
Revelstoke, B.C., Can. (rĕv'ĕl-stōk)	132-33	50°59'N	118°11'W
Revillagigedo, Islas, is., Mex. (ĕ's-läs-rĕ-vêl-yä-hĕ'gĕ-dô)	144-45	18°48'N	112°06'W
Revin, Fr. (rē-văn)	196-97	49°56'N	4°39'E
Rewa, India (rā'wä)	234-35	24°32'N	81°18'E
Rexburg, Id., U.S. (rĕks'bûrg)	112-13	43°50'N	111°47'W
Rey, Isla del, i., Pan. (ĕ's-lä-dĕl-rā'ē)	150	8°22'N	78°55'W
Rey, Laguna del, lk., Mex. (lä-gò'nä-dĕl-rā)	122-23	27°01'N	103°24'W
Reyes, Bol. (rā'yĕs)	166-67	14°19'S	67°22'W
Reyes, Point, c., Ca., U.S. (point rā'yĕs)	118-19	38°0'N	123°01'W
Reykjanes, pen., Ice. (rā'kyȧ-nĕs)	190a	63°49'N	22°43'W
Reykjavík, nat. cap., Ice. (rā'kyȧ-vēk)	190a	64°08'N	21°56'W
Reynosa, Mex. (rā-ē-nō'sä)	122-23	26°05'N	98°17'W
Reẓā'īyeh, Iran *see* Orūmīyeh	228-29	37°32'N	45°05'E
Rēzekne, Lat. (rå'zĕk-nĕ)	192-93	56°30'N	27°20'E
Rheims, Fr. *see* Reims	196-97	49°15'N	4°02'E
Rhein, stm., Eur. *see* Rhine	194-95	51°53'N	6°02'E
Rheine, Ger. (rī'nĕ)	194-95	52°17'N	7°27'E
Rhin, stm., Eur. *see* Rhine	194-95	51°53'N	6°02'E
Rhine, stm., Eur. (rīn)	194-95	51°53'N	6°02'E
Rhinelander, Wi., U.S. (rīn'lăn-dēr)	116-17	45°38'N	89°24'W
Rhir, Cap, c., Mor.	258-59	30°38'N	9°53'W
Rhode Island, state, U.S. (rōd ī'lănd)	108-09	41°40'N	71°30'W
Rhodes, Grc. *see* Ródos	200-01	36°26'N	28°14'E
Rhodes, i., Grc. (rôdz) *see* Ródos	200-01	36°10'N	28°00'E
Rhodesia, nation, Afr. *see* Zimbabwe	253	20°0'S	30°00'E
Rhône, stm., Eur. (rōn)	196-97	43°53'N	4°39'E
Riachão, Braz. (rē-ä-choun')	166-67	7°22'S	46°39'W
Riau, Kepulauan, is., Indon.	246-47	1°0'N	104°30'E
Ribe, Den. (rē'bĕ)	192-93	55°20'N	8°46'E
Ribeirão Preto, Braz. (rē-bā-roun-prĕ'tô)	172	21°10'S	47°48'W
Riberalta, Bol. (rē-bå-räl'tä)	166-67	11°00'S	66°05'W
Rib Lake, Wi., U.S. (rĭb lāk)	116-17	45°19'N	90°12'W
Rice Lake, Wi., U.S. (rīs lāk)	114-15	45°30'N	91°44'W
Rice Lake, lk., On., Can. (rīs lāk)	136-37	44°08'N	78°13'W
Richards Bay, S. Afr.	264-65	28°47'S	32°05'E
Richardson, Tx., U.S. (rĭch'ērd-sŭn)	120-21	32°58'N	96°44'W
Richardson Mountains, mts., Can. (rĭch'ērd-sŭn moun'tĭnz)	130-31	67°22'N	136°04'W
Richfield, Ut., U.S. (rĭch'fērd)	118-19	38°46'N	112°05'W
Rich Hill, Mo., U.S. (rĭch hĭl)	120-21	38°06'N	94°22'W
Richland, Ga., U.S. (rĭch'lănd)	124-25	32°05'N	84°40'W
Richland, Wa., U.S. (rĭch'lănd)	112-13	46°16'N	119°17'W
Richland Center, Wi., U.S. (rĭch'lănd sĕn'tēr)	114-15	43°20'N	90°23'W
Richmond, Austl. (rĭch'mŭnd)	277	20°44'S	143°08'E
Richmond, B.C., Can. (rĭch'mŭnd)	132-33	49°09'N	123°10'W
Richmond, Qc., Can. (rĭch'mŭnd)	136-37	45°40'N	72°09'W
Richmond, In., U.S. (rĭch'mŭnd)	116-17	39°49'N	84°54'W
Richmond, Ky., U.S. (rĭch'mŭnd)	116-17	37°45'N	84°18'W
Richmond, Mi., U.S. (rĭch'mŭnd)	116-17	42°49'N	82°45'W
Richmond, Mo., U.S. (rĭch'mŭnd)	120-21	39°17'N	93°59'W
Richmond, Va., U.S. (rĭch'mŭnd)	116-17	37°33'N	77°27'W
Richmond Hill, On., Can. (rĭch'mŭnd hĭl)	136-37	43°52'N	79°26'W
Richwood, La., U.S. (rĭch'wòd)	120-21	32°27'N	92°06'W
Richwood, W.V., U.S. (rĭch'wòd)	116-17	38°13'N	80°34'W
Ridā', Yemen	266	14°38'N	44°54'E
Ridder, Kaz.	226	50°21'N	83°30'E
Riding Mountain National Park, n.p., Mb., Can. (rīd'ĭng moun'tĭn năsh'ŭn-ăl pärk)	134-35	50°55'N	100°25'W
Riesa, Ger. (rē'zȧ)	194-95	51°18'N	13°18'E
Riesco, Isla, i., Chile	171	52°59'S	72°38'W
Rieti, Italy (rē-ā'tē)	200-01	42°24'N	12°52'E
Rif, mts., Mor.	258-59	35°0'N	4°00'W
Rift Valley, val., Afr. (rĭft văl'ē)	254	3°0'S	29°00'E
Rīga, nat. cap., Lat. (rē'gȧ)	192-93	56°57'N	24°06'E
Riga, Gulf of, b., Eur. (gŭlf ŭv rē'gȧ)	192-93	57°30'N	23°35'E
Rīgas jūras līcis, b., Eur. *see* Riga, Gulf of	192-93	57°30'N	23°35'E
Rigby, Id., U.S. (rĭg'bē)	112-13	43°40'N	111°56'W
Rīgestān, reg., Afg.	232-33	31°0'N	65°00'E
Rijeka, Cro. (rĭ-yĕ'kä)	200-01	45°20'N	14°27'E
Rijn, stm., Eur. *see* Rhine	194-95	51°53'N	6°02'E
Rima, stm., Nig.	260-61	13°04'N	5°07'E
Rimatara, i., Fr. Poly.	280-81	22°38'S	152°51'W
Rimavská Sobota, Slvk. (rē'màf-skä sô'bô-tȧ)	194-95	48°23'N	20°05'E
Rimbo, Swe. (rēm'bò)	192-93	59°45'N	18°22'E
Rimini, Italy (rē'mē-nē)	200-01	44°04'N	12°35'E
Rimouski, Qc., Can. (rē-mōōs'kē)	138-39	48°27'N	68°33'W
Rincón del Bonete, Lago Artificial de, res., Ur.	173	32°43'S	56°01'W
Rincón de Romos, Mex. (rēn-kōn dā rō-mōs')	146-47	22°14'N	102°18'W
Ringkøbing, Den. (rĭng'kûb-ĭng)	192-93	56°05'N	8°15'E
Ringsted, Den. (rĭng'stĕdh)	192-93	55°27'N	11°50'E
Ringvassøya, i., Nor. (rĭng'väs-ûê)	184-85	69°55'N	19°15'E
Rinjani, Gunung, vol., Indon.	248-49	8°24'S	116°28'E
Riobamba, Ec. (rē'ō-bäm-bä)	170	1°40'S	78°39'W

ăt; finăl; rāte; senâte; ärm; åsk; sofȧ; fâre; ch-choose; dh-as th in other; bē; ēvent; bĕt; recĕnt; cratēr; g-gō; gh-guttural g; bĭt; ĭ-short neutral; rīde; κ-guttural k as ch in German ich;

Feature (Pronunciation)	Page	Lat.	Long.
Rio Branco, Braz. (rē´ò brän´kò)	166-67	9°58'S	67°48'W
Río Branco, Ur. (rīô bräncô)	173	32°36'S	53°23'W
Rio Casca, Braz. (rē´ō-kà´s-kä)	172	20°14'S	42°39'W
Río Chico, Ven. (rê´ō chê´kǒ)	163b	10°18'N	65°59'W
Rio Claro, Braz. (rē´ò klä´rò)	172	22°26'S	47°33'W
Río Colorado, Arg.	173	38°60'S	64°07'W
Río Cuarto, Arg. (rē´ō kwär´tō)	173	33°08'S	64°21'W
Rio de Janeiro, Braz. (rē´ò dā zhä-nå´ê-rò)	172	22°54'S	43°14'W
Rio de Janeiro, state, Braz. (rē´ò dā zhä-nå´ê-rò)	172	22°0'S	42°30'W
Rio do Sul, Braz.	168-69	27°13'S	49°39'W
Río Gallegos, Arg. (rē´ō gä-lā´gōs)	171	51°38'S	69°13'W
Río Grande, Arg.	171	53°49'S	67°47'W
Rio Grande, Braz. (rē´ò grän´dĕ)	173	32°02'S	52°06'W
Río Grande, Mex. (rē´ō grän´dā)	146-47	15°59'N	97°27'W
Río Grande, Mex. (rē´ō grän´dā)	146-47	23°50'N	103°03'W
Rio Grande, stm., N.A. (rē´ō grän´dā)	110-11	25°57'N	97°09'W
Rio Grande do Sul, Braz. see Rio Grande	173	32°02'S	52°06'W
Rio Grande do Sul, state, Braz. (rē´ò grän´dĕ-dò-sōō´l)	173	30°0'S	54°00'W
Ríohacha, Col. (rē´ō-ä´chä)	164-65	11°33'N	72°55'W
Río Hato, Pan. (rê´ō-ä´tô)	150	8°23'N	80°10'W
Rio Largo, Braz.	163d	9°29'S	35°51'W
Riom, Fr. (rê-ôN´)	196-97	45°54'N	3°07'E
Río Mayo, Arg.	171	45°41'S	70°14'W
Rio Negro, Braz.	168-69	26°06'S	49°47'W
Ríonegro, Col. (rê´ō-nĕ´grō)	163c	6°08'N	75°23'W
Río Negro, state, Arg. (rē´ō nā´grō)	171	40°0'S	67°00'W
Rio Pardo, Braz.	168-69	29°59'S	52°22'W
Rio Pardo de Minas, Braz. (rē´ō pär´dō-dĕ-mē´näs)	168-69	15°37'S	42°33'W
Ríosucio, Col. (rē´ō-sōō´syô)	163c	5°25'N	75°42'W
Ríosucio, Col. (rē´ō-sōō´syô)	164-65	7°25'N	77°06'W
Río Tercero, Arg. (rê´ō dĕr-sĕ´rô)	173	32°11'S	64°07'W
Rio Tinto, Braz.	163d	6°48'S	35°05'W
Rio Verde, Braz. (rē´ō vĕr´dĕ)	168-69	17°47'S	50°55'W
Ríoverde, Mex. (rē´ō-vĕr´då)	146-47	21°56'N	99°59'W
Ripley, Ms., U.S. (rĭp´lê)	124-25	34°45'N	88°57'W
Ripley, Tn., U.S. (rĭp´lê)	124-25	35°45'N	89°32'W
Ripley, W.V., U.S. (rĭp´lê)	116-17	38°48'N	81°44'W
Ripoll, Spain (rê-pōl´)	198-99	42°12'N	2°12'E
Ripon, Wi., U.S. (rĭp´ŏn)	116-17	43°51'N	88°50'W
Rishiri-tō, i., Japan (rē-shē´rē tō)	244	45°11'N	141°15'E
Rising Sun, In., U.S. (rīz´ĭng sŭn)	116-17	38°57'N	84°52'W
Risør, Nor. (rēs´ûr)	192-93	58°43'N	9°14'E
Rittman, Oh., U.S. (rĭt´năn)	116-17	40°58'N	81°47'W
Ritzville, Wa., U.S. (rĭts´vĭl)	112-13	47°07'N	118°22'W
Rivas, Nic. (rē´väs)	149	11°27'N	85°52'W
Rivera, Ur. (rê-vā´rä)	173	30°54'S	55°33'W
River Falls, Wi., U.S. (rĭv´ēr fôlz)	114-15	44°52'N	92°37'W
Riverhead, N.Y., U.S. (rĭv´ēr hĕd)	116-17	40°55'N	72°40'W
Rivers, Mb., Can. (rĭv´ērz)	134-35	50°02'N	100°14'W
Riverside, Ca., U.S.	118-19	33°58'N	117°21'W
Rivers Inlet, B.C., Can.	132-33	51°42'N	127°15'W
Rivesaltes, Fr. (rēv´zält´)	196-97	42°46'N	2°52'E
Riviera Beach, Fl., U.S. (rĭv-ĭ-ēr´á bēch)	125a	26°46'N	80°04'W
Rivière-du-Loup, Qc., Can. (rê-vyâr´ dü lōō´)	138-39	47°50'N	69°32'W
Rivne, Ukr.	194-95	50°37'N	26°14'E
Riyadh, nat. cap., Sau. Ar. (rĭ-äd´)	230-31	24°38'N	46°43'E
Rize, Tur. (rĕ´zĕ)	227	41°01'N	40°31'E
Rjukan, Nor. (ryōō´kän)	192-93	59°53'N	8°35'E
Road Town, nat. cap., Br. Vir. Is. (rōd toun)	143b	18°26'N	64°37'W
Roanne, Fr. (rō-än´)	196-97	46°02'N	4°04'E
Roanoke, Al., U.S. (rō´á-nōk)	124-25	33°09'N	85°22'W
Roanoke, Va., U.S. (rō´á-nōk)	124-25	37°16'N	79°57'W
Roanoke, stm., U.S. (rō´á-nōk)	124-25	35°57'N	76°43'W
Roanoke Rapids, N.C., U.S. (rō´á-nōk răp´ĭdz)	124-25	36°28'N	77°39'W
Roan Plateau, plat., U.S. (rōn plä-tō´)	118-19	39°30'N	109°40'W
Roatán, Hond. (rō-ä-tän´)	149	16°20'N	86°32'W
Roatán, Isla de, i., Hond.	149	16°22'N	86°29'W
Roberval, Qc., Can. (rŏb´ēr-văl) (rô-bĕr-vál´)	136-37	48°31'N	72°14'W
Robinson, Il., U.S. (rŏb´ĭn-sŭn)	116-17	39°01'N	87°45'W
Robinvale, Austl. (rŏb-ĭn´văl)	276	34°36'S	142°46'E
Roblin, Mb., Can.	134-35	51°15'N	101°23'W
Roboré, Bol.	168-69	18°20'S	59°45'W
Robson, Mount, mtn., B.C., Can. (mount rŏb´sŭn)	132-33	53°07'N	119°09'W
Robstown, Tx., U.S. (rŏbz´toun)	122-23	27°47'N	97°40'W
Roca, Cabo da, c., Port. (ká´bō-dä-rō´kä)	198-99	38°47'N	9°29'W
Roca Partida, Isla, i., Mex.	144-45	19°00'N	112°04'W
Rocha, Ur. (rō´chás)	173	34°30'S	54°19'W
Rochefort, Fr. (rôsh-fōr´)	196-97	45°57'N	0°58'W
Rochelle, Il., U.S. (rô-shĕl´)	116-17	41°55'N	89°04'W
Rochester, In., U.S. (rŏch´ĕs-tēr)	116-17	41°04'N	86°12'W
Rochester, Mn., U.S. (rŏch´ĕs-tēr)	114-15	44°00'N	92°29'W
Rochester, N.H., U.S. (rŏch´ĕs-tēr)	116-17	43°18'N	70°59'W
Rochester, N.Y., U.S.	116-17	43°09'N	77°36'W
Rock, stm., U.S. (rŏk)	114-15	41°29'N	90°38'W
Rockdale, Tx., U.S. (rŏk´dāl)	122-23	30°39'N	97°00'W
Rockefeller Plateau, plat., Ant.	287	80°0'S	135°00'W
Rock Falls, Il., U.S. (rŏk fôlz)	116-17	41°47'N	89°41'W
Rockford, Il., U.S. (rŏk´fērd)	116-17	42°16'N	89°05'W
Rockford, Mi., U.S. (rŏk´fērd)	116-17	43°07'N	85°34'W
Rockhampton, Austl. (rŏk-hămp´tŭn)	277	23°23'S	150°31'E
Rock Hill, S.C., U.S. (rŏk hĭl)	124-25	34°56'N	81°02'W
Rockingham, N.C., U.S. (rŏk´ĭng-hăm)	124-25	34°56'N	79°46'W
Rock Island, Il., U.S. (rŏk ī´lănd)	114-15	41°30'N	90°34'W
Rockland, On., Can. (rŏk´lănd)	136-37	45°33'N	75°17'W
Rockland, Me., U.S.	117a	44°07'N	69°07'W
Rockport, In., U.S. (rŏk´pōrt)	116-17	37°53'N	87°03'W
Rockport, Tx., U.S. (rŏk´pōrt)	122-23	28°01'N	97°03'W
Rock Rapids, Ia., U.S. (rŏk răp´ĭdz)	114-15	43°26'N	96°10'W
Rocksprings, Tx., U.S. (rŏk springs)	122-23	30°01'N	100°12'W
Rock Springs, Wy., U.S. (rŏk springz)	112-13	41°35'N	109°13'W
Rockstone, Guy. (rŏk´stôn)	164-65	5°59'N	58°32'W
Rock Valley, Ia., U.S. (rŏk văl´ĭ văl´ê)	114-15	43°12'N	96°18'W
Rockville, In., U.S. (rŏk´vĭl)	116-17	39°45'N	87°14'W
Rockwell City, Ia., U.S. (rŏk´wĕl sĭ´tê)	114-15	42°24'N	94°38'W
Rockwood, Me., U.S. (rŏk-wŏŏd)	116-17	45°40'N	69°45'W
Rockwood, Tn., U.S. (rŏk-wŏŏd)	124-25	35°52'N	84°41'W
Rocky Ford, Co., U.S. (rŏk´-ē fôrd)	120-21	38°03'N	103°43'W
Rocky Island Lake, res., On., Can. (rŏk´-ē ī´lănd lāk)	136-37	46°56'N	82°57'W
Rocky Mount, N.C., U.S. (rŏk´-ē mount)	124-25	35°57'N	77°48'W
Rocky Mount, Va., U.S. (rŏk´-ē mount)	124-25	37°00'N	79°54'W
Rocky Mountain House, Ab., Can. (rŏk´-ē moun´tĭn hous)	132-33	52°23'N	114°56'W
Rocky Mountain National Park, n.p., Co., U.S. (rŏk´-ē moun´tĭn năsh´ŭn-ăl pärk)	112-13	40°21'N	105°42'W
Rocky Mountains, mts., N.A. (rŏk´-ē moun´tĭnz)	86	48°0'N	116°00'W
Rodeo, Arg.	168-69	30°12'S	69°06'W
Rodeo, Mex. (rô-dā´ō)	122-23	25°11'N	104°34'W
Rodez, Fr. (rô-dĕz´)	196-97	44°21'N	2°34'E
Rodniki, Russia (rôd´nê-kê)	186-87	57°06'N	41°44'E
Ródos, Grc.	200-01	36°26'N	28°14'E
Ródos, i., Grc.	200-01	36°10'N	28°00'E
Roebourne, Austl. (rō´bŭrn)	270-71	20°46'S	117°10'E
Rogagua, Laguna, lk., Bol.	166-67	13°42'S	67°07'W
Rogaguado, Laguna, lk., Bol. (rō´gō-ä-gwä-dō)	166-67	12°52'S	65°43'W
Rogers, Ar., U.S. (rŏj-ērz)	120-21	36°20'N	94°07'W
Rogers, Mount, mtn., Va., U.S.	124-25	36°39'N	81°33'W
Rogers City, Mi., U.S. (rŏj-ērz sĭ´tê)	116-17	45°25'N	83°49'W
Rohtak, India	234-35	28°53'N	76°36'E
Roi Georges, Îles du, is., Fr. Poly.	280-81	14°32'S	145°08'W
Rojas, Arg. (rō´häs)	173	34°12'S	60°44'W
Rojo, Cabo, c., Mex. (ká´bô rō´hō)	146-47	21°33'N	97°20'W
Rojo, Cabo, c., P.R. (ká´bô rō´hō)	142a	17°56'N	67°11'W
Rokan, stm., Indon.	246-47	1°50'N	100°55'E
Rokeby National Park, n.p., Austl. see Mungkan Kandju National Park	277	13°32'S	142°37'E
Rokycany, Czech Rep. (rô´kĭ´tsá-nĭ)	194-95	49°45'N	13°36'E
Rolândia, Braz.	168-69	23°18'S	51°23'W
Roldanillo, Col. (rôl-dä-nē´l-yō)	163c	4°24'N	76°09'W
Rolla, Mo., U.S.	120-21	37°57'N	91°46'W
Roma, Austl. (rō´má)	276	26°35'S	148°47'E
Roma, nat. cap., Italy (rō´má) see Rome	200-01	41°54'N	12°29'E
Romaine, stm., Can. (rô-mĕn´)	138-39	50°18'N	63°48'W
Roman, Rom. (rō´män)	194-95	46°56'N	26°57'E
Romang, Pulau, i., Indon.	248-49	7°34'S	127°26'E
Romania, nation, Eur. (rō-mā´nê-á)	174-75	46°0'N	25°30'E
Roman-Kosh, hora, mtn., Ukr.	202-03	44°37'N	34°15'E
Romano, Cape, c., Fl., U.S. (kāp rō-mā´nō)	125a	25°50'N	81°41'W
Romano, Cayo, i., Cuba (kä´yō-rō-má´nô)	142-43	22°04'N	77°50'W
Romblon, Phil. (rōm-blōn´)	250	12°34'N	122°16'E
Rome, Ga., U.S. (rōm)	124-25	34°16'N	85°10'W
Rome, N.Y., U.S. (rōm)	116-17	43°13'N	75°28'W
Rome, nat. cap., Italy (rōm)	200-01	41°54'N	12°29'E
Romeo, Mi., U.S. (rō´mê-ō)	116-17	42°48'N	83°00'W
Romilly-sur-Seine, Fr. (rô-mê-yē´sür-sān´)	196-97	48°31'N	3°44'E
Romny, Ukr. (rôm´nĭ)	202-03	50°45'N	33°29'E
Rømø, i., Den. (rûm´û)	192-93	55°08'N	8°31'E
Romorantin-Lanthenay, Fr. (rô-mô-räN-tăN´)	196-97	47°22'N	1°44'E
Rona, i., Scot., U.K.	184-85	59°07'N	5°49'W
Ronan, Mt., U.S. (rō´năn)	112-13	47°31'N	114°06'W
Roncador, Serra do, plat., Braz. (sĕr´rá dò rôn-kä-dôr´)	166-67	12°0'S	52°00'W
Ronda, Spain (rōn´dä)	198-99	36°44'N	5°10'W
Rondônia, state, Braz.	166-67	11°0'S	63°00'W
Rondonópolis, Braz.	168-69	16°28'S	54°38'W
Ronge, Lac la, lk., Sk., Can. (läk lä rŏnzh)	134-35	55°10'N	105°00'W
Rongelap, at., Marsh. Is.	280-81	11°20'N	166°50'E
Rongjiang, China (rôŋ-jyäŋ)	238-39	25°51'N	108°35'E
Rønne, Den. (rûn´ĕ)	194-95	55°06'N	14°42'E
Ronneby, Swe. (rōn´ĕ-bü)	192-93	56°12'N	15°18'E
Ronuro, stm., Braz.	166-67	11°56'S	53°33'W
Roorkee, India	234-35	29°52'N	77°53'E
Roosendaal, Neth. (rō´zĕn-däl)	190-91	51°32'N	4°28'E
Roosevelt, Ut., U.S. (rōz´´vĕlt)	118-19	40°19'N	109°59'W
Roosevelt, stm., Braz. (rô´sĕ-vĕlt)	166-67	7°34'S	60°41'W
Roper, stm., Austl. (rōp´ēr)	272-73	14°44'S	135°23'E
Roque Pérez, Arg. (rô´kĕ-pĕ´rĕz)	173	35°25'S	59°20'W
Roraima, state, Braz. (rô´rīy-mä)	166-67	1°0'N	61°00'W
Roraima, Monte, mtn., S.A. see Roraima, Mount	164-65	5°13'N	60°44'W
Roraima, Mount, mtn., S.A. (mount rô-rä-ē´mä)	164-65	5°13'N	60°44'W
Røros, Nor. (rûr´ôs)	184-85	62°35'N	11°23'E
Ros', stm., Ukr. (rôs)	202-03	49°41'N	31°36'E
Rosales, Mex. (rō-zä´lās)	122-23	28°12'N	105°33'W
Rosamorada, Mex. (rō´zä-mō-rä´dhä)	146-47	22°08'N	105°12'W
Rosario, Arg. (rō-zä´rê-ō)	173	32°57'S	60°40'W
Rosário, Braz. (rô-zä´rê-ò)	166-67	2°57'S	44°14'W
Rosario, Mex. (rô-zä´rê-ō)	146-47	23°00'N	105°52'W
Rosario, Para.	168-69	24°25'S	57°06'W
Rosario, Ur. (rô-zä´rê-ō)	173	34°19'S	57°21'W
Rosario de la Frontera, Arg.	168-69	25°48'S	64°58'W
Rosario de Lerma, Arg.	168-69	24°59'S	65°35'W
Rosário do Sul, Braz. (rô-zä´rê-ò-dô-sōō´l)	173	30°15'S	54°56'W
Rosário Oeste, Braz. (rô-zä´rê-ò ō´ĕst´ĕ)	166-67	14°50'S	56°25'W
Roscoe, Tx., U.S. (rôs´kō)	120-21	32°27'N	100°33'W
Roseau, Mn., U.S. (rô-zō´)	114-15	48°51'N	95°46'W
Roseau, nat. cap., Dom.	143b	15°18'N	61°23'W
Rosebud, stm., Ab., Can. (rōz´bŭd)	132-33	51°25'N	112°37'W
Rosebud Indian Reservation, ind. res., S.D., U.S. (rōz´bŭd ĭn´dĭ-ăn rĕ-sēr-vā´shĕn)	114-15	43°08'N	100°33'W
Roseburg, Or., U.S.	112-13	43°14'N	123°20'W
Rosenheim, Ger. (rō´zĕn-hīm)	194-95	47°52'N	12°08'E
Rosetown, Sk., Can. (rōz´toun)	134-35	51°32'N	108°01'W
Rosetta, Egypt	268b	31°24'N	30°25'E
Roseville, Mn., U.S. (rōz´vĭl)	114-15	45°01'N	93°10'W
Roșiori de Vede, Rom. (rô-shôr´ê dĕ vĕ-dĕ)	200-01	44°07'N	24°60'E
Roskilde, Den. (rôs´kêl-dĕ)	192-93	55°39'N	12°06'E
Roslavl', Russia (rôs´läv'l)	202-03	53°57'N	32°52'E
Rossano, Italy (rô-sä´nō)	200-01	39°35'N	16°39'E
Rossiya, nation, Eur. see Russia	174-75	60°0'N	100°00'E
Rossland, B.C., Can. (rôs´lănd)	132-33	49°05'N	117°48'W
Rosso, Maur.	258-59	16°31'N	15°48'W
Rossosh', Russia (rôs´sŭsh)	186-87	50°12'N	39°35'E
Ross River, Yk., Can.	128-29	62°00'N	132°26'W
Ross Sea, s., Ant. (rôs sē)	287	76°0'S	175°00'W
Rossville, Ga., U.S. (rôs´vĭl)	124-25	34°59'N	85°18'W
Rosthern, Sk., Can.	134-35	52°40'N	106°20'W
Rostock, Ger. (rôs´tŭk)	194-95	54°05'N	12°07'E
Rostov, Russia (rôstôv)	202-03	57°11'N	39°25'E
Rostov-na-Donu, Russia (rôstôv-nå-dô-nōō)	202-03	47°13'N	39°43'E
Roswell, Ga., U.S. (rôz´wĕl)	124-25	34°02'N	84°21'W
Roswell, N.M., U.S. (rôz´wĕl)	120-21	33°24'N	104°33'W
Rota, i., N. Mar. Is.	279c	14°10'N	145°12'E
Rotherham, Eng., U.K. (rŏdh´ēr-ăm)	190-91	53°25'N	1°23'W
Rothesay, Scot., U.K. (rôth´så)	190-91	55°50'N	5°03'W
Roti, Pulau, i., Indon. (pōō-lou rō´tê)	248-49	10°45'S	123°10'E
Rotorua, N.Z.	278	38°09'S	176°14'E
Rotterdam, Neth. (rôt´ēr-däm´)	190-91	51°55'N	4°28'E
Rottweil, Ger. (rōt´vīl)	194-95	48°10'N	8°38'E
Rotuma, i., Fiji	280-81	12°30'S	177°05'E

n-sing; ŋ-baŋk; N-nasalized n; nŏd; cŏmmit; ōld; ôbey; ôrder; oi-boil; fōōd; ŏŏ-as oo in foot; ou-out; s-soft; sh-dish; th-thin; pūre; ûnite; ûrn; stŭd; circŭs; ü-as in French tu; ´-indeterminate vowel.

Feature (Pronunciation)	Page	Lat.	Long.
Roubaix, Fr. (rōō-bĕ´)	196-97	50°41'N	3°10'E
Rouen, Fr. (rōō-äɴ´)	196-97	49°27'N	1°07'E
Rouge, stm., Qc., Can. (rōōzh)	136-37	45°38'N	74°42'W
Round Mountain, mtn., Austl.	276	30°27'S	152°14'E
Round Rock, Tx., U.S. (round rŏk)	122-23	30°30'N	97°41'W
Roundup, Mt., U.S. (round´ŭp)	112-13	46°27'N	108°33'W
Rouyn-Noranda, Qc., Can.	136-37	48°14'N	79°01'W
Rovaniemi, Fin. (rô´vá-nyĕ´mĭ)	184-85	66°30'N	25°42'E
Rovereto, Italy (rō-vå-rā´tô)	200-01	45°54'N	11°02'E
Rovigo, Italy (rô-vē´gô)	200-01	45°05'N	11°47'E
Rovinj, Cro. (rô´ēn')	200-01	45°05'N	13°38'E
Rovira, Col. (rô-vē´rä)	163c	4°14'N	75°15'W
Rovno, Ukr. see Rivne	194-95	50°37'N	26°14'E
Rovuma, stm., Afr.	264-65	10°31'S	40°24'E
Rowley Island, i., Nu., Can.	130-31	69°05'N	78°52'W
Roxas, Phil.	250	11°35'N	122°45'E
Roy, Ut., U.S. (roi)	112-13	41°10'N	112°01'W
Royale, Isle, i., Mi., U.S.	114-15	48°0'N	89°00'W
Royal Oak, Mi., U.S. (roi´ăl ōk)	116-17	42°30'N	83°08'W
Royal Tunbridge Wells, Eng., U.K.	190-91	51°08'N	0°16'E
Royan, Fr. (rwä-yäɴ´)	196-97	45°38'N	1°01'W
Rožňava, Slvk. (rôzh´nyà-và)	194-95	48°40'N	20°33'E
Rtishchevo, Russia ('r-tĭsh´chĕ-vô)	186-87	52°16'N	43°47'E
Ruaha National Park, n.p., Tan.	267	7°30'S	34°40'E
Ruapehu, Mount, vol., N.Z. (mount r´oo-à-pā´hōō)	278	39°17'S	175°34'E
Rub'al-Khali, des., Asia	220-21	20°0'N	51°00'E
Rubizhne, Ukr.	202-03	49°01'N	38°23'E
Rubondo Island, i., Tan.	267	2°20'S	31°52'E
Rubtsovsk, Russia	226	51°31'N	81°12'E
Ruby Mountains, mts., Nv., U.S. (rōō´bē moun´tĭnz)	118-19	40°25'N	115°31'W
Rudkøbing, Den. (rōōdh´kûb-ĭng)	194-95	54°56'N	10°44'E
Rūdnyy, Kaz.	226	52°59'N	63°07'E
Rudolf, Lake, lk., Afr. (lăk rōō´dŏlf)	267	3°30'N	36°00'E
Rudolf Hāyk', lk., Afr. see Rudolf, Lake	267	3°30'N	36°00'E
Ruffec, Fr. (rü-fĕk´)	196-97	46°01'N	0°12'E
Rufiji, stm., Tan. (rò-fē´jē)	262-63	7°58'S	39°25'E
Rufino, Arg.	173	34°16'S	62°42'W
Rugao, China (rōō-gou)	238-39	32°24'N	120°33'E
Rugby, Eng., U.K. (rŭg´bē)	190-91	52°23'N	1°16'W
Rugby, N.D., U.S.	114-15	48°22'N	99°60'W
Rügen, i., Ger. (rü´ghĕn)	194-95	54°25'N	13°24'E
Rugufu, stm., Tan.	267	5°30'S	30°01'E
Ruhengeri, Rw.	267	1°30'S	29°38'E
Rui'an, China (rwā-än)	238-39	27°50'N	120°35'E
Ruijin, China	238-39	25°52'N	116°00'E
Ruiz, Mex. (ròē´z)	146-47	21°57'N	105°09'W
Ruiz, Nevado del, vol., Col. (nĕ-vá´dô-dĕl-rōōē´z)	163c	4°53'N	75°20'W
Rūjiena, Lat. (rò´yĭ-ă-nà)	192-93	57°54'N	25°20'E
Rukwa, Lake, lk., Tan. (lăk rōōk-wä´)	267	8°0'S	32°25'E
Ruma, Serb. (rōō´mà)	200-01	45°00'N	19°49'E
Rumbek, Sudan (rŭm´bĕk)	262-63	6°48'N	29°41'E
Rum Cay, i., Bah. (rŭm kē)	142-43	23°41'N	74°53'W
Rumford, Me., U.S. (rŭm´fẽrd)	116-17	44°33'N	70°33'W
Rumoi, Japan	244	43°56'N	141°39'E
Runan, China (rōō-nän)	238-39	33°00'N	114°21'E
Runde, stm., Zimb.	264-65	21°18'S	32°24'E
Rundu, Nmb.	264-65	17°55'S	19°45'E
Rŭng, Kaôh, i., Camb.	246-47	10°44'N	103°14'E
Rungwa, stm., Tan.	267	7°37'S	31°49'E
Ruo, stm., China (rwô)	240-41	41°04'N	100°20'E
Ruoqiang, China	220-21	39°01'N	88°11'E
Rupat, Pulau, i., Indon. (pōō-lou rōō´pät)	246-47	1°50'N	101°35'E
Rupert, Id., U.S. (rōō´pẽrt)	112-13	42°38'N	113°41'W
Rurrenabaque, Bol.	166-67	14°28'S	67°30'W
Rurutu, i., Fr. Poly.	280-81	22°26'S	151°20'W
Rusape, Zimb.	264-65	18°32'S	32°08'E
Ruse, Blg. (rōō´sĕ) (rò´sĕ)	200-01	43°51'N	25°57'E
Rushville, Il., U.S. (rŭsh´vĭl)	120-21	40°07'N	90°33'W
Rushville, In., U.S. (rŭsh´vĭl)	116-17	39°36'N	85°27'W
Rushville, Ne., U.S. (rŭsh´vĭl)	114-15	42°43'N	102°28'W
Rusk, Tx., U.S. (rŭsk)	122-23	31°48'N	95°09'W
Russas, Braz. (rōō´s-säs)	166-67	4°56'S	37°58'W
Russell, Mb., Can. (rŭs´ĕl)	134-35	50°47'N	101°15'W
Russell, Ks., U.S. (rŭs´ĕl)	120-21	38°50'N	98°50'W
Russell, Ky., U.S. (rŭs´ĕl)	116-17	38°31'N	82°42'W
Russell Lake, lk., Mb., Can. (rŭs´ĕl lăk)	134-35	56°15'N	101°32'W
Russellville, Al., U.S. (rŭs´ĕl-vĭl)	124-25	34°30'N	87°44'W
Russellville, Ar., U.S. (rŭs´ĕl-vĭl)	120-21	35°17'N	93°09'W
Russellville, Ky., U.S. (rŭs´ĕl-vĭl)	124-25	36°51'N	86°53'W
Russia, nation, Eur. (rŭ´shå)	218-19	60°0'N	100°00'E
Rustavi, Geor.	227	41°32'N	45°02'E
Rustenburg, S. Afr. (rŭs´tĕn-bûrg)	269c	25°40'S	27°15'E
Ruston, La., U.S. (rŭs´tŭn)	120-21	32°32'N	92°38'W
Ruteng, Indon.	248-49	8°36'S	120°29'E
Rutherfordton, N.C., U.S. (rŭdh´ẽr-fẽrd-tŭn)	124-25	35°22'N	81°58'W
Rutland, Vt., U.S.	116-17	43°37'N	72°59'W
Rutog, China	234-35	33°26'N	79°42'E
Rutshuru, D.R.C. (rōōt-shōō´rōō)	267	1°11'S	29°27'E
Ruvuma, stm., Afr.	264-65	10°31'S	40°24'E
Ruwenzori Range, mts., Afr.	267	0°20'N	29°53'E
Ruzayevka, Russia	186-87	54°04'N	44°57'E
Rwanda, nation, Afr. (rü-än´då)	253	2°0'S	30°00'E
Ryazan', Russia (ryä-zän´')	202-03	54°38'N	39°44'E
Ryazhsk, Russia (ryäzh´sk')	186-87	53°42'N	40°05'E
Rybachiy, Poluostrov, pen., Russia	184-85	69°42'N	32°36'E
Rybachye, Kyrg. see Balykchy	226	42°28'N	76°12'E
Rybinsk, Russia	202-03	58°03'N	38°52'E
Rybnik, Pol. (rĭb´nēk)	194-95	50°06'N	18°33'E
Ryde, Eng., U.K. (rīd)	190-91	50°44'N	1°10'W
Ryeosu, Kor., S. see Yŏsu	243	34°44'N	127°44'E
Rylsk, Russia (rēl´'sk)	202-03	51°34'N	34°42'E
Ryojun, China see Lüshun	240-41	38°49'N	121°15'E
Ryōtsu, Japan (ryōt´sōō)	245	38°05'N	138°26'E
Ryukyu Islands, is., Japan (rē-kū´ĭ´lăndz)	244a	25°44'N	126°58'E
Rzeszów, Pol. (zhå-shôf)	194-95	50°03'N	22°01'E
Rzhev, Russia ('r-zhĕf)	202-03	56°17'N	34°19'E

S

Feature (Pronunciation)	Page	Lat.	Long.
Saale, stm., Ger. (sä-lĕ)	194-95	51°57'N	11°55'E
Saalfeld, Ger. (säl´fĕlt)	194-95	50°39'N	11°22'E
Saarbrücken, Ger. (zähr´brü-kĕn)	194-95	49°14'N	6°60'E
Saaremaa, i., Est.	192-93	58°25'N	22°30'E
Saavedra, Arg. (sä-ä-vā´drä)	173	37°46'S	62°21'W
Saba, i., Neth. Ant. (sä´bä)	143b	17°38'N	63°14'W
Šabac, Serb. (shä´bàts)	200-01	44°46'N	19°42'E
Sabadell, Spain (sä-bä-dhäl´)	198-99	41°33'N	2°06'E
Sabah, hist. reg., Malay.	248-49	5°20'N	117°10'E
Sabanagrande, Hond. (sä-bä´nä-grä´n-dĕ)	149	13°49'N	87°17'W
Sabanalarga, Col. (sä-bà´nä-lär´gä)	164-65	10°38'N	74°55'W
Sabancuy, Mex. (sä-bäŋ-kwē´)	148	18°58'N	91°11'W
Sabang, Indon. (sä´bäng)	248-49	0°13'N	119°53'E
Sabang, Indon. (sä´bäng)	246-47	5°53'N	95°20'E
Şāberī, Hāmūn-e, lk., Asia	232-33	31°30'N	61°20'E
Sabhā, Libya	258-59	27°01'N	14°28'E
Sabi, stm., Afr. (sä´bē) see Save	264-65	20°58'S	35°04'E
Sabinal, Cayo, i., Cuba (kä´yō sä-bē-näl´)	142-43	21°40'N	77°18'W
Sabinas, Mex.	122-23	27°51'N	101°07'W
Sabinas, stm., Mex. (sä-bē´näs)	122-23	26°51'N	99°35'W
Sabinas, stm., Mex. (sä-bē´näs)	122-23	27°29'N	100°40'W
Sabinas Hidalgo, Mex. (sä-bē´näs ē-däl´gô)	122-23	26°30'N	100°10'W
Sabine, stm., U.S.	110-11	30°00'N	93°46'W
Sable, Cape, c., N.S., Can. (kāp sā´b'l)	138-39	43°25'N	65°37'W
Sable, Cape, pen., Fl., U.S. (kāp sā´b'l)	125a	25°12'N	81°05'W
Sable, Île de, i., N. Cal.	272-73	19°15'S	159°56'E
Sable Island, i., N.S., Can.	138-39	43°56'N	59°56'W
Sablé-sur-Sarthe, Fr. (säb-lā-sür-särt´)	196-97	47°50'N	0°20'W
Sabor, stm., Port. (sä-bōr´)	198-99	41°11'N	7°07'W
Sabzevār, Iran	232-33	36°13'N	57°40'E
Sac, stm., Mo., U.S. (sôk)	120-21	38°01'N	93°44'W
Sac City, Ia., U.S. (sŏk sĭ´tē)	114-15	42°25'N	94°60'W
Sachigo, stm., On., Can.	134-35	55°04'N	88°59'W
Sachigo Lake, lk., On., Can. (săch´ĭ-gō lăk)	134-35	53°49'N	92°08'W
Sachsen, hist. reg., Ger. (zäk´sĕn) see Saxony	194-95	52°45'N	9°30'E
Sackville, N.B., Can. (săk´vĭl)	138-39	45°54'N	64°22'W
Saco, Me., U.S. (sô´kô)	116-17	43°30'N	70°27'W
Sacramento, Ca., U.S. (săk-rà-mĕn´tō)	118-19	38°35'N	121°29'W
Sacramento, stm., Ca., U.S. (săk-rà-mĕn´tō)	110-11	38°03'N	121°53'W
Sacramento Mountains, mts., N.M., U.S.	120-21	32°42'N	105°37'W
Şa'dah, Yemen	266	16°49'N	43°48'E
Sadiya, India (sŭ-dē´yä)	234-35	27°50'N	95°40'E
Sado, i., Japan (sä´dō)	245	38°0'N	138°25'E
Saeki, Japan (sä´å-kĕ) see Saiki	245	32°58'N	131°55'E
Safāga, Egypt	268b	26°45'N	33°56'E
Safford, Az., U.S. (săf´fẽrd)	118-19	32°50'N	109°43'W
Safi, Mor. (sä´fē) (äs´fē)	258-59	32°18'N	9°13'W
Safīd Koh, Selseleh-ye, mts., Afg.	232-33	34°30'N	63°30'E
Safonovo, Russia	202-03	55°07'N	33°15'E
Saga, China	234-35	29°29'N	85°09'E
Saga, Japan	245	33°15'N	130°18'E
Sagaing, Mya.	246-47	21°53'N	95°59'E
Sagami-nada, b., Japan (sä´gä´mē nä-dä)	245	34°60'N	139°30'E
Saganaga Lake, lk., N.A. (să-gà-nä´gȧ lăk)	134-35	48°14'N	90°52'W
Sāgar, India	234-35	23°50'N	78°45'E
Sagarmāthā, mtn., Asia see Everest, Mount	234-35	27°59'N	86°56'E
Sagavanirktok, stm., Ak., U.S.	126	70°21'N	148°11'W
Saginaw, Mi., U.S. (săg´ĭ-nô)	116-17	43°26'N	83°58'W
Saginaw Bay, b., Mi., U.S. (săg´ĭ-nô bā)	116-17	43°50'N	83°40'W
Sagua de Tánamo, Cuba (sä-gwä dĕ tá´nä-mō)	142-43	20°35'N	75°14'W
Sagua la Grande, Cuba (sä-gwä lä grä´n-dĕ)	142-43	22°49'N	80°04'W
Saguaro National Park, n.p., Az., U.S. (säg-wä´rō năsh´ŭn-ăl pärk)	118-19	32°16'N	111°12'W
Saguenay, stm., Qc., Can. (săg-ē-nā´)	138-39	48°08'N	69°41'W
Sagunt, Spain	198-99	39°41'N	0°16'W
Sagunto, Spain (sä-gòn´tō) see Sagunt	198-99	39°41'N	0°16'W
Sa'gya, China	234-35	28°54'N	88°04'E
Sahara, des., Afr. (sȧ-hä´rȧ)	258-59	26°0'N	13°00'E
Sahāranpur, India (sŭ-hä´rŭn-pōōr´)	234-35	29°58'N	77°33'E
Sahel, reg., Afr.	258-59	12°0'N	17°00'E
Sāḥil, reg., Afr. see Sahel	258-59	12°0'N	17°00'E
Sāhīwāl, Pak.	232-33	30°40'N	73°06'E
Şaḥrā', des., Afr. see Sahara	258-59	26°0'N	13°00'E
Saïda, Alg.	184-85	34°50'N	0°09'E
Saidpur, Bngl.	234-35	25°47'N	88°54'E
Saigon, Viet. see Ho Chi Minh City	246-47	10°45'N	106°40'E
Saiki, Japan	245	32°58'N	131°55'E
Saimaa, lk., Fin. (sä´ĭ-mä)	192-93	61°15'N	28°15'E
Saín Alto, Mex. (sä-ēn´ äl´tō)	146-47	23°35'N	103°13'W
Saint Albans, Eng., U.K. (sânt ôl´bănz)	190-91	51°45'N	0°21'W
Saint Albans, Vt., U.S. (sânt ôl´bănz)	116-17	44°49'N	73°05'W
Saint Albans, W.V., U.S. (sânt ôl´bănz)	116-17	38°23'N	81°50'W
Saint Albert, Ab., Can. (sânt ăl´bērt)	132-33	53°38'N	113°38'W
Saint-Amand-Mont-Rond, Fr. (săɴ´t á-mäɴ´ môɴ-rôɴ´)	196-97	46°43'N	2°30'E
Saint-André, Cap, c., Madag. see Vilanandro, Tanjona	264-65	16°12'S	44°28'E
Saint Andrews, Scot., U.K.	190-91	56°20'N	2°48'W
Saint-Anselme, Qc., Can. (săɴ´ tän-sĕlm´)	138-39	46°37'N	70°57'W
Saint Anthony, Nf., Can. (săn ăn´thō-nē)	138-39	51°22'N	55°37'W
Saint Anthony, Id., U.S. (sânt ăn´thō-nē)	112-13	43°58'N	111°41'W
Saint-Augustin, Qc., Can.	138-39	51°14'N	58°38'W
Saint Augustine, Fl., U.S. (sânt ô´gŭs-tēn)	124-25	29°54'N	81°19'W
Saint-Barthélemy, i., Guad.	143b	17°54'N	62°50'W
Saint Bees Head, c., Eng., U.K. (sânt bēz´hĕd)	190-91	54°31'N	3°38'W
Saint Bride, Mount, mtn., Ab., Can. (mount sânt brīd)	132-33	51°31'N	115°57'W
Saint-Brieuc, Fr. (săɴ´ brēs´)	196-97	48°31'N	2°45'W
Saint Catharines, On., Can. (sânt kăth´å-rĭnz)	136-37	43°10'N	79°14'W
Saint-Chamond, Fr. (săɴ´ shå-môɴ´)	196-97	45°29'N	4°31'E
Saint Charles, Il., U.S. (sânt chärlz´)	116-17	41°55'N	88°19'W
Saint Charles, Md., U.S. (sânt chärlz´)	116-17	38°35'N	76°57'W
Saint Charles, Mi., U.S. (sânt chärlz´)	116-17	43°18'N	84°08'W
Saint Charles, Mn., U.S. (sânt chärlz´)	114-15	43°58'N	92°03'W
Saint Charles, Mo., U.S. (sânt chärlz´)	120-21	38°48'N	90°29'W
Saint Christopher, i., St. K./N.	143b	17°20'N	62°45'W
Saint Christopher and Nevis, nation, N.A. see Saint Kitts and Nevis	140-41	17°20'N	62°45'W
Saint Clair, Mi., U.S. (sânt klâr)	116-17	42°50'N	82°29'W
Saint Clair, Mo., U.S. (sânt klâr)	120-21	38°21'N	90°59'W
Saint-Claude, Fr. (săɴ´ klōd´)	196-97	46°23'N	5°51'E
Saint Cloud, Fl., U.S. (sânt kloud´)	125a	28°15'N	81°17'W
Saint Cloud, Mn., U.S. (sânt kloud)	114-15	45°33'N	94°10'W
Saint Croix, i., V.I.U.S. (sânt kroi´)	143b	17°45'N	64°45'W
Saint Croix, stm., N.A. (sânt kroi´)	138-39	45°10'N	67°09'W
Saint Croix, stm., U.S. (sânt kroi´)	114-15	44°45'N	92°48'W
Saint-Denis, Fr. (săɴ´dē-nē´)	196-97	48°57'N	2°21'E
Saint-Denis, nat. cap., Reu. (săɴ´dē-nē´)	265a	20°52'S	55°28'E

ăt; finăl; rāte; senåte; ärm; åsk; sofȧ; fâre; ch-choose; dh-as th in other; bē; ēvent; bĕt; recĕnt; cratẽr; g-gō; gh-guttural g; bĭt; ĭ-short neutral; rīde; ᴋ-guttural k as ch in German ich;

Feature (Pronunciation)	Page	Lat.	Long.
Saint-Dizier, Fr. (săN dê-zyä')	196-97	48°39'N	4°57'E
Sainte-Agathe-des-Monts, Qc., Can.	136-37	46°03'N	74°17'W
Sainte-Foy, Qc., Can. (săNt fwä)	136-37	46°47'N	71°17'W
Sainte Genevieve, Mo., U.S. (sānt jĕn'ĕ-vēv)	120-21	37°59'N	90°03'W
Saint Elias, Mount, mtn., N.A. (mount sānt ê-lī'ăs)	126	60°18'N	140°55'W
Saint-Élie, Fr. Gu.	164-65	4°50'N	53°17'W
Sainte-Lucie, Canal de, strt., N.A. see Saint Lucia Channel	143b	14°09'N	60°57'W
Sainte-Marguerite, stm., Qc., Can.	138-39	50°09'N	66°36'W
Sainte-Marie, Cap, c., Madag. see Vohimena, Tanjona	264-65	25°36'S	45°09'E
Sainte Marie, Nosy, i., Madag.	264-65	16°50'S	49°57'E
Saint-Étienne, Fr.	196-97	45°26'N	4°24'E
Saint-Eustache, Qc., Can. (săN' tû-stásh')	136-37	45°34'N	73°55'W
Saint-Félicien, Qc., Can. (săN fā-lê-syăN')	136-37	48°39'N	72°27'W
Saint-Florent-sur-Cher, Fr. (săN' flô-răN'sür-shâr')	196-97	46°59'N	2°15'E
Saint-Flour, Fr. (săN flōōr')	196-97	45°02'N	3°05'E
Saint Francis, Cape, c., S. Afr.	264-65	34°11'S	24°50'E
Saint-Gaudens, Fr. (săN gō-dăNs')	196-97	43°07'N	0°44'E
Saint George, Austl. (sānt jôrj')	276	28°03'S	148°35'E
Saint George, N.B., Can. (săN jôrj')	138-39	45°08'N	66°49'W
Saint George, S.C., U.S. (sānt jôrj')	124-25	33°11'N	80°35'W
Saint George, Ut., U.S. (sānt jôrj')	118-19	37°06'N	113°34'W
Saint George, Cape, c., Nf., Can. (kāp sānt jôr-jĕz)	138-39	48°29'N	59°15'W
Saint George, Cape, c., Fl., U.S. (kāp sānt jôr-jĕz)	124-25	29°35'N	85°04'W
Saint George Island, i., Fl., U.S.	124-25	29°39'N	84°53'W
Saint-Georges, Fr. Gu.	164-65	3°57'N	51°48'W
Saint George's, nat. cap., Gren. (sānt jôrj'ĕs)	143b	12°04'N	61°45'W
Saint George's Bay, b., Nf., Can. (sānt jôr-jĕz bā)	138-39	48°20'N	59°00'W
Saint Georges Bay, b., N.S., Can. (sānt jôr-jĕz bā)	138-39	45°50'N	61°45'W
Saint George's Channel, strt., Eur. (sānt jôr-jĕz chăn'ĕl)	190-91	52°0'N	6°00'W
Saint-Girons, Fr. (săN zhē-rôN')	196-97	42°59'N	1°09'E
Saint Helena, dep., Afr. (sānt hē-lē'nȧ)	253	15°57'S	5°42'W
Saint Helena, i., St. Hel. (sānt hē-lē'nȧ)	254	15°57'S	5°43'W
Saint Helens, Or., U.S. (sānt hĕl'ĕnz)	112-13	45°52'N	122°48'W
Saint Helens, Mount, vol., Wa., U.S. (mount sānt hĕl'ĕnz)	112-13	46°12'N	122°11'W
Saint Helier, nat. cap., Jersey (sānt hyĕl'yĕr)	196-97	49°12'N	2°07'W
Saint-Hyacinthe, Qc., Can.	136-37	45°38'N	72°57'W
Saint Ignace, Mi., U.S. (sānt ĭg'nȧs)	116-17	45°52'N	84°44'W
Saint Ignace Island, i., On., Can. (sānt ĭg'nȧs ī'lȧnd)	136-37	48°48'N	87°56'W
Saint James, Mn., U.S. (sānt jāmz')	114-15	43°59'N	94°38'W
Saint James, Mo., U.S. (sānt jāmz')	120-21	37°60'N	91°37'W
Saint James, Cape, c., B.C., Can. (kāp sānt jāmz')	132-33	51°56'N	131°01'W
Saint-Jean, Lac, res., Qc., Can. (läk săN' zhäN')	136-37	48°35'N	72°05'W
Saint-Jean-d'Angély, Fr. (săN-zhäN'-däN-zhȧ-lē')	196-97	45°57'N	0°31'W
Saint-Jean-de-Luz, Fr. (săN-zhäN' dē lüz')	196-97	43°24'N	1°39'W
Saint-Jean-sur-Richelieu, Qc., Can.	136-37	45°19'N	73°16'W
Saint-Jérôme, Qc., Can. (săN zhā-rōm')	136-37	45°47'N	74°00'W
Saint John, N.B., Can. (sānt jŏn)	138-39	45°17'N	66°04'W
Saint John, i., V.I.U.S. (sānt jŏn)	143b	18°20'N	64°45'W
Saint John, stm., N.A. (sānt jŏn)	138-39	45°16'N	66°04'W
Saint John, Cape, c., Nf., Can. (kāp sānt jŏn)	138-39	49°59'N	55°32'W
Saint John's, Nf., Can. (sānt jŏns)	138-39	47°34'N	52°43'W
Saint Johns, Az., U.S. (sānt jŏnz)	118-19	34°30'N	109°22'W
Saint Johns, Mi., U.S. (sānt jŏnz)	116-17	42°60'N	84°33'W
Saint John's, nat. cap., Antig. (sānt jŏnz)	143b	17°07'N	61°51'W
Saint Johns, stm., Fl., U.S. (sānt jŏnz)	125a	30°24'N	81°23'W
Saint Johnsbury, Vt., U.S. (sānt jŏnz'bĕr-ē)	116-17	44°26'N	72°01'W
Saint Joseph, Mi., U.S. (sānt jō'sĕf)	116-17	42°05'N	86°29'W
Saint Joseph, Mo., U.S. (sānt jō'sĕf)	120-21	39°46'N	94°50'W
Saint Joseph, stm., U.S. (sānt jō'sĕf)	116-17	42°06'N	86°29'W
Saint Joseph, Lake, lk., On., Can.	134-35	51°03'N	90°52'W
Saint-Joseph-de-Beauce, Qc., Can. (sĕN zhō-zĕf' dē bōs)	138-39	46°18'N	70°52'W
Saint-Junien, Fr. (săN'zhü-nyăN')	196-97	45°53'N	0°54'E
Saint Kilda, i., Scot., U.K. (sānt kĭl'dȧ)	190-91	57°49'N	8°36'W
Saint Kitts, i., St. K./N. (sānt kĭtts) see Saint Christopher	143b	17°20'N	62°45'W
Saint Kitts and Nevis, nation, N.A. (sānt kĭts ănd nē'vĭs)	140-41	17°20'N	62°45'W
Saint-Laurent, stm., N.A. see Saint Lawrence	86	49°14'N	67°01'W
Saint-Laurent, Golfe du, b., Can. see Saint Lawrence, Gulf of	138-39	48°0'N	62°00'W
Saint-Laurent du Maroni, Fr. Gu.	164-65	5°28'N	54°02'W
Saint Lawrence, Nf., Can. (sānt lô'rĕns)	138-39	46°56'N	55°24'W
Saint Lawrence, stm., N.A. (sānt lô'rĕns)	86	49°14'N	67°01'W
Saint Lawrence, Gulf of, b., Can. (gŭlf ŭv sānt lô'rĕns)	138-39	48°0'N	62°00'W
Saint Lawrence Island, i., Ak., U.S. (sānt lô'rĕns ī'lȧnd)	126	63°30'N	170°30'W
Saint-Louis, Sen.	260-61	16°01'N	16°29'W
Saint Louis, Mi., U.S. (sānt lōō'ĭs)	116-17	43°24'N	84°36'W
Saint Louis, Mo., U.S. (sānt lōō'ĭs) (lōō'ē)	120-21	38°39'N	90°13'W
Saint Lucia, nation, N.A. (sānt lōō'-shȧ)	140-41	13°53'N	60°58'W
Saint Lucia, Lake, lk., S. Afr.	264-65	28°04'S	32°28'E
Saint Lucia Channel, strt., N.A. (sānt lū'shĭ-ȧ chăn'ĕl)	143b	14°09'N	60°57'W
Saint-Malo, Fr. (săN' mȧ-lō')	196-97	48°39'N	2°01'W
Saint-Marc, Haiti (săN' mȧrk')	142-43	19°07'N	72°41'W
Saint Maries, Id., U.S. (sānt mā'rēs)	112-13	47°19'N	116°34'W
Saint-Martin, i., N.A. (săN-mär'tĭn)	143b	18°04'N	63°04'W
Saint Martinville, La., U.S. (sānt mär'tĭn-vĭl)	124-25	30°08'N	91°50'W
Saint Marys, Austl. (sānt mā'rēz)	276	41°35'S	148°11'E
Saint Marys, Ga., U.S. (sānt mā'rēz)	124-25	30°44'N	81°33'W
Saint Marys, Oh., U.S. (sānt mā'rēz)	116-17	40°33'N	84°24'W
Saint Marys, Pa., U.S. (sānt mā'rēz)	116-17	41°25'N	78°35'W
Saint Marys, W.V., U.S. (sānt mā'rēz)	116-17	39°23'N	81°12'W
Saint Mary's, Cape, c., Nf., Can.	138-39	46°50'N	54°12'W
Saint Mary's Bay, b., Nf., Can.	138-39	46°50'N	53°47'W
Saint Matthew Island, i., Ak., U.S. (sānt măth'ū ī'lȧnd)	218-19	60°29'N	172°53'W
Saint Matthews, S.C., U.S. (sānt măth'ūz)	124-25	33°40'N	80°47'W
Saint Matthias Group, is., Pap. N. Gui.	277	1°36'S	149°47'E
Saint-Maurice, stm., Qc., Can. (săN' mô-rēs') (sānt mô'rĭs)	136-37	46°21'N	72°31'W
Saint Michael, Ak., U.S. (sānt mī'kĕl)	126	63°29'N	162°02'W
Saint-Mihiel, Fr. (săN' mē-yĕl')	196-97	48°54'N	5°32'E
Saint-Nazaire, Fr. (săN'nȧ-zâr')	196-97	47°17'N	2°13'W
Saint-Omer, Fr. (săN'tô-mâr')	196-97	50°45'N	2°16'E
Saint Paul, Ab., Can. (sānt pôl')	132-33	53°60'N	111°17'W
Saint-Paul, Reu.	265a	21°0'S	55°16'E
Saint Paul, Mn., U.S. (sānt pôl)	114-15	44°57'N	93°06'W
Saint Paul, Ne., U.S. (sānt pôl)	114-15	41°13'N	98°28'W
Saint Paul, stm., Lib.	260-61	6°25'N	10°44'W
Saint Pauls, N.C., U.S. (sānt pôls)	124-25	34°49'N	78°58'W
Saint Peter, Mn., U.S. (sānt pē'tēr)	114-15	44°20'N	93°58'W
Saint Peter Port, nat. cap., Guern. (sānt pē'tēr pôrt)	196-97	49°28'N	2°33'W
Saint Petersburg, Russia (sānt pē'tērz-bûrg)	192-93	59°57'N	30°15'E
Saint Petersburg, Fl., U.S. (sānt pē'tērz-bûrg)	125a	27°46'N	82°40'W
Saint-Pierre, Reu.	265a	21°19'S	55°29'E
Saint Pierre, i., Sey.	264-65	9°19'S	50°43'E
Saint-Pierre, nat. cap., St. P./M. (săN'pyâr')	138-39	46°47'N	56°12'W
Saint Pierre and Miquelon, dep., N.A. (sānt pē-âr' ănd mĭk-ē-lôn')	138-39	46°55'N	56°20'W
Saint-Pierre-et-Miquelon, dep., N.A. see Saint Pierre and Miquelon	138-39	46°55'N	56°20'W
Saint-Pol-de-Léon, Fr. (săN-pô'dē-lā-ôN')	196-97	48°41'N	3°59'W
Saint-Quentin, Fr. (săN'kän-tăN')	196-97	49°51'N	3°18'E
Saint-Sébastien, Cap, c., Madag. see Anorontany, Tanjona	264-65	12°26'S	48°45'E
Saint Stephen, N.B., Can. (sānt stē'vĕn)	138-39	45°12'N	67°17'W
Saint Thomas, On., Can. (sānt tŏm'ȧs)	136-37	42°47'N	81°11'W
Saint Thomas, i., V.I.U.S.	143b	18°21'N	64°55'W
Saint-Tropez, Fr. (săN trō-pĕ')	196-97	43°16'N	6°38'E
Saint Vincent, i., St. Vin.	143b	13°15'N	61°12'W
Saint-Vincent, Cap, c., Madag. see Ankaboa, Tanjona	264-65	21°55'S	43°18'E
Saint Vincent, Gulf, b., Austl. (gŭlf vĭn'sĕnt)	276	34°47'S	138°06'E
Saint Vincent and the Grenadines, nation, N.A. (sānt vĭn'sĕnt ănd thȧ grĕn'ȧ-dēnz)	140-41	13°15'N	61°12'W
Saipan, i., N. Mar. Is.	280-81	15°12'N	145°45'E
Saitama, state, Japan (sī'tä-mä)	245	36°0'N	139°30'E
Sajama, Nevado, mtn., Bol. (nĕ-vȧ'dô-sä-hä'mä)	168-69	18°06'S	68°54'W
Sak, stm., S. Afr.	264-65	30°06'S	20°42'E
Sakai, Japan (sä'kä-ē)	245	34°35'N	135°29'E
Sakākah, Sau. Ar.	228-29	29°58'N	40°13'E
Sakakawea, Lake, res., N.D., U.S.	114-15	47°44'N	102°18'W
Sakami, Lac, lk., Qc., Can.	130-31	53°15'N	76°45'W
Sakart'velo, nation, Asia see Georgia	227	42°0'N	44°00'E
Sakarya, Tur.	186-87	40°47'N	30°24'E
Sakarya, stm., Tur. (sȧ-kär'yȧ)	186-87	41°07'N	30°39'E
Sakata, Japan (sä'kä-tä)	244	38°55'N	139°51'E
Sakha, state, Russia see Yakutia	218-19	67°0'N	125°00'E
Sakhalin, i., Russia (sȧ-kȧ-lēn')	218-19	51°0'N	143°00'E
Šakiai, Lith. (shä'kĭ-ī)	192-93	54°58'N	23°04'E
Sakishima-shotō, is., Japan (sä'kē-shē'ma gòn'tō')	279a	24°33'N	124°26'E
Sal, i., C.V. (säal)	260-61	16°49'N	22°57'W
Sal, stm., Russia (sȧl)	186-87	47°31'N	40°44'E
Sal, Cay, i., Bah. (kē săl)	142-43	23°43'N	80°25'W
Sala, Swe. (sô'lä)	192-93	59°56'N	16°37'E
Salaberry-de-Valleyfield, Qc., Can.	136-37	45°15'N	74°08'W
Sala Consilina, Italy (sä'lä kôn-sē-lē'nä)	200-01	40°25'N	15°34'E
Salada, Laguna, lk., Mex. (lä-gô'nä-sä-lä'dä)	118-19	32°20'N	115°40'W
Saladas, Arg.	173	28°14'S	58°39'W
Saladillo, Arg. (sä-lä-dēl'yō)	173	35°38'S	59°47'W
Salado, stm., Arg. (sä-lä'dô)	168-69	31°41'S	60°44'W
Salado, stm., Arg. (sä-lä'dô)	173	35°45'S	57°23'W
Salado, stm., Arg. (sä-lä'dô)	171	38°49'S	64°59'W
Salado, stm., Mex. (sä-lä'dô)	122-23	26°52'N	99°19'W
Şalālah, Oman	220-21	17°01'N	54°06'E
Salamanca, Chile (sä-lä-mä'n-kä)	168-69	31°46'S	70°59'W
Salamanca, Mex. (sä-lä-mä'n-kä)	146-47	20°34'N	101°12'W
Salamanca, Spain (sä-lä-mä'n-kȧ)	198-99	40°58'N	5°39'W
Salamanca, N.Y., U.S. (sȧl-ȧ-măŋ'kȧ)	116-17	42°10'N	78°43'W
Salamat, Bahr, stm., Chad (bär sä-lä-mät')	262-63	9°27'N	18°06'E
Salamina, Col. (sä-lä-mē'-nä)	163c	5°25'N	75°29'W
Salatiga, Indon.	248-49	7°20'S	110°31'E
Salavat, Russia	186-87	53°22'N	55°56'E
Salaverry, Peru (sä-lä-vă'rē)	170	8°14'S	78°58'W
Salawati, i., Indon. (sä-lä-wä'tē)	224-25	1°07'S	130°52'E
Sala y Gómez, Isla, i., Chile	282-83	26°26'S	105°26'W
Saldanha, S. Afr.	264-65	32°60'S	17°57'E
Saldus, Lat. (sȧl'dòs)	192-93	56°40'N	22°30'E
Sale, Austl. (sāl)	276	38°07'S	147°04'E
Salé, Mor.	269a	34°03'N	6°48'W
Salebabu, Pulau, i., Indon.	248-49	3°56'N	126°42'E
Salekhard, Russia (sŭ-lyĭ-kärt)	218-19	66°32'N	66°37'E
Salem, India (sä'lĕm)	236	11°39'N	78°10'E
Salem, Il., U.S. (sā'lĕm)	116-17	38°37'N	88°57'W
Salem, In., U.S. (sā'lĕm)	116-17	38°36'N	86°06'W
Salem, Mo., U.S. (sā'lĕm)	120-21	37°39'N	91°32'W
Salem, Oh., U.S. (sā'lĕm)	116-17	40°54'N	80°51'W
Salem, Or., U.S.	112-13	44°56'N	123°01'W
Salem, S.D., U.S. (sā'lĕm)	114-15	43°44'N	97°23'W
Salem, Va., U.S. (sā'lĕm)	124-25	37°18'N	80°03'W
Salem, W.V., U.S. (sā'lĕm)	116-17	39°17'N	80°34'W
Salerno, Italy (sä-lĕr'nô)	200-01	40°41'N	14°47'E
Salerno, Golfo di, b., Italy (gôl-fô-dē-sä-lĕr'nô)	200-01	40°32'N	14°42'E
Salgótarján, Hung. (shôl'gô-tôr-yän)	194-95	48°06'N	19°50'E
Salida, Co., U.S. (sȧ-lī'dȧ)	118-19	38°32'N	105°60'W
Salīmah, Wāḥat, well, Sudan	266	21°22'N	29°19'E
Salina, Ks., U.S. (sȧ-lī'nȧ)	120-21	38°50'N	97°36'W
Salina, Ut., U.S. (sȧ-lī'nȧ)	118-19	38°58'N	111°52'W
Salina, Isola, i., Italy (ē'-sō-lä-sä-lē'nä)	200-01	38°34'N	14°50'E
Salina Cruz, Mex. (sä-lē'nä krōōz')	146-47	16°11'N	95°11'W
Salinas, Ec.	170	2°13'S	80°57'W
Salinas, Ca., U.S. (sȧ-lē'nȧs)	118-19	36°41'N	121°40'W
Salinas de Hidalgo, Mex.	146-47	22°38'N	101°44'W
Saline, stm., Ar., U.S. (sȧ-lēn')	120-21	33°09'N	92°08'W
Salisbury, Md., U.S.	116-17	38°22'N	75°36'W
Salisbury, Mo., U.S. (sôlz'bē-rē)	120-21	39°26'N	92°48'W
Salisbury, N.C., U.S. (sôlz'bē-rē)	124-25	35°40'N	80°28'W
Salisbury, nat. cap., Zimb. (sôlz'bē-rē) see Harare	264-65	17°50'S	31°03'E
Salisbury Island, i., Nu., Can.	130-31	63°30'N	76°60'W
Salliq, Nu., Can. see Coral Harbour	128-29	64°08'N	83°12'W
Sallisaw, Ok., U.S. (săl'ĭ-sô)	120-21	35°28'N	94°48'W

n-sing; ŋ-baŋk; N-nasalized n; nŏd; cŏmmit; ōld; ôbey; ôrder; oi-boil; fōōd; ò-as oo in foot; ou-out; s-soft; sh-dish; th-thin; pūre; ûnite; ûrn; stŭd; circŭs; ü-as in French tu; '-indeterminate vowel.

Feature (Pronunciation)	Page	Lat.	Long.
Salluit, Qc., Can.	128-29	62°13'N	75°36'W
Salmon, Id., U.S. (săm´ŭn)	112-13	45°11'N	113°54'W
Salmon, stm., B.C., Can. (săm´ŭn)	132-33	54°04'N	122°33'W
Salmon, stm., N.B., Can. (săm´ŭn)	138-39	46°04'N	65°55'W
Salmon, stm., Id., U.S. (săm´ŭn)	112-13	45°51'N	116°47'W
Salmon Arm, B.C., Can. (săm´ŭn ärm)	132-33	50°42'N	119°19'W
Salmon River Mountains, mts., Id., U.S. (săm´ŭn rĭv´ẽr moun´tĭnz)	112-13	44°58'N	114°52'W
Salon-de-Provence, Fr. (sȧ-lôN-dē-prô-väNs´)	196-97	43°39'N	5°05'E
Salonika, Grc. *see* Thessaloníki	200-01	40°38'N	22°59'E
Salsk, Russia (sälsk)	186-87	46°28'N	41°33'E
Salt, stm., Az., U.S. (sôlt)	118-19	33°23'N	112°17'W
Salta, Arg. (säl´tä)	168-69	24°48'S	65°25'W
Salta, state, Arg. (säl´tä)	168-69	25°0'S	64°30'W
Saltillo, Mex. (säl-tēl´yō)	122-23	25°26'N	101°00'W
Salt Lake City, Ut., U.S. (sôlt lāk sĭ´tĭ sĭ´tē)	112-13	40°47'N	111°54'W
Salto, Arg. (säl´tō)	173	34°18'S	60°15'W
Salto, Ur.	173	31°23'S	57°58'W
Salto Grande, Embalse, res., S.A.	173	30°55'S	57°54'W
Salto Grande, Embalse de, res., S.A. *see* Salto Grande, Embalse	173	30°55'S	57°54'W
Salton Sea, lk., Ca., U.S. (sôlt´ŭn sē)	118-19	33°19'N	115°50'W
Saltville, Va., U.S. (sôlt´vĭl)	124-25	36°53'N	81°46'W
Saluda, S.C., U.S. (sȧ-lōō´dȧ)	124-25	34°00'N	81°47'W
Salûm, Egypt	188-89	31°34'N	25°09'E
Saluzzo, Italy (sä-lōōt´sō)	200-01	44°39'N	7°29'E
Salvador, Braz. (säl-vä-dōr´)	166-67	12°59'S	38°30'W
Salvador, El, nation, N.A. *see* El Salvador	85	13°50'N	88°55'W
Salvador, Lake, lk., La., U.S. (lāk säl´-vä-dōr lāk)	124-25	29°45'N	90°15'W
Salvatierra, Mex. (säl-vä-tyĕr´rä)	146-47	20°13'N	100°54'W
Salyan, Azer.	227	39°35'N	48°58'E
Salzburg, Aus. (sälts´bŏrgh)	194-95	47°49'N	13°03'E
Salzwedel, Ger. (sälts-vā´dĕl)	194-95	52°51'N	11°09'E
Samâlût, Egypt (sä-mä-lōōt´)	268b	28°18'N	30°42'E
Samana Cay, i., Bah.	142-43	23°05'N	73°44'W
Samar, i., Phil. (sä´mär)	250	12°0'N	125°00'E
Samara, Russia (sȧ-mä´rȧ)	186-87	53°11'N	50°07'E
Samara, stm., Russia (sȧ-mä´rȧ)	186-87	53°10'N	50°04'E
Samara, stm., Ukr. (sȧ-mä´rȧ)	202-03	48°28'N	35°06'E
Samarai, Pap. N. Gui. (sä-mä-rä´ē)	277	10°36'S	150°42'E
Samarinda, Indon.	248-49	0°30'S	117°09'E
Samarqand, Uzb.	232-33	39°40'N	66°56'E
Sāmarrā', Iraq	228-29	34°11'N	43°53'E
Samaúna, Braz.	166-67	7°56'S	60°01'W
Sambalpur, India (sŭm´bŭl-pŏŏr)	234-35	21°28'N	83°59'E
Sambas, Indon.	246-47	1°19'N	109°16'E
Sambava, Madag.	264-65	14°16'S	50°09'E
Sambhal, India	234-35	28°35'N	78°34'E
Sāmbhar, India	234-35	26°54'N	75°13'E
Sambir, Ukr.	194-95	49°31'N	23°13'E
Samborombón, Bahía, b., Arg. (bä-ē´ä-säm-bô-rôm-bô´n)	173	36°0'S	57°12'W
Samch'ŏk, Kor., S.	243	37°27'N	129°10'E
Samch'ŏnp'o, Kor., S.	243	34°56'N	128°05'E
Same, Tan.	267	4°04'S	37°44'E
Samoa, nation, Oc. (sȧ-mō´ȧ)	279b	13°55'S	172°00'W
Samoa Islands, is., Oc. (sȧ-mō´ȧ ī´lăndz)	279b	14°0'S	171°00'W
Samoded, Russia	186-87	63°37'N	40°30'E
Samokov, Blg. (sä´mô-kôf)	200-01	42°20'N	23°34'E
Sámos, i., Grc. (să´mŏs)	200-01	37°42'N	26°50'E
Samothrace, i., Grc. *see* Samothráki	200-01	40°29'N	25°36'E
Samothráki, i., Grc.	200-01	40°29'N	25°36'E
Sampit, Indon.	248-49	2°33'S	112°57'E
Sam Rayburn Reservoir, res., Tx., U.S.	122-23	31°13'N	94°17'W
Samsun, Tur. (sȧm´sōōn´)	186-87	41°17'N	36°20'E
Samtredia, Geor. (sȧm´trĕ-dē)	227	42°10'N	42°21'E
Samui, Ko, i., Thai.	246-47	9°32'N	100°01'E
San, Mali (sän)	258-59	13°18'N	4°54'W
Sandoy, i., Far. Is.	190b	61°50'N	6°45'W
Şan'ā', nat. cap., Yemen (sän´ä) *see* Sanaa	266	15°21'N	44°12'E
Sanaa, nat. cap., Yemen (sän´ä)	266	15°21'N	44°12'E
Sanaga, stm., Camrn. (sä-nä´gä)	260-61	3°33'N	9°39'E
San Agustin, Cape, c., Phil.	250	6°18'N	126°12'E
Sanana, Pulau, i., Indon.	248-49	2°12'S	125°55'E
Sanandaj, Iran	228-29	35°19'N	47°00'E
San Andreas, Ca., U.S. (săn ăn´drē-ăs)	118-19	38°12'N	120°41'W
San Andrés, Col.	150	12°33'N	81°42'W
San Andrés, Isla de, i., Col. (ē´s-lä-dĕ-sän-än-drĕ´s)	164-65	12°33'N	81°43'W
San Andres Mountains, mts., N.M., U.S. (săn ăn´drē-ăs moun´tĭnz)	118-19	32°59'N	106°36'W
San Andrés Tuxtla, Mex. (sän-än-drā's-tōōs´tlä)	146-47	18°26'N	95°13'W
San Angelo, Tx., U.S. (săn ăn-jĕ-lō)	122-23	31°29'N	100°26'W
San Antonio, Chile (sän-ȧn-tō´nyō)	163e	33°36'S	71°36'W
San Antonio, Col. (sän-ȧn-tō´nyō)	163c	3°55'N	75°29'W
San Antonio, Tx., U.S. (săn ăn-tō´nē-ō)	122-23	29°25'N	98°29'W
San Antonio, stm., Tx., U.S. (săn ăn-tō´nē-ō)	122-23	28°30'N	96°53'W
San Antonio, Cabo, c., Arg.	173	36°40'S	56°42'W
San Antonio, Cabo de, c., Cuba (kȧ´bō-dĕ-sän-än-tō´nyō)	142-43	21°52'N	84°57'W
San Antonio Bay, b., Tx., U.S. (săn ăn-tō´nē-ō bā)	122-23	28°20'N	96°45'W
San Antonio de los Cobres, Arg. (sän-ȧn-tō´nyō dā lōs kō´brās)	168-69	24°13'S	66°19'W
San Antonio Oeste, Arg. (sän-nä-tō´nyō ō-ĕs´tā)	171	40°45'S	64°58'W
San Augustine, Tx., U.S. (săn ô´gŭs-tēn)	122-23	31°31'N	94°07'W
San Benedetto del Tronto, Italy (sän bā´nȧ-dĕt´tō dĕl trōn´tō)	200-01	42°58'N	13°53'E
San Benedicto, Isla, i., Mex.	144-45	19°19'N	110°49'W
San Benito, Guat.	148	16°55'N	89°54'W
San Benito, Tx., U.S. (săn bĕ-nē´tō)	122-23	26°08'N	97°38'W
San Bernardino, Ca., U.S. (săn bûr-när-dē´nō)	118-19	34°06'N	117°17'W
San Bernardino Strait, strt., Phil.	250	12°32'N	124°10'E
San Bernardo, Chile (sän bĕr-när´dō)	163e	33°36'S	70°42'W
San Blas, Mex. (sän bläs´)	146-47	21°33'N	105°17'W
San Blas, Mex. (sän bläs´)	144-45	26°05'N	108°46'W
San Blas, Cape, c., Fl., U.S. (kāp săn bläs´)	124-25	29°40'N	85°22'W
San Borja, Bol.	166-67	14°49'S	66°51'W
San Buenaventura, Mex. (sän bwā´nȧ-vĕn-tōō´rȧ)	122-23	27°04'N	101°33'W
San Buenaventura, Ca., U.S. *see* Ventura	118-19	34°17'N	119°17'W
San Carlos, Chile (sän-kȧ´r-lōs)	171	36°26'S	71°57'W
San Carlos, Mex. (sän kär´lōs)	122-23	29°01'N	100°51'W
San Carlos, Nic. (sän-kä´r-lōs)	149	11°07'N	84°47'W
San Carlos, Phil.	250	10°30'N	123°25'E
San Carlos, Phil.	250	15°56'N	120°21'E
San Carlos, Az., U.S. (săn kär´lōs)	118-19	33°21'N	110°27'W
San Carlos, Ven.	164-65	9°40'N	68°35'W
San Carlos, stm., C.R. (sän kär´lōs)	149	10°47'N	84°12'W
San Carlos de Bariloche, Arg.	171	41°09'S	71°18'W
San Carlos de Bolívar, Arg.	173	36°13'S	61°07'W
San Carlos del Zulia, Ven.	164-65	9°02'N	71°56'W
San Carlos de Río Negro, Ven.	164-65	1°55'N	67°04'W
San Carlos Indian Reservation, ind. res., Az., U.S. (săn kär´lōs ĭn´dĭ-ăn rĕ-sẽr-vā´shŭn)	118-19	33°23'N	110°09'W
San Cataldo, Italy (sän kä-täl´dō)	200-01	37°29'N	13°59'E
Sánchez, Dom. Rep. (sän´chĕz)	142-43	19°14'N	69°37'W
San Clemente, Monte, mtn., Chile *see* San Valentín, Monte	171	46°36'S	73°20'W
San Clemente Island, i., Ca., U.S. (săn klĕ-mĕn´tā ī´lănd)	118-19	32°54'N	118°29'W
San Cristóbal, Arg.	173	30°19'S	61°13'W
San Cristóbal, Dom. Rep. (sän krēs-tô´bäl)	142-43	18°25'N	70°06'W
San Cristóbal, Ven. (sän krēs-tô´bäl)	164-65	7°45'N	72°13'W
San Cristobal, i., Sol. Is.	279e	10°36'S	161°45'E
San Cristóbal, Isla, i., Ec.	170a	0°50'S	89°26'W
San Cristóbal de las Casas, Mex.	146-47	16°45'N	92°38'W
Sancti Spíritus, Cuba (säŋk´tē spē´rē-tōōs)	142-43	21°56'N	79°27'W
Sancti Spíritus, state, Cuba (säŋk´tē spē´rē-tōōs)	142-43	22°0'N	79°20'W
Sancy, Puy de, mtn., Fr. (pwē-dĕ-säN-sē´)	196-97	45°32'N	2°49'E
Sandakan, Malay. (sȧn-dä´kȧn)	250	5°51'N	118°06'E
Sandefjord, Nor. (sän´dĕ-fyôr´)	192-93	59°08'N	10°14'E
Sanders, Az., U.S. (săn´dẽrz)	118-19	35°14'N	109°20'W
Sanderson, Tx., U.S. (săn´dẽr-sŭn)	122-23	30°09'N	102°24'W
Sandersville, Ga., U.S. (săn´dẽrz-vĭl)	124-25	32°59'N	82°49'W
Sand Hills, hills, Ne., U.S. (sănd hĭlz)	114-15	42°0'N	101°00'W
Sandia, Peru	170	14°16'S	69°27'W
San Diego, Ca., U.S. (săn dē-ā´gō)	118-19	32°43'N	117°08'W
San Diego, Tx., U.S. (săn dē-ā´gō)	122-23	27°46'N	98°14'W
San Diego, Cabo, c., Arg.	171	54°39'S	65°08'W
San Diego de la Unión, Mex. (sän dē-ā-gō dā lä ōō-nyōn´)	146-47	21°28'N	100°52'W
Sandnes, Nor. (sänd´nĕs)	192-93	58°51'N	5°44'E
Sandomierz, Pol. (sȧn-dô´myĕzh)	194-95	50°41'N	21°46'E
San Donà di Piave, Italy (sän dô nȧ´ dē pyä´vĕ)	200-01	45°38'N	12°34'E
Sandoway, Mya. (sän-dô-wī´)	246-47	18°28'N	94°22'E
Sandpoint, Id., U.S. (sănd point)	112-13	48°17'N	116°33'W
Sand Springs, Ok., U.S. (sănd sprĭngz)	120-21	36°08'N	96°07'W
Sandstone, Mn., U.S. (sănd´stōn)	114-15	46°08'N	92°52'W
Sandusky, Mi., U.S. (săn-dŭs´kē)	116-17	43°25'N	82°49'W
Sandusky, Oh., U.S. (săn-dŭs´kē)	116-17	41°27'N	82°42'W
Sandwich, Il., U.S. (sănd´wĭch)	116-17	41°39'N	88°37'W
Sandy, Ut., U.S. (sănd´ē)	112-13	40°37'N	111°54'W
Sandy Cape, c., Austl.	277	24°42'S	153°16'E
Sandykgaçy, Turkmen.	232-33	36°33'N	62°33'E
Sandy Lake, lk., Nf., Can. (sănd´ē lāk)	138-39	49°16'N	57°00'W
Sandy Lake, lk., On., Can. (sănd´ē lāk)	134-35	53°02'N	93°00'W
Sandy Springs, Ga., U.S. (sănd´ē sprĭngz)	124-25	33°56'N	84°23'W
San Estanislao, Para. (săn ĕs-tä-nēs-lä´ō)	168-69	24°39'S	56°29'W
San Felipe, Chile (săn fĕ-lē´pĕ)	163e	32°45'S	70°43'W
San Felipe, Mex. (săn fĕ-lē´pĕ)	146-47	21°29'N	101°13'W
San Felipe, Mex. (săn fĕ-lē´pĕ)	144-45	31°02'N	114°51'W
San Felipe, Ven. (săn fĕ-lē´pĕ)	164-65	10°20'N	68°44'W
San Felipe, Cayos de, is., Cuba (kä´yōs-dĕ-sän-fĕ-lē´pĕ)	142-43	21°58'N	83°30'W
San Félix, Isla, i., Chile (ē´s-lä-dĕ-sän fā-lēks´)	159	26°17'S	80°06'W
San Fernando, Chile	163e	34°35'S	70°59'W
San Fernando, Mex. (sän fĕr-nän´dō)	122-23	24°51'N	98°10'W
San Fernando, Phil.	250	15°01'N	120°41'E
San Fernando, Phil.	250	16°37'N	120°19'E
San Fernando, Trin.	143b	10°17'N	61°27'W
San Fernando de Apure, Ven. (sän-fĕr-nä´n-dō-dĕ-ä-pōō´rä)	164-65	7°53'N	67°27'W
San Fernando de Atabapo, Ven. (sän-fĕr-nä´n-dō-dĕ-ä-tä-bä´pō)	164-65	4°02'N	67°41'W
San Fernando del Valle de Catamarca, Arg.	168-69	28°28'S	65°47'W
Sanford, Fl., U.S. (săn´fôrd)	124-25	28°47'N	81°17'W
Sanford, Me., U.S. (săn´fẽrd)	116-17	43°27'N	70°47'W
Sanford, N.C., U.S. (săn´fẽrd)	124-25	35°29'N	79°11'W
San Francisco, Arg. (sän frăn´sĭs´kō)	173	31°26'S	62°05'W
San Francisco, Ca., U.S. (săn frăn-sĭs´kō)	118-19	37°47'N	122°25'W
San Francisco del Oro, Mex. (săn frăn´sĭs´kō-dĕl ō´rō)	122-23	26°52'N	105°51'W
San Francisco del Rincón, Mex. (săn frăn´sĭs´kō-dĕl rēn-kōn´)	146-47	21°01'N	101°52'W
San Francisco de Macorís, Dom. Rep. (săn frăn´sĭs´kō-dā-mä-kō´rēs)	142-43	19°18'N	70°15'W
San Gabriel Chilac, Mex. (sän-gä-brē-ĕl-chē-läk´)	146-47	18°20'N	97°21'W
Sangar, Russia	218-19	63°55'N	127°29'E
Sangarius, stm., Tur. *see* Sakarya	186-87	41°07'N	30°39'E
Sangay, vol., Ec.	170	2°0'S	78°20'W
Sangeang, Pulau, i., Indon.	248-49	8°12'S	119°04'E
Sangerhausen, Ger. (säng´ẽr-hou-zĕn)	194-95	51°28'N	11°18'E
Sanggan, stm., China	240-41	40°21'N	115°25'E
Sanggau, Indon.	248-49	0°07'N	110°35'E
Sangha, stm., Afr.	260-61	1°12'S	16°50'E
Sangihe, Kepulauan, is., Indon.	248-49	3°0'N	125°30'E
Sangihe, Pulau, i., Indon.	248-49	3°35'N	125°32'E
San Gil, Col. (sän-kē´l)	164-65	6°33'N	73°08'W
San Giovanni in Fiore, Italy (sän jô-vän´nē ēn fyō´rä)	200-01	39°15'N	16°42'E
Sangju, Kor., S. (säng´jōō´)	243	36°25'N	128°10'E
Sāngli, India	236	16°52'N	74°34'E
San Gregorio, Ur.	173	32°38'S	55°50'W
Sangue, stm., Braz.	166-67	10°57'S	58°20'W
Sanibel Island, i., Fl., U.S. (săn´ĭ-bĕl ī´lănd)	125a	26°27'N	82°08'W
San Ignacio, Arg.	173	27°16'S	55°33'W
San Ignacio, Mex.	144-45	27°17'N	112°54'W
San Ignacio de Moxo, Bol.	166-67	14°56'S	65°37'W
San Ignacio de Velasco, Bol.	168-69	16°23'S	60°57'W
San Ildefonso, Cape, c., Phil. (kāp sän-ĕl-dĕ-fōn-sō)	250	16°02'N	122°00'E
San Ildefonso ó la Granja, Spain (sän-ĕl-dĕ-fōn-sō ō lä grän´khä)	198-99	40°54'N	4°00'W
San Isidro, Arg. (sän ē-sē´drō)	173	34°28'S	58°31'W
San Jacinto, Phil. (săn hä-sēn´tō)	250	12°34'N	123°44'E
San Javier, Arg.	173	30°34'S	59°56'W
San Javier, Bol.	168-69	16°20'S	62°38'W
San Joaquín, Bol.	166-67	13°04'S	64°49'W

ăt; finȧl; rāte; senāte; ärm; ȧsk; sofȧ; fâre; ch-choose; dh-as th in other; bē; ēvent; bĕt; recĕnt; cratẽr; g-gō; gh-guttural g; bĭt; ĭ-short neutral; rīde; K-guttural k as ch in German ich;

Feature (Pronunciation)	Page	Lat.	Long.
San Joaquín, stm., Bol.	166-67	13°08'S	63°41'W
San Joaquin Valley, val., Ca., U.S.	118-19	36°55'N	120°29'W
San Jorge, Golfo, b., Arg. (gôl-fô-sän-kô´r-kě)	171	46°0'S	67°00'W
San Jorge Island, i., Sol. Is.	279e	8°27'S	159°35'E
San Jose, Phil.	250	12°21'N	121°04'E
San Jose, Ca., U.S.	118-19	37°21'N	121°54'W
San José, nat. cap., C.R. (sän hô-sā´)	149	9°56'N	84°05'W
San José, Isla, i., Mex. (ē´s-lä-sän kô-sě´)	144-45	25°00'N	110°38'W
San José, Isla, i., Pan. (ē´s-lä-sän hô-sā´)	150	8°15'N	79°07'W
San José de Chiquitos, Bol.	168-69	17°50'S	60°44'W
San José de Feliciano, Arg. (sän kô-sě´ dā lä ěs-kě´nà)	173	30°23'S	58°45'W
San José de Jáchal, Arg.	168-69	30°14'S	68°45'W
San José del Cabo, Mex.	144-45	23°03'N	109°41'W
San José del Guaviare, Col.	164-65	2°34'N	72°38'W
San José de Mayo, Ur.	173	34°21'S	56°42'W
San Jose Island, i., Tx., U.S.	122-23	28°02'N	96°55'W
San Juan, Arg. (sän hwän´)	168-69	31°32'S	68°32'W
San Juan, state, Arg. (sän hwän´)	168-69	31°0'S	69°00'W
San Juan, nat. cap., P.R. (sän hwän´)	142a	18°28'N	66°07'W
San Juan, stm., Arg.	168-69	32°17'S	67°22'W
San Juan, stm., Mex. (sän-hōō-än´)	122-23	26°22'N	98°51'W
San Juan, stm., N.A.	149	10°56'N	83°43'W
San Juan, stm., U.S. (săn hwän´)	110-11	37°11'N	110°43'W
San Juan, Pico, mtn., Cuba (pē´kô-sän-kôà´n)	142-43	21°59'N	80°09'W
San Juan Bautista, Para. (sän hwän´ bou-tēs´tä)	173	26°53'S	57°01'W
San Juan de la Maguana, Dom. Rep.	142-43	18°48'N	71°13'W
San Juan del Norte, Nic.	149	10°55'N	83°42'W
San Juan de los Morros, Ven. (sän-hōō-än´dě-lôs-mô´r-rôs)	163b	9°55'N	67°21'W
San Juan del Río, Mex. (sän hwän del rē´ô)	146-47	20°23'N	100°00'W
San Juan del Río, Mex. (sän hwän del rē´ô)	122-23	24°48'N	104°27'W
San Juan del Sur, Nic. (sän hwän děl sōōr)	149	11°15'N	85°52'W
San Juan Evangelista, Mex. (sän-hōō-ä´n-å-văŋ-kå-lěs´ta´)	146-47	17°54'N	95°07'W
San Juanito, Isla, i., Mex.	146-47	21°46'N	106°41'W
San Juan Mountains, mts., Co., U.S. (san hwän´ moun´tĭnz)	118-19	37°32'N	107°31'W
San Justo, Arg. (sän hōōs´tô)	173	30°47'S	60°35'W
Sankt Michel, Fin. *see* Mikkeli	192-93	61°42'N	27°16'E
Sankt Pölten, Aus. (zäŋkt-pûl´těn)	194-95	48°12'N	15°37'E
Sankuru, stm., D.R.C. (sän-kōō´rōō)	262-63	4°17'S	20°24'E
San Lázaro, Cabo, c., Mex. (kä´bô sän-lä´zä-rō)	144-45	24°48'N	112°18'W
Şanlıurfa, Tur.	228-29	37°10'N	38°48'E
San Lorenzo, Arg. (sän lô-rěn´zô)	173	32°44'S	60°45'W
San Lorenzo, Ec.	170	1°15'N	78°50'W
San Lorenzo, Cabo, c., Ec.	170	1°04'S	80°54'W
San Lorenzo, Isla, i., Peru	163a	12°05'S	77°14'W
Sanlúcar de Barrameda, Spain (sän-lōō´kär)	198-99	36°47'N	6°21'W
San Lucas, Bol. (sän lōō´kås)	168-69	20°06'S	65°08'W
San Lucas, Cabo, c., Mex.	144-45	22°52'N	109°54'W
San Luis, Arg. (sän lò-ēs´)	171	33°18'S	66°21'W
San Luis, Guat. (sän lò-ēs´)	148	16°13'N	89°27'W
San Luis, state, Arg. (sän lò-ēs´)	171	34°0'S	66°00'W
San Luís, Laguna, lk., Bol.	166-67	13°45'S	64°00'W
San Luis de la Paz, Mex. (sän lò-ēs´ dā lä päz´)	146-47	21°18'N	100°31'W
San Luis Obispo, Ca., U.S. (săn lò-ěes´ ô-bĭs´pō)	118-19	35°17'N	120°40'W
San Luis Potosí, Mex.	146-47	22°09'N	100°59'W
San Luis Potosí, state, Mex.	146-47	22°30'N	100°30'W
San Luis Río Colorado, Mex.	144-45	32°28'N	114°46'W
San Marcos, Mex. (sän mär´kôs)	146-47	16°49'N	99°23'W
San Marcos, Tx., U.S. (săn mär´kôs)	122-23	29°53'N	97°56'W
San Marcos de Colón, Hond. (sän-má´r-kōs-dě-kô-lô´n)	149	13°26'N	86°49'W
San Marino, nation, Eur. (sän mēr-ē´nô)	200-01	43°56'N	12°25'E
San Martín, Arg.	163e	33°05'S	68°29'W
San Martín, Col. (sän mär-tē´n)	164-65	3°42'N	73°42'W
San Martín, stm., Bol.	166-67	13°08'S	63°47'W
San Martín, Lago, lk., S.A. (lä´gô sän mär-tē´n)	171	48°53'S	72°39'W
San Martín de los Andes, Arg.	171	40°10'S	71°22'W
San Mateo, Ca., U.S. (săn mä-tā´ô)	118-19	37°34'N	122°19'W
San Mateo, Ven. (sän må-tě´ô)	163b	9°45'N	64°33'W

Feature (Pronunciation)	Page	Lat.	Long.
San Matías, Golfo, b., Arg. (gôl-fô-sän-mä-tē´äs)	171	41°30'S	64°15'W
Sanmenxia, China	238-39	34°47'N	111°12'E
San Miguel, El Sal. (sän mê-gål´)	148	13°28'N	88°11'W
San Miguel, Mex. (sän mê-gål´)	122-23	29°10'N	101°28'W
San Miguel, Pan. (sän mê-gål´)	150	8°27'N	78°56'W
San Miguel, stm., Bol. (sän-mē-gěl´)	166-67	13°53'S	63°54'W
San Miguel, Golfo de, b., Pan. (gôl-fô-dě-sän mê-gål´)	150	8°22'N	78°17'W
San Miguel del Monte, Arg.	173	35°27'S	58°49'W
San Miguel de Tucumán, Arg.	168-69	26°49'S	65°13'W
San Miguel El Alto, Mex. (sän mê-gål´ ěl äl´tô)	146-47	21°01'N	102°19'W
Sannār, Sudan	266	13°34'N	33°33'E
San Nicolas, Phil. (sän nê-kô-läs´)	250	18°10'N	120°36'E
San Nicolás, stm., Mex. (sän nē-kô-lá´s)	146-47	19°38'N	105°13'W
San Nicolás, Canal de, strt., N.A. *see* Nicholas Channel	142-43	23°21'N	80°21'W
San Nicolás de los Arroyos, Arg.	173	33°20'S	60°14'W
Sanok, Pol. (sä´nôk)	194-95	49°34'N	22°13'E
San Pablo, Phil. (sän-pä-blô)	250	14°04'N	121°19'E
San Pedro, Arg. (sän pā´drô)	168-69	24°15'S	64°52'W
San Pedro, Arg. (sän pā´drô)	173	33°41'S	59°41'W
San Pedro, Chile (sän pě´drô)	163e	33°54'S	71°26'W
San-Pédro, C. Iv.	260-61	4°45'N	6°38'W
San Pedro, Punta, c., Chile	168-69	25°31'S	70°38'W
San Pedro, Volcán, vol., Chile	168-69	21°53'S	68°25'W
San Pedro de Jujuy, Arg. *see* San Pedro	168-69	24°15'S	64°52'W
San Pedro de las Colonias, Mex. (sän pā´drô dě-läs-kô-lô´nyäs)	122-23	25°46'N	102°59'W
San Pedro de Macorís, Dom. Rep. (sän-pě´drō-dā mä-kô-rēs´)	142-43	18°28'N	69°18'W
San Pedro de Ycuamandiyú, Para.	168-69	24°05'S	57°08'W
San Pedro Sula, Hond. (sän pā´drô sōō´lä)	149	15°30'N	88°02'W
San Pietro, Isola di, i., Italy (ē´sō-lä-dē-sän pyā´trô)	200-01	39°08'N	8°16'E
San Quintín, Cabo, c., Mex.	144-45	30°22'N	115°60'W
San Rafael, Arg. (sän rä-fä-āl´)	163e	34°37'S	68°20'W
San Ramón de la Nueva Orán, Arg.	168-69	23°09'S	64°20'W
San Remo, Italy (sän rā´mô)	200-01	43°50'N	7°46'E
San Roque, Punta, c., Mex.	144-45	27°11'N	114°25'W
San Saba, Tx., U.S. (săn să´bȧ)	122-23	31°12'N	98°43'W
San Saba, stm., Tx., U.S. (săn să´bȧ)	122-23	31°15'N	98°36'W
San Salvador, i., Bah. (săn săl´vȧ-dôr)	142-43	24°02'N	74°27'W
San Salvador, nat. cap., El Sal. (sän säl-vä-dōr´)	148	13°40'N	89°13'W
San Salvador, Isla, i., Ec. (ē´s-lä-sän säl-vä-dōr´) *see* Santiago, Isla	170a	0°14'S	90°45'W
San Salvador de Jujuy, Arg.	168-69	24°12'S	65°18'W
San Sebastián, Spain (sän så-bås-tyän´) *see* Donostia-San Sebastián	198-99	43°19'N	1°60'W
San Severo, Italy (sän sě-vā´rō)	200-01	41°41'N	15°23'E
Sanshui, China (sän-shwā)	238-39	23°11'N	112°53'E
San Simon, stm., Az., U.S. (sán sī-mōn´)	118-19	32°52'N	109°33'W
Santa, stm., Peru	170	9°01'S	78°38'W
Santa Ana, Bol.	166-67	13°45'S	65°35'W
Santa Ana, El Sal. (sän´tä ä´nä)	148	13°59'N	89°34'W
Santa Ana, Mex. (sän´tä ä´nä)	146-47	24°04'N	100°30'W
Santa Ana, Mex. (sän´tä ä´nä)	144-45	30°32'N	111°07'W
Santa Ana, Ca., U.S. (săn´tȧ ăn´ȧ)	118-19	33°45'N	117°53'W
Santa Anna, Tx., U.S. (săn´tȧ ăn´ȧ)	122-23	31°44'N	99°19'W
Santa Bárbara, Hond. (sän-tä-bä´r-bä-rä)	149	14°55'N	88°14'W
Santa Bárbara, Mex. (sän-tä-bä´r-bä-rä)	122-23	26°49'N	105°48'W
Santa Barbara, Ca., U.S. (săn-tȧ-bär´bȧ-rȧ)	118-19	34°25'N	119°42'W
Santa Catalina Island, i., Ca., U.S. (săn´tȧ kă-tȧ-lē´nȧ ī´lȧnd)	118-19	33°23'N	118°24'W
Santa Catarina, Mex. (sän´tä kä-tä-rē´nä)	122-23	25°41'N	100°28'W
Santa Catarina, state, Braz. (sän-tä-kä-tä-rē´nȧ)	168-69	27°0'S	50°00'W
Santa Catarina, Ilha de, i., Braz.	172	27°36'S	48°30'W
Santa Clara, Cuba (sän´tä klä´rä)	142-43	22°25'N	79°58'W
Santa Cruz, Braz. (sän-tä-krōō´s)	163d	6°13'S	36°01'W
Santa Cruz, Ca., U.S. (săn´tȧ krōōz´)	118-19	36°59'N	122°02'W
Santa Cruz, stm., Arg. (sän´tä krōōz´)	171	50°08'S	68°21'W
Santa Cruz, Isla, i., Ec. (ē´s-lä-sän-tä-krōō´z)	170a	0°38'S	90°23'W
Santa Cruz de la Palma, Spain	199d	28°41'N	17°46'W
Santa Cruz de la Sierra, Bol.	168-69	17°48'S	63°10'W
Santa Cruz del Sur, Cuba (sän-tä-krōō´s-děl-sô´r)	142-43	20°43'N	77°59'W

Feature (Pronunciation)	Page	Lat.	Long.
Santa Cruz de Tenerife, Spain (sän´tä krōōz dā tā-nå-rē´fā)	199d	28°28'N	16°15'W
Santa Cruz do Sul, Braz.	168-69	29°43'S	52°26'W
Santa Cruz Islands, is., Sol. Is.	272-73	10°60'S	166°15'E
Santa Fe, Arg. (sän´tä fā´)	173	31°38'S	60°42'W
Santa Fe, Spain (sän´tä-fā´)	198-99	37°11'N	3°43'W
Santa Fe, N.M., U.S. (săn´tȧ fā´)	118-19	35°41'N	105°59'W
Santa Fe, state, Arg. (sän´tä fā´)	173	31°0'S	61°00'W
Santa Fe de Bogotá, nat. cap., Col. *see* Bogotá	164-65	4°37'N	74°06'W
Santa Fé do Sul, Braz.	168-69	20°13'S	50°56'W
Santai, China (san-tī)	238-39	31°09'N	105°01'E
Santa Inés, Isla, i., Chile (ē´s-lä-sän´tä ē-nās´)	171	53°46'S	72°44'W
Santa Isabel, Arg.	171	36°15'S	66°56'W
Santa Isabel, i., Sol. Is.	279e	8°0'S	159°00'E
Santa Isabel, nat. cap., Eq. Gui. *see* Malabo	260-61	3°45'N	8°47'E
Santa Magdalena, Isla, i., Mex.	144-45	24°54'N	112°13'W
Santa Margarita, Isla, i., Mex. (ē´s-lä-sän´tä mär-gä-rē´tä)	144-45	24°27'N	111°51'W
Santa Maria, Braz. (sän´tä mä-rē´ä)	173	29°41'S	53°49'W
Santa Maria, Ca., U.S. (săn-tȧ mȧ-rē´ȧ)	118-19	34°57'N	120°26'W
Santa Maria, i., Port. (sän-tä-mä-rē´ä)	199c	36°58'N	25°06'W
Santa Maria, i., Vanuatu	279g	14°14'S	167°28'E
Santa María, stm., Mex. (sän´tä mä-rē´ä)	146-47	21°48'N	99°10'W
Santa Maria, Cabo de, c., Ang.	264-65	13°25'S	12°32'E
Santa Maria, Cabo de, c., Port. (kå´bō-dě-sän-tä-mä-rē´ä)	198-99	36°58'N	7°54'W
Santa María, Isla, i., Ec.	170a	1°17'S	90°26'W
Santa María del Oro, Mex. (sän´tä-mä-rē´ä-děl-ô-rô)	122-23	25°56'N	105°23'W
Santa Marta, Col. (sän´tä mär´tä)	164-65	11°15'N	74°12'W
Santa Monica, Ca., U.S. (săn´tȧ mŏn´ĭ-kȧ)	118-19	34°01'N	118°29'W
Santana do Livramento, Braz.	173	30°53'S	55°31'W
Santander, Col. (sän-tän-děr´)	163c	3°03'N	76°29'W
Santander, Phil.	250	9°25'N	123°20'E
Santander, Spain (sän-tän-dâr´)	198-99	43°28'N	3°48'W
Sant'Antioco, Isola di, i., Italy (ē´sō-lä-dē-sän-än-tyô´kô)	200-01	39°02'N	8°25'E
Santarém, Braz. (sän-tä-rěn´)	166-67	2°26'S	54°43'W
Santarém, Port.	198-99	39°14'N	8°41'W
Santaren Channel, strt., Bah. (săn-tȧ-rěn´ chăn´ěl)	142-43	24°0'N	79°30'W
Santa Rita, Hond.	149	15°10'N	87°54'W
Santa Rosa, Arg.	173	36°37'S	64°17'W
Santa Rosa, Braz.	173	27°52'S	54°26'W
Santa Rosa, Ec.	170	3°27'S	79°57'W
Santa Rosa, Ca., U.S.	118-19	38°26'N	122°43'W
Santa Rosa, N.M., U.S. (săn´tȧ rō´sȧ)	120-21	34°56'N	104°41'W
Santa Rosa de Copán, Hond.	149	14°46'N	88°47'W
Santa Rosalía, Mex. (sän´tä rô-zä´lē-ä)	144-45	27°20'N	112°17'W
Santa Rosa Range, mts., Nv., U.S. (săn´tȧ rō´zȧ rānj)	112-13	41°35'N	117°40'W
Santa Sylvina, Arg.	173	27°50'S	61°08'W
Santa Vitória do Palmar, Braz. (sän-tä-vē-tō´ryä-dô-päl-mår)	173	33°31'S	53°22'W
Santee, Ca., U.S. (săn tē´)	118-19	32°50'N	116°57'W
Santee, stm., S.C., U.S. (săn tē´)	124-25	33°14'N	79°28'W
Santiago, Braz. (sän-tyá´gô)	173	29°11'S	54°52'W
Santiago, Pan. (sän-tyá´gô)	150	8°06'N	80°58'W
Santiago, i., C.V.	260-61	15°02'N	23°39'W
Santiago, nat. cap., Chile (sän-tē-ä´gô)	171	33°27'S	70°40'W
Santiago, Isla, i., Ec.	170a	0°14'S	90°45'W
Santiago de Compostela, Spain	198-99	42°53'N	8°32'W
Santiago de Cuba, Cuba (sän-tyá´gô-dě kōō´bä)	142-43	20°02'N	75°49'W
Santiago de Cuba, state, Cuba (sän-tyá´gô-dě kōō´bä)	142-43	20°10'N	75°55'W
Santiago del Estero, Arg. (sän-tē-á´gô-děl ěs-tā-rô)	168-69	27°47'S	64°16'W
Santiago del Estero, state, Arg. (sän-tē-á´gô-děl ěs-tā-rô)	173	28°0'S	63°30'W
Santiago de los Caballeros, Dom. Rep.	142-43	19°27'N	70°42'W
Santiago Jamiltepec, Mex.	146-47	16°18'N	97°50'W
Santiago Papasquiaro, Mex.	122-23	25°03'N	105°25'W
Santiaguillo, Laguna, lk., Mex. (lä-oô´nä-sän-tē-a-gēl´yô)	122-23	24°45'N	104°48'W
Santo Amaro, Braz. (sän´tô ä-mä´rô)	166-67	12°32'S	38°42'W
Santo André, Braz.	172	23°40'S	46°31'W
Santo Ângelo, Braz. (sän-tô-á´n-zhě-lô)	173	28°16'S	54°16'W

n-sing; ŋ-baŋk; ɴ-nasalized n; nŏd; cŏmmit; ōld; ôbey; ôrder; oi-boil; fōōd; ò-as oo in foot; ou-out; s-soft; sh-dish; th-thin; pūre; ûnite; ûrn; stŭd; circŭs; ü-as in French tu; ´-indeterminate vowel.

Feature (Pronunciation)	Page	Lat.	Long.
Santo Antão, i., C.V. (sän´tô ä´n-zhě-lô)	**260-61**	17°03'N	25°07'W
Santo Antônio de Jesus, Braz.	**166-67**	12°57'S	39°14'W
Santo Antônio do Iça, Braz.	**166-67**	3°04'S	67°56'W
Santo Domingo, Nic. (sän-tô-dô-mě´n-gō)	**149**	12°16'N	85°05'W
Santo Domingo, i., N.A. see Hispaniola	**142-43**	19°0'N	71°00'W
Santo Domingo, nat. cap., Dom. Rep. (sän´tô dô-mĭn´gô)	**142-43**	18°30'N	69°53'W
Santoña, Spain (sän-tō´nyä)	**198-99**	43°26'N	3°27'W
Santorini, i., Grc. see Thíra	**200-01**	36°26'N	25°27'E
Santos, Braz. (sän´tozh)	**172**	23°56'S	46°20'W
Santos Dumont, Braz. (sän´tôs-dò-mô´nt)	**172**	21°28'S	43°33'W
Santo Tomé, Arg.	**173**	28°33'S	56°02'W
Santo Tomé de Guayana, Ven. see Ciudad Guayana	**164-65**	8°21'N	62°39'W
San Valentín, Monte, mtn., Chile (mô´n-tě-sän-vä-lěn-tē´n)	**171**	46°36'S	73°20'W
San Vicente, El Sal. (sän vê-sěn´tå)	**148**	13°38'N	88°47'W
San Vicente de Cañete, Peru	**163a**	13°05'S	76°24'W
San Vicente del Caguán, Col.	**164-65**	2°07'N	74°47'W
San Xavier Indian Reservation, ind. res., Az., U.S. (sän x-ā´vēr ĭn´dĭ-ăn rě-sěr-vā´shěn)	**118-19**	32°02'N	111°08'W
Sanya, China	**238-39**	18°14'N	109°30'E
Sanyuan, China	**238-39**	34°37'N	108°55'E
Sanza Pombo, Ang.	**262-63**	7°19'S	15°60'E
São Bento, Braz.	**166-67**	2°42'S	44°50'W
São Borja, Braz. (souɴ-bôr-zhä)	**173**	28°39'S	56°01'W
São Carlos, Braz. (souɴ kär´lōzh)	**172**	22°02'S	47°54'W
São Cristóvão, Braz. (souɴ-krěs-tō-vouɴ)	**163d**	11°01'S	37°12'W
São Domingos, Braz.	**166-67**	13°24'S	46°21'W
São Francisco, Braz. (souɴ frän-sěsh´kò)	**168-69**	15°57'S	44°52'W
São Francisco, stm., Braz. (souɴ frän-sěsh´kò)	**159**	10°30'S	36°24'W
São Francisco, Ilha de, i., Braz.	**172**	26°18'S	48°37'W
São Francisco do Sul, Braz. (souɴ frän-sěsh´kò-dò-sōō´l)	**172**	26°15'S	48°37'W
São Gabriel, Braz. (souɴ´gä-brê-ěl´)	**173**	30°20'S	54°19'W
São João da Barra, Braz. (souɴ-zhôuɴ-dä-bä´rä)	**172**	21°38'S	41°02'W
São João da Boa Vista, Braz. (souɴ-zhôuɴ-dä-bôä-vê´s-tä)	**172**	21°59'S	46°48'W
São João Del Rei, Braz. (souɴ zhô-ouɴ´děl-rā)	**172**	21°08'S	44°15'W
São Jorge, i., Port. (souɴ zhôr´zhě)	**199c**	38°38'N	28°03'W
São José do Rio Preto, Braz. (souɴ zhô-zě´dô-re´ô-prě-tō)	**168-69**	20°49'S	49°23'W
São José dos Campos, Braz. (souɴ zhô-zā´dōzh käɴ pōzh´)	**172**	23°11'S	45°53'W
São Leopoldo, Braz. (souɴ-lě-ô-pôl´dò)	**168-69**	29°46'S	51°08'W
São Lourenço do Sul, Braz.	**173**	31°22'S	51°58'W
São Luís, Braz.	**166-67**	2°31'S	44°16'W
São Luís Gonzaga, Braz.	**173**	28°24'S	54°57'W
São Manuel, stm., Braz.	**166-67**	7°21'S	58°08'W
São Mateus, Braz. (souɴ mä-tā´özh)	**172**	18°44'S	39°52'W
São Miguel, i., Port.	**199c**	37°47'N	25°30'W
Saona, Isla, i., Dom. Rep. (ě´s-lä-sä-ô´nä)	**142-43**	18°09'N	68°40'W
Saône, stm., Fr. (sōn)	**196-97**	45°43'N	4°50'E
São Nicolau, i., C.V. (souɴ´ ně-kô-louɴ´)	**260-61**	16°36'N	24°11'W
São Paulo, Braz. (souɴ´ pou´lò)	**172**	23°33'S	46°38'W
São Paulo, state, Braz. (souɴ´ pou´lò)	**172**	22°0'S	49°00'W
São Paulo de Olivença, Braz. (souɴ´pou´lòdå ô-lê-věn´sá)	**166-67**	3°28'S	68°57'W
São Raimundo Nonato, Braz. (souɴ´ rī-mò´n-do nô-nä´tò)	**166-67**	9°01'S	42°42'W
São Roque, Braz. (souɴ´ rō´kě)	**172**	23°32'S	47°08'W
São Roque, Cabo de, c., Braz. (kå´bō-dě-souɴ´ rō´kě)	**163d**	5°29'S	35°16'W
São Salvador, Braz. see Salvador	**166-67**	12°59'S	38°30'W
São Sebastião, Braz. (souɴ så-bäs-tê-ouɴ´)	**172**	23°49'S	45°25'W
São Sebastião, Ilha de, i., Braz.	**172**	23°51'S	45°20'W
São Sebastião, Ponta, c., Moz.	**264-65**	22°08'S	35°29'E
São Simão, Braz. (souɴ-sē-mouɴ)	**172**	21°29'S	47°33'W
São Simão, Represa de, res., Braz.	**168-69**	18°37'S	49°59'W
São Tiago, i., C.V. (souɴ tê-ä´gò) see Santiago	**260-61**	15°02'N	23°39'W
São Tomé, i., S. Tom./P.	**260-61**	0°12'N	6°36'E
São Tomé, nat. cap., S. Tom./P.	**260-61**	0°20'N	6°44'E
São Tomé, Cabo de, c., Braz.	**172**	21°59'S	40°59'W
Sao Tome and Principe, nation, Afr. (souɴ tòmä änd prēn´sê-pě)	**260-61**	1°0'N	7°00'E
São Tomé e Príncipe, nation, Afr. see Sao Tome and Principe	**260-61**	1°0'N	7°00'E
Saoura, Oued, stm., Alg.	**258-59**	29°01'N	0°57'W
São Vicente, Braz. (souɴ ve-se´n-tě)	**172**	23°58'S	46°22'W
São Vicente, i., C.V. (souɴ vê-sěn´tå)	**260-61**	16°49'N	24°55'W
São Vicente, Cabo de, c., Port. (kå´bō-dě-sän-vê-sě´n-tě)	**198-99**	37°01'N	8°59'W
Sap, Tonle, lk., Camb. (tôn´lā säp´)	**246-47**	13°0'N	104°00'E
Sapé, Braz.	**163d**	7°06'S	35°13'W
Sapele, Nig. (sä-pā´lā)	**260a**	5°54'N	5°40'E
Sapitwa, mtn., Malawi	**264-65**	15°57'S	35°36'E
Sapporo, Japan (säp-pô´rō)	**244**	43°04'N	141°21'E
Sapulpa, Ok., U.S. (sá-pŭl´pá)	**120-21**	36°00'N	96°06'W
Saqqez, Iran	**228-29**	36°14'N	46°18'E
Sarāb, Iran	**227**	37°56'N	47°31'E
Saragossa, Spain see Zaragoza	**198-99**	41°39'N	0°53'W
Sarajevo, nat. cap., Bos. (sä-rà-yěv´ô) (sá-rä´ya-vô)	**200-01**	43°52'N	18°25'E
Sarakhs, Iran	**232-33**	36°32'N	61°10'E
Saranac Lake, N.Y., U.S. (săr´á-năk lāk)	**116-17**	44°20'N	74°08'W
Sarandí Grande, Ur. (sä-rän´dē-grän´dě)	**173**	33°45'S	56°20'W
Sarang, Kaz.	**226**	49°46'N	72°52'E
Sarangani Islands, is., Phil.	**250**	5°25'N	125°26'E
Saransk, Russia (sá-ränsk´)	**186-87**	54°11'N	45°09'E
Sarapul, Russia (sä-räpôl')	**186-87**	56°28'N	53°48'E
Sarasota, Fl., U.S. (săr-á-sōtá)	**125a**	27°20'N	82°32'W
Saratoga, Wy., U.S. (săr-á-tō´gá)	**112-13**	41°28'N	106°48'W
Saratoga Springs, N.Y., U.S. (săr-á-tō´gá sprĭngz)	**116-17**	43°05'N	73°47'W
Saratov, Russia (sá rä´tôf)	**186-87**	51°34'N	45°60'E
Saratovskoye Vodokhranilishche, res., Russia	**186-87**	52°47'N	48°26'E
Saravan, Laos	**246-47**	15°43'N	106°25'E
Sarawak, hist. reg., Malay. (så-rä´wäk)	**248-49**	2°30'N	113°30'E
Sarayevo, nat. cap., Bos. see Sarajevo	**200-01**	43°52'N	18°25'E
Sardegna, i., Italy see Sardinia	**200-01**	40°0'N	9°00'E
Sardinia, i., Italy (sär-dĭn´ĭá)	**200-01**	40°0'N	9°00'E
Sardis Lake, res., Ms., U.S. (sär´dĭs lāk)	**124-25**	34°27'N	89°43'W
Sardis Lake, res., Ok., U.S. (sär´dĭs lāk)	**120-21**	34°42'N	95°21'W
Sargent, Ne., U.S. (sär´jěnt)	**114-15**	41°38'N	99°22'W
Sargodha, Pak.	**232-33**	32°05'N	72°40'E
Sarh, Chad (är-chaɴ-bô´)	**262-63**	9°09'N	18°23'E
Sārī, Iran	**232-33**	36°34'N	53°04'E
Sarina, Austl.	**277**	21°26'S	149°14'E
Sariqamish Kuli, lk., Asia see Sarygamysh köli	**226**	41°56'N	57°25'E
Sariwŏn, Kor., N.	**243**	38°30'N	125°46'E
Şarköy, Tur. (shär´kû-ê)	**200-01**	40°38'N	27°07'E
Sarmi, Indon.	**277**	1°51'S	138°42'E
Sarmiento, Arg.	**171**	45°35'S	69°05'W
Sarmiento de Gambia, Cerro, mtn., Chile	**171**	54°27'S	70°50'W
Särna, Swe.	**192-93**	61°41'N	13°08'E
Sarnia, On., Can. (sär´nē-á)	**136-37**	42°58'N	82°24'W
Sarny, Ukr. (sär´nê)	**194-95**	51°20'N	26°37'E
Sarpsborg, Nor. (särps´bôrg)	**192-93**	59°16'N	11°09'E
Sarrebourg, Fr. (sär-bōōr´)	**196-97**	48°44'N	7°03'E
Sarrebruck, Ger. see Saarbrücken	**194-95**	49°14'N	6°60'E
Sarreguemines, Fr. (sär-gē-mēn´)	**196-97**	49°07'N	7°04'E
Sartang, stm., Russia	**218-19**	67°27'N	133°15'E
Sárvár, Hung. (shär´vär)	**194-95**	47°15'N	16°56'E
Sarych, mys, c., Ukr. (mĭs så-rēch´)	**202-03**	44°25'N	33°45'E
Sarygamysh köli, lk., Asia	**226**	41°56'N	57°25'E
Sarysū, stm., Kaz. (sä´rê-sōō)	**226**	45°11'N	66°39'E
Sary-Tash, Kyrg.	**232-33**	39°44'N	73°15'E
Sāsarām, India (sŭs-ŭ-räm´)	**234-35**	24°57'N	84°01'E
Sasebo, Japan (sä´så-bô)	**245**	33°10'N	129°43'E
Saskatchewan, state, Can. (săs-kăch´ê-wän)	**128-29**	54°0'N	105°00'W
Saskatchewan, stm., Can. (săs-kăch´ê-wän)	**134-35**	53°16'N	98°50'W
Saskatoon, Sk., Can. (săs-ká-tōōn´)	**134-35**	52°08'N	106°39'W
Saskylakh, Russia	**206-07**	71°52'N	114°06'E
Sasovo, Russia (sás´ô-vô)	**186-87**	54°20'N	41°57'E
Sassandra, stm., C. Iv. (sás-sän´drá)	**260-61**	4°58'N	6°04'W
Sassari, Italy (säs´sä-rê)	**200-01**	40°43'N	8°33'E
Sata-misaki, c., Japan	**245**	30°60'N	130°40'E
Sātāra, India	**236**	17°41'N	74°00'E
Säter, Swe. (sĕ´tĕr)	**192-93**	60°21'N	15°45'E
Satilla, stm., Ga., U.S. (sá-tĭl´á)	**124-25**	30°59'N	81°29'W
Satīt, stm., Afr. see Tekezē	**266**	14°20'N	35°51'E
Satluj, stm., Asia see Sutlej	**234-35**	29°21'N	71°02'E
Satna, India	**234-35**	24°34'N	80°50'E
Sátoraljaújhely, Hung. (shä´tô-rô-lyô-ōō´yěl´)	**194-95**	48°24'N	21°41'E
Sattahip, Thai.	**246-47**	12°40'N	100°54'E
Satu Mare, Rom. (sá´tōō-má´rě)	**194-95**	47°47'N	22°53'E
Sauðárkrókur, Ice.	**190a**	65°45'N	19°41'W
Sauce, Arg.	**173**	30°05'S	58°47'W
Saucillo, Mex.	**122-23**	28°01'N	105°16'W
Saudi Arabia, nation, Asia (sá-ô´dĭ á-rä´bĭ-á)	**206-07**	25°0'N	45°00'E
Saugatuck, Mi., U.S. (sô´gá-tŭk)	**116-17**	42°40'N	86°11'W
Saujbulagh, Iran see Mahābād	**228-29**	36°46'N	45°44'E
Sauk Centre, Mn., U.S. (sôk sěn´tēr)	**114-15**	45°44'N	94°57'W
Sauk City, Wi., U.S. (sôk sĭ´tê)	**116-17**	43°16'N	89°43'W
Sauk Rapids, Mn., U.S. (sôk răp´ĭdz)	**114-15**	45°36'N	94°10'W
Saül, Fr. Gu.	**164-65**	3°38'N	53°12'W
Sault Sainte Marie, On., Can. (sōō sånt má-rē´)	**136-37**	46°31'N	84°20'W
Sault Sainte Marie, Mi., U.S. (sōō sånt má-rē´)	**114-15**	46°29'N	84°21'W
Saunders Island, i., Falk. Is.	**171**	51°23'S	60°13'W
Saurimo, Ang.	**264-65**	9°40'S	20°23'E
Sava, stm., Eur. (sä´vä)	**200-01**	44°50'N	20°27'E
Savai'i, i., Samoa	**279b**	13°35'S	172°25'W
Savanna, Il., U.S. (sá-văn´á)	**114-15**	42°05'N	90°08'W
Savannah, Ga., U.S. (sá-văn´á)	**124-25**	32°03'N	81°06'W
Savannah, Mo., U.S. (sá-văn´á)	**120-21**	39°56'N	94°50'W
Savannah, Tn., U.S. (sá-văn´á)	**124-25**	35°14'N	88°14'W
Savannah, stm., U.S. (sá-văn´á)	**110-11**	32°01'N	80°53'W
Savannakhét, Laos	**246-47**	16°34'N	104°45'E
Savanna-la-Mar, Jam. (sá-vän´á lá mär´)	**142-43**	18°14'N	78°08'W
Savè, Benin	**260a**	8°01'N	2°25'E
Save, stm., Afr. (sä´vě)	**264-65**	20°58'S	35°04'E
Sāveh, Iran	**232-33**	35°01'N	50°21'E
Saverne, Fr. (sá-věrn´)	**196-97**	48°45'N	7°22'E
Savo Island, i., Sol. Is.	**279e**	9°08'S	159°49'E
Savona, Italy (sä-nō´nä)	**200-01**	44°19'N	8°28'E
Savonlinna, Fin. (sä´vôn-lěn´nà)	**192-93**	61°52'N	28°54'E
Savran', Ukr. (säv-rän´)	**202-03**	48°08'N	30°06'E
Savu Sea, s., Indon. (sä-vōō sē)	**248-49**	9°40'S	122°00'E
Sawahlunto, Indon.	**246-47**	0°40'S	100°46'E
Sawāi Mādhopur, India	**234-35**	25°59'N	76°22'E
Sawākin, Sudan	**266**	19°06'N	37°20'E
Sawdā', Jabal, mtn., Sau. Ar.	**266**	18°18'N	42°22'E
Sawdā', Qurnat as-, mtn., Leb.	**228-29**	34°18'N	36°07'E
Sawu, Laut, s., Indon. see Savu Sea	**248-49**	9°40'S	122°00'E
Sawu, Pulau, i., Indon.	**248-49**	10°30'S	121°54'E
Saxony, hist. reg., Ger.	**194-95**	52°45'N	9°30'E
Sayan Mountains, mts., Asia (sŭ-hän´ moun´tĭnz)	**218-19**	53°32'N	94°50'E
Sayanogorsk, Russia	**218-19**	53°06'N	91°24'E
Sayany, mts., Asia see Sayan Mountains	**218-19**	53°32'N	94°50'E
Şaydā, Leb. see Sidon	**228-29**	33°34'N	35°23'E
Saylac, Som.	**266**	11°20'N	43°28'E
Saynshand, Mong. see Buyant-Uhaa	**240-41**	44°55'N	110°09'E
Sayre, Ok., U.S. (sā´ēr)	**120-21**	35°18'N	99°38'W
Sayre, Pa., U.S. (sā´ēr)	**116-17**	41°59'N	76°31'W
Sayula, Mex. (sä-yōō´lä)	**146-47**	19°53'N	103°36'W
Saywūn, Yemen	**220-21**	15°56'N	48°45'E
Scandinavia, reg., Eur.	**184-85**	62°30'N	15°00'E
Scappoose, Or., U.S. (skă-pōōs´)	**112-13**	45°45'N	122°52'W
Scarborough, Trin.	**143b**	11°11'N	60°44'W
Scarborough, Eng., U.K. (skär´bŭr-ô)	**190-91**	54°17'N	0°25'W
Schässburg, Rom. see Sighişoara	**194-95**	46°14'N	24°48'E
Schefferville, Qc., Can.	**128-29**	54°48'N	66°50'W
Schenectady, N.Y., U.S. (skě-něk´tá-dê)	**116-17**	42°48'N	73°56'W
Schiermonnikoog, i., Neth.	**190-91**	53°29'N	6°11'E
Schio, Italy (skē´ô)	**200-01**	45°43'N	11°21'E
Schleswig, Ger. (shěls´věgh)	**194-95**	54°32'N	9°33'E
Schneidemühl, Pol. see Piła	**194-95**	53°09'N	16°44'E
Schofield, Wi., U.S. (skō´fēld)	**116-17**	44°53'N	89°36'W
Schreiber, On., Can.	**136-37**	48°48'N	87°15'W
Schuyler, Ne., U.S. (slī´ler)	**114-15**	41°27'N	97°04'W
Schuylkill Haven, Pa., U.S. (skōōl´kĭl hā-věn)	**116-17**	40°38'N	76°10'W
Schwabach, Ger. (shvä´bäk)	**194-95**	49°20'N	11°02'E
Schwäbisch Hall, Ger. (shvă´běsh häl)	**194-95**	49°07'N	9°45'E
Schwaner, Pegunungan, mts., Indon. (skvän´ēr)	**248-49**	0°40'S	112°40'E

Feature (Pronunciation)	Page	Lat.	Long.
Schwarzwald, mts., Ger. (shvärts'väld)	194-95	48°21'N	8°11'E
Schwechat, Aus. (shvĕk'ät)	194-95	48°08'N	16°29'E
Schwedt, Ger. (shvĕt)	194-95	53°04'N	14°17'E
Schweinfurt, Ger. (shvīn'fòrt)	194-95	50°03'N	10°13'E
Schweiz, nation, Eur. *see* Switzerland	174-75	47°0'N	8°00'E
Schwerin, Ger. (shvĕ-rēn')	194-95	53°38'N	11°25'E
Sciacca, Italy (shê-äk'kä)	200-01	37°31'N	13°03'E
Scilly, Isles of, is., Eng., U.K. (īls ŏv sĭl'ê)	190-91	49°55'N	6°20'W
Scobey, Mt., U.S. (skō'bê)	112-13	48°48'N	105°25'W
Scotland, state, U.K. (skŏt'lănd)	190-91	57°0'N	4°00'W
Scotland Neck, N.C., U.S. (skŏt'lănd nĕk)	124-25	36°07'N	77°25'W
Scotstown, Qc., Can. (skŏts'toun)	138-39	45°31'N	71°16'W
Scott, Cape, c., B.C., Can. (kāp skŏt)	132-33	50°47'N	128°25'W
Scott City, Ks., U.S. (skŏt sĭ'tê)	120-21	38°29'N	100°54'W
Scottsbluff, Ne., U.S. (skŏts'blŭf)	114-15	41°52'N	103°40'W
Scottsboro, Al., U.S. (skŏts'bŭro)	124-25	34°41'N	86°01'W
Scottsburg, In., U.S. (skŏts'bûrg)	116-17	38°41'N	85°46'W
Scottsdale, Austl. (skŏts'dāl)	276	41°10'S	147°31'E
Scottsdale, Az., U.S.	118-19	33°35'N	111°52'W
Scottsville, Ky., U.S. (skŏts'vĭl)	124-25	36°45'N	86°11'W
Scottville, Mi., U.S. (skŏt'vĭl)	116-17	43°57'N	86°17'W
Scranton, Pa., U.S.	116-17	41°26'N	75°39'W
Scugog, Lake, lk., On., Can. (lāk skū'gôg)	136-37	44°10'N	78°50'W
Scunthorpe, Eng., U.K. (skŭn'thôrp)	190-91	53°36'N	0°40'W
Scutari, Alb. *see* Shkodër	200-01	42°04'N	19°31'E
Seaford, De., U.S. (sē'fērd)	116-17	38°39'N	75°37'W
Sea Islands, is., U.S. (sē ī'lăndz)	124-25	31°20'N	81°20'W
Seal Cays, is., T./C. Is. (sēl kēs)	142-43	21°10'N	71°38'W
Sealy, Tx., U.S. (sē'lê)	122-23	29°47'N	96°09'W
Searcy, Ar., U.S. (sûr'sê)	124-25	35°15'N	91°45'W
Seaside, Or., U.S. (sē'sīd)	112-13	45°59'N	123°55'W
Seattle, Wa., U.S. (sē-ăt''l)	112-13	47°36'N	122°20'W
Sébaco, Nic. (sĕ-bä'kô)	149	12°51'N	86°06'W
Sebastián Vizcaíno, Bahía, b., Mex.	144-45	28°0'N	114°30'W
Sebatik, Pulau, i., Asia	248-49	4°10'N	117°45'E
Sebewaing, Mi., U.S. (sē'bê-wăng)	116-17	43°44'N	83°26'W
Sebree, Ky., U.S. (sê-brē')	116-17	37°37'N	87°32'W
Sebring, Fl., U.S. (sē'brĭng)	125a	27°30'N	81°26'W
Sebuku, Pulau, i., Indon.	248-49	3°30'S	116°22'E
Sechura, Bahía de, b., Peru	170	5°39'S	81°01'W
Seda, China	238-39	32°20'N	100°41'E
Sedalia, Mo., U.S.	120-21	38°42'N	93°14'W
Sedan, Fr. (sē-däN)	196-97	49°42'N	4°56'E
Sedro-Woolley, Wa., U.S. (sē'drô-wŏŏl'ê)	112-13	48°30'N	122°14'W
Segama, stm., Malay.	248-49	5°31'N	118°48'E
Segamat, Malay. (sā'gá-mát)	246-47	2°30'N	102°49'E
Segesvár, Rom. *see* Sighişoara	194-95	46°14'N	24°48'E
Segezha, Russia	186-87	63°44'N	34°18'E
Ségou, Mali (sā-gōō')	258-59	13°26'N	6°16'W
Segovia, Spain (så-gō'vê-ä)	198-99	40°57'N	4°07'W
Segre, stm., Eur. (så'grā)	198-99	41°22'N	0°18'E
Seguin, Tx., U.S. (sĕ-gēn')	122-23	29°34'N	97°58'W
Segura, stm., Spain (sĕ-gū'lá)	198-99	38°07'N	0°39'W
Segura, Sierra de, mts., Spain (sē-ĕ'r-rä-dĕ sē-gū'lä)	198-99	38°0'N	2°43'W
Seiland, i., Nor.	184-85	70°25'N	23°15'E
Seinäjoki, Fin. (så'ê-nĕ-yô'kê)	184-85	62°47'N	22°51'E
Seine, stm., On., Can. (sån)	134-35	48°38'N	92°58'W
Seine, stm., Fr.	196-97	49°29'N	0°29'E
Seishin, Kor., N. *see* Ch'ŏngjin	243	41°47'N	129°48'E
Seixas, Ponta do, c., Braz.	163d	7°09'S	34°47'W
Şeki, Azer.	227	41°10'N	47°10'E
Sekondi, Ghana	260-61	4°59'N	1°43'W
Selaru, Pulau, i., Indon.	224-25	8°10'S	130°59'E
Selatan, Tanjung, c., Indon. (tän'jông så-lä'tän)	248-49	4°10'S	114°38'E
Selawik, Ak., U.S. (sē-lá-wĭk)	126	66°40'N	160°07'W
Selawik Lake, lk., Ak., U.S.	126	66°30'N	160°40'W
Selayar, Pulau, i., Indon.	248-49	6°05'S	120°30'E
Selemdzha, stm., Russia (så-lĕmt-zhä')	218-19	51°44'N	128°53'E
Selenga, stm., Asia (sĕ-lĕŋ-gä') *see* Selenge	240-41	52°17'N	106°16'E
Selenge, stm., Asia	240-41	52°17'N	106°16'E
Selennyakh, stm., Russia (sĕl-yĭn-yäk)	218-19	67°51'N	144°53'E
Sélestat, Fr. (sē-lĕ-stä')	196-97	48°15'N	7°27'E
Seliger, Ozero, lk., Russia (ô'zĕ-rô sĕl'lê-gĕr)	202-03	57°13'N	33°03'E
Selizharovo, Russia (så'lê-zhä'rô-vô)	202-03	56°51'N	33°28'E
Selkirk, Mb., Can. (sĕl'kûrk)	134-35	50°09'N	96°52'W
Selma, Al., U.S. (sĕl'mȧ)	124-25	32°24'N	87°01'W
Selma, Ca., U.S. (sĕl'mȧ)	118-19	36°35'N	119°37'W
Selma, N.C., U.S. (sĕl'mȧ)	124-25	35°32'N	78°17'W
Selva, Arg.	173	29°46'S	62°03'W
Selvas, reg., Braz.	166-67	5°0'S	68°00'W
Selwyn Lake, lk., Can. (sĕl'wĭn lāk)	130-31	59°55'N	104°22'W
Selwyn Mountains, mts., Can. (sĕl'wĭn moun'tĭnz)	130-31	63°10'N	130°20'W
Selwyn Range, mts., Austl.	277	21°35'S	140°35'E
Semara, W. Sah.	258-59	26°44'N	11°41'W
Semarang, Indon. (sĕ-mä'räng)	248-49	6°58'S	110°25'E
Semënov, Russia	186-87	56°47'N	44°29'E
Semeru, Gunung, vol., Indon.	248-49	8°06'S	112°55'E
Semey, Kaz.	226	50°24'N	80°14'E
Seminole, Ok., U.S. (sĕm'ĭ-nōl)	120-21	35°13'N	96°40'W
Seminole, Tx., U.S. (sĕm'ĭ-nōl)	120-21	32°43'N	102°39'W
Seminole, Lake, res., U.S. (lāk sĕm'ĭ-nōl)	124-25	30°46'N	84°50'W
Semliki, stm., Afr. (sĕm'lê-kē)	267	1°12'N	30°31'E
Semnān, Iran	232-33	35°34'N	53°24'E
Semporna, Malay.	248-49	4°28'N	118°36'E
Senador Pompeu, Braz. (sĕ-nä-dōr-pôm-pĕ'ŏ)	166-67	5°35'S	39°22'W
Sena Madureira, Braz.	166-67	9°04'S	68°40'W
Senatobia, Ms., U.S. (sĕ-nȧ-tō'bê-ȧ)	124-25	34°38'N	89°58'W
Sendai, Japan (sĕn-dī')	245	31°49'N	130°19'E
Sendai, Japan	245	38°15'N	140°53'E
Seneca, Ks., U.S. (sĕn'ĕ-kȧ)	120-21	39°50'N	96°04'W
Seneca, S.C., U.S. (sĕn'ĕ-kȧ)	124-25	34°41'N	82°57'W
Seneca Falls, N.Y., U.S. (sĕn'ĕ-kȧ fôlz)	116-17	42°54'N	76°48'W
Senegal, nation, Afr. (sĕn-ĕ-gôl')	253	14°0'N	14°00'W
Sénégal, stm., Afr.	258-59	15°48'N	16°32'W
Senekal, S. Afr. (sĕn'ê-kȧl)	269c	28°19'S	27°38'E
Senftenberg, Ger. (zĕnf'tĕn-bĕrgh)	194-95	51°32'N	14°00'E
Senhor do Bonfim, Braz. (sĕn-yôr dô bôN-fē'N)	166-67	10°27'S	40°11'W
Senigallia, Italy (så-nê-gäl'lyä)	200-01	43°43'N	13°13'E
Senj, Cro. (sĕn')	200-01	44°59'N	14°55'E
Senja, i., Nor. (sĕnyä)	184-85	69°20'N	17°30'E
Senneterre, Qc., Can.	136-37	48°23'N	77°14'W
Senqu, stm., Afr. *see* Orange	264-65	28°35'S	16°28'E
Sens, Fr. (säNs)	196-97	48°12'N	3°17'E
Senta, Serb. (sĕn'tä)	200-01	45°56'N	20°06'E
Senyavin Islands, is., Micron.	280-81	6°54'N	158°04'E
Seoni, India	234-35	22°05'N	79°33'E
Seoul, nat. cap., Kor., S. (sōl)	243	37°33'N	127°01'E
Sepanjang, Pulau, i., Indon.	248-49	7°11'S	115°50'E
Sepetiba, Baía de, b., Braz. (bäē'ä dĕ så-pâ-tē'bȧ)	172	23°0'S	43°48'W
Sepik, stm., (sĕp-ēk')	277	3°53'S	144°28'E
Sept-Îles, Qc., Can. (sĕ-tēl')	138-39	50°12'N	66°22'W
Sequoia National Park, n.p., Ca., U.S. (sê-kwoi'ȧ năsh'ŭn-ăl pärk)	118-19	36°31'N	118°34'W
Serafimovich, Russia	186-87	49°35'N	42°45'E
Seram, i., Indon. *see* Ceram	224-25	3°0'S	129°00'E
Seram, Laut, s., Indon. *see* Ceram Sea	224-25	2°30'S	128°00'E
Serang, Indon. (så-räng')	248-49	6°07'S	106°09'E
Serayevo, nat. cap., Bos. *see* Sarajevo	200-01	43°52'N	18°25'E
Serbia, nation, Eur. (sĕr'bê-ä)	174-75	44°0'N	21°00'E
Serdobsk, Russia (sĕr-dôpsk')	186-87	52°27'N	44°13'E
Seremban, Malay. (sĕr-ĕm-bän')	246-47	2°43'N	101°57'E
Serengeti National Park, n.p., Tan.	267	2°20'S	34°50'E
Serengeti Plain, pl., Tan.	267	2°50'S	35°00'E
Sergeyevka, Russia	244	43°20'N	133°21'E
Sergipe, state, Braz. (sĕr-zhē'pĕ)	166-67	10°30'S	37°30'W
Sergiyev Posad, Russia	202-03	56°19'N	38°09'E
Serian, Malay.	248-49	1°10'N	110°33'E
Sérifos, i., Grc.	200-01	37°10'N	24°29'E
Sermata, Pulau, i., Indon.	248-49	8°13'S	128°55'E
Serov, Russia (syĕ-rôf')	218-19	59°36'N	60°35'E
Serowe, Bots. (sĕ-rō'wĕ)	264-65	22°23'S	26°43'E
Serpukhov, Russia (syĕr'pò-kôf)	202-03	54°55'N	37°26'E
Serra do Navio, Braz.	166-67	0°55'N	52°01'W
Serra Talhada, Braz.	166-67	7°59'S	38°18'W
Sérres, Grc. (sĕr'rĕ) (sĕr'ĕs)	200-01	41°05'N	23°33'E
Serrinha, Braz. (sĕr-rēn'yȧ)	166-67	11°39'S	38°60'W
Sertã, Port. (sĕr'tȧ)	198-99	39°48'N	8°06'W
Sertânia, Braz. (sĕr-tȧ'nyä)	163d	8°05'S	37°16'W
Serutu, Pulau, i., Indon.	246-47	1°42'S	108°45'E
Sêrxü, China	238-39	33°08'N	97°55'E
Sesayap Lama, Indon.	248-49	3°35'N	116°60'E
Sese Islands, is., Ug.	267	0°20'S	32°20'E
Sesimbra, Port. (sĕ-sē'm-brä)	198-99	38°26'N	9°05'W
Sestri Levante, Italy (sĕs'trê lå-vän'tå)	200-01	44°16'N	9°24'E
Sestroretsk, Russia (sĕs-trô-rĕtsk)	192-93	60°06'N	29°58'E
Sète, Fr. (sĕt)	196-97	43°25'N	3°42'E
Sete Lagoas, Braz. (sĕ-tĕ lä-gô'äs)	172	19°28'S	44°15'W
Sétif, Alg.	269b	36°11'N	5°25'E
Seto-naikai, s., Japan (sĕ'tô nī'kī)	245	34°22'N	133°37'E
Settat, Mor. (sĕt-ät') (sē-tá')	269a	32°59'N	7°36'W
Settlers, S. Afr. (sĕt'lērs)	269c	25°01'S	28°28'E
Setúbal, Port. (så-tōō'bäl)	198-99	38°31'N	8°53'W
Setúbal, Baía de, b., Port. (bä-ē'ä-dĕ-så-tōō'bäl)	198-99	38°18'N	9°04'W
Seul, Lac, lk., On., Can. (läk sûl)	134-35	50°36'N	91°49'W
Sevana Lich, lk., Arm. (syĭ-vän')	227	40°18'N	45°19'E
Sevastopol', Ukr. (syĕ-väs-tô'pôl'')	202-03	44°36'N	33°32'E
Severn, stm., On., Can. (sĕv'ērn)	134-35	55°59'N	87°36'W
Severna Park, Md., U.S. (sĕv'ērn-á pärk)	116-17	39°04'N	76°33'W
Severnaya Dvina, stm., Russia	186-87	64°40'N	39°51'E
Severnaya Osetiya-Alaniya, state, Russia *see* North Ossetia	227	43°0'N	44°15'E
Severnaya Sos'va, stm., Russia	218-19	64°10'N	65°27'E
Severnaya Zemlya, is., Russia (sĕ-vyĭr-nīū zĭ-m'lyä')	218-19	79°30'N	98°00'E
Severnyye Uvaly, hills, Russia	186-87	59°28'N	48°13'E
Severodvinsk, Russia	186-87	64°34'N	39°50'E
Severo-Kuril'sk, Russia	218-19	50°42'N	156°07'E
Severomorsk, Russia	184-85	69°04'N	33°28'E
Severo-Sibirskaya Nizmennost', pl., Russia	218-19	73°0'N	100°00'E
Severouralsk, Russia (sĕ-vyĭ-rŭ-ōō-rälsk')	186-87	60°10'N	59°58'E
Severskiy Donets, stm., Eur. *see* Northern Donets	186-87	47°36'N	40°54'E
Sevier, stm., Ut., U.S. (sê-vēr')	118-19	39°02'N	113°06'W
Sevier Lake, lk., Ut., U.S. (sê-vēr' lāk)	118-19	38°56'N	113°09'W
Sevilla, Col. (sĕ-vê'l-yä)	163c	4°15'N	75°56'W
Sevilla, Spain (så-vēl'yä)	198-99	37°23'N	5°59'W
Seville, Spain *see* Sevilla	198-99	37°23'N	5°59'W
Sevsk, Russia (syĕfsk)	202-03	52°09'N	34°31'E
Seward, Ak., U.S. (sū'ård)	126	60°07'N	149°27'W
Seward, Ne., U.S. (sū'ård)	114-15	40°54'N	97°06'W
Seward Peninsula, pen., Ak., U.S. (sū'ård pĕ-nĭn'sūlȧ)	126	65°0'N	164°00'W
Sewell, Chile (sĕ'ò-ĕl)	163e	34°05'S	70°23'W
Seyðisfjörður, Ice. (sā'dês-fyûr-dòr)	190a	65°15'N	14°01'W
Seybaplaya, Mex. (sā-ê-bä-plä'yä)	148	19°40'N	90°40'W
Seychelles, nation, Afr. (sā-shĕl')	253	4°35'S	55°40'E
Seymchan, Russia	218-19	62°54'N	152°24'E
Seymour, In., U.S. (sē'mōr)	116-17	38°58'N	85°53'W
Seymour, Tx., U.S. (sē'mōr)	120-21	33°36'N	99°16'W
Sfax, Tun. (sfäks)	184-85	34°45'N	10°46'E
's-Gravenhage, nat. cap., Neth. ('s KRä'vĕn-hä'Kĕ) (hāg) *see* Hague, The	190-91	52°06'N	4°18'E
Sha, stm., China (shä)	238-39	33°37'N	114°38'E
Shabeelle, stm., Afr. (shä'bå-lē)	262-63	0°10'N	42°46'E
Shabunda, D.R.C.	262-63	2°42'S	27°21'E
Shache, China (shä-chŭ)	226	38°25'N	77°15'E
Shagonar, Russia	222-23	51°32'N	92°49'E
Shahdol, India	234-35	23°18'N	81°22'E
Shāhjahānpur, India (shä-jŭ-hän'pōōr)	234-35	27°53'N	79°54'E
Shahrisabz, Uzb.	232-33	39°03'N	66°50'E
Shāhrūd, Iran	232-33	36°25'N	54°58'E
Shaker Heights, Oh., U.S. (shā'kēr hīts)	116-17	41°29'N	81°36'W
Shakhty, Russia (shäk'tê)	186-87	47°42'N	40°13'E
Shakhunya, Russia	186-87	57°40'N	46°38'E
Shaki, Nig.	260-61	8°40'N	3°24'E
Shaktoolik, Ak., U.S.	126	64°20'N	161°09'W
Shala Hāyk', lk., Eth. (shä'lȧ)	269d	7°28'N	38°31'E
Shalqar, Kaz.	226	47°50'N	59°37'E
Shām, Bādiyat ash-, des., Asia *see* Syrian Desert	228-29	32°0'N	40°00'E
Shām, Jabal ash-, mtn., Oman	230-31	23°13'N	57°16'E
Shamokin, Pa., U.S. (shȧ-mō'kĭn)	116-17	40°47'N	76°35'W
Shamrock, Tx., U.S. (shăm'rŏk)	120-21	35°13'N	100°15'W
Shandī, Sudan	266	16°41'N	33°26'E
Shandong, state, China (shän-dôŋ)	240-41	36°0'N	118°00'E
Shandong Bandao, pen., China (shän-dôŋ bän-dou)	240-41	37°0'N	121°00'E
Shand uul, mtn., Mong.	240-41	43°28'N	104°03'E
Shangani, stm., Zimb.	264-65	18°31'S	27°12'E
Shangcheng, China (shäŋ-chŭŋ)	238-39	31°48'N	115°24'E
Shangdu, China (shäŋ-dōō)	240-41	41°34'N	113°31'E
Shanghai, China (shäng'hī')	238-39	31°14'N	121°28'E
Shanghai, state, China	238-39	31°10'N	121°30'E
Shanglin, China (shäŋ-lĭn)	238-39	23°30'N	108°32'E
Shangqiu, China (shäŋ-chyō)	238-39	34°27'N	115°39'E
Shangrao, China (shäŋ-rou)	238-39	28°26'N	117°58'E
Shangshui, China	238-39	33°33'N	114°34'E

n-sing; ŋ-baŋk; N-nasalized n; nŏd; cŏmmit; ōld; ôbey; ôrder; oi-boil; fōōd; ò-as oo in foot; ou-out; s-soft; sh-dish; th-thin; pūre; ûnite; ûrn; stŭd; circŭs; ü-as in French tu; '-indeterminate vowel.

Feature (Pronunciation)	Page	Lat.	Long.
Shangxian, China	238-39	33°52′N	109°56′E
Shangzhi, China (shäŋ-jr)	244	45°13′N	127°59′E
Shanhaiguan, China	240-41	40°01′N	119°45′E
Shannon, stm., Ire. (shăn′ŏn)	190-91	52°35′N	9°41′W
Shansi, state, China *see* Shanxi	240-41	37°0′N	112°00′E
Shantarskiye Ostrova, is., Russia (shän′tär-skyĕ ôs-trôf′)	218-19	54°54′N	137°33′E
Shantou, China (shän-tō)	238-39	23°21′N	116°40′E
Shantung, state, China *see* Shandong	240-41	36°0′N	118°00′E
Shantung Peninsula, pen., China *see* Shandong Bandao	240-41	37°0′N	121°00′E
Shanxi, state, China (shän-shyē)	240-41	37°0′N	112°00′E
Shanxian, China (shän shyĕn)	238-39	34°48′N	116°05′E
Shanyin, China	240-41	39°31′N	112°50′E
Shaoguan, China (shou-gŭän)	238-39	24°49′N	113°36′E
Shaowu, China	238-39	27°19′N	117°30′E
Shaoxing, China (shou-shyĭŋ)	238-39	29°59′N	120°34′E
Shaoyang, China	238-39	27°15′N	111°28′E
Shar, Kaz.	226	49°35′N	81°03′E
Sharjah, U.A.E.	230-31	25°22′N	55°24′E
Shark Bay, b., Austl. (shärk bā)	272-73	25°30′S	113°30′E
Sharktooth Mountain, mtn., B.C., Can.	130-31	58°35′N	127°57′W
Sharon, Pa., U.S. (shăr′ŏn)	116-17	41°13′N	80°30′W
Sharon Springs, Ks., U.S. (shăr′ŏn sprĭngz)	120-21	38°54′N	101°45′W
Sharonville, Oh., U.S. (shăr′ŏn vĭl)	116-17	39°16′N	84°25′W
Sharpsburg, Md., U.S. (shärps′bûrg)	116-17	39°27′N	77°45′W
Sharqīyah, Aṣ-Ṣaḥrā' ash-, des., Egypt *see* Arabian Desert	266	28°0′N	32°00′E
Sharya, Russia	186-87	58°22′N	45°31′E
Shashe, stm., Afr.	264-65	22°11′S	29°21′E
Shashi, China (shä-shē)	238-39	30°19′N	112°14′E
Shasta, Mount, vol., Ca., U.S. (mount shăs′tȧ)	112-13	41°25′N	122°13′W
Shasta Lake, res., Ca., U.S. (shăs′tȧ lāk)	112-13	40°46′N	122°22′W
Shatt al-Arab, stm., Asia *see* 'Arab, Shaṭṭ al-	228-29	29°57′N	48°33′E
Shattuck, Ok., U.S. (shăt′ŭk)	120-21	36°17′N	99°53′W
Shatura, Russia	202-03	55°34′N	39°32′E
Shaunavon, Sk., Can.	134-35	49°39′N	108°24′W
Shaw, Ms., U.S. (shô)	124-25	33°37′N	90°46′W
Shawano, Wi., U.S. (shȧ-wô′nô)	116-17	44°46′N	88°36′W
Shawinigan, Qc., Can.	136-37	46°33′N	72°45′W
Shawnee, Ks., U.S. (shô-nē′)	120-21	39°01′N	94°44′W
Shawnee, Ok., U.S. (shô-nē′)	120-21	35°20′N	96°55′W
Shawneetown, Il., U.S. (shô′nē-toun)	116-17	37°42′N	88°11′W
Shaybārā, i., Sau. Ar.	266	25°26′N	36°50′E
Shay Gap, Austl.	270-71	20°30′S	120°05′E
Shaykh, Jabal ash-, mtn., Asia *see* Hermon, Mount	228-29	33°25′N	35°51′E
Shchekino, Russia	202-03	54°01′N	37°31′E
Shchelkovo, Russia (shchĕl′kô-vô)	202-03	55°54′N	38°01′E
Shchigry, Russia (shchē′grē)	202-03	51°52′N	36°55′E
Shchors, Ukr. (shchôrs)	202-03	51°49′N	31°57′E
Shchūchīnsk, Kaz.	226	52°56′N	70°11′E
Sheberghān, Afg.	232-33	36°40′N	65°45′E
Sheboygan, Wi., U.S. (shē-boi′găn)	116-17	43°45′N	87°43′W
Sheboygan Falls, Wi., U.S. (shē-boi′găn fôlz)	116-17	43°44′N	87°48′W
Shediac, N.B., Can. (shĕ′dē-ăk)	138-39	46°12′N	64°34′W
Shedin Peak, mtn., B.C., Can. (shĕd′ĭn pēk)	132-33	55°55′N	127°32′W
Sheenjek, stm., Ak., U.S.	126	66°45′N	144°34′W
Sheffield, Eng., U.K.	190-91	53°23′N	1°28′W
Sheffield, Al., U.S. (shĕf′fēld)	124-25	34°45′N	87°42′W
Shekhūpura, Pak.	232-33	31°42′N	73°59′E
Sheki, Azer. *see* Şeki	227	41°10′N	47°10′E
Shelagyote Peak, mtn., B.C., Can.	132-33	55°58′N	127°12′W
Shelbina, Mo., U.S. (shĕl-bī′nȧ)	120-21	39°41′N	92°03′W
Shelburn, In., U.S. (shĕl′bŭrn)	116-17	39°11′N	87°24′W
Shelburne, N.S., Can.	138-39	43°46′N	65°19′W
Shelby, Mi., U.S. (shĕl′bē)	116-17	43°37′N	86°22′W
Shelby, Ms., U.S. (shĕl′bē)	124-25	33°57′N	90°46′W
Shelby, Mt., U.S. (shĕl′bē)	112-13	48°30′N	111°51′W
Shelby, N.C., U.S. (shĕl′bē)	124-25	35°18′N	81°32′W
Shelby, Oh., U.S. (shĕl′bē)	116-17	40°53′N	82°39′W
Shelbyville, Il., U.S. (shĕl′bē-vĭl)	116-17	39°24′N	88°48′W
Shelbyville, In., U.S. (shĕl′bē-vĭl)	116-17	39°31′N	85°46′W
Shelbyville, Ky., U.S. (shĕl′bē-vĭl)	116-17	38°13′N	85°13′W
Shelbyville, Tn., U.S. (shĕl′bē-vĭl)	124-25	35°29′N	86°27′W
Shelbyville, Lake, res., Il., U.S. (lāk shĕl′bē-vĭl)	116-17	39°30′N	88°43′W
Sheldon, Ia., U.S. (shĕl′dŭn)	114-15	43°11′N	95°51′W
Shelikhova, Zaliv, b., Russia	218-19	60°0′N	158°00′E
Shelikof Strait, strt., Ak., U.S. (shĕ′lē-kôf strāt)	126	57°18′N	155°41′W
Shellbrook, Sk., Can.	134-35	53°14′N	106°23′W
Shelley, Id., U.S. (shĕl′lē)	112-13	43°23′N	112°07′W
Shelton, Ct., U.S. (shĕl′tŭn)	116-17	41°19′N	73°05′W
Shelton, Wa., U.S. (shĕl′tŭn)	112-13	47°12′N	123°06′W
Shemonaīkha, Kaz.	226	50°39′N	81°54′E
Shenandoah, Ia., U.S. (shĕn-ăn-dō′ȧ)	114-15	40°46′N	95°23′W
Shenandoah, Pa., U.S. (shĕn-ăn-dō′ȧ)	116-17	40°49′N	76°12′W
Shenandoah, Va., U.S. (shĕn-ăn-dō′ȧ)	116-17	38°29′N	78°37′W
Shenandoah National Park, n.p., Va., U.S. (shĕn-ăn-dō′ȧ năsh′ŭn-ăl pärk)	116-17	38°34′N	78°20′W
Sheng-li Feng, mtn., Asia *see* Jengish Chokusu	226	42°02′N	80°05′E
Shenkursk, Russia (shĕn-kōōrsk′)	186-87	62°07′N	42°53′E
Shenxian, China (shŭn shyĕn)	240-41	38°01′N	115°33′E
Shenyang, China (shŭn-yäŋ)	243	41°48′N	123°24′E
Shenzhen, China	238-39	22°34′N	114°07′E
Shepetivka, Ukr.	194-95	50°11′N	27°04′E
Shepparton, Austl. (shĕp′âr-tŭn)	276	36°23′S	145°25′E
Sherbro Island, i., S.L.	260-61	7°34′N	12°43′W
Sherbrooke, Qc., Can.	136-37	45°24′N	71°54′W
Sheridan, Ar., U.S. (shĕr′ĭ-dăn)	120-21	34°18′N	92°24′W
Sheridan, Wy., U.S. (shĕr′ĭ-dăn)	112-13	44°48′N	106°58′W
Sherlovaya Gora, Russia	240-41	50°32′N	116°18′E
Sherman, Tx., U.S. (shĕr′măn)	120-21	33°35′N	96°36′W
Sherridon, Mb., Can.	134-35	55°07′N	101°05′W
Sherwood Park, Ab., Can.	132-33	53°31′N	113°18′W
Shetland Islands, is., Scot., U.K. (shĕt′lănd ī′lăndz)	190c	60°25′N	1°39′W
Shexian, China (shŭ shyĕn)	238-39	29°53′N	118°26′E
Sheyenne, stm., N.D., U.S. (shī-ĕn′)	114-15	47°01′N	96°50′W
Shiashkotan, Ostrov, i., Russia	218-19	48°52′N	154°10′E
Shibām, Yemen (shē′bäm)	220-21	15°54′N	48°40′E
Shidao, China	240-41	36°54′N	122°24′E
Shīeli, Kaz.	226	44°10′N	66°44′E
Shijiazhuang, China (shr-jyä-jûäŋ)	240-41	38°02′N	114°29′E
Shikārpur, Pak.	232-33	27°57′N	68°39′E
Shikoku, i., Japan (shē′kō′kōō)	245	33°45′N	133°30′E
Shikotan, Ostrov, i., Russia	218-19	43°47′N	146°45′E
Shikotan-tō, i., Russia *see* Shikotan, Ostrov	218-19	43°47′N	146°45′E
Shiliguri, India	234-35	26°43′N	88°26′E
Shilka, Russia	222-23	51°52′N	116°02′E
Shilka, stm., Russia (shĭl′kȧ)	222-23	53°21′N	121°27′E
Shillong, India (shĕl-lông′)	234-35	25°34′N	91°53′E
Shimanovsk, Russia	222-23	52°00′N	127°41′E
Shimber Berris, mtn., Som. *see* Shimbiris	262-63	10°44′N	47°15′E
Shimbiris, mtn., Som.	262-63	10°44′N	47°15′E
Shimian, China	238-39	29°16′N	102°17′E
Shimla, India	234-35	31°06′N	77°10′E
Shimoga, India	236	13°56′N	75°35′E
Shimonoseki, Japan	245	33°58′N	130°56′E
Shimono-shima, i., Japan	243	34°12′N	129°15′E
Shinano, stm., Japan (shē-nä′nō)	245	37°57′N	139°04′E
Shīndand, Afg.	232-33	33°18′N	62°08′E
Shingishū, Kor., N. *see* Sinŭiju	243	40°06′N	124°24′E
Shingū, Japan	245	33°43′N	136°00′E
Shinyanga, Tan. (shĭn-yäŋ′gä)	267	3°40′S	33°26′E
Shiono-misaki, c., Japan (shē-ō′nō mē′sä-kē)	245	33°26′N	135°46′E
Shiqizhen, China *see* Zhongshan	238-39	22°31′N	113°22′E
Shirati, Tan. (shē-rä′tē)	267	1°07′S	33°60′E
Shīrāz, Iran (shē-räz′)	230-31	29°36′N	52°32′E
Shire, stm., Afr. (shē′rȧ)	264-65	17°42′S	35°19′E
Shiretoko-misaki, c., Japan	244	44°21′N	145°20′E
Shishaldin Volcano, vol., Ak., U.S. (shī-shăl′dĭn vŏl-kā′nō)	126	54°45′N	163°57′W
Shively, Ky., U.S. (shīv′lē)	116-17	38°12′N	85°49′W
Shivpuri, India	234-35	25°25′N	77°39′E
Shizuoka, Japan (shē′zōō′ōkȧ)	245	34°58′N	138°23′E
Shkodër, Alb. (shkô′dûr) (skōō′tȧrē)	200-01	42°04′N	19°31′E
Shkodra, Alb. *see* Shkodër	200-01	42°04′N	19°31′E
Shmidta, Ostrov, i., Russia	208-09	81°08′N	90°48′E
Shoal Lake, lk., Can. (shōl lāk)	134-35	49°32′N	95°00′W
Shoals, In., U.S. (shōlz)	116-17	38°40′N	86°47′W
Shōdo-shima, i., Japan (shō′dō shē′mä)	245	34°30′N	134°17′E
Shortland Island, i., Sol. Is.	279e	7°04′S	155°43′E
Shoshone, Id., U.S. (shō-shōn′tē)	112-13	42°56′N	114°25′W
Shostka, Ukr. (shôst′kȧ)	202-03	51°52′N	33°29′E
Shouguang, China (shō-gûäŋ)	240-41	36°53′N	118°44′E
Shouxian, China (shō shyĕn)	238-39	32°34′N	116°46′E
Shpola, Ukr. (shpô′lȧ)	202-03	49°00′N	31°24′E
Shqipëria, nation, Eur. *see* Albania	174-75	41°0′N	20°00′E
Shreveport, La., U.S. (shrēv′pôrt)	120-21	32°30′N	93°45′W
Shrewsbury, Eng., U.K. (shrōōz′bēr-ĭ)	190-91	52°43′N	2°45′W
Shū, Kaz.	226	43°36′N	73°45′E
Shū, stm., Asia	226	45°00′N	67°45′E
Shuajingsi, China	238-39	32°00′N	103°17′E
Shuangcheng, China (shûäŋ-chŭŋ)	240-41	45°22′N	126°19′E
Shuangliao, China	240-41	43°30′N	123°30′E
Shuangyashan, China	244	46°35′N	131°19′E
Shubrâ el-Kheima, Egypt	268b	30°06′N	31°15′E
Shumagin Islands, is., Ak., U.S. (shōō′mȧ-gĕn ī′lăndz)	126	55°06′N	159°43′W
Shumen, Blg.	200-01	43°16′N	26°57′E
Shumerlya, Russia	186-87	55°29′N	46°25′E
Shunde, China (shòn-dŭ)	238-39	22°50′N	113°15′E
Shuqayyiqah, Nafūd, sand, Sau. Ar.	266	25°45′N	43°55′E
Shūshtar, Iran (shōōsh′tŭr)	228-29	32°03′N	48°51′E
Shuswap Lake, lk., B.C., Can. (shōōs′wŏp lăk)	132-33	50°57′N	119°15′W
Shuya, Russia (shōō′yȧ)	186-87	56°51′N	41°23′E
Shuyang, China (shōō yäng)	238-39	34°08′N	118°47′E
Shwangliao, China *see* Liaoyuan	240-41	42°55′N	125°08′E
Shwebo, Mya.	246-47	22°34′N	95°42′E
Shymkent, Kaz.	226	42°18′N	69°36′E
Shyok, stm., Asia	232-33	35°14′N	75°55′E
Siālkot, Pak. (sē-äl′kōt)	232-33	32°31′N	74°33′E
Siam, nation, Asia *see* Thailand	206-07	15°0′N	100°00′E
Siam, Gulf of, b., Asia *see* Thailand, Gulf of	246-47	10°0′N	101°00′E
Sian, China *see* Xi'an	238-39	34°15′N	108°52′E
Siargao Island, i., Phil.	250	9°53′N	126°02′E
Siasi Island, i., Phil.	250	5°33′N	120°51′E
Siau, Pulau, i., Indon.	248-49	2°46′N	125°23′E
Šiauliai, Lith. (shē-ou′lē-ī)	192-93	55°56′N	23°20′E
Sibay, Russia (sē′bäy)	226	52°42′N	58°40′E
Šibenik, Cro. (shē-bā′nēk)	200-01	43°44′N	15°54′E
Siberia, reg., Russia (sī-bĭr′ē-ȧ)	218-19	65°0′N	110°00′E
Sibi, Pak.	232-33	29°33′N	67°53′E
Sibir', reg., Russia *see* Siberia	218-19	65°0′N	110°00′E
Sibiryakova, Ostrov, i., Russia	218-19	72°50′N	79°00′E
Sibiti, Congo (sē-bē-tē′)	262-63	3°41′S	13°21′E
Sibiu, Rom. (sē-bĭ-ōō′)	194-95	45°47′N	24°09′E
Sibley, Ia., U.S. (sĭb′lē)	114-15	43°24′N	95°45′W
Sibolga, Indon. (sē-bō′gä)	246-47	1°45′N	98°47′E
Sibsāgar, India (sēb-sŭ′gŭr)	234-35	26°59′N	94°39′E
Sibu, Malay.	248-49	2°18′N	111°50′E
Sibut, C.A.R.	262-63	5°44′N	19°05′E
Sibutu Island, i., Phil.	250	4°46′N	119°29′E
Sibuyan Island, i., Phil. (sē-bōō-yän′ ī′lănd)	250	12°27′N	122°34′E
Sibuyan Sea, s., Phil. (sē-bōō-yän′ sē)	250	12°50′N	122°40′E
Sichuan, state, China (sz-chûän)	238-39	31°0′N	105°00′E
Sicilia, i., Italy *see* Sicily	200-01	37°30′N	14°00′E
Sicily, i., Italy (sĭs′ĭ-lē)	200-01	37°30′N	14°00′E
Sico Tinto, stm., Hond. (sē-kō tēn′tō)	149	15°50′N	85°03′W
Sicuani, Peru	170	14°16′S	71°13′W
Sidhi, India	234-35	24°24′N	81°53′E
Sīdi Barrâni, Egypt	188-89	31°37′N	25°56′E
Sidi Bel Abbès, Alg. (sē′dē-bĕl á-bĕs′)	198-99	35°12′N	0°11′W
Sidi-Bennour, Mor.	269a	32°39′N	8°25′W
Sidikalang, Indon.	246-47	2°44′N	98°20′E
Sidney, B.C., Can. (sĭd′nē)	132-33	48°39′N	123°24′W
Sidney, Mt., U.S. (sĭd′nē)	112-13	47°43′N	104°09′W
Sidney, Ne., U.S. (sĭd′nē)	114-15	41°09′N	102°59′W
Sidney, N.Y., U.S. (sĭd′nē)	116-17	42°19′N	75°23′W
Sidney, Oh., U.S. (sĭd′nē)	116-17	40°17′N	84°10′W
Sidney Lanier, Lake, res., Ga., U.S. (lăk sĭd′nē lăn′yēr)	124-25	34°15′N	83°57′W
Sidon, Leb.	228-29	33°34′N	35°23′E
Sidra, Gulf of, b., Libya (gŭlf ŭv sĭ′drȧ) *see* Surt, Khalīj	258-59	31°30′N	18°00′E
Siedlce, Pol. (syĕd′l-tsĕ)	194-95	52°10′N	22°17′E
Siegburg, Ger. (zēg′bōōrgh)	194-95	50°47′N	7°12′E
Siegen, Ger. (zē′ghĕn)	194-95	50°52′N	8°01′E
Siemiatycze, Pol. (syĕm′yä′tē-chĕ)	194-95	52°26′N	22°52′E
Siĕmréab, Camb.	246-47	13°22′N	103°51′E
Siena, Italy (sē-ĕn′ä)	200-01	43°19′N	11°20′E
Sienyang, China *see* Xianyang	238-39	34°20′N	108°42′E
Sieradz, Pol. (syĕ′rädz)	194-95	51°36′N	18°45′E
Sierpc, Pol. (syĕrpts)	194-95	52°51′N	19°40′E
Sierra Blanca, Tx., U.S. (sē-ĕ′rȧ blaŋ-kä)	122-23	31°11′N	105°21′W
Sierra Blanca Peak, mtn., N.M., U.S. (sē-ĕ′rä blăn′kȧ pēk)	120-21	33°23′N	105°48′W
Sierra Colorada, Arg.	171	40°36′S	67°45′W
Sierra Leone, nation, Afr. (sē-ĕr′rä lā-ō′nā)	253	8°30′N	11°30′W

Feature (Pronunciation)	Page	Lat.	Long.
Sierra Nevada, mts., Ca., U.S. see Nevada, Sierra	118-19	38°0'N	119°15'W
Sífnos, i., Grc.	200-01	36°58'N	24°43'E
Sighişoara, Rom. (sē-gē-shwä'rȧ)	194-95	46°14'N	24°48'E
Sigli, Indon.	246-47	5°23'N	95°57'E
Siglufjördur, Ice.	190a	66°09'N	18°55'W
Sigsig, Ec. (sēg-sēg')	170	3°00's	78°48'W
Siguatepeque, Hond. (sē-gwȧ'tē-pē-kĕ)	149	14°35'N	87°50'W
Sigüenza, Spain (sē-gwĕ'n-zä)	198-99	41°04'N	2°38'W
Siguiri, Gui. (sē-gē-rē')	260-61	11°26'N	9°10'W
Sihala, nation, Asia see Sri Lanka	206-07	7°0'N	81°00'E
Sihanoukville, Camb. see Kâmpóng Saôm	246-47	10°38'N	103°31'E
Sihong, China (sz-hôŋ)	238-39	33°28'N	118°12'E
Siirt, Tur. (sĭ-ērt')	227	37°56'N	41°57'E
Sīkar, India	234-35	27°36'N	75°08'E
Sikasso, Mali (sē-käs'sō)	258-59	11°19'N	5°40'W
Sikeston, Mo., U.S. (sīks'tŭn)	124-25	36°53'N	89°36'W
Sikhote-Alin', mts., Russia (se-kô'ta a-lēn')	218-19	48°0'N	138°00'E
Sikkim, state, India	234-35	27°35'N	88°35'E
Silao, Mex. (sē-lä'ō)	146-47	20°56'N	101°26'W
Silay, Phil.	250	10°48'N	122°59'E
Silchar, India (sĭl-chär')	234-35	24°49'N	92°48'E
Siler City, N.C., U.S. (sī'lēr sĭ'tĭ)	124-25	35°43'N	79°28'W
Silesia, hist. reg., Eur. (sĭ-lē'shȧ)	194-95	50°34'N	18°01'E
Siletitengiz köli, lk., Kaz.	226	53°15'N	73°15'E
Silifke, Tur.	228-29	36°22'N	33°56'E
Siling Co, lk., China	234-35	31°47'N	89°00'E
Silistra, Blg. (sē-lēs'trȧ)	200-01	44°07'N	27°16'E
Siljan, lk., Swe. (sēl'yän)	192-93	60°50'N	14°45'E
Silkeborg, Den. (sĭl'kĕ-bôr')	192-93	56°10'N	9°33'E
Siloam Springs, Ar., U.S. (sĭ-lōm spriṅgz)	120-21	36°11'N	94°33'W
Silsbee, Tx., U.S. (sĭlz' bē)	122-23	30°21'N	94°11'W
Silvânia, Braz. (sēl-vá'nyä)	168-69	16°42's	48°37'W
Silver Bank Passage, strt., N.A. (sĭl'vēr bǎnk pǎs'ĭj)	142-43	20°53'N	70°18'W
Silver Bay, Mn., U.S. (sĭl'vēr bā)	114-15	47°18'N	91°15'W
Silver City, N.M., U.S. (sĭl'vēr sĭ'tē)	118-19	32°47'N	108°17'W
Silver Creek, N.Y., U.S. (sĭl'vēr krēk)	116-17	42°33'N	79°10'W
Silverthrone Mountain, vol., B.C., Can. (sĭl'vēr-thrōn moun'tĭn)	132-33	51°31'N	126°06'W
Silverton, Or., U.S. (sĭl'vēr-tŭn)	112-13	45°01'N	122°47'W
Silves, Port. (sēl'vĕzh)	198-99	37°11'N	8°26'W
Simbo Island, i., Sol. Is.	279e	8°17's	156°31'E
Simcoe, On., Can. (sĭm'kō)	136-37	42°50'N	80°18'W
Simcoe, Lake, lk., On., Can. (lāk sĭm'kō)	136-37	44°28'N	79°19'W
Simeulue, Pulau, i., Indon.	246-47	2°37'N	96°04'E
Simferopol', Ukr.	202-03	44°57'N	34°05'E
Simití, Col.	164-65	7°56'N	73°57'W
Simojovel, Mex. (sē-mō-hō-vĕl')	146-47	17°07'N	92°39'W
Simonette, stm., Ab., Can. (sī-mŏn-ĕt')	132-33	55°09'N	118°16'W
Simonstad, S. Afr. see Simon's Town	264-65	34°15's	18°27'E
Simon's Town, S. Afr.	264-65	34°15's	18°27'E
Simoom Sound, B.C., Can.	132-33	50°46'N	126°26'W
Simplon Pass, p., Switz. (sĭm'plŏn pǎs) (sǎn-plôn' pǎs)	194-95	46°15'N	8°01'E
Simpson Desert, des., Austl. (sĭmp-sŭn dĕs'ērt)	272-73	25°0's	137°00'E
Simpson Desert National Park, n.p., Austl.	276	25°40's	138°15'E
Simpson Island, i., On., Can. (sĭmp-sŭn ī'lǎnd)	136-37	48°47'N	87°41'W
Simrishamn, Swe. (sēm'rēs-häm'n)	192-93	55°33'N	14°21'E
Simushir, Ostrov, i., Russia (ôs-trôf' se-mōō'shēr)	218-19	46°58'N	152°02'E
Sinai, pen., Egypt see Sinai Peninsula	266	29°30'N	34°00'E
Sinaia, Rom. (sĭ-nä'yȧ)	200-01	45°21'N	25°33'E
Sinai Peninsula, pen., Egypt (sī'nī pĕ-nĭn'sūlȧ)	266	29°30'N	34°00'E
Sinaloa, state, Mex. (sē-nä-lō-ä)	144-45	25°0'N	107°30'W
Sinan, China (sz-nän)	238-39	27°56'N	108°14'E
Sīnāwin, Libya	188-89	31°02'N	10°36'E
Sincelejo, Col. (sēn-sā-lā'hō)	164-65	9°18'N	75°24'W
Sindi, Est. (sēn'dē)	192-93	58°24'N	24°41'E
Sine, stm., Sen.	260-61	14°13'N	16°26'W
Sines, Port. (sē'nāzh)	198-99	37°57'N	8°52'W
Singapore, nation, Asia (sĭn'gȧ-pōr')	206-07	1°22'N	103°48'E
Singapore, nat. cap., Sing. (sĭn'gȧ-pōr')	246-47	1°18'N	103°49'E
Singaraja, Indon.	248-49	8°07's	115°06'E
Singida, Tan.	267	4°49's	34°44'E
Singkawang, Indon.	246-47	0°55'N	108°59'E
Singkep, Pulau, i., Indon.	246-47	0°30's	104°25'E
Singleton, Austl.	276	32°34's	151°10'E
Singora, Thai. see Songkhla	246-47	7°12'N	100°36'E
Sinj, Cro. (sēn')	200-01	43°42'N	16°38'E
Sinjah, Sudan	266	13°08'N	33°55'E
Sinjai, Indon.	248-49	5°07's	120°16'E
Sinkāt, Sudan	266	18°50'N	36°50'E
Sinkiang, state, China see Xinjiang	220-21	40°0'N	85°00'E
Sinmi-do, i., Kor., N.	243	39°33'N	124°53'E
Sinnamary, Fr. Gu.	164-65	5°23'N	52°57'W
Sinnûris, Egypt	268b	29°25'N	30°52'E
Sinop, Tur.	186-87	42°02'N	35°09'E
Sintang, Indon.	248-49	0°04'N	111°29'E
Sint Eustatius, i., Neth. Ant.	143b	17°30'N	62°59'W
Sint Maarten, i., N.A.	143b	18°04'N	63°04'W
Sinton, Tx., U.S. (sĭn'tŭn)	122-23	28°02'N	97°30'W
Sinú, stm., Col.	164-65	9°23'N	75°56'W
Sinŭiju, Kor., N. (sĭ'noĭ-jōō)	243	40°06'N	124°24'E
Siocon, Phil.	250	7°42'N	122°08'E
Sion, Switz. (sē'ôn')	194-95	46°14'N	7°21'E
Sioux City, Ia., U.S. (sōō sĭ'tē)	114-15	42°30'N	96°23'W
Sioux Falls, S.D., U.S. (sōō fôlz)	114-15	43°33'N	96°44'W
Sioux Lookout, On., Can.	134-35	50°06'N	91°56'W
Siping, China (sz-pĭŋ)	240-41	43°10'N	124°23'E
Sipiwesk Lake, lk., Mb., Can.	134-35	55°05'N	97°35'W
Sipsey, stm., Al., U.S. (sĭp'sē)	124-25	33°0'N	88°10'W
Siquia, stm., Nic. (sē-kē'ä)	149	12°11'N	84°17'W
Siquijor Island, i., Phil.	250	9°11'N	123°34'E
Siracusa, Italy (sē-rä-koo'sä)	200-01	37°04'N	15°17'E
Sirājganj, Bngl. (sĭ-räj'gŭnj)	234-35	24°27'N	89°42'E
Şir Banī Yās, i., U.A.E.	230-31	24°19'N	52°37'E
Sirdaryo, Uzb.	232-33	40°53'N	68°40'E
Sirdaryo, stm., Asia see Syr Darya	226	46°04'N	60°04'E
Sir Douglas, Mount, mtn., Can. (mount sûr dŭg'lǎs)	132-33	50°44'N	115°20'W
Sirḥān, Wādī as-, val., Sau. Ar.	228-29	30°58'N	37°41'E
Sir James MacBrien, Mount, mtn., N.T., Can.	130-31	62°07'N	127°41'W
Sirohi, India	234-35	24°53'N	72°51'E
Sirrah, Nafūd as-, sand, Sau. Ar.	266	23°01'N	44°34'E
Sir Sandford, Mount, mtn., B.C., Can. (mount sûr sǎnd'fērd)	132-33	51°40'N	117°52'W
Sirte, Gulf of, b., Libya see Surt, Khalīj	258-59	31°30'N	18°00'E
Širvintos, Lith. (shēr'vĭn-tōs)	192-93	55°03'N	24°57'E
Sir Wilfrid Laurier, Mount, mtn., B.C., Can. (mount sûr wĭl'frĭd lôr'yēr)	132-33	52°47'N	119°45'W
Sisaba, mtn., Tan.	267	6°09's	29°48'E
Sisak, Cro. (sē'sák)	200-01	45°29'N	16°23'E
Si Sa Ket, Thai.	246-47	15°08'N	104°20'E
Sishui, China (sz-shwā)	240-41	35°39'N	117°16'E
Sisseton, S.D., U.S. (sĭs'tŭn)	114-15	45°40'N	97°03'W
Sisteron, Fr. (sēst'rôn')	196-97	44°13'N	5°56'E
Sītāpur, India	234-35	27°34'N	80°41'E
Sitka, Ak., U.S. (sĭt'kȧ)	126	57°04'N	135°19'W
Sitten, Switz. see Sion	194-95	46°14'N	7°21'E
Sittoung, stm., Mya.	246-47	17°22'N	96°53'E
Sittwe, Mya.	246-47	20°09'N	92°54'E
Sivas, Tur. (sē'väs)	186-87	39°44'N	37°01'E
Siverek, Tur. (sē'vĕ-rĕk)	186-87	37°45'N	39°19'E
Sivers'kyi Donets', stm., Eur. see Northern Donets	186-87	47°36'N	40°54'E
Siwa, Egypt	188-89	29°12'N	25°31'E
Sjælland, i., Den. (shĕl'lán')	192-93	55°30'N	11°45'E
Skagen, Den. (skä'ghĕn)	192-93	57°43'N	10°35'E
Skagerrak, strt., Eur. (skä-ghĕ-räk')	192-93	57°45'N	9°00'E
Skagway, Ak., U.S. (skǎg-wā)	126	59°28'N	135°19'W
Skalistyy Golets, Gora, mtn., Russia	218-19	56°24'N	119°12'E
Skara, Swe. (skä'rȧ)	192-93	58°23'N	13°28'E
Skeena, stm., B.C., Can. (skē'nȧ)	130-31	54°08'N	130°07'W
Skeena Mountains, mts., B.C., Can. (skē'nȧ moun'tĭnz)	130-31	56°35'N	128°41'W
Skellefteå, Swe. (shĕl'ĕf-tē-a')	184-85	64°45'N	20°58'E
Skellefteälven, stm., Swe.	184-85	64°43'N	21°09'E
Skibbereen, Ire. (skĭb'ēr-ēn)	190-91	51°33'N	9°17'W
Skidegate Inlet, b., B.C., Can. (skĭ'-dē-gāt' ĭn'lĕt)	132-33	53°14'N	131°58'W
Skien, Nor. (skē'ĕn)	192-93	59°12'N	9°36'E
Skierniewice, Pol. (skyĕr-nyĕ-vēt'sĕ)	194-95	51°58'N	20°09'E
Skikda, Alg.	269b	36°53'N	6°55'E
Skive, Den. (skē'vĕ)	192-93	56°34'N	9°02'E
Skjálfandafljót, stm., Ice. (skyäl'fänd-ō)	190a	65°59'N	17°37'W
Škofja Loka, Slvn. (shkôf'yȧ lō'kȧ)	200-01	46°10'N	14°18'E
Skole, Ukr. (skô'lĕ)	194-95	49°02'N	23°29'E
Skopin, Russia (skô'pēn)	202-03	53°49'N	39°33'E
Skopje, nat. cap., Mac. (skôp'yĕ)	200-01	42°00'N	21°28'E
Skoplje, nat. cap., Mac. see Skopje	200-01	42°00'N	21°28'E
Skövde, Swe. (shûv'dĕ)	192-93	58°24'N	13°51'E
Skovorodino, Russia (skô'vô-rô'dĭ-nô)	222-23	53°59'N	123°56'E
Skowhegan, Me., U.S. (skou-hē'gǎn)	117a	44°47'N	69°43'W
Skunk, stm., Ia., U.S. (skŭnk)	114-15	40°42'N	91°07'W
Skuodas, Lith. (skwô'dás)	192-93	56°16'N	21°32'E
Skye, Island of, i., Scot., U.K. (ī'lǎnd ŏv skī)	190-91	57°25'N	6°28'W
Slamet, Gunung, vol., Indon. (gōō-nōng slä'mĕt)	248-49	7°14's	109°12'E
Slantsy, Russia	192-93	59°07'N	28°05'E
Śląsk, hist. reg., Eur. see Silesia	194-95	50°34'N	18°01'E
Slater, Mo., U.S. (slāt'ēr)	120-21	39°13'N	93°04'W
Slatina, Rom. (slä'tē-nä)	200-01	44°26'N	24°22'E
Slaton, Tx., U.S. (slā'tŭn)	120-21	33°26'N	101°38'W
Slave, stm., Can. (slāv)	130-31	61°16'N	113°35'W
Slave Lake, Ab., Can.	132-33	55°17'N	114°48'W
Slavgorod, Russia (sláf'gō-rôt)	226	53°00'N	78°38'E
Slavonski Brod, Cro. (skä-vôn'skē brôd)	200-01	45°10'N	18°00'E
Slavuta, Ukr. (slȧ-vōō'tȧ)	194-95	50°17'N	26°52'E
Slavyansk-na-Kubani, Russia	202-03	45°15'N	38°08'E
Sławno, Pol. (swav'nō)	194-95	54°22'N	16°42'E
Slayton, Mn., U.S. (slā'tŭn)	114-15	43°59'N	95°45'W
Sleaford, Eng., U.K. (slē'fērd)	190-91	53°00'N	0°25'W
Sleepy Eye, Mn., U.S. (slēp'ĭ ī)	114-15	44°18'N	94°44'W
Slezsko, hist. reg., Eur. see Silesia	194-95	50°34'N	18°01'E
Slidell, La., U.S. (slĭ-dĕl')	124-25	30°16'N	89°47'W
Sligeach, Ire. see Sligo	190-91	54°17'N	8°28'W
Sligo, Ire. (slī'gō)	190-91	54°17'N	8°28'W
Sliven, Blg. (slē'vĕn)	200-01	42°41'N	26°20'E
Slobodskoy, Russia	186-87	58°44'N	50°11'E
Slonim, Bela. (swō'nĕm)	194-95	53°05'N	25°19'E
Slovakia, nation, Eur. (slô-vák'ĕ-aȧ)	174-75	48°30'N	20°00'E
Slovenia, nation, Eur. (slô-vē'nĕ-aȧ)	174-75	46°15'N	15°10'E
Slovenija, nation, Eur. (slô-vē'nē-yä) see Slovenia	174-75	46°15'N	15°10'E
Slovensko, nation, Eur. see Slovakia	174-75	48°30'N	20°00'E
Slov'ians'k, Ukr.	202-03	48°52'N	37°37'E
Sluck, Bela.	194-95	53°01'N	27°33'E
Slunj, Cro. (slōn')	200-01	45°08'N	15°33'E
Słupsk, Pol. (swôpsk)	194-95	54°28'N	17°02'E
Slutsk, Bela. (slōtsk) see Sluck	194-95	53°01'N	27°33'E
Smackover, Ar., U.S. (smǎk'ō-vēr)	120-21	33°23'N	92°44'W
Smallwood Reservoir, res., Nf., Can.	130-31	54°09'N	64°24'W
Smederevska Palanka, Serb. (smĕ-dĕ-rĕv'skä pä-län'kä)	200-01	44°22'N	20°58'E
Smethport, Pa., U.S. (smĕth'pōrt)	116-17	41°49'N	78°27'W
Smidovich, Russia	240-41	48°36'N	133°49'E
Smila, Ukr.	202-03	49°13'N	31°53'E
Smiltene, Lat. (smēl'tē-nĕ)	192-93	57°26'N	25°54'E
Smithers, B.C., Can. (smĭth'ērs)	132-33	54°48'N	127°11'W
Smithfield, N.C., U.S. (smĭth'fēld)	124-25	35°30'N	78°21'W
Smithfield, Ut., U.S. (smĭth'fēld)	112-13	41°51'N	111°50'W
Smithfield, Va., U.S. (smĭth'fēld)	124-25	36°59'N	76°38'W
Smith Mountain Lake, res., Va., U.S. (smĭth moun'tĭn lāk)	124-25	37°07'N	79°39'W
Smiths Falls, On., Can. (smĭths fôlz)	136-37	44°54'N	76°01'W
Smithton, Austl. (smĭth'tŭn)	276	40°51's	145°07'E
Smithville, Tx., U.S. (smĭth'vĭl)	122-23	30°00'N	97°09'W
Smoke Creek Desert, des., Nv., U.S. (smōk krēk dĕs'ērt)	112-13	40°31'N	119°47'W
Smoky, stm., Ab., Can. (smōk'ĭ)	132-33	56°11'N	117°20'W
Smøla, i., Nor. (smûlä)	184-85	63°24'N	8°00'E
Smolensk, Russia (smô-lyĕnsk')	202-03	54°48'N	32°03'E
Smyrna, Tur. (smûr'nȧ) see İzmir	200-01	38°26'N	27°09'E
Smyrna, De., U.S. (smûr'nȧ)	116-17	39°18'N	75°36'W
Smyrna, Ga., U.S. (smûr'nȧ)	124-25	33°53'N	84°31'W
Smyrna, Tn., U.S. (smûr'nȧ)	124-25	35°59'N	86°31'W
Smythe, Mount, mtn., B.C., Can.	130-31	57°54'N	124°53'W
Snake, stm., U.S. (snāk)	110-11	46°11'N	119°01'W
Snares Islands, is., N.Z.	287	48°0's	166°30'E
Śniardwy, Jezioro, lk., Pol. (snyärt'vĭ)	194-95	53°46'N	21°44'E
Snøhetta, mtn., Nor. (snû-hĕttä)	184-85	62°20'N	9°17'E
Snøtinden, mtn., Nor.	184-85	66°38'N	14°00'E
Snov, stm., Eur. (snôf)	202-03	51°32'N	31°32'E
Snowdon, mtn., Wales, U.K.	190-91	53°04'N	4°05'W
Snowy Mountains, mts., Austl. (snō'ē moun'tĭnz)	276	36°15's	148°18'E
Snyder, Ok., U.S. (snī'dēr)	120-21	34°40'N	98°57'W
Snyder, Tx., U.S. (snī'dēr)	120-21	32°43'N	100°55'W
Soasiu, Indon. see Tidore	248-49	0°38'N	127°24'E
Sobinka, Russia (sô-bĭŋ'kȧ)	202-03	55°58'N	40°02'E
Sobradinho, Represa de, res., Braz.	166-67	9°40's	42°00'W
Sobral, Braz. (sô-brä'l)	166-67	3°42's	40°21'W

n-sing; ŋ-baŋk; n-nasalized n; nŏd; cŏmmit; ōld; ōbey; ôrder; oi-boil; fōōd; ò-as oo in foot; ou-out; s-soft; sh-dish; th-thin; pūre; ûnite; ûrn; stŭd; circŭs; ü-as in French tu; '-indeterminate vowel.

Feature (Pronunciation)	Page	Lat.	Long.
Sochaczew, Pol. (sô-ĸä´chĕf)	194-95	52°14'N	20°15'E
Sochi, Russia (sôch'ĭ)	227	43°35'N	39°44'E
Société, Archipel de la, is., Fr. Poly. see Society Islands	280-81	17°0'S	150°00'W
Society Islands, is., Fr. Poly. (sō-sī´ĕ-tê ī´lăndz)	280-81	17°0'S	150°00'W
Socoltenango, Mex. (sô-kôl-tĕ-näŋ´gō)	148	16°12'N	92°14'W
Socorro, Col. (sô-kôr´rō)	164-65	6°29'N	73°16'W
Socorro, N.M., U.S. (sō-kô´r-rō)	118-19	34°04'N	106°54'W
Socorro, Isla, i., Mex.	144-45	18°45'N	110°58'W
Socotra, i., Yemen (sô-kō´trȧ) see Suquṭrā	220-21	12°31'N	53°54'E
Soc Trang, Viet.	246-47	9°36'N	105°58'E
Socuéllamos, Spain (sô-kōō-äl´yä-môs)	198-99	39°17'N	2°47'W
Sodankylä, Fin.	184-85	67°25'N	26°34'E
Soda Springs, Id., U.S. (sō´dȧ sprĭngz)	112-13	42°40'N	111°36'W
Söderhamn, Swe. (sû-dĕr-häm´'n)	192-93	61°19'N	17°05'E
Södertälje, Swe. (sû-dĕr-tĕl´yĕ)	192-93	59°12'N	17°37'E
Sodo, Eth.	269d	6°52'N	37°46'E
Soe, Indon.	248-49	9°52'S	124°17'E
Soerabaja, Indon. see Surabaya	248-49	7°15'S	112°45'E
Sofia, nat. cap., Blg. (sô´fē-ȧ)	200-01	42°42'N	23°19'E
Sofia, stm., Madag.	264-65	15°25'S	47°14'E
Sofiya, nat. cap., Blg. (sô´fē-ȧ) see Sofia	200-01	42°42'N	23°19'E
Sogamoso, Col. (sô-gä-mô´sō)	164-65	5°44'N	72°56'W
Sognefjorden, b., Nor.	192-93	61°06'N	5°10'E
Sogo Nur, lk., China	240-41	42°17'N	101°14'E
Sog Xian, China	238-39	31°50'N	93°47'E
Sōhu Gan, i., Japan	244	29°49'N	140°21'E
Soissons, Fr. (swä-sôN´)	196-97	49°23'N	3°20'E
Sŏjosŏn-man, b., Kor., N.	243	39°20'N	124°50'E
Sokal', Ukr. (sô´käl')	194-95	50°29'N	24°17'E
Sokch'o, Kor., S.	243	38°11'N	128°34'E
Söke, Tur. (sû´kĕ)	200-01	37°45'N	27°24'E
Sokhumi, Geor.	227	43°00'N	41°00'E
Sokodé, Togo	260-61	8°59'N	1°09'E
Sokol, Russia	186-87	59°28'N	40°07'E
Sokółka, Pol. (sô-kōl´kȧ)	194-95	53°24'N	23°31'E
Sokołów Podlaski, Pol. (sô-kô-wôf´ pŭd-lä´skĭ)	194-95	52°24'N	22°15'E
Sokoto, Nig. (sō´kô-tō)	260-61	13°04'N	5°15'E
Sokoto, stm., Nig.	260-61	11°24'N	4°08'E
Solano, Phil. (sō-lä´nō)	250	16°31'N	121°11'E
Solāpur, India	236	17°41'N	75°54'E
Soledad, Col. (sō-lĕ-dä´d)	164-65	10°56'N	74°46'W
Soledad Díez Gutiérrez, Mex.	146-47	22°12'N	100°56'W
Solikamsk, Russia (sô-lē-kámsk´)	186-87	59°40'N	56°46'E
Sol'-Iletsk, Russia	186-87	51°09'N	55°00'E
Solimões, stm., S.A. see Amazon	164-65	0°04'S	49°15'W
Solingen, Ger. (zō´lĭng-ĕn)	194-95	51°10'N	7°05'E
Sollefteå, Swe.	184-85	63°11'N	17°16'E
Solnechnogorsk, Russia	202-03	56°11'N	36°59'E
Solo, Indon. see Surakarta	248-49	7°34'S	110°50'E
Solomon Islands, nation, Oc. (sŏ´lō-mŭn ī´lăndz)	279e	8°0'S	159°00'E
Solomon Sea, s., Oc. (sŏ´lō-mŭn sē)	277	8°0'S	155°00'E
Solon, China (swo-lōōn)	240-41	46°36'N	121°13'E
Solor, Pulau, i., Indon.	248-49	8°28'S	122°59'E
Solov'yëvsk, Russia	240-41	49°55'N	115°42'E
Soltau, Ger. (sôl´tou)	194-95	52°59'N	9°50'E
Sol'tsy, Russia (sôl´tsĕ)	192-93	58°07'N	30°20'E
Solvay, N.Y., U.S. (sŏl´vā)	116-17	43°04'N	76°14'W
Sölvesborg, Swe. (sûl´vĕs-bôrg)	192-93	56°03'N	14°35'E
Sol'vychegodsk, Russia (sôl´vē-chĕ-gôtsk´)	186-87	61°20'N	46°55'E
Solway Firth, b., U.K. (sŏl´wā fûrth´)	190-91	54°50'N	3°35'W
Solwezi, Zam.	264-65	12°11'S	26°25'E
Somalia, nation, Afr. (sō-ma´lē-ă)	253	6°0'N	48°00'E
Somaliland, nation, Afr. see Somalia	253	6°0'N	48°00'E
Somali Republic, nation, Afr. see Somalia	253	6°0'N	48°00'E
Sombor, Serb. (sôm´bôr)	200-01	45°47'N	19°07'E
Sombrerete, Mex. (sōm-brå-rā´tå)	146-47	23°41'N	103°39'W
Sombrero, i., St. K./N.	143b	18°36'N	63°26'W
Somerset, Ky., U.S. (sŭm´ĕr-sĕt)	124-25	37°05'N	84°37'W
Somerset, Oh., U.S. (sŭm´ĕr-sĕt)	116-17	39°48'N	82°18'W
Somerset East, S. Afr. (sŭm´ĕr-sĕt ēst)	264-65	32°44'S	25°35'E
Somersworth, N.H., U.S. (sŭm´ẽrz-wûrth)	116-17	43°16'N	70°52'W
Somerville, Tn., U.S. (sŭm´ẽr-vĭl)	124-25	35°15'N	89°21'W
Somerville, Tx., U.S. (sŭm´ẽr-vĭl)	122-23	30°20'N	96°32'W
Somoto, Nic. (sô-mō´tō)	149	13°28'N	86°35'W
Son, stm., India (sōn)	234-35	25°42'N	84°52'E
Sønderborg, Den. (sûn´'er-bôrgh)	194-95	54°55'N	9°48'E
Sonepur, India	234-35	20°49'N	83°54'E
Song Da, stm., Asia see Black	246-47	21°15'N	105°21'E
Songea, Tan. (sôn-gā´ȧ)	264-65	10°41'S	35°39'E
Songhua, stm., China	240-41	47°43'N	132°31'E
Songhua Hu, res., China	240-41	43°25'N	127°10'E
Songjiang, China	238-39	31°01'N	121°14'E
Sŏngjin, Kor., N. (sŭng´jĭn´) see Kimch'aek	243	40°41'N	129°12'E
Songkhla, Thai. (sông´ĸlä´)	246-47	7°12'N	100°36'E
Songnim, Kor., N.	243	38°44'N	125°38'E
Songo, Moz.	264-65	15°39'S	32°43'E
Sonid Youqi, China	240-41	42°44'N	112°40'E
Sonmiāni Bay, b., Pak.	232-33	25°15'N	66°30'E
Sonneberg, Ger. (sôn´ē-bĕrgh)	194-95	50°21'N	11°11'E
Sonora, Ca., U.S. (sô-nō´rȧ)	118-19	37°59'N	120°22'W
Sonora, Tx., U.S. (sō-nō´rȧ)	122-23	30°34'N	100°39'W
Sonora, state, Mex. (sô-nō´rȧ)	144-45	29°20'N	110°40'W
Sonora, stm., Mex. (sô-nō´rȧ)	144-45	29°05'N	110°54'W
Sonora, Desierto de, des., N.A. see Sonoran Desert	144-45	30°0'N	113°00'W
Sonoran Desert, des., N.A.	144-45	30°0'N	113°00'W
Sonsón, Col. (sôn-sôn´)	163c	5°43'N	75°18'W
Sonsonate, El Sal. (sōn-sō-nä´tå)	148	13°43'N	89°43'W
Sonsorol Islands, is., Palau (sŏn-sō-rōl´ ī´lăndz)	280-81	5°20'N	132°13'E
Son Tay, Viet.	246-47	21°08'N	105°30'E
Soomaaliya, nation, Afr. see Somalia	253	6°0'N	48°00'E
Soome laht, b., Eur. see Finland, Gulf of	192-93	60°0'N	27°00'E
Sora, Italy (sô´rä)	200-01	41°44'N	13°37'E
Sorell, Cape, c., Austl.	276	42°12'S	145°10'E
Sorel-Tracy, Qc., Can.	136-37	46°03'N	73°05'W
Soria, Spain (sō´rē-ä)	198-99	41°46'N	2°28'W
Sorocaba, Braz. (sô-rô-kä´bȧ)	172	23°30'S	47°28'W
Sorochinsk, Russia	186-87	52°26'N	53°10'E
Sorong, Indon. (sō-rông´)	224-25	0°53'S	131°15'E
Soroti, Ug. (sō-rō´tē)	267	1°43'N	33°36'E
Sørøya, i., Nor.	184-85	70°34'N	22°22'E
Sorrento, Italy (sôr-rĕn´tō)	200-01	40°38'N	14°22'E
Sor Rondane Mountains, mts., Ant.	287	72°0'S	25°00'E
Sorsogon, Phil. (sôr-sōgōn´)	250	12°59'N	124°01'E
Sortavala, Russia (sôr´tä-vä-lä)	192-93	61°42'N	30°40'E
Sosna, stm., Russia (sôs´nȧ)	202-03	52°42'N	38°55'E
Sosnogorsk, Russia	186-87	63°36'N	53°53'E
Sosnowiec, Pol. (sôs-nô´vyĕts)	194-95	50°18'N	19°08'E
Sos'va, stm., Russia (sôs´vȧ)	218-19	59°33'N	62°20'E
Soto la Marina, Barra, i., Mex.	146-47	24°10'N	97°44'W
Soufrière, vol., Guad. (sōō-frē-âr´)	143b	16°04'N	61°40'W
Sŏul, nat. cap., Kor., S. see Seoul	243	37°33'N	127°01'E
Sounding Creek, stm., Ab., Can. (soun´dĭng krēk)	132-33	52°06'N	110°28'W
Souris, Mb., Can. (sōō´rē´)	134-35	49°38'N	100°16'W
Souris, P.E., Can. (sōō´rē´)	138-39	46°21'N	62°15'W
Souris, stm., N.A. (sōō´rē´)	130-31	49°40'N	99°35'W
Sousa, Braz.	166-67	6°45'S	38°14'W
Sousse, Tun. (sōōs)	184-85	35°49'N	10°38'E
South, stm., N.C., U.S. (south)	124-25	34°35'N	78°16'W
South Africa, nation, Afr. (south ăf´rĭ-kă)	253	30°0'S	26°00'E
South America, cont., (south ȧ-mĕr´ĭ-kȧ)	159	15°0'S	60°00'W
Southampton, Eng., U.K. (south-ămp´tŭn)	190-91	50°55'N	1°24'W
Southampton Island, i., Nu., Can.	130-31	64°20'N	84°40'W
South Andaman, i., India (south ăn-dȧ-măn´)	246-47	11°48'N	92°44'E
South Australia, state, Austl. (south ôs-trā´lĭ-ȧ)	270-71	30°0'S	135°00'E
South Bend, In., U.S. (south bĕnd)	116-17	41°41'N	86°14'W
South Bend, Wa., U.S. (south bĕnd)	112-13	46°40'N	123°46'W
South Boston, Va., U.S. (south bôs´tŭn)	124-25	36°42'N	78°54'W
Southbridge, Ma., U.S. (south´brĭj)	116-17	42°05'N	72°03'W
South Carolina, state, U.S. (south kăr-ō-lī´nȧ)	108-09	34°0'N	81°00'W
South China Sea, s., Asia (south chī´nȧ sē)	224-25	10°0'N	113°00'E
South Dakota, state, U.S. (south dȧ-kō´tȧ)	108-09	44°15'N	100°00'W
South East Cape, c., Austl.	276	43°38'S	146°52'E
South East Point, c., Austl.	276	39°08'S	146°25'E
Southend-on-Sea, Eng., U.K. (south-ĕnd´-ŏn-sē)	190-91	51°33'N	0°45'E
Southern Alps, mts., N.Z. (sŭ-thûrn ălps)	278	43°30'S	170°30'E
Southern Bug, stm., Ukr. (sŭ-thûrn bōōg)	202-03	46°39'N	31°56'E
Southern Cook Islands, is., Cook Is.	280-81	20°0'S	159°00'W
Southern Cross, Austl.	270-71	31°14'S	119°19'E
Southern Indian Lake, lk., Mb., Can. (sŭth´ẽrn ĭn´dĭ-ăn lăk)	134-35	57°13'N	98°21'W
Southern Ocean, oc., (sŭ-thûrn ōshŭn)	20-21	50°0'S	135°00'E
Southern Pines, N.C., U.S. (sŭth´ẽrn pīnz)	124-25	35°10'N	79°24'W
Southern Ute Indian Reservation, ind. res., Co., U.S. (sŭth´ẽrn ūt ĭn´dĭ-ăn rĕ-sẽr-vā´shĕn)	118-19	37°05'N	107°45'W
South Georgia, i., S. Geor. (south jôr´jȧ)	287	54°15'S	36°45'W
South Georgia and the South Sandwich Islands, dep., S.A.	287	54°0'S	38°00'W
South Haven, Mi., U.S. (south hāv´'n)	116-17	42°24'N	86°16'W
South Henik Lake, lk., Nu., Can.	130-31	61°30'N	97°27'W
South Indian Lake, Mb., Can.	134-35	56°48'N	98°57'W
Southington, Ct., U.S. (sŭdh´ĭng-tŭn)	116-17	41°36'N	72°53'W
South Island, i., India	236	10°03'N	72°17'E
South Island, i., N.Z. (south ī´lănd)	278	43°0'S	171°00'E
South Korea, nation, Asia (south kô-rē´-ȧ)	206-07	36°30'N	128°00'E
South Luangwa National Park, n.p., Zam.	264-65	12°56'S	31°38'E
South Nahanni, stm., N.T., Can.	130-31	61°03'N	123°20'W
South Negril Point, c., Jam. (south nå-grēl´ point)	142-43	18°15'N	78°22'W
South Ogden, Ut., U.S. (south ŏg´dĕn)	112-13	41°12'N	111°59'W
South Orkney Islands, is., Ant.	287	60°35'S	44°07'W
South Paris, Me., U.S. (south păr´ĭs)	116-17	44°13'N	70°31'W
South Pittsburg, Tn., U.S. (south pĭs´bûrg)	124-25	35°01'N	85°43'W
South Platte, stm., U.S. (south plăt)	110-11	41°07'N	100°42'W
Southport, Austl. (south´pōrt)	276	27°58'S	153°25'E
Southport, Eng., U.K. (south´pôrt)	190-91	53°39'N	3°01'W
South River, On., Can.	136-37	45°50'N	79°22'W
South Sandwich Islands, is., S. Geor. (south sănd´wĭch ī´lăndz)	287	57°31'S	26°37'W
South Saskatchewan, stm., Can. (south săs-kach´ĕ-wän)	130-31	53°14'N	105°04'W
South Shetland Islands, is., Ant.	287	62°0'S	58°00'W
South Shields, Eng., U.K. (south shēldz)	190-91	54°60'N	1°25'W
South Sioux City, Ne., U.S. (south sōō sĭt´ē sĭ´tē)	114-15	42°27'N	96°25'W
South Thompson, stm., B.C., Can. (south tŏmp´sŭn)	132-33	50°41'N	120°20'W
South West Africa, nation, Afr. see Namibia	253	22°0'S	17°00'E
South West Cape, c., Austl.	276	43°33'S	146°04'E
South West Cape, c., N.Z.	278	47°17'S	167°28'E
Southwest Miramichi, stm., N.B., Can. (south-wĕst´ mĭr ȧ-mē´shē)	138-39	46°58'N	65°34'W
Southwest National Park, n.p., Austl.	276	43°05'S	146°09'E
Sovetsk, Russia (sô-vyĕtsk´)	192-93	55°05'N	21°53'E
Sovetsk, Russia (sô-vyĕtsk´)	186-87	57°35'N	48°58'E
Sovetskaya Gavan, Russia (sŭ-vyĕt´skĭ-u gä´vŭn')	222-23	48°58'N	140°18'E
Soweto, S. Afr.	269c	26°17'S	27°51'E
Sozopol, Blg. (sôz´ō-pôl')	200-01	42°25'N	27°42'E
Spa, Bel. (spä)	190-91	50°29'N	5°52'E
Spain, nation, Eur. (spān)	174-75	40°0'N	4°00'W
Spanish Fork, Ut., U.S. (spăn´ĭsh fôrk)	118-19	40°08'N	111°39'W
Spanish Sahara, dep., Afr. see Western Sahara	253	24°30'N	13°00'W
Spanish Town, Jam.	142-43	17°60'N	76°58'W
Sparks, Nv., U.S. (spärks)	118-19	39°32'N	119°44'W
Sparta, Grc. (spär´tȧ)	200-01	37°05'N	22°26'E
Sparta, Tn., U.S. (spär´tȧ)	124-25	35°56'N	85°28'W
Sparta, Wi., U.S. (spär´tȧ)	114-15	43°56'N	90°48'W
Spartanburg, S.C., U.S. (spär´tăn-bûrg)	124-25	34°57'N	81°56'W
Spartel, Cap, c., Mor. (kăp spär-tĕl´)	269a	35°48'N	5°55'W
Spárti, Grc. see Sparta	200-01	37°05'N	22°26'E
Spartivento, Capo, c., Italy (kä´pō spär-tē-vĕn´tô)	200-01	37°55'N	16°04'E
Spartivento, Capo, c., Italy (kä´pō spär-tē-vĕn´tô)	200-01	38°53'N	8°50'E
Spas-Demensk, Russia (spȧs dyĕ-mĕnsk´)	202-03	54°25'N	34°02'E
Spas-Klepiki, Russia (spȧs klĕp´ē-kē)	202-03	55°08'N	40°12'E
Spassk-Dal'niy, Russia (spŭsk´däl´nyē)	244	44°36'N	132°50'E
Spear, Cape, c., Nf., Can. (kăp spēr)	138-39	47°31'N	52°39'W
Spearfish, S.D., U.S. (spēr´fĭsh)	114-15	44°30'N	103°52'W
Speedway, In., U.S. (spēd´wā)	116-17	39°47'N	86°13'W
Spence Bay, Nu., Can. see Taloyoak	128-29	69°32'N	93°31'W
Spencer, Ia., U.S. (spĕn´sẽr)	114-15	43°09'N	95°09'W

ăt; fināl; rāte; senåte; ärm; åsk; sofȧ; fâre; ch-choose; dh-as th in other; bē; ėvent; bĕt; recĕnt; cratẽr; g-gō; gh-guttural g; bĭt; ĭ-short neutral; rīde; ĸ-guttural k as ch in German ich;

Feature (Pronunciation)	Page	Lat.	Long.
Spencer, In., U.S. (spěn´sẽr)	116-17	39°17'N	86°46'W
Spencer, W.V., U.S. (spěn´sẽr)	116-17	38°47'N	81°22'W
Spencer, Cape, c., Austl.	276	35°18'S	136°53'E
Spencer Gulf, b., Austl. (spěn´sẽr gŭlf)	272-73	34°0'S	137°00'E
Speyer, Ger. (shpī´ẽr)	194-95	49°20'N	8°26'E
Spezia, Italy *see* La Spezia	200-01	44°07'N	9°50'E
Spinazzola, Italy (spē-nät´zō-lä)	200-01	40°58'N	16°05'E
Spires, Ger. *see* Speyer	194-95	49°20'N	8°26'E
Spirit Lake, Ia., U.S. (spĭr´ĭt lāk)	114-15	43°26'N	95°06'W
Spirit Lake, Id., U.S. (spĭr´ĭt lāk)	112-13	47°58'N	116°53'W
Spišská Nová Ves, Slvk. (spēsh´skä nō´vä věs)	194-95	48°57'N	20°34'E
Spitsbergen, i., Nor. (spĭts´bûr-gěn)	218-19	78°45'N	16°00'E
Split, Cro. (splêt)	200-01	43°30'N	16°26'E
Split Lake, res., Mb., Can.	134-35	56°08'N	96°15'W
Spokane, Wa., U.S. (spōkăn´)	112-13	47°39'N	117°24'W
Spokane Indian Reservation, ind. res., Wa., U.S. (spōkăn´ ĭn´dĭ-ăn rĕ-sẽr-vā´shŭn)	112-13	47°55'N	118°00'W
Spoleto, Italy (spô-lā´tō)	200-01	42°44'N	12°44'E
Spooner, Wi., U.S. (spōōn´ẽr)	114-15	45°49'N	91°53'W
Spratly Islands, is., Asia	224-25	10°0'N	114°00'E
Springbok, S. Afr. (sprĭng´bŏk)	264-65	29°43'S	17°55'E
Springdale, Nf., Can. (sprĭng´dāl)	138-39	49°31'N	56°04'W
Springdale, Ar., U.S. (sprĭng´dāl)	120-21	36°11'N	94°09'W
Springer, N.M., U.S. (sprĭng´ẽr)	120-21	36°22'N	104°36'W
Springfield, Co., U.S. (sprĭng´fēld)	120-21	37°24'N	102°37'W
Springfield, Fl., U.S. (sprĭng´fēld)	124-25	30°12'N	85°37'W
Springfield, Il., U.S.	116-17	39°48'N	89°39'W
Springfield, Ky., U.S. (sprĭng´fēld)	116-17	37°41'N	85°13'W
Springfield, Ma., U.S.	116-17	42°07'N	72°35'W
Springfield, Mn., U.S. (sprĭng´fēld)	114-15	44°14'N	94°59'W
Springfield, Mo., U.S. (sprĭng´fēld)	120-21	37°13'N	93°17'W
Springfield, Oh., U.S. (sprĭng´fēld)	116-17	39°55'N	83°49'W
Springfield, Or., U.S. (sprĭng´fēld)	112-13	44°03'N	123°01'W
Springfield, Tn., U.S. (sprĭng´fēld)	124-25	36°30'N	86°53'W
Springfield, Vt., U.S. (sprĭng´fēld)	116-17	43°18'N	72°29'W
Springhill, N.S., Can. (sprĭng-hĭl´)	138-39	45°39'N	64°03'W
Springs, S. Afr. (sprĭngs)	269c	26°15'S	28°26'E
Springsure, Austl.	277	24°07'S	148°05'E
Spring Valley, Il., U.S. (sprĭng crēk văl´ē)	116-17	41°19'N	89°12'W
Spring Valley, Mn., U.S. (sprĭng văl´ē)	114-15	43°41'N	92°25'W
Spruce Grove, Ab., Can. (sprōōs grōv)	132-33	53°32'N	113°55'W
Spruce Knob, mtn., W.V., U.S.	116-17	38°42'N	79°32'W
Squamish, B.C., Can. (skwŏ´mĭsh)	132-33	49°42'N	123°08'W
Squamish, stm., B.C., Can. (skwŏ´mĭsh)	132-33	49°39'N	123°14'W
Srbija, nation, Eur. (sr bē-yä) *see* Serbia	174-75	44°0'N	21°00'E
Sredinny Khrebet, mts., Russia	218-19	56°0'N	158°00'E
Srednekolymsk, Russia (s'rĕd´nyĕ kô-lĕmsk´)	218-19	67°27'N	153°40'E
Srednerusskaya Vozvyshennost', plat., Russia	202-03	52°0'N	38°00'E
Śrem, Pol. (shrĕm)	194-95	52°05'N	17°02'E
Sremska Mitrovica, Serb. (srĕm´skä mē´trō-vē-tsä´)	200-01	44°59'N	19°37'E
Sri Aman, Malay.	248-49	1°13'N	111°28'E
Sri Jayewardenepura Kotte, nat. cap., Sri L.	236	6°54'N	79°54'E
Srīkākulam, India	236	18°18'N	83°54'E
Sri Lanka, nation, Asia (shrē´-län-kȧ) (srē´-län-kȧ)	206-07	7°0'N	81°00'E
Srīnagar, India	234-35	34°05'N	74°48'E
Staaten River National Park, n.p., Austl.	277	16°40'S	143°00'E
Stafford, Eng., U.K. (stăf´fẽrd)	190-91	52°48'N	2°07'W
Stafford, Va., U.S. (stăf´fẽrd)	116-17	38°25'N	77°24'W
Stakhanov, Ukr.	202-03	48°34'N	38°40'E
Stalin, Rom. *see* Brașov	194-95	45°39'N	25°37'E
Stambaugh, Mi., U.S. (stăm´bô)	114-15	46°05'N	88°38'W
Stamford, Eng., U.K. (stăm´fẽrd)	190-91	52°39'N	0°29'W
Stamford, Ct., U.S. (stăm´fẽrd)	116-17	41°03'N	73°33'W
Stamford, Tx., U.S. (stăm´fẽrd)	120-21	32°55'N	99°49'W
Stamps, Ar., U.S. (stămps)	120-21	33°22'N	93°30'W
Standerton, S. Afr. (stăn´dẽr-tŭn)	269c	26°57'S	29°15'E
Standing Rock Indian Reservation, ind. res., U.S. (stănd´ĭng rŏk ĭn´dĭ-ăn rĕ-sẽr-vā´shŭn)	114-15	45°50'N	101°10'W
Stanford, Ky., U.S. (stăn´fẽrd)	116-17	37°31'N	84°41'W
Stanisławów, Ukr. *see* Ivano-Frankivs'k	194-95	48°55'N	24°44'E
Stanley, N.D., U.S. (stăn´lē)	114-15	48°19'N	102°24'W
Stanley, nat. cap., Falk. Is. (stăn´lē)	171	51°43'S	57°49'W
Stanley Falls, wtfl., D.R.C.	262-63	0°29'N	25°13'E
Stanovoye Nagor'ye, mts., Russia	218-19	56°0'N	114°00'E
Stanovoy Khrebet, mts., Russia (stŭn-ȧ-voi´)	218-19	55°48'N	125°34'E
Stanovoy Mountains, mts., Russia (stŭn-ȧ-voi´ moun´tĭnz) *see* Stanovoye Nagor'ye	218-19	56°0'N	114°00'E
Stanovoy Range, mts., Russia (stŭn-ȧ-voi´ rānj) *see* Stanovoy Khrebet	218-19	55°48'N	125°34'E
Stanthorpe, Austl.	276	28°40'S	151°56'E
Stanton, Ky., U.S. (stăn´tŭn)	116-17	37°50'N	83°55'W
Stanton, Tx., U.S. (stăn´tŭn)	122-23	32°08'N	101°47'W
Staples, Mn., U.S. (stā´p'lz)	114-15	46°21'N	94°48'W
Staraya Russa, Russia (stä´rȧ-yȧ rōō´sȧ)	192-93	57°60'N	31°21'E
Stara Zagora, Blg. (stä´rä zä´gô-rȧ)	200-01	42°26'N	25°39'E
Starbuck, Mb., Can. (stär´bŭk)	134-35	49°46'N	97°37'W
Starbuck, i., Kir.	280-81	5°37'S	155°53'W
Staritsa, Russia (stä´rē-tsȧ)	202-03	56°30'N	34°56'E
Starke, Fl., U.S. (stärk)	124-25	29°57'N	82°07'W
Starkville, Ms., U.S. (stärk´vĭl)	124-25	33°27'N	88°49'W
Starodub, Russia (stä-rô-drōp´)	202-03	52°35'N	32°46'E
Starominskaya, Russia (stä´rô mĭn´skȧ-yȧ)	202-03	46°32'N	39°02'E
Start Point, c., Eng., U.K. (stärt point)	190-91	50°14'N	3°39'W
Staryy Oskol, Russia (stä´rē ôs-kôl´)	202-03	51°18'N	37°51'E
Staszów, Pol. (stä´shôf)	194-95	50°34'N	21°20'E
State College, Pa., U.S. (stāt kŏl´ĕj)	116-17	40°47'N	77°52'W
Staten Island, i., Arg. *see* Estados, Isla de los	171	54°48'S	64°33'W
Statesboro, Ga., U.S. (stāts´bŭr-ô)	124-25	32°27'N	81°47'W
Statesville, N.C., U.S. (stās´vĭl)	124-25	35°47'N	80°54'W
Staunton, Il., U.S. (stôn´tŭn)	120-21	39°01'N	89°47'W
Staunton, Va., U.S. (stôn´tŭn)	116-17	38°09'N	79°05'W
Staunton, stm., U.S. *see* Roanoke	124-25	35°57'N	76°43'W
Stavanger, Nor. (stä´väng´ẽr)	192-93	58°58'N	5°45'E
Stavropol', Russia	186-87	45°02'N	41°59'E
Stawell, Austl.	276	37°04'S	142°46'E
Steamboat Springs, Co., U.S. (stēm´bōt´ sprĭngz)	112-13	40°29'N	106°50'W
Steel, stm., On., Can. (stēl)	136-37	48°47'N	86°54'W
Steens Mountain, mts., Or., U.S. (stēnz moun´tĭn)	112-13	42°35'N	118°40'W
Stefanie, Lake, lk., Afr. *see* Ch'ew Bahir	267	4°40'N	36°50'E
Steinamanger, Hung. *see* Szombathely	194-95	47°14'N	16°38'E
Steinbach, Mb., Can.	134-35	49°31'N	96°41'W
Steinkjer, Nor. (stĕin-kyĕr)	184-85	64°01'N	11°29'E
Stellarton, N.S., Can. (stĕl´ȧr-tŭn)	138-39	45°33'N	62°39'W
Stendal, Ger. (shtĕn´däl)	194-95	52°36'N	11°51'E
Stephens Island, i., B.C., Can.	132-33	54°10'N	130°45'W
Stephens Lake, res., Mb., Can.	134-35	56°26'N	95°07'W
Stephenville, Nf., Can. (stē´vĕn-vĭl)	138-39	48°33'N	58°37'W
Sterling, Ak., U.S. (stûr´lĭng)	126	60°32'N	150°48'W
Sterling, Co., U.S. (stûr´lĭng)	114-15	40°37'N	103°13'W
Sterling, Il., U.S. (stûr´lĭng)	116-17	41°48'N	89°42'W
Sterlitamak, Russia (styĕr´lĕ-ta-mȧk´)	186-87	53°37'N	55°58'E
Šternberk, Czech Rep. (shtĕrn´bĕrk)	194-95	49°44'N	17°18'E
Stettin, Pol. *see* Szczecin	194-95	53°26'N	14°32'E
Steubenville, Oh., U.S. (stū´bĕn-vĭl)	116-17	40°22'N	80°38'W
Stevens Point, Wi., U.S.	116-17	44°31'N	89°34'W
Stevensville, Mt., U.S. (stē´vĕnz-vĭl)	112-13	46°30'N	114°05'W
Stewart, B.C., Can.	132-33	55°56'N	129°58'W
Stewart, Isla, i., Chile	171	54°52'S	71°12'W
Stewart Island, i., N.Z.	278	47°0'S	167°50'E
Steynsrus, S. Afr. (stīns´rōōs)	269c	27°57'S	27°34'E
Steyr, Aus. (shtīr)	194-95	48°03'N	14°25'E
Stikine, stm., N.A. (stĭ-kēn´)	130-31	56°41'N	132°14'W
Stillwater, Ok., U.S. (stĭl´wô-tẽr)	120-21	36°08'N	97°05'W
Stillwater Range, mts., Nv., U.S. (stĭl´wô-tẽr rānj)	118-19	39°53'N	118°06'W
Štip, Mac. (shtĭp)	200-01	41°45'N	22°12'E
Stirling, Scot., U.K. (stûr´lĭng)	190-91	56°07'N	3°56'W
Stjørdalshalsen, Nor. (styûr-däls-hälsĕn)	184-85	63°29'N	10°56'E
Stockholm, nat. cap., Swe. (stôk´hôlm)	192-93	59°20'N	18°03'E
Stockport, Eng., U.K. (stŏk´pôrt)	190-91	53°25'N	2°10'W
Stockton, Ca., U.S.	118-19	37°57'N	121°17'W
Stockton, Ks., U.S. (stŏk´tŭn)	120-21	39°26'N	99°16'W
Stockton Plateau, plat., Tx., U.S. (stŏk´tŭn plă-tō´)	122-23	30°30'N	102°30'W
Stœng Trêng, Camb. (stŏng´trĕng´)	246-47	13°31'N	105°58'E
Stoke-on-Trent, Eng., U.K. (stōk-ŏn-trĕnt)	190-91	52°60'N	2°10'W
Stolbovoy, Ostrov, i., Russia	218-19	74°05'N	136°00'E
Stolin, Bela. (stô´lĕn)	194-95	51°54'N	26°52'E
Stolp, Pol. *see* Słupsk	194-95	54°28'N	17°02'E
Stonehaven, Scot., U.K. (stōn´hā-v'n)	190-91	56°58'N	2°13'W
Stonewall, Mb., Can. (stōn´wôl)	134-35	50°08'N	97°19'W
Storm Bay, b., Austl.	276	43°10'S	147°32'E
Storm Lake, Ia., U.S.	114-15	42°39'N	95°13'W
Stornoway, Scot., U.K. (stôr´nô-wā)	190-91	58°13'N	6°24'W
Storsjøen, lk., Nor. (stôr-syûĕn)	192-93	60°21'N	11°41'E
Storsjön, lk., Swe.	184-85	63°12'N	14°18'E
Storuman, Swe.	184-85	65°05'N	17°05'E
Stosch, Isla, i., Chile	171	49°09'S	75°26'W
Strabane, N. Ire., U.K. (stră-băn´)	190-91	54°50'N	7°27'W
Strahan, Austl. (strā´ăn)	276	42°09'S	145°19'E
Strakonice, Czech Rep. (strä´kô-nyĕ-tsĕ)	194-95	49°15'N	13°55'E
Stralsund, Ger. (shräl´sŏnt)	194-95	54°19'N	13°05'E
Stranraer, Scot., U.K. (străn-rär´)	190-91	54°54'N	5°02'W
Strasbourg, Fr. (strȧs-bōōr´)	196-97	48°35'N	7°45'E
Stratford, On., Can. (străt´fẽrd)	136-37	43°22'N	80°58'W
Stratford, Ct., U.S. (străt´fẽrd)	116-17	41°13'N	73°08'W
Stratford, Tx., U.S. (străt´fẽrd)	120-21	36°20'N	102°04'W
Straubing, Ger. (strou´bĭng)	194-95	48°53'N	12°35'E
Strausberg, Ger. (strous´bĕrgh)	194-95	52°34'N	13°53'E
Streator, Il., U.S. (strē´tẽr)	116-17	41°08'N	88°49'W
Strehaia, Rom. (strĕ-ĸä´yȧ)	200-01	44°38'N	23°13'E
Streymoy, i., Far. Is.	190b	62°08'N	7°00'W
Strickland, stm., Pap. N. Gui. (strĭk´lănd)	277	7°35'S	141°23'E
Strongsville, Oh., U.S. (strôngz´vĭl)	116-17	41°18'N	81°50'W
Stronsay, i., Scot., U.K. (strŏn´sā)	190c	59°06'N	2°36'W
Stroudsburg, Pa., U.S. (stroudz´bûrg)	116-17	40°59'N	75°12'W
Strugi-Krasnyye, Russia (strōō´gĭ krä´s-ny´yĕ)	192-93	58°16'N	29°07'E
Strumica, Mac. (strōō´mĭ-tsȧ)	200-01	41°26'N	22°37'E
Stryi, Ukr.	194-95	49°15'N	23°51'E
Strzelce Opolskie, Pol. (stzhĕl´tsĕ ô-pŏl´skyĕ)	194-95	50°31'N	18°19'E
Strzelecki Creek, stm., Austl.	276	29°21'S	139°48'E
Stuart, Fl., U.S. (stū´ẽrt)	125a	27°12'N	80°15'W
Stuart, Ia., U.S. (stū´ẽrt)	114-15	41°30'N	94°20'W
Stuart, stm., B.C., Can.	132-33	53°59'N	123°33'W
Stuart Island, i., Ak., U.S. (stū´ẽrt ī´lănd)	126	63°35'N	162°31'W
Stuart Lake, lk., B.C., Can. (stū´ẽrt lāk)	132-33	54°32'N	124°35'W
Stuhlweissenburg, Hung. *see* Székesfehérvár	194-95	47°12'N	18°25'E
Stupino, Russia	202-03	54°54'N	38°05'E
Sturgeon, stm., On., Can. (stûr´jŭn)	136-37	46°16'N	79°56'W
Sturgeon Bay, Wi., U.S. (stûr´jŭn bā)	116-17	44°50'N	87°22'W
Sturgeon Bay, b., Mb., Can. (stûr´jŭn bā)	134-35	52°0'N	97°50'W
Sturgeon Falls, On., Can. (stûr´jŭn fôlz)	136-37	46°22'N	79°55'W
Sturt Stony Desert, des., Austl.	276	28°30'S	141°00'E
Stuttgart, Ger. (shtōōt´gärt)	194-95	48°48'N	9°11'E
Stuttgart, Ar., U.S. (stŭt´gärt)	124-25	34°30'N	91°33'W
Styr, stm., Eur. (stĕr)	194-95	52°07'N	26°36'E
Suduroy, i., Far. Is.	190b	61°32'N	6°50'W
Suao, Tai. (sōōōu)	225a	24°36'N	121°50'E
Subansiri, stm., Asia	238-39	26°46'N	93°45'E
Subarnarekha, stm., India	234-35	21°34'N	87°23'E
Sūbāţ, stm., Sudan	262-63	9°22'N	31°33'E
Subotica, Serb. (sōō´bô´tē-tsȧ)	200-01	46°06'N	19°41'E
Suceava, Rom. (sōō-chȧ-ȧ´vȧ)	194-95	47°40'N	26°17'E
Sucre, nat. cap., Bol. (sōō´krā)	168-69	19°02'S	65°16'W
Sudan, nation, Afr. (sōō-dän´)	253	15°0'N	30°00'E
Sudan, reg., Afr. (sōō-dän´) *see* Sahel	258-59	12°0'N	17°00'E
Sudbury, On., Can. (sŭd´bẽr-ē)	136-37	46°29'N	80°59'W
Sudd, reg., Sudan *see* As-Sudd	262-63	8°0'N	31°00'E
Sudost', stm., Eur. (sô-dôst´)	202-03	52°20'N	33°23'E
Sudzha, Russia (sôd´zhȧ)	202-03	51°11'N	35°18'E
Sue, stm., Sudan	262-63	7°40'N	28°02'E
Sueca, Spain (swā´kä)	198-99	39°12'N	0°19'W
Suez, Egypt (sōō-ĕz´)	268b	29°58'N	32°33'E
Suez, Gulf of, b., Egypt (gŭlf ŭv sōō-ĕz´)	268b	29°0'N	32°50'E
Suez Canal, can., Egypt (sōō-ĕz´ kȧ´năl)	268b	29°57'N	32°35'E
Suffolk, Va., U.S. (sŭf´ŭk)	124-25	36°44'N	76°35'W
Suhag, Egypt	268b	26°33'N	31°42'E
Şuḩār, Oman	230-31	24°20'N	56°44'E
Sühbaatar, Mong.	240-41	50°13'N	106°12'E
Suhl, Ger. (zōōl)	194-95	50°36'N	10°41'E
Suid-Afrika, nation, Afr. *see* South Africa	253	30°0'S	26°00'E
Suide, China (swā-dū)	240-41	37°31'N	110°15'E
Suifenhe, China (swā-fŭn-hŭ)	244	44°24'N	131°08'E
Suihua, China	240-41	46°39'N	126°59'E
Suining, China (sōō´ē-nĭng´)	238-39	30°30'N	105°35'E

n-sing; ŋ-baŋk; ɴ-nasalized n; nŏd; cŏmmit; ōld; ôbey; ôrder; oi-boil; fōōd; ŏ-as oo in foot; ou-out; s-soft; sh-dish; th-thin; pūre; ûnite; ûrn; stŭd; circŭs; ü-as in French tu; ´-indeterminate vowel.

Feature (Pronunciation)	Page	Lat.	Long.
Suipacha, Arg. (swē-pä'chä)	173	34°47'S	59°42'W
Suisse, nation, Eur. see Switzerland	174-75	47°0'N	8°00'E
Suixian, China (swā shyĕn)	238-39	34°26'N	115°04'E
Suizhong, China (swā-jōŋ)	240-41	40°20'N	120°20'E
Suizhou, China	238-39	31°42'N	113°22'E
Sukabumi, Indon.	248-49	6°55'S	106°55'E
Sukagawa, Japan (sōō'kä-gä'wä)	245	37°17'N	140°23'E
Sukarnapura, Indon. see Jayapura	277	2°32'S	140°43'E
Sukarno, Pegunungan, mtn., Indon. see Jaya, Puncak	224-25	4°05'S	137°11'E
Sukhinichi, Russia (sōō'kē'nē-chē)	202-03	54°07'N	35°22'E
Sukhona, stm., Russia (sò-ĸô'nà)	186-87	60°45'N	46°18'E
Sukhothai, Thai.	246-47	17°01'N	99°49'E
Sukhumi, Geor. (sò-kòm') see Sokhumi	227	43°00'N	41°00'E
Sukkozero, Russia	184-85	63°14'N	32°18'E
Sukkur, Pak. (sŭk'ŭr)	232-33	27°42'N	68°52'E
Sūknah, Libya	188-89	29°04'N	15°47'E
Sukumo, Japan (sōō'kò-mô)	245	32°56'N	132°44'E
Sula, i., Nor.	192-93	61°08'N	4°55'E
Sula, stm., Ukr. (sōō-lä')	202-03	49°38'N	32°43'E
Sula, Kepulauan, is., Indon.	248-49	1°52'S	125°22'E
Sulaimaniya, Iraq see As-Sulaymānīyah	228-29	35°34'N	45°27'E
Sulaimān Range, mts., Pak. (sò-lä-ē-män' rānj)	232-33	30°30'N	70°10'E
Sulawesi, i., Indon. see Celebes	248-49	2°0'S	121°00'E
Sulawesi, Laut, s., Asia see Celebes Sea	248-49	3°0'N	122°00'E
Sulina, Rom. (sōō-lē'nà)	202-03	45°09'N	29°40'E
Sulitelma, mtn., Eur. (sōō-lê-tyĕl'mà)	184-85	67°08'N	16°24'E
Sulitjelma, mtn., Eur. see Sulitelma	184-85	67°08'N	16°24'E
Sullana, Peru (sōō-lyä'nä)	170	4°54'S	80°41'W
Sulligent, Al., U.S. (sŭl'ĭ-jĕnt)	124-25	33°54'N	88°08'W
Sullivan, Il., U.S. (sŭl'ĭ-văn)	116-17	39°36'N	88°37'W
Sullivan, In., U.S. (sŭl'ĭ-văn)	116-17	39°05'N	87°24'W
Sullivan, Mo., U.S. (sŭl'ĭ-văn)	120-21	38°12'N	91°10'W
Sulmona, Italy (sōōl-mō'nä)	200-01	42°04'N	13°55'E
Sulphur, La., U.S. (sŭl'fŭr)	122-23	30°14'N	93°22'W
Sulphur, Ok., U.S. (sŭl'fŭr)	120-21	34°30'N	96°58'W
Sulphur Springs, Tx., U.S. (sŭl'fŭr sprĭngz)	120-21	33°09'N	95°36'W
Sultanabad, Iran see Arāk	232-33	34°05'N	49°41'E
Sulu, Laut, s., Asia see Sulu Sea	250	8°0'N	120°00'E
Sulu Archipelago, is., Phil. (sōō'lōō är'kĭ-pĕ'-â-gō)	250	6°0'N	121°00'E
Sulūq, Libya	188-89	31°40'N	20°15'E
Sulu Sea, s., Asia (sōō'lōō sē)	250	8°0'N	120°00'E
Sumatera, i., Indon. see Sumatra	246-47	0°05'S	102°00'E
Sumatra, i., Indon. (sò-mä-trà)	246-47	0°05'S	102°00'E
Sumba, i., Indon. (sŭm'bà)	248-49	10°0'S	120°00'E
Sumba, Île, i., D.R.C.	262-63	1°44'N	19°32'E
Sumbawa, i., Indon. (sòm-bä'wä)	248-49	8°49'S	117°56'E
Sumbawa Besar, Indon.	248-49	8°30'S	117°24'E
Sumbawanga, Tan.	267	7°60'S	31°38'E
Sumbe, Ang.	264-65	11°14'S	13°51'E
Sumenep, Indon.	248-49	7°00'S	113°52'E
Summerland, B.C., Can. (sŭ'mēr-lănd)	132-33	49°36'N	119°41'W
Summerside, P.E., Can. (sŭm'ēr-sīd)	138-39	46°24'N	63°47'W
Summerville, Ga., U.S. (sŭm'ēr-vĭl)	124-25	34°29'N	85°21'W
Summerville, S.C., U.S. (sŭm'ēr-vĭl)	124-25	33°01'N	80°11'W
Summit Lake, B.C., Can.	132-33	54°17'N	122°37'W
Summit Peak, mtn., Co., U.S. (sŭm'mĭt pēk)	118-19	37°21'N	106°42'W
Šumperk, Czech Rep. (shòm'pĕrk)	194-95	49°58'N	16°59'E
Sumqayıt, Azer.	227	40°35'N	49°38'E
Sumter, S.C., U.S. (sŭm'tēr)	124-25	33°55'N	80°21'W
Sumy, Ukr. (sōō'mĭ)	202-03	50°55'N	34°48'E
Sumzom, China	238-39	29°44'N	96°08'E
Sunchales, Arg.	173	30°56'S	61°34'W
Sunch'ŏn, Kor., S.	243	34°57'N	127°30'E
Sunda, Selat, strt., Indon. see Sunda Strait	248-49	6°00'S	105°46'E
Sundance, Wy., U.S. (sŭn'dăns)	114-15	44°24'N	104°23'W
Sunda Strait, strt., Indon. (sōōn'dȧ strāt)	248-49	6°00'S	105°46'E
Sunderland, Eng., U.K. (sŭn'dēr-lănd)	190-91	54°55'N	1°23'W
Sundsvall, Swe. (sònds'văl)	192-93	62°23'N	17°19'E
Sungaipenuh, Indon.	246-47	2°04'S	101°24'E
Sungari, stm., China see Songhua	240-41	47°43'N	132°31'E
Sungari Reservoir, res., China see Songhua Hu	240-41	43°25'N	127°10'E
Sunne, Swe. (sōōn'ĕ)	192-93	59°50'N	13°10'E
Sunnyvale, Ca., U.S. (sŭn-nē-vāl)	118-19	37°22'N	122°01'W
Sunset Crater Volcano National Monument, n.p., Az., U.S. (sŭn-sĕt krā'tēr vŏl-kā'nō năsh'ŭn-ăl mŏn'ū-mĕnt)	118-19	35°22'N	111°31'W
Suntar, Russia (sòn-tär')	218-19	62°10'N	117°38'E
Sun Valley, Id., U.S.	112-13	43°43'N	114°23'W
Sunyani, Ghana	260-61	7°21'N	2°20'W
Suomenlahti, b., Eur. see Finland, Gulf of	192-93	60°0'N	27°00'E
Suomi, nation, Eur. see Finland	174-75	64°0'N	26°00'E
Suomussalmi, Fin.	184-85	64°53'N	29°02'E
Superior, Az., U.S. (su-pē'rĭ-ēr)	118-19	33°18'N	111°06'W
Superior, Ne., U.S. (su-pē'rĭ-ēr)	120-21	40°01'N	98°04'W
Superior, Wi., U.S. (su-pē'rĭ-ēr)	114-15	46°43'N	92°05'W
Superior, Laguna, b., Mex. (lä-gò'nä sōō-pä-rē-ōr')	146-47	16°21'N	94°55'W
Superior, Lake, lk., N.A. (lăk su-pē'rĭ-ēr)	114-15	48°0'N	88°00'W
Suphan Buri, Thai.	246-47	14°28'N	100°08'E
Suqian, China (sōō-chyĕn)	238-39	33°57'N	118°18'E
Suquṭrā, i., Yemen	220-21	12°31'N	53°54'E
Ṣūr, Oman	230-31	22°34'N	59°30'E
Sura, stm., Russia	186-87	55°37'N	46°02'E
Surabaja, Indon. see Surabaya	248-49	7°15'S	112°45'E
Surabaya, Indon.	248-49	7°15'S	112°45'E
Surakarta, Indon.	248-49	7°34'S	110°50'E
Sūrat, India (sò'rŭt)	234-35	21°12'N	72°50'E
Surat Thani, Thai.	246-47	9°06'N	99°18'E
Surazh, Russia (sōō-rázh')	202-03	53°01'N	32°25'E
Surendranagar, India	234-35	22°43'N	71°38'E
Surgut, Russia (sòr-gòt')	218-19	61°16'N	73°12'E
Surigao, Phil.	250	9°46'N	125°29'E
Suriname, nation, S.A. (sōō-rē-näm')	158	4°0'N	56°00'W
Sūrīyah, nation, Asia see Syria	206-07	35°0'N	38°00'E
Sūrmaq, Iran	230-31	31°05'N	52°48'E
Surt, Libya	188-89	31°12'N	16°35'E
Surt, Khalīj, b., Libya	258-59	31°30'N	18°00'E
Suruga-wan, b., Japan (sōō'rōō-gä wän)	245	34°51'N	138°33'E
Susanville, Ca., U.S.	118-19	40°25'N	120°39'W
Susong, China (sōō-sòŋ)	238-39	30°09'N	116°07'E
Susquehanna, Pa., U.S. (sŭs'kwē-hăn'ȧ)	116-17	41°56'N	75°36'W
Susquehanna, stm., U.S. (sŭs'kwē-hăn'ȧ)	116-17	39°32'N	76°05'W
Susques, Arg.	168-69	23°25'S	66°30'W
Sussex, N.B., Can. (sŭs'ĕks)	138-39	45°43'N	65°31'W
Susuman, Russia	218-19	62°46'N	148°10'E
Sutlej, stm., Asia (sŭt'lĕj)	234-35	29°21'N	71°02'E
Sutton, W.V., U.S. (sŭt''n)	116-17	38°39'N	80°45'W
Sutton, Monts, mts., N.A. see Green Mountains	116-17	43°45'N	72°45'W
Suva, nat. cap., Fiji (sōō-vȧ)	279f	18°07'S	178°27'E
Suwałki, Pol. (sò-vou'kē)	194-95	54°06'N	22°56'E
Suwanose-jima, i., Japan	244	29°38'N	129°43'E
Suwarrow, at., Cook Is.	280-81	13°15'S	163°05'W
Suweis, Khalīg el-, b., Egypt see Suez, Gulf of	268b	29°0'N	32°50'E
Suweis, Qanâ el-, can., Egypt see Suez Canal	268b	29°57'N	32°35'E
Suwŏn, Kor., S.	243	37°16'N	127°01'E
Suzdal', Russia (sōōz'dȧl)	202-03	56°25'N	40°26'E
Suzhou, China (sōō-jō)	238-39	33°38'N	116°59'E
Suzhou, China (sōō-jō)	238-39	31°18'N	120°37'E
Svalbard, dep., Eur. (svăl'bärt)	208-09	78°0'N	17°00'E
Svay Riĕng, Camb.	246-47	11°04'N	105°49'E
Svelvik, Nor. (svĕl'vĕk)	192-93	59°37'N	10°24'E
Svendborg, Den. (svĕn-bôrgh)	194-95	55°04'N	10°37'E
Sverdlovs'k, Ukr.	202-03	48°05'N	39°39'E
Sverige, nation, Eur. see Sweden	174-75	62°0'N	15°00'E
Svetlaya, Russia (svyĕt'lá-yȧ)	244	46°34'N	138°20'E
Svetlograd, Russia	186-87	45°20'N	42°50'E
Svilengrad, Blg. (svĕl'ĕn-grát)	200-01	41°46'N	26°13'E
Svir', stm., Russia	186-87	60°30'N	32°48'E
Svishtov, Blg. (svĕsh'tôf)	200-01	43°37'N	25°21'E
Svizzera, nation, Eur. see Switzerland	174-75	47°0'N	8°00'E
Svobodnyy, Russia (svô-bôd'nĭ)	222-23	51°23'N	128°08'E
Svolvær, Nor. (svôl'vĕr)	184-85	68°15'N	14°33'E
Swainsboro, Ga., U.S. (swānz'bŭr-ô)	124-25	32°36'N	82°20'W
Swakop, stm., Nmb.	264-65	22°41'S	14°32'E
Swakopmund, Nmb. (svä'kôp-mònt) (swä'kôp-mònd)	264-65	22°40'S	14°32'E
Swan, stm., Can. (swŏn)	134-35	52°34'N	100°45'W
Swan Hill, Austl. (swŏn hĭl)	276	35°21'S	143°33'E
Swan Lake, lk., Mb., Can. (swŏn lāk)	134-35	52°31'N	100°45'W
Swan Range, mts., Mt., U.S. (swŏn rānj)	112-13	47°50'N	113°40'W
Swan River, Mb., Can. (swŏn rĭv'ēr)	134-35	52°05'N	101°16'W
Swansea, Wales, U.K. (swŏn'sē)	190-91	51°38'N	3°58'W
Swaziland, nation, Afr. (swä'zē-lănd)	253	26°30'S	31°30'E
Sweden, nation, Eur. (swē'dĕn)	174-75	62°0'N	15°00'E
Sweetwater, Tn., U.S. (swēt'wô-tēr)	124-25	35°36'N	84°28'W
Sweetwater, Tx., U.S. (swēt'wô-tēr)	120-21	32°28'N	100°24'W
Swellendam, S. Afr.	264-65	34°01'S	20°26'E
Świecie, Pol. (shvyăn'tsyĕ)	194-95	53°24'N	18°27'E
Swift Current, Sk., Can. (swĭft kûr'ĕnt)	134-35	50°17'N	107°47'W
Swindon, Eng., U.K. (swĭn'dŭn)	190-91	51°34'N	1°47'W
Swinemünde, Pol. see Świnoujście	194-95	53°54'N	14°15'E
Świnoujście, Pol. (shvĭ-nĭ-ô-wēsh'chyĕ)	194-95	53°54'N	14°15'E
Switzerland, nation, Eur. (swĭt'zēr-lănd)	174-75	47°0'N	8°00'E
Sycamore, Il., U.S. (sĭk'ȧ-mōr)	116-17	41°59'N	88°41'W
Sychëvka, Russia (sē-chôf'kȧ)	202-03	55°49'N	34°17'E
Sydney, Austl. (sĭd'nē)	276	33°52'S	151°13'E
Sydney, N.S., Can. (sĭd'nē)	138-39	46°09'N	60°12'W
Sydney Mines, N.S., Can. (sĭd'nē mīns)	138-39	46°15'N	60°15'W
Syktyvkar, Russia (sük-tüf'kär)	186-87	61°39'N	50°49'E
Sylacauga, Al., U.S. (sĭl-ȧ-kô'gȧ)	124-25	33°10'N	86°15'W
Sylhet, Bngl.	234-35	24°54'N	91°52'E
Sylvania, Ga., U.S. (sĭl-vā'nĭ-ȧ)	124-25	32°45'N	81°38'W
Sylvester, Ga., U.S. (sĭl-vĕs'tēr)	124-25	31°32'N	83°50'W
Syracuse, Ks., U.S. (sĭr'ȧ-kūs)	120-21	37°59'N	101°45'W
Syracuse, Ne., U.S. (sĭr'ȧ-kūs)	120-21	40°39'N	96°11'W
Syracuse, N.Y., U.S.	116-17	43°03'N	76°09'W
Syrdarīya, stm., Asia see Syr Darya	226	46°04'N	60°04'E
Syr Darya, stm., Asia (sĭr-dä'rē-ä)	226	46°04'N	60°04'E
Syria, nation, Asia (sĭr'ĭ-ȧ)	206-07	35°0'N	38°00'E
Syriam, Mya.	246-47	16°46'N	96°15'E
Syrian Desert, des., Asia	228-29	32°0'N	40°00'E
Sýros, i., Grc.	200-01	37°26'N	24°55'E
Syzran', Russia (sĕz-rän')	186-87	53°09'N	48°26'E
Szabadka, Serb. see Subotica	200-01	46°06'N	19°41'E
Szamotuły, Pol. (shȧ-mô-tōō'wē)	194-95	52°37'N	16°35'E
Szatmárnémeti, Rom. see Satu Mare	194-95	47°47'N	22°53'E
Szczecin, Pol. (shchĕ'tsĭn)	194-95	53°26'N	14°32'E
Szechwan, state, China see Sichuan	238-39	31°0'N	105°00'E
Szeged, Hung. (sĕ'gĕd)	194-95	46°16'N	20°10'E
Székesfehérvár, Hung. (sā'kĕsh-fĕ'hār-vär)	194-95	47°12'N	18°25'E
Szekszárd, Hung. (sĕk'särd)	194-95	46°21'N	18°43'E
Szentes, Hung. (sĕn'tĕsh)	194-95	46°39'N	20°16'E
Szolnok, Hung.	194-95	47°11'N	20°12'E
Szombathely, Hung. (sôm'bôt-hĕl')	194-95	47°14'N	16°38'E
Szydłowiec, Pol. (shid-wô'vyets)	194-95	51°14'N	20°52'E

T

Feature (Pronunciation)	Page	Lat.	Long.
Ta'izz, Yemen	266	13°35'N	44°01'E
Taal, Lake, lk., Phil. (lăk tä-äl')	250	13°60'N	121°01'E
Tabaco, Phil. (tä-bä'kō)	250	13°23'N	123°43'E
Tabar Islands, is., Pap. N. Gui.	277	2°45'S	151°57'E
Ṭabas, Iran	232-33	33°36'N	56°55'E
Tabasco, state, Mex. (tä-bäs'kô)	146-47	18°15'N	93°00'W
Taber, Ab., Can.	132-33	49°47'N	112°09'W
Tablas Island, i., Phil. (tä'bläs ī'lănd)	250	12°23'N	122°02'E
Tábor, Czech Rep. (tä'bôr)	194-95	49°25'N	14°41'E
Tabora, Tan. (tä-bō'rä)	267	5°01'S	32°50'E
Tabrīz, Iran (tȧ-brēz')	227	38°05'N	46°17'E
Tabuaeran, at., Kir.	280-81	3°51'N	159°18'W
Tabūk, Sau. Ar.	228-29	28°23'N	36°35'E
Tacheng, China (tä-chŭŋ)	226	46°45'N	82°58'E
Tacloban, Phil. (tä-klō'bän)	250	11°14'N	124°60'E
Tacna, Peru (täk'nä)	170	18°01'S	70°15'W
Tacoma, Wa., U.S. (tȧ-kō'mȧ)	112-13	47°15'N	122°26'W
Taconic Range, mts., U.S. (tȧ-kŏn'ĭk rānj)	116-17	42°30'N	73°20'W
Tacotalpa, stm., Mex. (tä-kô-täl'pä)	146-47	17°48'N	92°51'W
Tacuarembó, Ur.	173	31°42'S	55°59'W
Tademaït, Plateau du, plat., Alg. (plä-tō' dü tä-dē-mä'ēt)	258-59	28°20'N	2°47'E
Tadoussac, Qc., Can. (tȧ-dōō-sȧk')	138-39	48°10'N	69°42'W
Tādpatri, India	236	14°54'N	78°00'E
Tadzhikistan, nation, Asia see Tajikistan	232-33	39°0'N	71°00'E
T'aebaek-sanmaek, mts., Asia (tī-bĭk' sän-mīk')	243	37°30'N	128°31'E
Taedong-gang, stm., Kor., N. (tī-dŏng gäng')	243	38°43'N	125°07'E

ăt; finăl; rāte; senâte; ärm; ȧsk; sofȧ; fâre; ch-choose; dh-as th in other; bē; ēvent; bĕt; recĕnt; cratēr; g-gō; gh-guttural g; bĭt; ĭ-short neutral; rīde; ĸ-guttural k as ch in German ich;

Feature (Pronunciation)	Page	Lat.	Long.
Taegu, Kor., S. (tī'gōō')	243	35°52'N	128°35'E
Taehan-min'guk, nation, Asia see South Korea	206-07	36°30'N	128°00'E
Taejŏn, Kor., S.	243	36°20'N	127°26'E
Tafalla, Spain (tä-fäl'yä)	198-99	42°31'N	1°40'W
Tafassasset, Oued, stm., Afr.	258-59	21°52'N	9°59'E
Taft, Ca., U.S. (tȧft)	118-19	35°08'N	119°26'W
Taganrog, Russia (tȧ-gȧn-rôk')	202-03	47°14'N	38°54'E
Taganrogskiy Zaliv, b., Eur. (tȧ-gȧn-rôk'skĭ zä'lĭf)	202-03	47°0'N	38°23'E
Tagbilaran, Phil.	250	9°40'N	123°52'E
Tagdempt, Alg. see Tiaret	198-99	35°28'N	1°21'E
Tagtabazar, Turkmen.	232-33	35°58'N	62°55'E
Taguatinga, Braz.	166-67	12°24'S	46°27'W
Taguke, China	234-35	32°06'N	84°43'E
Tagula Island, i., Pap. N. Gui. (tä'gōō-lȧ ī'lănd)	277	11°30'S	153°30'E
Tagus, stm., Eur. (tā'gŭs)	198-99	38°51'N	8°57'W
Tahan, Gunong, mtn., Malay.	246-47	4°38'N	102°14'E
Tahanroz's'ka zatoka, b., Eur. see Taganrogskiy Zaliv	202-03	47°0'N	38°23'E
Tahat, mtn., Alg. (tä-hät')	258-59	23°17'N	5°32'E
Tahiti, i., Fr. Poly. (tä-hē'tē) (tä'ē-tē')	279d	17°37'S	149°27'W
Tahlequah, Ok., U.S. (tă-lĕ-kwä')	120-21	35°55'N	94°58'W
Tahoe, Lake, lk., U.S. (lāk tä'hō)	118-19	39°07'N	120°03'W
Tahoua, Niger (tä'ōō-ä)	258-59	14°53'N	5°16'E
Tahta, Egypt	268b	26°46'N	31°30'E
Tahulandang, Pulau, i., Indon.	248-49	2°20'N	125°25'E
Tahuna, Indon.	248-49	3°36'N	125°30'E
Tai'an, China (tī-än)	240-41	36°11'N	117°07'E
Taibai Shan, mtn., China (tī-bī shän)	238-39	33°54'N	107°46'E
Taibus Qi, China (tī-bōō-sz chyē)	240-41	41°53'N	115°17'E
T'aichung, Tai. (tī'chóng)	225a	24°09'N	120°41'E
Taiden, Kor., S. see Taejŏn	243	36°20'N	127°26'E
Taif, Sau. Ar. see Aṭ-Ṭā'if	266	21°16'N	40°25'E
Taigu, China (tī-gōō)	240-41	37°25'N	112°33'E
Taihang Shan, mts., China (tī-häŋ shän)	240-41	38°0'N	114°00'E
Taihe, China (tī-hŭ)	238-39	26°49'N	114°54'E
Taihoku, nat. cap., Tai. see T'aipei	225a	25°03'N	121°30'E
Tai Hu, lk., China (tī hōō)	238-39	31°13'N	120°11'E
Taikyu, Kor., S. see Taegu	243	35°52'N	128°35'E
Tailai, China (tī-lī)	240-41	46°23'N	123°25'E
Tailem Bend, Austl. (tā-lĕm bĕnd)	276	35°16'S	139°27'E
T'ainan, Tai. (tī'nan')	225a	23°0'N	120°12'E
Taínaro, Ákra, c., Grc.	200-01	36°23'N	22°29'E
Taining, China (tī'nĭng')	238-39	26°54'N	117°09'E
T'aipei, nat. cap., Tai. (tī'pā')	225a	25°03'N	121°30'E
Taiping, Malay.	246-47	4°51'N	100°44'E
Taira, Japan see Iwaki	245	37°03'N	140°55'E
Taishun, China	238-39	27°33'N	119°43'E
Taitao, Península de, pen., Chile	171	46°30'S	74°25'W
T'aitung, Tai. (tī'tōōng')	225a	22°45'N	121°08'E
Taiwan, nation, Asia (tī-wän)	206-07	23°30'N	121°00'E
T'ai-wan Hai-hsia, strt., Asia see Taiwan Strait	225a	24°0'N	119°00'E
Taiwan Haixia, strt., Asia see Taiwan Strait	225a	24°0'N	119°00'E
Taiwan Strait, strt., Asia (tī-wän strāt strāt)	225a	24°0'N	119°00'E
Taiyuan, China (tī-yůän)	240-41	37°52'N	112°33'E
Taizhao, China	238-39	30°02'N	92°57'E
Taizhou, China (tī-jō)	238-39	32°30'N	119°55'E
Tajikistan, nation, Asia (tä-jĕk'-ĭ-stän') (tä-jĭk'-ĭ-stän')	232-33	39°0'N	71°00'E
Tajo, stm., Eur. see Tagus	198-99	38°51'N	8°57'W
Tajumulco, Volcán, vol., Guat. (vôl-kä'n tä-hōō-mōōl'kō)	148	15°02'N	91°55'W
Tajuña, stm., Spain (tä-kōō'n-yä)	198-99	40°07'N	3°35'W
Tak, Thai.	246-47	16°53'N	99°09'E
Takamatsu, Japan	245	34°20'N	134°03'E
Takao, Tai. see Kaohsiung	225a	22°38'N	120°17'E
Takaoka, Japan (tä'kä'ō-kä')	245	36°45'N	137°01'E
Takasaki, Japan (tä'kät'sōō-kē')	245	36°19'N	139°01'E
Takatsuki, Japan (tä'kät'sōō-kē')	245	34°51'N	135°38'E
Takayama, Japan (tä'kä'yä'mä)	245	36°08'N	137°15'E
Takefu, Japan (tä'kĕ-fōō)	245	35°54'N	136°10'E
Takengon, Indon.	246-47	4°37'N	96°51'E
Takêv, Camb.	246-47	10°59'N	104°45'E
Takhli, Thai.	246-47	15°16'N	100°21'E
Takht-e Jamshīd, hist., Iran see Persepolis	230-31	29°57'N	52°52'E
Takla Lake, lk., B.C., Can.	132-33	55°25'N	125°54'W
Takla Makan Desert, des., China	222-23	39°0'N	83°00'E
Taklimakan Shamo, des., China see Takla Makan Desert	222-23	39°0'N	83°00'E
Tala, Mex. (tä'lä)	146-47	20°39'N	103°43'W
Talagante, Chile (tä-lä-gȧ'n-tĕ)	163e	33°39'S	70°55'W
Talara, Peru (tä-lä'rä)	170	4°35'S	81°16'W
Talas, Kyrg.	226	42°32'N	72°15'E
Talasea, Pap. N. Gui. (tä-lä-sā'ä)	277	5°18'S	150°02'E
Talaud, Kepulauan, is., Indon. (tä-lout')	248-49	4°20'N	126°50'E
Talavera de la Reina, Spain	198-99	39°58'N	4°49'W
Talca, Chile (täl'kä)	171	35°25'S	71°39'W
Talcahuano, Chile (täl-kä-wä'nō)	171	36°42'S	73°07'W
Taldom, Russia (täl-dôm)	202-03	56°44'N	37°32'E
Taldyqorghan, Kaz.	226	45°01'N	78°23'E
Talghar, Kaz.	226	43°18'N	77°14'E
Talkeetna, Ak., U.S. (tål-kēt'nȧ)	126	62°20'N	150°07'W
Tall 'Afar, Iraq	228-29	36°22'N	42°27'E
Talladega, Al., U.S. (tăl-ȧ-dē'gȧ)	124-25	33°26'N	86°06'W
Tallahassee, Fl., U.S. (tăl-ȧ-hăs'ē)	124-25	30°26'N	84°17'W
Tallapoosa, stm., U.S. (tăl-ȧ-pōō'sȧ)	124-25	32°30'N	86°16'W
Tallassee, Al., U.S. (tăl'ȧ-sē)	124-25	32°33'N	85°55'W
Tallinn, nat. cap., Est. (tål'lĕn) (rä'väl)	192-93	59°26'N	24°48'E
Tallulah, La., U.S. (tă-lōō'lȧ)	124-25	32°25'N	91°12'W
Talo, mtn., Eth.	262-63	10°44'N	37°54'E
Talok, Indon.	248-49	1°03'N	118°49'E
Taloyoak, Nu., Can.	128-29	69°32'N	93°31'W
Talpa de Allende, Mex. (täl'pä dā äl-yĕn'dȧ)	146-47	20°23'N	104°50'W
Talsi, Lat. (tal'sĭ)	192-93	57°15'N	22°37'E
Taltal, Chile (täl-täl')	168-69	25°24'S	70°29'W
Talurqjuak, Nu., Can. see Taloyoak	128-29	69°32'N	93°31'W
Tama, Ia., U.S. (tā'mä)	114-15	41°58'N	92°35'W
Tamale, Ghana (tä-mä'lå)	260-61	9°24'N	0°50'W
Taman', Russia (tȧ-män'')	202-03	45°12'N	36°43'E
Tamanrasset, Alg.	258-59	22°48'N	5°31'E
Tamaqua, Pa., U.S. (tȧ-mô'kwȧ)	116-17	40°48'N	75°58'W
Tamaulipas, state, Mex. (tä-mä-ōō-lē'päs')	146-47	24°0'N	98°45'W
Tamazunchale, Mex. (tä-mä-zòn-chä'lå)	146-47	21°16'N	98°47'W
Tambacounda, Sen. (täm-bä-kōōn'dä)	260-61	13°47'N	13°40'W
Tambelan, Kepulauan, is., Indon. (täm-bå-län')	246-47	1°0'N	107°30'E
Tambo, Austl. (tăm'bō)	277	24°53'S	146°15'E
Tambo, stm., Peru	170	17°09'S	71°49'W
Tambora, Gunung, vol., Indon.	248-49	8°14'S	117°55'E
Tambov, Russia (tåm-bôf')	186-87	52°43'N	41°25'E
Tambura, Sudan (täm-bōō'rä)	262-63	5°36'N	27°28'E
Tame, Col.	164-65	6°28'N	71°44'W
Tamiahua, Mex. (tä-myä-wä)	146-47	21°16'N	97°27'W
Tamiahua, Laguna de, lk., Mex. (lä-gò'nä-dĕ-tä-myä-wä)	146-47	21°35'N	97°35'W
Tamiami Canal, can., Fl., U.S. (tă-mī-ăm'ĭ kȧ'năl)	125a	25°46'N	80°11'W
Tamil Nādu, state, India	236	11°0'N	78°15'E
Tam Ky, Viet.	246-47	15°33'N	108°30'E
Tammerfors, Fin. see Tampere	192-93	61°30'N	23°46'E
Tammisaari, Fin. see Ekenäs	192-93	59°58'N	23°26'E
Tampa, Fl., U.S. (tăm'pȧ)	125a	27°58'N	82°27'W
Tampa Bay, b., Fl., U.S. (tăm'pȧ bā)	125a	27°45'N	82°35'W
Tampere, Fin. (tȧm'pĕ-rĕ)	192-93	61°30'N	23°46'E
Tampico, Mex. (täm-pē'kō)	146-47	22°13'N	97°51'W
Tamworth, Austl. (tăm'wûrth)	276	31°06'S	150°55'E
Tana, stm., Eur.	184-85	70°26'N	28°16'E
Tana, stm., Kenya (tä'nä)	262-63	2°31'S	40°31'E
Tanabe, Japan (tä-nä'bā)	245	33°44'N	135°24'E
T'ana Hāyk', lk., Eth.	262-63	11°57'N	37°17'E
Tanahjampea, Pulau, i., Indon.	248-49	7°05'S	120°42'E
Tanami Desert, des., Austl.	272-73	20°0'S	129°30'E
Tanana, Ak., U.S. (tă'nȧ-nô)	126	65°11'N	152°05'W
Tanana, stm., Ak., U.S. (tă'nȧ-nô)	126	65°09'N	152°04'W
Tananarive, nat. cap., Madag. see Antananarivo	264-65	18°55'S	47°32'E
Tanch'ŏn-ŭp, Kor., N.	243	40°27'N	128°54'E
Tancítaro, Pico de, mtn., Mex. (pē'kō-dĕ tän-sē'tä-rō)	146-47	19°23'N	102°13'W
Tandag, Phil.	250	9°04'N	126°12'E
Tandil, Arg. (tän-dēl')	173	37°19'S	59°08'W
Tanega-shima, i., Japan (tä'nå-gä' shē'mä)	244	30°40'N	131°00'E
Tang, stm., China (täŋ)	238-39	33°18'N	117°46'E
Tanga, Tan. (täŋ'gȧ)	262-63	5°04'S	39°06'E
Tanga Islands, is., Pap. N. Gui.	277	3°29'S	153°13'E
Tanganika, Lac, lk., Afr. see Tanganyika, Lake	262-63	6°0'S	29°30'E
Tanganyika, nation, Afr. see Tanzania	253	6°0'S	35°00'E
Tanganyika, Lac, lk., Afr. see Tanganyika, Lake	262-63	6°0'S	29°30'E
Tanganyika, Lake, lk., Afr. (lāk tăn'găn-yē'kȧ)	262-63	6°0'S	29°30'E
Tanger, Mor. (tăn-jĕr') see Tangier	269a	35°47'N	5°48'W
Tanggu, China (täŋ-gōō)	240-41	39°01'N	117°40'E
Tanggula Shan, mts., China (täŋ-gōō-lä shän)	238-39	33°0'N	92°00'E
Tangier, Mor. (tăn-jēr')	269a	35°47'N	5°48'W
Tangipahoa, stm., U.S. (tăn'jē-pȧ-hō'ȧ)	124-25	30°20'N	90°16'W
Tangra Yumco, lk., China (täŋ-rä yōōm-tswo)	234-35	31°01'N	86°34'E
Tangshan, China	240-41	39°37'N	118°12'E
Tanimbar, Kepulauan, is., Indon.	224-25	7°30'S	131°30'E
Tanjore, India see Thanjāvūr	236	10°47'N	79°09'E
Tanjungbalai, Indon. (tän'jông-bä'lå)	246-47	2°58'N	99°48'E
Tanjungkarang-Telukbetung, Indon. see Bandar Lampung	246-47	5°26'S	105°16'E
Tanjungpandan, Indon.	246-47	2°44'S	107°39'E
Tanjungpinang, Indon. (tän'jông-pē'näng)	246-47	0°55'N	104°28'E
Tanjungselor, Indon.	248-49	2°50'N	117°21'E
Tanna, i., Vanuatu	279g	19°30'S	169°20'E
Tannūrah, Ra's, c., Sau. Ar.	230-31	26°38'N	50°10'E
Tanout, Niger	258-59	14°58'N	8°53'E
Tanta, Egypt	268b	30°47'N	31°00'E
Tan-Tan, Mor.	258-59	28°26'N	11°06'W
Tantoyuca, Mex. (tän-tō-yōō'kä)	146-47	21°21'N	98°14'W
Tanzania, nation, Afr. (tăn-zä-nē'ȧ)	253	6°0'S	35°00'E
Tao, stm., China (tou)	240-41	35°55'N	103°20'E
Tao'er, stm., China (tou-är)	240-41	45°41'N	123°49'E
Taongi, at., Marsh. Is.	280-81	14°37'N	168°58'E
Taormina, Italy (tä-ôr-mē'nä)	200-01	37°51'N	15°17'E
Taos, N.M., U.S. (tä'ôs)	120-21	36°25'N	105°35'W
Taoyüan, Tai.	225a	24°59'N	121°18'E
Tapa, Est. (tá'pȧ)	192-93	59°16'N	25°58'E
Tapachula, Mex.	148	14°54'N	92°17'W
Tapajós, stm., Braz. (tä-pä-zhô's)	166-67	2°27'S	54°38'W
Tapalqué, Arg. (tä-päl-kĕ')	173	36°21'S	60°02'W
Tapanahoni, stm., Sur.	164-65	4°21'N	54°26'W
Tapauá, stm., Braz.	166-67	5°47'S	64°24'W
Tāpi, stm., India	234-35	21°09'N	72°44'E
Tapuruquara, Braz.	166-67	0°23'S	65°05'W
Taquari Novo, stm., Braz.	168-69	19°15'S	57°14'W
Tara, Russia (tä'rȧ)	218-19	56°54'N	74°22'E
Tara, stm., Russia (tä'rȧ)	218-19	56°42'N	74°36'E
Taraba, stm., Nig.	260-61	8°33'N	10°14'E
Ṭarābulus, Leb. (tȧ-rä'bò-lōōs) see Tripoli	228-29	34°26'N	35°51'E
Ṭarābulus, hist. reg., Libya see Tripolitania	258-59	31°0'N	15°00'E
Ṭarābulus, nat. cap., Libya see Tripoli	258-59	32°52'N	13°10'E
Tarakan, Indon.	248-49	3°19'N	117°35'E
Tarancón, Spain (tä-rän-kōn')	198-99	40°01'N	3°00'W
Taranto, Italy (tä'rän-tô)	200-01	40°28'N	17°15'E
Taranto, Golfo di, b., Italy (gôl-fô-dē tä'rän-tô)	200-01	40°10'N	17°20'E
Tarapoto, Peru (tä-rä-pô'tō)	170	6°30'S	76°24'W
Taraquá, Braz.	166-67	0°06'N	68°24'W
Tarare, Fr. (tȧ-rär')	196-97	45°54'N	4°26'E
Tarashcha, Ukr. (tä'råsh-chȧ)	202-03	49°34'N	30°31'E
Tarauacá, stm., Braz.	166-67	7°29'S	70°04'W
Tarawa, at., Kir.	280-81	1°21'N	173°08'E
Taraz, Kaz.	226	42°54'N	71°21'E
Tarazona, Spain (tä-rä-thō'nä)	198-99	41°55'N	1°43'W
Tarbagatai Shan, mts., Asia see Tarbagatay, khrebet	226	47°12'N	83°00'E
Tarbagatay, khrebet, mts., Asia	226	47°12'N	83°00'E
Tarbes, Fr. (tȧrb)	196-97	43°14'N	0°05'E
Tarboro, N.C., U.S. (tär'bŭr-ô)	124-25	35°54'N	77°33'W
Taree, Austl. (tȧ-rē')	276	31°54'S	152°28'E
Tarfaya, Mor.	258-59	27°57'N	12°55'W
Târgu Mureș, Rom.	194-95	46°33'N	24°34'E
Tari, Pap. N. Gui.	277	5°51'S	142°59'E
Tarija, Bol. (tär-rē'hä)	168-69	21°33'S	64°43'W
Tarim, stm., China (tä-rĭm')	222-23	39°32'N	88°26'E
Tarim Pendi, bas., China	222-23	39°0'N	83°00'E
Taritatu, stm., Indon.	277	2°55'S	138°28'E
Tarkhankut, mys, c., Ukr. (mĭs tȧr-kän'kòt)	202-03	45°21'N	32°30'E
Tarkio, Mo., U.S. (tär'kĭ-ō)	120-21	40°26'N	95°23'W
Tarko-Sale, Russia	218-19	64°56'N	77°47'E
Tarlac, Phil. (tär'läk)	250	15°29'N	120°36'E
Tarma, Peru (tär'mä)	163a	11°24'S	75°44'W
Tarnopol, Ukr. see Ternopil'	194-95	49°33'N	25°37'E
Tarnów, Pol. (tär'nôf)	194-95	50°01'N	21°01'E
Taroom, Austl.	276	25°39'S	149°48'E

n-sing; ŋ-baŋk; ɴ-nasalized n; nŏd; cŏmmit; ōld; ôbey; ôrder; oi-boil; fōōd; ò-as oo in foot; ou-out; s-soft; sh-dish; th-thin; pūre; ůnite; ûrn; stŭd; circŭs; ü-as in French tu; '-indeterminate vowel.

Feature (Pronunciation)	Page	Lat.	Long.
Tarpon Springs, Fl., U.S. (tär´pŏn sprĭngz)	125a	28°09'N	82°46'W
Tarquinia, Italy (tär-kwē´nē-ä)	200-01	42°15'N	11°45'E
Tarragona, Spain (tär-rä-gō´nä)	198-99	41°07'N	1°14'E
Tàrrega, Spain	198-99	41°39'N	1°09'E
Tárrega, Spain (tä rå-gä) see Tàrrega	198-99	41°39'N	1°09'E
Tarsus, Tur. (tȧr'sōs) (tär´sŭs)	228-29	36°54'N	34°55'E
Tartagal, Arg. (tär-tä-gä´l)	168-69	22°33'S	63°50'W
Tartu, Est. (tär´tōō)	192-93	58°23'N	26°43'E
Ṭarṭūs, Syria	228-29	34°53'N	35°54'E
Tarutao, Ko, i., Thai.	246-47	6°35'N	99°40'E
Tarutung, Indon.	246-47	2°01'N	98°58'E
Taseyeva, stm., Russia	218-19	58°05'N	94°01'E
Tashauz, Turkmen. see Daşoguz	226	41°50'N	59°58'E
Ţashk, Daryācheh-ye, lk., Iran	230-31	29°45'N	53°30'E
Tashkent, nat. cap., Uzb. (tȧsh´kĕnt)	232-33	41°19'N	69°17'E
Tāshkurghān, Afg. see Kholm	232-33	36°41'N	67°42'E
Tashtagol, Russia	226	52°46'N	87°53'E
Tasiilaq, Green. see Angmagssalik	284-85	65°35'N	37°50'W
Tasikmalaya, Indon.	248-49	7°20'S	108°13'E
Tasman Bay, b., N.Z. (tăz´măn bā)	278	41°0'S	173°20'E
Tasmania, state, Austl.	276	43°0'S	147°00'E
Tasman Peninsula, pen., Austl. (tăz´măn pĕ-nĭn´sūlă)	276	43°05'S	147°50'E
Tasman Sea, s., Oc. (tăz´măn sē)	282-83	40°0'S	163°00'E
Tatabánya, Hung.	194-95	47°34'N	18°26'E
Tataouine, Tun.	188-89	32°55'N	10°28'E
Tatarskiy Proliv, strt., Russia	218-19	50°0'N	141°15'E
Tatar Strait, strt., Russia (tȧ-tär´ strāt) see Tatarskiy Proliv	218-19	50°0'N	141°15'E
Tateyama, Japan (tä´tē-yä´mä)	245	34°59'N	139°52'E
Tathlina Lake, lk., N.T., Can.	130-31	60°32'N	117°32'W
Tatnam, Cape, c., Mb., Can.	134-35	57°14'N	90°54'W
Tatta, Pak.	232-33	24°45'N	67°56'E
Tatvan, Tur.	227	38°31'N	42°18'E
Tau, i., Am. Sam.	279b	14°15'S	169°29'W
Taunggyi, Mya.	246-47	20°47'N	97°02'E
Taupo, N.Z.	278	38°41'S	176°06'E
Taupo, Lake, lk., N.Z. (lăk tä´ōō-pō)	278	38°49'S	175°55'E
Tauragė, Lith. (tou´rá-gā)	192-93	55°15'N	22°17'E
Tauranga, N.Z.	278	37°42'S	176°09'E
Tauroa Point, c., N.Z.	278	35°10'S	173°04'E
Taurus Mountains, mts., Tur. (tôr´ŭs moun´tĭnz)	186-87	37°0'N	33°00'E
Tavastehus, Fin. see Hämeenlinna	192-93	60°58'N	24°31'E
Tavda, stm., Russia (tȧv-dȧ´)	218-19	57°48'N	67°15'E
Tavira, Port. (tä-vē´rȧ)	198-99	37°07'N	7°39'W
Tavoy, Mya. see Dawei	246-47	14°05'N	98°13'E
Tavşanlı, Tur. (tȧv´shän-lĭ)	200-01	39°32'N	29°29'E
Tawas City, Mi., U.S. (tô´wȧs sĭ´tĭ)	116-17	44°16'N	83°31'W
Tawau, Malay.	248-49	4°16'N	117°53'E
Tawitawi Island, i., Phil.	250	5°11'N	119°60'E
Ṭawkar, Sudan	266	18°25'N	37°44'E
Taxco de Alarcón, Mex. (täs´kō dĕ ä-lär-kō´n)	146-47	18°33'N	99°36'W
Taxkorgan Tajik Zizhixian, China	234-35	37°47'N	75°14'E
Tayabas Bay, b., Phil. (tä-yä´bäs bā)	250	13°45'N	121°45'E
Taylor, Tx., U.S. (tā´lẽr)	122-23	30°34'N	97°24'W
Taylorville, Il., U.S. (tā´lẽr-vĭl)	116-17	39°33'N	89°18'W
Taymura, stm., Russia	218-19	63°46'N	98°07'E
Taymyr, Ozero, lk., Russia (ō´zĕ-rô tī-mĭr´)	208-09	74°36'N	102°24'E
Taymyr, Poluostrov, pen., Russia (tī-mĭr´)	218-19	76°0'N	104°00'E
Taymyr Peninsula, pen., Russia (tī-mĭr´ pĕ-nĭn´sūlă) see Taymyr, Poluostrov	218-19	76°0'N	104°00'E
Tayshet, Russia (tī-shĕt´)	218-19	55°56'N	98°00'E
Taytay, Phil.	250	10°49'N	119°31'E
Taz, stm., Russia (tȧz)	218-19	67°30'N	78°44'E
Taza, Mor. (tä´zä)	184-85	34°14'N	4°01'W
Tazovskiy, Russia	218-19	67°29'N	78°42'E
Tbilisi, nat. cap., Geor. (´tbĭl-yē´sē)	227	41°44'N	44°47'E
Tchad, nation, Afr. see Chad	253	15°0'N	19°00'E
Tchad, Lac, lk., Afr. see Chad, Lake	258-59	13°03'N	14°33'E
Tchibanga, Gabon (chē-băŋ´gä)	260-61	2°51'S	11°01'E
Teapa, Mex. (tā-ä´pä)	146-47	17°34'N	92°58'W
Tébessa, Alg.	184-85	35°24'N	8°07'E
Tebingtinggi, Indon.	246-47	3°19'N	99°10'E
Tecalitlán, Mex. (tā-kä-lē-tlän´)	146-47	19°28'N	103°17'W
Techiman, Ghana	260-61	7°36'N	1°56'W
Tecka, Arg.	171	43°28'S	70°50'W
Tecomán, Mex. (tā-kō-män´)	146-47	18°55'N	103°52'W
Tecpan de Galeana, Mex. (tĕk-pän´ dā gä-lā-ä´nä)	146-47	17°13'N	100°36'W
Tecuala, Mex. (tĕ-kwä-lä)	146-47	22°24'N	105°28'W
Tecuci, Rom. (ta-kōoch')	202-03	45°51'N	27°26'E
Tecumseh, Mi., U.S. (tē-kŭm´sē)	116-17	41°60'N	83°56'W
Tecumseh, Ne., U.S. (tē-kŭm´sē)	120-21	40°22'N	96°12'W
Tecumseh, Ok., U.S. (tē-kŭm´sē)	120-21	35°15'N	96°56'W
Tees, stm., Eng., U.K. (tēz)	190-91	54°36'N	1°15'W
Tefé, Braz.	166-67	3°23'S	64°43'W
Tefé, stm., Braz.	166-67	3°31'S	64°57'W
Tegal, Indon.	248-49	6°52'S	109°08'E
Tégua, i., Vanuatu	279g	13°15'S	166°37'E
Tegucigalpa, nat. cap., Hond. (tā-gōō-sē-gäl´pä)	149	14°05'N	87°13'W
Tehek Lake, lk., Nu., Can.	130-31	64°56'N	95°37'W
Teheran, nat. cap., Iran see Tehrān	232-33	35°40'N	51°25'E
Tehrān, nat. cap., Iran (tĕ-hrän´)	232-33	35°40'N	51°25'E
Tehuacán, Mex. (tā-wä-kän´)	146-47	18°27'N	97°24'W
Tehuantepec, Golfo de, b., Mex. (gôl-fô dĕ tå-wän-tå-pĕk´)	146-47	15°60'N	94°50'W
Tehuantepec, Istmo de, isth., Mex. (ē´st-mô dĕ tå-wän-tå-pĕk´)	146-47	17°0'N	95°00'W
Teide, Pico del, mtn., Spain	199d	28°16'N	16°38'W
Tejen, Turkmen.	232-33	37°22'N	60°31'E
Tejen, stm., Asia	232-33	37°24'N	60°31'E
Tejo, stm., Eur. see Tagus	198-99	38°51'N	8°57'W
Tejupan, Punta, c., Mex. (pōō´n-tä-tĕ-κōō-pä´n)	146-47	18°20'N	103°30'W
Tejupilco de Hidalgo, Mex. (tå-hōō-pēl´kô dā ē-dhäl´gō)	146-47	18°54'N	100°09'W
Tekamah, Ne., U.S. (tē-kā´mȧ)	114-15	41°47'N	96°13'W
Tekeli, Kaz.	226	44°48'N	78°51'E
Tekezē, stm., Afr.	266	14°20'N	35°51'E
Tekirdağ, Tur.	200-01	40°60'N	27°31'E
Tekit, Mex. (tĕ-kē´t)	148	20°32'N	89°20'W
Tela, Hond. (tā´lä)	149	15°46'N	87°28'W
Tel Aviv-Jaffa, Isr. see Tel Aviv-Yafo	228-29	32°03'N	34°47'E
Tel Aviv-Yafo, Isr. (tĕl-ä-vēv´já´fȧ)	228-29	32°03'N	34°47'E
Telegraph Creek, B.C., Can. (tĕl´ē-gráf krēk)	128-29	57°55'N	131°10'W
Telén, Arg.	171	36°16'S	65°31'W
Telen, stm., Indon.	248-49	0°09'S	116°41'E
Telescope Peak, mtn., Ca., U.S. (tĕl´ē-skōp pēk)	118-19	36°10'N	117°05'W
Teletskoye Ozero, lk., Russia	226	51°38'N	87°40'E
Tell City, In., U.S. (tĕl sĭ´tē)	116-17	37°57'N	86°46'W
Tello, Col. (tĕ´l-yô)	163c	3°04'N	75°08'W
Telluride, Co., U.S. (tĕl´ū-rīd)	118-19	37°57'N	107°48'W
Teloloapan, Mex. (tā´lô-lô-ä´pän)	146-47	18°21'N	99°52'W
Telos, i., Grc. see Tílos	200-01	36°26'N	27°23'E
Telsen, Arg.	171	42°27'S	66°58'W
Telšiai, Lith. (tĕl´sha´ē)	192-93	55°59'N	22°15'E
Teluk Intan, Malay.	246-47	4°01'N	101°02'E
Tema, Ghana	260-61	5°38'N	0°01'E
Temagami, Lake, lk., On., Can.	136-37	47°0'N	80°05'W
Temax, Mex. (tĕ´mäx)	148	21°09'N	88°56'W
Tembenchi, stm., Russia	218-19	64°37'N	99°56'E
Tembesi, stm., Indon.	246-47	1°42'S	103°06'E
Tembilahan, Indon.	246-47	0°16'S	103°13'E
Temesvár, Rom. see Timişoara	200-01	45°45'N	21°13'E
Temirtau, Kaz.	226	50°03'N	72°57'E
Tempe, Az., U.S.	118-19	33°24'N	111°55'W
Tempio Pausania, Italy (tĕm´pē-ō pou-sä´nē-ä)	200-01	40°54'N	9°06'E
Temple, Tx., U.S. (tĕm´p'l)	122-23	31°06'N	97°21'W
Tempoal, stm., Mex. (tĕm-pô-ä´l)	146-47	21°46'N	98°27'W
Temryuk, Russia (tyĕm-ryŏk´)	202-03	45°16'N	37°22'E
Temuco, Chile (tå-mōō´kō)	171	38°44'S	72°36'W
Tena, Ec.	170	0°59'S	77°49'W
Tenāli, India	236	16°15'N	80°35'E
Tenasserim, Mya. (tĕn-ăs´ẽr-ĭm)	246-47	12°05'N	99°01'E
Ten Degree Channel, strt., India	246-47	10°0'N	93°00'E
Tendrara, Mor.	188-89	33°04'N	2°00'W
Ténéré, des., Niger	258-59	18°43'N	10°51'E
Tenerife, i., Spain (tå-nå-rē´fä) (tĕn-ẽr-ĭf´)	199d	28°19'N	16°34'W
Ténès, Alg. (tā-nĕs´)	198-99	36°30'N	1°18'E
Tengchong, China	238-39	25°01'N	98°30'E
Tenggara, Nusa, is., Asia see Lesser Sunda Islands	248-49	9°0'S	120°00'E
Tengiz köli, lk., Kaz.	226	50°22'N	68°56'E
Tengxian, China (tŭŋ shyĕn)	238-39	23°20'N	110°53'E
Tengxian, China (tŭŋ shyĕn)	240-41	35°05'N	117°09'E
Tennant Creek, Austl. (tĕn´ănt krēk)	270-71	19°39'S	134°11'E
Tennessee, state, U.S. (tĕn-ĕ-sē´)	108-09	35°50'N	85°30'W
Tennessee, stm., U.S. (tĕn-ĕ-sē´)	110-11	37°05'N	88°34'W
Teno, stm., Eur.	184-85	70°26'N	28°16'E
Tenom, Malay.	248-49	5°07'N	115°56'E
Tenosique, Mex. (tā-nō-sē´kå)	148	17°29'N	91°26'W
Tenryū, stm., Japan (tĕn´ryōō´)	245	34°40'N	137°48'E
Tensas, stm., La., U.S. (tĕn´sô)	124-25	31°37'N	91°48'W
Tenterfield, Austl. (tĕn´tẽr-fēld)	276	29°04'S	152°01'E
Teocaltiche, Mex. (tā´ō-käl-tē´chå)	146-47	21°26'N	102°34'W
Teófilo Otoni, Braz. (tĕ-ô´fē-lō-tô´nē)	172	17°53'S	41°31'W
Teotihuacán, hist., Mex.	146-47	19°44'N	98°50'W
Tepalcatepec, Mex. (tā´päl-kä-tå´pĕk)	146-47	19°11'N	102°51'W
Tepatitlán de Morelos, Mex. (tā-pä-tē-tlän´ dā mô-rā´los)	146-47	20°48'N	102°44'W
Tepeaca, Mex. (tā-på-ä´kä)	146-47	18°58'N	97°54'W
Tepic, Mex. (tā-pēk´)	146-47	21°30'N	104°54'W
Tequila, Mex. (tå-kē´lä)	146-47	20°52'N	103°50'W
Tequisquiapan, Mex. (tå-kēs-kē-ä´pän)	146-47	20°32'N	99°54'W
Téra, Niger	258-59	14°00'N	0°46'E
Teraina, i., Kir.	280-81	4°42'N	160°45'W
Teramo, Italy (tā´rä-mô)	200-01	42°40'N	13°42'E
Terceira, i., Port. (tĕr-sā´rä)	199c	38°43'N	24°13'W
Tercero, stm., Arg.	173	32°55'S	62°20'W
Terek, stm., Russia	227	43°44'N	46°33'E
Teresina, Braz. (tĕr-å-sē´nȧ)	166-67	5°05'S	42°49'W
Teresópolis, Braz. (tĕr-ā-sō´pō-lēzh)	172	22°26'S	42°59'W
Tergüün Bogd uul, mtn., Mong.	240-41	44°57'N	100°15'E
Teriběrka, Russia (tyĕr-ē-byôr´kȧ)	186-87	69°07'N	35°08'E
Términos, Laguna de, b., Mex. (lä-gô´nä dĕ ĕ´r-mē-nôs)	148	18°36'N	91°34'W
Termiz, Uzb.	232-33	37°14'N	67°16'E
Termoli, Italy (tĕr´mô-lē)	200-01	42°00'N	14°60'E
Ternate, Indon. (tĕr-nä´tā)	248-49	0°49'N	127°18'E
Terney, Russia	244	45°03'N	136°36'E
Terni, Italy (tĕr´nē)	200-01	42°34'N	12°39'E
Ternopil', Ukr.	194-95	49°33'N	25°37'E
Terpeniya, Mys, c., Russia (mĭs tĕr-pă´nĭ-yȧ)	218-19	48°39'N	144°44'E
Terpeniya, Zaliv, b., Russia (zä´lĭf tĕr-pă´nĭ-yȧ)	218-19	49°0'N	143°30'E
Terrace, B.C., Can. (tĕr´ĭs)	132-33	54°32'N	128°35'W
Terracina, Italy (tĕr-rä-chē´nä)	200-01	41°17'N	13°15'E
Terranova di Sicilia, Italy see Gela	200-01	37°04'N	14°15'E
Terrebonne, Qc., Can. (tĕr-bŏn´)	136-37	45°42'N	73°37'W
Terre Haute, In., U.S. (tĕr-ē hōt´)	116-17	39°27'N	87°25'W
Teruel, Spain (tå-rōō-ĕl´)	198-99	40°21'N	1°06'W
Tes, stm., Asia	222-23	50°29'N	93°03'E
Teseney, Erit.	266	15°08'N	36°42'E
Tes-Khem, stm., Asia see Tes	222-23	50°29'N	93°03'E
Teslin, Yk., Can. (tĕs-lĭn)	128-29	60°11'N	132°43'W
Teslin, stm., Can. (tĕs-lĭn)	130-31	61°34'N	134°53'W
Teslin Lake, lk., Can. (tĕs-lĭn lăk)	130-31	60°15'N	132°57'W
Tessalit, Mali	258-59	20°12'N	1°00'E
Tessaoua, Niger (tĕs-sä´ō-ä)	258-59	13°45'N	7°59'E
Tete, Moz. (tā´tē)	264-65	16°09'S	33°36'E
Tetepare Island, i., Sol. Is.	279e	8°43'S	157°33'E
Teterow, Ger. (tā´tē-rō)	194-95	53°46'N	12°34'E
Tetiaroa, at., Fr. Poly.	279d	17°00'S	149°34'W
Tetouan, Mor.	269a	35°35'N	5°22'W
Tetovo, Mac. (tā´tô-vô)	200-01	42°00'N	20°59'E
Teuco, stm., Arg.	168-69	25°39'S	60°10'W
Tevere, stm., Italy see Tiber	200-01	41°45'N	12°14'E
Texarkana, Ar., U.S. (tĕk-sär-kăn´ȧ)	120-21	33°26'N	94°03'W
Texarkana, Tx., U.S. (tĕk-sär-kăn´ȧ)	120-21	33°26'N	94°04'W
Texas, state, U.S. (tĕk´sŭs)	108-09	31°30'N	99°00'W
Texas City, Tx., U.S. (tĕk´sŭs sĭ´tĭ)	122-23	29°23'N	94°54'W
Texoma, Lake, res., U.S. (lăk tĕk´ō-mă)	120-21	33°54'N	96°37'W
Teykovo, Russia (tĕy-kô-vô)	202-03	56°51'N	40°33'E
Teziutlán, Mex. (tå-zē-ōō-tlän´)	146-47	19°49'N	97°21'W
Tezpur, India	234-35	26°37'N	92°48'E
Thabana-Ntlenyana, mtn., Leso.	264-65	29°28'S	29°16'E
Thabazimbi, S. Afr.	269c	24°37'S	27°24'E
Thai Lan, Vinh, b., Asia see Thailand, Gulf of	246-47	10°0'N	101°00'E
Thailand, nation, Asia (tī´ănd)	206-07	15°0'N	100°00'E
Thailand, Gulf of, b., Asia (gŭlf ŭv tī´ănd)	246-47	10°0'N	101°00'E
Thai Nguyen, Viet.	246-47	21°36'N	105°50'E
Thakhek, Laos see Muang Khammouan	246-47	17°25'N	104°49'E
Thal, Pak.	232-33	33°22'N	70°33'E
Thames, stm., On., Can. (tĕmz)	136-37	42°19'N	82°27'W
Thames, stm., Eng., U.K. (tĕmz)	190-91	51°27'N	0°21'E
Thāne, India	236	19°14'N	72°59'E
Thanh Hoa, Viet. (tän´hō´ä)	246-47	19°48'N	105°46'E
Thanh Pho Ho Chi Minh, Viet. see Ho Chi Minh City	246-47	10°45'N	106°40'E
Thanjāvūr, India	236	10°47'N	79°09'E
Thanlwin, stm., Asia see Salween	208-09	16°33'N	97°40'E

Feature (Pronunciation)	Page	Lat.	Long.
Thann, Fr. (tän)	**196-97**	47°49'N	7°05'E
Thar Desert, des., Asia (tär dĕs'ĕrt)	**232-33**	27°0'N	71°00'E
Thargomindah, Austl. (thár'gō-mĭn'dá)	**276**	28°0'S	143°49'E
Tharrawaddy, Mya.	**246-47**	17°39'N	95°47'E
Thásos, i., Grc. (thă'sôs)	**200-01**	40°39'N	24°40'E
Thayer, Mo., U.S. (thâ'ēr)	**124-25**	36°31'N	91°33'W
Thayetmyo, Mya.	**246-47**	19°19'N	95°11'E
Thazi, Mya.	**246-47**	20°51'N	96°04'E
Thebes, Grc. (thēbz) *see* Thíva	**200-01**	38°20'N	23°19'E
Thebes, hist., Egypt (thēbz)	**268b**	25°42'N	32°39'E
The Coorong, b., Austl. (thá kŏ'rŏng)	**276**	35°46'S	139°15'E
The Dalles, Or., U.S. (thá dălz)	**112-13**	45°36'N	121°11'W
The Hague, nat. cap., Neth. (thá hāg) *see* Hague, The	**190-91**	52°06'N	4°18'E
The Minch, strt., Scot., U.K.	**190-91**	58°10'N	5°50'W
Theodore, Austl. (thēō'dôr)	**277**	24°57'S	150°05'E
Theodore Roosevelt National Park (North Unit), n.p., N.D., U.S. (thē-ō-dôr rōō-sá-vĕlt năsh'ŭn-ăl pärk)	**114-15**	47°34'N	103°24'W
Theodore Roosevelt National Park (South Unit), n.p., N.D., U.S. (thē-ō-dôr rōō-sá-vĕlt năsh'ŭn-ăl pärk)	**114-15**	46°58'N	103°25'W
The Pas, Mb., Can. (thá pä)	**134-35**	53°49'N	101°13'W
Thermopolis, Wy., U.S. (thēr-mŏp'ō-lĭs)	**112-13**	43°39'N	108°13'W
The Snares, is., N.Z. *see* Snares Islands	**287**	48°0'S	166°30'E
Thessaloníki, Grc. (thĕs-sá-lô-nē'kê)	**200-01**	40°38'N	22°59'E
Thetford Mines, Qc., Can. (thĕt'fērd mīns)	**136-37**	46°05'N	71°18'W
The Valley, nat. cap., Anguilla	**143b**	18°13'N	63°04'W
Thibodaux, La., U.S. (tē-bô-dō')	**124-25**	29°48'N	90°49'W
Thief River Falls, Mn., U.S. (thēf rĭv'ēr fôlz)	**114-15**	48°07'N	96°11'W
Thiers, Fr. (tyâr)	**196-97**	45°51'N	3°32'E
Thiès, Sen. (tē-ĕs')	**260-61**	14°48'N	16°56'W
Thika, Kenya	**267**	1°03'S	37°04'E
Thimphu, nat. cap., Bhu. (tĭm-pōō')	**234-35**	27°28'N	89°39'E
Thingvellir, Ice.	**190a**	64°16'N	21°07'W
Thionville, Fr. (tyôN-vēl')	**196-97**	49°22'N	6°10'E
Thíra, i., Grc.	**200-01**	36°26'N	25°27'E
Thiruvananthapuram, India	**236**	8°31'N	76°57'E
Thisted, Den. (tēs'tĕdh)	**192-93**	56°57'N	8°42'E
Thíva, Grc.	**200-01**	38°20'N	23°19'E
Thjórsá, stm., Ice. (tyûr'sá)	**190a**	63°55'N	20°40'W
Thomas, Ok., U.S. (tŏm'ăs)	**120-21**	35°45'N	98°45'W
Thomaston, Ga., U.S. (tŏm'ăs-tŭn)	**124-25**	32°53'N	84°19'W
Thomasville, Al., U.S. (tŏm'ăs-vĭl)	**124-25**	31°54'N	87°45'W
Thomasville, Ga., U.S. (tŏm'ăs-vĭl)	**124-25**	30°50'N	83°59'W
Thomasville, N.C., U.S. (tŏm'ăs-vĭl)	**124-25**	35°53'N	80°05'W
Thompson, Mb., Can. (tŏm-sŏn)	**134-35**	55°44'N	97°51'W
Thompson, stm., B.C., Can. (tŏm-sŏn)	**132-33**	50°14'N	121°35'W
Thompson, stm., U.S. (tŏm-sŏn)	**120-21**	39°45'N	93°37'W
Thompson Falls, Mt., U.S. (tŏm-sŏn fôlz)	**112-13**	47°35'N	115°21'W
Thomson, stm., Austl. (tŏm-sŏn)	**277**	25°11'S	142°50'E
Thomson's Falls, Kenya (tŏm-sŏns fôlz) *see* Nyahururu Falls	**267**	0°02'N	36°22'E
Thonon-les-Bains, Fr. (tô-nôN'lā-băN')	**196-97**	46°23'N	6°29'E
Thorn, Pol. *see* Toruń	**194-95**	53°01'N	18°37'E
Thorshavn, nat. cap., Far. Is. *see* Tórshavn	**190b**	62°01'N	6°46'W
Thouars, Fr. (tōō-är')	**196-97**	46°59'N	0°13'W
Thrace, hist. reg., Eur. (thrās)	**200-01**	41°20'N	26°45'E
Thráki, hist. reg., Eur. *see* Thrace	**200-01**	41°20'N	26°45'E
Three Forks, Mt., U.S. (thrē fôrks)	**112-13**	45°53'N	111°34'W
Three Gorges Reservoir, res., China	**238-39**	31°0'N	110°30'E
Three Hummock Island, i., Austl.	**276**	40°26'S	144°55'E
Three Oaks, Mi., U.S. (thrē ōks)	**116-17**	41°48'N	86°36'W
Three Pagodas Pass, p., Asia	**246-47**	15°18'N	98°22'E
Three Points, Cape, c., Ghana	**260-61**	4°45'N	2°05'W
Three Rivers, Mi., U.S. (thrē rĭv'ērz)	**116-17**	41°56'N	85°37'W
Thrissur, India	**236**	10°31'N	76°13'E
Thu, Cu Lao, i., Viet.	**246-47**	10°32'N	108°57'E
Thule, Green.	**288**	76°41'N	68°51'W
Thunder Bay, On., Can. (thŭn'dēr bā)	**136-37**	48°24'N	89°15'W
Thunder Bay, b., On., Can. (thŭn'dēr bā)	**136-37**	48°24'N	89°00'W
Thursday Island, Austl.	**277**	10°36'S	142°15'E
Thurso, Scot., U.K.	**190-91**	58°35'N	3°32'W
Thysville, D.R.C. *see* Mbanza-Ngungu	**262-63**	5°14'S	14°53'E
Tiandong, China (tĭĕn-dôŋ)	**238-39**	23°36'N	107°08'E
Tianjin, China (tĭĕn-jyĭ)	**240-41**	39°08'N	117°11'E
Tianjin, state, China	**240-41**	39°30'N	117°15'E
Tianjun, China	**240-41**	37°20'N	98°57'E
Tianmen, China (tĭĕn-mŭn)	**238-39**	30°39'N	113°10'E

Feature (Pronunciation)	Page	Lat.	Long.
Tian Shan, mts., Asia (tĭĕn shän) *see* Tien Shan	**226**	42°0'N	80°00'E
Tianshui, China (tĭĕn-shwā)	**238-39**	34°32'N	105°54'E
Tiantai, China	**238-39**	29°08'N	121°00'E
Tianzhu, China	**240-41**	36°60'N	103°07'E
Tiaret, Alg.	**198-99**	35°28'N	1°21'E
Tibasti, Sarīr, des., Libya	**258-59**	24°0'N	17°00'E
Tibati, Camrn.	**260-61**	6°27'N	12°37'E
Tiber, stm., Italy (Itī'bēr)	**200-01**	41°45'N	12°14'E
Tiberias, Lake, lk., Isr. *see* Galilee, Sea of	**228-29**	32°48'N	35°35'E
Tibesti, mts., Afr. (tĭ-bĕs'-tē)	**258-59**	21°30'N	17°30'E
Tibet, state, China (tĭ-bĕt')	**234-35**	32°0'N	88°00'E
Tibet, Plateau of, plat., China (plä-tō' ŭv tĭ-bĕt')	**222-23**	33°0'N	92°00'E
Tibooburra, Austl.	**276**	29°26'S	142°01'E
Tiburón, Isla, i., Mex.	**144-45**	29°0'N	112°23'W
Tîchît, Maur.	**258-59**	18°29'N	9°28'W
Ticonderoga, N.Y., U.S. (tī-kŏn-dēr-ō'gá)	**116-17**	43°51'N	73°26'W
Ticul, Mex. (tē-kōō'l)	**148**	20°24'N	89°32'W
Tidaholm, Swe. (tē'dá-hōlm)	**192-93**	58°11'N	13°58'E
Tidjikja, Maur.	**258-59**	18°33'N	11°25'W
Tidore, Indon.	**248-49**	0°38'N	127°24'E
Tieli, China	**240-41**	46°59'N	128°04'E
Tieling, China (tĭĕ-lĭŋ)	**243**	42°18'N	123°51'E
Tien Giang, stm., Asia *see* Mekong	**246-47**	10°33'N	105°27'E
Tien Shan, mts., Asia (tĭĕn shän)	**226**	42°0'N	80°00'E
Tientsin, China *see* Tianjin	**240-41**	39°08'N	117°11'E
Tientsin, state, China *see* Tianjin	**240-41**	39°30'N	117°15'E
Tierp, Swe. (tyĕrp)	**192-93**	60°20'N	17°31'E
Tierra Blanca, Mex. (tyĕ'r-rä-blä'n-kä)	**146-47**	18°26'N	96°21'W
Tierra del Fuego, i., S.A. (tyĕr'rä dĕl fwā'gō)	**171**	54°0'S	69°00'W
Tietê, stm., Braz.	**168-69**	20°37'S	51°34'W
Tiffin, Oh., U.S. (tĭf'ĭn)	**116-17**	41°06'N	83°10'W
Tifton, Ga., U.S. (tĭf'tŭn)	**124-25**	31°27'N	83°30'W
Tiga, Île, i., N. Cal.	**279g**	21°08'S	167°48'E
Tighina, Mol.	**202-03**	46°50'N	29°29'E
Tigil', Russia	**218-19**	57°47'N	158°42'E
Tignish, P.E., Can. (tĭg'nĭsh)	**138-39**	46°58'N	64°02'W
Tigre, stm., Peru	**170**	4°29'S	74°05'W
Tigris, stm., Asia (tī-grĭs)	**208-09**	30°60'N	47°27'E
Tihuatlán, Mex. (tē-wä-tlän')	**146-47**	20°44'N	97°34'W
Tijuana, Mex. (tē-hwä'nä)	**144-45**	32°32'N	117°01'W
Tikal, hist., Guat. (tē-käl')	**148**	17°15'N	89°39'W
Tikei, Île, i., Fr. Poly.	**280-81**	14°58'S	144°33'W
Tikhoretsk, Russia (tē-κôr-yĕtsk')	**186-87**	45°51'N	40°08'E
Tikhvin, Russia (têκ-vēn')	**192-93**	59°39'N	33°32'E
Tikrīt, Iraq	**228-29**	34°36'N	43°42'E
Tiksi, Russia (têk-sē')	**218-19**	71°39'N	128°48'E
Tilburg, Neth. (tĭl'bŭrg)	**190-91**	51°34'N	5°05'E
Tilemsi, Vallée du, stm., Mali	**258-59**	16°18'N	0°01'E
Tillamook, Or., U.S. (tĭl'á-mŏk)	**112-13**	45°27'N	123°50'W
Tillsonburg, On., Can. (tĭl'sŭn-bûrg)	**136-37**	42°52'N	80°43'W
Tílos, i., Grc.	**200-01**	36°26'N	27°23'E
Tilpa, Austl.	**276**	30°57'S	144°24'E
Tim, Russia (têm)	**202-03**	51°38'N	37°07'E
Timan Ridge, hills, Russia *see* Timanskiy Kryazh	**186-87**	65°0'N	51°00'E
Timanskiy Kryazh, hills, Russia	**186-87**	65°0'N	51°00'E
Timaru, N.Z. (tĭm'á-rōō)	**278**	44°24'S	171°14'E
Timbalier Bay, b., La., U.S. (tĭm'bá-lēr bā)	**124-25**	29°10'N	90°20'W
Timbuktu, Mali *see* Tombouctou	**258-59**	16°47'N	3°01'W
Timimoun, Alg. (tē-mē-mōōn')	**188-89**	29°14'N	0°16'E
Timirist, Râs, c., Maur.	**258-59**	19°23'N	16°32'W
Timișoara, Rom.	**200-01**	45°45'N	21°13'E
Timmins, On., Can. (tĭm'ĭnz)	**136-37**	48°29'N	81°21'W
Timor, i., Asia (tē-mōr')	**248-49**	9°0'S	125°00'E
Timor, Laut, s., *see* Timor Sea	**272-73**	11°0'S	128°00'E
Timor-Leste, nation, Asia *see* East Timor	**248-49**	8°35'S	126°00'E
Timor Sea, s., (tē-mōr' sē)	**272-73**	11°0'S	128°00'E
Timor Timur, nation, Asia *see* East Timor	**248-49**	8°35'S	126°00'E
Timpanogos Cave National Monument, n.p., Ut., U.S. (tĭ-măn'ō-gŏz kāv năsh'ŭn-ăl mŏn'ū-mĕnt)	**118-19**	40°26'N	111°44'W
Tinaca Point, c., Phil.	**250**	5°34'N	125°20'E
Tindouf, Alg. (tēn-dōōf')	**258-59**	27°49'N	8°08'W
Tinghert, Ḥamādat, plat., Afr.	**258-59**	29°0'N	9°00'E
Tingo María, Peru (tē'ngô-mä-rē'ä)	**170**	9°10'S	75°56'W
Tingri, China *see* Dinggyê	**234-35**	28°35'N	86°37'E
Tingsryd, Swe. (tĭngs'rüd)	**192-93**	56°32'N	14°59'E
Tinian, i., N. Mar. Is.	**280-81**	15°00'N	145°38'E

Feature (Pronunciation)	Page	Lat.	Long.
Tinkisso, stm., Gui.	**260-61**	11°21'N	9°11'W
Tinogasta, Arg. (tē-nŏ-gäs'tä)	**168-69**	28°03'S	67°34'W
Tínos, i., Grc.	**200-01**	37°36'N	25°10'E
Tinrhert, Hamada de, plat., Afr.	**258-59**	29°0'N	9°00'E
Tintina, Arg.	**173**	27°02'S	62°43'W
Tioman, Pulau, i., Malay.	**246-47**	2°48'N	104°10'E
Tipitapa, Nic. (tē-pē-tä'pä)	**149**	12°12'N	86°06'W
Tip Top Mountain, mtn., On., Can.	**136-37**	48°16'N	85°59'W
Tīrān, i., Sau. Ar.	**228-29**	27°57'N	34°33'E
Tīrān, Maḍīq, strt., *see* Tiran, Strait of	**228-29**	27°58'N	34°28'E
Tiran, Strait of, strt.,	**228-29**	27°58'N	34°28'E
Tirana, nat. cap., Alb. *see* Tiranë	**200-01**	41°20'N	19°50'E
Tiranë, nat. cap., Alb. (tē-rä'nä)	**200-01**	41°20'N	19°50'E
Tirano, Italy (tē-rä'nō)	**200-01**	46°13'N	10°11'E
Tiraspol, Mol.	**202-03**	46°51'N	29°38'E
Tire, Tur. (tē'rĕ)	**200-01**	38°06'N	27°45'E
Tiree, i., Scot., U.K. (tī-rē')	**190-91**	56°31'N	6°52'W
Tîrgu Mureș, Rom. *see* Târgu Mureș	**194-95**	46°33'N	24°34'E
Tirich Mīr, mtn., Pak.	**232-33**	36°15'N	71°50'E
Tirreno, Mar, s., Eur. *see* Tyrrhenian Sea	**200-01**	40°0'N	12°00'E
Tiruchchirāppalli, India (tĭr'ō-chĭ-rä'pá-lĭ)	**236**	10°49'N	78°42'E
Tirunelveli, India	**236**	8°44'N	77°41'E
Tiruppur, India	**236**	11°06'N	77°21'E
Tisa, stm., Eur.	**200-01**	45°08'N	20°17'E
Tisdale, Sk., Can. (tĭz'dāl)	**134-35**	52°51'N	104°03'W
Tisisat Falls, wtfl., Eth.	**266**	11°29'N	37°35'E
T'īs Isat Fwafwatē, wtfl., Eth. *see* Tisisat Falls	**266**	11°29'N	37°35'E
Tīsta, stm., Asia	**234-35**	25°31'N	89°42'E
Tisza, stm., Eur. (tē'sä)	**200-01**	45°08'N	20°17'E
Titicaca, Lago, lk., S.A. (lä'gô-tē-tē-kä'kä)	**168-69**	15°50'S	69°20'W
Titograd, nat. cap., Mont. *see* Podgorica	**200-01**	42°27'N	19°16'E
Titov Veles, Mac. (tē'tôv vĕ'lĕs)	**200-01**	41°43'N	21°47'E
Titusville, Fl., U.S. (tī'tŭs-vĭl)	**125a**	28°37'N	80°49'W
Titusville, Pa., U.S. (tī'tŭs-vĭl)	**116-17**	41°38'N	79°41'W
Tivoli, Italy (tē'vô-lē)	**200-01**	41°58'N	12°48'E
Tiwanaku, hist., Bol.	**168-69**	16°33'S	68°41'W
Tizimín, Mex. (tē-zē-mē'n)	**148**	21°10'N	88°10'W
Tizi Ouzou, Alg. (tē'zē-ōō-zōō')	**269b**	36°48'N	4°02'E
Tiznit, Mor. (tēz-nēt)	**258-59**	29°42'N	9°43'W
Tjörn, i., Swe.	**192-93**	58°0'N	11°38'E
Tlacotalpan, Mex. (tlä-kô-täl'pän)	**146-47**	18°38'N	95°40'W
Tlacotepec, Mex. (tlä-kô-tå-pĕ'k)	**146-47**	17°47'N	99°59'W
Tlahualilo de Zaragoza, Mex.	**122-23**	26°06'N	103°26'W
Tlalnepantla, Mex. (tläl-nå-pán'tlä)	**146-47**	19°32'N	99°12'W
Tlaquepaque, Mex. (tlä-kĕ-pä'kĕ)	**146-47**	20°39'N	103°19'W
Tlaxcala, state, Mex.	**146-47**	19°25'N	98°10'W
Tlaxcala de Xicohténcatl, Mex.	**146-47**	19°19'N	98°14'W
Tlemcen, Alg.	**198-99**	34°53'N	1°18'W
Toamasina, Madag.	**264-65**	18°09'S	49°24'E
Tobago, i., Trin. (tô-bā'gō)	**143b**	11°15'N	60°40'W
Tobejuba, Isla, i., Ven.	**143b**	9°20'N	60°52'W
Tobelo, Indon.	**248-49**	1°44'N	128°00'E
Tobi, i., Palau	**280-81**	3°0'N	131°10'E
Tobol, stm., Asia (tô-bôl')	**218-19**	58°09'N	68°13'E
Tobol'sk, Russia (tô-bôlsk')	**218-19**	58°11'N	68°15'E
Tobruk, Libya	**258-59**	32°05'N	23°57'E
Tobyl, stm., Asia	**218-19**	58°09'N	68°13'E
Tocantinópolis, Braz. (tō-kän-tē-nŏ'pō-lēs)	**166-67**	6°19'S	47°25'W
Tocantins, state, Braz. (tō-kän-tēNs')	**166-67**	10°0'S	48°00'W
Tocantins, stm., Braz. (tō-kän-tēNs')	**166-67**	1°45'S	49°12'W
Toccoa, Ga., U.S. (tŏk'ō-á)	**124-25**	34°35'N	83°20'W
Tocoa, Hond. (tō-kō'ä)	**149**	15°38'N	86°01'W
Tocopilla, Chile (tō-kô-pēl'yä)	**168-69**	22°06'S	70°11'W
Tocuyo de la Costa, Ven. (tô-kōō'yō-dĕ-lä-kôs'tä)	**163b**	11°02'N	68°22'W
Todos Santos, Bol.	**168-69**	16°48'S	65°08'W
Toemoek Hoemak Gebergte, mts., S.A. *see* Tumuc-Humac Mountains	**164-65**	2°19'N	54°35'W
Tofino, B.C., Can. (tō-fē'nō)	**132-33**	49°08'N	125°54'W
Toga, i., Vanuatu	**279g**	13°25'S	166°41'E
Togian, Kepulauan, is., Indon.	**248-49**	0°20'S	122°00'E
Togliatti, Russia	**186-87**	53°32'N	49°26'E
Togo, nation, Afr. (tō'gō)	**253**	8°0'N	1°10'E
Tok, Ak., U.S.	**126**	63°20'N	143°00'W
Tokachi, stm., Japan (tō-kä'chē)	**244**	42°44'N	143°43'E
Tokat, Tur. (tô-kät')	**186-87**	40°19'N	36°34'E
Tokelau, dep., Oc. (tō-kē-lä'ō)	**280-81**	9°0'S	171°45'W
Tokmok, Kyrg.	**226**	42°50'N	75°18'E
Tokushima, Japan (tō'kō'shē-mä)	**245**	34°04'N	134°34'E
Tokuyama, Japan (tō'kō'yä-mä)	**245**	34°03'N	131°48'E

n-sing; ŋ-baŋk; N-nasalized n; nŏd; cŏmmit; ōld; ŏbey; ôrder; oi-boil; fōōd; ō-as oo in foot; ou-out; s-soft; sh-dish; th-thin; pūre; ûnite; ûrn; stŭd; circŭs; ü-as in French tu; ′-indeterminate vowel.

Feature (Pronunciation)	Page	Lat.	Long.
Tōkyō, nat. cap., Japan (tō′kē-ō)	245	35°42′N	139°47′E
Tôlañaro, Madag.	264-65	25°02′S	47°00′E
Toledo, Spain (tô-lĕ′dô)	198-99	39°53′N	4°03′W
Toledo, Ia., U.S. (tô-lē′dō)	114-15	41°60′N	92°35′W
Toledo, Oh., U.S. (tô-lē′dō)	116-17	41°39′N	83°33′W
Toledo, Or., U.S. (tô-lē′dō)	112-13	44°38′N	123°56′W
Toledo, Montes de, mts., Spain (mô′n-tĕs-dĕ-tô-lĕ′dô)	198-99	39°33′N	4°20′W
Toledo Bend Reservoir, res., U.S. (tô-lē′dō bĕnd rĕ′sĕr-vwär)	122-23	31°30′N	93°45′W
Toliara, Madag.	264-65	23°22′S	43°40′E
Tolima, Nevado del, vol., Col. (nĕ-vä-dô-dĕl-tô-lē′mä)	163c	4°40′N	75°19′W
Tolitoli, Indon.	248-49	1°02′N	120°49′E
Tolmezzo, Italy (tôl-mĕt′zô)	200-01	46°25′N	13°01′E
Tolo, Teluk, b., Indon. (tō′lō)	248-49	2°0′S	122°30′E
Tolosa, Spain (tô-lō′sä)	198-99	43°09′N	2°05′W
Tolsan-do, i., Kor., S.	243	34°38′N	127°45′E
Toluca, Il., U.S. (tô-lōō′kȧ)	116-17	40°60′N	89°08′W
Toluca, Nevado de, vol., Mex. (nĕ-vä-dô-dĕ-tô-lōō′kä)	146-47	19°05′N	99°44′W
Toluca de Lerdo, Mex.	146-47	19°17′N	99°39′W
Tolyatti, Russia *see* Togliatti	186-87	53°32′N	49°26′E
Tom′, stm., Russia	218-19	56°53′N	84°27′E
Tomah, Wi., U.S. (tō′mȧ)	114-15	43°59′N	90°30′W
Tomahawk, Wi., U.S. (tŏm′ȧ-hôk)	116-17	45°28′N	89°44′W
Tomakomai, Japan	244	42°38′N	141°36′E
Tomar, Port. (tō-mär′)	198-99	39°36′N	8°25′W
Tomaszów Lubelski, Pol. (tô-mä′shôf lōō-bĕl′skĭ)	194-95	50°27′N	23°25′E
Tomaszów Mazowiecki, Pol. (tô-mä′shôf mä-zô′vyĕt-skĭ)	194-95	51°33′N	20°01′E
Tomatlán, Mex. (tô-mä-tlä′n)	146-47	19°55′N	105°14′W
Tombador, Serra do, plat., Braz. (sĕr′rȧ dò tōm-bä-dôr′)	166-67	12°0′S	57°40′W
Tombigbee, stm., U.S. (tŏm-bĭg′bē)	110-11	31°04′N	87°58′W
Tombouctou, Mali	258-59	16°47′N	3°01′W
Tombstone, Az., U.S. (tōōm′stōn)	118-19	31°43′N	110°04′W
Tombstone Mountain, mtn., Yk., Can.	130-31	64°25′N	138°30′W
Tombua, Ang. (ȧ-lĕ-zhän′drĕ)	264-65	15°48′S	11°49′E
Tomé, Chile	171	36°36′S	72°57′W
Tomea, Pulau, i., Indon.	248-49	5°45′S	123°56′E
Tomelilla, Swe. (tô′mĕ-lēl-lä)	192-93	55°33′N	13°57′E
Tomelloso, Spain (tō-mål-lyō′sō)	198-99	39°09′N	3°01′W
Tomini, Indon.	248-49	0°32′N	120°32′E
Tomini, Teluk, b., Indon.	248-49	0°20′S	121°00′E
Tommot, Russia (tŏm-mŏt′)	218-19	58°58′N	126°18′E
Tomo, stm., Col.	164-65	5°19′N	67°50′W
Tom Price, Austl.	270-71	22°41′S	117°48′E
Tomsk, Russia (tŏmsk)	218-19	56°30′N	84°58′E
Tonalá, Mex.	146-47	16°05′N	93°45′W
Tondano, Indon. (tôn-dä′nō)	248-49	1°18′N	124°55′E
Tønder, Den. (tûn′nĕr)	194-95	54°56′N	8°52′E
Tone, stm., Japan (tô′nĕ)	245	35°45′N	140°51′E
Tonga, nation, Oc. (tŏŋ′gȧ)	280-81	20°0′S	175°00′W
Tonga Islands, is., Tonga (tŏŋ′gȧ ī′lȧndz)	280-81	20°0′S	175°00′W
Tong'an, China (tôŋ-än)	225a	24°44′N	118°09′E
Tongatapu, i., Tonga	280-81	21°10′S	175°10′W
Tongbei, China (tôŋ-bā)	240-41	47°46′N	126°46′E
Tongcheng, China	238-39	31°03′N	116°57′E
Tongchuan, China	238-39	35°04′N	109°04′E
Tongguan, China (tôŋ-gūän)	238-39	34°36′N	110°17′E
Tonghai, China	238-39	24°07′N	102°47′E
Tonghe, China (tôŋ-hŭ)	244	45°58′N	128°45′E
Tonghua, China (tôŋ-hwä)	243	41°43′N	125°56′E
Tongjiang, China (tôŋ-jyäŋ)	238-39	31°56′N	107°14′E
Tongjiang, China (tôŋ-jyäŋ)	240-41	47°38′N	132°30′E
Tongjosŏn-man, b., Kor., N.	243	39°30′N	128°00′E
Tongliao, China (tôŋ-lĭou)	240-41	43°37′N	122°17′E
Tongoy, Chile (tōn-goi′)	168-69	30°16′S	71°29′W
Tongren, China (tôŋ-rŭn)	238-39	27°43′N	109°11′E
Tongsa Dzong, Bhu.	234-35	27°31′N	90°30′E
Tongxian, China (tôŋ shyĕn)	240-41	39°54′N	116°39′E
Tongyu, China	240-41	44°48′N	123°05′E
Tongzi, China	238-39	28°09′N	106°49′E
Tonk, India (Tŏŋk)	234-35	26°10′N	75°48′E
Tonkawa, Ok., U.S. (tŏŋ kȧ-wô)	120-21	36°41′N	97°19′W
Tonkin, Gulf of, b., Asia (gŭlf ŭv tôn-kăn′)	246-47	20°0′N	108°00′E
Tônlé Sab, Bœng, lk., Camb. *see* Sap, Tonle	246-47	13°0′N	104°00′E
Tonneins, Fr. (tô-năN′)	196-97	44°23′N	0°19′E
Tonopah, Nv., U.S. (tō-nô-pä′)	118-19	38°05′N	117°13′W
Tønsberg, Nor. (tûns′bĕrgh)	192-93	59°16′N	10°26′E
Tonto National Monument, n.p., Az., U.S. (tôn′tô)	118-19	33°34′N	111°02′W
Tooele, Ut., U.S. (tò-ĕl ė)	118-19	40°32′N	112°18′W
Toowoomba, Austl. (tò wōōm′bȧ)	276	27°34′S	151°57′E
Topeka, Ks., U.S.	120-21	39°02′N	95°41′W
Topol'čany, Slvk. (tô-pôl′chä-nü)	194-95	48°34′N	18°10′E
Topolobampo, Mex. (tō-pō-lô-bä′m-pô)	144-45	25°36′N	109°03′W
Topozero, Ozero, lk., Russia	186-87	65°40′N	32°00′E
Toppenish, Wa., U.S. (tôp′ĕn-ĭsh)	112-13	46°23′N	120°19′W
Torawitan, Tanjung, c., Indon.	248-49	1°45′N	124°60′E
Torbat-e Ḥeydarīyeh, Iran	232-33	35°17′N	59°13′E
Torbat-e Jām, Iran	232-33	35°15′N	60°38′E
Torbay, Nf., Can. (tôr-bā′)	138-39	47°40′N	52°45′W
Torbay, Eng., U.K. *see* Torquay	190-91	50°28′N	3°32′W
Torch, stm., Sk., Can.	134-35	53°52′N	103°06′W
Torch Lake, lk., Mi., U.S. (tôrch lāk)	116-17	45°03′N	85°20′W
Torda, Rom. *see* Turda	194-95	46°34′N	23°47′E
Torez, Ukr.	202-03	48°02′N	38°38′E
Torghay, stm., Kaz.	226	48°02′N	62°34′E
Torghay üstirti, plat., Kaz.	226	51°0′N	64°00′E
Torino, Italy *see* Turin	200-01	45°03′N	7°41′E
Tori Sima, i., Japan	244	30°29′N	140°19′E
Torit, Sudan	267	4°24′N	32°34′E
Tormes, stm., Spain (tōr′mās)	198-99	41°18′N	6°27′W
Torneälven, stm., Eur.	184-85	65°49′N	24°09′E
Torneträsk, lk., Swe. (tôr′nĕ trĕsk)	184-85	68°20′N	19°23′E
Torngat, Monts, mts., Can. *see* Torngat Mountains	130-31	59°0′N	64°00′W
Torngat Mountains, mts., Can.	130-31	59°0′N	64°00′W
Tornio, Fin. (tôr′nĭ-ô)	184-85	65°51′N	24°10′E
Tornionjoki, stm., Eur.	184-85	65°49′N	24°09′E
Tornquist, Arg.	173	38°06′S	62°13′W
Toronto, On., Can. (tô-rŏn′tō)	136-37	43°38′N	79°24′W
Toropets, Russia (tô′rô-pyĕts)	192-93	56°30′N	31°40′E
Tororo, Ug.	267	0°42′N	34°11′E
Toros Dağları, mts., Tur. *see* Taurus Mountains	186-87	37°0′N	33°00′E
Torquay, Eng., U.K. (tôr-kē′)	190-91	50°28′N	3°32′W
Torrance, Ca., U.S. (tŏr′rănc)	118-19	33°51′N	118°20′W
Torrelavega, Spain (tôr-rā′lä-vā′gä)	198-99	43°21′N	4°03′W
Torremaggiore, Italy (tôr′rā mäd-jō′rā)	200-01	41°41′N	15°17′E
Torrens, Lake, lk., Austl. (lāk tŏr-ĕns)	276	31°03′S	137°51′E
Torreón, Mex. (tôr-rå-ōn′)	122-23	25°33′N	103°26′W
Torres, Îles, is., Vanuatu	279g	13°17′S	166°39′E
Torres Islands, is., Vanuatu (tôr′rĕs ī′lȧndz) (tŏr′ĕz ī′lȧndz) *see* Torres, Îles	279g	13°17′S	166°39′E
Torres Novas, Port. (tôr′rĕzh nō′väzh)	198-99	39°28′N	8°32′W
Torres Strait, strt., Oc. (tôr′rĕs strāt)	277	10°25′S	142°10′E
Torres Vedras, Port. (tôr′rĕsh vă′dräzh)	198-99	39°05′N	9°15′W
Torrevella, Spain	198-99	37°59′N	0°41′W
Torrevieja, Spain (tôr-rā-vyā′hä) *see* Torrevella	198-99	37°59′N	0°41′W
Torrington, Ct., U.S. (tŏr′ĭng-tŭn)	116-17	41°48′N	73°07′W
Torrington, Wy., U.S. (tŏr′ĭng-tŭn)	114-15	42°05′N	104°12′W
Torsby, Swe. (tôrs′bü)	192-93	60°08′N	13°01′E
Tórshavn, nat. cap., Far. Is. (tôrs-houn′)	190b	62°01′N	6°46′W
Tortola, i., Br. Vir. Is. (tôr-tō′lä)	143b	18°27′N	64°36′W
Tórtolas, Cerro de las, mtn., S.A. *see* Las Tórtolas, Cerro	168-69	29°57′S	69°53′W
Tortona, Italy (tôr-tō′nä)	200-01	44°54′N	8°52′E
Tortosa, Spain (tôr-tō′sä)	198-99	40°48′N	0°31′E
Tortue, Île de la, i., Haiti (ēl-dē-lä-tôr-tü′) *see* Tortuga Island	142-43	20°03′N	72°47′W
Tortuga Island, i., Haiti *see* Tortue, Île de la	142-43	20°03′N	72°47′W
Toruń, Pol.	194-95	53°01′N	18°37′E
Tõrva, Est. (t′r′vå)	192-93	58°01′N	25°56′E
Torzhok, Russia (tôr-zhôk)	202-03	57°03′N	34°58′E
Toscana, hist. reg., Italy (tôs-kä′nä) *see* Tuscany	200-01	43°25′N	11°00′E
Toshkent, nat. cap., Uzb. *see* Tashkent	232-33	41°19′N	69°17′E
Tosno, Russia (tôs′nô)	192-93	59°33′N	30°52′E
Tostado, Arg. (tôs-tä′dô)	173	29°14′S	61°46′W
Totana, Spain (tô-tä-nä)	198-99	37°46′N	1°30′W
Tot'ma, Russia (tôt′mȧ)	186-87	59°58′N	42°45′E
Totoras, Arg. (tô-tô′räs)	173	32°36′S	61°10′W
Totoya, i., Fiji	279f	18°56′S	179°51′W
Tottori, Japan (tô′tô-rē)	245	35°30′N	134°14′E
Toubkal, Jebel, mtn., Mor.	258-59	31°05′N	7°55′W
Toûil, Oued, stm., Alg. (wĕd tōō-ēl′)	269b	35°33′N	2°36′E
Toul, Fr. (tōōl)	196-97	48°41′N	5°53′E
Toulnustouc, stm., Qc., Can.	138-39	49°35′N	68°25′W
Toulon, Fr. (tōō-lôN′)	196-97	43°08′N	5°56′E
Toulouse, Fr. (tōō-lōōz′)	196-97	43°36′N	1°27′E
Toungoo, Mya. (tô-ôŋ-gōō′)	246-47	18°56′N	96°26′E
Tourane, Viet. *see* Da Nang	246-47	16°03′N	108°12′E
Tourcoing, Fr. (tòr-kwaN′)	196-97	50°43′N	3°09′E
Tours, Fr. (tōōr)	196-97	47°24′N	0°43′E
Toussidé, Pic, vol., Chad (pĭk tōō-sē-dā′)	258-59	21°02′N	16°28′E
Towner, N.D., U.S. (tou′nĕr)	114-15	48°21′N	100°24′W
Townsend, Mt., U.S. (toun′zĕnd)	112-13	46°19′N	111°31′W
Townshend Island, i., Austl.	277	22°15′S	150°30′E
Townsville, Austl. (tounz′vĭl)	277	19°16′S	146°48′E
Towson, Md., U.S. (tou′sŭn)	116-17	39°24′N	76°36′W
Towuti, Danau, lk., Indon. (tô-wōō′tē)	248-49	2°45′S	121°32′E
Toxkan, stm., China	226	41°07′N	80°12′E
Toyama, Japan (tō′yä-mä)	245	36°41′N	137°13′E
Toyohashi, Japan (tō′yô-hä′shē)	245	34°46′N	137°23′E
Tozeur, Tun. (tô-zûr′)	188-89	33°55′N	8°08′E
Trabzon, Tur. (tràb′zôn)	227	40°60′N	39°44′E
Tracy, Mn., U.S. (trā′sē)	114-15	44°14′N	95°37′W
Trafalgar, Cabo, c., Spain (kȧ′bô-trä-fäl-gä′r)	198-99	36°11′N	6°02′W
Trail, B.C., Can. (trāl)	132-33	49°06′N	117°42′W
Trakiya, hist. reg., Eur. *see* Thrace	200-01	41°20′N	26°45′E
Tranås, Swe. (trän′ôs)	192-93	58°03′N	14°59′E
Trancas, Arg.	168-69	26°13′S	65°17′W
Trang, Thai.	246-47	7°33′N	99°36′E
Trangan, Pulau, i., Indon. (pōō-lou träŋ′gän)	224-25	6°35′S	134°20′E
Trani, Italy (trä′nē)	200-01	41°16′N	16°25′E
Transylvania, hist. reg., Rom. (trăn-sĭl-vā′nĭ-ȧ)	194-95	46°44′N	23°37′E
Transylvanian Alps, mts., Rom. (trăn-sĭl-vā′nĭ-ăn ălps)	200-01	45°25′N	23°33′E
Trapani, Italy	200-01	38°01′N	12°31′E
Traralgon, Austl. (tră′răl-gŏn)	276	38°12′S	146°32′E
Traverse City, Mi., U.S. (trăv′ērs sĭ′tē)	116-17	44°45′N	85°37′W
Travnik, Bos. (träv′nēk)	200-01	44°14′N	17°40′E
Trebinje, Bos. (trå′bēn-yĕ)	200-01	42°43′N	18°23′E
Trebišov, Slvk. (trĕ′bē-shôf)	194-95	48°38′N	21°44′E
Trebizond, Tur. *see* Trabzon	227	40°60′N	39°44′E
Treinta y Tres, Ur. (trå-ēn′tä ē träs′)	173	33°14′S	54°23′W
Trelew, Arg. (trē′lū)	171	43°15′S	65°18′W
Trelleborg, Swe.	192-93	55°23′N	13°11′E
Tremblant, Mont, mtn., Qc., Can.	136-37	46°16′N	74°35′W
Trenčín, Slvk.	194-95	48°54′N	18°04′E
Trenque Lauquen, Arg. (trĕn′kĕ-lá′ò-kĕ′n)	173	35°58′S	62°45′W
Trent, Italy *see* Trento	200-01	46°04′N	11°08′E
Trent, stm., On., Can. (trĕnt)	136-37	44°06′N	77°34′W
Trento, Italy (trĕn′tô)	200-01	46°04′N	11°08′E
Trenton, N.S., Can. (trĕn′tŭn)	138-39	45°37′N	62°38′W
Trenton, On., Can. (trĕn′tŭn)	136-37	44°06′N	77°35′W
Trenton, Mo., U.S. (trĕn′tŭn)	120-21	40°05′N	93°37′W
Trenton, N.J., U.S.	116-17	40°13′N	74°45′W
Trenton, Tn., U.S. (trĕn′tŭn)	124-25	35°59′N	88°57′W
Tres Arroyos, Arg. (trās′är-rō′yōs)	173	38°22′S	60°16′W
Três Corações, Braz. (trĕ′s kō-rä-zô′ĕs)	172	21°42′S	45°15′W
Tres Esquinas, Col.	164-65	0°44′N	75°14′W
Três Lagoas, Braz. (trĕ′s lä-gô′ás)	168-69	20°47′S	51°43′W
Tres Marías, Islas, is., Mex.	146-47	21°32′N	106°32′W
Três Marias, Represa de, res., Braz.	172	18°14′S	45°16′W
Tres Picos, Cerro, mtn., Arg.	173	38°09′S	61°57′W
Tres Puntas, Cabo, c., Arg.	171	47°06′S	65°53′W
Três Rios, Braz. (trĕ′s rē′ōs)	172	22°07′S	43°12′W
Treviglio, Italy (trā-vē′lyô)	200-01	45°32′N	9°36′E
Treviso, Italy (trĕ-vē′sō)	200-01	45°40′N	12°14′E
Trichardt, S. Afr. (trĭ-kärt′)	269c	26°30′S	29°14′E
Trichinopoly, India *see* Tiruchchirāppalli	236	10°49′N	78°42′E
Trichūr, India *see* Thrissur	236	10°31′N	76°13′E
Trieste, Italy (trē-ĕs′tā)	200-01	45°40′N	13°46′E
Triglav, mtn., Slvn.	200-01	46°23′N	13°50′E
Trikora, Puncak, mtn., Indon.	277	4°18′S	138°40′E
Trincomalee, Sri L. (trĭŋ-kô-mȧ-lē′)	236	8°34′N	81°14′E
Trinidad, Bol. (trē-nē-dhädh′)	166-67	14°49′S	64°54′W
Trinidad, Col.	164-65	5°25′N	71°40′W
Trinidad, Cuba (trē-nē-dhädh′)	142-43	21°48′N	79°59′W
Trinidad, Co., U.S. (trĭn′ĭdăd)	120-21	37°10′N	104°30′W
Trinidad, Ur.	173	33°32′S	56°54′W
Trinidad, i., Trin. (trĭn′ĭ-dăd)	143b	10°30′N	61°15′W
Trinidad, Isla, i., Arg.	173	39°10′S	61°57′W
Trinidad and Tobago, nation, N.A. (trĭn′ĭ-dăd ănd tô-bā′gō)	140-41	11°0′N	61°00′W
Trinity, Tx., U.S. (trĭn′ĭ-tē)	122-23	30°56′N	95°23′W
Trinity, stm., Ca., U.S. (trĭn′ĭ-tē)	112-13	41°11′N	123°42′W

Feature (Pronunciation)	Page	Lat.	Long.
Trinity, stm., Tx., U.S. (trĭn´ĭ-tē)	**122-23**	29°46´N	94°41´W
Trinity Bay, b., Nf., Can. (trĭn´ĭ-tē bā)	**138-39**	47°59´N	53°31´W
Trinity Islands, is., Ak., U.S. (trĭn´ĭ-tē ī´lǎndz)	**126**	56°32´N	154°24´W
Tripoli, Leb.	**228-29**	34°26´N	35°51´E
Tripoli, nat. cap., Libya (trĭ´pō-lē)	**258-59**	32°52´N	13°10´E
Tripolitania, hist. reg., Libya	**258-59**	31°0´N	15°00´E
Tripura, state, India	**234-35**	24°0´N	92°00´E
Tristan da Cunha, i., St. Hel.	**284-85**	37°05´S	12°17´W
Trivandrum, India see Thiruvananthapuram	**236**	8°31´N	76°57´E
Trnava, Slvk. (t'r´nà-và)	**194-95**	48°23´N	17°36´E
Trobriand Islands, is., Pap. N. Gui. (trō-brē-ănd´ ī´lǎndz) see Kiriwina Islands	**277**	8°35´S	151°05´E
Trogir, Cro. (trô´gēr)	**200-01**	43°31´N	16°15´E
Trois-Rivières, Qc., Can. (trwä´rē-vyâ´)	**136-37**	46°21´N	72°33´W
Troitsk, Russia (trô´ĕtsk)	**226**	54°06´N	61°32´E
Troitsko-Pechorsk, Russia (trô´ĭtsk-ō-pyĕ-chôrsk´)	**186-87**	62°42´N	56°12´E
Trollhättan, Swe. (trôl´hĕt-ĕn)	**192-93**	58°17´N	12°18´E
Trombetas, stm., Braz.	**166-67**	1°54´S	55°37´W
Tromsø, Nor.	**184-85**	69°39´N	18°57´E
Tronador, Cerro, mtn., S.A. (sĕ´r-rō trō-nä´dōr) see Tronador, Monte	**171**	41°10´S	71°54´W
Tronador, Monte, mtn., S.A.	**171**	41°10´S	71°54´W
Troncoso, Mex. (trôn-kô´sō)	**146-47**	22°44´N	102°22´W
Trondheim, Nor. (trôn´hăm)	**184-85**	63°26´N	10°24´E
Trosa, Swe. (trô´sä)	**192-93**	58°54´N	17°34´E
Trout Lake, lk., N.T., Can. (trout lāk)	**130-31**	60°35´N	121°10´W
Trout Lake, lk., On., Can. (trout lāk)	**134-35**	51°13´N	93°20´W
Troy, Al., U.S. (troi)	**124-25**	31°49´N	85°58´W
Troy, Mi., U.S. (troi)	**116-17**	42°37´N	83°09´W
Troy, Mo., U.S. (troi)	**120-21**	38°59´N	90°59´W
Troy, Mt., U.S. (troi)	**112-13**	48°29´N	115°55´W
Troy, N.C., U.S. (troi)	**124-25**	35°21´N	79°54´W
Troy, N.Y., U.S.	**116-17**	42°44´N	73°41´W
Troy, Oh., U.S. (troi)	**116-17**	40°02´N	84°13´W
Troyes, Fr. (trwä)	**196-97**	48°18´N	4°04´E
Trst, Italy see Trieste	**200-01**	45°40´N	13°46´E
Trstenik, Serb. (t'r´stĕ-nēk)	**200-01**	43°37´N	20°60´E
Trubchevsk, Russia (tròp´chĕfsk)	**202-03**	52°35´N	33°48´E
Trucial States, nation, Asia see United Arab Emirates	**206-07**	24°0´N	54°00´E
Truckee, Ca., U.S. (trŭk´ē)	**118-19**	39°19´N	120°11´W
Trujillo, Col. (trò-ĸē´l-yō)	**163c**	4°10´N	76°18´W
Trujillo, Hond.	**149**	15°55´N	85°58´W
Trujillo, Peru (trò-ĸē´l-yō)	**170**	8°06´S	79°02´W
Trujillo, Spain (trōō-ĸē´l-yô)	**198-99**	39°27´N	5°53´W
Trujillo, Ven. (trò-ĸē´l-yō)	**164-65**	9°22´N	70°26´W
Truk Islands, is., Micron. see Chuuk	**280-81**	7°16´N	151°44´E
Trumann, Ar., U.S. (trōō´măn)	**124-25**	35°41´N	90°31´W
Truro, N.S., Can. (trōō´rō)	**138-39**	45°22´N	63°16´W
Truro, Eng., U.K. (trōō´rō)	**190-91**	50°16´N	5°03´W
Truth or Consequences, N.M., U.S. (trōōth ŏr kŏn´sē-kwĕn-sĭs)	**118-19**	33°08´N	107°15´W
Trutnov, Czech Rep. (tròt´nôf)	**194-95**	50°34´N	15°55´E
Trzcianka, Pol. (tchyän´kà)	**194-95**	53°02´N	16°28´E
Tsaidam Basin, bas., China (tsī-däm bā´s'n) see Qaidam Pendi	**222-23**	37°0´N	95°00´E
Tsaratanana, Madag.	**264-65**	16°46´S	47°37´E
Tsaritsyn, Russia see Volgograd	**186-87**	48°44´N	44°25´E
Tsavo East National Park, n.p., Kenya	**262-63**	2°31´S	38°44´E
Tsavo West National Park, n.p., Kenya	**267**	3°04´S	38°05´E
Tschenstochau, Pol. see Częstochowa	**194-95**	50°49´N	19°08´E
Tselinograd, nat. cap., Kaz. see Astana	**226**	51°12´N	71°27´E
Tsetserleg, Mong.	**240-41**	47°28´N	101°27´E
Tsévié, Togo	**260-61**	6°25´N	1°13´E
Tshabong, Bots.	**264-65**	26°02´S	22°25´E
Tshangalele, Lac, res., D.R.C.	**262-63**	10°55´S	27°03´E
Tshela, D.R.C. (tshā´là)	**262-63**	4°59´S	12°57´E
Tshikapa, D.R.C. (tshē-kä´pä)	**262-63**	6°24´S	20°48´E
Tshikapa, stm., Afr. see Chicapa	**262-63**	6°25´S	20°48´E
Tshuapa, stm., D.R.C.	**262-63**	0°17´S	20°45´E
Tshumbe, stm., Afr. see Chiumbe	**262-63**	6°59´S	21°11´E
Tshwane, nat. cap., S. Afr. see Pretoria	**269c**	25°45´S	28°11´E
Tsimlyanskoye Vodokhranilishche, res., Russia	**186-87**	48°0´N	43°00´E
Tsinan, China see Jinan	**240-41**	36°40´N	116°59´E
Tsinghai, state, China see Qinghai	**240-41**	36°0´N	96°00´E
Tsingtao, China see Qingdao	**240-41**	36°05´N	120°20´E
Tsiombe, Madag.	**264-65**	25°19´S	45°29´E
Tsiribihina, stm., Madag. (tsē´rē-bē-hē-nä´)	**264-65**	19°50´S	44°27´E
Tsiroanomandidy, Madag.	**264-65**	18°47´S	46°03´E
Tskhinvali, Geor.	**227**	42°12´N	43°59´E
Tsöh Gol, stm., Asia see Chikoy	**240-41**	51°02´N	106°38´E
Tsu, Japan (tsōō)	**245**	34°43´N	136°31´E
Tsuchiura, Japan (tsōō´chē-ōō-rä)	**245**	36°05´N	140°12´E
Tsugaru-kaikyō, strt., Japan	**244**	41°35´N	141°00´E
Tsumeb, Nmb. (tsōō´mĕb)	**264-65**	19°15´S	17°43´E
Tsuruga, Japan (tsōō´rò-gä)	**245**	35°39´N	136°04´E
Tsurugi-san, mtn., Japan (tsōō´rò-gē- sän´)	**245**	33°51´N	134°06´E
Tsuruoka, Japan (tsōō´rò-ō´kä)	**244**	38°43´N	139°50´E
Tsushima, is., Japan (tsōō-shē´mä)	**243**	34°30´N	129°22´E
Tsuyama, Japan (tsōō´yä-mä´)	**245**	35°03´N	134°00´E
Tsymlyansk Reservoir, res., Russia (tsēm-lyänsk´ rĕ´sĕr-vwär) see Tsimlyanskoye Vodokhranilishche	**186-87**	48°0´N	43°00´E
Tual, Indon.	**224-25**	5°40´S	132°43´E
Tuamotu, Îles, is., Fr. Poly.	**280-81**	19°0´S	142°00´W
Tuapse, Russia (tò´áp-sĕ)	**202-03**	44°07´N	39°05´E
Tubarão, Braz. (tōō-bä-rouɴ´)	**172**	28°29´S	49°03´W
Tübingen, Ger. (tü´bĭng-ĕn)	**194-95**	48°31´N	9°04´E
Ţubruq, Libya see Tobruk	**258-59**	32°05´N	23°57´E
Tubuai, i., Fr. Poly.	**280-81**	23°18´S	149°30´W
Tubuaï, Îles, is., Fr. Poly.	**280-81**	23°0´S	150°00´W
Tucacas, Ven. (tōō-kä´käs)	**163b**	10°48´N	68°19´W
Tucano, Braz.	**166-67**	10°58´S	38°46´W
Tucson, Az., U.S. (tōō-sŏn´)	**118-19**	32°13´N	110°59´W
Tucumán, Arg. (tōō-kōō-män´) see San Miguel de Tucumán	**168-69**	26°49´S	65°13´W
Tucumán, state, Arg. (tōō-kōō-män´)	**168-69**	27°0´S	65°30´W
Tucumcari, N.M., U.S. (tōō´kŭm-kâr-ē)	**120-21**	35°10´N	103°44´W
Tucupita, Ven. (tōō-kōō-pē´tä)	**143b**	9°03´N	62°02´W
Tucuruí, Braz.	**166-67**	3°43´S	49°43´W
Tucuruí, Represa de, res., Braz.	**166-67**	4°32´S	49°31´W
Tudela, Spain (tōō-dhā´lä)	**198-99**	42°04´N	1°36´W
Tudmur, Syria	**228-29**	34°33´N	38°17´E
Tugela, stm., S. Afr. (tōō-gel´ǎ)	**264-65**	29°13´S	31°30´E
Tuguegarao City, Phil.	**250**	17°37´N	121°43´E
Tuira, stm., Pan. (tōō-ē´rà)	**150**	8°21´N	78°04´W
Tukangbesi, Kepulauan, is., Indon.	**248-49**	5°40´S	123°50´E
Tukarak Island, i., Nu., Can.	**130-31**	56°18´N	78°45´W
Tūkrah, Libya	**188-89**	32°32´N	20°34´E
Tuktoyaktuk, N.T., Can.	**128-29**	69°26´N	133°01´W
Tuktut Nogait National Park, n.p., N.T., Can.	**128-29**	69°0´N	122°00´W
Tukums, Lat. (tò´kòms)	**192-93**	56°58´N	23°10´E
Tukuyu, Tan. (tōō-kōō´yà)	**264-65**	9°13´S	33°38´E
Tula, Mex. (tōō´lä)	**146-47**	23°00´N	99°42´W
Tula, Russia (tōō´là)	**202-03**	54°12´N	37°37´E
Tulach Mhór, Ire. see Tullamore	**190-91**	53°16´N	7°30´W
Tulaghi, Sol. Is.	**279e**	9°06´S	160°09´E
Tulancingo, Mex. (tōō-län-sĭŋ´gō)	**146-47**	20°05´N	98°23´W
Tulangbawang, stm., Indon.	**246-47**	4°24´S	105°51´E
Tulare, Ca., U.S. (tōō-lä´rà) (tul-âr´)	**118-19**	36°12´N	119°20´W
Tulcán, Ec. (tōōl-kän´)	**170**	0°48´N	77°43´W
Tulcea, Rom. (tòl´chà)	**202-03**	45°11´N	28°48´E
Tulemalu Lake, lk., Nu., Can.	**130-31**	62°58´N	99°25´W
Tulia, Tx., U.S. (tōō´lĭ-ǎ)	**120-21**	34°33´N	101°46´W
Tulita, N.T., Can.	**128-29**	64°54´N	125°34´W
Ţūlkarm, W.B. (tōōl kärm)	**228-29**	32°19´N	35°02´E
Tullahoma, Tn., U.S. (tŭl-ǎ-hō´mǎ)	**124-25**	35°22´N	86°12´W
Tullamore, Ire. (tŭl-ǎ-mōr´)	**190-91**	53°16´N	7°30´W
Tulle, Fr. (tül)	**196-97**	45°16´N	1°46´E
Tuloma, stm., Russia	**184-85**	69°03´N	33°03´E
Tulsa, Ok., U.S. (tŭl´sǎ)	**120-21**	36°09´N	95°59´W
Tuluá, Col.	**163c**	4°05´N	76°12´W
Tuluksak, Ak., U.S.	**126**	61°06´N	160°58´W
Tulum, Mex. (tōō-lò´m)	**148**	20°14´N	87°27´W
Tulun, Russia (tò-lōōn´)	**218-19**	54°34´N	100°34´E
Tuma, stm., Nic. (tōō´mä)	**149**	13°03´N	84°44´W
Tumaco, Col.	**164-65**	1°47´N	78°48´W
Tuman-gang, stm., Asia	**243**	42°17´N	130°41´E
Tumannaya, stm., Asia see Tumen	**243**	42°17´N	130°41´E
Tumbes, Peru (tōō´m-bĕs)	**170**	3°34´S	80°27´W
Tumbler Ridge, B.C., Can.	**132-33**	55°08´N	120°57´W
Tumen, China (tōō-mŭn)	**243**	42°57´N	129°51´E
Tumen, stm., Asia (tōō-mŭn)	**243**	42°17´N	130°41´E
Tumeremo, Ven. (tōō-må-rä´mō)	**164-65**	7°19´N	61°28´W
Tumkūr, India	**236**	13°20´N	77°06´E
Tumuc-Humac, Massif des, mts., S.A. see Tumuc-Humac Mountains	**164-65**	2°19´N	54°35´W
Tumuc-Humac Mountains, mts., S.A. (tōō-mòk´ōō-mäk´ moun´tĭnz)	**164-65**	2°19´N	54°35´W
Tumucumaque, Serra, mts., S.A. see Tumuc-Humac Mountains	**164-65**	2°19´N	54°35´W
Tumut, Austl.	**276**	35°18´S	148°13´E
Tunas de Zaza, Cuba (tōō´näs dĕ zä´zä)	**142-43**	21°38´N	79°33´W
Tunbridge Wells, Eng., U.K. (tŭn´brĭj welz´) see Royal Tunbridge Wells	**190-91**	51°08´N	0°16´E
Tungabhadra, stm., India	**236**	15°58´N	78°15´E
T'ungchou, China see Tongxian	**240-41**	39°54´N	116°39´E
Tung Hai, s., Asia see East China Sea	**222-23**	30°0´N	126°00´E
Tungsha Tao, i., Tai. see Pratas Island	**222-23**	20°42´N	116°43´E
Tunis, nation, Afr. see Tunisia	**253**	34°0´N	9°00´E
Tunis, nat. cap., Tun. (tū´nĭs)	**184-85**	36°48´N	10°11´E
Tunis, Golfe de, b., Tun. (gôlf-dĕ-tū´nĭs)	**258-59**	37°0´N	10°30´E
Tunis, Gulf of, b., Tun. (gŭlf ŭv tū´nĭs) see Tunis, Golfe de	**258-59**	37°0´N	10°30´E
Tunisia, nation, Afr. (tu-nĭzh´ē-ǎ)	**253**	34°0´N	9°00´E
Tunisie, nation, Afr. see Tunisia	**253**	34°0´N	9°00´E
Tunja, Col. (tōō´n-hä)	**164-65**	5°31´N	73°22´W
Tununak, Ak., U.S.	**126**	60°35´N	165°16´W
Tunuyán, Arg.	**163e**	33°33´S	69°00´W
Tunuyán, stm., Arg.	**171**	33°55´S	66°49´W
Tunxi, China see Huangshan	**238-39**	29°45´N	118°18´E
Tuo, stm., China	**238-39**	28°53´N	105°26´E
Tupã, Braz.	**168-69**	21°56´S	50°31´W
Tupaciguara, Braz.	**172**	18°36´S	48°41´W
Tupanciretã, Braz.	**173**	29°05´S	53°50´W
Tupelo, Ms., U.S. (tū´pĕ-lō)	**124-25**	34°15´N	88°42´W
Tupinambarana, Ilha, i., Braz.	**166-67**	3°0´S	58°00´W
Tupiza, Bol. (tōō-pē´zä)	**168-69**	21°25´S	65°44´W
Tupper Lake, N.Y., U.S. (tŭp´ēr lāk)	**116-17**	44°14´N	74°28´W
Tupungato, Cerro, mtn., S.A.	**163e**	33°25´S	69°45´W
Túquerres, Col. (tōō-kĕ´r-rĕs)	**164-65**	1°04´N	77°36´W
Tura, India	**234-35**	25°31´N	90°13´E
Tura, Russia (tòr´ǎ)	**218-19**	64°18´N	100°14´E
Tura, stm., Russia	**218-19**	57°13´N	66°57´E
Turbat, Pak.	**232-33**	25°60´N	63°04´E
Turbo, Col. (tōō´bō)	**164-65**	8°06´N	76°43´W
Turda, Rom. (tòr´dà)	**194-95**	46°34´N	23°47´E
Turfan Depression, depr., China	**222-23**	42°40´N	89°10´E
Turgay, stm., Kaz. see Torghay	**226**	48°02´N	62°34´E
Turia, stm., Spain (tōō´ryä)	**198-99**	39°27´N	0°19´W
Turin, Italy (tōō´rĭn)	**200-01**	45°03´N	7°41´E
Turka, Ukr. (tòr´kà)	**194-95**	49°09´N	23°03´E
Turkana, Lake, lk., Afr. (lāk tōōr-känǎ) see Rudolf, Lake	**267**	3°30´N	36°00´E
Turkey, nation, Asia (tûrk´ē)	**206-07**	39°0´N	35°00´E
Turkey, stm., Ia., U.S. (tûrk´ē)	**114-15**	42°41´N	90°56´W
Turkistan, Kaz.	**226**	43°18´N	68°16´E
Türkiye, nation, Asia see Turkey	**206-07**	39°0´N	35°00´E
Türkmenabat, Turkmen.	**232-33**	39°05´N	63°35´E
Türkmenbaşy, Turkmen.	**232-33**	40°01´N	52°58´E
Turkmenia, nation, Asia see Turkmenistan	**206-07**	40°0´N	60°00´E
Turkmenistan, nation, Asia (tûrk-mĕn´-ĭ-stän´)	**206-07**	40°0´N	60°00´E
Turkmeniya, nation, Asia see Turkmenistan	**206-07**	40°0´N	60°00´E
Turks and Caicos Islands, dep., N.A. (tûrks ănd kä´kōs ī´lǎndz) (tûrks ănd kī´kōs ī´lǎndz)	**140-41**	21°45´N	71°35´W
Turks Island Passage, strt., T./C. Is. (tûrks ī´lǎnd păs´ĭj)	**142-43**	21°25´N	71°18´W
Turks Islands, is., T./C. Is. (tûrks ī´lǎndz)	**142-43**	21°24´N	71°07´W
Turku, Fin. (tòrkò)	**192-93**	60°27´N	22°16´E
Turkwel, stm., Kenya	**267**	3°06´N	36°06´E
Turlock, Ca., U.S. (tûr´lŏk)	**118-19**	37°30´N	120°51´W
Turneffe Islands, is., Belize	**148**	17°22´N	87°51´W
Turnhout, Bel. (tŭrn-hout´)	**190-91**	51°19´N	4°57´E
Turnov, Czech Rep. (tòr´nôf)	**194-95**	50°35´N	15°09´E
Tŭrnovo, Blg. see Veliko Tŭrnovo	**200-01**	43°04´N	25°38´E
Turpan Pendi, depr., China see Turfan Depression	**222-23**	42°40´N	89°10´E
Turquino, Pico, mtn., Cuba (pē´kō tōōr-kē´nō)	**142-43**	19°59´N	76°50´W
Tursunzade, Taj.	**232-33**	38°31´N	68°14´E
Turukhansk, Russia (tōō-rōō-ĸänsk´)	**218-19**	65°49´N	87°55´E
Tuscaloosa, Al., U.S. (tŭs-kà-lōō´sǎ)	**124-25**	33°12´N	87°34´W
Tuscany, hist. reg., Italy	**200-01**	43°25´N	11°00´E
Tuscola, Il., U.S. (tŭs-kō-lǎ)	**116-17**	39°48´N	88°17´W
Tuscumbia, Al., U.S. (tŭs-kŭm´bĭ-ǎ)	**124-25**	34°43´N	87°42´W
Tuskegee, Al., U.S. (tŭs-kē´gē)	**124-25**	32°26´N	85°42´W
Tutayev, Russia (tōō-tà-yĕf´)	**202-03**	57°53´N	39°34´E
Tuticorin, India (tōō-tē-kô-rĭn´)	**236**	8°48´N	78°09´E
Tutóia, Braz. (tōō-tō´yǎ)	**166-67**	2°48´S	42°17´W
Tutuila, i., Am. Sam.	**279b**	14°18´S	170°42´W
Tutupaca, Volcán, vol., Peru	**170**	17°01´S	70°22´W

n-sing; ŋ-baŋk; ɴ-nasalized n; nŏd; cŏmmit; ōld; ōbey; ôrder; oi-boil; fōōd; ò-as oo in foot; ou-out; s-soft; sh-dish; th-thin; pūre; ûnite; ûrn; stŭd; circŭs; ü-as in French tu; ´-indeterminate vowel.

Feature (Pronunciation)	Page	Lat.	Long.
Tuul, stm., Mong.	**240-41**	48°56'N	104°48'E
Tuvalu, nation, Oc. (tōō-vä´-lōō)	**280-81**	8°0'S	178°00'E
Tuvuca, i., Fiji	**279f**	17°40'S	178°48'W
Ṭuwayq, Jabal, mts., Sau. Ar.	**220-21**	23°0'N	46°00'E
Tuxpan, Mex. (tōōs´pän)	**146-47**	21°56'N	105°17'W
Tuxpan de Rodríguez Cano, Mex.	**146-47**	20°58'N	97°24'W
Tuxtepec, Mex. (tòs-tå-pĕk´)	**146-47**	18°05'N	96°07'W
Tuxtla Gutiérrez, Mex. (tòs´tlä gōō-tyår´rĕs)	**146-47**	16°45'N	93°06'W
Tuyen Quang, Viet.	**246-47**	21°50'N	105°11'E
Tuy Hoa, Viet.	**246-47**	13°05'N	109°19'E
Tuymazy, Russia	**186-87**	54°36'N	53°43'E
Tuz Gölü, lk., Tur.	**186-87**	38°45'N	33°25'E
Tuzla, Bos. (tòz´là)	**200-01**	44°33'N	18°40'E
Tver', Russia	**202-03**	56°52'N	35°55'E
Tvertsa, stm., Russia (tvĕr´tsà)	**202-03**	56°52'N	35°56'E
Tweed, stm., U.K. (twēd)	**190-91**	55°46'N	1°60'W
Tweeling, S. Afr. (twē´lĭng)	**269c**	27°39'S	28°30'E
Twin Falls, Id., U.S. (twĭn fôlz)	**112-13**	42°34'N	114°28'W
Two Rivers, Wi., U.S. (tōō rĭv´ẽrz)	**116-17**	44°09'N	87°34'W
Tyan' Shan', mts., Asia *see* Tien Shan	**226**	42°0'N	80°00'E
Tyler, Mn., U.S. (tī´lẽr)	**114-15**	44°17'N	96°08'W
Tyler, Tx., U.S. (tī´lẽr)	**120-21**	32°21'N	95°19'W
Tylertown, Ms., U.S. (tī´lẽr-toun)	**124-25**	31°07'N	90°09'W
Tym, stm., Russia	**218-19**	59°26'N	80°01'E
Tymovskoye, Russia	**218-19**	50°51'N	142°38'E
Tynda, Russia	**218-19**	55°09'N	124°43'E
Tyndall, S.D., U.S. (tĭn´dǎl)	**114-15**	42°60'N	97°52'W
Tyrma, Russia	**240-41**	50°03'N	132°10'E
Tyrrhenian Sea, s., Eur. (tĭr-rē´nĭ-ǎn sē)	**200-01**	40°0'N	12°00'E
Tyrrhénienne, Mer, s., Eur. *see* Tyrrhenian Sea	**200-01**	40°0'N	12°00'E
Tyul'gan, Russia	**186-87**	52°24'N	56°14'E
Tyumen', Russia (tyōō-mĕn´)	**218-19**	57°10'N	65°33'E
Tyung, stm., Russia	**218-19**	63°46'N	121°32'E
Tyva, state, Russia	**222-23**	52°0'N	95°00'E
Tzaneen, S. Afr.	**269c**	23°49'S	30°10'E
Tzeliutsing, China *see* Zigong	**238-39**	29°22'N	104°45'E
Tzucacab, Mex. (tzōō-kä-kä´b)	**148**	20°04'N	89°02'W
Tzupo, China *see* Boshan	**240-41**	36°29'N	117°51'E

U

Feature (Pronunciation)	Page	Lat.	Long.
Uatumã, stm., Braz.	**166-67**	2°24'S	57°33'W
Uaupés, stm., S.A.	**164-65**	0°02'N	67°15'W
Ubá, Braz.	**172**	21°07'S	42°56'W
Ubangi, stm., Afr. (ōō-bäŋ´gē)	**262-63**	0°25'S	17°47'E
Ubatuba, Braz. (ōō-bå-tōō´bà)	**172**	23°26'S	45°04'W
Ube, Japan	**245**	33°57'N	131°15'E
Úbeda, Spain (ōō´bå-dä)	**198-99**	38°01'N	3°22'W
Uberaba, Braz. (ōō-bå-rä´bå)	**172**	19°46'S	47°56'W
Uberlândia, Braz. (ōō-bĕr-lá´n-dyä)	**172**	18°54'S	48°15'W
Ubon Ratchathani, Thai. (ōō´bŭn rä´chätä-nē)	**246-47**	15°14'N	104°52'E
Ubrique, Spain (ōō-brē´kå)	**198-99**	36°41'N	5°27'W
Ubsu-Nur, Ozero, lk., Asia *see* Uvs Lake	**222-23**	50°20'N	92°45'E
Ubundu, D.R.C.	**262-63**	0°21'S	25°25'E
Ucayali, stm., Peru (ōō´kä-yä´lē)	**170**	4°30'S	73°30'W
Uchaly, Russia (û-chä´lĭ)	**226**	54°18'N	59°27'E
Uchiura-wan, b., Japan (ōō´chē-ōō´rä wän)	**244**	42°20'N	140°40'E
Uchiza, Peru	**170**	8°25'S	76°25'W
Uchur, stm., Russia (ò-chòr´)	**218-19**	58°47'N	130°36'E
Uda, stm., Russia (ò´dà)	**222-23**	51°49'N	107°34'E
Uda, stm., Russia (ò´dà)	**218-19**	54°43'N	135°18'E
Uda, stm., Russia (ò´dà)	**218-19**	56°02'N	99°38'E
Udachnyy, Russia	**218-19**	66°29'N	112°15'E
Udagamandalam, India	**236**	11°25'N	76°42'E
Udai, stm., Ukr. (ò´dà)	**202-03**	50°04'N	33°07'E
Udaipur, India (ò-dŭ´ē-pōōr)	**234-35**	24°35'N	73°42'E
Uddevalla, Swe. (ōōd´dĕ-väl-å)	**192-93**	58°21'N	11°55'E
Udine, Italy (ōō´dē-nå)	**200-01**	46°04'N	13°15'E
Udmurtia, state, Russia	**186-87**	57°0'N	53°00'E
Udmurtiya, state, Russia *see* Udmurtia	**186-87**	57°0'N	53°00'E
Udon Thani, Thai.	**246-47**	17°24'N	102°47'E
Ueda, Japan (wä´dä)	**245**	36°24'N	138°15'E
Uele, stm., D.R.C. (wä´lå)	**262-63**	4°07'N	22°26'E
Uelen, Russia	**126**	66°09'N	169°48'W
Uelzen, Ger. (ült´sĕn)	**194-95**	52°58'N	10°34'E
Uere, stm., D.R.C.	**262-63**	3°33'N	25°15'E
Ufa, Russia (ò´fa)	**186-87**	54°42'N	55°58'E
Ufa, stm., Russia (ò´fa)	**186-87**	54°41'N	56°02'E
Ugab, stm., Nmb. (ōō´gäb)	**264-65**	21°11'S	13°38'E
Ugalla, stm., Tan. (ōō-gä´lä)	**267**	5°17'S	30°58'E
Uganda, nation, Afr. (ōō-gän´dä) (û-găn´dȧ)	**253**	1°0'N	32°00'E
Uglegorsk, Russia (ōō-glĕ-gôrsk)	**218-19**	49°04'N	142°03'E
Uglich, Russia (ōōg-lĕch´)	**202-03**	57°32'N	38°20'E
Ugoma, mtn., D.R.C.	**267**	4°0'S	28°45'E
Uhrichsville, Oh., U.S. (ū´rĭks-vĭl)	**116-17**	40°24'N	81°21'W
Uíge, Ang.	**262-63**	7°38'S	15°04'E
Uina, stm., Camrn. *see* Vina	**260-61**	7°52'N	15°46'E
Uitenhage, S. Afr.	**264-65**	33°40'S	25°27'E
Uji, Japan (ōō´jē)	**245**	34°54'N	135°49'E
Ujiji, Tan. (ōō-jē´jē)	**267**	4°55'S	29°41'E
Uji-yamada, Japan *see* Ise	**245**	34°30'N	136°42'E
Ujjain, India (ōō-jŭēn)	**234-35**	23°11'N	75°47'E
Ujungpandang, Indon. *see* Makassar	**248-49**	5°08'S	119°25'E
Újvidék, Serb. *see* Novi Sad	**200-01**	45°15'N	19°50'E
Ukara Island, i., Tan.	**267**	1°50'S	33°03'E
Ukerewe Island, i., Tan.	**267**	2°03'S	33°00'E
Ukhta, Russia (ōōk´tà)	**186-87**	63°34'N	53°44'E
Ukiah, Ca., U.S.	**118-19**	39°09'N	123°12'W
Ukiah, Or., U.S. (ū-kī´ȧ)	**112-13**	45°09'N	118°56'W
Ukkusiksalik National Park, n.p., Nu., Can.	**128-29**	66°0'N	90°00'W
Ukmergė, Lith. (òk´mĕr-ghå)	**192-93**	55°15'N	24°46'E
Ukraïna, nation, Eur. *see* Ukraine	**174-75**	49°0'N	32°00'E
Ukraine, nation, Eur. (yōō-krān´)	**174-75**	49°0'N	32°00'E
Ukyr, Russia	**240-41**	49°28'N	108°52'E
Ulaanbaatar, nat. cap., Mong. (ōō´län-bä´tôr)	**240-41**	47°55'N	106°56'E
Ulaangom, Mong.	**240-41**	49°59'N	92°04'E
Ulaan-Uul, Mong.	**240-41**	44°23'N	111°12'E
Ulan Bator, nat. cap., Mong. *see* Ulaanbaatar	**240-41**	47°55'N	106°56'E
Ulanhad, China *see* Chifeng	**240-41**	42°16'N	118°58'E
Ulanhot, China	**240-41**	46°04'N	122°04'E
Ulan-Ude, Russia (ōō´län ōō´då)	**222-23**	51°50'N	107°36'E
Ulawa Island, i., Sol. Is.	**279e**	9°47'S	161°57'E
Ulchin, Kor., S. (ōōl´chĕn´)	**243**	36°59'N	129°23'E
Uldz, stm., Asia	**240-41**	49°55'N	115°33'E
Uldza, stm., Asia *see* Uldz	**240-41**	49°55'N	115°33'E
Uleåborg, Fin. *see* Oulu	**184-85**	65°01'N	25°28'E
Ulhāsnagar, India	**236**	19°14'N	73°08'E
Uliast, Mong.	**240-41**	48°57'N	91°09'E
Uliastay, Mong.	**240-41**	47°44'N	96°51'E
Ulindi, stm., D.R.C. (ōō-lĭn´dē)	**262-63**	1°40'S	25°52'E
Ulithi, at., Micron.	**280-81**	9°55'N	139°42'E
Ülkenözen, stm., Eur.	**186-87**	48°60'N	49°59'E
Ulm, Ger. (òlm)	**194-95**	48°24'N	9°59'E
Ulóngué, Moz.	**264-65**	14°37'S	34°19'E
Ulricehamn, Swe. (òl-rē´sĕ-häm)	**192-93**	57°48'N	13°25'E
Ulsan, Kor., S. (ōōl´sän´)	**243**	35°33'N	129°19'E
Ulúa, stm., Hond. (ōō-lōō´ä)	**149**	15°52'N	87°44'W
Ulul, i., Micron.	**280-81**	8°36'N	149°40'E
Ulungur, stm., China (ōō-lōōn-gŭr)	**222-23**	46°59'N	87°26'E
Ulungur Hu, lk., China	**222-23**	47°13'N	87°16'E
Uluru, mtn., Austl.	**272-73**	25°20'S	130°60'E
Ulverstone, Austl. (ŭl´vẽr-stŭn)	**276**	41°10'S	146°11'E
Ulyanovsk, Russia (ōō-lyä´nôfsk)	**186-87**	54°19'N	48°22'E
Ulysses, Ks., U.S. (ū-lĭs´ēz)	**120-21**	37°35'N	101°21'W
Umán, Mex. (ōō-män´)	**148**	20°53'N	89°45'W
Uman', Ukr. (ò-màn´)	**202-03**	48°44'N	30°14'E
'Umān, nation, Asia *see* Oman	**206-07**	22°0'N	58°00'E
'Umān, Khalīj, b., Asia *see* Oman, Gulf of	**230-31**	24°30'N	58°30'E
Umarkot, Pak.	**232-33**	25°22'N	69°45'E
Umatilla Indian Reservation, ind. res., Or., U.S. (ū-má-tĭl´á ĭn´dĭ-ǎn rĕ-sẽr-vā´shŭn)	**112-13**	45°41'N	118°31'W
Umba, Russia	**186-87**	66°41'N	34°18'E
Umboi Island, i., Pap. N. Gui.	**277**	5°36'S	147°53'E
Umeå, Swe.	**184-85**	63°50'N	20°16'E
Umeälven, stm., Swe.	**184-85**	63°47'N	20°19'E
Umm Durmān, Sudan *see* Omdurman	**266**	15°39'N	32°29'E
Umm Lajj, Sau. Ar.	**266**	25°07'N	37°16'E
Umm Ruwābah, Sudan	**266**	12°54'N	31°12'E
Umm Urūmah, i., Sau. Ar.	**266**	25°46'N	36°33'E
Umnak Island, i., Ak., U.S. (ōōm´nå ī´lǎnd)	**126a**	53°25'N	168°10'W
Umpqua, stm., Or., U.S. (ŭmp´kwå)	**112-13**	43°42'N	124°05'W
'Umrān, Yemen	**266**	15°58'N	43°58'E
Umtata, S. Afr. (òm-tä´tä)	**264-65**	31°35'S	28°47'E
Umuarama, Braz.	**168-69**	23°46'S	53°19'W
Unalakleet, Ak., U.S. (ū-nå-lǎk´lēt)	**126**	63°53'N	160°47'W
Unalaska, Ak., U.S. (ū-nå-lǎs´kå)	**126a**	53°52'N	166°32'W
Unalaska Island, i., Ak., U.S.	**126a**	53°45'N	166°45'W
Unauna, Pulau, i., Indon.	**248-49**	0°10'S	121°35'E
'Unayzah, Sau. Ar.	**266**	26°05'N	43°59'E
Uncia, Bol. (ōōn´sē-ä)	**168-69**	18°26'S	66°35'W
Uncompahgre Peak, mtn., Co., U.S. (ŭn-kŭm-pä´grē pēk)	**118-19**	38°04'N	107°28'W
Unecha, Russia (ò-nĕ´chå)	**202-03**	52°51'N	32°42'E
Ungava, Baie d', b., Can. *see* Ungava Bay	**130-31**	59°30'N	67°30'W
Ungava, Péninsule d', pen., Qc., Can.	**130-31**	60°0'N	74°00'W
Ungava Bay, b., Can. (ŭŋ-gá´vå bā)	**130-31**	59°30'N	67°30'W
Ungava Peninsula, pen., Qc., Can. (ŭŋ-gá´vå pĕ-nĭn´sūlǎ) *see* Ungava, Péninsule d'	**130-31**	60°0'N	74°00'W
Ungvár, Ukr. *see* Uzhhorod	**194-95**	48°37'N	22°19'E
União, Braz.	**166-67**	4°35'S	42°52'W
União dos Palmares, Braz.	**163d**	9°10'S	36°02'W
Unimak Island, i., Ak., U.S. (ōō-nē-mäk´ ī´lǎnd)	**126**	54°43'N	164°27'W
Unini, stm., Braz.	**166-67**	1°41'S	61°31'W
Union, Mo., U.S. (ūn´yŭn)	**120-21**	38°27'N	91°01'W
Union, S.C., U.S. (ūn´yŭn)	**124-25**	34°43'N	81°37'W
Union City, In., U.S. (ūn´yŭn sĭ´tē)	**116-17**	40°11'N	85°00'W
Union City, Mi., U.S. (ūn´yŭn sĭ´tē)	**116-17**	42°04'N	85°09'W
Union City, Pa., U.S. (ūn´yŭn sĭ´tē)	**116-17**	41°54'N	79°50'W
Union City, Tn., U.S. (ūn´yŭn sĭ´tē)	**124-25**	36°25'N	89°03'W
Union Springs, Al., U.S. (ūn´yŭn sprĭngz)	**124-25**	32°09'N	85°43'W
Uniontown, Al., U.S. (ūn´yŭn-toun)	**124-25**	32°27'N	87°31'W
Uniontown, Pa., U.S.	**116-17**	39°54'N	79°44'W
Unionville, Mo., U.S. (ūn´yŭn-vĭl)	**120-21**	40°29'N	93°01'W
United Arab Emirates, nation, Asia (ū-nī´tĕd âr´ǎb ĕ´mĕr-ĕts)	**206-07**	24°0'N	54°00'E
United Arab Republic, nation, Afr. *see* Egypt	**253**	27°0'N	30°00'E
United Kingdom, nation, Eur. (ū-nī´tĕd kĭng´dŭm)	**174-75**	54°0'N	2°00'W
United States, nation, N.A. (ū-nī´tĕd stāts)	**85**	38°0'N	97°00'W
Unity, Sk., Can.	**134-35**	52°27'N	109°07'W
Upa, stm., Russia (ò´på)	**202-03**	54°02'N	36°21'E
Upata, Ven. (ōō-pä´tä)	**164-65**	8°01'N	62°24'W
Upemba, Lac, lk., D.R.C.	**262-63**	8°36'S	26°26'E
Upington, S. Afr. (ŭp´ĭng-tŭn)	**264-65**	28°27'S	21°14'E
Upland, In., U.S. (ŭp´lǎnd)	**116-17**	40°28'N	85°29'W
Upolu, i., Samoa	**279b**	13°55'S	171°45'W
Upolu Point, c., Hi., U.S. (ōō-pô´lōō point)	**127a**	20°16'N	155°51'W
Upper Arrow Lake, lk., B.C., Can. (ŭp´ẽr ăr´ō lāk)	**132-33**	50°31'N	117°56'W
Upper Kapuas Mountains, mts., Asia	**248-49**	1°15'N	113°30'E
Upper Klamath Lake, lk., Or., U.S. (ŭp´ẽr klăm´ǎth lāk)	**112-13**	42°24'N	121°54'W
Upper Red Lake, lk., Mn., U.S. (ŭp´ẽr rĕd lāk)	**114-15**	48°10'N	94°40'W
Upper Sandusky, Oh., U.S. (ŭp´ẽr săn-dŭs´kē)	**116-17**	40°49'N	83°17'W
Upper Volta, nation, Afr. *see* Burkina Faso	**253**	13°0'N	1°30'W
Uppsala, Swe. (ōōp´sá-lä)	**192-93**	59°52'N	17°38'E
Upsala, Swe. *see* Uppsala	**192-93**	59°52'N	17°38'E
Ural, stm., (ò-räl´´) (ū-rôl)	**176-77**	46°50'N	51°33'E
Ural Mountains, mts., Russia (ò-räl´´ moun´tĭnz) (ū-rôl moun´tĭnz)	**218-19**	60°0'N	60°00'E
Ural'skiye Gory, mts., Russia *see* Ural Mountains	**218-19**	60°0'N	60°00'E
Ura-Tyube, Taj. *see* Istaravshan	**232-33**	39°54'N	69°00'E
Urbana, Il., U.S. (ûr-băn´á)	**116-17**	40°07'N	88°13'W
Urbana, Oh., U.S. (ûr-băn´á)	**116-17**	40°07'N	83°45'W
Urbino, Italy (ōōr-bē´nô)	**200-01**	43°44'N	12°39'E
Urdinarrain, Arg. (ōōr-dē-när-rȧē´n)	**173**	32°41'S	58°54'W
Urfa, Tur. *see* Şanlıurfa	**228-29**	37°10'N	38°48'E
Urganch, Uzb.	**232-33**	41°33'N	60°38'E
Urgench, Uzb. *see* Urganch	**232-33**	41°33'N	60°38'E
Urla, Tur. (òr´lȧ)	**200-01**	38°20'N	26°46'E
Urmi, stm., Russia (òr´mē)	**240-41**	48°36'N	135°01'E
Urmia, Iran *see* Orūmīyeh	**228-29**	37°32'N	45°05'E
Urmia, Lake, lk., Iran (lāk òr´mēǎ) *see* Orūmīyeh, Daryācheh-ye	**227**	37°40'N	45°30'E
Urrao, Col. (ōōr-rá´ô)	**163c**	6°20'N	76°08'W
Uruapan del Progreso, Mex.	**146-47**	19°25'N	102°04'W
Urubamba, stm., Peru (ōō-rōō-bäm´bä)	**170**	10°44'S	73°44'W
Uruguai, stm., S.A.	**173**	34°10'S	58°18'W
Uruguaiana, Braz.	**173**	29°46'S	57°04'W

ăt; finǎl; rāte; senåte; ärm; åsk; sofȧ; fâre; ch-choose; dh-as th in other; bē; ĕvent; bĕt; recĕnt; cratẽr; g-gō; gh-guttural g; bĭt; ĭ-short neutral; rīde; ᴋ-guttural k as ch in German ich;

Feature (Pronunciation)	Page	Lat.	Long.
Uruguay, nation, S.A. (ōō-rōō-gwī′) (ū′rōō-gwā)	**158**	33°0′S	56°00′W
Uruguay, stm., S.A. (ōō-rōō-gwī′)	**173**	34°10′S	58°18′W
Urumchi, China *see* Ürümqi	**222-23**	43°48′N	87°35′E
Ürümqi, China (ů-rům-chyē)	**222-23**	43°48′N	87°35′E
Urundi, nation, Afr. *see* Burundi	**253**	3°15′S	30°00′E
Urup, Ostrov, i., Russia (ôs-trôf′ ō′rŏp′)	**218-19**	46°0′N	150°00′E
Uryupinsk, Russia (ŏr′yŏ-pēn-sk′)	**186-87**	50°48′N	42°01′E
Urzhum, Russia	**186-87**	57°07′N	50°01′E
Urziceni, Rom. (ŏ-zē-chĕn′′)	**202-03**	44°43′N	26°40′E
Usa, stm., Russia (ŏ′sȧ)	**186-87**	65°58′N	56°57′E
Uşak, Tur. (ōō′shȧk)	**200-01**	38°41′N	29°24′E
Usborne, Mount, mtn., Falk. Is.	**171**	51°41′S	58°50′W
Üshtöbe, Kaz.	**226**	45°14′N	77°58′E
Ushuaia, Arg. (ōō-shōō-ī′ä)	**171**	54°47′S	68°19′W
Usinsk, Russia	**186-87**	65°57′N	57°24′E
Üsküb, nat. cap., Mac. *see* Skopje	**200-01**	42°00′N	21°28′E
Usman′, Russia (ōōs-mȧn′)	**202-03**	52°03′N	39°45′E
Uspanapa, stm., Mex. (ōōs-pä-nä′pä)	**146-47**	17°56′N	94°28′W
Ussel, Fr. (üs′ĕl)	**196-97**	45°33′N	2°18′E
Ussuri, stm., Asia (ōō-sōō′rē)	**240-41**	48°27′N	135°04′E
Ussuriysk, Russia	**244**	43°48′N	131°59′E
Ust′-Barguzin, Russia	**218-19**	53°25′N	109°02′E
Ust-Bolsheretsk, Russia	**218-19**	52°49′N	156°17′E
Ust′-Ilimsk, Russia	**218-19**	58°00′N	102°40′E
Ústí nad Labem, Czech Rep.	**194-95**	50°40′N	14°02′E
Ustinov, Russia *see* Izhevsk	**186-87**	56°50′N	53°12′E
Üstirt, plat., Asia *see* Ust-Urt Plateau	**226**	43°0′N	56°00′E
Ust-Kamchatsk, Russia	**218-19**	56°13′N	162°29′E
Ust′-Kut, Russia	**218-19**	56°47′N	105°43′E
Ust′-Kuyga, Russia	**218-19**	69°60′N	135°35′E
Ust-Maya, Russia (ōst mȧ′yȧ)	**218-19**	60°25′N	134°30′E
Ust′-Nera, Russia	**218-19**	64°34′N	143°18′E
Ust′-Omchug, Russia	**218-19**	61°08′N	149°37′E
Ust-Tsilma, Russia (ōst tsĭl′mȧ)	**186-87**	65°25′N	52°05′E
Ust-Urt Plateau, plat., Asia (ōōst-ōōrt plä-tō′)	**226**	43°0′N	56°00′E
Ustyurt Platosi, plat., Asia *see* Ust-Urt Plateau	**226**	43°0′N	56°00′E
Ustyuzhna, Russia (yōōzh′nȧ)	**202-03**	58°51′N	36°28′E
Usu, China (ů-sōō)	**226**	44°26′N	84°41′E
Usulután, El Sal. (ōō-sōō-lä-tän′)	**148**	13°20′N	88°26′W
Usumacinta, stm., N.A. (ōō′sōō-mä-sēn′tō)	**148**	18°23′N	92°39′W
Usumbura, nat. cap., Bdi. *see* Bujumbura	**267**	3°23′S	29°22′E
Utah, state, U.S. (ū′taw)	**108-09**	39°30′N	111°30′W
Utah Lake, lk., Ut., U.S. (ū′taw lāk)	**118-19**	40°13′N	111°49′W
Utembo, stm., Ang.	**264-65**	17°04′S	21°58′E
Utena, Lith. (ōō′tā-nä)	**192-93**	55°30′N	25°37′E
Uthai Thani, Thai.	**246-47**	15°23′N	100°02′E
Utiariti, Braz.	**166-67**	13°02′S	58°17′W
Utica, N.Y., U.S.	**116-17**	43°06′N	75°15′W
Utiel, Spain (ōō-tyål′)	**198-99**	39°34′N	1°13′W
Utila, Isla de, i., Hond. (ē′s-lä-dĕ-ōō-tē′lä)	**149**	16°06′N	86°56′W
Uto, Japan (ōō′tō′)	**245**	32°41′N	130°40′E
Utrecht, Neth. (ü′trĕKt) (ū′trĕkt)	**190-91**	52°05′N	5°08′E
Utrecht, S. Afr.	**269c**	27°40′S	30°19′E
Utrera, Spain (ōō-trā′rä)	**198-99**	37°11′N	5°47′W
Utsunomiya, Japan (ōōt′sŏ-nŏ-mē-yȧ′)	**245**	36°33′N	139°54′E
Uttaradit, Thai.	**246-47**	17°38′N	100°06′E
Uttarakhand, state, India	**234-35**	30°0′N	79°30′E
Uttaranchal, state, India *see* Uttarakhand	**234-35**	30°0′N	79°30′E
Uttar Pradesh, state, India (ŏt-tär-prä-dĕsh)	**234-35**	27°0′N	80°00′E
Uummannarsuaq, c., Green. *see* Farewell, Cape	**86**	59°46′N	43°60′W
Uvá, stm., Col.	**164-65**	3°56′N	68°34′W
Uvalde, Tx., U.S. (ū-văl′dē)	**122-23**	29°13′N	99°47′W
Uvira, D.R.C. (ōō-vē′rä)	**267**	3°23′S	29°09′E
Uvs Lake, lk., Asia	**222-23**	50°20′N	92°45′E
Uvs nuur, lk., Asia *see* Uvs Lake	**222-23**	50°20′N	92°45′E
Uwajima, Japan (ōō-wä′jē-mä)	**245**	33°13′N	132°34′E
Uwayl, Sudan	**262-63**	8°46′N	27°24′E
'Uwaynāt, Jabal al-, mtn., Afr.	**258-59**	21°53′N	25°02′E
Uxmal, hist., Mex. (ōō′x-mä′l)	**148**	20°22′N	89°46′W
Uyuni, Bol. (ōō-yōō′nē)	**168-69**	20°28′S	66°50′W
Uyuni, Salar de, pl., Bol. (sä-lär-dĕ ōō-yōō′nē)	**168-69**	20°17′S	68°07′W
Uzbekistan, nation, Asia (ōōz-bĕk′-ĕ-stän′)	**232-33**	41°0′N	64°00′E
Ŭzbekiston, nation, Asia *see* Uzbekistan	**232-33**	41°0′N	64°00′E

Feature (Pronunciation)	Page	Lat.	Long.
Uzh, stm., Ukr. (ŏzh)	**202-03**	51°15′N	30°15′E
Uzhhorod, Ukr.	**194-95**	48°37′N	22°19′E
Užice, Serb. (ōō′zhĕ-tsĕ)	**200-01**	43°52′N	19°51′E
Uzlovaya, Russia	**202-03**	53°59′N	38°11′E

V

Feature (Pronunciation)	Page	Lat.	Long.
Vaal, stm., S. Afr. (väl)	**264-65**	29°04′S	23°38′E
Vaasa, Fin. (vä′sȧ)	**184-85**	63°06′N	21°37′E
Vache, Île à, i., Haiti	**142-43**	18°04′N	73°38′W
Vadodara, India	**234-35**	22°18′N	73°11′E
Vaduz, nat. cap., Liech. (vä′dŏts)	**194-95**	47°09′N	9°32′E
Vaga, stm., Russia (va′gȧ)	**186-87**	62°49′N	42°53′E
Vágar, i., Far. Is.	**190b**	62°05′N	7°17′W
Vaghena Island, i., Sol. Is.	**279e**	7°26′S	157°46′E
Váh, stm., Slvk. (väK)	**194-95**	47°45′N	18°09′E
Vaitupu, i., Tuvalu	**280-81**	7°28′S	178°41′E
Vakh, stm., Russia (vȧK)	**218-19**	60°49′N	76°48′E
Vākhān, hist. reg., Afg.	**232-33**	37°0′N	73°00′E
Vakhsh, stm., Taj.	**232-33**	37°07′N	68°19′E
Valcheta, Arg.	**171**	40°42′S	66°09′W
Valdai Hills, hills, Russia (vȧl-dī′ hĭlz) *see* Valdayskaya Vozvyshennost′	**202-03**	57°0′N	33°30′E
Valday, Russia (vȧl-dī′)	**202-03**	57°59′N	33°15′E
Valdayskaya Vozvyshennost′, hills, Russia *see* Valdai Hills	**202-03**	57°0′N	33°30′E
Valdepeñas, Spain (väl-dā-pän′yäs)	**198-99**	38°46′N	3°23′W
Valdés, Península, pen., Arg. (pĕ-nē′n-sōō-lä vȧl-dĕ′s)	**171**	42°30′S	64°00′W
Valdez, Ak., U.S. (văl′dĕz)	**126**	61°08′N	146°20′W
Valdivia, Chile (väl-dē′vä)	**171**	39°49′S	73°13′W
Val-d'Or, Qc., Can.	**136-37**	48°06′N	77°46′W
Valdosta, Ga., U.S. (văl-dŏs′tȧ)	**124-25**	30°50′N	83°16′W
Vale, Or., U.S. (vāl)	**112-13**	43°59′N	117°15′W
Valença, Braz. (vä-lĕN′sȧ)	**166-67**	13°22′S	39°05′W
Valença, Braz. (vä-lĕN′sȧ)	**172**	22°15′S	43°42′W
Valence, Fr.	**196-97**	44°56′N	4°54′E
València, Spain	**198-99**	39°28′N	0°22′W
Valencia, Spain *see* València	**198-99**	39°28′N	0°22′W
Valencia, Ven. (vä-lĕn′syä)	**163b**	10°11′N	68°00′W
Valenciennes, Fr. (vȧ-läN-syĕn′)	**196-97**	50°21′N	3°31′E
Valentine, Ne., U.S. (vȧ lăN-tē-nyĕ′)	**114-15**	42°53′N	100°33′W
Valera, Ven. (vä-lĕ′rä)	**164-65**	9°19′N	70°37′W
Valga, Est. (väl′gȧ)	**192-93**	57°47′N	26°03′E
Valjevo, Serb. (väl′yȧ-vŏ)	**200-01**	44°16′N	19°54′E
Valladolid, Mex. (väl-yä-dhō-lēdh′)	**148**	20°41′N	88°12′W
Valladolid, Spain (väl-yä-dhō-lēdh′)	**198-99**	41°39′N	4°43′W
Valle de Guanape, Ven. (vä′l-yĕ-dĕ-gwä-nä′pĕ)	**163b**	9°54′N	65°41′W
Valle de la Pascua, Ven. (väl′yā dā lä-pä′s-kōōä)	**163b**	9°13′N	66°00′W
Valle de Santiago, Mex. (väl′yā dā sän-tē-ä′gō)	**146-47**	20°24′N	101°12′W
Valledupar, Col. (väl-yā-dōō-pär′)	**164-65**	10°28′N	73°15′W
Vallegrande, Bol. (väl′yā grän′dā)	**168-69**	18°29′S	64°06′W
Vallenar, Chile (väl-yå-när′)	**168-69**	28°34′S	70°46′W
Valletta, nat. cap., Malta (väl-lĕt′ä)	**200b**	35°54′N	14°31′E
Valley City, N.D., U.S. (văl′ē sĭ′tĭ)	**114-15**	46°56′N	98°00′W
Valleyview, Ab., Can.	**132-33**	55°05′N	117°17′W
Vallimanca, Arroyo, stm., Arg. (är-rō′yō väl-yē-mä′n-kä)	**173**	35°44′S	60°08′W
Valls, Spain (väls)	**198-99**	41°17′N	1°15′E
Valmiera, Lat. (vål′myĕ-rȧ)	**192-93**	57°32′N	25°26′E
Valognes, Fr. (vȧ-lôn′y′)	**196-97**	49°31′N	1°28′W
Valona, Alb. *see* Vlorë	**200-01**	40°29′N	19°30′E
Vālpārai, India	**236**	10°19′N	76°54′E
Valparaíso, Chile (väl′pä-rä-ē′sō)	**163e**	33°03′S	71°37′W
Valparaíso, Mex.	**146-47**	22°46′N	103°35′W
Valparaiso, Fl., U.S. (văl-pȧ-rā′zō)	**124-25**	30°31′N	86°30′W
Valparaiso, In., U.S. (văl-pȧ-rā′zō)	**116-17**	41°28′N	87°03′W
Valréas, Fr. (vȧl-rȧ-ä′)	**196-97**	44°23′N	4°59′E
Vals, Tanjung, c., Indon.	**277**	8°24′S	137°38′E
Valuyki, Russia (vȧ-lŏ-ē′kē)	**202-03**	50°12′N	38°08′E
Valverde del Camino, Spain (väl-vĕr-dĕ-dĕl-kä-mē′nō)	**198-99**	37°34′N	6°45′W
Van, Tur. (vän)	**227**	38°30′N	43°24′E
Van, Lake, lk., Tur. *see* Van Gölü	**227**	38°33′N	42°46′E
Vanadzor, Arm.	**227**	40°48′N	44°29′E
Vanavara, Russia	**218-19**	60°21′N	102°16′E
Van Buren, Ar., U.S. (văn bū′rĕn)	**120-21**	35°27′N	94°22′W
Van Buren, Me., U.S. (văn bū′rĕn)	**117a**	47°10′N	67°57′W
Vanceburg, Ky., U.S. (văns′bûrg)	**116-17**	38°36′N	83°19′W
Vancouver, B.C., Can. (văn-kōō′vĕr)	**132-33**	49°17′N	123°07′W

Feature (Pronunciation)	Page	Lat.	Long.
Vancouver, Wa., U.S. (văn-kōō′vĕr)	**112-13**	45°38′N	122°39′W
Vancouver Island, i., B.C., Can. (văn-kōō′vĕr ī′lȧnd)	**130-31**	49°45′N	126°00′W
Vancouver Island Ranges, mts., B.C., Can. (văn-kōō′vĕr ī′lȧnd rānjĕz)	**132-33**	49°25′N	125°25′W
Vandalia, Il., U.S. (văn-dā′lĭ-ȧ)	**116-17**	38°58′N	89°06′W
Vandalia, Mo., U.S. (văn-dā′lĭ-ȧ)	**120-21**	39°19′N	91°30′W
Vandalia, Oh., U.S. (văn-dā′lĭ-ȧ)	**116-17**	39°54′N	84°12′W
Vanderbijlpark, S. Afr.	**269c**	26°42′S	27°50′E
Vanderhoof, B.C., Can.	**132-33**	54°01′N	124°06′W
Vanderlin Island, i., Austl.	**272-73**	15°44′S	137°02′E
Van Diemen Gulf, b., Austl. (văn dē′mĕn gŭlf)	**272-73**	11°50′S	132°00′E
Vanegas, Mex. (vä-nĕ′gäs)	**146-47**	23°53′N	100°56′W
Vänern, lk., Swe.	**192-93**	58°55′N	13°30′E
Vänersborg, Swe. (vĕ′nĕrs-bôr′)	**192-93**	58°23′N	12°19′E
Vangaindrano, Madag.	**264-65**	23°21′S	47°36′E
Van Gölü, lk., Tur.	**227**	38°33′N	42°46′E
Vanikolo, i., Sol. Is.	**272-73**	11°37′S	166°52′E
Vanimo, Pap. N. Gui.	**277**	2°44′S	141°20′E
Vankarem, Russia	**126**	67°50′N	175°50′W
Van Lear, Ky., U.S. (văn lēr′)	**116-17**	37°47′N	82°48′W
Vannes, Fr. (vån)	**196-97**	47°39′N	2°46′W
Van Rees, Pegunungan, mts., Indon.	**277**	2°35′S	138°15′E
Vanua Balavu, i., Fiji	**279f**	17°14′S	178°57′W
Vanua Lava, i., Vanuatu	**279g**	13°45′S	167°28′E
Vanua Levu, i., Fiji	**279f**	16°33′S	179°15′E
Vanuatu, nation, Oc. (vä-nōō-ä′-tōō)	**279g**	16°0′S	167°00′E
Van Wert, Oh., U.S. (văn wûrt′)	**116-17**	40°52′N	84°35′W
Vārānasi, India	**234-35**	25°20′N	82°59′E
Varaždin, Cro. (vä′räzh′dĕn)	**200-01**	46°18′N	16°20′E
Varberg, Swe. (vär′bĕrg)	**192-93**	57°06′N	12°16′E
Vardar, stm., Eur. (vär′där) *see* Axiós	**200-01**	40°31′N	22°43′E
Vardø, Nor.	**184-85**	70°21′N	31°01′E
Varėna, Lith. (vä-rā′nȧ)	**194-95**	54°13′N	24°35′E
Vareš, Bos. (vä′rĕsh)	**200-01**	44°09′N	18°19′E
Varese, Italy (vä-rā′sȧ)	**200-01**	45°49′N	8°50′E
Varginha, Braz. (vär-zhē′n-yä)	**172**	21°34′S	45°26′W
Varkaus, Fin. (vär′kous)	**184-85**	62°19′N	27°54′E
Varna, Blg. (vär′nȧ)	**200-01**	43°13′N	27°54′E
Värnamo, Swe. (vĕr′nȧ-mô)	**192-93**	57°11′N	14°03′E
Vasa, Fin. *see* Vaasa	**184-85**	63°06′N	21°37′E
Vaslui, Rom. (vȧs-lōō′ē)	**202-03**	46°38′N	27°45′E
Vassar, Mi., U.S. (văs′ẽr)	**116-17**	43°22′N	83°35′W
Västerås, Swe. (vĕs′tĕr-ôs)	**192-93**	59°37′N	16°33′E
Västervik, Swe. (vĕs′tĕr-vēk)	**192-93**	57°45′N	16°39′E
Vasto, Italy (väs′tô)	**200-01**	42°07′N	14°43′E
Vasyugan, stm., Russia (vȧs-yōō-gȧn′)	**218-19**	59°07′N	80°46′E
Vasyugan′ye, sw., Russia	**218-19**	58°0′N	77°00′E
Vatican City, nation, Eur. (văt′ĭkăn sĭ′tē)	**200-01**	41°54′N	12°27′E
Vaticano, Città del, nation, Eur. *see* Vatican City	**200-01**	41°54′N	12°27′E
Vatnajökull, ice, Ice. (vät′nȧ-yû-kôl)	**190a**	64°25′N	16°50′W
Vatra Dornei, Rom. (vät′rȧ dôr′nȧ′)	**194-95**	47°21′N	25°22′E
Vättern, lk., Swe.	**192-93**	58°24′N	14°36′E
Vatu-i-ra Channel, strt., Fiji	**279f**	17°17′S	178°31′E
Vaughn, N.M., U.S.	**120-21**	34°36′N	105°15′W
Vaupés, stm., S.A. (vá′ōō-pĕ′s)	**164-65**	0°02′N	67°15′W
Växjö, Swe. (vĕks′shû)	**192-93**	56°53′N	14°49′E
Vaygach, Ostrov, i., Russia (ôs-trôf′ vī-gäch′)	**186-87**	70°0′N	59°30′E
Vedea, stm., Rom. (vå′dyȧ)	**200-01**	43°43′N	25°33′E
Vedia, Arg. (vĕ′dyä)	**173**	34°30′S	61°33′W
Vega, i., Nor.	**184-85**	65°39′N	11°50′E
Vegreville, Ab., Can.	**132-33**	53°30′N	112°03′W
Vejle, Den. (vī′lĕ)	**192-93**	55°42′N	9°32′E
Velebit, mts., Cro. (vā′lĕ-bêt)	**200-01**	44°38′N	15°03′E
Vélez-Málaga, Spain (vĕ′lāth-mä′lä-gä)	**198-99**	36°47′N	4°06′W
Velhas, stm., Braz.	**172**	17°13′S	44°49′W
Velikaya, stm., Russia (vå-lē′kȧ-yȧ)	**192-93**	57°52′N	28°09′E
Velikaya, stm., Russia (vå-lē′kȧ-yȧ)	**218-19**	64°35′N	176°12′E
Veliki Bečkerek, Serb. *see* Zhovti Vody	**200-01**	45°23′N	20°24′E
Velikiye Luki, Russia (vyē-lē′-kyĕ lōō′ke)	**192-93**	56°20′N	30°33′E
Velikiy Ustyug, Russia (vå-lē′kĭ ōōs-tyŏg′)	**186-87**	60°45′N	46°19′E
Veliko Tŭrnovo, Blg.	**200-01**	43°04′N	25°38′E
Velizh, Russia (vå′lĕzh)	**192-93**	55°36′N	31°12′E
Vella Lavella, i., Sol. Is.	**279e**	7°45′S	156°40′E
Velletri, Italy (vĕl-lā′trē)	**200-01**	41°41′N	12°46′E
Vellore, India (vĕl-lōr′)	**236**	12°55′N	79°08′E
Vel'sk, Russia (vĕlsk)	**186-87**	61°04′N	42°06′E
Venadillo, Col. (vĕ-nä-dē′l-yō)	**163c**	4°43′N	74°55′W

n-sing; ŋ-baŋk; N-nasalized n; nŏd; cŏmmit; ōld; ôbey; ôrder; oi-boil; fōōd; ŏ-as oo in foot; ou-out; s-soft; sh-dish; th-thin; pūre; ůnite; ûrn; stŭd; circŭs; ü-as in French tu; ′-indeterminate vowel.

Feature (Pronunciation)	Page	Lat.	Long.
Venado Tuerto, Arg. (vĕ-nä´dô-tōō̆´r-tô)	173	33°45'S	61°58'W
Vendôme, Fr. (väɴ-dōm´)	196-97	47°47'N	1°04'E
Venëv, Russia (vĕn-ĕf´)	202-03	54°21'N	38°16'E
Venezia, Italy see Venice	200-01	45°26'N	12°20'E
Venezuela, nation, S.A. (vĕn-ĕ-zwē´lȧ)	158	8°0'N	66°00'W
Venezuela, Golfo de, b., S.A. (gôl-fō-dĕ vĕn-ĕ-zwē´lȧ)	164-65	11°30'N	71°00'W
Venezuela, Gulf of, b., S.A. (gŭlf ŭv vĕn-ĕ-zwē´lȧ) see Venezuela, Golfo de	164-65	11°30'N	71°00'W
Venice, Italy (vĕn´ĭs)	200-01	45°26'N	12°20'E
Venice, Fl., U.S. (vĕn´ĭs)	125a	27°06'N	82°27'W
Venta, stm., Eur. (vĕn´tȧ)	192-93	57°24'N	21°34'E
Ventersburg, S. Afr. (vĕn-tĕrs´bûrg)	269c	28°06'S	27°09'E
Ventersdorp, S. Afr. (vĕn-tĕrs´dôrp)	269c	26°19'S	26°51'E
Ventimiglia, Italy (vĕn-tē-mēl´yä)	200-01	43°48'N	7°36'E
Ventspils, Lat. (vĕnt´spēls)	192-93	57°24'N	21°35'E
Ventuari, stm., Ven. (vĕn-tōōá´rē)	164-65	3°58'N	67°03'W
Ventura, Ca., U.S. (vĕn-tōō´rȧ)	118-19	34°17'N	119°17'W
Venustiano Carranza, Mex. (vĕ-nōōs-tyä´nō-kär-rä´n-zä)	146-47	16°22'N	92°34'W
Venustiano Carranza, Mex. (vĕ-nōōs-tyä´nō-kär-rä´n-zä)	146-47	19°45'N	103°46'W
Vera, Arg. (vĕ-rä)	173	29°28'S	60°13'W
Vera, Spain (vā´rä)	198-99	37°15'N	1°52'W
Veracruz, Mex.	146-47	19°12'N	96°08'W
Veracruz, state, Mex. (vā-rä-krōōz´)	146-47	19°20'N	96°40'W
Verāval, India (vĕr´vŭ-väl)	234-35	20°55'N	70°22'E
Vercelli, Italy (vĕr-chĕl´lē)	200-01	45°20'N	8°25'E
Verde, stm., Braz.	168-69	21°12'S	51°53'W
Verde, Cape, c., Sen. see Vert, Cap	260-61	14°44'N	17°30'W
Verden, Ger. (fĕr´dĕn)	194-95	52°55'N	9°14'E
Verdun-sur-Meuse, Fr.	196-97	49°10'N	5°23'E
Vereeniging, S. Afr. (vĕ-rā´nĭ-gĭng)	269c	26°40'S	27°57'E
Vereshchagino, Russia	186-87	58°05'N	54°39'E
Vereya, Russia (vĕ-rå´yȧ)	202-03	55°21'N	36°12'E
Verín, Spain (vå-rēn´)	198-99	41°57'N	7°26'W
Verkhnetulomskoye Vodokhranilishche, res., Russia	186-87	68°30'N	31°05'E
Verkhneudinsk, Russia see Ulan-Ude	222-23	51°50'N	107°36'E
Verkhniy Baskunchak, Russia	186-87	48°14'N	46°43'E
Verkhnyaya Inta, Russia	186-87	65°59'N	60°20'E
Verkhoyansk, Russia (vyĕr-κô-yänsk´)	218-19	67°32'N	133°25'E
Verkhoyanskiy Khrebet, mts., Russia	218-19	67°0'N	129°00'E
Verkhoyansk Mountains, mts., Russia (vyĕr-κô-yänsk´ moun´tĭnz) see Verkhoyanskiy Khrebet	218-19	67°0'N	129°00'E
Vermilion, Ab., Can. (vĕr-mĭl´yŭn)	132-33	53°21'N	110°51'W
Vermilion, stm., Ab., Can. (vĕr-mĭl´yŭn)	132-33	53°39'N	110°20'W
Vermilion Bay, b., La., U.S. (vĕr-mĭl´yŭn bā)	124-25	29°40'N	92°00'W
Vermilion Lake, lk., Mn., U.S. (vĕr-mĭl´yŭn lāk)	114-15	47°53'N	92°25'W
Vermillion, S.D., U.S. (vĕr-mĭl´yŭn)	114-15	42°47'N	96°56'W
Vermillion, stm., S.D., U.S. (vĕr-mĭl´yŭn)	114-15	42°44'N	96°53'W
Vermont, state, U.S. (vĕr-mŏnt´)	108-09	43°50'N	72°45'W
Vernal, Ut., U.S. (vûr´nȧl)	112-13	40°28'N	109°33'W
Vernon, B.C., Can. (vĕr-nôn´)	132-33	50°16'N	119°16'W
Vernon, Tx., U.S. (vûr´nŭn)	120-21	34°10'N	99°17'W
Vero Beach, Fl., U.S. (vē´rô bēch)	125a	27°38'N	80°24'W
Verona, Italy (vā-rō´nä)	200-01	45°27'N	10°60'E
Versailles, Fr. (vĕr-sī´y')	196-97	48°48'N	2°08'E
Versailles, In., U.S. (vĕr-sālz´)	116-17	39°04'N	85°15'W
Versailles, Ky., U.S. (vĕr-sālz´)	116-17	38°03'N	84°44'W
Versec, Serb. see Vršac	200-01	45°07'N	21°18'E
Vershino-Shakhtaminskiy, Russia	240-41	51°18'N	117°52'E
Vert, Cap, c., Sen.	260-61	14°44'N	17°30'W
Verviers, Bel. (vĕr-vyā´)	190-91	50°35'N	5°52'E
Vesoul, Fr. (vē-sōōl´)	196-97	47°37'N	6°10'E
Vesterålen, is., Nor. (vĕs´tĕr ô´lĕn)	184-85	68°40'N	15°33'E
Vesterhavet, s., Eur. see North Sea	184-85	56°0'N	3°00'E
Vestfjorden, b., Nor.	184-85	68°08'N	15°00'E
Vestmannaeyjar, Ice. (vĕst´män-ä-ā´yär)	190a	63°26'N	20°17'W
Vestvågøya, i., Nor.	184-85	68°13'N	13°42'E
Vesuvio, vol., Italy (vĕ-sōō´vyä) see Vesuvius	200-01	40°49'N	14°26'E
Vesuvius, vol., Italy (vĕ-sōō´vy-ŭs)	200-01	40°49'N	14°26'E
Ves'yegonsk, Russia (vĕ-syĕ-gônsk´)	202-03	58°40'N	37°16'E
Veszprém, Hung. (vĕs´prām)	194-95	47°06'N	17°54'E
Vet, stm., S. Afr. (vĕt)	264-65	27°41'S	25°39'E
Vetlanda, Swe. (vĕt-län´dä)	192-93	57°26'N	15°05'E
Vetluga, Russia (vyĕt-lōō´gȧ)	186-87	57°51'N	45°47'E
Vevay, In., U.S. (vē´vā)	116-17	38°45'N	85°04'W
Viacha, Bol. (vēä´chȧ)	168-69	16°39'S	68°18'W
Vian, Ok., U.S. (vī´ăn)	120-21	35°30'N	94°58'W
Viana, Braz. (vē-ä´nä)	166-67	3°13'S	45°01'W
Viana do Castelo, Port. (vē-ä´nȧ dò käs-tā´lò)	198-99	41°42'N	8°50'W
Viangchan, nat. cap., Laos see Vientiane	246-47	17°57'N	102°37'E
Viareggio, Italy (vē-ä-rĕd´jô)	200-01	43°53'N	10°15'E
Viborg, Den. (vē´bôr)	192-93	56°27'N	9°25'E
Viborg, Russia	192-93	60°43'N	28°46'E
Vibo Valentia, Italy (vē´bô-vä-lĕ´n-tyä)	200-01	38°40'N	16°06'E
Vicebsk, Bela.	192-93	55°12'N	30°12'E
Vicente Guerrero, Presa, res., Mex.	146-47	23°57'N	98°46'W
Vicenza, Italy (vē-chĕnt´sä)	200-01	45°33'N	11°33'E
Vichada, stm., Col.	164-65	4°56'N	67°50'W
Vichadero, Ur.	173	31°48'S	54°42'W
Vichuga, Russia (vē-chōō´gȧ)	186-87	57°13'N	41°55'E
Vichy, Fr. (vē-shē´)	196-97	46°08'N	3°26'E
Vicksburg, Ms., U.S. (vĭks´bûrg)	124-25	32°22'N	90°52'W
Viçosa, Braz. (vē-sô´sä)	163d	9°24'S	36°14'W
Viçosa, Braz. (vē-sô´sä)	172	20°46'S	42°52'W
Victor Harbor, Austl.	276	35°33'S	138°37'E
Victoria, Arg. (vēk-tô´rēä)	173	32°36'S	60°09'W
Victoria, Braz. see Vitória	172	20°19'S	40°21'W
Victoria, B.C., Can.	132-33	48°26'N	123°22'W
Victoria, Chile (vēk-tô-rēä)	171	38°14'S	72°20'W
Victoria, China see Hong Kong	238-39	22°16'N	114°10'E
Victoria, Malay. see Labuan	248-49	5°17'N	115°15'E
Victoria, Tx., U.S. (vĭk-tō´rĭ-ȧ)	122-23	28°48'N	96°60'W
Victoria, Va., U.S. (vĭk-tō´rĭ-ȧ)	124-25	36°59'N	78°14'W
Victoria, state, Austl.	276	38°0'S	145°00'E
Victoria, stm., Austl.	272-73	15°07'S	129°40'E
Victoria, Lake, lk., Afr. (lăk vĭk-tō´rĭ-ȧ)	267	1°0'S	33°00'E
Victoria, Mount, mtn., Pap. N. Gui.	277	8°54'S	147°32'E
Victoria Falls, wtfl., Afr. (vĭk-tō´rĭ-ȧ fôlz)	264-65	17°55'S	25°51'E
Victoria Falls National Park, n.p., Zimb.	264-65	17°55'S	25°40'E
Victoria Island, i., Can. (vĭk-tō´rĭ-ȧ ī´lȧnd)	86	71°0'N	110°00'W
Victoria Lake, res., Nf., Can. (vĭk-tō´rĭ-ȧ lāk)	138-39	48°19'N	57°28'W
Victoria Land, reg., Ant. (vĭk-tō´rĭ-ȧ lănd)	287	75°0'S	163°00'E
Victoria Nile, stm., Ug. (vĭk-tō´rĭ-ȧ nīl)	267	2°14'N	31°26'E
Victoria Peak, mtn., Belize (vĕk-tōrĭ´ȧ pēk)	148	16°48'N	88°37'W
Victoria Peak, mtn., B.C., Can. (vĭk-tō´rĭ-ȧ pēk)	132-33	50°03'N	126°06'W
Victoriaville, Qc., Can. (vĭk-tō´rĭ-ȧ-vĭl)	136-37	46°03'N	71°57'W
Victoria West, S. Afr.	264-65	31°24'S	23°07'E
Vicuña Mackenna, Arg.	173	33°54'S	64°24'W
Vidalia, Ga., U.S. (vĭ-dā´lĭ-ȧ)	124-25	32°13'N	82°25'W
Vidalia, La., U.S. (vĭ-dā´lĭ-ȧ)	124-25	31°33'N	91°26'W
Vidin, Blg. (vĭ´dĕn)	200-01	43°60'N	22°53'E
Vidisha, India	234-35	23°31'N	77°49'E
Vidzy, Bela. (vĕ´dzĭ)	192-93	55°25'N	26°38'E
Viedma, Arg. (vyād´mä)	171	40°49'S	62°60'W
Viedma, Lago, lk., Arg.	171	49°35'S	72°35'W
Vienna, Ga., U.S. (vē-ĕn´ȧ)	124-25	32°05'N	83°47'W
Vienna, Il., U.S. (vē-ĕn´ȧ)	116-17	37°25'N	88°54'W
Vienna, W.V., U.S. (vē-ĕn´ȧ)	116-17	39°19'N	81°33'W
Vienna, nat. cap., Aus. (vē-ĕn´ȧ)	194-95	48°13'N	16°20'E
Vienne, Fr. (vyĕn´)	196-97	45°32'N	4°52'E
Vientiane, nat. cap., Laos (vyĕn´tän)	246-47	17°57'N	102°37'E
Vieques, Isla de, i., P.R. (ē´s-lä-dĕ-vyā´kås)	142a	18°08'N	65°25'W
Vierfontein, S. Afr. (vēr´fōn-tān)	269c	27°05'S	26°45'E
Vierzon, Fr. (vyâr-zôɴ´)	196-97	47°13'N	2°05'E
Viesca, Mex. (vē-ās´kä)	122-23	25°21'N	102°48'W
Vieste, Italy (vyĕs´tå)	200-01	41°53'N	16°11'E
Viet Nam, nation, Asia (vyĕt´näm´)	206-07	16°0'N	108°00'E
Vigan, Phil. (vēgän)	250	17°35'N	120°23'E
Vigevano, Italy (vē-jå-vä´nô)	200-01	45°19'N	8°52'E
Vigo, Spain (vē´gō)	198-99	42°14'N	8°43'W
Vihti, Fin. (vē´tĭ)	192-93	60°25'N	24°19'E
Vijayawāda, India	236	16°31'N	80°37'E
Vikna, i., Nor.	184-85	64°57'N	10°58'E
Vila Cabral, Moz. see Lichinga	264-65	13°17'S	35°15'E
Vila Coutinho, Moz. see Ulóngué	264-65	14°37'S	34°19'E
Vila do Conde, Port. (vē´lȧ dò kôn´dĕ)	198-99	41°21'N	8°45'W
Vila Franca de Xira, Port. (vē´lȧ-frän´kȧ dä shē´rȧ)	198-99	38°56'N	8°60'W
Vila Gouveia, Moz. see Cantandica	264-65	18°02'S	33°08'E
Vilanandro, Tanjona, c., Madag.	264-65	16°12'S	44°28'E
Vilāni, Lat. (vē´lȧ-nĭ)	192-93	56°34'N	26°57'E
Vilankulo, Moz.	264-65	21°60'S	35°19'E
Vila Nova de Gaia, Port. (vē´lȧ nō´vȧ dä gä´yä)	198-99	41°08'N	8°37'W
Vila Pery, Moz. see Chimoio	264-65	19°09'S	33°30'E
Vila Real, Port. (vē´lȧ rā-äl´)	198-99	41°18'N	7°45'W
Vila Velha, Braz.	172	20°20'S	40°17'W
Vila Viçosa, Port. (vē´lȧ-vē-sō´zȧ)	198-99	38°47'N	8°13'W
Vilejka, Bela.	192-93	54°30'N	26°55'E
Vileyka, Bela. (vē-lā´ē-kȧ) see Vilejka	192-93	54°30'N	26°55'E
Vilhelmina, Swe.	184-85	64°38'N	16°39'E
Vilhena, Braz.	166-67	12°43'S	60°07'W
Viljandi, Est. (vēl´yän-dē)	192-93	58°22'N	25°36'E
Vilkaviškis, Lith. (vēl-kȧ-vēsh´kēs)	192-93	54°39'N	23°02'E
Villa Ángela, Arg. (vē´l-yä à´n-κĕ-lä)	173	27°35'S	60°43'W
Villa Bella, Bol. (vē´l-yä-bĕ´l-yä)	166-67	10°26'S	65°24'W
Villacañas, Spain (vêl-yä-kän´yäs)	198-99	39°37'N	3°20'W
Villach, Aus. (fē´läκ)	194-95	46°36'N	13°50'E
Villacidro, Italy (vē-lä-chē´drô)	200-01	39°28'N	8°45'E
Villa Constitución, Arg. (vêl´yä-kōn-stē-tōō-syōn´)	173	33°14'S	60°20'W
Villa de Cura, Ven. (vēl´yä-ē-kōō´rä)	163b	10°02'N	67°29'W
Villa Dolores, Arg. (vēl´yä dô-lō´räs)	168-69	31°56'S	65°11'W
Villa Flores, Mex. (vēl´yä-flō´räs)	146-47	16°14'N	93°14'W
Villa Grove, Il., U.S. (vĭl´ȧ grōv´)	116-17	39°51'N	88°10'W
Villaguay, Arg. (vē´l-yä-gwī)	173	31°52'S	59°02'W
Villa Hayes, Para. (vēl´yä äyås)(hāz)	168-69	25°05'S	57°34'W
Villahermosa, Mex. (vēl´yä-ĕr-mō´sä)	146-47	17°59'N	92°55'W
Villa Hidalgo, Mex. (vēl´yäē-däl´gō)	146-47	21°40'N	102°36'W
Villaldama, Mex. (vēl-yäl-dä´mä)	122-23	26°30'N	100°25'W
Villa María, Arg. (vē´l-yä-mä-rē´ä)	173	32°25'S	63°14'W
Villa Mercedes, Arg. (vēl´yä-mĕr-sā´dås)	171	33°40'S	65°28'W
Villa Montes, Bol. (vē´l-yä-mô´n-tĕs)	168-69	21°15'S	63°29'W
Villanueva, Mex. (vēl´yä-nòē´vä)	146-47	22°20'N	102°52'W
Villanueva de la Serena, Spain (vēl-yä-nwĕ´vä-dä lä sā-rā´nä)	198-99	38°58'N	5°48'W
Villa Ocampo, Arg.	173	28°29'S	59°21'W
Villa Ocampo, Mex. (vēl´yä-ô-käm´pō)	122-23	26°28'N	105°33'W
Villa Regina, Arg.	171	39°06'S	67°05'W
Villarrica, Para. (vēl-yä-rē´kä)	168-69	25°47'S	56°28'W
Villarrobledo, Spain (vēl-yär-rō-blā´dhō)	198-99	39°16'N	2°36'W
Villa Unión, Arg.	173	29°24'S	62°47'W
Villa Unión, Mex. (vēl´yä-ōō-nyōn´)	146-47	23°10'N	106°12'W
Villavicencio, Col. (vē´l-yä-vē-sĕ´n-syō)	164-65	4°10'N	73°38'W
Villazón, Bol. (vē´l-yä-zô´n)	168-69	22°05'S	65°35'W
Villena, Spain (vē-lyā´nȧ)	198-99	38°38'N	0°52'W
Villeneuve-sur-Lot, Fr. (vēl´nûv´sür-lō´)	196-97	44°25'N	0°42'E
Ville Platte, La., U.S. (vēl plăt´)	122-23	30°41'N	92°16'W
Villers-Cotterêts, Fr. (vē-âr´kô-trā´)	196-97	49°15'N	3°06'E
Villeta, Col. (vē´l-yĕ´tȧ)	163c	4°60'N	74°30'W
Villeurbanne, Fr. (vēl-ûr-bän´)	196-97	45°45'N	4°52'E
Villiers, S. Afr. (vĭl´ĭ-ĕrs)	269c	27°02'S	28°36'E
Vilnius, nat. cap., Lith. (vĭl´nē-ŏs)	192-93	54°40'N	25°17'E
Vilyuy, stm., Russia (vēl´yĭ)	218-19	64°23'N	126°26'E
Vilyuysk, Russia (vē-lyōō´ĭsk')	218-19	63°45'N	121°37'E
Vilyuyskoye Vodokhranilishche, res., Russia	218-19	62°34'N	111°13'E
Vimmerby, Swe. (vĭm´ĕr-bü)	192-93	57°40'N	15°52'E
Vina, stm., Camrn.	260-61	7°52'N	15°46'E
Viña del Mar, Chile (vē´nyä dĕl mär´)	163e	33°01'S	71°33'W
Vincennes, In., U.S. (vĭn-zĕnz´)	116-17	38°41'N	87°32'W
Vincennes Bay, b., Ant.	287	66°18'S	108°49'E
Vindhya Range, mts., India (vĭnd´yä rānj)	234-35	23°0'N	77°00'E
Vineland, N.J., U.S. (vīn´lănd)	116-17	39°29'N	75°01'W
Vinh, Viet. (vĕn´y')	246-47	18°40'N	105°41'E
Vinh Long, Viet.	246-47	10°14'N	105°59'E
Vinita, Ok., U.S. (vĭ-nē´tȧ)	120-21	36°38'N	95°09'W
Vinkovci, Cro. (vēn´kôv-tsē)	200-01	45°17'N	18°49'E
Vinnitsa, Ukr. see Vinnytsia	202-03	49°14'N	28°32'E
Vinnytsia, Ukr.	202-03	49°14'N	28°32'E
Vinson Massif, mtn., Ant. (vĭn´sŭn mă-sēf)	287	78°32'S	85°14'W
Vinton, Ia., U.S. (vĭn´tŭn)	114-15	42°10'N	92°01'W
Vinton, La., U.S. (vĭn´tŭn)	122-23	30°11'N	93°35'W
Virac, Phil. (vē-räk´)	250	13°36'N	124°14'E
Virden, Mb., Can. (vûr´dĕn)	134-35	49°50'N	100°55'W
Virgin Gorda, i., Br. Vir. Is.	143b	18°30'N	64°24'W
Virginia, S. Afr. (vĕr-jĭn´yȧ)	269c	28°05'S	26°53'E
Virginia, Mn., U.S. (vĕr-jĭn´yȧ)	114-15	47°31'N	92°32'W
Virginia, state, U.S. (vĕr-jĭn´yȧ)	108-09	37°30'N	78°45'W

ăt; finȧl; rāte; senåte; ärm; ȧsk; sofȧ; fâre; ch-choose; dh-as th in other; bē; ēvent; bĕt; recĕnt; cratēr; g-gō; gh-guttural g; bĭt; ĭ-short neutral; rīde; κ-guttural k as ch in German ich;

Feature (Pronunciation) Page Lat. Long.

Virginia Beach, Va., U.S. (vẽr-jĭn´yȧ bēch) 124-25 36°52'N 75°59'W
Virginia City, Nv., U.S. 118-19 39°19'N 119°39'W
Virgin Islands, dep., N.A. (vûr´jĭn ī´lȧndz) 140-41 18°20'N 64°50'W
Viroqua, Wi., U.S. (vĭ-rō´kwȧ) 114-15 43°34'N 90°53'W
Virovitica, Cro. (vē-rô-vē´tē-tsȧ) 200-01 45°50'N 17°24'E
Virrat, Fin. (vĭr´ät) 192-93 62°15'N 23°45'E
Virserum, Swe. (vĭr´sĕ-rŏom) 192-93 57°19'N 15°36'E
Virudunagar, India 236 9°35'N 77°57'E
Vis, Otok, i., Cro. 200-01 43°02'N 16°11'E
Visalia, Ca., U.S. (vĭ-sā´lĭ-ȧ) 118-19 36°20'N 119°18'W
Visayan Sea, s., Phil. 250 11°35'N 123°51'E
Visby, Swe. (vĭs´bü) 192-93 57°38'N 18°19'E
Viscount Melville Sound, strt., Can. 86 74°10'N 108°00'W
Višegrad, Bos. (vē´shĕ-gräd) 200-01 43°47'N 19°18'E
Vishākhapatnam, India 236 17°43'N 83°19'E
Vishera, stm., Russia (vĭ´shĕ-rȧ) 186-87 59°54'N 56°26'E
Visoko, Bos. (vē´sô-kô) 200-01 43°59'N 18°11'E
Vistula, stm., Pol. (vĭs´tů-lȧ) 194-95 54°21'N 18°56'E
Vitarte, Peru 163a 12°02'S 76°56'W
Viterbo, Italy (vē-tĕr´bō) 200-01 42°25'N 12°06'E
Viti, nation, Oc. see Fiji 279f 18°0'S 178°00'E
Viti, nation, Oc. see Fiji 279f 18°0'S 178°00'E
Viti Levu, i., Fiji 279f 18°0'S 178°00'E
Vitim, stm., Russia (vē´tēm) 218-19 59°28'N 112°35'E
Vitória, Braz. (vē-tō´rē-ä) 166-67 2°53'S 52°00'W
Vitória, Braz. 172 20°19'S 40°21'W
Vitoria, Spain (vē-tô-ryä) see Gasteiz 198-99 42°51'N 2°40'W
Vitória da Conquista, Braz. 166-67 14°51'S 40°51'W
Vitry-le-François, Fr. (vē-trē´lē-frän-swȧ´) 196-97 48°44'N 4°36'E
Vivian, La., U.S. (vĭv´ĭ-ȧn) 120-21 32°53'N 93°59'W
Vizcaya, Golfo de, b., Eur. see Biscay, Bay of 196-97 44°0'N 4°00'W
Vize, Ostrov, i., Russia 218-19 79°33'N 76°50'E
Vizianagaram, India 236 18°07'N 83°25'E
Vladikavkaz, Russia 227 43°03'N 44°39'E
Vladimir, Russia (vlá-dyē´mēr) 202-03 56°08'N 40°24'E
Vladivostok, Russia (vlá-dē-vôs-tôk´) 240-41 43°08'N 131°56'E
Vlonë, Alb. see Vlorë 200-01 40°29'N 19°30'E
Vlora, Alb. see Vlorë 200-01 40°29'N 19°30'E
Vlorë, Alb. 200-01 40°29'N 19°30'E
Vogel Peak, mtn., Nig. see Dimlang 260-61 8°24'N 11°47'E
Voghera, Italy (vô-gā´rä) 200-01 44°60'N 9°01'E
Vohimena, Tanjona, c., Madag. 264-65 25°36'S 45°09'E
Voi, Kenya 262-63 3°23'S 38°34'E
Voinjama, Lib. 260-61 8°25'N 9°45'W
Voiron, Fr. (vwȧ-rôɴ´) 196-97 45°22'N 5°35'E
Volcano Islands, is., Japan (vŏl-kā´nō ī´lȧndz) see Kazan-rettō 280-81 25°0'N 141°00'E
Volga, stm., Russia (vôl´gä) 186-87 45°45'N 47°56'E
Volga Upland, plat., Russia (vôl´gä ŭp´lȧnd) see Privolzhskaya Vozvyshennost' 186-87 52°0'N 46°00'E
Volgodonsk, Russia 186-87 47°31'N 42°08'E
Volgograd, Russia (vŏl-gō-grä´t) 186-87 48°44'N 44°25'E
Volgograd Reservoir, res., Russia (vŏl-gō-grä´t rĕ´sĕr-vwär) see Volgogradskoye Vodokhranilishche 186-87 50°18'N 45°49'E
Volgogradskoye Vodokhranilishche, res., Russia 186-87 50°18'N 45°49'E
Volkhov, Russia (vôl´kôf) 192-93 59°55'N 32°19'E
Volksrust, S. Afr. 269c 27°22'S 29°54'E
Vologda, Russia (vô´lôg-dȧ) 186-87 59°14'N 39°55'E
Volokolamsk, Russia (vô-lô-kôlȧmsk) 202-03 56°02'N 35°58'E
Vólos, Grc. 200-01 39°22'N 22°57'E
Vol'sk, Russia (vôl´sk) 186-87 52°03'N 47°22'E
Volta, stm., Ghana (vôl´tȧ) 260-61 5°46'N 0°40'E
Volta Blanche, stm., Afr. (vôl´tȧ blänsh) see White Volta 260-61 8°57'N 1°10'W
Volta Lake, res., Ghana (vôl´tȧ lāk) 260-61 7°30'N 0°07'E
Volta Noire, stm., Afr. (vôl´tȧ nwár) see Black Volta 260-61 8°41'N 0°60'W
Volta Redonda, Braz. (vōl´tä-rä-dôn´dä) 172 22°32'S 44°07'W
Volzhsk, Russia 186-87 55°52'N 48°21'E
Volzhskiy, Russia 186-87 48°50'N 44°45'E
Vordingborg, Den. (vôr´dĭng-bôr) 194-95 55°01'N 11°55'E
Vóreioi Sporades, is., Grc. 200-01 39°15'N 23°55'E
Vorgashor, Russia 186-87 67°32'N 64°05'E
Vorkuta, Russia (vôr-kōō´tȧ) 186-87 67°29'N 64°03'E
Vormsi, i., Est. (vôrm´sĭ) 192-93 59°00'N 23°15'E
Vorona, stm., Russia (vô-rô´na) 186-87 51°21'N 42°02'E
Voronezh, Russia (vô-rô´nyĕzh) 202-03 51°40'N 39°10'E
Voronezh, stm., Russia (vô-rô´nyĕzh) 186-87 51°32'N 39°06'E
Voronya, stm., Russia (vô-rônyȧ) 186-87 69°00'N 35°42'E
Voroshilov, Russia see Ussuriysk 244 43°48'N 131°59'E
Voroshilovsk, Russia see Stavropol' 186-87 45°02'N 41°59'E
Võru, Est. (vô´rû) 192-93 57°50'N 27°01'E
Voskresensk, Russia (vôs-krĕ-sĕnsk´) 202-03 55°19'N 38°42'E
Voss, Nor. (vôs) 192-93 60°38'N 6°26'E
Vostochno-Sibirskoye More, s., Russia see East Siberian Sea 218-19 74°0'N 166°00'E
Vostok, i., Kir. 280-81 10°06'S 152°23'W
Votkinsk, Russia (vôt-kēnsk´) 186-87 57°03'N 53°59'E
Votuporanga, Braz. 168-69 20°26'S 49°58'W
Voyageurs National Park, n.p., Mn., U.S. 114-15 48°30'N 93°00'W
Voznesens'k, Ukr. 202-03 47°34'N 31°20'E
Vrangelya, Ostrov, i., Russia 218-19 71°14'N 179°21'W
Vranje, Serb. (vrän´yĕ) 200-01 42°34'N 21°55'E
Vratsa, Blg. (vrät´tsȧ) 200-01 43°12'N 23°34'E
Vrbas, Serb. (v'r´bäs) 200-01 45°34'N 19°39'E
Vrchlabí, Czech Rep. (v'r´chlä-bē) 194-95 50°37'N 15°37'E
Vrede, S. Afr. (vrĭ´dĕ)(vrēd) 269c 27°26'S 29°10'E
Vredefort, S. Afr. (vrĭ´dĕ-fôrt)(vrēd´fōrt) 269c 27°00'S 27°22'E
Vrindāvan, India 234-35 27°35'N 77°42'E
Vršac, Serb. (v'r´shȧts) 200-01 45°07'N 21°18'E
Vryburg, S. Afr. (vrī´bûrg) 264-65 26°58'S 24°44'E
Vryheid, S. Afr. (vrī´hīt) 264-65 27°46'S 30°48'E
Vsetín, Czech Rep. (fsĕt´yēn) 194-95 49°20'N 18°00'E
Vukovar, Cro. (vŏ´kô-vär) 200-01 45°21'N 19°00'E
Vulcano, Isola, i., Italy (ē´-sō-lä-vōōl-kä´nô) 200-01 38°24'N 14°58'E
Vung Tau, Viet. 246-47 10°21'N 107°05'E
Vyatka, Russia see Kirov 186-87 58°36'N 49°40'E
Vyatka, stm., Russia (vyát´kȧ) 186-87 55°35'N 51°29'E
Vyatskiye Polyany, Russia 186-87 56°14'N 51°05'E
Vyazemskiy, Russia (vyá-zĕm´skĭ) 240-41 47°33'N 134°46'E
Vyazma, Russia (vyáz´mȧ) 202-03 55°12'N 34°17'E
Vyazniki, Russia (vyáz´nē-kē) 186-87 56°15'N 42°08'E
Vychegda, stm., Russia (vē´chĕg-dȧ) 186-87 61°17'N 46°37'E
Vygozero, Ozero, lk., Russia 186-87 63°35'N 34°42'E
Vym', stm., Russia (vwēm) 186-87 62°13'N 50°24'E
Vyritsa, Russia (vē´rĭ-tsȧ) 192-93 59°24'N 30°20'E
Vyshniy Volochëk, Russia (vēsh´nyĭ vôl-ô-chĕk´) 202-03 57°35'N 34°34'E
Vyškov, Czech Rep. (vēsh´kôf) 194-95 49°17'N 16°60'E
Vysokogornyy, Russia 218-19 50°06'N 139°09'E
Vysokovsk, Russia (vĭ-sô´kôfsk) 202-03 56°19'N 36°34'E
Vytegra, Russia (vû´tĕg-rȧ) 186-87 61°00'N 36°28'E

W

Wa, Ghana 260-61 10°03'N 2°30'W
Wabana, Nf., Can. 138-39 47°39'N 52°57'W
Wabasca, stm., Ab., Can. 130-31 58°21'N 115°20'W
Wabasca-Desmarais, Ab., Can. 132-33 55°58'N 113°52'W
Wabash, In., U.S. (wô´băsh) 116-17 40°48'N 85°49'W
Wabash, stm., U.S. (wô´băsh) 110-11 37°48'N 88°01'W
Wabasha, Mn., U.S. (wä´bȧ-shô) 114-15 44°23'N 92°02'W
Wabē Gestro, stm., Eth. 262-63 4°17'N 42°03'E
Wabē Shebelē, stm., Afr. 262-63 0°10'N 42°46'E
Wabowden, Mb., Can. (wä-bō´d'n) 134-35 54°54'N 98°37'W
W.A.C. Bennett Dam, d., B.C., Can. 132-33 56°01'N 122°10'W
Waccasassa Bay, b., Fl., U.S. (wă-kȧ-sá´sȧ bā) 124-25 29°06'N 82°52'W
Waco, Tx., U.S. (wā´kō) 122-23 31°33'N 97°09'W
Waddān, Libya 188-89 29°10'N 16°10'E
Waddeneilanden, is., Eur. see Frisian Islands 190-91 53°27'N 5°50'E
Waddington, Mount, mtn., B.C., Can. (mount wŏd´dĭng-tŭn) 132-33 51°22'N 125°16'W
Wadena, Sk., Can. 134-35 51°56'N 103°47'W
Wadena, Mn., U.S. (wŏ-dē´nȧ) 114-15 46°26'N 95°09'W
Wadesboro, N.C., U.S. (wādz´bŭr-ô) 124-25 34°58'N 80°05'W
Wādī Ḥalfā', Sudan 266 21°48'N 31°20'E
Wadley, Ga., U.S. (wŭd´lē) 124-25 32°52'N 82°24'W
Wad Madanī, Sudan (wäd mĕ-dä´nē) 266 14°23'N 33°31'E
Wadsworth, Nv., U.S. (wŏdz´wûrth) 118-19 39°38'N 119°17'W
Wafangdian, China 240-41 39°37'N 122°01'E
Wagadugu, nat. cap., Burkina see Ouagadougou 260-61 12°23'N 1°32'W
Wager Bay, b., Nu., Can. (wā´jĕr bā) 130-31 65°26'N 88°40'W
Wagga Wagga, Austl. (wôg´ȧ wôg´ȧ) 276 35°07'S 147°21'E
Wagoner, Ok., U.S. (wăg´ŭn-ēr) 120-21 35°58'N 95°23'W
Wągrowiec, Pol. (vôŋ-grô´vyĕts) 194-95 52°49'N 17°13'E
Wāh Cantonment, Pak. 232-33 33°48'N 72°41'E
Wahoo, Ne., U.S. (wä-hōō´) 114-15 41°13'N 96°37'W
Wahpeton, N.D., U.S. (wô´pē-tŭn) 114-15 46°16'N 96°36'W
Wahrān, Alg. see Oran 198-99 35°41'N 0°39'W
Wai'anae, Hi., U.S. (wä´ē-á-nä´ā) 127a 21°27'N 158°11'W
Waigeo, Pulau, i., Indon. (pōō-lou wä-ē-gä´ô) 224-25 0°10'S 130°55'E
Waikabubak, Indon. 248-49 9°38'S 119°25'E
Waikato, stm., N.Z. (wä´ē-kä´to) 278 37°23'S 174°43'E
Waikerie, Austl. (wā´kĕr-ē) 276 34°11'S 139°59'E
Wailuku, Hi., U.S. (wä´ē-lōō´kōō) 127a 20°54'N 156°30'W
Waimea, Hi., U.S. (wä-ē-mā´ä) 127a 21°58'N 159°40'W
Waimea, Hi., U.S. (wä-ē-mā´ä) 127a 20°02'N 155°40'W
Waimea, Hi., U.S. (wä-ē-mā´ä) 127a 20°02'N 155°40'W
Wainganga, stm., India (wä-ēn-gŭŋ´gä) 234-35 19°37'N 79°48'E
Waingapu, Indon. 248-49 9°40'S 120°16'E
Wainwright, Ab., Can. (wān-rīt) 132-33 52°51'N 110°51'W
Wainwright, Ak., U.S. (wān-rīt) 126 70°39'N 159°59'W
Waitekere, N.Z. 278 36°55'S 174°40'E
Waitsburg, Wa., U.S. (wāts´bûrg) 112-13 46°16'N 118°09'W
Wajima, Japan (wä´jē-mȧ) 245 37°24'N 136°54'E
Wajir, Kenya 262-63 1°45'N 40°04'E
Waka, Eth. 269d 7°10'N 37°21'E
Wakamatsu, Japan see Aizu-wakamatsu 245 37°30'N 139°56'E
Wakasa-wan, b., Japan (wä´kä-sä wän) 245 35°45'N 135°40'E
Wakatipu, Lake, lk., N.Z. (läk wä-kä-tē´pōō) 278 45°05'S 168°34'E
Wakayama, Japan (wä-kä´yä-mä) 245 34°13'N 135°10'E
WaKeeney, Ks., U.S. (wô-kē´nē) 120-21 39°01'N 99°53'W
Wakefield, Ne., U.S. (wāk-fēld) 114-15 42°16'N 96°52'W
Wake Forest, N.C., U.S. (wāk fŏr´ĕst) 124-25 35°58'N 78°31'W
Wake Island, dep., Oc. (wāk ī´lȧnd) 280-81 19°17'N 166°36'E
Wakhān, hist. reg., Afg. see Vākhān 232-33 37°0'N 73°00'E
Wakkanai, Japan (wä´kä-nä´ē) 244 45°24'N 141°41'E
Wakkerstroom, S. Afr. (vák´ēr-strōm)(wăk´ēr-strōōm) 269c 27°20'S 30°08'E
Wałbrzych, Pol. (väl´bzhûk) 194-95 50°46'N 16°17'E
Waldenburg, Pol. see Wałbrzych 194-95 50°46'N 16°17'E
Waldorf, Md., U.S. (wăl´dōrf) 116-17 38°37'N 76°54'W
Wales, Ak., U.S. (wālz) 126 65°36'N 168°04'W
Wales, state, U.K. (wālz) 190-91 52°30'N 3°30'W
Wales Island, i., Nu., Can. 130-31 68°0'N 86°43'W
Walgett, Austl. (wôl´gĕt) 276 30°02'S 148°07'E
Walhalla, N.D., U.S. (wŭl-hăl´ȧ) 114-15 48°56'N 97°55'W
Walhalla, S.C., U.S. (wŭl-hăl´ȧ) 124-25 34°46'N 83°04'W
Walikale, D.R.C. 267 1°25'S 28°03'E
Walker, Mi., U.S. (wôk´ēr) 116-17 42°59'N 85°45'W
Walker, Mn., U.S. (wôk´ēr) 114-15 47°06'N 94°35'W
Walker Lake, lk., Mb., Can. (wôk´ēr lāk) 134-35 54°42'N 96°57'W
Walker Lake, lk., Nv., U.S. 118-19 38°44'N 118°43'W
Wallaceburg, On., Can. 136-37 42°36'N 82°23'W
Wallaroo, Austl. (wŏl-ȧ-rōō) 276 33°56'S 137°37'E
Walla Walla, Wa., U.S. (wŏl´á wŏl´á) 112-13 46°04'N 118°19'W
Wallis, Îles, is., Wal./F. 280-81 13°18'S 176°10'W
Wallis and Futuna, dep., Oc. (wŏl´ĭs ănd fōō-tōō´nȧ) 280-81 14°0'S 177°00'W
Wallis et Futuna, dep., Oc. see Wallis and Futuna 280-81 14°0'S 177°00'W
Wallowa Mountains, mts., Or., U.S. (wôl´ô-wȧ moun´tĭnz) 112-13 45°16'N 117°21'W
Walnut Creek, stm., Ks., U.S. (wôl´nŭt krēk) 120-21 38°21'N 98°41'W
Walnut Ridge, Ar., U.S. (wôl´nŭt rĭj) 124-25 36°04'N 90°58'W
Walsall, Eng., U.K. (wôl-sôl) 190-91 52°36'N 1°59'W
Walsenburg, Co., U.S. (wôl´sĕn-bûrg) 120-21 37°37'N 104°47'W
Walters, Ok., U.S. (wôl´tērz) 120-21 34°21'N 98°19'W
Walvisbaai, Nmb. see Walvis Bay 264-65 22°57'S 14°31'E
Walvis Bay, Nmb. (wôl´vĭs bā) 264-65 22°57'S 14°31'E
Walworth, Wi., U.S. (wôl´wûrth) 116-17 42°32'N 88°37'W
Wamba, D.R.C. 267 2°09'N 28°00'E
Wamego, Ks., U.S. (wŏ-mē´gō) 120-21 39°12'N 96°18'W
Wami, stm., Tan. (wä´mē) 262-63 6°15'S 38°51'E
Wanfoxia, China 240-41 40°05'N 95°55'E
Wanganui, N.Z. (wôŋ´gȧ-nōō´ē) 278 39°56'S 175°02'E
Wangaratta, Austl. (wôŋ´gȧ-răt´ȧ) 276 36°22'S 146°19'E
Wangiwangi, Pulau, i., Indon. 248-49 5°20'S 123°35'E
Wangpan Yang, b., China 238-39 30°30'N 121°46'E
Wanneroo, Austl. 270-71 31°45'S 115°48'E
Wanxian, China (wän-shyĕn) 238-39 30°49'N 108°22'E
Wanzai, China (wän-dzī) 238-39 28°05'N 114°27'E
Wapakoneta, Oh., U.S. (wä´pȧ-kô-nĕt´ȧ) 116-17 40°34'N 84°12'W
Wapawekka Lake, lk., Sk., Can. (wŏ´pä-wĕ´kȧ lăk) 134-35 54°55'N 104°40'W
Wapello, Ia., U.S. (wŏ-pĕl´ō) 114-15 41°10'N 91°12'W

n-sing; ŋ-baŋk; ɴ-nasalized n; nŏd; cŏmmit; ōld; ôbey; ôrder; oi-boil; fōōd; ŏo-as oo in foot; ou-out; s-soft; sh-dish; th-thin; pūre; ûnite; ûrn; stŭd; circŭs; ü-as in French tu; ´-indeterminate vowel.

Feature (Pronunciation)	Page	Lat.	Long.
Wapiti, stm., Can.	132-33	55°08'N	118°18'W
Wapusk National Park, n.p., Can.	128-29	58°0'N	93°30'W
Warangal, India (wŭ'rȧŋ-gȧl)	236	18°00'N	79°35'E
Warburton Creek, stm., Austl.	276	27°59'S	137°25'E
Warden, S. Afr. (wôr'dĕn)	269c	27°51'S	28°58'E
Wardha, India (wŭr'dä)	234-35	20°45'N	78°37'E
Wardha, stm., India	234-35	19°36'N	79°47'E
Warialda, Austl.	276	29°33'S	150°35'E
Warmbad, S. Afr. see Bela-Bela	269c	24°53'S	28°19'E
Warm Baths, S. Afr. see Bela-Bela	269c	24°53'S	28°19'E
Warm Springs Indian Reservation, ind. res., Or., U.S. (wôrm sprĭngz ĭn'dĭ-ăn rĕ-sẽr-vā'shĕn)	112-13	44°53'N	121°23'W
Warrego, stm., Austl. (wôr'ē-gō)	270-71	30°25'S	145°21'E
Warren, Ar., U.S. (wŏr'ĕn)	120-21	33°37'N	92°04'W
Warren, Mi., U.S. (wŏr'ĕn)	116-17	42°30'N	83°02'W
Warren, Mn., U.S. (wŏr'ĕn)	114-15	48°12'N	96°47'W
Warren, Oh., U.S. (wŏr'ĕn)	116-17	41°14'N	80°49'W
Warrensburg, Mo., U.S. (wŏr'ĕnz-bûrg)	120-21	38°46'N	93°44'W
Warrenton, S. Afr.	264-65	28°07'S	24°51'E
Warrenton, Mo., U.S. (wŏr'ĕn-tŭn)	120-21	38°49'N	91°09'W
Warrenton, Or., U.S. (wŏr'ĕn-tŭn)	112-13	46°10'N	123°55'W
Warrenton, Va., U.S. (wŏr'ĕn-tŭn)	116-17	38°43'N	77°48'W
Warri, Nig. (wär'ē)	260a	5°31'N	5°46'E
Warrnambool, Austl. (wôr'năm-bōōl)	276	38°23'S	142°29'E
Warroad, Mn., U.S. (wôr'rōd)	114-15	48°54'N	95°19'W
Warsaw, In., U.S. (wôr'sô)	116-17	41°14'N	85°51'W
Warsaw, Ky., U.S. (wôr'sô)	116-17	38°47'N	84°54'W
Warsaw, Mo., U.S. (wôr'sô)	120-21	38°15'N	93°23'W
Warsaw, N.C., U.S. (wôr'sô)	124-25	34°59'N	78°05'W
Warsaw, Va., U.S. (wôr'sô)	116-17	37°57'N	76°46'W
Warsaw, nat. cap., Pol. (wôr'sô)	194-95	52°15'N	21°00'E
Warszawa, nat. cap., Pol. (vár-shä'vá) see Warsaw	194-95	52°15'N	21°00'E
Warwick, Austl. (wŏr'ĭk)	276	28°13'S	152°02'E
Warwick, R.I., U.S. (wŏr'ĭk)	116-17	41°43'N	71°23'W
Wasco, Ca., U.S. (wäs'kō)	118-19	35°36'N	119°20'W
Waseca, Mn., U.S. (wô-sē'kȧ)	114-15	44°05'N	93°30'W
Washburn, N.D., U.S. (wŏsh'bŭrn)	114-15	47°17'N	101°02'W
Washburn, Wi., U.S. (wŏsh'bŭrn)	114-15	46°40'N	90°54'W
Washington, Ga., U.S. (wŏsh'ĭng-tŭn)	124-25	33°44'N	82°44'W
Washington, Ia., U.S. (wŏsh'ĭng-tŭn)	114-15	41°18'N	91°41'W
Washington, Il., U.S. (wŏsh'ĭng-tŭn)	116-17	40°42'N	89°25'W
Washington, In., U.S. (wŏsh'ĭng-tŭn)	116-17	38°39'N	87°10'W
Washington, Mo., U.S. (wŏsh'ĭng-tŭn)	120-21	38°33'N	91°01'W
Washington, N.C., U.S. (wŏsh'ĭng-tŭn)	124-25	35°33'N	77°04'W
Washington, state, U.S. (wŏsh'ĭng-tŭn)	108-09	47°30'N	120°30'W
Washington, nat. cap., D.C., U.S. (wŏsh'ĭng-tŭn)	116-17	38°53'N	77°02'W
Washington, Mount, mtn., N.H., U.S. (mount wŏsh'ĭng-tŭn)	116-17	44°16'N	71°18'W
Washington Island, i., Kir. see Teraina	280-81	4°42'N	160°45'W
Washington Island, i., Wi., U.S. (wŏsh'ĭng-tŭn ī'lȧnd)	116-17	45°22'N	86°54'W
Waskaganish, Qc., Can.	128-29	51°29'N	78°45'W
Waskaiowaka Lake, lk., Mb., Can. (wŏ'skă-yō'wō-kă lāk)	134-35	56°31'N	96°18'W
Watampone, Indon.	248-49	4°32'S	120°19'E
Wataru, i., Mald.	236	5°43'N	73°23'E
Waterberge, mts., S. Afr. (wôrtẽr'bûrg)	269c	24°28'S	27°58'E
Waterbury, Ct., U.S. (wô'tẽr-bĕr-ē)	116-17	41°33'N	73°02'W
Waterbury, Vt., U.S. (wô'tẽr-bĕr-ē)	116-17	44°20'N	72°45'W
Waterford, Ire. (wô'tẽr-fẽrd)	190-91	52°15'N	7°06'W
Waterhen Lake, lk., Mb., Can.	134-35	52°06'N	99°34'W
Waterloo, Bel. (wô-tẽr-lōō')	190-91	50°43'N	4°24'E
Waterloo, On., Can. (wô-tẽr-lōō')	136-37	43°28'N	80°30'W
Waterloo, Qc., Can. (wô-tẽr-lōō')	136-37	45°21'N	72°30'W
Waterloo, Ia., U.S. (wô-tẽr-lōō')	114-15	42°30'N	92°21'W
Waterloo, Il., U.S. (wô-tẽr-lōō')	120-21	38°20'N	90°09'W
Waterton Lakes National Park, n.p., Ab., Can.	132-33	49°06'N	114°01'W
Watertown, N.Y., U.S.	116-17	43°59'N	75°55'W
Watertown, S.D., U.S. (wô'tẽr-toun)	114-15	44°54'N	97°07'W
Watertown, Wi., U.S. (wô'tẽr-toun)	116-17	43°11'N	88°43'W
Water Valley, Ms., U.S. (văl'ē văl'ē)	124-25	34°10'N	89°38'W
Waterville, Me., U.S.	117a	44°33'N	69°38'W
Watervliet, N.Y., U.S. (wô'tẽr-vlēt')	116-17	42°44'N	73°43'W
Watford, Eng., U.K. (wŏt'fŏrd)	190-91	51°40'N	0°25'W
Watford City, N.D., U.S.	114-15	47°48'N	103°18'W
Watling Island, i., Bah. see San Salvador	142-43	24°02'N	74°27'W
Watonga, Ok., U.S. (wŏ-tôŋ'gȧ)	120-21	35°51'N	98°25'W
Watrous, Sk., Can.	134-35	51°41'N	105°27'W
Watsa, D.R.C. (wät'sä)	267	3°02'N	29°32'E
Watseka, Il., U.S. (wŏt-sē'kȧ)	116-17	40°46'N	87°44'W
Watson Lake, Yk., Can. (wŏt'sŭn lăk)	128-29	60°04'N	128°44'W
Watsonville, Ca., U.S. (wŏt'sŭn-vĭl)	118-19	36°55'N	121°45'W
Wauchula, Fl., U.S. (wô-chōō'lȧ)	125a	27°33'N	81°49'W
Waukegan, Il., U.S. (wŏ-kē'gȧn)	116-17	42°21'N	87°51'W
Waukesha, Wi., U.S. (wô'kê-shô)	116-17	43°01'N	88°14'W
Waukon, Ia., U.S. (wô kŏn)	114-15	43°16'N	91°29'W
Waupaca, Wi., U.S. (wô-păk'ȧ)	116-17	44°21'N	89°05'W
Waupun, Wi., U.S. (wô-pŭn')	116-17	43°38'N	88°44'W
Waurika, Ok., U.S. (wô-rē'kȧ)	120-21	34°10'N	97°60'W
Wausau, Wi., U.S. (wô'sô)	116-17	44°57'N	89°37'W
Wausaukee, Wi., U.S. (wô-sô'kē)	116-17	45°23'N	87°59'W
Wauseon, Oh., U.S. (wô'sē-ŏn)	116-17	41°33'N	84°08'W
Wautoma, Wi., U.S. (wô-tō'mȧ)	116-17	44°04'N	89°18'W
Waverly, Ia., U.S. (wā'vẽr-lē)	114-15	42°44'N	92°29'W
Waverly, Ne., U.S. (wā'vẽr-lē)	114-15	40°55'N	96°32'W
Waverly, Oh., U.S. (wā'vẽr-lē)	116-17	39°07'N	82°59'W
Waverly, Tn., U.S. (wā'vẽr-lē)	124-25	36°05'N	87°48'W
Wāw, Sudan	262-63	7°41'N	27°59'E
Wawa, On., Can.	136-37	47°59'N	84°47'W
Waxahachie, Tx., U.S. (wăk-sȧ-hăch'ē)	120-21	32°24'N	96°51'W
Waya, i., Fiji	279f	17°18'S	177°08'E
Wayabula, Indon.	248-49	2°18'N	128°12'E
Waycross, Ga., U.S.	124-25	31°13'N	82°22'W
Wayne, Ne., U.S. (wān)	114-15	42°14'N	97°01'W
Wayne, W.V., U.S. (wān)	116-17	38°13'N	82°27'W
Waynesboro, Ga., U.S. (wānz'bŭr-ō)	124-25	33°05'N	82°01'W
Waynesboro, Ms., U.S. (wānz'bŭr-ō)	124-25	31°40'N	88°39'W
Waynesboro, Pa., U.S. (wānz'bŭr-ō)	116-17	39°45'N	77°35'W
Waynesboro, Va., U.S. (wānz'bŭr-ō)	116-17	38°04'N	78°53'W
Waynesville, Mo., U.S. (wānz'vĭl)	120-21	37°50'N	92°12'W
Waynesville, N.C., U.S. (wānz'vĭl)	124-25	35°29'N	82°60'W
Waynoka, Ok., U.S. (wā-nō'kȧ)	120-21	36°35'N	98°53'W
Weagamow Lake, lk., On., Can. (wē'ăg-ă-mou lăk)	134-35	52°53'N	91°22'W
Weatherford, Ok., U.S. (wĕ-dhẽr-fẽrd)	120-21	35°32'N	98°43'W
Weatherford, Tx., U.S. (wĕ-dhẽr-fẽrd)	120-21	32°46'N	97°48'W
Weddell Island, i., Falk. Is.	171	51°53'S	61°05'W
Weddell Sea, s., Ant. (wĕd'ĕl sē)	287	72°0'S	45°00'W
Wedgeport, N.S., Can. (wĕj'pōrt)	138-39	43°45'N	65°60'W
Weed, Ca., U.S. (wēd)	112-13	41°25'N	122°23'W
Weenen, S. Afr. (vā'nĕn)	269c	28°51'S	30°05'E
Wei, stm., China (wā)	238-39	34°37'N	110°17'E
Wei, stm., China (wā)	240-41	36°49'N	115°41'E
Weichang, China (wā-chäŋ)	240-41	42°00'N	117°40'E
Weifang, China	240-41	36°42'N	119°06'E
Weihai, China (wa'hăī')	240-41	37°30'N	122°07'E
Weilheim, Ger. (vīl'hīm')	194-95	47°50'N	11°09'E
Weimar, Ger. (vī'mȧr)	194-95	50°59'N	11°19'E
Weinan, China	238-39	34°29'N	109°29'E
Weipa, Austl.	277	12°42'S	141°56'E
Weiser, Id., U.S. (wē'zẽr)	112-13	44°15'N	116°58'W
Weißenfels, Ger. (vī'sĕn-fĕlz)	194-95	51°12'N	11°58'E
Weixi, China (wā-shyē)	238-39	27°11'N	99°17'E
Welch, W.V., U.S. (wĕlch)	124-25	37°26'N	81°35'W
Welkom, S. Afr. (wĕl'kŏm)	269c	27°58'S	26°44'E
Welland, On., Can. (wĕl'ănd)	136-37	42°59'N	79°15'W
Wellesley Islands, is., Austl.	277	16°42'S	139°30'E
Wellington, Austl. (wĕl'lĭng-tŭn)	276	32°34'S	148°57'E
Wellington, Co., U.S. (wĕl'lĭng-tŭn)	120-21	40°42'N	104°60'W
Wellington, Ks., U.S. (wĕl'lĭng-tŭn)	120-21	37°16'N	97°24'W
Wellington, Oh., U.S. (wĕl'lĭng-tŭn)	116-17	41°10'N	82°13'W
Wellington, Tx., U.S. (wĕl'lĭng-tŭn)	120-21	34°51'N	100°13'W
Wellington, nat. cap., N.Z. (wĕl'lĭng-tŭn)	278	41°18'S	174°46'E
Wellington, Isla, i., Chile (ĕ's-lä-ŏĕ'lĕng-tŏn)	171	49°20'S	74°40'W
Wells, Mn., U.S. (wĕlz)	114-15	43°45'N	93°44'W
Wells, Nv., U.S. (wĕlz)	112-13	41°07'N	114°58'W
Wells, Lake, lk., Austl. (lăk wĕlz)	272-73	26°41'S	123°11'E
Wellsboro, Pa., U.S. (wĕlz'bŭ-rō)	116-17	41°45'N	77°17'W
Wellsburg, W.V., U.S. (wĕlz'bûrg)	116-17	40°16'N	80°36'W
Wellston, Oh., U.S. (wĕlz'tŭn)	116-17	39°07'N	82°32'W
Wellsville, N.Y., U.S. (wĕlz'vĭl)	116-17	42°07'N	77°56'W
Wellsville, Oh., U.S. (wĕlz'vĭl)	116-17	40°36'N	80°39'W
Wellsville, Ut., U.S. (wĕlz'vĭl)	112-13	41°39'N	111°56'W
Wels, Aus. (vĕls)	194-95	48°10'N	14°01'E
Welshpool, Wales, U.K. (wĕlsh'pōōl)	190-91	52°40'N	3°09'W
Wembere, stm., Tan.	267	4°09'S	34°11'E
Wenatchee, Wa., U.S. (wê-năch'ē)	112-13	47°25'N	120°19'W
Wenatchee Mountains, mts., Wa., U.S. (wê-năch'ê moun'tĭnz)	112-13	47°20'N	120°45'W
Wenchang, China (wŭn-chäŋ)	238-39	19°33'N	110°45'E
Wenchow, China see Wenzhou	238-39	28°01'N	120°38'E
Wendover, Ut., U.S.	112-13	40°44'N	114°02'W
Wenlock, stm., Austl.	277	12°15'S	141°56'E
Wenshan, China	238-39	23°30'N	104°28'E
Wentworth, Austl. (wĕnt'wûrth)	276	34°06'S	141°55'E
Wenzhou, China (wŭn-jō)	238-39	28°01'N	120°38'E
Werdēr, Eth.	262-63	6°58'N	45°21'E
Wesel, Ger. (vā'zĕl)	194-95	51°40'N	6°38'E
Weser, stm., Ger. (vā'zẽr)	194-95	53°32'N	8°34'E
Wesermünde, Ger. see Bremerhaven	194-95	53°32'N	8°36'E
Weslaco, Tx., U.S. (wĕs-lā'kō)	122-23	26°10'N	97°59'W
Wessel, Cape, c., Austl.	272-73	11°02'S	136°45'E
Wessington Springs, S.D., U.S. (wĕs'ĭng-tŭn sprĭngz)	114-15	44°05'N	98°34'W
West Allis, Wi., U.S. (wĕst ăl'ĭs)	116-17	43°01'N	88°01'W
West Bend, Ia., U.S. (wĕst bĕnd)	114-15	42°57'N	94°26'W
West Bend, Wi., U.S. (wĕst bĕnd)	116-17	43°25'N	88°10'W
West Bengal, state, India (wĕst bĕn-gôl')	234-35	24°0'N	88°00'E
West Branch, Ia., U.S. (wĕst brȧnch)	114-15	41°40'N	91°21'W
West Branch, Mi., U.S. (wĕst brȧnch)	116-17	44°16'N	84°14'W
Westbrook, Me., U.S. (wĕst'brŏŏk)	116-17	43°41'N	70°21'W
West Caicos, i., T./C. Is. (wĕst kī'kōs) (wĕst kăē'kō)	142-43	21°39'N	72°28'W
West Cape, c., N.Z. (wĕst kāp)	278	45°55'S	166°25'E
West Chester, Pa., U.S. (wĕst chĕs'tẽr)	116-17	39°58'N	75°36'W
West Columbia, S.C., U.S. (wĕst cŏl'ŭm-bē-ȧ)	124-25	33°59'N	81°05'W
West Columbia, Tx., U.S. (wĕst cŏl'ŭm-bē-ȧ)	122-23	29°09'N	95°39'W
West Des Moines, Ia., U.S. (wĕst dē moin')	114-15	41°34'N	93°44'W
West End, Bah. (wĕst ĕnd)	142-43	26°42'N	78°59'W
Westerly, R.I., U.S. (wĕs'tẽr-lē)	116-17	41°23'N	71°50'W
Western Australia, state, Austl. (wĕst'tẽrn ôs-trā'lĭ-ȧ)	270-71	25°0'S	122°00'E
Western Desert, des., Egypt (wĕst'tẽrn dĕs'ẽrt)	266	27°0'N	27°00'E
Western Dvina, stm., Eur.	192-93	57°04'N	24°03'E
Western Ghāts, mts., India (wĕst'tẽrn ghäts) (wĕst'tẽrn ghôts)	236	14°0'N	75°00'E
Westernport, Md., U.S. (wĕs'tẽrn pōrt)	116-17	39°29'N	79°03'W
Western Sahara, dep., Afr. (wĕst'tẽrn sȧ-hä'rȧ)	253	24°30'N	13°00'W
Western Samoa, nation, Oc. see Samoa	279b	13°55'S	172°00'W
Westerville, Oh., U.S. (wĕs'tẽr-vĭl)	116-17	40°07'N	82°55'W
West Falkland, i., Falk. Is.	171	51°50'S	59°60'W
Westfield, Ma., U.S. (wĕst'fēld)	116-17	42°08'N	72°45'W
Westfield, N.Y., U.S. (wĕst'fēld)	116-17	42°19'N	79°35'W
Westfield, Wi., U.S. (wĕst'fēld)	116-17	43°53'N	89°30'W
West Frankfort, Il., U.S. (wĕst frăŋk'fŭrt)	116-17	37°54'N	88°56'W
West Helena, Ar., U.S. (wĕst hĕl'ĕn-ȧ)	124-25	34°33'N	90°39'W
West Indies, is., (wĕst ĭn'dēz)	140-41	19°0'N	70°00'W
West Lafayette, In., U.S. (wĕst lä-fā-yĕt')	116-17	40°25'N	86°54'W
West Liberty, Ia., U.S. (wĕst lĭb'ẽr-tĭ)	114-15	41°34'N	91°16'W
West Liberty, Oh., U.S. (wĕst lĭb'ẽr-tĭ)	116-17	40°15'N	83°47'W
Westlock, Ab., Can. (wĕst'lŏk)	132-33	54°09'N	113°52'W
Westminster, Co., U.S. (wĕst'mĭn-stẽr)	120-21	39°51'N	105°04'W
West Nishnabotna, stm., Ia., U.S. (wĕst nĭsh-nȧ-bŏt'nȧ)	120-21	40°30'N	95°42'W
Weston, W.V., U.S. (wĕs'tŭn)	116-17	39°02'N	80°29'W
Weston-super-Mare, Eng., U.K. (wĕs'tŭn sū'pẽr-mā'rē)	190-91	51°21'N	2°58'W
West Palm Beach, Fl., U.S. (wĕst päm bēch)	125a	26°44'N	80°08'W
West Pensacola, Fl., U.S. (wĕst pĕn-sȧ-kō'lȧ)	124-25	30°25'N	87°16'W
West Plains, Mo., U.S. (wĕst-plānz')	124-25	36°44'N	91°52'W
West Point, Ga., U.S. (wĕst point)	124-25	32°54'N	85°09'W
West Point, Ms., U.S. (wĕst point)	124-25	33°36'N	88°39'W
West Point, Ne., U.S. (wĕst point)	114-15	41°51'N	96°43'W
West Point, N.Y., U.S. (wĕst point)	116-17	41°24'N	73°58'W
West Point, Va., U.S. (wĕst point)	116-17	37°32'N	76°48'W
West Point, c., Austl.	272-73	35°01'S	135°57'E
West Point Lake, res., U.S. (wĕst point lāk)	124-25	32°60'N	85°12'W

Feature (Pronunciation)	Page	Lat.	Long.
Westport, N.Z.	278	41°45'S	171°36'E
Westport, Wa., U.S. (wĕst´pôrt)	112-13	46°54'N	124°06'W
West Road, stm., B.C., Can. (wĕst rōd)	132-33	53°18'N	122°53'W
West Siberian Plain, pl., Russia (wĕst sī-bĭr´y´n plān)	218-19	60°0'N	75°00'E
West Union, Ia., U.S. (wĕst ūn´yŭn)	114-15	42°57'N	91°49'W
West Union, Oh., U.S. (wĕst ūn´yŭn)	116-17	38°47'N	83°33'W
Westville, N.S., Can. (wĕst´vĭl)	138-39	45°34'N	62°42'W
West Virginia, state, U.S. (wĕst vĕr-jĭn´ĭ-ȧ)	108-09	38°45'N	80°30'W
West Warwick, R.I., U.S. (wĕst wŏr´ĭk)	116-17	41°42'N	71°32'W
West Wyalong, Austl. (wĕst wīălông)	276	33°55'S	147°12'E
Wetar, Pulau, i., Indon. (pōō-lou wĕt´ȧr)	248-49	7°48'S	126°18'E
Wetaskiwin, Ab., Can. (wĕ-tăs´kē-wŏn)	132-33	52°58'N	113°22'W
Wete, Tan.	262-63	5°02'S	39°44'E
Wetumpka, Al., U.S. (wē-tŭmp´kȧ)	124-25	32°33'N	86°12'W
Wetzlar, Ger. (vets´lär)	194-95	50°33'N	8°29'E
Wewak, Pap. N. Gui. (wā-wäk´)	277	3°35'S	143°39'E
Wewoka, Ok., U.S. (wē-wō´kȧ)	120-21	35°10'N	96°30'W
Weyburn, Sk., Can. (wā´bûrn)	134-35	49°40'N	103°51'W
Weymouth, Eng., U.K. (wā´mŭth)	190-91	50°37'N	2°28'W
Whangarei, N.Z.	278	35°43'S	174°19'E
Whapmagoostui, Qc., Can.	128-29	55°17'N	77°45'W
Wharton, Tx., U.S. (hwôr´tŭn)	122-23	29°19'N	96°06'W
Wharton Lake, lk., Nu., Can.	130-31	64°01'N	99°52'W
Wheatland, Wy., U.S. (hwēt´lănd)	112-13	42°03'N	104°57'W
Wheaton, Md., U.S. (hwē´tŭn)	116-17	39°02'N	77°03'W
Wheaton, Mn., U.S. (hwē´tŭn)	114-15	45°48'N	96°30'W
Wheeler Peak, mtn., N.M., U.S.	120-21	36°34'N	105°25'W
Wheeling, W.V., U.S. (hwēl´ĭng)	116-17	40°04'N	80°41'W
Whitby, On., Can. (hwĭt´bē)	136-37	43°53'N	78°56'W
White, stm., On., Can. (hwīt)	136-37	48°33'N	86°16'W
White, stm., N.A.	126	63°11'N	139°35'W
White, stm., U.S. (hwīt)	110-11	33°53'N	91°04'W
White, stm., U.S. (hwīt)	114-15	43°42'N	99°27'W
White, stm., In., U.S. (hwīt)	116-17	38°25'N	87°45'W
White, East Fork, stm., In., U.S. (ēst fôrk hwīt)	116-17	38°32'N	87°14'W
White Bay, b., Nf., Can. (hwīt bā)	138-39	50°07'N	56°27'W
White Cloud, Mi., U.S. (hwīt kloud)	116-17	43°33'N	85°46'W
Whitecourt, Ab., Can. (hwīt´côrt)	132-33	54°08'N	115°43'W
White Earth Indian Reservation, ind. res., Mn., U.S. (hwīt ûrth ĭn´dĭ-ăn rĕ-sĕr-vā´shĕn)	114-15	47°18'N	95°50'W
Whitefish, Mt., U.S.	112-13	48°25'N	114°20'W
Whitefish Lake, lk., N.T., Can.	130-31	62°41'N	106°48'W
White Hall, Ar., U.S. (hwīt hôl)	120-21	34°16'N	92°07'W
Whitehall, Mi., U.S. (hwīt´hôl)	116-17	43°24'N	86°20'W
Whitehall, Mt., U.S. (hwīt´hôl)	112-13	45°52'N	112°06'W
Whitehall, N.Y., U.S. (hwīt´hôl)	116-17	43°33'N	73°24'W
Whitehaven, Eng., U.K. (hwīt´hā-vĕn)	190-91	54°33'N	3°35'W
Whitehorse, Yk., Can. (hwīt´hôrs)	128-29	60°43'N	135°08'W
White Lake, lk., On., Can. (hwīt lāk)	136-37	45°17'N	76°32'W
White Lake, lk., La., U.S. (hwīt lāk)	122-23	29°43'N	92°28'W
White Mountain Peak, mtn., Ca., U.S. (hwīt moun´tĭn pēk)	118-19	37°38'N	118°16'W
White Mountains, mts., N.H., U.S. (hwīt moun´tĭnz)	116-17	44°10'N	71°35'W
White Nile, stm., Sudan (hwīt nīl)	254	15°38'N	32°31'E
White Pass, p., N.A. (hwīt pās)	126	59°38'N	135°10'W
White Russia, nation, Eur. *see* Belarus	174-75	53°50'N	28°00'E
Whitesail Lake, res., B.C., Can. (hwīt´sāl lāk)	132-33	53°30'N	127°00'W
White Sands National Monument, n.p., N.M., U.S.	118-19	32°46'N	106°20'W
White Sea, s., Russia (hwīt sē sē)	186-87	65°37'N	37°52'E
White Sulphur Springs, Mt., U.S. (hwīt sŭl´fŭr sprĭngz)	112-13	46°33'N	110°55'W
White Sulphur Springs, W.V., U.S. (hwīt sŭl´fŭr sprĭngz)	116-17	37°48'N	80°18'W
Whiteville, N.C., U.S. (hwīt´vĭl)	124-25	34°20'N	78°42'W
White Volta, stm., Afr. (hwīt vôl´tȧ)	260-61	8°57'N	1°10'W
Whitewater, Wi., U.S. (hwīt-wŏt´ēr)	116-17	42°50'N	88°43'W
Whitewater Lake, lk., Mb., Can. (hwīt-wŏt´ēr lāk)	134-35	49°15'N	100°20'W
Whitewright, Tx., U.S. (hwīt´rīt)	120-21	33°31'N	96°24'W
Whitney, Lake, res., Tx., U.S. (lāk hwĭt´nē)	122-23	31°56'N	97°26'W
Whitney, Mount, mtn., Ca., U.S. (mount hwĭt´nē)	118-19	36°35'N	118°18'W
Whitsunday Island, i., Austl. (hwĭt´s'n-dā ī´lȧnd)	277	20°15'S	148°59'E
Whittle, Cap, c., Qc., Can.	138-39	50°11'N	60°10'W
Wholdaia Lake, lk., N.T., Can.	130-31	60°41'N	104°18'W
Whyalla, Austl. (hwī-ăl´ȧ)	276	33°02'S	137°34'E
Wiarton, On., Can. (wī´ȧr-tŭn)	136-37	44°44'N	81°08'W
Wichita, Ks., U.S. (wĭch´ĭ-tô)	120-21	37°41'N	97°19'W
Wichita Falls, Tx., U.S. (wĭch´ĭ-tô fôlz)	120-21	33°55'N	98°30'W
Wichita Mountains, mts., Ok., U.S. (wĭch´ĭ-tô moun´tĭnz)	120-21	34°45'N	98°40'W
Wick, Scot., U.K. (wĭk)	190-91	58°26'N	3°06'W
Wicklow Mountains, mts., Ire. (wĭk´lō moun´tĭnz)	190-91	53°02'N	6°24'W
Wieliczka, Pol. (vyĕ-lēch´kȧ)	194-95	49°59'N	20°04'E
Wien, nat. cap., Aus. (vēn) *see* Vienna	194-95	48°13'N	16°20'E
Wiener Neustadt, Aus. (vē´nĕr noi´shtät)	194-95	47°49'N	16°15'E
Wieprz, stm., Pol. (vyĕpzh)	194-95	51°33'N	21°50'E
Wiesbaden, Ger. (vēs´bä-dĕn)	194-95	50°05'N	8°14'E
Wiggins, Ms., U.S. (wĭg´ĭnz)	124-25	30°51'N	89°09'W
Wight, Isle of, i., Eng., U.K. (īl ŏv wīt)	190-91	50°40'N	1°20'W
Wilber, Ne., U.S. (wĭl´bēr)	120-21	40°29'N	96°58'W
Wilburton, Ok., U.S. (wĭl´bēr-tŭn)	120-21	34°56'N	95°19'W
Wilcannia, Austl. (wĭl-căn-ĭȧ)	276	31°34'S	143°23'E
Wildcat Hill, mtn., Sk., Can. (wīld´kăt hĭl)	134-35	53°17'N	102°30'W
Wildhay, stm., Ab., Can. (wīld´hā)	132-33	53°59'N	117°17'W
Wilge, stm., S. Afr. (wĭl´jē)	269c	27°02'S	28°21'E
Wilhelm, Mount, mtn., Pap. N. Gui.	277	5°47'S	145°00'E
Wilhelmina Peak, mtn., Indon. *see* Trikora, Puncak	277	4°18'S	138°40'E
Wilhelmshaven, Ger. (vēl-hĕlms-hä´fĕn)	194-95	53°32'N	8°07'E
Wilkes-Barre, Pa., U.S. (wĭlks´băr-ē)	116-17	41°15'N	75°53'W
Wilkes Land, reg., Ant.	287	69°0'S	120°00'E
Wilkie, Sk., Can. (wĭlk´ē)	134-35	52°25'N	108°40'W
Willamette, stm., Or., U.S.	112-13	45°39'N	122°46'W
Willard, Oh., U.S. (wĭl´ȧrd)	116-17	41°03'N	82°43'W
Willcox, Az., U.S. (wĭl´kŏks)	118-19	32°15'N	109°50'W
Willemstad, nat. cap., Neth. Ant. (vĭ´lĕm-stät)	140a	12°06'N	68°56'W
Williams, Az., U.S. (wĭl´yămz)	118-19	35°15'N	112°12'W
Williamsburg, Ia., U.S. (wĭl´yămz-bûrg)	114-15	41°40'N	92°01'W
Williamsburg, Ky., U.S. (wĭl´yămz-bûrg)	124-25	36°44'N	84°10'W
Williamsburg, Va., U.S. (wĭl´yămz-bûrg)	124-25	37°16'N	76°43'W
Williams Lake, B.C., Can. (wĭl´yămz lāk)	132-33	52°07'N	122°09'W
Williamson, W.V., U.S. (wĭl´yăm-sŭn)	116-17	37°40'N	82°17'W
Williamson Head, c., Ant.	287	69°12'S	157°47'E
Williamsport, Pa., U.S.	116-17	41°14'N	77°01'W
Williamston, N.C., U.S. (wĭl´yămz-tŭn)	124-25	35°51'N	77°04'W
Williamston, S.C., U.S. (wĭl´yămz-tŭn)	124-25	34°37'N	82°29'W
Williamstown, Ky., U.S. (wĭl´yămz-toun)	116-17	38°38'N	84°34'W
Williamstown, W.V., U.S. (wĭl´yămz-toun)	116-17	39°24'N	81°27'W
Willimantic, Ct., U.S. (wĭl-ĭ-măn´tĭk)	116-17	41°43'N	72°12'W
Willis, Tx., U.S. (wĭl´ĭs)	122-23	30°25'N	95°29'W
Williston, Fl., U.S. (wĭl´ĭs-tŭn)	124-25	29°23'N	82°27'W
Williston, N.D., U.S. (wĭl´ĭs-tŭn)	114-15	48°09'N	103°37'W
Williston, S.C., U.S. (wĭl´ĭs-tŭn)	124-25	33°24'N	81°26'W
Williston Lake, res., B.C., Can. (wĭl´ĭs-tŭn lāk)	130-31	56°00'N	123°54'W
Willmar, Mn., U.S. (wĭl´mär)	114-15	45°07'N	95°03'W
Willow, Ak., U.S. (wĭl´ō)	126	61°45'N	150°03'W
Willowmore, S. Afr. (wĭl´ō-môr)	264-65	33°18'S	23°29'E
Willows, Ca., U.S. (wĭl´ōz)	118-19	39°31'N	122°12'W
Willow Springs, Mo., U.S. (wĭl´ō sprĭngz)	124-25	36°60'N	91°58'W
Wills Point, Tx., U.S. (wĭlz point)	120-21	32°43'N	96°01'W
Wilmington, De., U.S.	116-17	39°45'N	75°32'W
Wilmington, N.C., U.S. (wĭl´mĭng-tŭn)	124-25	34°13'N	77°57'W
Wilmington, Oh., U.S. (wĭl´mĭng-tŭn)	116-17	39°26'N	83°50'W
Wilmore, Ky., U.S. (wĭl´mōr)	116-17	37°46'N	84°37'W
Wilna, nat. cap., Lith. *see* Vilnius	192-93	54°40'N	25°17'E
Wilson, N.C., U.S. (wĭl´sŭn)	124-25	35°44'N	77°55'W
Wilson, Ok., U.S. (wĭl´sŭn)	120-21	34°10'N	97°25'W
Wilson, Cape, c., Nu., Can.	130-31	67°01'N	81°30'W
Wilson, Mount, mtn., Ca., U.S. (mount wĭl´sŭn)	118-19	34°14'N	118°04'W
Wilson, Mount, mtn., Co., U.S. (mount wĭl´sŭn)	118-19	37°51'N	107°59'W
Wilsons Promontory, pen., Austl.	276	38°55'S	146°20'E
Wilton, N.D., U.S. (wĭl´tŭn)	114-15	47°09'N	100°47'W
Winamac, In., U.S. (wĭn´ȧ măk)	116-17	41°03'N	86°36'W
Winburg, S. Afr. (wĭm-bûrg)	269c	28°31'S	27°01'E
Winchester, In., U.S. (wĭn´chĕs-tēr)	116-17	40°10'N	84°59'W
Winchester, Ky., U.S. (wĭn´chĕs-tēr)	116-17	37°60'N	84°11'W
Winchester, Tn., U.S. (wĭn´chĕs-tēr)	124-25	35°11'N	86°06'W
Winchester, Va., U.S. (wĭn´chĕs-tēr)	116-17	39°11'N	78°10'W
Windau, Lat. *see* Ventspils	192-93	57°24'N	21°35'E
Wind Cave National Park, n.p., S.D., U.S. (wĭnd kāv năsh´ŭn-ăl pärk)	114-15	43°34'N	103°29'W
Windhoek, nat. cap., Nmb. (vĭnt´hök)	264-65	22°34'S	17°05'E
Windom, Mn., U.S. (wĭn´dŭm)	114-15	43°52'N	95°07'W
Windorah, Austl.	276	25°25'S	142°39'E
Wind River Indian Reservation, ind. res., Wy., U.S. (wĭnd rĭv´ēr ĭn´dĭ-ăn rĕ-sĕr-vā´shĕn)	112-13	43°26'N	109°00'W
Wind River Range, mts., Wy., U.S. (wĭnd rĭv´ēr rānj)	112-13	43°05'N	109°25'W
Windsor, Austl. (wĭn´zēr)	276	33°37'S	150°49'E
Windsor, N.S., Can. (wĭn´zēr)	138-39	44°59'N	64°08'W
Windsor, On., Can. (wĭn´zēr)	136-37	42°18'N	83°02'W
Windsor, Eng., U.K. (wĭn´zēr)	190-91	51°29'N	0°36'W
Windsor, Co., U.S. (wĭn´zēr)	120-21	40°28'N	104°53'W
Windsor, Mo., U.S. (wĭn´zēr)	120-21	38°32'N	93°32'W
Windsor, N.C., U.S. (wĭn´zēr)	124-25	35°60'N	76°57'W
Windsor, Vt., U.S. (wĭn´zēr)	116-17	43°29'N	72°23'W
Windward Islands, is., N.A. (wĭnd´wērd ī´lȧndz)	143b	13°0'N	61°00'W
Windward Passage, strt., N.A. (wĭnd´wērd păs´ĭj)	142-43	19°56'N	73°52'W
Winfield, Ks., U.S.	120-21	37°14'N	96°60'W
Wingham, On., Can.	136-37	43°53'N	81°18'W
Winisk, stm., On., Can.	130-31	55°16'N	85°07'W
Winisk Lake, lk., On., Can.	134-35	52°55'N	87°22'W
Winkler, Mb., Can. (wĭnk´lēr)	134-35	49°11'N	97°56'W
Winnebago, Mn., U.S. (wĭn´ē-bā´gō)	114-15	43°46'N	94°11'W
Winnebago, Lake, lk., Wi., U.S. (lāk wĭn´ē-bā´gō)	116-17	44°0'N	88°25'W
Winnebago Indian Reservation, ind. res., Ne., U.S. (wĭn´ē-bā´gō ĭn´dĭ-ăn rĕ-sĕr-vā´shĕn)	114-15	42°15'N	96°31'W
Winnemucca, Nv., U.S. (wĭn-ē-mŭk´ȧ)	112-13	40°58'N	117°44'W
Winner, S.D., U.S. (wĭn´ēr)	114-15	43°23'N	99°52'W
Winnfield, La., U.S. (wĭn´fēld)	122-23	31°55'N	92°38'W
Winnipeg, Mb., Can. (wĭn´ĭ-pĕg)	134-35	49°52'N	97°10'W
Winnipeg, stm., Can. (wĭn´ĭ-pĕg)	134-35	50°41'N	96°24'W
Winnipeg, Lake, lk., Mb., Can. (lāk wĭn´ĭ-pĕg)	134-35	52°0'N	97°00'W
Winnipegosis, Lake, lk., Mb., Can.	134-35	52°30'N	99°59'W
Winnsboro, La., U.S. (wĭnz´bŭr´ō)	124-25	32°10'N	91°43'W
Winnsboro, S.C., U.S. (wĭnz´bŭr´ō)	124-25	34°23'N	81°05'W
Winnsboro, Tx., U.S. (wĭnz´bŭr´ō)	120-21	32°58'N	95°17'W
Winona, Mi., U.S. (wĭ-nō´nȧ)	114-15	46°52'N	88°55'W
Winona, Mn., U.S. (wĭ-nō´nȧ)	114-15	44°03'N	91°38'W
Winona, Ms., U.S. (wĭ-nō´nȧ)	124-25	33°29'N	89°44'W
Winslow, Az., U.S. (wĭnz´lō)	118-19	35°02'N	110°42'W
Winsted, Ct., U.S. (wĭn´stĕd)	116-17	41°56'N	73°04'W
Winston-Salem, N.C., U.S. (wĭn stŭn-sā´lĕm)	124-25	36°06'N	80°14'W
Winter Garden, Fl., U.S. (wĭn´tēr gär´d'n)	125a	28°34'N	81°35'W
Winter Haven, Fl., U.S. (wĭn´tēr hā´vĕn)	125a	28°02'N	81°44'W
Winters, Tx., U.S. (wĭn´tērz)	122-23	31°57'N	99°58'W
Winterset, Ia., U.S. (wĭn´tēr-sĕt)	114-15	41°20'N	94°01'W
Winterthur, Switz. (vĭn´tēr-tōōr)	194-95	47°30'N	8°43'E
Winthrop, Me., U.S. (wĭn´thrŭp)	116-17	44°18'N	69°59'W
Winton, Austl. (wĭn-tŭn)	277	22°23'S	143°02'E
Wirāṭnagar, Nepal	234-35	26°28'N	87°17'E
Wīrgañj, Nepal	234-35	27°01'N	84°52'E
Wisby, Swe. *see* Visby	192-93	57°38'N	18°19'E
Wisconsin, state, U.S. (wĭs-kŏn´sĭn)	108-09	44°45'N	89°30'W
Wisconsin, stm., Wi., U.S. (wĭs-kŏn´sĭn)	114-15	42°59'N	91°09'W
Wisconsin Dells, Wi., U.S. (wĭs-kŏn´sĭn dĕlz)	116-17	43°38'N	89°45'W
Wisconsin Rapids, Wi., U.S. (wĭs-kŏn´sĭn răp´ĭdz)	116-17	44°23'N	89°49'W
Wishek, N.D., U.S. (wĭsh´ĕk)	114-15	46°16'N	99°33'W

Feature (Pronunciation)	Page	Lat.	Long.
Wisła, stm., Pol. (vēs′wȧ) *see* Vistula	194-95	54°21′N	18°56′E
Wisłoka, stm., Pol. (vēs-wô′kȧ)	194-95	50°27′N	21°24′E
Wismar, Ger. (vĭs′mär)	194-95	53°53′N	11°28′E
Wisner, Ne., U.S. (wĭz′nẽr)	114-15	41°59′N	96°56′W
Wissembourg, Fr. (vē-säN-bōōr′)	196-97	49°02′N	7°57′E
Witbank, S. Afr. (wĭt-băŋk)	269c	25°53′S	29°14′E
Withlacoochee, stm., U.S. (wĭth-lȧ-kōō′chē)	124-25	30°23′N	83°10′W
Witu Islands, is., Pap. N. Gui.	277	4°45′S	149°19′E
W.J. van Blommestein Meer, res., Sur.	164-65	4°49′N	55°04′W
Wkra, stm., Pol. (f′krȧ)	194-95	52°27′N	20°45′E
Włocławek, Pol. (vwô-tswä′vĕk)	194-95	52°39′N	19°04′E
Włodawa, Pol. (vwô-dä′vä)	194-95	51°33′N	23°34′E
Włoszczowa, Pol. (vwôsh-chô′vä)	194-95	50°51′N	19°58′E
Wodonga, Austl.	276	36°08′S	146°53′E
Wokam, Pulau, i., Indon.	224-25	5°37′S	134°30′E
Woleai, at., Micron.	280-81	7°21′N	143°53′E
Woleu, stm., Afr. *see* Mbini	260-61	1°35′N	9°38′E
Wolf, Volcán, vol., Ec.	170a	0°00′S	91°20′W
Wolf Point, Mt., U.S. (wo̤lf point)	112-13	48°05′N	105°37′W
Wolfsburg, Ger. (vōlfs′bo͝orgh)	194-95	52°26′N	10°47′E
Wolfville, N.S., Can. (wo̤lf′vĭl)	138-39	45°05′N	64°22′W
Wollaston, Islas, is., Chile	171	55°45′S	67°37′W
Wollaston Lake, lk., Sk., Can. (wo̤l′ȧs-tŭn lāk)	130-31	58°15′N	103°20′W
Wollaston Peninsula, pen., Can. (wo̤l′ȧs-tŭn pĕ-nĭn′sūlȧ)	130-31	70°0′N	115°00′W
Wollongong, Austl. (wo̤l′ŭn-gŏng)	276	34°25′S	150°54′E
Wołomin, Pol. (vô-wō′mēn)	194-95	52°20′N	21°15′E
Wolseley, Sk., Can.	134-35	50°25′N	103°16′W
Wolverhampton, Eng., U.K. (wo̤l′vẽr-hămp-tŭn)	190-91	52°35′N	2°08′W
Wondai, Austl.	276	26°19′S	151°53′E
Wŏnju, Kor., S.	243	37°21′N	127°57′E
Wŏnsan, Kor., N. (wŭn′sän′)	243	39°09′N	127°26′E
Wonthaggi, Austl. (wônt-hăg′ē)	276	38°37′S	145°35′E
Woodbine, Ia., U.S. (wo̤d′bīn)	114-15	41°44′N	95°43′W
Woodbridge, Va., U.S. (wo̤d′brĭj′)	116-17	38°39′N	77°15′W
Wood Buffalo National Park, n.p., Can. (wo̤d bŭf′ȧ-lō năsh′ŭn-ăl pärk)	128-29	59°06′N	112°58′W
Woodburn, Or., U.S. (wo̤d′bûrn)	112-13	45°08′N	122°51′W
Woodlark, i., Pap. N. Gui. (wo̤d′lärk) *see* Murua Island	277	9°06′S	152°45′E
Woodroffe, Mount, mtn., Austl. (mount wo̤d′rŭf)	272-73	26°20′S	131°45′E
Woodruff, S.C., U.S. (wo̤d′rŭf)	124-25	34°45′N	82°02′W
Woods, Lake of the, lk., N.A. (lāk ŭv thȧ wo̤dz)	134-35	49°15′N	94°45′W
Woodsfield, Oh., U.S. (wo̤dz-fēld)	116-17	39°46′N	81°07′W
Woodstock, N.B., Can. (wo̤d′stŏk)	138-39	46°09′N	67°34′W
Woodstock, On., Can. (wo̤d′stŏk)	136-37	43°08′N	80°45′W
Woodstock, Il., U.S. (wo̤d′stŏk)	116-17	42°19′N	88°26′W
Woodstock, N.Y., U.S. (wo̤d′stŏk)	116-17	42°03′N	74°07′W
Woodstock, Va., U.S. (wo̤d′stŏk)	116-17	38°53′N	78°30′W
Woodsville, N.H., U.S. (wo̤dz′vĭl)	116-17	44°09′N	72°02′W
Woodville, Ms., U.S. (wo̤d′vĭl)	124-25	31°07′N	91°18′W
Woodville, Tx., U.S. (wo̤d′vĭl)	122-23	30°46′N	94°25′W
Woodward, Ok., U.S. (wo̤d′wôrd)	120-21	36°27′N	99°23′W
Woomera, Austl. (wo͞om′ĕrȧ)	276	31°12′S	136°50′E
Woonsocket, R.I., U.S. (wo͞on-sŏk′ĕt)	116-17	42°01′N	71°31′W
Wooramel, stm., Austl.	272-73	25°51′S	114°16′E
Wooster, Oh., U.S. (wo̤s′tẽr)	116-17	40°48′N	81°56′W
Worcester, S. Afr. (wo͞os′tẽr)	264-65	33°39′S	19°27′E
Worcester, Eng., U.K. (wo̤′stẽr)	190-91	52°11′N	2°14′W
Worcester, Ma., U.S.	116-17	42°16′N	71°48′W
Worden, Mt., U.S. (wôr′dĕn)	112-13	45°58′N	108°13′W
Workington, Eng., U.K. (wûr′kĭng-tŭn)	190-91	54°38′N	3°34′W
Worksop, Eng., U.K. (wûrk′sŏp) (wûr′sŭp)	190-91	53°19′N	1°07′W
Worland, Wy., U.S. (wûr′lănd)	112-13	44°01′N	107°57′W
Worms, Ger. (vōrms)	194-95	49°38′N	8°21′E
Worthing, Eng., U.K. (wûr′dhĭng)	190-91	50°49′N	0°23′W
Worthington, In., U.S. (wûr′dhĭng-tŭn)	116-17	39°07′N	86°59′W
Worthington, Mn., U.S. (wûr′dhĭng-tŭn)	114-15	43°38′N	95°36′W
Wotho, at., Marsh. Is.	280-81	10°06′N	166°01′E
Wotje, at., Marsh. Is.	280-81	9°27′N	170°02′E
Wowoni, Pulau, i., Indon. (po͞o-lou wō-wō′nē)	248-49	4°08′S	123°06′E
Wrangel Island, i., Russia (răn′gĕl ī′lănd) *see* Vrangelya, Ostrov	218-19	71°14′N	179°21′W
Wrangell, Ak., U.S. (răn′gĕl)	126	56°29′N	132°22′W
Wrangell, Cape, c., Ak., U.S. (kāp răn′gĕl)	126a	52°55′N	172°30′E
Wrangell, Mount, mtn., Ak., U.S. (mount răn′gĕl)	126	62°0′N	144°06′W
Wrangell Mountains, mts., Ak., U.S. (răn′gĕl moun′tĭnz)	126	62°0′N	143°00′W
Wrangell-Saint Elias National Park and Preserve, n.p., Ak., U.S.	126	61°37′N	142°57′W
Wrath, Cape, c., Scot., U.K. (kāp răth)	190-91	58°38′N	4°60′W
Wray, Co., U.S. (rā)	120-21	40°05′N	102°14′W
Wrens, Ga., U.S. (rĕnz)	124-25	33°12′N	82°20′W
Wrexham, Wales, U.K. (rĕk′săm)	190-91	53°03′N	2°60′W
Wrightsville, Ga., U.S. (rīts′vĭl)	124-25	32°44′N	82°43′W
Wrigley, N.T., Can.	128-29	63°16′N	123°38′W
Wrocław, Pol. (vrôtsläv) (brĕs′lou)	194-95	51°07′N	17°02′E
Września, Pol. (vzhăsh′nyȧ)	194-95	52°20′N	17°35′E
Wu, stm., China (wo͞o′)	238-39	24°49′N	113°35′E
Wu, stm., China (wo͞o′)	238-39	27°11′N	109°48′E
Wuchang, China (wo͞o-chäŋ)	240-41	44°55′N	127°10′E
Wuchang, China *see* Wuhan	238-39	30°34′N	114°17′E
Wudaoliang, China	234-35	35°12′N	93°05′E
Wudu, China	238-39	33°25′N	104°51′E
Wugang, China	238-39	26°44′N	110°38′E
Wugong Shan, mts., China	238-39	27°21′N	113°50′E
Wuhai, China	240-41	39°40′N	106°48′E
Wuhan, China (wo͞o-hän′)	238-39	30°34′N	114°17′E
Wuhu, China (wo͞o′ho͞o)	238-39	31°21′N	118°22′E
Wüjang, China	234-35	33°37′N	79°48′E
Wukari, Nig.	260-61	7°53′N	9°47′E
Wuliang Shan, mts., China	238-39	24°29′N	100°39′E
Wuliaru, Pulau, i., Indon.	224-25	7°27′S	131°04′E
Wunnummin Lake, lk., On., Can.	134-35	52°55′N	89°10′W
Wupatki National Monument, n.p., Az., U.S.	118-19	35°32′N	111°26′W
Wuppertal, Ger. (vo̤p′ẽr-täl)	194-95	51°17′N	7°11′E
Würzburg, Ger. (vürts′bo̤rgh)	194-95	49°48′N	9°56′E
Wushan, China	238-39	31°06′N	109°50′E
Wushenqi, China	240-41	38°58′N	109°01′E
Wusuli, stm., Asia *see* Ussuri	240-41	48°27′N	135°04′E
Wutai, China	240-41	38°44′N	113°21′E
Wutai Shan, mtn., China	240-41	39°04′N	113°35′E
Wutongqiao, China	238-39	29°24′N	103°49′E
Wutsin, China *see* Changzhou	238-39	31°47′N	119°57′E
Wuvulu Island, i., Pap. N. Gui.	277	1°45′S	142°50′E
Wuwei, China (wo͞o′wā′)	238-39	31°18′N	117°54′E
Wuwei, China (wo͞o′wā′)	240-41	37°56′N	102°38′E
Wuxi, China (wo͞o-shyē)	238-39	31°22′N	109°33′E
Wuxi, China (wo͞o-shyē)	238-39	31°35′N	120°18′E
Wuxing, China (wo͞o-shyĭŋ) *see* Huzhou	238-39	30°52′N	120°06′E
Wuyi Shan, mts., China (wo͞o-yē shän)	238-39	27°42′N	117°09′E
Wuyuan, China	240-41	41°03′N	108°22′E
Wuzhong, China	240-41	37°59′N	106°12′E
Wuzhou, China (wo͞o-jō)	238-39	23°30′N	111°21′E
Wyandotte, Mi., U.S. (wī′ăn-dŏt)	116-17	42°13′N	83°09′W
Wyandra, Austl.	276	27°16′S	145°59′E
Wymore, Ne., U.S. (wī′mōr)	120-21	40°07′N	96°40′W
Wyndham, Austl. (wĭnd′ăm)	270-71	15°29′S	128°07′E
Wynne, Ar., U.S. (wĭn)	124-25	35°13′N	90°48′W
Wynnewood, Ok., U.S. (wĭn′wo̤d)	120-21	34°39′N	97°10′W
Wynyard, Sk., Can. (wĭn′yẽrd)	134-35	51°47′N	104°10′W
Wyoming, Mi., U.S. (wī-ō′mĭng)	116-17	42°55′N	85°43′W
Wyoming, state, U.S. (wī-ō′mĭng)	108-09	43°0′N	107°30′W
Wyong, Austl.	276	33°17′S	151°25′E
Wyszków, Pol. (vēsh′ko̤f)	194-95	52°36′N	21°28′E
Wytheville, Va., U.S. (wĭth′vĭl)	124-25	36°57′N	81°06′W

X

Feature (Pronunciation)	Page	Lat.	Long.
Xaafuun, Raas, c., Som.	262-63	10°26′N	51°25′E
Xaidulla, China	234-35	36°26′N	77°58′E
Xainza, China	234-35	30°55′N	88°40′E
Xai-Xai, Moz.	264-65	25°03′S	33°39′E
Xalapa, Mex.	146-47	19°32′N	96°55′W
Xam, stm., Asia *see* Chu	246-47	19°53′N	105°45′E
Xam Nua, Laos	246-47	20°25′N	104°03′E
Xankändi, Azer.	227	39°49′N	46°45′E
Xapuri, Braz.	166-67	10°39′S	68°31′W
Xar Moron, stm., China	240-41	43°25′N	120°45′E
Xau, Lake, pl., Bots.	264-65	21°18′S	24°44′E
Xäzär, Dänizi, lk., *see* Caspian Sea	226	41°18′N	50°59′E
Xcalak, Mex. (sä-lä′k)	148	18°16′N	87°50′W
Xenia, Oh., U.S. (zē′nĭ-ȧ)	116-17	39°41′N	83°56′W
Xeres, Spain *see* Jerez de la Frontera	198-99	36°42′N	6°08′W
Xi, stm., China (shyē)	238-39	22°20′N	113°18′E
Xi, stm., China (shyē)	240-41	42°25′N	100°55′E
Xiaguan, China *see* Dali	238-39	25°36′N	100°13′E
Xiahe, China	240-41	35°24′N	102°32′E
Xiamen, China	225a	24°27′N	118°07′E
Xi'an, China (shyē-än)	238-39	34°15′N	108°52′E
Xiangfan, China	238-39	32°02′N	112°09′E
Xianggang, China *see* Hong Kong	238-39	22°16′N	114°10′E
Xiangkhoang, Laos	246-47	19°20′N	103°22′E
Xiangquan, stm., Asia *see* Sutlej	234-35	29°21′N	71°02′E
Xiangride, China	240-41	35°60′N	97°59′E
Xiangtan, China (shyäŋ-tän)	238-39	27°51′N	112°54′E
Xiantao, China	238-39	30°22′N	113°27′E
Xianyang, China (shyĕn-yäŋ)	238-39	34°20′N	108°42′E
Xianyou, China	225a	25°22′N	118°40′E
Xiaogan, China	238-39	30°55′N	113°54′E
Xiao Hinggan Ling, mts., China *see* Lesser Khingan Range	240-41	48°45′N	127°00′E
Xiapu, China (shyä-po͞o)	238-39	26°52′N	120°01′E
Xibaxa, stm., Asia *see* Subansiri	238-39	26°46′N	93°45′E
Xichang, China	238-39	27°54′N	102°16′E
Xicoténcatl, Mex. (sē-kō-tĕn-kät′l)	146-47	23°00′N	98°56′W
Xifeng, China (shyē-fŭŋ)	240-41	42°44′N	124°43′E
Xigazê, China	234-35	29°16′N	88°54′E
Xilinhot, China	240-41	43°56′N	116°03′E
Ximiao, China	240-41	41°07′N	100°17′E
Xinchang, China (shyĭn-chäŋ)	238-39	29°31′N	120°53′E
Xing'an, China (shyĭŋ-än)	238-39	25°37′N	110°31′E
Xinghua, China (shyĭŋ-hwä)	238-39	32°56′N	119°50′E
Xingkai Hu, lk., Asia *see* Khanka, Lake	244	45°11′N	132°25′E
Xingtai, China (shyĭŋ-tī)	240-41	37°04′N	114°30′E
Xingu, stm., Braz. (zhĕŋ-gô′)	166-67	1°30′S	51°50′W
Xingyi, China	238-39	25°05′N	104°54′E
Xinhua, China (shyĭn-hwä)	238-39	27°37′N	111°02′E
Xining, China (shyē-nĭŋ)	240-41	36°38′N	101°50′E
Xinjiang, China	240-41	35°37′N	111°13′E
Xinjiang, state, China (shyĭn-jyäŋ)	220-21	40°0′N	85°00′E
Xinjiulong, China	238-39	22°21′N	114°10′E
Xinmin, China (shyĭn-mĭn)	243	41°59′N	122°50′E
Xinpu, China *see* Lianyungang	238-39	34°37′N	119°11′E
Xintai, China (shyĭn-tī)	240-41	35°54′N	117°46′E
Xinxian, China (shyĭn shyĕn)	240-41	38°24′N	112°44′E
Xinxiang, China (shyĭn-shyäŋ)	240-41	35°18′N	113°52′E
Xinyang, China (shyĭn-yäŋ)	238-39	32°07′N	114°04′E
Xinye, China (shyĭn-yŭ)	238-39	32°33′N	112°21′E
Xiping, China (shyē-pĭŋ)	238-39	33°23′N	114°01′E
Xique-Xique, Braz.	166-67	10°50′S	42°43′W
Xırdalan, Azer.	227	40°28′N	49°46′E
Xisha Qundao, is., China *see* Paracel Islands	224-25	15°46′N	112°17′E
Xishui, China (shyē-shwā)	238-39	30°28′N	115°15′E
Xixian, China (shyē shyĕn)	238-39	32°21′N	114°44′E
Xizang, state, China (shyē-dzäŋ) *see* Tibet	234-35	32°0′N	88°00′E
Xongka, stm., Asia *see* Ca	246-47	18°44′N	105°45′E
Xuancheng, China (shyủän-chŭŋ)	238-39	30°57′N	118°45′E
Xuanhua, China (shyủän-hwä)	240-41	40°36′N	115°02′E
Xuchang, China (shyo͞o-chäŋ)	238-39	34°02′N	113°49′E
Xun, stm., China (shyo̤n)	238-39	23°26′N	111°30′E
Xuwen, China	238-39	20°20′N	110°11′E
Xuyong, China	238-39	28°10′N	105°25′E
Xuzhou, China	238-39	34°16′N	117°11′E

Y

Feature (Pronunciation)	Page	Lat.	Long.
Yaan, China (yä-än)	238-39	30°01′N	103°04′E
Yablonovy Range, mts., Russia (yȧ-blô-nô-vē′ fänj) *see* Yablonovyy Khrebet	218-19	53°30′N	115°00′E
Yablonovyy Khrebet, mts., Russia	218-19	53°30′N	115°00′E
Yaco, stm., S.A. *see* Iaco	170	9°02′S	68°35′W
Yacuiba, Bol. (yȧ-ko͞o-ē′bȧ)	168-69	22°02′S	63°42′W
Yacyretá, Isla, i., Para.	173	27°25′S	56°30′W
Yadong, China	234-35	27°29′N	88°54′E
Yafran, Libya	188-89	32°04′N	12°31′E
Yagodnoye, Russia	218-19	62°32′N	149°37′E
Yaguajay, Cuba (yä-guä-hä′ē)	142-43	22°20′N	79°14′W
Yahualica, Mex. (yä-wä-lē′kä)	146-47	21°09′N	102°51′W
Yaitopya, nation, Afr. *see* Ethiopia	253	9°0′N	39°00′E
Yakima, Wa., U.S. (yăk′ĭmȧ)	112-13	46°36′N	120°30′W

ăt; finăl; rāte; senāte; ärm; ȧsk; sofȧ; fâre; ch-choose; dh-as th in other; bē; ēvent; bĕt; recĕnt; cratẽr; g-gō; gh-guttural g; bĭt; ĭ-short neutral; rīde; K-guttural k as ch in German ich;

Feature (Pronunciation)	Page	Lat.	Long.
Yakoma, D.R.C.	262-63	4°04'N	22°26'E
Yaku-shima, i., Japan (yä'kōō shē'mä)	244	30°20'N	130°30'E
Yakutat, Ak., U.S. (yăk'ô-tăt)	126	59°32'N	139°43'W
Yakutat Bay, b., Ak., U.S. (yōō-kū-tăt' bā)	126	59°40'N	140°00'W
Yakutia, state, Russia	218-19	67°0'N	125°00'E
Yakutsk, Russia (yá-kôtsk')	218-19	62°02'N	129°42'E
Yala, Thai.	246-47	6°33'N	101°17'E
Yalgoo, Austl.	270-71	28°21'S	116°41'E
Yalong, stm., China (yä-lôŋ)	238-39	26°36'N	101°48'E
Yalta, Ukr. (yäl'tá)	202-03	44°30'N	34°10'E
Yalu, stm., Asia	243	39°57'N	124°22'E
Yamagata, Japan	245	38°15'N	140°20'E
Yamaguchi, Japan	245	34°11'N	131°29'E
Yamal, Poluostrov, pen., Russia (yä-mäl')	218-19	70°0'N	70°00'E
Yamal Peninsula, pen., Russia (yŭ-mäl' pĕ-nĭn'sūlă) see Yamal, Poluostrov	218-19	70°0'N	70°00'E
Yamantau, Gora, mtn., Russia (gá-rä' yä'man-táw)	226	54°15'N	58°06'E
Yamarovka, Russia	240-41	50°34'N	110°25'E
Yambio, Sudan	267	4°34'N	28°24'E
Yambol, Blg. (yam'bôl)	200-01	42°29'N	26°31'E
Yamdena, Pulau, i., Indon.	224-25	7°36'S	131°25'E
Yamethin, Mya. (yŭ-mē'thēn)	246-47	20°28'N	96°09'E
Yamma Yamma, Lake, lk., Austl. (lāk yäm'á yäm'á)	276	26°20'S	141°25'E
Yamoussoukro, nat. cap., C. Iv. (yä-mōō-sōō'-krō)	260-61	6°49'N	5°17'W
Yamuna, stm., India	234-35	25°26'N	81°54'E
Yamzho Yumco, lk., China (yäm-jwo yōōm-tswo)	234-35	28°58'N	90°45'E
Yana, stm., Russia (yä'ná)	218-19	71°32'N	136°38'E
Yanac, Austl. (yăn'ăk)	276	36°09'S	141°25'E
Yanam, India (yŭnŭm')	236	16°44'N	82°15'E
Yan'an, China (yän-än)	240-41	36°35'N	109°29'E
Yanbu'al-Baḥr, Sau. Ar.	266	24°05'N	38°05'E
Yanchang, China	240-41	36°35'N	110°01'E
Yancheng, China (yän-chŭŋ)	238-39	33°24'N	120°09'E
Yanchi, China	240-41	37°47'N	107°23'E
Yandé, Île, i., N. Cal.	279g	20°03'S	163°48'E
Yangambi, D.R.C.	262-63	0°46'N	24°27'E
Yangchun, China (yäŋ-chòn)	238-39	22°11'N	111°47'E
Yanggu, China (yäŋ-gōō)	240-41	36°07'N	115°46'E
Yangiyŭl, Uzb.	232-33	41°09'N	69°07'E
Yangjiang, China (yäŋ-jyäŋ)	238-39	21°53'N	111°58'E
Yangon, nat. cap., Mya. (yän'gōn')	246-47	16°47'N	96°12'E
Yangquan, China (yäŋ-chyůän)	240-41	37°51'N	113°34'E
Yangtze, stm., China (yäng'tse)	238-39	31°24'N	121°54'E
Yangxin, China (yäŋ-shyĭn)	238-39	29°50'N	115°13'E
Yangzhou, China (yäŋ-jō)	238-39	32°24'N	119°25'E
Yanji, China (yän-jyē)	243	42°46'N	129°26'E
Yanji, China (yän-jyē)	243	42°54'N	129°30'E
Yankton, S.D., U.S. (yănk'tŭn)	114-15	42°52'N	97°24'W
Yanqi, China	222-23	42°03'N	86°34'E
Yanshan, China (yän-shän)	238-39	23°37'N	104°20'E
Yanshou, China (yän-shō)	244	45°26'N	128°21'E
Yantai, China	240-41	37°32'N	121°21'E
Yanzhou, China (yäŋ-jō)	240-41	35°33'N	116°49'E
Yaoundé, nat. cap., Camrn. (yá'-ōōn-dā')	260-61	3°52'N	11°31'E
Yap, i., Micron. (yăp)	280-81	9°31'N	138°06'E
Yapacaní, Bol.	168-69	16°45'S	64°18'W
Yapen, Pulau, i., Indon.	224-25	1°45'S	136°15'E
Yaponskoye More, s., Asia see Japan, Sea of	222-23	40°0'N	135°00'E
Yaque del Norte, stm., Dom. Rep. (yä'kå dĕl nôr'tå)	142-43	19°50'N	71°41'W
Yaqui, stm., Mex. (yä'kē)	144-45	27°40'N	110°38'W
Yaransk, Russia (yä-ränsk')	186-87	57°18'N	47°54'E
Yarensk, Russia	186-87	62°09'N	49°02'E
Yarí, stm., Col.	164-65	0°19'S	72°21'W
Yarkand, stm., China see Yarkant	226	40°28'N	80°51'E
Yarkant, China see Shache	226	38°25'N	77°15'E
Yarkant, stm., China	226	40°28'N	80°51'E
Yarlung, stm., Asia see Brahmaputra	234-35	24°02'N	91°00'E
Yarmouth, N.S., Can. (yär'mŭth)	138-39	43°50'N	66°06'W
Yaroslavl', Russia (yá-rô-släv''l)	202-03	57°37'N	39°52'E
Yar-Sale, Russia	218-19	66°51'N	70°53'E
Yartsevo, Russia (yär'tsyĕ-vô)	202-03	55°04'N	32°42'E
Yarumal, Col. (yä-rōō-mäl')	164-65	6°58'N	75°24'W
Yasawa, i., Fiji	279f	16°47'S	177°31'E
Yashiro-jima, i., Japan	245	33°55'N	132°15'E
Yass, Austl.	276	34°51'S	148°55'E
Yassy, Rom. see Iași	202-03	47°10'N	27°36'E
Yata, stm., Bol.	166-67	10°29'S	65°26'W
Yathkyed Lake, lk., Nu., Can. (yáth-kī-ĕd' lāk)	130-31	62°41'N	98°00'W
Yatsuga-take, mtn., Japan (yät'sōō-gä-dä'kä)	245	35°59'N	138°23'E
Yatsushiro, Japan (yät'sōō'shē-rô)	245	32°30'N	130°36'E
Yaundé, nat. cap., Camrn. see Yaoundé	260-61	3°52'N	11°31'E
Yautepec, Mex. (yä-ōō-tå-pĕk')	146-47	18°52'N	99°03'W
Yavarí, stm., S.A.	170	4°21'S	70°02'W
Yaví, Cerro, mtn., Ven.	164-65	5°32'N	65°59'W
Yawata, Japan (yä'wä-tä) see Kitakyūshū	245	33°54'N	130°51'E
Yawatahama, Japan (yä'wä'tä'hä-mä)	245	33°27'N	132°26'E
Yaxian, China (yä shyĕn) see Sanya	238-39	18°14'N	109°30'E
Yazd, Iran	232-33	31°54'N	54°22'E
Yazoo, stm., Ms., U.S. (yă'zōō)	124-25	32°23'N	91°00'W
Yazoo City, Ms., U.S. (yă'zōō sĭ'tĭ)	124-25	32°51'N	90°25'W
Ye, Mya. (yā)	246-47	15°15'N	97°52'E
Yecla, Spain (yā'klä)	198-99	38°37'N	1°07'W
Yefremov, Russia (yĕ-frā'môf)	202-03	53°09'N	38°07'E
Yegor'yevsk, Russia (yĕ-gôr'yĕfsk)	202-03	55°23'N	39°02'E
Yei, Sudan	267	4°06'N	30°40'E
Yei, stm., Sudan	262-63	6°15'N	30°13'E
Yekaterinburg, Russia	218-19	56°51'N	60°36'E
Yekaterinoslav, Ukr. see Dnipropetrovs'k	202-03	48°28'N	34°58'E
Yelabuga, Russia (yĕ-lä'bô-gá)	186-87	55°46'N	52°05'E
Yelizavety, Mys, c., Russia (mĭs yĕ-lyĕ-sá-vyĕ'tĭ)	218-19	54°24'N	142°42'E
Yellow, stm., China see Huang	222-23	37°49'N	118°53'E
Yellowhead Pass, p., Can. (yĕl'ô-hĕd pås)	132-33	52°54'N	118°22'W
Yellowknife, N.T., Can. (yĕl'ô-nīf)	128-29	62°27'N	114°21'W
Yellow Sea, s., Asia (yĕl'ô sē)	222-23	36°0'N	123°00'E
Yellowstone, stm., U.S. (yĕl'ô-stōn)	110-11	47°59'N	103°60'W
Yellowstone Lake, lk., Wy., U.S.	112-13	44°28'N	110°23'W
Yellowstone National Park, n.p., U.S. (yĕl'ô-stōn năsh'ŭn-ăl pärk)	112-13	44°30'N	110°35'W
Yel'nya, Russia (yĕl'nyá)	202-03	54°34'N	33°11'E
Yemen, nation, Asia (yĕm'ĕn)	206-07	15°0'N	44°00'E
Yenangyaung, Mya. (yā'nän-d oung)	246-47	20°27'N	94°53'E
Yen Bai, Viet.	246-47	21°42'N	104°52'E
Yendi, Ghana (yĕn'dē)	260-61	9°26'N	0°00'W
Yenisey, stm., Russia (yĕ-nĕ-sĕ'ē)	218-19	71°54'N	82°20'E
Yeo Lake, lk., Austl. (yō lăk)	272-73	27°58'S	124°25'E
Yeppoon, Austl.	277	23°08'S	150°45'E
Yerevan, nat. cap., Arm. (yĕ-rĕ-văn')	227	40°11'N	44°30'E
Yergeni, hills, Russia	186-87	47°0'N	44°00'E
Yerington, Nv., U.S. (yē'rĭng-tŭn)	118-19	38°59'N	119°09'W
Yershov, Russia	186-87	51°21'N	48°16'E
Yerupaja, Nevado, mtn., Peru	170	10°16'S	76°54'W
Yerushalayim, nat. cap., Isr. see Jerusalem	228-29	31°47'N	35°14'E
Yessentuki, Russia	227	44°02'N	42°51'E
Ye-u, Mya.	246-47	22°46'N	95°26'E
Yeu, Île d', i., Fr. (ēl dyû)	196-97	46°42'N	2°20'W
Yevlax, Azer.	227	40°37'N	47°09'E
Yevpatoriia, Ukr.	202-03	45°12'N	33°22'E
Yeya, stm., Russia (yă'yá)	186-87	46°40'N	38°36'E
Yeysk, Russia (yĕysk)	202-03	46°42'N	38°16'E
Yezd, Iran see Yazd	232-33	31°54'N	54°22'E
Ygatimí, Para.	168-69	24°05'S	55°24'W
Yi'an, China	240-41	47°53'N	125°18'E
Yibin, China (yē-bĭn)	238-39	28°46'N	104°37'E
Yichang, China (yē-chäŋ)	238-39	30°42'N	111°17'E
Yichun, China	238-39	27°48'N	114°23'E
Yichun, China	240-41	47°43'N	128°55'E
Yidu, China (yē-dōō)	238-39	30°24'N	111°26'E
Yilan, China (yē-län)	244	46°18'N	129°32'E
Yiliang, China	238-39	24°57'N	103°08'E
Yinchuan, China (yĭn-chůän)	240-41	38°28'N	106°16'E
Ying, stm., China	238-39	32°30'N	116°31'E
Yingkou, China (yĭŋ-kō)	240-41	40°40'N	122°14'E
Yingtan, China	238-39	28°14'N	117°02'E
Yining, China (yē-nĭŋ)	226	43°55'N	81°18'E
Yirga 'Alem, Eth.	269d	6°52'N	38°24'E
Yirol, Sudan	262-63	6°33'N	30°30'E
Yishui, China (yē-shwā)	240-41	35°47'N	118°38'E
Yisra'el, nation, Asia see Israel	206-07	31°30'N	34°45'E
Yitulihe, China	240-41	50°37'N	121°33'E
Yiyang, China (yē-yäŋ)	238-39	28°24'N	117°26'E
Yiyang, China (yē-yäŋ)	238-39	28°35'N	112°20'E
Yoakum, Tx., U.S. (yō'kŭm)	122-23	29°17'N	97°09'W
Yockanookany, stm., Ms., U.S. (yŏk'á-nōō-kä-nī)	124-25	32°40'N	89°41'W
Yog Point, c., Phil. (yŏg point)	250	14°06'N	124°12'E
Yogyakarta, Indon. (yŏg-yá-kär'tá)	248-49	7°48'S	110°22'E
Yokadouma, Camrn.	260-61	3°31'N	15°03'E
Yokkaichi, Japan (yô'kä'ē-chē)	245	34°58'N	136°39'E
Yokohama, Japan (yō'kô-hä'mä)	245	35°27'N	139°37'E
Yokosuka, Japan (yô-kō'sò-kä)	245	35°16'N	139°40'E
Yolöten, Turkmen.	232-33	37°17'N	62°22'E
Yom, stm., Thai.	246-47	15°52'N	100°16'E
Yonago, Japan (yō'nä-gō)	245	35°26'N	133°20'E
Yonezawa, Japan (yō'nĕ'zá-wä)	245	37°55'N	140°07'E
Yong'an, China (yôŋ-än)	238-39	25°58'N	117°22'E
Yongdeng, China	240-41	36°43'N	103°16'E
Yongding, China	238-39	24°44'N	116°44'E
Yongding, stm., China (yôŋ-dĭŋ)	240-41	39°16'N	117°04'E
Yŏngdŏk, Kor., S. (yŭng'dŭk')	243	36°26'N	129°23'E
Yongfeng, China	238-39	27°19'N	115°24'E
Yongnian, China (yôŋ-nĭĕn)	240-41	36°47'N	114°29'E
Yongren, China	238-39	26°06'N	101°48'E
Yongshan, China	238-39	28°09'N	103°32'E
Yongshun, China (yôŋ-shòn)	238-39	29°00'N	109°51'E
Yongzhou, China	238-39	26°13'N	111°37'E
Yonkers, N.Y., U.S. (yŏŋ'kẽrz)	116-17	40°56'N	73°54'W
York, Austl.	270-71	31°53'S	116°46'E
York, Eng., U.K.	190-91	53°58'N	1°05'W
York, Al., U.S. (yôrk)	124-25	32°30'N	88°18'W
York, Ne., U.S. (yôrk)	114-15	40°52'N	97°35'W
York, Pa., U.S.	116-17	39°58'N	76°44'W
York, S.C., U.S. (yôrk)	124-25	34°59'N	81°15'W
York, Cape, c., Austl. (kāp yôrk)	277	10°42'S	142°32'E
York Factory, Mb., Can.	134-35	57°03'N	92°15'W
Yorkton, Sk., Can. (yôrk'tŭn)	134-35	51°13'N	102°28'W
Yorktown, Tx., U.S. (yôrk'toun)	122-23	28°59'N	97°30'W
Yorktown, Va., U.S. (yôrk'toun)	124-25	37°14'N	76°31'W
Yoro, Hond. (yō'rô)	149	15°09'N	87°08'W
Yosemite National Park, n.p., Ca., U.S. (yō-sĕm'ĭ-tē năsh'ŭn-ăl pärk)	118-19	37°56'N	119°36'W
Yoshino, stm., Japan (yō'shē-nō)	245	34°04'N	134°37'E
Yoshkar-Ola, Russia (yôsh-kär'ô-lä')	186-87	56°39'N	47°52'E
Yösöbulag, Mong. see Altay	240-41	46°24'N	96°15'E
Yos Sudarso, Pulau, i., Indon.	277	7°50'S	138°30'E
Yŏsu, Kor., S. (yŭ'sōō')	243	34°44'N	127°44'E
You, stm., China (yō)	238-39	22°50'N	108°06'E
You, stm., China (yō)	225a	26°24'N	118°27'E
You, stm., China (yō)	238-39	28°27'N	110°23'E
Youghal, Ire. (yōō'ôl) (yôl)	190-91	51°57'N	7°51'W
Young, Austl. (yŭng)	276	34°19'S	148°18'E
Young, Ur. (yô-ōō'ng)	173	32°42'S	57°38'W
Youngstown, Oh., U.S.	116-17	41°06'N	80°39'W
Youssoufia, Mor.	269a	32°15'N	8°32'W
Youyang, China	238-39	28°58'N	108°41'E
Yozgat, Tur. (yŏz'gȧd)	186-87	39°49'N	34°48'E
Ypsilanti, Mi., U.S. (ĭp-sĭ-lăn'tĭ)	116-17	42°15'N	83°37'W
Yreka, Ca., U.S. (wī-rē'kă)	112-13	41°44'N	122°38'W
Ystad, Swe.	192-93	55°26'N	13°50'E
Ysyk-Köl, lk., Kyrg. see Issyk-Kul, Lake	226	42°25'N	77°15'E
Ytyk-Kyuyël', Russia	218-19	62°21'N	133°33'E
Yu, stm., China	238-39	23°24'N	110°06'E
Yuan, stm., Asia see Red	238-39	20°18'N	106°32'E
Yuan, stm., China (yůän)	238-39	28°45'N	111°20'E
Yuan'an, China (yůän-än)	238-39	31°04'N	111°25'E
Yuanling, China (yůän-lĭŋ)	238-39	28°20'N	110°16'E
Yuanmou, China	238-39	25°43'N	101°52'E
Yuba City, Ca., U.S. (yōō'bȧ sĭ'tĭ)	118-19	39°08'N	121°37'W
Yucatán, state, Mex. (yōō-kä-tän')	148	20°50'N	89°00'W
Yucatán, Canal de, strt., N.A. see Yucatan Channel	140-41	21°42'N	86°04'W
Yucatán, Península de, pen., N.A. see Yucatan Peninsula	148	19°30'N	89°00'W
Yucatan Channel, strt., N.A. (yōō-kä-tän' chăn'ĕl)	140-41	21°42'N	86°04'W
Yucatan Peninsula, pen., N.A. (yōō-kä-tän' pĕ-nĭn'sūlă)	148	19°30'N	89°00'W
Yuci, China (yōō-tsz)	240-41	37°41'N	112°44'E
Yudoma, stm., Russia (yōō-dō'mȧ)	218-19	59°10'N	135°14'E
Yueqing, China (yůĕ-chyĭn)	238-39	28°07'N	120°57'E
Yueyang, China (yůĕ-yäŋ)	238-39	29°22'N	113°06'E
Yug, stm., Russia (yòg)	186-87	60°43'N	46°19'E
Yukagirskoye Ploskogor'ye, plat., Russia	218-19	66°0'N	155°00'E
Yukhnov, Russia (yòk'nof)	202-03	54°44'N	35°15'E
Yukon, state, Can. (yōō'kŏn)	128-29	64°0'N	135°00'W
Yukon, stm., N.A. (yōō'kŏn)	126	62°36'N	164°49'W
Yulin, China (yōō-lĭn)	238-39	22°38'N	110°07'E

n-sing; ŋ-baŋk; N-nasalized n; nŏd; cŏmmit; ōld; ôbey; ôrder; oi-boil; fōōd; ò-as oo in foot; ou-out; s-soft; sh-dish; th-thin; pūre; ûnite; ûrn; stŭd; circŭs; ü-as in French tu; '-indeterminate vowel.

Feature (Pronunciation)	Page	Lat.	Long.
Yulin, China (yōō-lǐn)	240-41	38°17′N	109°45′E
Yuma, Az., U.S. (yōō′mä)	118-19	32°43′N	114°37′W
Yuma, Co., U.S. (yōō′mä)	120-21	40°07′N	102°44′W
Yumen, China (yōō-mǔn)	240-41	39°50′N	97°34′E
Yuncheng, China (yón-chǔn)	238-39	35°01′N	110°59′E
Yuncheng, China (yón-chǔn)	240-41	35°36′N	115°56′E
Yunnan, state, China (yun′nän′)	238-39	24°0′N	101°00′E
Yunxian, China (yón shyěn)	238-39	24°31′N	100°02′E
Yunxian, China (yón shyěn)	238-39	32°49′N	110°49′E
Yunxiao, China (yón-shyou)	238-39	24°04′N	117°19′E
Yurga, Russia	218-19	55°43′N	84°55′E
Yurimaguas, Peru (yōō-rē-mä′gwäs)	170	5°54′s	76°06′W
Yuruá, stm., S.A. see Juruá	166-67	2°35′s	65°47′W
Yuryev, Est. see Tartu	192-93	58°23′N	26°43′E
Yuscarán, Hond. (yōōs-kä-rän′)	149	13°56′N	86°50′W
Yü Shan, mtn., Tai.	225a	23°28′N	120°57′E
Yushu, China (yōō-shōō)	238-39	33°00′N	97°00′E
Yushu, China (yōō-shōō)	240-41	44°50′N	126°34′E
Yutian, China (yōō-tiēn) (kǔ-r-yä)	234-35	36°51′N	81°40′E
Yuty, Para. (yōō-tē′)	173	26°38′s	56°11′W
Yuxian, China (yōō shyěn)	238-39	34°10′N	113°28′E
Yuxian, China (yōō shyěn)	240-41	38°06′N	113°24′E
Yuzha, Russia (yōō′zhà)	186-87	56°35′N	42°01′E
Yuzhno-Sakhalinsk, Russia (yōōzh′nô-sä-kä-lĭnsk′)	244	46°58′N	142°43′E
Yuzovka, Ukr. see Donets′k	202-03	47°60′N	37°48′E
Yvetot, Fr. (ēv-tō′)	196-97	49°37′N	0°46′E

Z

Feature (Pronunciation)	Page	Lat.	Long.
Zaandam, Neth. (zän′dàm)	190-91	52°26′N	4°49′E
Zabaykal′sk, Russia	240-41	49°39′N	117°19′E
Zabīd, Yemen	266	14°11′N	43°19′E
Zābol, Iran	230-31	31°02′N	61°30′E
Zabrze, Pol. (zäb′zhě)	194-95	50°18′N	18°46′E
Zacapa, Guat. (sä-kä′pä)	148	14°58′N	89°32′W
Zacatecas, Mex. (sä-kä-tā′käs)	146-47	22°46′N	102°34′W
Zacatecas, state, Mex.	146-47	23°0′N	103°00′W
Zacatlán, Mex. (sä-kä-tlän′)	146-47	19°56′N	97°58′W
Zacoalco de Torres, Mex. (sä-kô-äl′kô dä tôr′rěs)	146-47	20°13′N	103°34′W
Zacualtipan, Mex. (sá-kò-äl-tē-pän′)	146-47	20°38′N	98°39′W
Zadar, Cro. (zä′där)	200-01	44°07′N	15°14′E
Zagazig, Egypt	268b	30°35′N	31°31′E
Zagreb, nat. cap., Cro. (zä′grěb)	200-01	45°49′N	15°58′E
Zāgros, Kūhhā-ye, mts., Iran see Zagros Mountains	220-21	33°03′N	48°33′E
Zagros Mountains, mts., Iran (zä′grôs moun′tĭnz)	220-21	33°03′N	48°33′E
Za′gya, stm., China	234-35	31°56′N	88°60′E
Zāhedān, Iran (zä′hå-dän)	230-31	29°30′N	60°52′E
Zaḥlah, Leb. (zä′lä′)	228-29	33°51′N	35°55′E
Zaḥodnjaja Dzvina, stm., Eur. see Western Dvina	192-93	57°04′N	24°03′E
Zaire, nation, Afr. see Congo, Democratic Republic of the.	253	4°0′s	25°00′E
Zaire, stm., Afr. see Congo	262-63	5°58′s	12°44′E
Zaječar, Serb. (zä′yě-chär′)	200-01	43°55′N	22°17′E
Zakamensk, Russia	240-41	50°23′N	103°16′E
Zakopane, Pol. (zá-kô-pä′ně)	194-95	49°18′N	19°58′E
Zákynthos, i., Grc.	200-01	37°47′N	20°47′E
Zalaegerszeg, Hung. (zŏ′lô-ě′gěr-sěg)	194-95	46°51′N	16°51′E
Zalantun, China	240-41	47°60′N	122°45′E
Zalingei, Sudan	262-63	12°55′N	23°29′E
Zambeze, stm., Afr. see Zambezi	264-65	18°49′s	36°15′E
Zambezi, stm., Afr.	264-65	18°49′s	36°15′E
Zambia, nation, Afr. (zăm′bě-å)	253	14°30′s	27°30′E
Zamboanga, Phil. (säm-bô-aŋ′gä)	250	6°54′N	122°04′E
Zamboanga Peninsula, pen., Phil.	250	7°32′N	122°16′E
Zambrów, Pol. (zäm′bróf)	194-95	52°58′N	21°15′E
Zamfara, stm., Nig.	260-61	12°02′N	4°03′E
Zamora, Spain (thä-mō′rä)	198-99	41°31′N	5°45′W
Zamora de Hidalgo, Mex.	146-47	19°59′N	102°17′W
Zanesville, Oh., U.S. (zänz′vĭl)	116-17	39°56′N	82°01′W
Zanjān, Iran	228-29	36°40′N	48°29′E
Zante, i., Grc. see Zákynthos	200-01	37°47′N	20°47′E
Zanzibar, Tan. (zän′zĭ-bär)	262-63	6°10′s	39°12′E
Zanzibar, i., Tan. (zän′zĭ-bär)	262-63	6°10′s	39°20′E
Zaozhuang, China (dzou-jůäŋ)	238-39	34°52′N	117°33′E
Zapadnaya Dvina, stm., Eur. see Western Dvina	192-93	57°04′N	24°03′E

Feature (Pronunciation)	Page	Lat.	Long.
Zapadno-Sibirskaya Ravnina, pl., Russia see West Siberian Plain	218-19	60°0′N	75°00′E
Zapala, Arg. (zä-pä′lä)	171	38°54′s	70°03′W
Zapata, Tx., U.S. (sä-pä′tä)	122-23	26°55′N	99°16′W
Zapata, Península de, pen., Cuba (pě-nē′n-sōō-lä-dě-zä-pá′tä)	142-43	22°20′N	81°35′W
Zapopan, Mex. (sä-pō′pän)	146-47	20°43′N	103°24′W
Zaporizhzhia, Ukr.	202-03	47°51′N	35°10′E
Zaporozhye, Ukr. see Zaporizhzhia	202-03	47°51′N	35°10′E
Zara, Cro. see Zadar	200-01	44°07′N	15°14′E
Zaragoza, Mex. (sä-rä-gō′sä)	146-47	23°56′N	99°46′W
Zaragoza, Mex. (sä-rä-gō′sä)	122-23	28°29′N	100°55′W
Zaragoza, Mex. (sä-rä-gō′sä)	122-23	31°43′N	106°23′W
Zaragoza, Spain (thä-rä-gō′thä)	198-99	41°39′N	0°53′W
Zaranj, Afg.	232-33	31°07′N	61°53′E
Zarasai, Lith. (zä-rä-sī′)	192-93	55°44′N	26°16′E
Zárate, Arg. (zä-rä′tä)	173	34°06′s	59°02′W
Zaraysk, Russia (zä-rä′ěsk)	202-03	54°45′N	38°53′E
Zard Kūh, mtn., Iran	232-33	32°22′N	50°04′E
Zarghon Shahr, Afg.	232-33	32°51′N	68°27′E
Zaria, Nig. (zä′rê-ä)	260-61	11°07′N	7°43′E
Zarzal, Col. (zär-zá′l)	163c	4°23′N	76°03′W
Žatec, Czech Rep. (zhä′těts)	194-95	50°20′N	13°33′E
Zavitinsk, Russia	240-41	50°07′N	129°27′E
Zawiercie, Pol. (zá-vyěr′tsyě)	194-95	50°30′N	19°26′E
Zaysan, Kaz. (zī′sán)	226	47°28′N	84°52′E
Zaza, stm., Cuba (zä′zá)	142-43	21°39′N	79°33′W
Zbarazh, Ukr. (zbä-räzh′)	194-95	49°40′N	25°48′E
Zbruch, stm., Ukr. (zbròch)	194-95	48°32′N	26°27′E
Zduńska Wola, Pol. (zdōōn′′skä vō′lä)	194-95	51°36′N	18°58′E
Zeehan, Austl.	276	41°53′s	145°20′E
Zeeland, Mi., U.S. (zē′lánd)	116-17	42°49′N	86°01′W
Zeerust, S. Afr.	269c	25°33′s	26°06′E
Zelěnodol′sk, Russia	186-87	55°50′N	48°32′E
Zelenogorsk, Russia (zě-lă′nô-gôrsk)	192-93	60°12′N	29°43′E
Zémio, C.A.R. (za-myô′)	262-63	5°02′N	25°08′E
Zenica, Bos. (zě′nět-sä)	200-01	44°12′N	17°54′E
Zernograd, Russia	186-87	46°50′N	40°18′E
Zeya, Russia (zá′yà)	218-19	53°44′N	127°15′E
Zeya, stm., Russia	218-19	50°14′N	127°36′E
Zeyskoye Vodokhranilishche, res., Russia	218-19	54°28′N	127°45′E
Zêzere, stm., Port. (zě′zå-rě)	198-99	39°28′N	8°20′W
Zgierz, Pol. (zgyězh)	194-95	51°52′N	19°25′E
Zhalpy Syrt, mts., Eur.	186-87	52°0′N	51°30′E
Zhambyl, Kaz. see Taraz	226	42°54′N	71°21′E
Zhangaözen, Kaz.	186-87	43°19′N	52°47′E
Zhangaqazaly, Kaz.	226	45°51′N	62°09′E
Zhangatas, Kaz.	226	43°69′N	69°44′E
Zhangdian, China see Zibo	240-41	36°47′N	118°03′E
Zhangjiakou, China	240-41	40°49′N	114°53′E
Zhangping, China	238-39	25°18′N	117°26′E
Zhangye, China (jäŋ-yu)	240-41	38°56′N	100°27′E
Zhangzhou, China (jäŋ-jō)	238-39	24°31′N	117°40′E
Zhänibek, Kaz.	186-87	49°26′N	46°50′E
Zhanjiang, China (jän-jyäŋ)	238-39	21°12′N	110°23′E
Zhao′an, China (jou-än)	238-39	23°44′N	117°09′E
Zhaodong, China (jou-dôŋ)	240-41	46°04′N	125°59′E
Zhaoqing, China	238-39	23°04′N	112°28′E
Zhaotong, China (jou-tôŋ)	238-39	27°21′N	103°43′E
Zhaoyuan, China	240-41	37°22′N	120°24′E
Zhaoyuan, China (jou-yuän)	240-41	45°31′N	125°09′E
Zharkent, Kaz.	226	44°10′N	79°60′E
Zhaxigang, China	234-35	32°31′N	79°41′E
Zhaysang köli, lk., Kaz.	226	48°0′N	84°00′E
Zhayyq, stm. see Ural	176-77	46°50′N	51°33′E
Zhdanov, Ukr. see Mariupol′	202-03	47°06′N	37°34′E
Zhejiang, state, China (jŭ-jyäŋ)	238-39	29°0′N	120°00′E
Zheleznogorsk-Ilimskiy, Russia	218-19	56°35′N	104°08′E
Zheltyye Vody, Ukr. see Zhovti Vody	202-03	48°21′N	33°31′E
Zhem, stm., Kaz.	226	46°43′N	53°08′E
Zhengding, China (jŭŋ-dǐŋ)	240-41	38°09′N	114°34′E
Zhengyang, China (jŭŋ-yäŋ)	238-39	32°36′N	114°23′E
Zhengzhou, China (jŭŋ-jō)	238-39	34°46′N	113°39′E
Zhenjiang, China (jŭn-jyäŋ)	238-39	32°12′N	119°25′E
Zhenping, China	238-39	33°08′N	112°19′E
Zhenyuan, China (jŭn-yůän)	238-39	26°52′N	108°19′E
Zhetiqara, Kaz.	226	52°11′N	61°12′E
Zhezqazghan, Kaz.	226	47°47′N	67°41′E
Zhidoi, China	238-39	33°08′N	94°50′E
Zhigansk, Russia (zhē-gánsk′)	218-19	66°48′N	123°21′E
Zhijiang, China (jr-jyäŋ)	238-39	27°26′N	109°40′E
Zhitomir, Ukr. see Zhytomyr	202-03	50°16′N	28°41′E
Zhob, stm., Pak.	232-33	31°21′N	69°27′E
Zhob, stm., Pak.	232-33	32°03′N	69°49′E

Feature (Pronunciation)	Page	Lat.	Long.
Zhongba, China	234-35	29°54′N	83°40′E
Zhongdian, China	238-39	27°49′N	99°42′E
Zhongghar Alataū zhotasy, mts., Asia see Alataw Shan	226	45°0′N	81°00′E
Zhongguo, nation, Asia see China	206-07	35°0′N	105°00′E
Zhongning, China	240-41	37°28′N	105°39′E
Zhongshan, China	238-39	22°31′N	113°22′E
Zhongwei, China (jŏn-wä)	240-41	37°31′N	105°11′E
Zhongxian, China (jŏŋ shyěn)	238-39	30°29′N	108°05′E
Zhongxiang, China	238-39	31°10′N	112°35′E
Zhosaly, Kaz.	226	45°29′N	64°06′E
Zhoucun, China (jŏ-tsōōn)	240-41	36°48′N	117°50′E
Zhoushan Dao, i., China	238-39	30°03′N	122°08′E
Zhoushan Qundao, is., China (jō-shän-chyòn-dou) see Choushan Islands	238-39	30°0′N	122°00′E
Zhovti Vody, Ukr.	202-03	48°21′N	33°31′E
Zhuanghe, China (jůäŋ-hŭ)	243	39°42′N	122°58′E
Zhucheng, China (jŏ-chŭŋ)	240-41	36°0′N	119°24′E
Zhuji, China (jōō-jyē) see Shangqiu	238-39	34°27′N	115°39′E
Zhuji, China (jōō-jyē)	238-39	29°43′N	120°15′E
Zhujiang Kou, est., Asia (jōō-jyäŋ kō)	238-39	22°36′N	113°44′E
Zhukovskiy, Russia (zhó-kôf′skī)	202-03	55°36′N	38°09′E
Zhuozhou, China	240-41	39°29′N	115°58′E
Zhushan, China	238-39	32°10′N	110°19′E
Zhuzhou, China	238-39	27°50′N	113°09′E
Zhytomyr, Ukr.	202-03	50°16′N	28°41′E
Zi, stm., China (dzě)	238-39	28°44′N	112°32′E
Zi, stm., China (dzě)	238-39	31°58′N	96°57′E
Zibo, China (dzě-bwo)	240-41	36°47′N	118°03′E
Zielona Góra, Pol. (zhyč-lô′nä gōō′rä)	194-95	51°56′N	15°31′E
Zigong, China	238-39	29°22′N	104°45′E
Ziguinchor, Sen.	260-61	12°34′N	16°17′W
Zihuatanejo, Mex.	146-47	17°39′N	101°33′W
Zile, Tur. (zě-lě′)	186-87	40°18′N	35°54′E
Žilina, Slvk. (zhě′lĭ-nä)	194-95	49°13′N	18°44′E
Zillah, Libya	258-59	28°34′N	17°34′E
Zima, Russia (zē′má)	218-19	53°55′N	102°04′E
Zimapán, Mex. (sē-mä′pän)	146-47	20°44′N	99°23′W
Zimbabwe, nation, Afr. (zĭm-bäb′-wä) (zĭm-bäb′-wē)	253	20°0′s	30°00′E
Zimbabwe Ruins, hist., Zimb.	264-65	20°17′s	30°57′E
Zimnicea, Rom. (zěm-nē′chá)	200-01	43°40′N	25°23′E
Zinder, Niger (zĭn′děr)	258-59	13°48′N	8°59′E
Zion, Il., U.S. (zī′ŭn)	116-17	42°27′N	87°50′W
Zion National Park, n.p., Ut., U.S.	118-19	37°18′N	113°02′W
Zipaquirá, Col.	163c	5°00′N	74°01′W
Zittau, Ger. (tsě′tou)	194-95	50°54′N	14°48′E
Ziway, Lake, lk., Eth.	269d	7°59′N	38°50′E
Ziway Hāyk′, lk., Eth. see Ziway, Lake	269d	7°59′N	38°50′E
Ziya, stm., China (dzě-yä)	240-41	39°09′N	117°10′E
Ziyun, China	238-39	25°43′N	106°05′E
Zizhong, China	238-39	29°47′N	104°50′E
Zlatoust, Russia (zlá-tô-òst′)	226	55°10′N	59°40′E
Zlynka, Russia (zlēŋ′ká)	202-03	52°25′N	31°44′E
Znaim, Czech Rep. see Znojmo	194-95	48°51′N	16°03′E
Znamenka, Ukr. see Znam′ianka	202-03	48°43′N	32°40′E
Znam′ianka, Ukr.	202-03	48°43′N	32°40′E
Znojmo, Czech Rep. (znoi′mô)	194-95	48°51′N	16°03′E
Zolotonosha, Ukr. (zŏ′lô-tô-nô′shá)	202-03	49°40′N	32°02′E
Zomba, Malawi (zŏm′bà)	264-65	15°23′s	35°19′E
Zongo, D.R.C. (zŏŋ′gô)	262-63	4°21′N	18°37′E
Zonguldak, Tur. (zŏn′gōōl′dák)	186-87	41°28′N	31°49′E
Zouérat, Maur.	258-59	22°40′N	12°27′W
Zrenjanin, Serb.	200-01	45°23′N	20°24′E
Zubtsov, Russia (zóp-tsôf′)	202-03	56°10′N	34°35′E
Zugdidi, Geor.	227	42°30′N	41°52′E
Zugspitze, mtn., Eur.	194-95	47°25′N	10°59′E
Zújar, stm., Spain (zōō′kär)	198-99	39°01′N	5°47′W
Zululand, hist. reg., S. Afr.	264-65	28°10′s	32°00′E
Zumbrota, Mn., U.S. (zŭm-brō′tà)	114-15	44°18′N	92°41′W
Zunhua, China (dzón-hwä)	240-41	40°11′N	117°57′E
Zunyi, China	238-39	27°42′N	106°56′E
Zürich, Switz. (tsü′rĭk)	194-95	47°23′N	8°32′E
Zuyevka, Russia	186-87	58°24′N	51°09′E
Zvishavane, Zimb.	264-65	20°20′s	30°03′E
Zvolen, Slvk. (zvô′lěn)	194-95	48°35′N	19°08′E
Zvornik, Bos. (zvôr′něk)	200-01	44°23′N	19°07′E
Zwedru, Lib.	260-61	6°04′N	8°07′W
Zweibrücken, Ger. (tsvī-brük′ěn)	194-95	49°15′N	7°22′E
Zwickau, Ger. (tsvĭkou)	194-95	50°43′N	12°30′E
Zwolle, Neth. (zvôl′ě)	190-91	52°31′N	6°06′E
Zyryanka, Russia (zě-ryän′ká)	218-19	65°45′N	150°51′E
Zyryanovsk, Kaz.	226	49°44′N	84°18′E